GEORGIA COURT RULES AND PROCEDURE

STATE

2007

Mat#40389109

This publication was created to provide you with accurate and authoritative information concerning the subject matter covered; however, this publication was not necessarily prepared by persons licensed to practice law in a particular jurisdiction. The publisher is not engaged in rendering legal or other professional advice, and this publication is not a substitute for the advice of an attorney. If you require legal or other expert advice, you should seek the services of a competent attorney or other professional.

ISBN—13 978–0–314–96346–8

ISBN—10 0–314–96346–4

PREFACE

This edition of the *Georgia Court Rules and Procedure, State, 2007*, replaces the 2006 edition. This volume provides, in convenient form, court rules governing state practice in Georgia and is current with amendments received through November 1, 2006.

Also included in this volume are selected provisions of Title 5 (Appeal and Error), Title 9 (Civil Practice), Title 17 (Criminal Procedure), Title 18 (Debtor and Creditor), Title 23 (Equity), Title 24 (Evidence), Title 40 (Motor Vehicles and Traffic) and Title 51 (Torts) as amended by the 2006 Regular Session of the Georgia General Assembly.

THE PUBLISHER

November, 2006

*

RELATED PRODUCTS FROM WEST

ALTERNATIVE DISPUTE RESOLUTION

Alternative Dispute Resolution: Practice and Procedure in Georgia
Douglas H. Yarn

Georgia Settlements Law and Strategies
H. Sol Clark and Fred S. Clark

BUSINESS/CORPORATIONS

Georgia Contracts—Law and Litigation
John K. Larkins, Jr.

***Kaplan's Nadler* Georgia Corporations, Limited Partnerships and Limited Liability Companies, with Forms**
Jerome L. Kaplan, B. Joseph Alley, Jr., Robert P. Finch, Scott A. Fisher, David A. Forehand, Jr., Hardy Gregory, Jr., David B. McAlister, Patricia T. Morgan, Shelli Willis de Roos

Georgia Securities Practice, with Forms
James S. Rankin, Jr.

CRIMINAL LAW

***Molnar's* Georgia Criminal Law, Crimes and Punishments**
Robert E. Cleary, Jr.

***Kurtz's* Criminal Offenses and Defenses in Georgia**
Robert E. Cleary, Jr.

***Daniel's* Georgia Criminal Trial Practice**
John J. Goger

***Daniel's* Georgia Criminal Trial Practice Forms**
John J. Goger

The Georgia DUI Trial Practice Manual
William C. Head

DAMAGES, REMEDIES AND COLLECTIONS

Georgia Legal Collections
Lewis N. Jones

Georgia Construction Mechanics' and Materialmen's Liens, with Forms
Daniel F. Hinkel

Georgia Law of Damages, with Forms
Eric James Hertz and Mark D. Link

Punitive Damages in Georgia
Eric James Hertz

Georgia Post-Judgment Collection, with Forms
Stuart Finestone

***Dobb's* Georgia Enforcement of Securities Interests in Personal Property, with Forms**
James S. Rankin, Jr.

RELATED PRODUCTS

ELDER LAW

Elder Care and Nursing Home Litigation in Georgia with Forms/Long-Term Health Care
Michael S. Reeves

EVIDENCE

Georgia Rules of Evidence
Paul S. Milich

Courtroom Handbook on Georgia Evidence
Paul S. Milich

***Daniel's* Georgia Handbook on Criminal Evidence**
Jack Goger

***Herman and McLaughlin* Admissibility of Evidence in Civil Cases—A Manual for Georgia Trial Lawyers**
Michael E. McLaughlin

***Green's* Georgia Law of Evidence**
Alexander Scherr

***Agnor's* Georgia Evidence**
D. Lake Rumsey, Jr.

Georgia Handbook on Foundations and Objections
Neal W. Dickert

Georgia Admissibility of Expert Testimony
Mary Donne Peters and James Willis Standard, Jr.

FORMS

***Ruskell's* Civil Pleading and Practice Forms for Use with West's Official Code of Georgia Annotated**
Richard C. Ruskell

Forms for Pleading Under the Georgia Civil Practice Act
Victoria C. Ferreira

***Brown's* Georgia Pleading, Practice and Legal Forms, Annotated**
Charles R. Adams III and Cynthia Trimboli Adams

Georgia Forms: Legal and Business

GENERAL

Georgia Automobile Insurance Law, Including Tort Law, with Forms
Frank E. Jenkins III and Wallace Miller III

Georgia Divorce, Alimony and Child Custody
Dan E. McConaughey

Georgia Employment Law
James W. Wimberly, Jr.

Handbook on Georgia Practice, with Forms
Charles R. Sheppard

Georgia Juvenile Practice and Procedure, with Forms
Mark H. Murphy

RELATED PRODUCTS

Georgia Law Enforcement Handbook

Georgia Magistrate Court Handbook, with Forms
Wayne M. Purdom

LANDLORD AND TENANT

Georgia Landlord and Tenant—Breach and Remedies, with Forms
William J. Dawkins

Georgia Landlord and Tenant—Leases, Forms and Causes
James A. Fleming

LITIGATION

Georgia Appellate Practice, with Forms
Christopher J. McFadden, Edward C. Brewer III and Charles R. Sheppard

Georgia Civil Discovery, with Forms
Wayne M. Purdom

***Davis and Shulman's* Georgia Practice and Procedure**
Richard C. Ruskell

Georgia Process and Service, with Forms
Phillip Weltner II

Trial Handbook for Georgia Lawyers
Ronald L. Carlson

PERSONAL INJURY AND TORTS

Medical Torts in Georgia: A Handbook on State and Federal Law
C. Ashley Royal, Preyesh K. Maniklal, Gary C. Christy and Jennifer Lewis Roberts

Premises Liability in Georgia, with Forms
Michael J. Gorby

Georgia Products Liability
Jane F. Thorpe, David R. Vanderbush and J. Kennard Neal

Soft Tissue Injuries in Georgia, Including Whiplash, with Forms
Houston D. Smith III

Georgia Law of Torts
Charles R. Adams III

Georgia Law of Torts—Forms
Eric James Hertz, Mark D. Link, Houston D. Smith III

Georgia Law of Torts, Preparation for Trial
Charles R. Adams III and Deron R. Hicks

***Eldridge's* Georgia Wrongful Death Actions, with Forms**
Robert E. Cleary, Jr.

PROBATE LAW AND TRUSTS

Georgia Guardian and Ward
Victoria Ferreira

Probate and Administration
Teresa E. Wise

RELATED PRODUCTS

***Redfearn's* Wills and Administration in Georgia**
Mary F. Radford

REAL PROPERTY

Georgia Eminent Domain
Daniel F. Hinkel

Georgia Real Estate Finance and Foreclosure Law, with Forms
Frank S. Alexander

***Pindar's* Georgia Real Estate Law and Procedure, with Forms**
Daniel F. Hinkel

***Abraham's* Georgia Real Estate Sales Contracts**
Daniel F. Hinkel

Georgia Real Estate Title Examinations and Closings, Including Drafting of Sales Contracts, with Forms
Daniel F. Hinkel

WORKERS' COMPENSATION

Georgia Workers' Compensation—Law and Practice
James B. Hiers, Jr. and Robert R. Potter

Workers' Compensation Claims, with Forms
Jack B. Hood and Benjamin A. Hardy, Jr.

Georgia Jurisprudence

West's Code of Georgia Annotated

Georgia Cases

Georgia Court Rules and Procedure—State and Federal

Georgia Digest 2d

Westlaw®

WESTCheck® and WESTMATE®

KeyCite®

West CD–ROM Libraries™

To order any of these Georgia practice tools, call your West Representative or **1–800–328–9352.**

NEED RESEARCH HELP?

You can get quality research results with free help—call the West Reference Attorneys when you have questions concerning Westlaw or West Publications at 1–800–733–2889.

RELATED PRODUCTS

INTERNET ACCESS

Contact the West Editorial Department directly with your questions and suggestions by e-mail at west.editor@thomson.com. Visit West's home page at west.thomson.com.

*

WESTLAW ELECTRONIC RESEARCH GUIDE

Westlaw—Expanding the Reach of Your Library

Westlaw is West's online legal research service. With Westlaw, you experience the same quality and integrity that you have come to expect from West books, plus quick, easy access to West's vast collection of statutes, case law materials, public records, and other legal resources, in addition to current news articles and business information. For the most current and comprehensive legal research, combine the strengths of West books and Westlaw.

When you research with westlaw.com you get the convenience of the Internet combined with comprehensive and accurate Westlaw content, including exclusive editorial enhancements, plus features found only in westlaw.com such as ResultsPlus™ or StatutesPlus.™

Accessing Databases Using the Westlaw Directory

The Westlaw Directory lists all databases on Westlaw and contains links to detailed information relating to the content of each database. Click **Directory** on the westlaw.com toolbar. There are several ways to access a database even when you don't know the database identifier. Browse a directory view. Scan the directory. Type all or part of a database name in the Search these Databases box. The Find a Database Wizard can help you select relevant databases for your search. You can access up to ten databases at one time for user-defined multibase searching.

Retrieving a Specific Document

To retrieve a specific document by citation or title on westlaw.com click **Find&Print** on the toolbar to display the Find a Document page. If you are unsure of the correct citation format, type the publication abbreviation, e.g., **xx st** (where xx is a state's two-letter postal abbreviation), in the Find this document by citation box and click **Go** to display a fill-in-the-blank template. To retrieve a specific case when you know one or more parties' names, click **Find a Case by Party Name**.

KeyCite®

KeyCite, the citation research service on Westlaw, makes it easy to trace the history of your case, statute, administrative decision or regulation to determine if there are recent updates, and to find other documents that cite your document. KeyCite will also find pending legislation relating to federal or state statutes. Access the powerful features of KeyCite from the westlaw.com toolbar, the **Links** tab, or KeyCite flags in a document display. KeyCite's red and yellow warning flags tell you at a glance whether your document has negative history. Depth-of-treatment stars help you focus on the most important citing references. KeyCite Alert allows you to monitor the status of your case, statute or rule, and automatically sends you updates at the frequency you specify.

ResultsPlus™

ResultsPlus is a Westlaw technology that automatically suggests additional information related to your search. The suggested materials are accessible by a set of links that appear to the right of your westlaw.com search results:

- Go directly to relevant ALR® articles and Am Jur® annotations.
- Find on-point resources by key number.
- See information from related treatises and law reviews.

StatutesPlus™

When you access a statutes database in westlaw.com you are brought to a powerful Search Center which collects, on one toolbar, the tools that are most useful for fast, efficient retrieval of statutes documents:

- Have a few key terms? Click **Statutes Index**.
- Know the common name? Click **Popular Name Table**.
- Familiar with the subject matter? Click **Table of Contents**.
- Have a citation or section number? Click **Find by Citation**.
- Interested in topical surveys providing citations across multiple state statutes? Click **50 State Surveys**.
- Or, simply search with **Natural Language** or **Terms and Connectors.**

When you access a statutes section, click on the **Links** tab for all relevant links for the current document that will also include a KeyCite section with a description of the KeyCite status flag. Depending on your document, links may also include administrative, bill text, and other sources that were previously only available by accessing and searching other databases.

Additional Information

Westlaw is available on the Web at www.westlaw.com.

For search assistance, call the West Reference Attorneys at
1–800–REF–ATTY (1–800–733–2889).

For technical assistance, call West Customer Technical Support at
1–800–WESTLAW (1–800–937–8529).

TABLE OF CONTENTS

GEORGIA STATUTES

GEORGIA RULES

TABLE OF CONTENTS

GEORGIA STATUTES

As Amended Through the 2006 Regular Session of the General Assembly

Table of Titles

TITLE 5

APPEAL AND ERROR

As Amended Through the 2006 Regular Session of the General Assembly

Research Note

Use Westlaw *to find cases citing a statute or to search for specific terms in a statute. See the Westlaw Directory Screens for lists of relevant databases.*

Table of Sections

CHAPTER 6. CERTIORARI AND APPEALS TO APPELLATE COURTS GENERALLY

Article 1. General Provisions

Article 2. Appellate Practice

CHAPTER 7. APPEAL OR CERTIORARI BY STATE IN CRIMINAL CASES

INDEX

See Index to Georgia Statutes, infra.

CHAPTER 1

GENERAL PROVISIONS [RESERVED]

CHAPTER 2

APPEALS TO JURY IN JUSTICE OF THE PEACE COURT

§§ 5-2-1 to 5-2-6. Repealed by Laws 1983, p. 884, § 4-2, eff. July 1, 1983

CHAPTER 3

APPEALS TO SUPERIOR COURT

Article 1

General Provisions

§ 5-3-1. Repealed by Laws 1983, p. 884, § 4-2, eff. July 1, 1983

§ 5-3-2. When appeal lies

(a) An appeal shall lie to the superior court from any decision made by the probate court, except an order appointing a temporary administrator.

(b) Notwithstanding subsection (a) of this Code section, no appeal from the probate court to the superior court shall lie from any civil case in a probate court which is provided for by Article 6 of Chapter 9 of Title 15.

Laws 1805, Cobb's 1851 Digest, p. 283; Laws 1823, Cobb's 1851 Digest, p. 497; Laws 1851-52, p. 49, § 1; Laws 1851-52, p. 91, § 19; Laws 1859, p. 33, § 5; Laws 1866, p. 24, § 1; Laws 1972, p. 738, § 6; Laws 1986, p. 982, § 1.

Formerly Code 1863, § 3530; Code 1868, § 3553; Code 1873, § 3611; Code 1882, § 3611; Civil Code 1895, § 4454; Civil Code 1910, § 4999; Code 1933, § 6-201.

§ 5-3-3. Attorneys authorized to enter appeals

An appeal may be entered by the plaintiff or defendant in person, or by his attorney at law or in fact and, if by the latter, he must be authorized in writing, which authority shall be filed in the court in which the case is pending at the time the appeal is entered; but if it is shown to the court that the authority exists, the court may allow a reasonable time to file the same. Upon failure to so file, the appeal shall be dismissed and execution shall issue without further order. If the authority is not filed within the time allowed, a ratification of an unauthorized appeal, if made in writing and filed in the clerk's office before the next term of the court, shall render the appeal valid.

Formerly Code 1863, § 3535; Code 1868, § 3558; Code 1873, § 3615; Code 1882, § 3615; Civil Code 1895, § 4457; Civil Code 1910, § 5002; Code 1933, § 6-104.

§ 5-3-4. One or more may appeal

When there is more than one party plaintiff or defendant, and one or more of the parties plaintiff or defendant desire to appeal, and the others refuse or fail to appeal, the party plaintiff or defendant desiring to appeal may enter an appeal in the manner provided by law.

Laws 1839, Cobb's 1851 Digest, p. 500; Laws 1995, p. 10, § 5.

Formerly Code 1863, § 3539; Code 1868, § 3562; Code 1873, § 3619; Code 1882, § 3619; Civil Code 1895, § 4461; Civil Code 1910, § 5006; Code 1933, § 6-110.

§ 5-3-5. All parties bound by final judgment

Upon the appeal of either party plaintiff or defendant, as provided in Code Section 5-3-4, the whole record shall be taken up and all shall be bound by the final judgment; but, in case damages are awarded upon such appeal, the damages shall only be recovered against the party appealing and his security, if any, and not against the party failing or refusing to appeal.

Laws 1839, Cobb's 1851 Digest, p. 500.

Formerly Code 1863, § 3540; Code 1868, § 3563; Code 1873, § 3620; Code 1882, § 3620; Civil Code 1895, § 4462; Civil Code 1910, § 5007; Code 1933, § 6-111.

§ 5-3-6. Liability and recourse of security on appeal

The security, if any, of the party appealing shall be bound for the judgment on the appeal; and, in case the security is compelled to pay off the debt or damages for which judgment is entered in the case, he shall have recourse only against the party for whom he became security.

Laws 1823, Cobb's 1851 Digest, p. 498; Laws 1839, Cobb's 1851 Digest, p. 500.

Formerly Code 1863, § 3541; Code 1868, § 3564; Code 1873, § 3621; Code 1882, § 3621; Civil Code 1895, § 4463; Civil Code 1910, § 5008; Code 1933, § 6-112.

§ 5-3-7. Suspension of judgment

An appeal shall suspend but not vacate a judgment and, if dismissed or withdrawn, the rights of all the parties shall be the same as if no appeal had been entered.

Formerly Code 1863, § 3549; Code 1868, § 3572; Code 1873, § 3628; Code 1882, § 3628; Civil Code 1895, § 4470; Civil Code 1910, § 5015; Code 1933, § 6-502.

§ 5-3-8. Consent to withdrawal of appeal

After an appeal has been entered, no person shall be allowed to withdraw the appeal without the consent of the adverse party.

Laws 1799, Cobb's 1851 Digest, p. 495.

Formerly Code 1863, § 3550; Code 1868, § 3573; Code 1873, § 3629; Code 1882, § 3629; Civil Code 1895, § 4471; Civil Code 1910, § 5016; Code 1933, § 6-503.

Article 2

Procedure

§ 5-3-20. When appeals entered

(a) Appeals to the superior court shall be filed within 30 days of the date the judgment, order, or decision complained of was entered.

(b) The date of entry of an order, judgment, or other decision shall be the date upon which it was filed in the court, agency, or other tribunal rendering same, duly signed by the judge or other official thereof.

(c) This Code section shall apply to all appeals to the superior court, any other law to the contrary notwithstanding.

Laws 1972, p. 738, § 1.

Formerly Code 1863, § 3533; Code 1868, § 3556; Code 1873, § 3613; Code 1882, § 3613; Civil Code 1895, § 4455; Civil Code 1910, § 5000; Code 1933, § 6-102.

§ 5-3-21. Notice of appeal

(a) An appeal to the superior court may be taken by filing a notice of appeal with the court, agency, or other tribunal appealed from. No particular form shall be necessary for the notice of appeal, but the following is suggested:

—(NAME OF INFERIOR JUDICATORY)—

—STATE OF GEORGIA—

__________________)
)
v.) (Case number
) designation)
)
__________________)

—APPEAL TO SUPERIOR COURT—

Notice is hereby given that _____, appellant herein, and _____, above-named, hereby appeals to the Superior (plaintiff, defendant, etc.)

Court of _____ County from the judgment (or order, decision, etc.) entered herein on (date), _____.

Dated: ______________.

____
Attorney For Appellant

____
Address

(b) A copy of the notice of appeal shall be served on all parties in the same manner prescribed by Code Section 5-6-32. Failure to perfect service on any party shall not work dismissal, but the superior court shall grant continuances and enter such other orders as may be necessary to permit a just and expeditious determination of the appeal.

Laws 1868, p. 131, § 2; Laws 1972, p. 738, § 3; Laws 1999, p. 81, § 5.

Formerly Code 1863, § 3534; Code 1868, § 3557; Code 1873, § 3614; Code 1882, § 3614; Civil Code 1895, § 4456; Civil Code 1910, § 5001; Code 1933, § 6-103.

§ 5-3-22. Appellant to pay accrued costs; supersedeas bond

(a) No appeal shall be heard in the superior court until any costs which have accrued in the court, agency, or tribunal below have been paid unless the appellant files with the superior court or with the court, agency, or tribunal appealed from an affidavit stating that because of his indigence he is unable to pay the costs on appeal. In all cases, no appeal shall be dismissed in the superior court because of nonpayment of the costs below until the appellant has been directed by the court to do so and has failed to comply with the court's direction.

(b) Filing of the notice of appeal and payment of costs or filing of an affidavit as provided in subsection (a) of this Code section shall act as supersedeas, and it shall not be necessary that a supersedeas bond be filed; provided, however, that the superior court upon motion may at any time require that supersedeas bond with good security be given in such amount as the court may deem necessary unless the appellant files with the court an affidavit stating that because of his indigence he is unable to give bond.

Laws 1799, Cobb's 1851 Digest, p. 494; Laws 1972, p. 738, § 4; Laws 1995, p. 10, § 5.

Formerly Code 1863, § 3536; Code 1868, § 3559; Code 1873, § 3616; Code 1882, § 3616; Civil Code 1895, § 4458; Civil Code 1910, § 5003; Code 1933, § 6-105.

§ 5-3-23. Attorney may sign appeal bond for principal

If an appeal is entered by the attorney at law or in fact, he may sign the name of the principal to the appeal bond, if required, and the principal shall be bound thereby as though he had signed it himself.

Formerly Code 1863, § 3537; Code 1868, § 3560; Code 1873, § 3617; Code 1882, § 3617; Civil Code 1895, § 4459; Civil Code 1910, § 5004; Code 1933, § 6-107.

§ 5-3-24. Appeal by executors, etc., without paying costs, etc., when

Executors, administrators, and other trustees, when defending an action as such or defending solely the title of the estate, may enter an appeal without paying costs and giving bond and security as required by Code Section 5-3-22; but, if a judgment should be obtained against such executor, administrator, or other trustee and not the assets of the estate, he must pay costs and give security as in other cases.

Laws 1799, Cobb's 1851 Digest, p. 495.

Formerly Code 1863, § 3542; Code 1868, § 3565; Code 1873, § 3622; Code 1882, § 3622; Civil Code 1895, § 4464; Civil Code 1910, § 5009; Code 1933, § 6-113.

§ 5-3-25. Appeals by partners, joint contractors, and corporations

When several partners or joint contractors bring or defend an action as such, any one of the partners or joint contractors may enter an appeal in the name of the firm or joint contractors and sign the name of the firm or joint contractors to a bond if required by the superior court, which shall be binding on the firm and the joint contractors as though they had signed it themselves. In the case of corporations, the appeal may be entered by the president or any agent thereof managing the case or by the attorney of record.

Laws 1838, Cobb's 1851 Digest, p. 589.

Formerly Code 1863, § 3538; Code 1868, § 3561; Code 1873, § 3618; Code 1882, § 3618; Civil Code 1895, § 4460; Civil Code 1910, § 5005; Code 1933, § 6-108.

§ 5-3-26. Repealed by Laws 1983, p. 884, § 4-2, eff. July 1, 1983

§ 5-3-27. Amendments and orders to cure defective appeals

No appeal shall be dismissed because of any defect in the notice of appeal, bond, or affidavit of indigence or because of the failure of the lower court, agency, or other tribunal to transmit the pleadings or other record; but the superior court shall at any time permit such amendments and enter such orders as may be necessary to cure the defect.

Laws 1972, p. 738, § 5.

Formerly Code 1933, § 6-115.

§ 5-3-28. Copy of pleadings and record to be transmitted to superior court

(a) Within ten days of the filing of the notice of appeal, it shall be the duty of the judge or other official of the court, agency, or tribunal appealed from to cause a true copy of the pleadings, if any, and all other parts of the record (and transcript of evidence and proceedings, where the appeal is not de novo) to be transmitted to the superior court.

(b) The superior court may issue such orders and writs as may be necessary in aid of its jurisdiction on appeal.

Laws 1972, p. 738, § 5.

Formerly Code 1933, § 6-114.

§ 5-3-29. Appeal as de novo investigation

An appeal to the superior court in any case where not otherwise provided by law is a de novo investigation. It brings up the whole record from the court below; and all competent evidence shall be admissible on the trial thereof, whether adduced on a former trial or not. Either party is entitled to be heard on the whole merits of the case.

Laws 1972, p. 738, § 8; Laws 1983, p. 884, § 3-1; Laws 1986, p. 982, § 2.

Formerly Code 1863, § 3548; Code 1868, § 3571; Code 1873, § 3627; Code 1882, § 3627; Civil Code 1895, § 4469; Civil Code 1910, § 5014; Code 1933, § 6-501.

§ 5-3-30. Nonjury trials of appeals; demand for jury trial

(a) Upon the filing of an appeal from magistrate court to superior court or state court, the appeal shall be placed upon the court's next calendar for nonjury trial. Such appeals from the magistrate court to superior court or state court shall be tried by the superior court or state court without a jury unless either party files a demand for a jury trial within 30 days of the filing of the appeal or the court orders a jury trial.

(b) Upon filing an appeal pursuant to subsection (a) of this Code section, the monetary limitations provided for in paragraph (5) of Code Section 15-10-2 shall no longer apply to any verdict and judgment entered by the superior or state court.

Laws 1805, Cobb's 1851 Digest, p. 183; Laws 1823, Cobb's 1851 Digest, p. 497; Laws 1988, p. 253, § 1; Laws 1998, p. 552, § 1; Laws 2001, p. 1223, § 1.

Formerly Code 1863, § 3551; Code 1868, § 3574; Code 1873, § 3630; Code 1882, § 3630; Civil Code 1895, § 4472; Civil Code 1910, § 5017; Code 1933, § 6-601.

§ 5-3-31. Damages for frivolous appeals

If upon the trial of any appeal it shall appear to the jury that the appeal was frivolous and intended for delay only, they shall assess damages against the appellant and his security, if any, in favor of the appellee for such delay, not exceeding 25 percent on the principal sum which they shall find due, which damages shall be specially noted in their verdict.

Laws 1799, Cobb's 1851 Digest, p. 495; Laws 1868, p. 132, § 2; Laws 1983, p. 884, § 3-2.

Formerly Code 1863, § 3552; Code 1868, § 3575; Code 1873, § 3631; Code 1882, § 3631; Civil Code 1895, § 4473; Civil Code 1910, § 5018; Code 1933, § 6-602.

CHAPTER 4

CERTIORARI TO SUPERIOR COURT

§ 5-4-1. When writ of certiorari will lie

(a) The writ of certiorari shall lie for the correction of errors committed by any inferior judicatory or any person exercising judicial powers, including the judge of the probate court, except in cases touching the probate of wills, granting letters testamentary, and of administration.

(b) Notwithstanding subsection (a) of this Code section, the writ of certiorari shall not lie in civil cases in the probate courts which are provided for by Article 6 of Chapter 9 of Title 15.

Laws 1986, p. 982, § 3.

Formerly Code 1863, § 3957; Code 1868, § 3977; Code 1873, § 4049; Code 1882, § 4049; Civil Code 1895, § 4634; Civil Code 1910, § 5180; Code 1933, § 19-101.

§ 5-4-2. To probate courts; petition

When either party in any case in any probate court lodges objections to any proceeding or decision in the case, affecting the real merits of the case, the party making the same shall offer the objections in writing, which shall be signed by himself or his attorney and, if the same are overruled by the court, the party may petition the superior court for a writ of certiorari, in which petition he shall plainly, fully, and distinctly set forth the errors complained of. If the court deems the objections to be sufficient, it shall forthwith issue a writ of certiorari, directed to the judge of the probate court, requiring him to certify and send up to the superior court, at the time specified in the writ, all the proceedings in the case.

Laws 1799, Cobb's 1851 Digest, p. 523.

Formerly Code 1863, § 3958; Code 1868, § 3978; Code 1873, § 4050; Code 1882, § 4050; Civil Code 1895, § 4635; Civil Code 1910, § 5181; Code 1933, § 19-201.

§ 5-4-3. To inferior judicatories; petition

When either party in any case in any inferior judicatory or before any person exercising judicial powers is dissatisfied with the decision or judgment in the case, the party may apply for and obtain a writ of certiorari by petition to the superior court for the county in which the case was tried, in which petition he shall plainly and distinctly set forth the errors complained of. On the filing of the petition in the office of the clerk of the superior court, with the sanction of the appropriate judge endorsed thereon, together with the bond or affidavit, as provided in Code Section 5-4-5, it shall be the duty of the clerk to issue a writ of certiorari, directed to the tribunal or person whose decision or judgment is the subject matter of complaint, requiring the tribunal or person to certify and send up all the proceedings in the case to the superior court, as directed in the writ of certiorari.

Laws 1850, Cobb's 1851 Digest, p. 529; Laws 1878-79, p. 153, § 7.

Formerly Code 1863, § 3960; Code 1868, § 3980; Code 1873, § 4052; Code 1882, § 4052; Civil Code 1895, § 4637; Civil Code 1910, § 5183; Code 1933, § 19-203.

§ 5-4-4. Repealed by Laws 1983, p. 884, § 4-2, eff. July 1, 1983

§ 5-4-5. Bond and security to be given

(a) Before any writ of certiorari shall issue, except as provided in subsection (c) of this Code section, the party applying for the same, his agent, or his attorney shall give bond and good security, conditioned to pay the adverse party in the case the sums sought as an award to be recovered, together with all future costs, and shall also produce a certificate from the officer whose decision or judgment is the subject matter of complaint that all costs which may have accrued on the trial below have been paid. The bond and certificate shall be filed with the petition for certiorari, and security on the bond shall be liable as securities on appeal.

(b) The person authorized to receive bond and security may compel the security tendered to swear upon oath the means by which he can fulfill the bond obligation. Such action shall exonerate from liability the person receiving the bond and security.

(c) If the party applying for the writ of certiorari makes and files with his petition a written affidavit that he is advised and believes that he has good cause for certiorari to the superior court and that because of his indigence he is unable to pay the costs or give security, as the case may be, the affidavit shall in every respect answer instead of the certificate and bond above-mentioned.

Laws 1811, Cobb's 1851 Digest, pp. 523, 524; Laws 1897, p. 33, § 1.

Formerly Code 1863, §§ 3962, 3963, 3964; Code 1868, §§ 3982, 3983, 3984; Code 1873, §§ 4054, 4055, 4056; Code 1882, §§ 4054, 4055, 4056; Civil Code 1895, §§ 4639, 4640, 4641; Civil Code 1910, §§ 5185, 5186, 5187; Code 1933, §§ 19-206, 19-207, 19-208.

§ 5-4-6. Must be applied for in 30 days; filing and service

(a) All writs of certiorari shall be applied for within 30 days after the final determination of the case in which the error is alleged to have been committed. Applications made after 30 days are not timely and shall be dismissed by the court.

(b) The certiorari petition and writ shall be filed in the clerk's office within a reasonable time after sanction by the superior court judge; and a copy shall be served on the respondent, within five days after such filing, by the sheriff or his deputy or by the petitioner or his attorney. A copy of the petition and writ shall also be served on the opposite party or his counsel or other legal representative, in person or by mail; and service shall be shown by acknowledgment or by certificate of the counsel or person perfecting the service.

Laws 1838, Cobb's 1851 Digest, p. 528; Laws 1850, Cobb's 1851 Digest, p. 529; Laws 1855-56, p. 233, § 16; Laws 1858, p. 88, § 1; Laws 1889, p. 84, § 1; Laws 1924, p. 59, §§ 1, 2; Laws 1961, p. 190, §§ 2, 3.

Formerly Code 1863, §§ 2861, 3965; Code 1868, §§ 2869, 3985; Code 1873, §§ 2920, 4057; Code 1882, §§ 2920, 4057; Civil Code 1895, §§ 3771, 4642; Civil Code 1910, §§ 4365, 5188; Code 1933, §§ 19-209, 19-210.

§ 5-4-7. Filing of answer; delivery of copy to petitioner

The answer to the writ of certiorari shall be filed in the clerk's office within 30 days after service thereof on the respondent unless further time is granted by the superior court. A copy of the answer shall be mailed or delivered to the petitioner by the respondent or by the clerk of the superior court. Failure to perfect service shall be grounds for continuance but shall not otherwise affect the validity of the proceedings.

Laws 1918, p. 124, §§ 1, 2; Laws 1961, p. 190, § 5.

Formerly Code 1863, § 3969; Code 1868, § 3989; Code 1873, § 4061; Code 1882, § 4061; Civil Code 1895, § 4646; Civil Code 1910, § 5195; Code 1933, § 19-301.

§ 5-4-8. Must not be written by party interested; verification

The answer shall not be written or dictated by either of the parties, or their attorneys, or any other person interested in the merits of the case. If made after the party making the same has retired from office, it shall be verified by affidavit.

Formerly Code 1863, § 3971; Code 1868, § 3991; Code 1873, § 4063; Code 1882, § 4063; Civil Code 1895, § 4648; Civil Code 1910, § 5197; Code 1933, § 19-303.

§ 5-4-9. Exceptions or traverse to answer

The petitioner or defendant in certiorari may traverse or except to the answer of the respondent, which exceptions or traverse shall be filed in writing, specifying the defects, within 15 days after the filing of the answer; and, if the traverse or exceptions are sustained, the answer shall be perfected as directed by the court.

Laws 1961, p. 190, § 6.

Formerly Code 1863, § 3970; Code 1868, § 3990; Code 1873, § 4062; Code 1882, § 4062; Civil Code 1895, § 4647; Civil Code 1910, § 5196; Code 1933, § 19-302.

§ 5-4-10. Amendability of certiorari proceedings

Certiorari proceedings shall be amendable at any stage, as to matters of form or substance, as to the petition, bond, answer, and traverse; and a valid bond may by amendment be substituted for a void bond or no bond at all.

Laws 1961, p. 190, § 9.

Formerly Code 1933, § 19-403.

§ 5-4-11. Hearing on writ; notice to opposite party; jury trial on demand

(a) Certiorari cases shall be heard by the court without a jury, in chambers or in open court, upon reasonable notice to the parties, at any time that the matters may be ready for hearing.

(b) Where a traverse to the answer has been filed and jury trial demanded, the matter may be tried at any time a jury is available therefor.

Laws 1961, p. 190, § 7.

Formerly Code 1863, § 3972; Code 1868, § 3992; Code 1873, § 4064; Code 1882, § 4064; Civil Code 1895, § 4649; Civil Code 1910, § 5198; Code 1933, § 19-401.

§ 5-4-12. Errors considered; scope of review; technical distinctions abolished

(a) No ground of error shall be considered which is not distinctly set forth in the petition.

(b) The scope of review shall be limited to all errors of law and determination as to whether the judgment or ruling below was sustained by substantial evidence.

(c) All technical distinctions as to what questions will be considered, such as questions concerning judgments absolutely void or assignments of error drawing in question the legal constitution or jurisdiction of the tribunal below, are abolished.

Laws 1961, p. 190, § 8.

Formerly Code 1863, § 3973; Code 1868, § 3993; Code 1873, § 4065; Code 1882, § 4065; Civil Code 1895, § 4650; Civil Code 1910, § 5199; Code 1933, § 19-402.

§ 5-4-13. Certiorari on ground that venue and time not proved

No judge of a superior court shall grant a writ of certiorari or sustain the writ in a criminal or quasi-criminal case on the ground that the venue was not proved in the trial court or that the time of the commission of the offense was not proved, unless there is a distinct allegation in the petition for the writ of failure to prove the venue or time and an allegation of error as to such matters.

Laws 1911, p. 149, § 1.

Formerly Code 1933, § 19-404.

§ 5-4-14. Certiorari may be dismissed or returned

(a) Upon the hearing of a writ of certiorari, the superior court may order the same to be dismissed or may return the same to the court from which it came with instructions.

(b) In all cases when the error complained of is an error in law which must finally govern the case, and the court is satisfied that there is no question of fact involved which makes it necessary to send the case back for a new hearing before the tribunal below, it shall be the duty of the judge of the superior court to make a final decision in the case without sending it back to the tribunal below.

Laws 1850, Cobb's 1851 Digest, p. 529.

Formerly Code 1863, § 3975; Code 1868, § 3995; Code 1873, § 4067; Code 1882, § 4067; Civil Code 1895, § 4652; Civil Code 1910, § 5201; Code 1933, § 19-501.

§ 5-4-15. New trial ordered, when

In all cases pending in the superior courts upon certiorari from any inferior judicatory or any person exercising judicial powers, if the judge or other officer before whom the case was tried dies before answering the writ of certiorari or answers that he cannot or does not remember or recollect what occurred at the trial of the case and he therefore cannot or does not make answer to the same, it shall be the duty of the judge who granted the writ of certiorari forthwith to order a new trial of the case in the court below.

Laws 1861, p. 63, § 1; Laws 1899, p. 38, § 1; Laws 1933, p. 113, § 1.

Formerly Code 1868, § 3996; Code 1873, § 4068; Code 1882, § 4068; Civil Code 1895, § 4653; Civil Code 1910, § 5202; Code 1933, § 19-502.

§ 5-4-16. If certiorari is sustained, judgment for plaintiff

If after the hearing the certiorari is sustained and a final decision thereon is made by the superior court, the plaintiff may have judgment entered for the amount recovered by him in the court below, the costs paid to obtain the certiorari, and the costs in the superior court. If the certiorari is returned to the court below for a new hearing, the plaintiff shall have judgment entered for the costs in the superior court only, leaving the costs paid to obtain the certiorari to be awarded upon the final trial below.

Formerly Code 1863, § 3977; Code 1868, § 3998; Code 1873, § 4070; Code 1882, § 4070; Civil Code 1895, § 4655; Civil Code 1910, § 5204; Code 1933, § 19-504.

§ 5-4-17. If certiorari is dismissed, judgment for defendant

If the certiorari is dismissed and a final decision is made in the case by the superior court, the defendant in certiorari may have judgment entered in the superior court against the plaintiff and his security for the sum recovered by him, together with the costs in the superior court; and if the case is sent back to the court below, and there is a judgment in the case in favor of the defendant in the court below the security on the certiorari bond shall then be included as in case of security on appeal.

Formerly Code 1863, § 3978; Code 1868, § 3999; Code 1873, § 4071; Code 1882, § 4071; Civil Code 1895, § 4656; Civil Code 1910, § 5205; Code 1933, § 19-505.

§ 5-4-18. Damage may be awarded where certiorari frivolous or for delay

If it shall be made to appear that a certiorari was frivolous and was applied for without good cause or only for the purpose of delay, the presiding judge before whom the writ was heard, on motion of the opposite party, may order that damages totaling not more than 20 percent of the sum adjudged to be due be recovered by the defendant in certiorari against the plaintiff in certiorari and his security; and judgment may be entered and execution issued accordingly.

Laws 1857, p. 104, § 2.

Formerly Code 1863, § 3976; Code 1868, § 3997; Code 1873, § 4069; Code 1882, § 4069; Civil Code 1895, § 4654; Civil Code 1910, § 5203; Code 1933, § 19-503.

§ 5-4-19. Supersedeas in civil cases

The writ of certiorari, when granted in civil cases, shall operate as a supersedeas of the judgment until the final hearing in the superior court.

Laws 1850, Cobb's 1851 Digest, p. 529.

Formerly Code 1863, § 3968; Code 1868, § 3988; Code 1873, § 4060; Code 1882, § 4060; Civil Code 1895, § 4645; Civil Code 1910, § 5191; Code 1933, § 19-213.

§ 5-4-20. Supersedeas in criminal cases; pauper affidavit; effect of supersedeas

(a) Any person who has been convicted of any criminal or quasi-criminal offense or violation of any ordinance, in any inferior judicatory by whatever name called, except constitutional city courts or state courts, exercising criminal or quasi-criminal jurisdiction, who desires a writ of certiorari to review and correct the judgment of conviction in the case shall be entitled to a supersedeas of the judgment if he files with the clerk of the court, or, if there is no clerk, with the judge thereof, or with the commissioners if it is a court presided over by commissioners with no clerk, a bond payable to the state, or, if the conviction is in a municipal court, payable to the municipality, in amount and with security acceptable to and to be approved by the clerk, judge, or majority of the commissioners, as the case may be, conditioned that the defendant will personally appear and abide the final judgment, order, or sentence upon him in the case. The bond, if payable to the state, may be forfeited in the same manner as any other criminal bond in any court having jurisdiction. If the bond is payable to the municipal corporation, it may be forfeited according to the procedure prescribed in the municipal ordinance or charter. Alternatively, an action may be brought on the bond in any court having jurisdiction. Upon the giving of bond the defendant shall be released from custody in like manner as defendants are released upon supersedeas bonds in criminal cases where a notice of appeal has been filed.

(b) If the defendant is unable because of his indigence to give bond and makes this fact appear by affidavit to be filed with the judge, clerk, or commissioners, as the case may be, the same shall operate as a supersedeas of the judgment; provided, however, that the defendant shall not be set at liberty unless he gives bond as prescribed in subsection (a) of this Code section.

(c) The supersedeas provided for in this Code section shall operate to suspend the judgment of conviction until the case is finally heard and determined by the superior court to which it is taken by certiorari or by the Court of Appeals upon appeal, provided that within the time prescribed by law the defendant shall apply for and procure the writs and remedies provided by law for reviewing the judgment complained of. The supersedeas shall be equally applicable whether the judge of the superior court to whom the petition for certiorari is presented sanctions it or refuses it, provided that within the time provided by law the defendant diligently files a notice of appeal.

(d) The object of this Code section is to provide a method by which a defendant may obtain a supersedeas so long as he is prosecuting or is entitled under the law to prosecute the proceeding brought or to be brought to review the conviction of which he is complaining, or any intermediate appellate judgment rendered thereon, in order that the defendant shall not be deprived of his right to apply to the courts by being compelled to serve his sentence or pay a fine before he has had the full opportunity allowed him by law of taking the necessary proceedings to correct and review his conviction.

Laws 1902, p. 105, § 1; Laws 1909, p. 148, §§ 1-3; Laws 1982, p. 3, § 5.

Formerly Civil Code 1910, §§ 5192, 5193, 5194; Code 1933, §§ 19-214, 19-215, 19-216.

CHAPTER 5

NEW TRIAL

Article 1

General Provisions

§ 5-5-1. Superior, state, juvenile, and probate courts and City Court of Atlanta may correct errors, etc.

(a) The superior, state, and juvenile courts and the City Court of Atlanta shall have power to correct errors and grant new trials in cases or collateral issues in any of the respective courts in such manner and under such rules as they may establish according to law and the usages and customs of courts.

(b) Probate courts shall have power to correct errors and grant new trials in civil cases provided for by Article 6 of Chapter 9 of Title 15 under such rules and procedures as apply to the superior courts.

Laws 1799, Cobb's 1851 Digest, p. 503; Laws 1986, p. 982, § 4; Laws 2000, p. 862, § 1.

Formerly Code 1863, § 3636; Code 1868, § 3661; Code 1873, § 3712; Code 1882, § 3712; Civil Code 1895, § 5474; Civil Code 1910, § 6079; Code 1933, § 70-102.

Article 2

Grounds

§ 5-5-20. Verdict contrary to evidence and principles of justice and equity

In any case when the verdict of a jury is found contrary to evidence and the principles of justice and equity, the judge presiding may grant a new trial before another jury.

Laws 1799, Cobb's 1851 Digest, p. 503.

Formerly Code 1863, § 3637; Code 1868, § 3662; Code 1873, § 3713; Code 1882, § 3713; Civil Code 1895, § 5477; Penal Code 1895, § 1057; Civil Code 1910, § 6082; Penal Code 1910, § 1084; Code 1933, § 70-202.

§ 5-5-21. Verdict against weight of evidence

The presiding judge may exercise a sound discretion in granting or refusing new trials in cases where the verdict may be decidedly and strongly against the weight of the evidence even though there may appear to be some slight evidence in favor of the finding.

Laws 1853-54, p. 46, § 3.

Formerly Code 1863, § 3641; Code 1868, § 3666; Code 1873, § 3717; Code 1882, § 3717; Civil Code 1895, § 5482; Penal Code 1895, § 1058; Civil Code 1910, § 6087; Penal Code 1910, § 1085; Code 1933, § 70-206.

§ 5-5-22. Illegal admission or exclusion of evidence

The courts may grant new trials in all cases when any material evidence may be illegally admitted to or illegally withheld from the jury over the objection of the movant.

Laws 1853-54, p. 46, § 1.

Formerly Code 1863, § 3638; Code 1868, § 3663; Code 1873, § 3714; Code 1882, § 3714; Civil Code 1895, § 5478; Penal Code 1895, § 1059; Civil Code 1910, § 6083; Penal Code 1910, § 1086; Code 1933, § 70-203.

§ 5-5-23. Newly-discovered evidence

A new trial may be granted in any case where any material evidence, not merely cumulative or impeaching in its character but relating to new and material facts, is discovered by the applicant after the rendition of a verdict against him and is brought to the notice of the court within the time allowed by law for entertaining a motion for a new trial.

Laws 1853–54, p. 46, § 1.

Formerly Code 1863, § 3640; Code 1868, § 3665; Code 1873, § 3716; Code 1882, § 3716; Civil Code 1895, §§ 5480, 5481; Penal Code 1895, § 1061; Civil Code 1910, §§ 6085, 6086; Penal Code 1910, § 1088; Code 1933, § 70–204.

§ 5–5–24. Requests to charge; time for objections; time for presentation of request; disposition of refused requests; appellate review of erroneous charges with or without objection

(a) Except as otherwise provided in this Code section, in all civil cases, no party may complain of the giving or the failure to give an instruction to the jury unless he objects thereto before the jury returns its verdict, stating distinctly the matter to which he objects and the grounds of his objection. Opportunity shall be given to make the objection out of the hearing of the jury. Objection need not be made with the particularity formerly required of assignments of error and need only be as reasonably definite as the circumstances will permit. This subsection shall not apply in criminal cases.

(b) In all cases, at the close of the evidence or at such earlier time during the trial as the court reasonably directs, any party may present to the court written requests that it instruct the jury on the law as set forth therein. Copies of requests shall be given to opposing counsel for their consideration prior to the charge of the court. The court shall inform counsel of its proposed action upon the requests prior to their arguments to the jury but shall instruct the jury after the arguments are completed. The trial judge shall file with the clerk all requests submitted to him, whether given in charge or not.

(c) Notwithstanding any other provision of this Code section, the appellate courts shall consider and review erroneous charges where there has been a substantial error in the charge which was harmful as a matter of law, regardless of whether objection was made hereunder or not.

Laws 1853–54, p. 46, § 1; Laws 1878–79, p. 150, § 1; Laws 1965, p. 18, § 17; Laws 1966, p. 493, § 6; Laws 1968, p. 1072, § 9.

Formerly Code 1863, § 3639; Code 1868, § 3664; Code 1873, § 3715; Code 1882, § 3715; Civil Code 1895, § 5479; Penal Code 1895, § 1060; Civil Code 1910, § 6084; Penal Code 1910, § 1087; Code 1933, § 70–207.

§ 5–5–25. Grant on other grounds; exercise of discretion by court

In all motions for a new trial on other grounds, not provided for in this Code, the presiding judge must exercise a sound legal discretion in granting or refusing the same according to the provisions of the common law and practice of the courts.

Formerly Code 1863, § 3642; Code 1868, § 3667; Code 1873, § 3718; Code 1882, § 3718; Civil Code 1895, § 5483; Penal Code 1895, § 1062; Civil Code 1910, § 6088; Penal Code 1910, § 1089; Code 1933, § 70–208.

Article 3

Procedure

§ 5–5–40. Time for motion for new trial; amendment; procedure where transcript of evidence required; hearing on motion; grant of new trial on motion of court

(a) All motions for new trial, except in extraordinary cases, shall be made within 30 days of the entry of the judgment on the verdict or entry of the judgment where the case was tried without a jury.

(b) The motion may be amended any time on or before the ruling thereon.

(c) Where the grounds of the motion require consideration of the transcript of evidence or proceedings, the court may in its discretion grant an extension of time, except in cases where the death penalty is imposed, for the preparation and filing of the transcript, which may be done any time on or before the hearing; or the court may in its discretion hear and determine the motion before the transcript of evidence and proceedings is prepared and filed.

(d) The grounds of the motion need not be approved by the court.

(e) The motion may be heard at any time; but, where it is not heard at the time specified in the order, it shall stand for hearing at such time as the court by order at any time may prescribe, unless sooner disposed of.

(f) Motions for new trial in cases in which the death penalty is imposed shall be given priority.

(g) On appeal, a party shall not be limited to the grounds urged in the motion or any amendment thereof.

(h) The court also shall be empowered to grant a new trial on its own motion within 30 days from entry of the judgment, except in criminal cases where the defendant was acquitted.

Laws 1889, p. 83, § 1; Laws 1965, p. 18, § 16; Laws 1973, p. 159, § 5.

Formerly Code 1863, § 3643; Code 1868, § 3668; Code 1873, § 3719; Code 1882, § 3719; Civil Code 1895, § 5484; Penal Code 1895, § 1063; Civil Code 1910, § 6089; Penal Code 1910, § 1090; Code 1933, § 70-301.

§ 5-5-41. Motion made after time expires

(a) When a motion for a new trial is made after the expiration of a 30 day period from the entry of judgment, some good reason must be shown why the motion was not made during such period, which reason shall be judged by the court. In all such cases, 20 days' notice shall be given to the opposite party.

(b) Whenever a motion for a new trial has been made within the 30 day period in any criminal case and overruled or when a motion for a new trial has not been made during such period, no motion for a new trial from the same verdict or judgment shall be made or received unless the same is an extraordinary motion or case; and only one such extraordinary motion shall be made or allowed.

(c)(1) Subject to the provisions of subsections (a) and (b) of this Code section, a person convicted of a serious violent felony as defined in Code Section 17-10-6.1 may file a written motion before the trial court that entered the judgment of conviction in his or her case, for the performance of forensic deoxyribonucleic acid (DNA) testing.

(2) The filing of the motion as provided in paragraph (1) of this subsection shall not automatically stay an execution.

(3) The motion shall be verified by the petitioner and shall show or provide the following:

(A) Evidence that potentially contains deoxyribonucleic acid (DNA) was obtained in relation to the crime and subsequent indictment, which resulted in his or her conviction;

(B) The evidence was not subjected to the requested DNA testing because the existence of the evidence was unknown to the petitioner or to the petitioner's trial attorney prior to trial or because the technology for the testing was not available at the time of trial;

(C) The identity of the perpetrator was, or should have been, a significant issue in the case;

(D) The requested DNA testing would raise a reasonable probability that the petitioner would have been acquitted if the results of DNA testing had been available at the time of conviction, in light of all the evidence in the case;

(E) A description of the evidence to be tested and, if known, its present location, its origin and the date, time, and means of its original collection;

(F) The results of any DNA or other biological evidence testing that was conducted previously by either the prosecution or the defense, if known;

(G) If known, the names, addresses, and telephone numbers of all persons or entities who are known or believed to have possession of any evidence described by subparagraphs (A) through (F) of this paragraph, and any persons or entities who have provided any of the information contained in petitioner's motion, indicating which person or entity has which items of evidence or information; and

(H) The names, addresses, and telephone numbers of all persons or entities who may testify for the petitioner and a description of the subject matter and summary of the facts to which each person or entity may testify.

(4) The petitioner shall state:

(A) That the motion is not filed for the purpose of delay; and

(B) That the issue was not raised by the petitioner or the requested DNA testing was not ordered in a prior proceeding in the courts of this state or the United States.

(5) The motion shall be served upon the district attorney and the Attorney General. The state shall file its response, if any, within 60 days of being served with the motion. The state shall be given notice and an opportunity to respond at any hearing conducted pursuant to this subsection.

(6)(A) If, after the state files its response, if any, and the court determines that the motion complies with the requirements of paragraphs (3) and (4) of this subsection, the court shall order a hearing to occur after the state has filed its response, but not more than 90 days from the date the motion was filed.

(B) The motion shall be heard by the judge who conducted the trial that resulted in the petitioner's conviction unless the presiding judge determines that the trial judge is unavailable.

(C) Upon request of either party, the court may order, in the interest of justice, that the petitioner be at the hearing on the motion. The court may receive additional memoranda of law or evidence from the parties for up to 30 days after the hearing.

(D) The petitioner and the state may present evidence by sworn and notarized affidavits or testimony; provided, however, any affidavit shall be served on the opposing party at least 15 days prior to the hearing.

(E) The purpose of the hearing shall be to allow the parties to be heard on the issue of whether the petitioner's motion complies with the requirements of paragraphs (3) and (4) of this subsection, whether upon consideration of all of the evidence there is a reasonable probability that the verdict would have been different if the results of the requested DNA testing had been available at the time of trial, and whether the requirements of paragraph (7) of this subsection have been established.

(7) The court shall grant the motion for DNA testing if it determines that the petitioner has met the requirements set forth in paragraphs (3) and (4) of this subsection and that all of the following have been established:

(A) The evidence to be tested is available and in a condition that would permit the DNA testing requested in the motion;

(B) The evidence to be tested has been subject to a chain of custody sufficient to establish that it has not been substituted, tampered with, replaced, or altered in any material respect;

(C) The evidence was not tested previously or, if tested previously, the requested DNA test would provide results that are reasonably more discriminating or probative of the identity of the perpetrator than prior test results;

(D) The motion is not made for the purpose of delay;

(E) The identity of the perpetrator of the crime was a significant issue in the case;

(F) The testing requested employs a scientific method that has reached a scientific state of verifiable certainty such that the procedure rests upon the laws of nature; and

(G) The petitioner has made a prima facie showing that the evidence sought to be tested is material to the issue of the petitioner's identity as the perpetrator of, or accomplice to, the crime, aggravating circumstance, or similar transaction that resulted in the conviction.

(8) If the court orders testing pursuant to this subsection, the court shall determine the method of testing and responsibility for payment for the cost of testing, if necessary, and may require the petitioner to pay the costs of testing if the court determines that the petitioner has the ability to pay. If the petitioner is indigent, the cost shall be paid from the fine and forfeiture fund as provided in Article 3 of Chapter 5 of Title 15.

(9) If the court orders testing pursuant to this subsection, the court shall order that the evidence be tested by the Division of Forensic Sciences of the Georgia Bureau of Investigation. In addition, the court may also authorize the testing of the evidence by a laboratory that meets the standards of the DNA advisory board established pursuant to the DNA Identification Act of 1994, Section 14131 of Title 42 of the United States Code, to conduct the testing. The court shall order that a sample of the petitioner's DNA be submitted to the Division of Forensic Sciences of the Georgia Bureau of Investigation and that the DNA analysis be stored and maintained by the bureau in the DNA data bank.

(10) If a motion is filed pursuant to this subsection the court shall order the state to preserve during the pendency of the proceeding all evidence that contains biological material, including, but not limited to, stains, fluids, or hair samples in the state's possession or control.

(11) The result of any test ordered under this subsection shall be fully disclosed to the petitioner, the district attorney, and the Attorney General.

(12) The judge shall set forth by written order the rationale for the grant or denial of the motion for new trial filed pursuant to this subsection.

(13) The petitioner or the state may appeal an order, decision, or judgment rendered pursuant to this Code section.

Laws 1873, p. 47, § 1; Laws 2003, Act 37, § 1, eff. May 27, 2003.

Formerly Code 1863, § 3645; Code 1868, § 3670; Code 1873, § 3721; Code 1882, § 3721; Civil Code 1895, § 5487; Penal Code 1895, § 1064; Civil Code 1910, § 6092; Penal Code 1910, § 1091; Code 1933, § 70-303.

§ 5-5-42. Form of motion for new trial

(a) The form for motion for new trial in civil cases prescribed in subsection (b) of this Code section shall be sufficient, but any other form substantially complying therewith shall also be sufficient.

(b) Form for motion for new trial in civil cases:

—IN THE _____ COURT OF _____ COUNTY—

—STATE OF GEORGIA—

________________	)
Plaintiff	)
	)
v.	) Civil Action
	) File no. ________
________________	)
Defendant	)
	)

—MOTION FOR NEW TRIAL—

Defendant moves the court to set aside the verdict returned herein on (date), _____, and the judgment entered thereon on (date), _____, and to grant a new trial on the following grounds:

(1) The verdict is contrary to law.

(2) The verdict is contrary to the evidence.

(3) The verdict is strongly against the weight of the evidence.

(4) The court erred in permitting witness Smith to testify as follows: _____.

(5) The court erred in failing to charge the jury on unavoidable accident as requested in writing by defendant.

(6) The court erred in charging the jury as follows: _____.

Dated: _____________.

____
Attorney for defendant

____
Address

—(Here set forth rule nisi and certificate of service.)—

(c) The form for motion for new trial in criminal cases in subsection (d) of this Code section is declared to be sufficient but any other form substantially complying therewith shall also be sufficient.

(d) Form for motion for new trial in criminal cases:

—IN THE _____ COURT OF _____ COUNTY—

—STATE OF GEORGIA—

____________________)
The State)
)
v.) Indictment
) Accusation
____________________)
Defendant) File no. _________

—MOTION FOR NEW TRIAL—

Defendant moves the court to set aside the verdict returned herein on (date), _____, and the sentence entered thereon on (date), _____, and to grant a new trial on the following grounds:

(1) The defendant should be acquitted and discharged due to the state's failure to prove guilt beyond a reasonable doubt.

(2) Although the state proved the defendant's guilt beyond a reasonable doubt, the evidence was sufficiently close to warrant the trial judge to exercise his discretion to grant the defendant a retrial.

(3) The court committed an error of law warranting a new trial.

Dated: _____________.

____
Attorney for defendant

____
Address

—(Here set forth rule nisi and certificate of service.)—

Laws 1965, p. 18, § 20; Laws 1983, p. 702, § 1; Laws 1984, p. 22, § 5; Laws 1999, p. 81, § 5.

§ 5-5-43. Grant by judge who did not try case

A judge who did not try the case may, if presented with a motion for new trial within 30 days from the date of the verdict or judgment sought to be set aside, allow the filing of, issue rule nisi thereon, and decide the motion either where he is presiding in the court in which the trial was had, or where he is named in the rule, or where he is otherwise authorized by law to do so.

Laws 1957, p. 224, § 13.

Formerly Code 1863, § 3644; Code 1868, § 3669; Code 1873, § 3720; Code 1882, § 3720; Civil Code 1895, § 5486; Civil Code 1910, § 6091; Code 1933, § 70-103.

§ 5-5-44. Rules nisi, service. Entry of motion on minutes of court

In all motions for a new trial the opposite party shall be served with a copy of the rule nisi unless such copy is waived. The clerks of the courts shall not be required, except by order of the presiding judge, to enter upon the minutes of the courts motions for new trial in cases tried therein; but the motions shall be filed in the clerk's office as are other papers and shall be recorded together with the other pleadings in the cases when the same are finally disposed of as required by law.

Laws 1878-79, p. 138, § 1.

Formerly Code 1863, § 3648; Code 1868, § 3673; Code 1873, § 3723; Code 1882, § 3723; Civil Code 1895, § 5475; Penal Code 1895, § 1065; Civil Code 1910, § 6080; Penal Code 1910, § 1092; Code 1933, § 70-306.

§ 5-5-45. Amendment of rule nisi

A rule nisi for a new trial may be amended by adding new grounds not taken at the time the motion was filed.

Formerly Code 1863, § 3432; Code 1868, § 3452; Code 1873, § 3503; Code 1882, § 3503; Civil Code 1895, § 5121; Civil Code 1910, § 5705; Code 1933, § 70-309.

§ 5-5-46. Rule nisi for new trial as supersedeas in criminal cases

(a) The rule nisi on a motion for a new trial in a criminal case shall not operate as a supersedeas unless it is so ordered by the court.

(b) When requested to do so by the defendant or his counsel, the judge trying the case shall grant an order superseding the sentence until the motion for a new trial is heard and decided.

Laws 1899, p. 77, § 1.

Formerly Code 1863, § 3649; Code 1868, § 3674; Code 1873, § 3724; Code 1882, § 3724; Penal Code 1895, § 1066; Penal Code 1910, § 1093; Code 1933, § 70-308.

§ 5-5-47. Supersedeas in criminal cases when motion for new trial filed; judge to assess amount of bond

(a) It shall be the right of any person convicted of a crime which is bailable under the law, and in which case a motion for a new trial has been filed as provided by law, to give a supersedeas bond immediately upon the filing of the motion for new trial without having to wait for the filing of a notice of appeal.

(b) The judge of the court having jurisdiction of the case, immediately upon the approval and filing of a motion for new trial therein, shall assess the amount of the bond, which shall be approved in the manner provided by law.

(c) The provisions of Code Section 5-6-45, relating to supersedeas and supersedeas bonds when a notice of appeal is filed, shall apply equally to cases when a motion for a new trial is filed.

Laws 1916, p. 157, §§ 1, 2; Laws 1984, p. 415, § 1.

Formerly Code 1933, §§ 6-1006, 6-1007.

§ 5-5-48. Time of new trial

When a new trial has been granted by the court, the case shall be placed on the docket for trial as though no trial had been had, subject to the rules for continuances provided in this Code.

Formerly Code 1863, § 3646; Code 1868, § 3671; Code 1873, § 3722; Code 1882, § 3722; Civil Code 1895, § 5489; Civil Code 1910, § 6094; Code 1933, § 70-401.

§ 5-5-49. Cases decided by Supreme Court or Court of Appeals returned, when; cases to be redocketed; discretion of judge as to retrial

(a) A case decided by the Supreme Court or Court of Appeals which is not finally disposed of by the decision shall stand for further hearing at the term next ensuing after the decision by the appellate court unless the lower court is in session when the decision is made, in which event it shall stand for trial during such term of the lower court.

(b) The clerk of the lower court, upon receipt of the remittitur of the appellate court, shall docket the case for trial in accordance with subsection (a) of this Code section.

(c) The judge presiding may in his discretion postpone the hearing of any such case to a day in the term as to him may seem reasonable; or, if necessary to give proper time for preparation, he may continue the case until the next term of the court.

Laws 1892, p. 103, §§ 1-3.

Formerly Civil Code 1895, §§ 5490, 5491, 5492; Civil Code 1910, §§ 6095, 6096, 6097; Code 1933, §§ 70-402, 70-403, 70-404.

§ 5-5-50. First grant of a new trial; disturbance

The first grant of a new trial shall not be disturbed by an appellate court unless the appellant shows that the judge abused his discretion in granting it and that the law and facts require the verdict notwithstanding the judgment of the presiding judge.

Formerly Civil Code 1895, § 5585; Civil Code 1910, § 6204; Code 1933, § 6-1608.

§ 5-5-51. When new trial based on exercise of judge's discretion, order to set forth reasons for exercise of such discretion

In all civil cases in which a new trial is granted, if the grant of a new trial is based on the discretion of the judge, the judge shall set forth by written order the reason or reasons for the exercise of his discretion. Such order shall not be required to conform to the provisions of Code Section 9-11-52, relating to findings by the court.

Laws 1985, p. 1312, § 1.

CHAPTER 6

CERTIORARI AND APPEALS TO APPELLATE COURTS GENERALLY

Article 1

General Provisions

§ 5-6-1. Third parties in interest to be heard

When a case is set for a hearing before the Supreme Court or the Court of Appeals and there are parties besides the plaintiffs and defendants, whether shown by the record or not, who have a direct interest in its result, upon the interest being made to appear the court shall allow the other parties to appear by counsel on equal terms with the parties directly before the court.

Laws 1870, p. 47, § 5.

Formerly Code 1873, § 4275; Code 1882, § 4275; Civil Code 1895, § 5581; Civil Code 1910, § 6196; Code 1933, § 6-1506.

§ 5-6-2. Transcripts not to be recorded

The transcript of the record shall not be recorded by the clerk of the appellate court but shall be carefully labeled and filed so as to be found easily when needed.

Laws 1847, Cobb's 1851 Digest, p. 454.

Formerly Code 1863, § 4185; Code 1868, § 4224; Code 1873, § 4289; Code 1882, § 4289; Civil Code 1895, § 5590; Civil Code 1910, § 6209; Code 1933, § 6-1701.

§ 5-6-3. Briefs where cases cannot be disposed of during term; cases deemed heard, when; additional argument; dismissal of case on noncompliance with order

(a) Whenever the appellate court may be unable to dispose of all cases on its docket for any term before the time fixed by law for the succeeding term to begin, the court may pass an order requiring counsel in all such cases to file their briefs in the clerk's office of the court on or before a certain day prior to the succeeding term. All cases in which briefs are thus filed shall be considered as heard at the term of the court to which returned. They shall be determined and the decision therein shall be announced by the court as soon after the briefs are filed as may be practicable. Should the court desire to hear argument in addition to that submitted in the briefs, the court may pass an order requiring counsel to submit further argument by brief or in open court at such time as may be prescribed in the order.

(b) Upon failure of counsel for the appellant to comply with the order of the court, where no sufficient excuse is shown for noncompliance, the case shall be dismissed for want of prosecution.

Laws 1878-79, p. 151, §§ 1-4.

Formerly Civil Code 1910, §§ 6198, 6199, 6200, 6201; Code 1933, §§ 6-1602, 6-1603, 6-1604, 6-1605.

§ 5-6-4. Amount of costs; payment; affidavit of indigence; reception of brief in absence of payment

The bill of costs for every application to the Supreme Court for a writ of certiorari or for applications for appeals filed in the Supreme Court or the Court of Appeals or appeals to the Supreme Court or the Court of Appeals shall be $80.00. The costs shall be paid by counsel for the applicant or appellant at the time of the filing of the application or, in the case of direct appeals, at the time of the filing of the original brief of the appellant. In those cases in which the writ of certiorari or an application for appeal is granted, there shall be no additional costs. Costs shall not be required in those instances when at the time the same are due counsel for the applicant or appellant shall file a statement that an affidavit of indigence has been duly filed or file an affidavit that he or she was appointed to represent the defendant by the trial court because of the defendant's indigency. The clerk is prohibited from receiving the application for appeal or the brief of the appellant unless the costs have been paid or a sufficient affidavit of indigence is filed or contained in the record.

Laws 1921, p. 239, § 1; Laws 1965, p. 650, § 1; Laws 1982, p. 1186, § 1; Laws 1991, p. 411, § 1.

Formerly Code 1933, § 6-1702.

§ 5-6-5. Judgment for costs on reversal

If there is a judgment of reversal, the appellant shall be entitled to a judgment for the amount of the costs in the appellate court against the appellee as soon as the remittitur is returned to the court below.

Laws 1845, Cobb's 1851 Digest, p. 251.

Formerly Code 1863, § 4186; Code 1868, § 4225; Code 1873, § 4290; Code 1882, § 4290; Civil Code 1895, § 5591; Civil Code 1910, § 6210; Code 1933, § 6-1704.

§ 5-6-6. Damages in cases of appeal taken for delay

When in the opinion of the court the case was taken up for delay only, 10 percent damages may be awarded by the appellate court upon any judgment for a sum certain which has been affirmed. The award shall be entered in the remittitur.

Laws 1845, Cobb's 1851 Digest, p. 450.

Formerly Code 1863, § 4182; Code 1868, § 4221; Code 1873, § 4286; Code 1882, § 4286; Civil Code 1895, § 5594; Civil Code 1910, § 6213; Code 1933, § 6-1801.

§ 5-6-7. Mode of announcing decisions. Publication

No decision shall be rendered ore tenus. The reporter shall publish in the official reports of the Supreme Court and the Court of Appeals all judgments, but only those opinions which the courts shall direct to be published.

Laws 1866, p. 46, § 5; Laws 1966, p. 493, § 9.

Formerly Code 1868, § 4210; Code 1873, § 4270; Code 1882, § 4270; Civil Code 1895, § 5583; Civil Code 1910, § 6202; Code 1933, § 6-1606.

§ 5-6-8. Decision entered on minutes. Directions to court below

The decision in each case shall be entered on the minutes. It shall be within the power of the appellate court rendering the decision in a case to make such order and to give such direction as to the final disposition of the case by the lower court as may be consistent with the law and justice of the case.

Formerly Code 1863, § 4180; Code 1868, § 4219; Code 1873, § 4284; Code 1882, § 4284; Civil Code 1895, § 5586; Penal Code 1895, § 1068; Civil Code 1910, § 6205; Penal Code 1910, § 1095; Code 1933, § 6-1610.

§ 5-6-9. When opinion is to be transmitted to court below

(a) Where a further hearing of the case is to follow in the lower court, the clerk of the appellate court shall transmit a copy of the opinion to the clerk of the lower court, without charge, as soon as the opinion is written out. The copy shall remain on file for the information of the court and the parties.

(b) The appellate court, on rendering its decision in any case, shall instruct the clerk whether the case comes within the terms of this Code section; and a note of such instructions shall be entered on the minutes of the court.

Laws 1887, p. 106, §§ 1, 2; Laws 1982, p. 3, § 5.

Formerly Civil Code 1895, §§ 5595, 5596; Civil Code 1910, §§ 6214, 6215; Code 1933, §§ 6-1802, 6-1803.

§ 5-6-10. Remittitur

The decision of the appellate court and any direction awarded in the case shall be certified by the clerk to the court below, under the seal of the court. The decision and direction shall be respected and carried into full effect in good faith by the court below. The remittitur shall contain nothing more, except the costs paid in the appellate court.

Laws 1845, Cobb's 1851 Digest, p. 450; Laws 1850, Cobb's 1851 Digest, p. 455.

Formerly Code 1863, § 4181; Code 1868, § 4220; Code 1873, § 4285; Code 1882, § 4285; Civil Code 1895, § 5597; Civil Code 1910, § 6216; Code 1933, § 6-1804.

§ 5-6-11. Remittitur in death sentence cases

In all cases where the Supreme Court of Georgia has affirmed the imposition of the death penalty in a case or has affirmed the denial of a petition for a writ of habeas corpus in any case in which the death penalty has been imposed, the remittitur shall not issue from that court for at least 90 days from the date of the court's decision, or from the date of the court's denial of a motion for a rehearing, if such motion is timely filed, whichever is later; provided, however, that this Code section shall not apply where the defendant has previously applied for a writ of habeas corpus which has been denied and the denial thereof has been affirmed by the Supreme Court of Georgia, or where the writ has been granted but the grant thereof has been reversed by the Supreme Court of Georgia.

Laws 1970, p. 691, § 1; Laws 1971, p. 212, § 1.

§ 5-6-12. Judgment affirmed, execution at once

If the judgment of the lower court is affirmed, upon the filing of the remittitur with the clerk of the court below, the supersedeas shall cease and execution shall issue at once for the amount of the original judgment.

Formerly Code 1863, § 4183; Code 1868, § 4222; Code 1873, § 4287; Code 1882, § 4287; Civil Code 1895, § 5598; Civil Code 1910, § 6217; Code 1933, § 6-1805.

§ 5-6-13. Contempt proceedings

(a) A judge of any trial court or tribunal having the power to adjudge and punish for contempt shall grant to any person convicted of or adjudged to be in contempt of court a supersedeas upon application and compliance with the provisions of law as to appeal and certiorari, where the person also submits, within the time prescribed by law, written notice that he intends to seek review of the conviction or adjudication of contempt. It shall not be in the discretion of any trial court judge to grant or refuse a supersedeas in cases of contempt.

(b) This Code section shall not apply to contempt in the presence of the court during the progress of a proceeding.

Laws 1939, p. 260, § 1.

§ 5–6–14. Extraordinary orders enforced by lower court, when

When judgments are rendered in the Supreme Court in injunction or other extraordinary cases, the judges of the superior courts may give immediate effect to such judgments.

Laws 1870, p. 405, § 5.

Formerly Code 1873, § 3215; Code 1882, § 3215; Civil Code 1895, § 5599; Civil Code 1910, § 6218; Code 1933, § 6–1806.

§ 5–6–15. When writ of certiorari will lie

The writ of certiorari shall lie from the Supreme Court to the Court of Appeals as provided by Article VI, Section VI, Paragraph V of the Constitution of this state.

Laws 1983, p. 3, § 47.

Formerly Code 1863, § 3957; Code 1868, § 3977; Code 1873, § 4049; Code 1882, § 4049; Civil Code 1895, § 4634; Civil Code 1910, § 5180; Code 1933, § 19–101.

§ 5–6–16. Death of party before appeal is entered; judgment where no appeal is entered; revival of suit by appeal; trial on appeal; administrator de bonis non may be made party

(a) When either the plaintiff or the defendant dies after a case has been tried and before the expiration of the time within which the party, if living, might have entered an appeal, and no appeal has been entered, the legal representative of the deceased party may enter an appeal within 30 days from the time he qualifies. If an appeal is not entered within the time prescribed in this Code section, judgment may be entered and execution issued as though the deceased party were alive, without making the representative a party.

(b) When an appeal is entered as provided in subsection (a) of this Code section, it shall not be necessary to revive the action, but it shall be revived by the appealing party giving notice to the adverse party within 30 days from the time of entering the appeal. When a defendant appeals, the case shall stand for trial on the appeal docket at the first term of the court after the expiration of six months from the qualification of the executor or administrator.

(c) In case of the death or removal from office of any executor or administrator pending such proceedings as are prescribed in subsections (a) and (b) of this Code section, an administrator de bonis non may be made a party in like manner.

Laws 1843, Cobb's 1851 Digest, pp. 474, 502.

Formerly Code 1863, §§ 3358, 3359, 3361; Code 1868, §§ 3377, 3378, 3380; Code 1873, §§ 3425, 3426, 3428; Code 1882, §§ 3425, 3426, 3428; Civil Code 1895, §§ 5023, 5024, 5026; Civil Code 1910, §§ 5605, 5606, 5608; Code 1933, §§ 3–408, 3–409, 3–411.

Article 2

Appellate Practice

§ 5–6–30. Intent; liberal construction

It is the intention of this article to provide a procedure for taking cases to the Supreme Court and the Court of Appeals, as authorized in Article VI, Sections V and VI of the Constitution of this state; to that end, this article shall be liberally construed so as to bring about a decision on the merits of every case appealed and to avoid dismissal of any case or refusal to consider any points raised therein, except as may be specifically referred to in this article.

Laws 1965, p. 18, § 23; Laws 1983, p. 3, § 47.

§ 5–6–31. "Entry of judgment" defined

The filing with the clerk of a judgment, signed by the judge, constitutes the entry of a judgment within the meaning of this article.

Laws 1965, p. 18, § 18B.

§ 5–6–32. Service of notice of appeal and motions

(a) Whenever under this article service or the giving of any notice is required or permitted to be made upon a party and the party is represented by an attorney, the service shall be made upon the attorney unless service upon the party himself is ordered by the court. Service of all notices and other papers hereunder and service of motions for new trial, motions in arrest, motions for judgment notwithstanding the verdict, and all other similar motions, orders, and proceedings may be made by the attorney or party filing the notice or paper, in person or by mail, and proof thereof shown by acknowledgment of the attorney or party served, or by certificate of the attorney, party, or other person perfecting service. Service of any paper, motion, or notice may be perfected either before or after filing with the clerk thereof; and when service is made by mail it shall be deemed to be perfected as of the day deposited in the mail. Where the address of any party is unknown and the party is not represented by an attorney of record, service of all notices and other papers referred to above may be perfected on the party by mail directed to the last known address of the party.

(b) Service of any notice, motion, or other paper provided for in this article may be waived or acknowledged either before or after filing.

Laws 1965, p. 18, § 18; Laws 1966, p. 493, § 7; Laws 1968, p. 1072, § 5.

§ 5-6-33. General right of appeal

(a)(1) Either party in any civil case and the defendant in any criminal proceeding in the superior, state, or city courts may appeal from any sentence, judgment, decision, or decree of the court, or of the judge thereof in any matter heard at chambers.

(2) Either party in any civil case in the probate courts provided for by Article 6 of Chapter 9 of Title 15 may appeal from any judgment, decision, or decree of the court, or of the judge thereof in any matter heard at chambers.

(b) This Code section shall not affect Chapter 7 of this title.

Laws 1880-81, p. 123, § 1; Laws 1887, p. 41, § 1; Laws 1965, p. 18, § 22; Laws 1986, p. 982, § 5.

Formerly Code 1863, § 4160; Code 1868, § 4192; Code 1873, § 4251; Code 1882, § 4251; Civil Code 1895, § 5527; Penal Code 1895, § 1070; Civil Code 1910, § 6139; Penal Code 1910, § 1097; Code 1933, § 6-901.

§ 5-6-34. Appeals from lower courts; finality of judgments; effect of appeal

(a) Appeals may be taken to the Supreme Court and the Court of Appeals from the following judgments and rulings of the superior courts, the constitutional city courts, and such other courts or tribunals from which appeals are authorized by the Constitution and laws of this state:

(1) All final judgments, that is to say, where the case is no longer pending in the court below, except as provided in Code Section 5-6-35;

(2) All judgments involving applications for discharge in bail trover and contempt cases;

(3) All judgments or orders directing that an accounting be had;

(4) All judgments or orders granting or refusing applications for receivers or for interlocutory or final injunctions;

(5) All judgments or orders granting or refusing applications for attachment against fraudulent debtors;

(6) Any ruling on a motion which would be dispositive if granted with respect to a defense that the action is barred by Code Section 16-11-184;

(7) All judgments or orders granting or refusing to grant mandamus or any other extraordinary remedy, except with respect to temporary restraining orders;

(8) All judgments or orders refusing applications for dissolution of corporations created by the superior courts;

(9) All judgments or orders sustaining motions to dismiss a caveat to the probate of a will; and

(10) All judgments or orders entered pursuant to subsection (c) of Code Section 17-10-6.2.

(b) Where the trial judge in rendering an order, decision, or judgment, not otherwise subject to direct appeal, including but not limited to the denial of a defendant's motion to recuse in a criminal case, certifies within ten days of entry thereof that the order, decision, or judgment is of such importance to the case that immediate review should be had, the Supreme Court or the Court of Appeals may thereupon, in their respective discretions, permit an appeal to be taken from the order, decision, or judgment if application is made thereto within ten days after such certificate is granted. The application shall be in the nature of a petition and shall set forth the need for such an appeal and the issue or issues involved therein. The applicant may, at his or her election, include copies of such parts of the record as he or she deems appropriate, but no certification of such copies by the clerk of the trial court shall be necessary. The application shall be filed with the clerk of the Supreme Court or the Court of Appeals and a copy of the application, together with a list of those parts of the record included with the application, shall be served upon the opposing party or parties in the case in the manner prescribed by Code Section 5-6-32, except that such service shall be perfected at or before the filing of the application. The opposing party or parties shall have ten days from the date on which the application is filed in which to file a response. The response may be accompanied by copies of the record in the same manner as is allowed with the application. The Supreme Court or the Court of Appeals shall issue an order granting or denying such an appeal within 45 days of the date on which the application was filed. Within ten days after an order is issued granting the appeal, the applicant, to secure a review of the issues, may file a notice of appeal as provided in Code Section 5-6-37. The notice of appeal shall act as a supersedeas as provided in Code Section 5-6-46 and the procedure thereafter shall be the same as in an appeal from a final judgment.

(c) In criminal cases involving a capital offense for which the death penalty is sought, a hearing shall be held as provided in Code Section 17-10-35.2 to determine if there shall be a review of pretrial proceedings by the Supreme Court prior to a trial before a jury. Review of pretrial proceedings, if ordered by the trial court, shall be exclusively as provided by Code Section 17-10-35.1 and no certificate of immediate review shall be necessary.

(d) Where an appeal is taken under any provision of subsection (a), (b), or (c) of this Code section, all judgments, rulings, or orders rendered in the case which are raised on appeal and which may affect the proceedings below shall be reviewed and determined by the appellate court, without regard to the appealability of the judgment, ruling, or order standing alone and without regard to whether the judgment, ruling, or order appealed from was final or was appealable by some other express provision of law contained in this Code section, or elsewhere. For purposes of review by the appellate court, one or more judgments, rulings, or orders by the trial court held to be erroneous on appeal shall not be deemed to have rendered all subsequent proceedings nugatory; but the appellate court shall in all cases review all judgments, rulings, or orders raised on appeal which may affect the proceedings below and which were rendered subsequent to the first judgment, ruling, or order held erroneous. Nothing in this subsection shall require the appellate court to pass upon questions which are rendered moot.

Laws 1890-91, p. 82, § 1; Laws 1965, p. 18, § 1; Laws 1968, p. 1072, § 1; Laws 1975, p. 757, § 1; Laws 1979, p. 619, §§ 1, 2; Laws 1984, p. 599, § 1; Laws 1988, p. 1437, § 1; Laws 1994, p. 347, § 1; Laws 2001, p. 88, § 1; Laws 2005, Act 8, § 2, eff. July 1, 2005; Laws 2005, Act 52, § 2, eff. Jan. 1, 2007; Laws 2006, Act 571, § 2, eff. July 1, 2006; Laws 2006, Act 650, § 1, eff. Jan. 1, 2007.

Formerly Code 1863, § 4159; Code 1868, § 4191; Code 1873, § 4250; Code 1882, § 4250; Civil Code 1895, § 5526; Penal Code 1895, § 1069; Civil Code 1910, § 6138; Penal Code 1910, § 1096; Code 1933, § 6-701.

§ 5-6-35. Appeals in certain specified cases

(a) Appeals in the following cases shall be taken as provided in this Code section:

(1) Appeals from decisions of the superior courts reviewing decisions of the State Board of Workers' Compensation, the State Board of Education, auditors, state and local administrative agencies, and lower courts by certiorari or de novo proceedings; provided, however, that this provision shall not apply to decisions of the Public Service Commission and probate courts and to cases involving ad valorem taxes and condemnations;

(2) Appeals from judgments or orders in divorce, alimony, child custody, and other domestic relations cases including, but not limited to, granting or refusing a divorce or temporary or permanent alimony, awarding or refusing to change child custody, or holding or declining to hold persons in contempt of such alimony or child custody judgment or orders;

(3) Appeals from cases involving distress or dispossessory warrants in which the only issue to be resolved is the amount of rent due and such amount is $ 2,500.00 or less;

(4) Appeals from cases involving garnishment or attachment, except as provided in paragraph (5) of subsection (a) of Code Section 5-6-34;

(5) Appeals from orders revoking probation;

(6) Appeals in all actions for damages in which the judgment is $ 10,000.00 or less;

(7) Appeals, when separate from an original appeal, from the denial of an extraordinary motion for new trial;

(8) Appeals from orders under subsection (d) of Code Section 9-11-60 denying a motion to set aside a judgment or under subsection (e) of Code Section 9-11-60 denying relief upon a complaint in equity to set aside a judgment;

(9) Appeals from orders granting or denying temporary restraining orders;

(10) Appeals from awards of attorney's fees or expenses of litigation under Code Section 9-15-14; and

(11) Appeals from decisions of the state courts reviewing decisions of the magistrate courts by de novo proceedings so long as the subject matter is not otherwise subject to a right of direct appeal.

(b) All appeals taken in cases specified in subsection (a) of this Code section shall be by application in the nature of a petition enumerating the errors to be urged on appeal and stating why the appellate court has jurisdiction. The application shall specify the order or judgment being appealed and, if the order or judgment is interlocutory, the application shall set forth, in addition to the enumeration of errors to be urged, the need for interlocutory appellate review.

(c) The applicant shall include as exhibits to the petition a copy of the order or judgment being appealed and should include a copy of the petition or motion which led directly to the order or judgment being appealed and a copy of any responses to the petition or motion. An applicant may include copies of such other parts of the record or transcript as he deems appropriate. No certification of such copies by the clerk of the trial court shall be necessary in conjunction with the application.

(d) The application shall be filed with the clerk of the Supreme Court or the Court of Appeals within 30 days of the entry of the order, decision, or judgment complained of and a copy of the application, together with a list of those parts of the record included with the application, shall be served upon the opposing party or parties as provided by law, except that the service shall be perfected at or before the filing of the application. When a motion for new trial, a motion in arrest of judgment, or a motion for judgment notwithstanding the verdict has been filed, the application shall be filed within 30 days after the entry of the order granting, overruling, or otherwise finally disposing of the motion.

(e) The opposing party or parties shall have ten days from the date on which the application is filed in which to file a response. The response may be accompanied by copies of the record in the same manner as is allowed with the application. The response may point out that the decision of the trial court was not error, or that the enumeration of error cannot be considered on appeal for lack of a transcript of evidence or for other reasons.

(f) The Supreme Court or the Court of Appeals shall issue an order granting or denying such an appeal within 30 days of the date on which the application was filed.

(g) Within ten days after an order is issued granting the appeal, the applicant, to secure a review of the issues, shall file a notice of appeal as provided by law. The procedure thereafter shall be the same as in other appeals.

(h) The filing of an application for appeal shall act as a supersedeas to the extent that a notice of appeal acts as supersedeas.

(i) This Code section shall not affect Code Section 9-14-52, relating to practice as to appeals in certain habeas corpus cases.

(j) When an appeal in a case enumerated in subsection (a) of Code Section 5-6-34, but not in subsection (a) of this Code section, is initiated by filing an otherwise timely application for permission to appeal pursuant to subsection (b) of this Code section without also filing a timely notice of appeal, the appellate court shall have jurisdiction to decide the case and shall grant the application. Thereafter the appeal shall proceed as provided in subsection (g) of this Code section.

Laws 1979, p. 619, §§ 3, 6; Laws 1982, p. 3, § 5; Laws 1984, p. 22, § 5; Laws 1984, p. 599, § 2; Laws 1986, p. 1591, § 2; Laws 1988, p. 1357, § 1; Laws 1991, p. 412, § 1; Laws 1994, p. 347, § 2; Laws 1997, p. 543, § 1.

§ 5-6-36. Motion for new trial as no condition precedent to appeal; availability of such motion; motion for judgment notwithstanding the verdict not necessary to review overruling of motion for directed verdict

(a) A motion for new trial need not be filed as a condition precedent to appeal or consideration of any judgment, ruling, or order in any case; but, in all cases where a motion for new trial is an available remedy, the party entitled thereto may elect to file the motion first or to appeal directly. However, where matters complained of arise or are discovered subsequent to verdict or judgment which otherwise would not appear in the record, such as newly discovered evidence, and in other like instances, a motion for new trial or other available procedure shall be filed and together with all proceedings thereon shall become a part of the record on appeal. Otherwise, the motion for new trial need not be transmitted as a part of the record on appeal; nor shall it be necessary that the overruling thereof be enumerated as error (subject to the exception last stated), as the appellate court may consider all questions included in the enumeration of errors provided for in Code Section 5-6-40. The entry of judgment on a verdict by the trial court constitutes an adjudication by the trial court as to the sufficiency of the evidence to sustain the verdict, affording a basis for review on appeal without further ruling by the trial court.

(b) A motion for judgment notwithstanding the verdict need not be filed as a condition precedent to review upon appeal of an order or ruling of the trial court overruling a motion for directed verdict; but, in all cases where the motion is an available remedy, the party may file the motion or appeal directly from the final judgment and enumerate as error the overruling of the motion for directed verdict.

Laws 1965, p. 18, § 2; Laws 1966, p. 493, § 1.

§ 5-6-37. Notice of appeal; contents; parties

Unless otherwise provided by law, an appeal may be taken to the Supreme Court or the Court of Appeals by filing with the clerk of the court wherein the case was determined a notice of appeal. The notice shall set forth the title and docket number of the case; the name of the appellant and the name and address of his attorney; a concise statement of the judgment, ruling, or order entitling the appellant to take an appeal; the court appealed to; a designation of those portions of the record to be omitted from the record on appeal; a concise statement as to why the appellate court appealed to has jurisdiction rather than the other appellate court; and, if the appeal is from a judgment of conviction in a criminal case, a brief statement of the offense and the punishment prescribed. The appeal shall not be dismissed nor denied consideration because of failure to include the jurisdictional statement or because of a designation of the wrong appellate court. In addition, the notice shall state whether or not any transcript of evidence and proceedings is to be transmitted as a part of the record on appeal. Approval by the court is not required as a condition to filing the notice. All parties to the proceedings in the lower court shall be parties on appeal and shall be served with a copy of the notice of appeal in the manner prescribed by Code Section 5–6–32.

Laws 1965, p. 18, § 4; Laws 1966, p. 493, § 2; Laws 1973, p. 303, § 1.

§ 5–6–38. Time for filing notice of appeal; cross appeals; contents; service

(a) A notice of appeal shall be filed within 30 days after entry of the appealable decision or judgment complained of; but when a motion for new trial, a motion in arrest of judgment, or a motion for judgment notwithstanding the verdict has been filed, the notice shall be filed within 30 days after the entry of the order granting, overruling, or otherwise finally disposing of the motion. In civil cases, the appellee may institute cross appeal by filing notice thereof within 15 days from service of the notice of appeal by the appellant; and the appellee may present for adjudication on the cross appeal all errors or rulings adversely affecting him; and in no case shall the appellee be required to institute an independent appeal on his own right, although the appellee may at his option file an independent appeal. The notice of cross appeal shall set forth the title and docket number of the case, the name of the appellee, the name and address of his attorney, and a designation of any portions of the record or transcript designated for omission by the appellant and which the appellee desires included and shall state that the appellee takes a cross appeal. In all cases where the notice of appeal did not specify that a transcript of evidence and proceedings was to be transmitted as a part of the record on appeal, the notice of cross appeal shall state whether such transcript is to be filed for inclusion in the record on appeal. A copy of the notice of cross appeal shall be served on other parties of record in the manner prescribed by Code Section 5–6–32.

(b) Where a cross appeal is filed, only one record and, where specified, only one transcript of evidence and proceedings need be prepared and transmitted to the appellate court; but the cross appellant may, at his election, require that such a separate record (and transcript, if required) be transmitted. Where a cross appeal is filed and only one record (and transcript, where required) is sent up, the court shall by order provide for the division of costs therefor between the parties if they are unable to do so by agreement.

(c) Notwithstanding subsection (a) of this Code section, where either the state or the defendant wishes to appeal any judgment, ruling, or order in the pretrial proceedings of a criminal case involving a capital offense for which the death penalty is sought, such appeal shall be brought as provided in Code Section 17–10–35.1.

Laws 1965, p. 18, § 5; Laws 1966, p. 493, § 3; Laws 1968, p. 1072, § 7; Laws 1988, p. 1437, § 2.

§ 5–6–39. Extension of time for filing notice of appeal and certain other papers

(a) Any judge of the trial court or any justice or judge of the appellate court to which the appeal is to be taken may, in his discretion, and without motion or notice to the other party, grant extensions of time for the filing of:

(1) Notice of appeal;

(2) Notice of cross appeal;

(3) Transcript of the evidence and proceedings on appeal or in any other instance where filing of the transcript is required or permitted by law;

(4) Designation of record referred to under Code Section 5–6–42; and

(5) Any other similar motion, proceeding, or paper for which a filing time is prescribed.

(b) No extension of time shall be granted for the filing of motions for new trial or for judgment notwithstanding the verdict.

(c) Only one extension of time shall be granted for filing of a notice of appeal and a notice of cross appeal, and the extension shall not exceed the time otherwise allowed for the filing of the notices initially.

(d) Any application to any court, justice, or judge for an extension must be made before expiration of the period for filing as originally prescribed or as extended by a permissible previous order. The order granting an extension of time shall be promptly filed with the clerk of the trial court, and the party securing it shall serve copies thereof on all other parties in the manner prescribed by Code Section 5–6–32.

Laws 1965, p. 18, § 6.

§ 5–6–40. Enumeration of errors; filing; sufficiency; service

The appellant and cross appellant shall file with the clerk of the appellate court, at such time as may be prescribed by its rules, an enumeration of the errors which shall set out separately each error relied upon. The enumeration shall be concise and need not set out or refer to portions of the record on appeal. It shall be served upon the appellee or cross appellee in the manner prescribed in Code Section 5–6–32, need not have approval of the trial court, and when filed shall become a part of the record on appeal. The appellate court, by rule, may permit the enumeration to be made a part of the brief.

Laws 1965, p. 18, § 14; Laws 1965, p. 240, § 2; Laws 1968, p. 1072, § 8.

§ 5–6–41. Preparation of record for appeal; reporting of evidence and other matter; when narrative form used

(a) In all felony cases, the transcript of evidence and proceedings shall be reported and prepared by a court reporter as provided in Code Section 17–8–5 or as otherwise provided by law.

(b) In all misdemeanor cases, the trial judge may, in the judge's discretion, require the reporting and transcribing of the evidence and proceedings by a court reporter on terms prescribed by the trial judge.

(c) In all civil cases tried in the superior and city courts and in any other court, the judgments of which are subject to review by the Supreme Court or the Court of Appeals, the trial judge thereof may require the parties to have the proceedings and evidence reported by a court reporter, the costs thereof to be borne equally between them; and, where an appeal is taken which draws in question the transcript of the evidence and proceedings, it shall be the duty of the appellant to have the transcript prepared at the appellant's expense. Where it is determined that the parties, or either of them, are financially unable to pay the costs of reporting or transcribing, the judge may, in the judge's discretion, authorize trial of the case unreported; and, when it becomes necessary for a transcript of the evidence and proceedings to be prepared, it shall be the duty of the moving party to prepare the transcript from recollection or otherwise.

(d) Where a trial in any civil or criminal case is reported by a court reporter, all motions, colloquies, objections, rulings, evidence, whether admitted or stricken on objection or otherwise, copies or summaries of all documentary evidence, the charge of the court, and all other proceedings which may be called in question on appeal or other posttrial procedure shall be reported; and, where the report is transcribed, all such matters shall be included in the written transcript, it being the intention of this article that all these matters appear in the record. Where matters occur which were not reported, such as objections to oral argument, misconduct of the jury, or other like instances, the court, upon motion of either party, shall require that a transcript of these matters be made and included as a part of the record. The transcript of proceedings shall not be reduced to narrative form unless by agreement of counsel; but, where the trial is not reported or the transcript of the proceedings for any other reason is not available and the evidence is prepared from recollection, it may be prepared in narrative form.

(e) Where a civil or criminal trial is reported by a court reporter and the evidence and proceedings are transcribed, the reporter shall complete the transcript and file the original and one copy thereof with the clerk of the trial court, together with the court reporter's certificate attesting to the correctness thereof. In criminal cases where the accused was convicted of a capital felony, an additional copy shall be filed for the Attorney General, for which the court reporter shall receive compensation from the Department of Law as provided by law. The original transcript shall be transmitted to the appellate court as a part of the record on appeal; and one copy will be retained in the trial court, both as referred to in Code Section 5–6–43. Upon filing by the reporter, the transcript shall become a part of the record in the case and need not be approved by the trial judge.

(f) Where any party contends that the transcript or record does not truly or fully disclose what transpired in the trial court and the parties are unable to agree thereon, the trial court shall set the matter down for a hearing with notice to both parties and resolve the difference so as to make the record conform to the truth. If anything material to either party is omitted from the record on appeal or is misstated therein, the parties by stipulation, or the trial court, either before or after the record is transmitted to the appellate court, on a proper suggestion or of its own initiative, may direct that the omission or misstatement shall be corrected and, if necessary, that a supplemental record shall be certified and transmitted by the clerk of the trial court. The trial court or the appellate court may at any time order the clerk of the trial court to send up any original papers or exhibits in the case, to be returned after final disposition of the appeal.

(g) Where a trial is not reported as referred to in subsections (b) and (c) of this Code section or where for any other reason the transcript of the proceedings is not obtainable and a transcript of evidence and proceedings is prepared from recollection, the agreement of the parties thereto or their counsel, entered thereon, shall entitle such transcript to be filed as a part of the record in the same manner and with the same binding effect as a transcript filed by the court reporter as referred to in subsection (e) of this Code section. In case of the inability of the parties to agree as to the correctness of such transcript, the decision of the trial judge thereon shall be final and not subject to review; and, if the trial judge is unable to recall what transpired, the judge shall enter an order stating that fact.

(h) Where any amendment or other pleading or paper which requires approval or sanction of the court in any proceeding before being filed of record is disallowed or sanction thereof is refused, the amendment, pleading, or paper may nevertheless be filed, with notation of disallowance thereon, and shall become part of the record for purposes of consideration on appeal or other procedure for review.

(i) In lieu of sending up a transcript of record, the parties may by agreement file a stipulation of the case showing how the questions arose and were decided in the trial court, together with a sufficient statement of facts to enable the appellate court to pass upon the questions presented therein. Before being transmitted to the appellate court, the stipulation shall be approved by the trial judge or the presiding judge of the court where the case is pending.

(j) In all cases, civil or criminal, any party may as a matter of right have the case reported at the party's own expense.

Laws 1965, p. 18, § 10; Laws 1993, p. 1315, § 1.

§ 5–6–42. Omission of matter from record; designation of addenda by opposite party; filing of transcript

If the appellant designates any matter to be omitted from the record on appeal as provided in Code Section 5–6–37, the appellee may, within 15 days of serving of the notice of appeal by appellant, file a designation of record designating that all or part of the omitted matters be included in the record on appeal. A copy of the designation shall be served on all other parties in the manner prescribed by Code Section 5–6–32. Where there is a transcript of evidence and proceedings to be included in the record on appeal, the appellant shall cause the transcript to be prepared and filed as provided by Code Section 5–6–41; but, when the appellant has designated that the transcript not be made a part of the record on appeal and its inclusion is by reason of a designation thereof by appellee, the appellee shall cause the transcript to be prepared and filed as referred to in Code Section 5–6–41 at his expense. The party having the responsibility of filing the transcript shall cause it to be filed within 30 days after filing of the notice of appeal or designation by appellee, as the case may be, unless the time is extended as provided in Code Section 5–6–39. In all cases, it shall be the duty of the trial judge to grant such extensions of time as may be necessary to enable the court reporter to complete his transcript of evidence and proceedings.

Laws 1965, p. 18, § 11.

§ 5–6–43. Duties of trial court clerk with reference to preparation of transcript of record on appeal; fees

(a) Within five days after the date of filing of the transcript of evidence and proceedings by the appellant or appellee, as the case may be, it shall be the duty of the clerk of the trial court to prepare a complete copy of the entire record of the case, omitting only those things designated for omission by the appellant and which were not designated for inclusion by the appellee, together with a copy of the notice of appeal and copy of any notice of cross appeal, with date of filing thereon, and transmit the same, together with the transcript of evidence and proceedings, to the appellate court, together with his certificate as to the correctness of the record. Where no transcript of evidence and proceedings is to be sent up, the clerk shall prepare and transmit the record within 20 days after the date of filing of the notice of appeal. If for any reason the clerk is unable to transmit the record and transcript within the time required in this subsection or when an extension of time was obtained under Code Section 5–6–39, he shall state in his certificate the cause of the delay and the appeal shall not be dismissed. The clerk need not recopy the transcript of evidence and proceedings to be sent up on appeal but shall send up the reporter's original and retain the copy, as referred to in Code Section 5–6–41; and it shall not be necessary that the transcript be renumbered as a part of the record on appeal. The clerk shall retain an exact duplicate copy of all records and the transcript sent up, with the same pagination, in his office as a permanent record.

(b) Where the accused in a criminal case was convicted of a capital felony, the clerk shall likewise furnish the Attorney General with an exact copy of the record on appeal, for which the clerk shall receive a fee as required by paragraph (6) of subsection (h) of Code Section 15–6–77, to be paid out of funds appropriated to the Department of Law.

(c) Where a defendant in a criminal case is confined in jail pending appeal, it shall be the duty of the clerk to state that fact in his certificate; and it shall be the duty of the appellate court to expedite disposition of the case.

(d) Where a transcript of evidence and proceedings is already on file at the time the notice of appeal is filed, as where the transcript was previously filed in connection with a motion for new trial or for judgment notwithstanding the verdict, the clerk shall cause the record and transcript (where specified for inclusion) to be transmitted as provided in subsection (a) of this Code section within 20 days after the filing of the notice of appeal.

Laws 1965, p. 18, § 12; Laws 1966, p. 493, § 5; Laws 1968, p. 1072, § 6; Laws 1981, p. 1396, § 15; Laws 1992, p. 6, § 5.

§ 5–6–44. Joint appeals; joinder of other motions

(a) Whenever two or more persons are defendants or plaintiffs in an action, and a judgment, verdict, or decree has been rendered against each of them, jointly or severally, or where two or more cases are tried together, the plaintiffs or defendants, as the case may be, shall be entitled, but not required, to file joint appeals, motions for new trial, motions in arrest, motions to set aside, and motions for judgment notwithstanding the verdict, without regard to whether the parties have a joint interest, or whether the cases were merely consolidated for purposes of trial, or whether the cases were simply tried together without an order of consolidation.

(b) Where joint appeals are filed, the appealing parties may nevertheless be entitled, but not required, to file separate enumerations of error in the appellate court.

(c) When separate appeals, motions for new trial, or motions for judgment notwithstanding the verdict are filed, only one transcript of evidence and proceedings (where required) and only one record need be prepared, filed, or transmitted to the appellate court (as the case may be).

(d) In such cases, the court shall by order specify the division of costs between the parties.

(e) This Code section shall apply to both civil and criminal cases.

Laws 1965, p. 18, § 15; Laws 1968, p. 1072, § 4.

§ 5–6–45. Supersedeas in criminal cases

(a) In all criminal cases, the notice of appeal filed as provided in Code Sections 5–6–37 and 5–6–38 shall serve as supersedeas in all cases where a sentence of death has been imposed or where the defendant is admitted to bail. If the sentence is bailable, the defendant may give bond in an amount prescribed by the presiding judge, with security approved by the clerk, conditioned upon the defendant's personal appearance to abide the final judgment or sentence of the court. If the judgment or sentence is or includes a fine which is unconditionally required to be paid, and is not required to be paid over a period of probation, nor as a condition of a suspended or probated sentence, nor as an alternative sentence, the bond may also be conditioned upon payment of the fine at the time the defendant appears to abide the final judgment or sentence.

(b) If the defendant is a corporation which has been convicted as provided in Code Section 17–7–92, the presiding judge, on the motion of the defendant, prosecuting attorney, or on its own motion, may order that supersedeas be conditioned upon the posting of a supersedeas bond. Said order may be entered either before or after the filing of a motion for a new trial or notice of appeal. The bond shall be in an amount prescribed by the presiding judge, with security approved by the clerk, conditioned upon the defendant's appearance, by and through a corporate officer, agent, or attorney at law, to satisfy the judgment, together with all costs and interest. If the corporation fails to make the bond as ordered, the prosecuting attorney or other proper officer may use any and all lawful process and procedures available to enforce and collect the judgment. Should final judgment be entered in favor of the defendant, the presiding judge shall order a refund of all amounts collected in satisfaction of the judgment. The State of Georgia, and its political subdivisions, district attorney, solicitor-general, sheriff, marshal, all other proper officers, and all agents and employees of the aforementioned persons shall be immune from all civil liability for acts and attempts to enforce and collect a judgment under this subsection.

(c) Any supersedeas bond may be reviewed by the presiding judge on the motion of defendant, prosecuting attorney, or on its own motion, and the court may require new or additional security, or order the bond strengthened, increased, reduced, or otherwise amended as justice may reasonably require.

Laws 1845, Cobb's 1851 Digest, pp. 449, 453; Laws 1965, p. 18, § 7; Laws 1984, p. 413, § 1; Laws 1992, p. 6, § 5; Laws 1996, p. 748, § 9.

Formerly Code 1863, § 4171; Code 1868, § 4203; Code 1873, § 4263; Code 1882, § 4263; Penal Code 1895, § 1077; Penal Code 1910, § 1104; Code 1933, § 6–1005.

§ 5–6–46. Supersedeas in civil cases; bond

(a) In civil cases, the notice of appeal filed as provided in Code Sections 5–6–37 and 5–6–38 shall serve as supersedeas upon payment of all costs in the trial court by the appellant and it shall not be necessary that a supersedeas bond or other form of security be filed; provided, however, that upon motion by the appellee, made in the trial court before or after the appeal is docketed in the appellate court, the trial court shall require that supersedeas bond or other form of security be given with such surety and in such amount as the court may require, conditioned for the satisfaction of the judgment in full, together with costs, interest, and damages for delay if the appeal is found to be frivolous. When the judgment is for the recovery of money not otherwise secured, the amount of the bond or other form of security shall be fixed at such sum as will cover the whole amount of the judgment remaining unsatisfied, costs on the appeal, interest, and damages for delay, unless the court after notice and hearing and for good cause shown fixes a lesser amount. When the judgment determines the disposition of the property in controversy as in real actions, trover, and actions to foreclose mortgages and other security instruments, or when such property is in the custody of the sheriff or other levying officer, or when the proceeds of such property or a bond for its value are in the custody or control of the court, the amount of the supersedeas bond or other form of security shall be fixed at such sum only as will secure the amount recovered for the use and detention of the property, the costs of the action, costs on appeal, interest, and damages for delay.

(b) Notwithstanding subsection (a) of this Code section, in any civil case under any legal theory, including cases involving individual, aggregated, class-action, or otherwise joined claims, the amount of supersedeas bond or other form of security to be furnished during the pendency of all appeals or discretionary reviews of any judgment granting legal, equitable, or any other form of relief or damages, including compensatory, special, punitive, exemplary, or other damages, in order to stay execution of the judgment during the entire course of appellate review by any court shall be set in accordance with applicable laws or court rules, but the total supersedeas bond or other form of security that is required of all appellants collectively shall not exceed $25 million regardless of the value of the judgment.

(c) If supersedeas bond or other form of security is not filed within the time specified by the judge, or if the bond or other form of security filed is found insufficient, a bond or other form of security may be filed at such time as may be fixed by the trial court.

(d) By entering into an appeal or supersedeas bond or other form of security given pursuant to this Code section, the surety submits himself or herself to the jurisdiction of the court and irrevocably appoints the clerk of the court as the surety's agent upon whom any papers affecting the surety's liability on the bond may be served. The surety's liability may be enforced on motion without the necessity of notice or an independent action.

(e) Nothing in this Code section shall deprive the superior courts of their separate power to grant supersedeas under paragraph (1) of Code Section 15–6–9 nor deprive the appellate courts of the power to grant supersedeas in such manner as they may determine to meet the ends of justice.

(f) If an appellee proves by a preponderance of the evidence that a party bringing an appeal, for whom the supersedeas bond or other form of security has been limited pursuant to subsection (b) of this Code section, is dissipating or secreting its assets, or diverting assets outside the ordinary course of business to avoid payment of a judgment, a court may require the appellant to post a bond or other form of security in an amount not to exceed the total amount of the judgment.

Laws 1845, Cobb's 1851 Digest, pp. 449, 453; Laws 1870, p. 416, § 1; Laws 1880–81, p. 120, § 1; Laws 1917, p. 63, § 1; Laws 1965, p. 18, § 8; Laws 1994, p. 346, § 1; Laws 2000, p. 228, § 2; Laws 2001, p. 4, § 5; Laws 2004, Act 778, § 1, eff. May 17, 2004; Laws 2005, Act 19, § 5, eff. April 7, 2005.

Formerly Code 1863, § 4171; Code 1868, § 4203; Code 1873, § 4263; Code 1882, § 4263; Civil Code 1895, § 5552; Civil Code 1910, § 6165; Code 1933, § 6–1002.

§ 5–6–47. Supersedeas where pauper's affidavit filed

(a) In all civil cases where the party taking an appeal files an affidavit stating that because of his indigence he is unable to pay costs or to post a supersedeas bond, if any, as may be required by the trial judge as provided in Code Section 5–6–46, the notice of appeal and affidavit of indigence shall act as supersedeas.

(b) Any party at interest or his agent or attorney may contest the truth of the affidavit of indigence by verifying affirmatively under oath that the same is untrue. The issue thereby formed shall be heard and determined by the trial court under the rules of the court. The judgment of the court on all issues of fact concerning the ability of a party to pay costs or give bond shall be final.

Laws 1965, p. 18, § 9; Laws 1966, p. 723, § 1.

§ 5–6–48. Dismissal of appeals generally prohibited; when permitted; effect of dismissal of appeal upon cross appeal

(a) Failure of any party to perfect service of any notice or other paper hereunder shall not work dismissal; but the trial and appellate courts shall at any stage of the proceeding require that parties be served in such manner as will permit a just and expeditious determination of the appeal and shall, when necessary, grant such continuance as may be required under the circumstances.

(b) No appeal shall be dismissed or its validity affected for any cause nor shall consideration of any enumerated error be refused, except:

(1) For failure to file notice of appeal within the time required as provided in this article or within any extension of time granted hereunder;

(2) Where the decision or judgment is not then appealable; or

(3) Where the questions presented have become moot.

(c) No appeal shall be dismissed by the appellate court nor consideration of any error therein refused because of failure of any party to cause the transcript of evidence and proceedings to be filed within the time allowed by law or order of court; but the trial court may, after notice and opportunity for hearing, order that the appeal be dismissed where there has been an unreasonable delay in the filing of the transcript and it is shown that the delay was inexcusable and was caused by such party. In like manner, the trial court may order the appeal dismissed where there has been an unreasonable delay in the transmission of the record to the appellate court, and it is seen that the delay was inexcusable and was caused by the failure of a party to pay costs in the trial court or file an affidavit of indigence; provided, however, that no appeal shall be dismissed for failure to pay costs if costs are paid within 20 days (exclusive of Saturdays, Sundays, and legal holidays) of receipt by the appellant of notice, mailed by registered or certified mail or statutory overnight delivery, of the amount of costs.

(d) At any stage of the proceedings, either before or after argument, the court shall by order, either with or without motion, provide for all necessary amendments, require the trial court to make corrections in the record or transcript or certify what transpired below which does not appear from the record on appeal, require that additional portions of the record or transcript of proceedings be sent up, or require that a complete transcript of evidence and proceedings be prepared and sent up, or take any other action to perfect the appeal and record so that the appellate court can and will pass upon the appeal and not dismiss it. If an error appears in the notice of appeal, the court shall allow the notice of appeal to be amended at any time prior to judgment to perfect the appeal so that the appellate court can and will pass upon the appeal and not dismiss it.

(e) Dismissal of the appeal shall not affect the validity of the cross appeal where notice therefor has been filed within the time required for cross appeals and where the appellee would still stand to receive benefit or advantage by a decision of his cross appeal.

(f) Where it is apparent from the notice of appeal, the record, the enumeration of errors, or any combination of the foregoing, what judgment or judgments were appealed from or what errors are sought to be asserted upon appeal, the appeal shall be considered in accordance therewith notwithstanding that the notice of appeal fails to specify definitely the judgment appealed from or that the enumeration of errors fails to enumerate clearly the errors sought to be reviewed. An appeal shall not be dismissed nor consideration thereof refused because of failure of the court reporter to file the transcript of evidence and proceedings within the time allowed by law or order of court unless it affirmatively appears from the record that the failure was caused by the appellant.

Laws 1965, p. 18, § 13; Laws 1965, p. 240, § 1; Laws 1966, p. 493, § 10; Laws 1968, p. 1072, §§ 2, 3; Laws 1972, p. 624, § 1; Laws 1978, p. 1986, § 1; Laws 2000, p. 1589, § 3.

§ 5–6–49. Bills of exceptions, exceptions pendente lite, and assignments of error abolished; contents of motions for new trial and for judgment notwithstanding the verdict

(a) Bills of exceptions, exceptions pendente lite, assignments of error, and all rules relating thereto are abolished.

(b) Motions for new trial and for judgment notwithstanding the verdict need not set out portions of the record or transcript of evidence and it shall not be necessary that the grounds thereof be complete in themselves or be approved by the court; provided, however, that the motions must be sufficiently definite to inform the opposite party of the contention of the movant.

Laws 1965, p. 18, § 3.

§ 5–6–50. Purpose of law; requirements as to bills of exceptions and writs of error superseded

The procedure provided in this article shall serve all purposes which a bill of exceptions or writ of error has served in the past; and, where under any law of force in this state provision is made for the taking of writs of error or bills of exception, the procedure prescribed in this article shall be deemed to apply in lieu thereof as to the procedure and as to all time requirements.

Laws 1965, p. 18, § 19.

§ 5–6–51. Suggested forms for appeal; declaration of sufficiency

The following suggested forms are declared to be sufficient, but any other form substantially complying therewith shall also be sufficient:

(1) NOTICE OF APPEAL—CIVIL CASES.

—IN THE ____ COURT OF ____ COUNTY—

—STATE OF GEORGIA—

________________	)
Plaintiffs	)
	)
v.	) Civil action
	) File no. ________
	)
________________	)
Defendants	)

—NOTICE OF APPEAL—

Notice is hereby given that ____ and ____, defendants above-named, hereby appeal to the ____ (Court of Appeals or Supreme Court) from the ____ (describe order or judgment) entered in this action on (date), ____.

Motion for new trial (or motion for judgment n.o.v., etc.) was filed and overruled (or granted, etc.) on (date), ____.

The clerk will please omit the following from the record on appeal:

1. ____
2. ____
3. ____

Transcript of evidence and proceedings will/will not be filed for inclusion in the record on appeal.

This court, rather than the (Court of Appeals or Supreme Court) has jurisdiction of this case on appeal for the reason that ____.

Dated: ________.

____
Attorney for appellants

____
Address

—(CERTIFICATE OF SERVICE)—

(2) NOTICE OF APPEAL—CRIMINAL CASES.

—IN THE ____ COURT OF ____ COUNTY—

—STATE OF GEORGIA—

________)
The State (etc.))
)
) (Indictment)
v.) (Accusation)
) No. ________
________)
Defendant)

—NOTICE OF APPEAL—

Notice is hereby given that ____, defendant above-named, hereby appeals to the ____ (Court of Appeals or Supreme Court) from the judgment of conviction and sentence entered herein on (date), ____.

The offense(s) for which defendant was convicted is (are) ____, and the sentence(s) imposed is (are) as follows: ____.

Motion for new trial (or motion in arrest of judgment, etc.) was filed and overruled on (date), ____.

The clerk will please omit the following from the record on appeal:

1. ____

2. ____

3. ____

Transcript of evidence and proceedings will/will not be filed for inclusion in the record on appeal.

This court, rather than the (Court of Appeals or Supreme Court) has jurisdiction of this case on appeal for the reason that ____.

Dated: ________.

____
Attorney for appellant

____
Address

—(CERTIFICATE OF SERVICE)—

(3) NOTICE OF CROSS APPEAL.

—IN THE ____ COURT OF ____ COUNTY—

—STATE OF GEORGIA—

________)
Plaintiffs)
)
)
v.) Civil action
) File no. ________
)
________)
Defendants)

—NOTICE OF CROSS APPEAL—

Notice is hereby given that ____, one of the defendants above-named, hereby cross appeals to the ____ (Court of Appeals or Supreme Court) from the ____ (describe order or judgment) entered in this action on (date), ____.

Notice of appeal was heretofore filed on (date), ____.

The clerk will please include the following in the record on appeal, all of which were designated for omission by appellant:

1. ____

2. ____

3. ____

Transcript of evidence and proceedings (will be filed) (will not be filed) (has already been designated to be filed by appellant) for inclusion in the record on appeal.

Dated: ________.

____
Attorney for cross appellant

____
Address

—(CERTIFICATE OF SERVICE)—

(4) ENUMERATION OF ERRORS.

—ENUMERATION OF ERRORS—

1. The court erred in charging the jury on gross negligence.

2. The court erred in admitting the testimony of witness Smith concerning his opinion as to how the collision happened.

3. The court erred in refusing to grant a mistrial because of the misconduct of plaintiff's attorney in oral argument.

4. The court erred in refusing to admit in evidence testimony of witness Jones concerning his estimate as to damages.

5. The court erred in denying defendant's motion for continuance.

Laws 1965, p. 18, § 20; Laws 1966, p. 493, §§ 8, 8A; Laws 1973, p. 303, § 2; Laws 1984, p. 22, § 5; Laws 1999, p. 81, § 5.

CHAPTER 7

APPEAL OR CERTIORARI BY STATE IN CRIMINAL CASES

§ 5–7–1. Appeal authorized in what instances

(a) An appeal may be taken by and on behalf of the State of Georgia from the superior courts, state courts, City Court of Atlanta, and juvenile courts and such other courts from which a direct appeal is authorized to the Court of Appeals of Georgia and the Supreme Court of Georgia in criminal cases and adjudication of delinquency cases in the following instances:

(1) From an order, decision, or judgment setting aside or dismissing any indictment, accusation, or petition alleging that a child has committed a delinquent act or any count thereof;

(2) From an order, decision, or judgment arresting judgment of conviction or adjudication of delinquency upon legal grounds;

(3) From an order, decision, or judgment sustaining a plea or motion in bar, when the defendant has not been put in jeopardy;

(4) From an order, decision, or judgment suppressing or excluding evidence illegally seized or excluding the results of any test for alcohol or drugs in the case of motions made and ruled upon prior to the impaneling of a jury or the defendant being put in jeopardy, whichever occurs first;

(5) From an order, decision, or judgment of a court where the court does not have jurisdiction or the order is otherwise void under the Constitution or laws of this state;

(6) From an order, decision, or judgment of a superior court transferring a case to the juvenile court pursuant to subparagraph (b)(2)(B) of Code Section 15–11–28;

(7) From an order, decision, or judgment of a superior court granting a motion for new trial or an extraordinary motion for new trial;

(8) From an order, decision, or judgment denying a motion by the state to recuse or disqualify a judge made and ruled upon prior to the defendant being put in jeopardy; or

(9) From an order, decision, or judgment issued pursuant to subsection (c) of Code Section 17–10–6.2.

(b) In any instance in which any appeal is taken by and on behalf of the State of Georgia in a criminal case, the defendant shall have the right to cross appeal. Such cross appeal shall be subject to the same rules of practice and procedure as provided for in civil cases under Code Section 5–6–38.

Laws 1973, p. 297, § 1; Laws 1984, p. 22, § 5; Laws 1994, p. 311, § 1; Laws 1994, p. 1012, § 28; Laws 2000, p. 20, § 3; Laws 2000, p. 862, § 2; Laws 2003, Act 37, § 2, eff. May 27, 2003; Laws 2005, Act 8, § 3, eff. July 1, 2005; Laws 2006, Act 571, § 3, eff. July 1, 2006.

§ 5–7–1.1. Repealed by Laws 2000, p. 862, § 3, eff. July 1, 2000

§ 5–7–2. Trial judge to certify that immediate review be had

Other than from an order, decision, or judgment sustaining a motion to suppress evidence illegally seized, in any appeal under this chapter where the order, decision, or judgment is not final, it shall be necessary that the trial judge certify within ten days of entry thereof that the order, decision, or judgment is of such importance to the case that an immediate review should be had.

Laws 1973, p. 297, § 2.

§ 5–7–3. Certiorari by state

A proceeding by certiorari may be taken by and on behalf of the State of Georgia from one court to another court of this state, where the right of certiorari is provided as a procedure for appealing a judgment, in the specified situations set forth in Code Sections 5–7–1 and 5–7–2.

Laws 1973, p. 297, § 3.

§ 5–7–4. Governing procedure

An appeal by the state, except as otherwise provided for in this chapter, and certiorari by the state, when authorized by this chapter, shall be governed by the same laws and provisions as to time and other procedures as apply to other appellants in criminal cases.

Laws 1973, p. 297, § 4.

§ 5–7–5. Release of accused on bail

In the event the state files an appeal as authorized in this chapter, the accused shall be entitled to be released on reasonable bail pending the disposition of the appeal, except in those cases punishable by death. The amount of the bail, to be set by the court, shall be reviewable on direct application by the court to which the appeal is taken.

Laws 1973, p. 297, § 5.

TITLE 9

CIVIL PRACTICE

As Amended Through the 2006 Regular Session of the General Assembly

Research Note

Use Westlaw *to find cases citing a statute or to search for specific terms in a statute. See the* Westlaw *Directory Screens for lists of relevant databases.*

Table of Sections

INDEX

See Index to Georgia Statutes, infra.

CHAPTER 1

GENERAL PROVISIONS [RESERVED]

CHAPTER 2

ACTIONS GENERALLY

Article 1

General Provisions

§ 9-2-1. Definitions

As used in this title, the term:

(1) "Action" means the judicial means of enforcing a right.

(2) "Civil action" means an action founded on private rights, arising either from contract or tort.

(3) "Penal action" means an action allowed in pursuance of public justice under particular laws.

Formerly Code 1863, §§ 3175, 3177, 3178; Code 1868, §§ 3186, 3188, 3189; Code 1873, §§ 3251, 3253, 3254; Code 1882, §§ 3251, 3253, 3254; Civil Code 1895, §§ 4930, 4932, 4933; Civil Code 1910, §§ 5507, 5509, 5510; Code 1933, §§ 3-101, 3-102, 3-103.

§ 9-2-2. Distinctions of actions abolished

(a) An action may be against the person, or against property, or both.

(b) Generally, a proceeding against the person shall bind the property also. A proceeding against property without service on the person shall bind only the particular property.

Laws 1982, p. 3, § 9.

Formerly Code 1863, § 3176; Code 1868, § 3187; Code 1873, § 3252; Code 1882, § 3252; Civil Code 1895, § 4931; Civil Code 1910, § 5508; Code 1933, § 3-104.

§ 9-2-3. Remedy provided for every right

For every right there shall be a remedy; every court having jurisdiction of the one may, if necessary, frame the other.

Formerly Code 1863, § 3174; Code 1868, § 3185; Code 1873, § 3250; Code 1882, § 3250; Civil Code 1895, § 4929; Civil Code 1910, § 5506; Code 1933, § 3-105.

§ 9-2-4. Consistent or inconsistent remedies, right to pursue

A plaintiff may pursue any number of consistent or inconsistent remedies against the same person or different persons until he shall obtain a satisfaction from some of them.

Laws 1967, p. 226, § 45.

Formerly Civil Code 1895, § 4945; Civil Code 1910, § 5522; Code 1933, § 3-114.

§ 9-2-5. Plaintiff required to elect between actions; exceptions

(a) No plaintiff may prosecute two actions in the courts at the same time for the same cause of action and against the same party. If two such actions are commenced simultaneously, the defendant may require the plaintiff to elect which he will prosecute. If two such actions are commenced at different times, the pendency of the former shall be a good defense to the latter.

(b) The rule requiring a plaintiff to elect shall not apply to a prior attachment against property where the defendant is subsequently served personally nor to an attachment obtained during the pendency of an action. However, the judgment in the case against the person shall set out the fact of its identity with the proceedings against the property.

Laws 1982, p. 3, § 9.

Formerly Code 1863, §§ 2835, 2836; Code 1868, §§ 2843, 2844; Code 1873, §§ 2894, 2895; Code 1882, §§ 2894, 2895; Civil Code 1895, §§ 3737, 3739; Civil Code 1910, §§ 4331, 4333; Code 1933, §§ 3-601, 3-605.

§ 9-2-6. Demand unnecessary to commence action

No demand shall be necessary before the commencement of an action, except in such cases as the law or the contract prescribes.

Formerly Code 1863, § 3179; Code 1868, § 3190; Code 1873, § 3255; Code 1882, § 3255; Civil Code 1895, § 4935; Civil Code 1910, § 5512; Code 1933, § 3-106.

§ 9-2-7. Implied obligations to pay

Ordinarily, when one renders service or transfers property which is valuable to another, which the latter accepts, a promise is implied to pay the reasonable value thereof. However, this presumption does not usually arise in cases between very near relatives.

Formerly Civil Code 1895, § 4936; Civil Code 1910, § 5513; Code 1933, § 3-107.

Article 2

Parties

§ 9-2-20. Parties to actions on contracts

(a) As a general rule, an action on a contract, whether the contract is expressed, implied, by parol, under seal, or of record, shall be brought in the name of the party in whom the legal interest in the contract is vested, and against the party who made it in person or by agent.

(b) The beneficiary of a contract made between other parties for his benefit may maintain an action against the promisor on the contract.

Laws 1949, p. 455, § 1.

Formerly Code 1863, § 3181; Code 1868, § 3192; Code 1873, § 3257; Code 1882, § 3257; Civil Code 1895, § 4939; Civil Code 1910, § 5516; Code 1933, § 3-108.

§ 9-2-21. Parties to actions for torts

(a) An action for a tort shall, in general, be brought in the name of the person whose legal right has been affected. In the case of an injury to property, a tort action shall be brought in the name of the person who was legally interested in the property at the time the injury thereto was committed or in the name of his assignee.

(b) An action for a tort shall be brought against the party committing the injury, either by himself, his servant, or an agent in his employ.

(c) If the person whose legal right has been affected has received medical assistance benefits pursuant to Chapter 4 of Title 49, prior to initiating recovery action, the representative or attorney who has actual knowledge of the receipt of said benefits shall notify the Department of Community Health of the claim. Mailing and deposit in a United States post office or public mail box of said notice addressed to the Department of Community Health with adequate postage affixed is adequate legal notice of the claim. Notice as provided in this subsection shall not be a condition precedent to the filing of any action for tort. Initiating recovery action shall include any communication with a party who may be liable or someone financially responsible for that liability with regard to recovery of a claim including but not limited to the filing of an action in court.

Laws 1993, p. 1080, § 1; Laws 1999, p. 296, § 24.

Formerly Code 1863, § 3182; Code 1868, § 3193; Code 1873, § 3258; Code 1882, § 3258; Civil Code 1895, § 4940; Civil Code 1910, § 5517; Code 1933, § 3-109.

§ 9-2-22. Joinder of claims arising out of deficiencies in improvements to real property

In any action arising out of alleged deficiencies in the construction of improvements on real property, the party plaintiff may join in one action, as parties defendants, all parties who allegedly contributed in the construction of the improvements as well as all bonding companies who bonded the performance of the parties defendant.

Laws 1964, p. 140, § 1.

Formerly Code 1933, § 3-110.1.

§ 9-2-23. Separate action by tenant in common

A tenant in common may bring an action separately for his own interest, and the judgment in such case shall affect only himself.

Formerly Code 1863, § 3183; Code 1868, § 3194; Code 1873, § 3259; Code 1882, § 3259; Civil Code 1895, § 4941; Civil Code 1910, § 5518; Code 1933, § 3-111.

§ 9-2-24. Actions by unincorporated associations

An action may be maintained by and in the name of any unincorporated organization or association.

Laws 1959, p. 44, § 1.

§ 9-2-25. Actions against unincorporated associations

(a) Actions may be maintained against and in the name of any unincorporated organization or association for any cause of action for or upon which the plaintiff therein may maintain such an action against the members of the organization or association.

(b) Service of process in the action against the organization or association shall be had by service upon any officer or official member of such organization or association, or upon any officer or official member of any branch or local of the organization or association, provided that any such organization or association may file with the Secretary of State a designated officer or agent upon whom service shall be had and his residence address within the state. If the designation is made and filed, service of process shall be had only on the officer or agent designated, if he can be found within the state.

(c) The organization or association shall be suable in any cause of action. The action may be maintained in any county where the organization or association does business or has in existence a branch or local organization.

(d) Where a judgment in such actions is rendered in favor of the plaintiff against the organizations or associations, the property of the organization or association shall be liable to the satisfaction of the judgment. No such judgment shall be enforced against the individual property of any member of an unincorporated association, unless the member has personally participated in the transaction for which the action was instituted and has been served with process as provided by law.

Laws 1959, p. 44, §§ 2-5.

§ 9-2-26. Several joint contractors or copartners sued in same action; representative made party in case of death

When two or more joint contractors, joint and several contractors, or copartners are defendants in the same action and service is perfected on one or more of the contractors or copartners and the officer serving the writ or process returns that the rest are not to be found, the plaintiff may proceed to judgment and execution against the defendants served with process in the same manner as if they were the sole defendants. If any of the defendants die pending the action, his representative may be made a party and the case may proceed to judgment and execution as in other cases against the representatives of deceased persons.

Laws 1820, Cobb's 1851 Digest, p. 485.

Formerly Code 1863, § 3263; Code 1868, § 3274; Code 1873, § 3350; Code 1882, § 3350; Civil Code 1895, § 5009; Civil Code 1910, § 5591; Code 1933, § 3-301.

§ 9-2-27. Actions against representative of obligor; accrual of right of action

Where any person is in possession, in his own right or in any other capacity, of any note, bill, bond, or other obligation in writing, signed by two or more persons, and one or more of the persons whose names are so signed dies before the payment of the money or the compliance with the conditions of such bond or obligation in writing, the person holding the bill, bond, note, or other obligation in writing shall not be compelled to bring an action against the survivors alone, but may at his discretion bring an action against (1) the survivor or survivors, (2) the representative or representatives of the deceased person or persons, or (3) the survivor or survivors and the representative or representatives of the deceased person or persons in the same action. However, nothing contained in this Code section shall authorize the bringing of an action against the representative of any estate until six months after the probate of the will or the granting of letters of administration on the estate or estates. This Code section shall be so construed as to embrace debts against copartners as well as debts against joint or joint and several contractors.

Laws 1818, Cobb's 1851 Digest, p. 483; Laws 1858, p. 86, § 1; Laws 1981; p. 852, § 1; Laws 1982, p. 3, § 9.

Formerly Code 1863, §§ 3261, 3262; Code 1868, §§ 3272, 3273; Code 1873, §§ 3348, 3349; Code 1882, §§ 3348, 3349; Civil Code 1895, §§ 5014, 5015; Civil Code 1910, §§ 5596, 5597; Code 1933, § 3-305.

§ 9-2-28. Actions by infant not void; amendments

An action commenced and prosecuted by an infant alone shall not be void. Although the action may be defective in wanting a guardian or next friend, the defect shall be amendable before verdict and cured by verdict.

Laws 1959, p. 79, § 1.

Formerly Code 1863, § 3187; Code 1868, § 3198; Code 1873, § 3263; Code 1882, § 3263; Civil Code 1895, § 4947; Civil Code 1910, § 5524; Code 1933, § 3-115.

§ 9-2-29. Penal action; party plaintiff

If no special officer is authorized to be the plaintiff in a penal action, the state, the Governor, the Attorney General, or a prosecuting attorney may be the plaintiff.

Formerly Code 1863, § 3178; Code 1868, § 3189; Code 1873, § 3254; Code 1882, § 3254; Civil Code 1895, § 4933; Civil Code 1910, § 5510; Code 1933, § 3-103.

§ 9-2-30. How parties made when year's support assigned

When a party plaintiff dies during litigation concerning any chose in action and the chose in action is assigned to the surviving spouse, the surviving spouse and children, or the children only of the decedent as any part of a year's support, the surviving spouse personally or for the use of the surviving spouse and the children, or, in the event of children only, a next friend for the children may be made a party plaintiff upon the same terms and in the same manner that administrators are made parties plaintiff to actions in favor of their intestate, upon the submission by the person to the court of a certified copy of the assignment; and the action shall proceed in the name of the parties so made.

Laws 1878-79, p. 148, § 1.

Formerly Code 1882, § 3424a; Civil Code 1895, § 5022; Civil Code 1910, § 5604; Code 1933, § 3-407.

Article 3

Abatement

§ 9-2-40. When action does not abate on death of party

No action shall abate by the death of either party, where the cause of action shall in any case survive to or against the legal representatives of the deceased party, either in the same or any other form of action.

Laws 1799, Cobb's 1851 Digest, p. 472.

Formerly Code 1863, § 3371; Code 1868, § 3390; Code 1873, § 3438; Code 1882, § 3438; Civil Code 1895, § 5035; Civil Code 1910, § 5617; Code 1933, § 3-501.

§ 9-2-41. Action for tort and certain causes of action not to abate by death of either party

No action for a tort shall abate by the death of either party, where the wrongdoer received any benefit from the tort complained of; nor shall any action or cause of action for the recovery of damages for homicide, injury to the person, or injury to property abate by the death of either party. The cause of action, in case of the death of the plaintiff and in the event there is no right of survivorship in any other person, shall survive to the personal representative of the deceased plaintiff. In case of the death of the defendant, the cause of action shall survive against said defendant's personal representative. However, in the event of the death of the wrongdoer before an action has been brought against him, the personal representative of the wrongdoer in such capacity shall be subject to the action just as the wrongdoer himself would have been during his life, provided that there shall be no punitive damages against the personal representative.

Laws 1889, p. 73, § 1; Laws 1935, p. 94, § 1; Laws 1952, p. 224, § 1.

Formerly Code 1863, § 2909; Code 1868, § 2916; Code 1873, § 2967; Code 1882, § 2967; Civil Code 1895, § 3825; Civil Code 1910, § 4421; Code 1933, § 3-505.

§ 9-2-42. Death of one of several defendants

In all actions against two or more defendants, one or more of whom have died or may die pending the action, the plaintiff may suggest the death of record and proceed against the surviving defendants to the extent of their respective liabilities.

Laws 1859, p. 49, § 1.

Formerly Code 1863, § 3377; Code 1868, § 3396; Code 1873, § 3444; Code 1882, § 3444; Civil Code 1895, § 5041; Civil Code 1910, § 5623; Code 1933, § 3-506.

§ 9-2-43. Abatement where one of several defendants not liable

An action against several persons shall not abate where it appears that some of the defendants are not liable but may proceed against those who are liable.

Formerly Code 1863, § 3375; Code 1868, § 3394; Code 1873, § 3442; Code 1882, § 3442; Civil Code 1895, § 5039; Civil Code 1910, § 5621; Code 1933, § 3-504.

§ 9-2-44. Former recovery and pendency of former action

(a) A former recovery or the pendency of a former action for the same cause of action between the same parties in the same or any other court having jurisdiction shall be a good cause of abatement. However, if the first action is so defective that no recovery can possibly be had, the pendency of a former action shall not abate the latter.

(b) Parol evidence shall be admissible to show that a matter apparently covered by the judgment was not passed upon by the court.

Laws 1982, p. 3, § 9.

Formerly Code 1863, §§ 2838, 2839, 3407; Code 1868, §§ 2846, 2847, 3426; Code 1873, §§ 2897, 2898, 3476; Code 1882, §§ 2897, 2898, 3476; Civil Code 1895, §§ 3741, 3743, 5094; Civil Code 1910, §§ 4335, 4337, 5678; Code 1933, §§ 3-607, 3-608.

§ 9-2-45. Pendency of action in another state, effect

The pendency of a prior action in another state shall not abate an action between the same parties for the same cause in this state.

Formerly Civil Code 1895, § 3738; Civil Code 1910, § 4332; Code 1933, § 3-602.

§ 9-2-46. Setting cases involved in proceedings in other states; continuing and postponing cases

(a) Whenever it is made to appear to the judge of any court that any party to a case pending in the court, after the case has been commenced, has instituted proceedings in any court of any other state involving the same controversy or cause of action, or in which the judgment which might be rendered in the other state might be pleadable in the case in this state as affecting the relief sought, it shall be the duty of the judge of the court in which the case is pending to set the case specially and ahead of all other business for trial as the first case at the next ensuing term of the court, except for other cases having precedence for the same reason.

(b) No case so assigned for trial shall be continued or postponed for more than 30 days for any cause whatsoever at the instance of the party who has instituted the case or proceedings in the foreign state. The case may be postponed from day to day for good cause for not exceeding 30 days at the instance of such party, but after being postponed for the 30 days it shall not be further postponed at his instance. If the term of court ends within the 30 days and the case has not been continued for the term, it shall stand for trial as the first case at the next ensuing term. This Code section shall not be applied so as to set any case for trial before proper times have elapsed for notice, the filing of defensive pleadings, and discovery. Proper time limits for discovery shall be in the discretion of the judge.

Laws 1922, p. 96, §§ 1, 2.

Formerly Code 1933, §§ 3-603, 3-604.

§ 9-2-47. Actions by informers, precedence in

In the case of actions by informers to recover any fine, forfeiture, or penalty, the first filed in the clerk's office shall have precedence for the same cause of action and the latter filed actions shall abate.

Formerly Code 1863, § 2837; Code 1868, § 2845; Code 1873, § 2896; Code 1882, § 2896; Civil Code 1895, § 3740; Civil Code 1910, § 4334; Code 1933, § 3-606.

Article 4

Dismissal and Renewal

§ 9-2-60. Dismissal of action where no order taken for five years

(a) For the purposes of this Code section, an order of continuance will be deemed an order and the word "proceedings" shall be held to include, but shall not be limited to, an appeal from an award of assessors or a special master in a condemnation proceeding.

(b) Any action or other proceeding filed in any of the courts of this state in which no written order is taken for a period of five years shall automatically stand dismissed with costs to be taxed against the party plaintiff.

(c) When an action is dismissed under this Code section, if the plaintiff recommences the action within six months following the dismissal then the renewed action shall stand upon the same footing, as to limitation, with the original action.

Laws 1953, Nov.-Dec. Sess., p. 342, §§ 1, 2; Laws 1967, p. 557, § 1; Laws 1984, p. 597, § 1.

§ 9-2-61. Discontinuance or dismissal

(a) When any case has been commenced in either a state or federal court within the applicable statute of limitations and the plaintiff discontinues or dismisses the same, it may be recommenced in a court of this state or in a federal court either within the original applicable period of limitations or within six months after the discontinuance or dismissal, whichever is later, subject to the requirement of payment of costs in the original action as required by subsection (d) of Code Section 9-11-41; provided, however, if the dismissal or discontinuance occurs after the expiration of the applicable period of limitation, this privilege of renewal shall be exercised only once.

(b) This Code section shall not apply to contracts for the sale of goods covered by Article 2 of Title 11.

(c) The provisions of subsection (a) of this Code section granting a privilege of renewal shall apply if an action is discontinued or dismissed without prejudice for lack of subject matter jurisdiction in either a court of this state or a federal court in this state.

Laws 1847, Cobb's 1851 Digest, p. 569; Laws 1855-56, p. 233, § 33; Laws 1962, p. 156, § 1; Laws 1967, p. 226, § 39; Laws

1985, p. 1446, § 1; Laws 1989, p. 419, § 1; Laws 1990, p. 876, § 1; Laws 1998, p. 862, § 1.

Formerly Code 1863, § 2873; Code 1868, § 2881; Code 1873, § 2932; Code 1882, § 2932; Civil Code 1895, § 3786; Civil Code 1910, § 4381; Code 1933, § 3-808.

§ 9-2-62. How retraxit differs from dismission or discontinuance

A retraxit differs from a dismissal or discontinuance in that a retraxit is the open, public, and voluntary renunciation by the plaintiff in open court of his action or cause of action. It is positive and conclusive of the plaintiff's right of action. Where a retraxit is entered by the plaintiff and a judgment is entered thereon by the defendant, the plaintiff's right of action shall be forever gone. A dismissal or discontinuance is negative, and the plaintiff may recommence his action on the payment of costs.

Laws 1967, p. 226, § 38.

Formerly Code 1863, §§ 3378, 3379; Code 1868, §§ 3397, 3398; Code 1873, §§ 3445, 3446; Code 1882, §§ 3445, 3446; Civil Code 1895, §§ 5042, 5043; Civil Code 1910, §§ 5624, 5625; Code 1933, §§ 3-507, 3-508.

§ 9-2-63. Renewal of actions in forma pauperis

When any action is dismissed or discontinued and the plaintiff desires to recommence his action, if he will make and file with his complaint, summons, or other proceedings an affidavit in writing stating that he is advised and believes that he has good cause for recommencing his action and that because of his indigence he is unable to pay the costs that have accrued in the case, he shall have the right to renew the action without payment of the cost as aforesaid.

Laws 1901, p. 80, § 1.

Formerly Civil Code 1910, § 5626; Code 1933, § 3-509.

CHAPTER 3

LIMITATIONS OF ACTIONS

Article 1

General Provisions

§ 9-3-1. Limitations to operate against the state

Except as otherwise provided by law, the state shall be barred from bringing an action if, under the same circumstances, a private person would be barred.

Laws 1855-56, p. 233, § 38.

Formerly Code 1873, § 2925a; Code 1882, § 2925a; Civil Code 1895, § 3777; Civil Code 1910, § 4371; Code 1933, § 3-715.

§ 9-3-2. Municipal claims; executions

Any claim or demand held by any municipality not in the nature of a special contract or not reduced to execution shall be barred by the general statutes of limitation of force, and all executions issued by any municipality shall be subject to the same laws relating to the statutes of limitation governing other executions.

Laws 1899, p. 60, § 1.

Formerly Civil Code 1910, § 4372; Code 1933, § 3-716.

§ 9-3-3. Limitations in equity; laches

Unless otherwise provided by law, limitation statutes shall apply equally to all courts. In addition, courts of equity may interpose an equitable bar whenever, from the lapse of time and laches of the complainant, it would be inequitable to allow a party to enforce his legal rights.

Laws 1855-56, p. 233, §§ 28, 39.

Formerly Code 1863, § 2865; Code 1868, § 2873; Code 1873, § 2924; Code 1882, § 2924; Civil Code 1895, § 3775; Civil Code 1910, § 4369; Code 1933, § 3-712.

§ 9-3-4. Repealed by Laws 1991, p. 810, § 3, eff. July 1, 1991

§ 9-3-5. Trustee barred, beneficiaries barred

Where a trustee is barred, the beneficiaries of the estate represented by him shall also be barred.

Formerly Civil Code 1895, § 3773; Civil Code 1910, § 4367; Code 1933, § 3-710.

§ 9-3-6. Setoffs

The statute of limitations applies to the subject matter of setoff as well as to the plaintiff's demand.

Formerly Code 1863, § 3399; Code 1868, § 3418; Code 1873, § 3470; Code 1882, § 3470; Civil Code 1895, § 5089; Civil Code 1910, § 5673; Code 1933, § 3-708.

§ 9-3-7. Mutual accounts

The statute of limitations for a mutual account begins to run on the date of the last item thereof. A mutual account must include an indebtedness on both sides. Mere entries of credits of partial payments shall not be sufficient.

Formerly Civil Code 1895, § 3769; Civil Code 1910, § 4363; Code 1933, § 3-707.

Article 2

Specific Periods of Limitation

§ 9-3-20. Actions upon foreign judgments

All actions upon judgments obtained outside this state, except judgments for child support or spousal support, or both, shall be brought within five years after such judgments have been obtained.

Laws 1805, Cobb's 1851 Digest, p. 564; Laws 1855-56, p. 233, § 7; Laws 1997, p. 1613, § 1.

Formerly Code 1863, § 2854; Code 1868, § 2862; Code 1873, § 2913; Code 1882, § 2913; Civil Code 1895, § 3760; Civil Code 1910, § 4354; Code 1933, § 3-701.

§ 9-3-21. Repealed by Laws 1986, p. 294, § 2, eff. July 1, 1986

§ 9-3-22. Statutory rights; recovery of wages, overtime, etc.

All actions for the enforcement of rights accruing to individuals under statutes or acts of incorporation or by operation of law shall be brought within 20 years after the right of action has accrued; provided, however, that all actions for the recovery of wages, overtime, or damages and penalties accruing under laws respecting the payment of wages and overtime shall be brought within two years after the right of action has accrued.

Laws 1855-56, p. 233, § 12; Laws 1943, p. 333, § 1.

Formerly Code 1863, § 2857; Code 1868, § 2865; Code 1873, § 2916; Code 1882, § 2916; Civil Code 1895, § 3766; Civil Code 1910, § 4360; Code 1933, § 3-704.

§ 9-3-23. Actions on bond or instruments under seal

Actions upon bonds or other instruments under seal shall be brought within 20 years after the right of action has accrued. No instrument shall be considered under seal unless so recited in the body of the instrument.

Laws 1806, Cobb's 1851 Digest, p. 566; Laws 1855-56, p. 233, § 11.

Formerly Code 1863, § 2856; Code 1868, § 2864; Code 1873, § 2915; Code 1882, § 2915; Civil Code 1895, § 3765; Civil Code 1910, § 4359; Code 1933, § 3-703.

§ 9-3-24. Simple contracts in writing

All actions upon simple contracts in writing shall be brought within six years after the same become due and payable. However, this Code section shall not apply to actions for the breach of contracts for the sale of goods under Article 2 of Title 11 or to negotiable instruments under Article 3 of Title 11.

Laws 1962, p. 156, § 1; Laws 1996, p. 1306, § 15.

Formerly Code 1863, § 2858; Code 1868, § 2866; Code 1873, § 2917; Code 1882, § 2917; Civil Code 1895, § 3767; Civil Code 1910, § 4361; Code 1933, § 3-705.

§ 9-3-25. Open accounts; breach of contract not under hand of party; implied promise

All actions upon open account, or for the breach of any contract not under the hand of the party sought to be charged, or upon any implied promise or undertaking shall be brought within four years after the right of action accrues. However, this Code section shall not apply to actions for the breach of contracts for the sale of goods under Article 2 of Title 11.

Laws 1809, Cobb's 1851 Digest, p. 566; Laws 1855-56, p. 233, § 10; Laws 1962, p. 156, § 1.

Formerly Code 1863, § 2859; Code 1868, § 2867; Code 1873, § 2918; Code 1882, § 2918; Civil Code 1895, § 3768; Civil Code 1910, § 4362; Code 1933, § 3-706.

§ 9-3-26. Other actions ex contractu

All other actions upon contracts express or implied not otherwise provided for shall be brought within four years from the accrual of the right of action. However, this Code section shall not apply to actions for the breach of contracts for the sale of goods under Article 2 of Title 11.

Laws 1855-56, p. 233, § 18; Laws 1962, p. 156, § 1.

Formerly Code 1863, § 2864; Code 1868, § 2872; Code 1873, § 2923; Code 1882, § 2923; Civil Code 1895, § 3774; Civil Code 1910, § 4368; Code 1933, § 3-711.

§ 9-3-27. Actions against executors, administrators, or guardians of action accrues.

All actions against executors, administrators, or guardians, except on their bonds, shall be brought within ten years after the right of action accrues.

Laws 1991, p. 810, § 4.

Formerly Code 1863, § 2863; Code 1868, § 2871; Code 1873, § 2922; Code 1882, § 2922; Civil Code 1895, § 3772; Civil Code 1910, § 4366; Code 1933, § 3-709.

§ 9–3–28. Actions by informers

All actions by informers to recover any fine, forfeiture, or penalty shall be commenced within one year from the time the defendant's liability thereto is discovered or by reasonable diligence could have been discovered.

Laws 1767, Cobb's 1851 Digest, p. 563.

Formerly Code 1863, § 2866; Code 1868, § 2874; Code 1873, § 2925; Code 1882, § 2925; Civil Code 1895, § 3776; Civil Code 1910, § 4370; Code 1933, § 3–714.

§ 9–3–29. Limitations as to actions for breach of covenant restricting use of land

(a) All actions for breach of any covenant restricting lands to certain uses shall be brought within two years after the right of action accrues, excepting violations for failure to pay assessments or fees, which shall be governed by subsection (b) of this Code section. This Code section shall apply to rights of action which may accrue as a result of the violation of a building set-back line.

(b) In actions for breach of covenant which accrue as a result of the failure to pay assessments or fees, the action shall be brought within four years after the right of action accrues.

(c) For the purpose of this Code section, the right of action shall accrue immediately upon the violation of the covenant restricting lands to certain uses or the violation of a set-back line provision. This Code section shall not be construed so as to extend any applicable statute of limitations affecting actions in equity.

Laws 1953, Jan.-Feb. Sess., p. 238, §§ 1, 2; Laws 1991, p. 665, § 1; Laws 1995, p. 727, § 1.

§ 9–3–30. Trespass upon or damage to realty; damage to dwelling due to synthetic exterior siding

(a) All actions for trespass upon or damage to realty shall be brought within four years after the right of action accrues.

(b)(1) The causes of action specified in Code Section 51–1–11 and subsection (a) of Code Section 9–3–51 for recovery of damages to a dwelling due to the manufacture of or the negligent design or installation of synthetic exterior siding shall accrue when the damage to the dwelling is discovered or, in the exercise of reasonable diligence, should have been discovered, whichever first occurs. In any event, such cause of action shall be brought within the time limits provided in Code Sections 51–1–11 and 9–3–51, respectively.

(2) This subsection shall apply to causes of action which had not expired under the former law before March 28, 2000. This subsection shall not revive any cause of action which was barred by former law before March 28, 2000.

Laws 1767, Cobb's 1851 Digest, p. 562; Laws 1805, Cobb's 1851 Digest, p. 564; Laws 1855–56, p. 233, § 3; Laws 2000, p. 212, § 1.

Formerly Code 1863, § 2990; Code 1868, § 3003; Code 1873, § 3058; Code 1882, § 3058; Civil Code 1895, § 3898; Civil Code 1910, § 4495; Code 1933, § 3–1001.

§ 9–3–30.1. Revival of actions against manufacturer or supplier of asbestos or material containing asbestos

(a) Notwithstanding the provisions of Code Section 9–3–30 or any other law, every action against a manufacturer or supplier of asbestos or material containing asbestos brought by or on behalf of any person or entity, public or private; or brought by or on behalf of this state or any agency, department, political subdivision, authority, board, district, or commission of the state; or brought by or on behalf of any municipality, county, or any state or local school board or local school district to recover for:

(1) Removal of asbestos or materials containing asbestos from any building owned or used by such entity;

(2) Other measures taken to correct or ameliorate any problem related to asbestos in such building;

(3) Reimbursement for such removal, correction, or amelioration related to asbestos in such building; or

(4) Any other claim for damage to real property allowed by law relating to asbestos in such building

which might otherwise be barred prior to July 1, 1990, as a result of expiration of the applicable period of limitation, is revived or extended. Any action thereon shall be commenced no later than July 1, 1990.

(b) The enactment of this Code section shall not be construed to imply that any action against a manufacturer or supplier of asbestos or material containing asbestos is now barred by an existing limitations period.

(c) Nothing in this Code section shall be construed to revive, extend, change, or otherwise affect the applicable period of limitation for persons or entities not set forth and provided for in subsection (a) of this Code section.

(d) Nothing contained in this Code section shall be construed to have any effect on actions for personal injury or any other claim except as specifically provided in this Code section.

Laws 1988, p. 1996, § 1.

Validity

This section was declared unconstitutional by the Supreme Court of Georgia in the case of Celotex Corp. v. St. Joseph Hospital, 259 Ga. 108, 376 S.E.2d 880 (1989), answer to certified question conformed to 874 F.2d 764 (1989), rehearing denied 887 F.2d 1093 (1989), certiorari denied 110 S.Ct. 1138, 493 U.S. 1081, 107 L.Ed.2d 1043 (1990).

§ 9-3-30.2. Actions against persons engaged in the practice of land surveying

(a) As used in this Code section, the term "land surveying" shall have the same meaning as provided by paragraph (6) of Code Section 43-15-2.

(b) No action to recover damages for any deficiency, defect, omission, error, or miscalculation in a survey or plat shall be brought against registered surveyors or their employees engaged in the practice of land surveying who performed or furnished such survey or plat more than six years from the date of the survey or plat. The cause of action in such cases shall accrue when such services are rendered as shown from the date on the survey or plat. Any such action not instituted within the six-year period provided by this subsection shall be forever barred.

Laws 1998, p. 178, § 1.

§ 9-3-31. Injuries to personalty

Actions for injuries to personalty shall be brought within four years after the right of action accrues.

Laws 1767, Cobb's 1851 Digest, p. 562; Laws 1805, Cobb's 1851 Digest, p. 564; Laws 1855-56, p. 233, § 4.

Formerly Code 1863, § 2991; Code 1868, § 3004; Code 1873, § 3059; Code 1882, § 3059; Civil Code 1895, § 3899; Civil Code 1910, § 4496; Code 1933, § 3-1002.

§ 9-3-32. Recovery of personalty and damages for its conversion or destruction

Actions for the recovery of personal property, or for damages for the conversion or destruction of the same, shall be brought within four years after the right of action accrues.

Laws 1855-56, p. 233, § 2.

Formerly Code 1933, § 3-1003.

§ 9-3-33. Injuries to the person

Actions for injuries to the person shall be brought within two years after the right of action accrues, except for injuries to the reputation, which shall be brought within one year after the right of action accrues, and except for actions for injuries to the person involving loss of consortium, which shall be brought within four years after the right of action accrues.

Laws 1767, Cobb's 1851 Digest, p. 562; Laws 1805, Cobb's 1851 Digest, p. 564; Laws 1855-56, p. 233, § 5; Laws 1964, p. 763, § 1.

Formerly Code 1863, § 2992; Code 1868, § 3005; Code 1873, § 3060; Code 1882, § 3060; Civil Code 1895, § 3900; Civil Code 1910, § 4497; Code 1933, § 3-1004.

§ 9-3-33.1. Childhood sexual abuse

(a) As used in this Code section, the term "childhood sexual abuse" means any act committed by the defendant against the plaintiff which act occurred when the plaintiff was under the age of 18 years and which act would have been proscribed by Code Section 16-6-1, relating to rape; Code Section 16-6-2, relating to sodomy and aggravated sodomy; Code Section 16-6-3, relating to statutory rape; Code Section 16-6-4, relating to child molestation and aggravated child molestation; Code Section 16-6-5, relating to enticing a child for indecent purposes; Code Section 16-6-12, relating to pandering; Code Section 16-6-14, relating to pandering by compulsion; Code Section 16-6-15, relating to solicitation of sodomy; Code Section 16-6-22, relating to incest; Code Section 16-6-22.1, relating to sexual battery; or Code Section 16-6-22.2, relating to aggravated sexual battery, or any prior laws of this state of similar effect which were in effect at the time the act was committed.

(b) Any civil action for recovery of damages suffered as a result of childhood sexual abuse shall be commenced within five years of the date the plaintiff attains the age of majority.

Laws 1992, p. 2473, § 1.

§ 9-3-34. Actions for medical malpractice excluded

This article shall not apply to actions for medical malpractice as defined in Code Section 9-3-70.

Laws 1976, p. 1363, § 2.

Formerly Code 1933, § 3-718.

§ 9-3-35. Actions by creditors seeking relief under Uniform Fraudulent Transfers Act

An action by a creditor seeking relief under the provisions of Article 4 of Chapter 2 of Title 18, known as the "Uniform Fraudulent Transfers Act," shall be brought within the applicable period set out in Code Section 18-2-79.

Laws 2002, p. 141, § 1.

Article 3

Limitations on Recovery for Deficiencies Connected with Improvements to Realty and Resulting Injuries

§ 9-3-50. Definitions

As used in this article, the term:

(1) "Person" means an individual, corporation, partnership, business trust, unincorporated organization, association, or joint-stock company.

(2) "Substantial completion" means the date when construction was sufficiently completed, in accordance with the contract as modified by any change order agreed to by the parties, so that the owner could occupy the project for the use for which it was intended.

Laws 1968, p. 127, §§ 5, 6.

§ 9-3-51. Deficiencies in connection with improvements to real property

(a) No action to recover damages:

(1) For any deficiency in the survey or plat, planning, design, specifications, supervision or observation of construction, or construction of an improvement to real property;

(2) For injury to property, real or personal, arising out of any such deficiency; or

(3) For injury to the person or for wrongful death arising out of any such deficiency

shall be brought against any person performing or furnishing the survey or plat, design, planning, supervision or observation of construction, or construction of such an improvement more than eight years after substantial completion of such an improvement.

(b) Notwithstanding subsection (a) of this Code section, in the case of such an injury to property or the person or such an injury causing wrongful death, which injury occurred during the seventh or eighth year after such substantial completion, an action in tort to recover damages for such an injury or wrongful death may be brought within two years after the date on which such injury occurred, irrespective of the date of death, but in no event may such an action be brought more than ten years after the substantial completion of construction of such an improvement.

Laws 1968, p. 127, §§ 1, 2.

§ 9-3-52. Improvements to real property; when limitations prescribed by this law may not be asserted as a defense

The limitation prescribed by this article shall not be asserted as a defense by any person who would otherwise be entitled to its benefits but who is in actual possession or control, as owner, tenant, or otherwise, of such an improvement at the time any deficiency of such an improvement constitutes the proximate cause of the injury or death for which it is proposed to bring an action.

Laws 1968, p. 127, § 4.

§ 9-3-53. Improvements to real property; no extension of period of limitations prescribed by other law

Nothing in this article shall extend the period of limitations prescribed by the law of this state for the bringing of any action or shall postpone the time as of which a cause of action accrues.

Laws 1968, p. 127, § 3.

Article 4

Limitations for Malpractice Actions

§ 9-3-70. "Action for medical malpractice" defined

As used in this article, the term "action for medical malpractice" means any claim for damages resulting from the death of or injury to any person arising out of:

(1) Health, medical, dental, or surgical service, diagnosis, prescription, treatment, or care rendered by a person authorized by law to perform such service or by any person acting under the supervision and control of the lawfully authorized person; or

(2) Care or service rendered by any public or private hospital, nursing home, clinic, hospital authority, facility, or institution, or by any officer, agent, or employee thereof acting within the scope of his employment.

Laws 1976, p. 1363, § 1.

Formerly Code 1933, § 3-1101.

§ 9-3-71. General limitations

(a) Except as otherwise provided in this article, an action for medical malpractice shall be brought within two years after the date on which an injury or death arising from a negligent or wrongful act or omission occurred.

(b) Notwithstanding subsection (a) of this Code section, in no event may an action for medical malpractice be brought more than five years after the date on which the negligent or wrongful act or omission occurred.

(c) Subsection (a) of this Code section is intended to create a two-year statute of limitations. Subsection (b) of this Code section is intended to create a five-year statute of ultimate repose and abrogation.

(d) Nothing contained in subsection (a) or (b) of this Code section shall be construed to repeal Code Section 9-3-73, which shall be deemed to apply either to the applicable statutes of limitation or repose.

Laws 1976, p. 1363, § 1; Laws 1985, p. 556, § 1.

Formerly Code 1933, § 3-1102.

§ 9-3-72. Foreign objects left in body

The limitations of Code Section 9-3-71 shall not apply where a foreign object has been left in a patient's body, but in such a case an action shall be brought within one year after the negligent or wrongful act or omission is discovered. For the purposes of this Code section, the term "foreign object" shall not include a chemical compound, fixation device, or prosthetic aid or device.

Laws 1976, p. 1363, § 1; Laws 1985, p. 556, § 2.

Formerly Code 1933, § 3-1103.

§ 9-3-73. Certain disabilities and exceptions applicable

(a) Except as provided in this Code section, the disabilities and exceptions prescribed in Article 5 of this chapter in limiting actions on contracts shall be allowed and held applicable to actions, whether in tort or contract, for medical malpractice.

(b) Notwithstanding Article 5 of this chapter, all persons who are legally incompetent because of mental retardation or mental illness and all minors who have attained the age of five years shall be subject to the periods of limitation for actions for medical malpractice provided in this article. A minor who has not attained the age of five years shall have two years from the date of such minor's fifth birthday within which to bring a medical malpractice action if the cause of action arose before such minor attained the age of five years.

(c) Notwithstanding subsections (a) and (b) of this Code section, in no event may an action for medical malpractice be brought by or on behalf of:

(1) A person who is legally incompetent because of mental retardation or mental illness more than five years after the date on which the negligent or wrongful act or omission occurred; or

(2) A minor:

(A) After the tenth birthday of the minor if such minor was under the age of five years on the date on which the negligent or wrongful act or omission occurred; or

(B) After five years from the date on which the negligent or wrongful act or omission occurred if such minor was age five or older on the date of such act or omission.

(d) Subsection (b) of this Code section is intended to create a statute of limitations and subsection (c) of this Code section is intended to create a statute of repose.

(e) The limitations of subsections (b) and (c) of this Code section shall not apply where a foreign object has been left in a patient's body. Such cases shall be governed by Code Section 9-3-72.

(f) The findings of the General Assembly under this Code section include, without limitation, that a reasonable relationship exists between the provisions, goals, and classifications of this Code section and the rational, legitimate state objectives of providing quality health care, assuring the availability of physicians, preventing the curtailment of medical services, stabilizing insurance and medical costs, preventing stale medical malpractice claims, and providing for the public safety, health, and welfare as a whole.

(g) No action which, prior to July 1, 1987, has been barred by provisions relating to limitations of actions shall be revived by this article, as amended. No action which would be barred before July 1, 1987, by the provisions of this article, as amended, but which would not be so barred by the provisions of this article and Article 5 of this chapter in force immediately prior to July 1, 1987, shall be barred until July 1, 1989.

Laws 1976, p. 1363, § 1; Laws 1987, p. 887, § 2.

Formerly Code 1933, § 3-1104.

§ 9-3-74. Certain actions not revived

No action for medical malpractice which, prior to July 1, 1976, has been barred by the provisions of this chapter relating to actions shall be revived by this article.

Laws 1976, p. 1363, § 1.

Formerly Code 1933, § 3-1105.

Article 5

Tolling of Limitations

§ 9-3-90. Persons under disability

(a) Minors and persons who are legally incompetent because of mental retardation or mental illness, who are such when the cause of action accrues, shall be entitled to the same time after their disability is removed to bring an action as is prescribed for other persons.

(b) No action accruing to a person imprisoned at the time of its accrual which, prior to July 1, 1984, has been barred by the provisions of this chapter relating to limitations of actions shall be revived by this chapter, as amended. No action accruing to a person imprisoned at the time of its accrual which would be barred before July 1, 1984, by the provisions of this chapter, as amended, but which would not be so barred by the provisions of this chapter in force immediately prior to July 1, 1984, shall be barred until July 1, 1985.

Laws 1805, Cobb's 1851 Digest, p. 564; Laws 1806, Cobb's 1851 Digest, p. 565; Laws 1817, Cobb's 1851 Digest, p. 567; Laws 1855–56, p. 233, § 19; Laws 1984, p. 580, § 1.

Formerly Code 1863, § 2867; Code 1868, § 2875; Code 1873, § 2926; Code 1882, § 2926; Civil Code 1895, § 3779; Civil Code 1910, § 4374; Code 1933, § 3–801.

§ 9-3-91. Disabilities occurring after accrual of right

If any person suffers a disability specified in Code Section 9–3–90 after his right of action has accrued and the disability is not voluntarily caused or undertaken by the person claiming the benefit thereof, the limitation applicable to his cause of action shall cease to operate during the continuance of the disability.

Laws 1817, Cobb's 1851 Digest, p. 567; Laws 1855–56, p. 233, § 20.

Formerly Code 1863, § 2868; Code 1868, § 2876; Code 1873, § 2927; Code 1882, § 2927; Civil Code 1895, § 3780; Civil Code 1910, § 4375; Code 1933, § 3–802.

§ 9-3-92. Unrepresented estate

The time between the death of a person and the commencement of representation upon his estate or between the termination of one administration and the commencement of another shall not be counted against his estate in calculating any limitation applicable to the bringing of an action, provided that such time shall not exceed five years. At the expiration of the five years the limitation shall commence, even if the cause of action accrued after the person's death.

Laws 1855–56, p. 235, §§ 21, 40.

Formerly Code 1863, § 2869; Code 1868, § 2877; Code 1873, § 2928; Code 1882, § 2928; Civil Code 1895, § 3781; Civil Code 1910, § 4376; Code 1933, § 3–803.

§ 9-3-93. Creditors of unrepresented estate

The time between the death of a person and the commencement of representation upon his estate or between the termination of one administration and the commencement of another shall not be counted against creditors of his estate, provided that such time does not exceed five years. At the expiration of the five years the limitation shall commence.

Laws 1882–83, p. 104, § 1.

Formerly Civil Code 1895, § 3782; Civil Code 1910, § 4377; Code 1933, § 3–804.

§ 9-3-94. Absence of defendant from state

Unless otherwise provided by law, if a defendant removes from this state, the time of his absence from the state until he returns to reside shall not be counted or estimated in his favor.

Laws 1805, Cobb's 1851 Digest, p. 564; Laws 1806, Cobb's 1851 Digest, p. 565; Laws 1817, Cobb's 1851 Digest, p. 567; Laws 1839, Cobb's 1851 Digest, p. 568; Laws 1851–52, p. 239, § 1; Laws 1855–56, p. 233, § 23.

Formerly Code 1863, § 2870; Code 1868, § 2878; Code 1873, § 2929; Code 1882, § 2929; Civil Code 1895, § 3783; Civil Code 1910, § 4378; Code 1933, § 3–805.

§ 9-3-95. Joint action; party under disability

Where there is a joint right of action and one or more of the persons having the right is under any of the disabilities specified in Code Section 9–3–90, the terms of limitation shall not be computed against the joint action until all the disabilities are removed. However, if the action is severable so that each person may bring an action for his own share, those free from disability shall be barred after the running of the applicable statute of limitations, and only the rights of those under disability shall be protected.

Laws 1855–56, p. 233, § 24.

Formerly Code 1863, § 2871; Code 1868, § 2879; Code 1873, § 2930; Code 1882, § 2930; Civil Code 1895, § 3784; Civil Code 1910, § 4379; Code 1933, § 3–806.

§ 9-3-96. Fraud

If the defendant or those under whom he claims are guilty of a fraud by which the plaintiff has been debarred or deterred from bringing an action, the period of limitation shall run only from the time of the plaintiff's discovery of the fraud.

Laws 1855-56, p. 233, § 30.

Formerly Code 1863, § 2872; Code 1868, § 2880; Code 1873, § 2931; Code 1882, § 2931; Civil Code 1895, § 3785; Civil Code 1910, § 4380; Code 1933, § 3-807.

§ 9-3-97. Extension of limitation period with respect to counterclaims and cross-claims

The limitations of time within which various actions may be commenced and pursued within this state to enforce the rights of the parties are extended, only insofar as the enforcement of rights which may be instituted by way of counterclaim and cross-claim, so as to allow parties, up to and including the last day upon which the answer or other defensive pleadings should have been filed, to commence the prosecution and enforcement of rights by way of counterclaim and cross-claim, provided that the final date allowed by such limitations for the commencement of such actions shall not have expired prior to filing of the main action.

Laws 1964, p. 165, § 1; Laws 1967, p. 226, § 37.

§ 9-3-97.1. Tolling of limitation period for bringing medical malpractice action

(a) The periods of limitation for bringing an action for medical malpractice as provided in Code Sections 9-3-71 and 9-3-72 shall be tolled if:

(1) The injured person or his duly appointed attorney makes a request by certified or registered mail or statutory overnight delivery, return receipt requested, upon any physician, hospital, or other health care provider for medical records in their custody or control relating to such injured person's health or medical treatment which medical records the injured person is entitled by law to receive;

(2) The request, if made by an injured person's duly appointed attorney, has enclosed therewith a properly executed medical authorization authorizing release of the requested information to said attorney;

(3) Such request expressly requests that the medical records be mailed to the injured person or his attorney by certified or registered mail or statutory overnight delivery, return receipt requested and states therein that the requested records are needed by the injured person for possible use in a medical malpractice action;

(4) The injured person or his attorney has promptly paid all fees and costs charged by such physician, hospital, or other health care provider for compiling, copying, and mailing such medical records; and

(5) Such medical records or a letter of response stating that the provider does not have custody or control of the medical records has not been received by the injured person or his attorney within 21 days of the date of receiving such request.

Such periods of limitation shall cease to run on the twenty-second day following the day such request was received and shall resume on the day following the date such medical records, or response stating that the provider does not have custody or control of the medical records, are actually received by such injured person or his attorney; provided, however, that such periods of limitation shall be tolled only once for any cause of action.

(b) Any action filed in reliance upon a tolling of the statute of limitations as authorized by this Code section shall contain in the complaint as first filed allegations showing that the plaintiff is entitled to rely upon the provisions of this Code section, and said complaint as first filed shall have attached thereto as exhibits copies of the request, medical release, and evidence of mailing and receipt by certified or registered mail or statutory overnight delivery.

(c) Notwithstanding any other provision of this Code section, no period of limitation shall be tolled for a period exceeding 90 days except as provided in this subsection. In the event the procedure set forth in subsection (a) of this Code section has been followed by an injured person but the requested records or a letter of response stating that the provider does not have custody or control of the medical records have not been received within 85 days, the injured person shall have the right to petition the court for an order tolling the period of limitation beyond the 90 days and requiring the delivery of the medical records originally requested or a letter of response stating that the provider does not have custody or control of the medical records.

(d) It is intended that the provisions of this Code section tolling the statute of limitations for medical malpractice under certain circumstances be strictly complied with and strictly construed.

Laws 1989, p. 419, § 2; Laws 2000, p. 1589, § 4.

§ 9-3-98. Application to tort and contract actions

This article shall apply to tort actions as well as actions on contracts.

Formerly Code 1863, § 2993; Code 1868, § 3006; Code 1873, § 3061; Code 1882, § 3061; Civil Code 1895, § 3901; Civil Code 1910, § 4498; Code 1933, § 3-1005.

§ 9-3-99. Tolling of limitation period for tort arising from a crime

The running of the period of limitations with respect to any cause of action in tort that may be brought by the victim of an alleged crime which arises out of the facts and circumstances relating to the commission of such alleged crime committed in this state shall be tolled from the date of the commission of the alleged crime or the act giving rise to such action in tort until the prosecution of such crime or act has become final or otherwise terminated, provided that such time does not exceed six years.

Laws 2005, Act 20, § 2, eff. July 1, 2005.

Article 6

Revival

§ 9-3-110. New promise; necessity of writing

A new promise, in order to renew a right of action already barred or to constitute a point from which the limitation shall commence running on a right of action not yet barred, shall be in writing, either in the party's own handwriting or subscribed by him or someone authorized by him.

Laws 1855-56, p. 233, § 25.

Formerly Code 1863, § 2875; Code 1868, § 2883; Code 1873, § 2934; Code 1882, § 2934; Civil Code 1895, § 3788; Civil Code 1910, § 4383; Code 1933, § 3-901.

§ 9-3-111. Effect of discharge in bankruptcy

No promise made after discharge in bankruptcy to pay a debt provable in bankruptcy from the liability of which the debtor has been discharged shall be valid or binding upon the debtor or promisor unless the same is made in writing and signed by the party making the same or to be charged therewith, or by someone duly authorized by him.

Laws 1905, p. 101, § 1.

Formerly Civil Code 1910, § 4384; Code 1933, § 3-902.

§ 9-3-112. Effect of payment or written acknowledgment of liability

A payment entered upon a written evidence of debt by the debtor or upon any other written acknowledgment of the existing liability shall be equivalent to a new promise to pay.

Formerly Code 1863, § 2876; Code 1868, § 2884; Code 1873, § 2935; Code 1882, § 2935; Civil Code 1895, § 3789; Civil Code 1910, § 4385; Code 1933, § 3-903.

§ 9-3-113. Effect of new promise

A new promise shall revive or extend the original liability; it shall not create a new one.

Formerly Code 1863, § 2877; Code 1868, § 2885; Code 1873, § 2936; Code 1882, § 2936; Civil Code 1895, § 3790; Civil Code 1910, § 4386; Code 1933, § 3-904.

§ 9-3-114. New promise by joint contractor

In cases of joint or joint and several contracts, a new promise by one of the contractors shall operate only against the promisor.

Laws 1855-56, p. 233, § 27.

Formerly Code 1863, § 2879; Code 1868, § 2887; Code 1873, § 2938; Code 1882, § 2938; Civil Code 1895, § 3792; Civil Code 1910, § 4388; Code 1933, § 3-906.

§ 9-3-115. New promise by partner

After the dissolution of a partnership, a new promise by one partner shall revive or extend a partnership debt only as to the promisor and not as to his copartner or copartners.

Laws 1855-56, p. 233, § 26.

Formerly Code 1863, § 2878; Code 1868, § 2886; Code 1873, § 2937; Code 1882, § 2937; Civil Code 1895, § 3791; Civil Code 1910, § 4387; Code 1933, § 3-905.

CHAPTER 4
DECLARATORY JUDGMENTS

§ 9-4-1. Purpose of Chapter

The purpose of this chapter is to settle and afford relief from uncertainty and insecurity with respect to rights, status, and other legal relations; and this chapter is to be liberally construed and administered.

Laws 1945, p. 137, § 13.

§ 9-4-2. Power of superior courts to declare rights and legal relations; cases in which power can be exercised; effect of other adequate remedy

(a) In cases of actual controversy, the respective superior courts of this state shall have power, upon petition or other appropriate pleading, to declare rights and other legal relations of any interested party petitioning for such declaration, whether or not further relief is or could be prayed; and the declaration shall have the force and effect of a final judgment or decree and be reviewable as such.

(b) In addition to the cases specified in subsection (a) of this Code section, the respective superior courts of this state shall have power, upon petition or other appropriate pleading, to declare rights and other legal relations of any interested party petitioning for the declaration, whether or not further relief is or could be prayed, in any civil case in which it appears to the court that the ends of justice require that the declaration should be made; and the declaration shall have the force and effect of a final judgment or decree and be reviewable as such.

(c) Relief by declaratory judgment shall be available, notwithstanding the fact that the complaining party has any other adequate legal or equitable remedy or remedies.

Laws 1945, p. 137, § 1; Laws 1959, p. 236, § 1; Laws 1982, p. 3, § 9.

§ 9–4–3. Further relief; damages; injunction; mandamus; quo warranto; service of process; procedure

(a) Further plenary relief, legal or equitable, including but not limited to damages, injunction, mandamus, or quo warranto, may be sought in a petition seeking declaratory judgment, and in such case, the action shall be governed as to process, service, and procedure by Code Section 9–4–5. In all such cases, the court shall award to the petitioning party such relief as the pleadings and evidence may show him to be entitled; and the failure of the petition to state a cause of action for declaratory relief shall not affect the right of the party to any other relief, legal or equitable, to which he may be entitled.

(b) The court, in order to maintain the status quo pending the adjudication of the questions or to preserve equitable rights, may grant injunction and other interlocutory extraordinary relief in substantially the manner and under the same rules applicable in equity cases.

Laws 1945, p. 137, § 2; Laws 1959, p. 236, § 2; Laws 1982, p. 3, § 9.

§ 9–4–4. Rights of persons interested in estates or trusts; effect of enumeration of powers on general powers conferred in Section 9–4–2

(a) Without limiting the generality of Code Sections 9–4–2, 9–4–3, 9–4–5 through 9–4–7, and 9–4–9, any person interested as or through an executor, administrator, trustee, guardian, or other fiduciary, creditor, devisee, legatee, heir, ward, next of kin, or beneficiary in the administration of a trust or of the estate of a decedent, a minor, a person who is legally incompetent because of mental illness or mental retardation, or an insolvent may have a declaration of rights or legal relations in respect thereto and a declaratory judgment:

(1) To ascertain any class of creditors, devisees, legatees, heirs, next of kin, or others;

(2) To direct the executor, administrator, or trustee to do or abstain from doing any particular act in his fiduciary capacity; or

(3) To determine any question arising in the administration of the estate or trust, including questions of construction of wills and other writings.

(b) The enumeration in subsection (a) of this Code section does not limit or restrict the exercise of general powers conferred in Code Section 9–4–2 in any proceeding covered thereby where declaratory relief is sought in which a judgment or decree will terminate the controversy or remove the uncertainty.

Laws 1945, p. 137, §§ 7, 8.

§ 9–4–5. Filing of proceeding; service; time of trial

A proceeding instituted under this chapter shall be filed and served as are other cases in the superior courts of this state and may be tried at any time designated by the court not earlier than 20 days after the service thereof, unless the parties consent in writing to an earlier trial. If there is an issue of fact which requires a submission to a jury, the jury may be drawn, summoned, and sworn either in regular term or specially for the pending case.

Laws 1945, p. 137, § 4.

§ 9–4–6. Jury trials; special verdict; instructions by court

When a declaration of right or the granting of further relief based thereon involves the determination of issues of fact triable by a jury and jury trial is not waived, the issues shall be submitted to a jury of 12 in the form of interrogatories, with proper instructions by the court, whether a general verdict is required or not. The instructions by the court shall in all respects be governed by the laws of this state relating to instructions or charges by a court to a jury.

Laws 1945, p. 137, § 3.

§ 9–4–7. Rights of persons not parties; state and municipalities made parties

(a) No declaration shall prejudice the rights of persons not parties to the proceeding.

(b) In any proceeding involving the validity of a municipal ordinance or franchise, the municipality shall be made a party and shall be entitled to be heard as a party.

(c) If a statute of the state, any order or regulation of any administrative body of the state, or any franchise granted by the state is alleged to be unconstitutional, the Attorney General of the state shall be served with a copy of the proceeding and shall be entitled to be heard.

Laws 1945, p. 137, § 6.

§ 9-4-8. Refusal of judgment not terminating uncertainty or controversy

The court may refuse to render or enter a declaratory judgment or decree where the judgment or decree, if rendered or entered, would not terminate the uncertainty or controversy giving rise to the proceeding.

Laws 1945, p. 137, § 9.

§ 9-4-9. Costs

In any proceeding under this chapter the court may make such award or division of costs as may seem equitable and just.

Laws 1945, p. 137, § 5.

§ 9-4-10. Effect on equity jurisdiction

Nothing in this chapter is intended to impair the equity jurisdiction of the superior courts of the state.

Laws 1945, p. 137, § 10.

CHAPTER 5

INJUNCTIONS

§ 9-5-1. Purposes for which issued in general; inadequate remedy at law

Equity, by a writ of injunction, may restrain proceedings in another or the same court, a threatened or existing tort, or any other act of a private individual or corporation which is illegal or contrary to equity and good conscience and for which no adequate remedy is provided at law.

Formerly Code 1863, § 3137; Code 1868, § 3149; Code 1873, § 3210; Code 1882, § 3210; Civil Code 1895, § 4913; Civil Code 1910, § 5490; Code 1933, § 55-101.

§ 9-5-2. Administration of criminal laws, interference by equity

Equity will take no part in the administration of the criminal law. It will neither aid criminal courts in the exercise of their jurisdiction, nor will it restrain or obstruct them.

Formerly Civil Code 1895, § 4914; Civil Code 1910, § 5491; Code 1933, § 55-102.

§ 9-5-3. Enjoining proceedings or processes of court of law

(a) Equity will not enjoin the proceedings and processes of a court of law, absent some intervening equity or other proper defense of which a party, without fault on his part, cannot avail himself at law.

(b) Writs of injunction may be issued by judges of the superior courts to enjoin sales by sheriffs, at any time before a sale takes place, in any proper case made by application for injunction.

Laws 1878-79, p. 139, § 1.

Formerly Code 1863, § 3140; Code 1868, § 3152; Code 1873, § 3218; Code 1882, § 3218; Civil Code 1895, § 4915; Civil Code 1910, § 5492; Code 1933, § 55-103.

§ 9-5-4. Restraining trespasses; avoidance of circuity and multiplicity of actions

Equity will not interfere to restrain a trespass, unless the injury is irreparable in damages, or the trespasser is insolvent, or other circumstances exist which, in the discretion of the court, render the interposition of the writ necessary and proper, among which shall be the avoidance of circuity and multiplicity of actions.

Laws 1842, Cobb's 1851 Digest, p. 528.

Formerly Code 1863, § 3141; Code 1868, § 3153; Code 1873, § 3219; Code 1882, § 3219; Civil Code 1895, § 4916; Civil Code 1910, § 5493; Code 1933, § 55-104.

§ 9-5-5. Waste not enjoined when title in dispute

Equity will not interfere by injunction to restrain waste when the petitioner's title is not clear. Such relief shall be granted only when the title is free from dispute.

Formerly Civil Code 1895, § 4917; Civil Code 1910, § 5494; Code 1933, § 55-105.

§ 9-5-6. Creditors without lien, rights of

Creditors without liens may not, as a general rule, enjoin their debtors from disposing of property nor obtain injunctions or other extraordinary relief in equity.

Formerly Civil Code 1895, § 4918; Civil Code 1910, § 5495; Code 1933, § 55-106.

§ 9-5-7. Restraining breach of contract for personal services

Generally an injunction will not issue to restrain the breach of a contract for personal services unless the services are of a peculiar merit or character and cannot be performed by others.

Formerly Civil Code 1895, § 4919; Civil Code 1910, § 5496; Code 1933, § 55-107.

§ 9-5-8. Discretion of judge; caution to be exercised

The granting and continuing of injunctions shall always rest in the sound discretion of the judge, according to the circumstances of each case. This power shall be prudently and cautiously exercised and, except in clear and urgent cases, should not be resorted to.

Formerly Code 1863, § 3141; Code 1868, § 3153; Code 1873, § 3220; Code 1882, § 3220; Civil Code 1895, §§ 4902, 4920; Civil Code 1910, §§ 5477, 5497; Code 1933, § 55-108.

§ 9-5-9. Second injunction granted in discretion of judge

A second injunction may be granted in the discretion of the judge.

Laws 1842, Cobb's 1851 Digest, p. 528.

Formerly Code 1863, § 3144; Code 1868, § 3156; Code 1873, § 3223; Code 1882, § 3223; Civil Code 1895, § 4921; Civil Code 1910, § 5498; Code 1933, § 55-109.

§ 9-5-10. Perpetual injunction

A perpetual injunction shall be granted only after hearing and upon a final decree.

Formerly Code 1863, § 3146; Code 1868, § 3158; Code 1873, § 3225; Code 1882, § 3225; Civil Code 1895, § 4923; Civil Code 1910, § 5500; Code 1933, § 55-111.

§ 9-5-11. Enjoining transactions outside State

Equity may enjoin the defendant as to transactions involving fraud, trust, or contracts beyond the limits of this state.

Formerly Civil Code 1895, § 4854; Civil Code 1910, § 5427; Code 1933, § 55-112.

CHAPTER 6

EXTRAORDINARY WRITS

Article 1

General Provisions

§ 9-6-1. Appeal; finality of judgment in mandamus, quo warranto, and prohibition

No appeal as to any ruling or decision in a mandamus or quo warranto proceeding or in a case involving a writ of prohibition may be taken to the Supreme Court until there has been a final judgment in the trial court. The grant of a new trial shall be treated as a final judgment in these cases and subject to review as in other cases.

Laws 1882-83, p. 103, § 3; Laws 1946, p. 726, § 1.

Formerly Civil Code 1895, § 4874; Civil Code 1910, § 5447; Code 1933, § 64-110.

Article 2

Mandamus

§ 9-6-20. Enforcement of official duty; inadequacy of legal remedy

All official duties should be faithfully performed; and whenever, from any cause, a defect of legal justice would ensue from a failure to perform or from improper performance, the writ of mandamus may issue to compel a due performance, if there is no other specific legal remedy for the legal rights.

Formerly Code 1863, § 3130; Code 1868, § 3142; Code 1873, § 3198; Code 1882, § 3198; Civil Code 1895, § 4867; Civil Code 1910, § 5440; Code 1933, § 64-101.

§ 9–6–21. Lies not as private remedy; exception

(a) Mandamus shall not lie as a private remedy between individuals to enforce private rights nor to a public officer who has an absolute discretion to act or not to act unless there is a gross abuse of such discretion. However, mandamus shall not be confined to the enforcement of mere ministerial duties.

(b) On the application of one or more citizens of any county against the county board of commissioners where by law supervision and jurisdiction is vested in such commissioners over the public roads of such counties and the overseers of the public roads complained of; or against the judge of the probate court where by law supervision, control, and jurisdiction over such public roads is vested in the judge and the overseers of the public roads that may be complained of; or against either, both, or all of the named parties, as the facts and methods of working the public roads in the respective counties may justify, which application or action for mandamus shall show that one or more of the public roads of the county of the plaintiff's residence are out of repair; do not measure up to the standards and do not conform to the legal requirements as prescribed by law; and are in such condition that ordinary loads, with ordinary ease, cannot be hauled over such public roads, the judges of the superior courts are authorized and given jurisdiction and it is made their duty, upon such showing being made, to issue the writ of mandamus against the parties having charge of and supervision over the public roads of the county; and to compel by such proceedings the building, repairing, and working of the public roads as are complained of, up to the standard required by law, so that ordinary loads, with ordinary ease and facility, can be continuously hauled over such public roads. The judges of the superior courts shall, by proper order, in the same proceedings compel the work done necessary to build, repair, and maintain such public roads up to the standard so prescribed.

Laws 1903, p. 41, § 1.

Formerly Code 1863, § 3131; Code 1868, § 3143; Code 1873, § 3199; Code 1882, § 3199; Civil Code 1895, § 4868; Civil Code 1910, § 5441; Code 1933, § 64–102.

§ 9–6–22. Mandamus against clerk, sheriff, or other officer

If any sheriff, clerk, or other officer fails to discharge any duty required of him by any provision of Title 5, upon petition the appellate court or the superior, state, or city court, as the case may be, may compel the performance of such duty by mandamus. No party shall lose any right by reason of the failure of the officer to discharge his duties when the party has been guilty of no fault himself and has exercised ordinary diligence to secure the discharge of such duties.

Laws 1845, Cobb's 1851 Digest, p. 450.

Formerly Code 1863, § 4172; Code 1868, § 4204; Code 1873, § 4264; Code 1882, § 4264; Civil Code 1895, § 5555; Civil Code 1910, § 6169; Code 1933, § 6–918.

§ 9–6–23. Mandamus by private person

A private person may by mandamus enforce the performance by a corporation of a public duty as to matters in which he has a special interest.

Formerly Civil Code 1895, § 4869; Civil Code 1910, § 5442; Code 1933, § 64–103.

§ 9–6–24. No special interest necessary for plaintiff to enforce public right

Where the question is one of public right and the object is to procure the enforcement of a public duty, no legal or special interest need be shown, but it shall be sufficient that a plaintiff is interested in having the laws executed and the duty in question enforced.

Formerly Code 1933, § 64–104.

§ 9–6–25. Prerequisite to enforcement of private right by mandamus

In order for a plaintiff to enforce a private right by mandamus he must show pecuniary loss for which he cannot be compensated in damages.

Formerly Code 1933, § 64–105.

§ 9–6–26. Writ denied where nugatory or fruitless; suspicion or fear

Mandamus will not be granted when it is manifest that the writ would, for any cause, be nugatory or fruitless, nor will it be granted on a mere suspicion or fear, before a refusal to act or the doing of a wrongful act.

Formerly Code 1863, § 3132; Code 1868, § 3144; Code 1873, § 3200; Code 1882, § 3200; Civil Code 1895, § 4870; Civil Code 1910, § 5443; Code 1933, § 64–106.

§ 9–6–27. Time of trial; facts in issue, how and when tried

(a) Upon the presentation of an application for mandamus, if the mandamus nisi is granted the judge shall cause the same to be returned for trial not less than ten nor more than 30 days from such date. The defendant shall be served at least five days before the time fixed for the hearing.

(b) If no issue of fact is raised by the application and answer, the case shall be heard and determined by the court without the intervention of a jury.

(c) If an issue of fact is involved, it may be heard by the judge upon the consent of all parties. Otherwise, the case shall be set for trial upon the first day of the next term of the superior court as other jury cases are tried. However, if the court has a scheduled session for jury trials which will occur before the next term, the case shall stand for trial at the present term.

Laws 1882–83, p. 103, §§ 1, 2, 4.

Formerly Civil Code 1895, §§ 4871, 4872, 4873; Civil Code 1910, §§ 5444, 5445, 5446; Code 1933, §§ 64–107, 64–108, 64–109.

§ 9–6–28. Appeal

(a) Upon refusal of the court to grant the mandamus nisi, the applicant may appeal to the Supreme Court, as in other cases. Either party dissatisfied with the judgment on the hearing of the answer to the mandamus nisi may likewise appeal.

(b) Mandamus cases shall be heard in the Supreme Court under the same laws and rules as apply to injunction cases.

Laws 1882–83, p. 103, §§ 3, 5; Laws 1946, p. 726, § 1.

Formerly Civil Code 1895, §§ 4874, 4875; Civil Code 1910, §§ 5447, 5448; Code 1933, §§ 64–110, 64–111.

Article 3

Prohibition

§ 9–6–40. Grounds for issuance of writ; when issued

The writ of prohibition is the counterpart of mandamus, to restrain subordinate courts and inferior judicial tribunals from exceeding their jurisdiction, where no other legal remedy or relief is given. The granting or refusal thereof is governed by the same principles of right, necessity, and justice as apply to mandamus.

Formerly Code 1863, § 3136; Code 1868, § 3148; Code 1873, § 3209a; Code 1882, § 3209a; Civil Code 1895, § 4885; Civil Code 1910, § 5458; Code 1933, § 64–301.

§ 9–6–41. Prohibition may be granted at any time; return; trial of fact issue

The writ of prohibition may be granted at any time, on proper showing made. The return must be in term. Any issue of fact made thereon must be tried as in equity cases.

Formerly Code 1863, §§ 3133, 3136; Code 1868, §§ 3145, 3148; Code 1873, §§ 3201, 3209a; Code 1882, §§ 3201, 3209a; Civil Code 1895, §§ 4876, 4885; Civil Code 1910, §§ 5449, 5458; Code 1933, §§ 64–301, 64–302.

§ 9–6–42. Prohibition lies to executive officers, except Governor, and to military officers

The writ of prohibition will not lie to the duly inaugurated Governor, but it lies to all other executive or military officers when acting as a judicial or quasi-judicial tribunal.

Formerly Code 1863, § 3134; Code 1868, § 3146; Code 1873, § 3202; Code 1882, § 3202; Civil Code 1895, § 4877; Civil Code 1910, § 5450; Code 1933, § 64–303.

Article 4

Quo Warranto

§ 9–6–60. Grounds for issuance; at whose instance issued

The writ of quo warranto may issue to inquire into the right of any person to any public office the duties of which he is in fact discharging. It may be granted only after the application by some person either claiming the office or interested therein.

Formerly Code 1863, § 3135; Code 1868, § 3147; Code 1873, § 3203; Code 1882, § 3203; Civil Code 1895, § 4878; Civil Code 1910, § 5451; Code 1933, § 64–201.

§ 9–6–61. Quo warranto lies to executive officers, except Governor, and to military officers

The question of who is the lawful Governor of this state may not be tried by quo warranto, but the writ of quo warranto will lie to all other civil or military officers.

Laws 1871–72, p. 41, § 1; Laws 1875, p. 104, § 1.

Formerly Code 1863, § 3134; Code 1868, § 3146; Code 1873, §§ 3202, 3206; Code 1882, §§ 3202, 3206, 3208a; Civil Code 1895, §§ 4877, 4881, 4883; Civil Code 1910, §§ 5450, 5454, 5456; Code 1933, §§ 64–208, 64–209.

§ 9-6-62. Quo warranto may be granted at any time. Trial of fact issue

The writ of quo warranto may be granted at any time, on proper showing made. Any issue of fact made thereon must be tried as in equity cases.

Formerly Code 1863, § 3133; Code 1868, § 3145; Code 1873, § 3201; Code 1882, § 3201; Civil Code 1895, § 4876; Civil Code 1910, § 5449; Code 1933, § 64-205.

§ 9-6-63. Writ of quo warranto; service of process

(a) As used in this Code section, the term "personal service" means service by placing a copy of the writ and process in the quo warranto proceeding in the hands of the defendant.

(b) The writ and process in a quo warranto proceeding shall be served on the defendant personally.

(c) Service of the writ and process in such proceeding upon a resident of this state who is temporarily residing or sojourning outside this state may be perfected in the same manner as is provided for service of process by publication as set forth in paragraph (1) of subsection (f) of Code Section 9-11-4 or personal service outside the state as set forth in paragraph (2) of subsection (f) of Code Section 9-11-4. When service is perfected upon any such person as provided for in the aforesaid Code section, then the person shall be bound by the final decision of the proceedings as fully as though the person had been personally served within this state.

Laws 1964, p. 766, § 1; Laws 2000, p. 1225, § 2.

Formerly Code 1933, § 64-202.1.

§ 9-6-64. Proceedings in cases of quo warranto; exceptions to decision

(a) In all applications for writs of quo warranto, of informations in the nature of quo warranto, or of proceedings by such writs to determine the right to hold office, where the case presented by the applicant involves only questions of law, the same may be determined, as are equitable proceedings, by the judge of the superior court before whom the case was begun; and the judge shall so order all the proceedings connected with and usual in such cases that the final determination shall be had by him within ten days from the commencement of the action, application, or proceeding. If either party to the application or proceeding desires to except to the final decision of the judge of the superior court, he shall file an appeal as in other cases, and the duties of the clerk shall be the same as in other cases.

(b) All the provisions of subsection (a) of this Code section are extended to proceedings quo warranto, or writs of that nature, involving issues of fact to be tried by a jury, when the same can be applied; but nothing in the subsection shall be construed to affect any rights or remedies in this class of cases which are not covered thereby.

Laws 1871-72, p. 41, §§ 1, 2; Laws 1946, p. 746, § 1.

Formerly Code 1873, §§ 3206, 3208; Code 1882, §§ 3206, 3208; Civil Code 1895, §§ 4881, 4882; Civil Code 1910, §§ 5454, 5455; Code 1933, §§ 64-206, 64-207.

§ 9-6-65. Issue of fact, how tried; notice to parties; continuance

In cases where the facts alleged are denied by the defendant or defendants on oath, the judge shall forthwith, in the usual manner, draw a jury of 12 to try the issue of fact, and the judge shall have the power to fix a day for trial of the issue of fact with an order that the sheriff shall notify the parties of the time and place of trial. The date fixed for the trial shall not be less than ten nor more than 30 days from the date of the order. The judge shall have the discretion to continue the hearing from day to day, as provided for in other cases.

Laws 1868, p. 130, § 2.

Formerly Code 1873, § 3205; Code 1882, § 3205; Civil Code 1895, § 4880; Civil Code 1910, § 5453; Code 1933, § 64-204.

§ 9-6-66. Judgment to dispose of books and papers

Whenever the right to any office is decided, the judgment fixing the right shall further provide for the delivery to the person held to be entitled to the office of all the books and papers of every sort belonging to the office, which judgment shall be enforced as decrees in equity are enforced.

Laws 1871-72, p. 41, § 2.

Formerly Code 1873, § 3209; Code 1882, § 3209; Civil Code 1895, § 4884; Civil Code 1910, § 5457; Code 1933, § 64-202.

CHAPTER 7

AUDITORS

§ 9-7-1. Auditor instead of master in superior court

The duties heretofore performed by a master in the superior court shall be performed by an auditor.

Laws 1894, p. 123, § 3; Laws 1895, p. 47, § 1.

Formerly Civil Code 1895, § 4581; Civil Code 1910, § 5127; Code 1933, § 10-101.

§ 9-7-2. Referral to auditor

Upon application of either party, after notice to the opposite party, the judge of the superior court, in equitable proceedings if the case shall require it, may refer any part of the facts to an auditor to investigate and report the result to the court. Furthermore, the judge may, upon his own motion, when in his judgment the facts and circumstances of any such case require it, refer the same to an auditor.

Laws 1894, p. 123, § 3; Laws 1895, p. 47, § 1.

Formerly Civil Code 1895, § 4581; Civil Code 1910, § 5127; Code 1933, § 10-101.

§ 9-7-3. Auditor to investigate matters of account

In all cases in the superior, state or city courts involving matters of account, if the case shall require it, the judge may appoint an auditor to investigate the matters of account and report the result to the court upon the application of either party and after notice to the opposite party, or upon his own motion when in his judgment the facts and circumstances of any such case require it.

Laws 1895, p. 47, § 1.

Formerly Civil Code 1895, § 4582; Civil Code 1910, § 5128; Code 1933, § 10-102.

§ 9-7-4. Where parties agree on person to be appointed

In all cases where the parties agree upon the person to be appointed as auditor, the court shall appoint such person.

Laws 1894, p. 123, § 23.

Formerly Civil Code 1895, § 4603; Civil Code 1910, § 5147; Code 1933, § 10-502.

§ 9-7-5. Place and notice of hearing; oath

Except by the written consent of all parties, the auditor shall not hear evidence or argument outside the county in which the case is proceeding. He shall give both parties or their counsel reasonable notice of the time and place of hearing and shall be sworn to render a true report according to the law and the evidence without favor or affection to either party.

Laws 1894, p. 123, § 4.

Formerly Civil Code 1895, § 4584; Civil Code 1910, § 5130; Code 1933, § 10-104.

§ 9-7-6. Powers of auditor

In all cases, unless modified by the order of appointment, in addition to the matter specially referred, the auditor shall have power to hear motions, allow amendments, and pass upon all questions of law and fact. He shall have power to subpoena and swear witnesses and compel the production of papers.

Laws 1894, p. 123, § 3.

Formerly Civil Code 1895, § 4583; Civil Code 1910, § 5129; Code 1933, § 10-103.

§ 9-7-7. Contempt

In cases of contempt by either party, a witness, or other persons, upon application to the court making the appointment, the judge thereof shall take such proceedings and impose such penalty as the facts authorize or require.

Laws 1894, p. 123, § 3.

Formerly Civil Code 1895, § 4583; Civil Code 1910, § 5129; Code 1933, § 10-103.

§ 9-7-8. Rulings and conclusions reported

After hearing the evidence and argument, the auditor shall file the evidence and a report in which he shall clearly and separately state all rulings made by him, classify and state his findings, and report his conclusions upon the law and facts.

Laws 1894, p. 123, § 7.

Formerly Civil Code 1895, § 4587; Civil Code 1910, § 5133; Code 1933, § 10-203.

§ 9-7-9. Contents of report

The auditor shall make an accurate report of all motions made before him and of his rulings thereon, and either the auditor or a party shall have the evidence and proceedings recorded by a court reporter. Any original document introduced in evidence shall be properly identified and attached to the report.

Laws 1894, p. 123, § 5.

Formerly Civil Code 1895, § 4585; Civil Code 1910, § 5131; Code 1933, § 10-201.

§ 9-7-10. Evidence inadmissible to be reported

All evidence offered but deemed inadmissible by the auditor shall nevertheless be reported by the auditor; and if, upon exception filed to his ruling thereon, the evidence is adjudged to be admissible, the same may be considered upon the trial of exceptions of fact.

Laws 1894, p. 123, § 6.

Formerly Civil Code 1895, § 4586; Civil Code 1910, § 5132; Code 1933, § 10-202.

§ 9-7-11. Notice of filing report

Upon filing his report, the auditor shall give both parties or their counsel written notice thereof.

Laws 1894, p. 123, § 8.

Formerly Civil Code 1895, § 4588; Civil Code 1910, § 5134; Code 1933, § 10-204.

§ 9-7-12. Exception to report

The report of the auditor shall be prima facie the truth, either party having the liberty to except thereto.

Laws 1894, p. 123, § 3; Laws 1895, p. 47, § 1.

Formerly Civil Code 1895, § 4581; Civil Code 1910, § 5127; Code 1933, § 10-101.

§ 9-7-13. Report may be recommitted, when

(a) For indefiniteness, omissions, errors of calculation, failure to report evidence, errors of law, or other proper cause, the judge may recommit the report for such further action as may be proper.

(b) In such cases, the evidence shall be confined to such issues as the judge, in the order of recommitment, may indicate. If ordered to be taken de novo, the parties may agree as to what portion of the original report shall be retained in lieu of reintroduction.

Laws 1894, p. 123, § 13.

Formerly Civil Code 1895, § 4593; Civil Code 1910, § 5139; Code 1933, § 10-305.

§ 9-7-14. Time for filing; specification of errors

(a) Within 20 days after the report is filed and notice is given to the parties, either party may file exceptions to be classified separately as "exceptions of law" and "exceptions of fact."

(b) The trial judge may, in his discretion, on application of any party and without notice to the other party or parties, grant and issue an order extending the time for filing exceptions to an auditor's report. Extensions shall be freely granted in cases involving complicated facts or accounts, complicated issues of law, or lengthy records, so as to allow adequate time for preparation of exceptions thereto. All applications for extensions of time must be made before the expiration of the period of time for filing exceptions as originally prescribed or as extended by previous order of the court. The order granting any extension of time shall be promptly filed with the clerk of the trial court who shall promptly give notice thereof to all other parties involved in the case.

(c) Exceptions to auditors' reports need not set out therein portions of the record in the original case, nor of the auditor's report, nor of the evidence reported by the auditor. It shall not be necessary that the grounds of any exceptions be complete in themselves. It shall be sufficient, for purposes of this Code section, if the exceptions point out by title and paragraph number such part of the pleadings, and by page number such part of the auditor's report, and such parts of the evidence reported by the auditor as are necessary to an understanding of the errors complained of.

Laws 1894, p. 123, § 9; Laws 1964, p. 697, § 1.

Formerly Civil Code 1895, § 4589; Civil Code 1910, § 5135; Code 1933, § 10-301.

§ 9-7-15. Exceptions as to matters not in record; objections; certification; mandamus nisi; petition; service of writ; hearing; effect

(a) Exceptions as to any matter not appearing on the face of the record, in the transcript of the evidence and proceedings, or in the report itself, shall be certified to be true by the auditor within 40 days after the report is filed. If the auditor determines that any such exception is not true or does not contain all of the necessary facts, he shall return the same within ten days to the party or his attorney with his objections in writing. If these objections are met and removed within ten days, he may then certify the same, specifying the cause of delay.

(b) If for any cause the exceptions are not certified by the auditor, without fault of the party or his attorney, the party or his attorney may apply to the judge of the superior court within 30 days from the tendering of the exceptions and on petition obtain a mandamus nisi directed to the auditor.

(c) The petition for a mandamus nisi shall set out a substantial copy of the exceptions, and shall be verified by the party or his counsel, or supported by other proof as to the truth of the facts stated therein. The mandamus nisi shall be served upon the auditor within ten days after the same is signed by the judge and shall be made returnable not more than 30 days after signing. The opposite party shall have notice of the time and place of hearing the mandamus nisi and may resist the application for a mandamus absolute. If there is a traverse filed to the answer, the same shall be determined by a jury. If the mandamus is made absolute, the order shall have the effect, to that extent, of amending the report of the auditor.

Laws 1894, p. 123, §§ 10, 11.

Formerly Civil Code 1895, §§ 4590, 4591, 4592; Civil Code 1910, §§ 5136, 5137, 5138; Code 1933, §§ 10-302, 10-303, 10-304.

§ 9-7-16. Exceptions of law for judges

Exceptions of law shall be for the exclusive consideration of the judge.

Laws 1894, p. 123, § 14.

Formerly Civil Code 1895, § 4594; Civil Code 1910, § 5140; Code 1933, § 10-401.

§ 9-7-17. Jury trial, when; burden of proof; right to open and conclude

In all law cases where an auditor is appointed, exceptions of fact to his report shall be passed upon by the jury as in other issues of fact, and in equity cases by the jury when approved by the judge. The burden of proving error in the report of the auditor shall be upon the party making the exceptions, who shall have the right to open and conclude the argument. In all cases where both parties file exceptions of fact, the party against whom judgment would be rendered if the report were approved shall be entitled to open and conclude the argument.

Laws 1894, p. 123, §§ 15-17; Laws 1895, p. 47, § 3.

Formerly Civil Code 1895, §§ 4595, 4596, 4597; Civil Code 1910, §§ 5141, 5142, 5143; Code 1933, §§ 10-402, 10-403, 37-1103.

§ 9-7-18. Determination where exceptions of fact submitted to jury, etc.; what evidence to be read to jury

In all cases where exceptions of fact are submitted to the jury, the same shall be determined upon the testimony reported by the auditor. Only so much of the evidence as is material and pertinent to the issue then on trial shall be read to the jury. Admissible material evidence introduced and not reported and evidence improperly excluded shall also be submitted to the jury and all inadmissible evidence shall be excluded from their consideration.

Laws 1894, p. 123, §§ 18, 20.

Formerly Civil Code 1895, §§ 4598, 4600; Civil Code 1910, §§ 5144, 5146; Code 1933, §§ 10-404, 10-406.

§ 9-7-19. When new testimony may be considered

(a) No new testimony shall be considered, except in those cases where, according to the principles of law, a new trial would be granted for newly discovered evidence.

(b) Application to introduce such original and newly discovered evidence shall be made to the judge before the argument on the exceptions, if the same is then known, with a statement of the party and his attorney setting out the expected testimony and facts authorizing it to be admitted as newly discovered evidence.

(c) The opposite party shall be served with notice of the application. If the same is admitted, the opposite party shall be entitled to a continuance. On the trial he shall be entitled to introduce original testimony in rebuttal of the newly discovered evidence.

Laws 1894, p. 123, § 19.

Formerly Civil Code 1895, § 4599; Civil Code 1910, § 5145; Code 1933, § 10-405.

§ 9-7-20. Jury verdict

In all cases the jury shall find for or against each exception submitted, seriatim.

Laws 1894, p. 123, § 20.

Formerly Civil Code 1895, § 4600; Civil Code 1910, § 5146; Code 1933, § 10-406.

§ 9-7-21. Proceedings when report not excepted to; when exceptions made

(a) If the auditor's report is not excepted to, the court shall frame a judgment or decree thereon as may be proper.

(b) If exceptions are filed, after the same have been considered and passed upon by the court or the jury, or both, as the case may be, the court shall order a judgment or a decree in accordance with the report and the changes made by the court or the jury, unless the same shall require a recommitment.

Laws 1894, p. 123, § 21.

Formerly Civil Code 1895, § 4601; Civil Code 1910, § 5147; Code 1933, § 10-407.

§ 9-7-22. Amount; where parties agree on person to be appointed; fixing amount in advance

(a) The fees of an auditor to whom a case, whether legal or equitable, has been referred shall be determined and fixed by the trial judge making the referral or by any other judge having jurisdiction of the case and serving in the place and stead of the trial judge. The fees so determined and fixed may be apportioned between and among the parties at the discretion of the judge.

(b) The court with consent of the parties may fix the fees of the auditor in advance and incorporate the same in the order making the appointment.

(c) The fees of an auditor, as determined and fixed by the judge, shall be included in and made a part of the judgment of the court. The fees of the auditor shall be assessed as court costs and shall be paid prior to the filing of any appeal from the judgment of the court; provided, however, that if such fees have not been determined and assessed at the time of filing any such appeal, the same shall be paid within 30 days from the date of assessment.

Laws 1894, p. 123, § 22; Laws 1963, p. 620, § 1; Laws 1982, p. 3, § 9; Laws 1988, p. 408, § 1.

Formerly Civil Code 1895, §§ 4602, 4603; Civil Code 1910, §§ 5148, 5149; Code 1933, §§ 10-501, 10-502.

§ 9-7-23. Compensation of court reporter

(a) The compensation of the court reporter for recording the evidence and proceedings in all cases before an auditor shall be as provided by law for civil cases.

(b) The court reporter shall be compensated as provided by law for furnishing transcripts of the evidence and proceedings. The compensation shall be paid by the parties to the case. The reporter, for additional transcripts of evidence and proceedings furnished by him, shall be paid by the party requesting the same as agreed between the parties and, in the event of a disagreement, shall be paid as provided by law.

Laws 1963, p. 349, § 1.

Formerly Code 1933, § 10-503.

CHAPTER 8

RECEIVERS

§ 9-8-1. Grounds for appointment. When officer of court

When any fund or property is in litigation and the rights of either or both parties cannot otherwise be fully protected or when there is a fund or property having no one to manage it, a receiver of the same may be appointed by the judge of the superior court having jurisdiction thereof.

Laws 1855-56, p. 219, § 2.

Formerly Code 1863, § 271; Code 1868, § 265; Code 1873, § 274; Code 1882, § 274; Civil Code 1895, § 4900; Civil Code 1910, § 5475; Code 1933, § 55-301.

§ 9-8-2. Protection of property in danger of destruction and loss

Equity may appoint receivers to take possession of and protect trust or joint property and funds whenever the danger of destruction and loss shall require such interference.

Formerly Code 1863, § 3031; Code 1868, § 3043; Code 1873, § 3098; Code 1882, § 3098; Civil Code 1895, § 4901; Civil Code 1910, § 5476; Code 1933, § 55-302.

§ 9-8-3. Appointment, in order to protect assets of debtor; notice; discretion as to terms

Equity may appoint a receiver to take possession of and hold, subject to the direction of the court, any assets charged with the payment of debts where there is manifest danger of loss, destruction, or material injury to those interested. Under extraordinary circumstances, a receiver may be appointed before and without notice to the trustee or other person having charge of the assets. The terms on which a receiver is appointed shall be in the discretion of the court.

Formerly Code 1863, § 3080; Code 1868, § 3092; Code 1873, § 3149; Code 1882, § 3149; Civil Code 1895, § 4904; Civil Code 1910, § 5479; Code 1933, § 55-305.

§ 9-8-4. Power of appointment to be cautiously exercised

The power of appointing receivers should be prudently and cautiously exercised and except in clear and urgent cases should not be resorted to.

Formerly Civil Code 1895, § 4902; Civil Code 1910, § 5477; Code 1933, § 55-303.

§ 9-8-5. Intervention in equitable proceedings

Where property has been placed in the hands of a receiver, all persons properly seeking to assert equitable remedies against such assets shall become parties to the case by intervention and shall prosecute their remedies therein.

Formerly Civil Code 1895, § 4903; Civil Code 1910, § 5478; Code 1933, § 55-304.

§ 9-8-6. Liens divested by receiver's sale

Persons holding liens on property in the hands of a receiver may be made parties to the case at any time. Unless otherwise provided in the order, liens upon the property held by any parties to the record, shall be dissolved by the receiver's sale and transferred to the funds arising from the sale of the property.

Formerly Civil Code 1895, § 4911; Civil Code 1910, § 5486; Code 1933, § 55-312.

§ 9-8-7. When fund may be invested

The presiding judge, in his discretion under the law, may order any funds, in the hands of a receiver or any other officer of court, while awaiting the termination of protracted litigation, to be invested as provided in the case of executors and administrators.

Formerly Code 1863, § 272; Code 1868, § 266; Code 1873, § 275; Code 1882, § 275; Civil Code 1895, § 4905; Civil Code 1910, § 5480; Code 1933, § 55-306.

§ 9-8-8. Receiver as officer of court; removal of receiver

(a) The receiver is an officer and servant of the court appointing him, is responsible to no other tribunal than the court, and must in all things obey its direction.

(b) The receiver shall discharge his trust according to the orders or decrees of the court appointing him. He is at all times subject to its orders and may be brought to account and removed at its pleasure.

Formerly Code 1863, §§ 273, 3081; Code 1868, §§ 267, 3093; Code 1873, §§ 276, 3150; Code 1882, §§ 276, 3150; Civil Code 1895, §§ 4906, 4908; Civil Code 1910, §§ 5481, 5483; Code 1933, §§ 55-307, 55-309.

§ 9-8-9. Returns, how made

Receivers of corporations shall be amenable to and shall make their returns to the superior court of the county where they reside at the time of the appointment.

Formerly Code 1863, § 275; Code 1868, § 269; Code 1873, § 278; Code 1882, § 278; Civil Code 1895, § 4912; Civil Code 1910, § 5487; Code 1933, § 55-313.

§ 9-8-10. Bonds required in discretion of court

The judge of the superior court, in his discretion, may require a receiver to give bond conditioned for the faithful discharge of the trust reposed. If bond is so required, the judge shall fix the amount thereof and shall determine the sufficiency of the security. The judge shall also regulate the compensation paid to the receiver.

Formerly Code 1863, § 274; Code 1868, § 268; Code 1873, § 277; Code 1882, § 277; Civil Code 1895, § 4907; Civil Code 1910, § 5482; Code 1933, § 55-308.

§ 9-8-11. Receiver liable for money in bank, when

Where funds are in the hands of a receiver pending a final disposition, the receiver may deposit the funds into a bank or trust company which is insured by the Federal Deposit Insurance Corporation, Federal Savings and Loan Insurance Corporation, or successor entities. If the receiver fails to utilize such an insured bank or trust company, he shall be personally liable for any resulting loss.

Formerly Civil Code 1895, § 4909; Civil Code 1910, § 5484; Code 1933, § 55-310.

§ 9-8-12. Garnishment of receivers

A receiver shall not be subject to the process of garnishment.

Formerly Code 1863, § 3475; Code 1868, § 3495; Code 1873, § 3553; Code 1882, § 3553; Civil Code 1895, § 4910; Civil Code 1910, § 5485; Code 1933, § 55-311.

§ 9-8-13. Receiver's and attorney's fees

(a) In all cases where a receiver is appointed under the laws of this state to take charge of the assets of any person, firm, or corporation and a fund is brought into court for distribution, the court having jurisdiction thereof shall award to counsel filing the petition and representing the moving creditor or creditors, out of the fund, no greater sum as fees for services rendered in filing the petition and bringing the fund into court than the services are actually worth, taking as a basis therefor the amount represented by the counsel in the original petition and the assets brought into the hands of the receiver by the services of counsel not including the assets turned over to the receiver by defendants under order of the court.

(b) In all cases where a receiver is appointed to take charge of the assets of any person, firm, or corporation, the court having jurisdiction thereof shall award to the receiver as full compensation for his services, out of the fund coming into his hands, not more than 8 percent of the first $1,000.00, 4 percent of the excess up to $5,000.00, 3 percent of the amount above $5,000.00 and not exceeding $10,000.00, and 2 percent of all sums over $10,000.00. Where the business of an insolvent person, firm, or corporation is continued and conducted by a receiver, the judge may allow such compensation as may be reasonable for such services in lieu of commissions, not exceeding the compensation paid by persons in the usual and regular conduct of such business.

(c) In all cases, the presiding judge or other competent tribunal shall allow such compensation to the attorney or attorneys filing the original petition and to the receiver or receivers appointed thereunder as their services are reasonably worth.

Laws 1897, p. 55, §§ 1, 2; Laws 1898, p. 86, §§ 1, 2.

Formerly Civil Code 1910, §§ 5488, 5489; Code 1933, §§ 55-314, 55-315.

§ 9-8-14. Expenses of giving bond allowable

(a) Receivers who are required by law to give bond as such who have given as security on such bonds one or more guaranty companies, surety companies, fidelity insurance companies, or fidelity and deposit companies, as authorized by law, may include as part of their lawful expenses or costs of administration such reasonable sum or sums paid to the company or companies for the suretyship not exceeding 1 percent per annum on the amount of the bond as the court, judge, or other officer by whom they were appointed allows.

(b) Any court, judge, or other officer whose duty it is to pass upon the account of any person or corporation required to execute a bond with surety or sureties, whenever the person or corporation has given any such company or companies as security as provided in subsection (a) of this Code section, shall allow in the settlement of the account a reasonable sum for the expenses and premiums incurred in securing the surety, not exceeding the amounts specified in the subsection.

Laws 1903, p. 75, § 1.

Formerly Civil Code 1910, §§ 4071, 4072; Code 1933, §§ 55-316, 55-317.

CHAPTER 9

ARBITRATION

Article 1

General Provisions

Part 1

Arbitration Code

§ 9-9-1. Short title

This part shall be known and may be cited as the "Georgia Arbitration Code."

Laws 1978, p. 2270, § 1; Laws 1988, p. 903, § 1.

Formerly Code 1933, § 7-301; Code 1981, § 9-9-80.

§ 9-9-2. Applicability

(a) Part 3 of Article 2 of this chapter, as it existed prior to July 1, 1988, applies to agreements specified in subsection (b) of this Code section made between July 1, 1978, and July 1, 1988. This part applies to agreements specified in subsection (b) of this Code section made on or after July 1, 1988, and to disputes arising on or after July 1, 1988, in agreements specified in subsection (c) of this Code section.

(b) Part 3 of Article 2 of this chapter, as it existed prior to July 1, 1988, shall apply to construction contracts, contracts of warranty on construction, and contracts involving the architectural or engineering design of any building or the design of alterations or additions thereto made between July 1, 1978, and July 1, 1988, and on and after July 1, 1988, this part shall apply as provided in subsection (a) of this Code section and shall provide the exclusive means by which agreements to arbitrate disputes arising under such contracts can be enforced.

(c) This part shall apply to all disputes in which the parties thereto have agreed in writing to arbitrate and shall provide the exclusive means by which agreements to arbitrate disputes can be enforced, except the following, to which this part shall not apply:

(1) Agreements coming within the purview of Article 2 of this chapter, relating to arbitration of medical malpractice claims;

(2) Any collective bargaining agreements between employers and labor unions representing employees of such employers;

(3) Any contract of insurance, as defined in paragraph (1) of Code Section 33–1–2; provided, however, that nothing in this paragraph shall impair or prohibit the enforcement of or in any way invalidate an arbitration clause or provision in a contract between insurance companies;

(4) Any other subject matters currently covered by an arbitration statute;

(5) Any loan agreement or consumer financing agreement in which the amount of indebtedness is $ 25,000.00 or less at the time of execution;

(6) Any contract for the purchase of consumer goods, as defined in Title 11, the "Uniform Commercial Code," under subsection (1) of Code Section 11–2–105 and subsection (a) of Code Section 11–9–102;

(7) Any contract involving consumer acts or practices or involving consumer transactions as such terms are defined in paragraphs (2) and (3) of subsection (a) of Code Section 10–1–392, relating to definitions in the "Fair Business Practices Act of 1975";

(8) Any sales agreement or loan agreement for the purchase or financing of residential real estate unless the clause agreeing to arbitrate is initialed by all signatories at the time of the execution of the agreement. This exception shall not restrict agreements between or among real estate brokers or agents;

(9) Any contract relating to terms and conditions of employment unless the clause agreeing to arbitrate is initialed by all signatories at the time of the execution of the agreement;

(10) Any agreement to arbitrate future claims arising out of personal bodily injury or wrongful death based on tort.

Laws 1978, p. 2270, § 1; Laws 1979, p. 393, § 1; Laws 1988, p. 903, § 1; Laws 1997, p. 1556, § 1; Laws 2001, p. 362, § 25.

Formerly Code 1933, § 7–302; Code 1981, § 9–9–81.

§ 9–9–3. Enforcement of agreements to arbitrate without regard to justiciability of controversy

A written agreement to submit any existing controversy to arbitration or a provision in a written contract to submit any controversy thereafter arising to arbitration is enforceable without regard to the justiciable character of the controversy and confers jurisdiction on the courts of the state to enforce it and to enter judgment on an award.

Laws 1978, p. 2270, § 1; Laws 1988, p. 903, § 1.

Formerly Code 1933, § 7–303; Code 1981, § 9–9–82.

§ 9–9–4. Venue; orders for attachment and preliminary injunctions

(a)(1) Any application to the court under this part shall be made to the superior court of the county where venue lies, unless the application is made in a pending court action, in which case it shall be made to the court hearing that action. Subsequent applications shall be made to the court hearing the initial application unless the court otherwise directs.

(2) All applications shall be by motion and shall be heard in the manner provided by law and rule of court for the making or hearing of motions, provided that the motion shall be filed in the same manner as a complaint in a civil action.

(b) Venue for applications to the court shall lie:

(1) In the county where the agreement provides for the arbitration hearing to be held; or

(2) If the hearing has already been held, in the county where it was held; or

(3) In the county where any party resides or does business; or

(4) If there is no county as described in paragraph (1), (2), or (3) of this subsection, in any county.

(c)(1) A demand for arbitration shall be served on the other parties by registered or certified mail or statutory overnight delivery, return receipt requested.

(2) The initial application to the court shall be served on the other parties in the same manner as a complaint under Chapter 11 of this title.

(3) All other papers required to be served by this part shall be served in the same manner as pleadings subsequent to the original complaint and other papers are served under Chapter 11 of this title.

(d) In determining any matter arising under this part, the court shall not consider whether the claim with respect to which arbitration is sought is tenable nor otherwise pass upon the merits of the dispute.

(e) The superior court in the county in which an arbitration is pending, or, if not yet commenced, in a county specified in subsection (b) of this Code section, may entertain an application for an order of attachment or for a preliminary injunction in connection with an arbitrable controversy, but only upon the ground that the award to which the applicant may be entitled may be rendered ineffectual without such provisional relief.

Laws 1978, p. 2270, § 1; Laws 1988, p. 903, § 1; Laws 2000, p. 1589, § 3.

Formerly Code 1933, § 7–305; Code 1981, § 9–9–84.

§ 9-9-5. Court discretion in applying bar of limitation of time; waiver of limitation of time; time for asserting limitation of time as bar

(a) If a claim sought to be arbitrated would be barred by limitation of time had the claim sought to be arbitrated been asserted in court, a party may apply to the court to stay arbitration or to vacate the award, as provided in this part. The court has discretion in deciding whether to apply the bar. A party waives the right to raise limitation of time as a bar to arbitration in an application to stay arbitration by that party's participation in the arbitration.

(b) Failure to make this application to the court shall not preclude a party from asserting before the arbitrators limitation of time as a bar to the arbitration. The arbitrators, in their sole discretion, shall decide whether to apply the bar. This exercise of discretion shall not be subject to review of the court on an application to confirm, vacate, or modify the award except upon the grounds hereafter specified in this part for vacating or modifying an award.

Laws 1978, p. 2270, § 1; Laws 1988, p. 903, § 1.

Formerly Code 1933, § 7-306; Code 1981, § 9-9-85.

§ 9-9-6. Procedures for applications to compel arbitration

(a) A party aggrieved by the failure of another to arbitrate may apply for an order compelling arbitration. If the court determines there is no substantial issue concerning the validity of the agreement to submit to arbitration or compliance therewith and the claim sought to be arbitrated is not barred by limitation of time, the court shall order the parties to arbitrate. If a substantial issue is raised or the claim is barred by limitation of time, the court shall summarily hear and determine that issue and, accordingly, grant or deny the application for an order to arbitrate. If an issue claimed to be arbitrable is involved in an action pending in a court having jurisdiction to hear a motion to compel arbitration, the application shall be made by motion in that action. If the application is granted, the order shall operate to stay a pending or subsequent action, or so much of it as is referable to arbitration.

(b) Subject to subsections (c) and (d) of this Code section, a party who has not participated in the arbitration and who has not made an application to compel arbitration may apply to stay arbitration on the grounds that:

(1) No valid agreement to submit to arbitration was made;

(2) The agreement to arbitrate was not complied with; or

(3) The arbitration is barred by limitation of time.

(c) A party may serve upon another party a demand for arbitration. This demand shall specify:

(1) The agreement pursuant to which arbitration is sought;

(2) The name and address of the party serving the demand;

(3) That the party served with the demand shall be precluded from denying the validity of the agreement or compliance therewith or from asserting limitation of time as a bar in court unless he makes application to the court within 30 days for an order to stay arbitration; and

(4) The nature of the dispute or controversy sought to be arbitrated; provided, however, that the demand for arbitration may be amended by either party to include disputes arising under the same agreement after the original demand is served.

(d) After service of the demand, or any amendment thereof, the party served must make application within 30 days to the court for a stay of arbitration or he will thereafter be precluded from denying the validity of the agreement or compliance therewith or from asserting limitation of time as a bar in court. Notice of this application shall be served on the other parties. The right to apply for a stay of arbitration may not be waived, except as provided in this Code section.

(e) Unless otherwise provided in the arbitration agreement, a party to an arbitration agreement may petition the court to consolidate separate arbitration proceedings, and the court may order consolidation of separate arbitration proceedings when:

(1) Separate arbitration agreements or proceedings exist between the same parties or one party is a party to a separate arbitration agreement or proceeding with a third party;

(2) The disputes arise from the same transactions or series of related transactions; and

(3) There is a common issue or issues of law or fact creating the possibility of conflicting rulings by more than one arbitrator or panel of arbitrators.

(f) If all the applicable arbitration agreements name the same arbitrator, arbitration panel, or arbitration tribunal, the court, if it orders consolidation under subsection (e) of this Code section, shall order all matters to be heard before the arbitrator, panel, or tribunal agreed to by the parties. If the applicable arbitration agreements name separate arbitrators, panels, or tribunals, the court, if it orders consolidation under subsection (e) of this Code section, shall, in the absence of an agreed method of selection by all parties to the consolidated arbitration, appoint an arbitrator.

(g) In the event that the arbitration agreements in proceedings consolidated under subsection (e) of this

Code section contain inconsistent provisions, the court shall resolve such conflicts and determine the rights and duties of various parties.

(h) If the court orders consolidation under subsection (e) of this Code section, the court may exercise its discretion to deny consolidation of separate arbitration proceedings only as to certain issues, leaving other issues to be resolved in separate proceedings.

Laws 1978, p. 2270, § 1; Laws 1988, p. 903, § 1.

Formerly Code 1933, § 7-307; Code 1981, § 9-9-86.

§ 9-9-7. Appointment of arbitrators

(a) If the arbitration agreement provides for a method of appointment of arbitrators, that method shall be followed. If there is only one arbitrator, the term "arbitrators" shall apply to him.

(b) The court shall appoint one or more arbitrators on application of a party if:

(1) The agreement does not provide for a method of appointment;

(2) The agreed method fails;

(3) The agreed method is not followed for any reason; or

(4) The arbitrators fail to act and no successors have been appointed.

(c) An arbitrator appointed pursuant to subsection (b) of this Code section shall have all the powers of one specifically named in the agreement.

Laws 1978, p. 2270, § 1; Laws 1988, p. 903, § 1.

Formerly Code 1933, § 7-308; Code 1981, § 9-9-87.

§ 9-9-8. Hearing before arbitrators

(a) The arbitrators, in their discretion, shall appoint a time and place for the hearing notwithstanding the fact that the arbitration agreement designates the county in which the arbitration hearing is to be held and shall notify the parties in writing, personally or by registered or certified mail or statutory overnight delivery, not less than ten days before the hearing. The arbitrators may adjourn or postpone the hearing. The court, upon application of any party, may direct the arbitrators to proceed promptly with the hearing and determination of the controversy.

(b) The parties are entitled to be heard; to present pleadings, documents, testimony, and other matters; and to cross-examine witnesses. The arbitrators may hear and determine the controversy upon the pleadings, documents, testimony, and other matters produced notwithstanding the failure of a party duly notified to appear.

(c) A party has the right to be represented by an attorney and may claim such right at any time as to any part of the arbitration or hearings which have not taken place. This right may not be waived. If a party is represented by an attorney, papers to be served on the party may be served on the attorney.

(d) The hearing shall be conducted by all the arbitrators unless the parties otherwise agree; but a majority may determine any question and render and change an award, as provided in this part. If during the course of the hearing, an arbitrator for any reason ceases to act, the remaining arbitrator or arbitrators appointed to act as neutrals may continue with the hearing and determination of the controversy.

(e) The arbitrators shall maintain a record of all pleadings, documents, testimony, and other matters introduced at the hearing. The arbitrators or any party to the proceeding may have the proceedings transcribed by a court reporter.

(f) Except as provided in subsection (c) of this Code section, a requirement of this Code section may be waived by written consent of the parties or by continuing with the arbitration without objection.

Laws 1978, p. 2270, § 1; Laws 1988, p. 903, § 1; Laws 2000, p. 1589, § 3.

Formerly Code 1933, § 7-309; Code 1981, § 9-9-88.

§ 9-9-9. Subpoenas; notices to produce; list of witnesses; compensation of witnesses

(a) The arbitrators may issue subpoenas for the attendance of witnesses and for the production of books, records, documents, and other evidence. These subpoenas shall be served and, upon application to the court by a party or the arbitrators, enforced in the same manner provided by law for the service and enforcement of subpoenas in a civil action.

(b) Notices to produce books, writings, and other documents or tangible things; depositions; and other discovery may be used in the arbitration according to procedures established by the arbitrators.

(c) A party shall have the opportunity to obtain a list of witnesses and to examine and copy documents relevant to the arbitration.

(d) Witnesses shall be compensated in the same amount and manner as witnesses in the superior courts.

Laws 1978, p. 2270, § 1; Laws 1988, p. 903, § 1.

Formerly Code 1933, § 7-310; Code 1981, § 9-9-89.

§ 9-9-10. Award

(a) The award shall be in writing and signed by the arbitrators joining in the award. The arbitrators shall deliver a copy of the award to each party personally or by registered or certified mail or statutory overnight delivery, return receipt requested, or as provided in the agreement.

(b) An award shall be made within the time fixed therefor by the agreement or, if not so fixed, within 30 days following the close of the hearing or within such time as the court orders. The parties may extend in writing the time either before or after its expiration. A party waives the objection that an award was not made within the time required unless he notifies in writing the arbitrators of his objection prior to the delivery of the award to him.

Laws 1978, p. 2270, § 1; Laws 1988, p. 903, § 1; Laws 2000, p. 1589, § 3.

Formerly Code 1933, § 7-311; Code 1981, § 9-9-90.

§ 9-9-11. Change of award

(a) Pursuant to the procedure described in subsection (b) of this Code section, the arbitrators may change the award upon the following grounds:

(1) There was a miscalculation of figures or a mistake in the description of any person, thing, or property referred to in the award;

(2) The arbitrators have awarded upon a matter not submitted to them and the award may be corrected without affecting the merits of the decision upon the issues submitted; or

(3) The award is imperfect in a matter of form, not affecting the merits of the controversy.

(b)(1) An application to the arbitrators for a change in the award shall be made by a party within 20 days after delivery of the award to the applicant. Written notice of this application shall be served upon the other parties.

(2) Objection to a change in the award by the arbitrators must be made in writing to the arbitrators within ten days of service of the application to change. Written notice of this objection shall be served upon the other parties.

(3) The arbitrators shall dispose of any application made under this Code section in a written, signed order within 30 days after service upon them of objection to change or upon the expiration of the time for service of this objection. The parties may extend, in writing, the time for this disposition by the arbitrators either before or after its expiration.

(4) An award changed under this Code section shall be subject to the provisions of this part concerning the confirmation, vacation, and modification of awards by the court.

Laws 1978, p. 2270, § 1; Laws 1988, p. 903, § 1.

Formerly Code 1933, § 7-312; Code 1981, § 9-9-91.

§ 9-9-12. Confirmation of award

The court shall confirm an award upon application of a party made within one year after its delivery to him, unless the award is vacated or modified by the court as provided in this part.

Laws 1978, p. 2270, § 1; Laws 1988, p. 903, § 1.

Formerly Code 1933, § 7-313; Code 1981, § 9-9-92.

§ 9-9-13. Vacation of award

(a) An application to vacate an award shall be made to the court within three months after delivery of a copy of the award to the applicant.

(b) The award shall be vacated on the application of a party who either participated in the arbitration or was served with a demand for arbitration if the court finds that the rights of that party were prejudiced by:

(1) Corruption, fraud, or misconduct in procuring the award;

(2) Partiality of an arbitrator appointed as a neutral;

(3) An overstepping by the arbitrators of their authority or such imperfect execution of it that a final and definite award upon the subject matter submitted was not made;

(4) A failure to follow the procedure of this part, unless the party applying to vacate the award continued with the arbitration with notice of this failure and without objection; or

(5) The arbitrator's manifest disregard of the law.

(c) The award shall be vacated on the application of a party who neither participated in the arbitration nor was served with a demand for arbitration or order to compel arbitration if the court finds that:

(1) The rights of the party were prejudiced by one of the grounds specified in subsection (b) of this Code section;

(2) A valid agreement to arbitrate was not made;

(3) The agreement to arbitrate has not been complied with; or

(4) The arbitrated claim was barred by limitation of time, as provided by this part.

(d) The fact that the relief was such that it could not or would not be granted by a court of law or equity is not ground for vacating or refusing to confirm the award.

(e) Upon vacating an award, the court may order a rehearing and determination of all or any of the issues either before the same arbitrators or before new arbitrators appointed as provided by this part. In any provision of an agreement limiting the time for a hearing or award, time shall be measured from the date of such order or rehearing, whichever is appropriate, or a time may be specified by the court. The court's ruling or order under this Code section shall constitute a final judgment and shall be subject to appeal in accordance with the appeal provisions of this part.

Laws 1978, p. 2270, § 1; Laws 1988, p. 903, § 1; Laws 2003, Act 363, § 2, eff. July 1, 2003.

Formerly Code 1933, § 7-314; Code 1981, § 9-9-93.

§ 9-9-14. Modification of award

(a) An application to modify the award shall be made to the court within three months after delivery of a copy of the award to the applicant.

(b) The court shall modify the award if:

(1) There was a miscalculation of figures or a mistake in the description of any person, thing, or property referred to in the award;

(2) The arbitrators awarded on a matter not submitted to them and the award may be corrected without affecting the merits of the decision upon the issues submitted; or

(3) The award is imperfect in a manner of form, not affecting the merits of the controversy.

(c) If the court modifies the award, it shall confirm the award as modified. If the court denies modification, it shall confirm the award made by the arbitrators.

Laws 1978, p. 2270, § 1; Laws 1988, p. 903, § 1.

Formerly Code 1933, § 7-315; Code 1981, § 9-9-94.

§ 9-9-15. Judgment

(a) Upon confirmation of the award by the court, judgment shall be entered in the same manner as provided by Chapter 11 of this title and be enforced as any other judgment or decree.

(b) The judgment roll shall consist of the following:

(1) The agreement and each written extension of time within which to make the award;

(2) The award;

(3) A copy of the order confirming, modifying, or correcting the award; and

(4) A copy of the judgment.

Laws 1978, p. 2270, § 1; Laws 1988, p. 903, § 1.

Formerly Code 1933, § 7-316; Code 1981, § 9-9-95.

§ 9-9-16. Appeal of judgment

Any judgment or any order considered a final judgment under this part may be appealed pursuant to Chapter 6 of Title 5.

Laws 1978, p. 2270, § 1; Laws 1988, p. 903, § 1.

Formerly Code 1933, § 7-317; Code 1981, § 9-9-96.

§ 9-9-17. Expenses and fees of arbitrators

Unless otherwise provided in the agreement to arbitrate, the arbitrators' expenses and fees, together with other expenses, not including counsel fees, incurred in the conduct of the arbitration, shall be paid as provided in the award.

Laws 1978, p. 2270, § 1; Laws 1988, p. 903, § 1.

Formerly Code 1933, § 7-318; Code 1981, § 9-9-97.

§ 9-9-18. Effect of death or incompetency of party in arbitration

Where a party dies or becomes incompetent after making a written agreement to arbitrate, the proceedings may be begun or continued upon the application of, or upon notice to, his executor or administrator or trustee or guardian or, where it relates to real property, his distributee or devisee who has succeeded to his interest in the real property. Upon the death or incompetency of a party, the court may extend the time within which an application to confirm, vacate, or modify the award or to stay arbitration must be made. Where a party has died since an award was delivered, the proceedings thereupon are the same as where a party dies after a verdict.

Laws 1988, p. 903, § 1.

Part 2

International Transactions

§ 9-9-30. Purpose

In order to encourage the use of arbitration in the resolution of conflicts arising out of international transactions effectuating the policy of the state to provide a conducive environment for international business and trade, this part supplements Part 1 of this article and shall be used concurrently with the provisions of Part 1 of this article whenever an arbitration is within the scope of this part.

Laws 1988, p. 903, § 2.

§ 9-9-31. Applicability

(a) This part shall apply to arbitrations within its scope notwithstanding provisions in Part 1 of this article to the contrary.

(b) This part shall apply only to the arbitration of disputes between:

(1) Two or more persons at least one of whom is domiciled or established outside the United States; or

(2) Two or more persons all of whom are domiciled or established in the United States if the dispute bears some relation to property, contractual performance, investment, or other activity outside the United States.

(c) Notwithstanding the provisions of subsection (b) of this Code section, this part shall not apply to the arbitration of any of the exceptions set forth in Part 1 of this article.

Laws 1988, p. 903, § 2.

§ 9-9-32. Agreements in writing

For purposes of this part, in particular, an agreement is in writing if it is contained in a document signed by the parties or in an exchange of letters, telex, telegrams, or other means of telecommunication which provide a record of the agreement, or in an exchange of statements of claim and defense in which the existence of an agreement is alleged by one party and not denied by another. The reference in a contract to a document containing an arbitration clause constitutes an arbitration agreement, provided that the contract is in writing and the reference is such as to make that clause part of the contract.

Laws 1988, p. 903, § 2.

§ 9-9-33. Persons not precluded from acting as arbitrators by reason of nationality

No person shall be precluded by reason of his nationality from acting as an arbitrator, unless otherwise agreed by the parties.

Laws 1988, p. 903, § 2.

§ 9-9-34. Arbitrators may rule on their own jurisdiction

The arbitrators may rule on their own jurisdiction, including any objections with respect to the existence or validity of the arbitration agreement. For that purpose, an arbitration clause which forms part of a contract shall be treated as an agreement independent of the other terms of the contract. A decision by the arbitrators that the contract is null and void shall not thereby invalidate the arbitration clause.

Laws 1988, p. 903, § 2.

§ 9-9-35. Interim relief

The arbitrators may grant such interim relief as they consider appropriate and, in so doing, may require a party to post bond or give other security. The power conferred in this Code section upon the arbitrators is without prejudice to the right of a party to request interim relief directly from any court, tribunal, or other governmental authority, inside or outside this state, and to do so without prior authorization of the arbitrators.

Laws 1988, p. 903, § 2.

§ 9-9-36. Selection of law governing arbitration

Selection of this state as the place of arbitration shall not in itself constitute selection of the procedural or substantive law of that place as the law governing the arbitration.

Laws 1988, p. 903, § 2.

§ 9-9-37. Language or languages to be used in arbitral proceedings

(a) The parties are free to agree on the language or languages to be used in the arbitral proceedings. Failing such agreement, the arbitrators shall determine the language or languages to be used in the proceedings. This agreement or determination, unless otherwise specified therein, shall apply to any written statement by a party, any hearing, and any award, decision, or other communication by the arbitrators.

(b) The arbitrators may order that any documentary evidence shall be accompanied by a translation into the language or languages agreed upon by the parties or determined by the arbitrators.

Laws 1988, p. 903, § 2.

§ 9-9-38. Experts

(a) Unless otherwise agreed by the parties, the arbitrators:

(1) May appoint one or more experts to report on specific issues to be determined by the arbitrators; and

(2) May require a party to give the expert any relevant information or to produce, or to provide access to, any relevant documents, goods, or other property for his inspection.

(b) Unless otherwise agreed by the parties, if a party so requests or if the arbitrators consider it necessary, the expert shall, after delivery of his written or oral report, participate in a hearing where the parties have the opportunity to put questions to him and to present expert witnesses in order to testify on the points at issue.

Laws 1988, p. 903, § 2.

§ 9-9-39. Statement of reasons for award; interpretation of award; fees and expenses

(a) A written statement of the reasons for an award shall be issued if the parties agree to the issuance thereof or the arbitrators determine that a failure to do so could prejudice recognition or enforcement of the award.

(b) If so agreed by the parties, a party, with notice to the other party, may request the arbitrators to give an interpretation of a specific point or part of the award. The interpretation shall form part of the award.

(c) The arbitrators may award reasonable fees and expenses actually incurred, including, without limitation, fees and expenses of legal counsel to any party to the arbitration and shall allocate the costs of the arbitration among the parties as it determines appropriate.

Laws 1988, p. 903, § 2.

§ 9-9-40. Confirmation or vacation of award

The courts of this state shall confirm or vacate a final award, notwithstanding the fact that it grants relief in a currency other than United States dollars.

Laws 1988, p. 903, § 2.

§ 9-9-41. Confirmation or vacation of award which has been reduced to judgment, etc.

If a final award has been reduced to judgment or made the subject of official action by any court, tribunal, or other governmental authority outside the United States, the courts of this state shall confirm or vacate the award without regard to any term or condition of the foreign judgment or official action and without regard to whether the award may be deemed merged into judgment.

Laws 1988, p. 903, § 2.

§ 9-9-42. Recognition of awards on basis of reciprocity

An arbitration award irrespective of where it was made, on the basis of reciprocity, shall be recognized as binding and shall be enforceable in the courts of this state subject to the grounds for vacating an award under Part 1 of this article and providing that the award is not contrary to the public policy of this state with respect to international transactions. Reciprocity in the recognition and enforcement of foreign arbitral awards shall be in accordance with applicable federal laws, international conventions, and treaties.

Laws 1988, p. 903, § 2.

§ 9-9-43. Time limitations

For arbitrations arising under this part, time periods set forth in the following Code sections of Part 1 of this article shall be modified as follows:

(1) The time periods referred to in subsections (c) and (d) of Code Section 9-9-6 and in Code Section 9-9-11 shall be doubled;

(2) The time period contained in subsection (b) of Code Section 9-9-10 shall not be applicable; and

(3) The ten-day time period in subsection (a) of Code Section 9-9-8 shall be 30 days.

Laws 1988, p. 903, § 2.

Article 2

Medical Malpractice

§ 9-9-60. Medical malpractice claims defined

For the purposes of this article, the term "medical malpractice claim" means any claim for damages resulting from the death of or injury to any person arising out of:

(1) Health, medical, dental, or surgical service, diagnosis, prescription, treatment, or care, rendered by a person authorized by law to perform such service or by any person acting under the supervision and control of a lawfully authorized person; or

(2) Care or service rendered by any public or private hospital, nursing home, clinic, hospital authority, facility, or institution, or by any officer, agent, or employee thereof acting within the scope of his employment.

Laws 1978, p. 2270, § 2; Laws 1988, p. 903, § 3.

Formerly Code 1933, § 7-401; Code 1981, § 9-9-110.

§ 9–9–61. Medical malpractice arbitration authorized

In addition to any other legal procedure for the resolution of medical malpractice claims, the parties to a medical malpractice claim may submit the claim for arbitration in accordance with this article.

Laws 1978, p. 2270, § 2; Laws 1988, p. 903, § 3.

Formerly Code 1933, § 7–402; Code 1981, § 9–9–111.

§ 9–9–62. Arbitration order

If the parties to a medical malpractice claim agree in writing to arbitrate the claim pursuant to this article, they shall file a petition in the superior court of the county where any party resides for an order authorizing the arbitration of the claim in accordance with this article and for the appointment of a referee for the arbitration. If the judge determines that the claim is a medical malpractice claim subject to this article, within 30 days of the filing of the petition for such order he shall issue an order authorizing the arbitration and appointing a referee. However, no agreement to arbitrate shall be enforceable unless the agreement was made subsequent to the alleged malpractice and after a dispute or controversy has occurred and unless the claimant is represented by an attorney at law at the time the agreement is entered into.

Laws 1978, p. 2270, § 2; Laws 1988, p. 903, § 3.

Formerly Code 1933, § 7–403; Code 1981, § 9–9–112.

§ 9–9–63. Tolling of statute of limitations; circumstances in which suit permitted after petition for arbitration filed

(a) The filing of the petition for an order authorizing arbitration as provided in Code Section 9–9–62 shall toll any applicable statute of limitations, and the statute of limitations shall remain tolled until the earliest of:

(1) Thirty days after the filing of the petition, when the judge has failed within the 30 days to issue an order authorizing arbitration as provided in Code Section 9–9–62;

(2) Sixty days after the issuance of the judge's order authorizing arbitration, when the parties or their representatives have failed by such time to sign the arbitration submission as provided in Code Section 9–9–65; or

(3) The date the arbitration submission is revoked as provided in Code Section 9–9–65.

(b) If any of the contingencies listed in subsection (a) of this Code section occur and if the statute of limitations has not yet run, the medical malpractice claim may be brought in any court of this state having jurisdiction.

Laws 1978, p. 2270, § 2; Laws 1988, p. 903, § 3.

Formerly Code 1933, § 7–404; Code 1981, § 9–9–113.

§ 9–9–64. Reporter; duties; compensation

The judge of the superior court of the county in which was issued the order authorizing arbitration shall appoint a reporter to attend the proceedings of the medical malpractice arbitration panel and to record exactly and truly the testimony and proceedings in the case being arbitrated, except the arguments of counsel. All provisions relating to court reporter fees, compensation, contingent expenses, and travel allowance, as well as those relating to the furnishing of transcripts and the style and form of transcripts, shall be the same for reporters appointed to attend the arbitration panel proceedings as those applicable to reporters of the superior court of the county in which the arbitration was authorized.

Laws 1978, p. 2270, § 2; Laws 1988, p. 903, § 3.

Formerly Code 1933, § 7–405; Code 1981, § 9–9–114.

§ 9–9–65. Arbitration submission

(a) The referee shall meet with the parties or their representatives, or both, prior to the arbitration. The referee shall assist the parties in preparing an arbitration submission which shall contain the following:

(1) A clear and accurate statement of the matters in controversy;

(2) An agreement as to the payment of the costs of the arbitration;

(3) The procedure to be followed in the arbitration;

(4) A list of the witnesses whose testimony the parties desire to present to the arbitrators;

(5) The names of the arbitrators chosen by each party;

(6) The time and place of meeting of the arbitrators; and

(7) Any other matters that may be pertinent to the arbitration.

(b) The submission shall be in writing and shall be signed by the parties or their representatives. When signed, the submission shall be irrevocable except by consent of all the parties.

Laws 1978, p. 2270, § 2; Laws 1988, p. 903, § 3.

Formerly Code 1933, § 7–407; Code 1981, § 9–9–115.

§ 9-9-66. Qualifications of referee

The referee shall be an attorney who is an active member of the State Bar of Georgia. The referee shall be a nonvoting member of the arbitration panel.

Laws 1978, p. 2270, § 2; Laws 1988, p. 903, § 3.

Formerly Code 1933, § 7-406; Code 1981, § 9-9-116.

§ 9-9-67. Arbitrators, choosing of

(a) Every arbitration pursuant to this article shall be conducted by three arbitrators, one of whom shall be chosen by each of the parties prior to the execution of the submission provided for in Code Section 9-9-65 and one of whom shall be chosen by the arbitrators named in the submission. The third arbitrator shall be chosen after the parties sign the submission provided in Code Section 9-9-65 and before arbitration begins.

(b) If the arbitrators chosen by the parties are unable to agree upon the third arbitrator as provided in subsection (a) of this Code section, the judge authorizing the arbitration and appointing the referee or the judge's successor shall appoint the third arbitrator.

(c) In cases involving a medical malpractice claim where there are multiple plaintiffs or defendants, there shall be only one arbitrator chosen by each side. The plaintiff parties shall have the right to choose one arbitrator and the defendant parties shall have the right to choose one arbitrator.

Laws 1978, p. 2270, § 2; Laws 1988, p. 903, § 3.

Formerly Code 1933, § 7-408; Code 1981, § 9-9-117.

§ 9-9-68. Vacancies

If an arbitrator selected by one of the parties should cease to serve for any reason, the party who chose the arbitrator shall then choose another in his place. If the arbitrator chosen by the other arbitrators shall cease to serve for any reason, the arbitrators chosen by the parties shall choose another in his place. If the arbitrators chosen by the parties are unable to agree upon the third arbitrator, the third arbitrator shall be appointed as provided in subsection (b) of Code Section 9-9-67. An arbitrator chosen pursuant to this Code section shall have all the powers of the original arbitrator.

Laws 1978, p. 2270, § 2; Laws 1988, p. 903, § 3.

Formerly Code 1933, § 7-409; Code 1981, § 9-9-118.

§ 9-9-69. Arbitrators to be sworn

(a) Before the arbitrators begin the arbitration, they shall be sworn by the referee to determine impartially the matters submitted to them according to law and the justice and equity of the case without favor or affection to either party.

(b) Each arbitrator selected under this article shall sign the following affidavit before the selection is effective and before acting as an arbitrator:

State of Georgia

__________ County

I, _____, first being duly sworn, make this affidavit:

I, _____, agree to serve as arbitrator in the case of _____ v. _____ and will decide any issue put before me without favor or affection to any party and without prejudice for or against any party. I will follow and apply the law as given to me by the referee and will accept and abide by all decisions of the referee. I also agree not to discuss this case or any issue with any person except when all other arbitrators and the referee are present.

______________________________, L. S.

Laws 1978, p. 2270, § 2; Laws 1988, p. 903, § 3.

Formerly Code 1933, § 7-410; Code 1981, § 9-9-119.

§ 9-9-70. Postponement of arbitration

When, upon the meeting of the arbitrators, either party is not ready for trial, the referee may postpone the hearing of the case to a future day, which day shall be as early as may be consistent with the ends of justice, considering all the circumstances of the case. If one party is not ready for trial at the time appointed for the hearing of the case and the party has previously required two or more postponements of the trial, the referee shall determine whether the arbitration panel shall nonetheless hear the case or whether another postponement shall be granted, the determination to be consistent with the ends of justice, considering all the circumstances of the case.

Laws 1978, p. 2270, § 2; Laws 1988, p. 903, § 3.

Formerly Code 1933, § 7-411; Code 1981, § 9-9-120.

§ 9-9-71. Adjournment by arbitrators

After the arbitrators have commenced their investigations, they may adjourn from day to day or for a longer time, if the ends of justice require it, until their investigations are completed and they have made up their award. The arbitrators shall not meet or discuss the case or any issue except as a group and with the referee present.

Laws 1978, p. 2270, § 2; Laws 1988, p. 903, § 3.

Formerly Code 1933, § 7-412; Code 1981, § 9-9-121.

§ 9-9-72. Discovery

The parties to the arbitration may obtain discovery in the same manner as provided by law for discovery in civil cases in the superior courts.

Laws 1978, p. 2270, § 2; Laws 1988, p. 903, § 3.

Formerly Code 1933, § 7-413; Code 1981, § 9-9-122.

§ 9-9-73. Powers of referee to compel attendance of witnesses; compensation of witnesses

The referee shall have all the powers of the superior courts to compel the attendance of witnesses before the arbitrators, to compel witnesses to testify, and to issue subpoenas requiring the attendance of witnesses at the time and place of the meeting of the arbitrators. Subpoenas shall be served in the manner provided by law for the service of subpoenas in cases pending in the superior courts. Witnesses shall be entitled to the same compensation as witnesses in the superior courts, and the compensation may be collected in the same manner.

Laws 1978, p. 2270, § 2; Laws 1988, p. 903, § 3.

Formerly Code 1933, § 7-414; Code 1981, § 9-9-123.

§ 9-9-74. Powers of the referee to compel the production of books, etc.

The referee shall have all the powers of the superior courts to compel parties to produce books and all other papers which may be deemed necessary and proper for the investigation of the matters submitted to arbitration, giving to the party, his agent, or his attorney, from whom the production is required, such notice as is required in the superior courts for the production of papers.

Laws 1978, p. 2270, § 2; Laws 1988, p. 903, § 3.

Formerly Code 1933, § 7-415; Code 1981, § 9-9-124.

§ 9-9-75. Competency of witnesses

All persons who are competent as witnesses in the superior courts shall be competent in all cases before the arbitrators.

Laws 1978, p. 2270, § 2; Laws 1988, p. 903, § 3.

Formerly Code 1933, § 7-416; Code 1981, § 9-9-125.

§ 9-9-76. Rules governing examination of witnesses and admission of evidence

The examination of witnesses and the admission of evidence shall be governed by the rules applicable to the superior courts.

Laws 1978, p. 2270, § 2; Laws 1988, p. 903, § 3.

Formerly Code 1933, § 7-417; Code 1981, § 9-9-126.

§ 9-9-77. Administration of oaths by referee

The referee shall have power to administer oaths to witnesses and to administer all other oaths that may be necessary for carrying this article into full effect.

Laws 1978, p. 2270, § 2; Laws 1988, p. 903, § 3.

Formerly Code 1933, § 7-418; Code 1981, § 9-9-127.

§ 9-9-78. Findings

The arbitrators shall make a written finding on each of the matters in controversy contained in the submission. If the arbitrators shall fail to agree on any finding, then any two of them may make the finding, which shall have the same force and effect as if made by all.

Laws 1978, p. 2270, § 2; Laws 1988, p. 903, § 3.

Formerly Code 1933, § 7-419; Code 1981, § 9-9-128.

§ 9-9-79. Copy of findings to be given to parties, original returned to court; record; effect

After the arbitrators have made their findings, the referee shall furnish each of the parties with a copy thereof. The original shall be entered on the minutes of the court authorizing the arbitration; it shall have all the force and effect of a judgment or decree of the court and may be enforced in the same manner at any time after the adjournment of the court. For the entering of the findings upon the minutes of the court, the clerk shall be entitled to the same fees allowed by law for the entering of judgments in other cases, to be paid by the parties as provided in the submission.

Laws 1978, p. 2270, § 2; Laws 1988, p. 903, § 3.

Formerly Code 1933, § 7-420; Code 1981, § 9-9-129.

§ 9-9-80. Finality of findings; appeals to superior court

(a) All findings of the arbitrators with respect to which no application for a review thereof is filed in due time shall be final and conclusive between the parties as to all matters submitted to the arbitrators; but either party to the dispute may, within 30 days from the date the findings are entered upon the minutes of the court authorizing the arbitration, appeal from the findings to the superior court of the county in which the arbitration was authorized. When an appeal is made, all findings shall be final and conclusive between the parties as to all matters submitted to the arbitrators only upon the final disposition of the appeal as provided by this article.

(b) The party conceiving himself to be aggrieved may file an application in writing to the referee of the arbitration panel asking for an appeal from the findings, stating generally the grounds upon which the appeal is sought. In the event the appeal is filed as provided in this Code section, the referee shall, within 30 days from the filing of the same, cause a true copy of the submission, findings, and all other parts of the record, including a transcript of evidence and proceedings, to be transmitted to the clerk of the superior court to which the case is appealable. The case so appealed may thereupon be brought on for a hearing before the superior court upon such record by either party on ten days' written notice to the other; subject, however, to an assignment of the same for hearing by the court.

(c) The findings of fact made by the arbitrators shall, in the absence of fraud, be conclusive but, upon the hearing, the court shall set aside the findings if it is found that:

(1) The findings were procured by fraud;

(2) There is no evidence to support the findings of fact by the arbitrators; or

(3) The findings are contrary to law.

(d) No findings shall be set aside by the court upon any grounds other than one or more of the grounds above-stated. If not set aside upon one or more of the stated grounds, the court shall affirm the findings so appealed from. Upon the setting aside of any such findings, the court may recommit the controversy to the arbitration panel for further hearing or proceeding in conformity with the judgment and opinion of the court or the court may enter the proper judgment upon the findings, as the nature of the case may demand. The decree of the court shall have the same effect and all proceedings in relation thereto shall thereafter be the same as though rendered in an action heard and determined by the court.

(e) An appeal from the decision of the arbitration panel shall operate as a supersedeas and no defendant shall be required to make payment of the amount involved in the submission in the case so appealed until the question at issue therein has been fully determined in accordance with this article. The defendant may voluntarily make payment, however, prior to final disposition of the appeal.

Laws 1978, p. 2270, § 2; Laws 1988, p. 903, § 3.

Formerly Code 1933, § 7–421; Code 1981, § 9–9–130.

§ 9-9-81. Costs; how taxed

The arbitrators shall return in their award the costs of the case, which they shall tax against the parties in accordance with the submission.

Laws 1978, p. 2270, § 2; Laws 1988, p. 903, § 3.

Formerly Code 1933, § 7–422; Code 1981, § 9–9–131.

§ 9-9-82. Compensation of arbitrators and referee

The arbitrators and referee shall have such compensation for their services as may be agreed upon by the parties in the submission.

Laws 1978, p. 2270, § 2; Laws 1988, p. 903, § 3.

Formerly Code 1933, § 7–423; Code 1981, § 9–9–132.

§ 9-9-83. Civil and criminal immunity

An arbitrator shall not be civilly or criminally liable for libel, slander, or defamation of any of the parties to the arbitration for any statement or action taken within the official capacity of the arbitrator during the arbitration.

Laws 1978, p. 2270, § 2; Laws 1988, p. 903, § 3.

Formerly Code 1933, § 7–424; Code 1981, § 9–9–133.

§ 9-9-84. Repealed by Laws 1990, p. 573, § 1, eff. Dec. 1, 1990

CHAPTER 10

CIVIL PRACTICE AND PROCEDURE GENERALLY

Article 1

General Provisions

§ 9-10-1. Preference in trial of cases when state is party

Where civil cases are pending in the superior courts, the Court of Appeals, or the Supreme Court in which the state is a party plaintiff, preference shall be given to such cases over all other cases so pending; and the judges or Justices, as the case may be, shall use all the power vested in them by law to bring the cases to a speedy trial and, whenever required to do so by counsel for the state, shall take up the cases for trial and proceed to try the same, unless the defendant shows some good cause for continuance, when the case shall be continued to a future time in the same term, or to the next term, in the discretion of the court. Nothing in this Code section shall affect the right of the state to a continuance on a proper showing.

Laws 1876, p. 104, § 1; Laws 1984, p. 22, § 9.

Formerly Code 1882, § 22a; Civil Code 1895, § 24; Civil Code 1910, § 24; Code 1933, § 81-1005.

§ 9-10-2. State as party; notice to Attorney General

Any verdict, decision, judgment, decree, order, ruling, or other judicial action by any court in this state in any matter in which this state or an official of this state in his official capacity is a party defendant, intervenor, respondent, appellee, or plaintiff in fi. fa. shall be void unless it affirmatively appears as a matter of record either:

(1) That the Attorney General was given five days' advance written notice by the adverse party or his attorney of the time set for the particular trial, hearing, or other proceeding as a result of which the verdict, decision, judgment, decree, order, ruling, or other judicial action was entered; or

(2) That the Attorney General or an assistant attorney general was present in person at the trial, hearing, or other proceeding; or

(3) That the Attorney General or an assistant attorney general has, in writing, waived the notice.

Laws 1956, p. 625, § 1.

§ 9-10-3. Exclusion of public from courtroom when evidence vulgar, etc.

During the trial in any court of any case in which the evidence is vulgar and obscene or relates to improper sexual acts and tends to debauch the morals of the young, the presiding judge shall have the right, in his discretion and on his own motion, or on motion of the plaintiff or the defendant or their attorneys, to hear and try the case after clearing the courtroom of all or any portion of the audience.

Laws 1890-91, p. 111, § 1; Laws 1895, p. 49, § 1; Laws 1982, p. 3, § 9.

Formerly Civil Code 1895, § 5296; Civil Code 1910, § 5885; Code 1933, § 81-1006.

§ 9-10-4. Collateral issues to be tried by jury

All collateral issues in the superior, state, or city courts, unless otherwise directed by law, shall be tried by jury.

Formerly Code 1863, § 3532; Code 1868, § 3555; Code 1873, § 3612; Code 1882, § 3612; Civil Code 1895, § 4948; Civil Code 1910, § 5525; Code 1933, § 81-1010.

§ 9-10-5. Judges to write out charges on request when official reporter not present; judges authorized to reduce charges to writing and to send them out with jury; charges to be filed; certified copies

(a) The judges of the superior, state, and city courts, when counsel for either party requests it before argument begins, shall write out their charges and read them to the jury; and it shall be error to give any other or additional charge than that so written and read; provided, however, that this Code section shall not apply when there is an official court reporter in attendance thereon who records the full charge of the trial judge in the case upon the direction of the court.

(b) In any civil action, upon motion by a party, upon request by the jury, or sua sponte, a judge of a superior, state, or city court is authorized, but shall not be required, to reduce all of the charge to the jury to writing and send all of the charge so reduced to writing out with the jury during its deliberation.

(c) Any charge reduced to writing under subsection (a) or (b) of this Code section shall be filed with the clerk of the court in which it was given and shall be accessible to all persons interested in it. The clerk shall give certified copies of the charge to any person applying therefor, upon payment of the usual fee.

Laws 1860, p. 42, §§ 1, 2; Laws 1877, p. 13, § 1; Laws 1878-79, p. 150, § 1; Laws 1897, p. 41, § 1; Laws 1943, p. 262, § 1; Laws 1982, p. 3, § 9; Laws 1983, p. 884, § 3-3; Laws 1986, p. 320, § 1.

Formerly Code 1863, §§ 240, 241; Code 1868, §§ 234, 235; Code 1873, §§ 244, 245; Code 1882, §§ 244, 245; Civil Code 1895, §§ 4318, 4319; Penal Code 1895, §§ 1030, 1031; Civil Code 1910, §§ 4847, 4848; Penal Code 1910, §§ 1056, 1057; Code 1933, §§ 81-1102, 81-1103.

§ 9-10-6. Juror not to act on private knowledge

A juror shall not act on his private knowledge respecting the facts, witnesses, or parties unless sworn and examined as a witness in the case.

Formerly Civil Code 1895, § 5337; Civil Code 1910, § 5932; Code 1933, § 110-108.

§ 9-10-7. Expression of opinion on facts, error

It is error for any judge, during the progress of any case, or in his charge to the jury, to express or intimate his opinion as to what has or has not been proved. Should any judge violate this Code section, the violation shall be held by the Supreme Court or Court of Appeals to be error, the decision in the case shall be reversed, and a new trial shall be granted in the court below with such directions as the Supreme Court or the Court of Appeals may lawfully give.

Laws 1850, Cobb's 1851 Digest, p. 462.

Formerly Code 1863, § 3172; Code 1868, § 3183; Code 1873, § 3248; Code 1882, § 3248; Civil Code 1895, § 4334; Penal Code 1895, § 1032; Civil Code 1910, § 4863; Penal Code 1910, § 1058; Code 1933, § 81–1104.

§ 9–10–8. Expression of judge in open court re verdict forbidden; commending or complimenting jury forbidden; disqualification of judge to preside at new trial

(a) No judge of any court shall either directly or indirectly express in open court his approval or disapproval of the verdict of any jury in any case tried before him, except as provided in this Code section; nor may the judge discharge any jury upon the ground that the verdict rendered in any case does not meet with his approval.

(b) No judge of any court may commend or compliment a jury during the term of any court for discharging its duty if the commendation or compliment has the effect of approving a verdict.

(c) If any judge of any court either directly or indirectly expresses in open court his approval or disapproval of the verdict of the jury in any case tried before him, he shall be disqualified from presiding in the case in the event a new trial is granted.

(d) Nothing in this Code section shall have the effect of prohibiting a judge of any court from approving or disapproving the verdict of a jury in any case tried before him in hearing a motion for a new trial that comes on before him; however, the approval or disapproval on the hearing of a motion for new trial shall be expressed in the formal order of the judge in granting or overruling the motion and not otherwise.

Laws 1918, p. 168, §§ 1–3.

Formerly Code 1933, §§ 110–201, 110–202, 110–203.

§ 9–10–9. Jurors may sustain but not impeach verdict

The affidavits of jurors may be taken to sustain but not to impeach their verdict.

Formerly Civil Code 1895, § 5338; Civil Code 1910, § 5933; Code 1933, § 110–109.

§ 9–10–10. Posting of cash bonds permitted; receipt; docket

(a) Any party, litigant, or other person required or permitted by law to give or post bond or bail as surety or security for the happening of any event or act in all civil matters may discharge the requirement by depositing cash in the amount of the bond so required with the appropriate person, official, or other depository.

(b) Any official or other person receiving any such bond shall give a receipt therefor and shall cause the fact of the receipt to be entered and recorded on the docket of the case in which it was given. If bond is given in a matter not appearing as a separate court case on a docket, a docket shall be prepared, maintained, and kept of all such transactions. The name and address of the person giving or making the bond, the date of the receipt of the bond, the name of the person receiving the bond, the amount of the bond, and a description of the cause for giving the bond, together with any and all other desirable information concerning the bond, shall be a part of the record in that separate docket.

Laws 1969, p. 41, §§ 1, 2; Laws 1982, p. 3, § 9.

§ 9–10–11. Forfeiture of appearance bond avoided where attendance of principal prevented by physical disability or where principal confined in another jurisdiction; forfeiture set aside upon proper showing

(a) No judgment decreeing the forfeiture of any appearance bond shall be rendered:

(1) If it is shown to the satisfaction of the court by the sworn statement of a reputable physician that the principal in the bond was prevented from attending by some physical disability; or

(2) If it is shown to the satisfaction of the court that the principal in the bond was prevented from attending because he was detained in a penal institution in another jurisdiction. A sworn affidavit of the warden or other responsible officer of the penal institution in which the principal is being detained shall be considered adequate proof of the principal's detention.

(b) If adequate proof is furnished within 60 days of the forfeiture of an appearance bond that the principal failed to appear on the date of forfeiture for one of the reasons set forth in subsection (a) of this Code section, the forfeiture shall be set aside.

Laws 1965, p. 266, §§ 1–3.

§ 9–10–12. "Certified mail" sufficient compliance with "registered mail" requirement; compliance with "statutory overnight delivery" requirement

(a) Whenever any law, statute, Code section, ordinance, rule, or regulation of this state or any officer, department, agency, municipality, or governmental subdivision thereof provides that a notice shall be given by "registered mail," the notice may be given by "certified mail."

(b) Whenever any law, statute, Code section, ordinance, rule, or regulation of this state or any officer, department, agency, municipality, or governmental subdivision thereof provides that a notice may be given by "statutory overnight delivery," it shall be sufficient compliance if:

(1) Such notice is delivered through the United States Postal Service or through a commercial firm which is regularly engaged in the business of document delivery or document and package delivery;

(2) The terms of the sender's engagement of the services of the United States Postal Service or commercial firm call for the document to be delivered not later than the next business day following the day on which it is received for delivery by the United States Postal Service or the commercial firm; and

(3) The sender receives from the United States Postal Service or the commercial firm a receipt acknowledging receipt of the document which receipt is signed by the addressee or an agent of the addressee.

Laws 1967, p. 560, § 1; Laws 2000, p. 1589, § 2.

§ 9-10-13. Effect of judgment on party vouched into court

Where a defendant may have a remedy over against another person and vouches him into court by giving notice of the pendency of the action, the judgment rendered therein shall be conclusive upon the person vouched, as to the amount and right of the plaintiff to recover.

Formerly Civil Code 1895, § 5234; Civil Code 1910, § 5821; Code 1933, § 38-624.

§ 9-10-14. Forms for use by inmates of penal and correctional institutions in actions against state and local governments and government agencies and officers

(a) The Administrative Office of the Courts shall, with the approval of the Supreme Court, promulgate and from time to time amend as necessary a form or forms for use by inmates of state and local penal and correctional institutions in actions against the state and local governments and government agencies and officers. In addition to any other appropriate provisions, such form or forms shall clearly identify the nature of the action, the subject matter and disposition of all previous actions filed against any unit or officer of government by the inmate during his incarceration, the law and facts on which the action is based, the parties to be served, the parties against whom relief is requested, and the specific relief requested against each party. If an affidavit of indigency accompanies the pleading, it shall include a sworn financial statement which shall include but not be limited to any custodial account of the inmate with the institution wherein he is incarcerated.

(b) No clerk of any court shall accept for filing any action by an inmate of a state or local penal or correctional institution against the state or a local government or against any agency or officer of state or local government unless the complaint or other initial pleading is on a form or forms promulgated by the Administrative Office of the Courts and such form or forms are appropriately and legibly completed. Any inmate filing such an action may submit with the complaint or other initial pleading any additional matter in any form if the pleading includes the form or forms required by this Code section. If the pleading is accompanied by an affidavit of indigency, the clerk shall not accept the pleading for filing unless the pleading is also accompanied by a certification from the institution wherein the inmate is incarcerated that the financial statement correctly states the amount of funds in any and all custodial accounts of the inmate with the institution.

(c) Upon request of an inmate or the order of a court wherein an inmate has filed an action subject to this Code section, the officials in charge of a state or local institution may remit to the court amounts from an inmate's custodial account for payment of court costs, deposits, or filing fees. Such officials shall upon request of an inmate provide the certification required by subsection (b) of this Code section.

(d) The Administrative Office of the Courts shall cause to be printed such number of the forms provided for in this Code section as is necessary to furnish such forms to attorneys and to the Department of Corrections and local penal and correctional institutions for use by their inmates. Such forms shall be distributed to such institutions by the Administrative Office of the Courts without cost, and such forms shall be provided in reasonable numbers to inmates without cost. The cost of printing and distributing such forms shall be paid from funds appropriated to the judicial branch of government.

Laws 1985, p. 883, § 1.

Article 2

Venue

Part 1

General Provisions

§ 9-10-30. Equitable proceedings

All actions seeking equitable relief shall be filed in the county of the residence of one of the defendants against whom substantial relief is prayed, except in cases of injunctions to stay pending proceedings, when the action may be filed in the county where the proceedings are pending, provided no relief is prayed as to matters not included in such litigation, and except in divorce cases, venue in which is governed by Article VI, Section II, Paragraph I of the Constitution of this state.

Laws 1962, p. 659, § 1; Laws 1983, p. 3, § 48.

Formerly Code 1863, § 4095; Code 1868, § 4124; Code 1873, § 4183; Code 1882, § 4183; Civil Code 1895, § 4950; Civil Code 1910, § 5527; Code 1933, § 3-202.

§ 9-10-31. Joint obligors, joint tort-feasors, joint promisors, copartners, joint trespassers; medical malpractice claims

(a) The General Assembly finds that Paragraph IV of Section II of Article VI of the Georgia Constitution permits a trial and entry of judgment against a resident of Georgia in a county other than the county of the defendant's residence only if the Georgia resident defendant is a joint obligor, joint tort-feasor, joint promisor, copartner, or joint trespasser.

(b) Subject to the provisions of Code Section 9-10-31.1, joint tort-feasors, obligors, or promisors, or joint contractors or copartners, residing in different counties, may be subject to an action as such in the same action in any county in which one or more of the defendants reside.

(c) In any action involving a medical malpractice claim as defined in Code Section 9-9-60, a nonresident defendant may require that the case be transferred to the county of that defendant's residence if the tortious act upon which the medical malpractice claim is based occurred in the county of that defendant's residence.

(d) If all defendants who reside in the county in which an action is pending are discharged from liability before or upon the return of a verdict by the jury or the court hearing the case without a jury, a nonresident defendant may require that the case be transferred to a county and court in which venue would otherwise be proper. If venue would be proper in more than one county, the plaintiff may elect from among the counties in which venue is proper the county and the court in which the action shall proceed.

(e) Nothing in this Code section shall be deemed to alter or amend the pleading requirements of Chapter 11 of this title relating to the filing of complaints or answers.

Laws 1999, p. 734, § 1; Laws 2001, p. 4, § 9; Laws 2005, Act 1, § 2, eff. Feb. 16, 2005.

Formerly Code 1863, § 3315; Code 1868, § 3327; Code 1873, § 3404; Code 1882, § 3404; Civil Code 1895, § 4952; Civil Code 1910, § 5529; Code 1933, § 3-204.

Validity

This section has been held unconstitutional in the case of EHCA Cartersville, LLC v. Turner, 2006, 280 Ga. 333, 626 S.E.2d 482.

§ 9-10-31.1. Forum non conveniens

(a) If a court of this state, on written motion of a party, finds that in the interest of justice and for the convenience of the parties and witnesses a claim or action would be more properly heard in a forum outside this state or in a different county of proper venue within this state, the court shall decline to adjudicate the matter under the doctrine of forum non conveniens. As to a claim or action that would be more properly heard in a forum outside this state, the court shall dismiss the claim or action. As to a claim or action that would be more properly heard in a different county of proper venue within this state, the venue shall be transferred to the appropriate county. In determining whether to grant a motion to dismiss an action or to transfer venue under the doctrine of forum non conveniens, the court shall give consideration to the following factors:

(1) Relative ease of access to sources of proof;

(2) Availability and cost of compulsory process for attendance of unwilling witnesses;

(3) Possibility of viewing of the premises, if viewing would be appropriate to the action;

(4) Unnecessary expense or trouble to the defendant not necessary to the plaintiff's own right to pursue his or her remedy;

(5) Administrative difficulties for the forum courts;

(6) Existence of local interests in deciding the case locally; and

(7) The traditional deference given to a plaintiff's choice of forum.

(b) A court may not dismiss a claim under this Code section until the defendant files with the court or with the clerk of the court a written stipulation that, with respect to a new action on the claim commenced by the plaintiff, all the defendants waive the right to assert a statute of limitations defense in all other states of the United States in which the claim was not barred by limitations at the time the claim was filed in this state as necessary to effect a tolling of the limitations periods in those states beginning on the date the claim was filed in this state and ending on the date the claim is dismissed.

Laws 2005, Act 1, § 2, eff. Feb. 16, 2005.

§ 9-10-32. When maker and endorser of note reside in different counties; service of process

Where the maker and endorser of a promissory note who reside in different counties are subjected to an action in the county where the maker resides, as provided by Article VI, Section II, Paragraph V of the Constitution of this state, service of a copy of the original pleading and process on the endorser, as provided in the case of joint obligors and promisors, shall be deemed sufficient.

Laws 1983, p. 3, § 48.

Formerly Code 1863, § 3266; Code 1868, § 3277; Code 1873, § 3353; Code 1882, § 3353; Civil Code 1895, § 5012; Civil Code 1910, § 5594; Code 1933, § 3-303.

§ 9-10-33. Citizens of another state

A person who is not a citizen of this state, passing through or sojourning temporarily in the state, may be subject to an action in any county thereof in which he may be found at the time when the action is brought.

Formerly Code 1863, § 3318; Code 1868, § 3339; Code 1873, § 3416; Code 1882, § 3416; Civil Code 1895, § 4954; Civil Code 1910, § 5531; Code 1933, § 3-206.

§ 9-10-34. Claim of defending party against third-party defendant

(a) As used in this Code section, the term:

(1) "Defending party" means a party to a civil action who is:

(A) A defendant who contends that a person or entity not a party to the action is or may be liable to the defendant for all or part of a plaintiff's claim against the defendant;

(B) A plaintiff who contends that a person or entity not a party to the action is or may be liable to the plaintiff for all or part of another party's claim against the plaintiff; or

(C) A third-party defendant who contends that a person or entity not a party to the action is or may be liable to the third-party defendant for all or part of a claim made in the action against the third-party defendant.

(2) "Third-party defendant" means any person or entity whom a defending party contends may be liable to the defending party for all or part of the claim made against the defending party in the action.

(b) The claim of a defending party against a third-party defendant may be tried in the county where the action in which the claim for which the third-party defendant may be wholly or partially liable to the defending party is pending; and such claim may be tried in such county even though the third-party defendant is not a resident of such county.

(c) The venue established under this Code section against a third-party defendant is dependent upon the venue over the defending party who brought the third-party defendant into the action, and if venue is lost over said defending party, whether through dismissal or otherwise, venue shall likewise be lost as to the third-party defendant.

Laws 1984, p. 1149, § 1; Laws 1985, p. 149, § 9.

Part 2

Change of Venue

§ 9-10-50. Change of venue; grounds; how county selected

(a) Whenever, by an examination voir dire of the persons whose names are on the jury list and who are compellable to serve on the jury, the presiding judge is satisfied that an impartial jury cannot be obtained in the county where any civil case is pending, the civil case may be transferred to any county that may be agreed upon by the parties or their counsel.

(b) In the event the parties or their counsel fail or refuse to agree upon any county in which to try the case pending, the judge may select the county in which the same shall be tried and have the case transferred accordingly.

(c) When any civil case has been once transferred, the judge may again change the venue from the county to which the transfer was first made to any other county, in the same manner as the venue was first changed from the county in which the civil case was originally commenced.

Laws 1884-85, p. 35, § 1.

Formerly Civil Code 1895, §§ 4955, 4956; Civil Code 1910, §§ 5532, 5533; Code 1933, §§ 3-207, 3-208.

§ 9–10–51. Suits by county against county

In all actions brought by one county against another county in the defending county, the judge shall change the venue to a county adjoining the one in which the action is brought, on the motion of the plaintiff, supported by the oath of the chairman or presiding official of the county governing authority of the county bringing the action, that in his opinion a fair and impartial trial cannot be had in the county in which the action is brought.

Laws 1898, p. 88, § 1.

Formerly Civil Code 1910, § 5537; Code 1933, § 3–212.

§ 9–10–52. Transcript of order and record

The clerk of the court from which a case has been transferred shall send a true transcript of the order for the change of venue, together with the original record in the case, including depositions and orders and all pleadings, to the court of the county to which the case has been transferred.

Laws 1884–85, p. 35, § 2.

Formerly Civil Code 1895, § 4957; Civil Code 1910, § 5534; Code 1933, § 3–209.

§ 9–10–53. Further proceedings after transfer

After a case has been transferred, all further proceedings shall be conducted as if the case had been originally commenced in the court to which the same was transferred.

Laws 1884–85, p. 35, § 3.

Formerly Civil Code 1895, § 4958; Civil Code 1910, § 5535; Code 1933, § 3–210.

§ 9–10–54. Costs

All costs which have accrued at the time of the transfer of a case shall, at the termination of the case, be paid by the party or parties against whom the same are assessed to the proper officers of the county from which the case was transferred.

Laws 1884–85, p. 35, § 4.

Formerly Civil Code 1895, § 4959; Civil Code 1910, § 5536; Code 1933, § 3–211.

Article 3

Service

§ 9–10–70. Service of process upon minor 14 years of age or older where such minor is temporarily outside state

(a) Anything to the contrary notwithstanding, in all instances where a minor, 14 years of age or older, is a legal resident of the county wherein the legal proceeding concerning such service is sought to be made but is temporarily residing or sojourning outside this state or outside the United States, service may be perfected upon the minor by registered or certified United States mail with return receipt attached or by statutory overnight delivery.

(b) When service is to be perfected by registered or certified mail or statutory overnight delivery, as provided for in subsection (a) of this Code section, the clerk or the judge of the court in which the matter is proceeding shall enclose a copy of the petition, order, or other document sought to be served on the minor in an envelope addressed to the minor at his or her last known address and shall mail the same forthwith with postage prepaid, noting on the records of the court the date and hour of mailing, or shall send the same by statutory overnight delivery as provided in Code Section 9–10–12. When a receipt therefor is returned or if the sealed envelope in which the notice was mailed to the minor is returned to the sender by the appropriate postal authorities or commercial delivery company marked "Refused," giving the date of refusal, and the notation of refusal is signed or initialed by a postal employee or mail carrier or commercial delivery company employee to whom the refusal was made, then the clerk or judge shall attach the same to the original papers in the case or shall otherwise file it as a part of the records in the case and it shall be prima-facie evidence of service on the minor.

(c) When service upon a minor is perfected as set forth in subsections (a) and (b) of this Code section, the minor shall have 60 days from the date of receipt of the registered letter or statutory overnight delivery or the refusal thereof as shown on the receipt of refusal in which to file such defensive pleadings as may be necessary. No judgment or decree shall be rendered in the proceeding which shall adversely affect the interest of the minor until the 60 day period has elapsed unless the judgment or decree is expressly agreed or consented to by the duly appointed guardian ad litem of the minor as being in the best interest of the minor and unless the 60 day period provided for in this subsection has been expressly waived by the guardian ad litem. Each process issued in such cases shall be conformed to the 60 day provision set forth in this subsection.

(d) When the return of service provided for in this Code section is made to the proper court and an order is taken to appoint for the minor a guardian ad litem, and the guardian ad litem agrees to serve in writing, all of which shall be shown in the proceedings of the court, the minor shall be considered a party to the proceedings.

(e) In cases concerning minors 14 years of age or older who are temporarily sojourning or living outside this state or the United States, where the minor has a statutory or testamentary guardian or trustee representing the interest of the minor to be affected by a legal proceeding, service as usual on the guardian or trustee shall be sufficient to bind the minor's interest in his control to be affected by the proceedings.

Laws 1964, p. 301, § 1; Laws 2000, p. 1589, § 5.

Formerly Code 1933, § 81-212.1.

§ 9-10-71. Service by publication; nonresidents or unknown owners or claimants

(a) Where any nonresident or person unknown claims or owns title to or an interest, present or contingent, in any real or personal property in this state, service on the nonresident or unknown owner or claimant may be made by publication in cases affecting such property in proceedings brought:

(1) To remove a cloud therefrom or quiet title thereto;

(2) To cancel or set aside deeds, mortgages, liens, or encumbrances thereon;

(3) To establish, enforce, or foreclose liens thereon;

(4) To enforce, by decree for specific performance, any contract in reference thereto;

(5) To order the partition thereof by division or sale;

(6) To make any decree or order in which the subject of the action is real or personal property in this state in which a nonresident or unknown person has or may have or claims an interest, actual or contingent, and in which the relief demanded consists wholly or in part in excluding him from an interest therein;

(7) Where a nonresident or person unknown has or may have or may claim a present, future, or contingent interest in any property in this state; or

(8) Where a nonresident or person unknown may have or claim any interest in any trust estate in this state and it becomes necessary or proper or advantageous to order a sale of the whole or any part of the property.

(b) This Code section shall be supplemental to the other provisions in this Code providing for service by publication.

Laws 1895, p. 42, § 1.

Formerly Civil Code 1895, §§ 4976, 4977; Civil Code 1910, §§ 5554, 5555; Code 1933, § 81-205.

§ 9-10-72. Second original if defendants reside out of county

If the defendant or any of the defendants reside outside the county where the action is filed, the clerk shall issue a second original and copy for such other county or counties and forward the same to the sheriff, who shall serve the copy and return the second original, with his entry thereon, to the clerk of the court from which the same issued.

Laws 1984, p. 966, § 1.

Formerly Code 1863, § 3254; Code 1868, § 3265; Code 1873, § 3341; Code 1882, § 3341; Civil Code 1895, § 4989; Civil Code 1910, § 5567; Code 1933, § 81-215.

§ 9-10-73. Process and service may be waived

The defendant may acknowledge service or waive process by a writing signed by the defendant or someone authorized by him.

Laws 1840, Cobb's 1851 Digest, p. 363.

Formerly Code 1863, § 3250; Code 1868, § 3261; Code 1873, § 3337; Code 1882, § 3337; Civil Code 1895, § 4983; Civil Code 1910, § 5561; Code 1933, § 81-211.

Article 4
Personal Jurisdiction over Nonresidents

§ 9-10-90. "Nonresident" defined

As used in this article, the term "nonresident" includes an individual, or a partnership, association, or other legal or commercial entity (other than a corporation) not residing, domiciled, organized, or existing in this state at the time a claim or cause of action under Code Section 9-10-91 arises, or a corporation which is not organized or existing under the laws of this state and is not authorized to do or transact business in this state at the time a claim or cause of action under Code Section 9-10-91 arises. The term "nonresident" shall also include an individual, or a partnership, association, or other legal or commercial entity (other than a corporation) who, at the time a claim or cause of action arises under Code Section 9-10-91, was residing, domiciled, organized, or existing in this state and subsequently becomes a resident, domiciled, organized, or existing outside of this state as of the date of perfection of service of process as provided by Code Section 9–10–94.

Laws 1968, p. 1419, § 2; Laws 1977, p. 586, § 1.

§ 9–10–91. Personal jurisdiction over nonresidents of state

A court of this state may exercise personal jurisdiction over any nonresident or his executor or administrator, as to a cause of action arising from any of the acts, omissions, ownership, use, or possession enumerated in this Code section, in the same manner as if he were a resident of the state, if in person or through an agent, he:

(1) Transacts any business within this state;

(2) Commits a tortious act or omission within this state, except as to a cause of action for defamation of character arising from the act;

(3) Commits a tortious injury in this state caused by an act or omission outside this state if the tort-feasor regularly does or solicits business, or engages in any other persistent course of conduct, or derives substantial revenue from goods used or consumed or services rendered in this state;

(4) Owns, uses, or possesses any real property situated within this state; or

(5) With respect to proceedings for alimony, child support, or division of property in connection with an action for divorce or with respect to an independent action for support of dependents, maintains a matrimonial domicile in this state at the time of the commencement of this action or, if the defendant resided in this state preceding the commencement of the action, whether cohabiting during that time or not. This paragraph shall not change the residency requirement for filing an action for divorce.

Laws 1966, p. 343, § 1; Laws 1970, p. 443, § 1; Laws 1983, p. 1304, § 1.

§ 9–10–92. Effect of appearance

Where personal jurisdiction is based solely upon this article, an appearance does not confer such jurisdiction with respect to causes of action not arising from the conduct enumerated in Code Section 9–10–91.

Laws 1966, p. 343, § 2; Laws 1970, p. 443, § 2.

§ 9–10–93. Venue of actions

Venue in cases under this article shall lie in any county wherein a substantial part of the business was transacted, the tortious act, omission, or injury occurred, or the real property is located. Where an action is brought against a resident of this state, any nonresident of this state who is involved in the same transaction or occurrence and who is suable under the provisions of this article may be joined as a defendant in the county where a resident defendant is suable. Under such circumstances, jurisdiction and venue of the court of and over such nonresident defendant shall not be affected or lost if at trial a verdict or judgment is returned in favor of such resident defendant. If such resident defendant is dismissed from the action prior to commencement of the trial, the action against the nonresident defendant shall not abate but shall be transferred to a court in a county where venue is proper.

Laws 1966, p. 343, § 4; Laws 1968, p. 1419, § 1; Laws 1970, p. 443, § 3; Laws 1997, p. 480, § 1.

§ 9–10–94. Service beyond the state

A person subject to the jurisdiction of the courts of the state under Code Section 9–10–91, or his executor or administrator, may be served with a summons outside the state in the same manner as service is made within the state by any person authorized to make service by the laws of the state, territory, possession, or country in which service is made or by any duly qualified attorney, solicitor, barrister, or the equivalent in such jurisdiction.

Laws 1966, p. 343, § 3.

Article 5

Verification

§ 9–10–110. How petition for extraordinary equitable relief verified; support by proof

Petitions for a restraining order, injunction, receiver, or other extraordinary equitable relief shall be verified positively by the petitioner or supported by other satisfactory proofs.

Laws 1982, p. 3, § 9.

Formerly Civil Code 1895, § 4966; Civil Code 1910, § 5544; Code 1933, § 81–110.

§ 9-10-111. Verified petition requires verified plea or answer

In all cases where the plaintiff files a pleading with an affidavit attached to the effect that the facts stated in the pleading are true to the best of his knowledge and belief, the defendant shall in like manner verify any answer. If the defendant is a corporation, the affidavit may be made by the president, vice-president, superintendent, or any officer or agent who knows, or whose official duty it is to know, about the matters set out in the answer.

Laws 1895, p. 44, § 1.

Formerly Civil Code 1895, § 5055; Civil Code 1910, § 5638; Code 1933, § 81-401.

§ 9-10-112. Pleas in suits on open accounts

Whenever an action is brought on an open account and the same is verified by the plaintiff as provided by law, the answer either shall deny that the defendant is indebted in any sum or shall specify the amount in which the defendant admits he may be indebted and it shall be verified as required by law.

Laws 1901, p. 55, § 1.

Formerly Civil Code 1910, § 4728; Code 1933, § 81-410.

§ 9-10-113. Sufficiency of verification

All affidavits, petitions, answers, defenses, or other proceedings required to be verified or sworn to under oath shall be held to be sufficient when the same are sworn to before any notary public, magistrate, judge of any court, or any other officer of the state or county where the oath is made who is authorized by the laws thereof to administer oaths. The oath if made outside this state shall have the same force and effect as if it had been made before an officer of this state authorized to administer the same. The official attestation of the officer before whom the oath or affidavit is made shall be prima facie evidence of the official character of the officer and that he was authorized by law to administer oaths. However, this Code section shall not apply to such affidavits as may be expressly required by statute to be made before some particular officer within the state.

Laws 1853-54, p. 50, § 1; Laws 1870, p. 415, §§ 1, 2; Laws 1905, p. 103, § 1; Laws 1913, p. 56, § 1; Laws 1983, p. 884, § 4-1.

Formerly Code 1863, § 4108; Code 1868, § 4139; Code 1873, §§ 3450, 4198; Code 1882, §§ 3450, 4198; Civil Code 1895, §§ 5060, 5062; Civil Code 1910, §§ 5643, 5645, 5646; Code 1933, §§ 81-407, 81-408, 81-409.

§ 9-10-114. Verified answer as evidence

The defendant shall always have the privilege of filing an answer under oath for the purpose of using the same as evidence on any motion to dissolve an injunction or to set aside any extraordinary process or remedy granted. A sworn answer may be amended at any time, by leave of the court, as other pleadings; but an admission made in the answer shall always be evidence when offered by the other party.

Formerly Code 1863, § 4105; Code 1868, § 4136; Code 1873, § 4195; Code 1882, § 4195; Civil Code 1895, § 5056; Civil Code 1910, § 5639; Code 1933, § 81-402.

Article 6

Amendments

§ 9-10-130. Affidavits

All affidavits for the foreclosure of liens, including mortgages, all affidavits that are the foundation of legal proceedings, and all counter affidavits shall be amendable to the same extent as ordinary pleadings and with only the restrictions, limitations, and consequences of ordinary pleadings.

Laws 1887, p. 59, § 1; Laws 1889, p. 110, § 1.

Formerly Code 1863, § 3433; Code 1868, § 3453; Code 1873, § 3504; Code 1882, § 3504; Civil Code 1895, § 5122; Civil Code 1910, § 5706; Code 1933, § 81-1203.

§ 9-10-131. Bonds in judicial proceedings

All bonds taken under requirement of law in the course of a judicial proceeding may be amended and new security given if necessary.

Formerly Code 1863, § 3434; Code 1868, § 3454; Code 1873, § 3505; Code 1882, § 3505; Civil Code 1895, § 5123; Civil Code 1910, § 5707; Code 1933, § 81-1204.

§ 9-10-132. Misnomers amendable instanter

All misnomers, whether in the Christian name or surname, made in writs, pleadings, or other civil judicial proceedings, shall, on motion, be amended and corrected instanter without working unnecessary delay to the party making the same.

Laws 1850, Cobb's 1851 Digest, p. 493.

Formerly Code 1863, § 3413; Code 1868, § 3433; Code 1873, § 3483; Code 1882, § 3483; Civil Code 1895, § 5102; Civil Code 1910, § 5686; Code 1933, § 81-1206.

§ 9-10-133. Mistakes of clerks or ministerial officers

The mistake or misprision of a clerk or other ministerial officer shall in no case work to the injury of a party where by amendment justice may be promoted.

Laws 1799, Cobb's 1851 Digest, p. 480.

Formerly Code 1863, § 3436; Code 1868, § 3456; Code 1873, § 3507; Code 1882, § 3507; Civil Code 1895, § 5125; Civil Code 1910, § 5709; Code 1933, § 81-1205.

§ 9-10-134. Amending party put upon terms, when

If a party must apply for leave to amend his pleadings and has been negligent or dilatory in respect to the subject of the amendment, the court may order the party to pay to his adversary the cost of any proceedings which he proposes by amendment and, in the court's discretion, may order reasonable and equitable terms for amendment not affecting the merits of the case.

Laws 1853-54, p. 48, § 1.

Formerly Code 1863, § 3412; Code 1868, § 3432; Code 1873, § 3482; Code 1882, § 3482; Civil Code 1895, § 5101; Civil Code 1910, § 5685; Code 1933, § 81-1207.

§ 9-10-135. Amendment of pleadings as not waiving objections

Either party who amends or attempts to amend his complaint or other pleadings in response to an order or other ruling of the court shall not be held to have waived his objection to the order or ruling but may thereafter take exception thereto as in other cases.

Laws 1946, p. 761, § 1; Laws 1952, p. 243, § 1; Laws 1953, Nov.-Dec. Sess., p. 82, § 1; Laws 1962, p. 682, § 1; Laws 1966, p. 451, § 1; Laws 1966, p. 609, § 135; Laws 1967, p. 226, § 42.

Formerly Civil Code 1895, § 5045; Civil Code 1910, § 5628; Code 1933, § 81-1001.

Article 7

Continuances

§ 9-10-150. Membership in General Assembly by party or counsel

A member of the General Assembly who is a party to or the attorney for a party to a case, or any member of the staff of the Lieutenant Governor, the Speaker of the House of Representatives, the President Pro Tempore of the Senate, the Speaker Pro Tempore of the House of Representatives, or the chairperson of the Judiciary Committee or Special Judiciary Committee of either the Senate or the House of Representatives who is the lead counsel for a party to a case pending in any trial or appellate court or before any administrative agency of this state, shall be granted a continuance and stay of the case. The continuance and stay shall apply to all aspects of the case, including, but not limited to, the filing and serving of an answer to a complaint, the making of any discovery or motion, or of any response to any subpoena, discovery, or motion, and appearance at any hearing, trial, or argument. Unless a shorter length of time is requested by the member, the continuance and stay shall last the length of any regular or extraordinary session of the General Assembly and during the first three weeks following any recess or adjournment including an adjournment sine die of any regular or extraordinary session. A continuance and stay shall also be granted for such other times as the member of the General Assembly or staff member certifies to the court that his or her presence elsewhere is required by his or her duties with the General Assembly. Notwithstanding any other provision of law, rule of court, or administrative rule or regulation, the time for doing any act in the case which is delayed by the continuance provided by this Code section shall be automatically extended by the same length of time as the continuance or stay covered.

Laws 1905, p. 93, § 1; Laws 1952, p. 26, § 1; Laws 1973, p. 478, § 1; Laws 1977, p. 760, § 1; Laws 1991, p. 376, § 1; Laws 1996, p. 112, § 1; Laws 2002, p. 403, § 1; Laws 2006, Act 608, § 1, eff. July 1, 2006.

Formerly Civil Code 1910, § 5711; Code 1933, § 81-1402.

§ 9-10-151. Absence of party or counsel on meeting of Board of Regents of University System of Georgia or State Board of Education

Should any member of the Board of Regents of the University System of Georgia or any member of the State Board of Education be engaged, at the time of any meeting of the board, as counsel or party in any case pending in the courts of this state and should the case be called for trial during the regular session of the board, the absence of the member to attend the session shall be good ground for a postponement or continuance of the case until the session of the board has come to an end.

Laws 1931, p. 7, § 56; Laws 1985, p. 1406, § 1.

Formerly Code 1933, § 81-1404.

§ 9-10-152. Absence of party or counsel on meeting of Board of Human Resources

Should any member of the Board of Human Resources be engaged, at the time of any meeting of the board, as counsel or party in any case pending in the courts of this state and should the case be called for trial during the regular session of the board, the absence of the member to attend the session shall be good ground for a postponement or a continuance of the case until the session of the board has come to an end.

Laws 1933, p. 7, § 1.

Formerly Code 1933, § 81-1405.

§ 9-10-153. Absence of parties or leading counsel for National Guard duty

It shall be the duty of any judge of a court of this state, on or without motion, to continue any case in the court when the case is reached and any party thereto or his leading counsel is absent from the court by reason of his service in the armed forces when such service directly prevents his attendance in court or by reason of his attendance as a member of the National Guard upon any duty prescribed by the Governor or the adjutant general, unless the party, in the absence of his leading counsel, or the leading counsel, in the absence of the party, on the call of the case, announces ready for trial. If counsel is absent it shall be necessary for his client to make oath that he cannot safely go to trial without the absent counsel; and, if the party plaintiff or defendant is absent, his counsel shall state in his place that he cannot safely go to trial without the client.

Laws 1925, p. 149, § 1; Laws 1991, p. 404, § 1.

Formerly Code 1933, § 81-1406.

§ 9-10-154. Absence of a party as cause for continuance

If either party is providentially prevented from attending the trial of a case, and the counsel of the absent party will state in his place that he cannot go safely to trial without the presence of the absent party, the case shall be continued, provided the continuances of the party have not been exhausted.

Formerly Code 1863, § 3453; Code 1868, § 3473; Code 1873, § 3524; Code 1882, § 3524; Civil Code 1895, § 5131; Civil Code 1910, § 5717; Code 1933, § 81-1412.

§ 9-10-155. Absence or illness of counsel as cause for continuance

The illness or absence, from providential cause, of counsel where there is but one, or of the leading counsel where there are more than one, shall be a sufficient ground for continuance, provided that the party making the application for a continuance will swear that he cannot go safely to trial without the services of the absent counsel, that he expects his services at the next term, and that the application is not made for delay only.

Formerly Code 1863, § 3454; Code 1868, § 3474; Code 1873, § 3525; Code 1882, § 3525; Civil Code 1895, § 5132; Penal Code 1895, § 964; Civil Code 1910, § 5718; Penal Code 1910, § 990; Code 1933, § 81-1413.

§ 9-10-156. Continuance of cases called during sessions of the General Assembly or within 15 days before or after such sessions when Attorney General is of counsel

When any case pending in the courts of this state in which the Attorney General is of counsel is scheduled to be called for any purpose during sessions of the General Assembly or during a period of 15 days preceding or following sessions of the General Assembly, on motion of the Attorney General or an assistant attorney general, it shall be a good ground for continuance that the Attorney General and his staff are occupied in aid of the business of the General Assembly.

Laws 1956, p. 700, § 1.

§ 9-10-157. Amending party, when entitled to continuance

The party amending pleadings or other proceedings in any of the courts of this state shall not be entitled to delay or continuance on account of the amendment, except by leave of the court to enable him to make the amendment.

Formerly Code 1863, § 3449; Code 1868, § 3469; Code 1873, § 3520; Code 1882, § 3520; Civil Code 1895, § 5127; Civil Code 1910, § 5713; Code 1933, § 81-1408.

§ 9-10-158. Continuance charged to amending party, when

When a pleading is amended, if the opposite party makes oath or his counsel states in his place that he is surprised and not fully prepared for trial because of the amendment, upon a showing of the manner of unpreparedness and that surprise is not claimed for the purpose of delay, the case may be continued and the continuance charged to the amending party.

Formerly Code 1863, § 3450; Code 1868, § 3470; Code 1873, § 3521; Code 1882, § 3521; Civil Code 1895, § 5128; Civil Code 1910, § 5714; Code 1933, § 81-1409.

§ 9-10-159. Member of General Assembly as witness

Any person summoned as a witness in any case shall be excused by the judge from attending the court by reason of his attendance as a legislator in the General Assembly. In all civil cases it shall be the right of either party thereto to take the deposition, as provided by law, of any person desired to be used as a witness in the case who is a member of the General Assembly when the session of the General Assembly conflicts with the session of the court in which such case is to be tried.

Laws 1905, p. 93, § 2.

Formerly Civil Code 1910, § 5712; Code 1933, § 81-1407.

§ 9-10-160. Absence of witnesses; showing required

All applications for continuances upon the ground of the absence of a witness shall show to the court:

(1) That the witness is absent;

(2) That he has been subpoenaed;

(3) That he does not reside outside of the state;

(4) That his testimony is material;

(5) That the witness is not absent by the permission, directly or indirectly, of the applicant;

(6) That the applicant expects he will be able to procure the testimony of the witness at the next term of the court;

(7) That the application is not made for the purpose of delay but to enable the party to procure the testimony of the absent witness; and

(8) The facts expected to be proved by the absent witness.

Laws 1959, p. 342, § 1; Laws 1991, p. 376, § 2.

Formerly Code 1863, § 3451; Code 1868, § 3471; Code 1873, § 3522; Code 1882, § 3522; Civil Code 1895, § 5129; Penal Code 1895, § 962; Civil Code 1910, § 5715; Penal Code 1910, § 987; Code 1933, § 81-1410.

§ 9-10-161. Admission of facts as ground for denial of continuance because of absence of witness

No continuance shall be allowed in any court on account of the absence of a witness or for the purpose of procuring testimony when the opposite party is willing to admit and does not contest the truth of the facts expected to be proved by the testimony of the witness. The court shall order the admission to be reduced to writing.

Laws 1853-54, p. 52, § 1.

Formerly Code 1863, § 3452; Code 1868, § 3472; Code 1873, § 3523; Code 1882, § 3523; Civil Code 1895, § 5130; Penal Code 1895, § 963; Civil Code 1910, § 5716; Penal Code 1910, § 989; Code 1933, § 81-1411.

§ 9-10-162. Cases sent back from appellate court

When any case is sent back for trial by the Supreme Court or the Court of Appeals, the same shall be in order for trial; and, if the continuances of a party are exhausted, the trial court may grant one continuance to the party as the ends of justice may require.

Laws 1851-52, p. 216, § 6.

Formerly Code 1863, § 3456; Code 1868, § 3476; Code 1873, § 3527; Code 1882, § 3527; Civil Code 1895, § 5134; Civil Code 1910, § 5720; Code 1933, § 81-1415.

§ 9-10-163. Continuance on appeal

No appeal case shall be continued more than twice by the same party, except for providential cause, for which it may be continued as often as justice may require.

Formerly Code 1863, § 3459; Code 1868, § 3479; Code 1873, § 3530; Code 1882, § 3530; Civil Code 1895, § 5137; Civil Code 1910, § 5723; Code 1933, § 81-1418.

§ 9-10-164. Continuance for no longer than one term

A continuance requested by a party in a pending case in any court shall not be granted for longer than one term.

Laws 1799, Cobb's 1851 Digest, p. 486.

Formerly Code 1863, § 3448; Code 1868, § 3468; Code 1873, § 3519; Code 1882, § 3519; Civil Code 1895, § 5126; Civil Code 1910, § 5710; Code 1933, § 81-1401.

§ 9-10-165. Case not reached at trial term

A case not reached at the trial term stands over as continued.

Formerly Code 1863, § 3455, Code 1868, § 3475; Code 1873, § 3526; Code 1882, § 3526; Civil Code 1895, § 5133; Civil Code 1910, § 5719; Code 1933, § 81-1414.

§ 9-10-166. Diligence required of applicants

In all cases, the party making an application for a continuance must show that he has used due diligence.

Formerly Code 1863, § 3457; Code 1868, § 3477; Code 1873, § 3528; Code 1882, § 3528; Civil Code 1895, § 5135; Penal Code 1895, § 965; Civil Code 1910, § 5721; Penal Code 1910, § 991; Code 1933, § 81-1416.

§ 9-10-167. Counter-showing and discretion of court

(a) All applications for continuances are addressed to the sound legal discretion of the court and, if not expressly provided for, shall be granted or refused as the ends of justice may require.

(b) In all cases the presiding judge may, in his discretion, admit a countershowing to a motion for a continuance and, after a hearing, may decide whether the motion shall prevail.

Laws 1871-72, p. 49, § 1; Laws 1872, p. 41, § 1.

Formerly Code 1863, § 3460; Code 1868, § 3480; Code 1873, § 3531; Code 1882, § 3531; Civil Code 1895, § 5138; Penal Code 1895, § 966; Civil Code 1910, § 5724; Penal Code 1910, § 992; Code 1933, § 81-1419.

§ 9-10-168. No continuance for term, when

No continuance shall be granted in any of the courts in this state which have a continuous session for 30 days or more, over the objection of the adverse party, where the cause for the same can be obviated by a postponement to a later day during the term. It shall be the duty of the presiding judge, whenever a motion and a proper showing for a continuance are made by either party at any time, to set the case down for a later day during the same term if it is practicable thereby to avoid the continuance of the case.

Laws 1893, p. 56, § 1.

Formerly Civil Code 1895, § 5139; Civil Code 1910, § 5725; Code 1933, § 81-1420.

§ 9-10-169. Public announcement of continuance

Continuances of cases in the superior, state, county, and city courts and the dates thereof shall be entered on the docket. Upon the call of the calendar which includes such case, the judge shall announce the continuance.

Laws 1895, p. 41, § 1.

Formerly Civil Code 1895, § 5140; Penal Code 1895, § 968; Civil Code 1910, § 5726; Penal Code 1910, § 994; Code 1933, § 81-1421.

Article 8

Argument and Conduct of Counsel

§ 9-10-180. Time limit of argument

Counsel shall be limited in their arguments to two hours on a side.

Laws 1924, p. 75, §§ 2, 3; Laws 1983, p. 884, § 3-4.

Formerly Code 1933, § 81-1007.

§ 9-10-181. Extension of time, when allowed

If counsel on either side, before argument begins, applies to the court for extension of the time prescribed for argument and states in his place or on oath, in the discretion of the court, that he or they cannot do the case justice within the time prescribed and that it will require for that purpose additional time, stating how much additional time will be necessary, the court shall grant such extension of time as may seem reasonable and proper.

Laws 1924, p. 75, § 4.

Formerly Code 1933, § 81-1008.

§ 9-10-182. Number of counsel who may argue case

Not more than two counsel for each side shall be permitted to argue any case, except by express leave of the court; and in no case shall more than one counsel be heard in conclusion.

Laws 1924, p. 75, § 1.

Formerly Code 1933, § 81-1004.

§ 9-10-183. Use in argument by counsel of blackboard, models and similar devices

In the trial of any civil action, counsel for either party shall be permitted to use a blackboard and models or similar devices in connection with his argument to the jury for the purpose of illustrating his contentions with respect to the issues which are to be decided by the jury, provided that counsel shall not in writing present any argument that could not properly be made orally.

Laws 1960, p. 1037, § 1; Laws 1982, p. 3, § 9.

§ 9–10–184. Argument of counsel with respect to monetary value of pain and suffering

In the trial of a civil action for personal injuries, counsel shall be allowed to argue the worth or monetary value of pain and suffering to the jury; provided, however, that any such argument shall conform to the evidence or reasonable deductions from the evidence in the case.

Laws 1960, p. 174, § 1.

§ 9–10–185. Improper conduct by counsel; duty of court

Where counsel in the hearing of the jury make statements of prejudicial matters which are not in evidence, it is the duty of the court to interpose and prevent the same. On objection made, the court shall also rebuke counsel and by all needful and proper instructions to the jury endeavor to remove the improper impression from their minds. In its discretion, the court may order a mistrial if the plaintiff's attorney is the offender.

Formerly Civil Code 1895, § 4419; Civil Code 1910, § 4957; Code 1933, § 81–1009.

§ 9–10–186. Which parties are entitled to opening and concluding arguments; admission of prima facie case

In civil actions, where the burden of proof rests with the plaintiff, the plaintiff is entitled to the opening and concluding arguments except that if the defendant introduces no evidence or admits a prima-facie case, the defendant shall be entitled to open and conclude. In civil actions for personal injuries, the defendant shall be deemed not to have admitted a prima-facie case if such defendant introduces any evidence as to the extent of damages, other than cross-examination of the plaintiff and witnesses called by the plaintiff.

Laws 1997, p. 951, § 1.

Article 9

General Civil Forms

§ 9–10–200. Form of action to recover real estate and mesne profits

The form of an action for the recovery of real estate and mesne profits may be as follows:

—IN THE ____ COURT OF ____ COUNTY—
—STATE OF GEORGIA—

A.B.,   )
  Plaintiff   ) Civil action
) File no. ________
v.   ) (Clerk will insert
) number.)
C.D.,   )
  Defendant   )

—COMPLAINT—

The defendant herein named is a resident of ____ (street), ____ (city), ____ County, Georgia, and is subject to the jurisdiction of this court.

1.

Defendant C.D. of said county is in possession of a certain tract of land in said county (here describe the land) to which plaintiff claims title.

2.

Defendant has received the profits of said land since the ____ day of ____, ____, of the yearly value of $____ and refuses to deliver said land to plaintiff or to pay him the profits thereof.

Wherefore, plaintiff demands judgment against defendant (here list the relief prayed for).

____
Attorney for plaintiff

____
Address

Laws 1999, p. 81, § 9.

Formerly Code 1863, § 3301; Code 1868, § 3313; Code 1873, § 3389; Code 1882, § 3389.

§ 9–10–201. Form of action to recover personal property

The form of an action for the recovery of personal property may be as follows:

—IN THE ____ COURT OF ____ COUNTY
STATE OF GEORGIA—

A.B.,   )
  Plaintiff   ) Civil action
) File no. ________
v.   ) (Clerk will insert
) number.)
C.D.,   )
  Defendant   )

—COMPLAINT—

The defendant herein named is a resident of _____ (street), _____ (city), _____ County, Georgia, and is subject to the jurisdiction of this court.

—1.—

Defendant C. D. is in possession of a certain (here describe the property) of the value of $_____, to which plaintiff claims title.

—2.—

Defendant refuses to deliver the said _____ to plaintiff or to pay plaintiff the profits thereof.

Wherefore, plaintiff demands judgment against defendant (here list the relief prayed for).

____
Attorney for plaintiff

____
Address

Formerly Code 1863, § 3302; Code 1868, § 3314; Code 1873, § 3390; Code 1882, § 3390.

§ 9-10-202. Form of action to recover money on a judgment

The form of an action to recover money on a judgment may be as follows:

—IN THE _____ COURT OF _____ COUNTY—

—STATE OF GEORGIA—

A.B.,)
Plaintiff) Civil action
) File no. _________
v.) (Clerk will insert
) number.)
C.D.,)
Defendant)

—COMPLAINT—

The defendant herein named is a resident of _____ (street), _____ (city), _____ County, Georgia, and is subject to the jurisdiction of this court.

1.

Defendant C.D. is indebted to plaintiff in the sum of $_____, plus interest, on a judgment obtained by plaintiff against defendant.

2.

Said judgment was obtained in the (name of court) held on the _____ day of _____, _____, in (county, city, or town and state), as fully appears in the properly authenticated certified copies of the proceeding attached to this complaint as Exhibit A.

3.

Said judgment has not been satisfied and defendant C.D. has not paid the same.

Wherefore, plaintiff demands judgment against defendant (here list the relief prayed for).

____
Attorney for plaintiff

____
Address

Laws 1999, p. 81, § 9.

Formerly Code 1863, § 3305; Code 1868, § 3317; Code 1873, § 3394; Code 1882, § 3394.

§ 9-10-203. Form of action for breach of warranty in deed

The form of an action for a breach of warranty in a deed may be as follows:

—IN THE _____ COURT OF _____ COUNTY—

—STATE OF GEORGIA—

A.B.,)
Plaintiff) Civil action
) File no. _________
v.) (Clerk will insert
) number.)
C.D.,)
Defendant)

—COMPLAINT—

The defendant herein named is a resident of _____ (street), _____ (city), _____ County, Georgia, and is subject to the jurisdiction of this court.

1.

On the _____ day of _____, _____, defendant C.D. executed to plaintiff a warranty deed to a certain tract of land (here describe the land), for the sum of $_____, paid by plaintiff to defendant C.D.

2.

Plaintiff has been evicted from said lot of land and defendant refuses to indemnify plaintiff from his damages in that behalf.

3.

Because of said eviction, plaintiff has suffered damages in the amount of $_____, for which defendant is indebted to plaintiff.

Wherefore, plaintiff demands judgment against defendant (here list the relief prayed for).

____
Attorney for plaintiff

____
Address

Laws 1999, p. 81, § 9.

Formerly Code 1863, § 3306; Code 1868, § 3318; Code 1873, § 3395; Code 1882, § 3394.

§ 9–10–204. Form of action for words

The form of an action for words may be as follows:

—IN THE ____ COURT OF ____ COUNTY—

—STATE OF GEORGIA—

A.B.,	)
Plaintiff	) Civil action
	) File no. ________
v.	) (Clerk will insert
	) number.)
C.D.,	)
Defendant	)

—COMPLAINT—

The defendant herein named is a resident of ____ (street), ____ (city), ____ County, Georgia, and is subject to the jurisdiction of this court.

Defendant C.D. has injured and damaged plaintiff in the sum of $____, by falsely and maliciously saying of and concerning plaintiff, on the ____ day of ____, ____, the following false and malicious words to ____ (name of person): (here give the words).

Wherefore, plaintiff demands judgment against defendant (here list the relief prayed for).

____
Attorney for plaintiff

____
Address

Laws 1984, p. 22, § 9; Laws 1999, p. 81, § 9.

Formerly Code 1863, § 3307; Code 1868, § 3319; Code 1873, § 3396; Code 1882, § 3396.

CHAPTER 11

CIVIL PRACTICE ACT

Article 1

Scope of Rules and Form of Action

§ 9–11–1. Scope of chapter

This chapter governs the procedure in all courts of record of this state in all actions of a civil nature whether cognizable as cases at law or in equity, with the exceptions stated in Code Section 9–11–81. This chapter shall be construed to secure the just, speedy, and inexpensive determination of every action. This chapter shall also apply to courts which are not courts of record to the extent that no other rule governing a particular practice or procedure of such courts is prescribed by general or local law applicable to such courts.

Laws 1966, p. 609, § 1.

§ 9–11–2. One form of action

There shall be one form of action, to be known as "civil action."

Laws 1966, p. 609, § 2.

Article 2

Commencement of Action and Service

§ 9–11–3. Commencement of action

(a) A civil action is commenced by filing a complaint with the court.

(b) At the time of filing the complaint for a civil action in superior court or state court, the plaintiff shall file the appropriate civil case filing form with the clerk of the court. The form shall contain complete information and shall be substantially in the form prescribed in Code Section 9–11–133. The filing of the complaint shall not be delayed for the filing of the case filing form. If, after a civil action has been filed, the court presiding over the civil action decides that the civil case filing form has not been filed or has been filed incorrectly, the court shall require the plaintiff to file the civil case filing form or an amended form. In no case shall the failure to accurately complete the civil case filing form required by this Code section provide a basis to dismiss a civil action.

Laws 1966, p. 609, § 3; Laws 2000, p. 850, § 1; Laws 2001, p. 4, § 9; Laws 2006, Act 660, § 1, eff. July 1, 2006.

§ 9-11-4. Process

(a) *Summons—Issuance.* Upon the filing of the complaint, the clerk shall forthwith issue a summons and deliver it for service. Upon request of the plaintiff, separate or additional summons shall issue against any defendants.

(b) *Summons—Form.* The summons shall be signed by the clerk; contain the name of the court and county and the names of the parties; be directed to the defendant; state the name and address of the plaintiff's attorney, if any, otherwise the plaintiff's address; and state the time within which this chapter requires the defendant to appear and file appropriate defensive pleadings with the clerk of the court, and shall notify the defendant that in case of the defendant's failure to do so judgment by default will be rendered against him or her for the relief demanded in the complaint.

(c) *Summons—By whom served.* Process shall be served by the sheriff of the county where the action is brought or where the defendant is found, or by such sheriff's deputy, or by the marshal or sheriff of the court, or by such official's deputy, or by any citizen of the United States specially appointed by the court for that purpose, or by someone who is not a party and is not younger than 18 years of age and has been appointed as a permanent process server by the court in which the action is brought. Where the service of process is made outside of the United States, after an order of publication, it may be served either by any citizen of the United States or by any resident of the country, territory, colony, or province who is specially appointed by the court for that purpose. When service is to be made within this state, the person making such service shall make the service within five days from the time of receiving the summons and complaint; but failure to make service within the five-day period will not invalidate a later service.

(d) *Waiver of service.*

(1) A defendant who waives service of a summons does not thereby waive any objection to the venue or to the jurisdiction of the court over the person of the defendant.

(2) Upon receipt of notice of an action in the manner provided in this subsection, the following defendants have a duty to avoid unnecessary costs of serving the summons:

(A) A corporation or association that:

(i) Is subject to service under paragraph (1) or (2) of subsection (e) of this Code section; and

(ii) Receives notice of such action by an agent other than the Secretary of State; and

(B) A natural person who:

(i) Is not a minor; and

(ii) Has not been judicially declared to be of unsound mind or incapable of conducting his or her own affairs.

(3) To avoid costs, the plaintiff may notify such a defendant of the commencement of the action and request that the defendant waive service of a summons. The notice and request shall:

(A) Be in writing and shall be addressed directly to the defendant, if an individual, or else to an officer or managing or general agent or other agent authorized by appointment to receive service of process for a defendant subject to service under paragraph (1) or (2) of subsection (e) of this Code section;

(B) Be dispatched through first-class mail or other reliable means;

(C) Be accompanied by a copy of the complaint and shall identify the court in which it has been filed;

(D) Make reference to this Code section and shall inform the defendant, by means of the text prescribed in subsection (*l*) of this Code section, of the consequences of compliance and of failure to comply with the request;

(E) Set forth the date on which the request is sent;

(F) Allow the defendant a reasonable time to return the waiver, which shall be at least 30 days from the date on which the request is sent, or 60 days from that date if the defendant is addressed outside any judicial district of the United States; and

(G) Provide the defendant with an extra copy of the notice and request, as well as a prepaid means of compliance in writing.

(4) If a defendant located within the United States that is subject to service inside or outside the state under this Code section fails to comply with a request for a waiver made by a plaintiff located within the United States, the court shall impose the costs subsequently incurred in effecting service on the defendant unless good cause for the failure is shown.

(5) A defendant that, before being served with process, returns a waiver so requested in a timely manner is not required to serve an answer to the complaint until 60 days after the date on which the request for waiver of service was sent, or 90 days after that date if the defendant was addressed outside any judicial district of the United States.

(6) When the plaintiff files a waiver of service with the court, the action shall proceed, except as

provided in paragraph (5) of this subsection, as if a summons and complaint had been served at the time of filing the waiver, and no proof of service shall be required.

(7) The costs to be imposed on a defendant under paragraph (4) of this subsection for failure to comply with a request to waive service of summons shall include the costs subsequently incurred in effecting service, together with the costs, including a reasonable attorney's fee, of any motion required to collect the costs of service.

(e) *Summons—Personal service.* Except for cases in which the defendant has waived service, the summons and complaint shall be served together. The plaintiff shall furnish the clerk of the court with such copies as are necessary. Service shall be made by delivering a copy of the summons attached to a copy of the complaint as follows:

(1) If the action is against a corporation incorporated or domesticated under the laws of this state or a foreign corporation authorized to transact business in this state, to the president or other officer of the corporation, secretary, cashier, managing agent, or other agent thereof, provided that when for any reason service cannot be had in such manner, the Secretary of State shall be an agent of such corporation upon whom any process, notice, or demand may be served. Service on the Secretary of State of any such process, notice, or demand shall be made by delivering to and leaving with him or her or with any other person or persons designated by the Secretary of State to receive such service a copy of such process, notice, or demand, along with a copy of the affidavit to be submitted to the court pursuant to this Code section. The plaintiff or the plaintiff's attorney shall certify in writing to the Secretary of State that he or she has forwarded by registered mail or statutory overnight delivery such process, service, or demand to the last registered office or agent listed on the records of the Secretary of State, that service cannot be effected at such office, and that it therefore appears that the corporation has failed either to maintain a registered office or to appoint a registered agent in this state. Further, if it shall appear from such certification that there is a last known address of a known officer of the corporation outside the state, the plaintiff shall, in addition to and after such service upon the Secretary of State, mail or cause to be mailed to the known officer at the address by registered or certified mail or statutory overnight delivery a copy of the summons and a copy of the complaint. Any such service by certification to the Secretary of State shall be answerable not more than 30 days from the date the Secretary of State receives such certification;

(2) If the action is against a foreign corporation or a nonresident individual, partnership, joint-stock company, or association, doing business and having a managing or other agent, cashier, or secretary within this state, to such agent, cashier, or secretary or to an agent designated for service of process;

(3) If against a minor, to the minor, personally, and also to such minor's father, mother, guardian, or duly appointed guardian ad litem unless the minor is married, in which case service shall not be made on the minor's father, mother, or guardian;

(4) If against a person residing within this state who has been judicially declared to be of unsound mind or incapable of conducting his or her own affairs and for whom a guardian has been appointed, to the person and also to such person's guardian and, if there is no guardian appointed, then to his or her duly appointed guardian ad litem;

(5) If against a county, municipality, city, or town, to the chairman of the board of commissioners, president of the council of trustees, mayor or city manager of the city or to an agent authorized by appointment to receive service of process. If against any other public body or organization subject to an action, to the chief executive officer or clerk thereof;

(6) If the principal sum involved is less than $ 200.00 and if reasonable efforts have been made to obtain personal service by attempting to find some person residing at the most notorious place of abode of the defendant, then by securely attaching the service copy of the complaint in a conspicuously marked and waterproof packet to the upper part of the door of the abode and on the same day mailing by certified or registered mail or statutory overnight delivery an additional copy to the defendant at his or her last known address, if any, and making an entry of this action on the return of service; or

(7) In all other cases to the defendant personally, or by leaving copies thereof at the defendant's dwelling house or usual place of abode with some person of suitable age and discretion then residing therein, or by delivering a copy of the summons and complaint to an agent authorized by appointment or by law to receive service of process.

(f) *Summons—Other service.*

(1) SERVICE BY PUBLICATION.

(A) General. When the person on whom service is to be made resides outside the state, or has departed from the state, or cannot, after due diligence, be found within the state, or conceals himself or herself to avoid the service of the summons, and the fact shall appear, by affidavit, to the satisfaction of the judge or clerk of the court, and it shall appear, either by affidavit or by a verified complaint on file, that a claim exists against the defendant in respect to whom the service is to be made, and that he or she is a necessary or proper party to the action, the judge or clerk may grant an order that the service be made by the publication of summons, provided that when the affidavit is based on the fact that the party on whom service is to be made resides outside the state, and the present address of the party is unknown, it shall be a sufficient showing of such fact if the affiant shall state generally in the affidavit that at a previous time such person resided outside this state in a certain place (naming the place and stating the latest date known to affiant when the party so resided there); that such place is the last place in which the party resided to the knowledge of affiant; that the party no longer resides at the place; that affiant does not know the present place of residence of the party or where the party can be found; and that affiant does not know and has never been informed and has no reason to believe that the party now resides in this state; and, in such case, it shall be presumed that the party still resides and remains outside the state, and the affidavit shall be deemed to be a sufficient showing of due diligence to find the defendant. This Code section shall apply to all manner of civil actions, including those for divorce.

(B) Property. In any action which relates to, or the subject of which is, real or personal property in this state in which any defendant, corporate or otherwise, has or claims a lien or interest, actual or contingent, or in which the relief demanded consists wholly or in part of excluding such defendant from any interest therein, where the defendant resides outside the state or has departed from the state, or cannot, after due diligence, be found within the state, or conceals himself or herself to avoid the service of summons, the judge or clerk may make an order that the service be made by publication of summons. The service by publication shall be made in the same manner as provided in all cases of service by publication.

(C) Publication. When the court orders service by publication, the clerk shall cause the publication to be made in the paper in which sheriff's advertisements are printed, four times within the ensuing 60 days, publications to be at least seven days apart. The party obtaining the order shall, at the time of filing, deposit the cost of publication. The published notice shall contain the name of the parties plaintiff and defendant, with a caption setting forth the court, the character of the action, the date the action was filed, the date of the order for service by publication, and a notice directed and addressed to the party to be thus served, commanding him or her to file with the clerk and serve upon the plaintiff's attorney an answer within 60 days of the date of the order for service by publication and shall bear teste in the name of the judge and shall be signed by the clerk of the court. Where the residence or abiding place of the absent or nonresident party is known, the party obtaining the order shall advise the clerk thereof; and it shall be the duty of the clerk, within 15 days after filing of the order for service by publication, to enclose, direct, stamp, and mail a copy of the notice, together with a copy of the order for service by publication and complaint, if any, to the party named in the order at his or her last known address, if any, and make an entry of this action on the complaint or other pleadings filed in the case. The copy of the notice to be mailed to the nonresident shall be a duplicate of the one published in the newspaper but need not necessarily be a copy of the newspaper itself. When service by publication is ordered, personal service of a copy of the summons, complaint, and order of publication outside the state in lieu of publication shall be equivalent to serving notice by publication and to mailing when proved to the satisfaction of the judge or otherwise. The defendant shall have 30 days from the date of such personal service outside the state in which to file defensive pleadings.

(2) Personal service outside the state. Personal service outside the state upon a natural person may be made: (A) in any action where the person served is a resident of this state, and (B) in any action affecting specific real property or status, or in any other proceeding in rem without regard to the residence of the person served. When such facts shall appear, by affidavit, to the satisfaction of the court and it shall appear, either by affidavit or by a verified complaint on file, that a claim is asserted against the person in respect to whom the service is to be made, and that he or she is a necessary or proper party to the action, the court may grant an order that the service be made by personal service outside the state. Such service shall be made by delivering a copy of the process together with a copy of the complaint in person to the persons served.

(3) Service upon persons in a foreign country. Unless otherwise provided by law, service upon a person from whom a waiver has not been obtained and filed, other than an infant or an incompetent person, may be effected in a place not within the United States:

(A) By any internationally agreed means reasonably calculated to give notice, such as those means authorized by the Hague Convention on the Service Abroad of Judicial and Extrajudicial Documents;

(B) If there is no internationally agreed means of service or the applicable international agreement allows other means of service, provided that service is reasonably calculated to give notice:

(i) In the manner prescribed by the law of the foreign country for service in that country in an action in any of its courts of general jurisdiction;

(ii) As directed by the foreign authority in response to a letter rogatory or letter of request; or

(iii) Unless prohibited by the law of the foreign country, by:

(I) Delivery to the person of a copy of the summons and the complaint; or

(II) Any form of mail requiring a signed receipt, to be addressed and dispatched by the clerk of the court to the party to be served; or

(C) By other means not prohibited by international agreement as may be directed by the court.

(g) *Territorial limits of effective service.* All process may be served anywhere within the territorial limits of the state and, when a statute so provides, beyond the territorial limits of the state.

(h) *Return.* The person serving the process shall make proof of service thereof to the court promptly and, in any event, within the time during which the person served must respond to the process. Proof of service shall be as follows:

(1) If served by a sheriff or marshal, or such official's deputy, the affidavit or certificate of the sheriff, marshal, or deputy;

(2) If by any other proper person, such person's affidavit;

(3) In case of publication, the certificate of the clerk of court certifying to the publication and mailing; or

(4) The written admission or acknowledgment of service by the defendant.

In the case of service otherwise than by publication, the certificate or affidavit shall state the date, place, and manner of service. Failure to make proof of service shall not affect the validity of the service.

(i) *Amendment.* At any time in its discretion and upon such terms as it deems just, the court may allow any process or proof of service thereof to be amended, unless it clearly appears that material prejudice would result to the substantial rights of the party against whom the process issued.

(j) *Alternative service.* The methods of service provided in this Code section are cumulative and may be utilized with, after, or independently of other methods of service. Whenever a statute provides for another method of service, service may be made under the circumstances and in the manner prescribed by the statute or under any other methods prescribed in this Code section. The provisions for service by publication provided in this Code section shall apply in any action or proceeding in which service by publication may be authorized by law; and, where by law special provision is made for service by publication, the procedure for such service by publication provided in this Code section may be utilized in lieu thereof. In all cases or special proceedings where the requirements or procedure for service, or both, are not prescribed by law and in any situation where the provisions therefor are not clear or certain, the court may prescribe service according to the exigencies of each case, consistent with the Constitution.

(k) *Service in probate courts and special statutory proceedings.* The methods of service provided in this Code section may be used as alternative methods of service in proceedings in the probate courts and in any other special statutory proceedings and may be used with, after, or independently of the method of service specifically provided for in any such proceeding; and, in any such proceeding, service shall be sufficient when made in accordance with the statutes relating particularly to the proceeding or in accordance with this Code section.

(*l*) *Forms.*

—NOTICE OF LAWSUIT AND REQUEST FOR WAIVER OF SERVICE OF SUMMONS—

TO: (Name of individual defendant or name of officer or agent of corporate defendant) as (title, or other relationship of individual to corporate defendant) of (name of corporate defendant to be served, if any)

A lawsuit has been commenced against you (or the entity on whose behalf you are addressed). A copy of the complaint is attached to this notice. The complaint has been filed in the (court named on the complaint) for the State of Georgia in and for the County of (county) and has been assigned (case number of action).

This is not a formal summons or notification from the court, but rather my request pursuant to Code Section 9-11-4 of the Official Code of Georgia Annotated that you sign and return the enclosed Waiver of Service in order to save the cost of serving you with a judicial summons and an additional copy of the complaint. The cost of service will be avoided if I receive a signed copy of the waiver within 30 days (or 60 days if located outside any judicial district of the United States) after the date designated below as the date on which this Notice of Lawsuit and Request for Waiver of Service of Summons is sent. I enclose a stamped and addressed envelope (or other means of cost-free return) for your use. An extra copy of the Waiver of Service is also attached for your records. YOU ARE ENTITLED TO CONSULT WITH YOUR ATTORNEY REGARDING THIS MATTER.

If you comply with this request and return the signed Waiver of Service, the waiver will be filed with the court and no summons will be served on you. The action will then proceed as if you had been served on the date the waiver is filed except that you will not be obligated to answer or otherwise respond to the complaint within 60 days from the date designated below as the date on which this notice is sent (or within 90 days from that date if your address is not in any judicial district of the United States).

If you do not return the signed waiver within the time indicated, I will take appropriate steps to effect formal service in a manner authorized by the Georgia Rules of Civil Procedure and then, to the extent authorized by those rules, I will ask the court to require you (or the party on whose behalf you are addressed) to pay the full cost of such service. In that connection, please read the statement concerning the duty of parties to avoid unnecessary costs of service of summons, which is set forth on the Notice of Duty to Avoid Unnecessary Costs of Service of Summons enclosed herein.

I affirm that this Notice of Lawsuit and Request for Waiver of Service of Summons is being sent to you on behalf of the Plaintiff on this _____ day of _____.

____
Signature of plaintiff's attorney
or
Unrepresented plaintiff

—WAIVER OF SERVICE OF SUMMONS—

To: (Name of plaintiff's attorney or unrepresented plaintiff)

I acknowledge receipt of your request that I waive service of a summons in the action of (caption of action), which is case number (docket number) in the (name of court) of the State of Georgia in and for the County of (county). I have also received a copy of the complaint in the action, two copies of this instrument, and a means by which I can return the signed waiver to you without cost to me. I understand that I am entitled to consult with my own attorney regarding the consequences of my signing this waiver.

I agree to save the cost of service of a summons and an additional copy of the complaint in this lawsuit by not requiring that I (or the entity on whose behalf I am acting) be served with judicial process in the manner provided by the Georgia Rules of Civil Procedure.

I (or the entity on whose behalf I am acting) will retain all defenses or objections to the lawsuit or to the jurisdiction or venue of the court except for objections based on a defect in the summons or in the service of the summons.

I understand that a judgment may be entered against me (or the entity on whose behalf I am acting) if an answer is not served upon you within 60 days after the date this waiver was sent, or within 90 days after that date if the request for the waiver was sent outside the United States.

This _____ day of _____, _____.

(Signed)

____
(Printed or typed name of defendant)

as (title) ________________________________
of (name of corporate defendant, if any)

—NOTICE OF DUTY TO AVOID UNNECESSARY COSTS OF SERVICE OF SUMMONS—

Subsection (d) of Code Section 9-11-4 of the Official Code of Georgia Annotated requires certain parties to cooperate in saving unnecessary costs of service of the summons and the pleading. A defendant located in the United States who, after being notified of an action and asked by a plaintiff located in the United States to waive service of a summons, fails to do so will be required to bear the cost of such service unless good cause be shown for such defendant's failure to sign and return the waiver.

It is not good cause for a failure to waive service that a party believes that the complaint is unfounded, or that the action has been brought in an improper place or in a court that lacks jurisdiction over the subject matter of the action or over its person or property. A party who waives service of the summons retains all defenses and objections (except any relating to the summons or to the service of the summons), and may later object to the jurisdiction of the court or to the place where the action has been brought.

A defendant who waives service must, within the time specified on the waiver form, serve on the plaintiff's attorney (or unrepresented plaintiff) a response to the complaint and also must file a signed copy of the response with the court. If the answer is not served within this time, a default judgment may be taken against that defendant. By waiving service, a defendant is allowed more time to answer than if the summons had been actually served when the request for waiver of service was received.

Laws 1966, p. 609, § 4; Laws 1967, p. 226, §§ 1–3, 51; Laws 1968, p. 1036, § 1; Laws 1968, p. 1104, §§ 1, 2; Laws 1969, p. 487, § 1; Laws 1972, p. 689, §§ 1–3; Laws 1980, p. 1124, § 1; Laws 1982, p. 3, § 9; Laws 1984, p. 22, § 9; Laws 1989, p. 364, § 1; Laws 1991, p. 626, § 1; Laws 1993, p. 91, § 9; Laws 2000, p. 1225, § 1; Laws 2000, p. 1589, §§ 3, 4; Laws 2002, p. 1244, § 1.

§ 9-11-5. Service and filing of pleadings subsequent to the original complaint and other papers

(a) *Service—When required.* Except as otherwise provided in this chapter, every order required by its terms to be served, every pleading subsequent to the original complaint unless the court otherwise orders because of numerous defendants, every written motion other than one which may be heard ex parte, and every written notice, appearance, demand, offer of judgment, and similar paper shall be served upon each of the parties. However, the failure of a party to file pleadings in an action shall be deemed to be a waiver by him or her of all notices, including notices of time and place of trial and entry of judgment, and all service in the action, except service of pleadings asserting new or additional claims for relief, which shall be served as provided by subsection (b) of this Code section.

(b) *Same—How made.* Whenever under this chapter service is required or permitted to be made upon a party represented by an attorney, the service shall be made upon the attorney unless service upon the party himself is ordered by the court. Service upon the attorney or upon a party shall be made by delivering a copy to him or by mailing it to him at his last known address or, if no address is known, by leaving it with the clerk of the court. As used in this Code section, the term "delivery of a copy" means handing it to the attorney or to the party, or leaving it at his office with his clerk or other person in charge thereof or, if the office is closed or the person to be served has no office, leaving it at his dwelling house or usual place of abode with some person of suitable age and discretion then residing therein. Service by mail is complete upon mailing. Proof of service may be made by certificate of an attorney or of his employee, by written admission, by affidavit, or by other proof satisfactory to the court. Failure to make proof of service shall not affect the validity of service.

(c) *Same—Numerous defendants.* In any action in which there are unusually large numbers of defendants, the court, upon motion or of its own initiative, may order that service of the pleadings of the defendants and replies thereto need not be made as between the defendants, and that any cross-claim, counterclaim, or matter constituting an avoidance or affirmative defense contained therein shall be deemed to be denied or avoided by all other parties, and that the filing of any such pleading and service thereof upon the plaintiff constitutes due notice of it to the parties. A copy of every such order shall be served upon the parties in such manner and form as the court directs.

(d) *Filing.* All papers after the complaint required to be served upon a party shall be filed with the court within the time allowed for service.

(e) *"Filing with the court" defined.* The filing of pleadings and other papers with the court as required by this chapter shall be made by filing them with the clerk of the court, except that the judge may permit the papers to be filed with him, in which event he shall note thereon the filing date and forthwith transmit them to the office of the clerk.

Laws 1966, p. 609, § 5; Laws 1967, p. 226, § 4; Laws 2001, p. 854, § 1.

§ 9–11–6. Time

(a) *Computation.* In computing any period of time prescribed or allowed by this chapter, by the rules of any court, by order of court, or by an applicable statute, the computation rules prescribed in paragraph (3) of subsection (d) of Code Section 1–3–1 shall be used.

(b) *Extension of time.* When by this chapter or by a notice given thereunder or by order of court an act is required or allowed to be done at or within a specified time, the parties, by written stipulation of counsel filed in the action, may extend the period, or the court for cause shown may at any time in its discretion (1) with or without motion or notice, order the period extended if request therefor is made before the expiration of the period originally prescribed or as extended by a previous order, or (2) upon motion made after the expiration of the specified period, permit the act to be done where the failure to act was the result of excusable neglect; provided, however, that no extension of time shall be granted for the filing of motions for new trial or for judgment notwithstanding the verdict.

(c) *Unaffected by expiration of term.* The period of time provided for the doing of any act or the taking of any proceeding is not affected or limited by the continued existence or expiration of a term of court, except as otherwise specifically provided by law. The continued existence or expiration of a term of court in no way affects the power of a court to do any act or take any proceeding in any civil action which has been pending before it, except as otherwise specifically provided by law.

(d) *For motions; for affidavits.* A written motion, other than one which may be heard ex parte, and notice of the hearing thereof shall be served not later than five days before the time specified for the hearing, unless a different period is fixed by this chapter or by order of the court. Such an order may for cause shown be made on ex parte application. When a motion is supported by affidavit, the affidavit shall be served with the motion. Opposing affidavits may be served not later than one day before the hearing, unless the court permits them to be served at some other time.

(e) *Additional time after service by mail.* Whenever a party has the right or is required to do some act or take some proceedings within a prescribed period after the service of a notice or other paper, other than process, upon him, and the notice or paper is served upon him by mail, three days shall be added to the prescribed period.

Laws 1966, p. 609, § 6; Laws 1967, p. 226, §§ 5, 6; Laws 1985, p. 648, § 2.

Article 3

Pleadings and Motions

§ 9–11–7. Pleadings allowed; form of motions

(a) *Pleadings.* There shall be a complaint and an answer; a third-party complaint, if a person who is not an original party is summoned under Code Section 9–11–14; and a third-party answer, if a third-party complaint is served. There may be a reply to a counterclaim denominated as such and an answer to a cross-claim, if the answer contains a cross-claim. No other pleading shall be allowed, except that the court may order a reply to an answer or a third-party answer.

(b) *Motions and other papers.*

(1) An application to the court for an order shall be by motion which, unless made during a hearing or trial, shall be made in writing, shall state with particularity the grounds therefor, and shall set forth the relief or order sought. The requirement of writing is fulfilled if the motion is stated in a written notice of the hearing of the motion.

(2) The rules applicable to captions, signing, and other matters of form of pleadings apply to all motions and other papers provided for by this chapter.

(c) *Demurrers, pleas, etc., abolished.* Demurrers, pleas, and exceptions for insufficiency of a pleading shall not be used.

Laws 1966, p. 609, § 7; Laws 1967, p. 226, § 7.

§ 9–11–8. General rules of pleading

(a) *Claims for relief.*

(1) "ACTION FOR MEDICAL MALPRACTICE" DEFINED. As used in this Code section, the term "action for medical malpractice" means any claim for damages resulting from the death of or injury to any person arising out of:

(A) Health, medical, dental, or surgical service, diagnosis, prescription, treatment, or care rendered by a person authorized by law to perform such services or by any person acting under the supervision and control of a lawfully authorized person; or

(B) Care or service rendered by any public or private hospital, nursing home, clinic, hospital authority, facility, or institution, or by any officer, agent, or employee thereof acting within the scope of his employment.

(2) FORM OF COMPLAINT, GENERALLY; ACTION FOR MALPRACTICE. An original complaint shall contain facts upon which the court's venue depends; and any pleading which sets forth a claim for relief, whether an original claim, counterclaim, a cross-claim, or a third-party claim, shall contain:

(A) A short and plain statement of the claims showing that the pleader is entitled to relief; and

(B) A demand for judgment for the relief to which the pleader deems himself entitled; provided, however, that in actions for medical malpractice, as defined in this Code section, in which a claim for unliquidated damages is made for $10,000.00 or less, the pleadings shall contain a demand for judgment in a sum certain; and, in actions for medical malpractice in which a claim for unliquidated damages is made for a sum exceeding $10,000.00, the demand for judgment shall state that the pleader "demands judgment in excess of $10,000.00," and no further monetary amount shall be stated. Relief in the alternative or of several different types may be demanded.

(3) SANCTIONS. If the provisions of subparagraph (B) of paragraph (2) of this subsection are violated, the court in which the action is pending shall, upon a proper motion, strike the improper portion of the demand for judgment and may impose such other sanctions, including disciplinary action against the attorney, found in Code Section 9–11–37 as are appropriate.

(b) *Defenses; form of denials.* A party shall state in short and plain terms his defenses to each claim asserted and shall admit or deny the averments upon which the adverse party relies. If he is without knowledge or information sufficient to form a belief as to the truth of an averment, he shall so state, and this has the effect of a denial. Denials shall fairly meet the substance of the averments denied. When a pleader intends in good faith to deny only a part or a qualification of an averment, he shall specify so much of it as is true and material and shall deny only the remainder. Unless the pleader intends in good faith to controvert all the averments of the preceding pleading, he may make his denials as specific denials of designated averments or paragraphs, or he may generally deny all the averments except such designated averments or paragraphs as he expressly admits; but, when he does so intend to controvert all its averments, he may do so by general denial subject to the obligations set forth in Code Section 9–11–11.

(c) *Affirmative defenses.* In pleading to a preceding pleading, a party shall set forth affirmatively accord and satisfaction, arbitration and award, discharge in bankruptcy, duress, estoppel, failure of consideration, fraud, illegality, injury by fellow servant, laches, license, payment, release, res judicata, statute of frauds, statute of limitations, and waiver. When a party has mistakenly designated a defense as a counterclaim or a counterclaim as a defense, the court on terms, if justice so requires, shall treat the pleadings as if there had been a proper designation.

(d) *Effect of failure to deny.* Averments in a pleading to which a responsive pleading is required, other than those as to the amount of damage, are admitted when not denied in the responsive pleading. Averments in a pleading to which no responsive pleading is required or permitted shall be taken as denied or avoided.

(e) *Pleading to be concise and direct; alternative statements.*

(1) Each averment of a pleading shall be simple, concise, and direct. No technical forms of pleading or motions are required.

(2) A party may set forth two or more statements of a claim or defense alternatively or hypothetically, either in one count or defense or in separate counts or defenses. When two or more statements are made in the alternative and one of them, if made independently, would be sufficient, the pleading is not made insufficient by the insufficiency of one or more of the alternative statements. A party may also state as many separate claims or defenses as he has, regardless of consistency and whether based on legal or on equitable grounds or on both. All statements shall be made subject to the obligations set forth in Code Section 9–11–11.

(f) *Construction of pleadings.* All pleadings shall be so construed as to do substantial justice.

Laws 1966, p. 609, § 8; Laws 1967, p. 226, § 8; Laws 1976, p. 1047, § 1.

§ 9–11–9. Pleading special matters

(a) *Capacity.* It is not necessary to aver the capacity of a party to bring or defend an action, the authority of a party to bring or defend an action in a representative capacity, or the legal existence of an organized association of persons that is made a party. When a party desires to raise an issue as to the legal existence of any party, the capacity of any party to bring or defend an action, or the authority of a party to bring or defend an action in a representative capacity, he shall do so by specific negative averment, which shall include such supporting particulars as are peculiarly within the pleader's knowledge.

(b) *Fraud, mistake, condition of the mind.* In all averments of fraud or mistake, the circumstance constituting fraud or mistake shall be stated with particularity. Malice, intent, knowledge, and other condition of mind of a person may be averred generally.

(c) *Conditions precedent.* In pleading the performance or occurrence of conditions precedent, it is sufficient to aver generally that all conditions precedent have been performed or have occurred. A denial of performance or occurrence shall be made specifically and with particularity.

(d) *Official document or act.* In pleading an official document or official act it is sufficient to aver that the document was issued or the act done in compliance with law.

(e) *Judgment.* In pleading a judgment or decision of a domestic or foreign court, of a judicial or quasi-judicial tribunal, or of a board or officer, it is sufficient to aver the judgment or decision without setting forth matter showing jurisdiction to render it.

(f) *Time and place.* For the purpose of testing the sufficiency of a pleading, averments of time and place are material and shall be considered like all other averments of material matter.

(g) *Special damage.* When items of special damage are claimed, they shall be specifically stated.

Laws 1966, p. 609, § 9.

§ 9–11–9.1. Affidavit of expert to be filed with complaint in action for damages alleging professional malpractice

(a) In any action for damages alleging professional malpractice against a professional licensed by the State of Georgia and listed in subsection (d) of this Code section or against any licensed health care facility alleged to be liable based upon the action or inaction of a health care professional licensed by the State of Georgia and listed in subsection (d) of this Code section, the plaintiff shall be required to file with the complaint an affidavit of an expert competent to testify, which affidavit shall set forth specifically at least one negligent act or omission claimed to exist and the factual basis for each such claim.

(b) If a plaintiff files an affidavit which is allegedly defective, and the defendant to whom it pertains alleges, with specificity, by motion to dismiss filed on or before the close of discovery, that said affidavit is defective, the plaintiff's complaint is subject to dismissal for failure to state a claim, except that the plaintiff may cure the alleged defect by amendment pursuant to Code Section 9–11–15 within 30 days of service of the motion alleging that the affidavit is defective. The trial court may, in the exercise of its discretion, extend the time for filing said amendment or response to the motion, or both, as it shall determine justice requires.

(c) If a plaintiff fails to file an affidavit as required by this Code section and the defendant raises the failure to file such an affidavit by motion to dismiss filed contemporaneously with its initial responsive pleading, such complaint shall not be subject to the renewal provisions of Code Section 9–2–61 after the expiration of the applicable period of limitation, unless a court determines that the plaintiff had the requisite affidavit within the time required by this Code section and the failure to file the affidavit was the result of a mistake.

(d) The professions to which this Code section applies are:

(1) Architects;
(2) Attorneys at law;
(3) Audiologists;
(4) Certified public accountants;
(5) Chiropractors;
(6) Clinical social workers;
(7) Dentists;
(8) Dietitians;
(9) Land surveyors;
(10) Marriage and family therapists;
(11) Medical doctors;
(12) Nurses;
(13) Occupational therapists;
(14) Optometrists;
(15) Osteopathic physicians;
(16) Pharmacists;
(17) Physical therapists;
(18) Physicians' assistants;
(19) Podiatrists;
(20) Professional counselors;
(21) Professional engineers;
(22) Psychologists;
(23) Radiological technicians;
(24) Respiratory therapists;
(25) Speech–language pathologists; or
(26) Veterinarians.

Laws 1987, p. 887, § 3; Laws 1989, p. 419, § 3; Laws 1997, p. 916, § 1; Laws 2005, Act 1, § 3, eff. Feb. 16, 2005; Laws 2006, Act 453, § 9(1), eff. April 14, 2006.

§ 9–11–9.2. Medical authorization form filed with complaint

(a) In any action for damages alleging medical malpractice against a professional licensed by the State of Georgia and listed in subsection (d) of Code Section 9–11–9.1, against a professional corporation or other legal entity that provides health care services through a professional licensed by the State of Georgia and listed in subsection (d) of Code Section 9–11–9.1, or against any licensed health care facility alleged to be liable based upon the action or inaction of a health care professional licensed by the State of Georgia and listed in subsection (d) of Code Section 9–11–9.1, contemporaneously with the filing of the complaint, the plaintiff shall be required to file a medical authorization form. Failure to provide this authorization shall subject the complaint to dismissal.

(b) The authorization shall provide that the attorney representing the defendant is authorized to obtain and disclose protected health information contained in medical records to facilitate the investigation, evaluation, and defense of the claims and allegations set forth in the complaint which pertain to the plaintiff or, where applicable, the plaintiff's decedent whose treatment is at issue in the complaint. This authorization includes the defendant's attorney's right to discuss the care and treatment of the plaintiff or, where applicable, the plaintiff's decedent with all of the plaintiff's or decedent's treating physicians.

(c) The authorization shall provide for the release of all protected health information except information that is considered privileged and shall authorize the release of such information by any physician or health care facility by which health care records of the plaintiff or the plaintiff's decedent would be maintained.

Laws 2005, Act 1, § 4, eff. Feb. 16, 2005.

Validity

This section has been held preempted by federal law in the case of Northlake Medical Center, LLC vs. Queen, 2006 634 S.E.2d 486.

§ 9–11–10. Form of pleadings

(a) *Caption; names of parties.* Every pleading shall contain a caption setting forth the name of the court and county, the title of the action, the file number, and a designation as in subsection (a) of Code Section 9–11–7. In the complaint the title of the action shall include the names of all the parties, but in other pleadings it is sufficient to state the name of the first party on each side with an appropriate indication of other parties. A party whose name is not known may be designated by any name; and, when his true name is discovered, the pleading may be amended accordingly.

(b) *Paragraphs; separate statements.* All averments of claim or defense shall be made in numbered paragraphs, the contents of each of which shall be limited as far as practicable to a statement of a single set of circumstances; and a paragraph may be referred to by number in all succeeding pleadings. Each claim founded upon a separate transaction or occurrence and each defense other than denials shall be stated in a separate count or defense whenever a separation facilitates the clear presentation of the matters set forth.

(c) *Adoption by reference; exhibits.* Statements in a pleading may be adopted by reference in a different part of the same pleading or in another pleading or in any motion. A copy of any written instrument which is an exhibit to a pleading is a part thereof for all purposes.

Laws 1966, p. 609, § 10; Laws 1967, p. 226, § 47.

§ 9–11–11. Signing of pleadings

(a) Every pleading of a party represented by an attorney shall be signed by at least one attorney of record in his individual name, whose address shall be stated. A party who is not represented by an attorney shall sign his pleading and state his address. The signature of an attorney constitutes a certificate by him that he has read the pleading and that it is not interposed for delay.

(b) Except when otherwise specifically provided by rule or statute, pleadings need not be verified or accompanied by affidavit.

(c) The rule in equity that the averments of an answer under oath must be overcome by the testimony of two witnesses or of one witness sustained by corroborating circumstances is abolished.

Laws 1966, p. 609, § 11.

§ 9-11-11.1. Certification that claim arising from act in furtherance of right of free speech or to petition government for redress of grievances is well grounded in fact and warranted by law

(a) The General Assembly of Georgia finds and declares that it is in the public interest to encourage participation by the citizens of Georgia in matters of public significance through the exercise of their constitutional rights of freedom of speech and the right to petition government for redress of grievances. The General Assembly of Georgia further finds and declares that the valid exercise of the constitutional rights of freedom of speech and the right to petition government for a redress of grievances should not be chilled through abuse of the judicial process.

(b) For any claim asserted against a person or entity arising from an act by that person or entity which could reasonably be construed as an act in furtherance of the right of free speech or the right to petition government for a redress of grievances under the Constitution of the United States or the Constitution of the State of Georgia in connection with an issue of public interest or concern, both the party asserting the claim and the party's attorney of record, if any, shall be required to file, contemporaneously with the pleading containing the claim, a written verification under oath as set forth in Code Section 9-10-113. Such written verification shall certify that the party and his or her attorney of record, if any, have read the claim; that to the best of their knowledge, information, and belief formed after reasonable inquiry it is well grounded in fact and is warranted by existing law or a good faith argument for the extension, modification, or reversal of existing law; that the act forming the basis for the claim is not a privileged communication under paragraph (4) of Code Section 51-5-7; and that the claim is not interposed for any improper purpose such as to suppress a person's or entity's right of free speech or right to petition government, or to harass, or to cause unnecessary delay or needless increase in the cost of litigation. If the claim is not verified as required by this subsection, it shall be stricken unless it is verified within ten days after the omission is called to the attention of the party asserting the claim. If a claim is verified in violation of this Code section, the court, upon motion or upon its own initiative, shall impose upon the persons who signed the verification, a represented party, or both an appropriate sanction which may include dismissal of the claim and an order to pay to the other party or parties the amount of the reasonable expenses incurred because of the filing of the pleading, including a reasonable attorney's fee.

(c) As used in this Code section, "act in furtherance of the right of free speech or the right to petition government for a redress of grievances under the Constitution of the United States or the Constitution of the State of Georgia in connection with an issue of public interest or concern" includes any written or oral statement, writing, or petition made before or to a legislative, executive, or judicial proceeding, or any other official proceeding authorized by law, or any written or oral statement, writing, or petition made in connection with an issue under consideration or review by a legislative, executive, or judicial body, or any other official proceeding authorized by law.

(d) All discovery and any pending hearings or motions in the action shall be stayed upon the filing of a motion to dismiss or a motion to strike made pursuant to subsection (b) of this Code section. The motion shall be heard not more than 30 days after service unless the emergency matters before the court require a later hearing. The court, on noticed motion and for good cause shown, may order that specified discovery or other hearings or motions be conducted notwithstanding this subsection.

(e) Nothing in this Code section shall affect or preclude the right of any party to any recovery otherwise authorized by common law, statute, law, or rule.

(f) Attorney's fees and expenses under this Code section may be requested by motion at any time during the course of the action but not later than 45 days after the final disposition, including but not limited to dismissal by the plaintiff, of the action.

Laws 1996, p. 260, § 1; Laws 1998, p. 862, § 2.

§ 9-11-12. Defenses and objections—when and how presented

(a) *When answer presented.* A defendant shall serve his answer within 30 days after the service of the summons and complaint upon him, unless otherwise provided by statute. A cross-claim or counterclaim shall not require an answer, unless one is required by order of the court, and shall automatically stand denied.

(b) *How defenses and objections presented.* Every defense, in law or fact, to a claim for relief in any pleading, whether a claim, counterclaim, cross-claim, or third-party claim, shall be asserted in the responsive pleading thereto if one is required, except that the following defenses may, at the option of the pleader, be made by motion in writing:

(1) Lack of jurisdiction over the subject matter;

(2) Lack of jurisdiction over the person;

(3) Improper venue;

(4) Insufficiency of process;

(5) Insufficiency of service of process;

(6) Failure to state a claim upon which relief can be granted;

(7) Failure to join a party under Code Section 9-11-19.

A motion making any of these defenses shall be made before or at the time of pleading if a further pleading is permitted. No defense or objection is waived by being joined with one or more other defenses or objections in a responsive pleading or motion. If a pleading sets forth a claim for relief to which the adverse party is not required to serve a responsive pleading, he may assert at the trial any defense in law or fact to that claim for relief. If, on a motion to dismiss for failure of the pleading to state a claim upon which relief can be granted, matters outside the pleading are presented to and not excluded by the court, the motion shall be treated as one for summary judgment and disposed of as provided in Code Section 9-11-56, and all parties shall be given reasonable opportunity to present all material made pertinent to such a motion by Code Section 9-11-56.

(c) *Motion for judgment on the pleadings.* After the pleadings are closed but within such time as not to delay the trial, any party may move for judgment on the pleadings. If, on a motion for judgment on the pleadings, matters outside the pleadings are presented to and not excluded by the court, the motion shall be treated as one for summary judgment and disposed of as provided in Code Section 9-11-56, and all parties shall be given reasonable opportunity to present all material made pertinent to such a motion by Code Section 9-11-56.

(d) *Preliminary hearings.* The defenses specifically enumerated in paragraphs (1) through (7) of subsection (b) of this Code section, whether made in a pleading or by motion, and the motion for judgment mentioned in subsection (c) of this Code section shall be heard and determined before trial on application of any party unless the court orders that the hearing and determination thereof be deferred until the trial.

(e) *Motion for more definite statement.* If a pleading to which a responsive pleading is permitted is so vague or ambiguous that a party cannot reasonably be required to frame a proper responsive pleading, he shall nevertheless answer or respond to the best of his ability, and he may move for a more definite statement. The motion shall point out the defects complained of and the details desired. If the motion is granted and the order of the court is not obeyed within 15 days after notice of the order, or within such other time as the court may fix, the court may strike the pleading to which the motion was directed or make such order as it deems just.

(f) *Motion to strike.* Upon motion made by a party within 30 days after the service of the pleading upon him, or upon the court's own initiative at any time, the court may order stricken from any pleading any insufficient defense or any redundant, immaterial, impertinent, or scandalous matter.

(g) *Consolidation of defenses in motion.* A party who makes a motion under this Code section may join with it any other motions provided for in this Code section and then available to him. If a party makes a motion under this Code section but omits therefrom any defense or objection then available to him which this Code section permits to be raised by motion, he shall not thereafter make a motion based on the defense or objection so omitted, except a motion as provided in paragraph (2) of subsection (h) of this Code section on any of the grounds there stated.

(h) *Waiver or preservation of certain defenses.*

(1) A defense of lack of jurisdiction over the person, improper venue, insufficiency of process, or insufficiency of service of process is waived:

(A) If omitted from a motion in the circumstances described in subsection (g) of this Code section; or

(B) If it is neither made by motion under this Code section nor included in a responsive pleading, as originally filed.

(2) A defense of failure to state a claim upon which relief can be granted, a defense of failure to join a party indispensable under Code Section 9-11-19, and an objection of failure to state a legal defense to a claim may be made in any pleading permitted or ordered under subsection (a) of Code Section 9-11-7, or by motion for judgment on the pleadings, or at the trial on the merits.

(3) Whenever it appears, by suggestion of the parties or otherwise, that the court lacks jurisdiction of the subject matter, the court shall dismiss the action.

(i) *Officer's defense of service.* The officer making service of process and the principal officer in charge of service made by a deputy need not be made a party to any action or motion where the defense or defenses under paragraph (2), (4), or (5) of subsection (b) of this Code section are asserted by motion or by answer. Any party to the action may give notice of the objection to the service, made pursuant to such paragraphs, to the officer making the service and to the principal officer in case of service made by a deputy, and the court shall afford the officer or officers opportunity to defend the service, in which case the decision on the question of service shall be conclusive on the officer and on his principal in case of service by a deputy.

Laws 1966, p. 609, § 12; Laws 1967, p. 226, § 9; Laws 1968, p. 1104, § 3; Laws 1972, p. 689, §§ 4, 5; Laws 1993, p. 91, § 9.

§ 9–11–13. Counterclaim and cross-claim

(a) *Compulsory counterclaims.* A pleading shall state as a counterclaim any claim which at the time of serving the pleading the pleader has against any opposing party, if it arises out of the transaction or occurrence that is the subject matter of the opposing party's claim and does not require for its adjudication the presence of third parties of whom the court cannot acquire jurisdiction. But the pleader need not state the claim if (1) at the time the action was commenced the claim was the subject of another pending action, or (2) the opposing party brought an action upon his claim by attachment or other process by which the court did not acquire jurisdiction to render a personal judgment on that claim, and the pleader is not stating any counterclaim under this Code section, or (3) the claim is not within the jurisdiction of the court.

(b) *Permissive counterclaims.* A pleading may state as a counterclaim any claim against an opposing party not arising out of the transaction or occurrence that is the subject matter of the opposing party's claim. But any such permissive counterclaim shall be separated for the purposes of trial, unless the parties otherwise agree.

(c) *Counterclaim exceeding opposing claim.* A counterclaim may or may not diminish or defeat the recovery sought by the opposing party. It may claim relief exceeding in amount or different in kind from that sought in the pleading of the opposing party.

(d) *Counterclaim against the state.* This Code section shall not be construed to enlarge beyond the limits fixed by law the right to assert counterclaims or to claim credits against the state or an officer or agency thereof.

(e) *Counterclaim maturing or acquired after pleading.* A claim which either matured or was acquired by the pleader after serving his pleading may, with the permission of the court, be presented as a counterclaim by supplemental pleading.

(f) *Omitted counterclaim.* When a pleader fails to set up a counterclaim through oversight, inadvertence, or excusable neglect, or when justice requires, he may by leave of court set up the counterclaim by amendment.

(g) *Cross-claim against coparty.* A pleading may state as a cross-claim any claim by one party against a coparty arising out of the transaction or occurrence that is the subject matter either of the original action or of a counterclaim therein or relating to any property that is the subject matter of the original action. The cross-claim may include a claim that the party against whom it is asserted is or may be liable to the cross-claimant for all or part of a claim asserted in the action against the cross-claimant.

(h) *Additional parties may be brought in.* When the presence of parties other than those to the original action is required for the granting of complete relief in the determination of a counterclaim or cross-claim, the court shall order them to be brought in as defendants as provided in this chapter, if jurisdiction of them can be obtained.

(i) *Separate trials; separate judgments.* If the court orders separate trials as provided in subsection (b) of Code Section 9–11–42, judgment on a counterclaim or cross-claim may be rendered in accordance with the terms of subsection (b) of Code Section 9–11–54 when the court has jurisdiction to do so, even if the claims of the opposing party have been dismissed or otherwise disposed of.

Laws 1966, p. 609, § 13.

§ 9–11–14. Third-party practice

(a) *When defendant may bring in third party.* At any time after commencement of the action a defendant, as a third-party plaintiff, may cause a summons and complaint to be served upon a person not a party to the action who is or may be liable to him for all or part of the plaintiff's claim against him. The third-party plaintiff need not obtain leave to make the service if he files the third-party complaint not later than ten days after he serves his original answer. Otherwise he must obtain leave on motion upon notice to all parties to the action. The person served with the summons and third-party complaint, hereinafter called the third-party defendant, shall make his defenses to the third-party plaintiff's claim as provided in Code Section 9–11–12 and his counterclaims against the third-party plaintiff and cross-claims against other third-party defendants as provided in Code Section 9–11–13. The third-party defendant may assert against the plaintiff any defenses which the third-party plaintiff has to the plaintiff's claim. The third-party defendant may also assert any claim against the plaintiff arising out of the transaction or occurrence that is the subject matter of the plaintiff's claim against the third-party plaintiff. The plaintiff may assert any claim against the third-party defendant arising out of the transaction or occurrence that is the subject matter of the plaintiff's claim against the third-party plaintiff, and the third-party defendant thereupon shall assert his defenses as provided in Code Section 9–11–12 and his counterclaims and cross-claims as provided in Code Section 9–11–13. Any party may move to strike the third-party claim, or for its severance or separate trial. A third-party defendant may proceed under this Code section against any person not a party to the action who is or may be liable to him for all or part of the claim made in the action against the third-party defendant.

(b) *When plaintiff may bring in third party.* When a counterclaim is asserted against a plaintiff, he may cause a third party to be brought in under circumstances which under this Code section would entitle a defendant to do so.

(c) *Exhibits attached to third-party complaint.* Any third-party complaint filed shall have attached thereto, as exhibits, a true and correct copy of the original complaint in the action and all other pleadings which have been filed in the action prior to the filing of the third-party complaint.

Laws 1966, p. 609, § 14; Laws 1969, p. 979, § 1; Laws 1984, p. 22, § 9.

§ 9-11-15. Amended and supplemental pleadings

(a) *Amendments.* A party may amend his pleading as a matter of course and without leave of court at any time before the entry of a pretrial order. Thereafter the party may amend his pleading only by leave of court or by written consent of the adverse party. Leave shall be freely given when justice so requires. A party may plead or move in response to an amended pleading and, when required by an order of the court, shall plead within 15 days after service of the amended pleading, unless the court otherwise orders.

(b) *Amendments to conform to the evidence.* When issues not raised by the pleadings are tried by express or implied consent of the parties, they shall be treated in all respects as if they had been raised in the pleadings. Such amendment of the pleadings as may be necessary to cause them to conform to the evidence and to raise these issues may be made upon motion of any party at any time, even after judgment; but failure so to amend does not affect the result of the trial of these issues. If evidence is objected to at the trial on the ground that it is not within the issues made by the pleadings, the court may allow the pleadings to be amended and shall do so freely when the presentation of the merits of the action will be subserved thereby and the objecting party fails to satisfy the court that the admission of the evidence would prejudice him in maintaining his action or defense upon the merits. The court may grant a continuance to enable the objecting party to meet the evidence.

(c) *Relation back of amendments.* Whenever the claim or defense asserted in the amended pleading arises out of the conduct, transaction, or occurrence set forth or attempted to be set forth in the original pleading, the amendment relates back to the date of the original pleading. An amendment changing the party against whom a claim is asserted relates back to the date of the original pleadings if the foregoing provisions are satisfied, and if within the period provided by law for commencing the action against him the party to be brought in by amendment (1) has received such notice of the institution of the action that he will not be prejudiced in maintaining his defense on the merits, and (2) knew or should have known that, but for a mistake concerning the identity of the proper party, the action would have been brought against him.

(d) *Supplemental pleadings.* Upon motion of a party the court may, upon reasonable notice and upon such terms as are just, permit him to serve a supplemental pleading setting forth transactions or occurrences or events which have happened since the date of the pleading sought to be supplemented. Permission may be granted even though the original pleading is defective in its statement of a claim for relief or defense. If the court deems it advisable that the adverse party plead to the supplemental pleading, it shall so order, specifying the time therefor.

Laws 1966, p. 609, § 15; Laws 1968, p. 1104, § 4; Laws 1972, p. 689, § 6.

§ 9-11-16. Pre-trial procedure; formulating issues

(a) Upon the motion of any party, or upon its own motion, the court shall direct the attorneys for the parties to appear before it for a conference to consider:

(1) The simplification of the issues;

(2) The necessity or desirability of amendments to the pleadings;

(3) The possibility of obtaining admissions of fact and of documents which will avoid unnecessary proof;

(4) The limitation of the number of expert witnesses; and

(5) Such other matters as may aid in the disposition of the action.

(b) The court shall make an order which recites the action taken at the conference and the agreements made by the parties as to any of the matters considered and which limits the issues for trial to those not disposed of by admissions or agreements of counsel. The order, when entered, controls the subsequent course of the action unless modified at the trial to prevent manifest injustice. After entry of the pretrial order, it shall be within the discretion of the court to permit or disallow the presentation of testimony from any expert witness whose name is not contained in the pretrial order; provided, however, that if the additional expert witness is permitted to testify, any opposing party shall be permitted reasonable time to take the deposition of the additional expert witness. The court, in its discretion, may establish by rule a pretrial calendar on which actions may be placed for consideration as provided in subsection (a) of this Code section and may either confine the calendar to jury actions or to nonjury actions or extend it to all actions.

Laws 1966, p. 609, § 16; Laws 1967, p. 226, § 10; Laws 1968, p. 1104, § 5; Laws 1993, p. 91, § 9; Laws 2002, p. 1244, § 1.1.

Article 4

Parties

§ 9-11-17. Parties plaintiff and defendant; capacity

(a) *Real party in interest.* Every action shall be prosecuted in the name of the real party in interest. An executor, an administrator, a guardian, a bailee, a trustee of an express trust, a party with whom or in whose name a contract has been made for the benefit of another, or a party authorized by statute may bring an action in his own name without joining with him the party for whose benefit the action is brought; and, when a statute so provides, an action for the use or benefit of another shall be brought in the name of the state. No action shall be dismissed on the ground that it is not prosecuted in the name of the real party in interest until a reasonable time has been allowed after objection for ratification of commencement of the action by, or joinder or substitution of, the real party in interest; and such ratification, joinder, or substitution shall have the same effect as if the action had been commenced in the name of the real party in interest.

(b) *Capacity to bring or defend an action.* The capacity of an individual, including one acting in a representative capacity, to bring or defend an action shall be determined by the law of this state. The capacity of a corporation to bring or defend an action shall be determined by the law under which it was organized, unless a statute of this state provides to the contrary.

(c) *Infants or incompetent persons.* Whenever an infant or incompetent person has a representative, such as a general guardian, committee, conservator, or other like fiduciary, the representative may bring or defend an action on behalf of the infant or incompetent person. If an infant or incompetent person does not have a duly appointed representative, he may bring an action by his next friend or by a guardian ad litem. The court shall appoint a guardian ad litem for an infant or incompetent person not otherwise represented in an action or shall make such other order as it deems proper for the protection of the infant or incompetent person. No next friend shall be permitted to receive the proceeds of any personal action, in the name and on behalf of an infant, or incompetent person, until such next friend shall have entered into a sufficient bond to the Governor, for the use of the infant and the infant's representatives, conditioned well and fully to account for and concerning such trust, which bond may be sued on by order of the court in the name of the Governor and for the use of the infant. Such bond shall be approved by the court in which the action is commenced and such approval shall be filed in such clerk's office.

Laws 1966, p. 609, § 17; Laws 1968, p. 1104, § 6; Laws 1985, p. 656, § 1.

§ 9-11-18. Joinder of claims and remedies

(a) *Joinder of claims.* A party asserting a claim to relief as an original claim, counterclaim, cross-claim, or third-party claim may join, either as independent or as alternate claims, as many claims, legal or equitable, as he has against an opposing party.

(b) *Joinder of remedies; fraudulent conveyances.* Whenever a claim is one heretofore cognizable only after another claim has been prosecuted to a conclusion, the two claims may be joined in a single action; but the court shall grant relief in that action only in accordance with the relative substantive rights of the parties. In particular, a plaintiff may state a claim for money and a claim to have set aside a conveyance fraudulent as to him without first having obtained a judgment establishing the claim for money.

Laws 1966, p. 609, § 18; Laws 1968, p. 1104, § 7.

§ 9-11-19. Joinder of persons needed for just adjudication

(a) *Persons to be joined if feasible.* A person who is subject to service of process shall be joined as a party in the action if:

(1) In his absence complete relief cannot be afforded among those who are already parties; or

(2) He claims an interest relating to the subject of the action and is so situated that the disposition of the action in his absence may:

(A) As a practical matter impair or impede his ability to protect that interest; or

(B) Leave any of the persons who are already parties subject to a substantial risk of incurring double, multiple, or otherwise inconsistent obligations by reason of his claimed interest.

If he has not been so joined, the court shall order that he be made a party. If he should join as a plaintiff but refuses to do so, he may be made a defendant or, in a proper case, an involuntary plaintiff. If the joined party objects to venue and his joinder would render the venue of the action improper, he shall be dismissed from the action.

(b) *Determination by court whenever joinder not feasible.* If a person, as described in paragraphs (1) and (2) of subsection (a) of this Code section, cannot be made a party, the court shall determine whether in equity and good conscience the action should proceed among the parties before it or should be dismissed, the absent person being thus regarded as indispensable. The factors to be considered by the court include:

(1) To what extent a judgment rendered in the person's absence might be prejudicial to him or to those already parties;

(2) The extent to which, by protective provisions in the judgment, by the shaping of relief, or by other measures, the prejudice can be lessened or avoided;

(3) Whether a judgment rendered in the person's absence will be adequate;

(4) Whether the plaintiff will have an adequate remedy if the action is dismissed for nonjoinder; and

(5) Whether and by whom prejudice might have been avoided or may, in the future, be avoided.

(c) *Pleading reasons for nonjoinder.* A pleading asserting a claim for relief shall state the names, if known to the pleader, of any persons, as described in paragraphs (1) and (2) of subsection (a) of this Code section, who are not joined and the reasons why they are not joined.

(d) *Exception of class actions.* This Code section shall be subject to Code Section 9-11-23.

Laws 1966, p. 609, § 19; Laws 1972, p. 689, § 7.

§ 9-11-20. Permissive joinder of parties

(a) *Permissive joinder.* All persons may join in one action as plaintiffs if they assert any right to relief jointly, severally, or in the alternative in respect of or arising out of the same transaction, occurrence, or series of transactions or occurrences and if any question of law or fact common to all of them will arise in the action. All persons may be joined in one action as defendants if there is asserted against them jointly, severally, or in the alternative any right to relief in respect of or arising out of the same transaction, occurrence, or series of transactions or occurrences and if any question of law or fact common to all of them will arise in the action. A plaintiff or defendant need not be interested in obtaining or defending against all the relief demanded. Judgment may be given for one or more of the plaintiffs according to their respective rights to relief and against one or more of the defendants according to their respective liabilities.

(b) *Separate trials.* The court may make such orders as will prevent a party from being embarrassed, delayed, or put to expense by the inclusion of a party against whom he asserts no claim and who asserts no claim against him and may order separate trials or make other orders to prevent delay or prejudice.

Laws 1966, p. 609, § 20.

§ 9-11-21. Misjoinder and nonjoinder of parties

Misjoinder of parties is not ground for dismissal of an action. Parties may be dropped or added by order of the court on motion of any party or of its own initiative at any stage of the action and on such terms as are just. Any claim against a party may be severed and proceeded with separately.

Laws 1966, p. 609, § 21.

§ 9-11-22. Interpleader

(a) Persons having claims against the plaintiff may be joined as defendants and required to interplead when their claims are such that the plaintiff is or may be exposed to double or multiple liability. It is not ground for objection to the joinder that the claims of the several claimants or the titles on which their claims depend do not have a common origin or are not identical but are adverse to and independent of one another or that the plaintiff avers that he is not liable in whole or in part to any or all of the claimants. A defendant exposed to similar liability may obtain such interpleader by way of cross-claim or counterclaim. This Code section supplements and does not in any way limit the joinder of parties permitted in Code Section 9-11-20.

(b) The remedy provided in this Code section is in addition to and in no way supersedes or limits the remedy of equitable interpleader provided for in Code Sections 23-3-90 through 23-3-92.

Laws 1966, p. 609, § 22; Laws 1967, p. 226, § 11.

§ 9-11-23. Class actions

(a) One or more members of a class may sue or be sued as representative parties on behalf of all only if:

(1) The class is so numerous that joinder of all members is impracticable;

(2) There are questions of law or fact common to the class;

(3) The claims or defenses of the representative parties are typical of the claims or defenses of the class; and

(4) The representative parties will fairly and adequately protect the interests of the class.

(b) An action may be maintained as a class action if the prerequisites of subsection (a) of this Code section are satisfied, and, in addition:

(1) The prosecution of separate actions by or against individual members of the class would create a risk of:

(A) Inconsistent or varying adjudications with respect to individual members of the class which would establish incompatible standards of conduct for the party opposing the class; or

(B) Adjudications with respect to individual members of the class which would as a practical matter be dispositive of the interests of the other members not parties to the adjudications or substantially impair or impede their ability to protect their interests;

(2) The party opposing the class has acted or refused to act on grounds generally applicable to the class, thereby making appropriate final injunctive relief or corresponding declaratory relief with respect to the class as a whole; or

(3) The court finds that the questions of law or fact common to the members of the class predominate over any questions affecting only individual members, and that a class action is superior to other available methods for the fair and efficient adjudication of the controversy. The matters pertinent to the findings include:

(A) The interest of members of the class in individually controlling the prosecution or defense of separate actions;

(B) The extent and nature of any litigation concerning the controversy already commenced by or against members of the class;

(C) The desirability or undesirability of concentrating the litigation of the claims in the particular forum; and

(D) The difficulties likely to be encountered in the management of a class action.

(c)(1) As soon as practicable after the commencement of an action brought as a class action, the court shall determine by order whether it is to be so maintained. An order under this subsection may be conditional, and may be altered or amended before the decision on the merits.

(2) In any class action maintained under paragraph (3) of subsection (b) of this Code section, the court shall direct to the members of the class the best notice practicable under the circumstances, including individual notice to all members who can be identified through reasonable effort. The notice shall advise each member that:

(A) The court will exclude the member from the class if the member so requests by a specified date;

(B) The judgment, whether favorable or not, will include all members who do not request exclusion; and

(C) Any member who does not request exclusion may, if the member desires, enter an appearance through counsel.

(3) The judgment in an action maintained as a class action under paragraph (1) or (2) of subsection (b) of this Code section, whether or not favorable to the class, shall include and describe those whom the court finds to be members of the class. The judgment in an action maintained as a class action under paragraph (3) of subsection (b) of this Code section, whether or not favorable to the class, shall include and specify or describe those to whom the notice provided in paragraph (2) of subsection (b) of this Code section was directed, and who have not requested exclusion, and whom the court finds to be members of the class.

(4) When appropriate:

(A) An action may be brought or maintained as a class action with respect to particular issues; or

(B) A class may be divided into subclasses and each subclass treated as a class, and the provisions of this rule shall then be construed and applied accordingly.

(d) In the conduct of actions to which this rule applies, the court may make appropriate orders:

(1) Determining the course of proceedings or prescribing measures to prevent undue repetition or complication in the presentation of evidence or argument;

(2) Requiring, for the protection of the members of the class or otherwise for the fair conduct of the action, that notice be given in such manner as the court may direct to some or all of the members of any step in the action, or of the proposed extent of the judgment, or of the opportunity of members to signify whether they consider the representation fair and adequate, to intervene and present claims or defenses, or otherwise to come into the action;

(3) Imposing conditions on the representative parties or on intervenors; and

(4) Requiring that the pleadings be amended to eliminate therefrom allegations as to representation of absent persons, and that the action proceed accordingly.

The orders may be combined with other orders, and may be altered or amended by the court as may be desirable from time to time.

(e) A class action shall not be dismissed or compromised without the approval of the court, and notice of the proposed dismissal or compromise shall be given to all members of the class in such manner as the court directs.

(f)(1) After the commencement of an action in which claims or defenses are purported to be asserted on behalf of or against a class, the court shall hold a conference among all named parties to the action for the purpose of establishing a schedule for any discovery germane to the issue of whether the requested class should or should not be certified. At this conference, the court shall set a date for a hearing on the issue of class certification. Except for good cause shown, such hearing may not be set sooner than 90 days nor later than 180 days after the date on which the court issues its scheduling order pursuant to the conference. If evidence is presented by affidavit, the parties shall have an opportunity to cross-examine affiants as to such testimony offered by affidavit.

(2) Except for good cause shown, the court shall stay all discovery directed solely to the merits of the claims or defenses in the action until the court has issued its written decision regarding certification of the class.

(3) When deciding whether a requested class is to be certified, the court shall enter a written order addressing whether the factors required by this Code section for certification of a class have been met and specifying the findings of fact and conclusions of law on which the court has based its decision with regard to whether each such factor has been established. In so doing, the court may treat a factor as having been established if all parties to the action have so stipulated on the record.

(4) Nothing in this Code section shall affect, or be construed to affect, any provision of Code Section 9-11-12 or Code Section 9-11-56.

(g) A court's order certifying a class or refusing to certify a class shall be appealable in the same manner as a final order to the appellate court which would otherwise have jurisdiction over the appeal from a final order in the action. The appellate courts shall expedite resolution of any appeals taken under this Code section. Such appeal may only be filed within 30 days of the order certifying or refusing to certify the class. During the pendency of any such appeal, the action in the trial court shall be stayed in all respects.

Laws 1966, p. 609, § 23; Laws 1989, p. 946, § 75; Laws 1996, p. 1203, § 1; Laws 2003, Act 363, § 3, eff. July 1, 2003; Laws 2005, Act 56, § 1, eff. April 22, 2005.

§ 9-11-24. Intervention

(a) *Intervention of right.* Upon timely application anyone shall be permitted to intervene in an action:

(1) When a statute confers an unconditional right to intervene; or

(2) When the applicant claims an interest relating to the property or transaction which is the subject matter of the action and he is so situated that the disposition of the action may as a practical matter impair or impede his ability to protect that interest, unless the applicant's interest is adequately represented by existing parties.

(b) *Permissive intervention.* Upon timely application anyone may be permitted to intervene in an action:

(1) When a statute confers a conditional right to intervene; or

(2) When an applicant's claim or defense and the main action have a question of law or fact in common.

In exercising its discretion the court shall consider whether the intervention will unduly delay or prejudice the adjudication of the rights of the original parties.

(c) *Procedure.* A person desiring to intervene shall serve a motion to intervene upon the parties as provided in Code Section 9-11-5. The motion shall state the grounds therefor and shall be accompanied by a pleading setting forth the claim or defense for which intervention is sought. The same procedure shall be followed when a statute gives a right to intervene.

Laws 1966, p. 609, § 24; Laws 1967, p. 226, § 12; Laws 1968, p. 1104, § 8.

§ 9-11-25. Substitution of parties

(a) *Death.*

(1) If a party dies and the claim is not thereby extinguished, the court may order substitution of the proper parties. The motion for substitution may be made by any party or by the successors or representative of the deceased party and, together with the notice of the hearing, shall be served on the parties as provided in Code Section 9-11-5 and upon persons not parties in the manner provided in Code Section 9-11-4 for the service of a summons. Unless the motion for substitution is made not later than 180 days after the death is suggested upon the record by service of a statement of the fact of the death, the action shall be dismissed as to the deceased party.

(2) In the event of the death of one or more of the plaintiffs or of one or more of the defendants in an action in which the right sought to be enforced survives only to the surviving plaintiffs or only against the surviving defendants, the action does not abate. The death shall be suggested upon the record and the action shall proceed in favor of or against the surviving parties.

(b) *Incompetency.* If a party becomes incompetent, the court, upon motion served as provided in subsection (a) of this Code section, may allow the action to be continued by or against his representative.

(c) *Transfer of interest.* In case of any transfer of interest, the action may be continued by or against the original party unless the court, upon motion, directs the person to whom the interest is transferred to be substituted in the action or joined with the original party. Service of the motion shall be made as provided in subsection (a) of this Code section.

(d) *Public officers; death or separation from office.*

(1) When a public officer is a party to an action in his official capacity and during its pendency dies, resigns, or otherwise ceases to hold office, the action does not abate, and his successor is automatically substituted as a party. Proceedings following the substitution shall be in the name of the substituted party, but any misnomer not affecting the substantial rights of the parties shall be disregarded. An order of substitution may be entered at any time, but the omission to enter such an order shall not affect the substitution.

(2) When a public officer brings or defends an action in his official capacity, he may be described as a party by his official title rather than by name; but the court may require his name to be added.

Laws 1966, p. 609, § 25.

Article 5

Depositions and Discovery

§ 9-11-26. General provisions governing discovery

(a) *Discovery methods.* Parties may obtain discovery by one or more of the following methods: depositions upon oral examination or written questions; written interrogatories; production of documents or things or permission to enter upon land or other property for inspection and other purposes; physical and mental examinations; and requests for admission. Unless the court orders otherwise under subsection (c) of this Code section, the frequency of use of these methods is not limited.

(b) *Scope of discovery.* Unless otherwise limited by order of the court in accordance with this chapter, the scope of discovery is as follows:

(1) IN GENERAL. Parties may obtain discovery regarding any matter, not privileged, which is relevant to the subject matter involved in the pending action, whether it relates to the claim or defense of the party seeking discovery or to the claim or defense of any other party, including the existence, description, nature, custody, condition, and location of any books, documents, or other tangible things and the identity and location of persons having knowledge of any discoverable matter. It is not ground for objection that the information sought will be inadmissible at the trial if the information sought appears reasonably calculated to lead to the discovery of admissible evidence;

(2) INSURANCE AGREEMENTS. A party may obtain discovery of the existence and contents of any insurance agreement under which any person carrying on an insurance business may be liable to satisfy part or all of a judgment which may be entered in the action or to indemnify or reimburse for payments made to satisfy the judgment. Information concerning the insurance agreement is not by reason of disclosure admissible in evidence at trial. For purposes of this paragraph, an application for insurance shall not be treated as part of an insurance agreement;

(3) TRIAL PREPARATION; MATERIALS. Subject to paragraph (4) of this subsection, a party may obtain discovery of documents and tangible things otherwise discoverable under paragraph (1) of this subsection and prepared in anticipation of litigation or for trial by or for another party or by or for that other party's representative (including his attorney, consultant, surety, indemnitor, insurer, or agent) only upon a showing that the party seeking discovery has substantial need of the materials in the preparation of his case and that he is unable without undue hardship to obtain the substantial equivalent of the materials by other means. In ordering discovery of such materials when the required showing has been made, the court shall protect against disclosure of the mental impressions, conclusions, opinions, or legal theories of an attorney or other representative of a party concerning the litigation. A party may obtain, without the required showing, a statement concerning the action or its subject matter previously made by that party. Upon request, a person not a party may obtain, without the required showing, a statement concerning the action or its subject matter previously made by that person. If the request is refused, the person may move for a court order. Paragraph (4) of subsection (a) of Code Section 9-11-37 applies to the award of expenses incurred in relation to the motion. For purposes of this paragraph, a "statement previously made" is (A) a written statement signed or otherwise adopted or approved by the person making it, or (B) a stenographic, mechanical, electrical, or other recording, or a transcription thereof, which is a substantially verbatim recital of an oral statement by the person making it and contemporaneously recorded; and

(4) TRIAL PREPARATION; EXPERTS. Discovery of facts known and opinions held by experts, otherwise discoverable under paragraph (1) of this subsection and acquired or developed in anticipation of litigation or for trial, may be obtained only as follows:

(A)(i) A party may, through interrogatories, require any other party to identify each person whom the other party expects to call as an expert witness at trial, to state the subject matter on which the expert is expected to testify, and to state the substance of the facts and opinions to which the expert is expected to testify and a summary of the grounds for each opinion.

(ii) A party may obtain discovery under Code Section 9-11-30, 9-11-31, or 9-11-34 from any expert described in this paragraph, the same as any other witness, but the party obtaining discovery of an expert hereunder must pay a reasonable fee for the time spent in responding to discovery by that expert, subject to the right of the expert or any party to obtain a determination by the court as to the reasonableness of the fee so incurred;

(B) A party may discover facts known or opinions held by an expert who has been retained or specially employed by another party in anticipation of litigation or preparation for trial and who is not expected to be called as a witness at trial, only as provided in subsection (b) of Code Section 9-11-35 or upon a showing of exceptional circumstances under which it is impracticable for the party seeking discovery to obtain facts or opinions on the same subject by other means; and

(C) Unless manifest injustice would result:

(i) The court shall require the party seeking discovery to pay the expert a reasonable fee for time spent in responding to discovery under subparagraph (B) of this paragraph; and

(ii) With respect to discovery obtained under division (ii) of subparagraph (A) of this paragraph, the court may require, and with respect to discovery obtained under subparagraph (B) of this paragraph the court shall require, the party seeking discovery to pay the other party a fair portion of the fees and expenses reasonably incurred by the latter party in obtaining facts and opinions from the expert.

(c) *Protective orders.* Upon motion by a party or by the person from whom discovery is sought and for good cause shown, the court in which the action is pending or, alternatively, on matters relating to a deposition, the court in the county where the deposition is to be taken may make any order which justice requires to protect a party or person from annoyance, embarrassment, oppression, or undue burden or expense, including one or more of the following:

(1) That the discovery not be had;

(2) That the discovery may be had only on specified terms and conditions, including a designation of the time or place;

(3) That the discovery may be had only by a method of discovery other than that selected by the party seeking discovery;

(4) That certain matters not be inquired into or that the scope of the discovery be limited to certain matters;

(5) That discovery be conducted with no one present except persons designated by the court;

(6) That a deposition, after being sealed, be opened only by order of the court;

(7) That a trade secret or other confidential research, development, or commercial information not be disclosed or be disclosed only in a designated way; or

(8) That the parties simultaneously file specified documents or information enclosed in sealed envelopes to be opened as directed by the court.

If the motion for a protective order is denied in whole or in part, the court may, on such terms and conditions as are just, order that any party or person provide or permit discovery. Paragraph (4) of subsection (a) of Code Section 9-11-37 applies to the award of expenses incurred in relation to the motion.

(d) *Sequence and timing of discovery.* Unless the court, upon motion, for the convenience of parties and witnesses and in the interests of justice, orders otherwise, methods of discovery may be used in any sequence; and the fact that a party is conducting discovery, whether by deposition or otherwise, shall not operate to delay any other party's discovery.

(e) *Supplementation of responses.* A party who has responded to a request for discovery with a response that was complete when made is under no duty to supplement his response to include information thereafter acquired, except as follows:

(1) A party is under a duty seasonably to supplement his response with respect to any question directly addressed to:

(A) The identity and location of persons having knowledge of discoverable matters; and

(B) The identity of each person expected to be called as an expert witness at trial, the subject matter on which he is expected to testify, and the substance of his testimony.

(2) A party is under a duty seasonably to amend a prior response if he obtains information upon the basis of which:

(A) He knows that the response was incorrect when made; or

(B) He knows that the response, though correct when made, is no longer true and the circumstances are such that a failure to amend the response is, in substance, a knowing concealment.

(3) A duty to supplement responses may be imposed by order of the court, agreement of the parties, or at any time prior to trial through new requests for supplementation of prior responses.

Laws 1966, p. 609, § 26; Laws 1967, p. 226, § 13; Laws 1972, p. 510, § 1; Laws 1984, p. 22, § 9; Laws 1987, p. 3, § 9; Laws 1993, p. 91, § 9.

§ 9-11-27. Depositions before action or pending appeal

(a) *Before action.*

(1) PETITION. A person who desires to perpetuate such person's own testimony or that of another person regarding any matter that may be cognizable in any court may file a verified petition in the superior court of the county where the witness resides. The petition shall be entitled in the name of the petitioner and shall show that the petitioner expects to be a party to litigation but is presently unable to bring it or cause it to be brought, the subject matter of the expected action and the petitioner's interest therein, the facts which the petitioner desires to establish by the proposed testimony and the petitioner's reasons for desiring to perpetuate it, the names or a description of the persons the petitioner expects will be adverse parties and their addresses so far as known, and the names and addresses of the persons to be examined and the substance of the testimony which the petitioner expects to elicit from each, and shall ask for an order authorizing the petitioner to take the depositions of the persons to be examined named in the petition, for the purpose of perpetuating their testimony.

(2) NOTICE AND SERVICE. The petitioner shall thereafter serve a notice upon each person named in the petition as an expected adverse party, together with a copy of the petition, stating that the petitioner will apply to the court at a time and place named therein for the order described in the petition. At least 20 days before the date of hearing the notice shall be served either within or outside the county in the manner provided for service of summons; but, if such service cannot with due diligence be made upon any expected adverse party named in the petition, the court may make such order as is just for service by publication or otherwise and shall appoint, for persons not served, an attorney who shall represent them and, in case they are not otherwise represented, shall cross-examine the deponent. The court may make such order as is just requiring the petitioner to pay a reasonable fee to an attorney so appointed. If any expected adverse party is a minor or an incompetent person and does not have a general guardian, the court shall appoint a guardian ad litem.

(3) ORDER AND EXAMINATION. If the court is satisfied that the perpetuation of the testimony may prevent a failure or delay of justice, it shall make an order designating or describing the persons whose depositions may be taken and specifying the subject matter of the examination and whether the depositions shall be taken upon oral examination or written interrogatories. The depositions may then be taken by a certified court reporter, or as otherwise provided by the rules of the Board of Court Reporting, in accordance with this chapter; and the court may make orders of the character provided for by Code Sections 9-11-34 and 9-11-35. For the purpose of applying this chapter to depositions for perpetuating testimony, each reference therein to the court in which the action is pending shall be deemed to refer to the court in which the petition for such deposition was filed.

(4) USE OF DEPOSITION. If a deposition to perpetuate testimony is taken under this Code section or if, although not so taken, it would be otherwise admissible under the laws of this state, it may be used in any action involving the same parties and the same subject matter subsequently brought.

(b) *Pending appeal.* If an appeal has been taken from a judgment of a trial court or before the taking of an appeal if the time therefor has not expired, the court in which the judgment was rendered may allow the taking of the depositions of witnesses to perpetuate their testimony for use in the event of further proceedings in the trial court. In such case the party who desires to perpetuate the testimony may make a motion in the trial court for leave to take the depositions, upon the same notice and service thereof as if the action were pending in the court. The motion shall show the names and addresses of persons to be examined, the substance of the testimony which the movant expects to elicit from each, and the reasons for perpetuating their testimony. If the court finds that the perpetuation of the testimony is proper to avoid a failure or delay of justice, it may make an order allowing the depositions to be taken and may make orders of the character provided for by Code Sections 9-11-34 and 9-11-35; and thereupon the depositions may be taken before a certified court reporter, or as otherwise provided by the rules of the Board of Court Reporting, and used in the same manner and under the same conditions as are prescribed in this chapter for depositions taken in actions pending in court.

(c) *Perpetuation by action.* This Code section does not limit the power of a court to entertain an action to perpetuate testimony.

Laws 1966, p. 609, § 27; Laws 1993, p. 1315, § 2.

§ 9-11-28. Persons before whom depositions may be taken

(a) *Within the United States and its possessions.* Within the United States or within a territory or insular possession subject to the dominion of the United States, depositions shall be taken before an officer authorized to administer oaths by the laws of the United States or by the laws of the place where the examination is held or before a court reporter appointed by the court in which the action is pending or, if within this state, before a certified court reporter or as otherwise provided by the rules of the Board of Court Reporting. A person so appointed has power to administer oaths and take testimony.

(b) *In foreign countries.* In a foreign state or country depositions shall be taken on notice before a secretary of embassy or legation, consul general, consul, vice-consul, or consular agent of the United States, or before such person or officer as may be appointed by commission or under letters rogatory. A commission or letters rogatory shall be issued only when necessary or convenient, on application and notice, and on such terms and with such directions as are just and appropriate. Officers may be designated in notices or commissions either by name or by descriptive title and letters rogatory may be addressed "To the Appropriate Judicial Authority in (here name the country)."

(c) *Disqualification for interest.* No deposition shall be taken before a court reporter who is a relative, employee, attorney, or counsel of any of the parties, or who is a relative or employee of such attorney or counsel, or who is financially interested in the action, excepting that a deposition may be taken before a court reporter who is a relative of a party or of an attorney or counsel of a party if all parties represented at the deposition enter their explicit consent to the same upon the record of the deposition.

Laws 1966, p. 609, § 28; Laws 1993, p. 1315, § 3; Laws 1994, p. 1007, § 1; Laws 1999, p. 848, § 1.

§ 9-11-29. Stipulation regarding discovery procedure

Unless the court orders otherwise, the parties may, by written stipulation:

(1) Provide that depositions may be taken before any person, at any time or place, upon any notice, and in any manner and, when so taken, may be used like other depositions; and

(2) Modify the procedures provided by this chapter for other methods of discovery.

Laws 1966, p. 609, § 29; Laws 1972, p. 510, § 2.

§ 9-11-29.1. When depositions and discovery materials required to be filed with court

(a) Depositions and other discovery material otherwise required to be filed with the court under this chapter shall not be required to be so filed unless:

(1) Required by local rule of court;

(2) Ordered by the court;

(3) Requested by any party to the action;

(4) Relief relating to discovery material is sought under this chapter and said material has not previously been filed under some other provision of this chapter, in which event copies of the material in dispute shall be filed by the movant contemporaneously with the motion for relief; or

(5) Such material is to be used at trial or is necessary to a pretrial or posttrial motion and said material has not previously been filed under some other provision of this chapter, in which event the portions to be used shall be filed with the clerk of the court at the outset of the trial or at the filing of the motion, insofar as their use can be reasonably anticipated by the parties having custody thereof, but a party attempting to file and use such material which was not filed with the clerk at the outset of the trial or at the filing of the motion shall show to the satisfaction of the court, before the court may authorize such filing and use, that sufficient reasons exist to justify that late filing and use and that the late filing and use will not constitute surprise or manifest injustice to any other party in the proceedings.

(b) Until such time as discovery material is filed under paragraphs (1) through (5) of subsection (a) of this Code section, the original of all depositions shall be retained by the party taking the deposition and the original of all other discovery material shall be retained by the party requesting such material, and the person thus retaining the deposition or other discovery material shall be the custodian thereof.

Laws 1982, p. 2374, § 1.

§ 9-11-30. Depositions upon oral examination

(a) *When depositions may be taken.* After commencement of the action, any party may take the testimony of any person, including a party, by deposition upon oral examination. Leave of court, granted with or without notice, must be obtained only if the plaintiff seeks to take a deposition prior to the expiration of 30 days after service of the summons and complaint upon any defendant or service made under subsection (f) of Code Section 9-11-4, except that leave is not required if a defendant has served a notice of taking deposition or otherwise sought discovery or if special notice is given as provided in paragraph (2) of subsection (b) of this Code section. The attendance of witnesses may be compelled by subpoena as provided in Code Section 9-11-45. The deposition of a person confined in a penal institution may be taken only by leave of court on such terms as the court prescribes.

(b) *Notice of examination.*

(1) GENERAL REQUIREMENTS. A party desiring to take the deposition of any person upon oral examination shall give reasonable notice in writing to every other party to the action. The notice shall state the time and place for taking the deposition, the means by which the testimony shall be recorded, and the name and address of each person to be examined, if known, and, if the name is not known, a general description sufficient to identify the person to be examined or the particular class or group to which he or she belongs. If a subpoena for the production of documentary and tangible evidence is to be served on the person to be examined, the designation of the materials to be produced, as set forth in the subpoena, shall be attached to, or included in, the notice.

(2) SPECIAL NOTICE. Leave of court is not required for the taking of a deposition by plaintiff if the notice:

(A) States that the person to be examined is about to go out of the county where the action is pending and more than 150 miles from the place of trial, or is about to go out of the United States, or is bound on a voyage to sea, and will be unavailable for examination unless the deposition is taken before expiration of the 30 day period; and

(B) Sets forth facts to support the statement.

The plaintiff's attorney shall sign the notice, and said attorney's signature constitutes a certification by him or her that, to the best of his or her knowledge, information, and belief, the statement and supporting facts are true. If a party shows that, when he or she was served with notice under this paragraph, he or she was unable through the exercise of diligence to obtain counsel to represent him or her at the taking of the deposition, the deposition may not be used against such party.

(3) TIME REQUIREMENTS. The court may, for cause shown, enlarge or shorten the time for taking the deposition.

(4) RECORDING OF DEPOSITION. Unless the court orders otherwise, the testimony at a deposition must be recorded by stenographic means, and may also be recorded by sound or sound and visual means in addition to stenographic means, and the party taking the deposition shall bear the costs of the recording. A deposition shall be conducted before an officer appointed or designated under Code Section 9–11–28. Upon motion of a party or upon its own motion, the court may issue an order designating the manner of recording, preserving, and filing of a deposition taken by nonstenographic means, which order may include other provisions to assure that the recorded testimony will be accurate and trustworthy. Any party may arrange for a transcription to be made from the recording of a deposition taken by nonstenographic means. With prior notice to the deponent and other parties, any party may designate another method to record the deponent's testimony in addition to the methods specified by the person taking the deposition. The additional record or transcript shall be made at that party's expense unless the court otherwise orders. The appearance or demeanor of deponents or attorneys shall not be distorted through camera or sound-recording techniques. Notwithstanding the foregoing provisions of this paragraph, a deposition may be taken by telephone or other remote electronic means only upon the stipulation of the parties or by order of the court. For purposes of the requirements of this chapter, a deposition taken by telephone or other remote electronic means is taken in the state and at the place where the deponent is to answer questions.

(5) PRODUCTION OF DOCUMENTS AND THINGS. The notice to a party deponent may be accompanied by a request made in compliance with Code Section 9–11–34 for the production of documents and tangible things at the taking of the deposition. The procedure of Code Section 9–11–34 shall apply to the request.

(6) DEPOSITION OF ORGANIZATION. A party may, in his or her notice, name as the deponent a public or private corporation or a partnership or association or a governmental agency and designate with reasonable particularity the matters on which examination is requested. The organization so named shall designate one or more officers, directors, or managing agents, or other persons who consent to testify on its behalf, and may set forth, for each person designated, the matters on which he or she will testify. The persons so designated shall testify as to matters known or reasonably available to the organization. This paragraph does not preclude taking a deposition by any other procedure authorized in this chapter.

(c) *Examination and cross-examination; record of examination; oath; objections.*

(1) Examination and cross-examination of witnesses may proceed as permitted at the trial under the rules of evidence. The authorized officer or court reporter before whom the deposition is to be taken shall put the witness on oath and shall personally, or by someone acting under the direction and in the presence of the authorized officer or court reporter, record the testimony of the witness.

(2) All objections made at the time of the examination to the qualifications of the officer taking the deposition, or to the manner of taking it, or to the evidence presented, or to the conduct of any party, and any other objection to the proceedings shall be noted by the officer upon the deposition. Evidence objected to shall be taken subject to the objections. In lieu of participating in the oral examination, parties may serve written questions in a sealed

envelope on the party taking the deposition, and said party shall transmit them to the officer, who shall propound them to the witness and record the answers verbatim.

(3) Unless otherwise ordered by the court or agreed by the parties, the officer shall retain the record of each deposition until the later of (A) five years after the date on which the deposition was taken, or (B) two years after the date of final disposition of the action for which the deposition was taken and any appeals of such action. The officer may preserve the record through storage of the original paper, notes, or recordings or an electronic copy of the notes, recordings, or the transcript on computer disks, cassettes, backup tape systems, optical or laser disk systems, or other retrieval systems.

(d) *Motion to terminate or limit examination.* At any time during the taking of the deposition, on motion of a party or of the deponent and upon a showing that the examination is being conducted in bad faith or in such manner as unreasonably to annoy, embarrass, or oppress the deponent or party, the court in which the action is pending or the court in the county where the deposition is being taken may order the officer conducting the examination to cease forthwith from taking the deposition or may limit the scope and manner of the taking of the deposition as provided in subsection (c) of Code Section 9–11–26. If the order made terminates the examination, it shall be resumed thereafter only upon the order of the court in which the action is pending. Upon demand of the objecting party or deponent, the taking of the deposition shall be suspended for the time necessary to make a motion for an order. Paragraph (4) of subsection (a) of Code Section 9–11–37 applies to the award of expenses incurred in relation to the motion.

(e) *Review by witness; changes; signing.* If requested by the deponent or a party before completion of the deposition, the deponent shall have 30 days after being notified by the officer that the transcript or recording is available in which to review the transcript or recording and, if there are changes in form or substance, to sign a statement reciting such changes and the reasons given by the deponent for making them. The officer shall indicate in the certificate prescribed by paragraph (1) of subsection (f) of this Code section whether any review was requested and, if so, shall append any changes made by the deponent during the period allowed. If the deposition is not reviewed and signed by the witness within 30 days of its submission to him or her, the officer shall sign it and state on the record that the deposition was not reviewed and signed by the deponent within 30 days. The deposition may then be used as fully as though signed unless, on a motion to suppress under paragraph (4) of subsection (d) of Code Section 9–11–32, the court holds that the reasons given for the refusal to sign require rejection of the deposition in whole or in part.

(f) *Certification and filing by officer; inspection and copying of exhibits; copy of deposition.*

(1)(A) The officer shall certify that the witness was duly sworn by the officer and that the deposition is a true record of the testimony given by the witness. This certificate shall be in writing and accompany the record of the deposition. The officer shall then securely seal the deposition in an envelope marked with the title of the action, the court reporter certification number, and "Deposition of (here insert name of witness)" and shall promptly file it with the court in which the action is pending or deliver it to the party taking the deposition, as the case may be, in accordance with Code Section 9–11–29.1.

(B) Documents and things produced for inspection during the examination of the witness shall, upon the request of a party, be marked for identification and annexed to and returned with the deposition and may be inspected and copied by any party, except that the person producing the materials may substitute copies to be marked for identification, if he or she affords to all parties fair opportunity to verify the copies by comparison with the originals; and, if the person producing the materials requests their return, the officer shall mark them, give each party an opportunity to inspect and copy them, and return them to the person producing them, and the materials may then be used in the same manner as if annexed to and returned with the deposition. Any party may move for an order that the original be annexed to and returned with the deposition to the court, pending final disposition of the case.

(2) Upon payment of reasonable charges therefor, the officer shall furnish a copy of the deposition to any party or to the deponent.

(g) *Failure to attend or to serve subpoena; expenses.*

(1) If the party giving the notice of the taking of a deposition fails to attend and proceed therewith and another party attends in person or by attorney pursuant to the notice, the court may order the party giving the notice to pay to such other party the reasonable expenses incurred by him and his attorney in attending, including reasonable attorney's fees.

(2) If the party giving the notice of the taking of a deposition of a witness fails to serve a subpoena upon him and the witness, because of such failure, does not attend and if another party attends in person or by attorney because he expects the deposition of that witness to be taken, the court may order the party giving the notice to pay to such other party the reasonable expenses incurred by

him and his attorney in attending, including reasonable attorney's fees.

(h) *Form of presentation.* Except as otherwise directed by the court, a party offering deposition testimony may offer it in stenographic or nonstenographic form, but if in nonstenographic form, the party shall also provide the court with a transcript of the portions so offered. On request of any party in a case tried before a jury, deposition testimony offered other than for impeachment purposes shall be presented in nonstenographic form, if available, unless the court for good cause orders otherwise.

Laws 1966, p. 609, § 30; Laws 1967, p. 226, § 14; Laws 1972, p. 510, § 3; Laws 1993, p. 1315, § 4; Laws 1996, p. 266, § 1; Laws 2000, p. 1225, § 3.

§ 9–11–31. Depositions upon written questions

(a) *Serving questions; notice.*

(1) After commencement of the action, any party may take the testimony of any person, including a party, by deposition upon written questions. The attendance of witnesses may be compelled by the use of subpoena as provided in Code Section 9–11–45. The deposition of a person confined in a penal institution may be taken only by leave of court on such terms as the court prescribes.

(2) A party desiring to take a deposition upon written questions shall serve them upon every other party with a notice stating the name and address of the person who is to answer them, if known, and, if the name is not known, a general description sufficient to identify him or the particular class or group to which he belongs and the name or descriptive title and address of the officer before whom the deposition is to be taken. A deposition upon written questions may be taken of a public or private corporation or a partnership or association or governmental agency in accordance with paragraph (6) of subsection (b) of Code Section 9–11–30.

(3) Within 30 days after the notice and written questions are served, a party may serve cross-questions upon all other parties. Within ten days after being served with cross-questions, a party may serve redirect questions upon all other parties. Within ten days after being served with redirect questions, a party may serve recross-questions upon all other parties. The court may, for cause shown, enlarge or shorten the time.

(b) *Officer to take responses and prepare record.* A copy of the notice and copies of all questions served shall be delivered by the party taking the deposition to the officer designated in the notice, who shall proceed promptly, in the manner provided by subsections (c), (e), and (f) of Code Section 9–11–30, to take the testimony of the witness in response to the questions and to prepare, certify, and file or mail the deposition, attaching thereto the copy of the notice and the questions received by him.

Laws 1966, p. 609, § 31; Laws 1967, p. 226, § 15; Laws 1972, p. 510, § 4.

§ 9–11–32. Use of depositions in court proceedings; effect of errors and irregularities in depositions

(a) *Use of depositions.* At the trial or upon the hearing of a motion or an interlocutory proceeding, any part or all of a deposition, so far as admissible under the rules of evidence applied as though the witness were then present and testifying, may be used against any party who was present or represented at the taking of the deposition or who had reasonable notice thereof, in accordance with any of the following provisions:

(1) Any deposition may be used by any party for the purpose of contradicting or impeaching the testimony of the deponent as a witness;

(2) The deposition of a party or of anyone who, at the time of taking the deposition, was an officer, director, or managing agent or a person designated under paragraph (6) of subsection (b) of Code Section 9–11–30 or subsection (a) of Code Section 9–11–31 to testify on behalf of a public or private corporation, a partnership or association, or a governmental agency which is a party may be used by an adverse party for any purpose;

(3) The deposition of a witness, whether or not a party, may be used by any party for any purpose if the court finds:

(A) That the witness is dead;

(B) That the witness is out of the county, unless it appears that the absence of the witness was procured by a party offering the deposition;

(C) That the witness is unable to attend or testify because of age, illness, infirmity, or imprisonment;

(D) That the party offering the deposition has been unable to procure the attendance of the witness by subpoena;

(E) That because of the nature of the business or occupation of the witness it is not possible to secure his personal attendance without manifest inconvenience to the public or third persons; or

(F) That the witness will be a member of the General Assembly and that the session of the General Assembly will conflict with the session of the court in which the case is to be tried;

(4) The deposition of a witness, whether or not a party, taken upon oral examination, may be used in the discretion of the trial judge, even though the witness is available to testify in person at the trial. The use of the deposition shall not be a ground for

excluding the witness from testifying orally in open court; or

(5) If only part of a deposition is offered in evidence by a party, an adverse party may require him to introduce all of it which is relevant to the part introduced, and any party may introduce any other parts. Substitution of parties does not affect the right to use depositions previously taken; and, when an action in any court of the United States or of any state has been dismissed and another action involving the same subject matter is afterward brought between the same parties or their representatives or successors in interest, all depositions lawfully taken and duly filed in the former action may be used in the latter as if originally taken therefor.

(b) *Objections to admissibility.* Subject to paragraph (3) of subsection (d) of this Code section, objection may be made at the trial or hearing to receiving in evidence any deposition or part thereof for any reason which would require the exclusion of the evidence if the witness were then present and testifying.

(c) *Effect of taking or using depositions.* A party does not make a person his own witness for any purpose by taking his deposition. The introduction in evidence of the deposition or any part thereof for any purpose other than that of contradicting or impeaching the deponent makes the deponent the witness of the party introducing the deposition; but this shall not apply to the use by an adverse party of a deposition under paragraph (2) of subsection (a) of this Code section. At the trial or hearing any party may rebut any relevant evidence contained in a deposition whether introduced by him or by any other party.

(d) *Effect of errors and irregularities in depositions.*

(1) AS TO NOTICE. All errors and irregularities in the notice for taking a deposition are waived unless written objection is promptly served upon the party giving the notice.

(2) AS TO DISQUALIFICATION OF OFFICER. Objection to taking a deposition because of disqualification of the officer before whom it is to be taken is waived unless made before the taking of the deposition begins or as soon thereafter as the disqualification becomes known or could be discovered with reasonable diligence.

(3) AS TO TAKING OF DEPOSITION.

(A) Objections to the competency of a witness or to the competency, relevancy, or materiality of testimony are not waived by failure to make them before or during the taking of the deposition, unless the ground of the objection is one which might have been obviated or removed if presented at that time.

(B) Errors and irregularities occurring at the oral examination in the manner of taking the deposition, in the form of the questions or answers, in the oath or affirmation, or in the conduct of parties, and errors of any kind which might be obviated, removed, or cured if promptly presented are waived unless seasonable objection thereto is made at the taking of the deposition.

(C) Objections to the form of written questions submitted under Code Section 9-11-31 are waived unless served in writing upon the party propounding them within the time allowed for serving the succeeding cross or other questions and within five days after service of the last questions authorized.

(4) AS TO COMPLETION AND RETURN OF DEPOSITION. Errors and irregularities in the manner in which the testimony is transcribed or the deposition is prepared, signed, certified, sealed, endorsed, transmitted, filed, or otherwise dealt with by the officer under Code Sections 9-11-30 and 9-11-31 are waived unless a motion to suppress the deposition or some part thereof is made with reasonable promptness after such defect is, or with due diligence might have been, ascertained.

Laws 1966, p. 609, § 32; Laws 1972, p. 510, § 5; Laws 1984, p. 22, § 9.

§ 9-11-33. Interrogatories to parties

(a) *Availability; procedures for use.*

(1) Any party may serve upon any other party written interrogatories to be answered by the party served or, if the party served is a public or private corporation or a partnership or association or a governmental agency, by any officer or agent, who shall furnish such information as is available to the party. Interrogatories may, without leave of court, be served upon the plaintiff after commencement of the action and upon any other party with or after service of the summons and complaint upon that party; provided, however, that no party may serve interrogatories containing more than 50 interrogatories, including subparts, upon any other party without leave of court upon a showing of complex litigation or undue hardship incurred if such additional interrogatories are not permitted.

(2) Each interrogatory shall be answered separately and fully in writing under oath, unless it is objected to, in which event the reasons for objection shall be stated in lieu of an answer. The answers are to be signed by the person making them, and the objections signed by the attorney making them. The party upon whom the interrogatories have been served shall serve a copy of the answers, and objections if any, within 30 days after the service of the interrogatories, except that a defendant may serve answers or objections within 45 days after service of the summons and complaint upon that defendant. The court may allow a shorter or longer time. The

party submitting the interrogatories may move for an order under subsection (a) of Code Section 9-11-37 with respect to any objection to or other failure to answer an interrogatory.

(b) *Scope; use at trial.*

(1) Interrogatories may relate to any matters which can be inquired into under subsection (b) of Code Section 9-11-26, and the answers may be used to the extent permitted by the rules of evidence.

(2) An interrogatory otherwise proper is not necessarily objectionable merely because an answer to the interrogatory involves an opinion or contention that relates to fact or to the application of law to fact; but the court may order that such an interrogatory need not be answered until after designated discovery has been completed or until a pretrial conference or other later time.

(c) *Option to produce business records.* Where the answer to an interrogatory may be derived or ascertained from the business records of the party upon whom the interrogatory has been served or from an examination, audit, or inspection of such business records, or from a compilation, abstract, or summary based thereon, and the burden of deriving or ascertaining the answer is substantially the same for the party serving the interrogatory as for the party served, it is a sufficient answer to the interrogatory to specify the records from which the answer may be derived or ascertained and to afford to the party serving the interrogatory reasonable opportunity to examine, audit, or inspect such records and to make copies, compilations, abstracts, or summaries.

Laws 1966, p. 609, § 33; Laws 1972, p. 510, § 6; Laws 1980, p. 938, § 1.

§ 9-11-34. Production of documents and things and entry upon land for inspection and other purposes

(a) *Scope.* Any party may serve on any other party a request:

(1) To produce and permit the party making the request, or someone acting on his behalf, to inspect and copy any designated documents (including writings, drawings, graphs, charts, photographs, phonorecords, and other data compilations from which information can be obtained, translated, if necessary, by the respondent through detection devices into reasonably usable form), or to inspect and copy, test, or sample any tangible things which constitute or contain matters within the scope of subsection (b) of Code Section 9-11-26 and which are in the possession, custody, or control of the party upon whom the request is served; or

(2) To permit entry upon designated land or other property in the possession or control of the party upon whom the request is served for the purpose of inspection and measuring, surveying, photographing, testing, or sampling the property or any designated object or operation thereon, within the scope of subsection (b) of Code Section 9-11-26.

(b) *Procedure.*

(1) The request may, without leave of court, be served upon the plaintiff after commencement of the action and upon any other party with or after service of the summons and complaint upon that party. The request shall set forth the items to be inspected, either by individual item or by category, and describe each item and category with reasonable particularity. The request shall specify a reasonable time, place, and manner of making the inspection and performing the related acts.

(2) The party upon whom the request is served shall serve a written response within 30 days after the service of the request, except that a defendant may serve a response within 45 days after service of the summons and complaint upon that defendant. The court may allow a shorter or longer time. The response shall state, with respect to each item or category, that inspection and related activities will be permitted as requested, unless the request is objected to, in which event the reasons for objection shall be stated. If objection is made to part of an item or category, the part shall be specified. The party submitting the request may move for an order under subsection (a) of Code Section 9-11-37 with respect to any objection to or other failure to respond to the request or any part thereof, or any failure to permit inspection as requested.

(c) *Applicability to nonparties.*

(1) This Code section shall also be applicable with respect to discovery against persons, firms, or corporations who are not parties, in which event a copy of the request shall be served upon all parties of record; or, upon notice, the party desiring such discovery may proceed by taking the deposition of the person, firm, or corporation on oral examination or upon written questions under Code Section 9-11-30 or 9-11-31. The nonparty or any party may file an objection as provided in subsection (b) of this Code section. If the party desiring such discovery moves for an order under subsection (a) of Code Section 9-11-37 to compel discovery, he or she shall make a showing of good cause to support his or her motion. The party making a request under this Code section shall, upon request from any other party to the action, make all reasonable efforts to cause all information produced in response to the nonparty request to be made available to all parties. A reasonable document copying charge may be required.

(2) This Code section shall also be applicable with respect to discovery against a nonparty who is a practitioner of the healing arts or a hospital or health care facility, including those operated by an

agency or bureau of the state or other governmental unit. Where such a request is directed to such a nonparty, a copy of the request shall be served upon the person whose records are sought by certified mail or statutory overnight delivery, return receipt requested, or, if known, that person's counsel, and upon all other parties of record in compliance with Code Section 9–11–5; where such a request to a nonparty seeks the records of a person who is not a party, a copy of the request shall be served upon the person whose records are sought by certified mail or statutory overnight delivery, return receipt requested, or, if known, that person's counsel by certified mail or statutory overnight delivery, return receipt requested, and upon all parties of record in compliance with Code Section 9–11–5; or, upon notice, the party desiring such discovery may proceed by taking the deposition of the person, firm, or corporation on oral examination or upon written questions under Code Section 9–11–30 or 9–11–31. The nonparty, any party, or the person whose records are sought may file an objection with the court in which the action is pending within 20 days of service of the request and shall serve a copy of such objection on the nonparty to whom the request is directed, who shall not furnish the requested materials until further order of the court, and on all other parties to the action. Upon the filing of such objection, the party desiring such discovery may move for an order under subsection (a) of Code Section 9–11–37 to compel discovery and, if he or she shall make a showing of good cause to support his or her motion, discovery shall be allowed. If no objection is filed within 20 days of service of the request, the nonparty to whom the request is directed shall promptly comply therewith.

(3) For any discovery requested from a nonparty pursuant to paragraph (2) of this subsection or a subpoena requesting records from a nonparty pursuant to Code Section 9–11–45, when the nonparty to whom the discovery request is made is not served with an objection and the nonparty produces the requested records, the nonparty shall be immune from regulatory, civil, or criminal liability or damages notwithstanding that the produced documents contained confidential or privileged information.

(d) *Confidentiality.* The provisions of this Code section shall not be deemed to repeal the confidentiality provided by Code Sections 37–3–166 concerning mental illness treatment records, 37–4–125 concerning mental retardation treatment records, 37–7–166 concerning alcohol and drug treatment records, 24–9–40.1 concerning the confidential nature of AIDS information, and 24–9–47 concerning the disclosure of AIDS information; provided, however, that a person's failure to object to the production of documents as set forth in paragraph (2) of subsection (c) of this Code section shall waive any right of recovery for damages as to the nonparty for disclosure of the requested documents.

Laws 1966, p. 609, § 34; Laws 1967, p. 226, § 16; Laws 1972, p. 510, § 7; Laws 1979, p. 1041, § 1; Laws 1986, p. 1277, § 1; Laws 1988, p. 375, § 1; Laws 1998, p. 152, § 1; Laws 2006, Act 608, § 2, eff. July 1, 2006.

§ 9–11–35. Physical and mental examination of persons

(a) *Order for examination.* When the mental or physical condition (including the blood group) of a party, or of a person in the custody or under the legal control of a party, is in controversy, the court in which the action is pending may order the party to submit to a physical examination by a physician or to submit to a mental examination by a physician or a licensed psychologist or to produce for examination the person in his custody or legal control. The order may be made only on motion for good cause shown and upon notice to the person to be examined and to all parties and shall specify the time, place, manner, conditions, and scope of the examination and the person or persons by whom it is to be made.

(b) *Report of examining physician or psychologist.*

(1) If requested by the party against whom an order is made under subsection (a) of this Code section or by the person examined, the party causing the examination to be made shall deliver to him a copy of a detailed written report of the examining physician or psychologist setting out his findings, including results of all tests made, diagnoses, and conclusions, together with like reports of all earlier examinations of the same condition.

(2) Any party shall be entitled, upon request, to receive from the party whose physical or mental condition is in issue, or who is in control of, or has legal custody of, a person whose physical or mental condition is in issue, a report of any and every examination, previously or thereafter made, of the condition in issue, unless, in the case of a report of examination of a person not a party, the party shows that he is unable to obtain it.

(3) The court, on motion, may make an order against a party requiring delivery of a report under paragraph (1) or (2) of this subsection on such terms as are just; and, if a physician or psychologist fails or refuses to make a report, the court may exclude his testimony if offered at the trial.

(4) By requesting and obtaining a report of the examination so ordered or by taking the deposition of the examiner, the party examined waives any privilege he may have in that action, or any other action involving the same controversy, regarding the testimony of every other person who has examined or may thereafter examine him in respect to the same mental or physical condition.

(5) Paragraphs (1) through (4) of this subsection apply to examinations made by agreement of the parties, unless the agreement expressly provides otherwise. Paragraphs (1) through (4) of this subsection do not preclude discovery of a report of an examining physician or psychologist or the taking of a deposition of the physician or psychologist in accordance with any other Code section of this chapter.

Laws 1966, p. 609, § 35; Laws 1972, p. 510, § 8; Laws 2001, p. 808, § 1.

§ 9-11-36. Request for admission

(a) *Scope; service; answer or objection; motion to determine sufficiency.*

(1) A party may serve upon any other party a written request for the admission, for purposes of the pending action only, of the truth of any matters within the scope of subsection (b) of Code Section 9-11-26 which are set forth in the request and that relate to statements or opinions of fact or of the application of law to fact, including the genuineness of any documents described in the request. Copies of documents shall be served with the request unless they have been or are otherwise furnished or made available for inspection and copying. The request may, without leave of court, be served upon the plaintiff after commencement of the action and upon any other party with or after service of the summons and complaint upon that party.

(2) Each matter of which an admission is requested shall be separately set forth. The matter is admitted unless, within 30 days after service of the request or within such shorter or longer time as the court may allow, the party to whom the request is directed serves upon the party requesting the admission a written answer or objection addressed to the matter, signed by the party or by his attorney; but unless the court shortens the time, a defendant shall not be required to serve answers or objections before the expiration of 45 days after service of the summons and complaint upon him. If objection is made, the reasons therefor shall be stated. The answer shall specifically deny the matter or set forth in detail the reasons why the answering party cannot truthfully admit or deny the matter. A denial shall fairly meet the substance of the requested admission; and, when good faith requires that a party qualify his answer or deny only a part of the matter of which an admission is requested, he shall specify so much of it as is true and qualify or deny the remainder. An answering party may not give lack of information or knowledge as a reason for failure to admit or deny unless he states that he has made reasonable inquiry and that the information known or readily obtainable by him is insufficient to enable him to admit or deny. A party who considers that a matter of which an admission has been requested presents a genuine issue for trial may not, on that ground alone, object to the request; he may, subject to subsection (c) of Code Section 9-11-37, deny the matter or set forth reasons why he cannot admit or deny it.

(3) The party who has requested the admissions may move to determine the sufficiency of the answers or objections. Unless the court determines that an objection is justified, it shall order that an answer be served. If the court determines that an answer does not comply with the requirements of this subsection, it may order either that the matter is admitted or that an amended answer be served. The court may, in lieu of these orders, determine that final disposition of the request be made at a pretrial conference or at a designated time prior to trial. Paragraph (4) of subsection (a) of Code Section 9-11-37 shall apply to the award of expenses incurred in relation to the motion.

(b) *Effect of admission.* Any matter admitted under this Code section is conclusively established unless the court, on motion, permits withdrawal or amendment of the admission. Subject to Code Section 9-11-16 governing amendment of a pretrial order, the court may permit withdrawal or amendment when the presentation of the merits of the action will be subserved thereby and the party who obtained the admission fails to satisfy the court that withdrawal or amendment will prejudice him in maintaining his action or defense on the merits. Any admission made by a party under this Code section is for the purpose of the pending action only and is not an admission by him for any other purpose, nor may it be used against him in any other proceeding.

Laws 1966, p. 609, § 36; Laws 1967, p. 226, §§ 17, 18A; Laws 1972, p. 510, § 9.

§ 9-11-37. Failure to make discovery

(a) *Motion for order compelling discovery.* A party, upon reasonable notice to other parties and all persons affected thereby, may apply for an order compelling discovery as follows:

(1) APPROPRIATE COURT. An application for an order to a party may be made to the court in which the action is pending or, on matters relating to a deposition, to the court in the county where the deposition is being taken. An application for an order to a deponent who is not a party shall be made to the court in the county where the deposition is being taken;

(2) MOTION; PROTECTIVE ORDER. If a deponent fails to answer a question propounded or submitted under Code Section 9-11-30 or 9-11-31, or a corporation or other entity fails to make a designation under paragraph (6) of subsection (b) of Code Section 9-11-30 or subsection (a) of Code Section 9-11-31, or a party fails to answer an interrogatory

submitted under Code Section 9–11–33, or if a party, in response to a request for inspection submitted under Code Section 9–11–34, fails to respond that inspection will be permitted as requested or fails to permit inspection as requested, the discovering party may move for an order compelling an answer, or a designation, or an order compelling inspection in accordance with the request. When taking a deposition on oral examination, the proponent of the question may complete or adjourn the examination before he applies for an order. If the court denies the motion in whole or in part, it may make such protective order as it would have been empowered to make on a motion made pursuant to subsection (c) of Code Section 9–11–26;

(3) EVASIVE OR INCOMPLETE ANSWER. For purposes of the provisions of this chapter which relate to depositions and discovery, an evasive or incomplete answer is to be treated as a failure to answer; and

(4) AWARD OF EXPENSES OF MOTION.

(A) If the motion is granted, the court shall, after opportunity for hearing, require the party or deponent whose conduct necessitated the motion or the party or attorney advising such conduct or both of them to pay to the moving party the reasonable expenses incurred in obtaining the order, including attorney's fees, unless the court finds that the opposition to the motion was substantially justified or that other circumstances make an award of expenses unjust.

(B) If the motion is denied, the court shall, after opportunity for hearing, require the moving party or the attorney advising the motion or both of them to pay to the party or deponent who opposed the motion the reasonable expenses incurred in opposing the motion, including attorney's fees, unless the court finds that the making of the motion was substantially justified or that other circumstances make an award of expenses unjust.

(C) If the motion is granted in part and denied in part, the court may apportion the reasonable expenses incurred in relation to the motion among the parties and persons in a just manner.

(b) *Failure to comply with order.*

(1) SANCTIONS BY COURT IN COUNTY WHERE DEPOSITION IS TAKEN. If a deponent fails to be sworn or to answer a question after being directed to do so by the court in the county in which the deposition is being taken, the failure may be considered a contempt of that court.

(2) SANCTIONS BY COURT IN WHICH ACTION IS PENDING. If a party or an officer, director, or managing agent of a party or a person designated under paragraph (6) of subsection (b) of Code Section 9–11–30 or subsection (a) of Code Section 9–11–31 to testify on behalf of a party fails to obey an order to provide or permit discovery, including an order made under subsection (a) of this Code section or Code Section 9–11–35, the court in which the action is pending may make such orders in regard to the failure as are just and, among others, the following:

(A) An order that the matters regarding which the order was made or any other designated facts shall be taken to be established for the purposes of the action in accordance with the claim of the party obtaining the order;

(B) An order refusing to allow the disobedient party to support or oppose designated claims or defenses, or prohibiting him from introducing designated matters in evidence;

(C) An order striking out pleadings or parts thereof, or staying further proceedings until the order is obeyed, or dismissing the action or proceeding or any part thereof, or rendering a judgment by default against the disobedient party;

(D) In lieu of any of the foregoing orders, or in addition thereto, an order treating as a contempt of court the failure to obey any orders except an order to submit to a physical or mental examination; or

(E) Where a party has failed to comply with an order under subsection (a) of Code Section 9–11–35 requiring him to produce another for examination, such orders as are listed in subparagraphs (A), (B), and (C) of this paragraph, unless the party failing to comply shows that he is unable to produce such person for examination.

In lieu of any of the foregoing orders, or in addition thereto, the court shall require the party failing to obey the order or the attorney advising him, or both, to pay the reasonable expenses, including attorney's fees, caused by the failure, unless the court finds that the failure was substantially justified or that other circumstances make an award of expenses unjust.

(c) *Expenses on failure to admit.* If a party fails to admit the genuineness of any document or the truth of any matter as requested under Code Section 9–11–36 and if the party requesting the admissions thereafter proves the genuineness of the document or the truth of the matter, he may apply to the court for an order requiring the other party to pay him the reasonable expenses incurred in making that proof, including reasonable attorney's fees. The court shall make the order unless it finds that the request was held objectionable pursuant to subsection (a) of Code Section 9–11–36, or the admission sought was of no substantial importance, or the party failing to admit had reasonable ground to believe that he might prevail on the matter, or there was other good reason for the failure to admit.

(d) *Failure of party to attend at own deposition or serve answers to interrogatories or respond to request for inspection.*

(1) If a party or an officer, director, or managing agent of a party or a person designated under paragraph (6) of subsection (b) of Code Section 9-11-30 or subsection (a) of Code Section 9-11-31 to testify on behalf of a party fails to appear before the officer who is to take his deposition, after being served with a proper notice, or fails to serve answers or objections to interrogatories submitted under Code Section 9-11-33, after proper service of the interrogatories, or fails to serve a written response to a request for inspection submitted under Code Section 9-11-34, after proper service of the request, the court in which the action is pending on motion may make such orders in regard to the failure as are just; and, among others, it may take any action authorized under subparagraphs (b)(2)(A) through (b)(2)(C) of this Code section. In lieu of any order, or in addition thereto, the court shall require the party failing to act or the attorney advising him, or both, to pay the reasonable expenses, including attorney's fees, caused by the failure, unless the court finds that the failure was substantially justified or that other circumstances make an award of expenses unjust.

(2) The failure to act described in the provisions of this chapter which relate to depositions and discovery may not be excused on the ground that the discovery sought is objectionable unless the party failing to act has applied for a protective order as provided by subsection (c) of Code Section 9-11-26.

Laws 1966, p. 609, § 37; Laws 1967, p. 226, § 18; Laws 1970, p. 157, § 1; Laws 1972, p. 510, § 10; Laws 1984, p. 22, § 9; Laws 1992, p. 6, § 9.

Article 6

Trials

§ 9-11-38. Jury trial of right

The right of trial by jury as declared by the Constitution of the state or as given by a statute of the state shall be preserved to the parties inviolate.

Laws 1966, p. 609, § 38.

§ 9-11-39. Trial by jury or by the court

(a) The parties or their attorneys of record, by written stipulation filed with the court or by an oral stipulation made in open court and entered in the record, may consent to trial by the court sitting without a jury.

(b) In all actions not triable of right by a jury, or where jury trial has been expressly waived, the court may nevertheless order a trial with a jury whose verdict will have the same effect as if trial by jury had been a matter of right or had not been waived.

Laws 1966, p. 609, § 39.

§ 9-11-40. Trial

(a) *Time of trial.* All civil cases, including divorce and other domestic relations cases, shall be triable any time after the last day upon which defensive pleadings were required to be filed therein; provided, however, that the court shall in all cases afford to the parties reasonable time for discovery procedures, subsequent to the date that defensive pleadings were required to be filed; provided, further, that, in divorce cases involving service by publication, service shall occur on the date of the first publication of notice following the order for service of publication pursuant to subparagraph (f)(1)(C) of Code Section 9-11-4, and such divorce cases shall be triable any time after 60 days have elapsed since the date of the first publication of notice.

(b) *Trial in chambers.* The judges of any courts of record may, on reasonable notice to the parties, at any time and at chambers in any county in the circuit, hear and determine by interlocutory or final judgment any matter or issue where a jury trial is not required or has been waived. However, nothing in this subsection shall authorize the trial of any divorce case by consent or otherwise until after the last day upon which defensive pleadings were required by law to be filed therein.

(c) *Assignment of cases for trial.* The courts shall provide for the placing of actions upon the trial calendar:

(1) Without request of the parties but upon notice to the parties; or

(2) Upon request of a party and notice to the other parties.

Except for cause, cases shall be placed upon the calendar in chronological order in accordance with filing dates. Precedence shall be given to actions entitled thereto by any statute.

Laws 1966, p. 609, § 40; Laws 1967, p. 226, § 41; Laws 1968, p. 1104, § 9; Laws 1976, p. 1677, § 1; Laws 1993, p. 91, § 9; Laws 2000, p. 1225, § 4.

§ 9-11-41. Dismissal of actions

(a) *Voluntary dismissal; effect:*

(1) BY PLAINTIFF; BY STIPULATION. Subject to the provisions of subsection (e) of Code

Section 9-11-23, Code Section 9-11-66, and any statute, an action may be dismissed by the plaintiff, without order or permission of court:

(A) By filing a written notice of dismissal at any time before the first witness is sworn; or

(B) By filing a stipulation of dismissal signed by all parties who have appeared in the action.

(2) BY ORDER OF COURT. Except as provided in paragraph (1) of this subsection, an action shall not be dismissed upon the plaintiff's motion except upon order of the court and upon the terms and conditions as the court deems proper. If a counterclaim has been pleaded by a defendant prior to the service upon him or her of the plaintiff's motion to dismiss, the action shall not be dismissed against the defendant's objection unless the counterclaim can remain pending for independent adjudication by the court.

(3) EFFECT. A dismissal under this subsection is without prejudice, except that the filing of a second notice of dismissal operates as an adjudication upon the merits.

(b) *Involuntary dismissal; effect thereof.* For failure of the plaintiff to prosecute or to comply with this chapter or any order of court, a defendant may move for dismissal of an action or of any claim against him. After the plaintiff, in an action tried by the court without a jury, has completed the presentation of his evidence, the defendant, without waiving his right to offer evidence in the event the motion is not granted, may move for dismissal on the ground that upon the facts and the law the plaintiff has shown no right to relief. The court as trier of the facts may then determine the facts and render judgment against the plaintiff or may decline to render any judgment until the close of all the evidence. The effect of dismissals shall be as follows: (1) A dismissal for failure of the plaintiff to prosecute does not operate as an adjudication upon the merits; and (2) Any other dismissal under this subsection and any dismissal not provided for in this Code section, other than a dismissal for lack of jurisdiction or for improper venue or for lack of an indispensable party, does operate as an adjudication upon the merits unless the court in its order for dismissal specifies otherwise.

(c) *Dismissal of counterclaim, cross-claim, or third-party claim.* This Code section also applies to the dismissal of any counterclaim, cross-claim, or third-party claim.

(d) *Cost of previously dismissed action.* If a plaintiff who has dismissed an action in any court commences an action based upon or including the same claim against the same defendant, the plaintiff shall first pay the court costs of the action previously dismissed.

(e) *Dismissal for want of prosecution; recommencement.* Any action in which no written order is taken for a period of five years shall automatically stand dismissed, with costs to be taxed against the party plaintiff. For the purposes of this Code section, an order of continuance will be deemed an order. When an action is dismissed under this subsection, if the plaintiff recommences the action within six months following the dismissal then the renewed action shall stand upon the same footing, as to limitation, with the original action.

Laws 1966, p. 609, § 41; Laws 1982, p. 784, §§ 1, 2; Laws 1984, p. 597, § 2; Laws 1985, p. 546, § 1; Laws 1986, p. 816, § 1; Laws 2003, Act 363, § 4, eff. July 1, 2003.

§ 9-11-42. Consolidation; separate trials

(a) *Consolidation.* When actions involving a common question of law or fact are pending before the court, if the parties consent, the court may order a joint hearing or trial of any or all the matters in issue in the actions; it may order all the actions consolidated; and it may make such orders concerning proceedings therein as may tend to avoid unnecessary costs or delay.

(b) *Separate trials.* The court, in furtherance of convenience or to avoid prejudice, may order a separate trial of any claim, cross-claim, counterclaim, or third-party claim, or of any separate issue, or of any number of claims, cross-claims, counterclaims, third-party claims, or issues.

Laws 1966, p. 609, § 42.

§ 9-11-43. Evidence

(a) *Evidence on trials.* In all trials the testimony of witnesses shall be taken orally in open court unless otherwise provided by this chapter or by statute.

(b) *Evidence on motions.* When a motion is based on facts not appearing of record, the court may hear the matter on affidavits presented by the respective parties, but the court may direct that the matter be heard wholly or partly on oral testimony or depositions; provided, however, that this provision shall not limit the right of parties to use depositions where they would otherwise be entitled to do so.

(c) *Determination of the law of other jurisdictions.* A party who intends to raise an issue concerning the law of another state or of a foreign country shall give notice in his pleadings or other reasonable written notice. The court, in determining such law, may consider any relevant material or source, including testimony, whether or not submitted by a party or admissible under the rules of evidence. The court's determination shall be treated as a ruling on a question of law.

Laws 1966, p. 609, § 43; Laws 1968, p. 1104, § 10.

§ 9–11–44. Official record

(a) *Proof of lack of record.* A written statement, signed by an officer having the custody of an official record or by his deputy, that after diligent search no record or entry of a specified tenor is found to exist in the records of his office, accompanied by a certificate attesting to his custody of the official record relating to such matters, is admissible as evidence that the records of his office contain no such record or entry.

(b) *Other proof.* This Code section does not prevent the proof of official records or of entry or lack of entry therein by any method authorized by any applicable statutes or by the rules of evidence at common law.

Laws 1967, p. 226, § 20.

§ 9–11–45. Subpoena for taking depositions; place of examination

(a)(1)(A) The clerk of the superior court of the county in which the action is pending or the clerk of any court of record in the county where the deposition is to be taken shall issue subpoenas for the persons sought to be deposed, upon request.

(B) Upon agreement of the parties, an attorney, as an officer of the court, may issue and sign a subpoena for the person sought to be deposed on behalf of a court in which the attorney is authorized to practice or a court for a venue in which a deposition is compelled by the subpoena, if the deposition pertains to an action pending in a court in which the attorney is authorized to practice.

(C) Subpoenas issued pursuant to this paragraph shall be issued and served in accordance with law governing issuance of subpoenas for attendance at court, except as to issuance by an attorney. The subpoena may command the person to whom it is directed to produce and permit inspection and copying of designated books, papers, documents, or tangible things which constitute or contain matters within the scope of the examination permitted by subsection (b) of Code Section 9–11–26, but in that event the subpoena will be subject to subsection (c) of Code Section 9–11–26; or the court, upon motion made promptly and in any event at or before the time specified in the subpoena for compliance therewith, may quash or modify the subpoena if it is unreasonable and oppressive, or condition denial of the motion upon the advancement by the person in whose behalf the subpoena is issued of the reasonable cost of producing the books, papers, documents, or tangible things.

(2) The person to whom the subpoena is directed may, within ten days after the service thereof or on or before the time specified in the subpoena for compliance, if such time is less than ten days after service, serve upon the attorney designated in the subpoena written objection to inspection or copying of any or all of the designated materials. If objection is made, the party serving the subpoena shall not be entitled to inspect and copy the materials except pursuant to an order of the court from which the subpoena was issued. The party serving the subpoena may, if objection has been made, move, upon notice to the deponent, for an order at any time before or during the taking of the deposition, provided that nothing in this Code section shall be construed as requiring the issuance of a subpoena to compel a party to attend and give his deposition or produce documents at the taking of his deposition where a notice of deposition under Code Section 9–11–30 has been given or a request under Code Section 9–11–34 has been served, such notice or request to a party being enforceable by motion under Code Section 9–11–37.

(b) A person who is to give a deposition may be required to attend an examination:

(1) In the county wherein he resides or is employed or transacts his business in person;

(2) In any county in which he is served with a subpoena while therein; or

(3) At any place which is not more than 30 miles from the county seat of the county wherein the witness resides, is employed, or transacts his business in person.

Laws 1967, p. 226, § 19; Laws 1972, p. 510, § 11; Laws 1997, p. 457, § 1.

§ 9–11–46. Exceptions unnecessary

(a) Formal exceptions to rulings or orders of the court are unnecessary. For all purposes for which an exception has heretofore been necessary, it is sufficient that a party, at the time the ruling or order of the court is made or sought, makes known to the court the action which he desires the court to take or his objection to the action of the court and his grounds therefor; and, if a party has no opportunity to object to a ruling or order at the time it is made, the absence of an objection does not thereafter prejudice him.

(b) When motion for mistrial or other like relief is made, the question is thereby presented as to whether the moving party is entitled to the relief therein sought or to any lesser relief, and where such motion is denied in whole or in part, it shall not be necessary that the moving party thereafter renew his motion or otherwise seek further ruling by the court.

Laws 1966, p. 609, § 46.

§ 9–11–47. Jurors

(a) The parties may by written stipulation, filed of record, stipulate that the jury shall consist of any number less than that fixed by statute.

(b) The court may direct that one or two jurors in addition to the regular panel be called and impaneled to sit as alternate jurors. Alternate jurors in the order in which they are called shall replace jurors who become or are found to be unable or disqualified to perform their duties. Alternate jurors shall be drawn in the same manner, shall have the same qualifications, shall be subject to the same examination and challenges, shall take the same oath, and shall have the same functions, powers, facilities, and privileges as the principal jurors. An alternate juror who does not replace a principal juror may be discharged. However, if the court deems it advisable, it may direct that one or more of the alternate jurors be kept in the custody of one or more court officers, separate and apart from the regular jurors, until the jury has agreed upon a verdict. If one or two alternate jurors are called, each party is entitled to one peremptory challenge in addition to those otherwise allowed by law. The additional peremptory challenge may be used only against an alternate juror, and the other peremptory challenges allowed by law shall not be used against the alternates.

Laws 1966, p. 609, § 47; Laws 1967, p. 226, § 34; Laws 1989, p. 243, § 1; Laws 1993, p. 91, § 9.

§ 9-11-48. Reserved

§ 9-11-49. Special verdicts

(a) The court may require a jury to return only a special verdict in the form of a special written finding upon each issue of fact. In that event the court may submit to the jury written questions susceptible of categorical or other brief answer or may submit written forms of several special findings which might properly be made under the pleadings and evidence; or it may use such other method of submitting the issues and requiring the written findings thereon as it deems most appropriate. The court shall give to the jury such explanation and instruction concerning the matter thus submitted as may be necessary to enable the jury to make its findings upon each issue. If in so doing the court omits any issue of fact raised by the pleadings or by the evidence, each party waives his right to a trial by jury of the issues so omitted unless before the jury retires he demands its submission to the jury. As to an issue omitted without such demand, the court may make a finding; or, if it fails to do so, it shall be deemed to have made a finding in accordance with the judgment on the special verdict.

(b) Upon written request by any party made on or before the call of the case for trial, it shall be the duty of the court to require the jury to return only a special verdict, as provided in subsection (a) of this Code section, in any case involving equitable relief, mandamus, quo warranto, prohibition, a declaratory judgment, and in any other case or proceeding where special verdicts may be specifically required by law. The court shall prescribe the form of the questions for submission to the jury.

Laws 1966, p. 609, § 49; Laws 1967, p. 226, § 21; Laws 1972, p. 689, § 8; Laws 1993, p. 91, § 9.

§ 9-11-50. Motion for a directed verdict and for judgment notwithstanding the verdict

(a) *Motion for directed verdict; when made; effect.* A motion for a directed verdict may be made at the close of the evidence offered by an opponent or at the close of the case. A party who moves for a directed verdict at the close of the evidence offered by an opponent may offer evidence in the event that a motion is not granted without having reserved the right to do so and to the same extent as if the motion had not been made. A motion for a directed verdict which is not granted is not a waiver of trial by jury even though all parties to the action have moved for directed verdicts. A motion for a directed verdict shall state the specific grounds therefor. The order of the court granting a motion for a directed verdict is effective without any assent of the jury. If there is no conflict in the evidence as to any material issue and the evidence introduced, with all reasonable deductions therefrom, shall demand a particular verdict, such verdict shall be directed.

(b) *Motion for judgment notwithstanding the verdict--When made; new trial motion.* Whenever a motion for a directed verdict made at the close of all the evidence is denied or for any reason is not granted, the court is deemed to have submitted the action to the jury subject to a later determination of the legal questions raised by the motion. Not later than 30 days after entry of judgment, a party who has moved for a directed verdict may move to have the verdict and any judgment entered thereon set aside and to have judgment entered in accordance with his motion for a directed verdict; or, if a verdict was not returned, such party, within 30 days after the jury has been discharged, may move for judgment in accordance with his motion for a directed verdict. A motion for a new trial may be joined with this motion, or a new trial may be prayed for in the alternative. If a verdict was returned, the court may allow the judgment to stand or may reopen the judgment and either order a new trial or direct the entry of judgment as if the requested verdict had been directed. If no verdict was returned, the court may direct the entry of judgment as if the requested verdict had been directed or may order a new trial.

(c) *Same--Conditional rulings on grant of motion; motion for new trial by losing party.*

(1) If the motion for judgment notwithstanding the verdict provided for in subsection (b) of this Code section is granted, the court shall also rule on the motion for a new trial, if any, by determining whether it should be granted if the judgment is

thereafter vacated or reversed and shall specify the grounds for granting or denying the motion for the new trial. If the motion for a new trial is thus conditionally granted, the order thereon does not affect the finality of the judgment. In case the motion for a new trial has been conditionally granted and the judgment is reversed on appeal, the new trial shall proceed unless the appellate court has otherwise ordered. In case the motion for a new trial has been conditionally denied, the appellee on appeal may assert error in that denial; and, if the judgment is reversed on appeal, subsequent proceedings shall be in accordance with the order of the appellate court.

(2) The party whose verdict has been set aside on motion for judgment notwithstanding the verdict may serve a motion for a new trial not later than 30 days after entry of the judgment notwithstanding the verdict.

(d) *Same--Denial of motion.* If the motion for judgment notwithstanding the verdict is denied, the party who prevailed on that motion may, as appellee, assert grounds entitling him to a new trial in the event the appellate court concludes that the trial court erred in denying the motion for judgment notwithstanding the verdict. If the appellate court reverses the judgment, nothing in this Code section precludes it from determining that the appellee is entitled to a new trial or from directing the trial court to determine whether a new trial shall be granted.

(e) *Erroneous denial of directed verdict.* Where error is enumerated upon an order denying a motion for directed verdict and the appellate court determines that the motion was erroneously denied, it may direct that judgment be entered below in accordance with the motion or may order that a new trial be had, as the court may determine necessary to meet the ends of justice under the facts of the case.

Laws 1966, p. 609, § 50; Laws 1967, p. 226, §§ 22, 43, 48.

§ 9-11-51. Reserved

§ 9-11-52. Findings by the court

(a) In ruling on interlocutory injunctions and in all nonjury trials in courts of record, the court shall upon request of any party made prior to such ruling, find the facts specially and shall state separately its conclusions of law. If an opinion or memorandum of decision is filed, it will be sufficient if the findings and conclusions appear therein. Findings shall not be set aside unless clearly erroneous, and due regard shall be given to the opportunity of the trial court to judge the credibility of the witnesses.

(b) This Code section shall not apply to actions involving uncontested divorce, alimony, and custody of minors, nor to motions except as provided in subsection (b) of Code Section 9-11-41. The requirements of subsection (a) of this Code section may be waived in writing or on the record by the parties.

(c) Upon motion made not later than 20 days after entry of judgment, the court may make or amend its findings or make additional findings and may amend the judgment accordingly. If the motion is made with a motion for new trial, both motions shall be made within 20 days after entry of judgment. The question of the sufficiency of the evidence to support the findings may be raised on appeal whether or not the party raising the question has made in the trial court an objection to findings or a motion for judgment. When findings or conclusions are not made prior to judgment to the extent necessary for review, failure of the losing party to move therefor after judgment shall constitute a waiver of any ground of appeal which requires consideration thereof.

Laws 1969, p. 645, § 1; Laws 1970, p. 170, § 1; Laws 1987, p. 1057, § 1.

Formerly Code 1933, § 81A-152.

§ 9-11-53. Reserved

Article 7

Judgment

§ 9-11-54. Judgments

(a) *Definition.* The term "judgment," as used in this chapter, includes a decree and any order from which an appeal lies.

(b) *Judgment upon multiple claims or involving multiple parties.* When more than one claim for relief is presented in an action, whether as a claim, counterclaim, cross-claim, or third-party claim, or when multiple parties are involved, the court may direct the entry of a final judgment as to one or more but fewer than all of the claims or parties only upon an express determination that there is no just reason for delay and upon an express direction for the entry of judgment. In the absence of such determination and direction, any order or other form of decision, however designated, which adjudicates fewer than all the claims or the rights and liabilities of fewer than all the parties shall not terminate the action as to any of the claims or parties, and the order or other form of decision is subject to revision at any time before the entry of judgment adjudicating all the claims and the rights and liabilities of all the parties.

(c) *Relief granted.*

(1) A judgment by default shall not be different in kind from or exceed in amount that prayed for in the demand for judgment. Except as to a party against whom a judgment is entered by default, every final judgment shall grant the relief to which the party in whose favor it is rendered is entitled, even if the party has not demanded such relief in his pleadings; but the court shall not give the successful party relief, though he may be entitled to it, where the propriety of the relief was not litigated and the opposing party had no opportunity to assert defenses to such relief.

(2) As used in this subsection, the term "action for medical malpractice" means any claim for damages resulting from the death of or injury to any person arising out of:

(A) Health, medical, dental, or surgical service, diagnosis, prescription, treatment, or care rendered by a person authorized by law to perform such services or by any person acting under the supervision and control of a lawfully authorized person; or

(B) Care or service rendered by any public or private hospital, nursing home, clinic, hospital authority, facility, or institution, or by any officer, agent, or employee thereof acting within the scope of his employment.

(3) Notwithstanding paragraph (1) of this subsection, where a claim in an action for medical malpractice does not exceed $10,000.00, a judgment by default shall not be different in kind from or exceed in amount that prayed for in the demand for judgment. Where the claim exceeds $10,000.00, a judgment by default may be rendered for the amount determined upon a trial of the issue of damages, provided notice of the trial is served upon the defaulting party at least three days prior to that trial.

(d) *Costs.* Except where express provision therefor is made in a statute, costs shall be allowed as a matter of course to the prevailing party unless the court otherwise directs; but costs against this state and its officers, agencies, and political subdivisions shall be imposed only to the extent permitted by the law.

Laws 1966, p. 609, § 54; Laws 1976, p. 1047, § 2.

§ 9–11–55. Default

(a) *When case in default; opening as matter of right; judgment.* If in any case an answer has not been filed within the time required by this chapter, the case shall automatically become in default unless the time for filing the answer has been extended as provided by law. The default may be opened as a matter of right by the filing of such defenses within 15 days of the day of default, upon the payment of costs. If the case is still in default after the expiration of the period of 15 days, the plaintiff at any time thereafter shall be entitled to verdict and judgment by default, in open court or in chambers, as if every item and paragraph of the complaint or other original pleading were supported by proper evidence, without the intervention of a jury, unless the action is one ex delicto or involves unliquidated damages, in which event the plaintiff shall be required to introduce evidence and establish the amount of damages before the court without a jury, with the right of the defendant to introduce evidence as to damages and the right of either to move for a new trial in respect of such damages; provided, however, in the event a defendant, though in default, has placed damages in issue by filing a pleading raising such issue, either party shall be entitled, upon demand, to a jury trial of the issue as to damages. An action based upon open account shall not be considered one for unliquidated damages within the meaning of this Code section.

(b) *Opening default.* At any time before final judgment, the court, in its discretion, upon payment of costs, may allow the default to be opened for providential cause preventing the filing of required pleadings or for excusable neglect or where the judge, from all the facts, shall determine that a proper case has been made for the default to be opened, on terms to be fixed by the court. In order to allow the default to be thus opened, the showing shall be made under oath, shall set up a meritorious defense, shall offer to plead instanter, and shall announce ready to proceed with the trial.

Laws 1966, p. 609, § 55; Laws 1967, p. 226, § 24; Laws 1981, p. 769, § 1; Laws 1982, p. 3, § 9.

§ 9–11–56. Summary judgment

(a) *For claimant.* A party seeking to recover upon a claim, counterclaim, or cross-claim or to obtain a declaratory judgment may, at any time after the expiration of 30 days from the commencement of the action or after service of a motion for summary judgment by the adverse party, move with or without supporting affidavits for a summary judgment in his favor upon all or any part thereof.

(b) *For defending party.* A party against whom a claim, counterclaim, or cross-claim is asserted or a declaratory judgment is sought may, at any time, move with or without supporting affidavits for a summary judgment in his favor as to all or any part thereof.

(c) *Motion and proceedings thereon.* The motion shall be served at least 30 days before the time fixed for the hearing. The adverse party prior to the day of hearing may serve opposing affidavits. The judgment sought shall be rendered forthwith if the pleadings, depositions, answers to interrogatories, and admissions on file, together with the affidavits, if any, show that there is no genuine issue as to any material fact and that the moving party is entitled to a judgment as a matter of law; but nothing in this Code section shall be construed as denying to any party the right to trial by jury where there are substantial issues of fact to be determined. A summary judgment may be rendered on the issue of liability alone although there is a genuine issue as to the amount of damage.

(d) *Case not fully adjudicated on motion.* If on motion under this Code section judgment is not rendered upon the whole case or for all the relief asked and a trial is necessary, the court at the hearing of the motion, by examining the pleadings and the evidence before it and by interrogating counsel shall, if practicable, ascertain what material facts exist without substantial controversy and what material facts are actually and in good faith controverted. It shall thereupon make an order specifying the facts that appear without substantial controversy, including the extent to which the amount of damages or other relief is not in controversy, and directing such proceedings in the action as are just. Upon the trial of the action the facts so specified shall be deemed established, and the trial shall be conducted accordingly.

(e) *Form of affidavits; further testimony; defense required.* Supporting and opposing affidavits shall be made on personal knowledge, shall set forth such facts as would be admissible in the evidence, and shall show affirmatively that the affiant is competent to testify to the matters stated therein. Sworn or certified copies of all papers or parts thereof referred to in an affidavit shall be attached thereto or served therewith. The court may permit affidavits to be supplemented or opposed by depositions, answers to interrogatories, or further affidavits. All affidavits shall be filed with the court and copies thereof shall be served on the opposing parties. When a motion for summary judgment is made and supported as provided in this Code section, an adverse party may not rest upon the mere allegations or denials of his pleading, but his response, by affidavits or as otherwise provided in this Code section, must set forth specific facts showing that there is a genuine issue for trial. If he does not so respond, summary judgment, if appropriate, shall be entered against him.

(f) *When affidavits are unavailable.* Should it appear from the affidavits of a party opposing the motion that he cannot, for reasons stated, present by affidavits facts essential to justify his opposition, the court may refuse the application for judgment, or may order a continuance to permit affidavits to be obtained or depositions to be taken or discovery to be had, or may make such other order as is just.

(g) *Affidavits made in bad faith.* Should it appear to the satisfaction of the court at any time that any of the affidavits presented pursuant to this Code section are presented in bad faith or solely for the purpose of delay, the court shall forthwith order the party employing them to pay to the other party the amount of the reasonable expenses which the filing of the affidavits caused him to incur, including reasonable attorney's fees, and any offending party may be adjudged guilty of contempt.

(h) *Appeal.* An order granting summary judgment on any issue or as to any party shall be subject to review by appeal. An order denying summary judgment shall be subject to review by direct appeal in accordance with subsection (b) of Code Section 5–6–34.

Laws 1966, p. 609, § 56; Laws 1967, p. 226, § 25; Laws 1975, p. 757, § 3.

§ 9–11–57. Reserved

§ 9–11–58. Entry of judgment

(a) *Signing.* Except when otherwise specifically provided by statute, all judgments shall be signed by the judge and filed with the clerk. The signature of the judge shall be followed by the spelling of the judge's name and title legibly typed, printed, or stamped. The failure of the judgment to have the typed, printed, or stamped name of the judge shall not invalidate the judgment.

(b) *When judgment entered.* The filing with the clerk of a judgment, signed by the judge, with the fully completed civil case disposition form constitutes the entry of the judgment, and, unless the court otherwise directs, no judgment shall be effective for any purpose until the entry of the same, as provided in this subsection. As part of the filing of the final judgment, a civil case disposition form shall be filed by the prevailing party or by the plaintiff if the case is settled, dismissed, or otherwise disposed of without a prevailing party; provided, however, that the amount of a sealed or otherwise confidential settlement agreement shall not be disclosed on the civil case disposition form. The form shall be substantially in the form prescribed in Code Section 9–11–133. If any of the information required by the form is sealed by the court, the form shall state that fact and the information under seal shall not be provided. The entry of the judgment shall not be made by the clerk of the court until the civil case disposition form is filed. The entry of the judgment shall not be delayed for the taxing of costs. This subsection shall not apply to actions brought pursuant to Code Sections 44–7–50 through 44–7–59.

Laws 1966, p. 609, § 58; Laws 1993, p. 91, § 9; Laws 2000, p. 850, § 2; Laws 2006, Act 660, § 2, eff. July 1, 2006.

§ 9–11–59. Reserved

§ 9–11–60. Relief from judgments

(a) *Collateral attack.* A judgment void on its face may be attacked in any court by any person. In all other instances, judgments shall be subject to attack only by a direct proceeding brought for that purpose in one of the methods prescribed in this Code section.

(b) *Methods of direct attack.* A judgment may be attacked by motion for a new trial or motion to set aside. Judgments may be attacked by motion only in the court of rendition.

(c) *Motion for new trial.* A motion for new trial must be predicated upon some intrinsic defect which does not appear upon the face of the record or pleadings.

(d) *Motion to set aside.* A motion to set aside may be brought to set aside a judgment based upon:

(1) Lack of jurisdiction over the person or the subject matter;

(2) Fraud, accident, or mistake or the acts of the adverse party unmixed with the negligence or fault of the movant; or

(3) A nonamendable defect which appears upon the face of the record or pleadings. Under this paragraph, it is not sufficient that the complaint or other pleading fails to state a claim upon which relief can be granted, but the pleadings must affirmatively show no claim in fact existed.

(e) *Complaint in equity.* The use of a complaint in equity to set aside a judgment is prohibited.

(f) *Procedure; time of relief.* Reasonable notice shall be afforded the parties on all motions. Motions to set aside judgments may be served by any means by which an original complaint may be legally served if it cannot be legally served as any other motion. A judgment void because of lack of jurisdiction of the person or subject matter may be attacked at any time. Motions for new trial must be brought within the time prescribed by law. In all other instances, all motions to set aside judgments shall be brought within three years from entry of the judgment complained of.

(g) *Clerical mistakes.* Clerical mistakes in judgments, orders, or other parts of the record and errors therein arising from oversight or omission may be corrected by the court at any time of its own initiative or on the motion of any party and after such notice, if any, as the court orders.

(h) *Law of the case rule.* The law of the case rule is abolished; but generally judgments and orders shall not be set aside or modified without just cause and, in setting aside or otherwise modifying judgments and orders, the court shall consider whether rights have vested thereunder and whether or not innocent parties would be injured thereby; provided, however, that any ruling by the Supreme Court or the Court of Appeals in a case shall be binding in all subsequent proceedings in that case in the lower court and in the Supreme Court or the Court of Appeals as the case may be.

Laws 1966, p. 609, § 60; Laws 1967, p. 226, §§ 26, 27, 30; Laws 1974, p. 1138, § 1; Laws 1984, p. 22, § 9; Laws 1986, p. 294, § 1; Laws 1987, p. 564, § 1.

§ 9-11-61. Harmless error

No error in either the admission or the exclusion of evidence and no error or defect in any ruling or order or in anything done or omitted by the court or by any of the parties is ground for granting a new trial or for setting aside a verdict or for vacating, modifying, or otherwise disturbing a judgment or order, unless refusal to take such action appears to the court inconsistent with substantial justice. The court at every stage of the proceeding must disregard any error or defect in the proceeding which does not affect the substantial rights of the parties.

Laws 1966, p. 609, § 61.

§ 9-11-62. Stay of proceedings to enforce a judgment

(a) *Stay upon entry of judgment.* No execution shall issue upon a judgment nor shall proceedings be taken for its enforcement until the expiration of ten days after its entry, except that, in the case of a default judgment, execution may issue and enforcement proceedings may be taken at any time after entry of judgment and except that, in any case in which both the plaintiff or plaintiffs and the defendant or defendants agree, in writing, and file a copy of such agreement with the clerk of the court, execution may issue and enforcement proceedings may be taken at any time after entry of judgment. Unless otherwise ordered by the court, an interlocutory or final judgment in an action for an injunction or in a receivership action shall not be stayed during the period after its entry and until an appeal is taken or during the pendency of an appeal. Subsection (c) of this Code section governs the suspending, modifying, restoring, or granting of an injunction during the pendency of an appeal.

(b) *Stay on motion for new trial or for judgment.* The filing of a motion for a new trial or motion for judgment notwithstanding the verdict shall act as supersedeas unless otherwise ordered by the court; but the court may condition supersedeas upon the giving of bond with good security in such amounts as the court may order.

(c) *Injunction pending appeal.* When an appeal is taken from an interlocutory or final judgment granting, dissolving, or denying an injunction, the court in its discretion may suspend, modify, restore, or grant an injunction during the pendency of the appeal upon such terms as to bond or otherwise as it considers proper for the security of the rights of the adverse party.

(d) *Stay in favor of the state or agency thereof.* When an appeal is taken by the state or by any county, city, or town within the state, or an officer or agency thereof, and the operation or enforcement of the judgment is stayed, no bond, obligation, or other security shall be required from the appellant.

(e) *Power of appellate court not limited.* The provisions in this Code section do not limit any power of an appellate court or of a judge or justice thereof to stay proceedings during the pendency of an appeal or to suspend, modify, restore, or grant an injunction during the pendency of an appeal or to make any order appropriate to preserve that status quo or the effectiveness of the judgment subsequently to be entered.

(f) *Stay of judgment as to multiple claims or multiple parties.* When a court has ordered a final judgment under the conditions stated in subsection (b) of Code Section 9–11–54, the court may stay enforcement of that judgment until the entering of a subsequent judgment or judgments and may prescribe such conditions as are necessary to secure the benefit thereof to the party in whose favor the judgment is entered.

Laws 1966, p. 609, § 62; Laws 1967, p. 226, § 28; Laws 1970, p. 550, § 1; Laws 1972, p. 689, § 9; Laws 1973, p. 693, § 1.

Article 8

Provisional and Final Remedies and Special Proceedings

§ 9–11–63. Reserved

§ 9–11–64. Reserved

§ 9–11–65. Injunctions; restraining orders

(a) *Interlocutory injunction.*

(1) NOTICE. No interlocutory injunction shall be issued without notice to the adverse party.

(2) CONSOLIDATION OF HEARING WITH TRIAL ON MERITS. Before or after the commencement of the hearing of an application for an interlocutory injunction, the court may order the trial of the action on the merits to be advanced and consolidated with the hearing of the application. Even when this consolidation is not ordered, any evidence received upon an application for an interlocutory injunction which would be admissible upon the trial on the merits shall become a part of the record on the trial and need not be repeated upon the trial. This paragraph shall be construed and applied so as to save any rights of the parties which they may have to trial by jury.

(b) *Temporary restraining order; when granted without notice; duration; hearing; application to dissolve or modify.* A temporary restraining order may be granted without written or oral notice to the adverse party or his attorney only if:

(1) It clearly appears from specific facts shown by affidavit or by the verified complaint that immediate and irreparable injury, loss, or damage will result to the applicant before the adverse party or his attorney can be heard in opposition; and

(2) The applicant's attorney certifies to the court, in writing, the efforts, if any, which have been made to give the notice and the reasons supporting the party's claim that notice should not be required.

Every temporary restraining order granted without notice shall be endorsed with the date and hour of issuance, shall be filed forthwith in the clerk's office and entered of record, and shall expire by its terms within such time after entry, not to exceed 30 days, as the court fixes, unless the party against whom the order is directed consents that it may be extended for a longer period. In case a temporary restraining order is granted without notice, the motion for an interlocutory injunction shall be set down for hearing at the earliest possible time and shall take precedence over all matters except older matters of the same character; when the motion comes on for hearing, the party who obtained the temporary restraining order shall proceed with the application for an interlocutory injunction; and, if he does not do so, the court shall dissolve the temporary restraining order. On two days' notice to the party who obtained the temporary restraining order without notice or on such shorter notice to that party as the court may prescribe, the adverse party may appear and move its dissolution or modification; and in that event the court shall proceed to hear and determine the motion as expeditiously as the ends of justice require.

(c) *Security.* As a prerequisite to the issuance of a restraining order or an interlocutory injunction, the court may require the giving of security by the applicant, in such sum as the court deems proper, for the payment of such costs and damages as may be incurred or suffered by any party who is found to have been enjoined or restrained wrongfully. A surety upon a bond or undertaking under this Code section submits himself to the jurisdiction of the court and irrevocably appoints the clerk of the court as his agent upon whom any papers affecting his liability on the bond or undertaking may be served. His liability may be enforced on motion without the necessity of an independent action. The motion and such notice of the motion as the court prescribes may be served on the clerk of the court, who shall forthwith mail copies to the persons giving the security if their addresses are known.

(d) *Form and scope of injunction or restraining order.* Every order granting an injunction and every restraining order shall be specific in terms; shall describe in reasonable detail, and not by reference to the complaint or other document, the act or acts sought to be restrained; and is binding only upon the parties to the action, their officers, agents, servants, employees, and attorneys, and upon those persons in active concert or participation with them who receive notice of the order by personal service or otherwise.

(e) *When inapplicable.* This Code section is not applicable to actions for divorce, alimony, separate maintenance, or custody of children. In such actions, the court may make prohibitive or mandatory orders, with or without notice or bond, and upon such terms and conditions as the court may deem just.

Laws 1966, p. 609, § 65; Laws 1967, p. 226, § 31; Laws 1972, p. 689, §§ 10, 11.

§ 9-11-66. Receivers

An action wherein a receiver has been appointed shall not be dismissed except by order of the court.

Laws 1966, p. 609, § 66.

§ 9-11-67. Deposit in court

In an action in which any part of the relief sought is a judgment for a sum of money or the disposition of any other thing capable of delivery, a party, upon notice to every other party, and by leave of court, may deposit with the court all or any part of such sum or thing to be held by the clerk of the court, subject to withdrawal, in whole or in part, at any time thereafter upon order of the court, upon posting of sufficient security. Where the thing deposited is money, interest thereupon shall abate.

Laws 1966, p. 609, § 67.

§ 9-11-68. Written offers to settle tort claims; liability of refusing party for attorney's fees and expenses

(a) At any time more than 30 days after the service of a summons and complaint on a party but not less than 30 days (or 20 days if it is a counteroffer) before trial, either party may serve upon the other party, but shall not file with the court, a written offer, denominated as an offer under this Code section, to settle a tort claim for the money specified in the offer and to enter into an agreement dismissing the claim or to allow judgment to be entered accordingly. Any offer under this Code section must:

(1) Be in writing and state that it is being made pursuant to this Code section;

(2) Identify the party or parties making the proposal and the party or parties to whom the proposal is being made;

(3) Identify generally the claim or claims the proposal is attempting to resolve;

(4) State with particularity any relevant conditions;

(5) State the total amount of the proposal;

(6) State with particularity the amount proposed to settle a claim for punitive damages, if any;

(7) State whether the proposal includes attorney's fees or other expenses and whether attorney's fees or other expenses are part of the legal claim; and

(8) Include a certificate of service and be served by certified mail or statutory overnight delivery in the form required by Code Section 9-11-5.

(b)(1) If a defendant makes an offer of settlement which is rejected by the plaintiff, the defendant shall be entitled to recover reasonable attorney's fees and expenses of litigation incurred by the defendant or on the defendant's behalf from the date of the rejection of the offer of settlement through the entry of judgment if the final judgment is one of no liability or the final judgment obtained by the plaintiff is less than 75 percent of such offer of settlement.

(2) If a plaintiff makes an offer of settlement which is rejected by the defendant and the plaintiff recovers a final judgment in an amount greater than 125 percent of such offer of settlement, the plaintiff shall be entitled to recover reasonable attorney's fees and expenses of litigation incurred by the plaintiff or on the plaintiff's behalf from the date of the rejection of the offer of settlement through the entry of judgment.

(c) Any offer made under this Code section shall remain open for 30 days unless sooner withdrawn by a writing served on the offeree prior to acceptance by the offeree, but an offeror shall not be entitled to attorney's fees and costs under subsection (b) of this Code section to the extent an offer is not open for at least 30 days (unless it is rejected during that 30 day period). A counteroffer shall be deemed a rejection but may serve as an offer under this Code section if it is specifically denominated as an offer under this Code section. Acceptance or rejection of the offer by the offeree must be in writing and served upon the offeror. An offer that is neither withdrawn nor accepted within 30 days shall be deemed rejected. The fact that an offer is made but not accepted does not preclude a subsequent offer. Evidence of an offer is not admissible except in proceedings to enforce a settlement or to determine reasonable attorney's fees and costs under this Code section.

(d)(1) The court shall order the payment of attorney's fees and expenses of litigation upon receipt of proof that the judgment is one to which the provisions of either paragraph (1) or paragraph (2) of subsection (b) of this Code section apply; provided, however, that if an appeal is taken from such judgment, the court shall order payment of such attorney's fees and expenses of litigation only upon remittitur affirming such judgment.

(2) If a party is entitled to costs and fees pursuant to the provisions of this Code section, the court may determine that an offer was not made in good faith in an order setting forth the basis for such a determination. In such case, the court may disallow an award of attorney's fees and costs.

(e) Upon motion by the prevailing party at the time that the verdict or judgment is rendered, the moving party may request that the finder of fact determine whether the opposing party presented a frivolous claim or defense. In such event, the court shall hold a separate bifurcated hearing at which the finder of fact shall make a determination of whether such frivolous claims or defenses were asserted and to award damages, if any, against the party presenting such frivolous claims or defenses. Under this subsection:

(1) Frivolous claims shall include, but are not limited to, the following:

(A) A claim, defense, or other position that lacks substantial justification or that is not made in good faith or that is made with malice or a wrongful purpose, as those terms are defined in Code Section 51-7-80;

(B) A claim, defense, or other position with respect to which there existed such a complete absence of any justiciable issue of law or fact that it could not be reasonably believed that a court would accept the asserted claim, defense, or other position; and

(C) A claim, defense, or other position that was interposed for delay or harassment;

(2) Damages awarded may include reasonable and necessary attorney's fees and expenses of litigation; and

(3) A party may elect to pursue either the procedure specified in this subsection or the procedure specified in Code Section 9-15-14, but not both.

Laws 2005, Act 1, § 5, eff. Feb. 16, 2005; Laws 2006, Act 589, § 1, eff. April 27, 2006.

§ 9-11-69. Discovery in aid of execution

Process to enforce a judgment for the payment of money shall be a writ of execution unless the court directs otherwise. In aid of the judgment or execution, the judgment creditor, or his successor in interest when that interest appears of record, may do any or all of the following:

(1) Examine any person, including the judgment debtor by taking depositions or propounding interrogatories;

(2) Compel the production of documents or things; and

(3) Upon a showing of reasonable necessity, obtain permission from a court of competent jurisdiction to enter upon that part of real property belonging to or lawfully occupied by the debtor which is not used as a residence and which property is not bona fide in the lawful possession of another;

in the manner provided in this chapter for such discovery measures prior to judgment.

Laws 1966, p. 609, § 69; Laws 1967, p. 226, § 32; Laws 1987, p. 816, § 1.

§ 9-11-70. Judgment for specific acts; vesting title

A decree for specific performance shall operate as a deed to convey land or other property without any conveyance being executed by the vendor. The decree, certified by the clerk, shall be recorded in the registry of deeds in the county where the land lies and shall stand in the place of a deed. In all other cases where a judgment directs a party to perform other specific acts and the party fails to comply within the time specified, the court may direct the acts to be done at the cost of the disobedient party by some other person appointed by the court; and acts when so done have like effect as if done by the party. The court may also in proper cases adjudge the party in contempt. If real or personal property is within the state, the court in lieu of directing a conveyance thereof may enter a judgment divesting the title of any party and vesting it in others; and the judgment has the effect of a conveyance executed in due form of law. When any order or judgment is for the delivery of possession, the party in whose favor it is entered is entitled to a writ of execution upon oral or written application to the clerk.

Laws 1966, p. 609, § 70.

Article 9

General Provisions

§§ 9-11-71 to 9-11-77. Reserved

§ 9-11-78. Motion day

Unless local conditions make it impracticable, each court shall establish regular times and places, at intervals sufficiently frequent for the prompt dispatch of business, at which motions requiring notice and hearing may be heard and disposed of; but the judge at any time or place and on such notice, if any, as is reasonable may make orders for the advancement, conduct, and hearing of actions.

Laws 1966, p. 609, § 78.

§ 9-11-79. Reserved

§ 9-11-80. Reserved

§ 9-11-81. Applicability

This chapter shall apply to all special statutory proceedings except to the extent that specific rules of practice and procedure in conflict herewith are expressly prescribed by law; but, in any event, the provisions of this chapter governing the sufficiency of pleadings, defenses, amendments, counterclaims, cross-claims, third-party practice, joinder of parties and causes, making parties, discovery and depositions, interpleader, intervention, evidence, motions, summary judgment, relief from judgments, and the effect of judgments shall apply to all such proceedings.

Laws 1966, p. 609, § 81; Laws 1967, p. 226, § 33; Laws 1968, p. 1104, § 12.

§ 9-11-82. Jurisdiction and venue unaffected

This chapter shall not be construed to extend or limit the jurisdiction of the courts or the venue of actions therein.

Laws 1966, p. 609, § 82.

§ 9-11-83. Local court rules

Each court by action of a majority of the judges thereof may from time to time make and amend rules governing its practice not inconsistent with this chapter or any other statute.

Laws 1966, p. 609, § 83.

§ 9-11-84. Forms

The forms contained in Code Sections 9-11-101 through 9-11-132 are sufficient under this chapter and are intended to indicate the simplicity and brevity of statement which this chapter contemplates.

Laws 1966, p. 609, § 84; Laws 1967, p. 226, § 49.

§ 9-11-85. Title

This chapter may be known and cited as the "Georgia Civil Practice Act."

Laws 1966, p. 609, § 85.

Article 10

Forms

§ 9-11-100. Reserved

§ 9-11-101. Form of summons

IN THE ____ COURT OF ____ COUNTY

STATE OF GEORGIA

A.B.,)
)
Plaintiff)
)
)
)
v.) Civil action
) File no. _____
)
C.D.,) (Clerk will insert
Defendant) number.)

SUMMONS

To the above-named defendant:

You are hereby summoned and required to file with the clerk of said court and serve upon _____, plaintiff's attorney, whose address is _____, an answer to the complaint which is herewith served upon you, within 30 days after service of this summons upon you, exclusive of the day of service. If you fail to do so, judgment by default will be taken against you for the relief demanded in the complaint.

____
Clerk of court

Laws 1966, p. 609, § 101.

§ 9-11-102. Reserved

§ 9-11-103. Form of complaint on a promissory note

IN THE ____ COURT OF ____ COUNTY

STATE OF GEORGIA

A.B.,)
)
Plaintiff)
)
)
v.) Civil action
) File no. _____
C.D.,) (Clerk will insert
Defendant) number.)

COMPLAINT

The defendant C.D., herein named, is a resident of _____ (street), _____ (city), _____ County, Georgia, and is subject to the jurisdiction of this court.

—1.—

Defendant on or about June 1, 1965, executed and delivered to plaintiff a promissory note in the following words and figures: (here set out the note verbatim); (a copy of which is hereto annexed as Exhibit A); whereby defendant promised to pay to plaintiff or order on June 1, 1966, the sum of $10,000.00 with interest thereon at the rate of 6 percent per annum.

—2.—

Defendant owes to plaintiff the amount of said note and interest.

Wherefore, plaintiff demands judgment against defendant for the sum of $10,000.00, interest, costs, and attorney fees (where applicable).

____
Attorney for plaintiff

____
Address

Laws 1966, p. 609, § 103; Laws 1980, p. 649, § 1.

§ 9-11-104. Form of complaint on an account

IN THE _____ COURT OF _____ COUNTY

STATE OF GEORGIA

A.B.,)
)
Plaintiff)
)
)
v.) Civil action
) File no. _____
C.D.,) (Clerk will insert
Defendant) number.)

—COMPLAINT—

The defendant C.D., herein named, is a resident of _____ (street), _____ (city), _____ County, Georgia, and is subject to the jurisdiction of this court.

Defendant owes plaintiff $10,000.00 according to the account hereto annexed as Exhibit A.

Wherefore, plaintiff demands judgment against defendant for the sum of $10,000.00, interest, costs, and attorney fees (where applicable).

____
Attorney for plaintiff

____
Address

Laws 1966, p. 609, § 104; Laws 1980, p. 649, § 2.

§ 9-11-105. Form of complaint for goods sold and delivered

IN THE _____ COURT OF _____ COUNTY

STATE OF GEORGIA

A.B.,)
)
Plaintiff)
)
)
v.) Civil action
) File no. _____
C.D.,) (Clerk will insert
Defendant) number.)

—COMPLAINT—

The defendant C.D., herein named, is a resident of _____ (street), _____ (city), _____ County, Georgia, and is subject to the jurisdiction of this court.

Defendant owes plaintiff $10,000.00 for goods sold and delivered by plaintiff to defendant between June 1, 1966, and December 1, 1966.

Wherefore, plaintiff demands judgment against defendant for the sum of $10,000.00, interest, costs, and attorney fees (where applicable).

____
Attorney for plaintiff

____
Address

Laws 1966, p. 609, § 105; Laws 1980, p. 649, § 3.

§ 9-11-106. Form of complaint for money lent

IN THE _____ COURT OF _____ COUNTY

STATE OF GEORGIA

A.B.,)
)
Plaintiff)
)
)
v.) Civil action
) File no. _____
C.D.,) (Clerk will insert
Defendant) number.)

—COMPLAINT—

The defendant C.D., herein named, is a resident of ____ (street), ____ (city), ____ County, Georgia, and is subject to the jurisdiction of this court.

Defendant owes plaintiff $10,000.00 for money lent by plaintiff to defendant on June 1, 1966.

Wherefore, plaintiff demands judgment against defendant for the sum of $10,000.00, interest, costs, and attorney fees (where applicable).

____
Attorney for plaintiff

____
Address

Laws 1966, p. 609, § 106; Laws 1980, p. 649, § 4.

§ 9-11-107. Form of complaint for money paid by mistake

IN THE ____ COURT OF ____ COUNTY

STATE OF GEORGIA

A.B.,)
)
Plaintiff)
)
)
v.) Civil action
) File no. ____
C.D.,) (Clerk will insert
Defendant) number.)

—COMPLAINT—

The defendant C.D., herein named, is a resident of ____ (street), ____ (city), ____ County, Georgia, and is subject to the jurisdiction of this court.

Defendant owes plaintiff $10,000.00 for money paid by plaintiff to defendant by mistake on June 1, 1966, under the following circumstances: (Here state the circumstances with particularity).

Wherefore, plaintiff demands judgment against defendant for the sum of $10,000.00, interest, costs, and attorney fees (where applicable).

____
Attorney for plaintiff

____
Address

Laws 1966, p. 609, § 107; Laws 1980, p. 649, § 5.

§ 9-11-108. Form of complaint for money had and received

IN THE ____ COURT OF ____ COUNTY

STATE OF GEORGIA

A.B.,)
)
Plaintiff)
)
)
v.) Civil action
) File no. ____
C.D.,) (Clerk will insert
Defendant) number.)

—COMPLAINT—

The defendant C.D., herein named, is a resident of ____ (street), ____ (city), ____ County, Georgia, and is subject to the jurisdiction of this court.

Defendant owes plaintiff $10,000.00 for money had and received from one G.H. on June 1, 1966, to be paid by defendant to plaintiff.

Wherefore, plaintiff demands judgment against defendant for the sum of $10,000.00, interest, costs, and attorney fees (where applicable).

____
Attorney for plaintiff

____
Address

Laws 1966, p. 609, § 108; Laws 1980, p. 649, § 6.

§ 9-11-109. Form of complaint for negligence

IN THE ____ COURT OF ____ COUNTY

STATE OF GEORGIA

A.B.,)
)
Plaintiff)
)
)
v.) Civil action
) File no. ____
C.D.,) (Clerk will insert
Defendant) number.)

—COMPLAINT—

The defendant C.D., herein named, is a resident of ____ (street), ____ (city), ____ County, Georgia, and is subject to the jurisdiction of this court.

—1.—

On June 1, 1966, on a public highway called Broad Street in Athens, Georgia, defendant negligently drove a motor vehicle against plaintiff who was then crossing said highway.

—2.—

As a result plaintiff was thrown down and had his leg broken and was otherwise injured, was prevented from transacting his business, suffered great pain of body and mind, and incurred expenses for medical attention and hospitalization in the sum of $1,000.00.

Wherefore, plaintiff demands judgment against defendant in the sum of $10,000.00 and costs.

____
Attorney for plaintiff

____
Address

Laws 1966, p. 609, § 109; Laws 1980, p. 649, § 7.

§ 9-11-110. Form of complaint for negligence where plaintiff is unable to determine definitely whether the person responsible is C. D. or E. F. or whether both are responsible and where his evidence may justify a finding of wilfulness or of recklessness or of negligence

IN THE ____ COURT OF ____ COUNTY

STATE OF GEORGIA

A.B.,)
)
Plaintiff)
)
)
v.) Civil action
) File no. ____
C.D. and E.F.,) (Clerk will insert
Defendant) number.)

—COMPLAINT—

The defendant C.D., herein named, is a resident of ____ (street), ____ (city), ____ County, Georgia, and is subject to the jurisdiction of this court. (Add appropriate statement about domicile of defendant E.F.)

—1.—

On June 1, 1966, on a public highway called Broad Street in Athens, Georgia, defendant C.D. or defendant E.F., or both defendants C.D. and E.F., willfully or recklessly or negligently drove or caused to be driven a motor vehicle against plaintiff who was then crossing said highway.

—2.—

As a result plaintiff was thrown down and had his leg broken and was otherwise injured, was prevented from transacting his business, suffered great pain of body and mind, and incurred expenses for medical attention and hospitalization in the sum of $1,000.00.

Wherefore, plaintiff demands judgment against C.D. or against E.F. or against both in the sum of $10,000.00 and costs.

____
Attorney for plaintiff

____
Address

Laws 1966, p. 609, § 110; Laws 1980, p. 649, § 8.

§ 9-11-111. Form of complaint for conversion

IN THE ____ COURT OF ____ COUNTY

STATE OF GEORGIA

A.B.,)
)
Plaintiff)
)
)
v.) Civil action
) File no. ____
C.D.,) (Clerk will insert
Defendant) number.)

—COMPLAINT—

The defendant C.D., herein named, is a resident of ____ (street), ____ (city), ____ County, Georgia, and is subject to the jurisdiction of this court.

On or about December 1, 1966, defendant converted to his own use ten bonds of the ____ Company (here insert brief identification as by number and issue) of the value of $10,000.00, the property of plaintiff.

Wherefore, plaintiff demands judgment against defendant in the sum of $10,000.00, interest, and costs.

____
Attorney for plaintiff

____
Address

Laws 1966, p. 609, § 111; Laws 1980, p. 649, § 9; Laws 1984, p. 22, § 9.

§ 9-11-112. Form of complaint for specific performance of contract to convey land

IN THE ____ COURT OF ____ COUNTY

STATE OF GEORGIA

A.B.,)
)
Plaintiff)
)
)
v.) Civil action
) File no. ____
C.D.,) (Clerk will insert
Defendant) number.)

—COMPLAINT—

The defendant C.D., herein named, is a resident of ____ (street), ____ (city), ____ County, Georgia, and is subject to the jurisdiction of this court.

—1.—

On or about December 1, 1966, plaintiff and defendant entered into an agreement in writing, a copy of which is hereto annexed as Exhibit A.

—2.—

In accordance with said agreement, plaintiff tendered to defendant the purchase price and requested a conveyance of the land, but defendant refused to accept the tender and refused to make the conveyance.

—3.—

Plaintiff now offers to pay the purchase price.

Wherefore, plaintiff demands:

(1) That defendant be required specifically to perform said agreement,

(2) Damages in the sum of $1,000.00, and

(3) That, if specific performance is not granted, plaintiff have judgment against defendant in the sum of $10,000.00.

____
Attorney for plaintiff

____
Address

Laws 1966, p. 609, § 112; Laws 1980, p. 649, § 10.

§ 9-11-113. Form of complaint on claim for debt and to set aside fraudulent conveyance under section 9-11-18

IN THE ____ COURT OF ____ COUNTY

STATE OF GEORGIA

A.B.,)
)
Plaintiff)
)
)
v.) Civil action
) File no. ____
C.D. and E.F.,) (Clerk will insert
Defendant) number.)

—COMPLAINT—

The defendant C.D., herein named, is a resident of ____ (street), ____ (city), ____ County, Georgia, and is subject to the jurisdiction of this court. (Add appropriate statement about domicile of defendant E.F.)

—1.—

Defendant C.D. on or about ____ executed and delivered to plaintiff a promissory note in the following words and figures: (here set out the note verbatim); (a copy of which is hereto annexed as Exhibit A); whereby defendant C.D. promised to pay to plaintiff or order on ____ the sum of $5,000.00 with interest thereon at the rate of ____ percent per annum.

—2.—

Defendant C.D. owes to plaintiff the amount of said note and interest.

—3.—

Defendant C.D. on or about ____ conveyed all his property, real and personal (or specify and describe), to defendant E.F. for the purpose of defrauding plaintiff and hindering and delaying the collection of the indebtedness evidenced by the note above-referred to.

Wherefore, plaintiff demands:

(1) That plaintiff have judgment against defendant C.D. for $10,000.00 and interest;

(2) That the aforesaid conveyance to defendant E.F. be declared void and the judgment herein be declared a lien on said property;

(3) That plaintiff have judgment against the defendants for costs.

____
Attorney for plaintiff

____
Address

Laws 1966, p. 609, § 113; Laws 1980, p. 649, § 11.

§ 9-11-114. Form of complaint for negligence under Federal Employers' Liability Act

IN THE ____ COURT OF ____ COUNTY

STATE OF GEORGIA

A.B.,)
)
Plaintiff)
)
)
v.) Civil action
) File no. ____
C.D.,) (Clerk will insert
Defendant) number.)

—COMPLAINT—

The defendant C.D., herein named, is a resident of ____ (street), ____ (city), ____ County, Georgia, and is subject to the jurisdiction of this court.

—1.—

During all the times herein mentioned defendant owned and operated in interstate commerce a railroad which passed through a tunnel located at _____ and known as Tunnel No. _____.

—2.—

On or about June 1, 1966, defendant was repairing and enlarging the tunnel in order to protect interstate trains and passengers and freight from injury and in order to make the tunnel more conveniently usable for interstate commerce.

—3.—

In the course of thus repairing and enlarging the tunnel on said day, defendant employed plaintiff as one of its workmen and negligently put plaintiff to work in a portion of the tunnel which defendant had left unprotected and unsupported.

—4.—

By reason of defendant's negligence in thus putting plaintiff to work in that portion of the tunnel, plaintiff was, while so working pursuant to the defendant's orders, struck and crushed by a rock which fell from the unsupported portion of the tunnel and was (here describe plaintiff's injuries).

—5.—

Prior to these injuries, plaintiff was a strong, able-bodied man, capable of earning $_____ per day. By these injuries he has been made incapable of any gainful activity, has suffered great physical and mental pain, and has incurred expense in the amount of $_____ for medicine, medical attendance, and hospitalization.

Wherefore, plaintiff demands judgment against defendant in the sum of $_____ and costs.

____

Attorney for plaintiff

____

Address

Laws 1966, p. 609, § 114; Laws 1980, p. 649, § 12.

§§ 9–11–115 to 9–11–117. Reserved

§ 9–11–118. Form of complaint for interpleader and declaratory relief

IN THE _____ COURT OF _____ COUNTY

STATE OF GEORGIA

A.B.,	)	
	)	
Plaintiff	)	
	)	
	)	
v.	)	Civil action
	)	File no. _____
C.D., E.F., and X.Y.,	)	(Clerk will insert
Defendant	)	number.)

—COMPLAINT—

The defendant C.D., herein named, is a resident of _____ (street), _____ (city), _____ County, Georgia, and is subject to the jurisdiction of this court. (Add appropriate statement about domicile of remaining defendants.)

—1.—

On or about June 1, 1965, plaintiff issued to G.H. a policy of life insurance whereby plaintiff promised to pay to K.L. as beneficiary the sum of $10,000.00 upon the death of G.H. The policy required the payment by G.H. of a stipulated premium on June 1, 1966, and annually thereafter as a condition precedent to its continuance in force.

—2.—

No part of the premium due June 1, 1966, was ever paid and the policy ceased to have any force or effect after July 1, 1966.

—3.—

Thereafter, on September 1, 1966, G.H. and K.L. died as the result of a collision between a locomotive and the automobile in which G.H. and K.L. were riding.

—4.—

Defendant C.D. is the duly appointed and acting executor of the will of G.H., defendant E.F. is the duly appointed and acting executor of the will of K.L., and defendant X.Y. claims to have been duly designated as beneficiary of said policy in place of K.L.

—5.—

Each of the defendants, C.D., E.F., and X.Y., is claiming that the above-mentioned policy was in full force and effect at the time of the death of G.H.; each of them is claiming to be the only person entitled to receive payment of the amount of the policy and has made demand for payment thereof.

—6.—

By reason of these conflicting claims of the defendants, plaintiff is in great doubt as to which defendant is entitled to be paid the amount of the policy if it was in force at the time of death of G.H.

Wherefore, plaintiff demands that the court adjudge:

(1) That none of the defendants is entitled to recover from plaintiff the amount of said policy or any part thereof.

(2) That each of the defendants be restrained from instituting any action against plaintiff for the recovery of the amount of said policy or any part thereof.

(3) That, if the court shall determine that said policy was in force at the death of G.H., the defendants be required to interplead and settle between themselves their rights to the money due under said policy and that plaintiff be discharged from all liability in the premises except to the person whom the court shall adjudge entitled to the amount of said policy.

(4) That plaintiff recover its costs.

____
Attorney for plaintiff

____
Address

Laws 1966, p. 609, § 120; Laws 1980, p. 649, § 13; Laws 1984, p. 22, § 9; Laws 2006, Act 453, § 9, eff. April 14, 2006.

§ 9-11-119. Form of motion to dismiss, presenting defense of failure to state a claim

—IN THE ____ COURT OF ____ COUNTY—

—STATE OF GEORGIA—

A.B.,)
Plaintiff)
) Civil action
v.) File no. ________
)
C.D.,)
Defendant)

—MOTION TO DISMISS—

The defendant moves the court as follows:

1.

To dismiss the action because the complaint fails to state a claim against defendant upon which relief can be granted.

2.

(Additional defenses under subsection (b) of Code Section 9-11-12.)

____
Attorney for defendant

____
Address

—NOTICE OF MOTION—

To: ____________________
Attorney for plaintiff

Please take notice that the undersigned will bring the above motion on for hearing before this court at ____, on the ____ day of ____, ____, at ____: ____ ____.M. or as soon thereafter as counsel can be heard.

____
Attorney for defendant

____
Address

Laws 1966, p. 609, § 121; Laws 1980, p. 649, § 14; Laws 1999, p. 81, § 9.

§ 9-11-120. Form of answer presenting defenses under section 9-11-12(b)

IN THE ____ COURT OF ____ COUNTY

STATE OF GEORGIA

A.B.,)
)
Plaintiff)
)
)
v.) Civil action
) File no. ____
C.D.,)
Defendant)

—ANSWER—

—First Defense—

The complaint fails to state a claim against defendant upon which relief can be granted.

—Second Defense—

If defendant is indebted to plaintiff for the goods mentioned in the complaint, he is indebted to him jointly with G.H. G.H. is alive, is subject to the jurisdiction of the court, and has not been made a party.

—Third Defense—

Defendant admits the allegations contained in paragraphs 1 and 4 of the complaint, alleges that he is without knowledge or information sufficient to form a belief as to the truth of the allegations contained in paragraph 2 of the complaint, and denies each and every other allegation contained in the complaint.

—Fourth Defense—

The right of action set forth in the complaint did not accrue within six years next before the commencement of this action.

—COUNTERCLAIM—

(Here set forth any claim as a counterclaim in the manner in which a claim is pleaded in a complaint.)

—CROSS-CLAIM AGAINST DEFENDANT M.N.—

(Here set forth the claim constituting a cross-claim against defendant M.N. in the manner in which a claim is pleaded in a complaint.)

____
Attorney for defendant

____
Address

Laws 1966, p. 609, § 122; Laws 1980, p. 649, § 15.

§ 9-11-121. Form of answer to complaint set forth in section 9-11-108, with counterclaim for interpleader

IN THE ____ COURT OF ____ COUNTY

STATE OF GEORGIA

A.B.,)
)
Plaintiff)
)
)
v.) Civil action
) File no. ____
C.D.,)
Defendant)

—ANSWER—

—Defense—

Defendant denies the allegations stated to the extent set forth in the counterclaim herein.

—COUNTERCLAIM FOR INTERPLEADER—

—1.—

Defendant received the sum of $10,000.00 as a deposit from E.F.

—2.—

Plaintiff has demanded the payment of such deposit to him by virtue of an assignment of it which he claims to have received from E.F.

—3.—

E.F. has notified the defendant that he claims such deposit, that the purported assignment is not valid, and that he holds the defendant responsible for the deposit.

Wherefore, defendant demands:

(1) That the court order E.F. to be made a party defendant to respond to the complaint and to this counterclaim.

(2) That the court order the plaintiff and E.F. to interplead their respective claims.

(3) That the court adjudge whether the plaintiff or E.F. is entitled to the sum of money.

(4) That the court discharge defendant from all liability in the premises except to the person it shall adjudge entitled to the sum of money.

(5) That the court award to the defendant its costs and attorney's fees.

____
Attorney for defendant

____
Address

Laws 1966, p. 609, § 123; Laws 1980, p. 649, § 16.

§ 9-11-122. Form of summons and complaint against third-party defendant

IN THE ____ COURT OF ____ COUNTY

STATE OF GEORGIA

A.B.,)
)
Plaintiff)
)
)
v.) Civil action
) File no. ____
C.D.,)
)
Defendant and)
Third-Party)
Plaintiff)
v.)
)
)
E.F.,)
)
Third-Party)
Defendant)

—SUMMONS—

To the above-named third-party defendant:

You are hereby summoned and required to file with the clerk of said court and serve upon ____, plaintiff's attorney whose address is ____, and upon ____, who is attorney for C.D., defendant and third-party plaintiff, and whose address is ____, an answer to the third-party complaint which is herewith served upon you, within 30 days after the service of this summons upon you exclusive of the day of service. If you fail to do so, judgment by default will be taken against you for the relief demanded in the third-party complaint. There is also served upon you herewith a copy of the complaint of the plaintiff which you may but are not required to answer.

____
Clerk of court

____

IN THE _____ COURT OF _____ COUNTY

STATE OF GEORGIA

A.B.,
Plaintiff
v. Civil action
File no. _____
C.D.,
Defendant and Third-Party Plaintiff
v.
E.F.,
Third-Party Defendant

—THIRD-PARTY COMPLAINT—

—1.—

Plaintiff, A.B., has filed against defendant, C.D., a complaint, a copy of which is hereto attached as "Exhibit A." A copy of all other pleadings filed prior to the filing of this third-party complaint is hereto attached as "Exhibit B."

—2.—

(Here state the grounds upon which C.D. is entitled to recover from E.F. all or part of what A.B. may recover from C.D. The statements should be framed as in an original complaint.)

Wherefore, C.D. demands judgment against third-party defendant E.F. for all sums that may be adjudged against defendant C.D. in favor of plaintiff A.B.

____
Attorney for C.D., third-party plaintiff

____
Address

Laws 1966, p. 609, § 124; Laws 1969, p. 979, § 2.

§ 9-11-123. Form of motion to intervene as a defendant under section 9-11-24

IN THE _____ COURT OF _____ COUNTY

STATE OF GEORGIA

A.B.,
Plaintiff
v. Civil action
C.D., File no. _____
Defendant
E.F.,
Applicant for Intervention

—MOTION TO INTERVENE AS A DEFENDANT—

E.F. moves for leave to intervene as a defendant in this action, in order to assert the defenses set forth in his proposed answer, of which a copy is hereto attached, on the ground that _____.

____
Attorney for E.F., applicant for intervention

____
Address

—NOTICE OF MOTION—

—(Contents the same as in Code Section 9-11-119)—

IN THE _____ COURT OF _____ COUNTY

STATE OF GEORGIA

A.B.,
Plaintiff
v. Civil action
C.D., File no. _____
Defendant
E.F.,
Intervenor

—INTERVENOR'S ANSWER—

—First Defense—

Intervenor admits the allegations stated in paragraphs 1 and 4 of the complaint, denies the allegations in paragraph 3, and denies the allegations in paragraph 2 insofar as they assert the _____.

—Second Defense—

(Set forth defenses)

____
Attorney
for E.F., intervenor

____
Address

(Like form if intervention is as plaintiff).

Laws 1966, p. 609, § 125; Laws 1984, p. 22, § 9.

§ 9–11–124. Form of motion for production of documents, etc., under section

—IN THE ____ COURT OF ____ COUNTY—

—STATE OF GEORGIA—

A.B., Plaintiff
v.) Civil action) File no. ________
C.D., Defendant

—MOTION FOR PRODUCTION OF DOCUMENTS—

Plaintiff A.B. moves the court for an order requiring defendant C.D.:

1.

To produce and to permit plaintiff to inspect and to copy each of the following documents: (Here list the documents and describe each of them).

2.

To produce and to permit plaintiff to inspect and to photograph each of the following objects: (Here list the objects and describe each of them).

3.

To permit plaintiff to enter (here describe property to be entered) and to inspect and to photograph (here describe the portion of the real property and the objects to be inspected and photographed).

Defendant C.D. has the possession, custody, or control of each of the foregoing documents and objects and of the above-mentioned real estate. Each of them constitutes or contains evidence relevant and material to a matter involved in this action, as is more fully shown in Exhibit A hereto attached.

____
Attorney for plaintiff

____
Address

—NOTICE OF MOTION—

—(Contents the same as in Code Section 9–11–119)—

—EXHIBIT A—

—AFFIDAVIT—

State of ____,

County of ____

A.B., being first duly sworn says:

1.

(Here set forth all that plaintiff knows which shows that defendant has the papers or objects in his possession or control.)

2.

(Here set forth all that plaintiff knows which shows that each of the above-mentioned items is relevant to some issue in the action.)

Sworn to and subscribed before me this ____ day of ____, ____.

____
A.B.,

____
Address

Laws 1966, p. 609, § 126; Laws 1980, p. 649, § 17; Laws 1999, p. 81, § 9.

§ 9–11–125. Form of request for admission under section 9–11–36

IN THE ____ COURT OF ____ COUNTY

STATE OF GEORGIA

A.B., Plaintiff
v.) Civil action) File no. ____
C.D., Defendant

—REQUEST FOR ADMISSION OF FACTS AND GENUINENESS OF DOCUMENTS—

Plaintiff A.B. requests defendant C.D. within ____ days after service of this request to make the following admissions for the purpose of this action only and subject to all pertinent objections to admissibility which may be interposed at the trial:

—1.—

That each of the following documents exhibited with this request is genuine: (Here list the documents and describe each document).

—2.—

That each of the following statements is true: (Here list the statements).

____
Attorney for plaintiff

____
Address

Laws 1966, p. 609, § 127; Laws 1980, p. 649, § 18.

§§ 9–11–126 to 9–11–130. Reserved

§ 9–11–131. Form of judgment on jury verdict

—IN THE _____ COURT OF _____ COUNTY—

—STATE OF GEORGIA—

A.B.,)
Plaintiff)
) Civil action
v.) File no. __________
)
C.D.,)
Defendant)

—JUDGMENT—

This action came on for trial before the court and a jury, Honorable John Marshall, presiding, and the issue having been duly tried and the jury having duly rendered its verdict,

It Is Ordered and Adjudged

(That the plaintiff A.B. recover of the defendant C.D. the sum of $ _____, with interest thereon at the rate of _____ percent as provided by law, and his costs of action.)

or

(That the plaintiff take nothing, that the action be dismissed on the merits, and that the defendant C.D. recover of the plaintiff A.B. his costs of action.)

Dated at _____, Georgia, this _____ day of _____, _____.

____
Judge

Laws 1966, p. 609, § 133; Laws 1980, p. 649, § 19; Laws 1999, p. 81, § 9.

§ 9–11–132. Form of judgment on decision by the court

—IN THE _____ COURT OF _____ COUNTY—

—STATE OF GEORGIA—

A.B.,)
Plaintiff)
) Civil action
v.) File no. __________
)
C.D.,)
Defendant)

—JUDGMENT—

This action came on for (trial) (hearing) before the court, Honorable John Marshall, presiding, and the issues having been duly (tried) (heard) and a decision having been duly rendered,

It Is Ordered and Adjudged

(That the plaintiff A.B. recover of the defendant C.D. the sum of $ _____, with interest thereon at the rate of _____ percent as provided by law, and his costs of action.)

or

(That the plaintiff take nothing, that the action be dismissed on the merits, and that the defendant C.D. recover of the plaintiff A.B. his costs of action.)

Dated at _____, Georgia, this _____ day of _____, _____.

____
Judge

Laws 1966, p. 609, § 134; Laws 1980, p. 649, § 20; Laws 1982, p. 3, § 9; Laws 1999, p. 81, § 9.

§ 9–11–133. Civil case filing and disposition forms

(a) The forms set out in subsections (b), (c), (d) and (e) or forms substantially similar to such forms are sufficient to meet the requirements for civil case filing and disposition forms. The civil case forms set out in Exhibit F of the "Report and Recommendations of the 1997–1998 Court Filings Committee" published by the State Bar of Georgia and dated May 15, 1998, are substantially similar to the forms set out in this Code section.

(b) *General Civil Case Filing Information Form.*

—GENERAL CIVIL CASE FILING—

—INFORMATION FORM—

—(NONDOMESTIC)—

Court
___ Superior County ______________ Date filed ____________
___ State mm-dd-yyyy

Docket no. ______________________________

Plaintiff(s) (last, suffix, first, middle initial, maiden)
1. ____________________
2. ____________________
3. ____________________
4. ____________________

Defendant(s) (last, suffix, first, middle initial, maiden)
1. ____________________
2. ____________________
3. ____________________
4. ____________________

Plaintiff/petitioner's attorney
____________________ ___ Pro Se

Bar #
____

No. of plaintiffs ____________ No. of defendants ____________

CHECK PRIMARY CASE TYPE:
(Check only ONE)
___ Contract/Account
___ Wills/Estate
___ Real Property
___ Dispossessory/Distress
___ Personal Property
___ Equity
___ Habeas Corpus
___ Appeals, Reviews
___ Postjudgment Garnishment, Attachment, or Other Relief
___ Nondomestic Contempt
___ Tort (If tort, fill in right column)
___ Other General Civil (specify) ____________

IF TORT IS CASE TYPE:
(Check no more than TWO)
___ Auto Accident
___ Premises Liability
___ Medical Malpractice
___ Other Professional Negligence
___ Product Liability
___ Other (specify) ___
____

Are punitive damages pleaded?
___ Yes ___ No

(c) *Domestic Relations Case Filing Information Form.*

—DOMESTIC RELATIONS CASE FILING—

—INFORMATION FORM—

Court
___ Superior County ______________ Date filed ____________
mm-dd-yyyy

Docket no. ______________________________

Plaintiff(s) (last, suffix, first, middle initial, maiden)
1. ____________________
2. ____________________

Defendant(s) (last, suffix, first, middle initial, maiden)
1. ____________________
2. ____________________

Plaintiff/Petitioner's attorney
____________________ ___ Pro Se

Bar #
____

CHECK CASE TYPE:
(one or more)
___ Divorce (includes annulment)
___ Separate Maintenance
___ Adoption
___ Paternity (includes legitimation)
___ Interstate Support Enforcement Action
___ Domestication of Foreign Custody Decree

FAMILY VIOLENCE
Additional information-Ex Parte Relief
____

Did the initial pleading include a request for relief:
1. From alleged family violence?
___ Yes ___ No
2. Was ex parte relief requested?
___ Yes ___ No
3. Was ex parte relief granted?

___ Family Violence Act Petition

MODIFICATION
___ Modification—Custody and/or Visitation
___ Modification—Child Support and Alimony
___ Modification—Child Support
___ Modification—Alimony

CONTEMPT
___ Contempt—Custody and/or Visitation
___ Contempt—Child Support and Alimony
___ Contempt—Child Support
___ Contempt—Alimony
___ Other Domestic Contempt

___ Yes ___ No

(d) *General Civil Case Final Disposition Form.*

—GENERAL CIVIL CASE FINAL—

—DISPOSITION FORM—

—(NONDOMESTIC)—

Court
___ Superior County ____________ Date disposed: ____________
___ State mm-dd-yyyy

Docket no. ______________________________

Reporting party ______________ ______________
(Name) (Title)

Name of plaintiff/petitioner(s)
____

Plaintiff/petitioner's attorney ___ Pro Se
____

Bar #
____

Name of defendant/respondent(s)
____

Defendant/respondent's attorney ___ Pro Se
____

Bar #
____

TYPE OF DISPOSITION
1. ___Pretrial Dismissal (specify which type)
 A. ___Involuntary
 B. ___Voluntary (without prejudice)
 C. ___Voluntary (with prejudice)
2. ___Pretrial Settlement
3. ___Default Judgment
4. ___Summary Judgment
5. ___Transferred/Consolidated

6. ___Bench Trial
7. ___Jury Trial (specify outcome further)
 A. ___Dismissal after jury selected
 B. ___Settlement during trial
 C. ___Judgment on Verdict
 D. ___Directed Verdict or JNOV

____

1. Judgment on verdict. Was the verdict:
 A. ___For plaintiff(s) (all)

AWARD
1. If verdict for plaintiff, how much was awarded?
 ________ compensatory
 ________ punitive
2. If verdict on cross or counter claims, how much was awarded?
 $ ________ compensatory
 $ ________ punitive
3. Did the court modify the award?
 ___ Yes ___ No
4. Were attorneys fees awarded?
 ___ Yes ___ No

____

ADR
1. Was ADR utilized?
 ___ Yes ___ No
2. If yes, was it (check if applicable):
 _____ court annexed?
 _____ court mandated?
3. Did the matter settle after trial for other than judgment? (If known at

B. ___For defendant(s) (all)
C. ___Other: (explain) ___
___
___

the time of this submission)
___ Yes ___ No

(e) *Domestic Relations Case Final Disposition Information form.*

—DOMESTIC RELATIONS CASE FINAL—

—DISPOSITION INFORMATION FORM—

Court
___ Superior County ___ Date disposed ___
mm-dd-yyyy

Docket no. ___
Reporting party ___ ___
(Name) (Title)

Name of plaintiff/petitioner(s)
___

Plaintiff/petitioner's attorney ___ Pro Se
___

Bar #
___

Name of defendant/respondent(s)
___

Defendant/respondent's attorney ___ Pro Se
___

Bar #
___

TYPE OF DISPOSITION

1. Dismissed Without Final Order
   A. ___Voluntary (by parties)
   B. ___Involuntary (by court)
2. ___ Pretrial Settlement
3. ___ Judgment on the Pleadings
4. ___ Summary Judgment
5. ___ Trial
   A. Bench Trial
   B. Jury Trial
      1. ___Dismissal after jury selected
      2. ___Settlement during trial
   3. ___ Judgment on Verdict
   4. ___ Directed Verdict or JNOV

RELIEF GRANTED
(Check all that apply)

1. ___Ex Parte Relief
2. ___Temporary Relief
3. ___Final Relief
   A. ___Divorce/Annulment/ Separate Maintenance
   B. ___Child Custody
   C. ___Visitation
   D. ___Child Support
   E. ___Legitimation/ Paternity
   F. ___Alimony
   G. ___Contempt
   H. ___Equitable Division
   I. ___Restraining Order
      ___ Person ___ Property
   J. ___Adoption
   K. ___Other (specify) ___
   ___
4. ___ Dismissed prior to granting of relief.

___

ADR

1. Was mediation utilized?
   ___ Yes ___ No
2. If yes, was it (check if applicable):
   ___ court annexed?
   ___ court mandated?

Laws 2000, p. 850, § 3.

CHAPTER 12

VERDICT AND JUDGMENT

Article 1

General Provisions

§ 9-12-1. Verdict to cover issues

The verdict shall cover the issues made by the pleadings and shall be for the plaintiff or for the defendant.

Formerly Code 1863, § 3479; Code 1868, § 3501; Code 1873, § 3559; Code 1882, § 3559; Civil Code 1895, § 5329; Civil Code 1910, § 5924; Code 1933, § 110-101.

§ 9-12-2. Instructions by judge as to form of verdict

In the trial of all civil cases, the judge upon request of the jury shall furnish the jury with written instructions as to the form of their verdict.

Laws 1880-81, p. 115, § 1.

Formerly Code 1863, § 3480; Code 1868, § 3502; Code 1873, § 3560; Code 1882, § 3560; Civil Code 1895, § 5330; Civil Code 1910, § 5925; Code 1933, § 110-103.

§ 9-12-3. Verdicts received, how

Verdicts shall be received only in open court in the absence of agreement of the parties.

Formerly Code 1863, § 3486; Code 1868, § 3509; Code 1873, § 3567; Code 1882, § 3567; Civil Code 1895, § 5336; Civil Code 1910, § 5931; Code 1933, § 110-107.

§ 9-12-4. Construction of verdicts

Verdicts shall have a reasonable intendment and shall receive a reasonable construction. They shall not be avoided unless from necessity.

Formerly Code 1863, § 3481; Code 1868, § 3503; Code 1873, § 3561; Code 1882, § 3561; Civil Code 1895, § 5332; Civil Code 1910, § 5927; Code 1933, § 110-105.

§ 9-12-5. Molding verdicts

In a proper case, the superior court may mold the verdict so as to do full justice to the parties in the same manner as a decree in equity.

Formerly Code 1863, § 3482; Code 1868, § 3504; Code 1873, § 3562; Code 1882, § 3562; Civil Code 1895, § 5333; Civil Code 1910, § 5928; Code 1933, § 110-106.

§ 9-12-6. Amendment of verdict to conform to pleadings

A verdict may be so amended as to make it conform to the pleadings if the error plainly appears upon the face of the record.

Formerly Code 1863, § 3421; Code 1868, § 3441; Code 1873, § 3491; Code 1882, § 3491; Civil Code 1895, § 5110; Civil Code 1910, § 5694; Code 1933, § 110-110.

§ 9-12-7. Amendment of verdict after dispersion of jury

A verdict may be amended in mere matter of form after the jury has dispersed. However, after a verdict has been received and recorded and the jury has dispersed, it may not be amended in matter of substance either by what the jurors say they intended to find or otherwise.

Formerly Code 1863, § 3422; Code 1868, § 3442; Code 1873, § 3492; Code 1882, § 3492; Civil Code 1895, § 5111; Civil Code 1910, § 5695; Code 1933, § 110-111.

§ 9-12-8. Amendment of verdict where part is legal and part illegal

If a part of a verdict is legal and a part illegal, the court will construe the verdict and order it amended by entering a remittitur as to that part which is illegal and giving judgment for the balance.

Formerly Code 1863, § 3423; Code 1868, § 3443; Code 1873, § 3493; Code 1882, § 3493; Civil Code 1895, § 5112; Civil Code 1910, § 5696; Code 1933, § 110-112.

§ 9-12-9. Judgment to follow verdict

Judgment and execution shall conform to the verdict.

Formerly Code 1863, § 3482; Code 1868, § 3504; Code 1873, § 3562; Code 1882, § 3562; Civil Code 1895, § 5333; Civil Code 1910, § 5928; Code 1933, § 110-301.

§ 9-12-10. Judgment for principal and interest

In all cases where judgment is obtained, the judgment shall be entered for the principal sum due, with interest, provided the claim upon which it was obtained draws interest. No part of the judgment shall bear interest except the principal which is due on the original debt.

Laws 1814, Cobb's 1851 Digest, p. 393.

Formerly Code 1863, § 3489; Code 1868, § 3512; Code 1873, § 3570; Code 1882, § 3570; Civil Code 1895, § 5341; Civil Code 1910, § 5936; Code 1933, § 110-304.

§ 9-12-11. Judgments against sureties and endorsers

In all judgments against sureties or endorsers on any draft, promissory note, or other instrument in writing, the plaintiff or his attorney shall designate and identify the relation of the parties under the contract on which the judgment is rendered.

Laws 1845, Cobb's 1851 Digest, p. 598; Laws 1850, Cobb's 1851 Digest, p. 600.

Formerly Code 1863, § 3491; Code 1868, § 3514; Code 1873, § 3572; Code 1882, § 3572; Civil Code 1895, § 5343; Civil Code 1910, § 5938; Code 1933, § 110-306.

§ 9-12-12. Judgment for costs against executors, etc.

When the verdict of a jury is against an executor, administrator, or other trustee in his representative character, a judgment for costs shall be entered against him in the same character.

Formerly Code 1863, § 3493; Code 1868, § 3516; 1873, § 3574; Code 1882, § 3574; Civil Code 1895, § 5344; Civil Code 1910, § 5939; Code 1933, § 110-307.

§ 9-12-13. Judgment on bonds

All judgments entered against the obligors on any bond, whether official or voluntary, shall be for the amount of damages found by the verdict of the jury and not for the penalty thereof.

Laws 1847, Cobb's 1851 Digest, p. 502.

Formerly Code 1863, § 3494; Code 1868, § 3517; Code 1873, § 3575; Code 1882, § 3575; Civil Code 1895, § 5345; Civil Code 1910, § 5940; Code 1933, § 110-308.

§ 9-12-14. Amendment of judgments

A judgment may be amended by order of the court to conform to the verdict upon which it is predicated, even after an execution issues.

Laws 1902, p. 55, § 1.

Formerly Code 1863, § 3424; Code 1868, § 3444; Code 1873, § 3494; Code 1882, § 3494; Civil Code 1895, § 5113; Civil Code 1910, § 5697; Code 1933, § 110-311.

§ 9-12-15. Amendable defects not ground for arrest

A judgment may not be set aside for any defect in the pleadings or the record that is aided by verdict or amendable as a matter of form.

Laws 1984, p. 22, § 9.

Formerly Code 1863, § 3509; Code 1868, § 3532; Code 1873, § 3590; Code 1882, § 3590; Civil Code 1895, § 5365; Civil Code 1910, § 5960; Code 1933, § 110-705.

§ 9-12-16. Judgments void because of want of jurisdiction of court

The judgment of a court having no jurisdiction of the person or the subject matter or which is void for any other cause is a mere nullity and may be so held in any court when it becomes material to the interest of the parties to consider it.

Formerly Code 1863, § 3513; Code 1868, § 3536; Code 1873, § 3594; Code 1882, § 3594; Civil Code 1895, § 5369; Civil Code 1910, § 5964; Code 1933, § 110-709.

§ 9-12-17. Judgments attacked by creditors or bona fide purchasers, when

Creditors or bona fide purchasers may attack a judgment for any defect appearing on the face of the record or the pleadings or for fraud or collusion, whenever and wherever it interferes with their rights, either at law or in equity.

Formerly Code 1863, § 3515; Code 1868, § 3538; Code 1873, § 3596; Code 1882, § 3596; Civil Code 1895, § 5371; Civil Code 1910, § 5966; Code 1933, § 110-711.

§ 9-12-18. Where and when confession of judgment allowed

(a) Either party has a right to confess judgment without the consent of his adversary and to appeal from such confession without reserving the right to do so in cases where an appeal is allowed by law.

(b) No confession of judgment shall be entered except in the county where the defendant resided at the commencement of the action unless expressly provided for by law. The action must have been regularly filed and docketed as in other cases. However, a judge of a superior court or a magistrate may confess judgment in his own court.

Laws 1799, Cobb's 1851 Digest, p. 495; Laws 1983, p. 884, § 4-1.

Formerly Code 1863, §§ 3518, 3519, 3520; Code 1868, §§ 3541, 3542, 3543; Code 1873, §§ 3600, 3601, 3602; Code 1882, §§ 3600, 3601, 3602; Civil Code 1895, §§ 5359, 5360, 5361; Civil Code 1910, §§ 5954, 5955, 5956; Code 1933, §§ 110-601, 110-602, 110-603.

§ 9-12-19. Appeal suspends judgment

Where a judgment is entered and, within the time allowed for entering an appeal, an appeal is entered, the judgment shall be suspended.

Formerly Code 1863, § 3488; Code 1868, § 3511; Code 1873, § 3569; Code 1882, § 3569; Civil Code 1895, § 5340; Civil Code 1910, § 5935; Code 1933, § 110-303.

§ 9-12-20. Judgment on appeals

In all cases of appeal where security has been given, the plaintiff or his attorney may enter judgment against the principal and his surety jointly and severally.

Laws 1826, Cobb's 1851 Digest, p. 498.

Formerly Code 1863, § 3490; Code 1868, § 3513; Code 1873, § 3571; Code 1882, § 3571; Civil Code 1895, § 5342; Civil Code 1910, § 5937; Code 1933, § 110-305.

§ 9-12-21. Right to transfer; rights and liabilities of transferees

A person in whose favor a judgment has been entered or a person to whom a judgment has been transferred may bona fide and for a valuable consideration transfer any judgment to a third person. In all such cases the transferee of any judgment shall have the same rights and shall be subject to the same equities and to the same defenses as was the original holder of the judgment.

Laws 1829, Cobb's 1851 Digest, p. 499.

Formerly Code 1863, § 3516; Code 1868, § 3539; Code 1873, § 3597; Code 1882, § 3597; Civil Code 1895, § 5374; Civil Code 1910, § 5969; Code 1933, § 110-901.

§ 9-12-22. Transfer by attorney of record; estoppel to deny transaction by ratification

The transfer of a judgment by the attorney of record of the person in whose favor the judgment was entered shall be good to pass the title thereto as against every person except the person in whose favor judgment was entered or his assignee without notice. Ratification by the plaintiff shall estop him also from denying the transfer. Receipt of the money from the transfer shall be such a ratification.

Formerly Code 1863, § 3517; Code 1868, § 3540; Code 1873, § 3598; Code 1882, § 3598; Civil Code 1895, § 5375; Civil Code 1910, § 5970; Code 1933, § 110-902.

§ 9-12-23. Consent to judgment

The consent of the parties to a judgment has the effect of removing any issuable defenses previously filed. After such a consent the court may render judgment without the verdict of a jury.

Laws 1982, p. 1262, § 1.

Article 2

Effect of Judgments

§ 9-12-40. Conclusiveness of judgments

A judgment of a court of competent jurisdiction shall be conclusive between the same parties and their privies as to all matters put in issue or which under the rules of law might have been put in issue in the cause wherein the judgment was rendered until the judgment is reversed or set aside.

Formerly Code 1863, § 3496; Code 1868, § 3519; Code 1873, § 3577; Code 1882, § 3577; Civil Code 1895, §§ 3742, 5348; Civil Code 1910, §§ 4336, 5943; Code 1933, § 110-501.

§ 9-12-41. Judgments in rem

A judgment in rem is conclusive upon everyone.

Formerly Code 1863, § 3750; Code 1868, § 3774; Code 1873, § 3827; Code 1882, § 3827; Civil Code 1895, § 5372; Civil Code 1910, § 5967; Code 1933, § 110-502.

§ 9-12-42. Former judgment not a bar, when

Where the merits were not and could not have been in question, a former recovery on purely technical grounds shall not be a bar to a subsequent action brought so as to avoid the objection fatal to the first. For a former judgment to be a bar to subsequent action, the merits of the case must have been adjudicated.

Formerly Civil Code 1895, § 5095; Civil Code 1910, § 5679; Code 1933, § 110-503.

§ 9-12-43. Parol evidence to show matter covered by judgment

Parol evidence shall be admissible to show that a matter apparently covered by a judgment was not really passed upon by the court.

Formerly Code 1863, § 2839; Code 1868, § 2847; Code 1873, § 2898; Code 1882, § 2898; Civil Code 1895, § 3743; Civil Code 1910, § 4337; Code 1933, § 3-608.

Article 3

Dormancy and Revival of Judgments

§ 9-12-60. Dormancy of judgments

(a) A judgment shall become dormant and shall not be enforced:

(1) When seven years shall elapse after the rendition of the judgment before execution is issued thereon and is entered on the general execution docket of the county in which the judgment was rendered;

(2) Unless entry is made on the execution by an officer authorized to levy and return the same and the entry and the date thereof are entered by the clerk on the general execution docket within seven years after issuance of the execution and its record; or

(3) Unless a bona fide public effort on the part of the plaintiff in execution to enforce the execution in the courts is made and due written notice of such effort specifying the time of the institution of the action or proceedings, the nature thereof, the names of the parties thereto, and the name of the court in which it is pending is filed by the plaintiff in execution or his attorney at law with the clerk and is entered by the clerk on the general execution docket, all at such times and periods that seven years will not elapse between such entries of such notices or between such an entry and a proper entry made as prescribed in paragraph (2) of this subsection.

(b) The record of the execution made as prescribed in paragraph (1) of subsection (a) of this Code section or of every entry as prescribed in paragraph (2) or (3) of subsection (a) of this Code section shall institute a new seven-year period within which the judgment shall not become dormant, provided that when an entry on the execution or a written notice of public effort is filed for record, the execution shall be recorded or rerecorded on the general execution docket with all entries thereon. It shall not be necessary in order to prevent dormancy that such execution be entered or such entry be recorded on any other docket.

(c) When an entry on an execution or a written notice of public effort is filed for record and the original execution is recorded in a general execution docket other than the current general execution docket, the original execution shall be rerecorded in the current general execution docket with all entries thereon. When an original execution is so rerecorded, a notation shall be made upon the original execution which states that it has been rerecorded and gives the book and page number where the execution has been rerecorded. When an original execution is so rerecorded in the current general execution docket, it shall be indexed in the current general execution docket in the same manner as if it were an original execution. Nothing in this subsection shall affect the priority of any judgment or lien; and no judgment or lien shall lose any priority because an execution is rerecorded.

(d) The provisions of subsection (a) of this Code section shall not apply to judgments or orders for child support or spousal support.

Laws 1823, Cobb's 1851 Digest, p. 498; Laws 1855–56, p. 233, § 8; Laws 1884–85, p. 95, § 1; Laws 1910, p. 121, § 1; Laws 1920, p. 81, §§ 1, 3; Laws 1955, p. 417, § 1; Laws 1965, p. 272, § 1; Laws 1984, p. 22, § 9; Laws 1984, p. 912, § 1; Laws 1997, p. 1613, § 2.

Formerly Code 1863, § 2855; Code 1868, § 2863; Code 1873, § 2914; Code 1882, § 2914; Civil Code 1895, §§ 3761, 3762, 3763; Civil Code 1910, §§ 4355, 4356, 4357; Code 1933, § 110–1001.

§ 9–12–61. Manner of renewal of dormant judgments; limitations

When any judgment obtained in any court becomes dormant, the same may be renewed or revived by an action or by scire facias, at the option of the holder of the judgment, within three years from the time it becomes dormant.

Laws 1823, Cobb's 1851 Digest, p. 498; Laws 1910, p. 121, § 1.

Formerly Code 1863, §§ 2855, 3522; Code 1868, §§ 2863, 3545; Code 1873, §§ 2914, 3604; Code 1882, §§ 2914, 3604; Civil Code 1895, §§ 3761, 5378; Civil Code 1910, §§ 4355, 5973; Code 1933, §§ 110–1002, 110–1003.

§ 9–12–62. Scire facias to revive

Scire facias to revive a judgment is not an original action but is the continuation of the action in which the judgment was obtained.

Formerly Code 1863, § 3524; Code 1868, § 3547; Code 1873, § 3606; Code 1882, § 3606; Civil Code 1895, § 5380; Civil Code 1910, § 5975; Code 1933, § 110–1005.

§ 9–12–63. Issuance, return, direction, service, etc., of scire facias

A scire facias to revive a dormant judgment in the courts must issue from and be returnable to the court of the county in which the judgment was obtained. It shall be directed to all and singular the sheriffs of this state and shall be signed by the clerk of such court who shall make out copies thereof. An original and a copy shall issue for each county in which any party to be notified resides. A copy shall be served by the sheriff of the county in which the party to be notified resides 20 days before the sitting of the court to which the scire facias is made returnable and the original shall be returned to the clerk of the court from which it issued.

Formerly Code 1863, § 3525; Code 1868, § 3548; Code 1873, § 3607; Code 1882, § 3607; Civil Code 1895, § 5381; Civil Code 1910, § 5976; Code 1933, § 110–1006.

§ 9–12–64. Judgment of revival, when taken; trial by jury

In all cases of scire facias to revive a judgment, when service has been perfected, the judgment may be revived on motion at the first term without the intervention of a jury unless the person against whom judgment was entered files an issuable defense under oath, in which case the defendant in judgment shall be entitled to a trial by jury as in other cases.

Formerly Code 1863, § 3527; Code 1868, § 3550; Code 1873, § 3609; Code 1882, § 3609; Civil Code 1895, § 5383; Civil Code 1910, § 5978; Code 1933, § 110–1008.

§ 9–12–65. Scire facias in favor of transferee

When a judgment has been transferred, the scire facias shall issue in the name of the original holder of the judgment for the use of the transferee.

Laws 1982, p. 3, § 9.

Formerly Code 1863, § 3528; Code 1868, § 3551; Code 1873, § 3610; Code 1882, § 3610; Civil Code 1895, § 5384; Civil Code 1910, § 5979; Code 1933, § 110–1009.

§ 9–12–66. Actions to renew judgments, where brought

An action to renew a dormant judgment shall be brought in the county where the defendant in judgment resides at the commencement of the action.

Formerly Code 1863, § 3523; Code 1868, § 3546; Code 1873, § 3605; Code 1882, § 3605; Civil Code 1895, § 5379; Civil Code 1910, § 5974; Code 1933, § 110–1004.

§ 9–12–67. Revival of judgments against nonresidents

If the defendant in judgment or other party to be notified resides outside this state, a dormant judgment may be revived against such defendant or his representative by such process as is issued in cases in which the defendant resides in this state, provided that the defendant in judgment or other party to be notified shall be served with scire facias by publication in the newspaper in which the official advertisements of the county are published, twice a month for two months previous to the term of the court at which it is intended to revive the judgment, which service shall be as effectual in all cases as if the defendant or person to be notified had been personally served.

Laws 1850, Cobb's 1851 Digest, p. 502; Laws 1982, p. 3, § 9; Laws 1984, p. 22, § 9.

Formerly Code 1863, § 3526; Code 1868, § 3549; Code 1873, § 3608; Code 1882, § 3608; Civil Code 1895, § 5382; Civil Code 1910, § 5977; Code 1933, § 110-1007.

§ 9-12-68. Dormant decrees; revival

Decrees for the payment of money shall become dormant like other judgments when not enforced and may be revived as provided by law for other judgments.

Formerly Code 1863, § 4128; Code 1868, § 4160; Code 1873, § 4219; Code 1882, § 4219; Civil Code 1895, § 4861; Civil Code 1910, § 5434; Code 1933, § 37-1211.

Article 4

Judgment Liens

§ 9-12-80. Dignity and binding effect of judgments

All judgments obtained in the superior courts, magistrate courts, or other courts of this state shall be of equal dignity and shall bind all the property of the defendant in judgment, both real and personal, from the date of such judgments except as otherwise provided in this Code.

Laws 1799, Cobb's 1851 Digest, p. 494; Laws 1810, Cobb's 1851 Digest, p. 495; Laws 1983, p. 884, § 4-1.

Formerly Code 1863, § 3499; Code 1868, § 3522; Code 1873, § 3580; Code 1882, § 3580; Civil Code 1895, § 5351; Civil Code 1910, § 5946; Code 1933, § 110-507.

§ 9-12-81. General execution docket

(a) The clerk of the superior court of each county shall be required to keep a general execution docket.

(b) As against the interest of third parties acting in good faith and without notice who have acquired a transfer or lien binding the property of the defendant in judgment, no money judgment obtained within the county of the defendant's residence in any court of this state or federal court in this state shall create a lien upon the property of the defendant unless the execution issuing thereon is entered upon the execution docket. When the execution has been entered upon the docket, the lien shall date from such entry.

Laws 1889, p. 106, § 2; Laws 1921, p. 115, § 1; Laws 1955, p. 425, § 1.

Formerly Civil Code 1895, § 2779; Civil Code 1910, § 3321; Code 1933, § 39-701.

§ 9-12-82. Judgments take effect against property out of county, when; lien against defendant not resident of county

As against bona fide purchasers for value without actual notice of a judgment or other third parties acting in good faith and without notice who have acquired a transfer or lien binding the defendant's property, no money judgment obtained in any court of this state or federal court in this state outside the county of the defendant's residence shall create a lien upon the property of the defendant located in any county other than that where obtained unless the execution issuing thereon is entered upon the general execution docket of the county of the defendant's residence within 30 days from the date of the judgment. When the execution is entered upon the docket after the 30 days, the lien shall date from such entry.

Laws 1822, Cobb's 1851 Digest, p. 497; Laws 1851-52, p. 238, § 1; Laws 1878-79, p. 143, § 2; Laws 1889, p. 1006, § 3.

Formerly Code 1863, § 3502; Code 1868, § 3525; Code 1873, § 3583; Code 1882, § 3583; Civil Code 1895, §§ 2780, 5356; Civil Code 1910, §§ 3322, 5951; Code 1933, §§ 39-702, 110-512.

§ 9-12-83. Judgments as lien on land in county other than where obtained

No money judgment obtained in any court of this state or federal court in this state shall create any lien on land in any county other than that in which it was obtained as against the interests of third parties acting in good faith and without notice who have acquired a transfer or lien binding defendant's property unless at the time of the transfer or the acquisition of the lien the execution was recorded on the general execution docket in the county in which such land is located.

Laws 1914, p. 98, § 2.

Formerly Code 1933, § 39-703.

§ 9-12-84. Judgment against nonresidents recorded on general execution docket; creation of lien

(a) As against the interests of third parties acting in good faith and without notice who have acquired a transfer or lien binding any real estate situated in this state owned by a nonresident, no money judgment obtained in any court of this state or federal court in this state against the nonresident shall create a lien upon the real estate of the nonresident unless the execution issuing thereon is entered upon the general execution docket of the county in which the real estate is situated. When the execution is entered upon the docket, the lien shall date from such entry.

(b) Nothing in this Code section shall be construed to affect the validity or force of any judgment as between the parties thereto.

Laws 1890–91, p. 207, §§ 1, 2.

Formerly Civil Code 1895, §§ 2783, 2784; Civil Code 1910, §§ 3325, 3326; Code 1933, §§ 39–706, 39–707.

§ 9–12–85. Validity of lien as between parties unaffected

Nothing in Code Sections 9–12–81 and 9–12–82 shall be construed to affect the validity or force of any deed, mortgage, judgment, or other lien of any kind as between the parties thereto.

Laws 1889, p. 106, § 4.

Formerly Civil Code 1895, § 2781; Civil Code 1910, § 3323; Code 1933, § 39–704.

§ 9–12–86. Necessity for filing and indexing judgments, decrees or orders, or writs of fieri facias issued thereunder, before title to real property is affected

(a) For purposes of this Code section, the term "applicable records" shall include deed books, lis pendens dockets, federal tax lien dockets, general execution dockets, and attachment dockets.

(b) No judgment, decree, or order or any writ of fieri facias issued pursuant to any judgment, decree, or order of any superior court, city court, magistrate court, municipal court, or any federal court shall in any way affect or become a lien upon the title to real property until the judgment, decree, order, or writ of fieri facias is recorded in the office of the clerk of the superior court of the county in which the real property is located and is entered in the indexes to the applicable records in the office of the clerk. Such entries and recordings must be requested and paid for by the plaintiff or the defendant, or his attorney at law.

(c) The recording and indexing required by this Code section shall be in addition to and supplemental to all other recording of judgments, decrees, and orders required by law.

(d) This Code section shall only apply to judgments, decrees, or orders rendered after March 25, 1958.

Laws 1958, p. 379, §§ 1–5; Laws 1966, p. 142, §§ 1–3; Laws 1983, p. 884, § 3–5.

§ 9–12–87. Judgments at same term considered of equal date; no preference

(a) All judgments signed on verdicts rendered at the same term of court shall be considered, held, and taken to be of equal date.

(b) In the case of judgments signed on verdicts rendered at the same term of the court, no execution shall be entitled to any preference by reason of being first placed in the hands of the levying officer.

Laws 1822, Cobb's 1851 Digest, p. 497.

Formerly Code 1863, § 3497; Code 1868, § 3520; Code 1873, § 3578; Code 1882, § 3578; Civil Code 1895, § 5349; Civil Code 1910, § 5944; Code 1933, §§ 39–112, 110–505.

§ 9–12–88. First judgment prevents alienation in cases of appeal

In all cases in which a judgment is rendered and an appeal is entered from the judgment, the property of the defendant in judgment shall not be bound by the judgment except so far as to prevent the alienation by the defendant of his property between its signing and the signing of the judgment on the appeal, but the property shall be bound from the signing of the judgment on the appeal.

Laws 1812, Cobb's 1851 Digest, p. 496.

Formerly Code 1863, § 3500; Code 1868, § 3523; Code 1873, § 3581; Code 1882, § 3581; Civil Code 1895, § 5352; Civil Code 1910, § 5947; Code 1933, § 110–508.

§ 9–12–89. Rank of judgments affirmed by appellate court

A judgment in the trial court which is taken to the Supreme Court or the Court of Appeals and is affirmed loses no lien or priority by the proceeding in the appellate court.

Formerly Code 1863, § 3498; Code 1868, § 3521; Code 1873, § 3579; Code 1882, § 3579; Civil Code 1895, § 5350; Civil Code 1910, § 5945; Code 1933, § 110–506.

§ 9–12–90. Rank of judgments in actions for damages arising out of common disaster or occurrence

(a) Liens of all judgments obtained in actions for damages growing out of a common disaster or occurrence shall be equal in rank or priority regardless of the date of the rendition of the verdict or the entering of the judgment. However, this Code section shall apply only to judgments obtained in actions which are filed within 12 months from the date of the happening of the disaster or occurrence giving rise to the cause of action.

(b) This Code section applies to all actions filed in the courts of this state in which damages are sought to be recovered on account of injuries sustained in or death resulting from a common disaster or occurrence.

Laws 1947, p. 1138, §§ 1, 2.

§ 9-12-91. Judgment not lien on promissory notes

A judgment creates no lien upon promissory notes in the hands of the defendant.

Formerly Code 1863, § 3501; Code 1868, § 3524; Code 1873, § 3582; Code 1882, § 3582; Civil Code 1895, § 5353; Code 1910, § 5948; Code 1933, § 110-509.

§ 9-12-92. Lien of judgment on property removed from state

When a judgment lien has attached to personal property which is removed to another state and sold, the property shall be subject to the judgment lien if brought back to this state.

Formerly Code 1863, § 3503; Code 1868, § 3526; Code 1873, § 3584; Code 1882, § 3584; Civil Code 1895, § 5357; Civil Code 1910, § 5952; Code 1933, § 110-513.

§ 9-12-93. Lien of judgment on transferred property, when discharged

When any person has bona fide and for a valuable consideration purchased real or personal property and has been in the possession of the real property for four years or of the personal property for two years, such property shall be discharged from the lien of any judgment against the person from whom it was purchased or against any predecessor in title of real or personal property. Nothing contained herein shall be construed to otherwise affect the validity or enforceability of such judgment, except to discharge such property from any such lien of judgment.

Laws 1822, Cobb's 1851 Digest, p. 497; Laws 1851-52, p. 238, § 1; Laws 1994, p. 310, § 1.

Formerly Code 1863, § 3502; Code 1868, § 3525; Code 1873, § 3583; Code 1882, § 3583; Civil Code 1895, § 5355; Civil Code 1910, § 5950; Code 1933, § 110-511.

§ 9-12-94. Clerk's fees

For entering an execution upon the general execution docket, the clerk shall be entitled to the fees enumerated in Code Section 15-6-77.

Laws 1889, p. 106, § 5; Laws 1950, p. 107, § 1; Laws 1971, p. 699, § 3.

Formerly Civil Code 1895, § 2782; Civil Code 1910, § 3324; Code 1933, § 39-705.

Article 5

Georgia Foreign Money Judgments Recognition Act

§ 9-12-110. Short title

This article may be cited as the "Georgia Foreign Money Judgments Recognition Act."

Laws 1975, p. 479, § 8.

§ 9-12-111. Definitions

As used in this article, the term:

(1) "Foreign judgment" means any judgment of a foreign state granting or denying recovery of a sum of money other than a judgment for taxes, a fine or other penalty, or a judgment for support in matrimonial or family matters.

(2) "Foreign state" means any governmental unit other than:

(A) The United States;

(B) Any state, district, commonwealth, territory, or insular possession of the United States; or

(C) The Trust Territory of the Pacific Islands.

Laws 1975, p. 479, § 1.

§ 9-12-112. Applicability

This article applies to any foreign judgment that is final, conclusive, and enforceable where rendered even though an appeal therefrom is pending or it is subject to appeal.

Laws 1975, p. 479, § 2.

§ 9-12-113. Recognition and enforcement

Except as provided in Code Sections 9-12-114 and 9-12-115, a foreign judgment meeting the requirements of Code Section 9-12-112 is conclusive between the parties to the extent that it grants or denies recovery of a sum of money. The foreign judgment is enforceable in the same manner as the judgment of a sister state which is entitled to full faith and credit.

Laws 1975, p. 479, § 3.

§ 9-12-114. Grounds for nonrecognition

A foreign judgment shall not be recognized if:

(1) The judgment was rendered under a system which does not provide impartial tribunals or procedures compatible with the requirements of due process of law;

(2) The foreign court did not have personal jurisdiction over the defendant;

(3) The foreign court did not have jurisdiction over the subject matter;

(4) The defendant in the proceedings in the foreign court did not receive notice of the proceedings in sufficient time to enable him to defend;

(5) The judgment was obtained by fraud;

(6) The cause of action on which the judgment is based is repugnant to the public policy of this state;

(7) The judgment conflicts with another final and conclusive judgment;

(8) The proceedings in the foreign court were contrary to an agreement between the parties under which the dispute in question was to be settled otherwise than by proceedings in that court;

(9) In the case of jurisdiction based only on personal service, the foreign court was a seriously inconvenient forum for the trial of the action; or

(10) The party seeking to enforce the judgment fails to demonstrate that judgments of courts of the United States and of states thereof of the same type and based on substantially similar jurisdictional grounds are recognized and enforced in the courts of the foreign state.

Laws 1975, p. 479, § 4.

§ 9-12-115. Personal jurisdiction

(a) A foreign judgment shall not be refused recognition for lack of personal jurisdiction if:

(1) The defendant was served personally in the foreign state;

(2) The defendant voluntarily appeared in the proceedings other than for the purpose of protecting property seized or threatened with seizure in the proceedings or of contesting the jurisdiction of the court over him;

(3) Prior to the commencement of the proceedings, the defendant had agreed expressly in writing to submit to the jurisdiction of the foreign court, with respect to the subject matter involved in such proceedings, in an action by the party seeking to enforce the judgment;

(4) The defendant was domiciled in the foreign state when the proceedings were instituted or, being a body corporate, then had its principal place of business or was incorporated in the foreign state;

(5) The defendant had a business office in the foreign state and the proceedings in the foreign court involved a cause of action arising out of business done by the defendant through that office in the foreign state; provided, however, that a business office in the foreign state which it maintained for the transaction of business by a subsidiary corporation of the defendant but which is not held out as a business office of the defendant shall not be deemed to be a business office of the defendant; or

(6) The defendant operated a motor vehicle or airplane in the foreign state and the proceedings involved a cause of action arising out of such operation.

(b) The courts of this state may recognize other bases of personal jurisdiction; provided, however, that if the proceedings in the foreign court involved a cause of action arising out of business activities in the foreign state, the judgment shall not be recognized unless there is a basis for personal jurisdiction as specified in subsection (a) of this Code section.

Laws 1975, p. 479, § 5.

§ 9-12-116. Stay in case of appeal

If the defendant satisfies the court either that an appeal is pending or that he is entitled and intends to appeal from the foreign judgment, the court may stay the proceedings until the appeal has been determined or until the expiration of a period of time sufficient to enable the defendant to prosecute the appeal.

Laws 1975, p. 479, § 6.

§ 9-12-117. Saving clause

This article does not prevent the recognition of a foreign judgment in situations not covered by this article.

Laws 1975, p. 479, § 7.

Article 6

Enforcement of Foreign Judgments

§ 9-12-130. Short title

This article may be cited as the "Uniform Enforcement of Foreign Judgments Law."

Laws 1986, p. 380, § 1.

§ 9-12-131. Definition of foreign judgment

As used in this article, the term "foreign judgment" means a judgment, decree, or order of a court of the

United States or of any other court that is entitled to full faith and credit in this state.

Laws 1986, p. 380, § 1.

§ 9-12-132. Filing, status, and effect

A copy of any foreign judgment authenticated in accordance with an act of Congress or statutes of this state may be filed in the office of the clerk of any court of competent jurisdiction of this state. The clerk shall treat the foreign judgment in the same manner as a judgment of the court in which the foreign judgment is filed. A filed foreign judgment has the same effect and is subject to the same procedures, defenses, and proceedings for reopening, vacating, staying, enforcing, or satisfying as a judgment of the court in which it is filed and may be enforced or satisfied in like manner.

Laws 1986, p. 380, § 1.

§ 9-12-133. Affidavit and notice of filing

(a) At the time a foreign judgment is filed, the judgment creditor or the judgment creditor's attorney shall make and file with the clerk of the court an affidavit showing the name and last known post office address of the judgment debtor and the judgment creditor.

(b) The clerk shall promptly mail notice of the filing of the foreign judgment to the judgment debtor at the address given and shall note the mailing in the docket. The notice must include the name and post office address of the judgment creditor and, if the judgment creditor has an attorney in this state, the attorney's name and address. The judgment creditor may mail a notice of the filing of the judgment to the judgment debtor and may file proof of mailing with the clerk. Lack of mailing notice of filing by the clerk does not affect the enforcement proceedings if proof of mailing by the judgment creditor has been filed.

Laws 1986, p. 380, § 1.

§ 9-12-134. Stay of enforcement; security pending stay

(a) If the judgment debtor shows the court that an appeal from the foreign judgment is pending or will be taken or that a stay of execution has been granted and proves that the judgment debtor has furnished the security for the satisfaction of the judgment required by the state in which it was rendered, the court shall stay enforcement of the foreign judgment until the appeal is concluded, the time for appeal expires, or the stay of execution expires or is vacated.

(b) If the judgment debtor shows the court any ground on which enforcement of a judgment of the court of this state would be stayed, including the ground that an appeal from the foreign judgment is pending or will be taken or that the time for taking such an appeal has not yet expired, the court shall stay enforcement of the foreign judgment for an appropriate period until all available appeals are concluded or the time for taking all appeals has expired and require the same security for satisfaction of the judgment that is required in this state, subject to the provisions of subsections (b) and (f) of Code Section 5-6-46.

Laws 1986, p. 380, § 1; Laws 2000, p. 228, § 3; Laws 2004, Act 778, § 2, eff. May 17, 2004.

§ 9-12-135. Fees

A person filing a foreign judgment shall pay to the clerk of court the same sums as in civil cases in superior court as provided in Code Section 15-6-77. Fees for other enforcement proceedings shall be as otherwise provided by law.

Laws 1986, p. 380, § 1; Laws 1988, p. 320, § 1; Laws 1991, p. 1324, § 3.

§ 9-12-136. Optional procedures

The judgment creditor retains the right to bring an action to enforce a judgment instead of proceeding under this article.

Laws 1986, p. 380, § 1.

§ 9-12-137. Construction

This article shall be interpreted and construed to achieve its general purposes to make the law of those states which enact it uniform.

Laws 1986, p. 380, § 1.

§ 9-12-138. Applicability

This article shall apply to foreign judgments of other states only if those states have adopted the "Uniform Enforcement of Foreign Judgments Act" in substantially the same form as this article.

Laws 1986, p. 380, § 1.

CHAPTER 13
EXECUTIONS AND JUDICIAL SALES

Article 1
General Provisions

§ 9-13-1. When execution to issue

No execution shall issue until judgment is entered and signed by the party in whose favor verdict was rendered or by his attorney, or by the presiding judge or justice.

Laws 1799, Cobb's 1851 Digest, p. 494.

Formerly Code 1863, § 3487; Code 1868, § 3510; Code 1873, § 3568; Code 1882, § 3568; Civil Code 1895, § 5339; Civil Code 1910, § 5934; Code 1933, § 39-102.

§ 9-13-2. Time of issuance; suspension by appeal

If execution is issued before the expiration of the time allowed for entering an appeal, the execution will be suspended on the entering of an appeal by either party.

Formerly Code 1863, § 3556; Code 1868, § 3579; Code 1873, § 3634; Code 1882, § 3634; Civil Code 1895, § 5415; Civil Code 1910, § 6020; Code 1933, § 39-115.

§ 9-13-3. Execution to follow the judgment

Every execution shall follow the judgment upon which it issued and shall describe the parties thereto as described in the judgment.

Formerly Code 1863, § 3558; Code 1868, § 3581; Code 1873, § 3636; Code 1882, § 3636; Civil Code 1895, § 5417; Civil Code 1910, § 6022; Code 1933, § 39-104.

§ 9-13-4. Judge may frame executions

The judge of any superior court may frame and cause to be issued by the clerk thereof any writ of execution to carry into effect any lawful judgment or decree rendered in his court.

Formerly Code 1863, § 3561; Code 1868, § 3584; Code 1873, § 3639; Code 1882, § 3639; Civil Code 1895, § 5420; Civil Code 1910, § 6025; Code 1933, § 39-105.

§ 9-13-5. Amendment to conform to judgment

A writ of fieri facias may be amended so as to conform to the judgment upon which it issued and to the time of its return; and such amendments shall in no manner affect the validity of the writ of fieri facias, nor shall the levy of the writ fall or be in any manner invalidated thereby.

Laws 1890-91, p. 76, § 1.

Formerly Code 1863, § 3425; Code 1868, § 3445; Code 1873, § 3495; Code 1882, § 3495; Civil Code 1895, § 5114; Civil Code 1910, § 5698; Code 1933, § 39-109.

§ 9-13-6. Amendment to conform to amended judgment

Where a judgment has been amended by order of the court in conformity to the verdict upon which it is predicated and execution has previously issued thereon, the clerk of the court in which the judgment was rendered shall have power to amend the execution at any time so as to make it conform to the amended judgment; and such amendment shall not cause any levy on the execution to fall.

Laws 1902, p. 55, § 1.

Formerly Code 1863, § 3424; Code 1868, § 3444; Code 1873, § 3494; Code 1882, § 3494; Civil Code 1895, § 5113; Civil Code 1910, § 5697; Code 1933, § 39-110.

§ 9-13-7. Mistakes in execution amendable

(a) When the clerk of any court has made any mistake in issuing an execution, the clerk or any of his successors in office may correct the mistake by amending the execution and shall note and certify on the execution the fact that the amendment was made by him.

(b) Alternatively, the clerk may issue an alias execution to be signed and dated by him at the time it is issued instead of the execution in which the mistake was made. The clerk shall note the fact of the issuing of the alias on the original, which original shall remain on file in his office, and shall likewise make a memorandum thereof on the execution docket; he shall also transcribe upon the alias all the entries and credits from the original. No order of court shall be necessary in the cases contemplated by this Code section.

Laws 1869, p. 137, § 1.

Formerly Code 1873, § 3496; Code 1882, § 3496; Civil Code 1895, § 5115; Civil Code 1910, § 5699; Code 1933, § 39-111.

§ 9-13-8. When execution lost, alias may issue

(a) When an execution which was regularly issued from a court is lost or destroyed, the judge or justice of the court from which the same was issued may at any time, upon proper application and proof of the facts by the affidavit of the applicant, his agent, or his attorney or by any other satisfactory proof, grant an order for the issuing of an alias execution in lieu of the lost original execution. The alias execution shall have all the legal force and effect of the lost or destroyed original execution.

(b) When an execution which was regularly issued by an officer of the state as authorized by law is lost or destroyed, the state officer or the successor to the state officer by whom the same was issued may at any time issue an alias execution in lieu of the lost original execution. The alias execution shall be dated the same date as the original execution and the officer shall endorse the word "alias" on the alias execution. The alias execution shall have all the legal force and effect of the lost or destroyed original execution.

(c) When an execution which was regularly issued by an officer of a county or local government as authorized by law is lost or destroyed, the judge of the probate court of the county in which the original execution was issued may issue an alias execution upon the filing by the party having the right to control the original execution of a statement under oath of the loss or destruction of such original execution. The judge shall endorse the word "alias" on the alias execution. The alias execution shall have all the legal force and effect of the lost or destroyed original execution.

Laws 1857, p. 104, § 1; Laws 1985, p. 1243, § 1.

Formerly Code 1863, § 3892; Code 1868, § 3912; Code 1873, § 3988; Code 1882, § 3988; Civil Code 1895, § 4752; Civil Code 1910, § 5321; Code 1933, § 63-210.

§ 9-13-9. Term of court to which execution returnable

All executions, except as otherwise provided by this Code, shall be made returnable to the next term of the court from which they issued.

Formerly Code 1863, § 3557; Code 1868, § 3580; Code 1873, § 3635; Code 1882, § 3635; Civil Code 1895, § 5416; Civil Code 1910, § 6021; Code 1933, § 39-125.

§ 9-13-10. How executions issued, directed, and levied

Except as otherwise provided by law, executions shall be issued by the clerk of the court in which judgment is obtained, shall bear teste in the name of the judge of such court, shall bear date from the time of their issuing, shall be directed "To all and singular the sheriffs of this state and their lawful deputies," and may be levied on all the estate of the defendant, both real and personal, which is subject to levy and sale.

Laws 1799, Cobb's 1851 Digest, p. 510.

Formerly Code 1863, § 3553; Code 1868, § 3576; Code 1873, § 3632; Code 1882, § 3632; Civil Code 1895, § 5413; Civil Code 1910, § 6018; Code 1933, § 39-101.

§ 9-13-11. When sheriff is a party, how directed and executed

All executions, orders, decrees, attachments for contempt, and final process issued by the clerks of the courts in favor of or against any sheriff shall be directed to the coroner of the county in which the sheriff resides and to all and singular the sheriffs of the state, except the sheriff of the county in which the interested sheriff resides, and may be levied, served, and returned by the coroner, other sheriff, or constable of the county at the option of the plaintiff or the party seeking the remedy.

Laws 1847, Cobb's 1851 Digest, p. 517.

Formerly Code 1863, § 3554; Code 1868, § 3577; Code 1873, § 3633; Code 1882, § 3633; Civil Code 1895, § 5414; Civil Code 1910, § 6019; Code 1933, § 39-114.

§ 9-13-12. Form of entry of levy

The officer making a levy shall enter the same on the process by virtue of which levy is made and in the entry shall plainly describe the property levied on and the amount of the interest of defendant therein.

Formerly Code 1863, § 3569; Code 1868, § 3592; Code 1873, § 3640; Code 1882, § 3640; Civil Code 1895, § 5421; Civil Code 1910, § 6026; Code 1933, § 39-103.

§ 9-13-13. Notice of levy on land

(a) In all cases of levying on land, written notice of the levy must be given personally or delivered by certified mail or statutory overnight delivery to the tenant in possession and to the defendant if not in possession.

(b) The officer levying on land under an execution, within five days thereafter, shall leave a written notice of the levy with the tenant in possession of the land, if any; and, if the defendant is not in possession, the officer shall also leave a written notice with the defendant if he is in the county or shall transmit the notice by mail to the defendant within the time aforesaid.

Laws 1808, Cobb's 1851 Digest, p. 509; Laws 1847, Cobb's 1851 Digest, p. 516; Laws 1990, p. 298, § 1; Laws 2000, p. 1589, § 3.

Formerly Code 1863, §§ 3572, 3573; Code 1868, §§ 3595, 3596; Code 1873, §§ 3643, 3644; Code 1882, §§ 3643, 3644; Civil Code 1895, §§ 5426, 5428; Civil Code 1910, §§ 6031, 6033; Code 1933, §§ 39-120, 39-122.

§ 9-13-14. Bonds taken by executing officers, valid; rights of plaintiffs not affected by taking of bond

(a) All bonds taken by sheriffs or other executing officers from defendants in execution for the delivery of property, on the day of sale or any other time, which they may have levied on by virtue of any fi. fa. or other legal process from any court shall be good and valid in law and recoverable in any court having jurisdiction thereof.

(b) No bond taken in conformity with subsection (a) of this Code section shall in any case prejudice or affect the rights of the plaintiff in execution; the bond shall relate to and have effect solely between the officer to whom it is given and the defendant in execution. The officer shall in no case excuse himself for not having made the money on an execution by having taken the bond but shall be liable to be ruled as prescribed by law.

Laws 1829, Cobb's 1851 Digest, pp. 534, 535.

Formerly Code 1863, §§ 3599, 3600; Code 1868, §§ 3623, 3624; Code 1873, §§ 3673, 3674; Code 1882, §§ 3673, 3674; Civil Code 1895, §§ 5436, 5437; Civil Code 1910, §§ 6041, 6042; Code 1933, §§ 39-302, 39-303.

§ 9-13-15. Measure of damages on forthcoming bond

Whenever personal property is levied upon under any judicial process from the courts of this state and a forthcoming bond is given for the same, the measure of damages to be recovered upon the bond shall be the value of the property at the time of its delivery under the bond, with interest thereon; and, if the property deteriorates in value by reason of being used by the person giving the bond or otherwise and is then delivered to the officer making the seizure, the officer or the plaintiff in execution may recover on the bond the difference between the value at the time of the delivery of the property under the bond and its value when turned over to the officer making the levy, with interest thereon. The amount of damages shall in no case exceed the amount due on the execution levied.

Laws 1893, p. 123, § 1.

Formerly Civil Code 1895, § 5438; Civil Code 1910, § 6043; Code 1933, § 39-304.

§ 9-13-16. Fraudulent levies

Any person who fraudulently causes any process, attachment, distress, or execution to be levied on any estrayed animal, lot of land, or other property, knowing that the same is not subject to the process or writ, shall, for the first offense, be guilty of a misdemeanor. For any subsequent conviction, the person shall be sentenced to confinement for not less than two nor more than four years.

Laws 1837, Cobb's 1851 Digest, pp. 849, 850; Laws 1865-66, p. 233, § 14.

Formerly Code 1863, § 4333; Code 1868, § 4369; Code 1873, § 4436; Code 1882, § 4436; Penal Code 1895, § 218; Penal Code 1910, § 215; Code 1933, § 39-9901.

Article 2

Parties in Execution

§ 9-13-30. Execution against sureties and endorsers

When, in a judgment against sureties or endorsers on a draft, promissory note, or other instrument in writing, the plaintiff or his attorney has designated and identified the relation of the parties under the contract on which the judgment was rendered, execution shall issue accordingly.

Laws 1845, Cobb's 1851 Digest, p. 598; Laws 1850, Cobb's 1851 Digest, p. 600.

Formerly Code 1863, § 3491; Code 1868, § 3514; Code 1873, § 3572; Code 1882, § 3572; Civil Code 1895, § 5343; Civil Code 1910, § 5938; Code 1933, § 39-107.

§ 9-13-31. Execution against principal and surety on appeal

In all cases of appeal where security has been given and judgment has been entered against the principal and surety, jointly and severally, execution shall issue accordingly and shall proceed against either or both at the option of the plaintiff until his debt is satisfied.

Formerly Code 1863, § 3490; Code 1868, § 3513; Code 1873, § 3571; Code 1882, § 3571; Civil Code 1895, § 5342; Civil Code 1910, § 5937; Code 1933, § 39-106.

§ 9-13-32. Execution against deceased defendants

On the death of a defendant after final judgment when no execution has been issued prior to such death, execution may issue as though the death had not taken place.

Laws 1873, p. 21, § 1.

Formerly Code 1863, § 3370; Code 1868, § 3389; Code 1873, § 3437; Code 1882, § 3437; Civil Code 1895, § 5034; Civil Code 1910, § 5616; Code 1933, § 3–419.

§ 9–13–33. Executions in favor of or against partners

Executions issued in favor of or against partners, where the partnership style is used therein instead of the individual names of the persons composing the firm, shall be valid.

Formerly Code 1863, § 3495; Code 1868, § 3518; Code 1873, § 3576; Code 1882, § 3576; Civil Code 1895, § 5346; Civil Code 1910, § 5941; Code 1933, § 39–108.

§ 9–13–34. Right to transfer; rights and liabilities of transferees

Any plaintiff in judgment or transferee may in good faith and for a valuable consideration transfer any execution to a third person. In all cases the transferee of any execution shall have the same rights and shall be subject to the same equities and the same defenses as was the original plaintiff in judgment.

Laws 1829, Cobb's 1851 Digest, p. 499.

Formerly Code 1863, § 3516; Code 1868, § 3539; Code 1873, § 3597; Code 1882, § 3597; Civil Code 1895, § 5374; Civil Code 1910, § 5969; Code 1933, § 39–401.

§ 9–13–35. Transfer by attorney of record; estoppel to deny transaction by ratification

The transfer of an execution by the attorney of record shall be good to pass the title thereto as against every person except the plaintiff in execution or his assignee without notice. Ratification by the plaintiff shall estop him also from denying the transfer. Receipt of the money from the transfer shall be such a ratification.

Formerly Code 1863, § 3517; Code 1868, § 3540; Code 1873, § 3598; Code 1882, § 3598; Civil Code 1895, § 5375; Civil Code 1910, § 5970; Code 1933, § 39–402.

§ 9–13–36. Transfer of execution upon payment by third party; exceptions

(a) Except as otherwise provided for in subsection (b) of this Code section, whenever any person other than the person against whom the same has issued pays any execution, issued without the judgment of a court, under any law, the officer whose duty it is to enforce the execution, upon the request of the party paying the same, shall transfer the execution to the party. The transferee shall have the same rights as to enforcing the execution and priority of payment as might have been exercised or claimed before the transfer, provided that the transferee shall have the execution entered on the general execution docket of the superior court of the county in which the same was issued and, if the person against whom the same was issued resides in a different county, also in the county of such person's residence within 30 days from the transfer; in default thereof the execution shall lose its lien upon any property which has been transferred bona fide and for a valuable consideration before the recordation and without notice of the existence of the execution.

(b) This Code section shall not be applicable to tax executions. Tax executions shall be governed exclusively by Chapters 3 and 4 of Title 48.

Laws 1872, p. 75, § 1; Laws 1875, p. 119, § 1; Laws 1894, p. 37, § 1; Laws 2006, Act 759, § 1, eff. July 1, 2006.

Formerly Code 1873, § 891a; Code 1882, § 891a; Civil Code 1895, § 888; Civil Code 1910, § 1145; Code 1933, § 39–403.

Article 3
Property against which Execution Levied

§ 9–13–50. On what property execution first levied

(a) The defendant in execution shall be at liberty to point out what part of his property he may think proper to be levied on, which property the sheriff or other officer shall be bound to take and sell first if the same is, in the opinion of the levying officer, sufficient to satisfy the judgment and costs.

(b) When a defendant in execution shall point out property on which to levy the execution which is in the possession of a person not a party to the judgment from which the execution issued, the sheriff or other officer shall not levy thereon but shall proceed to levy on such property as may be found in the possession of the defendant.

Laws 1811, Cobb's 1851 Digest, p. 510.

Formerly Code 1863, § 3570; Code 1868, § 3593; Code 1873, § 3641; Code 1882, § 3641; Civil Code 1895, § 5423; Civil Code 1910, § 6028; Code 1933, § 39–116.

§ 9–13–51. Sale of separate parcels subject to lien

Where property is subject to a lien and part of it is sold by the debtor, the part remaining shall be first applied to the payment of the lien. If the property subject to the lien is sold in several parcels at different times, the parcels shall be charged in the inverse order of their alienation.

Formerly Civil Code 1895, § 5424; Civil Code 1910, § 6029; Code 1933, § 39-118.

§ 9-13-52. Officer not to sell land out of his county

A sheriff or other levying officer shall not sell land outside the county in which he is sheriff or such officer except when the defendant in execution owns a tract or tracts of land divided by the line of the county of his residence, in which case the land may be sold in the county of his residence; if such tract of land is in a county other than that of the defendant's residence, it may be levied on and sold in either county.

Laws 1808, Cobb's 1851 Digest, p. 509; Laws 1847, Cobb's 1851 Digest, p. 516.

Formerly Code 1863, § 3573; Code 1868, § 3596; Code 1873, § 3644; Code 1882, § 3644; Civil Code 1895, § 5428; Civil Code 1910, § 6033; Code 1933, § 39-122.

§ 9-13-53. Constable may levy on land, when

No constable, except as provided by this Code, shall be authorized to levy on any real estate unless there is no personal property to be found sufficient to satisfy the debt or unless the real estate, being in the possession of the defendant, was pointed out by the defendant. In such event the constable is authorized to levy on such real estate, if in his county, and to deliver over the execution to the sheriff of the county a return of the property levied upon; and the sheriff shall proceed to advertise and sell the same as in case of levies made by himself.

Formerly Code 1863, § 3574; Code 1868, § 3597; Code 1873, § 3645; Code 1882, § 3645; Civil Code 1895, § 5429; Civil Code 1910, § 6034; Code 1933, § 39-121.

§ 9-13-54. Growing crop to be sold, how

No sheriff or other officer shall levy on any growing crop of corn, wheat, oats, rye, rice, cotton, potatoes, or any other crop usually raised or cultivated by planters or farmers nor sell the same until the crop has matured and is fit to be gathered. However, this Code section shall not prevent any levying officer from levying on and selling crops in cases where the defendant in execution absconds or removes himself from the county or state, or from selling growing crops with the land.

Laws 1836, Cobb's 1851 Digest, p. 514.

Formerly Code 1863, § 3571; Code 1868, § 3594; Code 1873, § 3642; Code 1882, § 3642; Civil Code 1895, § 5425; Civil Code 1910, § 6030; Code 1933, § 39-119.

§ 9-13-55. Seizure of personalty

To authorize a sale of personal property there shall be an actual or constructive seizure.

Formerly Code 1863, § 2581; Code 1868, § 2583; Code 1873, § 2625; Code 1882, § 2625; Civil Code 1895, § 5452; Civil Code 1910, § 6057; Code 1933, § 39-1310.

§ 9-13-56. Seizure of future interest in personalty

A future interest in personalty may not be seized and sold but the lien of judgments shall attach thereto so as to prevent alienation before the right to present possession accrues.

Formerly Code 1863, § 2581; Code 1868, § 2583; Code 1873, § 2625; Code 1882, § 2625; Civil Code 1895, § 5452; Civil Code 1910, § 6057; Code 1933, § 39-1310.

§ 9-13-57. Levy on choses in action

Choses in action are not liable to be seized and sold under execution, unless made so specially by statute.

Formerly Code 1863, § 3501; Code 1868, § 3524; Code 1873, § 3582; Code 1882, § 3582; Civil Code 1895, § 5353; Civil Code 1910, § 5948; Code 1933, § 39-113.

§ 9-13-58. Levy on stock; disclosure of information

Upon demand by any sheriff, constable, or other levying officer having in his hands any execution against any person who is the owner of any shares of stock of a bank or corporation upon the president, superintendent, manager, or other officer having access to the books of the bank or corporation, the president, superintendent, manager, or other officer aforesaid shall disclose to the levying officer the number of shares and the par value thereof owned by the defendant in execution and, on refusal to do so, shall be considered in contempt of court and punished accordingly.

Laws 1822, Cobb's 1851 Digest, p. 511; Laws 1890-91, p. 73, § 1; Laws 1894, p. 45, § 1.

Formerly Code 1863, § 2582; Code 1868, § 2584; Code 1873, § 2626; Code 1882, § 2626; Civil Code 1895, § 5430; Civil Code 1910, § 6035; Code 1933, § 39-123.

§ 9-13-59. Property of joint contractors or of partnership

Where, in an action against two or more joint contractors, joint and several contractors, or partners, service is perfected on only part of the contractors or partners and the officer serving the writ returns that the others are not to be found, the judgment obtained shall bind, and execution may be levied on, the joint or partnership property as well as the individual property, real and personal, of the defendant or defendants who have been served with a copy of the process. However, the judgment shall not bind nor shall execution be levied on the individual property of the defendant or defendants not served with process.

Laws 1820, Cobb's 1851 Digest, p. 485.

Formerly Code 1863, §§ 3263, 3264; Code 1868, §§ 3274, 3275; Code 1873, §§ 3350, 3351; Code 1882, §§ 3350, 3351; Civil Code 1895, §§ 5009, 5010; Civil Code 1910, §§ 5591, 5592; Code 1933, § 39–117.

§ 9–13–60. Where person other than vendor, etc., has judgment; notice of levy and sale must be given

(a) Where any person other than the vendor or other than the holder or assignee of the purchase money or secured debt has a judgment against a defendant in execution who does not hold legal title to property but has an interest or equity therein, such plaintiff in execution may take up the debt necessary to be paid by the defendant in order to give the defendant legal title to the property by paying the debt with interest to date if due and interest to maturity if not due; and thereupon a conveyance to the defendant in execution or, if he is dead, to his executor or administrator shall be made by the vendor or holder of title given to secure the debt or, if dead, by the executor or administrator thereof. When the conveyance has been filed and recorded, the property may be levied on and sold as property of the defendant.

(b) In all cases provided for in subsection (a) of this Code section, notice of the levy and time of sale shall be given by the levying officer to the vendor or holder of the title given to secure the debt, if known, and also to the defendant in execution and, in case of death, to their legal representatives. Depositing a properly addressed and stamped letter into the United States mail shall be deemed sufficient notice under this subsection.

(c) The proceeds of the sale shall be applied first to the payment of liens superior to the claims taken up by the plaintiff in execution, next to the payment of principal advanced by the plaintiff in execution to put title in defendant, with interest to date of sale, and the balance to the execution under which the property was sold, and to other liens according to priority, to be determined as provided by law.

Laws 1847, Cobb's 1851 Digest, p. 517; Laws 1850, Cobb's 1851 Digest, p. 518; Laws 1868, p. 16, § 1; Laws 1877, p. 21, § 1; Laws 1894, p. 100, §§ 2, 3.

Formerly Code 1863, § 3581; Code 1868, § 3604; Code 1873, § 3654; Code 1882, § 3654; Civil Code 1895, §§ 5433, 5434; Civil Code 1910, §§ 6038, 6039; Code 1933, §§ 39–201, 39–202.

Article 4

Satisfaction or Discharge of Judgment and Execution

§ 9–13–70. How execution stayed

(a) In all cases in which a verdict or judgment is rendered, the party against whom the same is entered may, either in open court or in the clerk's office, within four days after the adjournment of court, enter into bond with good and sufficient security for the payment of the verdict or judgment and costs within 60 days.

(b) When bond and security have been given as provided in this Code section, the verdict and judgment, or the execution thereon, shall be suspended for the 60 days. If the party fails to pay the verdict or judgment within that time, execution shall issue against the party and his security without further proceedings thereon.

Laws 1799, Cobb's 1851 Digest, p. 494.

Formerly Code 1863, §§ 3588, 3589; Code 1868, §§ 3611, 3612; Code 1873, §§ 3661, 3662; Code 1882, §§ 3661, 3662; Civil Code 1895, §§ 5439, 5440; Civil Code 1910, §§ 6044, 6045; Code 1933, §§ 39–501, 39–502.

§ 9–13–71. Effect of unexplained levy on personalty or dismissal of levy

A levy upon personal property sufficient to pay the debt, which levy is unaccounted for, shall be prima facie evidence of satisfaction to the extent of the value of the property. The unexplained dismissal of the levy shall be an abandonment of the lien so far as third persons are concerned.

Formerly Code 1863, § 3584; Code 1868, § 3607; Code 1873, § 3657; Code 1882, § 3657; Civil Code 1895, § 5442; Civil Code 1910, § 6047; Code 1933, § 39–601.

§ 9–13–72. Release of property subject to execution

If the plaintiff in execution, for a valuable consideration, releases property which is subject to execution, the release shall be a satisfaction of the execution to the extent of the value of the property so released insofar as purchasers and creditors are concerned. However, nothing in this Code section shall apply to any such release made by the transferee of any execution issued for taxes due the state or any county or municipality therein or of any execution issued by any municipality on account of assessments made against real estate for street or other improvements. In all such cases the execution shall be discharged or satisfied only to the extent of the amount of taxes or other assessments owing by the parcel released.

Laws 1929, p. 172, § 1.

Formerly Code 1863, § 3585; Code 1868, § 3608; Code 1873, § 3658; Code 1882, § 3658; Civil Code 1895, § 5443; Civil Code 1910, § 6048; Code 1933, § 39-602.

§ 9-13-73. Allowing fund to be applied to younger lien, effect of

If an execution creditor having the older lien on a fund in the hands of the sheriff or other officer allows the fund by his consent to be applied to a younger writ of execution, it shall be considered an extinguishment pro tanto of the creditor's lien insofar as third persons may be concerned.

Formerly Code 1863, § 3586; Code 1868, § 3609; Code 1873, § 3659; Code 1882, § 3659; Civil Code 1895, § 5444; Civil Code 1910, § 6049; Code 1933, § 39-603.

§ 9-13-74. Contract not to enforce execution, effect of

An agreement for a valuable consideration never to enforce a judgment or execution shall release the judgment or execution.

Formerly Code 1863, § 3587; Code 1868, § 3610; Code 1873, § 3660; Code 1882, § 3660; Civil Code 1895, § 5445; Civil Code 1910, § 6050; Code 1933, § 39-604.

§ 9-13-75. Setoff of judgments. Rights of assignees

One judgment may be set off against another, on motion, whether in the hands of an original party or an assignee. The balance on the larger is collectable under execution. The rights of an assignee shall not be interfered with if bona fide and for value.

Laws 1993, p. 91, § 9.

Formerly Code 1863, §§ 2843, 3396; Code 1868, §§ 2851, 3415; Code 1873, §§ 2902, 3467; Code 1882, §§ 2902, 3467; Civil Code 1895, §§ 3748, 5086; Civil Code 1910, §§ 4342, 5670; Code 1933, § 39-605.

§ 9-13-76. Excess of setoff

In all cases of mutual debts and setoffs where the jury finds a balance for the defendant, the defendant may enter judgment for the amount and take out execution in the manner as plaintiffs may do by this Code, provided that the defendant at the time of filing his answer files therewith a true copy or copies of the subject matter of such setoffs.

Laws 1799, Cobb's 1851 Digest, p. 487.

Formerly Code 1863, § 3398; Code 1868, § 3417; Code 1873, § 3469; Code 1882, § 3469; Civil Code 1895, § 5088; Civil Code 1910, § 5672; Code 1933, § 39-606.

§ 9-13-77. Security to have control, when

The security paying off an execution shall have control thereof.

Laws 1826, Cobb's 1851 Digest, p. 593.

Formerly Code 1863, § 3590; Code 1868, § 3613; Code 1873, § 3663; Code 1882, § 3663; Civil Code 1895, § 5441; Civil Code 1910, § 6046; Code 1933, § 39-607.

§ 9-13-78. Joint debtors may control execution, when

When judgments have been obtained against several persons and one of them has paid more than his just proportion of the same, he may have full power to control and use the execution as securities in execution control the same against principals or cosureties by having this payment entered on the execution issued to enforce the judgment, and he shall not be compelled to bring an action against the codebtors for the excess of payment on the judgment.

Laws 1871-72, p. 54, § 1.

Formerly Code 1873, § 3599; Code 1882, § 3599; Civil Code 1895, § 5376; Civil Code 1910, § 5971; Code 1933, § 39-608.

§ 9-13-79. Entry of partial payments on execution

When a payment on an execution is made which does not entirely satisfy the judgment upon which the execution has been issued, the plaintiff in execution or his attorney shall authorize the clerk to enter the amount of the payments upon the execution.

Laws 1966, p. 408, § 1.

Formerly Code 1933, § 39-609.

§ 9-13-80. Cancellation of executions; right of action for noncompliance; affidavit of satisfaction; filing; fraudulent affidavits, classification and punishment

(a) Upon the satisfaction of the entire debt upon which an execution has been issued, the plaintiff in execution or his or her attorney shall timely direct the clerk to cancel the execution and mark the judgment satisfied. Such direction shall be delivered to the clerk not later than 30 days following the date upon which the execution was fully satisfied.

(b)(1) A private right of action shall be granted to a judgment debtor upon the failure of such plaintiff or counsel to comply with the provisions of subsection (a) of this Code section.

(2) Failure to direct cancellation and satisfaction within 60 days after satisfaction of the entire debt shall be prima-facie evidence of untimeliness.

(3) Recovery may be had by way of motion in the action precipitating the judgment and execution or by separate action in any court of competent jurisdiction.

(4) Damages shall be presumed in the amount of $100.00 and the court may award reasonable attorney's fees. Actual damages may be recovered, but in no event shall recovery exceed $500.00; provided, however, the court may also award reasonable attorney's fees.

(c) In order to authorize the clerk of superior court to make an entry of satisfaction with respect to an execution on the general execution docket, there shall be presented for filing on the general execution docket:

(1) A satisfaction upon the original execution or alias execution itself;

(2) A satisfaction as provided in subsection (d) of this Code section; or

(3) A satisfaction as provided in subsection (e) of this Code section.

Any clerk of superior court who cancels of record any execution in the manner authorized in this subsection shall be immune from any civil liability, either in such clerk's official capacity or personally, for so canceling of record such security deed.

(d) Proof of satisfaction of an execution, the original of which has been lost, stolen, or otherwise mislaid, may be made based upon an affidavit executed by the plaintiff in execution or owner or holder of record of such execution and who so swears in such affidavit, which affidavit shall be recorded in the execution docket and shall be in the following form:

__________ County, Georgia

Affidavit for Satisfaction of Execution

The original execution having been lost or destroyed and the indebtedness, penalties, and interest referred to in that certain writ of fi. fa. styled __________ v. __________, dated __________, and of record in General Execution Docket Book __________, Page ____, in the office of the clerk of the Superior Court of __________ County, Georgia, having been satisfied in full and the undersigned being the present owner of such writ of fi. fa. by virtue of being the plaintiff in fi. fa. or the heir, assign, transferee, or devisee of the original plaintiff in fi. fa., the clerk of such superior court is authorized and directed to make an entry of satisfaction with respect to such writ of fi. fa.

In witness whereof, the undersigned has set his or her hand and seal, this __________ day of __________, ____.

__________(SEAL)
Signature

Signed, sealed, and
delivered on the
date above shown

____
Notary Public

(SEAL)

My commission expires: __________.

(e) In the event that a plaintiff in execution or any person that owns or holds an execution has failed to properly transmit a legally sufficient satisfaction or cancellation to authorize and direct the clerk or clerks to cancel the execution of record within 60 days after a written notice mailed to such plaintiff in execution or owner or holder of record by registered or certified mail or statutory overnight delivery, return receipt requested, the clerk or clerks are authorized and directed to cancel the execution upon recording an affidavit by the attorney for the judgment debtor against whom the execution was issued or any attorney who has caused the indebtedness and other obligations under the execution to be paid in full or any attorney who has actual knowledge that the indebtedness has been paid in full. The notice shall be mailed to the plaintiff in execution or owner or holder of record, shall identify the execution, and shall include a recital or explanation of this subsection. The affidavit shall include a recital of actions taken to comply with this subsection. Such affidavit shall include as attachments the following items:

(1) A written verification which was given at the time of payment by the plaintiff in execution or owner or holder of record of the amount necessary to pay off such obligations; and

(2) Any one of the following:

(A) Copies of the front and back of a canceled check to the plaintiff in execution or owner or holder of record showing payment of such obligations;

(B) Confirmation of a wire transfer to the owner or holder of record showing payment of such obligations; or

(C) A bank receipt showing payment to the plaintiff in execution or owner or holder of record of such obligations.

(f) Any person who files an affidavit in accordance with subsection (d) or (e) of this Code section which affidavit is fraudulent shall be guilty of a felony and shall be punished by imprisonment for not less than one year nor more than three years or by a fine of not less than $1,000.00 nor more than $5,000.00, or both.

Laws 1966, p. 408, § 1; Laws 1996, p. 1093, § 1; Laws 1997, p. 143, § 9; Laws 2004, Act 494, § 1, eff. July 1, 2004.

Formerly Code 1933, § 39-610.

Article 5

Claims

§ 9-13-90. Claims to be on oath

When any sheriff or other officer shall levy an execution or other process on property claimed by a third person not a party to the execution, the person, his agent, or his attorney may make oath claiming the property.

Laws 1839, Cobb's 1851 Digest, p. 535; Laws 1877, p. 22, § 1.

Formerly Code 1863, § 3650; Code 1868, § 3675; Code 1873, § 3725; Code 1882, § 3725; Civil Code 1895, § 4611; Civil Code 1910, § 5157; Code 1933, § 39-801.

§ 9-13-91. Bond and security for damages

The person claiming the property levied on, or his agent or attorney, shall give bond to the sheriff or other levying officer, with good and sufficient security in a sum not larger than double the amount of the execution levied, made payable to the plaintiff in execution. Where the property levied on is of less value than the execution, the amount of the bond shall be double the value of the property levied upon, at a reasonable valuation to be judged by the levying officer, conditioned to pay the plaintiff in execution all damages which the jury on the trial of the claim may assess against the person claiming the property in case it appears that the claim was made for the purpose of delay only.

Laws 1821, Cobb's 1851 Digest, p. 533; Laws 1872, p. 41, § 1.

Formerly Code 1863, §§ 3651, 3654; Code 1868, §§ 3676, 3679; Code 1873, §§ 3726, 3729; Code 1882, §§ 3726, 3729; Civil Code 1895, §§ 4612, 4615; Civil Code 1910, §§ 5158, 5161; Code 1933, § 39-802.

§ 9-13-92. Claims may be made in forma pauperis

In all claim cases where claimants are unable to give bond and security as required in this article, the claimants may file, in addition to the oath required in Code Section 9-13-90, an affidavit as follows:

"I, A.B., do swear that I do not interpose this claim for delay only; that I bona fide claim the right and title to the same; that I am advised and believe that the claim will be sustained; and that because of my indigence I am unable to give bond and security as required by law."

When the affidavit has been made and delivered to the levying officer, it shall suspend the sale in the same manner as if bond and security had been given.

Laws 1870, p. 411, § 1.

Formerly Code 1873, § 3733; Code 1882, § 3733; Civil Code 1895, § 4618; Civil Code 1910, § 5164; Code 1933, § 39-807.

§ 9-13-93. Sale to be postponed, when

When affidavit and bond have been made and delivered as required in Code Sections 9-13-90 and 9-13-91, it shall be the duty of the sheriff or other levying officer to postpone the sale of the property until otherwise ordered.

Laws 1821, Cobb's 1851 Digest, p. 532.

Formerly Code 1863, § 3652; Code 1868, § 3677; Code 1873, § 3727; Code 1882, § 3727; Civil Code 1895, § 4613; Civil Code 1910, § 5159; Code 1933, § 39-803.

§ 9-13-94. Forthcoming bond may be given, etc.; bond recoverable on failure

(a) In all cases where a levy is made upon property that is claimed by a third person and the person desires the possession thereof, it shall be the duty of the sheriff or other levying officer to take bond, made payable to the sheriff with good security for a sum equal to double the value of the property levied on to be estimated by the levying officer, for the delivery of the property at the time and place of sale, provided the property so levied upon shall be found subject to the execution. However, it shall not be lawful to require or take a forthcoming bond for real estate.

(b) When bond and security have been given as provided in this Code section, it shall be the duty of the sheriff or other levying officer to leave the property in the possession of the claimant. In the event that the claimant or his security fails to deliver the property after it has been found to be subject to execution, the bond shall be made recoverable in any court having cognizance of the same.

Laws 1811, Cobb's 1851 Digest, p. 532; Laws 1841, Cobb's 1851 Digest, p. 536; Laws 1872, p. 40, § 1.

Formerly Code 1863, §§ 3653, 3654, 3655; Code 1868, §§ 3678, 3679, 3680; Code 1873, §§ 3728, 3729, 3730; Code 1882, §§ 3728, 3729, 3730; Civil Code 1895, §§ 4614, 4615, 4616; Civil Code 1910, §§ 5160, 5161, 5162; Code 1933, §§ 39-804, 39-805.

§ 9-13-95. Partner or joint owner may claim and execute bond for all

One of several partners or persons jointly interested may make the affidavit and execute the bond in the name of the firm or persons jointly interested, who shall be bound thereby as though each individual had signed it himself.

Laws 1838, Cobb's 1851 Digest, p. 589.

Formerly Code 1863, § 3656; Code 1868, § 3681; Code 1873, § 3731; Code 1882, § 3731; Civil Code 1895, § 4617; Civil Code 1910, § 5163; Code 1933, § 39-806.

§ 9-13-96. Forthcoming bond not given; delivery to plaintiff; compensation for keeping property

If the claimant to personal property levied on is unable to give a forthcoming bond, it shall be the privilege of the plaintiff in execution to give the bond, to be approved by the levying officer, and, upon the bond being given and approved, it shall be the duty of the levying officer to deliver the property to the plaintiff. However, in no event shall the plaintiff be allowed any compensation for keeping the property.

Laws 1870, p. 411, § 2.

Formerly Code 1873, § 3734; Code 1882, § 3734; Civil Code 1895, § 4619; Civil Code 1910, § 5165; Code 1933, § 39-808.

§ 9-13-97. Disposition of property where no bond is given

In the event the claimant is unable, and the plaintiff neglects or refuses, to give bond for the forthcoming of the property, the claimant may apply to the judge of the probate court and procure an order for the sale of the same; and, when the order has been granted, it shall be the duty of the levying officer to advertise the time and place of sale at not less than three public places, to be selected in different parts of the county in which the sale is to take place, for 15 days immediately preceding the time of sale. On the day of sale, between the hours of 10:00 A.M. and 4:00 P.M., the property shall be sold; and the money arising from the sale shall remain in the hands of the levying officer subject to the order of court upon the final hearing of the claim.

Laws 1870, p. 411, § 3.

Formerly Code 1873, § 3735; Code 1882, § 3735; Civil Code 1895, § 4620; Civil Code 1910, § 5166; Code 1933, § 39-809.

§ 9-13-98. Where claim to be returned

When an execution issued from a court is levied upon personal property and claimed by a person not a party to the execution, it shall be the duty of the levying officer to return the same, together with the execution, to the next term of the court from which the execution issued. Where an execution is levied upon real property and the same is claimed in the manner aforesaid, it shall be the duty of the officer making the levy to return the same, together with the execution and claim, to the next term of the superior court of the county in which the land so levied upon lies.

Laws 1821, Cobb's 1851 Digest, p. 532.

Formerly Code 1863, § 3658; Code 1868, § 3683; Code 1873, § 3736; Code 1882, § 3736; Civil Code 1895, § 4621; Civil Code 1910, § 5167; Code 1933, § 39-901.

§ 9-13-99. Claims and illegalities against executions from probate court

Whenever an execution issued from a probate court is levied upon personal property and a claim to the property or an affidavit of illegality is interposed, it shall be the duty of the sheriff or other levying officer to return the same, together with the execution and all the other papers, to the next term of the superior court of the county from which the execution was issued. If the levy has been made upon realty, the execution, with the claim or illegality papers, shall be returned by the levying officer to the next term of the superior court of the county where the land lies and the issue shall be tried as is provided for the trial of claim and illegality cases.

Laws 1876, p. 100, § 1.

Formerly Code 1882, § 3742a; Civil Code 1895, § 4628; Civil Code 1910, § 5174; Code 1933, § 39-908.

§ 9-13-100. Trial by jury

The court to which a claim is returned shall cause the right of property to be decided by a jury at the first term thereof, unless continued in the same manner as other cases.

Laws 1821, Cobb's 1851 Digest, pp. 532, 533.

Formerly Code 1863, § 3660; Code 1868, § 3684; Code 1873, § 3737; Code 1882, § 3737; Civil Code 1895, § 4622; Civil Code 1910, § 5168; Code 1933, § 39-902.

§ 9-13-101. Oath of jurors in claim cases; damages where claim made for delay

Every juror on the trial of the claim of property either real or personal shall be sworn, in addition to the oath usually administered, to give such damages as may seem reasonable and just, in an amount not less than 10 percent of the amount due upon the execution when the value of the property in dispute exceeds the amount of the execution, or of the value of the property when the value of the property is less than the execution levied, to the plaintiff against the claimant in case it shall be shown that the claim was made for delay only. The jury may give a verdict in the manner aforesaid and judgment may be entered thereon against the claimant and his security for the damages so assessed and the costs of the trial.

Laws 1821, Cobb's 1851 Digest, p. 533.

Formerly Code 1863, § 3661; Code 1868, § 3685; Code 1873, § 3738; Code 1882, § 3738; Civil Code 1895, § 4623; Civil Code 1910, § 5169; Code 1933, § 39-903.

§ 9-13-102. Burden of proof on plaintiff

Upon the trial of all claims provided for in this article, the burden of proof shall lie upon the plaintiff in execution in all cases where the property levied on is not in possession of the defendant in execution at the time of the levy.

Laws 1821, Cobb's 1851 Digest, p. 533.

Formerly Code 1863, § 3662; Code 1868, § 3686; Code 1873, § 3739; Code 1882, § 3739; Civil Code 1895, § 4624; Civil Code 1910, § 5170; Code 1933, § 39-904.

§ 9-13-103. Withdrawal or discontinuance of claim

Whenever a claim of property is made in terms of this article and is returned to the proper court by the sheriff or other levying officer, the claimant shall not be permitted to withdraw or discontinue his claim more than once without the consent of the plaintiff in execution or some person duly authorized to represent the plaintiff; rather, the court shall proceed to the trial of the claim of the property and it shall be the duty of the jury to assess damages accordingly.

Laws 1821, Cobb's 1851 Digest, p. 533.

Formerly Code 1863, § 3663; Code 1868, § 3687; Code 1873, § 3740; Code 1882, § 3740; Civil Code 1895, § 4625; Civil Code 1910, § 5171; Code 1933, § 39-905.

§ 9-13-104. Damages where claim is discontinued or dismissed

Whenever a claim is dismissed for insufficiency or is withdrawn, the plaintiff in execution may have a case made up and submitted to the jury charging that the claim was filed for the purpose of delay. Upon proof of the same, defendant and claimant having the same power to resist the case as in claim cases where damages are claimed, the jury, under instructions from the court, may give damages as in cases where the claim is not withdrawn but is submitted for trial to the jury. The cases so submitted shall be tried at the time of the disposal of the claim if the parties are ready, but continuances shall be granted as in other cases.

Laws 1871-72, p. 52, § 1.

Formerly Code 1873, § 3741; Code 1882, § 3741; Civil Code 1895, § 4626; Civil Code 1910, § 5172; Code 1933, § 39-906.

§ 9-13-105. How damages are to be assessed

Upon the trial of claims to property which may be pending in the court, when damages are found by the jury, the damages shall be assessed upon the whole amount then due upon the execution when the value of the property in dispute exceeds the amount of the execution and upon the value of the property when the value of the property is less than the execution levied.

Laws 1821, Cobb's 1851 Digest, p. 534.

Formerly Code 1863, § 3664; Code 1868, § 3688; Code 1873, § 3742; Code 1882, § 3742; Civil Code 1895, § 4627; Civil Code 1910, § 5173; Code 1933, § 39-907.

§ 9-13-106. Original execution in claim cases may be withdrawn

The plaintiff in execution in all claim cases shall have the right to withdraw the original execution from the files of the court by making application therefor, in person or by attorney, to the clerk of the court if there is a clerk or to the court if there is no clerk. Upon application being made, the clerk or court shall make a true copy of the execution with all the entries thereon and shall certify the same to be true, which certified copy shall be filed with the claim papers in lieu of the original execution; and an entry of the filing shall be made thereon.

Laws 1887, p. 62, § 1.

Formerly Civil Code 1895, § 4629; Civil Code 1910, § 5175; Code 1933, § 39-909.

Article 6

Illegality

§ 9-13-120. Illegality, how taken

When an execution against the property of any person issues illegally, or is proceeding illegally, and the execution is levied on such property, the person may make oath in writing, stating the cause of the illegality, and deliver the same to the sheriff or other executing officer together with bond and good security for the forthcoming of the property, as provided by this article.

Laws 1799, Cobb's 1851 Digest, p. 509; Laws 1838, Cobb's 1851 Digest, p. 514.

Formerly Code 1863, § 3591; Code 1868, § 3614; Code 1873, § 3664; Code 1882, § 3664; Civil Code 1895, § 4736; Civil Code 1910, § 5305; Code 1933, § 39-1001.

§ 9-13-121. When illegality may not go behind judgment

If the defendant was not served and did not appear, he may take advantage of the defect by affidavit of illegality. However, if he has had his day in court, he may not go behind the judgment by an affidavit of illegality.

Formerly Code 1863, § 3597; Code 1868, § 3621; Code 1873, § 3671; Code 1882, § 3671; Civil Code 1895, § 4742; Civil Code 1910, § 5311; Code 1933, § 39-1009.

§ 9-13-122. Illegality not remedy for excessive levy

An affidavit of illegality shall not be a remedy for an excessive levy except where authorized by statute.

Formerly Code 1933, § 39-1004.

§ 9-13-123. Who may file affidavit of illegality

An affidavit of illegality may be filed by an attorney in fact or by an executor, administrator, or other trustee.

Formerly Code 1863, § 3596; Code 1868, § 3620; Code 1873, § 3670; Code 1882, § 3670; Civil Code 1895, § 4741; Civil Code 1910, § 5310; Code 1933, § 39-1002.

§ 9-13-124. Affidavit of illegality not to be received until after levy

No affidavit of illegality shall be received by any sheriff or other executing officer until a levy has been made.

Laws 1838, Cobb's 1851 Digest, p. 514.

Formerly Code 1863, § 3592; Code 1868, § 3615; Code 1873, § 3665; Code 1882, § 3665; Civil Code 1895, § 4737; Civil Code 1910, § 5306; Code 1933, § 39-1003.

§ 9-13-125. Amendment of affidavits of illegality

Affidavits of illegality are, upon motion and leave of court, amendable instanter by the insertion of new and independent grounds, provided that the defendant shall swear that he did not know of such grounds when the original affidavit was filed.

Laws 1850, Cobb's 1851 Digest, p. 518.

Formerly Code 1863, § 3430; Code 1868, § 3450; Code 1873, § 3501; Code 1882, § 3501; Civil Code 1895, § 5120; Civil Code 1910, § 5704; Code 1933, § 39-1005.

§ 9-13-126. Forthcoming bond when illegality filed

When an execution is levied on personal property and an affidavit of illegality is filed thereto and the party filing the illegality desires to take or keep possession of the property, he shall deliver to the sheriff or other levying officer a bond payable to the levying officer, with good security in a sum equal to double the value of the property so levied upon, to be judged of by the levying officer, conditioned for the delivery of the property levied upon at the time and place of sale in the event that the illegality is dismissed by the court or withdrawn, which bond shall be recoverable in any court having cognizance thereof.

Formerly Code 1863, § 3598; Code 1868, § 3622; Code 1873, § 3672; Code 1882, § 3672; Civil Code 1895, § 5435; Civil Code 1910, § 6040; Code 1933, § 39-301.

§ 9-13-127. How illegality returned and tried; continuance

When levy has been made and affidavit and bond delivered to the levying officer, it shall be the duty of the officer to suspend further proceedings on the execution and to return the execution, affidavit, and bond to the next term of the court from which the execution issued. It shall be the duty of the court to make a determination thereon at the first term thereof unless the plaintiff or his attorney desires to controvert the facts contained in the affidavit, in which case an issue shall be joined and tried by a jury at the same term unless good cause is shown for a continuance.

Formerly Code 1863, § 3593; Code 1868, § 3616; Code 1873, § 3666; Code 1882, § 3666; Civil Code 1895, § 4738; Civil Code 1910, § 5307; Code 1933, § 39-1006.

§ 9-13-128. Damages for delay only

Upon the trial of an issue formed on an affidavit of illegality, the jury trying the case shall have power to assess such damages as may seem reasonable and just, not exceeding 25 percent of the principal debt, where it is made to appear that the illegality was interposed for delay only. Whenever an illegality is dismissed for insufficiency or informality or is withdrawn, plaintiff in execution may proceed as is provided in cases where claims are dismissed or withdrawn.

Laws 1859, p. 49, § 1; Laws 1871–72, p. 52, § 1.

Formerly Code 1863, § 3594; Code 1868, § 3617; Code 1873, § 3667; Code 1882, § 3667; Civil Code 1895, § 4739; Civil Code 1910, § 5308; Code 1933, § 39–1007.

§ 9-13-129. Property may be sold under other executions; release of bond

When an execution has been levied on property and an affidavit of illegality has been filed to stay proceedings thereon, the property so levied on shall be subject to levy and sale under other executions. The officer making the first levy shall claim, receive, hold, and retain the amount of the proceeds of the sale as the court deems sufficient to pay the execution first levied, including interest up to the time of the court at which the illegality shall be determined. Any bond given by the defendant on filing the affidavit shall be released and discharged so far as relates to the property sold.

Laws 1845, Cobb's 1851 Digest, p. 516.

Formerly Code 1863, § 3595; Code 1868, § 3619; Code 1873, § 3669; Code 1882, § 3669; Civil Code 1895, § 4740; Civil Code 1910, § 5309; Code 1933, § 39–1008.

Article 7

Judicial Sales

Part 1

Advertisement

§ 9-13-140. Sales, how advertised

(a) The sheriff, coroner, or other officer shall publish weekly for four weeks in the legal organ for the county, or if there is no newspaper designated as such, then in the nearest newspaper having the largest general circulation in such county, notice of all sales of land and other property executed by the officer. In the advertisement the officer shall give a full and complete description of the property to be sold, making known the names of the plaintiff, the defendant, and any person who may be in the possession of the property. In the case of real property, such advertisement shall include the legal description of such real property and may include the street address of such real property, if available, but provided that no foreclosure shall be invalidated by the failure to include a street address or by the insertion of an erroneous street address.

(b) However, horses, hogs, and cattle may be sold at any time by the consent of the defendant, in which case it shall be the duty of the officer to give the plaintiff ten days' notice thereof and also to advertise the same at three or more public places in the county where the property may be at least ten days before the sale.

Laws 1799, Cobb's 1851 Digest, p. 509; Laws 1850, Cobb's 1851 Digest, p. 580; Laws 1851–52, p. 78, § 1; Laws 1866, p. 163, § 1; Laws 1995, p. 931, § 1; Laws 1998, p. 213, § 1; Laws 1999, p. 6, § 1.

Formerly Code 1863, § 3576; Code 1868, § 3599; Code 1873, § 3647; Code 1882, § 3647; Civil Code 1895, § 5457; Civil Code 1910, § 6062; Code 1933, § 39–1101.

§ 9-13-141. Notices published once a week for four weeks

In all cases where the law requires citations, notices, or advertisements by probate court judges, clerks, sheriffs, county bailiffs, administrators, executors, guardians, trustees, or others to be published in a newspaper for 30 days or for four weeks or once a week for four weeks, it shall be sufficient and legal to publish the same once a week for four weeks, that is, one insertion each week for each of the four weeks, immediately preceding the term or day when the order is to be granted or the sale is to take place. The number of days between the date of the first publication and the term or day when the order is to be granted or the sale is to take place, whether more or less than 30 days, shall not in any manner invalidate or render irregular the notice, citation, advertisement, order, or sale.

Laws 1876, p. 99, § 1; Laws 1890–91, p. 241, § 1.

Formerly Code 1882, § 2628a; Civil Code 1895, § 5458; Civil Code 1910, § 6063; Code 1933, § 39–1102.

§ 9-13-142. Selection of official organ; notice of change must be given

(a) No journal or newspaper published in this state shall be declared, made, or maintained as the official organ of any county for the publication of sheriff's sales, citations of probate court judges, or any other advertising commonly known in terms of "official or legal advertising" and required by law to be published in such county official newspaper unless the newspaper shall meet and maintain the following qualifications:

(1) "Newspaper" as used in this Code section means a printed product of multiple pages containing not greater than 75 percent advertising content in no more than one-half of its issues during the previous 12 months, excluding separate advertising supplements inserted into but separately identifiable from any regular issue or issues of the newspaper;

(2) The newspaper shall be published within the county and continuously at least weekly for a period of two years or is the direct successor of such a newspaper. Failure to publish for not more than two weeks in any calendar year shall not disqualify a newspaper otherwise qualified;

(3) For a period of two years prior to designation and thereafter, the newspaper shall have and maintain at least 75 percent paid circulation as established by an independent audit. Paid circulation shall not include newspapers that are distributed free or in connection with a service or promotion at no additional charge to the ultimate recipient. For circulation to be considered paid, the recipient of the newspaper or such recipient's employer or household must pay reasonable and adequate consideration for the newspaper. No rules of circulation of audit companies, the United States Postal Service, or accounting principles may be considered in determining paid circulation if they are inconsistent with the provisions of this subsection;

(4) Based on the published results of the 1990 United States decennial census or any future such census, the newspaper shall have and maintain at least the following paid circulation within the county for which it is designated as the legal organ newspaper:

(A) Five hundred copies per issue in counties having a population of less than 20,000;

(B) Seven hundred fifty copies per issue in counties having a population of at least 20,000 but less than 100,000; or

(C) One thousand five hundred copies per issue in counties having a population of 100,000 or greater; and

(5) For purposes of this Code section, paid circulation shall include home or mail delivery subscription sales, counter, vendor and newsrack sales, and sales to independent newspaper contract carriers for resale. Paid circulation shall not include multiple copies purchased by one entity unless the multiple copies are purchased for and distributed to the purchaser's officers, employees, or agents, or within the purchaser's household.

(b) However, in counties where no journal or newspaper meets the qualifications set forth in subsection (a) of this Code section, the official organ may be designated by the judge of the probate court, the sheriff, and the clerk of the superior court, a majority of these officers governing from among newspapers otherwise qualified to be a legal organ that meet the minimum circulation in the preceding subsection for the county, or if there is no such newspaper, then the newspaper having the greatest general paid circulation in the county.

(c) Any selection or change in the official organ of any county shall be made upon the concurrent action of the judge of the probate court, the sheriff, and the clerk of the superior court of the county or a majority of the officers. No change in the official legal organ shall be effective without the publication for four weeks of notice of the decision to make a change in the newspaper in which legal advertisements have previously been published. All changes in the official legal organ shall be made effective on January 1 unless a change has to be made where there is no other qualified newspaper.

(d) Notwithstanding the other provisions of this Code section, an official organ of any county meeting the qualifications under the statute in force at the time of its appointment and which was appointed prior to July 1, 1999, may remain the official organ of that county until a majority of the judge of the probate court, the sheriff, and the clerk of the superior court determine to appoint a new official organ for the county.

(e) During the month of December in each year, the judge of the probate court of each county shall notify the Secretary of State, on a form supplied by the Secretary of State, of the name and mailing address of the journal or newspaper currently serving as the official organ of the county. The judge of the probate court shall also likewise notify the Secretary of State of any change in the official organ of the county at the time that such change is made. The Secretary of State shall maintain at all times a current listing of the names and addresses of all county organs and shall make such list available to any person upon request.

Laws 1850, Cobb's 1851 Digest, p. 580; Laws 1910, p. 87, § 1; Laws 1953, Nov.-Dec. Sess., p. 271, § 1; Laws 1989, p. 1248, § 1; Laws 1992, p. 1035, § 1; Laws 1997, p. 528, § 1; Laws 1999, p. 6, § 2.

Formerly Code 1863, § 3577; Code 1868, § 3600; Code 1873, § 3650; Code 1882, § 3650; Civil Code 1895, § 5460; Code 1910, § 6065; Code 1933, §§ 39–1103, 39–1107.

§ 9–13–143. Fees for advertising

(a) The rates to be allowed to publishers for publishing legal advertisements shall be as follows:

(1) For each 100 words, not more than the sum of $ 10.00 for each insertion for the first four insertions; and

(2) For each subsequent insertion, not more than the sum of $ 9.00 per 100 words.

In all cases fractional parts shall be charged for at the same rates.

(b) For the purpose of the computation in subsection (a) of this Code section, a block of numbers or a block of letters and numbers shall be counted as one word. If the block of numbers or letters or any combination thereof contains a hyphen, a semicolon, a colon, or other similar character or punctuation mark, the block shall still be counted as one word, provided there are no intervening spaces. When an intervening space does occur, this space shall mark the start of a new word.

(c) No judge of the probate court, sheriff, coroner, clerk, marshal, or other officer shall receive or collect from the parties, plaintiff or defendant, other or greater rates than set forth in this Code section.

Laws 1878–79, p. 81, § 1; Laws 1920, p. 86, § 1; Laws 1949, p. 566, § 1; Laws 1953, Nov.-Dec. Sess., p. 271, § 2; Laws 1964, p. 77, § 1; Laws 1965, p. 174, § 1; Laws 1968, p. 126, § 1; Laws 1975, p. 52, § 1; Laws 1981, p. 1808, § 1; Laws 1985, p. 1042, § 1; Laws 1989, p. 325, § 1; Laws 1993, p. 91, § 9; Laws 1995, p. 992, § 1; Laws 1996, p. 6, § 9.

Formerly Code 1882, § 3704a; Civil Code 1895, § 5461; Civil Code 1910, § 6066; Code 1933, § 39–1105.

§ 9–13–144. Officer to make contracts

(a) If the judge of the probate court, the sheriff, or other officer is unable to procure advertisements at the rate prescribed in Code Section 9–13–143 in a newspaper published at the county site of the county, he may have the advertisements published in any newspaper in this state having the largest general circulation in the county, provided that any paper published in the county shall be next entitled to the public advertisements and provided, further, that the rates shall be agreed upon.

(b) If contracts cannot be made with newspapers at the rates prescribed, then the sheriff and the judge of the probate court or other advertising officers shall post their advertisements at the courthouse and in a public place in each militia district in the county for the length of time required by law for advertising in newspapers.

Laws 1878–79, p. 81, § 3; Laws 1899, p. 40, § 1.

Formerly Code 1882, § 3704c; Civil Code 1895, § 5462; Civil Code 1910, § 6067; Code 1933, § 39–1104.

§ 9–13–145. Advertising fee to be paid in advance, when; pauper affidavit

No sheriff or deputy sheriff shall be required to advertise the property of any defendant in execution for sale until the cost of the advertisement shall have been first paid by the plaintiff in execution, his agent, or his attorney, provided that when any such party plaintiff, or his agent or attorney for him, shall make and file an affidavit in writing that because of his indigence he is unable to pay such cost, it shall be the duty of the sheriff or his deputy to proceed as required by law.

Laws 1872, p. 42, § 1.

Formerly Code 1873, § 3649; Code 1882, § 3649; Civil Code 1895, § 5459; Civil Code 1910, § 6064; Code 1933, § 39–1106.

Part 2

Conduct and Effect

§ 9–13–160. Hours for conducting public sales

(a) For the purposes of this Code section, the term "public sale" means any sale, the notice of which must by law in any manner be given to the public.

(b) All public sales conducted within this state shall be between the hours of 10:00 A.M. and 4:00 P.M. eastern standard time or eastern daylight time, whichever is applicable, on the date fixed for the sale.

Laws 1963, p. 366, § 1; Laws 1979, p. 833, § 1.

§ 9–13–161. Place, time and manner of sales

(a) Unless otherwise provided, sales of property taken under execution shall be made by the sheriffs or coroners only at the courthouse of the county where the levy was made on the first Tuesday in each month, between the hours of 10:00 A.M. and 4:00 P.M., and at public outcry; provided, however, that, should the first Tuesday of the month fall on New Year's Day or Independence Day, such sales shall take place on the immediately following Wednesday. A change in the time of such sales from the first Tuesday of the month to the first Wednesday of the month as provided in this subsection shall also apply to all public sales within the county required to be conducted at the time of the sheriff's sales.

(b) In all cases where any sheriff, coroner, or other levying officer shall levy any execution or other legal process upon any corn, lumber, timber of any kind, bricks, machinery, or other articles difficult and expensive to transport, the officer may sell the property without carrying and exposing the same at the courthouse door on the day of sale, but the levying officer shall give a full description of the property and the place where it is located in the advertisement of the sale.

(c) By general order of the presiding judge of the superior court of the county, published in the official newspaper of the county and entered on the minutes of the court, all sales of property under execution within a county may be held at a place other than at the courthouse when, in the opinion of the judge, the holding of such sales before the courthouse door would create an undue traffic hazard or unnecessarily endanger the person or property of persons using the public streets. However, no such property shall be sold at a place different from that shown in the advertisement of the sale. Any change in the place of such sales within any county, as provided in this Code section, shall also apply to all public sales within the county required to be conducted in the manner of sheriff's sales.

Laws 1799, Cobb's 1851 Digest, p. 509; Laws 1821, Cobb's 1851 Digest, p. 511; Laws 1871–72, p. 49, § 1; Laws 1956, p. 701, § 1; Laws 1990, p. 1731, § 1; Laws 1993, p. 91, § 9.

Formerly Code 1863, § 3575; Code 1868, § 3598; Code 1873, § 3646; Code 1882, § 3646; Civil Code 1895, § 5455; Civil Code 1910, § 6060; Code 1933, § 39–1201.

§ 9–13–161.1. Place of sales in certain counties

(a) In any county of this state having a population of 600,000 or more according to the United States decennial census of 1990 or any future such census, the chief judge of the superior court shall be authorized and empowered to provide, by general order published in the official newspaper of the county and also in two other newspapers having general circulation in such county and entered upon the minutes of the court, that all sales of personal property by the sheriff of such county may be held at a place other than at the courthouse where, in the opinion of the chief judge, the holding of such sales before the courthouse door would create an undue traffic hazard or unnecessarily endanger the person or property of persons using the public streets.

(b) No such property shall be sold at a place different from that shown in the advertisement of the sale.

(c) After the issuance of the first general order as provided in subsection (a) of this Code section, the chief judge may from time to time change the place of holding such sales by another general order published as provided in subsection (a) of this Code section.

(d) This Code section shall be supplemental to other provisions of law, with a view towards efficient and orderly handling of sheriff's sales.

(e) Nothing in this Code section shall be construed to affect the time, manner, or place of any sale not made by the sheriff but required to be made at the same time, manner, or place as sheriff's sales.

Laws 1965, p. 3260, §§ 1–5; Laws 1982, p. 2107, § 3; Laws 1992, p. 1229, § 1.

§ 9–13–162. Sale may continue from day to day

Any sheriff, coroner, constable, tax collector, guardian, trustee, or any other officer of this state, when selling property at public sale by virtue of any law of this state, may continue the sale from day to day until the sale is completed, provided that the trustee or other officer has given notice of the intended continuance in the advertisement of the sale.

Laws 1851–52, p. 242, § 1.

Formerly Code 1882, § 3646a; Civil Code 1895, § 5456; Civil Code 1910, § 6061; Code 1933, § 39–1202.

§ 9–13–163. Sale of perishable property

Whenever any personal property which is of a perishable nature or liable to deteriorate from keeping or the keeping of which is attended by expense is levied on by virtue of any fi. fa., attachment, or other process, and the defendant fails to recover possession of the same and it remains in the hands of the levying officer, upon the facts being made plainly to appear to the judge of the court from which the process has issued or to the judge of the superior court of the county or to the judge of the probate court of the county in which the levy has been made during the absence of the judge of the superior court, it shall be the duty of the judge to order a sale of the property. The sale shall be at the usual place of holding sheriff's sales for the county where the property is located.

Laws 1873, p. 48, § 1; Laws 1880–81, p. 60, § 1; Laws 1983, p. 884, § 3–6.

Formerly Code 1873, § 3648; Code 1882, § 3648; Civil Code 1895, § 5463; Civil Code 1910, § 6068; Code 1933, § 39–1203.

§ 9–13–164. How perishable property sold

(a) The time and place of holding a sale under Code Section 9–13–163 shall be advertised at the courthouse and at two other public places at least ten days before the day of sale.

(b) The judge or judge of the probate court may order a sale of livestock, fruit, or other personal property in a perishable condition, after three days' notice.

(c) No judicial officer shall grant any order for the sale of personal property where the defendant in execution or other process or his attorney has not had at least two days' notice of applicant's intention to apply for such order, which notice shall specify the time and place of hearing. In cases of attachment for purchase money falling within this Code section, like notice shall be furnished the plaintiff or his attorney. In no case shall the notice be dispensed with, except where it is made to appear that it is impracticable to have the notice perfected or where the case is an urgent one, in which latter event the court may, in the exercise of a sound discretion, grant the order without notice.

(d) The money arising from the sale shall be held by the officer making the same, subject to the order of the court having jurisdiction of the same.

Laws 1873, p. 48, § 1; Laws 1880–81, p. 60, § 1; Laws 1983, p. 884, § 3–7.

Formerly Code 1873, § 3648; Code 1882, § 3648; Civil Code 1895, § 5464; Civil Code 1910, § 6069; Code 1933, § 39–1204.

§ 9–13–165. Sale of perishable property under tax fi. fas., etc.

Whenever a tax fi. fa. is levied on property which is of a perishable nature or is liable to deteriorate in value from keeping or which is attended with expense in keeping, the same may be sold under Code Sections 9–13–163 and 9–13–164.

Laws 1873, p. 48, § 1; Laws 1983, p. 884, § 3–8.

Formerly Code 1882, § 3648a; Civil Code 1895, § 5465; Civil Code 1910, § 6070; Code 1933, § 39–1205.

§ 9–13–166. Purchasers at judicial sales may tender cashier's or certified check instead of cash

Purchasers at judicial sales need not tender cash but, as an alternative, may tender a cashier's or certified check which is drawn for the amount of the purchase price and which is issued by or certified by any financial institution insured by the Federal Deposit Insurance Corporation or the Federal Savings and Loan Insurance Corporation.

Laws 1976, p. 367, § 1.

§ 9–13–167. Caveat emptor, fraud, warranty

(a) The purchaser shall look for himself as to the title and soundness of all property sold under judicial process.

(b) Actual fraud or misrepresentation by the officer or his agent may bind the officer personally. No covenant of warranty shall bind him individually unless made with that intention and for a valuable consideration.

Laws 1853–54, p. 56, § 1.

Formerly Code 1863, § 2578; Code 1868, § 2580; Code 1873, § 2622; Code 1882, § 2622; Civil Code 1895, § 5449; Civil Code 1910, § 6054; Code 1933, § 39–1307.

§ 9–13–168. Purchaser need not trace funds

The purchaser at a judicial sale shall not be bound to look to the appropriation of the proceeds of the sale nor to the returns made by the officer, nor shall he be required to see that the officer has complied fully with all regulations prescribed in such cases. All such irregularities shall create questions and liabilities between the officer and the parties interested in the sale. An innocent purchaser shall be bound only to see that the officer has competent authority to sell and that he is apparently proceeding to sell under the prescribed forms.

Formerly Code 1863, § 2584; Code 1868, § 2586; Code 1873, § 2628; Code 1882, § 2628; Civil Code 1895, § 5454; Civil Code 1910, § 6059; Code 1933, § 39–1311.

§ 9–13–169. Memorandum unnecessary to charge person at judicial sale

No note or memorandum in writing shall be necessary to charge any person at a judicial sale.

Laws 1831, Cobb's 1851 Digest, p. 514.

Formerly Code 1863, § 2577; Code 1868, § 2579; Code 1873, § 2621; Code 1882, § 2621; Civil Code 1895, § 5448; Civil Code 1910, § 6053; Code 1933, § 39–1306.

§ 9–13–170. Purchaser's liability; form of action against purchaser

(a) Any person who becomes the purchaser of any real or personal property at any sale made at public outcry by any executor, administrator, or guardian or by any sheriff or other officer under and by virtue of any execution or other legal process, who fails or refuses to comply with the terms of the sale when requested to do so, shall be liable for the amount of the purchase money. It shall be at the option of the sheriff or other officer either to proceed against the purchaser for the full amount of the purchase money or to resell the real or personal property and then proceed against the first purchaser for any deficiency arising from the sale.

(b) The action provided for in subsection (a) of this Code section may be brought in the name of the sheriff or other officer making the sale for the use of the plaintiff or defendant in execution or any other person in interest, as the case may be.

Laws 1831, Cobb's 1851 Digest, p. 514; Laws 1982, p. 3, § 9.

Formerly Code 1863, §§ 3582, 3583; Code 1868, §§ 3605, 3606; Code 1873, §§ 3655, 3656; Code 1882, §§ 3655, 3656; Civil Code 1895, §§ 5466, 5467; Civil Code 1910, §§ 6071, 6072; Code 1933, §§ 39-1301, 39-1302.

§ 9-13-171. Defendant, when bound by void sale

Where property is sold under void process and the proceeds are applied to valid liens against the defendant or the defendant receives the benefit thereof, he shall be bound thereby if he is present and does not object to the sale.

Formerly Civil Code 1895, § 5472; Civil Code 1910, § 6077; Code 1933, § 39-1315.

§ 9-13-172. Setting aside execution sale

Courts shall have full power over their officers making execution sales. Whenever the court is satisfied that a sale made under process is infected with fraud, irregularity, or error to the injury of either party, the court shall set aside the sale.

Formerly Civil Code 1895, § 5427; Civil Code 1910, § 6032; Code 1933, § 39-1316.

§ 9-13-172.1. Limitation of damages when eligible sale of property rescinded

(a) As used in this Code section, "eligible sale" means a judicial or nonjudicial sale that was conducted in the usual manner of a sheriff's sale and that was rescinded by the seller within 30 days after the sale but before the deed or deed under power has been delivered to the purchaser.

(b) Upon recision of an eligible sale, the seller shall return to the purchaser, within five days of the recision, all bid funds paid by the purchaser.

(c) Where the eligible sale was rescinded due to an automatic stay pursuant to the filing of bankruptcy by a person with an interest in the property, the damages that may be awarded to the purchaser in any civil action shall be limited to the amount of the bid funds tendered at the sale.

(d) Where the eligible sale was rescinded due to:

(1) The statutory requirements for the sale not being fulfilled;

(2) The default leading to the sale being cured prior to the sale; or

(3) The plaintiff in execution and the defendant in execution having agreed prior to the sale to cancel the sale based upon an enforceable promise by the defendant to cure the default,

the damages that may be awarded to the purchaser in any civil action shall be limited solely to the amount of the bid funds tendered at the sale plus interest on the funds at the rate of 18 percent annually, calculated daily. Notwithstanding any other provision of law, specific performance shall not be a remedy available under this Code section.

Laws 2003, Act 173, § 1, eff. July 1, 2003.

§ 9-13-173. Judicial sale passes title

A sale regularly made by virtue of judicial process issuing from a court of competent jurisdiction shall convey the title as effectually as if the sale were made by the person against whom the process was issued.

Formerly Code 1863, § 2575; Code 1868, § 2577; Code 1873, § 2619; Code 1882, § 2619; Civil Code 1895, § 5446; Civil Code 1910, § 6051; Code 1933, § 39-1303.

§ 9-13-174. Titles made by successor of sheriff

If a sheriff fails to make titles to a purchaser, his successor in office may make them in the same manner as if he had sold the property.

Laws 1799, Cobb's 1851 Digest, p. 576.

Formerly Code 1863, § 2583; Code 1868, § 2585; Code 1873, § 2627; Code 1882, § 2627; Civil Code 1895, § 5453; Civil Code 1910, § 6058; Code 1933, § 39-1304.

§ 9-13-175. Officer shall put purchaser in possession

When any sheriff or other officer sells any real estate or present interest in land by virtue of and under any execution or otherwise, it shall be his duty, upon application, to place the purchaser or his agent or attorney in possession of the real estate. To this end, the officer may dispossess the defendant, his heirs, his tenants, or his lessees, vendees, or assignees since the judgment. However, he may not dispossess other persons claiming under an independent title.

Laws 1811, Cobb's 1851 Digest, p. 510; Laws 1823, Cobb's 1851 Digest, p. 512.

Formerly Code 1863, §§ 2580, 3578; Code 1868, §§ 2582, 3601; Code 1873, §§ 2624, 3651; Code 1882, §§ 2624, 3651; Civil Code 1895, §§ 5451, 5468; Civil Code 1910, §§ 6056, 6073; Code 1933, §§ 39-1309, 39-1312.

§ 9-13-176. Possession, how obtained

If the purchaser of real estate at sheriff's and other sales under execution fails to make application for possession thereof until the next term of the superior court after the sale has taken place or until the officer making the sale has gone out of office, the possession may be obtained only under an order of the superior court.

Formerly Code 1863, § 3579; Code 1868, § 3602; Code 1873, § 3652; Code 1882, § 3652; Civil Code 1895, § 5469; Civil Code 1910, § 6074; Code 1933, § 39-1313.

§ 9-13-177. Purchaser has covenants of warranty running with land

The purchaser at a judicial sale may enforce any covenants of warranty running with the land which are incorporated in the previous title deeds.

Formerly Code 1863, § 2578; Code 1868, § 2581; Code 1873, § 2623; Code 1882, § 2623; Civil Code 1895, § 5450; Civil Code 1910, § 6055; Code 1933, § 39-1308.

§ 9-13-178. Title of purchaser is original

In all controversies in the courts of this state, the purchaser at a judicial sale shall not be required to show title deeds prior to his purchase unless it is necessary for his case to show good title in the person whose interest he purchased.

Formerly Code 1863, § 2576; Code 1868, § 2578; Code 1873, § 2620; Code 1882, § 2620; Civil Code 1895, § 5447; Civil Code 1910, § 6052; Code 1933, § 39-1305.

CHAPTER 14

HABEAS CORPUS

Article 1

General Provisions

§ 9-14-1. Who may sue out writ

(a) Any person restrained of his liberty under any pretext whatsoever, except under sentence of a state court of record, may seek a writ of habeas corpus to inquire into the legality of the restraint.

(b) Any person alleging that another person in whom for any cause he is interested is kept illegally from the custody of the applicant may seek a writ of habeas corpus to inquire into the legality of the restraint.

(c) Any person restrained of his liberty as a result of a sentence imposed by any state court of record may seek a writ of habeas corpus to inquire into the legality of the restraint.

Cobb's 1851 Digest, pp. 1131-1134; Laws 1967, p. 835, § 2.

Formerly Code 1863, § 3909; Code 1868, § 3933; Code 1873, § 4009; Code 1882, § 4009; Penal Code 1895, § 1210; Penal Code 1910, § 1291; Code 1933, § 50-101.

§ 9-14-2. Detention of spouse or child

In all writs of habeas corpus sought on account of the detention of a spouse or child, the court on hearing all the facts may exercise its discretion as to whom the custody of the spouse or child shall be given and shall have the power to give the custody of a child to a third person.

Laws 1845, Cobb's 1851 Digest, p. 335; Laws 1976, p. 1050, § 2.

Formerly Code 1863, § 3925; Code 1868, § 3948; Code 1873, § 4024; Code 1882, § 4024; Civil Code 1895, § 2453; Penal Code 1895, § 1226; Civil Code 1910, § 2972; Penal Code 1910, § 1307; Code 1933, § 50-121.

§ 9-14-3. Application; how made and what to contain

The application for the writ of habeas corpus shall be by petition in writing, signed by the applicant, his attorney or agent, or some other person in his behalf, and shall state:

(1) The name or description of the person whose liberty is restrained;

(2) The person restraining, the mode of restraint, and the place of detention as nearly as practicable;

(3) The cause or pretense of the restraint. If the restraint is under the pretext of legal process, a copy of the process must be annexed to the petition if this is within the power of the applicant;

(4) A distinct averment of the alleged illegality in the restraint or of any other reason why the writ of habeas corpus is sought; and

(5) A prayer for the writ of habeas corpus.

Formerly Code 1863, § 3910; Code 1868, § 3934; Code 1873, § 4010; Code 1882, § 4010; Penal Code 1895, § 1211; Penal Code 1910, § 1292; Code 1933, § 50-102.

§ 9-14-4. Petition, how verified and to whom presented

The petition for the writ of habeas corpus must be verified by the oath of the applicant or some other person in his behalf. It may be presented to the judge of the superior court of the circuit in which the illegal detention exists who may order the party restrained of his liberty to be brought before him from any county in his circuit, or it may be presented to the judge of the probate court of the county, except in cases of capital felonies or in which a person is held for extradition under warrant of the Governor.

Cobb's 1851 Digest, p. 543; Laws 1868, p. 128, § 1; Laws 1872, p. 44, § 1; Laws 1884-85, p. 50, § 1; Laws 1884-85, p. 470, § 10.

Formerly Code 1863, § 3911; Code 1868, § 3935; Code 1873, § 4011; Code 1882, § 4011; Penal Code 1895, § 1212; Penal Code 1910, § 1293; Code 1933, § 50-103.

§ 9-14-5. When writ must be granted

When upon examination of the petition for a writ of habeas corpus it appears to the judge that the restraint of liberty is illegal, he shall grant the writ, requiring the person restraining the liberty of another or illegally detaining such person in his custody to bring the person before him at a time and place to be specified in the writ for the purpose of an examination into the cause of the detention.

Formerly Code 1863, § 3912; Code 1868, § 3936; Code 1873, § 4012; Code 1882, § 4012; Penal Code 1895, § 1213; Penal Code 1910, § 1294; Code 1933, § 50-104.

§ 9-14-6. Form of writ

The writ of habeas corpus may be substantially as follows:

—IN THE ____ COURT OF ____ COUNTY—

—STATE OF GEORGIA—

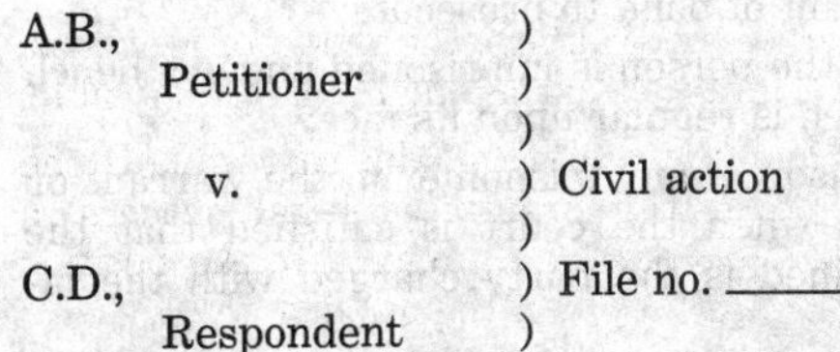

A.B.,)
Petitioner)
)
v.) Civil action
)
C.D.,) File no. ____
Respondent)

—WRIT OF HABEAS CORPUS—

To C.D.:

You are hereby commanded to produce the body of ____, alleged to be illegally detained by you, together with the cause of the detention, before me on the ____ day of ____, ____, at ____: ____ ____.M., then and there to be disposed of as the law directs.

Given under my hand and official signature, this ____ day of ____, ____.

____
Judge

Laws 1999, p. 81, § 9.

Formerly Code 1863, § 3913; Code 1868, § 3937; Code 1873, § 4013; Code 1882, § 4013; Penal Code 1895, § 1214; Penal Code 1910, § 1295; Code 1933, § 50-106.

§ 9-14-7. Return day of the writ

The return day of the writ of habeas corpus in civil cases shall always be within 20 days after the presentation of the petition therefor. The return day of the writ in criminal cases shall always be within eight days after the presentation of the petition therefor.

Laws 1956, p. 374, § 1.

Formerly Code 1863, § 3914; Code 1868, § 3938; Code 1873, § 4014; Code 1882, § 4014; Penal Code 1895, § 1215; Penal Code 1910, § 1296; Code 1933, § 50-107.

§ 9-14-8. How and by whom the writ shall be served

The writ of habeas corpus shall be served by delivery of a copy thereof by any officer authorized to make a return of any process or by any other citizen. The entry of the officer or the affidavit of the citizen serving the writ shall be sufficient evidence of the service. The person serving the writ shall exhibit the original if required to do so. If personal service cannot be effected, the writ may be served by leaving a copy at the house, jail, or other place in which the party in whose behalf the writ issues is detained.

Formerly Code 1863, § 3915; Code 1868, § 3939; Code 1873, § 4015; Code 1882, § 4015; Penal Code 1895, § 1216; Penal Code 1910, § 1297; Code 1933, § 50-108.

§ 9-14-9. When and how the party detained may be arrested

If the affidavit of the applicant to the effect that he has reason to apprehend that the party detaining or holding another in custody will remove him beyond the limits of the county or conceal him from the officers of the law is filed with the petition, the judge granting the writ shall at the same time issue his warrant directed to the sheriff, deputy sheriff, coroner, or any lawful constable of the county requiring the officers to search for and arrest the body of the person detained and to bring him before the judge to be disposed of as he may direct.

Formerly Code 1863, § 3916; Code 1868, § 3940; Code 1873, § 4016; Code 1882, § 4016; Penal Code 1895, § 1217; Penal Code 1910, § 1298; Code 1933, § 50-109.

§ 9-14-10. Within what time return to writ must be made

The return of the party served with the writ shall be made at the time and place specified by the court. Two days from the time of service shall be allowed for every 20 miles which the party has to travel from the place of detention to the place appointed for the hearing. If service has not been made a sufficient time before the hearing to cover the time allowed in this Code section to reach the place of hearing, the return shall be made within the time so allowed immediately after the service.

Formerly Code 1863, § 3917; Code 1868, § 3941; Code 1873, § 4017; Code 1882, § 4017; Penal Code 1895, § 1218; Penal Code 1910, § 1299; Code 1933, § 50-110.

§ 9-14-11. Return to be under oath, and body produced

Every return to a writ of habeas corpus shall be under oath. If the custody or detention of the party on whose behalf the writ issues is admitted, his body shall be produced unless prevented by providential cause or prohibited by law.

Formerly Code 1863, § 3918; Code 1868, § 3942; Code 1873, § 4018; Code 1882, § 4018; Penal Code 1895, § 1219; Penal Code 1910, § 1300; Code 1933, § 50-111.

§ 9-14-12. Transfer of custody must be stated in return

If the return denies the custody or detention of the person in question, it shall further state distinctly the latest date, if ever, at which custody was had and when and to whom custody was transferred. If it appears that a transfer of custody was made to avoid the writ of habeas corpus, the party making the return may be imprisoned, in the discretion of the judge hearing the case, until the body of the party kept or detained is produced.

Formerly Code 1863, § 3920; Code 1868, § 3944; Code 1873, § 4020; Code 1882, § 4020; Penal Code 1895, § 1221; Penal Code 1910, § 1302; Code 1933, § 50-113.

§ 9-14-13. When process must be produced

In every case in which detention is justified under legal process, the legal process shall be produced and submitted to the judge at the hearing of the return.

Formerly Code 1863, § 3919; Code 1868, § 3943; Code 1873, § 4019; Code 1882, § 4019; Penal Code 1895, § 1220; Penal Code 1910, § 1301; Code 1933, § 50-112.

§ 9-14-14. Trial of issue on the return

If the return denies any of the material facts stated in the petition or alleges other facts upon which issue is taken, the judge hearing the return may in a summary manner hear testimony as to the issue. To that end, he may compel the attendance of witnesses and the production of papers, may adjourn the examination of the question, or may exercise any other power of a court which the principles of justice may require.

Formerly Code 1863, § 3922; Code 1868, § 3945; Code 1873, § 4021; Code 1882, § 4021; Penal Code 1895, § 1222; Penal Code 1910, § 1303; Code 1933, § 50-114.

§ 9-14-15. Notice of the hearing

If the person who is the subject of a petition for the writ of habeas corpus is detained upon a criminal charge and the district attorney is in the county, he shall be notified of the hearing. If he is not, the notice shall be given to the prosecutor of the criminal charge.

Laws 1851-52, p. 236, § 1.

Formerly Code 1863, § 3931; Code 1868, § 3954; Code 1873, § 4030; Code 1882, § 4030; Penal Code 1895, § 1233; Penal Code 1910, § 1314; Code 1933, § 50-120.

§ 9-14-16. When party shall not be discharged

No person shall be discharged upon the hearing of a writ of habeas corpus in the following cases:

(1) When he is imprisoned under lawful process issued from a court of competent jurisdiction unless his case is one in which bail is allowed and proper bail is tendered;

(2) By reason of any irregularity in the warrant or commitment where the same substantially conforms to the requirements of law;

(3) For want of bond to prosecute;

(4) When the person is imprisoned under a bench warrant which is regular upon its face;

(5) By reason of any misnomer in the warrant or commitment when the court is satisfied that the person detained is the party charged with the offense;

(6) When the person is in custody for a contempt of court and the court has not exceeded its jurisdiction in the length of the imprisonment imposed; or

(7) In any other case in which it appears that the detention is authorized by law.

Formerly Code 1863, § 3924; Code 1868, § 3947; Code 1873, § 4023; Code 1882, § 4023; Penal Code 1895, § 1224; Penal Code 1910, § 1305; Code 1933, § 50-116.

§ 9-14-17. No discharge for defect in proceedings

If the person in question is detained upon a criminal charge and it appears to the court that there is probable cause for his detention, he shall not be discharged for any defect in the affidavit, warrant, or commitment until a reasonable time has been given to the prosecutor to remedy the defect by a new proceeding.

Laws 1808, Cobb's 1851 Digest, p. 856.

Formerly Code 1863, § 3926; Code 1868, § 3949; Code 1873, § 4025; Code 1882, § 4025; Penal Code 1895, § 1227; Penal Code 1910, § 1308; Code 1933, § 50-117.

§ 9-14-18. Offense committed in another state

If a person is arrested on suspicion of the commission of an offense in another state and the suspicion is reasonable, the person shall not be discharged until a sufficient time has been given for a demand to be made on the Governor for his rendition.

Formerly Code 1863, § 3926; Code 1868, § 3949; Code 1873, § 4025; Code 1882, § 4025; Penal Code 1895, § 1228; Penal Code 1910, § 1309; Code 1933, § 50-118.

§ 9-14-19. Powers of court in other cases

In cases other than those specified in Code Sections 9-14-16, 9-14-17, and 9-14-18, the judge hearing the return shall discharge, remand, or admit the person in question to bail or shall deliver him to the custody of the officer or person entitled thereto, as the principles of law and justice may require.

Formerly Code 1863, § 3927; Code 1868, § 3950; Code 1873, § 4026; Code 1882, § 4026; Penal Code 1895, § 1229; Penal Code 1910, § 1310; Code 1933, § 50-119.

§ 9-14-20. Proceedings must be recorded

In all habeas corpus cases, the proceedings shall be returned to the clerk of the superior court of the county the judge of which heard the same or to the probate court if the case was heard by the judge of the probate court and shall be recorded by such officer as are other cases. For such services, the officer shall receive the fees provided by Code Section 15-6-77.

Laws 1970, p. 497, § 5.

Formerly Code 1863, § 3930; Code 1868, § 3953; Code 1873, § 4029; Code 1882, § 4029; Penal Code 1895, § 1232; Penal Code 1910, § 1313; Code 1933, § 50-124.

§ 9-14-21. Costs; discretion; execution

The judge hearing the return to a writ of habeas corpus may in his discretion award the costs of the proceeding against either party and may order execution to issue therefor by the clerk.

Formerly Code 1863, § 3929; Code 1868, § 3952; Code 1873, § 4028; Code 1882, § 4028; Penal Code 1895, § 1231; Penal Code 1910, § 1312; Code 1933, § 50-125.

§ 9-14-22. Practice as to appeals; hearing in habeas corpus cases

(a) Appeals in habeas corpus cases shall be governed, in all respects where applicable, by the laws in reference to appeals in other cases regarding the practice in the lower courts and in the Supreme Court relating to the time and manner of signing, filing, serving, transmitting, and hearing.

(b) It shall be the duty of the Supreme Court to give a speedy hearing and determination in habeas corpus cases either under existing rules or under special rules to be formulated by the court for such purpose.

(c) If the judgment of the court below is affirmed by the Supreme Court, the clerk of the Supreme Court shall promptly transmit the remittitur to the clerk of the court from which the appeal was taken. Upon the receipt of the remittitur, the clerk shall notify the judge of the court who shall have full power to pass an order, sentence, or judgment necessary to carry into execution the judgment of the court.

Laws 1897, p. 53, § 1; Laws 1946, p. 726, § 1.

Formerly Penal Code 1910, § 1316; Code 1933, § 50-126.

§ 9-14-23. Disobedience of the writ, how punished

Any person disregarding the writ of habeas corpus in any manner whatever shall be liable to attachment for contempt, issued by the judge granting the writ, under which attachment the person may be imprisoned until he complies with the legal requirements of the writ.

Formerly Code 1863, § 3923; Code 1868, § 3946; Code 1873, § 4022; Code 1882, § 4022; Penal Code 1895, § 1223; Penal Code 1910, § 1304; Code 1933, § 50-115.

Article 2

Procedure for Persons under Sentence of State Court of Record

§ 9-14-40. Findings of General Assembly

(a) The General Assembly finds that:

(1) Expansion of the scope of habeas corpus in federal court by decisions of the United States Supreme Court together with other decisions of the court substantially curtailing the doctrine of waiver of constitutional rights by an accused and limiting the requirement of exhaustion of state remedies to those currently available have resulted in an increasingly large number of convictions of the courts of this state being collaterally attacked by federal habeas corpus based upon issues and contentions not previously presented to or passed upon by courts of this state;

(2) The increased reliance upon federal courts tends to weaken state courts as instruments for the vindication of constitutional rights with a resultant deterioration of the federal system and federal-state relations; and

(3) To alleviate such problems, it is necessary that the scope of state habeas corpus be expanded and the state doctrine of waiver of rights be modified.

(b) The General Assembly further finds that expansion of state habeas corpus to include many sharply contested issues of a factual nature requires that only the superior courts have jurisdiction of such cases.

Laws 1967, p. 835, § 1.

§ 9-14-41. Exclusive procedure for suing out writ of habeas corpus for persons whose liberty is being restrained by virtue of sentence imposed against them by state court of record

Notwithstanding the other provisions of this chapter, this article provides the exclusive procedure for seeking a writ of habeas corpus for persons whose liberty is being restrained by virtue of a sentence imposed against them by a state court of record.

Laws 1967, p. 835, § 3.

Formerly Code 1933, § 50-127.

§ 9-14-42. Denial of constitutional or other rights; waiver of objections

(a) Any person imprisoned by virtue of a sentence imposed by a state court of record who asserts that in the proceedings which resulted in his conviction there was a substantial denial of his rights under the Constitution of the United States or of this state may institute a proceeding under this article.

(b) The right to object to the composition of the grand or trial jury will be deemed waived under this Code section unless the person challenging the sentence shows in the petition and satisfies the court that cause exists for his being allowed to pursue the objection after the conviction and sentence have otherwise become final.

(c) Any action brought pursuant to this article shall be filed within one year in the case of a misdemeanor, except as otherwise provided in Code Section 40-13-33, or within four years in the case of a felony, other than one challenging a conviction for which a death sentence has been imposed or challenging a sentence of death, from:

(1) The judgment of conviction becoming final by the conclusion of direct review or the expiration of the time for seeking such review; provided, however, that any person whose conviction has become final as of July 1, 2004, regardless of the date of conviction, shall have until July 1, 2005, in the case of a misdemeanor or until July 1, 2008, in the case of a felony to bring an action pursuant to this Code section;

(2) The date on which an impediment to filing a petition which was created by state action in violation of the Constitution or laws of the United States or of this state is removed, if the petitioner was prevented from filing such state action;

(3) The date on which the right asserted was initially recognized by the Supreme Court of the United States or the Supreme Court of Georgia, if that right was newly recognized by said courts and made retroactively applicable to cases on collateral review; or

(4) The date on which the facts supporting the claims presented could have been discovered through the exercise of due diligence.

(d) At the time of sentencing, the court shall inform the defendant of the periods of limitation set forth in subsection (c) of this Code section.

Laws 1967, p. 835, § 3; Laws 1975, p. 1143, § 1; Laws 1982, p. 786, §§ 1, 3; Laws 1984, p. 22, § 9; Laws 2004, Act 661, § 1, eff. July 1, 2004.

Formerly Code 1933, § 50-127.

§ 9-14-43. Exclusive jurisdiction in superior court in county in which petitioner detained

A petition brought under this article must be filed in the superior court of the county in which the petitioner is being detained. The superior courts of such counties shall have exclusive jurisdiction of habeas corpus actions arising under this article. If the petitioner is not in custody or is being detained under the authority of the United States, any of the several states other than Georgia, or any foreign state, the petition must be filed in the superior court of the county in which the conviction and sentence which is being challenged was imposed.

Laws 1967, p. 835, § 3; Laws 2004, Act 661, § 2, eff. July 1, 2004.

Formerly Code 1933, § 50-127.

§ 9-14-44. Contents and verification of petition

A petition brought under this article shall identify the proceeding in which the petitioner was convicted, give the date of rendition of the final judgment complained of, clearly set forth the respects in which the petitioner's rights were violated, and state with specificity which claims were raised at trial or on direct appeal, providing appropriate citations to the trial or appellate record. The petition shall have attached thereto affidavits, records, or other evidence supporting its allegations or shall state why the same are not attached. The petition shall identify any previous proceedings that the petitioner may have taken to secure relief from his or her conviction and, in the case of prior habeas corpus petitions, shall state which claims were previously raised. Argument and citations of authorities shall be omitted from the petition; however, a brief may be submitted in support of the petition setting forth any applicable argument. The petition must be verified by the oath of the applicant or of some other person in his or her behalf.

Laws 1967, p. 835, § 3; Laws 1995, p. 381, § 3.

Formerly Code 1933, § 50-127.

§ 9-14-45. Service of petition

Service of a petition brought under this article shall be made upon the person having custody of the petitioner. If the petitioner is being detained under the custody of the Department of Corrections, an additional copy of the petition shall be served on the Attorney General. If the petitioner is being detained under the custody of some authority other than the Department of Corrections, an additional copy of the petition shall be served upon the district attorney of the county in which the petition is filed. Service upon the Attorney General or the district attorney may be had by mailing a copy of the petition and a proper certificate of service.

Laws 1967, p. 835, § 3; Laws 1985, p. 283, § 1.

Formerly Code 1933, § 50-127.

§ 9-14-46. Custody, control and production of petitioner

Custody and control of the petitioner shall be retained by the Department of Corrections or other authority having custody of the petitioner. It shall be the duty of the department or authority to produce the petitioner at such times and places as the court may direct.

Laws 1967, p. 835, § 3; Laws 1985, p. 283, § 1.

Formerly Code 1933, § 50-127.

§ 9-14-47. Time for answer or motion to dismiss, and hearing

Except as otherwise provided in Code Section 9-14-47.1 with respect to petitions challenging for the first time state court proceedings resulting in a sentence of death, within 20 days after the filing and docketing of a petition under this article or within such further time as the court may set, the respondent shall answer or move to dismiss the petition. The court shall set the case for a hearing on the issues within a reasonable time after the filing of defensive pleadings.

Laws 1967, p. 835, § 3; Laws 1995, p. 381, § 4.

Formerly Code 1933, § 50-127.

§ 9-14-47.1. Procedures for challenging for first time state court proceedings resulting in death sentence; establishment by uniform court rules of time periods and schedules

(a) In petitions filed under this article challenging for the first time state court proceedings resulting in a death sentence, the provisions of this article shall apply except as specifically provided otherwise in this Code section.

(b) Within ten days of the filing of a petition challenging for the first time state court proceedings resulting in a death sentence, the superior court clerk of the county where the petition is filed shall give written notice to The Council of Superior Court Judges of Georgia of the filing of the petition which shall serve as a request for judicial assistance under paragraph (3) of subsection (b) of Code Section 15-1-9.1. Within 30 days of receipt of such notice, the president of the council shall, under guidelines promulgated by the executive committee of the council, assign the case to a judge of a circuit other than the circuit in which the conviction and sentence were imposed.

(c) The Council of Superior Court Judges of Georgia shall establish, by uniform court rules, appropriate time periods and schedules applicable to petitions filed on or after January 1, 1996, challenging for the first time state court proceedings resulting in a sentence of death. Such rules shall be adopted by the Supreme Court of Georgia on or before December 31, 1995. Such new time periods and schedules shall include, but specifically not be limited to, the following:

(1) Respondent's filing of an answer or motion to dismiss the petition;

(2) Petitioner's filing of any amendments to the petition;

(3) Filing by either party of motions and responses to motions;

(4) Scheduling and conducting of evidentiary hearings; and

(5) Date of final order.

(d) In petitions filed under this article challenging for a second or subsequent time a state court proceeding resulting in a death sentence, the petitioner shall not be entitled to invoke any of the provisions set forth in this Code section to delay the proceedings. To the extent the court deems it necessary to have an evidentiary hearing on any such petition, the court shall expedite the proceedings and the time limits shall not exceed those set for initial petitions.

Laws 1995, p. 381, § 5; Laws 1996, p. 6, § 9.

§ 9-14-48. Proof; depositions; affidavits; order of court

(a) The court may receive proof by depositions, oral testimony, sworn affidavits, or other evidence. No other forms of discovery shall be allowed except upon leave of court and a showing of exceptional circumstances.

(b) The taking of depositions or depositions upon written questions by either party shall be governed by Code Sections 9-11-26 through 9-11-32 and 9-11-37; provided, however, that the time allowed in Code Section 9-11-31 for service of cross-questions upon all other parties shall be ten days from the date the notice and written questions are served.

(c) If sworn affidavits are intended by either party to be introduced into evidence, the party intending to introduce such an affidavit shall cause it to be served upon the opposing party at least ten days in advance of the date set for a hearing in the case. The affidavit so served shall include the address and telephone number of the affiant, home or business, if known, to provide the opposing party a reasonable opportunity to contact the affiant; failure to include this information in any affidavit shall render the affidavit inadmissible. The affidavit shall also be accompanied by a notice of the party's intention to introduce it into evidence. The superior court judge considering the petition for writ of habeas corpus may resolve disputed issues of fact upon the basis of sworn affidavits standing by themselves.

(d) The court shall review the trial record and transcript of proceedings and consider whether the petitioner made timely motion or objection or otherwise complied with Georgia procedural rules at trial and on appeal and whether, in the event the petitioner had new counsel subsequent to trial, the petitioner raised any claim of ineffective assistance of trial counsel on appeal; and absent a showing of cause for noncompliance with such requirement, and of actual prejudice, habeas corpus relief shall not be granted. In all cases habeas corpus relief shall be granted to avoid a miscarriage of justice. If the court finds in favor of the petitioner, it shall enter an appropriate order with respect to the judgment or sentence challenged in the proceeding and such supplementary orders as to rearraignment, retrial, custody, or discharge as may be necessary and proper.

(e) A petition, other than one challenging a conviction for which a death sentence has been imposed or challenging a sentence of death, may be dismissed if there is a particularized showing that the respondent has been prejudiced in its ability to respond to the petition by delay in its filing unless the petitioner shows by a preponderance of the evidence that it is based on grounds of which he or she could not have had knowledge by the exercise of reasonable diligence before the circumstances prejudicial to the respondent occurred. This subsection shall apply only to convictions had before July 1, 2004.

Laws 1967, p. 835, § 3; Laws 1975, p. 1143, § 2; Laws 1982, p. 786, §§ 2, 4; Laws 1995, p. 381, § 6; Laws 2004, Act 661, § 3, eff. July 1, 2004.

Formerly Code 1933, § 50-127.

§ 9-14-49. Written findings of facts and conclusions of law

After reviewing the pleadings and evidence offered at the trial of the case, the judge of the superior court hearing the case shall make written findings of fact and conclusions of law upon which the judgment is based. The findings of fact and conclusions of law shall be recorded as part of the record of the case.

Laws 1967, p. 835, § 3.

Formerly Code 1933, § 50-127.

§ 9–14–50. Transcription of trial

All trials held under this article shall be transcribed by a court reporter designated by the superior court hearing the case.

Laws 1967, p. 835, § 3.

Formerly Code 1933, § 50–127.

§ 9–14–51. Waiver of ground not raised, exception

All grounds for relief claimed by a petitioner for a writ of habeas corpus shall be raised by a petitioner in his original or amended petition. Any grounds not so raised are waived unless the Constitution of the United States or of this state otherwise requires or unless any judge to whom the petition is assigned, on considering a subsequent petition, finds grounds for relief asserted therein which could not reasonably have been raised in the original or amended petition.

Laws 1967, p. 835, § 3; Laws 1973, p. 1315, § 1.

Formerly Code 1933, § 50–127.

§ 9–14–52. Appeals

(a) Appeals in habeas corpus cases brought under this article shall be governed by Chapter 6 of Title 5 except that as to final orders of the court which are adverse to the petitioner no appeal shall be allowed unless the Supreme Court of this state issues a certificate of probable cause for the appeal.

(b) If an unsuccessful petitioner desires to appeal, he must file a written application for a certificate of probable cause to appeal with the clerk of the Supreme Court within 30 days from the entry of the order denying him relief. The petitioner shall also file within the same period a notice of appeal with the clerk of the concerned superior court. The Supreme Court shall either grant or deny the application within a reasonable time after filing. In order for the Supreme Court to consider fully the request for a certificate, the clerk of the concerned superior court shall forward, as in any other case, the record and transcript, if designated, to the clerk of the Supreme Court when a notice of appeal is filed. The clerk of the concerned superior court need not prepare and retain and the court reporter need not file a copy of the original record and a copy of the original transcript of proceedings. The clerk of the Supreme Court shall return the original record and transcript to the clerk of the concerned superior court upon completion of the appeal if the certificate is granted. If the Supreme Court denies the application for a certificate of probable cause, the clerk of the Supreme Court shall return the original record and transcript and shall notify the clerk of the concerned superior court and the parties to the proceedings below of the determination that probable cause does not exist for appeal.

(c) If the trial court finds in favor of the petitioner, no certificate of probable cause need be obtained by the respondent as a condition precedent to appeal. A notice of appeal filed by the respondent shall act as a supersedeas and shall stay the judgment of the superior court until there is a final adjudication by the Supreme Court; provided, however, that, while such case is on appeal, the petitioner may be released on bail as is provided in criminal cases except when the petitioner has been convicted of a crime which the Supreme Court has jurisdiction to consider on direct appeal. The right to bail and the amount of bond shall be within the discretion of the judge of the superior court in which the sentence successfully challenged under this article was originally imposed.

Laws 1967, p. 835, § 3; Laws 1975, p. 1143, § 3.

Formerly Code 1933, § 50–127.

§ 9–14–53. Reimbursement of counties for court costs for writs of habeas corpus sought by indigent petitioners

Each county of this state shall be reimbursed from state funds for court costs both at the trial level and in any appellate court for each writ of habeas corpus sought in the superior court of the county by indigent petitioners when the granting of the writ is denied or when the court costs are cast upon the respondent, but such reimbursement shall not exceed $ 10,000.00 per annum total for each county. By not later than September 1 of each calendar year, the clerk of the superior court of each county shall send a certified list to the commissioner of administrative services of each writ of habeas corpus sought in the superior court of the county during the 12 month period immediately preceding July 1 of that calendar year by indigent petitioners for which the granting of the writ was denied or for which the court costs were cast upon the respondent; and such list shall include the court costs both at the trial level and in any appellate court for each such writ of habeas corpus. By not later than December 15 of each calendar year, the commissioner shall pay to the county from funds appropriated or otherwise made available for the operation of the superior courts the reimbursement as set forth in the certified list, subject to the maximum reimbursement provided for in this Code section. The list sent to the commissioner as provided in this paragraph shall be certified as correct by the governing authority of the county and by the judge of the superior court of the county. The commissioner is authorized to devise and make available to the counties such forms as may be reasonably necessary to carry out this paragraph and to establish such procedures as may be reasonably necessary for such purposes. This Code section shall not be construed to amend or repeal the provisions of

Code Section 15-6-28 or any other provision of law for funds for any judicial circuit.

Laws 1978, p. 2051, § 1; Laws 1985, p. 283, § 1; Laws 1993, p. 1402, § 19; Laws 1994, p. 97, § 9; Laws 1999, p. 660, § 1.

Formerly Code 1933, § 50-128.

CHAPTER 15

COURT AND LITIGATION COSTS

§ 9-15-1. Who shall pay costs

In all civil cases in any of the courts of this state, except as otherwise provided, the party who dismisses, loses, or is cast in the action shall be liable for the costs thereof.

Formerly Code 1863, § 3601; Code 1868, § 3625; Code 1873, § 3675; Code 1882, § 3675; Civil Code 1895, § 5385; Civil Code 1910, § 5980; Code 1933, § 24-3401.

§ 9-15-2. Pauper's affidavit in lieu of payment of costs; traverse by opposite party

(a)(1) When any party, plaintiff or defendant, in any action or proceeding held in any court in this state is unable to pay any deposit, fee, or other cost which is normally required in the court, if the party shall subscribe an affidavit to the effect that because of his indigence he is unable to pay the costs, the party shall be relieved from paying the costs and his rights shall be the same as if he had paid the costs.

(2) Any other party at interest or his agent or attorney may contest the truth of an affidavit of indigence by verifying affirmatively under oath that the same is untrue. The issue thereby formed shall be heard and determined by the court, under the rules of the court. The judgment of the court on all issues of fact concerning the ability of a party to pay costs or give bond shall be final.

(b) In the absence of a traverse affidavit contesting the truth of an affidavit of indigence, the court may inquire into the truth of the affidavit of indigence. After a hearing, the court may order the costs to be paid if it finds that the deposit, fee, or other costs can be paid and, if the costs are not paid within the time permitted in such order, may deny the relief sought.

(c) The adjudication of the issue of indigence shall not affect a decision on the merits of the pending action.

(d) When a civil action is presented for filing under this Code section by a party who is not represented by an attorney, the clerk of court shall not file the matter but shall present the complaint or other initial pleading to a judge of the court. The judge shall review the pleading and, if the judge determines that the pleading shows on its face such a complete absence of any justiciable issue of law or fact that it cannot be reasonably believed that the court could grant any relief against any party named in the pleading, then the judge shall enter an order denying filing of the pleading. If the judge does not so find, then the judge shall enter an order allowing filing and shall return the pleading to the clerk for filing as in other cases. An order denying filing shall be appealable in the same manner as an order dismissing an action.

Laws 1955, p. 584, §§ 1, 2; Laws 1982, p. 933, § 1; Laws 1983, p. 3, § 7; Laws 1984, p. 22, § 9; Laws 1985, p. 1256, § 1.

§ 9-15-3. When costs payable

The several officers of court are prohibited from demanding the costs in any civil case or any part thereof until after judgment in the same, except as otherwise provided by law.

Laws 1834, Cobb's 1851 Digest, p. 506; Laws 1842, Cobb's 1851 Digest, p. 507.

Formerly Code 1863, § 3609; Code 1868, § 3634; Code 1873, § 3684; Code 1882, § 3684; Civil Code 1895, § 5393; Civil Code 1910, § 5991; Code 1933, § 24-3409.

§ 9-15-4. Deposit of cost required in civil cases

(a) A clerk of the superior court shall not be required to file any civil case or proceeding until the fee required by Code Section 15-6-77 and Code Section 15-6-77.2, relating to fees of clerks of the superior courts, has been paid to the clerk. The fee shall not be required if the party desiring to file the case or proceeding is unable because of his indigence to pay the fee and the party files with the clerk an affidavit to such effect.

(b) The deposit required to be filed by this Code section shall not affect any other law which requires a deposit in excess of or in addition to the deposit of cost required by this Code section.

(c) Nothing contained in this Code section shall be deemed to require a deposit of cost by the state, its agencies, or its political subdivisions; and, without limiting the generality of the foregoing, no clerk of any court shall be authorized to require any deposit of costs in any action or proceeding for the collection of criminal penalties as authorized under Code Section 42–8–34.2.

Laws 1890–91, p. 100, § 1; Laws 1945, p. 207, § 1; Laws 1957, p. 405, § 2; Laws 1958, p. 398, § 1; Laws 1970, p. 497, § 4; Laws 1971, p. 214, § 2; Laws 1972, p. 664, § 5; Laws 1981, p. 1396, § 2; Laws 1986, p. 1002, § 4; Laws 1991, p. 1051, § 2.

Formerly Civil Code 1895, § 5398; Civil Code 1910, § 5986; Code 1933, § 24–3406.

§ 9–15–5. Repealed by Laws 1981, p. 1396, § 23, eff. July 1, 1981

§ 9–15–6. Costs when attorney or client or both are nonresident

(a) When any attorney institutes an action in any of the courts of this state for any person who resides outside this state, the attorney shall be liable to pay all costs of the officers of court in the event that the action is dismissed or the plaintiff is cast in the action.

(b) When the plaintiff and his attorney both reside outside the limits of this state, the proper officers may demand their full costs before they shall be bound to perform any service in any case commenced by the nonresident attorney or plaintiff.

Laws 1812, Cobb's 1851 Digest, p. 505; Laws 1839, Cobb's 1851 Digest, p. 507.

Formerly Code 1863, §§ 3603, 3605; Code 1868, §§ 3627, 3629; Code 1873, §§ 3677, 3679; Code 1882, §§ 3677, 3679; Civil Code 1895, §§ 5387, 5389; Civil Code 1910, § 5982; Code 1933, § 24–3403.

§ 9–15–7. Attorney liable for costs when negligent

If any plaintiff is involuntarily dismissed or cast in the action by reason of the willful neglect or misconduct of his attorney, his attorney shall be liable for the costs which may have accrued in the case. In like manner, if any defendant is cast in the action by reason of the willful neglect or misconduct of his attorney, his attorney shall be liable for the costs thereof.

Laws 1799, Cobb's 1851 Digest, p. 505.

Formerly Code 1863, § 3602; Code 1868, § 3626; Code 1873, § 3676; Code 1882, § 3676; Civil Code 1895, § 5386; Civil Code 1910, § 5981; Code 1933, § 24–3402.

§ 9–15–8. Costs of witnesses of adverse party

No party plaintiff or defendant shall be liable for the costs of any witness of the adverse party unless the witness is subpoenaed, sworn, and examined on the trial of the case or unless the plaintiff voluntarily dismisses his case before trial. No party shall be liable for the costs of more than two witnesses to the same point unless the court certifies that the question at issue was of such a character as rendered a greater number of witnesses necessary.

Laws 1799, Cobb's 1851 Digest, p. 277.

Formerly Code 1863, § 3608; Code 1868, § 3632; Code 1873, § 3682; Code 1882, § 3682; Civil Code 1895, § 5392; Civil Code 1910, § 5990; Code 1933, § 24–3408.

§ 9–15–9. Costs when recovery is less than $50 in action ex contractu

When any action ex contractu is brought in the superior or state court and the verdict of the jury, unreduced by setoff or payment pending the action, is for a sum under $50.00, the defendant shall not be charged with more costs than would have necessarily accrued if the case had been heard before a magistrate. The remainder of the court costs shall be paid by the plaintiff and may be retained out of the sum recovered by the plaintiff and, if that is insufficient, judgment shall be entered by the court against the plaintiff for the balance.

Laws 1809, Cobb's 1851 Digest, p. 505; Laws 1983, p. 884, § 4–1.

Formerly Code 1863, § 3604; Code 1868, § 3628; Code 1873, § 3678; Code 1882, § 3678; Civil Code 1895, § 5388; Civil Code 1910, § 5983; Code 1933, § 24–3404.

§ 9–15–10. Costs when recovery is less than $10.00 in slander or other personal action

(a) In all actions for slanderous words, in any court having jurisdiction of the same, if the jury renders a verdict under $10.00, the plaintiff shall have and recover no more costs than damages.

(b) In actions of assault and battery and in all other personal actions wherein the jury upon the trial thereof finds the damages to be less than $10.00, the plaintiff shall recover no more costs than damages unless the judge, at the trial thereof, finds and certifies on the record that an aggravated assault and battery was proved.

Laws 1767, Cobb's 1851 Digest, p. 504.

Formerly Code 1863, §§ 3606, 3607; Code 1868, §§ 3630, 3631; Code 1873, §§ 3680, 3681; Code 1882, §§ 3680, 3681; Civil Code 1895, §§ 5390, 5391; Civil Code 1910, § 5984; Code 1933, § 24–3405.

§ 9–15–11. How costs taxed

When a case is disposed of, the costs, including fees of witnesses, shall be included in the judgment against the party voluntarily dismissing, being involuntarily dismissed, or cast in the action. It shall be the duty of the clerk of the court, of the magistrate, or of any other officer who may issue an execution to endorse on the execution at the time it is issued the date and amount of the judgment, the items of the bill of cost, written in words, and the amount of each item distinctly stated in figures. No costs or items of costs shall in any case be demanded by any officer unless they are itemized and endorsed as provided in this Code section.

Laws 1870, p. 67, § 1; Laws 1983, p. 884, § 4-1.

Formerly Code 1863, § 3610; Code 1868, § 3635; Code 1873, § 3685; Code 1882, § 3685; Civil Code 1895, § 5394; Civil Code 1910, § 5992; Code 1933, § 24-3410.

§ 9-15-12. Liability of plaintiff and attorney on return of nulla bona

If execution issues on a judgment recovered by the plaintiff against the defendant and the executing officer returns the same marked "No property to be found," a fi. fa. may issue against the plaintiff for the purpose of recovering the costs from him; and, if the plaintiff resides outside the state, the fi. fa. shall issue against his attorney also.

Laws 1842, Cobb's 1851 Digest, p. 507.

Formerly Code 1863, § 3611; Code 1868, § 3636; Code 1873, § 3686; Code 1882, § 3686; Civil Code 1895, § 5395; Civil Code 1910, § 5993; Code 1933, § 24-3411.

§ 9-15-13. Judgment and execution against attorney for costs

In all cases in which it is made to appear that an attorney is liable for costs, the court shall, on motion, order a judgment and execution against him for the same.

Formerly Code 1863, § 3612; Code 1868, § 3637; Code 1873, § 3687; Code 1882, § 3687; Civil Code 1895, § 5396; Civil Code 1910, § 5994; Code 1933, § 24-3412.

§ 9-15-14. Attorney's fees and expenses of litigation where attorney brings or defends action lacking substantial justification

(a) In any civil action in any court of record of this state, reasonable and necessary attorney's fees and expenses of litigation shall be awarded to any party against whom another party has asserted a claim, defense, or other position with respect to which there existed such a complete absence of any justiciable issue of law or fact that it could not be reasonably believed that a court would accept the asserted claim, defense, or other position. Attorney's fees and expenses so awarded shall be assessed against the party asserting such claim, defense, or other position, or against that party's attorney, or against both in such manner as is just.

(b) The court may assess reasonable and necessary attorney's fees and expenses of litigation in any civil action in any court of record if, upon the motion of any party or the court itself, it finds that an attorney or party brought or defended an action, or any part thereof, that lacked substantial justification or that the action, or any part thereof, was interposed for delay or harassment, or if it finds that an attorney or party unnecessarily expanded the proceeding by other improper conduct, including, but not limited to, abuses of discovery procedures available under Chapter 11 of this title, the "Georgia Civil Practice Act." As used in this Code section, "lacked substantial justification" means substantially frivolous, substantially groundless, or substantially vexatious.

(c) No attorney or party shall be assessed attorney's fees as to any claim or defense which the court determines was asserted by said attorney or party in a good faith attempt to establish a new theory of law in Georgia if such new theory of law is based on some recognized precedential or persuasive authority.

(d) Attorney's fees and expenses of litigation awarded under this Code section shall not exceed amounts which are reasonable and necessary for defending or asserting the rights of a party. Attorney's fees and expenses of litigation incurred in obtaining an order of court pursuant to this Code section may also be assessed by the court and included in its order.

(e) Attorney's fees and expenses under this Code section may be requested by motion at any time during the course of the action but not later than 45 days after the final disposition of the action.

(f) An award of reasonable and necessary attorney's fees or expenses of litigation under this Code section shall be determined by the court without a jury and shall be made by an order of court which shall constitute and be enforceable as a money judgment.

(g) Attorney's fees and expenses of litigation awarded under this Code section in a prior action between the same parties shall be treated as court costs with regard to the filing of any subsequent action.

(h) This Code section shall not apply to proceedings in magistrate courts. However, when a case is appealed from the magistrate court, the appellee may seek litigation expenses incurred below if the appeal lacks substantial justification.

Laws 1986, p. 1591, § 1; Laws 1987, p. 397, § 1; Laws 1989, p. 437, § 1; Laws 1994, p. 856, § 2; Laws 1997, p. 689, § 1; Laws 2001, p. 967, § 1.

§ 9-15-15. Attorney's fees and expenses in actions brought against judicial officers and arising out of performance of official duties where action lacks substantial justification

(a) When any civil action is brought against a judicial officer, other than an action for quo warranto, mandamus, or an action brought under Title 42, Section 1983 of the United States Code, and such action arises out of the performance of the judicial officer's official duties, the plaintiff shall be liable for all attorney's fees and expenses incurred in the defense of the action if the action is concluded in favor of the judicial officer, and the court finds that an attorney or party brought an action that lacked substantial justification or that the action, or any part of the action, was interposed for delay or harassment. As used in this Code section, "lacked substantial justification" means substantially frivolous, substantially groundless, or substantially vexatious. For purposes of this Code section, judicial officers shall include justices and judges of the appellate courts of Georgia and judges of the superior, state, probate, juvenile, magistrate, and municipal courts.

(b) The provisions of subsection (a) of this Code section shall apply both with respect to actions brought against a judicial officer in his or her official capacity and with respect to actions brought against a judicial officer in his or her individual capacity where the action arises out of the performance of the judicial officer's official duties.

(c) Recovery may be had under subsection (a) of this Code section by the state or by a unit of local government with respect to attorney's fees and expenses incurred by the state or by the unit of local government. Where recovery by a governmental unit is so authorized, recovery shall be authorized for attorney's fees paid to outside counsel as well as for compensation paid to counsel employed by the governmental unit. Recovery may also be had under subsection (a) of this Code section with respect to attorney's fees and expenses personally incurred by a judicial officer. Recovery under subsection (a) of this Code section shall include any attorney's fees and expenses incurred in appellate proceedings arising out of an action subject to this Code section.

(d) When a civil action against a judicial officer, other than an action for quo warranto, mandamus, or an action brought under Title 42, Section 1983 of the United States Code, which action arises out of the performance of the judicial officer's official duties is presented for filing, the clerk of court shall file the matter but shall present the complaint or other initial pleading to the district court administrator for the judicial circuit where the action was filed, to assign to a superior court judge of that circuit. If the action is filed against a judge or justice of an appellate court, the chief judge or justice shall assign the matter to a member of that court. The judge shall review the pleading, and, if the judge determines that the pleading shows on its face such a complete absence of any justiciable issue of law or fact that it cannot be reasonably believed that the court could grant any relief against any party named in the pleading, then the judge shall enter an order dismissing the pleading. An order dismissing the pleading shall be appealable in the same manner as an order dismissing an action.

(e) Attorney's fees and expenses under this Code section may be requested by motion at any time during the course of the action but not later than 45 days after the final disposition of the action.

(f) An award of reasonable and necessary attorney's fees or expenses of litigation under this Code section shall be determined by the court without a jury and shall be made by an order of court which shall constitute and be enforceable as a money judgment.

Laws 1998, p. 862, § 3; Laws 1999, p. 81, § 9.

TITLE 17

CRIMINAL PROCEDURE

As Amended Through the 2006 Regular Session of the General Assembly

Research Note

Use Westlaw *to find cases citing a statute or to search for specific terms in a statute. See the Westlaw Directory Screens for lists of relevant databases.*

Table of Sections

INDEX

See Index to Georgia Statutes, infra.

CHAPTER 1
GENERAL PROVISIONS

§ 17–1–1. Service and filing of pleadings and other papers

(a) Unless otherwise provided by law or by order of the court, every pleading subsequent to the entry of the initial indictment or accusation upon which the defendant is to be tried; every order not entered in open court; every written motion, unless it is one as to which a hearing ex parte is authorized; and every written notice, demand, and similar paper shall be served upon each party.

(b)(1) Where service is required to be made, the service shall be made upon the party's attorney unless service upon the party himself is ordered by the court. Service upon the attorney or upon a party shall be made by delivering a copy to him or by mailing it to him at his last known address or, if no address is known, by leaving it with the clerk of the court.

(2) As used in this subsection, delivering a copy means:

(A) Handing it to the attorney or to the party;

(B) Leaving it at his office with his clerk or other person in charge thereof; or

(C) If the office is closed or the person to be served has no office, leaving it at his dwelling house or usual place of abode with some person of suitable age and discretion then residing therein.

(3) Service by mail shall be deemed complete upon mailing.

(c) All original papers, copies of which are required to be served upon parties, shall be filed with the court either before service or immediately thereafter.

(d) The filing of pleadings and other papers with the court shall be made by filing them with the clerk of the court unless the judge permits the papers to be filed with him, in which event he shall note thereon the filing date and transmit them to the office of the clerk.

(e)(1) Proof of service may be made by certificate of an attorney or of his employee, written admission, affidavit, or other proof satisfactory to the court. Failure to make proof of service shall not affect the validity of service.

(2) When an attorney executes a certificate, which shall be attached to the original of the paper to be served, certifying as to the service thereof, the certificate shall be taken as prima-facie proof of such service.

(3) The certificate of service provided for in this subsection shall read substantially as follows:

—Certificate of Service—

I do certify that (copy) (copies) hereof have been furnished to (here insert name or names) by (delivery) (mail) this _____ day of _____, _____.

____
Attorney

Laws 1981, Ex. Sess., p. 8; Laws 1999, p. 81, § 17.

§ 17–1–2. Penal action defined; party plaintiff

A "penal action" is an action allowed in pursuance of public justice under particular laws. If no special officer is authorized to be the plaintiff therein, the state, the Governor, the Attorney General, or the prosecuting attorney may be the plaintiff.

Formerly Code 1863, § 3178; Code 1868, § 3189; Code 1873, § 3254; Code 1882, § 3254; Civil Code 1895, § 4933; Civil Code 1910, § 5510; Code 1933, § 3–103.

§ 17–1–3. Mistakes of clerks or ministerial officers

The mistake or misprision of a clerk or other ministerial officer shall in no case work to the injury of a party where by amendment justice may be promoted.

Laws 1799, Cobb's 1851 Digest, p. 480.

Formerly Code 1863, § 3436; Code 1868, § 3456; Code 1873, § 3507; Code 1882, § 3507; Civil Code 1895, § 5125; Civil Code 1910, § 5709; Code 1933, § 81–1205.

§ 17–1–4. Judgments, etc., obtained by perjury

Any judgment, verdict, rule, or order of court which may have been obtained or entered shall be set aside and be of no effect if it appears that the same was entered in consequence of corrupt and willful perjury. It shall be the duty of the court in which the verdict, judgment, rule, or order was obtained or entered to cause the same to be vacated upon motion and notice to the adverse party; but it shall not be lawful for the court to do so unless the person charged with perjury shall have been duly convicted thereof and unless it appears to the court that the verdict, judgment, rule, or order could not have been obtained and entered without the evidence of the perjured person, saving always to third persons innocent of such perjury the rights which they may lawfully have acquired under the verdict, judgment, rule, or order before the same shall have been actually vacated.

Laws 1833, Cobb's 1851 Digest, p. 804.

Formerly Code 1863, § 3510; Code 1868, § 3533; Code 1873, § 3591; Code 1882, § 3591; Civil Code 1895, § 5366; Civil Code 1910, § 5961; Code 1933, § 110–706.

CHAPTER 2

JURISDICTION AND VENUE

§ 17–2–1. Jurisdiction

(a) It is the policy of this state to exercise its jurisdiction over crime and persons charged with the commission of crime to the fullest extent allowable under, and consistent with, the Constitution of this state and the Constitution of the United States.

(b) Pursuant to this policy, a person shall be subject to prosecution in this state for a crime which he commits, while either within or outside the state, by his own conduct or that of another for which he is legally accountable, if:

(1) The crime is committed either wholly or partly within the state;

(2) The conduct outside the state constitutes an attempt to commit a crime within the state; or

(3) The conduct within the state constitutes an attempt to commit in another jurisdiction a crime under the laws of both this state and the other jurisdiction.

(c) A crime is committed partly within this state if either the conduct which is an element of the crime or the result which is such an element occurs within the state. In homicide, the "result" is either the act which causes death or the death itself; and, if the body of a homicide victim is found within this state, the death is presumed to have occurred within the state.

(d) A crime which is based on an omission to perform a duty imposed by the law of this state is committed within the state, regardless of the location of the accused at the time of the omission.

Laws 1968, p. 1249, § 1.

Formerly Code 1933, § 26–301.

§ 17–2–2. Venue

(a) *In general.* Criminal actions shall be tried in the county where the crime was committed, except as otherwise provided by law.

(b) *Crime committed on boundary line of two counties.* If a crime is committed on, or immediately adjacent to, the boundary line between two counties, the crime shall be considered as having been committed in either county.

(c) *Criminal homicide.* Criminal homicide shall be considered as having been committed in the county in which the cause of death was inflicted. If it cannot be determined in which county the cause of death was inflicted, it shall be considered that it was inflicted in the county in which the death occurred. If a dead body is discovered in this state and it cannot be readily determined in what county the cause of death was inflicted, it shall be considered that the cause of death was inflicted in the county in which the dead body was discovered.

(d) *Crime commenced outside the state.* If the commission of a crime under the laws of this state commenced outside the state is consummated within this state, the crime shall be considered as having been committed in the county where it is consummated.

(e) *Crime committed while in transit.* If a crime is committed upon any railroad car, vehicle, watercraft, or aircraft traveling within this state and it cannot readily be determined in which county the crime was committed, the crime shall be considered as having been committed in any county in which the crime could have been committed through which the railroad car, vehicle, watercraft, or aircraft has traveled.

(f) *Crime committed on water boundaries of two counties.* Whenever a stream or body of water is the boundary between two counties, the jurisdiction of each county shall extend to the center of the main channel of the stream or the center of the body of water; and, if a crime is committed on the stream or body of water and it cannot be readily determined in which county the crime was committed, the crime shall be considered as having been committed in either county.

(g) *Crime committed on water boundaries of two states.* Whenever a crime is committed on any river or body of water which forms a boundary between this state and another state, the accused shall be tried in the county of this state which is situated opposite the point where the crime is committed. If it cannot be readily determined on which side of the line a crime was committed between two counties which border the river or body of water, the crime shall be considered as having been committed in either county.

(h) *Crime in more than one county.* If in any case it cannot be determined in what county a crime was committed, it shall be considered to have been committed in any county in which the evidence shows beyond a reasonable doubt that it might have been committed.

(i) *Cumulative effect of Code section.* This Code section is cumulative and shall not supersede venue provisions found in other parts of this Code.

Laws 1833, Cobb's 1851 Digest, p. 840; Laws 1855–56, p. 265, § 1; Laws 1895, p. 70, § 1; Laws 1968, p. 1249, § 1.

Formerly Code 1863, §§ 39, 40, 4556, 4557, 4558; Code 1868, §§ 37, 38, 4576, 4577, 4578; Code 1873, §§ 35, 36, 4570, 4571, 4572, 4686; Code 1882, §§ 35, 36, 4570, 4571, 4572, 4686, 5172; Penal Code 1895, §§ 23, 24, 26, 27, 28, 29; Penal Code 1910, §§ 23, 24, 26, 27, 28, 29; Code 1933, §§ 27-1101, 27-1102, 27-1103, 27-1104, 27-1105, 27-1106; Code 1933, § 26-302.

§ 17-2-3. Boundary lines of the state; determination of question of jurisdiction

This state claims jurisdiction of an offense committed on any of her boundary lines with other states for the county bordering on that part of the line where the offense was committed and, if doubtful as to which of two counties as set forth in subsection (g) of Code Section 17-2-2, for either county, and will proceed to arrest, indict, try, and punish unless the other state makes a demand for the accused person as a fugitive from justice, in which event the progress of the case shall be suspended by order of the Governor until the question of jurisdiction is settled.

Formerly Code 1863, § 41; Code 1868, § 39; Code 1873, § 37; Code 1882, § 37; Penal Code 1895, § 25; Penal Code 1910, § 25; Code 1933, § 27-1107.

§ 17-2-4. Transfer to county where defendant has been arrested, held, or is present to plead guilty, guilty but mentally ill, guilty but mentally retarded, or nolo contendere

(a) A defendant arrested, held, or present in a county other than that in which an indictment or accusation is pending against that defendant may state in writing a wish to plead guilty, guilty but mentally ill, guilty but mentally retarded, or nolo contendere; to waive trial in the county in which the indictment or accusation is pending; and to consent to disposition of the case in the county in which the defendant was arrested, held, or present, subject to the approval of the prosecuting attorney for each county. Upon receipt of the defendant's statement and the written approval of the prosecuting attorney for each county, the clerk of the court in which the indictment or accusation is pending shall transmit the papers in the proceeding or certified copies thereof to the clerk of the court for the county in which the defendant was arrested, held, or present, and the prosecution shall continue in that county.

(b) A defendant arrested, held, or present in a county other than the county in which a complaint or arrest warrant is pending against that defendant may state in writing a wish to plead guilty, guilty but mentally ill, guilty but mentally retarded, or nolo contendere; to waive venue and trial in the county in which the complaint or warrant was issued; and to consent to disposition of the case in the county in which the defendant was arrested, held, or present, subject to the approval of the prosecuting attorney for each county. Upon receipt of the defendant's statement and the written approval of the prosecuting attorney for each county, the clerk of the court in which the complaint or arrest warrant is pending shall transmit the papers in the proceeding or certified copies thereof to the clerk of the court for the county in which the defendant was arrested, held, or present, and the prosecution shall continue in that county.

(c) If after the proceeding has been transferred pursuant to subsection (a) or (b) of this Code section the defendant pleads not guilty or not guilty by reason of insanity, the clerk shall return the papers to the court in which the prosecution was commenced and the proceeding shall be restored to the docket of that court. A defendant's statement that the defendant wishes to plead guilty, guilty but mentally ill, guilty but mentally retarded, or nolo contendere shall not be used against the defendant.

Laws 1995, p. 1250, § 1.

CHAPTER 3

LIMITATIONS ON PROSECUTION

§ 17–3–1. Limitation of prosecutions

(a) A prosecution for murder may be commenced at any time.

(b) Prosecution for other crimes punishable by death or life imprisonment must be commenced within seven years after the commission of the crime except as provided by subsection (c.1) of this Code section; provided, however, that prosecution for the crime of forcible rape must be commenced within 15 years after the commission of the crime.

(c) Prosecution for felonies other than those specified in subsections (a), (b), and (c.1) of this Code section must be commenced within four years after the commission of the crime, provided that prosecution for felonies committed against victims who are at the time of the commission of the offense under the age of 18 years must be commenced within seven years after the commission of the crime.

(c.1) A prosecution for the following offenses may be commenced at any time when deoxyribonucleic acid (DNA) evidence is used to establish the identity of the accused:

(1) Armed robbery, as defined in Code Section 16–8–41;

(2) Kidnapping, as defined in Code Section 16–5–40;

(3) Rape, as defined in Code Section 16–6–1;

(4) Aggravated child molestation, as defined in Code Section 16–6–4;

(5) Aggravated sodomy, as defined in Code Section 16–6–2; or

(6) Aggravated sexual battery, as defined in Code Section 16–6–22.2;

provided, however, that a sufficient portion of the physical evidence tested for DNA is preserved and available for testing by the accused and provided, further, that, if the DNA evidence does not establish the identity of the accused, the limitation on prosecution shall be as provided in subsections (b) and (c) of this Code section.

(d) Prosecution for misdemeanors must be commenced within two years after the commission of the crime.

Laws 1968, p. 1249, § 1; Laws 1987, p. 330, § 1; Laws 1996, p. 1115, § 4; Laws 2002, p. 650, § 1.

Formerly Code 1933, § 26–502.

§ 17–3–2. Periods excluded from limitation

The period within which a prosecution must be commenced under Code Section 17–3–1 or other applicable statute does not include any period in which:

(1) The accused is not usually and publicly a resident within this state;

(2) The person committing the crime is unknown or the crime is unknown;

(3) The accused is a government officer or employee and the crime charged is theft by conversion of public property while such an officer or employee; or

(4) The accused is a guardian or trustee and the crime charged is theft by conversion of property of the ward or beneficiary.

Laws 1968, p. 1249, § 1; Laws 1969, p. 857, § 17.

Formerly Code 1933, § 26–503.

§ 17–3–2.1. Periods excluded from limitation of prosecution for certain offenses

(a) If the victim of a violation of:

(1) Code Section 16–5–70, relating to cruelty to children;

(2) Code Section 16–6–1, relating to rape;

(3) Code Section 16–6–2, relating to sodomy and aggravated sodomy;

(4) Code Section 16–6–3, relating to statutory rape;

(5) Code Section 16–6–4, relating to child molestation and aggravated child molestation;

(6) Code Section 16–6–5, relating to enticing a child for indecent purposes; or

(7) Code Section 16–6–22, relating to incest,

is under 16 years of age on the date of the violation, the applicable period within which a prosecution must be commenced under Code Section 17–3–1 or other applicable statute shall not begin to run until the victim has reached the age of 16 or the violation is reported to a law enforcement agency, prosecuting attorney, or other governmental agency, whichever occurs earlier. Such law enforcement agency or other governmental agency shall promptly report such allegation to the appropriate prosecuting attorney.

(b) This Code section shall apply to any offense designated in paragraphs (1) through (7) of subsection (a) of this Code section occurring on or after July 1, 1992.

Laws 1992, p. 2973, § 1.

§ 17-3-2.2. Periods excluded from limitation of prosecution where victim is 65 years of age or older

In addition to any periods excluded pursuant to Code Section 17-3-2, if the victim is a person who is 65 years of age or older, the applicable period within which a prosecution must be commenced under Code Section 17-3-1 or other applicable statute shall not begin to run until the violation is reported to or discovered by a law enforcement agency, prosecuting attorney, or other governmental agency, whichever occurs earlier. Such law enforcement agency or other governmental agency shall promptly report such allegation to the appropriate prosecuting attorney. Except for prosecutions for crimes for which the law provides a statute of limitations longer than 15 years, prosecution shall not commence more than 15 years after the commission of the crime.

Laws 2000, p. 1085, § 5.

§ 17-3-3. Extended limitations

If an indictment is found within the time provided for in Code Section 17-3-1 or 17-3-2, or other applicable statute, and is quashed or a nolle prosequi entered, the limitation shall be extended six months from the time the first indictment is quashed or the nolle prosequi entered.

Laws 1968, p. 1249, § 1.

Formerly Code 1933, § 26-504.

CHAPTER 4

ARREST OF PERSONS

Article 1

General Provisions

§ 17-4-1. What constitutes an arrest

An actual touching of a person with a hand is not essential to constitute a valid arrest. If the person voluntarily submits to being considered under arrest or yields on condition of being allowed his freedom of locomotion, under the discretion of the officer, the arrest is complete.

Formerly Code 1863, § 4609; Code 1968, § 4631; Code 1873, § 4728; Code 1882, § 4728; Penal Code 1895, § 893; Penal Code 1910, § 914; Code 1933, § 27-201.

§ 17-4-2. Privilege of members of militia and military forces

The members of the organized militia or military forces shall in all cases, except treason, felony, or breach of the peace, be privileged from arrest during their attendance at drills, parades, meetings, encampments, and the election of officers and going to, during, and returning from the performance of any active duty as such members.

Laws 1884-85, p. 74, § 11.

Formerly Penal Code 1895, § 892; Penal Code 1910, § 913; Code 1933, § 27-204.

§ 17-4-3. Breaking open doors

In order to arrest under a warrant charging a crime, the officer may break open the door of any house where the offender is concealed.

Formerly Code 1863, § 4610; Code 1868, § 4632; Code 1873, § 4729; Code 1882, § 4729; Penal Code 1895, § 894; Penal Code 1910, § 915; Code 1933, § 27-205.

Article 2

Arrest by Law Enforcement Officers Generally

§ 17–4–20. Arrest without warrant; use of deadly force; training recommendations; authority of nuclear power facility security officers

(a) An arrest for a crime may be made by a law enforcement officer either under a warrant or without a warrant if the offense is committed in such officer's presence or within such officer's immediate knowledge; if the offender is endeavoring to escape; if the officer has probable cause to believe that an act of family violence, as defined in Code Section 19–13–1, has been committed; if the officer has probable cause to believe that an offense involving physical abuse has been committed against a vulnerable adult, who shall be for the purposes of this subsection a person 18 years old or older who is unable to protect himself or herself from physical or mental abuse because of a physical or mental impairment; or for other cause if there is likely to be failure of justice for want of a judicial officer to issue a warrant.

(b) Sheriffs and peace officers who are appointed or employed in conformity with Chapter 8 of Title 35 may use deadly force to apprehend a suspected felon only when the officer reasonably believes that the suspect possesses a deadly weapon or any object, device, or instrument which, when used offensively against a person, is likely to or actually does result in serious bodily injury; when the officer reasonably believes that the suspect poses an immediate threat of physical violence to the officer or others; or when there is probable cause to believe that the suspect has committed a crime involving the infliction or threatened infliction of serious physical harm. Nothing in this Code section shall be construed so as to restrict such sheriffs or peace officers from the use of such reasonable nondeadly force as may be necessary to apprehend and arrest a suspected felon or misdemeanant.

(c) Nothing in this Code section shall be construed so as to restrict the use of deadly force by employees of state and county correctional institutions, jails, and other places of lawful confinement or by peace officers of any agency in the State of Georgia when reasonably necessary to prevent escapes or apprehend escapees from such institutions.

(d) No law enforcement agency of this state or of any political subdivision of this state shall adopt or promulgate any rule, regulation, or policy which prohibits a peace officer from using that degree of force to apprehend a suspected felon which is allowed by the statutory and case law of this state.

(e) Each peace officer shall be provided with a copy of this Code section. Training regarding elder abuse, abuse of vulnerable adults, and the requirements of this Code section should be offered as part of at least one in-service training program each year conducted by or on behalf of each law enforcement department and agency in this state.

(f) A nuclear power facility security officer, including a contract security officer, employed by a federally licensed nuclear power facility or licensee thereof for the purpose of securing that facility shall have the authority to:

(1) Threaten or use force against another in defense of a federally licensed nuclear power facility and the persons therein as provided for under Code Sections 16–3–21 and 16–3–23;

(2) Search any person on the premises of the nuclear power facility or the properties adjacent to the facility if the facility is under imminent threat or danger pursuant to a written agreement entered into with the local enforcement agency having jurisdiction over the facility for the purpose of determining if such person possesses unauthorized weapons, explosives, or other similarly prohibited material; provided, however, that if such person objects to any search, he or she shall be detained as provided in paragraph (3) of this subsection or shall be required to immediately vacate the premises. Any person refusing to submit to a search and refusing to vacate the premises of a facility upon the request of a security officer as provided for in this Code section shall be guilty of a misdemeanor; and

(3) In accordance with a nuclear security plan approved by the United States Nuclear Regulatory Commission or other federal agency authorized to regulate nuclear facility security, detain any person located on the premises of a nuclear power facility or on the properties adjacent thereto if the facility is under imminent threat or danger pursuant to a written agreement entered into with the local law enforcement agency having jurisdiction over the facility, where there is reasonable suspicion to believe that such person poses a threat to the security of the nuclear power facility, regardless of whether such prohibited act occurred in the officer's presence. In the event of such detention, the law enforcement agency having jurisdiction over the facility shall be immediately contacted. The detention shall not exceed the amount of time reasonably necessary to allow for law enforcement officers to arrive at the facility.

Laws 1975, p. 1209, § 1; Laws 1981, p. 880, § 6; Laws 1981, p. 1393, § 1; Laws 1986, p. 490, § 1; Laws 1986, p. 657, § 1;

Laws 1988, p. 1251, § 1; Laws 1991, p. 624, § 1; Laws 1997, p. 700, § 1; Laws 2006, Act 767, § 3, eff. May 3, 2006.

Formerly Code 1863, § 4603; Code 1868, § 4626; Code 1873, § 4723; Code 1882, § 4723; Penal Code 1895, § 896; Penal Code 1910, § 917; Code 1933, § 27-207.

§ 17-4-20.1. Investigation of and arrests in incidents of family violence

(a) Whenever a law enforcement officer responds to an incident in which an act of family violence, as defined in Code Section 19-13-1, has been committed, the officer shall not base the decision of whether to arrest and charge a person on the specific consent of the victim or on a request by the victim solely or on consideration of the relationship of the parties. No officer investigating an incident of family violence shall threaten, suggest, or otherwise indicate the arrest of all parties for the purpose of discouraging requests for law enforcement intervention.

(b) Where complaints of family violence are received from two or more opposing parties, the officer shall evaluate each complaint separately to attempt to determine who was the primary aggressor. If the officer determines that one of the parties was the primary physical aggressor, the officer shall not be required to arrest any other person believed to have committed an act of family violence during the incident. In determining whether a person is a primary physical aggressor, an officer shall consider:

(1) Prior family violence involving either party;

(2) The relative severity of the injuries inflicted on each person;

(3) The potential for future injury; and

(4) Whether one of the parties acted in self-defense.

(c) Whenever a law enforcement officer investigates an incident of family violence, whether or not an arrest is made, the officer shall prepare and submit to the supervisor or other designated person a written report of the incident entitled "Family Violence Report." Forms for such reports shall be designed and provided by the Georgia Bureau of Investigation. The report shall include the following:

(1) Name of the parties;

(2) Relationship of the parties;

(3) Sex of the parties;

(4) Date of birth of the parties;

(5) Time, place, and date of the incident;

(6) Whether children were involved or whether the act of family violence was committed in the presence of children;

(7) Type and extent of the alleged abuse;

(8) Existence of substance abuse;

(9) Number and types of weapons involved;

(10) Existence of any prior court orders;

(11) Type of police action taken in disposition of case, the reasons for the officer's determination that one party was the primary physical aggressor, and mitigating circumstances for why an arrest was not made;

(12) Whether the victim was apprised of available remedies and services; and

(13) Any other information that may be pertinent.

(d) The report provided for in subsection (c) of this Code section shall be considered as being made for statistical purposes only and where no arrests are made shall not be subject to the provisions of Article 4 of Chapter 18 of Title 50. However, upon request, a defendant who has been arrested for an act of family violence or the victim shall be entitled to review and copy any report prepared in accordance with this Code section relating to the defendant.

(e) Each police department, including local precincts and county sheriff departments, shall report, according to rules and regulations of the Georgia Crime Information Center, all family violence incidents, both arrests and nonarrests, to the Georgia Bureau of Investigation, which shall compile and analyze statistics of family violence crimes and cause them to be published annually in the Georgia Uniform Crime Reports. An offense shall be counted for each incident reported to the police. A zero shall be reported if no incidents have occurred during the reporting period.

Laws 1991, p. 1778, § 1; Laws 1992, p. 2939, § 1; Laws 1995, p. 1186, § 1.

§ 17-4-21. Taking arrested person before judicial officer; selection of judge to try cause

The arresting officer shall take the arrested person before the most convenient and accessible judicial officer authorized to hear the case unless the arrested person requests otherwise, in which case, if there is no suspicion of improper motive, the arresting officer shall take him before some other judicial officer. An arrested person has no right to select the judicial officer before whom he shall be tried.

Formerly Code 1863, § 4599; Code 1868, § 4621; Code 1873, § 4718; Code 1882, § 4718; Penal Code 1895, § 897; Penal Code 1910, § 918; Code 1933, § 27-208.

§ 17-4-22. Authority of peace officers to make arrests not denied because of race, creed, or national origin

No peace officer of this state or of any political subdivision thereof shall be denied the authority to arrest any person because of the race, creed, or national origin of the peace officer nor because of the race, creed, or national origin of the person who is being arrested.

Laws 1969, p. 732, § 1.

§ 17-4-23. Arrests for motor vehicle violations may be made by citation; warrants for failure to appear

(a) A law enforcement officer may arrest a person accused of violating any law or ordinance governing the operation, licensing, registration, maintenance, or inspection of motor vehicles by the issuance of a citation, provided the offense is committed in his presence or information constituting a basis for arrest concerning the operation of a motor vehicle was received by the arresting officer from a law enforcement officer observing the offense being committed, except that, where the offense results in an accident, an investigating officer may issue citations regardless of whether the offense occurred in the presence of a law enforcement officer. The arresting officer shall issue to such person a citation which shall enumerate the specific charges against the person and the date upon which the person is to appear and answer the charges. Whenever an arresting officer makes an arrest concerning the operation of a motor vehicle based on information received from another law enforcement officer who observed the offense being committed, the citation shall list the name of each officer and each must be present when the charges against the accused person are heard.

(b) If the accused person fails to appear as specified in the citation, the judicial officer having jurisdiction of the offense may issue a warrant ordering the apprehension of the person and commanding that he be brought before the court to answer the charge contained within the citation and the charge of his failure to appear as required. The person shall then be allowed to make a reasonable bond to appear on a given date before the court.

Laws 1969, p. 759, § 1; Laws 1975, p. 874, §§ 1–4.

§ 17-4-24. Execution of penal warrants; summoning of posse

Every law enforcement officer is bound to execute the penal warrants given to him to execute. He may summon to his assistance, either in writing or orally, any of the citizens of the neighborhood or county to assist in the execution of such warrants. The acts of the citizens formed as a posse by such officer shall be subject to the same protection and consequences as official acts.

Laws 1997, p. 143, § 17.

Formerly Code 1863, § 4602; Code 1868, § 4625; Code 1873, § 4722; Code 1882, § 4722; Penal Code 1895, § 895; Penal Code 1910, § 916; Code 1933, § 27-206.

§ 17-4-25. Officer may make arrest in any county. Duty to carry prisoner to county in which offense committed

(a) Under a warrant issued by a judicial officer, an arresting officer may, in any county without regard to the residence of the arresting officer, arrest any person charged with a crime. It is the duty of the arresting officer to take the accused, with the warrant under which he was arrested, to the county in which the offense is alleged to have been committed, for examination before any judicial officer of that county.

(b) The county where the offense is alleged to have been committed shall pay the expenses of the arresting officer in taking the arrested person to the county. The arresting officer may hold or imprison the arrested person in a county other than the county in which the offense is alleged to have been committed long enough to enable him to prepare to take the arrested person to the county in which the offense is alleged to have been committed.

(c) Should the county in which the offense is alleged to have been committed be a member of a regional jail authority created under Article 5 of Chapter 4 of Title 42, known as the "Regional Jail Authorities Act," the arresting officer shall transport the prisoner to the regional jail. The judicial officer of the county in which the offense is alleged to have been committed may conduct the examination of the accused required by subsection (a) of this Code section in the county in which the offense is alleged to have been committed or in facilities available at the regional jail or by audio-visual communication between the two locations and between the accused, the court, the attorneys, and the witnesses.

Laws 1865–66, p. 38, §§ 1, 2; Laws 1895, p. 34, § 1; Laws 1996, p. 742, § 1.

Formerly Code 1863, § 4607; Code 1868, § 4624; Code 1873, § 4721; Code 1882, § 4721; Penal Code 1895, § 898; Penal Code 1910, § 919; Code 1933, § 27-209.

§ 17-4-25.1. Transportation of arrested persons for certain purposes

(a) As provided in subsection (e) of this Code section, a sworn law enforcement officer from a county or municipality in which an offense is alleged to have been committed shall be authorized to transport an arrested person, with the warrant under which such person was arrested, from one jurisdiction to the county or municipality in which the offense is alleged to have been committed for examination before any judicial officer of that county or municipality.

(b) Unless otherwise provided by contract, the agency transporting the arrested person pursuant to subsection (a) of this Code section shall be responsible for all costs associated with the transport. Such officer may hold or imprison the arrested person in a jurisdiction other than where the offense is alleged to have been committed long enough to enable such officer to prepare to take the arrested person to the jurisdiction in which the offense is alleged to have been committed.

(c) A sworn law enforcement officer from a county or municipality shall be authorized to transport a prisoner who is lawfully in the custody of such officer to a medical facility, youth development center, or court appearance outside such county or municipality or to transport such prisoner to a location outside such county or municipality for any lawfully required or necessary purpose.

(d) This Code section shall not be construed to provide any general state-wide police powers or authority for county or municipal law enforcement officers or expand the arrest powers of such officers outside their properly authorized jurisdiction.

(e) Sheriffs and, with the approval of its governing authority, municipal or other law enforcement agency heads are authorized to enter into a contract for the purposes of transporting arrested individuals from the jurisdiction of the arrest to an appropriate detention facility where the alleged crime is to have occurred. In the absence of a written contract between the sheriff and municipal or other law enforcement agency head, the sheriff or his or her designee has the right of first refusal, as evidenced in writing, of transporting persons arrested on a warrant to an appropriate detention facility where the crime is alleged to have occurred. Any responsibility arising as a result of the transportation of an arrested individual as authorized in this Code section shall be that of the agency whose employee is transporting the arrested individual.

Laws 1993, p. 710, § 1.

§ 17-4-26. Arresting officer must bring person before judicial officer within 72 hours of arrest; notice of commitment hearing

Every law enforcement officer arresting under a warrant shall exercise reasonable diligence in bringing the person arrested before the judicial officer authorized to examine, commit, or receive bail and in any event to present the person arrested before a committing judicial officer within 72 hours after arrest. The accused shall be notified as to when and where the commitment hearing is to be held. An arrested person who is not notified before the hearing of the time and place of the commitment hearing shall be released.

Laws 1956, p. 796, § 1; Laws 1995, p. 932, § 1.

Formerly Code 1863, § 4606; Code 1868, § 4629; Code 1873, § 4726; Code 1882, § 4726; Penal Code 1895, § 899; Penal Code 1910, § 920; Code 1933, § 27-210.

§ 17-4-27. Names, addresses and ages of persons arrested to be recorded by sheriffs, police chiefs, and heads of other law enforcement agencies

It shall be the duty of all sheriffs, chiefs of police, and the heads of any other law enforcement agencies of this state to obtain, or cause to be obtained, the name, address, and age of each person arrested by law enforcement officers under the supervision of such sheriffs, chiefs of police, or heads of any other law enforcement agencies of this state, when any such person is charged with an offense against the laws of this state, any other state, or the United States. The information shall be placed on appropriate records which each law enforcement agency shall maintain. The records shall be open for public inspection unless otherwise provided by law.

Laws 1967, p. 839, § 1.

§ 17-4-28. Arresting officer advising dismissal of warrant

Any arresting officer who advises or encourages the dismissal or settlement of any criminal warrant placed in his hands for execution, either before or after an arrest is made on the warrant, or who procures or encourages the dismissal or settlement of such warrants by threats, duress, intimidation, promises, or any other artifice or means shall be guilty of a misdemeanor.

Laws 1897, p. 98, § 1.

Formerly Penal Code 1910, § 923; Code 1933, § 27-9901.

§ 17-4-29. Arresting officer receiving costs before return of warrant

(a) Any arresting officer who collects or receives any costs or other charges of a prosecutor or defendant in a case made on a state's warrant, or of anyone acting in the interest of either of them, before the warrant is returned to the court to which it is made returnable, shall be guilty of a misdemeanor.

(b) Nothing in this Code section or in Code Section 17-4-28 shall be construed as prohibiting arresting officers from receiving from prosecutors sums of money sufficient to defray their expenses in going beyond the limits of the jurisdiction of such arresting officer to search for or to make the arrest of the accused person.

Laws 1897, p. 98, § 2.

Formerly Penal Code 1910, § 924; Code 1933, § 27-9902.

Article 3

Warrants for Arrest

§ 17–4–40. Who may issue warrants for arrest

(a) Any judge of a superior, city, state, or magistrate court or any municipal officer clothed by law with the powers of a magistrate may issue a warrant for the arrest of any offender against the penal laws, based on probable cause either on the judge's or officer's own knowledge or on the information of others given to the judge or officer under oath. Any retired judge or judge emeritus of a state court may likewise issue arrest warrants if authorized in writing to do so by an active judge of the state court of the county wherein the warrants are to be issued.

(b)(1) If application is made for a warrant by a person other than a peace officer or law enforcement officer and the application alleges the commission of an offense against the penal laws, the judge or other officer shall schedule a warrant application hearing as provided in this subsection unless the person accused has been taken into custody by a peace officer or law enforcement officer or except as provided in paragraph (6) of this subsection.

(2) Except as otherwise provided in paragraph (6) of this subsection, a warrant application hearing shall be conducted only after attempting to notify the person whose arrest is sought by any means approved by the judge or other officer which is reasonably calculated to apprise such person of the date, time, and location of the hearing.

(3) If the person whose arrest is sought does not appear for the warrant application hearing, the judge or other officer shall proceed to hear the application and shall note on the warrant application that such person is not present.

(4) At the warrant application hearing, the rules regarding admission of evidence at a commitment hearing shall apply. The person seeking the warrant shall have the customary rights of presentation of evidence and cross-examination of witnesses. The person whose arrest is sought may cross-examine the person or persons applying for the warrant and any other witnesses testifying in support of the application at the hearing. The person whose arrest is sought may present evidence that probable cause does not exist for his or her arrest. The judge or other officer shall have the right to limit the presentation of evidence and the cross-examination of witnesses to the issue of probable cause.

(5) At the warrant application hearing, a determination shall be made whether or not probable cause exists for the issuance of a warrant for the arrest of the person whose arrest is sought. If the judge or other officer finds that probable cause exists, the warrant may issue instanter.

(6) Nothing in this subsection shall be construed as prohibiting a judge or other officer from immediately issuing a warrant for the arrest of a person upon application of a person other than a peace officer or law enforcement officer if the judge or other officer determines from the application or other information available to the judge or other officer that:

(A) An immediate or continuing threat exists to the safety or well-being of the affiant or a third party;

(B) The person whose arrest is sought will attempt to evade arrest or otherwise obstruct justice if notice is given;

(C) The person whose arrest is sought is incarcerated or otherwise in the custody of a local, state, or federal law enforcement agency;

(D) The person whose arrest is sought is a fugitive from justice;

(E) The offense for which application for a warrant is made is deposit account fraud under Code Section 16–9–20, and the person whose arrest is sought has previously been served with the ten-day notice as provided in paragraph (2) of subsection (a) of Code Section 16–9–20; or

(F) The offense for which application for the warrant is made consists of an act of family violence as defined in Code Section 19–13–1.

In the event that the judge or officer finds such circumstances justifying dispensing with the requirement of a warrant application hearing, the judge or officer shall note such circumstances on the face of the warrant application.

(7) No warrant shall be quashed nor evidence suppressed because of any irregularity in proceedings conducted pursuant to this subsection not affecting the substantial rights of the accused under the Constitution of this state or of the United States.

(c) Any warrant for the arrest of a peace officer, law enforcement officer, teacher, or school administrator for any offense alleged to have been committed while in the performance of his or her duties may be issued only by a judge of a superior court, a judge of a state court, or a judge of a probate court.

Laws 1974, p. 1230, § 1; Laws 1983, p. 884, § 3–17; Laws 1985, p. 1105, § 1; Laws 1990, p. 8, § 17; Laws 2000, p. 1702, § 1.

Formerly Code 1863, § 4595; Code 1868, § 4616; Code 1873, § 4713; Code 1882, § 4713; Penal Code 1895, § 882; Penal Code 1910, § 903; Code 1933, § 27–102.

§ 17–4–41. What affidavit and warrant for arrest must state

(a) An affidavit made or warrant issued for the arrest of a person who is accused of violating the penal laws of this state shall include, as nearly as practicable, the following facts:

(1) The offense, including the time, date, place of occurrence, against whom the offense was committed, and a statement describing the offense; and

(2) The county in which the offense was committed.

(b) When the offense charged is theft, the affidavit made or warrant issued shall state, in addition to the requirements of subsection (a) of this Code section, the following facts:

(1) Name of the property alleged to have been stolen, with a description thereof, including its value; and

(2) Name of the owner of the property and the person from whose possession such property was taken.

(c) It is the intent of these requirements that the accused person shall be informed of the specific charge against him and of all basic pertinent particulars pertaining thereto.

Laws 1865–66, p. 235, § 1; Laws 1962, p. 668, § 1.

Formerly Code 1868, § 4617; Code 1873, § 4714; Code 1882, § 4714; Penal Code 1895, § 883; Penal Code 1910, § 904; Code 1933, § 27–103; Code 1933, § 27–103.1.

§ 17–4–42. Special warrant for arrest

No judicial officer except a judge of the superior court shall issue a special warrant for arrest returnable only before himself; nor shall any superior court judge issue such warrant outside of his own judicial circuit. If issued outside the judicial circuit, the warrant shall be treated as a general arrest warrant.

Formerly Code 1863, § 4598; Code 1868, § 4620; Code 1873, § 4717; Code 1882, § 4717; Penal Code 1895, § 886; Penal Code 1910, § 907; Code 1933, § 27–106.

§ 17–4–43. Officer may require bond to prosecute

The judicial officer issuing a warrant for arrest upon any sufficient grounds may first require the applicant to file a bond, with sufficient sureties, to prosecute the case in the event of a committal.

Formerly Code 1863, § 4600; Code 1868, § 4622; Code 1873, § 4719; Code 1882, § 4719; Penal Code 1895, § 887; Penal Code 1910, § 908; Code 1933, § 27–107.

§ 17–4–44. Warrant for arrest issued in any county and executed without backing

A warrant for arrest may be issued in any county, though the crime was committed in another county. A warrant, once issued, may be executed in any county without being backed or endorsed by a judicial officer in the county where the warrant is executed.

Laws 1865–66, p. 38, §§ 1, 3.

Formerly Code 1863, § 4601; Code 1868, § 4623; Code 1873, § 4720; Code 1882, § 4720; Penal Code 1895, § 888; Penal Code 1910, § 909; Code 1933, § 27–108.

§ 17–4–45. Form of affidavit for arrest

An affidavit for an arrest warrant substantially complying with the following form shall in all cases be sufficient:

Georgia, _____ County.

Personally came (name of affiant), who on oath says that, to the best of his knowledge and belief, (name of person against whom the warrant is sought) did, on the _____ day of _____, _____, in the county aforesaid, commit the offense of (insert here all information describing offense as required by Code Section 17–4–41) and this affiant makes this affidavit that a warrant may issue for his arrest.

____
(Signature of the affiant)

Sworn to and subscribed before me, this _____ day of _____, _____.

____
Judicial officer

Laws 1982, p. 3, § 17; Laws 1999, p. 81, § 17.

Formerly Code 1863, § 4596; Code 1868, § 4618; Code 1873, § 4715; Code 1882, § 4715; Penal Code 1895, § 884; Penal Code 1910, § 905; Code 1933, § 27–104.

§ 17–4–46. Form of warrant for arrest

An arrest warrant substantially complying with the following form shall in all cases be sufficient:

Georgia, _____ County.

To any sheriff, deputy sheriff, coroner, constable, or marshal of said state—Greetings:

(Name of the affiant) makes oath before me that on the _____ day of _____, in the year _____, in the county aforesaid, (name of person against whom the warrant is sought) did commit the offense of (insert here all information describing offense as required by Code Section 17–4–41). You are therefore commanded to arrest (name of person against whom the warrant is sought) and bring him before me, or some other judicial officer of this state, to be dealt with as the law directs. You will also levy on a sufficiency of the property of (name of person against whom the warrant is sought) to pay the costs in the event of his final conviction. Herein fail not.

____
Judicial officer

Laws 1962, p. 668, § 3; Laws 1999, p. 81, § 17.

Formerly Code 1863, § 4597; Code 1868, § 4619; Code 1873, § 4716; Code 1882, § 4716; Penal Code 1895, § 885; Penal Code 1910, § 906; Code 1933, § 27–105.

§ 17–4–47. Conduct of applications for issuance of arrest warrants by video conference

(a) A judge of any court in this state authorized to issue arrest warrants pursuant to Code Section 17–4–40 may, as an alternative to other laws relating to the issuance of arrest warrants, conduct such applications for the issuance of arrest warrants by video conference.

(b) Arrest warrant applications heard by video conference shall be conducted in a manner to ensure that the judge conducting the hearing has visual and audible contact with all affiants and witnesses giving testimony.

(c) The affiant participating in an arrest warrant application by video conference shall sign the affidavit for an arrest warrant and any related documents by any reasonable means which identifies the affiant, including, but not limited to, his or her typewritten name, signature affixed by electronic stylus, or any other reasonable means which identifies the person signing the affidavit and any related documents. The judge participating in an arrest warrant application by video conference shall sign the affidavit for an arrest warrant, the arrest warrant, and any related documents by any reasonable means which identifies the judge, including, but not limited to, his or her typewritten name, signature affixed by electronic stylus, or any other reasonable means which identifies the judicial officer signing the affidavit and warrant and any related documents. Such authorization shall be deemed to comply with the signature requirements provided for in Code Sections 17–4–45 and 17–4–46.

(d) A judge may also utilize a video conference to conduct hearings relating to the issuance of an initial bond connected with an offense for which an arrest warrant is issued provided that the setting of such bond is within the jurisdiction of that court.

(e) A judge hearing matters pursuant to this Code section shall administer an oath to any person testifying by means of a video conference.

Laws 1998, p. 872, § 1; Laws 1999, p. 81, § 17.

Article 4

Arrest by Private Persons

§ 17–4–60. Arrest by private person

A private person may arrest an offender if the offense is committed in his presence or within his immediate knowledge. If the offense is a felony and the offender is escaping or attempting to escape, a private person may arrest him upon reasonable and probable grounds of suspicion.

Formerly Code 1863, § 4604; Code 1868, § 4627; Code 1873, § 4724; Code 1882, § 4724; Penal Code 1895, § 900; Penal Code 1910, § 921; Code 1933, § 27–211.

§ 17–4–61. Procedures subsequent to arrest by private person

(a) A private person who makes an arrest pursuant to Code Section 17–4–60 shall, without any unnecessary delay, take the person arrested before a judicial officer, as provided in Code Section 17–4–62, or deliver the person and all effects removed from him to a peace officer of this state.

(b) A peace officer who takes custody of a person arrested by a private person shall immediately proceed in accordance with Code Section 17–4–62.

(c) A peace officer who in good faith and within the scope of his authority takes custody of a person arrested by a private person pursuant to this Code section shall not be liable at law for false arrest or false imprisonment arising out of the arrest.

Laws 1977, p. 902, § 1.

Formerly Code 1933, § 27–211.1.

§ 17–4–62. Duty of person arresting without warrant

In every case of an arrest without a warrant, the person arresting shall, without delay, convey the offender before the most convenient judicial officer authorized to receive an affidavit and issue a warrant as provided for in Code Section 17–4–40. No such imprisonment shall be legal beyond a reasonable time allowed for this purpose; and any person who is not brought before such judicial officer within 48 hours of arrest shall be released.

Laws 1956, p. 796, § 2.

Formerly Code 1863, § 4605; Code 1868, § 4628; Code 1873, § 4725; Code 1882, § 4725; Penal Code 1895, § 901; Penal Code 1910, § 922; Code 1933, § 27-212.

CHAPTER 5

SEARCHES AND SEIZURES

Article 1

Searches without Warrants

§ 17-5-1. Search without warrant

(a) When a lawful arrest is effected a peace officer may reasonably search the person arrested and the area within the person's immediate presence for the purpose of:

(1) Protecting the officer from attack;

(2) Preventing the person from escaping;

(3) Discovering or seizing the fruits of the crime for which the person has been arrested; or

(4) Discovering or seizing any instruments, articles, or things which are being used or which may have been used in the commission of the crime for which the person has been arrested.

(b) When the peace officer is in the process of effecting a lawful search, nothing in this Code section shall be construed to preclude him from discovering or seizing any stolen or embezzled property, any item, substance, object, thing, or matter, the possession of which is unlawful, or any item, substance, object, thing, or matter, other than the private papers of any person, which is tangible evidence of the commission of a crime against the laws of this state.

Laws 1966, p. 567, § 1.

§ 17-5-2. Inventory of things seized

An inventory of all instruments, articles, or things seized in a search without a search warrant shall be given to the person arrested and a copy thereof delivered to the judicial officer before whom the person arrested is taken. If the person arrested is released without a charge being preferred against him, all instruments, articles, or things seized, other than contraband or stolen property, shall be returned to him upon release.

Laws 1966, p. 567, § 2.

Article 2

Searches with Warrants

§ 17-5-20. Application for search warrant

(a) A search warrant may be issued only upon the application of an officer of this state or its political subdivisions charged with the duty of enforcing the criminal laws or a currently certified peace officer engaged in the course of official duty, whether said officer is employed by a law enforcement unit of:

(1) The state or a political subdivision of the state; or

(2) A university, college, or school.

(b) A search warrant shall not be issued upon the application of a private citizen or for his aid in the enforcement of personal, civil, or property rights.

Laws 1966, p. 567, § 14; Laws 1990, p. 1980, § 1.

§ 17-5-21. Grounds for search warrant

(a) Upon the written complaint of any certified peace officer of this state or its political subdivisions charged with the duty of enforcing the criminal laws and otherwise as authorized in Code Section 17-5-20 under oath or affirmation, which states facts sufficient to show probable cause that a crime is being committed or has been committed and which particularly describes the place or person, or both, to be searched and things to be seized, any judicial officer authorized to hold a court of inquiry to examine into an arrest of an offender against the penal laws, referred to in this Code section as "judicial officer," may issue a search warrant for the seizure of the following:

(1) Any instruments, articles, or things, including the private papers of any person, which are designed, intended for use, or which have been used in the commission of the offense in connection with which the warrant is issued;

(2) Any person who has been kidnapped in violation of the laws of this state, who has been kidnapped in another jurisdiction and is now concealed within this state, or any human fetus or human corpse;

(3) Stolen or embezzled property;

(4) Any item, substance, object, thing, or matter, the possession of which is unlawful; or

(5) Any item, substance, object, thing, or matter, other than the private papers of any person, which is tangible evidence of the commission of the crime for which probable cause is shown.

(b) When the peace officer is in the process of effecting a lawful search, nothing in this Code section shall be construed to preclude him from discovering or seizing any stolen or embezzled property, any item, substance, object, thing, or matter, the possession of which is unlawful, or any item, substance, object, thing, or matter, other than the private papers of any person, which is tangible evidence of the commission of a crime against the laws of this state.

(c) Any retired judge or judge emeritus of a state court may issue search warrants as authorized by this Code section if authorized in writing to do so by an active judge of the state court of the county wherein the warrants are to be issued.

(d) Notwithstanding any provisions of Code Section 17–5–20 or other provisions of this Code section to the contrary, with respect to the execution of a search warrant by a certified peace officer employed by a university, college, or school, which search warrant will be executed beyond the arrest jurisdiction of a campus policeman pursuant to Code Section 20–3–72, the execution of such search warrant shall be made jointly by the certified peace officer employed by a university, college, or school and a certified peace officer of a law enforcement unit of the political subdivision wherein the search will be conducted.

Laws 1966, p. 567, § 3; Laws 1985, p. 1105, § 2; Laws 1990, p. 1980, §§ 2, 3.

§ 17–5–21.1. Search warrant application by video conference

(a) A judge of any court in this state authorized to issue search warrants pursuant to Code Section 17–5–21 may, as an alternative to other laws relating to the issuance of search warrants, conduct such applications for the issuance of search warrants by video conference.

(b) Search warrant applications heard by video conference shall be conducted in a manner to ensure that the judge conducting the hearing has visual and audible contact with all affiants and witnesses giving testimony.

(c) The affiant participating in a search warrant application by video conference shall sign the affidavit for a search warrant and any related documents by any reasonable means which identifies the affiant, including, but not limited to, his or her typewritten name, signature affixed by electronic stylus, or any other reasonable means which identifies the person signing the affidavit and any related documents. The judge participating in a search warrant application by video conference shall sign the affidavit for a search warrant, the search warrant, and any related documents by any reasonable means which identifies the judge, including, but not limited to, his or her typewritten name, signature affixed by electronic stylus, or any other reasonable means which identifies the judicial officer signing the affidavit and warrant and any related documents. Such applications shall be deemed to be written within the meaning of Code Section 17–5–21. Such authorization shall be deemed to comply with the issuance requirements provided for in Code Section 17–5–22.

(d) A judge hearing matters pursuant to this Code section shall administer an oath to any person testifying by means of a video conference.

(e) A video recording of the application hearing and any documents submitted in conjunction with the application shall be maintained as part of the record.

Laws 2001, p. 300, § 1.

§ 17–5–22. Issuance of search warrant

All warrants shall state the time and date of issuance and are the warrants of the judicial officer issuing the same and not the warrants of the court in which he is then sitting. Such warrants need not bear the seal of the court or clerk thereof. The warrant, the complaint on which the warrant is issued, the affidavit or affidavits supporting the warrant, and the returns shall be filed with the clerk of the court of the judicial officer issuing the same, or with the court if there is no clerk, at the time the warrant has been executed or has been returned "not executed"; provided, however, the judicial officer shall keep a docket record of all warrants issued by him and upon issuing any warrant he shall immediately record the same, within a reasonable time, on the docket.

Laws 1966, p. 567, § 4; Laws 1992, p. 1328, § 1.

§ 17–5–23. Command of search warrant

The search warrant shall command the officer directed to execute the same to search the place or person particularly described in the warrant and to seize the instruments, articles, or things particularly described in the search warrant.

Laws 1966, p. 567, § 7.

§ 17-5-24. Persons authorized to execute search warrants

The search warrant shall be issued in duplicate and shall be directed for execution to all peace officers of this state. However, the judicial officer may direct the search warrant to be executed by any peace officer named specially therein.

Laws 1966, p. 567, § 5.

§ 17-5-25. Execution of search warrants

The search warrant shall be executed within ten days from the time of issuance. If the warrant is executed, the duplicate copy shall be left with any person from whom any instruments, articles, or things are seized; or, if no person is available, the copy shall be left in a conspicuous place on the premises from which the instruments, articles, or things were seized. Any search warrant not executed within ten days from the time of issuance shall be void and shall be returned to the court of the judicial officer issuing the same as "not executed."

Laws 1966, p. 567, § 6.

§ 17-5-26. When warrant may be executed

The search warrant may be executed at any reasonable time.

Laws 1966, p. 567, § 11.

§ 17-5-27. Use of force in execution of search warrant

All necessary and reasonable force may be used to effect an entry into any building or property or part thereof to execute a search warrant if, after verbal notice or an attempt in good faith to give verbal notice by the officer directed to execute the same of his authority and purpose:

(1) He is refused admittance;

(2) The person or persons within the building or property or part thereof refuse to acknowledge and answer the verbal notice or the presence of the person or persons therein is unknown to the officer; or

(3) The building or property or part thereof is not then occupied by any person.

Laws 1966, p. 567, § 8.

Formerly Code 1863, § 4636; Code 1868, § 4660; Code 1873, § 4758; Code 1882, § 4758; Penal Code 1895, § 1244; Penal Code 1910, § 1326; Code 1933, § 27-301.

§ 17-5-28. Detention and search of persons on premises

In the execution of the search warrant the officer executing the same may reasonably detain or search any person in the place at the time:

(1) To protect himself from attack; or

(2) To prevent the disposal or concealment of any instruments, articles, or things particularly described in the search warrant.

Laws 1966, p. 567, § 9.

§ 17-5-29. Return to court of things seized

A written return of all instruments, articles, or things seized shall be made without unnecessary delay before the judicial officer named in the warrant or before any court of competent jurisdiction. An inventory of any instruments, articles, or things seized shall be filed with the return and signed under oath by the officer executing the warrant. The judicial officer or court shall, upon request, deliver a copy of the inventory to the persons from whom or from whose premises the instruments, articles, or things were taken and to the applicant for the warrant.

Laws 1966, p. 567, § 10.

§ 17-5-30. Motion to suppress evidence illegally seized

(a) A defendant aggrieved by an unlawful search and seizure may move the court for the return of property, the possession of which is not otherwise unlawful, and to suppress as evidence anything so obtained on the grounds that:

(1) The search and seizure without a warrant was illegal; or

(2) The search and seizure with a warrant was illegal because the warrant is insufficient on its face, there was not probable cause for the issuance of the warrant, or the warrant was illegally executed.

(b) The motion shall be in writing and state facts showing that the search and seizure were unlawful. The judge shall receive evidence out of the presence of the jury on any issue of fact necessary to determine the motion; and the burden of proving that the search and seizure were lawful shall be on the state. If the motion is granted the property shall be restored, unless otherwise subject to lawful detention, and it shall not be admissible in evidence against the movant in any trial.

(c) The motion shall be made only before a court with jurisdiction to try the offense. If a criminal accusation is filed or if an indictment or special presentment is returned by a grand jury, the motion shall be made only before the court in which the accusation, indictment, or special presentment is filed and pending.

Laws 1966, p. 567, § 13.

§ 17-5-31. No warrant quashed for technicality

No search warrant shall be quashed or evidence suppressed because of a technical irregularity not affecting the substantial rights of the accused.

Laws 1966, p. 567, § 12; Laws 1990, p. 8, § 17.

§ 17-5-32. Searches and seizures of documentary evidence in possession of an attorney

(a) As used in this Code section, the term "documentary evidence" includes but is not limited to writings, documents, blueprints, drawings, photographs, computer printouts, microfilms, X-rays, files, diagrams, ledgers, books, tapes, audio and video recordings, and papers of any type or description.

(b) Notwithstanding any other provision of law, no search and seizure without a warrant shall be conducted and no search warrant shall be issued for any documentary evidence in the possession of an attorney who is not a criminal suspect, unless the application for the search warrant specifies that the place to be searched is in the possession or custody of an attorney and also shows that there is probable cause to believe that the documentary evidence will be destroyed or secreted in the event a search warrant is not issued. This Code section shall not impair the ability to serve search warrants in cases in which the search is directed against an attorney if there is probable cause to suspect such attorney has committed a crime. This Code section shall not impair the ability to serve subpoenas on nonsuspect attorneys.

(c) In any case in which there is probable cause to believe that documentary evidence will be destroyed or secreted if a search warrant is not issued, no search warrant shall be issued or be executed for any documentary evidence in the possession or custody of an attorney who is not a criminal suspect unless:

(1) At the time the warrant is issued the court shall appoint a special master to accompany the person who will serve the warrant. The special master shall be an attorney who is a member in good standing of the State Bar of Georgia and who has been selected from a list of qualified attorneys maintained by the State Bar of Georgia. Upon service of the warrant, the special master shall inform the party served of the specific items being sought and that the party shall have the opportunity to provide the items requested. If the party, in the judgment of the special master, fails to provide the items requested, the special master shall conduct a search for the items in the areas indicated in the search warrant;

(2) If the party who has been served states that an item or items should not be disclosed, such item or items shall be sealed by the special master and taken to the superior court for a hearing. At the hearing the party whose premises has been searched shall be entitled to raise any issues which may be raised pursuant to Code Section 17-5-30 as well as claims that the item or items are privileged or claims that the item or items are inadmissible because they were obtained in violation of this Code section. Any such hearing shall be held in the superior court;

(3) Any such warrant must, whenever practicable, be served during normal business hours. The law enforcement officer or prosecutor serving the warrant shall not participate in the search but may accompany the special master when the special master is conducting the search;

(4) Any such warrant must be served upon a party who appears to have possession or control of the items sought. If, after reasonable efforts, the party serving the warrant is unable to locate any such person, the special master shall seal and return to the court for determination by the court any items which appear to be privileged;

(5) Any such warrant shall be issued only by the superior court. At the time of applying for such a warrant, the law enforcement officer or prosecutor shall submit a written search plan designed to minimize the intrusiveness of the search. When the warrant is executed, the special master carrying out the search shall have a duty to make reasonable efforts to minimize the intrusiveness of the search.

(d) Notwithstanding any provision of law to the contrary, evidence obtained in violation of this Code section shall be excluded and suppressed from the prosecution's case in chief or in rebuttal, and such evidence shall not be admissible either as substantive evidence or for impeachment purposes.

Laws 1989, p. 1687, § 1.

Article 3

Disposition of Property Seized

§ 17-5-50. Return of articles

(a) The clerk or person having charge of the property section for any police department, sheriff's office, or other law enforcement agency in this state shall enter in a suitable book a description of every article of property alleged to be stolen, embezzled, or otherwise unlawfully obtained and brought into the office or taken from the person of a prisoner and shall attach a number to each article and make a corresponding entry thereof.

(b) (1) Any person claiming ownership of such allegedly stolen, embezzled, or otherwise unlawfully obtained property may make application to the law enforcement agency for the return of such property. Upon such an application being filed, the clerk or person in charge of the property section shall serve upon the person from whom custody of the property was taken a copy of such application. Such person from whom custody of the property was taken shall have a reasonable opportunity to claim ownership of such property and to request a hearing on forms provided by the person in charge of the property section.

(2) If the person from whom custody of the property was taken fails to assert a claim to such property, upon any applicant furnishing satisfactory proof of ownership of such property and presentation of proper personal identification, the person in charge of the property section may deliver such property to the applicant. The person to whom property is delivered shall sign, under penalty of false swearing, a declaration of ownership, which shall be retained by the person in charge of the property section. Such declaration, absent any other proof of ownership, shall be deemed satisfactory proof of ownership for the purposes of this Code section; provided, however, that, in the case of motor vehicles, trailers, tractors, or motorcycles which are required to be registered with the state revenue commissioner, any such stolen vehicle shall be returned to the person evidencing ownership of such vehicle through a certificate of title, tag receipt, bill of sale, or other such evidence. The stolen vehicle shall be returned to the person evidencing ownership within two days after such person makes application for the return of such vehicle unless a hearing on the ownership of such vehicle is required under this Code section or unless law enforcement needs the stolen vehicle for further criminal investigation purposes. Prior to such delivery, such person in charge of the property section shall make and retain a complete photographic record of such property. Such delivery shall be without prejudice to the state or to the person from whom custody of the property was taken or to any other person who may have a claim against the property.

(3) If the person from whom custody of the property was taken asserts a claim to such property and requests a hearing, the court which examines the charge against the person accused of stealing, embezzling, or otherwise unlawfully obtaining the property, or the court before whom the trial is had for stealing, embezzling, or otherwise unlawfully obtaining the property shall conduct the hearing to determine the ownership of such property.

(4) The provisions of this subsection shall not apply to any contraband or property subject to forfeiture under any provision of law.

(c) Photographs, video tapes, or other identification or analysis of the property involved, duly identified in writing by the law enforcement officer originally taking custody of the property as accurately representing such property, shall be admissible at trial in lieu of the original property.

(d) In the case of unknown or unapprehended defendants or defendants willfully absent from the jurisdiction, the court shall have discretion to appoint a guardian ad litem to represent the interest of the unknown or absent defendants.

(e) Statements made by the defendant or a person representing the defendant at a hearing provided for in subsection (b) of this Code section shall not be admissible for use against the defendant at trial.

Laws 1978, p. 2260, § 1; Laws 1979, p. 761, § 1; Laws 1982, p. 2336, § 1; Laws 1986, p. 158, § 1; Laws 2002, p. 415, § 17; Laws 2005, Act 68, § 7-1, eff. July 1, 2005.

Formerly Code 1863, § 4637; Code 1868, § 4661; Code 1873, § 4759; Code 1882, § 4759; Penal Code 1895, § 1245; Penal Code 1910, § 1327; Code 1933, § 27-302.

§ 17-5-51. Weapons declared contraband; forfeiture; motor vehicles excepted

Any device which is used as a weapon in the commission of any crime against any person or any attempt to commit any crime against any person, any weapon the possession or carrying of which constitutes a crime or delinquent act, and any weapon for which a person has been convicted of the crime of carrying a concealed weapon, as provided for by Code Section 16-11-126, are declared to be contraband and are forfeited. For the purposes of this article, a motor vehicle shall not be deemed to be a weapon or device and shall not be contraband or forfeited under this article; provided, however, this exception shall not be construed to prohibit the seizure, condemnation, and sale of motor vehicles used in the illegal transportation of alcoholic beverages.

Laws 1967, p. 749, § 1; Laws 1977, p. 1131, § 1; Laws 1994, p. 963, § 1.

§ 17–5–52. Sale or destruction of weapons; proceeds of sale

(a) When a final judgment is entered finding a defendant guilty of the commission or attempted commission of a crime against any person or guilty of the commission of a crime or delinquent act involving the illegal possession or carrying of a weapon, any device which was used as a weapon in the commission of the crime or delinquent act shall be turned over by the person having custody of the device to the sheriff of the county wherein the device was confiscated when the device is no longer needed for evidentiary purposes. Within 90 days after receiving the device, the sheriff shall retain the device for use in law enforcement, destroy the same, or advertise it for sale in such manner as other sheriff's sales are advertised and shall sell the device to the highest bidder at the next sheriff's sale conducted after the completion of the advertisements, provided that, if the device used as a weapon in the crime is not the property of the defendant, there shall be no forfeiture of such weapon.

(b) The proceeds derived from all sales of such devices, after deducting the costs of the advertising and the sale, shall be turned in to the treasury of the county wherein the sale is made; provided, however, that if the device was used in the commission of a crime within a municipal corporation, the proceeds derived from the sale of the device, after deducting the costs of the advertising and the sale, shall be turned in to the treasury of the municipality wherein the crime was committed.

Laws 1967, p. 749, § 3; Laws 1976, p. 167, § 1; Laws 1994, p. 963, § 2.

§ 17–5–53. Weapons valuable for historical or instructional purposes

(a) After a forfeiture of a device used in a crime, in the event the director of the Division of Archives and History or the commissioner of public safety, in that order or priority, shall desire to receive and retain a device described in Code Section 17–5–51 for historical or instructional purposes of his or her division or department and gives written notice thereof to the sheriff, either prior to the sheriff's advertisement of the device for sale or within ten days thereafter, the sheriff shall forthwith deliver the device to the requesting division or department which shall retain the device for such purposes. A device delivered to either the division or the department in accordance with this Code section shall become the property of the state.

(b) This Code section shall prevail over Code Section 17–5–52.

Laws 1976, p. 749, § 4; Laws 2002, p. 532, § 5.

§ 17–5–54. Disposition of personal property in custody of law enforcement agencies

(a)(1) Except as provided in Code Sections 17–5–55 and 17–5–56 and subsections (d), (e), and (f) of this Code section, when a law enforcement agency assumes custody of any personal property which is the subject of a crime or has been abandoned or is otherwise seized, a disposition of such property shall be made in accordance with the provisions of this Code section. When a final verdict and judgment is entered finding a defendant guilty of the commission of a crime, any personal property used as evidence in the trial shall be returned to the rightful owner of the property. All personal property in the custody of a law enforcement agency, including personal property used as evidence in a criminal trial, which is unclaimed after a period of 90 days following its seizure, or following the final verdict and judgment in the case of property used as evidence, and which is no longer needed in a criminal investigation or for evidentiary purposes in accordance with Code Section 17–5–55 or 17–5–56 shall be subject to disposition by the law enforcement agency. The sheriff, chief of police, or other executive officer of a law enforcement agency shall make application to the superior court for an order to retain, sell, or discard such property. In the application the officer shall state each item of personal property to be retained, sold, or discarded. Upon the superior court's granting an order for the law enforcement agency to retain such property, the law enforcement agency shall retain such property for official use. Upon the superior court's granting an order which authorizes that the property be discarded, the law enforcement agency shall dispose of the property as other salvage or nonserviceable equipment. Upon the superior court's granting an order for the sale of personal property, the officer shall provide for a notice to be placed once a week for four weeks in the legal organ of the county specifically describing each item and advising possible owners of items of the method of contacting the law enforcement agency; provided, however, that miscellaneous items having an estimated fair market value of $75.00 or less may be advertised or sold, or both, in lots. Such notice shall also stipulate a date, time, and place said items will be placed for public sale if not claimed. Such notice shall also stipulate whether said items or groups of items are to be sold in blocks, by lot numbers, by entire list of items, or separately.

(2) Items not claimed by the owners shall be sold at a sale which shall be conducted not less than seven nor more than 15 days after the final advertised notice has been run. The sale shall be to the highest bidder.

(3) If property has not been bid on in two successive sales, the law enforcement agency may retain the property for official use or the property will be considered as salvage and disposed of as other county or municipal salvage or nonserviceable equipment.

(4) With respect to unclaimed perishable personal property or animals or other wildlife, the officer may make application to the superior court for an order authorizing the disposition of such property prior to the expiration of 90 days.

(5) With respect to a seized motor vehicle which is not the subject of forfeiture proceedings, the law enforcement agency shall be required to contact the Georgia Crime Information Center to determine if such motor vehicle has been stolen and to follow generally the procedures of Code Section 40-11-2 to ascertain the registered owner of such vehicle.

(b) Records will be maintained showing the manner in which each item came into possession of the law enforcement agency, a description of the property, all efforts to locate the owner, any case or docket number, the date of publication of any newspaper notices, and the date on which the property was retained by the law enforcement agency, sold, or discarded.

(c) The proceeds from the sale of personal property by the sheriff or other county law enforcement agency pursuant to this Code section shall be paid into the general fund of the county treasury. The proceeds from the sale of personal property by a municipal law enforcement agency pursuant to this Code section shall be paid into the general fund of the municipal treasury.

(d) The provisions of this Code section shall not apply to personal property which is the subject of forfeiture proceedings as otherwise provided by law.

(e) The provisions of this Code section shall not apply to any property which is the subject of a disposition pursuant to Code Sections 17-5-50 through 17-5-53.

(f) The provisions of this Code section shall not apply to any abandoned motor vehicle for which the provisions of Chapter 11 of Title 40 are applicable.

Laws 1991, p. 944, § 1; Laws 1995, p. 909, § 1; Laws 2004, Act 539, § 1, eff. July 1, 2004.

§ 17-5-55. Custody of property; evidence in criminal cases

(a) In all criminal cases, the court shall designate either the clerk of court, the court reporter, or any other officer of the court to be the custodian of any property that is introduced into evidence during the pendency of the case. Property introduced into evidence shall be identified or tagged with an exhibit number. After verdict and judgment has been entered in any criminal case, the person who has custody of the physical evidence introduced in the case shall inventory the evidence and create an evidence log within 30 days of the entry of the judgment. Within 30 days following the creation of the evidence log, physical evidence shall be returned to the rightful owner of the property unless the physical evidence itself is necessary for the appeal of the case, for a new trial, or for purposes of complying with this Code section or Code Section 17-5-56. The evidence log shall contain the case number, style of the case, description of the item, exhibit number, the name of the person creating the evidence log, and the location where the physical evidence is stored. After the evidence log is completed, the judge shall designate the clerk of court, the prosecuting attorney, or the law enforcement agency involved in prosecuting the case to obtain and store the evidence, and a notation shall appear in the evidence log indicating the transfer of evidence. If evidence is transferred to any other party, the evidence log shall be annotated to show the identity of the person or entity receiving the evidence, the date of the transfer, and the location of the evidence. The signature of any person or entity to which physical evidence is transferred shall be captured through electronic means that will be linked to the evidence log or the use of a property transfer form that will be filed with the evidence log. When physical evidence, other than audio or video recordings, is transferred to any person or entity, a photograph or other visual image of the evidence shall be made and placed in the case file.

(b) Physical evidence classified as dangerous or contraband by state or federal law, including, but not limited to, items described by state or federal law as controlled substances, dangerous drugs, explosives, weapons, ammunition, biomedical waste, hazardous substances, or hazardous waste shall be properly secured in a manner authorized by state or federal law. This evidence may be transferred to a government agency authorized to store or dispose of the material.

(c) Documents, photographs, and similar evidence shall be maintained and disposed of in accordance with records retention schedules adopted in accordance with Article 5 of Chapter 18 of Title 50, known as the "Georgia Records Act." Other physical evidence that contains biological material, including, but not limited to, stains, fluids, or hair samples that relate to the identity of the perpetrator of the crime, shall be maintained in accordance with Code Section 17-5-56. A party to an extraordinary motion for new trial or a habeas corpus action in which DNA testing is sought that was filed prior to the expiration of the time prescribed for the preservation of evidence by this Code section may apply to the court in which the defendant was convicted for an order directing that the evidence be preserved beyond the time period prescribed by this Code section and until judgment in the action shall become final.

(d) Except as is otherwise provided in subsections (b) and (c) of this Code section or by law, following the expiration of the period of time set forth in subsections (b) and (c) of this Code section, physical evidence may be disposed of in accordance with the provisions of Article 5 of Chapter 12 of Title 44, known as the "Disposition of Unclaimed Property Act," or, in the case of property of historical or instructional value, as provided in Code Section 17–5–53.

Laws 2003, Act 37, § 3, eff. May 27, 2003; Laws 2004, Act 539, § 2, eff. July 1, 2004.

§ 17–5–56. Preservation of physical evidence collected at the scene of the crime

(a) Except as otherwise provided in Code Section 17–5–55, on or after May 27, 2003, governmental entities in possession of any physical evidence in a criminal case, including, but not limited to, a law enforcement agency or a prosecuting attorney, shall maintain any physical evidence collected at the time of the crime that contains biological material, including, but not limited to, stains, fluids, or hair samples that relate to the identity of the perpetrator of the crime as provided in this Code section. Biological samples collected directly from any person for use as reference materials for testing or collected for the purpose of drug or alcohol testing shall not be preserved.

(b) In a case in which the death penalty is imposed, the evidence shall be maintained until the sentence in the case has been carried out. In a case that involves the prosecution of a serious violent felony as defined by Code Section 17–10–6.1, the evidence that contains biological material, including but not limited to, stains, fluids, or hair samples that relate to the identity of the perpetrator of the crime shall be maintained for ten years after judgment in the criminal case becomes final or ten years after May 27, 2003, whichever is later. Evidence in all other felony and misdemeanor cases may be purged.

Laws 2003, Act 37, § 3, eff. May 27, 2003.

CHAPTER 6

BONDS AND RECOGNIZANCES

Article 1

General Provisions

§ 17–6–1. Before whom offenses are bailable; when person charged with misdemeanor may be bailed

(a) The following offenses are bailable only before a judge of the superior court:

(1) Treason;

(2) Murder;

(3) Rape;

(4) Aggravated sodomy;

(5) Armed robbery;

(6) Aircraft hijacking and hijacking a motor vehicle;

(7) Aggravated child molestation;

(8) Aggravated sexual battery;

(9) Manufacturing, distributing, delivering, dispensing, administering, or selling any controlled substance classified under Code Section 16–13–25 as Schedule I or under Code Section 16–13–26 as Schedule II;

(10) Violating Code Section 16–13–31, relating to trafficking in cocaine, methamphetamine, or marijuana;

(11) Kidnapping, arson, aggravated assault, or burglary if the person, at the time of the alleged kidnapping, arson, aggravated assault, or burglary, had previously been convicted of, was on probation or parole with respect to, or was on bail for kidnapping, arson, aggravated assault, burglary, or one or more of the offenses listed in paragraphs (1) through (10) of this subsection; and

(12) Aggravated stalking.

(b)(1) All offenses not included in subsection (a) of this Code section are bailable by a court of inquiry. Except as provided in subsection (g) of this Code section, at no time, either before a court of inquiry, when indicted or accused, after a motion for new trial is made, or while an appeal is pending, shall any person charged with a misdemeanor be refused bail.

(2) Except as otherwise provided in this chapter:

(A) A person charged with violating Code Section 40–6–391 whose alcohol concentration at the time of arrest, as determined by any method authorized by law, violates that provided in paragraph (5) of subsection (a) of Code Section 40–6–391 may be detained for a period of time up to six hours after booking and prior to being released on bail or on recognizance; and

(B) When an arrest is made by a law enforcement officer without a warrant upon an act of family violence pursuant to Code Section 17-4-20, the person charged with the offense shall not be eligible for bail prior to the arresting officer or some other law enforcement officer taking the arrested person before a judicial officer pursuant to Code Section 17-4-21.

(3)(A) Notwithstanding any other provision of law, a judge of a court of inquiry may, as a condition of bail or other pretrial release of a person who is charged with violating Code Section 16-5-90 or 16-5-91, prohibit the defendant from entering or remaining present at the victim's school, place of employment, or other specified places at times when the victim is present or intentionally following such person.

(B) If the evidence shows that the defendant has previously violated the conditions of pretrial release or probation or parole which arose out of a violation of Code Section 16-5-90 or 16-5-91, the judge of a court of inquiry may impose such restrictions on the defendant which may be necessary to deter further stalking of the victim, including but not limited to denying bail or pretrial release.

(c)(1) In the event a person is detained in a facility other than a municipal jail for an offense which is bailable only before a judge of the superior court, as provided in subsection (a) of this Code section, and a hearing is held pursuant to Code Section 17-4-26 or 17-4-62, the presiding judicial officer shall notify the superior court in writing within 48 hours that the arrested person is being held without bail. If the detained person has not already petitioned for bail as provided in subsection (d) of this Code section, the superior court shall notify the district attorney and shall set a date for a hearing on the issue of bail within 30 days after receipt of such notice.

(2) In the event a person is detained in a municipal jail for an offense which is bailable only before a judge of the superior court as provided in subsection (a) of this Code section for a period of 30 days, the municipal court shall notify the superior court in writing within 48 hours that the arrested person has been held for such time without bail. If the detained person has not already petitioned for bail as provided in subsection (d) of this Code section, the superior court shall notify the district attorney and set a date for a hearing on the issue of bail within 30 days after receipt of such notice.

(3) Notice sent to the superior court pursuant to paragraph (1) or (2) of this subsection shall include any incident reports and criminal history reports relevant to the detention of such person.

(d) A person charged with any offense which is bailable only before a judge of the superior court as provided in subsection (a) of this Code section may petition the superior court requesting that such person be released on bail. The court shall notify the district attorney and set a date for a hearing within ten days after receipt of such petition.

(e) A court shall be authorized to release a person on bail if the court finds that the person:

(1) Poses no significant risk of fleeing from the jurisdiction of the court or failing to appear in court when required;

(2) Poses no significant threat or danger to any person, to the community, or to any property in the community;

(3) Poses no significant risk of committing any felony pending trial; and

(4) Poses no significant risk of intimidating witnesses or otherwise obstructing the administration of justice.

However, if the person is charged with a serious violent felony and has already been convicted of a serious violent felony, or of an offense under the laws of any other state or of the United States which offense if committed in this state would be a serious violent felony, there shall be a rebuttable presumption that no condition or combination of conditions will reasonably assure the appearance of the person as required or assure the safety of any other person or the community. As used in this subsection, the term "serious violent felony" means a serious violent felony as defined in Code Section 17-10-6.1.

(f)(1) Except as provided in subsection (a) of this Code section or as otherwise provided in this subsection, the judge of any court of inquiry may by written order establish a schedule of bails and unless otherwise ordered by the judge of any court, a person charged with committing any offense shall be released from custody upon posting bail as fixed in the schedule.

(2) For offenses involving an act of family violence, as defined in Code Section 19-13-1, the schedule of bails provided for in paragraph (1) of this subsection shall require increased bail and shall include a listing of specific conditions which shall include, but not be limited to, having no contact of any kind or character with the victim or any member of the victim's family or household, not physically abusing or threatening to physically abuse the victim, the immediate enrollment in and participation in domestic violence counseling, substance abuse therapy, or other therapeutic requirements.

(3) For offenses involving an act of family violence, the judge shall determine whether the schedule of bails and one or more of its specific conditions shall be used, except that any offense involving an act of family violence and serious injury to the victim shall be bailable only before a judge when the judge or the arresting officer is of the opinion that the danger of further violence to or harassment

or intimidation of the victim is such as to make it desirable that the consideration of the imposition of additional conditions as authorized in this Code section should be made. Upon setting bail in any case involving family violence, the judge shall give particular consideration to the exigencies of the case at hand and shall impose any specific conditions as he or she may deem necessary. As used in this Code section, the term "serious injury" means bodily harm capable of being perceived by a person other than the victim and may include, but is not limited to, substantially blackened eyes, substantially swollen lips or other facial or body parts, substantial bruises to body parts, fractured bones, or permanent disfigurements and wounds inflicted by deadly weapons or any other objects which, when used offensively against a person, are capable of causing serious bodily injury.

(4) If probable cause is shown that the offense charged is in furtherance of a pattern of criminal gang activity as defined by Code Section 16-15-3, the court shall require increased bail and shall include as a condition of bail or pretrial release that the defendant shall not have contact of any kind or character with any other member or associate of a criminal street gang and that the defendant shall not have contact of any kind or character with the victim or any member of the victim's family or household.

(5) For offenses involving violations of Code Section 40-6-393, bail or other release from custody shall be set by a judge on an individual basis and not a schedule of bails pursuant to this Code section.

(g) No appeal bond shall be granted to any person who has been convicted of murder, rape, aggravated sodomy, armed robbery, aggravated child molestation, child molestation, kidnapping, trafficking in cocaine or marijuana, aggravated stalking, or aircraft hijacking and who has been sentenced to serve a period of incarceration of five years or more. The granting of an appeal bond to a person who has been convicted of any other felony offense or of any misdemeanor offense involving an act of family violence as defined in Code Section 19-13-1, or of any offense delineated as a high and aggravated misdemeanor or of any offense set forth in Code Section 40-6-391, shall be in the discretion of the convicting court. Appeal bonds shall terminate when the right of appeal terminates, and such bonds shall not be effective as to any petition or application for writ of certiorari unless the court in which the petition or application is filed so specifies.

(h) Except in cases in which life imprisonment or the death penalty may be imposed, a judge of the superior court by written order may delegate the authority provided for in this Code section to any judge of any court of inquiry within such superior court judge's circuit. However, such authority may not be exercised outside the county in which said judge of the court of inquiry was appointed or elected. The written order delegating such authority shall be valid for a period of one year, but may be revoked by the superior court judge issuing such order at any time prior to the end of that one-year period.

(i) As used in this Code section, the term "bail" shall include the releasing of a person on such person's own recognizance.

(j) For all persons who have been authorized by law or the court to be released on bail, sheriffs and constables shall accept such bail; provided, however, that the sureties tendered and offered on the bond are approved by the sheriff of the county in which the offense was committed.

Laws 1922, p. 51, § 1; Laws 1973, p. 454, § 1; Laws 1980, p. 1359, § 1; Laws 1982, p. 910, § 1; Laws 1983, p. 3, § 14; Laws 1983, p. 358, § 1; Laws 1983, p. 452, § 1; Laws 1984, p. 22, § 17; Laws 1984, p. 679, § 1; Laws 1984, p. 760, § 1; Laws 1985, p. 416, § 1; Laws 1986, p. 166, §§ 1, 2; Laws 1988, p. 358, § 1; Laws 1989, p. 1714, § 1; Laws 1990, p. 8, § 17; Laws 1991, p. 416, § 1; Laws 1991, p. 1401, § 1; Laws 1992, p. 1150, § 1; Laws 1992, p. 2527, § 1; Laws 1993, p. 91, § 17; Laws 1993, p. 1534, § 2; Laws 1994, p. 532, § 1; Laws 1994, p. 1270, § .5; Laws 1994, p. 1625, § 5; Laws 1995, p. 379, §§ 1, 2; Laws 1995, p. 989, §§ 1, 2; Laws 1996, p. 1233, § 1; Laws 1996, p. 1624, § 1; Laws 1997, p. 143, § 17; Laws 1998, p. 270, § 9; Laws 1999, p. 391, § 3; Laws 2000, p. 1171, § 1; Laws 2006, Act 571, § 18, eff. July 1, 2006.

Formerly Code 1863, § 4625; Code 1868, § 4649; Code 1873, § 4747; Code 1882, § 4747; Penal Code 1895, § 933; Penal Code 1910, § 958; Code 1933, § 27-901.

§ 17-6-2. Amount of bail in misdemeanor cases; acceptance by sheriffs and constables

(a) (1) In all cases wherein a licensed driver of this state has been arrested, incarcerated, and charged with a violation of state law and where said violation is a misdemeanor, the sheriff of the county wherein the violation occurred shall be authorized, unless otherwise ordered by a judicial officer, after the individual has been incarcerated for not less than five days, to accept that individual's driver's license as collateral for any bail which has been set in the case, up to and including the amount of $ 1,000.00, provided such license is not under suspension or has not expired or been revoked.

(2) The individual posting a license as collateral pursuant to this subsection shall execute an acknowledgment and agreement between the individual and the State of Georgia as bond wherein the individual agrees to appear in court to answer the charges made against the individual and acknowledges that failure to appear in court when the case is scheduled for hearing, trial, or plea shall result in a forfeiture of the individual's license through suspension by operation of law effective upon the date

of the individual's scheduled appearance. The individual shall also be notified that failure to appear in court as required may result in criminal prosecution for bail jumping as provided in Code Section 16-10-51. After execution of the agreement, except as otherwise provided by law, the license shall be returned to the individual and the original agreement shall be delivered to the prosecuting attorney for filing with the accusation, citation, or dismissal. Whenever an individual has been charged with a violation of Code Section 40-6-391, relating to driving under the influence of alcohol or drugs, then the provisions of Code Section 40-5-67 shall apply.

(3) A failure to appear by the individual who has been charged with a misdemeanor offense and who posted that individual's license as bail pursuant to this subsection shall, by operation of law, cause that individual's license to be suspended by the Department of Driver Services effective immediately, and the clerk of the court within five days after that failure to appear shall forward a copy of the agreement to the Department of Driver Services which shall enter the suspension upon the individual's driver history record. The posting of a license as provided in this subsection shall also be considered as bail for the purposes of Code Section 16-10-51. Where the original court date has been continued by the judge, clerk, or other officer of the court and there has been actual notice given to the defendant in open court or in writing by a court official or officer of the court or by mailing such notice to the defendant's last known address, then the provisions of this paragraph shall apply to the new court appearance date.

(4) A license suspended pursuant to this subsection shall only be reinstated when the individual shall pay to the Department of Driver Services a restoration fee of $25.00 together with a certified notice from the clerk of the originating court that the case has either been disposed of or has been rescheduled and a deposit of sufficient collateral approved by the sheriff of the county wherein the charges were made in an amount to satisfy the original bail amount has been paid. The court wherein the charges are pending shall be authorized to require payment of costs by the defendant in an amount not to exceed $100.00 to reschedule the case.

(5) Upon the trial of any individual charged with the offense of driving with a suspended license where such license was suspended as provided in this subsection, a copy of the acknowledgment and agreement executed by the individual together with certification by the clerk of the court of the individual's failure to appear shall be prima-facie evidence of actual notice to the individual that the individual's license was suspended.

(b) In all other misdemeanor cases, sheriffs and constables shall accept bail in such reasonable amount as may be just and fair for any person or persons charged with a misdemeanor, provided that the sureties tendered and offered on the bond are approved by the sheriff in the county where the offense was committed.

Laws 1921, p. 241, § 1; Laws 1966, p. 428, § 1; Laws 1989, p. 448, § 1; Laws 1990, p. 8, § 17; Laws 1991, p. 94, § 17; Laws 2002, p. 415, § 17; Laws 2005, Act 68, § 7-2, eff. July 1, 2005.

Formerly Code 1933, § 27-902.

§ 17-6-3. Amount of bail in misdemeanor cases; recognizance bond for persons in military service

(a) In the case of any person engaged in military service who is charged with a misdemeanor and whose bond has been fixed at not more than $400.00 plus costs, any sheriff shall be allowed to accept, in lieu of bail, a recognizance bond executed and signed by the commanding officer of the person or the officer's lawfully delegated subordinates. Any person so charged may be taken into custody on behalf of the military installation by his commanding officer or by persons designated by the commanding officer of the military installation under the following terms and conditions:

(1) Immediately following his release he will be returned by the military police or other designated authority directly to the military installation and delivered to the duty officer of the command to which he is attached;

(2) He then will be restrained as appropriate in each case. The restraint will be for a minimum of 12 hours in all cases involving consumption of alcoholic beverages. He normally will be restricted to the limits of the military installation until such time as the charges are dismissed or his case has been adjudicated;

(3) He will not be transferred, granted leave, or discharged from the military service without 36 hours' notice to the sheriff or his deputy sheriff;

(4) He will be delivered to the sheriff or his deputy on demand; and

(5) These terms or conditions will be withdrawn only upon his posting the required bond or otherwise being released by the sheriff, his deputy, or the appropriate court.

(b) The recognizance bond shall be of the following type:

In consideration of the release of _____ (name of person charged) charged with _____ (name or description of offense) it is agreed that the aforementioned prisoner will be restrained at the _____ (appropriate military installation) in whatever degree considered to be appropriate by his commanding officer. This restraint will be for a minimum of 12 hours in all cases involving consumption of alcoholic beverages. It is further agreed that he will not be transferred, granted leave, or discharged from the ____ (appropriate service) without notice to the sheriff or his deputy and will be delivered to the sheriff or his deputy upon demand. These terms and conditions will be withdrawn only upon his posting of the required personal bond or upon the release by the sheriff, his deputy, or the appropriate court.

Signed ______________
Official title ______________

Laws 1921, p. 241, § 1; Laws 1966, p. 428, § 1; Laws 1982, p. 3, § 17; Laws 1983, p. 884, § 3–18; Laws 1984, p. 22, § 17.

Formerly Code 1933, § 27–902.

§ 17–6–4. Posting of cash bonds permitted; disposition of unclaimed bonds

(a) Any party, defendant, accused, or other person required or permitted by law to give or post bond (or bail) as surety or security for the happening of any event or act in criminal matters may discharge the requirement by depositing cash in the amount of the bond so required with the appropriate person, official, or other depository.

(b) Any official or other person receiving any such bond shall give a receipt therefor and shall cause the fact of the receipt to be entered and recorded on the docket of the case in which it was given. If bond is given in a matter not appearing as a separate court case on a docket, a docket shall be prepared, maintained, and kept of all such transactions and the name and address of the person giving or making the bond, the date of the receipt of the bond, the name of the person receiving the bond, the amount of the bond, and a description of the cause for giving the bond, together with any and all other information desirable concerning the bond, shall be a part of the record in that separate docket.

(c) In the event that any cash bail posted pursuant to this Code section or Code Section 17–6–5 is not later claimed by the surety on such bond after a period of seven years from the later of either the date on which the defendant was required to appear in court or the date of disposition of the case by the prosecutor or the court, including any appeal of a verdict or sentence, then the cash shall be paid into the general fund of the county having trial venue of the case, as in the case of forfeited cash bonds, provided that the officer who accepted such cash bail shall first have notified the surety, by mailing notice to such surety at the last address given by such surety, that such funds shall be forfeited if they are not claimed within 90 days following the date of mailing of such notice. Any claim by a surety for refund of a cash bail shall include acceptable documentary proof of disposition of the case from the prosecuting official or appropriate court records or such other documentation as may be acceptable to the official holding such cash bail as proof that the case has been settled.

Laws 1969, p. 41, §§ 1, 2; Laws 1991, p. 749, § 1.

§ 17–6–5. Cash bonds in motor vehicle, game, boating violation or litter cases; authorization by court

Any sheriff, deputy sheriff, county peace officer, or other county officer charged with the duty of enforcing the laws of this state relating to (1) traffic or the operation or licensing of motor vehicles or operators; (2) the width, height, or length of vehicles and loads; (3) motor common carriers and motor contract carriers; (4) road taxes on motor carriers as provided in Article 2 of Chapter 9 of Title 48; (5) game and fish; (6) boating; or (7) litter control who makes an arrest outside the corporate limits of any municipality of this state for a violation of said laws and who is authorized, as provided herein by a court of record having jurisdiction over such offenses, to accept cash bonds may accept a cash bond from the person arrested in lieu of a statutory bond or recognizance. No such officer shall accept a cash bond unless he is authorized to receive cash bonds in such cases by an order of the court having jurisdiction over such offenses and unless such order has been entered on the minutes of the court. Any such order may be granted, revoked, or modified by the court at any time.

Laws 1953, Jan.-Feb. Sess., p. 331, § 1; Laws 1962, p. 530, § 1; Laws 1975, p. 845, § 1; Laws 1982, p. 1136, §§ 1, 4.

§ 17–6–6. Receipt book; distribution of copies of receipts

Other laws to the contrary notwithstanding, when an order is passed as provided for in Code Section 17–6–5 authorizing an officer to accept cash bonds, it shall be the duty of the clerk of the court, if there is one, or, if there is no clerk, the judge passing the order to furnish the officer or officers authorized under the order with a book of blank receipts, consecutively numbered in triplicate and readily distinguishable and identifiable. The receipts shall be completed by the officers when making an arrest and accepting a cash bond so as to show the name of the person arrested, date of arrest, nature of the offense, amount of the cash bond given, and the name of the arresting officer. The arresting officer or the person receiving the cash bond shall deliver a copy of the receipt to the person arrested at the time the cash bond is given and shall file the original receipt together with the cash bond with the clerk, or judge, as the case may be, of the court having jurisdiction of the offense not later than the next succeeding business day of such clerk or judge following the date of issuance of the receipt. The remaining copy of the receipt shall be mailed to the commissioner of public safety.

Laws 1953, Jan.-Feb. Sess., p. 331, § 2; Laws 1978, p. 1493, § 1.

§ 17–6–7. Duty of arresting officer to account for receipts; personal liability; contempt of court for failure

All receipts issued to arresting officers and all cash bonds received under Code Sections 17–6–5 and 17–6–6 shall be accounted for by the receiving officers to the court from which the receipts were issued and, in the event that any such officer fails to account for same, he shall be personally liable for any default and may be punished as for contempt by the court, in addition to any other penalties which are provided for by law in such cases.

Laws 1953, Jan.-Feb. Sess., p. 331, § 3.

§ 17–6–8. Forfeiture; distribution of proceeds; subsequent prosecution

If any person arrested for a misdemeanor arising out of a violation of the laws of this state relating to (1) traffic or the operation or licensing of motor vehicles or operators; (2) the width, height, or length of vehicles and loads; (3) motor common carriers and motor contract carriers; (4) road taxes on motor carriers as provided in Article 2 of Chapter 9 of Title 48; (5) game and fish; (6) boating; or (7) litter control gives a cash bond for his appearance as provided in Code Section 17–6–5 and fails to appear on the date, time, and place specified in the citation or summons without legal excuse, the court may order said cash bond forfeited without the necessity of complying with the statutory procedure provided for in the forfeiture of statutory bail bonds. A judgment ordering the case disposed of and settled may be entered by the court and the proceeds shall be applied in the same manner as fines. If the court does not enter a judgment ordering the case disposed of and settled, the forfeiture of the cash bond shall not be a bar to subsequent prosecution of the person charged with the violation of such laws.

Laws 1953, Jan.-Feb. Sess., p. 331, § 4; Laws 1962, p. 530, § 2; Laws 1975, p. 845, § 2; Laws 1982, p. 1136, §§ 2, 5.

§ 17–6–9. Law enforcement officers and officials of political subdivisions authorized to accept cash bonds for violation of litter laws

Any law enforcement officer or official of a political subdivision of this state who is authorized to enforce Part 2 of Article 2 of Chapter 7 of Title 16 and who is authorized by the judge having jurisdiction of the offense to accept cash bonds may accept a cash bond for the personal appearance at trial of the person arrested in lieu of a statutory bond or recognizance. The procedures connected with such cash bonds, including, but not limited to, duties of the arresting officer, forfeiture, distribution of proceeds, and discretion of court as to disposal of the cash bond, shall be the same procedures applicable to arrest by a sheriff for a violation of any litter law.

Laws 1975, p. 845, § 3; Laws 2006, Act 538, § 3–7, eff. July 1, 2006.

§ 17–6–10. Offenses against municipalities; cash bonds

(a) All mayors or chief governing officers or their designated official or officials of municipalities are authorized to accept a cash bond for the personal appearance in court of any person charged with a violation of an ordinance or other offense against the municipality. The officer assessing and accepting a cash bond shall issue a receipt for the bond to the person charged with the violation.

(b) When any mayor or chief governing officer of any municipality of this state designates any municipal official to accept cash bonds under subsection (a) of this Code section, the delegation of authority shall be in writing and filed in the records of the municipality.

(c) Any person charged with a violation of an ordinance or other offense against a municipality who gives a cash bond for his personal appearance in court at a designated time and place and who fails to appear at said time and place shall forfeit the cash bond upon the call of the case for trial. It shall not be necessary for the municipality to take any further action to forfeit the cash bond. Forfeiture of a cash bond shall not be a bar to a subsequent prosecution of the accused for the violation.

(d) This Code section shall not apply to municipalities having provisions in their charters with reference to the subject matter of this Code section.

Laws 1952, p. 182, §§ 1–4, 4A.

§ 17–6–11. Display of driver's license in motor vehicle violation apprehensions; suspension of license; organ donations; rules and regulations

(a) Any other laws to the contrary notwithstanding, any person who is apprehended by an officer for the violation of the laws of this state or ordinances relating to: (1) traffic, including any offense under Code Section 40–5–72 or 40–6–10, but excepting any other offense for which a license may be suspended for a first offense by the commissioner of driver services, any offense covered under Code Section 40–5–54, or any offense covered under Article 15 of Chapter 6 of

Title 40; (2) the licensing and registration of motor vehicles and operators; (3) the width, height, and length of vehicles and loads; (4) motor common carriers and motor contract carriers; or (5) road taxes on motor carriers as provided in Article 2 of Chapter 9 of Title 48 upon being served with the official summons issued by such apprehending officer, in lieu of being immediately brought before the proper magistrate, recorder, or other judicial officer to enter into a formal recognizance or make direct the deposit of a proper sum of money in lieu of a recognizance ordering incarceration, may display his or her driver's license to the apprehending officer in lieu of bail, in lieu of entering into a recognizance for his or her appearance for trial as set in the aforesaid summons, or in lieu of being incarcerated by the apprehending officer and held for further action by the appropriate judicial officer. The apprehending officer shall note the driver's license number on the official summons. The summons duly served as provided in this Code section shall give the judicial officer jurisdiction to dispose of the matter.

(b) Upon display of the driver's license, the apprehending officer shall release the person so charged for his or her further appearance before the proper judicial officer as required by the summons. The court in which the charges are lodged shall immediately forward to the Department of Driver Services of this state the driver's license number if the person fails to appear and answer to the charge against him or her. The commissioner of driver services shall, upon receipt of a license number forwarded by the court, suspend the driver's license and driving privilege of the defaulting person until notified by the court that the charge against the person has been finally adjudicated. Such person's license shall be reinstated if the person submits proof of payment of the fine from the court of jurisdiction and pays to the Department of Driver Services a restoration fee of $50.00 or $25.00 when such reinstatement is processed by mail.

(b.1) It shall be the duty of a law enforcement officer or emergency medical technician responding to the scene of any motor vehicle accident or other accident involving a fatal injury to examine immediately the driver's license of the victim to determine the victim's wishes concerning organ donation. If the victim has indicated that he or she wishes to be an organ donor, it shall be the duty of such law enforcement officer or emergency medical technician to take appropriate action to ensure, if possible, that the victim's organs shall not be imperiled by delay in verification by the donor's next of kin.

(c) Nothing in this Code section bars any law enforcement officer from arresting or from seizing the driver's license of any individual possessing a fraudulent license or a suspended license or operating a motor vehicle while his or her license is suspended, outside the scope of a driving permit, or without a license.

(d) The commissioner of driver services shall be authorized to promulgate reasonable rules and regulations to carry out the purposes of this Code section and to establish agreements with other states whereby a valid license from that state may be accepted for purposes of this Code section.

Laws 1973, p. 435, §§ 1, 2; Laws 1976, p. 213, § 1; Laws 1979, p. 759, § 1; Laws 1982, p. 1136, §§ 3, 6; Laws 1986, p. 1607, § 1; Laws 1987, p. 542, § 3; Laws 1990, p. 8, § 17; Laws 1991, p. 94, § 17; Laws 1991, p. 1776, § 1; Laws 1996, p. 1624, § 2; Laws 2000, p. 951, § 12-1; Laws 2005, Act 68, § 7-3, eff. July 1, 2005.

§ 17-6-12. Release of person charged with crime on his own recognizance only; arrest where person fails to appear for trial

(a) In addition to other laws regarding the release of an accused person, the judge of any court having jurisdiction over a person charged with committing an offense against the criminal laws of this state shall have authority, in his sound discretion and in appropriate cases, to authorize the release of the person upon his own recognizance only.

(b) Upon the failure of a person released on his own recognizance only to appear for trial, if the release is not otherwise conditioned by the court, the court may summarily issue an order for his arrest which shall be enforced as in cases of forfeited bonds.

Laws 1969, p. 72, §§ 1, 2.

§ 17-6-13. Number of times bail may be permitted for same offense

Except as otherwise provided in this chapter, each person who is entitled to bail under this article shall be permitted one bail for the same offense as a matter of right. Subsequent bails shall be in the discretion of the court.

Laws 1832, Cobb's 1851 Digest, p. 862; Laws 1878-79, p. 55, § 1; Laws 1971, p. 408, § 1; Laws 1983, p. 452, § 2.

Formerly Code 1863, § 4625; Code 1868, § 4649; Code 1873, § 4747; Code 1882, § 4747; Penal Code 1895, § 934; Penal Code 1910, § 959; Code 1933, § 27-903.

§ 17-6-14. Preliminary hearing bond valid to insure presence at trial; exception of bail set higher; limitations

(a) When a person posts bail bond prior to a preliminary or commitment hearing and is later bound over to another court for trial, the original bail bond shall not terminate but shall be valid to provide for the person's appearance at the trial of the case unless the amount of the bail is set higher by lawful authority, in which case new bail bond shall be posted.

(b) Nothing contained in subsection (a) of this Code section shall apply to any proceedings in which any federal court or United States commissioner is involved. Subsection (a) of this Code section shall apply only to those instances wherein the person required to post a bail bond shall be bound over to a court or grand jury of the same county wherein the committing court exercised its jurisdiction. Subsection (a) of this Code section shall not apply to those instances where a person is bound over to two or more courts or grand juries.

(c) Nothing contained in subsection (a) of this Code section shall be construed to require an additional bail bond in the event the court to which the person has been committed requires a lesser bail bond than the bond originally posted.

Laws 1971, p. 407, §§ 1, 2.

§ 17-6-15. Bail

(a) After arrest, if bail is tendered and accepted, no regular commitment need be entered, but a simple memorandum of the fact of bail being taken shall be sufficient.

(b)(1) A reasonable opportunity shall be allowed the accused person to give bail; and, even after commitment and imprisonment, the committing court may order the accused person brought before it to receive bail. No person shall be imprisoned under a felony commitment when bail has been fixed, if the person tenders and offers to give bond in the amount fixed, with sureties acceptable to the sheriff of the county in which the alleged offense occurred; provided, however, the sheriff shall publish and make available written rules and regulations defining acceptable sureties and prescribing under what conditions sureties may be accepted. If the sheriff determines that a professional bonding company is an acceptable surety, the rules and regulations shall require, but shall not be limited to, the following:

(A) Complete documentation showing the composition of the company to be an individual, a trust, or a group of individuals, whether or not formed as a partnership or other legal entity, or a corporation or a combination of individuals, trusts, and corporations;

(B) Complete documentation for all employees, agents, or individuals authorized to sign or act on behalf of the bonding company;

(C) Complete documentation showing that the company holds a valid business license in the jurisdiction where bonds will be written;

(D) Fingerprints and background checks of every individual who acts as a professional bondsperson as defined in Code Section 17-6-50 for the professional bonding company seeking approval;

(E) Establishment of a cash escrow account or other form of collateral in a sum and upon terms and conditions approved by the sheriff;

(F) Establishment of application, approval, and reporting procedures for the professional bonding company deemed appropriate by the sheriff which satisfy all rules and regulations required by the laws of this state and the rules and regulations established by the sheriff;

(G) Applicable fees to be paid by the applicant to cover the cost of copying the rules and regulations and processing and investigating all applications and all other costs relating thereto; or

(H) Additional criteria and requirements for approving and regulating bonding companies to be determined at the discretion of the sheriff.

(2) This Code section shall not be construed to require a sheriff to accept a professional bonding company or bondsperson as a surety.

(3) This Code section shall not be construed to prevent the posting of real property bonds and the sheriff may not prohibit the posting of property bonds. Additional requirements for the use of real property may be determined at the discretion of the sheriff. The sheriff shall not prohibit a nonresident of the county from posting a real property bond if such real property is located in the county in which it is offered as bond and if such property has sufficient unencumbered equity to satisfy the sheriff's posted rules and regulations as to acceptable sureties.

(c) This Code section shall not abrogate or repeal the common-law authority of the judge having jurisdiction.

Laws 1977, p. 346, § 1; Laws 1994, p. 532, § 2.

Formerly Code 1863, § 4620; Code 1868, § 4644; Code 1873, § 4742; Code 1882, § 4742; Penal Code 1895, § 922; Penal Code 1910, § 947; Code 1933, § 27-418.

§ 17-6-16. Waiver of hearing; memorandum entered on warrant; supersedeas

If the accused person waives a commitment hearing and tenders bail, a memorandum of these facts shall be entered on the warrant by the person authorized to accept bail; and this waiver may be done by the person charged before arrest and, when done, shall operate as a supersedeas.

Formerly Code 1863, § 4621; Code 1868, § 4645; Code 1873, § 4743; Code 1882, § 4743; Penal Code 1895, § 923; Penal Code 1910, § 948; Code 1933, § 27-419.

§ 17-6-17. Conditions of bail bond and recognizance

In addition to all other requirements prescribed for appearance bonds or recognizances, the appearance bond or recognizance given by a person accused of the commission of a crime shall be conditioned upon the person presenting himself before the court at the time fixed for his arraignment. Upon failure of a person charged with a penal offense to appear before the court at the time fixed for his arraignment, the prosecuting attorney may proceed to forfeit the bond or recognizance.

Laws 1966, p. 430, § 2; Laws 1977, p. 179, § 1.

Formerly Code 1933, § 27–1402.

§ 17–6–18. Amendment of bonds in judicial proceedings

All bonds taken under requisition of law in the course of a judicial proceeding may be amended and new security given if necessary.

Formerly Code 1863, § 3434; Code 1868, § 3454; Code 1873, § 3505; Code 1882, § 3505; Civil Code 1895, § 5123; Civil Code 1910, § 5707; Code 1933, § 81–1204.

Article 2

Sureties

Part 1

General Provisions

§ 17–6–30. Fees of sureties

(a) Sureties on criminal bonds in any court shall not charge or receive more than 12 percent of the face amount of the bond set in the amount of $10,000.00 or less, which amount includes the principal and all applicable surcharges, and shall not charge or receive more than 15 percent of the face amount of the bond set in an amount in excess of $10,000.00, which amount includes the principal and all applicable surcharges, as compensation from defendants or from anyone acting for defendants.

(b) Any person who violates subsection (a) of this Code section shall be guilty of a misdemeanor.

Laws 1921, p. 243, §§ 1, 8; Laws 1958, p. 120, § 1; Laws 1982, p. 1254, § 1; Laws 1999, p. 546, § 1; Laws 2006, Act 581, § 1, eff. July 1, 2006.

Formerly Code 1933, §§ 27–501, 27–9903.

§ 17–6–31. Surety surrendering principal; release of surety from liability

(a) When the court is not in session, a surety on a bond may surrender the surety's principal to the sheriff or to the responsible law enforcement officer of the jurisdiction in which the case is pending in order to be released from liability.

(b) When the court is in session, a surety on a bond may surrender the surety's principal in open court.

(c) The principal shall also be considered surrendered by plea of guilty or nolo contendere to the court or if the principal is present in person when the jury or judge, if tried without a jury, finds the principal guilty or if the judge dead dockets the case prior to entry of judgment and, upon such plea or finding of guilty or dead docketing, the surety shall be released from liability.

(d)(1) Furthermore, the surety shall be released from liability if, prior to entry of judgment, there is:

(A) A deferred sentence;

(B) A presentence investigation;

(C) A court ordered pretrial intervention program;

(D) A court ordered educational and rehabilitation program;

(E) A fine;

(F) A dead docket; or

(G) Death of the principal.

(2) Furthermore, the surety may be released from liability at the discretion of the court if:

(A) The principal used a false name when he or she was bound over and committed to jail or a correctional institution and was subsequently released from such facility unless the surety knew or should have known that the principal used a false name; and

(B) The surety shows to the satisfaction of the court that he or she acted with due diligence and used all practical means to secure the attendance of the principal before the court.

(e) If the prosecuting attorney does not try the charges against a defendant within a period of two years in the case of felonies and one year in the case of misdemeanors after the date of posting bond, then judgment rendered after such period may not be enforced against the surety on the bond and the surety shall thereafter be relieved of liability on the bond. This subsection shall not apply where the prosecuting attorney's failure to try the charges is due to the fault of the principal.

(f) No judgment shall be rendered on any appearance bond if it is shown to the satisfaction of the court that the surety was prevented from returning the principal to the jurisdiction because such principal was on active military duty.

Laws 1943, p. 282, § 1; Laws 1982, p. 1224, § 1; Laws 1986, p. 1588, § 1; Laws 1987, p. 1342, § 1; Laws 1992, p. 2933, § 1; Laws 1997, p. 973, § 2.

Formerly Code 1863, § 4624; Code 1868, § 4648; Code 1873, § 4746; Code 1882, § 4746; Penal Code 1895, § 935; Penal Code 1910, § 960; Code 1933, § 27-904.

Part 2

Professional Bondsmen

§ 17-6-50. Professional bondsmen; definition

(a) Bondsmen or persons who hold themselves out as signers or sureties of bonds for compensation are declared to be professional bondsmen.

(b) A professional bondsperson is one who holds himself or herself out as a signer or surety of bonds for compensation who must meet the following qualifications:

(1) Is 18 years of age or over;

(2) Is a resident of the State of Georgia for at least one year before making application to write bonds;

(3) Is a person of good moral character and has not been convicted of a felony or any crime involving moral turpitude; and

(4) Is approved by the sheriff and remains in good standing with respect to all applicable federal, state, and local laws and all rules and regulations established by the sheriff in the county where the bonding business is conducted.

(c) The sheriff of the county in which the bonding business is conducting business or is seeking approval to conduct business shall initiate a criminal background investigation to ensure that a professional bondsman has not been convicted of a felony or a crime involving moral turpitude in this state or any other jurisdiction. The sheriff shall require the professional bondsman to furnish two full sets of fingerprints which the sheriff shall submit to the Georgia Crime Information Center. The center shall submit a full set of fingerprints to the Federal Bureau of Investigation for a national criminal history record check.

Laws 1921, p. 243, § 5; Laws 1994, p. 532, § 3; Laws 2002, p. 942, § A.

Formerly Code 1933, § 27-502.

§ 17-6-50.1. Continuing education programs for professional bondsmen

(a) The Georgia Association of Professional Bondsmen shall approve continuing education programs offered by professional associations, educational institutions, government agencies, and others as deemed appropriate for professional bondsmen to attend.

(b) The fee for continuing education programs for professional bondsmen shall not exceed $ 125.00 annually.

(c) Professional bondsmen shall be required to obtain eight hours of continuing education annually.

(d) On or before January 31 of each year, each professional bondsman shall submit a certificate of completion of eight hours of approved continuing education to the individual or department which is responsible for issuing bail bonds for each jurisdiction in which he or she is doing business.

Laws 2002, p. 791, § 1.

§ 17-6-51. Suggesting employment of attorneys

Professional bondsmen, their agents, or representatives shall not suggest or advise the employment of or name for employment any attorney or attorneys to represent a defendant, during the negotiations for the bondsmen to sign the bond or subsequent thereto.

Laws 1921, p. 243, § 2.

Formerly Code 1933, § 27-503.

§ 17-6-52. Soliciting business by bondsmen and attorneys

Professional bondsmen, their agents, or employees shall not solicit business as bondsmen or loiter about or around jails, places where prisoners are confined, or the courts for the purpose of engaging in or soliciting business as such bondsmen. No state or municipal law enforcement officer or keeper or employee of a penal institution may suggest to or give advice to, in any manner whatsoever, any prisoner regarding the services of a professional bondsman to write a criminal bond for the appearance of a prisoner in any court at any time.

Laws 1921, p. 243, § 3.

Formerly Code 1933, § 27-504.

§ 17–6–53. Participation in defense prohibited

Professional bondsmen, their agents, or employees shall not advise defendants who are principals in bonds signed by them or give any directions in the defense or disposition of the cases in which they sign bonds.

Laws 1921, p. 243, § 4.

Formerly Code 1933, § 27–505.

§ 17–6–54. Payments to and by; forfeiture of bond; surrender of custody of defendant

(a) No professional bondsman or his or her agents or employees who receive compensation for becoming the surety on a criminal bond shall thereafter receive any other sum in the case. If the surety surrenders a defendant into the custody of the court, the sheriff, or another law enforcement officer in the jurisdiction where the bond was made before final disposition of the case, the surety is required to return to the principal the compensation received for signing the bond as surety if such surrender of the defendant is for reasons other than:

(1) The defendant's arrest for a crime other than a traffic violation or misdemeanor;

(2) The defendant's cosigner attests in writing the desire to be released from the bond;

(3) The defendant fails to provide to the court and the surety the defendant's change of address;

(4) The defendant fails to pay any fee due to the surety after being notified by certified mail or statutory overnight delivery that the same is past due;

(5) The defendant fails to notify the court and the surety upon leaving the jurisdiction of the court; or

(6) The defendant provides false information to the surety.

(b) In the event of a forfeiture on the bond by the defendant, the surety shall have the right to surrender into custody the defendant who is the principal on the bond without returning any compensation paid by the defendant for the signing of the bond.

Laws 1921, p. 243, §§ 6, 7; Laws 1996, p. 1233, § 2; Laws 2000, p. 1589, § 3.

Formerly Code 1933, §§ 27–506, 27–507.

§ 17–6–55. Violations relating to sureties on criminal bonds

Any person who violates any Code section in this part shall be guilty of a misdemeanor.

Laws 1921, p. 243, § 8.

Formerly Code 1933, § 27–9903.

§ 17–6–56. Qualifications and registration of bail recovery agents

(a) As used in this Code section and Code Sections 17–6–57 and 17–6–58, the term "bail recovery agent" means any person who performs services or takes action for the purpose of apprehending the principal on a bail bond granted in this state or capturing a fugitive who has escaped from bail in this state for gratuity, benefit, or compensation.

(b) A bail recovery agent must be a United States citizen, 25 years of age or older, and must obtain a license pursuant to Code Section 16–11–129.

(c) Any sheriff of a county shall require any professional bondsman who is a resident of or doing business in the sheriff's county to register his or her bail recovery agents in that county. The professional bondsman must submit to the sheriff, in a form and manner to be determined by the sheriff, a list of all bail recovery agents whose services may be used by such bondsman.

Laws 1999, p. 546, § 1.1.

§ 17–6–56.1. Continuing education programs for bail recovery agents

(a) The Georgia Association of Professional Bondsmen shall approve continuing education programs offered by professional associations, educational institutions, government agencies, and others as deemed appropriate for bail recovery agents to attend.

(b) The fee for continuing education programs for bail recovery agents shall not exceed $ 125.00 annually.

(c) Bail recovery agents shall be required to obtain eight hours of continuing education annually.

(d) On or before January 31 of each year, each bail recovery agent shall submit a certificate of completion of eight hours of approved continuing education to the individual or department which is responsible for issuing bail bonds for each jurisdiction in which he or she is doing business.

Laws 2002, p. 791, § 2.

§ 17–6–57. Notification of sheriff and police chief when action to be taken by bail recovery agent; out-of-state bail recovery agents; uniform identification cards

(a) Any bail recovery agent who enters any local police jurisdiction in pursuit of and for the purpose of apprehending the principal on a bail bond or capturing a fugitive or engaging in surveillance of such principal or fugitive shall, prior to taking any action in his or her capacity as a bail recovery agent in that local police jurisdiction, notify by facsimile transmission or telephone the sheriff and police chief of the local police jurisdiction in which the surveillance, apprehension, or capture is to take place unless it is to take place in public.

(b) An out-of-state bail recovery agent shall submit proof to the sheriff or police chief that he or she is qualified to be a bail recovery agent under the requirements of his or her home state. An out-of-state bail recovery agent shall deliver a certified copy of the bail bond or of the forfeiture or failure to appear to the sheriff or chief of police. Such out-of-state bail recovery agent, if not qualified in his or her home state or if his or her home state does not require bail recovery agents to be qualified, shall employ a Georgia bail recovery agent who is lawfully registered pursuant to this part.

(c) Each professional bondsman shall issue a uniform identification card to each bail recovery agent registered by the professional bondsman which identification card shall include the bail recovery agent's name, height, weight, address, photograph, and signature. The identification card shall also include the signature of the professional bondsman who has registered the bail recovery agent as required in subsection (c) of Code Section 17–6–56. A bail recovery agent shall be required to carry such identification card while acting in the capacity as a bail recovery agent.

Laws 1999, p. 546, § 1.1.

§ 17–6–58. Penalties for bail recovery agents and for bondsmen; civil liability

(a) Any bail recovery agent who fails to register with the local sheriff or who is otherwise unqualified to act as a bail recovery agent but who nonetheless attempts to apprehend or capture a principal on a bail bond or a fugitive or who succeeds in apprehending or capturing such person shall be guilty of a misdemeanor upon conviction for the first violation and shall be guilty of a felony upon conviction for the second and all subsequent violations punishable by imprisonment for not less than one nor more than five years.

(b) Any bondsman or bonding company owner, surety, or agent who hires a bail recovery agent who is not qualified to act as a bail recovery agent pursuant to Code Sections 17–6–56 and 17–6–57 shall be guilty of a misdemeanor upon conviction for the first violation and shall be guilty of a felony upon conviction for the second and all subsequent violations punishable by imprisonment for not less than one nor more than five years, or a fine of not more than $ 10,000.00, or both.

(c) No bail recovery agent shall wear, carry, or display any uniform, badge, shield, card, or other item with any printing, insignia, or emblem that purports to indicate that such bail recovery agent is an employee, officer, or agent of any state or federal government or any political subdivision of any state or federal government. A violation of this subsection shall be punished upon conviction as a felony punishable by imprisonment for not less than one nor more than five years, or a fine of not more than $ 10,000.00, or both.

(d) A bail recovery agent who enters the wrong property, causes damage to said property, or causes injury to anyone thereon is liable for all damages.

Laws 1999, p. 546, § 1.1.

Article 3

Proceedings for Forfeiture of Bonds or Recognizances

§ 17–6–70. Bond forfeiture proceedings

(a) A bond forfeiture occurs at the end of the court day upon the failure of appearance of a principal of any bond or recognizance given for the appearance of that person.

(b) An appearance bond shall not be forfeited unless the clerk of the court gave the surety at least 72 hours' written notice, exclusive of Saturdays, Sundays, and legal holidays, before the time of the required appearance of the principal. Notice shall not be necessary if the time for appearance is within 72 hours from the time of arrest, provided the time for appearance is stated on the bond, or where the principal is given actual notice in open court.

Laws 1831, Cobb's 1851 Digest, p. 861; Laws 1878–79, p. 57, § 1; Laws 1966, p. 430, § 1; Laws 1982, p. 1224, § 2; Laws 1986, p. 1588, § 2; Laws 1987, p. 1342, § 2; Laws 1990, p. 8, § 17; Laws 1992, p. 6, § 17; Laws 1992, p. 2933, § 2.

Formerly Code 1863, § 4584; Code 1868, § 4605; Code 1873, § 4702; Code 1882, § 4702; Penal Code 1895, § 936; Penal Code 1910, § 961; Code 1933, § 27–905.

§ 17–6–70.1. Repealed by Laws 1983, p. 1203, § 1, eff. March 29, 1983

§ 17–6–71. Hearings; notice; orders

(a) The judge shall, at the end of the court day, upon the failure of the principal to appear, forfeit the bond and order an execution hearing not sooner than 120 days but not later than 150 days after such failure to appear. Notice of the execution hearing shall be served within ten days of such failure to appear by certified mail or statutory overnight delivery to the surety at the address listed on the bond or by personal service to the surety within ten days of such failure to appear at its home office or to its designated registered agent. Service shall be considered complete upon the mailing of such certified notice.

(b) If at the execution hearing it is determined that judgment should be entered, the judge shall so order and a writ of fieri facias shall be filed in the office of the clerk of the court where such judgment is entered. The provisions of this subsection shall apply to all bail bonds, whether returnable to superior court, state court, probate court, magistrate court, or municipal court.

Laws 1831, Cobb's 1851 Digest, p. 862; Laws 1943, p. 282, § 2; Laws 1953, Jan.-Feb. Sess., p. 452, § 1; Laws 1982, p. 1224, § 2; Laws 1983, p. 1203, § 2; Laws 1986, p. 1588, § 3; Laws 1987, p. 1342, § 3; Laws 1989, p. 556, § 1; Laws 1990, p. 8, § 17; Laws 1990, p. 2336, § 1; Laws 1992, p. 2933, § 3; Laws 2000, p. 1589, § 3.

Formerly Code 1863, § 4585; Code 1868, § 4606; Code 1873, § 4703; Code 1882, § 4703; Penal Code 1895, § 937; Penal Code 1910, § 962; Code 1933, § 27–906.

§ 17–6–72. Forfeiture of appearance bond avoided; avoidance where principal confined in another jurisdiction

(a) No judgment shall be rendered on a forfeiture of any appearance bond if it is shown to the satisfaction of the court by the written statement of a licensed physician that the principal on the bond was prevented from attending by some mental or physical disability.

(b) No judgment shall be rendered on a forfeiture of any appearance bond if it is shown to the satisfaction of the court that the principal on the bond was prevented from attending because he or she was detained by reason of arrest, sentence, or confinement in a penal institution or jail in the State of Georgia, or so detained in another jurisdiction, or because he or she was involuntarily confined or detained pursuant to court order in a mental institution in the State of Georgia or in another jurisdiction. An official written notice of the holding institution in which the principal is being detained or confined shall be considered proof of the principal's detention or confinement and such notice may be sent from the holding institution by mail or delivered by hand or by facsimile machine. Upon the presentation of such written notice to the clerk of the proper court, the prosecuting attorney, and the sheriff or other law enforcement officer having jurisdiction over the case, along with a letter of intent to pay all costs of returning the principal to the jurisdiction of the court, such notice and letter shall serve as the surety's request for a detainer or hold to be placed on the principal. Should there be a failure to place a detainer or hold within 15 days, excluding Saturdays, Sundays, and legal holidays, and after such presentation of such notice and letter of intent to pay costs, the surety shall then be relieved of the liability for the appearance bond without further order of the court.

(c) No judgment shall be rendered on a forfeiture of any appearance bond if it is shown to the satisfaction of the court that prior to the entry of the judgment on the forfeiture the principal on the bond is in the custody of the sheriff or other responsible law enforcement agency. An official written notice of the holding institution in which the principal is being detained or confined shall be considered proof of the principal's detention or confinement and such notice may be sent from the holding institution by mail or delivered by hand or by facsimile machine. Upon presentation of such written notice to the clerk of the proper court, the prosecuting attorney, and the sheriff or other law enforcement officer having jurisdiction over the case along with a letter of intent to pay all costs of returning the principal to the jurisdiction of the court, such notice and letter shall serve as the surety's request for a detainer or hold to be placed against the principal. Should there be a failure to place a detainer or hold within 15 days, excluding Saturdays, Sundays, and legal holidays, and after presentation of such notice and letter of intent to pay costs, the surety shall then be relieved of the liability for the appearance bond without further order of the court.

(d) In cases in which paragraph (3) of this subsection is not applicable, on application filed within 120 days from the payment of judgment, the court shall order remission under the following conditions:

(1) Provided the bond amount has been paid within 120 days after judgment and the delay has not prevented prosecution of the principal and upon application to the court with prior notice to the prosecuting attorney of such application, said court shall direct remission of 95 percent of the bond amount remitted to the surety if the surety locates the principal in the custody of the sheriff in the jurisdiction where the bond was made or in another jurisdiction causing the return of the principal to the jurisdiction where the bond was made, apprehends, surrenders, or produces the principal, if the apprehension or surrender of the principal was substantially procured or caused by the surety, or if the location of the principal by the surety caused the adjudication of the principal in the jurisdiction in which the bond was made. Should the surety, within two years of the principal's failure to appear, locate the principal in the custody of the sheriff in the jurisdiction where the bond was made or in another jurisdiction causing the return of the principal to the jurisdiction where the bond was made, apprehend, surrender, or produce the principal, if the apprehension or surrender of the principal is substantially procured or caused by the surety, or if the location of the principal by the surety causes the

adjudication of the principal in the jurisdiction in which the bond was made, the surety shall be entitled to a refund of 50 percent of the bond amount. The application for 50 percent remission shall be filed no later than 30 days following the expiration of the two-year period following the date of judgment;

(2) Remission shall be granted upon condition of the payment of court costs and of the expenses of returning the principal to the jurisdiction by the surety; or

(3) If, within 120 days after judgment, the surety surrenders the principal to the sheriff or responsible law enforcement officer, or said surrender has been denied by the sheriff or responsible law enforcement officer, or surety locates the principal in custody in another jurisdiction, the surety shall only be required to pay costs and 5 percent of the face amount of the bond, which amount includes all surcharges. If it is shown to the satisfaction of the court, by the presentation of competent evidence from the sheriff or the holding institution, that said surrender has been made or denied or that the principal is in custody in another jurisdiction or that said surrender has been made and that 5 percent of the face amount of the bond and all costs have been tendered to the sheriff, the court shall direct that the judgment be marked satisfied and that the writ of execution, fi. fa., be canceled.

Laws 1965, p. 266, §§ 1–3; Laws 1982, p. 1224, § 2; Laws 1982, p. 1658, § 2; Laws 1983, p. 3, § 14; Laws 1983, p. 1203, § 3; Laws 1985, p. 982, § 1; Laws 1986, p. 1588, § 4; Laws 1987, p. 1342, § 4; Laws 1989, p. 556, § 2; Laws 1990, p. 2336, § 2; Laws 1992, p. 2933, § 4; Laws 1996, p. 1233, § 3.

§ 17–6–73. Mailing address of principal and surety

Every bond or recognizance given to secure the appearance of any person in any criminal proceeding shall have entered thereon the mailing address of the principal and each surety.

Laws 1982, p. 1224, § 2.

Article 4

Bonds for Good Behavior and to Keep the Peace

Part 1

Bonds for Good Behavior

§ 17–6–90. Authority to require bond

(a) Any judicial officer authorized to hold a court of inquiry may, upon the information of others under oath or upon his own motion, issue a warrant against any person in the county whose conduct is such as to justify the belief that the safety of any one or more persons in the county or the peace or property of the same is in danger of being injured or disturbed thereby. Upon the return of the warrant and upon sufficient cause being shown, the court may require from the person a bond with sureties for his good behavior until the next term of the superior court of the county or for a period of 60 days, whichever is greater. Any person against whom a warrant issues must, within 24 hours, be brought for a hearing before the court which issued the warrant or be released on bond by the sheriff, the amount and reasonable conditions of such bond to be set by the court which issued the warrant.

(b) All bonds posted under this Code section shall be returnable in the court which issued the warrant and shall be amendable in the court's discretion. Within seven days after being released on bond by the sheriff, the person shall be entitled to a hearing before the court which issued the warrant. The court may, on its own motion, require a hearing.

(c) If it is determined at a hearing that there was not sufficient cause for the warrant to have been issued, the affiant who caused the warrant to be issued shall pay all court costs.

Laws 1974, p. 322, § 1; Laws 1978, p. 1924, § 1; Laws 1986, p. 1151, § 1.

Formerly Code 1863, § 4627; Code 1868, § 4651; Code 1873, § 4749; Code 1882, § 4749; Penal Code 1895, § 1235; Penal Code 1910, § 1317; Code 1933, § 76–101.

§ 17–6–91. Spouse may require bond

A person may require a bond for good behavior against the spouse of such person.

Formerly Code 1863, § 4634; Code 1868, § 4658; Code 1873, § 4756; Code 1882, § 4756; Penal Code 1895, § 1242; Penal Code 1910, § 1324; Code 1933, § 76–104.

§ 17–6–92. Suit for breach of bond; disposition of recovery

For a violation of a bond posted pursuant to Code Section 17–6–90, an action may be brought at the instance of any person in the county. The recovery on the bond shall be paid to the person bringing the action.

Laws 1981, p. 622, § 1.

Formerly Code 1863, § 4628; Code 1868, § 4652; Code 1873, § 4750; Code 1882, § 4750; Penal Code 1895, § 1236; Penal Code 1910, § 1318; Code 1933, § 76-102.

§ 17-6-93. Extension from term to term

A bond for good behavior posted pursuant to Code Section 17-6-90 may be extended from term to term by the superior or state court, as the case may be, or for additional 60 day periods by the court which issued the warrant, whichever is greater, in its discretion. The sureties on the bond shall have the privilege of surrendering their principal as in other cases of bail.

Laws 1986, p. 1151, § 2.

Formerly Code 1863, § 4629; Code 1868, § 4653; Code 1873, § 4751; Code 1882, § 4751; Penal Code 1895, § 1237; Penal Code 1910, § 1319; Code 1933, § 76-103.

§ 17-6-94. Contempt proceedings for violation of bonds

Upon oral or written complaint by the injured party or upon motion by the prosecuting attorney, the court may, in its discretion, issue a rule for contempt against a party who violates the bond posted pursuant to Code Section 17-6-90. Upon hearing the rule, if the court finds that there has been a violation of the bond, the court may, in addition to the remedy provided in Code Section 17-6-92, impose a sentence for contempt of court. If it should appear to the court from the evidence and the court finds that the violation of the bond was provoked or brought about by the conduct of the prosecuting witness, the witness may be ruled for contempt of court and sentenced as provided by law.

Laws 1986, p. 1151, § 3.

Part 2

Bonds to Keep the Peace

§ 17-6-110. Authority to require bond

(a) Upon the information of any person, under oath, that he is in fear of bodily harm to himself or his family, or of violent injury to his property, from another person, any judicial officer authorized to hold a court of inquiry may issue his warrant requiring the arrest of such other person. If, after the return of the warrant and upon hearing the evidence of both parties, the court is satisfied that probable cause for such fear exists, the court may require the accused to give bond, with good security, to keep the peace as against the person, family, or property of the affiant. If the accused fails to give bond, the court shall commit him to jail. Any person against whom a warrant issues must, within 24 hours, be brought for a hearing before the court which issued the warrant or be released on bond by the sheriff.

(b) Nothing in this Code section shall prohibit the sheriff from releasing the person at any time prior to the hearing after posting bond. The amount of the bond shall be set by the sheriff but in no event shall the amount set by the sheriff exceed $1,000.00. Such bond shall contain the same conditions as a bond required after a hearing by the court of inquiry, except that, in counties in which a state court is established, all bonds posted under this Code section shall be returnable in the state court rather than in the superior court. Within five days after being released on bond by the sheriff, the person shall be entitled to a hearing before the court of inquiry.

(c) If it is determined at the hearing that there was not sufficient cause for the warrant to have been issued, the affiant who caused the warrant to be issued shall pay all court costs.

(d) A judicial officer shall not be required to issue the warrant provided for in this Code section until the person requesting the issuance of the warrant deposits with the judicial officer a sum, not to exceed $12.00, to be applied against the total cost in the proceedings. At the termination of the proceedings, any part of the deposit remaining because of dismissal or because the costs are assessed against another party shall be refunded to the depositor. If the person requesting the issuance of the warrant is unable to pay any deposit, fee, or other cost which would normally be required in the court and subscribes an affidavit to the effect that because of his indigence he is unable to pay these costs, the person shall be relieved from paying the costs and his rights shall be the same as if he had paid the costs.

Laws 1850, Cobb's 1851 Digest, p. 865; Laws 1962, p. 121, § 1; Laws 1974, p. 322, § 2; Laws 1978, p. 1924, § 2; Laws 1990, p. 8, § 17.

Formerly Code 1863, § 4630; Code 1868, § 4654; Code 1873, § 4752; Code 1882, § 4752; Penal Code 1895, § 1238; Penal Code 1910, § 1320; Code 1933, § 76-201.

§ 17-6-111. Spouse may require bond

A person may require a bond to keep the peace against the spouse of such person.

Formerly Code 1863, § 4634; Code 1868, § 4658; Code 1873, § 4756; Code 1882, § 4756; Penal Code 1895, § 1242; Penal Code 1910, § 1324; Code 1933, § 76-205.

§ 17–6–112. Breach of the peace; right of action

(a) Actual violence, a threat of violence, or any other act intended and calculated to excite alarm or to provoke a breach of the peace shall be a violation of the bond posted pursuant to Code Section 17–6–110. For every such act, the party at whose instance the bond was required shall have a right of action.

(b) In counties having a population of not less than 200,000 nor more than 250,000 according to the United States decennial census of 1950 or any future such census in which there is located a municipal court, upon oral or written complaint by the injured party, the court may in its discretion issue a rule for contempt against the offending defendant. Upon hearing the rule, if the court finds that there has been a violation of the bond, the court may, in addition to the remedy provided in subsection (a) of this Code section, impose a sentence for contempt of court. If it should appear to the court from the evidence and the court finds that the breach of the peace was provoked or brought about by the conduct of the prosecuting witness, the witness may be ruled for contempt of court and sentenced as provided by law.

Laws 1959, p. 3085, § 1; Laws 1982, p. 2107, § 16.

Formerly Code 1863, § 4631; Code 1868, § 4655; Code 1873, § 4753; Code 1882, § 4753; Penal Code 1895, § 1239; Penal Code 1910, § 1321; Code 1933, § 76–202.

§ 17–6–113. Provoking breach of bond; effect

If the person who required the bond provokes a violation thereof by the person who posted the bond, no recovery shall be had.

Formerly Code 1863, § 4632; Code 1868, § 4656; Code 1873, § 4754; Code 1882, § 4754; Penal Code 1895, § 1240; Penal Code 1910, § 1322; Code 1933, § 76–203.

§ 17–6–114. Discharge or extension of bond

The superior or state court, as the case may be, may discharge the bond at any time unless a motion is made to extend it, accompanied by evidence to satisfy the court of the necessity of the extension.

Formerly Code 1863, § 4633; Code 1868, § 4657; Code 1873, § 4755; Code 1882, § 4755; Penal Code 1895, § 1241; Penal Code 1910, § 1323; Code 1933, § 76–204.

CHAPTER 7

PRETRIAL PROCEEDINGS

Article 1

General Provisions

§ 17–7–1. County sending prisoner to jail in adjoining county liable for fees

When there is no secure jail in a county or when it is deemed necessary by the sheriff, any person committing an offense in the county may be sent to a jail in another county determined to be suitable by the sheriff. The county where the offense is committed shall be primarily liable for jail fees and costs and shall pay the same monthly in advance to the county holding the prisoner. For the purpose of raising funds to pay the costs, the county governing authority may levy and collect an additional tax.

Laws 1865–66, p. 40, §§ 1–3; Laws 1995, p. 291, § 1.

Formerly Code 1868, § 4642; Code 1873, § 4740; Code 1882, § 4740; Penal Code 1895, § 920; Penal Code 1910, § 945; Code 1933, § 27–416.

§ 17–7–2. Receipt of prisoner from another county

The sheriff shall not be bound to receive a prisoner from another county until the jail fees and costs are provided for as set forth in Code Section 17–7–1.

Laws 1865–66, p. 40, § 2.

Formerly Code 1868, § 4643; Code 1873, § 4741; Code 1882, § 4741; Penal Code 1895, § 921; Penal Code 1910, § 946; Code 1933, § 27–417.

§ 17–7–3. Detention facilities required to provide weekly lists of juveniles detained pending trial; information to be included

The official in charge of any facility in which a child is detained pending trial in the superior, state, or juvenile courts, including but not limited to sheriffs, regional jail authorities, and the Department of Juvenile Justice, shall furnish at least once a week a list of all children so detained to the chief judge, or his or her designee, and the prosecuting attorney for the court or courts having jurisdiction to adjudicate the case against the child. The list shall include the following information pertaining to each child:

(1) The child's name;

(2) The date of arrest;

(3) The offense charged or other reason for being held;

(4) The amount of the bond, if known; and

(5) Whether the child is represented by an attorney and, if represented, the name of the attorney.

Laws 2006, Act 475, § 1, eff. July 1, 2006.

Article 2

Commitment Hearings

§ 17-7-20. Who may hold courts of inquiry

Any judge of a superior or state court, judge of the probate court, magistrate, or officer of a municipality who has the criminal jurisdiction of a magistrate may hold a court of inquiry to examine into an accusation against a person legally arrested and brought before him or her. The time and place of the inquiry shall be determined by such judicial officer. Should the county in which the offense is alleged to have been committed be a member of a regional jail authority created under Article 5 of Chapter 4 of Title 42, the "Regional Jail Authorities Act," the judge may order the court of inquiry to be conducted alternatively in the county in which the offense is alleged to have been committed or in facilities available at the regional jail or by audiovisual communication between the two locations and between the accused, the court, the attorneys, and the witnesses.

Laws 1982, p. 493, §§ 1, 2; Laws 1983, p. 884, § 3-19; Laws 1996, p. 742, § 2.

Formerly Code 1863, § 4611; Code 1868, § 4633; Code 1873, § 4730; Code 1882, § 4730; Penal Code 1895, § 906; Penal Code 1910, § 931; Code 1933, § 27-401.

§ 17-7-21. Associates of officer holding court of inquiry

The judicial officer before whom the accused is brought may associate with him, in the investigation, one or more magistrates, in which event a majority shall decide all questions. If there are only two presiding, the original officer shall determine all the questions where the court is not in agreement.

Laws 1984, p. 22, § 17.

Formerly Code 1863, § 4612; Code 1868, § 4634; Code 1873, § 4731; Code 1882, § 4731; Penal Code 1895, § 907; Penal Code 1910, § 932; Code 1933, § 27-402.

§ 17-7-22. Courts of municipal corporations may commit offenders

Any mayor, recorder, or other proper officer presiding in any court of a municipal corporation shall have authority to bind over or commit to jail offenders against any criminal law whenever, in the course of an investigation before such officer, a proper case therefor is made out by the evidence.

Laws 1880-81, p. 176, § 2.

Formerly Code 1882, § 786c; Penal Code 1895, § 927; Penal Code 1910, § 952; Code 1933, § 27-423.

§ 17-7-23. Rule of decision; commitment of accused; limited jurisdiction of certain courts

(a) The duty of a court of inquiry is simply to determine whether there is sufficient reason to suspect the guilt of the accused and to require him to appear and answer before the court competent to try him. Whenever such probable cause exists, it is the duty of the court to commit.

(b) Any court, other than a superior court or a state court, to which any charge of a violation of Code Section 16-11-126 or Code Section 16-11-128 is referred for the determination required by this Code section shall thereafter have and exercise only the jurisdiction of a court of inquiry with respect to the charge and with respect to any other criminal violation arising from the transaction on which the charge was based and shall not thereafter be competent to try the accused for the charge or for any other criminal violation arising from the transaction on which the charge was based, irrespective of the jurisdiction that the court otherwise would have under any other law.

Laws 1980, p. 415, § 1.

Formerly Code 1863, § 4618; Code 1868, § 4640; Code 1873, § 4738; Code 1882, § 4738; Penal Code 1895, § 912; Penal Code 1910, § 937; Code 1933, § 27-407.

§ 17-7-24. Time granted parties for preparation of case; bail

A reasonable time shall be given to the defendant and prosecutor for the preparation of the case. In no event shall the defendant be forced to attend the hearing without the aid of counsel if there is a reasonable probability of his securing counsel without too great delay. Where the hearing is postponed to a future day at the instance of either party or the court, it shall not be necessary to commit the defendant to jail pending the hearing; but he shall have the right to give bail for appearance at the hearing before the court of inquiry if the offense is bailable under the authority of the court.

Laws 1865–66, p. 236, § 1.

Formerly Code 1863, § 4613; Code 1868, § 4635; Code 1873, § 4732; Code 1882, § 4732; Penal Code 1895, § 908; Penal Code 1910, § 933; Code 1933, § 27–403.

§ 17-7-25. Attendance of witnesses

A court of inquiry shall have the same power to compel the attendance of witnesses as in other criminal cases, as set forth in and subject to all of the provisions of Chapter 10 of Title 24, at any location where the court shall conduct a hearing, provided that notice is given at least 24 hours prior to the hearing. A court of inquiry may order the arrest of witnesses if required to compel their attendance.

Laws 1996, p. 742, § 3.

Formerly Code 1863, § 4617; Code 1868, § 4639; Code 1873, § 4736; Code 1882, § 4736; Penal Code 1895, § 909; Penal Code 1910, § 934; Code 1933, § 27–404.

§ 17-7-26. Binding over witnesses

In the event of a commitment of the accused person, the court, in its discretion, may require the witnesses, on behalf of the state or others, to give suitable bonds to secure their appearance at court, with or without sureties, as the circumstances seem to demand.

Formerly Code 1863, § 4616; Code 1868, § 4638; Code 1873, § 4735; Code 1882, § 4735; Penal Code 1895, § 915; Penal Code 1910, § 940; Code 1933, § 27–410.

§ 17-7-27. Amount of bonds for appearance of witnesses; sureties

The sheriffs and constables shall accept bond in such reasonable amount as may be just and fair to secure the appearance of any witness to attend the courts, provided the sureties tendered and offered on the bond are approved by a sheriff of any county.

Laws 1921, p. 241, § 1.

Formerly Code 1933, § 27–411.

§ 17-7-28. Evidence; testimony of defendant

The court of inquiry shall hear all legal evidence submitted by either party. If the defendant wishes to testify and announces in open court before the court of inquiry his intention to do so, he may testify in his own behalf. If he so elects, he shall be sworn as any other witness and may be examined and cross-examined as any other witness, except that no evidence of general bad character or prior convictions shall be admissible unless and until the defendant first puts his character into issue. The failure of a defendant to testify shall create no presumption against him, and no comment may be made because of such failure.

Laws 1962, p. 453, § 1; Laws 1973, p. 292, § 1.

Formerly Code 1863, § 4614; Code 1868, § 4636; Code 1873, § 4733; Code 1882, § 4733; Penal Code 1895, § 910; Penal Code 1910, § 935; Code 1933, § 27–405.

§ 17-7-29. Committing for different offense

A court of inquiry may commit the defendant for a different offense than that stated in the warrant if the evidence requires it.

Formerly Code 1863, § 6422; Code 1868, § 4646; Code 1873, § 4744; Code 1882, § 4744; Penal Code 1895, § 913; Penal Code 1910, § 938; Code 1933, § 27–408.

§ 17-7-30. Form of commitment

The following form, or one in substance the same, shall be deemed to be a sufficient commitment:

Georgia, _____ County.

_____ (name of the defendant) having been arrested on a warrant for the offense of _____ and brought before me, after hearing evidence it is ordered that he be committed for trial for the offense of _____. The jailer of said county (or any other county, if necessary) is required to receive and safely keep him until discharged by due process of law.

Witness my hand and seal, this _____ day of _____, _____.

____
Judicial officer (Seal)

Laws 1999, p. 81, § 17.

Formerly Code 1863, § 4619; Code 1868, § 4641; Code 1873, § 4739; Code 1882, § 4739; Penal Code 1895, § 914; Penal Code 1910, § 939; Code 1933, § 27–409.

§ 17-7-31. State's witnesses to be named on warrants

Whenever any judicial officer sitting as a court of inquiry binds over a defendant to appear at an appropriate court to answer any charge, it shall be the duty of the judicial officer to write on the warrant the names of each witness for the state who appeared at the commitment hearing.

Laws 1873, p. 31, § 1.

Formerly Code 1873, § 4737; Code 1882, § 4737; Penal Code 1895, § 916; Penal Code 1910, § 941; Code 1933, § 27–412.

§ 17-7-32. Disposition of papers

The commitment form shall be delivered to the officer in whose charge the accused person is placed, and the officer shall deliver it with the accused person to the sheriff or the other person in charge of the jail. A memorandum of the commitment shall be entered on the warrant by the judicial officer. The warrant and all other papers shall be forwarded to the clerk of the appropriate court having jurisdiction over the offense for delivery to the prosecuting attorney.

Formerly Code 1863, § 4623; Code 1868, § 4647; Code 1873, § 4745; Code 1882, § 4745; Penal Code 1895, § 924; Penal Code 1910, § 949; Code 1933, § 27-420.

§ 17-7-33. Repealed by Laws 1983, p. 884, § 4-2, eff. July 1, 1983

§ 17-7-34. Informality no ground of discharge

No defendant shall be discharged on a writ of habeas corpus because of informality in the commitment or in the proceedings prior thereto, provided there has been substantial compliance with this article.

Cobb's 1851 Digest, p. 856.

Formerly Code 1863, § 4626; Code 1868, § 4650; Code 1873, § 4748; Code 1882, § 4748; Penal Code 1895, § 926; Penal Code 1910, § 951; Code 1933, § 27-422.

Article 3

Indictments

§ 17-7-50. Persons refused bail entitled to grand jury hearing

Any person who is arrested for a crime and who is refused bail shall, within 90 days after the date of confinement, be entitled to have the charge against him or her heard by a grand jury having jurisdiction over the accused person; provided, however, that if the person is arrested for a crime for which the death penalty is being sought, the superior court may, upon motion of the district attorney for an extension and after a hearing and good cause shown, grant one extension to the 90 day period not to exceed 90 additional days; and, provided, further, that if such extension is granted by the court, the person shall not be entitled to have the charge against him or her heard by the grand jury until the expiration of such extended period. In the event no grand jury considers the charges against the accused person within the 90 day period of confinement or within the extended period of confinement where such an extension is granted by the court, the accused shall have bail set upon application to the court.

Laws 1973, p. 291, § 1; Laws 1996, p. 1233, § 4.

Formerly Code 1933, § 27-701.1.

§ 17-7-50.1. Juvenile arrested and subject to the jurisdiction of the superior court entitled to grand jury hearing; failure to return indictment within 180 days; extensions and exceptions

(a) Any child who is charged with a crime that is within the jurisdiction of the superior court, as provided in Code Section 15-11-28 or 15-11-30.2, who is detained shall within 180 days of the date of detention be entitled to have the charge against him or her presented to the grand jury. The superior court shall, upon motion for an extension of time and after a hearing and good cause shown, grant one extension to the original 180 day period, not to exceed 90 additional days.

(b) If the grand jury does not return a true bill against the detained child within the time limitations set forth in subsection (a) of this Code section, the detained child's case shall be transferred to the juvenile court and shall proceed thereafter as provided in Chapter 11 of Title 15.

(c) The provisions of this Code section shall not apply to any case in which the prosecuting attorney files notice with the court that the detained child is a codefendant to a case in which an adult is charged with committing the same offense and the state has filed a notice of its intention to seek the death penalty.

Laws 2006, Act 475, § 2, eff. July 1, 2006.

§ 17-7-51. Presentments treated as indictments; entry upon minutes

All special presentments by the grand jury charging defendants with violations of the penal laws shall be treated as indictments. It shall not be necessary for the clerk of the court to enter the special presentments in full upon the minutes, but only the statement of the case and finding of the grand jury as in cases of indictments. It shall not be necessary for the district attorney to frame bills of indictment on the special presentments, but he may arraign defendants upon the special presentments and put them on trial in like manner as if the presentments were bills of indictment.

Laws 1873, p. 51, § 1.

Formerly Code 1863, § 4520; Code 1868, § 4539; Code 1873, § 4632; Code 1882, § 4632; Penal Code 1895, § 931; Penal Code 1910, § 956; Code 1933, § 27-703.

§ 17-7-52. Indictment against peace officer; procedure

(a) Before an indictment against a present or former peace officer charging the officer with a crime which is alleged to have occurred while he or she was in the performance of his or her duties is returned by a grand jury, the officer shall be notified of the contemplated action by the district attorney of the county wherein the grand jury shall convene and the officer shall be afforded the rights provided in Code Section 45-11-4.

(b) The requirements of subsection (a) of this Code section shall apply to all prosecutions, whether for misdemeanors or felonies, and no such prosecution shall proceed either in state or superior court without a grand jury indictment.

Laws 1975, p. 607, § 1; Laws 1997, p. 879, § 1; Laws 2001, p. 487, § 5.

§ 17-7-53. Two returns of "no bill" as bar to prosecution

Two returns of "no bill" by grand juries on the same charge or allegation shall be a bar to any future prosecution of a person for the same offense under the same or another name; provided, however, that, if the returns have been procured by the fraudulent conduct of the person charged or there is newly discovered evidence, upon proof, the judge may allow a third bill to be presented, found, and prosecuted.

Laws 1850, Cobb's 1851 Digest, p. 864.

Formerly Code 1863, § 4591; Code 1868, § 4612; Code 1873, § 4708; Code 1882, § 4708; Penal Code 1895, § 930; Penal Code 1910, § 955; Code 1933, § 27-702.

§ 17-7-53.1. Quashing of second grand jury indictment or presentment bars further prosecution

If, upon the return of two "true bills" of indictments or presentments by a grand jury on the same offense, charge, or allegation, the indictments or presentments are quashed for the second time, whether by ruling on a motion, demurrer, special plea or exception, or other pleading of the defendant or by the court's own motion, such actions shall be a bar to any future prosecution of such defendant for the offense, charge, or allegation.

Laws 1987, p. 529, § 1.

§ 17-7-54. Form

(a) Every indictment of the grand jury which states the offense in the terms and language of this Code or so plainly that the nature of the offense charged may easily be understood by the jury shall be deemed sufficiently technical and correct. The form of every indictment shall be substantially as follows:

Georgia, _____ County.

The grand jurors selected, chosen, and sworn for the County of _____, to wit: _____, in the name and behalf of the citizens of Georgia, charge and accuse (name of the accused) of the county and state aforesaid with the offense of _____; for that the said (name of the accused) (state with sufficient certainty the offense and the time and place of committing the same), contrary to the laws of said state, the good order, peace, and dignity thereof.

(b) If there should be more than one count, each additional count shall state:

And the jurors aforesaid, in the name and behalf of the citizens of Georgia, further charge and accuse (name of the accused) with having committed the offense of _____; for that the said (name of the accused) (state with sufficient certainty the offense and the time and place of committing the same) contrary to the laws of said state, the good order, peace, and dignity thereof.

Laws 1833, Cobb's 1851 Digest, p. 833.

Formerly Code 1863, § 4516; Code 1868, § 4535; Code 1873, § 4628; Code 1882, § 4628; Penal Code 1895, § 929; Penal Code 1910, § 954; Code 1933, § 27-701.

§ 17-7-55. Concurrent grand juries

In any term of court when the public interest requires it, the court may empanel one or more concurrent grand juries in accordance with Part 1 of Article 4 of Chapter 12 of Title 15.

Laws 2003, Act 26, § 1, eff. May 14, 2003.

Article 4

Accusations

§ 17-7-70. Trial on accusation; waiver of indictment

(a) In all felony cases, other than cases involving capital felonies, in which defendants have been bound over to the superior court, are confined in jail or released on bond pending a commitment hearing, or are in jail having waived a commitment hearing, the district attorney shall have authority to prefer accusations, and such defendants shall be tried on such accusations, provided that defendants going to trial under such accusations shall, in writing, waive indictment by a grand jury.

(b) Judges of the superior court may open their courts at any time without the presence of either a grand jury or a trial jury to receive and act upon pleas of guilty in misdemeanor cases and in felony cases, except those punishable by death or life imprisonment, when the judge and the defendant consent thereto. The judge may try the issues in such cases without a jury upon an accusation filed by the district attorney where the defendant has waived indictment and consented thereto in writing and counsel is present in court representing the defendant either by virtue of his employment or by appointment by the court.

Laws 1915, p. 32, § 1; Laws 1935, p. 116, § 1; Laws 1972, p. 386, § 1; Laws 1972, p. 623, § 1; Laws 1980, p. 452, § 1.

Formerly Code 1933, § 27-704.

§ 17-7-70.1. Trial upon accusation in certain felony cases without necessity of waiving indictment

(a) (1) In felony cases involving violations of the following:

(A) Code Sections 16-8-2, 16-8-14, 16-8-18, 16-9-1, 16-9-2, 16-9-20, 16-9-31, 16-9-33, 16-9-37, 16-10-52, and 40-5-58;

(B) Article 1 of Chapter 8 of Title 16, relating to theft;

(C) Chapter 9 of Title 16, relating to forgery and fraudulent practices;

(D) Article 3 of Chapter 10 of Title 16, relating to escape and other offenses related to confinement; or

(E) Code Section 16-11-131, relating to possession of a firearm by a convicted felon or first offender probationer,

in which defendants have either been bound over to the superior court based on a finding of probable cause pursuant to a commitment hearing under Article 2 of this chapter or have expressly or by operation of law waived a commitment hearing, the district attorney shall have authority to prefer accusations, and the defendants shall be tried on such accusations according to the same rules of substantive and procedural laws relating to defendants who have been indicted by a grand jury.

(2) All laws relating to rights and responsibilities attendant to indicted cases shall be applicable to cases brought by accusations signed by the district attorney.

(3) The accusation need not be supported by an affidavit except in those cases in which the defendant has not been previously arrested in conjunction with the transaction charged in the accusation.

(a.1) The provisions of subsection (a) of this Code section shall apply to violations of Code Section 16-13-30 whenever there has been a finding of probable cause pursuant to a commitment hearing under Article 2 of this chapter or the accused has waived either expressly or by operation of law the right to this hearing.

(b) Judges of the superior court may open their courts at any time without the presence of either a grand jury or a trial jury to receive and act upon pleas of guilty or nolo contendere in felony and misdemeanor cases. The judge of the superior court may try the issues in such cases without a jury upon an indictment or upon an accusation filed by the district attorney where the defendant has waived trial by jury.

(c) An accusation substantially complying with the form provided in subsections (d) and (e) of Code Section 17-7-71 shall in all cases be sufficient.

(d) The district attorney may not bring an accusation pursuant to this Code section in those cases where the grand jury has heard evidence or conducted an investigation or in which a no bill has been returned.

(e) Notwithstanding the above provisions, nothing in this Code section shall affect the rights of police officers and public officials to appear before a grand jury as provided in Code Sections 17-7-52, 45-11-4, and 45-15-11.

Laws 1992, p. 1808, § 1; Laws 1996, p. 678, § 1; Laws 1998, p. 208, § 1.

§ 17-7-71. Trial of misdemeanors upon accusations; form of accusations; amendment

(a) In all misdemeanor cases, the defendant may be tried upon an accusation framed and signed by the prosecuting attorney of the court. The accusation need not be supported by an affidavit except in those cases where the defendant has not been previously arrested in conjunction with the transaction charged in the accusation and where the accusation is to be used as the basis for the issuance of a warrant for the arrest of the defendant.

(b) (1) In all misdemeanor cases arising out of violations of the laws of this state, relating to (A) the operation and licensing of motor vehicles and operators; (B) the width, height, and length of vehicles and loads; (C) motor common carriers and motor contract carriers; or (D) road taxes on motor carriers as provided in Article 2 of Chapter 9 of Title 48, the defendant may be tried upon the uniform traffic citation and complaint provided for in Article 1 of Chapter 13 of Title 40.

(2) In all misdemeanor cases arising out of violations of the laws of this state relating to game, fish,

or boating, the defendant may be tried upon the summons provided for in Code Section 27-1-35.

(c) Every accusation which states the offense in the terms and language of the law or so plainly that the nature of the offense charged may be easily understood by the jury shall be deemed sufficiently technical and correct.

(d) An accusation substantially complying with the following form shall in all cases be sufficient:

IN THE ____ COURT OF ____ COUNTY
STATE OF GEORGIA

On behalf of the people of the State of Georgia, the undersigned, as prosecuting attorney for the county and state aforesaid, does hereby charge and accuse (name of accused) with the offense of ____; for that the said (name of accused) (state with sufficient certainty the offense and the time and place it occurred) contrary to the laws of this state, the good order, peace, and dignity thereof.

/s/ ____________________
(District attorney)
(Solicitor-general)

(e) If there should be more than one count, each additional count shall state:

The undersigned, as prosecuting attorney, does further charge and accuse the said (name of accused) with the offense of ____ (the offense as before); for that the said (name of accused) (state with sufficient certainty the offense and the time and place it occurred), contrary to the laws of this state, the good order, peace, and dignity thereof.

(f) Prior to trial, the prosecuting attorney may amend the accusation, summons, or any citation to allege or to change the allegations regarding any offense arising out of the same conduct of the defendant which gave rise to any offense alleged or attempted to be alleged in the original accusation, summons, or citation. A copy of any such amendment shall be served upon the defendant or his or her counsel and the original filed with the clerk of the court. On motion, the court shall grant the defendant a continuance which is reasonably necessitated by an amendment. If any additional charges against the defendant are made the judge shall advise the defendant that he or she has an automatic right to a continuance.

Laws 1980, p. 452, § 2; Laws 1981, p. 828, § 1; Laws 1982, p. 3, § 17; Laws 1996, p. 748, § 14; Laws 2002, p. 627, § 2.

Formerly Code 1933, § 27-705.

§ 17-7-72. Trial of certain misdemeanor cases upon summons or citation in lieu of accusation

In probate courts which have jurisdiction over misdemeanor possession of marijuana in accordance with Code Sections 16-13-2 and 16-13-30 and certain misdemeanor violations of Code Section 3-3-23 pursuant to Code Section 15-9-30.6, the following offenses may be tried upon a summons or citation without an accusation:

(1) Possession of one ounce or less of marijuana, in accordance with Code Sections 16-13-2 and 16-13-30; and

(2) Any violation of paragraph (2) of subsection (a) of Code Section 3-3-23 which is punishable as a misdemeanor, but not violations punishable as high and aggravated misdemeanors.

Laws 1996, p. 1298, § 2.

§ 17-7-73. Violations relating to littering and related environmental offenses that are punishable as misdemeanors; trial upon summons or citation with or without accusation

In probate, magistrate, and municipal courts that have jurisdiction over violations of Part 2, Part 3, or Part 3A of Article 2 of Chapter 7 of Title 16 or Code Section 32-6-51 or 40-6-248.1 that are punishable as misdemeanors in accordance with Code Section 15-9-30.7, 15-10-2.1, or 36-32-10.3 such offenses may be tried upon a summons or citation with or without an accusation.

Laws 2006, Act 538, § 3-8, eff. July 1, 2006.

Article 5

Arraignment and Pleas Generally

§ 17-7-90. Bench warrant; definition; execution; who may take bail

A bench warrant is a warrant issued by a judge for the arrest of a person accused of a crime by a grand jury or for the arrest of a person charged with a crime who has failed to appear in court after actual notice to the person in open court or notice to the person by mailing to his or her last known address or otherwise being notified personally in writing by a court official or officer of the court of the time and place to appear or for the arrest of a person charged with a crime upon the filing by the prosecutor of an accusation supported by affidavit. Every officer is bound to execute the warrant within his or her jurisdiction, and every person so arrested must be committed to jail until bail is tendered. Any judicial officer or the sheriff of the county where the charge was returned may receive the bail, fix the amount of the bond, and approve the sureties unless it is a case that is bailable only before some particular judicial officer.

Laws 1989, p. 623, § 2; Laws 2004, Act 564, § 17, eff. May 13, 2004.

Formerly Code 1863, § 4608; Code 1868, § 4630; Code 1873, § 4727; Code 1882, § 4727; Penal Code 1895, § 932; Penal Code 1910, § 957; Code 1933, § 27-801.

§ 17-7-91. Notice of date of arraignment; time for trial

(a) In all criminal cases the court shall fix a date on which the defendant shall be arraigned. The clerk of the court, at least five days prior to the date set therefor, shall mail to the accused and his attorney of record, if known, notice of the date which has been fixed for arraignment. For such first service of notice, the clerk shall receive the fee prescribed in Code Section 15-6-77. This notice may be served by the sheriff of the county in which the court is situated or his lawful deputies. If the defendant has posted a bond or recognizance, a copy of the notice shall be mailed to each surety on the bond.

(b) On the date fixed by the court the accused shall be arraigned. The court shall receive the plea of the accused and enter the plea as provided for in this chapter. In those cases in which a plea of not guilty is entered, the court shall set the case down for trial at such time as shall be determined by the court.

(c) The appearance and entering of a plea by the accused shall be a waiver of the notice required in this Code section.

Laws 1966, p. 430, § 2; Laws 1977, p. 1098, § 5; Laws 1982, p. 1224, § 3; Laws 1989, p. 223, § 1; Laws 1990, p. 8, § 17.

Formerly Code 1933, § 27-1401.

§ 17-7-92. Service of notice of filing of indictment or presentment against corporation; plea; judgment for fine and costs

Whenever an indictment, special presentment, or accusation against a corporation doing business in this state is returned or filed in any court having jurisdiction over the offense, the clerk of the court shall issue an original and copy notice to the defendant corporation of the filing of the indictment, special presentment, or accusation, which copy notice shall be served by a sheriff upon any officer of the corporation who is found in his county; or, if there is no such officer in his county, then service shall be upon any agent of the corporation. The sheriff serving the copy notice shall make an entry of such service on the original notice and return the same to the court from which it issued. Such service shall be deemed service upon the corporation. Upon the return of the notice, executed as provided for in this Code section, the indictment, special presentment, or accusation shall stand for trial. At the trial, if the defendant corporation fails to appear, or appearing, fails to plead, the judge shall cause a plea of not guilty to be entered, and the trial shall proceed as though the defendant had appeared and pleaded. Upon the conviction of any corporation in any such trial, there shall be rendered against it a judgment for the fine imposed, together with the costs of the prosecution. Upon judgment, an execution shall issue against the property of the defendant.

Laws 1889, p. 120, §§ 1, 2.

Formerly Penal Code 1895, § 938; Penal Code 1910, § 963; Code 1933, § 27-1001.

§ 17-7-93. Form of arraignment; plea of "guilty"; withdrawal of plea; understanding effect on immigration status

(a) Upon the arraignment of a person accused of committing a crime, the indictment or accusation shall be read to him and he shall be required to answer whether he is guilty or not guilty of the offense charged, which answer or plea shall be made orally by the accused person or his counsel.

(b) If the person pleads "guilty," the plea shall be immediately recorded on the minutes of the court by the clerk, together with the arraignment; and the court shall pronounce the judgment of the law upon the person in the same manner as if he had been convicted of the offense by the verdict of a jury. At any time before judgment is pronounced, the accused person may withdraw the plea of "guilty" and plead "not guilty"; and the former plea shall not be admissible as evidence against him at his trial.

(c) In addition to any other inquiry by the court prior to acceptance of a plea of guilty, the court shall determine whether the defendant is freely entering the plea with an understanding that if he or she is not a citizen of the United States, then the plea may have an impact on his or her immigration status. This subsection shall apply with respect to acceptance of any plea of guilty to any state offense in any court of this state or any political subdivision of this state.

Laws 1833, Cobb's 1851 Digest, p. 834; Laws 2000, p. 808, § 1.

Formerly Code 1863, § 4524; Code 1868, § 4543; Code 1873, § 4636; Code 1882, § 4636; Penal Code 1895, § 946; Penal Code 1910, § 971; Code 1933, § 27-1404.

§ 17-7-94. Standing mute or pleading "not guilty"

If the person accused of committing a crime, upon being arraigned, pleads "not guilty" or stands mute, the clerk shall immediately record upon the minutes of the court the plea of "not guilty," together with the arraignment; and the arraignment and plea shall constitute the issue between the accused and the state.

Laws 1833, Cobb's 1851 Digest, p. 834.

Formerly Code 1863, § 4525; Code 1868, § 4544; Code 1873, § 4638; Code 1882, § 4638; Penal Code 1895, § 947; Penal Code 1910, § 972; Code 1933, § 27-1405.

§ 17-7-95. Plea of nolo contendere; right to enter with consent of judge; imposition of sentence; subsequent use against defendant

(a) The defendant in all criminal cases other than capital felonies in any court of this state, whether the offense charged is a felony or a misdemeanor, may, with the consent and approval of the judge of the court, enter a plea of nolo contendere instead of a plea of guilty or not guilty.

(b) Should the judge allow a plea of nolo contendere to be entered, he shall thereupon be authorized to impose such sentence as may be authorized by law as to the offense charged.

(c) Except as otherwise provided by law, a plea of nolo contendere shall not be used against the defendant in any other court or proceedings as an admission of guilt or otherwise or for any purpose; and the plea shall not be deemed a plea of guilty for the purpose of effecting any civil disqualification of the defendant to hold public office, to vote, to serve upon any jury, or any other civil disqualification imposed upon a person convicted of any offense under the laws of this state. The plea shall be deemed and held to put the defendant in jeopardy within the meaning of Article I, Section I, Paragraph XVIII of the Constitution of this state after sentence has been imposed.

Laws 1946, p. 142, §§ 1-3; Laws 1982, p. 3, § 17; Laws 1983, p. 3, § 51.

§ 17-7-96. Arraignment and plea to be entered on the indictment or accusation

The arraignment and plea of the person accused of committing a crime shall be entered on the indictment or accusation by the prosecuting attorney or other person acting as prosecuting officer on the part of the state.

Laws 1833, Cobb's 1851 Digest, p. 835.

Formerly Code 1863, § 4528; Code 1868, § 4547; Code 1873, § 4641; Code 1882, § 4641; Penal Code 1895, § 949; Penal Code 1910, § 974; Code 1933, § 27-1407.

§ 17-7-97. Issue may be recorded afterward

If the clerk of the court shall fail or neglect to record the arraignment and plea of the person accused of committing a crime at the time the arraignment and plea are made, the recordation may be done at any time afterward by order of the court; and this shall cure the error or omission of the clerk.

Laws 1833, Cobb's 1851 Digest, p. 835.

Formerly Code 1863, § 4527; Code 1868, § 4546; Code 1873, § 4640; Code 1882, § 4640; Penal Code 1895, § 948; Penal Code 1910, § 973; Code 1933, § 27-1406.

Article 6

Demurrers, Motions, and Special Pleas and Exceptions

Part 1

General Provisions

§ 17-7-110. Filing of pretrial motions; time limitation

All pretrial motions, including demurrers and special pleas, shall be filed within ten days after the date of arraignment, unless the time for filing is extended by the court.

Laws 2003, Act 26, § 2, eff. May 14, 2003.

§ 17-7-111. Demurrers and special pleas to be in writing; right to plead "not guilty"

If the defendant, upon being arraigned, demurs to the indictment, pleads to the jurisdiction of the court, pleads in abatement, or enters any other special plea in bar, the demurrer or plea shall be made in writing. If the demurrer or plea is decided against the defendant, he may nevertheless plead and rely on the general issue of "not guilty."

Laws 1833, Cobb's 1851 Digest, p. 834.

Formerly Code 1863, § 4526; Code 1868, § 4545; Code 1873, § 4639; Code 1882, § 4639; Penal Code 1895, § 950; Penal Code 1910, § 975; Code 1933, § 27-1501.

§ 17-7-112. Misnomer, plea of

A plea of misnomer should state the true name of the accused person, that he had never been known by any other name than that, and that he was not known and called by the name which was contained in the indictment or accusation.

Formerly Penal Code 1895, § 954; Penal Code 1910, § 979; Code 1933, § 27-1505.

§ 17-7-113. Time for making exception

All exceptions which go merely to the form of an indictment or accusation shall be made before trial. Laws 1833, Cobb's 1851 Digest, p. 833.

Formerly Code 1863, § 4517; Code 1868, § 4536; Code 1873, § 4629; Code 1882, § 4629; Penal Code 1895, § 955; Penal Code 1910, § 980; Code 1933, § 27-1601.

Part 2

Insanity and Mental Incompetency

§ 17-7-130. Plea of mental incompetency to stand trial

(a) Whenever a plea is filed that a defendant in a criminal case is mentally incompetent to stand trial, it shall be the duty of the court to cause the issue of the defendant's mental competency to stand trial to be tried first by a special jury. If the special jury finds the defendant mentally incompetent to stand trial, the court shall retain jurisdiction over the defendant but shall transfer the defendant to the Department of Human Resources.

(b) Within 90 days after the Department of Human Resources has received actual custody of a person pursuant to subsection (a) of this Code section, the person shall be evaluated and a diagnosis made as to whether the person is presently mentally incompetent to stand trial and, if so, whether there is a substantial probability that the person will attain mental competency to stand trial in the foreseeable future. If the person is found to be mentally competent to stand trial, the department shall immediately report that finding and the reasons therefor to the committing court; and the person shall be returned to the court as provided for in subsection (e) of this Code section.

(c) If the person is found to be mentally incompetent to stand trial by the Department of Human Resources and there is not a substantial probability that the person will attain competency in the foreseeable future, the department shall report that finding and the reasons therefor to the committing court. If the person meets the criteria for civil commitment, he shall thereupon be civilly committed to a state institution pursuant to Chapter 3 or 4 of Title 37, whichever is applicable. If the person does not meet the criteria for civil commitment or if the person after having been committed becomes mentally competent to stand trial, the committing court shall be notified and the person shall be returned to the court as provided for in subsection (e) of this Code section.

(d) If the person is found to be mentally incompetent to stand trial but there is a substantial probability that the person will attain competency in the foreseeable future, by the end of the 90 day period, or at any prior time, the department shall report that finding and the reasons therefor to the committing court and shall retain custody over the person for the purpose of continued treatment for an additional period not to exceed nine months. If, by the end of the nine-month period or at any prior time if the person's condition warrants, the person is still found not to be competent to stand trial, irrespective of the probability of recovery in the foreseeable future, the department shall report that finding and the reasons therefor to the committing court. If the person meets the criteria for civil commitment, he shall thereupon be civilly committed to a state institution pursuant to Chapter 3 or 4 of Title 37, whichever is applicable. If the person does not meet the criteria for civil commitment or if the person after having been committed becomes mentally competent to stand trial, the committing court shall be notified and the person shall be returned to the court as provided for in subsection (e) of this Code section.

(e)(1) A person who is found by the Department of Human Resources to be mentally competent to stand trial shall be discharged into the custody of a law enforcement officer of the jurisdiction of the court which committed the person to the department unless the court has dismissed the charges which led to the commitment, in which case the person shall be discharged. In the event a law enforcement officer does not appear and take custody of the person within 20 days after notice to the appropriate law enforcement official in the jurisdiction of the committing court, the presiding judge of the committing court, and the prosecuting attorney for the court, the department shall itself return the person to one of the committing court's detention facilities; and the cost of returning the person shall be paid by the county in which the committing court is located. All notifications shall be sent by certified mail or statutory overnight delivery, return receipt requested. With the concurrence of the appropriate court and upon the recommendation of the attending physician, any person discharged as competent to stand trial may be held by the department instead of at the court's detention facilities whenever, in the attending physician's opinion, such detention in the court's facilities would be detrimental to the well-being of the person so committed. Such alternative detention shall continue only until the date of the person's trial.

(2) The physical custody of a person who is found by the Department of Human Resources to be mentally incompetent to stand trial and for whom there is no substantial probability that he or she will attain competency in the foreseeable future shall be returned to the committing court. The committing court shall retain custody of the person and may order an independent evaluation of the person by a court appointed licensed clinical psychologist or psychiatrist who shall report to the court in writing as to the current mental and emotional condition of the person. Then the court shall conduct a hearing at which the court shall hear evidence and consider all psychiatric and psychological reports submitted to the court and determine whether the state has proved by clear and convincing evidence that the person meets the criteria for involuntary civil commitment pursuant to Chapter 3 or Chapter 4 of Title 37, whichever is applicable. If the person is found to meet the criteria for involuntary civil commitment, the judge may issue an order committing the person to a state institution. If the person does not meet the criteria for involuntary civil commitment, the person shall be released subject to provisions of bond and other conditions set by the committing court. A person committed under the provisions of this paragraph may only be discharged from that commitment by order of the committing court in accordance with the procedures specified in paragraphs (1) through (3) of subsection (f) of Code Section 17–7–131 except that the burden of proof in such release hearing shall be on the state and if the committed person cannot afford a physician or licensed clinical psychologist of the person's choice, the person may petition the court and the court may order such cost be paid by the county. This paragraph applies to those persons:

(A) Accused of committing the following crimes:

(i) Murder;

(ii) Rape;

(iii) Aggravated sodomy;

(iv) Armed robbery;

(v) Aggravated assault;

(vi) Hijacking of a motor vehicle or an aircraft;

(vii) Aggravated battery;

(viii) Aggravated sexual battery;

(ix) Aggravated child molestation; or

(x) Aggravated stalking;

(B) Who are an obvious threat to society as determined by the Department of Human Resources or the assigned judge; or

(C) Who have been convicted of or committed for three or more felonies.

(f) Any person returned to the court as provided in subsection (e) of this Code section shall again be entitled to file a special plea as provided for in this Code section.

(g) If a person is found to be mentally incompetent to stand trial, whether or not committed to a state institution under this Code section, the state may file at any time a motion for rehearing on the issue of the person's mental competency. The court shall grant said motion upon a showing by the state that there are reasonable grounds to believe that the person's mental condition has changed. If this motion is granted, the case shall proceed as provided in subsection (a) of this Code section.

Laws 1977, p. 1293, § 3; Laws 1982, p. 3, § 17; Laws 1995, p. 1250, §§ 1.1, 1.2; Laws 2000, p. 1589, § 3.

Formerly Code 1863, § 4195; Code 1868, § 4234; Code 1873, § 4299; Code 1882, § 4299; Penal Code 1895, § 951; Penal Code 1910, § 976; Code 1933, § 27–1502.

§ 17–7–130.1. Evidence of sanity or insanity; appointment of medical witnesses

At the trial of a criminal case in which the defendant intends to interpose the defense of insanity, evidence may be introduced to prove the defendant's sanity or insanity at the time at which he is alleged to have committed the offense charged in the indictment or information. When notice of an insanity defense is filed, the court shall appoint at least one psychiatrist or licensed psychologist to examine the defendant and to testify at the trial. This testimony shall follow the presentation of the evidence for the prosecution and for the defense, including testimony of any medical experts employed by the state or by the defense. The medical witnesses appointed by the court may be cross-examined by both the prosecution and the defense, and each side may introduce evidence in rebuttal to the testimony of such a medical witness.

Laws 1985, p. 637, § 1.

§ 17–7–131. Insanity and incompetency

(a) For purposes of this Code section, the term:

(1) "Insane at the time of the crime" means meeting the criteria of Code Section 16–3–2 or Code Section 16–3–3. However, the term shall not include a mental state manifested only by repeated unlawful or antisocial conduct.

(2) "Mentally ill" means having a disorder of thought or mood which significantly impairs judgment, behavior, capacity to recognize reality, or ability to cope with the ordinary demands of life. However, the term "mental illness" shall not include

a mental state manifested only by repeated unlawful or antisocial conduct.

(3) "Mentally retarded" means having significantly subaverage general intellectual functioning resulting in or associated with impairments in adaptive behavior which manifested during the developmental period.

(b)(1) In all cases in which the defense of insanity is interposed, the jury, or the court if tried by it, shall find whether the defendant is:

(A) Guilty;

(B) Not guilty;

(C) Not guilty by reason of insanity at the time of the crime;

(D) Guilty but mentally ill at the time of the crime, but the finding of guilty but mentally ill shall be made only in felony cases; or

(E) Guilty but mentally retarded, but the finding of mental retardation shall be made only in felony cases.

(2) A plea of guilty but mentally ill at the time of the crime or a plea of guilty but mentally retarded shall not be accepted until the defendant has undergone examination by a licensed psychologist or psychiatrist and the court has examined the psychological or psychiatric reports, held a hearing on the issue of the defendant's mental condition, and is satisfied that there is a factual basis that the defendant was mentally ill at the time of the offense or mentally retarded to which the plea is entered.

(2.1) A plea of not guilty by reason of insanity at the time of the crime shall not be accepted and the defendant adjudicated not guilty by reason of insanity by the court without a jury until the defendant has undergone examination by a licensed psychologist or psychiatrist and the court has examined the psychological or psychiatric reports, has held a hearing on the issue of the defendant's mental condition, and the court is satisfied that the defendant was insane at the time of the crime according to the criteria of Code Section 16-3-2 or 16-3-3.

(3) In all cases in which the defense of insanity is interposed, the trial judge shall charge the jury, in addition to other appropriate charges, the following:

(A) I charge you that should you find the defendant not guilty by reason of insanity at the time of the crime, the defendant will be committed to a state mental health facility until such time, if ever, that the court is satisfied that he or she should be released pursuant to law.

(B) I charge you that should you find the defendant guilty but mentally ill at the time of the crime, the defendant will be placed in the custody of the Department of Corrections which will have responsibility for the evaluation and treatment of the mental health needs of the defendant, which may include, at the discretion of the Department of Corrections, referral for temporary hospitalization at a facility operated by the Department of Human Resources.

(C) I charge you that should you find the defendant guilty but mentally retarded, the defendant will be placed in the custody of the Department of Corrections, which will have responsibility for the evaluation and treatment of the mental health needs of the defendant, which may include, at the discretion of the Department of Corrections, referral for temporary hospitalization at a facility operated by the Department of Human Resources.

(c) In all criminal trials in any of the courts of this state wherein an accused shall contend that he was insane or otherwise mentally incompetent under the law at the time the act or acts charged against him were committed, the trial judge shall instruct the jury that they may consider, in addition to verdicts of "guilty" and "not guilty," the additional verdicts of "not guilty by reason of insanity at the time of the crime," "guilty but mentally ill at the time of the crime," and "guilty but mentally retarded."

(1) The defendant may be found "not guilty by reason of insanity at the time of the crime" if he meets the criteria of Code Section 16-3-2 or 16-3-3 at the time of the commission of the crime. If the court or jury should make such finding, it shall so specify in its verdict.

(2) The defendant may be found "guilty but mentally ill at the time of the crime" if the jury, or court acting as trier of facts, finds beyond a reasonable doubt that the defendant is guilty of the crime charged and was mentally ill at the time of the commission of the crime. If the court or jury should make such finding, it shall so specify in its verdict.

(3) The defendant may be found "guilty but mentally retarded" if the jury, or court acting as trier of facts, finds beyond a reasonable doubt that the defendant is guilty of the crime charged and is mentally retarded. If the court or jury should make such finding, it shall so specify in its verdict.

(d) Whenever a defendant is found not guilty by reason of insanity at the time of the crime, the court shall retain jurisdiction over the person so acquitted and shall order such person to be detained in a state mental health facility, to be selected by the Department of Human Resources, for a period not to exceed 30 days from the date of the acquittal order, for evaluation of the defendant's present mental condition. Upon completion of the evaluation, the proper officials of the mental health facility shall send a report of the defendant's present mental condition to the trial judge, the prosecuting attorney, and the defendant's attorney, if any.

(e)(1) After the expiration of the 30 days' evaluation period in the state mental health facility, if the evaluation report from the Department of Human Resources indicates that the defendant does not meet the inpatient commitment criteria of Chapter 3 of Title 37 or Chapter 4 of Title 37, the trial judge may issue an order discharging the defendant from custody without a hearing.

(2) If the defendant is not so discharged, the trial judge shall order a hearing to determine if the defendant meets the inpatient commitment criteria of Chapter 3 of Title 37 or Chapter 4 of Title 37. If such criteria are not met, the defendant must be discharged.

(3) The defendant shall be detained in custody until completion of the hearing. The hearing shall be conducted at the earliest opportunity after the expiration of the 30 days' evaluation period but in any event within 30 days after receipt by the prosecuting attorney of the evaluation report from the mental health facility. The court may take judicial notice of evidence introduced during the trial of the defendant and may call for testimony from any person with knowledge concerning whether the defendant is currently a mentally ill person in need of involuntary treatment or currently mentally retarded and in need of being ordered to receive services, as those terms are defined by paragraph (12) of Code Section 37-3-1 and Code Section 37-4-40. The prosecuting attorney may cross-examine the witnesses called by the court and the defendant's witnesses and present relevant evidence concerning the issues presented at the hearing.

(4) If the judge determines that the defendant meets the inpatient commitment criteria of Chapter 3 of Title 37 or Chapter 4 of Title 37, the judge shall order the defendant to be committed to the Department of Human Resources to receive involuntary treatment under Chapter 3 of Title 37 or to receive services under Chapter 4 of Title 37. The defendant is entitled to the following rights specified below and shall be notified in writing of these rights at the time of his admission for evaluation under subsection (d) of this Code section. Such rights are:

(A) A notice that a hearing will be held and the time and place thereof;

(B) A notice that the defendant has the right to counsel and that the defendant or his representatives may apply immediately to the court to have counsel appointed if the defendant cannot afford counsel and that the court will appoint counsel for the defendant unless he indicates in writing that he does not desire to be represented by counsel;

(C) The right to confront and cross-examine witnesses and to offer evidence;

(D) The right to subpoena witnesses and to require testimony before the court in person or by deposition from any person upon whose evaluation the decision of the court may rest;

(E) Notice of the right to have established an individualized service plan specifically tailored to the person's treatment needs, as such plans are defined in Chapter 3 of Title 37 and Chapter 4 of Title 37; and

(F) A notice that the defendant has the right to be examined by a physician or a licensed clinical psychologist of his own choice at his own expense and to have that physician or psychologist submit a suggested service plan for the patient which conforms with the requirements of Chapter 3 of Title 37 or Chapter 4 of Title 37, whichever is applicable.

(5)(A) If a defendant appears to meet the criteria for outpatient involuntary treatment as defined in Part 3 of Article 3 of Chapter 3 of Title 37, which shall be the criteria for release on a trial basis in the community in preparation for a full release, the court may order a period of conditional release subject to certain conditions set by the court. The court is authorized to appoint an appropriate community service provider to work in conjunction with the Department of Human Resources to monitor the defendant's compliance with these conditions and to make regular reports to the court.

(B) If the defendant successfully completes all requirements during this period of conditional release, the court shall discharge the individual from commitment at the end of that period. Such individuals may be referred for community mental health, mental retardation, or substance abuse services as appropriate. The court may require the individual to participate in outpatient treatment or any other services or programs authorized by Chapter 3, 4, or 7 of Title 37.

(C) If the defendant does not successfully complete any or all requirements of the conditional release period, the court may:

(i) Revoke the period of conditional release and return the defendant to a state hospital for inpatient services; or

(ii) Impose additional or revise existing conditions on the defendant as appropriate and continue the period of conditional release.

(D) For any decision rendered under subparagraph (C) of this paragraph, the defendant may request a review by the court of such decision within 20 days of the order of the court.

(E) The Department of Human Resources and any community services providers, including the employees and agents of both, providing supervision or treatment during a period of conditional release shall not be held criminally or civilly liable for any acts committed by a defendant placed by the committing court on a period of conditional release.

(f) A defendant who has been found not guilty by reason of insanity at the time of the crime and is ordered committed to the Department of Human Resources under subsection (e) of this Code section may only be discharged from that commitment by order of the committing court in accordance with the procedures specified in this subsection:

(1) Application for the release of a defendant who has been committed to the Department of Human Resources under subsection (e) of this Code section upon the ground that he does not meet the civil commitment criteria under Chapter 3 of Title 37 or Chapter 4 of Title 37 may be made to the committing court, either by such defendant or by the superintendent of the state hospital in which the said defendant is detained;

(2) The burden of proof in such release hearing shall be upon the applicant. The defendant shall have the same rights in the release hearing as set forth in subsection (e) of this Code section; and

(3) If the finding of the court is adverse to release in such hearing held pursuant to this subsection on the grounds that such defendant does meet the inpatient civil commitment criteria, a further release application by the defendant shall not be heard by the court until 12 months have elapsed from the date of the hearing upon the last preceding application. The Department of Human Resources shall have the independent right to request a release hearing once every 12 months.

(g)(1) Whenever a defendant is found guilty but mentally ill at the time of a felony or guilty but mentally retarded, or enters a plea to that effect that is accepted by the court, the court shall sentence him or her in the same manner as a defendant found guilty of the offense, except as otherwise provided in subsection (j) of this Code section. A defendant who is found guilty but mentally ill at the time of the felony or guilty but mentally retarded shall be committed to an appropriate penal facility and shall be evaluated then treated, if indicated, within the limits of state funds appropriated therefor, in such manner as is psychiatrically indicated for his or her mental illness or mental retardation.

(2) If at any time following the defendant's conviction as a guilty but mentally ill or guilty but mentally retarded offender it is determined that a temporary transfer to the Department of Human Resources is clinically indicated for his or her mental illness or mental retardation, then the defendant shall be transferred to the Department of Human Resources pursuant to procedures set forth in regulations of the Department of Corrections and the Department of Human Resources. In all such cases, the legal custody of the defendant shall be retained by the Department of Corrections. Upon notification from the Department of Human Resources to the Department of Corrections that hospitalization at a Department of Human Resources facility is no longer clinically indicated for his or her mental illness or mental retardation, the Department of Corrections shall transfer the defendant back to its physical custody and shall place such individual in an appropriate penal institution.

(h) If a defendant who is found guilty but mentally ill at the time of a felony or guilty but mentally retarded is placed on probation under the "State-wide Probation Act," Article 2 of Chapter 8 of Title 42, the court may require that the defendant undergo available outpatient medical or psychiatric treatment or seek similar available voluntary inpatient treatment as a condition of probation. Persons required to receive such services may be charged fees by the provider of the services.

(i) In any case in which the defense of insanity is interposed or a plea of guilty but mentally ill at the time of the felony or a plea of guilty but mentally retarded is made and an examination is made of the defendant pursuant to Code Section 17-7-130.1 or paragraph (2) of subsection (b) of this Code section, upon the defendant's being found guilty or guilty but mentally ill at the time of the crime or guilty but mentally retarded, a copy of any such examination report shall be forwarded to the Department of Corrections with the official sentencing document. The Department of Human Resources shall forward, in addition to its examination report, any records maintained by such department that it deems appropriate pursuant to an agreement with the Department of Corrections, within ten business days of receipt by the Department of Human Resources of the official sentencing document from the Department of Corrections.

(j) In the trial of any case in which the death penalty is sought which commences on or after July 1, 1988, should the judge find in accepting a plea of guilty but mentally retarded or the jury or court find in its verdict that the defendant is guilty of the crime charged but mentally retarded, the death penalty shall not be imposed and the court shall sentence the defendant to imprisonment for life.

Laws 1952, p. 205, § 1; Laws 1972, p. 848, § 1; Laws 1977, p. 1293, § 2; Laws 1982, p. 1476, §§ 1, 2; Laws 1984, p. 22, § 17; Laws 1985, p. 283, § 1; Laws 1985, p. 637, §§ 2-4; Laws 1988, p. 1003, § 1; Laws 1989, p. 14, § 17; Laws 1991, p. 780, §§ 1-3; Laws 1992, p. 1328, §§ 2, 3; Laws 2006, Act 754, § 1, eff. July 1, 2006.

Formerly Code 1863, § 1314; Code 1868, § 1395; Code 1873, § 1374; Code 1882, § 1374; Penal Code 1895, § 952; Penal Code 1910, § 977; Code 1933, § 27-1503.

Part 3

Change of Venue

§ 17-7-150. When and how venue changed; appeals from denial of change of venue

(a)(1) The defendant, in any criminal case in which a trial by jury is provided, may move in writing for a change of venue, whenever, in the defendant's or defense counsel's judgment, an impartial jury cannot be obtained in the county where the crime is alleged to have been committed. Upon the hearing of the motion it shall not be necessary to examine all persons in the county liable to serve on juries, but the judge shall hear evidence by affidavit or oral testimony in support of or against the motion. If, from the evidence submitted, the judge is satisfied that an impartial jury cannot be obtained to try the case, the judge shall grant a change in venue; the judge shall transfer the case to any county that may be agreed upon by the prosecuting attorney and the defendant or the defense counsel, to be tried in the county agreed upon. The judge has the discretion to reject any county agreed upon; if a county is not thus agreed upon, or if the judge, in the exercise of discretion, rejects a county agreed upon, the judge shall select such county as in the judge's judgment will afford a fair and impartial jury to try the case and have it transferred accordingly.

(2) In the exercise of such discretion, the judge shall consult with the chief superior court judge of the circuit in which a county of transfer lies and consider the following factors:

(A) The existing criminal and civil trial calendars of the transfer county;

(B) The frequency of use as a transfer county;

(C) The estimated length of trial;

(D) The proposed date of trial;

(E) Whether or not the jury is to be sequestered;

(F) Which county shall be responsible for court security, prisoner security, bailiffs, jailers, and clerks of court personnel;

(G) Jury transportation;

(H) Securing hotel accommodations in the event of jury sequestration;

(I) Securing of meals for jurors and other court personnel;

(J) Which county will guarantee and pay vendors for services rendered;

(K) The necessity for deposit or prepayment of expenses by the county of the crime venue; and

(L) All other matters which reasonably may affect the orderly administration of justice in the transfer county. In the event of disagreement between the trial judge and the chief judge of the transfer circuit, the district administrative judge for the proposed transfer of venue shall have final responsibility for resolving the dispute.

(3) Either by the agreement of the defense counsel, the prosecuting attorney, and the judge or by the exercise of discretion by the judge the trial jury may be selected from qualified jurors of the transfer county, although the trial of the criminal case may take place in the county of the venue of the alleged crime. In the exercise of discretion, to select the jury in the transfer county but to try the case in the county of venue of the alleged crime, the judge shall consult with the chief superior court judge of the circuit in which the county of transfer lies and consider all of the factors provided in subparagraphs (A) through (L) of paragraph (2) of this subsection as well as the following factors:

(A) The hardship of sequestration a distance from home on the jurors;

(B) The comparison of court space available;

(C) The comparison of security, jail, clerical, and support staff;

(D) The costs to conduct the trial in each place;

(E) The impact of trial on the orderly administration of justice in each county;

(F) The impact on witnesses;

(G) The availability of hotel accommodations and meals for jurors in each county;

(H) The effect on the prosecuting attorney and defense counsel in each county; and

(I) All other matters which would afford a fair trial and the orderly administration of justice.

In the event of disagreement between the trial judge and the chief judge of the transfer circuit, the district administrative judge for the proposed transfer of venue shall have final responsibility for resolving the dispute.

(b) The judge of the court in whose jurisdiction a crime is alleged to have been committed may change the venue for trial of the case on his own motion whenever, in his judgment, there is danger of violence being committed on the defendant, if carried back to, or allowed to remain in the county where the crime is alleged to have been committed. If a motion is made by the defendant for a change of venue, the judge shall hear the motion at such time and place as the judge may direct. If the evidence submitted shall reasonably show that there is probability or danger of violence, it shall be mandatory on the judge to change the venue to such other county as, in his judgment, will reasonably avoid violence.

(c) Notwithstanding other laws, the denial of a motion to change venue shall be appealable immediately only with a certificate of immediate review. Otherwise, the denial shall be appealed with the merits of the case.

Laws 1895, p. 70, § 2; Laws 1911, p. 74, § 1; Laws 1972, p. 536, § 1; Laws 1995, p. 1292, § 12.

Formerly Penal Code 1895, § 939; Penal Code 1910, § 964; Code 1933, § 27-1201; Code 1933, §§ 27-1201, 27-1202.

§ 17-7-151. Clerk to transmit papers, etc.; subpoenas for witnesses

Whenever a change of venue is made, the clerk of the court from which the case has been transferred shall send to the court to which the case has been transferred a transcript of the order for the change of venue, the evidence before the court of inquiry, a list of all the witnesses subpoenaed in the case, and all other papers connected with the case. The clerk of the court selected to try the case shall issue subpoenas to the witnesses and such others as may be applied for by either party.

Laws 1895, p. 70, § 4; Laws 1972, p. 536, § 1.

Formerly Penal Code 1895, § 940; Penal Code 1910, § 965; Code 1933, § 27-1202; Code 1933, § 27-1203.

§ 17-7-152. Subsequent change of venue

If, on motion, the judge presiding in the court to which a case has been transferred is satisfied that a fair and impartial jury cannot be obtained therein, he shall, in the manner prescribed in subsection (a) of Code Section 17-7-150, transfer the case to some other county where a fair and impartial jury can be obtained.

Laws 1895, p. 70, § 5; Laws 1972, p. 536, § 1.

Formerly Penal Code 1895, § 941; Penal Code 1910, § 966; Code 1933, § 27-1203; Code 1933, § 27-1204.

Article 7

Demand for Trial; Announcement of Readiness for Trial

§ 17-7-170. Demand in noncapital cases

(a) Any defendant against whom a true bill of indictment or an accusation is filed with the clerk for an offense not affecting the defendant's life may enter a demand for speedy trial at the court term at which the indictment or accusation is filed or at the next succeeding regular court term thereafter; or, by special permission of the court, the defendant may at any subsequent court term thereafter demand a speedy trial. In either case, the demand for speedy trial shall be filed with the clerk of court and served upon the prosecutor and upon the judge to whom the case is assigned or, if the case is not assigned, upon the chief judge of the court in which the case is pending. A demand for speedy trial filed pursuant to this Code section shall be filed as a separate, distinct, and individual document and shall not be a part of any other pleading or document. Such demand shall clearly be titled "Demand for Speedy Trial"; reference this Code section within the pleading; and identify the indictment number or accusation number for which such demand is being made. The demand for speedy trial shall be binding only in the court in which the demand for speedy trial is filed, except where the case is transferred from one court to another without a request from the defendant.

(b) If the defendant is not tried when the demand for speedy trial is made or at the next succeeding regular court term thereafter, provided that at both court terms there were juries impaneled and qualified to try the defendant, the defendant shall be absolutely discharged and acquitted of the offense charged in the indictment or accusation. For purposes of computing the term at which a misdemeanor must be tried under this Code section, there shall be excluded any civil term of court in a county in which civil and criminal terms of court are designated; and for purposes of this Code section it shall be as if such civil term was not held.

(c) Any demand for speedy trial filed pursuant to this Code section shall expire at the conclusion of the trial or upon the defendant entering a plea of guilty or nolo contendere.

(d) If a case in which a demand for speedy trial has been filed, as provided in this Code section, is reversed on direct appeal, a new demand for speedy trial shall be filed within the term of court in which the remittitur from the appellate court is received by the clerk of court or at the next succeeding regular court term thereafter.

(e) If the case in which a demand for speedy trial has been filed as provided in this Code section results in a mistrial, the case shall be tried at the next succeeding regular term of court.

Laws 1859, p. 60, § 1; Laws 1985, p. 637, § 5; Laws 1987, p. 841, § 1; Laws 2003, Act 26, § 3, eff. May 14, 2003; Laws 2006, Act 879, § 1, eff. July 1, 2006.

Formerly Code 1863, § 4534; Code 1868, § 4554; Code 1873, § 4648; Code 1882, § 4648; Penal Code 1895, § 958; Penal Code 1910, § 983; Code 1933, § 27-1901.

§ 17-7-171. Demand in capital cases

(a) Any person accused of a capital offense may enter a demand for speedy trial at the term of court at which the indictment is found or at the next succeeding regular term thereafter; or, by special permission of the court, the defendant may at any subsequent term thereafter demand a speedy trial. The demand for speedy trial shall be filed with the clerk of court and served upon the prosecutor and upon the judge to whom the case is assigned or, if the case is not assigned, upon the chief judge of the court in which the case is pending. A demand for trial filed pursuant to this Code section shall be filed as a separate, distinct, and individual document and shall not be a part of any other pleading or document. Such demand shall clearly be titled "Demand for Speedy Trial"; reference this Code section within the pleading; and identify the indictment number or accusation number for which such demand is being made. The demand for speedy trial shall be binding only in the court in which such demand is filed, except where the case is transferred from one court to another without a request from the defendant.

(b) If more than two regular terms of court are convened and adjourned after the term at which the demand for speedy trial is filed and the defendant is not given a trial, then the defendant shall be absolutely discharged and acquitted of the offense charged in the indictment, provided that at both terms there were juries impaneled and qualified to try the defendant and provided, further, that the defendant was present in court announcing ready for trial and requesting a trial on the indictment.

(c) In cases involving a capital offense for which the death penalty is sought, if a demand for speedy trial is entered, the counting of terms under subsection (b) of this Code section shall not begin until the convening of the first term following the completion of pretrial review proceedings in the Supreme Court under Code Section 17-10-35.1.

Laws 1952, p. 299, §§ 1, 2; Laws 1983, p. 452, § 3; Laws 1988, p. 1437, § 3; Laws 1990, p. 8, § 17; Laws 2006, Act 879, § 2, eff. July 1, 2006.

§ 17-7-172. Announcement by state of ready or not ready for trial

The state shall be required in every case to announce ready or not ready for trial, except in those cases where the defendant is entitled by law to demand a speedy trial, before the defendant shall be called on to make such announcement.

Laws 1862-63, p. 138, § 1; Laws 2006, Act 879, § 3, eff. July 1, 2006.

Formerly Code 1868, § 4613; Code 1873, § 4710; Code 1882, § 4710; Penal Code 1895, § 959; Penal Code 1910, § 984; Code 1933, § 27-1902.

Article 8

Procedure for Securing Attendance of Witnesses at Grand Jury or Trial Proceedings

§ 17-7-190. Attendance of witness before grand jury

When any person accused of a criminal offense before a court of inquiry is bound over or committed for trial in superior court, the judicial officer holding the court of inquiry shall, at the time of the commitment hearing, give a subpoena to all material witnesses examined for the state to appear and testify before the grand jury at the term to which the defendant is committed or bound to appear; and, after the hearing and commitment or binding over, the prosecutor may apply to the clerk of the superior court and obtain a subpoena for any person deemed by him to be a material witness for the state before the grand jury. The subpoenas issued under this Code section shall be effectual in compelling the attendance of the witnesses to appear and give evidence before the grand jury. The judicial officer holding the court of inquiry and the clerk of the superior court shall, on the first day of the term of court to which the defendant is committed or bound to appear, furnish the prosecuting officers with a complete list of all persons so subpoenaed.

Laws 1873, p. 33, §§ 1, 2.

Formerly Code 1873, § 3846; Code 1882, § 3846; Penal Code 1895, § 917; Penal Code 1910, § 942; Code 1933, § 27-413.

§ 17-7-191. Attendance of witnesses for accused

The defendant may, upon application to the committing judicial officer or to the clerk of the court to which he is committed or bound to appear for trial, obtain subpoenas for such witnesses as he deems material for his defense. The judicial officer or the clerk of the court shall issue such subpoenas requiring the witnesses to appear at the term of the court to which the defendant is committed or bound to appear and until his case is ended. The subpoenas so issued shall have the power and authority to compel the attendance of the witnesses at the court but shall not extend to witnesses for the defendant who reside outside the county until a true bill of indictment is found or an accusation is filed against the defendant.

Laws 1873, p. 33, § 3.

Formerly Code 1873, § 3847; Code 1882, § 3847; Penal Code 1895, § 918; Penal Code 1910, § 943; Code 1933, § 27-414.

§ 17-7-192. Continuance for nonattendance of witness refused

A defendant who fails to use the subpoena power provided for in Code Section 17-7-191, when it is within his power to do so, shall not be entitled to a continuance because a witness material to his defense is not in attendance at the term of the court when his case is called for trial, if he is prosecuted for the same criminal act.

Laws 1873, p. 33, § 3.

Formerly Code 1873, § 3848; Code 1882, § 3848; Penal Code 1895, § 919; Penal Code 1910, § 944; Code 1933, § 27-415.

Article 9

Discovery

§§ 17-7-210, 17-7-211. Repealed by Laws 1994, p. 1895, § 1, eff. January 1, 1995

CHAPTER 8

TRIAL

Article 1

General Provisions

§ 17-8-1. Cases called in order in which they stand on docket

The cases on the criminal docket shall be called in the order in which they stand on the docket unless the defendant is in jail or, otherwise, in the sound discretion of the court.

Laws 1862-63, p. 139, § 1.

Formerly Code 1863, § 4592; Code 1868, § 4613; Code 1873, § 4710; Code 1882, § 4710; Penal Code 1895, § 942; Penal Code 1910, § 967; Code 1933, § 27-1301.

§ 17-8-2. Approval of settlement by court

All indictments or special presentments shall be submitted to and passed upon by a jury under the direction of the presiding judge unless there is a settlement of the case between the prosecutor and the defendant, which settlement shall be valid only by the approval and order of the court on examination into the merits of the case.

Laws 1850, Cobb's 1851 Digest, p. 864; Laws 1870, p. 422, § 2.

Formerly Code 1863, § 4588; Code 1868, §§ 4609, 4610; Code 1873, § 4706; Code 1882, § 4706; Penal Code 1895, § 956; Penal Code 1910, § 981; Code 1933, § 27-1701.

§ 17-8-3. Nolle prosequi; when and how allowed; notice to defendant and defendant's attorney

After an examination of the case in open court and before it has been submitted to a jury, the prosecuting attorney may enter a nolle prosequi with the consent of the court. After the case has been submitted to a jury, a nolle prosequi shall not be entered except by the consent of the defendant. The prosecuting attorney shall notify the defendant and the defendant's attorney of record within 30 days of the entry of a nolle prosequi either personally or in writing; such written notice shall be sent by regular mail to the defendant at the defendant's last known address and to the defendant's attorney of record.

Laws 1833, Cobb's 1851 Digest, p. 836; Laws 1870, p. 422, § 1; Laws 1877, p. 108, § 1; Laws 1989, p. 585, § 1.

Formerly Code 1863, § 4535; Code 1868, § 4555; Code 1873, § 4649; Code 1882, § 4649; Penal Code 1895, § 957; Penal Code 1910, § 982; Code 1933, § 27-1801.

§ 17-8-4. Joint or separate trials

(a) When two or more defendants are jointly indicted for a capital offense, any defendant so electing shall be separately tried unless the state shall waive the death penalty. When indicted for a capital felony when the death penalty is waived, or for a felony less than capital, or for a misdemeanor, such defendants may be tried jointly or separately in the discretion of the trial court. In any event, a jointly indicted defendant may testify for another jointly indicted defendant or on behalf of the state. When separate trials are ordered in any case, the defendants shall be tried in the order requested by the state. If the offense requires joint action and concurrence of two or more persons, acquittal or conviction of one defendant shall not operate as acquittal or conviction of others not tried.

(b) When two or more defendants are tried jointly for a crime or offense, such defendants shall be entitled to the same number of strikes as a single defendant if tried separately. The strikes shall be exercised jointly by the defendants or shall be apportioned among the defendants in the manner the court shall direct. In the event two or more defendants are tried jointly, the court, upon request of the defendants, shall allow an equal number of additional strikes to the defendants, not to exceed five each, as the court shall deem necessary, to the ends that justice may prevail. The court may allow the state additional strikes not to exceed the number of additional strikes as are allowed to the defendants.

Laws 1836, Cobb's Digest, p. 841; Laws 1855–56, p. 266, § 1; Laws 1858, p. 99, § 1; Laws 1878–79, p. 59, § 1; Laws 1971, p. 891, § 1; Laws 1972, p. 618, § 1; Laws 2005, Act 8, § 9, eff. July 1, 2005.

Formerly Code 1863, § 4574; Code 1868, § 4595; Code 1873, § 4692; Code 1882, § 4692; Penal Code 1895, § 969; Penal Code 1910, § 995; Code 1933, § 27-2101.

§ 17-8-5. Stenographic notes; entry of testimony on minutes of court; transcript or brief

(a) On the trial of all felonies the presiding judge shall have the testimony taken down and, when directed by the judge, the court reporter shall exactly and truly record or take stenographic notes of the testimony and proceedings in the case, except the argument of counsel. In the event of a verdict of guilty, the testimony shall be entered on the minutes of the court or in a book to be kept for that purpose. In the event that a sentence of death is imposed, the transcript of the case shall be prepared within 90 days after the sentence is imposed by the trial court. Upon petition by the court reporter, the Chief Justice of the Supreme Court of Georgia may grant an additional period of time for preparation of the transcript, such period not to exceed 60 days. The requirement that a transcript be prepared within a certain period in cases in which a sentence of death is imposed shall not inure to the benefit of a defendant.

(b) In the event that a mistrial results from any cause in the trial of a defendant charged with the commission of a felony, the presiding judge may, in his discretion, either with or without any application of the defendant or state's counsel, order that a brief or transcript of the testimony in the case be duly filed by the court reporter in the office of the clerk of the superior court in which the mistrial occurred. If the brief or transcript is ordered, it shall be the duty of the judge, in the order, to provide for the compensation of the reporter and for the transcript to be paid for as is provided by law for payment of transcripts in cases in which the law requires the testimony to be transcribed, at a rate not to exceed that provided in felony cases.

Laws 1833, Cobb's 1851 Digest, p. 841; Laws 1876, p. 133, § 1; Laws 1925, p. 101, § 1; Laws 1973, p. 159, § 6; Laws 1976, p. 991, § 1.

Formerly Code 1863, § 4578; Code 1868, § 4599; Code 1873, § 4696; Code 1882, § 4696; Penal Code 1895, § 981; Penal Code 1910, § 1007; Code 1933, § 27-2401.

§ 17-8-6. Municipal court judges authorized to seal criminal records under certain circumstances

(a) Any judge of a municipal court of any municipality of this state or any judge hearing cases for any such court wherein a municipal court is a court of first instance in criminal cases shall have the authority to seal, to all persons except criminal justice officials, all criminal records of the municipality, including, but not limited to, records of arrest, fingerprints, and photographs, whether maintained in the police agency of the municipality or elsewhere in the municipality, related to any individual, upon a finding by such a judge that one of the following conditions exists:

(1) When, upon the call of a case for trial, criminal charges against the individual are dismissed either:

(A) Upon the motion of the arresting officer; or

(B) Because of the lack of prosecution of such charges by the arresting officer or the municipality; or

(2) When criminal charges against the individual are the subject of a pretrial disposition by the municipal prosecutor, provided that the terms and conditions of the pretrial disposition are satisfied.

(b) Any order sealing the records of an individual, as provided for in subsection (a) of this Code section, shall in no way constitute an adjudication of any illegal or wrongful action on the part of the arresting officer or the municipality.

Laws 1980, p. 1683, § 1.

Article 2

Continuances

§ 17-8-20. Diligence required of applicants

In all cases, the party making an application for a continuance must show that he has used due diligence.

Formerly Code 1863, § 3457; Code 1868, § 3477; Code 1873, § 3528; Code 1882, § 3528; Civil Code 1895, § 5135; Penal Code 1895, § 965; Civil Code 1910, § 5721; Penal Code 1910, § 991; Code 1933, § 81-1416.

§ 17-8-21. When showing for continuance is required of state

In all cases in which the defendant cannot, according to law, demand a speedy trial, a continuance shall not be granted to the state, except upon a reasonable showing therefor.

Laws 1862-63, p. 138, § 1; Laws 2006, Act 879, § 4, eff. July 1, 2006.

Formerly Code 1863, § 4592; Code 1868, § 4613; Code 1873, § 4710; Code 1882, § 4710; Penal Code, § 960; Penal Code, § 985; Code 1933, § 27-2001.

§ 17-8-22. Counter-showing and discretion of court

All applications for continuances are addressed to the sound legal discretion of the court and, if not expressly provided for, shall be granted or refused as the ends of justice may require. In all cases the presiding judges may, in their discretion, admit a counter-showing to a motion for a continuance and, after a hearing, may decide whether the motion shall prevail.

Laws 1871-72, p. 49, § 1; Laws 1872, p. 41, § 1.

Formerly Code 1863, § 3460; Code 1868, § 3480; Code 1873, § 3531; Code 1882, § 3531; Civil Code 1895, § 5138; Penal Code 1895, § 966; Civil Code 1910, § 5724; Penal Code 1910, § 992; Code 1933, § 81-1419.

§ 17-8-23. Absence of a party as cause for continuance

If either party is providentially prevented from attending the trial of any case and the counsel of the absent party will state in his place that he cannot go safely to trial without the presence of the absent party, the case shall be continued, provided his continuances are not exhausted.

Formerly Code 1863, § 3453; Code 1868, § 3473; Code 1873, § 3524; Code 1882, § 3524; Civil Code 1895, § 5131; Civil Code 1910, § 5717; Code 1933, § 81-1412.

§ 17-8-24. Absence or illness of counsel as cause for continuance

The illness or absence, from providential cause, of counsel where there is but one, or of the leading counsel where there are more than one, shall be a sufficient ground for continuance, provided that the party making the application will swear that he cannot go safely to trial without the services of the absent counsel, that he expects his services at the next term, and that the application is not made for delay only.

Formerly Code 1863, § 3454; Code 1868, § 3474; Code 1873, § 3525; Code 1882, § 3525; Civil Code 1895, § 5132; Penal Code 1895, § 964; Civil Code 1910, § 5718; Penal Code 1910, § 990; Code 1933, § 81-1413.

§ 17-8-25. Absence of witnesses; showing required

In all applications for continuances upon the ground of the absence of a witness, it shall be shown to the court that the witness is absent; that he has been subpoenaed; that he does not reside more than 100 miles from the place of trial by the nearest practical route; that his testimony is material; that the witness is not absent by the permission, directly or indirectly, of the applicant; that the applicant expects he will be able to procure the testimony of the witness at the next term of the court; that the application is not made for the purpose of delay but to enable the applicant to procure the testimony of the absent witness; and the application must state the facts expected to be proved by the absent witness.

Laws 1959, p. 342, § 1.

Formerly Code 1863, § 3451; Code 1868, § 3471; Code 1873, § 3522; Code 1882, § 3522; Civil Code 1895, § 5129; Penal Code 1895, § 962; Civil Code 1910, § 5715; Penal Code 1910, § 987; Code 1933, § 81-1410.

§ 17-8-26. Membership in General Assembly by party or counsel

(a) A member of the General Assembly who is a party to or the attorney for a party to a case which is pending in any trial or appellate court or before any administrative agency of this state shall be granted a continuance and stay of the case. The continuance and stay shall apply to all aspects of the case, including, but not limited to, the filing and serving of an answer to a complaint, the making of any discovery or motion, or of any response to any subpoena, discovery, or motion, and appearance at any hearing, pretrial appearance, arraignment, plea or motion calendar, trial, or argument. When a case, motion, hearing, or argument is called and is subject to a continuance or stay under this Code section due to the party's attorney's membership in the General Assembly, the party shall not be required to be present at the call of the case, motion, hearing, or argument. Unless a shorter length of time is requested by the member, the continuance and stay shall last the length of any regular or extraordinary session of the General Assembly and during the first three weeks following any recess or adjournment, including an adjournment sine die of any regular or extraordinary session. Notwithstanding any other provision of law, rule of court, or administrative rule or regulation, and to the extent permitted by the Constitutions of the United States and of the State of Georgia, the time for doing any act in the case which is delayed by the continuance or stay provided by this Code section shall be automatically extended by the same length of time as the continuance or stay covered.

(b) A continuance and stay shall also be granted for such other times as the member of the General Assembly or staff member certifies to the court that his or her presence elsewhere is required by his or her duties with the General Assembly.

Laws 1905, p. 93, § 1; Laws 1952, p. 26, § 1; Laws 1973, p. 478, § 1; Laws 1977, p. 760, § 1; Laws 1983, p. 675, § 1; Laws 1996, p. 112, § 2; Laws 2002, p. 403, § 2; Laws 2006, Act 749, § 3, eff. May 3, 2006.

Formerly Civil Code 1910, § 5711; Code 1933, § 81-1402.

§ 17-8-27. Continuance of case when Attorney General occupied in aid of General Assembly

When any case pending in the courts of this state in which the Attorney General is of counsel is scheduled to be called for any purpose during sessions of the General Assembly or during a period of 15 days preceding or following sessions of the General Assembly, on motion of the Attorney General or an assistant attorney general, it shall be a good ground for continuance that the Attorney General and his staff are occupied in aid of the business of the General Assembly.

Laws 1956, p. 700, § 1.

§ 17-8-28. When witness is in attendance upon General Assembly

(a) Any person summoned to serve as a witness in a criminal case shall be excused by the judge from attendance at the court by reason of his attendance as a legislator at the General Assembly.

(b) In all criminal cases, it shall be the duty of the presiding judge, on motion of either the state or the defendant, to continue the case when it appears that a material witness is absent from the court by reason of his attendance at the General Assembly.

Laws 1905, p. 93, § 3.

Formerly Civil Code 1910, § 5712; Penal Code 1910, § 988; Code 1933, §§ 27-2003, 81-1407.

§ 17-8-29. Absence of party or counsel on meeting of Board of Regents of University System of Georgia or State Board of Education

Should any member of the Board of Regents of the University System of Georgia or any member of the State Board of Education be engaged at the time of any meeting of the board as counsel or party in any case pending in the courts of this state and should the case be called for trial during the regular session of the board, the member's absence from attending the session shall be good ground for a postponement or continuance of the case until the session of the board has ended.

Laws 1931, p. 7, § 56; Laws 1985, p. 1406, § 2; Laws 1997, p. 143, § 17.

Formerly Code 1933, § 81-1404.

§ 17-8-30. Absence of party or counsel on meeting of Board of Human Resources

Should any member of the Board of Human Resources be engaged at the time of any meeting of the board as counsel or party in any case pending in the courts of this state and should the case be called for trial during the regular session of the board, his absence to attend the session shall be good ground for a postponement or a continuance of the case until the session of the board has ended.

Laws 1933, p. 7, § 1.

Formerly Code 1933, § 81-1405.

§ 17-8-31. Absence of parties or leading attorney by reason of active duty in the armed forces

(a) It shall be the duty of any judge of the courts of this state to continue any case in the court on or without motion when any party thereto or his or her leading attorney is absent from court when the case is reached by reason of his or her attendance on active duty as a member of the National Guard or a reserve or active component of the armed forces of the United States. The case may proceed if the party, in the absence of his or her leading attorney, or the leading attorney, in the absence of the party, announces ready for trial on the call of the case. If counsel is absent, it shall be necessary for his or her client to make oath that he or she cannot safely go to trial without the absent attorney and, if a party is absent, his or her counsel shall state in his or her place that he or she cannot safely go to trial without the client.

(b) It shall be the duty of any judge of the courts of this state to continue any case in the court upon a showing by the state or the defendant that a material and necessary witness is unavailable by reason of being on active duty as a member of the National Guard or as a member of a reserve or active component of the armed forces of the United States.

(c) In cases in which a demand for speedy trial has been filed in accordance with Code Section 17-7-170 or 17-7-171, the court shall grant the continuance if the party moving for a continuance pursuant to subsection (b) of this Code section establishes by testimony, affidavits, or other evidence that:

(1) The witness is material and necessary;

(2) The witness is located outside the territorial limits of the state;

(3) The party has submitted a request to the proper military authorities for the testimony of the witness in accordance with Section 301 of Title 5 of the United States Code and federal regulations or directives issued by the armed forces pursuant thereto; and

(4) The witness will not be available within the time limits prescribed by Code Section 17-7-170 or 17-7-171.

This continuance shall toll the running of the demand for speedy trial and shall continue the trial until the witness is released from active duty or the military makes the witness available to testify. If the witness only becomes available to testify within the last two weeks of the term of court in which the case must be tried, the case may be tried at the next succeeding term of court.

(d) In any case in which the court grants the state a continuance pursuant to subsection (c) of this Code section, the defendant shall have bail set upon application to the court, except in those cases punishable by death or imprisonment for life without parole. In any case in which the defendant is accused of committing a serious violent felony, as defined by subsection (a) of Code Section 17-10-6.1, the court shall consider but shall not be required to set bail.

Laws 1925, p. 149, § 1; Laws 2003, Act 26, § 4, eff. May 14, 2003; Laws 2004, Act 564, 17, eff. May 13, 2004; Laws 2006, Act 879, § 5, eff. July 1, 2006.

Formerly Code 1933, § 81-1406.

§ 17-8-32. Admission of facts as ground for denial of continuance because of absence of witness

No continuance shall be allowed in any court on account of the absence of a witness or for the purpose of procuring testimony when the opposite party is willing to admit, and does not contest the truth of, the facts expected to be proved; and the court shall order such admission to be reduced to writing.

Laws 1853-54, p. 52, § 1.

Formerly Code 1863, § 3452; Code 1868, § 3472; Code 1873, § 3523; Code 1882, § 3523; Civil Code 1895, § 5130; Penal Code 1895, § 963; Civil Code 1910, § 5716; Penal Code 1910, § 989; Code 1933, § 81-1411.

§ 17-8-33. When case tried and when continued

(a) Every person against whom a true bill of indictment is found or an accusation is made shall be tried at the term of the court at which the indictment is found or the accusation is made unless the absence of a material witness or the principles of justice should require a continuance of the case, in which case the court shall allow a continuance until the next term of the court. The court shall have power to allow the continuance of criminal cases from term to term, as often as the principles of justice may require, upon sufficient cause shown under oath.

(b) No continuance shall be granted over the objection of the adverse party in any court which has a continuous session for 30 days or more where the cause for the continuance can be obviated by a postponement to a later day during the term. Whenever a motion and a proper showing for a continuance is made by either party, the presiding judge, at any time, shall set the case down for a later day during the same term if it shall be practicable thereby to avoid a continuance of the case until the next term.

Laws 1833, Cobb's 1851 Digest, p. 835; Laws 1893, p. 56, § 1.

Formerly Code 1863, § 4533; Code 1868, § 4553; Code 1873, § 4647; Code 1882, § 4647; Penal Code 1895, § 961; Penal Code 1910, § 986; Code 1933, § 27-2002.

§ 17-8-34. Cases sent back from appellate court

When a case is sent back for trial to a superior, state, or city court by the Supreme Court or Court of Appeals, the case shall be in order for trial; and, if the continuances of either party are exhausted, the trial court may grant one continuance to the party, as the ends of justice may require.

Laws 1851-52, p. 214, § 6.

Formerly Code 1863, § 3456; Code 1868, § 3476; Code 1873, § 3527; Code 1882, § 3527; Civil Code 1895, § 5134; Civil Code 1910, § 5720; Code 1933, § 81-1415.

§ 17–8–35. Continuance by codefendant; effect

The continuance of a case by one of several defendants indicted jointly shall not operate as a continuance as to the other defendants objecting thereto.

Laws 1858, p. 99, § 2.

Formerly Code 1863, § 4575; Code 1868, § 4596; Code 1873, § 4693; Code 1882, § 4693; Penal Code 1895, § 967; Penal Code 1910, § 993; Code 1933, § 27–2004.

§ 17–8–36. Public announcement of continuance

The judges of the superior, state, and city courts shall, upon the continuance of any case, enter the date of the continuance upon their dockets opposite the case and in open court make public announcement of the continuance.

Laws 1895, p. 41, § 1; Laws 1983, p. 884, § 3–20.

Formerly Civil Code 1895, § 5140; Penal Code 1895, § 968; Civil Code 1910, § 5726; Penal Code 1910, § 994; Code 1933, § 81–1421.

§ 17–8–37. Length of continuance

When a court grants a continuance of a pending case for whatever cause, the continuance shall extend until the next term of court only.

Laws 1799, Cobb's 1851 Digest, p. 486.

Formerly Code 1863, § 3448; Code 1868, § 3468; Code 1873, § 3519; Code 1882, § 3519; Civil Code 1895, § 5126; Civil Code 1910, § 5710; Code 1933, § 81–1401.

§ 17–8–38. Case not reached at trial term

A case not reached at the trial term stands over as continued.

Formerly Code 1863, § 3455; Code 1868, § 3475; Code 1873, § 3526; Code 1882, § 3526; Civil Code 1895, § 5133; Civil Code 1910, § 5719; Code 1933, § 81–1414.

Article 3

Conduct of Proceedings

§ 17–8–50. Trials for escapees from state or county correctional institutions; witnesses

The trial of inmates escaping from a state or county correctional institution shall take place in the superior court of the county in which the escape occurs, and inmates so escaping shall remain in the correctional institution after their apprehension and shall be treated as are other inmates until the trial takes place. At the trial, the copies of the records transmitted to the superintendent or warden of the state or county correctional institution, relative to the former trials of such inmates, shall be produced and filed of record in the superior court; and any other inmate not included in the same indictment shall be a competent witness.

Laws 1833, Cobb's 1851 Digest, p. 837; Laws 1968, p. 1249, § 1.

Formerly Code 1863, § 4545; Code 1868, § 4565; Code 1873, § 4659; Code 1882, § 4659; Penal Code 1895, § 318; Penal Code 1910, § 323; Code 1933, § 26–4511; Code 1933, § 26–9902.

§ 17–8–51. Convict witnesses on trial for mutiny

At the trial of an inmate of a penal institution for the crime of mutiny, any other inmate not included in the same indictment shall be a competent witness, and the infamy of his character and of the crime of which he has been convicted shall be exceptions to his credit only.

Laws 1833, Cobb's 1851 Digest, p. 840; Laws 1968, p. 1249, § 1.

Formerly Code 1863, § 4563; Code 1868, § 4583; Code 1873, § 4677; Code 1882, § 4677; Penal Code 1895, § 331; Penal Code 1910, § 336; Code 1933, § 26–4803; Code 1933, § 26–9903.

§ 17–8–52. Witnesses' oath in criminal cases

(a) The following oath shall be administered to witnesses in criminal cases:

"Do you solemnly swear or affirm that the evidence you shall give to the court and jury in the matter now pending before the court shall be the truth, the whole truth, and nothing but the truth? So help you God."

(b) Any oath given that substantially complies with the language in this Code section shall subject the witness to the provisions of Code Section 16–10–70.

Laws 1833, Cobb's 1851 Digest, p. 836; Laws 1997, p. 1499, § 2.

Formerly Code 1863, § 4537; Code 1868, § 4557; Code 1873, § 4651; Code 1882, § 4651; Penal Code 1895, § 980; Penal Code 1910, § 1006; Code 1933, § 38–1702.

§ 17–8–53. Exclusion of public from courtroom when evidence vulgar

During a trial in a court of any case in which the evidence is vulgar and obscene or relates to the improper acts of the sexes, and tends to debauch the morals of the young, the presiding judge shall have the right in his discretion and on his own motion, or on motion of a party or his attorney, to hear and try the case after clearing the courtroom of all or any portion of the audience.

Laws 1890–91, p. 111, § 1; Laws 1895, p. 49, § 1.

Formerly Civil Code 1895, § 5296; Civil Code 1910, § 5885; Code 1933, § 81–1006.

§ 17–8–54. Exclusion of persons from courtroom when person under 16 years of age testifies in sex offense case

In the trial of any criminal case, when any person under the age of 16 is testifying concerning any sex offense, the court shall clear the courtroom of all persons except parties to the cause and their immediate families or guardians, attorneys and their secretaries, officers of the court, jurors, newspaper reporters or broadcasters, and court reporters.

Laws 1985, p. 1190, § 1.

§ 17–8–55. Closed circuit television testimony of sex offense victims under 10 years of age

(a) In all proceedings involving the criminal charges specified in this Code section, the court may order that the testimony of a child ten years of age or younger who has been the victim of any violation of Code Section 16–5–70, Code Section 16–6–1, Code Section 16–6–2, Code Section 16–6–4, or Code Section 16–6–5.1 be taken outside the courtroom and shown in the courtroom by means of a two-way closed circuit television. An order may be granted in such cases only if:

(1) The testimony is taken during the criminal trial proceeding for such violation; and

(2) The judge determines that testimony by the child victim in the courtroom will result in the child's suffering serious emotional distress such that the child cannot reasonably communicate.

(b) Only the prosecuting attorney, the attorney for the defendant, and the judge may question the child who testifies by two-way closed circuit television.

(c) The operators of the two-way closed circuit television shall make every effort to be unobtrusive.

(d) Only the following persons may be in the room with the child when the child testifies by two-way closed circuit television:

(1) The prosecuting attorney;

(2) The attorney for the defendant;

(3) The operators of the two-way closed circuit television equipment;

(4) The judge; and

(5) In the court's discretion, any person whose presence, in the opinion of the court, contributes to the well-being of the child, including a person who has dealt with the child in a therapeutic setting concerning the crime. The defendant and defendant's counsel shall be notified at least 24 hours before the closed circuit testimony as to the prosecution's representatives and any other persons who shall be present in the room with the child victim during the child's testimony.

(e) During the child's testimony by two-way closed circuit television, the defendant shall be in the courtroom.

(f) The defendant shall be allowed to communicate with the persons in the room where the child is testifying by any appropriate electronic method.

(g) The provisions of this Code section do not apply if the defendant is an attorney pro se.

(h) This Code section may not be interpreted to preclude, for purposes of identification of a defendant, the presence of both the child victim and the defendant in the courtroom at the same time.

Laws 1985, p. 1190, § 1; Laws 1990, p. 8, § 17; Laws 1991, p. 1377, § 1.

§ 17–8–56. Judges to write out charges on request when official reporter not present; charges to be filed; certified copies

(a) The judges of the superior, state, and city courts shall, when the counsel for either party requests it before argument begins, write out their charges and read them to the jury; and it shall be error to give any other or additional charge than that so written and read.

(b) The charge so written out and read shall be filed with the clerk of the court in which it was given and shall be accessible to all persons interested in it. The clerk shall give certified copies of the charge to any person applying therefor, upon payment of the usual fee.

(c) This Code section shall not apply when there is an official stenographer or reporter of the court in attendance thereon who takes down in shorthand and writes out the full charge of the trial judge in the case upon the direction of court.

Laws 1860, p. 42, §§ 1, 2; Laws 1877, p. 13, § 1; Laws 1878–79, p. 150, § 1; Laws 1897, p. 41, § 1; Laws 1943, p. 262, § 1; Laws 1983, p. 884, § 3–21; Laws 1985, p. 1190, § 1.

Formerly Code 1863, §§ 240, 241; Code 1868, §§ 234, 235; Code 1873, §§ 244, 245; Code 1882, §§ 244, 245; Civil Code

1895, §§ 4318, 4319; Penal Code 1895, §§ 1030, 1031; Civil Code 1910, §§ 4847, 4848; Penal Code 1910, §§ 1056, 1057; Code 1933, §§ 81-1102, 81-1103.

§ 17-8-57. Expression of opinion on facts, error

It is error for any judge in any criminal case, during its progress or in his charge to the jury, to express or intimate his opinion as to what has or has not been proved or as to the guilt of the accused. Should any judge violate this Code section, the violation shall be held by the Supreme Court or Court of Appeals to be error and the decision in the case reversed, and a new trial granted in the court below with such directions as the Supreme Court or Court of Appeals may lawfully give.

Laws 1850, Cobb's 1851 Digest, p. 462; Laws 1985, p. 1190, § 1.

Formerly Code 1863, § 3172; Code 1868, § 3183; Code 1873, § 3248; Code 1882, § 3248; Civil Code 1895, § 4334; Penal Code 1895, § 1032; Civil Code 1910, § 4863; Penal Code 1910, § 1058; Code 1933, § 81-1104; Code 1981, § 17-8-55.

Article 4

Conduct and Argument of Counsel

§ 17-8-70. Number of counsel who may argue case

Not more than two counsel shall be permitted to argue any case for each side, except by express leave of the court. In no case shall more than one counsel for each side be heard in conclusion.

Laws 1924, p. 75, § 1.

Formerly Code 1933, § 27-2202.

§ 17-8-71. Order of argument

After the evidence is closed on both sides, the prosecuting attorney shall open and conclude the argument to the jury. The defendant shall be entitled to make a closing argument prior to the concluding argument of the prosecuting attorney.

Laws 1851-52, p. 242, § 1; Laws 2005, Act 8, § 10, eff. July 1, 2005.

Formerly Code 1868, § 4551; Code 1873, § 4645; Code 1882, § 4645; Penal Code 1895, § 1029; Penal Code 1910, § 1055; Code 1933, § 27-2201.

§ 17-8-72. Limit of one-half hour in cases below felony

In all misdemeanor cases and cases brought up from inferior judicatories, counsel for either party shall not occupy more than one-half hour in the whole discussion of the case after the evidence is closed without obtaining special leave of the court before the argument is opened.

Laws 1924, p. 75, § 2.

Formerly Code 1933, § 27-2203.

§ 17-8-73. Time limits for closing argument in capital and noncapital felony cases

In felony cases other than those involving capital felonies, counsel shall be limited in their closing arguments to one hour for each side. In cases involving capital felonies, counsel shall be limited to two hours for each side.

Laws 1924, p. 75, § 3.

Formerly Code 1933, § 27-2204.

§ 17-8-74. Extension of time, when allowed

If, before argument begins, counsel on either side applies to the court for an extension of the time prescribed for argument and states in his place or on oath, in the discretion of the court, that he cannot do the case justice within the time prescribed and that it will require for that purpose additional time, stating how much additional time will be necessary, the court shall grant such extension of time as may seem reasonable and proper, provided that the extension of time granted in misdemeanor cases or cases brought up from inferior judicatories shall not exceed 30 minutes.

Laws 1924, p. 75, § 4; Laws 1982, p. 3, § 17.

Formerly Code 1933, § 27-2205.

§ 17-8-75. Improper conduct by counsel; duty of court

Where counsel in the hearing of the jury make statements of prejudicial matters which are not in evidence, it is the duty of the court to interpose and prevent the same. On objection made, the court shall also rebuke the counsel and by all needful and proper instructions to the jury endeavor to remove the improper impression from their minds; or, in his discretion, he may order a mistrial if the prosecuting attorney is the offender.

Formerly Civil Code 1895, § 4419; Civil Code 1910, § 4957; Code 1933, § 81–1009.

§ 17–8–76. Counsel prohibited from arguing possibility of executive clemency; mistrial for violation of rule

(a) No attorney at law in a criminal case shall argue to or in the presence of the jury that a defendant, if convicted, may not be required to suffer the full penalty imposed by the court or jury because pardon, parole, or clemency of any nature may be granted by the Governor, the State Board of Pardons and Paroles, or other proper authority vested with the right to grant clemency.

(b) If counsel for either side in a criminal case argues to or in the presence of the jury as provided in subsection (a) of this Code section, opposing counsel shall have the right immediately to request the court to declare a mistrial, in which case it shall be mandatory upon the court to declare a mistrial. Failure to declare a mistrial shall constitute reversible error.

(c) This Code section shall be construed as setting forth requirements in addition to other requirements of law.

Laws 1955, p. 191, §§ 1–3.

CHAPTER 9

VERDICT AND JUDGMENT GENERALLY

Article 1

General Provisions

§ 17–9–1. Direction of verdict of acquittal

(a) Where there is no conflict in the evidence and the evidence introduced with all reasonable deductions and inferences therefrom shall demand a verdict of acquittal or "not guilty" as to the entire offense or to some particular count or offense, the court may direct the verdict of acquittal to which the defendant is entitled under the evidence and may allow the trial to proceed only as to the counts or offenses remaining, if any.

(b) The defendant shall be entitled to move for a directed verdict at the close of the evidence offered by the prosecuting attorney or at the close of the case, even if he fails to introduce any evidence at the trial. A defendant who moves for a directed verdict at the close of the evidence offered by the prosecuting attorney may offer evidence in the event that the motion is not granted, without having reserved the right to do so and to the same extent as if the motion had not been made. A motion for a directed verdict which is not granted shall not be deemed to be a waiver of the right to trial by jury. The order of the court granting a motion for a directed verdict of acquittal is effective without any assent of the jury.

Laws 1971, p. 460, § 1; Laws 1982, p. 3, § 17.

Formerly Code 1933, § 27–1802.

§ 17–9–2. Jury judges of law and facts; general verdict; form and construction of verdicts

The jury shall be the judges of the law and the facts in the trial of all criminal cases and shall give a general verdict of "guilty" or "not guilty." Upon a verdict of "guilty," the sentence shall be imposed by the judge, unless otherwise provided by law. Verdicts are to have a reasonable intendment, are to receive a reasonable construction, and are not to be avoided unless from necessity.

Laws 1833, Cobb's 1851 Digest, p. 835; Laws 1974, p. 352, § 1.

Formerly Code 1863, §§ 3481, 4532; Code 1868, §§ 3503, 4552; Code 1873, §§ 3561, 4646; Code 1882, §§ 3561, 4646; Penal Code 1895, § 1033; Penal Code 1910, § 1059; Code 1933, § 27–2301.

§ 17–9–3. Recommendation for mercy

In all capital cases, other than those of homicide, when the verdict is "guilty," with a recommendation for mercy, it shall be legal and shall mean imprisonment for life. When the verdict is "guilty," without a recommendation for mercy, it shall be legal and shall mean that the convicted person shall be sentenced to death. When it is shown that a person convicted of a capital offense without a recommendation for mercy had not reached his seventeenth birthday at the time of the commission of the offense, the punishment of such person shall not be death but shall be imprisonment for life.

Laws 1875, p. 106, § 2; Laws 1963, p. 122, § 2; Laws 1974, p. 352, § 2.

Formerly Code 1882, § 4646a; Penal Code 1895, § 1034; Penal Code 1910, § 1060; Code 1933, § 27–2302.

§ 17-9-4. Judgments void because of want of jurisdiction of court

The judgment of a court having no jurisdiction of the person or subject matter, or void for any other cause, is a mere nullity and may be so held in any court when it becomes material to the interest of the parties to consider it.

Formerly Code 1863, § 3513; Code 1868, § 3536; Code 1873, § 3594; Code 1882, § 3594; Civil Code 1895, § 5369; Civil Code 1910, § 5964; Code 1933, § 110-709.

Article 2

Rendition and Receipt of Verdict

§ 17-9-20. Juror not to act on private knowledge

A juror shall not act on his private knowledge respecting the facts, witnesses, or parties unless he is sworn and examined as a witness in the case.

Formerly Civil Code 1895, § 5337; Civil Code 1910, § 5932; Code 1933, § 110-108.

§ 17-9-21. Receipt of verdict

Verdicts shall be received only in open court, in the absence of agreement of the parties.

Formerly Code 1863, § 3486; Code 1868, § 3509; Code 1873, § 3567; Code 1882, § 3567; Civil Code 1895, § 5336; Civil Code 1910, § 5931; Code 1933, § 110-107.

§ 17-9-22. Expression in open court of approval or disapproval of verdict or discharge of jury forbidden

(a) No judge of any court shall either directly or indirectly express in open court his approval or disapproval of the verdict of any jury in any case tried before him, except as provided in subsection (c) of this Code section; nor may any judge discharge any jury upon the ground that the verdict rendered in any case does not meet with his approval.

(b) If any judge of any court either directly or indirectly expresses in open court his approval or disapproval of the verdict of the jury in any case tried before him, he shall be disqualified from presiding in the case in the event a new trial is granted.

(c) Nothing in this Code section shall have the effect of prohibiting a judge of any court from approving or disapproving the verdict of a jury in any case tried before him in hearing a motion for a new trial that comes on before him; but the approval or disapproval on the hearing of a motion for new trial shall be expressed in the formal order of the judge in granting or overruling the motion and not otherwise.

Laws 1918, p. 168, §§ 1, 2.

Formerly Code 1933, §§ 110-201, 110-202.

§ 17-9-23. Commending or complimenting jury forbidden

No judge of any court may commend or compliment a jury during the term of any court for discharging its duty if the commendation or compliment has the effect of approving of a verdict.

Laws 1918, p. 168, § 3.

Formerly Code 1933, § 110-203.

Article 3

Amendment and Impeachment of Verdict

§ 17-9-40. Amendment of verdict after dispersion of jury

A verdict may be amended in mere matter of form after the jury have dispersed; but, after it has been received, recorded, and the jury dispersed, it may not be amended in matter of substance, either by what the jurors say they intended to find or otherwise.

Formerly Code 1863, § 3422; Code 1868, § 3442; Code 1873, § 3492; Code 1882, § 3492; Civil Code 1895, § 5111; Civil Code 1910, § 5695; Code 1933, § 110-111.

§ 17-9-41. Jurors may sustain but not impeach verdict

The affidavits of jurors may be taken to sustain but not to impeach their verdict.

Formerly Civil Code 1895, § 5338; Civil Code 1910, § 5933; Code 1933, § 110-109.

Article 4

Motions in Arrest

§ 17-9-60. Motion in arrest of judgment; notice of motion

All motions to arrest a judgment must be made to the court by which the judgment was rendered, and the opposite party must have reasonable notice of such motions.

Formerly Code 1863, § 3511; Code 1868, § 3534; Code 1873, § 3592; Code 1882, § 3592; Civil Code 1895, § 5367; Civil Code 1910, § 5962; Code 1933, § 110-707.

§ 17-9-61. Grounds and time for motion in arrest

(a) When a judgment has been rendered, either party may move in arrest thereof for any defect not amendable which appears on the face of the record or pleadings.

(b) A motion in arrest of judgment must be made during the term at which the judgment was obtained.

Formerly Code 1863, §§ 3506, 3507; Code 1868, §§ 3529, 3530; Code 1873, §§ 3587, 3588; Code 1882, §§ 3587, 3588; Civil Code 1895, §§ 5362, 5363; Civil Code 1910, §§ 5957, 5958; Code 1933, §§ 110-702, 110-703.

§ 17-9-62. Amendable defects not ground for arrest

A judgment may not be arrested for any defect in the pleadings or record that is aided by verdict or amendable as a matter of form.

Formerly Code 1863, § 3509; Code 1868, § 3532; Code 1873, § 3590; Code 1882, § 3590; Civil Code 1895, § 5365; Civil Code 1910, § 5960; Code 1933, § 110-705.

§ 17-9-63. Motion not granted for matters not affecting real merits of offense charged

No motion in arrest of judgment shall be granted for any matter not affecting the real merits of the offense charged in the indictment or accusation.

Laws 1833, Cobb's 1851 Digest, p. 833.

Formerly Code 1863, § 4517; Code 1868, § 4536; Code 1873, § 4629; Code 1882, § 4629; Penal Code 1895, § 955; Penal Code 1910, § 980; Code 1933, § 27-1601.

CHAPTER 10

SENTENCE AND PUNISHMENT

Article 1

Procedure for Sentencing and Imposition of Punishment

§ 17-10-1. Determinate sentences

(a)(1) Except in cases in which life imprisonment, life without parole, or the death penalty may be imposed, upon a verdict or plea of guilty in any case involving a misdemeanor or felony, and after a presentence hearing, the judge fixing the sentence shall prescribe a determinate sentence for a specific number of months or years which shall be within the minimum and maximum sentences prescribed by law as the punishment for the crime. The judge imposing the sentence is granted power and authority to suspend or probate all or any part of the entire sentence under such rules and regulations as the judge deems proper, including service of a probated sentence in the sentencing options system, as provided by Article 9 of Chapter 8 of Title 42, and including the authority to revoke the suspension or probation when the defendant has violated any of the rules and regulations prescribed by the court, even before the probationary period has begun, subject to the conditions set out in this subsection; provided, however, that such action shall be subject to the provisions of Code Sections 17-10-6.1 and 17-10-6.2.

(2) Probation supervision shall terminate in all cases no later than two years from the commencement of probation supervision unless specially extended or reinstated by the sentencing court upon notice and hearing and for good cause shown; provided, however, in those cases involving the collection of fines, restitution, or other funds, the period of supervision shall remain in effect for so long as any such obligation is outstanding, or until termination of the sentence, whichever first occurs. Probation supervision shall not be required for defendants sentenced to probation while the defendant is in the legal custody of the Department of Corrections or the State Board of Pardons and Paroles.

(3)(A) Any part of a sentence of probation revoked for a violation other than a subsequent commission of any felony, a violation of a special condition, or a misdemeanor offense involving physical violence resulting in bodily injury to an innocent victim which in the opinion of the trial court constitutes a danger to the community or a serious infraction occurring while the defendant is assigned to an alternative probation confinement facility shall be served in a probation detention center, probation boot camp, diversion center, weekend lock up, or confinement in a local jail or detention facility, or other community correctional alternatives available to the court or provided by the Department of Corrections.

(B) A parolee or probationer charged with a misdemeanor involving physical injury or an attempt to commit physical injury or terroristic threats or with a new felony shall not be entitled to bond pending a hearing on the revocation of his or her parole or probation, except by order of a judge of the superior, state, or magistrate court wherein the alleged new offense occurred after a hearing and upon determination of the superior, state, or magistrate court that the parolee or probationer does not constitute a threat to the community; provided, however, that this subparagraph does not authorize state or magistrate court judges to grant bail for a person charged with any offense listed in subsection (a) of Code Section 17-6-1.

(4) In cases of imprisonment followed by probation, the sentence shall specifically provide that the period of probation shall not begin until the defendant has completed service of the confinement portion of the sentence. No revocation of any part of a probated sentence shall be effective while a defendant is in the legal custody of the State Board of Pardons and Paroles.

(5)(A) Where a defendant has been sentenced to probation, the court shall retain jurisdiction throughout the period of the probated sentence as provided for in subsection (g) of Code Section 42-8-34. Without limiting the generality of the foregoing, the court may shorten the period of probation on motion of the defendant or on its own motion, if the court determines that probation is no longer necessary or appropriate for the ends of justice, the protection of society, and the rehabilitation of the defendant. Prior to entering any order for shortening a period of probation, the court shall afford notice to the victim or victims of all sex related offenses or violent offenses resulting in serious bodily injury or death, and, upon request of the victim or victims so notified, shall afford notice and an opportunity for hearing to the defendant and the prosecuting attorney.

(B) The Department of Corrections shall establish a form document which shall include the elements set forth in this Code section concerning notification of victims and shall make copies of such form available to prosecuting attorneys in the state. When requested by the victim, the form document shall be provided to the victim by the prosecuting attorney. The form shall include the address of the probation office having jurisdiction over the case and contain a statement that the victim must maintain a copy of his or her address with the probation office and must notify the office of any change of address in order to maintain eligibility for notification by the Department of Corrections as required in this Code section.

(6)(A) Except as otherwise authorized by law, no court shall modify, suspend, probate, or alter a previously imposed sentence so as to reduce or eliminate a period of incarceration or probation and impose a financial payment which:

(i) Exceeds the statutorily specified maximum fine, plus all penalties, fees, surcharges, and restitution permitted or authorized by law; or

(ii) Is to be made to an entity which is not authorized by law to receive fines, penalties, fees, surcharges, or restitution.

(B) The prohibitions contained in this paragraph shall apply regardless of whether a defendant consents to the modification, suspension, probation, or alteration of such defendant's sentence and the imposition of such payment.

(C) Nothing in this paragraph shall prohibit or prevent a court from requiring, as a condition of suspension, modification, or probation of a sentence in a criminal case involving child abandonment, that the defendant pay all or a portion of child support which is owed to the custodial parent of a child which is the subject of such case.

(b) The judge, in fixing the sentence as prescribed in subsection (a) of this Code section, may make a determination as to whether the person being sentenced should be considered for parole prior to the completion of any requirement otherwise imposed by law relating to the completion of service of any specified time period before parole eligibility. In the event that the judge so determines, he may specify in the sentence that the person is sentenced under this subsection and may provide that the State Board of Pardons and Paroles, acting in its sole discretion, may consider and may parole any person so sentenced at any time prior to the completion of any minimum requirement otherwise imposed by law, rule, or regulation for the service of sentences or portions thereof. The determination allowed in this subsection shall be applicable to first offenders only.

(c) In any case in which a minor defendant who has not achieved a high school diploma or the equivalent is placed under a probated or suspended sentence, the court may require as a condition of probation or suspension of sentence that the defendant pursue a course of study designed to lead to achieving a high school diploma or the equivalent; and, in any case in which such a condition of probation may be imposed, the court shall give express consideration to whether such a condition should be imposed.

(d) In any case involving a misdemeanor or a felony in which the defendant has been punished in whole or in part by a fine, the sentencing judge shall be authorized to allow the defendant to satisfy such fine through community service as defined in paragraph (2) of Code Section 42–8–70. One hour of community service shall equal the dollar amount of one hour of paid labor at the minimum wage under the federal Fair Labor Standards Act of 1938,[1] as now or hereafter amended, unless otherwise specified by the sentencing judge. A defendant shall be required to serve the number of hours in community service which equals the number derived by dividing the amount of the fine by the federal minimum hourly wage or by the amount specified by the sentencing judge. Prior to or subsequent to sentencing, a defendant may request the court that all or any portion of a fine may be satisfied under this subsection.

(e) In any case involving a felony in which the defendant previously appeared before a juvenile court, the records of the dispositions of the defendant as well as any evidence used in any juvenile court hearing shall be available to the district attorney, the defendant, and the superior court judge in determining sentencing as provided in Code Section 15–11–79.1.

(f) Within one year of the date upon which the sentence is imposed, or within 120 days after receipt by the sentencing court of the remittitur upon affirmance of the judgment after direct appeal, whichever is later, the court imposing the sentence has the jurisdiction, power, and authority to correct or reduce the sentence and to suspend or probate all or any part of the sentence imposed. Prior to entering any order correcting, reducing, or modifying any sentence, the court shall afford notice and an opportunity for a hearing to the prosecuting attorney. Any order modifying a sentence which is entered without notice and an opportunity for a hearing as provided in this subsection shall be void. This subsection shall not limit any other jurisdiction granted to the court in this Code section or as provided for in subsection (g) of Code Section 42–8–34.

(g)(1)(A) In sentencing a defendant convicted of a felony to probated confinement, the sentencing judge may make the defendant's participation in a work release program operated by a county a condition of probation, provided that such program is available and the administrator of such program accepts the inmate.

(B) Any defendant accepted into a county work release program shall thereby be transferred into the legal custody of the administrator of said program; likewise, any defendant not accepted shall remain in the legal custody of the Department of Corrections.

(2) Work release status granted by the court may be revoked for cause by the sentencing court in its discretion or may be revoked by the state or local authority operating the work release program for any reason for which work release status would otherwise be revoked.

(3) The provisions of this subsection shall not limit the authority of the commissioner to authorize work release status pursuant to Code Section 42–5–59 or apply to or affect the authority to authorize work release of county prisoners, which shall be as provided for in Code Sections 42–1–4 and 42–1–9 or as otherwise provided by law.

(4) This subsection shall not apply with respect to any violent felony or any offense for which the work release status is specifically prohibited by law, including but not limited to serious violent felonies as specified in Code Section 17–10–6.1.

Laws 1919, p. 387, § 1; Laws 1950, p. 352, § 3; Laws 1964, p. 483, §§ 2, 4; Laws 1974, p. 352, §§ 3, 4; Laws 1981, p. 1024, § 1; Laws 1982, p. 3, § 17; Laws 1984, p. 894, § 2; Laws 1986, p. 842, § 1; Laws 1988, p. 463, § 1; Laws 1991, p. 310, § 1; Laws 1992, p. 3221, § 1; Laws 1993, p. 1654, § 1; Laws 1994, p. 1959, § 9; Laws 1995, p. 1043, § 1; Laws 1996, p. 1257, § 1; Laws 1998, p. 842, § 6; Laws 2000, p. 20, § 7; Laws 2001, p. 94, § 5; Laws 2001, p. 1030, § 1; Laws 2004, Act 595, § 1, eff. July 1, 2004; Laws 2005, Act 19, § 17, eff. April 7, 2005; Laws 2006, Act 571, § 19, eff. July 1, 2006; Laws 2006, Act 739, § 7, eff. July 1, 2006.

Formerly Code 1933, § 27–2502.

[1] 29 U.S.C.A. § 201 et seq.

§ 17–10–1.1. Victim impact form

(a) A prosecuting attorney bringing charges against a defendant shall notify, where practical, the alleged victim or, when the victim is no longer living, a member of the victim's family of his or her right to submit a victim impact form.

(b)(1) A victim impact form shall identify the victim of the offense and the perpetrator.

(2) A victim impact form may itemize any economic loss suffered by the victim as a result of the offense and may:

(A) Identify any physical injury suffered by the victim as a result of the offense along with its seriousness and permanence;

(B) Describe any change in the victim's personal welfare or familial relationships as a result of the offense; and

(C) Contain any other information related to the impact of the offense upon the victim or the victim's family that the victim wishes to include.

(c) The Prosecuting Attorneys' Council of Georgia shall establish forms which are designed to obtain the information specified by subsection (b) of this Code section. The Prosecuting Attorneys' Council of Georgia shall make copies of such form available to prosecuting attorneys in the state. It shall be the duty of the prosecuting attorney or his or her designee to make such forms available to crime victims.

(d) The victim may complete a victim impact form and submit such form to the appropriate prosecuting attorney charged with the prosecution of the case. If the victim is unable to do so because of such victim's mental, emotional, or physical incapacity, or because of such victim's age, the victim's attorney or a family member may complete the victim impact form on behalf of the victim.

(e)(1) If, prior to trial, the defendant engages in discussion with the prosecuting attorney for the purpose of reaching a plea agreement or other pretrial disposition of his or her case, the prosecuting attorney shall, upon the request of the defendant, provide the defendant with a copy of the victim impact form relating to the defendant's case within a reasonable time prior to such discussions.

(2) If the prosecuting attorney intends to present information from a victim impact form to the court at any hearing at which sentencing or a determination of restitution will be considered by the court, the prosecuting attorney shall furnish a copy of the victim impact form to the defendant not less than five days prior to any such hearing. The defendant shall have the right to rebut the information contained in the victim impact form.

(3) The court shall consider the victim impact form that is presented to the court prior to imposing a sentence or making a determination as to the amount of restitution.

(f) If for any reason a victim was not allowed an opportunity to make a written victim impact statement, the victim may submit a victim impact statement to the State Board of Pardons and Paroles in any case prior to consideration of parole.

(g) No sentence shall be invalidated because of failure to comply with the provisions of this Code section. This Code section shall not be construed to create any cause of action or any right of appeal on behalf of any person.

Laws 1985, p. 739, § 1; Laws 1992, p. 2419, § 2; Laws 1993, p. 1660, § 1; Laws 2005, Act 20, § 3, eff. July 1, 2005.

§ 17-10-1.2. Admissibility of certain evidence subsequent to adjudication of guilt

(a)(1) In all cases in which the death penalty may be imposed, subsequent to an adjudication of guilt and in conjunction with the procedures in Code Section 17-10-30, the court may allow evidence from the family of the victim, or such other witness having personal knowledge of the victim's personal characteristics and the emotional impact of the crime on the victim, the victim's family, or the community. Such evidence shall be given in the presence of the defendant and of the jury and shall be subject to cross-examination. The admissibility of such evidence shall be in the sole discretion of the judge and in any event shall be permitted only in such a manner and to such a degree as not to inflame or unduly prejudice the jury.

(2) In all cases other than those in which the death penalty may be imposed, prior to fixing of the sentence as provided for in Code Section 17-10-1 or the imposing of life imprisonment as mandated by law, and before rendering the appropriate sentence, including any order of restitution, the court, within its discretion, may allow evidence from the victim, the family of the victim, or such other witness having personal knowledge of the impact of the crime on the victim, the family of the victim, or community. Such evidence shall be given in the presence of the defendant and shall be subject to cross-examination.

(b) In presenting such evidence, the victim, the family of the victim, or such other witness having personal knowledge of the impact of the crime on the victim, the victim's family, or the community shall, if applicable:

(1) Describe the nature of the offense;

(2) Itemize any economic loss suffered by the victim or the family of the victim, if restitution is sought;

(3) Identify any physical injury suffered by the victim as a result of the offense along with its seriousness and permanence;

(4) Describe any change in the victim's personal welfare or familial relationships as a result of the offense;

(5) Identify any request for psychological services initiated by the victim or the victim's family as a result of the offense; and

(6) Include any other information related to the impact of the offense upon the victim, the victim's family, or the community that the court inquires of.

(c) The court shall allow the defendant the opportunity to cross-examine and rebut the evidence presented of the victim's personal characteristics and the emotional impact of the crime on the victim, the victim's family, or the community, and such cross-examination and rebuttal evidence shall be subject to the same discretion set forth in paragraph (1) of subsection (a) of this Code section.

(d) No sentence shall be invalidated because of failure to comply with the provisions of this Code section. This Code section shall not be construed to create any cause of action or any right of appeal on behalf of any person.

Laws 1985, p. 739, § 1; Laws 1993, p. 1660, § 2.

§ 17–10–2. Presentence hearings in felony cases

(a)(1) Except in cases in which the death penalty or life without parole may be imposed, upon the return of a verdict of "guilty" by the jury in any felony case, the judge shall dismiss the jury and shall conduct a presentence hearing at which the only issue shall be the determination of punishment to be imposed. In the hearing the judge shall hear additional evidence in extenuation, mitigation, and aggravation of punishment, including the record of any prior criminal convictions and pleas of guilty or nolo contendere of the defendant, or the absence of any prior conviction and pleas.

(2) The judge shall also hear argument by the defendant or the defendant's counsel and the prosecuting attorney, as provided by law, regarding the punishment to be imposed. Except in cases where the death penalty may be imposed, the prosecuting attorney shall open and conclude the argument. In cases where the death penalty may be imposed, the prosecuting attorney shall open and the defendant or the defendant's counsel shall conclude the argument.

(3) Upon the conclusion of the evidence and arguments, the judge shall impose the sentence or shall recess the trial for the purpose of taking the sentence to be imposed under advisement. The judge shall fix a sentence within the limits prescribed by law.

(b) In cases in which the death penalty or life without parole may be imposed, the judge, when sitting without a jury, in addition to the procedure set forth in subsection (a) of this Code section, shall follow the procedures provided for in Code Sections 17–10–30 and 17–10–30.1.

(c) In all cases tried by a jury in which the death penalty or life without parole may be imposed, upon a return of a verdict of "guilty" by the jury, the court shall resume the trial and conduct a presentence hearing before the jury. The hearing shall be conducted in the same manner as presentence hearings conducted before the judge as provided for in subsection (a) of this Code section. Upon the conclusion of the evidence and arguments, the judge shall give the jury appropriate instructions, and the jury shall retire to determine whether any mitigating or aggravating circumstances, as defined in Code Section 17–10–30, exist and whether to recommend mercy for the defendant. Upon the findings of the jury, the judge shall fix a sentence within the limits prescribed by law.

(d) If the trial court is reversed on appeal because of error only in the presentence hearing, the new trial which may be ordered shall apply only to the issue of punishment.

Laws 1974, p. 352, § 7; Laws 1990, p. 8, § 17; Laws 1993, p. 1654, § 2; Laws 2005, Act 8, § 11, eff. July 1, 2005.

Formerly Code 1933, § 27–2503.

§ 17–10–3. Misdemeanors, how punished

(a) Except as otherwise provided by law, every crime declared to be a misdemeanor shall be punished as follows:

(1) By a fine not to exceed $1,000.00 or by confinement in the county or other jail, county correctional institution, or such other places as counties may provide for maintenance of county inmates, for a total term not to exceed 12 months, or both;

(2) By confinement under the jurisdiction of the Board of Corrections in a state probation detention center or diversion center pursuant to Code Sections 42–8–35.4 and 42–8–35.5, for a determinate term of months which shall not exceed a total term of 12 months; or

(3) If the crime was committed by an inmate within the confines of a state correctional institution, by confinement under the jurisdiction of the Board of Corrections in a state correctional institution or such other institution as the Department of Corrections may direct for a term which shall not exceed 12 months.

(b) Either the punishment provided in paragraph (1) or (2) of subsection (a) of this Code section, but not both, may be imposed in the discretion of the sentencing judge. Misdemeanor punishment imposed under either paragraph may be subject to suspension or probation. The sentencing courts shall retain jurisdiction to amend, modify, alter, suspend, or probate sentences under paragraph (1) of subsection (a) of this Code section at any time, but in no instance shall any sentence under the paragraph be modified in a manner to place a county inmate under the jurisdiction of the Board of Corrections, except as provided in paragraph (2) of subsection (a) of this Code section.

(c) In all misdemeanor cases in which, upon conviction, a six-month sentence or less is imposed, it is within the authority and discretion of the sentencing judge to allow the sentence to be served on weekends by weekend confinement or during the nonworking hours of the defendant. A weekend shall commence and shall end in the discretion of the sentencing judge, and the nonworking hours of the defendant shall be determined in the discretion of the sentencing judge; provided, however, that the judge shall retain plenary control of the defendant at all times during the sentence period. A weekend term shall be counted as serving two days of the full sentence. Confinement during the nonworking hours of a defendant during any day may be counted as serving a full day of the sentence.

(d) In addition to or instead of any other penalty provided for the punishment of a misdemeanor involving a traffic offense, or punishment of a municipal ordinance involving a traffic offense, with the exception of habitual offenders sentenced under Code Section 17–10–7, a judge may impose any one or more of the following sentences:

(1) Reexamination by the Department of Driver Services when the judge has good cause to believe that the convicted licensed driver is incompetent or otherwise not qualified to be licensed;

(2) Attendance at, and satisfactory completion of, a driver improvement course meeting standards approved by the court;

(3) Within the limits of the authority of the charter powers of a municipality or the punishment prescribed by law in other courts, imprisonment at times specified by the court or release from imprisonment upon such conditions and at such times as may be specified; or

(4) Probation or suspension of all or any part of a penalty upon such terms and conditions as may be prescribed by the judge. The conditions may include driving with no further motor vehicle violations during a specified time unless the driving privileges have been or will be otherwise suspended or revoked by law; reporting periodically to the court or a specified agency; and performing, or refraining from performing, such acts as may be ordered by the judge.

(e) Any sentence imposed under subsection (d) of this Code section shall be reported to the Department of Driver Services as prescribed by law.

(f) The Department of Corrections shall lack jurisdiction to supervise misdemeanor offenders, except when the sentence is made concurrent to a probated felony sentence or when the sentence is accepted pursuant to Code Section 42–9–71. Except as provided in this subsection, the Department of Corrections shall lack jurisdiction to confine misdemeanor offenders.

(g) This Code section will have no effect upon any offender convicted of a misdemeanor offense prior January 1, 2001, and sentenced to confinement under the jurisdiction of the Board of Corrections or to the supervision of the Department of Corrections.

Laws 1865–66, p. 233, § 2; Laws 1878–79, p. 54, § 1; Laws 1895, p. 63, § 2; Laws 1908, p. 1119, § 1; Laws 1956, p. 161, § 4; Laws 1957, p. 477, § 5; Laws 1964, p. 485, § 1; Laws 1970, p. 236, § 10; Laws 1972, p. 600, § 1; Laws 1974, p. 361, § 1; Laws 1974, p. 631, § 1; Laws 1976, p. 210, § 1; Laws 1985, p. 283, § 1; Laws 1992, p. 3221, § 2; Laws 1997, p. 1526, § 1; Laws 2000, p. 1643, § 1; Laws 2001, p. 1030, § 2; Laws 2002, p. 415, § 17; Laws 2005, Act 68, § 7–4, eff. July 1, 2005.

Formerly Code 1863, § 4209; Code 1868, §§ 4245, 4608; Code 1873, §§ 4310, 4705; Code 1882, §§ 4310, 4705; Penal Code 1895, § 1039; Penal Code 1910, § 1065; Code 1933, § 27–2506.

§ 17–10–3.1. Service of sentence by persons convicted of violating Code Section 40–6–391(k)

(a) In any case where a person is sentenced to a period of imprisonment under Code Section 40–6–391 upon conviction for violating subsection (k) of said Code section, it is within the authority and discretion of the sentencing judge in cases involving the first such violation to allow the sentence to be served on weekends by weekend confinement or during the nonworking hours of the defendant. A weekend shall commence and shall end in the discretion of the sentencing judge, and the nonworking hours of the defendant shall be determined in the discretion of the sentencing judge; provided, however, that the judge shall retain plenary control of the defendant at all times during the sentence period. Confinement during the nonworking hours of a defendant during any day may be counted as serving a full day of the sentence.

(b) Any confinement of a person pursuant to a sentence to a period of imprisonment under Code Section 40–6–391 upon conviction for violating subsection (k) of said Code section shall be served in a county jail, provided that for the first such violation such person shall be kept segregated from all offenders other than those confined for violating subsection (k) of Code Section 40–6–391.

Laws 1997, p. 760, § 2; Laws 1999, p. 391, § 4.

§ 17–10–4. Punishment for misdemeanor of a high and aggravated nature

(a) A person who is convicted of a misdemeanor of a high and aggravated nature shall be punished by a fine not to exceed $ 5,000.00 or by confinement in the county or other jail, county correctional institution, or such other places as counties may provide for maintenance of county inmates, for a term not to exceed 12 months, or both; provided, however, that a person convicted of a misdemeanor of a high and aggravated nature which was committed by an inmate within the confines of a state correctional institution and sentenced to confinement as a result of such offense shall be sentenced to confinement under the jurisdiction of the Board of Corrections in a state correctional institution or such other institution as the Department of Corrections may direct for a term which shall not exceed 12 months. In all cases of a conviction of a misdemeanor of a high and aggravated nature, the sentencing court shall retain jurisdiction to amend, modify, alter, suspend, or probate sentences imposed under this Code section at any time; but in no instance shall a sentence imposed under this Code section be modified in such a manner as to increase the amount of fine or the term of confinement.

(b) Notwithstanding any laws to the contrary, a person sentenced for a misdemeanor of a high and aggravated nature may earn no more than four days per month earned time allowance.

Laws 1970, p. 236, § 11; Laws 1985, p. 283, § 1; Laws 1997, p. 1526, § 2; Laws 2000, p. 1111, § 1.

Formerly Code 1933, § 27–2506.1.

§ 17–10–5. Reducible felonies

When a defendant is found guilty of a felony punishable by imprisonment for a maximum term of ten years or less, the judge may, in his discretion, impose punishment as for a misdemeanor.

Laws 1968, p. 1249, § 1.

Formerly Code 1933, § 26–3101.

§ 17–10–6. Review of sentences

(a) In any case, except cases in which the death penalty is imposed or cases involving a serious violent felony as defined in subsection (a) of Code Section 17–10–6.1, in which a sentence of 12 or more years, or several consecutive sentences which total 12 or more years, has been fixed and imposed by a judge, without a jury, the defendant shall have the right to have the sentence or sentences reviewed by a panel of three superior court judges to determine whether the sentence or sentences so imposed are excessively harsh. Consideration shall be given in the review to the nature of the crime for which the defendant has been convicted and to the defendant's prior criminal record. Any defendant seeking a review of such sentence or sentences shall make application therefor within 30 days of the date on which the sentence was imposed by a judge of the superior court or after the remittitur from the Court of Appeals or Supreme Court affirming the conviction is made the judgment of the sentencing court, whichever occurs last. The application shall be filed with the clerk of the superior court in which the sentence was imposed. Upon the filing of an application the clerk shall transmit the same to the three-judge panel created under this Code section within ten days of the date on which the application was filed. For such service, the clerk shall receive the fees prescribed in Code Section 15–6–77 from the funds of the county, except where the clerk is on a salary. It shall be the duty of the judge imposing the sentence and any probation officer to transmit, within ten days of the filing of an application for review of a sentence, a copy of any presentence or postsentence report prepared by the probation officer, including the record of the defendant, to the three-judge panel.

(b) For the purpose of reviewing sentences, as provided by this Code section, there is created a panel of three superior court judges, to be appointed by the superior court judge then serving as president of The Council of Superior Court Judges of Georgia. Judges so appointed shall serve for a term of three months and until their successors are duly appointed and qualified. Judges so appointed shall receive their actual expenses incurred in the performance of their duties on the panel but shall receive no additional compensation. The expenses shall be paid from funds appropriated to, or otherwise available to, the judicial branch of state government. The panel shall be furnished offices, supplies, materials, and secretarial assistance required for the performance of their duties by the state. The panel shall meet at the state capital at such times as may be required for the review of sentences, provided that all applications for review of sentences shall be heard within three months from the date on which they are filed. No judge appointed to a panel shall review a sentence which he has imposed on the trial of the case in the superior court or participate in any such review. If such a case is brought before the panel, the president of The Council of Superior Court Judges of Georgia shall have the authority to appoint an additional superior court judge as a member of the panel for the review of the case.

(c) The three-judge panel provided for by this Code section shall have the authority to review sentences upon application of the defendants in such cases. In the review of the sentences the defendant and the district attorney shall have the right to present written argument relative to the sentence imposed and the harshness or justification thereof. If, in the opinion of the panel, the sentence imposed by the trial judge is too harsh or severe in light of all of the circumstances surrounding the case and the defendant, and in light of the defendant's past history, the panel shall have the authority to issue an order reducing the sentence originally imposed by the trial judge. The panel shall not have the authority, however, to reduce any sentence to probation or to suspend any sentence. The panel shall not be required to file written opinions but shall file a copy of any order or remittitur reducing a sentence with the superior court which originally imposed the sentence.

(d) The reduction of a sentence or the refusal to reduce a sentence by the panel shall not be reviewable. The provisions for review of sentences provided by this Code section shall not be deemed to affect the right to appeal or any practices, procedures, or time limitations relative to appeals to appellate courts. A defendant shall not have the right to file more than one application for a review of a sentence, and any order issued by the panel reducing or refusing to reduce any sentence covered by an application shall be binding on the defendant and the superior court which imposed the sentence.

(e) This Code section shall not apply to cases in which the death penalty is imposed.

(f) This Code section shall not apply to sentences imposed in misdemeanor cases or cases in which a life sentence is imposed for murder.

Laws 1974, p. 352, § 8; Laws 1977, p. 1098, § 6; Laws 1982, p. 1271, §§ 1, 2; Laws 1993, p. 705, § 1; Laws 1994, p. 1959, § 10.

Formerly Code 1933, § 27-2511.1.

§ 17-10-6.1. Sentencing of persons convicted of serious violent felonies

(a) As used in this Code section, the term "serious violent felony" means:

(1) Murder or felony murder, as defined in Code Section 16-5-1;

(2) Armed robbery, as defined in Code Section 16-8-41;

(3) Kidnapping, as defined in Code Section 16-5-40;

(4) Rape, as defined in Code Section 16-6-1;

(5) Aggravated child molestation, as defined in subsection (c) of Code Section 16-6-4, unless subject to the provisions of paragraph (2) of subsection (d) of Code Section 16-6-4;

(6) Aggravated sodomy, as defined in Code Section 16-6-2; or

(7) Aggravated sexual battery, as defined in Code Section 16-6-22.2.

(b)(1) Notwithstanding any other provisions of law to the contrary, any person convicted of the serious violent felony of kidnapping involving a victim who is 14 years of age or older or armed robbery shall be sentenced to a mandatory minimum term of imprisonment of ten years and no portion of the mandatory minimum sentence imposed shall be suspended, stayed, probated, deferred, or withheld by the sentencing court and shall not be reduced by any form of pardon, parole, or commutation of sentence by the State Board of Pardons and Paroles.

(2) Notwithstanding any other provisions of law to the contrary, the sentence of any person convicted of the serious violent felony of:

(A) Kidnapping involving a victim who is less than 14 years of age;

(B) Rape;

(C) Aggravated child molestation, as defined in subsection (c) of Code Section 16-6-4, unless subject to the provisions of paragraph (2) of subsection (d) of Code Section 16-6-4;

(D) Aggravated sodomy, as defined in Code Section 16-6-2; or

(E) Aggravated sexual battery, as defined in Code Section 16-6-22.2

shall, unless sentenced to life imprisonment, be a split sentence which shall include a mandatory minimum term of imprisonment of 25 years, followed by probation for life. No portion of the mandatory minimum sentence imposed shall be suspended, stayed, probated, deferred, or withheld by the sentencing court and shall not be reduced by any form of pardon, parole, or commutation of sentence by the State Board of Pardons and Paroles.

(3) No person convicted of a serious violent felony shall be sentenced as a first offender pursuant to Article 3 of Chapter 8 of Title 42, relating to probation for first offenders, or any other provision of Georgia law relating to the sentencing of first offenders. The State of Georgia shall have the right to appeal any sentence which is imposed by the superior court which does not conform to the provisions of this subsection in the same manner as is provided for other appeals by the state in accordance with Chapter 7 of Title 5, relating to appeals or certiorari by the state.

(c)(1) Except as otherwise provided in subsection (c) of Code Section 42-9-39, for a first conviction of a serious violent felony in which the defendant has been sentenced to life imprisonment, that person shall not be eligible for any form of parole or early release administered by the State Board of Pardons and Paroles until that person has served a minimum of 30 years in prison. The minimum term of imprisonment shall not be reduced by any earned time, early release, work release, leave, or other sentence-reducing measures under programs administered by the Department of Corrections.

(2) For a first conviction of a serious violent felony in which the defendant has been sentenced to death but the sentence of death has been commuted to life imprisonment, that person shall not be eligible for any form of parole or early release administered by the State Board of Pardons and Paroles until that person has served a minimum of 30 years in prison. The minimum term of imprisonment shall not be reduced by any earned time, early release, work release, leave, or other sentence-reducing measures under programs administered by the Department of Corrections.

(3) Any sentence imposed for the first conviction of any serious violent felony other than a sentence of life imprisonment or life without parole or death shall be served in its entirety as imposed by the sentencing court and shall not be reduced by any form of parole or early release administered by the State Board of Pardons and Paroles or by any earned time, early release, work release, leave, or other sentence-reducing measures under programs

administered by the Department of Corrections, the effect of which would be to reduce the period of incarceration ordered by the sentencing court.

(d) For purposes of this Code section, a first conviction of any serious violent felony means that the person has never been convicted of a serious violent felony under the laws of this state or of an offense under the laws of any other state or of the United States, which offense if committed in this state would be a serious violent felony. Conviction of two or more crimes charged on separate counts of one indictment or accusation, or in two or more indictments or accusations consolidated for trial, shall be deemed to be only one conviction.

Laws 1994, p. 1959, § 11; Laws 1998, p. 180, § 2; Laws 2006, Act 571, § 20, eff. July 1, 2006.

§ 17-10-6.2. Sentencing of persons convicted of a sexual offense

(a) As used in this Code section, the term "sexual offense" means:

(1) Aggravated assault with the intent to rape, as defined in Code Section 16-5-21;

(2) False imprisonment, as defined in Code Section 16-5-41, if the victim is not the child of the defendant and the victim is less than 14 years of age;

(3) Sodomy, as defined in Code Section 16-6-2, unless subject to the provisions of subsection (d) of Code Section 16-6-2;

(4) Statutory rape, as defined in Code Section 16-6-3, if the person convicted of the crime is 21 years of age or older;

(5) Child molestation, as defined in subsection (a) of Code Section 16-6-4, unless subject to the provisions of paragraph (2) of subsection (b) of Code Section 16-6-4;

(6) Enticing a child for indecent purposes, as defined in Code Section 16-6-5, unless subject to the provisions of subsection (c) of Code Section 16-6-5;

(7) Sexual assault against persons in custody, as defined in Code Section 16-6-5.1;

(8) Incest, as defined in Code Section 16-6-22;

(9) A second or subsequent conviction for sexual battery, as defined in Code Section 16-6-22.1; or

(10) Sexual exploitation of children, as defined in Code Section 16-12-100.

(b) Except as provided in subsection (c) of this Code section, and notwithstanding any other provisions of law to the contrary, any person convicted of a sexual offense shall be sentenced to a split sentence which shall include the minimum term of imprisonment specified in the Code section applicable to the offense. No portion of the mandatory minimum sentence imposed shall be suspended, stayed, probated, deferred, or withheld by the sentencing court and such sentence shall include, in addition to the mandatory imprisonment, an additional probated sentence of at least one year. No person convicted of a sexual offense shall be sentenced as a first offender pursuant to Article 3 of Chapter 8 of Title 42, relating to probation for first offenders, or any other provision of Georgia law relating to the sentencing of first offenders.

(c)(1) In the court's discretion, the court may deviate from the mandatory minimum sentence as set forth in subsection (b) of this Code section, or any portion thereof, provided that:

(A) The defendant has no prior conviction of an offense prohibited by Chapter 6 of Title 16 or Part 2 of Article 3 of Chapter 12 of Title 16, nor a prior conviction for any offense under federal law or the laws of another state or territory of the United States which consists of the same or similar elements of offenses prohibited by Chapter 6 of Title 16 or Part 2 of Article 3 of Chapter 12 of Title 16;

(B) The defendant did not use a deadly weapon or any object, device, or instrument which when used offensively against a person would be likely to or actually did result in serious bodily injury during the commission of the offense;

(C) The court has not found evidence of a relevant similar transaction;

(D) The victim did not suffer any intentional physical harm during the commission of the offense;

(E) The offense did not involve the transportation of the victim; and

(F) The victim was not physically restrained during the commission of the offense.

(2) If the court deviates in sentencing pursuant to this subsection, the judge shall issue a written order setting forth the judge's reasons. Any such order shall be appealable by the defendant pursuant to Code Section 5-6-34, or by the State of Georgia pursuant to Code Section 5-7-1.

(d) If the court imposes a probated sentence, the defendant shall submit to review by the Sexual Offender Registration Review Board for purposes of risk assessment classification within ten days of being sentenced and shall otherwise comply with Article 2 of Chapter 1 of Title 42.

Laws 2006, Act 571, § 21, eff. July 1, 2006.

§ 17-10-7. Repeat offenders

(a) Except as otherwise provided in subsection (b) of this Code section, any person convicted of a felony offense in this state or having been convicted under the laws of any other state or of the United States of a crime which if committed within this state would be a felony and sentenced to confinement in a penal institution, who shall afterwards commit a felony punishable by confinement in a penal institution, shall be sentenced to undergo the longest period of time prescribed for the punishment of the subsequent offense of which he or she stands convicted, provided that, unless otherwise provided by law, the trial judge may, in his or her discretion, probate or suspend the maximum sentence prescribed for the offense.

(b)(1) As used in this subsection, the term "serious violent felony" means a serious violent felony as defined in subsection (a) of Code Section 17–10–6.1.

(2) Any person who has been convicted of a serious violent felony in this state or who has been convicted under the laws of any other state or of the United States of a crime which if committed in this state would be a serious violent felony and who after such first conviction subsequently commits and is convicted of a serious violent felony for which such person is not sentenced to death shall be sentenced to imprisonment for life without parole. Any such sentence of life without parole shall not be suspended, stayed, probated, deferred, or withheld, and any such person sentenced pursuant to this paragraph shall not be eligible for any form of pardon, parole, or early release administered by the State Board of Pardons and Paroles or for any earned time, early release, work release, leave, or any other sentence-reducing measures under programs administered by the Department of Corrections, the effect of which would be to reduce the sentence of life imprisonment without possibility of parole, except as may be authorized by any existing or future provisions of the Constitution.

(c) Except as otherwise provided in subsection (b) of this Code section, any person who, after having been convicted under the laws of this state for three felonies or having been convicted under the laws of any other state or of the United States of three crimes which if committed within this state would be felonies, commits a felony within this state other than a capital felony must, upon conviction for such fourth offense or for subsequent offenses, serve the maximum time provided in the sentence of the judge based upon such conviction and shall not be eligible for parole until the maximum sentence has been served.

(d) For the purpose of this Code section, conviction of two or more crimes charged on separate counts of one indictment or accusation, or in two or more indictments or accusations consolidated for trial, shall be deemed to be only one conviction.

(e) This Code section is supplemental to other provisions relating to recidivous offenders.

Laws 1833, Cobb's 1851 Digest, p. 840; Laws 1953, Nov.-Dec. Sess., p. 289, § 1; Laws 1974, p. 352, § 5; Laws 1983, p. 3, § 14; Laws 1984, p. 760, § 2; Laws 1994, p. 1959, § 12.

Formerly Code 1863, § 4562; Code 1868, § 4582; Code 1873, § 4676; Code 1882, § 4676; Penal Code 1895, § 1042; Penal Code 1910, § 1068; Code 1933, § 27–2511.

§ 17–10–8. Payment of fine as condition precedent to probation in felony cases

In any case where the judge may, by any law so authorizing, place on probation a person convicted of a felony, the judge may in his discretion impose a fine on the person so convicted as a condition to such probation. The fine shall not exceed $100,000.00 or the amount of the maximum fine which may be imposed for conviction of such a felony, whichever is greater. In any case where probation is revoked, the defendant shall not be entitled to any rebate or refund of any part of the fine so paid.

Laws 1957, p. 477, § 1; Laws 1964, p. 496, § 1; Laws 1979, p. 848, § 1; Laws 1990, p. 1408, § 1.

§ 17–10–8.1. Payment of legal defense application fee as condition of probation

In any case in which a defendant receives legal defense services pursuant to Chapter 12 of Title 17 where the defendant has not paid the application fee required by Code Section 15–21A–6 and the court has not waived such fee at the time of sentencing, the court shall impose such fee as a condition of probation.

Laws 2006, Act 749, § 2, eff. May 3, 2006.

§ 17–10–9. Time from which sentences run

In the imposition of sentence for violation of the penal laws, it shall be the duty of the judge to specify that the term of service under the sentence shall be computed from the date of sentence if the defendant is confined in jail or otherwise incarcerated and has no appeal or motion for new trial pending. In cases which are appealed to the Georgia Court of Appeals or the Georgia Supreme Court for reversal of the conviction, the sentence shall be computed from the date the remittitur of the appellate court is made the judgment of the court in which the conviction is had, provided the defendant is not at liberty under bond but is incarcerated or in custody of the sheriff of the county where convicted. If a defendant has been convicted and sentenced but, because of his failure or inability to post bond or bail for any reason, he has been incarcerated pending the prosecution of an appeal to any court, the time of the original imposition of his sentence until the time when the remittitur of the appellate court is made the judgment of the court in which the conviction is had shall be counted as time spent under sentence for all purposes.

Laws 1931, p. 165, § 1; Laws 1965, p. 230, § 1.

Formerly Code 1933, § 27–2505.

§ 17–10–9.1. Release of defendants

(a) When a defendant who pleads nolo contendere or guilty or is convicted of an offense against the laws of this state other than:

(1) Treason;

(2) Murder;

(3) Rape;

(4) Aggravated sodomy;

(5) Armed robbery;

(6) Aircraft hijacking and hijacking of a motor vehicle;

(7) Aggravated child molestation;

(8) Manufacturing, distributing, delivering, dispensing, administering, selling, or possessing with intent to distribute any controlled substance classified under Code Section 16–13–25 as Schedule I or under Code Section 16–13–26 as Schedule II;

(9) Violating Code Section 16–13–31, relating to trafficking in cocaine or marijuana;

(10) Kidnapping, arson, or burglary if the person, at the time such person was charged, has previously been convicted of, was on probation or parole with respect to, or was on bail for kidnapping, arson, aggravated assault, burglary, or one or more of the offenses listed in paragraphs (1) through (9) of this subsection;

(11) Child molestation;

(12) Robbery;

(13) Aggravated assault; or

(14) Voluntary manslaughter

is sentenced to a term of confinement in a county jail or a correctional institution operated by or under the jurisdiction and supervision of the Department of Corrections, the sentencing judge may release the defendant pending the defendant's surrendering to a county jail or to a correctional institution designated by the Department of Corrections as authorized in this Code section. The sentencing court may release the defendant on bond or may release the defendant on the defendant's personal recognizance. This Code section shall not be construed to limit the court's authority in prescribing conditions of probation.

(b) Any defendant who has been released on bond and who has complied with all of the conditions of the bond and any other defendant who, in the opinion of the sentencing judge, is deemed worthy of the procedure to surrender voluntarily, may be eligible to participate in the program. However, the sentencing judge shall be the sole and final arbiter concerning eligibility and the defendant shall have no right to appeal such decision.

(c) When a defendant submits a request to the sentencing judge to be allowed to surrender voluntarily to a county jail or a correctional facility, the judge may consider the request and if, taking into the consideration the crime for which the defendant is being sentenced, the history of the defendant, and any other factors which may aid in the decision, the judge determines that the granting of the request will pose no threat to society, the defendant shall be remanded to the supervision of a probation officer by the judge and ordered to surrender voluntarily to a county jail designated by the court or to a correctional institution as thereafter designated by the Department of Corrections. The surrender date shall be a date thereafter specified as provided in subsection (d) of this Code section. The sentence of any defendant who is released pursuant to this Code section shall not begin to run until such person surrenders to the facility designated by the court or by the department, provided that such person will receive credit toward his sentence for time spent in confinement awaiting trial as provided in Code Section 17–10–11.

(d) In the event the defendant is ordered to surrender voluntarily to a county jail, the court shall designate the date on which the defendant shall surrender, which date shall not be more than 120 days after the date of conviction. When the sentencing judge issues an order requiring a defendant to surrender voluntarily to a correctional institution, the Department of Corrections shall authorize the commitment and designate the correctional institution to which the defendant shall report and the date on which the defendant is to report, which date shall not be more than 120 days after the date of conviction. Upon such designation, the department shall notify the supervising probation officer who shall notify the defendant accordingly. Subsistence and transportation expenses en route to the correctional institution shall be borne by the defendant.

(e) The provisions of this Code section shall not apply to any defendant convicted of a capital felony.

(f) If the defendant fails to surrender voluntarily as directed and required, the defendant may be charged with the offense of bail jumping pursuant to subsection (a) of Code Section 16–10–51 or the offense of escape pursuant to paragraph (3) of subsection (a) of Code Section 16–10–52 and, if convicted of such crimes, shall be punished as provided by law; or may be cited for contempt of court by the sentencing judge and, if convicted of contempt, the defendant shall be punished as provided in Code Section 15–6–8.

(g) The Department of Corrections is authorized and directed to promulgate such rules and regulations as may be necessary to effectuate the purposes of this Code section.

Laws 1989, p. 607, § 1; Laws 1994, p. 1625, § 6.

§ 17–10–10. Sentences, whether concurrent or successive

(a) Where at one term of court a person is convicted on more than one indictment or accusation, or on more than one count thereof, and sentenced to imprisonment, the sentences shall be served concurrently unless otherwise expressly provided therein.

(b) Where a person is convicted on more than one indictment or accusation at separate terms of court, or in different courts, and sentenced to imprisonment, the sentences shall be served concurrently, one with the other, unless otherwise expressly provided therein.

(c) This Code section shall apply alike to felony and misdemeanor offenses.

(d) This Code section shall govern and shall be followed by the Department of Corrections in the computation of time that sentences shall run.

Laws 1833, Cobb's 1851 Digest, p. 836; Laws 1956, p. 161, § 3; Laws 1964, p. 494, §§ 1, 2; Laws 1985, p. 283, § 1.

Formerly Code 1863, § 4539; Code 1868, § 4559; Code 1873, § 4653; Code 1882, § 4653; Penal Code 1895, § 1041; Penal Code 1910, § 1067; Code 1933, § 27-2510.

§ 17-10-11. Credit for time spent awaiting trial or resulting from court order applied to sentence and parole

(a) Each person convicted of a crime in this state shall be given full credit for each day spent in confinement awaiting trial and for each day spent in confinement, in connection with and resulting from a court order entered in the criminal proceedings for which sentence was imposed, in any institution or facility for treatment or examination of a physical or mental disability. The credit or credits shall be applied toward the convicted person's sentence and shall also be considered by parole authorities in determining the eligibility of the person for parole.

(b) This Code section applies to sentences for all crimes, whether classified as violations, misdemeanors, or felonies, and to all courts having criminal jurisdiction located within the boundaries of this state, except juvenile courts.

Laws 1970, p. 692, §§ 1, 2; Laws 1972, p. 742, § 1.

§ 17-10-12. Affidavit of custodian specifying number of days spent in custody

(a) The custodian of the defendant shall be required to make an affidavit specifying the number of days which the defendant has spent in confinement in his custody and furnish the affidavit to the clerk of the court within five days after sentence is imposed if the defendant is convicted. The affidavit of the custodian of the defendant shall be made a part of the official record of the trial.

(b) The clerk of the court shall transmit a copy of the custodian's affidavit to the Department of Corrections when the defendant has been sentenced to the custody of the department. The Department of Corrections shall give the defendant credit for the number of days spent in confinement prior to conviction and sentence, as reflected in the custodian's affidavit, before forwarding the record to the State Board of Pardons and Paroles.

(c) Where the defendant has been sentenced to the custody of an official other than the commissioner of corrections, the clerk of the court shall transmit the custodian's affidavit to the proper authorities who shall give the defendant credit for the number of days spent in custody prior to conviction and sentence.

(d) For service under this Code section, the clerk shall receive the fee prescribed in Code Section 15-6-77 from the funds of the county, except where the clerk is on a salary.

Laws 1970, p. 692, §§ 3, 4; Laws 1972, p. 742, §§ 2, 3; Laws 1977, p. 1098, § 7; Laws 1985, p. 283, § 1; Laws 1990, p. 8, § 17.

§ 17-10-13. Conviction in court having jurisdiction must precede punishment

The punishments prescribed by this Code shall be assessed only after a legal adjudication of guilt in a court having jurisdiction.

Formerly Penal Code 1895, § 20; Penal Code 1910, § 20; Code 1933, § 27-2509.

§ 17-10-14. Sentences of persons under the age of 17 sentenced as adults

(a) Notwithstanding any other provisions of this article and except as otherwise provided in subsections (b) and (c) of this Code section, in any case where a person under the age of 17 years is convicted of a felony and sentenced as an adult to life imprisonment or to a certain term of imprisonment, such person shall be committed to the Department of Juvenile Justice to serve such sentence in a detention center of such department until such person is 17 years of age at which time such person shall be transferred to the Department of Corrections to serve the remainder of the sentence. This Code section shall apply to any person convicted on or after July 1, 1987, and to any person convicted prior to such date who has not been committed to an institution operated by the Department of Corrections.

(b) If a child is transferred to superior court according to subsection (b) of Code Section 15-11-30.2 and convicted of aggravated assault as defined in Chapter 5 of Title 16, the court may sentence such child to the Department of Corrections. Such child shall be housed in a designated youth confinement unit until such person is 17 years of age, at which time such person may be housed in any other unit designated by the Department of Corrections.

(c) In any case where a child 13 to 17 years of age is convicted of a felony provided under subparagraph (b)(2)(A) of Code Section 15-11-28, such child shall be committed to the custody of the Department of Corrections and shall be housed in a designated youth confinement unit until such person is 17 years of age, at which time such person may be housed in any other unit designated by the Department of Corrections.

Laws 1987, p. 1335, § 1; Laws 1990, p. 1930, § 7; Laws 1992, p. 1983, § 19; Laws 1994, p. 1012, § 27; Laws 1997, p. 1453, § 1; Laws 2000, p. 20, § 8.

§ 17-10-15. HIV testing upon arrest, verdict, or plea of guilty or nolo contendere to AIDS transmitting crime; failure or refusal to submit to test; test results

(a) Any term used in this Code section and defined in Code Section 31-22-9.1 shall have the meaning provided for such term in Code Section 31-22-9.1.

(b) A victim or the parent or legal guardian of a minor or incompetent victim of a sexual offense as defined in Code Section 31-22-9.1 or other crime which involves significant exposure as defined by subsection (g) of this Code section may request that the agency responsible for prosecuting the alleged offense request that the person arrested for such offense submit to a test for the human immunodeficiency virus and consent to the release of the test results to the victim. If the person so arrested declines to submit to such a test, the judge of the superior court in which the criminal charge is pending, upon a showing of probable cause that the person arrested for the offense committed the alleged crime and that significant exposure occurred, may order the test to be performed in compliance with the rules adopted by the Department of Human Resources. The cost of the test shall be borne by the victim or by the arrested person, in the discretion of the court.

(c) Upon a verdict or plea of guilty or a plea of nolo contendere to any AIDS transmitting crime, the court in which that verdict is returned or plea entered shall require the defendant in such case to submit to an HIV test within 45 days following the date of such verdict or plea. The clerk of the court in such case shall mail, within three days following the date of that verdict or plea, a copy of that verdict or plea to the Department of Human Resources.

(d) The Department of Human Resources, within 30 days following receipt of the court's order under subsection (b) of this Code section or within 30 days following receipt of the copy of the verdict or plea under subsection (c) of this Code section, shall arrange for the HIV test for the person required to submit thereto.

(e) Any person required under this Code section to submit to the HIV test who fails or refuses to submit to the test arranged pursuant to subsection (d) of this Code section shall be subject to such measures deemed necessary by the court in which the order was entered, verdict was returned, or plea was entered to require involuntary submission to the HIV test, and submission thereto may also be made a condition of suspending or probating any part of that person's sentence for the AIDS transmitting crime.

(f) If a person is required by this Code section to submit to an HIV test and is thereby determined to be infected with HIV, that determination and the name of the person shall be reported to:

(1) The Department of Human Resources, which shall disclose the name of the person as necessary to provide counseling to each victim of that person's AIDS transmitting crime if that crime is other than one specified in subparagraph (a)(3)(J) of Code Section 31-22-9.1 or to any parent or guardian of any such victim who is a minor or incompetent person;

(2) The court which ordered the HIV test, which court shall make that report a part of that person's criminal record. That report shall be sealed by the court; and

(3) The officer in charge of any penal institution or other facility in which the person has been confined by order or sentence of the court for purposes of enabling that officer to confine the person separately from those not infected with HIV.

(g) For the purpose of subsection (b) of this Code section, "significant exposure" means contact of the victim's ruptured or broken skin or mucous membranes with the blood or body fluids of the person arrested for such offense, other than tears, saliva, or perspiration, of a magnitude that the Centers for Disease Control have epidemiologically demonstrated can result in transmission of the human immunodeficiency virus.

(h) The state may not use the fact that a medical procedure or test was performed on a person under this Code section or use the results of the procedure or test in any criminal proceeding arising out of the alleged offense.

Laws 1988, p. 1799, § 4; Laws 1991, p. 974, § 1.

§ 17-10-16. Sentence of death, life imprisonment without parole, or life imprisonment; ineligibility for parole, work release, or leave programs

(a) Notwithstanding any other provision of law, a person who is convicted of an offense committed after May 1, 1993, for which the death penalty may be imposed under the laws of this state may be sentenced to death, imprisonment for life without parole, or life imprisonment as provided in Article 2 of this chapter.

(b) Notwithstanding any other provision of law, any person who is convicted of an offense for which the death penalty may be imposed and who is sentenced to imprisonment for life without parole shall not be eligible for any form of parole during such person's natural life unless the State Board of Pardons and

Paroles or a court of this state shall, after notice and public hearing, determine that such person was innocent of the offense for which the sentence of imprisonment for life without parole was imposed. Such person shall not be eligible for any work release program, leave, or any other program administered by the Department of Corrections the effect of which would be to reduce the term of actual imprisonment to which such person was sentenced.

Laws 1993, p. 1654, § 3.

§ 17-10-17. Enhanced sentence where defendant intentionally selected victim or property as object of offense because of bias or prejudice

(a) Subject to the notice requirement provided in Code Section 17-10-18 and in enhancement of the penalty imposed, if the trier of fact determines beyond a reasonable doubt that the defendant intentionally selected any victim or any property of the victim as the object of the offense because of bias or prejudice, the judge imposing sentence shall:

(1) If the offense for which the defendant was convicted is a misdemeanor, increase the sentence and the fine normally imposed by the court through court policy or voluntary sentencing guidelines by 50 percent up to the maximum authorized by law;

(2) If the offense for which the defendant was convicted is a misdemeanor of a high and aggravated nature, increase the sentence and fine normally imposed by the court through court policy or voluntary sentencing guidelines by 50 percent up to the maximum authorized by law; or

(3) If the offense for which the defendant was convicted is a felony, increase the sentence normally imposed by the court through court policy or voluntary sentencing guidelines by up to five years, not to exceed the maximum authorized by law.

(b) The judge shall state when the judge imposes the sentence the amount of the increase of the sentence based on the application of subsection (a) of this Code section.

(c) Any person convicted of a felony and given an enhanced sentence under this Code section shall not be eligible for any form of parole or early release until such person has served at least 90 percent of the sentence imposed by the sentencing court.

Laws 2000, p. 224, § 1.

Validity

This section has been held unconstitutional in the case of Botts v. State, 2004, 278 Ga. 538, 604 S.E.2d 512.

§ 17-10-18. Notice to defendant of intention to seek enhanced sentence

At any time after the filing of an indictment or accusation but not later than the arraignment, the state shall notify the defendant of its intention to seek the enhanced penalty or penalties authorized by Code Section 17-10-17. The notice shall be in writing and shall allege the specific factor or factors authorizing an enhanced sentence in the case pursuant to Code Section 17-10-17.

Laws 2000, p. 224, § 1.

§ 17-10-19. Procedure for imposing enhanced sentence

(a) In a case where notice has been given pursuant to Code Section 17-10-18, the trier of fact shall initially determine the defendant's guilt on the charge or charges. If the trier of fact finds the defendant guilty of such charge or charges, the trial shall immediately be recommenced to receive evidence as is relevant to determine whether the defendant intentionally selected the victim or the property of the victim as the object of the offense as set forth in the notice given pursuant to Code Section 17-10-18.

(b) If the trier of fact determines beyond a reasonable doubt that the defendant so acted, the judge shall enhance the sentence imposed in accordance with the provisions of Code Section 17-10-17.

Laws 2000, p. 224, § 1.

§ 17-10-20. Fine or restitution as part of sentence

(a) In any case in which a fine or restitution is imposed as part of the sentence, such fine and restitution shall constitute a judgment against the defendant. Upon the request of the prosecuting attorney, it shall be the duty of the clerk of the sentencing court to issue a writ of fieri facias thereon and enter it on the general execution docket of the superior court of the county in which such sentence was imposed. Such fieri facias may also be entered on the general execution docket in any county in which the defendant owns real property.

(b) If, in imposing sentence, the court sets a time certain for such fine or restitution to be paid in full, no execution shall issue upon the writ of fieri facias against the property of the defendant until such time as the time set by the court for payment of the fine or restitution shall have expired.

(c) If the fine or restitution is not paid in full, such judgment may be enforced by instituting any procedure for execution upon the writ of fieri facias through levy, foreclosure, garnishment, and all other actions provided for the enforcement of judgments in the State of Georgia and in other states and foreign nations where such judgment is afforded full faith and credit under the Uniform Foreign Money Judgments Act or domestication thereof.

(d) If the fine is not paid in full by the expiration of the time set by the court for payment of the fine, the governing authority of the county or municipality entitled to such fine may institute procedures to enforce such judgment as provided by subsection (c) of this Code section.

(e) If the restitution is not paid in full by the expiration of the time set by the court for payment of the restitution, the prosecuting attorney or the victim entitled to receive such restitution may institute procedures to enforce such judgment as provided by subsection (c) of this Code section.

(f) Notwithstanding the provisions of Code Section 9-12-60, a judgment entered on the general execution docket pursuant to this Code section shall not become dormant during any period when the defendant is incarcerated and for seven years thereafter. Such judgment shall be subject to revival in the same manner as provided for dormant judgments under Code Section 9-12-60.

(g) No fees, costs, or other charges authorized by law in civil cases shall be charged by a clerk of superior court for entering a judgment arising out of a criminal case on the general execution docket or for any action brought by the state to enforce such judgment.

(h) The provisions of this Code section shall be supplemental to any other provision of law applicable to the collection of fines or restitution in criminal cases.

Laws 2005, Act 20, § 4, eff. July 1, 2005.

Article 2

Death Penalty Generally

§ 17-10-30. Mitigating and aggravating circumstances; death penalty

(a) The death penalty may be imposed for the offenses of aircraft hijacking or treason in any case.

(b) In all cases of other offenses for which the death penalty may be authorized, the judge shall consider, or he shall include in his instructions to the jury for it to consider, any mitigating circumstances or aggravating circumstances otherwise authorized by law and any of the following statutory aggravating circumstances which may be supported by the evidence:

(1) The offense of murder, rape, armed robbery, or kidnapping was committed by a person with a prior record of conviction for a capital felony;

(2) The offense of murder, rape, armed robbery, or kidnapping was committed while the offender was engaged in the commission of another capital felony or aggravated battery, or the offense of murder was committed while the offender was engaged in the commission of burglary or arson in the first degree;

(3) The offender, by his act of murder, armed robbery, or kidnapping, knowingly created a great risk of death to more than one person in a public place by means of a weapon or device which would normally be hazardous to the lives of more than one person;

(4) The offender committed the offense of murder for himself or another, for the purpose of receiving money or any other thing of monetary value;

(5) The murder of a judicial officer, former judicial officer, district attorney or solicitor-general, or former district attorney, solicitor, or solicitor-general was committed during or because of the exercise of his or her official duties;

(6) The offender caused or directed another to commit murder or committed murder as an agent or employee of another person;

(7) The offense of murder, rape, armed robbery, or kidnapping was outrageously or wantonly vile, horrible, or inhuman in that it involved torture, depravity of mind, or an aggravated battery to the victim;

(8) The offense of murder was committed against any peace officer, corrections employee, or firefighter while engaged in the performance of his official duties;

(9) The offense of murder was committed by a person in, or who has escaped from, the lawful custody of a peace officer or place of lawful confinement;

(10) The murder was committed for the purpose of avoiding, interfering with, or preventing a lawful arrest or custody in a place of lawful confinement, of himself or another; or

(11) The offense of murder, rape, or kidnapping was committed by a person previously convicted of rape, aggravated sodomy, aggravated child molestation, or aggravated sexual battery.

(c) The statutory instructions as determined by the trial judge to be warranted by the evidence shall be given in charge and in writing to the jury for its deliberation. The jury, if its verdict is a recommendation of death, shall designate in writing, signed by the foreman of the jury, the aggravating circumstance or circumstances which it found beyond a reasonable doubt. In nonjury cases the judge shall make such designation. Except in cases of treason or aircraft hijacking, unless at least one of the statutory aggravating circumstances enumerated in subsection (b) of this Code section is so found, the death penalty shall not be imposed.

Laws 1973, p. 159, § 3; Laws 1996, p. 748, § 15; Laws 2002, p. 660, § 4; Laws 2002, p. 1259, § 11; Laws 2006, Act 571, § 22, eff. July 1, 2006.

Formerly Code 1933, § 27-2534.1.

§ 17-10-30.1. Mitigating and aggravating circumstances; sentence of life imprisonment without parole

(a) Imprisonment for life without parole can be imposed in any murder case in which there is found by the court or jury one or more statutory aggravating circumstances as defined by Code Section 17-10-30.

(b) In all cases for which life without parole may be authorized, the judge shall consider, or shall include in the judge's instructions to the jury for it to consider, any mitigating circumstances or any of the statutory aggravating circumstances specified by Code Section 17-10-30 which may be supported by the evidence.

(c) The statutory instructions as determined by the trial judge to be warranted by the evidence shall be given in charge and in writing to the jury for its deliberation. The jury, if its verdict is a recommendation of life without parole, shall designate in writing, signed by the foreman of the jury, the statutory aggravating circumstance or circumstances which it found beyond a reasonable doubt. In nonjury cases the judge shall make such designation. Unless at least one of the statutory aggravating circumstances enumerated in Code Section 17-10-30 is so found, life without parole shall not be imposed.

Laws 1993, p. 1654, § 4.

§ 17-10-31. Capital felonies; jury verdict and sentence

Where, upon a trial by jury, a person is convicted of an offense which may be punishable by death, a sentence of death shall not be imposed unless the jury verdict includes a finding of at least one statutory aggravating circumstance and a recommendation that such sentence be imposed. Where a statutory aggravating circumstance is found and a recommendation of death is made, the court shall sentence the defendant to death. Where a sentence of death is not recommended by the jury, the court shall sentence the defendant to imprisonment as provided by law. Unless the jury trying the case makes a finding of at least one statutory aggravating circumstance and recommends the death sentence in its verdict, the court shall not sentence the defendant to death, provided that no such finding of statutory aggravating circumstance shall be necessary in offenses of treason or aircraft hijacking. This Code section shall not affect a sentence when the case is tried without a jury or when the judge accepts a plea of guilty.

Laws 1968, p. 1249, § 1; Laws 1969, p. 809, § 1; Laws 1973, p. 159, § 7.

Formerly Code 1933, § 26-3102.

§ 17-10-31.1. Murder conviction; sentence of life imprisonment without parole

(a) Where, upon a trial by jury, a person is convicted of murder, a sentence of death or life without parole shall not be imposed unless the jury verdict includes a finding of at least one statutory aggravating circumstance and a recommendation that such sentence be imposed.

(b) Where a statutory aggravating circumstance is found and a recommendation of life without parole is made, the court shall sentence the defendant to imprisonment for life without parole as provided in Code Section 17-10-16.

(c) Where a jury has been impaneled to determine sentence and the jury has unanimously found the existence of at least one statutory aggravating circumstance but is unable to reach a unanimous verdict as to sentence, the judge shall dismiss the jury and shall impose a sentence of either life imprisonment or imprisonment for life without parole. In imposing sentence, the judge may sentence the defendant to imprisonment for life without parole only if the court finds beyond a reasonable doubt that the defendant committed at least one statutory aggravating circumstance and the trial court has been informed by the jury foreman that upon their last vote, a majority of the jurors cast their vote for a sentence of death or for a sentence of life imprisonment without parole; provided, however, that the trial judge may impose a sentence of life imprisonment as provided by law.

(d) Notwithstanding any other provision of law, during the sentencing phase before a jury, counsel for the state and the accused may present argument and the trial judge may instruct the jury:

(1) That "life without parole" means that the defendant shall be incarcerated for the remainder of his or her natural life and shall not be eligible for parole unless such person is subsequently adjudicated to be innocent of the offense for which he or she was sentenced; and

(2) That "life imprisonment" means that the defendant will be incarcerated for the remainder of his

or her natural life but will be eligible for parole during the term of such sentence.

Laws 1993, p. 1654, § 5.

§ 17-10-32. Sentence of life imprisonment or lesser punishment on plea of guilty to an offense punishable by death

Any person who has been indicted for an offense punishable by death may enter a plea of guilty at any time after his indictment, and the judge of the superior court having jurisdiction may, in his discretion, sentence the person to life imprisonment or to any other punishment authorized by law for the offense named in the indictment; provided, however, that the judge must find one of the statutory aggravating circumstances provided in Code Section 17-10-30 before imposing the death penalty, except in cases of treason or aircraft hijacking.

Laws 1956, p. 737, § 1; Laws 1973, p. 159, § 8.

§ 17-10-32.1. Sentence of life imprisonment or lesser punishment on plea of guilty to an offense punishable by death or life without parole

(a) Subject to the provisions of subsection (b) of this Code section, any person who has been indicted for an offense for which the death penalty or life without parole may be imposed may enter a plea of guilty at any time after indictment, and the judge of the superior court having jurisdiction may, in the judge's discretion, sentence the person to life imprisonment or to any other punishment authorized by law for the offense named in the indictment.

(b) Unless the district attorney has given notice that the state intends to seek the death penalty pursuant to the Uniform Rules of the Superior Courts, the judge shall sentence the defendant to life imprisonment. In cases where such notice has been given, the judge may sentence the defendant to death or life without parole only if the judge finds beyond a reasonable doubt the existence of at least one statutory aggravating circumstance as provided in Code Section 17-10-30.

Laws 1993, p. 1654, § 6.

§ 17-10-33. Sentence of death; copy of sentence; time and mode of conveying prisoner to penitentiary; expenses

Upon a judgment of death made by a judge, it shall be the duty of the judge to sentence the defendant to death and to indicate the sentence in writing, which writing shall be filed with the papers in the case against the defendant. A certified copy of the sentence shall be sent by the clerk of the court in which the sentence is pronounced to the defendant's attorney of record, to the Attorney General, and to the superintendent of the state correctional institution where the execution is to take place, not less than ten days prior to the time fixed in the sentence of the court for the execution of the defendant. In all cases it shall be the duty of the sheriff of the county in which the defendant is sentenced, together with one deputy or more if in the sheriff's judgment it is necessary, and provided that in all cases the number of guards shall be approved by the trial judge or, if the trial judge is not available, by the judge of the probate court of the county in which the defendant is sentenced, to convey the defendant to the appropriate state correctional institution, not more than 20 days nor less than two days prior to the time fixed in the judgment for the execution of the defendant, unless otherwise directed by the Governor or unless a stay of execution has been caused by an appeal, granting of a new trial, or other order of a court of competent jurisdiction. The expense for transporting the defendant to the state correctional institution for the purpose of execution of the death sentence shall be paid by the county governing authority of the county in which the defendant was convicted, out of any funds on hand in the treasury of the county.

Laws 1924, p. 195, § 3; Laws 1973, p. 159, § 9; Laws 1983, p. 665, § 1; Laws 2000, p. 947, § 2.

Formerly Code 1933, § 27-2514.

§ 17-10-34. Sentence to specify time period for execution; pregnant females

When a person is sentenced to the punishment of death, the court shall specify the time period for the execution in the sentence. The time period for the execution fixed by the court shall be seven days in duration and shall commence at noon on a specified date and shall end at noon on a specified date. The time period shall commence not less than 20 days nor more than 60 days from the date of sentencing. However, if the person is a female who is pregnant at the time of sentencing, the court shall appoint a time period for execution after the female is no longer pregnant.

Laws 1833, Cobb's 1851 Digest, p. 840; Laws 1985, p. 1463, § 1.

Formerly Code 1863, § 4555; Code 1868, § 4575; Code 1873, § 4669; Code 1882, § 4669; Penal Code 1895, § 1044; Penal Code 1910, § 1070; Code 1933, § 27-2519.

§ 17-10-35. Review of death sentences

(a) Whenever the death penalty is imposed, upon the judgment becoming final in the trial court, the sentence shall be reviewed on the record by the Supreme Court of Georgia. The clerk of the trial court, within ten days after receiving the transcript, shall transmit the entire record and transcript to the Supreme Court together with a notice prepared by the clerk and a report prepared by the trial judge. The notice shall set forth the title and docket number of the case, the name of the defendant and the name and address of his attorney, a narrative statement of the judgment, the offense, and the punishment prescribed. The report shall be in the form of a standard questionnaire prepared and supplied by the Supreme Court.

(b) The Supreme Court shall consider the punishment as well as any errors enumerated by way of appeal.

(c) With regard to the sentence, the court shall determine:

(1) Whether the sentence of death was imposed under the influence of passion, prejudice, or any other arbitrary factor;

(2) Whether, in cases other than treason or aircraft hijacking, the evidence supports the jury's or judge's finding of a statutory aggravating circumstance as enumerated in subsection (b) of Code Section 17-10-30; and

(3) Whether the sentence of death is excessive or disproportionate to the penalty imposed in similar cases, considering both the crime and the defendant.

(d) Both the defendant and the state shall have the right to submit briefs within the time provided by the court and to present oral argument to the court.

(e) The court shall include in its decision a reference to those similar cases which it took into consideration. In addition to its authority regarding correction of errors, the court, with regard to review of death sentences, shall be authorized to:

(1) Affirm the sentence of death; or

(2) Set the sentence aside and remand the case for resentencing by the trial judge based on the record and argument of counsel. The records of those similar cases referred to by the Supreme Court in its decision and the extracts prepared as provided for in subsection (a) of Code Section 17-10-37 shall be provided to the resentencing judge for his consideration.

(f) The sentence review shall be in addition to direct appeal, if taken, and the review and appeal shall be consolidated for consideration. The court shall render its decision on legal errors enumerated, the factual substantiation of the verdict, and the validity of the sentence.

Laws 1973, p. 159, § 4.

Formerly Code 1933, § 27-2537.

§ 17-10-35.1. Review of pretrial proceedings in cases in which death sentence sought

(a) In cases in which the death penalty is sought, there may be a review of all pretrial proceedings by the Supreme Court upon a determination by the trial judge under Code Section 17-10-35.2 that such review is appropriate. The review shall be initiated by the trial judge's filing in the office of the clerk of superior court and delivering to the parties a report certifying that all pretrial proceedings in the case have been completed and that the case stands ready for trial. Within ten days after the filing of the report or the receipt of transcripts of the proceedings, whichever is later, the prosecutor and the defendant may each file with the clerk of superior court and serve upon the opposing party a report identifying all areas of the pretrial proceedings with respect to which reversible error may arguably have occurred. Either party may consolidate with such report an application for appeal with respect to any order, decision, or judgment entered in the case. Any such application for appeal shall be in the form otherwise appropriate under subsection (b) of Code Section 5-6-34, but:

(1) Any such application for appeal shall be filed with the clerk of superior court rather than the clerk of the Supreme Court;

(2) The opposing party shall not be required or permitted to respond to such an application for appeal; and

(3) No certificate of immediate review shall be required for the filing of such application for appeal.

(b) The reports of the trial judge, prosecutor, and defendant under subsection (a) of this Code section shall be in the form of standard questionnaires prepared and supplied by the Supreme Court. Such questionnaires shall be designed to determine whether there is arguably any existence of reversible error with respect to any of the following matters:

(1) Any proceedings with respect to change of venue;

(2) Any proceedings with respect to recusal of the trial judge;

(3) Any challenge to the jury array;

(4) Any motion to suppress evidence;

(5) Any motion for psychiatric or other medical evaluation; and

(6) Any other matter deemed appropriate by the Supreme Court.

(c) Upon the filing of the reports of the parties, the clerk of superior court shall transmit to the Supreme Court the report of the trial judge, the transcripts of proceedings, and the reports of the parties together with any application for appeal consolidated therewith. A copy of all of the foregoing shall also be delivered by the clerk of superior court to the Attorney General.

(d) The Supreme Court shall issue an order granting review of the pretrial proceedings, or portions thereof, or denying review within 20 days of the date on which the case was received. The order of the Supreme Court shall identify the matters which shall be subject to review, and such matters may include, but need not be limited to, any matters called to the court's attention in any of the reports or in any application for appeal. No notice of appeal shall be required to be filed if review of the pretrial proceedings is granted. An order granting review of pretrial proceedings shall specify the period of time within which each party shall file briefs and reply briefs with respect to the matters identified in the Supreme Court's order granting review. The Supreme Court may order oral argument or may render a decision on the record and the briefs.

(e) If requested by the district attorney, the Attorney General shall assist in the review and appeal provided for in this Code section.

(f) Review of any matter under this Code section shall, as to any question passed on in such review, be res judicata as to such question and shall be deemed to be the law of the case.

(g) The procedure under this Code section shall not apply to any ruling or order made, invoked, or sought subsequent to the filing of the report of the trial judge.

(h) The failure of either party to assert the rights given in this Code section, or the failure of the Supreme Court to grant review, shall not waive the right to posttrial review of any question review of which could be sought under this Code section and shall not constitute an adjudication as to such question.

Laws 1988, p. 1437, § 4.

§ 17-10-35.2. Hearing to determine whether interim appellate review of pretrial rulings is appropriate

Prior to the filing of a report by the trial judge under Code Section 17-10-35.1 certifying that pretrial proceedings are complete, the court shall conduct a hearing to determine if an interim appellate review of pretrial rulings is appropriate. The court shall hear from the state and the defense as to whether the delay to be caused by interim appellate review outweighs the need for such review. The court shall order such review and initiate the procedure contained in Code Section 17-10-35.1 unless the court concludes and enters an order to the effect that interim appellate review would not serve the ends of justice in the case. An order obviating interim appellate review shall not be appealable.

Laws 1988, p. 1437, § 4.

§ 17-10-36. Unified review of conviction, sentence, and detention when death sentence imposed; habeas corpus not affected

(a) The Supreme Court of Georgia shall establish, by rules, a new unified review procedure to provide for the presentation to the sentencing court and to the Supreme Court of all possible challenges to the trial, conviction, sentence, and detention of defendants upon whom the sentence of death has been or may be imposed, which challenges before July 1, 1988, have been presented for review by the former unified review procedure under this subsection. Such new unified review procedure shall govern both pretrial and posttrial appellate review of death penalty cases.

(b) The Supreme Court shall establish, by rules, a series of check lists to be utilized by the trial court, the prosecuting attorney, and defense counsel prior to, during, and after the trial of cases in which the death penalty is sought to make certain that all possible matters which could be raised in defense have been considered by the defendant and defense counsel and either asserted in a timely and correct manner or waived in accordance with applicable legal requirements, so that, for purposes of any pretrial review and the trial and posttrial review, the record and transcript of proceedings will be complete for a review by the sentencing court and the Supreme Court of all possible challenges to the trial, conviction, sentence, and detention of the defendant.

(c) Nothing in this Code section or in the rules of the Supreme Court shall limit or restrict the grounds of review or suspend the rights or remedies available through the procedures governing the writ of habeas corpus.

(d) The procedures governing the writ of habeas corpus may be employed to assert rights or seek remedies if the procedures established in the rules of the Supreme Court as applied to the petitioner are inadequate or ineffective in any constitutional sense.

Laws 1980, p. 390, § 1; Laws 1988, p. 1437, § 5.

Formerly Code 1933, § 27-2538.

§ 17-10-37. Review of death sentences; assistant to Supreme Court

(a) There shall be an assistant to the Supreme Court who shall be an attorney appointed by the Chief Justice and who shall serve at the pleasure of the court. The court shall accumulate the records of all capital felony cases in which sentence was imposed after January 1, 1970, or such earlier date as the court may deem appropriate. The assistant shall provide the court with whatever extracted information it desires with respect thereto, including, but not limited to, a synopsis or brief of the facts in the record concerning the crime and the defendant.

(b) The court shall be authorized to employ an appropriate staff and such methods to compile such data as are deemed by the Chief Justice to be appropriate and relevant to the statutory questions concerning the validity of the sentence reviewed in accordance with Code Section 17-10-35.

(c) The office of the assistant shall be attached for administrative purposes to the office of the clerk of the Supreme Court of Georgia.

Laws 1973, p. 159, § 4.

Formerly Code 1933, § 27-2537.

§ 17-10-38. Lethal injection; place of execution; physician not required to participate

(a) All persons who have been convicted of a capital offense and have had imposed upon them a sentence of death shall suffer such punishment by lethal injection. Lethal injection is the continuous intravenous injection of a substance or substances sufficient to cause death into the body of the person sentenced to death until such person is dead.

(b) In all cases in which the defendant is sentenced to death, it shall be the duty of the trial judge in passing sentence to direct that the defendant be delivered to the Department of Corrections for execution of the death sentence at a state correctional institution designated by the department.

(c) Notwithstanding any other provision of law, prescription, preparation, compounding, dispensing, or administration of a lethal injection authorized by a sentence of death by a court of competent jurisdiction shall not constitute the practice of medicine or any other profession relating to health care which is subject by law to regulation, licensure, or certification.

(d) No state agency, department, or official may, through regulation or otherwise, require or compel a physician to participate in the execution of a death sentence. "To participate in the execution of a death sentence" means any of the following actions: selecting injection sites; starting an intravenous line or lines as a port for a lethal injection device; prescribing, preparing, administering, or supervising injection drugs or their doses or types; inspecting, testing, or maintaining lethal injection devices; or consulting with or supervising lethal injection personnel.

Laws 1924, p. 195, § 1; Laws 1937-38, Ex. Sess., p. 330, § 1; Laws 1985, p. 283, § 1; Laws 2000, p. 947, § 3.

Formerly Code 1933, § 27-2512.

§ 17-10-39. Suspension of sentence when defendant is pregnant

After a sentence of death has been imposed, if a female defendant so sentenced is believed to be pregnant, the sheriff of the county in which the defendant is imprisoned, with the concurrence and assistance of the judge of the probate court, shall select one or more physicians who shall conduct an examination. If the female is found to be pregnant, the sheriff shall suspend the execution of the sentence and make a report of the examination and suspension of execution to the presiding judge of the circuit, who shall cause the report and suspension to be entered on the minutes of the superior court of the county where the sentence was imposed. When the defendant is no longer pregnant, the judge shall issue a new order as provided in Code Section 17-10-40 directing the sheriff to execute the sentence at such date and place as the judge may appoint and direct in the order, which the sheriff shall be bound to do accordingly. The judge shall cause the new order and other proceedings in the case to be entered on the minutes of the court in which the sentence was imposed.

Laws 1833, Cobb's 1851 Digest, p. 839; Laws 1874, p. 30.

Formerly Code 1863, § 4553; Code 1868, § 4573; Code 1873, § 4667; Code 1882, § 4667; Penal Code 1895, § 1045; Penal Code 1910, § 1071; Code 1933, § 27-2520.

§ 17-10-40. Fixing of new time period for execution where original time period has passed

(a) Where the time period for the execution of any convicted person in a capital case has passed by reason of a supersedeas incident to appellate review, a stay of execution by the State Board of Pardons and Paroles, or for any other reason, a judge of the superior court of the county where the case was tried shall have the power and authority to pass an order fixing a new time period for the execution of the original sentence without requiring the convicted person to be brought before him by a writ of habeas corpus. The order shall be recorded on the minutes of the court and a certified copy of the order shall be sent immediately to the convicted person's attorney of record, to the Attorney General, and to the superintendent of the state correctional institution at the place of execution.

(b) The new time period for the execution shall be seven days in duration and shall commence at noon on a specified date and shall end at noon on a specified date. The new time period for the execution fixed by the judge shall commence not less than ten nor more than 20 days from the date of the order.

(c) The Department of Corrections shall set the day and time for execution within the time period designated by the judge of the superior court. If the execution is not carried out on the day and at the time originally set by the Department of Corrections, the Department of Corrections is authorized to set new dates and times for execution within the period designated by the judge of the superior court.

Laws 1924, p. 195, § 7; Laws 1983, p. 665, § 2; Laws 1985, p. 1463, § 2.

Formerly Code 1933, § 27-2518.

§ 17-10-41. Who shall be present at execution

There shall be present at the execution of a convicted person the superintendent of the state correctional institution or a deputy superintendent thereof, at least three executioners, two physicians to determine when death supervenes, and other correctional officers, assistants, technicians, and witnesses as determined by the commissioner of corrections. In addition, the convicted person may request the presence of his or her counsel, a member of the clergy, and a reasonable number of relatives and friends, provided that the total number of witnesses appearing at the request of the convicted person shall be determined by the commissioner of corrections.

Laws 1924, p. 195, § 4; Laws 1956, p. 161, § 32; Laws 1988, p. 252, § 1; Laws 2000, p. 947, § 4.

Formerly Code 1933, § 27-2515.

§ 17-10-42. Certificate of execution

The executioner and attending physicians shall certify the fact of the execution to the clerk of the superior court of the county in which the sentence was imposed, which certificate shall be filed by the clerk with the papers in the case.

Laws 1924, p. 195, § 5.

Formerly Code 1933, § 27-2516.

§ 17-10-42.1. Participating physicians or medical professionals not subject to challenge, suspension, or revocation of license

Participation in any execution of any convicted person carried out under this article shall not be the subject of any licensure challenge, suspension, or revocation for any physician or medical professional licensed in the State of Georgia.

Laws 2006, Act 537, § 1, eff. July 1, 2006.

§ 17-10-43. Disposition of body; expenses of transporting body

The body of an executed person shall be delivered to the relatives of the person if they so desire; and, in case no claim is made by relatives for the body, it shall be disposed of in the same manner as bodies of inmates dying in a state correctional institution. If the nearest relatives of the person executed desire that the body be transported to the former home of the executed person, if in this state, the expenses of transportation shall be paid by the county governing authority of the county where the person was convicted, from any funds on hand in the treasury.

Laws 1924, p. 195, § 6.

Formerly Code 1933, § 27-2517.

§ 17-10-44. Place for execution and apparatus

The Department of Corrections shall provide a place for execution of the death sentence and all necessary apparatus, machinery, and appliances for inflicting the penalty of death.

Laws 1924, p. 195, § 2; Laws 1956, p. 161, § 28; Laws 1985, p. 283, § 1; Laws 2000, p. 947, § 5.

Formerly Code 1933, § 27-2513.

Article 3

Mentally Incompetent to Be Executed

§ 17-10-60. "Mentally incompetent to be executed" defined

As used in this article, the term "mentally incompetent to be executed" means that because of a mental condition the person is presently unable to know why he or she is being punished and understand the nature of the punishment.

Laws 1988, p. 1003, § 2.

§ 17-10-61. When person sentenced to death shall not be executed

A person under sentence of death shall not be executed when it is determined under the provisions of this article that the person is mentally incompetent to be executed as defined in Code Section 17-10-60.

Laws 1988, p. 1003, § 2.

§ 17-10-62. Exclusive procedure

Notwithstanding any other provision of this Code, this article provides the exclusive procedure for challenging mental competency to be executed when such challenge is made subsequent to the time of conviction and sentence.

Laws 1988, p. 1003, § 2.

§ 17-10-63. Filing and contents of application

(a) An application brought under this article must be filed in the superior court of the county in which the applicant is being detained. The named respondent shall be the person having actual custody of the applicant.

(b) An application brought under this article shall identify the proceeding in which the applicant was convicted, give the date of the rendition and the final judgment complained of, set forth the fact that a time period for execution has been set, give the date of the signing of the order and the dates of the designated time period for execution, and shall clearly set forth alleged facts in support of the assertion that the applicant is presently mentally incompetent to be executed. The application shall have attached thereto affidavits, records, or other evidence supporting its allegations or shall state why the same are not attached. The application shall identify any previous proceedings that the applicant may have taken challenging his mental competency to be executed or challenging his mental condition in relation to the conviction and sentence in question. Arguments and citations of authority shall be omitted from the application. The application must be verified with the oath of the applicant or of some other person in his behalf.

Laws 1988, p. 1003, § 2.

§ 17-10-64. Service of application

Service of an application brought under this article shall be made upon the person having custody of the applicant. If the applicant is being detained under the custody of the Department of Corrections, an additional copy of the application shall be served upon the Attorney General. If the applicant is being detained under the custody of some authority other than the Department of Corrections, an additional copy of the petition shall be served upon the district attorney of the county in which the application is filed.

Laws 1988, p. 1003, § 2.

§ 17-10-65. Answer; schedule of case

As soon as possible after the filing and docketing of the application under this article, the respondent shall answer the application. The court may schedule a case for a hearing prior to the filing of responsive pleadings but, in any event, shall schedule the case for a hearing as soon as possible so that the proceedings may move expeditiously.

Laws 1988, p. 1003, § 2.

§ 17-10-66. Examination of applicant for purposes of assessing mental competency to be executed

(a) By filing an application under this article, the applicant specifically consents to submit to a state examination for the purposes of assessing mental competency to be executed.

(b) Simultaneously with the filing of the application, the applicant, if he or she wishes the court to consider any request for appointment of an expert, shall file such a request and shall state specific facts in support of that request so that the court may determine if the applicant's mental competency to be executed is in fact a significant issue. The applicant shall further submit with the motion a specific statement as to the particular expert requested, the nature of the examination to be conducted, the time period within which an examination can be conducted, and an estimate of the expenses to be incurred.

(c) If the applicant has filed a request for an examination as provided in subsection (b) of this Code section and the applicant makes a sufficient showing that his or her mental competency to be executed is a significant issue, the court shall appoint an expert to make an examination of the applicant, with such examination to be conducted as soon as possible. Payment for such expert shall be made by the Department of Corrections unless otherwise designated by the General Assembly.

Laws 1988, p. 1003, § 2.

§ 17-10-67. When application may be filed

An application under this article shall not be filed until completion of direct appeal and until an order has been signed by a judge of the trial court setting a time period for the execution.

Laws 1988, p. 1003, § 2.

§ 17-10-68. Pleadings and evidence; findings

(a) The court may receive proof by depositions, oral testimony, sworn affidavits, or other evidence.

(b) The taking of depositions shall be governed by Code Sections 9-11-26 through 9-11-32 and 9-11-37.

(c) If a sworn affidavit is to be introduced into evidence by either party, the party intending to introduce such an affidavit shall cause it to be served upon the opposing party at least five days in advance of the date set for a hearing in the case or, in the event a hearing is set less than five days from the date of the filing of the application, as soon as possible so that opposing counsel has the opportunity to review the affidavit prior to the hearing. The affidavit so served shall be accompanied by notice of the party's intention to introduce it into evidence. The superior court judge considering the application may resolve disputed issues of fact upon the basis of sworn affidavits standing by themselves.

(d) After reviewing the pleadings and evidence offered at the hearing, the judge of the superior court hearing the case shall make written findings of fact and conclusions of law upon which the judgment is based. The findings of fact and conclusions of law shall be recorded as part of the record in the case.

(e) If the court finds in favor of the applicant by finding that the applicant has proven his or her mental incompetence to be executed by a preponderance of the evidence, the court shall enter an appropriate order with respect to any scheduled execution time period and shall enter such supplementary orders as necessary and proper. If the court denies the application, the court shall direct that immediate telephonic notification be given to the parties and any stay presently entered under this article shall be dissolved instanter.

Laws 1988, p. 1003, § 2.

§ 17–10–69. Prior adjudication of mental competency

If an applicant is determined to have previously filed an application under this article and has previously been determined to be mentally competent to be executed, such prior adjudication shall act as a presumption of mental competency and the applicant shall not be entitled to a new hearing on the question of mental competency to be executed absent the applicant's making a prima-facie showing of a substantial change in circumstances sufficient to raise a significant question as to the applicant's mental competency to be executed at the time of filing of any subsequent applications.

Laws 1988, p. 1003, § 2.

§ 17–10–70. Appeals

(a) Appeals in cases brought under this article shall be governed by Chapter 6 of Title 5 except that as to final orders of the court which are adverse, to the applicant, no appeal shall be ordered unless the Supreme Court of this state issues a certificate of probable cause for the appeal.

(b) If an unsuccessful applicant desires to appeal, he or she must file a written application for a certificate of probable cause to appeal with the clerk of the Supreme Court within three days of the entry of the order denying relief. The applicant shall also file within the same period a notice of appeal with the clerk of the concerned superior court. The Supreme Court shall either grant or deny the application within a reasonable time after filing. In order for the Supreme Court to consider fully the request for a certificate, the clerk of the concerned superior court shall forward, as in any other case, the record and transcript, if designated, to the clerk of the Supreme Court when a notice of appeal is filed. The clerk of the concerned superior court need not prepare and retain and the court reporter need not file a copy of the original record and a copy of the original transcript of proceedings. The clerk of the Supreme Court shall return the original record and transcript to the clerk of the concerned superior court upon completion of the appeal if the certificate is granted. If the Supreme Court denies the application for a certificate of probable cause, the clerk of the Supreme Court shall return the original record and transcript and shall notify the clerk of the concerned superior court and the parties to the proceedings below of the determination that probable cause does not exist for appeal.

(c) If the trial court finds in favor of the applicant, no certificate of probable cause need be obtained by the respondent as a condition precedent to appeal. A notice of appeal filed by the respondent shall act as a supersedeas and shall stay the judgment of the superior court until there is a final adjudication by the Supreme Court.

Laws 1988, p. 1003, § 2.

§ 17–10–71. Regaining of mental competency

If a convicted person under sentence of death who is found to be mentally incompetent to be executed under this article regains his or her mental competency, the fact shall be certified at once by the appropriate mental health official to the court initially making the finding of mental incompetency. Upon such certification, that court shall enter an appropriate order noting receipt of certification and vacating any previously entered stay of execution. A copy of such order shall be sent to the sentencing court, at which time the sentencing court shall fix a new time period for execution as provided in Code Section 17–10–40. The judge of the court which made the determination on the issue of mental competency shall cause the new order and other proceedings in the case to be presented on the minutes of the court.

Laws 1988, p. 1003, § 2.

CHAPTER 11
ASSESSMENT AND PAYMENT OF COSTS OF CRIMINAL PROCEEDINGS

Article 1
General Provisions

§ 17-11-1. When defendant shall pay costs

The costs of a prosecution, except the fees of his own witnesses, shall not be demanded of a defendant until after trial and conviction. If convicted, judgment may be entered against the defendant for all costs accruing in the committing and trial courts and by any officer pending the prosecution. The judgment shall be a lien from the date of his arrest on all the property of the defendant. The clerk shall issue an execution on the judgment against the property.

Laws 1816, Cobb's 1851 Digest, p. 857; Laws 1820, Cobb's 1851 Digest, p. 859; Laws 1826, Cobb's 1851 Digest, p. 859; Laws 1830, Cobb's 1851 Digest, p. 860.

Formerly Code 1863, § 4581; Code 1868, § 4602; Code 1873, § 4699; Code 1882, § 4699; Penal Code 1895, § 1078; Penal Code 1910, § 1105; Code 1933, § 27-2801.

§ 17-11-2. Liability of defendant for costs of witnesses

No defendant shall be liable for the costs of any witness of the state, unless such witness was subpoenaed, sworn, and examined during the trial, nor for the costs of more than two witnesses testifying on the same point, unless the court shall certify that the question at issue was of such a character as to require the testimony of more than two witnesses.

Laws 1799, Cobb's 1851 Digest, p. 277.

Formerly Code 1863, § 3608; Code 1868, § 3632; Code 1873, § 3682; Code 1882, § 3682; Penal Code 1895, § 1079; Penal Code 1910, § 1106; Code 1933, § 27-2802.

§ 17-11-3. Cost of inquest when defendant is convicted of murder or manslaughter

Any person convicted of murder or manslaughter in a case where an inquest has been held concerning the cause of death of the victim shall be charged for the costs of the inquest as part of the costs of prosecution.

Formerly Code 1863, § 572; Code 1868, § 636; Code 1873, § 595; Code 1882, § 595; Penal Code 1895, § 1080; Penal Code 1910, § 1107; Code 1933, § 27-2803.

§ 17-11-4. When the prosecutor shall pay costs

(a) The prosecutor's name shall be endorsed on every indictment, and he shall be compelled to pay all costs and jail fees upon the acquittal or discharge of the person accused when:

(1) The grand jury, by its foreman, on returning "no bill," expresses as its opinion that the prosecution was unfounded or malicious;

(2) A jury on the trial of the prosecution finds it to be malicious; or

(3) The prosecution is abandoned before trial. When it is thus abandoned, the officer who issued the warrant shall enter a judgment against the prosecutor for all the costs and enforce it by an execution in the name of the state or by an attachment for contempt.

(b) A magistrate may, in his discretion, assess costs and jail fees against the person who instigated the prosecution when, at a committal hearing, the action is dismissed for want of probable cause and the magistrate finds that the complaint was unfounded and malicious. This subsection shall not apply to law enforcement personnel.

Laws 1833, Cobb's 1851 Digest, p. 833; Laws 1871-72, p. 53, § 1; Laws 1982, p. 3, § 17; Laws 1986, p. 282, § 1.

Formerly Code 1863, § 4518; Code 1868, § 4537; Code 1873, § 4630; Code 1882, § 4630; Penal Code 1895, § 1082; Penal Code 1910, § 1109; Code 1933, § 27-2805.

§ 17-11-5. Payment of costs and expenses when venue is changed

(a) When the venue in a case is changed, the whole costs of the case, jail fees of the person to be tried, and expenses of the trial in the county to which it was transferred shall be paid by the county from which the case was removed.

(b) The entire court costs, including the costs of the sheriff, bailiff, clerks, and jurors, shall also be paid by the county from which the case was removed and shall have the same priority as jail fees. The county in which the case is tried shall be reimbursed after paying the court costs incurred.

Laws 1871-72, p. 49, § 1; Laws 1895, p. 70, § 4.

Formerly Code 1873, § 4689; Code 1882, § 4689; Penal Code 1895, § 1083; Penal Code 1910, § 1110; Code 1933, § 27-2806.

Article 2

Reimbursement of Counties for Expenses of Capital Felony Prosecutions

§ 17-11-20. Short title

This article shall be known and may be cited as the "Capital Felony Expense Act."

Laws 1979, p. 504, § 1.

§ 17-11-21. Definitions

As used in this article, the term:

(1) "Capital felony case" means a criminal case in which the death penalty may be imposed upon the defendant under the laws of this state.

(2) "Capital felony expenses" means expenses incurred by a county and paid from county funds as a direct result of a capital felony case being tried by a superior court. The term includes expenses from the date of the arrest of the defendant to the date of the superior court conviction, expenses from the date of the conviction until the date of the last appellate court affirmance of the conviction, expenses from the last appellate court reversal to any subsequent superior court convictions or retrials, expenses from any retrials to the last appellate court action on the conviction, expenses from the date of the arrest of the defendant to the date of the defendant's release if there is no conviction or if the conviction is reversed and there is no retrial, or expenses during any combination of these periods. The term shall not include the following expenses:

(A) Any expenses reimbursed by or pursuant to state law;

(B) The salaries, compensation, and expenses of all county officers and employees, except for any compensation and expenses of temporary employees employed as a direct result of the capital felony case or extraordinary expenses incurred by county officers and employees as a direct result of the capital felony case; and

(C) County paid supplements to the salaries or compensation of state officers and employees.

(3) "Commissioner" means the commissioner of community affairs.

(4) "County revenue" means the most current available total of adjusted taxes as determined from the annual financial report relating to local government finances filed by the county with the Department of Community Affairs pursuant to Code Section 36-81-8.

Laws 1979, p. 504, § 2; Laws 1983, p. 395, § 1; Laws 1988, p. 1859, § 1.

§ 17-11-22. Basis for reimbursement of capital felony expenses

(a) Each county which is responsible for the costs of a capital felony case will be reimbursed for capital felony expenses as provided in this Code section. With respect to one or more capital felony cases, expenses from the date of arrest will be accumulated. When one or more capital felony cases result in capital felony expenses, the accumulation of which is more than 5 percent of county revenue for the calendar year in which the superior court conviction occurs or in which the defendant is released if not convicted, the county will be reimbursed for all such accumulated capital felony expenses in excess of the 5 percent level. After a county has qualified or been reimbursed for capital felony expenses for any calendar year, the county shall be eligible for any capital felony expenses resulting from such case or cases in subsequent calendar years prior to the appeal of such case or cases. County revenues shall not be applicable in determining the amount of reimbursement for capital felony expenses occurring in such subsequent years prior to the appeal of the case or cases.

(b) If one or more capital felony cases are appealed, expenses from the date of the superior court conviction will be accumulated. When the appeal of one or more capital felony cases results in capital felony expenses, the accumulation of which is more than 5 percent of county revenue for the calendar year in which the last appellate court action on the conviction occurs, the county will be reimbursed for all such capital felony expenses in excess of the 5 percent level. If the county chooses not to seek reimbursement for capital felony expenses from the date of arrest to the date of the superior court conviction and instead seeks reimbursement for its capital felony expenses through the last appellate court action, the county will be reimbursed for all accumulated capital felony expenses in excess of the 5 percent level.

(c) If a capital felony case is appealed and the conviction is reversed, capital felony expenses for any subsequent retrial and appeals will be handled in accordance with the provisions of subsections (a) and (b) of this Code section.

(d) No capital felony expenses for which reimbursement has already been made will again be included in any subsequent calculations or reimbursement requests.

Laws 1979, p. 504, § 3; Laws 1983, p. 395, § 2; Laws 1988, p. 1859, § 2.

§ 17-11-23. Reimbursement payments

(a)(1) Reimbursement payments for eligible capital felony expenses under this article will be made to the governing authority of each county incurring capital felony expenses. The payments will be made during the second quarter of a calendar year for capital felony expenses eligible for reimbursement during the immediately preceding calendar year; provided, however, that, if a county is reimbursed during the second quarter of a calendar year and has additional capital felony expenses eligible for reimbursement during the remainder of such calendar year resulting from the same case or cases, payments will be made during the fourth quarter of such calendar year for the additional capital felony expenses eligible for reimbursement.

(2) Reimbursement payments shall be made from funds appropriated for such purpose pursuant to subsection (a) of Code Section 17-11-24, and no payments are required to be made if funds are not available or have not been appropriated.

(b)(1) In the event that requests for reimbursement exceed the amount appropriated for this article, the commissioner shall have the right to reduce each request proportionally so that the total amount of requests shall not exceed the total amount of funds available for reimbursement payments at the time of the request.

(2) Notwithstanding any other provisions of this Code section, during the first payment cycle of a state fiscal year (fourth quarter of a calendar year) not more than one-half of the funds available for reimbursement will be expended for reimbursement purposes.

Laws 1979, p. 504, § 5; Laws 1983, p. 395, § 3; Laws 1988, p. 1859, § 3.

§ 17-11-24. Administration

(a) The commissioner shall administer this article and shall make payments to counties for the reimbursement of capital felony expenses as provided by this article. The payments shall be made from funds appropriated to the Department of Community Affairs specifically for the purpose of making reimbursements pursuant to this article.

(b) The commissioner shall adopt rules and regulations for the administration of this article. The rules and regulations shall be distributed to the county governing authorities and to the clerks of the superior courts.

(c) The clerks of the superior courts will be the local administrators of this article; and, consistent with rules and regulations promulgated by the commissioner as provided by subsection (b) of this Code section, the clerks will maintain records of capital felony expenses for the purposes of this article. Based on such records, the clerk of each superior court will certify to the commissioner, during the first quarter of each calendar year, capital felony expenses eligible for reimbursement during the preceding calendar year.

Laws 1979, p. 504, § 4; Laws 1983, p. 395, § 4.

CHAPTER 12

LEGAL DEFENSE FOR INDIGENTS

Revision of Chapter 12

Laws 2003, Act 32, § 1, amended Title 17 by striking Chapter 12, consisting of Code Sections 17-12-1 to 17-12-97, relating to legal defense of indigents, and adding a new Chapter 12, consisting of Code Sections 17-12-1 to 17-12-128. Section 10(a) of Laws 2003, Act 32, provides: "Section 1 of the Act shall become effective as set forth in said section."

Article 1

Georgia Public Defender Standards Council

Revision of Chapter 12

Laws 2003, Act 32, § 1, added this article effective December 31, 2003. See § 17–12–13.

Former Article 1, Local Indigent Defense Programs Generally, consisting of §§ 17–12–1 to 17–12–14, was repealed by Laws 2003, Act 32, § 1, effective December 31, 2003.

§ 17–12–1. Short title; independent agency of judicial branch; responsibility of council

(a) This chapter shall be known and may be cited as the "Georgia Indigent Defense Act of 2003."

(b) The Georgia Public Defender Standards Council shall be an independent agency within the judicial branch of state government.

(c) The council shall be responsible for assuring that adequate and effective legal representation is provided, independently of political considerations or private interests, to indigent persons who are entitled to representation under this chapter.

Laws 2003, Act 32, § 1, eff. Dec. 31, 2003.

§ 17–12–2. Definitions

As used in this chapter, the term:

(1) "Assistant public defender" means an attorney who is employed by any circuit public defender or conflict defender office.

(2) "Circuit public defender" means the head of a public defender office providing indigent defense representation within any given judicial circuit of this state.

(3) "Circuit public defender office" means the office of any of the several circuit public defenders.

(4) "Council" means the Georgia Public Defender Standards Council.

(5) "Indigent person" or "indigent defendant" means:

(A) A person charged with a misdemeanor, violation of probation, or a municipal, county, or juvenile offense punishable by imprisonment who earns or, in the case of a juvenile, whose parents earn, less than 125 percent of the federal poverty guidelines unless there is evidence that the person has other resources that might reasonably be used to employ a lawyer without undue hardship on the person or his or her dependents; and

(B) A person charged with a felony who earns or, in the case of a juvenile, whose parents earn, less than 150 percent of the federal poverty guidelines unless there is evidence that the person has other resources that might reasonably be used to employ a lawyer without undue hardship on the person or his or her dependents.

In no case shall a person whose maximum income level exceeds 150 percent of the federal poverty level or, in the case of a juvenile, whose household income exceeds 150 percent of the federal poverty level be an indigent person or indigent defendant.

(6) "Public defender" means an attorney who is employed in a circuit public defender office or conflict defender office or who represents an indigent person pursuant to this chapter.

Laws 2003, Act 32, § 1, eff. Dec. 31, 2003; Laws 2006, Act 749, § 4, eff. May 3, 2006.

§ 17–12–3. Creation of council; appointment of members; effective date

(a) There is created the Georgia Public Defender Standards Council to be composed of 11 members.

(b) Ten members of the council shall be appointed as follows:

(1) Two members shall be appointed by the Governor, the Lieutenant Governor, the Speaker of the House of Representatives, the Chief Justice of the Supreme Court of Georgia, and the Chief Judge of the Georgia Court of Appeals as further set forth in paragraph (2) of this subsection. The members of the council shall be individuals with significant experience working in the criminal justice system or who have demonstrated a strong commitment to the provision of adequate and effective representation of indigent defendants. The members shall serve terms of four years; provided, however, that the members appointed from the even-numbered judicial administration circuits shall serve initial terms of six years and thereafter shall serve terms of four years;

(2) The members appointed pursuant to paragraph (1) of this subsection shall be chosen so that each of the ten judicial administration districts in the state is represented and so that each appointing authority shall rotate the particular judicial administration district for which he or she is responsible for appointing. The appointments shall be as follows:

(A) For the initial appointments:

(i) The Governor shall appoint one person who resides in judicial administration district 1 and one person who resides in judicial administration district 2;

(ii) The Lieutenant Governor shall appoint one person who resides in judicial administration district 3 and one person who resides in judicial administration district 4;

(iii) The Speaker of the House of Representatives shall appoint one person who resides in judicial administration district 5 and one person who resides in judicial administration district 6;

(iv) The Chief Justice of the Supreme Court of Georgia shall appoint one person who resides in judicial administration district 7 and one person who resides in judicial administration district 8; and

(v) The Chief Judge of the Georgia Court of Appeals shall appoint one person who resides in judicial administration district 9 and one person who resides in judicial administration district 10;

(B) For the first subsequent council appointments:

(i) The Governor shall appoint one person who resides in judicial administration district 3 and one person who resides in judicial administration district 4;

(ii) The Lieutenant Governor shall appoint one person who resides in judicial administration district 5 and one person who resides in judicial administration district 6;

(iii) The Speaker of the House of Representatives shall appoint one person who resides in judicial administration district 7 and one person who resides in judicial administration district 8;

(iv) The Chief Justice of the Supreme Court of Georgia shall appoint one person who resides in judicial administration district 9 and one person who resides in judicial administration district 10; and

(v) The Chief Judge of the Georgia Court of Appeals shall appoint one person who resides in judicial administration district 1 and one person who resides in judicial administration district 2;

(C) For the second subsequent council appointments:

(i) The Governor shall appoint one person who resides in judicial administration district 5 and one person who resides in judicial administration district 6;

(ii) The Lieutenant Governor shall appoint one person who resides in judicial administration district 7 and one person who resides in judicial administration district 8;

(iii) The Speaker of the House of Representatives shall appoint one person who resides in judicial administration district 9 and one person who resides in judicial administration district 10;

(iv) The Chief Justice of the Supreme Court of Georgia shall appoint one person who resides in judicial administration district 1 and one person who resides in judicial administration district 2; and

(v) The Chief Judge of the Georgia Court of Appeals shall appoint one person who resides in judicial administration district 3 and one person who resides in judicial administration district 4;

(D) For the third subsequent council appointments:

(i) The Governor shall appoint one person who resides in judicial administration district 7 and one person who resides in judicial administration district 8;

(ii) The Lieutenant Governor shall appoint one person who resides in judicial administration district 9 and one person who resides in judicial administration district 10;

(iii) The Speaker of the House of Representatives shall appoint one person who resides in judicial administration district 1 and one person who resides in judicial administration district 2;

(iv) The Chief Justice of the Supreme Court of Georgia shall appoint one person who resides in judicial administration district 3 and one person who resides in judicial administration district 4; and

(v) The Chief Judge of the Georgia Court of Appeals shall appoint one person who resides in judicial administration district 5 and one person who resides in judicial administration district 6; and

(E) For the fourth subsequent council appointments:

(i) The Governor shall appoint one person who resides in judicial administration district 9 and one person who resides in judicial administration district 10;

(ii) The Lieutenant Governor shall appoint one person who resides in judicial administration district 1 and one person who resides in judicial administration district 2;

(iii) The Speaker of the House of Representatives shall appoint one person who resides in judicial administration district 3 and one person who resides in judicial administration district 4;

(iv) The Chief Justice of the Supreme Court of Georgia shall appoint one person who resides in judicial administration district 5 and one person who resides in judicial administration district 6; and

(v) The Chief Judge of the Georgia Court of Appeals shall appoint one person who resides in judicial administration district 7 and one person who resides in judicial administration district 8.

All subsequent appointments shall continue on, with the entire cycle starting over again as specified in subparagraph (A) of this paragraph;

(3) In addition, the eleventh member shall be one circuit public defender who shall serve on the council. After the initial appointments as set forth in paragraph (4) of this subsection, the circuit public defender to serve on the council shall be elected by a majority vote of all the circuit public defenders. The circuit public defender councilmember shall serve terms of two years;

(4) All initial appointments shall be made to become members of the council on July 1, 2003, and their successors shall become members of the council on July 1 following their appointment. The initial appointees from the even-numbered judicial administration circuits shall serve until June 30, 2009. Notwithstanding the provisions of paragraph (3) of this subsection, the initial member representing the circuit public defenders shall be made by the Supreme Court of Georgia. The person representing the circuit defender position on the initial council shall be engaged on a full-time basis in the provision of criminal defense to the indigent;

(5) Any vacancy for a member appointed pursuant to paragraphs (1) and (2) of this subsection shall be filled by the appointing authority, and such appointee shall serve the balance of the vacating member's unexpired term; and

(6) Any vacancy for a member appointed pursuant to paragraph (3) of this subsection shall be the successor to the circuit public defender as set forth in subsection (d) of Code Section 17–12–20.

(c) In making these appointments, the appointing authorities shall seek to identify and appoint persons who represent a diversity of backgrounds and experience and shall solicit suggestions from the State Bar of Georgia, state and local bar associations, the Georgia Association of Criminal Defense Lawyers, the councils representing the various categories of state court judges in Georgia, and the Prosecuting Attorneys' Council of the State of Georgia, as well as from the public and other interested organizations and individuals within the state. The appointing authorities shall not appoint a prosecuting attorney as defined in paragraph (6) of Code Section 19–13–51, any employee of a prosecuting attorney's office, or an employee of the Prosecuting Attorneys' Council of the State of Georgia to serve on the council.

(d) This Code section shall become effective on July 1, 2003, for purposes of making the initial appointments to the council.

Laws 2003, Act 32, § 1, eff. Dec. 31, 2003; Laws 2004, Act 564, § 17, eff. May 13, 2004; Laws 2004, Ex. Sess., Act 4, § 11, eff. June 15, 2004; Laws 2006, Act 749, § 5, eff. May 3, 2006.

§ 17–12–4. Legal entity; powers

(a) The council:

(1) Shall be a legal entity;

(2) Shall have perpetual existence;

(3) May contract;

(4) May own property;

(5) May accept funds, grants, and gifts from any public or private source, which shall be used to defray the expenses incident to implementing its purposes;

(6) May adopt and use an official seal;

(7) May establish a principal office;

(8) Shall appoint a director;

(9) May hire such administrative and clerical personnel as may be necessary and appropriate to fulfill its purposes; and

(10) Shall have such other powers, privileges, and duties as may be reasonable and necessary for the proper fulfillment of its purposes.

(b) The council shall establish auditing procedures as may be required in connection with the handling of public funds. The state auditor is authorized and directed to make an annual audit of the transactions of the council and to make a complete report of the same to the General Assembly. The report shall disclose all moneys received by the council and all expenditures made by the council, including administrative expense. The state auditor shall also make an audit of the affairs of the council at any time when requested to do so by a majority of the council or by the Chief Justice of the Supreme Court of Georgia.

(c) The council may not provide compensation from its funds to any administrative or clerical personnel employed by the council if the personnel are then receiving retirement compensation from any retirement or pension fund created by Title 47 to provide compensation for past services as a judicial officer, prosecuting attorney, indigent defense attorney, court officer, or law enforcement officer except for county or municipal retirement funds.

Laws 2003, Act 32, § 1, eff. Dec. 31, 2003.

§ 17–12–5. Director

(a) To be eligible for appointment as the council's director, a candidate shall be a member in good standing of the State Bar of Georgia with at least three years' experience in the practice of law. The director shall be selected on the basis of training and experience and such other qualifications as the council deems appropriate. The director shall serve at the pleasure of the council and may be removed by a majority vote of the entire council. The council shall establish the director's salary.

(b)(1) The director shall work with and provide support services and programs for circuit public defender offices and other attorneys representing indigent persons in criminal or juvenile cases in order to improve the quality and effectiveness of legal representation of such persons and otherwise fulfill the purposes of this chapter. Such services and programs shall include, but shall not be limited to, technical, research, and administrative assistance; educational and training programs for attorneys, investigators, and other staff; assistance with the representation of indigent defendants with mental disabilities; assistance with the representation of juveniles; and assistance with appellate advocacy.

(2) The director, with the consent of the council, may establish divisions within the office to administer the services and programs as may be necessary to fulfill the purposes of this chapter.

(3) The director may hire such staff employees and may contract with outside consultants on behalf of the office as may be necessary to provide the services contemplated by this chapter.

(c) The director shall:

(1) Prepare and submit to the council a proposed budget for the council. Said budget shall not contain any request for funding for the operation of the circuit public defender offices until the budget submission for Fiscal Year 2005. The director shall also prepare and submit an annual report containing pertinent data on the operations, costs, and needs of the council and such other information as the council may require;

(2) Develop such rules, policies, procedures, regulations, and standards as may be necessary to carry out the provisions of this chapter and comply with all applicable laws, standards, and regulations, and submit these to the council for approval;

(3) Administer and coordinate the operations of the council and supervise compliance with rules, policies, procedures, regulations, and standards adopted by the council;

(4) Maintain proper records of all financial transactions related to the operation of the council;

(5) At the director's discretion, solicit and accept on behalf of the council any funds that may become available from any source, including government, nonprofit, or private grants, gifts, or bequests;

(6) Coordinate the services of the council with any federal, county, or private programs established to provide assistance to indigent persons in cases subject to this chapter and consult with professional bodies concerning the implementation and improvement of programs for providing indigent services;

(7) Provide for the training of attorneys and other staff involved in the legal representation of persons subject to this chapter;

(8) Attend all council meetings, except those meetings or portions thereof that address the question of appointment or removal of the director;

(9) Ensure that the expenditures of the council are not greater than the amounts budgeted or available from other revenue sources; and

(10) Perform other duties as the council may assign.

Laws 2003, Act 32, § 1, eff. Dec. 31, 2003; Laws 2004, Act 564, § 17, eff. May 13, 2004.

§ 17-12-6. Assistance to public defenders; fiscal officer; records and statistics

(a) The council shall assist the public defenders throughout the state in their efforts to provide adequate legal defense to the indigent. Assistance may include:

(1) The preparation and distribution of a basic defense manual and other educational materials;

(2) The preparation and distribution of model forms and documents employed in indigent defense;

(3) The promotion of and assistance in the training of indigent defense attorneys;

(4) The provision of legal research assistance to public defenders; and

(5) The provision of such other assistance to public defenders as may be authorized by law.

(b) The council:

(1) Shall be the fiscal officer for the circuit public defender offices; and

(2) Shall collect, maintain, review, and publish records and statistics for the purpose of evaluating the delivery of indigent defense representation in Georgia.

Laws 2003, Act 32, § 1, eff. Dec. 31, 2003.

§ 17-12-7. Actions in best interest of indigent defendants; voting; term; quorum; meetings; chairperson; compensation

(a) All members of the council shall at all times act in the best interest of indigent defendants who are receiving legal representation under the provisions of this chapter.

(b) All members of the council shall be entitled to vote on any matter coming before the council unless otherwise provided by law or by rules adopted by the council concerning conflicts of interest.

(c) Each member of the council shall serve until a successor has been appointed. Removal of council members shall be for cause and shall be in accordance with policies and procedures adopted by the council.

(d) Unless otherwise provided in this article, a quorum shall be a majority of the members of the council who are then in office, and decisions of the council shall be by majority vote of the members present, except that a majority of the entire council must approve the appointment or removal of the chairperson or removal of a circuit public defender for cause pursuant to Code Section 17–12–20 and an alternative delivery system pursuant to Code Section 17–12–36 and other matters as set forth in Code Section 17–12–36.

(e) The council shall meet at least quarterly and at such other times and places as it deems necessary or convenient for the performance of its duties.

(f) The council shall elect a chairperson and such officers from the members of the council as it deems necessary and shall adopt such rules for the transaction of its business as it desires. The chairperson and officers shall serve for a term of two years and may be removed without cause by a vote of two-thirds of the members of the entire council and for cause by a majority vote of the entire council. The chairperson shall retain a vote on all matters except those in which the chairperson has a conflict of interest or the removal of the chairperson for cause. The council shall keep and maintain minutes of all council meetings.

(g) The members of the council shall receive no compensation for their services but shall be reimbursed for their actual expenses incurred in the performance of their duties as members of the council. Any expenses incurred by the council shall be paid from the general operating budget of the council.

Laws 2003, Act 32, § 1, eff. Dec. 31, 2003.

§ 17–12–8. Approval and implementation of programs, services, rules, procedures, regulations; standards

(a) The council shall approve the development and improvement of programs which provide legal representation to indigent persons and juveniles.

(b) The council shall approve and implement programs, services, rules, policies, procedures, regulations, and standards as may be necessary to fulfill the purposes and provisions of this article and to comply with all applicable laws governing the rights of indigent persons accused of violations of criminal law. Standards shall include, but shall not be limited to, the following:

(1) Standards for maintaining and operating circuit defender offices, including requirements regarding qualifications, training, and size of the legal and supporting staff of such offices;

(2) Standards prescribing minimum experience, training, and other qualifications for appointed counsel where a conflict of interest arises between the public defender and an indigent person;

(3) Standards for assistant public defender and appointed counsel caseloads;

(4) Standards for the performance of assistant public defenders and appointed counsel representing indigent persons;

(5) Standards and procedures for the appointment of independent, competent, and efficient counsel for representation in both the trial and appellate courts of indigent persons whose cases present conflicts of interest;

(6) Standards for providing and compensating experts, investigators, and other persons who provide services necessary for the effective representation of indigent persons;

(7) Standards for qualifications and performance of counsel representing indigent persons in capital cases;

(8) Standards for collecting the costs of legal representation and related services;

(9) Standards for compensation of attorneys appointed to represent indigent persons under this article;

(10) Standards for removing a circuit public defender for cause pursuant to Code Section 17–12–20;

(11) Standards for a uniform definition of a "case" for purposes of determining caseload statistics; and

(12) Standards for accepting contractual indigent defense representation.

(c) The initial minimum standards promulgated by the council pursuant to this Code section which are determined by the General Oversight Committee for the Georgia Public Defender Standards Council to have a fiscal impact shall be submitted by the council to the General Assembly at the regular session for 2005 and shall become effective only when ratified by joint resolution of the General Assembly and upon the approval of the resolution by the Governor or upon its becoming law without such approval. The power of the council to promulgate such initial minimum standards shall be deemed to be dependent upon such ratification; provided, however, the minimum standards promulgated by the council shall be utilized as a guideline prior to ratification. Any subsequent amendments or additions to the initial minimum standards promulgated by the council pursuant to this Code section which are determined by the General Oversight Committee for the Georgia Public Defender

Standards Council to have a fiscal impact shall be ratified at the next regular session of the General Assembly and shall become effective only when ratified by joint resolution of the General Assembly and upon the approval of the resolution by the Governor or upon its becoming law without such approval.

(d) All standards that are promulgated by the council shall be publicly available for review and shall be posted on the council's website. Each standard shall identify the date upon which the standard took effect, and if the standard is subject to ratification by the General Assembly as provided by subsection (c) of this Code section, the status of the standard with respect to ratification.

Laws 2003, Act 32, § 1, eff. Dec. 31, 2003; Laws 2004, Ex. Sess., Act 4, § 12, eff. June 15, 2004; Laws 2005, Act 19, § 17, eff. April 7, 2005; Laws 2005, Act 281, § 1, eff. May 6, 2005; Laws 2006, Act 749, § 6, eff. May 3, 2006.

§ 17-12-9. Legal education and training programs; reimbursement

The council shall be authorized to conduct or approve for credit or reimbursement, or both, basic and continuing legal education courses or other appropriate training programs for the circuit public defenders or their staff members. The council, in accordance with such rules as it shall adopt, shall be authorized to provide reimbursement, in whole or in part, for the actual expenses incurred by any circuit public defender or their staff members in attending any approved course or training program from funds as may be appropriated or otherwise made available to the council. Notwithstanding any other provision of law, the circuit public defenders or their staff members shall be authorized to receive reimbursement for actual expenses incurred in attending approved courses or training programs, provided that no person shall be entitled to claim reimbursement under both this Code section and Code Section 17-12-26. The council shall adopt rules governing the approval of courses and training programs for credit or reimbursement as may be necessary to administer this Code section properly.

Laws 2003, Act 32, § 1, eff. Dec. 31, 2003.

§ 17-12-10. Report of activities; analysis of grants and funds

(a) The council shall prepare annually a report of its activities in order to provide the General Assembly, the Governor, and the Supreme Court of Georgia with an accurate description and accounting of the preceding year's expenditures and accomplishments.

(b) The council shall also provide to the General Assembly, the Governor, and the Supreme Court of Georgia a detailed analysis of all grants and funds, whether public or private, applied for or granted, together with how and in what manner the same are to be utilized and expended.

Laws 2003, Act 32, § 1, eff. Dec. 31, 2003.

§ 17-12-10.1. General Oversight Committee; creation; membership; powers and duties

(a) There is created the General Oversight Committee for the Georgia Public Defender Standards Council which shall be composed of eight persons: three members of the House of Representatives appointed by the Speaker of the House of Representatives, three members of the Senate appointed by the Senate Committee on Assignments or such person or entity as established by Senate rule, and one member of the House of Representatives and one member of the Senate appointed by the Governor. The members of such committee shall be selected within ten days after the convening of the General Assembly in each odd-numbered year and shall serve until their successors are appointed.

(b) The Speaker of the House of Representatives shall appoint a member of the committee to serve as chairperson and the Senate Committee on Assignments or such person or entity as established by Senate rule shall appoint one member of the committee to serve as vice chairperson during each even-numbered year. The Senate Committee on Assignments or such person or entity as established by Senate rule shall appoint a member of the committee to serve as chairperson and the Speaker of the House of Representatives shall appoint one member to serve as vice chairperson during each odd-numbered year. Such committee shall meet at least six times each year and, upon the call of the chairperson, at such additional times as deemed necessary by the chairperson.

(c) It shall be the duty of such committee to review and evaluate the following:

(1) Information on new programs submitted by the council;

(2) Information on standards proposed by the council;

(3) The strategic plans for the council;

(4) Program evaluation reports and budget recommendations of the council;

(5) The fiscal impact of fees and fines on counties;

(6) The reports submitted pursuant to Code Section 15-21A-7 in order to identify, among other things, opportunities to reduce or consolidate fees, fines, and surcharges; and

(7) Such other information or reports as deemed necessary by such committee.

(d) The council shall cooperate with such committee and provide such information or reports as requested by the committee for the performance of its functions.

(e) Notwithstanding subsection (c) of Code Section 45-12-78, the council shall submit its budget estimate to the director of the Office of Planning and Budget prior to submitting its budget estimate to the Judicial Council of Georgia. The council's budget estimate included in the Governor's budget report as provided in subsection (d) of Code Section 45-12-78 shall be as submitted by the Judicial Council of Georgia; provided, however, that the Governor shall be authorized to analyze the council's budget estimate and include such analysis as a part of the Governor's budget report.

(f) The committee shall make an annual report of its activities and findings to the membership of the General Assembly and the Governor within one week of the convening of each regular session of the General Assembly. The chairperson of the committee shall deliver written executive summaries of such report to the members of the General Assembly prior to the adoption of the General Appropriations Act each year.

(g) The members of the committee shall receive the allowances authorized for legislative members of legislative committees. The funds necessary to pay such allowances shall come from funds appropriated to the House of Representatives and the Senate.

(h) The committee shall be authorized to request that a performance audit of the council be conducted.

Laws 2004, Ex. Sess., Act 4, § 13, eff. June 15, 2004.

§ 17-12-10.2. Member liability

The members of the council as created by this article, the members of the circuit public defender selection panel created by Article 2 of this chapter, and other policy-making or administrative personnel acting in a policy-making or administrative capacity shall not be subject to civil liability resulting from any act or failure to act in the implementation and carrying out of the purposes of this article and Article 2 of this chapter.

Laws 2004, Ex. Sess., Act 4, § 14, eff. June 15, 2004.

§ 17-12-11. Assumption of powers, duties, and obligations of Georgia Indigent Defense Council; distribution of funds; transfer of employees

(a) On December 31, 2003, the Georgia Public Defender Standards Council shall assume all powers, duties, and obligations of the Georgia Indigent Defense Council created by former Code Section 17-12-32, and all references in this Code to the Georgia Indigent Defense Council shall be deemed to be references to the Georgia Public Defender Standards Council. Such powers shall include, without limitation, making grants and distributions to the counties.

(b) At least 90 percent of all state appropriated funds to the former Georgia Indigent Defense Council or the Georgia Public Defender Standards Council for grants to counties shall be distributed to counties for the January 1, 2004, through December 31, 2004, time period, based upon previous year expenditures for the provision of defense services at the local level.

(c) On December 31, 2003, the employees in good standing, assets, and resources of the Georgia Indigent Defense Council shall be transferred to the Georgia Public Defender Standards Council, and the council shall assume any executory contractual obligations of the Georgia Indigent Defense Council, provided that allocated funding resources for such obligations are also transferred. All full-time employees of the Georgia Public Defender Standards Council shall be state employees in the unclassified service of the State Merit System of Personnel Administration with all of the benefits of appointed state employees provided by law.

Laws 2003, Act 32, § 1, eff. Dec. 31, 2003; Laws 2004, Ex. Sess., Act 4, § 15, eff. June 15, 2004.

§ 17-12-12. Transition and governing provisions

From January 1, 2005, through December 31, 2005, the Georgia Public Defender Standards Council shall coordinate the transition from the procedures for providing criminal defense to indigent persons in effect on December 31, 2004, in each county to the procedures provided in Article 2 of this chapter. On and after January 1, 2005, the provisions of Article 2 of this chapter shall govern the public provision of criminal defense to indigent persons in the courts of this state.

Laws 2003, Act 32, § 1, eff. Dec. 31, 2003.

§ 17-12-13. Effective date of article

This article shall become effective on December 31, 2003, except as specified in Code Section 17-12-3.

Laws 2003, Act 32, § 1, eff. Dec. 31, 2003.

§ 17-12-14. Repealed by Laws 2003, Act 32, § 1, eff. Dec. 31, 2003

Article 1A

Local Indigent Defense Programs [Repealed]

Revision of Chapter 12

Laws 2004, Ex. Sess., Act 4, § 16, added this article effective June 15, 2004, and repealed it effective December 31, 2004.

§§ 17-12-19.1 to 17-12-19.14. Repealed by Laws 2004, Ex. Sess., Act 4, § 16, eff. December 31, 2004 (§ 17-12-19.14)

Article 2

Public Defenders

Revision of Chapter 12

Laws 2003, Act 32, § 1, added this article effective January 1, 2005, and provided that the council and circuit public defender selection panels were authorized to take necessary and appropriate action for phase-in full implementation of this article on or after December 31, 2003. See § 17-12-37.

Former Article 2, State Funded Local Indigent Defense Programs, consisting of §§ 17-12-30 to 17-12-51, was repealed by Laws 2003, Act 32, § 1, effective January 1, 2005.

§ 17-12-20. Circuit public defender selection panel; membership; powers

(a) There is created in each judicial circuit in the state a circuit public defender selection panel to be composed of five members. The membership shall be composed of one member each appointed by the Governor, the Lieutenant Governor, the Speaker of the House of Representatives, the Chief Justice of the Supreme Court of Georgia, and the chief judge of the superior court of the circuit. Members of the circuit public defender selection panel shall be individuals with significant experience working in the criminal justice system or who have demonstrated a strong commitment to the provision of adequate and effective representation of indigent defendants. A prosecuting attorney as defined in paragraph (6) of Code Section 19-13-51, any employee of a prosecuting attorney's office, or an employee of the Prosecuting Attorneys' Council of the State of Georgia shall not serve as a member of the circuit public defender selection panel after July 1, 2005. Members of the circuit public defender selection panel shall reside in the judicial circuit in which they serve. The circuit public defender selection panel members shall serve for a term of five years. Any vacancy for an appointed member shall be filled by the appointing authority.

(b) By majority vote of its membership, the circuit public defender selection panel shall appoint the circuit public defender in the circuit as provided in this article. The first such appointments shall be made to take office on January 1, 2005, for terms of up to four years. The initial appointments shall be for a term of up to four years.

(c) A circuit public defender may be removed for cause by a majority vote of the council.

(d) If a vacancy occurs for the position of circuit public defender, the chief judge of the superior court of the circuit shall appoint an interim circuit public defender to serve until the circuit public defender selection panel has appointed a replacement to serve out the unexpired term of office. The circuit public defender selection panel shall appoint a replacement circuit public defender within three months of the occurring of the vacancy.

Laws 2003, Act 32, § 1, eff. Jan. 1, 2005; Laws 2004, Act 564, § 17, eff. Jan. 1, 2005; Laws 2004, Ex. Sess., Act 4, § 17, eff. Jan. 1, 2005.

§ 17-12-21. Eligibility

To be eligible to fill the position of circuit public defender, a person must:

(1) Have attained the age of 25 years;

(2) Have been duly admitted and licensed to practice law in the superior courts for at least three years;

(3) Be a member in good standing of the State Bar of Georgia; and

(4) If previously disbarred from the practice of law, have been reinstated as provided by law.

Laws 2003, Act 32, § 1, eff. Jan. 1, 2005.

§ 17-12-22. Conflicts of interest

(a) The council shall establish a procedure for providing legal representation in cases where the circuit public defender office has a conflict of interest. This procedure may be by appointment of individual counsel on a case-by-case basis or by the establishment of a conflict defender office in those circuits where the volume of cases may warrant a separate conflict defender office.

(b) Attorneys who seek appointment in conflict cases must have such experience or training in the defense of criminal cases as is necessary in light of the complexity of the case to which they are appointed and must meet such qualifications and standards for the representation of indigent defendants as are established by the council.

(c) The circuit public defender shall establish a method for identifying conflicts of interest at the earliest possible opportunity.

Laws 2003, Act 32, § 1, eff. Jan. 1, 2005.

§ 17-12-23. Representation in actions and proceedings; time of entitlement to services; juveniles; contracts with cities or counties

(a) The circuit public defender shall provide representation in the following actions and proceedings:

(1) Any case prosecuted in a superior court under the laws of the State of Georgia in which there is a possibility that a sentence of imprisonment or probation or a suspended sentence of imprisonment may be adjudged;

(2) A hearing on a revocation of probation in a superior court;

(3) Any juvenile court case where the juvenile may face a disposition of confinement, commitment, or probation; and

(4) Any direct appeal of any of the proceedings enumerated in paragraphs (1) through (3) of this subsection.

(b) In each of the actions and proceedings enumerated in subsection (a) of this Code section, entitlement to the services of counsel begins as soon as is feasible and no more than 72 hours after the indigent person is taken into custody or service is made upon him or her of the charge, petition, notice, or other initiating process.

(c) Each circuit public defender shall establish a juvenile division within the circuit public defender office to specialize in the defense of juveniles.

(d) A city or county may contract with the circuit public defender office for the provision of criminal defense for indigent persons accused of violating city or county ordinances or state laws. If a city or county does not contract with the circuit public defender office, the city or county shall be subject to all applicable standards adopted by the council for representation of indigent persons in this state.

Laws 2003, Act 32, § 1, eff. Jan. 1, 2005; Laws 2006, Act 739, § 5, eff. July 1, 2006.

§ 17-12-24. Determination of financial eligibility; administration of operations; records

(a) The circuit public defender and any other person or entity providing indigent defense services shall determine the financial eligibility of any person or juvenile arrested, detained, or charged in any manner in accordance with the definition of an indigent person set forth in Code Section 17-12-2 that would entitle him or her to representation under this chapter.

(b) The circuit public defenders shall administer and coordinate the day-to-day operations of their respective offices and shall supervise the assistant public defenders and other staff serving in the office.

(c) The circuit public defender shall keep and maintain appropriate records, which shall include the number of persons represented under this article, including cases assigned to other counsel based on conflict of interest; the offenses charged; the outcome of each case; the expenditures made in carrying out the duties imposed by this article; and any other information requested by the council.

Laws 2003, Act 32, § 1, eff. Jan. 1, 2005; Laws 2006, Act 749, § 7, eff. May 3, 2006.

§ 17-12-25. Salary and cost-of-living adjustments; supplementation; private practice of law

(a) Each circuit public defender shall receive an annual salary of $87,593.58 and cost-of-living adjustments as may from time to time be granted to employees of the executive, judicial, and legislative branches of government from state funds.

(b) The county or counties comprising the judicial circuit may supplement the salary of the circuit public defender in an amount as is or may be authorized by local Act or in an amount as may be determined by the governing authority of the county or counties, whichever is greater.

(c) No circuit public defender shall engage in the private practice of law for profit.

Laws 2003, Act 32, § 1, eff. Jan. 1, 2005; Laws 2004, Ex. Sess., Act 4, § 18, eff. Jan. 1, 2005.

§ 17-12-26. Annual budget; administrative support; expenses; travel budget; expense reimbursement

(a) The council shall prepare and submit to the Judicial Council of Georgia an annual proposed budget necessary for fulfilling the purposes of this article in accordance with Code Section 45-12-78. The budget request shall be based on the previous year's expenditures and budget requests submitted by each circuit public defender, the Office of the Georgia Capital Defender, and the office of the mental health advocate. The council's total budget request for funding for the operations of the circuit public defender offices and the council's programs shall not exceed the amount of funds collected for indigent defense pursuant to Code Sections 15-21-73 and 15-21A-6. For fiscal years beginning prior to July 1, 2006, such funds collected for indigent defense may be estimated by the council based on actual monthly collections received prior to the council's budget request submission. The council is also authorized to seek, solicit, apply for, and utilize funds from any public or private source to use in fulfilling the purposes of this article.

(b) The budget of the council shall include the budget of all circuit public defenders and other offices and entities, including conflict defender offices and appointed attorneys providing indigent defense representation under the authority of this article and the Office of the Georgia Capital Defender and the office of the mental health advocate.

(c)(1) Subject to the provisions of paragraphs (3) and (4) of this subsection, expenses paid by the council pursuant to this Code section shall be paid out of funds as may be appropriated by the General Assembly.

(2) On or before June 1 of each year, the council shall establish and furnish to each circuit public defender and the state auditor the travel budget for each judicial circuit based on the amount appropriated by the General Assembly for travel.

(3) In determining the travel budget for each judicial circuit, the council shall consider the budget request submitted by the circuit public defender of each judicial circuit, the geographic size and the caseload of each circuit, and other facts as may be relevant. The council is authorized to establish a contingency reserve of not more than 3 percent of the total amount appropriated by the General Assembly in order to meet any expenses which could not be reasonably anticipated. The council shall submit to each circuit public defender, the state auditor, and the legislative budget analyst a monthly report showing the budget amount of expenditures made under the travel budget. The council may periodically review and adjust the travel budget as may be necessary to carry out the purposes of this subsection.

(4) Neither the circuit public defender nor any personnel compensated by the state pursuant to the provisions of this article shall be reimbursed from state funds for any expenses for which the person has been reimbursed from funds other than state funds; provided, however, that the governing authority of the county or counties comprising the judicial circuit are authorized to provide travel advances or to reimburse expenses which may be incurred by the person in the performance of his or her official duties to the extent the expenses are not reimbursed by the state as provided in this Code section.

Laws 2003, Act 32, § 1, eff. Jan. 1, 2005; Laws 2004, Ex. Sess., Act 4, § 19, eff. Jan. 1, 2005; Laws 2006, Act 453, § 17, eff. April 14, 2006; Laws 2006, Act 749, § 8, eff. May 3, 2006.

§ 17-12-27. Assistant public defenders

(a) Subject to the provisions of this Code section, the circuit public defender in each judicial circuit is authorized to appoint:

(1) One assistant public defender for each superior court judge authorized for the circuit, excluding the chief judge and senior judges; and

(2) Subject to funds being appropriated by the General Assembly or otherwise available, additional assistant public defenders as may be authorized by the council. In authorizing additional assistant public defenders, the council shall consider the caseload, present staff, and resources available to each circuit public defender and shall make authorizations as will contribute to the efficiency of individual circuit public defenders and the effectiveness of providing adequate legal defense for indigent defendants.

(b) Each assistant public defender appointed pursuant to subsection (a) of this Code section shall be classified based on education, training, and experience. The jobs of assistant public defenders and the minimum qualifications required for appointment or promotion to each job shall be established by the council based on education, training, and experience and in accordance with the provisions of Code Sections 17-12-30 and 17-12-34.

(c) Each assistant public defender appointed pursuant to this Code section shall be compensated based on a salary range established in accordance with subsection (c) of Code Section 17-12-30. The salary range for each job established in accordance with subsection (b) of this Code section shall be as follows:

(1) Assistant public defender I. Not less than $38,124.00 nor more than 65 percent of the compensation of the circuit public defender;

(2) Assistant public defender II. Not less than $40,884.00 nor more than 70 percent of the compensation of the circuit public defender;

(3) Assistant public defender III. Not less than $45,108.00 nor more than 80 percent of the compensation of the circuit public defender; and

(4) Assistant public defender IV. Not less than $52,176.00 nor more than 90 percent of the compensation of the circuit public defender.

(d) All personnel actions involving attorneys appointed pursuant to this Code section shall be made by the circuit public defender in writing in accordance with the provisions of Code Section 17–12–30.

(e)(1) All salary advancements shall be based on quality of work, education, and performance.

(2) The salary of an assistant public defender appointed pursuant to this Code section may be increased at the first of the calendar month following the anniversary of his or her appointment.

(3) The salary of any assistant public defender who, subsequent to his or her appointment pursuant to this Code section, is awarded an LL.M. or S.J.D. degree by a law school recognized by the State Bar of Georgia from which a graduate of or student enrolled therein is permitted to take the bar examination or by a law school accredited by the American Bar Association or the Association of American Law Schools may be increased effective on the first day of the calendar month following the award of the degree, provided that such advancement does not exceed the maximum of the salary range applicable to the attorney's job classification.

(f) Any assistant public defender appointed pursuant to this Code section may be promoted to the next highest job at any time the attorney meets the minimum qualifications for such job, but in order to be eligible for promotion, the attorney shall have served not less than 12 months in the job from which the attorney is to be promoted. When an assistant public defender is promoted to the next highest job, the assistant public defender shall enter the higher job at an annual salary greater than the annual salary the assistant public defender was receiving immediately prior to the promotion.

(g) All full-time state paid employees of the office of the circuit public defender shall be state employees in the unclassified service of the State Merit System of Personnel Administration with all benefits of such appointed state employees as provided by law. A circuit public defender, assistant public defender, or local public defender may be issued an employee identification card by his or her employing agency; provided, however, no employer of any such public defender shall issue nor shall any public defender display, wear, or carry any badge, shield, card, or other item that is similar to a law enforcement officer's badge or that could be reasonably construed to indicate that the public defender is a peace officer or law enforcement official.

(h) Notwithstanding the provisions of subsection (g) of this Code section, an employee of a local public defender office who was an employee of the office on June 30, 2004, and who becomes a circuit public defender or an employee of a circuit public defender office before July 1, 2005, may elect, with the consent of the former employer and the consent of the council, to remain an employee of the entity for which the employee worked as a local public defender; and such entity shall be his or her employer for all purposes, including, without limitation, compensation and employee benefits. The right to make an election pursuant to this subsection shall expire on July 1, 2005. The council shall reimburse the appropriate entity for compensation, benefits, and employer contributions under the federal Social Security Act, but the total payment from the council to the entity on behalf of the employee shall not exceed the amount otherwise payable to or for the employee under the circumstance where the employee had become a state employee.

Laws 2003, Act 32, § 1, eff. Jan. 1, 2005; Laws 2004, Act 564, § 17, eff. Jan. 1, 2005; Laws 2004, Ex. Sess., Act 4, § 20, eff. Jan. 1, 2005; Laws 2005, Act 19, § 17, eff. April 7, 2005; Laws 2006, Act 749, § 9, eff. May 3, 2006.

§ 17–12–28. Investigators

(a) Subject to the provisions of this Code section, the circuit public defender in each judicial circuit is authorized to appoint one investigator to assist the circuit public defender in the performance of his or her official duties in the preparation of cases for trial. Subject to funds being appropriated by the General Assembly or otherwise available, the circuit public defender in each judicial circuit may appoint additional investigators as may be authorized by the council. In authorizing additional investigators, the council shall consider the caseload, present staff, and resources available to each circuit public defender and shall make authorizations as will contribute to the efficiency of individual circuit public defenders and the effectiveness of circuit public defenders throughout the state in providing adequate legal defense for indigent defendants.

(b) An investigator appointed pursuant to this Code section shall be not less than 21 years of age and shall serve at the pleasure of the circuit public defender.

(c) An investigator appointed pursuant to this Code section shall:

(1) Assist the attorneys within the office of the circuit public defender in the preparation of cases for preliminary hearings, pretrial hearings, and trial; and

(2) Perform other duties as are required by the circuit public defender.

(d) Each investigator appointed pursuant to this Code section shall be compensated based on a salary range established pursuant to Code Section 17–12–30.

The salary range for the investigator appointed pursuant to this Code section shall be not less than $30,828.00 nor more than 70 percent of the compensation of the circuit public defender from state funds.

(e)(1) Except as otherwise provided in this subsection, an investigator appointed pursuant to this Code section shall be appointed initially to the entry grade of the job on the state-wide pay ranges.

(2) Any person who is employed in a nonstate paid investigator's position within the office of the circuit public defender may be transferred to a state paid position. Such transfer shall be to the job and salary range commensurate with the education and experience of the employee.

(3) Any person who is employed as a peace officer by an agency of the executive branch of state government who is appointed as an investigator pursuant to this Code section without a break in service may be appointed to an annual salary at least equal to the annual salary the person received on the last day of employment immediately preceding said appointment.

(4) Any person who was a certified peace officer employed on a full-time basis by this state, the United States or any of the several states, or a political subdivision or authority thereof may be appointed to the salary that gives the officer credit for experience as a full-time certified peace officer.

(f) Personnel appointed pursuant to this Code section shall be reimbursed for actual expenses incurred in the performance of their official duties in accordance with the provisions of Code Section 17-12-26.

Laws 2003, Act 32, § 1, eff. Jan. 1, 2005; Laws 2004, Act 564, § 17, eff. Jan. 1, 2005; Laws 2004, Ex. Sess., Act 4, § 21, eff. Jan. 1, 2005.

§ 17-12-29. Administrative, clerical, and paraprofessional personnel

(a) Each circuit public defender is authorized to employ administrative, clerical, and paraprofessional personnel as may be authorized by the council based on funds appropriated by the General Assembly or otherwise available; provided, however, that each circuit public defender shall be authorized not less than two such personnel. In authorizing administrative, clerical, and paraprofessional personnel, the council shall consider the caseload, present staff, and resources available to each circuit public defender and shall make authorizations as will contribute to the efficiency of individual circuit public defenders in providing effective criminal defense for indigent defendants.

(b) Personnel appointed pursuant to this Code section shall be compensated based on a salary range developed in accordance with Code Section 17-12-30.

(c) All personnel actions involving personnel appointed pursuant to this Code section shall be in accordance with the provisions of Code Section 17-12-30.

Laws 2003, Act 32, § 1, eff. Jan. 1, 2005; Laws 2004, Act 564, § 17, eff. Jan. 1, 2005; Laws 2004, Ex. Sess., Act 4, § 22, eff. Jan. 1, 2005.

§ 17-12-30. State paid personnel

(a) All state paid personnel employed by the circuit public defenders pursuant to this article shall be employees of the judicial branch of state government in accordance with Article VI, Section VIII of the Constitution of Georgia and shall be in the unclassified service of the State Merit System of Personnel Administration.

(b) Personnel employed by the circuit public defenders pursuant to this article shall have the authority, duties, powers, and responsibilities as are authorized by law or as assigned by the circuit public defender and shall serve at the pleasure of the circuit public defender.

(c)(1) The council shall establish salary ranges for each state paid position authorized by this article or any other provision of law. Salary ranges shall be similar to the state-wide and senior executive ranges adopted by the State Merit System of Personnel Administration and shall provide for minimum, midpoint, and maximum salaries not to exceed the maximum allowable salary. In establishing the salary ranges, all amounts will be rounded off to the nearest whole dollar. The council may, from time to time, revise the salary ranges to include across-the-board increases which the General Assembly may from time to time authorize in the General Appropriations Act.

(2) The circuit public defender shall fix the compensation of each state paid employee appointed pursuant to this article in accordance with the job to which the person is appointed and the appropriate salary range.

(3) All salary advancements shall be based on quality of work, training, and performance. The salary of state paid personnel appointed pursuant to this article may be increased at the first of the calendar month following the annual anniversary of the person's appointment. No employee's salary shall be advanced beyond the maximum established in the applicable pay range.

(4) Any reduction in salary shall be made in accordance with the salary range for the position and the policies, rules, or regulations adopted by the council.

(5) The compensation of state paid personnel appointed pursuant to this article shall be paid in equal installments by the Department of Administrative Services or the Administrative Office of the Courts, as determined by the council, as provided

by this subsection from funds appropriated for such purpose. The council may, with the consent of the Department of Administrative Services or the Administrative Office of the Courts, authorize employees compensated pursuant to this Code section to participate in voluntary salary deductions as provided by Article 3 of Chapter 7 of Title 45.

(6) The governing authority of the county or counties comprising a judicial circuit may supplement the salary or fringe benefits of any state paid position appointed pursuant to this article.

(7) The governing authority of any municipality within the judicial circuit may, with the approval of the circuit public defender, supplement the salary or fringe benefits of any state paid position appointed pursuant to this article.

Laws 2003, Act 32, § 1, eff. Jan. 1, 2005; Laws 2004, Ex. Sess., Act 4, § 23, eff. Jan. 1, 2005.

§ 17–12–31. Employment of additional assistant or deputy circuit public defenders, other employees, or independent contractors

(a) The circuit public defender in each judicial circuit may employ additional assistant circuit public defenders, deputy circuit public defenders, or other attorneys, investigators, paraprofessionals, clerical assistants, and other employees or independent contractors as may be provided for by local law or as may be authorized by the governing authority of the county or counties comprising the judicial circuit. The circuit public defender shall define the duties and fix the title of any attorney or other employee of the office of the circuit public defender.

(b) Personnel employed by the circuit public defender pursuant to this Code section shall serve at the pleasure of the circuit public defender and shall be compensated by the county or counties comprising the judicial circuit, the manner and amount of compensation to be paid to be fixed either by local Act or by the circuit public defender with the approval of the county or counties comprising the judicial circuit.

Laws 2003, Act 32, § 1, eff. Jan. 1, 2005.

§ 17–12–32. County or city contracts with council to provide additional personnel

The governing authority of any county or municipality within the judicial circuit which provides additional personnel for the office of circuit public defender may contract with the council to provide such additional personnel in the same manner as is provided for state paid personnel in this article. Any such personnel shall be considered state employees and shall be entitled to the same fringe benefits as other state paid personnel employed by the circuit public defender pursuant to this article. The governing authority of such county or municipality shall transfer to the council such funds as may be necessary to cover the compensation, benefits, travel, and other expenses for such personnel.

Laws 2003, Act 32, § 1, eff. Jan. 1, 2005; Laws 2006, Act 749, § 10, eff. May 3, 2006.

§ 17–12–33. Assistant public defenders or other attorneys; private practice of law; admission to practice; powers and duties

(a) Any assistant public defender or other attorney at law employed full time by the circuit public defender who is compensated in whole or in part by state funds shall not engage in the private practice of law for profit.

(b) Any assistant public defender or any other attorney at law employed by the circuit public defender shall be a member of the State Bar of Georgia and shall be admitted to practice before the appellate courts of this state. The assistant public defender shall serve at the pleasure of the circuit public defender and shall have such authority, powers, and duties as may be assigned by the circuit public defender.

Laws 2003, Act 32, § 1, eff. Jan. 1, 2005; Laws 2004, Act 564, § 17, eff. Jan. 1, 2005.

§ 17–12–34. Offices, utilities, telephone expenses, materials, and supplies

The governing authority of the county shall provide, in conjunction and cooperation with the other counties in the judicial circuit and in a pro rata share according to the population of each county, appropriate offices, utilities, telephone expenses, materials, and supplies as may be necessary to equip, maintain, and furnish the office or offices of the circuit public defender in an orderly and efficient manner. The provisions of an office, utilities, telephone expenses, materials, and supplies shall be subject to the budget procedures required by Article 1 of Chapter 81 of Title 36.

Laws 2003, Act 32, § 1, eff. Jan. 1, 2005.

§ 17–12–35. Public or private contracts, funds, and grants

A circuit public defender office may contract with and may accept funds and grants from any public or private source.

Laws 2003, Act 32, § 1, eff. Jan. 1, 2005.

§ 17–12–36. Alternative delivery systems for judicial circuits composed of a single county

(a) The council may permit a judicial circuit composed of a single county to continue in effect an alternative delivery system to the one set forth in this article if:

(1) The delivery system:

(A) Has a full-time director and staff and had been fully operational for at least two years on July 1, 2003; or

(B) Is administered by the county administrative office of the courts or the office of the court administrator of the superior court and had been fully operational for at least two years on July 1, 2003;

(2) The council, by majority vote of the entire council, determines that the delivery system meets or exceeds its standards, including, without limitation, caseload standards, as the council adopts;

(3) The governing authority of the county comprising the judicial circuit enacts a resolution expressing its desire to continue its delivery system and transmits a copy of such resolution to the council not later than September 30, 2004; and

(4) The governing authority of the county comprising the judicial circuit enacts a resolution agreeing to fully fund its delivery system.

(b) A judicial circuit composed of a single county may request an alternative delivery system only one time; provided, however, that if such judicial circuit's request for an alternative delivery system was disapproved on or before December 31, 2004, such judicial circuit may make one further request on or before September 1, 2005. The council shall allow such judicial circuit to have a hearing on such judicial circuit's request.

(c) The council shall make a determination with regard to continuation of an alternative delivery system not later than December 1, 2005, and if the council determines that such judicial circuit's alternative delivery system does not meet the standards as established by the council, the council shall notify such judicial circuit of its deficiencies in writing and shall allow such judicial circuit an opportunity to cure such deficiencies. The council shall make a final determination with regard to continuation of an alternative delivery system on or before December 31, 2005. Initial and subsequent approvals of alternative delivery systems shall be by a majority vote of the entire council.

(d) Any circuit whose alternative delivery system is disapproved at any time shall be governed by the provisions of this article other than this Code section.

(e) In the event an alternative delivery system is approved, the council shall annually review the operation of such system and determine whether such system is meeting the standards as established by the council and is eligible to continue operating as an approved alternative delivery system. In the event the council determines that such system is not meeting the standards as established by the council, the council shall provide written notice to such system of the deficiencies and shall provide such system an opportunity to cure such deficiencies.

(f) In the event an alternative delivery system is approved, it shall keep and maintain appropriate records, which shall include the number of persons represented; the offenses charged; the outcome of each case; the expenditures made in providing services; and any other information requested by the council.

(g) In the event the council disapproves an alternative delivery system either in its initial application or annual review, such system may appeal such decision to the Supreme Court of Georgia under such rules and procedures as shall be prescribed by the Supreme Court.

Laws 2003, Act 32, § 1, eff. Jan. 1, 2005; Laws 2004, Ex. Sess., Act 4, § 24, eff. Jan. 1, 2005; Laws 2005, Act 281, § 2, eff. May 6, 2005.

§ 17-12-37. Effective date of article

This article shall become effective on January 1, 2005; provided, however, that the council and the circuit public defender selection panels shall be authorized to take administrative actions as may be necessary or appropriate to prepare for and phase-in full implementation of this article on or after December 31, 2003.

Laws 2003, Act 32, § 1, eff. Jan. 1, 2005.

§§ 17-12-38 to 17-12-39. Repealed by Laws 2003, Act 32, § 1, eff. January, 1, 2005

Article 2A

Reimbursement for Legal Services

In 2006, the Code Commission redesignated this Article, added as Article 2A, consisting of §§ 17-12-50 through 17-12-52, by Laws 2006, Act 739, § 6, as Article 3A.

Article 3

Assistance by Third-Year Law Student or Staff Instructors

Revision of Chapter 12

Laws 2003, Act 32, § 1, added this article effective January 1, 2005. See § 17–12–45.

Former Article 3, Defense of Indigents in Capital Cases, consisting of §§ 17–12–60 to 17–12–62, was repealed by Laws 2003, Act 32, § 1, effective January 1, 2005.

§ 17–12–40. Definitions

As used in this article, the term:

(1) "Circuit public defender" means any circuit public defender of this state or assistants of such officer.

(2) "Criminal proceeding" means any investigation, trial, juvenile proceeding, adjudicatory hearing, or other legal proceeding by which a person's liability for a crime is investigated or determined, commencing with the investigation and including the final disposition of the case.

(3) "Law school" means a law school within or outside this state which is approved by the American Bar Association or which is authorized to operate under Code Section 20–3–250.8.

(4) "Staff instructor" means a full-time professional staff instructor of a law school in this state who has been admitted to the bar of another state but who has not yet been admitted to the bar of this state.

(5) "Third-year law student" means a student regularly enrolled and in good standing in a law school within or outside this state who has satisfactorily completed at least two-thirds of the requirements for the first professional degree in law (J.D. or its equivalent) in not less than four semesters or six quarters of residence.

Laws 2003, Act 32, § 1, eff. Jan. 1, 2005.

§ 17–12–41. Assistance in criminal proceedings

An authorized third-year law student or staff instructor, when under the supervision of a circuit public defender, may assist in criminal proceedings within this state as if admitted and licensed to practice law in this state except that all pleadings and other entries of record must be signed by a circuit public defender or by his or her duly appointed assistant and that, in the conduct of a trial or other criminal proceeding, a circuit public defender or his or her duly appointed assistant must be physically present.

Laws 2003, Act 32, § 1, eff. Jan. 1, 2005.

§ 17–12–42. Authorization to assist circuit public defender; certification

A third-year law student or staff instructor may be authorized to assist a circuit public defender in such form and manner as the judge of the court may prescribe, taking care that the requirements of this article and the good moral character of the third-year law student or staff instructor are properly certified by the dean of the law school.

Laws 2003, Act 32, § 1, eff. Jan. 1, 2005.

§ 17–12–43. File of certificates, oaths, orders; time of authorization

As to each third-year law student or staff instructor authorized to assist a circuit public defender, there shall be kept on file in the office of the clerk of the court in the county where such authority is to be exercised the dean's certificate, the student's and instructor's oaths, and the judge's order as contemplated under Code Section 17–12–42. The authority to assist a circuit public defender as allowed under this Code section shall extend for no longer than 18 months. If during this period any change occurs in the status of the student or instructor at the law school in which he or she was enrolled or employed, that is, if the student ceases his or her enrollment, is suspended, or is expelled or if the instructor ceases his or her employment or is released by the school, any such authority shall terminate and be revoked.

Laws 2003, Act 32, § 1, eff. Jan. 1, 2005.

§ 17–12–44. Qualifications not required

Any third-year law student or staff instructor authorized to assist a circuit public defender under this article is not required to possess the qualifications for appointment to the office of circuit public defender or appointment as an assistant circuit public defender as provided in Article 1 of this chapter.

Laws 2003, Act 32, § 1, eff. Jan. 1, 2005.

§ 17–12–45. Effective date of article

This article shall become effective on January 1, 2005.

Laws 2003, Act 32, § 1, eff. Jan. 1, 2005.

§§ 17–12–46 to 17–12–49. Repealed by Laws 2003, Act 32, § 1, eff. January, 1, 2005

Article 3A

Reimbursement for Legal Services

In 2006, the Code Commission redesignated this Article, added as Article 2A, consisting of §§ 17–12–50 through 17–12–52, by Laws 2006, Act 739, § 6, as Article 3A.

§ 17–12–50. Definitions

As used in this article, the term:

(1) "Paid in part" means payment by a county or municipality for a part of the cost of the provision of indigent defense services pursuant to a contract with a circuit public defender office as set forth in subsection (d) of Code Section 17–12–23. The term does not include payment by a county or municipality for office space and other supplies as set forth in Code Section 17–12–34.

(2) "Public defender" means an attorney employed by a circuit public defender office, an attorney who is a conflict defender, or any other attorney who is paid from public funds to represent an indigent person in a criminal case.

Laws 2006, Act 739, § 6, eff. July 1, 2006.

§ 17–12–51. Repayment of costs of legal representation as condition of probation; financial hardship

(a) When a defendant who is represented by a public defender, who is paid in part or in whole by a county, enters a plea of nolo contendere, first offender, or guilty or is otherwise convicted, the court may impose as a condition of probation repayment of all or a portion of the cost for providing legal representation and other expenses of the defense if the payment does not impose a financial hardship upon the defendant or the defendant's dependent or dependents. The defendant shall make the payment through the probation department to the county.

(b) When a defendant who is represented by a public defender, who is paid in part or in whole by a municipality, enters a plea of nolo contendere, first offender, or guilty or is otherwise convicted, the court may impose as a condition of probation repayment of all or a portion of the cost for providing legal representation and other expenses of the defense if the payment does not impose a financial hardship upon the defendant or the defendant's dependent or dependents. The defendant shall make the payment through the probation department to the municipality.

(c) If a defendant who is represented by a public defender, who is paid for entirely by the state, enters a plea of nolo contendere, first offender, or guilty or is otherwise convicted, the court may impose as a condition of probation repayment of all or a portion of the cost for providing legal representation and other costs of the defense if the payment does not impose a financial hardship upon defendant or the defendant's dependent or dependents. The defendant shall make the payment through the probation department to Georgia Public Defender Standards Council for payment to the general fund of the state treasury. It is the intent of the General Assembly that all funds collected under this subsection shall be made available through the general appropriations process and may be appropriated for purposes of funding indigent defense.

(d) In determining whether or not a payment imposed under this Code section imposes a financial hardship upon a defendant or defendant's dependent or dependents and in determining the amount of the payment to impose, the court shall consider the factors set forth in Code Section 17–14–10. The public defender may provide the court with an estimate of the cost for providing to the defendant the legal representation and other expenses of the defense. If requested by the defendant, the court shall hold a hearing to determine the amount to be paid.

(e) This Code section shall not apply to a disposition involving a child pursuant to Chapter 11 of Title 15, relating to juvenile proceedings.

Laws 2006, Act 739, § 6, eff. July 1, 2006.

§ 17–12–52. Reimbursement to county or municipality for legal assistance

(a) A county or municipality may recover payment or reimbursement from a person who has received legal assistance from a public defender paid in part or in whole by the county or municipality:

(1) If the person was not eligible to receive such legal assistance; or

(2) If the person has been ordered to pay for the legal representation and other expenses of the defense pursuant to Code Section 17–12–51 and has not paid for the legal services.

(b) An action shall be brought within four years after the date on which the legal services were received.

(c) In determining the amount of the payment imposed under this Code section, the court shall consider the factors set forth in Code Section 17-14-10. The public defender may provide the court with an estimate of the cost for providing to the defendant the legal representation and other expenses of the defense.

(d) This Code section shall not apply to proceedings involving a child pursuant to Chapter 11 of Title 15, relating to juvenile proceedings.

Laws 2006, Act 739, § 6, eff. July 1, 2006.

§§ 17-12-60 to 17-12-62. Repealed by Laws 2003, Act 32, § 1, eff. January, 1, 2005

§ 17-12-70 to 17-12-72. Repealed by Laws 2003, Act. 32, § 1, eff. December 31, 2003

Article 4

Mental Health Advocacy for Insane

Chapter 12 Revision

Laws 2003, Act 32, § 1, added this article effective December 31, 2003. See § 17-12-88.

Former Article 4, Public Defenders, consisting of §§ 17-12-70 to 17-12-72, was repealed by Laws 2003, Act 32, § 1, effective December 31, 2003.

§ 17-12-80. Definitions

As used in this article, the term "office" means the office of mental health advocacy created by this article.

Laws 2003, Act 32, § 1, eff. Dec. 31, 2003; Laws 2004, Act 564, § 17, eff. May 13, 2004.

§ 17-12-81. Creation of office; successor to mental health advocacy division; powers, duties, assets, employees

There is created the office of mental health advocacy for the purpose of undertaking the representation of indigent persons found not guilty by reason of insanity at the time of the crime in any court in this state. The office shall serve all counties of this state. The office shall be a direct successor of the mental health advocacy division of the Georgia Indigent Defense Council created by former Code Section 17-12-45 and all powers, duties, and obligations of such division shall become the powers, duties, and obligations of the office. The employees, assets, and resources of the mental health advocacy division of the Georgia Indigent Defense Council shall be transferred to the office. All references in this Code to the mental health advocacy division of the Georgia Indigent Defense Council shall be deemed to be references to the office.

Laws 2003, Act 32, § 1, eff. Dec. 31, 2003.

§ 17-12-82. Legal entity; powers

The office shall be a legal entity; shall have perpetual existence; may contract; may own property; may accept funds, grants, and gifts from any public or private source, which funds shall be used to defray the expenses incident to implementing its purposes; and may establish a principal office.

Laws 2003, Act 32, § 1, eff. Dec. 31, 2003.

§ 17-12-83. Management

The council shall be responsible for management of the office. Managerial duties shall include, but are not limited to, the following:

(1) Appointment of the mental health advocate;

(2) Establishing the salaries of the mental health advocate and the office's staff;

(3) Approving the level of staffing and establishing policy consistent with the intent of this chapter; and

(4) Preparing an annual budget for the office, administering the funds made available to the office, and overseeing the expenditure of such funds.

Laws 2003, Act 32, § 1, eff. Dec. 31, 2003.

§ 17-12-84. Budget

The council shall prepare an annual budget showing all anticipated expenses of the office for the following fiscal year, which shall be the same as the fiscal year of this state. Such budget shall be submitted by the mental health advocate to the council.

Laws 2003, Act 32, § 1, eff. Dec. 31, 2003.

§ 17-12-85. Mental health advocate; appointment, qualifications, and compensation

The mental health advocate shall be appointed by and shall serve at the pleasure of the council. The mental health advocate must be a member in good standing of the State Bar of Georgia with at least three years' experience in the practice of law and must be competent to counsel and represent a person found not guilty by reason of insanity at the time of the crime. The salary of the mental health advocate shall be established by the council.

Laws 2003, Act 32, § 1, eff. Dec. 31, 2003.

§ 17-12-86. Employment of personnel

The mental health advocate shall employ, with the advice and consent of the council and in the manner and at the compensation prescribed by the council, as many assistant attorneys, clerks, investigators, paraprofessionals, administrative assistants, and any other persons as may be necessary for carrying out the responsibilities assigned to the office by law. A person employed under this Code section serves at the pleasure of the mental health advocate.

Laws 2003, Act 32, § 1, eff. Dec. 31, 2003.

§ 17-12-87. Representation of persons prior to and after finding of not guilty by reason of insanity at time of crime

(a) Whenever any person has been found not guilty by reason of insanity at the time of the crime pursuant to Code Section 17-7-131 and has been determined to be indigent, as provided in Article 1 of this chapter, the court in which such charges are pending shall notify the office and the office may assume the defense and representation of such persons in all matters pursuant to Code Section 17-7-131 if the resources, funding, and staffing of the office allow; provided, however, that the circuit public defender or other attorney who represented the indigent at the time of the finding of not guilty by reason of insanity at the time of the crime shall have the option to retain responsibility for the representation of any such person.

(b) Nothing in this Code section shall prevent the circuit public defender, the court, or the court appointed attorney from requesting the participation of the office prior to a finding of not guilty by reason of insanity at the time of the crime. The circuit public defender, the court, or the court appointed attorney may request that the office assist in the case prior to a plea being entered and accepted by the court.

(c) If for any reason the office is unable to represent any indigent person found not guilty by reason of insanity at the time of the crime, such representation shall be provided as otherwise provided by law.

Laws 2003, Act 32, § 1, eff. Dec. 31, 2003.

§ 17-12-88. Effective date of article

This article shall become effective on December 31, 2003.

Laws 2003, Act 32, § 1, eff. Dec. 31, 2003.

§§ 17-12-90 to 17-12-97. Repealed by Laws 2003, Act. 32, § 1, eff. December 31, 2003

Article 5

Office of Multicounty Public Defender [Repealed]

Revision of Chapter 12

Laws 2003, Act 32, § 1, added this article effective December 31, 2003, consisting of §§ 17-12-100 to 17-12-108, and repealed it effective December 31, 2004.

Former Article 5, Office of Multicounty Public Defender, consisting of §§ 17-12-90 to 17-12-97, was repealed by Laws 2003, Act 32, § 1, effective December 31, 2003.

§§ 17-12-100 to 17-12-108. Repealed by Laws 2003, Act 32, § 1, eff. Dec. 31, 2004

Article 6

Georgia Capital Defender

Revision of Chapter 12

Laws 2003, Act 32, § 1, added this article effective January 1, 2005. See § 17-12-128.

§ 17-12-120. Definitions

As used in this article, the term "office" means the Office of the Georgia Capital Defender created by this article.

Laws 2003, Act 32, § 1, eff. Jan. 1, 2005.

§ 17-12-121. Creation of office

There is created the Office of the Georgia Capital Defender to undertake the defense of all indigent persons charged with a capital felony for which the death penalty is being sought in any court in this state and to be the successor to the office of the multicounty public defender. The office shall serve all counties of this state.

Laws 2003, Act 32, § 1, eff. Jan. 1, 2005.

§ 17-12-122. Nature and powers of office

The Office of the Georgia Capital Defender shall be a legal entity, shall have perpetual existence, may contract, may own property, may accept funds, grants, and gifts from any public or private source, which funds shall be used to defray the expenses incident to implementing its purposes, and may establish a principal office.

Laws 2003, Act 32, § 1, eff. Jan. 1, 2005.

§ 17-12-123. Management of office

The council shall be responsible for management of the office. Managerial duties shall include, but not be limited to, the following:

(1) Appointing the capital defender;

(2) Establishing the salaries of the capital defender and the office's staff;

(3) Approving the level of staffing and establishing policy consistent with the intent of this article; and

(4) Preparing an annual budget for the office, administering the funds made available to the office, and overseeing the expenditure of such funds.

Laws 2003, Act 32, § 1, eff. Jan. 1, 2005; Laws 2004, Act 564, § 17, eff. Jan. 1, 2005.

§ 17-12-124. Annual budget

The council shall prepare an annual budget showing all anticipated expenses of the office for the following fiscal year, which shall be the same as the fiscal year of this state. The budget shall be submitted by the capital defender to the council and for Fiscal Year 2005 and thereafter shall include the proposed budget for representation of all indigent persons accused of a capital felony for which the death penalty is or is likely to be sought.

Laws 2003, Act 32, § 1, eff. Jan. 1, 2005; Laws 2006, Act 749, § 11, eff. May 3, 2006.

§ 17-12-125. Appointment, qualifications, and compensation of capital defender

The capital defender shall be appointed by and shall serve at the pleasure of the council. The capital defender must have been licensed to practice law in this state for at least five years and must be competent to counsel and defend a person charged with a capital felony. The salary of the capital defender shall be established by the council.

Laws 2003, Act 32, § 1, eff. Jan. 1, 2005.

§ 17-12-126. Staffing of office; competency of primary counsel

(a) The capital defender shall employ, with the advice and consent of the council and in the manner and at the compensation prescribed by the council, as many assistant attorneys, clerks, investigators, paraprofessionals, administrative assistants, and other persons as may be necessary for carrying out his or her responsibilities under this article. A person employed under this Code section serves at the pleasure of the capital defender.

(b) No person may be assigned the primary responsibility of representing an indigent person accused of a capital offense for which the death penalty is sought unless the person is authorized to practice law in this state and is otherwise competent to counsel and defend a person charged with a capital felony.

Laws 2003, Act 32, § 1, eff. Jan. 1, 2005.

§ 17-12-127. Duties and responsibilities of office

(a) Whenever any person accused of a capital felony for which the death penalty is being sought has been determined to be indigent, as provided in Article 2 of this chapter, the court in which the charges are pending shall notify the office, and the office shall assume the defense of the person if there is no conflict of interest.

(b) If for any reason the office is unable to defend any indigent person accused of a capital felony for which the death penalty is being sought, the presiding judge of the superior court in which the case is pending shall appoint an attorney or attorneys to represent the defendant. Counsel appointed pursuant to this subsection shall be paid with state funds appropriated to the council for use by the office. The council with the assistance of the office shall establish guidelines for attorney's fees and expense requests.

(c) The office or appointed counsel's defense of a defendant shall include all proceedings in the trial court and any appeals to the Supreme Court of Georgia. Neither the office nor appointed counsel shall assist with any petition for a writ of habeas corpus in federal court.

Laws 2003, Act 32, § 1, eff. Jan. 1, 2005.

§ 17-12-127.1. Continuation of representation

On and after January 1, 2005, any attorney appointed pursuant to Article 5 of this chapter shall continue to represent a defendant under this article and shall be paid for services pursuant to this article.

Laws 2003, Act 32, § 1; Laws 2004, Act 564, § 17, eff. Dec. 31, 2004.

Formerly 1981 Code § 17-12-108.

§ 17-12-128. Effective date of article

This article shall become effective on January 1, 2005.

Laws 2003, Act 32, § 1, eff. Jan. 1, 2005.

CHAPTER 13

CRIMINAL EXTRADITION

Article 1

General Provisions

§ 17-13-1. Rules to be observed by applicants for requisitions

In addition to rules adopted by the Governor, the following rules shall be observed as a condition precedent to obtaining a requisition by him for the extradition of any fugitive from the justice of this state:

(1) The application for a requisition shall be made to the Governor by a district attorney, prosecuting attorney of a state court, judge of a city or state court, or the mayor of any municipal corporation of this state and must show the full name of the fugitive for whom extradition is asked, the crime charged, the state or territory to which he has fled, the full name of the person suggested to act as agent of this state to receive and convey the fugitive to this state, the agent in no case to be the prosecutor; but the Governor may, in his discretion, appoint some other suitable person as agent of this state to receive and convey the fugitive. The application must also show that the ends of public justice require that the fugitive shall be brought back to this state for trial and that the requisition is not wanted for the purpose of enforcing the collection of a debt or for any private purpose whatever but solely for the purpose of a criminal prosecution as provided by law;

(2) The application shall be accompanied by the affidavit of the prosecutor, if any, stating that the requisition is wanted for the sole purpose of punishing the accused and not in any way to collect a debt or money or to enforce the payment thereof;

(3) If the fugitive has been indicted, two certified copies of the indictment or presentment shall be forwarded to the Governor with the application; and

(4) If no indictment has been preferred and an affidavit is the basis of the requisition, the affidavit shall describe the crime committed, with all the particularity required in an indictment, and two certified copies of the affidavit shall accompany the petition for the requisition.

Laws 1884-85, p. 141, § 1; Laws 1983, p. 884, § 3-22.

Formerly Penal Code 1895, § 1275; Penal Code 1910, § 1357; Code 1933, § 44-101.

§ 17-13-2. Duty of Governor

When an application is made as provided in Code Section 17-13-1 and in accordance with other rules adopted by the Governor, he shall make his requisition for the extradition of the fugitive under the seal of the office of the Governor, according to law.

Laws 1884-85, p. 141, § 2; Laws 1983, p. 649, § 1.

Formerly Penal Code 1895, § 1276; Penal Code 1910, § 1358; Code 1933, § 44-102.

§ 17–13–3. Expense authorized by county governing authority

Before any expenses shall be incurred by any officer or duly authorized agent of the state for bringing back to the county where the crime was committed any fugitive from the justice of this state, who may be beyond the limits of the state, so as to become a charge upon any county where the crime was committed, the incurring of any such expense and the amount thereof shall be first authorized by the county governing authority.

Laws 1914, p. 123, § 1.

Formerly Code 1933, § 44–201.

§ 17–13–4. Fugitives from foreign countries

Whenever a fugitive from justice from a foreign country is found within this state, and by the treaty stipulations of the United States the person is to be surrendered to the authorities of the foreign country upon requisition from the proper officers, the Governor, by his warrant, shall cause him to be arrested and delivered over to such authorities.

Formerly Code 1863, § 60; Code 1868, § 56; Code 1873, § 53; Code 1882, § 53; Penal Code 1895, § 1270; Penal Code 1910, § 1352; Code 1933, § 44–301.

§ 17–13–5. Officers must execute warrants for the arrest of fugitives

When the Governor or other officer issues a warrant of arrest, it is the duty of the sheriffs, their deputies, coroners, and constables to execute it when placed in their hands.

Formerly Code 1863, § 64; Code 1868, § 60; Code 1873, § 57; Code 1882, § 57; Penal Code 1895, § 1274; Penal Code 1910, § 1356; Code 1933, § 44–305.

Article 2

Uniform Criminal Extradition Act

§ 17–13–20. Short title

This article shall be known and may be cited as the "Uniform Criminal Extradition Act."

Laws 1951, p. 726, § 32; Laws 2004, Act 564, § 17, eff. May 13, 2004.

§ 17–13–21. Definitions

As used in this article, the term:

(1) "Executive authority" includes the Governor and any person performing the functions of governor in a state other than this state.

(2) "Governor" includes any person performing the functions of governor by authority of the laws of this state.

(3) "State," referring to a state other than this state, includes the District of Columbia and any other state or territory, organized or unorganized, of the United States of America.

Laws 1951, p. 726, § 1; Laws 1978, p. 1754, § 1.

§ 17–13–22. Fugitives from justice; duty of Governor

Subject to this article, the Constitution of the United States, and any and all acts of Congress enacted in pursuance thereof, it is the duty of the Governor of this state to have arrested and delivered up to the executive authority of any other state any person charged in that state with treason, felony, or other crime, who has fled from justice and is found in this state.

Laws 1951, p. 726, § 2.

§ 17–13–23. Form of demand

No demand for the extradition of a person charged with a crime in another state shall be recognized by the Governor unless in writing, alleging, except in cases arising under Code Section 17–13–25, that the accused was present in the demanding state at the time of the commission of the alleged crime and that thereafter he fled from the state, and accompanied by a copy of an indictment found, or by information supported by affidavit in the state having jurisdiction of the crime, or by a copy of an affidavit made before a magistrate there, together with a copy of any warrant which was issued thereupon, or by a copy of a judgment of conviction or of a sentence imposed in execution thereof, together with a statement by the executive authority of the demanding state that the person claimed has escaped from confinement or has broken the terms of his bail, probation, or parole. The indictment, information, or affidavit made before the magistrate must substantially charge the person demanded with having committed a crime under the law of the state; and the copy of the indictment, information, affidavit, judgment of conviction, or sentence must be authenticated by the executive authority making the demand.

Laws 1951, p. 726, § 3.

§ 17-13-24. Extradition of person imprisoned or awaiting trial in another state or who has left the demanding state under compulsion

(a) When it is desired to have returned to this state a person charged in this state with a crime, and such person is imprisoned or is held under criminal proceedings then pending against him in another state, the Governor of this state may agree with the executive authority of the other state for the extradition of the person before the conclusion of the proceedings or of his term of sentence in the other state, upon condition that the person be returned to the other state, at the expense of this state, as soon as the prosecution in this state is terminated.

(b) The Governor of this state may also surrender, on demand of the executive authority of any other state, any person in this state who is charged in the manner provided in Code Section 17-13-43 with having violated the laws of the state whose executive authority is making the demand, even though such person left the demanding state involuntarily.

Laws 1951, p. 726, § 5; Laws 1955, p. 587, § 3.

§ 17-13-25. Extradition of persons not present in demanding state at time of commission of crime

The Governor of this state may also surrender, on demand of the executive authority of any other state, any person in this state charged in such other state in the manner provided in Code Section 17-13-23 with committing an act in this state, or in a third state, intentionally resulting in a crime in the state whose executive authority is making the demand and the provisions of this article not otherwise inconsistent shall apply to such cases, even though the accused was not in that state at the time of the commission of the crime and has not fled therefrom.

Laws 1951, p. 726, § 6.

§ 17-13-26. Governor may investigate case

When a demand for the surrender of a person charged with a crime shall be made upon the Governor of this state by the executive authority of another state, the Governor may call upon the Attorney General or any prosecuting officer in this state to investigate or assist in investigating the demand, to report to him the situation and circumstances of the person so demanded, and to advise whether he ought to be surrendered.

Laws 1951, p. 726, § 4.

§ 17-13-27. Warrant of arrest; issuance by Governor

If the Governor decides that the demand should be complied with, he shall sign a warrant of arrest, which shall be sealed with the seal of the office of the Governor and directed to any peace officer or other person whom he may think fit to entrust with the execution thereof. The warrant must substantially recite the facts necessary to the validity of its issuance.

Laws 1951, p. 726, § 7; Laws 1983, p. 649, § 2.

§ 17-13-28. Manner and place of execution

The warrant shall authorize the peace officer or other person to whom directed to arrest the accused at any time and any place where he may be found within the state, to command the aid of all peace officers or other persons in the execution of the warrant, and to deliver the accused, subject to other provisions of this article, to the duly authorized agent of the demanding state.

Laws 1951, p. 726, § 8.

§ 17-13-29. Authority of arresting officer

Every peace officer or other person empowered to make the arrest shall have the same authority, in arresting the accused, to command assistance therein as peace officers have by law in the execution of any criminal process directed to them, with like penalties against those who refuse their assistance.

Laws 1951, p. 726, § 9.

§ 17-13-30. Rights of accused person; application for writ of habeas corpus; penalty

(a) No person arrested upon a warrant shall be delivered over to the agent whom the executive authority demanding him shall have appointed to receive him unless he shall first be taken forthwith before a judge of a court of record in this state, who shall inform him of the demand made for his surrender, of the crime with which he is charged, and that he has the right to demand and procure legal counsel. If the prisoner or his counsel shall state that he or they desire to test the legality of his arrest, the judge of the court of record shall fix a reasonable time to be allowed him within which to apply for a writ of habeas corpus. When the writ is applied for, notice thereof, and of the time and place of hearing thereon, shall be given to the prosecuting officer of the county in which the arrest is made and in which the accused is in custody and to the agent of the demanding state.

(b) Any officer who shall deliver to the agent for extradition of the demanding state a person in his custody under the Governor's warrant, in willful disobedience of subsection (a) of this Code section, shall be guilty of a misdemeanor and, upon conviction, shall be fined not more than $1,000.00 or be imprisoned not more than six months, or both.

Laws 1951, p. 726, §§ 10, 11.

§ 17-13-31. District attorneys to defend habeas corpus actions

The district attorney shall answer and defend any habeas corpus action brought under this article, which action contests the issuance, execution, or validity of a Governor's warrant of arrest, unless the Governor shall direct the Attorney General to answer and defend the habeas corpus action.

Laws 1979, p. 412, § 1.

§ 17-13-32. Confinement in jail when necessary

(a) The officer or persons executing the Governor's warrant of arrest or the agent of the demanding state to whom the prisoner may have been delivered may, when necessary, confine the prisoner in the jail of any county or city through which he may pass; and the keeper of the jail must receive and safely keep the prisoner until the officer or person having charge of him is ready to proceed on his route, such officer or person being chargeable with the expense of keeping.

(b) The officer or agent of a demanding state to whom a prisoner may have been delivered following extradition proceedings in another state, or to whom a prisoner may have been delivered after waiving extradition in such other state, and who is passing through this state with such a prisoner for the purpose of immediately returning the prisoner to the demanding state may, when necessary, confine the prisoner in the jail of any county or city through which he may pass; and the keeper of the jail must receive and safely keep the prisoner until the officer or agent having charge of him is ready to proceed on his route, the officer or agent, however, being chargeable with the expense of keeping; provided, however, that the officer or agent shall produce and show to the keeper of the jail satisfactory written evidence of the fact that he is actually transporting the prisoner to the demanding state after a requisition by the executive authority of the demanding state. The prisoner shall not be entitled to demand a new requisition while in this state.

Laws 1951, p. 726, § 12.

§ 17-13-33. Arrest prior to requisition

Whenever any person within this state shall be charged, on the oath of any credible person before any judge or magistrate of this state, with the commission of any crime in any other state and, except in cases arising under Code Section 17-13-25, with having fled from justice, or with having been convicted of a crime in that state and having escaped from confinement, or with having broken the terms of his bail, probation, or parole, or whenever complaint shall have been made before any judge or magistrate in this state setting forth, on the affidavit of any credible person in another state, that a crime has been committed in such other state and that the accused has been charged in such state with the commission of the crime and, except in cases arising under Code Section 17-13-25, has fled from justice, or with having been convicted of a crime in that state and having escaped from confinement, or with having broken the terms of his bail, probation, or parole, and is believed to be in this state, the judge or magistrate shall issue a warrant directed to any peace officer, commanding him to apprehend the person named therein, wherever he may be found in this state, and to bring him before the same or any other judge, magistrate, or court who or which may be available in or convenient of access to the place where the arrest may be made, to answer the charge or complaint and affidavit. A certified copy of the sworn charge or complaint and affidavit upon which the warrant is issued shall be attached to the warrant.

Laws 1951, p. 726, § 13.

§ 17-13-34. Arrest without a warrant

The arrest of a person may be lawfully made by any peace officer or private person, without a warrant, upon reasonable information that the accused stands charged in the courts of a state with a crime punishable by death or imprisonment for a term exceeding one year, but when so arrested, the accused must be taken before a judge or magistrate with all practicable speed and complaint must be made against him under oath, setting forth the ground for the arrest, as provided in Code Section 17-13-33; and thereafter the answer of the accused shall be heard as if he had been arrested on a warrant.

Laws 1951, p. 726, § 14; Laws 1990, p. 8, § 17.

§ 17-13-35. Commitment to await requisition; bail

If from the examination before the judge or magistrate it appears that the person held is the person charged with having committed the crime alleged and, except in cases arising under Code Section 17-13-25, that he has fled from justice, the judge or magistrate must, by a warrant reciting the accusation, commit him to the county jail for such a time, not exceeding 30 days and which time must be specified in the warrant, as will enable the arrest of the accused to be made under a warrant of the Governor on a requisition of the executive authority of the state having jurisdiction of the offense, unless the accused gives bail, as provided in Code Section 17-13-36, or until he shall be legally discharged.

Laws 1951, p. 726, § 15.

§ 17-13-36. Bail; in what cases; conditions of bond

Unless the offense with which the prisoner is charged is shown to be an offense punishable by death or life imprisonment under the laws of the state in which it was committed, a judge or magistrate in this state may admit the prisoner to bail by bond, with sufficient sureties, in such sum as he deems proper, conditioned for the prisoner's appearance before the judge or magistrate at a time specified in such bond and for the prisoner's surrender to be arrested upon the warrant of the Governor of this state.

Laws 1951, p. 726, § 16.

§ 17-13-37. Extension of time of commitment

If the accused is not arrested under warrant of the Governor by the expiration of the time specified in the warrant or bond, a judge or magistrate may discharge him or may recommit him for a further period not to exceed 60 days, or a judge or magistrate may again take bail for his appearance and surrender as provided for in Code Section 17-13-36, but within a period not to exceed 60 days after the date of such new bond.

Laws 1951, p. 726, § 17.

§ 17-13-38. Forfeiture of bail

If the prisoner is admitted to bail and fails to appear and surrender himself according to the conditions of his bond, the judge or magistrate, by proper order, shall declare the bond forfeited and order his immediate arrest without warrant if he is within the state. Recovery may be had on the bond in the name of the state as in the case of other bonds given by the accused in criminal proceedings within this state.

Laws 1951, p. 726, § 18.

§ 17-13-39. Persons under criminal prosecution in this state at time of demand

The Governor may, in his discretion, surrender, upon demand of the executive authority of another state, any person found in this state, notwithstanding the fact that a criminal prosecution or charges under the laws of this state are pending against the person, that the person has already been convicted in this state and is serving a sentence in any jail or penal institution of this state or of any county or municipality thereof, or that the person is serving a suspended or probationary sentence. The Governor may condition the release of the prisoner to the demanding state upon such terms as he may stipulate, including the condition that the prisoner be returned to this state immediately after trial and before commencing the service of sentence, if any, in the demanding state. In no case shall surrender of the prisoner be construed as a complete relinquishment of jurisdiction by this state, but the prisoner shall forthwith be returned to the custody of this state at the expense of the demanding state immediately after trial in the demanding state or the completion of sentence therein, as the case may be, except where the sentence of death has been executed in the demanding state.

Laws 1951, p. 726, § 19; Laws 1955, p. 587, § 2.

§ 17-13-40. Guilt or innocence of accused; when inquired into

The guilt or innocence of the accused as to the crime of which he is charged may not be inquired into by the Governor or in any proceeding after the demand for extradition accompanied by a charge or crime in legal form as provided for in this article shall have been presented to the Governor, except as it may be involved in identifying the person held as the person charged with the crime.

Laws 1951, p. 726, § 20.

§ 17-13-41. Governor may recall warrant or issue another warrant

The Governor may recall his warrant of arrest or may issue another warrant whenever he deems proper.

Laws 1951, p. 726, § 21.

§ 17-13-42. Fugitives from this state; duty of Governor

Whenever the Governor of this state shall demand a person charged with a crime or with escaping from confinement or breaking the terms of his bail, probation, or parole in this state, from the executive authority of any other state, or from the chief justice or an associate justice of the Supreme Court of the District of Columbia authorized to receive such demand under the laws of the United States, he shall issue a warrant under the seal of the office of the Governor to some agent, commanding him to receive the person so charged if delivered to him and convey him to the proper officer of the county in this state in which the offense was committed.

Laws 1951, p. 726, § 22; Laws 1983, p. 649, § 3.

§ 17-13-43. Application for issuance of demand; by whom made; contents

(a) When the return to this state of a person charged with crime in this state is required, the prosecuting attorney shall present to the Governor his written application, in which application shall be stated the name of the person so charged, the crime charged against him, the approximate time, place, and circumstance of its commission, the state in which he is believed to be, including the location of the accused therein at the time the application is made, and certifying that, in the opinion of the prosecuting attorney, the ends of justice require the arrest and return of the accused to this state for trial and that the proceeding is not instituted to enforce a private claim.

(b) When the return to this state is required of a person who has been convicted of a crime in this state and who has escaped from confinement or broken the terms of his bail, probation, or parole, the prosecuting attorney of the county in which the offense was committed, the State Board of Pardons and Paroles, or the warden of the institution or sheriff of the county from which escape was made shall present to the Governor a written application for a requisition for the return of such person. The application shall state the name of the person, the crime of which he was convicted, the circumstances of his escape from confinement or of the breach of the terms of his bail, probation, or parole and the state in which he is believed to be, including the location of the person therein at the time application is made.

(c) The application shall be verified by affidavit, executed in duplicate, and accompanied by two certified copies of the indictment returned, information and affidavit filed, or of the complaint made to the judge or magistrate, stating the offense with which the accused is charged, or of the judgment of conviction or of the sentence. The prosecuting officer, parole board, warden, or sheriff may also attach such further affidavits and other documents in duplicate as he shall deem proper to be submitted with such application. One copy of the application, with the action of the Governor indicated by endorsement thereon, and one of the certified copies of the indictment, complaint, information and affidavits, or of the judgment of conviction or of the sentence shall be filed in the office of the Governor, to remain of record in that office. The other copies of all papers shall be forwarded with the Governor's requisition.

Laws 1951, p. 726, § 23; Laws 1983, p. 649, § 4.

§ 17–13–44. Costs and expenses

When the punishment of the crime shall be the confinement of the person in a penal institution, the expenses shall be paid out of the state treasury on the certificate of the Governor and warrant of the state auditor; and in all other cases the expenses shall be paid out of the county treasury in the county wherein the crime is alleged to have been committed. The expenses shall be the fees paid to the officers of the state on whose governor the requisition is made and shall not exceed 8¢ per mile for all necessary travel in returning such prisoner.

Laws 1951, p. 726, § 24.

§ 17–13–45. Immunity from service of process in certain civil actions

A person brought into this state by or after waiver of extradition based on a criminal charge shall not be subject to service of personal process in civil actions arising out of the same facts as the criminal proceedings to answer which he is being or has been returned until he has been convicted in the criminal proceeding; or, if acquitted, until he has had reasonable opportunity to return to the state from which he was extradited.

Laws 1951, p. 726, § 25.

§ 17–13–46. Written waiver of extradition proceedings

(a) Any person arrested in this state charged with having committed any crime in another state or alleged to have escaped from confinement, or broken the terms of his bail, probation, or parole, may waive the issuance and service of the warrant provided for in Code Sections 17–13–27 and 17–13–28 and all other procedure incidental to extradition proceedings, by executing or subscribing in the presence of a judge of any court of record within this state a writing which states that he consents to return to the demanding state; provided, however, that before the waiver shall be executed or subscribed by the person it shall be the duty of the judge to inform the person of his rights to the issuance or service of a warrant of extradition and to obtain a writ of habeas corpus as provided in Code Section 17–13–30.

(b) If and when the consent has been duly executed, it shall forthwith be forwarded to the office of the Governor of this state and filed therein. The judge shall direct the officer having the person in custody to deliver forthwith the person to the duly accredited agent or agents of the demanding state and shall deliver or cause to be delivered to the agent or agents a copy of the consent. Nothing in this Code section shall be deemed to limit the rights of the accused person to return voluntarily and without formality to the demanding state; nor shall this waiver procedure be deemed to be an exclusive procedure or to limit the powers, rights, or duties of the officers of the demanding state or of this state.

Laws 1951, p. 726, § 26; Laws 1982, p. 3, § 17.

§ 17–13–47. Non-waiver by this state

Nothing in this article contained shall be deemed to constitute a waiver by this state of its right, power, or privilege to try a person demanded for extradition by another state for crimes committed within this state or of its right, power, or privilege to regain custody of the person by extradition proceedings or otherwise for the purpose of trial, sentence, or punishment for any crime committed within this state; nor shall any proceedings had under this article result in, or fail to result in, extradition, be deemed a waiver by this state of any of its rights, privileges, or jurisdiction in any way whatsoever.

Laws 1951, p. 726, § 27.

§ 17-13-48. No immunity from other criminal prosecutions while in this state

After a person has been brought back to this state by, or after waiver of, extradition proceedings, he may be tried in this state for other crimes which he may be charged with having committed here as well as that specified in the requisition for his extradition.

Laws 1951, p. 726, § 28.

§ 17-13-49. Interpretation

This article shall be so interpreted and construed as to effectuate the general purposes to make uniform the laws of those states which enact it.

Laws 1951, p. 726, § 29.

CHAPTER 14

RESTITUTION AND DISTRIBUTION OF PROFITS TO VICTIMS OF CRIMES

Article 1

Restitution

§ 17-14-1. Policy

It is declared to be the policy of this state that restitution to their victims by those found guilty of crimes or adjudicated as having committed delinquent acts is a primary concern of the criminal justice system and the juvenile justice system.

Laws 1980, p. 1382, § 1; Laws 2005, Act 20, § 5, eff. July 1, 2005.

Formerly Code 1933, § 27-3001.

§ 17-14-2. Definitions

As used in this article, the term:

(1) "Conviction" means an adjudication of guilt of or a plea of guilty or nolo contendere to the commission of an offense against the laws of this state. Such term includes any such conviction or plea, notwithstanding the fact that sentence was imposed pursuant to Article 3 of Chapter 8 of Title 42. Such term also includes the adjudication or plea of a juvenile to the commission of an act which, if committed by an adult, would constitute a crime under the laws of this state.

(2) "Damages" means all special damages which a victim could recover against an offender in a civil action, including a wrongful death action, based on the same act or acts for which the offender is sentenced, except punitive damages and damages for pain and suffering, mental anguish, or loss of consortium. Such special damages shall not be limited by any law which may cap economic damages. Special damages may include the reasonably determined costs of transportation to and from court proceedings related to the prosecution of the crime.

(3) "Offender" means any natural person, firm, partnership, association, public or private corporation, or other legal entity that has been sentenced for any crime or any juvenile who has been adjudged delinquent.

(4) "Ordering authority" means:

(A) A court of competent jurisdiction;

(B) The State Board of Pardons and Paroles;

(C) The Department of Corrections;

(D) The Department of Juvenile Justice; or

(E) Any combination thereof, as is required by the context.

(5) "Parent" means a person who is the legal mother as defined in paragraph (10.2) of Code Section 15-11-2, the legal father as defined in paragraph (10.1) of Code Section 15-11-2, or the legal guardian. Such term shall not include a foster parent.

(6) "Relief" means any parole or other conditional release from incarceration; the awarding of earned time allowances; reduction in security status; or placement in prison rehabilitation programs, including, but not limited to, those in which the offender receives monetary compensation.

(7) "Restitution" means any property, lump sum, or periodic payment ordered to be made by any offender or other person to any victim by any ordering authority. Where the victim is a public corporation or governmental entity or where the offender is a juvenile, restitution may also be in the

form of services ordered to be performed by the offender.

(8) "Restitution order" means any order, decree, or judgment of an ordering authority which requires an offender to make restitution.

(9) "Victim" means any:

(A) Natural person or his or her personal representative or, if the victim is deceased, his or her estate; or

(B) Any firm, partnership, association, public or private corporation, or governmental entity suffering damages caused by an offender's unlawful act; provided, however, that the term "victim" shall not include any person who is concerned in the commission of such unlawful act as defined in Code Section 16-2-20.

Laws 1980, p. 1382, § 1; Laws 1985, p. 283, § 1; Laws 2005, Act 20, § 5, eff. July 1, 2005.

Formerly Code 1933, § 27-3002.

§ 17-14-3. Court-ordered restitution

(a) Subject to the provisions of Code Section 17-14-10, notwithstanding the provisions contained in Chapter 11 of Title 15, and in addition to any other penalty imposed by law, a judge of any court of competent jurisdiction shall order an offender to make full restitution to any victim.

(b) If the offender is placed on probation, including probation imposed pursuant to Chapter 11 of Title 15 or Article 3 of Chapter 8 of Title 42, or sentence is suspended, deferred, or withheld, restitution ordered under this Code section shall be a condition of that probation, sentence, or order.

(c) If the offender is granted relief by the Department of Juvenile Justice, Department of Corrections, or the State Board of Pardons and Paroles, the terms of any court order requiring the offender to make restitution to a victim shall be a condition of such relief in addition to any other terms or conditions which may apply to such relief.

Laws 1980, p. 1382, § 1; Laws 2005, Act 20, § 5, eff. July 1, 2005.

Formerly Code 1933, § 27-3003.

§ 17-14-4. Pardons and paroles

Notwithstanding any provision of Code Section 42-9-45 to the contrary, the State Board of Pardons and Paroles may grant parole prior to the completion of one-third of the sentence if restitution is ordered as a condition of the parole.

Laws 1980, p. 1382, § 1; Laws 2005, Act 20, § 5, eff. July 1, 2005.

Formerly Code 1933, § 27-3004.

§ 17-14-5. Juveniles

(a) It is declared to be the policy of this state to recognize that restitution is consistent with the goal of rehabilitation of delinquent juveniles and to provide restitution in such cases.

(b) Notwithstanding any provision of Chapter 11 of Title 15, the juvenile courts shall order restitution in any case involving delinquent juveniles in the same manner as is authorized by this article for adult offenders.

(c) For purposes of ensuring compliance with the restitution order, the juvenile courts are authorized to retain jurisdiction over a juvenile subject to such restitution order until the juvenile reaches 21 years of age. If the juvenile court retains jurisdiction of such offender as provided in this Code section and the terms of the restitution order are not completed before the offender's twenty-first birthday, the juvenile court shall transfer the restitution order to the superior court.

(d) As an alternative to subsection (c) of this Code section, the juvenile courts are authorized to transfer to the superior courts, and the superior courts are authorized to accept, jurisdiction over enforcement of restitution orders against juveniles who, since entry of the order, have attained 18 years of age.

(e) If the court determines that a juvenile is or will be unable to pay all of the restitution ordered, after notice to the juvenile's parent or parents and an opportunity for the parent or parents to be heard, the court may order the parent or parents to pay any portion of the restitution ordered that is outstanding where the court or a jury finds by clear and convincing evidence that the parent or parents knew or should have known of the juvenile's propensity to commit such acts and the acts are due to the parent's or parents' negligence or reckless disregard for the juvenile's propensity to commit such acts. Upon the eighteenth birthday of the juvenile, the parental obligation to pay restitution shall be terminated.

(f) If the court orders a parent to pay restitution under subsection (e) of this Code section, the court shall take into account the considerations identified in Code Section 17-14-10. If the parent or parents are required to pay restitution under subsection (e) of this Code section, the court shall provide for payment to be made in specified installments and within a specified period of time.

Laws 1980, p. 1382, § 1; Laws 2005, Act 20, § 5, eff. July 1, 2005.

Formerly Code 1933, § 27-3005.

§ 17-14-6. Past restitution considered

(a) Where an offender has made total or partial restitution to a victim, the ordering authority shall set off any such amounts and reduce the amount payable to the victim.

(b) The ordering authority shall not order restitution to be paid to a victim or victim's estate if the victim or victim's estate has received or is to receive full compensation for that loss from the offender as a result of a civil proceeding.

(c) Any amount paid to a victim or victim's estate under a restitution order shall reduce the amount payable to a victim or a victim's estate by an award from the Georgia Crime Victims Compensation Board made prior to or after a restitution order under this article.

(d) The ordering authority shall order restitution be paid to the Georgia Crime Victims Compensation Board, other governmental entities, or any individuals, partnerships, corporations, associations, or other legal entities acting on behalf of a governmental entity that have compensated the victim or the victim's estate for a loss incurred by the victim to the extent of the compensation paid for that loss. The ordering authority shall also order restitution for the costs of services provided to persons or entities that have provided services to the victim as a result of the crime. Services that are subject to restitution under this subsection include, but are not limited to, shelter, food, clothing, and transportation. However, a restitution order shall require that all restitution to a victim or victim's estate under the restitution order be made before any restitution to any other person or entity under that restitution order is made.

(e) In the event the ordering authority provides for a setoff or priority in terms of payment of restitution, the ordering authority shall state on the record with specificity the reasons for its action.

Laws 1980, p. 1382, § 1; Laws 2005, Act 20, § 5, eff. July 1, 2005; Laws 2006, Act 453, § 17, eff. April 14, 2006.

Formerly Code 1933, § 27–3006.

§ 17–14–7. Voluntary restitution plans; restitution hearing; joint liability; multiple victims; waiver of restitution

(a) Any offender may offer a restitution plan to the ordering authority. If a plan is offered, it shall be the duty of the ordering authority to consider the factors stated in Code Section 17–14–10 and to make the plan part of a restitution order if acceptable to the ordering authority.

(b) If the parties have not agreed on the amount of restitution prior to sentencing, the ordering authority shall set a date for a hearing to determine restitution. Any dispute as to the proper amount or type of restitution shall be resolved by the ordering authority by the preponderance of the evidence. The burden of demonstrating the amount of the loss sustained by a victim as a result of the offense shall be on the state. The burden of demonstrating the financial resources of the offender or person being ordered to pay restitution and the financial needs of his or her dependents shall be on the offender or person being ordered to pay restitution. The burden of demonstrating such other matters as the ordering authority deems appropriate shall be upon the party designated by the ordering authority as justice requires.

(c) If the ordering authority finds that more than one offender has contributed to the loss of a victim, the court may make each offender liable for payment of the full amount of restitution or may apportion liability among the offenders to reflect the level of contribution to the victim's loss and economic circumstances of each offender.

(d) If the ordering authority finds that more than one victim has sustained a loss requiring restitution by an offender, the court may provide for a different payment schedule for each victim based on the type and amount of each victim's loss and accounting for the economic circumstances of each victim. In any case in which the state or any of its political subdivisions is a victim and thus is due restitution, the ordering authority shall ensure that any other victim receives full restitution before the state or a political subdivision receives restitution.

(e) A victim may waive his or her right to obtain restitution pursuant to this article. Any such waiver shall be made in writing and filed with the court or ordering authority having jurisdiction over the criminal case. Such waiver shall not affect any other rights or remedies that the victim may have against the offender under the laws of this state or the United States or any of the several states.

Laws 1980, p. 1382, § 1; Laws 2005, Act 20, § 5, eff. July 1, 2005; Laws 2006, Act 453, § 17, eff. April 14, 2006.

Formerly Code 1933, § 27–3007.

§ 17–14–8. Partial payment of restitution; time of payment

(a) In any case in which a court sentences an offender to pay restitution and a fine, if the court permits the offender to pay such restitution and fine in other than a lump sum, the clerk of any superior court of this state, probation officer or parole officer, or other official who receives such partial payments shall apply not less than one-half of each payment to the restitution before paying any portion of such fine or any forfeitures, costs, fees, or surcharges provided for by law to any agency, department, commission, committee, authority, board, or bureau of state or local government.

(b) The clerk of any court of this state, probation officer or parole officer, or other official who receives partial payments for restitution shall pay the restitution amount to the victim as provided in the restitution order not later than the last day of each month, provided that the amount exceeds $100.00. If the amount does not exceed $100.00, the clerk of any court of this state, probation officer or parole officer, or other official may allow the amount of restitution to accumulate until such time as it exceeds $100.00 or until the end of the next calendar quarter, whichever occurs first.

Laws 1980, p. 1382, § 1; Laws 2005, Act 20, § 5, eff. July 1, 2005.

Formerly Code 1933, § 27-3008.

§ 17-14-9. Restitution not to exceed damages

The amount of restitution ordered shall not exceed the victim's damages.

Laws 1980, p. 1382, § 1; Laws 2005, Act 20, § 5, eff. July 1, 2005.

Formerly Code 1933, § 27-3009.

§ 17-14-10. Factors considered

(a) In determining the nature and amount of restitution, the ordering authority shall consider:

(1) The financial resources and other assets of the offender or person ordered to pay restitution including whether any of the assets are jointly controlled;

(2) The earnings and other income of the offender or person ordered to pay restitution;

(3) Any financial obligations of the offender or person ordered to pay restitution, including obligations to dependents;

(4) The amount of damages;

(5) The goal of restitution to the victim and the goal of rehabilitation of the offender;

(6) Any restitution previously made;

(7) The period of time during which the restitution order will be in effect; and

(8) Other factors which the ordering authority deems to be appropriate.

(b) If, subsequent to restitution being ordered pursuant to this article, a victim is convicted of a crime for which restitution is ordered, the ordering authority shall consider the previously ordered restitution as part of the financial resources of such victim.

Laws 1980, p. 1382, § 1; Laws 2005, Act 20, § 5, eff. July 1, 2005.

Formerly Code 1933, § 27-3010.

§ 17-14-11. Civil actions

An order for restitution shall not bar any civil action against the offender. However, any payments made by an offender to a victim under an order for restitution may be a setoff against any judgment awarded to the victim in a civil action based on the same facts for which restitution was ordered. The fact of restitution or a restitution order under this article shall not be placed before the jury on the issue of liability. If the amount of restitution made is in dispute and liability is established, the court shall order further appropriate proceedings to determine the amount of setoff.

Laws 1980, p. 1382, § 1; Laws 2005, Act 20, § 5, eff. July 1, 2005.

Formerly Code 1933, § 27-3011.

§ 17-14-12. Modification

The ordering authority shall retain jurisdiction to modify a restitution order at any time before the expiration of the relief ordered.

Laws 1980, p. 1382, § 1; Laws 2005, Act 20, § 5, eff. July 1, 2005.

Formerly Code 1933, § 27-3012.

§ 17-14-13. Enforcement

(a) A restitution order shall be enforceable as is a civil judgment by execution as provided in Code Section 17-10-20.

(b) If an offender or other person ordered to pay restitution willfully refuses to comply with a restitution order, the order, in the discretion of the court, may be enforced by attachment for contempt, upon the application of the prosecuting attorney or the victim.

(c) Failure to comply with a restitution order may, in the discretion of the ordering authority, be grounds to revoke or cancel the relief at any time the restitution order is in effect. Where the relief is earned time allowances, the Department of Corrections may suspend the offender from earning earned time allowances for a specified period of time.

Laws 1980, p. 1382, § 1; Laws 1982, p. 3, § 17; Laws 1985, p. 231, § 1; Laws 2005, Act 20, § 5, eff. July 1, 2005.

Formerly Code 1933, § 27-3013.

§ 17-14-14. Payments; wage assignment; review of case; interest

(a) Payments pursuant to an order for restitution shall be made to the clerk of the court or to any other person, for the benefit of the victim or victims, as the ordering authority shall order.

(b) In each case in which payment of restitution is ordered as a condition of probation or parole, the ordering authority may require any employed offender to execute a wage assignment to pay the restitution.

(c) Until such time as the restitution has been paid or the sentence has been completed, the clerk of court or the probation or parole officer assigned to the case, whoever is responsible for collecting restitution, shall review the case not less frequently than twice yearly to ensure that restitution is being paid as ordered. If the restitution was ordered to be made within a specific period of time, the case shall be reviewed at the end of the specific period of time to determine if the restitution has been paid in full. The final review shall be conducted before the sentence or probationary or parole period expires. If it is determined at any review that restitution is not being paid as ordered, a written report of the violation shall be filed with the court on a form prescribed by the Council of Superior Court Clerks of Georgia.

(d) If the ordering authority permits the offender to pay restitution in other than a lump sum, the ordering authority may require the offender to pay interest on the amount of restitution due the victim or the victim's estate. Such interest shall be set at the same rate as is provided by Code Section 7-4-12 for judgments.

Laws 1980, p. 1382, § 1; Laws 2005, Act 20, § 5, eff. July 1, 2005.

Formerly Code 1933, § 27-3014.

§ 17-14-15. Peonage; denial of benefits because of poverty

(a) Nothing in this article shall authorize peonage; and this article shall be construed and diligently administered to prevent peonage.

(b) No offender shall be denied any benefit, relief, or privilege to which he or she might otherwise be entitled or eligible solely because he or she is financially unable and cannot become financially able to make restitution.

Laws 1980, p. 1382, § 1; Laws 2005, Act 20, § 5, eff. July 1, 2005.

Formerly Code 1933, § 27-3016.

§ 17-14-16. Copy of restitution order to department

If an offender who is ordered to pay restitution under this article is remanded to the jurisdiction of the Department of Corrections or the Department of Juvenile Justice, the court shall provide a copy of the restitution order to such department when the offender is remanded to such department's jurisdiction.

Laws 1980, p. 1382, § 1; Laws 2005, Act 20, § 5, eff. July 1, 2005.

Formerly Code 1933, § 27-3015.

§ 17-14-17. Action pursuant to the Uniform Fraudulent Transfers Act

(a) The state or the victim of a crime may institute an action against an offender pursuant to Article 4 of Chapter 2 of Title 18, the "Uniform Fraudulent Transfers Act," to set aside a transfer of real, personal, or other property made voluntarily by the offender on or after the date of the crime committed by the offender against the victim with the intent to:

(1) Conceal the crime or the fruits of the crime;

(2) Hinder, delay, or defraud any victim; or

(3) Avoid the payment of restitution.

(b) Any such action shall be filed within four years of the date the crime was committed.

Laws 1998, p. 549, § 1; Laws 2005, Act 20, § 5, eff. July 1, 2005.

§ 17-14-18. Deposit of unclaimed restitution in victim's fund

If a person or entity entitled to restitution cannot be located or refuses to claim such restitution within two years after the date on which he or she could have claimed such restitution, the restitution paid to such person or entity shall be deposited in the Crime Victims Emergency Fund created pursuant to Chapter 15 of Title 17 or its successor fund. However, a person or entity entitled to such restitution may claim such restitution any time within five years of the date on which he or she could have claimed such restitution by applying in writing to Georgia Crime Victims Compensation Board. Upon receipt of such application and verification that the person making the claim is in fact entitled to such restitution, the Georgia Crime Victims Compensation Board shall pay such restitution to the person or entity.

Laws 2005, Act 20, § 5, eff. July 1, 2005.

§ 17-14-19. Court, agency, or board power not limited

This article shall not be construed to limit or abrogate any power of any court, agency, or board to place other conditions, limits, terms, rules, or regulations on any relief in the nature of suspension of sentence, probation, parole, pardon, or restoration of rights.

Laws 2005, Act 20, § 5, eff. July 1, 2005.

Article 2
Distribution of Profits of Crimes

§ 17-14-30. Definitions

As used in this article, the term:

(1) "Board" means the Board of Corrections.

(2) "Convicted person" includes a person found not guilty by reason of insanity.

Laws 1979, p. 1262, § 1; Laws 1985, p. 283, § 1.

§ 17-14-31. Distribution of moneys received as a result of the commission of crime

(a)(1) Every person, firm, corporation, partnership, association, or other legal entity contracting with any person or with the representative or assignee of any person who has been accused or convicted of a crime in this state with respect to the reenactment of the crime by way of a movie, book, magazine article, tape recording, phonograph record, radio or television presentation, or live entertainment of any kind or with respect to the expression of the accused or convicted person's thoughts, feelings, opinions, or emotions regarding the crime shall submit a copy of the contract to the board and shall pay over to the board any moneys which would otherwise, by the terms of the contract, be owing to the accused or convicted person or to his representatives.

(2) The board shall deposit such moneys in an escrow account for the benefit of and payable to any victim or the legal representative of any victim of crimes committed by the accused or convicted person.

(3) Payments may be made pursuant to paragraph (2) of this subsection only if the accused person is eventually convicted or enters a plea of guilty of the crime and if the victim, within five years of the date of the establishment of the escrow account, brings a civil action in a court of competent jurisdiction and recovers a money judgment for damages against the convicted or accused person or his representatives.

(4) It shall be the duty of the victim, the victim's attorney, or the victim's representative to notify the board within 30 days of the filing of any claim under this article.

(b) At least once every six months for five years from the date it receives such moneys, the board shall cause to have published a legal notice in newspapers of general circulation in the county in which the crime was committed and in counties contiguous to such county, advising victims of the crime that escrow moneys are available to satisfy money judgments pursuant to this Code section.

(c) Upon dismissal of charges or acquittal of any accused person, the board shall immediately pay over to the accused person the moneys in the escrow account established on behalf of the accused person.

(d) Upon a showing by any convicted person that five years have elapsed from the establishment of the escrow account and that no actions are pending against the convicted person pursuant to this Code section, the board shall immediately pay over any moneys in the escrow account to the person or his legal representatives.

(e) Whenever it is found that a person accused of a crime is unfit to proceed to trial as a result of insanity because the person lacks capacity to understand the proceedings against him or to assist in his own defense, the board shall bring an action of interpleader to determine the disposition of the escrow account.

(f) Any excess which remains in the escrow account or is deposited into the account after all money judgments have been satisfied shall be paid over into the state treasury as compensation for the establishment, administration, and execution of this article.

(g) The board shall make payments from the escrow account to any person accused or convicted of crime, upon the order of a court of competent jurisdiction, after a showing by the person that the moneys shall be used for the exclusive purpose of retaining legal representation at any stage of the proceedings against the person, including the appeals process.

(h) The board shall disburse payments from the escrow account on a pro rata basis of all claims filed, according to the amount of money in the escrow account as compared to the amount of each claim. The sums are not to be disbursed until all pending claims have been settled or reduced to judgment.

(i) Any action taken by a person who is accused or convicted of a crime or who enters a plea of guilty, whether by way of execution of a power of attorney, creation of corporate entities, or otherwise, to defeat the purpose of this Code section shall be null and void as against the public policy of this state.

Laws 1979, p. 1262, § 1.

§ 17-14-32. Penalties

(a) It shall be unlawful for any person, firm, corporation, partnership, association, or other legal entity to fail to comply with this article.

(b) Any person, firm, corporation, partnership, association, or other legal entity violating this article shall be guilty of a misdemeanor.

(c) Each day that a person, firm, corporation, partnership, association, or other legal entity continues in violation of this article shall constitute a separate offense.

Laws 1979, p. 1262, § 1.

CHAPTER 15

VICTIM COMPENSATION

§ 17-15-1. Declaration of purpose

The General Assembly recognizes that many innocent persons suffer personal physical injury, severe financial hardship, or death as a result of criminal acts. The General Assembly finds and determines that there is a need for assistance for such victims of crime. Accordingly, it is the General Assembly's intent that under certain circumstances aid, care, and assistance be provided by the state for such victims of crime.

Laws 1988, p. 591, § 1.

§ 17-15-2. Definitions

As used in this chapter, the term:

(1) "Board" means the Criminal Justice Coordinating Council.

(2) "Claimant" means any person filing a claim pursuant to this chapter.

(3) "Crime" means:

(A) An act which constitutes hit and run as defined in Code Section 40-6-270, homicide by vehicle as defined in Code Section 40-6-393, serious injury by vehicle as defined in Code Section 40-6-394, or any act which constitutes a violent crime as defined by state or federal law which results in physical injury or death to the victim and which is committed:

(i) In this state;

(ii) In a state which does not have a victims' compensation program, if the victim is a resident of this state; or

(iii) In a state which has compensated the victim in an amount less than the victim would be entitled to pursuant to this chapter, if the victim is a resident of this state;

(B) An act which constitutes international terrorism as defined in 18 U.S.C. Section 2331 which results in physical injury or death to the victim, if the victim is a resident of this state and is outside the territorial boundaries of the United States when such act is committed; or

(C) An act of mass violence which results in physical injury or death to the victim, if the victim is a resident of this state and is outside the territorial boundaries of the United States when such act is committed.

(4) "Direct service provider" means a public or nonprofit entity which provides aid, care, and assistance to a victim.

(5) "Director" means the director of the Criminal Justice Coordinating Council.

(6) "Fund" means the Georgia Crime Victims Emergency Fund.

(7) "Investigator" means an investigator of the board.

(8) "Victim" means a person who is injured physically, who dies, or who suffers financial hardship as a result of being injured physically as a direct result of a crime.

Laws 1988, p. 591, § 1; Laws 1990, p. 8, § 17; Laws 1994, p. 1800, § 1; Laws 1997, p. 481, § 1; Laws 2002, p. 843, § 2.

§ 17-15-3. Georgia Crime Victims Compensation Board; abolition and recreation

(a) The five-member Georgia Crime Victims Compensation Board in existence on June 30, 1992, is abolished.

(b) There is created the Georgia Crime Victims Compensation Board. The Criminal Justice Coordinating Council created under Chapter 6A of Title 35 shall serve as the Georgia Crime Victims Compensation Board.

(c) The Governor shall appoint the director of the Criminal Justice Coordinating Council to carry out the provisions of this chapter.

Laws 1988, p. 591, § 1; Laws 1992, p. 2426, § 1; Laws 1994, p. 1800, § 2.

§ 17-15-4. Powers and duties of board

(a) The board shall have the following powers and duties:

(1) To promulgate suitable rules and regulations to carry out the provisions and purposes of this chapter;

(2) To request from the Attorney General, the Department of Public Safety, the Georgia Bureau of Investigation, district attorneys, solicitors-general, judges, county and municipal law enforcement agencies, and any other agency or department such assistance and data as will enable the board to determine the needs state wide for victim compen-

sation and whether, and the extent to which, a claimant qualifies for an award. Any person, agency, or department listed in this paragraph is authorized to provide the board with the information requested upon receipt of a request from the board. Any provision of law providing for confidentiality of records does not apply to a request of the board pursuant to this Code section; provided, however, that the board shall preserve the confidentiality of any such records received;

(3) To hear and determine all appeals of denied claims for awards filed with the board pursuant to this chapter and to reinvestigate or reopen cases as the board deems necessary;

(4) To apply for funds from, and to submit all necessary forms to, any federal agency participating in a cooperative program to compensate victims of crime and to receive and administer federal funds for the purposes of this chapter;

(5) To render awards to victims of crimes or to those other persons entitled to receive awards in the manner authorized by this chapter. Victim compensation payments may be made directly to direct service providers who are not the recipients of local, state, federal, or private grant funds awarded for purposes of providing direct services to crime victims. A victim or claimant may be paid directly in the case of lost wages, loss of support, and instances where the victim or claimant has paid the direct service provider and is filing for reimbursement. In all cases where the victim has incurred out-of-pocket expenses, such as lost wages or loss of support or in cases where the victim or claimant has paid the direct service provider directly and is filing for reimbursement, the victim or claimant shall be paid first before any third party;

(6) To carry out programs designed to inform the public of the purposes of this chapter; and

(7) To render each year to the Governor and to the General Assembly a written report of its activities pursuant to this chapter.

(b) The board shall assist applicants with their claims for compensation through educational programs and administrative assistance.

Laws 1988, p. 591, § 1; Laws 1990, p. 8, § 17; Laws 1992, p. 2426, § 2; Laws 1994, p. 1800, § 3; Laws 1996, p. 748, § 16.

§ 17-15-5. Procedures for making claims for awards

(a) A claim may be filed by a person eligible to receive an award, as provided in Code Section 17-15-7, or, if such person is a minor, by his parent or guardian. In any case in which the person entitled to make a claim is mentally incompetent, the claim may be filed on his behalf by his guardian or such other individual authorized to administer his estate.

(b) A claim must be filed by the claimant not later than one year after the occurrence of the crime upon which such claim is based or not later than one year after the death of the victim; provided, however, that, upon good cause shown, the board may extend that time for filing for a period not exceeding three years after such occurrence. Claims shall be filed in the office of the board in person or by mail.

(c) The claim shall be verified and shall contain the following:

(1) A description of the date, nature, and circumstances of the crime;

(2) A complete financial statement, including, but not limited to, the cost of medical care or burial expense, the loss of wages or support the victim has incurred or will incur, any other emergency expenses incurred by the victim, and the extent to which the victim has been or may be indemnified for these expenses from any source;

(3) When appropriate, a statement indicating the extent of any disability resulting from the injury incurred;

(4) An authorization permitting the board to verify the contents of the application; and

(5) Such other information as the board may require.

Laws 1988, p. 591, § 1; Laws 1997, p. 481, § 2; Laws 2005, Act 20, § 6, eff. July 1, 2005.

§ 17-15-6. Investigation of claims; decision of director; review of decision by board

(a) A claim, once accepted for filing and completed, must be assigned to an investigator. The investigator shall examine the papers filed in support of the claim and cause an investigation to be conducted into the validity of the claim. The investigation shall include, but not be limited to, an examination of law enforcement, court, and official records and reports concerning the crime and an examination of medical, financial, and hospital reports relating to the injury or loss upon which the claim is based. All claims arising from the death of an individual as a direct result of a crime must be considered together by a single investigator.

(b) Claims must be investigated and determined regardless of whether the alleged criminal has been apprehended, prosecuted, or convicted of any crime based upon the same incident or whether the alleged criminal has been acquitted or found not guilty of the crime in question.

(c) The investigator conducting the investigation shall file with the director a written report setting forth a recommendation and the investigator's reason therefor. The director shall render a decision and furnish the victim or claimant with a copy of the report if so requested. In cases where an investigative report is provided, information deemed confidential in nature shall be excluded.

(d) The claimant may, within 30 days after receipt of the report of the decision of the director, make an application in writing to the director for review of the decision.

(e) Upon receipt of an application for review pursuant to subsection (d) of this Code section, the director shall forward all relevant documents and information to the board. The board shall review the records and affirm or modify the decision of the director. If considered necessary by the board or if requested by the claimant, the board shall order a hearing prior to rendering a decision. At the hearing, any relevant evidence not legally privileged is admissible. The board shall render a decision within 90 days after completion of the investigation. If the director receives no application for review pursuant to subsection (d) of this Code section, the director's decision becomes final.

(f) The board, for purposes of this chapter, may subpoena witnesses, administer or cause to be administered oaths, and examine such parts of the books and records of the parties to proceedings as relate to questions in dispute.

(g) The director shall, within ten days after receipt of the board's final decision, make a report to the claimant including a copy of the final decision and the reasons why the decision was made.

Laws 1988, p. 591, § 1; Laws 1990, p. 8, § 17; Laws 1994, p. 1800, § 4.

§ 17–15–7. Eligibility for awards

(a) Except as otherwise provided in this Code section, the following persons are eligible for awards pursuant to this chapter:

(1) A victim;

(2) A dependent spouse or child of a victim;

(2.1) For purposes of an award under subsection (k) of Code Section 17–15–8, any member of the immediate family of a victim of homicide by vehicle caused by a violation of Code Section 40–6–391;

(3) Any person who goes to the aid of another and suffers physical injury or death as a direct result of acting, not recklessly, to prevent the commission of a crime, to apprehend lawfully a person reasonably suspected of having committed a crime, or to aid the victim of a crime or any person who is injured or killed while aiding or attempting to aid a law enforcement officer in the prevention of crime or apprehension of a criminal at the officer's request;

(4) Any person who is a victim of family violence as defined by Code Section 19–13–1 and anyone who is a victim as a result of a violation of Code Section 40–6–391; or

(5) Any person who is not a direct service provider and who assumes the cost of an eligible expense of a victim regardless of such person's relationship to the victim or whether such person is a dependent of the victim.

(b)(1) Victims may be legal residents or nonresidents of this state. A surviving spouse, parent, or child who is legally dependent for his or her principal support upon a deceased victim is entitled to file a claim under this chapter if the deceased victim would have been so entitled, regardless of the residence or nationality of the surviving spouse, parent, or child.

(2) Victims of crimes occurring within this state who are subject to federal jurisdiction shall be compensated on the same basis as resident victims of crime.

(c) No award of any kind shall be made under this chapter to a victim injured while confined in any federal, state, county, or municipal jail, prison, or other correctional facility.

(d) No award of any kind shall be made under this chapter to a victim of a crime which occurred prior to July 1, 1989.

(e) A person who is criminally responsible for the crime upon which a claim is based or is an accomplice of such person shall not be eligible to receive an award with respect to such claim.

(f) There shall be no denial of compensation to a victim based on that victim's familial relationship with the person who is criminally responsible for the crime.

(g) No award of any kind shall be made under this chapter to a victim of a crime for loss of property.

(h) A victim or claimant who has been convicted of a felony involving criminally injurious conduct and who is currently serving a sentence therefor shall not be considered eligible to receive an award under this chapter. For purposes of this subsection, "criminally injurious conduct" means an act which occurs or is attempted in this state that results in personal injury or death to a victim, which act is punishable by fine, imprisonment, or death. Such term shall not include acts arising out of the operation of motor vehicles, boats, or aircraft unless the acts were committed with the intent to inflict injury or death or unless the acts committed were in violation of Code Section 40–6–391. For the purposes of this subsection, a person shall be deemed to have committed criminally injurious conduct notwithstanding that by reason of age, insanity, drunkenness, or other reason, he or she was legally incapable of committing a crime.

Laws 1988, p. 591, § 1; Laws 1992, p. 2426, § 3; Laws 1994, p. 1800, § 5; Laws 1997, p. 481, § 3; Laws 2004, Act 570, § 3, eff. July 1, 2004.

§ 17–15–8. Limitations on awards; determination of amount of award

(a) No award may be made unless the board or director finds that:

(1) A crime was committed;

(2) The crime directly resulted in the victim's physical injury, financial hardship as a result of the victim's physical injury, or the victim's death;

(3) Police records show that the crime was promptly reported to the proper authorities. In no case may an award be made where the police records show that such report was made more than 72 hours after the occurrence of such crime unless the board, for good cause shown, finds the delay to have been justified; and

(4) The applicant has pursued restitution rights against any person who committed the crime unless the board or director determines that such action would not be feasible.

The board, upon finding that any claimant or award recipient has not fully cooperated with all law enforcement agencies, may deny, reduce, or withdraw any award.

(b) Any award made pursuant to this chapter may be in an amount not exceeding actual expenses, including indebtedness reasonably incurred for medical expenses, loss of wages, funeral expenses, mental health counseling, or support for dependents of a deceased victim necessary as a direct result of the injury or hardship upon which the claim is based.

(c)(1) Notwithstanding any other provisions of this chapter, no award made under the provisions of this chapter shall exceed $ 1,000.00 in the aggregate; provided, however, with respect to any claim filed with the board as a result of a crime occurring on or after July 1, 1994, no award made under the provisions of this chapter payable to a victim and to all other claimants sustaining economic loss because of injury to or death of such victim shall exceed $ 5,000.00 in the aggregate; provided, however, with respect to any claim filed with the board as a result of a crime occurring on or after July 1, 1995, no award made under the provisions of this chapter payable to a victim and to all other claimants sustaining economic loss because of injury to or death of such victim shall exceed $ 10,000.00 in the aggregate; provided, further, with respect to any claim filed with the board as a result of a crime occurring on or after July 1, 2002, no award made under the provisions of this chapter payable to a victim and to all other claimants sustaining economic loss because of injury to or death of such victim shall exceed $ 25,000.00 in the aggregate.

(2) No award under this chapter for the following losses shall exceed the maximum amount authorized:

Category	Maximum Award
Lost Wages	$10,000.00
Funeral Expenses	3,000.00
Financial Hardship or Loss of Support	10,000.00
Medical	15,000.00
Counseling	3,000.00
Crime Scene Sanitization	1,500.00

(d) In determining the amount of an award, the director and board shall determine whether because of his or her conduct the victim of such crime contributed to the infliction of his or her injury or financial hardship, and the director and board may reduce the amount of the award or reject the claim altogether in accordance with such determination.

(e) The director and board may reject an application for an award when the claimant has failed to cooperate in the verification of the information contained in the application.

(f) Any award made pursuant to this chapter may be reduced by or set off by the amount of any payments received or to be received as a result of the injury:

(1) From or on behalf of the person who committed the crime; and

(2) From any other private or public source, including an award of workers' compensation pursuant to the laws of this state,

provided that private sources shall not include contributions received from family members or persons or private organizations making charitable donations to a victim.

(g) No award made pursuant to this chapter is subject to garnishment, execution, or attachment other than for expenses resulting from the injury which is the basis for the claim.

(h) An award made pursuant to this chapter shall not constitute a payment which is treated as ordinary income under either the provisions of Chapter 7 of Title 48 or, to the extent lawful, under the United States Internal Revenue Code.

(i) Notwithstanding any other provisions of this chapter to the contrary, no awards from state funds shall be paid prior to July 1, 1989.

(j) In any case where a crime results in death, the spouse, children, parents, or siblings of such deceased victim may be considered eligible for an award for the cost of psychological counseling which is deemed necessary as a direct result of said criminal incident. The maximum award for said counseling expenses shall not exceed $ 3,000.00 in the aggregate.

(k)(1) In addition to any other award authorized by this Code section, in any case where a deceased was a victim of homicide by vehicle caused by a violation of

Code Section 40-6-391 on any road which is part of the state highway system, upon request of the next of kin of the deceased, an award of compensation in the form of a memorial sign erected by the Department of Transportation as provided by this subsection shall be paid to an eligible claimant.

(2) The provisions of paragraph (4) of subsection (a) of this Code section shall not apply for purposes of eligibility for awards made under this subsection, and the value of any award paid to a claimant under this subsection shall not apply toward or be subject to any limitation on award amounts paid to any claimant under other provisions of this Code section.

(3) The Department of Transportation, upon receiving payment for the cost of materials and labor from the board, shall upon request of the next of kin of the deceased erect a sign memorializing the deceased on the right of way of such public highway at the location of the accident or as near thereto as safely and reasonably possible and shall maintain such sign for a period of five years from the date the sign is erected unless its earlier removal is requested in writing by the next of kin. Such sign shall be 24 inches wide by 36 inches high and depict a map of the State of Georgia, with a dark blue background and a black outline of the state boundaries. A border of white stars shall be placed on the inside of the state boundaries, and the sign shall contain the words "In Memory of (name), DUI Victim (date of accident)."

(4) In the event of multiple such claims arising out of a single motor vehicle accident, the names of all deceased victims for whom such claims are made and for whom a request has been made by the next of kin of the deceased may be placed on one such sign or, if necessary, on one such sign and a plaque beneath of the same color as the sign. In the event of multiple claims relating to the same deceased victim, no more than one such sign shall be paid for and erected for such victim.

Laws 1988, p. 591, § 1; Laws 1992, p. 2426, §§ 4, 5; Laws 1994, p. 1800, § 6; Laws 1995, p. 385, § 1; Laws 1997, p. 481, § 4; Laws 2002, p. 843, § 3; Laws 2004, Act 564, § 17, eff. May 13, 2004; Laws 2004, Act 570, § 4, eff. July 1, 2004.

§ 17-15-9. Payment of awards

Notwithstanding any other provision of this chapter to the contrary, where an award under this chapter has been authorized but there are not sufficient funds in the Georgia Crime Victims Emergency Fund to pay or continue paying the award, then the award or the remaining portion thereof must not be paid unless and until sufficient funds become available from the fund and at such time awards which have not been paid must begin to be paid in chronological order with the oldest award being paid first. In the event an award was to be paid in installments and some remaining installments have not been paid due to a lack of funds, then when funds due become available that award must be paid in full when its appropriate time for payment comes on the chronological list before any other postdated award must be paid. Any award under this chapter is specifically not a claim against the state if it cannot be paid due to a lack of funds in the Georgia Crime Victims Emergency Fund.

Laws 1988, p. 591, § 1.

§ 17-15-10. Georgia Crime Victims Emergency Fund; creation; purpose of fund and moneys paid into or disbursed from fund

(a) There is created a fund to be known as the Georgia Crime Victims Emergency Fund. The custodian of the fund shall be the board. The director shall administer the fund and may invest the resources of the fund in the same manner and fashion that an insurer authorized to issue contracts of life insurance is authorized to invest its resources. The board is specifically authorized to contract with any person or organization, public or private, to administer the fund, assume the powers of the director, and carry out the duties of the board relating to the fund.

(b)(1) The fund shall consist of all moneys received pursuant to Article 7 of Chapter 21 of Title 15 from the assessment of additional penalties in cases involving a violation of Code Section 40-6-391, relating to driving under the influence of alcohol or drugs, or a violation of an ordinance of a political subdivision of this state which has adopted by reference Code Section 40-6-391 pursuant to Article 14 of Chapter 6 of Title 40.

(2) The funds placed in the fund shall also consist of all moneys appropriated by the General Assembly, if any, for the purpose of compensating claimants under this chapter and money recovered on behalf of the state pursuant to this chapter by subrogation or other action, recovered by court order, received from the federal government, received from additional court costs, received from specific tax proceeds allocated to the fund, received from other assessments or fines, or received from any other public or private source pursuant to this chapter.

(c) All funds appropriated to or otherwise paid into the fund shall be presumptively concluded to have been committed to the purpose for which they have been appropriated or paid and shall not lapse.

(d) The board is authorized, subject to the limitations contained in this chapter, to pay the appropriate compensation to the persons eligible for compensation under this chapter from the proceeds of the Georgia Crime Victims Emergency Fund.

(e) After determining that an award should be paid and the method of payment, the board or director, within five days, shall be authorized to draw a warrant or warrants upon the Georgia Crime Victims Emergency Fund to pay the amount of the award from such fund.

Laws 1988, p. 591, § 1; Laws 1992, p. 1836, § 2; Laws 1993, p. 91, § 17.

§ 17-15-11. Unlawful to file false claims for awards

Any person who asserts a false claim under the provisions of this chapter shall be guilty of a misdemeanor and, upon conviction thereof, shall be punished as for a misdemeanor and shall further forfeit any benefit received and shall reimburse and repay the state for payments received or paid on his behalf pursuant to any of the provisions of this chapter.

Laws 1988, p. 591, § 1.

§ 17-15-12. Subrogation; pursuit of civil remedies

(a) Acceptance of an award made pursuant to this chapter shall subrogate the state, to the extent of such award, to any right or right of action occurring to the claimant or the victim to recover payments on account of losses resulting from the crime with respect to which the award is made.

(b) Acceptance of an award made pursuant to this chapter based on damages from a criminal act shall constitute an agreement on the part of the recipient reasonably to pursue any and all civil remedies arising from any right of action against the person or persons responsible for or committing the act.

Laws 1988, p. 591, § 1.

§ 17-15-13. Restitution from persons convicted of crimes

(a) Any award or payment of benefits to, or on behalf of, a victim or eligible family member under this chapter shall create a debt due and owing to the state by any person found in a court of competent jurisdiction of this state to have committed such criminal act.

(b) A court, when placing on probation any person who owes a debt to the state as a consequence of a criminal act, may set as a condition of probation the payment of the debt or a portion of the debt to the state. The court may also set the schedule or amounts of payments subject to modification based on change of circumstances.

(c) The State Board of Pardons and Paroles shall also have the right to make payment of the debt or a portion of the debt to the state a condition of parole.

(d) When a child is adjudicated delinquent in a juvenile court proceeding involving a crime upon which a claim under this chapter can be made, the juvenile court in its discretion may order that the child pay the debt to the state as an adult would have to pay had an adult committed the crime. Any assessments so ordered may be made a condition of probation as provided in paragraph (2) of subsection (a) of Code Section 15-11-66.

(e) Payments authorized or required under this Code section shall be paid into the Georgia Crime Victims Emergency Fund. The board shall coordinate the development of policies and procedures for the State Board of Pardons and Paroles and the Administrative Office of the Courts to assure that victim restitution programs are administered in an effective manner to increase payments into the fund.

(f) In every case where an individual is serving under active probation supervision and paying a supervision fee, $ 9.00 per month shall be added to any supervision fee collected by any entity authorized to collect such fees and shall be paid into the Georgia Crime Victims Emergency Fund. This subsection shall apply to probationers supervised under either Code Section 42-8-20 or 42-8-100. The probation supervising entity shall collect and forward the $ 9.00 fee to the Georgia Crime Victims Compensation Board by the end of each month.

Laws 1988, p. 591, § 1; Laws 1998, p. 840, § 1; Laws 2000, p. 20, § 9; Laws 2002, p. 843, § 4.

§ 17-15-14. Spending of funds for public information purposes

The board shall be authorized to designate and expend not more than 10 percent of the moneys collected and paid into the fund pursuant to paragraph (1) of subsection (b) of Code Section 17-15-10 and Code Section 17-15-13 to provide funding to victim service providers for the purpose of disseminating materials regarding the availability of compensation for victims of crime and public information purposes regarding the victim compensation program provided in this chapter.

Laws 1994, p. 1800, § 7.

CHAPTER 15A

COMPENSATION FOR CRIMINALLY INFLICTED PROPERTY DAMAGE

§ 17–15A–1. Additional remedy

The provisions of this chapter are enacted pursuant Article III, Section VI, Paragraph VI(f) of the Constitution and are in addition to those provisions for compensation of innocent victims of other crimes under Chapter 15 of this title.

Laws 2003, Act 38, § 1, eff. July 1, 2003.

§ 17–15A–2. Definitions

As used in this chapter, the term "graffiti" means any inscriptions, words, figures, paintings, or other defacements that are written, marked, etched, scratched, sprayed, drawn, painted, or engraved on or otherwise affixed to any surface of real property or improvements thereon without prior authorization of the owner or occupant of the property by means of any aerosol paint container, broad–tipped marker, gum label, paint stick, graffiti stick, etching equipment, brush, or other device capable of scarring or leaving a visible mark on any surface.

Laws 2003, Act 38, § 1, eff. July 1, 2003.

§ 17–15A–3. Declaration of purpose

The General Assembly finds and declares that:

(1) Criminal street gang activity is a serious and continuing public safety concern;

(2) Criminal trespass and criminal damage to property in the second degree caused by graffiti being placed unlawfully upon private property are crimes frequently associated with criminal street gang activity; and

(3) It is in the public interest, not only in the pursuit of justice but also as a means of combating such criminal street gang activity and of contributing to the general public welfare by improving the esthetics of public views, to compensate as provided in this chapter those private property owners who are the innocent victims of such criminal trespass or criminal damage to property in the second degree by using inmate labor to remove or obliterate graffiti unlawfully placed on private properties when such graffiti is visible from public roads or other public property.

Laws 2003, Act 38, § 1, eff. July 1, 2003.

§ 17–15A–4. Powers and duties of Board of Corrections and political subdivisions

(a) In order to provide a form of compensation by the state to innocent victims of criminal trespass in violation of Code Section 16–7–21 or criminal damage to property in the second degree in violation of Code Section 16–7–23, either of which crime involved the unlawful placement of graffiti upon private property by a person who was not the owner of such property, the Board of Corrections or any political subdivision of this state may authorize the use of labor by inmates from any penal institution or jail under its authority to remove or obliterate such unlawfully placed graffiti when such graffiti is visible from any public road or other public property. Any such authorization and related supervision of inmates shall be a discretionary function within the meaning of paragraph (2) of Code Section 50–21–24 for purposes of sovereign immunity, and the sovereign immunity of neither the state nor any political subdivision thereof is waived for any loss arising out of such authorization or related supervision of inmates. The Board of Corrections shall provide rules and regulations governing such use of labor by inmates from institutions under its jurisdiction.

(b) No graffiti removal program operated by any political subdivision of this state shall charge any fee to any property owner or operator for removal of graffiti from such property.

Laws 2003, Act 38, § 1, eff. July 1, 2003.

CHAPTER 16

DISCOVERY

Article 1

Definitions; Felony Cases

§ 17–16–1. Definitions

As used in this chapter, the term:

(1) "Possession, custody, or control of the state or prosecution" means an item which is within the possession, custody, or control of the prosecuting

attorney or any law enforcement agency involved in the investigation of the case being prosecuted.

(2) "Statement of a witness" means:

(A) A written or recorded statement, or copies thereof, made by the witness that is signed or otherwise adopted or approved by the witness;

(B) A substantially verbatim recital of an oral statement made by the witness that is recorded contemporaneously with the making of the oral statement and is contained in a stenographic, mechanical, electrical, or other recording or a transcription thereof; or

(C) A summary of the substance of a statement made by a witness contained in a memorandum, report, or other type of written document but does not include notes or summaries made by counsel.

(3) "Witness" does not include the defendant.

Laws 1994, p. 1895, § 4; Laws 1995, p. 1250, § 2.

§ 17–16–2. Applicability of law

(a) This article shall apply to all criminal cases in which at least one felony offense is charged in the event that at or prior to arraignment, or at such time as the court permits, the defendant provides written notice to the prosecuting attorney that such defendant elects to have this article apply to the defendant's case. When one defendant in a multidefendant case demands discovery under this article, the provisions of this article shall apply to all defendants in the case, unless a severance is granted.

(b) Except as provided in subsection (c) of this Code section, this article shall not apply to juvenile court proceedings.

(c) This article shall be deemed to have been automatically invoked, without the written notice provided for in subsection (a) of this Code section, when a defendant has sought discovery pursuant to Chapter 11 of Title 9, the "Georgia Civil Practice Act," pursuant to Code Section 15–11–75, or pursuant to the Uniform Rules for the Juvenile Courts of Georgia where such discovery material is the same as the discovery material that may be provided under this article when a written notice is filed pursuant to subsection (a) of this Code section.

(d) Except as provided under Code Section 17–16–8, this article is not intended to authorize discovery or inspection of attorney work product.

(e) This article shall apply also to all criminal cases in which at least one felony offense is charged which was docketed, indicted, or in which an accusation was returned prior to January 1, 1995, if both the prosecuting attorney and the defendant agree in writing that the provisions of this article shall apply to the case.

(f) Except as provided in paragraph (3) of subsection (b) of Code Section 17–16–4, if a defendant has elected to have the provisions of this article apply, the provisions of this article shall also apply to sentencing hearings and the sentencing phase of a death penalty trial.

Laws 1994, p. 1895, § 4; Laws 1995, p. 1250, § 2; Laws 2005, Act 8, § 12, eff. July 1, 2005; Laws 2005, Act 79, § 1, eff. July 1, 2005.

§ 17–16–3. Copy of indictment or accusation and list of witnesses furnished accused

Prior to arraignment, every person charged with a criminal offense shall be furnished with a copy of the indictment or accusation and a list of witnesses that may be supplemented pursuant to the other provisions of this article.

Laws 1994, p. 1895, § 4; Laws 1995, p. 1250, § 2.

§ 17–16–4. Disclosure of evidence by prosecution and defendants

(a)(1) The prosecuting attorney shall, no later than ten days prior to trial, or at such time as the court orders, disclose to the defendant and make available for inspection, copying, or photographing any relevant written or recorded statements made by the defendant, or copies thereof, within the possession, custody, or control of the state or prosecution and that portion of any written record containing the substance of any relevant oral statement made by the defendant, whether before or after arrest, in response to interrogation by any person then known to the defendant to be a law enforcement officer or member of the prosecuting attorney's staff. The prosecuting attorney shall also disclose to the defendant the substance of any other relevant oral statement made by the defendant, before or after arrest, in response to interrogation by any person then known by the defendant to be a law enforcement officer or member of the prosecuting attorney's staff if the state intends to use that statement at trial. The prosecuting attorney shall also disclose to the defendant the substance of any other relevant written or oral statement made by the defendant while in custody, whether or not in response to interrogation. Statements of coconspirators that are attributable to the defendant and arguably admissible against the defendant at trial also shall be disclosed under this Code section. Where the defendant is a corporation, partnership, association, or labor union, the court may grant the defendant, upon its motion, discovery of any similar such statement of any witness who was:

(A) At the time of the statement, so situated as an officer or employee as to have been legally able to bind the defendant in respect to conduct constituting the offense; or

(B) At the time of the offense, personally involved in the alleged conduct constituting the offense and so situated as an officer or employee as to have been legally able to bind the defendant in respect to that alleged conduct in which the witness was involved.

(2) The prosecuting attorney shall, no later than ten days prior to trial, or as otherwise ordered by the court, furnish to the defendant a copy of the defendant's Georgia Crime Information Center criminal history, if any, as is within the possession, custody, or control of the state or prosecution. Nothing in this Code section shall affect the provisions of Code Section 17-10-2.

(3) The prosecuting attorney shall, no later than ten days prior to trial, or as otherwise ordered by the court, permit the defendant at a time agreed to by the parties or ordered by the court to inspect and copy or photograph books, papers, documents, photographs, tangible objects, audio and visual tapes, films and recordings, or copies or portions thereof and to inspect and photograph buildings or places which are within the possession, custody, or control of the state or prosecution and are intended for use by the prosecuting attorney as evidence in the prosecution's case-in-chief or rebuttal at the trial or were obtained from or belong to the defendant. Evidence that is within the possession, custody, or control of the Forensic Sciences Division of the Georgia Bureau of Investigation or other laboratory for the purpose of testing and analysis may be examined, tested, and analyzed at the facility where the evidence is being held pursuant to reasonable rules and regulations adopted by the Forensic Sciences Division of the Georgia Bureau of Investigation or the laboratory where the evidence is being held.

(4) The prosecuting attorney shall, no later than ten days prior to trial, or as otherwise ordered by the court, permit the defendant at a time agreed to by the parties or ordered by the court to inspect and copy or photograph a report of any physical or mental examinations and of scientific tests or experiments, including a summary of the basis for the expert opinion rendered in the report, or copies thereof, if the state intends to introduce in evidence in its case-in-chief or in rebuttal the results of the physical or mental examination or scientific test or experiment. If the report is oral or partially oral, the prosecuting attorney shall reduce all relevant and material oral portions of such report to writing and shall serve opposing counsel with such portions no later than ten days prior to trial. Nothing in this Code section shall require the disclosure of any other material, note, or memorandum relating to the psychiatric or psychological treatment or therapy of any victim or witness.

(5) The prosecuting attorney shall, no later than ten days prior to trial, or at such time as the court orders but in no event later than the beginning of the trial, provide the defendant with notice of any evidence in aggravation of punishment that the state intends to introduce in sentencing.

(b)(1) The defendant within ten days of timely compliance by the prosecuting attorney but no later than five days prior to trial, or as otherwise ordered by the court, shall permit the prosecuting attorney at a time agreed to by the parties or as ordered by the court to inspect and copy or photograph books, papers, documents, photographs, tangible objects, audio and visual tapes, films and recordings, or copies or portions thereof and to inspect and photograph buildings or places, which are within the possession, custody, or control of the defendant and which the defendant intends to introduce as evidence in the defense's case-in-chief or rebuttal at the trial.

(2) The defendant shall within ten days of timely compliance by the prosecuting attorney but no later than five days prior to trial, or as otherwise ordered by the court, permit the prosecuting attorney at a time agreed to by the parties or as ordered by the court to inspect and copy or photograph a report of any physical or mental examinations and of scientific tests or experiments, including a summary of the basis for the expert opinion rendered in the report, or copies thereof, if the defendant intends to introduce in evidence in the defense's case-in-chief or rebuttal the results of the physical or mental examination or scientific test or experiment. If the report is oral or partially oral, the defendant shall reduce all relevant and material oral portions of such report to writing and shall serve opposing counsel with such portions no later than five days prior to trial. Nothing in this Code section shall require the disclosure of any other material, note, or memorandum relating to the psychiatric or psychological treatment or therapy of any defendant or witness.

(3)(A) The defendant shall, no later than the announcement of the verdict of the jury or if the defendant has waived a jury trial at the time the verdict is published by the court, serve upon the prosecuting attorney all books, papers, documents, photographs, tangible objects, audio and visual tapes, films and recordings, or copies or portions thereof and to inspect and photograph buildings or places which are within the possession, custody, or control of the defendant and which the defendant intends to introduce as evidence in the presentence hearing.

(B) The defendant shall, no later than the announcement of the verdict of the jury or if the defendant has waived a jury trial at the time the verdict is published by the court, serve upon the prosecuting attorney all reports of any physical or mental examinations and scientific tests or experiments, including a summary of the basis for the expert opinions rendered in the reports, or copies thereof, if the defendant intends to introduce in evidence in the presentence hearing the results of the physical or mental examination or scientific test or experiment. If the report is oral or partially oral, the defendant shall reduce all relevant and material oral portions of such report to writing and shall serve opposing counsel with such portions.

(C) The defendant shall, no later than five days before the trial commences, serve upon the prosecuting attorney a list of witnesses that the defendant intends to call as a witness in the presentence hearing. No later than the announcement of the verdict of the jury or if the defendant has waived a jury trial at the time the verdict is published by the court, the defendant shall produce for the opposing party any statement of such witnesses that is in the possession, custody, or control of the defendants or the defendant's counsel that relates to the subject matter of the testimony of such witnesses unless such statement is protected from disclosure by the privilege contained in paragraph (5), (6), (7), or (8) of Code Section 24–9–21.

(c) If prior to or during trial a party discovers additional evidence or material previously requested or ordered which is subject to discovery or inspection under this article, such party shall promptly notify the other party of the existence of the additional evidence or material and make this additional evidence or material available as provided in this article.

(d) Upon a sufficient showing that a discovery required by this article would create a substantial threat of physical or economic harm to a witness, the court may at any time order that the discovery or inspection be denied, restricted, or deferred or make such other order as is appropriate. Upon motion by a party, the court may permit the party to make such showing, in whole or in part, in the form of a written statement to be inspected by the judge alone. If the court enters an order granting relief following such an ex parte showing, the entire text of the party's statement shall be sealed and preserved in the records of the court subject to further order of the court and to be made available to the appellate court in the event of an appeal.

(e) Discovery with respect to alibi witnesses shall be as provided for in Code Section 17–16–5.

Laws 1994, p. 1895, § 4; Laws 1995, p. 1250, § 2; Laws 2003, Act 26, §§ 5, 6, eff. May 14, 2003; Laws 2005, Act 8, § 13, eff. July 1, 2005.

§ 17–16–5. Procedure where defendant intends to offer a defense of alibi

(a) Upon written demand by the prosecuting attorney within ten days after arraignment, or at such time as the court permits, stating the time, date, and place at which the alleged offense was committed, the defendant shall serve within ten days of the demand of the prosecuting attorney or ten days prior to trial, whichever is later, or as otherwise ordered by the court, upon the prosecuting attorney a written notice of the defendant's intention to offer a defense of alibi. Such notice by the defendant shall state the specific place or places at which the defendant claims to have been at the time of the alleged offense and the names, addresses, dates of birth, and telephone numbers of the witnesses, if known to the defendant, upon whom the defendant intends to rely to establish such alibi unless previously supplied.

(b) The prosecuting attorney shall serve upon the defendant within five days of the defendant's written notice but no later than five days before trial, whichever is later, a written notice stating the names, addresses, dates of birth, and telephone numbers of the witnesses, if known to the state, upon whom the state intends to rely to rebut the defendant's evidence of alibi unless previously supplied.

(c) If prior to or during trial, a party learns of an additional witness whose identity, if known, should have been included in the information furnished under subsection (a) or (b) of this Code section, the party shall promptly notify the other party of the existence and identity of such additional witness.

(d) Upon a showing that a disclosure required by this Code section would create a substantial threat of physical or economic harm to a witness, the court may grant an exception to any of the requirements of subsections (a) through (c) of this Code section.

(e) If the defendant withdraws the notice of intention to rely upon an alibi defense, the notice and intention to rely upon an alibi defense are not admissible. However the prosecuting attorney may offer any other evidence regarding alibi.

Laws 1994, p. 1895, § 4; Laws 1995, p. 1250, § 2.

§ 17–16–6. Court orders with respect to failure of state or defendant to comply

If at any time during the course of the proceedings it is brought to the attention of the court that the state has failed to comply with the requirements of this article, the court may order the state to permit the discovery or inspection, interview of the witness, grant a continuance, or, upon a showing of prejudice and bad faith, prohibit the state from introducing the evidence not disclosed or presenting the witness not disclosed, or may enter such other order as it deems just under the circumstances. If at any time during the course of the proceedings it is brought to the attention of the court that the defendant has failed to comply with the requirements of this article, the court may order the defendant to permit the discovery or inspection, interview of the witness, grant a continuance, or, upon a showing of prejudice and bad faith, prohibit the defendant from introducing the evidence not disclosed or presenting the witness not disclosed, or may enter such other order as it deems just under the circumstances. The court may specify the time, place, and manner of making the discovery, inspection, and interview and may prescribe such terms and conditions as are just.

Laws 1994, p. 1895, § 4; Laws 1995, p. 1250, § 2.

§ 17-16-7. Production of statements of witnesses

No later than ten days prior to trial or at such time as the court permits, or at the time of any post-indictment pretrial evidentiary hearing other than a bond hearing, the prosecution or the defendant shall produce for the opposing party any statement of any witness that is in the possession, custody, or control of the state or prosecution or in the possession, custody, or control of the defendant or the defendant's counsel that relates to the subject matter concerning the testimony of the witness that the party in possession, custody, or control of the statement intends to call as a witness at trial or at such post-indictment pretrial evidentiary hearing.

Laws 1994, p. 1895, § 4; Laws 1995, p. 1250, § 2.

§ 17-16-8. Furnishing of witness information; certain information regarding law enforcement officers not required

(a) The prosecuting attorney, not later than ten days before trial, and the defendant's attorney, within ten days after compliance by the prosecuting attorney but no later than five days prior to trial, or as otherwise ordered by the court, shall furnish to the opposing counsel as an officer of the court, in confidence, the names, current locations, dates of birth, and telephone numbers of that party's witnesses, unless for good cause the judge allows an exception to this requirement, in which event the counsel shall be afforded an opportunity to interview such witnesses prior to the witnesses being called to testify.

(b) Nothing in this Code section shall be construed to require the prosecuting attorney to furnish the home address, date of birth, or home telephone number of a witness who is a law enforcement officer. Instead, in such cases, the prosecuting attorney shall furnish to the defense attorney the law enforcement officer's current work location and work phone number.

Laws 1994, p. 1895, § 4; Laws 1995, p. 1250, § 2; Laws 1996, p. 1624, § 4.

§ 17-16-9. Reimbursement for costs incurred in providing documents

Any party providing documents or statements to another party under this article shall be reimbursed for the actual cost incurred in providing such documents. If the court has determined the defendant to be indigent, the court shall determine the means of reimbursement.

Laws 1994, p. 1895, § 4; Laws 1995, p. 1250, § 2.

§ 17-16-10. Information previously provided to defendant or prosecuting attorney need not be included in subsequent information furnished

The defendant need not include in materials and information furnished to the prosecuting attorney under this article any material or information which the prosecuting attorney has already furnished to the defendant under this article. The prosecuting attorney need not include in materials and information furnished to the defendant under this article any material or information which that defendant has already furnished to the prosecuting attorney under this article. Either party may call as a witness any person listed on either the prosecuting attorney's or defendant's witness list.

Laws 1995, p. 1250, § 2.

Article 2

Misdemeanor Cases

§ 17-16-20. Applicability of law

The provisions of this article shall apply only to misdemeanor cases or to felony cases docketed, indicted, or in which an accusation was returned prior to January 1, 1995, if the prosecuting attorney and the defendant do not agree in writing that the provisions of Article 1 of this chapter shall apply.

Laws 1994, p. 1895, § 4; Laws 1995, p. 1250, § 3.

§ 17-16-21. Copy of indictment or accusation and list of witnesses furnished accused

Prior to arraignment, every person charged with a criminal offense shall be furnished with a copy of the indictment or accusation and, on demand, with a list of the witnesses on whose testimony the charge against such person is founded. Without the consent of the defendant, no witness shall be permitted to testify for the state whose name does not appear on the list of witnesses as furnished to the defendant unless the prosecuting attorney shall state that the evidence sought to be presented is newly discovered evidence which the state was not aware of at the time of its furnishing the defendant with a list of the witnesses.

Laws 1994, p. 1895, § 4.

§ 17-16-22. Discovery of defendant's statements

(a) At least ten days prior to the trial of the case, the defendant shall be entitled to have a copy of any statement given by the defendant while in police custody. The defendant may make such request for a copy of any such statement, in writing, within any reasonable period of time prior to trial.

(b) If the defendant's statement is oral or partially oral, the prosecution shall furnish, in writing, all relevant and material portions of the defendant's statement.

(c) Failure of the prosecution to comply with a defendant's timely written request for a copy of such defendant's statement, whether written or oral, shall result in such statement being excluded and suppressed from the prosecution's use in its case-in-chief or in rebuttal.

(d) If the defendant's statement is oral, no relevant and material, incriminating or inculpatory, portion of the statement of the defendant may be used against the defendant unless it has been previously furnished to the defendant, if a timely written request for a copy of the statement has been made by the defendant.

(e) This Code section shall not apply to evidence discovered after a request has been filed. If a request has been filed, such evidence shall be produced as soon as possible after it has been discovered.

Laws 1994, p. 1895, § 4.

§ 17-16-23. Discovery of scientific reports

(a) As used in this Code section, the term "written scientific reports" includes, but is not limited to, reports from the Division of Forensic Sciences of the Georgia Bureau of Investigation; an autopsy report by the coroner of a county or by a private pathologist; blood alcohol test results done by a law enforcement agency or a private physician; and similar types of reports that would be used as scientific evidence by the prosecution in its case-in-chief or in rebuttal against the defendant.

(b) In all criminal trials the defendant shall be entitled to have a complete copy of any written scientific reports in the possession of the prosecution which will be introduced in whole or in part against the defendant by the prosecution in its case-in-chief or in rebuttal. The request for a copy of any written scientific reports shall be made by the defendant in writing at arraignment or within any reasonable time prior to trial. If such written request is not made at arraignment, it shall be within the sound discretion of the trial judge to determine in each case what constitutes a reasonable time prior to trial. If the scientific report is in the possession of or available to the prosecuting attorney, the prosecuting attorney must comply with this Code section at least ten days prior to the trial of the case.

(c) Failure by the prosecution to furnish the defendant with a copy of any written scientific report, when a proper and timely written demand has been made by the defendant, shall result in such report being excluded and suppressed from evidence in the prosecution's case-in-chief or in rebuttal.

Laws 1994, p. 1895, § 4.

CHAPTER 17

CRIME VICTIMS' BILL OF RIGHTS

§ 17-17-1. Legislative findings

The General Assembly hereby finds and declares it to be the policy of this state that victims of crimes should be accorded certain basic rights just as the accused are accorded certain basic rights.

Laws 1995, p. 385, § 2.

§ 17-17-2. Short title

This chapter shall be known and may be cited as the "Crime Victims' Bill of Rights."

Laws 1995, p. 385, § 2.

§ 17-17-3. Definitions

As used in this chapter, the term:

(1) "Accused" means a person suspected of and subject to arrest for, arrested for, or convicted of a crime against a victim.

(2) "Arresting law enforcement agency" means any law enforcement agency, other than the investigating law enforcement agency, which arrests the accused.

(3) "Compensation" means awards granted by the Georgia Crime Victims Compensation Board pursuant to Chapter 15 of this title.

(4) "Crime" means an act committed in this state which constitutes any violation of Chapter 5 of Title 16, relating to crimes against persons; Chapter 6 of Title 16, relating to sexual offenses; Article 1 or Article 3 of Chapter 7 of Title 16, relating to burglary and arson; Article 1 or Article 2 of Chapter 8 of Title 16, relating to offenses involving theft and armed robbery; Code Section 16-12-100, relating to sexual exploitation of children; Code Section 40-6-393, relating to homicide by vehicle; Code Section 40-6-393.1, relating to feticide by vehicle; or Code Section 40-6-394, relating to serious injury by vehicle.

(5) "Custodial authority" means a warden, sheriff, jailer, deputy sheriff, police officer, correctional officer, officer or employee of the Department of Corrections or the Department of Juvenile Justice, or any other law enforcement officer having actual custody of the accused.

(6) "Investigating law enforcement agency" means the law enforcement agency responsible for the investigation of the crime.

(7) "Notice," "notification," or "notify" means a written notice when time permits or, failing such, a documented effort to reach the victim by telephonic or other means.

(8) "Person" means an individual.

(9) "Prompt notice," "prompt notification," or "promptly notify" means notification given to the victim as soon as practically possible so as to provide the victim with a meaningful opportunity to exercise his or her rights pursuant to this chapter.

(10) "Prosecuting attorney" means the district attorney, the solicitor-general of a state court or the solicitor of any other court, the Attorney General, a county attorney opposing an accused in a habeas corpus proceeding, or the designee of any of these.

(11) "Victim" means:

(A) A person against whom a crime has been perpetrated; or

(B) In the event of the death of the crime victim, the following relations if the relation is not either in custody for an offense or the defendant:

(i) The spouse;

(ii) An adult child if division (i) does not apply;

(iii) A parent if divisions (i) and (ii) do not apply;

(iv) A sibling if divisions (i) through (iii) do not apply; or

(v) A grandparent if divisions (i) through (iv) do not apply; or

(C) A parent, guardian, or custodian of a crime victim who is a minor or a legally incapacitated person except if such parent, guardian, or custodian is in custody for an offense or is the defendant.

Laws 1995, p. 385, § 2; Laws 1996, p. 748, § 17; Laws 1997, p. 1453, § 1.

§ 17-17-4. Designation of persons to act in place of victim during duration of physical disability

If a victim is physically unable to exercise privileges and rights under this chapter, the victim may designate by written instrument his or her spouse, adult child, parent, sibling, or grandparent to act in place of the victim during the duration of the physical disability. During the physical disability, notices to be provided under this chapter to the victim shall continue to be afforded only to the victim.

Laws 1995, p. 385, § 2.

§ 17-17-5. Victims entitled to notification of accused's arrest, release from custody, and any proceeding at which release of accused considered

(a) All victims, wherever practicable, shall be entitled to notification as defined by paragraph (7) of Code Section 17-17-3 of the accused's arrest, of the accused's release from custody, and of any judicial proceeding at which the release of the accused will be considered. No such notification shall be required unless the victim provides a landline telephone number other than a pocket pager or electronic communication device number to which such notice can be directed.

(b) The investigating law enforcement agency, prosecuting attorney, or custodial authority who is required to provide notification pursuant to this chapter shall advise the victim of his or her right to notification and of the requirement of the victim's providing a landline telephone number other than a pocket pager or electronic communication device number to which the notification shall be directed. Such victim shall transmit the telephone number described in this subsection to the appropriate investigating law enforcement agency, prosecuting attorney, or custodial authority as provided for in this chapter.

Laws 1995, p. 385, § 2.

§ 17-17-6. Information to be made available to victim upon initial contact by law enforcement and court personnel

(a) Upon initial contact with a victim, all law enforcement and court personnel shall make available to the victim the following information written in plain language:

(1) The possibility of pretrial release of the accused, the victim's rights and role in the stages of the criminal justice process, and the means by which additional information about these stages can be obtained;

(2) The availability of victim compensation; and

(3) The availability of community based victim service programs.

(b) The Criminal Justice Coordinating Council is designated as the coordinating entity between various law enforcement agencies, the courts, and social service delivery agencies. The Criminal Justice Coordinating Council shall develop and disseminate written information upon which law enforcement personnel may rely in disseminating the information required by this chapter.

Laws 1995, p. 385, § 2.

§ 17-17-7. Notification of victim by investigating law enforcement agency, prosecuting attorney, and custodial authority

(a) Whenever possible, the investigating law enforcement agency shall give to a victim prompt notification as defined in paragraph (9) of Code Section 17-17-3 of the arrest of an accused.

(b) The arresting law enforcement agency shall promptly notify the investigating law enforcement agency of the accused's arrest.

(c) Whenever possible, the prosecuting attorney shall notify the victim prior to any proceeding in which the release of the accused will be considered.

(d) Whenever possible, the prosecuting attorney shall offer the victim the opportunity to express the victim's opinion on the release of the accused pending judicial proceedings.

(e) Whenever possible, the custodial authority shall give prompt notification to a victim of the release of the accused.

(1) Prompt notification of release from a county or municipal jail is effected by placing a telephone call to the telephone number provided by the victim and giving notice to the victim or any person answering the telephone who appears to be sui juris or by leaving an appropriate message on a telephone answering machine.

(2) Notification of release from the custody of the state or any county correctional facility shall be in the manner provided by law.

(f) If the court has granted a pretrial release or supersedeas bond, the victim shall have the right to file a written complaint with the prosecuting attorney asserting acts or threats of physical violence or intimidation by the accused or at the accused's direction against the victim or the victim's immediate family. Based on the victim's written complaint or other evidence, the prosecuting attorney may move the court that the bond or personal recognizance of an accused be revoked.

Laws 1995, p. 385, § 2.

§ 17-17-8. Information to be made available to victim upon initial contact by prosecuting attorney

(a) Upon initial contact with a victim, a prosecuting attorney shall give prompt notification to the victim of the following:

(1) The procedural steps in processing a criminal case;

(2) The rights and procedures of victims under this chapter;

(3) Suggested procedures if the victim is subjected to threats or intimidation; and

(4) The names and telephone numbers of contact persons at both the office of the custodial authority and in the prosecuting attorney's office.

(b) If requested in writing by the victim and to the extent possible, the prosecuting attorney shall give prompt advance notification of any scheduled court proceedings and notice of any changes to that schedule. Court proceedings shall include, but not be limited to, pretrial commitment hearings, arraignment, motion hearings, trial, sentencing, appellate review, and post-conviction relief. The prosecuting attorney shall notify all victims of the requirement to make such request in writing.

Laws 1995, p. 385, § 2.

§ 17-17-9. Separation of victims from accuseds and related parties during court proceedings

The victim shall have the right to wait in an area separate from the accused, from the family and friends of the accused, and from witnesses for the accused during any judicial proceeding involving the accused, provided that such separate area is available and its use in such a manner practical. If such a separate area is not available or practical, the court, upon request of the victim made through the prosecuting attorney, shall attempt to minimize the victim's contact with the accused, the accused's relatives and friends, and witnesses for the accused during any such judicial proceeding.

Laws 1995, p. 385, § 2.

§ 17-17-10. Information concerning victim's address, telephone number, or place of employment not to be transmitted to defendant

As a condition of permitting a response to an inquiry as to the victim's current address, telephone number, or place of employment, the court may require counsel or any other officer of the court, including but not limited to counsel for the defendant, not to transmit or permit transmission to the defendant of the victim's current address, telephone number, or place of employment by the counsel or officer of the court or any employee, agent, or other representative of the counsel or officer of the court.

Laws 1995, p. 385, § 2.

§ 17-17-11. Victim's right to express opinion as to disposition of accused's case

The prosecuting attorney shall offer the victim the opportunity to express the victim's opinion on the disposition of an accused's case, including the views of the victim regarding:

(1) Plea or sentence negotiations; and

(2) Participation in pretrial or post-conviction diversion programs.

This provision shall not limit any other right created pursuant to state law.

Laws 1995, p. 385, § 2.

§ 17-17-12. Notification of victim of appellate proceedings by prosecuting attorney

(a) Upon the written request of the victim, the prosecuting attorney shall notify the victim of the following:

(1) That the accused has filed a motion for new trial, an appeal of his or her conviction, or an extraordinary motion for new trial;

(2) Whether the accused has been released on bail or other recognizance pending the disposition of the motion or appeal;

(3) The time and place of any appellate court proceedings relating to the motion or appeal and any changes in the time or place of those proceedings; and

(4) The result of the motion or appeal.

(b) Upon the written request of the victim as defined in paragraph (11) of Code Section 17-17-3, in cases in which the accused is convicted of a capital offense and receives the death penalty, it shall be the duty of the Attorney General to:

(1) Notify the victim of the filing and disposition of all collateral attacks on such conviction which are being defended by the Attorney General including, but not limited to, petitions for a writ of habeas corpus, and the time and place of any such proceedings and any changes in the time or place of those proceedings; and

(2) Provide the victim with a report on the status of all pending appeals, collateral attacks, and other litigation concerning such conviction which is being defended by the Attorney General at least every six months until the accused dies or the sentence or conviction is overturned or commuted or otherwise reduced to a sentence other than the death penalty.

(c) In the event the accused is granted a new trial or the conviction is reversed or remanded and the case is returned to the trial court for further proceedings, the victim shall be entitled to request the rights and privileges provided by this chapter.

Laws 1995, p. 385, § 2; Laws 2002, p. 1093, § 1; Laws 2003, Act 37, § 4, eff. May 27, 2003.

§ 17-17-13. Notification of victim prior to consideration of pardon, parole, or other clemency by State Board of Pardons and Paroles

The State Board of Pardons and Paroles shall give 20 days' advance notification to a victim whenever it considers making a final decision to grant parole or any other manner of executive clemency action to release a defendant for a period exceeding 60 days; and the board shall provide the victim with an opportunity to file a written objection to such action. No notification need be given unless the victim has expressed objection to release or has expressed a desire for such notification and has provided the State Board of Pardons and Paroles with a current address and telephone number.

Laws 1995, p. 385, § 2.

§ 17-17-14. Responsibility of victim to keep certain persons informed of victim's current address and phone number

(a) It is the right and responsibility of the victim who desires notification under this chapter or under any other notification statute to keep the following informed of the victim's current address and phone number:

(1) The investigating law enforcement agency;

(2) The prosecuting attorney, until final disposition or completion of the appellate and post-conviction process, whichever occurs later; and

(3) As directed by the prosecuting attorney, the sheriff if the accused is in the sheriff's custody for pretrial, trial, or post-conviction proceedings; the Department of Corrections if the accused is in the custody of the state; or any county correctional facility if the defendant is sentenced to serve time in a facility which is not a state facility; and

(4) The State Board of Pardons and Paroles.

(b) Current addresses and telephone numbers of victims and their names provided for the purposes of notification pursuant to this chapter or any other notification statute shall be confidential and used solely for the purposes of this chapter and shall not be subject to disclosure under Article 4 of Chapter 18 of Title 50, relating to inspection of public records.

Laws 1995, p. 385, § 2.

§ 17-17-15. Failure to provide information or notifications

(a) Failure to provide or to timely provide any of the information or notifications required by this chapter shall not subject the person responsible for such notification or that person's employer to any liability for damages.

(b) Failure to provide a victim with any of the rights required by law shall not give an accused a basis for error in either an appellate action or a post-conviction writ of habeas corpus.

(c) This chapter does not confer upon a victim any standing to participate as a party in a criminal proceeding or to contest the disposition of any charge.

(d) The enumeration of these rights shall not be construed to deny or diminish other notification rights granted by state law.

(e) The victim may waive any of the information or notification or other rights provided for by this chapter.

Laws 1995, p. 385, § 2.

§ 17-17-16. Temporary restraining orders and protective orders prohibiting harassment of victims or witnesses

(a) As used in this Code section, the term:

(1) "Course of conduct" spans a series of acts over a period of time, however short, indicating a continuity of purpose.

(2) "Harassment" means a course of conduct directed at a specific person that causes substantial emotional distress in such person.

(b)(1) A superior court, upon application of a prosecuting attorney, shall issue a temporary restraining order prohibiting harassment of a victim or witness in a criminal case if the court finds from specific facts shown by affidavit or by verified complaint that there are reasonable grounds to believe that harassment of an identified victim or witness in a criminal case exists or that such order is necessary to prevent and restrain an offense under Code Section 16-10-32 or 16-10-93.

(2)(A) A temporary restraining order may be issued under this Code section without written or oral notice to the adverse party or such party's attorney in a civil action under this Code section if the court finds, upon written certification of facts by the prosecuting attorney, that such notice should not be required and that there is a reasonable probability that the state will prevail on the merits.

(B) A temporary restraining order issued without notice under this Code section shall be endorsed with the date and hour of issuance and be filed forthwith in the office of the clerk of the court issuing the order.

(C) A temporary restraining order issued under this Code section shall expire at such time, not to exceed ten days from issuance, as the court directs. The court, for good cause shown before expiration of such order, may extend the expiration date of the order for up to ten days or for such longer period agreed to by the adverse party.

(D) When a temporary restraining order is issued without notice, the motion for a protective order shall be set down for hearing at the earliest possible time and takes precedence over all matters except older matters of the same character; and at the hearing, if the prosecuting attorney does not proceed with the application for a protective order, the court shall dissolve the temporary restraining order.

(E) If on two days' notice to the prosecuting attorney or on such shorter notice as the court may prescribe, the adverse party appears and moves to dissolve or modify the temporary restraining order, the court shall proceed to hear and determine such motion as expeditiously as the ends of justice require.

(F) A temporary restraining order shall set forth the reasons for the issuance of such order, be specific in terms, and describe in reasonable detail and not by reference to the complaint or other document the act or acts being restrained.

(c)(1) A superior court, upon motion of the prosecuting attorney, shall issue a protective order prohibiting harassment of a victim or witness in a criminal case if the court, after a hearing, finds by a preponderance of the evidence that harassment of an identified victim or witness in a criminal case exists or that such order is necessary to prevent and restrain an offense under Code Section 16-10-32 or 16-10-93.

(2) At the hearing referred to in paragraph (1) of this subsection, any adverse party named in the complaint shall have the right to present evidence and cross-examine witnesses.

(3) A protective order shall set forth the reasons for the issuance of such order, be specific in terms, and describe in reasonable detail and not by reference to the complaint or other document the act or acts being restrained.

(4) The court shall set the duration of effect of the protective order for such period as the court

determines necessary to prevent harassment of the victim or witness but in no case for a period in excess of three years from the date of such order's issuance. The prosecuting attorney may, at any time within 90 days before the expiration of such order, apply for a new protective order under this Code section.

(d) Article 5 of Chapter 11 of Title 9, relating to depositions and discovery, shall not apply to actions brought pursuant to this Code section.

Laws 1998, p. 270, § 10.

CHAPTER 18

WRITTEN STATEMENTS OF INFORMATION TO VICTIMS OF RAPE OR FORCIBLE SODOMY

§ 17-18-1. Certain information to be provided to persons believed to be victims of rape or aggravated sodomy

When any employee of the Department of Human Resources, a law enforcement agency, or a court has reason to believe that he or she in the course of official duties is speaking to an adult who is or has been a victim of a violation of Code Section 16-6-1, relating to rape, or Code Section 16-6-2, relating to aggravated sodomy, such employee shall offer or provide such adult a written statement of information for victims of rape or aggravated sodomy. Such written statement shall, at a minimum, include the information set out in Code Section 17-18-2 and may include additional information regarding resources available to victims of sexual assault. Information for victims of rape or aggravated sodomy may be provided in any language.

Laws 1996, p. 1115, § 5.

§ 17-18-2. Information to be provided set out

The following information in substantially the form set out in this Code section shall be provided to adult victims of rape or aggravated sodomy in accordance with Code Section 17-18-1:

—INFORMATION FOR VICTIMS OF RAPE OR FORCIBLE SODOMY—

If you are the victim of rape or forcible sodomy, you have certain rights under the law.

Rape or forcible sodomy by a stranger or a person known to you, including rape or forcible sodomy by a person married to you, is a crime. You can ask the government's lawyer to prosecute a person who has committed a crime. The government pays the cost of prosecuting for crimes.

If you are the victim of rape or forcible sodomy you should contact a local police department or other law enforcement agency immediately. A police officer will come to take a report and collect evidence. You should keep any clothing you were wearing at the time of the crime as well as any other evidence such as bed sheets. Officers will take you to the hospital for a medical examination. You should not shower or douche before the examination. The law requires that the police department or law enforcement agency investigating the crime pay for the medical examination to the extent of the cost for the collection of evidence of the crime.

Laws 1996, p. 1115, § 5.

TITLE 18

DEBTOR AND CREDITOR

As Amended Through the 2006 Regular Session of the General Assembly

Research Note

Use Westlaw *to find cases citing a statute or to search for specific terms in a statute. See the Westlaw Directory Screens for lists of relevant databases.*

Table of Sections

CHAPTER 3. ATTACHMENT PROCEEDINGS

Article 1. General Provisions

CHAPTER 4. GARNISHMENT PROCEEDINGS

Article 1. General Provisions

INDEX

See Index to Georgia Statutes, infra.

CHAPTER 3
ATTACHMENT PROCEEDINGS

Article 1
General Provisions

§ 18–3–1. Grounds of attachment

Attachments may issue when the debtor:

(1) Resides out of the state;

(2) Moves or is about to move his domicile outside the limits of the county;

(3) Absconds;

(4) Conceals himself;

(5) Resists legal arrest; or

(6) Is causing his property to be removed beyond the limits of the state.

Laws 1799, Cobb's 1851 Digest, p. 69; Laws 1855–56, p. 25, § 1.

Formerly Code 1863, § 3188; Code 1868, § 3199; Code 1873, § 3264; Code 1882, § 3264; Civil Code 1895, § 4510; Civil Code 1910, § 5055; Code 1933, § 8–101.

§ 18–3–2. Money demands

In all cases of money demands, whether arising ex contractu or ex delicto, the plaintiff shall have the right to seek attachment when the defendant places himself in such situation as will authorize a plaintiff to seek attachment.

Laws 1857, p. 23, § 1.

Formerly Code 1863, § 3199; Code 1868, § 3210; Code 1873, § 3278; Code 1882, § 3278; Civil Code 1895, § 4524; Civil Code 1910, § 5069; Code 1933, § 8–102.

§ 18–3–3. Issuance when debt is not due; stay of execution

When the debt is not due, the debtor shall be subject to attachment in the same manner and to the same extent as in cases where the debt is due, except that, where the debt does not become due before final judgment, execution upon the judgment shall be stayed until the debt is due.

Laws 1816, Cobb's 1851 Digest, p. 75.

Formerly Code 1863, § 3197; Code 1868, § 3208; Code 1873, § 3275; Code 1882, § 3275; Civil Code 1895, § 4521; Civil Code 1910, § 5066; Code 1933, § 8–103.

§ 18–3–4. Issuance when suit is pending

In all cases where the plaintiff has commenced an action for the recovery of a debt and the defendant, during the pendency of such action, shall become subject to attachment, the plaintiff may have an attachment against the defendant; and all the proceedings in relation to the same shall be as prescribed in relation to attachments where no action is pending. A satisfaction of the judgment in the common-law action shall satisfy the judgment in attachment, and a satisfaction of the judgment in attachment shall satisfy the judgment in the common-law action.

Laws 1855–56, p. 25, § 28.

Formerly Code 1863, § 3201; Code 1868, § 3212; Code 1873, § 3280; Code 1882, § 3280; Civil Code 1895, § 4526; Civil Code 1910, § 5071; Code 1933, § 8–104.

§ 18–3–5. Issuance against administrator or executor

Process of attachment may issue against an administrator of an estate or the executor of the last will and testament of any deceased person, as in other cases, when the administrator or executor actually removes or is about to remove the property of the deceased person outside the limits of any county, provided that final judgment shall not be entered against such administrator or executor until after the expiration of two years from the granting of letters of administration or letters testamentary, as the case may be.

Laws 1857, p. 24, § 1.

Formerly Code 1863, § 3199; Code 1868, § 3210; Code 1873, § 3277; Code 1882, § 3277; Civil Code 1895, § 4523; Civil Code 1910, § 5068; Code 1933, § 8–105.

§ 18–3–6. Joint contractors and partners subject to attachment

In cases of joint contractors and partners, where any one of them shall render himself liable to attachment according to law, an attachment may issue against him, upon the plaintiff, his agent, or his attorney at law complying with this article. The proceeding against such joint contractor or partner shall be in all respects as in other cases of attachment, except that such attachment shall be levied only upon the separate property of such joint contractor or partner.

Laws 1851–52, p. 19, § 1; Laws 1855–56, p. 25, § 26.

Formerly Code 1863, § 3198; Code 1868, § 3209; Code 1873, § 3276; Code 1882, § 3276; Civil Code 1895, § 4522; Civil Code 1910, § 5067; Code 1933, § 8–106.

§ 18–3–7. Foreign corporations subject to attachment

Attachments may issue against nonresident corporations transacting business within the state under the same rules and regulations as are prescribed in relation to issuing attachments and garnishments in other cases.

Laws 1855–56, p. 25, § 33.

Formerly Code 1863, § 3202; Code 1868, § 3213; Code 1873, § 3281; Code 1882, § 3281; Civil Code 1895, § 4527; Civil Code 1910, § 5072; Code 1933, § 8–108.

§ 18–3–8. Right of security or endorser against principal

(a) In all cases where a person is surety or endorser upon an instrument of writing and the principal shall become subject to attachment according to Code Section 18–3–1, such surety or endorser may, upon complying with this chapter, have attachment against his principal. The proceedings shall be in all respects the same as in other cases of attachment, and the money raised by the attachment shall be paid to the person holding the instrument of writing.

(b) If the surety or endorser has paid the debt, then the money raised upon the attachment or so much thereof as will pay the amount the surety or endorser has paid shall be paid to the surety or endorser.

(c) In case the debt is not due at the time judgment is rendered against the principal, execution shall be stayed until the debt is due.

Laws 1820, Cobb's 1851 Digest, p. 75; Laws 1842, Cobb's 1851 Digest, p. 88; Laws 1855-56, p. 25, § 27.

Formerly Code 1863, § 3200; Code 1868, § 3211; Code 1873, § 3279; Code 1882, § 3279; Civil Code 1895, § 4525; Civil Code 1910, § 5070; Code 1933, § 8-107.

§ 18-3-9. Application; necessity and contents; judicial supervision

(a) When the plaintiff contends one or more of the grounds set forth in Code Section 18-3-1 exist, prior to obtaining judgment against the defendant, the plaintiff may make application to a judge of any court of record, other than the probate court, in the county of the residence of the defendant, if known, and, if not known, in the county wherein the property sought to be attached is located, for an order authorizing issuance of a writ of attachment. The application shall be made in writing, under oath, and shall set forth the specific facts that show the existence of one or more of such grounds, the basis and nature of the claim, and the amount of indebtedness claimed therein by the plaintiff.

(b) Upon presentation of plaintiff's sworn application for a writ of attachment, it shall be the duty of the judge to inquire into the facts alleged, going beyond mere conclusions of fact alleged by the plaintiff and clearly setting forth the facts entitling the creditor to a writ of attachment as set forth in Code Section 18-3-1. Upon consideration of the inquiry, the judge shall have the discretion to grant or deny the issuance of a writ of attachment. Any order by a judge granting the issuance of a writ of attachment shall be subject to approval of a bond by the clerk of the court, pursuant to Code Section 18-3-10, prior to filing of the writ of attachment.

Laws 1855-56, p. 25, § 2; Laws 1893, p. 117, § 1; Laws 1968, p. 1013, § 1; Laws 1980, p. 1065, § 1.

Formerly Code 1863, § 3189; Code 1868, § 3200; Code 1873, § 3265; Code 1882, § 3265; Civil Code 1895, § 4511; Civil Code 1910, § 5056; Code 1933, § 8-109.

§ 18-3-10. Plaintiff to give bond as security

No writ of attachment shall issue unless accompanied by a bond with good security, conditioned to pay the defendant all costs and damages that he may sustain in consequence of the issuance of the writ of attachment in the event that the amount claimed to be due was not due, that no lawful ground for issuance of the attachment existed, or that the property sought to be attached was not subject to attachment. The bond shall be in a sum equal to twice the amount claimed due in the plaintiff's application. The bond shall be presented to the clerk of the court where the application provided for in Code Section 18-3-9 is sought to be filed for approval by such clerk prior to filing of the writ of attachment.

Laws 1833, Cobb's 1851 Digest, p. 83; Laws 1855-56, p. 25, § 3; Laws 1892, p. 56, § 1; Laws 1980, p. 1065, § 2.

Formerly Code 1863, § 3190; Code 1868, § 3201; Code 1873, § 3266; Code 1882, § 3266; Civil Code 1895, § 4512; Civil Code 1910, § 5057; Code 1933, § 8-111.

§ 18-3-10.1. Suit on attachment bond of plaintiff; service of process

When a person who has been a defendant in attachment desires to bring an action against the plaintiff for damages, and the plaintiff in attachment does not reside in this state, it shall be sufficient to serve the complaint and summons on the security to the bond given by the plaintiff, and the action may proceed against both principal and security.

Laws 1855-56, p. 25, § 54.

Formerly Code 1863, § 3267; Code 1868, § 3278; Code 1873, § 3354; Code 1882, § 3354; Civil Code 1895, § 5013; Civil Code 1910, § 5595; Code 1933, § 3-304.

§ 18-3-11. Affidavit by partner, joint creditor, agent, or attorney

When the debt, for the recovery of which the attachment is sought, is due to a partnership or is due to several persons jointly, any one of the partners or joint creditors, his agent, or his attorney at law may make the affidavit and give the bond as prescribed and sign the names of the other partners or joint creditors to said bond; and the partners or joint creditors shall be bound thereby in the same manner as though they had signed it themselves.

Laws 1855-56, p. 25, § 4.

Formerly Code 1863, § 3191; Code 1868, § 3202; Code 1873, § 3267; Code 1882, § 3267; Civil Code 1895, § 4513; Civil Code 1910, § 5058; Code 1933, § 8-110.

§ 18-3-12. Who shall be surety on bond

No person shall be taken as security or surety on any attachment bond who is an attorney for the plaintiff or a nonresident, except such nonresident who is possessed of real estate in the county where the attachment issues which is the value of the amount of such bond.

Laws 1873, p. 29, § 1.

Formerly Code 1873, § 3268; Code 1882, § 3268; Civil Code 1895, § 4514; Civil Code 1910, § 5059; Code 1933, § 8-112.

§ 18-3-13. Sufficiency of bond, how contested

When any attachment shall be issued and levied upon the property of the defendant, the defendant, his agent, or his attorney may file an affidavit stating that he has a good defense to the action, that the bond given in the action is not a good bond, and stating the ground of its insufficiency. When the affidavit is made and delivered to the levying officer, the officer shall return such attachment together with the affidavit forthwith to the judge issuing the attachment. The judge issuing the attachment shall without delay hear testimony as to the sufficiency of the bond and may in his discretion require additional security or a new bond to be given within such time as he may prescribe. If the plaintiff fails to provide such additional security or new bond, the judge shall dismiss the levy made under the attachment.

Laws 1873, p. 29, § 2; Laws 1892, p. 56, § 2; Laws 1899, p. 37, § 1; Laws 1980, p. 1065, § 3.

Formerly Code 1873, § 3271; Code 1882, § 3271; Civil Code 1895, § 4517; Civil Code 1910, § 5062; Code 1933, § 8-113.

§ 18-3-14. Notice to defendant

(a) The defendant shall be given notice of the attachment issued against his property by any one or more of the following methods:

(1) The plaintiff, at the time the attachment is filed with the clerk, shall commence procedures to effectuate the service of a copy of the writ of attachment on the defendant; and service thereafter shall be made on the defendant as soon as is reasonably practicable. Service pursuant to this paragraph shall be made pursuant to Code Section 9-11-4;

(2) The plaintiff, after issuance of the writ of attachment and not more than three business days after levy upon the property of the defendant, shall cause a written notice to be sent to the defendant at defendant's last known address by registered or certified mail or statutory overnight delivery, return receipt requested. Either the return receipt indicating receipt by the defendant or the envelope bearing the official notification from the United States Postal Service of the defendant's refusal to accept delivery or failure to claim such registered or certified mail or statutory overnight delivery shall be filed with the clerk of the court in which the attachment is pending. The defendant's refusal to accept or failure to claim such registered or certified mail or statutory overnight delivery addressed to defendant shall be deemed notice to defendant;

(3) The plaintiff, after the issuance of the writ of attachment and not more than three business days after levy upon the property of the defendant, shall cause a written notice to be delivered personally to the defendant by the plaintiff or by plaintiff's attorney at law or other agent. A certification by the person making the delivery shall be filed with the clerk;

(4) When the defendant resides out of the state or has departed the state or cannot, after due diligence, be found within the state or conceals his place of residence from the plaintiff and the fact shall appear, by affidavit, to the satisfaction of the judge or clerk of the court, the levy and attachment shall constitute sufficient notice to the defendant, provided such levy and attachment without more shall constitute sufficient notice, unless the plaintiff has actual knowledge of the defendant's address, in which case, to provide sufficient notice, the plaintiff shall also mail a written notice of attachment to the defendant at said address or, not having actual knowledge of the defendant's address but the address at which the defendant was last known to reside, to provide sufficient notice, the plaintiff shall also mail a written notice of attachment to the defendant at said address. A mailing of the written notice provided in this paragraph shall be made after the issuance of the writ of attachment and not more than three business days after levy upon the property of the defendant, and a certificate of such mailing shall be filed with the clerk by the person mailing the notice;

(5) Where it shall appear by affidavit that a defendant in the attachment action is not a resident of this state or has departed from this state or, after due diligence, cannot be found in this state or that the defendant conceals his place of residence from the plaintiff, notice may be given by causing two publications of the written notice in the paper in which advertisements are printed by the sheriff in each county in which a writ of attachment is served. Such publications must be at least six days apart and the second publication must be made not more than 21 days after levy upon the property of the defendant. A certification by the person causing the notice to be published shall be filed with the clerk, provided such publication shall constitute sufficient notice alone, unless the plaintiff has actual knowledge of the defendant's address, in which case, to provide sufficient notice, the plaintiff shall also mail a written notice of attachment to the defendant at said address. A mailing of the written notice provided in this paragraph shall be made after the issuance of the writ of attachment and not more than three business days after levy upon the property of the defendant, and a certificate of such mailing shall be filed with the clerk by the person mailing the notice; or

(6) Where the defendant's address is known, the plaintiff, after issuance of the attachment and not more than three business days after levy upon the property of the defendant, shall send a written notice of the attachment to the defendant at such

known address by ordinary mail. A certification by the person mailing the notice shall be filed with the clerk.

(b) The receiving by the defendant of actual timely notice of the attachment and levy shall constitute notice.

(c) "Written notice," as referred to in paragraphs (2) through (6) of subsection (a) of this Code section, shall consist of a copy of the affidavit and bond for attachment or of a document which includes the names of the plaintiff and the defendant, the amount claimed in the affidavit for attachment, and the court wherein the proceeding is filed.

(d) The methods of notification specified in subsection (a) of this Code section are cumulative and may be used in any sequence or combination. Where it appears that a plaintiff has reasonably, diligently, and in good faith attempted to use one method, another method thereafter may be utilized and, for the time during which the attempt was being made, the time limit shall be tolled for the subsequent method.

Laws 1799, Cobb's 1851 Digest, p. 70; Laws 1855–56, p. 25, § 5; Laws 1980, p. 1065, § 4; Laws 1991, p. 94, § 18; Laws 2000, p. 1589, § 3.

Formerly Code 1863, § 3192; Code 1868, § 3203; Code 1873, § 3269; Code 1882, § 3269; Civil Code 1895, § 4515; Civil Code 1910, § 5060; Code 1933, § 8-114.

§ 18-3-15. Defendant's right to post seizure hearing

When a writ of attachment is issued against the property of the defendant, the defendant may at any time traverse the plaintiff's affidavit upon which the attachment was obtained, stating that the affidavit is untrue or legally insufficient. Upon filing of the traverse, the court shall issue a show cause order to the plaintiff requiring him to appear at a specified time, which shall not be more than ten days from the filing of the traverse, to prove the grounds for the issuance of the attachment. If the plaintiff shall fail to carry the burden of proof, the order authorizing the attachment shall be revoked.

Laws 1980, p. 1065, § 5.

Formerly Code 1933, § 8-114.1.

§ 18-3-16. Issuance and levy on Sunday

Attachments may issue and be levied on Sunday when the plaintiff, his agent, or his attorney at law shall state, in his sworn application for a writ of attachment, that he has reason to believe the debt will not be satisfied unless process of attachment shall issue on Sunday and shall also comply with the other provisions of this chapter.

Laws 1834, Cobb's 1851 Digest, p. 482; Laws 1855–56, p. 25, § 23.

Formerly Code 1863, § 3196; Code 1868, § 3207; Code 1873, § 3274; Code 1882, § 3274; Civil Code 1895, § 4520; Civil Code 1910, § 5065; Code 1933, § 8-115.

§ 18-3-17. Where attachments returnable, general rules of practice and procedure applicable in certain cases

(a) Attachments shall be returnable to the court of record in which filed pursuant to subsection (a) of Code Section 18-3-9 and shall be governed by the rules of procedure and practice governing ordinary civil actions, as respects appearance day, trial term, and judgment pursuant to default, and by any and all other rules relating to procedure and practice.

(b) The plaintiff shall file his declaration in attachment within 15 days after the levy of attachment and the declaration shall thereafter be governed by the rules governing ordinary civil actions as provided for in subsection (a) of this Code section. Notice of the declaration shall be given pursuant to Code Section 18-3-14.

Laws 1799, Cobb's 1851 Digest, pp. 70, 638; Laws 1855–56, p. 25, § 6; Laws 1857, p. 117, § 1; Laws 1962, p. 520, § 1; Laws 1980, p. 1065, § 6.

Formerly Code 1863, § 3194; Code 1868, § 3205; Code 1873, § 3272; Code 1882, § 3272; Civil Code 1895, § 4518; Civil Code 1910, § 5063; Code 1933, § 8-117.

§ 18-3-18. Pleading, defenses and procedures in attachment

All pleadings, defenses, and procedures subsequent to the filing of the declaration in attachment shall be governed by Chapter 10 of Title 9.

Laws 1838, Cobb's 1851 Digest, p. 86; Laws 1855–56, p. 25, § 20; Laws 1962, p. 520, § 2; Laws 1980, p. 1065, § 12.

Formerly Code 1863, § 3221; Code 1868, § 3232; Code 1873, § 3308; Code 1882, § 3308; Civil Code 1895, § 4556; Civil Code 1910, § 5102; Code 1933, § 8-601.

§ 18-3-19. Forms of affidavit, bond and attachment and order

In all cases of attachment, the form of the affidavit, bond, attachment, and order authorizing the issuance thereof may be as follows:

(1) Affidavit for attachment.

—AFFIDAVIT—

STATE OF GEORGIA

COUNTY OF ________

Personally appeared ____ who on oath says that he is attorney at law for ____ and that ____ is indebted to said plaintiff in the sum of $____ and that said defendant ____.

____
Affiant

Sworn to and subscribed
before me this ________
day of ________, ____.

____
Judge

(2) Bond.

—BOND—

STATE OF GEORGIA

COUNTY OF ________

We, ____, principal, and ____, security, jointly and severally acknowledge ourselves bound unto the foregoing defendant in the sum of $____, subject to the following conditions:

The said principal is seeking attachment against the said defendant which is now about to be sued out in the ____ Court of ____ County.

Now, if the said plaintiff shall pay all damages that the defendant may sustain, and also all costs that may be incurred by him in consequence of suing out such attachment, in the event that the said plaintiff shall fail to recover in said case, then this bond shall be void.

________ (SEAL)

________ (SEAL)

Witnessed and approved
this ________ day of
________, ____.

____
Deputy Clerk,
____ Court of ____ County

(3) Attachment.

—ATTACHMENT—

STATE OF GEORGIA

COUNTY OF ________

To the marshal of said court or his lawful deputies, to all and singular the sheriffs or their lawful deputies, and to all lawful constables of said state:

You are commanded to seize so much of the property of the foregoing defendant as will make the sum of $____ and all costs, and to serve such summons of garnishment as may be placed in your hands, and that you make return of this attachment with your actions entered thereon to the ____ term, ____, of the ____ Court of ____ County, to which court this attachment is hereby made returnable.

This ____ day of ____, ____.

________ (SEAL)
________ Court of ________ County

(4) Order.

IN THE ____ COURT OF ____ COUNTY

STATE OF GEORGIA

________	)	
Plaintiff	)	
v.	)	Civil action
	)	File no. ________
________	)	
Defendant	)	
	)	

—ORDER—

Upon application of the plaintiff for a writ of attachment, and having considered the affidavit with bond attached, and inquiring into the grounds and circumstances herein, it is the determination of this court that the plaintiff is (or is not) entitled to a writ of attachment, and it is

ORDERED that a writ of attachment issue upon the property of the defendant (or that a writ of attachment be denied).

This ____ day of ____, ____.

____
Judge,
________ Court of ________ County

Laws 1855–56, p. 25, § 42; Laws 1980, p. 1065, § 7; Laws 1999, p. 81, § 18.

Formerly Code 1863, § 3205; Code 1868, § 3216; Code 1873, § 3283; Code 1882, § 3283; Civil Code 1895, § 4529; Civil Code 1910, § 5074; Code 1933, § 8–119.

§ 18-3-20. Compliance in substance sufficient

A substantial compliance in all matters of form shall be held sufficient in all applications for attachment and in all attachments issued as provided by this chapter.

Laws 1855–56, p. 25, § 43.

Formerly Code 1863, § 3204; Code 1868, § 3215; Code 1873, § 3282; Code 1882, § 3282; Civil Code 1895, § 4528; Civil Code 1910, § 5073; Code 1933, § 8–118.

Article 2

Levy and Replevy of Property Generally

§ 18–3–30. Duty of officer to whom attachment is directed; following property

It shall be the duty of any one of the officers to whom an attachment is directed to levy the attachment upon real or personal property of the defendant which is necessary to satisfy the claim of the plaintiff and which may be found in the county of which he is an officer. It shall be the duty of any one of the officers to whom an attachment is directed, where the defendant has removed his property beyond the limits of the county in which the attachment is issued and returnable, to follow the property into any county of the state, levy the attachment upon such property of the defendant which is necessary to satisfy the claim of the plaintiff, and return the property to the county in which the attachment is returnable.

Laws 1799, Cobb's 1851 Digest, p. 70; Laws 1841, Cobb's 1851 Digest, p. 87; Laws 1855–56, p. 25, § 10.

Formerly Code 1863, § 3206; Code 1868, § 3217; Code 1873, § 3284; Code 1882, § 3284; Civil Code 1895, § 4530; Civil Code 1910, § 5075; Code 1933, § 8–201.

§ 18–3–31. Officer must levy in order in which received; entry on docket

In all cases it shall be the duty of the officer levying attachments to levy them in the order in which they come into his hands, and it shall be his duty to enter upon the same the year, month, day, and hour on which he made the levy. Where the levy is upon land, the attachment must be entered on the execution or attachment docket by the clerk of the superior court in order to be good against third persons acting in good faith and without actual notice.

Laws 1855–56, p. 25, § 19; Laws 1892, p. 58, § 1.

Formerly Code 1863, § 3208; Code 1868, § 3219; Code 1873, § 3286; Code 1882, § 3286; Civil Code 1895, § 4532; Civil Code 1910, § 5077; Code 1933, § 8–203.

§ 18–3–32. Property in a different county, how levied upon

When the plaintiff in attachment wishes to levy his attachment upon property in a different county from that in which the same is returnable, it shall be the duty of the judge issuing the attachment, upon the request of the plaintiff, his agent, or his attorney at law, to make out a copy or copies of the original attachment, bond, and affidavit and certify the same officially to be true copies. Upon delivery of the copies of the attachment, bond, and affidavit, as directed, to any officer of the county in which the property of the defendant is located, it shall be the duty of the officer forthwith to levy the attachment upon the property of the defendant located in that county and to return the attachment, with his actings and doings entered thereon, to the court to which the original attachment is returnable.

Laws 1799, Cobb's 1851 Digest, p. 73; Laws 1855–56, p. 25, § 10; Laws 1980, p. 1065, § 8.

Formerly Code 1863, § 3193; Code 1868, § 3204; Code 1873, § 3270; Code 1882, § 3270; Civil Code 1895, § 4516; Civil Code 1910, § 5061; Code 1933, § 8–210.

§ 18–3–33. Right of defendant to replevy property; bond; officer's duty

(a) When an attachment has been levied upon the property of a defendant, it shall be the duty of the officer levying the attachment to deliver the property levied upon to the defendant upon his giving bond, with good security, payable to the plaintiff in attachment, obligating himself to pay the plaintiff the amount of the judgment and costs that he may recover in the case.

(b) Where the value of the property levied upon, as appraised by the levying officer, is equal to or exceeds the claim of the plaintiff, the bond shall be fixed in an amount equal to the amount claimed to be due. Where the value of the property levied upon, as appraised by the levying officer, is less than the claim of the plaintiff, the bond shall be fixed in an amount equal to twice the value of the property levied upon.

(c) The officer taking the bond shall return the bond with the attachment to the court to which the attachment is returnable, and the plaintiff shall be entitled to entry of judgment against the defendant and his sureties upon the bond for the amount of the judgment and costs entered against the defendant in the case.

Laws 1799, Cobb's 1851 Digest, p. 71; Laws 1816, Cobb's 1851 Digest, p. 74; Laws 1855–56, p. 25, § 11; Laws 1872, p. 8, § 1.

Formerly Code 1863, § 3232; Code 1868, § 3243; Code 1873, § 3319; Code 1882, § 3319; Civil Code 1895, § 4567; Civil Code 1910, § 5113; Code 1933, § 8–701.

§ 18–3–34. Levy on property of foreign corporation; bond; judgment

When an attachment is levied on the property of a foreign corporation, any agent of the corporation may recover the property levied upon by giving a bond, with good security, conditioned to pay the amount of judgment and costs that the plaintiff in attachment may recover in the case. The officer taking the bond shall return the bond with the attachment to the court to which the attachment is made returnable; and the plaintiff shall be entitled to entry of judgment against the corporation and its sureties upon the bond for the amount of the judgment and costs entered against the corporation in the case.

Laws 1855–56, p. 25, § 33.

Formerly Code 1863, § 3233; Code 1868, § 3244; Code 1873, § 3320; Code 1882, § 3320; Civil Code 1895, § 4568; Civil Code 1910, § 5114; Code 1933, § 8–702.

Article 3
Third–Party Claims

§ 18–3–50. How claims interposed; bond

(a) When property is levied on by virtue of an attachment and the same is claimed by any person not a party to the attachment, it shall be the duty of the person claiming the same, his agent, or his attorney at law to make an oath before some person authorized by law to administer an oath that the property levied on is the property of the claimant and is not subject to the attachment according to the best of his knowledge and belief.

(b) The claimant shall give bond, with good security, payable to the plaintiff in attachment in a sum not larger than double the amount of the attachment levied and, where the property attached is of less value than the attachment, in the judgment of the levying officer, then in double the value of the property conditioned to pay the plaintiff all damages which the jury, on the trial of the right of property, may assess against him in case it should be made to appear that the claim was made for the purpose of delay; and, in case the claim is interposed by the agent or attorney at law of the claimant, the agent or attorney at law shall have power to sign the name of the claimant to the bond, and the claimant shall be bound in the same manner as though he had signed it himself. It shall be the duty of the levying officer taking the affidavit and bond to return the same to the court to which the attachment is returnable, unless the property levied on should be real estate, in which case it shall be his duty to return the same to the superior court of the county where the land lies, provided that, if the claimant is unable to give such bond and security, he may interpose his claim as provided in Code Section 9–15–2.

Laws 1814, Cobb's 1851 Digest, p. 72; Laws 1855–56, p. 25, § 34; Laws 1887, p. 40, § 1.

Formerly Code 1863, § 3235; Code 1868, § 3246; Code 1873, § 3322; Code 1882, § 3322; Civil Code 1895, § 4569; Civil Code 1910, § 5115; Code 1933, § 8–801.

§ 18–3–51. Right of claimant, his agent, or attorney to replevy; bond

The claimant, his agent, or his attorney at law may give bond, with good security, payable to the levying officer, in a sum equal to double the value of the property claimed, the value to be judged by the levying officer, conditioned to deliver the property at the time and place of sale, provided the same should be found subject to the attachment; and, upon the delivery of the bond to the levying officer, it shall be his duty to deliver such property to the claimant, his agent, or his attorney at law; and it shall be the duty of the levying officer to return the bond, together with the affidavit and claim bond, to the court to which the attachment is returnable; and, when the claim is interposed by the agent or attorney at law of the claimant, the agent or attorney at law shall have power to sign the name of the claimant to the bond, who shall be bound thereby in the same manner as though he had signed it himself.

Laws 1836, Cobb's 1851 Digest, p. 84; Laws 1855–56, p. 25, § 36.

Formerly Code 1863, § 3237; Code 1868, § 3248; Code 1873, § 3324; Code 1882, § 3324; Civil Code 1895, § 4571; Civil Code 1910, § 5117; Code 1933, § 8–803.

§ 18–3–52. How claim to be tried

The third-party claim shall be tried in the same manner and subject to the same rules and regulations as are prescribed by law for the trial of other claims in the court to which it is returned.

Laws 1855–56, p. 25, § 35.

Formerly Code 1863, § 3236; Code 1868, § 3247; Code 1873, § 3323; Code 1882, § 3323; Civil Code 1895, § 4570; Civil Code 1910, § 5116; Code 1933, § 8–802.

§ 18–3–53. Proceeding on failure of claimant to deliver property

Upon the failure of the claimant to deliver the property according to the conditions of the bond, the levying officer may immediately sue the claimant and security upon the bond and recover the full value of the property claimed and also all damages, costs, and charges that the plaintiff may have sustained in consequence of the failure of the claimant to deliver the property.

Laws 1836, Cobb's 1851 Digest, p. 84; Laws 1855–56, p. 25, § 37.

Formerly Code 1863, § 3238; Code 1868, § 3249; Code 1873, § 3325; Code 1882, § 3325; Civil Code 1895, § 4572; Civil Code 1910, § 5118; Code 1933, § 8–804.

§ 18–3–54. Liability of claimant and security for hire or use of property

(a) In cases where the claimant shall deliver the property and upon selling the same a sufficient amount shall not be raised to pay the debt and costs of the plaintiff, the plaintiff may institute an action against the claimant and his securities upon his bond and recover the full value of the hire or use of the property while the same has been in the possession of the claimant and also full damages for any deterioration of the value of the property, by use or otherwise, while the same has been in the possession of the claimant, provided such recovery shall not exceed the amount of the debt that may remain due from the defendant in attachment to the plaintiff.

(b) The remedy provided in this Code section is and shall be extended to all other claims in the cases herein provided for.

Laws 1855–56, p. 25, § 38; Laws 1873, p. 42, § 1.

Formerly Code 1863, § 3239; Code 1868, § 3250; Code 1873, § 3326; Code 1882, § 3326; Civil Code 1895, § 4573; Civil Code 1910, § 5119; Code 1933, § 8–805.

§ 18–3–55. Time when claim may be interposed

In cases of attachment, the claim may be interposed either before or after judgment.

Formerly Code 1863, § 3240; Code 1868, § 3251; Code 1873, § 3327; Code 1882, § 3327; Civil Code 1895, § 4574; Civil Code 1910, § 5120; Code 1933, § 8–806.

Article 4

Judgment, Execution, and Levy

§ 18–3–70. When judgment binds defendant's property

When the defendant has given bond and security, or when he has appeared and made defense by himself or attorney at law without raising a valid defense of lack of jurisdiction over the person, the judgment rendered against him in such case shall bind all his property and shall have the same force and effect as when there has been personal service, and execution shall issue accordingly, but it shall be first levied upon the property attached. In all other cases, the judgment on the attachment shall only bind the property attached and the judgment shall be entered only against such property.

Laws 1982, p. 1578, § 1; Laws 1982, p. 1578, § 2.

Formerly Code 1933, § 8–901.

§ 18–3–71. Judgment may be set aside for fraud or want of consideration

A judgment in attachment may be set aside in a court of law upon an issue suggesting fraud or want of consideration, tendered by a judgment creditor of the defendant in attachment.

Laws 1982, p. 1578, § 1; Laws 1982, p. 1578, § 2.

Formerly Code 1933, § 8–902.

§ 18–3–72. Executions must issue on all judgments; property on which levied

After the judgment has been obtained in any case of attachment, execution shall issue as in cases at common law, which execution shall be levied in the same manner as executions issuing at common law; and the proceedings in all respects shall be the same, except that when the judgment only binds the property levied on by the attachment, as aforesaid, the execution shall be issued against such property only and that property only shall be levied on and sold.

Laws 1982, p. 1578, § 1; Laws 1982, p. 1578, § 2.

Formerly Code 1933, § 8–903.

§ 18–3–73. Application of money raised by sale of property

All money raised by the sale of defendant's property or otherwise, by virtue of this chapter, shall be paid over to the creditors of the defendant, according to the priority of the lien of their judgments, except that as between attaching creditors the attachment first levied shall be first satisfied to the entire exclusion of any attachment of younger levy.

Laws 1982, p. 1578, § 1; Laws 1982, p. 1578, § 2.

Formerly Code 1933, § 8–904.

§ 18-3-74. Lien of attachments; priorities

The lien of an attachment is created by the levy and not the judgment in the attachment; and in case of a conflict between attachments, the first levied shall be first satisfied; but in a contest between attachments and ordinary judgments or suits, it is the judgment and not the levy which fixes the lien. However, the lien of an attachment shall have priority over the lien of an ordinary judgment that has been obtained upon a suit filed after the levy of the attachment.

Laws 1982, p. 1578, § 1; Laws 1982, p. 1578, § 2.

Formerly Code 1933, § 8-905.

§ 18-3-75. Lien on realty only after entry on docket

As against the interests of third parties acting in good faith and without notice who may have acquired a transfer or lien binding any real estate, no attachment levied upon real estate shall be a lien on the same from the levy thereof unless said attachment is entered upon the attachment docket of the county in which the real estate is situated within five days from said levy. When the attachment is entered upon the docket after the five days, the lien shall date from such entry; and it shall be the duty of the sheriff to have said entry made within the five days. Nothing in this Code section shall be construed to affect the validity or force of any attachment as between the parties thereto.

Laws 1982, p. 1578, § 1; Laws 1982, p. 1578, § 2.

Formerly Code 1933, § 8-906.

CHAPTER 4

GARNISHMENT PROCEEDINGS

Article 1

General Provisions

§ 18-4-1. Practice and procedure

The procedure in garnishment cases shall be uniform in all courts throughout this state; and, except as otherwise provided in this chapter, Chapter 11 of Title 9 shall apply in garnishment proceedings.

Laws 1976, p. 1608, § 1; Laws 1982, p. 3, § 18.

Formerly Code 1933, § 46-305.

§ 18-4-2. Discovery

Discovery in a garnishment proceeding shall be made in the manner provided for in Chapter 11 of Title 9.

Laws 1976, p. 1608, § 1; Laws 1982, p. 3, § 18.

Formerly Code 1933, § 46-601.

§ 18-4-3. Amendment

Unless otherwise provided in this chapter, any affidavit, bond, or pleading required or permitted by this chapter shall be amendable at any time before judgment thereon.

Laws 1976, p. 1608, § 1.

Formerly Code 1933, § 46-602.

§ 18-4-4. Judge to act where no clerk

Where this chapter makes the performance of any function the duty of the clerk, the function shall be performed by the judge if the court in which the proceedings are filed has no clerk.

Laws 1976, p. 1608, § 1.

Formerly Code 1933, § 46-604.

§ 18-4-5. Challenge to sufficiency of bond

(a) Any party of record to a proceeding under this chapter who may be affected materially thereby may challenge the sufficiency of any bond required or permitted by this chapter. Such challenge shall be made by motion to require additional security; and, if upon hearing the same the court shall determine that the security upon the bond is inadequate for the purposes for which the bond is filed, an order shall be entered requiring the person filing the bond to furnish additional security within seven days of the date of the order.

(b) The original surety shall not be discharged from his liability on the bond until another surety is approved.

Laws 1976, p. 1608, § 1.

Formerly Code 1933, § 46-603.

§ 18-4-6. Release of summons of garnishment

It shall be the duty of the clerk of the court in which garnishment proceedings are pending to issue a release of garnishment if:

(1) The plaintiff or his attorney so requests in writing;

(2) The amount claimed due together with the costs of the garnishment proceeding are paid into court;

(3) A dissolution bond is filed by the defendant and approved by the clerk as provided for in this chapter;

(4) A judge shall enter an order, after a hearing required by this chapter, directing that the garnishment be released; or

(5) The garnishment is dismissed.

Laws 1976, p. 1608, § 1.

Formerly Code 1933, § 46-307.

§ 18-4-7. Restriction on discharge from employment by reason of garnishment

No employer may discharge any employee by reason of the fact that his earnings have been subjected to garnishment for any one indebtedness, even though more than one summons of garnishment may be served upon such employer with respect to the indebtedness.

Laws 1976, p. 1608, § 1.

Formerly Code 1933, § 46-303.

Article 2

Property and Persons Subject to Garnishment

§ 18-4-20. What is subject to garnishment

(a) As used in this Code section, the term:

(1) "Disposable earnings" means that part of the earnings of an individual remaining after the deduction from those earnings of the amounts required by law to be withheld.

(2) "Earnings" means compensation paid or payable for personal services, whether denominated as wages, salary, commission, bonus, or otherwise, and includes periodic payments pursuant to a pension or retirement program.

(b) All debts owed by the garnishee to the defendant at the time of service of the summons of garnishment upon the garnishee and all debts accruing from the garnishee to the defendant from the date of service to the date of the garnishee's answer shall be subject to process of garnishment; and no payment made by the garnishee to the defendant or to his order, or by any arrangement between the defendant and the garnishee, after the date of the service of the summons of garnishment upon the garnishee, shall defeat the lien of such garnishment.

(c) All property, money, or effects of the defendant in the possession or control of the garnishee at the time of service of the summons of garnishment upon the garnishee or coming into the possession or control of the garnishee at any time from the date of service of the summons of garnishment upon the garnishee to the date of the garnishee's answer shall be subject to process of garnishment except, in the case of collateral securities in the hands of a creditor, such securities shall not be subject to garnishment so long as there is an amount owed on the debt for which the securities were given as collateral.

(d)(1) Notwithstanding subsection (a) of this Code section, the maximum part of the aggregate disposable earnings of an individual for any work week which is subject to garnishment may not exceed the lesser of:

(A) Twenty-five percent of his disposable earnings for that week; or

(B) The amount by which his disposable earnings for that week exceed 30 times the federal minimum hourly wage prescribed by Section 6(a)(1) of the Fair Labor Standards Act of 1938, U.S.C. Title 29, Section 206(a)(1), in effect at the time the earnings are payable.

(2) In case of earnings for a period other than a week, a multiple of the federal minimum hourly wage equivalent in effect to that set forth in subparagraph (B) of paragraph (1) of this subsection shall be used.

(e) The limitation on garnishment set forth in subsection (d) of this Code section shall apply although the garnishee may receive a summons of garnishment in more than one garnishment case naming the same defendant unless the garnishee has received a summons of garnishment based on a judgment for alimony or the support of a dependent, in which case the limitation on garnishment set forth in subsection (f) of this Code section shall apply although the garnishee may receive a summons of garnishment in more than one garnishment case naming the same defendant. No garnishee shall withhold from the disposable earnings of the defendant any sum greater than the amount prescribed by subsection (d) or subsection (f) of this

Code section, as applicable, regardless of the number of summonses served upon the garnishee.

(f) The exemption provided by subsection (d) of this Code section shall not apply if the judgment upon which the garnishment is based is a judgment for alimony or for the support of any dependent of the defendant, provided the summons of garnishment shall contain a notice to the garnishee that the garnishment is based on the judgment for alimony or the support of a dependent. In any case in which the garnishment is based on the judgment, the maximum part of the aggregate disposable earnings of an individual for any workweek which is subject to garnishment shall be 50 percent of the individual's disposable earnings for that week.

(g) Except as provided in Article 7 of this chapter for a summons of continuing garnishment for support, the summons of garnishment, including a summons of continuing garnishment pursuant to Article 6 of this chapter, shall on its face state the total amount claimed to be due at the time of the summons and the amount subject to garnishment shall not exceed the amount so shown on the summons of garnishment.

(h) The summons of garnishment, including a summons of continuing garnishment, may on its face set forth, if known, the social security number of the defendant.

(i) A summons of garnishment upon a financial institution, or an attachment thereto, shall state with particularity all of the following information, to the extent reasonably available to the plaintiff:

(1) The name of the defendant, and, to the extent such would reasonably enable the garnishee to answer properly the summons, all known configurations, nicknames, aliases, former or maiden names, trade names, or variations thereof;

(2) The service address and the current addresses of the defendant and, to the extent such would reasonably enable the garnishee to answer properly the summons of garnishment and such is reasonably available to the plaintiff, the past addresses of the defendant;

(3) The social security number or federal tax identification number of the defendant; and

(4) Account, identification, or tracking numbers known or suspected by the plaintiff to be used by the garnishee in the identification or administration of the defendant's funds or property.

A misspelling of any information required by paragraph (1) or (2) of this subsection, other than the surname of a natural person defendant, shall not invalidate a summons of garnishment, so long as such information is not misleading in a search of the garnishee's records.

Laws 1976, p. 1608, § 1; Laws 1977, p. 159, § 3; Laws 1980, p. 1769, §§ 2–4; Laws 1984, p. 370, § 1; Laws 1985, p. 149, § 18; Laws 1985, p. 785, § 1; Laws 1985, p. 1632, § 1; Laws 1997, p. 941, § 1.

Formerly Code 1933, § 46–301.

§ 18–4–21. Salaries of officials and employees of State and its subdivision made subject

(a) Money due officials or employees of a municipal corporation or county of this state or of the state government, or any department or institution thereof, as salary for services performed for or on behalf of the municipal corporation or county of this state, or the state, or any department or institution thereof, shall be subject to garnishment, except in no event may the officials' or employees' salary for services performed for or on behalf of any municipal corporation or county of this state, or the state, or any department or institution thereof, be garnisheed where the judgment serving as a basis for the issuance of the summons of garnishment arises out of the liability incurred in the scope of the officials' or employees' governmental employment while responding to an emergency. In such cases, the summons shall be directed to such political entity and served upon the person authorized by law to draw the warrant on the treasury of the government or to issue a check for such salary due, or upon the chief administrative officer of the political subdivision, department, agency, or instrumentality; and such entity is required to answer the summons in accordance with the mandate thereof and as provided by this chapter.

(b) For purposes of this Code section only, the state and its political subdivisions, departments, agencies, and instrumentalities shall be deemed private persons; and jurisdiction for the purpose of issuing a summons of garnishment shall be restricted to a court located in the county in which the warrant is drawn on the treasury of the government or in which the check is issued for the salary due the official or employee of the state or its political subdivisions, departments, agencies, or instrumentalities.

Laws 1976, p. 1608, § 1; Laws 1977, p. 634, § 1; Laws 1980, p. 1769, § 6.

Formerly Code 1933, § 46–306.

§ 18–4–22. Pension and retirement funds and benefits exemption

(a) Funds or benefits from a pension or retirement program as defined in 29 U.S.C. Section 1002(2)(A) or funds or benefits from an individual retirement account as defined in Section 408 or 408A of the United States Internal Revenue Code of 1986, as amended, shall be exempt from the process of garnishment until paid or otherwise transferred to a member of such program or beneficiary thereof. Such funds or benefits, when paid or otherwise transferred to the member or beneficiary, shall be exempt from the process of garnishment only to the extent provided in Code Section 18-4-20 for other disposable earnings, unless a greater exemption is otherwise provided by law.

(b) The exemption provided by this Code section shall not apply when the garnishment is based upon a judgment for alimony or for child support, in which event such funds or benefits shall then be subject to the process of garnishment to the extent provided in subsection (f) of Code Section 18-4-20.

(c) Nothing in this Code section shall prohibit the attachment or alienation of welfare benefits as defined in 29 U.S.C. Section 1002(1) in the control of an administrator or trustee.

Laws 1976, p. 1608, § 1; Laws 1980, p. 1769, § 5; Laws 1983, p. 683, § 1; Laws 1990, p. 360, § 1; Laws 2006, Act 459, § 1, eff. April 18, 2006.

Formerly Code 1933, § 46-302.

§ 18-4-22.1. Repealed by Laws 1990, p. 360, § 2, eff. July 1, 1990

§ 18-4-23. Service of summons of garnishment upon corporation

Service of a summons of garnishment shall be made by serving the agent in charge of the office or other place of business where the defendant is employed. In the event that such service cannot be made, then service of a summons of garnishment upon the agent in charge of either the registered office or the principal place of business of a corporation shall be sufficient.

Laws 1976, p. 1608, § 1; Laws 1984, p. 1319, § 2.

Formerly Code 1933, § 46-304.

Article 3

Prejudgment Garnishment Proceedings Generally

§ 18-4-40. Right to writ before judgment

In cases where an action is pending against the defendant, garnishment may issue prior to judgment only in the following cases:

(1) When the defendant resides outside the limits of the state;

(2) When the defendant is actually removing, or about to remove, outside the limits of the county;

(3) When the defendant is causing his property to be removed beyond the limits of the state;

(4) When the defendant has transferred, has threatened to transfer, or is about to transfer property to defraud or delay his creditors; or

(5) When the defendant is insolvent.

Laws 1976, p. 1608, § 1.

Formerly Code 1933, § 46-201.

§ 18-4-41. Application to be made to judge; contents

When the plaintiff contends one or more of the grounds set forth in Code Section 18-4-40 exist, the plaintiff may, prior to obtaining judgment against the defendant, make application to a judge of any court of record, other than the probate court, in the county of residence of the garnishee having jurisdiction over the garnishee, for an order authorizing the issuance of summons of garnishment. Such application shall be made in writing, under oath, and shall set forth the specific facts that show the existence of one or more such grounds as well as the name of the court where the action is pending, the case number of such action, and the amount claimed therein by the plaintiff.

Laws 1976, p. 1608, § 1.

Formerly Code 1933, § 46-202.

§ 18-4-42. Order authorizing garnishment prior to judgment

After considering plaintiff's application, if the judge to whom same is made finds that the facts alleged show the existence of one or more of the grounds set forth in Code Section 18-4-40, he may enter an order authorizing garnishment prior to judgment. The entry of such order shall authorize the clerk of the court in which the garnishment proceedings are pending to issue summons of garnishment from time to time without a further showing until the case is terminated or until further order of the court.

Laws 1976, p. 1608, § 1.

Formerly Code 1933, § 46-203.

§ 18-4-43. Bond in proceedings to secure garnishment prior to judgment

No summons of garnishment prior to judgment shall issue unless accompanied by a bond with good security, conditioned to pay the defendant all costs and damages that he may sustain in consequence of the issuance of the summons of garnishment in the event that the amount claimed to be due was not due, or that no lawful ground for the issuance of such garnishment prior to judgment existed, or that the property sought to be garnisheed was not subject to garnishment. Such bond shall be in a sum equal to twice the amount claimed due in the plaintiff's application. The bond shall be presented to the clerk of the court where the application provided for in this article is sought to be filed, for approval by the clerk prior to making application to the judge of the court for the writ of garnishment.

Laws 1976, p. 1608, § 1.

Formerly Code 1933, § 46-204.

§ 18-4-44. Service upon defendant

Upon the entry of an order authorizing the issuance of garnishment prior to judgment, summons of garnishment shall issue and be served as provided in Code Section 18-4-62. A copy of the order and of each summons of garnishment issued pursuant thereto shall be served upon the defendant in any manner prescribed for the service of original summons and complaints.

Laws 1976, p. 1608, § 1.

Formerly Code 1933, § 46-205.

§ 18-4-45. Defendant's right to hearing; procedure

When summons of garnishment shall issue before judgment against the defendant, the defendant may at any time traverse the plaintiff's affidavit upon which the garnishment was obtained, stating that the affidavit is untrue or legally insufficient. Upon filing of the traverse, the court from which the garnishment issued shall issue a show cause order to the plaintiff requiring him to appear at a specified time, which shall not be more than ten days from the filing of the traverse, to prove the grounds for the issuance of the garnishment. If the plaintiff shall fail to carry the burden of proof, the order authorizing the garnishment prior to judgment shall be revoked.

Laws 1976, p. 1608, § 1.

Formerly Code 1933, § 46-206.

§ 18-4-46. Personal earnings of defendant not subject to garnishment prior to judgment

Any other provisions of this chapter to the contrary notwithstanding, no part of the personal earnings of the defendant shall be subject to garnishment prior to judgment, whether such earnings be denominated as salary, wages, commissions, or otherwise; and each summons of garnishment which is issued pursuant to this article shall state the substance of this Code section upon the face thereof.

Laws 1976, p. 1608, § 1.

Formerly Code 1933, § 46-207.

§ 18-4-47. Funds to be held by clerk pending judgment

When funds or other property are paid into court or subject to garnishment under this article, the funds or other property shall be held by the clerk of the court in which the garnishment proceedings are pending until final judgment is entered against the defendant in the main proceedings; provided, however, that, if the garnishment is released by filing of the bond provided for by Code Section 18-4-81, such funds or other property shall be delivered to the defendant if no claim has been filed pursuant to Code Section 18-4-95 at the time the bond is approved and filed with the clerk of the court.

Laws 1976, p. 1608, § 1.

Formerly Code 1933, § 46-208.

§ 18-4-48. Proceedings subsequent to judgment

After final judgment is entered in an action in which a summons of garnishment was issued prior to judgment, the garnishment proceedings shall continue in accordance with Article 4 of this chapter. The plaintiff shall not have judgment against the garnishee until he obtains final judgment against the defendant.

Laws 1976, p. 1608, § 1.

Formerly Code 1933, § 46-209.

Article 4

Postjudgment Garnishment Proceedings Generally

§ 18-4-60. Right to writ after judgment

In all cases where a money judgment shall have been obtained in a court of this state or in a federal court sitting in this state, the plaintiff shall be entitled to the process of garnishment.

Laws 1976, p. 1608, § 1; Laws 1980, p. 1769, § 1.

Formerly Code 1933, § 46-101.

§ 18–4–61. Affidavit; necessity and contents; judicial supervision

The plaintiff, the plaintiff's attorney at law, or the plaintiff's agent shall make, on personal knowledge, an affidavit setting forth that the plaintiff has a judgment against a named defendant, the amount claimed to be due on the judgment, the name of the court which rendered the judgment, and the case number thereof. Upon the filing of the affidavit with the clerk of any court having jurisdiction over the garnishee, the clerk shall cause a summons of garnishment to issue forthwith; provided, however, that the affidavit shall first be made and be approved as containing the information required by this Code section in one of the following ways:

(1) The affidavit may be made before and approved by a judge of the court in which the garnishment proceeding is filed;

(2) The affidavit may be made before and approved by a judge of the court that rendered the judgment upon which the garnishment is based;

(3) The affidavit may be made before and approved by a judge of any court of record;

(4) The affidavit may be made before any officer authorized to administer oaths, including a notary public, provided that the affidavit is then submitted by mail or in person to any judge of a court specified in paragraph (1), (2), or (3) of this Code section and is approved by him; or

(5) The affidavit may be made before the clerk or deputy clerk of the court in which the garnishment is filed or before any officer authorized to administer oaths, including a notary public, and may be approved by the clerk or deputy clerk if the judge or judges of the court promulgate rules supervising the initiation of the garnishment proceedings and the affidavit is made and approved pursuant to such rules. No court rule or practice shall preclude a plaintiff from proceeding pursuant to paragraph (1), (2), (3), or (4) of this Code section.

Laws 1976, p. 1608, § 1; Laws 1977, p. 159, § 1; Laws 1996, p. 317, § 1.

Formerly Code 1933, § 46–102.

§ 18–4–62. Summons of garnishment

(a) The summons of garnishment shall be directed to the garnishee, commanding him to file an answer stating what money or other property is subject to garnishment. Except as provided in subsection (b) or (c) of this Code section, the answer must be filed with the court issuing the summons not sooner than 30 days and not later than 45 days after the service of the summons and must be accompanied by the money or other property subject to garnishment. Upon the affidavit and summons being delivered to the sheriff, marshal, constable, or like officer of the court issuing the summons, it shall be his duty to serve the summons of garnishment upon the person to whom it is directed and to make his entry of service upon the affidavit and return the affidavit to the court. The summons of garnishment shall state that, if the garnishee fails to answer the summons, a judgment by default will be entered against the garnishee for the amount claimed by plaintiff against the defendant.

(b) Under circumstances where the defendant has been an employee of the garnishee, and if the defendant is no longer employed by the garnishee, and if the garnishee has no money or property of the defendant subject to garnishment, the garnishee may immediately file an answer; however, such answer shall be filed not later than 45 days after the service of the summons.

(c) If the garnishee is a bank or other financial institution and if the defendant does not have an active account with, and is not the owner of any money or property in the possession of, the bank or financial institution then the garnishee may immediately file an answer; however, such answer shall be filed not later than 45 days after the service of the summons.

Laws 1976, p. 1608, § 1; Laws 1983, p. 454, § 1.

Formerly Code 1933, § 46–103.

§ 18–4–63. Additional summons

(a) Summons of garnishment may issue from time to time on the same affidavit until the judgment is paid or the garnishment proceeding is otherwise terminated in accordance with this chapter.

(b) In the event no summons of garnishment has been issued on an affidavit for two years or more, the garnishment proceeding based on that affidavit shall automatically stand dismissed.

Laws 1976, p. 1608, § 1; Laws 1981, p. 383, § 1.

Formerly Code 1933, § 46–104.

§ 18–4–64. Notice to judgment defendant

(a) In a garnishment based on a judgment, the defendant shall be given notice of the filing of the first summons of garnishment on an affidavit for garnishment and of the issuance of an additional summons of garnishment on such affidavit when no notice has been given to the defendant within 90 days immediately preceding the issuance of such additional summons, using any one or more of the following methods:

(1) The plaintiff, at the time the garnishment is filed with the clerk, shall commence procedures to effectuate the service of a copy of the summons of garnishment on the defendant; and service thereafter shall be made on the defendant as soon as is

reasonably practicable. Service pursuant to this paragraph shall be made pursuant to Code Section 9–11–4;

(2) The plaintiff, after issuance of the summons of garnishment and not more than three business days after service of the summons of garnishment on the garnishee, shall cause a written notice to be sent to the defendant at the defendant's last known address by registered or certified mail or statutory overnight delivery, return receipt requested. Either the return receipt indicating receipt by the defendant or the envelope bearing the official notification from the United States Postal Service of the defendant's refusal to accept delivery of such registered or certified mail or statutory overnight delivery shall be filed with the clerk of the court in which the garnishment is pending. The defendant's refusal to accept such registered or certified mail or statutory overnight delivery addressed to defendant shall be deemed notice to defendant;

(3) The plaintiff, after the issuance of the summons of garnishment and not more than three business days after service of the summons of garnishment on the garnishee, shall cause a written notice to be delivered personally to the defendant by the plaintiff or by the plaintiff's attorney at law or other agent. A certification by the person making the delivery shall be filed with the clerk;

(4)(A) When the defendant resides out of the state, has departed the state, cannot, after due diligence, be found within the state, or conceals his place of residence from the plaintiff and the fact shall appear, by affidavit, to the satisfaction of the judge or clerk of the court, the levy and attachment of the lien of the garnishment shall constitute sufficient notice to the defendant, provided such levy and attachment of the lien of garnishment alone shall constitute sufficient notice, unless the plaintiff has actual knowledge of the defendant's address, in which case, to provide sufficient notice, the plaintiff shall also mail a written notice of garnishment to the defendant at said address; or, not having such actual knowledge of the defendant's address but the address at which the defendant was served being shown on the return of service in the action resulting in the judgment, to provide sufficient notice, the plaintiff shall also mail a written notice of garnishment to the defendant at said address.

(B) A mailing of the written notice provided for in this Code section shall be made after the issuance of the summons of garnishment and not more than three business days after service of the summons of garnishment on the garnishee; and a certificate of such mailing shall be filed with the clerk by the person mailing the notice;

(5) (A) Where it shall appear by affidavit that a defendant in the garnishment action is not a resident of this state or has departed from this state, or after due diligence cannot be found in this state, or conceals his place of residence from the plaintiff, notice may be given by causing two publications of the written notice in the paper in which advertisements are printed by the sheriff in each county in which a summons of garnishment is served. Such publications must be at least six days apart; and the second publication must be made not more than 21 days after the service of the summons of garnishment on the garnishee. A certification by the person causing the notice to be published shall be filed with the clerk, provided such publication shall constitute sufficient notice alone, unless the plaintiff has actual knowledge of the defendant's address, in which case, to provide sufficient notice, the plaintiff shall also mail a written notice of garnishment to the defendant at said address.

(B) A mailing of the written notice provided for in this Code section shall be made after the issuance of the summons of garnishment and not more than three business days after service of the summons of garnishment on the garnishee; and a certificate of such mailing shall be filed with the clerk by the person mailing the notice;

(6) After issuance of the summons of garnishment and not more than three business days after service of the summons of garnishment on the garnishee, the plaintiff shall send by ordinary mail a written notice of the garnishment to the defendant at the address at which the defendant was served in the action resulting in the judgment on which the garnishment proceeding is based; provided, however, this paragraph may be used only when the garnishment proceeding is commenced within 60 days after the judgment upon which the garnishment is based was obtained. A certification by the person mailing the notice shall be filed with the clerk;

(7) Where the defendant's address is known, the plaintiff, after issuance of the summons of garnishment and not more than three business days after service of the summons of garnishment on the garnishee, shall send to the defendant at such known address by ordinary mail a written notice of the garnishment. A certification by the person mailing the notice shall be filed with the clerk.

(b) The receiving by the defendant of actual timely notice of a summons of garnishment shall constitute notice.

(c) "Written notice," as referred to in paragraphs (2) through (7) of subsection (a) of this Code section, shall consist of a copy of the summons of garnishment or of a document which includes the names of the plaintiff and the defendant, the amount claimed in the affidavit of garnishment, a statement that a garnishment against the property and credits of the defendant has been or will be served on the garnishee, and the name of the court issuing the summons of garnishment.

(d) The methods of notification specified in subsection (a) of this Code section are cumulative and may be used in any sequence or combination. Where it appears that a plaintiff has reasonably, diligently, and in good faith attempted to use one method, another method thereafter may be utilized; and, for the time during which the attempt was being made, the time limit shall be tolled for the subsequent method.

(e) No money or other property delivered to the court by the garnishee shall be distributed; nor shall any judgment be rendered against the garnishee until after the expiration of ten days from the date of compliance with at least one method of notification provided by subsection (a) of this Code section.

Laws 1977, p. 159, § 2; Laws 2000, p. 1589, § 3.

Formerly Code 1933, § 46-105.

§ 18-4-65. Issues defendant may raise by traverse

(a) When garnishment proceedings are based upon a judgment, the defendant, by traverse of the plaintiff's affidavit, may challenge the existence of the judgment or the amount claimed due thereon. The defendant may plead any other matter in bar of the judgment, except as provided in subsection (b) of this Code section.

(b) The validity of the judgment upon which a garnishment is based may only be challenged in accordance with Chapter 11 of Title 9; and no such challenge shall be entertained in the garnishment case. However, where the court finds that the defendant has attacked the validity of the judgment upon which the garnishment is based in an appropriate forum, the judge may order the garnishment released and stayed until the validity of the judgment has been determined in such forum.

(c) If the garnishment proceedings are based upon a pending action, the case shall proceed in accordance with Code Section 18-4-45.

Laws 1976, p. 1608, § 1; Laws 1982, p. 3, § 18.

Formerly Code 1933, § 46-403.

§ 18-4-66. Forms for post-judgment garnishment

For the purpose of Articles 1 through 5 of this chapter, the following forms are declared to be sufficient for garnishment after judgment, provided that nothing in this Code section shall be construed to require the use of particular forms in any proceeding under this article:

(1) Garnishment affidavit.

IN THE _____ COURT OF _____ COUNTY

STATE OF GEORGIA

_______________)
Plaintiff)
)
v.) Civil action
) File no. _____
)
Defendant)
)
_______________)
Garnishee)
)
_______________)
Address)

—GARNISHMENT AFFIDAVIT—

Personally appeared the undersigned affiant who on oath says that he is the above plaintiff, his agent, or his attorney at law and that the above defendant is indebted to said plaintiff on a judgment described as follows:

_____ is the case number in the _____ Court of _____ County which rendered the judgment against the defendant, $_____ being the balance thereon.

____
Affiant

Sworn to and subscribed before me this _____ day of _____, _____.

____
Plaintiff's attorney

(2) Summons of garnishment.

IN THE _____ COURT OF _____ COUNTY

STATE OF GEORGIA

_______________)
Plaintiff)
)
v.) Civil action
) File no. _____
_______________)
Defendant)
Social security)
number)
)
_______________)
Garnishee)
)
_______________)
Address)

SUMMONS OF GARNISHMENT

To: _______________ Garnishee

Amount claimed due by plaintiff $_____
(To be completed by plaintiff)

Plus court costs due on the summons $____
(To be completed by the clerk)

YOU ARE HEREBY COMMANDED to hold immediately all property, money, wages, except what is exempt, belonging to the defendant, or debts owed to the defendant named above at the time of service of this summons and between the time of service of this summons and the time of making your answer. Not sooner than 30 days but not later than 45 days after you are served with this summons, you are commanded to file your answer in writing with the clerk of this court and serve a copy upon the plaintiff or his attorney named below. Money or other property subject to this summons should be delivered to the court with your answer. Should you fail to answer this summons, a judgment will be rendered against you for the amount the plaintiff claims due by the defendant.

Witness the Honorable ____, Judge of said Court.

This ____ day of ____, ____.

____
Clerk,

____ Court of ____ County

____
Plaintiff's attorney

____
Address

Service perfected on garnishee, this ________ day of ________, ____.

____
Deputy marshal, sheriff, or constable

(3) Defendant's traverse and order thereon.

IN THE ____ COURT OF ____ COUNTY

STATE OF GEORGIA

________ Plaintiff	)	
v.	)	Civil action File no. ____
________ Defendant	)	
________ Garnishee	)	

—TRAVERSE OF DEFENDANT—

Now comes the defendant in the above-styled case and traverses the plaintiff's affidavit by saying the same is untrue or legally insufficient.

____
Defendant or his attorney at law

—ORDER—

It is hereby ordered that a hearing be held upon the defendant's traverse before this court on the ____ day of ____, ____, at ____: ____.M., and that a copy of the defendant's traverse and this order be served as provided by law.

This ____ day of ____, ____.

____
Judge,
____ Court of ____ County

—(CERTIFICATE OF SERVICE)—

(4) Answer of garnishee.

IN THE ____ COURT OF ____ COUNTY

STATE OF GEORGIA

________ Plaintiff	)	
v.	)	Civil action File no. ____
________ Defendant	)	
________ Garnishee	)	

—ANSWER OF GARNISHEE—

—1.—

At the time of service or from the time of service to the time of this answer, garnishee had in his possession the following described property of the defendant: ____ ____

—2.—

At the time of service or from the time of service to the time of this answer, all debt accruing from garnishee to defendant is in the amount of $____.

—3.—

$____ of the amount named in paragraph 2 was wages earned at the rate of $____ per ____ for the period beginning (date), ____, through the time of making this answer. The amount of wages which is subject to this garnishment is computed as follows:

$____ Gross earnings
$____ Total social security and withholding tax
$____ Total disposable earnings
$____ Amount of wages subject to garnishment

—4.—

Garnishee further states: ____.

____
Garnishee or his attorney at law

—(CERTIFICATE OF SERVICE)—

(5) Plaintiff's traverse.

IN THE _____ COURT OF _____ COUNTY

STATE OF GEORGIA

______________ Plaintiff	)))	
v.	)))	Civil action File no. _____
______________ Defendant	)))	
______________ Garnishee	))	

—TRAVERSE OF PLAINTIFF—

Now comes the plaintiff in the above-styled case and traverses the garnishee's answer by saying the same is untrue or legally insufficient.

____
Plaintiff or his attorney at law

—(CERTIFICATE OF SERVICE)—

(6) Release of garnishment.

IN THE _____ COURT OF _____ COUNTY

STATE OF GEORGIA

______________ Plaintiff	)))	
v.	)))	Civil action File no. _____
______________ Defendant	)))	
______________ Garnishee	)))	
______________ Address	))	

—RELEASE OF GARNISHMENT—

To: _____ Garnishee

This is to notify you that you have been released from filing an answer to any and all summons of garnishment pending as of this date in the above-styled case.

This release authorizes you to deliver to the defendant in garnishment any money or other property in your possession belonging to the defendant.

This release does not terminate the garnishment proceedings, nor does this release relieve you of any obligation placed on you by the service of a summons of garnishment subsequent to this date.

This _____ day of _____, _____.

____
Clerk,
_____ Court of _____ County

(7) Attachment to summons of garnishment upon a financial institution.

IN THE _____ COURT OF _____ COUNTY

STATE OF GEORGIA

______________ Plaintiff	)))	
v.	))	Civil action File no. _____
______________ Defendant	)))	
______________ Other known names of Defendant	)))	
______________ Current and past addresses of Defendant	)))	
______________ Social security number or federal tax identification number of Defendant	))))))	
______________ Account or identification numbers of Defendant used by Garnishee	)))))	
______________ Other allegations	)))	
______________ Garnishee	))	

Laws 1976, p. 1608, § 1; Laws 1984, p. 370, § 2; Laws 1985, p. 1632, § 2; Laws 1997, p. 941, § 2; Laws 1999, p. 81, § 18.

Formerly Code 1933, § 46-605.

Article 5

Answer by Garnishee and Subsequent Proceedings

§ 18–4–80. Effect of release

A release of summons of garnishment shall relieve the garnishee from any obligation to file an answer to any summons of garnishment pending on the date of the release and shall authorize the garnishee to deliver to the defendant in garnishment any money or other property in the garnishee's possession belonging to the defendant. A release shall not operate as a dismissal of the garnishment proceedings.

Laws 1976, p. 1608, § 1.

Formerly Code 1933, § 46–308.

§ 18–4–81. Effect of defendant's traverse on garnishee; substitution by bond

When the defendant files his traverse, the garnishee is not relieved of filing an answer, nor is the garnishee relieved of delivering the money or other property of the defendant which is subject to the garnishment to the court, unless the defendant files in the clerk's office of the court where the garnishment is pending a bond with good security, in favor of the plaintiff, conditioned for the payment of any judgment that may be entered in the proceeding. The bond shall be subject to approval by the clerk of the court; and, upon receipt of a bond deemed acceptable by the clerk, it shall be his duty to issue a release of any summons of garnishment pending in the garnishment proceeding. If the plaintiff shall prevail in the proceeding, he shall be entitled to entry of judgment upon such bond against the principal and securities therein, as judgment may be entered against securities upon appeal. Where the defendant files a bond, no further garnishment process may be filed in any court by the plaintiff against the defendant until the issues raised by the defendant's pleadings are decided.

Laws 1976, p. 1608, § 1.

Formerly Code 1933, § 46–402.

§ 18–4–82. Contents of answer

Within the time prescribed by Code Section 18–4–62, the garnishee shall file his answer describing what money or other property is subject to garnishment under Code Section 18–4–20. If the garnishee owes the defendant any sum for wages, the answer shall also state specifically when the wages were earned by defendant and whether they were earned as daily, weekly, or monthly wages. If the garnishee has been served with summons in more than one garnishment case involving the same defendant, the garnishee shall state in each answer that the money or other property is being delivered to the court subject to the claims of all the cases and shall give the numbers of all such cases in each answer. If the garnishee shall be unable to answer as provided for in this Code section, his inability shall appear in his answer, together with all the facts plainly, fully, and distinctly set forth, so as to enable the court to give judgment thereon.

Laws 1976, p. 1608, § 1.

Formerly Code 1933, § 46–501.

§ 18–4–83. Service of answer

All answers by the garnishee shall, concurrently with filing, be served upon the plaintiff or his attorney. Service may be shown by the written acknowledgment of the plaintiff or his attorney, or by the certificate of the garnishee or his attorney, attached to the garnishee's answer, that a copy of the answer was mailed to the plaintiff or his attorney; provided, however, no service shall be required unless the name and address of the plaintiff or his attorney shall appear on the face of the summons of garnishment; provided, further, that, if the garnishee fails to serve the plaintiff, the plaintiff shall be allowed 15 days from the time the plaintiff receives actual notice of the answer to traverse the same.

Laws 1976, p. 1608, § 1.

Formerly Code 1933, § 46–502.

§ 18–4–84. Delivery of property to court; procedure where property in safe-deposit box

Along with the answer, the garnishee shall deliver to the court the money or other property admitted in the answer to be subject to garnishment. If in answering the summons of garnishment, as provided in Code Section 18–4–82, the garnishee shall state that the property of the defendant includes property in a safe-deposit box or similar property, the garnishee shall answer to the court issuing the summons of garnishment as to the existence of such safe-deposit box and shall hold any contents of such safe-deposit box until the earlier of:

(1) Further order of said court either releasing the garnishment or specifically requiring the garnishee to open such safe-deposit box and deliver any contents thereof to said court upon conditions prescribed by said court; or

(2) The elapsing of 120 days from the date of filing of the answer to the summons of garnishment unless such time has been extended by the court.

Laws 1976, p. 1608, § 1; Laws 1997, p. 941, § 3.

Formerly Code 1933, § 46-503.

§ 18-4-85. Traverse of answer of garnishee

If the garnishee serves his answer on the plaintiff as provided for in Code Section 18-4-83, the plaintiff or claimant must traverse the answer within 15 days after it is served or the garnishee is automatically discharged from further liability with respect to the summons so answered.

Laws 1976, p. 1608, § 1.

Formerly Code 1933, § 46-504.

§ 18-4-86. Contents of traverse

The traverse of the garnishee's answer shall be a statement by the plaintiff or his attorney, or by a claimant or his attorney, that the garnishee's answer is untrue or legally insufficient. Such statement places in issue all questions of law and fact concerning the garnishee's answer.

Laws 1976, p. 1608, § 1.

Formerly Code 1933, § 46-505.

§ 18-4-87. Service of traverse

A traverse shall be served in the same manner as is provided for in subsection (b) of Code Section 9-11-5 for the service of subsequent pleadings.

Laws 1976, p. 1608, § 1.

Formerly Code 1933, § 46-506.

§ 18-4-88. Order of trial after answer

After the garnishee's answer is filed, the defendant's traverse shall be tried first, the plaintiff's traverse shall be tried second, and claims shall be tried last; provided, however, the court shall retain the money or other property subject to garnishment until trial of all claims which are filed under this chapter.

Laws 1976, p. 1608, § 1.

Formerly Code 1933, § 46-511.

§ 18-4-89. Proceedings after answer

If no traverse or claim has been filed within 15 days after the garnishee's answer is filed:

(1) If money is delivered to the court by the garnishee, the clerk shall pay the money to the plaintiff or his attorney on his application;

(2) If other property is delivered to the court by the garnishee, the sheriff, marshal, constable, or like officer of the court shall sell the property in the manner provided by law for the sale of property levied under an execution; and the proceeds of the sale shall be delivered to the plaintiff or his attorney on his application; or

(3) If money or other property admitted to be subject to the garnishment is not delivered to the court, judgment shall be entered for the plaintiff and against the garnishee for the money or other property and execution shall issue on the judgment.

Laws 1976, p. 1608, § 1.

Formerly Code 1933, § 46-510.

§ 18-4-90. Default judgment against garnishee on failure to answer

In case the garnishee fails or refuses to file an answer by the forty-fifth day after service of the summons, the garnishee shall automatically be in default. The default may be opened as a matter of right by the filing of an answer within 15 days of the day of default and payment of costs. If the case is still in default after the expiration of the period of 15 days, judgment by default may be entered at any time thereafter against the garnishee for the amount claimed to be due on the judgment obtained against the defendant.

Laws 1976, p. 1608, § 1.

Formerly Code 1933, § 46-508.

§ 18-4-91. Relief from default judgment

When a judgment is rendered against a garnishee under Code Section 18-4-90, on a motion filed not later than 60 days from the date the garnishee receives actual notice of the entry of the judgment against him, he may, upon payment of all accrued costs of court, have the judgment modified so that the amount of the judgment shall be reduced to an amount equal to the greater of $ 50.00 or $ 50.00 plus 100 percent of the amount by which the garnishee was indebted to the defendant from the time of service of the summons of garnishment through and including the last day on which a timely answer could have been made for all money, other property, or effects belonging to the defendant which came into the garnishee's hands from the time of service of the summons through and including the last day on which a timely answer could have been made and, in the case of garnishment of wages, less any exemption allowed the defendant by law. Notice to the garnishee by certified mail or statutory overnight delivery shall be sufficient notice as required in this Code section. On the trial of the motion, the burden of proof shall be upon any plaintiff who objects to the timeliness of the motion to establish that the motion was not filed within the time provided for by this Code section.

Laws 1976, p. 1608, § 1; Laws 1977, p. 783, § 1; Laws 1980, p. 1769, § 7; Laws 2000, p. 1589, § 3.

Formerly Code 1933, § 46-509.

§ 18-4-92. Trial of plaintiff's traverse; judgment against garnishee

On the trial of the plaintiff's traverse, if the court finds the garnishee has failed to answer properly the summons of garnishment, the court shall disallow any expenses claimed by the garnishee and enter a judgment for any money or other property delivered to the court with the garnishee's answer, plus any money or other property the court finds subject to garnishment which the garnishee has failed to deliver to the court; provided, however, that the total amount of such judgment shall in no event exceed the amount claimed due by the plaintiff, together with the costs of the garnishment proceeding.

Laws 1976, p. 1608, § 1.

Formerly Code 1933, § 46-514.

§ 18-4-92.1. Relief from liability for failure to answer, for attaching liens, and for freezing, paying, or delivering into court of certain property or money

(a) A garnishee may be relieved from liability for failure to answer properly the summons of garnishment if the plaintiff failed to provide the information required by subsection (i) of Code Section 18-4-20 that would reasonably enable the garnishee to answer properly the summons of garnishment and a good faith effort to locate the requested property was made by the garnishee based on the information provided by the plaintiff. In determining whether a garnishee may be relieved of liability imposed by Code Section 18-4-92, the court shall consider and compare the accuracy and quantity of the information supplied by the plaintiff pursuant to subsection (i) of Code Section 18-4-20 with the manner in which the garnishee maintains and locates its records, the compliance by the garnishee with its own procedures, and the conformity of the record systems and procedures with reasonable commercial standards prevailing in the area in which the garnishee is located.

(b) A garnishee and a plaintiff shall not be subject to liability to any party or nonparty to the garnishment at issue arising from the attachment of a lien, the freezing, payment, or delivery into court of property, money, or effects reasonably believed to be that of the defendant if such attachment, freezing, payment, or delivery is reasonably required by a good faith effort to comply with the summons of garnishment. In determining whether such compliance by a garnishee is reasonable, the court shall proceed in the manner prescribed in subsection (a) of this Code section by comparing the efforts of the plaintiff to comply with subsection (i) of Code Section 18-4-20 and the garnishee's record system and procedures.

(c)(1) As used in this subsection, the term:

(A) "Association account" means any account, or any safe-deposit box or similar property, maintained by a corporation, statutory close corporation, limited liability company, partnership, limited partnership, limited liability partnership, foundation, trust, a national, state, or local government or quasi-government entity, or any other incorporated or unincorporated association.

(B) "Fiduciary account" means any account, or any safe-deposit box, maintained by any party in a fiduciary capacity for any other party other than the defendant in garnishment. Without limiting the foregoing, for purposes of this subsection, the term fiduciary account shall include any "trust account" as defined in Code Section 7-1-810, any account created pursuant to a transfer governed by Code Section 44-5-119, and any agency account or safe-deposit box governed by a power of attorney or other written designation of authority.

(2)(A) A garnishee shall not be liable for failure to deliver to the court property, money, or effects in an association account that may be subject to garnishment by reason of the fact that a defendant is an authorized signer on such association account, unless the summons of garnishment alleges that the association account is being used by the defendant for an improper or unlawful purpose.

(B) A garnishee shall not be liable for failure to deliver to the court property, money, or effects in a fiduciary account that may be subject to garnishment if such account specifically is exempted from garnishment by the laws of this state.

(C) A garnishee shall not be liable for failure to deliver to the court property, money, or effects in a fiduciary account that may be subject to garnishment by reason of the fact that a defendant is a fiduciary of the fiduciary account, unless the summons of garnishment is against the defendant in the defendant's capacity as a fiduciary of the fiduciary account or the summons of garnishment alleges that the fiduciary account is being used by the defendant for an improper or unlawful purpose.

Laws 1997, p. 941, § 4.

§ 18-4-93. Defendant may become a party

A garnishment proceeding is an action between the plaintiff and the garnishee; but, at any time before a judgment is entered on the garnishee's answer or before money or other property subject to garnishment is distributed, the defendant may become a party to the garnishment for the purposes set out in Code Section 18-4-65 by filing a traverse to the plaintiff's affidavit stating that the affidavit is untrue or legally insufficient; and he shall be a party to all proceedings thereafter. Upon the filing of the defendant's traverse, and at the defendant's application therefor, a judge of the court in which the case is pending shall order a hearing to be held not more than ten days from the date the traverse is filed. The hearing shall be available to the defendant as a matter of right after filing his traverse; and no further summons of garnishment may issue nor may any money or other property delivered to the court as subject to garnishment be disbursed until the hearing shall be held.

Laws 1976, p. 1608, § 1.

Formerly Code 1933, § 46-401.

§ 18-4-94. Procedure where defendant prevails; claims

(a) Where the defendant prevails upon the trial of the issues made by his traverse, the garnishment case shall be dismissed by the court; and any money or other property belonging to the defendant in the possession of the court shall be restored to the defendant unless a claim thereto has been filed.

(b) If a claim has been filed, all parties of record may introduce evidence to establish their respective interests in the money or other property in court; and the court shall direct that the money or other property be distributed in accordance with the laws governing priority of claims.

Laws 1976, p. 1608, § 1.

Formerly Code 1933, § 46-512.

§ 18-4-95. Claimants may become a party

At any time before judgment is entered on the garnishee's answer or money or other property subject to garnishment is distributed, any person may file a claim in writing under oath stating that he has a claim superior to that of the plaintiff to the money or other property in the hands of the garnishee subject to the process of garnishment; and the claimant shall be a party to all further proceedings upon the garnishment.

Laws 1976, p. 1608, § 1.

Formerly Code 1933, § 46-404.

§ 18-4-96. Conflicting claims of cases

Where money or other property in court is subject to the claims of more than one garnishment case, any interested party to any one of the garnishment cases may make a motion to the court in his case for the distribution of the money or other property. Each party of interest in each case and the clerk of the court shall be served with a copy of the motion. Upon hearing the motion, the court shall enter an order directing that the clerk be paid the court cost of each garnishment proceeding first, and all remaining money or other property shall be distributed in accordance with the law governing the relative priorities of claims, judgments, and liens.

Laws 1976, p. 1608, § 1.

Formerly Code 1933, § 46-513.

§ 18-4-97. Garnishee's expenses

(a) The garnishee shall be entitled to his actual reasonable expenses, including attorney's fees, in making a true answer of garnishment. The amount so incurred shall be taxed in the bill of costs and shall be paid by the party upon whom the cost is cast, as costs are cast in other cases. The garnishee may deduct $25.00 or 10 percent of the amount paid into court, whichever is greater, not to exceed $50.00, as reasonable attorney's fees or expenses.

(b) If the garnishee can show that his actual attorney's fees or expenses exceed the amount provided for in subsection (a) of this Code section, he must petition the court for a hearing at the time of making his answer without deducting from the amount paid into court. Upon hearing from the parties, the court may enter an order for payment of actual attorney's fees or expenses proven by the garnishee to have been incurred reasonably in making his answer.

(c) In the event the garnishee makes the deduction permitted in subsection (a) of this Code section but the costs are later cast upon the garnishee, the garnishee shall forthwith refund to the defendant the funds deducted; and, if the costs are later cast against the plaintiff, the court shall enter judgment in favor of the defendant and against the plaintiff for the amount of the deductions made by the garnishee.

(d) Nothing in this Code section shall limit the reimbursement of costs incurred by a financial institution as provided by Code Section 7-1-237.

Laws 1976, p. 1608, § 1; Laws 1985, p. 1632, § 3; Laws 1997, p. 941, § 5.

Formerly Code 1933, § 46-507.

Article 6

Continuing Garnishment Proceedings

§ 18-4-110. Additional remedy

In addition to garnishment proceedings otherwise available under this chapter, in cases where a money judgment shall have been obtained in a court of this state or a federal court sitting in this state, the plaintiff shall be entitled to the process of continuing garnishment against any garnishee who is an employer of the defendant against whom the judgment has been obtained. Unless otherwise specifically provided in this article, the methods, practices, and procedures for continuing garnishment shall be the same as for any other garnishment as provided in this chapter, including, but not limited to, those proceedings after answer as provided in Code Section 18-4-89.

Laws 1980, p. 1769, § 8; Laws 1981, p. 383, § 2; Laws 1985, p. 1632, § 4.

Formerly Code 1933, § 46-701.

§ 18-4-111. What subject to continuing garnishment

(a) All debts owed by the garnishee to the defendant at the time of service of summons of continuing garnishment upon the garnishee and all debts accruing from the garnishee to the defendant from such date of service to and including the one hundred seventy-ninth day thereafter shall be subject to process of continuing garnishment; and no payment made by the garnishee to the defendant or to his order or by any arrangement between the defendant and the garnishee after the date of the service of the summons of continuing garnishment upon the garnishee shall defeat the lien of such garnishment.

(b) All property, money, or effects of the defendant in the possession or control of the garnishee at the time of service of the summons of continuing garnishment upon the garnishee or coming into the possession or control of the garnishee at any time from the date of such service to and including the one hundred seventy-ninth day thereafter shall be subject to process of continuing garnishment, except in the case of collateral securities in the hands of a creditor. Such securities shall not be subject to continuing garnishment so long as there is an amount owed on the debt for which such securities were given as collateral.

(c) Notwithstanding this Code section, the exemptions from garnishment required or allowed by law, including, but not limited to, exemptions provided by Code Sections 18-4-20 and 18-4-22, shall be applicable to a continuing garnishment.

Laws 1980, p. 1769, § 8.

Formerly Code 1933, § 46-702.

§ 18-4-112. Affidavit; summons; notice

(a) In addition to the information required by Code Section 18-4-61, an affidavit for continuing garnishment shall state that the plaintiff believes that the garnishee is or may be an employer of the defendant and subject to continuing garnishment and shall request that a summons of continuing garnishment shall issue. Upon the filing of the affidavit with the clerk of any court having jurisdiction over the garnishee, the clerk shall cause a summons of continuing garnishment to issue forthwith, provided that the affidavit shall first be made and approved as containing the information required by Code Section 18-4-61 and by this Code section in one of the ways provided for in Code Section 18-4-61.

(b) Only one summons of continuing garnishment may issue on one affidavit for continuing garnishment, and the defendant shall be given notice of the issuance of the summons using any method provided for in Code Section 18-4-64.

(c) The plaintiff, using either forms provided by the court or forms prepared by himself, shall cause forms sufficient for seven answers to a summons of continuing garnishment to be served on the garnishee along with the summons.

Laws 1980, p. 1769, § 8.

Formerly Code 1933, § 46-703.

§ 18-4-113. Answer; payments

(a) The summons of continuing garnishment shall be directed to the garnishee, who shall be required:

(1) To file a first answer no later than 45 days after service of summons of continuing garnishment, which answer shall state what property, money, or other effects of the defendant are subject to continuing garnishment from the time of service through and including the day of the first answer;

(2) To file further answers for the remaining period covered by the summons of continuing garnishment. Further answers shall be filed no later than 45 days after the previous answer date. Further answers shall state what property, money, or other effects of the defendant are subject to continuing garnishment from the previous answer date through and including the date on which that next answer is filed. No subsequent answers shall be required on a summons of continuing garnishment if the last answer filed states what property, money, or other effects of the defendant are subject to continuing garnishment from the previous answer date to and including the one hundred seventy-ninth

day after service of summons of continuing garnishment. The last answer shall be filed, notwithstanding the other provisions of this paragraph, no later than the one hundred ninety-fifth day after service. For purposes of this paragraph, "previous answer date" means the date upon which the immediately preceding answer to the summons of continuing garnishment was filed as provided in this subsection; and

(3) To accompany all such answers with any property, money, or other effects of the defendant admitted in the answer to be subject to continuing garnishment.

(b) The summons of continuing garnishment shall state the requirements of subsection (a) of this Code section and shall inform the garnishee that failure to comply with such requirements may result in a judgment against the garnishee for the entire amount claimed due on the judgment against the defendant.

Laws 1980, p. 1769, § 8.

Formerly Code 1933, § 46-704.

§ 18-4-114. Traverse of answer of garnishee

If the garnishee serves his answer on the plaintiff as provided in Code Section 18-4-83, the plaintiff must traverse the answer within 15 days after it is served or the garnishee is automatically discharged from further liability with respect to such answer.

Laws 1980, p. 1769, § 8.

Formerly Code 1933, § 46-707.

§ 18-4-115. Default judgment and relief therefrom

(a) If the garnishee fails or refuses to file an answer at least once every 45 days, the garnishee shall automatically become in default. The default may be opened as a matter of right by the filing of the required answer within 15 days after the day of default upon payment of costs. If the case is still in default after the expiration of such period of 15 days, judgment by default may be entered at any time thereafter against garnishee for the amount claimed to be due on the judgment obtained against the defendant.

(b) The garnishee may obtain relief from default judgment entered as provided in subsection (a) of this Code section upon the same conditions as provided in Code Section 18-4-91.

Laws 1980, p. 1769, § 8.

Formerly Code 1933, § 46-708.

§ 18-4-116. Defendant may become party

(a) In a continuing garnishment proceeding, upon the filing of a traverse by defendant pursuant to Code Section 18-4-93, no further summons of garnishment may issue nor may any money delivered to the court as subject to garnishment be disbursed until the hearing is held upon defendant's traverse. The filing of a traverse by the defendant does not relieve the garnishee of the duties of filing an answer, of withholding property, money, or other effects subject to continuing garnishment or of delivering to the court any property, money, or other effects subject to continuing garnishment.

(b) Nothing in this Code section shall affect the right of the defendant to file bond under this chapter.

Laws 1980, p. 1769, § 8.

Formerly Code 1933, § 46-705.

§ 18-4-117. Termination of employment relationship

Notwithstanding the requirements of Code Section 18-4-113, if the employment relationship between the garnishee and the defendant does not exist at the time of the service of summons of continuing garnishment or terminates during the continuing garnishment, in any answer required by this article the garnishee may state that the employment relationship between the garnishee and defendant does not exist or has been terminated, giving the date of termination if terminated on or after service of this summons of continuing garnishment. If no traverse is filed within 15 days after the answer is served as provided in Code Section 18-4-83, the garnishee is automatically discharged from further liability and obligation under Code Section 18-4-113 for that summons with respect to the period of continuing garnishment remaining after the employment relationship is terminated.

Laws 1980, p. 1769, § 8.

Formerly Code 1933, § 46-706.

§ 18-4-118. Forms for continuing garnishment

For purposes of this article, the following forms are declared to be sufficient, along with those provided in Code Section 18-4-66, for continuing garnishment, provided that nothing in this Code section shall be construed to require the use of particular forms in any proceeding under this article:

(1) Affidavit of continuing garnishment.

IN THE ____ COURT OF ____ COUNTY

STATE OF GEORGIA

______________)

Plaintiff)
)
v.) Civil action
) File no. ____
____________)
Defendant)
)
____________)
Garnishee)
)
____________)
Address)

—AFFIDAVIT OF CONTINUING GARNISHMENT—

Personally appeared the undersigned affiant who on oath says that he is the above plaintiff, his agent, or his attorney at law and that the above defendant is indebted to said plaintiff on a judgment described as follows:

____ is the case number in the ____ Court of ____ County which rendered the judgment against the defendant, $____ being the balance thereon.

Affiant further states that affiant believes that garnishee is or may be an employer of the defendant and subject to continuing garnishment.

____
Affiant

Sworn to and subscribed before me this ______ day of __________, ____.

____
Plaintiff's attorney

(2) Summons of continuing garnishment.

IN THE ____ COURT OF ____ COUNTY

STATE OF GEORGIA

____________)
Plaintiff)
)
v.) Civil action
) File no. ____
____________)
Defendant)
Social security)
number)
____________)
Garnishee)
)
____________)
Address)

SUMMONS OF CONTINUING GARNISHMENT

To: ____________ Garnishee

Amount claimed due by plaintiff $____
(To be completed by plaintiff)

Plus court costs due on this summons $____
(To be completed by clerk)

YOU ARE HEREBY COMMANDED to hold immediately all property, money, wages, except what is exempt, belonging to the defendant, or debts owed to the defendant named above at the time of service of this summons and between the time of service of this summons to and including the one hundred seventy-ninth day thereafter. Not later than 45 days after you are served with this summons, you are commanded to file your answer in writing with the clerk of this court and serve a copy upon the plaintiff or his attorney named below. This answer shall state what property, money, and wages, except what is exempt, belonging to the defendant, or debts owed to the defendant, you hold or owe at the time of service of this summons and between the time of such service and the time of making your first answer. Thereafter, you are required to file further answers no later than 45 days after your last answer. Every further answer shall state what property, money, and wages, except what is exempt, belonging to the defendant or debts owed to the defendant, you hold or owe at and from the time of the last answer to the time of the current answer. The last answer required by this summons shall be filed no later than the one hundred ninety-fifth day after you receive this summons. Money or other property admitted in an answer to be subject to continuing garnishment must be delivered to the court with your answers. Should you fail to file answers as required by this summons, a judgment will be rendered against you for the amount the plaintiff claims due by the defendant.

Witness the Honorable ____, Judge of said Court.

This ____ day of ____, ____.

____
Clerk,
____ Court of ____ County

____
Plaintiff's attorney

____
Address

Service perfected on garnishee, this ____ day of ____, ____.

____
Deputy marshal, sheriff, or constable

(3) Answer of continuing garnishment.

IN THE ____ COURT OF ____ COUNTY

STATE OF GEORGIA

____________)

Plaintiff)
)
v.) Civil action
) File no. ______
______________)
Defendant)
)
______________)
Garnishee)
______________)
Address)

—ANSWER OF CONTINUING GARNISHMENT—

—1.—

From the time of service of this summons of continuing garnishment, if this is the first answer to such summons, otherwise from the time of the last answer to this summons of continuing garnishment, until the time of this answer, garnishee had in his possession the following described property of the defendant: ______.

—2.—

From the time of service of this summons of continuing garnishment, if this is the first answer to such summons, otherwise from the time of the last answer to this summons of continuing garnishment, until the time of this answer, all debts accruing from garnishee to the defendant are in the amount of $______.

—3.—

$______ of the amount named in paragraph 2 was wages earned at the rate of $______ per ______ for the period beginning (date), ______, through the time of making this answer. The amount of wages which is subject to this garnishment is computed as follows:

$______ Gross earnings
$______ Total social security and withholding tax
$______ Total disposable earnings
$______ Amount of wages subject to continuing garnishment

—4.—

( ) If checked, defendant is not presently employed by this garnishee and, if employed by garnishee on or after service of this summons of continuing garnishment, was most recently terminated as of the ______ day of ______, ______.

—5.—

( ) If checked, this is the last answer this garnishee is required to file to the presently pending summons of continuing garnishment in the above-styled case.

—6.—

Garnishee further states: ______.

____
Garnishee or his attorney at law

—(CERTIFICATE OF SERVICE)—

Laws 1980, p. 1769, § 8; Laws 1985, p. 1632, § 5; Laws 1999, p. 81, § 18.

Formerly Code 1933, § 46–709.

Article 7

Continuing Garnishment for Support

§ 18–4–130. Additional remedy

In addition to garnishment proceedings otherwise available in this chapter, a writ of garnishment shall issue for the continuing withholding of earnings for the enforcement of a judgment for periodic support of a family member. Unless otherwise specifically provided in this article, the methods, practices, and procedures for continuing garnishment for support shall be the same as for any other garnishment as provided in this chapter, including, but not limited to, procedures relative to default of a garnishee and relief from default and provisions relative to fees and expenses.

Laws 1985, p. 785, § 2.

§ 18–4–131. Definitions

As used in this article, the term:

(1) "Accruing on a daily basis" means the amount of support computed by conversion of the periodic amount to an annual sum, divided by 365.

(2) "Department" means the Department of Human Resources.

(3) "Earnings" means any periodic form of payment due to an individual, regardless of source, including without limitation wages, salary, commission, bonus, workers' compensation, disability, payments pursuant to a pension or retirement program, and interest.

(4) "Family member" means any minor child of the defendant or a spouse or former spouse of the defendant.

(5) "Judgment" means any order or judgment of a court of this state, any order or judgment of a court of another state which has been registered pursuant to Code Section 19–11–77 or otherwise, any order of a court of this state entered pursuant

to a proceeding under Chapter 10 of Title 19, any final administrative order for support issued by the department, or any final administrative order issued by another state.

(6) "Periodic support" means support required by the terms of a court order or judgment or an administrative order to be paid regularly on a daily, weekly, monthly, or other similar specified frequency.

Laws 1985, p. 785, § 2; Laws 1997, p. 1613, § 5.

§ 18–4–132. Affidavit

(a) The contents of the affidavit for continuing garnishment for support shall be substantially identical to those set forth in Code Section 18–4–112, but in addition thereto, the plaintiff shall attach a certified copy of the judgment to be enforced and shall also state the following in the affidavit:

(1) That the defendant is in arrears on the obligation of support in an amount equal to or in excess of one month's obligation as decreed in said judgment;

(2) The amount of arrearage which exists under said judgment as of the date of the execution of the affidavit;

(3) The periodic amount of support due under the judgment for each obligee named therein, taking into account the possible attainment of majority or emancipation or death of any minor child named in the judgment; and

(4) The date of the termination of the obligation of support of each obligee named in the order or judgment of support, based upon the terms of said order or judgment, or, as to any obligee who is a minor child, the date each such obligee shall attain the age of 18 years.

(b) Such affidavit may be amended from time to time by subsequent affidavits of any party showing a modification or other amendment to the original judgment sought to be enforced. Such amended or subsequent affidavits shall include a certified copy of any such modification or amendment and shall contain the information required by paragraphs (1) through (4) of subsection (a) of this Code section.

Laws 1985, p. 785, § 2.

§ 18–4–133. Summons; answer; payments

(a) The summons of continuing garnishment for support shall be directed to the garnishee who shall be required to file a first answer no later than 45 days after service, which answer shall state what earnings were payable to the defendant from the time of service through and including the day of the first answer and the basis for the computation of same, including the rate of pay and hours worked, or salaries, commissions, or other basis of compensation.

(b) The garnishee shall accompany such initial answer with money of the defendant admitted in the answer to be subject to continuing garnishment for support. In computing the amounts subject to this article, the provisions of subsection (f) of Code Section 18–4–20 shall control.

(c) The money paid into court with the initial answer, after deduction for costs, shall be first applied to the periodic support payment accrued on a daily basis from the date of the affidavit of the plaintiff to the date of the initial answer. All sums in excess of such periodic payment shall be applied to the original arrearage. Original arrearage shall mean those arrears existing as of the date of the making of the plaintiff's affidavit, plus any amounts includable pursuant to subsection (b) of Code Section 18–4–134.

Laws 1985, p. 785, § 2.

§ 18–4–134. Further answers; payments

(a) If the amount claimed as original arrearage as of the date of the making of the plaintiff's affidavit is not satisfied by the money payable into court under the initial answer of the garnishee, after application of the funds as set forth in subsection (c) of Code Section 18–4–133, the garnishee shall file further answers no later than 45 days after the previous answer date, stating the earnings accrued and the basis of their accrual and tendering such money accruing in such answer period. The amounts paid into court pursuant to subsequent answers, over and above the periodic payment accruing within such answer period, shall be applied to the original arrearage until the same is retired.

(b) If the earnings paid into court pursuant to any answer by the garnishee are less than the sums due under the periodic support requirement accruing over the same period of time, after allowance for any costs deductible from same, the resulting difference shall be added to the amount due as original arrearage until the same is retired by subsequent payments.

(c) The garnishee shall file additional answers until the original arrearage is retired and all periodic support payments are current.

(d) Upon the termination of employment of the defendant by the garnishee, the garnishee shall be required to file a final answer stating the date and reason for the defendant's termination from employment and stating, to the best of the garnishee's information, the defendant's present residential address and employer.

Laws 1985, p. 785, § 2.

§ 18–4–135. Termination

The writ of garnishment described in this article shall attach for so long as the defendant is employed by the garnishee and shall not terminate until the original arrearage is retired. The garnishee may rely upon the information as to the termination date of the duty of support of any individual claimed in the affidavit of garnishment, the amount of the duty of periodic support to be paid, any sums paid by the defendant between the date of the filing of the plaintiff's affidavit and the date of the initial answer of the garnishee, and the amount of the original arrearage existing as of the date of the affidavit of garnishment, unless the same are traversed by the defendant and the court enters any finding otherwise.

Laws 1985, p. 785, § 2.

TITLE 23

EQUITY

As Amended Through the 2006 Regular Session of the General Assembly

Research Note

Use Westlaw *to find cases citing a statute or to search for specific terms in a statute. See the Westlaw Directory Screens for lists of relevant databases.*

Table of Sections

INDEX

See Index to Georgia Statutes, infra.

CHAPTER 1

GENERAL PROVISIONS

§ 23-1-1. Courts vested with equity jurisdiction

All equity jurisdiction shall be vested in the superior courts of the several counties.

Laws 1799, Cobb's 1851 Digest, p. 467.

Formerly Code 1863, § 3013; Code 1868, § 3025; Code 1873, § 3080; Code 1882, § 3080; Civil Code 1895, § 3921; Civil Code 1910, § 4518; Code 1933, § 37-101.

§ 23-1-2. Extent of jurisdiction

Generally, equity jurisprudence embraces the same matters of jurisdiction and modes of remedy as were allowed and practiced in England.

Formerly Code 1863, § 3033; Code 1868, § 3045; Code 1873, § 3100; Code 1882, § 3100; Civil Code 1895, § 3945; Civil Code 1910, § 4542; Code 1933, § 37-124.

§ 23-1-3. Grounds for relief

Equity jurisdiction is established and allowed for the protection and relief of parties where, from any peculiar circumstances, the operation of the general rules of law would be deficient in protecting from anticipated wrong or relieving for injuries done.

Formerly Code 1863, § 3014; Code 1868, § 3026; Code 1873, § 3081; Code 1882, § 3081; Civil Code 1895, § 3922; Civil Code 1910, § 4519; Code 1933, § 37-102.

§ 23-1-4. Common law remedy

Equity will not take cognizance of a plain legal right where an adequate and complete remedy is provided by law; but the mere privilege of a party to bring an action at law or the existence of a common-law remedy not as complete or effectual as the equitable relief shall not deprive equity of jurisdiction.

Formerly Code 1863, § 3028; Code 1868, § 3040; Code 1873, § 3095; Code 1882, § 3095; Civil Code 1895, § 3941; Civil Code 1910, § 4538; Code 1933, § 37-120.

§ 23-1-5. Concurrent jurisdiction

Where law and equity have concurrent jurisdiction, whichever first takes jurisdiction shall retain it, unless a good reason shall be given for the interference of equity.

Formerly Code 1863, § 3029; Code 1868, § 3041; Code 1873, § 3096; Code 1882, § 3096; Civil Code 1895, § 3943; Civil Code 1910, § 4540; Code 1933, § 37-122.

§ 23-1-6. Equity follows the law

Equity is ancillary, not antagonistic, to the law; hence, equity follows the law where the rule of law is applicable and follows the analogy of the law where no rule is directly applicable.

Formerly Code 1863, § 3016; Code 1868, § 3028; Code 1873, § 3083; Code 1882, § 3083; Civil Code 1895, § 3923; Civil Code 1910, § 4520; Code 1933, § 37-103.

§ 23-1-7. Complete justice

Equity seeks always to do complete justice. Hence, having the parties before the court rightfully, it will proceed to give full relief to all parties in reference to the subject matter of the action, provided the court has jurisdiction for that purpose.

Formerly Code 1863, § 3018; Code 1868, § 3030; Code 1873, § 3085; Code 1882, § 3085; Civil Code 1895, § 3925; Civil Code 1910, § 4522; Code 1933, § 37-105.

§ 23-1-8. What ought to be done is considered done

Equity considers that done which ought to be done and directs its relief accordingly.

Formerly Code 1863, § 3019; Code 1868, § 3031; Code 1873, § 3086; Code 1882, § 3086; Civil Code 1895, § 3926; Civil Code 1910, § 4523; Code 1933, § 37-106.

§ 23-1-9. Equality is equity

In many cases, equality is equity in the distribution of equitable assets.

Formerly Code 1863, § 3023; Code 1868, § 3035; Code 1873, § 3090; Code 1882, § 3090; Civil Code 1895, § 3930; Civil Code 1910, § 4527; Code 1933, § 37-110.

§ 23-1-10. Complainant must do equity

He who would have equity must do equity and must give effect to all equitable rights of the other party respecting the subject matter of the action.

Formerly Code 1863, § 3017; Code 1868, § 3029; Code 1873, § 3084; Code 1882, § 3084; Civil Code 1895, § 3924; Civil Code 1910, § 4521; Code 1933, § 37-104.

§ 23-1-11. Where equities equal

Where equities are equal, the law shall prevail. If equities are unequal, the superior equity shall prevail.

Superior diligence as to time will create such inequality.

Formerly Code 1863, § 3020; Code 1868, § 3032; Code 1873, § 3087; Code 1882, § 3087; Civil Code 1895, § 3927; Civil Code 1910, § 4524; Code 1933, § 37–107.

§ 23–1–12. Party misled

The equity of a party who has been misled is superior to that of the person who willfully misleads such party.

Formerly Code 1863, § 3022; Code 1868, § 3034; Code 1873, § 3089; Code 1882, § 3089; Civil Code 1895, § 3929; Civil Code 1910, § 4526; Code 1933, § 37–109.

§ 23–1–13. Volunteers

The equity under trust or contract for value is superior to that of a mere volunteer.

Formerly Code 1863, § 3021; Code 1868, § 3033; Code 1873, § 3088; Code 1882, § 3088; Civil Code 1895, § 3928; Civil Code 1910, § 4525; Code 1933, § 37–108.

§ 23–1–14. Which of two innocent persons shall bear loss

When one of two innocent persons must suffer by the act of a third person, he who put it in the power of the third person to inflict the injury shall bear the loss.

Formerly Civil Code 1895, § 3940; Civil Code 1910, § 4537; Code 1933, § 37–113.

§ 23–1–15. Both parties at fault

When both parties are equally at fault, equity will not interfere but will leave them where it finds them. The rule is otherwise if the fault of one decidedly overbalances that of the other.

Formerly Code 1863, § 3026; Code 1868, § 3038; Code 1873, § 3093; Code 1882, § 3093; Civil Code 1895, § 3937; Civil Code 1910, § 4534; Code 1933, § 37–112.

§ 23–1–16. Notice

He who takes with notice of an equity takes subject to that equity.

Formerly Code 1863, § 3024; Code 1868, § 3036; Code 1873, § 3091; Code 1882, § 3091; Civil Code 1895, § 3932; Civil Code 1910, § 4529; Code 1933, § 37–115.

§ 23–1–17. Notice extends to facts discoverable

Notice sufficient to excite attention and put a party on inquiry shall be notice of everything to which it is afterwards found that such inquiry might have led. Ignorance of a fact due to negligence shall be equivalent to knowledge in fixing the rights of parties.

Formerly Civil Code 1895, § 3933; Civil Code 1910, § 4530; Code 1933, § 37–116.

§ 23–1–18. Lis pendens, notice by

Decrees ordinarily bind only parties and their privies; but a pending action shall be a general notice of an equity or claim to all the world from the time the action is filed and docketed. If the same is duly prosecuted and is not collusive, one who purchases pending the final outcome of the litigation shall be affected by the decree rendered therein.

Formerly Civil Code 1895, § 3936; Civil Code 1910, § 4533; Code 1933, § 37–117.

§ 23–1–19. Purchaser without notice from one with notice, and vice versa

If one with notice sells to one without notice, the latter shall be protected. If one without notice sells to one with notice, the latter shall be protected, as otherwise a bona fide purchaser might be deprived of selling his property for full value.

Formerly Civil Code 1895, § 3938; Civil Code 1910, § 4535; Code 1933, § 37–114.

§ 23–1–20. Bona fide purchaser, interference with

A bona fide purchaser for value without notice of an equity will not be interfered with by equity.

Formerly Code 1863, § 3025; Code 1868, § 3037; Code 1873, § 3092; Code 1882, § 3092; Civil Code 1895, § 3934; Civil Code 1910, § 4531; Code 1933, § 37–111.

§ 23–1–21. Compelling persons to litigate

Equity will not force persons to litigate in order to have done what they ought to do and are willing to do voluntarily.

Formerly Civil Code 1895, § 3935; Civil Code 1910, § 4532; Code 1933, § 37–118.

§ 23–1–22. Equity not to interfere with creditor

A diligent creditor shall not needlessly be interfered with in the prosecution of his legal remedies.

Formerly Civil Code 1895, § 3942; Civil Code 1910, § 4539; Code 1933, § 37–121.

§ 23-1-23. Rule of construction as to conditions; relief against forfeitures

Where the rules of construction will allow, equity seeks always to construe conditions subsequent into covenants and to relieve against forfeitures.

Formerly Code 1863, § 3048; Code 1868, § 3060; Code 1873, § 3115; Code 1882, § 3115; Civil Code 1895, § 3971; Civil Code 1910, § 4568; Code 1933, § 37-216.

§ 23-1-24. When case of election arises

A case of election arises whenever a person is entitled to one of two benefits, to each of which he has legal title; but the enforcement of both would be unconscionable and inequitable to others having claims upon the same property or fund. In such cases equity may compel an election.

Formerly Code 1863, § 3092; Code 1868, § 3104; Code 1873, § 3161; Code 1882, § 3161; Civil Code 1895, § 4012; Civil Code 1910, § 4609; Code 1933, § 37-501.

§ 23-1-25. Laches

Equity gives no relief to one whose long delay renders the ascertainment of the truth difficult, even when no legal limitation bars the right.

Formerly Code 1863, § 3027; Code 1868, § 3039; Code 1873, § 3094; Code 1882, § 3094; Civil Code 1895, § 3939; Civil Code 1910, § 4536; Code 1933, § 37-119.

CHAPTER 2

GROUNDS FOR EQUITABLE RELIEF

Article 1

General Provisions

§ 23-2-1. Repealed by Laws 1986, p. 294, § 3, eff. March 26, 1986

§ 23-2-2. Inadequacy of consideration

Great inadequacy of consideration, joined with great disparity of mental ability in contracting a bargain, may justify equity in setting aside a sale or other contract.

Formerly Code 1863, § 3110; Code 1868, § 3122; Code 1873, § 3179; Code 1882, § 3179; Civil Code 1895, § 4033; Civil Code 1910, § 4630; Code 1933, § 37-710.

§ 23-2-3. Payment of lost bonds or notes

In cases of lost bonds or negotiable securities, the court may decree that payment shall be made, provided indemnity is given against liability or loss resulting from such payment.

Formerly Code 1863, § 3046; Code 1868, § 3058; Code 1873, § 3113; Code 1882, § 3113; Civil Code 1895, § 3969; Civil Code 1910, § 4566; Code 1933, § 37-214.

Article 2

Accident and Mistake

§ 23-2-20. What is accident

An accident relievable in equity is an occurrence, not the result of negligence or misconduct of the party seeking relief in relation to a contract, as was not anticipated by the parties when the contract was entered into, which gives an undue advantage to one of them over another in a court of law.

Formerly Code 1863, § 3045; Code 1868, § 3057; Code 1873, § 3112; Code 1882, § 3112; Civil Code 1895, § 3968; Civil Code 1910, § 4565; Code 1933, § 37-201.

§ 23-2-21. What is mistake

(a) A mistake relievable in equity is some unintentional act, omission, or error arising from ignorance, surprise, imposition, or misplaced confidence.

(b) Mistakes may be either of law or of fact.

(c) The power to relieve mistakes shall be exercised with caution; to justify it, the evidence shall be clear, unequivocal, and decisive as to the mistake.

Formerly Code 1863, §§ 3050, 3053; Code 1868, §§ 3062, 3065; Code 1873, §§ 3117, 3120; Code 1882, §§ 3117, 3120; Civil Code 1895, §§ 3973, 3977; Civil Code 1910, §§ 4570, 4574; Code 1933, §§ 37-202, 37-203.

§ 23–2–22. Mistake of law by parties

An honest mistake of the law as to the effect of an instrument on the part of both contracting parties, when the mistake operates as a gross injustice to one and gives an unconscionable advantage to the other, may be relieved in equity.

Formerly Code 1863, § 3055; Code 1868, § 3067; Code 1873, § 3122; Code 1882, § 3122; Civil Code 1895, § 3979; Civil Code 1910, § 4576; Code 1933, § 37–204.

§ 23–2–23. Mistake of law by draftsman or agent

A mistake of law by the draftsman or other agent, by which the contract, as executed, does not fulfill or violates the manifest intention of the parties to the agreement, may be relieved in equity.

Formerly Code 1863, § 3056; Code 1868, § 3068; Code 1873, § 3123; Code 1882, § 3123; Civil Code 1895, § 3980; Civil Code 1910, § 4577; Code 1933, § 37–205.

§ 23–2–24. Mistake of fact

In all cases of a mistake of fact material to the contract or other matter affected by it, if the complaining party applies within a reasonable time, equity will grant relief.

Formerly Code 1863, § 3058; Code 1868, § 3070; Code 1873, § 3125; Code 1882, § 3125; Civil Code 1895, § 3983; Civil Code 1910, § 4580; Code 1933, § 37–206.

§ 23–2–25. Error in form of conveyance

If the form of conveyance is, by accident or mistake, contrary to the intention of the parties in their contract, equity shall interfere to make it conform thereto.

Formerly Code 1863, § 3047; Code 1868, § 3059; Code 1873, § 3114; Code 1882, § 3114; Civil Code 1895, § 3970; Civil Code 1910, § 4567; Code 1933, § 37–215.

§ 23–2–26. Execution of power; remedy

Accident or mistake in the execution of a power or causing the defective execution of the power will be remedied in equity.

Formerly Code 1863, § 3061; Code 1868, § 3073; Code 1873, § 3128; Code 1882, § 3128; Civil Code 1895, § 3986; Civil Code 1910, § 4583; Code 1933, § 37–218.

§ 23–2–27. Ignorance of law

Mere ignorance of the law on the part of the party himself, where the facts are all known and there is no misplaced confidence and no artifice, deception, or fraudulent practice is used by the other party either to induce the mistake of law or to prevent its correction, shall not authorize the intervention of equity.

Formerly Code 1863, § 3054; Code 1868, § 3066; Code 1873, § 3121; Code 1882, § 3121; Civil Code 1895, § 3978; Civil Code 1910, § 4575; Code 1933, § 37–209.

§ 23–2–28. Mutual ignorance of fact, etc.

Ignorance of a fact by both parties shall not justify the interference of equity; nor shall a mistake in judgment or opinion merely as to the value of property authorize such interference.

Formerly Code 1863, § 3060; Code 1868, § 3072; Code 1873, § 3127; Code 1882, § 3127; Civil Code 1895, § 3985; Civil Code 1910, § 4582; Code 1933, § 37–210.

§ 23–2–29. Negligence and concealment

If a party, by reasonable diligence, could have had knowledge of the truth, equity shall not grant relief; nor shall the ignorance of a fact known to the opposite party justify an interference if there has been no misplaced confidence, misrepresentation, or other fraudulent act.

Formerly Code 1863, § 3059; Code 1868, § 3071; Code 1873, § 3126; Code 1882, § 3126; Civil Code 1895, § 3984; Civil Code 1910, § 4581; Code 1933, § 37–211.

§ 23–2–30. Reforming or executing contract in case of mistake

A distinction exists between reforming a contract and executing a contract in case of mistake. To authorize the former, the court shall be satisfied by the evidence that the mistake was mutual; but the court may refuse to act in the latter case if the mistake is confined to the party refusing to execute.

Formerly Code 1863, § 3057; Code 1868, § 3069; Code 1873, § 3124; Code 1882, § 3124; Civil Code 1895, § 3981; Civil Code 1910, § 4578; Code 1933, § 37–208.

§ 23–2–31. Cancellation of contract for mistake of one party, when

Equity will not reform a written contract unless the mistake is shown to be the mistake of both parties; but it may rescind and cancel upon the ground of mistake of fact material to the contract of one party only.

Formerly Civil Code 1895, § 3982; Civil Code 1910, § 4579; Code 1933, § 37–207.

§ 23–2–32. Relief in equity in cases of negligence by complainant

(a) The negligence of the complaining party, preventing relief in equity, is that want of reasonable prudence, the absence of which would be a violation of legal duty.

(b) Relief may be granted even in cases of negligence by the complainant if it appears that the other party has not been prejudiced thereby.

Formerly Civil Code 1895, § 3974; Civil Code 1910, § 4571; Code 1933, § 37-212.

§ 23-2-33. Volunteers

Equity will not interfere to relieve against accidents or mistakes of mere volunteers; but, if a contract is actually executed, all the rights growing out of it against or in favor of any one will be enforced.

Formerly Code 1863, § 3049; Code 1868, § 3061; Code 1873, § 3116; Code 1882, § 3116; Civil Code 1895, § 3972; Civil Code 1910, § 4569; Code 1933, § 37-217.

§ 23-2-34. Against whom equity relieves

Equity will grant relief as between the original parties or their privies in law, in fact, or in estate, except bona fide purchasers for value without notice.

Formerly Code 1863, § 3052; Code 1868, § 3064; Code 1873, § 3119; Code 1882, § 3119; Civil Code 1895, § 3976; Civil Code 1910, § 4573; Code 1933, § 37-213.

Article 3

Fraud

§ 23-2-50. Jurisdiction over fraud

In all cases of fraud, except fraud in the execution of a will, equity has concurrent jurisdiction with the law.

Formerly Code 1863, § 3103; Code 1868, § 3115; Code 1873, § 3172; Code 1882, § 3172; Civil Code 1895, § 4024; Civil Code 1910, § 4621; Code 1933, § 37-701.

§ 23-2-51. Actual and constructive fraud; definitions

(a) Fraud may be actual or constructive.

(b) Actual fraud consists of any kind of artifice by which another is deceived. Constructive fraud consists of any act of omission or commission, contrary to legal or equitable duty, trust, or confidence justly reposed, which is contrary to good conscience and operates to the injury of another.

(c) Actual fraud implies moral guilt; constructive fraud may be consistent with innocence.

Formerly Code 1863, § 3104; Code 1868, § 3116; Code 1873, § 3173; Code 1882, § 3173; Civil Code 1895, § 4025; Civil Code 1910, § 4622; Code 1933, § 37-702.

§ 23-2-52. Misrepresentation

Misrepresentation of a material fact, made willfully to deceive or recklessly without knowledge and acted on by the opposite party or made innocently and mistakenly and acted on by the opposite party, constitutes legal fraud.

Formerly Code 1863, § 3105; Code 1868, § 3117; Code 1873, § 3174; Code 1882, § 3174; Civil Code 1895, § 4026; Civil Code 1910, § 4623; Code 1933, § 37-703.

§ 23-2-53. Suppression of the truth

Suppression of a material fact which a party is under an obligation to communicate constitutes fraud. The obligation to communicate may arise from the confidential relations of the parties or from the particular circumstances of the case.

Formerly Code 1863, § 3106; Code 1868, § 3118; Code 1873, § 3175; Code 1882, § 3175; Civil Code 1895, § 4027; Civil Code 1910, § 4624; Code 1933, § 37-704.

§ 23-2-54. Surprise

Anything which happens without the agency or fault of the party affected by it, tending to disturb and confuse his judgment or to mislead him, of which the opposite party takes an undue advantage, is in equity a surprise and is a form of fraud for which relief is granted.

Formerly Code 1863, § 3111; Code 1868, § 3123; Code 1873, § 3180; Code 1882, § 3180; Civil Code 1895, § 4034; Civil Code 1910, § 4631; Code 1933, § 37-711.

§ 23-2-55. Fraudulent trademarks, etc.

Any attempt to encroach upon the business of a trader or other person by the use of similar trademarks, names, or devices, with the intention of deceiving and misleading the public, is a fraud for which equity will grant relief.

Formerly Code 1863, § 3112; Code 1868, § 3124; Code 1873, § 3181; Code 1882, § 3181; Civil Code 1895, § 4035; Civil Code 1910, § 4632; Code 1933, § 37-712.

§ 23-2-56. How fraud consummated

Fraud may be consummated by signs or tricks, or through agents employed to deceive, or by any other unfair way used to cheat another.

Formerly Code 1863, § 3107; Code 1868, § 3119; Code 1873, § 3176; Code 1882, § 3176; Civil Code 1895, § 4028; Civil Code 1910, § 4625; Code 1933, § 37-705.

§ 23–2–57. Presumption; slight circumstances sometimes sufficient

Fraud may not be presumed but, being in itself subtle, slight circumstances may be sufficient to carry conviction of its existence.

Formerly Code 1863, § 2715; Code 1868, § 2709; Code 1873, § 2751; Code 1882, § 2751; Civil Code 1895, § 4029; Civil Code 1910, § 4626; Code 1933, § 37–706.

§ 23–2–58. Confidential relations

Any relationship shall be deemed confidential, whether arising from nature, created by law, or resulting from contracts, where one party is so situated as to exercise a controlling influence over the will, conduct, and interest of another or where, from a similar relationship of mutual confidence, the law requires the utmost good faith, such as the relationship between partners, principal and agent, etc.

Formerly Code 1863, § 3108; Code 1868, § 3120; Code 1873, § 3177; Code 1882, § 3177; Civil Code 1895, § 4030; Civil Code 1910, § 4627; Code 1933, § 37–707.

§ 23–2–59. Confidential relations preventing acquisition of adverse rights

Where, by the act or consent of parties or the act of a third person or of the law, one person is placed in such relation to another that he becomes interested for him or with him in any subject or property, he is prohibited from acquiring rights in that subject or property which are antagonistic to the person with whose interest he has become associated.

Formerly Civil Code 1895, § 4031; Civil Code 1910, § 4628; Code 1933, § 37–708.

§ 23–2–60. Fraud annuls conveyances

Fraud will authorize equity to annul conveyances, however solemnly executed.

Laws 1986, p. 294, § 4.

Formerly Code 1863, § 3109; Code 1868, § 3121; Code 1873, § 3178; Code 1882, § 3178; Civil Code 1895, § 4032; Civil Code 1910, § 4629; Code 1933, § 37–709.

Article 4

Accounting of Contribution; Apportionment; Setoff

§ 23–2–70. Account

Equity jurisdiction over matters of account shall extend to:

(1) Mutual accounts growing out of privity of contract;

(2) Cases where accounts are complicated and intricate;

(3) Cases where a discovery or writ of ne exeat is prayed and granted;

(4) Cases where the account is of a trust fund;

(5) Accounts between partners or tenants in common; and

(6) Cases where a multiplicity of actions would render a trial difficult, expensive, and unsatisfactory at law.

Formerly Code 1863, § 3063; Code 1868, § 3075; Code 1873, § 3130; Code 1882, § 3130; Civil Code 1895, § 3989; Civil Code 1910, § 4586; Code 1933, § 37–301.

§ 23–2–71. Contribution

In cases of joint, joint and several, or several liabilities of two or more persons, where all are equally bound to bear the common burden and one has paid more than his share, he shall be entitled to contribution from the others; and whenever the circumstances are such that an action at law will not give a complete remedy, equity may entertain jurisdiction.

Formerly Code 1863, § 3065; Code 1868, § 3077; Code 1873, § 3132; Code 1882, § 3132; Civil Code 1895, § 3991; Civil Code 1910, § 4588; Code 1933, § 37–303.

§ 23–2–72. Apportionment

Apportionment of a contract or of rent or hire may, from peculiar circumstances rendering the common-law remedy incomplete, become the subject of equitable jurisdiction.

Formerly Code 1863, § 3067; Code 1868, § 3079; Code 1873, § 3134; Code 1882, § 3134; Civil Code 1895, § 3993; Civil Code 1910, § 4590; Code 1933, § 37–305.

§ 23–2–73. Discharge of encumbrances

Where several persons are interested in an estate as tenants for years, or for life, or in remainder or reversion, and encumbrances are to be discharged, the equitable division of the burden, according to the several interests, shall be a question for equitable interference.

Formerly Code 1863, § 3066; Code 1868, § 3078; Code 1873, § 3133; Code 1882, § 3133; Civil Code 1895, § 3992; Civil Code 1910, § 4589; Code 1933, § 37–304.

§ 23-2-74. Mingling of goods

If a party who has charge of the property of others shall so confound it with his own that the line of distinction cannot be drawn, all the inconvenience shall be thrown upon him who causes the confusion; and he shall distinguish his own property or lose it.

Formerly Code 1863, § 3064; Code 1868, § 3076; Code 1873, § 3131; Code 1882, § 3131; Civil Code 1895, § 3990; Civil Code 1910, § 4587; Code 1933, § 37-302.

§ 23-2-75. Offer to pay balance

A petition for an accounting need not offer to pay a balance if found against the complainant.

Formerly Code 1863, § 3069; Code 1868, § 3081; Code 1873, § 3136; Code 1882, § 3136; Civil Code 1895, § 3995; Civil Code 1910, § 4592; Code 1933, § 37-307.

§ 23-2-76. Equitable setoff

Regarding a setoff, equity generally follows the law; but, if there is an intervening equity not reached by the law or if the setoff is of an equitable nature, equity shall take jurisdiction to enforce the setoff.

Formerly Code 1863, § 3072; Code 1868, § 3084; Code 1873, § 3141; Code 1882, § 3141; Civil Code 1895, § 3996; Civil Code 1910, § 4593; Code 1933, § 37-308.

Article 5
Administration of Assets Generally

§ 23-2-90. Legal and equitable assets

(a) Assets are either legal or equitable. Legal assets are such as may be reached by the ordinary process of law. Equitable assets are such as can be reached only through the intervention of equity.

(b) Legal assets, when properly before the court, shall be distributed according to legal liens and priorities. Equitable assets shall be distributed according to justice and right in the particular case, the general rule being that equality is equity.

(c) Sometimes assets are partly legal and partly equitable. In such cases, while the above rule shall be adhered to as to the legal assets, equity shall so administer the equitable assets as to produce general equality.

Formerly Code 1863, §§ 3073, 3074; Code 1868, §§ 3085, 3086; Code 1873, §§ 3142, 3143; Code 1882, §§ 3142, 3143; Civil Code 1895, §§ 3997, 3998; Civil Code 1910, §§ 4594, 4595; Code 1933, §§ 37-401, 37-402.

§ 23-2-91. Interfering with administration of estates

Equity will not interfere with the regular administration of estates, except upon:

(1) Application of the representative:

(A) For construction and direction; or

(B) For marshaling the assets; or

(2) Application of any person interested in the estate where there is danger of loss or other injury to his interests.

Formerly Code 1863, § 3075; Code 1868, § 3087; Code 1873, § 3144; Code 1882, § 3144; Civil Code 1895, § 3999; Civil Code 1910, § 4596; Code 1933, § 37-403.

§ 23-2-92. Petitions for direction

In cases of difficulty in construing wills, in distributing estates, in ascertaining the persons entitled, or in determining under what law property should be divided, the representative may ask the direction of the court, but not on imaginary difficulties or from excessive caution.

Formerly Code 1863, § 3076; Code 1868, § 3088; Code 1873, § 3145; Code 1882, § 3145; Civil Code 1895, § 4000; Civil Code 1910, § 4597; Code 1933, § 37-404.

§ 23-2-93. Marshaling assets

In all cases where legal difficulties arise as to the distribution of assets in payment of debts or where from any circumstances the ordinary process of law would interfere with the due administration of an estate, without fault on the part of the representative of the estate, a petition to marshal the assets shall be maintained at the instance of the representative.

Formerly Code 1863, § 3077; Code 1868, § 3089; Code 1873, § 3146; Code 1882, § 3146; Civil Code 1895, § 4001; Civil Code 1910, § 4598; Code 1933, § 37-405.

§ 23-2-94. Election, compelling

In marshaling assets, the court shall look to the equities of the creditors and, where cases arise for election, shall compel the parties to elect.

Formerly Code 1863, § 3078; Code 1868, § 3090; Code 1873, § 3147; Code 1882, § 3147; Civil Code 1895, § 4002; Civil Code 1910, § 4599; Code 1933, § 37-406.

§ 23-2-95. Creditors' petitions

Creditors' petitions may be filed at the instance of any creditor, the privilege being extended to all to appear and become parties within a reasonable time.

Formerly Code 1863, § 3079; Code 1868, § 3091; Code 1873, § 3148; Code 1882, § 3148; Civil Code 1895, § 4003; Civil Code 1910, § 4600; Code 1933, § 37-407.

§ 23-2-96. Equitable assets for creditor

Equitable assets may be reached by a creditor in every case where he shows that there is danger of not being satisfied out of legal assets.

Formerly Code 1863, § 3084; Code 1868, § 3096; Code 1873, § 3153; Code 1882, § 3153; Civil Code 1895, § 4004; Civil Code 1910, § 4601; Code 1933, § 37-408.

§ 23-2-97. Time limit for intervention where assets are being disposed of by court

(a) In all equity cases in which assets of either or both parties are being administered, marshaled, or otherwise disposed of by the court, upon motion of either party or of the court at least 60 days before the term for trial, an order shall be passed bearing the title of the case and addressed to all persons concerned, requiring all persons claiming an interest in the assets to intervene in the case by not later than a certain date to be fixed by the court. The date shall be not less than 60 days nor more than 90 days from the date on which the order is filed. After filing, the order shall be published twice each month for two consecutive months in the official organ for legal advertisements in the county in which the case is pending.

(b) After the passage of the last date for intervention fixed in the published order, no person interested in the assets of the case shall be allowed to intervene.

Laws 1939, p. 344, §§ 1, 2.

§ 23-2-98. Joint and individual assets

Joint assets shall be applied to joint debts, and individual assets to individual debts; but, when the joint assets are exhausted, the joint debts may come upon individual assets, the individual debts, without regard to relative dignity as compared with the joint debts, being first advanced the pro rata amount received on the joint debts from joint assets.

Formerly Code 1863, § 3085; Code 1868, § 3097; Code 1873, § 3154; Code 1882, § 3154; Civil Code 1895, § 4005; Civil Code 1910, § 4602; Code 1933, § 37-409.

Article 6

Exercise of Powers of Appointment, and Sale

§ 23-2-110. Jurisdiction over powers

Powers, especially of appointment, being always founded on trust or confidence, are peculiarly subjects of equitable supervision.

Formerly Code 1863, § 3097; Code 1868, § 3109; Code 1873, § 3166; Code 1882, § 3166; Civil Code 1895, § 4017; Civil Code 1910, § 4614; Code 1933, § 37-601.

§ 23-2-111. Discretionary powers

Equity may not compel a party, having a discretion, to exercise a power of appointment.

Formerly Code 1863, § 3098; Code 1868, § 3110; Code 1873, § 3167; Code 1882, § 3167; Civil Code 1895, § 4018; Civil Code 1910, § 4615; Code 1933, § 37-602.

§ 23-2-112. Cases of no discretion, or discretion abused

In all cases where no discretion is allowed or the discretion allowed is abused, equity may compel a faithful execution of the power.

Formerly Code 1863, § 3102; Code 1868, § 3114; Code 1873, § 3171; Code 1882, § 3171; Civil Code 1895, § 4022; Civil Code 1910, § 4619; Code 1933, § 37-606.

§ 23-2-113. Discretionary powers; collusive execution; illusory appointment

(a) As used in this Code section, the term:

(1) "Collusive execution" means every execution whereby the person exercising a power uses it by contrivance for his own benefit, he not being legitimately an intended beneficiary.

(2) "Illusory appointment" means an appointment whereby a nominal benefit only is given to one of a class, to all of whom a substantial benefit was intended.

(b) Equity may relieve against mistaken or defective executions, collusive executions, and illusory appointments.

Formerly Code 1863, §§ 3098, 3099, 3100; Code 1868, §§ 3110, 3111, 3112; Code 1873, §§ 3167, 3168, 3169; Code 1882, §§ 3167, 3168, 3169; Civil Code 1895, §§ 4018, 4019, 4020; Civil Code 1910, §§ 4615, 4616, 4617; Code 1933, §§ 37-602, 37-603, 37-604.

§ 23-2-114. Power of sale in deeds of trust, etc.

Powers of sale in deeds of trust, mortgages, and other instruments shall be strictly construed and shall be fairly exercised. In the absence of stipulations to the contrary in the instrument, the time, place, and manner of sale shall be that pointed out for public sales. Unless the instrument creating the power specifically provides to the contrary, a personal representative, heir, heirs, legatee, devisee, or successor of the grantee in a mortgage, deed of trust, deed to secure debt, bill of sale to secure debt, or other like instrument, or an assignee thereof, or his personal representative, heir, heirs, legatee, devisee, or successor may exercise any power therein contained; and such powers may so be exercised regardless of whether or not the transfer specifically includes the powers or conveys title to the property described. A power of sale not revocable by death of the grantor or donor may be exercised after his death in the same manner and to the same extent as though the grantor or donor were in life; and it shall not be necessary in the exercise of the power to advertise or sell as the property of the estate of the deceased nor to make any mention of or reference to the death.

Laws 1937, p. 481, § 1; Laws 1967, p. 735, § 1.

Formerly Civil Code 1895, § 4023; Civil Code 1910, § 4620; Code 1933, § 37–607.

§ 23–2–115. Power of sale as authorizing private sale

Unless expressly limited in a will, deed, or other instrument creating a power of sale or unless specifically otherwise provided in such instrument, a power of sale conferred upon an executor, trustee, guardian, or attorney in fact shall authorize a private sale by the executor, trustee, guardian, or attorney in fact, with or without advertisement and on such terms and conditions as the donee of the power may deem advisable, without the necessity of applying for leave to sell or obtaining any order therefor from any court; provided, however, that this Code section shall not apply to powers of sale in security deeds, mortgages, trust deeds, bills of sale, and other instruments conveying property or creating a lien thereon, to secure a debt or debts.

Laws 1955, p. 430, § 1.

§ 23–2–116. Power of sale as authorizing sale by successor administrator, trustee, etc.

Unless expressly limited in an instrument creating a power of sale or unless specifically otherwise provided in the instrument, the power of sale conferred upon an executor, trustee, or guardian may be exercised and executed by an administrator with the will annexed or by a successor administrator, trustee, or guardian. If the power is conferred upon more than one executor, trustee, or guardian, the surviving or remaining executor or executors, trustee or trustees, or guardian or guardians may exercise and execute the power.

Laws 1955, p. 430, § 2.

§ 23–2–117. Release of powers of appointment; extent of authority to execute

Any person holding a power of appointment, general or special, whether exercisable by deed or by will only or otherwise, and whether reserved by the holder of the power or conferred upon him by another, may, as to all or any part of the property covered by the power of appointment, release or relinquish the power completely, or may release or relinquish the right to exercise the power except among a limited class set out in the release or relinquishment, or may covenant that the power will be exercised only in favor of the members of a limited class; and any such release, relinquishment, or covenant executed and delivered as provided in Code Sections 23–2–118 and 23–2–119 shall be valid and binding, whether with or without a consideration, provided that no such release, relinquishment, or covenant shall have the effect of permitting the property to be appointed to a person not permitted by the original power.

Laws 1945, p. 340, § 1.

§ 23–2–118. Release, relinquishment, or covenant; writing, delivery, record

Any release, relinquishment, or covenant referred to in Code Section 23–2–117 shall be in writing, signed by the person holding the power, and delivered to anyone interested in the power, including any person in the limited class, or to any fiduciary holding the property or any part thereof, or recorded in the office of the clerk of the superior court of the county in which the property or any part thereof Is located.

Laws 1945, p. 340, § 2.

§ 23–2–119. Release, relinquishment, or covenant; notice to fiduciaries and bona fide purchasers

No fiduciary holding or distributing any property subject to a power of appointment as referred to in Code Section 23–2–117 shall be deemed to have notice of the release, relinquishment, or covenant or be bound thereby unless and until a copy thereof is delivered to the fiduciary. No bona fide purchaser purchasing the property shall be affected by the release, relinquishment, or covenant unless he has notice thereof or unless the release, relinquishment, or covenant has been recorded in the office of the clerk of the superior court of the county in which the property is located.

Laws 1945, p. 340, § 3.

§ 23–2–120. Provisions declaratory of existing law; applicability to releases previously executed

Code Sections 23–2–117 through 23–2–119 are declaratory of existing law and apply to all such releases, relinquishments, and covenants, whenever executed.

Laws 1945, p. 340, § 4.

Article 7

Nonperformance of Contract

§ 23-2-130. When specific performance decreed

Specific performance of a contract, if within the power of the party, will be decreed, generally, whenever the damages recoverable at law would not be an adequate compensation for nonperformance.

Formerly Code 1863, § 3118; Code 1868, § 3130; Code 1873, § 3186; Code 1882, § 3186; Civil Code 1895, § 4036; Civil Code 1910, § 4633; Code 1933, § 37-801.

§ 23-2-131. Parol contract as to land

(a) The specific performance of a parol contract as to land shall be decreed if the defendant admits the contract or if the contract has been so far executed by the party seeking relief and at the instance or by the inducements of the other party that if the contract were abandoned he could not be restored to his former position.

(b) Full payment alone accepted by the vendor, or partial payment accompanied with possession, or possession alone with valuable improvements, if clearly proved in each case to have been done with reference to the parol contract, shall be sufficient part performance to justify a decree.

Formerly Code 1863, § 3119; Code 1868, § 3131; Code 1873, § 3187; Code 1882, § 3187; Civil Code 1895, § 4037; Civil Code 1910, § 4634; Code 1933, § 37-802.

§ 23-2-132. Specific performance of voluntary promises

Specific performance will not be decreed of a voluntary agreement or merely gratuitous promise. If, however, possession of lands has been given under such an agreement, upon a meritorious consideration, and valuable improvements have been made upon the faith thereof, equity will decree the performance of the agreement.

Formerly Code 1863, § 3121; Code 1868, § 3133; Code 1873, § 3189; Code 1882, § 3189; Civil Code 1895, § 4039; Civil Code 1910, § 4636; Code 1933, § 37-804.

§ 23-2-133. Inadequacy of price; effect as to specific performance

Mere inadequacy of price, though not sufficient to rescind a contract, may justify a court in refusing to decree a specific performance, as may any other fact showing the contract to be unfair, unjust, or against good conscience.

Formerly Code 1863, § 3122; Code 1868, § 3134; Code 1873, § 3190; Code 1882, § 3190; Civil Code 1895, § 4040; Civil Code 1910, § 4637; Code 1933, § 37-805.

§ 23-2-134. Ability of complainant vendor to comply

The vendor seeking specific performance shall show an ability to comply substantially with his contract in every part and as to all the property. However, a vendor's want of title or other inability as to part of the property shall not be a good answer to the vendee seeking performance who is willing to accept title to part of the property, receiving compensation for the other part. If the defects in the vendor's title are trifling or comparatively small, equity shall decree at his instance, granting compensation for such defects.

Formerly Code 1863, § 3123; Code 1868, § 3135; Code 1873, § 3191; Code 1882, § 3191; Civil Code 1895, § 4041; Civil Code 1910, § 4638; Code 1933, § 37-806.

§ 23-2-135. Damages for breach of contract

If, for any cause, specific performance is impossible or if the vendee declines to accept a performance in part, the court may proceed to assess damages for the breach of the contract.

Formerly Code 1863, § 3124; Code 1868, § 3136; Code 1873, § 3192; Code 1882, § 3192; Civil Code 1895, § 4042; Civil Code 1910, § 4639; Code 1933, § 37-807.

§ 23-2-136. Possession of personalty; damages or specific performance

Any good reason in equity and good conscience why the complainant should have the possession of specific personalty to which he has title shall sustain an action for specific performance or delivery and, unless rebutted by other equitable reasons, shall justify a decree. The jury in such cases may decree either damages or specific delivery.

Formerly Code 1863, § 3120; Code 1868, § 3132; Code 1873, § 3188; Code 1882, § 3188; Civil Code 1895, § 4038; Civil Code 1910, § 4635; Code 1933, § 37-803.

CHAPTER 3

EQUITABLE REMEDIES AND PROCEEDINGS GENERALLY

Article 1

General Provisions

§ 23-3-1. Equitable or legal rights, remedies applied

The superior courts, on the trial of any civil case, shall give effect to all the rights of the parties, legal, equitable, or both, and apply remedies or relief, legal, equitable, or both, in favor of either party, as the nature of the case may allow or require.

Laws 1887, p. 64, § 1.

Formerly Civil Code 1895, § 4833; Civil Code 1910, § 5406; Code 1933, § 37-901.

§ 23-3-2. Proceedings to obtain equitable relief, in general

Any person may, in any civil action, claim equitable relief by appropriate and sufficient pleadings and obtain the equitable relief proper in the case.

Laws 1884-85, p. 36, § 1.

Formerly Civil Code 1895, § 4834; Civil Code 1910, § 5407; Code 1933, § 37-902.

§ 23-3-3. Extraordinary remedies in aid of suit, right to

A person who asserts a claim for equitable relief may at any time, by proper pleading and proof, also apply for and obtain any of the extraordinary remedies available from the court in its exercise of equitable powers.

Laws 1884-85, p. 36, § 1.

Formerly Civil Code 1895, § 4836; Civil Code 1910, § 5409; Code 1933, § 37-904.

§ 23-3-4. Extraordinary remedies for defendant

Any defendant may, by proper pleadings and sufficient evidence, obtain the benefit of extraordinary remedies allowed in equitable proceedings by the superior court.

Laws 1884-85, p. 36, § 2.

Formerly Civil Code 1895, § 4838; Civil Code 1910, § 5411; Code 1933, § 37-906.

Article 2

Ne Exeat

§ 23-3-20. Ne exeat issued in what cases

The writ of ne exeat shall issue to restrain a person from leaving the jurisdiction of the state. The writ may be granted in the following cases:

(1) In favor of an obligor, promisor, or partner, against his co-obligor, joint promisor, or copartner equally or partly responsible with him for any duty to be performed;

(2) Against persons illegally removing the property of a decedent or of a minor, at the instance of any person interested therein, or of a next friend of the minor;

(3) At the instance of a remainderman or reversioner against anyone attempting to remove the property in which the remainder or reversion exists or may contingently exist;

(4) At the instance of a mortgagee against a person holding the equity of redemption;

(5) At the instance of any person interested legally or equitably in property about to be removed, where no adequate remedy is afforded at law.

Laws 1814, Cobb's 1851 Digest, p. 526.

Formerly Code 1863, § 3147; Code 1868, § 3159; Code 1873, § 3226; Code 1882, § 3226; Civil Code 1895, § 4886; Civil Code 1910, § 5459; Code 1933, § 37-1401.

§ 23-3-21. Complainant's showing in application for writ of ne exeat

In every case of application for a writ of ne exeat, the complaining party shall show that no adequate remedy is afforded at law, and that the defendant is removing or about to remove himself, his property, or the specific property to which the complainant claims title or an interest.

Formerly Code 1863, § 3148; Code 1868, § 3160; Code 1873, § 3227; Code 1882, § 3227; Civil Code 1895, § 4887; Civil Code 1910, § 5460; Code 1933, § 37-1402.

§ 23-3-22. Affidavit and bond of complainant

(a) In every application for a writ of ne exeat, the petition or motion must be verified by one or more of the complainants.

(b) The judge may, in his discretion, require the complainant to give bond and security for the payment of any damages which the defendant may recover from him for obtaining the writ, before granting an order for the issuing of the same, and may require a verification by all or any of the complainants.

Laws 1855-56, p. 219, § 4; Laws 1857, p. 109, § 1.

Formerly Code 1863, § 3151; Code 1868, § 3163; Code 1873, § 3230; Code 1882, § 3230; Civil Code 1895, § 4890; Civil Code 1910, § 5463; Code 1933, § 37-1405.

§ 23-3-23. Defendant's bond; sufficiency of security

The defendant may relieve himself, his property, or the specific property from the restraint imposed by giving bond in double the value of plaintiff's claim, with good security, to the officer serving the process, for the forthcoming of each or either, according to the tenor of the writ, to answer to complainant's claim or abide by the order and decree of the court. The judge granting the writ may, in his discretion, require a larger bond. An officer receiving insufficient security shall be held surety himself, and the sureties on his bond may be held responsible therefor.

Laws 1830, Cobb's 1851 Digest, p. 527.

Formerly Code 1863, § 3149; Code 1868, § 3161; Code 1873, § 3228; Code 1882, § 3228; Civil Code 1895, § 4888; Civil Code 1910, § 5461; Code 1933, § 37-1403.

§ 23-3-24. Court's decision as to disposition of property

If the defendant fails or refuses to replevy the property, the court may, in its discretion, make such disposition of it as shall appear most advantageous to all parties.

Formerly Code 1863, § 3150; Code 1868, § 3162; Code 1873, § 3229; Code 1882, § 3229; Civil Code 1895, § 4889; Civil Code 1910, § 5462; Code 1933, § 37-1404.

§ 23-3-25. When writ of ne exeat issued without sanction

In cases of emergency, upon the affidavit of the complainant that he cannot obtain the sanction of the judge in time to remedy the mischief, the writ of ne exeat may issue at once, to continue until the first term of the court to which it is returnable, unless earlier heard by order of the judge.

Formerly Code 1863, § 3152; Code 1868, § 3164; Code 1873, § 3231; Code 1882, § 3231; Civil Code 1895, § 4891; Civil Code 1910, § 5464; Code 1933, § 37-1406.

Article 3

Quia Timet

Part 1

Conventional Quia Timet

§ 23-3-40. Proceeding quia timet

The proceeding quia timet is sustained in equity for the purpose of causing to be delivered and canceled any instrument which has answered the object of its creation or any forged or other iniquitous deed or other writing which, though not enforced at the time, either casts a cloud over the complainant's title or otherwise subjects him to future liability or present annoyance, and the cancellation of which is necessary to his perfect protection.

Formerly Code 1863, § 3153; Code 1868, § 3165; Code 1873, § 3232; Code 1882, § 3232; Civil Code 1895, § 4892; Civil Code 1910, § 5465; Code 1933, § 37-1407.

§ 23-3-41. In what cases quia timet proceeding sustained; costs

(a) In all proceedings quia timet or proceedings to remove clouds upon titles to real estate, if a proper case is made, the relief sought shall be granted to any complainant irrespective of whether the invalidity of the instrument sought to be canceled appears upon the face of the instrument or whether the invalidity appears or arises solely from facts outside of the instrument.

(b) In such cases the costs shall be taxed against the litigants in the discretion of the court.

Laws 1905, p. 102, §§ 1, 2.

Formerly Civil Code 1910, §§ 5466, 5467; Code 1933, §§ 37-1408, 37-1409.

§ 23-3-42. Removing cloud on title

An instrument which, by itself or in connection with proof of possession by a former occupant or other extrinsic facts, gives the claimant thereunder an apparent right in or to the property may constitute a cloud on the title of the true owner; and the latter may proceed to have the same removed upon proof:

(1) That he cannot immediately or effectually maintain or protect his rights by any other course of proceeding open to him;

(2) That the instrument sought to be canceled is such as would operate to throw a cloud or suspicion upon his title and might be vexatiously or injuriously used against him;

(3) That he either suffers some present injury by reason of the hostile claim of right or, though the claim has not been asserted adversely or aggressively, he has reason to apprehend that the evidence upon which he relies to impeach or invalidate the same as a claim upon his title may be lost or impaired by lapse of time.

Formerly Civil Code 1895, § 4893; Civil Code 1910, § 5468; Code 1933, § 37-1410.

§ 23-3-43. Submission to special master at option of complainant

At the option of the complainant as prayed for in the complaint, the court, upon receipt of the complaint, shall submit the same to a special master as provided for in Code Sections 23-3-63 through 23-3-68, except that as in other equity cases there shall be no right to a jury trial.

Laws 2000, p. 1408, § 1.

§ 23-3-44. Removing cloud on title caused by equity of redemption following tax sale

Proceedings quia timet may be used to remove clouds on title caused by equities of redemption following tax sales; provided, however, that the length of time for redemption shall remain as provided by law and nothing in this Code section shall preclude the necessity of giving all parties at interest notice of this proceeding.

Laws 2000, p. 1408, § 1; Laws 2001, p. 4, § 23.

Part 2

Quia Time Against All the World

§ 23-3-60. Purpose of part

The purpose of this part is to create a procedure for removing any cloud upon the title to land, including the equity of redemption by owners of land sold at tax sales, and for readily and conclusively establishing that certain named persons are the owners of all the interests in land defined by a decree entered in such proceeding, so that there shall be no occasion for land in this state to be unmarketable because of any uncertainty as to the owner of every interest therein.

Laws 1966, p. 443, § 11.

§ 23-3-61. Proceedings in rem against all the world to establish title; removal of clouds upon title; who may bring action

Any person, which term shall include a corporation, partnership, or other association, who claims an estate of freehold present or future or any estate for years of which at least five years are unexpired, including persons holding lands under tax deeds, in any land in this state, whether in the actual and peaceable possession thereof or not and whether the land is vacant or not, may bring a proceeding in rem against all the world to establish his title to the land and to determine all adverse claims thereto or to remove any particular cloud or clouds upon his title to the land, including an equity of redemption, which proceeding may be against all persons known or unknown who claim or might claim adversely to him, whether or not the petition discloses any known or possible claimants.

Laws 1966, p. 443, § 1.

§ 23-3-62. Petition, contents, attachments; lis pendens notice

(a) The proceeding in rem shall be instituted by filing a petition in the superior court of the county in which the land is situated.

(b) The petition shall be verified by the petitioner and shall contain a particular description of the land to be involved in the proceeding, a specification of the petitioner's interest in the land, a statement as to whether the interest is based upon a written instrument (whether same be a contract, deed, will, or otherwise) or adverse possession or both, a description of all adverse claims of which petitioner has actual or constructive notice, the names and addresses, so far as known to the petitioner, of any possible adverse claimant, and, if the proceeding is brought to remove a particular cloud or clouds, a statement as to the grounds upon which it is sought to remove the cloud or clouds.

(c) With the petition there shall be filed (1) a plat of survey of the land, (2) a copy of the immediate instrument or instruments, if any, upon which the petitioner's interest is based, and (3) a copy of the immediate instrument or instruments of record or otherwise known to the petitioner, if any, upon which any person might base an interest in the land adverse to the petitioner.

(d) Upon the filing of the petition, the petitioner shall contemporaneously file with the clerk of the court a notice for record in the lis pendens docket pursuant to Code Sections 44-14-610 through 44-14-613.

Laws 1966, p. 443, § 2.

§ 23-3-63. Submission to special master

The court, upon receipt of the petition together with the plat and instruments filed therewith, shall submit the same to a special master who shall be a person who is authorized to practice law in this state and is a resident of the judicial circuit wherein the action is brought.

Laws 1966, p. 443, § 3.

§ 23-3-64. Examination of pleadings by master; order to file further evidence

The master shall examine the petition, plat, and all documents filed therewith and may require other evidence to be filed, including, but not limited to, an abstract of title.

Laws 1966, p. 443, § 4.

§ 23-3-65. Preliminary determinations by master; service; responsive pleadings; guardians ad litem

(a) Upon the filing of all evidence with him, the master shall:

(1) Determine who is entitled to notice, including, but not limited to, all adjacent landowners and all adverse claimants as to whose adverse claims petitioner has actual or constructive notice;

(2) Cause process to issue, directed to all persons who are entitled to notice and to all other persons whom it may concern.

(b) Process shall be served upon known persons whose residence is ascertainable by the sheriff or his deputy as provided by law. In all cases where service by publication is permitted under the laws and where the respondent or other party resides outside this state or whose residence is unknown and it is necessary to perfect service upon such person by publication, upon the fact being made to appear to the judge or clerk of the court in which the action is pending, the judge or clerk may order service to be perfected by publication in the paper in which sheriffs' advertisements are printed, four times within the ensuing 30 days, publications to be weekly. The published notice shall contain the name of the petitioner and respondent with a caption setting forth the court, the character of the action, the date the action was filed, the date of the order for service by publication, and a notice directed and addressed to the party to be thus served, commanding him to be and appear at the court in which the action is pending within 30 days of the date of the order for service by publication, and shall bear teste in the name of the judge and shall be signed by the clerk of the court. The date upon which the nonresident or party whose residence is unknown is called upon to appear shall be the appearance day of the case.

(c) Any adverse party shall be entitled to have at least 30 days after completion of service to file any pleading he desires in the matter before the court.

(d) If, upon the filing of the petition or of the evidence required by him, the master finds that there are persons under a disability, or minors, or persons not in being, unascertained, or unknown who may have an interest, he shall appoint a disinterested person, in the nature of a guardian ad litem, who shall be served with copies of the notice prescribed and who shall represent these interests.

Laws 1966, p. 443, § 5.

§ 23-3-66. Jurisdiction of master; report to superior court; jury trial upon demand or on order of master

Upon reasonable notice to the parties, after proof of serving notice as required by this article has been filed and after the appointment of the disinterested person as representative where required, the special master shall have complete jurisdiction within the scope of the pleadings to ascertain and determine the validity, nature, or extent of petitioner's title and all other interests in the land, or any part thereof, which may be adverse to the title claimed by the petitioner, or to remove any particular cloud or clouds upon the title to the land and to make a report of his findings to the judge of the court; provided, however, any party to this proceeding may demand a trial by a jury of any question of fact; provided, further, that the master on his own initiative may require a trial by a jury of any question of fact.

Laws 1966, p. 443, § 6.

§ 23-3-67. Decrees; entries upon records

Upon the receipt of the master's report or upon a jury verdict, the court shall issue a decree which shall be recorded in the office of the clerk of the superior court of the county or counties wherein the land affected lies and which, when recorded, shall operate to bind the land affected according to the tenor thereof and shall be conclusive upon and against all persons named therein, known or unknown. A marginal reference to the recorded judgments and decree shall be entered upon any recorded instrument stated to be affected thereby.

Laws 1966, p. 443, § 7.

§ 23-3-68. Compensation of master and representatives

The court shall fix a reasonable compensation, not less than $50.00, to be paid to the master appointed under this part and shall fix the compensation to be paid to any representative in the nature of a guardian ad litem appointed under this part. These fees are to be taxed in the discretion of the court as a part of the costs.

Laws 1966, p. 443, § 8.

§ 23-3-69. Intervention

At any time within 30 days from the entering of the final decree, any person not previously a party who claims an interest in the land may intervene, in which event the case shall be reopened as to that party so that his rights may be adjudicated.

Laws 1966, p. 443, § 9.

§ 23-3-70. Joinder of actions; separate trials permitted

(a) Two or more persons having separate and distinct parcels of land in the same county and holding under the same source of title or persons having separate and distinct interests in the same parcel or parcels may join in a petition under this part against the same supposed claimants.

(b) A petitioner may join separate causes of action in one petition; but, if they cannot be conveniently disposed of together, the court may order separate trials.

Laws 1966, p. 443, § 10.

§ 23-3-71. Construction of part

This part shall be liberally construed.

Laws 1966, p. 443, § 12.

§ 23-3-72. Cumulative nature of remedy

The remedy provided by this part is intended to be cumulative and not exclusive.

Laws 1966, p. 443, § 13.

§ 23-3-73. Standing

All municipalities, counties, and housing authorities shall have standing pursuant to this article.

Laws 2006, Act 444, § 18, eff. April 4, 2006.

Article 4

Equitable Interpleader

§ 23-3-90. Grounds for grant of interpleader

(a) Whenever a person is possessed of property or funds or owes a debt or duty, to which more than one person lays claim of such a character as to render it doubtful or dangerous for the holder to act, he may apply to equity to compel the claimants to interplead.

(b) If the person bringing the action has to make or incur any expenses in so doing, including attorney's fees, the amount so incurred shall be taxed in the bill of costs, under the approval of the court, the court in its discretion determining the amount of the attorney's fees, and shall be paid by the parties cast in the action as other costs are paid.

Laws 1952, p. 90, § 1.

Formerly Code 1863, § 3156; Code 1868, § 3168; Code 1873, § 3235; Code 1882, § 3235; Civil Code 1895, § 4896; Civil Code 1910, § 5471; Code 1933, § 37-1503.

§ 23-3-91. Affidavit to petition for interpleader

Every petition for interpleader shall be verified and shall show that the petitioner is not in collusion with any party claiming the property.

Formerly Civil Code 1895, § 4897; Civil Code 1910, § 5472; Code 1933, § 37-1504.

§ 23-3-92. Collateral interpleading

If, in the progress of any proceeding in equity, the court perceives the necessity for parties to interplead, it may order such interpleader as collateral and ancillary to the main case.

Formerly Code 1863, § 3157; Code 1868, § 3169; Code 1873, § 3236; Code 1882, § 3236; Civil Code 1895, § 4898; Civil Code 1910, § 5473; Code 1933, § 37-1505.

Article 5

Bills of Peace

§ 23-3-110. When bill of peace will be entertained

(a) It being the interest of this state that there shall be an end of litigation, equity will entertain a bill of peace:

(1) To confirm some right which has been previously satisfactorily established by more than one legal trial and is likely to be litigated again;

(2) To avoid a multiplicity of actions by establishing a right, in favor of or against several persons, which is likely to be the subject of legal controversy; or

(3) In other similar cases.

(b) As ancillary to this jurisdiction, equity will grant perpetual injunctions.

Formerly Code 1863, §§ 3154, 3155; Code 1868, §§ 3166, 3167; Code 1873, §§ 3233, 3234; Code 1882, §§ 3233, 3234; Civil Code 1895, §§ 4894, 4895; Civil Code 1910, §§ 5469, 5470; Code 1933, §§ 37-1501, 37-1502.

CHAPTER 4

EQUITY PROCEDURE

Article 1

General Provisions

§ 23-4-1. Multiplicity ground for consolidation, when

Where there is one common claim to be asserted by or against several, and one is asserting the claim against many, or many against one, the court may utilize equitable powers to consolidate and determine the whole matter in one action.

Formerly Civil Code 1895, § 4846; Civil Code 1910, § 5419; Code 1933, § 37-1007.

§ 23-4-2. Extraordinary remedies in aid of suit or defense, how obtained

A claim for extraordinary relief or remedy to aid an action or defense may be asserted either by original pleading or by amendment.

Laws 1887, p. 64, § 4.

Formerly Civil Code 1895, § 4839; Civil Code 1910, § 5412; Code 1933, § 37-907.

§ 23-4-3. Equitable relief for defendants; pleading and evidence

A defendant to any action in the superior court, whether the action is for legal or equitable relief, may claim legal or equitable relief, or both, by framing proper pleadings for that purpose and sustaining them by sufficient evidence.

Laws 1884-85, p. 36, § 2.

Formerly Civil Code 1895, § 4837; Civil Code 1910, § 5410; Code 1933, § 37-905.

§ 23-4-4. Proceedings by petition

All ex parte proceedings or proceedings for the execution of the protective powers of equity over trust estates or the estates of wards of equity shall be initiated by presenting a petition to the court. The court may order such other proceedings as the necessity of each case demands.

Formerly Code 1863, § 4130; Code 1868, § 4162; Code 1873, § 4221; Code 1882, § 4221; Civil Code 1895, § 4863; Civil Code 1910, § 5436; Code 1933, § 37-1301.

§ 23-4-5. What may be done at chambers; record of proceedings

The judge may receive and act upon the petitions described in Code Section 23-4-4 at chambers, always transmitting the entire proceedings to the clerk to be entered on the minutes or other records of the court.

Laws 1853-54, p. 59, § 1.

Formerly Code 1863, § 4131; Code 1868, § 4163; Code 1873, § 4222; Code 1882, § 4222; Civil Code 1895, § 4864; Civil Code 1910, § 5437; Code 1933, § 37-1302.

Article 2

Parties

§ 23–4–20. Who may sue

Any person who may not bring an action at law may complain in equity and every person who is remediless elsewhere may claim the protection and assistance of equity to enforce any right recognized by the law.

Formerly Code 1863, § 4090; Code 1868, § 4119; Code 1873, § 4178; Code 1882, § 4178; Civil Code 1895, § 4841; Civil Code 1910, § 5414; Code 1933, § 37–1001.

Article 3

Decrees

§ 23–4–30. Definition; signature; entry on minutes of court

A decree is the judgment of the judge in equitable proceedings upon the facts ascertained and should be signed by him and entered on the minutes of the court.

Formerly Code 1863, § 4122; Code 1868, § 4153; Code 1873, § 4212; Code 1882, § 4212; Civil Code 1895, § 4851; Civil Code 1910, § 5424; Code 1933, § 37–1201.

§ 23–4–31. Moulding decrees and enforcement thereof

A superior court shall have full power to mold its decrees so as to meet the exigencies of each case and shall have full power to enforce its decrees when rendered.

Formerly Code 1863, § 4123; Code 1868, § 4154; Code 1873, § 4213; Code 1882, § 4213; Civil Code 1895, § 4853; Civil Code 1910, § 5426; Code 1933, § 37–1203.

§ 23–4–32. Extraterritorial effect of decree

Equity may decree in cases of fraud, trust, or contract, although property not within the jurisdiction may be affected by the decree.

Formerly Civil Code 1895, § 4854; Civil Code 1910, § 5427; Code 1933, § 37–1204.

§ 23–4–33. Decree in will and contract cases

When it becomes impossible to carry out any last will and testament in whole or in part, and in all matters of contract, the judges of the superior courts shall have power to render any decree that may be necessary and legal, provided that all parties in interest shall consent thereto in writing and there shall be no issue as to the facts or, if there is such an issue, that there shall be a like consent in writing that the judge presiding may hear and determine such facts, subject to a review by the Supreme Court, as in other cases. In all cases where minors are interested, the consent of the guardian at law or the guardian ad litem shall be obtained before the decree is rendered.

Laws 1865–66, p. 221, § 1; Laws 1882–83, p. 69, § 1.

Formerly Code 1868, § 4155; Code 1873, § 4214; Code 1882, § 4214; Civil Code 1895, § 4855; Civil Code 1910, § 5428; Code 1933, § 37–1205.

§ 23–4–34. Interlocutory decrees and orders

At any stage in the progress of an action seeking equitable relief, if any portion of the same is ready for or requires a decree, the court may hear and determine such matters and pass such interlocutory decree or order as may advance the cause and expedite a final hearing. If no issue of fact is involved, the verdict of a jury shall be unnecessary.

Formerly Code 1863, § 4111; Code 1868, § 4142; Code 1873, § 4201; Code 1882, § 4201; Civil Code 1895, § 4847; Civil Code 1910, § 5420; Code 1933, § 37–1101.

§ 23–4–35. Confirmation of sale under decree

Sales under decrees in equity shall be subject to confirmation by the judge, who has a large discretion vested in him in reference thereto. Such sales shall not be consummated until confirmed by him.

Formerly Civil Code 1895, § 4856; Civil Code 1910, § 5429; Code 1933, § 37–1206.

§ 23–4–36. Transfer of decree; lien

A decree shall be transferable like other judgments and, when for money, shall constitute a like lien.

Formerly Code 1863, § 4126; Code 1868, § 4158; Code 1873, § 4217; Code 1882, § 4217; Civil Code 1895, § 4859; Civil Code 1910, § 5432; Code 1933, § 37–1209.

§ 23-4-37. Attachment and execution on decrees

Every decree or order of a superior court in equitable proceedings may be enforced by attachment against the person for contempt. Decrees for money may be enforced by execution against the property. If a decree is partly for money and partly for the performance of a duty, the former may be enforced by execution and the latter by attachment or other process.

Formerly Code 1863, §§ 3032, 4125; Code 1868, §§ 3044, 4157; Code 1873, §§ 3099, 4216; Code 1882, §§ 3099, 4216; Civil Code 1895, §§ 3944, 4858; Civil Code 1910, §§ 4541, 5431; Code 1933, §§ 37-123, 37-1208.

§ 23-4-38. Attachment to enforce extraordinary remedies

Injunction, ne exeat, prohibition, and other extraordinary remedies may be enforced by attachment for contempt.

Formerly Code 1863, §§ 3157, 4127; Code 1868, §§ 3169, 4159; Code 1873, §§ 3237, 4218; Code 1882, §§ 3237, 4218; Civil Code 1895, §§ 4860, 4899; Civil Code 1910, §§ 5433, 5474; Code 1933, § 37-1210.

TITLE 24

EVIDENCE

As Amended Through the 2006 Regular Session of the General Assembly

Research Note

Use Westlaw *to find cases citing a statute or to search for specific terms in a statute. See the Westlaw Directory Screens for lists of relevant databases.*

Table of Sections

INDEX

See Index to Georgia Statutes, infra.

CHAPTER 1

GENERAL PROVISIONS

§ 24-1-1. Definitions

As used in this title, the term:

(1) "Competent evidence" means evidence which is admissible.

(2) "Cumulative evidence" means evidence which is additional to other evidence already obtained.

(3) "Direct evidence" means evidence which immediately points to the question at issue.

(4) "Indirect evidence" or "circumstantial evidence" means evidence which only tends to establish the issue by proof of various facts, sustaining by their consistency the hypothesis claimed.

(5) "Preponderance of evidence" means that superior weight of evidence upon the issues involved, which, while not enough to free the mind wholly from a reasonable doubt, is yet sufficient to incline a reasonable and impartial mind to one side of the issue rather than to the other.

(6) "Presumptive evidence" means evidence which consists of inferences drawn by human experience from the connection of cause and effect and from observations of human conduct.

(7) "Sufficient evidence" means evidence which is satisfactory for the purpose.

Formerly Code 1863, § 3671; Code 1868, § 3695; Code 1873, § 3748; Code 1882, § 3748; Civil Code 1895, §§ 5143, 5145; Penal Code 1895, § 983; Civil Code 1910, §§ 5729, 5731; Penal Code 1910, § 1009; Code 1933, §§ 38-102, 38-106.

§ 24-1-2. Object of evidence

The object of all legal investigation is the discovery of truth. The rules of evidence are framed with a view to this prominent end, seeking always for pure sources and the highest evidence.

Formerly Code 1863, § 3670; Code 1868, § 3694; Code 1873, § 3747; Code 1882, § 3747; Civil Code 1895, § 5142; Penal Code 1895, § 982; Civil Code 1910, § 5728; Penal Code 1910, § 1008; Code 1933, § 38-101.

§ 24-1-3. Same rule in all courts and cases

The rules of evidence shall be the same in all courts and in all trials unless otherwise expressly provided by statute.

Formerly Code 1863, § 3673; Code 1868, § 3697; Code 1873, § 3750; Code 1882, § 3750; Civil Code 1895, § 5147; Civil Code 1910, § 5733; Code 1933, § 38-108.

§ 24-1-4. Matters judicially recognized

The existence and territorial extent of states, their forms of government, symbols of nationality, the laws of nations, all laws and resolutions of the General Assembly and the journals of each branch thereof as published by authority, the laws of the United States and of the several states thereof as published by authority, general customs of merchants, the admiralty and maritime courts of the world and their seals, the political constitution and history of our own government as well as the local divisions of our own state, the seals of the several departments of the government of the United States and of the several states of the Union, and all similar matters of public knowledge shall be judicially recognized without the introduction of proof.

Laws 1819, Cobb's 1851 Digest, p. 272.

Formerly Code 1863, §§ 3674, 3738, 3747; Code 1868, §§ 3698, 3762, 3771; Code 1873, §§ 3751, 3815, 3824; Code 1882, §§ 3751, 3815, 3824; Civil Code 1895, §§ 5148, 5210, 5231; Civil Code 1910, §§ 5734, 5797, 5818; Code 1933, § 38-112.

§ 24–1–5. Procedure where hearing impaired persons arrested for violations of criminal laws

In the event a hearing impaired person is arrested for any alleged violation of a criminal law of this state, the arresting officer shall comply with the provisions of Article 5 of Chapter 9 of this title.

Laws 1974, p. 484, § 2; Laws 1983, p. 852, § 1.

CHAPTER 2

RELEVANCY

§ 24–2–1. Evidence must be relevant

Evidence must relate to the questions being tried by the jury and bear upon them either directly or indirectly. Irrelevant matter should be excluded.

Formerly Code 1863, § 3679; Code 1868, § 3703; Code 1873, § 3756; Code 1882, § 3756; Civil Code 1895, § 5158; Civil Code 1910, § 5744; Code 1933, § 38–201.

§ 24–2–2. Character and conduct of parties, relevancy

The general character of the parties and especially their conduct in other transactions are irrelevant matter unless the nature of the action involves such character and renders necessary or proper the investigation of such conduct.

Formerly Code 1863, § 3680; Code 1868, § 3704; Code 1873, § 3757; Code 1882, § 3757; Civil Code 1895, § 5159; Penal Code 1895, § 993; Civil Code 1910, § 5745; Penal Code 1910, § 1019; Code 1933, § 38–202.

§ 24–2–3. Matters not relevant in prosecution for rape

(a) In any prosecution for a violation of Code Section 16–6–1, relating to rape; Code Section 16–6–2, relating to aggravated sodomy; Code Section 16–6–4, relating to aggravated child molestation; or Code Section 16–6–22.2, relating to aggravated sexual battery, evidence relating to the past sexual behavior of the complaining witness shall not be admissible, either as direct evidence or on cross–examination of the complaining witness or other witnesses, except as provided in this Code section. For the purposes of this Code section, evidence of past sexual behavior includes, but is not limited to, evidence of the complaining witness's marital history, mode of dress, general reputation for promiscuity, nonchastity, or sexual mores contrary to the community standards.

(b) In any prosecution for a violation of Code Section 16–6–1, relating to rape; Code Section 16–6–2, relating to aggravated sodomy; Code Section 16–6–4, relating to aggravated child molestation; or Code Section 16–6–22.2, relating to aggravated sexual battery, evidence relating to the past sexual behavior of the complaining witness may be introduced if the court, following the procedure described in subsection (c) of this Code section, finds that the past sexual behavior directly involved the participation of the accused and finds that the evidence expected to be introduced supports an inference that the accused could have reasonably believed that the complaining witness consented to the conduct complained of in the prosecution.

(c) The procedure for introducing evidence as described in subsection (b) of this Code section shall be as follows:

(1) At the time the defense shall seek to introduce evidence which would be covered by subsection (b) of this Code section, the defense shall notify the court of such intent, whereupon the court shall conduct an in camera hearing to examine into the defendant's offer of proof;

(2) At the conclusion of the hearing, if the court finds that any of the evidence introduced at the hearing is admissible under subsection (b) of this Code section or is so highly material that it will substantially support a conclusion that the accused reasonably believed that the complaining witness consented to the conduct complained of and that justice mandates the admission of such evidence, the court shall by order state what evidence may be introduced by the defense at the trial of the case and in what manner the evidence may be introduced; and

(3) The defense may then introduce evidence pursuant to the order of the court.

Laws 1976, p. 741, § 1; Laws 1989, p. 272, § 1; Laws 2005, Act 8, § 13.1, eff. July 1, 2005.

Formerly Code 1933, § 38–202.1.

§ 24-2-4. Part of paper introduced, balance admissible if relevant

Where either party introduces part of a document or record, the opposite party may read so much of the balance as is relevant.

Formerly Civil Code 1895, § 5241; Civil Code 1910, § 5830; Code 1933, § 38-703.

CHAPTER 3

HEARSAY

Article 1

General Provisions

§ 24-3-1. Definition; when and why admitted

(a) Hearsay evidence is that which does not derive its value solely from the credit of the witness but rests mainly on the veracity and competency of other persons.

(b) Hearsay evidence is admitted only in specified cases from necessity.

Formerly Code 1863, § 3693; Code 1868, § 3717; Code 1873, § 3770; Code 1882, § 3770; Civil Code 1895, § 5175; Civil Code 1910, § 5762; Code 1933, § 38-301.

§ 24-3-2. Original evidence, when

When, in a legal investigation, information, conversations, letters and replies, and similar evidence are facts to explain conduct and ascertain motives, they shall be admitted in evidence not as hearsay but as original evidence.

Formerly Code 1863, § 3694; Code 1868, § 3718; Code 1873, § 3771; Code 1882, § 3771; Civil Code 1895, § 5176; Penal Code 1895, § 997; Civil Code 1910, § 5763; Penal Code 1910, § 1023; Code 1933, § 38-302.

§ 24-3-3. Res gestae

Declarations accompanying an act, or so nearly connected therewith in time as to be free from all suspicion of device or afterthought, shall be admissible in evidence as part of the res gestae.

Formerly Code 1863, § 3696; Code 1868, § 3720; Code 1873, § 3773; Code 1882, § 3773; Civil Code 1895, § 5179; Penal Code 1895, § 998; Civil Code 1910, § 5766; Penal Code 1910, § 1024; Code 1933, § 38-305.

§ 24-3-4. Statements for purposes of medical diagnosis or treatment

Statements made for purposes of medical diagnosis or treatment and describing medical history, or past or present symptoms, pain, or sensations, or the inception or general character of the cause or external source thereof insofar as reasonably pertinent to diagnosis or treatment shall be admissible in evidence.

Laws 1977, p. 226, § 1.

Formerly Code 1933, § 38-315.

§ 24-3-5. Declarations by conspirators

After the fact of conspiracy is proved, the declarations by any one of the conspirators during the pendency of the criminal project shall be admissible against all.

Formerly Code 1863, § 3698; Code 1868, § 3722; Code 1873, § 3775; Code 1882, § 3775; Penal Code 1895, § 999; Penal Code 1910, § 1025; Code 1933, § 38-306.

§ 24-3-6. Dying declarations

Declarations by any person in the article of death, who is conscious of his condition, as to the cause of his death and the person who killed him, shall be admissible in evidence in a prosecution for the homicide.

Formerly Code 1863, § 3704; Code 1868, § 3728; Code 1873, § 3781; Code 1882, § 3781; Penal Code 1895, § 1000; Penal Code 1910, § 1026; Code 1933, § 38-307.

§ 24-3-7. Declarations by persons in possession

(a) Declarations by a person in possession of property in disparagement of his own title shall be admissible in evidence in favor of anyone and against privies of the declarant.

(b) Declarations by a person in favor of his own title shall be admissible to prove his adverse possession.

Formerly Code 1863, § 3697; Code 1868, § 3721; Code 1873, § 3774; Code 1882, § 3774; Civil Code 1895, § 5180; Civil Code 1910, § 5767; Code 1933, § 38-308.

§ 24-3-8. Declarations and entries by deceased persons

Declarations and entries made by a person since deceased against his interest and not made with a view to pending litigation shall be admissible in evidence in any case.

Formerly Code 1863, § 3699; Code 1868, § 3723; Code 1873, § 3776; Code 1882, § 3776; Civil Code 1895, § 5181; Civil Code 1910, § 5768; Code 1933, § 38-309.

§ 24-3-9. Matters of public interest; ancient rights

Declarations of deceased persons as to ancient rights made before the litigation arose shall be admissible to prove matters of public interest in which the whole community is supposed to take interest and to have knowledge.

Formerly Code 1863, § 3701; Code 1868, § 3725; Code 1873, § 3778; Code 1882, § 3778; Civil Code 1895, § 5183; Civil Code 1910, § 5770; Code 1933, § 38-311.

§ 24-3-10. Testimony of witness on former trial

The testimony of a witness since deceased, disqualified, or inaccessible for any cause which was given under oath on a former trial upon substantially the same issue and between substantially the same parties may be proved by anyone who heard it and who professes to remember the substance of the entire testimony as to the particular matter about which he testifies.

Formerly Code 1863, § 3705; Code 1868, § 3729; Code 1873, § 3782; Code 1882, § 3782; Civil Code 1895, § 5186; Penal Code 1895, § 1001; Civil Code 1910, § 5773; Penal Code 1910, § 1027; Code 1933, § 38-314.

§ 24-3-11. Ancient documents

Ancient documents purporting to be a part of the transaction to which they relate shall be admissible in evidence.

Formerly Code 1863, § 3702; Code 1868, § 3726; Code 1873, § 3779; Code 1882, § 3779; Civil Code 1895, § 5184; Civil Code 1910, § 5771; Code 1933, § 38-312.

§ 24-3-12. Pedigree, how proved

Pedigree, including descent, relationship, birth, marriage, and death, may be proved by the declarations of deceased persons related by blood or marriage, by general repute in the family, or by genealogies, inscriptions, "family trees," and similar evidence.

Formerly Code 1863, § 3695; Code 1868, § 3719; Code 1873, § 3772; Code 1882, § 3772; Civil Code 1895, § 5177; Civil Code 1910, § 5764; Code 1933, § 38-303.

§ 24-3-13. Ancient boundaries and landmarks

Traditional evidence as to ancient boundaries and landmarks shall be admissible in evidence, the weight to be determined by the jury according to the source from which it comes.

Formerly Code 1863, § 3703; Code 1868, § 3727; Code 1873, § 3780; Code 1882, § 3780; Civil Code 1895, § 5185; Civil Code 1910, § 5772; Code 1933, § 38-313.

§ 24-3-14. Writings, records, entries, and memoranda made in regular course of business

(a) As used in this Code section, the term "business" shall include every kind of business, profession, occupation, calling, or operation of institutions, whether carried on for profit or not.

(b) Any writing or record, whether in the form of an entry in a book or otherwise, made as a memorandum or record of any act, transaction, occurrence, or event shall be admissible in evidence in proof of the act, transaction, occurrence, or event, if the trial judge shall find that it was made in the regular course of any business and that it was the regular course of such business to make the memorandum or record at the time of the act, transaction, occurrence, or event or within a reasonable time thereafter.

(c) All other circumstances of the making of the writing or record, including lack of personal knowledge by the entrant or maker, may be shown to affect its weight; but they shall not affect its admissibility.

(d) This Code section shall be liberally interpreted and applied.

Laws 1952, p. 177, §§ 1, 2, 3.

§ 24-3-15. Definitions

The term "admissions" usually refers to civil cases. The term "confessions" usually refers to criminal cases.

Formerly Code 1863, § 3706; Code 1868, § 3730; Code 1873, § 3783; Code 1882, § 3783; Civil Code 1895, § 5187; Penal Code 1895, § 1002; Civil Code 1910, § 5774; Penal Code 1910, § 1028; Code 1933, § 38-401.

§ 24-3-16. Statements made by child under age of 14 years describing acts of sexual contact or physical abuse

A statement made by a child under the age of 14 years describing any act of sexual contact or physical abuse performed with or on the child by another or performed with or on another in the presence of the child is admissible in evidence by the testimony of the person or persons to whom made if the child is available to testify in the proceedings and the court finds that the circumstances of the statement provide sufficient indicia of reliability.

Laws 1986, p. 668, § 1; Laws 1995, p. 937, § 1.

Validity

This section has been held unconstitutional in the case of Woodard v. State, 1998, 269 Ga. 317, 496 S.E.2d 896.

§ 24-3-17. Copies of records of Department of Public Safety or comparable agencies in other states

(a) A certified copy of any record of the Department of Public Safety or the Department of Driver Services or comparable agency in any other state is admissible in any judicial proceedings or administrative hearing in the same manner as the original of the record.

(b) Any court may receive and use as evidence in any case information otherwise admissible from the records of the Department of Public Safety or the Department of Driver Services obtained from any terminal lawfully connected to the Georgia Crime Information Center without the need for additional certification of those records.

(c) Any court may receive and use as evidence for the purpose of imposing a sentence in any criminal case information otherwise admissible from the records of the Department of Driver Services obtained from a request made in accordance with a contract with the Georgia Technology Authority for immediate on-line electronic furnishing of information.

Laws 1988, p. 470, § 2; Laws 1989, p. 1080, § 1; Laws 2005, Act 68, § 10A-1, eff. July 1, 2005.

§ 24-3-18. Medical reports

(a) Upon the trial of any civil case involving injury or disease, any medical report in narrative form which has been signed and dated by an examining or treating licensed medical doctor, dentist, orthodontist, podiatrist, physical or occupational therapist, doctor of chiropractic, psychologist, advanced practice nurse, social worker, professional counselor, or marriage and family therapist shall be admissible and received in evidence insofar as it purports to represent the history, examination, diagnosis, treatment, prognosis, or interpretation of tests or examinations, including the basis therefor, by the person signing the report, the same as if that person were present at trial and testifying as a witness; provided, however, that such report and notice of intention to introduce such report must first be provided to the adverse party at least 60 days prior to trial. A statement of the qualifications of the person signing the report may be included as part of the basis for providing the information contained therein, and the opinion of the person signing the report with regard to the etiology of the injury or disease may be included as part of the diagnosis. Any adverse party may object to the admissibility of any portion of the report, other than on the ground that it is hearsay, within 15 days of being provided with the report. Further, any adverse party shall have the right to cross-examine the person signing the report and provide rebuttal testimony. The party tendering the report may also introduce testimony of the person signing the report for the purpose of supplementing the report or otherwise.

(b) The medical narrative shall be presented to the jury as depositions are presented to the jury and shall not go out with the jury as documentary evidence.

Laws 1997, p. 945, § 1.

Article 2

Admissions

§ 24-3-30. Admissions in pleadings, how far evidence

Without offering the same in evidence, either party may avail himself of allegations or admissions made in the pleadings of the other.

Formerly Civil Code 1895, § 5188; Civil Code 1910, § 5775; Code 1933, § 38-402.

§ 24-3-31. Admissions by parties to record

The admission by a party to the record shall be admissible in evidence when offered by the other side, except in the following cases:

(1) Admissions of a mere nominal party or naked trustee;

(2) Admissions of one of several parties with no joint interest, unless the issue is of such a character that the effect of the admission can be confined to the one party alone;

(3) Admissions of a trustee before he is clothed with the trust;

(4) Admissions of defendants in execution in claim cases, after the pendency of litigation.

Formerly Code 1863, § 3707; Code 1868, § 3731; Code 1873, § 3784; Code 1882, § 3784; Civil Code 1895, § 5189; Civil Code 1910, § 5776; Code 1933, § 38-403.

§ 24-3-32. Admissions by privies

Admissions by privies in blood, privies in estate, and privies in law shall be admissible as against the parties themselves. However, declarations by privies in estate after the title shall have passed out of them shall not be received.

Formerly Code 1863, § 3711; Code 1868, § 3735; Code 1873, § 3788; Code 1882, § 3788; Civil Code 1895, § 5193; Civil Code 1910, § 5780; Code 1933, § 38-407.

§ 24-3-33. Admissions by agents

Admissions by an agent or attorney in fact, during the existence and in pursuance of his agency, shall be admissible against the principal.

Formerly Code 1863, § 3710; Code 1868, § 3734; Code 1873, § 3787; Code 1882, § 3787; Civil Code 1895, § 5192; Civil Code 1910, § 5779; Code 1933, § 38-406.

§ 24-3-34. Admissions by real parties in interest, though not of record

Admissions by a real party in interest shall be admissible, even if he is not of record, subject to the exceptions stated in Code Section 24-3-31.

Formerly Code 1863, § 3708; Code 1868, § 3732; Code 1873, § 3785; Code 1882, § 3785; Civil Code 1895, § 5190; Civil Code 1910, § 5777; Code 1933, § 38-404.

§ 24-3-35. Admissions by strangers to suit

The following admissions by third persons, strangers to a suit, shall be received in evidence:

(1) Statements made when a party refers another to such third person for information;

(2) Admissions by a third person which are against his interest, as to a fact collateral to the main issue between the litigants but essential to the adjudication of the cause;

(3) Statements by an interpreter where from any cause he cannot be sworn.

Formerly Code 1863, § 3709; Code 1868, § 3733; Code 1873, § 3786; Code 1882, § 3786; Civil Code 1895, § 5191; Civil Code 1910, § 5778; Code 1933, § 38-405.

§ 24-3-36. Effect of acquiescence or silence

Acquiescence or silence, when the circumstances require an answer, a denial, or other conduct, may amount to an admission.

Formerly Code 1863, § 3713; Code 1868, § 3737; Code 1873, § 3790; Code 1882, § 3790; Civil Code 1895, § 5195; Penal Code 1895, § 1003; Civil Code 1910, § 5782; Penal Code 1910, § 1029; Code 1933, § 38-409.

§ 24-3-37. Admissions improperly obtained or made with view to compromise

Admissions obtained by constraint, by fraud, or by drunkenness induced for the purpose or admissions or propositions made with a view to a compromise are not proper evidence.

Formerly Code 1863, § 3712; Code 1868, § 3736; Code 1873, § 3789; Code 1882, § 3789; Civil Code 1895, § 5194; Civil Code 1910, § 5781; Code 1933, § 38-408.

§ 24-3-37.1. Statements or activities constituting offers of assistance or expressions of regret, mistake, etc.; not admission of liability

(a) The General Assembly finds that conduct, statements, or activity constituting voluntary offers of assistance or expressions of benevolence, regret, mistake, error, sympathy, or apology between or among parties or potential parties to a civil action should be encouraged and should not be considered an admission of liability. The General Assembly further finds that such conduct, statements, or activity should be particularly encouraged between health care providers and patients experiencing an unanticipated outcome resulting from their medical care. Regulatory and accreditation agencies are in some instances requiring health care providers to discuss the outcomes of their medical care and treatment with their patients, including unanticipated outcomes, and studies have shown such discussions foster improved communications and respect between provider and patient, promote quicker recovery by the patient, and reduce the incidence of claims and lawsuits arising out of such unanticipated outcomes. The General Assembly therefore concludes certain steps should be taken to promote such conduct, statements, or activity by limiting their admissibility in civil actions.

(b) As used in this Code section, the term:

(1) "Health care provider" means any person licensed under Chapter 9, 10A, 11, 11A, 26, 28, 30, 33, 34, 35, 39, or 44 of Title 43 or any hospital, nursing home, home health agency, institution, or medical facility licensed or defined under Chapter 7 of Title 31. The term shall also include any corporation, professional corporation, partnership, limited liability company, limited liability partnership, authority,

or other entity comprised of such health care providers.

(2) "Unanticipated outcome" means the outcome of a medical treatment or procedure, whether or not resulting from an intentional act, that differs from an expected or intended result of such medical treatment or procedure.

(c) In any claim or civil action brought by or on behalf of a patient allegedly experiencing an unanticipated outcome of medical care, any and all statements, affirmations, gestures, activities, or conduct expressing benevolence, regret, apology, sympathy, commiseration, condolence, compassion, mistake, error, or a general sense of benevolence which are made by a health care provider or an employee or agent of a health care provider to the patient, a relative of the patient, or a representative of the patient and which relate to the unanticipated outcome shall be inadmissible as evidence and shall not constitute an admission of liability or an admission against interest.

Laws 2005, Act 1, § 6, eff. Feb. 16, 2005; Laws 2006, Act 453, § 24, eff. April 14, 2006.

§ 24-3-38. Entire conversation admissible when admission given in evidence

When an admission is given in evidence by one party, it shall be the right of the other party to have the whole admission and all the conversation connected therewith admitted into evidence.

Formerly Code 1863, § 3714; Code 1868, § 3738; Code 1873, § 3791; Code 1882, § 3791; Civil Code 1895, § 5196; Penal Code 1895, § 1004; Civil Code 1910, § 5783; Penal Code 1910, § 1030; Code 1933, § 38-410.

Article 3

Confessions

§ 24-3-50. Confessions must be voluntary

To make a confession admissible, it must have been made voluntarily, without being induced by another by the slightest hope of benefit or remotest fear of injury.

Formerly Code 1863, § 3716; Code 1868, § 3740; Code 1873, § 3793; Code 1882, § 3793; Penal Code 1895, § 1006; Penal Code 1910, § 1032; Code 1933, § 38-411.

§ 24-3-51. Confessions under spiritual exhortation or promise of secrecy or collateral benefit

The fact that a confession has been made under a spiritual exhortation, a promise of secrecy, or a promise of collateral benefit shall not exclude it.

Formerly Code 1863, § 3717; Code 1868, § 3741; Code 1873, § 3794; Code 1882, § 3794; Penal Code 1895, § 1007; Penal Code 1910, § 1033; Code 1933, § 38-412.

§ 24-3-52. Confession by joint offender or conspirator

The confession of one joint offender or conspirator made after the enterprise is ended shall be admissible only against himself.

Formerly Code 1863, § 3719; Code 1868, § 3743; Code 1873, § 3796; Code 1882, § 3796; Penal Code 1895, § 1009; Penal Code 1910, § 1035; Code 1933, § 38-414.

§ 24-3-53. Weight of admissions or confessions

All admissions shall be scanned with care, and confessions of guilt shall be received with great caution. A confession alone, uncorroborated by any other evidence, shall not justify a conviction.

Formerly Code 1863, § 3715; Code 1868, § 3739; Code 1873, § 3792; Code 1882, § 3792; Civil Code 1895, § 5197; Penal Code 1895, § 1005; Civil Code 1910, § 5784; Penal Code 1910, § 1031; Code 1933, § 38-420.

CHAPTER 4

PROOF GENERALLY

Article 1

General Provisions

§ 24-4-1. Burden of proof

The burden of proof generally lies upon the party who is asserting or affirming a fact and to the existence of whose case or defense the proof of such fact is essential. If a negation or negative affirmation is essential to a party's case or defense, the proof of such negation or negative affirmation lies on the party so affirming it.

Formerly Code 1863, § 3681; Code 1868, § 3705; Code 1873, § 3758; Code 1882, § 3758; Civil Code 1895, § 5160;

Penal Code 1895, § 994; Civil Code 1910, § 5746; Penal Code 1910, § 1020; Code 1933, § 38–103.

§ 24–4–2. Changing burden of proof

What amount of evidence will change the onus or burden of proof is a question to be decided in each case by the sound discretion of the court.

Formerly Code 1863, § 3682; Code 1868, § 3706; Code 1873, § 3759; Code 1882, § 3759; Civil Code 1895, § 5161; Penal Code 1895, § 995; Civil Code 1910, § 5747; Penal Code 1910, § 1021; Code 1933, § 38–104.

§ 24–4–3. Amount of mental conviction; preponderance of evidence

Moral and reasonable certainty is all that can be expected in legal investigation. In all civil cases a preponderance of evidence is considered sufficient to produce mental conviction. In criminal cases a greater strength of mental conviction is held necessary to justify a verdict of guilty.

Formerly Code 1863, § 3672; Code 1868, § 3696; Code 1873, § 3749; Code 1882, § 3749; Civil Code 1895, § 5144; Penal Code 1895, § 986; Civil Code 1910, § 5730; Penal Code 1910, § 1012; Code 1933, § 38–105.

§ 24–4–4. Determination of where preponderance of evidence lies

In determining where the preponderance of evidence lies, the jury may consider all the facts and circumstances of the case, the witnesses' manner of testifying, their intelligence, their means and opportunity for knowing the facts to which they testified, the nature of the facts to which they testified, the probability or improbability of their testimony, their interest or want of interest, and their personal credibility so far as the same may legitimately appear from the trial. The jury may also consider the number of the witnesses, though the preponderance is not necessarily with the greater number.

Formerly Civil Code 1895, § 5146; Civil Code 1910, § 5732; Code 1933, § 38–107.

§ 24–4–5. When evidence warrants conviction; reasonable doubt

Whether dependent upon direct or circumstantial evidence, the true question in criminal cases is not whether it is possible that the conclusion at which the evidence points may be false, but whether there is sufficient evidence to satisfy the mind and conscience beyond a reasonable doubt.

Formerly Penal Code 1895, § 987; Penal Code 1910, § 1013; Code 1933, § 38–110.

§ 24–4–6. Circumstantial evidence, when sufficient in criminal prosecution

To warrant a conviction on circumstantial evidence, the proved facts shall not only be consistent with the hypothesis of guilt, but shall exclude every other reasonable hypothesis save that of the guilt of the accused.

Formerly Penal Code 1895, § 984; Penal Code 1910, § 1010; Code 1933, § 38–109.

§ 24–4–7. Positive and negative testimony

The existence of a fact testified to by one positive witness is to be believed, rather than that such fact did not exist because many other witnesses who had the same opportunity of observation swear that they did not see or know of its having existed. This rule shall not apply when two parties have equal facilities for seeing or hearing a thing and one swears that it occurred while the other swears that it did not.

Formerly Civil Code 1895, § 5165; Penal Code 1895, § 985; Civil Code 1910, § 5751; Penal Code 1910, § 1011; Code 1933, § 38–111.

§ 24–4–8. Number of witnesses necessary

The testimony of a single witness is generally sufficient to establish a fact. However, in certain cases, including prosecutions for treason, prosecutions for perjury, and felony cases where the only witness is an accomplice, the testimony of a single witness is not sufficient. Nevertheless, corroborating circumstances may dispense with the necessity for the testimony of a second witness, except in prosecutions for treason.

Formerly Code 1863, § 3678; Code 1868, § 3702; Code 1873, § 3755; Code 1882, § 3755; Civil Code 1895, § 5156; Penal Code 1895, § 991; Civil Code 1910, § 5742; Penal Code 1910, § 1017; Code 1933, § 38–121.

§ 24–4–9. Inference of existence of certain facts

In arriving at a verdict, the jury, from facts proved, and sometimes from the absence of counter evidence, may infer the existence of other facts reasonably and logically consequent on those proved.

Formerly Civil Code 1895, § 5157; Civil Code 1910, § 5743; Code 1933, § 38–123.

Article 2

Presumptions and Estoppel

§ 24–4–20. Presumptions of law and fact

Presumptions are either of law or of fact. Presumptions of law are conclusions and inferences which the law draws from given facts. Presumptions of fact are exclusively questions for the jury, to be decided by the ordinary test of human experience.

Formerly Code 1863, § 3675; Code 1868, § 3699; Code 1873, § 3752; Code 1882, § 3752; Civil Code 1895, § 5149; Penal Code 1895, § 988; Civil Code 1910, § 5735; Penal Code 1910, § 1014; Code 1933, § 38–113.

§ 24–4–21. Prima facie presumptions

Certain presumptions of law, such as the presumption of innocence, in some cases the presumption of guilt, the presumption of continuance of life for seven years, the presumption of a mental state once proved to exist, and all similar presumptions, may be rebutted by proof.

Formerly Code 1863, § 3677; Code 1868, § 3701; Code 1873, § 3754; Code 1882, § 3754; Civil Code 1895, § 5154; Penal Code 1895, § 990; Civil Code 1910, § 5740; Penal Code 1910, § 1016; Code 1933, § 38–118.

§ 24–4–22. Presumption arising from failure to produce evidence

If a party has evidence in his power and within his reach by which he may repel a claim or charge against him but omits to produce it, or if he has more certain and satisfactory evidence in his power but relies on that which is of a weaker and inferior nature, a presumption arises that the charge or claim against him is well founded; but this presumption may be rebutted.

Formerly Civil Code 1895, § 5163; Penal Code 1895, § 989; Civil Code 1910, § 5749; Penal Code 1910, § 1015; Code 1933, § 38–119.

§ 24–4–23. Presumption arising from failure to answer letter

In the ordinary course of business, when good faith requires an answer, it is the duty of the party receiving a letter from another to answer within a reasonable time. Otherwise he is presumed to admit the propriety of the acts mentioned in the letter of his correspondent and to adopt them.

Formerly Civil Code 1895, § 5155; Civil Code 1910, § 5741; Code 1933, § 38–120.

§ 24–4–23.1. Presumption of payment of check

(a) As used in this Code section:

(1) "Bank" means any person engaged in the business of banking and includes, in addition to a commercial bank, a savings and loan association, savings bank, or credit union; and

(2) "Check" means a draft, other than a documentary draft, payable on demand and drawn on a bank, even though it is described by another term, such as "share draft" or "negotiable order of withdrawal."

(b) In any dispute concerning payment by means of a check, a copy of the check produced in accordance with Code Section 24–5–26, together with the original bank statement that reflects payment of the check by the bank on which it was drawn or a copy thereof produced in the same manner, creates a presumption that the check has been paid.

Laws 1996, p. 1306, § 16.

§ 24–4–24. Estoppels

(a) Conclusive presumptions of law are termed estoppels; averments to the contrary of such presumptions shall not be allowed. Estoppels are not generally favored.

(b) Estoppels include presumptions in favor of:

(1) A record or judgment unreversed;

(2) The proper conduct of courts and judicial officers acting within their legitimate spheres;

(3) The proper conduct of other officers of the law after the lapse of time has rendered it dangerous to open the investigation of their acts in regard to mere formalities of the law;

(4) Ancient deeds and other instruments more than 30 years old, when they come from proper custody and possession has been held in accordance with them;

(5) Recitals in deeds, except payment of purchase money, as against a grantor, sui juris, acting in his own right, and his privies in estate, blood, and in law;

(6) A landlord's title as against his tenant in possession;

(7) Solemn admissions made in judicio;

(8) Admissions upon which other parties have acted, either to their own injury or to the benefit of the persons making the admissions.

Estoppels also include all similar cases where it would be more unjust and productive of evil to hear the truth than to forbear investigation.

Formerly Code 1863, § 3676; Code 1868, § 3700; Code 1873, § 3753; Code 1882, § 3753; Civil Code 1895, § 5150; Civil Code 1910, § 5736; Code 1933, § 38-114.

§ 24-4-25. Estoppel as to title to real estate

(a) Where an estoppel relates to the title to real estate, the party claiming to have been influenced by the other party's acts or declarations must not only have been ignorant of the true title, but also ignorant of any convenient means of acquiring such knowledge.

(b) Where both parties have equal knowledge or equal means of obtaining the truth, there shall be no estoppel.

Formerly Civil Code 1895, § 5151; Civil Code 1910, § 5737; Code 1933, § 38-115.

§ 24-4-26. Trustees estopped to claim title adverse to estate

Trustees and other representatives with custody of papers have ample opportunities to discover defects in the title of property in their care and are estopped from setting up title adverse to their trust.

Formerly Civil Code 1895, § 5153; Civil Code 1910, § 5739; Code 1933, § 38-117.

§ 24-4-27. Equitable estoppel

In order for an equitable estoppel to arise, there must generally be some intended deception in the conduct or declarations of the party to be estopped, or such gross negligence as to amount to constructive fraud, by which another has been misled to his injury.

Formerly Civil Code 1895, § 5152; Civil Code 1910, § 5738; Code 1933, § 38-116.

Article 3

Particular Matters of Proof

§ 24-4-40. Proof of identity

(a) Concordance of name alone is some evidence of identity. Residence, vocation, ownership of property, and other like facts may be proved. Reasonable certainty is all that can be required.

(b) In civil actions parties are generally relieved from the onus of proving identity, as it is a fact generally more easily disproved than established.

Formerly Civil Code 1895, § 5178; Civil Code 1910, § 5765; Code 1933, § 38-304.

§ 24-4-41. Officer de facto, proving

An officer de facto may be proved to be such by his acts, without the production of his commission or appointment.

Formerly Code 1863, § 3687; Code 1868, § 3711; Code 1873, § 3764; Code 1882, § 3764; Civil Code 1895, § 5168; Civil Code 1910, § 5754; Code 1933, § 38-207.

§ 24-4-42. Admissibility and effect of judgment as evidence

A judgment shall be admissible between any parties to show the fact of the rendition thereof; between parties and privies it is conclusive as to the matter directly in issue, until reversed or set aside.

Formerly Code 1863, § 3749; Code 1868, § 3773; Code 1873, § 3826; Code 1882, § 3826; Civil Code 1895, § 5233; Civil Code 1910, § 5820; Code 1933, § 38-623.

§ 24-4-43. Stern's United States and Stafford's office calendars

Stern's United States calendar and Stafford's office calendar shall be admissible in proof of dates for the space of time covered by them respectively without further proof.

Laws 1882-83, p. 135, § 1; Laws 1897, p. 87, § 1.

Formerly Civil Code 1895, § 5169; Civil Code 1910, § 5755; Code 1933, § 38-208.

§ 24-4-44. American Experience Mortality Tables admissible to show life expectancy

In all civil cases where the life expectancy of a person shall be an issue, the American Experience Mortality Tables shall be admissible as evidence of the life expectancy of such person.

Laws 1956, p. 68, § 1.

§ 24-4-45. The Commissioners 1958 Standard Ordinary Mortality Tables and Annuity Mortality Table for 1949, Ultimate admissible in actions involving wrongful death or permanent personal injury

(a) In addition to any other lawful methods of computing the value of the life of a decedent in wrongful death cases or of determining the present value of future due earnings or amounts in cases involving permanent personal injuries, there shall be admissible in evidence, as competent evidence in such cases, either or both of the following mortality tables:

(1) The Commissioners 1958 Standard Ordinary Mortality Table;

(2) Annuity Mortality Table for 1949, Ultimate.

(b) In addition to the provisions set out in subsection (a) of this Code section, the jury or court shall be authorized in cases of wrongful death or permanent personal injuries to use any table determined by the jury or court, whichever is the trier of fact, to be accurate in showing the value of annuities on single lives according to the mortality tables listed in subsection (a) of this Code section.

(c) The admissible evidence provided for in subsections (a) and (b) of this Code section shall not be the exclusive method which the jury or court hereafter is required to use in such cases but shall be supplementary to other lawful and allowable evidence and method for such purpose otherwise obtaining in this state.

Laws 1970, p. 168, §§ 1, 3, 4; Laws 1995, p. 10, § 24.

§ 24-4-46. United States Department of Agriculture inspection certificates as prima facie evidence

All inspection certificates issued by the United States Department of Agriculture over the signature of any inspector thereof which are admissible in courts of the United States as prima-facie evidence of the truth of the statements therein contained shall be admissible in all courts of the State of Georgia as prima-facie evidence of the truth of the statements therein contained.

Laws 1939, p. 315, § 1.

§ 24-4-47. Written findings evidence of facts stated

(a) A written finding of presumed death made by officers or employees of the United States authorized to make such findings pursuant to any law of the United States or a duly certified copy of such finding shall be received in any court, office, or other place in this state as evidence of the death of the person therein found to be dead, and the date, circumstances, and place of his disappearance.

(b) An official written report, record, or duly certified copy thereof, that a person is missing, missing in action, interned in a neutral country, beleaguered, besieged, or captured by an enemy, dead, or alive, made by an officer or employee of the United States authorized by any law of the United States to make the same shall be received in any court, office, or other place in this state, as evidence that such person is missing, missing in action, interned in a neutral country, beleaguered, besieged, or captured by an enemy, dead, or alive, as the case may be.

(c) For the purposes of subsections (a) and (b) of this Code section, any finding, report, record, or duly certified copy thereof, purporting to have been signed by an officer or employee of the United States as is described in this Code section shall prima facie be deemed to have been signed and issued by such an officer or employee pursuant to law, and the person signing same shall prima facie be deemed to have acted within the scope of his authority. If a copy purports to have been certified by a person authorized by law to certify the same, such certified copy shall be prima-facie evidence of his authority so to certify.

Laws 1945, p. 417, §§ 1-3.

§ 24-4-48. Admissibility of photographs, motion pictures, videotapes, and audio recordings when necessitated by unavailability of witness

(a) For purposes of this Code section, "unavailability of a witness" includes situations in which the authenticating witness:

(1) Is exempted by ruling of the court on the ground of privilege from testifying concerning the subject matter of the authentication;

(2) Persists in refusing to testify concerning the subject matter of the authentication despite an order of the court to do so;

(3) Testifies to a lack of memory of the subject matter of the authentication;

(4) Is unable to be present or to testify at the hearing because of death or then existing physical or mental illness or infirmity; or

(5) Is absent from the hearing and the proponent of the authentication has been unable to procure the attendance of the authenticating witness by process or other reasonable means.

An authenticating witness is not unavailable as a witness if his or her exemption, refusal, claim of lack of memory, inability, or absence is due to the procurement or wrongdoing of the proponent of an authentication for the purpose of preventing the witness from attending or testifying.

(b) Subject to any other valid objection, photographs, motion pictures, videotapes, and audio recordings shall be admissible in evidence when necessitated by the unavailability of a witness who can provide personal authentication and when the court determines, based on competent evidence presented to the court, that such items tend to show reliably the fact or facts for which the items are offered.

(c) Subject to any other valid objection, photographs, motion pictures, videotapes, and audio recordings produced at a time when the device producing the items was not being operated by an individual person or was not under the personal control or in the presence of an individual operator shall be admissible in evidence when the court determines, based on competent evidence presented to the court, that such items tend to show reliably the fact or facts for which the items are offered, provided that prior to the admission of such evidence the date and time of such photograph, motion picture, or videotape recording shall be contained on such evidence and such date and time shall be shown to have been made contemporaneously with the events depicted in the photograph, videotape, or motion picture.

(d) This Code section shall not be the exclusive method of introduction into evidence of photographs, motion pictures, videotapes, and audio recordings but shall be supplementary to any other statutes and lawful methods existing in this state.

Laws 1996, p. 443, § 1; Laws 1997, p. 143, § 24.

Article 4

DNA Analysis upon Conviction of Certain Sex Offenses

§ 24–4–60. Samples required; storage in DNA data bank

(a) As used in this Code section, the term "state correctional facility" means a penal institution under the jurisdiction of the Department of Corrections, including inmate work camps and inmate boot camps; provided, however, that such term shall not include a probation detention center, probation diversion center, or probation boot camp under the jurisdiction of the Department of Corrections.

(b) Any person convicted of a criminal offense defined in Code Section 16–6–1, relating to the offense of rape; Code Section 16–6–2, relating to the offense of sodomy or aggravated sodomy; Code Section 16–6–3, relating to the offense of statutory rape; Code Section 16–6–4, relating to the offense of child molestation or aggravated child molestation; Code Section 16–6–5, relating to the offense of enticing a child for indecent purposes; Code Section 16–6–5.1, relating to the offense of sexual assault against persons in custody, sexual assault against a person detained or a patient in a hospital or other institution, or sexual assault by a practitioner of psychotherapy against a patient; Code Section 16–6–6, relating to the offense of bestiality; Code Section 16–6–7, relating to the offense of necrophilia; or Code Section 16–6–22, relating to the offense of incest, shall have a sample of his or her blood, an oral swab, or a sample obtained from a noninvasive procedure taken for DNA (deoxyribonucleic acid) analysis to determine identification characteristics specific to the person. In addition, on and after July 1, 2000, any person convicted of a felony and incarcerated in a state correctional facility shall at the time of entering the prison system have a sample of his or her blood, an oral swab, or a sample obtained from a noninvasive procedure taken for DNA (deoxyribonucleic acid) analysis to determine identification characteristics specific to the person. The provisions and requirements of this Code section shall also apply to any person who has been convicted of a felony prior to July 1, 2000, and who currently is incarcerated in a state correctional facility in this state for such offense. The provisions and requirements of this Code section shall also apply to any person who has been convicted of a felony in this state on or after July 1, 2000, and who is incarcerated in a private correctional facility in this state for such offense pursuant to a contract with the Department of Corrections upon entering the facility, and for any person convicted of a felony prior to July 1, 2000, and who is incarcerated in a private correctional facility in this state pursuant to contract with the Department of Corrections. The analysis shall be performed by the Division of Forensic Sciences of the Georgia Bureau of Investigation. The division shall be authorized to contract with individuals or organizations for services to perform such analysis. The identification characteristics of the profile resulting from the DNA analysis shall be stored and maintained by the bureau in a DNA data bank and shall be made available only as provided in Code Section 24–4–63.

Laws 1992, p. 2034, § 1; Laws 2000, p. 1075, § 1; Laws 2004, Act 523, § 1, eff. July 1, 2004; Laws 2005, Act 19, § 24, eff. April 7, 2005.

§ 24–4–61. Time and procedures for withdrawal of samples

(a) Each sample required pursuant to Code Section 24–4–60 from persons who are to be incarcerated shall be withdrawn within the first 30 days of incarceration at the receiving unit or at such other place as is designated by the Department of Corrections. Each sample required pursuant to Code Section 24–4–60 from persons who are to be released from a state correctional facility or private correctional facility shall be withdrawn within the 12 months preceding such person's release at a place designated by the Department of Corrections. The required samples from persons who are not sentenced to a term of confinement shall be withdrawn as a condition of probation. The Division of Forensic Sciences of the Georgia Bureau of Investigation shall publish in its quality manuals the procedures for the collection and transfer of samples to such division pursuant to Code Section 35–3–154. Personnel at a Department of Corrections facility shall implement the provisions of this

Code section as part of the regular processing of offenders.

(b) Samples collected by oral swab or by a noninvasive procedure may be collected by any individual who has been trained in the procedure. Only a correctional health nurse technician, physician, registered professional nurse, licensed practical nurse, graduate laboratory technician, or phlebotomist shall withdraw any sample of blood to be submitted for analysis. No civil liability shall attach to any person authorized to take a sample as provided in this article as a result of the act of taking a sample from any person submitting thereto, provided the sample was taken according to recognized medically accepted procedures. However, no person shall be relieved from liability for negligence in the withdrawing of any blood sample.

(c) Chemically clean sterile disposable needles shall be used for the withdrawal of all samples of blood. The containers for blood samples, oral swabs, and the samples obtained by noninvasive procedures shall be sealed and labeled with the subject's name, social security number, date of birth, race, and gender plus the name of the person collecting the sample and the date and place of collection. The containers shall be secured to prevent tampering with the contents. The steps set forth in this subsection relating to the taking, handling, identification, and disposition of samples are procedural and not substantive. Substantial compliance therewith shall be deemed to be sufficient. The samples shall be transported to the Division of Forensic Sciences of the Georgia Bureau of Investigation not more than 15 days following withdrawal and shall be analyzed and stored in the DNA data bank in accordance with Code Sections 24-4-62 and 24-4-63.

Laws 1992, p. 2034, § 1; Laws 2000, p. 1075, § 2.

§ 24-4-62. Procedures for conducting DNA analysis of samples

Whether or not the results of an analysis are to be included in the data bank, the bureau shall conduct the DNA analysis in accordance with procedures adopted by the bureau to determine identification characteristics specific to the individual whose sample is being analyzed. The director of the Georgia Bureau of Investigation or his or her designated representative shall complete and maintain on file a form indicating the name of the person whose sample is to be analyzed, the date and by whom the sample was received and examined, and a statement that the seal on the container containing the sample had not been broken or otherwise tampered with. The remainder of a sample submitted for analysis and inclusion in the data bank pursuant to Code Section 24-4-60 may be divided, if possible, labeled as provided for the original sample, and securely stored by the bureau in accordance with specific procedures of the bureau to ensure the integrity and confidentiality of the samples. All or part of the remainder of that sample may be used only to create a statistical data base provided no identifying information on the individual whose sample is being analyzed is included or for retesting by the bureau to validate or update the original analysis. A report of the results of a DNA analysis conducted by the bureau as authorized, including the identifying information, shall be made and maintained at the bureau. Except as specifically provided in this Code section and Code Section 24-4-63, the results of the analysis shall be securely stored and shall remain confidential.

Laws 1992, p. 2034, § 1; Laws 2000, p. 1075, § 3.

§ 24-4-63. Procedures governing dissemination of information

(a) It shall be the duty of the bureau to receive samples and to analyze, classify, and file the results of DNA identification characteristics of samples submitted pursuant to Code Section 24-4-60 and to make such information available as provided in this Code section. The results of an analysis and comparison of the identification of the characteristics from two or more biological samples shall be made available directly to federal, state, and local law enforcement officers upon a request made in furtherance of an official investigation of any criminal offense. A request may be made by personal contact, mail, or electronic means. The name of the requestor and the purpose for which the information is requested shall be maintained on file with the bureau.

(b) (1) Upon his or her request, a copy of the request for search shall be furnished to any person identified and charged with an offense as the result of a search of information in the data bank. Only when a sample or DNA profile supplied by the requestor satisfactorily matches the requestor's profile in the data bank shall the existence of data in the data bank be confirmed or identifying information from the data bank be disseminated.

(2) The name of the convicted offender whose profile is contained in the data bank may be related to any other data bases which are constructed for law enforcement purposes and may be disseminated only for law enforcement purposes.

(3) Upon a showing by the defendant in a criminal case that access to the DNA data bank is material to the investigation, preparation, or presentation of a defense at trial or in a motion for a new trial, a superior court having proper jurisdiction over such criminal case shall direct the bureau to compare a DNA profile which has been generated by the defendant through an independent test against the data bank, provided that such DNA profile has been generated in accordance with standards for forensic DNA analysis adopted pursuant to 42 U.S.C. Section 14131, as amended.

(c) The bureau shall develop procedures governing the methods of obtaining information from the data bank in accordance with this Code section and procedures for verification of the identity and authority of the requestor. The bureau shall specify the positions in that agency which require regular access to the data bank and samples submitted as a necessary function of the job.

(d) The bureau may create a separate statistical data base comprised of DNA profiles of samples of persons whose identity is unknown. Nothing in this Code section or Code Section 24-4-64 shall prohibit the bureau from sharing or otherwise disseminating the information in the statistical data base with law enforcement or criminal justice agencies within or outside the state.

(e) The bureau may charge a reasonable fee to search and provide a comparative analysis of DNA profiles in the data bank to any authorized law enforcement agency outside of the state.

Laws 1992, p. 2034, § 1; Laws 2000, p. 1075, § 4.

§ 24-4-64. Penalties for unauthorized use of information

(a) Any person who, without authority, disseminates information contained in the data bank shall be guilty of a misdemeanor. Any person who disseminates, receives, or otherwise uses or attempts to so use information in the data bank, knowing that such dissemination, receipt, or use is for a purpose other than as authorized by law, shall be guilty of a misdemeanor of a high and aggravated nature.

(b) Except as authorized by law, any person who, for purposes of having DNA analysis performed, obtains or attempts to obtain any sample submitted to the Division of Forensic Sciences for analysis shall be guilty of a felony.

Laws 1992, p. 2034, § 1.

§ 24-4-65. Expungement of records

A person whose DNA profile has been included in the data bank pursuant to this article may request that it be expunged on the grounds that the conviction on which the authority for including his or her DNA profile was based has been reversed and the case dismissed. The bureau shall purge all records and identifiable information in the data bank pertaining to the person and destroy all samples from the person upon receipt of a written request that such data be expunged, pursuant to this Code section, and a certified copy of the court order reversing and dismissing the conviction.

Laws 1992, p. 2034, § 1; Laws 2000, p. 1075, § 5.

CHAPTER 5

BEST EVIDENCE RULE

Article 1

General Provisions

§ 24-5-1. Primary and secondary evidence defined

(a) Primary evidence is such as in itself does not indicate the existence of other and better proof.

(b) Secondary evidence is such as from necessity in some cases is substituted for stronger and better proof.

Formerly Code 1863, § 3684; Code 1868, § 3708; Code 1873, § 3761; Code 1882, § 3761; Civil Code 1895, § 5164; Civil Code 1910, § 5750; Code 1933, § 38-204.

§ 24-5-2. Secondary evidence admitted when

In order to admit secondary evidence, it shall appear that the primary evidence for some sufficient cause is not accessible to the diligence of the party. This showing shall be made to the court, who shall hear the party himself on the question of diligence and the inaccessibility of the primary evidence.

Formerly Code 1863, § 3690; Code 1868, § 3714; Code 1873, § 3767; Code 1882, § 3767; Civil Code 1895, § 5172; Civil Code 1910, § 5759; Code 1933, § 38-212.

§ 24-5-3. Exceptions to general rule

Cases of necessity or manifest convenience, resting on principles of reason and justice, may be made exceptions to the general rule requiring the production of primary evidence.

Formerly Code 1863, § 3689; Code 1868, § 3713; Code 1873, § 3766; Code 1882, § 3766; Civil Code 1895, § 5171; Civil Code 1910, § 5758; Code 1933, § 38-211.

§ 24–5–4. Best evidence, necessity of producing; written evidence as best evidence

(a) The best evidence which exists of a writing sought to be proved shall be produced, unless its absence shall be satisfactorily accounted for.

(b) Written evidence of a writing is considered of higher proof than oral evidence. In all cases where the parties have reduced their contract, agreement, or stipulation to writing and have assented thereto, such writing is the best evidence of the same.

Formerly Code 1863, §§ 3683, 3685; Code 1868, §§ 3707, 3709; Code 1873, §§ 3760, 3762; Code 1882, §§ 3760, 3762; Civil Code 1895, §§ 5162, 5166; Civil Code 1910, §§ 5748, 5752; Code 1933, §§ 38–203, 38–205.

§ 24–5–5. Degrees in secondary evidence

There are degrees in secondary evidence. The best secondary evidence should always be produced. A duplicate is better than a copy and an examined copy is better than oral evidence.

Formerly Code 1863, § 3691; Code 1868, § 3715; Code 1873, § 3768; Code 1882, § 3768; Civil Code 1895, § 5173; Civil Code 1910, § 5760; Code 1933, § 38–213.

Article 2

Copies of Writings

§ 24–5–20. Exemplifications primary evidence, when; facsimile transmissions

(a) Exemplifications made by public officers of records, documents, papers, or other matters in their respective offices, pursuant to Code Sections 24–7–20 and 24–7–21 or in the manner set out in subsection (b) of this Code section, shall be primary evidence as to all records or other things required by law to remain in such offices, but only secondary evidence as to such documents as by law properly remain in the possession of the party.

(b) As an alternative to an exemplification made by any public officer of the records, documents, papers, or other matters in the office of such public officer in accordance with Code Sections 24–7–20 and 24–7–21, an exemplification transmitted by facsimile or a copy of an exemplification transmitted by facsimile is admissible if:

(1) The certification by the public officer includes a statement that the certified document is being transmitted by facsimile and the telephone number and location of the facsimile machine transmitting the facsimile; and

(2) Each page of the document shows the telephone number of the transmitting facsimile machine to be identical to the telephone number shown as a part of the certification by the public officer.

This subsection shall not be construed to require public officers to obtain or maintain facsimile equipment. Public officers are authorized to collect the usual cost of providing exemplifications as provided by law and a reasonable fee for the cost of telephone facsimile transmission. Public officers are authorized to maintain a record of facsimile exemplifications, which may but is not required to include the retention of the exemplification as transmitted by facsimile.

Laws 1993, p. 1078, § 1.

Formerly Code 1863, § 3740; Code 1868, § 3764; Code 1873, § 3817; Code 1882, § 3817; Civil Code 1895, § 5212; Civil Code 1910, § 5799; Code 1933, § 38–602.

§ 24–5–21. Proof in case of loss; diligence

If a paper shall have been lost or destroyed, proof of the fact to the court shall admit secondary evidence. The question of diligence is one for the sound discretion of the court.

Formerly Code 1863, § 3755; Code 1868, § 3779; Code 1873, § 3832; Code 1882, § 3832; Civil Code 1895, § 5240; Civil Code 1910, § 5829; Code 1933, § 38–702.

§ 24–5–22. Certified copy of lost or destroyed paper

(a) If the properly registered original of any paper is lost or destroyed, a certified copy from the registry shall be deemed good secondary evidence.

(b) The official entry of the proper officer on a paper shall be sufficient evidence of its registry.

Formerly Code 1863, §§ 3742, 3743; Code 1868, §§ 3766, 3767; Code 1873, §§ 3819, 3820; Code 1882, §§ 3819, 3820; Civil Code 1895, §§ 5218, 5219; Civil Code 1910, §§ 5805, 5806; Code 1933, §§ 38–608, 38–609.

§ 24–5–23. Proof of destroyed records; presumption of proper probate

(a) When a record has been burned or otherwise destroyed, its contents may be proved by secondary evidence which does not disclose the existence of other and better evidence.

(b) If the registry has also been destroyed before a copy of an original paper has been made and certified, any secondary evidence shall be admissible to prove the original and its registry which does not disclose the existence of other and better evidence.

(c) If the original is found to have been recorded and it does not appear whether it was done on proper probate, the court shall presume, until the contrary appears, that the same was done on proper probate.

Laws 1855–56, p. 138, § 2; Laws 1858, p. 53, § 1.

Formerly Code 1863, §§ 3741, 3744, 3745; Code 1868, §§ 3765, 3768, 3769; Code 1873, §§ 3818, 3821, 3822; Code 1882, §§ 3818, 3821, 3822; Civil Code 1895, §§ 5217, 5220, 5221; Civil Code 1910, §§ 5804, 5807, 5808; Code 1933, §§ 38-607, 38-610, 38-611.

§ 24-5-24. Paper rerecorded, when; second record admissible in evidence, when

(a) Whenever the book containing the record of any deed, will, execution, or other paper, the record of which is provided for by law, is destroyed or lost, or when the record of such paper shall have been incorrectly made or destroyed, the person whose duty it is to record the paper shall, upon receiving the fees provided for such cases, record the paper together with the certificate or certificates of former record thereof.

(b) In case of the loss or inaccessibility of such original paper, such records, or certified copies thereof, shall be admitted as evidence in all cases where the original record, if had, would be admissible.

Laws 1882–83, p. 96, §§ 1, 2.

Formerly Civil Code 1895, §§ 5229, 5230; Civil Code 1910, §§ 5816, 5817; Code 1933, §§ 38-620, 38-621.

§ 24-5-25. Proof of existence of original as essential to admission of copy

The existence of a genuine original is essential to the admissibility of a copy. The amount of evidence to show such existence must vary with the circumstances of each case. Where no direct issue is made upon the fact, slight evidence shall be sufficient.

Formerly Code 1863, § 3692; Code 1868, § 3716; Code 1873, § 3769; Code 1882, § 3769; Civil Code 1895, § 5174; Penal Code 1895, § 996; Civil Code 1910, § 5761; Penal Code 1910, § 1022; Code 1933, § 38-214.

§ 24-5-26. Photostats, microphotographs, photographs, and optical image reproductions of original writings

Any photostatic, microphotographic, photographic, or optical image reproduction of any original writing or record made in the regular course of business to preserve the writing or record shall be admissible in evidence in any proceeding in any court of this state and in any proceeding before any board, bureau, department, commission, or agency of the state, in lieu of and without accounting for the original of such writing or record, if such reproduction accurately reproduces or forms a durable medium for reproducing the original. Any enlargement or facsimile of such reproduction shall likewise be admissible if the original of the reproduction is in existence and available for inspection under direction of the court or the agency conducting the proceeding.

Laws 1950, p. 73, § 1; Laws 1991, p. 787, § 1; Laws 1993, p. 1078, § 2.

§ 24-5-27. Certified copy of deed as evidence

A certified copy of a deed or any other instrument affecting real property which has been properly recorded in the office of the clerk of the superior court of the county or counties in which said property is situated shall be admissible in evidence under the same rules which would apply to the original without the necessity of accounting for the original instrument.

Laws 1965, p. 250, § 1.

§ 24-5-28. Certified copy of 30-year-old deed as evidence

A certified copy of a deed more than 30 years old, where the deed has been recorded more than 30 years and possession has been consistent with the deed, shall be admissible in evidence without proof of execution.

Laws 1952, p. 169, § 1.

§ 24-5-29. Extracts from books of incorporated companies

(a) When any portion of the contents of the books or records of any incorporated company located in this state is material and competent evidence in any civil cause, the party desiring to use the same in evidence, upon procuring a correct transcript from such books, certified under the hand of the chief officer in charge of the office where the books are located, that the extract is a true and complete transcript of all that appears upon the books in the office relative to that subject matter, may use the extract in evidence, in lieu of the books themselves, provided that he first serves the opposite party with a copy of the extract 20 days before court and with notice that the same will be offered in evidence.

(b) Nothing in this Code section shall be construed to impair or diminish the right of either party to compel the production of books and papers, by notice, where in the hands of the opposite party, or by subpoena for the production of evidence, where in the hands of third persons.

Laws 1873, p. 35, § 1.

Formerly Code 1873, § 3830; Code 1882, § 3830; Civil Code 1895, § 5236; Civil Code 1910, § 5823; Code 1933, § 38-626.

§ 24-5-30. Copies of letters of administration, etc., as primary evidence

Copies of letters testamentary, letters of administration, and letters of guardianship shall be primary evidence of the fact of administration and guardianship to the same extent as the original letters, provided that such copy letters shall have been duly certified from the proper record of the proper officer.

Laws 1878-79, p. 151, § 1.

Formerly Code 1882, § 3817a; Civil Code 1895, § 5213; Civil Code 1910, § 5800; Code 1933, § 38-603.

§ 24-5-31. Wills and records; copies

Copies of records of judicial proceedings and wills admitted to probate shall be admitted as primary evidence, when properly authenticated. In all other cases a copy shall be secondary evidence.

Formerly Code 1863, § 3686; Code 1868, § 3710; Code 1873, § 3763; Code 1882, § 3763; Civil Code 1895, § 5167; Civil Code 1910, § 5753; Code 1933, § 38-206.

§ 24-5-32. Inscriptions on monuments, etc., proof by copies

Inscriptions on walls, monuments, and other fixed objects may be proved by copies established as such.

Formerly Code 1863, § 3688; Code 1868, § 3712; Code 1873, § 3765; Code 1882, § 3765; Civil Code 1895, § 5170; Civil Code 1910, § 5757; Code 1933, § 38-210.

§ 24-5-33. Certified copy of soldiers' discharge certificates as evidence

A certified copy of any discharge from the military service of the United States, when the original is lost or destroyed, shall be admitted in evidence in any of the courts of this state without further proof of the original.

Laws 1921, p. 184, § 3.

Formerly Code 1933, § 38-613.

CHAPTER 6

PAROL EVIDENCE RULE

§ 24-6-1. Admissibility of parol contemporaneous evidence

Parol contemporaneous evidence is generally inadmissible to contradict or vary the terms of a valid written instrument.

Formerly Code 1863, § 3723; Code 1868, § 3747; Code 1873, § 3800; Code 1882, § 3800; Civil Code 1895, § 5201; Civil Code 1910, § 5788; Code 1933, § 38-501.

§ 24-6-2. Admissibility where part only of stipulations is in writing

If the writing does not purport to contain all the stipulations of the contract, parol evidence shall be admissible to prove other portions thereof not inconsistent with the writing; so collateral undertakings between parties of the same part among themselves would not properly be looked for in the writing.

Formerly Code 1863, § 3726; Code 1868, § 3750; Code 1873, § 3803; Code 1882, § 3803; Civil Code 1895, § 5204; Civil Code 1910, § 5791; Code 1933, § 38-504.

§ 24-6-3. Explanation of ambiguities

(a) All contemporaneous writings shall be admissible to explain each other.

(b) Parol evidence shall be admissible to explain all ambiguities, both latent and patent.

Formerly Code 1863, § 3724; Code 1868, § 3748; Code 1873, § 3801; Code 1882, § 3801; Civil Code 1895, § 5202; Civil Code 1910, § 5789; Code 1933, § 38-502.

§ 24-6-4. Surrounding circumstances

The surrounding circumstances are always proper subjects of proof to aid in the construction of contracts.

Formerly Code 1863, § 3727; Code 1868, § 3751; Code 1873, § 3804; Code 1882, § 3804; Civil Code 1895, § 5205; Civil Code 1910, § 5792; Code 1933, § 38-505.

§ 24-6-5. Usage

Evidence of known and established usage shall be admissible to aid in the construction of contracts as well as to annex incidents.

Formerly Code 1863, § 3728; Code 1868, § 3752; Code 1873, § 3805; Code 1882, § 3805; Civil Code 1895, § 5206; Civil Code 1910, § 5793; Code 1933, § 38-506.

§ 24-6-6. Rebuttal of equity; discharge of contract; subsequent agreement; enlargement of time; change of place of performance

Parol evidence shall be admissible to rebut an equity, to discharge an entire contract, to prove a new and distinct subsequent agreement, to enlarge the time of performance, or to change the place of performance.

Formerly Code 1863, § 3729; Code 1868, § 3753; Code 1873, § 3806; Code 1882, § 3806; Civil Code 1895, § 5207; Civil Code 1910, § 5794; Code 1933, § 38-507.

§ 24-6-7. Mistake in deed or contract in writing

Parol evidence is admissible to prove a mistake in a deed or any other contract required by law to be in writing.

Formerly Code 1863, § 3051; Code 1868, § 3063; Code 1873, § 3118; Code 1882, § 3118; Civil Code 1895, § 3975; Civil Code 1910, § 4572; Code 1933, § 38-510.

§ 24-6-8. Showing invalidity of writing

Parol evidence shall be admissible to show that a writing either was originally void or subsequently became so.

Formerly Code 1863, § 3725; Code 1868, § 3749; Code 1873, § 3802; Code 1882, § 3802; Civil Code 1895, § 5203; Civil Code 1910, § 5790; Code 1933, § 38-503.

§ 24-6-9. Denial or explanation of receipts for money

Receipts for money are always only prima-facie evidence of payment and may be denied or explained by parol.

Formerly Code 1863, § 3730; Code 1868, § 3754; Code 1873, § 3807; Code 1882, § 3807; Civil Code 1895, § 5208; Civil Code 1910, § 5795; Code 1933, § 38-508.

§ 24-6-10. Blank endorsements, explanation of

Blank endorsements of negotiable paper may always be explained between the parties themselves or those taking with notice of dishonor or of the actual facts of such endorsements.

Formerly Code 1863, § 3731; Code 1868, § 3755; Code 1873, § 3808; Code 1882, § 3808; Civil Code 1895, § 5209; Civil Code 1910, § 5796; Code 1933, § 38-509.

CHAPTER 7

AUTHENTICATION OF WRITINGS

Article 1

In General

§ 24-7-1. Production; proof of execution

Generally, an original writing shall be produced and its execution proved. Exceptions are prescribed by law.

Formerly Code 1863, § 3754; Code 1868, § 3778; Code 1873, § 3831; Code 1882, § 3831; Civil Code 1895, § 5239; Civil Code 1910, § 5828; Code 1933, § 38-701.

§ 24-7-2. Explaining alteration in paper offered in evidence

If a paper appears to have been altered materially, unless it is the paper sued on and no plea of non est factum is filed, the party offering it in evidence shall explain the alteration unless the paper comes from the custody of the opposite party.

Formerly Code 1863, § 3758; Code 1868, § 3782; Code 1873, § 3835; Code 1882, § 3835; Civil Code 1895, § 5242; Civil Code 1910, § 5831; Code 1933, § 38-704.

§ 24-7-3. Production of paper by opposite party as dispensing with proof

The production of a paper by the opposite party, if he claims any benefit under it, dispenses with the necessity of proof. The notice to produce shall dispense with proof as against the party giving the notice.

Formerly Code 1863, § 3759; Code 1868, § 3783; Code 1873, § 3836; Code 1882, § 3836; Civil Code 1895, § 5243; Civil Code 1910, § 5832; Code 1933, § 38-705.

§ 24-7-4. Subscribing witness, production of; exceptions

The subscribing witness shall be produced in all cases except the following:

(1) Ancient writings which prove themselves;

(2) If from any cause the witness cannot be produced or sworn;

(3) Office bonds required by law to be approved or tested by a particular functionary;

(4) If the paper is only incidentally or collaterally material to the case; or

(5) If the party executing the written instrument testifies to its execution.

Laws 1895, p. 31, § 1.

Formerly Code 1863, § 3760; Code 1868, § 3784; Code 1873, § 3837; Code 1882, § 3837; Civil Code 1895, § 5244; Civil Code 1910, § 5833; Code 1933, § 38-706.

§ 24-7-5. Proof where subscribing witnesses dead, insane, incompetent, inaccessible, or without memory of transaction

Whenever the subscribing witnesses to an instrument in writing are dead, insane, incompetent, or inaccessible or, being produced, do not recollect the transaction, proof of the actual signing by or the handwriting of the alleged maker shall be received as primary evidence of the fact of execution. If such evidence shall not be attainable, the court may admit evidence of the handwriting of the subscribing witnesses or other secondary evidence to establish the fact of execution.

Laws 1895, p. 90, § 1.

Formerly Code 1863, § 3761; Code 1868, § 3785; Code 1873, § 3838; Code 1882, § 3838; Civil Code 1895, § 5245; Civil Code 1910, § 5834; Code 1933, § 38-707.

§ 24-7-6. Handwriting, proof of

Proof of handwriting may be resorted to in the absence of direct evidence of execution. In such case, any witness who shall swear that he knows or would recognize the handwriting shall be competent to testify as to his belief. The source of his knowledge shall be a question for investigation and shall go entirely to the credit and weight of his evidence.

Formerly Code 1863, § 3762; Code 1868, § 3786; Code 1873, § 3839; Code 1882, § 3839; Civil Code 1895, § 5246; Penal Code 1895, § 1016; Civil Code 1910, § 5835; Penal Code 1910, § 1042; Code 1933, § 38-708.

§ 24-7-7. Comparison of writings

Other writings proved or acknowledged to be genuine may be admitted in evidence for the purpose of comparison by the jury. Such other papers, when intended to be introduced, shall be submitted to the opposite party before he announces himself ready for trial.

Formerly Code 1863, § 3763; Code 1868, § 3787; Code 1873, § 3840; Code 1882, § 3840; Civil Code 1895, § 5247; Civil Code 1910, § 5836; Code 1933, § 38-709.

§ 24-7-8. Authentication of medical records

(a) As used in this Code section, the term "medical records" means all written clinical information which relates to the treatment of individuals, when such information is kept in an institution.

(b) Medical records or reproductions thereof, when duly certified by their custodians, need not be identified at the trial and may be used in any manner in which records identified at the trial by the custodian could be used.

Laws 1971, p. 441, §§ 1, 2.

§ 24-7-9. Competency to identify medical bills, etc.

(a) Upon the trial of any civil case involving injury or disease, the patient or the member of his family or other person responsible for the care of the patient shall be a competent witness to identify bills for expenses incurred in the treatment of the patient upon a showing by such witness that the expenses were incurred in connection with the treatment of the injury, disease, or disability involved in the subject of litigation at trial and that the bills were received from:

(1) A hospital;

(2) An ambulance service;

(3) A pharmacy, drugstore, or supplier of therapeutic or orthopedic devices; or

(4) A licensed practicing physician, chiropractor, dentist, orthotist, podiatrist, or psychologist.

(b) Such items of evidence need not be identified by the one who submits the bill, and it shall not be necessary for an expert witness to testify that the charges were reasonable and necessary. However, nothing in this Code section shall be construed to limit the right of a thorough and sifting cross-examination as to such items of evidence.

Laws 1970, p. 225, § 1; Laws 1983, p. 525, § 1; Laws 1987, p. 3, § 24.

Formerly Code 1933, § 38-706.1.

Article 2

Public Records

§ 24-7-20. Exemplifications

The certificate or attestation of any public officer, either of this state or any county thereof, shall give sufficient validity or authenticity to any copy or transcript of any record, document, paper of file, or other matter or thing in his respective office, or pertaining thereto, to admit the same in evidence.

Laws 1819, Cobb's 1851 Digest, p. 272; Laws 1830, Cobb's 1851 Digest, p. 273; Laws 1855-56, p. 143, § 1.

Formerly Code 1863, § 3739; Code 1868, § 3763; Code 1873, § 3816; Code 1882, § 3816; Civil Code 1895, § 5211;

Penal Code 1895, § 1015; Civil Code 1910, § 5798; Penal Code 1910, § 1041; Code 1933, § 38–601.

§ 24–7–21. Exemplification of municipal records, etc.

Exemplifications of the records and minutes of municipal corporations of this state, when certified under seal by the clerks or keepers of such records, shall be admitted in evidence under the same rules and regulations as exemplifications of the records of the courts of record of this state.

Laws 1890–91, p. 109, § 1.

Formerly Civil Code 1895, § 5216; Civil Code 1910, § 5803; Code 1933, § 38–606.

§ 24–7–22. Authentication of ordinances and resolutions of counties and municipal corporations

When certified by a public officer, clerk, or keeper of the county or municipal records specified in Code Section 24–7–20 or 24–7–21 and in the absence of contrary evidence, judicial notice may be taken of a copy of any ordinance or resolution included within a general codification required by paragraph (1) of subsection (b) of Code Section 36–80–19 as representing an ordinance or resolution duly approved by the governing authority and currently in force as presented. Any such certified copy shall be self-authenticating and shall be admissible as prima-facie proof of any such ordinance or resolution before any court or administrative body.

Laws 2001, p. 1219, § 1.

§ 24–7–23. Notarial acts; proof by certificate

All notarial acts of notaries public in relation to bills of exchange, drafts, and promissory notes, required to be done by law, may be proved by the certificate of such notary under his hand and seal, provided that such certificate is filed in the trial court at its first term and permitted to remain there until the trial.

Laws 1836, Cobb's 1851 Digest, p. 273.

Formerly Code 1863, § 3753; Code 1868, § 3777; Code 1873, § 3829; Code 1882, § 3829; Civil Code 1895, § 5235; Civil Code 1910, § 5822; Code 1933, § 38–625.

§ 24–7–24. Laws and judicial proceedings of other states, how proved

(a)(1) The acts of the legislature of any other state, territory, or possession of the United States shall be authenticated by affixing the seal of such state, territory, or possession thereto; provided, however, nothing herein shall be construed as repealing or modifying Code Section 9–11–43. The records and judicial proceedings, or copies thereof, of any court of any such state, territory, or possession shall be proved or admitted in other courts within this state by the attestation of the clerk and seal of the court annexed, if a seal exists, together with a certificate of a judge of the court that the attestation is in proper form.

(2) Such acts, records, and judicial proceedings, or copies thereof, so authenticated, shall have the same full faith and credit in every court within this state as they have by law or usage in the courts of such state, territory, or possession from which they are taken.

(b) In lieu of the above, the records and judicial proceedings, or copies thereof, of any court, tribunal, or quasi-judicial agency of any such state, territory, or possession may also be proved or admitted in any court, tribunal, office, or agency in this state when certified under the hand and seal, if any, of the judge, clerk, or other official of such court, tribunal, or quasi-judicial agency and shall be given the same full faith and credit as provided in subsection (a) of this Code section.

Laws 1973, p. 299, § 1; Laws 1995, p. 10, § 24.

Formerly Civil Code 1895, § 5237; Civil Code 1910, § 5824; Code 1933, § 38–627.

§ 24–7–25. Nonjudicial books and records of other states, how proved

(a)(1) All nonjudicial records or books, or copies thereof, kept in any public office of any state, territory, or possession of the United States shall be proved or admitted in any court or office in this state by the attestation of the custodian of the records or books, and the seal of his office annexed, if there is a seal, together with a certificate of a judge of a court of record of the county, parish, or district in which such office may be kept, or a certificate of the governor, the secretary of state, the chancellor, or the keeper of the great seal of the state, territory, or possession that the attestation is in due form and by the proper officers.

(2) If the certificate is given by a judge, it shall be further authenticated by the clerk or prothonotary of the court, who shall certify under his hand and the seal of his office that the judge is duly commissioned and qualified; or, if given by the governor, secretary of state, chancellor, or keeper of the great seal, the certificate shall be under the great seal of the state, territory, or possession in which it is made.

(3) Such records or books, or copies thereof, so authenticated, shall have the same full faith and credit in every court and office within this state as they have by law or usage in the courts or offices of the state, territory, or possession from which they are taken.

(b) In lieu of the above, the nonjudicial records or books, or copies thereof, kept in any public office of any state, territory, or possession of the United States may also be proved or admitted in evidence in any court, tribunal, office, or agency in this state when certified under the hand and seal, if any, by the officer or other official having custody or possession of the original thereof and shall be given the same full faith and credit as provided in subsection (a) of this Code section.

Laws 1973, p. 299, § 2; Laws 1995, p. 10, § 24.

Formerly Civil Code 1895, § 5238; Civil Code 1910, § 5827; Code 1933, § 38–630.

§ 24–7–26. Judgments and proceedings of justices' courts in other states

(a) The official certificate of a justice of the peace of any state of the United States to any judgment, and the preliminary proceedings before him, with the official certificate of the clerk of any court of record within the county in which the justice resides, under the seal of such court of record, stating that the justice is an acting justice of the peace of that county and that the signature to his certificate is genuine, shall be prima-facie evidence of the proceedings and judgment.

(b) When the term of office of a justice of the peace of another state has expired or when for any reason the office has been vacated, the official certificate of the successor in office of the justice to any judgment and the preliminary proceedings before the retired justice, stating that he is the successor in office of the retired justice and the proper custodian of the judgment and preliminary proceedings, the same being in his custody, with the official certificate of the clerk of any court of record within the county in which the justice making the certificate resides, under the seal of such court of record, stating that the justice making the certificate is an acting justice of the peace of that county and the successor in office of the justice before whom the proceedings were had and by whom the judgment was rendered and that the signature to his certificate is genuine, shall be prima-facie evidence of such proceedings and judgment.

Laws 1900, p. 78, §§ 1, 2.

Formerly Civil Code 1910, §§ 5825, 5826; Code 1933, §§ 38–628, 38–629.

§ 24–7–27. Records of Department of Corrections, how proved

Records of the Department of Corrections, or authenticated copies thereof, when certified in accordance with the terms of subsection (d) of Code Section 42–5–36, shall be admissible as evidence in any civil or criminal proceeding as proof of the contents thereof.

Laws 1997, p. 851, § 3.

CHAPTER 8

ESTABLISHMENT OF LOST RECORDS

Article 1

Public Records

§ 24–8–1. Establishment of mutilated, destroyed, or lost public records

Where any public records have been lost, mutilated, stolen, or destroyed, the superior court of the county where the records belong may establish copies. When so established, such records shall be in all respects evidence as the original records would have been.

Laws 1887, p. 112, § 1.

Formerly Civil Code 1895, § 5223; Civil Code 1910, § 5810; Code 1933, § 38–614.

§ 24–8–2. Proceedings; discretion of court

The judge of the probate court of the county may bring a petition which may be heard and determined at the first term after or during which the same may be filed. The superior court shall give precedence to the case and proceed with the same as speedily as possible. Upon the hearing it shall be discretionary with the court to order the whole or any part of such records established.

Laws 1887, p. 112, § 2.

Formerly Civil Code 1895, § 5224; Civil Code 1910, § 5811; Code 1933, § 38–615.

§ 24–8–3. Petition to contain what

The petition shall set forth the fact that some portion of the records has been lost, mutilated, stolen, or destroyed, specifying as nearly as may be possible the books or parts of the books in which they existed, and shall pray for the establishment of the same. The copies so established, as nearly as may be possible, shall specify and conform to the original book and pages of the same on which they originally existed.

Laws 1887, p. 112, § 3.

Formerly Civil Code 1895, § 5225; Civil Code 1910, § 5812; Code 1933, § 38-616.

§ 24-8-4. Auditor to hear evidence

The court or the judge thereof may appoint an auditor in all cases where he shall deem it proper, who shall hear evidence, summon witnesses, and compel the production of books and papers, under such rules and regulations as are now practiced in the courts. The auditor shall make his report of such copies of such lost, stolen, mutilated, or destroyed records; when such report is filed, it shall be made the judgment of the court, unless objections are filed to the same or some part thereof as being incorrect, which objections, if any, shall be heard and determined by the court without the intervention of a jury.

Laws 1887, p. 112, § 4.

Formerly Civil Code 1895, § 5226; Civil Code 1910, § 5813; Code 1933, § 38-617.

§ 24-8-5. Fee of auditor

The auditor shall receive for his services such compensation as may be allowed by the court, to be paid out of the public funds of the county.

Laws 1887, p. 112, § 5.

Formerly Civil Code 1895, § 5227; Civil Code 1910, § 5814; Code 1933, § 38-618.

§ 24-8-6. Exception to auditor's report

Any person who is adversely interested in the report of the auditor or who claims that there is any mistake in the report shall have the right to file objections thereto as specified in Code Section 24-8-4. Said objections shall be filed within 30 days after the filing of the report and shall be heard and determined in the manner prescribed in Code Section 24-8-4.

Laws 1887, p. 112, § 6.

Formerly Civil Code 1895, § 5228; Civil Code 1910, § 5815; Code 1933, § 38-619.

Article 2

Private Papers

§ 24-8-20. Copy of office papers established instanter on motion

(a) Upon the loss of any original pleading, declaration, bill of indictment, special presentment, or other office paper, a copy may be established instanter on motion.

(b) An instrument on which an action has been brought shall be deemed an office paper after the case has gone to trial.

Laws 1799, Cobb's 1851 Digest, p. 463.

Formerly Code 1863, §§ 3884, 3885; Code 1868, §§ 3904, 3905; Code 1873, §§ 3980, 3981; Code 1882, §§ 3980, 3981; Civil Code 1895, §§ 4743, 4744; Civil Code 1910, §§ 5312, 5313; Code 1933, §§ 63-201, 63-202.

§ 24-8-21. Summary establishment; petition; citation or notice; order; defense; record; appeal; bond for costs

(a) The owner, agent of the owner, or legal representative of the owner of any bond, bill, note, draft, check, or other evidence of indebtedness which has been lost or destroyed may establish a copy of the same in a summary manner by filing a petition with the judge of the probate court of the county of the residence of the alleged debtor or maker, if he is a resident of this state; and the judge of the probate court is deemed as judicial officer for the purpose of this Code section. The petition shall be sworn to by the party applying and shall contain as full and accurate a description as possible of the lost paper, of the loss and mode of loss, of the inability to find the same and why, along with a prayer for the establishment of a copy setting forth the copy desired to be established.

(b) Upon the filing of a petition, the judge shall issue a citation or notice, to the alleged debtor or maker, requiring him to appear at a day not more than ten days distant and show cause, if he has any, why the copy should not be established in lieu of the lost original. The citation or notice shall be personally served by either the sheriff or bailiff or by a person specially appointed by the judge for the purpose, at least five days before the time of hearing.

(c) If no successful defense is made at the time and place appointed, the judge shall proceed to establish, by an order entered on the petition, the copy so prayed to be established, which shall have all the effect of the original. The petition, notice, and order shall be entered in a book of record specially prepared for the purpose.

(d) If the debtor or maker so served files a defense under oath to the effect that the original never existed as claimed, the judge shall decide, after giving the parties time for preparation and hearing, not to exceed 20 days, upon the case so made. If the judge's decision is in favor of the applicant and no appeal is entered as provided in subsection (e) of this Code section, the decision shall be entered on the petition and the copy so established shall have the same effect as an original. If the judge's decision is in favor of the alleged debtor or maker, the judge shall also enter his decision on the petition. In all cases the proceedings shall be recorded as provided in subsection (c) of this Code section.

(e) Except as provided in Article 6 of Chapter 9 of Title 15, if either party to the proceedings provided for in this Code section is dissatisfied, he may appeal upon giving the usual bond and security for costs, as in cases of appeal from the probate court to the superior court. The appeal shall be tried in the superior court from all the pleadings and proceedings as were before the judge of the probate court. In the superior court the case shall be tried and determined as provided in Code Sections 24-8-24 through 24-8-27.

(f) This Code section shall not apply to evidences of indebtedness to which Title 11 is applicable.

Laws 1876, p. 101, § 1; Laws 1986, p. 982, § 8.

Formerly Code 1882, § 3995a; Civil Code 1895, § 4757; Civil Code 1910, § 5326; Code 1933, § 63-101.

§ 24-8-22. Nonresidents, how served

When the person alleged to be a debtor or maker of a lost or destroyed paper as set forth in Code Section 24-8-21 does not reside in this state, the alleged debtor or maker may be made a party to the proceedings by publication, in a newspaper to be designated by the judge of the probate court, twice a month for two months. When the person has been made a party, this article shall apply in his case, except as otherwise provided.

Laws 1876, p. 101, § 2.

Formerly Code 1882, § 3995b; Civil Code 1895, § 4758; Civil Code 1910, § 5327; Code 1933, § 63-102.

§ 24-8-23. Repealed by Laws 1983, p. 884, § 4-2, eff. July 1, 1983

§ 24-8-24. Establishment in superior court; how other papers established; petition; rule nisi

(a) The owner of a lost or destroyed paper which is not an office paper as defined in Code Section 24-8-20 who desires to establish the same shall present to the clerk of the superior court of the county where the maker of the paper resides, if the maker is a resident of this state, a petition in writing, together with a copy, in substance, of the paper lost or destroyed, as nearly as he can recollect, which copy shall be sworn to by the petitioner, his agent, or his attorney.

(b) Thereupon, the clerk shall issue a rule nisi in the name of the judge of the superior court, calling upon the opposite party to show cause, if he has any, why the copy sworn to should not be established in lieu of the lost or destroyed original. The rule shall be served personally upon the respondent by the sheriff, his deputy, or any constable of this state, if the respondent is found in this state, 20 days before the sitting of the court to which the rule nisi is made returnable. If the respondent cannot be found in this state, the rule shall be published in some public newspaper twice a month for two months before the final hearing of the rule.

Laws 1855-56, p. 238, §§ 1, 2; Laws 1983, p. 884, § 3-23.

Formerly Code 1863, § 3886; Code 1868, § 3906; Code 1873, § 3982; Code 1882, § 3982; Civil Code 1895, § 4745; Civil Code 1910, § 5314; Code 1933, § 63-203.

§ 24-8-25. Continuance, when granted

In a proceeding to establish lost papers under Code Section 24-8-24, no continuance shall be granted unless it appears reasonable and just to the court; nor shall a continuance be allowed to the same party more than once, except for providential cause.

Laws 1855-56, p. 238, § 4.

Formerly Code 1863, § 3887; Code 1868, § 3907; Code 1873, § 3983; Code 1882, § 3983; Civil Code 1895, § 4746; Civil Code 1910, § 5315; Code 1933, § 63-204.

§ 24-8-26. Rule absolute

When a rule nisi has been duly served as provided in Code Section 24-8-24, the court shall grant a rule absolute establishing the copy of the lost or destroyed paper sworn to, unless good and sufficient cause is shown why the rule absolute should not be granted.

Laws 1855-56, p. 238, § 3.

Formerly Code 1863, § 3888; Code 1868, § 3908; Code 1873, § 3984; Code 1882, § 3984; Civil Code 1895, § 4747; Civil Code 1910, § 5316; Code 1933, § 63-205.

§ 24-8-27. Certified endorsement of copy

When the copy of the lost or destroyed paper is established, the clerk of the court in which it is done shall furnish the copy to the party who had it established, with a certified endorsement thereon of the day and term of the court when the rule absolute was granted, provided all costs of the proceeding have been paid.

Laws 1855-56, p. 238, § 5.

Formerly Code 1863, § 3889; Code 1868, § 3909; Code 1873, § 3985; Code 1882, § 3985; Civil Code 1895, § 4748; Civil Code 1910, § 5317; Code 1933, § 63-206.

§ 24-8-28. Action on lost paper

(a) If the paper which has been lost or destroyed is a note, bill, bond, or other instrument upon which an action may be brought, the owner may institute an action thereon as soon as the rule nisi has been issued as provided for in Code Section 24–8–24. The complaint shall set forth that the paper upon which the action is based is lost or destroyed. In no case shall a judgment be entered in the action until it is determined whether the application to establish the paper is granted or not. If the application is granted, then judgment shall be entered as in other cases.

(b) In an action as provided for in subsection (a) of this Code section, production of the paper upon which the action is based shall not be demanded until the time for rendition of judgment in the action; at that time, if the plaintiff produces a copy of the paper with a certified endorsement thereon by the clerk of the court in which it was established, as provided in Code Section 24–8–27, it shall be taken and considered as the original.

(c) This Code section shall not apply to instruments to which Title 11, the "Uniform Commercial Code," is applicable.

Laws 1855–56, p. 238, §§ 6–8; Laws 1995, p. 10, § 24.

Formerly Code 1863, §§ 3890, 3891; Code 1868, §§ 3910, 3911; Code 1873, §§ 3986, 3987; Code 1882, §§ 3986, 3987; Civil Code 1895, §§ 4750, 4751; Civil Code 1910, §§ 5319, 5320; Code 1933, §§ 63–208, 63–209.

§ 24–8–29. Who may be party

In all cases for the purpose of establishing any lost or destroyed paper other than an office paper as defined in Code Section 24–8–20, any person whose interest will be affected by the establishment of the lost paper shall, upon motion, by order of the court, be made a party respondent in the proceeding and shall be allowed all the rights of defense against the establishment of the paper as fully as if he were the maker of the lost paper.

Laws 1866, p. 139, § 1.

Formerly Code 1868, § 3916; Code 1873, § 3992; Code 1882, § 3992; Civil Code 1895, § 4756; Civil Code 1910, § 5325; Code 1933, § 63–303.

§ 24–8–30. Applicability of article

Other than Code Section 24–8–20, this article shall not apply to lost or destroyed papers to which Title 11 is applicable.

CHAPTER 9

WITNESSES GENERALLY

Article 1

Competency

§ 24–9–1. Competency of witnesses to testify

(a) No person offered as a witness shall be excluded by reason of incapacity, for crime or interest or from being a party, from giving evidence, either in person or by deposition, according to the practice of the court, on the trial of any issue joined, or of any matter or question, or on any inquiry arising in any suit, action, or proceeding, civil or criminal, in any court or before any judge, jury, sheriff, coroner, magistrate, officer, or party having by law or consent of parties authority to hear, receive, and examine evidence; but every person so offered shall be competent and compellable to give evidence on behalf of either or any of the parties to the suit, action, or other proceeding.

(b) This Code section, as revised by an Act approved April 17, 1979 (Ga. L. 1979, p. 1261), shall apply to transactions or occurrences which take place on or after July 1, 1979, and this Code section, as it existed prior to July 1, 1979, shall apply to transactions or occurrences which took place prior to July 1, 1979.

Laws 1866, p. 138, § 1; Laws 1889, p. 85, § 1; Laws 1890–91, p. 107, §§ 1, 2; Laws 1893, p. 53, § 1; Laws 1897, p. 53, § 1; Laws 1900, p. 57, § 1; Laws 1924, p. 62, § 1; Laws 1953, Nov.-Dec. Sess., p. 319, § 1; Laws 1979, p. 1261, §§ 1, 2; Laws 1992, p. 6, § 24.

Formerly Code 1868, § 3798; Code 1873, § 3854; Code 1882, § 3854; Civil Code 1895, §§ 5269, 5270; Civil Code 1910, §§ 5858, 5859; Code 1933, § 38–1603.

§ 24–9–2. Testimony of husband and wife as to adultery of other

In any civil proceeding a husband and wife shall each be competent to testify to the adultery of the other; and a party shall be competent to testify to his or her innocence of adultery in such proceeding.

Laws 1866, p. 138, § 3; Laws 1935, p. 120, § 1; Laws 1951, p. 596, § 1; Laws 1976, p. 1014, § 2; Laws 1982, p. 1187, §§ 1, 2.

Formerly Code 1868, § 3799; Code 1873, § 3855; Code 1882, § 3855; Civil Code 1895, § 5272; Civil Code 1910, § 5861; Code 1933, § 38–1606.

§ 24–9–3. Religious belief

Religious belief shall go only to the credit of a witness.

Laws 1841, p. 144, § 1; Cobb's 1851 Digest, p. 280.

Formerly Code 1863, § 3772; Code 1868, § 3797; Code 1873, § 3853; Code 1882, § 3853; Civil Code 1895, § 5268; Civil Code 1910, § 5857; Code 1933, § 38–1602.

§ 24–9–4. Evidence through interpreter

No physical defect in any of the senses shall incapacitate a witness. An interpreter may explain the evidence of such witness.

Formerly Code 1863, § 3774; Code 1868, § 3802; Code 1873, § 3858; Code 1882, § 3858; Civil Code 1895, § 5275; Penal Code 1895, § 1014; Civil Code 1910, § 5864; Penal Code 1910, § 1040; Code 1933, § 38–1609.

§ 24–9–5. Persons who do not have the use of reason

(a) Except as provided in subsection (b) of this Code section, persons who do not have the use of reason, such as idiots, lunatics during lunacy, and children who do not understand the nature of an oath, shall be incompetent witnesses.

(b) Notwithstanding the provisions of subsection (a) of this Code section, in all cases involving deprivation as defined by Code Section 15–11–2, or in criminal cases involving child molestation, and in all other criminal cases in which a child was a victim of or a witness to any crime, any such child shall be competent to testify, and his credibility shall be determined as provided in Article 4 of this chapter.

Laws 1866, p. 138, § 4; Laws 1989, p. 1639, § 1; Laws 1990, p. 1795, § 1.

Formerly Code 1868, § 3800; Code 1873, § 3856; Code 1882, § 3856; Civil Code 1895, § 5273; Penal Code 1895, § 1012; Civil Code 1910, § 5862; Penal Code 1910, § 1038; Code 1933, § 38–1607.

§ 24–9–6. Drunkenness

Drunkenness, which dethrones reason and memory, shall incapacitate during its continuance.

Formerly Code 1863, § 3775; Code 1868, § 3801; Code 1873, § 3857; Code 1882, § 3857; Civil Code 1895, § 5274; Penal Code 1895, § 1013; Civil Code 1910, § 5863; Penal Code 1910, § 1039; Code 1933, § 38–1608.

§ 24–9–7. Court decides competency; objections to competency; restoration to competency

(a) The competency of a witness shall be decided by the court. The court shall by examination decide upon the capacity of one alleged to be incompetent from idiocy, lunacy, insanity, drunkenness, or infancy.

(b) If an objection to competency is known, it shall be taken before the witness is examined at all. It may be proved by the witness himself or by other testimony. If proved by other testimony, the witness shall be incompetent to explain it away.

(c) Any fact which in the judgment of the court removes the ground of incompetency shall restore the competency of the witness.

Formerly Code 1863, §§ 3772, 3776, 3784, 3785; Code 1868, §§ 3796, 3803, 3804, 3805; Code 1873, §§ 3852, 3859, 3860, 3861; Code 1882, §§ 3852, 3859, 3860, 3861; Civil Code 1895, §§ 5267, 5276, 5277, 5278; Civil Code 1910, §§ 5856, 5865, 5866, 5867; Code 1933, §§ 38–1601, 38–1610, 38–1611, 38–1612.

Article 2
Privilege

Part 1
General Provisions

§ 24–9–20. Person not compellable to testify for or against self; testimony of defendant in criminal case

(a) No person who is charged in any criminal proceeding with the commission of any indictable offense or any offense punishable on summary conviction shall be compellable to give evidence for or against himself.

(b) If a defendant in a criminal case wishes to testify and announces in open court his or her intention to do so, the defendant may so testify in his or her own behalf. If a defendant testifies, he or she shall be sworn as any other witness and may be examined and cross–examined as any other witness. The failure of a defendant to testify shall create no presumption against him or her, and no comment shall be made because of such failure.

Laws 1866, p. 138, § 2; Laws 1868, p. 24, § 1; Laws 1874, p. 22, § 1; Laws 1878–79, p. 53, § 1; Laws 1962, p. 133, § 2; Laws 1973, p. 292, § 2; Laws 2005, Act 8, § 14, eff. July 1, 2005.

Formerly Code 1868, § 3798; Code 1873, §§ 3854, 4637; Code 1882, §§ 3854, 4637; Penal Code 1895, §§ 1010, 1011; Penal Code 1910, §§ 1036, 1037; Code 1933, §§ 38–415, 38–416.

§ 24-9-21. Confidential communications, etc.

There are certain admissions and communications excluded on grounds of public policy. Among these are:

(1) Communications between husband and wife;

(2) Communications between attorney and client;

(3) Communications among grand jurors;

(4) Secrets of state;

(5) Communications between psychiatrist and patient;

(6) Communications between licensed psychologist and patient as provided in Code Section 43-39-16;

(7) Communications between patient and a licensed clinical social worker, clinical nurse specialist in psychiatric/mental health, licensed marriage and family therapist, or licensed professional counselor during the psychotherapeutic relationship; and

(8) Communications between or among any psychiatrist, psychologist, licensed clinical social worker, clinical nurse specialist in psychiatric/mental health, licensed marriage and family therapist, and licensed professional counselor who are rendering psychotherapy or have rendered psychotherapy to a patient, regarding that patient's communications which are otherwise privileged by paragraph (5), (6), or (7) of this Code section.

As used in this Code section, the term "psychotherapeutic relationship" means the relationship which arises between a patient and a licensed clinical social worker, a clinical nurse specialist in psychiatric/mental health, a licensed marriage and family therapist, or a licensed professional counselor using psychotherapeutic techniques as defined in Code Section 43-10A-3 and the term "psychotherapy" means the employment of "psychotherapeutic techniques."

Laws 1959, p. 190, § 1; Laws 1978, p. 1657, § 1; Laws 1995, p. 858, § 1.

Formerly Code 1863, § 3720; Code 1868, § 3744; Code 1873, § 3797; Code 1882, § 3797; Civil Code 1895, § 5198; Civil Code 1910, § 5785; Code 1933, § 38-418.

§ 24-9-22. Communications to ministers, priests and rabbis

Every communication made by any person professing religious faith, seeking spiritual comfort, or seeking counseling to any Protestant minister of the Gospel, any priest of the Roman Catholic faith, any priest of the Greek Orthodox Catholic faith, any Jewish rabbi, or to any Christian or Jewish minister, by whatever name called, shall be deemed privileged. No such minister, priest, or rabbi shall disclose any communications made to him by any such person professing religious faith, seeking spiritual guidance, or seeking counseling, nor shall such minister, priest, or rabbi be competent or compellable to testify with reference to any such communication in any court.

Laws 1951, p. 468, §§ 1, 2; Laws 1986, p. 1277, § 2.

§ 24-9-23. Husband and wife as witnesses for and against each other in criminal proceedings

(a) Husband and wife shall be competent but shall not be compellable to give evidence in any criminal proceeding for or against each other.

(b) The privilege created by subsection (a) of this Code section or by corresponding privileges in paragraph (1) of Code Section 24-9-21 or subsection (a) of Code Section 24-9-27 shall not apply in proceedings in which the husband or wife is charged with a crime against the person of a minor child, but such person shall be compellable to give evidence only on the specific act for which the defendant is charged.

Laws 1866, p. 138, § 2; Laws 1880-81, p. 121, § 1; Laws 1927, p. 145, § 1; Laws 1957, p. 53, § 1; Laws 1987, p. 1155, § 1.

Formerly Code 1868, § 3798; Code 1873, § 3854; Code 1882, § 3854; Penal Code 1895, § 1011; Penal Code 1910, § 1037; Code 1933, § 38-1604.

§ 24-9-24. Communications to attorney by client

Communications to any attorney or to his employee to be transmitted to the attorney pending his employment or in anticipation thereof shall never be heard by the court. The attorney shall not disclose the advice or counsel he may give to his client, nor produce or deliver up title deeds or other papers, except evidences of debt left in his possession by his client. This Code section shall not exclude the attorney as a witness to any facts which may transpire in connection with his employment.

Laws 1850, Cobb's 1851 Digest, p. 280; Laws 1859, p. 18, § 1.

Formerly Code 1863, § 3721; Code 1868, § 3745; Code 1873, § 3798; Code 1882, § 3798; Civil Code 1895, § 5199; Civil Code 1910, § 5786; Code 1933, § 38-419.

§ 24-9-25. Testimony of attorneys as against clients

No attorney shall be competent or compellable to testify for or against his client to any matter or thing, the knowledge of which he may have acquired from his client by virtue of his employment as attorney or by reason of the anticipated employment of him as attorney. However, an attorney shall be both competent and compellable to testify for or against his client as to any matter or thing, the knowledge of which he may have acquired in any other manner.

Laws 1866, p. 138, § 2; Laws 1887, p. 30, § 1.

Formerly Code 1868, § 3798; Code 1873, § 3854; Code 1882, § 3854; Civil Code 1895, § 5271; Penal Code 1895, § 1011; Civil Code 1910, § 5860; Penal Code 1910, § 1037; Code 1933, § 38–1605.

§ 24–9–26. Law enforcement officers testifying in criminal proceedings not compelled to reveal home address

Law enforcement officers testifying before any court in any criminal proceedings shall not be compelled to reveal their home address but may be required to divulge the business address of their employer, except that the court may require any officer to answer questions as to his home address whenever such fact may be material to any issue in the case.

Laws 1973, p. 547, § 1.

§ 24–9–27. Privilege of party or witness

(a) No party or witness shall be required to testify as to any matter which may criminate or tend to criminate himself or which shall tend to bring infamy, disgrace, or public contempt upon himself or any member of his family.

(b) Except in proceedings in which a judgment creditor or his successor in interest seeks post-judgment discovery involving a judgment debtor pursuant to Code Section 9–11–69, no party or witness shall be required to testify as to any matter which shall tend to work a forfeiture of his estate.

(c) No party or witness shall be required to make discovery of the advice of his professional advisers or his consultation with them.

(d) No official persons shall be called on to disclose any state matters of which the policy of the state and the interest of the community require concealment.

Laws 1978, p. 2000, § 1.

Formerly Code 1863, §§ 3035, 3737, 3794; Code 1868, §§ 3047, 3761, 3814; Code 1873, §§ 3102, 3814, 3870; Code 1882, §§ 3102, 3814, 3870; Civil Code 1895, §§ 3947, 3957, 5288; Civil Code 1910, §§ 4544, 4554, 5877; Code 1933, §§ 38–1102, 38–1205, 38–1711.

§ 24–9–28. Immunity from prosecution for persons ordered to testify or produce evidence in criminal prosecutions; contempt

(a) Whenever in the judgment of the Attorney General or any district attorney the testimony of any person or the production of evidence of any kind by any person in any criminal proceeding before a court or grand jury is necessary to the public interest, the Attorney General or the district attorney may request the superior court in writing to order that person to testify or produce the evidence. Upon order of the court that person shall not be excused on the basis of his privilege against self-incrimination from testifying or producing any evidence required; but no testimony or other evidence required under the order or any information directly or indirectly derived from such testimony or evidence may be used against the person in any proceedings or prosecution for a crime or offense concerning which he testified or produced evidence under court order. However, he may nevertheless be prosecuted or subjected to penalty or forfeiture for any perjury, false swearing, or contempt committed in testifying or failing to testify, or in producing or failing to produce evidence in accordance with the order but shall not be required to produce evidence that can be used in any other courts, including federal courts. Any order entered under this Code section shall be entered of record in the minutes of the court so as to afford a permanent record thereof; and any testimony given by a person pursuant to such order shall be transcribed and filed for permanent record in the office of the clerk of the court.

(b) If a person refuses to testify after being granted immunity from prosecution and after being ordered to testify as aforesaid, he may be adjudged in contempt and committed to the county jail until such time as he purges himself of contempt by testifying as ordered without regard to the expiration of the grand jury. If the grand jury before which he was ordered to testify has been dissolved, he may purge himself by testifying before the court.

Laws 1975, p. 727, §§ 1, 2.

§ 24–9–29. Confidential communications; veterinarians

No veterinarian licensed under Chapter 50 of Title 43 shall be required to disclose any information concerning the veterinarian's care of an animal except on written authorization or other waiver by the veterinarian's client or on appropriate court order or subpoena. Any veterinarian releasing information under written authorization or other waiver by the client or under court order or subpoena shall not be liable to the client or any other person. The privilege provided by this Code section shall be waived to the extent that the veterinarian's client or the owner of the animal places the veterinarian's care and treatment of the animal or the nature and extent of injuries to the animal at issue in any civil or criminal proceeding.

Laws 1986, p. 1090, § 1.

§ 24–9–30. Qualified privilege for persons, companies, or other entities engaged in news gathering or dissemination

Any person, company, or other entity engaged in the gathering and dissemination of news for the public through a newspaper, book, magazine, or radio or television broadcast shall have a qualified privilege against disclosure of any information, document, or item obtained or prepared in the gathering or dissemination of news in any proceeding where the one asserting the privilege is not a party, unless it is shown that this privilege has been waived or that what is sought:

(1) Is material and relevant;

(2) Cannot be reasonably obtained by alternative means; and

(3) Is necessary to the proper preparation or presentation of the case of a party seeking the information, document, or item.

Laws 1990, p. 167, § 1.

Part 2

Medical Information

§ 24–9–40. Confidential communications; physicians; pharmacists

(a) No physician licensed under Chapter 34 of Title 43 and no hospital or health care facility, including those operated by an agency or bureau of the state or other governmental unit, shall be required to release any medical information concerning a patient except to the Department of Human Resources, its divisions, agents, or successors when required in the administration of public health programs pursuant to Code Section 31–12–2 and where authorized or required by law, statute, or lawful regulation; or on written authorization or other waiver by the patient, or by his or her parents or duly appointed guardian ad litem in the case of a minor, or on appropriate court order or subpoena; provided, however, that any physician, hospital, or health care facility releasing information under written authorization or other waiver by the patient, or by his or her parents or guardian ad litem in the case of a minor, or pursuant to law, statute, or lawful regulation, or under court order or subpoena shall not be liable to the patient or any other person; provided, further, that the privilege shall be waived to the extent that the patient places his care and treatment or the nature and extent of his injuries at issue in any civil or criminal proceeding. This Code section shall not apply to psychiatrists or to hospitals in which the patient is being or has been treated solely for mental illness.

(b) No pharmacist licensed under Chapter 4 of Title 26 shall be required to release any medical information concerning a patient except on written authorization or other waiver by the patient, or by his or her parents or duly appointed guardian ad litem in the case of a minor, or upon appropriate court order or subpoena; provided, however, that any pharmacist releasing information under written authorization or other waiver by the patient, or by his or her parents or duly appointed guardian ad litem in the case of a minor, or upon appropriate court order or subpoena shall not be liable to the patient or any other person; provided, further, that the privilege shall be waived to the extent that the patient places his or her care and treatment or the nature and extent of his or her injuries at issue in any administrative, civil, or criminal proceeding.

Laws 1978, p. 1657, § 1; Laws 1982, p. 1077, §§ 1, 3; Laws 1986, p. 1277, § 3; Laws 1993, p. 1050, § 1.

Formerly Code 1933, § 38–418.

§ 24–9–40.1. AIDS confidential information

AIDS confidential information as defined in Code Section 31–22–9.1 and disclosed or discovered within the patient-physician relationship shall be confidential and shall not be disclosed except as otherwise provided in Code Section 24–9–47.

Laws 1988, p. 1799, § 6.

§ 24–9–40.2. Confidentiality of raw research data

(a) The General Assembly finds and declares that protecting the confidentiality of research data from disclosure in administrative proceedings, civil and criminal judicial proceedings, and quasi-judicial proceedings is essential to safeguarding the integrity of research in this state, guaranteeing the privacy of individuals who participate in research projects, and ensuring the continuation of research in science, medicine, and other fields that benefits the citizens and institutions of Georgia and other states. The protection of such research data has more than local significance, is of equal importance to all citizens of the state, is of state-wide concern, and consequently is properly a matter for regulation under the police power of the state.

(b) As used in this Code section, the term "confidential raw research data" means medical information, interview responses, reports, statements, memoranda, or other data relating to the condition, treatment, or characteristics of any person which is gathered by or provided to a researcher:

(1) In support of a research study approved by an appropriate research oversight committee of a hospital, health care facility, or educational institution; and

(2) With the objective to develop, study, or report aggregate or anonymous information not intended to be used in any way in which the identity of an individual is material to the results.

The term does not include published compilations of the raw research data created by the researcher or the researcher's published summaries, findings, analyses, or conclusions related to the research study.

(c) Confidential raw research data in a researcher's possession shall not be subject to subpoena, otherwise discoverable, or deemed admissible as evidence in any administrative, civil, criminal, or other judicial proceeding in any court except as otherwise provided in subsection (d) of this Code section.

(d) Confidential raw research data may be released, disclosed, subject to subpoena, otherwise discoverable, or deemed admissible as evidence in a judicial or quasi-judicial proceeding as follows:

(1) Confidential raw research data related to a person may be disclosed to that person or to another person on such person's behalf where the authority is otherwise specifically provided by law;

(2) Confidential raw research data related to a person may be disclosed to any person or legal entity designated to receive that information when that designation is made in writing by the research participant or where a designation is made in writing by a person authorized by law to act for the participant;

(3) Confidential raw research data related to a person may be disclosed to any agency or department of the federal government, this state, or any political subdivision of this state if those data are required by law or regulation to be reported to that agency or department;

(4) Confidential raw research data may be disclosed in any proceeding in which a party was a participant, researcher, or sponsor in the underlying research study, including but not limited to any judicial or quasi-judicial proceeding in which a research participant places his or her care, treatment, injuries, insurance coverage, or benefit plan coverage at issue; provided, however, that the identity of any research participant other than the party to the judicial or quasi-judicial proceeding shall not be disclosed, unless the researcher or sponsor is a defendant in the case;

(5) Confidential raw research data may be disclosed in any proceeding in which the researcher has either volunteered to testify or has been hired to testify as an expert by one of the parties to the proceeding; and

(6) In a criminal proceeding, the court shall order the production of confidential raw research data if the data are relevant to any issue in the proceeding, impose appropriate safeguards against unauthorized disclosure of the data, and admit confidential raw research data into evidence if the data are material to the defense or prosecution.

(e) Nothing in this Code section shall be construed to permit, require, or prohibit the disclosure of confidential raw research data in any setting other than an administrative, judicial, or quasi-judicial proceeding that is governed by the requirements of this title.

(f) Any disclosure of confidential raw research data authorized or required by this Code section or any other law shall in no way destroy the confidential nature of that data except for the purpose for which the authorized or required disclosure is made.

Laws 1999, p. 516, § 1; Laws 2000, p. 1372, § 1.

§ 24-9-41. Disclosure of confidential or privileged medical records in certain circumstances; definitions

As used in this Code section and Code Sections 24-9-42 through 24-9-45, the term:

(1) "Confidential or privileged" means the protection afforded by law from unauthorized disclosure, whether the protection is afforded by law as developed and applied by the courts, by statute or lawful regulations, or by the requirements of the Constitutions of the State of Georgia or the United States. The term "confidential or privileged" also includes protection afforded by law from compulsory process or testimony.

(2) "Disclosure" means the act of transmitting or communicating medical matter to a person who would not otherwise have access thereto.

(3) "Health care facility" means any institution or place in which health care is rendered to persons, which health care includes but is not limited to medical, psychiatric, acute, intermediate, rehabilitative, and long-term care.

(4) "Laws requiring disclosure" means laws and statutes of the State of Georgia and of the United States and lawful regulations issued by any department or agency of the State of Georgia or of the United States which require the review, analysis, or use of medical matter by persons not originally having authorized access thereto. The term "laws requiring disclosure" also includes any authorized practice of disclosure for purposes of evaluating claims for reimbursement for charges or expenses under any public or private reimbursement or insurance program.

(5) "Limited consent to disclosure" means proper authorization given by or on behalf of a person entitled to protection from disclosure of medical

matter and given for a specific purpose related to such person's health or related to such person's application for insurance or like benefits.

(6) "Medical matter" means information respecting the medical or psychiatric condition, including without limitation the physical and the mental condition, of a natural person or persons, however recorded, obtained, or communicated.

(6.1) "Nurse" means a person authorized by license issued under Chapter 26 of Title 43 as a registered professional nurse or licensed practical nurse to practice nursing.

(7) "Physician" means any person lawfully licensed in this state to practice medicine and surgery pursuant to Chapter 34 of Title 43.

Laws 1974, p. 595, § 1; Laws 1995, p. 10, § 24; Laws 2004, Act 519, § 5, eff. July 1, 2004.

§ 24-9-42. Confidential or privileged character not destroyed

The disclosure of confidential or privileged medical matter constituting all or part of a record kept by a health care facility, a nurse, or a physician, pursuant to laws requiring disclosure or pursuant to limited consent to disclosure, shall not serve to destroy or in any way abridge the confidential or privileged character thereof, except for the purpose for which such disclosure is made.

Laws 1974, p. 595, § 2; Laws 1995, p. 10, § 24; Laws 2004, Act 519, § 6, eff. July 1, 2004.

§ 24-9-43. Utilization of matter

Persons to whom confidential or privileged medical matter is disclosed in the circumstances described in Code Section 24-9-42 shall utilize such matter only in connection with the purpose or purposes of such disclosure and thereafter shall keep such matter in confidence. However, nothing in Code Sections 24-9-41 and 24-9-42, this Code section, and Code Sections 24-9-44 and 24-9-45 shall prohibit the use of such matter where otherwise authorized by law.

Laws 1974, p. 595, § 3; Laws 1995, p. 10, § 24.

§ 24-9-44. Immunity from liability

Any person, corporation, authority, or other legal entity acting in good faith shall be immune from liability for the transmission, receipt, or use of medical matter disclosed pursuant to laws requiring disclosure or pursuant to limited consent to disclosure.

Laws 1974, p. 595, § 4.

§ 24-9-45. Use in connection with medical and public education

Nothing in Code Sections 24-9-41 through 24-9-44 and this Code section shall be construed to prevent the customary and usual audit, discussion, and presentation of cases in connection with medical and public education.

Laws 1974, p. 595, § 5; Laws 1995, p. 10, § 24.

§ 24-9-46. Confidential nature of library records of library which identify user of library materials

(a) Circulation and similar records of a library which identify the user of library materials shall not be public records but shall be confidential and may not be disclosed except:

(1) To members of the library staff in the ordinary course of business;

(2) Upon written consent of the user of the library materials or the user's parents or guardian if the user is a minor or ward; or

(3) Upon appropriate court order or subpoena.

(b) Any disclosure authorized by subsection (a) of this Code section or any unauthorized disclosure of materials made confidential by that subsection (a) shall not in any way destroy the confidential nature of that material, except for the purpose for which an authorized disclosure is made. A person disclosing material as authorized by subsection (a) of this Code section shall not be liable therefor.

Laws 1987, p. 595, § 1.

§ 24-9-47. Disclosure of AIDS confidential information

(a) Any term used in this Code section and defined in Code Section 31-22-9.1 shall have the meaning provided for such term in Code Section 31-22-9.1.

(b) Except as otherwise provided in this Code section:

(1) No person or legal entity which receives AIDS confidential information pursuant to this Code section or which is responsible for recording, reporting, or maintaining AIDS confidential information shall:

(A) Intentionally or knowingly disclose that information to another person or legal entity; or

(B) Be compelled by subpoena, court order, or other judicial process to disclose that information to another person or legal entity; and

(2) No person or legal entity which receives AIDS confidential information which that person or

legal entity knows was disclosed in violation of paragraph (1) of this subsection shall:

(A) Intentionally or knowingly disclose that information to another person or legal entity; or

(B) Be compelled by subpoena, court order, or other judicial process to disclose that information to another person or legal entity.

(c) AIDS confidential information may be disclosed to the person identified by that information or, if that person is a minor or incompetent person, to that person's parent or legal guardian.

(d) AIDS confidential information may be disclosed to any person or legal entity designated to receive that information when that designation is made in writing by the person identified by that information or, if that person is a minor or incompetent person, by that person's parent or legal guardian.

(e) AIDS confidential information may be disclosed to any agency or department of the federal government, this state, or any political subdivision of this state if that information is authorized or required by law to be reported to that agency or department.

(f) The results of an HIV test may be disclosed to the person, or that person's designated representative, who ordered such tests of the body fluids or tissue of another person.

(g) When the patient of a physician has been determined to be infected with HIV and that patient's physician reasonably believes that the spouse or sexual partner or any child of the patient, spouse, or sexual partner is a person at risk of being infected with HIV by that patient, the physician may disclose to that spouse, sexual partner, or child that the patient has been determined to be infected with HIV, after first attempting to notify the patient that such disclosure is going to be made.

(h)(1) An administrator of an institution licensed as a hospital by the Department of Human Resources or a physician having a patient who has been determined to be infected with HIV may disclose to the Department of Human Resources:

(A) The name and address of that patient;

(B) That such patient has been determined to be infected with HIV; and

(C) The name and address of any other person whom the disclosing physician or administrator reasonably believes to be a person at risk of being infected with HIV by that patient.

(2) When mandatory and nonanonymous reporting of confirmed positive HIV tests to the Department of Human Resources is determined by that department to be reasonably necessary, that department shall establish by regulation a date on and after which such reporting shall be required. On and after the date so established, each health care provider, health care facility, or any other person or legal entity which orders an HIV test for another person shall report to the Department of Human Resources the name and address of any person thereby determined to be infected with HIV. No such report shall be made regarding any confirmed positive HIV test provided at any anonymous HIV test site operated by or on behalf of the Department of Human Resources.

(3) The Department of Human Resources may disclose that a person has been reported, under paragraph (1) or (2) of this subsection, to have been determined to be infected with HIV to the board of health of the county in which that person resides or is located if reasonably necessary to protect the health and safety of that person or other persons who may have come in contact with the body fluids of the HIV infected person. The Department of Human Resources or county board of health to which information is disclosed pursuant to this paragraph or paragraph (1) or (2) of this subsection:

(A) May contact any person named in such disclosure as having been determined to be an HIV infected person for the purpose of counseling that person and requesting therefrom the name of any other person who may be a person at risk of being infected with HIV by that HIV infected person;

(B) May contact any other person reasonably believed to be a person at risk of being infected with HIV by that HIV infected person for the purposes of disclosing that such infected person has been determined to be infected with HIV and counseling such person to submit to an HIV test; and

(C) Shall contact and provide counseling to the spouse of any HIV infected person whose name is thus disclosed if both persons are reasonably likely to have engaged in sexual intercourse or any other act determined by the department likely to have resulted in the transmission of HIV between such persons within the preceding seven years and if that spouse may be located and contacted without undue difficulty.

(i) Any health care provider authorized to order an HIV test may disclose AIDS confidential information regarding a patient thereof if that disclosure is made to a health care provider or health care facility which has provided, is providing, or will provide any health care service to that patient and as a result of such provision of service that health care provider or facility:

(1) Has personnel or patients who may be persons at risk of being infected with HIV by that patient, if that patient is an HIV infected person and such disclosure is reasonably necessary to protect any such personnel or patients from that risk; or

(2) Has a legitimate need for that information in order to provide that health care service to that patient.

(j) A health care provider or any other person or legal entity authorized but not required to disclose AIDS confidential information pursuant to this Code section shall have no duty to make such disclosure and shall not be liable to the patient or any other person or legal entity for failing to make such disclosure. A health care provider or any other person or legal entity which discloses information as authorized or required by this Code section or as authorized or required by law or rules or regulations made pursuant thereto shall have no civil or criminal liability therefor.

(k) When any person or legal entity is authorized or required by this Code section or any other law to disclose AIDS confidential information to a person at risk of being infected with HIV and that person at risk is a minor or incompetent person, such disclosure may be made to any parent or legal guardian of the minor or incompetent person, to the minor or incompetent person, or to both the minor or incompetent person and any parent or legal guardian thereof.

(*l*) When an institutional care facility is the site at which a person is at risk of being infected with HIV and as a result of that risk a disclosure of AIDS confidential information to any person at risk at that site is authorized or required under this Code section or any other law, such disclosure may be made to the person at risk or to that institutional care facility's chief administrative or executive officer, or such officer's designee, in which case that officer or designee is authorized to make such disclosure to the person at risk.

(m) When a disclosure of AIDS confidential information is authorized or required by this Code section to be made to a physician, health care provider, or legal entity, that disclosure may be made to employees of that physician, health care provider, or legal entity who have been designated thereby to receive such information on behalf thereof. Those designated employees may thereafter disclose to and provide for the disclosure of that information among such other employees of that physician, health care provider, or legal entity, but such disclosures among those employees are only authorized when reasonably necessary in the ordinary course of business to carry out the purposes for which that disclosure is authorized or required to be made to that physician, health care provider, or legal entity.

(n) Any disclosure of AIDS confidential information authorized or required by this Code section or any other law and any unauthorized disclosure of such information shall in no way destroy the confidential nature of that information except for the purpose for which the authorized or required disclosure is made.

(*o*) Any person or legal entity which violates subsection (b) of this Code section shall be guilty of a misdemeanor.

(p) Nothing in this Code section or any other law shall be construed to authorize the disclosure of AIDS confidential information if that disclosure is prohibited by federal law, or regulations promulgated thereunder, nor shall anything in this Code section or any other law be construed to prohibit the disclosure of information which would be AIDS confidential information except that such information does not permit the identification of any person.

(q) A public safety agency or district attorney may obtain the results from an HIV test to which the person named in the request has submitted under Code Section 15–11–66.1, 17–10–15, 42–5–52.1, or 42–9–42.1, notwithstanding that the results may be contained in a sealed record.

(r) Any person or legal entity required by an order of a court to disclose AIDS confidential information in the custody or control of such person or legal entity shall disclose that information as required by that order.

(s) AIDS confidential information may be disclosed as medical information pursuant to Code Section 24–9–40, relating to the release of medical information, or pursuant to any other law which authorizes or requires the disclosure of medical information if:

(1) The person identified by that information:

(A) Has consented in writing to that disclosure; or

(B) Has been notified of the request for disclosure of that information at least ten days prior to the time the disclosure is to be made and does not object to such disclosure prior to the time specified for that disclosure in that notice; or

(2) A superior court in an in camera hearing finds by clear and convincing evidence a compelling need for the information which cannot be accommodated by other means. In assessing compelling need, the court shall weigh the public health, safety, or welfare needs or any other public or private need for the disclosure against the privacy interest of the person identified by the information and the public interest which may be disserved by disclosures which may deter voluntary HIV tests. If the court determines that disclosure of that information is authorized under this paragraph, the court shall order that disclosure and impose appropriate safeguards against any unauthorized disclosure. The records of that hearing otherwise shall be under seal.

(t)(1) A superior court of this state may order a person or legal entity to disclose AIDS confidential information in its custody or control to:

(A) A prosecutor in connection with a prosecution for the alleged commission of reckless conduct under subsection (c) of Code Section 16-5-60;

(B) Any party in a civil cause of action; or

(C) A public safety agency or the Department of Human Resources if that agency or department has an employee thereof who has, in the course of that employment, come in contact with the body fluids of the person identified by the AIDS confidential information sought in such a manner reasonably likely to cause that employee to become an HIV infected person and provided the disclosure is necessary for the health and safety of that employee,

and for purposes of this subsection the term "petitioner for disclosure" means any person or legal entity specified in subparagraph (A), (B), or (C) of this paragraph.

(2) An order may be issued against a person or legal entity responsible for recording, reporting, or maintaining AIDS confidential information to compel the disclosure of that information if the petitioner for disclosure demonstrates by clear and convincing evidence a compelling need for the information which cannot be accommodated by other means. In assessing compelling need, the court shall weigh the public health, safety, or welfare needs or any other public or private need for the disclosure against the privacy interest of the person identified by the information and the public interest which may be disserved by disclosures which may deter voluntary HIV tests.

(3) A petition seeking disclosure of AIDS confidential information under this subsection shall substitute a pseudonym for the true name of the person concerning whom the information is sought. The disclosure to the parties of that person's true name shall be communicated confidentially, in documents not filed with the court.

(4) Before granting any order under this subsection, the court shall provide the person concerning whom the information is sought with notice and a reasonable opportunity to participate in the proceedings if that person is not already a party.

(5) Court proceedings as to disclosure of AIDS confidential information under this subsection shall be conducted in camera unless the person concerning whom the information is sought agrees to a hearing in open court.

(6) Upon the issuance of an order that a person or legal entity be required to disclose AIDS confidential information regarding a person named in that order, that person or entity so ordered shall disclose to the ordering court any such information which is in the control or custody of that person or entity and which relates to the person named in the order for the court to make an in camera inspection thereof. If the court determines from that inspection that the person named in the order is an HIV infected person, the court shall disclose to the petitioner for disclosure that determination and shall impose appropriate safeguards against unauthorized disclosure which shall specify the persons who may have access to the information, the purposes for which the information shall be used, and appropriate prohibitions on future disclosure.

(7) The record of the proceedings under this subsection shall be sealed by the court.

(8) An order may not be issued under this subsection against the Department of Human Resources, any county board of health, or any anonymous HIV test site operated by or on behalf of that department.

(u) A health care provider, health care facility, or other person or legal entity who, in violation of this Code section, unintentionally discloses AIDS confidential information, notwithstanding the maintenance of procedures thereby which are reasonably adopted to avoid risk of such disclosure, shall not be civilly or criminally liable, unless such disclosure was due to gross negligence or wanton and willful misconduct.

(v) AIDS confidential information may be disclosed when that disclosure is otherwise authorized or required by Code Section 42-1-6, if AIDS or HIV infection is the communicable disease at issue, or when that disclosure is otherwise authorized or required by any law which specifically refers to "AIDS confidential information," "HIV test results," or any similar language indicating a legislative intent to disclose information specifically relating to AIDS or HIV.

(w) A health care provider who has received AIDS confidential information regarding a patient from the patient's health care provider directly or indirectly under the provisions of subsection (i) of this Code section may disclose that information to a health care provider which has provided, is providing, or will provide any health care service to that patient and as a result of that provision of service that health care provider:

(1) Has personnel or patients who may be persons at risk of being infected with HIV by that patient, if that patient is an HIV infected person and such disclosure is reasonably necessary to protect any such personnel or patients from that risk; or

(2) Has a legitimate need for that information in order to provide that health care service to that patient.

(x) Neither the Department of Human Resources nor any county board of health shall disclose AIDS confidential information contained in its records unless such disclosure is authorized or required by this Code section or any other law, except that such information in those records shall not be a public record and shall not be subject to disclosure through subpoena, court order, or other judicial process.

(y) The protection against disclosure provided by Code Section 24-9-40.1 shall be waived and AIDS confidential information may be disclosed to the extent that the person identified by such information, his heirs, successors, assigns, or a beneficiary of such person, including but not limited to an executor, administrator, or personal representative of such person's estate:

(1) Files a claim or claims other entitlements under any insurance policy or benefit plan or is involved in any civil proceeding regarding such claim;

(2) Places such person's care and treatment, the nature and extent of his injuries, the extent of his damages, his medical condition, or the reasons for his death at issue in any civil or criminal proceeding; or

(3) Is involved in a dispute regarding coverage under any insurance policy or benefit plan.

(z) AIDS confidential information may be collected, used, and disclosed by an insurer in accordance with the provisions of Chapter 39 of Title 33, relating to the collection, use, and disclosure of information gathered by insurance institutions.

(aa) In connection with any civil or criminal action in which AIDS confidential information is disclosed as authorized or required by this Code section, the party to whom that information is thereby disclosed may subpoena any person to authenticate such AIDS confidential information, establish a chain of custody relating thereto, or otherwise testify regarding that information, including but not limited to testifying regarding any notifications to the patient regarding results of an HIV test. The provisions of this subsection shall apply as to records, personnel, or both of the Department of Human Resources or a county board of health notwithstanding Code Section 50-18-72, but only as to test results obtained by a prosecutor under subsection (q) of this Code section and to be used thereby in a prosecution for reckless conduct under subsection (c) of Code Section 16-5-60.

(bb) AIDS confidential information may be disclosed as a part of any proceeding or procedure authorized or required pursuant to Chapter 3, 4, or 7 of Title 37, regarding a person who is alleged to be or who is mentally ill, mentally retarded, or alcoholic or drug dependent, or as a part of any proceeding or procedure authorized or required pursuant to Title 29, regarding the guardianship of a person or that person's estate, as follows:

(1) Any person who files or transmits a petition or other document which discloses AIDS confidential information in connection with any such proceeding or procedure shall provide a cover page which contains only the type of proceeding or procedure, the court in which the proceeding or procedure is or will be pending, and the words "CONFIDENTIAL INFORMATION" without in any way otherwise disclosing thereon the name of any individual or that such petition or other document specifically contains AIDS confidential information;

(2) AIDS confidential information shall only be disclosed pursuant to this subsection after disclosure to and with the written consent of the person identified by that information, or that person's parent or guardian if that person is a minor or has previously been adjudicated as being incompetent, or by order of court obtained in accordance with subparagraph (C) of paragraph (3) of this subsection;

(3) If any person files or transmits a petition or other document in connection with any such proceeding or procedure which discloses AIDS confidential information without obtaining consent as provided in paragraph (2) of this subsection, the court receiving such information shall either obtain written consent as set forth in that paragraph (2) for any further use or disclosure of such information or:

(A) Return such petition or other document to the person who filed or transmitted same, with directions against further filing or transmittal of such information in connection with such proceeding or procedure except in compliance with this subsection;

(B) Delete or expunge all references to such AIDS confidential information from the particular petition or other document; or

(C)(i) If the court determines there is a compelling need for such information in connection with the particular proceeding or procedure, petition a superior court of competent jurisdiction for permission to obtain or disclose that information. If the person identified by the information is not yet represented by an attorney in the proceeding or procedure in connection with which the information is sought, the petitioning court shall appoint an attorney for such person. The petitioning court shall have both that person and that person's attorney personally served with notice of the petition and time and place of the superior court hearing thereon. Such hearing shall not be held sooner than 72 hours after service, unless the information is to be used in connection with an emergency guardianship proceeding under Code Section 29-4-14, in which event the hearing shall not be held sooner than 48 hours after service.

(ii) The superior court in which a petition is filed pursuant to division (i) of this subparagraph shall hold an in camera hearing on such petition. The purpose of the hearing shall be to determine whether there is clear and convincing evidence of a compelling need for the AIDS confidential information sought in connection with the particular proceeding or procedure which cannot be accommodated by other means. In assessing compelling need, the superior court shall weigh the public health, safety, or welfare needs or any other public or private need for the disclosure against the privacy interest of the person identified by the information and the public interest which may be disserved by disclosures which may deter voluntary HIV tests. If the court determines that disclosure of that information is authorized under this subparagraph, the court shall order that disclosure and impose appropriate safeguards against any unauthorized disclosure. The records of that hearing otherwise shall be under seal; and

(4) The court having jurisdiction over such proceeding or procedure, when it becomes apparent that AIDS confidential information will likely be or has been disclosed in connection with such proceeding or procedure, shall take such measures as the court determines appropriate to preserve the confidentiality of the disclosed information to the maximum extent possible. Such measures shall include, without being limited to, closing the proceeding or procedure to the public and sealing all or any part of the records of the proceeding or procedure containing AIDS confidential information. The records of any appeals taken from any such proceeding or procedure shall also be sealed. Furthermore, the court may consult with and obtain the advice of medical experts or other counsel or advisers as to the relevance and materiality of such information in such proceedings or procedures, so long as the identity of the person identified by such information is not thereby revealed.

Laws 1988, p. 1799, § 6; Laws 1989, p. 14, § 24; Laws 1990, p. 705, § 1; Laws 2000, p. 20, § 19; Laws 2004, Act 460, § 5, eff. July 1, 2005.

Article 3

Examination

§ 24-9-60. Oath or affirmation, necessity of

The sanction of an oath or affirmation equivalent thereto shall be necessary to the reception of any oral evidence. The court may frame such affirmation according to the religious faith of the witness.

Formerly Code 1863, § 3786; Code 1868, § 3806; Code 1873, § 3862; Code 1882, § 3862; Civil Code 1895, § 5279; Civil Code 1910, § 5868; Code 1933, § 38-1701.

§ 24-9-61. Separate examinations; effect of mere irregularity

Except as otherwise provided in Code Section 24-9-61.1, in all cases either party shall have the right to have the witnesses of the other party examined out of the hearing of each other. The court shall take proper care to effect this object as far as practicable and convenient, but no mere irregularity shall exclude a witness.

Laws 1985, p. 744, § 1.

Formerly Code 1863, § 3787; Code 1868, § 3807; Code 1873, § 3863; Code 1882, § 3863; Civil Code 1895, § 5280; Penal Code 1895, § 1017; Civil Code 1910, § 5869; Penal Code 1910, § 1043; Code 1933, § 38-1703.

§ 24-9-61.1. Victim of criminal offense may be entitled to be present in court during prosecution of such offense

(a) The victim of a criminal offense may be entitled to be present in any court exercising jurisdiction over such offense. It shall be within the sole discretion of the judge to implement the provisions of this Code section and determine when to allow such victim to be present in such court and, if such victim is permitted to be present, to determine the order in which the testimony of such victim shall be given.

(b) The failure of a victim to exercise any right granted by this Code section shall not be a cause or ground for an appeal of a conviction by a defendant or for any court to set aside, reverse, or remand a criminal conviction.

Laws 1985, p. 744, § 2.

§ 24-9-62. Protection of witnesses

It shall be the right of a witness to be examined only as to relevant matter and to be protected from improper questions and from harsh or insulting demeanor.

Formerly Civil Code 1895, § 5281; Civil Code 1910, § 5870; Code 1933, § 38-1704.

§ 24-9-63. Leading questions; discretion of court

Leading questions are generally allowed only in cross-examination. However, the court may exercise discretion in granting the right to the party calling the witness and in refusing it to the opposite party when, from the conduct of the witness or other reason, justice shall require it.

Formerly Code 1863, § 3789; Code 1868, § 3809; Code 1873, § 3865; Code 1882, § 3865; Civil Code 1895, § 5283; Penal Code 1895, § 1019; Civil Code 1910, § 5872; Penal Code 1910, § 1045; Code 1933, § 38–1706.

§ 24-9-64. Cross-examination of witnesses, right of

The right of a thorough and sifting cross-examination shall belong to every party as to the witnesses called against him. If several parties to the same case have distinct interests, each may exercise this right.

Formerly Code 1863, § 3788; Code 1868, § 3808; Code 1873, § 3864; Code 1882, § 3864; Civil Code 1895, § 5282; Penal Code 1895, § 1018; Civil Code 1910, § 5871; Penal Code 1910, § 1044; Code 1933, § 38–1705.

§ 24-9-65. Opinions of witness admissible, when

Where the question under examination, and to be decided by the jury, shall be one of opinion, any witness may swear to his opinion or belief, giving his reasons therefor. If the issue shall be as to the existence of a fact, the opinions of witnesses shall be generally inadmissible.

Formerly Code 1863, § 3791; Code 1868, § 3811; Code 1873, § 3867; Code 1882, § 3867; Civil Code 1895, § 5285; Penal Code 1895, § 1021; Civil Code 1910, § 5874; Penal Code 1910, § 1047; Code 1933, § 38–1708.

§ 24-9-66. Market value, how proved

Direct testimony as to market value is in the nature of opinion evidence. One need not be an expert or dealer in the article in question but may testify as to its value if he has had an opportunity for forming a correct opinion.

Formerly Civil Code 1895, § 5286; Civil Code 1910, § 5875; Code 1933, § 38–1709.

§ 24-9-67. Expert opinions; admissibility; criminal cases

In criminal cases, the opinions of experts on any question of science, skill, trade, or like questions shall always be admissible; and such opinions may be given on the facts as proved by other witnesses.

Laws 2005, Act 1, § 7, eff. Feb. 16, 2005.

Formerly Code 1863, § 3792; Code 1868, § 3812; Code 1873, § 3868; Code 1882, § 3868; Civil Code 1895, § 5287; Penal Code 1895, § 1022; Civil Code 1910, § 5876; Penal Code 1910, § 1048; Code 1933, § 38–1710.

§ 24-9-67.1. Expert opinions; admissibility; civil actions

(a) The provisions of this Code section shall apply in all civil actions. The opinion of a witness qualified as an expert under this Code section may be given on the facts as proved by other witnesses. The facts or data in the particular case upon which an expert bases an opinion or inference may be those perceived by or made known to the expert at or before the hearing or trial. If of a type reasonably relied upon by experts in the particular field in forming opinions or inferences upon the subject, the facts or data need not be admissible in evidence in order for the opinion or inference to be admitted. Facts or data that are otherwise inadmissible shall not be disclosed to the jury by the proponent of the opinion or inference unless the court determines that their probative value in assisting the jury to evaluate the expert's opinion substantially outweighs their prejudicial effect.

(b) If scientific, technical, or other specialized knowledge will assist the trier of fact in any cause of action to understand the evidence or to determine a fact in issue, a witness qualified as an expert by knowledge, skill, experience, training, or education may testify thereto in the form of an opinion or otherwise, if:

(1) The testimony is based upon sufficient facts or data which are or will be admitted into evidence at the hearing or trial;

(2) The testimony is the product of reliable principles and methods; and

(3) The witness has applied the principles and methods reliably to the facts of the case.

(c) Notwithstanding the provisions of subsection (b) of this Code section and any other provision of law which might be construed to the contrary, in professional malpractice actions, the opinions of an expert, who is otherwise qualified as to the acceptable standard of conduct of the professional whose conduct is at issue, shall be admissible only if, at the time the act or omission is alleged to have occurred, such expert:

(1) Was licensed by an appropriate regulatory agency to practice his or her profession in the state in which such expert was practicing or teaching in the profession at such time; and

(2) In the case of a medical malpractice action, had actual professional knowledge and experience in the area of practice or specialty in which the opinion is to be given as the result of having been regularly engaged in:

(A) The active practice of such area of specialty of his or her profession for at least three of the last five years, with sufficient frequency to establish an appropriate level of knowledge, as determined by the judge, in performing the procedure, diagnosing the condition, or rendering the treatment which is alleged to have been performed or rendered negligently by the defendant whose conduct is at issue; or

(B) The teaching of his or her profession for at least three of the last five years as an employed member of the faculty of an educational institution accredited in the teaching of such profession, with sufficient frequency to establish an appropriate level of knowledge, as determined by the judge, in teaching others how to perform the procedure, diagnose the condition, or render the treatment which is alleged to have been performed or rendered negligently by the defendant whose conduct is at issue; and

(C) Except as provided in subparagraph (D) of this paragraph:

(i) Is a member of the same profession;

(ii) Is a medical doctor testifying as to the standard of care of a defendant who is a doctor of osteopathy; or

(iii) Is a doctor of osteopathy testifying as to the standard of care of a defendant who is a medical doctor; and

(D) Notwithstanding any other provision of this Code section, an expert who is a physician and, as a result of having, during at least three of the last five years immediately preceding the time the act or omission is alleged to have occurred, supervised, taught, or instructed nurses, nurse practitioners, certified registered nurse anesthetists, nurse midwives, physician's assistants, physical therapists, occupational therapists, or medical support staff, has knowledge of the standard of care of that health care provider under the circumstances at issue shall be competent to testify as to the standard of that health care provider. However, a nurse, nurse practitioner, certified registered nurse anesthetist, nurse midwife, physician's assistant, physical therapist, occupational therapist, or medical support staff shall not be competent to testify as to the standard of care of a physician.

(d) Upon motion of a party, the court may hold a pretrial hearing to determine whether the witness qualifies as an expert and whether the expert's testimony satisfies the requirements of subsections (a) and (b) of this Code section. Such hearing and ruling shall be completed no later than the final pretrial conference contemplated under Code Section 9–11–16.

(e) An affiant must meet the requirements of this Code section in order to be deemed qualified to testify as an expert by means of the affidavit required under Code Section 9–11–9.1.

(f) It is the intent of the legislature that, in all civil cases, the courts of the State of Georgia not be viewed as open to expert evidence that would not be admissible in other states. Therefore, in interpreting and applying this Code section, the courts of this state may draw from the opinions of the United States Supreme Court in Daubert v. Merrell Dow Pharmaceuticals, Inc., 509 U.S. 579 (1993); General Electric Co. v. Joiner, 522 U.S. 136 (1997); Kumho Tire Co. Ltd. v. Carmichael, 526 U.S. 137 (1999); and other cases in federal courts applying the standards announced by the United States Supreme Court in these cases.

Laws 2005, Act 1, § 7, eff. Feb. 16, 2005.

§ 24–9–68. State of feeling and relationship

The state of a witness's feelings toward the parties and his relationship to them may always be proved for the consideration of the jury.

Laws 1995, p. 10, § 24.

Formerly Code 1863, § 3800; Code 1868, § 3820; Code 1873, § 3876; Code 1882, § 3876; Civil Code 1895, § 5289; Penal Code 1895, § 1023; Civil Code 1910, § 5878; Penal Code 1910, § 1049; Code 1933, § 38–1712.

§ 24–9–69. Memorandum in aid of witness' memory

A witness may refresh and assist his memory by the use of any written instrument or memorandum, provided he shall finally speak from his recollection thus refreshed or shall be willing to swear positively from the paper.

Formerly Code 1863, § 3790; Code 1868, § 3810; Code 1873, § 3866; Code 1882, § 3866; Civil Code 1895, § 5284; Penal Code 1895, § 1020; Civil Code 1910, § 5873; Penal Code 1910, § 1046; Code 1933, § 38–1707.

§ 24–9–70. Waiver of objection made on direct examination

If on direct examination of a witness objection is made to the admissibility of evidence, neither cross-examination of the witness on the same subject matter nor the introduction of evidence on the same subject matter shall constitute a waiver of the objection made on direct examination.

Laws 1971, p. 460, § 1.

Formerly Code 1933, § 38–1713.

Article 4

Credibility

§ 24-9-80. Credibility of witnesses as question for jury

The credibility of a witness is a matter to be determined by the jury under proper instructions from the court.

Formerly Civil Code 1895, § 5294; Penal Code 1895, § 1028; Civil Code 1910, § 5883; Penal Code 1910, § 1054; Code 1933, § 38-1805.

§ 24-9-81. Impeaching own witness

Any party, including the party calling the witness, may attack the credibility of a witness. In the trial of all civil cases, either plaintiff or defendant shall be permitted to make the opposite party, or anyone for whose immediate benefit the action is prosecuted or defended, or any agent of said party, or agent of any person for whose immediate benefit such action is prosecuted or defended, or officer or agent of a corporation when a corporation is such party or for whose benefit such action is prosecuted or defended a witness, with the privilege of subjecting such witness to a thorough and sifting examination and with the further privilege of impeachment, as if the witness had testified in his or her own behalf and were being cross-examined.

Laws 1890-91, p. 78, § 1; Laws 1945, p. 227, § 1; Laws 1947, p. 568, § 1; Laws 2005, Act 8, § 15, eff. July 1, 2005.

Formerly Code 1863, § 3793; Code 1868, § 3813; Code 1873, § 3869; Code 1882, § 3869; Civil Code 1895, § 5290; Penal Code 1895, § 1024; Civil Code 1910, § 5879; Penal Code 1910, § 1050; Code 1933, § 38-1801.

§ 24-9-82. Disproving facts testified to

A witness may be impeached by disproving the facts testified to by him.

Formerly Code 1863, § 3795; Code 1868, § 3815; Code 1873, § 3871; Code 1882, § 3871; Civil Code 1895, § 5291; Penal Code 1895, § 1025; Civil Code 1910, § 5880; Penal Code 1910, § 1051; Code 1933, § 38-1802.

§ 24-9-83. Contradictory statements. Proof of general good character

A witness may be impeached by contradictory statements previously made by him as to matters relevant to his testimony and to the case. Before contradictory statements may be proved against him, unless they are written statements made under oath in connection with some judicial proceedings, the time, place, person, and circumstances attending the former statements shall be called to his mind with as much certainty as possible. If the contradictory statements are in writing and in existence, they shall be shown to him or read in his hearing. To lay this foundation, the witness may be recalled at any time. When thus impeached, the witness may be sustained by proof of general good character, the effect of the evidence to be determined by the jury.

Formerly Code 1863, §§ 3795, 3796, 3799; Code 1868, §§ 3815, 3816, 3819; Code 1873, §§ 3871, 3872, 3875; Code 1882, §§ 3871, 3872, 3875; Civil Code 1895, § 5292; Penal Code 1895, § 1026; Civil Code 1910, § 5881; Penal Code 1910, § 1052; Code 1933, § 38-1803.

§ 24-9-84. Proof of general bad character; particular transactions

Any party may impeach the credibility of a witness by offering evidence of the witness's bad character in the form of reputation, but subject to the following limitations:

(1) The evidence may refer only to character for truthfulness or untruthfulness;

(2) Evidence of truthful character is admissible only after the character of the witness for truthfulness has been attacked by reputation evidence or otherwise;

(3) In a criminal case, the character for untruthfulness of the defendant may be introduced in evidence only if the defendant testifies and offers evidence of his or her truthful character; and

(4) The character witness should first be questioned as to his or her knowledge of the general character of the witness, next as to what that character is, and lastly the character witness may be asked if from that character he or she would believe him or her on his or her oath. The witness may be sustained by similar proof of character. The particular transactions or the opinions of single individuals shall not be inquired of on either side, except upon cross-examination in seeking for the extent and foundation of the witness's knowledge.

Laws 2005, Act 8, § 16, eff. July 1, 2005.

Formerly Code 1863, §§ 3795, 3797, 3798; Code 1868, §§ 3815, 3817, 3818; Code 1873, §§ 3871, 3873, 3874; Code 1882, §§ 3871, 3873, 3874; Civil Code 1895, § 5293; Penal Code 1895, § 1027; Civil Code 1910, § 5882; Penal Code 1910, § 1053; Code 1933, § 38-1804.

§ 24-9-84.1. Evidence of criminal conviction; effect of pardon or annulment; juvenile adjudications

(a) *General rule.* For the purpose of attacking the credibility of a witness, or of the defendant, if the defendant testifies:

(1) Evidence that a witness has been convicted of a crime shall be admitted if the crime was punishable by death or imprisonment of one year or more under the law under which the witness was convicted if the court determines that the probative value of admitting the evidence outweighs its prejudicial effect to the witness;

(2) Evidence that the defendant has been convicted of a crime shall be admitted if the crime was punishable by death or imprisonment of one year or more under the law under which the defendant was convicted if the court determines that the probative value of admitting the evidence substantially outweighs its prejudicial effect to the defendant; and

(3) Evidence that any witness or the defendant has been convicted of a crime shall be admitted if it involved dishonesty or making a false statement, regardless of the punishment that could be imposed for such offense.

(b) *Time limit.* Evidence of a conviction under subsection (a) of this Code section is not admissible if a period of more than ten years has elapsed since the date of the conviction or of the release of the witness or the defendant from the confinement imposed for that conviction, whichever is the later date, unless the court determines, in the interest of justice, that the probative value of the conviction supported by specific facts and circumstances substantially outweighs its prejudicial effect. However, evidence of a conviction more than ten years old, as calculated in this subsection, is not admissible unless the proponent gives to the adverse party sufficient advance written notice of intent to use such evidence to provide the adverse party with a fair opportunity to contest the use of such evidence.

(c) *Effect of pardon or annulment.* Evidence of a conviction is not admissible under this Code section if:

(1) The conviction has been the subject of a pardon or annulment based on a finding of the rehabilitation of the person convicted and such person has not been convicted of a subsequent crime that was punishable by death or imprisonment for one year or more; or

(2) The conviction has been the subject of a pardon, annulment, or other equivalent procedure based on a finding of innocence.

(d) *Juvenile adjudications.* An adjudication of delinquency in juvenile court shall be inadmissible against a defendant in a criminal case. An adjudication of delinquency in juvenile court shall be presumed to be inadmissible against a witness in a criminal case; however, this presumption may be rebutted only if it is shown that:

(1) The factual basis for the proven allegations of delinquency would have constituted a crime under the laws of the state of the juvenile court if committed by an adult at the time they were committed by the juvenile:

(2) The probative value of the evidence substantially outweighs the prejudicial effect of its admission; and

(3) The court finds that admission of the adjudication into evidence is necessary for a fair determination of the issue of guilt or innocence of the defendant.

(e) *Pendency of appeal.* The pendency of an appeal from a conviction does not render evidence of a conviction inadmissible. Evidence of the pendency of an appeal shall be admissible.

Laws 2005, Act 8, § 16, eff. July 1, 2005; Laws 2006, Act 453, § 24, eff. April 14, 2006.

§ 24-9-85. What credit to impeached witness; question for jury

(a) When a witness shall be successfully contradicted as to a material matter, his credit as to other matters shall be for the jury. The credit to be given a witness's testimony where impeached for general bad character or for contradictory statements out of court shall be for the jury to determine.

(b) If a witness shall willfully and knowingly swear falsely, his testimony shall be disregarded entirely, unless corroborated by circumstances or other unimpeached evidence.

Formerly Civil Code 1895, § 5295; Civil Code 1910, § 5884; Code 1933, § 38-1806.

Article 5

Use of Sign Language and Intermediary Interpreter in Administrative and Judicial Proceedings

§ 24-9-100. Policy of state

It is the policy of the State of Georgia to secure the rights of hearing impaired persons who, because of impaired hearing, cannot readily understand or communicate in spoken language and who consequently cannot equally participate in or benefit from proceedings, programs, and activities of the courts, legislative bodies, administrative agencies, licensing commission, departments, and boards of the state and its subdivisions unless qualified interpreters are available to assist them.

Laws 1983, p. 852, § 2.

§ 24-9-101. Definitions

As used in this article, the term:

(1) "Agency" means any agency, authority, board, bureau, committee, commission, court, department, or jury of the legislative, judicial, or executive branch of government of the state or any political subdivision thereof.

(2) "Department" means the Department of Human Resources.

(3) "Hearing impaired person" means any person whose hearing is totally impaired or whose hearing is so seriously impaired as to prohibit the person from understanding oral communications when spoken in a normal conversational tone.

(4) "Intermediary interpreter" means any person, including any hearing impaired person, who is able to assist in providing an accurate interpretation between spoken English and sign language or between the variance of sign language by acting as an intermediary between a hearing impaired person and a qualified interpreter.

(5) "Proceeding" means any meeting, hearing, trial, investigation, or other proceeding of any nature conducted by an agency.

(6) "Qualified interpreter" means any person certified as an interpreter by the National Registry of Interpreters for the Deaf or approved as an interpreter by the Georgia Registry of Interpreters for the Deaf.

Laws 1983, p. 852, § 2.

§ 24-9-102. When interpreter shall be provided by agency

(a) The agency conducting any proceeding shall provide a qualified interpreter to the hearing impaired person:

(1) Whenever the hearing impaired person is a party to the proceeding or a witness before the proceeding; or

(2) Whenever a person below the age of 18 years whose parents are hearing impaired persons is a party to the proceeding or a witness before the proceeding conducted by an agency.

(b) The hearing impaired person shall notify the agency not less than ten days, excluding weekends and holidays, prior to the date of the proceeding of the need for a qualified interpreter. If the hearing impaired person receives notice of the proceeding less than ten days, excluding weekends and holidays, prior to the proceeding, he shall notify the agency as soon as practicable after receiving such notice. Upon receiving a request for a qualified interpreter, the agency shall immediately forward such request to the department. Upon receiving a request from an agency, the department shall provide a qualified interpreter for the proceeding specified in the request.

Laws 1983, p. 852, § 2; Laws 1985, p. 149, § 24.

§ 24-9-103. Procedures for providing interpreter by arresting law enforcement agency

(a) The arresting law enforcement agency shall provide a qualified interpreter to any hearing impaired person whenever the hearing impaired person is taken into custody for allegedly violating any criminal law or ordinance of the state or any political subdivision thereof.

(b)(1) Except as provided in paragraph (2) of this subsection, the law enforcement agency shall immediately request a qualified interpreter from the department, and the department shall provide a qualified interpreter. No interrogation, warning, informing of rights, taking of statements, or other investigatory procedures shall be undertaken until a qualified interpreter has been provided; and no answer, statement, admission, or other evidence acquired from the hearing impaired person shall be admissible in any criminal or quasi-criminal proceeding unless such was knowingly and voluntarily given through and in the presence of a qualified interpreter. No hearing impaired person who has been taken into custody and who is otherwise eligible for release shall be detained because of the unavailability of a qualified interpreter.

(2) If a qualified interpreter is not available one hour after the hearing impaired person has been taken into custody and a request has been forwarded to the department, the arresting officer may interrogate or take a statement from such person, provided that such interrogation and answers thereto shall be in writing and shall be preserved and turned over to the court in the event such person is tried for the alleged offense.

Laws 1983, p. 852, § 2.

§ 24-9-104. Procedures for providing interpreter by court

(a) A court shall provide a qualified interpreter to any hearing impaired person whenever the hearing impaired person has been provided with a court appointed legal counsel. The court shall request a qualified interpreter from the department, and the department shall provide a qualified interpreter.

(b) The qualified interpreter authorized by this Code section shall be present at all times when the hearing impaired person is consulting with legal counsel.

Laws 1983, p. 852, § 2.

§ 24-9-105. Waiver of right to use of interpreter

Whenever a hearing impaired person shall be authorized a qualified interpreter, such person may waive the right to the use of such interpreter. Any such waiver shall be in writing and shall be approved by the agency, law enforcement agency, or court before which the hearing impaired person is to appear. In no event shall the failure of a hearing impaired person to request an interpreter be deemed to be a waiver.

Laws 1983, p. 852, § 2.

§ 24-9-106. Determination that interpreter is able to communicate with hearing impaired person

(a) Whenever a hearing impaired person shall be authorized a qualified interpreter, the agency, law enforcement agency, or court shall determine whether the qualified interpreter so provided is able to communicate accurately with and translate information to and from the hearing impaired person. If it is determined that the qualified interpreter cannot perform these functions, the agency, law enforcement agency, or court shall request another qualified interpreter from the department or shall appoint an intermediary interpreter to assist the qualified interpreter in communicating with the hearing impaired person.

(b) The department shall prepare and maintain a list of qualified interpreters and qualified intermediary interpreters from which such interpreters shall be provided.

Laws 1983, p. 852, § 2.

§ 24-9-107. Oath; privilege

(a) Prior to providing any service to a hearing impaired person, any qualified interpreter or intermediary interpreter shall subscribe to an oath that he will interpret all communications in an accurate manner to the best of his skill and knowledge.

(b) Whenever a hearing impaired person communicates with any other person through the use of an interpreter and under circumstances which make such communications privileged, the presence of the interpreter shall not vitiate such privilege and the interpreter shall not be required to disclose the contents of such communication.

(c) Whenever an interpreter is required by this article, the agency, law enforcement agency, or court shall not begin the proceeding or take any action until the interpreter is in full view of and spatially situated so as to assure effective communication with the hearing impaired person.

(d) The agency, law enforcement agency, or court may, upon its own motion or upon motion of any party, witness, or participant, order that the testimony of the hearing impaired person be electronically and visually taped or filmed. Any such tape or film may be used to verify the testimony given by the hearing impaired person.

Laws 1983, p. 852, § 2.

§ 24-9-108. Compensation

(a) Any qualified interpreter or intermediary interpreter providing service under this article shall be compensated by the agency, law enforcement agency, or court requesting such service. Compensation shall be as provided in the fee schedule developed by the department.

(b) The department shall develop a fee schedule to be used in determining the compensation to be paid interpreters under this article. The schedule shall include reasonable fees commensurate with the services provided and shall include travel expenses and subsistence allowances as are authorized for state employees.

(c) The expenses of providing a qualified interpreter or intermediary interpreter in any civil proceeding may be assessed by the court or agency as costs in such proceeding.

Laws 1983, p. 852, § 2.

CHAPTER 10

SECURING ATTENDANCE OF WITNESSES AND PRODUCTION AND PRESERVATION OF EVIDENCE

Article 1

General Provisions

§ 24–10–1. Freedom of witnesses from arrest

A witness shall not be arrested on any civil process while going to or returning from and attending on any court. An officer who holds him imprisoned after seeing his subpoena or being satisfied of the fact shall be liable for false imprisonment.

Laws 1799, Cobb's 1851 Digest, p. 463.

Formerly Code 1863, § 3770; Code 1868, § 3794; Code 1873, § 3850; Code 1882, § 3850; Civil Code 1895, § 5265; Civil Code 1910, § 5854; Code 1933, § 38–1506.

§ 24–10–2. Attendance of female witnesses in civil cases

Female witnesses in civil cases pending in the courts of this state shall be required to attend in person under the same conditions and requirements that apply to male witnesses.

Laws 1953, Nov.-Dec. Sess., p. 212, § 1.

§ 24–10–2.1. Costs to witness after continuance

A witness in making a claim or proof of a claim for fees for attendance shall indicate the date on which he attended and, in the event of a continuance, shall not claim or receive fees for any day after the date to which the docket shows the case was continued nor for any day before the continuance was granted on which he did not attend.

Laws 1895, p. 41, § 2.

Formerly Civil Code 1895, § 5141; Civil Code 1910, § 5727; Code 1933, § 81–1422.

§ 24–10–3. Fees where cause continued for witnesses' absence

(a) A witness shall not receive any fees whatever for attendance on a subpoena if he is absent from the trial, or if the trial is continued at any time for his absence, where his absence did not arise from providential cause.

(b) No witness shall receive fees from both parties in the same case; the fees of a witness for both parties shall be apportioned equally between the parties unless the costs are all taxed against one party.

Formerly Code 1863, § 3771; Code 1868, § 3795; Code 1873, § 3851; Code 1882, § 3851; Civil Code 1895, § 5266; Civil Code 1910, § 5855; Code 1933, § 38–1507.

§ 24–10–4. Excessive claim by witness; forfeiture

A witness who claims more than is due to him shall forfeit all his fees and shall pay to the injured party, in addition thereto, four times the amount so unjustly claimed.

Formerly Code 1863, § 3766; Code 1868, § 3790; Code 1873, § 3843; Code 1882, § 3843; Civil Code 1895, § 5262; Civil Code 1910, § 5851; Code 1933, § 38–1503.

§ 24–10–5. When transcript of books may be used

When any person is served with a subpoena for the production of evidence or a notice to produce, seeking books in his possession to be used as testimony on the trial of any cause, if the person makes oath that he cannot produce the books required without suffering a material injury in his business and also makes or causes to be made out a full transcript from the books of all the accounts and dealings with the opposite party, has the transcript examined and sworn to by an impartial witness, and produces the same in court, he shall be deemed to have complied with the notice to produce or subpoena for the production of evidence.

Formerly Code 1863, § 3446; Code 1868, § 3466; Code 1873, § 3517; Code 1882, § 3517; Civil Code 1895, § 5258; Civil Code 1910, § 5847; Code 1933, § 38–1001.

§ 24–10–6. When books may be examined by commission

When the transcript provided for in Code Section 24–10–5 is produced in court, if the adverse party is dissatisfied therewith and swears that he believes that the books contain entries material to him which do not appear in the transcript, the court will grant him a commission directed to certain persons named by the parties and approved by the court. The commission shall cause the person with possession of the books to produce the books required, the person swearing that the books produced are all that he has or had that answer to the description in the subpoena or notice to produce. The commission shall examine the books and transmit to the court a full and fair statement of the accounts and entries between the parties under their hand. When received by the court, the statement of the commission shall be deemed a compliance with the notice to produce or subpoena for the production of evidence.

Formerly Code 1863, § 3447; Code 1868, § 3467; Code 1873, § 3518; Code 1882, § 3518; Civil Code 1895, § 5259; Civil Code 1910, § 5848; Code 1933, § 38-1002.

§ 24-10-7. Withdrawal of documentary evidence; substitution of copies

Parties interested and participating in the trial of all cases tried in the courts are authorized and empowered, on the order of the court trying the case, to withdraw from the court and record of the case all original deeds, maps, blueprints, notes, papers, and documents belonging to them and which are introduced in evidence on the trial, on substituting therefor, when required by the court, copies thereof, verified as such by the parties or their agents, representatives, or attorneys. However, if any such deeds, maps, blueprints, notes, papers, or documents shall be attacked by any party to the case as forgeries, or as not being genuine originals, it shall be in the discretion of the court to require the original deeds, maps, blueprints, notes, papers, or documents so attacked to remain on file in the court as a part of the record in the case.

Laws 1919, p. 235, § 1; Laws 1995, p. 10, § 24.

Formerly Code 1933, § 38-1003.

Article 2

Subpoenas and Notice to Produce

Part 1

In General

§ 24-10-20. Issuance of subpoenas

(a) Every subpoena shall be issued by the clerk under the seal of the court, shall state the name of the court and the title of the action, and shall command each person to whom it is directed to attend and give testimony at a time and place therein specified.

(b) The clerk shall issue a subpoena, or a subpoena for the production of documentary evidence, signed and sealed but otherwise in blank, to a party requesting it, who shall fill it in before service.

Laws 1792, Cobb's 1851 Digest, p. 353; Laws 1799, Cobb's 1851 Digest, p. 276; Laws 1873, p. 25, § 1; Laws 1953, Nov.-Dec. Sess., p. 484, § 1; Laws 1966, p. 502, § 1.

Formerly Code 1863, § 3764; Code 1868, § 3788; Code 1873, § 3841; Code 1882, § 3841; Civil Code 1895, § 5260; Civil Code 1910, § 5849; Code 1933, § 38-1501.

§ 24-10-21. Subpoenas; request for issuance; place of service

At the request of any party, subpoenas for attendance at a hearing or trial shall be issued by the clerk of the court in which the hearing or trial is held. A subpoena requiring the attendance of a witness at a hearing or trial may be served at any place within the state.

Laws 1966, p. 502, § 1; Laws 1980, p. 70, § 2.

§ 24-10-22. Subpoenas; for production of documents

(a) A subpoena may also command the person to whom it is directed to produce the books, papers, documents, or tangible things designated therein.

(b) The court, upon written motion made promptly and in any event at or before the time specified in the subpoena for compliance therewith, may:

(1) Quash or modify the subpoena if it is unreasonable and oppressive; or

(2) Condition denial of the motion upon the advancement by the person in whose behalf the subpoena is issued of the reasonable cost of producing the books, papers, documents, or tangible things.

Laws 1829, Cobb's 1851 Digest, p. 278; Laws 1877, p. 21, § 1; Laws 1880-81, p. 78, § 1; Laws 1892, p. 60, § 1; Laws 1966, p. 502, § 1.

Formerly Code 1863, §§ 3443, 3444; Code 1868, §§ 3463, 3464; Code 1873, §§ 3514, 3515; Code 1882, §§ 3514, 3515; Civil Code 1895, §§ 5255, 5256; Civil Code 1910, §§ 5844, 5845; Code 1933, §§ 38-901, 38-902.

§ 24-10-23. Subpoenas; service of

A subpoena may be served by any sheriff, by his deputy, or by any other person not less than 18 years of age. Proof may be shown by return or certificate endorsed on a copy of the subpoena. Subpoenas may also be served by registered or certified mail or statutory overnight delivery, and the return receipt shall constitute prima-facie proof of service. Service upon a party may be made by serving his counsel of record.

Laws 1792, Cobb's 1851 Digest, p. 353; Laws 1799, Cobb's 1851 Digest, p. 276; Laws 1873, p. 25, § 1; Laws 1966, p. 502, § 1; Laws 2000, p. 1589, § 3.

Formerly Code 1863, § 3764; Code 1868, § 3788; Code 1873, § 3841; Code 1882, § 3841; Civil Code 1895, § 5260; Civil Code 1910, § 5849; Code 1933, § 38–1501.

§ 24–10–24. Subpoenas; witness fees

The witness fee shall be $25.00 per diem, and execution shall be issued by the clerk upon affidavit of the witness to enforce payment thereof. The payment of fees shall not be demanded as a condition precedent to attendance; but, when a witness resides outside the county where the testimony is to be given, service of the subpoena, to be valid, must be accompanied by tender of the fee for one day's attendance plus mileage of 20¢ per mile for traveling expenses for going from and returning to his or her place of residence by the nearest practical route. Tender of fees and mileage may be made by United States currency, postal money order, cashier's check, certified check, or the check of an attorney or law firm. When the subpoena is issued on behalf of the state, or an officer, agency, or political subdivision thereof, or a defendant in a criminal case, fees and mileage need not be tendered.

Laws 1799, Cobb's 1851 Digest, p. 277; Laws 1842, Cobb's 1851 Digest, p. 280; Laws 1878–79, p. 66, § 1; Laws 1893, p. 38, § 1; Laws 1894, p. 49, § 1; Laws 1907, p. 58, § 1; Laws 1966, p. 502, § 1; Laws 1980, p. 70, § 1; Laws 2000, p. 1166, § 1.

Formerly Code 1863, §§ 3765, 3768; Code 1868, §§ 3789, 3792; Code 1873, §§ 3842, 3845; Code 1882, §§ 3842, 3845; Civil Code 1895, § 5261; Penal Code 1895, § 1115; Civil Code 1910, § 5850; Penal Code 1910, § 1144; Code 1933, §§ 38–1502, 38–1902.

§ 24–10–25. Subpoenas; enforcement

(a) Subpoenas may be enforced by attachment for contempt and by a fine not exceeding $300.00 and imprisonment not exceeding 20 days. In all cases under this Code section, the court shall consider whether under the circumstances of each case the subpoena was served within a reasonable time, but in any event not less than 24 hours prior to the time that appearance thereunder was required.

(b) The court may also in appropriate cases grant continuance of the cause. Where subpoenas were issued in blank, no continuance shall be granted because of failure to respond thereto when the party obtaining them fails to present to the clerk the name and address of the witness so subpoenaed at least six hours before appearance is required.

(c) When books, papers, or documents are unsuccessfully sought, secondary evidence thereof shall be admissible.

Laws 1799, Cobb's 1851 Digest, p. 276; Laws 1966, p. 502, § 1; Laws 1995, p. 10, § 24.

Formerly Code 1863, § 3767; Code 1868, § 3791; Code 1873, § 3844; Code 1882, § 3844; Civil Code 1895, § 5263; Civil Code 1910, § 5852; Code 1933, § 38–1504.

§ 24–10–26. Notices to produce

Where a party desires to compel production of books, writings, or other documents or tangible things in the possession, custody, or control of another party, in lieu of serving a subpoena under this article, the party desiring the production may serve a notice to produce upon counsel for the other party. Service may be perfected in accordance with Code Section 24–10–23, but no fees or mileage shall be allowed therefor. Such notices may be enforced in the manner prescribed by Code Section 24–10–25, and Code Section 24–10–22 shall also apply to such notices. The notice shall be in writing, signed by the party seeking production of the evidence, or his attorney, and shall be directed to the opposite party or his attorney.

Laws 1799, Cobb's 1851 Digest, p. 463; Laws 1841, Cobb's 1851 Digest, p. 465; Laws 1880–81, p. 78, § 1; Laws 1966, p. 502, § 1.

Formerly Code 1863, §§ 3437, 3438, 3439, 3440, 3441, 3442, 3757; Code 1868, §§ 3457, 3458, 3459, 3460, 3461, 3462, 3781; Code 1873, §§ 3508, 3509, 3510, 3511, 3512, 3513, 3834; Code 1882, §§ 3508, 3509, 3510, 3511, 3512, 3513, 3834; Civil Code 1895, §§ 5248, 5249, 5250, 5251, 5252, 5253, 5254; Civil Code 1910, §§ 5837, 5838, 5839, 5840, 5841, 5842, 5843; Code 1933, §§ 38–801, 38–802, 38–803, 38–804, 38–805, 38–806, 38–807.

§ 24–10–27. Witness fees of members of municipal or county police forces, deputy sheriffs, and campus policemen

(a) Notwithstanding any other provision in this article, any member of a municipal or county police force or any deputy sheriff or any campus policeman as defined in Code Section 20–8–1 or a member of a local fire department who shall be required by writ of subpoena to attend any superior court, other courts having jurisdiction to enforce the penal laws of this state, municipal court having jurisdiction to enforce the penal laws of this state as provided by Code Section 40–13–21, juvenile court, or grand jury, or hearing or inquest held or called by a coroner, or magistrate court involving any criminal matter, as a witness on behalf of the state during any hours except the regular duty hours to which the officer is assigned, may be paid for such attendance at a fixed rate to be established by the governing authority, but not less than $20.00 per diem. The claim for the witness fees shall be endorsed on the subpoena showing the dates of attendance and stating that attendance was required during the hours other than the regular duty hours to which the claimant was assigned. The claimant shall verify this statement. The dates of attendance shall be certified by the judge or the prosecuting attorney of the court attended. The chief of police, the sheriff, the director of public safety of a college or university, or the local fire chief shall certify that the claimant has not received any overtime pay for his attendance and that his attendance was required during hours other than regular duty hours. The amount due may be paid by the governing body authorized to dispense public funds for the operation of the court. However, no such officer may claim or receive more than one witness fee per day for attendance in any court or before the grand jury regardless of the number of subpoenas which the officer may have received requiring him to appear in such court or before the grand jury on any one day.

(b)(1) Notwithstanding any other provision in this article except paragraph (2) of this subsection, any member of a municipal or county police force or any deputy sheriff or any campus policeman as defined in Code Section 20–8–1 or any arson investigator of the state fire marshal's office or a member of a local fire department who shall be required by writ of subpoena to attend any court of this state with respect to any civil case, as a witness concerning any matter relative to the law enforcement duties of such officer during any hours except the regular duty hours to which the officer is assigned, may be paid for such attendance at a fixed rate to be established by the governing authority, but not less than $20.00 per diem. Any such officer shall also be entitled to the mileage allowance provided in Code Section 24–10–24 when such officer resides outside the county where the testimony is to be given. The claim for the witness fees shall be endorsed on the subpoena showing the dates of attendance and stating that attendance was required during the hours other than the regular duty hours to which the claimant was assigned. The claimant shall verify this statement. The dates of attendance shall be certified by the party obtaining the subpoena. The chief of police, the sheriff, the director of public safety of a college or university, or the local fire chief shall certify that the claimant has not received any overtime pay for his attendance and that his attendance was required during hours other than regular duty hours.

(2) Any officer covered by paragraph (1) of this subsection who is required by writ of subpoena to attend any court with respect to any civil case, as a witness concerning any matter which is not related to the duties of such officer, shall be compensated as provided in Code Section 24–10–24.

(c) The fee specified by subsections (a) and (b) of this Code section shall not be paid if the officer receives any overtime pay for time spent attending such court pursuant to the writ of subpoena.

(d) For the purposes of this Code section, the term "regular duty hours" means the daily shift of duty to which such officer is assigned and shall not include paid or unpaid vacation, paid or unpaid sick leave, paid or unpaid holiday or any other paid or unpaid leave status established pursuant to the personnel regulations or scheduling practices of the employing agency.

Laws 1968, p. 434, § 1; Laws 1978, p. 925, § 1; Laws 1980, p. 439, § 1; Laws 1982, p. 982, §§ 1, 2; Laws 1983, p. 3, § 17; Laws 1983, p. 884, § 3–24; Laws 1984, p. 964, § 1; Laws 1985, p. 407, § 1; Laws 1987, p. 3, § 24; Laws 1987, p. 404, § 1; Laws 1987, p. 834, § 1; Laws 1989, p. 332, § 1; Laws 1990, p. 1446, §§ 1, 2; Laws 1991, p. 773, § 1.

§ 24–10–27.1. Witness fees of members of Georgia State Patrol, Georgia Bureau of Investigation, correctional officers, Department of Natural Resources law enforcement officers, and arson investigators

(a) Notwithstanding any other provision in this article, any member of the Georgia State Patrol or Georgia Bureau of Investigation, any correctional officer, any person employed by the Department of Natural Resources as a law enforcement officer, or any arson investigator of the state fire marshal's office who shall be required by writ of subpoena to attend any superior court, other courts having jurisdiction to enforce the penal laws of this state, municipal court having jurisdiction to enforce the penal laws of this state as provided by Code Section 40–13–21, juvenile court, or grand jury, or hearing or inquest held or called by a coroner, or magistrate court involving any criminal matter, as a witness on behalf of the state during any hours except the regular duty hours to which the officer is assigned, shall be paid for such attendance at a fixed rate to be established by the governing authority, but not less than $ 20.00 per diem. The claim for the witness fees shall be endorsed on the subpoena showing the dates of attendance and stating that attendance was required during the hours other than the regular duty hours to which the claimant was assigned. The claimant shall verify this statement. The dates of attendance shall be certified by the judge or the prosecuting attorney of the court attended. The director of the Georgia Bureau of Investigation or his or her designees, the commanding officer of the Georgia State Patrol or his or her designees, the commissioner of natural resources or his or her designees, the superintendent of the institution, or the state fire marshal shall certify that the claimant has not received any overtime pay for his or her attendance and that his or her attendance was required during hours other than regular duty hours. The amount due shall be paid by the governing body authorized to dispense public funds for the operation of the court. However, no such officer may claim or receive more than one witness fee per day for attendance in any court or before the grand jury regardless of the number of subpoenas which the officer may have received requiring him or her to appear in such court or before the grand jury on any one day.

(b) (1) Notwithstanding any other provision in this article except paragraph (2) of this subsection, any member of the Georgia State Patrol, Georgia Bureau of Investigation, any correctional officer, any person employed by the Department of Natural Resources as a law enforcement officer, or any arson investigator of the state fire marshal's office who shall be required by writ of subpoena to attend any court of this state with respect to any civil case, as a witness concerning any matter relative to the law enforcement duties of such officer during any hours except the regular duty hours to which the officer is assigned, shall be paid for such attendance at a fixed rate to be established by the governing authority, but not less than $20.00 per diem. Any such officer shall also be entitled to the mileage allowance provided in Code Section 24-10-24 when such officer resides outside the county where the testimony is to be given. The claim for the witness fees shall be endorsed on the subpoena showing the dates of attendance and stating that attendance was required during the hours other than the regular duty hours to which the claimant was assigned. The claimant shall verify this statement. The dates of attendance shall be certified by the party obtaining the subpoena. The director of the Georgia Bureau of Investigation or his or her designees, the commanding officer of the Georgia State Patrol or his or her designees, the commissioner of natural resources or his or her designees, the superintendent of the institution, or the state fire marshal shall certify that the claimant has not received any overtime pay for his or her attendance and that his or her attendance was required during hours other than regular duty hours.

(2) Any officer covered by paragraph (1) of this subsection who is required by writ of subpoena to attend any court with respect to any civil case, as a witness concerning any matter which is not related to the duties of such officer, shall be compensated as provided in Code Section 24-10-24.

Laws 1991, p. 773, § 2; Laws 1996, p. 315, § 1.

§ 24-10-28. Exemptions as to members of General Assembly

No member of the General Assembly of Georgia shall be compelled to attend and give testimony at any hearing or trial or to produce books, papers, documents, or other tangible things while the General Assembly is in regular or extraordinary session.

Laws 1968, p. 1200, § 1.

§ 24-10-29. Applicability

This article shall apply to all civil cases and, insofar as consistent with the Constitution, to all criminal cases.

Laws 1966, p. 502, § 2.

Part 2

Securing Testimony of Witnesses in Cases Tried on Affidavits

§ 24-10-40. Testimony obtained how; cross-examination

(a) Any party to an application for injunction, motion for new trial, or other case tried only on affidavits who desires to introduce into evidence the affidavit of any witness not a party to the record and who is unwilling to make affidavit may apply to the clerk of the superior court where the action is pending for a subpoena to compel the attendance of such witness at the hearing, subject to the rules applicable to the case of ordinary witnesses. Written questions may be prepared by the party desiring the evidence; and the witness shall answer such questions in the presence of the judge or of some person to be designated as commissioner by the judge, who may swear the witness to testify truly in answer to the questions propounded. The answers of the witness shall be written down, sworn to, and subscribed by the witness at the hearing. If the witness at the hearing consents, an affidavit containing the facts may be prepared and may then be sworn to by the witness. No cross-examination shall be allowed.

(b) When any application for injunction, motion for new trial, or other case tried only on affidavits is heard in any county other than the county in which the action is pending, any party to such injunction, motion for new trial, or other case who desires to introduce into evidence the affidavit of any witness not a party to the record and unwilling to make affidavit may prepare written questions to elicit the information he desires. On application, the clerk of the superior court of the county in which the action is pending and in which the witness resides shall issue a subpoena requiring the witness to attend before some officer of the county named therein, authorized to administer oaths, on a day therein fixed, to answer the questions. The answers shall be reduced to writing and sworn to by the officer who shall forward or deliver the questions and answers to the clerk of the court in which the case is pending, as in the case of interrogatories. It shall be the duty of the clerk to enter on the questions and on the answers a certificate of the date of receipt and from whom or in what manner he received them, to sign the same, and, on application of the party or his counsel interrogating the witness, to deliver the same to him.

Laws 1882–83, p. 96, § 1; Laws 1921, p. 119, § 1.

Formerly Civil Code 1895, § 5323; Civil Code 1910, § 5918; Code 1933, § 38-2401.

§ 24-10-41. Procedure when witness resides out of county

If the witness whose affidavit is desired resides out of the county in which the case is pending or falls within any of the classes for whom interrogatories must be taken in ordinary cases, the party desiring to use such witness's testimony in the cases referred to in Code Section 24-10-40 may prepare written questions to elicit the information he desires. On application, the clerk of the superior court of the county in which the witness resides shall issue a subpoena requiring the witness to attend before some officer of the county, named therein, authorized to administer oaths, on a day therein fixed, to answer the questions. The answers shall be reduced to writing and sworn to before the officer who shall forward or deliver the questions and answers to the clerk of the court where the case is pending, as in cases of interrogatories.

Laws 1882–83, p. 96, § 2.

Formerly Civil Code 1895, § 5324; Civil Code 1910, § 5919; Code 1933, § 38-2402.

§ 24-10-42. Procedure when attendance inconvenient

If, due to the condition of his health or the nature of his business, it is not possible to secure the attendance of the witness without manifest inconvenience to the public and to himself, on the day named in the subpoena the officer shall proceed to the residence of the witness and take the answers to the questions.

Laws 1882–83, p. 96, § 2; Laws 1953, Nov.-Dec. Sess., p. 288, § 2.

Formerly Civil Code 1895, § 5325; Civil Code 1910, § 5920; Code 1933, § 38-2403.

§ 24-10-43. Fees

The fees of the officer shall be paid by the party desiring the testimony and may be taxed against the party against whom costs are taxed on the final trial.

Laws 1882–83, p. 96, § 2.

Formerly Civil Code 1895, § 5326; Civil Code 1910, § 5921; Code 1933, § 38-2404.

§ 24-10-44. Notices to produce books

The provisions of this chapter in relation to subpoenas for the production of evidence and notices to produce shall be applicable to the cases specified in Code Section 24-10-40.

Laws 1882–83, p. 96, § 3.

Formerly Civil Code 1895, § 5327; Civil Code 1910, § 5922; Code 1933, § 38-2405.

§ 24-10-45. Defaulting witness

Any witness summoned under Code Sections 24-10-40 through 24-10-44 who fails or refuses to obey the subpoena shall be liable for the penalties prescribed in the case of defaulting witnesses in the superior court.

Laws 1882–83, p. 96, § 4.

Formerly Civil Code 1895, § 5328; Civil Code 1910, § 5923; Code 1933, § 38-2406.

Article 3
Securing Attendance of Prisoners

§ 24-10-60. How prisoners may be produced as witnesses; costs and expenses

(a) When a prisoner confined in any state prison, county correctional institution, or other penal institution under the jurisdiction of the Board of Corrections, other than a prisoner under a death sentence, is needed as a witness in any civil or criminal proceeding in any court of record in this state or when it is desired that such person stand trial on an indictment or accusation charging him with commission of a felony or misdemeanor, the judge of the court wherein the proceeding is pending is authorized to and shall issue an ex parte order, directed to the Board of Corrections, requiring his delivery to the sheriff of the county where the prisoner is desired as a witness or defendant. The sheriff or his deputies shall take custody of the prisoner on the date named in the order, safely keep him pending the proceeding, and shall return him to the original place of detention after his discharge by the trial judge.

(b) If the prisoner was desired as a witness by the state in a criminal proceeding or if the prisoner's release to the sheriff was for the purpose of standing trial on criminal charges, the county wherein the case was pending shall pay all expenses of transportation and keeping, including per diem and mileage of the sheriff, jail fees, and any other proper expense approved by the trial judge.

(c) If the prisoner was desired as a witness by the defendant in a criminal proceeding, or by either party to a civil proceeding, the costs and expenses referred to in subsection (b) of this Code section shall be borne by the person requesting the prisoner as a witness. The court shall require a deposit of money sufficient to defray same, except where the judge, after examining into the matter, determines that the prisoner's presence is required by the ends of justice and that the party requesting it is financially unable to make the deposit, in which case the expenses shall be taxed as costs of court.

(d) If a prisoner under a death sentence is needed as a witness for either the prosecution or the defense in any felony case, the requesting party may interview the proposed witness. Following such interview, the requesting party may move for a writ of habeas corpus ad testificandum. Such motion shall be accompanied by a proffer of the testimony of the proposed witness. The requesting party shall make such motion and proffer as soon as possible but shall not make such motion later than 20 days prior to the date of the trial. Nothing in this Code section shall limit the right of a party from presenting a material witness at a hearing or trial and to have compulsory process for that purpose.

Laws 1882–83, p. 106, §§ 1, 2; Laws 1956, p. 161, § 31; Laws 1969, p. 607, § 1; Laws 1985, p. 283, § 1; Laws 1988, p. 1732, § 1.

Formerly Penal Code 1895, §§ 1187, 1188, 1189, 1190, 1191; Penal Code 1910, §§ 1180, 1181, 1182, 1183, 1184; Code 1933, §§ 38–2001, 38–2002, 38–2003, 38–2004, 38–2005.

§ 24–10–61. How imprisoned witnesses may be brought into court

Any judge of the superior court may issue his order to any officer having a lawfully imprisoned person in his custody, requiring the production of such person before his court for the purpose of giving evidence in any criminal cause pending therein, without any formal application or writ of habeas corpus for that purpose.

Formerly Code 1863, § 3928; Code 1868, § 3951; Code 1873, § 4027; Code 1882, § 4027; Penal Code 1895, § 1230; Penal Code 1910, § 1311; Code 1933, § 50–123.

§ 24–10–62. Witnesses in imprisonment; habeas corpus ad testificandum

The writ of habeas corpus ad testificandum may be issued by the superior court to cause the production in court of any witness under legal imprisonment.

Formerly Code 1863, § 3769; Code 1868, § 3793; Code 1873, § 3849; Code 1882, § 3849; Civil Code 1895, § 5264; Civil Code 1910, § 5853; Code 1933, § 38–1505.

Article 4
Production of Medical Records

§ 24–10–70. Definitions

As used in this article, the term:

(1) "Institution" shall have the meaning set forth in paragraph (1) of Code Section 31–7–1 and shall also include a psychiatric hospital as defined in paragraph (7) of Code Section 37–3–1.

(2) "Medical records" means all written clinical information which relates to the treatment of individuals when such information is kept in an institution.

(3) "Patient" means any natural person to whom information contained in medical records relates directly, whether or not the person has been discharged from the institution keeping medical records.

Laws 1971, p. 441, § 1; Laws 1984, p. 22, § 24; Laws 1991, p. 94, § 24.

§ 24–10–71. Use at trial; reproductions

(a) Where it appears that medical records for which a subpoena or order for production has been issued should be kept in an institution as reasonably necessary for the treatment of a patient, the court in which admission is sought shall order that reproduction of the medical records shall be made, the reproduction when duly certified to be admissible in place of the medical records.

(b) Where it does not so appear that medical records should be kept in an institution, an institution upon request at any time shall be permitted to substitute reproductions for medical records, provided such reproductions shall be accompanied by a certificate executed by the person responsible for keeping medical records that the reproductions are true and accurate copies of the medical records.

(c) A court upon good cause shown may order that available medical records be produced to determine the accuracy of reproductions made pursuant to this Code section.

Laws 1971, p. 441, § 2.

§ 24–10–72. Use at trial; subpoenas

(a) An institution, as such, and its personnel shall be in compliance with a subpoena or order for production if it shows timely delivery of the medical records or substitutes and certificate to the clerk of court or other authorized person (by way of illustration, counsel seeking production in discovery proceedings) by any means, including, but not limited to, certified or registered mail or statutory overnight delivery.

(b) A certificate signed before a notary public or other officer authorized to administer oaths shall excuse the personal appearance of any person responsible for keeping medical records. No sanction or remedy for contempt shall be applied against any such person or institution unless a subpoena or order expressly commanding the person's presence has been issued by authority of the court or body for good cause shown, such cause and authority appearing of record and on the face of the subpoena or order.

Laws 1971, p. 441, § 2; Laws 2000, p. 1589, § 4.

§ 24–10–73. Costs

The court or agency compelling the production of medical records or of reproductions thereof pursuant to subsections (a) and (c) of Code Section 24–10–71 shall in civil cases and administrative proceedings, except upon pauper's affidavit, provide for payment in advance to the institution keeping the records of the reasonable costs of reproduction and reasonable costs incident to the transportation of the records. No institution or person shall be held in contempt or otherwise penalized for failure of production unless it appears of record that the costs provided in this Code section have been established and tendered. When the institution, at the time of service of a subpoena or order for production, is a party to the proceeding, the court or agency may in its discretion defer such costs and award them with the other costs in the proceeding.

Laws 1971, p. 441, § 2.

§ 24–10–74. Custody

When medical records are removed from any institution to the custody of a court pursuant to a subpoena or order, the records so removed shall be kept in the custody of the clerk of the court or the clerk or secretary of an administrative agency and shall be open to inspection according to the terms of the subpoena or order or modification thereof. Upon completion of the necessity for their use, the records shall be promptly returned by the party compelling production to the institution from which they came.

Laws 1971, p. 441, § 2.

§ 24–10–75. Applicability

This article applies to all situations for which subpoenas may issue or for which production may be sought, including, but not limited to, trials, hearings, and discovery.

Laws 1971, p. 441, § 3.

§ 24–10–76. Construction

(a) Nothing in this article shall be deemed to restrict the admissibility of evidence heretofore determined admissible by law nor to be in derogation of the right of a person on trial for an alleged criminal offense to confront and cross-examine witnesses against him when such right is asserted.

(b) Nothing contained in this article shall be deemed to abrogate or repeal any law or rule of evidence respecting the use of confidences, such as that provided in Code Section 24–9–21, relating to communications between psychiatrist and patient.

Laws 1971, p. 441, §§ 4, 5.

Article 5
Uniform Act to Secure the Attendance of Witnesses from without the State

§ 24–10–90. Short title

This article shall be known and may be cited as "The Uniform Act to Secure the Attendance of Witnesses from Without the State."

Laws 1976, p. 1366, § 1; Laws 1995, p. 10, § 24.

§ 24–10–91. Definitions

As used in this article, the term:

(1) "Penal institution" means a jail, prison, penitentiary, house of correction, or other place of penal detention.

(2) "State" means any state or territory of the United States and the District of Columbia.

(3) "Summons" means a subpoena, order, or other notice requiring the appearance of a witness.

(4) "Witness" means a person whose testimony is desired in any proceeding or investigation by a grand jury or in a criminal action, prosecution, or proceeding held by the prosecution or the defense, including a person who is confined in a penal institution in any state.

Laws 1976, p. 1366, § 2.

§ 24–10–92. Summoning witness in this State to testify in another State

(a) If a judge of a court of record in any state which by its laws has made provision for commanding persons within that state to attend and testify in this state certifies under the seal of such court that there is a criminal prosecution pending in such court or that a grand jury investigation has commenced or is about to commence, that a person within this state is a material witness in such prosecution or grand jury investigation, and that his presence will be required for a specified number of days, upon presentation of such certificate to any judge of a court of record in the county in which the person is found, such judge shall fix a time and place for a hearing and shall make an order directing the witness to appear at a time and place certain for the hearing. The witness shall at all times be entitled to counsel.

(b) If at a hearing the judge determines that the witness is material and necessary, that it will not cause undue hardship to the witness to be compelled to attend and testify in the prosecution or a grand jury investigation in the other state, and the laws of the state in which the prosecution is pending, or grand jury investigation has commenced or is about to commence, will give to him protection from arrest and the service of civil and criminal process, he shall issue a summons, with a copy of the certificate attached, directing the witness to attend and testify in the court where the prosecution is pending or, where a grand jury investigation has commenced or is about to commence, at a time and place specified in the summons. In any such hearing the certificate shall be prima-facie evidence of all the facts stated therein.

(c) If such certificate recommends that the witness be taken into immediate custody and delivered to an officer of the requesting state to assure his attendance in the requesting state, such judge may, in lieu of notification of the hearing, direct that the witness be forthwith brought before him for the hearing; and the judge at the hearing being satisfied of the desirability of such custody and delivery, for which determination the certificate shall be prima-facie proof of such desirability, may, in lieu of issuing subpoena or summons, order that the witness be forthwith taken into custody and delivered to an officer of the requesting state.

(d) If the witness, who is summoned as above provided, after being paid or tendered by some properly authorized person the sum of 12¢ a mile for each mile by the ordinarily traveled route to and from the court where the prosecution is pending and $25.00 for each day that he is required to travel and attend as a witness, fails without good cause to attend and testify as directed in the summons, he shall be punished in the manner provided for the punishment of any witness who disobeys a summons issued from a court of record in this state.

Laws 1976, p. 1366, § 3.

§ 24-10-93. Summoning of a prisoner in this State to testify in another State

(a) A judge of a state court of record in another state which by its laws has made provision for commanding persons confined in penal institutions within that state to attend and testify in this state may certify that there is a criminal proceeding or investigation by a grand jury or a criminal action pending in the court, that a person who is confined in a penal institution in this state is a material witness in the proceeding, investigation, or action, and that his presence will be required during a specified time. Upon presentation of the certificate to any judge having jurisdiction over the person confined and upon notice to the Attorney General, the judge in this state shall fix a time and place for a hearing and shall make an order directed to the person having custody of the prisoner requiring that the prisoner be produced before him at the hearing.

(b) If at the hearing the judge determines that the witness is material and necessary, that his attending and testifying are not adverse to the interest of this state or to the health and legal rights of the witness, that the laws of the state in which he is required to testify will give him protection from arrest and the service of civil and criminal process because of any act committed prior to his arrival in the state under the order, and that as a practical matter the possibility is negligible that the witness may be subject to arrest or to the service of civil or criminal process in any state through which he will be required to pass, the judge shall issue an order, with a copy of the certificate attached, directing the witness to attend and testify, directing the person having custody of the witness to produce him in the court where the criminal action is pending or where the grand jury investigation is pending at a time and place specified in the order, and prescribing such conditions as the judge shall determine. The judge, in lieu of directing the person having custody of the witness to produce him in the requesting jurisdiction's court, may direct and require in his order that the requesting jurisdiction shall come to the Georgia penal institution in which the witness is confined to accept custody of the witness for physical transfer to the requesting jurisdiction; that the requesting jurisdiction shall provide proper safeguards on his custody while in transit; that the requesting jurisdiction shall be liable for and shall pay all expenses incurred in producing and returning the witness, including, but not limited to, food, lodging, clothing, and medical care; and that the requesting jurisdiction shall promptly deliver the witness back to the same or another Georgia penal institution as specified by the Department of Corrections at the conclusion of his testimony.

(c) The order to the witness and to the person having custody of the witness shall provide for the return of the witness at the conclusion of his testimony, proper safeguards on his custody, and proper financial reimbursement or prepayment by the requesting jurisdiction for all expenses incurred in the production and return of the witness and may prescribe such other conditions as the judge thinks proper or necessary. If the judge directs and requires the requesting jurisdiction to accept custody of the witness at the Georgia penal institution in which the witness is confined and to deliver the witness back to the same or another Georgia penal institution at the conclusion of his testimony, no prepayment of expenses shall be necessary. The order shall not become effective until the judge of the state requesting the witness enters an order directing compliance with the conditions prescribed.

(d) This Code section does not apply to any person in this state confined as insane or mentally ill or under sentence of death.

Laws 1976, p. 1366, § 4; Laws 1977, p. 847, § 1; Laws 1985, p. 283, § 1.

§ 24–10–94. Witness from another state summoned to testify in this state

(a) If a person in any state which by its laws has made provision for commanding persons within its borders to attend and testify in criminal prosecutions, or grand jury investigations commenced or about to commence, in this state is a material witness in a prosecution pending in a court of record in this state or in a grand jury investigation which has commenced or is about to commence, a judge of such court may issue a certificate under the seal of the court stating these facts and specifying the number of days the witness will be required. The certificate may include a recommendation that the witness be taken into immediate custody and delivered to an officer of this state to assure his attendance in this state. This certificate shall be presented to a judge of a court of record in the county in which the witness is found.

(b) If the witness is summoned to attend and testify in this state, he shall be tendered the sum of 12¢ a mile for each mile by the ordinarily traveled route to and from the court where the prosecution is pending and $25.00 for each day that he is required to travel and attend as a witness. A witness who has appeared in accordance with the provisions of the summons shall not be required to remain within this state for a longer period of time than the period mentioned in the certificate, unless otherwise ordered by the court. If such witness, after coming into this state, fails without good cause to attend and testify as directed in the summons, he shall be punished in the manner provided for the punishment of any witness who disobeys a summons issued from a court of record in this state.

Laws 1976, p. 1366, § 5.

§ 24–10–95. Prisoner from another State summoned to testify in this State

(a) If a person confined in a penal institution in any other state is a material witness in a criminal action pending in a court of record or in a grand jury investigation in this state, a judge of the court may certify that there is a criminal proceeding or investigation by a grand jury or a criminal action pending in the court, that a person who is confined in a penal institution in the other state is a material witness in the proceeding, investigation, or action, and that his presence will be required during a specified time. The certificate shall be presented to a judge of a court of record in the other state having jurisdiction over the prisoner confined, and a notice shall be given to the attorney general of the state in which the prisoner is confined.

(b) The judge of the court in this state may enter an order directing compliance with the terms and conditions prescribed by the judge of the state in which the witness is confined.

Laws 1976, p. 1366, § 6.

§ 24–10–96. Exemption from arrest and service of process

(a) If a person comes into this state in obedience to a summons directing him to attend and testify in this state, he shall not while in this state pursuant to such summons be subject to arrest or the service of process, civil or criminal, in connection with matters which arose before his entrance into this state under the summons.

(b) If a person passes through this state while going to another state in obedience to a summons to attend and testify in that state or while returning therefrom, he shall not while so passing through this state be subject to arrest or the service of process, civil or criminal, in connection with matters which arose before his entrance into this state under the summons.

Laws 1976, p. 1366, § 7.

§ 24–10–97. Uniformity of interpretation

This article shall be so interpreted and construed as to effectuate its general purpose to make uniform the law of the states which enact it and shall be applicable only to such state as shall enact reciprocal powers to this state relative to the matter of securing attendance of witnesses as provided in this article.

Laws 1976, p. 1366, § 8.

Article 6

Uniform Foreign Depositions Act

§ 24-10-110. Short title

This article may be cited as the "Uniform Foreign Depositions Act."

Laws 1959, p. 311, § 3.

§ 24-10-111. Compelling testimony of witnesses upon foreign mandates, writs and commissions

Whenever any mandate, writ, or commission is issued out of any court of record in any other state, territory, district, or foreign jurisdiction, or whenever upon notice or agreement it is required to take the testimony of a witness or witnesses in this state, witnesses may be compelled to appear and testify in the same manner and by the same process and proceeding as may be employed for the purpose of taking testimony in proceedings pending in this state.

Laws 1959, p. 311, § 1.

§ 24-10-112. Construction

This article shall be so interpreted and construed as to effectuate its general purposes to make uniform the law of those states which enact it.

Laws 1959, p. 311, § 2.

Article 7

Depositions to Preserve Testimony in Criminal Proceedings

§ 24-10-130. When and for what reasons depositions to be taken; motion to take a deposition; notice of hearing; order of court

(a)(1) At any time after a defendant has been charged with an offense against the laws of this state or an ordinance of any political subdivision or authority thereof, upon motion of the state or the defendant, the court having jurisdiction to try the offense charged may, after notice to the parties, order that the testimony of a prospective material witness of a party be taken by deposition and that any designated book, paper, document, record, recording, or other material not privileged be produced at the same time and place.

(2) At any time after a defendant has been charged with an offense of child molestation, aggravated child molestation, or physical or sexual abuse of a child, upon motion of the state or the defendant, the court having jurisdiction to try the offense charged may, after notice to the parties, order that the testimony of any physician whose testimony is relevant to such charge be taken by deposition and that any designated book, paper, document, record, recording, or other material not privileged be produced at the same time and place.

(b) The court shall not order the taking of the witness's testimony, except as provided in paragraph (2) of subsection (a) of this Code section, unless it appears to the satisfaction of the court that the testimony of the witness is material to the case and the witness:

(1) Is in imminent danger of death;

(2) Has been threatened with death or great bodily harm because of the witness's status as a potential witness in a criminal trial or proceeding;

(3) Is about to leave the state and there are reasonable grounds to believe that such witness will be unable to attend the trial;

(4) Is so sick or infirm as to afford reasonable grounds to believe that such witness will be unable to attend the trial; or

(5) Is being detained as a material witness and there are reasonable grounds to believe that the witness will flee if released from detention.

(c) A motion to take a deposition of a material witness, or a physician as provided in paragraph (2) of subsection (a) of this Code section, shall be verified and must state:

(1) The nature of the offense charged;

(2) The status of the criminal proceedings;

(3) The name of the witness and an address in Georgia where the witness may be contacted;

(4) That the testimony of the witness is material to the case or that the witness is a physician as provided in paragraph (2) of subsection (a) of this Code section; and

(5) The basis for taking the deposition as provided in subsection (b) of this Code section.

(d) A motion to take a deposition shall be filed in the court having jurisdiction to try the defendant for the offense charged; provided, however, if the defendant is charged with multiple offenses, only the court having jurisdiction to try the most serious charge against the defendant shall have jurisdiction to hear and decide the motion to take a deposition.

(e) The party moving the court for an order pursuant to this Code section shall give not less than one day's notice of the hearing to the opposite party. A copy of the motion shall be sent to the opposing party or his or her counsel by any means which will reasonably ensure timely delivery including transmission by facsimile or by digital or electronic means. A copy of the notice shall be attached to the motion and filed with the clerk of court.

(f) If the court is satisfied that the examination of the witness is authorized by law and necessary, the court shall enter an order setting a time period of not more than 30 days during which the deposition shall be taken.

(g) On motion of either party, the court may designate a judge who will be available to rule on any objections to the interrogation of the witness or before whom the deposition shall be taken. The judge so designated may be a judge of any court of this state who is otherwise qualified to preside over the trial of criminal cases in the court having jurisdiction over the offense charged.

Laws 1980, p. 426, § 1; Laws 1994, p. 1895, § 5; Laws 1995, p. 10, § 24; Laws 1995, p. 1360, § 1; Laws 1996, p. 795, §§ 1, 2; Laws 1996, p. 1233, §§ 5, 6.

Formerly Code 1933, § 38-1301a.

§ 24-10-131. Notice of time and place of taking deposition

(a) The party at whose instance a deposition is to be taken shall give to every party reasonable written notice of the time and place for taking the deposition. The notice shall state the name and address of each person to be examined.

(b) On motion of a party upon whom the notice is served, the court for cause shown may extend or shorten the time or change the place for taking the deposition.

(c) The officer having custody of a defendant shall be notified of the time and place set for the examination and shall, unless the defendant waives in writing the right to be present, produce the defendant at the examination and keep the defendant in the presence of the witness during the examination unless, after being warned by the judge that disruptive conduct will cause the defendant's removal from the place where the deposition is being taken, the defendant persists in conduct which would justify exclusion from that place.

(d) A defendant not in custody shall have the right to be present at the examination; but failure of the defendant, absent good cause shown, to appear, after notice and tender of expenses, shall constitute a waiver of that right and of any objection to the taking and use of the deposition based upon that right.

(e) Notwithstanding the provisions of subsections (c) and (d) of this Code section, if the witness is a child, the court may order that the deposition be taken in accordance with Code Section 17-8-55.

Laws 1980, p. 426, § 1; Laws 1994, p. 1895, § 6.

Formerly Code 1933, § 38-1301a.

§ 24-10-132. Right to counsel; costs

(a) If a defendant is financially unable to employ counsel, the court shall appoint counsel as provided in the uniform rules of the courts, unless the defendant elects to proceed without counsel.

(b) Whenever a deposition is taken at the instance of the state, the cost of any such deposition shall be paid by the state in the same manner as is provided by law for the payment of costs in the appellate courts.

(c) Depositions taken at the instance of a defendant shall be paid for by the defendant; provided, however, that, whenever a deposition is taken at the instance of a defendant who is eligible for the appointment of counsel as provided in the uniform rules of the courts, the court shall direct that the reasonable expenses for the taking of the deposition and of travel and subsistence of the defendant and the defendant's attorney, not to exceed the limits established pursuant to Article 2 of Chapter 7 of Title 45, for attendance at the examination be paid for out of the fine and forfeiture fund of the county where venue is laid.

Laws 1980, p. 426, § 1; Laws 1994, p. 1895, § 7.

Formerly Code 1933, § 38-1301a.

§ 24-10-133. Scope of examination; written interrogatories; objections

Except as provided in Code Section 24-10-137, a deposition shall be taken and filed in the manner provided in civil actions, provided that (1) in no event shall a deposition be taken of a party defendant without his or her consent and (2) the scope of examination and cross-examination shall be such as would be allowed in the trial itself. On request or waiver by the defendant, the court may direct that a deposition be taken on written interrogatories in the manner provided in civil actions. Such request shall constitute a waiver by the defendant of any objection to the taking and use of the deposition based upon its being so taken. If a judge has been designated to rule on objections or to preside over the deposition, objections to interrogation of the witness shall be made to and ruled on by such judge in the same manner as at the trial of a criminal case.

Laws 1980, p. 426, § 1; Laws 1994, p. 1895, § 8.

Formerly Code 1933, § 38–1301a.

§ 24–10–134. Taking and use of depositions; certain statements to be made available to defendants

The state shall make available to the defendant, for his examination and use at the taking of the deposition, any statement of the witness being deposed which is in the possession of the state and which the state would be required to make available to the defendant if the witness were testifying at the trial.

Laws 1980, p. 426, § 1.

Formerly Code 1933, § 38–1301a.

§ 24–10–135. Use as evidence, when allowed

At the trial or upon any hearing, a part or all of a deposition, so far as otherwise admissible under the rules of evidence, may be used if the witness is unavailable. Any deposition may also be used by any party for the purpose of contradicting or impeaching the testimony of the deponent as a witness. If only a part of a deposition is offered in evidence by a party, an adverse party may require the offering of all of it which is relevant to the part offered and any party may offer other parts. A witness is not unavailable if the exemption, refusal to testify, claim of lack of memory, inability, or absence of such witness is due to the procurement or wrongdoing of the party offering the deposition at the hearing or trial for the purpose of preventing the witness from attending or testifying.

Laws 1980, p. 426, § 1; Laws 1994, p. 1895, § 9.

Formerly Code 1933, § 38–1301a.

§ 24–10–136. Taking and use of depositions; use as evidence; objections

Objections to receiving in evidence a deposition or part thereof may be made as provided in civil actions.

Laws 1980, p. 426, § 1.

Formerly Code 1933, § 38–1301a.

§ 24–10–137. Use of audio-visual equipment

(a) Any party shall have the right to require that the deposition be recorded and preserved by the use of audio-visual equipment in addition to a stenographic record. The audio-visual recording shall be transmitted to the clerk of the court which ordered the deposition and shall be made available for viewing and copying only to the prosecuting attorney and defendant's attorney prior to trial. An audio-visual recording made pursuant to this Code section shall not be available for inspection or copying by the public until such audio-visual recording has been admitted into evidence during a trial or hearing in the case in which such deposition is made.

(b) An audio-visual recording made pursuant to this Code section may be admissible at trial or hearing as an alternative to the stenographic record of the deposition.

(c) A stenographic record of the deposition contemplated in this Code section shall be made pursuant to Code Section 9–11–28.

Laws 1980, p. 426, § 1; Laws 1994, p. 1895, § 10.

Formerly Code 1933, § 38–1301a.

§ 24–10–138. Taking of deposition by agreement of parties with consent of court not precluded

Nothing in this article shall preclude the taking of a deposition, orally or upon written questions, or the use of a deposition by agreement of the parties with the consent of the court.

Laws 1994, p. 1895, § 11.

§ 24–10–139. Legislative intent

It is the intent of the General Assembly that depositions shall be taken in criminal cases only in exceptional circumstances when it is in the interest of justice that the testimony of a prospective witness be taken and preserved for use at trial. If the court finds that any party or counsel for a party is using the procedures set forth in this article for the purpose of harassment or delay, such conduct may be punished as contempt of court.

Laws 1994, p. 1895, § 11.

Article 8

Perpetuation of Testimony

§ 24-10-150. Cases in which proceedings may be entertained

Superior courts may entertain proceedings for the perpetuation of testimony in all cases in which the fact to which the testimony relates cannot immediately be made the subject of investigation at law and in which, for any cause, the common-law proceeding authorized under this Code is not as available, or as completely available, as a proceeding in equity.

Formerly Code 1863, § 3041; Code 1868, § 3053; Code 1873, § 3108; Code 1882, § 3108; Civil Code 1895, § 3958; Civil Code 1910, § 4555; Code 1933, § 38-1301.

§ 24-10-151. Discovery and perpetuating testimony; grounds

A petition for discovery merely or to perpetuate testimony shall not be sustained unless some reason is shown why the usual proceeding at law is inadequate.

Formerly Code 1863, § 4094; Code 1868, § 4123; Code 1873, § 4182; Code 1882, § 4182; Civil Code 1895, § 3959; Civil Code 1910, § 4556; Code 1933, § 38-1302.

§ 24-10-152. Possession immaterial

The possession of the property is immaterial; nor shall the proceeding be denied though all parties in interest cannot be ascertained or reached.

Formerly Code 1863, § 3042; Code 1868, § 3054; Code 1873, § 3109; Code 1882, § 3109; Civil Code 1895, § 3960; Civil Code 1910, § 4557; Code 1933, § 38-1303.

§ 24-10-153. When testimony may be used

Testimony taken in the proceedings contemplated under Code Section 24-10-150 shall be used only from the necessity of the case, but in such case may be used against all persons, whether parties to the proceeding or not.

Formerly Code 1863, § 3043; Code 1868, § 3055; Code 1873, § 3110; Code 1882, § 3110; Civil Code 1895, § 3961; Civil Code 1910, § 4558; Code 1933, § 38-1304.

§ 24-10-154. Costs; liability of complainant

The complainant shall in all cases be taxed with the costs of proceedings to perpetuate testimony.

Formerly Code 1863, § 3044; Code 1868, § 3056; Code 1873, § 3111; Code 1882, § 3111; Civil Code 1895, § 3962; Civil Code 1910, § 4559; Code 1933, § 38-1305.

TITLE 40
MOTOR VEHICLES AND TRAFFIC

As Amended Through the 2006 Regular Session of the General Assembly

---

Research Note

Use Westlaw *to find cases citing a statute or to search for specific terms in a statute. See the Westlaw Directory Screens for lists of relevant databases.*

Table of Sections

INDEX

See Index to Georgia Statutes, infra.

CHAPTER 13

PROSECUTION OF TRAFFIC OFFENSES

Article 1

Uniform Traffic Citation and Complaint Form

§ 40–13–1. Authorization for development of form; contents; identifying number

The commissioner of driver services shall develop a uniform traffic citation and complaint form for use by all law enforcement officers who are empowered to enforce the traffic laws and ordinances in effect in this state. Such form shall serve as the citation, summons, accusation, or other instrument of prosecution of the offense or offenses for which the accused is charged, and as the record of the disposition of the matter by the court before which the accused is brought, and shall contain such other matter as the commissioner shall provide. Each such form shall have a unique identifying number which shall serve as the docket number for the court having jurisdiction of the accused.

Laws 1972, p. 1148, § 1; Laws 1985, p. 149, § 40; Laws 2005, Act 68, § 22–1, eff. July 1, 2005.

§ 40–13–2. Rules and regulations

The Board of Public Safety, by rule and regulation, shall establish a system of accountability for all traffic citations and complaints, and it shall also provide the procedures governing the use and issuance of such citations and complaints.

Laws 1972, p. 1148, § 3.

§ 40–13–2.1. Traffic citation signature requirements

(a) A person who is issued a citation as provided in this chapter or Code Section 17–6–11, relating to display of driver's license in lieu of bail, shall sign the citation to acknowledge receipt of the citation and of his or her obligation to appear for trial. The officer shall advise the person that signing the citation is not an admission of guilt and that failure to sign will result in the person having to post a cash bond. If the person refuses to sign the citation, it shall constitute reasonable cause to believe that the person will not appear at trial and the officer may bring the person before a judicial officer or traffic violations bureau to post a bond as is otherwise provided by law.

(b) The provisions of subsection (a) of Code Section 17–6–11 shall not apply to a person in possession of a driver's license issued by a state or foreign country that has not entered into a reciprocal agreement regarding the operation of motor vehicles with this state as provided in Chapter 5 of Title 40, which provides for the suspension of a driver's license by the other state or foreign country of a person who fails to appear for trial of a traffic offense committed in this state.

Laws 2000, p. 1313, § 5.

§ 40–13–3. Indictment or accusation unnecessary to bring accused to trial, when; report of disposition of case

Except for offenses tried in the superior courts, all other courts having jurisdiction of the offense may proceed with the adjudication of the offenses contained within the complaint without the necessity of filing an indictment or other accusation in order to bring the accused to trial. The judge or clerk of each court before whom a person accused of such an offense is brought shall promptly report the final disposition of the case to the Department of Driver Services. Notwithstanding the reporting requirements of this Code section, the Department of Driver Services may by rule or regulation relieve the judge or clerk of each such court of the responsibility of reporting those offenses which do not result in convictions or adjudications of guilt or pleas of nolo contendere.

Laws 1972, p. 1148, §§ 2, 4; Laws 1992, p. 1118, § 2; Laws 1992, p. 2785, § 29; Laws 2000, p. 951, § 7A–1; Laws 2005, Act 68, § 22–2, eff. July 1, 2005.

§ 40–13–4. Fees not precluded

Nothing contained in this article shall be construed to prohibit or to deny to any officer or official of any court any fees prescribed for his duties and services in connection with the offenses provided for in this article.

Laws 1972, p. 1148, § 4.

Article 2

Arrests, Trials, and Appeals

§ 40–13–20. Municipal courts defined

As used in this article, the term "municipal courts" shall be construed to include municipal courts of the incorporated municipalities of this state.

Laws 1937–38, Ex. Sess., p. 558, § 3; Laws 1987, p. 3, § 40; Laws 1994, p. 604, § 1.

§ 40–13–21. Jurisdiction of probate courts and municipal courts

(a) The probate courts and municipal courts of the incorporated towns and cities of this state, acting by and through the judges or presiding officers thereof, shall have the right and power to conduct trials, receive pleas of guilty, and impose sentence, in the manner required by law, upon defendants violating any and all criminal laws of this state relating to traffic upon the public roads, streets, and highways of this state where the penalty for the offense does not exceed that of the grade of misdemeanor.

(b) The probate court shall have jurisdiction to issue warrants, try cases, and impose sentence thereon in all misdemeanor cases arising under the traffic laws of this state in all counties of this state in which there is no city, county, or state court, provided the defendant waives a jury trial. Notwithstanding any provision of law to the contrary, all municipal courts are granted jurisdiction to try and dispose of misdemeanor traffic offenses arising under state law except violations of Code Section 40–6–393 and to impose any punishment authorized for such offenses under general state law, whether or not there is a city, county, or state court in such county, if the defendant waives a jury trial and the offense arises within the territorial limits of the respective jurisdictions as now or hereafter fixed by law.

(c) In any traffic misdemeanor trial, a judge of the probate court, upon his or her own motion, may request the assistance of the district attorney of the circuit in which the court is located or solicitor-general of the state court of the county to conduct the trial on behalf of the state. If, for any reason, the district attorney or solicitor-general is unable to assist, the district attorney or solicitor-general may designate a member of his or her staff to conduct the trial on behalf of the state.

Laws 1937–38, Ex. Sess., p. 558, §§ 1–3; Laws 1953, Nov.-Dec. Sess., p. 83, § 2; Laws 1962, p. 3146, § 2; Laws 1971, p. 2299, § 1; Laws 1982, p. 2107, § 44; Laws 1987, p. 3, § 40; Laws 1989, p. 354, § 1; Laws 1989, p. 604, § 1; Laws 1992, p. 909, § 1; Laws 1992, p. 980, § 1; Laws 1996, p. 748, § 21.

§ 40–13–22. Operating motor vehicle without license

(a) Notwithstanding any provision of the law to the contrary, any person, firm, or corporation charged with an offense under Code Section 40–2–8 may be tried in any municipal court of any municipality if the offense occurred within the corporate limits of such municipality. Such courts are granted the jurisdiction to try and dispose of such cases. The jurisdiction of such courts shall be concurrent with the jurisdiction of any other courts within the county having jurisdiction to try and dispose of such cases. Any fines and forfeitures arising from the prosecution of such cases shall be retained by the municipality and shall be paid into the treasury of such municipality. Any person, firm, or corporation charged with any offense under this Code section shall be entitled to request to have the case against him transferred to the court having general misdemeanor jurisdiction in the county wherein the alleged offense occurred.

(b) Nothing in this Code section shall be construed to give any municipality the right to impose a fine or punish by imprisonment in excess of the limits as set forth in the municipality's charter.

Laws 1931, p. 213, § 2; Laws 1977, p. 1039, § 1; Laws 1987, p. 3, § 40.

Formerly Code 1933, § 68–9901.

§ 40–13–23. Waiver of jury trial necessary

(a) No court defined in this article shall have the power to dispose of traffic misdemeanor cases as provided in this article unless the defendant shall first waive in writing a trial by jury. If the defendant wishes a trial by jury, he shall notify the court and, if reasonable cause exists, he shall be immediately bound over to the court in the county having jurisdiction to try the offense, wherein a jury may be impaneled. Where a cash bond, property bond, or driver's license in lieu of bond has been posted, the bond shall be transferred to the court assuming jurisdiction, and the defendant shall not be required to post a new bond by the court assuming jurisdiction.

(b) No waiver of a trial by jury may be withdrawn when such waiver has been interposed for the purpose of delay. Except with approval of the court, no waiver of a trial by jury may be withdrawn after the commencement of the trial or the filing of motions on behalf of the defendant, whichever comes first.

Laws 1937–38, Ex. Sess., p. 558, § 4; Laws 1985, p. 149, § 40; Laws 1987, p. 329, § 1; Laws 1992, p. 2785, § 29; Laws 1996, p. 1279, § 1.

§ 40–13–24. Citation and complaint; dockets

An indictment or accusation shall not be required against a defendant under this article, but a citation and complaint specifically setting out the charge shall be issued. The court shall keep a docket on which shall be plainly kept the name and address of the defendant, the nature of the offense in brief, the date when brought before the court, and the final disposition of the case with the date thereof. Such docket shall be the same in each probate court handling traffic misdemeanor cases and shall be on a form to be prescribed by the Department of Law. Such docket shall be paid for from the treasury of the county in which such court is located. Municipal courts may use the dockets ordinarily in use by them in the trial of other cases or, in the discretion of the court, may adopt the docket provided in this Code section for probate courts.

Laws 1937–38, Ex. Sess., p. 558, § 6; Laws 1987, p. 3, § 40.

§ 40–13–25. Costs

The costs in any case disposed of under this article shall be as provided in Code Section 15–9–60. In case a defendant refuses to waive a trial by jury and is bound over to another court, the costs shall await the final disposition of the case.

Laws 1937–38, Ex. Sess., p. 558, § 5.

§ 40–13–26. Sentences, costs, fines, fees; urban interstate system violations

Text of section effective until June 30, 2011

(a) Defendants who plead guilty or who are convicted under this article shall be required to serve their sentences in such manner as is provided for by law in misdemeanor cases. In case a fine is imposed and paid, the officers of court, where on fee basis, shall first be paid their costs arising in such case. After the payment of all costs, the remainder of such fine shall be paid into the county treasury in the event the case is disposed of by the probate court; if the case is disposed of by the municipal court of an incorporated municipality, the remainder of such fine or fines shall be paid into the treasury of the municipality where the court is located, except that where such courts have jurisdiction beyond the corporate limits of a municipality, and the offense occurs outside the municipality, the fine shall be paid into the county treasury; provided, however, that in any case where a fine was imposed for violation of any traffic offense provided in or authorized by Chapter 6 of this title on any "urban interstate system" if the arrest or citation in such case was made or issued by a member of the Uniform Division of the Department of Public Safety's motorcycle enforcement unit, the remainder of such fine shall be remitted to the Department of Public Safety for the maintenance and enhancement of the Department's motorcycle program. The judge of the probate court or the person presiding over the municipal court must pay into the county treasury, municipal treasury, or Department of Public Safety by the fifteenth day of each month the remainder of all fines for the preceding month. Such payment must be accompanied by a list showing the name of the defendant in each case, the fine imposed in each case, the costs in each case and to whom paid, and the balance which is being paid into the treasury. The official making such payment must be given a written receipt by the person receiving the payment. No officer receiving a salary will receive any fees for arresting or attending court in any case arising under this article, but the usual fees must be assessed, and, if the arresting officer is not entitled to the costs, they must go to the county or city to which the fine is paid or Department of Public Safety as required by this Code section.

(b) As used in this Code section, the term "urban interstate system" means a portion of the national system of interstate and defense highways which:

(1) Is located entirely within any part of this state; and

(2) Includes a single numbered interstate highway which forms a closed loop or perimeter.

Where these conditions exist, the urban interstate system shall consist of the interstate highway constituting the closed loop or perimeter and all interstate highways or portions thereof located within such loop or perimeter, not including any portion of any interstate highway outside of the loop or perimeter.

Laws 1937–38, Ex. Sess., p. 558, § 7; Laws 1953, Jan.-Feb. Sess., p. 416, § 1; Laws 1953, Nov.-Dec. Sess., p. 207, § 1; Laws 1985, p. 149, § 40; Laws 1987, p. 3, § 40; Laws 2006, Act 470, § 2, eff. July 1, 2006.

For text of section effective June 30, 2011, see § 40–13–26, post

§ 40–13–26. Sentences, costs, fines, fees

Text of section effective June 30, 2011

Defendants who plead guilty or who are convicted under this article shall be required to serve their sentences in such manner as is provided for by law in misdemeanor cases. In case a fine is imposed and paid, the officers of court, where on fee basis, shall first be paid their costs arising in such case. After the payment of all costs, the remainder of such fine shall be paid into the county treasury in the event the case is disposed of by the probate court; if the case is disposed of by the municipal court of an incorporated municipality, the remainder of such fine or fines shall be paid into the treasury of the municipality where the court is located, except that where such courts have jurisdiction beyond the corporate limits of a municipality, and the offense occurs outside the municipality, the fine shall be paid into the county treasury. The judge of the probate court or the person presiding over the municipal court must pay into the county treasury or municipal treasury by the fifteenth day of each month the remainder of all fines for the preceding month. Such payment must be accompanied by a list showing the name of the defendant in each case, the fine imposed in each case, the costs in each case and to whom paid, and the balance which is being paid into the treasury. The official making such payment must be given a written receipt by the person receiving the payment. No officer receiving a salary will receive any fees for arresting or attending court in any case arising under this article, but the usual fees must be assessed, and, if the arresting officer is not entitled to the costs, they must go to the county or city to which the fine is paid.

Laws 1937–38, Ex. Sess., p. 558, § 7; Laws 1953, Jan.-Feb. Sess., p. 416, § 1; Laws 1953, Nov.-Dec. Sess., p. 207, § 1; Laws 1985, p. 149, § 40; Laws 1987, p. 3, § 40; Laws 2006, Act 470, § 2, eff. July 1, 2006.

For text of section effective until June 30, 2011, see § 40–13–26, ante

§ 40–13–27. Record to be kept for public inspection

A written record is required to be kept of every case made or disposed of under this article. Such record shall be accessible at all times for public inspection and official audit and shall be kept and remain as a part of the permanent records of the court.

Laws 1937–38, Ex. Sess., p. 558, § 8.

§ 40–13–28. Appeals to superior court; bail; hearing

Any defendant convicted under this article shall have the right of appeal to the superior court. The provisions of Code Sections 5–3–29 and 5–3–30 shall not apply to appeals under this Code section. Otherwise, the appeal shall be entered as appeals are entered from the probate court to the superior court, provided that the defendant shall be entitled to bail and shall be released from custody upon giving the bond as is provided for appearances in criminal cases in the courts of this state. Such bond shall have the same conditions as appearance bonds in criminal cases. The appeal to the superior court shall not be a de novo investigation before a jury but shall be on the record of the hearing as certified by the judge of that court who presided at the hearing below.

Laws 1937–38, Ex. Sess., p. 558, § 10; Laws 1986, p. 982, § 15.

§ 40–13–29. Jurisdiction, when exclusive

In all counties except those having city, county, or state courts, the judge of the probate court shall have exclusive jurisdiction of all traffic misdemeanor cases originating in the county outside of municipal corporations, and the judge of the municipal court in each municipal corporation shall have exclusive jurisdiction of traffic misdemeanor cases originating inside the corporate limits of municipalities.

Laws 1937–38, Ex. Sess., p. 558, § 11; Laws 1987, p. 3, § 40; Laws 1992, p. 2785, § 29.

§ 40–13–30. Arrests by Officers of the Georgia State Patrol or any arresting officer

Officers of the Georgia State Patrol and any other officer of this state or of any county or municipality thereof having authority to arrest for a criminal offense of the grade of misdemeanor shall have authority to prefer charges and bring offenders to trial under this article, provided that officers of an incorporated municipality shall have no power to make arrests beyond the corporate limits of such municipality unless such jurisdiction is given by local or other law.

Laws 1937–38, Ex. Sess., p. 558, § 9; Laws 1992, p. 2785, § 29.

§ 40–13–31. Sheriffs entitled to arresting fees for arrests

The sheriffs of the several counties of this state are entitled to an arresting fee, as provided by law, in every case in which the sheriff or his lawful deputy arrests, assists in arresting, or takes custody of any person charged with a crime who has been apprehended by an officer of the Georgia State Patrol and delivered to the sheriff or his lawful deputy. If the sheriff is upon a salary, the fee shall be paid into the county treasury.

Laws 1943, p. 571, § 1; Laws 1992, p. 2785, § 29.

§ 40–13–32. Procedures for modifying sentences or judgments

(a) No court having jurisdiction over cases arising out of the traffic laws of this state or the traffic laws of any county or municipal government shall change or modify a traffic law sentence or judgment rendered pursuant to a conviction, plea of guilty, or plea of nolo contendere after 90 days from the date of judgment, except for the purpose of correcting clerical errors therein, unless there is strict compliance with all of the following requirements:

(1) A motion to change or modify the sentence or judgment is made by the defendant to the court rendering the judgment;

(2) Notice, including a copy of the motion and rule nisi, is given to the prosecuting official who brought the original charge at least ten days prior to the motion hearing; and

(3) A hearing is held with opportunity for the state to be heard.

(b) If the original judgment is changed or modified pursuant to this Code section, the judge shall certify to the Department of Driver Services that such change or modification is a true and correct copy of the change or modification and that the requirements set forth in paragraphs (1) through (3) of subsection (a) of this Code section have been met.

(c) Except for orders correcting clerical errors, the Department of Driver Services shall not recognize as valid any change or modification order nor make any changes to a driver's history unless such change or modification as submitted to the department is in strict compliance with the requirements set forth in subsections (a) and (b) of this Code section.

(d) In the case of municipal courts, notice to the city attorney, or to the solicitor in those cases where the municipal court has a solicitor, shall be deemed to be notice as provided for in this Code section.

(e) In all cases wherein notice is required in this Code section, same shall be deemed sufficient if sent by certified mail or statutory overnight delivery, return receipt requested, with adequate postage thereon, to the correct address of the prosecuting official.

(f) Notwithstanding other laws and specifically notwithstanding Code Section 17–7–93, a motion to change or modify a traffic law sentence or judgment may, at any time prior to the expiration of the term of court following the term at which judgment and sentence were pronounced or within 90 days of the time judgment and sentence were pronounced, whichever time period is greater, be made by the defendant and accepted by the court as provided in this Code section.

Laws 1984, p. 1144, § 1; Laws 1985, p. 149, § 40; Laws 1988, p. 1893, § 4; Laws 1989, p. 14, § 40; Laws 2000, p. 951, § 7A–2; Laws 2000, p. 1589, § 3; Laws 2005, Act 68, § 22–3, eff. July 1, 2005.

§ 40–13–33. Challenges to misdemeanor convictions of traffic laws

(a) Any challenge to a misdemeanor conviction of any of the traffic laws of this state or the traffic laws of any county or municipal government which may be brought pursuant to Chapter 14 of Title 9 must be filed within 180 days of the date the conviction becomes final.

(b) Any challenge to a conviction specified in subsection (a) of this Code section which became final before March 28, 1986, must be filed within 180 days following March 28, 1986.

(c) When the commissioner of driver services is named as the respondent, all such petitions must be brought in the Superior Court of Fulton County.

(d) Failure to file the challenge within the time prescribed in this Code section shall divest the court of jurisdiction.

Laws 1986, p. 444, § 1; Laws 1992, p. 2785, § 29; Laws 2000, p. 951, § 7A–3; Laws 2005, Act 68, § 22–4, eff. July 1, 2005.

Article 3

Traffic Violations Bureaus

§ 40–13–50. Power of judges to establish traffic violations bureau

In every court of this state having jurisdiction over the violation of traffic laws or traffic ordinances, the judge, or the judges where there is more than one judge, may provide by written order for the establishment of a traffic violations bureau for the handling or disposition of certain traffic cases in substantial compliance with this article. The court shall promulgate and provide to the clerk of the traffic violations bureau a list of the traffic offenses which shall be handled and disposed of by the traffic violations bureau. However, nothing in this article shall authorize the judge of such court to employ any person or persons to administer this article.

Laws 1966, p. 381, § 1; Laws 1992, p. 2785, § 29.

§ 40–13–51. Clerk appointed to receive money; bond

(a) The court may appoint a clerk or deputy clerk or deputy clerks, who shall be named in the order establishing the traffic violations bureau, for the purpose of receiving money as provided in this article. Any deputy clerk so appointed shall be under the direct supervision of and attached to the office of the clerk of the court.

(b) Such person or persons, except where such person is the clerk of the court and is already under bond, shall be bonded in the sum of $2,500.00.

Laws 1966, p. 381, § 2.

§ 40–13–52. Traffic offense cards; contents

The court may, in its order, provide that there shall be maintained in the office of the traffic violations bureau cards known as "traffic offense cards." Upon each traffic offense card shall appear: the name and address of the person charged with a traffic offense; the date of the birth of such person; the sex of such person; and his driver's license number. The card shall be numbered so that it may show any previous traffic offense, giving the date of the offense, the trial date, the citation number, the disposition of the case, and the amount of any fine paid.

Laws 1966, p. 381, § 5.

§ 40–13–53. Release of offenders upon citation and complaint; excepted offenses

(a) Subject to the exceptions set out in subsection (b) of this Code section, any officer who arrests any person for the violation of a traffic law or traffic ordinance alleged to have been committed outside the corporate limits of any municipality shall permit such person to be released upon being served with a citation and complaint and agreeing to appear, as provided in this article. If such officer has reasonable and probable grounds to believe that the person will not obey such citation and agreement to appear, the officer may require such person to surrender his driver's license in accordance with Code Section 17–6–11.

(b) The following offenses shall not be handled or disposed of by a traffic violations bureau:

(1) Any offense for which a driver's license may be suspended by the commissioner of driver services;

(2) Any motor vehicle registration violation;

(3) A violation of Code Section 40–5–20;

(4) Speeding in excess of 30 miles per hour over the posted speed limit; or

(5) Any offense which would otherwise be a traffic violations bureau offense but which arose out of the same conduct or occurred in conjunction with an offense which is excluded from the jurisdiction of the traffic violations bureau. Any such offense shall be subject to the maximum punishment set by law.

Laws 1966, p. 381, § 3; Laws 1983, p. 1000, § 16; Laws 1992, p. 2785, § 29; Laws 2000, p. 951, § 7A–4; Laws 2005, Act 68, § 22–5, eff. July 1, 2005.

§ 40–13–54. Disposition of original and copies of citations

The original citation and complaint shall be sent by the officer issuing it to the traffic violations bureau of the court within 24 hours of the arrest. The defendant named in the citation shall be given the second copy. The officer issuing the citation and complaint shall retain one copy for himself or herself, and the court may, by order, provide that an additional copy shall be made for the use of any municipality in the county or the Department of Driver Services.

Laws 1966, p. 381, §§ 7, 8; Laws 2000, p. 951, § 7A–5; Laws 2005, Act 68, § 22–6, eff. July 1, 2005.

§ 40–13–55. Cash bonds to be accepted

Any person cited for any traffic offense under the jurisdiction of the traffic violations bureau of the court shall be permitted to give a cash bond for his appearance under the terms and conditions as set forth upon the citation and complaint given to him at the time he is cited by the arresting officer for a traffic violation.

Laws 1966, p. 381, § 10.

§ 40–13–56. Officers prohibited from accepting cash bonds

No officer giving a citation and complaint to a defendant for a traffic violation shall accept a cash bond himself.

Laws 1966, p. 381, § 11.

§ 40–13–57. Discretion of arresting officer to bring offender before bureau; cash bond

In the event an officer has authority to issue citation and complaint as set forth in Code Section 40–13–53 but declines to do so because of his belief that such person will not obey the citation and agreement to appear, such officer may bring such person to the traffic violations bureau and such person may be allowed to post a cash bond for his appearance in accordance with the schedule established by the court.

Laws 1966, p. 381, § 4; Laws 1992, p. 2785, § 29.

§ 40–13–58. Cash bonds; effect of forfeiture

Where a defendant cited for a traffic violation posts a cash bond according to the schedule set up by court order and fails to appear in court at the term of court and on the day set in the original citation and complaint, then and in that event, such failure shall be construed as an admission of guilt and the cash bond may be forfeited without the necessity for the statutory procedure provided for the forfeiture of statutory bail bonds. A judgment of guilty may be entered accordingly, ordering the case disposed of and settled. The proceeds of the cash bond shall be applied and distributed as any fine imposed by said court would be. Nothing in this Code section shall be construed as preventing the judge from ordering the defendant to appear and stand trial.

Laws 1966, p. 381, § 10.

§ 40–13–59. Information to be recorded on summons and driver history cards; filing citation and complaint; recording of forfeiture order

(a) The traffic violations bureau of the court shall record on the prescribed form, as set out in Code Section 40–13–52, the driving record of the defendant. If there is no previous record of the driver's history, the citation appearing on the original citation and complaint shall be entered on the driver's traffic offense card; and each traffic offense thereafter shall be entered thereon, with the disposition thereof, up to a period of four years.

(b) All the pending cases which appear on the citation and complaint issued by the arresting officer, as provided for in this article, shall be filed at the cashier's desk in the traffic violations bureau of the court and shall be retained there up until 72 hours, or such other period of time as the judge shall fix by order, prior to the time the case is set for trial in the court. If cash bond is posted according to the schedules prescribed by order of the judge at any time up to 72 hours, or such other period of time as the judge shall fix by order, prior to the date of the court appearance, as specified in the citation and complaint, the same shall be entered on the driver's traffic offense card and an entry shall be made thereon that the driver has posted a cash bond.

(c) Within 72 hours after the date set for a hearing in the court on the citation and complaint given, where the defendant has posted a cash bond and has failed to appear for the hearing, the court shall enter an order that the cash bond has been forfeited in accordance with this article. Such order shall be recorded on the back of the citation and complaint which is maintained in the traffic violations bureau of the court and shall also be recorded on the defendant's traffic offense card.

Laws 1966, p. 381, § 11.

§ 40–13–60. Traffic violations distinguished from misdemeanors; handling of cases

Any traffic violation under the jurisdiction of the traffic violations bureau shall be characterized and classified as a traffic violation and shall not be considered as a misdemeanor. Whenever any traffic violation is transferred from another court to a court which has a traffic violations bureau, if such offense is classified as a traffic violation on the traffic violations bureau schedule of the receiving court, such violation shall be handled and disposed of by such traffic violations bureau. Where a defendant demands a trial on a traffic violation, it shall be tried before a judge of the court which established the traffic violations bureau. The request for a trial shall not result in a loss of jurisdiction by the traffic violations bureau.

Laws 1966, p. 381, § 12; Laws 1992, p. 2785, § 29.

Validity

This section has been held unconstitutional in the case of Geng v. State, 2003, 276 Ga. 428, 578 S.E.2d 115.

§ 40–13–61. Maintenance of records; accusations not entered on misdemeanor docket; failure to post bond or appear as grounds for accusation

All records other than those excepted in this article shall be maintained at the traffic violations bureau of the court. No accusation of an offense for which citation and complaint may be issued shall be entered on the misdemeanor docket maintained by the clerk of the court. No accusation for any offense coming under the jurisdiction of the traffic violations bureau of the court shall be taken by the prosecuting attorney of the court or maintained in his office unless said person to whom the said summons was issued fails to post a cash bond as defined in this article or fails to appear on the date specified in the summons to answer said complaint.

Laws 1966, p. 381, § 9; Laws 1985, p. 149, § 40.

§ 40–13–62. Procedure on failure of person cited to appear

When any person cited for a traffic violation pursuant to this article fails to appear in court on the date specified in the citation and in accordance with his written promise to appear, unless such person has posted a cash bond as provided in this article, the traffic violations bureau thereupon loses jurisdiction and the citation shall be forwarded to the prosecuting attorney of the court who shall have an accusation issued against such person. Upon motion of the prosecuting attorney, a bench warrant shall issue based on the accusation for the arrest of the defendant. The defendant's case shall be docketed by the clerk of the court and handled as all other misdemeanors.

Laws 1966, p. 381, § 12; Laws 1992, p. 2785, § 29.

§ 40–13–63. Penalty for failure of person cited to appear

The willful failure of any person to appear in accordance with the written promise contained on the citation and complaint and served upon such person shall constitute an offense which shall be punishable by fine in an amount not to exceed $200.00 or by confinement in jail for a period not to exceed three days.

Laws 1966, p. 381, § 13; Laws 1999, p. 334, § 4.

§ 40–13–64. Bureau to have charge of suspended sentence division of court

The court may provide that its traffic violations bureau, in addition to the duties set out in this article, shall have charge of what shall be called and designated in the court as the "Suspended Sentence Division of the ____ Court." This division of the court shall be responsible for collecting fines imposed upon persons convicted in the court, where the sentence is suspended upon the payment of a fine. The person or persons in the division shall be authorized, where the judge imposing the sentence stipulates the same therein, to permit such persons receiving suspended sentences, in addition to the other conditions imposed in the suspended sentence, to pay the suspended sentence fine in installments. The person or persons responsible for the administration of the suspended sentence division shall be responsible for collecting the suspended sentence fine by installments and shall also be responsible for the arrest of persons who fail in this respect to comply with the conditions of the suspended sentence.

Laws 1966, p. 381, § 14.

TITLE 51

TORTS

As Amended Through the 2006 Regular Session of the General Assembly

Research Note

Use Westlaw *to find cases citing a statute or to search for specific terms in a statute. See the* Westlaw *Directory Screens for lists of relevant databases.*

Table of Sections

INDEX

See Index to Georgia Statutes, infra.

CHAPTER 7

FALSE ARREST, FALSE IMPRISONMENT, MALICIOUS PROSECUTION, AND ABUSIVE LITIGATION

Article 5

Abusive Litigation

§ 51–7–80. Definitions

As used in this article, the term:

(1) "Civil proceeding" includes any action, suit, proceeding, counterclaim, cross-claim, third-party claim, or other claim at law or in equity.

(2) "Claim" includes any allegation or contention of fact or law asserted in support of or in opposition to any civil proceeding, defense, motion, or appeal.

(3) "Defense" includes any denial of allegations made by another party in any pleading, motion, or other paper submitted to the court for the purpose of seeking affirmative or negative relief, and any affirmative defense or matter asserted in confession or avoidance.

(4) "Good faith," when used with reference to any civil proceeding, claim, defense, motion, appeal, or other position, means that to the best of a person's or his or her attorney's knowledge, information, and belief, formed honestly after reasonable inquiry, that such civil proceeding, claim, defense, motion, appeal, or other position is well grounded in fact and is either warranted by existing law or by reasonable grounds to believe that an argument for the extension, modification, or reversal of existing law may be successful.

(5) "Malice" means acting with ill will or for a wrongful purpose and may be inferred in an action if the party initiated, continued, or procured civil proceedings or process in a harassing manner or used process for a purpose other than that of securing the proper adjudication of the claim upon which the proceedings are based.

(6) "Person" means an individual, corporation, company, association, firm, partnership, society,

joint-stock company, or any other entity, including any governmental entity or unincorporated association of persons with capacity to sue or be sued.

(7) "Without substantial justification," when used with reference to any civil proceeding, claim, defense, motion, appeal, or other position, means that such civil proceeding, claim, defense, motion, appeal, or other position is:

(A) Frivolous;

(B) Groundless in fact or in law; or

(C) Vexatious.

(8) "Wrongful purpose" when used with reference to any civil proceeding, claim, defense, motion, appeal, or other position results in or has the effect of:

(A) Attempting to unjustifiably harass or intimidate another party or witness to the proceeding; or

(B) Attempting to unjustifiably accomplish some ulterior or collateral purpose other than resolving the subject controversy on its merits.

Laws 1989, p. 408, § 2.

§ 51-7-81. "Abusive litigation" defined

Any person who takes an active part in the initiation, continuation, or procurement of civil proceedings against another shall be liable for abusive litigation if such person acts:

(1) With malice; and

(2) Without substantial justification.

Laws 1989, p. 408, § 2.

§ 51-7-82. Defenses to claim for abusive litigation

(a) It shall be a complete defense to any claim for abusive litigation that the person against whom a claim of abusive litigation is asserted has voluntarily withdrawn, abandoned, discontinued, or dismissed the civil proceeding, claim, defense, motion, appeal, civil process, or other position which the injured person claims constitutes abusive litigation within 30 days after the mailing of the notice required by subsection (a) of Code Section 51-7-84 or prior to a ruling by the court relative to the civil proceeding, claim, defense, motion, appeal, civil process, or other position, whichever shall first occur; provided, however, that this defense shall not apply where the alleged act of abusive litigation involves the seizure or interference with the use of the injured person's property by process of attachment, execution, garnishment, writ of possession, lis pendens, injunction, restraining order, or similar process which results in special damage to the injured person.

(b) It shall be a complete defense to any claim for abusive litigation that the person against whom a claim of abusive litigation is asserted acted in good faith; provided, however, that good faith shall be an affirmative defense and the burden of proof shall be on the person asserting the actions were taken in good faith.

(c) It shall be a complete defense to any claim for abusive litigation that the person against whom a claim of abusive litigation is asserted was substantially successful on the issue forming the basis for the claim of abusive litigation in the underlying civil proceeding.

Laws 1989, p. 408, § 2.

§ 51-7-83. Damages, costs, and expenses

(a) A plaintiff who prevails in an action under this article shall be entitled to all damages allowed by law as proven by the evidence, including costs and expenses of litigation and reasonable attorney's fees.

(b) If the abusive litigation is in a civil proceeding of a court of record and no damages other than costs and expenses of litigation and reasonable attorney's fees are claimed, the procedures provided in Code Section 9-15-14 shall be utilized instead.

(c) No motion filed under Code Section 9-15-14 shall preclude the filing of an action under this article for damages other than costs and expenses of litigation and reasonable attorney's fees. Any ruling under Code Section 9-15-14 is conclusive as to the issues resolved therein.

Laws 1989, p. 408, § 2.

§ 51-7-84. Notice of claim; time of bringing action

(a) As a condition precedent to any claim for abusive litigation, the person injured by such act shall give written notice by registered or certified mail or statutory overnight delivery or some other means evidencing receipt by the addressee to any person against whom such injured person intends to assert a claim for abusive litigation and shall thereby give the person against whom an abusive litigation claim is contemplated an opportunity to voluntarily withdraw, abandon, discontinue, or dismiss the civil proceeding, claim, defense, motion, appeal, civil process, or other position. Such notice shall identify the civil proceeding, claim, defense, motion, appeal, civil process, or other position which the injured person claims constitutes abusive litigation.

(b) An action or claim under this article requires the final termination of the proceeding in which the alleged abusive litigation occurred and must be brought within one year of the date of final termination.

Laws 1989, p. 408, § 2; Laws 2000, p. 1589, § 3.

§ 51–7–85. Exclusive remedy

On and after April 3, 1989, no claim other than as provided in this article or in Code Section 9–15–14 shall be allowed, whether statutory or common law, for the torts of malicious use of civil proceedings, malicious abuse of civil process, nor abusive litigation, provided that claims filed prior to such date shall not be affected. This article is the exclusive remedy for abusive litigation.

Laws 1989, p. 408, § 2.

*

INDEX TO GEORGIA STATUTES

STATE COURT RULES

Table of Features

STATE COURT RULES

Table of Contents

RULES OF THE SUPREME COURT OF GEORGIA

Effective May 22, 1995

Including Amendments Received Through November 1, 2006

Research Note

Use WESTLAW *to find cases citing a rule. In addition, use* WESTLAW *to search for specific terms or to update a rule; see the GA–RULES and GA–ORDERS Scope screens for further information.*

Amendments to these rules are published, as received, in the South Eastern Reporter 2d *and* Georgia Cases *advance sheets.*

Table of Rules

I. GENERAL

RULE 1. OFFICE HOURS

Filings and communications relating to cases shall be directed to the Clerk's office during office hours. The Clerk's office shall be open Monday through Friday from 8:30 a.m. to 4:30 p.m. E.S.T./E.D.T. The address is Clerk, Supreme Court of Georgia, Room 572, 244 Washington Street, Atlanta, Georgia 30334. The telephone number is (404) 656–3470. The fax number is 404) 656–2253. See Rule 2. The Court's website is www.gasupreme.us.

Adopted effective May 22, 1995; amended effective September 1, 2001; January 5, 2005.

RULE 2. FILING BY FACSIMILE

No filing, except requests for an extension of time, oral argument, extra time, or extra pages, will be accepted by facsimile without the prior permission of the Court. When such permission is granted, a filing received by facsimile will be filed as of the date of receipt of the facsimile, but only after the original has been received by mail. An original need not be provided for the 4 requests listed above. Service upon the opposing party must be shown on the facsimile. See Rule 14.

The Clerk's office will not transmit documents by facsimile, except when ordered by the Court.

Adopted effective May 22, 1995; amended effective September 1, 2001; January 5, 2005.

RULE 3. TERMS OF COURT

The Supreme Court has three terms each year as follows:

(1) January term beginning the first Monday in January;

(2) April term beginning the third Monday in April; and

(3) September term beginning the first Monday in September.

Adopted effective May 22, 1995; amended effective September 1, 2001.

RULE 4. ATTORNEYS

An attorney must be in good standing and admitted in the Supreme Court in order to make an appearance. A visiting attorney from a foreign jurisdiction may participate in a particular case with permission of the Court. The visiting attorney's motion seeking such permission shall include a current certificate of good standing from the highest court of the foreign jurisdiction.

(1) Law students authorized to practice under the third-year practice act, see Rules 91–96, or the law school graduate rules, see Rules 97–103, may not make oral argument, but may co-author briefs, and shall indicate their status on the signature line.

(2) Any member of the State Bar of Georgia may be admitted to practice in this Court upon written application, and the certificate of at least two members of the Bar of this Court, attesting that the applicant is of good private and professional character. See Rule 55 (2) regarding proper attire. The oath which is required to be taken, in open Court or before a Justice, and which shall be subscribed in a book to be kept by the Clerk and known as the "Roll Book," is as follows:

> "I do solemnly swear (or affirm) that I will *conduct* myself as an attorney or counselor of this Court truly and honestly, justly and uprightly, and according to law; and that I will support the Constitution of the State of Georgia and the Constitution of the United States. So help me God."

(3) The fee for admission is $30.00, payable to the Clerk, Supreme Court of Georgia, who will issue a license under the seal of the Court.

(4) A certificate of good standing will be issued to members of the Supreme Court bar upon written request if accompanied by a check for $3.00, payable to the Clerk, Supreme Court of Georgia. Orders may be placed by credit card through the Court's website. See Rule 1.

(5) Any withdrawal, discharge or substitution of attorneys of record in the Court shall be communicated to the Court in writing and shall include the name and number of the case in this Court and the name and address of counsel's client. Telephonic or other immediate notification to the Court, in addition to written notification, is required where the withdrawal, discharge or substitution occurs prior to oral argument in cases where oral argument has been requested.

Counsel shall provide a copy of the notification to the client, substituted counsel, and opposing counsel including the Attorney General where required by law.

(6) If during the pendency of any proceeding, counsel of record for either party change their address, they shall notify the Clerk by letter of this change and show service on opposing counsel. Upon receipt of the notification, the Clerk will amend the Court's docket accordingly, and all subsequent notices from the Court will be mailed to counsel's new address.

Failure of counsel to receive notice of Court action shall not be grounds to reinstate or reconsider any matter adverse to counsel or parties if counsel failed to properly notify the Court of any change of address or telephone number.

(7) The words "counsel" or "attorney" as used in these rules include pro se parties.

Adopted effective May 22, 1995; amended effective March 13, 1997; April 24, 1997; September 1, 2001; July 11, 2002; January 5, 2005.

RULE 5. COSTS

Costs in all cases are $80.00, unless pauper's status has been granted in the trial court and the record so reflects. Costs shall be paid upon filing, except in direct appeals when the costs, which accrue on docketing, shall be paid upon filing of the original brief. Costs need not be paid again where a discretionary or interlocutory application, an application for interim review or for a certificate of probable cause, or a petition for certiorari has been granted. Costs are not required for certified questions or in disciplinary cases.

Attorneys are liable for costs. Failure to pay costs subjects the offender to sanctions. See Rule 7.

Former Rule 6 adopted effective May 22, 1995; amended effective May 22, 1997; renumbered as Rule 5 effective September 1, 2001.

RULE 6. FRIVOLOUS APPEAL

The Court may, with or without a motion, impose a penalty not to exceed $2,500 against any party and/or party's counsel in any civil case in which there is a direct appeal, application for discretionary appeal, application for interlocutory appeal, petition for certiorari, or motion which the Court determines to be frivolous. The party or party's counsel may respond to such a motion within 10 days or, if no motion was filed, file a motion for reconsideration within 10 days of receipt of the order. This rule applies only to those cases in which there has been no money judgment, as money judgments are subject to the penalties outlined in OCGA § 5–6–6. The imposition of such penalty shall constitute a money judgment in favor of appellee against appellant or appellant's counsel or in favor of appellant against appellee or appellee's counsel, as the Court directs. Upon filing of the remittitur in the trial court, the penalty may be collected as are other money judgments.

Former Rule 8 adopted effective May 22, 1995; renumbered as Rule 6 effective September 1, 2001; amended effective February 5, 2003; January 5, 2005.

RULE 7. SANCTIONS

Breach of any of these rules may subject the offender to contempt and revocation of the license to practice in the Supreme Court.

Former Rule 9 adopted effective May 22, 1995; renumbered as Rule 7 effective September 1, 2001.

II. FILINGS

RULE 8. NOTICE OF DOCKETING

The Clerk shall notify all attorneys and all pro se parties of the docketing dates of all appeals, petitions for certiorari, and applications for appeal.

Former Rule 10 adopted effective May 22, 1995; renumbered as Rule 8 effective September 1, 2001; amended effective January 5, 2005.

RULE 9. SUPERSEDEAS

The Court may issue supersedeas or other orders whenever deemed necessary. Service of motions for supersedeas shall be made on the opposing party or attorney before filing and so certified. A copy of the order being appealed and a copy of the Notice of Appeal must be included with the motion.

Former Rule 11 adopted effective May 22, 1995; renumbered as Rule 9 effective September 1, 2001.

RULE 10. BRIEFS: TIME OF FILING

Appellant's and cross–appellant's briefs shall be filed within 20 days after the case is docketed (see also Rules 50 and 51, regarding requests for oral argument). Appellee's and cross–appellee's briefs shall be filed within 40 days after the case is docketed or 20 days after the filing of appellant's or cross appellant's briefs, whichever is later. Appeal and cross appeal may be argued in one brief, but this shall not extend the time for filing.

Failure to comply with an order of the Court directing the filing of a brief may cause the appeal to be dismissed and may subject the offender to sanctions. See Rule 7.

Former Rule 12 adopted effective May 22, 1995; renumbered as Rule 10 effective September 1, 2001; amended effective January 5, 2005.

RULE 11. DUE DATE

To determine the due date for filing, start counting with the day after docketing, including weekends and holidays. When an expiration date falls on a Saturday, Sunday, or an official state or federal holiday, the time for filing is extended to the next business day.

Former Rule 13 adopted effective May 22, 1995; renumbered as Rule 11 effective September 1, 2001.

RULE 12. EXTENSION OF TIME.

Extensions of time for filing petitions for certiorari, applications, and motions for reconsideration will be granted only in unusual circumstances and only if the request is filed before the time for filing the pleading has expired.

Requests for extension of time for filing briefs should be directed by letter to the Clerk sufficiently in advance of the due date so that if the request is denied the briefs can still be filed within the time fixed by these rules.

Requests not showing service on the opposing party will not be honored.

A copy of the letter or order granting the extension must be included as an exhibit to the document for which the extension was granted.

Former Rule 14 adopted effective May 22, 1995; renumbered as Rule 12 effective September 1, 2001; amended effective January 5, 2005.

RULE 13. FILING BY MAIL

Except as provided hereafter, the contents of properly addressed mail shall be deemed filed as of the date such mail is received in the Clerk's office. The contents of properly addressed, registered or certified mail shall be deemed filed on the official United States Postal Service postmark date. If there is no clear official or cancellation date stamped, the filing date shall be the date the filing is received. Alternatively, a document will be deemed filed as of the date on which it is delivered to the United States Postal Service or a commercial delivery company for overnight delivery as evidenced by the receipt provided by the Post Office or commercial delivery company.

Former Rule 15 adopted effective May 22, 1995; amended effective June 22, 2000; renumbered as Rule 13 effective September 1, 2001.

RULE 14. SERVICE

Prior to filing, including filing by facsimile, service on opposing attorneys or pro se parties, stating their names and addresses, shall be certified. Briefs, petitions for certiorari, applications for appeal, and all motions and requests not so certified will not be accepted for filing.

In appeals involving death penalties, murder, aircraft hijacking, and treason, copies of the notice of appeal, briefs, motions, and all other filings must be served on the Attorney General, the District Attorney, and the attorney for the accused.

Former Rule 16 adopted effective May 22, 1995; renumbered as Rule 14 effective September 1, 2001.

RULE 15. NUMBER OF COPIES

An original and seven copies shall be filed of briefs, petitions for certiorari, applications for appeal, motions, and responses.

Former Rule 17 adopted effective May 22, 1995; renumbered as Rule 15 effective September 1, 2001.

RULE 16. TYPE.

All filings shall be printed or typed with not less than double-spacing between the lines, except in block quotations or footnotes. Margins shall be no less than one inch at the top, bottom and sides. The type size shall not be smaller than 12–point courier font or 14–point Times New Roman.

Former Rule 18 adopted effective May 22, 1995; renumbered as Rule 16 effective September 1, 2001; amended effective January 5, 2005.

RULE 17. DOCUMENTS: FORMAT.

Except for requests which should be made by letter to the Clerk, see Rules 12, 20 and 51, petitions, applications and motions shall be on letter size (8 ½" × 11") paper with a back cover of recyclable paper that is heavier than regular stationery and shall be STAPLED at the top.

Responses should be filed as briefs, see Rule 18.

Former Rule 19 adopted effective May 22, 1995; renumbered as Rule 17 effective September 1, 2001; amended effective January 5, 2005.

RULE 18. BRIEFS: FORMAT

All briefs and responses shall be typed or printed on letter size (8 ½" × 11") paper with covers on the front and back, STAPLED on the left-hand side in booklet form. Covers shall be of recyclable paper, heavier than regular stationery, and shall bear the style of the case, the case number, and the name or names of the persons preparing the brief, along with their bar numbers, if attorneys.

Former Rule 20 adopted effective May 22, 1995; renumbered as Rule 18 effective September 1, 2001.

RULE 19. BRIEFS: ENUMERATION OF ERRORS

The enumeration of errors (which shall contain a statement of jurisdiction as to why the Supreme Court, and not the Court of Appeals, has jurisdiction) shall be stated as a separate part of, and shall be incorporated in, the brief.[1]

1. The Court prescribes no particular arrangement for briefs, motions, applications for appeal, petitions for certiorari, or other papers. However, Rules specifying certain paper, size, and spacing must be complied with and page references to the record (R-) and transcript (T-) are essential. The volume of cases necessarily requires that all matters be presented succinctly. Inclusion of extraneous facts and frivolous issues tends to obscure critical issues.

Generally, a presentation by the moving party in the following order, where applicable, is the most efficient: Type of case showing Supreme Court jurisdiction, the judgment appealed, and date of entry; a brief statement of the facts showing the general nature of the case; the enumeration of errors; the argument in sequence with the enumeration of errors, including additional facts where essential, and citation of authorities; and the certification of service. Replies in the same order as presented by appellant are desirable.

Adopted effective September 1, 2001.

RULE 20. BRIEFS: PAGE LIMITATION

Briefs, petitions for certiorari, applications for appeal, motions, and responses shall be limited to 30 pages in civil cases, except upon written request directed by letter to the Clerk and authorized by the Court prior to the due date of the filing.

Former Rule 21 adopted effective May 22, 1995; renumbered as Rule 20 effective September 1, 2001.

RULE 21. BRIEFS: PAGE NUMBERING

The pages of each brief shall be sequentially numbered with arabic numbers.

Adopted effective September 1, 2001.

RULE 22. BRIEFS: ARGUMENT AND AUTHORITY

Any enumerated error not supported by argument or citation of authority in the brief shall be deemed abandoned. All citations of authority must be full and complete. Georgia citations must include the volume and page number of the official Georgia reporters (Harrison, Darby or Lexis). Cases not yet reported shall be cited by the Supreme Court or Court of Appeals case number and date of decision. The enumeration of errors shall be deemed to include and present for review all judgments necessary for a determination of the errors specified.

Adopted effective May 22, 1995; amended effective September 1, 2001; January 5, 2005.

RULE 23. AMICUS BRIEFS

Amicus curiae briefs may be filed without prior permission and shall disclose the identity and interest of the persons on whose behalf the briefs are filed. Amici do not have standing to file motions for reconsideration, but may submit briefs in support of a motion made by a party.

Adopted effective May 22, 1995; amended effective September 1, 2001.

RULE 24. SUPPLEMENTAL BRIEFS

Supplemental briefs may be filed at any time before decision. Any such briefs which serve only to circumvent the limitation on pages for civil cases set out in Rule 20 will not be considered.

Adopted effective May 22, 1995; amended effective June 5, 1997; September 1, 2001.

RULE 25. SUPPLEMENTAL RECORD

In the event a record is supplemented pursuant to OCGA § 5–6–41 (f) or § 5–6–48 (d), any party wishing to present an issue in this Court relating to the trial court proceeding wherein the record was supplemented must first raise the issue before the trial court and then file additional enumerations of error and a brief within 10 days after docketing of the supplemental record in this Court or after the trial court rules on the issue raised, whichever date is later.

Opposing parties may file a supplemental brief within 20 days after docketing or after the trial court rules on the issue raised, whichever date is later.

Adopted effective May 22, 1995; amended effective September 1, 2001.

RULE 26. MOTIONS

Any motions may be filed while a matter is pending in the Court. Motions should comply with Rules 15, 16, and 17. Responses to motions may be filed at any time. See Rule 18.

Adopted effective May 22, 1995; amended effective September 1, 2001.

RULE 27. MOTIONS FOR RECONSIDERATION

A motion for reconsideration may be filed regarding any matter in which the Court has ruled within 10 days from the date of decision. A copy of the opinion or disposition to be reconsidered shall be attached. See Rule 61, regarding motions to stay the remittitur. No second or subsequent motion for reconsideration by the same party after a first motion has been denied shall be filed except by permission of the Court. The Clerk may receive any later motion and deliver it to the Court for direction as to whether it shall be filed.

Former Rule 26(1) adopted effective May 22, 1995; renumbered as Rule 27 effective September 1, 2001; amended effective January 5, 2005.

RULE 28. SUGGESTION OF DEATH

The death of a party to a pending appeal may be suggested at any time. The Court may then take appropriate action to substitute the legal representative of the deceased party.

Former Rule 26(2) adopted effective May 22, 1995; renumbered as Rule 28 effective September 1, 2001; amended effective January 5, 2005.

RULE 29. PERSONAL REMARKS

Personal remarks which are discourteous or disparaging to opposing counsel or to any judge are strictly forbidden, whether oral or written.

Former Rule 28 adopted effective May 22, 1995; renumbered as Rule 29 effective September 1, 2001.

III. INTERLOCUTORY APPEALS

RULE 30. REQUIREMENTS

Applications for interlocutory appeal shall contain a jurisdictional statement and have attached a copy of the trial court's order to be appealed and a stamped copy of the certificate of immediate review showing the date of filing. A certified transcript is not necessary, but affidavits, exhibits and relevant portions of the transcript should be attached to the application to demonstrate to the Court what the record will show if the application is granted. See Rule 17.

Responses, due within 10 days of docketing, are encouraged and should be filed as briefs. See Rule 18.

Former Rule 29 adopted effective May 22, 1995; renumbered as Rule 30 effective September 1, 2001.

RULE 31. STANDARD FOR GRANTING

An application for leave to appeal an interlocutory order will be granted only when:

(1) The issue to be decided appears to be dispositive of the case;

(2) The order appears erroneous and will probably cause a substantial error at trial; or

(3) The establishment of a precedent is desirable.

Former Rule 30 adopted effective May 22, 1995; renumbered as Rule 31 effective September 1, 2001.

RULE 32. TRANSFERS

Applications to appeal interlocutory orders of which the Court of Appeals has jurisdiction will be transferred to that Court.

Former Rule 31 adopted effective May 22, 1995; renumbered as Rule 32 effective September 1, 2001.

IV. DISCRETIONARY APPEALS

RULE 33. REQUIREMENTS

Applications for discretionary appeal shall contain a jurisdictional statement and have attached a stamped copy of the trial court's order to be appealed, showing the date of filing. A transcript is not necessary, but affidavits, exhibits and relevant portions of the transcript should be attached to the application to demonstrate to the Court what the record will show if the application is granted. See Rule 17.

Responses, due within 10 days of docketing, are encouraged and should be filed as briefs. See Rule 18.

Former Rule 32 adopted effective May 22, 1995; renumbered as Rule 33 effective September 1, 2001.

RULE 34. STANDARD FOR GRANTING

An application for leave to appeal a final judgment in cases subject to appeal under OCGA § 5–6–35 shall be granted when:

(1) Reversible error appears to exist;

(2) The establishment of a precedent is desirable; or

(3) Further development of the common law, particularly in divorce cases, is desirable.

Former Rule 33 adopted effective May 22, 1995; renumbered as Rule 34 effective September 1, 2001.

RULE 35. TRANSFERS

Discretionary applications to appeal, of which the Court of Appeals has jurisdiction, will be transferred to that Court.

Adopted effective September 1, 2001.

V. POST–CONVICTION HABEAS CORPUS APPEALS

RULE 36. STANDARD FOR GRANTING

A certificate of probable cause to appeal a final judgment in a habeas corpus case involving a criminal conviction will be issued where there is arguable merit, provided there has been compliance with *Fulwood v. Sivley*, 271 Ga. 248 (517 SE2d 511) (1999); *Hicks v. Scott, Warden*, 273 Ga. 358 (541 SE2d 27) (2001).

Adopted effective May 22, 1995; amended effective September 1, 2001; January 5, 2005.

VI. INTERIM APPELLATE REVIEW

RULE 37. ISSUES FOR REVIEW

The questionnaire required by OCGA § 17–10–35.1 may be found in the Unified Appeal, Section II, F.

(1) Once any reports and applications have been filed in the trial court, the trial court shall determine whether justice will be served by allowing the application(s) to appeal, as required by OCGA § 17–10–35.2, and, if so, shall certify the questions which might appropriately be addressed by this Court. The trial court clerk shall transmit the entire record to this Court, as set out in OCGA § 17–10–35.1 (c).

(2) Opposing parties may file in this Court, but not in the trial court, a response to the order of the trial court certifying the questions appropriate for review within 7 days of the docketing here of the interim review.

(3) This Court will issue an order upon the entire record either denying interim review or granting review and setting out the issues to be briefed by the parties. Thereafter, the case will proceed as any other appeal.

(4) Upon completion, the record will be returned to the trial court.

Adopted effective May 22, 1995; amended effective September 1, 2001.

VII. CERTIORARI TO COURT OF APPEALS

RULE 38. REQUIREMENTS

Compliance with the requirements of this rule governing petitions for certiorari is mandatory.

(1) Notice of intention to apply for certiorari shall be given to the Clerk of the Court of Appeals within 10 days after the date of entry of judgment or the date of the disposition of the motion for reconsidera-

tion, if one is filed. A copy of the notice of intent is not to be filed in the Supreme Court.

(2) The petition for certiorari shall be filed with the Clerk of the Supreme Court within 20 days after the date of entry of judgment or the date of the disposition of the motion for reconsideration, if one is filed, along with payment of costs when required by Rule 5.

Adopted effective May 22, 1995; amended effective September 1, 2001.

RULE 39. COURT OF APPEALS' OPINION

A copy of the Court of Appeals' opinion or order shall be attached to each copy of the petition.

Adopted effective May 22, 1995; amended effective September 1, 2001.

RULE 40. STANDARD FOR GRANTING

A review on certiorari is not a right. In all appeals from criminal convictions, a litigant shall not be required to petition for rehearing and certiorari following an adverse decision of the Court of Appeals in order to be deemed to have exhausted all available state remedies respecting a claim of error. When the claim has been presented to the Court of Appeals, and relief has been denied, the litigant shall be deemed to have exhausted all available state remedies. A petition for the writ will be granted only in cases of great concern, gravity, or importance to the public.

Certiorari generally will not be granted to review the sufficiency of evidence.

Adopted effective May 22, 1995; amended effective September 1, 2001; November 16, 2004; January 5, 2005.

RULE 41. FORMAT

See Rule 17. Any brief of facts and law prepared in connection with a petition for certiorari should be included as part of the petition and not filed as a separate document.

Adopted effective May 22, 1995; amended effective September 1, 2001.

RULE 42. RESPONSES

Responses to petitions for certiorari, filed within 20 days of the filing of the petition, are encouraged. See Rule 18. Failure to file a response shall be deemed to be an acknowledgment by respondent that the requirements of the rules for the granting of the petition for certiorari have been met, provided, however, that such acknowledgment shall not be binding on the Court.

Adopted effective May 22, 1995; amended effective September 1, 2001.

RULE 43. RECORD

Upon receiving a copy of the notice of docketing of the petition for certiorari from the Clerk of this Court, the Clerk of the Court of Appeals shall transmit a certified copy of the Court of Appeals' opinion and judgment to the Supreme Court. Upon the request of the Supreme Court or upon the grant of certiorari, the Clerk of the Court of Appeals shall prepare the record of the case for use by the Supreme Court. Upon disposition, the record shall be returned to the Court of Appeals.

Adopted effective May 22, 1995; amended effective September 1, 2001.

RULE 44. APPEAL BOND

In criminal cases, the filing of a petition for certiorari does not automatically extend the applicant's appeal bond; application must be made to the Supreme Court for extension of the appeal bond.

Adopted effective May 22, 1995; amended effective September 1, 2001.

RULE 45. GRANTED CERTIORARI

In the event a petition for certiorari is granted, appellant and appellee shall file briefs only in response to the question or questions posed by the Court in its order granting certiorari. The briefing schedule set forth in Rule 10 shall be followed, counting from the date of the order granting certiorari.

Adopted effective May 22, 1995; amended effective September 1, 2001.

VIII. CERTIFIED QUESTIONS

RULE 46. FEDERAL COURTS

When it shall appear to the Supreme Court of the United States, or to any District Court or Circuit Court of Appeals of the United States, or to any state appellate court, that there are involved in any proceeding before it questions or propositions of the laws of this State which are determinative of said cause and there are no clear controlling precedents in the appellate court decisions of this State, such court may certify such questions or propositions of the laws of Georgia to this Court for instructions.

Adopted effective May 22, 1995; amended effective September 1, 2001; January 5, 2005.

RULE 47. QUESTION PRESENTED

The Court certifying to this Court a question of law shall formulate the question and cause the question to be certified and transmitted to this Court, together with copies of such parts of the record and briefs in the case as the certifying Court deems relevant.

Adopted effective May 22, 1995; amended effective September 1, 2001.

RULE 48. PROCEDURE

Such questions shall be docketed by the Clerk like other cases and the rules relating to oral arguments, briefs, motions, etc., in direct appeals shall apply.

Adopted effective May 22, 1995; amended effective September 1, 2001.

IX. DISCIPLINARY, JQC, AND BAR ADMISSIONS

RULE 49. PROCEDURE

Filings should be in compliance with the Disciplinary, JQC, or Bar Admissions rules and with the Supreme Court Rules, especially Rules 8—29, as appropriate.

Adopted effective May 22, 1995; amended effective September 1, 2001.

X. ORAL ARGUMENT

RULE 50. ORAL ARGUMENT

Oral argument will be scheduled by the Court as follows:

(1) Direct appeals from judgments imposing the death penalty will be placed on the calendar automatically and oral argument in such cases is mandatory;

(2) All granted writs of certiorari will be placed on the calendar automatically unless disposed of summarily by the Court and oral argument in such cases is mandatory; and

(3) Other cases will be placed on the calendar upon the request of either party within 20 days from the date the case is docketed in this Court. See Rule 51. No extensions for requesting oral argument will be granted. Oral argument by counsel in appeals other than where the death penalty is imposed or where certiorari is granted is never mandatory, and argument may be submitted by briefs only. Argument will not be permitted to parties or attorneys whose briefs have not been timely filed. The Court may deny or limit oral argument where appropriate.

Adopted effective May 22, 1995; amended effective October 17, 1996; September 1, 2001; June 7, 2006.

RULE 51. REQUESTS

A request for oral argument shall be filed by letter directed to the Clerk, and shall certify that the opposing parties or their attorneys have been notified of the intention to argue the case orally and that inquiry has been made whether they intend also to argue orally. The request shall further certify that the opponents do or do not desire to argue orally, and shall show service of the letter upon such opponents.

A request for oral argument must be renewed upon transfer of an appeal to this Court from the Court of Appeals.

Adopted effective May 22, 1995; amended effective September 1, 2001.

RULE 52. APPEARANCE

Attorneys appearing for oral argument should notify the Clerk of their presence upon arrival at the courtroom. Argument is waived unless attorneys are ready to argue in the sequence presented on the calendar.

Adopted effective May 22, 1995; amended effective September 1, 2001.

RULE 53. ORDER OF ARGUMENT

Appellant opens the argument. Appellee (or cross-appellant) replies. Rebuttal is restricted to one attorney, representing appellant, who shall confine his or her arguments to matters covered in argument of opposing counsel.

Adopted effective May 22, 1995; amended effective September 1, 2001.

RULE 54. TIME

Unless otherwise provided by the Court, oral argument is limited to 20 minutes for each side except in direct appeals of judgments imposing the death penalty, which are limited to 30 minutes for each side. Appeals, cross appeals, and companion cases shall be considered to be one case for purpose of oral argument. Parties must divide the allotted time by agreement among themselves. The yellow podium light indicates 5 minutes of argument time remain; the red podium light indicates that time has expired.

Adopted effective May 22, 1995; amended effective September 1, 2001; January 5, 2005.

RULE 55. COURTROOM DECORUM

(1) Talking, reading newspapers or other material, and audibly studying briefs and arranging papers are prohibited in the courtroom without the express permission of the Court. The lawyers' lounge has been provided for these purposes.

(2) All counsel appearing before the Court must be properly attired.

Adopted effective September 1, 2001.

XI. OPINIONS AND JUDGMENTS

RULE 56. PARTICIPATION OF JUSTICES

Each judgment shall show on its face the vote, nonparticipation, or disqualification of each Justice.

Adopted effective May 22, 1995; amended effective September 1, 2001.

RULE 57. DISQUALIFIED OR NOT PARTICIPATING

A disqualified or nonparticipating Justice shall be replaced by a senior appellate justice or judge, a judge of the Court of Appeals or a judge of a superior court whenever deemed necessary. A disqualified or nonparticipating Justice does not participate in any motion or decisions or the opinion on the merits and is not present when discussions regarding the case take place. Neither briefs and motions nor copies of bench briefs, draft opinions or other memoranda are circulated to the disqualified or nonparticipating Justice.

Adopted effective May 22, 1995; amended effective September 1, 2001.

RULE 58. JUDGMENTS

When a Justice concurs, he or she agrees with the opinion and judgment of either the opinion or the order. When a Justice concurs specially or in the judgment only, he or she does not agree with all that is said in the opinion or the order. A dissenting Justice disagrees with the opinion and judgment.

Adopted effective May 22, 1995; amended effective September 1, 2001.

RULE 59. AFFIRMANCE WITHOUT OPINION

An affirmance without opinion may be rendered in any civil case when the Court determines one or more of the following circumstances exist and is dispositive of the appeal:

(1) The evidence supports the judgment;

(2) No harmful error of law, properly raised and requiring reversal appears; or

(3) The judgment of the court below adequately explains the decision and an opinion would have no precedential value.

Rule 59 cases have no precedential value.

Adopted effective May 22, 1995; amended effective September 1, 2001.

RULE 60. REMITTITUR

A remittitur shall be transmitted to the Court from which the case was received as follows:

(1) In death sentences as provided by Georgia Laws 1971, p. 212 (OCGA § 5–6–11); and

(2) In other cases as soon as practicable after the expiration of 10 days after the entry of the judgment or upon the denial of a motion for reconsideration, see Rule 27, unless otherwise ordered.

Adopted effective May 22, 1995; amended effective September 1, 2001.

RULE 61. STAY OF REMITTITUR

Any party desiring to have the remittitur stayed in this Court in order to appeal to, or seek a writ of certiorari in, the United States Supreme Court shall file in this Court a motion to stay the remittitur with a concise statement of the issues to be raised on appeal or in the petition for certiorari. Such notice shall be filed at the time of filing a motion for reconsideration or, if no motion for reconsideration is filed, within the time allowed for the filing of the same. See Rule 27.

A stay of remittitur will not be granted by this Court from the denial of a petition for certiorari.

Adopted effective May 22, 1995; amended effective September 1, 2001.

XII. THE PARENTAL NOTIFICATION ACT

INTRODUCTION

Rules 62 through 66 are adopted to provide for the expedited consideration of appeals under the "Parental Notification Act" (OCGA § 15–11–110 et seq.) for a minor seeking an abortion.

Adopted effective May 22, 1995; amended effective September 1, 2001.

RULE 62. CERTIORARI TO THE COURT OF APPEALS

(1) Any minor to whom a juvenile court has denied a waiver of notice under OCGA § 15–11–114 (c) and whose appeal to the Court of Appeals has been denied may obtain expedited treatment of a petition for certiorari by filing a petition in this Court.

(2) A notice of intention to apply for certiorari shall be filed with the Clerk of the Court of Appeals within twenty-four hours after the judgment of the Court of Appeals affirming the disposition of the juvenile court, and the petition shall be filed within 48 hours after the judgment.

(3) Within twenty-four hours after notice, the Clerk of the Court of Appeals shall prepare the record of the case and a certified copy of the Court of Appeals' opinion and judgment for use by the Supreme Court.

(4) Time shall be computed as set out in Rule 11.

(5) The requirements of Rules 38, 40, 42, 43, 44, and 45 are not applicable. The requirement for payment of costs is waived.

(6) Upon receipt of the petition, any response, the record of the case, and a certified copy of the Court of Appeals' opinion, this Court shall take the petition under consideration and shall grant or deny the petition within 2 days of receipt of the record and certified opinion.

(7) If certiorari is granted, this Court will render a decision within 5 days following the grant of certiorari.

(8) If the decision of this Court or the denial of the petition for certiorari has the effect of affirming the judgment of the juvenile court, the minor may file a motion for reconsideration and the same will be governed by Rule 27, except that such a motion shall be filed within 5 days from the date of the decision of this Court and may be filed out of term. Any such motion will be decided by the Court within 5 days of the filing thereof.

Adopted effective May 22, 1995; amended effective September 1, 2001; January 5, 2005.

RULE 63. DIRECT APPEAL

(1) A minor seeking an expedited appeal to this Court shall file a notice of appeal and a certified copy of the order denying waiver of notice with the Clerk of this Court. In order to invoke the special procedures of this rule, the notice of appeal must be filed within 5 days of receipt by the minor of the juvenile court's order.

The name, address, and telephone number of the guardian ad litem and any counsel of record must be included with the notice of appeal.

(2) A copy of the notice of appeal must also be filed with the juvenile court.

(3) Upon receipt of the notice of appeal, this Court will issue an order to the juvenile court directing that the record be transmitted to and received by this Court within 5 days from the date of filing of the notice of appeal with this Court. The record of the juvenile court shall be certified by the clerk of the juvenile court and transmitted to this Court under seal.

(4) A brief may be filed within the time period for the filing of the record. No filing fee is required. A response may be filed within 2 days thereafter.

(5) This Court shall issue its decision within 5 days of receipt of the record.

(6) If the decision of this Court affirms the judgment of the juvenile court, the minor may file a motion for reconsideration and the same will be governed by Rule 27, except that such a motion shall be filed within 5 days from the date of the decision of this Court and may be filed out of term. Any such motion will be decided by the Court within five days of the filing thereof.

Adopted effective May 22, 1995; amended effective September 1, 2001.

RULE 64. REMITTITUR

If the decision of this Court reverses the judgment of the Court of Appeals or the juvenile court, the remittitur will be forwarded to the Clerk of the Court of Appeals or the clerk of the juvenile court immediately after the rendition of the decision. If the decision of this Court or the denial of the petition for certiorari has the effect of affirming the judgment of the juvenile court, the remittitur shall be transmitted to the Clerk of the Court of Appeals or the clerk of the juvenile court as soon as practicable after the expiration of 5 days from the date of the judgment unless otherwise ordered or unless a motion for reconsideration has been filed.

Adopted effective May 22, 1995; amended effective September 1, 2001.

RULE 65. EXPEDITING

Upon good cause shown, the Court will enter such orders as will further expedite the processing of these cases.

Adopted effective May 22, 1995; amended effective September 1, 2001.

RULE 66. RECORD UNDER SEAL

All pleadings, briefs, orders, transcripts, exhibits, and any other written or recorded materials that are part of the record shall be considered and treated by the Court as confidential. Upon conclusion of the appellate proceedings, the record will be resealed, and the contents of the record shall not be disclosed, except upon order of this Court.

Adopted effective May 22, 1995; amended effective September 1, 2001.

XIII. RECORDS AND TRANSCRIPTS

RULE 67. RECORDS AND TRANSCRIPTS

The clerk of the trial court shall certify and transmit to the Clerk of this Court the original transcript and copies of all records as required within the time prescribed by statute. In habeas corpus appeals after criminal convictions, the original record in its entirety shall be certified and transmitted. Transmittal shall be by the clerk or deputy personally or by United States mail or express mail, or by a commercial delivery company, charges prepaid. Transmittal by a party or attorney is prohibited.

Adopted effective May 22, 1995; amended effective September 1, 2001.

RULE 68. FORMAT

Records and transcripts shall be written or printed on one side of white paper not less than letter size of good quality with ample spacing (at least double spaced) and margins so that they may be read easily. The margin at the top shall be of sufficient space so that the transcript may be read when folded over at the top. Metal fasteners which cover the top center are prohibited.

Adopted effective May 22, 1995; amended effective September 1, 2001.

RULE 69. SEQUENCE

The record with pages numbered at the bottom and a manuscript cover shall be arranged as follows:

(1) Index (including page references and dates of filing);

(2) Notice of Appeal;

(3) Other items in chronological order; and

(4) Clerk's certificate.

Voluminous records may be bound in separate parts but each part shall be certified separately.

Adopted effective May 22, 1995; amended effective September 1, 2001.

RULE 70. COURT REPORTER'S TRANSCRIPT

The transcript (original) shall be a separate document and not attached to the record. It should show the style of the case and an index, including page references, of witnesses and exhibits. Voluminous transcripts may be bound in separate parts. The court reporter and clerk shall certify each part. Court reporters should try to submit an electronic copy of the transcript, as set out by administrative order of this Court, directly to the Supreme Court or to the trial court for transmittal to the Supreme Court. The electronic copy will not be an official record of the Supreme Court of Georgia.

Adopted effective May 22, 1995; amended effective September 1, 2001; January 5, 2005.

RULE 71. EVIDENCE

Where a party relies upon physical evidence on appeal that was proffered at trial, the party shall see that a description or a photograph of the physical evidence, together with an explanation of it, if helpful, is included within the transcript, in lieu of sending the original evidence.

(1) If the party who is relying upon physical evidence deems the original evidence to be of such importance that a photograph or a description cannot suffice to demonstrate the party's contention, application may be made to the trial court for an order directing the transmission of the original evidence to this Court, or application may be made to this Court for such an order if it cannot be obtained from the trial court after a bona fide effort.

(2) Where the admissibility of photographs is attacked, the originals or exact duplicates, to be furnished by appellant, shall be included in the transcript.

(3) The court reporter and clerk shall certify the exhibits.

Adopted effective May 22, 1995; amended effective September 1, 2001.

RULE 72. PROHIBITED EVIDENCE

Unless directed by this Court, no physical evidence or exhibits shall be sent to this Court that do not fit within the transcript or are bulky, cumbersome or expensive to transport, or which, by reason of their nature, are dangerous to handle.

Adopted effective May 22, 1995; amended effective September 1, 2001.

RULE 73. RETURN OF EVIDENCE

Original evidence or exhibits received by this Court pursuant to Rules 71 or 72 shall be offered back to the trial court clerk and to the parties within 90 days after the remittitur is returned to the lower court.

Evidence or exhibits not reclaimed will be destroyed.

Adopted effective May 22, 1995; amended effective September 1, 2001.

RULE 74. WAIVER

Appellee shall be deemed to have waived any failure of the appellant to comply with the provisions of the Appellate Practice Act relating to the filing of the transcript of the evidence and proceedings or transmittal of the record to this Court unless objection thereto was made and ruled upon in the trial court prior to transmittal, and such order is appealed as provided by law.

Adopted effective May 22, 1995; amended effective September 1, 2001.

XIV. MEDIA RULES

RULE 75.

Proceedings in the Supreme Court may be broadcast by television and radio, recorded electronically, and photographed by still news photographers, if in compliance with the provisions of this plan and the Code of Judicial Conduct.

Adopted effective May 22, 1995; amended effective September 1, 2001.

RULE 76.

No broadcasting, recording, or photographing shall distract from the dignity of the Court proceedings.

Adopted effective May 22, 1995; amended effective September 1, 2001.

RULE 77.

No more than 4 still photographers and 4 television cameras will be permitted in the courtroom for coverage at any time while a proceeding is in session. However, the Court will allow all photographers and television stations to pool or divide the time, so that all will be allowed to participate. The positioning and removal of cameras shall be done only when the Court is in recess. Any pooling arrangements among those seeking to provide camera coverage shall be the sole responsibility of media persons. Neither the Clerk nor the Public Information Officer is responsible for resolving disputes regarding the same.

Adopted effective May 22, 1995; amended effective September 1, 2001; January 5, 2005.

RULE 78.

The Court, upon request, will permit persons to obtain audio from the Court's public address system on a first-come, first-served basis.

Adopted effective May 22, 1995; amended effective September 1, 2001.

RULE 79.

Persons desiring to cover a proceeding must furnish their own equipment and shall be responsible for it.

Former Rule 80 adopted effective May 22, 1995; renumbered as Rule 79 effective September 1, 2001.

RULE 80.

All television cameras are restricted to the alcove of the Courtroom. Television cameras or still cameras which produce distracting noise or sound may not be used.

Former Rule 81 adopted effective May 22, 1995; renumbered as Rule 80 effective September 1, 2001.

RULE 81.

During sessions of the Court, still news photographers may sit anywhere in the courtroom designated for use by the public, and may take pictures. However, if they wish to take pictures while standing they must do so from behind the back rows of spectator seats or from the alcove. No flashbulbs or noisy motor drives or battery-operated film advances may be used in the courtroom.

Former Rule 82 adopted effective May 22, 1995; renumbered as Rule 81 effective September 1, 2001.

RULE 82.

During the time the Court is in session, television personnel will be limited in their movements to the alcove area of the courtroom. They and still news photographers will be permitted to enter and leave the courtroom through the back doors of the alcove into the lawyer's lounge.

Former Rule 83 adopted effective May 22, 1995; renumbered as Rule 82 effective September 1, 2001.

RULE 83.

All persons covering a hearing or event will remain in the areas designated by the Court and will avoid activity that might disrupt the proceedings.

Former Rule 84 adopted effective May 22, 1995; renumbered as Rule 83 effective September 1, 2001.

RULE 84.

This plan shall not affect the coverage of any judicial proceeding by a news reporter or other person who is not using a camera, broadcast, or recording device but who is taking notes or making sketches.

Former Rule 85 adopted effective May 22, 1995; renumbered as Rule 84 effective September 1, 2001.

RULE 85.

Attorneys appearing before the Supreme Court may not give interviews in the courtroom or in the Judicial Building, and media representatives shall not seek interviews in the courtroom or in the Judicial Building, without permission of the Court.

Former Rule 86 adopted effective May 22, 1995; renumbered as Rule 85 effective September 1, 2001.

RULE 86.

All media representatives who cover a judicial proceeding are subject to this plan and thereby agree to observe the rules and objectives set out herein.

Former Rule 87 adopted effective May 22, 1995; renumbered as Rule 86 effective September 1, 2001.

RULE 87.

In the event that the Court holds judicial sessions at places other than in the courtroom of the Judicial Building in Atlanta, the spirit of this plan shall be followed to the extent possible.

Former Rule 88 adopted effective May 22, 1995; renumbered as Rule 87 effective September 1, 2001.

RULE 88.

The restrictions under this plan are not to be applied to the coverage of ceremonial or non-judicial proceedings.

Former Rule 89 adopted effective May 22, 1995; renumbered as Rule 88 effective September 1, 2001.

RULE 89.

The Supreme Court reserves the right in any particular proceeding to modify by court order any of the above rules and provisions, whether on its own motion or on the written request of any member of the media affected by the rules and provisions.

Former Rule 90 adopted effective May 22, 1995; renumbered as Rule 89 effective September 1, 2001.

RULE 90.

The Supreme Court shall retain the exclusive authority to limit, restrict, prohibit, and terminate the photographing, recording, and broadcasting of any judicial session.

Former Rule 91 adopted effective May 22, 1995; renumbered as Rule 90 effective September 1, 2001.

XV. THIRD–YEAR LAW STUDENTS

RULE 91.

An authorized third-year law student, when under the supervision of a district attorney, a solicitor general of a state court, a solicitor of a municipal court, a public defender, or a licensed practicing attorney who works or volunteers for a court or for a not-for-profit organization which provides free legal representation to indigent persons or children may assist in proceedings within this state as if admitted and licensed to practice law in this state.

Former Rule 92 adopted effective May 22, 1995; amended effective June 5, 1997; renumbered as Rule 91 effective September 1, 2001; amended effective January 5, 2005.

RULE 92.

All pleadings and other entries of record must also be signed by the district attorney, solicitor general, solicitor, public defender, or duly appointed assistant district attorney, assistant solicitor general, assistant solicitor, assistant public defender, or licensed practicing attorney as described in Rule 91. In the conduct of any grand jury investigation, administrative proceeding, hearing, trial, or other proceeding, such district attorney, solicitor general, solicitor, public defender, or duly appointed assistant district attorney, assistant solicitor general, assistant solicitor, assistant public defender, or licensed practicing attorney as described in Rule 91 must be physically present.

Former Rule 93 adopted effective May 22, 1995; amended effective June 5, 1997; renumbered as Rule 92 effective September 1, 2001; amended effective January 5, 2005.

RULE 93.

An eligible third-year law student is a student regularly enrolled and in good standing in a law school in this state, or an accredited law school located outside of this state, who has satisfactorily completed at least two-thirds of the requirements for the first professional degree in law, a J.D. or its equivalent, in not less than four semesters or six quarters of residence.

Any third-year law student eligible to assist a district attorney, solicitor general, solicitor, or public defender under this Rule is not required to possess the qualifications for appointment to the office of district attorney, solicitor general, solicitor, public defender, or assistant district attorney, assistant solicitor general, assistant solicitor, or assistant public defender.

Former Rule 94 adopted effective May 22, 1995; amended effective June 5, 1997; renumbered as Rule 93 effective September 1, 2001; amended effective January 5, 2005.

RULE 94.

An eligible third-year law student may be authorized to participate in the proceedings in such form and manner as the judge of the court where such authority is to be exercised may prescribe, if these requirements and the good moral character of the third-year law student are properly certified by the dean of the student's law school. Before entering an order authorizing a student to assist the district attorney, solicitor general, solicitor, or public defender, the judge shall further require of the student an oath similar to the oath required by a district attorney, a solicitor general, a solicitor, or a public defender.

As to each third-year law student authorized to assist a district attorney, solicitor general, solicitor, public defender or licensed practicing attorney as described in Rule 91, there shall be kept on file in the office of the clerk of the court where such authority is to be exercised, the dean's certificate, the student's oath if required, and the judge's order.

Former Rule 95 adopted effective May 22, 1995; amended effective June 5, 1997; renumbered as Rule 94 effective September 1, 2001.

RULE 95.

The authority to assist a district attorney, solicitor general, solicitor, public defender, or licensed practicing attorney as described in Rule 91 shall extend for no longer than one year. If during this period any change occurs in the student's law school enrollment status, such authority shall terminate and be revoked.

Former Rule 96 adopted effective May 22, 1995; amended effective June 5, 1997; renumbered as Rule 95 effective September 1, 2001; amended effective January 5, 2005.

RULE 96.

A licensed practicing attorney as described in Rule 91, who is supervising law students under this Rule, shall ensure that at all times the student is covered by an adequate amount of malpractice insurance.

Former Rule 97 adopted effective May 22, 1995; renumbered as Rule 96 effective September 1, 2001.

XVI. LAW SCHOOL GRADUATES

RULE 97.

A law school graduate certified under these rules, when under the supervision of the Attorney General, a district attorney, a solicitor general of a state court, a solicitor of a municipal court, a public defender, or a licensed practicing attorney who works or volunteers for a court or for a not-for-profit organization which provides free legal representation to indigent persons or children, may assist in proceedings within this state as if admitted and licensed to practice law in this state.

Former Rule 98 adopted effective June 5, 1997; amended effective October 21, 1997; renumbered as Rule 97 effective September 1, 2001; amended effective January 5, 2005.

RULE 98.

All pleadings and other entries of record must also be signed by the Attorney General, a district attorney, solicitor general, solicitor, public defender, or duly appointed assistant attorney general, assistant district attorney, assistant solicitor general, assistant solicitor, assistant public defender, or licensed practicing attorney as described in Rule 97. In the conduct of any grand jury investigation, administrative proceeding, hearing, trial, or other proceeding, such Attorney General, district attorney, solicitor general, solicitor, public defender, or duly appointed assistant district attorney, assistant solicitor general, assistant solicitor, assistant public defender, or licensed practicing attorney as described in Rule 97, must be physically present.

Former Rule 99 adopted effective June 5, 1997; amended effective October 21, 1997; renumbered as Rule 98 effective September 1, 2001.

RULE 99.

An eligible law–school graduate is a recent graduate of a Georgia law school or of an accredited law school from another state who has not yet received the results of his or her *first* taking of any bar examination. Such graduate shall file a petition to practice as a law–school graduate with the Clerk of the Supreme Court, setting out the graduate's name, address, the name of the law school from which he or she graduated and the date thereof, and the name, title and signature of the Attorney General, district attorney, solicitor general, solicitor, public defender, or licensed practicing attorney as described in Rule 97, whom the graduate intends to assist. If available, evidence of certification of fitness to practice law from the Board to Determine Fitness of Bar Applicants issued under Part A, Section 11 of the Rules Governing Admission to the Practice of Law, or similar certification from another state, shall be attached to the petition. If not available, the status of the graduate's fitness application in Georgia or any other state, if any, shall be set out in the petition. A graduate who has been denied or tentatively denied certification of fitness to practice law in Georgia, or any other state, shall not be eligible to practice under this Rule.

Application for a certificate of fitness to take the bar examination is not a prerequisite to eligibility to practice as a graduate.

Any graduate eligible to assist the Attorney General, a district attorney, solicitor general, solicitor, or public defender under this Rule is not required to possess the qualifications for appointment to the office of Attorney General, district attorney, solicitor general, solicitor, public defender, or assistant attorney general, assistant district attorney, assistant solicitor general, assistant solicitor, or assistant public defender.

Former Rule 100 adopted effective June 5, 1997; amended effective October 21, 1997; renumbered as Rule 99 effective September 1, 2001; amended effective January 5, 2005; June 7, 2006.

RULE 100.

Upon receiving and examining the petition of the graduate, the Court shall register the graduate as eligible to practice under these rules until the end of the month (October or May) in which the results of the first Georgia Bar examination for which the petitioner is eligible will be published. The Court shall issue a certificate to the graduate setting out the petitioner's status as a graduate and the duration of his or her eligibility to practice under these rules.

Former Rule 101 adopted effective June 5, 1997; renumbered as Rule 100 effective September 1, 2001.

RULE 101.

The graduate shall present such certificate to the judge of the trial court where the graduate intends to assist in proceedings. The graduate may be authorized to participate in the proceedings in such form and manner as the judge of the court where such authority is to be exercised may prescribe. Before entering an order authorizing a graduate to assist the Attorney General, district attorney, solicitor general, solicitor, or public defender, the judge shall further require of the graduate an oath similar to the oath required by a district attorney, a solicitor general, a solicitor, or a public defender.

As to each graduate authorized to assist the Attorney General, a district attorney, solicitor general, solicitor, public defender, or licensed practicing attorney as described in Rule 97, there shall be kept on file in the office of the clerk of the court where such authority is to be exercised, a copy of this Court's certificate, the graduate's oath if required, and the judge's order.

Former Rule 102 adopted effective June 5, 1997; amended effective October 21, 1997; renumbered as Rule 101 effective September 1, 2001; amended effective January 5, 2005.

RULE 102.

If during this period the Board to Determine Fitness of Bar Applicants, or a similar board from another state, denies or tentatively denies the graduate's application, the graduate shall notify the judge of the trial court where he or she is assisting in proceedings immediately and such authority to practice as a graduate shall terminate and be revoked.

Former Rule 103 adopted effective June 5, 1997; renumbered as Rule 102 effective September 1, 2001.

RULE 103.

A licensed practicing attorney as described in Rule 97, who is supervising law graduates under this Rule, shall ensure that at all times the graduate is covered by an adequate amount of malpractice insurance.

Former Rule 104 adopted effective June 5, 1997; renumbered as Rule 103 effective September 1, 2001.

XVII. PROPOSED AMENDMENTS TO THE UNIFORM RULES

RULE 104.

Any request to the Court to amend the Uniform Rules of the five classes of trial courts, or to adopt rules that deviate from the uniform rules, emergency rules, or experimental rules, shall be filed with the Clerk of the Supreme Court. Internal operating procedures must also be filed with the Clerk of the

Supreme Court but do not require the Court's approval.

Former Rule 98 adopted effective May 22, 1995; renumbered as Rule 105 effective June 5, 1997; amended effective June 1, 1998; renumbered as Rule 104 effective September 1, 2001.

RULE 105.

Any proposal submitted, except submissions of internal operating procedures, shall contain a statement that a copy of the proposed rule has been forwarded to the State Bar for comment. In the case of an experimental rule, the proposal shall also contain a statement that the rule has been advertised to the local bar for 30 days prior to filing.

Former Rule 99 adopted effective May 22, 1995; renumbered as Rule 106 effective June 5, 1997; amended effective June 1, 1998; renumbered as Rule 105 effective September 1, 2001.

RULE 106.

Any submission, including submissions of internal operating procedures, shall explain the reasons for the proposal, the ways that it differs from existing rules and procedures, and the specific changes sought, with additional material underlined and deleted material stricken through.

Former Rule 100 adopted effective May 22, 1995; renumbered as Rule 107 effective June 5, 1997; amended effective June 1, 1998; renumbered as Rule 106 effective September 1, 2001.

XVIII. DEFEATED SENIOR JUDGES

Rule 107.

Any defeated senior judge who has properly obtained senior status in accordance with OCGA § 15–1–9.2 or OCGA § 15–1–9.3, may seek this Court's approval of such service by filing a petition for service that includes proof of senior status, and an affidavit executed by the defeated senior judge that attests to his or her good standing with the State Bar and general good character, and that the defeated senior judge has not been found guilty of any malfeasance while serving as an active or senior judge.

Adopted effective March 5, 2003; amended effective June 7, 2006.

Rule 108.

If the Court approves the defeated senior judge's petition for service, it will issue an order to that effect, at which time the defeated senior judge may begin to comply with the requests to serve made in accordance with OCGA § 15–1–9.2 or OCGA § 15–1–9.3.

Adopted effective March 5, 2003; amended effective January 5, 2005.

Rule 109.

This Court periodically may review its approval of any defeated senior judge's petition for service, but once having been approved, the defeated senior judge may continue to serve until such approval is withdrawn or revoked.

Adopted effective March 5, 2003.

XIX. CONTINUING JUDICIAL EDUCATION

RULE 110.

Each Justice of the Supreme Court of Georgia shall complete a minimum of 12 hours of instruction in an approved continuing judicial or legal education activity during each calendar year. If a Justice completes more than twelve hours in a year, the excess credit may be carried forward and applied to the education requirement for the succeeding year only.

Each Justice shall complete during each year a minimum of 1 hour of continuing judicial or legal education activity in the area of legal or judicial ethics and 1 hour in an activity of the Institute of Continuing Legal Education in the area of professionalism. These hours are to be included in, and not in addition to, the twelve-hour requirement. If a Justice completes more than 1 hour in either or both of these areas during a year, the excess may be carried forward to a maximum of 2 hours in either or both areas and be applied to the ethics and/or professionalism requirement for succeeding years.

The Supreme Court may exempt a Justice from the continuing judicial education requirements but not from the reporting requirements of this rule for a period of not more than one year upon a finding by the Court of special circumstances unique to that member constituting undue hardship.

Former Rule 101 adopted effective May 22, 1995; renumbered as Rule 108 effective June 5, 1997; renumbered as Rule 107 effective September 1, 2001; renumbered as Rule 110 effective March 5, 2003.

RULE 111.

On or before January 31 of each year, each Justice shall make and file with the Clerk of the Supreme

Court evidence of compliance with the requirements of the program for mandatory continuing judicial education.

Former Rule 102 adopted effective May 22, 1995; renumbered as Rule 109 effective June 5, 1997; renumbered as Rule 108 effective September 1, 2001; renumbered as Rule 111 effective March 5, 2003.

RULE 112.

Continuing education programs for which a Justice may receive qualifying credit shall include: (1) programs of the Appellate Judges Conference sponsored by the American Bar Association; (2) programs sponsored by the Institute of Continuing Judicial Education of Georgia; (3) programs of continuing legal education accredited by the Commission on Continuing Lawyer Competency of the State Bar of Georgia, including all programs of the Institute of Continuing Legal Education; (4) programs sponsored by any law school accredited by the American Bar Association; and (5) such other programs of continuing judicial or legal education as may be approved by the Supreme Court of Georgia.

For teaching in a program qualifying under (1)-(5), above, a Justice shall be given three hours of credit for each hour of instructional responsibility when no handout paper is required but preparation is necessary and is conducted, and six hours of credit for each hour of instructional responsibility when a handout paper is required and prepared. When the same lecture or instructional activity is repeated in a single year, additional credit shall be given equivalent to the actual time spent in delivering that presentation.

Former Rule 103 adopted effective May 22, 1995; renumbered as Rule 110 effective June 5, 1997; renumbered as Rule 109 effective September 1, 2001; renumbered as Rule 112 effective March 5, 2003.

RULE 113.

In the event a Justice shall fail to comply with the requirements of the rules for Mandatory Continuing Judicial Education at the end of an applicable period, such Justice may submit to the Supreme Court a specific plan for making up the deficiency of necessary hours within 60 days after the last day for the reporting of activities for the preceding year.

In the event such plan is not submitted, or in the event a plan is submitted but not complied with during the 60–day period, the Supreme Court shall administer a reprimand to the noncomplying Justice and the fact of such reprimand may be noted and published in the Supreme Court Reports.

Former Rule 104 adopted effective May 22, 1995; renumbered as Rule 111 effective June 5, 1997; renumbered as Rule 110 effective September 1, 2001; renumbered as Rule 113 effective March 5, 2003.

INDEX TO RULES OF THE SUPREME COURT OF GEORGIA

*

RULES OF THE COURT OF APPEALS OF THE STATE OF GEORGIA

Effective January 6, 2005

Including Amendments Received Through November 1, 2006

Research Note

Use WESTLAW *to find cases citing a rule. In addition, use* WESTLAW *to search for specific terms or to update a rule; see the GA–RULES and GA–ORDERS Scope screens for further information.*

Amendments to these rules are published, as received, in the South Eastern Reporter 2d *and* Georgia Cases *advance sheets.*

Table of Rules

Note

These rules are not intended to reiterate all applicable laws. Where the word "counsel" has been used, this will include pro se parties.

I. GENERAL

Rule 1. [Document Requirements.]

(a) Requirement for Written and Signed Documents.

All filings, documents, motions, briefs, requests and communications relating to appeals shall be in writing, shall be filed with the Clerk's office, shall be signed by an attorney of record, an attorney granted courtesy appearance or pro se parties, and shall include the mailing address and telephone number of the attorney or pro se party signing the document, and shall show that copies have been furnished to opposing counsel. Documents with conformed signatures by law firm staff or an attorney's employee will not be accepted. All signed documents shall include the State Bar of Georgia membership number of all submitting attorneys.

(b) Communications with the Court.

There shall be no communications relating to pending cases to any judge or member of the judge's staff.

(c) Documents.

All documents filed with the Court shall be typed or printed on non–transparent, letter size (8 ½" x 11") white paper and bound at the top with staples or fasteners (round head or Acco) and all matters contained therein, including quotations and footnotes, shall have no less than double spacing between the lines. Letter spacing and type or font size shall be no smaller than Courier 10 cpi, 12 point (or equivalent). Notwithstanding the ten (10) characters per inch requirement, the Court will accept in lieu thereof Times New Roman Regular 14pt (Western). Any documents which the Court deems inappropriate as to type size, type style and/or form may be returned to counsel after filing by the Court, and counsel may be ordered to redact and recast such documents. All documents filed with this Court shall have a non–glossy, white back of recyclable paper, heavier than regular stationery–type paper.

(d) Counsel.

All reference to counsel in these rules shall include pro se parties.

(e) Facsimile Filing.

The Court does not accept facsimile filings.

Adopted effective January 6, 2005.

Rule 2. [Clerk's Office; Filing Fees; Stamped Copies.]

(a) Clerk's Office Hours of Operation and Location.

The Clerk's office shall be open Monday through Friday from 8:30 a.m. to 4:30 p.m. E.S.T./E.D.T. The address is: Clerk, Court of Appeals of Georgia, 47 Trinity Avenue, Suite 501, Atlanta, Georgia 30334. The telephone number is (404) 656–3450.

(b) Filing Fees.

All filings requiring fees must be accompanied by a check or money order or a sufficient pauper's affidavit. The Clerk's office cannot be responsible for filings accompanied by cash.

(c) Stamped "Filed" Copy.

If a return stamped "filed" copy of a filed document is needed, parties filing such documents must include an extra copy and a pre–addressed stamped envelope with sufficient postage to have the document returned.

Adopted effective January 6, 2005; amended effective November 1, 2006.

Rule 3. Expiration Date.

When an expiration date falls on Saturday, Sunday, or an official state or national holiday, the time is extended to the next business day.

Adopted effective January 6, 2005.

Rule 4. Filing.

(a) Drop Box.

The Clerk's office has provided a drop box for filing documents after business hours. Any items placed in the drop box after 4:30 p.m., Monday through Friday, will be docketed to the date the documents were placed in the drop box. The Judicial Building is open from 7:00 a.m. until generally 5:00 p.m. Since the building hours of operation are controlled by the Georgia Building Authority, check the court web site at www.gaappeals.us for current hours. Court personnel will remove the documents the morning of the following business day and clock documents to the present time and date and file the documents to the date they were placed in the drop box.

(b) Motions for Reconsideration.

Motions for reconsideration are deemed filed only on the date they are physically received in the Clerk's office. See Rule 37.

(c) Other Documents.

Any other document shall be deemed filed on the date:

(1) It is physically delivered to the Clerk's office, with sufficient costs, if applicable, and clocked in by the Clerk's office staff;

(2) It is deposited in the United States Postal Service registered or certified mail, the United States Postal Service postmark date on the envelope or container, and with sufficient costs, if applicable; or

(3) It is delivered to the United States Postal Service or a commercial delivery company, with sufficient costs, if applicable, for overnight delivery.

(d) Proof of Filing.

The United States Postal Service or commercial delivery company receipt must be submitted to the Clerk's office upon request. An office or private postage meter date is not sufficient.

Adopted effective January 6, 2005.

Rule 5. Costs.

Costs in all cases are $80.00 unless a sufficient pauper's affidavit is filed with the Court or contained in the record. Costs shall be paid upon filing of applications or, in direct appeals, upon filing of appellant's brief. Costs are incurred and appellant and appellant's counsel are liable for costs when the case is docketed. The Clerk shall not file any matter unless the costs have been paid or a sufficient pauper's affidavit has been filed.

Adopted effective January 6, 2005.

Rule 6. Copies and Certificate of Service.

All documents filed with the Clerk shall include an original and two copies. All documents shall show copies have been furnished to opposing counsel. Service shall be shown by written acknowledgment, certificate of counsel or affidavit of server, to include the mailing address of all opposing counsel. Service shall be made before filing. Any document without a Certificate of Service will not be accepted for filing. (The Certificate of Service shall be attached to the document filed.)

Adopted effective January 6, 2005.

Rule 7. Contempt.

Breach of any rule of the Court of Appeals or failure to comply with an order of this Court subjects the offending party and/or attorney to contempt and may subject the appeal to dismissal or cause appellee's brief to be stricken. The Court may, upon a finding of conduct constituting contempt, impose a fine not to exceed $1,000.00 against each contemner or revoke the license to practice in this Court, or both.

Adopted effective January 6, 2005.

Rule 8. Notice of Cause for Disqualification or Recusal.

Cause for disqualification or recusal of a judge of this Court shall be brought to the attention of the Clerk as soon as practicable. See Rule 44.

Adopted effective January 6, 2005.

II. ATTORNEYS

Rule 9. Attorneys.

(a) Application and Oath.

Any member of the State Bar of Georgia may be admitted to practice in this Court upon written application, and the certificate of at least two attorneys of this Court, that such member is of good private and professional character. The oath, which is required to be taken in open Court or before a Judge in Chambers, and which shall be subscribed in a book to be kept by the Clerk and known as the "Roll Book," is as follows:

"I do solemnly swear (or affirm) that I will conduct myself as an attorney or counselor of this Court truly and honestly, justly and uprightly, and according to law; and that I will support the Constitution of the State of Georgia and the Constitution of the United States. So help me God."

(b) Fee.

The fee for admission is $30.00, payable to the Clerk, who will issue a license under the seal of the Court as evidence of applicant's authority to practice.

(c) Appearance by Courtesy.

As a matter of professional courtesy, a visiting attorney from another state, or from a district or territory, if admitted to practice in the highest court of the state, district, or territory of such attorney's residence, by leave of court, may be heard as associate counsel or counsel in a single case, without being admitted as a regular practitioner in this Court. A resident attorney, who is not a member of the State Bar of Georgia, may petition this Court for courtesy appearance by showing that the attorney is certified in good–standing in the Bar of the highest court of another state.

(d) Withdrawal or Substitution of Counsel.

Any withdrawal or substitution of attorneys of record in the Court shall be communicated to the Court by written motion with a copy to substituted counsel, opposing counsel and the withdrawing or substituting attorney's client. A Motion to Withdraw as Counsel shall contain the address of the withdrawing counsel's client, or if the address is unknown, the motion shall contain a statement that the client's address is unknown and shall contain the client's last known address.

(e) Change of Address or Telephone Number.

If during the pendency of any appeal or application counsel for either party has a change of address or telephone number, counsel shall file a notification of change of address or telephone number with the Court, notifying the Court of counsel's correct address and telephone number, and the effective date of such change.

The notification of change of address or telephone number shall be filed as a separate document, an original and two copies, with service made to opposing counsel.

Upon receipt of the notification of change of address or telephone number, the Clerk will enter the change of address or telephone number on the Court's docket and all further notices generated from the Court will be to counsel's new address.

Failure of counsel to properly notify the Court of any change of address or telephone number, which may result in counsel not receiving notification of Court action, shall not be grounds to reinstate or reconsider any matter adverse to counsel or parties because of the failure of counsel to receive notification from the Court.

(f) The Court of Appeals does not recognize, nor grant, Leaves of Court or Leaves of Absence.

Adopted effective January 6, 2005.

Rule 10. Personal Remarks.

Opposing Counsel or Judge.

Personal remarks, whether oral or written, which are discourteous or disparaging to opposing counsel, to any judge or the Court, are strictly forbidden.

Adopted effective January 6, 2005.

III. DOCKETS; CALENDARS; HEARINGS

Rule 11. Appeals, How Entered.

(a) Docketing.

No appeal shall be docketed until the notice of appeal and a record, and transcript, if requested, are filed in the Clerk's office. Each notice of appeal will be docketed as a separate case.

(b) Transfer of Cases.

Whenever an appeal or application filed in this Court is within the jurisdiction of the Supreme Court, such appeal or application shall be transferred by order to that court.

(c) Transferred Cases.

Appeals or applications transferred to this Court from the Supreme Court shall be docketed as of the date they are received in this Court.

(d) Premature Docketing.

Any case docketed prior to the entire record coming to the Court, as requested by the parties, may be remanded to the trial court until such time as the record is so prepared and delivered to the Court.

Adopted effective January 6, 2005.

Rule 12. Closing of the Dockets.

The docket for the January, April, and September terms shall close at noon on the 15th day of December, April and August, respectively. By order, a closed docket may be opened when expedient for the docketing of a case or cases so that a judgment may be rendered by the Court at the earliest practicable date.

Adopted effective January 6, 2005.

Rule 13. Notice of Docketing.

Upon the docketing of every appeal and application for appeal, the Clerk shall mail notice of the docketing date and schedule for briefing to all counsel. The notice shall include a statement that failure to file the enumeration of errors and appellant's brief within the time required, except as extended upon motion for good cause shown, may subject the appeal to dismissal. The notice shall also state that: Failure to timely file responsive briefs may result in their non–consideration; a brief shall be filed by the appellee in all criminal appeals when the State is the appellee; and upon failure to file such brief, the State's representative may be subject to contempt. Failure of counsel to receive the docketing notice shall not relieve counsel of the responsibility to file briefs timely. See Rule 23.

Adopted effective January 6, 2005.

Rule 14. Notice of Call.

(a) Calendars to be Mailed.

The Clerk shall mail the calendar to counsel in each appeal to be orally argued at least 14 days prior to the date set for oral argument at the addresses shown on the notice of appeal unless the Court is otherwise advised under Rule 9(e).

(b) Non–Receipt of Calendar.

Counsel not receiving a calendar at least 10 days prior to the tentative oral argument dates should contact the Clerk's office to inquire about oral argument dates.

(c) Conflicts—State and Federal Court.

(1) Counsel shall not be deemed to have a conflict unless such counsel:

(i) Is lead counsel in two or more of the actions affected; and

(ii) Certifies that the matters cannot be adequately handled by other counsel.

(2) When there is an apparent conflict:

(i) Appellate arguments prevail over trials, hearings and conferences.

(ii) The action first filed takes precedence.

(iii) Felony actions prevail over civil actions.

(iv) Misdemeanors stand on equal footing with civil actions.

(v) The courts are assigned the following priorities:

(aa) United States Supreme Court.

(bb) Supreme Court of the State of Georgia.

(cc) Federal Courts of Appeal and State Courts of Appeal.

(dd) United States District Courts and Superior Courts.

(ee) Federal Magistrate Courts and State Courts.

(ff) Probate, Juvenile and Magistrate Courts.

(3) The Clerk shall resolve conflicts so as to accommodate all parties insofar as possible.

(4) Using the above criteria, the only time a conflict exists is when the actions are in courts of equal priority, are of the same type and were filed on the same day. When such conflict exists, counsel shall give prompt written notice of the conflict to opposing counsel and to the clerk of each court.

(5) When it is evident that counsel's presence is required in more than one court on the same day and no conflict actually exists under the above criteria, counsel shall nevertheless inform all courts concerned, giving the style of the case and the date of filing.

Adopted effective January 6, 2005.

Rule 15. No Prosecution, Frivolous Appeals and Penalties.

(a) On the call of the case for argument, if the appellant does not appear, and has not filed a brief, the Court may dismiss the appeal for want of prosecution. If the appellee or appellee's counsel shall appear, such appellee or counsel may move to reopen the record and insist upon an affirmance of the judgment below.

(b) The panel of the Court ruling on a case, with or without motion, may by majority vote impose a penalty not to exceed $1,000.00 against any party and/or party's counsel in any civil case in which there is a direct appeal, application for discretionary appeal, application for interlocutory appeal, or motion which is determined to be frivolous.

(c) The imposition of such penalty shall constitute a money judgment in favor of appellee against appellant or appellant's counsel or in favor of appellant against appellee or appellee's counsel, as the Court directs. Upon filing of the remittitur in the trial court, the penalty may be collected as are other money judgments.

Adopted effective January 6, 2005.

IV. EXTENSION OF TIME FOR NOTICE OF APPEAL, ETC.

Rule 16. Extension of Time for Filing.

(a) Pursuant to the provisions of O.C.G.A. § 5–6–39, requests for extensions of time, which must be in writing, may be made only upon showing a bona fide effort has been made to obtain the extension from the trial court and the reason it could not be obtained. Any motion for extension of time to file a Notice of Appeal made in this Court shall be accompanied by an $80.00 filing fee or sufficient pauper's affidavit.

(b) Extensions of time to file briefs must be requested by motion and shall be subject to the Court's discretion. All extensions shall be by written order and no oral extension shall be recognized.

Failure to request an extension of time to file a brief prior to the date the brief is due may result in the non–consideration of the motion and/or the dismissal of the appeal.

(c) No extension of time shall be granted for filing interlocutory or discretionary applications or filing responses thereto.

Adopted effective January 6, 2005.

V. RECORDS AND TRANSCRIPTS

Rule 17. Duty of Trial Court Clerks.

The clerk of the trial court shall certify and transmit to the Clerk of this Court the original transcript and copies of all records as required within the time prescribed by statute. Trial court orders included in the record must contain the signature of the trial court judge. Conformed signatures will not be accepted. Transmittal shall be by the clerk or deputy personally or by first class United States mail, or express mail, or commercial courier or delivery service, charges prepaid. Transmittal by a party or attorney is prohibited.

Adopted effective January 6, 2005.

Rule 18. Preparation and Arrangement of Records and Transcripts.

(a) Records and transcripts, to include depositions, shall be printed on one side of white paper not less than letter size of good quality with ample spacing (at least double spaced) and margins so that they may be easily read. The margin at the top shall be of sufficient space so that the transcript may be read when folded over at the top. Type size shall not be smaller than Courier 10 cpi, 12 point (or equivalent). Notwithstanding the 10 characters per inch requirement, the Court will accept in lieu thereof Times New Roman Regular 14pt (Western).

(b) Any records or transcripts delivered to this Court from the trial court, and sealed by the trial court, with an order of the trial court attached to the record, shall remain sealed until a motion is made to unseal the record and/or the record is unsealed by this Court. Counsel for any party may move this Court for an order to unseal or seal any record in the Court.

Adopted effective January 6, 2005.

Rule 19. Transmission of Transcript.

The original transcript shall be a separate document and not attached to the record. It should show the style of the case and an index. Voluminous transcripts may be bound in separate parts. The court reporter and trial court clerk shall certify each part.

Adopted effective January 6, 2005.

Rule 20. Objections to Records or Transcripts; Waiver.

Appellee shall be deemed to have waived any failure of the appellant to comply with the provisions of the Appellate Practice Act relating to the filing of the transcript of the evidence and proceedings or transmittal of the record to this Court, unless objection thereto was made and ruled upon in the trial court prior to transmittal and such order is appealed as provided by law.

Adopted effective January 6, 2005.

Rule 21. Physical Evidence—Original Evidence.

Any party relying on physical evidence may include as a part of the transcript or record a photograph, a videotape or an audiotape of the evidence, together with an explanation or description if deemed necessary, in lieu of transmitting the original evidence. No original evidence or exhibits shall be transmitted to the Court unless the Court directs the clerk of the trial court to transmit such original evidence or exhibits, or upon the grant of a written motion of the party or parties desiring such original evidence or exhibits to be transmitted to the Court. The motion shall be specific as to what original evidence or exhibits shall be transmitted to the Court and the reason such original evidence or exhibits are necessary for the determination of the appeal. After the remittitur has been issued from the Court to the trial court, all original evidence or exhibits shall be returned to the clerk of the trial court. In no event, unless directed by this Court, shall physical evidence be transmitted to the Court which is bulky, cumbersome, or expensive to transport, or which, by reason of its nature, is dangerous to handle, or which is contraband.

Adopted effective January 6, 2005.

VI. ENUMERATION OF ERRORS

Rule 22. Filing.

(a) Time of Filing.

Pursuant to O.C.G.A. § 5–6–40, the enumeration of errors, which shall be Part 2 of the appellant's brief, shall be filed within 20 days after the case is docketed. A separate enumeration of errors is not required.

(b) Jurisdictional Statement.

The enumeration of errors shall contain a statement of jurisdiction as to why this Court, and not the Supreme Court, has jurisdiction.

Adopted effective January 6, 2005.

VII. BRIEFS

Rule 23. Time of Filing; Contempt; Dismissal; Service.

(a) Appellant's brief, which shall contain as Part 2 an enumeration of errors, shall be filed within 20 days after the appeal is docketed. Failure to file within that time, unless extended upon motion for good cause shown, may subject the appeal to dismissal, and may subject the offender to contempt. See Rule 7 and Rule 13.

Appellant's motion for extension of time to file brief and enumeration of errors must be filed prior to the date the documents are due or the Court may dismiss the appeal.

(b) Appellee's brief shall be filed within 40 days after the appeal is docketed or 20 days after the filing of appellant's brief, whichever is later. Failure to timely file may result in non–consideration of the brief and may subject counsel to contempt. See also Rule 13.

(c) Appellant may file a reply brief within 20 days from the date of filing of appellee's brief. Appellee has no right to respond to appellant's reply brief except as permitted under Rule 27.

Adopted effective January 6, 2005.

Rule 24. Preparation.

(a) Briefs shall be limited to an initial appellant's brief, a responding appellee's brief and a reply brief of the appellant. Other briefs will be accepted only if filed as an Amicus Curiae brief (Rule 26) or in accordance with Rule 27. Briefs will not be accepted unless filed by a pro se party, a member of the State Bar of Georgia admitted to the Court or an attorney granted a courtesy appearance in accordance with Rule 9 (c).

(b) Paper, Spacing.

All briefs shall be filed in conformity with Rule 1 (a) and (c) and Rule 6. Electronic briefs will not be accepted by the Court unless a motion requesting permission to file has been filed and granted by the Court. Such motion must indicate the medium, file format and any software required to view the brief. Permission to file in an electronic form does not relieve the party from filing the required number of paper copies.

(c) Margins.

Writing shall be on only one side of each sheet with a margin of not less than two inches at the top and a margin of at least one inch on the sides and bottom of each page.

(d) Citations.

All citations of cases shall be by name of the case as well as by volume, page and year of the Official Report. Cases not yet reported shall be cited by the Court of Appeals or Supreme Court case number and date of decision.

(e) Pages to be Numbered.

The pages of each brief shall be sequentially numbered with Arabic numerals.

(f) Limitation as to Length.

Briefs and responsive briefs shall be limited to 30 pages in civil cases and 50 pages in criminal cases including indexes, exhibits and appendices, except upon written application directed to the Clerk and approved by the Court. Appellant's reply brief shall be limited to 15 pages. See Rule 27 for additional briefs.

(g) Attachments and Exhibits.

Documents attached to an appellate brief, which have not been certified by the clerk of the trial court as a part of the appellate record and forwarded to this Court, will not be considered on appeal.

(h) Address of Defendant.

Counsel for defendant shall include the address of the defendant in a criminal case on the face of the brief and shall notify the Court of any change of address.

Adopted effective January 6, 2005.

Rule 25. Structure and Content.

(a) Appellant.

The brief of appellant shall consist of three parts:

(1) Part One shall contain a succinct and accurate statement of the proceedings below and the material facts relevant to the appeal and the citation of such parts of the record or transcript essential to a consideration of the errors complained of, and a statement of the method by which each enumeration of error was preserved for consideration. Record and transcript citations must be to the volume or part of the record or transcript and the page numbers that appear on the appellate records or transcript as sent from the court below.

(2) Part Two shall consist of the enumeration of errors.

(3) Part Three shall contain the argument and citation of authorities. It shall also include a concise statement of the applicable standard of review with supporting authority for each issue presented in the brief.

(b) Appellee.

The brief of appellee shall be divided in the following manner:

(1) Part One shall point out any material inaccuracy or incompleteness of appellant's statement of facts and any additional statement of facts deemed necessary, plus such additional parts of the record or transcript deemed material. Failure to do so shall constitute consent to a decision based on the appellant's statement of facts. Except as controverted, appellant's statement of facts may be accepted by this Court as true.

(2) Part Two shall contain appellee's argument and the citation of authorities as to each enumeration of error. It shall also include the standard of review if different from that contended by the appellant.

(c) General Provisions.

(1) Sequence of Argument.

The sequence of arguments in the briefs shall follow the order of the enumeration of errors, and shall be numbered accordingly.

(2) Unsupported Claim of Error Treated as Abandoned.

Any enumeration of error which is not supported in the brief by citation of authority or argument may be deemed abandoned.

(3) References to Record or Transcript.

(i) Each enumerated error shall be supported in the brief by specific reference to the record or transcript. In the absence of such reference, the Court will not search for or consider such enumeration.

(ii) A contention that certain matters are not supported by the record may be answered by reference to particular pages where they appear.

(iii) Reference to the record should be indicated by specific volume or part of the record and by (R–Page Number of the Record). Reference to the transcript should be indicated by specific volume or part of the transcript and by (T–Page Number of the Transcript). Reference to a motion transcript should be indicated by (MT–Page Number of the Transcript and date of the hearing).

(iv) No briefs or motions shall be filed under seal unless counsel has moved the Court for permission to file under seal and the Court has granted such motion.

Adopted effective January 6, 2005.

Rule 26. Amicus Curiae Briefs.

Amicus Curiae briefs may be filed without leave of Court, disclosing the identity and interest of the person or group on whose behalf the brief is filed and limited to issues properly raised by the parties. Only members of the Bar of this Court or attorneys appearing by courtesy may file Amicus Curiae briefs.

Adopted effective January 6, 2005.

Rule 27. Supplemental Briefs.

(a) Briefs shall be limited to an appellant's brief, an appellee's brief, and an appellant's reply brief. Supplemental briefs may be filed only by leave of the Court. Counsel may file a motion for permission to file supplemental briefs. Contemporaneously with filing a motion, counsel may file, as a separate document, an original and two copies of the supplemental brief, not to exceed 15 pages.

(b) Parties are not permitted to file letter briefs nor letter cites. Any communication with the Court regarding recent authority which comes to the attention of a party subsequent to the filing of such party's brief or after oral argument, but before decision, must be filed in compliance with (a) above as a supplemental brief, an original and two copies, with a Certificate of Service, and service must be made on opposing counsel. Any response shall be made promptly and in accordance with this rule.

Adopted effective January 6, 2005.

VIII. ARGUMENT

Rule 28. [Oral Argument.]

(a) Request and Time.

(1) Unless expressly ordered by the Court, oral argument is never mandatory and argument may be submitted by briefs only. A case will be placed on the calendar for oral argument only upon the granting of the request of either party.

A request for oral argument shall be filed within 20 days from the date the case is docketed in this Court. The request must be a separate document, an original and two copies, directed to the Clerk, certifying that opposing counsel has been notified of the request and that opposing counsel desires, or does not desire, to argue orally. The request shall identify counsel who is scheduled to argue, and any change shall be communicated to the Clerk as soon as practicable.

An extension of time to file brief and enumeration of errors does not extend the time to request oral argument.

A request shall contain a brief statement demonstrating that the decisional process will be significantly aided by oral argument. The request should be self–contained and should convey the specific reason or reasons oral argument would be beneficial to the Court. Counsel should not assume the brief will be considered in ruling on the request for oral argument.

After either side has been granted oral argument, it may be waived by either side, but waiver by the requester does not remove the case from the oral argument calendar. Argument will not be allowed on behalf of any party whose brief has not been timely filed, unless permission is granted by the Court. Counsel requesting extension of time to file briefs waive oral argument if the extension is beyond the end of the term.

(2) Argument is limited to 30 minutes for each case, 15 minutes on each side, unless by special leave an extension of time is granted. No additional time will be granted except on application made in writing at least 5 days before the date set for the call of the case. If additional time is granted, the case will be placed at the end of the calendar unless otherwise ordered by the Court. Appeals, cross appeals, companion cases, and related cases shall be considered to be one case for purpose of oral argument. In the discretion of the Court, a companion case may be treated as a separate case for oral argument if counsel so requests by written motion at least 5 days before the date set for oral argument. Where there are third parties or additional parties with divergent interests, additional time may be requested and granted as set out above.

(3) Appeals in which oral argument has been granted pursuant to Rule 28 (a) will be assigned to the calendar in the order in which they appear on the docket, unless otherwise ordered. When a case has been reached in its order on the calendar, it will not be postponed except for good reason shown. Postponements of oral argument are not favored, and no postponement shall be granted under any circumstances that would allow oral argument to take place during a term of the Court subsequent to the term for which the case was docketed.

(4) If either counsel decides to waive oral argument after it has been granted, waiving counsel must notify other counsel and the Court of that fact.

(b) Number of Arguments.

Ordinarily, when both sides of an appeal are argued, only two counsel on each side will be heard. When only one side of an appeal is argued, or when arguments are to be made on behalf of more than two parties, no more than one counsel per party shall be heard. For exception, see Rule 28(h).

(c) Opening and Concluding; Rebuttal.

Appellant has the right to open and conclude the arguments.

(d) Courtroom Decorum.

(1) Counsel appearing for oral argument shall check in with the Clerk in the courtroom at 9:30 a.m. on the date of oral argument specifying who will argue and for how long.

(2) Talking, reading newspapers or other material, and audibly studying briefs and arranging papers are prohibited in the courtroom. The lawyers' lounge has been provided for this purpose.

(3) All counsel appearing before the Court must be properly attired.

(e) Presence of Counsel.

Oral argument is waived if counsel is not actually inside the courtroom when the case is formally called in its order for argument.

(f) Time of Argument.

Counsel may request 5, 10 or 15 minutes for argument. If counsel do not agree on the length of oral argument, the longer time requested shall prevail and each counsel shall be given the same amount of time. Ordinarily, cases will be argued in the following order: first, 5 minute cases; second, 10 minute cases; and third, 15 minute cases.

(g) Oral Argument Open to the Public.

Unless ordered by the Court, oral argument is open to the public. Counsel may move the Court to exclude the public for a good cause shown. Such motion shall be filed not later than 24 hours prior to oral argument.

News media are permitted to photograph or videotape oral argument pursuant to the Court's standing order regarding media in the courtroom.

(h) Procedural Questions.

The Presiding Judge shall decide all questions or issues arising at oral argument.

Adopted effective January 6, 2005; amended effective October 18, 2005.

Rule 29. Hearing by Quorum.

(a) Whenever a Division of the Court is on the bench for the purpose of hearing oral argument, and a quorum (two judges) is present, the Division shall proceed with the call of the docket.

(b) Oral arguments shall be tape recorded for the use and benefit of the Court.

Adopted effective January 6, 2005.

IX. APPLICATION FOR INTERLOCUTORY APPEALS

Rule 30. Interlocutory Applications.

(a) An application for leave to appeal an interlocutory order will be granted only when it appears from the documents submitted that:

(1) The issue to be decided appears to be dispositive of the case; or

(2) The order appears erroneous and will probably cause a substantial error at trial or will adversely affect the rights of the appealing party until entry of final judgment in which case the appeal will be expedited; or

(3) The establishment of precedent is desirable.

(b) Applications for interlocutory appeal shall contain a jurisdictional statement and have attached a stamped "filed" copy of the court's order to be appealed and a stamped "filed" copy of the certificate of immediate review. The trial court's order and certificate of immediate review must contain the signature of the trial court judge. Conformed signatures will not be accepted.

(c) The clerk is prohibited from receiving the application without the $80.00 filing fee or sufficient pauper's affidavit.

(d) Applications for interlocutory appeal pursuant to OCGA § 5–6–34 (b) should have copies of all materials from the record tabbed and indexed and shall be securely bound at the top with staples or fasteners (round head or Acco). If not tabbed, indexed and securely bound at the top, the petition is subject to dismissal or return for preparation according to the Court's rules. The materials must be sufficient to apprise the Court of the appellate issues, in context, and support the arguments advanced. Applications are limited to 30 pages in civil cases and 50 pages in criminal cases, exclusive of attached exhibits and parts of the record, and should follow the general format of briefs as to margins.

(e) No application for interlocutory appeal shall be filed under seal unless counsel has moved the Court for permission to file under seal and the Court has granted such motion.

(f) No extension of time shall be granted for filing of interlocutory applications or responses to interlocutory applications.

(g) Responses are due within 10 days of docketing. No response is required, unless ordered by the Court.

(h) If an interlocutory application is granted, appellant must file a notice of appeal in the trial court within 10 days of the date of the order granting the application.

Adopted effective January 6, 2005.

X. APPLICATION FOR DISCRETIONARY APPEAL

Rule 31. Discretionary Applications.

(a) An application for leave to appeal a final judgment in cases subject to appeal under O.C.G.A. § 5–6–35 will be granted only when:

(1) Reversible error appears to exist; or

(2) The establishment of a precedent is desirable.

(b) Applications for discretionary appeal pursuant to O.C.G.A. § 5–6–35 should have copies of all material from the record tabbed and indexed and shall be securely bound at the top with staples or fasteners (round head or Acco). If not tabbed, indexed and securely bound at the top, the petition is subject to dismissal or return for preparation according to the Court's rules. The material must be sufficient to apprise the Court of the appellate issues, in context, and support the arguments advanced. Applications are limited to 30 pages in civil cases and 50 pages in criminal cases, exclusive of attached exhibits and parts of the record, and should follow the general format of briefs as to margins.

(c) The clerk is prohibited from receiving the application without the $80.00 filing fee or sufficient pauper's affidavit.

(d) Discretionary appeals must contain a stamped "filed" copy of the trial court's order from which the appeal is sought. The stamped "filed" copy of the trial court's order must contain the signature of the trial court judge. Conformed signatures will not be accepted.

(e) No application for discretionary appeal shall be filed under seal unless counsel has moved the Court for permission to file under seal and the Court has granted such motion.

(f) No extensions of time will be granted in filing discretionary applications or responses to discretionary applications.

(g) Responses are due within 10 days of docketing. No response is required, unless ordered by the Court.

(h) If the discretionary application is granted, appellant must file a notice of appeal in the trial court within 10 days of the date of the order granting the application.

Adopted effective January 6, 2005.

XI. TIME OF FILING APPLICATIONS

Rule 32. Time of Filing.

(a) An application for interlocutory appeal shall be filed in this Court within 10 days of the entry of the trial court's order granting the certificate for immediate review. Entry of the trial court's order shall be the date it is filed with the trial court clerk.

(b) An application for discretionary appeal shall be filed in this Court generally within 30 days of the date of the entry of the trial court's order being appealed. Pursuant to O.C.G.A. § 44–7–56, a discretionary application involving a dispossessory action must be filed within 7 days of the entry of the trial court's order. Entry of the trial court's order shall be the date it is filed with the trial court clerk.

(c) Applications to appeal interlocutory or discretionary orders of which the Supreme Court has jurisdiction shall be transferred to that Court, if timely filed.

Adopted effective January 6, 2005.

XII. OPINIONS AND JUDGMENTS

Rule 33. Showing of Concurrence or Dissent.

Each judgment shall show on its face the votes, non–participation, or disqualification of each judge.

(a) Judgment as Precedent.

A judgment in which all judges of the Division fully concur is a binding precedent; if there is a special concurrence without a statement of agreement with all that is said in the opinion or a concurrence in the judgment only, the opinion is a physical precedent only. If the appeal is decided by a seven or twelve judge Court, a full concurrence by a majority of judges is a binding precedent, but if the judgment is made only by special concurrences without a statement of agreement with all that is said in the opinion or by concurrence in the judgment only, there being general concurrence by less than a majority of the Judges, it is a physical precedent only.

(b) Unreported Opinion.

An unreported opinion is neither a physical nor binding precedent but establishes the law of the case as provided by O.C.G.A. § 9–11–60 (h).

Adopted effective January 6, 2005.

Rule 34. Reporting of Opinions.

Opinions are reported except as otherwise designated by the Court.

The official reports shall list the cases in which opinions were written but not officially reported and shall indicate the authors and participants in the opinions.

Adopted effective January 6, 2005.

Rule 35. Copies of Opinions.

As soon as practicable after judgment, the Clerk shall furnish, without charge, a copy of the opinion to counsel for each party and to the trial judge. Additional copies cost $1.00 per page, with a minimum cost of $5.00 per opinion.

Adopted effective January 6, 2005.

Rule 36. Affirmance Without Opinion, When Rendered.

Cases in which:

(1) The evidence supports the judgment;

(2) No reversible error of law appears and an opinion would have no precedential value;

(3) The judgment of the court below adequately explains the decision;

and/or

(4) The issues are controlled adversely to the appellant for the reasons and authority given in the appellee's brief

may be affirmed without opinion. Rule 36 cases have no precedential value.

Adopted effective January 6, 2005.

XIII. RECONSIDERATION

Rule 37. Motions for Reconsideration.

(a) Physical Preparation.

Motions for reconsideration shall be prepared in accordance with Rule 24.

(b) Time of Filing.

Motions for reconsideration must be filed within 10 days from the rendition of the judgment or dismissal. Motions for reconsideration must be physically received in the Court for filing within 10 days of the order or judgment for which reconsideration is sought. The certified mail and commercial overnight delivery rules do not apply to motions for reconsideration. See Rule 4. No extension of time shall be granted except for providential cause on written application made before the expiration of 10 days. No response to a motion for reconsideration is required, but any party wishing to respond must do so expeditiously.

(c) Time May be Limited.

The Court may by special order in any case direct that the remittitur be transmitted to the clerk of the trial court immediately after the rendition of the decision and judgment, or at any other time, without awaiting the expiration of 10 days, and may by special order limit the time within which a motion for reconsideration may be filed to any period less than 10 days.

(d) Second Motion.

No party shall file a second motion for reconsideration unless permitted by order of the Court. The filing of a motion for permission to file a second motion for reconsideration does not toll the 10 days for filing a notice of intent to apply for certiorari with the Supreme Court of Georgia.

(e) Basis for Granting.

A reconsideration will be granted on motion of the requesting party, only when it appears that the Court overlooked a material fact in the record, a statute or a decision which is controlling as authority and which would require a different judgment from that rendered, or has erroneously construed or misapplied a provision of law or a controlling authority.

(f) Opinion May be Revised Without Grant of Motion.

If, upon the consideration of a motion for reconsideration, the Court decides its judgment as rendered is correct but that some revision of the opinion is appropriate, it may revise the opinion accordingly, without granting reconsideration.

(g) Voting on Motions, Effect.

A motion for reconsideration shall be voted on by the judges who voted on the original opinion. If there is a dissent on the motion for reconsideration on a three judge case, the motion shall be voted on by seven judges, or should the Court deem it appropriate, 12 judges.

Adopted effective January 6, 2005.

XIV. CERTIORARI

Rule 38. [To the Supreme Court of Georgia or To the Supreme Court of the United States.]

(a) Supreme Court of Georgia.

(1) Notice of intention to petition for certiorari shall be filed with the Clerk of this Court within 10 days after the judgment or, if motion for reconsideration is filed, within 10 days after the order ruling on reconsideration. Filing a motion for reconsideration is not a prerequisite for petition for certiorari.

(2) Petition for writ of certiorari to the Supreme Court of Georgia is governed by the rules of that Court. Notice of filing a petition for certiorari shall be filed in this Court simultaneously with the filing of the petition in the Supreme Court.

(b) Supreme Court of the United States.

(1) Notice of intention to petition for certiorari shall be filed with the Clerk of this Court within 20 days after denial of a writ of certiorari by the Supreme Court of Georgia.

(2) Notice of filing a petition shall be filed in this Court simultaneously with the filing of a petition in the Supreme Court of the United States.

Adopted effective January 6, 2005.

XV. REMITTITUR

Rule 39. Transmittal.

(a) Remittiturs shall be transmitted to the clerk of the trial court as soon as practicable after the expiration of 10 days from the date of the judgment unless otherwise ordered or unless a motion for reconsideration or notice of intention to apply to the Supreme Court of Georgia for writ of certiorari has been filed.

(b) Notice of intention to apply to the Supreme Court of the United States for writ of certiorari generally will not stay the remittitur.

Adopted effective January 6, 2005.

XVI. SUPERSEDEAS

Rule 40. Supersedeas.

(a) Civil Cases.

The notice of appeal filed as provided in O.C.G.A. §§ 5–6–37 and 5–6–38 shall serve as supersedeas upon payment of all costs in the trial court by the appellant. See O.C.G.A. § 5–6–46. Upon motion by the appellee, made in the trial court before or after the appeal is docketed in the appellate court, the trial court may require supersedeas bond to be given with such surety and in such amount as the trial court may require. The filing of an application for discretionary appeal shall act as a supersedeas to the extent that a notice of appeal acts as a supersedeas. See O.C.G.A. § 5–6–35 (h).

(b) Emergencies.

In the exercise of its inherent power this Court may issue such orders or give such direction to the trial court as may be necessary to preserve jurisdiction of an appeal or to prevent the contested issue from becoming moot. This power will be exercised sparingly. Generally, no order will be made or direction given in an appeal until it has been docketed in this Court.

A Rule 40 (b) motion must:

(i) Contain an explanation why an order of this Court is necessary and why the action requested is time sensitive;

(ii) Contain a stamped "filed" copy of the order being appealed;

(iii) Contain a copy of the notice of appeal, if such has been filed in the trial court;

(iv) Show that service has been perfected upon the opposing party before filing the motion with the Court;

(v) Be accompanied by an $80.00 filing fee or a sufficient pauper's affidavit, unless the motion is filed in a pending case already docketed with the Court.

Adopted effective January 6, 2005.

XVII. MOTIONS

Rule 41. Preparation and Filing.

(a) Filing in Triplicate.

Motions shall be filed as an original and two copies as set out in Rule 6. Motions, not letters, should be filed whenever counsel wish the Court to take any action.

(b) Form and Physical Preparation.

All motions shall be filed as separate documents, and shall not be filed as compound motions or alternative motions. No motions shall be filed in the body of briefs, applications or responses. Motions shall be prepared in accordance with Rule 24. Failure to comply with this rule may result in non–consideration of such motions.

(c) Motions to Dismiss.

Notice of a motion to dismiss and of the grounds thereof shall be given in writing to counsel for the appellant by service made and shown as required in Rule 1 (a). If such notice cannot be given, the motion will be entertained and the Court in its discretion will give such direction as may seem proper. Whenever it appears the Court has no jurisdiction of a pending appeal, it will be dismissed or transferred to the Supreme Court, as the facts and/or law require.

(d) Response Time to Motions.

Responses to motions should be made as soon as possible since the Court generally acts on motions quickly. There is no 10 day rule for time to respond to motions.

(e) Reconsideration.

See Rule 37.

(f) Motion to Withdraw Appeal.

(1) Whenever appellant decides not to pursue an appeal, such party shall promptly file a motion for permission to withdraw the appeal.

(2) In a criminal case, unless the state is the appellant, the motion shall include an affidavit from defendant agreeing to the withdrawal of the appeal. Should the defendant refuse to provide such affidavit, that fact shall be made known to the Court and the grounds for the withdrawal of the appeal shall be stated in the motion.

Adopted effective January 6, 2005.

XVIII. OFFICE PAPERS

Rule 42. Access and Retention of Office Papers.

(a) Papers shall not be taken from the Clerk's office without leave of the Court. When leave is granted, the party receiving the paper shall receipt the Clerk therefor. The Clerk may deliver records to the Clerk of the Supreme Court.

(b) One year after the remittitur has gone out, the party paying for the record and transcript may claim them. Otherwise all records and transcripts will be recycled, unless the parties notify the Clerk, in writing, that the record should be maintained, and the reason therefor.

(c) If the parties anticipate that the case will return to the Court or be appealed to the United States Supreme Court, the parties must notify the Clerk, in writing, to hold the record.

Adopted effective January 6, 2005.

XIX. PARTIES

Rule 43. Parties, How Made.

(a) Suggestion of Death of Party.

The death of a party in a pending appeal may be suggested by counsel for either side at any time.

(b) Legal Representative May Volunteer.

The legal representative of the deceased party may voluntarily become a party to the appeal at any time.

(c) Temporary Administrator.

A temporary administrator is regarded as a competent party.

(d) Substituted Party.

Whenever a party is substituted, counsel for the substituting party shall notify the Clerk and opposing counsel of such substitution.

Adopted effective January 6, 2005.

XX. DISQUALIFICATIONS

Rule 44. Disqualifications and Recusals.

(a) Any motion to recuse or disqualify a judge in a particular case shall be filed in writing, and shall contain such evidence and affidavits which shall fully assert the facts upon which the motion is founded. Such motion shall be filed within 20 days of the date of docketing, unless good cause is shown for failure to meet such time requirements.

(b) The affidavit shall clearly state the facts and reasons for the belief that bias or prejudice exists, being definite and specific as to time, place, persons and circumstances which demonstrate either bias in favor of any adverse party or prejudice against the moving party or systematic pattern of prejudicial conduct. Allegations consisting of conclusions and opinions are not legally sufficient to support the motion or warrant further proceedings.

(c) The determination of the recusal motion shall be made upon the written record and no hearing or oral argument shall be permitted.

Adopted effective January 6, 2005.

XXI. EXPEDITED APPEALS UNDER THE PARENTAL NOTIFICATION ACT

Rule 45. [Expedited Appeals Under the Parental Notification Act.]

(a) This rule is adopted under the authority of the Georgia Constitution, Article 6, § 1, ¶ 4 (1983); O.C.G.A. §§ 15–1–5 and 15–11–114 (e) to provide for the expedited consideration of appeals under the "Parental Notification Act." (O.C.G.A. § 15–11–110 et seq.)

(b) Any minor to whom a juvenile court has denied a waiver of notice under O.C.G.A. § 15–11–114 (d) may obtain an expedited appeal to this Court. For the purpose of this rule, in computing time, Saturdays, Sundays and holidays shall be included. Rule 3 shall govern in the event an expiration date falls on such a date.

(c) A minor seeking an expedited appeal shall file a notice of appeal and a certified copy of the order denying waiver of notice with the Clerk of this Court. A copy of the notice of appeal must also be filed with the juvenile court. The name, address and telephone number of the Guardian Ad Litem and any Counsel of Record must be included with the notice of appeal. Upon receipt of the notice of appeal, this Court will issue an order to the juvenile court directing that the record and transcript of the hearing be transmitted to and received by this Court within 5 days from the date of filing of the notice of appeal with this Court. An enumeration of errors shall be filed within the time period for the filing of the record. If a brief is desired, it shall also be filed within the time period for the filing of the record. No filing fee is required.

(d) The record of the juvenile court shall be certified by the clerk of the juvenile court and transmitted to this Court under seal.

(e) The Clerk shall assign the appeal to a panel of this Court, who shall take the matter under consideration and shall issue its decision within 5 days of receipt of the record.

(f) In order to expedite further appellate review, a motion for reconsideration shall not be required. However, if the decision of this Court affirms the judgment of the juvenile court, the minor may file a motion for reconsideration and the same will be governed by Rule 37, except that such a motion shall be filed within 5 days from the date of the decision of this Court and may be filed out of term. Any motion for reconsideration will be decided by the Court within 5 days of filing thereof.

(g) If the decision of this Court reverses the judgment of the juvenile court, the remittitur will be forwarded to the clerk of the juvenile court immediately after the rendition of the decision. If the decision of this Court affirms the judgment of the juvenile court, the remittitur shall be transmitted to the clerk of the juvenile court as soon as practicable after the expiration of 5 days from the date of the judgment unless otherwise ordered or unless a motion for reconsideration or notice of intention to apply to the Supreme Court for writ of certiorari has been filed.

(h) Upon good cause shown, the Court will enter such orders as will further expedite the processing of these cases.

(i) In order to invoke the foregoing special procedures, the notice of appeal must be filed within 5 days of receipt by the minor of the juvenile court's order.

(j) All pleadings, briefs, orders, transcripts, exhibits and any other written or recorded material that are part of the record shall be considered and treated by the Court as confidential. Upon conclusion of the appellate proceedings, the record will be sealed, and the contents of the record shall not be disclosed, except upon order of this Court or the Supreme Court of Georgia.

Adopted effective January 6, 2005.

*

INDEX TO RULES OF THE COURT OF APPEALS OF GEORGIA

*

UNIFIED APPEAL

Effective January 27, 2000

Including Amendments Received Through November 1, 2006

Research Note

Use WESTLAW *to find cases citing a rule. In addition, use* WESTLAW *to search for specific terms or to update a rule; see the GA–RULES and GA–ORDERS Scope screens for further information.*

Amendments to these rules are published, as received, in the South Eastern Reporter 2d *and* Georgia Cases *Advance Sheets.*

Table of Rules

OUTLINE OF PROCEEDINGS

INTRODUCTION

The revised Unified Appeal [effective January 27, 2000] should be followed in all cases for which the notice that the state intends to seek the death penalty is given after the effective date.

The proceedings outlined here shall be applicable only in cases in which the death penalty is sought.

NOTE

All proceedings in the Superior Court shall be recorded and transcribed. The defendant shall be present during all proceedings in the Superior Court.

RULE I. STATEMENT OF PURPOSES

A. Purposes of the Outline of Proceedings. The Outline of Proceedings is a procedure to be followed before, during and after trial, having as its purposes:

1. Insuring that all legal issues which ought to be raised on behalf of the defendant have been considered by the defendant and defense counsel and asserted in a timely and correct manner.

2. Minimizing the occurrence of error and correcting as promptly as possible any error that nonetheless may occur.

3. Making certain that the record and transcripts of the proceedings are complete for unified review by the sentencing court and by the Supreme Court.

B. Purposes of the Checklist.

1. Appended to the Outline of Proceedings is a *Checklist* of legal issues which may arise in a death-penalty case. Its purpose is to remind the court, defense counsel and the prosecuting attorney of these issues and to provide a quick reference to case authority on them. The parties may raise any issue, whether or not it is listed on the checklist. The checklist shall be revised and updated periodically.

2. Proper use of the *Checklist* as a means of avoiding or promptly correcting error will require the court to schedule conferences (see Sections II and III) during which defense counsel and the prosecuting attorney will be given an opportunity to present, or to schedule for presentation, issues which would be waived if not asserted in the proper and timely fashion. These conferences shall be transcribed by the official court reporter.

Adopted effective September 1, 1989; amended effective January 27, 2000.

RULE II. PRE–TRIAL PROCEEDINGS

A. Qualifications of Appointed Counsel. In order to insure that persons are adequately represented in death penalty cases, any attorney appointed to serve as either lead or co-counsel is required to meet the following minimum qualifications:

1. *Trial.* Two attorneys shall be appointed to handle matters in death penalty cases:

a. Lead Counsel.

(1) must be a member in good standing of the State Bar or admitted to practice pro hac vice, and must have at least five years criminal litigation experience as a defense attorney or a prosecuting attorney; and

(2) must have been lead counsel on at least one death-penalty murder trial to verdict or three capital (non-death penalty) trials to verdict, one of which must have been a murder case, or been co-counsel on two death penalty cases; and

(3) must be familiar with the unified appeal procedures; and

(4) must be familiar with and experienced in the utilization of expert witnesses and evidence, including, but not limited to, psychiatric and forensic evidence; and

(5) must have attended within twelve months previous to appointment at least ten hours of specialized training or educational programs in death-penalty defense or, upon appointment agree to take ten hours of such training or educational programs and maintain annually during the pendency of the case ten hours of such training or educational programs. This requirement may be met by viewing video-tape instruction and written materials and certifying to the trial court that the materials have been reviewed; and

(6) must have demonstrated the necessary proficiency and commitment which exemplify the quality of representation appropriate to capital cases.

b. Co-counsel.

(1) must be a member in good standing of the State Bar with combined three years criminal trial experience either as a criminal defense attorney or prosecuting attorney; and

(2) must have been lead or co-counsel in at least one (non-death penalty) murder trial to verdict, or in at least two felony jury trials; and

(3) must have attended within twelve months previous to appointment at least ten hours of specialized training or educational programs in death-penalty defense or, upon appointment, agree to take ten hours of such training or educational programs and maintain annually during the pendency of the case 10 hours of such training or educational programs. This requirement may be met by viewing video-tape instruction and written materials and certifying to the trial court that the materials have been reviewed.

2. *Direct Appeal.* It is recommended that two attorneys be appointed to handle matters on a direct appeal, unless the appointing authority decides for good cause that it is not necessary to have co-counsel.

a. Lead Counsel.

(1) must be a member in good standing of the State Bar or admitted to practice pro hac vice and must have at least five years criminal litigation experience as a defense attorney or a prosecuting attorney; and

(2) must have been co-counsel, or have actively assisted in the direct appeal of at least one death penalty case and have been counsel of record in at least three felony appeals; and

(3) must have attended within twelve months previous to appointment at least ten hours of specialized training or educational programs relating to post-conviction appeals and appellate procedures relating to post-conviction appeals, or upon appointment agree to take ten hours of such training or educational programs and maintain annually during the pendency of the case ten hours of such training or educational programs. This requirement may be met by viewing video-tape instruction and written materials and certifying to the trial court that the materials have been reviewed.

b. Co-counsel.

(1) must be a member in good standing of the State Bar with combined three years criminal trial experience either as a criminal defense attorney or prosecuting attorney; and

(2) must have experience as counsel of record in three felony appeals either as a defense attorney or prosecuting attorney; and

(3) must have attended within twelve months previous to appointment at least ten hours of specialized training or educational programs relating to post-conviction appeals and appellate procedures relating to post-conviction appeals, or upon appointment agree to take ten hours of such

training or educational programs and maintain annually during the pendency of the case ten hours of such training or educational programs. This requirement may be met by viewing videotape instruction and written materials and certifying to the trial court that the materials have been reviewed.

3. *Exceptions for Good Cause.* The enforcement of these minimum qualifications rests with the trial courts and the Supreme Court. If a trial judge finds that an attorney is otherwise competent but does not meet these standards, the judge shall petition the Supreme Court prior to the First Proceeding (Part II, B) under the Unified Appeal Procedure for authorization to appoint the attorney by specifying the attorney's qualifications and stating the reasons the trial judge has determined that the attorney is competent to serve as either lead or co-counsel.

B. Fees for Appointed Counsel.

1. Attorneys handling appointed cases shall receive reasonable and adequate compensation for their labor, based on hourly rates and time spent as documented in records submitted by the attorneys, and in addition shall be reimbursed for all expenses, reasonable and necessary to the individual case. Local indigent defense committees, or the judge or judges of a multi-judge circuit in those circuits without an indigent defense committee, shall set a standard hourly fee schedule and shall give due weight to the following factors in determining the hourly fee to be paid to attorneys handling appointed cases:

a. Attorneys' hourly overhead. "Overhead" is intended to include those expenses inherent in running the attorney's office on a daily basis, including but not limited to rent, utilities, support staff compensation and benefits, insurance, bar and professional association membership dues, office supplies, amortized capital expenditures and maintenance. Overhead does not include the expense of expert witnesses, investigators, record retrieval, travel, or other expenses incurred only in conjunction with a particular case.

b. Hourly rates in fee-paying cases for attorneys handling similar work and practicing in the general geographic area where the appointment is made.

c. The rate of inflation, as measured by an objective index such as the Consumer Price Index or other generally accepted measure of inflation.

2. In no case shall the hourly rates set pursuant to this rule be less than the minimum schedule set out in Georgia Indigent Defense Guideline 2.6. In individual cases, the judge or committee may deviate upward from the standard fee schedule set in the circuit, in order to take into account the particular seriousness or complexity of the case, or other factors deemed relevant by the court or the committee. Reasonable and necessary expenses incurred in conjunction with a particular case, including but not limited to fees for expert witnesses, investigators, record retrieval, and travel, shall be calculated and paid separately from the compensation which is paid to the attorney in return for the attorney's labor. Attorneys shall be required to submit itemized statements for payment and reimbursement. In instances where the invoice submitted by an attorney for payment is reduced, the judge, administrator, or committee shall indicate in writing the reason(s) for the reduction.

3. Compensation for a **capital felony case in which the death penalty** is sought shall be set at a higher rate than the rate in non-death penalty cases, in consideration of the seriousness, complexity, and longevity of death penalty cases. Each case shall be examined by the court, and the fee total shall be based on a complete examination of the individual case. Counsel in death penalty cases shall be compensated for attorney fees and, **if necessary,** reimbursed for expenses on no less than a monthly basis throughout the case, and special attention shall be given to continuing counsel obligations in death penalty cases when conviction and imposition of the death penalty occur.

4. In counties that do not have local indigent defense committees, the court may establish a committee composed of a designee of the chief judge, the local county governing authority and the local bar association to perform the functions of establishing fee guidelines and approval of fees.

C. First Proceeding. At the earliest possible opportunity after indictment and before arraignment, the court shall confer with the prosecuting attorney and defense counsel. The defendant shall be present during the conference. The conference shall be recorded and transcribed.

The following matters shall be concluded during the first proceeding:

1. The prosecuting attorney shall state whether he or she intends to seek the death penalty. If the prosecuting attorney intends to seek the death penalty, a written notice of such intentions shall be prepared and filed with the clerk of the superior court. Within ten days of receiving this notice, the clerk of the superior court shall send a copy to the clerk of the Supreme Court. (If the prosecuting attorney does not seek the death penalty, these procedures and the checklist are not applicable. If the prosecuting attorney later abandons seeking the death penalty or the sentencing jury returns a verdict of life imprisonment, these procedures and the checklist are no longer applicable.)

2. Defense counsel shall be identified and it shall be made a matter of record whether they are retained or appointed, and, if appointed, the qualifications required by Section II, part A(1), or that an exception for good cause has been granted under Section II, part A(3) shall be specifically reported.

3. The Unified Appeal Procedure, as amended, shall be published in the Georgia Court and Bar Rules. Copies of this procedure shall be given to the defendant, defense counsel and the prosecuting attorney, all of whom shall be instructed to read and adhere to its provisions. A copy also shall be given to the reporter for inclusion in the record. The reporter shall be reminded that the trial shall be completely transcribed as set forth in Rule IV(A). Counsel for the defense shall be instructed that the outline and checklist are intended to assist them in protecting the defendant's rights, but it remains the responsibility of defense counsel to protect those rights; the outline and checklist do not take the place of diligent counsel actively representing the defendant.

4. Defense counsel shall be reminded of defendant's option to invoke the provisions of Georgia's Criminal Procedure Discovery Act, OCGA § 17–16–1 et seq. If defendant elects to participate in reciprocal discovery, both parties shall be reminded that the information provided shall be accurate and complete.

5. The court shall determine whether the defendant intends to challenge the arrays of the grand or traverse juries. Challenges to the composition of the boxes from which the grand or traverse jury is drawn, and challenges to the manner in which the grand or traverse jury is drawn, shall be presented and heard at the earliest possible time consistent with the court's calendar and with the right of the defendant to seek a continuance. If a challenge is presented, the court shall hear the asserted factual and legal basis of challenge although under law the right to challenge may have been waived.

6. Whether or not a challenge is presented, the court shall nonetheless review the grand and traverse jury lists to determine whether all of the cognizable groups in that county are fairly represented.

a. To establish a "cognizable group" under the sixth amendment, the defendant must show (1) that the group is defined and limited by some factor; (2) that a common thread or basic similarity in attitude, ideas, or experience runs through the group; and (3) that there is a community of interest among members of the group such that the group's interests cannot adequately be represented if the group is excluded from the jury selection process. Whether a "cognizable group" exists is a question of fact, which is dependent upon the time and location of the trial. *Potts v. State*, 259 Ga. 812, 813 (1990), quoting *Willis v. Zant*, 720 F.2d 1212, 1216 (11th Cir. 1983), cert. denied, 467 U.S. 1256 (1984).

b. The court shall compare the percentages of each cognizable group in the county, according to the most recent official decennial census figures, with the percentages represented on the grand and traverse jury lists. Significant under-representation of any such group on either jury list shall be corrected prior to trial. This rule shall not be construed to deprive the defendant of any rights under the constitutions of the United States and the State of Georgia or OCGA § 15–12–40.

The court's findings shall be included in the trial judge's report in the form specified by Rule II (C).

7. The court shall give the defendant an opportunity to state any objections to defense counsel or to the manner in which defense counsel have conducted or are conducting the defense.

8. The court shall review Section I of the checklist with defense counsel and the prosecuting attorney to determine which pre-trial issues the defendant intends to raise. Hearings shall be scheduled for any issues the defense wishes to present. The defendant shall be reminded that issues not raised may be waived if not timely presented.

9. The court shall instruct defense counsel to locate and interview all persons whose testimony might be helpful in discovering or supporting available theories of (1) defense or in (2) mitigation of punishment.

10. The court shall schedule for an appropriate time an arraignment and plea on the merits of the indictment.

D. Motion Hearing. At an appropriate time consistent with the court's calendar and with the right of the defendant to seek a continuance, the court shall conduct a motion hearing. The defendant shall be present, accompanied by defense counsel. The hearing shall be recorded and transcribed. The hearing shall precede trial of the case.

The following matters shall be concluded during the motion hearing:

1. All motions previously filed shall be heard.

2. The court shall review Section I of the checklist with defense counsel and the prosecuting attorney to determine if there are possible pre-trial issues that have not been raised. The court shall determine during this conference whether defense counsel intend to allow the deadline for raising of any such issue to pass without presenting the issue for decision. If so, the court shall question defense counsel in the presence of the defendant to determine whether defense counsel have explained the defendant's rights regarding that issue and whether defense counsel and the defendant have agreed not to assert the issue.

3. The court shall remind defense counsel to be prepared to present evidence during the sentencing phase as well as the guilt-innocence phase of the trial.

4. The court shall give the defendant an opportunity to state any objections to defense counsel or to the manner in which defense counsel have conducted or are conducting the defense.

5. The court reporter shall be advised that all pretrial proceedings and hearings should be transcribed prior to trial.

E. Forms for Required Jury Certificates. The grand and traverse jury certificates required by Rule II(B)(6) shall comply with the following forms, and shall be included in the trial judge's report specified by OCGA § 17–10–35 (a).

(Note: To convert a decimal number to percentage notation, move the decimal point two places to the right. Example: .055 = 5.5%)

Grand Jury Certificate

This court has reviewed the Grand Jury List for______County from which the grand jury was selected that rendered the indictment in this case. This Grand Jury List was last revised in the year ______.

The following categories are "cognizable groups" in this county within the meaning of the Unified Appeal and current state and federal law:

A. Males B. Females C. African Americans D. Whites

E. ______ F. ______

The total county population according to the most recent decennial census is ______.

The total county population over 18 years old, according to the most recent census is ______.

The total number of persons on the grand jury list is ______.

For each "cognizable group" listed above, calculate the percentage of the over–18 population of the county represented by the cognizable group, as follows:

A. Males

1. The total population over 18 years old in the county is ______.

2. The total population of cognizable group A (males) is ______.

3. Divide answer 2 by answer 1, move the decimal 2 places to the right: ______%

4. The number of people on the grand jury list is ______.

5. The number of males on the grand jury list is ______.

6. Divide answer 5 by answer 4, move the decimal 2 places to the right: ______%

7. Subtract the larger from the smaller; the difference must be less than 5%: ______%

B. Females

1. The total population over 18 years old in the county is ______

2. The total population of cognizable group B (females) is ______

3. Divide answer 2 by answer 1, move the decimal 2 places to the right: ______%

4. The number of people on the grand jury list is ______.

5. The number of females on the grand jury list is ______.

6. Divide answer 5 by answer 4, move the decimal 2 places to the right: ______%

7. Subtract the larger from the smaller; the difference must be less than 5%: ______%

C. African Americans

1. The total population over 18 years old in the county is ______

2. The total population of cognizable group C (African Americans) is ______

3. Divide answer 2 by answer 1, move the decimal 2 places to the right: ______%

4. The number of people on the grand jury list is ______.

5. The number of African Americans on the grand jury list is ______.

6. Divide answer 5 by answer 4, move the decimal 2 places to the right: ______%

7. Subtract the larger from the smaller; the difference must be less than 5%: ______%

D. Whites

1. the total population over 18 years old in the county is ______

2. the total population of cognizable group D (whites) is ______

3. Divide answer 2 by answer 1, move the decimal 2 places to the right: ______%

4. The number of people on the grand jury list is ______.

5. The number of whites on the grand jury list is ______.

6. Divide answer 5 by answer 4, move the decimal 2 places to the right: ______%

7. Subtract the larger from the smaller; the difference must be less than 5%: ______%

E. ____________

1. The total population over 18 years old in the county is ______

2. The total population of cognizable group E is ______

3. Divide answer 2 by answer 1, move the decimal 2 places to the right: ______%

4. The number of people on the grand jury list is ______.

5. The number of cognizable group E on the grand jury list is ______.

6. Divide answer 5 by answer 4, move the decimal 2 places to the right: ______%

7. Subtract the larger from the smaller; the difference must be less than 5%: ______%

F. ______________

1. The total population over 18 years old in the county is ______.

2. The total population of cognizable group F is ______.

3. Divide answer 2 by answer 1, move the decimal 2 places to the right: ______%

4. The number of people on the grand jury list is ______.

5. The number of cognizable group F on the grand jury list is ______.

6. Divide answer 5 by answer 4, move the decimal 2 places to the right: ______%

7. Subtract the larger from the smaller; the difference must be less than 5%: ______%

This court is satisfied that the identified cognizable groups are adequately represented on the grand jury list.

Traverse Jury Certificate

This court has reviewed the Traverse Jury List for ______ County from which the defendant's traverse jury panel will be selected. This Traverse Jury List was last revised in the year ______.

The following categories are "cognizable groups" in this county within the meaning of the Unified Appeal and current state and federal law:

A. Males B. Females C. African Americans D. Whites

E. ______ F. ______

The total county population according to the most recent decennial census is ______.

The total county population over 18 years old, according to the most recent census is ______.

The total number of persons on the traverse jury list is ______.

For each "cognizable group" listed above, calculate the percentage of the over–18 population of the county represented by the cognizable group, as follows:

A. Males

1. The total population over 18 years old in the county is ______.

2. The total population of cognizable group A (males) is ______.

3. Divide answer 2 by answer 1, move the decimal 2 places to the right: ______%

4. The number of people on the traverse jury list is ______.

5. The number of males on the traverse jury list is ______.

6. Divide answer 5 by answer 4, move the decimal 2 places to the right: ______%

7. Subtract the larger from the smaller; the difference must be less than 5%: ______%

B. Females

1. The total population over 18 years old in the county is ______

2. The total population of cognizable group B (females) is ______

3. Divide answer 2 by answer 1, move the decimal 2 places to the right: ______%

4. The number of people on the traverse jury list is ______.

5. The number of females on the traverse jury list is ______.

6. Divide answer 5 by answer 4, move the decimal 2 places to the right: ______%

7. Subtract the larger from the smaller; the difference must be less than 5%: ______%

C. African Americans

1. The total population over 18 years old in the county is ______

2. The total population of cognizable group C (African Americans) is ______

3. Divide answer 2 by answer 1, move the decimal 2 places to the right: ______%

4. The number of people on the traverse jury list is ______.

5. The number of African Americans on the traverse jury list is ______.

6. Divide answer 5 by answer 4, move the decimal 2 places to the right: ______%

7. Subtract the larger from the smaller; the difference must be less than 5%: ______%

D. Whites

1. the total population over 18 years old in the county is ______

2. the total population of cognizable group D (whites) is ______

3. Divide answer 2 by answer 1, move the decimal 2 places to the right: ______%

4. The number of people on the traverse jury list is ______.

5. The number of whites on the traverse jury list is ______.

6. Divide answer 5 by answer 4, move the decimal 2 places to the right: ______%

7. Subtract the larger from the smaller; the difference must be less than 5%: ______%

E. ______________

1. The total population over 18 years old in the county is ______.

2. The total population of cognizable group E is ______.

3. Divide answer 2 by answer 1, move the decimal 2 places to the right: ______%

4. The number of people on the traverse jury list is ______.

5. The number of cognizable group E on the traverse jury list is ______.

6. Divide answer 5 by answer 4, move the decimal 2 places to the right: ______%

7. Subtract the larger from the smaller; the difference must be less than 5%: ______%

F. ______________

1. The total population over 18 years old in the county is ______.

2. The total population of cognizable group F is ______.

3. Divide answer 2 by answer 1, move the decimal 2 places to the right: ______%

4. The number of people on the traverse jury list is ______.

5. The number of cognizable group F on the traverse jury list is ______.

6. Divide answer 5 by answer 4, move the decimal 2 places to the right: ______%

7. Subtract the larger from the smaller; the difference must be less than 5%: ______%

This court is satisfied that the identified cognizable groups are adequately represented on the traverse jury list.

F. Pre-trial Review Hearing.

1. After the completion of all pre-trial proceedings, the court shall conduct a hearing to determine if an interim appellate review of pre-trial rulings is appropriate. The court shall hear from the state and the defense as to whether the delay to be caused by interim appellate review outweighs the need for such review. If the court concludes that interim appellate review would not serve the ends of justice in the case, the court shall enter an order so stating and declaring the case stands ready for trial. An order obviating interim appellate review shall not be appealable. See OCGA § 17–10–35.1.

2. If the court concludes that interim appellate review of the pre-trial proceedings is appropriate, the court shall order such review and initiate the procedure by filing in the office of the clerk of superior court and deliver to the parties a report certifying that all pre-trial proceedings in the case have been completed. The report of the trial judge shall state whether there is arguably any reversible error with respect to any of the following matters:

a. Any proceedings with respect to change of venue;

b. Any proceedings with respect to recusal of the trial judge;

c. Any challenge to the jury array;

d. Any motion to suppress evidence;

e. Any motion to exclude statements by the defendant;

f. Any motion for psychiatric or other mental or physical evaluation;

g. Any motion for additional legal, investigative, or expert assistance; and

h. Any other pre-trial matter which may arguably result in reversible error.

i. If the trial judge determines that there is arguably any reversible error with respect to any ex parte proceedings, the report of the trial judge shall so state and shall identify the issue in a manner which does not disclose ex parte communications.

3. Within 10 days after the filing of the report or the filing of the transcripts of the proceedings, whichever is later, the prosecutor and the defendant may each seek review of any areas of the pre-trial proceedings in which reversible error may arguably have occurred by filing with the clerk of the Supreme Court an application to appeal any order, decision, or judgment entered in the case. The application for appeal shall be in the form of a petition and shall set forth the need for such an appeal and the issue or issues to be resolved.

a. The applicant shall identify with specificity those portions of the record which pertain to each of the issues as to which review is sought;

b. The applicant shall file an original and seven copies, which shall also include copies of the order or orders to be reviewed;

c. No certificate of immediate review shall be required for the filing of such application for appeal.

d. Copies of the application shall be served upon the opposing party and the Attorney General in the manner prescribed by OCGA § 5–6–32 except that such service shall be perfected at or before the filing of the application. A copy shall also be filed in the superior court.

4. The opposing party may file with the clerk of the Supreme Court an original response and seven copies within ten days from the date on which the application is filed in the Supreme Court. The re-

sponse shall include specific reference to any additional portions of the record which the respondent deems pertinent to the issues addressed. Service shall be perfected as described above.

5. Any application for appeal which seeks review of any order, decision, or judgment entered ex parte shall so state and shall identify the issue in a manner which does not disclose confidential information. Such application shall be accompanied by a separate ex parte application in the form described above. Copies of the separate ex parte application shall not be served on the opposing party or the Attorney General, but a copy thereof shall be filed under seal in the superior court.

6. Upon the filing of a copy of the application, the clerk of superior court shall immediately transmit to the Supreme Court the report of the trial judge and the portions of the record relevant to the issues to be addressed. A copy of all of the foregoing shall also be delivered by the clerk of superior court to the Attorney General. The clerk of the superior court shall transmit to the Supreme Court under seal any ex parte proceedings in the record without furnishing a copy to the Attorney General.

G. Forms for Pre-trial Reports.

Report of the__________(Judge, District Attorney, or Defense Attorney)

Is there arguably reversible error with respect to any of the following matters? If so, describe the pertinent factual and legal issues:

(1) Any proceedings with respect to change of venue;

(2) Any proceedings with respect to recusal of the trial judge;

(3) Any challenge to the jury array;

(4) Any motion to suppress evidence;

(5) Any motion to exclude statements by the defendant;

(6) Any motion for psychiatric or other mental or physical evaluation;

(7) Any motion for additional legal, investigative, or expert assistance;

(8) Any other pre-trial matter which may arguably result in reversible error.

(9) If the trial judge determines that there is arguably any reversible error with respect to any ex parte proceedings, the report of the trial judge shall so state and shall identify the issue in a manner which does not disclose ex parte communications.

H. Pre-trial Review in the Supreme Court.

1. The Supreme Court shall issue an order granting review of the pre-trial proceedings, or portions thereof, or denying review within 20 days of the date on which the case is docketed. The order of the Supreme Court shall identify the matters which shall be subject to review, and such matters may include, but need not be limited to, any matters called to the court's attention in any of the reports or in any application for appeal. If such review is granted, no notice of appeal need be filed. The order granting review shall specify the period of time within which each party shall file briefs and responsive briefs as to matters identified in the order granting review. Oral argument must be requested and shall be discretionary with the court.

2. If requested by the district attorney, the Attorney General shall assist in the review and appeal.

3. Pre-trial review of any matter as provided for herein, as to any question passed on in such review, shall be res judicata as to such question and shall be deemed to be the law of the case.

4. This pre-trial review procedure shall not apply to any ruling or order made, invoked, or sought subsequent to the filing of the report of the trial judge.

5. The failure of either party to assert their rights under this pre-trial review procedure, or the failure of the Supreme Court to grant review, shall not waive the right to post-trial review of any question which could be raised under this procedure, and shall not constitute an adjudication as to such question.

Adopted effective September 1, 1989; amended effective June 18, 1992; January 27, 2000.

RULE III. TRIAL PROCEEDINGS

A. Guilt–Innocence Phase.

1. *Before Commencement of Trial.* Immediately before trial, the court shall confer with the prosecuting attorney and defense counsel. The defendant shall be present during the conference. The conference shall be recorded and transcribed.

The following matters shall be concluded during the conference:

a. All pending motions shall be heard.

b. The court shall determine whether there are any last-minute motions the defense wishes to present and give the prosecuting attorney and defense counsel an opportunity to present any stipulations to which they have agreed.

c. The court shall ascertain whether counsel for both sides have reviewed Part II (A) through (H) of the checklist and are prepared to raise any possible trial issues in a timely manner.

d. The court shall give the defendant an opportunity to state any objections he or she may have to defense counsel or to the manner in which defense counsel have conducted or are conducting the defense.

2. *After Close of the Evidence.* After close of the evidence, but before closing arguments, the court shall confer with the prosecuting attorney and defense counsel. The defendant shall be present during the conference. The conference shall be recorded and transcribed.

The following matters shall be concluded during the conference after close of the evidence:

a. Written requests to charge shall be presented to the court for rulings.

b. The court shall make a final ruling on any issues as to which a tentative ruling or no ruling was made during presentation of the evidence.

c. The court shall hear any timely and otherwise proper motions or objections the defense wishes to present. Defense counsel shall be given an opportunity to perfect the record by making a tender of proof as to any evidence that was excluded by the court.

d. The court shall ascertain whether the parties have reviewed Part II (I) through (Q) of the checklist and are prepared to raise these issues in a timely manner. Defense counsel shall be advised that objections to the state's closing argument will be waived if not raised as soon as grounds for such objection arise, unless explicit permission is granted to reserve objection until the conclusion of argument.

e. The court shall give the defendant an opportunity to state any objections he or she may have to defense counsel, or to the manner in which defense counsel have conducted or are conducting the defense.

3. *After Charge of the Court.* After charge of the court, the court shall confer with the prosecuting attorney and defense counsel. The defendant shall be present during the conference. The conference shall be recorded and transcribed.

The following matters shall be concluded during the conference after charge of the court:

a. Any issue as to arguments of counsel or as to the charge of the court shall be presented and decided.

b. The court shall hear any timely and otherwise proper motions or objections the defense wishes to present.

c. The court shall give the defendant an opportunity to state any objections he or she may have to defense counsel, or to the manner in which defense counsel have conducted or are conducting the defense.

B. Sentencing Phase.

1. *Before Commencement of Sentencing Phase.* Immediately before the commencement of the sentencing phase of the trial, the court shall confer with the prosecuting attorney and defense counsel. The defendant shall be present during the conference. The conference shall be recorded and transcribed.

The following matters shall be taken up during the conference:

a. All pending motions shall be heard.

b. The court shall review Part III of the checklist with defense counsel and the prosecuting attorney. Defense counsel shall be given the opportunity to raise in limine any objections to the state's anticipated evidence in aggravation. However, failure to object in limine shall not amount to a waiver of otherwise timely objections to the introduction of evidence. The court shall give the prosecuting attorney and defense counsel an opportunity to present any stipulations to which they have agreed.

c. In the event of a retrial as to sentence, the court shall also review Part VI of the checklist with defense counsel and the prosecuting attorney.

2. *After Close of the Evidence.* After the close of the evidence, but before closing arguments, the court shall confer with the prosecuting attorney and defense counsel. The defendant shall be present during the conference. The conference shall be recorded and transcribed.

The following matters shall be concluded during the conference:

a. Written requests to charge shall be presented to the court for rulings.

b. The court shall make a final ruling on any issues raised during the sentencing phase of the trial as to which a tentative ruling or no ruling was made during the presentation of the evidence.

c. The court shall again review Part III of the checklist with defense counsel and the prosecuting attorney and shall hear any timely and otherwise proper motions or objections the defense wishes to present. Defense counsel shall be given an opportunity to perfect the record by making a tender of proof as to any evidence that was excluded by the court. If the court determines that a mistake was made in the exclusion of potentially-mitigating evidence, the court shall reopen the evidence and allow its presentation to the jury.

d. Defense counsel shall be advised that objections to the state's sentencing phase closing argument will be waived if not raised as soon as grounds for such objection arise, unless explicit permission is granted to reserve objection until the conclusion of argument.

e. The court shall give the defendant an opportunity to state any objections he or she may have to defense counsel or to the manner in which defense counsel have conducted or are conducting the defense.

3. *After Charge of the Court.* After charge of the court at the sentencing phase of the trial, the court

shall confer with the prosecuting attorney and defense counsel. The defendant shall be present during the conference. The conference shall be recorded and transcribed.

The following matters shall be concluded during the conference after the charge of the court:

a. The court shall review Part III (C) and (D) with the prosecuting attorney and defense counsel. Any issue as to arguments of counsel or as to the charge of the court shall be presented and decided. Defense counsel shall be advised that any such issue not timely raised shall be waived. Reservations of objections to the sentencing-phase charge will not be permitted.

b. The court shall also review Part III (E) of the checklist with the prosecuting attorney and defense counsel. Defense counsel shall be advised that objections to the form of the verdict must be raised when the verdict is returned. The court shall note that a poll of the jurors is required.

c. The court shall give the defendant an opportunity to state any objections he or she may have to defense counsel or to the manner in which defense counsel have conducted or are conducting the defense.

Adopted effective September 1, 1989; amended effective January 27, 2000.

RULE IV. REVIEW PROCEEDINGS

A. In the Superior Court.

1. Within forty-five (45) days from the jury's verdict in the sentencing phase of the proceedings, the court reporter shall file with the superior court a *complete transcript* of all phases of the case unless the reporter has obtained an extension of time in writing from the judge who imposed the death sentence. No extension of time for filing the transcript shall exceed fifteen (15) days. For purposes of this rule, the term "complete transcript" shall include a complete transcription of: all pre-trial hearings; the selection of the jurors, including challenges for cause; the voir dire examination and the striking; the opening statements and closing arguments of counsel; the examination of the witnesses; all documentary evidence, including photographs; all oral motions (whether pre-trial, during trial or after trial) and all hearings on oral and written motions; all oral objections and all hearings on oral and written objections; all conferences and hearings of every description and for every purpose conducted between court and counsel, including all bench and chamber conferences; all oral stipulations of counsel; the charges of the court to the jury during the guilt-innocence and sentencing phases of the proceedings; the publication of the verdict and the polling of the jury; the pronouncement of sentence; and all oral comments, instructions, directions, admonitions, rulings and orders of the court in the case from the first proceeding through conclusion of the trial.

a. The filing of a motion for new trial is not a procedural prerequisite for review by the superior court and Supreme Court. A defendant may, but is not required to file a motion for new trial. A defendant may elect to proceed either by motion for new trial or direct appeal, or may allow the case to be presented directly to the Supreme Court for review. The case nevertheless shall be considered by the Supreme Court.

b. These rules shall not be construed so as to limit or restrict the grounds of review available through motion for new trial, motion to withdraw a guilty plea, direct appeal, writ of habeas corpus, or any other writ, motion, or proceeding cognizable in the courts of this state. It is, however, the purpose of these rules to insure that as many issues as possible which heretofore could be raised by writ of habeas corpus or other post-trial procedure are timely raised before or during trial.

c. The procedures governing the writ of habeas corpus may be employed by any defendant to assert rights and seek remedies if the procedures established by these rules are inadequate or ineffective in any constitutional sense.

d. It is not the intent of these rules to permit any issues to be raised or presented in the superior court or the Supreme Court that previously have been waived, procedurally defaulted, or abandoned pursuant to the laws of this state or of the United States.

2. *Motion for New Trial.* The sole function of a motion for new trial shall be to bring to the attention of the superior court after imposition of sentence such grounds as defense counsel may wish the trial court to decide.

a. When the court reporter files the complete transcript, as described above, he or she shall notify the trial judge and counsel. The hearing on the motion for new trial shall be taken down and transcribed by the reporter.

b. Additional evidence may be heard under the rules applicable to extraordinary motions for new trial or otherwise as necessary to perfect the record and to rule upon the motion for new trial.

c. The hearing on the motion for new trial shall not be limited to the grounds asserted by the defendant.

d. Every defendant shall have the right to be represented by appointed or retained counsel in all matters and at all times during the pendency of a motion for new trial.

e. Within twenty (20) days of the hearing by the trial court, the court reporter shall file with the trial court a complete transcript of the proceedings on the motion for new trial, unless the reporter has obtained an extension of time in writing from the judge who imposed the death sentence. No extension of time for filing the transcript shall exceed fifteen (15) days.

3. *Transmission to the Supreme Court.*

a. It shall be the duty of the superior court to transmit the entire record, the trial judge's questionnaire required by OCGA § 17–10–35(a) (*attached as appendix B to these rules*) and the complete transcript, as defined in Section IV(A) above, to the Supreme Court for review regardless of whether a notice of appeal has been filed.

(1) If no review proceedings have been commenced in the superior court, the superior court shall transmit the case to the Supreme Court for review within ten (10) days of the filing by the official reporter of the complete transcript of trial.

(2) The superior court shall transmit the case to the Supreme Court for review within thirty (30) days from entry of an order denying a motion for new trial.

b. Except as provided in these rules, the appeal shall be presented, heard and determined in accordance with the rules of the Supreme Court and the Appellate Practice Act.

B. In the Supreme Court. Review proceedings in the Supreme Court shall be conducted in accordance with the following rules:

1. At any time after the case is docketed in the Supreme Court, the superior court may be directed by the Supreme Court to conduct further hearings, to hold additional conferences for specified purposes, or to make additional findings of facts or conclusions of law in respect to issues raised by the parties on appeal or perceived by the Supreme Court although not asserted by the defendant or the state. Any such matter may be referred to the superior court for disposition according to a timetable established by order of the Supreme Court. The Supreme Court shall retain jurisdiction of the entire appeal, unless otherwise specified by order, notwithstanding the referral to the superior court, and may take such actions in respect thereto as are necessary or proper pending a decision by the superior court on the matter or matters referred.

2. In all cases, the Supreme Court shall determine whether the verdicts are supported by the evidence according to law. The Supreme Court shall review each of the assertions of error timely raised by the defendant during the proceedings in the trial court regardless of whether an assertion of error was presented to the trial court by motion for new trial and regardless of whether error is enumerated in the Supreme Court. However, except in cases of plain error, assertions of error not raised on appeal shall be waived. The Supreme Court may direct defense counsel and the state to brief and argue any or all additional grounds.

Adopted effective September 1, 1989; amended effective January 27, 2000.

CHECKLIST

Categories of Some Possible Errors

PART I. PRE–TRIAL

Some possible errors arising or complained of prior to trial:

A. Arrest: OCGA Title 17, Chapter 4.

1. *With Warrant.* OCGA § 17–4–40; Devier v. State, 253 Ga. 604 (5) (323 SE2d 150)(1984)

2. *Without Warrant.* OCGA § 17–4–20; Durden v. State, 250 Ga. 325 (1) (297 SE2d 237)(1982)

a. In public place: United States v. Watson, 423 US 411 (96 SC 820, 46 LE2d 598) (1976); Ellis v. State, 248 Ga. 414 (283 SE2d 870)(1981)

b. In home: Payton v. New York, 445 US 573 (100 SC 1371, 63 LE2d 639)(1980); Carranza v. State, 266 Ga. 263 (467 SE2d 315)(1996)

3. *Investigative Detentions.*

a. Must be supported by reasonable and articulable suspicion: Vansant v. State, 264 Ga. 319 (2) (443 SE2d 474) (1994); Lee v. State, 270 Ga. 798 (7) (514 SE2d 1) (1999)

b. Limited in Scope: Terry v. Ohio, 392 US 1 (88 SC 1868, 20 LE2d 889) (1968); Smith v. State, 216 Ga. App. 453 (2) (454 SE2d 635) (1995)

B. Search and Seizure: OCGA Title 17, Chapter 5.

1. *With warrant.*

a. Sufficiency of description: Anderson v. State, 249 Ga. 132 (5) (287 SE2d 195) (1982)

b. Sufficiency of probable cause: Illinois v. Gates, 462 US 213 (103 SC 2317, 76 LE2d 527) (1983); DeYoung v. State, 268 Ga. 780 (7) (493 SE2d 157) (1997)

c. Scope of permissible search: Landers v. State, 250 Ga. 808 (301 SE2d 633) (1983)

2. *Without Warrant.*

a. Expectation of privacy—standing: Rakas v. Illinois, 439 US 128 (99 SC 421, 58 LE2d 387)

(1978); Barnes v. State, 269 Ga. 345 (4) (496 SE2d 674) (1998); Sears v. State, 268 Ga. 759 (4) (493 SE2d 180) (1997)

b. Search of person

(1) Incident to arrest: United States v. Robertson, 414 US 21 (94 SC 467, 38 LE2d 427) (1973); Chimel v. California, 395 US 752 (89 SC 2034, 23 LE2d 685) (1969); Paxton v. State, 160 Ga. App. 19 (1) (285 SE2d 741) (1981); Banks v. State, 246 Ga. 178 (2) (269 SE2d 450) (1980); Batton v. State, 260 Ga. 127 (3) (391 SE2d 914) (1990)

(2) Inventory search of personal effects prior to incarceration: Illinois v. Lafayette, 462 US 640 (103 SC 2605, 77 LE2d 65) (1983)

(3) Limited search during investigative detention: Florida v. Royer, 460 US 491 (103 SC 1319, 75 LE2d 229) (1983)

(4) Consent search: Schneckloth v. Bustamante, 412 US 218 (93 SC 2041, 36 LE2d 854) (1973)

c. Search of vehicle

(1) Protective search during lawful investigative stop: Michigan v. Long, 463 US 1032 (103 SC 3469, 77 LE2d 1201) (1983)

(2) The "plain view" doctrine: Texas v. Brown, 460 US 730 (103 SC 1535, 75 LE2d 502) (1983); United States v. Ross, 456 US 798 (102 SC 2157, 72 LE2d 572) (1982); State v. David, 269 Ga. 533 (501 SE2d 494) (1998); Pickens v. State, 225 Ga. App. 792 (484 SE2d 731) (1997)

(3) Incident to arrest: New York v. Belton, 453 US 454 (101 SC 2860, 69 LE2d 768) (1981); Banks v. State, 246 Ga. 178 (2) (269 SE2d 450) (1980)

(4) Inventory search of seized automobile: South Dakota v. Opperman, 428 US 364(96 SC 3092, 49 LE2d 1000) (1976); Hansen v. State, 168 Ga. App. 304 (3) (308 SE2d 643) (1983)

d. Search of premises

(1) Incident to arrest: Chimel v. California, 395 US 752 (89 SC 2034, 23 LE2d 685) (1969); Maryland v. Buie, 494 US 325 (110 SC 1093, 108 LE2d 276) (1990)

(2) Probable cause and exigent circumstances: Warden v. Hayden, 387 US 294 (87 SC 1642, 18 LE2d 782) (1967); Cates v. State, 232 Ga. App. 262 (501 SE2d 262) (1998); Clare v. State, 135 Ga. App. 281 (217 SE2d 638) (1975)

(3) Arrest warrant for third party: Steagald v. United States, 451 US 204 (101 SC 1642, 68 LE2d 38) (1981); King v. State, 217 Ga. App. 889 (459 SE2d 605) (1995)

3. *Electronic Surveillance.*

a. Federal Statutes: 18 USCA 2516 et seq.

b. Georgia statutes: OCGA Title 16, Ch. 11, Art. 3, Part 1

(1) By law enforcement: OCGA § 16–11–64; State v. Toomey, 134 Ga. App. 343 (214 SE2d 421) (1975); Dobbins v. State, 262 Ga. 161 (2) (a) (415 SE2d 168) (1992)

(2) By private party: OCGA § 16–11–62; Mitchell v. State, 239 Ga. 3 (235 SE2d 509) (1977)

4. *Motion to suppress: OCGA § 17–5–30.*

a. Scope: State v. Johnston, 249 Ga. 413 (291 SE2d 543) (1982)

b. File before trial if grounds known: Thomas v. State, 118 Ga. App. 359 (163 SE2d 850) (1968)

c. Should be in writing: Hiatt v. State, 132 Ga. App. 289 (208 SE2d 163) (1974)

d. Sufficiency of form of motion: Lavelle v. State, 250 Ga. 224 (3) (297 SE2d 234) (1982)

C. Identification of Defendant.

1. *Reliability/Admissibility.* Manson v. Brathwaite, 432 US 98 (97 SC 2243, 53 LE2d 140) (1977); Neil v. Biggers, 409 US 188 (93 SC 375, 34 LE2d 401) (1972); Thomason v. State, 268 Ga. 298 (3) (486 SE2d 861) (1997)

a. Of defendant's voice: Jefferson v. State, 206 Ga. App. 544 (2) (425 SE2d 915) (1992)

D. Confessions and Admissions.

1. *Applicability Of.* Miranda v. Arizona, 384 US 436 (86 SC 1602, 16 LE2d 694) (1966): Cook v. State, 270 Ga. 820 (2) (514 SE2d 657) (1999); Findley v. State, 251 Ga. 222 (1) (304 SE2d 898) (1983)

2. *Assertion of Right to Counsel.* Davis v. United States, 512 US 450 (114 SC 2350, 129 LE2d 362) (1994); Edwards v. Arizona, 451 US 477 (101 SC 1880, 68 LE2d 378) (1981); Jordan v. State, 267 Ga. 442 (1) (480 SE2d 18) (1997); Allen v. State, 259 Ga. 63 (377 SE2d 150) (1989); Gissendaner v. State, 269 Ga. 495 (500 SE2d 577) (1998)

3. *Invocation of Right to Remain Silent.* Michigan v. Mosley, 423 US 96 (96 SC 321, 46 LE2d 313) (1975); Fields v. State, 266 Ga. 241 (1) (466 SE2d 202) (1996); Hatcher v. State, 259 Ga. 274 (2) (379 SE2d 775) (1989)

4. *Confessions and Admissions of Co-Conspirators.* OCGA § 24–3–52; Bruton v. United States, 391 US 123 (88 SC 1620, 20 LE2d 476) (1968); Hanifa v. State, 269 Ga. 797 (2) (505 SE2d 731) (1998); Gray v. Maryland, 523 US 185 (118 SC 1151, 140 LE2d 294) (1998)

5. *Confessions and Admissions During Psychiatric Examination.* Estelle v. Smith, 451 US 454 (101 SC 1866, 68 LE2d 359) (1981); Hicks v. State, 256 Ga. 715 (14) (352 SE2d 762) (1987); Stephens v. State, 270 Ga. 354 (4) (309 SE2d 605) (1998)

6. *Confessions Obtained After Illegal Arrest.* Dunaway v. New York, 442 US 200 (99 SC 2248, 60 LE2d 824) (1979); Devier v. State, 253 Ga. 604 (7) (323 SE2d 150) (1984)

7. *Voluntariness of Confession.* OCGA § 24–3–50; Lee v. State, 270 Ga. 798 (2) (514 SE2d 1) (1999); State v. Ritter, 268 Ga. 108 (485 SE2d 492) (1997)

E. Bail: OCGA Title 17, Chapter 6.

1. Ayala v. State, 262 Ga. 704 (425 SE2d 282) (1993); Lane v. State, 247 Ga. 387 (276 SE2d 644) (1981)

F. Representation by Counsel.

1. *Right to Counsel.* OCGA Title 17, Chapter 12; Gideon v. Wainwright, 372 US 335 (83 SC 792, 9 LE2d 799) (1963)

2. *Right of Self-Representation.* Faretta v. California, 422 US 806 (95 SC 2525, 45 LE2d 562) (1975); Thaxton v. State, 260 Ga. 141 (2) (390 SE2d 841) (1990); Seagraves v. State, 259 Ga. 36 (376 SE2d 670) (1989)

3. *No Absolute Right of Indigent to Appointment of Attorney of Own Choosing.* Lipham v. State, 257 Ga. 808 (2) (364 SE2d 840) (1988); Kesler v. State, 249 Ga. 462 (12) (291 SE2d 497) (1982)

4. *Appointment of Counsel.* Amadeo v. State, 259 Ga. 469 (384 SE2d 181) (1989); Clarke v. Zant, 247 Ga. 194 (275 SE2d 49) (1981)

5. *Effective Assistance of Counsel.*

a. General standard: Strickland v. Washington, 466 US 668 (104 SC 2052, 80 LE2d 674) (1984); Smith v. Francis, 253 Ga. 782 (1) (325 SE2d 362) (1985)

b. Includes meaningful access to attorney: Wright v. State, 250 Ga. 570 (1) (300 SE2d 147) (1983)

c. Conflicts of interest: Chapel v. State, 264 Ga. 267 (443 SE2d 271) (1994); Sallie v. State, 269 Ga. 446 (499 SE2d 897) (1998)

G. Demurrers, Motions to Quash and Special Pleas: OCGA §§ 17–7–111, 17–7–113, 17–9–63.

1. *Special Versus General Demurrers.* Bramblett v. State, 239 Ga. 336 (1) (236 SE2d 580) (1977)

H. Arraignment: OCGA § 17–7–5.

1. *Notice.* OCGA § 17–7–91; Smith v. State, 235 Ga. 620 (221 SE2d 41) (1975)

2. *Guilty Plea.*

a. Competency: Boykin v. Alabama, 395 US 238 (89 SC 1709, 23 LE2d 274) (1969); Godinez v. Moran, 509 US 389 (113 SC 2680, 125 LE2d 321) (1993); Goodman v. Davis, 249 Ga. 11 (287 SE2d 26) (1982); State v. Germany, 245 Ga. 326 (265 SE2d 13) (1980)

b. Plea to lesser offense: Wharton v. Anderson, 270 Ga. 22 (504 SE2d 670) (1998); Breland v. Smith, 247 Ga. 690 (279 SE2d 204) (1981)

c. Jury trial as to sentence after guilty plea: Browner v. State, 257 Ga. 321 (357 SE2d 559) (1987)

d. Withdrawal of plea: Henry v. State, 269 Ga. 851 (2) (507 SE2d 419) (1998); Browner v. State, 257 Ga. 321 (357 SE2d 559) (1987); Fair v. State, 245 Ga. 868 (8) (268 SE2d 316) (1980)

I. Pleas in Bar.

1. *Double Jeopardy.* 1983 Const., Art 1, Sec. 1, Par. XVII; OCGA § 16–1–8 (c); Blockburger v. United States, 284 US 299 (52 SC 180, 76 LE2d 306) (1932); Torres v. State, 270 Ga. 79 (1) (508 SE2d 171) (1998)

a. Denial of timely-filed plea of double jeopardy appealable prior to trial: Patterson v. State, 248 Ga. 875 (287 SE2d 7) (1982)

b. Aggravating circumstances: OCGA § 17–10–30; Spraggins v. State, 255 Ga. 195 (336 SE2d 227) (1985)

2. *Statute of Limitations.* OCGA § 17–3–1, 2; Hall v. Hopper, 234 Ga. 625 (1) (216 SE2d 839) (1975)

3. *Speedy Trial.*

a. OCGA § 17–7–171

b. US Constitution, Amendments 6 and 14: Barker v. Wingo, 407 US 574 (92 SC 2182, 33 LE2d 101) (1972); Pruitt v. State, 270 Ga. 745 (3) (514 SE2d 639)(1999); Brown v. State, 264 Ga. 803 (2) (450 SE2d 821) (1994)

4. *Prevent Seeking of Death Penalty Due to Alleged Racial or Gender Bias.* Rower v. State, 264 Ga. 323 (1) (443 SE2d 839) (1994); Perkins v. State, 269 Ga. 791 (2) (505 SE2d 16) (1998)

J. Defendant's Mental Condition.

1. *Motion for Independent Mental Examination.* Ake v. Oklahoma, 470 US 68 (105 SC 1087, 84 LE2d 53) (1985); Bright v. State, 265 Ga. 265 (2) (455 SE2d 37) (1995) (to develop mitigation evidence); Holloway v. State, 257 Ga. 620 (361 SE2d 794) (1987); Lindsey v. State, 254 Ga. 444 (330 SE2d 563) (1985)

2. *Defendant's Competence to Stand Trial.* OCGA § 17–7–130; Pate v. Robinson, 383 US 375 (86 SC 836, 15 LE2d 815) (1966); Meders v. State, 260 Ga. 49 (1) (238 SE2d 334) (1990); Holloway v. State, 257 Ga. 620 (361 SE2d 794) (1987)

3. *Defendant's Mental Condition at Time of Offense.*

a. Presumption of sanity: Durham v. State, 239 Ga. 697 (1) (238 SE2d 334) (1977)

b. Insane at time of crime defined: OCGA § 17–7–131 (a) (1); OCGA § 16–3–2 and 3; Clark v. State, 245 Ga. 629 (1) (266 SE2d 466) (1980)

c. "Mentally ill" defined: OCGA § 17–7–131 (a) (2)

d. "Mentally retarded" defined: OCGA § 17–7–131 (a) (3); Fleming v. Zant, 259 Ga. 687 (386 SE2d 339) (1989); Burgess v. State, 264 Ga. 777 (36) (450 SE2d 680) (1994)

e. Charge/form of verdict: OCGA § 17–7–131 (b) and (c); Spraggins v. State, 258 Ga. 32 (364 SE2d 861) (1988)

f. Burden of proof as to sanity: Brown v. State, 250 Ga. 66 (2) (295 SE2d 727) (1982)

g. Burden of proof as to mental retardation: Burgess v. State, 264 Ga. 777 (36) (450 SE2d 680) (1994); Stephens v. State, 270 Ga. 354 (2) (509 SE2d 605) (1998)

K. Discovery.

1. *Generally.* OCGA § 17–16–1 et seq.; State v. Lucious, 271 Ga.361 (518 SE2d 677) (1999)

2. *State's Disclosure of Evidence Favorable to Defendant.* Brady v. Maryland, 373 US 83 (83 SC 1194, 10 LE2d 215) (1963); United States v. Agurs, 427 US 97 (96 SC 2392, 49 LE2d 342) (1976); Williams v. State, 250 Ga. 463 (298 SE2d 492) (1983); Mize v. State, 269 Ga. 646 (2) (501 SE2d 219) (1998); Gulley v. State, 271 Ga. 337 (5) (519 SE2d 655) (1999)

3. *Witness List.* OCGA § 17–16–8

4. *Witness Statements.* OCGA §§ 17–16–4 (a) (1), 17–16–7

a. Plea arrangements with witness: Giglio v. United States, 405 US 150 (92 S. Ct. 763, 31 LE2d 104) (1972); Owen v. State, 265 Ga. 67 (2) (453 SE2d 728) (1995); Patillo v. State, 258 Ga. 255 (4) (368 SE2d 493) (1988)

5. *Failure to Preserve Evidence—Bad Faith.* Arizona v. Youngblood, 488 US 51 (109 SC 333, 102 LE2d 281) (1988)

6. *In-camera Inspection by Trial Court.* Reed v. State, 249 Ga. 52 (3) (287 SE2d 205)(1982); Tribble v. State, 248 Ga. 274 (280 SE2d 352) (1981)

7. *Discovery of the Defendant's Statements.* OCGA §§ 17–16–4 (a) (1), 17–16–7; Walraven v. State, 250 Ga. 401 (2) (297 SE2d 278) (1982)

a. Statements made by co-defendant: OCGA § 17–16–4 (a) (1); OCGA § 17–16–7

8. *Scientific Reports.* OCGA § 17–16–4 (a) (4) and (b) (2); Brady v. State, 233 Ga. App. 287 (2) (503 SE2d 906) (1998)

9. *Notice to Produce.* OCGA §§ 24–10–26, 24–10–29; Wilson v. State, 246 Ga. 62 (1) (268 SE2d 895) (1980)

10. *Independent Examination of Evidence By a Defense Expert.* OCGA § 17–16–4 (a) (3)

L. Motion for Severance.

1. *Severance of Co-Defendant's Case a Matter of Right When Death Penalty Sought.* OCGA § 17–8–4

2. *Severance of Offenses.* OCGA § 16–1–7 (c); Cooper v. State, 253 Ga. 736 (3) (325 SE2d 137) (1985); Jarrell v. State, 234 Ga. 410 (1) (216 SE2d 258) (1975)

M. Other Pre-Trial Motions.

1. *Bruton motion.* Bruton v. United States, 391 US 123 (88 SC 1620, 20 LE2d 476) (1968); Hanifa v. State, 269 Ga. 797 (2) (505 SE2d 731) (1998)

2. *Motion to disclose plea bargain agreements between state and its witnesses.* Giglio v. United States, 405 US 150 (92 SC 763, 31 LE2d 104) (1972); Owens v. State, 251 Ga. 313 (1) (305 SE2d 102) (1983);

3. *Motions in limine—discretion of court to rule on admissibility of evidence prior to trial.* State v. Johnston, 249 Ga. 413 (3) (291 SE2d 543) (1982)

N. Motion to Recuse.

1. *Judge.* Pope v. State, 257 Ga. 32 (354 SE2d 429) (1987); Romine v. State, 251 Ga. 208 (2) (305 SE2d 93) (1983); Smith v. State, 250 Ga. 438 (1) (298 SE2d 492) (1983); Speed v. State, 270 Ga. 688 (55) (512 SE2d 896) (1999)

2. *Prosecutor.* Frazier v. State, 257 Ga. 690 (9) (362 SE2d 357) (1987); Rutledge v. State, 245 Ga. 768 (1) (267 SE2d 199) (1980); Pruitt v. State, 270 Ga. 745 (19)(514 SE2d 639) (1999)

O. Continuances: OCGA § 17–8–2.

1. *Absence of Witness.* OCGA § 17–8–25; Wilson v. State, 250 Ga. 630 (8) (300 SE2d 640) (1983); Romine v. State, 251 Ga. 208 (11) (298 SE2d 492) (1983)

2. *Absence of Attorney.* OCGA § 17–8–24; Putman v. State, 251 Ga. 605 (5) (308 SE2d 145) (1983); Shaw v. State, 251 Ga. 109 (303 SE2d 448) (1983)

3. *Other Reasons.* OCGA § 17–8–22; Johnson v. State, 271 Ga. 375 (8) (519 SE2d 221) (1999)

P. Motions Regarding Publicity.

1. *Change of Venue.* OCGA § 17–7–150; Kesler v. State, 249 Ga. 462 (7) (291 SE2d 497) (1982); Jenkins v. State, 269 Ga. 282 (3) (498 SE2d 502) (1998); Barnes v. State, 269 Ga. 345 (2) (496 SE2d 674) (1998)

2. *"Gag Orders".* Nebraska Press Assn. v. Stuart, 427 US 539 (96 SC 2791, 49 LE2d 683) (1976)

3. *Motion for Closed Hearing.* R. W. Page Corp. v. Lumpkin, 249 Ga. 576 (292 SE2d 815) (1982); Rockdale Citizen Publishing Co. v. State, 266 Ga. 579 (468 SE2d 764) (1996)

Q. Jury Challenges (to the Array.)

1. *Distinguish Challenges to the "Poll".* Jordan v. State, 247 Ga. 328 (6) (276 SE2d 224) (1981)

2. *Statutory Fair Cross-Section Requirement.* OCGA § 15–12–40

a. Applicable to grand and traverse jury pools: Devier v. State, 250 Ga. 652 (300 SE2d 480) (1983)

b. Violation of OCGA § 15–12–40 regarding grand jury pool is not cured by subsequent conviction by properly constituted traverse jury: West v. State, 252 Ga. 156 (1) (313 SE2d 67) (1984)

3. *Sixth Amendment.*

a. Requires that traverse jury array constitute a fair cross-section of the community: Duren v. Missouri, 439 US 357 (99 SC 664, 58 LE2d 579) (1979)

b. Purposeful discrimination irrelevant: Walraven v. State, 250 Ga. 401 (3) (297 SE2d 278) (1982)

4. *Equal Protection Clause of Fourteenth Amendment.*

a. Applicable to grand and traverse jury venires: Castaneda v. Partida; 430 US 482 (97 SC 1272, 51 LE2d 498) (1977)

b. Substantial under representation of race or identifiable group, resulting from purposeful discrimination, is a denial of equal protection: Swain v. Alabama, 380 US 202 (85 SC 824, 13 LE2d 759) (1965)

c. Violation of equal protection regarding the grand jury is not cured by subsequent conviction by properly constituted traverse jury: Vasquez v. Hillery, 474 US 254 (106 SC 617, 88 LE2d 598) (1986)

5. *Measuring Under Representation.* Cook v. State, 255 Ga. 565 (11) (340 SE2d 843) (1986); Mobley v. State, 262 Ga 808 (1) (426 SE2d 150) (1993)

6. *Cognizability of Under Represented Group.* Parks v. State, 254 Ga. 403 (6)(b) (330 SE2d 686) (1985); Bryant v. State, 268 Ga 664 (2) (492 SE2d 868) (1997)

7. *Time for Interposing Challenge.*

a. Announcement of intention to challenge should be made at first hearing: Unified Appeal Procedure, Rule II (B) (5); Walraven v. State, 250 Ga. 401 (1) (297 SE2d 278) (1982)

b. After trial is too late: Young v. State, 232 Ga. 285 (206 SE2d 439) (1974)

8. *Prospective Jurors May be Excused from Jury Duty by Trial Court.* OCGA § 15–12–1 (a)

a. Disregard of this code section may vitiate the array: Joyner v. State, 251 Ga. 84 (303 SE2d 106) (1983)

Adopted effective September 1, 1990; amended effective January 27, 2000.

PART II. TRIAL PROCEEDINGS: GUILT–INNOCENCE PHASE

A. Voir Dire.

1. *Individual Voir Dire.* OCGA § 15–12–133; State v. Hutter, 251 Ga. 615 (307 SE2d 910) (1983)

2. *Sequestered Voir Dire Discretionary.* Sanborn v. State, 251 Ga. 169(3) (304 SE2d 377) (1983)

3. *Scope of Examination.* Curry v. State, 255 Ga. 215(2)(b) (336 SE2d 762) (1985): Henderson v. State, 251 Ga. 398 (306 SE2d 645) (1983)

4. *Challenges for Cause.*

a. Generally: Jordan v. State, 247 Ga. 328(6) (276 SE2d 224) (1981); OCGA § 15–12–163

b. Death penalty bias—for or against: Greene v. State, 268 Ga. 47 (485 SE2d 741) (1997); Wainwright v. Witt, 469 US 412 (105 SC 844, 83 LE2d 841) (1985); Alderman v. State, 254 Ga. 206(4) (327 SE2d 168) (1985)

c. Required disqualification of police officers upon defense motion: Hutcheson v. State, 246 Ga. 13 (268 SE2d 643) (1980); Mosher v. State, 268 Ga. 555(2) (491 SE2d 348) (1997)

d. Pretrial publicity: Speed v. State, 270 Ga. 688(4) (512 SE2d 896) (1999); Norton v. State, 263 Ga. 448(2) (435 SE2d 30) (1993)

5. *Peremptory Challenges.*

a. Parties entitled to panel of 42 qualified jurors: Harris v. State, 255 Ga. 464 (339 SE2d 712) (1986)

b. Racial discrimination: Georgia v. McCollum, 505 US 42 (112 SC 2348, 120 LE2d 33) (1992); Powers v. Ohio, 499 US 400 (111 SC 1364, 113 LE2d 411) (1991); Barnes v. State, 269 Ga. 345(6) (496 SE2d 674) (1998); Batson v. Kentucky, 476 US 79 (106 SC 1712, 90 LE2d 69) (1986); Gamble v. State, 257 Ga. 325(2) (357 SE2d 792) (1987)

c. Gender discrimination: JEB v. Alabama, 511 US 127 (114 SC 1419, 128 LE2d 89) (1994); Tedder v. State, 265 Ga. 900(2) (463 SE2d 697) (1995)

B. Opening Statements.

1. *Order.* Berryhill v. State, 235 Ga. 549 (221 SE2d 185) (1975)

2. *Comments by State.* Alexander v. State, 270 Ga. 346(2) (509 SE2d 56) (1998)

C. Sequestration of Witnesses: OCGA § 24–9–61.

1. *On Request, Invocation of Rule Mandatory.* Poultryland v. Anderson, 200 Ga. 549(2) (37 SE2d 745) (1956)

a. Rule need not be invoked until presentation of evidence: Putman v. State, 251 Ga. 605(6) (308 SE2d 145) (1983)

b. Court may allow exceptions to the Rule: Hill v. State, 250 Ga. 277(8) (295 SE2d 518) (1982); Barnes v. State, 269 Ga. 345(17) (496 SE2d 674) (1998)

2. *Violation of the Rule by a Witness Does Not Render Witness Incompetent.* Jordan v. State, 247 Ga. 328(10) (276 SE2d 224) (1981)

3. *Violation of the Rule Outside the Courtroom is Relevant to the Credibility of the Violator.* Childress v. State, 266 Ga. 425(2) (467 SE2d 865) (1996)

D. Hearings Outside the Presence of the Jury.

1. *Admissibility of Defendant's Statement.*

a. Upon objection by defendant to admissibility of custodial statement, trial court must conduct hearing outside the presence of the jury: Peinado v. State, 223 Ga. App. 271(1) (477 SE2d 408) (1996); Jackson v. Denno, 378 US 368 (84 SC 1774, 12 LE2d 908) (1964)

(1) Trial court's ruling on voluntariness of statement must be clear: Walraven v. State, 250 Ga. 401(4)(a) (297 SE2d 278) (1982)

2. *Motion to Quash In-Court Identification.* Holcomb v. State, 128 Ga. App. 238 (196 SE2d 330) (1973)

3. *Hearing Outside Presence of Jury Contemplated by Motion in Limine Made Prior to Trial.* State v. Johnson, 249 Ga. 413(3) (291 SE2d 543) (1982)

E. Issues Which May Arise Regarding Admissibility of Evidence.

1. *Relevancy Defined.* Williams v. State, 153 Ga. App. 890(1) (267 SE2d 305) (1980); Smith v. State, 270 Ga. 240(4) (510 SE2d 1) (1998)

2. *Videotapes.*

a. Motion pictures: Beasley v. State, 269 Ga. 620(2) (502 SE2d 235) (1998) (motive, state of mind); Rushin v. State, 269 Ga. 599(2)(502 SE2d 454)(1998) (bent of mind)

b. Reenactment videos: Pickren v. State, 269 Ga. 453 (2) (500 SE2d 566)(1998)

3. *Audiotapes.* Robertson v. State, 268 Ga. 772(3)(493 SE2d 697)(1997) (enhanced copies, use of certified copies, partly inaudible); Washington v. State, 268 Ga. 598(3) (492 SE2d 197)(1997) (certified court reporter did not prepare transcript); Johnson v. State, 271 Ga. 375(4)(519 SE2d 221)(1999) (break in audiotape); Page v. State, 249 Ga. 648(26)(292 SE2d 850)(1982)

4. *Photographs.*

a. Authentication: Bryan v. State, 206 Ga. 73 (2)(55 SE2d 547)(1949)

b. Autopsy photographs: Jenkins v. State, 269 Ga. 282(20)(498 SE2d 502)(1998); Sears v. State, 268 Ga. 759(14)(493 SE2d 180)(1997); Drane v. State, 265 Ga. 255(10)(455 SE2d 27)(1995) (post-incision photographs sometimes admissible); Brown v. State, 250 Ga. 862(5)(302 SE2d 347)(1983)

c. Trial court has discretion to exclude photos with marginal probative value: Hicks v. State, 256 Ga. 715(13)(352 SE2d762)(1987)

5. *Documents.*

a. Public: OCGA Title 24, Chapter 7, Article 2

b. Private: OCGA Title 24, Chapter 7, Article 1

c. Handwriting: OCGA § 24–7–6

6. *Tangible Objects.*

a. Chain of custody: Mize v. State, 269 Ga. 646(5)(501 SE2d 219)(1998); Stephens v. State, 259 Ga. 820(3)(388 SE2d 519)(1990); Harper v. State, 251 Ga. 183(1) (304 SE2d 693)(1983)

7. *Best Evidence Rule.* OCGA § 24–5–1; Howard v. State, 204 Ga. App. 743(1)(420 SE2d 594)(1992) (certified copy of conviction); In the Interest of F.L.P, 184 Ga. App. 164(2)(361 SE2d 43)(1987) (BER does not apply to a tape recorded statement); Merrill Lynch v. Zimmerman, 248 Ga. 580(285 SE2d 181)(1981)

8. *Character Evidence.* OCGA § 24–2–2 (character of parties usually not admissible); Walraven v. State, 250 Ga. 401(4)(b)(297 SE2d 278)(1982)

a. Relevant evidence not inadmissible simply because it reflects defendant's bad character: Mize v. State, 269 Ga. 646(3)(501 SE2d 219)(1998); Earnest v. State, 262 Ga. 494(1)(422 SE2d 188)(1992)

b. Victim's character: Brown v. State, 270 Ga. 601(2)(512 SE2d 260)(1999)(not admissible if not relevant); Owens v. State, 270 Ga. 199(2)(509 SE2d 905)(1999) (admissible if relevant to justification defense)

c. Placing character "in issue": Head v. State, 195 Ga. App. 445(2)(393 SE2d 730) (1990); Jones v. State, 257 Ga. 753 (323 SE2d 529)(1988)

9. *Scientific Evidence.*

a. Admissibility: Carr v. State, 267 Ga. 701(1)(482 SE2d 314)(1997); Caldwell v. State, 260 Ga. 278(393 SE2d 436)(1990)(DNA); Harper v. State, 249 Ga. 519 (1)(292 SE2d 389)(1982)

b. Polygraph evidence: State v. Chambers, 240 Ga. 76(239 SE2d 324)(1977)

10. *Opinion Evidence.*

a. Lay witnesses: OCGA § 24–9–65; Johnson v. Knebel, 267 Ga 853(1)(485 SE2d 451)(1997)

(1) Emotional states: Travelers Ins. Co. v. Sheppard, 85 Ga. 751(8)(12 SE2d 18) (1890)

(2) Lay testimony of defendant's mental condition: Dix v. State, 238 Ga. 209(2) (232 SE2d 47)(1977); Speed v. State, 270 Ga. 688(37)(512 SE2d 896)(1999)

b. Expert witnesses: OCGA 24–9–67; Barlow v. State, 270 Ga. 54(507 SE2d 416) (1998); Smith v. State, 247 Ga. 612 (277 SE2d 678)(1981)

11. *Hearsay.*

a. Definition: OCGA § 24–3–1; Hurston v. State, 194 Ga. App. 226 (390 SE2d 119) (1990); Reed v. State, 249 Ga. 52(4) n.3 (287 SE2d 205)(1982)

b. Explanation of conduct: OCGA § 24–3–2; Mincey v. State, 251 Ga. 255(12)(304 SE2d 882)(1983)

c. Declarations of co-conspirators: OCGA § 24–3–5; Copeland v. State, 266 Ga. 664 (2) (469 SE2d 672) (1996); Castell v. State, 250 Ga. 776 (1) (301 SE2d 234) (1983)

d. Business records: OCGA § 24–3–14

12. *Privileged Communications.* OCGA §§ 24–9–21, 24–9–23, 24–9–24, 43–39–16; Sweat v. State, 226 Ga. App. 88 (2) (485 SE2d 259) (1997) (defendant cannot call witness knowing he will plead 5th); Brown v. State, 199 Ga. App. 188 (1) (404 SE2d 469) (1991) (husband and wife)

F. Examination of Witnesses.

1. *Competency of Witnesses.*

a. Generally: OCGA § 24–9–1

b. Children: OCGA § 24–9–5; Smith v. State, 247 Ga. 511 (277 SE2d 53) (1981); Sizemore v. State, 262 Ga. 214 (416 SE2d 500) (1992); Norton v. State, 263 Ga. 448 (3) (435 SE2d 30) (1993)

c. Interpreters: OCGA § 24–9–4; Reed v. State, 249 Ga. 52 (1) (287 SE2d 205) (1982)

2. *Direct Examination.*

a. Leading questions

(1) Definition: Ealey v. State, 139 Ga. App. 110 (227 SE2d 902) (1976)

(2) Discretion to allow: Hayes v. State, 268 Ga. 809 (6) (493 SE2d 169) (1997); OCGA § 24–9–63; Hamby v. State, 158 Ga. App. 265 (1) (279 SE2d 715) (1981)

3. *Cross Examination.* OCGA § 24–9–64

a. Cross examination of state witnesses regarding pending criminal charges: Byrd v. State, 262 Ga. 426 (2) (420 SE2d 748) (1992); Beam v. State, 265 Ga. 853 (4) (463 SE2d 347) (1995); Davis v. Alaska, 415 US 308 (94 SC 1105, 39 LE2d 347) (1974); Kinsman v. State, 259 Ga. 89 (7)(b) (376 SE2d 845) (1989)

b. Right to thorough and sifting cross examination not an exception to the hearsay rule: Willett v. State, 223 Ga. App. 866 (4) (479 SE2d 132) (1996); Bell v. State, 71 Ga. App. 430 (2) (31 SE2d 109) (1944)

4. *Redirect/Recross Examination.* Mincey v. State, 251 Ga. 255 (15) (304 SE2d 882) (1983)

5. *Impeachment by Prior Inconsistent Statement.*

a. Not hearsay: Gibbons v. State, 248 Ga. 858 (286 SE2d 717) (1982)

b. Showing of surprise unnecessary to impeach own witness: Williams v. State, 251 Ga. 749 (13) (312 SE2d 408) (1983); Ranger v. State, 249 Ga. 315 (2) (290 SE2d 63) (1982); Davis v. State, 249 Ga. 309 (3) (290 SE2d 273) (1982)

c. Impeachment of defendant's testimony with statements taken in violation of Miranda

(1) *Permissible if Statement Voluntary.* Harris v. New York, 401 US 222 (91 SC 643, 28 LE2d 1) (1971); Jones v. State, 265 Ga. 84 (3) (453 SE2d 716) (1995)

(2) *Not Permissible if Statement Involuntary.* Mincey v. Arizona, 437 US 385 (98 SC 2408, 57 LE2d 290) (1978)

G. Motions for Mistrial and for Curative Instructions.

1. *Time for Motion.* Cochran v. State, 213 Ga. 706 (5) (100 SE2d 919) (1957)

2. *Discretion of the Trial Court.* White v. State, 268 Ga. 28, 32 (486 SE2d 338) (1997); Sabel v. State, 250 Ga. 640 (5) (300 SE2d 663) (1983)

H. Motion for Directed Verdict (Sufficiency of the Evidence).

1. OCGA § 17–9–1; Brown v. State, 269 Ga. 67 (1) (495 SE2d 289) (1998); State v. Royal, 247 Ga. 309 (1) (275 SE2d 646) (1981); Graham v. State, 250 Ga. 473 (1) (298 SE2d 499) (1983)

I. Reopening the Evidence.

1. Carruth v. State, 267 Ga. 221 (476 SE2d 739) (1996); Castell v. State, 250 Ga. 776 (9) (301 SE2d 234) (1983); State v. Roberts, 247 Ga. 456 (277 SE2d 644) (1981)

J. Closing Argument. OCGA § 17–8–70 thru 17–8–76.

1. *In General.* Conner v. State, 251 Ga. 113 (6) (303 SE2d 266) (1983)

2. *Injection by State of Matters not in Evidence.* Bell v. State, 263 Ga. 776 (439 SE2d 480) (1994)

3. *Restriction of Argument of Defense Counsel.* Hayes v. State, 268 Ga. 809 (7) (493 SE2d 169) (1997)

4. *Prosecutorial Comment on Pre-Trial Silence of Accused.* Mallory v. State, 261 Ga. 625 (5) (409 SE2d 839) (1991); Barnes v. State, 269 Ga. 345 (12) (496 SE2d 674) (1998)

5. *Prosecutorial Comment on Defendant's Failure to Testify.* Ranger v. State, 249 Ga. 315 (3) (290 SE2d 63) (1982); Shirley v. State, 245 Ga. 616 (1) (266 SE2d 218) (1980)

6. *Prosecutorial Comment on the Failure of the Defendant's Wife to Testify.* OCGA § 24–9–23; Ferry v. State, 161 Ga. App. 795 (1) (287 SE2d 732) (1982)

7. *Expression of Personal Opinion as to Defendant's Guilt.* McClain v. State, 267 Ga. 378 (3) (b) (477 SE2d 814) (1996); Hoerner v. State, 246 Ga. 374 (4) (271 SE2d 458) (1980)

8. *Reference to the Possibility of Parole or Other Clemency.* OCGA § 17–8–76

9. *Reading Law.* Kirkland v. State, 271 Ga. 217 (3) (518 SE2d 687) (1999); Conklin v. State, 254 Ga. 558 (10) (b) (331 SE2d 532) (1985)

10. *Defendant's Failure to Object to Improper Argument by the State in Death Penalty Cases.* Mullins v. State, 270 Ga. 450 (2) (511 SE2d 165) (1999)

11. *Improper to Argue Future Dangerousness.* McClain v. State, 267 Ga. 378 (3) (a) (477 SE2d 814) (1996); Sterling v. State, 267 Ga. 209 (2) (477 SE2d 807) (1996)

12. *Time Allowed.* OCGA § 17–8–73; Hayes v. State, 268 Ga. 809 (7) (493 SE2d 169) (1997)

13. *Order of Argument.* Kennebrew v. State, 267 Ga. 400 (4) (480 SE2d 1) (1996)

14. *"Golden Rule" Violation (Asking Jury to Assume Victim's Position).* Horne v. State, 192 Ga. App. 528 (2) (385 SE2d 704) (1989); McClain v. State, 267 Ga. 378 (3) (477 SE2d 814) (1996)

K. Charge of the Court.

1. *Requests to Charge.*

a. Trial court must inform counsel of its charge before closing argument: OCGA § 5–5–24 (b); Speed v. State, 270 Ga. 688 (42) (512 SE2d 896) (1999)

b. Trial court shall file with clerk all written requests to charge: OCGA § 5–5–24 (b)

2. *Lesser Included Offenses.*

a. Failure to charge not error absent request: State v. Stonaker, 236 Ga. 1 (222 SE2d 354) (1976)

b. Or when evidence fails to warrant such a charge: Hopper v. Evans, 456 US 605 (102 SC 2049, 72 LE2d 367) (1982); Edwards v. State, 264 Ga. 131 (442 SE2d 444) (1994)

c. Defined: State v. Estevez, 232 Ga. 316 (206 SE2d 475) (1974); Haynes v. State, 249 Ga. 119 (288 SE2d 185) (1982); State v. Burgess, 263 Ga. 143 (429 SE2d 252) (1993)

d. Improper sequential charges: Hill v. State, 269 Ga. 23 (3) (499 SE2d 661) (1998); Edge v. State, 261 Ga. 865 (2) (414 SE2d 463) (1992)

3. *Presumptions.*

a. Except for sanity and innocence, charge should not be cast in terms of presumptions: Rose v. State, 249 Ga. 628 (3) (292 SE2d 678) (1982); State v. Moore, 237 Ga. 269 (227 SE2d 241) (1976)

b. Mandatory presumptions: Bridges v. State, 268 Ga. 700 (2) (492 SE2d 877) (1997); Francis v. Franklin, 471 US 307 (105 SC 1965, 85 LE2d 344) (1985); Sandstrom v. Montana, 442 US 510 (99 SC 2450, 61 LE2d 39) (1979); See Doyel, Burden Shifting Criminal Jury Instructions in Georgia, 38 Mercer Law Review 1 (1986).

c. Permissible inferences: Williamson v. State, 248 Ga. 47 (281 SE2d 512) (1981)

d. Sanity presumed, burden to prove contrary on defendant: Brown v. State, 250 Ga. 66 (2) (295 SE2d 727) (1982)

4. *Charges on Confessions and Admissions.*

a. Word "confession" best avoided: Golden v. State, 250 Ga. 428 (4) (297 SE2d 479) (1982)

b. Definitions: Lowe v. State, 267 Ga. 180 (4) (476 SE2d 583) (1996)

5. *Exceptions to Charges.*

a. Generally: Freeman v. State, 269 Ga. 337 (1) (d) (496 SE2d 558) (1998); McCoy v. State, 262 Ga. 699 (2) (425 SE2d 646) (1993)

b. "Substantial error" in charge reviewable, regardless of whether objection entered: OCGA § 5–5–24 (c); Medina v. State, 234 Ga. App. 13 (2) (505 SE2d 558) (1998); Parker v. State, 230 Ga. App. 578 (2) (497 SE2d 62) (1998)

c. General reservation of objections for appeal and/or new trial: McCoy v. State, 262 Ga. 699 (2) (425 SE2d 646) (1993)

L. Conduct of the Judge: See ABA Standards for Criminal Justice—Trial by Jury 5.6.

1. *Expression of Opinion by Trial Court.* OCGA § 17–8–57; Sims v. State, 266 Ga. 417 (2) (467 S.E.2d 574) (1996) (general reservation of right to object to jury charge preserves for review alleged OCGA § 17–8–57 violation which occurs during the charge); Cook v. State, 270 Ga. 820 (6) (514 SE2d 657) (1999); Barnes v. State, 269 Ga. 345 (16) (496 SE2d 674) (1998)

2. *Control of Counsel.*

a. Correction of misstatement of law by defense counsel: Davis v. State, 234 Ga. 730 (2) (218 SE2d 20) (1975)

b. Rebuke of counsel for improper conduct: Defreese v. State, 232 Ga. 739 (14) (208 SE2d 832) (1974)

3. *Physical Control of Defendant.* OCGA § 15–1–3 (1), (4); Young v. State, 269 Ga. 478 (2) (499 SE2d 60) (1998) (shock belt); Pace v. State, 212 Ga. App. 489 (442 SE2d 307) (1994) (shackles); Illinois v. Allen, 397 US 337 (90 SC 1057, 25 LE2d 353) (1970); Potts v. State, 259 Ga. 96 (3) (376 SE2d 881) (1989)

4. *Examination of the Witness by the Trial Court.* Ashley v. State, 263 Ga. 820 (3) (439 SE2d 914) (1994); Thomas v. State, 240 Ga. 393 (3) (242 SE2d 1) (1977)

5. *Coercion of Jury.* Sears v. State, 270 Ga. 834 (1) (514 SE2d 426) (1999); Riggins v. State, 226 Ga. 381 (3) (174 SE2d 908) (1970)

6. *Comments on Post-Trial Remedies.* Hollis v. State, 215 Ga. App. 35 (6) (450 SE2d 247) (1994); Floyd v. State, 135 Ga. App. 217 (2) (217 SE2d 452) (1975)

7. *Judicial Comment on the Defendant's Failure to Testify.* Earnest v. State, 262 Ga. 494 (4) (422 SE2d 188) (1992); OCGA § 24–9–20

8. *Power of the Court.* OCGA § 15–1–3 and 4; In the Matter of Inquiry Concerning a Judge No. 94–70, 265 Ga. 326 (454 SE2d 780) (1995) (judicial discipline)

a. Summary contempt power: Farmer v. Strickland, 652 F2d 427 (5th Cir. 1981); Martin v. Waters, 151 Ga. App. 149 (259 SE2d 153) (1979)

M. Conduct of Counsel.

1. *Duties of Attorneys.* OCGA § 15–19–4

2. *Attorney-Client Privilege.* OCGA § 24–9–21, 24, 25; Williams v. State, 258 Ga. 281 (5) (368 SE2d 742) (1988); Cazanas v. State, 270 Ga. 130 (1) (508 SE2d 412) (1998)

N. Conduct of Jurors.

1. *Jury's Knowledge of Co-Defendant's Guilty Plea.* Hayes v. State, 136 Ga. App. 746(1) (222 SE2d 193) (1975); Hendrix v. State, 202 Ga. App. 54 (4) (413 SE2d 232) (1991)

2. *Communications With Non-Jurors.* Maltbie v. State, 139 Ga. App. 342 (1) (228 SE2d 368) (1976); Wellmaker v. State, 124 Ga. App. 37 (1) (183 SE2d 62) (1971); McIlwain v. State, 264 Ga. 382 (3) (445 SE2d 261) (1994) (with bailiff); Hanifa v. State, 269 Ga. 797 (6) (505 SE2d 731) (1998) (communications with judge outside presence of counsel)

3. *Unauthorized Dispersal of Jurors.* Huey v. State, 263 Ga. 840 (6) (439 SE2d 656) (1994); Legare v. State, 243 Ga. 744 (11) (257 SE2d 247) (1979)

4. *Waiver of Jury Sequestration.* Jones v. State, 243 Ga. 820 (3) (256 SE2d 907) (1979)

5. *Jurors not Permitted to Directly Question Witness.* Matchett v. State, 257 Ga. 785 (2) (364 SE2d 565) (1988); State v. Williamson, 247 Ga. 685 (279 SE2d 203) (1981)

6. *Jury Request to Rehear Evidence.* Johns v. State, 239 Ga. 681 (2) (238 SE2d 372) (1977); Stephens v. State, 261 Ga. 467 (4) (405 SE2d 483) (1991)

7. *Jury Request to be Recharged.* Williams v. State, 263 Ga. 135 (4) (429 SE2d 512) (1993); Williams v. State, 249 Ga. 6 (6) (287 SE2d 31) (1982)

8. *Alternate Jurors not to Deliberate with Jury.* OCGA § 15–12–171, 172; Lonchar v. State, 258 Ga. 447 (5) (369 SE2d 749) (1988); Jarrells v. State, 258 Ga. 833 (6) (375 SE2d 842) (1989)

O. Conduct of Witness.

1. *Violation of the Rule of Sequestration Does Not Render the Witness Incompetent.* OCGA § 24–9–61; Jordan v. State, 247 Ga. 328 (10) (276 SE2d 224) (1981); Johnson v. State, 258 Ga. 856(4) (376 SE2d 356) (1989); Childress v. State, 266 Ga. 425(2) (467 SE2d 865) (1996)

P. Conduct of the Defendant.

1. *Voluntary Absence of the Defendant.* Speed v. State, 270 Ga. 688(2) (512 SE2d 896) (1999); Lonchar v. State, 258 Ga. 447(2) (369 SE2d 749) (1988); State v. Phillips, 247 Ga. 246 (275 SE2d 323) (1981)

2. *Disruptive Defendant.* Illinois v. Allen, 397 US 337 (90 SC 1057, 25 LE2d 353) (1970)

3. *Right to Assist in the Defense.* Cargill v. State, 255 Ga. 616(3) (340 SE2d 891) (1986); Johnson v. State, 266 Ga. 775(9) (470 SE2d 637) (1996); Miller v. State, 219 Ga. App. 213(1) (464 SE2d 621) (1995)

Q. Verdict.

1. *Form.* Rucker v. State, 270 Ga. 431(5) (510 SE2d 816) (1999)

2. *Poll of Jurors.* Maddox v. State, 233 Ga. 874(2) (213 SE2d 654) (1975)

Adopted effective September 1, 1990; amended effective January 27, 2000.

PART III. TRIAL PROCEEDINGS: SENTENCING PHASE

A. Issues Which May Arise Regarding the Admissibility of Evidence.

1. *General Considerations Applicable to Evidence in Mitigation and Aggravation.*

a. Jury may consider all facts and circumstances of the case: Spivey v. State, 241 Ga. 477(2) (246 SE2d 288) (1978); Everheart v. State, 232 Ga. 247, 253–54 (206 SE2d 12) (1974)

b. Evidence may not be excluded because it could have been presented in guilt-innocence phase: Brown v. State, 235 Ga. 644(3) (220 SE2d 922) (1975)

c. Evidence may not be excluded as only relevant to guilt or innocence: Blankenship v. State, 251 Ga. 621 (308 SE2d 369) (1983)

2. *Admissibility of Proffered Mitigation Evidence.*

a. Generally: Barnes v. State, 269 Ga. 345(27) (496 SE2d 674) (1998); Woodson v. North Carolina, 428 US 280 (96 SC 2978, 49 LE2d 944) (1976); Lockett v. Ohio, 438 US 586 (98 SC 2954, 57 LE2d 973) (1978); Eddings v. Oklahoma, 455 US 104 (102 SC 869, 71 LE2d 1) (1982)

b. Testimony of friend or relative asking for mercy: Barnes v. State, 269 Ga. 345 (27) (496 SE2d 674) (1998); Childs v. State, 257 Ga. 243 (19)(b) (357 SE2d 48) (1987); Romine v. State, 251 Ga. 208(11) (305 SE2d 93) (1983)

c. Examples of testimony or other evidence irrelevant at sentencing phase

(1) Death Penalty is Not a Deterrent. Stevens v. State, 247 Ga. 698(24) (278 SE2d 398) (1981);

Fleming v. State, 265 Ga. 541 (458 SE2d 638) (1995)

(2) Religious/Philosophical Approaches to Death Penalty. Franklin v. State, 245 Ga. 141(7) (263 SE2d 666) (1980)

(3) Mechanics of Electrocution. Horton v. State, 249 Ga. 871(5) (295 SE2d 281) (1982)

(4) Penalties Imposed by Juries in Similar Cases. OCGA § 17–10–35(c)(3); Wilson v. State, 250 Ga. 630(12) (300 SE2d 640) (1983); Blake v. State, 239 Ga. 292 (3) (236 SE2d 637) (1977)

3. *Admissibility of Aggravating Evidence.*

a. Notice: OCGA § 17–10–2

b. Non-statutory aggravating circumstances may be shown and considered by the jury: Zant v. Stephens, 250 Ga. 97(2) (297 SE2d 1) (1982)

c. Matters relevant in aggravation: Fair v. State, 245 Ga. 868(4) (268 SE2d 316) (1980); Simpkins v. State, 268 Ga. 219(2) (486 SE2d 833) (1997)

d. Proof of prior crimes: Jefferson v. State, 256 Ga. 821(8) (353 SE2d 468) (1987); Bishop v. State, 268 Ga. 286(16) (486 SE2d 887) (1997); Devier v. State, 253 Ga. 604(9) (323 SE2d 150) (1984)

e. Prior convictions based on guilty pleas: Mize v. State, 269 Ga. 646(15) (501 SE2d 219) (1998); Pope v. State, 256 Ga. 195 (17) (345 SE2d 831) (1986)

f. Victim-impact evidence: OCGA § 17–10–1.2; Turner v. State, 268 Ga. 213 (2) (486 SE2d 839) (1997); Pickren v. State, 269 Ga. 453 (1) (500 SE2d 566) (1998)

B. Issues Concerning Specific Statutory Aggravating Circumstances—OCGA § 17–10–30 (b).

1. *Aggravating Circumstance (b)(1).*

a. Notice of prior convictions: Franklin v. State, 245 Ga. 141 (5) (263 SE2d 666) (1980)

b. Invalid prior convictions: Johnson v. Mississippi, 486 US 578 (108 SC 1981, 100 LE2d 575) (1988)

c. (b)(1) status determined at time of sentencing rather than time of offense: Stephens v. Hopper, 241 Ga. 596 (4) (247 SE2d 92) (1978)

2. *Aggravating Circumstance (b)(2).*

a. Phrase "Capital Felony" in (b)(2) Defined: Waters v. State, 248 Ga. 355 (13) (283 SE2d 238) (1981)

b. Aggravated battery—must be separate from act causing instantaneous death: Davis v. State, 255 Ga. 588 (3)(c) (340 SE2d 862) (1986)

c. A finding of the (b)(2) circumstance does not require separate conviction of the capital felony: Jones v. State, 249 Ga. 605 (6) (293 SE2d 708) (1982); Fair v. State, 245 Ga. 868 (2) (268 SE2d 316) (1980)

d. The supporting felony should be specified: Rivers v. State, 250 Ga. 303 (8) (a) (298 SE2d 1) (1982); Burger v. State, 245 Ga. 458 (4) (265 SE2d 796) (1980)

e. Mutually supporting aggravating circumstances resulting from a double murder renders one aggravating circumstance invalid: Jenkins v. State, 269 Ga. 282 (23) (a) (498 SE2d 502) (1998); Putman v. State, 251 Ga. 605 (12) (308 SE2d 145) (1983)

f. Continuous course of conduct may establish "in commission of" element of (b) (2) aggravating circumstance: Romine v. State, 251 Ga. 208 (8) (305 SE2d 93) (1983)

3. *Aggravating Circumstance (b)(3).*

a. Application: Harrison v. State, 257 Ga. 528 (6) (361 SE2d 149) (1987); Pope v. State, 256 Ga.195 (18) (345 SE2d 831) (1986); Philpot v. State, 268 Ga. 168 (486 SE2d 158) (1997)

b. Jury Instructions: Philpot v. State, 268 Ga. 168 (3) (486 SE2d 158) (1997)

4. *Aggravating Circumstance (b)(4).*

a. Distinction between (b)(4) and (b)(2) aggravating circumstances: Simpkins v. State, 268 Ga. 219 (2) (486 SE2d 833) (1997); Jenkins v. State, 269 Ga. 282 (23) (d) (498 SE2d 502) (1998)

5. *Aggravating circumstance (b)(5).*

6. *Aggravating Circumstance (b)(6).* Mize v. State, 269 Ga. 646 (14) (501 SE2d 219) (1998); Whittington v. State, 252 Ga. 168 (313 SE2d 73) (1984)

7. *Aggravating Circumstance (b)(7).*

a. Scope: McMichen v. State, 265 Ga. 598 (2) (404 SE2d 255) (1995); Hance v. State, 245 Ga. 856 (3) (268 SE2d 339) (1980); Whittington v. State, 252 Ga. 168 (313 SE2d 73) (1984)

b. Suggested Charge on (b)(7): Taylor v. State, 261 Ga. 287 (13) (404 SE2d 255) (1991); West v. State, 252 Ga. 156 (313 SE2d 67) (1984)

8. *Aggravating Circumstance (b)(8).*

9. *Aggravating Circumstance (b)(9).*

a. Evidence to prove lawful custody or confinement: Franklin v. State, 245 Ga. 141 (6) (263 SE2d 666) (1980)

10. *Aggravating Circumstance (b)(10).*

C. Issues Which May Arise in Connection With Closing Argument.

1. *Scope of Closing Argument Generally.* Conner v. State, 251 Ga. 113 (5), (6) (303 SE2d 266) (1983); Brooks v. Kemp, 762 F2d 1383 (11th Cir. 1985)

2. *Prosecutorial Reference to Appellate Review.* Smith v. State, 270 Ga. 240 (11) (510 SE2d 1) (1998); Caldwell v. Mississippi, 472 US 320 (105 SC 2653, 86 LE2d 231) (1985); Prevatte v. State, 233 Ga. 929 (6) (214 SE2d 365) (1975)

3. *Reading Law.* Kirkland v. State, 271 Ga. 217 (3) (518 SE2d 687) (1999); Conklin v. State, 254 Ga. 558 (10) (331 SE2d 532) (1985)

4. *Arguments Regarding Lack of Remorse, Future Dangerousness and Deterrence.* Jenkins v. State, 269 Ga. 282 (27) (c) (498 SE2d 502) (1998); Pye v. State, 269 Ga. 779 (19) (505 SE2d 4) (1998); McClain v. State, 267 Ga. 378 (4) (a) (477 SE2d 814) (1996)

5. *Parole Argument Permissible.* OCGA § 17–10–31.1; Jenkins v. State, 265 Ga. 539 (1) (458 SE2d 477) (1995)

D. Issues Which May Arise in Connection With the Court's Charge.

1. *Charge on Mitigating Circumstances.*

a. Generally: Romine v. State, 251 Ga. 208 (10) (305 SE2d 93) (1983)

b. Jury can consider all the evidence presented in both phases of the trial: Spivey v. State, 241 Ga. 477, 481 (246 SE2d 288) (1978)

c. Jury should be instructed that it is authorized to consider mitigating evidence but the trial court is not required to identify specific mitigating circumstances: Jenkins v. State, 269 Ga. 282 (24), (25) (498 SE2d 502) (1998); Hawes v. State, 240 Ga. 327 (9) (240 SE2d 833) (1977)

d. Jury should be informed that it may recommend a life sentence even if it finds one or more statutory aggravating circumstances: Fleming v. State, 240 Ga. 142 (7) (240 SE2d 37) (1977); Jenkins v. State, 269 Ga. 282 (24) (498 SE2d 502) (1998)

e. Charge that jury should not base its verdict on sympathy disapproved: Legare v. State, 250 Ga. 875 (2) (302 SE2d 351) (1983)

2. *Necessity to Define Legal Words of Art.* Rivers v. State, 250 Ga. 303 (8) (a), (b) (298 SE2d 1) (1982); Gilreath v. State, 247 Ga. 814 (16) (279 SE2d 650) (1981)

3. *"Allen" Charge.* Romine v. State, 256 Ga. 521 (1) (350 SE2d 446) (1986); Sears v. State, 270 Ga. 834 (1) (514 SE2d 426) (1999)

4. *Statutory Instructions to be Provided to Jury in Writing.* OCGA § 17–10–30 (c); Spraggins v. State, 243 Ga. 73 (2) (252 SE2d 620) (1979)

E. Issues Which May Arise in Connection With the Verdict.

1. *Form.* Potts v. State, 259 Ga. 96 (22) (376 SE2d 851) (1989); Romine v. State, 251 Ga. 208 (7) (305 SE2d 93) (1983); Ledford v. State, 264 Ga. 60 (22) (430 SE2d 917) (1994) ((b) (7) aggravating circumstance)

2. *Substance.* Gibson v. State, 236 Ga. 874 (2) (226 SE2d 63) (1976)

3. *Poll of Jurors.*

Adopted effective September 1, 1990; amended effective January 27, 2000.

PART IV. MOTION FOR NEW TRIAL

A. Necessity for Presence of Defendant at Hearing.

1. Brown v. State, 250 Ga. 66 (7) (295 SE2d 727) (1982)

B. Supplementation of the Record.

1. Rule IV(A)(5)(b) of the Unified Appeal Procedure; Romine v. State, 251 Ga. 208 (11) (305 SE2d 93) (1983); Castell v. State, 250 Ga. 776 (11) (301 SE2d 234) (1983); Carr v. State, 267 Ga. 547 (2) (480 SE2d 583) (1997)

C. Newly Discovered Evidence Regarding Sentence.

1. Mincey v. State, 251 Ga. 255 (18) (304 SE2d 882) (1983); Horton v. State, 249 Ga. 871 (9) (295 SE2d 281) (1982)

Adopted effective September 1, 1990; amended effective January 27, 2000.

PART V. REVIEW IN THE SUPREME COURT

A. Superior Court Can Be Directed to Conduct Further Hearings.

1. Hammond v. State, 260 Ga. 591 (10) (398 SE2d 168) (1990)

B. "Plain Error" Review in Death Penalty Cases.

1. Lynd v. State, 262 Ga. 58 (8) (414 SE2d 5) (1992)

C. Mandatory Review of Sentence Whenever Death Penalty Imposed.

1. OCGA § 17–10–35

Adopted effective September 1, 1990; amended effective January 27, 2000.

PART VI. RETRIAL AS TO SENTENCE

A. When Permitted.

1. *Permitted.* Brooks v. State, 259 Ga. 562 (1) (385 SE2d 81) (1989); Griffin v. State, 266 Ga. 115 (3) (464 SE2d 371) (1995)

2. *Not Permitted.* Bullington v. Missouri, 451 US 430 (101 SC 1852, 68 LE2d 270) (1981); Hill v. State, 250 Ga. 821 (301 SE2d 269) (1983)

B. Evidence.

1. *State not Limited to Statutory Aggravating Circumstances Found at First Trial.* Spraggins v.

State, 255 Ga. 195 (336 SE2d 227) (1985); Poland v. Arizona, 476 US 147 (106 SC 1749, 90 LE2d 123)(1986)

2. Defendant May Introduce Exculpatory Evidence Even Though He Stands Convicted. *Blankenship v. State, 251 Ga. 621 (308 SE2d 369) (1983)*

Adopted effective September 1, 1990; amended effective January 27, 2000.

REPORT OF TRIAL JUDGE

REPORT OF THE TRIAL JUDGE
OF THE
SUPERIOR COURT OF _____ COUNTY, GEORGIA

THE STATE v. ____________________
(A case in which the death penalty was imposed)

A. DATA CONCERNING THE DEFENDANT

1. Name ______________________ (Last / First / Middle)
2. Date of Birth __________ (MM/DD/YY)

3. Sex: M [ ] F [ ]
4. Race: African American [ ] White [ ] Other __________

5. Marital Status: Never married [ ] Separated [ ] Spouse deceased [ ] Married [ ] Divorced [ ]

6. Number of children: _____; and ages: ____________________.

7. Father living: Yes [ ] No [ ], died 19_____.
   Mother living: Yes [ ] No [ ], died 19_____.

8. Number of brothers and sisters _______.

9. Education completed: ________________.

10. Intelligence level:

(IQ below 70)	Low	[ ]
(IQ 70 to 100)	Medium	[ ]
(IQ above 100)	High	[ ]

11. Psychiatric evaluation performed? Yes [ ] No [ ]
    If performed is defendant:

	Yes	No
a. Able to distinguish right from wrong?	[ ]	[ ]
b. Able to adhere to the right?	[ ]	[ ]
c. Able to cooperate intelligently in his own defense?	[ ]	[ ]

12. If examined, were character or behavior disorders found?
    Yes [ ] No [ ]

13. What other pertinent psychiatric (and psychological) information was revealed?
    ____
    ____
    ____

14. Prior work record of defendant:

	Type job	Salary	Dates held	Reason for termination
a.				
b.				
c.				
d.				
e.				

B. DATA CONCERNING THE TRIAL

1. How did the defendant plead? ____________________
2. Was the guilt-phase of the case tried before a jury? ____________
3. Was the sentencing phase tried before a jury? ____________

C. OFFENSE RELATED DATA

1. Offense(s) for which the defendant received a death sentence:
   a.____________________ b.____________________
   c.____________________ d.____________________

2. If other offenses were tried in the same trial list those offenses:
   a.____________________ b.____________________
   c.____________________ d.____________________

3. Which of the following statutory aggravating circumstances were instructed and which were found?

	Instructed	Found
a. The offense of murder, rape, armed robbery, or kidnapping was committed by a person with a prior record of conviction for a capital felony.	[ ]	[ ]
b. (1) The offense of murder, rape, armed robbery or kidnapping was committed while the offender was engaged in the commission of another capital felony or aggravated battery or	[ ]	[ ]
(2) The offense of murder was committed while the offender was engaged in the commission of burglary or arson in the first degree.	[ ]	[ ]
c. The offender by his act of murder, armed robbery or kidnapping knowingly created a great risk of death to more than one person in a public place by means of a weapon or device which would normally be hazardous to the lives of more than one person.	[ ]	[ ]
d. The offender committed the offense of murder for himself or another, for the purpose of receiving money or any other thing of monetary value.	[ ]	[ ]
e. The murder of a judicial officer, former judicial officer, district attorney or solicitor-general or former district attorney or solicitor-general during or because of the exercise of his official duty.	[ ]	[ ]
f. The offender caused or directed another to commit murder or committed murder as an agent or employee of another person.	[ ]	[ ]
g. The offense of murder, rape, armed robbery, or kidnapping was outrageously or wantonly vile, horrible or inhuman in that it involved torture, depravity of mind, or an aggravated battery to the victim.	[ ]	[ ]

	Instructed	Found
h. The offense of murder was committed against any peace officer, corrections employee or fireman while engaged in the performance of his official duties.	[ ]	[ ]
i. The offense of murder was committed by a person in, or who has escaped from, the lawful custody of a peace officer or place of lawful confinement.	[ ]	[ ]
j. The murder was committed for the purpose of avoiding, interfering with, or preventing, a lawful arrest or custody in a place of lawful confinement, of himself or another.	[ ]	[ ]

4. List significant nonstatutory aggravating circumstances indicated by the evidence:
   a.______________________________
   b.______________________________
   c.______________________________
   d.______________________________

5. Which, if any, of the following mitigating circumstances was in evidence?

   a. The defendant has no significant history of prior criminal activity. [ ]

   b. The murder was committed while the defendant was under the influence of extreme mental or emotional disturbance. [ ]

   c. The victim was a participant in the defendant's homicidal conduct or consented to the homicidal act. [ ]

   d. The murder was committed under circumstances which the defendant believed to provide a moral justification or extenuation for his conduct. [ ]

   e. The defendant was an accomplice in a murder committed by another person and his participation in the homicidal act was relatively minor. [ ]

   f. The defendant acted under duress or under the domination of another person. [ ]

   g. At the time of the murder, the capacity of the defendant to appreciate the criminality (wrongfulness) of his conduct or to conform his conduct to the requirements of law was impaired as a result of mental disease or defect or intoxication. [ ]

   h. The youth of the defendant at the time of the crime. [ ]

   i. The evidence, although sufficient to sustain the conviction, does not foreclose all doubt respecting the defendant's guilt. [ ]

   j. Other [ ]
   Please explain if (j) is checked:____________________
   ____
   ____

6. If tried with a jury, was the jury instructed to consider mitigating circumstances? Yes [ ] No. [ ]

7. Does the defendant's physical or mental condition call for special consideration? Yes [ ] No. [ ]

8. Was the victim related by blood or marriage to defendant? Yes [ ] No. [ ]
If yes, what relationship?________________

9. Was the victim an employer or employee of defendant? No [ ]
Employer [ ] Employee [ ]

10. Was the victim acquainted with the defendant? No [ ]
Casual acquaintance [ ] Friend [ ]

11. Was the victim a local resident or transient in the community?
Resident [ ] Transient [ ]

12. Was the victim the same race as defendant? Yes [ ] No. [ ]

13. Was the victim the same sex as the defendant? Yes [ ] No. [ ]

14. Was the victim held hostage during the crime? No [ ]
yes = less than an hour [ ] yes = more than an hour [ ]

15. The victim's reputation in the community was:
Good [ ] Bad [ ] Unknown [ ]

16. Was the victim tortured? Yes [ ] No. [ ]
If yes, state extent of torture:________________
____
____

17. What was the age of the victim? ______

18. If a weapon was used in commission of the crime, was it:

No weapon used	[ ]	Blunt instrument	[ ]	Poison	[ ]
Motor vehicle	[ ]	Sharp instrument	[ ]	Firearm	[ ]

19. Does the defendant have a record of prior convictions? Yes [ ] No. [ ]

20. If answer is yes, list the offenses, the dates of the offenses, and the sentences imposed.

	Offense	Date of offense	Sentence imposed
a.			
b.			
c.			
d.			

21. Was there evidence the defendant was under the influence of narcotics or dangerous drugs at the time of the offense? Yes [ ] No [ ]

D. REPRESENTATION OF DEFENDANT
(If more than one counsel served, answer these questions as to each counsel and attach to this report.)

1. Date counsel secured:_____________

2. How was counsel secured: a. retained by defendant [ ]
b. appointed by court [ ]

3. If counsel was appointed by court was it because

a. Defendant was unable to afford counsel? [ ]
b. Defendant refused to secure counsel? [ ]
c. Other (explain)____

4. How many years has counsel practiced law?
a. 0 to 5 [ ] b. 5 to 10 [ ] c. over 10 [ ]

5. What is the nature of counsel's practice?
a. mostly civil [ ] b. general [ ] c. mostly criminal [ ]

6. Did the same counsel serve throughout the trial? Yes [ ] No [ ]

7. If not, explain in detail. ____

E. GENERAL CONSIDERATIONS

1. Did race appear as an issue in the trial? Yes [ ] No [ ]

2. Was there extensive publicity in the community concerning the case?
Yes [ ] No [ ]

3. Was the jury impermissibly influenced by passion, prejudice, or any other arbitrary factor when imposing sentence? Yes [ ] No [ ]

4. In answer is yes, explain:____

5. In your opinion, was the death sentence imposed in this case appropriate?
Yes [ ] No [ ]
General comments concerning your answer:____

F. FORMS FOR REQUIRED JURY CERTIFICATES

These certificates are required by Rule II (A)(6) of the Unified Appeal Procedure.

(NOTE: To convert a decimal number to percentage notation, move the decimal point two places to the right. Example: .055 = 5.5%)

Grand Jury Certificate

This court has reviewed the Grand Jury List for___________County from which the grand jury was selected that rendered the indictment in this case. This Grand Jury List was last revised in the year________.

The following categories are "cognizable groups" in this county within the meaning of the Unified Appeal and current state and federal law:

A. Males B. Females C. African Americans D. Whites
E. _______________ F. _______________

The total county population according to the most recent decennial census is ______.

The total county population over 18 years old, according to the most recent census is ______.

The total number of persons on the grand jury list is ______.

For each "cognizable group" listed above, calculate the percentage of the over–18 population of the county represented by the cognizable group, as follows:

A. Males

1. The total population over 18 years old in the county is ____.
2. The total population of cognizable group A (males) is ____.
3. Divide answer 2 by answer 1, move the decimal 2 places to the right: ____%
4. The number of people on the grand jury list is ____.
5. The number of males on the grand jury list is ____.
6. Divide answer 5 by answer 4, move the decimal 2 places to the right: ____%
7. Subtract the larger from the smaller; the difference must be less than 5%: ____%

B. Females

1. The total population over 18 years old in the county is ____
2. The total population of cognizable group B (females) is ____
3. Divide answer 2 by answer 1, move the decimal 2 places to the right: ____%
4. The number of people on the grand jury list is ____.
5. The number of females on the grand jury list is ____.
6. Divide answer 5 by answer 4, move the decimal 2 places to the right: ____%
7. Subtract the larger from the smaller; the difference must be less than 5%: ____%

C. African Americans

1. The total population over 18 years old in the county is ____
2. The total population of cognizable group C (African Americans) is ____
3. Divide answer 2 by answer 1, move the decimal 2 places to the right: ____%
4. The number of people on the grand jury list is ____.
5. The number of African Americans on the grand jury list is ____.
6. Divide answer 5 by answer 4, move the decimal 2 places to the right: ____%
7. Subtract the larger from the smaller; the difference must be less than 5%: ____%

D. Whites

1. the total population over 18 years old in the county is ____
2. the total population of cognizable group D (whites) is ____
3. Divide answer 2 by answer 1, move the decimal 2 places to the right: ____%

4. The number of people on the grand jury list is _____.
5. The number of whites on the grand jury list is _____.
6. Divide answer 5 by answer 4, move the decimal 2 places to the right: _____%
7. Subtract the larger from the smaller; the difference must be less than 5%: _____%

E. ______________
1. The total population over 18 years old in the county is _____
2. The total population of cognizable group E is _____
3. Divide answer 2 by answer 1, move the decimal 2 places to the right: _____%
4. The number of people on the grand jury list is _____.
5. The number of cognizable group E on the grand jury list is _____.
6. Divide answer 5 by answer 4, move the decimal 2 places to the right: _____%
7. Subtract the larger from the smaller; the difference must be less than 5%: _____%

F. ______________
1. The total population over 18 years old in the county is _____.
2. The total population of cognizable group F is _____.
3. Divide answer 2 by answer 1, move the decimal 2 places to the right: _____%
4. The number of people on the grand jury list is _____.
5. The number of cognizable group F on the grand jury list is _____.
6. Divide answer 5 by answer 4, move the decimal 2 places to the right: _____%
7. Subtract the larger from the smaller; the difference must be less than 5%: _____%

This court is satisfied that the identified cognizable groups are adequately represented on the grand jury list.

Traverse Jury Certificate

This court has reviewed the Traverse Jury List for__________County from which the defendant's traverse jury panel will be selected. This Traverse Jury List was last revised in the year _______.

The following categories are "cognizable groups" in this county within the meaning of the Unified Appeal and current state and federal law:

A. Males B. Females C. African Americans D. Whites
E. ______________ F. ______________

The total county population according to the most recent decennial census is _______.

The total county population over 18 years old, according to the most recent census is _______.

The total number of persons on the traverse jury list is _______.

For each "cognizable group" listed above, calculate the percentage of the over–18 population of the county represented by the cognizable group, as follows:

A. Males

1. The total population over 18 years old in the county is _____.
2. The total population of cognizable group A (males) is _____.
3. Divide answer 2 by answer 1, move the decimal 2 places to the right: _____%
4. The number of people on the traverse jury list is _____.
5. The number of males on the traverse jury list is _____.
6. Divide answer 5 by answer 4, move the decimal 2 places to the right: _____%
7. Subtract the larger from the smaller; the difference must be less than 5%: _____%

B. Females

1. The total population over 18 years old in the county is _____
2. The total population of cognizable group B (females) is _____
3. Divide answer 2 by answer 1, move the decimal 2 places to the right: _____%
4. The number of people on the traverse jury list is _____.
5. The number of females on the traverse jury list is _____.
6. Divide answer 5 by answer 4, move the decimal 2 places to the right: _____%
7. Subtract the larger from the smaller; the difference must be less than 5%: _____%

C. African Americans

1. The total population over 18 years old in the county is _____.
2. The total population of cognizable group C (African Americans) is _____.
3. Divide answer 2 by answer 1, move the decimal 2 places to the right: _____%
4. The number of people on the traverse jury list is _____.
5. The number of African Americans on the traverse jury list is _____.
6. Divide answer 5 by answer 4, move the decimal 2 places to the right: _____%
7. Subtract the larger from the smaller; the difference must be less than 5%: _____%

D. Whites

1. the total population over 18 years old in the county is _____.
2. the total population of cognizable group D (whites) is _____.
3. Divide answer 2 by answer 1, move the decimal 2 places to the right: _____%
4. The number of people on the traverse jury list is _____.
5. The number of whites on the traverse jury list is _____.
6. Divide answer 5 by answer 4, move the decimal 2 places to the right: _____%
7. Subtract the larger from the smaller; the difference must be less than 5%: _____%

E. _______________

1. The total population over 18 years old in the county is _____.
2. The total population of cognizable group E is _____.

3. Divide answer 2 by answer 1, move the decimal 2 places to the right: _____%
4. The number of people on the traverse jury list is _____.
5. The number of cognizable group E. on the traverse jury list is _____.
6. Divide answer 5 by answer 4, move the decimal 2 places to the right: _____%
7. Subtract the larger from the smaller; the difference must be less than 5%: _____%

F. _______________

1. The total population over 18 years old in the county is _____.
2. The total population of cognizable group F is _____.
3. Divide answer 2 by answer 1, move the decimal 2 places to the right: _____%
4. The number of people on the traverse jury list is _____.
5. The number of cognizable group F on the traverse jury list is _____.
6. Divide answer 5 by answer 4, move the decimal 2 places to the right: _____%
7. Subtract the larger from the smaller; the difference must be less than 5%: _____%

This court is satisfied that the identified cognizable groups are adequately represented on the traverse jury list.

G. CHRONOLOGY OF CASE

			Elapsed Days
1.	Date of offense	________	
2.	Date of arrest	________	________
3.	Date trial began	________	________
4.	Date sentence imposed	________	________
5.	Date motion for new trial ruled on	________	________
6.	Date trial judge's report completed	________	________
7.	Date received by Supreme Court [1]	________	________
8.	Date sentence review completed	________	________
9.	Total elapsed days [1]	________	________

([1]To be completed by Supreme Court.)

This report was submitted to the defendant's counsel for such comments as counsel desired to make concerning the factual accuracy of the report, and

1. Defense counsel's comments are attached [ ]
2. Defense counsel offered no comments [ ]
3. Defense counsel has not responded [ ]

________________________ (Date)

________________________ Judge, Superior Court of

________________________ County

Adopted effective January 27, 2000.

RULES FOR THE SUPERIOR COURTS SENTENCE REVIEW PANEL OF GEORGIA

Effective July 1, 1985

Including Amendments Received Through November 1, 2006

Research Note

Use WESTLAW *to find cases citing a rule. In addition, use* WESTLAW *to search for specific terms or to update a rule; see the GA–RULES and GA–ORDERS Scope screens for further information.*

Amendments to these rules are published, as received, in the South Eastern Reporter 2d *and* Georgia Cases *advance sheets.*

Table of Rules

I. GENERAL

RULE 1.

Pursuant to OCGA § 17–10–6, the President of the Council of Superior Court Judges shall appoint one or more panels of three Superior Court Judges to serve as members of the Sentence Review Panel and shall designate the Chairman of each Panel. The President of the Council of Superior Court Judges shall also appoint another Superior Court Judge for a like term to serve as a supernumerary member when one of the regular members is disqualified or unable to serve. No Judge appointed to a Panel shall review a sentence which he has imposed or participate in any such review. The Panel shall serve 3-month terms (January through March; April through June; July through September; October through December).

RULE 2.

The President of the Council of Superior Court Judges shall appoint annually a Committee of three Superior Court Judges to consider and review the operations of the Panel.

Amended effective May 11, 2000.

RULE 3.

The Clerk and support staff shall be employed by the Council of Superior Court Judges.

Amended effective May 11, 2000.

RULE 4.

The Panel shall not review death penalty cases, life sentences for murder or misdemeanors. Cases involving a serious violent felony as defined in subsection (a) of Code Section 17–10–6.1 shall not be eligible for review by the Panel.

Amended effective May 11, 2000.

RULE 5.

Sentences eligible for review are felony sentences of 12 or more years, including probated sentences, split sentences, sentences imposed under the First Offender Act and sentences imposed under the Youthful Offender Act. The Panel is not authorized to review probation revocations except sentences imposed under the First Offender Act. If a First Offender Act sentence is revoked and a sentence of 12 or more years is imposed, that sentence is reviewable even if the original First Offender Act sentence has already been reviewed by the Panel.

RULE 6.

Felony sentences of less than 12 years are eligible for review only when they are to be served consecutively for a total of 12 or more years and were imposed in the same county within the same term of court.

RULE 7.

The Panel shall not have the authority to suspend or reduce fines or to reduce a sentence below the statutory minimum. The Panel shall not have the authority to reduce an entire sentence to probation, suspend a sentence, reverse the conviction or change the charge for which the applicant has been sentenced. In reducing any sentence, the Panel shall not have the authority to impose or increase a fine or to prescribe more onerous conditions of probation than those contained in the original sentence.

Amended effective July 28, 1986.

RULE 8.

Negotiated sentences will be reduced only in extraordinary cases. The sentencing court is required to identify such sentences on the face thereof.

RULE 9. [Reserved]

RULE 10.

Filings and communications relating to cases pending before the Panel shall be directed to the Clerk of the Panel, and not to the Judges directly, and shall show that copies thereof have been served on opposing counsel.

RULE 11.

The Clerk's office shall be open Monday through Friday from 8:30 a.m. to 4:30 p.m. E.S.T./E.D.T. The address is: Clerk, Superior Courts Sentence Review Panel of Georgia, Legislative Office Building, Suite 108, 18 Capitol Square, Atlanta, Georgia 30334. Telephone: (404) 656–5159.

RULE 12.

When an expiration date falls on a Saturday, Sunday or official holiday, the time is extended through the next business day.

RULE 13.

The contents of properly addressed registered or certified mail shall be deemed filed on the official postmark date.

RULE 14.

There are no costs payable to the Clerk of the Panel.

RULE 15.

No paper belonging to the office of the Clerk of the Panel shall be taken therefrom, except that the Clerk of the Panel may release the records to the Judges of the Panel for their respective official uses.

RULE 16.

The Clerk of the Panel shall not provide photocopies of documents, but the Clerk of the Panel is authorized to furnish certified copies of records for use in other pending judicial proceedings.

RULE 17.

Wherever in these rules the word "Clerk" shall appear, the same shall include the lawful deputies of said Clerk.

RULES 18 and 19. [Reserved]

II. FILING THE APPLICATION FOR REVIEW OF SENTENCE

RULE 20.

Applications for Review of Sentence must include applicant's name, county in which sentence was imposed, all indictment numbers of cases to be reviewed and the complete name and mailing address of the filing party, all of which must be typed or printed legibly in ink. If applicant is represented by more than one counsel, said application shall designate the name of the counsel to whom notices shall be sent.

RULE 21.

Application for Review of Sentence forms may be obtained from the Superior Court Clerk or the Clerk of the Panel; however a form is not mandatory. A written request to the Clerk of Superior Court, including the requirements specified in Rule 20, is sufficient.

RULE 22.

All Applications for Review of Sentence must be filed in the office of the Clerk of Superior Court where the sentence was imposed within 30 days of the date of the following, *whichever occurs last*:

(1) the sentencing order is filed in the office of the Clerk of Superior Court; or

(2) disposition of timely-filed motion for new trial *if* no subsequent appeal is made to a Georgia appellate court; or

(3) Georgia Court of Appeals or Supreme Court remittitur affirming the conviction is made the judgment of the sentencing court.

RULE 23.

Post-sentence motions for modification of sentence filed in the sentencing court, habeas corpus actions, and federal appeals do not toll the 30-day filing limit specified in Rule 22.

RULE 24.

Out-of-time Applications for Review of Sentence will be granted only when the Panel is ordered to do so by a court of competent jurisdiction or if the sentencing judge certifies to the Panel that an appropriate and timely explanation of the right of sentence review was not made to the defendant; however the sentencing judge shall have the right to grant a discretionary out-of-time review. In the event the sentencing judge is no longer available, then any other judge of that court shall make said certification.

RULES 25 and 26. [Reserved]

III. RECORDS—TRANSMITTAL BY CLERK OF SUPERIOR COURT

RULE 27.

The Clerk of Superior Court shall certify and transmit to the Clerk of the Panel, within 10 days after filing of the Application for Review of Sentence, one copy of the following:

(1) Application;

(2) Sentence(s);

(3) Indictment(s), plea(s), court/jury verdict(s);

(4) Criminal record, if any, of applicant;

(5) Pre-sentence or post-sentence report, if any;

(6) Eligibility Determination Form if the Application for Review of Sentence is not timely filed;

(7) Clerk's certification.

Amended effective May 11, 2000.

RULE 28.

The Clerk of Superior Court shall not send the transcript of the plea or sentencing phase of the case unless the sentencing court prescribes by order or rule that said transcript shall be forwarded to the Panel.

RULE 29.

Transmittal of records shall be by Clerk or deputy personally or by mail or express, charges prepaid. Transmittal by a party or attorney is prohibited.

RULE 30.

Records shall be written or printed on one side of white paper not less than letter size. Thin paper which shows the following page and indistinct photocopies are unacceptable. Blue backings are prohibited unless the Clerk's certification is preprinted thereon.

RULE 31.

Following transmittal of a case to the Panel, the Clerk of the Superior Court shall forward to the Clerk of the Panel copies of subsequent filings of any amendment to the sentence.

Amended effective May 11, 2000.

RULES 32 and 33. [Reserved]

IV. DOCKETING

RULE 34.

All applications shall be consecutively numbered and entered upon the docket in the order of their filing in the office of the Clerk of the Panel.

RULE 35.

The Clerk of the Panel shall give notice of docketing by mail to the sentencing judge, applicant and district attorney. The Clerk shall make an entry on the docket indicating when the notice was mailed and it shall be conclusive evidence that notice was properly and timely sent.

RULE 36.

If the Application for Review of Sentence appears on its face to be ineligible for review, the docketing notice shall so indicate.

RULE 37. [Reserved]

V. WRITTEN ARGUMENTS

RULE 38.

Oral arguments, videotapes or tape recordings are prohibited.

RULE 39.

Applicant and district attorney shall have the right to submit only written argument relative to the sentence imposed and the harshness or justification thereof. Said argument shall be postmarked to the Panel within 15 days of the docketing date.

RULE 40.

Arguments shall be typed or printed (double spaced) on paper not less than letter size (8½″ × 11″). The docket number assigned by the Sentence Review Panel must appear on the first page. Only one side of a sheet may be used. Pages must have margins of 2″ at the top, not less than 1½″ at the left and not less than 1½″ at the bottom. No documents submitted in argument will be returned. Blue backings are prohibited.

RULE 41.

Original and 3 copies of the entire argument shall be filed with the Clerk of the Panel. Indistinct photocopies are unacceptable. Service on opposing party, stating the name and address, shall be certified. Parties failing to comply with this rule shall be instructed to do so by the Clerk of the Panel.

RULE 42.

The plea or sentencing transcript is not a statutory requirement. A party desiring such transcript included in the review shall submit 4 copies to the Clerk of the Panel.

RULE 43.

The sentencing judge may submit a memorandum supporting his position and stating what facts, if any, he wishes to make available to the Panel. Original and 3 copies of such memorandum shall be submitted to the Clerk of the Panel and a copy shall be served on counsel for the parties by the sentencing judge.

RULE 44.

There are exceptional cases in which the record does not reflect the uniqueness of the case. When a Superior Court Judge, because of the seriousness or uniqueness of a case, makes a brief statement for the court reporter to attach to the sentence pointing out reasons why the sentence should not be reduced, then the Panel shall give such recommendation serious consideration.

RULES 45 and 46. [Reserved]

VI. JUDGMENTS

RULE 47.

The Superior Courts Sentence Review Panel shall be in continuous session and shall meet at such times as may be necessary to dispose of all cases within 90 days after they are ripe for consideration. The Chairman shall call the meetings. A case shall be considered ripe for consideration if the 15 days for submission of written argument have elapsed and all documents pertinent to the review of the case have been received.

Amended effective May 11, 2000.

RULE 48.

The Panel shall dismiss without further consideration all docketed applications which are not eligible for review.

RULE 49.

Factors to be considered in the review shall be the nature and circumstances of the crime, prior criminal record, age, disparity of sentences between codefendants, negotiated sentences, aggravating circumstances and mitigating circumstances. Members of the Panel shall not base their decision upon what sentence the Panel members would have imposed, but shall reduce a sentence or sentences only if they determine that the sentence under review is excessively harsh.

RULE 50.

The Panel shall not issue written opinions.

RULE 51.

Each judgment shall show on its face the votes, nonparticipation or disqualification of each Judge. Each Judge of the reviewing Panel shall sign the order and remittitur.

RULE 52.

As soon as it is practicable after the entry of the judgment, the Clerk of the Panel shall transmit the order and remittitur to the Clerk of the Superior Court from which the case was received. If the sentence is affirmed or the application is dismissed, a copy of the order and remittitur will be mailed to the applicant. If the sentence is reduced, a copy of the order and remittitur will be mailed to the sentencing judge, applicant, district attorney, probation office, parole office and the Department of Corrections. The Clerk of the Panel shall forward a copy of any reduction order to the Georgia Crime Information Center showing the defendant's state identification number, social security number and date of birth on the face of the order.

Amended effective May 11, 2000.

RULE 53.

The Panel will not entertain motions for reconsideration. The decision of the Panel shall not be reviewable. Applicant shall not have the right to file more than one application for a review of a sentence. Any order issued by the Panel shall be binding on all parties.

RULES 54 and 55. [Reserved]

VII. EFFECTIVE DATE

RULE 56.

These Rules shall be in effect as of July 1, 1985.

*

ALTERNATIVE DISPUTE RESOLUTION RULES

Effective April 15, 1993

Including Amendments Received Through November 1, 2006

Research Note

Use WESTLAW *to find cases citing a rule. In addition, use* WESTLAW *to search for specific terms or to update a rule; see the GA–RULES and GA–ORDERS Scope screens for further information.*

Amendments to these rules are published, as received, in the South Eastern Reporter 2d *and* Georgia Cases *advance sheets.*

Table of Rules

INTRODUCTION

The Georgia Constitution of 1983 mandates that the judicial branch of government provide "speedy, efficient, and inexpensive resolution of disputes and prosecutions." As part of a continuing effort to carry out this constitutional mandate the Supreme Court of Georgia established a Commission on Alternative Dispute Resolution under the joint leadership of the Chief Justice of the Georgia Supreme Court and the President of the State Bar of Georgia on September 26, 1990.

The Supreme Court charged the Commission to explore the feasibility of using court-annexed or court-referred alternative dispute resolution (ADR) processes to complement existing dispute resolution methods. The order creating the Commission directed that the Commission gather information, implement experimental pilot programs, and prepare recommendations for a statewide, comprehensive ADR system.

This court has now received the recommendations of the Commission and promulgates the following rules to establish a statewide plan for the use of alternative dispute mechanisms by the courts of Georgia.

Adopted effective April 15, 1993.

RULE I. DEFINITIONS

The term Alternative Dispute Resolution (ADR) refers to any method other than litigation for resolution of disputes. A definition of some common ADR terms follows.

Neutral. The term "neutral" as used in these rules refers to an impartial person who facilitates discussions and dispute resolution between disputants in mediation, case evaluation or early neutral evaluation, and arbitration, or who presides over a summary jury trial or mini trial. Thus, mediators, case evaluators, and arbitrators are all classified as "neutrals."

Mediation. Mediation is a process in which a neutral facilitates settlement discussions between parties. The neutral has no authority to make a decision or impose a settlement upon the parties. The neutral attempts to focus the attention of the parties upon their needs and interests rather than upon rights and positions. Although in court-annexed or court-referred mediation programs the parties may be ordered to attend a mediation session, any settlement is entirely voluntary. In the absence of settlement the parties lose none of their rights to a jury trial.

Arbitration. Arbitration differs from mediation in that an arbitrator or panel of arbitrators renders a decision after hearing an abbreviated version of the evidence. In non-binding arbitration, either party may demand a trial within a specified period. The essential difference between mediation and arbitration is that arbitration is a form of adjudication, whereas mediation is not.

Case Evaluation or Early Neutral Evaluation. Case evaluation or early neutral evaluation is a process in which a lawyer with expertise in the subject matter of the litigation acts as a neutral evaluator of the case. Each side presents a summary of its legal theories and evidence. The evaluator assesses the strength of each side's case and assists the parties in narrowing the legal and factual issues in the case. This conference occurs early in the discovery process and is designed to "streamline" discovery and other pretrial aspects of the case. The early neutral evaluation of the case may also provide a basis for settlement discussions.

Multi-door Courthouse. The multi-door courthouse is a concept rather than a process. It is based on the premise that the justice system should make a wide range of dispute resolution processes available to disputants. In practice, skilled intake workers direct disputants to the most appropriate process or series of processes, considering such factors as the relationship of the parties, the amount in controversy, anticipated length of trial, number of parties, and type of relief sought. Mediation, arbitration, case evaluation or early neutral evaluation, summary jury trial, mini trial, and various combinations of these ADR processes would all be available in the multi-door courthouse.

Summary Jury Trial. The summary jury trial is a non-binding abbreviated trial by mock jurors chosen from the jury pool. A judge or magistrate presides. Principals with authority to settle the case attend. The advisory jury verdict which results is intended to provide the starting point for settlement negotiations.

Mini Trial. The mini trial is similar to the summary jury trial in that it is an abbreviated trial usually presided over by a neutral. Attorneys present their best case to party representatives with authority to settle. Generally, no decision is announced by the neutral. After the hearing, the party representatives begin settlement negotiations, perhaps calling on the neutral for an opinion as to how a court might decide the case.

Settlement Week. During a settlement week there is a moratorium on litigation. Mediation is the ADR process most often used during settlement week. Appropriate cases are selected by the court and submitted to mediation. Lawyers and others who have undergone mediation training often act as volunteer mediators for these cases.

Adopted effective April 15, 1993.

RULE II. CENTRAL ORGANIZATION

A. There is hereby created the Georgia Commission on Dispute Resolution.

1. The Georgia Commission on Dispute Resolution will consist of the current Chief Justice of the Georgia Supreme Court or the Chief Justice's designee, a judge of the Georgia Court of Appeals, a designee of the President of the State Bar of Georgia, three superior court judges, and two judges to be drawn from the other four classes of trial courts in Georgia. The remaining members of the Commission will be one member from the Georgia General Assembly, four members of the State Bar of Georgia, and three non-lawyer public members. All members of the Commission shall be appointed by the Georgia Supreme Court. The chair of the Commission and a chair-elect of the Commission shall be designated by the Georgia Supreme Court.

2. The Commission is charged with the following duties and responsibilities:

a. To administer a statewide comprehensive ADR program;

b. To oversee the development and ensure the quality of all court-annexed or court-referred ADR programs;

c. To approve court programs;

d. To develop guidelines for court-annexed or court-referred programs;

e. To develop criteria for training and qualifications of neutrals;

f. To establish standards of conduct for neutrals;

g. To establish and register with the Georgia Secretary of State a nonprofit organization, The Georgia Commission on Dispute Resolution, Inc. This corporation shall qualify at all times as a tax exempt organization under sections 501(a) and 501(c)(3) of the Internal Revenue Code. This corporation shall be governed by a board of directors made up of at least three and no more than five directors appointed by the Georgia Supreme Court in cooperation with the President of the State Bar of Georgia from members of the Georgia Commission on Dispute Resolution. This nonprofit organization shall be established for the sole purpose of receiving and disbursing money from private grants and donations as a tax-exempt organization.

3. The first Commission will be appointed to serve terms as follows: the first term for three members will be one year, the first term for three members will be two years, the first term for four members will be three years, the first term for three members will be four years, the first term for three members will be five years. Thereafter, the term for Commission members will be five years. A Commission member shall not succeed himself or herself, except that Commission members originally appointed to a term of two years or less would be eligible for reappointment to one additional five-year term. If the status of a Commission member chosen to represent a particular category changes during his or her term, the member will continue to serve-out his or her term.

4. Members of the Commission shall receive no compensation for their services but shall be entitled to reimbursement for expenses and mileage for travel in connection with Commission business.

B. There is hereby created the Georgia Office of Dispute Resolution under the Georgia Supreme Court.

1. The Georgia Office of Dispute Resolution will be administered by a director who will serve at the pleasure of the Commission and be directly accountable to the Commission. The director's salary will be paid from the budget of the Georgia Supreme Court.

2. The Georgia Office of Dispute Resolution will implement the policies of the Commission. The responsibilities of the Georgia Office of Dispute Resolution will include the following:

a. To serve as a resource for ADR education and research;

b. To provide technical assistance to new and existing court-annexed or court-referred programs at no charge;

c. To develop the capability of providing training to neutrals in courts throughout the state at no charge;

d. To implement the Commission's policies regarding qualification of neutrals and quality of programs;

e. To register neutrals and remove neutrals from the registry if necessary;

f. To collect statistics from court-annexed or court-referred programs in order to monitor the effectiveness of various programs throughout the state.

3. Funding for the activities of the Georgia Office of Dispute Resolution will be provided in part by fees derived from registration and reregistration of neutrals.

Adopted effective April 15, 1993; amended effective December 30, 1993; February 9, 1995; March 5, 1998.

RULE III. FUNDING

The funding of court-annexed and court-referred ADR programs is primarily a public responsibility. Permanent funding for the Commission's work will be sought through a filing fee surcharge and fees for registration and reregistration of neutrals. Appropriate legislation will be sought to authorize permanent funding.

Adopted effective April 15, 1993; amended effective December 30, 1993.

RULE IV. COURT PROGRAMS

The Georgia Supreme Court encourages every court in Georgia to consider the use of ADR processes to provide a system of justice which is more efficient and less costly in human and monetary terms. The Georgia Supreme Court strongly urges that courts with established mediation programs cooperate with courts seeking to establish new programs. Courts should assist new programs by providing information and by allowing mediator trainees from new programs to observe veteran mediators mediating in established programs for the purpose of completing training requirements.

Any court desiring to develop an ADR program shall apply to the Commission for approval by making its application to the Georgia Office of Dispute Resolution in accordance with rules and guidelines promulgated by the Commission. Applications for programs shall include the following:

1. A description of existing dispute resolution services and resources in the area.

2. A demonstration of need, of coordination with existing social services, support of the bench and bar, and community support.

3. A description of the program.

4. A budget for the program.

5. A demonstration of the administrative capacity of the applicant.

Although existing court-annexed or court-referred programs must be approved under these rules, the above requirements should not be construed to prevent existing dispute resolution programs from applying for approval. Review and action of the Commission will be accomplished as efficiently as possible, and every effort will be made to avoid imposing unnecessary burdens upon any court. Funding obtained through local collection of filing fee surcharges will be used for the administration and development of local programs and payment of staff. Appropriate administrative fees may be charged by the Georgia Office of Dispute Resolution for technical assistance and training.

Neutrals serving in court programs must meet the requirements of the Georgia Commission on Dispute Resolution for registration. Although these requirements are threshold requirements for neutrals serving in court programs, courts are free to impose higher qualifications for neutrals who serve in their programs.

Uniform rules governing these programs appear as Appendix A to this rule.

Commentary

The Georgia Supreme Court strongly recommends that the program have a full-time administrator.

Adopted effective April 15, 1993; amended effective December 30, 1993.

RULE V. QUALIFICATION AND TRAINING OF NEUTRALS

The qualification and training requirements for various kinds of neutrals differ according to the process or program involved. Requirements for qualification and training of neutrals will be established by the Georgia Commission on Dispute Resolution and subject to review by the Georgia Supreme Court. All training for neutrals in court-annexed or court-referred programs will be in training programs approved by the Georgia Office of Dispute Resolution according to guidelines established by the Georgia Commission on Dispute Resolution. The Georgia Office of Dispute Resolution shall develop specific training programs for neutrals in accordance with requirements set by the Commission and subject to review by the Georgia Supreme Court.

Requirements for qualification and training of neutrals established by the Georgia Commission on Dispute Resolution will appear as Appendix B to this rule and will be published from time to time as amended. Ethical Standards for Neutrals established by the Georgia Commission on Dispute Resolution will appear as Appendix C to this rule and will be published from time to time as amended.

The Georgia Commission on Dispute Resolution will develop procedures to handle complaints against neutrals and ADR programs. The Georgia Commission on Dispute Resolution will have the authority to publish opinions resulting from the resolution of complaints and may, from time to time, publish advisory opinions as well.

Persons who have met the Commission's criteria as to qualifications and training may apply to the Georgia Office of Dispute Resolution for registration as a neutral. The Commission may set the amount of a registration fee which will accompany each application. The Commission may provide for periodic renewal of registration. Neutrals who have been trained prior to the promulgation of these rules may apply to the Georgia Office of Dispute Resolution for registration.

Adopted effective April 15, 1993; amended effective December 30, 1993; January 11, 1996; December 19, 1996.

RULE VI. COMPENSATION OF NEUTRALS

There shall be no uniform, state-wide compensation system at this time. Local courts will have the responsibility for developing and testing a variety of approaches to compensation consistent with guidelines that may be established by the Commission. However, every court program in which neutrals are compensated by the parties must provide ADR services free of charge to indigent parties. All compensated neutrals should contribute some pro bono hours to the program.

Commentary

Although the contribution of volunteers to ADR programs throughout the country is inestimable, the Georgia Supreme Court believes that the comprehensive system of statewide ADR services envisioned by these rules cannot be handled entirely by unpaid volunteers. This court is convinced that in order to build and maintain a statewide system of ADR services of the extent and quality desired, there must be mechanisms for compensating neutrals at appropriate levels. This court also believes that the Georgia ADR program will require a combination of volunteers, salaried in-house neutrals, and free market neutrals in order to meet the highly varied demands and circumstances of courts in urban, rural, and suburban areas.

Adopted effective April 15, 1993.

RULE VII. CONFIDENTIALITY AND IMMUNITY

A. The Extent of Confidentiality. Any statement made during a court-annexed or court-referred mediation or case evaluation or early neutral evaluation conference or as part of intake by program staff in preparation for a mediation, case evaluation or early neutral evaluation is confidential, not subject to disclosure, may not be disclosed by the neutral or program staff, and may not be used as evidence in any subsequent administrative or judicial proceeding. Unless a court's ADR rules provide otherwise, the confidentiality herein applies to non-binding arbitration conferences as well. A written and executed agreement or memorandum of agreement resulting from a court-annexed or court-referred ADR process is not subject to the confidentiality described above.

Any document or other evidence generated in connection with a court-annexed or court-referred mediation or case evaluation, early neutral evaluation or, unless otherwise provided by court ADR rules, a non-binding arbitration, is not subject to discovery. A written and executed agreement or memorandum of agreement resulting from a court-annexed or court-referred ADR process is discoverable unless the parties agree otherwise in writing. Otherwise discoverable material is not rendered immune from discovery by use in a mediation, case evaluation or early neutral evaluation or a non-binding arbitration.

Neither the neutral nor any observer present with permission of the parties in a court-annexed or court-referred ADR process may be subpoenaed or otherwise required to testify concerning a mediation or case evaluation or early neutral evaluation conference or, unless otherwise provided by court ADR rules, a non-binding arbitration, in any subsequent administrative or judicial proceeding. A neutral's notes or records are not subject to discovery. Notes and records of a court ADR program are not subject to discovery to the extent that such notes or records pertain to cases and parties ordered or referred by a court to the program.

B. Exceptions to Confidentiality. Confidentiality on the part of program staff or the neutral does not extend to the issue of appearance. Confidentiality does not extend to a situation in which a) there are threats of imminent violence to self or others; or b) the mediator believes that a child is abused or that the safety of any party or third person is in danger. Confidentiality does not extend to documents or communications relevant to legal claims or disciplinary complaints brought against a neutral or an ADR program and arising out of an ADR process. Documents or communications relevant to such claims or complaints may be revealed only to the extent necessary to protect the neutral or ADR program. Nothing in the above rule negates any statutory duty of a neutral to report information. Parties should be informed of limitations on confidentiality at the beginning of the conference. Collection of information necessary to monitor the quality of a program is not considered a breach of confidentiality.

C. Immunity. No neutral in a court-annexed or court-referred program shall be held liable for civil damages for any statement, action, omission or decision made in the course of any ADR process unless that statement, action, omission or decision is 1) grossly negligent and made with malice or 2) is in willful disregard of the safety or property of any party to the ADR process.

Adopted effective April 15, 1993; amended effective March 23, 1995; December 19, 1996; May 24, 1999.

RULE VIII. EDUCATION

In order to educate the bar about the benefits of ADR and the specifics of ADR processes, each member of the State Bar of Georgia shall be required to complete a one-time mandatory three-hour CLE credit in dispute resolution. The ADR requirement shall be completed before March 31, 1996. Lawyers admitted to the bar after July 31, 1995, may satisfy this requirement by attending the Bridge-the-Gap seminar conducted by the Institute of Continuing Legal Education in Georgia.

Lawyers who have taken a class essentially devoted to the study of ADR in law school are deemed to have satisfied the above requirement. Lawyers who have been trained as a neutral in a training which was approved for CLE credit or would not be eligible for CLE credit are deemed to have satisfied the above requirement. Lawyers who have previously taken an approved CLE seminar devoted to ADR are deemed to have satisfied the above requirement. The Georgia

Commission on Dispute Resolution will review requests for exemption from the CLE requirement on the basis of law school coursework.

The Georgia Supreme Court recommends that the Bridge the Gap seminar required for every new member of the State Bar of Georgia incorporate an introduction to ADR processes. This court further recommends that information concerning ADR be incorporated into CLE ethics and professionalism seminars. Sponsors and seminars designed to satisfy the ADR CLE requirement must be approved by the Commission on Continuing Lawyer Competency and the Georgia Commission on Dispute Resolution.

Adopted effective April 15, 1993; amended effective February 22, 1996.

APPENDIX A. UNIFORM RULES FOR DISPUTE RESOLUTION PROGRAMS

As amended by the Georgia Supreme Court, April 28, 2002

INTRODUCTION

The following rules apply to those courts which have elected to use the alternative dispute resolution (hereinafter referred to as ADR) processes of mediation, non-binding arbitration, case evaluation or early neutral evaluation, summary jury trial, mini trial or combinations thereof in a court-annexed or court-referred program.

Adopted effective April 15, 1993.

RULE 1. GENERAL RULES

1.1 The court will make information about ADR options available to all litigants.

Adopted effective April 15, 1993.

RULE 2. REFERRAL TO ADR

2.1 Any contested civil case, criminal case, or juvenile case may be referred to mediation by the judge to whom the case is assigned. Any contested civil case may be referred to non-binding arbitration, case evaluation or early neutral evaluation or multi-door program by the judge to whom the case is assigned. If cases are referred on a case-by-case basis, the time of referral is within the discretion of the referring judge.

2.2 Cases may be referred to an ADR process by category. If cases are referred by category, the court may provide for the timing of diversion by rule.

2.3 Courts should develop mechanisms to provide some individual review of cases sent to an ADR process. Cases shall be screened by the judge or the program to determine (1) whether the case is appropriate for the process; (2) whether the parties are able to compensate the neutral if compensation is required; and (3) whether a need for emergency relief makes referral inappropriate until the request for relief is heard by the court.

2.4 If court personnel other than judges are involved in ADR referral decisions, these individuals will receive appropriate training and will work within clearly stated written policies, procedures and criteria for referral.

2.5 Any party to a dispute may petition the court to refer the case to mediation, non-binding arbitration, case evaluation or early neutral evaluation, summary jury trial, mini trial or some combination thereof.

2.6 Parties may be ordered to attend a mediation session, a case evaluation or early neutral evaluation conference, or a non-binding arbitration. However, the order mandating attendance must clearly state that compliance does not require settlement or acceptance of an arbitration award.

2.7 If parties in a case have submitted the matter to an approved ADR process before filing suit, the case will not be referred to a duplicative ADR process by the court. If parties are required by statute to submit a dispute to an ADR process before filing suit, the court will not require submission to a successive ADR process.

2.8 In actions brought by state agencies seeking to enjoin activities injurious to the public interest, the agency may within 10 days of service of the action make a showing to the trial court that referral to ADR would adversely affect the public interest. Upon a showing of reasonable probability of such adverse effect, the court will proceed with emergency measures provided by law. Later referral to an ADR process may be appropriate if the emergency measures do not bring the case to conclusion.

Commentary

The Georgia Supreme Court recommends that cases be referred to ADR processes on a case by case basis. The indiscriminate use of ADR processes may result in increased obstacles for litigants and in further expense, overcrowding, and delay. However, courts may find it convenient to refer cases by category. The Georgia Supreme Court strongly recommends that if cases are referred by category, some appropriate review procedure be established.

The timing of referral should be late enough in the discovery process for the parties to have developed a realistic understanding of the strengths and weaknesses of the case and early enough to save discovery costs where possible. For example, where consistent with this premise, the time of diversion of a case selected for arbitration might be no later than the end of the six month discovery period. The time of diversion to case evaluation or early neutral evaluation and mediation might be within 60 days after the last responsive pleading. The court would retain the discretion to shorten or lengthen the time before diversion.

Although the Georgia Supreme Court believes that mandatory participation is an essential element of an effective court-annexed or court-referred ADR program, this court recommends that parties be allowed input into the referral decision wherever possible. For example, if parties or attorneys believe that mediation would be more helpful than arbitration in a specific case, this opinion should be considered by the referring court.

Adopted effective April 15, 1993; amended effective December 30, 1993.

RULE 3. EXEMPTION FROM ADR

3.1 Any party to a dispute may petition the court to have the case removed from mediation, non-binding arbitration, or case evaluation or early neutral evaluation.

3.2 Any party to a dispute may petition the court to refer the case to an ADR process other than the process to which it has been referred.

Adopted effective April 15, 1993.

RULE 4. APPEARANCE AT AN ADR CONFERENCE OR HEARING

4.1 The appearance of all parties and their attorneys is required at non-binding arbitration hearings and case evaluation or early neutral evaluation conferences. The appearance of all parties is required at mediation conferences. In every process, the presence of a representative with authority to settle without further consultation is required if the decision to settle depends upon an entity other than a party.

4.2 Failure to appear in the manner described above may subject a party to citation for contempt and to the imposition of sanctions permitted by law.

4.3 Attorneys are not required to attend mediation conferences but should be allowed and encouraged to do so. Attorneys of record should never be excluded from any process. The mediator may meet and consult privately with any party or any attorney during a mediation conference.

Adopted effective April 15, 1993.

RULE 5. QUALIFICATIONS AND TRAINING FOR NEUTRALS

5.1 All neutrals in a court-annexed or court-referred ADR program must be registered by the Georgia Office of Dispute Resolution.

5.2 All neutrals should attend an orientation program on court procedures given by the court in which they will serve.

5.3 All neutrals should attend continuing education seminars. The Commission will establish the standards for continuing education of neutrals.

5.4 All neutrals must be competent.

Adopted effective April 15, 1993; amended effective December 30, 1993; April 28, 2002.

RULE 6. CONFIDENTIALITY AND IMMUNITY

6.1 All parties in a court-annexed or court-referred ADR process are entitled to confidentiality to the extent described by the Georgia Supreme Court in the order to which these rules are appended.

6.2 Neutrals acting in a court-annexed or court-referred ADR process are entitled to immunity to the extent described by the Georgia Supreme Court in the order to which these rules are appended.

Adopted effective April 15, 1993; amended effective December 30, 1993.

RULE 7. COMMUNICATIONS BETWEEN NEUTRALS, THE PROGRAM, AND THE COURT

7.1 If any communication between the court and a neutral is necessary, the communication shall be in writing or through the program administrator. Copies of any written communication with the court should be given to parties and their attorneys.

7.2 Once an ADR process is underway in a given case, contact between the administrator of an ADR program and the court concerning that case should be limited to

a. Communicating with the court about the failure of a party to attend;

b. Communicating with the court with the consent of the parties concerning procedural action on the part of the court which might facilitate the ADR process;

c. Communicating to the court the neutral's assessment that the case is inappropriate for that process;

d. Communicating any request for additional time to complete the mediation, non-binding arbitration, or case evaluation or early neutral evaluation;

e. Communicating information that the case has settled or has not settled and whether agreement has been reached as to any issues in the case;

f. Communicating the contents of a written and executed agreement or memorandum of agreement unless the parties agree in writing that the agreement should not be disclosed;

g. Communicating with the consent of the parties any discovery, pending motions or action of any party which, if resolved or completed, would facilitate the possibility of settlement.

Adopted effective April 15, 1993; amended effective December 30, 1993; May 24, 1999.

RULE 8. ENFORCEABILITY OF AGREEMENTS

Written and executed agreements or memoranda of agreement reached as a result of a court-connected ADR process are enforceable to the same extent as any other agreements. Oral agreements shall not be enforceable.

Adopted effective April 15, 1993; amended effective May 24, 1999.

RULE 9. SELECTION OF NEUTRALS

9.1 Disputants outside of the court setting are always entitled to choose their own neutrals. Nothing in these rules will infringe upon the right of parties to choose any third party to assist in dispute resolution prior to filing a case with the court. However, when the parties have been referred to an ADR process by the court, the court is responsible for the integrity of the process. For this reason, neutrals in a court-annexed or court-referred ADR process will be chosen from neutrals registered by the Georgia Office of Dispute Resolution.

9.2 If parties referred by the court to an ADR process are unable to agree upon a neutral within a reasonable time, the neutral will be selected by the court. In either event, the neutral will be selected from the roster of registered neutrals.

9.3 Any party may petition the court for the appointment of another neutral on the ground that the neutral selected by the court is disqualified because of a conflict or because the party feels that the objectivity of the neutral is in question.

9.4 A neutral registered by the Georgia Office of Dispute Resolution is registered to serve as a neutral anywhere in the state.

9.5 Nothing in these rules is intended to discourage courts from using a co-mediation model where appropriate.

Adopted effective April 15, 1993; amended effective December 30, 1993.

RULE 10. EVALUATION

10.1 Evaluation of the Program. Sufficient data will be collected on an ongoing basis to ensure the quality of the program. Such data will include evaluation by parties and attorneys of the ADR process as applied to their case, the performance of the neutral in the case, and ways to improve the effectiveness of the ADR program. Courts will use the data to improve the quality of programs. It is inappropriate to use data concerning settlement rate as the sole basis for program funding or program evaluation.

10.2 Evaluation of Neutrals.

a. Courts must establish procedures to monitor the performance of neutrals on an ongoing basis. It is inappropriate to use data concerning settlement rate as the sole basis for evaluation of a neutral.

b. Procedures should be established to remove incompetent, ineffective, or unethical neutrals from the roster. These procedures should also include reporting removal to the Georgia Office of Dispute Resolution so that registration may be reconsidered.

Adopted effective April 15, 1993; amended effective December 30, 1993.

RULE 11. LOCAL PROGRAM RULES OF PROCEDURE FOR ADR

Courts may present local program rules of procedure to the Georgia Commission on Dispute Resolution for approval. Approval of local program rules of procedure will be filed with the Georgia Supreme Court. Approved programs will be considered experimental pilot projects for one year under Uniform Superior Court Rule 1.2. It is the intention of the Georgia Supreme Court to work toward uniformity so that variations between programs will be eventually minimized. In order to assist lawyers and parties in discerning differences between the rules of different courts, the rules will be submitted with the following format:

1. Referral:
2. Timing of ADR processes:
3. Exemption:
4. Appointment of neutrals:
5. Qualifications of neutrals:
6. Compensation of neutrals:
7. Immunity:
8. Confidentiality:
9. Appearance:
10. Sanctions for failing to appear without good cause:
11. Communication with parties:
12. Communication with the court:
13. Completion of ADR processes:

Adopted effective April 15, 1993; amended effective December 30, 1993.

APPENDIX B. REQUIREMENTS FOR QUALIFICATION AND TRAINING OF NEUTRALS

**Established by the
Georgia Commission on Dispute Resolution**

As amended by the Georgia Commission on Dispute Resolution, January 18, 2005

I. REQUIREMENTS FOR QUALIFICATION AND TRAINING OF NEUTRALS

The Georgia Commission on Dispute Resolution is dedicated to the principle that neutrals serving in court programs must be of the highest possible caliber in training and experience. All neutrals serving in Georgia programs must be of good moral character.

A. Mediation: Although mediators do not necessarily need subject matter expertise, they must have process expertise. Mediators are frequently called upon to operate outside of their area of expertise. For this reason, training of mediators must be more extensive than for other neutrals. Training for mediators who seek registration in the category of general mediation shall be no less than twenty-eight hours of classroom training (including role play and other participatory exercises), plus observation of or co-mediation with a registered mediator in at least five general civil mediations. In lieu of five observations and/or comediations, prospective mediators may substitute an approved general mediation practicum. Individuals must complete approved twenty-eight hour general mediation training prior to taking an approved practicum or performing their observations. New mediators should be observed several times before mediating alone.

Mediators should be drawn from a variety of disciplines and should reflect the racial, ethnic and cultural diversity of our society. Prospective mediators should be screened carefully for qualities such as the ability to listen actively, to isolate issues, and to focus discussion on issues.

Competencies for mediators include: (1) Skill in interacting with others and in helping others with their problems; (2) As guardian of the integrity of the mediation process, capacity to maintain the fairness of the process; (3) Capacity to assist parties in identifying their needs and interests, developing options for resolution, and realistically assessing their options for settlement; (4) Protecting the balance of the process by having the capacity to (a) remain neutral in the presence of significant interpersonal conflict between others, (b) understand the points of view of all parties to the dispute, and (c) demonstrate respect for all participants in the mediation conference; (5) Honoring the self-determination of the parties by (a) having the capacity to thoroughly explain the process to the parties, (b) having the capacity to assess the parties' capacity to participate in the mediation conference, (c) having the capacity to assure that the parties have sufficient capacity and information to bargain effectively and to participate in the development of any resolution reached; (d) having the ability to honor the right of parties to develop their own resolution free from any coercion of the mediator, and (e) having the ability to honor the boundaries between the role of mediator and any other professional capacity in which the mediator operates, scrupulously guarding against giving professional advice; and (6) having the capacity to guard the confidentiality of the process.

Mediators in divorce and custody cases shall have at least a baccalaureate degree from an accredited four-year college. An individual whose graduate degree was obtained after waiver of the requirement that the baccalaureate be completed shall be deemed to have completed the baccalaureate degree. Mediators in divorce and custody cases must satisfy the requirements for general mediators prior to taking domestic relations mediation training. The required domestic relations training is at least 40 hours of training which substantially meets the standards of the Family Section of the Association for Conflict Resolution. Mediators in divorce and custody cases shall receive special training in the subject of domestic violence. Mediators who seek registration in the category of domestic relations must observe at least one mediation of a divorce or custody case and participate in at least two co-mediations of divorce or custody cases. In lieu of one observation and two co-mediations of divorce or custody cases, prospective domestic relations mediators may substitute an approved domestic relations mediation practicum. Individuals must complete approved forty-hour domestic relations mediation training prior to taking an approved domestic relations practicum or doing the observation and co-mediations of divorce or custody cases.

Mediators who handle cases involving allegations of domestic violence must be currently registered as domestic relations mediators prior to taking specialized domestic violence training. Specialized domestic violence training shall be no less than fourteen hours of classroom training (including role plays and other participatory exercises) approved by the Georgia Office of Dispute Resolution.

Specific training requirements for mediators in juvenile court cases shall be developed by the Commission.

B. Arbitration: Arbitration in court-annexed or court-referred non-binding arbitration programs may be conducted by panels of lawyers, panels made up of lawyers and experts, or by individual lawyers. If the arbitration is conducted by a panel, the chief of the panel shall be a lawyer with five years experience. Where the arbitration is conducted by a single arbitrator, that arbitrator shall be a lawyer with five years experience. All arbitrators shall receive at least six hours of training in a program which qualifies for CLE credits or, for judges and persons with acceptable experience as an arbitrator, such other training, experience, or education as approved by the Chair of the Committee on Training and Credentials and the Director of the Georgia Office of Dispute Resolution.

C. Case Evaluation or Early Neutral Evaluation: Case evaluators or early neutral evaluators shall be lawyers with extensive subject matter expertise in the area of the litigation in question. Case evaluators or early neutral evaluators shall receive at least six hours training for their role. The Commission recommends, but does not require, twenty-eight hours general mediation training for case evaluators or early neutral evaluators.

Adopted effective January 1, 1994; amended effective December 1, 1994; June 1, 1995; October 1, 1995; April 30, 1998; September 20, 2000; February 28, 2002; amended August 20, 2002, eff. July 1, 2003; amended effective March 27, 2003; May 11, 2004; January 18, 2005.

II. REGISTRATION OF NEUTRALS

All neutrals working in court programs must be registered with the Georgia Office of Dispute Resolution. The application and training guidelines attached to this appendix set forth the specific requirements for registration. Neutrals must have registration in the appropriate categories for the cases in which they serve.

An individual who completed an approved general mediation training prior to July 1, 2003 shall apply for registration by December 31, 2004. Effective July 1, 2003, an applicant for registration as a general mediator shall apply for registration within eighteen (18) months after completing an approved general mediation training.

Specialized Domestic Violence Mediation. Effective January 1, 2005, mediators who handle cases involving allegations of domestic violence must be registered in the category of specialized domestic violence. To be eligible to register in the category of specialized domestic violence, one must be: 1) registered as a domestic relations mediator; 2) have taken an approved 14 hour specialized domestic violence mediation training after June 1, 2004; and, 3) provide a letter of recommendation from a director of a superior court ADR program who is familiar with the mediator's work as a domestic relations mediator.

A mediator who has had specialized domestic violence training prior to June 1, 2004, may apply for registration in the specialized domestic category if the mediator: (1) has had at least six hours of advanced domestic violence training provided by an approved domestic relations trainer in Georgia; and has been mediating domestic violence cases for court-connected programs for at least two years prior to June 1, 2004; and has mediated at least five domestic violence cases; and is recommended by a director of a court-connected program for which he or she has been mediating domestic violence cases; OR (2) has taken an advanced domestic violence training of at least twelve hours provided by an approved Georgia domestic relations mediation training provider and is recommended by the director of a court-connected program for which she or he has mediated domestic relations cases; OR (3) has taken one of the specialized domestic violence trainings sponsored by the Georgia Office of Dispute Resolution in 2003.

Until January 1, 2005, the Director of the Georgia Office of Dispute Resolution, in consultation with the Commission's Training and Credentials Committee, shall have the discretion to permit registration of registered domestic relations mediators who have had domestic violence training provided by a court-connected ADR program and provide certification from a program director that the applicant has the necessary skills level.

Veteran Mediators: Mediators who were actively working in court programs at the time that registration was instituted, January 1, 1994, have had an opportunity to be "grandfathered" into registration as general or domestic mediators even if they did not meet all requirements of Appendix B if, in the judgment of the Director of the Georgia Office of Dispute Resolution, their training substantially met the qualifications set forth above. Registration has been underway since the winter of 1994, and these candidates have had ample opportunity to come forward to seek registration. In the future, applications to be grandfathered into registration as a general mediator will be granted only rarely. Grandfathering of domestic mediators will be granted only in the most unusual circumstances.

Candidates for grandfathering may petition the Office of Dispute Resolution to be accepted for registration. Candidates may demonstrate their competence in the field by (1) describing the training they have received; (2) providing three letters of recommendation from a mediation program, clients, court personnel, registered mediators, or other professionals with whom the applicant has worked; and (3) providing evidence of having completed a minimum of five mediations or ten hours of mediation in the twelve months preceding the registration request. Compliance with this procedure does not guarantee registration.

Mediators from Other States: A mediator from another state who (1) has received training which meets that state's qualifications and, at the discretion of the Director, has had substantially similar training to that approved in Georgia, (2) has mediated for one year, (3) has completed a minimum of five mediations or ten hours of mediation during that time, and (4) meets the educational requirements of Appendix B may ask to be waived in for Georgia registration on the basis of that training. A mediator from another state who is waived in must be observed by a staff member of the court in which he or she intends to serve or submit a letter from the office of dispute resolution or director of the court program for which he or she served in the other state before applying for registration by the Georgia Office of Dispute Resolution.

Continuing Education of Neutrals: All registered neutrals are required to take six (6) hours of continuing education in a two-year registration renewal cycle in order to maintain their registration; provided, however, that in the first renewal cycle after initial registration a neutral is only required to take three (3) hours of continuing education. This six (6) hour requirement applies regardless of the number of categories for which a neutral is registered. A neutral may carry over up to three (3) hours of continuing education to the next renewal cycle. There must be a nexus between the continuing education attended and enhancement of the neutral's skill, substantive knowledge and/or professionalism as a neutral. Any neutral who fails to meet the continuing education requirement is subject to being removed from the registry of the Georgia Office of Dispute Resolution.

Registration Period and Renewal of Registration: A neutral is registered for a period not to exceed two years unless the neutral relinquishes or loses registration as part of an adverse action taken by the Commission on Dispute Resolution's Committee on Ethics. Neutrals who wish to continue their registration with the Georgia Office of Dispute Resolution shall file an application for registration renewal by December 31st every other year. The first two-year renewal cycle for a neutral shall begin on the date the neutral is approved for registration and shall end at midnight, December 31st of the following year, *provided that* neutrals whose initial registration is approved in December of any year shall have their initial registration period extend until midnight, December 31st two years later. Each subsequent renewal cycle shall begin January 1st and continue through midnight on December 31st twenty-four months later. Neutrals seeking continued registration shall file a renewal application in the form provided by the Georgia Office of Dispute Resolution and pay the following nonrefundable fees:

Neutrals who, in the preceding two years, have earned less than $2500 from the provision of ADR neutral services $25.00

Neutrals who, in the preceding two years, have earned $2500 or more from the provision of ADR neutral services $125.00

Renewal applications shall be postmarked or submitted online no later than midnight, December 31st of the year the renewal application is due.

Lapsed Status: Neutrals who file a renewal application after midnight, December 31st of the year they must renew, or who fail to file a renewal application shall be placed in a lapsed status. A lapsed neutral may file a renewal application between 12:01 a.m. January 1st the year after the renewal application is due through midnight, April 30th of that year upon payment of an additional nonrefundable late fee equal to the applicable neutral renewal fee. For example, a neutral who must pay a renewal fee of $25 must pay $50 to renew registration between January 1st and April 30th. A neutral who must pay a renewal fee of $125 must pay $250 to renew registration between January 1st and April 30th. Neutrals may continue to serve in court-connected programs while in a lapsed status.

Inactive Status: After April 30th, all lapsed neutrals shall be placed in inactive status and may not provide services in court-connected cases. Neutrals in inactive status shall be required to take eight hours of appropriate CE in order to renew their registration status, and shall also be required to pay a late fee equal to their renewal fee in addition to their regular renewal fee. A neutral who is in an inactive status may remain in that status for up to two years from the date registration should have been renewed. Inactive neutrals who apply for renewal of registration after day 730 shall be required to meet the initial requirements for registration, including completion of an approved training course in each category for which they desire to renew their registration, observations or practicums that may be required for each category of registration for which they are seeking renewal, and requisite recommendation letter(s).

Failure to Meet CE Requirements: In the event a neutral has not met the continuing education requirement for a renewal cycle and postmarks or submits the renewal application online on or before midnight, December 31st of the year of renewal, the neutral shall be in a "lapsed" status until the deficiency in CE hours is cured or until April 30th, whichever comes first. If the renewal application is timely filed, the neutral shall have until midnight, April 30th to provide information that substantiates that this deficiency has been cured, at no additional cost. The neutral shall be placed in an inactive status if the deficiency is not cured by April 30th.

Hardship Exception: In cases of extraordinary hardship (e.g. military deployment or extreme illness or injury), a neutral may request an extension of time for renewal, and/or a waiver of the continuing education requirement, and/or any penalties by submitting such a request in writing to the Director of the Georgia Office of Dispute Resolution. The Director shall issue a written response. If such request is denied, an appeal may be taken to the Training and Credentials Committee of the Commission on Dispute Resolution within thirty (30) days of receipt of the Director's denial of the request for waiver. A decision of the Training and Credentials Committee shall be final.

Delayed Payment: A neutral who submits a renewal application online by midnight, December 31st of the year that renewal is due, but who chooses to submit the renewal fee through regular mail rather than online, shall mail the appropriate renewal fee so that it is received by GODR within ten (10) days of the submission of the application. If GODR does not receive payment within ten (10) days of submission, the neutral shall be placed in a lapsed status.

Adopted effective October 1, 1995; amended effective April 1, 1998; amended August 20, 2002, eff. January 1, 2003; amended effective May 20, 2003; January 15, 2004; May 11, 2004; August 24, 2004.

III. APPEAL FROM ADVERSE DECISIONS OF THE OFFICE OF DISPUTE RESOLUTION

A. Registration decisions are made by the Georgia Office of Dispute Resolution. Applicants who are denied registration for any reason other than that described in § IV may appeal within thirty days of that denial to the Georgia Commission on Dispute Resolution's Committee on Training and Credentials, which may grant a hearing to the applicant. The Committee on Training and Credentials will make a determination as to whether the applicant should be registered.

B. An adverse decision of the Committee on Training and Credentials may be appealed to the full Commission within thirty days of the date of such decision. The Commission may grant a hearing to the applicant.

Adopted effective June 1, 1995.

IV. PROCEDURE FOR APPLICANTS FOR REGISTRATION OR RENEWAL OF REGISTRATION WHO HAVE BEEN CONVICTED OF OR PLED GUILTY OR NOLO CONTENDERE TO A VIOLATION OF THE LAW, WHO HAVE BEEN DISCIPLINED BY A PROFESSIONAL ORGANIZATION, WHO HAVE HAD PROFESSIONAL PRIVILEGES CURTAILED, AND/OR WHO HAVE RELINQUISHED ANY PROFESSIONAL PRIVILEGE OR LICENSE WHILE UNDER INVESTIGATION AND/OR WHO DO NOT MEET COMPETENCY STANDARDS

A. Applicants for registration with the Georgia Office of Dispute Resolution must acknowledge the following information: (1) convictions of, guilty pleas to, or nolo contendere pleas to violations of the law, including traffic violations resulting in suspension or revocation of a driver's license and DUI offenses; (2) discipline by a professional organization; (3) curtailment of professional privileges, (4) relinquishment of any professional privilege or license while under investigation. An applicant against whom any of the above actions are pending shall likewise acknowledge this fact.

B. Upon request of the Georgia Office of Dispute Resolution, the applicant must amend his/her application to provide (1) information concerning the background of the offense which led to conviction, plea, discipline, curtailment of professional privileges and/or relinquishment of professional privilege or license; (2) information concerning the length of time which has elapsed since the conviction, plea, discipline, curtailment and/or relinquishment; (3) the age of the applicant at the time of the conviction, plea, discipline, curtailment and/or relinquishment; and (4) evidence of rehabilitation since the conviction, plea, discipline, curtailment and/or relinquishment.

C. The applicant may be asked to appear before the Committee on Ethics of the Georgia Commission on Dispute Resolution to discuss the information contained within the application. The Committee on Ethics will make a determination as to whether the applicant should be registered or have registration renewed.

D. If an applicant for registration or renewal of registration fails to acknowledge (1) that he/she has been convicted of or pled guilty or nolo contendere to a violation of the law, including traffic violations resulting in suspension or revocation of a driver's license and DUI offenses; (2) that he/she has been disciplined by a professional organization; (3) that he/she has had his/her professional privileges curtailed; (4) that he/she has relinquished any professional privilege or license while under investigation; or (5) that any such actions are pending, the Georgia Office of Dispute Resolution will immediately notify the applicant for registration or renewal of registration that he/she will be denied registration or renewal of registration or, if currently registered, removed from registration by the Georgia Office of Dispute Resolution.

E. An adverse decision of the Committee on Ethics may be appealed to the full Commission within thirty days of the date of such decision. The Commission may grant a hearing to the applicant.

Adopted effective June 1, 1995; amended effective October 1, 1995; April 1, 1998; December 3, 1998; September 30, 1999; February 28, 2002.

V. REMOVAL FROM REGISTRATION

A. A neutral who (1) has been convicted of or pled guilty or nolo contendere to a violation of the law, including traffic violations resulting in suspension or revocation of a driver's license and DUI offenses; (2) has been disciplined by a professional organization; (3) has had his/her professional privileges curtailed; and/or (4) has relinquished any professional privilege or license while under investigation, may be removed from the registry of approved neutrals maintained by the Georgia Office of Dispute Resolution. A grievance concerning the ethical behavior of a neutral may result in that neutral being removed from the registry of approved neutrals maintained by the Georgia Office of Dispute Resolution.

B. Upon receiving information that a neutral has been convicted of or pled guilty or nolo contendere to a violation of the law as described above, been disciplined by a professional organization, had his/her professional privileges curtailed, or has relinquished any professional privilege or license while under investigation, or upon receiving a grievance concerning the behavior of a neutral, the Georgia Office of Dispute Resolution or the Georgia Commission on Dispute Resolution will refer the matter to the Committee on Ethics of the Georgia Commission on Dispute Resolution.

C. Both the neutral and the complainant may be asked to appear before the Committee on Ethics of the Georgia Commission on Dispute Resolution to discuss the complaint. The Committee on Ethics will make a determination as to whether the neutral should be removed from the registry. The Committee on Ethics will make written findings which will inform the neutral and the Commission of the basis of its decision.

D. An adverse decision of the Committee on Ethics may be appealed to the full Commission within thirty days of the date of such decision. The Commission may grant a hearing to the applicant.

Adopted effective June 1, 1995.

APPENDIX C

As amended by the Georgia Commission on Dispute Resolution, November 29, 2005

CHAPTER 1. ETHICAL STANDARDS FOR NEUTRALS

A.[1] ETHICAL STANDARDS FOR MEDIATORS

[1] Chapter 1 contained no Part B.

PREFACE

In June, 1994, The Georgia Commission on Dispute Resolution turned its attention to the development of a code of ethical behavior for mediators serving court programs in Georgia. We initiated a dialogue with practicing mediators in the state. This dialogue served as the starting point for the development of the code.

The code consists of two parts. The first part contains standards of practice, the foundation of ethical behavior by mediators. Because the Commission is cognizant of the limited guidance provided through mere articulation of standards, commentary, including specific examples from practice, accompanies each standard, enhancing and strengthening this foundation.

Specific practice rules, treating matters of conduct which are settled and do not lend themselves to the exercise of discretion on the part of the mediator, appear as Part V. Rules of Fair Practice.

Adopted effective September 28, 1995.

INTRODUCTION

The Georgia Commission on Dispute Resolution believes that ethical standards for mediators can be most easily understood in the context of the three fundamental promises that the mediator makes to the parties in explaining the process: 1) the mediator will protect the self-determination of the parties; 2) the mediator will protect the confidentiality of the mediation process; 3) the mediator is a neutral who is impartial and is without bias or prejudice toward any party. Besides maintaining fidelity to these principles, a mediator acts as guardian of the overall fairness of the process.

Adopted effective September 28, 1995.

I. SELF-DETERMINATION/VOLUNTARINESS

Where the court orders that parties participate in a dispute resolution process other than trial, the process must be non-binding so as not to interfere with parties' constitutional right to trial. To that extent, all court-ordered ADR processes are voluntary. However, the self-determination of the parties which is a hallmark of mediation is of a different and far more subtle order.

Commentary

The Georgia Commission on Dispute Resolution accepts the proposition that self-determination of the parties is the most critical principle underlying the mediation process. Control of the outcome by the parties is the source of the power of the mediation process. Further, it is the characteristic which may lead to an outcome superior to an adjudicated outcome.

Self-determination is a difficult goal in our society in which people seem often unwilling to assume responsibility for their own lives, anxious for someone else to make the decisions for them. Mediation is antithetical to this attitude.

A. In order for parties to exercise self-determination they must understand the mediation process and be willing to participate in the process. A principal duty of the mediator is to fully explain the mediation process. This explanation should include:

1. An explanation of the role of the mediator as a neutral person who will facilitate the discussion between the parties but who will not coerce or control the outcome;

2. An explanation of the procedure which will be followed during the mediation session;

3. An explanation of the pledge of confidentiality which binds the mediator and any limitations upon the extent of confidentiality;

4. An explanation of the fact that the mediator will not give legal or financial advice and that if expert advice is needed, parties will be expected to refer to outside experts;

5. An explanation that where participation is mandated by the court, the participation of the parties is all that is required and settlement cannot be mandated;

6. An explanation that the mediation can be terminated at any time by the mediator or the parties;

7. An explanation that parties who participate in mediation are expected to negotiate in an atmosphere of good faith and full disclosure of matters material to any agreement reached;

8. An explanation that the parties are free to consult legal counsel at any time and are encouraged to have any agreement reviewed by independent counsel prior to signing;

9. An explanation that a mediated agreement, once signed, can have a significant effect upon the rights of the parties and upon the status of the case.

B. The mediator has an obligation to assure that every party has the capacity to participate in the mediation conference. Where an incapacity cannot be redressed, the mediation should be rescheduled or cancelled.

Self-determination includes the ability to bargain for oneself alone or with the assistance of an attorney. Although the mediator has a duty to make every effort to address a power imbalance, this may be impossible. At some point the balance of power may be so skewed that the mediation should be terminated.

Commentary

Georgia mediators are confident of their ability to recognize serious incapacity. Situations in which there is a subtle incapacity are more troubling. Several mediators expressed concern about situations in which they questioned capacity to bargain but felt certain that the agreement in question would be in the best interest of the party and that going to court would be very traumatic. Should the mediation be terminated because of suspected incapacity if mediation is the gentler forum for a fragile person and the agreement which the other party is willing to make is favorable? Does the mediator's substituting his or her judgment for the judgment of the party destroy any possibility of self-determination? Is self-determination and the empowerment which it offers a rigid requirement in every mediation? Does it make a difference whether the suspected incapacity is temporary—i.e. a party is intoxicated—so the mediation could be rescheduled?

Example 1: *The husband, who is a doctor, is also an alcoholic. The mediator notes, "She could have said anything and he would have said yes. He just wanted to get it over with. It was really hard keeping him here. I had to make two pots of coffee during each session to keep him going. He was just ready to get out and go get a drink or something." The wife is represented, but he is not represented. Both parties are concerned about preserving his assets, and they both agree that she should get a large portion of the assets. There seems to be danger that the assets will disappear because of his alcoholism. The mediator is concerned that the husband is agreeing too readily and is worried about the balance of power. The party is not presently incapacitated—except to the extent that his desire to complete the mediation is interfering with his giving careful thought to the process. It may be that the level of self-determination which he is exhibiting is the highest level that is possible for him. Should this person be deprived of the benefits which he might derive from mediation because he is not able to bargain as effectively as the other party?*

Example 2: *During the mediation it becomes apparent to the mediator that one party is well-represented and the other party is not being adequately represented. What, if anything, should the mediator do? If the mediator interferes in the attorney-client relationship a number of issues are raised. Would interference infringe upon the self-determination of the party who has retained the attorney? Is neutrality compromised? Is the mediator crossing a line and in effect giving legal advice? If the mediator is compensated, will the mediator's action or inaction be influenced by the desire to maintain good relationships with attorneys for business reasons?*

Recommendation: Where a party is laboring under an incapacity which makes him or her incapable of effective bargaining, the mediator should terminate the mediation. Mediation is not an appropriate forum for the protection of the rights of a person who cannot bargain for him or herself.

If the incapacity is temporary—i.e. intoxication—the mediation should be rescheduled.

If there is a serious imbalance of power between parties, the mediator should consider whether the presence of an attorney, family member, or friend would give the needed support.

An obvious example of a power imbalance occurs when there is a history of domestic violence. Although the Commission has drawn up guidelines to assist court programs in identifying those cases which are not appropriate for mediation, information about a history of domestic violence may surface for the first time during the mediation. The questions the mediator faces are whether to terminate the mediation and, if so, how to safely terminate it. Factors which should be considered are whether there was more than one incident, when the incident or incidents occurred, whether the information surfaces during a joint session or during caucus, whether the alleged victim is intimidated. If the mediator has any concern that the safety of any person will be jeopardized by continuing the mediation, the mediation should be terminated.

If one party is simply unable to bargain as effectively as another, it is probably inappropriate to deny those parties the benefits of the mediation process because of that factor.

If the imbalance occurs because of disparity in the ability of the parties' attorneys, the principle of self-determination, in this case in relation to the selection of an attorney, again prevails.

One mediator expressed his view this way: "I am reluctant to withdraw where there is an imbalance in power because I always try to look at the alternative. The alternative usually is that person is going to be no better off in litigation. I understand that there's a judge there that can look after the parties, but still my practical experience in litigation teaches me that most parties are not going to be much better off in litigation rather than mediation if lack of power is their problem."

C. Parties cannot bargain effectively unless they have sufficient information. Informed consent to an agreement implies that parties not only knowingly agree to every term of the agreement but that they have had sufficient information to bargain effectively in reaching that agreement. Self-determination of the parties in a mediation includes not only informed consent to any agreement reached but participation in crafting the agreement as well.

Commentary

One mediator suggested that the parties who are operating without full information be asked to reconvene with attorneys present. This mediator said, "I have been more and more impressed with how effective a subsequent session can be with the attorneys present and everyone having prepared for it."

Example 1: *One party says that there are assets which have been hidden and the other party denies the existence of the assets. The mediator faces the question of whether to push them forward on the facts that are established or give any credence to these alleged facts.*

Recommendation: The question is resolved in favor of terminating or rescheduling the mediation if there has not been sufficient discovery or the party claiming that assets have been hidden feels that she or he cannot bargain effectively. The closer question comes if there is unsubstantiated suspicion—i.e. "He must have made more than he reported on his income taxes in 1992, so where is it?"

Domestic relations mediators who work in court-annexed or court-referred programs may not have the luxury of several sessions so that parties can be assigned "homework." As long as the information on assets and budgets is available, the actual preparation of lists of assets and liabilities and the preparation of budgets may provide an important opportunity for collaborative work by the parties.

Example 2: *In a divorce mediation the wife is clearly dependent on the lawyer, as she had been on her husband while they were married. The lawyer is not cooperative in the mediation. At each session the lawyer comes in with a totally new agenda and without promised information. The mediator finds that she is spending an inordinate amount of time dealing with the lawyer. The mediator offers to meet with the parties alone, but the lawyers will not allow that.*

Recommendation: The mediator may caucus with the lawyers alone and confront the lawyer who is obstructing the mediation. The mediator may also raise questions in caucus with the lawyer and the client which may alert the client to the need to control the lawyer. Beyond this, it is difficult to resolve this situation without compromising the self-determination of the client or compromising neutrality.

Commentary

Yet another variation on the issue of missing information is the missing issue—should the mediator bring up issues which the parties have not identified? As one mediator expressed this: "What's our role when people say we want you to mediate this case? Are we to mediate the issues that they bring to us or are we to create issues for them to discuss and decide about? I guess that a lot of the conflict that we're talking about here is what do we as mediators have to initiate or inform people or educate people about: all the issues that can be and probably ought to be discussed in the context of a divorce mediation? You're potentially opening up all these cans of worms for people who don't necessarily want them opened." On the other hand, have the parties had an opportunity to mediate from a position of full information if they have not considered every relevant issue? Beyond this, will the agreement hold up if it is not made in the context of all issues in the dispute?

D. The mediator must guard against any coercion of parties in obtaining a settlement.

Commentary

Many mediators discussed the question of when to declare impasse. One mediator said that she loved the point of impasse because the parties have "gone through the conflict" to get to impasse. She felt that the moment of impasse is a moment of great opportunity. At some point, however, persistence becomes coercion. The question of when to terminate the mediation will be discussed further under the topic of fairness.

E. It is improper for a lawyer/mediator, therapist/mediator, or mediator who has any professional expertise in another area to offer professional advice to a party. If the mediator feels that a party is acting without sufficient information, the mediator should raise the possibility of the party's consulting an expert to supply that information.

Commentary

Conversations with Georgia mediators who are trained as lawyers confirmed that this concept is extremely difficult for lawyer/mediators. Lawyers, having been trained to protect others, agonize over the perception that missing information, poor representation, ignorance of a defense, etc. may place a party in danger.

Recommendation: The line between information and advice can be very difficult to find. However, failure to honor the maxim that a mediator never offers professional advice can lead to an invasion of the parties' right to self-determination and a real or perceived breach of neutrality.

Adopted effective September 28, 1995.

II. CONFIDENTIALITY

Confidentiality is the attribute of the mediation process which promotes candor and full disclosure. Without the protection of confidentiality, parties would be unwilling to communicate freely, and the discussion necessary to resolve disputes would be seriously curtailed. Statements made during the conference and documents and other material, including a mediator's notes, generated in connection with the conference are not subject to disclosure or discovery and may not be used in a subsequent administrative or judicial proceeding. A written and executed agreement or memorandum of agreement resulting from a court-annexed or court-referred ADR process is discoverable unless the parties agree otherwise in writing. Any exceptions to the promise of confidentiality such as a statutory duty to report certain information must be revealed to the parties in the opening statement. Information given to a mediator in confidence by one party must never be revealed to another party absent permission of the first party.

Example 1: *A party reveals to the mediator in caucus that he has cancer and that he does not want his ex-wife to know about it. He is not sure how long he will be working because of his illness. This information could be very important to the wife. She may need to make other plans for the time when that money is not coming in. Because of the confidentiality, the mediator feels that she cannot say anything.*

Recommendation: This presents the classic dilemma of the collision between the promise of confidentiality and the need of the parties for complete information if they're to enter into an agreement voluntarily. The mediator is placed in the position of keeping a confidence of one party at the expense of the self-determination of the other party. If the mediation is terminated, there is no guarantee that the husband's condition would be revealed at trial, and the parties may lose the opportunity for a more creative agreement than the verdict imposed after a return to court.

The first tactic of the mediator is to encourage the person keeping the crucial secret to share it with the other party or allow the mediator to reveal the secret. If the secret is central to the creation of a solid agreement, and if the mediator cannot persuade the party with the crucial secret to share it, she may have no alternative but to terminate the mediation.

One mediator discussed the problem of information which, if made part of an agreement, might constitute a fraud upon the court. He felt that the ethical requirement that a lawyer is always an officer of the court would require that the lawyer/mediator not draft an agreement if there were a secret which made the agreement a fraud on the parties or on the court. "In other words, if one party says as soon as we sign this custody agreement I'm going to take my kids across the country, that would put me in an impossible conflict of interest. I would feel that I would be perpetrating a fraud on the other side if I allowed them to enter into an agreement."

Example 2: *A deceptively simple example of this problem can occur in jurisdictions where a "warrant fee" must be paid even if the warrant is not served or is dropped. As the parties enter into the mediation of this sub-issue after the mediation of the dispute which resulted in the warrant is completed, both parties refuse to pay a penny, saying that it is the responsibility of the other party. In caucus, one party says, "I'll pay half of it but don't tell them that." Or someone will say, "I think I should only have to pay half of it, but I'd pay it all to be finished with this, but don't tell them." The mediator has been given a piece of information that would make a difference in the settlement of perhaps the entire case and instructed not to tell.*

Recommendation: When the secret information is something that would foster settlement rather than something that would prevent settlement, the mediator is remiss if he or she does not push the parties toward revelation.

Commentary

An interesting problem intersecting self-determination and confidentiality occurs because of the increasing use of guardians ad litem to represent the interests of the child in disputed custody cases. If the guardian is present at the mediation, should he or she be privy to the entire mediation, including caucuses? The interests of the child are not necessarily synonymous with the positions of parties. One solution to the issue would be to caucus separately with each party and with the guardian. Another question is whether the guardian, who has an obligation to report to the court, can be bound by confidentiality.

Recommendation: The mediator's opening statement should include an explanation that the guardian ad litem is a party to the mediation whose interests may be separate from those of the other parties. Parties should be informed of the limits on confidentiality presented by the guardian ad litem's presence in the joint session. The mediator should caucus with the guardian ad litem separately. The guardian ad litem should not be present when the mediator conducts a caucus with a party.

Adopted effective September 28, 1995.

III. IMPARTIALITY

A. A mediator must demonstrate impartiality in word and deed. A mediator must scrupulously avoid any appearance of partiality. Impartiality means freedom from favoritism, bias or prejudice.

Example 1: *As one mediator expressed this problem: "I had a big case once upon a time where I thought the plaintiffs, who were represented by three attorneys, had made a very poor presentation of their case and this was a case that went on for multiple sessions. I don't remember whether it was the opening presentation. I think it may not have been the opening presentation, but a subsequent presentation, and it may have been on just a few issues or something like that. I felt like they did not present their case in as strong a form as they could have. Maybe that they were holding back some evidence. In caucus I just did some coaching. I don't mean to be so presumptuous as to say that I knew how to do it better than they did but I pointed out some things to them that I think they agreed with. They went back and made a more forceful, more cogent presentation and I think were able to move things along better. Because by making a weak presentation of their case, they were not going to be able to get what they knew or believed they were entitled to. So it was a matter of helping the other side see the strengths of the plaintiff's case that they had not been able to see through the original presentation."*

Recommendation: Several mediators discussed the problem of dealing with a party who is unable to bargain effectively and puzzled over an ethical way to coach that party while retaining neutrality. Helping a party to present his or her needs and interests in a way that can be heard by the other side is not a breach of neutrality but is, rather, an important part of the mediator's role. When the mediator helps each side to communicate effectively, the mediator is assisting the parties in establishing the common ground upon which a solid agreement can be based.

Commentary

Mediators gave very few examples of situations in which they felt such antipathy for a party that they were unable to remain neutral. Many mediators discussed the fact that when they began to search for needs and interests of a party they were able to reach a sufficient level of understanding that neutrality was not an issue.

Although the classic dilemma regarding impartiality occurs when the mediator feels great sympathy or antipathy toward one party or another, the problem is more complicated when the loss of impartiality occurs because of behavior of someone other than a party.

Example 1: *During a mediation the attorneys begin to fight with each other to the extent that it is difficult to control the mediation. It is also difficult for the mediator to keep an open mind about how to deal with it because, as he expressed his own emotion, his stomach is churning. The mediator is faced not only with controlling the situation but in dealing with his own reaction to it. The mediation did not result in an agreement although the matter was settled before trial. The mediator wondered in hindsight if it might have been better if he had said "Look, because of the way I'm reacting to your fight, I can't be an effective mediator for you. You need a different personality to help you mediate."*

B. A mediator may not accept anything of value from a party or attorney for a party before, during, or after the mediation, other than the compensation agreed upon. Mediators should be sensitive to the fact that future business dealings with parties may give the appearance of impropriety. However, it is not improper for a mediator to receive referrals from parties or attorneys.

C. CONFLICTS OF INTEREST/BIAS

a. A mediator shall avoid a conflict of interest or the appearance of a conflict of interest during and after a mediation. A conflict of interest can arise from involvement by a mediator with the subject matter of the dispute or from any relationship between a mediator and any mediation participant, whether past or present, personal or professional, that reasonably raises a question of a mediator's impartiality. Mediators should avoid any dual relationship with a party which would cause any question about the mediator's impartiality.

b. A mediator shall make a reasonable inquiry to determine whether there are any facts that a reasonable individual would consider likely to create a potential or actual conflict of interest for a mediator. A mediator's actions necessary to accomplish a reasonable inquiry into potential conflicts of interest may vary based on practice context.

c. A mediator shall disclose, as soon as practicable, all actual and potential conflicts of interest that are reasonably known to the mediator and could reasonably be seen as raising a question about the mediator's impartiality. After disclosure, if all parties agree, the mediator may proceed with the mediation.

d. If a mediator learns of any fact after accepting a mediation that raises a question with respect to that mediator's service creating a potential or actual conflict of interest, the mediator shall disclose it as quickly as practicable. After disclosure, if all parties agree, the mediator may proceed with the mediation.

e. If a mediator's conflict of interest might reasonably be viewed as undermining the integrity of the mediation, a mediator shall withdraw from or decline to proceed with the mediation regardless of the expressed desire or agreement of the parties to the contrary.

f. Subsequent to a mediation, a mediator shall not establish another relationship with any of the participants in any matter that would raise questions about the integrity of the mediation. When a mediator develops personal or professional relationships with parties, other individuals or organizations following a mediation in which they were involved, the mediator should consider factors such as time elapsed following the mediation, the nature of the relationships established, and services offered when determining whether the relationships might create a perceived or actual conflict of interest.

Commentary

How a mediator conducts a conflicts check varies by practice context. For a complex case that comes to a mediator through his or her law firm, best practice consists of making a firm-wide conflicts check at the pre-mediation phase. By contrast, for a mediator of a matter outside the mediator or firm's area of practice, making an inquiry of the parties and participants at the time of the mediation regarding potential conflicts of interest may be sufficient.

In performing the mediator's role, an individual displays multiple analytical and interpersonal skills which may well lead a mediation participant to consider employing the mediator again. If a mediation participant, be it a party, party representative, witness or any other participant, wishes to employ the mediator in a subsequent mediation, or in another role (such as personal lawyer, therapist, or consultant), then the mediator must make certain that entering into such a new relationship does not cast doubt on the integrity of the mediation process.

Example 1: *A divorce mediation results in a full agreement. The parties do not want to take the agreement and spend the extra money on an attorney. And they ask the mediator to take the agreement to court and help them obtain an uncontested divorce. As the mediator described the problem, "I told them that technically I could but no I won't because I've been your mediator and must be neutral. I think it would be a conflict for me to go from mediator to attorney in the same case for the purpose of getting you your divorce and making it legal. They said that they really didn't want to go pay anybody else and asked me to prepare the papers. So I charged them an additional fee to prepare the papers, the decree and separation agreement, without my name on it and I told them to file it pro se. They were satisfied with that and I could sleep with that decision."*

Recommendation: The ethical problems that arise in the area of subsequent contact with parties have to do with neutrality and the perception that the mediator might capitalize upon the mediation experience to create a future business relationship with one or the other party. Here the mediator did legal work for both parties so that there was no question of a breach of neutrality. There was no question that the dual representation was clearly explained and understood by the parties. Further, the mediator tried to distance himself by refusing to represent the parties in court, acting more as a scribe than a representative. He acted with great reluctance and only because the parties requested that they not be placed in a position of incurring additional expense. This mediator said that specific rules in this area would be helpful. It is the Commission's recommendation that a lawyer/mediator never accept any legal work arising out of the mediation. In the context of the example above, this recommendation is more for the protection of the mediator than for the parties.

Adopted effective September 28, 1995; amended effective November 29, 2005.

IV. FAIRNESS

The mediator is the guardian of fairness of the process. In that context, the mediator must assure that the conference is characterized by overall fairness and must protect the integrity of the process.

A. A mediator should not be a party to an agreement which is illegal or impossible to execute. The mediator should alert parties to the effect of the agreement upon third parties who are not part of the mediation. The mediator should alert the parties to the problems which may arise if the effectiveness of the agreement depends upon the commitment of persons who are not parties to the agreement. A mediator may refuse to draft or sign an agreement which seems fundamentally unfair to one party.

Commentary

Georgia mediators expressed two concerns related to the fairness of a mediated agreement: How to handle the situation in which the parties agree to something which the mediator feels is unworkable; how to separate out the mediator's own bias that a party could have done better from the agreement which seems fundamentally unfair to the party.

Example 1: *As one mediator expressed the tension, "You know, have you done this or that? Why don't we come back? 'No, I just want to get it over with.' God, you're paying such a price just to get it over with. But then, maybe they just really need to get it over with. I don't know how many times I've heard that, that I just want to get it over with. I don't care what it takes, I want it done, nobody's going to abide by this anyway. Whatever that whole bundle of things may be. That's my bugaboo. I don't know what advice to give other people about it. You can create some type of abstract standard [for mediators to handle this situation]."*

Example 2: *In a juvenile court case the parties are working toward agreement and the mediator realizes that the child is agreeing to anything in order to get out of the room. The mediator also realizes that if the agreement is breached, the child will have to answer for the breach in court. The mediator's reality testing is to no avail.*

Example 3: *The mediator is concerned about the tax consequences of a property transfer, and the parties are unwilling to consult an outside expert. As one mediator set forth the problem: "So they come in with a house to sell or a business as part of their marital assets and you're talking about transferring all this property and then what about the taxes. Have you thought about the tax implications? They say no, and you say well you ought to go see a CPA and get this information. And they don't want to because they don't want to spend any more money and all of a sudden you're taking what appeared to be a simple situation and you're making it more complex and you're making it more expensive and where does it stop. That's our question."*

Example 4: *The parties have been married twenty-two years and have grown children. They come to mediation having settled everything but who is to get the Volvo, which is for them their most prestigious material possession. The husband suggests the solution of just selling the car, a solution which would make it possible to finalize the divorce. The wife, who is not ready for finality begins to cry hysterically and then says "Just write it up and I'll sign anything."*

Recommendation: The mediator's tension may result from his or her concern that the agreement is not the best possible agreement. On the other end of the continuum, the mediator feels that the agreement is unconscionable. This is an area in which the mediator's sense of fairness may collide with the fundamental principle of self-determination of the parties. On the other end of the contin-

uum, the mediator may feel that the agreement is unfair in that one party is not fully informed. In other words, the process by which agreement was reached was unfair because one party was not bargaining from a position of knowledge. An underlying question is whose yardstick should be used in measuring fairness.

The mediator has an obligation to test the parties' understanding of the agreement by making sure that they understand all that it involves and the ramifications of the agreement. The mediator has an obligation to make sure that the parties have considered the effect of the agreement upon third parties. If after testing the agreement the mediator is convinced that the agreement is so unfair that he or she cannot participate, the mediator should withdraw without drafting the agreement. Parties should be informed that they are, of course, free to enter into any agreement that they wish notwithstanding the withdrawal of the mediator.

B. A mediator is the guardian of the integrity of the mediation process.

Commentary

Georgia mediators expressed concern about confusion of parties and neutrals as to the difference between various ADR processes. This confusion may result in the parties' not knowing what to expect of the mediation process. While there is room for variation in mediation style from the more directive to the more therapeutic, the mediator should recognize the line between mediation and a more evaluative process and be prepared to refer the party to another process if that would be more appropriate.

Another concern mentioned by many Georgia mediators was how to recognize impasse and, perhaps more difficult, how to recognize when parties come to the table unwilling to bargain in good faith. Another variation on this theme is the attorney who has come to the table merely intending to benefit from free discovery or use mediation as a dilatory tactic. Yet another variation on this theme was the expectation of lawyers that the mediation could be completed in one session. These problems are experienced differently whether the mediator is being compensated on an hourly basis, per session, or is a volunteer. Many mediators and program directors struggle with the issue of good faith and the question of whether lack of good faith can ever be reported to the court.

Recommendation: When a mediator realizes that a party is not bargaining in good faith, he or she often experiences an understandable frustration and a desire to report the bad faith to the court. The pledge of confidentiality extends to the question of conduct in the mediation, excepting of course threatened or actual violence. The possible damage to the process by reporting more than offsets the benefit in a given case. Further, if the lodestar of mediation is the principle of self-determination, the unwillingness of a party to bargain in good faith is consistent with that party's right to refuse the benefits of mediation.

Adopted effective September 28, 1995.

V. RULES OF FAIR PRACTICE

Referrals. Mediators should observe the same care to be impartial in their business dealings that they observe in the mediation session. In this regard, mediators should not refer parties to any entity in which they have any economic interest. As a corollary to this principle, mediators should avoid referrals to professionals from whom the mediator expects to receive future business. Similarly, mediators should avoid an ongoing referral relationship with an attorney that would interfere with that attorney's independent judgment.

It is not improper to receive referrals from attorneys or parties. However, mediators should be aware that their impartiality or appearance of impartiality may be compromised by referrals from parties or attorneys for whom they act as mediators on more than one occasion.

Fees. Mediators who are compensated by parties must be scrupulous in disclosing all fees and costs at the earliest opportunity. Fees may be based on an hourly rate, a sliding scale, or a set fee for an entire mediation as long as the fee structure has been carefully explained to the parties and they have consented to the arrangement.

Fees may never be contingent upon a specific result. It is imperative that the mediator have no "stake" in the outcome.

Mediators who serve for compensation in court programs are obligated to provide some pro bono hours in order to serve parties who are indigent.

Competence. Mediators are obligated to disclose their training and background to parties who request such information. Mediators are obligated not to undertake cases for which their training or expertise is inadequate. Mediators shall meet the competency standards of Appendix B. § 1.

Mediators who serve in court programs or receive referrals from courts must be registered with the Georgia Office of Dispute Resolution and must be in compliance with the Alternative Dispute Resolution Rules of the Supreme Court of Georgia. Any mediator who receives a court referral without being in compliance with the Supreme Court Rules is subject to being removed from the registry of the Georgia Office of Dispute Resolution. Further, the immunity protection of the Supreme Court Rules is not available to mediators who receive court referrals without being in compliance with said rules.

Advertising. Mediators are permitted to advertise. Mediators have an obligation to the integrity of the mediation process. In that regard, all statements as to qualifications must be truthful. Mediators may never claim that they will guarantee a specific result. It is important to the public perception of mediation that advertisements by mediators are not only accurate, clear, and truthful, but that they are in no way misleading.

Diligence. Mediators will exercise diligence in scheduling the mediation, drafting the agreement if requested to do so, and returning completed necessary paperwork to the court or referring agency.

Mediation may be terminated by either the mediator or the parties at any time. Mediators will be sensitive to the need to terminate the mediation if an impasse has been reached. However, mediators must be courageous in declaring impasse only when there is no possibility of progress.

Adopted effective September 28, 1995; amended effective February 28, 2002.

CHAPTER 2. ETHICS PROCEDURES

These Ethics Procedures describe the steps for handling questions of a neutral's fitness that involve his/her character or allegedly unethical conduct. Thus, "complaint," as used here, refers only to formal objections to a neutral's fitness that involve his/her character or allegedly unethical conduct. Questions of a neutral's fitness that do not involve character or allegedly unethical conduct will be referred to the Committee on Training and Credentials of the Georgia Commission on Dispute Resolution.

I. PROCEDURE FOR APPLICANTS FOR REGISTRATION OR RENEWAL OF REGISTRATION WHO HAVE BEEN CONVICTED OF OR PLED GUILTY OR NOLO CONTENDERE TO A VIOLATION OF THE LAW, WHO HAVE BEEN DISCIPLINED BY A PROFESSIONAL ORGANIZATION, WHO HAVE HAD PROFESSIONAL PRIVILEGES CURTAILED, AND/OR WHO HAVE RELINQUISHED ANY PROFESSIONAL PRIVILEGE OR LICENSE WHILE UNDER INVESTIGATION

A. Applicants for registration with the Georgia Office of Dispute Resolution must acknowledge the following information: (1) convictions of, guilty pleas to, or nolo contendere pleas to violations of the law, including traffic violations resulting in suspension or revocation of a driver's license and DUI offenses; (2) discipline by a professional organization; (3) curtailment of professional privileges; (4) relinquishment of any professional privilege or license while under investigation. An applicant against whom any of the above actions are pending shall likewise acknowledge this fact.

B. Upon request of the Georgia Office of Dispute Resolution, the applicant must amend his/her application to provide (1) information concerning the background of the offense which led to conviction, plea, discipline, curtailment of professional privileges and/or relinquishment of professional privilege or license; (2) information concerning the length of time which has elapsed since the conviction, plea, discipline, curtailment and/or relinquishment; (3) the age of the applicant at the time of the conviction, plea, discipline, curtailment and/or relinquishment; and (4) evidence of rehabilitation since the conviction, plea, discipline, curtailment and/or relinquishment.

C. The Georgia Office of Dispute Resolution conducts a background check on every applicant for registration or renewal of registration. If the background check reveals an arrest but no disposition, the applicant will be contacted by the Office for further information. Until there is a response from the applicant, the application will not be processed further. If there is no response from the applicant within six months of a request for information, the file will be closed. Any fee received beyond the $25.00 non-refundable administrative fee will be returned to the applicant if requested. Once the Office is satisfied that no conviction followed the arrest and the case is closed, the application process will continue.

D. If an applicant for registration or renewal of registration fails to acknowledge (1) that he/she has been convicted of or pled guilty or nolo contendere to a violation of the law, including traffic violations resulting in suspension or revocation of a driver's license and DUI offenses; (2) that he/she has been disciplined by a professional organization; (3) that he/she has had his/her professional privileges curtailed; (4) that he/she has relinquished any professional privilege or license while under investigation; or (5) that any such actions are pending, the Georgia Office of Dispute Resolution has the discretion to immediately notify the applicant for registration or renewal of registration that he/she will be denied registration or renewal of registration. If currently registered, a neutral may be summarily removed from registration by the Georgia Office of Dispute Resolution under these circumstances.

E. The Committee on Ethics of the Georgia Commission on Dispute Resolution will identify categories of cases in which the Director of the Office of Dispute Resolution may exercise his/her discretion in permitting registration without referral to the Committee. In other cases, the applicant may be asked to appear before the Committee to discuss the information contained within the application. The Committee will make a determination as to whether the applicant should be registered or have registration renewed.

F. The hearing is private and is not open to the public. The hearing is informal, and rules of civil procedure and rules of evidence do not apply. The rules of evidence may serve as a guide for the Committee. The standard of proof is a preponderance of the evidence. The applicant may bring counsel or a support person to the hearing. Although witnesses are not generally necessary in the hearing on an application, witnesses may be presented with permission of the Committee. If the applicant fails to appear or participate in good faith, the Committee will deny the application. The record in the case will consist of the application and any correspondence or documents gathered by the Committee or the Georgia Office of Dispute Resolution in connection with the application. The Committee will record the hearing. A copy of the tape will be made available to the applicant upon request.

G. An adverse decision of the Committee on Ethics may be appealed to the full Commission within thirty days of the date of such decision. The Commission may grant a hearing to the applicant. Hearings before the Commission are private. A decision of the Commission is final.

(1) The review by the Commission is ordinarily confined to the record, which will consist of the material described in Section F above and the tape of the hearing before the Committee. However, if good cause is shown before the review, the Commission may grant leave to present additional evidence. The Commission will, upon request, receive briefs and hear oral argument.

(2) The Commission will not substitute its judgment for that of the Committee in regard to the weight of the evidence or facts but may reverse or modify the original decision upon a finding that substantial rights of the appellant have been prejudiced because the Committee's findings, inferences, conclusions, or decisions are:

(a) In violation of constitutional or statutory provisions;

(b) Beyond the authority of the Committee in either substance or procedure;

(c) Clearly erroneous;

(d) Arbitrary or capricious or characterized by abuse of discretion or clearly unwarranted discretion.

(3) The review will proceed as follows:

(a) The Commission will hear an opening statement and argument from the appellant/ respondent and the counsel for appellant/respondent, if there be counsel.

(b) The Commission may hear additional evidence if good cause is shown.

(c) The Commission may question the Committee as to the basis of its decision.

(d) The Commission will deliberate outside the presence of the Committee and parties.

Adopted effective May 24, 1999; amended effective September 30, 1999; September 20, 2000.

II. PROCEDURES FOR PROCESSING COMPLAINTS OR INFORMATION REGARDING A NEUTRAL'S CONDUCT OR VIOLATION OF SOME PROFESSIONAL STANDARD; COMPLAINTS REGARDING AN APPROVED TRAINING PROGRAM; OR COMPLAINTS REGARDING A COURT–CONNECTED ADR PROGRAM

A. Receipt of Information that a Neutral (1) Has Been Convicted of or Pled Guilty or Nolo Contendere to a Violation of the Law; (2) Has Been Disciplined by a Professional Organization; (3) Has Had His/Her Professional Privileges Curtailed; (4) Has Relinquished Any Professional Privilege or License While Under Investigation; or (5) Who is a Mediator Who Does not Meet Competency Standards. Upon receipt of information that a neutral has (1) been convicted of or pled guilty or nolo contendere to a violation of the law, including traffic violations resulting in suspension or revocation of a driver's license and DUI offenses; (2) been disciplined by a professional organization; (3) had his/her professional privileges curtailed; and/or (4) relinquished any professional privilege or license while under investigation, and/or who is a mediator who does not meet competency standards, the Director of the Georgia Office of Dispute Resolution will begin an investigation even in the absence of a formal complaint. The procedures for considering such information will be the same as those set out below for processing complaints against neutrals.

B. Complaints: A complaint against a neutral may be made by anyone having knowledge of the subject matter of the complaint. A complaint against a court program may be made by anyone having knowledge of the subject matter of the complaint. A complaint against an approved training program or any person responsible for conducting, administering, or promoting such a training program may be made by anyone having knowledge of the subject matter of the complaint.

Complaints may be made to or referred to the Georgia Office of Dispute Resolution. A complaint need not take any particular form but shall be made in writing and signed by the complaining party. Until made in writing and signed by the complaining party, it will be considered only a grievance, and the Office will neither inform the neutral, court program or training program of the complaint, nor investigate it, nor refer it to the Ethics Committee of the Georgia Commission on Dispute Resolution.

Complaints regarding character or conduct will be handled in the first instance by the Georgia Office of Dispute Resolution and thereafter by the Committee on Ethics.

A complaint regarding a training program which is not approved by the Georgia Office of Dispute Resolution is not within the jurisdiction of the Commission. However, if such a training course is advertised as approved, the Commission will undertake appropriate action to correct the false impression that the course is approved.

C. Notice of a Formal Complaint: Once a complaint is made in writing and signed by the complaining party, it is considered a formal complaint. The Office will send the complaint to the neutral, training program, or court program by certified mail and regular mail.

D. Response: A neutral, training program, or court program will be asked to respond to the Director of the Georgia Office of Dispute Resolution (the Director) within twenty (20) days of receiving a formal complaint.

E. Preliminary Review of the Complaint: The Director will make a preliminary review of the complaint to consider whether the allegations, if true, would constitute a violation of (1) the Georgia Supreme Court's Alternative Dispute Resolution Rules; (2) the Ethical Standards for Mediators contained in Appendix C of the Supreme Court ADR Rules; (3) the requirement in Appendix B of the Supreme Court ADR Rules that "[all] neutrals serving in Georgia programs must be of good moral character"; or (4) training guidelines set forth by the Georgia Commission on Dispute Resolution. Complaints that do not rise to that level of seriousness will not be forwarded to the Ethics Committee. The Director will, however, report all formal complaints to the Chair of the Committee, who may determine that the complaint should be reviewed by the Committee.

F. Investigation: The Director will make an initial inquiry into the complaint by telephone conversation with the complainant, the neutral, other parties to the mediation, the program director, or the director of the training program, and any other person whose observations may be relevant to the complaint.

G. Director's Discretion to Conduct Facilitated Meeting: If the Director concludes that the complaint has arisen primarily from a misunderstanding that might be addressed in a facilitated meeting between the parties, she has the discretion to invite the necessary participants to such a meeting. If the Director concludes that the complaint does not rise to that level of seriousness required for Committee review as described in Section E above, she has the discretion to invite the necessary participants to such a meeting.

H. Suspension of a Neutral or Training Program Pending Hearing: Upon receipt of sufficient evidence demonstrating that conduct complained of poses a threat of harm to parties in mediation or to the public, the Georgia Office of Dispute Resolution or the Committee on Ethics may petition the Georgia Commission on Dispute Resolution for suspension of a neutral or training program pending disciplinary proceedings predicated upon the conduct causing such complaint.

I. Right to Hearing: A neutral, program director or training program director against whom a complaint is lodged (the respondent) has the right to a hearing before the Committee on Ethics. The respondent will receive a letter from the Chair of the Committee on Ethics advising him or her as to the time and place of the hearing. The respondent will also be advised in the letter of any information that would assist him or her in preparing for the hearing. The respondent has a right to review at the Office of Dispute Resolution in advance of the hearing any relevant written material submitted to the Committee by any person. With the approval of the Director, copies of relevant documents and evidence may be mailed to a requesting party. This in no way limits the right of the complainant or the respondent to submit additional written material or to call witnesses at the hearing before the Committee.

J. The Hearing: The hearing is private and is not open to the public. The hearing is informal, and rules of civil procedure and rules of evidence do not apply. The rules of evidence may serve as a guide for the Committee. The standard of proof is a preponderance of the evidence. The neutral and the complainant may bring counsel or a support person to the hearing. Testimony may be made by telephone, if good cause is shown to the Committee. The Committee may elect to sequester witnesses, if appropriate. Witnesses may be subpoenaed by the Committee as in civil cases in state courts of record. Witnesses will be entitled to receive the fees and mileage provided by law for witnesses in civil cases. If any witness so subpoenaed fails to appear, the Commission may apply to the superior court of the county where the matter is being heard for an order requiring obedience. Failure to comply with such order shall be cause for punishment as for contempt of court. If any party fails to appear or to participate in good faith, the Committee may proceed on the evidence before it. If the complainant fails to appear, the Committee may dismiss the complaint for want of prosecution. The record of any contested case will include the complaint, the response, and all correspondence. The Committee will record the hearing. A copy of the tape will be made available to the respondent upon request.

K. In the Event That the Committee Finds That:

(1) a neutral has violated (a) the Ethical Standards for Mediators contained in Appendix C of the Supreme Court ADR Rules or (b) the requirement in Appendix B of the Supreme Court ADR Rules that "[all] neutrals serving in Georgia programs must be of good moral character," or that

(2) a neutral has been convicted of or pled guilty or nolo contendere to a violation of the law, including traffic violations resulting in suspension or revocation of a driver's license and DUI offenses; has been disciplined by a professional organization; had his/her professional privileges curtailed; has relinquished any professional privilege or license while under investigation, for behavior which would constitute a violation of (a) the Ethical Standards for Mediators contained in Appendix C of the Supreme Court ADR Rules or (b) the requirement in Appendix B of the Supreme Court ADR Rules that "[all] neutrals serving in Georgia programs must be of good moral character," or that

(3) a training program is in violation of guidelines promulgated by the Georgia Commission on Dispute Resolution,

the Committee may impose sanctions.

L. Sanctions: Unless the conduct complained of involves moral turpitude, is potentially injurious to the public, involves gross incompetence, or has been the subject of repeated complaints, education and mentoring requirements may be imposed as sanctions. Where there are repeated complaints, gross incompetence, or conduct which rises to the level of moral turpitude or is potentially injurious to the public, removal from registration would be appropriate.

The Committee may recommend imposition of one or more appropriate sanctions upon the neutral, including the following:

(a) Additional training

(b) Restriction of types of cases to be mediated in the future

(c) Continuing education

(d) Mentoring by an experienced mediator/mentor

(e) Suspension for a specified term

(f) Removal from registration

Failure of a respondent to comply with sanctions imposed by the Committee may result in removal from registration. Where a complaint against a court program or training program is found to be meritorious, sanctions may range from technical assistance and mentoring to removal of approval.

M. The Decision of the Committee on Ethics: The Committee will make written findings which will inform the neutral, director of training program, or ADR program and the Georgia Commission on Dispute Resolution (the Commission) of the basis of its decision. In lieu of a decision, the Committee may elect to issue an advisory opinion.

N. Review of a Decision of the Committee on Ethics:

(1) A respondent may appeal an adverse decision of the Committee to the full Commission within thirty (30) days of the date of such decision. The Commission may grant a hearing to the appellant/respondent. Hearings before the Commission are private. A decision of the Commission is final.

(2) The review by the Commission is ordinarily confined to the record, which will consist of correspondence between the parties and the Georgia Office of Dispute Resolution, any evidence considered by the Committee, and the recording of the hearing before the Committee. However, if good cause is shown before the review, the Commission may grant leave to present additional evidence. The Commission will, upon request, receive briefs and hear oral argument. Witnesses may be subpoenaed by the Commission as in civil cases in state courts of record. Witnesses will be entitled to receive the fees and mileage provided for by law for witnesses in civil cases. If any witness so subpoenaed fails to appear, the Commission may apply to the superior court of the county where the matter is being heard for an order requiring obedience. Failure to comply with such order shall be cause for punishment as for contempt of court.

(3) The Commission will not substitute its judgment for that of the Committee in regard to the weight of the evidence or facts but may reverse or modify the original decision upon a finding that substantial rights of the appellant have been prejudiced because the Committee's findings, inferences, conclusions, or decision are:

(a) In violation of constitutional or statutory provisions;

(b) Beyond the authority of the Committee in either substance or procedure;

(c) Clearly erroneous;

(d) Arbitrary or capricious or characterized by abuse of discretion or clearly unwarranted discretion.

(4) The review will proceed as follows:

(a) The Commission will hear an opening statement and argument from the appellant/respondent and the counsel for appellant/respondent, if there be counsel.

(b) The Commission may hear a statement from the complainant and may hear additional evidence if good cause is shown.

(c) The Commission may question the Committee as to the basis of its decision.

(d) The Commission will deliberate outside the presence of the Committee and parties.

Adopted effective May 24, 1999; amended effective February 28, 2002.

III. CONFIDENTIALITY

A. A mere grievance will be kept confidential.

B. The Director will make a preliminary review of a formal complaint against a neutral to consider whether the allegations, if true, would constitute a violation of either (1) the Ethical Standards for Mediators contained in Appendix C of the Supreme Court ADR Rules, or (2) the requirement in Appendix B of the Supreme Court ADR Rules that "[all] neutrals serving in Georgia programs must be of good moral character." Complaints that do not rise to that level of seriousness will not be forwarded to the Committee on Ethics and will remain confidential except that the Director will report all formal complaints to the Chair of the Committee, who may determine that the complaint should be reviewed by the Committee.

C. Once a complaint is forwarded to the Committee on Ethics, the existence of the complaint is no longer confidential. After a complaint has been forwarded to the Committee on Ethics, the Office of Dispute Resolution will accept inquiries about the existence of a complaint but will not make available the complaint or response of the neutral until after an opinion is rendered by the Committee on Ethics.

D. If a neutral is suspended from the registry of neutrals (before or after a final opinion of the Committee on Ethics) or is removed from the registry of neutrals after a final opinion of the Committee on Ethics, the Office of Dispute Resolution will disseminate this information to program directors throughout the state.

E. If a training program is suspended or permanently removed from the list of approved training programs, the Office of Dispute Resolution will remove that program from the list of approved training programs disseminated in response to inquiries concerning training.

F. Once a final opinion is rendered in regard to a complaint, the complaint, response, and opinion will be treated as a matter of public record. A synopsis of the case may be published in the Office of Dispute Resolution's *Symposium*. The name of the neutral will not be included in the synopsis.

G. The confidentiality of a mediation, arbitration, or case evaluation session is deemed waived by the parties to the extent necessary to allow the complainant to fully present his/her case and to allow the neutral to fully respond to the complaint. The waiver relates only to information necessary to deal with the complaint. The Commission, the Committee, and the Office will be sensitive to the need to protect the privacy of all parties to an ADR process to the fullest extent possible commensurate with fairness to the neutral and protection of the public.

H. Information concerning procedures intended to remain confidential, such as a private letter of reprimand in lawyer discipline, will be kept confidential. Neutrals or applicants for registration or renewal of registration who have received private professional discipline will be asked to sign a release so that the surrounding circumstances can be reviewed. This information, as well as information obtained through a criminal background check, will be used only to determine an individual's eligibility for registration or continued registration.

I. Hearings before the Committee and the Commission are private. Any statement made during an ethics hearing before the Committee or the Commission or as part of investigation by the Georgia Office of Dispute Resolution in preparation for a hearing is confidential, not subject to disclosure, and may not be used as evidence in any subsequent administrative or judicial proceeding. Members of the Committee, the Commission, and staff of the Georgia Office of Dispute Resolution may not be subpoenaed or otherwise required to testify concerning an ethics investigation or hearing. Notes and records of members of the Committee, the Commission, or the staff of the Georgia Office of Dispute Resolution are not subject to discovery to the extent that such notes or records pertain to investigation or hearing of an ethical complaint. Documents considered by the Committee, the Commission, and the Office in connection with any ethical proceeding concerning a registered neutral or applicant for registration or renewal of registration may not be subpoenaed from the Committee, the Commission, or the Office. The recording made of the hearing before the Committee is for the benefit of the Committee, the Commission, and the respondent or applicant for registration or renewal of registration and is not available for any other purpose.

Adopted effective May 24, 1999.

IV. IMMUNITY

No member of the Committee on Ethics, the Georgia Commission on Dispute Resolution, the staff of the Georgia Office of Dispute Resolution, or individual reporting to or testifying before the Committee, Commission, or Office will be held liable for civil damages for any statement, action, omission or decision made in the course of any investigation or hearing of an ethics matter unless that statement, action, omission or decision is grossly negligent and made with malice.

Adopted effective May 24, 1999.

UNIFORM SUPERIOR COURT RULES

Effective July 1, 1985

Including Amendments Received Through November 1, 2006

Research Note

Use WESTLAW *to find cases citing a rule. In addition, use* WESTLAW *to search for specific terms or to update a rule; see the GA–RULES and GA–ORDERS Scope screens for further information.*

Amendments to these rules are published, as received, in the South Eastern Reporter 2d *and* Georgia Cases *advance sheets.*

Table of Rules

RULE 1. PREAMBLE

Pursuant to the inherent powers of the Court and Article VI, Section IX, Paragraph I of the Georgia Constitution of 1983, and in order to provide for the speedy, efficient and inexpensive resolution of disputes and prosecutions, these rules are promulgated. It is not the intention, nor shall it be the effect, of these rules to conflict with the Constitution or substantive law, either per se or in individual actions and these rules shall be so construed and in case of conflict shall yield to substantive law.

Amended September 19, 1986.

1.1 Repeal of Local Rules

All local rules of the superior courts except those relating to drawing of jurors by mechanical or electronic means pursuant to OCGA §§ 15–12–40(b) and 15–12–42(b) et seq. shall expire effective December 31, 1994. If any superior court by action of its judges (or failing this, by action of its chief judge) proposes to prevent any local rule from expiring pursuant to Rule 1.1 then a proposal to prevent the local rule from expiring must be presented to the Supreme Court for approval 30 days prior to the expiration date as stated in Rule 1.1. Only those rules reapproved by the Supreme Court on or after December 31, 1994, shall remain in effect after that date. Rules timely resubmitted shall remain in effect until action by the Supreme Court.

Amended effective May 5, 1994.

1.2 Authority to Enact Rules Which Deviate From the Uniform Superior Court Rules

(A) The term "local rules" will no longer be used in the context of the Uniform Superior Court Rules.

(B) Each superior court by action of a majority of its judges (or failing this, by action of its chief judge), from time to time, may propose to make and amend rules which deviate from the Uniform Superior Court Rules provided such proposals are not inconsistent with the Georgia Civil Practice Act, general laws, these Uniform Superior Court Rules, or any directive of the Supreme Court of Georgia. Any such proposals shall be filed with the clerk of the Supreme Court; proposals so submitted shall take effect 30 days after approval by the Supreme Court. It is the intendment of these rules that rules which deviate from the Uniform Superior Court Rules be restricted in scope.

(C) Notwithstanding the expiration of previously approved local rules December 31, 1994 courts may continue to promulgate rules which relate only to internal procedure and do not affect the rights of any party substantially or materially, either to unreasonably delay or deny such rights. These rules, which will be designated "internal operating procedures," do not require the approval of the Supreme Court. "Internal operating procedures," as used in these Uniform Superior Court Rules, are defined as rules which relate to case management, administration, and operation of the court or govern programs which relate to case management, administration, and operation of the court.

(D) The above provisions notwithstanding, each superior court may retain or adopt without specific Supreme Court approval a local rule relating to drawing of jurors by mechanical or electronic means pursuant to OCGA §§ 15–12–40(b) and 15–12–42(b) et seq. and an order establishing guidelines governing excuses from jury duty pursuant to OCGA § 15–12–10.

(E) Notwithstanding these uniform rules, a majority of judges in a circuit may adopt experimental rules applicable to pilot projects, upon approval of the Supreme Court, adequately advertised to the local bar, with copies to the State Bar of Georgia, not to exceed a period of one year, subject to extension for one additional year upon approval of the circuit judges and the Supreme Court. At the end of the second year, any such pilot projects will either be approved by the Supreme Court or will be allowed to sunset. Programs developed under the Alternative Dispute Resolution Rules of the Supreme Court will be approved by the Georgia Commission on Dispute Resolution before attaining permanent status under these rules.

(F) Rules which are approved as deviations from the Uniform Superior Court Rules and internal operating procedures of courts shall be published by the judicial circuit in which the rules are effective. Copies must be made available through the clerk of the superior court of each county in the judicial circuit where the rules are effective. Any amendments to deviations from the Uniform Superior Court Rules or to internal operating procedures must be published and made available through each superior court clerk's office within 15 days of the effective date of the amendment or change.

(G) Internal operating procedures effective in any court must be filed with the Supreme Court even though Supreme Court approval is not needed for these rules.

(H) Any internal operating procedure or proposed deviation from the Uniform Superior Court Rules, or any amendment of either, filed with the Supreme Court shall be accompanied by an explanation of changes sought, with additional material underlined and deleted material stricken through. The submission shall clearly state whether it is intended to be a deviation or an internal operating procedure. The submission shall also explain why it is needed and how it differs from existing rule or procedure.

Amended effective May 5, 1994; April 3, 1998.

1.3 Repeal of Earlier "Rules of the Superior Court"

Each of the "Rules of the Superior Court" set out in (former) Ga.Code Ann. §§ 24–3301 through 24–3389, inclusive, not earlier repealed is hereby expressly repealed.

1.4 Matters of Statewide Concern

The following rules, to be known as "Uniform Superior Court Rules," are to be given statewide application.

1.5 Deviation

These rules are not subject to local deviation except as provided herein. A specific rule may be superseded in a specific action or case or by an order of the court entered in such case explaining the necessity for deviation and served upon the attorneys in the case.

1.6 Amendments

The Council of Superior Court Judges shall have a permanent committee to recommend to the Supreme Court such changes and additions to these rules as may from time to time appear necessary or desirable.

The State Bar of Georgia and the Uniform Rules committee chairpersons for the other classes of courts shall receive notice of the proposed changes and additions and be given the opportunity to comment.

Amended effective March 9, 1989.

1.7 Publication of Rules and Amendments

These rules and any amendments to these rules shall be published in the advance sheets to the Georgia Reports. Unless otherwise provided, the effective date of any amendment to these rules is the date of publication in the advance sheets to the Georgia Reports.

Amended effective June 7, 1990.

RULE 2. DEFINITIONS

2.1 Attorney

The word "attorney" as used in these rules refers to any person admitted to practice in the superior courts of Georgia, and to any person who is permitted, in accordance with law, to represent a party in an action pending in a superior court of the State of Georgia, and to any person proceeding pro se in an action pending in a superior court of this state. The word "attorney" is synonymous with "counsel" in these rules.

Amended effective October 9, 1997.

2.2 Judge

The word "judge" as used in these rules refers to any of the several active judges of the superior courts of Georgia, and to any senior or other judge authorized to serve as a judge of a superior court of this state.

2.3 Clerk

The word "clerk" as used in these rules refers to the clerk of any of the several superior courts in this state and to staff members serving as deputy clerks.

Amended effective October 9, 1997.

2.4 Calendar Clerk

The term "calendar clerk" as used in these rules refers to that person who is charged with the responsibility of setting and scheduling all hearings and trials in actions assigned to a particular judge. Each calendar clerk carries out those duties under the supervision of the assigned judge, or the designee of that judge.

Amended effective October 9, 1997.

2.5 Assigned Judge

The term "assigned judge" as used in these rules refers to the judge to whom an action is assigned in accordance with these rules; or, if the context permits, in circuits having approved local rules permitting a general calendaring system, to the trial judge responsible for the matter at any particular time.

2.6 Non-sexist Pronouns [Deleted]

Deleted effective October 9, 1997.

RULE 3. ASSIGNMENT OF CASES AND ACTIONS

3.1 Method of Assignment

In multi-judge circuits, unless a majority of the judges in a circuit elect to adopt a different system, all actions, civil and criminal, shall be assigned by the clerk of each superior court according to a plan approved by such judges to the end that each judge is allocated an equal number of cases. The clerk shall have no power or discretion in determining the judge to whom any case is assigned; the clerk's duties are ministerial only in this respect and the clerk's responsibility is to carry out the method of assignment established by the judges. The assignment system is designed to prevent any persons choosing the judge to whom an action is to be assigned; all persons are directed to refrain from attempting to affect such assignment in any way. If the order or the timing of filing is a factor in determining case assignment, neither the clerk nor any member of the clerk's staff shall disclose to any person the judge to whom a case is or will be assigned until such time as the case is in fact filed and assigned.

Amended effective October 9, 1997; October 26, 2006.

3.2 Companion and Related Actions

When practical, all actions involving substantially the same parties, or substantially the same subject matter, or substantially the same factual issues, whether pending simultaneously or not, shall be assigned to the same judge. Whenever such action is refiled, or a derivative or companion action is filed or refiled, or a defendant is reindicted on a previous charge, or is indicted on a subsequent charge while still under charges or serving a confinement or probated sentence on a previous action, or co-defendants are indicted separately, such actions shall be assigned to the judge to whom the original action was or is assigned. Generally, such actions will be assigned to the judge to whom the action with the lower action number is assigned.

3.3 Exclusive Control

The judge to whom any action is assigned shall have exclusive control of such action, except as provided in these rules, and no person shall change any assignment except by order of the judge affected and as provided in these rules. In this regard an assigned judge may transfer an assigned action to another judge with the latter's consent in which event the latter becomes the assigned judge.

Amended effective March 9, 1989.

3.4 Local Authority

The method of assignment and the procedures necessary for an orderly transition from one calendaring system to another shall be established by local rules of each multi-judge circuit. All such rules shall be adequately published to the local bar; copies shall be filed with the respective clerk(s) and with the Supreme Court of Georgia.

RULE 4. ATTORNEYS—APPEARANCE, WITHDRAWAL AND DUTIES

4.1 Prohibition on Ex Parte Communications

Except as authorized by law or by rule, judges shall neither initiate nor consider ex parte communications by interested parties or their attorneys concerning a pending or impending proceeding.

4.2 Entry of Appearance and Pleadings

No attorney shall appear in that capacity before a superior court until the attorney has entered an appearance by filing a signed entry of appearance form or by filing a signed pleading in a pending action. An entry of appearance and all pleadings shall state:

(1) the style and number of the case;

(2) the identity of the party for whom the appearance is made; and

(3) the name, assigned state bar number, and current office address and telephone number of the attorney.

The filing of any pleading shall contain the information required by this paragraph and shall constitute an appearance by the person(s) signing such pleading, unless otherwise specified by the court. The filing of a signed entry of appearance alone shall not be a substitute for the filing of an answer or any other required pleading. The filing of an indictment or accusation shall constitute an entry of appearance by the district attorney.

Any attorney who has been admitted to practice in this state but who fails to maintain active membership in good standing in the State Bar of Georgia and who makes or files any appearance or pleading in a superior court of this state while not in good standing shall be subject to the contempt powers of the court.

Within forty-eight hours after being retained, an attorney shall mail to the court and opposing counsel or file with the court the entry of appearance in the pending matter. Failure to timely file shall not prohibit the appearance and representation by said counsel.

Amended effective March 9, 1989; May 26, 1994.

4.3 Withdrawal

(1) An attorney appearing of record in any action pending in any superior court, who wishes to withdraw as counsel for any party therein, shall submit a written request to an appropriate judge of the court for an order of court permitting such withdrawal. Such request shall state that the attorney has given due written notice to the affected client respecting such intention to withdraw 10 days (or such lesser time as the court may permit in any specific instance) prior to submitting the request to the court or that such withdrawal is with the client's consent. Such request will be granted unless in the judge's discretion to do so would delay the trial of the action or otherwise interrupt the orderly operation of the court or be manifestly unfair to the client. The attorney requesting an order permitting withdrawal shall give notice to opposing counsel and shall file with the clerk in each such action and serve upon the client, personally or at that client's last known address, a notice which shall contain at least the following information:

(A) That the attorney wishes to withdraw;

(B) That the court retains jurisdiction of the action;

(C) That the client has the burden of keeping the court informed respecting where notices, pleadings or other papers may be served;

(D) That the client has the obligation to prepare for trial or hire other counsel to prepare for trial when the trial date has been set;

(E) That if the client fails or refuses to meet these burdens, the client may suffer adverse consequences, including, in criminal cases, bond forfeiture and arrest;

(F) The dates of any scheduled proceedings, including trial, and that holding of such proceedings will not be affected by the withdrawal of counsel;

(G) That service of notices may be made upon the client at the client's last known address, and,

(H) If the client is a corporation, that a corporation may only be represented in court by an attorney, that an attorney must sign all pleadings submitted to the court, and that a corporate officer may not represent the corporation in court unless that officer is also an attorney licensed to practice law in the state of Georgia;

(I) Unless the withdrawal is with the client's consent, the client's right to object within 10 days of the date of the notice.

The attorney seeking to withdraw shall prepare a written notification certificate stating that the above notification requirements have been met, the manner by which such notification was given to the client and the client's last known address and telephone number. The notification certificate shall be filed with the court and a copy mailed to the client and all other parties. The client shall have 10 days prior to entry of an order permitting withdrawal or such lesser time as the court may permit within which to file objections to the withdrawal. After the entry of an order permitting withdrawal, the client shall be notified by the withdrawing attorney of the effective date of the withdrawal; thereafter all notices or other papers may be served on the party directly by mail at the last known address of the party until new counsel enters an appearance.

(2) When an attorney has already filed an entry of appearance and the client wishes to substitute counsel, it will not be necessary for the former attorney to comply with rule 4.3(a). Instead, the former attorney may file with the clerk of court a notice of substitution of counsel signed by the party and the former attorney. The notice shall contain the style of the case, the name, address, phone number and bar number of the substitute counsel. A copy of the notice shall be served on the substitute counsel, opposing counsel or

party if unrepresented, and the assigned judge. No other or further action shall be required by the former attorney to withdraw from representing the party. The substitution shall not delay any proceeding or hearing in the case.

The notice may be in substantially the following form:

IN THE SUPERIOR COURT OF ______ COUNTY
STATE OF GEORGIA

SAM SPADE,)
)
Plaintiff,)
) CIVIL ACTION
v.)
) FILE NO. 99–CV–0000
DAVID ROBICHEAUX,)
)
Defendant.)

NOTICE OF SUBSTITUTION OF COUNSEL

Please substitute (name of substitute counsel) as counsel for (name of party) in this case.

Substitute counsel's address, phone number and bar number are as follows:

____

All further pleadings, orders and notices should be sent to substitute counsel.

This ______ day of ______, ____.

signature	signature
Name of former attorney	Name of party
Address	Address
Phone number	Phone number

CERTIFICATE OF SERVICE

Certificate of service on: substitute counsel, opposing counsel or party, assigned judge.

Amended effective October 9, 1997; amended November 4, 1999, effective December 16, 1999.

4.4 Admission Pro Hac Vice

A. Definitions

1. A "Domestic Lawyer" is a person not admitted to practice law in this state but who is admitted in another state or territory of the United States or of the District of Columbia and not disbarred or suspended from practice in any jurisdiction.

2. A Domestic Lawyer is "eligible" for admission *pro hac vice* if that lawyer:

a. lawfully practices solely on behalf of the lawyer's employer and its commonly owned organizational affiliates, regardless of where such lawyer may reside or work; or

b. neither resides nor is regularly employed at an office in this state; or

c. resides in this state but (i) lawfully practices from offices in one or more other states and (ii) practices no more than temporarily in this state, whether pursuant to admission *pro hac vice* or in other lawful ways.

3. A "client" is a person or entity for whom the Domestic Lawyer has rendered services or by whom the lawyer has been retained prior to the lawyer's performance of services in this state.

4. "This state" refers to Georgia. This Rule does not govern proceedings before a federal court or federal agency located in this state unless that body adopts or incorporates this Rule.

B. Authority of Court To Permit Appearance By Domestic Lawyer

1. Court Proceeding. A court of this state may, in its discretion, admit an eligible Domestic Lawyer retained to appear in a particular proceeding pending before such court to appear *pro hac vice* as counsel in that proceeding.

C. In–State Lawyer's Duties. When a Domestic Lawyer appears for a client in a proceeding pending in this state, either in the role of co-counsel of record with the in-state lawyer, or in an advisory or consultative role, the in-state lawyer who is co-counsel or counsel of record for that client in the proceeding remains responsible to the client and responsible for the conduct of the proceeding before the court or agency. It is the duty of the in-state lawyer to advise the client of the in-state lawyer's independent judgment on contemplated actions in the proceeding if that judgment differs from that of the Domestic Lawyer.

D. Application Procedure

1. Verified Application. An eligible Domestic Lawyer seeking to appear in a proceeding pending in this state as counsel *pro hac vice* shall file a verified application with the court where the litigation is filed. The application shall be served on all parties who have appeared in the case and the Office of General Counsel of the State Bar of Georgia. The application shall include proof of service. The court has the discretion to grant or deny the application summarily if there is no opposition.

2. Objection to Application. The Office of General Counsel of the State Bar of Georgia or a party to the proceeding may file an objection to the application or seek the court's imposition of conditions to its being granted. The Office of General Counsel or objecting party must file with its objection a verified affidavit containing or describing information establishing a factual basis for the objection. The Office of General Counsel or objecting party may seek denial of the application or modification of it. If the application has already been granted, the Office of General Counsel

or objecting party may move that the *pro hac vice* admission be withdrawn.

3. Standard for Admission and Revocation of Admission. The court has discretion as to whether to grant applications for admission *pro hac vice* and to set the terms and conditions of such admission. An application ordinarily should be granted unless the court or agency finds reason to believe that such admission:

a. may be detrimental to the prompt, fair and efficient administration of justice,

b. may be detrimental to legitimate interests of parties to the proceedings other than the client(s) the applicant proposes to represent,

c. one or more of the clients the applicant proposes to represent may be at risk of receiving inadequate representation and cannot adequately appreciate that risk,

d. the applicant has engaged in such frequent appearances as to constitute regular practice in this state, or

e. should be denied, if that applicant had, prior to the application, filed or appeared in an action in the courts of this State without having secured approval pursuant to the Uniform Superior Court Rules.

4. Revocation of Admission. Admission to appear as counsel *pro hac vice* in a proceeding may be revoked for any of the reasons listed in Section D.3 above.

E. Application

1. Required Information. An application shall state the information listed on Appendix A to this rule. The applicant may also include any other matters supporting admission *pro hac vice*.

2. Application Fee. An applicant for permission to appear as counsel *pro hac vice* under this Rule shall pay a non-refundable fee as set by the Investigative Panel of the State Bar of Georgia at the time of filing the application.

3. Exemption for *Pro Bono* Representation. An applicant shall not be required to pay the fee established by E.2 above if the applicant will not charge an attorney fee to the client(s) and is:

a. employed or associated with a *pro bono* project or nonprofit legal services organization in a civil case involving the client(s) of such programs; or

b. involved in a criminal case or a *habeas* proceeding for an indigent defendant.

F. Authority of the Office of General Counsel of the State Bar of Georgia and Court: Application of Ethical Rules, Discipline, Contempt, and Sanctions

1. Authority over Domestic Lawyer and Applicant.

a. During pendency of an application for admission *pro hac vice* and upon the granting of such application, a Domestic Lawyer submits to the authority of the courts and the Office of General Counsel of the State Bar of Georgia of this state for all conduct relating in any way to the proceeding in which the Domestic Lawyer seeks to appear. The applicant or Domestic Lawyer who has obtained *pro hac vice* admission in a proceeding submits to this authority for all that lawyer's conduct (i) within the state while the proceeding is pending or (ii) arising out of or relating to the application or the proceeding. An applicant or Domestic Lawyer who has *pro hac vice* authority for a proceeding may be disciplined in the same manner as an in-state lawyer.

b. The court's and Office General Counsel's authority includes, without limitation, the court's and State Bar of Georgia's rules of professional conduct, contempt and sanctions orders, local court rules, and court policies and procedures.

2. Familiarity With Rules. An applicant shall become familiar with the Georgia Rules of Professional Conduct, local court rules, and policies and procedures of the court before which the applicant seeks to practice.

G. Temporary Practice. An out-of-state lawyer will only be eligible for admission *pro hac vice*, or to practice in another lawful way only on a temporary basis.

H. The conflicts of the domestic lawyer shall not delay any deadlines, depositions, mediation, hearings, or trials in connection with the case for which admission has been granted.

APPENDIX A

The Domestic Lawyer's application shall include:

1. the applicant's residence and business address;

2. the name, address and phone number of each client sought to be represented;

3. the courts before which applicant has been admitted to practice and the respective period(s) of admission;

4. whether the applicant (a) has been denied admission *pro hac vice* in this state, (b) had admission *pro hac vice* revoked in this state, or (c) has otherwise formally been disciplined or sanctioned by any court in this state. If so, specify the nature of the allegations; the name of the authority bringing such proceedings; the caption of the proceedings, the date filed, and what findings were made and what action was taken in connection with those proceedings;

5. whether any formal, written disciplinary proceeding has ever been brought against the applicant by a disciplinary authority in any other jurisdiction within the last five (5) years and, as to each such proceeding: the nature of the allegations; the name of

the person or authority bringing such proceedings; the date the proceedings were initiated and finally concluded; the style of the proceedings; and the findings made and actions taken in connection with those proceedings;

6. whether the applicant has been held formally in contempt or otherwise sanctioned by any court in a written order in the last five (5) years for disobedience to its rules or orders, and, if so: the nature of the allegations; the name of the court before which such proceedings were conducted; the date of the contempt order or sanction, the caption of the proceedings, and the substance of the court's rulings (a copy of the written order or transcript of the oral rulings shall be attached to the application);

7. the name and address of each court or agency and a full identification of each proceeding in which the applicant has filed an application to appear *pro hac vice* in this state within the preceding two years; the date of each application; and the outcome of the application;

8. an averment as to the applicant's familiarity with the Georgia Rules of Professional Conduct, local rules and court procedures of the court before which the applicant seeks to practice; and

9. the name, address, telephone number and bar number of an active member in good standing of the bar of this state who will sponsor the applicant's *pro hac vice* request. The bar member shall appear of record together with the Domestic Lawyer.

The Domestic Lawyer's application may provide the following optional information:

10. the applicant's prior or continuing representation in other matters of one or more of the clients the applicant proposes to represent and any relationship between such other matter(s) and the proceeding for which applicant seeks admission.

11. any special experience, expertise, or other factor deemed to make it particularly desirable that the applicant be permitted to represent the client(s) the applicant proposes to represent in the particular cause.

Amended effective October 9, 1997; November 10, 2005.

4.5 Entries of Appearance and Withdrawals by Members or Employees of Law Firms or Professional Corporations

The entry of an appearance or request for withdrawal by an attorney who is a member or an employee of a law firm or professional corporation shall relieve the other members or employees of the same law firm or professional corporation from the necessity of filing additional entries of appearance or requests for withdrawal in the same action.

4.6 To Notify of Representation

In any matter pending in a superior court, promptly upon agreeing to represent any client, the new attorney shall notify the appropriate calendar clerk in writing (and, in criminal actions, the district attorney; and, in civil actions the opposing attorney(s)) of the fact of such representation, the name of the client, the name and number of the action, the attorney's firm name, office address and telephone number.

Each such attorney shall notify the calendar clerk (and, in criminal actions, the district attorney; and, in civil actions, the opposing attorney(s)) immediately upon any change of representation, name, address or telephone number.

4.7 To Utilize Assigned Judge

Attorneys shall not present to any judge any matter or issue in any action which has been assigned to another judge, except under the most compelling circumstances. In that event, any attorney doing so shall first advise the judge to whom the matter is presented that the action is assigned to another judge. Counsel shall also inform the assigned judge as soon as possible that the matter was presented to another judge.

4.8 To Notify of Related Cases

At any time an attorney is counsel in any action which the attorney knows is or may be related to another action either previously or presently pending in and assigned to a particular judge of a superior court in the same circuit involving some or all of the same subject matter, or some or all of the same factual issues, such attorney immediately shall so advise the judges involved, who will then make an appropriate determination as to which judge the action or actions should be assigned.

Amended effective October 9, 1997.

4.9 To Notify of Previous Presentation to Another Judge

Attorneys shall not present to a judge any matter which has been previously presented to another judge without first advising the former of the fact and result of such previous presentation.

4.10 To Notify of Settlements and Dismissals

Immediately upon the settlement or dismissal of any civil action the involved attorneys shall notify the assigned judge and, where appropriate, the calendar clerk of such event.

4.11 Attorneys: Appearance, Withdrawal and Duties; to Attend and Remain

Subject to the provisions of Rule 17, attorneys having matters on calendars, or who are otherwise directed to do so, unless excused by the court, are required to be in court at the call of the matter and to remain until otherwise directed by the court. Should the judge excuse counsel from the courtroom before the matter is concluded such attorney(s) shall return as directed. So that the court can provide timely direction, counsel shall contact the trial court daily during the remainder of any ongoing calendar. Failure of any attorney in this respect shall subject that attorney to the contempt powers of the court.

Amended effective October 9, 1997; November 10, 2005.

4.12 Binding Authority

Attorneys of record have apparent authority to enter into agreements on behalf of their clients in civil actions. Oral agreements, if established, are enforceable.

Amended effective October 9, 1997.

RULE 5. DISCOVERY IN CIVIL ACTIONS[1]

[1] Rule 5 shall not be applied in any case prior to January 1, 1986.

5.1 Prompt Completion

In order for a party to utilize the court's compulsory process to compel discovery, any desired discovery procedures must first be commenced promptly, pursued diligently and completed without unnecessary delay and within 6 months after the filing of the answer. At any time, the court, in its discretion, may extend, reopen or shorten the time to utilize the court's compulsory process to compel discovery.

Amended effective January 18, 1990; January 31, 1991; designated as Rule 5.1 effective November 12, 1992.

5.2 Filing Requirements

(1) Depositions and other original discovery material shall not be filed with the court unless or until required by the provisions of OCGA § 9–11–29.1(a)(1)–(5).

(2) A party serving Interrogatories, Requests for Production of Documents, Requests for Admission and Answers or responses thereto upon counsel, a party or a non-party shall file with the court a certificate indicating the pleading which was served, the date of service (or that the same has been delivered for service with the summons) and the persons served.

Adopted effective November 12, 1992.

5.3 Depositions Upon Oral Examination—Duration

Unless otherwise authorized by the court or stipulated by the parties, a deposition is limited to one day of seven hours. The court must allow additional time if needed for a fair examination of the deponent or if the deponent or another person or other circumstance impedes or delays the examination.

Adopted effective May 8, 2003.

RULE 6. MOTIONS IN CIVIL ACTIONS

6.1 Filing

In civil actions every motion made prior to trial, except those consented to by all parties, when filed shall include or be accompanied by citations of supporting authorities and, where allegations of unstipulated fact are relied upon, supporting affidavits, or citations to evidentiary materials of record. In circuits utilizing an individual assignment system, the clerk shall promptly upon filing furnish a copy provided by the attorney of such motions and related materials to the judge.

6.2 Reply

Unless otherwise ordered by the judge, each party opposing a motion shall serve and file a response, reply memorandum, affidavits, or other responsive material not later than 30 days after service of the motion.

[In State Court, see State Court Rule 6.2.]

6.3 Hearing

Unless otherwise ordered by the court, all motions in civil actions, including those for summary judgment, shall be decided by the court without oral hearing, except motions for new trial and motions for judgment notwithstanding the verdict.

However, oral argument on a motion for summary judgment shall be permitted upon written request made in a separate pleading bearing the caption of the case and entitled "Request for Oral Hearing," and provided that such pleading is filed with the motion for summary judgment or filed not later than five (5) days after the time for response.

Amended May 7, 1987; amended effective November 9, 1995.

6.4 Failure to Make Discovery and Motions to Compel Discovery

(A) Motions to compel discovery in accordance with OCGA § 9–11–37 shall:

(1) Quote verbatim or attach a copy as an exhibit of each interrogatory, request for admission, or request for production to which objection is taken;

(2) Include the specific objection or response said to be insufficient;

(3) Include the grounds assigned for the objection (if not apparent from the objection); and,

(4) Include the reasons assigned as supporting the motion. Such objections and grounds shall be addressed to the specific interrogatory, request for admission, or request for production and may not be made generally.

(B) Prior to filing any motion seeking resolution of a discovery dispute, counsel for the moving party shall confer with counsel for the opposing party in a good faith effort to resolve the matters involved. At the time of filing the motion, counsel shall also file a statement certifying that such conference has occurred and that the effort to resolve by agreement the issues raised failed. This rule also applies to motions to quash, motions for protective order and cases where no discovery has been provided.

Amended effective November 28, 1996.

6.5 Motions for Summary Judgment

Upon any motion for summary judgment pursuant to the Georgia Civil Practice Act, there shall be annexed to the notice of motion a separate, short and concise statement of each theory of recovery and of each of the material facts as to which the moving party contends there is no genuine issue to be tried. The response shall include a separate, short and concise statement of each of the material facts as to which it is contended there exists a genuine issue to be tried.

6.6 Time for Filing Summary Judgment Motions

Motions for summary judgment shall be filed sufficiently early so as not to delay the trial. No trial shall be continued by reason of the delayed filing of a motion for summary judgment.

6.7 Motions in Emergencies

Upon written notice and good cause shown, the assigned judge may shorten or waive the time requirement applicable to emergency motions, except motions for summary judgment, or grant an immediate hearing on any matter requiring such expedited procedure. The motion shall set forth in detail the necessity for such expedited procedure.

RULE 7. PRE–TRIAL CONFERENCES

7.1 Civil

The assigned judge may set pre-trial conferences sua sponte or upon motion. In scheduling actions for pre-trial conferences the court shall give consideration to the nature of the action, its complexity and the reasonable time requirement for preparation for pre-trial. In the event a pre-trial conference is ordered, the following shall apply.

A calendar will be published or a written order issued specifying the time and place for the pre-trial conference. The court will consider the issues stated in Rule 16 of the Civil Practice Act (OCGA § 9–11–16) among others. Subject to the provisions of Rule 17, the pre-trial hearing shall be attended by the attorneys who will actually try the action; with the consent of the court, another attorney of record in the action may attend if authorized to define the issues and enter into stipulations. At the commencement of the pre-trial conference, or prior thereto upon written order of the court, counsel for each party shall present to the court a written proposed pre-trial order in substantially the form required by the rules. Failure of counsel to appear at the pre-trial conference without legal excuse or to present a proposed pre-trial order shall authorize the court to remove the action from any trial calendar, enter such pre-trial order as the court shall deem appropriate, or impose any other appropriate sanction, except dismissal of the action with prejudice.

7.2 Civil Pre-Trial Order

At the pre-trial conference, or prior to that day if specified in the pre-trial calendar, counsel for each party shall have prepared and shall file with the court a proposed pre-trial order in substantially the following form:

IN THE SUPERIOR COURT OF ______
COUNTY
STATE OF GEORGIA

(STYLE OF CASE) CIVIL ACTION, CASE NO. ____

PRE–TRIAL ORDER

The following constitutes a Pre-Trial Order entered in the above-styled case after conference with counsel for the parties:

(1) The name, address and phone number of the attorneys who will conduct the trial are as follows:

Plaintiff ______________________

Defendant ______________________

Other ______________________

(2) The estimated time required for trial is ______

(3) There are no motions or other matters pending for consideration by the court except as follows: ______

(4) The jury will be qualified as to relationship with the following: ______

(5) a. All discovery has been completed, unless otherwise noted, and the court will not consider any further motions to compel discovery except for good cause shown. The parties, however, shall be permitted to take depositions of any person(s) for the preservation of evidence for use at trial.

b. Unless otherwise noted, the names of the parties as shown in the caption to this order are correct and complete and there is no question by any party as to the misjoinder or nonjoinder of any parties.

(6) The following is the Plaintiff's brief and succinct outline of the case and contentions: (USE SPACE AS NEEDED) ______

(7) The following is the Defendant's brief and succinct outline of the case and contentions: (USE SPACE AS NEEDED) ______

(8) The issues for determination by the jury are as follows: ______

(9) Specifications of negligence including applicable code sections are as follows: ______

(10) If the case is based on a contract, either oral or written, the terms of the contract are as follows (or, the contract is attached as an Exhibit to this order): ______

(11) The types of damages and the applicable measure of those damages are stated as follows: ______

(12) If the case involves divorce, each party shall present to the court at the pre-trial conference the affidavits required by Rule 24.2.

(13) The following facts are stipulated: ______

(14) The following is a list of all documentary and physical evidence that will be tendered at the trial by the Plaintiff or Defendant. Unless noted, the parties have stipulated as to the authenticity of the documents listed and the exhibits listed may be admitted without further proof of authenticity. All exhibits shall be marked by counsel prior to trial so as not to delay the trial before the jury.

a. By the Plaintiff: ______

b. By the Defendant: ______

(15) Special authorities relied upon by Plaintiff relating to peculiar evidentiary or other legal questions are as follows: ______

(16) Special authorities relied upon by Defendant relating to peculiar evidentiary or other legal questions are as follows: ______

(17) All requests to charge anticipated at the time of trial will be filed in accordance with Rule 10.3.

(18) The testimony of the following persons may be introduced by depositions: ______

Any objection to the depositions or questions or arguments in the depositions shall be called to the attention of the court prior to trial.

(19) The following are lists of witnesses the

a. Plaintiff will have present at trial: ______

b. Plaintiff may have present at trial: ______

c. Defendant will have present at trial: ______

d. Defendant may have present at trial: ______

Opposing counsel may rely on representation that the designated party will have a witness present unless notice to the contrary is given in sufficient time prior to trial to allow the other party to subpoena the witness or obtain his testimony by other means.

(20) The form of all possible verdicts to be considered by the jury are as follows: ______

(21) a. The possibilities of settling the case are: ______

b. The parties do/do not want the case reported.

c. The cost of take-down will be paid by: ______

d. Other matters:

Submitted by:

______

______

It is hereby ordered that the foregoing, including the attachments thereto, constitutes the PRE–TRIAL ORDER in the above case and supersedes the pleadings which may not be further amended except by order of the court to prevent manifest injustice.

This _____ day of _____, 19____.

____
Judge, Superior Court
_______ Judicial Circuit

Amended effective October 9, 1997.

7.3 Interpreters

Any proposed pre-trial order submitted by any party shall designate any witnesses whose testimony will need the services of an interpreter and the language, including sign language for the deaf, for which the interpreter is required. If known, the name, address, and telephone number of the interpreter or interpreting service intended to be used shall be listed. If this information is not known at the time the pre-trial order is signed, it shall be promptly provided to court and opposing counsel once known. Where notice is not provided, the Court may, among other sanctions, refuse the use of any non-certified interpreter and then exclude the use of the witness's testimony if the witness cannot readily communicate in English.

Adopted effective November 8, 2001.

7.4 Criminal Matters

At or after the arraignment, pre-trial conferences may be scheduled as the judge deems appropriate. Such pre-trial conferences shall be attended by the attorneys who will actually try the case. At the pre-trial conference:

(A) All motions, special pleas and demurrers not previously determined shall be presented to and heard by the judge. Any and all pending motions not called to the judge's attention at the pre-trial conference shall be deemed to have been abandoned and waived; however, at the judge's discretion and for good cause, such matters may subsequently be heard. At the discretion of the judge, the disposition of any matter brought before the court may be postponed.

(B) To the extent possible without revealing confidential trial strategies, the attorneys shall inform the judge of probable evidentiary problems known to them or any other matter which might delay the trial so the judge may take any necessary action before the trial to avoid a delay.

(C) If possible, the judge shall set a firm trial date.

(D) Counsel are encouraged to enter into reasonable stipulations.

Amended effective October 9, 1997; renumbered from 7.3 effective November 8, 2001.

RULE 8. CIVIL JURY TRIAL CALENDAR

8.1 Scheduling Trials

The assigned judge has the sole responsibility for setting hearings in all actions assigned to that judge, for the scheduling of all trials in such actions and for the publication of all necessary calendars in advance of trial dates. In scheduling actions for trial the assigned judge shall give consideration to the nature of the action, its complexity and the reasonable time requirements of the action for trial. It is the intendment of these rules that no matter be allowed to languish, and the assigned judge is responsible for the orderly movement and disposition of all assigned matters.

Amended effective October 9, 1997.

8.2 Ready List

All actions ready for trial in accordance with OCGA § 9–11–40 shall be placed upon a list of actions ready for final jury trial to be maintained as a "ready list" by the calendar clerk.

Actions may be placed on the ready list by:

(A) The assigned judge upon notice to the parties; or

(B) A party, after the entry of a pre-trial order, upon notice to the other parties.

Except for cause, actions shall be placed on the ready list in chronological order in accordance with filing dates, except that actions previously on the ready list shall retain their superior position; however, actions entitled thereto by statute shall be given precedence.

8.3 Trial Calendar

The calendar clerk shall prepare a trial calendar from the actions appearing on the ready list, in the order appearing on such list. The calendar shall state the place of trial and the date and time during which the actions shall be tried. The trial calendar shall be delivered to the clerk of the court and distributed or published a sufficient period of time, but not less than 20 days, prior to the session of court at which the actions listed thereon are to be tried. [In State Court, see State Court Rule 8.3.]

8.4 Trial Date

The parties and counsel in the first 10 actions on the published trial calendar shall appear ready for trial on the date specified unless otherwise directed by the assigned judge. Parties in all other actions on the calendar are expected to be ready for trial but may contact the calendar clerk to obtain:

(A) A specific date and time for trial during the trial term specified in the calendar; or

(B) Permission to await the call by the calendar clerk of the action for trial upon reasonable notice to counsel.

Amended effective March 9, 1989.

8.5 Continuance After Scheduled for Trial

Continuances will not be granted merely by agreement of counsel. Actions will not be removed from a published trial calendar except by court direction upon such terms as reasonably may be imposed, including the possible imposition of a penalty of up to $50 upon the moving party if, absent statutory grounds or good cause, a motion for continuance of an action is first made within 5 days of the trial week scheduled.

8.6 Special Settings

Special settings of actions for jury trial are not favored.

RULE 9. TELEPHONE AND VIDEO–CONFERENCING

9.1 Telephone Conferencing

The trial court on its own motion or upon the request of any party may in its discretion conduct pre–trial or post–trial proceedings in civil actions by telephone conference with attorneys for all affected parties. The trial judge may specify:

(A) The time and the person who will initiate the conference;

(B) The party which is to incur the initial expense of the conference call, or the apportionment of such costs among the parties, while retaining the discretion to make an adjustment of such costs upon final resolution of the case by taxing same as part of the costs; and

(C) Any other matter or requirement necessary to accomplish or facilitate the telephone conference.

Adopted effective July 15, 2004.

9.2. Video–Conferencing

(A) The following matters may be conducted by video–conference:

1. Determination of indigence and appointment of counsel;
2. Hearings on appearance and appeal bonds;
3. Initial appearance hearings;
4. Probable cause hearings;
5. Applications for arrest warrants;
6. Applications for search warrants;
7. Arraignment or waiver of arraignment;
8. Pretrial diversion and post–sentencing compliance hearings;
9. Entry of pleas in criminal cases;
10. Impositions of sentences upon pleas of guilty or *nolo contendere*;
11. Probation revocation hearings in felony cases in which the probationer admits the violation and in all misdemeanor cases;
12. Post–sentencing proceedings in criminal cases;
13. Acceptance of special pleas of insanity (incompetency to stand trial);
14. Situations involving inmates with highly sensitive medical problems or who pose a high security risk; and
15. Testimony of youthful witnesses;
16. *Ex–parte* applications for Temporary Protective Orders under the Family Violence Act and the Stalking Statute;
17. Appearances of interpreters;

Notwithstanding any other provisions of this rule, a judge may order a defendant's personal appearance in court for any hearing.

(B) Confidential Attorney–Client Communication. Provision shall be made to preserve the confidentiality of attorney–client communications and privilege in accordance with Georgia law. In all criminal proceedings, the defendant and defense counsel shall be provided with a private means of communications when in different locations.

(C) Witnesses. In any pending matter, a witness may testify via video conference. Any party desiring to call a witness by video conference shall file a notice of intention to present testimony by video conference at least thirty (30) days prior to the date scheduled for such testimony. Any other party may file an objection to the testimony of a witness by video conference within ten (10) days of the filing of the notice of intention. In civil matters, the discretion to allow testimony via video conference shall rest with the trial judge. In any criminal matter, a timely objection shall be sustained; however, such objection shall act as a motion for continuance and a waiver of any speedy trial demand.

(D) Recording of Hearings. A record of any proceedings conducted by video conference shall be made in the same manner as all such similar proceedings not conducted by video conference. However, upon the consent of all parties, that portion of the proceedings conducted by video conference may be recorded by an audio–visual recording system and such recording shall be part of the record of the case and transmitted to courts of appeal as if part of a transcript.

(E) Technical Standards. Any video–conferencing system utilized under this rule must conform to the following minimum requirements:

1. All participants must be able to see, hear, and communicate with each other simultaneously;

2. All participants must be able to see, hear, and otherwise observe any physical evidence or exhibits presented during the proceeding, either by video, facsimile, or other method;

3. Video quality must be adequate to allow participants to observe each other's demeanor and nonverbal communications; and

4. The location from which the trial judge is presiding shall be accessible to the public to the same extent as such proceeding would if not conducted by video conference. The court shall accommodate any request by interested parties to observe the entire proceeding.

Adopted effective July 15, 2004.

RULE 10. TRIALS

10.1 Voir Dire

The court may propound, or cause to be propounded by counsel such questions of the jurors as provided in OCGA § 15–12–133; however, the form, time required and number of such questions is within the discretion of the court. The court may require that questions be asked once only to the full array of the jurors, rather than to every juror—one at a time—provided that the question be framed and the response given in a manner that will provide the propounder with an individual response prior to the interposition of challenge. Hypothetical questions are discouraged, but may be allowed in the discretion of the court. It is improper to ask how a juror would act in certain contingencies or on a certain hypothetical state of facts. No question shall be framed so as to require a response from a juror which might amount to a prejudgment of the action. Questions calling for an opinion by a juror on matters of law are improper. The court will exclude questions which have been answered in substance previously by the same juror. It is discretionary with the court to permit examination of each juror without the presence of the remainder of the panel. Objections to the mode and conduct of voir dire must be raised promptly or they will be regarded as waived.

In cases in which the death penalty is sought, the trial judge shall address all *Witherspoon* and reverse–*Witherspoon* questions to prospective jurors individually. Prior to ruling upon any motion to strike a juror under *Witherspoon*, the trial judge shall confer with counsel for the state and for the accused as to any additional inquiries. Failure to object to the court's ruling on whether or not a juror is qualified shall be a waiver of any such objection.

Amended effective October 9, 1997.

10.2 Opening Statements in Criminal Matters

The district attorney may make an opening statement prior to the introduction of evidence. This statement shall be limited to expected proof by legally admissible evidence. Defense counsel may make an opening statement immediately after the state's opening statement and prior to introduction of evidence, or following the conclusion of the state's presentation of evidence. Defense counsel's statement shall be restricted to expected proof by legally admissible evidence, or the lack of evidence.

10.3 Requests and Exceptions to Charge

All requests to charge shall be numbered consecutively on separate sheets of paper and submitted to the court in duplicate by counsel for all parties at the commencement of trial, unless otherwise provided by pre-trial order; provided, however, that additional requests may be submitted to cover unanticipated points which arise thereafter.

10.4 Excusals from Courtroom

During the course of a proceeding no one except the judge may excuse from the courtroom a party, a witness (including one who has testified), or counsel.

RULE 11. SELECTION OF JURIES

After completion of the examination of jurors upon their voir dire, the parties and their counsel shall be entitled, upon request, to 15 minutes to prepare for jury selection; thereafter, during the selection of jurors, the court in its discretion, upon first warning counsel, may restrict to not less than 1 minute the time within which each party may exercise a peremptory challenge; a party shall forfeit a challenge by failing to exercise it within the time allowed.

Amended effective October 9, 1997.

RULE 12. VOLUNTARY DISMISSAL OF ACTIONS

If a civil action is voluntarily dismissed (other than as a result of final settlement agreement, the terms of which are dictated, in court or in chambers, into the record) after the trial jury has been empaneled, all court costs including juror fees incurred for all panels from which the trial jury was selected shall be taxed against the dismissing party.

RULE 13. ARGUMENTS

13.1 Time Limitations

Counsel shall be limited in their arguments as follows:

(A) Felony cases punishable by the death penalty or life in prison—2 hours each side.

(B) Any other felony case—1 hour each side.

(C) Misdemeanor case—30 minutes each side.

(D) Civil cases other than appeals from magistrate courts—1 hour each side.

(E) Appeals from magistrate courts—30 minutes each side.

Amended effective Sept. 2, 1999.

13.2 Extensions

Before arguments begin, counsel may apply to the court for an extension of the time prescribed for argument. The applicant shall state the reason that additional time is needed; the court in its discretion may grant extensions.

13.3 Number of Arguments

Not more than two attorneys shall be permitted to argue any case for any party except by leave of court; in no event shall more than one attorney for each party be heard in concluding argument.

13.4 Conclusion

In civil actions, where the burden of proof rests with the plaintiff, the plaintiff is entitled to the opening and concluding arguments except that if the defendant introduces no evidence or admits a prima facie case, then the defendant shall be entitled to open and conclude.

Amended effective October 9, 1997.

RULE 14. DISMISSAL

On its own motion or upon motion of the opposite party, the court may dismiss without prejudice any civil action, or where appropriate, any pleading filed on behalf of any party upon the failure to properly respond to the call of the action for trial or other proceeding. In civil actions or criminal cases the court may adjudge any attorney in contempt for failure to appear without legal excuse upon the call of any proceeding.

RULE 15. DEFAULT JUDGMENTS

The party seeking entry of a default judgment in any action shall certify to the court the date and type of service effected and that no defensive pleading has been filed by the defendant as shown by court records. This certificate shall be in writing and must be attached to the proposed default judgment when presented to the judge for signature. [In State Court, see State Court Rule 15.

Amended effective May 8, 2003.

15.1 Garnishments

In accordance with OCGA § 18–4–61(5), the clerk of superior court is authorized to supervise initiation of the garnishment proceedings and the affidavit, provided the clerk determines:

(A) That the affidavit is on personal knowledge and contains all elements required by Georgia law;

(B) That the garnishment proceedings are carried out through the use of proper forms in the filing of garnishments and in accord with Georgia law;

(C) That any questionable matter concerning these procedures be presented to the presiding judge for determination and in all cases a judge's facsimile signature may be affixed to an affidavit of garnishment as determined by the presiding judge.

Rule 15.1 adopted effective January 31, 1991.

RULE 16. LEAVES OF ABSENCE

16.1 Leaves for Thirty (30) Calendar Days or Less

An attorney of record shall be entitled to a leave of absence for thirty days or less from court appearance in pending matters which are neither on a published calendar for court appearance, nor noticed for a hearing during the requested time, by submitting to the clerk of the court at least thirty (30) calendar days prior to the effective date for the proposed leave, a written notice containing:

(a) a list of the actions to be protected, including the action numbers;

(b) the reason for leave of absence; and

(c) the duration of the requested leave of absence.

A copy of the notice shall be sent, contemporaneously, to the judge before whom an action is pending and all opposing counsel. Unless opposing counsel files a written objection within ten (10) days with the clerk of the court, with a copy to the court and all counsel of record, or the court responds denying the leave, such leave will stand granted without entry of an order. If objection is filed, the court, upon request of any counsel, will conduct a conference with all counsel to determine whether the court will, by order, grant the requested leave of absence.

The clerk of the court shall retain leave of absence notices in a chronological file two (2) calendar years; thereafter, the notices may be discarded.

16.2 Leaves for More Than Thirty (30) Calendar Days or Those Either on a Published Calendar, Noticed for a Hearing, or Not Meeting the Time Requirements of 16.1

Application for leaves of absence for more than thirty (30) days, or those either on a published calendar, noticed for a hearing, or not submitted within the time limits contained in 16.1 above, must be in writing, filed with the clerk of the court, and served upon opposing counsel at least ten (10) days prior to submission to the appropriate judge of the court in which an action pends. This time period may be waived if opposing counsel consents in writing to the application. This procedure permits opposing counsel to object or to consent to the grant of the application, but the application is addressed to the discretion of the court. Such application for leave of absence shall contain:

(a) a list of the actions to be protected, including the action numbers;

(b) the reason for leave of absence; and

(c) the duration of the requested leave of absence.

16.3 16.1 or 16.2 Leave

A 16.1 or 16.2 leave when granted shall relieve any attorney from all trials, hearings, depositions and other legal proceedings in that matter. This rule shall not extend any deadline set by law or the court.

16.4 Denial of Application for Leave

Any application for leave not filed in conformance with this rule will be denied. Notice shall be provided substantially as on the attached form.

To: All Judges, Clerk of Court, and Counsel of Record
From: Name of Attorney
RE: **Notice of Leave of Absence**
Date:

Comes now (attorney's name) and respectfully notifies all judges before whom s/he has cases pending, all affected clerks of court, and all opposing counsel, that s/he will be on leave pursuant to Georgia Uniform Court Rule 16.

1. The period of leave during which time Applicant will be away from the practice of law, is: (dates of leave). The purpose of the leave is:

2. All affected judges and opposing counsel shall have ten days from the date of this Notice to object to it. If no objections are filed, the leave shall be granted.

name of attorney
Bar no.
address of attorney
phone number of attorney

CERTIFICATE OF SERVICE

This is to certify that I have this date served a copy of the foregoing Notice of Leave of Absence upon all judges, clerks and opposing counsel listed on the attached Exhibit A, by depositing the same in the U.S. Mail with adequate postage affixed thereto.

This ____ day of ______, _____.

____
Name of attorney

EXHIBIT A
(Sample)

Name of Case Case Number	Name of Judge Court/County	Opposing Counsel
Jones v. Jones 98–3333	Brown DeKalb/Superior	opp. atty. A (address)
Smith v. Exxon 97A–454545	Black Cobb/State	opp. atty. B (address)
Schwartz v. Craig & Co. E–6789	Grey Fulton/Superior	opp. atty. C (address)

Amended September 23, 1998.

RULE 17. CONFLICTS—STATE AND FEDERAL COURTS

17.1 Method of Resolution

(A) An attorney shall not be deemed to have a conflict unless:

(1) the attorney is lead counsel in two or more of the actions affected; and,

(2) the attorney certifies that the matters cannot be adequately handled, and the client's interest adequately protected, by other counsel for the party in the action or by other attorneys in lead counsel's firm; certifies that in spite of compliance with this rule, the attorney has been unable to resolve these conflicts; and certifies in the notice a proposed resolution by list of such cases in the order of priority specified by this rule.

(B) When an attorney is scheduled for a day certain by trial calendar, special setting or court order to appear in two or more courts (trial or appellate; state or federal), the attorney shall give prompt written notice as specified in (A) above of the conflict to opposing counsel, to the clerk of each court and to the judge before whom each action is set for hearing (or, to an appropriate judge if there has been no designation of a presiding judge). The written notice shall contain the attorney's proposed resolution of the appearance conflicts in accordance with the priorities established by this rule and shall set forth the order of cases to be tried with a listing of the date and data required by (B)(1)–(4) as to each case arranged in the order in which the cases should prevail under this rule. In the absence of objection from opposing counsel or the courts affected, the proposed order of conflict resolution shall stand as offered. Should a judge wish to change the order of cases to be tried, such notice shall be given promptly after agreement is reached between the affected judges. Attorneys confronted by such conflicts are expected to give written notice such that it will be received at least seven (7) days prior to the date of conflict. Absent agreement, conflicts shall be promptly resolved by the judge or the clerk of each affected court in accordance with the following order of priorities:

(1) Criminal (felony) actions shall prevail over civil actions;

(2) Jury trials shall prevail over non-jury matters, including trials and administrative proceedings;

(3) Trials shall prevail over appellate arguments, hearings and conferences;

(4) Within each of the above categories only, the action which was first filed shall take precedence.

(C) Conflict resolution shall not require the continuance of the other matter or matters not having priority. In the event any matter listed in the letter notice is disposed of prior to the scheduled time set for any other matter listed or subsequent to the scheduled time set but prior to the end of the calendar, the attorney shall immediately notify all affected parties, including the court affected, of the disposal and shall, absent good cause shown to the court, proceed with the remaining case or cases in which the conflict was resolved by the disposal in the order of priorities as set forth heretofore.

Amended effective March 9, 1989; October 9, 1997.

17.2 Attorneys Serving as Part-time Judges

A judge presiding in a civil matter shall give prompt consideration to resolving scheduling conflicts resulting from an attorney's serving as a part-time judge of a court of record. The presiding judge should be mindful of the strict time limitations of juvenile proceedings. See, e.g., *Ga. Unif. Juvenile Court Rules 6.8, 7.3 and 23.5*. However, a continuance by reason of such scheduling conflicts should not be granted in a scheduled Superior Court civil matter involving the safety of a child or the need of a custodial parent for temporary support.

Adopted effective Sept. 2, 1999.

RULE 18. RULES FOR SERVICE OF SENIOR JUDGES

18.1 Definitions

For the purposes of this section of the uniform rules, the following definitions shall apply:

(A) "Active judge" means a superior court judge in active service.

(B) "Senior judge" means a superior court judge retired from active service, yet authorized by law to serve as a superior court judge.

(C) "Defeated senior judge" means a senior judge who retired from active service after failing to be reelected at a primary or election.

18.2 Requests for Assistance

The chief judge of any superior court of this state may make a written request for assistance to the chief judge of any other superior court, a senior judge of the superior court, a retired judge, or a judge emeritus of any court. The request by the chief judge may be made if one of the following circumstances arise:

(A) A judge of the requesting court is disqualified for any cause from presiding in any matter pending before the court;

(B) A judge of the requesting court is unable to preside because of disability, illness, or absence; or,

(C) A majority of the judges of the requesting court determines that the business of the court requires the temporary assistance of an additional judge or additional judges. OCGA § 15–1–9.1(b).

An active judge may, except as hereinafter provided, call upon a senior judge to serve in an emergency or when the volume of cases or other unusual circumstances cause such service to be necessary in order to provide for the speedy and efficient disposition of the business of the circuit.

18.3 Certificate of Need

Except in cases of emergency, having determined the necessity for the service of a senior judge, the requesting judge shall certify the reason such service is required, which shall include an order of appointment giving the scope and tenure of such requested service as in the discretion of the requesting judge is necessary to meet the need. Such certificate and order shall be filed in the office of clerk of superior court of the county in which service is to be performed and with the district administrative judge of such district.

18.4 Emergency Requests

In case of an unforeseen emergency requiring the immediate service of a senior judge, the requesting judge may act without prior certificate or order of appointment, later ratifying such designation of service by an appropriate order.

18.5 Residence of Senior Judge

No active judge shall call to serve any senior judge who is not a bona fide resident of and domiciled in this state.

18.6 Defeated Senior Judges

Any active judge, with the concurrence of the district administrative judge, or any district administrative judge alone where the need arises, may request the service of any defeated senior judge under the same circumstances and procedures as heretofore set out for active judges requesting the service of undefeated senior judges, except that no judge shall request the services of a defeated senior judge unless such defeated senior judge shall be first approved for such service by the Supreme Court of Georgia pursuant to rules promulgated by the Supreme Court. Such approval shall be reviewed periodically by the Supreme Court, but after once having been approved by the Supreme Court, a defeated senior judge could continue to serve until such approval is withdrawn or revoked.

Amended effective October 9, 1997.

18.7 Fiscal Eligibility. [Deleted]

Deleted September 23, 1998.

18.8 Election of Ineligibility

In view of the foregoing limitations upon service and compensation of senior judges, senior judges may elect to declare themselves ineligible to serve as judges and may engage in the private practice of law if and when authorized by law. Such election shall be made in writing delivered to the Supreme Court. Senior judges electing to practice law shall be entitled to draw their earned retirement pay but shall not be entitled to additional compensation for serving as judges. A senior judge who has elected to practice law shall not thereafter be eligible to serve as a judge except upon petition showing good cause to and with the approval of the Supreme Court. Having once been reinstated as eligible to serve as judge by the Supreme Court, no second such petition shall be granted.

No judge shall call upon any senior judge to serve who is exercising the right to practice law and no senior judge who is exercising the right to practice law shall agree to serve as a judge.

The practice of law as described in this section shall not include service as an arbitrator, mediator, or any other neutral in an alternative dispute process. This is true whether or not senior judges are compensated for their services as neutrals.

Amended effective November 12, 1992.

RULE 19. TRANSFER/CHANGE OF VENUE

19.1 Civil

(A) Subject to the provisions of OCGA § 9–11–12 and section (C) of this rule, a timely motion in any pending civil action or proceeding (1) by any party, that jurisdiction is lacking or that venue is improper, or (2) by the court, sua sponte, that subject matter jurisdiction is lacking, shall be treated as a motion to transfer the action to another court, whether in the same or another county of this state.

(B) The moving party shall specify the court(s) having jurisdiction and in which venue properly would lie.

(C) If the basis of the motion is that a party necessary to the court's jurisdiction has been dismissed during or at the conclusion of the trial, the motion shall be made immediately and orally; any opposition shall be made orally. Should the motion to transfer be granted as to the remaining parties the claim against the party dismissed shall be severed, so that the order of dismissal will be final for purposes of appeal.

(D) Unless otherwise ordered by the court, notice of a written motion to transfer shall be served upon all parties, including any who failed to file pleadings in the matter at least 10 days before the motion is heard. A party opposing a written motion to transfer shall notify the court and all other parties in writing within 10 days after service upon that party of the motion to transfer; such notice shall designate the basis upon which it is claimed that the court in which the action pends has jurisdiction and upon which venue is claimed to be proper.

(E) When a motion to transfer is filed, the court may stay all other proceedings in the pending action until determination of the motion.

(F) No action or proceeding may be transferred except upon written order of the court in which the action pends (transferor court), reasonable notice of which shall be given to all parties. This order shall specify the court to which the matter is to be transferred (transferee court) and shall state that unless plaintiff pays all accrued court costs within 20 days of mailing or delivery of the cost bill to plaintiff, the action shall automatically stand dismissed without prejudice.

The court ruling upon a motion to transfer may award reasonable attorney's fees to the prevailing party; if the court grants the motion, transfer costs of $50 shall be taxed, unless the court expressly determines otherwise, in its discretion.

(G) When an order transferring an action is filed with the clerk of the court entering such order, the clerk shall promptly compute the court costs, including the costs incident to preparing and transferring the record as provided in subparagraph (H) of this rule, and shall notify counsel for plaintiff (or, the plaintiff, if there is no counsel of record) in writing of the amount of the court costs. Plaintiff shall pay the costs within 20 days of mailing or delivery of the cost bill; if costs are not paid within that time, the action shall automatically stand dismissed, without prejudice.

(H) Upon timely payment of costs, the clerk of the transferor court shall make and retain copies of (1) the complaint or initial pleading, (2) the motion to transfer if in writing, and (3) the order of transfer. The originals of all pleadings, orders, depositions and other papers on file shall be indexed and certified by the clerk of the transferor court and transmitted, with the transfer cost (if applicable), to the clerk of the transferee court in the manner provided by law for transmittal of records to appellate courts.

(I) Upon receipt of the items specified in subparagraph (H) of this rule, the clerk of the transferee court shall assign the action an appropriate number and notify all parties and their respective counsel of record thereof. The action thereafter shall continue in the transferee court as though initially commenced there; all items specified in subparagraph (H) of this rule shall be deemed amended accordingly. It shall not be necessary that service of process be perfected a second time upon parties defendant, except that any publication required to be made in a newspaper in the proper venue shall be republished. Any interlocutory or other order theretofore entered in the action, upon the motion of any party, shall be reviewed, and thereafter reissued or vacated by the court to which the action was transferred.

Amended effective October 9, 1997.

19.2 Criminal

When a criminal action is to be transferred to the superior court of a county different from that in which initially brought, the superior court judge granting the venue change, unless disqualified, shall continue as presiding judge in the action.

19.3 Contested Election Results

In respect of actions contesting election results, venue change is not limited to the county adjoining that in which the action commenced, but may be made to an appropriate court in any county of the state; costs incident to the further handling and trial of such action shall be borne by the transferor county.

Amended effective March 14, 1996.

RULE 20. PEREMPTORY CALENDAR

Periodically the assigned judge may cause to be delivered to the clerk of the court and published a list of pending civil actions in which the discovery period has expired or criminal cases upon reasonable notice requiring the parties (including the state) or their attorneys to announce whether the actions or cases appearing thereon are ready for trial and when trial should be scheduled. Failure to appear at the calendar sounding or otherwise to advise the judge or appropriate calendar clerk may result in the following disposition:

(A) In civil actions, the dismissal without prejudice of plaintiff's action or defendant's answer, counterclaim, or cross-claim; and,

(B) In criminal cases, the acquitting of the accused defendant or the dead docketing of the case.

RULE 21. LIMITATION OF ACCESS TO COURT FILES

All court records are public and are to be available for public inspection unless public access is limited by law or by the procedure set forth below.

21.1 Motions and Orders

Upon motion by any party to any civil action, after hearing, the court may limit access to court files respecting that action. The order of limitation shall specify the part of the file to which access is limited, the nature and duration of the limitation, and the reason for limitation.

21.2 Finding of Harm

An order limiting access shall not be granted except upon a finding that the harm otherwise resulting to the privacy of a person in interest clearly outweighs the public interest.

21.3 Ex Parte Orders

Under compelling circumstances, a motion for temporary limitation of access, not to exceed 30 days, may be granted, ex parte, upon motion accompanied by supporting affidavit.

21.4 Review

An order limiting access may be reviewed by interlocutory application to the Supreme Court.

Amended effective May 15, 1997.

21.5 Amendments

Upon notice to all parties of record and after hearing, an order limiting access may be reviewed and amended by the court entering such order or by the Supreme Court at any time on its own motion or upon the motion of any person for good cause.

RULE 22. ELECTRONIC AND PHOTOGRAPHIC NEWS COVERAGE OF JUDICIAL PROCEEDINGS

Unless otherwise provided by rule of the Supreme Court or otherwise ordered by the assigned judge after appropriate hearing (conducted after notice to all parties and counsel of record) and findings, representatives of the print and electronic public media may be present at and unobtrusively make written notes and sketches pertaining to any judicial proceedings in the superior courts. However, due to the distractive nature of electronic or photographic equipment, representatives of the public media utilizing such equipment are subject to the following restrictions and conditions:

(A) Persons desiring to broadcast/record/photograph official court proceedings must file a timely written request (form attached as Exhibit "A") with the judge involved prior to the hearing or trial, specifying the particular calendar/case or proceedings for which such coverage is intended; the type equipment to be used in the courtroom; the trial, hearing or proceeding to be covered; and the person responsible for installation and operation of such equipment.

(B) Approval of the judge to broadcast/record/photograph a proceeding, if granted, shall be granted without partiality or preference to any person, news agency, or type of electronic or photographic coverage, who agrees to abide by and conform to these rules, up to the capacity of the space designated therefor in the courtroom. Violation of these rules will be grounds for a reporter/technician to be removed or excluded from the courtroom and held in contempt.

(C) The judge may exercise discretion and require pooled coverage which would allow only one still photographer, one television camera and attendant, and one radio or tape recorder outlet and attendant. Photographers, electronic reporters and technicians shall be expected to arrange among themselves pooled coverage if so directed by the judge and to present the judge with a schedule and description of the pooled coverage. If the covering persons cannot agree on such a schedule or arrangement, the schedule and arrangements for pooled coverage may be designated at the judge's discretion.

(D) The positioning and removal of cameras and electronic devices shall be done quietly and, if possible, before or after the court session or during recesses; in no event shall such disturb the proceedings of the court. In every such case, equipment should be in place and ready to operate before the time court is scheduled to be called to order.

(E) Overhead lights in the courtroom shall be switched on and off only by court personnel. No other lights, flashbulbs, flashes or sudden light changes may be used unless the judge approves beforehand.

(F) No adjustment of central audio system shall be made except by persons authorized by the judge. Audio recordings of the court proceedings will be from one source, normally by connection to the court's central audio system. Upon prior approval of the court, other microphones may be added in an unobtrusive manner to the court's public address system.

(G) All television cameras, still cameras and tape recorders shall be assigned to a specific portion of the public area of the courtroom or specially designed access areas, and such equipment will not be permitted to be removed or relocated during the court proceedings.

(H) Still cameras must have quiet functioning shutters and advancers. Movie and television cameras and broadcasting and recording devices must be quiet running. If any equipment is determined by the judge to be of such noise as to be distractive to the court proceedings, then such equipment can be excluded from the courtroom by the judge.

(I) Pictures of the jury, whether by still, movie, or television cameras, shall not be taken except where the jury happens to be in the background of other topics being photographed. Audio recordings of the jury foreperson's announcement of the verdict, statements or questions to the judge may be made. Photographs and televising of the public and the courtroom are allowed, if done without disruption to the court proceedings.

(J) Reporters, photographers, and technicians must have and produce upon request of court officials credentials identifying them and the media company for which they work.

(K) Court proceedings shall not be interrupted by a reporter or technician with a technical or an equipment problem.

(L) Reporters, photographers, and technicians should do everything possible to avoid attracting attention to themselves. Reporters, photographers, and technicians will be accorded full right of access to court proceedings for obtaining public information within the requirements of due process of law, so long as it is done without detracting from the dignity and decorum of the court.

(M) Other than as permitted by these rules and guidelines, there will be no photographing, radio or television broadcasting, including videotaping pertaining to any judicial proceedings on the courthouse floor where the trial, hearing or proceeding is being held or any other courthouse floor whereon is located a superior court courtroom, whether or not the court is actually in session.

(N) No interviews pertaining to a particular judicial proceeding will be conducted in the courtroom except with the permission of the judge.

(O) All media plans heretofore approved by the Supreme Court for superior courts are hereby repealed.

(P) A request for installation and use of electronic recording, transmission, videotaping or motion picture or still photography of any judicial proceeding shall be evaluated pursuant to the standards set forth in OCGA § 15–1–10.1.

Amended effective May 15, 1997; October 9, 1997.

EXHIBIT A

IN THE SUPERIOR COURT OF ______
COUNTY
STATE OF GEORGIA

(STYLE OF CASE) CASE NO. ______

REQUEST TO INSTALL RECORDING AND/OR PHOTOGRAPHING EQUIPMENT PURSUANT TO RULES AND GUIDELINES FOR ELECTRONIC AND PHOTOGRAPHIC NEWS COVERAGE OF JUDICIAL PROCEEDINGS.

Pursuant to Rule 22 of the Electronic and Photographic News Coverage of Judicial Proceedings in the Uniform Superior Court Rules, the undersigned hereby requests permission to install equipment in courtroom ______ in order to record, photograph or televise all or portions of the proceedings in the above-captioned case.

Consistent with the provisions of the rules and guidelines, the undersigned desires to install the following described equipment: ______ in the following locations: ______. The proceedings that the undersigned desires to record, photograph or televise commence on ______ (date). Subject to direction from the court regarding possible pooled coverage, the undersigned wishes to install this equipment in the courtroom on ______ (date). The personnel who will be responsible for the installation and operation of this equipment during its use are: ______ (identify appropriate personnel).

The undersigned hereby certifies that the equipment to be installed and the locations and operation of such equipment will be in conformity with the rules and guidelines issued by the court.

This ______ day of ______, 19__.

______
(Individual Signature)

______
(Representing/Firm)

______
(Position)

______
(Address)

______
(Telephone Number)

APPROVED:

______
Judge, Superior Court
______ Judicial Circuit

RULE 23. WITHDRAWAL OF FUNDS FROM COURT

Upon any order being presented to a judge requiring the court clerk to pay out funds from the registry of the court, except in garnishment proceedings, counsel for the parties presenting the order shall at the same time submit to the court the following certificate executed by counsel:

I hereby certify that the order presented in case no. ____ on this the ______ day of ______, 19____, to draw down funds from the registry of court, is done with written consent of all parties, or their counsel, who have filed claims of record in this case, and whose interest has not previously been foreclosed by judicial decree. In condemnation matters only, I further certify that provision is made in this order for the payment of all local, state and federal government taxes, or assessments of record.

I understand that the truth of the statements contained in this certificate is a condition precedent to the issuance of a valid order to pay the funds from the registry of the court.

Date ______

Signed ______

Attorney for ______

RULE 24. DOMESTIC RELATIONS

24.1 Scope of Domestic Relations Actions

Domestic relations actions shall include actions for divorce, alimony, equitable division of assets and liabilities, child custody, child support, legitimation, annulment, paternity actions, termination of parental rights in connection with adoption proceedings filed in superior court, contempt proceedings relating to enforcement of decrees and orders, petitions in respect to modification of decrees and orders, actions under the Family Violence Act, actions on foreign judgments based on alimony or child support, and adoptions. Domestic relations actions shall also include any direct or collateral attacks on judgments or orders entered in any such actions.

Amended effective May 15, 1997.

24.2 Financial Data Required

Every action for temporary or permanent child support, alimony, equitable division of property, modification of child support or alimony or attorneys' fees shall be accompanied by an affidavit specifying the party's financial circumstances. The affidavit shall be served at the same time that the notice of interlocutory hearing is served. The opposing party shall make an affidavit regarding his or her financial circumstances and shall serve it upon opposing counsel at least five days prior to the interlocutory hearing. If the parties are ordered to participate in mediation at any time prior to trial, each shall serve the affidavit upon the other at least five days prior to the mediation. Each shall furnish the mediator with a copy at the time of the mediation.

If no application for a temporary award is made and the parties do not participate in mediation prior to trial, then the parties shall make and serve the affidavits at least ten days before trial. If a party is not represented by an attorney, sufficient time will be allowed the party to prepare the required affidavit at hearing or trial. On the request of either party, and good cause shown to the court, the affidavits and any other financial information may be sealed, upon order of the court.

Failure of any party to furnish the above affidavit, in the discretion of the court, may subject the offending party to the penalties of contempt and result in continuance of the hearing until such time as the required affidavit is furnished.

The affidavit shall be under oath and in substantially the following form:

IN THE SUPERIOR COURT OF
_______ COUNTY, GEORGIA

___________, PLAINTIFF

VS CIVIL ACTION NO. _____

_________, DEFENDANT

DOMESTIC RELATIONS FINANCIAL AFFIDAVIT

1. AFFIANT'S NAME _______________ Age ____
   Spouse's Age _______________
   Date of Marriage ______ Date of Separation ______
   Names and birth dates of children of this marriage:
   Name Date of Birth Resides With

   ____
   ____
   ____

   Names and birth dates of children of prior marriage residing with Affiant:
   Name Date of Birth

   ____
   ____

2. SUMMARY OF AFFIANT'S INCOME AND NEEDS
   (a) Gross monthly income (from Item 3A) $____
   (b) Net monthly income (from Item 3C) ____
   (c) Average monthly expenses (Item 5A) $____
   Monthly payments to creditors (Item 5B) +____
   Total monthly expenses and payments to creditors (Item 5C) ____
   (d) Amount of spousal/child support needed by Affiant $____
   (e) Amount of child support indicated by Child Support Guidelines $____
3. A. AFFIANT'S GROSS MONTHLY INCOME
   (All income must be entered based on monthly average regardless of date of receipt. Where applicable, income should be annualized.)
   Salary $____
   Bonuses, commissions, allowances, overtime, tips and similar payments (based on past 12-month average or time of employment if less than 1 year) ATTACH SHEET ITEMIZING THIS INCOME. $____
   Business income from sources such as self employment, partnership, close corporations and/or independent contracts (gross receipts minus ordinary and necessary expenses required to produce income) ATTACH SHEET ITEMIZING THIS INCOME. $____
   Disability/unemployment/worker's compensation ____
   Pension, retirements or annuity payments ____
   Social security benefits ____
   Other public benefits (specify) ____
   Spousal or child support from prior marriage ____
   Interest and dividends ____
   Rental income (gross receipts minus ordinary and necessary expenses required to produce income) ATTACH SHEET ITEMIZING THIS INCOME. ____
   Income from royalties, trusts or estates ____
   Gains derived from dealing in property (not including non-recurring gains) ____
   Other income of a recurring nature (specify source) ____

   GROSS MONTHLY INCOME $____

   B. List and describe all benefits of employment, e.g., automobile and/or auto allowance, insurance (auto, life, disability, etc.) deferred compensation, employer contribution to retirement or stock, club memberships and reimbursed expenses (to the extent they reduce personal living expenses) ATTACH SHEET, IF NECESSARY.

   ____
   ____

____

C. Net monthly income from employment (deducting only state and federal taxes and FICA) $_____

Affiant's pay period (i.e., weekly, monthly, etc.) ______

Number of exemptions claimed ______

4. ASSETS

(If you claim or agree that all or part of an asset is non-marital, indicate the non-marital portion under the appropriate spouse's column. The total value of each asset must be listed in the "value" column. "Value" means what you feel the item of property would be worth if it were offered for sale.)

Description	Value	Separate Asset of Husband	Separate Asset of Wife
Cash	$____	____	____
Stocks, bonds	$____	____	____
CD's/Money Market Accounts	$____	____	____
Real estate: home	$____	____	____
other	$____	____	____
Automobiles	$____	____	____
Money owed you	$____	____	____
Retirement/IRA	$____	____	____
Furniture/furnishings	$____	____	____
Jewelry	$____	____	____
Life insurance (cash value)	$____	____	____
Collectibles	$____	____	____
Bank accounts	$____	____	____
(List each account)	$____	____	____
	$____	____	____
Other assets	$____	____	____
____	$____	____	____
____	$____	____	____
TOTAL ASSETS	$____	____	____

5. A. AVERAGE MONTHLY EXPENSES

HOUSEHOLD

Mortgage or rent payments ____
Property taxes ____
Insurance ____
Electricity ____
Water ____
Garbage & sewer ____
Telephone ____
Gas ____
Repairs & maintenance ____
Lawn care ____
Pest control ____
Cable TV ____
Miscellaneous household and grocery items ____
Meals outside home ____
Other ____

AUTOMOBILE

Gasoline and oil ____
Repairs ____
Auto tags and license ____
Insurance ____

CHILDREN'S EXPENSES

Child care ____
School tuition ____
School supplies/expenses ____
Lunch money ____
Allowance ____
Clothing ____
Diapers ____
Medical, dental, prescription ____
Grooming/hygiene ____
Gifts ____
Entertainment ____
Activities ____

OTHER INSURANCE

Health ____
Life ____
Disability ____
Other (specify) ____

AFFIANT'S OTHER EXPENSES

Dry cleaning and laundry ____
Clothing ____
Medical/dental ____
Affiant's gifts (special holidays) ____
Entertainment ____
Vacations ____
Publications ____
Dues, clubs ____
Religious and charities ____
Miscellaneous (attach sheet) ____
Other (attach sheet) ____
Alimony paid to former spouse ____
Child support paid to former spouse ____

TOTAL ABOVE EXPENSES $____

B. PAYMENTS TO CREDITORS

To Whom	Balance Due	Monthly Payments
____	____	____
____	____	____
____	____	____
____	____	____
____	____	____
____	____	____

Total Monthly Payments to Creditors $____

C. TOTAL MONTHLY EXPENSES $____

This ______ day of ______, 19____.

____

Notary Public Affiant

Amended effective January 18, 1990; October 28, 1993; amended November 4, 1999, effective December 16, 1999; amended effective August 12, 2004.

24.3 Acknowledgment and Waivers

All acknowledgments of service must be witnessed by an official attesting officer or the parties' counsel. Consent of the parties must be signed by both parties and each signature witnessed in the same manner as required for acknowledgments of service.

Amended effective March 9, 1989.

24.4 Temporary Hearing, Scheduling

Notice of the date of the temporary hearing on alimony and custody matters shall be served upon the adverse party at least 5 days before the date of the hearing, unless otherwise ordered by the court.

24.5 Witnesses in Domestic Relations Actions

(A) At temporary hearings the parties involved and one additional witness for each side may give oral testimony. Additional witnesses must testify by deposition or affidavit unless otherwise ordered by the court. Any affidavit shall be served on opposing counsel at least 24 hours prior to hearing.

(B) Except by leave of court, the minor child/children of the parties shall not be permitted to give oral testimony at temporary hearings; such child/children will be excluded from the courtroom or other place of hearing. When custody is in dispute, if directed by the court, minor child/children of the parties shall be available for consultation with the court. At any such consultation, attorneys for both parties may be in attendance but shall not interrogate such child/children except by express permission from the court. Upon request, the proceedings in chambers shall be recorded.

24.6 Uncontested Divorce Actions

Uncontested divorce actions may be heard at times agreeable to counsel and the court, subject to the following rules:

(A) By written consent of both parties to a hearing a divorce may be granted any time 31 days after service or filing acknowledgment of service.

(B) In an unanswered action, a divorce may be granted any time 46 days after service, unless the time for response has been extended by court order.

(C) A divorce action served by publication may be granted any time suitable to the judge and attorneys 61 days or more after date of the first publication.

(D) All divorce actions with orders for publication or acknowledgments of service should be filed prior to or contemporaneously with the signing of the order or acknowledgment.

24.7 Contested Divorce Actions

Although the court may, in appropriate cases, grant judgment on the pleadings or summary judgment that the moving party is entitled to a divorce as a matter of law, no divorce decree shall be granted unless all contestable issues in the case have been finally resolved.

24.8 Court Mandated Programs in Domestic Relations Cases

(A) There may be established by any superior court circuit a program designed to educate the parties to domestic relations actions in regard to the effects of divorce on minor children of the marriage. Establishment of the program shall be by majority vote of the judges of the circuit or by the chief judge, in the event of a tie vote by all judges.

(B) The superior court judges, under whose authority the program shall function, may require any or all parties to attend an educational seminar of no more than four hours in any domestic relations action before the court. The program may be administered by the court or by contract with a private agency. The seminar shall be conducted by qualified personnel whose professional and educational experiences include a knowledge of children and families.

(C) The seminar shall focus on the effects of divorce on children, specifically as it relates to the parents' actions during and after the separation, and as it relates to the children at different developmental stages. Specific attention should be given to the effects of the economics of divorce on children.

(D) The court or contracted agency may charge each participant a fee, provided there is a fee waiver procedure in cases of indigent parties. The fee may be assessed in addition to court costs against either party in the discretion of the judge. The program shall be non-profit.

(E) The mandate of attendance shall be by court order with the assigned judge retaining the discretion to waive attendance for good cause shown. Such good cause may include: a party's non-residence in Georgia or in the county in which the action is pending or the reasonable availability of a similar program to the party or other such reasonable causes which indicate to the court that a party should not be required to complete the program. The court may, in its discretion, accept alternative counseling covering the subject matter of the required seminar. Unless waived, the failure to successfully complete the seminar shall be cause for appropriate action by the assigned judge, including but not limited to, withholding the final decree of divorce, attachment for contempt and award of attorneys' fees and costs.

(F) The assigned judge may, as a discretionary matter, grant a final decree of divorce before completion of the seminar, but shall retain authority to impose sanctions upon either party who fails or refuses to comply with the order to attend and complete the seminar.

(G) The various courts which have established a seminar may make reciprocal agreements which would allow a party to attend an approved out-of-county seminar as a substitute for attending the seminar held in the county in which the action is pending.

Rule 24.8 adopted effective May 26, 1994.

24.9 Appointment, Qualification and Role of a *Guardian ad Litem*

1. Appointment

The Guardian ad Litem ("GAL") is appointed to assist in a domestic relations case by the superior court judge assigned to hear that particular case, or otherwise having the responsibility to hear such case. The appointing judge has the discretion to appoint any person as a GAL so long as the person so selected has been trained as a GAL or is otherwise familiar with the role, duties, and responsibilities as determined by the judge. The GAL may be selected through an intermediary.

2. Qualifications

A GAL shall receive such training as provided by or approved by the Circuit in which the GAL serves. This training should include, but not be limited to, instruction in the following subjects: domestic relations law and procedure, including the appropriate standard to be applied in the case; domestic relations courtroom procedure; role, duties, and responsibilities of a GAL; recognition and assessment of a child's best interests; methods of performing a child custody/visitation investigation; methods of obtaining relevant information concerning a child's best interest; the ethical obligations of a GAL, including the relationship between the GAL and counsel, the GAL and the child, and the GAL and the court; recognition of cultural and economic diversity in families and communities; base child development, needs, and abilities at different ages; interviewing techniques; communicating with children; family dynamics and dysfunction, domestic violence and substance abuse; recognition of issues of child abuse; and available services for child welfare, family preservation, medical, mental health, educational, and special needs, including placement/evaluation/diagnostic treatment services.

3. Role and Responsibilities

The GAL shall represent the best interests of the child. The GAL is an officer of the court and shall assist the court and the parties in reaching a decision regarding child custody, visitation and child-related issues. Should the issue of child custody and/or visitation be tried, the GAL shall be available to offer testimony in accordance with provision 6 and 7 herein.

The GAL holds a position of trust with respect to the minor child at issue, and must exercise due diligence in the performance of his/her duties. A GAL should be respectful of, and should become educated concerning, cultural and economic diversity as may be relevant to assessing a child's best interests.

A GAL's appointment, unless ordered otherwise by the Court for a specific designated period, terminates upon final disposition of all matters pertaining to child custody, visitation and child-related issues. The GAL shall have the authority to bring a contempt action, or other appropriate remedy, to recover court-ordered fees for the GAL's services.

4. Duties

By virtue of the order appointing a GAL, a GAL shall have the right to inspect all records relating to the minor child maintained by the Clerk of the Court in this and any other jurisdiction, other social and human service agencies, the Department of Family and Children Services, and the Juvenile Court. Upon written release and/or waiver by a party or appropriate court order, the GAL shall have the right to examine all records maintained by any school, financial institution, hospital, doctor or other mental health provider, any other social or human services agency or financial institution pertaining to the child which are deemed confidential by the service provider. The GAL shall have the right to examine any residence wherein any person seeking custody or visitation rights proposes to house the minor child. The GAL may request the court to order examination of the child, parents or anyone seeking custody of the child, by a medical or mental health professional, if appropriate. The GAL shall be entitled to notice of, and shall be entitled to participate in all hearings, trials, investigations, depositions, settlement negotiations, or other proceedings concerning the child.

5. Release to GAL of a Party's Confidential Information from Non–Parties

A GAL's right to request and receive documents and information from mental health professionals, counselors, and others with knowledge of a confidential nature concerning a party is conditional upon the party agreeing to sign a release allowing the GAL access to such records and information.

Upon receipt of a party's signed waiver/release form, the GAL shall have the right to inspect all records, documents and information relating to the minor child(ren) and/or the parties maintained by any mental health professionals, counselors and others with knowledge of a confidential nature concerning a party or minor child.

6. Written Report

Unless otherwise directed by the appointing judge, the GAL shall submit to the parties or counsel and to the Court a written report detailing the GAL's findings and recommendations at such time as may be directed by the assigned judge. At trial, the report shall be admitted into evidence for direct evidence and impeachment purposes, or for any other purposes allowed by the laws of this state. The court will consider the report, including the recommendations, in making its decision. However, the recommendations of the GAL are not a substitute for the court's independent discretion and judgment, nor is the report a substitute for the GAL's attendance and testimony at the final hearing, unless all parties otherwise agree.

a. *Contents of Report*

The report shall summarize the GAL's investigation, including identifying all sources the GAL contacted or relied upon in preparing the report. The

GAL shall offer recommendations concerning child custody, visitation, and child–related issues and the reasons supporting those recommendations.

b. *Release of Report to Counsel and Parties*

The Report shall be released to counsel (including counsel's staff and experts) and parties only, and shall not be further disseminated unless otherwise ordered by the Court.

c. *Release of GAL's File to Counsel*

If ordered by the Court, the parties and their counsel shall be allowed to review and/or copy (and shall pay the cost of same) the contents of the GAL's file.

d. *Unauthorized Dissemination of GAL's Report and Contents of File*

Any unauthorized dissemination of the GAL's Report, its contents or the contents of the GAL's file by a party or counsel to any person, shall be subject to sanctions, including a finding of contempt by the Court.

e. *Sealing of Written Report*

If filed, the Report shall be filed under seal by the Clerk of Superior Court in order to preserve the security, privacy, and best interests of the children at issue.

7. Role at Hearing and Trial

It is expected that the GAL shall be called as the Court's witness at trial unless otherwise directed by the Court. The GAL shall be subject to examination by the parties and the court. The GAL is qualified as an expert witness on the best interest of the child(ren) in question. The GAL may testify as to the foundation provided by witnesses and sources, and the results of the GAL's investigation, including a recommendation as to what is in a child's best interest. The GAL shall not be allowed to question witnesses or present argument, absent exceptional circumstances and upon express approval of the Court.

8. General and Miscellaneous Provisions

a. *Requesting Mental Fitness and Custody Evaluations*

Based upon the facts and circumstances of the case, a GAL may request the Court to order the parties to undergo mental fitness and/or custody evaluations to be performed by a mental health expert approved by the Court. The Court shall provide for the parties' responsibility for payment of fees to the appointed experts.

b. *Filing Motions and Pleadings*

If appropriate, the GAL may file motions and pleadings if the GAL determines that the filing of such motion or pleading is necessary to preserve, promote, or protect the best interest of a child. This would include the GAL's right to file appropriate discovery requests and request the issuance of subpoenas. Upon the filing of any such motions or pleadings, the GAL shall promptly serve all parties with copies of such filings.

c. *Right to Receive Notice of Mediations, Hearings and Trials*

Counsel shall notify the GAL of the date and time of all mediations, depositions, hearings and trials or other proceedings concerning the children(ren). Counsel shall serve the GAL with proper notice of all legal proceedings, court proceedings wherein the child(ren)'s interests are involved and shall provide the GAL with proper and timely written notice of all non–court proceedings involving the child(ren)'s interests.

d. *Approval of Settlement Agreements*

If the parties reach an Agreement concerning issues affecting the best interest of a child, the GAL shall be so informed and shall have the right and opportunity to make objections to the Court to any proposed settlement of issues relating to the children prior to the Court approving the Agreement.

e. *Communications Between GAL and Counsel*

A GAL may communicate with a party's counsel without including the other counsel in the same conversation, meeting or, if by writing, notice of the communication. When communicating with the GAL, counsel is not required to notify opposing counsel of the communication or, if in writing, provide opposing counsel with a copy of the communication to the GAL.

f. *Ex Parte Communication Between GAL and the Court*

The GAL shall not have *ex parte* communications with the Court except in matters of emergency concerning the child's welfare or upon the consent of the parties or counsel. Upon making emergency concerns known to the Court, the GAL may request an immediate hearing to address the emergency. Notification shall be provided immediately to the parties and counsel of the nature of the emergency and time of hearing.

g. *Payment of GAL Fees and Expenses*

It shall be within the Court's discretion to determine the amount of fees awarded to the GAL, and how payment of the fees shall be apportioned between the parties. The GAL's requests for fees shall be considered, upon application properly served upon the parties and after an opportunity to be heard, unless waived. In the event the GAL determines that extensive travel outside of the circuit in which the GAL is appointed or other extraordinary expenditures are necessary, the GAL may petition the Court in advance for payment of such expenses by the parties.

h. *Removal of GAL from the Case*

Upon motion of either party or upon the court's own motion, the court may consider removing the GAL from the case for good cause shown.

Adopted effective May 19, 2005.

RULE 25. RECUSAL

25.1 Motions

All motions to recuse or disqualify a judge presiding in a particular case or proceeding shall be timely filed in writing and all evidence thereon shall be presented by accompanying affidavit(s) which shall fully assert the facts upon which the motion is founded. Filing and presentation to the judge shall be not later than five (5) days after the affiant first learned of the alleged grounds for disqualification, and not later than ten (10) days prior to the hearing or trial which is the subject of recusal or disqualification, unless good cause be shown for failure to meet such time requirements. In no event shall the motion be allowed to delay the trial or proceeding.

Amended effective January 31, 1991.

25.2 Affidavit

The affidavit shall clearly state the facts and reasons for the belief that bias or prejudice exists, being definite and specific as to time, place, persons and circumstances of extra-judicial conduct or statements, which demonstrate either bias in favor of any adverse party, or prejudice toward the moving party in particular, or a systematic pattern of prejudicial conduct toward persons similarly situated to the moving party, which would influence the judge and impede or prevent impartiality in that action. Allegations consisting of bare conclusions and opinions shall not be legally sufficient to support the motion or warrant further proceedings.

Adopted effective January 31, 1991.

25.3 Duty of the Trial Judge

When a judge is presented with a motion to recuse, or disqualify, accompanied by an affidavit, the judge shall temporarily cease to act upon the merits of the matter and shall immediately determine the timeliness of the motion and the legal sufficiency of the affidavit, and make a determination, assuming any of the facts alleged in the affidavit to be true, whether recusal would be warranted. If it is found that the motion is timely, the affidavit sufficient and that recusal would be authorized if some or all of the facts set forth in the affidavit are true, another judge shall be assigned to hear the motion to recuse. The allegations of the motion shall stand denied automatically. The trial judge shall not otherwise oppose the motion.

Former Rule 25.2 renumbered as Rule 25.3 and amended effective January 31, 1991.

25.4 Procedure Upon a Motion for Disqualification

The motion shall be assigned for hearing to another judge, who shall be selected in the following manner:

(A) If within a single-judge circuit, the district administrative judge shall select the judge;

(B) If within a two-judge circuit, the other judge, unless disqualified, shall hear the motion;

(C) If within a multi-judge circuit, composed of three (3) or more judges, selection shall be made by use of the circuit's existing random, impartial case assignment method. If the circuit does not have random, impartial case assignment rules, then assignment shall be made as follows:

(1) The chief judge of the circuit shall select a judge within the circuit to hear the motion, unless the chief judge is the one against whom the motion is filed; or

(2) In the event the chief judge is the one against whom the motion is filed, the assignment shall be made by the judge of the circuit who is most senior in terms of service other than the chief judge and who is not also a judge against whom the motion is filed; or

(3) When the motion pertains to all active judges in the circuit, the district administrative judge shall select a judge outside the circuit to hear the motion.

(D) If the district administrative judge is the one against whom the motion is filed, the available judge within the district senior in time of service (or next senior in time of service, if the administrative judge is the one senior in the time of service) shall serve in the selection process instead of the district administrative judge.

(E) If all judges within a judicial administrative district are disqualified, including the administrative judge, the matter shall be referred by the disqualified administrative judge to the administrative judge of an adjacent district for the appointment of a judge who is not a member of the district to preside over the motion or case.

If the motion is sustained, the selection of another judge to hear the case shall follow the same procedure as outlined above.

Former Rule 25.4 deleted effective January 31, 1991. Former Rule 25.3 renumbered as Rule 25.4 effective January 31, 1991; amended effective May 19, 2005.

25.5 Selection of Judge

In the instance of any hearing on a motion to recuse or disqualify a judge, the challenged judge shall neither select nor participate in the selection of the judge to hear the motion; if recused or disqualified, the recused or disqualified judge shall not select nor participate in the selection of the judge assigned to hear further proceedings in the involved action.

25.6 Findings and Ruling

The judge assigned may consider the motion solely upon the affidavits, but may, in the exercise of discretion, convene an evidentiary hearing. After consideration of the evidence, the judge assigned shall rule on the merits of the motion and shall make written findings and conclusions. If the motion is sustained, the selection of another judge to hear the case shall follow the same procedure as established in Rule 25.4 above. Any determination of disqualification shall not be competent evidence in any other case or proceedings.

Adopted effective January 31, 1991.

25.7 Voluntary Recusal

If a judge, either on the motion of one of the parties or the judge's own motion, voluntarily disqualifies, another judge, selected by the procedure set forth in Rule 25.4 above, shall be assigned to hear the matter involved. A voluntary recusal shall not be construed as either an admission or denial to any allegations which have been set out in the motion.

Adopted effective January 31, 1991.

RULE 26. PRE-INDICTMENT PROCEEDINGS

26.1 Bonds and First Appearance

Immediately following any arrest but not later than 48 hours if the arrest was without a warrant, or 72 hours following an arrest with a warrant, unless the accused has made bond in the meantime, the arresting officer or the law officer having custody of the accused shall present the accused in person before a magistrate or other judicial officer for first appearance.

At the first appearance, the judicial officer shall:

(A) Inform the accused of the charges;

(B) Inform the accused of the right to remain silent, that any statement made may be used against the accused, and of the right to the presence and advice of an attorney, either retained or appointed;

(C) Determine whether or not the accused desires and is in need of an appointed attorney and, if appropriate, advise the accused of the necessity for filing a written application;

(D) Inform the accused of his or her right to a later pre-indictment commitment hearing, unless the first appearance covers the commitment hearing issues, and inform the accused that giving a bond shall be a waiver of the right to a commitment hearing;

(E) In the case of warrantless arrest, make a fair and reliable determination of the probable cause for the arrest unless a warrant has been issued before the first appearance;

(F) Inform the accused of the right to grand jury indictment in felony cases and the right to trial by jury, and when the next grand jury will convene; [In state court, see State Court Rule 26.1(F).]

(G) Inform the accused that if he or she desires to waive these rights and plead guilty, then the accused shall so notify the judge or the law officer having custody, who shall in turn notify the judge.

(H) Set the amount of bail if the offense is not one bailable only by a superior court judge, or so inform the accused if it is.

Amended effective October 28, 1993; October 9, 1997.

26.2 Commitment Hearing by Court of Inquiry

(A) At the commitment hearing by the court of inquiry, the judicial officer shall perform the following duties:

(1) Explain the probable cause purpose of the hearing;

(2) Repeat to the accused the rights explained at the first appearance;

(3) Determine whether the accused intends to plead "guilty" or "not guilty," or waives the commitment hearing;

(4) If the accused intends to plead guilty or waives the hearing, the court shall immediately bind the entire case over to the court having jurisdiction of the most serious offense charged;

(5) If the accused pleads "not guilty" the court shall immediately proceed to conduct the commitment hearing unless, for good cause shown, the hearing is continued to a later scheduled date;

(6) Cause an accurate record to be made of the testimony and proceeding by any reliable method.

(7) The judicial officer shall bind the entire case over to the court having jurisdiction of the most serious offense for which probable cause has been shown by sufficient evidence and dismiss any charge for which probable cause has not been shown.

(8) On each case which is bound over, a memorandum of the commitment shall be entered on the warrant by the judicial officer. The warrant, bail

bond and all other papers pertaining to the case shall be forwarded to the clerk of the appropriate court having jurisdiction over the offense for delivery to the district attorney. Each bail bond shall contain the full name, telephone number, residence, business and mailing address(es) of the accused and any surety.

(9) A copy of the record of any testimony and the proceedings of the first appearance and the commitment hearing shall be provided to the proper prosecuting officer and to the accused upon payment of the reasonable cost for preparation of the record.

(10) A judicial officer, conducting a commitment hearing, is without jurisdiction to make final disposition of the case or cases at the hearing by imposing any fine or punishment, except where the only charge arising out of the transaction at issue is the violation of a county ordinance.

(B) At the commitment hearing, the following procedures shall be utilized:

(1) The rules of evidence shall apply except that hearsay may be allowed;

(2) The prosecuting entity shall have the burden of proving probable cause; and may be represented by a law enforcement officer, a district attorney, a solicitor, a private attorney or otherwise as is customary in that court;

(3) The accused may be represented by an attorney or may appear pro se; and

(4) The accused shall be permitted to introduce evidence.

Amended effective October 28, 1993.

26.3 Delayed Indictments

The district attorney shall notify the chief judge in writing of the name of any unindicted accused who has been in custody under criminal felony charges for 45 days within 2 business days after said 45-day period has run. The chief judge may take any action deemed necessary or appropriate under the circumstances.

RULE 27. PRE-TRIAL RELEASE PROGRAM

This program may be established in any county by the superior court judges of the circuit within which that county lies and the appropriate county governing authorities.

27.1 Structure

The superior court judges, under whose authority the program shall function, shall appoint a director, setting the qualifications deemed necessary and appropriate for the office. The director shall:

(A) Be responsible for the supervision and execution of the duties enumerated hereinafter in connection with the program;

(B) Receive such compensation as may be set by the superior court judges from time to time subject to the approval of the governing authority;

(C) Hold office at the pleasure of the superior court judges;

(D) Employ such assisting and clerical staff as may be authorized and assign them as needed to discharge the functions of the program; and,

(E) Develop and promulgate rules, regulations and procedures pertaining to conditional release under the program, subject to the approval of the superior court judges, including such as pertain to the issuance of a bench warrant for the arrest of any individual released under the program who fails to comply with the conditions of the release.

27.2 Duties

The duties involved in the proper functioning of the program shall include:

(A) Securing pertinent data and providing reports containing verified information respecting an accused who has agreed to be considered for release under the program;

(B) Conducting such investigation and interviews as may be necessary for the compilation of such reports and submitting the reports to an appropriate judicial officer;

(C) Monitoring and reporting to the court the compliance or noncompliance of an accused released under the program with the conditions of release;

(D) Providing appropriate documentation to the court respecting performance by an accused complying with the conditions of release so that upon full performance by the accused the sheriff shall return to the party posting deposit bail that portion of the deposit not retained to defray administrative costs; and,

(E) Providing appropriate documentation to the court respecting performance by an accused not complying with the conditions of release so that the court having jurisdiction may:

(1) enter an order declaring the bond forfeit and requiring that any deposit held in escrow by the sheriff be paid into the county general fund;

(2) issue a bench warrant for the arrest of the accused.

27.3 Release Under the Program.

(A) After reviewing available reports provided pursuant to Rule 27.2(B), upon determination of eligibility, a judicial officer having bail jurisdiction may order an accused person released conditionally and/or released under supervision in lieu of requiring the accused to post a money bond or equivalent security; alternatively the judicial officer may require the accused, prior to release, to deposit with the sheriff a sum of money or equivalent security equal to 10% of the principal amount of the bond which otherwise would be required, referred to hereinafter as "10% bail."

(B) No person may receive compensation for acting as surety in respect of posting 10% bail under Rule 27.

(C) Of the amount deposited as 10% bail under Rule 27, $10.00 or 10%, whichever is greater, will be transferred immediately to the general fund of the county to defray administrative costs; the amount remaining will be held by the sheriff in an escrow account pending final disposition as provided in Rule 27.2(D) and (E).

27.4 Security Bail Other Than 10% Bail.

In lieu of the bail deposit provided for above, any person for whom bail has been set may execute the bail bond with or without sureties which bond may be secured by:

(1) Cash—by a deposit with the sheriff of an amount equal to the required cash bail; or

(2) Property—by real estate located within the State of Georgia with unencumbered equity, not exempted, owned by the accused or surety, valued at double the amount of bail set in the bond; or

(3) Professional—by a professional bail bondsman authorized by the sheriff and in compliance with the rules and regulations for execution of a surety bail bond.

27.5 Exoneration of Bondsman After Forfeiture.

The surety in an appearance bond shall not be relieved from the liability of said bond except upon the filing of a written motion and the entering of an order by the court or one of the judges thereof exonerating said bondsman and payment of all accrued costs. The bondsman shall be responsible for informing the district attorney, in writing, of the reason for failure to produce the body of the defendant as provided in the bond.

RULE 28. JAIL CENSUS

The sheriff or court administrator of each county shall furnish to the chief judge, or designee, and the district attorney at least once a week, a list of all prisoners in the county jail or held elsewhere at the sheriff's direction. Such lists shall include, as to each prisoner:

(A) The prisoner's name;

(B) The date of arrest;

(C) The offense charged, or other reason for being held;

(D) The amount of bond;

(E) Whether or not the prisoner is represented by counsel, and if so, the name of such counsel; and

(F) If not represented by counsel, whether such confined person desires appointed counsel.

Amended effective October 9, 1997.

RULE 29. APPOINTMENT OF COUNSEL FOR INDIGENT DEFENDANTS

29.1 Counties to Which This Rule Is Applicable

Pursuant to OCGA § 17–12–1 et seq., the following rule is promulgated to provide representation by competent legal counsel of indigent persons in criminal proceedings for those counties not receiving state funds under "The Georgia Indigent Defense Act" (Ga. L. 1979, p. 367, § 1; OCGA § 17–12–30 et seq.).

29.2 Application and Appointment of Counsel

When an accused person, contending to be financially unable to employ an attorney to defend against pending criminal charges or to appeal a conviction, desires to have an attorney appointed, the accused shall make a request in writing to the court or its designee for an attorney to be appointed. The request shall be in the form of an application for appointment of counsel and certificate of financial resources, made under oath and signed by the accused which shall contain information as to the accused's assets, liabilities, employment, earnings, other income, number and ages of dependents, the charges against the accused and such other information as shall be required by the court. The purpose of the application and certification is to provide the court or its designee with sufficient information from which to determine the financial ability of the accused to employ counsel.

The determination of indigency or not shall be made by a judge of a superior court or designee.

Upon a determination of indigency the court shall, in writing, authorize the appointment of counsel for the indigent accused. The original authorization of appointment shall be filed with the indictment or warrant in the case; a copy of the authorization shall be forwarded to the clerk, court administrator, public defender or such other person designated by the court to assign an attorney to an indigent defendant. Such person shall notify the accused, the appointed attorney, the sheriff and the district attorney of the appointment. [In State Court, see State Court Rule 29.2.]

29.3 The Role of Law Enforcement

Any law enforcement authority having custody of any person shall:

(A) Allow a person claiming to be indigent and without counsel to immediately complete an application for an attorney and certificate of financial resources and forward such to the court or its designee, for a determination of indigency or not;

(B) Clearly advise detained persons of their right to have counsel and that if they cannot afford a lawyer one will be provided to assist them;

(C) Accomplish the above procedures as soon as possible after detention; and,

(D) Complete an application for an attorney and certificate of financial resources in substantially the following form:

IN THE SUPERIOR COURT OF ______
COUNTY
STATE OF GEORGIA

State of Georgia) Indictment No.
v.) Charge(s):
________________)

APPLICATION FOR APPOINTMENT OF COUNSEL AND CERTIFICATE OF FINANCIAL RESOURCES

I am the defendant in the above-styled action. I am charged with the offense(s) of ________, which is/are a felony/misdemeanor. I can/cannot afford to hire a lawyer to assist me. I do/do not want the court to provide me with a lawyer. I understand that I am providing this information in this declaration in order for the court to determine my eligibility for a court-appointed lawyer, paid by ______ County, to defend me on the above charges.

In jail _____ Out on bond _____ Arrest Date _____

1. Name __________ Telephone No. ________
Mailing address ____________________
Birth date __________ Age ____________
Soc. Sec. No. ____________________
Highest grade in school completed ______

2. If employed, employer is ____________
Net take home pay is (gross pay minus state, federal and social security taxes): ______ (weekly) ______ (monthly)

3. If unemployed, how long? ______ List other sources of income such as unemployment compensation, welfare or disability income and the amounts received per week or month: ______

4. Are you married? ______ Is spouse employed? ________________
If yes, by whom ______ Spouse's net income (week) ______

5. Number of children living in home: ______ Ages ________________

6. Dependents (other than spouse or children) in home, names, relationship, amount contributed to their support ________________

7. Do you own a motor vehicle? ______ Year and model ________________
How much do you owe on it? ______

8. Do you own a home? ______ Value ______ How much do you owe on it? ______

9. Amount of house payment or rent payment each month ________________

10. List checking or savings accounts or other deposits with any bank or financial institution and the amount of deposits: ________________

11. List other assets or property, including real estate, jewelry, notes, bonds or stocks ______

12. List indebtedness and amount of payments ______

13. List any extraordinary living expenses and amount (such as regularly occurring medical expenses) ________________

14. Child support payable under any court order ________________

15. Do you understand that whether you are convicted or acquitted ______ County may seek reimbursement of attorney's fees paid for you if you become financially able to pay or reimburse the county but refuse to do so?

I have read (had read to me) the above questions and answers and they are correct and true.

The undersigned swears that the information given herein is true and correct and understands that a false answer to any item may result in a charge of perjury.

The ______ day of ______, 19__.

____
Defendant's Signature

Sworn to and subscribed before me this ______ day of ______, 19__.
____

Notary Public

My Commission Expires ______________

ORDER

Having considered the above matter, it is the finding of this court that the above-named defendant is/is not indigent under criteria of the Georgia Criminal Justice Act and appropriate court rules and is/is not entitled to have appointed counsel.

It is ordered that the clerk, panel administrator, or court administrator assign an attorney practicing in this county to represent the defendant in the above case.

Let the defendant and the assigned attorney be notified hereof and furnished a copy of this application and order.

This ______ day of ______, 19__.

____
Superior Court Judge
______ Judicial Circuit

29.4 Responsibility for Determination of Eligibility

The financial eligibility of a person for publicly provided counsel should be determined by the court or its designee. The court may appoint counsel in cases where the defendant does not qualify and cannot be provided counsel under provisions of the above.

29.5 Uniform Eligibility Guidelines

Income eligibility—Eligible accused persons include all applicants for an attorney with net income below a level set by the applicable superior court and revised periodically.

The following special needs of a family unit may be deducted from net income in determining eligibility:

(1) Child care expenses for working custodial parents; and,

(2) Legally required support payments to dependents, including alimony for the support of a child/children.

"Net income" shall include only a client's take-home pay, which is the gross income earned by a client minus those deductions required by law or as a condition of employment.

"Family unit" includes the defendant, a spouse, if the couple lives together, any minors who are unemployed and unmarried, and any infirm or permanently disabled person living with the defendant and for whom the defendant has assumed financial responsibility. The income of a minor who is attending school full time, but has after-school employment or does odd jobs, shall not be attributed to that of the family unit. No other persons, even if living within the same household, will be deemed members of the family unit.

In the event an accused person is discovered to have been ineligible at the time of the appointment of an attorney, the court shall be notified. The court may discharge the appointed attorney and refer the matter to the private bar. The attorney should be paid for the time spent on the case and recoupment sought from the ineligible person.

Regardless of the prima facie eligibility on the basis of income, a person who has sufficient assets that are easily converted to cash by sale or mortgage may not be qualified for representation.

The court may appoint counsel for representation for any accused person who is unable to obtain counsel due to special circumstances such as emergency, hardship, or documented refusal of the case by members of the private bar because of financial inability to pay for counsel.

If the accused is determined to be eligible for defense services in accordance with approved financial eligibility criteria and procedures, and if, at the time that the determination is made, the accused is able to provide a cash contribution to offset defense costs without imposing a substantial financial hardship either personally or upon dependents, such contribution may be required as a condition of continued representation at public expense. The court should determine the amount to be contributed. The contribution shall be paid directly to the fund for indigent defense of the affected county.

Amended effective October 9, 1997.

29.6 Standards of Performance for Appointed Attorneys [Reserved]

29.7 County May Select Method of Providing Counsel

A county may use a public defender system, legal aid and defender society, agency for indigent defense, a panel of private attorneys, a combination of the above, or other means, to provide adequate legal defense for indigents accused of felonies.

29.8 Assignment of Cases to Private Attorneys

(A) Appointments of private attorneys shall be made on an impartial and equitable basis;

(B) The cases shall be distributed among the attorneys to ensure balanced workloads through a rotation system;

(C) More difficult or complex cases shall be assigned to attorneys with sufficient levels of experience and competence to afford adequate representation;

(D) Less experienced attorneys should be assigned cases which are within their capabilities, but should be given the opportunity to expand their experience under supervision; and,

(E) Cases in which the death penalty is sought shall be assigned only to attorneys of sufficient experience, skill and competence to render effective assistance of counsel to defendants in such cases.

Amended effective October 9, 1997.

29.9 Fees Paid to Lawyers Under a Panel Program.

The judge or judges of a multi-judge circuit shall determine the method of compensation to be paid under a panel program.

Each program shall prescribe minimum fees to be paid as a total fee, regardless of hours, in certain categories of cases, governed by these rules. In prescribing such minimums, the court shall take into consideration the complexity of the case categories and the corresponding fee that is presently being obtained by competent members of the local bar for such representation where privately retained. While the fee paid under the panel program need not equate that of a corresponding fee obtained by a private practitioner, there should be a reasonable relationship.

Compensation for a capital felony case in which the death penalty is sought shall be at the same hourly rate as other cases, but each case should be examined by the court and the fee total should be based on a complete examination of the individual case. Special attention should be given to continuing counsel obligations in death penalty cases when conviction and imposition of the death penalty occur.

The court may establish a committee composed of a designee of the chief judge, the local county governing authority and the local bar association to perform the functions of establishing fee guidelines and approval of fees.

29.10 Fee Disputes.

All fee vouchers or requests from panel attorneys shall be submitted to the judge assigned the case or a person or committee designated to review fee requests prior to their submission to the county for payment.

29.11 Independence of Counsel.

Any indigent defense program shall operate independently and be structured to preserve independence. Independent counsel shall be politically autonomous and free from influence, guidance or control from any other authority in the discharge of professional duties, within the bounds of the law and the Code of Professional Responsibility.

RULE 30. ARRAIGNMENT

30.1 Calendar

The judge, or the judge's designee, shall set the time of arraignment unless arraignment is waived either by the defendant or by operation of law. Notice of the date, time, and place of arraignment shall be delivered to the clerk of the court and sent to attorneys of record, defendants, and bondsmen.

Amended effective October 9, 1997.

30.2 Call for Arraignment

Before arraignment the court shall inquire whether the accused is represented by counsel and, if not, inquire into the defendant's desires and financial circumstances. If the defendant desires an attorney and is indigent, the court shall authorize the immediate appointment of counsel.

Upon the call of a case for arraignment, unless continued for good cause, the accused, or the attorney for the accused, shall answer whether the accused pleads "guilty," "not guilty" or desires to enter a plea of *nolo contendere* to the offense or offenses charged; a plea of not guilty shall constitute the joining of the issue.

Upon arraignment, the attorney, if any, who announces for or on behalf of an accused, or who is entered as counsel of record, shall represent the accused in that case throughout the trial, unless other counsel and the defendant notify the judge prior to trial that such other counsel represents the accused and is ready to proceed, or counsel is otherwise relieved by the judge.

Amended effective October 9, 1997.

30.3 List of Witnesses

Upon request of defense counsel, the district attorney shall furnish to defense counsel as an officer of the court, in confidence, the addresses and telephone numbers of the state's witnesses to the extent such are within the knowledge of the district attorney, unless for good cause the judge allows an exception to this requirement, in which event defense counsel shall be afforded an opportunity to interview such witnesses prior to the witness being called to testify.

RULE 31. MOTIONS, DEMURRERS, SPECIAL PLEAS, AND SIMILAR ITEMS IN CRIMINAL MATTERS

31.1 Time for Filing; Requirements.

All motions, demurrers, and special pleas shall be made and filed at or before the time set by law unless time therefor is extended by the judge in writing prior to trial. Notices of the states intention to present evidence of similar transactions or occurrences and notices of the intention of the defense to raise the issue of insanity or mental illness, or the intention of the defense to introduce evidence of specific acts of violence by the victim against third persons, shall be given and filed at least ten [10] days before trial unless the time is shortened or lengthened by the judge. Such filing shall be in accordance with the following procedures.

Amended effective December 30, 1993; amended November 4, 1999, effective December 16, 1999; amended effective August 12, 2004.

31.2 Time for Hearing

All such motions, demurrers, special pleas and notices shall be heard and considered at such time, date, and place as set by the judge. Generally, such will be heard at or after the time of arraignment and prior to the time at which such case is scheduled for trial.

31.3 Notice of Prosecution's Intent to Present Evidence of Similar Transactions

(A) The prosecution may, upon notice filed in accordance with section 31.1 of these rules, request of the court in which the accusation or indictment is pending leave to present during the trial of the pending case evidence of similar transactions or occurrences.

(B) The notice shall be in writing, served upon the defendant's counsel, and shall state the transaction, date, county, and the name(s) of the victim(s) for each similar transaction or occurrence sought to be introduced. Copies of accusations or indictments, if any, and guilty pleas or verdicts, if any, shall be attached to the notice. The judge shall hold a hearing at such time as may be appropriate, and may receive evidence on any issue of fact necessary to determine the request, out of the presence of the jury. The burden of proving that the evidence of similar transactions or occurrences should be admitted shall be upon the prosecution. The state may present during the trial evidence of only those similar transactions or occurrences specifically approved by the judge.

(C) Evidence of similar transactions or occurrences not approved shall be inadmissible. In every case, the prosecuting attorney and defense attorney shall instruct their witnesses not to refer to similar crimes, transactions or occurrences, or otherwise place the defendant's character in issue, unless specifically authorized by the judge.

(D) If upon the trial of the case the defense places the defendant's character in issue, evidence of similar transactions or occurrences, as shall be admissible according to the rules of evidence, shall be admissible, the above provisions notwithstanding.

(E) Nothing in this rule is intended to prohibit the state from introducing evidence of similar transactions or occurrences which are lesser included alleged offenses of the charge being tried, or are immediately related in time and place to the charge being tried, as part of a single, continuous transaction. Nothing in this rule is intended to alter the rules of evidence relating to impeachment of witnesses.

(F) This rule shall not apply to sentencing hearings.

31.4 Motion and Order for Evaluation Regarding Mental Incompetency to Stand Trial

(A) In pending superior court cases, except in proceedings for involuntary treatment under OCGA Title 37, or proceedings for the appointment of a guardian under Title 29, where the mental competency of an accused is brought into question, the judge may, upon a proper showing, exercise discretion and require a mental evaluation at public expense. A motion for mental evaluation may be filed in writing, setting out allegations and grounds for such motion, praying for a court-ordered evaluation. The judge may enter an order requiring a mental evaluation of the defendant for the purposes of evaluating competency to stand trial. The judge may direct the Department of Human Resources to perform the evaluation at a time and place to be set by the department in cooperation with the county sheriff. A copy of the order shall be forwarded to the department accompanied by a copy of the indictment, accusation or specification of charges, a copy of the police arrest report, where available, and a brief summary of any known or alleged previous mental health treatment or hospitalization involving this particular person. Any other background information available to the court shall also be forwarded to the evaluating department to assist in performing adequately the requested services. Unless otherwise ordered by the court the department shall submit its report to the requesting judge, the defendant's attorney and the prosecuting attorney.

(B) Upon the filing of a Plea of Mental Incompetency to Stand Trial, the judge shall determine from the prosecuting attorney and the defense attorney whether a specially empaneled jury is required to determine the issue of mental incompetency to stand trial ahead of the trial of the case on the merits.

(C) Copies of suggested orders are attached as Specimen Order for Mental Evaluation Re: Competency to Stand Trial, and Specimen Judgment and Order of the Court on the Defendant's Plea of Mental Incompetency to Stand Trial.

IN THE SUPERIOR COURT OF
_____________ COUNTY

STATE OF GEORGIA

THE STATE OF GEORGIA INDICTMENT NO.
V. _________________ CHARGE(S):

ORDER FOR MENTAL EVALUATION
re: COMPETENCY TO STAND TRIAL

WHEREAS the mental competency to stand trial of the above defendant has been called into question, and evidence presented in the matter, and this court has found that it is appropriate for evaluation to be conducted at public expense;

IT IS HEREBY ORDERED that the Department of Human Resources conduct an evaluation of said defendant, provide treatment of the defendant, if appropriate, and provide to this court, a report of diagnosis, prognosis and its findings, with respect to:

Competency to Stand Trial. Whether the accused is capable of understanding the nature and object of the proceedings; whether the accused comprehends his or her own condition in reference to such proceedings; and, whether the accused is capable of rendering to counsel assistance in providing a proper defense.

IT IS FURTHER ORDERED that the department arrange with the county sheriff, or the sheriff's lawful deputies, for the prompt evaluation of said defendant, either at the county jail or at a designated hospital, with transportation of the defendant to be provided by the sheriff, where necessary, with transportation costs to be borne by the county. Upon completion of the evaluation, the evaluating facility shall notify the sheriff, who shall promptly reassume custody of the defendant. Unless otherwise ordered by the court the department shall submit its report to the requesting judge, the defendant's attorney and the prosecuting attorney.

Observed behaviors that led to this request are: __

____

____

Copies of documents supporting this request are attached hereto, as follows:

( ) Indictment/Accusation

( ) Summary of previous mental health treatment and prior mental health records

( ) Copy of arrest report

( ) Other ____________________

So ordered, this the ___ day of ___, 20___.

____
JUDGE, SUPERIOR COURT

____
JUDICIAL CIRCUIT, GEORGIA

SPECIMEN ORDER FOR MENTAL EVALUATION
RE: COMPETENCY TO STAND TRIAL

IN THE SUPERIOR COURT OF
____________ COUNTY
STATE OF GEORGIA

THE STATE OF GEORGIA INDICTMENT NO.
V. ____________ CHARGE(S):

JUDGMENT AND ORDER OF THE COURT ON THE DEFENDANT'S PLEA OF MENTAL INCOMPETENCY TO STAND TRIAL

The above stated case came on regularly before the undersigned for trial this date. The defendant was represented by counsel.

After a hearing on defendant's plea of mental incompetency and due consideration, the plea of Mental Incompetency to Stand Trial is sustained.

IT IS, THEREFORE, THE ORDER of this court that the defendant be now delivered to the sheriff of this County and that the defendant be delivered by the sheriff, or the sheriff's lawful deputy, to the Department of Human Resources, as provided by OCGA § 17–7–130.

IT IS FURTHER ORDERED that at such time as it is determined that the defendant is capable of understanding the nature and object of the proceedings, comprehends his or her own condition in reference to such proceedings, and is capable of rendering to counsel assistance in providing a proper defense, the defendant be delivered by the Department of Human Resources to the sheriff of this county, or the sheriff's lawful deputy, with transportation costs to be borne by the county.

IT IS FURTHER ORDERED that, should it be determined in light of present day medical knowledge that recovery of the defendant's legal mental competency to stand trial is not expected at any time in the foreseeable future, the defendant shall be dealt with by the Department of Human Resources as provided in OCGA § 17–7–130.

SO ORDERED, this the ________ day of ________, 20___.

____
JUDGE, SUPERIOR COURT

____
JUDICIAL CIRCUIT, GEORGIA

SPECIMEN ORDER ON THE DEFENDANT'S PLEA OF MENTAL INCOMPETENCY TO STAND TRIAL

Amended effective October 9, 1997; November 10, 2005.

31.5 Notice of Intention of Defense to Raise Issue of Insanity, Mental Illness or Mental Retardation at the Time of the Act

(A) If, in any criminal proceeding, the defense intends to raise the issue that the defendant or accused was insane, mentally ill or mentally retarded at the time of the act or acts charged against the accused, such intention must be stated, in writing, in a pleading denominated as "Notice of Intent of Defense to Raise Issue of Insanity, Mental Illness or Mental Retardation." This notice shall be filed and served upon the prosecuting attorney in accordance with section 31.1 of these rules. Upon the filing of such notice, the judge shall determine from the prosecuting attorney and the defense attorney whether such issue requires any further mental examination of the accused *or* any further non-jury hearing relative to this issue.

Upon defense motion, the judge may enter an order requiring a mental evaluation of the defendant for the purposes of evaluating the degree of criminal responsibility or insanity at the time of the act in question. The judge may direct the Department of Human Resources to perform the evaluation at a time and place to be set by the department in cooperation with the county sheriff. A copy of the order shall be forwarded to the department accompanied by a copy of the indictment, accusation or specification of charges, a copy of the police arrest report, where available, a copy of the defendant's Notice of Intent to Raise Issue of Insanity if filed, and a brief summary of any known or alleged previous mental health treatment or hospitalization involving this particular person. Any other background information available to the court shall also be forwarded to the evaluating department to assist in performing adequately the requested services. Unless otherwise ordered by the court the department shall submit its report to the requesting judge and the defendant's attorney. Contemporaneous with filing the Notice of Intent of Defense to Raise Issue of Insanity, defendant's attorney shall provide a copy of the Report to the prosecuting attorney and shall so certify in writing attached to the Notice of Intent of Defense to Raise Issue of Insanity.

(B) Except for good cause shown, the issue of insanity shall not be raised in the trial on the merits unless notice has been filed and served ahead of trial as provided in these rules.

(C) A copy of a suggested order is attached as Specimen Order for Mental Evaluation re: Degree of Criminal Responsibility or Insanity at the Time of the Act.

IN THE SUPERIOR COURT OF
________________ COUNTY

STATE OF GEORGIA

THE STATE OF GEORGIA INDICTMENT NO.
V. ________________ CHARGE(S):

ORDER FOR MENTAL EVALUATION re: DEGREE OF CRIMINAL RESPONSIBILITY OR INSANITY AT THE TIME OF THE ACT

WHEREAS, the defendant's sanity at the time of the act has been called into question, and evidence presented in the matter, and this court has found that it is appropriate for an evaluation to be conducted at public expense;

IT IS HEREBY ORDERED that the Department of Human Resources conduct an evaluation of the defendant, provide treatment of the defendant, if appropriate, and provide to this court a report of diagnosis, prognosis and its findings, with respect to:

Degree of Criminal Responsibility or Insanity at the Time of the Act. Whether or not the accused had the mental capacity to distinguish right from wrong in relation to the alleged act; whether or not the presence of a delusional compulsion overmastered the accused's will to resist committing the alleged act.

IT IS FURTHER ORDERED that the department arrange with the county sheriff, or the sheriff's lawful deputies, for the prompt evaluation of said defendant, either at the county jail or at a specified hospital, with transportation costs to be borne by the county. Upon completion of the evaluation, the evaluating facility shall notify the sheriff, who shall promptly reassume custody of the accused. The department shall submit its report to the requesting judge and the defendant's attorney. Contemporaneous with filing the Notice of Intent of Defense to Raise Issue of Insanity, defendant's attorney shall provide a copy of the Report to the prosecuting attorney and shall so certify in writing attached to the Notice of Intent of Defense to Raise Issue of Insanity.

Copies of documents supporting this request are attached hereto, as follows:

( ) Indictment/Accusation

( ) Summary of previous mental health treatment and prior mental health records

( ) Copy of arrest report

( ) Other ________________

So ordered, this the ________ day of ________, 20__.

____
JUDGE, SUPERIOR COURT

____
JUDICIAL CIRCUIT, GEORGIA

SPECIMEN ORDER FOR MENTAL EVALUATION RE: DEGREE OF CRIMINAL RESPONSIBILITY OR INSANITY AT THE TIME OF THE ACT

Amended effective October 9, 1997; November 10, 2005.

31.6 Notice of Intention of Defense to Present Evidence of Acts of Violence by the Victim

(A) The defense may, upon notice filed ill accordance with Rule 31.1, claim justification and present during the trial of the pending case evidence of relevant specific acts of violence by the victim against third persons.

(B) The notice shall be in writing, served upon the state's counsel, and shall state the act of violence, date, county and the name, address and telephone number of the person for each specific act of violence sought to be introduced. The judge shall hold a hearing at such time as may be appropriate and may receive evidence on any issue of fact necessary to determine the request, out of the presence of the jury. The burden of proving that the evidence of specific acts of violence by the victim should be admitted shall be upon the defendant. The defendant may present during the trial evidence of only those specific acts of violence by the victim specifically approved by the judge.

(C) Notice of the state's intention to introduce evidence in rebuttal of the defendant's evidence of the victim's acts of violence and of the nature of such evidence, together with the name, address and telephone number of any witness to be called for such rebuttal, shall be given defendant's counsel and filed within five days before trial unless the time is shortened or lengthened by the judge.

Adopted effective December 30, 1993; amended November 4, 1999, effective December 16, 1999.

RULE 32. CRIMINAL TRIAL CALENDAR

32.1 Calendar Preparation

All indictments and special presentments shall be set for trial within a reasonable time after arraignment. The judge or designee shall prepare a trial calendar, shall deliver a copy thereof to the clerk of court, and shall give notice in person or by mail to each counsel of record, the bondsman (if any) and the defendant at the last address indicated in court records, not less than 7 days before the trial date or dates. The calendar shall list the dates that cases are set for trial, the cases to be tried at that session of court, the case numbers, the names of the defendants and the names of the defense counsel.

Amended effective October 9, 1997.

32.2 Removal from Calendar

No case shall be postponed or removed from the calendar except by the judge.

RULE 33. PLEADING BY DEFENDANT

33.1 Alternatives

(A) A defendant may plead guilty, not guilty, or in the discretion of the judge, nolo contendere. A plea of guilty or nolo contendere should be received only from the defendant personally in open court, except when the defendant is a corporation, in which case the plea may be entered by counsel or a corporate officer.

(B) A defendant may plead nolo contendere only with the consent of the judge. Such a plea should be accepted by the judge only after due consideration of the views of the parties and the interest of the public in the effective administration of justice. Procedurally, a plea of nolo contendere should be handled under these rules in a manner similar to a plea of guilty. [In State Court, see State Court Rule 33.1.]

33.2 Aid of Counsel—Time for Deliberation

(A) A defendant shall not be called upon to plead before having an opportunity to retain counsel, or if defendant is eligible for appointment of counsel, until counsel has been appointed or right to counsel waived. A defendant with counsel shall not be required to enter a plea if counsel makes a reasonable request for additional time to represent the defendant's interest, or if the defendant has not had a reasonable time to consult with counsel.

(B) A defendant without counsel should not be called upon to plead to any offense without having had a reasonable time to consider this decision. When a defendant without counsel tenders a plea of guilty or nolo contendere to an offense, the court should not accept the plea unless it is reaffirmed by the defendant after a reasonable time for deliberation, following the advice from the court required in section 33.8.

Amended effective October 9, 1997.

33.3 Propriety of Plea Discussions and Plea Agreements

(A) In cases in which it appears that the interests of the public in the effective administration of criminal justice (as stated in section 33.6) would thereby be served, the prosecuting attorney may engage in plea discussions for the purpose of reaching a plea agreement. The prosecuting attorney should engage in plea discussions or reach a plea agreement with the defendant only through defense counsel, except when the defendant is not eligible for or does not desire appointment of counsel and has not retained counsel.

(B) The prosecuting attorney, in reaching a plea agreement, may agree to one or more of the following, as dictated by circumstances of the individual case:

(1) to make or not to oppose favorable recommendations as to the sentence which should be imposed if the defendant enters a plea of guilty or nolo contendere;

(2) to seek or not to oppose dismissal of the offense charged if the defendant enters a plea of guilty or nolo contendere to another offense reasonably related to defendant's conduct; or,

(3) to seek or not to oppose dismissal of other charges or potential charges against the defendant if the defendant enters a plea of guilty or nolo contendere.

Amended effective October 9, 1997.

33.4 Relationship Between Defense Counsel and Client

(A) Defense counsel should conclude a plea agreement only with the consent of the defendant, and should ensure that the decision to enter or not enter a plea of guilty or nolo contendere is ultimately made by the defendant.

(B) To aid the defendant in reaching a decision, defense counsel, after appropriate investigation, should advise the defendant of the alternatives available and of considerations deemed important by him in reaching a decision.

33.5 Responsibilities of the Trial Judge

(A) The trial judge should not participate in plea discussions.

(B) If a tentative plea agreement has been reached, upon request of the parties, the trial judge may permit the parties to disclose the tentative agreement and the reasons therefor in advance of the time for the tendering of the plea. The judge may then indicate to the prosecuting attorney and defense counsel whether the judge will likely concur in the proposed disposition if the information developed in the plea hearing or presented in the presentence report is consistent with the representations made by the parties. If the trial judge concurs but the final disposition differs from that contemplated by the plea agreement, then the judge shall state for the record what information in the presentence report or hearing contributed to the decision not to sentence in accordance with the plea agreement.

(C) When a plea of guilty or nolo contendere is tendered or received as a result of a plea agreement, the trial judge should give the agreement due consideration, but notwithstanding its existence, must reach an independent decision on whether to grant charge or sentence leniency under the principles set forth in section 33.6 of these rules.

Amended effective October 9, 1997.

33.6 Consideration of Plea in Final Disposition

(A) It is proper for the judge to grant charge and sentence leniency to defendants who enter pleas of guilty or nolo contendere where the interests of the public in the effective administration of criminal justice are thereby served. Among the considerations which are appropriate in determining this question are:

(1) that the defendant by entering a plea has aided in ensuring the prompt and certain application of correctional measures;

(2) that the defendant has acknowledged guilt and shown a willingness to assume responsibility for conduct;

(3) that the leniency will make possible alternative correctional measures which are better adapted to achieving rehabilitative, protective, deterrent or other purposes of correctional treatment, or will prevent undue harm to the defendant from the form of conviction;

(4) that the defendant has made public trial unnecessary when there are good reasons for not having the case dealt with in a public trial;

(5) that the defendant has given or offered cooperation when such cooperation has resulted or may result in the successful prosecution of other offenders engaged in equally serious or more serious criminal conduct;

(6) that the defendant by entering a plea has aided in avoiding delay (including delay due to crowded dockets) in the disposition of other cases and thereby has increased the probability of prompt and certain application of correctional measures to other offenders.

(B) The judge should not impose upon a defendant any sentence in excess of that which would be justified by any of the rehabilitative, protective, deterrent or other purposes of the criminal law merely because the defendant has chosen to require the prosecution to prove the defendant's guilt at trial rather than to enter a plea of guilty or nolo contendere.

Amended effective October 9, 1997.

33.7 Determining Voluntariness of Plea

The judge shall not accept a plea of guilty or nolo contendere without first determining, on the record, that the plea is voluntary. By inquiry of the prosecuting attorney and defense counsel, the judge should determine whether the tendered plea is the result of prior plea discussions and a plea agreement, and, if it is, what agreement has been reached. If the prosecuting attorney has agreed to seek charge or sentence leniency which must be approved by the judge, the judge must advise the defendant personally that the recommendations of the prosecuting attorney are not binding on the judge. The judge should then address the defendant personally and determine whether any other promises or any force or threats were used to obtain the plea.

Amended effective October 9, 1997.

33.8 Defendant to Be Informed

The judge should not accept a plea of guilty or nolo contendere from a defendant without first:

(A) Determining on the record that the defendant understands the nature of the charge(s);

(B) Informing the defendant on the record that by entering a plea of guilty or nolo contendere one waives:

(1) the right to trial by jury;

(2) the presumption of innocence;

(3) the right to confront witnesses against oneself;

(4) the right to subpoena witnesses;

(5) the right to testify and to offer other evidence;

(6) the right to assistance of counsel during trial;

(7) the right not to incriminate oneself; and that by pleading not guilty or remaining silent and not entering a plea, one obtains a jury trial; and

(C) Informing the defendant on the record:

(1) of the terms of any negotiated plea;

(2) that a plea of guilty may have an impact on his or her immigration status if the defendant is not a citizen of the United States;

(3) of the maximum possible sentence on the charge, including that possible from consecutive sentences and enhanced sentences where provided by law; and/or

(4) of the mandatory minimum sentence, if any, on the charge. This information may be developed by questions from the judge, the district attorney or the defense attorney, or a combination of any of these.

Amended effective March 22, 2001.

33.9 Determining Accuracy of Plea

Notwithstanding the acceptance of a plea of guilty, judgment should not be entered upon such plea without such inquiry on the record as may satisfy the judge that there is a factual basis for the plea.

Amended effective October 9, 1997.

33.10 Stating Intention to Reject the Plea Agreement

If the trial court intends to reject the plea agreement, the trial court shall, on the record, inform the defendant personally that (1) the trial court is not bound by any plea agreement; (2) the trial court intends to reject the plea agreement presently before it; (3) the disposition of the present case may be less favorable to the defendant than that contemplated by the plea agreement; and (4) that the defendant may then withdraw his or her guilty plea as a matter of right. If the plea is not then withdrawn, sentence may be pronounced.

33.11 Record of Proceedings

A verbatim record of the proceedings at which a defendant enters a plea of guilty or nolo contendere shall be made and preserved. The record should include:

(A) The inquiry into the voluntariness of the plea (as required in section 33.7);

(B) The advice to the defendant (as required in section 33.8);

(C) The inquiry into the accuracy of the plea (as required in section 33.9), and, if applicable;

(D) The notice to the defendant that the trial court intends to reject the plea agreement and the defendant's right to withdraw the guilty plea before sentence is pronounced. [In State Court, see State Court Rule 33.11.]

33.12 Plea Withdrawal

(A) After sentence is pronounced, the judge should allow the defendant to withdraw a plea of guilty or nolo contendere whenever the defendant, upon a timely motion for withdrawal, proves that withdrawal is necessary to correct a manifest injustice.

(B) In the absence of a showing that withdrawal is necessary to correct a manifest injustice, a defendant may not withdraw a plea of guilty or nolo contendere as a matter of right once sentence has been pronounced by the judge.

Amended effective October 9, 1997.

RULE 34. UNIFIED APPEAL

Publisher's Note

The Unified Appeal is set forth following the Rules of the Court of Appeals of the State of Georgia, supra.

RULE 35. POST–SENTENCE INFORMATION

35.1 Notification to Department of Corrections

As soon as practical after the imposition of the sentence or modification of an earlier disposition, the clerk shall notify the commissioner of the Department of Corrections of the sentence, and shall mail to such department the documentation required by law. Disposition reports shall be forwarded to the Georgia

Crime Information Center (GCIC) not more than 30 days after disposition decisions.

Amended effective March 9, 1989.

35.2 Sentencing and Sentence Review

Sentences shall be imposed and reviewed in accordance with OCGA § 17–10–1 et seq., as amended from time to time.

RULE 36. FILING AND PROCESSING

36.1 Preparation of Documents

To the extent practical, all materials presented for filing in any superior court shall be typed, legibly written or printed on one side only in blue or black ink suitable for reproduction, on opaque white paper measuring 8½″ × 11″, of a good quality, grade and weight. Manuscript covers and backings shall be omitted wherever practical. [In State Court, see State Court Rule 36.1.]

Amended effective December 22, 2005.

36.2 Time of Docketing

Actions shall be entered by the clerk in the proper docket immediately or within a reasonable period after being received in the clerk's office.

36.3 Caption

Every document or pleading presented for filing in a superior court shall bear a caption which sets out the *exact* nature of the pleading or the type of complaint.

36.4 Signatures

All judgments, orders, pleadings and other documents shall bear the signature of the responsible attorney or party who prepared the document, with the preparer's name, proper address and telephone number typed or printed underneath.

Amended effective October 9, 1997.

36.5 Location of Original

All original documents, petitions and pleadings in both civil and criminal matters shall remain in the custody of the clerk except as provided by the judge, these rules, or as otherwise provided by law; provided, however, that this rule shall not prohibit an attorney of record's checking the file out for transportation to the judge for a hearing.

36.6 Minutes and Final Record

There shall be one or more books or microfilm records (combined "Minutes Book", "Writ or Pleading Record" and "Final Record") called *Minutes and Final Record* in which each entire matter shall be recorded after completion. (This does not include adoptions.) After recording, the original may be destroyed according to the state retention schedule or stored off premises as provided by law. [In State Court, see State Court Rule 36.6.]

36.7 Filing of Transcripts

Transcripts in all matters shall be filed as provided by law and the clerk shall not be required to record or preserve these in a bound book or on microfilm.

36.8 File Categories

The categories of files to be established by the clerk shall be civil, criminal, and adoptions. [In State Court, see State Court Rule 36.8.]

36.9 Identification

Each matter, civil, criminal, adoption, or otherwise, shall be identified by year of filing, type of case, consecutive case number and judge assignment where required. The sequence shall be as follows: year of filing—type of case—consecutive case number—judge assignment.

36.10 Filing Requirements—Civil

Complaints or petitions presented to the clerk for filing shall be filed only when accompanied by the proper filing fee, fee for sheriff service or a pauper's affidavit, a civil case initiation form, and, when applicable, any forms required by law or rule to be completed by the parties. The attorney or party filing the complaint shall furnish the necessary service copies. Judgments, settlements, dismissals and other dispositions presented to the clerk for filing shall be filed only when accompanied by a civil case disposition form. [In State Court, see State Court Rule 36.10.]

Amended effective January 18, 1990.

36.11 Return of Service—Civil

Entry of return of service shall be made by the sheriff or other authorized person on a form provided by the clerk and filed with the clerk.

36.12 Advance Costs—Civil

Advance costs paid upon filing shall be the minimum costs in a case.

36.13 Filing Requirements—Criminal

All indictments, no bills, and accusations presented to the clerk shall be filed and should be accompanied by all applicable documents including arrest warrants, if issued, and the Georgia Crime Information Center OBTS form, if the offense is one for which an OBTS form is applicable.

36.14 Filing of No Bills

The clerk shall prepare a list of all no bills, a copy of which shall be recorded in the Minutes and Final Records. No bills shall be filed chronologically by date of filing.

36.15 Assessment of Costs—Criminal

When costs are assessed the minimum amount assessed as court costs in the disposition of any criminal offense shall be $100.00. Any surcharge provided for by law shall be in addition. [In State Court, see State Court Rule 36.15.]

RULE 37. COURT ADMINISTRATORS

(A) The district court administrator performs such district administrative duties as are prescribed from time to time.

(B) The courts of various counties may, with the consent of local governing authorities, appoint a local court administrator, with such compensation, duties, and term as may be specified in such appointment. The local court administrator may perform general administrative and managerial supervision over the administrative activities and functions of the court and the personnel connected therewith, except the staff of any elected official.

The court administrator may be responsible for the enforcement of the courts' administrative policies and procedures and may directly supervise and direct the employees who are necessary to the operation of the courts.

RULE 38. FILING OF REMITTITUR AND JUDGMENT

After receiving the remittitur and judgment of an appellate court, a copy of the notice of appeal, the remittitur and the index of each appeal shall be filed with the original action and the balance of the copy of the record destroyed, although the original shall be retained. If two or more cases are involved in one appeal, the above-referenced material shall be placed in one of the case files and a cross-reference to that file shall be noted in the remaining file(s).

RULE 39. DOCKETING AND INDEXING

39.1 Dockets to Be Maintained

Each clerk shall maintain the dockets as provided in this Rule 39 of the following, each of which shall include the information required under these rules. Each docket shall bear the name of the docket, the county, and a unique consecutive number. No other dockets shall be required to be kept except those relating to real estate.

39.2 The Civil Docket

The Civil Docket shall contain separate case number entries for all civil actions filed in the office of the clerk including: complaints, motions, URESA's, domestic relations, contempt actions, modifications on closed civil actions, and all other actions civil in nature, except adoptions. Each action in the civil docket shall be indexed by the names of all parties to the action number or the civil docket book and page number. This docket shall contain entries of the following information:

(A) Action Number—a unique case number shall be assigned to each action as prescribed in Rule 36.9;

(B) Cause of Action—an entry of the specific type of action filed;

(C) Names of all attorneys of record;

(D) Names of all parties;

(E) Date of filing;

(F) Advance cost paid;

(G) Additional costs paid;

(H) Date of service;

(I) Type of service, including whether a second original is sent and where;

(J) The date and type of specific disposition of the action, including clear entries for:

(1) Dismissals (with or without prejudice);

(2) Settlements;

(3) Judgments and the type of judgment, i.e., summary, default, on the pleadings, consent, on the verdict, notwithstanding the verdict, directed and so forth. In the event the case is a divorce, enter final decree and the type of judgment.

(4) Five-year or other administrative termination; and

(5) Transfer to court with proper jurisdiction and venue.

(K) Whether the verdict or judgment is for the plaintiff or the defendant;

(L) Whether there was a mistrial;

(M) The date of the trial, if any;

(N) Whether the case was tried (with or without jury);

(O) The name of the judge making the final disposition of the case;

(P) Date a Fi. Fa. was issued;

(Q) A cross-reference to the minutes and final record and page number;

(R) A cross-reference to the records storage area and box number if the case file is stored off-site; and

(S) A summary of all pleadings in the case and the dates of their filings, transcripts filed, motions for new trial, notices of appeal, and remittiturs.

39.2.1 Civil Case Initiation Form

The clerk shall require the attorney filing a civil action to complete the civil case initiation form. The clerk shall enter the action number for the case on the civil case initiation form and the form shall become part of the file for the case. The clerk shall use the cause(s) of action indicated by the attorney completing the form to enter cause(s) of action upon the civil docket of the court, unless it appears to the satisfaction of the clerk by an inspection of the pleadings that the cause(s) of action has been recorded in error by the attorney. If the wrong cause(s) of action has been recorded, the clerk shall correct the civil case initiation form and enter the correct cause(s) of action upon the civil docket of the court.

Adopted effective January 18, 1990.

39.2.2 Modification of the Civil Case Initiation Form

If additional information is deemed necessary by the court at filing, the civil case initiation form may be modified to include new items by using the blank space available at the bottom of the form.

Adopted effective January 18, 1990.

39.2.3 Civil Case Disposition Form

Any order disposing of a civil action presented for consideration to a judge by any attorney or party shall be accompanied by a completed civil case disposition form. If the order is prepared or reframed by the court, the court shall cause the civil case disposition form to be completed or corrected, if necessary. The civil case disposition form shall be sent to the clerk along with the relevant order to become part of the file for the case. The clerk shall require any attorney or party filing a voluntary dismissal or settlement of a civil action to complete a civil case disposition form. The form shall become part of the file for the case. The clerk shall use the specific type of disposition found on the completed civil case disposition form to enter the specific type of disposition upon the civil docket of the court, unless it appears to the satisfaction of the clerk by an inspection of the order that the type of disposition has been recorded in error. If the wrong type of disposition has been recorded, the clerk shall correct the civil case disposition form and enter the correct type of disposition upon the civil docket of the court.

Adopted effective January 18, 1990.

39.2.4 Modification of the Civil Case Disposition Form

If additional information is deemed necessary by the court at disposition, the civil case disposition form may be modified to include new items by using the blank space available at the bottom of the form.

Adopted effective January 18, 1990.

39.3 The Criminal Docket

The Criminal Docket shall contain a record of all criminal indictments in which true bills are rendered and all accusations filed in the office of the clerk of superior court and a summary of the pleadings in each case. Entries shall be made of the following information:

(A) Number—a unique number shall be assigned to each indictment which receives a true bill or accusation filed pursuant to Rule 36.9;

(B) Date of filing;

(C) Names of defendants and their OBTS numbers (the pre-printed Offender Tracking No. found on the GCIC final disposition report);

(D) Names of defense attorneys;

(E) An enumeration of the specific types of offenses (counts);

(F) Whether the case was brought by accusation or indictment;

(G) Whether each count is a felony or misdemeanor, or a traffic ticket, and if a traffic ticket, the citation number;

(H) The name of the judge making the final disposition of the case;

(I) The plea and date of plea for each count in the case, including whether the plea was guilty, not guilty, nolo contendere, mentally incompetent to stand trial, and whether or not the plea was negotiated;

(J) Whether the case was tried with or without a jury;

(K) The disposition for each count in the case and the date of disposition including whether the count was dismissed, a nolle prosequi entered, a verdict of guilty was rendered, a verdict of not guilty was rendered, a verdict of not guilty by reason of insanity, or a verdict of guilty but mentally ill;

(L) A listing of the dates and types of proceedings in the case including motions for new trials;

(M) The date and type of sentence including term, conditions, and amount of costs, fines or restitution for each defendant;

(N) The date of issuance of a bench warrant and officer's return;

(O) The date of issuance of a judgment absolute;

(P) The date of issuance of scire facias;

(Q) The date the transcript was filed;

(R) The date application was made for sentence review;

(S) The date notice of appeal was filed;

(T) The date the remittitur was filed;

(U) A cross-reference to the minutes and final record and page number; and

(V) A cross-reference to the records storage area and box number if the case file is stored off-site.

39.4 Lis Pendens Docket

The Lis Pendens Docket shall contain all lis pendens filed with the clerk and shall be properly indexed by the names of the parties.

39.5 General Execution Docket

The General Execution Docket shall contain all Fi. Fas. The information to be entered shall be:

(A) Names of the parties and attorneys of record;

(B) Names of county and court in which judgment was issued;

(C) The date of judgment;

(D) The date of issuance of the Fi. Fa.;

(E) The date of the recording of the Fi. Fa. on the General Execution Docket;

(F) The number of the case on which the judgment was rendered; and

(G) The amount of principal, costs, attorney fees, interest, penalties, and total amount of the Fi. Fa. on the case.

Nulla Bona's and satisfactions are to be noted on the original entry. Re-issued Fi. Fas. shall be recorded as a new Fi. Fa. in the General Execution Docket. A cross-reference to that new entry shall be made on the original entry of the Fi. Fa. or the last renewal of the Fi. Fa. which is less than seven years old. (In State Court, see State Court Rule 39.5.)

39.6 Adoption Docket

The original files shall suffice as the Adoption Docket. Each adoption shall be given a unique consecutive case number pursuant to Rule 36.9. The adoption index shall contain the names of the petitioners. All adoptions shall be recorded in a separate adoption minutes and final record which shall be properly indexed. All adoption records, including the index, shall be kept sealed and locked and shall be confidential unless otherwise ordered by the judge.

39.7 Required Forms [1]

The forms listed below shall be required for use in all superior courts in this state:

SC–1 Summons
SC–2 Sheriff's Entry of Service
SC–3 Service by Publication
SC–4 Notice of Publication
SC–5 Writ of Fieri Facias
SC–6 Final Disposition Form (Criminal)
SC–6.1 First Offender Sentence Form
SC–6.2 Youthful Offender Sentence Form
SC–7 Exemplification
SC–8 Witness Subpoena
SC–9 Subpoena for the Production of Evidence
SC–9.1 Subpoena for the Production of Evidence at a Deposition
SC–13 Civil Case Initiation Form
SC–14 Civil Case Disposition Form

(In State Court, see State Court Rule 39.7.)

Amended effective January 18, 1990.

[1] For information regarding the availability of sample and preprinted forms, please contact the Administrative Office of the Courts.

Publisher's Note

Forms SC–1 through SC–9.1, SC–13 and SC–14 are set forth in Uniform Court Rules Appendix A: Forms, infra.

39.8 Suggested Forms [1]

The forms listed below are suggested for use in all superior courts:

SC–10 Civil Docket Form (space-saver size 8½″ × 11″)
SC–11 Civil Docket Form (space-saver size 8½″ × 11″)
SC–12 Criminal Docket Form (space-saver size 8½″ × 11″)

[1] For information regarding the availability of sample and preprinted forms, please contact the Administrative Office of the Courts.

Publisher's Note

Forms SC–10 through SC–12 are set forth in Uniform Court Rules Appendix A: Forms, infra.

39.9 Court Information

The chief judge of each circuit may require the superior court clerk of each county of that circuit to furnish to the chief judge within 10 days after the end of each month, a general civil, domestic relations and a criminal caseload management report. The Chief Justice of the Georgia Supreme Court may request copies of the information that is furnished to the Chief Judges of the circuits pursuant to this rule.

The case types, events types and disposition methods used in these reports will conform to Judicial Council guidelines for reporting caseload. Each such report shall include the following:

(A) the number of cases filed by case type in the prior month and year-to-date;

(B) the number of cases disposed by case type and disposition method in the prior month and year-to-date;

(C) the number and type of pending cases;

(D) a list of cases more than 120 days old (criminal) and 180 days old (civil/domestic relations) to include the following data:

(i) case number,

(ii) style,

(iii) case type,

(iv) filing date,

(v) next event scheduled,

(vi) date of that event; and

(E) any other information the Chief Judge requests that is contained within court standardized computer programs.

Rule 39.9 adopted effective March 13, 1997.

RULE 40. COMPUTER APPLICATIONS AND STANDARDS

When the clerk of a superior court elects to store for computer retrieval any or all records, the same data elements used in a manual system shall be used, and the same integrity and security maintained.

RULE 41. MOTIONS FOR NEW TRIAL

41.1 Time for Hearing

In order to reduce delay between the conclusion of the trial and the filing of the notice of appeal, the trial court may hear motions for new trial immediately after filing and prior to the preparation of the transcript of proceedings. In any event, the motion for new trial shall be heard and decided as promptly as possible.

41.2 Transcript Preparation

In criminal cases, the transcript shall be prepared as promptly as possible.

41.3 Transcript Costs

Except where leave to proceed in forma pauperis has been granted, an attorney who files a motion for new trial, or a notice of appeal which specifies that the transcript of evidence or hearing shall be included in the record, shall be personally responsible for compensating the court reporter for the cost of transcription. The filing of such motion or notice shall constitute a certificate by the attorney that the transcript has been ordered from the court reporter. The filing of such motion or notice prior to ordering the transcript from the reporter shall subject the attorney to disciplinary action by the court.

RULE 42. SPECIAL COUNSEL

42.1 Private Special Prosecutors

Private special prosecutors retained by the family or relatives of one named as a victim in an indictment or accusation may not participate in the prosecution of a criminal case. Special assistant district attorneys appointed by the district attorney including attorneys from personnel of public agencies may prosecute criminal cases.

42.2 Appointment of Counsel to Assist Retained Counsel

During the pendency of a criminal case, the trial judge may appoint additional counsel to assist retained counsel in the representation of a defendant prior to, during, or after trial.

RULE 43. MANDATORY CONTINUING JUDICIAL EDUCATION (MCJE)

43.1 Program Requirements

(A) Every superior court judge, including senior superior court judges, shall attend approved creditable judicial education programs or activities, totaling a minimum of twelve hours every year. At least one hour of the mandated twelve hours per year shall be devoted to the topic of legal or judicial ethics or legal or judicial professionalism. If a judge completes more than twelve hours for credit in any calendar year, the excess credit shall be carried over and credited to the education requirements for the next succeeding year only.

(B) Each new judge must attend the pertinent Institute of Continuing Judicial Education (ICJE) in-state program of instruction for new judges or its locally administered individual new judge orientation course. Either activity must be attended as soon as possible after the judge's election or appointment and, preferably, before hearing cases, but in any event, within one year after assuming office. Each new judge is also encouraged to attend a nationally-based basic course for general jurisdiction trial judges.

(C) Additionally, every judge is encouraged to attend national or regional specialty, graduate or advanced programs of judicial and legal education.

(D) Qualifying creditable judicial education programs and activities shall include:

(1) Programs sponsored by the Institute of Continuing Judicial Education of Georgia;

(2) Programs of continuing legal education accredited by the State Bar of Georgia's Commission on Continuing Lawyer Competency, such as all Institute of Continuing Legal Education (ICLE) programs;

(3) Additional programs approved on behalf of the Council of Superior Court Judges by its Committee on Mandatory Continuing Judicial Education;

(4) Courses at a Georgia-based law school, whether for credit or not, that qualify an individual for a degree or to sit for the Georgia bar examination;

(5) Teaching any of the above;

(6) Service on the Judicial Qualifications Commission (JQC) or the State Bar Disciplinary Board for legal or judicial ethics or legal or judicial professionalism credit.

(E) For teaching, the following credits shall be given:

(1) Three additional hours for each hour of instructional responsibility as a lecturer when no handout paper is prepared, and six hours for each hour of lecture when a handout paper is required.

(2) Two hours for each hour as a panelist or mock trial judge.

(3) When the same lecture or other instructional activity is repeated in a single calendar year, additional credit shall be given equivalent to the actual time spent.

Adopted effective October 28, 1993; amended effective Sept. 2, 1999.

43.2 Administration of the Program

Administrative implementation of this program of mandatory continuing judicial education shall be conducted solely by the Council of Superior Court Judges.

Adopted effective October 28, 1993.

43.3 Council of Superior Court Judges Committee on Mandatory Continuing Judicial Education

The President of the Council of Superior Court Judges shall appoint a Committee on Mandatory Continuing Judicial Education, including at least one member of ICJE, which shall on behalf of the Council approve for credit judicial educational programs not otherwise automatically accredited by the MCJE rule, regardless of whether sponsored by a legal or judicial organization; and the committee shall impose the prescribed private and public sanctions on judges who fail to comply with the mandatory training plan.

Adopted effective October 28, 1993.

43.4 Sanctioning Procedures

(1) In December of each year, the Committee on Mandatory Continuing Judicial Education will receive a report from the Council of Superior Court Judges detailing the creditable participation of judges in MCJE activities for that year. At the same time, every superior court judge will also receive from the Council of Superior Court Judges a report on his or her creditable activity.

Judges failing to attain the required twelve hours in any year will be notified by the committee chair that they have not met the MCJE participation requirement for that year. Following receipt of such notice, a judge shall submit a plan for making up any deficiency in education requirements. Education credit hours earned thereafter shall first be credited to the deficiency for any prior year.

(2) Judges who fail to earn a minimum of twenty-four hours over a two-year period shall receive a private administrative admonition issued from the Committee on Mandatory Continuing Education of the Council of Superior Court Judges detailing the consequences of failure to fulfill the training requirements.

(3) Upon a judge's failure to fulfill the training requirements at the end of three years, the President of the Council of Superior Court Judges shall issue a public reprimand, with a copy spread upon the minutes of each county in the circuit where the judge serves.

Adopted effective October 28, 1993; amended effective Sept. 2, 1999.

43.5 Exemptions

The Committee on Mandatory Continuing Judicial Education of the Council of Superior Court Judges shall receive and act upon requests for exemptions to MCJE requirements of these rules.

Adopted effective October 28, 1993.

RULE 44. HABEAS CORPUS PROCEEDINGS IN DEATH SENTENCE CASES

44.1 Application

This rule shall apply to all petitions seeking, for the first time, a writ of habeas corpus in state court proceedings for those cases in which the petitioner has received a sentence of death. OCGA § 9–14–47.1.

Adopted effective January 11, 1996.

44.2 Request for Judicial Assignment

Within ten days of the filing of such a petition, the superior court clerk of the county where the petition is filed shall serve a copy of the petition upon the Executive Director of the Council of Superior Court Judges of Georgia. This service may be effected by mail and will constitute a request for judicial assistance under OCGA § 15–1–9.1(b)(3).

Adopted effective January 11, 1996.

44.3 Respondent's Answer or Motion to Dismiss

The respondent shall answer or move to dismiss the petition within 20 days after the filing of the petition or within such further time as the court may set for good cause shown.

Adopted effective January 11, 1996.

44.4 Assignment of Judge for Habeas Corpus Proceedings

(A) The Executive Committee of the Council of Superior Court Judges shall promulgate guidelines for the assignment of such cases to the various superior court judges throughout Georgia, and shall provide that the case will not be assigned to a judge within the circuit in which the sentence was imposed. Within 30 days after the Executive Director receives the petition, the president of the council shall assign the case to a judge in accordance with the guidelines.

(B) Pending assignment of a judge, or during a later vacancy of an assigned judge, a presiding judge of the court in which the petition is filed shall be authorized to act on emergency matters unless otherwise disqualified by Uniform Superior Court Rule 25.

Adopted effective January 11, 1996.

44.5 Preliminary Conference and Scheduling

The assigned judge may wish to consider scheduling a preliminary conference with counsel for the petitioner and respondent as soon as practical. This conference may be conducted by telephone. The court may also wish to enter a scheduling order establishing specific dates in accordance with the guidelines set forth in this rule. The court may on its own or on motion of either party shorten any time period set forth hereinafter, and may extend such time period for good cause.

Adopted effective January 11, 1996.

44.6 Motions

Within 60 days after the filing of the petition, the petitioner may file pretrial motions. Within 90 days after the filing of the petition, the respondent may file any motions. Responses to motions shall be governed by Rule 6.2.

Adopted effective January 11, 1996.

44.7 Amendments to the Petition; Discovery

No later than 120 days after the filing of the petition, the petitioner may amend the petition, and if discovery is allowed pursuant to OCGA § 9–14–48 it shall be completed.

Adopted effective January 11, 1996.

44.8 Pretrial Conference

The court may wish to schedule a pretrial conference with counsel for the petitioner and the respondent and enter an appropriate pretrial order for proceedings in the case. This conference may be conducted with counsel only and by telephone if appropriate.

Adopted effective January 11, 1996.

44.9 Evidentiary Hearing

Within 180 days after the filing of the petition, the court shall conduct an evidentiary hearing as provided by OCGA §§ 9–14–47 and 9–14–48.

Adopted effective January 11, 1996.

44.10 Preparation of Transcript

The evidentiary hearing shall be transcribed by a court reporter designated by the court hearing the case as set forth in OCGA § 9–14–50. Within 30 days after the evidentiary hearing, the transcript of the evidentiary hearing shall be made available to the parties and the court.

Adopted effective January 11, 1996.

44.11 Briefing

Within 60 days after the evidentiary hearing, the petitioner may file any brief and if so directed by the court shall file proposed findings of fact and conclusions of law and a proposed order. Within 90 days after the evidentiary hearing, the respondent may file any responsive brief and if so directed by the court shall file proposed findings of fact and conclusions of law and a proposed order. Within 100 days after the evidentiary hearing, the petitioner may file any additional responsive brief.

Adopted effective January 11, 1996.

44.12 Ruling on Petition

Within 90 days of the filing of the respondent's brief, or the petitioner's reply brief if one is filed, the court shall issue its ruling on the petition and its written findings of fact and conclusions of law as required by OCGA § 9–14–49.

Adopted effective January 11, 1996.

44.13 Effect of Rule

Upon application of any party, the Supreme Court may order such relief as it finds necessary to assure compliance with this Rule. This Rule provides procedural guidelines and no substantive rights are hereby conferred upon any person. No violation of this Rule shall be the basis of any grant of habeas corpus relief.

Adopted effective January 11, 1996.

RULE 45. COURT EMERGENCY MEASURES

Courts within a judicial circuit shall prepare for emergencies and disruptions in court business by adopting and periodically reviewing a consolidated plan addressing the safety and security of employees and the public, continuity of operations and their immediate response to crises.

a. Court Security and Facilities

In coordination with local and/or state public safety officials, courts shall develop and annually update court security policies and procedures and a short–term emergency response program that anticipates safeguarding lives and property.

b. Court Operations

At a minimum, each plan for the continuity of court operations shall identify:

i. Essential activities and functions to be performed;

ii. Vital records, systems and equipment, and provide for their protection;

iii. Automatic succession of leadership and delegation of authority;

iv. One or more relocation sites, and provide for their preparation;

v. Employees to perform essential activities and functions, and provide for their training;

vi. Means for warning employees, the public and the media of potential threats and recommended actions;

vii. Means for identifying the location and status of employees following an emergency;

viii. Means for communicating with employees and the public subsequent to an emergency;

ix. Means for restoring normal functions as soon as is feasible and prudent; and

x. Regular training for employees with specific emergency responsibilities and for all employees that may be affected by disruptions to operations.

c. Court Emergency Order

Upon his or her own motion or after consideration of a request by another judge or court official, the chief judge of a court experiencing an emergency or disruption in operations may issue an order authorizing relief from time deadlines imposed by statute or court rule until the restoration of normal court operations or as specified. The order shall contain (1) the identity and position of the judge, (2) the time, date and place executed, (3) the jurisdiction affected, (4) the nature of the emergency, (5) the period of duration, and (6) other information relevant to the suspension or restoration of court operations.

The duration of a court emergency order is limited to a maximum of thirty days. The order may be extended no more than twice by the issuing judge for additional thirty-day periods, and any extensions shall contain information required in the original order.

The court emergency order may designate one or more facilities as temporary courthouses which shall be suitable for court business and located as near as possible to the county seat.

Adopted effective December 2, 2004.

INDEX TO UNIFORM SUPERIOR COURT RULES

*

UNIFORM STATE COURT RULES

Effective July 1, 1985

Including Amendments Received Through November 1, 2006

Research Note

Use WESTLAW *to find cases citing a rule. In addition, use* WESTLAW *to search for specific terms or to update a rule; see the GA–RULES and GA–ORDERS Scope screens for further information.*

Amendments to these rules are published, as received, in the South Eastern Reporter 2d *and* Georgia Cases *advance sheets.*

The Uniform Rules for the Superior Courts shall be applicable in State Courts except as follows:

A. Wherever the words "superior court" or "superior courts" appear in the Uniform Superior Court Rules, the word "state" shall apply in lieu of the word "superior."

B. Wherever the words "district attorney" appear in the Uniform Superior Court Rules, the words "prosecuting attorney" shall apply in lieu of "district attorney."

C. Wherever the word "felony" appears, the words "or misdemeanor" shall be added.

D. Wherever the words "indictment" or "grand jury indictment" appear, the word "accusation" shall apply in lieu thereof.

E. The following Uniform State Court Rules shall read as follows:

RULE 6. MOTIONS IN CIVIL ACTIONS

6.2 Reply. Unless otherwise ordered by the judge, each party opposing a motion shall serve and file a response, reply memorandum, affidavits, or other responsive material not later than 30 days after service of the motion, or on the date of the hearing (if one is held) whichever occurs sooner.

RULE 8. CIVIL JURY TRIAL CALENDAR

8.3 Trial Calendar. The calendar clerk shall prepare a trial calendar from the actions appearing on the ready list, in the order appearing on such list. The calendar shall state the place of trial and the date and time during which the actions shall be tried. The trial calendar shall be delivered to the clerk of the court and distributed or published a sufficient period of time, but not less than 20 days, prior to the session of court at which the actions listed thereon are to be tried, except that the trial calendar for dispossessories, foreclosures, mechanics liens, garnishments and distress warrants shall be published at least twenty-four hours in advance of the hearing and shall be available at the clerk's office.

RULE 15. DEFAULT JUDGMENTS

The party seeking entry of a default judgment in any action shall certify to the court the date and type of service effected as shown by court records and that there has been no defensive pleading from the party against whom the judgment is sought. This certificate shall be in writing and must be attached to the proposed default judgment when presented to the judge for signature.

If a claim is for a liquidated amount, default judgment may be entered without a certificate when service has been perfected, the matter stands in default, and judgment is otherwise appropriate.

RULE 17. CONFLICTS—STATE AND FEDERAL COURTS

17.2 Notice of Resolution. The judges or clerks of the courts in which such conflicts exist shall give prompt written notice to all counsel of the manner in which the conflicts have been resolved; provided, however, that if the conflict is resolved by the court seven days or less in advance of the conflict, oral notice shall suffice.

RULE 26. PRE–INDICTMENT PROCEEDINGS

26.1 Bonds and First Appearance.

(F) Inform the accused that he has the right to accusation in misdemeanor cases or to Uniform Traffic Citation in traffic cases, and the right to trial by jury;

RULE 29. APPOINTMENT OF COUNSEL FOR INDIGENT DEFENDANTS

29.2 Application and Appointment of Counsel. When an accused person, contending to be financially unable to employ an attorney to defend against pending criminal charges or to appeal a conviction, desires to have an attorney appointed, the accused shall make a request in writing to the court or its designee for an attorney to be appointed. The request shall be in the form of an application for appointment of counsel and certificate of financial resources, made under oath and signed by the accused which shall contain information as to the accused's assets, liabilities, employment, earnings, other income, number and ages of dependents, the charges against the accused and such other information as shall be required by the court. The purpose of the application and certificate is to provide the court or its designee with sufficient information from which to determine the financial ability of the accused to employ counsel. The court may appoint an attorney for an indigent defendant without a written request.

The determination of indigency or not shall be made by a judge of a state court or designee.

Upon a determination of indigency the court shall, in writing, authorize the appointment of counsel for the indigent accused. The original authorization of appointment shall be filed with the accusation or warrant in the case; a copy of the authorization shall be forwarded to the clerk, court administrator, public defender or such other person designated by the court to assign an attorney to an indigent defendant. Such person shall notify the accused, the appointed attorney, the sheriff and the prosecuting attorney of the appointment.

RULE 33. PLEADING BY DEFENDANT

33.1 Alternatives.

(A) A defendant may plead guilty, not guilty, or in the discretion of the judge, nolo contendere. A plea of guilty or nolo contendere should be received only from the defendant personally in open court, except when the defendant is a corporation, in which case the plea may be entered by counsel or a corporate officer. In misdemeanor cases, upon the request of a defendant who has made, in writing, a knowing, intelligent and voluntary waiver of his right to be present, the court may accept a plea of guilty in absentia.

(B) A defendant may plead nolo contendere only with the consent of the judge. Such a plea should be accepted by the judge only after due consideration of the views of the parties and the interest of the public in the effective administration of justice. Procedurally, a plea of nolo contendere should be handled under these rules in a manner similar to a plea of guilty.

33.11 Record of Proceedings. A record of the proceedings at which a defendant enters a plea of guilty or nolo contendere shall be made and preserved. The record should include:

(A) the inquiry into the voluntariness of the plea (as required in section 33.7);

(B) the advice to the defendant (as required in section 33.8);

(C) the inquiry into the accuracy of the plea (as required in section 33.9), and, if applicable;

(D) the notice to the defendant that the trial court intends to reject the plea agreement and the defendant's right to withdraw the guilty plea before sentence is pronounced.

RULE 36. FILING AND PROCESSING

36.1 Preparation of Documents. To the extent practical, all materials presented for filing in any state court shall be typed, legibly written or printed in black ink suitable for reproduction, on opaque white paper measuring 8½″ × 11″ of a good quality, grade and weight.

36.6 Minutes and Final Record. There shall be one or more books or microfilm records (combined "Minutes Book", "Writ or Pleading Record" and "Final Record") called Minutes and Final Record in which each entire matter (except traffic and T.V.B. cases) shall be recorded after completion. After recording, the original may be destroyed according to the state retention schedule or stored off premises as provided by law.

36.8 File Categories. The categories of files to be established by the clerk shall be civil and criminal, and such subcategories as the clerk may establish.

36.10 Filing Requirements—Civil. Complaints or petitions presented to the clerk for filing shall be filed only when accompanied by the proper filing fee, fee for sheriff service or a pauper's affidavit, and when applicable, any forms required by law or rule to be completed by the parties. The attorney or party filing the complaint shall furnish the necessary service copies, and shall fill out and attach the appropriate backing sheets.

36.15 Assessment of Costs—Criminal. When costs are assessed the minimum amount assessed as court costs in the disposition of any criminal offense shall be $50.00. Any surcharge provided for by law shall be in addition.

RULE 39. DOCKETING AND INDEXING

39.5 General Execution Docket. The General Execution Docket shall contain all Fi. Fas. All state court judgments shall be forwarded to the superior court to be recorded in the General Execution Docket, with costs of recording being added to advanced costs. The information to be entered shall be:

(A) Names of the parties and attorneys of record;

(B) Names of county and court in which judgment was issued;

(C) The date of judgment;

(D) The date of issuance of the Fi. Fa.;

(E) The date of the recording of the Fi. Fa. on the General Execution Docket;

(F) The number of the case on which the judgment was rendered; and

(G) The amount of principal, costs, attorney fees, interest, penalties, and total amount of the Fi. Fa. on the case.

Nulla Bona's and satisfactions are to be noted on the original entry. Re-issued Fi. Fas. shall be recorded as a new Fi. Fa. in the General Execution Docket. A cross-reference to that new entry shall be made on the original entry of the

Fi. Fa. or the last renewal of the Fi. Fa. which is less than seven years old.

39.7 Suggested Forms. [1] The forms below are suggested for use in all state courts in this state.

[1] For information regarding the availability of sample and preprinted forms, please contact the Administrative Office of the Courts.

Publisher's Note

The suggested forms are set forth in Uniform Court Rules Appendix A: Forms, infra.

39.9 Court Information. The chief judge of each State Court may require the clerk of that court to furnish to the chief judge within 10 days after the end of each month, a general civil and a criminal (including traffic violation bureau offenses, OCGA § 40–13–50 et seq.) caseload management report. The Chief Justice of the Supreme Court of Georgia may request copies of the information that is furnished to the Chief Judges of the State Courts pursuant to this rule.

The case types, events types and disposition methods used in these reports will conform to Judicial Council guidelines for reporting caseload. Each such report shall include the following:

(A) the number of cases filed by case type in the prior month and year-to-date;

(B) the number of cases disposed by case type and disposition method in the prior month and year-to-date;

(C) the number and type of pending cases;

(D) a list of cases more than 120 days old (criminal) and 180 days old (civil) to include the following data:

(1) case number,

(2) style,

(3) case type,

(4) filing date,

(5) next event scheduled,

(6) date of that event; and

(E) any other information the chief judge requests that is contained within the court's standardized computer programs.

Rule 39.9 adopted October 9, 1997.

RULE 43. CONTINUING JUDICIAL EDUCATION

A. Every state court judge (including senior judges who serve more than 30 days a year and any pro hac vice judge serving for more than 30 days a year, or any person serving as a state court judge for more than 30 days a year) shall attend approved MCJE courses and/or MCLE courses approved by ICJE for credit for judges, or other educational programs or activities approved by ICJE for credit for judges, totaling a minimum of 24 hours every two (2) years. At least two hours of the mandated 24 hours shall be approved ICJE "ethics studies."

B. It is recommended that judges acquire the judicial study at the rate of 12 hours per year, but sanctions do not apply if this annual recommendation is not met. It is further recommended that at least one of the two hours required in "ethics" be in the area of judicial ethics, but this is not mandated. For sitting judges, the two-year period shall begin January 1, 1988, and end December 31, 1989, and each two-year period thereafter. Any judge coming on the bench shall acquire pro rata educational credits as required. (For example, a judge coming on the bench in March, 1988, will be required to accumulate 21 credits before December 31, 1989). A judge coming on the bench within the last five months of the educational period shall not be required to acquire credits for the remainder of the period, except for the educational requirements of new judges.

C. Each new judge must attend the pertinent Institute of Continuing Judicial Education (ICJE) in-state program of instruction for new judges or its locally administered individual new judge orientation course. Either activity must be attended as soon as possible after the judge's election or appointment, but, in any event, within one year after assuming office. Each new judge is also encouraged to attend a nationally-based basic course for general jurisdiction trial judges, as set forth in Paragraph D below.

ICJE's program of orientation for new judges is periodically available as a group-oriented, participative, instructional activity (usually in December of each election year), and is always available for self-study by use of audio or videotapes. Credit for new judges studies shall also apply to the requirement in Paragraph A above to the extent ICJE approves credits.

D. Additionally, every judge is encouraged to attend national or regional specialty, graduate or advanced programs of judicial and legal education and shall receive such credits as mandated by ICJE.

E. Sanctioning Procedures.

(1) Judges who fail to earn a minimum of 24 hours over a two-year period may receive a private administrative admonition issued from the Education Committee of the State Court Judges Council detailing the consequences of failure to fulfill the training requirements.

In December of each year, the Committee on Mandatory Continuing Judicial Education will receive a report from ICJE detailing the creditable participation of judges in MCJE activities for that year. At the same time, every state court judge will also receive from ICJE a report on his or her creditable activity.

Persons failing to attain the required 12 hours in any year will be notified by that committee chair that they have not met the MCJE participation requirement for that year, and a copy of this notice will be furnished to the pertinent chief judge of the judicial administrative district.

Persons failing to earn 24 credit hours over any period of two successive years or, regardless of total hours, failing to earn two (2) hours credit in judicial ethics over any period of two successive years, will be notified by the committee chair that they have not met MCJE participation requirements and may receive a private letter of admonition issued from the committee detailing any deficiencies and consequences. A copy of this notice or admonition will be furnished to the pertinent chief judge of the judicial administrative district, and the President of the State Court Judges Council.

(2) Upon a judge's failure to fulfill the training requirements at the end of three years, the President of the State Court Judges Council shall issue a public reprimand, *with a copy spread upon the minutes of each county in the circuit where the judge serves.*

One month prior to the issuance of a public reprimand, the committee shall issue to any applicable judge a request as to why a public reprimand should not be issued.

Adopted December 14, 1987.

F. The following Uniform Superior Court Rules shall not be applicable in state courts:

Rules 24.1 through 24.7—Domestic Relations.

Rules 34.1 through 34.5—Unified Appeal.

UNIFORM COURT RULES
APPENDIX A: FORMS

Including Amendments Received Through November 1, 2006

Research Note

Use WESTLAW *to find cases citing a rule. In addition, use* WESTLAW *to search for specific terms or to update a rule; see the GA–RULES and GA–ORDERS Scope screens for further information.*

Amendments to these rules are published, as received, in the South Eastern Reporter 2d *and* Georgia Cases *advance sheets.*

Table of Forms

FORM SC–1. SUMMONS

IN THE SUPERIOR COURT OF (Your County) COUNTY

STATE OF GEORGIA

______________________ CIVIL ACTION,
NUMBER ______________________

____

____
PLAINTIFF

VS.

____

____

____
DEFENDANT

SUMMONS

TO THE ABOVE NAMED DEFENDANT:

You are hereby summoned and required to file with the Clerk of said court and serve upon the Plaintiff's attorney, whose name and address is:

an answer to the complaint which is herewith served upon you, within 30 days after service of this summons upon you, exclusive of the day of service. If you fail to do so, judgment by default will be taken against you for the relief demanded in the complaint.

This ________ day of ________________, 19___.

(Your Name)
Clerk of Superior Court

By ______________________
Deputy Clerk

Instructions: Attach addendum sheet for additional parties if needed, make notation on this sheet if addendum sheet is used.

SC-1 Rev. 85

FORM SC–2. SHERIFF'S ENTRY OF SERVICE

Civil Action No. ____________________ Superior Court ☐

Date Filed ____________________ State Court ☐

Georgia, (Your County) COUNTY

____

Attorney's Address ____________________

Plaintiff

VS.

____

Name and Address of Party to be Served ____________________

Defendant

____

____

____

Garnishee

SHERIFF'S ENTRY OF SERVICE

I have this day served the defendant ____________ personally with a copy of the within action and summons.
I have this day served the defendant ____________ by leaving a copy of the action and summons at his most notorious place of abode in this County. Delivered same into hands of ____________ described as follows: age, about ____ years; weight, about ____ pounds; height, about ____ feet and ____ inches, domiciled at the residence of defendant.
Served the defendant ____________, a corporation, by leaving a copy of the within action and summons with ____________ in charge of the office and place of doing business of said Corporation in this County.
I have this day served the above styled affidavit and summons on the defendant(s) by posting a copy of the same to the door of the premises designated in said affidavit, and on the same day of such posting by depositing a true copy of same in the United States Mail, First Class in an envelope properly addressed to the defendant(s) at the address shown in said summons, with adequate postage affixed thereon containing notice to the defendant(s) to answer said summons at the place stated in the summons.
Diligent search made and defendant ____________ not to be found in the jurisdiction of this Court.

This ________ day of ________, 19___.

____

DEPUTY

SHERIFF DOCKET ______ PAGE ______

SC-2 Rev. 85

FORM SC-3. ORDER OF PUBLICATION; RETURN OF SERVICE; ORDER PERFECTING SERVICE

IN THE SUPERIOR COURT OF (Your County) COUNTY
STATE OF GEORGIA

______________________ CIVIL ACTION NO. ______________
______________________ SERVICE BY PUBLICATION DATES:
PLAINTIFF

____

VS.

____

____

____
DEFENDANT ______________________

NAME OF PARTY TO BE SERVED:
____

ORDER OF PUBLICATION

It appearing by Affidavit, that the above named defendant on whom service is to be made in this case resides out of the State, or has departed from the State, or cannot after due diligence, be found within the State, or conceals (him)(her)self to avoid service of the Summons, and it further appearing, either by Affidavit or by verified Complaint on file, that a claim exists against the defendant in respect to whom service is to be made, and that (he)(she) is a necessary or proper party to the action.

IT IS HEREBY CONSIDERED, ORDERED AND DECREED THAT: Service be made by publication as provided by law.

SO ORDERED this ______________ day of ______________, 19___.

____
JUDGE/CLERK SUPERIOR COURT
OF (Your County) COUNTY, GA.

RETURN OF SERVICE

I hereby certify that a Notice in the Manner and form prescribed in the foregoing Order was published, and that I have enclosed, directed, stamped and mailed a copy of the said Notice together with a copy of the Order for Service by Publication and Complaint (if any), to the above named defendant.

This the ______________ day of ______________, 19___.

(Your Name)
Clerk of Superior Court

By ______________________
DEPUTY CLERK

ORDER PERFECTING SERVICE

It appearing to the Court that service upon the above named party has been perfected by publication of notice on the above stated dates in the legal organ of this County, and by enclosing, directing, stamping, and mailing a copy of the notice together with a copy of the order for Publication and the Complaint (if any) to said defendant at (his) (her) last known address.

IT IS HEREBY ORDERED that said service by publication be, and is approved.

____
JUDGE, (Your County) SUPERIOR COURT

PUBLICATION DATES OK: This the ______________ day of ______________, 19___.

(Your Name)
Clerk of Superior Court

____
DEPUTY CLERK

SC-3 Rev. 85

FORM SC–4. NOTICE OF PUBLICATION

IN THE SUPERIOR COURT OF (Your County) COUNTY

STATE OF GEORGIA

______________________ PLAINTIFF	:	CIVIL ACTION NO. ______________
______________________ DEFENDANT	:	
TO: ______________________	:	
______________________	:	
______________________	:	

NOTICE OF PUBLICATION

By Order for service by publication dated the ______________________ day of ______________________, 19___, you are hereby notified that on the ________ day of ______________________, 19___, ______________________ filed suit against you for ______________________.

You are required to file with the Clerk of the Superior Court, and to serve upon plaintiff's attorney, ______________________ an Answer in writing within sixty (60) days of the date of the order for publication.

WITNESS, the Honorable ______________________, Judge of this Superior Court.

This the ________ day of ______________, 19___.

____
DEPUTY CLERK, SUPERIOR COURT
FOR: (Your Name and address)

SC-4 Rev. 85

FORM SC-5. WRIT OF FIERI FACIAS

WRIT OF FIERI FACIAS
IN THE SUPERIOR COURT OF (Your County) COUNTY, GEORGIA

CIVIL ACTION NUMBER ____________

JUDGMENT DATE ____________

Plaintiff's Attorney—Name, Address & Telephone

Name: ____________

Address: ____________

____

____

Telephone & Area Code: ____________

Fi. Fa. in Hands of: ____________

____

____

____

____

Plaintiff(s)

VS.

____

____

____

Defendant(s)

To all and singular the sheriffs of the State and their lawful deputies:

In the above styled case, and on the judgment date set out, the plaintiff(s) named above recovered against the defendant(s) named above, judgment in the following sums:

Principal	$________
Interest	$________
Interest—Other	$________
Attorney's Fees	$________
Court Costs	$________
Total	$________

NOTE: ____________

____

with future interest upon said principal amount from the date of judgment at the legal rate.

Therefore, YOU ARE COMMANDED, that of the goods and chattels, lands and tenements of said defendant(s), and ESPECIALLY/ONLY of the following described property, to wit:

CANCELLATION

The within and foregoing Fi. Fa. having been paid in full the Clerk of Superior Court is hereby directed to cancel it of record this ________ day of ______, 19____.

Signature: ____________

Title: ____________

YOU cause to be made the several sums set out in the foregoing recital of the judgment in this case and have the said several sums of money before the Superior Court of this County at the next term of court, with this Writ to render to said plaintiff(s) the principal, interest, attorney fees and costs aforesaid.

Witness the Honorable ____________ Judge of Said Court, this the ____________ day of ____________, 19____.

(Your Name), CLERK

By: ____________

Deputy Clerk

Entered on General Execution Docket ______, at Page ______ this ______ day of ______, 19____.

SC-5 Rev. 85

A diligent search was made and no property of the defendant(s) ______________________________

has been found in this County, on which to levy this Fi. Fa.

This the ________ day of __________, 19___

____
Deputy Sheriff

STATE OF GEORGIA, COUNTY OF (Your County):

I have this day executed the within Fi. Fa. by levying upon and seizing the following described property of defendant(s), to-wit:

Levied at ______________________________
Georgia, this ________ day of __________, 19___

____
Deputy Sheriff

THE PROPERTY DESCRIBED IN LEVY WAS KNOCKED DOWN TO

____

Sheriff's Service $________
Sheriff's Commission $________
Sheriff's Deed $________
Sheriff's Levy $________
Advertising Fee $________
Other $________
Total $________
Net Proceeds $________

____
Sheriff

STATE OF GEORGIA, COUNTY OF (Your County):

I have this day executed the within Fi. Fa. by levying upon and seizing the following described property of defendant(s), to-wit:

Levied at ______________________________
Georgia, this ________ day of __________, 19___

____
Deputy Sheriff

THE PROPERTY DESCRIBED IN LEVY WAS KNOCKED DOWN TO

____

Sheriff's Service $________
Sheriff's Commission $________
Sheriff's Deed $________
Sheriff's Levy $________
Advertising Fee $________
Other $________
Total $________
Net Proceeds $________

____
Sheriff

FORM SC–6. FINAL DISPOSITION (FELONY/MISDEMEANOR)

IN THE SUPERIOR COURT OF ______ COUNTY, GEORGIA FINAL DISPOSITION

CRIMINAL ACTION NO. ______

VS

OFFENSE(S) ______

______

______ TERM, 19___

☐ PLEA:
☐ NEGOTIATED
☐ GUILTY ON COUNT(S) ______
☐ NOLO CONTENDERE ON COUNT(S) ______
☐ TO LESSER INCLUDED OFFENSE(S) ______
ON COUNT(S) ______

☐ JURY
☐ NON-JURY

☐ VERDICT:
☐ GUILTY ON COUNT(S) ______
☐ NOT GUILTY ON COUNT(S) ______
☐ GUILTY OF INCLUDED OFFENSE(S) OF ______ ON COUNT(S) ______

☐ OTHER DISPOSITION:
☐ NOLLE PROSEQUI ORDER ON COUNT(S) ______
☐ DEAD DOCKET ORDER ON COUNT(S) ______
(SEE SEPARATE ORDER)

☐ DEFENDANT WAS ADVISED OF HIS/HER RIGHT TO HAVE THIS SENTENCE REVIEWED BY THE SUPERIOR COURTS SENTENCE REVIEW PANEL

☐ FELONY SENTENCE ☐ MISDEMEANOR SENTENCE

WHEREAS, the above-named defendant has been found guilty of the above-stated offense, WHEREUPON, it is ordered and adjudged by the Court that: The said defendant is hereby sentenced to confinement for a period of ______ in the State Penal System or such other institution as the Commissioner of the State Department of Corrections or Court may direct, to be computed as provided by law. HOWEVER, it is further ordered by the Court:

☐ 1) THAT the above sentence may be served on probation.
☐ 2) THAT upon service of ______ of the above sentence, the remainder of ______ may be served on probation PROVIDED that the said defendant complies with the following general and other conditions herein imposed by the Court as a part of this sentence.

☐ GENERAL CONDITIONS OF PROBATION

The defendant, having been granted the privilege of serving all or part of the above-stated sentence on probation, hereby is sentenced to the following general conditions of probation:

☐ 1) Do not violate the criminal laws of any governmental unit.
☐ 2) Avoid injurious and vicious habits—especially alcoholic intoxication and narcotics and other dangerous drugs unless prescribed lawfully.
☐ 3) Avoid persons or places of disreputable or harmful character.
☐ 4) Report to the Probation-Parole Supervisor as directed and permit such Supervisor to visit him (her) at home or elsewhere.
☐ 5) Work faithfully at suitable employment insofar as may be possible.
☐ 6) Do not change his (her) present place of abode, move outside the jurisdiction of the Court, or leave the State for any period of time without prior permission of the Probation Supervisor.
☐ 7) Support his (her) legal dependents to the best of his (her) ability.

☐ OTHER CONDITIONS OF PROBATION

IT IS FURTHER ORDERED that the defendant pay a fine in the amount of ______ plus $50 or 10%, whichever is less pursuant to O.C.G.A. § 15–21–70, and pay restitution in the amount of ______.

______

______

______

IT IS THE FURTHER ORDER of the Court, and the defendant is hereby advised that the Court may, at any time, revoke any conditions of this probation and/or discharge the defendant from probation. The probationer shall be subject to arrest for violation of any condition of probation herein granted. If such probation is revoked, the Court may order the execution of the sentence which was originally imposed or any portion thereof in the manner provided by law after deducting therefrom the amount of time the defendant has served on probation.

The defendant was represented by the Honorable ______ Attorney at Law, ______ County, by (Employment) (Appointment).

By the Court ______, 19___

So ordered this ______ day of ______, 19___.

______
Judge, Superior Court

SC-6 Rev. 85

FORM SC–6.1. FINAL DISPOSITION (FIRST OFFENDER)

IN THE SUPERIOR COURT OF __________ COUNTY, GEORGIA FINAL DISPOSITION

CRIMINAL ACTION NO. __________

VS

OFFENSE(S) __________

__________ TERM, 19__

☐ PLEA

___ NEGOTIATED __________
___ GUILTY ON COUNT(S) __________
___ NOLO CONTENDERE ON COUNT(S) __________
___ TO LESSER INCLUDED OFFENSE(S) __________ ON COUNT(S) __________

☐ VERDICT ___ JURY ___ NON-JURY

___ GUILTY ON COUNT(S) __________
___ NOT GUILTY ON COUNT(S) __________
___ GUILTY OF INCLUDED OFFENSE(S) OF __________ ON COUNT(S) __________

☐ OTHER DISPOSITION

___ NOLLE PROSEQUI ORDER ON COUNT(S) __________
___ DEAD DOCKET ORDER ON COUNT(S) __________
(SEE SEPARATE ORDER)

___ DEFENDANT WAS ADVISED OF THE RIGHT TO HAVE THIS SENTENCE REVIEWED BY THE SUPERIOR COURTS SENTENCE REVIEW PANEL

FIRST OFFENDER TREATMENT

WHEREAS, no adjudication of guilt has been made subsequent to the entry of the plea or verdict shown above, and

WHEREAS, the Court has reviewed the defendant's criminal record on file with the Georgia Crime Information Center, and

WHEREAS, the defendant has not previously been convicted of a felony or used the provisions of the First Offender Act (Ga. Laws 1968, p. 324).

NOW, THEREFORE, the defendant consenting hereto, it is the judgment of the Court that no judgment of guilt be imposed at this time but that further proceedings are deferred and the defendant is hereby sentenced to confinement for the period of __________;

HOWEVER, it is further ordered by the Court:

___ That the sentence may be served on probation;
___ That upon service of __________ of the sentence, the remainder of __________ may be served on probation;

PROVIDED, that the defendant complies with the following general and special conditions herein imposed by the Court as part of the sentence.

PROVIDED, further, that upon violation of the terms of probation, upon conviction for another crime during the period of probation, or upon the Court's determination that the defendant is or was not eligible for sentencing under the First Offender Act, the Court may enter an adjudication of guilt and proceed to sentence the defendant to the maximum sentence as provided by law.

IT IS THE FURTHER ORDER of the Court, and the defendant is hereby advised, that the Court may, at any time, revoke any conditions of this probation and/or discharge the defendant from probation. The probationer shall be subject to arrest for violation of any condition of probation herein granted. If such probation is revoked, the Court may enter an adjudication of guilt and proceed to sentence the defendant to the maximum sentence authorized by law with or without credit for time served on probation.

Upon fulfillment of the terms of this sentence, or upon release of the defendant by the Court prior to the termination of this sentence, the defendant shall stand discharged of said offense without court adjudication of guilt and shall be completely exonerated of guilt of said offense charged.

Let a copy of this Order be forwarded to the office of the State Probation System of Georgia and the Identification Division of the Federal Bureau of Investigation.

__________ __________
Initials of Probation Officer Initials of Defendant

Page 1 of 2
SC-6.1 (Rev. 10/89)

IN THE SUPERIOR COURT OF ________ COUNTY, GEORGIA FINAL DISPOSITION

VS CRIMINAL ACTION NO. ________

____

FIRST OFFENDER TREATMENT (Page 2)

GENERAL CONDITIONS OF PROBATION

The defendant having been granted the privilege of serving all or part of the above-stated sentence on probation, hereby is sentenced to the following general conditions of probation:

___ 1) Do not violate the criminal laws of any governmental unit.
___ 2) Avoid injurious and vicious habits — especially alcoholic intoxication and narcotics and other dangerous drugs unless prescribed lawfully.
___ 3) Avoid persons or places of disreputable or harmful character.
___ 4) Report to the Probation Officer as directed and permit such officer to visit you at home or elsewhere.
___ 5) Work faithfully at suitable employment insofar as may be possible.
___ 6) Do not change your present place of abode, move outside the jurisdiction of the Court, or leave the State for any period of time without prior permission of the Probation Supervisor.
___ 7) Support your legal dependents to the best of your ability.

OTHER CONDITIONS OF PROBATION

IT IS FURTHER ORDERED, that the defendant pay a FINE of ________ plus COURT COST of ________ plus $50 or 10%, whichever is less pursuant to OCGA § 15-21-70 and pay RESTITUTION in the amount of ________ and pay ATTORNEY'S FEE of ________.

To be paid to ________________________

____

Pay $________ Probation Fees to be paid at the rate of $________ each month beginning ________.

OTHER SPECIAL CONDITIONS

____

The defendant was represented by the Honorable ________________, Attorney at Law, ________________ County, by (Employment) (Appointment).

SO ORDERED, this ______ day of ________, 19___.

________________ Judge   Superior Court

Certificate of Service — This is to certify that a true and correct copy of both pages of this Final Disposition has been delivered in person and the defendant has been duly instructed regarding the conditions as set forth.

This ______ day of ________, 19___.

________________ Probation Officer   ________________ Defendant

Filed in this office this ________ day of ________, 19___. ________________ Deputy Clerk

Page 2 of 2
SC-6.1 (Rev. 10/89)

Amended effective January 18, 1990.

FORM SC–6.2. FINAL DISPOSITION (YOUTHFUL OFFENDER)

IN THE SUPERIOR COURT OF ______ COUNTY, GEORGIA FINAL DISPOSITION

CRIMINAL ACTION NO. ______

VS

OFFENSE(S) ______

______ TERM, 19____

☐ PLEA:
☐ NEGOTIATED ☐ JURY
☐ GUILTY ON COUNT(S) ____ ☐ NON-JURY
☐ NOLO CONTENDERE ON COUNT(S) ______
☐ TO LESSER INCLUDED ______ ON COUNT(S) ______

☐ VERDICT:
☐ GUILTY ON COUNT(S) ______
☐ NOT GUILTY ON COUNT(S) ______
☐ GUILTY OF INCLUDED ON COUNT(S) ______

☐ OTHER DISPOSITION:
☐ NOLLE PROSEQUI ORDER ON COUNT(S) ______
☐ DEAD DOCKET ORDER ON COUNT(S) ______
(SEE SEPARATE ORDER)

☐ DEFENDANT WAS ADVISED OF HIS/HER RIGHT TO HAVE THIS SENTENCE REVIEWED BY THE SUPERIOR COURTS SENTENCE REVIEW PANEL

☐ YOUTHFUL OFFENDER SENTENCE

WHEREAS, the above-named defendant has been found guilty of the above-stated offense. WHEREUPON, IT IS CONSIDERED, ORDERED, AND ADJUDGED THAT THE SAID DEFENDANT BE TREATED PURSUANT TO THE PROVISIONS OF THE Georgia Youthful Offender Act of 1972 (Georgia Laws 1972, pp. 592-599), and said defendant is hereby remanded to the State Department of Corrections.
☐ for an indefinite period of time for confinement, treatment and supervision
☐ for not less than ______ years for confinement, treatment and supervision

☐ GENERAL CONDITIONS OF PROBATION

The defendant, having been granted the privilege of serving all or part of the above-stated sentence on probation, hereby is sentenced to the following general conditions of probation:
☐ 1) Do not violate the criminal laws of any governmental unit.
☐ 2) Avoid injurious and vicious habits—especially alcoholic intoxication and narcotics and other dangerous drugs unless prescribed lawfully.
☐ 3) Avoid persons or places of disreputable or harmful character.
☐ 4) Report to the Probation-Parole Supervisor as directed and permit such Supervisor to visit him (her) at home or elsewhere.
☐ 5) Work faithfully at suitable employment insofar as may be possible.
☐ 6) Do not change his (her) present place of abode, move outside the jurisdiction of the Court, or leave the State for any period of time without prior permission of the Probation Supervisor.
☐ 7) Support his (her) legal dependents to the best of his (her) ability.

☐ OTHER CONDITIONS OF PROBATION

IT IS FURTHER ORDERED that the defendant pay a fine in the amount of ______ plus $50 or 10%, whichever is less pursuant to O.C.G.A. § 15–21–70, and pay restitution in the amount of ______

______

______

______

IT IS THE FURTHER ORDER of the Court, and the defendant is hereby advised that the Court may, at any time, revoke any conditions of this probation and/or discharge the defendant from probation. The probationer shall be subject to arrest for violation of any condition of probation herein granted. If such probation is revoked, the Court may order the execution of the sentence which was originally imposed by committing the offender to the custody of the State Department of Corrections. The defendant was represented by the Honorable ______ Attorney at Law, ______ County, by (Employment) (Appointment).

By the Court ______, 19____

So ordered this ______ day of ______, 19____

______
Judge Superior Court

SC-6.2 Rev.85

FORM SC-7. EXEMPLIFICATION

EXEMPLIFICATION

Georgia, County

I, ______________, Clerk of the Superior Court of ______________ County, do hereby certify that I have compared the foregoing copy of ____
____
____
____
____
____
with the original record thereof, now remaining in this office, and the same is a correct transcript therefrom, and the whole of such original record, and that said Court is a Court of Record.

IN TESTIMONY WHEREOF, I have thereunto set my hand and affixed the seal of said Court, this the ______________ day of ______________ 19____.

____
, Clerk
Superior Court of ______________ County, Georgia

Georgia, County

I, ______________________________________, do certify that I am Judge of the Superior Court of said county, and that I am the presiding Judge of said Court and that the above attestation, subscribed by Clerk of said Court, is sufficient and in due form of law, and that his signature thereto is genuine.

Witness my hand and official signature, this the ______________ day of ______________ 19____.

____
Judge,
Superior Court of ______________ County, Georgia

Georgia, County

I, ______________ Clerk of the Superior Court in and for said County, hereby certify that the above attestation of Hon. ______________________________, Judge of the Superior Court of ______________ County, Georgia, is his genuine signature, and that he is Judge of said Court, and said certificate is in due form of law.

Given under my hand and seal of office, this the ______________ day of ______________ 19____.

____
Clerk
Superior Court of ______________ County, Georgia

SC-7 Rev. 85

FORM SC–8. WITNESS SUBPOENA

STATE OF GEORGIA
(Your County) COUNTY

WITNESS SUBPOENA

TO

YOU ARE HEREBY COMMANDED, that laying all other business aside you be and appear at the (Your County) County Superior Court, Civil/Criminal Division, before ____________________, Judge of the Superior Court, in Room ______ of the (Your County) County Courthouse at ______ o'clock A.M./P.M. on the __________ day of __________ 19___, to be sworn as a witness for the ____ in the case of ____________________ vs. ____________________ Case No. ____.

You are required to attend from day to day and from time to time until the matter is disposed of.

HEREIN FAIL NOT, under the penalty of law by authority of ____________________, Judge of said Court this __________ day of ____________________ 19___.

If you have questions contact Attorney For Plaintiff/Defendant

____
____
____
Phone: ________________________

(Your Name), Clerk
Superior Court

____

SC-8 Rev. 85

Amended effective April 13, 1988.

FORM SC-9. SUBPOENA FOR THE PRODUCTION OF EVIDENCE

SUBPOENA FOR THE PRODUCTION OF EVIDENCE

STATE OF GEORGIA
(Your County) COUNTY

TO:

You are hereby required to be and appear at the (Your County) County Superior Court before ______________________________, Judge of Superior Court, in Room ______ of the (Your County) County Courthouse at ______ o'clock A.M./P.M. on the ________ day of ______________ 19___, and to bring with you into said Court certain ______________ to be used as evidence by ______________ in a certain case pending in said Court between ______________ and ______________, Case No. ______.

The following are hereby subpoenaed: ______________________________

____

____

____

____

____

____

____

____

____

Herein fail not, under penalty of the law.

Witness, ______________________________, Judge of said Court this ______________ day of ______________ 19___.

If you have questions contact Attorney For Plaintiff/Defendant

____

____

____

Phone: ______________________________

(Your Name), Clerk
Superior Court

____

SC-9 Rev. 85

FORM SC–9.1. SUBPOENA FOR THE PRODUCTION OF EVIDENCE AT A DEPOSITION

IN THE SUPERIOR COURT OF ________________ COUNTY, GEORGIA

TO: ______________________ CIVIL ACTION NO. ______________

______________________ ______________, PLAINTIFF

______________________ VS

______________, DEFENDANT

SUBPOENA FOR THE PRODUCTION OF EVIDENCE AT A DEPOSITION

Pursuant to the provisions of OCGA §§ 9–11–30 and 9–11–45 you are hereby required to be and appear at ____

at ______ o'clock A.M./P.M. on the ____________ day of ____________, 19___, to give your deposition upon oral examination in the case pending in the Superior Court of ______________ County, Case No. ______________, and to bring with you ______
____
____
____
____.

Herein fail not, under penalty of law.

Witness, ______________________, Judge of said Court this ______ day of ____________, 19___.

______________, Clerk

______________, Court

______________, County

Inquiries should be directed to:

____

____

Attorney for Plaintiff/Defendant

SC-9.1 (7/89)

Adopted effective January 18, 1990.

FORM SC-10. CIVIL DOCKET

CIVIL DOCKET **COURT OF** **COUNTY,** **TERM 19**

CAUSE OF ACTION:		PROCEEDINGS:	Minute and Final Record Book ____ Page ____ Storage Box #	Case No.
ATTORNEYS	NAME OF PARTIES		Date of Filing / / Advance Cost Paid $ Service / / Additional Cost Paid $ Type: ☐ Personal ☐ Substitute ☐ Publication Second Original: County ____ / / Dismissed: ☐ With Prejudice ☐ W/O Prejudice / / Settlement: / / Interlocutory Order / / Trial: ☐ With Jury ☐ W/O Jury ☐ Mistrial / / Verdict For: ☐ Plaintiff ☐ Defendant / / Judgment For: ☐ Plaintiff ☐ Defendant / / Final Decree / / Fi.fa. Issued / / PROCEEDINGS	

SC-10 [D5157]

FORM SC–11. SUPERIOR COURT CIVIL DOCKET

SUPERIOR COURT CIVIL DOCKET

CAUSE OF ACTION CASE NUMBER

ATTORNEYS PARTIES

JUDGE

FILING DATE __/__/__ COST DEPOSIT $______ ADD'L COST PAID $______ SERVICE __/__/__ ☐ PERSONAL ☐ PUBLICATION ☐ SUBSTITUTE SECOND ORIGINAL TO ______

DISMISSED __/__/__ ☐ W/PREJUDICE ☐ W/O PREJUDICE SETTLEMENT __/__/__ INTERLOCUTORY ORDER __/__/__ TRIAL __/__/__ ☐ MISTRIAL ☐ W/JURY ☐ W/O JURY STORAGE BOX # ______

MINUTES AND FINAL RECORDS BOOK PAGE

VERDICT __/__/__ ☐ PLAINTIFF ☐ DEFENDANT

JUDGMENT __/__/__ ☐ PLAINTIFF ☐ DEFENDANT

FINAL DECREE __/__/__

FI.FA. ISSUED __/__/__

CONTINUED ON PAGE ______

SC-11

FORM SC-12. CRIMINAL DOCKET

CRIMINAL DOCKET **COURT OF** **COUNTY,**

ATTORNEYS	NAMES OF PARTIES	OFFENSE(S)	☐ ACCUSATION ☐ INDICTMENT	CASE NO.
	THE STATE VS.		STORAGE BOX #	
	1.		☐ FELONY ☐ MISDEMEANOR	☐ TRAFFIC TICKET NO. ______
	2.		JUDGE	
	3.		MINUTES & FINAL RECORD	BOOK ______ PAGE ______ BOOK ______ PAGE ______ BOOK ______ PAGE ______ BOOK ______ PAGE ______
	4.			

DATE	PROCEEDINGS	DATE	PROCEEDINGS (Cont.)

1. TRIAL / /	☐ WITH JURY	☐ WITHOUT JURY
2. TRIAL / /	☐ WITH JURY	☐ WITHOUT JURY
3. TRIAL / /	☐ WITH JURY	☐ WITHOUT JURY
4. TRIAL / /	☐ WITH JURY	☐ WITHOUT JURY

	1	2	3	4
PLEA (G) Guilty (NG) Not Guilty (NC) Nolo Contendere	G NG NC / /	G NG NC / /	G NG NC / /	G NG NC / /
(D) Dismissed (NP) Nol Prossed	D NP / /	D NP / /	D NP / /	D NP / /
Bond Forfeiture (Amount)	$	$	$	$
Judgment of Court 1 ☐ 2 ☐ 3 ☐ 4 ☐	/ /	/ /	/ /	/ /
Scire Facias	/ /	/ /	/ /	/ /
Judgment Absolute	/ /	/ /	/ /	/ /
Bench Warrant Issued	/ /	/ /	/ /	/ /
Arrest Warrant Issued	/ /	/ /	/ /	/ /
VERDICT: (G) Guilty (NG) Not Guilty	G NG / /	G NG / /	G NG / /	G NG / /

☐ FIRST OFFENDER STATUS	SENTENCE
1 DATE: ☐	
2 DATE: ☐	
3 DATE: ☐	
4 DATE: ☐	

Transcript Filed	/ /	/ /	/ /	/ /
Sentence Review Application	/ /	/ /	/ /	/ /
Notice of Appeal	/ /	/ /	/ /	/ /
Date of Parole	/ /	/ /	/ /	/ /

SC-12 [D5159]

FORM SC–13. CIVIL CASE INITIATION FORM

CIVIL CASE INITIATION FORM

(Please type or print legibly)

SUPERIOR COURT

_______________ COUNTY

GEORGIA

FOR OFFICIAL USE ONLY

CASE NUMBER

☐☐☐☐☐☐☐☐☐☐-☐☐

DATE OF FIRST SERVICE

☐☐-☐☐-☐☐

DATE FILED ☐☐-☐☐-☐☐

PLAINTIFF(S) (Last Name, First, Middle Initial)

DEFENDANT(S) (Last Name, First, Middle Initial)

ATTORNEY(S) (Name, Address, Phone, Bar#)

ATTORNEY(S) (Name, Address, Phone, Bar#)

CAUSE OF ACTION

(Please check an action)

DOMESTIC RELATIONS

☐ ADOPTION (001)
☐ DIVORCE/ALIMONY (002)
☐ SUPPORT/CUSTODY (003)
☐ MODIFICATIONS (004)
☐ FAMILY VIOLENCE (005)
☐ LEGITIMATION (006)
☐ CONTEMPT (007)

OTHER CIVIL ACTIONS

☐ CONTRACT/ACCOUNT (008)
☐ TORT/NEGLIGENCE (009)
☐ HABEAS CORPUS (010)
☐ APPEALS/REVIEW (011)
☐ TITLE TO LAND/ CONDEMNATION (012)
☐ POST–JUDGMENT GARNISHMENT/ ATTACHMENT (013)
☐ CONDEMNATION/FORECLOSURE (PERSONAL PROPERTY) (014)
☐ DISPOSSESSORY/DISTRESS (015)
☐ NON-DOMESTIC CONTEMPT (016)
☐ DOMESTICATION OF FOREIGN JUDGMENT (017)

☐ OTHER CAUSE OF ACTION (Cite Ga. statute or give brief description) (018)

SC-13 (7/89)

Adopted effective January 18, 1990.

FORM SC-14. CIVIL CASE DISPOSITION FORM

CIVIL CASE DISPOSITION FORM

(Please type or print legibly)

SUPERIOR COURT

________________ COUNTY

GEORGIA

FOR OFFICIAL USE ONLY
CASE NUMBER
☐☐☐☐☐☐☐☐☐☐-☐☐

ATTORNEY(S) (Name, Address, Phone, Bar#)

____

____

DISPOSITION DATE ☐☐-☐☐-☐☐

PRE-TRIAL DISPOSITIONS
For: ☐ Plaintiff
☐ Defendant

- ☐ SETTLED/DISMISSED (001)
- ☐ DEFAULT JUDGMENT (002)
- ☐ SUMMARY JUDGMENT (003)
- ☐ CONSENT JUDGMENT (004)
- ☐ JUDGMENT ON PLEADINGS (005)
- ☐ OTHER PRE-TRIAL (006)
  (Please specify) ________________

BENCH TRIAL
For: ☐ Plaintiff
☐ Defendant

- ☐ JUDGMENT FOR PLAINTIFF/ DEFENDANT (007)
  (Record a bench trial when the parties appear before a judge who hears issues and evidence, including testimony, then makes a determination without a jury.)

JURY TRIAL
For: ☐ Plaintiff
☐ Defendant

- ☐ JUDGMENT ON VERDICT (008)
- ☐ DIRECTED VERDICT (009)
- ☐ JUDGMENT N/W VERDICT (010)

SC-14 (7/89)

Adopted effective January 18, 1990.

FORM SC–15. FAMILY VIOLENCE EX PARTE PROTECTIVE ORDER

ORI Number ______

THE SUPERIOR COURT FOR THE COUNTY OF ________

STATE OF GEORGIA

________________________,	:	
Petitioner,	:	Civil Action File
v.	:	No. ________
________________________,	:	
Respondent.	:	

FAMILY VIOLENCE EX PARTE PROTECTIVE ORDER

The Petitioner having prayed pursuant to O.C.G.A. §§ 19–13–1 et seq., that a Protective Order be issued; and alleged that Respondent has committed acts of Family Violence and that Petitioner is in reasonable fear of the Petitioner's safety and the safety of Petitioner's child/ren; and it appearing to the Court that probable cause exists that family violence has occurred in the past and may occur in the future, IT IS HEREBY ORDERED AND ADJUDGED:

1. That these proceedings be filed in the office of the Clerk of this Court.

2. That this Order applies in every county throughout the state and it shall be the duty of every court and every law enforcement official to enforce and carry out the provisions of this Order pursuant to O.C.G.A. § 19–13–4(d). Law enforcement officers may use their arrest powers pursuant to O.C.G.A. §§ 19–13–6 and 17–4–20 to enforce the terms of this Order.

3. That a copy of this Order be given to law enforcement and the Respondent be served with a copy of this Order and Petition for Temporary Protective Order instanter.

CIVIL ACTION FILE NO.______

4. That the Respondent appear before this Court, on the ________ day of ________, ____ at ______ __.m. in room ________ of the ______________ County Courthouse at ______________ to show cause why the requests of the Petitioner should not be granted.

5. [pco01] That Respondent is hereby enjoined and restrained from doing, or attempting to do, or threatening to do, any act of injury, maltreating, molesting, following, harassing, harming or abusing the Petitioner and/or the minor child/ren in any manner. Respondent is not to interfere with Petitioner's travel, transportation, or communication. Respondent shall not follow, place under surveillance, or contact the Petitioner at any place of the Petitioner for the purpose of harassing and intimidating the Petitioner.

6. [pco02] That the Respondent is enjoined and restrained from doing or threatening to do any act of injury, maltreating, molesting, harassing, harming, or abusing the Petitioner's family or household.

7. That this Court determined that it had jurisdiction over the parties and the subject matter under the laws of the State of Georgia and the Court ordered that the Respondent be given reasonable notice and opportunity to be heard sufficient to protect the Respondent's due process rights. This Order shall be presumed valid and pursuant to 18 U.S.C. § 2265(a) shall be accorded **full faith and credit** by any other state or local jurisdiction and shall be enforced as if an Order of the enforcing state or jurisdiction.

ONLY THE FOLLOWING THAT ARE INITIALED BY THE JUDGE SHALL APPLY.

____ 8. [pco03] That until further Order by this Court, Petitioner is awarded sole and exclusive use of the family residence at ______________________.

____ 9. Respondent is ordered to leave the family residence immediately and law enforcement ______________ (sheriff or police department) is ordered to assist Petitioner in returning to the family residence and the removal of the Respondent. Respondent is to immediately surrender to law enforcement ______________ (sheriff or police department) all and any keys, garage door openers and other security devices to the family residence and law enforcement is to insure that these are given to the Petitioner.

____ 10. Respondent is ordered to provide suitable alternate housing for Petitioner and/or Petitioner's child/ren by __________.

CIVIL ACTION FILE NO. ______

____ 11. Petitioner's address is ordered to be kept confidential.

____ 12. [pco04] Respondent is ordered to stay away from Petitioner's and Petitioner's minor child/ren's residence at ______________ and workplace at ______________ or school and any subsequent residence or workplace or school of Petitioner and/or Petitioner's minor child/ren.

____ 13. [pco01,04] That until further Order of this Court, Respondent is restrained and enjoined from approaching within ____ yards of Petitioner and/or Petitioner's minor child/ren.

____ 14. [pco05] Respondent is ordered not to have any contact, direct, indirect or through another person with Petitioner, by telephone, pager, fax, e-mail or any other means of communication except as specified in this Order.

____ 15. [pco09] That Petitioner is awarded temporary custody of the minor child/ren, namely:

______________ DOB ____ sex ____
______________ DOB ____ sex ____
______________ DOB ____ sex ____
______________ DOB ____ sex ____

Respondent is ordered not to interfere with the physical custody of the child/ren.

____ [pco06] Check here ***only if Respondent*** is awarded temporary custody of child/ren.

____ 16. That Respondent is ordered to pay temporary child support for the minor child/ren to Petitioner in the amount of $______ every ______ beginning ______.

All payments shall be made by or to:
____ income deduction order
____ child support receiver
____ by mail directly to the Petitioner
or____ ______________

____ 17. That Respondent is ordered to pay temporary support for the Petitioner in the amount of $______ every ______ beginning ______

All payments shall be made by or to:
____ income deduction order
____ child support receiver
____ by mail directly to the Petitioner
or____ ______________

CIVIL ACTION FILE NO. ______

____ 18. That Respondent, **only when accompanied by local law enforcement,** shall be able to remove his/her clothing and personal items from the residence as follows: ____

On ______, 20__ at ______ ___.m.

____ 19. That (Respondent)(Petitioner)(both Respondent and Petitioner) [strike through appropriate] is/are ordered not to sell, encumber, trade, damage, contract to sell, or otherwise dispose of or remove from the jurisdiction of this Court any of the property or pets of the Petitioner or joint property or pets of the parties except in the ordinary course of business.

____ 20. That (Respondent)(Petitioner)(both Respondent and Petitioner) [strike through appropriate] is/are ordered not to disconnect or have disconnected the home utilities, change or have changed and/or cancel or have canceled auto, health or life insurance for Respondent, Petitioner, and/or Petitioner's child/ren or interfere with Respondent, Petitioner's and/or Petitioner's child/ren's mail.

____ 21. That Petitioner is awarded temporary sole possession of the vehicle: Make ______ Model ______ Year ______ Color ______. Respondent shall immediately surrender all keys, proof of insurance, and registration to this vehicle to law enforcement and law enforcement shall immediately turn over said items to Petitioner.

____ 22. That Petitioner shall be allowed to remove the following property from the family residence for Petitioner and/or Petitioner's child/ren's use ____.

On ______, 20__ at ______ and law enforcement ______(sheriff or police department) is hereby ordered to assist the Petitioner during this removal.

____ 23. That Respondent shall be required to return the following property for Petitioner and/or Petitioner's child/ren's use ________________________________. On ______, 20__ at ______ and law enforcement __________ (sheriff or police department) is hereby ordered to assist the Petitioner with this return.

CIVIL ACTION FILE NO. ______

____ 24. It is further Ordered
[pco08] ____
____

SO ORDERED this ____ day of __________, ____.

____
JUDGE, SUPERIOR COURT
________________ County
____
Print or stamp Judge's name

Violation of the above Order may be punishable by arrest.

NOTICE TO RESPONDENT

1. **Violation of this Order may result in immediate arrest and criminal prosecution that may result in jail time and/or fines and/or may subject you to prosecution and penalties for contempt of court.**
2. **This Order shall remain in effect unless specifically superceded by a subsequent signed and filed Order, by operation of law, or by Order of dismissal, whichever occurs first. Only this Court can void, modify or dismiss this Order. Either party may ask this Court to change or dismiss this Order.**
3. **A person commits the offense of Aggravated Stalking when such person, in violation of a temporary or permanent protective Order prohibiting this behavior follows, places under surveillance, or contacts Petitioner on public or private property for the purpose of harassing and intimidating the other person. This activity can subject the Respondent to arrest and prosecution for felony Aggravated Stalking, which carries penalties of imprisonment for not less than 1 year nor more than 10 years and a fine of up to $10,000.00.**

CIVIL ACTION FILE NO. ______

Pursuant to O.C.G.A. Section 19–13–3,
Petitioner assisted by

Name: ______________________
Address: ______________________
____
Telephone: ______________________

Note to Judges: This form is promulgated as a Uniform Superior Court Rule under the auspices of O.C.G.A. § 19–13–53. To order a specific provision, please initial in the space provided. The court should delete or otherwise make inoperative any provision in the standardized form which is not supported by the evidence in the case and in order to comply with the court's application of the law and facts to an individual case.

CIVIL ACTION FILE NO. ______

RESPONDENT'S IDENTIFYING FACT SHEET

(please complete as much as possible; one of these must be provided to have the order placed in the National Crime Information Center registry: Respondent's date of birth OR social security number)

Respondent's social security number is __________, date of birth is ______, sex ___, color of hair ________, color of eyes ________, height ______, weight ______. Respondent's race is ________, ethnic background __________. Respondent has distinguishing marks (tattoos, scars, etc.) __________. Respondent drives a __________, license tag number __________ and has a ____ (state) driver's license number __________. Respondent's home address ______________ and is employed by ______________ at ______________ and works from ____ to ____ on (days) __________.

PETITIONER'S IDENTIFYING INFORMATION

Protected parties ______________ DOB ____ sex ____ race ____
______________ DOB ____ sex ____ race ____
______________ DOB ____ sex ____ race ____
______________ DOB ____ sex ____ race ____

☐ Transmitted to Georgia Protective Order Registry Date ______ Clerk ______

Rev'd 10/1/04

Adopted effective September 6, 2001; amended effective December 2, 2004.

FORM SC–16. FAMILY VIOLENCE PROTECTIVE ORDER

ORI Number ______

THE SUPERIOR COURT FOR THE COUNTY OF ________

STATE OF GEORGIA

_________________________________,	:	
Petitioner,	:	Civil Action File
v.	:	No. ____________
_________________________________,	:	
Respondent.	:	

FAMILY VIOLENCE PROTECTIVE ORDER

A hearing was held on this matter on ____________, ___ for which the Respondent had notice as required by law and at which the Respondent appeared and/or had the opportunity to be heard and the Petitioner requested that the Protective Order entered in this case be continued. Having heard the evidence presented, reviewed the petition and the entire record concerning this case and for good cause shown, IT IS HEREBY ORDERED AND ADJUDGED:

1. That these proceedings be filed in the office of the Clerk of this Court.

2. That this Order applies in every county throughout the state and it shall be the duty of every court and every law enforcement official to enforce and carry out the provisions of this Order pursuant to O.C.G.A. § 19–13–4(d). Law enforcement officers may use their arrest powers pursuant to O.C.G.A. §§ 19–13–6 and 17–4–20 to enforce the terms of this Order.

3. This Order shall be in effect for up to twelve (12) months from ___________ until ___________

4. That the Respondent has violated the Family Violence Act, at [pco01] O.C.G.A. § 19–13–1 et seq., by committing family violence, has placed the Petitioner in reasonable fear for Petitioner's safety, and represents a credible threat to the physical safety of Petitioner and/or Petitioner's child/ren. Respondent is hereby enjoined and restrained from doing, or attempting to do, or threatening to do, any act of injury, maltreating, molesting, following, harassing, harming, or abusing the Petitioner and/or the minor child/ren in any manner. Respondent is not to interfere with Petitioner's travel, transportation, or communication. Respondent shall not follow, place under surveillance, or contact the Petitioner at any place of the Petitioner for the purpose of harassing and intimidating the Petitioner.

CIVIL ACTION FILE NO. ______

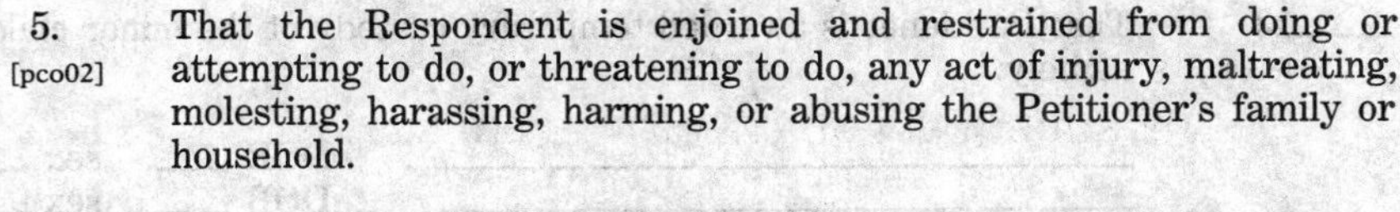
5. [pco02] That the Respondent is enjoined and restrained from doing or attempting to do, or threatening to do, any act of injury, maltreating, molesting, harassing, harming, or abusing the Petitioner's family or household.

6. That this Court determined that it had jurisdiction over the parties and the subject matter under the laws of the State of Georgia and Respondent received reasonable notice and had the opportunity to be heard before this Order was issued sufficient to protect the Respondent's due process rights and this Order shall be presumed valid and pursuant to 18 U.S.C. § 2265(a) shall be accorded **full faith and credit** by any other state or local jurisdiction and shall be enforced as if an Order of the enforcing state or jurisdiction.

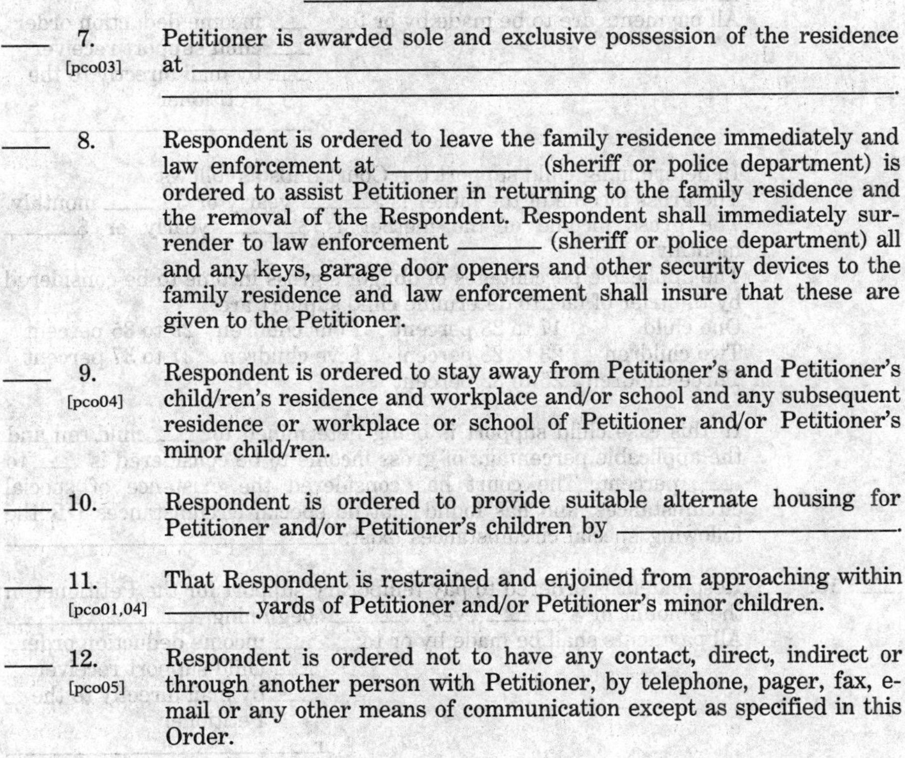
ONLY THE FOLLOWING THAT ARE INITIALED BY THE JUDGE SHALL APPLY

____ 7. [pco03] Petitioner is awarded sole and exclusive possession of the residence at ____.

____ 8. Respondent is ordered to leave the family residence immediately and law enforcement at ____________ (sheriff or police department) is ordered to assist Petitioner in returning to the family residence and the removal of the Respondent. Respondent shall immediately surrender to law enforcement ________ (sheriff or police department) all and any keys, garage door openers and other security devices to the family residence and law enforcement shall insure that these are given to the Petitioner.

____ 9. [pco04] Respondent is ordered to stay away from Petitioner's and Petitioner's child/ren's residence and workplace and/or school and any subsequent residence or workplace or school of Petitioner and/or Petitioner's minor child/ren.

____ 10. Respondent is ordered to provide suitable alternate housing for Petitioner and/or Petitioner's children by ____________________.

____ 11. [pco01,04] That Respondent is restrained and enjoined from approaching within ________ yards of Petitioner and/or Petitioner's minor children.

____ 12. [pco05] Respondent is ordered not to have any contact, direct, indirect or through another person with Petitioner, by telephone, pager, fax, e-mail or any other means of communication except as specified in this Order.

CIVIL ACTION FILE NO. ______

____13 [pco09]. That Petitioner is awarded temporary custody of the minor child/ren, namely:

________________________________ DOB ____ sex ____
________________________________ DOB ____ sex ____
________________________________ DOB ____ sex ____
________________________________ DOB ____ sex ____

Respondent is ordered not to interfere with the physical custody of the minor child/ren.

____ [pco06] Check here ***only if Respondent*** is awarded temporary custody of child/ren.

____ 14. Respondent is ordered to pay to the Petitioner support for the minor child/ren in the amount of $______ every ______ beginning the ______ of ______, ______.

All payments are to be made by or to: ___ income deduction order
___ child support receiver
___ by mail directly to the Petitioner
or___ ______________

In determining child support the Court finds as follows:
The gross income of the father is $______ yearly or $______ monthly.
The gross income of the mother is $______ yearly or $______ monthly.
The applicable percentages of obligor's gross income to be considered by the trier of fact to determine child support are:

One child	17 to 23 percent	Four children	29 to 35 percent
Two children	23 to 28 percent	Five children	31 to 37 percent
Three children	25 to 32 percent		

In this case child support is being determined for ___ child/ren and the applicable percentage of gross income to be considered is ____ to ____ percent. The court has considered the existence of special circumstances, and has found that no special circumstances **OR** the following special circumstances exist: ______________

____ 15. Respondent is ordered to pay temporary support for the Petitioner in the amount of $______ every ______ beginning ______________.

All payments shall be made by or to: ___ income deduction order
___ child support receiver
___ by mail directly to the Petitioner
or___ ______________

CIVIL ACTION FILE NO. ______

____ 16. Respondent shall have visitation with the minor child/ren according to the following schedule, beginning ________:

____ no visitation
____ no visitation until ________
____ supervised visitation, supervised by a third party as follows: ________________________________
____
____ visitation every other weekend from Friday at 6 p.m. until Sunday at 6 p.m., beginning ________, ___
____ other visitation ________________
____ circumstances concerning how Respondent shall pick up and return the minor child/ren shall be ____________

Strict compliance with this visitation provision shall not be a violation of the restraining provisions of this Order.

____ 17. Respondent, **only when accompanied by local law enforcement**, shall be able to remove his/her clothing and personal items from the residence as follows: ________________________________
____

On ______, 20__ at ______ ___ m.

____ 18. (Respondent)(Petitioner)(both Respondent and Petitioner) [strike through appropriate] is/are ordered not to sell, encumber, trade, damage, contract to sell, or otherwise dispose of or remove from the jurisdiction of this Court any of the property or pets of the Petitioner or joint property or pets of the parties except in the ordinary course of business.

____ 19. (Respondent)(Petitioner)(both Respondent and Petitioner) [strike through appropriate] is/are ordered not to disconnect or have disconnected home utilities, change or have changed and/or cancel or have canceled auto, health or life insurance for Respondent, Petitioner, and/or Petitioner's child/ren or interfere with Respondent, Petitioner's and/or Petitioner's child/ren's mail.

____ 20. Petitioner shall have sole, exclusive temporary possession of the vehicle: Make ______ Model ______ Year______ Color ______. Respondent shall immediately surrender all keys, proof of insurance, and registration to this vehicle to law enforcement and law enforcement shall immediately turn over said items to Petitioner.

CIVIL ACTION FILE NO. ______

____ 21. Petitioner shall be allowed to remove the following property from the family residence for Petitioner and/or Petitioner's child/ren's use ____

On ______, 20__ at ______ and law enforcement ______ (sheriff or police department) is hereby ordered to assist the Petitioner during this removal.

____ 22. Respondent is ordered to undergo a batterer's intervention program and follow the recommended treatment.

____ 23. Respondent is ordered to undergo alcohol/drug abuse evaluation and follow the recommended treatment.

____ 24. That Respondent shall be required to return the following property for Petitioner and/or Petitioner's child/ren's use ______________ ______________________________ on ______, 20__ at ______ and law enforcement ______ (sheriff or police department) is hereby ordered to assist the Petitioner during this return.

____ 25. Petitioner is awarded costs and attorney fees in the amount of ____.

____ 26. [pco07] Petitioner/protected party is either a spouse, former spouse, parent of a common child, child of Petitioner, child of Respondent, cohabitates or has cohabited with Respondent and qualifies for 18 U.S.C. 922(g).

____ 27. [pco08] It is further Ordered ______________________________________.

SO ORDERED this ____ day of ______, ___.

____
JUDGE, SUPERIOR COURT
______________ County
____
Print or stamp Judge's name

Violation of the above Order may be punishable by arrest.

CIVIL ACTION FILE NO. ______

NOTICE TO RESPONDENT

1. **Violation of this Order may result in immediate arrest and criminal prosecution that may result in jail time and/or fines and/or may subject you to prosecution and penalties for contempt of court.**
2. **This Order shall remain in effect unless specifically superceded by a subsequent Order signed and filed, by operation of law, or by Order of dismissal, whichever occurs first. Only this Court can void, modify or dismiss this Order. Either party may ask this Court to change or dismiss this Order.**
3. **If after a hearing, of which the Respondent received notice and opportunity to participate, a protective order is issued which restrains Respondent from harassing, stalking or threatening an intimate partner, Respondent is prohibited from possessing, receiving, or transporting a firearm or ammunition which has been shipped or transported in interstate or foreign commerce for the duration of the Order. 18 U.S.C. § 922(g).**
4. **A person commits the offense of Aggravated Stalking when such person, in violation of a temporary or permanent protective Order prohibiting this behavior follows, places under surveillance, or contacts another person on public or private property for the purpose of harassing and intimidating the other person. This activity can subject the Respondent to arrest and prosecution for felony aggravated stalking, which carries penalties of imprisonment for not less that 1 year nor more than 10 years and a fine of up to $10,000.00**

CIVIL ACTION FILE NO. ______

Pursuant to O.C.G.A. Section 19–13–3,
Petitioner assisted by

Name: ______________________
Address: ______________________
____
Telephone: ______________________

Note to Judges: This form is promulgated as a Uniform Superior Court Rule under the auspices of O.C.G.A. § 19–13–53. To order a specific provision, please initial in the space provided. The court should delete or otherwise make inoperative any provision in the standardized form which is not supported by the evidence in the case and in order to comply with the court's application of the law and facts to an individual case.

CIVIL ACTION FILE NO. ______

RESPONDENT'S IDENTIFYING FACT SHEET

(please complete as much as possible; one of these must be provided to have the order placed in the National Crime Information Center registry: Respondent's date of birth OR social security number)

Respondent's social security number is ________, date of birth is ______, sex ___, color of hair ______, color of eyes ______, height ______, weight ______. Respondent's race is ______, ethnic background ________. Respondent has distinguishing marks (tattoos, scars, etc.) ________. Respondent drives a ________, license tag number ________ and has a ____ (state) driver's license number ______. Respondent's home address ________ and is employed by ________ at ________ and works from ____ to ____ on (days) ______.

PETITIONER'S IDENTIFYING INFORMATION

Protected parties ________ DOB ____ sex ____ race ____
________ DOB ____ sex ____ race ____
________ DOB ____ sex ____ race ____
________ DOB ____ sex ____ race ____

☐ **Transmitted to Georgia Protective Order Registry** **Date** ____ **Clerk** ____

Rev'd 10/1/04

Adopted effective September 6, 2001; amended effective December 2, 2004.

FORM SC-17. STALKING EX PARTE TEMPORARY PROTECTIVE ORDER

ORI Number ______

THE SUPERIOR COURT FOR THE COUNTY OF ______

STATE OF GEORGIA

______________________,	:	
Petitioner,	:	Civil Action File
v.	:	No. ______
______________________,	:	
Respondent.	:	

STALKING EX PARTE TEMPORARY PROTECTIVE ORDER

Upon proceedings before me, the Petitioner having demanded pursuant to O.C.G.A. § 16–5–94 that a Protective Order be issued; and alleged that Respondent has knowingly and willfully committed or attempted to commit acts in violation of O.C.G.A. § 16–5–90 *et seq.*, and such acts were not at the home of the Respondent, had no legitimate purpose and that Petitioner is in reasonable fear of her/his safety and/or the safety of her/his immediate family; and it appearing to the Court that probable cause exists to believe that similar events will occur in the future, IT IS HEREBY ORDERED AND ADJUDGED:

1. [pco01,02] That Respondent is enjoined and restrained from any acts directly or indirectly which harass and/or intimidate the Petitioner or her/his immediate family.

2. [pco01,04] That Respondent is enjoined from approaching within ___ yards of Petitioner.

3. That Respondent have no contact of any type, direct or indirect, or through another person with Petitioner, or her/his immediate family, including but not limited to telephone, pager, fax, e-mail, mail or any other means of communication.

4. **That the Respondent appear before ______________, Judge, on the ________ day of ________, 20__ at ______________ in room _______ of the ______________ County court house at _______ to show cause why the demands of the Petitioner should not be granted.**

5. That a copy of this Order be given to local law enforcement and the Respondent be served with a copy of this Order and Petition for Stalking Temporary Protective Order instanter.

CIVIL ACTION FILE NO. ______

6. That this Order applies in every county throughout the state and it shall be the duty of every court and every law enforcement official to enforce and carry out the provisions of this Order pursuant to O.C.G.A. §§ 16–5–94(e) and 19–13–4(d). Law Enforcement may use their arrest powers pursuant to O.C.G.A. §§ 16–5–91 and 17–4–20 to enforce the terms of this Order.

7. That these proceedings be filed in the office of the Clerk of this Court.

8. That this Court determined that it had jurisdiction over the parties and the subject matter under the laws of the State of Georgia and the Court ordered that the Respondent be given reasonable notice and opportunity to be heard sufficient to protect the Respondent's due process rights and this Order shall be presumed valid and pursuant to 18 U.S.C. § 2265(a) shall be accorded **full faith and credit** by any other state or local jurisdiction and shall be enforced as ordered as if an Order of the enforcing state or jurisdiction.

SO ORDERED this ____ day of __________, 20___.

____
JUDGE, SUPERIOR COURT
____________________ County

____
Print or stamp Judge's name

Violation of the above Order may be punishable by arrest.

CIVIL ACTION FILE NO. ______

NOTICE TO RESPONDENT

1. **Violation of this Order may result in immediate arrest and criminal prosecution that may result in jail time and/or fines and/or may subject you to prosecution and penalties for contempt of court.**
2. **This Order shall remain in effect unless specifically superceded by a subsequent signed and filed Order, by operation of law, or by Order of dismissal, whichever occurs first. Only this Court can void, modify or dismiss this Order. Either party may ask this Court to change or dismiss this Order.**
3. **A person commits the offense of Aggravated Stalking when such person, in violation of a temporary or permanent protective Order prohibiting this behavior follows, places under surveillance, or contacts Petitioner on public or private property for the purpose of harassing and intimidating the other person. This activity can subject the Respondent to arrest and prosecution for felony Aggravated Stalking, which carries penalties of imprisonment for not less that 1 year nor more than 10 years and a fine of up to $10,000.00**

CIVIL ACTION FILE NO. ______

Pursuant to O.C.G.A. Section 9–13–3,
Petitioner assisted by

Name: ______________________
Address: ____________________
____
Telephone: __________________

Note to Judges: This form is promulgated as a Uniform Superior Court Rule under the auspices of O.C.G.A. § 19–13–53. To order a specific provision, please initial in the space provided. The court should delete or otherwise make inoperative any provision in the standardized form which is not supported by the evidence in the case and in order to comply with the court's application of the law and facts to an individual case.

CIVIL ACTION FILE NO. ______

RESPONDENT'S IDENTIFYING INFORMATION

(please complete as much as possible; one of these must be provided to have the order place in the National Crime Information Center registry: Respondent's date of birth, social security number, or driver's license number)

Respondent's social security number is ________, date of birth is ______, sex ___, color of hair ________, color of eyes ________, height ______, weight ____. Respondent's race is ____, ethnic background ________. Respondent has distinguishing marks (tattoos, scars, etc.) __________. Respondent drives a ________, license tag number ________ and has a ___ (state) driver's license number ______. Respondent's home address __________ and is employed by ________ at ________ and works from ___ to ___ on (days) ______.

PETITIONER'S IDENTIFYING INFORMATION

Protected parties ____________ DOB ___ sex ___ race ___
____________ DOB ___ sex ___ race ___
____________ DOB ___ sex ___ race ___
____________ DOB ___ sex ___ race ___

☐ Transmitted to Georgia Protective Order Registry Date ______ Clerk ______

Rev'd 7/1/02

Adopted effective September 6, 2001.

FORM SC–18. STALKING PROTECTIVE ORDER

ORI Number ______

THE SUPERIOR COURT FOR THE COUNTY OF ________

STATE OF GEORGIA

______________________________,	:	
Petitioner,	:	Civil Action File
v.	:	
______________________________,	:	No. ________
Respondent.	:	

STALKING PROTECTIVE ORDER

A hearing was held on this matter on ________, 20__ at which the Respondent appeared and/or was provided with the opportunity to be heard and the Petitioner requested that the Protective Order entered in this case be continued. Having heard the evidence presented, reviewed the petition and the record concerning this case and for good cause shown, IT IS HEREBY ORDERED AND ADJUDGED:

1. The Respondent has knowingly and wilfully violated O.C.G.A.
[pco01] § 16–5–90 *et seq.* and placed the Petitioner in reasonable fear for the
[pco02] Petitioner's safety. Respondent is hereby enjoined and restrained from doing or attempting to do, or threatening to do any act constituting a violation of O.C.G.A. § 16–5–90 *et seq.* and of harassing, interfering, or intimidating the Petitioner or Petitioner's immediate family. Specifically Respondent is hereby enjoined and restrained from ______________________ which is a violation of O.C.G.A. § 16–5–90 *et seq.* and that any future acts committed by the Respondent towards the Petitioner which are in violation of this statute and this Protective Order can amount to AGGRAVATED STALKING, pursuant to O.C.G.A. § 16–5–91, which is a felony. A person convicted of Aggravated Stalking shall be punished by imprisonment for not less than one nor more than ten years and by a fine of not more than $10,000.00.

2. Respondent is enjoined and restrained from approaching within ______
[pco04] yards of Petitioner and/or Petitioner's immediate family, and/or residence, place of employment, or school.

3. Respondent is not to have any contact of any type, direct, indirect, or
[pco05] through another person with the Petitioner or her/his immediate family, including but not limited to telephone, fax, e-mail, voice mail, mail, or any other type of contact.

4. That these proceedings be filed in the office of the Clerk of this Court.

CIVIL ACTION FILE NO. ______

5. This Order shall remain in effect for up to twelve (12) months from this date. This Order expires on __________, ___.

6. That this Order applies in every county throughout the state and it shall be the duty of every court and every law enforcement official to enforce and carry out the provisions of this Order pursuant to O.C.G.A. §§ 16–5–94(e) and 19–13–4(d). Law enforcement may use their arrest powers pursuant to O.C.G.A. §§ 16–5–91 and 17–4–20 to enforce the terms of this Order.

7. That this Court determined that it had jurisdiction over the parties and the subject matter under the laws of the State of Georgia and Respondent received reasonable notice and had the opportunity to be heard before this Order was issued sufficient to protect the Respondent's due process rights and this Order shall be presumed valid and pursuant to 18 U.S.C. § 2265(a) shall be accorded **full faith and credit** by any other state or local jurisdiction and shall be enforced as if an Order of the enforcing state or jurisdiction.

ONLY the following that are initialed by the JUDGE shall apply:

_____ 8. Respondent is to receive appropriate psychiatric or psychological services.

_____ 9. Petitioner is awarded costs and attorney fees in the amount of _____.

_____ 10. Petitioner/protected party is either a spouse, former spouse, parent of a [pco07] common child, child of Petitioner, child of Respondent, cohabitates or has cohabited with Respondent and qualifies for 18 U.S.C. § 922(g)

SO ORDERED this ____ day of __________, ____.

____
JUDGE, SUPERIOR COURT
______________ County

____
Print or stamp Judge's name

Violation of the above Order may be punishable by arrest.

CIVIL ACTION FILE NO. ______

NOTICE TO RESPONDENT

1. **Violation of this Order may result in immediate arrest and criminal prosecution that may result in jail time and/or fines and/or may subject you to prosecution and penalties for contempt of court.**
2. **This Order shall remain in effect unless specifically superceded by a subsequent Order signed and filed, by operation of law, or by Order of dismissal, whichever occurs first. Only this Court can void, modify or dismiss this Order. Either party may ask this Court to change or dismiss this Order.**
3. **If after a hearing, of which the Respondent received notice and opportunity to participate, a protective order is issued which restrains Respondent from harassing, stalking or threatening an intimate partner, Respondent is prohibited from possessing, receiving, or transporting a firearm or ammunition which has been shipped or transported in interstate or foreign commerce for the duration of the Order. 18 U.S.C. § 922(g).**
4. **A person commits the offense of Aggravated Stalking when such person, in violation of a temporary or permanent protective Order prohibiting this behavior follows, places under surveillance, or contacts another person on public or private property for the purpose of harassing and intimidating the other person. This activity can subject the Respondent to arrest and prosecution for felony aggravated stalking, which carries penalties of imprisonment for not less that 1 year nor more than 10 years and a fine of up to $10,000.00**

CIVIL ACTION FILE NO. ______

Pursuant to O.C.G.A. Section 19–13–3,
Petitioner assisted by

Name: ____________________
Address: ____________________
____
Telephone: ____________________

Note to Judges: This form is promulgated as a Uniform Superior Court Rule under the auspices of O.C.G.A. § 19–13–53. To order a specific provision, please initial in the space provided. The court may delete or otherwise make inoperative any provision in the standardized form which is not supported by the evidence in the case and in order to comply with the court's application of the law and facts to an individual case.

CIVIL ACTION FILE NO. _____

RESPONDENT'S IDENTIFYING INFORMATION

(please complete as much as possible; one of these must be provided to have the order placed in the National Crime Information Center registry: Respondent's date of birth OR social security number)

Respondent's social security number is __________, date of birth is ______, sex ___, color of hair ______, color of eyes ______, height ______, weight ______. Respondent's race is ______. Ethnic background ______ Respondent drives a __________, license tag number __________ and has a ____ (state) driver's license number ________. Respondent has distinguishing marks (tattoos, scars, etc.) __________. Respondent's home address ______________.

and is employed by __________ at __________ and works from ____ to ____ on (days) ________.

PETITIONER'S IDENTIFYING INFORMATION

Protected parties ______________ DOB ____ sex ____ race ____
______________ DOB ____ sex ____ race ____
______________ DOB ____ sex ____ race ____
______________ DOB ____ sex ____ race ____
______________ DOB ____ sex ____ race ____

☐ Transmitted to Georgia Protective Order Registry Date ______ Clerk ______

Rev'd 10/1/04

Adopted effective September 6, 2001; amended effective December 2, 2004.

FORM SC–19. DISMISSAL OF TEMPORARY PROTECTIVE ORDER

ORI Number ______

THE SUPERIOR COURT FOR THE COUNTY OF ________

STATE OF GEORGIA

____________________,	]	
Petitioner,	]	Civil Action File
v.	]	No. ________
____________________,	]	
Respondent.	]	

DISMISSAL OF TEMPORARY PROTECTIVE ORDER

IT IS HEREBY ORDERED, ADJUDGED, and DECREED that the (Petition)(Counter–Petition)(both Petition and Counter–Petition)[strike through appropriate] for Temporary Protective Order filed on the ___ day of ________, 20___ is hereby dismissed without prejudice:

[ ] on (Petitioner's)(Respondent's)(both Petitioner's and Respondent's) motion to dismiss.

[ ] on (Petitioner's)(Respondent's)(both Petitioner's and Respondent's) failure to appear and proceed.

[ ] on (Petitioner's)(Respondent's)(both Petitioner's and Respondent's) failure to prove by a preponderance of the evidence the allegations contained in the (Petition)(Counter–Petition)(both Petition and Counter–Petition) for Temporary Protective Order.

[ ] due to lack of service on (Petitioner)(Respondent)(both Petitioner and Respondent).

[ ] OTHER:

This ______ day of ________, 20___.

____
JUDGE, SUPERIOR COURT
__________________ County

____
Print or stamp Judge's name

☐ Transmitted to Georgia Protective Order Registry Date ______ Clerk ______

Rev'd 10/1/04

Adopted effective September 6, 2001; amended effective December 2, 2004.

FORM SC–20. ORDER FOR CONTINUANCE OF HEARING AND EX PARTE PROTECTIVE ORDER

ORI ________

THE SUPERIOR COURT FOR THE COUNTY OF __________
STATE OF GEORGIA

____________________________,	]	
	]	
Petitioner,	]	Civil Action File
v.	]	
	]	
____________________________,	]	No. ___________
	]	
Respondent.	]	

ORDER FOR CONTINUANCE OF HEARING AND EX PARTE PROTECTIVE ORDER

IT IS ORDERED that the hearing for a Protective Order in the above styled case be continued and rescheduled to _________, 20 ___.

IT IS FURTHER ORDERED that the Ex Parte Protective Order issued on _________, 20 ___ in the above styled case is continued until the hearing date of _________, 20 ___ and all provisions of the Ex Parte Protective Order shall remain in full effect with the following modifications ______________________________
____
____.

This ___ day of _________, 20 ___.

____
JUDGE, SUPERIOR COURT
________________________ County

____
Print or stamp Judge's name

☐ TRANSMITTED TO GEORGIA PROTECTIVE ORDER REGISTRY DATE _____ CLERK _____

Rev'd 1/10/03

REMOVE THIS PAGE FROM ORDER

Pursuant to O.C.G.A. Section 19–13–3,
Petitioner assisted by:

Name: ______________________
Address: ______________________
____
Telephone: ______________________

Adopted effective December 19, 2002.

FORM SC–21. ORDER TO MODIFY PRIOR PROTECTIVE ORDER

ORI ________

THE SUPERIOR COURT FOR THE COUNTY OF ________
STATE OF GEORGIA

______________________________,	]	
	]	
Petitioner,	]	Civil Action File
v.	]	
	]	
______________________________,	]	No. ____________
	]	
Respondent.	]	

ORDER TO MODIFY PRIOR PROTECTIVE ORDER

IT IS HEREBY ORDERED, ADJUDGED and DECREED that the prior Family Violence Protective Order issued __________, 20 ___ is modified as follows: ______
____
____
the remaining parts of the Protective Order issued __________, 20 ___ remains unmodified and in full effect.

This ___ day of __________, 20 ___.

____
JUDGE, SUPERIOR COURT
__________________________ County

____
Print or stamp Judge's name

☐ TRANSMITTED TO GEORGIA PROTECTIVE ORDER REGISTRY DATE _____ CLERK _____

Rev'd 1/10/03

REMOVE THIS PAGE FROM ORDER

Pursuant to O.C.G.A. Section 19–13–3,
Petitioner assisted by:

Name: ______________________________
Address: ____________________________
____
Telephone: ___________________________

Adopted effective December 19, 2002.

FORM SC–22. THREE YEAR/PERMANENT FAMILY VIOLENCE PROTECTIVE ORDER

ORI ________

THE SUPERIOR COURT FOR THE COUNTY OF ________

STATE OF GEORGIA

________________,	]	
	]	
Petitioner,	]	Civil Action File
v.	]	
	]	
________________,	]	No. ________
	]	
Respondent.	]	

THREE YEAR/PERMANENT FAMILY VIOLENCE PROTECTIVE ORDER

A hearing was held on this matter on ________, 20 ___ for which the Respondent had notice as required by law and at which the Respondent appeared and/or had the opportunity to be heard and the Petitioner requested that the Protective Order entered in this case be converted to a Permanent Family Violence Protective Order. This Court has determined that it had jurisdiction over the subject matter and the parties. Having heard the evidence presented, reviewed the Motion and the entire record concerning this case and for good cause shown, IT IS HEREBY ORDERED AND ADJUDGED:

1. That these proceedings be filed in the office of the Clerk of this Court.

2. That this Order applies in every county throughout the state and it shall be the duty of every court and every law enforcement official to enforce and carry out the provisions of this Order pursuant to O.C.G.A. § 19–13–4(d). Law enforcement officers may use their arrest powers pursuant to O.C.G.A. §§ 19–13–6, 17–4–20 to enforce the terms of this Order.

3. This Order and the Order issued ________, 20 ___ shall be permanent pursuant to O.C.G.A. § 19–13–4(c) and have NO expiration date.

OR

3.1 This Order shall be in effect for three (3) years and shall expire on ________, 20__.

4. [pco01] That the Respondent has violated the Family Violence Act, at O.C.G.A. § 19–13–1 et seq., by committing family violence, has placed the Petitioner in reasonable fear for Petitioner's safety, and represents a credible threat to the physical safety of Petitioner and/or Petitioner's child/ren. Respondent is hereby enjoined and restrained from doing, or attempting to do, or threatening to do, any act of injury, maltreating, molesting, following, harassing, harming, or abusing the Petitioner and/or the minor child/ren in any manner. Respondent is not to interfere with Petitioner's travel, transportation, or communication. Respondent shall not follow, place under surveillance, or contact the Petitioner at any place of the Petitioner for the purpose of harassing and intimidating the Petitioner.

CIVIL ACTION FILE NO. ____________

5. [pco02] That the Respondent is enjoined and restrained from doing or attempting to do, or threatening to do, any act of injury, maltreating, molesting, harassing, harming, or abusing the Petitioner's family or household.

6. That this Court determined that it had jurisdiction over the parties and the subject matter under the laws of the State of Georgia and Respondent received reasonable notice and had the opportunity to be heard before this Order was issued sufficient to protect the Respondent's due process rights and this Order shall be presumed valid and pursuant to 18 U.S.C. § 2265(a) shall be accorded full faith and credit by any other state or local jurisdiction and shall be enforced as if an Order of the enforcing state or jurisdiction.

ONLY THE FOLLOWING THAT ARE INITIALED BY THE JUDGE SHALL APPLY

____ 7. [pco04] Respondent is ordered to stay away from Petitioner's and Petitioner's child/ren's residence and workplace and/or school and any subsequent residence or workplace or school of Petitioner and/or Petitioner's minor child/ren.

____ 8. [pco01,04] That Respondent is restrained and enjoined from approaching within ___ yards of Petitioner and/or Petitioner's minor child/ren.

____ 9. [pco05] Respondent is ordered not to have any contact, direct, indirect or through another person with Petitioner, by telephone, pager, fax, e-mail or any other means of communication except as specified in this Order.

____ 10. [pco09] That Petitioner is awarded temporary custody of the minor child/ren, namely:

__________________________ DOB ____ sex ____
__________________________ DOB ____ sex ____
__________________________ DOB ____ sex ____
__________________________ DOB ____ sex ____

Respondent is ordered not to interfere with the physical custody of the minor child/ren.

____ [pco06] Check here ***only if Respondent*** is awarded temporary custody of child/ren.

____ 11. Respondent is ordered to pay to the Petitioner support for the minor child/ren in the amount of $ ______ every ______ beginning the ______ of ______, ___.

All payments are to be made by or to:
____ income deduction order
____ child support receiver
____ by mail directly to the Petitioner
or____ ______________

CIVIL ACTION FILE NO. ______________

In determining child support the Court finds as follows:

The gross income of the father is $ _____ yearly or $ _____ monthly. The gross income of the mother is $ _____ yearly or $ _____ monthly.
The applicable percentages of obligor's gross income to be considered by the trier of fact to determine child support are:

One child	17 to 23 percent	Four children	29 to 35 percent
Two children	23 to 28 percent	Five children	31 to 37 percent
Three children	25 to 32 percent		

In this case child support is being determined for ___ child/ren and the applicable percentage of gross income to be considered is ____ to ____ percent. The court has considered the existence of special circumstances, and has found that no special circumstances **OR** the following special circumstances exist: ______________________________

_____ 12. Respondent is ordered to pay temporary support for the Petitioner in the amount of $_______ every _______ beginning _________.
All payments are to be made by or to: _____ income deduction order
_____ child support receiver
_____ by mail directly to the Petitioner
or_____ ______________

_____ 13. Respondent shall have visitation with the minor child/ren according to the following schedule, beginning __________:

_____ no visitation
_____ no visitation until ______________
_____ supervised visitation, supervised by a third party as follows: ______________________________
____
_____ visitation every other weekend from Friday at 6 p.m. until Sunday at 6 p.m., beginning ___________, _______
_____ other visitation ______________________________
_____ circumstances concerning how Respondent shall pick up and return the minor child/ren shall be ______________

Strict compliance with this visitation provision shall not be a violation of the restraining provisions of this Order.

_____ 14. (Respondent)(Petitioner)(both Petitioner and Respondent)[strike through appropriate] is/are ordered not to sell, encumber, trade, damage, contract to sell, or otherwise dispose of or remove from the jurisdiction of this Court any of the property or pets of the Petitioner or joint property or pets of the parties except in the ordinary course of business.

CIVIL ACTION FILE NO. ______________

____ 15. (Respondent)(Petitioner)(both Petitioner and Respondent) [strike through appropriate] is/are ordered not to disconnect or have disconnected home utilities, change or have changed and/or cancel or have canceled auto, health or life insurance for Respondent, Petitioner, and/or Petitioner's child/ren or interfere with, Respondent's, Petitioner's and/or Petitioner's child/ren's mail.

____ 16. Petitioner is awarded costs and attorney fees in the amount of __________.

____ 17. [pco07] Petitioner/protected party is either a spouse, former spouse, parent of a common child, child of Petitioner, child of Respondent, cohabitates or has cohabited with Respondent.

____ 18. [pco08] It is further Ordered ____
____.

SO ORDERED this ___ day of __________, 20 ___.

____
JUDGE, SUPERIOR COURT
______________________ County

____
Print or stamp Judge's name

Violation of the above Order may be punishable by arrest.

CIVIL ACTION FILE NO. ______________

NOTICE TO RESPONDENT

1. **Violation of this Order may result in immediate arrest and criminal prosecution that may result in jail time and/or fines and/or may subject you to prosecution and penalties for contempt of court.**
2. **This Order shall remain in effect unless specifically superceded by a subsequent signed and filed Order, by operation of law, or by Order of dismissal, whichever occurs first. Only this Court can void, modify or dismiss this Order. Either party may ask this Court to change or dismiss this Order.**
3. **A person commits the offense of Aggravated Stalking when such person, in violation of a temporary or permanent protective Order prohibiting this behavior follows, places under surveillance, or contacts Petitioner on public or private property for the purpose of harassing and intimidating the other person. This activity can subject the Respondent to arrest and prosecution for felony Aggravated Stalking, which carries penalties of imprisonment for not less than 1 year nor more than 10 years and a fine of up to $10,000.00.**

CIVIL ACTION FILE NO. ______________

Pursuant to O.C.G.A. Section 19-13-3,
Petitioner assisted by
Name: ______________________________
Address: ____________________________
____
Telephone: __________________________

Note to Judges: This form is promulgated as a Uniform Superior Court Rule under the auspices of O.C.G.A. § 19–13–53. To order a specific provision, please initial in the space provided. The court should delete or otherwise make inoperative any provision in the standardized form which is not supported by the evidence in the case and in order to comply with the court's application of the law and facts to an individual case.

CIVIL ACTION FILE NO. ____________

RESPONDENT'S IDENTIFYING FACT SHEET

(please complete as much as possible; one of these must be provided to have the order placed in the National Crime Information Center registry: Respondent's date of birth OR social security number)

Respondent's social security number is ____________, date of birth is ________, sex ___, color of hair ________, color of eyes ________, height _______, weight _______. Respondent's race is ________, ethnic background ___________. Respondent has distinguishing marks (tattoos, scars, etc.) ___________. Respondent drives a ___________, license tag number ___________ and has a ____ (state) driver's license number ________. Respondent's home address ________________ and is employed by ______________ at ________ and works from ____ to ____ on (days) ___________.

PETITIONER'S IDENTIFYING INFORMATION

Protected parties ________________ DOB ____ sex ____ race ____
________________ DOB ____ sex ____ race ____
________________ DOB ____ sex ____ race ____
________________ DOB ____ sex ____ race ____

☐ Transmitted to Georgia Protective Order Registry Date _____ Clerk _____

Rev'd 10/1/04

Adopted effective December 19, 2002; amended effective December 2, 2004.

FORM SC–23. STALKING PERMANENT PROTECTIVE ORDER PURSUANT TO CRIMINAL CONVICTION

ORI ________

THE SUPERIOR COURT FOR THE COUNTY OF ________

STATE OF GEORGIA

State of Georgia]
]
] Accusation
v.]
]
____________,] No. ________
]
Defendant.]

STALKING PERMANENT PROTECTIVE ORDER PURSUANT TO CRIMINAL CONVICTION

Defendant appeared before this Court and was convicted of stalking O.C.G.A. § 16–5–90. Pursuant to O.C.G.A. § 16–5–90(d) a permanent restraining order is issued to protect the victim and the members of the victim's immediate family; therefore IT IS HEREBY ORDERED AND ADJUDGED:

1. [pco01,02] Defendant is hereby enjoined and restrained from doing or attempting to do, or threatening to do any act constituting a violation of O.C.G.A. §§ 16–5–90 *et seq.* and of harassing, interfering, or intimidating ________ or his/her immediate family. Any future acts committed by the Defendant towards ________ which are in violation of this statute and this Protective Order can amount to AGGRAVATED STALKING, pursuant to O.C.G.A. § 16–5–91, which is a felony. A person convicted of Aggravated Stalking shall be punished by imprisonment for not less than one nor more than ten years and by a fine of not more than $10,000.00.

2. [pco01,04] Defendant is enjoined and restrained from approaching within _____ yards of ____________ and/or her/his immediate family, and/or residence, place of employment, or school and any subsequent residence, workplace or school.

3. [pco05] Defendant is not to have any contact of any type, direct, indirect, or through another person with ________ or her/his immediate family, including but not limited to telephone, fax, e-mail, voice mail, mail, or any other type of contact.

4. That this Order be filed in the office of the Clerk of this Court.

ACCUSATION NO. ________

5. This Order shall remain in effect permanently and shall not terminate unless modified by the Court.

6. That this Order applies in every county throughout the state and it shall be the duty of every court and every law enforcement official to enforce and carry out the provisions of this Order pursuant to O.C.G.A. §§ 16–5–94(e) and 19–13–4(d). Law Enforcement may use their arrest powers pursuant to O.C.G.A. §§ 16–5–91 and 17–4–20 to enforce the terms of this Order.

7. That this Court determined that it had jurisdiction over the parties and the subject matter under the laws of the State of Georgia and Defendant received reasonable notice and had the opportunity to be heard before this Order was issued sufficient to protect the Defendant's due process rights and this Order shall be presumed valid and pursuant to 18 U.S.C. § 2265(a) shall be accorded **full faith and credit** by any other state or local jurisdiction and shall be enforced as if an Order of the enforcing state or jurisdiction.

ONLY the following that are initialed by the JUDGE shall apply:

____ 8. Defendant is to receive appropriate psychiatric or psychological services.

____ 9. [pco07] Protected party is either a spouse, former spouse, parent of a common child, child of a protected party, child of Defendant, cohabitates or has cohabited with Defendant and qualifies for 18 U.S.C. § 922(g).

SO ORDERED this ___ day of ________, ___.

____
JUDGE, SUPERIOR COURT
________________ County

____
Print or stamp Judge's name

Violation of the above Order may be punishable by arrest.

Note to Judges: This form is promulgated as a Uniform Superior Court Rule under the auspices of O.C.G.A. § 19–13–53. To order a specific provision, please initial in the space provided. The court should delete or otherwise make inoperative any provision in the standardized form which is not supported by the evidence in the case and in order to comply with the court's application of the law and facts to an individual case.

ACCUSATION NO. ________

NOTICE TO DEFENDANT

1. **Violation of this Order may result in immediate arrest and criminal prosecution that may result in jail time and/or fines and/or may subject you to prosecution and penalties for contempt of court.**
2. **This Order shall remain in effect unless specifically superceded by a subsequent Order signed and filed, by operation of law, or by Order of dismissal, whichever occurs first. Only this Court can void, modify or dismiss this Order. Either party may ask this Court to change or dismiss this Order.**
3. **If after a hearing, of which the Defendant received notice and opportunity to participate, a protective order is issued which restrains Defendant from harassing, stalking or threatening an intimate partner, Defendant is prohibited from possessing, receiving, or transporting a firearm or ammunition which has been shipped or transported in interstate or foreign commerce for the duration of the Order. 18 U.S.C. § 922(g).**
4. **A person commits the offense of Aggravated Stalking when such person, in violation of a temporary or permanent protective Order prohibiting this behavior follows, places under surveillance, or contacts another person on public or private property for the purpose of harassing and intimidating the other person. This activity can subject the Defendant to arrest and prosecution for felony aggravated stalking, which carries penalties of imprisonment for not less than 1 year nor more than 10 years and a fine of up to $10,000.00.**

DEFENDANT'S IDENTIFYING INFORMATION

(please complete as much as possible; one of these must be provided to have the order placed in the National Crime Information Center registry: Defendant's date of birth OR social security number)

Defendant's social security number is ________, date of birth is ______, sex ___, color of hair ________, color of eyes ______, height ______, weight ______. Defendant's race is ______. Ethnic background ________ Defendant drives a ____________, license tag number ________ and has a ____ (state) driver's license number ________. Defendant has distinguishing marks (tattoos, scars, etc.) ________. Defendant's home address ____________.

PETITIONER'S IDENTIFYING INFORMATION

Protected parties ____________ DOB ____ sex ____ race ____
____________ DOB ____ sex ____ race ____
____________ DOB ____ sex ____ race ____
____________ DOB ____ sex ____ race ____
____________ DOB ____ sex ____ race ____

☐ Transmitted to Georgia Protective Order Registry Date ____ Clerk ____

Rev'd 10/1/04

Adopted effective December 19, 2002; amended effective December 2, 2004.

FORM SC-24. STALKING THREE YEAR/PERMANENT PROTECTIVE ORDER

ORI ________

THE SUPERIOR COURT FOR THE COUNTY OF ________
STATE OF GEORGIA

________________,	]	
	]	
Petitioner,	]	Civil Action File
v.	]	
	]	
________________,	]	No. ________
	]	
Respondent.	]	

STALKING THREE YEAR/PERMANENT PROTECTIVE ORDER

A civil hearing was held on this matter on ________, 20 ___ at which the Respondent appeared and/or was provided with the opportunity to be heard and the Petitioner requested, pursuant to O.C.G.A. §§ 16–5–94 (e) and 19–13–4 (c), that a permanent Protective Order be issued. Having heard the evidence presented, reviewed the petition and the record concerning this case and for good cause shown, IT IS HEREBY ORDERED AND ADJUDGED:

1. [pco01,02] The Respondent has knowingly and wilfully violated O.C.G.A. §§ 16–5–90 *et seq.* and placed the Petitioner in reasonable fear for the Petitioner's safety, because ____.

   Respondent is hereby enjoined and restrained from doing or attempting to do, or threatening to do any act constituting a violation of O.C.G.A. §§ 16–5–90 *et seq.* and of harassing, interfering, or intimidating the Petitioner or Petitioner's immediate family. Any future acts committed by the Respondent towards the Petitioner which are in violation of this statute and this Protective Order can amount to AGGRAVATED STALKING, pursuant to O.C.G.A. § 16–5–91, which is a felony. A person convicted of Aggravated Stalking shall be punished by imprisonment for not less than one nor more than ten years and by a fine of not more than $10,000.00.

2. [pco01,04] Respondent is permanently enjoined and restrained from approaching within _____ yards of Petitioner and/or Petitioner's immediate family, and/or residence, place of employment, or school or subsequent residence, place of employment or school.

3. [pco05] Respondent is not to have any contact of any type, direct, indirect, or through another person with the Petitioner or her/his immediate family, including but not limited to telephone, fax, e-mail, voice mail, mail, or any other type of contact.

CIVIL ACTION FILE NO. ______

4. That this order be filed in the office of the Clerk of this Court.

5. This Order shall remain in effect permanently and shall not terminate unless modified by the Court.

6. That this Order applies in every county throughout the state and it shall be the duty of every court and every law enforcement official to enforce and carry out the provisions of this Order pursuant to O.C.G.A. §§ 16–5–94(e) and 19–13–4(d). Law enforcement may use their arrest powers pursuant to O.C.G.A. §§ 16–5–91 and 17–4–20 to enforce the terms of this Order.

7. That this Court determined that it had jurisdiction over the parties and the subject matter under the laws of the State of Georgia and Respondent received reasonable notice and had the opportunity to be heard before this Order was issued sufficient to protect the Respondent's due process rights and this Order shall be presumed valid and pursuant to 18 U.S.C. § 2265(a) shall be accorded **full faith and credit** by any other state or local jurisdiction and shall be enforced as if an Order of the enforcing state or jurisdiction.

ONLY the following that are initialed by the JUDGE shall apply:

_____ 8. Respondent is to receive appropriate psychiatric or psychological services.

_____ 9. Petitioner is awarded costs and attorney fees in the amount of ________.

_____ 10. Petitioner/protected party is either a spouse, former spouse, parent of a common child, child of Petitioner, child of Respondent, cohabitates or has cohabited with Respondent and qualifies for 18 U.S.C. § 922(g)

[pco07]

SO ORDERED this ___ day of __________, 20 ___.

____
JUDGE, SUPERIOR COURT
______________ County

____
Print or stamp Judge's name

Violation of the above Order may be punishable by arrest.

CIVIL ACTION FILE NO. ______

NOTICE TO RESPONDENT

1. **Violation of this Order may result in immediate arrest and criminal prosecution that may result in jail time and/or fines and/or may subject you to prosecution and penalties for contempt of court.**
2. **This Order shall remain in effect unless specifically superceded by a subsequent signed and filed Order, by operation of law, or by Order of dismissal, whichever occurs first. Only this Court can void, modify or dismiss this Order. Either party may ask this Court to change or dismiss this Order.**
3. **If after a hearing, of which the Defendant received notice and opportunity to participate, a protective order is issued which restrains Defendant from harassing, stalking or threatening an intimate partner, Defendant is prohibited from possessing, receiving, or transporting a firearm or ammunition which has been shipped or transported in interstate or foreign commerce for the duration of the Order. 18 U.S.C. § 922(g).**
4. **A person commits the offense of Aggravated Stalking when such person, in violation of a temporary or permanent protective Order prohibiting this behavior follows, places under surveillance, or contacts Petitioner on public or private property for the purpose of harassing and intimidating the other person. This activity can subject the Respondent to arrest and prosecution for felony Aggravated Stalking, which carries penalties of imprisonment for not less than 1 year nor more than 10 years and a fine of up to $10,000.00.**

Note to Judges: This form is promulgated as a Uniform Superior Court Rule under the auspices of O.C.G.A. § 19–13–53. To order a specific provision, please initial in the space provided. The court should delete or otherwise make inoperative any provision in the standardized form which is not supported by the evidence in the case and in order to comply with the court's application of the law and facts to an individual case.

RESPONDENT'S IDENTIFYING FACT SHEET

(please complete as much as possible; one of these must be provided to have the order placed in the National Crime Information Center registry: Respondent's date of birth OR social security number)

Respondent's social security number is ____________, date of birth is ________, sex ___, color of hair _______, color of eyes _______, height ________, weight ______. Respondent's race is ________, ethnic background ___________. Respondent has distinguishing marks (tattoos, scars, etc.) _______________. Respondent drives a _______________, license tag number ____________ and has a ____ (state) driver's license number _________. Respondent's home address ____________________ and is employed by _______________ at _______________ and works from ____ to ____ on (days) __________.

PETITIONER'S IDENTIFYING INFORMATION

Protected parties _________________ **DOB** ____ **sex** ____ **race** ____
_________________ **DOB** ____ **sex** ____ **race** ____
_________________ **DOB** ____ **sex** ____ **race** ____
_________________ **DOB** ____ **sex** ____ **race** ____

☐ TRANSMITTED TO GEORGIA PROTECTIVE ORDER REGISTRY DATE _____ CLERK _____

Rev'd 10/1/04

REMOVE THIS PAGE FROM ORDER

Pursuant to O.C.G.A. Section 19-13-3,
Petitioner assisted by
Name: ______________________________
Address: ____________________________
____
Telephone: __________________________

Adopted effective December 19, 2002; amended effective December 2, 2004.

*

UNIFORM RULES FOR THE JUVENILE COURTS

Effective July 1, 1985

Including Amendments Received Through November 1, 2006

Research Note

Use WESTLAW *to find cases citing a rule. In addition, use* WESTLAW *to search for specific terms or to update a rule; see the GA–RULES and GA–ORDERS Scope screens for further information.*

Amendments to these rules are published, as received, in the South Eastern Reporter 2d *and* Georgia Cases *advance sheets.*

Table of Rules

SECTION 1. PRELIMINARY PROVISIONS

RULE 1.1. SCOPE

These are rules of practice and procedure for the juvenile courts of Georgia. It is recognized that it is difficult to adopt a stringent set of uniform rules for the juvenile courts of Georgia due to the diversity of the juvenile court system of this State. Great differences in population, in rural and urban courts, full-time judges as opposed to part-time judges, independent probation staff as opposed to state court service workers, as well as regional versus local Youth Development Centers near and far from the courts make a stringent set of uniform rules impractical. However, in an effort to provide general uniformity to the juvenile courts of this state, these rules will be broad. This will leave opportunities for each individual court to narrow these by means of local guidelines as they find necessary.

These rules are established by the Georgia Supreme Court with the advice and consent of the Council of Juvenile Court Judges as provided in the Constitution of 1983; Art. VI; Sec. IX; Par. I.

Insofar as these rules may add to existing statutory provisions relating to the same subject matter, they shall be construed so as to implement the purposes of the Juvenile Court Code.

Amended effective December 31, 1992.

RULE 1.2. LOCAL OPERATING PROCEDURES

Courts exercising jurisdiction over juveniles may adopt local operating procedures governing proceedings in the juvenile court if the procedures are not inconsistent with these rules, the Constitution or statutory law.

RULE 1.3. CERTIFICATION OF JUDICIAL OFFICERS

For the purposes of this rule judicial officers shall include judges and associate judges. Each judicial officer exercising juvenile court jurisdiction shall become certified after participation in at least one seminar established by the Council of Juvenile Court Judges each year. Any judge pro tempore who sits as juvenile court judge for at least thirty (30) days during a calendar year, in order to serve in the capacity in the following calendar year, must become certified by attending at least one seminar of the type described above. Superior court judges may meet this requirement by attending seminars held in conjunction with the seminars for superior court judges provided by the Institute of Continuing Judicial Education. Judicial officers shall not exercise juvenile court jurisdiction after January 1st of each year unless their Council certifies to the Administrative Office of the Courts that annual training has been accomplished or unless the judicial officer is in the first year of his or her initial appointment. The Council of Juvenile Court Judges shall certify the attendance of juvenile court judicial officers; the Council of Superior Court Judges shall certify the attendance of superior court judges who sit as juvenile court judges. Determination of certification will be based upon the completion of the requirements for certification set out in OCGA § 15–11–20. Each Council shall notify each judicial officer of that class of courts of his or her status relative to certification. The period of certification shall begin on January 1st of the year following completion of the requirements and shall extend through December 31st of that same year. If, on January 1st of each year, certification has not been attained by a judicial officer, the appropriate Council of Judges may grant an extension of 120 days for the judicial officers to become certified, upon good cause shown.

Amendment authorized effective July 10, 1987 and required effective September 1, 1987; amended effective March 21, 1991; December 31, 1992; August 16, 2001.

RULE 1.4. JUDGES PRACTICING IN OTHER COURTS

Attorneys who practice law and who are appointed or elected to serve as juvenile court judges shall not practice law in any juvenile court in the State of Georgia. This rule, however, shall not apply to custody cases in which the action was originally filed in superior court and is subsequently transferred by the judge thereof to the juvenile court pursuant to OCGA § 15–11–28 (c).

Rule authorized effective July 10, 1987 and required effective September 1, 1987; amended effective December 31, 1992; August 16, 2001.

RULE 1.5. NEW JUDGE ORIENTATION TRAINING

Each person serving as juvenile court judge or associate juvenile court judge shall attend a new judge orientation program established by the Council of Juvenile Court Judges (hereinafter referred to as the "Council") and presented in conjunction with the Institute of Continuing Judicial Education. The orientation program shall include a minimum of 16 hours of training in curriculum areas specified by the Council standing committee on education and certification. New judges shall complete the training as soon as possible following their appointment, but in any event within two (2) years of becoming subject to the certification requirement provided in Rule 1.3. Any person serving as juvenile court judge or associate juvenile court judge prior to the effective date of this rule shall be exempt from its requirements. No judge pro tempore shall be required to attend the new judge orientation program except those who are subject to the certification requirement provided in Rule 1.3. The new judge orientation program shall be administered by the Council standing committee on education and certification in keeping with this rule and any additional guidelines established by such standing committee in order to implement the purposes of this rule.

Adopted effective March 16, 2006.

SECTION 2. OFFICERS OF THE COURT AND COURT PERSONNEL

RULE 2.1. APPOINTMENTS BY THE JUDGE

See OCGA §§ 15–11–24 and 15–11–24.3.

(a) Appointment of Associate Judge. See OCGA § 15–11–21.

(b) Appointment of Judge Pro Tempore. See OCGA § 15–11–23.

Amendment authorized effective July 10, 1987 and required effective September 1, 1987; amended effective March 21, 1991; December 31, 1992; August 16, 2001.

RULE 2.2. CLERK OF THE COURT

See OCGA § 15–11–24. The judge of juvenile court shall notify the executive director of the Council of Juvenile Court Judges of the name, address, and telephone number of the clerk of juvenile court within thirty (30) days of his or her appointment as clerk.

(a) Duties. The clerk of the court, or a person designated by the clerk, shall record all proceedings of the court, issue and sign summonses and subpoenas and maintain all records within the court system. Any and all subpoenas for records shall be addressed to the clerk of juvenile court. The clerk shall also receive and safely maintain all evidence brought to the court and properly dispose of same. The clerk shall prepare and transmit copies of court records to proper appellate courts upon notification that a case has been appealed. The clerk shall certify court documents or records when transmitted to other courts or agencies and insure proper recording and safekeeping of transcripts of hearings, including adjudicatory, probable cause, detention and transfer hearings. Upon transfer of a delinquent child to criminal court for prosecution as an adult under the provisions of OCGA § 15–11–30.2, the clerk of the juvenile court shall forward a copy of all court documents relating to the case to the office of the prosecuting attorney. The clerk shall also perform other duties as directed by the judge.

(b) Deputy Clerks. See OCGA § 15–11–24.

Amended effective March 21, 1991; December 31, 1992; August 16, 2001.

RULE 2.3. COURT REPORTERS

The court reporter who is appointed by the judge shall attend all hearings as required by the judge, or at the request of any party, provided appropriate financial arrangements are made with said reporter in advance. The court reporter shall take down a verbatim record of the proceedings unless waived by the child and the child's parent, guardian or attorney. The proceedings shall be recorded by stenographic notes or by electronic, mechanical or other appropriate means.

Amended effective August 16, 2001.

RULE 2.4. PROBATION OFFICERS

The judge may appoint one or more probation officers whose powers and duties shall be as stated in OCGA § 15–11–24.2, or the judge may designate a court service worker of the Department of Juvenile Justice to perform the duties of a probation officer. Probation officers' salaries shall be fixed by the judge with the approval of the governing authority of the county or counties for which they are appointed unless a court service worker fills this position in which case compensation will be fixed by the State. Probation officers shall be given an appropriate oath of office.

A probation or non-judicial intake officer shall not conduct an accusatory proceeding against any child. For purposes of this rule, an accusatory proceeding is any hearing or court proceeding in which the child stands accused of violating the law or an order of the court and is subject to court sanctions as a result thereof. Probation or non-judicial intake officers shall not participate in such a proceeding either as the trier of facts or in a prosecutorial role, but may give testimony as to any violation of a valid order of probation or supervision of which he or she has personal knowledge.

Amendment authorized effective July 10, 1988 and required effective September 1, 1988; amended effective October 9, 1997; August 16, 2001.

RULE 2.5. INTAKE OFFICERS

Officers assigned to conduct intake shall receive, screen and examine all properly executed complaints filed pursuant to Uniform Rule 4.1 concerning delinquent, unruly or deprived children who are received by the court. Said officers shall, by authority of the judge, informally adjust those cases which are appropriate for such action. The intake officer shall compile on a regular basis the case files or a report on those cases that were informally adjusted for review by the juvenile court judge. Intake officers shall only be court-employed intake or probation officers, court service workers or other Department of Juvenile Justice staff designated by the judge or judges or associate judges exercising juvenile court jurisdiction.

Amended effective March 21, 1991; November 12, 1992; December 31, 1992; October 9, 1997.

RULE 2.6. LANGUAGE LINE SERVICE INTERPRETERS

The Language Line Service is authorized for use in the juvenile courts whenever interpreting is needed in a juvenile proceeding, and such service is economically more feasible than the hiring of personal interpreters.

Adopted effective August 8, 1996; amended effective August 16, 2001.

RULE 2.7. TELEPHONE AND VIDEO CONFERENCING

2.7–1 Telephone Conferencing. The trial court on its own motion or upon the request of any party may in its discretion conduct pre–trial or post–trial proceedings in civil actions by telephone conference with attorneys for all affected parties. The trial judge may specify:

(A) The time and the person who will initiate the conference;

(B) The party which is to incur the initial expense of the conference call, or the apportionment of such costs among the parties, while retaining the discretion to make an adjustment of such costs upon final resolution of the case by taxing same as part of the costs; and

(C) Any other matter or requirement necessary to accomplish or facilitate the telephone conference.

2.7–2 Video–Conferencing.

(A) At the discretion of the court, any Juvenile Court matters may be conducted by video–conference with the following exceptions:

1. Formal adjudicatory hearings on Petitions alleging the delinquency or unruliness of a child; and

2. Hearings alleging the violation of a juvenile court protective order which may result in the loss of liberty of the person alleging to have violated the protective order.

Notwithstanding any other provisions of this rule, a judge may order a party's personal appearance in court for any hearing. Furthermore, in civil matters transferred from the superior court to the juvenile court, the court may require compliance with Uniform Superior Court Rule 9.2.

(B) Confidential Attorney–Client Communication. Provision shall be made to preserve the confidentiality of attorney-client communications and privilege in accordance with Georgia law. In all delinquency, unruliness and traffic offense proceedings, the child and his or her attorney shall be provided with a private means of communications when in different locations.

(C) Witnesses. In any pending matter, a witness may testify via video–conference.

1. Any party desiring to call a witness by video–conference shall file a notice of intention to present testimony by video–conference.

a. For a proceeding that occurs prior to the filing of the petition, the notice shall be provided as soon as practicable before such proceeding.

b. For a ten–day adjudicatory hearing, notice shall be provided at least five (5) days prior to the hearing.

c. For a hearing regarding the termination of parental rights, notice shall be provided at least fifteen (15) days prior to the hearing.

d. For all other proceedings, notice shall be provided at least ten (10) days prior to the proceeding.

2. Any other party may file an objection to the testimony of a witness by video–conference within three (3) days of the filing of the notice of intention if the child is in detention or within five (5) days of the filing of the notice of intention otherwise. In a

delinquency or unruliness matter, such objection by the child shall be sustained; however, such objection shall act as a motion for continuance and shall toll the applicable time limits; furthermore, no such continuance or tolling shall exceed ten (10) days from the date of the objection if the child is in detention or thirty (30) days from the date of the objection otherwise.

3. The court may modify these requirements upon a showing of good cause. The discretion to allow testimony via video–conference shall rest with the judge.

(D) Recording of Hearings. A record of any proceedings conducted by video–conference shall be made in the same manner as all such similar proceedings not conducted by video–conference. However, upon the consent of all parties, that portion of the proceedings conducted by video conference may be recorded by an audio–visual recording system and such recording shall be part of the record of the case and transmitted to courts of appeal as if part of a transcript.

(E) Technical Standards. Any video–conferencing system utilized under this rule must conform to the following minimum requirements:

1. All participants must be able to see, hear, and communicate with each other simultaneously;

2. All participants must be able to see, hear, and otherwise observe any physical evidence or exhibits presented during the proceedings, either by video, facsimile, or other method;

3. Video quality must be adequate to allow participants to observe each other's demeanor and nonverbal communications; and

4. If the proceeding is one from which the general public may not be excluded as provided by O.C.G.A § 15–11–78(b), the location from which the judge is presiding shall be accessible to the public to the same extent as such proceeding would if not conducted by video conference. In any such case, the court shall accommodate any request by interested parties to observe the entire proceeding.

Adopted effective July 15, 2004.

SECTION 3. COURT RECORDS

RULE 3.1. COURT RECORDS

The court shall make and keep records of all cases brought before it including cases dismissed, informally adjusted or adjudicated. Such records shall be preserved in accordance with records retention schedules established by the State Records Committee and approved by the Administrative Office of the Courts. The court shall make official minutes, which may be the case files, consisting of all petitions and orders filed in a case and any other pleadings, certificates, proofs of publication, summonses, notices, warrants and other writs which may be filed therein and shall make social records, consisting of records of investigation and treatment and other confidential information. All complaints, summonses, orders, notices and pleadings shall be filed with the clerk of juvenile court with the date and time received noted thereon by the clerk.

(a) Making Records Available to the Council. All records required to be made available to the Council pursuant to these Rules shall be kept in the manner set forth in the Guidelines for Maintaining a Juvenile Court Docket for the Council of Juvenile Court Judges (hereinafter referred to as the "Guidelines"). A current copy of the Guidelines shall be maintained in the Clerk's Office.

Amended effective November 12, 1992; November 28, 1996.

RULE 3.2(a). COMPLAINT

Upon the receipt and filing of a complaint, consistent with Rule 4.1, the clerk of the juvenile court shall forward a copy of said complaint to the Council of Juvenile Court Judges or shall furnish the Council with the same data as that on the complaint form by means of computer tape or other electronic means in a record format approved by the Council of Juvenile Court Judges.

Adopted effective November 12, 1992.

RULE 3.2(b). DOCKET

Each juvenile court clerk shall keep a separate juvenile docket book. The juvenile court clerk shall use the uniform docket form JUV–16 and follow the instructions in the Guidelines for completing the docket form. The clerk shall make the docket book available for review by a representative of the Council of Juvenile Court Judges upon the Council's request. In lieu of maintaining a separate juvenile docket book, the clerk may furnish the Council, upon the Council's request, with the same data as that on the uniform docket by means of computer tape or other electronic means in a record format approved by the Council of Juvenile Court Judges.

Former Rule 3.2 redesignated as new Rule 3.2(b) effective November 12, 1992; amended effective November 28, 1996.

RULE 3.3. REMOVAL OF PAPERS FROM CLERK'S OFFICE

Attorneys, court reporters and other persons allowed to have access to official court records shall remove such records from the clerk's office only upon written order of the judge. Probation officers and intake staff may have access to official court records only under conditions prescribed by the judge under a general order.

RULE 3.4. INITIATION OF PROCEEDINGS FOR SEALING OF RECORDS

See O.C.G.A. § 15–11–79.2. The court shall give reasonable notice of the hearing to:

1. Any court or agency to which any information or records have been disseminated; and

2. Any court to which a case or records have been transferred for supervision, disposition or otherwise.

Amended effective July 1, 1986; December 31, 1992; August 16, 2001; April 15, 2004.

RULE 3.5. HEARINGS

See O.C.G.A. § 15–11–79.2. Copies of the order shall be sent to each agency or official therein named and the deputy director of the Georgia Crime Information Center. Sealed records shall be destroyed in accordance with approved court records retention schedules.

Amended effective December 31, 1992; October 5, 1998; August 16, 2001; April 17, 2003.

RULE 3.6. EFFECT

Upon the entry of the order, the proceeding shall be treated as if it never occurred. All index references, including computer and micrographic records, shall be deleted and the person, the court, the law enforcement officers and departments shall properly reply that no record exists with respect to the person upon inquiry in any matter.

The records shall be sealed in an envelope which is identified on the outside by the applicant's social security number and the date of birth of the applicant. All references to the case outside of the sealed envelope shall be removed completely.

Amended effective October 5, 1998.

RULE 3.7. REOPENING OF SEALED RECORDS

Inspection of sealed files and records may be permitted by an order of the court upon petition by the person who is the subject of the records and only by that person named in the order or to criminal justice officials upon petition to the court for official judicial enforcement or criminal justice purposes. After the record is reopened and the proceeding to reopen the record is terminated, the Court shall order that the record be resealed.

Amended effective October 5, 1998.

RULE 3.8. FORMS

All courts shall use the forms prescribed by these rules. Use of the Complaint Form, JUV–2, shall be required. All other forms listed below shall be used as provided or in another form which is in substantial conformity with the one provided below:

1. Delinquent/Unruly Petition, JUV–3;
2. Standard Deprived Petition, JUV–4;
3. Motion for Extension of Order, JUV–6.
4. Summons and Process, JUV–7;
5. Subpoena, JUV–8;
6. Subpoena to Produce, JUV–9;
7. Notice of Transfer to Adult Criminal Court, JUV–10;
8. Application for Bond, JUV–11;
9. Affidavit and Warrant, JUV–12;
10. Order of Detention, JUV–13;
11. Adult Commitment Order, JUV–14;
12. Order of Commitment, JUV–15;
13. Juvenile Court Docket Sheet, JUV–16;
14. Informal Adjustment Agreement, JUV–17;
15. Parental Notification of Abortion Petition, JUV–18;
16. Order for Shelter Care, JUV–19;
17. Pre–Trial Juvenile Rights Form, JUV–20;
18. Social History Face Sheet and Format, JUV–21;
19. Motion for Access to a Juvenile Court Proceeding, JUV–22;
20. Court Order in Response to a Motion for Access to a Juvenile Court Proceeding (granting motion), JUV–23;
21. Court Order in Response to a Motion for Access to a Juvenile Court Proceeding (denying motion), JUV–24;
22. Request to Install Recording And/Or Photographic Equipment Pursuant to Rules and Guidelines for Electronic and Photographic News Coverage of Juvenile Court Proceedings, JUV–25;
23. Court Order in Response to a Request to Install Recording And/Or Photographic Equipment Pursuant to Rules and Guidelines for Electronic and Photographic News Coverage of Juvenile Court Proceedings (approval of motion), JUV–26;
24. Court Order in Response to a Request to Install Recording And/Or Photographic Equipment Pursuant to Rules and Guidelines for Electronic and Photographic News Coverage of Juvenile Court Proceedings (denial of motion), JUV–27;

25. Parental Notification Certificate: Hearing Not Held/More Than 24 Hours Elapsed, JUV–28;

26. Parental Notification Certificate: Hearing Not Held/Failure to Appear/No Motion for Continuance, JUV–29;

27. Parental Notification Certificate: Hearing Held/No Decision Rendered Within 24 Hours, JUV–30.

(a) Form size. All prescribed forms, written reports, briefs, pleadings, and other documentary evidence used in the juvenile courts shall be on letter size paper, 8 ½″ × 11″ in size.

(b) Style of Pleadings, Motions and Briefs. Any pleadings, motions or briefs not filed on the forms adopted herein shall be styled in the same manner and shall contain the same information as contained on the petition forms prescribed under these rules.

(c) Maintenance of Prescribed Forms. It shall be incumbent upon the clerk of the juvenile court to order and maintain a supply of all forms prescribed by Rule 3.8. The forms shall be paid for out of county funds and purchased through a local vendor.

Amended effective July 1, 1986; amendment authorized effective July 10, 1987 and required effective September 1, 1987; amendment authorized effective July 10, 1988 and required effective September 1, 1988; amended effective March 21, 1991; December 31, 1992; October 28, 1993; November 28, 1996; April 15, 2004.

COMPLAINT, JUV–2
IN THE JUVENILE COURT OF
____________________ COUNTY, GEORGIA

Case Number:

Name: (Last, F.M.) Age:
AKA: DOB: / /

Race: Lives With: Res.: ________
Sex: Bus.:

(Name) (Phone)

Child's Address:

(Street) (Apt. #) (City) (County) (State) (Zip)

Mother's Name: Res.: ________
Phone: Bus.:

(Include Mother's Maiden Name In Parentheses)

Mother's Address:

(Street) (Apt. #) (City) (County) (State) (Zip)

Father's Name: Res.: ________
Phone: Bus.:

Father's Address:

(Street) (Apt. #) (City) (County) (State) (Zip)

Legal Custodian: Res.: ________
Phone: Bus.:

Custodian's Address:

(Street) (Apt. #) (City) (County) (State) (Zip)

Complaint: / /
(Code Section) (Misd./Fel.) Date of Offense

Complaint: / /
(Code Section) (Misd./Fel.) Date of Offense

Complaint: / /
(Code Section) (Misd./Fel.) Date of Offense

Taken Into Custody: Yes ( ) No ( )
By Whom:
(Name) (Agency)

Placement of Deprived Child: Date: / /
Time:

Person notified: Date: / /
By: VIA: Time:

Detained: Yes ( ) No ( ) Place Detained: Date: / /
Time:
Authorized by:

Released To: Date: / /
Relation: Time:

Co-perpetrator:

(Name and Age)

Co-perpetrator:

(Name and Age)

Victim's Name: Phone #:

Victim's Address:		
Victim's Name:		Phone #:
Victim's Address:		
Give Complete Details of Offense(s) or Complaint(s) and Apprehension:		
Investigating Agency:		
Officer:	P.D. Report #:	Phone #:
Complainant's Name: ____________________	Complainant's Address:	
Signature:	Date:	Phone:

Rev. 01/2001 JUV–2

Amended effective July 1, 1986; use of amended form authorized effective July 1, 1986 and required effective January 1, 1987; renumbered as JUV–93–2 effective October 28, 1993; renumbered as JUV–2 and amended effective November 28, 1996; amended effective August 16, 2001.

DELINQUENT/UNRULY PETITION, JUV–3
PETITION
(DELINQUENT/UNRULY)
IN THE JUVENILE COURT OF
__________COUNTY, GEORGIA

In the interest of ____________________ A Child

CASE NUMBER __________
SEX __________
DOB __________ AGE ______

TO THE JUVENILE COURT OF ________ COUNTY, GEORGIA:

1. Your petitioner alleges the child named above to be of the sex and age and to have the name there set forth; that the father of said child is ________________, who resides at ________________________________ the mother is ____________________, who resides at ____________________; said child resides at ________________________________

(Address)

in said county and state, and is in the custody and control of ______________,

(Name)

who resides at said place; that the said child is subject to the jurisdiction of this Court.

2. That the within petition is filed in the best interest of the public and the within named child.

3. That said child has violated the section of the code cited below and is a delinquent/unruly child by reason of the facts set forth below:

A.

4. That said child is in need of supervision, treatment or rehabilitation. That said child is/is not currently in detention in the ______ Center, having been placed there at ______ on ______ 20 ______.

Petitioner prays that process issue, directed to the parties hereto, requiring them to show cause why said child should not be dealt with according to law.

____
(Petitioner)

Subscribed and sworn to before me, on information and belief, this ____ day of ______, 20____.

____
(Attesting Officer)

The above petition is approved to be filed in the best interest of the public and the named child.

This ____ day of ______, 20____.

____
(Court Designee)

ORDER OF DISMISSAL

The foregoing petition having come before me for consideration, and is hereby dismissed for the following reason(s):

____
____
____
____

This ______ day of __________, 20____.

____

Judge/Associate Judge of
________ County Juvenile Court

ORDER OF WITHDRAWAL

The foregoing petition having come before me for consideration, it is hereby found that withdrawal of the petition is in the best interest of the public and the child and the petition is withdrawn.

This ______ day of ________, 20____.

____

Judge/Associate Judge of

________ County Juvenile Court

ADMISSION/DENIAL

After having been fully advised of my rights to remain silent, to a hearing before the Judge and my right to have legal counsel, I, _______, understand the nature of the charges against me and hereby admit/deny the following allegations contained in this petition:

____

____

I do further assert that I have not been promised anything or been threatened or forced to enter this admission and that this admission is entered freely and voluntarily.

This ______ day of __________, 20____.

______________________________ ______________________________
(Attorney's Signature) (Child's Signature)

____
(Parent or Guardian's Signature)

ORDER OF ADJUDICATION

The foregoing petition having come on before me for hearing and consideration, it is hereby found that the allegations of the petition are true (as admitted), that the acts attributed to or admitted by the child were, in fact, committed by said child, and that such acts constitute acts of delinquency (felony/misd.) / unruliness within the meaning of the law. It is further found that the child's admission was entered knowingly, freely and voluntarily.

It is further found upon hearing the evidence that said child is in need of treatment or rehabilitation (and/or supervision) as a delinquent/unruly child. Said child is hereby ordered released into the custody of _______/ detained or held in custody until further order of this court.

This ______ day of ______, 20 ______.

____

Judge/Associate Judge of

________ County Juvenile Court

Rev. 01/2001 JUV–3

Amended effective July 1, 1986; use of amended form authorized effective July 1, 1986 and required effective January 1, 1987; renumbered as JUV–93–3 effective October 28, 1993; amended effective August 8, 1996; renumbered as JUV–3 and amended effective November 28, 1996; amended effective October 5, 1998; August 16, 2001.

STANDARD DEPRIVATION PETITION, JUV-4

PETITION
(DEPRIVATION)

IN THE JUVENILE COURT OF
_________ COUNTY, GEORGIA
In the interest of

_______________	SEX ___	AGE ___	DOB ___	CASE # _____
_______________	SEX ___	AGE ___	DOB ___	CASE # _____
_______________	SEX ___	AGE ___	DOB ___	CASE # _____
_______________	SEX ___	AGE ___	DOB ___	CASE # _____

A child/children under 18 years of age.

Your petitioner alleges the child(ren) named above to be of the sex(es) and age(s) and to have the name(s) there set forth above; that the (putative) father of said child(ren) is ______, who resides at ______; the mother is ______, who resides at ______; said child(ren) reside(s) at ______, in said county and state, and is/are in the custody and control of ______, who resides at said place; that the said child(ren) is/are subject to the jurisdiction of this Court; that said child(ren) is/are in need of protection of this Court and is/are deprived (O.C.G.A. § 15–11–2(8)) due to the following condition(s):

That said child(ren) was/were (not) taken into custody under the provisions of O.C.G.A. § 15–11–45(a)(4).

That it is in the best interest of the child(ren) and the public that this proceeding be brought.

That said child(ren) is/are, is not/are not currently in shelter care facilities under the supervision of the ______ County Department of Family and Children Services, having been placed there at ____ m., on ______, 20____.

Petitioner prays that process issue, directed to the parties hereto, requiring them to appear before this Court to answer the allegations of this petition.

____

(Petitioner)

Subscribed and sworn to before me, on information and belief this ______ day of ________, 20____.

____

(Attesting Officer)

The above petition is approved to be filed in the best interest of the public and the named child(ren).

This ______ day of ______, 20____.

____

(Court Designee)

Rev. 01/2001 JUV–4

Renumbered as JUV–93–4 effective October 28, 1993; renumbered as JUV–4 and amended effective November 28, 1996; amended effective August 16, 2001.

MOTION FOR EXTENSION OF JUVENILE COURT ORDER, JUV–6

IN THE JUVENILE COURT OF

_____ COUNTY, GEORGIA

In the interest of

_______________ SEX _____ AGE_____ DOB _____ CASE # _____
_______________ SEX _____ AGE _____ DOB _____ CASE # _____
_______________ SEX _____ AGE _____ DOB _____ CASE # _____
_______________ SEX _____ AGE _____ DOB _____ CASE # _____

A child/children.

ADDRESS:

MOTHER:

FATHER:

IN CUSTODY OF:

DATE OF ORDER: ORIGINAL CASE NUMBER _______

FACTUAL BASIS FOR MOTION:

MOTION

Now comes _____, and moves the Court to extend the order of the Juvenile Court of _____ County, Georgia, dated _____, for an additional two year period, from the date of expiration of said order, in accordance with O.C.G.A. § 15–11–58.

This _____ day of _____, 20____.

____

Signature of Movant

NOTICE OF HEARING

The within and foregoing Motion filed and the said matter to come on for a review in the Juvenile Court of_____ County, Georgia, on _____ at _____, the interested parties should be present in Court to show cause why said motion should not be granted.

This _____ day of _____, 20____.

____

Clerk/Deputy Clerk of

_____ County Juvenile Court

Summons attached

ORDER TO EXTEND

The foregoing motion having come on before me for hearing and consideration, it is hereby ordered and adjudged that the previous order of this court dated the _____ day of _____ 20_____ be and the same hereby is extended for _____ under the provisions of O.C.G.A. § 15–11–58.

This _____ day of _____, 20____.

____

Judge/Associate Judge of

_____ County Juvenile Court

Motion denied this, the _____ day of _____, 20____.

____

Judge/Associate Judge of

______ County Juvenile Court

Rev. 01/2001 JUV–6

Amended effective July 1, 1986; use of amended form authorized effective July 1, 1986 and required effective January 1, 1987; renumbered as JUV–93–6 effective October 28, 1993; renumbered as JUV–6 and amended effective November 28, 1996; amended effective October 5, 1998; August 16, 2001.

SUMMONS AND PROCESS, JUV–7

IN THE JUVENILE COURT OF
_______ COUNTY, GEORGIA

To: ____________________ and ____________________
Child Parent

____________________ ____________________
Street Address Street Address

____________________ ____________________
City State Zip City State Zip

In the interest of:

Name DOB

____________________ CASE #__________
____________________ CASE #__________
____________________ CASE #__________
____________________ CASE #__________

Child(ren).

A petition has been filed in this court concerning the above child(ren). A copy of that petition is attached to this summons.

This is a summons requiring you to be in court. If you fail to come to court as required you may be held in contempt of court and punished accordingly.

Now therefore, you, the parties named above, are commanded to be and appear on the date and time stated below, and to remain in attendance from hour to hour, day to day, month to month, year to year, and time to time, as said case may be continued, and until discharged by the court, and you are commanded to lay any and all business aside and to be and appear before the Juvenile Court of _______ County, Georgia, located at _______ on the _______ day of _______, 20_______ at _______ o'clock ____.m., and you the said parent, guardian or legal custodian are likewise hereby commanded to be and appear with the aforesaid child(ren) in said court at the time and place above stated, each of you then and there to make defense thereto and to show cause why the said child(ren) and all parties named herein should not be dealt with according to the provisions of the law.

WITNESS the Honorable _______, Judge of said Court, this the _______ day of _______, 20____.

____

Clerk/Deputy Clerk of

_______ County Juvenile Court

READ CAREFULLY

This Summons requires you to be present at a formal hearing in the Juvenile Court.

The child or children and other parties involved may be represented by a lawyer at all stages of these proceedings.

If you want a lawyer, you may choose and hire your own lawyer. If you want to lure a lawyer, please contact your lawyer immediately.

If you want a lawyer but are not able to hire a lawyer without undue financial hardship, you may ask for a lawyer to be appointed to represent you. The Court would inquire into your financial circumstances and if the Court finds you to be financially unable to hire a lawyer, then a lawyer will be appointed to represent you.

If you want a lawyer appointed to represent you, you must let the Court or the officer of this Court handling this case know that you want a lawyer immediately.

PROOF OF SERVICE TO CHILD

I hereby certify that on the ______ day of ______, 20______, I personally served a true copy of the within summons and process and a true copy of the attached petition on ______, child in this case.

____

Authorized Signature

PROOF OF SERVICE TO PARENT OR LEGAL CUSTODIAN

I have this ______ day of ______ 20______, served a true copy of the within summons and process and a true copy of the attached petition by delivering to and leaving same with ______.

____

Authorized Signature

RETURN OF NO SERVICE

I, the undersigned officer, after making diligent search, was unable to find the persons within named, to-wit: ______, within the jurisdiction of said court, and service of said summons and process upon said person was therefore not made. This ______ day of ______, 20___.

____

Authorized Signature

ORDER TO TAKE CHILD INTO IMMEDIATE CUSTODY

It appearing to the court, from the allegations of the sworn petition and otherwise, that the welfare of the within named child ______ requires that the custody of same be immediately assumed,

IT IS ORDERED that the officer serving this summons and process shall at once take said child into immediate custody and deliver said child without delay to ______ there to be held pending further order of the court or its authority. So ordered this ______ day of ______ 20___.

____

Judge/Associate Judge of

______ County Juvenile Court

RETURN OF OFFICER TAKING CHILD INTO IMMEDIATE CUSTODY

Pursuant to the order of court, I did, on the ______ day of ______, 20___, take the within named child ______ into custody and delivered this child to ______
____
____
____.

____

Authorized Signature

Rev. 01/2001 JUV–7

Renumbered as JUV–93–7 effective October 28, 1993; renumbered as JUV–7 and amended effective November 28, 1996; amended effective August 16, 2001.

SUBPOENA, JUV–8
IN THE JUVENILE COURT OF
______ COUNTY, GEORGIA

In the Interest of CASE NUMBER ____________
SEX __________________
DOB _________ AGE _________

______________________________,
A Child.

TO______ GREETING:

You are hereby commanded, that, laying all other business aside, you be and appear at the JUVENILE COURT OF ________________ COUNTY, GEORGIA, for a hearing to be held at ___________________________ on ______ 20____ at ______ o'clock ____m., and thereafter from day to day until discharged, then and there to be sworn as a witness in the above stated matter. Herein fail not under penalty of the law, including a fine of up to $300 and/or possible confinement of up to twenty (20) days in the common jail of said county.
Address

WITNESS the Honorable ______, Judge of said court, this the ______ day of ______, 20____.

____
Clerk/Deputy Clerk of

______ County Juvenile Court

PROOF OF SERVICE

I have this ______ day of ______, 20______, served the within subpoena by delivering to and leaving same with

____

____

____

____
Authorized Signature

Rev. 01/2001 JUV–8

Amended effective July 1, 1986; use of amended form authorized effective July 1, 1986 and required effective January 1, 1987; renumbered as JUV–93–8 effective October 28, 1993; renumbered as JUV–8 and amended effective November 28, 1996; amended effective August 16, 2001.

SUBPOENA TO PRODUCE DOCUMENTS OR OTHER EVIDENCE, JUV–9
IN THE JUVENILE COURT OF
______ COUNTY, GEORGIA

In the Interest of

CASE NUMBER ______
SEX ______
DOB ______ AGE ______

______,
A Child.

You are hereby commanded, that, laying all other business aside, you be and appear at the JUVENILE COURT OF ______ COUNTY, GEORGIA, for a hearing to be held at ______
Address
______ Georgia, on the ______ day of ______, 20____, at ______ o'clock ____m., and thereafter from day to day until discharged, then and there to be sworn as a witness in the above stated matter.

You are further required and commanded to bring with you into said Court:
______
______
______

Herein fail not under penalty of law, including a fine of up to $300 and/or possible confinement for up to twenty (20) days in the common jail of said county.

WITNESS, the Honorable ______, Judge of said Court, this ______ day of ______, 20______.

______
Clerk/Deputy Clerk of
______ County Juvenile Court

PROOF OF SERVICE

I have this ______ day of ______, 20____, served the within subpoena by delivering to and leaving same with ______
______
______

______
Authorized Signature

Rev. 01/2001 JUV–9

Amended effective July 1, 1986; use of amended form authorized July 1, 1986 and required effective January 1, 1987; renumbered as JUV–93–9 effective October 28, 1993; renumbered as JUV–9 and amended effective November 28, 1996; amended effective August 16, 2001.

NOTICE OF TRANSFER TO ADULT CRIMINAL COURT, JUV–10

IN THE JUVENILE COURT OF

______ COUNTY, GEORGIA

In the Interest of:

______________________________, A Child.

CASE NUMBER ______________

SEX ______________

DOB ________ AGE ________

TO: ______________________ Child

______________________ Street Address

______________________ City State Zip

AND: ______________________ Parent, Guardian, Custodian

______________________ Street Address

______________________ City State Zip

You are hereby put on notice that before the hearing on the attached petition on its merits, and at the time and place designated for hearing in the summons hereto attached, the Court will consider transfer of the offense(s) to the appropriate Adult Criminal Court having jurisdiction of the offense(s). This notice is given as required in O.C.G.A. § 15–11–30.2.

This ______ day of ______ 20____.

____

Clerk/Deputy Clerk of

______ County Juvenile Court

PROOF OF SERVICE

Notice of transfer hearing, as required in O.C.G.A. § 15–11–30.2, was personally served on ______, child and ______, parent, by me.

This ______ day of ______ 20____.

____

Authorized Signature

Rev. 01/2001 JUV–10

Amended effective July 1, 1986; use of amended form authorized effective July 1, 1986 and required effective January 1, 1987; renumbered as JUV–93–10 effective October 28, 1993; renumbered as JUV–10 and amended effective November 28, 1996; amended effective August 16, 2001.

APPLICATION FOR BOND, JUV–11
IN THE JUVENILE COURT OF
______ COUNTY, GEORGIA

In the interest of:

CASE NUMBER________________
________________________________, SEX________________
Child DOB ________ AGE ________

Now comes ____,
(Name)
parent/guardian/legal custodian of ____,
(Juvenile)

being held in the ________________________ charged with the offense(s) of ____________________ and respectfully requests that the within named child be released on bond returnable to this juvenile court in the custody of the undersigned, to be returned to this Court at a date and time to be specified.

This ______ day of ______ 20____.

____
(Name)

____
(Street)

____
(City, State, Zip Code)

Witness:

____

Application denied/approved and bond set in the amount of $______

This ______ day of ______ 20____.

____
Judge/Associate Judge of

______ County Juvenile Court

Amended effective July 1, 1986; use of amended form authorized effective July 1, 1986 and required effective January 1, 1987; renumbered as JUV–93–11 effective October 28, 1993; renumbered as JUV–11 and amended effective November 28, 1996; amended effective October 5, 1998; August 16, 2001.

AFFIDAVIT AND WARRANT, JUV–12
IN THE JUVENILE COURT OF
______ COUNTY, GEORGIA

CASE NUMBER ______
SEX ______
D.O.B. ______ AGE ______

In the interest of
______ address ______
A child

personally comes to a duly authorized officer of this Court and, on oath, says that to the best of ______ knowledge and belief the above-named child did on the ______ day of ______, 20____, commit the offense of ______ in that said child
______
______
______
______

and this deponent makes this affidavit so that a warrant may issue for ______ arrest.

(Deponent Sign)______

Sworn to and subscribed before me, this ______ day of ______, 20____.

______

Court Designee

______**WARRANT** ______

To any Sheriff, Deputy Sheriff, or any peace officer of this State or any duly authorized officer of this Court:

Greetings:

______ having made oath before this Court that on the ____ day of ______, 20____, ______ did commit the offense as stated in the above affidavit,

You are therefore commanded to take into custody said child and bring ______ before me to be dealt with as the law directs.

Witness my hand an official signature, as Judge, this ____ day of ______, 20____.

______

Judge/Associate Judge of

______ County Juvenile Court

Executed by ______ Date ______

Rev. 01/2001 JUV–12

Amended effective July 1, 1986; use of amended form authorized effective July 1, 1986 and required effective January 1, 1987; use of amended form authorized effective July 10, 1987 and required effective September 1, 1987; renumbered as JUV–93–12 effective October 28, 1993; renumbered as JUV–12 and amended effective November 28, 1996; amended effective August 16, 2001.

ORDER FOR DETENTION, JUV–13
IN THE JUVENILE COURT OF
_____ COUNTY, GEORGIA

In the interest of:

____

A Child.

CASE NUMBER ____________
SEX ____________
DOB ________ AGE ________

WHEREAS a complaint has been made to the court concerning the above-named child and the court finding from information brought before it that it is necessary for the protection of said child and/or society that he or she be detained,

It is therefore ordered that said child be detained in the custody of the court until further order of the court or until released by a person duly authorized by the court.

Said child is being detained pursuant to O.C.G.A. § 15–11–46 for the following reason(s):

( ) to protect the person or property of others or of the child;

( ) the child may abscond or be removed from the jurisdiction of the court;

( ) because the child has no parent, guardian, or custodian or other person able to provide supervision and care for him or her and return him or her to the court when required;

( ) an order for the child's detention or shelter care has been made by the court pursuant to the Juvenile Proceedings Code.

It is further ordered that the place of detention shall be the

____

____

____

ORDERED AND ADJUDGED

This ______ day of ______, 20___.

____

Judge/Associate Judge of

_____ County Juvenile Court

Rev. 01/2001 JUV–13

Amended form authorized effective July 1, 1986 and required effective January 1, 1987; amended form authorized effective July 1, 1988 and required effective September 1, 1988; renumbered as JUV–93–13 effective October 28, 1993; renumbered as JUV–13 and amended effective November 28, 1996; amended effective August 16, 2001.

ADULT COMMITMENT ORDER, JUV–14
IN THE JUVENILE COURT OF
______ COUNTY, GEORGIA

In the interest of: CASE NUMBER ______
SEX ______
DOB ______ AGE ______

______________________,
A Child.

______ having appeared before the undersigned during the course of a juvenile court proceeding and the Court, after hearing evidence, finding that there is probable cause to believe that______ has committed the offense of ______, said ______ is hereby bound over to the ______ Court of ______ County for the offense of ______, pursuant to the provisions of O.C.G.A. § 15–11–4 and other applicable laws.

The sheriff of ______ County, Georgia is required to receive and safely keep ______ until discharged by due process of law.

Bond is hereby act in the amount of $______.

SO ORDERED, this ______ day of ______, 20___.

____
Judge/Associate Judge of
______ County Juvenile Court

Rev. 01/2001 JUV–14

Amended effective July 1, 1986; use of amended form authorized effective July 1, 1986 and required effective January 1, 1987; renumbered as JUV–93–14 effective October 28, 1993; renumbered as JUV–14 and amended effective November 28, 1996; amended effective August 16, 2001.

ORDER OF COMMITMENT, JUV–15
IN THE JUVENILE COURT OF
_____ COUNTY, GEORGIA

In the interest of: CASE NUMBER __________
SEX __________
__________________ DOB __________ AGE ______
A Child

Petition(s) having been filed in this court and after hearing evidence in this court, this court has determined that the above-named child is subject to the jurisdiction and protection of this court as provided by law; and

After hearing evidence or upon the recommendation of the associate judge no appeal having been timely filed, the court finds that the child committed the act(s) alleged in said petition(s), to wit: ________________

____

____

____

and that said child is hereby found to be in a state of (Place an "X" in appropriate space).

________ delinquency and in need of treatment or rehabilitation.

________ unruliness and in need of treatment, rehabilitation, or supervision. The court also finds that the child is not amenable to treatment or rehabilitation pursuant to O.C.G.A. § 15–11–66(a)(1)-(3).

The court further finds that reasonable efforts have been made to prevent the unnecessary removal of the child from the child's home, and that removal is in the best interest of the child at this time.

It is further ordered that said child be and hereby is committed to the Department of Juvenile Justice, for care, supervision and planning as provided in O.C.G.A. § 49–4A–8. The undersigned judge hereby recommends that the child be: ______

____

____

The said Department of Juvenile Justice is authorized to provide such medical treatment, hospitalization and/or surgery as is considered necessary by competent medical authorities for said child.

It is further ordered that said child be released into the custody of ________ /detained in the ________ pending placement by the Department of Juvenile Justice.

Considered, Ordered, and Adjudged

This ________ day of ________, 20 ___.

____

Judge/Associate Judge of

________ County Juvenile Court

________ COUNTY JUVENILE COURT

FILED IN THE CLERK'S OFFICE ON THE ___ DAY OF ________, 20 ___.

____

CLERK/DEPUTY CLERK

Rev. 03/2002 JUV–15

Amended effective July 1, 1986; use of amended form authorized effective July 1, 1986 and required effective January 1, 1987; renumbered as JUV–93–15 effective October 28, 1993; renumbered as JUV–15 and amended effective November 28, 1996; amended effective October 9, 1997; August 16, 2001; March 21, 2002.

JUVENILE COURT DOCKET SHEET, JUV–16
JUVENILE COURT OF
______ COUNTY

Case Number: __________

Name:
Address:
Race: ( ) White ( ) Black ( ) Am. Indian ( ) Hispanic ( ) Asian ( ) Other
Age: DOB: / / Sex: ( ) Male ( ) Female
Complaint:

( ) Delinquency __Fel. __Misd.
( ) Unruly ( ) Deprivation ( ) Termination of Parental Rights ( ) Traffic ( ) Special Proceedings
Referral Source:

Attorney Type: ( ) Pub. Defender ( ) Private Appointed ( ) Private Retained
( ) County Attorney ( ) None
/ / Date of Bond Type: Amount: $
/ / Date Complaint Received
/ / Date Child Taken Into Custody
/ / Date Detained or Placed ( ) RYDC ( ) Attention Home ( ) Foster Care
/ / Detention Hearing Date ( ) Shelter ( ) Other:
Released To:
/ / Date Petition Filed
/ / Date of Arraignment, if held
/ / Dismissed or Withdrawn Prior to Adjudication
/ / Date Continuation of Adjudicatory Hearing is Granted
/ / Adjudicatory Hearing Date:

OFFENSE DISPOSITION

( ) Adjudicated ( ) Amended/Reduced ( ) Dismissed
( ) Transferred to Another Juvenile Court
( ) Transferred to Superior Court
( ) Informal Adjustment ( ) Order Entered ( ) Granted
( ) Denied

CASE DISPOSITION

/ / Date of Disposition
( ) Informal Adjustment
( ) Probation/Supervision
( ) Probation – Detention under OCGA § 15–11–35(b)
( ) Detention under OCGA § 15–11–35(b)
( ) Committed to DJJ
( ) Committed – Designated Felony
Restrictive Custody For: Months
( ) Committed – Detention under OCGA § 15–11–35(b)
( ) Committed – DHR
( ) Traffic Fine
( ) Dismissed
( ) Custody Other Name/Relationship:
( ) Custody To DFCS
( ) Transferred to Other Juvenile Court

( ) Transferred to Superior Court
( ) Granted
( ) Denied
( ) Review Order Entered

Disposition By: ( ) Judge, Name:
( ) Associate Judge, Name:
( ) Officer of the Court, Name:

Appealed ( ) Yes ( ) No Date of Notice: / /

Date of Remittitur: / / Findings:

Motions, Remarks:

Rev. 01/2001 JUV–16

Renumbered as JUV–93–16 effective October 28, 1993; renumbered as JUV–16 and amended effective November 28, 1996; amended effective October 9, 1997; August 16, 2001.

INFORMAL ADJUSTMENT AGREEMENT, JUV–17
IN THE JUVENILE COURT OF
______ COUNTY, GEORGIA

In the interest of: CASE NUMBER ____________
SEX ____________
______________________, DOB ________ AGE ________

The above-named child having been charged with

and;

The child and his parent/guardian having acknowledged the following:

(1) That the admitted facts bring the case within the jurisdiction of the Court;

(2) That the child has been advised that he/she has a right to have an attorney represent him/her in this matter and that if he/she is unable to afford to hire an attorney, one will be supplied free of charge;

(3) That he/she does not have to make any statement if he/she chooses not to;

(4) That this matter could be heard formally before a judge rather than by an officer of the Court.

The child and parent do hereby elect to have an attorney ____ not to have an attorney ____ and to proceed with this informal handling.

______________________ ______________________
Signature of Child Signature of Parent/Guardian

______________________ ______________________
Date Date

This Court having determined that the above-named child is subject to the jurisdiction and protection of this court as provided by law, and;
This Court having found that counsel and advice without an adjudication is in the best interest of the public and the child, and;
The child and his/her parent(s) or guardian having consented to the informal adjustment with knowledge that consent is not obligatory.
It is therefore agreed that the case of the above-named child is informally adjusted under the conditions and stipulations attached hereto and incorporated in this informal adjustment by reference.
Further, the above-named child and his/her parent(s) or guardian acknowledge that they have been advised, by a copy of this informal adjustment, and agree that any violation of any provision of this adjustment may result in the filing of a petition at any time during the term or period of this informal adjustment or any extension thereof.

Consented to by: Recommended by:

______________________ ______________________
Child Officer of Juvenile Court

____
Parent/Guardian

____
Attorney

Approved, this ____ day of ______, 20____.

____
Judge/Associate Judge of
________ County Juvenile Court

Rev. 01/2001 JUV–17

Adopted effective July 1, 1986; use of amended form authorized effective July 1, 1986 and required effective January 1, 1987; renumbered as JUV–93–17 effective October 28, 1993; renumbered as JUV–17 and amended effective November 28, 1996; amended effective August 16, 2001.

PETITION (PARENTAL NOTIFICATION), JUV–18
IN THE JUVENILE COURT OF
______ COUNTY, GEORGIA

In the Interest of ______ CASE NUMBER ______
SEX ______
______ DOB ______ AGE ______
An Unemancipated Minor

To the Juvenile Court of ______ County, Georgia:

1. Your petitioner alleges that the court has jurisdiction in that the minor is under the age of 18 and

2. That the within petition is filed in the best interest of the said minor, and

3. Said minor states that she desires to have her pregnancy terminated by approved medical procedures and asks that the court waive the requirements of O.C.G.A. § 15–11–112 and asks the court to consider her request under the provisions of O.C.G.A. § 15–11–114. A statement from a licensed medical doctor confirming the pregnancy and current trimester of gestation is attached and made a part of this petition by reference, and

4. Said minor further alleges:

______ that she is mature and sufficiently well-informed to make an intelligent decision on her own concerning an abortion;

or

______ that notice to a parent or guardian pursuant to O.C.G.A. § 15–11–112 would not be in her best interest, particulars being:

Therefore, petitioner prays for relief under the provisions of Article 3 of the Official Code of Georgia, Chapter 11 of Title 15.

______
(Petitioner: Minor/Next Friend)

Subscribed and sworn to before me this ______ day of ______, 20____.

______
(Attesting Officer)

Notice of Hearing

Petition having been filed in this court, a hearing is hereby scheduled to determine the merits of the petition on the ______ day of ______, 20____ at ______ at the ______ Juvenile Court, located at ______.

Notice of Right to Counsel

Said minor is hereby notified that she has a right to court appointed counsel and that the court will provide such minor with counsel upon request or if such minor is not already adequately represented.

Pursuant to the above, the undersigned minor hereby requests that the court appoint legal counsel to represent her in this matter.

______
(Minor)

Waiver of Counsel

I, the aforementioned minor, having been explained my right to counsel, hereby waive that right and elect to proceed without benefit of legal counsel.

____

(Minor)

Appointment of Guardian Ad Litem

Pursuant to Rule 23.2 of the Uniform Rules for Juvenile Courts, the Court hereby appoints _______ as guardian ad litem to protect the interests of the minor.

This _______ day of _______, 20____.

____

Judge or Court Designee

Rev. 01/2001 JUV–18

Adopted effective July 10, 1987; use of amended form authorized effective July 10, 1987 and required effective September 1, 1987; amended effective July 1, 1988; renumbered as JUV–93–18 effective October 28, 1993; renumbered as JUV–18 and amended effective November 28, 1996; amended effective August 16, 2001.

ORDER FOR SHELTER CARE, JUV–19
IN THE JUVENILE COURT OF
______ COUNTY, GEORGIA

In the interest of: SEX ________________________
DOB ________________________
______________________________ FILE # ______ CASE # ______
A Child

A complaint has been made to the Court concerning the above-named child. The Court finds from information brought before it that continuation in the home at this time would be contrary to the welfare of said child. It is necessary for the protection of said child that that he/she be placed in shelter care because ______
____

The Court also finds that pursuant to O.C.G.A. § 15–11–58(a):

( ) reasonable efforts have been made by the Department to preserve and reunify the family prior to the placement of the child in foster care, to prevent or eliminate the need for removal of the child from the child's home and to make it possible for said child to remain safely in the home, to wit: ________________
____
____

( ) reasonable efforts by the Department to preserve and reunify the family prior to the placement of the child in foster care, to prevent or eliminate the need for removal of the child from the child's home and to make it possible for said child to remain safely in the home were not required pursuant to O.C.G.A. § 15–11–58(a)(4)(A–C) because: ________________________
____

( ) the Department failed to make reasonable efforts to preserve and reunify the family prior to the placement of the child in foster care, to prevent or eliminate the need for removal of the child from the child's home and to make it possible for said child to remain safely in the home. The following efforts would have been reasonable to prevent or eliminate the need for removal: ________________
____

IT IS THEREFORE ORDERED that said child be placed in the custody of:
_________ until further order of the Court or until released by a person duly authorized by the Court. Said child is being placed pursuant to O.C.G.A. § 15–11–46 for the following reasons:

( ) to protect the person or property of others or of the child;

( ) the child may abscond or be removed from the jurisdiction of the Court;

( ) because the child has no parent, guardian, or custodian or other person able to provide supervision and care for him or her and return him or her to the Court when required; or

( ) an order for the child's detention or shelter care has been made by the Court pursuant to the Juvenile Proceedings Code.

Pursuant to O.C.G.A. § 15–11–48(f), the Court approves the following physical placement of the child: _________
_________ pending the 72 Hour Hearing on _________ at _________, _________ .m.

It is further ordered that the custodian be and hereby is authorized to obtain a physical examination, ordinary medical care, and such additional medical treatment and care which, in the opinion of a licensed physician, requires prompt treatment for the care of the said child while said child is in his/her/its custody.

ORDERED AND ADJUDGED this ___ day of _________, 20 ___.

____
Judge/Associate Judge of
_________ County Juvenile Court

Rev. 03/2002 JUV–19

Form authorized effective July 1, 1988 and required effective September 1, 1988; amended effective December 31, 1992; renumbered as JUV–93–19 effective October 28, 1993; renumbered as JUV–19 and amended effective November 28, 1996; amended effective October 5, 1998; August 16, 2001; March 21, 2002.

PRE–TRIAL JUVENILE RIGHTS FORM, JUV–20

IN THE JUVENILE COURT OF
_____ COUNTY, GEORGIA

In the interest of: CASE NUMBER ______________
SEX ______________
______________________ DOB ________ AGE ________

A Child.

ACKNOWLEDGEMENT OF RIGHTS

The above named child, along with the undersigned parent/guardian and/or attorney, states as follows:

I understand that I have been charged with ________________ and that I am here today to answer to that charge(s). I have had explained and further understand the following:

1. I do not have to admit to the charges against me or even say anything at all, and that if I choose not to say anything it will not be used against me.
2. I have the right to have the charges against me served upon me in writing within a reasonable time.
3. I have a right to have a lawyer represent me, and if I cannot afford to hire a lawyer, the Court will provide one for me.
4. I understand that a lawyer is trained to understand court procedure and proceedings, knows how to conduct trials and how to properly introduce evidence and exclude improper evidence, knows how the law applies to the circumstances of my case, and knows how my rights and liberties may be affected by the court proceedings and how to protect my rights and liberties, and how to present my case and all matters favorable to me to the court, all of which I may not know.
5. I have had my right to be represented by a lawyer explained to me and I understand the danger of proceeding without a lawyer.
6. I have been told of the possible dispositions which the court can order if I admit to the charge(s) or if I am found to have committed a delinquent or unruly act(s), and those dispositions may include but are not limited to dismissal, informal adjustment, probation, commitment to the Department of Human Resources, commitment to the Department of Juvenile Justice not to exceed sixty months, placement in an institution, placement in the custody of the Division of Family and Children Services, community service, suspension of driving license privileges, requiring school attendance, and restitution.
7. I have talked with my parents/guardian and/or lawyer about this case and have had all of the above explained to me and had the opportunity to ask questions and have had all my questions answered.
8. I have the right to have a trial before the judge, I can have witnesses there to testify for me, and I can question anyone who might testify against me. I have the right to an appeal from the trial, if I disagree with the decision, and I have a right to receive a record and/or transcript of the proceedings in the event of an appeal.

After having been advised of the above, I do hereby:

( ) Elect to have a lawyer ( ) Elect not to have a lawyer

BY SIGNATURE HEREIN, I ACKNOWLEDGE RECEIPT OF A COPY HEREOF.

THIS ____ day of _______, 20___.

Signature of Child	Signature of Parent
Signature of Person Advising Rights	Signature of Attorney/GAL

Rev. 07/97 JUV–20

Form authorized effective July 1, 1988 and required effective September 1, 1988; amended effective January 18, 1990; renumbered as JUV–93–20 effective October 28, 1993; renumbered as JUV–20 and amended effective November 28, 1996; amended effective October 9, 1997; August 16, 2001.

SOCIAL HISTORY FORMAT AND FACE SHEET, JUV–21
SOCIAL HISTORY FORMAT

IN THE JUVENILE COURT OF ______
COUNTY, GEORGIA

Child's Name: ______________________________ D.O.B. ____________________
Court Officer: ______________________________

I. OFFENSE DATA:

A. Prior Offenses

Discuss previous contacts with the Juvenile Court in this county as well as any contacts with courts in other counties.

B. Current Offense

List the current complaint which brings the child before the Court and discuss any relative information which would shed light on the circumstances surrounding the offense.

II. FAMILY DATA:

Describe the family constellation in which the child is living. Which family members are regularly in the household?

A. Father—Absent or present in the home? Is there a stepfather? Explain and define roles. Describe either or both along the following dimensions: (a) role in the home-relationship with spouse, type and consistency of discipline (b) employment—type of job, income, hours worked (c) role in community. Are there any outstanding problems: medical, emotional, drug/alcohol?

B. Mother/Stepmother or Other Female Care-taker—Define roles. Describe either or both along the same dimensions as father above.

C. Other Significant Adults—Age, sex, relationship to child.

D. Siblings—Are any of the siblings positive resources for the child? Have any been involved with court?

E. Home Life—Describe housing, neighborhood. Have there been any traumatic experiences (deaths, illness, divorces, etc.)? Describe basic feelings of family members toward each other (caring, hostile, indifferent). Has the family been referred to or involved in, counseling?

F. Discuss how the child perceives the present situation and how the court involvement has impacted upon the lives of the family members. Is the child remorseful and willing to face whatever the court decides or is the child hostile and difficult to work with? Will the family resist efforts by the court to help or are they willing to cooperate with the worker? If there has been any prior Court involvement, what was the child and family's reaction to it?

III. CHILD'S PERSONAL HISTORY AND ADJUSTMENT:

A. Physical Health

1. Medical History—Give a general physical description. Discuss in detail any serious illness or handicaps.

2. Drug/Alcohol Involvement—Is the use/abuse of drugs or alcohol involved in the child's offense(s)?

B. School—Academic and Vocational Aptitude—Discuss school attendance, achievement, behavior and extra curricular activities. Has the youth any career goals, work experience or vocational interests?

C. Leisure Time—Has the child any special interest, talents, or activities?

D. Treatment Efforts—Has the youth been referred to or evaluated by psychologists, mental health clinics, etc.? Has the child been previously placed in a Youth Development Center or other DJJ residential program or non-residential program? What other agencies are now or have been involved with child?

IV. RECOMMENDATIONS:

These should be well thought-out and reasoned recommendations which include justification for each recommendation. It should contain goals and the recommendations should be the means to achieve those ends. If the recommendation is for probation you should state what your goals are for the child and relate how you intend to help the child reach those goals. If you recommend restitution you should specify how much, to whom it should be paid, how it should be paid and how the victim should receive it. (Should the child be required to deliver it in person or pay it into the clerk of the Court?)

SOCIAL HISTORY FACE SHEET

Worker ____________________
County ____________________
Name ____________________ Case #__________ Date ________
Address ____
Social Security #________ Race/Sex ______ DOB ______ Phone #________
School ____________________ Phone #________ Grade ________

	Father	Mother	Other Male	Other Female
Full Name				
Address: If different from child				
Marital Status				
Occupation				
Income				
Highest Grade				

Siblings' Name(s)	Age	Siblings' Address(es)	Marital Status	Occupation	Highest Grade

Has a psychological or psychiatric evaluation been done? Date: __/__/__
By Whom: ____________________

Other agencies involved with family: ____________________
Current Offense: ____________________

History of Prior Dispositions				
Informally adjusted or adjudicated offenses	Comp. Date	Disposition	Date Disposed	Date Discharged

Rev. 01/2001 JUV–21

Form authorized effective July 1, 1988 and required effective September 1, 1988; renumbered as JUV–93–21 effective October 28, 1993; renumbered as JUV–21 and amended effective November 28, 1996; amended effective October 9, 1997; August 16, 2001.

MOTION FOR ACCESS TO A JUVENILE COURT PROCEEDING, JUV–22

IN THE JUVENILE COURT OF

______ COUNTY, GEORGIA

In the Interest of:

______________________________ CASE NUMBER __________________

A Child. AGE _________________________

SEX _________________________

DOB _________________________

MOTION FOR ACCESS TO A JUVENILE COURT PROCEEDING

Now comes ______________________________ (Name) and moves the Court to permit the above-named to attend the juvenile court proceeding on ________ (date), related to the above-referenced case, and all subsequent proceedings related to the above-referenced case, and to declare that such proceeding be open. Movant is of the opinion and belief that the state's and/or child's interest in a closed hearing in this instance is overridden by the public's interest in a public hearing and cites the following as support for this contention:

____

____

____

____.

This ____ day of _______, 19____.

____

Signature of Movant

NOTICE OF HEARING

The within and foregoing motion filed and the said matter to come on for a review in the Juvenile Court of______, County, Georgia, on ______ at ______, all interested parties should be present in Court to show cause, if any, why said motion should or should not be granted.

This ______ day of ______, 20____.

____

Clerk/Deputy Clerk of

______ County Juvenile Court

Rev. 01/2001 JUV–22

Adopted effective March 21, 1991; renumbered as JUV–93–22 effective October 28, 1993; renumbered as JUV–22 and amended effective November 28, 1996; amended effective August 16, 2001.

COURT ORDER IN RESPONSE TO A MOTION FOR ACCESS TO A JUVENILE COURT PROCEEDING (GRANTING MOTION), JUV–23

IN THE JUVENILE COURT OF
______ COUNTY, GEORGIA

In the Interest of:

______________________ CASE NUMBER ______________
A Child. SEX ______________
DOB ______________

ORDER

A Motion for Access to a Juvenile Court Proceeding having been filed in this court for the above-referenced case and after a hearing on this motion and full review by this court, this court has determined that the state's and/or child's interest in a closed hearing is overridden in this instance by the public's interest in a public hearing and orders that such motion be granted. This court cites the following reasons for granting such motion:

____

____

____

____.

SO ORDERED this, the ______ day of ______, 20____.

____

Judge/Associate Judge of

______ County Juvenile Court

Rev. 01/2001 JUV–23

Adopted effective March 21, 1991; renumbered as JUV–93–23 effective October 28, 1993; renumbered as JUV–23 and amended effective November 28, 1996; amended effective August 16, 2001.

COURT ORDER IN RESPONSE TO A MOTION FOR ACCESS TO A JUVENILE COURT PROCEEDING (DENYING MOTION), JUV–24

IN THE JUVENILE COURT OF
______ COUNTY, GEORGIA

In the Interest of:

________________________ CASE NUMBER ____________
A Child. SEX ____________
DOB ____________

ORDER

A Motion for Access to a Juvenile Court Proceeding having been filed in this court for the above-referenced case and after a hearing on this motion and full review by this court, this court has decided to deny such motion, finding that the state's and/or child's interest in a closed hearing in this case overrides the public's interest in a public hearing. This court cites the following reasons for denying such motion: ____
____
____
____.

SO ORDERED this, the ______ day of ______, 20__.

____

Judge/Associate Judge of

______ County Juvenile Court

Rev. 01/2001 JUV–24

Adopted effective March 21, 1991; renumbered as JUV–93–24 effective October 28, 1993; renumbered as JUV–24 and amended effective November 28, 1996.; amended effective August 16, 2001.

REQUEST TO INSTALL RECORDING AND/OR PHOTOGRAPHING EQUIPMENT PURSUANT TO RULES AND GUIDELINES FOR ELECTRONIC AND PHOTOGRAPHIC NEWS COVERAGE OF JUVENILE COURT PROCEEDINGS, JUV–25

IN THE JUVENILE COURT OF
______ COUNTY, GEORGIA

In the Interest of:

_______________________ CASE NUMBER ______________

A Child. SEX ______________

DOB ______________

Pursuant to Rule 26.2, Electronic and Photographic News Coverage of Juvenile Court Proceeding in the Uniform Rules for the Juvenile Courts of Georgia, the undersigned hereby respectfully requests permission to install equipment in courtroom ______ in order to record, photograph or televise all or portions of the proceedings in the above-captioned case.

Consistent with the provisions of the rules and guidelines, the undersigned desires to install the following described equipment: ________ in the following locations: ______________. The proceedings that the undersigned desires to record, photograph or televise commence on ________.
(date)

Subject to direction from the court regarding possible pooled coverage, the undersigned wishes to install this equipment in the courtroom on ________.
(date)

The personnel who will be responsible for the installation and operation of this equipment during its use are:

______________________.
(identify appropriate personnel)

The undersigned hereby certifies that the equipment to be installed and the locations and operation of such equipment will be in conformity with the rules and guidelines issued by the court.

This ______ day of ______, 20__.

____

(Individual Signature)

or

____

(Attorney's Signature)

Representing: ______

____

(Address)

____

(Telephone Number)

Rev. 01/2001 JUV–25

Adopted effective March 21, 1991; renumbered as JUV–93–25 effective October 28, 1993; renumbered as JUV–25 and amended effective November 28, 1996; amended effective August 16, 2001.

COURT ORDER IN RESPONSE TO A REQUEST TO INSTALL RECORDING AND/OR PHOTOGRAPHING EQUIPMENT PURSUANT TO RULES AND GUIDELINES FOR ELECTRONIC AND PHOTOGRAPHIC NEWS COVERAGE OF JUVENILE COURT PROCEEDINGS (APPROVAL OF MOTION), JUV–26

IN THE JUVENILE COURT OF
______ COUNTY, GEORGIA

In the Interest of:

______________________________ A Child.

CASE NUMBER ________________
SEX ________________________
DOB ________________________

ORDER

Pursuant to Rule 26.2 of the Uniform Rules for the Juvenile Courts of Georgia, a Request to Install Recording and/or Photographic Equipment for Electronic and Photographic News Coverage of Juvenile Court Proceedings having been filed in this court for media coverage of the juvenile court proceeding for the above-referenced case to commence on ______ (date), and after review by this court, this court has decided to approve such request, subject to the following special conditions:

____
____
____
____.

So approved and confirmed this, the ______ day of ______, 20__.

____

Judge/Associate Judge of

______ County Juvenile Court

Rev. 01/2001 JUV–26

Adopted effective March 21, 1991; renumbered as JUV–93–26 effective October 28, 1993; renumbered as JUV–26 and amended effective November 28, 1996; amended effective August 16, 2001.

COURT ORDER IN RESPONSE TO A REQUEST TO INSTALL RECORDING AND/OR PHOTOGRAPHING EQUIPMENT PURSUANT TO RULES AND GUIDELINES FOR ELECTRONIC AND PHOTOGRAPHIC NEWS COVERAGE OF JUVENILE COURT PROCEEDINGS (DENIAL OF MOTION), JUV–27

IN THE JUVENILE COURT OF
______ COUNTY, GEORGIA

In the Interest of:

____________________________ CASE NUMBER ________________
A Child. SEX ______________________
DOB ______________________

ORDER

Pursuant to Rule 26.2 of the Uniform Rules for the Juvenile Courts of Georgia, a Request to Install Recording and/or Photographic Equipment for Electronic and Photographic News Coverage of Juvenile Court Proceedings having been filed in this court for media coverage of the juvenile court proceeding for the above-referenced case to commence on ________ (date), and after review by this court, this court has decided to deny such request, for the following reason(s):

and after review by this court, this court has decided to deny such request, for the following reason(s):

____
____
____
____.

SO ORDERED this, the ______ day of ______, 20__.

____

Judge/Associate Judge of

______ County Juvenile Court

Rev. 01/2001 JUV–27

Adopted effective March 21, 1991; renumbered as JUV–93–27 effective October 28, 1993; renumbered as JUV–27 and amended effective November 28, 1996; amended effective August 16, 2001.

PARENTAL NOTIFICATION CERTIFICATE: HEARING NOT HELD/MORE THAN 24 HOURS ELAPSED, JUV–28

IN THE JUVENILE COURT OF
_______ COUNTY, GEORGIA

IN THE INTEREST OF: CASE NUMBER ______________
______________________________, SEX ______________
An Unemancipated Minor DOB __________ AGE__________

CERTIFICATE

I hereby certify that according to the record in this case, a hearing was scheduled to be heard on the __ day of ______, 20__, at __ o'clock __.m. The court did not conduct the hearing, and more than twenty-four (24) hours have elapsed since the time of the scheduled hearing.

This __ day of ______, 20__, at ____, o'clock __.m.

____

Clerk or Designated Deputy

(Seal of Court)

Rev. 01/2001 JUV–28

Adopted effective December 31, 1992; renumbered as JUV–93–28 effective October 28, 1993; renumbered as JUV–28 and amended effective November 28, 1996; amended effective August 16, 2001.

PARENTAL NOTIFICATION CERTIFICATE: HEARING NOT HELD/FAILURE TO APPEAR/NO MOTION FOR CONTINUANCE, JUV–29

IN THE JUVENILE COURT OF
______ COUNTY, GEORGIA

IN THE INTEREST OF:	CASE NUMBER ________
______________________,	SEX ________
An Unemancipated Minor	DOB ______ AGE______

CERTIFICATE

I hereby certify that according to the record in this case, a hearing was scheduled to be heard on the ___ day of ______, 20__, at __ o'clock __.m. The hearing was not held because the petitioner failed to appear at the appointed time, and there was no motion for a continuance. The case was dismissed as evidenced by the Court Order attached hereto.

This __ day of ______, 20__.

____

Clerk or Designated Deputy

(Seal of Court)

Rev. 01/2001 JUV–29

Adopted effective December 31, 1992; renumbered as JUV–93–29 effective October 28, 1993; renumbered as JUV–29 and amended effective November 28, 1996; amended effective August 16, 2001.

PARENTAL NOTIFICATION CERTIFICATE: HEARING HELD/NO DECISION RENDERED WITHIN 24 HOURS, JUV–30

IN THE JUVENILE COURT OF
_______ COUNTY, GEORGIA

IN THE INTEREST OF: CASE NUMBER _______________
_________________________, SEX _______________
An Unemancipated Minor DOB __________ AGE __________

CERTIFICATE

I hereby certify that according to the record in this case, the hearing was heard on the ______ day of ______, 20____, and was concluded on the ______ day of ______, 20____, at ______ o'clock ____.m. The Court did not render and file its decision within twenty-four (24) hours after the conclusion of the hearing.

This ______ day of ______, 20____, at ______ o'clock ____.m.

____

Clerk or Designated Deputy

(Seal of Court)

Rev. 01/2001 JUV–30

Adopted effective December 31, 1992; renumbered as JUV–93–30 effective October 28, 1993; renumbered as JUV–30 and amended effective November 28, 1996; amended effective August 16, 2001.

RULE 3.9. SHARING OF COURT RECORDS AMONG JUVENILE COURTS

There is established a statewide system for providing juvenile court legal case information on individuals to juvenile courts for the sole purpose of ensuring effective rehabilitation, disposition, supervision and treatment of juveniles. The Council of Juvenile Court Judges, through its presiding judge and executive director, shall ensure that information disseminated on individuals is used solely for these purposes. It is the express intent of the Council that individuals' prior juvenile court histories shall not be used for investigative purposes.

For purposes of this rule the term "legal case information" means information contained in petitions, complaints and allegations related to cases within the jurisdiction of the juvenile court. "Legal case information" shall also mean demographic data on the subject child or children in whose interest a complaint or petition has been filed.

The Council may receive legal case information from juvenile courts for the purpose of compiling and maintaining a statewide database on children referred to juvenile court. Juvenile courts shall submit through their clerks case information to the Council, in a timely fashion and in a manner and form prescribed by the Council of Juvenile Court Judges.

Upon request, the Council may provide data from any or all juvenile courts on a child's prior juvenile court cases to individual juvenile courts in which a complaint or petition has been filed. Such data shall only be used for the purposes of making intake and detention decisions and appropriate dispositions of current cases. Such statewide information shall only be:

Child's I.D. #
Case #
File #
County #
Child's Name and AKA's
Child's Age, DOB, Sex, Race
With Whom The Child Lives (parents, relatives, etc.)
Child's Phone Number (residence and business)
Child's Address
Mother's Name
Mother's Address (if different from child)
Mother's Phone Number (residence and business)
Father's Name
Father's Address (if different from Child)
Father's Phone Number (residence and business)
Legal Custodian's Name (if different from parent)
Legal Custodian's Address, Phone Number
Complaint(s)
Complaint(s) Types
Date Offense Committed
Date Complaint Filed
Referral Source
Detained or Placed (location, date, time)
If Released: Date, Time
Date Petition Filed
Complaint or Petition Amended
Date of Adjudicatory Hearing
Results of Adjudicatory Hearing; Offense and Type
Disposition Date
Disposition(s)
Person Who Made Disposition
Whether Case is Appealed
Findings on Appeal

Such statewide information shall be requested from the Council only by officers of the court designated by the chief judge and approved by the Council's executive director. Each officer, thus approved, shall be given a unique identifier which shall be registered in a log kept by the Council and which must be used in requesting information. Officers of the court who may be approved to request such information are limited to the judge, the clerk of the court or employees of the clerk of court, a court-employed intake or probation officer, or a court service worker assigned to provide probation or intake services to the court. Unique identifiers shall be changed periodically and whenever designated court officers or employees of the Council authorized to release statewide information are terminated. Information from cases in which the child has been acquitted shall not be released to any court other than the reporting court. This shall also apply to an adjudicated offense overturned by an appeals court.

Legal case information transmitted to the court shall be filed with the clerk of the juvenile court, who shall be ordered to maintain a record of such information. Such information shall not be open to public inspection; but inspection of the record shall only be permitted to the judge, intake officer, probation officer, or court service worker assigned to the case. Dissemination of such information to unauthorized parties or use of such information for purposes other than authorized in this rule shall be grounds for termination of employment with the Council, user agency, or the court. Intentional dissemination or receipt of legal case information for purposes not authorized in this rule shall be punishable by the civil contempt power of the court.

When it appears to the Council that any court has not instituted sufficient procedural safeguards to ensure the privacy and security of juvenile court histories, the Council, through its presiding judge and executive director, shall not release any further information until that court demonstrates that adequate safeguards have been instituted.

After a child has been committed to the Department of Juvenile Justice, a copy of the legal case information of the person committed may be furnished to the agency receiving custody of the person for the sole purpose of establishing treatment or rehabilitation plans. Such information shall remain confidential.

The Council may permit authorized representatives of recognized organizations compiling statistics for appropriate purposes to inspect and make abstracts from prior juvenile court histories under conditions to be determined by the Council. Statistical information thus released shall not include a child's name nor the names of the child's parents or legal custodian.

All juvenile prior histories shall be destroyed within six months after a child reaches age 25.

Amended effective December 31, 1992; October 9, 1997; August 16, 2001.

RULE 3.10. RECORDS OF CITIZEN REVIEW PANELS

All findings, reports, documents, recommendations, and other records created for or by judicial citizen review panels constituted pursuant to OCGA § 15–11–58, other than records which are a part of a child's court record as defined in Rule 3.2, shall be maintained by the Court as judicial citizen review panel records. With respect to each child, these judicial citizen review panel records may be destroyed by the Court after two years have elapsed since the date of the most recent record pertaining to that child or after the child becomes 18 years of age, whichever occurs first.

Adopted effective December 31, 1992; amended effective August 16, 2001.

SECTION 4. COMMENCEMENT OF PROCEEDINGS

RULE 4.1. RECEIPT OF COMPLAINT AND PETITION

(a) Initiation of Proceedings. In all proceedings over which the juvenile court has jurisdiction, such proceedings shall be initiated in the juvenile court upon the receipt of a written juvenile complaint form, petition, transfer from another court, a uniform traffic citation, or a Georgia Natural Resources/Game and Fish Division Notice of Summons which shall be submitted to the court and shall be referred to an intake officer of the court.

(b) Preliminary Determination as to Filing Petition. The intake officer shall not have the authority to refuse to accept a complaint. However, the intake officer shall make a preliminary determination as to whether a petition shall be filed. If the allegations appear to be legally sufficient for the filing of a petition, and it further appears that judicial action is in the best interest of the public and the child within guidelines established by the court, the intake officer may endorse a petition. The intake officer may elect to informally adjust, divert, or recommend dismissing the case, within guidelines established by the court.

(c) Filing of Complaints and Petitions. All complaints or petitions shall be filed and docketed with the clerk of juvenile court. The clerk shall record the date and time of filing upon each and every copy of the complaint form.

(d) Completion of Form JUV–2 Required. The complaint alleging delinquency, deprivation, or unruliness may be made by any person, including a law enforcement officer, who has knowledge of the facts alleged or is informed and believes they are true. However, in all cases in which a proceeding is initiated by other than a complaint, the form JUV–2 shall be completed by the person bringing the action and shall accompany the initiating document. In all cases where a petition references a prior court order, a copy of such prior court order shall be attached to the petition. For uniform traffic citations and Georgia Natural Resources/Game and Fish Division Notice of Summonses, the form JUV–2 shall be completed by court personnel designated by the judge.

Amended effective July 1, 1986; amendment authorized effective July 10, 1987 and required effective September 1, 1987; amended effective November 12, 1992; December 31, 1992; November 28, 1996; August 16, 2001.

RULE 4.2. SCREENING PROCESS

Before a petition is filed, the intake officer shall screen the complaint. This may result in a decision to recommend dismissal to the judge or associate judge, to make a referral to another agency for services, if appropriate, to informally adjust the case, to file a petition, or to take other appropriate action. Factors involved in the process of screening the complaint shall include:

1. Whether the complaint is one over which the court has jurisdiction;

2. Whether the complaint is frivolous;

3. Whether the child should be detained pending a hearing and, if so, where he or she should be detained;

4. Whether the child's case can be informally adjusted;

5. Whether the child should be diverted to an agency that meets his or her needs; and

6. If a petition should be filed with the court.

Amended effective July 1, 1986; March 21, 1991.

RULE 4.3. INFORMAL ADJUSTMENT

In cases where a child is alleged to have committed a delinquent act which is not of a serious nature, or has been alleged to have committed an unruly act, but appears to be amenable to informal handling, the intake officer may withhold the filing of a petition with a view toward first seeking an informal adjustment of the matter, where it is in the best interest of the child and the community. If, after the filing of a petition, it appears that informal adjustment best suits the need of the child and the public, the judge may direct the withdrawal of the petition so the matter may proceed to informal adjustment.

(a) Prerequisites. In order for informal adjustment to occur:

1. The admitted facts must bring the child within the jurisdiction of the court.

2. It must be determined that counsel and advice without an adjudication would be in the best interest of the public and the child; and

3. The child and the child's parents, guardian, or other custodian must consent to the informal adjustment with knowledge that consent is not obligatory.

4. If the child is alleged to have committed a designated felony act as defined in OCGA § 15–11–63, the case shall not be subject to informal adjustment, counsel, or advice without the prior written notification of the district attorney or his or her authorized representative.

(b) Informal Adjustment Alternatives. After a conference with the child and the child's parents or guardian concerning the complaint, the intake officer may do any of the following:

1. *Counseling and adjustment.* If the intake officer feels that a satisfactory adjustment of the problem has been accomplished through counseling with the child and the child's parents at the informal hearing or conference and that there is no further need to see the child or the child's family, the informal adjustment may be considered complete.

2. *Counsel and advice.* Where there is an apparent need for follow-up services by the intake officer on a less formal basis than actual probation, the child shall be placed on counsel and advice for a period not to exceed three months from the day of the informal hearing or conference at which the counsel and advice was commenced. The court may extend the counsel and advice for a period not to exceed an additional three months. A child may not be detained during the period of counsel and advice unless otherwise permitted by law.

3. *Referral to counseling resource.* The child may be placed on counsel and advice pending successful completion of the recommended counseling.

4. The intake officer may style individualized agreements which are appropriate to the offense and circumstances. Such agreements may include, but are not limited to, letters of apology, book reports, essays, traffic school and volunteer work with a community service organization. The child should be placed on counsel and advice until the requirements of the disposition have been met. Failure to comply with such agreements may result in the filing of a petition on the complaint.

(c) Disposition by Informal Adjustment. After completion of informal adjustment, the court or its designee shall inform the clerk of court of the disposition of the case.

(d) Notification of Judge. The case files or a report of informally adjusted cases shall be sent by the intake officer or intake supervisor for review to the juvenile court judge on a regular basis.

(e) Incriminating Statements. See OCGA § 15–11–69 (c).

(f) Informal Adjustment Agreement. An informal adjustment agreement shall be prepared on each case adjusted by a court officer, and filed with the clerk of juvenile court by the officer adjusting the case. A copy of said agreement shall be furnished to the child and the child's attorney and/or legal guardian.

Amended effective July 1, 1986; December 31, 1992; October 9, 1997; August 16, 2001.

RULE 4.4. DISMISSAL OF COMPLAINT

A complaint may be dismissed by the judge, or by the associate judge if he or she presided over a detentional/arraignment hearing on the complaint, prior to the filing of the petition upon the recommendation of the intake officer, if the judge or associate judge feels that such dismissal is warranted and it is in the best interest of the child and community.

Amended effective July 1, 1986; March 21, 1991; August 16, 2001.

RULE 4.5. MOTION FOR EXTENSION

A motion for the court to extend its previous order pursuant to O.C.G.A. § 15–11–58(n), § 15–11–58.1 or § 15–11–70 shall be treated as a new proceeding in the court and shall be subject to the provisions of Rule 4.1 regarding the filing of a complaint form, JUV–2. The motion shall not be filed in the office of the clerk of juvenile court unless it is accompanied by a properly completed complaint form. The case shall be entered into the juvenile court docket and treated as any other new proceeding.

Adopted effective July 1, 1986; amended effective November 28, 1996; August 16, 2001; April 15, 2004.

RULE 4.6. COMMENCEMENT OF PROCEEDING FOR CHILD ON AFTERCARE TO DEPARTMENT OF JUVENILE JUSTICE

Aftercare is a nonjudicial administrative status granted to a child who is under an order of commitment to the Department of Juvenile Justice and has been released from confinement under the supervision of an employee of the Department. If such a child commits a new delinquent or an unruly offense, the case shall be handled by the juvenile court like any other complaint filed pursuant to the provisions of Sections 4 and 5 of the Uniform Rules for Juvenile Courts; provided, however, that the court officer handling the case may consult with the employee of the Department of Juvenile Justice for providing supervision of the child for input prior to making a disposition of the case. If a child who is on aftercare violates the conditions of that aftercare and the violation does not constitute a delinquent or unruly offense, the child shall not be referred to the juvenile court for said violation. Violation of aftercare is not an offense and, therefore, is to be handled administratively by the Department of Juvenile Justice.

Rule authorized effective July 10, 1988 and required effective September 1, 1988; amended effective December 31, 1992; October 9, 1997.

RULE 4.7. JUVENILE RIGHTS FORM

After a case has been referred to the court prior to beginning the initial conference between a child and a non-judicial officer of the court at which the allegations of a delinquency or unruly complaint are discussed, an officer of the court shall fully explain the child's rights and fill out the Pre-trial Juvenile Rights Form JUV–20 with the child and parent. The judge or associate judge may use this form in lieu of another form or methodology in advising the child of his or her rights before proceeding with any hearing. The signed form shall be filed with the clerk of the court and made a part of the permanent file.

Rule authorized effective July 10, 1988 and required effective September 1, 1988; amended effective January 18, 1990; March 21, 1991; November 28, 1996; amended effective August 16, 2001.

SECTION 5. COMMENCEMENT OF FORMAL PROCEEDINGS

RULE 5.1. METHODS

See OCGA § 15–11–35.

Amendment authorized effective July 10, 1987 and required effective September 1, 1987; amended effective November 12, 1992; December 31, 1992; August 16, 2001.

RULE 5.2. TRANSFER OF CUSTODY AND SUPPORT QUESTIONS FROM SUPERIOR COURT

Courts of record, in handling divorce, alimony, or habeas corpus cases involving the custody of a child or children, may transfer the question of the determination of custody and support to the juvenile court for investigation and report back to the superior court or for investigation and determination. If the referral is for investigation and determination, then the juvenile court shall proceed to handle the matter in the same manner as though the action originated under Article 1 of the Juvenile Proceedings Code, in compliance with the order of the superior court. At any time prior to the determination of such question, the juvenile court may transfer the jurisdiction of the question back to the referring superior court. Following the matter of an investigation and a report back, the juvenile court clerk shall send a copy of the report and record of the investigation to the referring superior court judge. Following the matter of an investigation and determination, the juvenile court clerk shall file the original order of the juvenile court, shall make a certified copy thereof for filing with the clerk of superior court and shall also furnish a copy of the final order to the referring superior court judge.

(a) Docketing the Transfer Order. Upon receiving the order of transfer, the clerk shall docket said order and incorporate it as a part of the juvenile court record.

(b) Assessment of Costs for Investigations in Custody and Support Matters. The judge of the juvenile court may assess reasonable costs against the party or parties for conducting investigations in custody and support matters as referred by the Superior Court.

(c) Filing of Complaint Form in Custody or Support Matters. In all cases referred to the juvenile court by the Superior Court for investigation and report or determination, the clerk of superior court shall, within ten days of the date of the order, forward to the clerk of the juvenile court the order of transfer together with the superior court file or a certified copy thereof in its entirety. In modifications and habeas corpus cases, in addition to the foregoing, the form JUV–2 shall be completed by and filed by the plaintiff's attorney. Upon the receipt of the above stated documents, the juvenile court clerk shall file the transfer.

Amendment authorized effective July 10, 1987 and required effective September 1, 1987; amended effective October 28, 1993; November 28, 1996.

RULE 5.3. INTRASTATE TRANSFER OF CASES AMONG JUVENILE COURTS

Documents in all cases to be transferred between juvenile courts shall be prepared and forwarded only by the clerk of juvenile court of the transferring court and shall be forwarded to the clerk of juvenile court of the receiving court.

(a) Pre–Adjudication Transfer of Non–Deprivation Cases. If an in-state non-resident child as defined in OCGA § 15–11–30 (a) (2) is referred to the juvenile court for an offense for which that court would not normally commence formal proceedings, the court may transfer the matter to the juvenile court of the county of the child's residence. The clerk of the transferring court shall forward original citations and a copy of all police reports as well as certified copies of all legal documents which have been filed relating to the transferred case. If the child's county of residence changes again before the transfer order is received, the receiving court shall transfer jurisdiction to the new county of residence, and shall notify the original transferring court.

(b) Post–Adjudication Transfer of Non–Deprivation Cases for Disposition. If transfer is made pursuant to the provisions of OCGA § 15–11–30, the clerk of the transferring court shall forward a certified copy of all legal documents relating to the transferred case as well as any social or psychological information prepared by the transferring court or its agent within the twelve (12) months prior to the transfer including, but not limited to, social history reports, supervision summaries, psychological or psychiatric evaluations, and any record of restitution paid to or owed to the court. If the child's county of residence changes again before the transfer order is received, the receiving court shall transfer jurisdiction to the new county of residence, and shall notify the original transferring court.

(c) Post–Disposition Transfer of Non–Deprivation Cases for Supervision. In the event that the residence of a child changes while an order of probation is in effect, the court may order transfer of the supervision of that child to the juvenile court of the new county of residence. The receiving court shall docket the transfer pursuant to Rule 4.1 and shall enforce the conditions of probation contained in the original order and may make such other conditions as it sees fit pursuant to OCGA § 15–11–40. If the original order of probation requires the child to pay restitution and at the time of transfer that restitution has not been fully paid, the enforcement of that condition is also transferred to the juvenile court of the new county of residence which shall enforce it pursuant to OCGA § 15–11–66 (a) (5). The clerk of the transferring court shall forward a certified copy of all legal documents relating to the transferred case as well as any social or psychological information prepared by the transferring court or its agent within twelve (12) months prior to the transfer including, but not limited to, social history reports, supervision summaries, psychological or psychiatric evaluations, and any record of restitution paid to or owed to the court. If the child's county of residence changes again before the transfer order is received, the receiving court shall transfer supervision to the new county of residence, and shall notify the original transferring court.

(d) Pre–Adjudication Transfer of Deprivation Cases. In the event that a deprivation proceeding is brought in the county in which the child is present when it is commenced, the juvenile court may transfer the proceeding for the convenience of the parties and witnesses pursuant to OCGA § 15–11–29 to the county in which the child resides. If the proceeding is transferred, the clerk shall forward certified copies of all legal and social documents and records pertaining to the proceeding.

(e) Post–Disposition Transfer of Deprivation Cases. If transfer is made to the juvenile court of the residence of the parent or parents to whom reunification is directed pursuant to the provisions of OCGA § 15–11–30.5, the clerk of the transferring court shall forward certified copies of the transfer order, adjudication order, disposition order, case plan, and such other documents deemed necessary by the transferring court to the receiving court within 30 days of the filing of the transfer order.

Amendment authorized effective July 10, 1987 and required effective September 1, 1987; amended effective October 27, 1994; October 5, 1998; August 16, 2001.

RULE 5.4. TRANSFER OF DELINQUENCY CASE FROM SUPERIOR COURT

(a) Prior to Indictment. Whenever the prosecution of delinquency charges are to be lodged in the juvenile court by the district attorney pursuant to the discretion provided in OCGA § 15–11–28 (b) (2) (C), the district attorney shall commence the case in the juvenile court by filing with the clerk of the juvenile court a fully completed complaint form and a written memorandum of the district attorney's transfer of the case to the juvenile court.

(b) After Indictment. Whenever the prosecution of delinquency charges are to be lodged in the juvenile court by order of the superior court, the clerk of superior court shall within three (3) working days of the entry of the order, file with the clerk of the juvenile court certified copies of the order of transfer, indictment, and all motions, orders and other pleadings and documents contained in the file. The clerk of the juvenile court shall cause a fully completed complaint form to be filed within 24 hours of receipt of the documents from the clerk of the superior court.

Adopted effective November 28, 1996; amended effective August 16, 2001.

SECTION 6. FILING OF PETITION

RULE 6.1. WHEN MAY A PETITION BE FILED

A petition may be filed only when the petition is in proper form and it has been properly endorsed by the court or a designee thereof.

RULE 6.2. DEFINITION OF FILING

The filing of a petition shall consist of the act of presenting to the clerk of the juvenile court, or to a deputy clerk if authorized, a petition in proper form (verified and endorsed) which said clerk or deputy clerk shall accept and note thereon by rubber stamp, automatic date/time stamp or other means, the exact date and time of filing.

RULE 6.3. PRELIMINARY DETERMINATION

A petition alleging delinquency, deprivation or unruliness of a child shall not be filed unless the court or its designee has determined and endorsed upon the petition that the filing of the petition is in the best interest of the public and the child.

RULE 6.4. STYLE OF THE PETITION

The petition and all other documents in the proceeding shall be styled "In the interest of . . ., a child," except upon appeal, in which event the anonymity of the child shall be preserved by appropriate use of the initials.

RULE 6.5. CONTENT OF PETITION

See OCGA § 15–11–38.1.

Amendment authorized effective July 10, 1988 and required effective September 1, 1988; amended effective December 31, 1992; August 16, 2001.

RULE 6.6. AMENDMENT TO PETITION

A petition may be amended at any time prior to adjudication, provided that the court shall grant the parties such additional time to prepare as may be required to ensure a full and fair hearing. Amendments shall be freely permitted in the interest of justice and the welfare of the child. When the amended petition constitutes or adds additional charges the petition shall be served in accordance with OCGA §§ 15–11–39 and 15–11–39.1. Where the child is detained amendments to the petition shall not delay the hearing more than ten (10) days beyond the time originally fixed for the hearing unless a continuance is requested by the child or the child's attorney.

Amendment authorized effective July 10, 1987 and required effective September 1, 1987; amended effective December 31, 1992; August 16, 2001.

RULE 6.7. WITHDRAWAL OF PETITION

If it appears after a petition has been filed that an informal adjustment rather than an adjudication would be in the best interest of the child, petitioner may file a motion to withdraw the petition. The petition shall be withdrawn upon approval by the judge. Such approval does not result in a dismissal of the case, but only in the substitution of informal adjustment for a formal adjudication.

RULE 6.8. TIME LIMITATIONS

If a child who is alleged to be delinquent or deprived is detained or placed in shelter care, a detention hearing shall be held within 72 hours from the moment the child is placed in detention or shelter care to determine whether detention or shelter care is required, provided that if the 72 hour time period expires on a Saturday, Sunday or legal holiday, the hearing shall be held on the next day which is not a Saturday, Sunday, or legal holiday. With respect to any child alleged to be unruly, the informal detention hearing shall be held promptly and not later than 72 hours. If a child is not detained and the case is to be further prosecuted other than by informal adjustment, a petition must be made and filed with the court within 30 days from the date of the child's release. If a child who is alleged to be delinquent or unruly is not released from detention, a petition must be made and filed within 72 hours of the detention hearing. If a child who is alleged to be deprived is not released from detention, a petition must be made and filed within five days of the detention hearing. After the petition has been filed, the court shall fix a time for a hearing thereon, which, if the child is in detention, shall not be later than ten (10) days after the filing of the petition. In the event the child is not in detention, the court shall fix a time for a hearing thereon which shall be not later than sixty (60) days from the date of the filing of the petition.

Any child who is the subject of a delinquency or unruly proceeding or any party in a deprivation or termination of parental rights proceeding may request a rehearing of an associate judge's findings and recommendations in said proceeding. A written request for a rehearing before the judge on an associate judge's findings and recommendations shall be made within five (5) days of the date of receiving notice of the findings and recommendations, unless the fifth day falls on a weekend or legal holiday, in which event the time shall be extended to the next working day.

Amendment authorized effective July 10, 1987 and required effective September 1, 1987; amended effective December 31, 1992; November 28, 1996.

RULE 6.9. RESPONSIVE PLEADINGS AND MOTIONS

No answer to the petition or any other pleading need be filed by any child, parent or legal guardian. A party may file a written pleading or motion to the allegations of the petition before the hearing. Copies of such pleadings shall be made available to the other parties to the case.

SECTION 7. DISCOVERY AND MOTIONS

RULE 7.1. WHEN DISCOVERY IS PERMITTED

Discovery may be allowed in all cases where deprivation is alleged, or where the termination of parental rights is requested or in cases where matters of custody have been referred to the juvenile court by a superior court. Any discovery so permitted shall be at the discretion of the judge to whom the case is assigned, and any such discovery allowed shall be made in conformance with Article V of the Civil Practice Act, O.C.G.A. §§ 9–11–26 through 9–11–37, except as modified by these rules. Discovery in any case in which delinquency is alleged shall be as provided by O.C.G.A. § 15–11–75.

Amended effective April 15, 2004.

RULE 7.2. HOW DISCOVERY MAY BE MADE

Any request for discovery shall be made in writing and shall state with particularity the type of discovery requested.

1. If the request is for answers to written interrogatories, such request shall include the questions to be answered and include the name of the person or persons who are to respond to those interrogatories.

2. If the request is for the taking of a deposition, such request should name the person or persons who are to be deposed and their addresses, and such request should also include the subject matter areas which the deposition would embrace.

3. If the request is for admissions of a party to a proceeding, such request should include the exact admissions requested and the party to whom directed.

4. If the request is for production of documents, such request shall state the documents requested and the name of the individual from whom the documents are sought.

5. If the request is for physical or mental examination of a parent, guardian, custodian or child, such request shall state the name of the person or persons to be examined and the reason why such examination is necessary.

(a) **Rule Nisi.** All written requests for discovery shall include a Rule Nisi order setting down a time and place for a hearing for the entry of an order by the court as to the scope of discovery to be allowed and the time for the completion of such discovery.

(b) **Objections.** Any and all objections to any of the requests for discovery so made shall be made at such hearing or all objections are waived unless otherwise allowed by discretion of the court.

(c) **Notice and Service.**

1. The written motion and notice of the hearing thereof shall be served not later than three (3) days, excluding weekends and holidays, before the time specified for the hearing, unless specifically ordered otherwise by the court on ex parte application for good cause shown. All requests for discovery shall be served as required by these rules upon all parties, including parents, child or legal custodian and any other person to whom the court directs, or their legal counsel, if so represented.

2. If the child is alleged to be a deprived child, or the subject of an action to terminate parental rights, in which it is alleged that the child was the victim of conduct by the parent or guardian which is a violation of the criminal laws of this state, and such parent or guardian has been charged as a defendant with the commission of such offense against the child, a request for discovery made by or on behalf of such parent or guardian shall also be served upon the district attorney having jurisdiction over the criminal case against the parent or guardian. The district attorney shall have an opportunity to be heard prior to entry of an order allowing discovery.

Amended effective March 16, 2006.

RULE 7.3. TIME PERIODS

Any request for discovery must be filed within forty-eight (48) hours of the filing of the petition where the child is in detention. Otherwise, the request must be filed within fifteen (15) days of the filing of the petition. The court may modify these requirements upon a showing of good cause for the lack of filing within these time periods.

Any such discovery permitted shall be completed within fifteen (15) days of the date of the order permitting such discovery where the child is in detention. In all other cases, such discovery shall be completed within thirty (30) days from the date of the order permitting such discovery. These time periods may be either extended or abbreviated at the discretion of the court for legal cause shown.

If the child is in detention and a request for discovery is made by any party, such request shall simultaneously act as request for a continuance as pertains to the time provisions of OCGA § 15–11–39 (a) regarding time period for adjudicatory hearings. The adjudicatory hearing shall then be reset to be heard within seven (7) days, excluding weekends and holidays, of the date that such discovery is ordered to be completed by the court.

Amended effective August 16, 2001.

RULE 7.4. HEARING ON THE MOTION

At the hearing set to determine whether discovery is to be allowed, the court shall enter an order outlining the discovery to be allowed and time for completion of such discovery and setting the date for the adjudicatory hearing.

Any motions for orders to compel discovery, requests for sanctions or request for expenses as a result thereof, shall be made to the judge issuing the original order allowing discovery. Any such motion shall be made prior to the adjudicatory hearing and in conformance with the procedures set out herein for filing motions.

RULE 7.5. PRETRIAL PROCEDURE

Upon the motion of any party, or upon its own motion, the court shall direct the attorneys for the parties to appear before it for a conference to consider:

1. The simplification of the issues;
2. The necessity or desirability of amendments to the pleadings;
3. The possibility of obtaining admissions of fact and of documents which will avoid unnecessary proof;
4. The limitation of the number of expert witnesses; and
5. Such other matters as may aid in the disposition of the action.

The court shall make an order which recites the action taken at the conference and the agreements made by the parties as to any of the matters considered and which limits the issues for trial to those not disposed of by admissions or agreements of counsel. The order, when entered, controls the subsequent course of the action unless modified at the trial to prevent manifest injustice.

RULE 7.6. RESPONSIVE PLEADINGS

Responsive pleadings in all proceedings before the juvenile court are permissible and encouraged. However, they are not mandatory. If filed, such responsive pleadings must be in writing and served upon all parties. Responsive pleadings may be filed any time prior to the adjudicatory hearing.

RULE 7.7. CONTINUANCES

Except as provided for in Rules 7.3 and 8.6, any request for continuance shall be made in conformance with OCGA § 9–10–150 et seq. through or on stipulation of counsel alone. Permission of the court is required for all continuances.

Amended effective December 31, 1992; amended effective August 16, 2001.

RULE 7.8. FILING

All pleadings made pursuant to any proceeding of the juvenile court shall be filed with the clerk of juvenile court and stamped with the date and time of filing along with a certificate of service showing to whom copies have been served.

RULE 7.9. OTHER MOTIONS

All other pretrial motions must be made in writing and filed not later than three (3) days, excluding weekends and holidays, before the adjudicatory hearing unless otherwise permitted by the court. If any such motions necessitate an evidentiary hearing, the procedures in Rule 7.2(c) concerning notice and service must be followed.

Amended effective April 15, 2004.

SECTION 8. DETENTION HEARING

RULE 8.1. PURPOSE

The purposes of the detention hearing are to determine whether a child who has been taken into custody shall be released or detained pending further court proceedings, and if reasonable grounds exist to believe that the allegations in the complaint or petition are true. The detention hearing shall be informal and hearsay may be allowed.

Amended effective October 28, 1993.

RULE 8.2. NOTICE

The person taking a child into custody shall promptly give notice thereof, together with a statement of the reason for taking the child into custody, to a parent, guardian or other custodian and to the court. Any temporary detention or questioning of the child necessary to comply with this rule shall conform to the procedures and conditions prescribed by the Juvenile Proceedings Code and guidelines of the court.

RULE 8.3. COMMENCEMENT OF HEARING

Prior to the commencement of the detention hearing the court shall inform the parties of their right to counsel and their right to have counsel appointed by the court if they are indigent. The child shall also be informed of his or her right to remain silent with respect to any allegation of delinquent or unruly conduct.

Amended effective August 16, 2001.

RULE 8.4. CONDITIONAL RELEASE

If a child is released from detention without bond pending further hearings on the charges, the court may specify certain conditions of release (e.g., curfews, school attendance).

RULE 8.5. VIOLATION OF CONDITIONS

If a court officer finds that the child has violated his or her conditional release from detention, the officer may take the child into custody and return the child to detention. If the child is detained, the officer shall file a complaint stating what the child did to violate the conditional release and give a copy of the complaint to the intake worker at the detention center. Said child is entitled to a hearing on whether the child has violated the conditions of release.

Amended effective August 16, 2001.

RULE 8.6. CONTINUANCE

On the motion of the court or that of a party, the court may continue a detention hearing for a reasonable period to receive reports and other evidence bearing on the need to detain the child. In this event, the court shall make an appropriate order for detention of the child or release of the child from detention subject to supervision of the court during the period of continuance.

In scheduling investigations and hearings, the court shall give priority to proceedings in which a child is in detention or has otherwise been removed from home before an order of disposition has been made. A request for continuation by a party or a party's counsel beyond these limits shall be considered as a waiver of the right to a hearing within the appropriate time limits.

Amended effective August 16, 2001.

SECTION 9. BOND HEARING

RULE 9.1. APPLICATION

If a child is placed in detention pending a hearing, the child's parents or legal guardian may make application for bond by filing a written request with the clerk of the court, who shall schedule a hearing in the event one is needed.

Amended effective August 16, 2001.

RULE 9.2. HEARING

The judge, associate judge, or authorized officer of the court shall determine if the circumstances permit the child's release from detention as well as the amount of the bond. All children subject to the jurisdiction of the juvenile court and alleged to be delinquent or unruly, on application of the parent or guardian, shall have the same right to bail as adults and the judge shall admit to bail all children under his or her jurisdiction in the same manner and under the same circumstances and procedures as are applicable to adults accused of the commission of crimes.

Amended effective March 21, 1991; August 16, 2001.

SECTION 10. ARRAIGNMENT HEARING

RULE 10.1. NATURE AND PURPOSE

The arraignment hearing is an optional formal hearing which may be conducted in conjunction with the detention hearing or in a separate hearing. The purpose of the arraignment hearing is to formally advise the child of his or her rights to counsel, to remain silent and to a hearing before the judge; to advise the child of the allegations as they are stated in the petition; and to offer the child an opportunity to enter an admission or a denial to the charges.

Amended effective August 16, 2001.

RULE 10.2. NOTICE

On appearance at the detention hearing, a party may waive service of summons to allow the judge, associate judge, or authorized officer of the court to proceed with the arraignment hearing in conjunction with the detention hearing.

Amended effective March 21, 1991.

RULE 10.3. WAIVER

Counsel for a child, or the child's parent (if their interests are not in conflict) may waive in writing the formal arraignment hearing and proceed to an adjudicatory hearing on the merits of the petition or may enter an admission to the charges and proceed to a dispositional hearing.

RULE 10.4. PLEAS

(a) Admissions. If the child admits the allegations, the judge, associate judge or authorized officer of the court shall then hear information as to the particulars of the act and determine whether the admission is accepted by the court.

The child shall sign a waiver of his or her right to a contested hearing on the merits of the petition. The matter may be disposed of at that time, or it may be scheduled for a dispositional hearing at a later time.

(b) Denials. If the allegations of the petition are denied by the child, the case shall be scheduled for an adjudicatory hearing on the merits of the petition.

Amended effective March 21, 1991; August 16, 2001.

SECTION 11. ADJUDICATORY HEARING

RULE 11.1. NATURE AND PURPOSE

The purpose of the adjudicatory hearing is to determine if the allegations contained in the petition are true.

RULE 11.2. DISMISSAL

In matters involving delinquency and/or unruliness, if the court finds that the petitioner has not met the burden of proof, it shall dismiss the proceeding, discharge the child from detention or other restrictions previously ordered by the court and enter an order of acquittal. In matters involving deprivation or termination of parental rights, the court shall dismiss the petition, with findings of fact and conclusions of law, if the evidence fails to sustain the allegations by clear and convincing evidence.

Former Rule 11.4 renumbered as new Rule 11.2 effective December 31, 1992.

RULE 11.3. CONTINUANCE

On the motion of the court or that of a party, the court may continue a hearing for a reasonable time upon good cause shown. However, in cases involving allegations of deprivation the granting of continuances beyond the statutory limitations as defined in OCGA § 15–11–39 (a) shall be by written order and the specific reason for the continuance must be stated therein.

Formal Rule 11.5 amended effective July 1, 1986; renumbered as new Rule 11.3 effective December 31, 1992; amended effective August 16, 2001.

RULE 11.4. SOCIAL HISTORY

The social history of the child shall not be presented to the judge until after said child is adjudicated to have committed the delinquent or unruly act.

Former Rule 11.7 renumbered as new Rule 11.4 effective December 31, 1992.

SECTION 12. DISPOSITIONAL HEARING; CONTINUANCE

RULE 12.1. CONTINUANCE

See O.C.G.A. § 15–11–56(b) and § 15–11–65(c).

Former Rule 12.3 renumbered as new Rule 12.1 and amended effective December 31, 1992; amended effective August 16, 2001; April 15, 2004.

SECTION 13. JUVENILE TRAFFIC OFFENSES

See OCGA § 15–11–73.

Forfeiture of cash bonds will not be accepted as disposition of a case which the Department of Public Safety considers a serious traffic offense as defined in OCGA § 40–5–54 or § 40–5–70 or where an accident is involved, except for out-of-state residents and, by judicial discretion, for those in-state residents for whom return to the court would present a hardship for the child and parent.

Amended effective December 31, 1992; August 16, 2001.

SECTION 14. COURT OF INQUIRY

See OCGA § 15–11–4.

Amended effective December 31, 1992; August 16, 2001.

SECTION 15. LIMITATIONS OF TIME ON ORDERS OF DISPOSITION

RULE 15.1. TERMINATION OF PARENTAL RIGHTS

See OCGA § 15–11–93.

Amended effective December 31, 1992; August 16, 2001.

RULE 15.2. OTHER ORDERS OF DISPOSITION

Any other order of disposition in a proceeding including delinquency, unruliness and deprivation, except in an order involving the appointment of a guardian of the person or property of a child, continues in force for not more than two years. Provided, however, that an order placing a deprived child in foster care under the supervision of the Department of Human Resources shall continue in force for 12 months after the date the child is considered to have entered foster care or until the court sooner terminates its order. A child is considered to have entered foster care on the date of the first judicial finding that the child has been subjected to child abuse or neglect or the date that is 60 days after the date on which the child is removed from the home, whichever is earlier. The court may sooner terminate its order or extend its duration for further periods as provided by OCGA §§ 15–11–58 and 15–11–70.

Former Rule 15.3 renumbered as new Rule 15.2 effective December 31, 1992; amended effective November 28, 1996; October 5, 1998; August 16, 2001.

RULE 15.3. TERMINATION OF ORDER

Except as provided in OCGA § 15–11–70, the court may terminate an order of disposition or extension prior to its expiration, on or without an application of a party, if it appears to the court that the purposes of the order have been accomplished.

Except as otherwise provided by law, when the child reaches 21 years of age, all orders affecting the child then in force terminate and the child is discharged from future obligation or control.

Former Rule 15.4 renumbered as new Rule 15.3 and amended effective December 31, 1992; amended effective August 16, 2001.

RULE 15.4. EARLY TERMINATION OF PROBATION

The probation officer, with the approval of the probation supervisor, may submit a request for early termination of probation to the judge asking that a child be released early from probation. The recommendation should include a history of the child's involvement with the court, an account of the child's conduct and progress during probation and the reason for making the request. If the early termination is approved by the judge, the probation officer shall notify the child and his or her parents.

Former Rule 15.4(a) redesignated as new Rule 15.4 effective December 31, 1992; amended effective August 16, 2001.

SECTION 16. MODIFICATION OR VACATION OF ORDER

RULE 16.1. GROUNDS FOR MODIFICATION OR VACATION OF ORDER

See OCGA § 15–11–40.

Amended effective December 31, 1992; August 16, 2001.

RULE 16.2. MODIFICATION OF PROBATION RULES

A probation officer may submit a request to the judge that a condition of a child's probation be changed if that rule of probation has become inappropriate to the child's situation. The parent and child shall be notified of the proposed modifications and be given an opportunity to appear and object thereto or may agree in writing to the proposed changes and waive objections. Upon the written approval of the change by the judge, the child and his or her parents shall be served with a copy of the modification order.

Amended effective August 16, 2001.

RULE 16.3. PETITION FOR MODIFICATION OR VACATION

See OCGA § 15–11–40 (c).

Amended effective December 31, 1992; August 16, 2001.

RULE 16.4. HEARING

See OCGA § 15–11–40 (d).

Amended effective December 31, 1992; August 16, 2001.

SECTION 17. ENTRY OF JUDGMENT

RULE 17.1. SIGNING

Except when otherwise specifically provided by statute, all judgments shall be signed by the judge and filed with the clerk, and, for purposes of appeal, shall not be considered as entry of judgment until stamped as filed by the clerk.

SECTION 18. CONTEMPT ORDERS

RULE 18.1. CONTEMPT OF COURT

See OCGA § 15–11–5.

Amended effective March 21, 1991; December 31, 1992; August 16, 2001.

RULE 18.2. RULE NISI

Upon the filing of a petition alleging that a party has willfully and intentionally failed to abide by an order of the court, or on the court's own motion, the court shall issue a show cause order, or rule nisi, commanding the party to appear before the court at a designated time to show cause why said party should not be held in contempt of court.

SECTION 19. APPEALS; SUPERSEDEAS

RULE 19.1. APPEALS AND SUPERSEDEAS

See OCGA § 15–11–3.

Amended effective December 31, 1992; August 16, 2001.

RULE 19.2. APPEALS FROM ASSOCIATE JUDGE'S DECISION

A rehearing of an associate judge's order under OCGA § 15–11–21 (e) will be by a review by the juvenile court judge of the pleadings, recorded, electronic, or written transcript and evidence of the original proceeding to be obtained at the request and expense of the party appealing said ruling of the associate judge. The standard of proof for such review shall be the same as for the original case.

Adopted effective July 1, 1986; amended effective March 21, 1991; October 5, 1998; August 16, 2001.

SECTION 20. PHYSICAL AND MENTAL EXAMINATIONS

RULE 20.1. BY COURT ORDER

See OCGA § 15–11–12 (b).

Amended effective December 31, 1992; August 16, 2001.

RULE 20.2. COSTS

See OCGA § 15–11–8 (a) (1) and Rule 21.

Amended effective December 31, 1992; August 16, 2001.

RULE 20.3. DISPOSITION OF MENTALLY ILL OR MENTALLY RETARDED CHILD

See OCGA § 15–11–149 et seq.

Amended effective December 31, 1992; August 16, 2001.

SECTION 21. COURT COSTS

RULE 21.1. CARE OF CHILD

See OCGA §§ 15–11–8, 15–11–71 and 24–9–100 et seq.

Amended effective December 31, 1992; August 16, 2001.

RULE 21.2. APPEALS

Appellant shall pay all costs for transcribing the recording of a case on appeal. However, upon filing of a pauper's affidavit with the clerk and showing to the court that the appellant is unable without undue financial hardship to pay the cost of transcribing the record, the court shall authorize payment of such costs from county funds.

SECTION 22. UNIFORM RULES COMMITTEE

RULE 22.1. CREATION AND DUTIES

There shall be a standing committee of the Council of Juvenile Court Judges designated as the Uniform Rules Committee. The membership of said committee and the chairperson thereof shall be appointed by the president of the Council of Juvenile Court Judges on an annual basis, and such members may be reappointed in the discretion of the president.

The duties of this standing committee shall be to propose for the Council's vote, after study, any amendments to the uniform rules which may be desirable or which may become necessary as a result of legislative changes in statutory law, to be submitted to the Supreme Court as provided by law.

These rules and any amendments to these rules shall be published in the advance sheets to the Georgia Reports. Unless otherwise provided, the effective date of any amendment to these rules is the date of publication in the advance sheets to the Georgia Reports.

See Section XVII of the Rules of the Supreme Court of Georgia.

Amended effective June 7, 1990; August 16, 2001.

SECTION 23. PARENTAL NOTIFICATION OF ABORTION

RULE 23.1. STYLE OF THE CASE

The petition and all other documents in a proceeding under Article 3, Chapter 11, Title 15 of the Official Code of Georgia shall be as provided for in Rule 6.4 relating to cases under appeal.

Adopted effective July 1, 1987.

RULE 23.2. APPOINTMENT OF GUARDIAN AD LITEM

Whenever an unemancipated minor petitions the court for relief under Article 3, Chapter 11, Title 15 of the Official Code of Georgia, the court shall appoint a guardian ad litem to protect the interests of the unemancipated minor.

Adopted effective July 1, 1987; amended effective December 31, 1992.

RULE 23.3. RELATION TO OTHER UNIFORM RULES

All rules in conflict with the provisions of Article 3, Chapter 11, Title 15 of the Official Code of Georgia are subrogated to the provisions of that article for the purpose of implementing the intent of the article.

Adopted effective July 1, 1987.

RULE 23.4. HEARING CONDUCTED BY JUDGE

In order to insure the expeditious disposition of the procedures, the hearing provided for in OCGA § 15–11–113 shall be conducted by a judge in all instances.

Adopted effective July 1, 1987.

RULE 23.5. NOTIFICATION OF HEARING

The unemancipated minor, her attorney or next friend shall be notified of the date, time, and place of the hearing in proceedings under this article at the time of the filing of the petition. The hearing shall be held within three days of the date of filing, excluding Saturdays, Sundays, and holidays. Upon filing the petition, the clerk shall provide a certified copy thereof to the unemancipated minor, her attorney or next friend with the date, time, and place of the hearing recorded thereon.

Adopted effective July 1, 1987; amended effective November 12, 1992; December 31, 1992.

RULE 23.6. COURT ORDER

Upon conclusion of the hearing to be held pursuant to O.C.G.A. § 15–11–113, the court shall issue a written order stating specific factual findings and legal conclusions supporting its decision. The order shall be styled in the same manner as the petition and shall contain a physical description of the unemancipated minor for purposes of identifying the unemancipated minor to the physician who is asked to perform the abortion. The court shall prepare a certified copy of the order which shall be furnished only to the unemancipated minor, her attorney or next friend within 24 hours of the hearing. In the event that no hearing is held or more than 24 hours have elapsed since the time of the hearing and the court has not entered an order, the unemancipated minor may request the Clerk of Court to issue a certificate indicating such.

Adopted effective July 1, 1987; amended effective July 1, 1988; November 12, 1992; December 31, 1992.

RULE 23.7. RECORD AND TRANSCRIPT

The name of the unemancipated minor shall not appear in any public record, including the transcript of the hearing provided for in Rule 23.4. Should reference be made to the unemancipated minor, the clerk shall obliterate or render illegible the name and substitute initials.

Adopted effective July 1, 1987; amended effective December 31, 1992.

RULE 23.8. DISCLOSURE OF INFORMATION GENERALLY

The court shall not disclose any information concerning a case arising under Article 3, Chapter 11, Title 15 of the Official Code of Georgia, or permit access to any such file except to the unemancipated minor who is the subject of the proceeding, the next friend, or the unemancipated minor's attorney.

Adopted effective July 1, 1988; amended effective December 31, 1992.

RULE 23.9. DISCLOSURE OF INFORMATION ON APPEAL

In the event of an expedited appeal as provided for in OCGA § 15–11–114(e), the juvenile court shall insure complete anonymity of the unemancipated minor by using her initials only to identify her in the complete record sent to the appellate court and shall not disclose her name, address, birth date or social security number in any part of the record.

Adopted effective July 1, 1988; amended effective December 31, 1992.

SECTION 24. JUDICIAL CITIZEN REVIEW FOR CHILDREN IN FOSTER CARE

RULE 24.1. CASE REVIEW OF CHILDREN IN FOSTER CARE; GENERALLY

All cases of children in foster care in the custody of the Division of Family and Children Services of the Department of Human Resources (hereinafter referred to as "DFCS") shall be initially reviewed within ninety (90) days of the entering of the dispositional order but no later than six (6) months following the child's placement in temporary foster care. Such review shall be conducted by the juvenile court judge, or a properly designated associate judge or judge pro tempore, or by judicial citizen review panels established by the court. After the initial review, each case shall be reviewed at least every six (6) months.

Adopted effective July 1, 1991; amended effective October 5, 1998.

RULE 24.2. CREATION OF JUDICIAL CITIZEN REVIEW PANELS

A chief judge of a juvenile court or a chief superior court judge in a county where a superior court judge has juvenile court jurisdiction may elect to create judicial citizen review panels. If a judge elects to create judicial citizen review panels, he or she shall file a statement of intent with the Council of Juvenile Court Judges (hereinafter referred to as the "Council"). The Council shall then determine if there are adequate staff and resources available for the creation and operation of a judicial citizen review panel program and shall notify the court in writing of its determination within a reasonable time from receiving the statement of intent. If the Council determines that there are adequate resources to establish judicial citizen review panels, the Council shall notify the court in writing of this, and such written notice shall serve as the formal creation of a judicial citizen review panel program. Such panels shall be conducted in the manner set forth in OCGA § 15–11–58 and shall employ the standards and procedures as mandated by such statute, these rules, and program guidelines approved by the Council standing committee on permanency planning (hereinafter referred to as "Program Guidelines"). Only those courts which agree to operate under such terms and conditions shall be deemed to be in compliance with OCGA § 15–11–58.

Adopted effective July 1, 1991; amended effective October 28, 1993; October 5, 1998; August 16, 2001.

RULE 24.3. PROGRAM GUIDELINES

A current copy of the Program Guidelines shall be maintained in the clerk's office of every court that has a judicial citizen review panel program in place and shall be available for review upon request during the court's normal business hours.

Adopted effective July 1, 1991; amended effective October 5, 1998; August 16, 2001.

RULE 24.4. APPOINTMENTS; TERM OF SERVICE; VACANCIES; AND REMOVAL FROM OFFICE

(a) Appointments. The judge shall screen, select and appoint individuals to serve on local judicial citizen review panels. The judge shall seek to select persons who represent a cross-section of the community with respect to race, economic status, gender, and ethnic background. Any person employed by DFCS, any juvenile court except for the person designated by the judge as the local program coordinator, or any person who serves as a legal guardian or custodian of a child in temporary foster care shall not be eligible to serve on any local judicial citizen review panels; provided, however, that any person serving as a member of a local judicial citizen review panel on July 1, 1991, who would be ineligible to serve under these rules may continue to do so until the judge appoints a qualified replacement.

(b) Term of Service. Judicial citizen review panel members shall serve at the pleasure of the judge for a term of one (1) year. The panel member may continue to serve as long as the panel member meets the requirements of the Program Guidelines.

(c) Vacancies. In the event that a vacancy arises, the judge shall appoint a qualified individual to serve the remainder of the unexpired term.

(d) Removal from Office. The judge may remove a panel member for: (1) failure to meet the certification requirements as provided in the Program Guidelines; (2) displaying any behavior which hinders the overall effectiveness of the panel; (3) violating the oath of confidentiality; or (4) conviction of a crime involving moral turpitude.

Adopted effective July 1, 1991; amended effective October 5, 1998; August 16, 2001.

RULE 24.5. TRAINING AND CERTIFICATION

Before any person may serve on a judicial citizen review panel, they shall successfully complete an initial training course provided by professional staff employed by the Council. Each year thereafter, judicial citizen review panel members are required to complete additional training as prescribed by the Program Guidelines. Council staff shall certify completion of the required training to the court and the Council standing committee on permanency planning.

Adopted effective July 1, 1991; amended effective October 5, 1998.

RULE 24.6. PANEL COMPOSITION; QUORUM; AND EMERGENCY SUBSTITUTION PROCEDURE

(a) Panel Composition. Each citizen review panel shall be set up in accordance with the Program Guidelines.

(b) Quorum. A quorum shall be as defined in the Program Guidelines.

(c) Emergency Substitution Procedure. Emergency substitution procedures shall be handled as provided in the Program Guidelines.

Adopted effective July 1, 1991; amended effective October 5, 1998.

RULE 24.7. DUTIES OF THE JUDICIAL CITIZEN REVIEW PANELS

Each judicial citizen review panel participating in foster care reviews shall submit findings and recommendations to the court which, at a minimum, shall address the following issues:

1. The necessity and appropriateness of the current placement;

2. Whether reasonable efforts have been made to obtain permanency for the child;

3. The degree of compliance with the specific goals and action steps set out in the case plan;

4. Whether any progress has been made in improving the conditions that caused the child's removal from the home; and

5. Any specific changes that need to be made in the case plan, including a change in the permanency goal and the projected date when permanency for the child is likely to be achieved.

Judicial citizen review panels, if designated by the court, may assist DFCS, in a consultant-like capacity, in the preparation of the initial thirty (30) day case plan. Such assistance shall be provided during a face-to-face meeting between the primary caseworker, the parents and child(ren) when available, and members of the judicial citizen review panel.

Judicial citizen review panels may also perform such other duties and functions as provided by law.

Adopted effective July 1, 1991; amended effective October 5, 1998.

RULE 24.8. CONFIDENTIALITY OF PROCEEDINGS

All information discussed during a judicial citizen review panel review related to the cases reviewed shall remain confidential. The release of any case-related information must first be approved by the court.

Adopted effective July 1, 1991; amended effective October 5, 1998.

RULE 24.9. CONFLICT OF INTEREST

Whenever a judicial citizen review panel member has a potential conflict of interest in a case being reviewed, the panel member shall advise the other panel members and persons present of the potential conflict prior to participating in the case review. If any party to the case believes that the potential conflict may prevent the panel member from fairly and objectively reviewing the case, such panel member shall be excused from participating in the review. The potential conflict of interest shall be duly recorded in the panel's findings and recommendations.

Adopted effective July 1, 1991; amended effective October 5, 1998.

RULE 24.10. NOTICE OF CASE REVIEWS

The local DFCS office shall furnish the local program coordinator with a master calendar of foster care cases to be reviewed on a quarterly basis and a list of individuals to be invited to each review at least twenty (20) working days prior to the date of the scheduled review. Advance written notice shall be provided to all interested parties in a uniform manner as set forth in the Program Guidelines.

Adopted effective March 21, 1991; amended effective October 5, 1998.

RULE 24.11. WORKLOAD OF THE PANELS

The workload of the panels at any given time may not exceed the maximum or fall below the minimum number set forth in the Program Guidelines.

Adopted effective March 21, 1991; amended effective October 1, 1998.

RULE 24.12. ACCESS TO CASE INFORMATION; TIME FRAMES

(a) Access to Case Information. Each judicial citizen review panel, each juvenile court, and Council staff shall have access to all records and information of the court and the local DFCS office that is pertinent to the case being reviewed.

(b) Time Frames. DFCS shall submit progress reports and updated case information to the local program coordinator at least five (5) working days before the date of the judicial citizen review panel review. Any supplemental information requested by the judicial citizen review panels from the local DFCS office must be submitted within five (5) working days from the date the request is received. All other information requested by judicial citizen review panels from other individuals and agencies shall be submitted within the time frames set forth in the Program Guidelines.

Adopted effective March 21, 1991; amended effective October 5, 1998; August 16, 2001.

RULE 24.13. PANEL REVIEWS

(a) Case Review. A judicial citizen review panel may elect to hear from any person who formally requests to be heard during a foster care case review, as long as such person has specific knowledge of the case and can assist the panel in the review process. Parents and children may be accompanied to the review by a representative of their choice and such representative may be permitted to provide information.

(b) Presence of the Child. In the case where a child is present, any panel member may request of the chairperson that the panel members, Council staff, and other persons meet privately with the child if it is determined that this would facilitate the child's ability to communicate with the panel members.

(c) Persons Who Shall Receive Notice of Reviews. The following persons shall be given written notice of the judicial citizen review panel reviews: the parents, the child, Council staff, DFCS staff, any preadoptive parent or relative providing care for the child, and foster parents.

(d) Persons Who May Participate in Reviews. The following persons may participate in judicial citizen review panel reviews at the invitation of the panel: family members of the child, legal counsel retained by the parent(s) or appointed by the court for the child, and professionals and other citizens having specific knowledge of the case or special expertise which would benefit the panel review process.

(e) Exclusion From the Review. The panel chairperson may remove any person from any review on his or her initiative or at the request of any participant if the panel chairperson determines that such removal is necessary for an orderly and thorough review of the case.

(f) Oath of Confidentiality. Prior to participating in a judicial citizen review panel review, each person shall affirm by oath that he or she shall keep confidential all information disclosed during the panel review and any information related to the case and that such information may be disclosed only when authorized by law. In the event that any person violates the oath of confidentiality, such person shall be subject to the contempt powers of the court as provided by law.

Adopted effective July 1, 1991; amended effective December 31, 1992; October 5, 1998.

RULE 24.14. PLACEMENT AGENCY ATTENDANCE

Unless excused from doing so by the judicial citizen review panel, DFCS and any other agency directly responsible for the placement, care, and custody of the child whose case is under review shall require the presence of the employee designated as responsible under the case plan or his or her immediate supervisor. The citizen review panel may request the presence of other specific employees of the DFCS office or other agency at the panel review.

Adopted effective July 1, 1991; amended effective October 5, 1998.

RULE 24.15. ADDITIONAL PROCEDURES AND PRACTICES

The Council may adopt such other administrative practices and procedures not inconsistent with the provisions of law and these rules as may be necessary from time to time for the operation of judicial citizen review panels.

Adopted effective July 1, 1991; amended effective October 5, 1998.

RULE 24.16. MAINTENANCE OF RECORDS

See Rule 3.10.

Adopted effective July 1, 1991.

SECTION 25. ATTORNEYS

RULE 25.1. LEAVES OF ABSENCE

This rule shall be in conformity with Superior Court Rule 16.

Adopted effective March 21, 1991; amended effective August 16, 2001.

RULE 25.2. WITHDRAWAL OF COUNSEL

This rule shall be in conformity with Superior Court Rule 4.3.

Adopted effective March 21, 1991.

RULE 25.3. ENTRY OF APPEARANCE

No attorney shall appear in that capacity before a juvenile court until he or she has entered an appearance by filing a signed entry of appearance form or by filing a signed pleading in a pending action, except those representing the state or appointed by the court. An entry of appearance and all pleadings shall include:

(1) the style and number of the case;

(2) the identity of the party for whom the appearance is made;

(3) the name, assigned state bar number, and current office address and telephone number of the attorney; and

(4) an affidavit or verified petition attached to the pleadings disclosing any related matters pending before another court and acknowledging the on–going obligation, as provided by Rule 25.5, to notify the court regarding any such related matters.

The filing of any pleading shall contain the information required by this paragraph and shall constitute an appearance by the person(s) signing such pleading, unless otherwise specified by the court.

Any attorney who has been admitted to practice in this state but who fails to maintain active membership in good standing in the State Bar of Georgia and who makes or files any appearance or pleading in a juvenile court of this state while not in good standing shall be subject to the contempt powers of the court.

Within forty-eight (48) hours after being retained, an attorney shall mail to the court and opposing counsel or file with the court the entry of his or her appearance in the pending matter. Failure to timely file shall not prohibit the appearance and representation by said counsel.

Adopted effective March 21, 1991; amended effective March 16, 2006.

RULE 25.4. CONFLICTS

This rule shall be in conformity with Superior Court Rule 17.

Adopted effective April 15, 2004.

SECTION 26. ACCESS TO JUVENILE COURT PROCEEDINGS

RULE 26.1. ACCESS TO JUVENILE COURT PROCEEDINGS

Whether a hearing is generally open to public access or generally closed to public access is governed by OCGA § 15–11–78. Any person seeking access to any juvenile court proceeding shall file a written motion for access in substantial conformity with Juvenile Form JUV–22. Said motion shall be timely filed prior to any hearing at which access is sought. The court shall expeditiously set the motion for hearing. The movant shall expeditiously serve the motion and notice of hearing on all parties.

Adopted effective March 21, 1991; amended effective August 8, 1996; November 28, 1996; amended effective August 16, 2001.

RULE 26.2. ELECTRONIC AND PHOTOGRAPHIC NEWS COVERAGE OF JUVENILE COURT PROCEEDINGS

In any hearing open to public access by operation of law or by court order, representatives of the print and electronic public media may be present at and unobtrusively make written notes and sketches pertaining to such proceedings. However, due to the distractive nature of electronic or photographic equipment, representatives of the public media utilizing such equipment are subject to the following restrictions and conditions:

(A) Persons desiring to broadcast/record/photograph juvenile court proceedings must file a timely written request (Juvenile Form JUV–25) with the judge involved prior to the proceeding, specifying the particular case for which such coverage is intended; the type of equipment to be used in the courtroom; the proceeding to be covered; and the person responsible for installation and operation of such equipment.

(B) Approval of the judge to broadcast/record/photograph a proceeding, if granted, shall be granted without partiality or preference to any person, news agency, or type of electronic or photographic coverage, who agrees to abide by and conform to these rules, up to the capacity of the space designated therefor in the courtroom. Violation of these rules will be grounds for a reporter/technician to be removed or excluded from the courtroom and held in contempt.

(C) The judge, in his or her discretion, may require pooled coverage which would allow only one still photographer, one television camera and attendant, and one radio or tape recorder outlet and attendant. Photographers, electronic reporters and technicians shall be expected to arrange themselves pooled coverage if so directed by the judge and to present the judge with a schedule and description of the pooled coverage. If the covering persons cannot agree on such a schedule or arrangement, the judge may, in his or her discretion, designate the schedule and arrangements for pooled coverage.

(D) The positioning and removal of cameras and electronic devices shall be done quietly and, if possible, before or after the court session or during recesses; in no event shall such disturb the proceedings of the court. In every such case, equipment should be in place and ready to operate before the time court is scheduled to be called to order.

(E) Overhead lights in the courtroom shall be switched on and off only by court personnel. No other lights, flashbulbs, flashes or sudden light changes may be used unless the judge approves before-hand.

(F) No adjustment of the central audio system shall be made except by persons authorized by the judge. Audio recordings of the court proceedings will be from one source, normally by connection to the court's central audio system. Upon prior approval of the court, other microphones may be added in an unobtrusive manner to the court's public address system.

(G) All television cameras, still cameras and tape recorders shall be assigned to a specific portion of the public area of the courtroom or specially designated access areas, and such equipment will not be permitted to be removed or relocated during the court proceedings.

(H) Still cameras must have quiet functioning shutters and advancers. Movie and television cameras and broadcasting and recording devices must be quiet running. If any equipment is determined by the judge to be of such noise as to be distractive to the court proceedings, then such equipment can be excluded from the courtroom by the judge.

(I) Pictures of the child, whether by still, movie, or television cameras, shall not be taken. Photographs and televising of the public and courtroom are allowed, if done without disruption of the court proceedings.

(J) Reporters, photographers, and technicians must have and produce upon request of court officials credentials identifying them and the media company for which they work.

(K) Court proceedings shall not be interrupted by a reporter or technician with a technical or an equipment problem.

(L) Reporters, photographers, and technicians should do everything possible to avoid attracting attention to themselves. Reporters, photographers, and technicians will be accorded full right of access to court proceedings for obtaining public information within the requirements of due process of law, so long as it is done without detracting from the dignity and decorum of the court.

(M) Other than as permitted by these rules and guidelines, there will be no photographing, radio or television broadcasting, including videotaping pertaining to any judicial proceedings on the courthouse floor whereon is located a juvenile court courtroom, whether or not the court is actually in session.

(N) No interviews pertaining to a particular judicial proceeding will be conducted in the courtroom except with the permission of the judge.

Adopted effective March 21, 1991; amended effective August 8, 1996; November 28, 1996; August 16, 2001.

SECTION 27. RECUSAL

RULE 27.1. MOTIONS

All motions to recuse or disqualify a judge presiding in a particular case or proceeding shall be timely filed in writing and all evidence thereon shall be presented by accompanying affidavit(s) which shall fully assert the facts upon which the motion is founded. Filing and presentation to the judge shall be not later than 5 days after the affiant first learned of the alleged grounds for disqualification, and not later than 10 days prior to the hearing or trial which is the subject of recusal or disqualification, unless good cause be shown for failure to meet such time requirements. In no event shall the motion be allowed to delay the trial or proceeding.

Adopted effective December 31, 1992.

RULE 27.2. AFFIDAVIT

The affidavit shall clearly state the facts and reasons for the belief that bias or prejudice exists, being definite and specific as to time, place, persons and circumstances of extra-judicial conduct or statements, which demonstrate either bias in favor of any adverse party, or prejudice toward the moving party in particular, or a systematic pattern of prejudicial conduct toward persons similarly situated to the moving party, which would influence the judge and impede or prevent impartiality in that action. Allegations consisting of bare conclusions and opinions shall not be legally sufficient to support the motion or warrant further proceedings.

Adopted effective December 31, 1992.

RULE 27.3. DUTY OF THE TRIAL JUDGE

When a judge is presented with a motion to recuse, or disqualify, accompanied by an affidavit, the judge shall temporarily cease to act upon the merits of the matter and shall immediately determine the timeliness of the motion and the legal sufficiency of the affidavit, and make a determination, assuming any of the facts alleged in the affidavit are true, whether recusal would be warranted. If it is found that the motion is timely, the affidavit sufficient and that recusal would be authorized if some or all of the facts set forth in the affidavit are true, another judge shall be assigned to hear the motion to recuse. The allegations of the motion shall stand denied automatically. The trial judge shall not otherwise oppose the motion.

Adopted effective December 31, 1992.

RULE 27.4. PROCEDURE UPON A MOTION FOR DISQUALIFICATION

The motion shall be assigned for hearing to another judge, who shall be selected in the following manner:

(A) If within a single-judge court, the President of the Council of Juvenile Court Judges shall select the judge;

(B) If within a two-judge court, the other judge, unless disqualified, shall hear the motion. If the other judge is disqualified, then the President of the Council of Juvenile Court Judges shall select the judge;

(C) If within a multi-judge court, the presiding judge of the court shall assign the judge to hear the motion unless the judge sought to be recused is the presiding judge, in which case the next senior judge of the court not otherwise recused shall select the judge to hear the motion; or

(D) If the Judge against whom the motion is filed is the President of the Council of Juvenile Court Judges or if the President of the Council of Juvenile Court Judges is absent or disqualified for any reason, then the immediate Past President of the Counsel of Juvenile Court Judges shall select the judge to hear the motion.

Adopted effective December 31, 1992; amended effective March 13, 1997.

RULE 27.5. SELECTION OF JUDGE

In the instance of any hearing on a motion to recuse or disqualify a judge, the challenged judge shall neither select nor participate in the selection of the judge to hear the motion; if recused or disqualified, the recused or disqualified judge shall not select nor participate in the selection of the judge assigned to hear further proceedings in the involved action.

Adopted effective December 31, 1992.

RULE 27.6. FINDINGS AND RULING

The judge assigned may consider the motion solely upon the affidavits, but may, in the exercise of discretion, convene an evidentiary hearing. After consideration of the evidence, the judge assigned shall rule on the merits of the motion and shall make written findings and conclusions. If the motion is sustained, the selection of another judge to hear the case shall follow the same procedure as established in Rule 27.4 above. Any determination of disqualification shall not be competent evidence in any other case or proceedings.

Adopted effective December 31, 1992.

RULE 27.7. VOLUNTARY RECUSAL

If a judge, either on the motion of one of the parties or the judge's own motion, voluntarily disqualifies, another judge, selected by the procedure set forth in Rule 27.4 above, shall be assigned to hear the matter involved. A voluntary recusal shall not be construed as either an admission or denial to any allegations which have been set out in the motion.

Adopted effective December 31, 1992.

SECTION 28. CENTRAL CHILD ABUSE REGISTRY

RULE 28.1. CREATION

See O.C.G.A. Section 49–5–180, et seq.

Adopted effective October 28, 1993.

Publisher's Note

Section 49–5–180 et seq. has been held unconstitutional in the case of State vs. Jackson, 1996, 269 Ga. 308, 496 S.E.2d 912.

Rule 28.2. Initiation of Proceedings to Expunge [Deleted]

Deleted effective August 8, 1996.

Rule 28.3. Hearings [Deleted]

Deleted effective August 8, 1996.

Rule 28.4. Order [Deleted]

Deleted effective August 8, 1996.

SECTION 29. ELECTRONIC FILING

RULE 29.1. ELECTRONIC FILING GENERALLY

(a) Except as otherwise provided, this rule shall be construed in accordance with Georgia's Electronic Records and Signatures Act, O.C.G.A. §§ 10–12–1 *et. seq.*

(b) A juvenile court may adopt local rules permitting electronic court filing and service of documents subject to this rule.

(c) Subject to paragraph (f), below, electronic filing is not mandatory, but permissive. Parties in a case who opt to file electronically shall deal with parties who do not file electronically in accordance with traditional, paper-based rules and procedure in keeping with the Juvenile Court Code and the Uniform Rules For Juvenile Courts.

(d) When a document to be filed requires a signature by a person but such signature is not submitted under penalty of perjury the document shall be deemed to have been signed by that person if filed electronically.

(e) When a document to be filed requires a signature of any person and such signature is submitted under the penalty of perjury the document shall be deemed to be signed by that person if any one of the following conditions is met:

(i) The clerk of the court accepting the document for filing swears that the person whose signature is required signed or intended to sign the document. The clerk of the court may keep a paper or electronic copy of the signed document as a record of the signer's intent.

(ii) A faxed copy of the signed document is delivered to the court.

(iii) An electronic image of the signed document is delivered to the court.

(f) A judge may require all parties in a case to file electronically.

(g) A judge may alter these rules in any case in the interest of justice.

Adopted effective April 17, 2003.

RULE 29.2. COURT AND COURT AGENTS

Except as otherwise provided, "court" means the juvenile court or an authorized agent of the juvenile court.

Adopted effective April 17, 2003.

RULE 29.3. DOCUMENT FORMAT OF PLEADINGS, MOTIONS, BRIEFS, AND EXHIBITS

(a) A pleading, motion, brief, or other similar document filed electronically into a court shall be filed in Adobe Portable Document Format ("PDF") using the Legal XML Court Filing Standard as modified for Georgia Courts.

(b) A pleading, motion, brief, or other similar document may be delivered to an authorized agent of the court in any format, provided that the document is ultimately delivered to the court as an Adobe PDF document.

Adopted effective April 17, 2003.

RULE 29.4. FILING OF COMPLAINT, PETITION, OR OTHER DOCUMENT REQUIRING SERVICE OF PROCESS

(a) An electronically filed petition or other document requiring service of process may be served in any of the following ways:

(i) The clerk of court may print the electronic summons and petition and the sheriff or the sheriff's designee shall serve the documents in such manner as required by Georgia law for the specific pleading; or

(ii) The clerk of court may deliver the electronic summons and petition to the sheriff or the sheriff's designee; the sheriff or the sheriff's designee shall print the summons and petition and shall serve the documents in such manner as required by Georgia law for the specific pleading; or

(iii) The clerk of court may deliver the electronic summons and petition to a private process server approved by the court; the private process server shall then print the summons and petition and shall serve the documents in the manner required by Georgia law for the specific pleading.

(b) In all cases, the summons and petition shall have affixed or logically associated to it the court's seal, signature, or some other evidence of authenticity.

(c) Except for service of a petition or other document requiring personal service, electronic service is complete at the time of successful transmission, but any period of notice or any right or duty to do any act or make any response within any period or on a date certain after the service of the document, which time period or date is prescribed by statute or rule of court, shall be extended after service by electronic transmission by two business days. This extension applies in the absence of a specific exception provided for by any other statute or rule of court.

Adopted effective April 17, 2003.

RULE 29.5. EXHIBITS

Exhibits or other attachments shall accompany the document being filed in one of the following ways:

(i) As a paper document filed over the counter into the court,

(ii) As a facsimile transmission in accordance with local court rules, or

(iii) As an electronically filed image in Adobe PDF format.

Adopted effective April 17, 2003.

RULE 29.6. TIME OF FILING, CONFIRMATION OF FILING, NOTICES, SERVICE INTERRUPTIONS

(a) Any document that is electronically filed with the court after the close of business on any day, but before midnight, shall be deemed to have been filed on the same business day.

(b) "Close of business" as used in paragraph (a) shall mean 12:00 noon or the time at which the court would not accept a filing at the court's counter, whichever is earlier.

(c) The precise time of filing of an electronically filed document is when the document is first received without error by the court or the court's agent, whichever entity receives it first, provided the received document is eventually accepted by the court and filed.

(d) The court receiving a document filed electronically shall issue one or more confirmations that the document has been received and filed. The confirmation or confirmations shall serve as proof that the document has been received or filed, as the case may be.

(e) Notice of an electronically filed document shall be given to other parties in the following ways:

(i) An electronic filer may give non-electronic filers notice in accordance with traditional paper-based rules and procedure; or

(ii) Either the court or the electronic filer may give notice to other electronic filers by sending electronic mail to the registered email address of the electronic filers requiring notice. Whether the filer or the court is responsible for sending notice shall be determined by local court rule. Parties opting to use electronic filing shall be responsible for registering their email address with the court and shall immediately notify the court and other parties if the address changes. Attorneys shall also register their email address with the State Bar of Georgia.

Adopted effective April 13, 2003.

RULE 29.7. SERVICE INTERRUPTION

A service interruption occurs when the system used for electronic filing is not operational for more than one hour in a given day after 12:00 noon. In the case of a service interruption, a filing due on the day of the service interruption that was not filed solely because of the service interruption shall be due on the following business day. Delayed filings shall be accompanied by a declaration or affidavit attesting to the filer's failed attempts to file electronically at least two times after 12:00 noon separated by at least one hour on each day of delay due to the service interruption.

Adopted effective April 17, 2003.

RULE 29.8. PRIVACY

Consistent with O.C.G.A. § 15–11–79 and other applicable laws, sufficient procedural safeguards shall be exercised to ensure the privacy and security of documents filed electronically.

Adopted effective April 13, 2003.

APPENDIX. GUIDELINES FOR MAINTAINING A JUVENILE COURT DOCKET FOR THE COUNCIL OF JUVENILE COURT JUDGES OF GEORGIA

JUVENILE DOCKET SHEET INSTRUCTIONS

Prepared: March 1, 1991

Uniform Juvenile Court Rule 3.2 requires that each juvenile court clerk keep a juvenile docket book. The juvenile docket book must contain a completed Form JUV–16 for each new case referred to the court. Rule 3.1 (a) requires the clerk to follow the instructions below in completing the docket forms and maintaining the docket book.

The clerk shall make the docket book available for review by a representative of the Council of Juvenile Court Judges upon the Council's request. In lieu of maintaining a juvenile docket book and making such available to the Council for review, the clerk may furnish the Council, upon the Council's request, with the same data as that on the uniform docket by means of computer tape or other electronic means in a record format approved by the Council of Juvenile Court Judges.

Docket Entries

1. Case Number

A. Procedure. Enter the case number assigned by the court for each child referred to the juvenile court by way of a complaint in the appropriate space at the top right hand corner of the docket page. A case is opened when an offense or a group of offenses are referred to the court against or on behalf of the child on the same day by the same referring entity. A case contains all offenses arising out of the same conduct, transaction, or event within the same jurisdiction, regardless of the number of offenses involving the same child. A case is opened to resolve any postdispositional motion.

B. Specific Information and Examples.

(1) Several children who participate in one or more offenses together should be counted separately. Make a separate case entry for each child. Each child is assigned a separate case number.

(2) Multiple offenses within the same case must be docketed. For example, Adam Smith is charged with two counts of burglary. One docket sheet should be filled out completely listing all information pertinent to count one, #101–A. The next case entry on the docket sheet should contain all information pertinent to count two, #101–B. It is not necessary to duplicate the preliminary information for count two; however, it is important to enter the relevant dates for each count on the docket sheet.

(3) In deprivation and custody cases involving more than one child, separate case entries and case numbers are assigned for each child even though the children are listed on the same petition. This enables one to track individual case dispositions on each child in the docket book.

(4) Violations of probation are considered new cases and complete dispositional information must be provided on the docket sheet. Always assign new case numbers rather than assigning the same number as the case from which the offense originated.

(5) It is not necessary to inform the Council of a termination of probation order. This is not considered a new case.

(6) Postdispositional motions for contempt constitute a new case. Predispositional motions for contempt do not constitute a new case.

(7) A judicial review of a deprived case constitutes a new case. A judicial citizen review panel review of a deprived case does not constitute a new case, but an appeal of a judicial citizen review panel report constitutes a new case.

2. Name. Enter the full name of the child in the following order: last name, first name, and middle name.

3. Address. Enter the child's complete address.

4. Race. Mark the appropriate box.

5. Age. Enter the age of the child as shown on the complaint form.

6. Date of Birth ("DOB"). Enter the child's date of birth. This information is extremely important. The child's current age is calculated by subtracting the DOB from the date the complaint was filed.

7. Sex. Mark the appropriate box.

8. Complaint. The complaint includes proceedings against or on behalf of a child, regardless of whether a petition has been filed.

A. Procedure. Enter the written description of the offense and reference the relevant code section of the Official Code of Georgia, local ordinance or federal statute.

B. Example. Theft by taking OCGA § 16–8–2.

9. Type of Case.

A. Procedure. Mark the appropriate box which classifies the case type. All cases must be classified as one of the following case types: 1) delinquency; 2) unruly; 3) deprivation; 4) termination of parental rights; 5) special proceedings; or 6) traffic. If the "delinquency" box is checked, also indicate whether the offense is a felony or misdemeanor.

B. Case Type Classifications.

(1) The following occurrences will result in the opening of a delinquency case:

a. A complaint alleging delinquency is filed.

b. A Georgia Natural Resources/Game and Fish Division Notice of Summons is filed.

c. A delinquency case is received from the superior court by superior court order or transfer by the district attorney pursuant to OCGA § 15–11–28 (b) (2) (B) for either adjudication or disposition.

d. A delinquency case is received from another juvenile court (within Georgia or another state) for disposition. OCGA §§ 15–11–87, 15–11–88.

e. A delinquency case is received from another juvenile court (within Georgia or another state) for supervision of probation. OCGA §§ 15–11–87, 15–11–90.

f. A case alleging delinquency is received from another juvenile court for adjudication.

g. A petition to modify/vacate a previous order arising out of a delinquency case is filed. OCGA § 15–11–40.

h. A motion to extend commitment arising out of a delinquency case is filed. OCGA § 15–11–70.

i. A motion to extend probation arising out of a delinquency case is filed. O.C.G.A. § 15–11–70.

j. Any postdispositional motion arising out of a delinquency case is filed excluding motions for contempt.

(2) The following occurrences will result in the opening of an unruly case:

a. A complaint alleging unruly conduct is filed.

b. An unruly case is received from another juvenile court (within Georgia or another state) for disposition. OCGA §§ 15–11–87, 15–11–88.

c. An unruly case is received from another juvenile court (within Georgia or another state) for supervision of probation/supervision. OCGA §§ 15–11–87, 15–11–90.

d. A case alleging unruly conduct is received from another juvenile court for adjudication.

e. A petition to modify/vacate a previous order arising out of an unruly case is filed. OCGA § 15–11–40.

f. A motion to extend commitment arising out of an unruly case is filed. OCGA § 15–11–70.

g. A motion to extend probation arising out of an unruly case is filed. O.C.G.A. 15–11–70.

h. Any postdispositional motion arising out of an unruly case is filed excluding motions for contempt.

(3) The following occurrences will result in the opening of a deprivation case:

a. A complaint alleging deprivation is filed or on motion of the court.

b. A petition to modify/vacate a previous order arising out of a deprivation case is filed. OCGA § 15–11–40.

c. A motion to modify/extend custody arising out of a deprivation case is filed. OCGA § 15–11–58.

d. Any postdispositional motion arising out of a deprivation case is filed excluding motions for contempt.

e. A deprivation case is received from another juvenile court. OCGA §§ 15–11–29, 15–11–30.5.

(4) The following occurrences will result in the opening of a termination of parental rights case:

a. A petition for termination of parental rights is filed. OCGA § 15–11–94.

b. A petition to modify/vacate a previous order arising out of a termination of parental rights case is filed. OCGA § 15–11–40.

c. Annual review by the court to determine what efforts have been made to assure the child's adoption. OCGA § 15–11–103 (d).

d. Any postdispositional motion arising out of a termination of parental rights case is filed excluding motions for contempt.

(5) The following occurrences will result in the opening of a special proceedings case:

a. An application to marry is filed. OCGA § 15–11–28 (a) (2) (A).

b. An application to enlist in the military is filed. OCGA § 15–11–28 (a) (2) (A).

c. An application to seal a child's record is filed or on court's own motion. OCGA § 15–11–79.2.

d. An application to unseal a child's previously sealed record is filed. OCGA § 15–11–79.2.

e. A petition for waiver of the parental notification requirement for an abortion is filed. OCGA § 15–11–112.

f. The court orders a child committed to a mental health facility. OCGA § 15–11–149.

g. A petition for access to law enforcement records is filed. OCGA § 15–11–79.

h. An application for the appointment of a guardian is filed.

i. Any postdispositional motion for contempt order is filed. Predispositional contempt actions do not constitute a new case. OCGA § 15–11–5.

j. An application for protective order is filed or on court's own motion. OCGA § 15–11–11.

k. A petition to modify/vacate a previous order is filed. OCGA § 15–11–40.

l. A case is transferred to juvenile court pursuant to § 15–11–28 (c) for determination or investigation of custody or support.

m. A petition for return of personal property is filed.

n. A request for research is filed.

o. A petition for legitimation is filed.

p. A legitimation petition is transferred to the juvenile court by order of the superior court.

q. A petition to proceed against a parent or guardian pursuant to OCGA § 20–2–766.1 is filed by a local school board. OCGA § 15–11–28 (a) (2) (E).

r. A request for dissolution of a temporary guardianship is received upon transfer from a probate court. OCGA § 29–4–4.1.

(6) The following occurrences result in the opening of a traffic case:

a. A uniform traffic citation is issued or a complaint alleging a traffic violation is filed. OCGA § 15–11–73.

b. A petition to modify/vacate a previous order arising out of a traffic case is filed. OCGA § 15–11–40.

C. Examples

(1) A charge of burglary would be entered as:

(x) delinquency (x) felony

(2) A truancy charge would be entered as:

(x) unruly

(3) If the complaint is "violation of probation," the type of case is the same as that of the original offense. For example, if a child was placed on probation for truancy, an unruly offense, the violation of probation would also be classified as an "unruly" offense. If a child was placed on probation for criminal trespass, a misdemeanor, the violation of probation would be classified as delinquent—misdemeanor.

10. Referral Source. Enter the referral source for the complaint, such as Atlanta PD, DFCS, Parent, Court, etc. This information is also contained on the complaint form under "complainant."

11. Child's Attorney Type. Indicate the child's attorney type by checking the appropriate box.

12. Date of Bond, Type, Amount. If the court sets bond for the child, indicate the date, type, and amount. For example, Date: 01/10/91 Type: Cash Amount: $150.00.

13. Date Complaint Received. Enter the date the complaint was physically received by the court.

14. Date Child Taken Into Custody. Enter the date that the child was physically taken into custody by law enforcement. If the child was not taken into custody, leave the space blank.

15. Date When and Location Where Child Was Detained or Placed. Enter the date the child was detained or placed, and place an "x" in the appropriate box: ( ) RYDC, ( ) Detention Home, ( ) Foster Care, ( ) Shelter Care, ( ) Other.

16. Detention Hearing Date. If a detention hearing was held, enter the date.

17. Released To. If the child was taken into custody, enter the date and to whom the child was released, regardless of whether or not there was a detention hearing.

Example: 04/11/91—Date child was taken into custody

Released to—Joan DeWitt
Relationship—Mother

18. Date Petition Filed. Enter the date the petition was filed in the clerk's office.

19. Date of Arraignment, If Held, Enter the date of the arraignment if applicable. If the court has a judicial process, other than a formal arraignment hearing, in which the child is informed of the charge(s) against him/her, his/her rights are explained, and a plea is entered, this can be considered an arraignment for practical purposes and the date of that proceeding should be entered.

Dismissed or Withdrawn Prior to Adjudication. If the case is dismissed or withdrawn prior to adjudication, enter the date.

20. Adjudicatory Hearing Date. Enter the date of the adjudicatory hearing.

21. Date of Disposition. Enter the date the court makes a final disposition. If the court orders that the child be placed on probation, enter the date the child is placed as the date of disposition. The case is legally closed since the court rendered a final disposition. In deprivation cases, do not hold the cases "open" until a termination order is given.

22. Offense Disposition. Check the appropriate box to indicate the offense disposition or court action for each offense.

A. If the case type is delinquency or unruly, the offense disposition will be one of the following:

(1) Adjudicated—Check this option if the court finds the child committed the offense.

(2) Amended/reduced—Check this option if the court amends or reduces the offense. For example, if the court reduces a charge of aggravated battery to battery, this option should be selected.

(3) Dismissed—Check this option if the complaint or petition is dismissed for any reason prior to trial or the court finds at trial that the child is not delinquent or unruly. Check this option if the case is diverted.

(4) Transferred to another juvenile court—Check this option if the court transfers the case to another juvenile court for trial.

(5) Transferred to superior court—Check this option if the court transfers the case to the superior court for trial.

(6) Informal adjustment—Check this box if the offense is disposed of informally and no petition is filed. If this option is selected, the "case disposition" will also be "informally adjusted."

B. If the case type is deprivation, the offense disposition will be one of the following:

(1) Adjudicated—Check this option if the court finds the child is deprived.

(2) Dismissed—Check this option if the court dismisses the case for any reason prior to trial or finds that the child is not deprived at trial.

(3) Order entered—Check this option if the court enters an order following a judicial review of a deprivation case or an appeal of a judicial citizen review panel report conducted pursuant to OCGA § 15–11–58.

C. If the case type is termination of parental rights, the offense disposition will be one of the following:

(1) Granted—Check this option if the court grants the petition for termination of parental rights.

(2) Denied—Check this option if the court denies the petition for termination of parental rights.

(3) Dismissed—Check this option if the petition for termination of parental rights is dismissed for any reason prior to trial. Example: petition is withdrawn by DFCS.

(4) Order Entered—Check this option if the court enters an order following an annual review by the court to determine what efforts have been made to assure the child's adoption pursuant to OCGA § 15–11–103.

D. If the case type is special proceedings, the offense disposition will be one of the following:

(1) Granted—Check this option if the court grants the petition.

(2) Denied—Check this option if the court denies the petition.

(3) Dismissed—Check this option if the court dismisses the petition for any reason prior to hearing the petition on the merits.

E. If the case type is traffic, leave the offense disposition blank.

23. Case Disposition. Mark the appropriate box to indicate the type of disposition for each offense.

Informal Adjustment. Check this box if the case is informally adjusted and no petition is filed. An informal adjustment may include the following: (1) counsel and advice for a period of up to 90 days under OCGA § 15–11–69 before a petition is filed; (2) warning; (3) reprimand; or (4) probation with no official court action.

Probation/Supervision. Check this box if probation or supervision with official court action is ordered by the judge. This box should also be marked if the judge orders restitution without ordering probation or supervision.

Probation—Detention under OCGA § 15–11–66 (b). Check this box if the court places the child on probation and further orders that the child be detained for up to 90 days in a YDC.

Detention under OCGA § 15–11–66 (b). Check this box if the court orders that the child be detained for up to 90 days in a YDC. Do not check this box if the court further orders that the child be placed on probation or be committed to DJJ.

Committed. Check this box if the child is committed to DJJ, regardless of whether the child is placed in a YDC or alternative placement with the exception that if the child is committed under the designated felony statute, check the box "Committed—Designated Felony."

Committed—Designated Felony. Check this box if the child is committed to DJJ as a designated felon. Enter the number of months of restrictive custody ordered by the court.

Committed—Detention under OCGA § 15–11–66 (b). Check this box if the child is committed to DJJ, and the court in addition orders the child detained for up to 90 days in a YDC.

Committed—DHR. Check this box if the child is committed to the Division of Mental Health as a mentally ill or mentally retarded child. This box should only be checked when the commitment is a final disposition of the case and not when the child is referred for evaluation.

Traffic Fine. Check this box if the court orders the child to pay a fine as the disposition for committing a traffic offense or a traffic related delinquency offense.

Dismissed. Check this box if the case was ultimately dismissed by the court. Examples: 1) If the court found the child delinquent but found that the child was not in need of rehabilitation and dismissed the case. 2) If the court held the disposition open for a period of time and eventually dismissed the case. 3) If the court diverted the case.

Custody Other. Check this box if custody is granted to a person or agency other than DFCS and indicate the name of the person or agency to whom custody is granted. If custody is granted to a person, specify his/her relationship to the child.

Custody to DFCS. Check this box if the court orders that the child be placed in the custody of the Department of Family and Children Services.

Transferred to other Juvenile Court. Check this box if final disposition is to transfer the case to another juvenile court. If the case is transferred to another juvenile court, enter the name of the court, e.g., Fulton County Juvenile Court.

Transferred to Superior Court. Check this box if the court orders that the case be transferred to the superior court.

Granted. Check this box in termination of parental rights or special proceedings cases only where the "offense disposition" was marked "granted" to indicate that the petition was granted by the court.

Denied. Check this box in termination of parental rights or special proceedings cases only where the "offense disposition" was marked "denied" to indicate that the petition was denied by the court.

Review Order Entered. Check this box if the court enters an order following a judicial review of a deprived case or an appeal of a judicial citizen review panel report pursuant to OCGA § 15–11–58 or following an annual review to determine what efforts have been made toward a child's adoption pursuant to OCGA § 15–11–103.

Appealed. Check whether or not the disposition was appealed and enter the date the notice of appeal was filed with the court.

Date of Remittitur. Enter date the remittitur is received if case is being appealed.

Findings. Enter the findings on appeal. Example: Affirmed in part.

Motions/Remarks. Enter pre-judgment or post-judgment motions or remarks which are pertinent to the case disposition.

Amended effective November 28, 1996; October 9, 1997; August 16, 2001; April 15, 2004.

*

INDEX TO UNIFORM RULES FOR THE JUVENILE COURTS

UNIFORM PROBATE COURT RULES

Effective July 1, 1985

Including Amendments Received Through November 1, 2006

Research Note

Use WESTLAW *to find cases citing a rule. In addition, use* WESTLAW *to search for specific terms or to update a rule; see the GA–RULES and GA–ORDERS Scope screens for further information.*

Amendments to these rules are published, as received, in the South Eastern Reporter 2d *and* Georgia Cases *advance sheets.*

Table of Rules

RULE 1. PREAMBLE

Pursuant to the inherent powers of the Court and Article VI, Section IX, Paragraph I of the Georgia Constitution of 1983, and in order to provide for the speedy, efficient and inexpensive resolution of disputes and prosecutions, these rules are promulgated. It is not the intention, nor shall it be the effect, of these rules to conflict with the Constitution or substantive law, either per se or in individual actions and these rules shall be so construed and in case of conflict shall yield to substantive law.

1.1. Repeal of local rules. All local rules of the probate courts except those relating to drawing of jurors by mechanical or electronic means pursuant to OCGA §§ 15–12–40(b) and 15–12–42(b) et seq. in effect as of the effective date of this Rule are hereby repealed.

1.2. Authority to enact rules which deviate from the Uniform Probate Court Rules.

(A) The term "local rules" will no longer be used in the context of the Uniforms Probate Court Rules.

(B) Each probate judge, from time to time, may propose to make and amend rules which deviate from the Uniform Probate Court Rules provided such proposals are not inconsistent with the Georgia Civil Practice Act, general laws, these Uniform Probate Court Rules, or any directive of the Supreme Court of Georgia. Any such proposals shall be filed with the clerk of the Supreme Court; proposals so submitted shall take effect 30 days after approval by the Supreme Court. It is the intendment of these rules that rules which deviate from the Uniform Probate Court Rules be restricted in scope.

(C) Notwithstanding the repeal of local rules pursuant to Rule 1.1 courts may continue to promulgate rules which relate only to internal procedure and do not affect the rights of any party substantially or materially, either to unreasonably delay or deny such rights. These rules, which will be designated "internal operating procedures," do not require the approval of the Supreme Court. "Internal operating procedures," as used in these Uniform Probate Court Rules, are defined as rules which relate to case management, administration, and operation of the court or govern programs which relate to case management, administration, and operations of the court.

(D) The above provisions notwithstanding, each probate court defined in and governed under OCGA §§ 15–9–120 et seq. may retain or adopt without specific Supreme Court approval a local rule relating to drawing of jurors by mechanical or electronic means pursuant to OCGA §§ 15–12–40(b) and 15–12–42(b) et seq. and an order establishing guidelines governing excuses from jury duty pursuant to OCGA § 15–12–10.

(E) Notwithstanding these uniform rules, a probate judge may adopt experimental rules applicable to pilot projects, upon approval of the Supreme Court, adequately advertised to the local bar, with copies to the State Bar of Georgia, not to exceed a period of one year, subject to extension for one additional year upon approval of the circuit judges and the Supreme Court. An the end of the second year, any such pilot projects will either be approved by the Supreme Court or will be allowed to sunset. Programs developed under the Alternative Dispute Resolutions Rules of the Supreme Court will be approved by the Georgia Commission on Dispute Resolution before attaining permanent status under these rules.

(F) Rules which are approved as deviations from the Uniform Probate Court Rules and internal operating procedures of courts shall be published by the probate court in which the rules are effective. Copies must be made available through the clerk of the probate court for such county where the rules are effective. Any amendments to deviations from the Uniform Probate Court Rules or to internal operating procedures must be published and made available through each probate court clerk within 15 days of the effective date of the amendment or change.

(G) Internal operating procedures effective in any court must be filed with the Supreme Court even though Supreme Court approval is not needed for these rules.

Amended June 5, 1987; amended effective July 1, 1988; July 1, 1994; June 7, 1990; December 2, 2004.

Publisher's Note

See Appendix A for Uniform Probate Court Rule amendments applicable to certain counties with a population of more than 96,000 persons.

RULE 2. DEFINITIONS

2.1 Attorney. The word "attorney" as used in these rules refers to any person who is an active member in good standing of the State Bar of Georgia, and to any person who is permitted, as provided below in Rule 4.4, to represent a party in an action pending in a probate court of the State of Georgia, and to any person representing himself pro se in an action pending in a probate court of this state. The word "attorney" is synonymous with "counsel" in these rules.

2.2 Judge. The word "judge" as used in these rules refers to any of the several active judges of the probate courts of Georgia, and to any other person who may at the time be performing a judicial function of the probate court of this state in accordance with law.

2.3 Clerk. The word "clerk" as used in these rules refers to any clerk or deputy clerk of any of the several probate courts in this state.

2.4 Plaintiff/Defendant/Petition. The term "plaintiff" includes petitioner, applicant or propounder, and the term "defendant" includes caveator or respondent. "Petition" includes any application to the court for an order.

2.5 Non-sexist Pronouns. for the sake of brevity only, the pronoun "he" shall include "she" and vice versa, unless the context clearly indicates otherwise; the pronoun "her" shall include "him" and vice versa, unless the context clearly indicates otherwise.

Publisher's Note

See Appendix A for Uniform Probate Court Rule amendments applicable to certain counties with a population of more than 96,000 persons.

RULE 3. APPOINTMENT OF ATTORNEY TO ACT IN JUDGE'S ABSENCE

Whenever a judge of the probate court appoints an attorney to act in his stead pursuant to OCGA § 15–9–13(a), said appointment shall be by written order which shall specify the cases or time period covered and shall be recorded in the minutes of the court. Whenever the attorney so appointed signs an order while acting as judge, there shall appear following such signature: "Exercising the jurisdiction of the probate court pursuant to order of Judge ______, dated ______, as provided by OCGA § 15–9–13(a)." It shall not be necessary for the probate judge to confirm any such order when the judge resumes his jurisdiction. However, if the appointment was for an indefinite period, the judge shall enter and record an order terminating the appointment when he resumes jurisdiction. The foregoing is not intended to imply that § 15–9–13(a) is the only allowable method of providing a substitute, but only to establish a uniform procedure when § 15–9–13(a) is used.

Publisher's Note

See Appendix A for Uniform Probate Court Rule amendments applicable to certain counties with a population of more than 96,000 persons.

RULE 4. ATTORNEYS—APPEARANCE, WITHDRAWAL AND DUTIES

4.1 Prohibition on Ex Parte Communications. Except as authorized by law or by rule, judges shall neither initiate nor consider ex parte communications by interested parties or their attorneys concerning a pending or impending proceeding.

4.2 Entry of Appearance. No attorney shall appear in that capacity before a probate court until he has entered an appearance by filing a signed entry of appearance form or by filing a signed pleading in a pending action. An entry of appearance shall state (1) the style and number; (2) the identity of the party for whom the appearance is made; and, (3) the name and current office address and telephone number of the attorney. The filing of any pleading, unless otherwise specified by the court, shall constitute an appearance by the person(s) signing such pleading.

Any attorney who has been admitted to practice in this state but who fails to maintain active membership in good standing in the State Bar of Georgia and who makes or files any appearance or pleading in a probate court of this state while not in good standing shall be subject to the contempt powers of the court.

4.3 Withdrawal. An attorney appearing of record in any action pending in any probate court, who wishes to withdraw as counsel for any party therein, shall submit a written request to the judge of said court for an order of court permitting such withdrawal. Such request shall state that the attorney has given due written notice to his client respecting such intention to withdraw 10 days (or such lesser time as the court may permit in any specific instance) prior to submitting the request to the court or that such withdrawal is with the client's consent. Such request will be granted unless in the judge's discretion to do so would delay the trial of the action or otherwise interrupt the orderly operation of the court or be manifestly unfair to the client. The attorney requesting an order permitting withdrawal shall give notice to opposing counsel and shall file with the clerk in each such action and serve upon his client, personally or at his last known address, a notice which shall contain at least the following information:

(A) That the attorney wishes to withdraw;

(B) That the court retains jurisdiction of the action;

(C) That the client has the burden of keeping the court informed respecting where notices, pleadings or other papers may be served;

(D) That the client has the obligation to prepare for trial or hire other counsel to prepare for trial when the trial date has been set;

(E) That if the client fails or refuses to meet these burdens, the client may suffer adverse consequences;

(F) The dates of any scheduled proceedings, including trial, and that holding of such proceedings will not be affected by the withdrawal of counsel;

(G) That service of notices may be made upon the client at his last known address; and,

(H) Unless the withdrawal is with the client's consent, the client's right to object within 10 days of the date of the notice.

The attorney seeking to withdraw shall prepare a written notification certificate stating that the above notification requirements have been met, the manner by which such notification was given to the client and the client's last known address and telephone number. The notification certificate shall be filed with the court and a copy mailed to the client and all other parties. The client shall have 10 days prior to entry of an order permitting withdrawal or such lesser time as the court may permit within which to file objections to the withdrawal. After the entry of an order permitting withdrawal, the client shall be notified by the withdrawing attorney of the effective date of the withdrawal; thereafter all notices or other papers may be served on the party directly by mail at the last known address of the party until new counsel enters an appearance.

4.4 Special Admission of Attorneys From Other States.

(A) When permitted by law or rules, any attorney admitted to practice in the courts of record of another state who desires to be specially admitted to practice in a specific action pending in a probate court of Georgia shall make application for such special admission to the judge of the probate court in which the action is pending or is to be brought. Such application shall contain the following information:

(1) Name, current address and telephone number of the attorney making such application;

(2) A listing of the state or states in which such attorney is duly licensed to practice;

(3) That he has associated in the action an attorney who is a resident of Georgia, and who is an active member in good standing of the State Bar of Georgia;

(4) The name and current office address and telephone number maintained by the associated attorney.

The requirements of (3) and (4) above may be waived in writing by the judge.

(B) Service may be had upon the associated attorney in all matters connected with said action with the same effect as though personally made upon the out of state attorney specially admitted to practice in the action. The out of state attorney so admitted to practice in such action shall be subject to the orders of the court of this state and amenable to disciplinary action as though he were regularly admitted to practice in the State of Georgia.

4.5 Entries of Appearance and Withdrawals by Members or Employees of Law Firms or Professional Corporations. The entry of an appearance or request for withdrawal by an attorney who is a member or an employee of a law firm or professional corporation shall relieve the other members or employees of the same law firm or professional corporation from the necessity of filing additional entries of appearance or requests for withdrawal in the same action.

4.6 To Notify of Representation. In any matter pending in a probate court, promptly upon agreeing to represent any client, the new attorney shall notify the appropriate court and the opposing attorney(s) in writing of the fact of such representation, the name of the client, the name and number of the action, the attorney's firm name, office address and telephone number.

Each such attorney shall notify the court and the opposing attorney(s) in writing immediately upon any change of representation, name, address or telephone number.

4.7 To Notify of Settlements and Dismissals. Immediately upon the settlement or dismissal of any civil action the involved attorneys shall notify the judge in writing of such event.

4.8 To Attend and Remain. Subject to the provisions of Rule 15, attorneys having matters on calendars, or who are otherwise directed to do so, unless excused by the court, are required to be in court at the call of the matter and to remain until otherwise directed by the court. Should the judge excuse counsel from the courtroom before the matter is concluded such attorney(s) shall return as directed. Failure of any attorney in this respect shall subject him to the contempt powers of the court.

4.9 Binding Authority. An attorney of record has apparent authority to enter into agreements on behalf of his client(s). Oral agreements, if established, are enforceable.

Publisher's Note

See Appendix A for Uniform Probate Court Rule amendments applicable to certain counties with a population of more than 96,000 persons.

RULE 5. DISCOVERY

In order for a party to utilize the court's compulsory process to compel discovery, any desired discovery procedures must first be commenced promptly, pursued diligently and completed without unnecessary delay and within 2 months after the filing of the answer unless for cause shown the time has been extended or shortened by court order.

Effective January 1, 1986.

Publisher's Note

See Appendix A for Uniform Probate Court Rule amendments applicable to certain counties with a population of more than 96,000 persons.

RULE 6. MOTIONS

6.1 Filing. Every motion made prior to trial, except those consented to by all parties, when filed shall include or be accompanied by citations of supporting authorities and, where allegations of unstipulated fact are relied upon, supporting affidavits, or citations to evidentiary materials of record. The clerk shall promptly upon filing furnish a copy provided by the attorney of such motions and related materials to the judge.

6.2 Reply. Unless otherwise ordered by the judge, each party opposing a motion shall serve and file a response, reply memorandum, affidavits, or other responsive material not later than 30 days after service of the motion.

6.3 Hearing. Unless otherwise ordered by the court all motions in civil actions shall be decided by the court without oral hearing, except motions for new trial and motions for summary judgment. Oral argument on any motion shall be permitted upon written request.

6.4 Failure to Make Discovery and Motion to Compel Discovery.

(A) Motions to compel discovery in accordance with OCGA § 9–11–37 shall:

(1) Quote verbatim or attach a copy as an exhibit of each interrogatory, request for admission, or request for production to which objection is taken;

(2) Include the specific objection or response said to be insufficient;

(3) Include the grounds assigned for the objection (if not apparent from the objection); and,

(4) Include the reasons assigned as supporting the motion. Such objections and grounds shall be addressed to the specific interrogatory, request for admission, or request for production and may not be made generally.

(B) Prior to filing a motion to compel discovery, counsel for the moving party shall confer with counsel for the opposing party in a good faith effort to resolve the matters involved. At the time of filing the motion, counsel shall also file a statement certifying that such conference has occurred and that the effort to resolve by agreement the issues raised failed. If certain of the issues have been resolved by agreement, the statement shall specify the issues remaining unresolved.

6.5 Motions for Summary Judgment. Upon any motion for summary judgment pursuant to the Georgia Civil Practice Act, there shall be annexed to the notice of motion a separate, short and concise statement of each theory of recovery and of each of the material facts as to which the moving party contends there is no genuine issue to be tried. The response shall include a separate, short and concise statement of each of the material facts as to which it is contended there exists a genuine issue to be tried.

6.6 Time for Filing Summary Judgment Motions. Motions for summary judgment shall be filed sufficiently early so as not to delay the trial. No trial shall be continued by reason of the delayed filing of a motion for summary judgment.

6.7 Motions in Emergencies. Upon written notice and good cause shown, the judge may shorten or waive the time requirement applicable to emergency motions, except motions for summary judgment, or grant an immediate hearing on any matter requiring such expedited procedure. The motion shall set forth in detail the necessity for such expedited procedure.

Publisher's Note

See Appendix A for Uniform Probate Court Rule amendments applicable to certain counties with a population of more than 96,000 persons.

RULE 7. PRE–TRIAL CONFERENCES

7.1 Procedures. The judge may set pre-trial conferences sua sponte or upon motion. In scheduling actions for pre-trial conferences the court shall give consideration to the nature of the action, its complexity and the reasonable time requirements for preparation for pre-trial. In the event a pre-trial conference is ordered, the following shall apply.

A calendar will be published or a written order issued specifying the time and place for the pre-trial conference. The court will consider the issues stated in Rule 16 of the Civil Practice Act (OCGA § 9–11–16) among others. Subject to the provisions of Rule 15, the pre-trial hearing shall be attended by the attorneys who will actually try the action; with the consent of the court, another attorney of record in the action may attend if authorized to define the issues and enter into stipulations. At the commencement of the pre-trial conference, or prior thereto upon written order of the court, counsel for each party shall present to the court a written proposed pre-trial order in substantially the form required by the rules. Failure of counsel to appear at the pre-trial conference without legal excuse or to present a proposed pre-trial order shall authorize the court to remove the action from any trial calendar, enter such pre-trial order as the court shall deem appropriate, or impose any other appropriate sanction, except dismissal of the action with prejudice.

7.2 Pre-trial Order. At the pre-trial conference, or prior to that day if specified in the pre-trial calendar, counsel for each party shall have prepared and shall file with the court a proposed pre-trial order in substantially the following form:

IN THE PROBATE COURT OF ______ COUNTY
STATE OF GEORGIA

(STYLE OF CASE) ESTATE NO. ________

PRE–TRIAL ORDER

The following constitutes a Pre-Trial Order entered in the above-styled case after conference with counsel for the parties:

(1) The name, address and phone number of the attorneys who will conduct the trial are as follows:

Plaintiff ______________________________

Defendant ______________________________

Other ______________________________

(2) The estimated time required for trial is ____

(3) There are no motions or other matters pending for consideration by the court except as follows: ___

(4) a. All discovery has been completed, unless otherwise noted, and the court will not consider any further motions to compel discovery except for good cause shown. The parties, however, shall be permitted to take depositions of any person(s) for the preservation of evidence for use at trial.

b. Unless otherwise noted, the names of the parties as shown in the caption to this order are correct and complete and there is no question by any party as to the misjoinder or nonjoinder of any parties.

(5) The following is the Plaintiff's brief and succinct outline of the case and contentions: (USE SPACE AS NEEDED) ______________________________

(6) The following is the Defendant's brief and succinct outline of the case and contentions: (USE SPACE AS NEEDED) ______________________________

(7) The issues for determination by the court are as follows: ______________________________

(8) The following facts are stipulated: ________

(9) The following is a list of all documentary and physical evidence that will be tendered at the trial by the Plaintiff or Defendant. Unless noted, the parties have stipulated as to the authenticity of the documents listed and the exhibits listed may be admitted without further proof of authenticity. All exhibits shall be marked by counsel prior to trial so as not to delay the trial.

a. By the Plaintiff: ______________________

b. By the Defendant: ______________________

(10) Special authorities relied upon by Plaintiff relating to peculiar evidentiary or other legal questions are as follows: ______________________

(11) Special authorities relied upon by Defendant relating to peculiar evidentiary or other legal questions are as follows: ______________________

(12) The testimony of the following persons may be introduced by depositions: ______________________

Any objection to the depositions or questions or arguments in the depositions shall be called to the attention of the court prior to trial.

(13) The following are lists of witnesses the

a. Plaintiff *will* have present at trial: ______

b. Plaintiff *may* have present at trial: ______

c. Defendant *will* have present at trial: ______

d. Defendant *may* have present at trial: ______

Opposing counsel may rely on representation by the designated party that he *will* have a witness present unless notice to the contrary is given in sufficient time prior to trial to allow the other party to subpoena the witness or obtain his testimony by other means.

(14) a. The possibilities of settling the case are: ______________________

b. The parties do/do not want the case reported. If they do, ______ will arrange for the reporter.

c. The cost of take-down will be paid by: ______

d. Other matters:

Submitted by:

____

____

It is hereby ordered that the foregoing, including the attachments thereto, constitutes the PRE-TRIAL ORDER in the above case and supersedes the pleadings which may not be further amended except by order of the court to prevent manifest injustice.

This ______ day of ______, 19__.

____
Judge, Probate Court
______ County

Publisher's Note

See Appendix A for Uniform Probate Court Rule amendments applicable to certain counties with a population of more than 96,000 persons.

RULE 8. TELEPHONE AND VIDEO CONFERENCING

8.1 Telephone Conferencing. The trial court on its own motion or upon the request of any party may in its discretion conduct pre-trial or post-trial proceedings in civil actions by telephone conference with attorneys for all affected parties. The trial judge may specify:

(A) The time and the person who will initiate the conference;

(B) The party which is to incur the initial expense of the conference call, or the apportionment of such costs among the parties, while retaining the discretion to make an adjustment of such costs upon final resolution of the case by taxing same as part of the costs; and

(C) Any other matter or requirement necessary to accomplish or facilitate the telephone conference.

8.2 Video-Conferencing.

(A) The following matters may be conducted by video-conference:

1. Determination of indigence and appointment of counsel;
2. Hearings on appearance and appeal bonds;
3. Initial appearance hearings;
4. Probable cause hearings;
5. Applications for arrest warrants;
6. Applications for search warrants;
7. Arraignment or waiver of arraignment;
8. Pretrial diversion and post-sentencing compliance hearings;
9. Entry of pleas in criminal cases;
10. Impositions of sentences upon pleas of guilty or *nolo contendere*;
11. Probation revocation hearings in felony cases in which the probationer admits the violation and in all misdemeanor cases;
12. Post-sentencing proceedings in criminal cases;
13. Acceptance of special pleas of insanity (incompetency to stand trial);

14. Situations involving inmates with highly sensitive medical problems or who pose a high security risk; and

15. Testimony of youthful witnesses;

16. *Ex-parte* applications for Temporary Protective Orders under the Family Violence Act and the Stalking Statute;

17. Appearances of interpreters;

18. All mental health, alcohol and drug hearings held by the Probate Court pursuant to Title 37 of the Official Code of Georgia provided that the confidentiality prescribed by Title 37 be preserved.

Notwithstanding any other provisions of this rule, a judge may order a defendant's personal appearance in court for any hearing.

(B) Confidential Attorney–Client Communication. Provision shall be made to preserve the confidentiality of attorney-client communications and privilege in accordance with Georgia law. In all criminal proceedings, the defendant and defense counsel shall be provided with a private means of communications when in different locations.

(C) Witnesses. In any pending matter, a witness may testify via video conference. Any party desiring to call a witness by video conference shall file a notice of intention to present testimony by video conference at least thirty (30) days prior to the date scheduled for such testimony. Any other party may file an objection to the testimony of a witness by video conference within ten (10) days of the filing of the notice of intention. In civil matters, the discretion to allow testimony via video conference shall rest with the trial judge. In any criminal matter, a timely objection shall be sustained; however, such objection shall act as a motion for continuance and a waiver of any speedy trial demand.

(D) Recording of Hearings. A record of any proceedings conducted by video conference shall be made in the same manner as all such similar proceedings not conducted by video conference. However, upon the consent of all parties, that portion of the proceedings conducted by video conference may be recorded by an audio–visual recording system and such recording shall be part of the record of the case and transmitted to courts of appeal as if part of a transcript.

(E) Technical Standards. Any video–conferencing system utilized under this rule must conform to the following minimum requirements:

1. All participants must be able to see, hear, and communicate with each other simultaneously;

2. All participants must be able to see, hear, and otherwise observe any physical evidence or exhibits presented during the proceeding, either by video, facsimile, or other method;

3. Video quality must be adequate to allow participants to observe each other's demeanor and nonverbal communications; and

4. The location from which the trial judge is presiding shall be accessible to the public to the same extent as such proceeding would if not conducted by video conference. The court shall accommodate any request by interested parties to observe the entire proceeding.

Adopted effective July 15, 2004.

Publisher's Note

See Appendix A for Uniform Probate Court Rule amendments applicable to certain counties with a population of more than 96,000 persons.

RULE 9. HEARINGS

9.1 Setting Contested Hearings. Hearings on contested matters shall be set by the court upon the request of any interested party, at the next available hearing date, and notice shall be given by first class mail at least ten (10) days in advance to all interested parties. An interested party represented by an attorney shall be notified by giving notice to his attorney.

9.2 Continuances. An attorney requesting a continuance shall contact the other attorney to determine whether or not the other attorney objects. If the other attorney does not object, then the attorney requesting the continuance shall make his request known to the court, and the request will normally be granted. The request should be made immediately by telephone, and be followed up with a letter stating that the other party has consented to the continuance, with a copy to the other attorney. If the adverse party does not consent to the continuance, then a proper motion for continuance must be filed, and will be scheduled by the court in accordance with law.

9.3 Appeals—Probate Court Transcript Not Transmitted. The record which is transmitted to the superior court in connection with any de novo appeal from the probate court shall include certified copies of all documents which will be recorded in the official record books of the probate court. In addition, a certified copy of any alleged will which is denied probate will be transmitted even though it will not be recorded on the probate court records. No exhibits, transcript of hearing, depositions, interrogatories, notices to produce documents, or any other materials which reflect the evidence presented in the probate court shall be transmitted to the superior court in connection with a de novo appeal. Instead, any such materials in the possession of the court (other than documents required by law to be kept on file with the probate court) shall be returned to the attorney who presented them, if the probate court is requested to do so or does so on its own motion, and the attorney may then present them at the superior court hearing if he desires.

Publisher's Note

See Appendix A for Uniform Probate Court Rule amendments applicable to certain counties with a population of more than 96,000 persons.

RULE 10. EXCUSALS FROM COURTROOM

During the course of a proceeding no one except the judge may excuse from the courtroom a party, a witness (including one who has testified), or counsel.

Publisher's Note

See Appendix A for Uniform Probate Court Rule amendments applicable to certain counties with a population of more than 96,000 persons.

RULE 11. ARGUMENT

11.1 Number of Arguments. Not more than two attorneys shall be permitted to argue any case for any party except by leave of court; in no event shall more than one attorney for each party be heard in concluding argument.

11.2 Conclusion. Where the burden of proof rests with the plaintiff, the plaintiff is entitled to the opening and concluding arguments except that if the defendant introduces no evidence or admits a prima facie case, he shall be entitled to open and conclude.

Publisher's Note

See Appendix A for Uniform Probate Court Rule amendments applicable to certain counties with a population of more than 96,000 persons.

RULE 12. DISMISSAL

On its own motion or upon motion of the opposite party, the court may dismiss without prejudice any action, or where appropriate, any pleading filed on behalf of any party upon the failure to properly respond to the call of the action for trial or other proceeding. The court may adjudge any attorney in contempt for failure to appear without legal excuse upon the call of any proceeding.

Publisher's Note

See Appendix A for Uniform Probate Court Rule amendments applicable to certain counties with a population of more than 96,000 persons.

RULE 13. DEFAULT JUDGMENTS

Default judgments may be entered, or defaults may be opened, by the court pursuant to O.C.G.A. § 15–9–47 as set forth below:

(A) If required by the court, the party seeking entry of a default judgment in any action shall certify to the court the date and type of service effected as shown by court records and that there has been no defensive pleading from any party against whom the default judgment is sought. When required, any such certificate shall be in writing and must be attached to the proposed default judgment when presented to the judge for signature.

(B) Any party seeking to open a default must make the showing required by O.C.G.A. § 15–9–47 in writing under oath. The court may then enter an order, without notice or hearing, granting or denying the request to open the default.

Amended effective August 15, 1991; June 18, 1992.

Publisher's Note

See Appendix A for Uniform Probate Court Rule amendments applicable to certain counties with a population of more than 96,000 persons.

RULE 14. LEAVES OF ABSENCE

Application for leaves of absence must be in writing and shall be served upon opposing counsel at least 5 days (if such service is made personally) prior to submission to the judge of the court in which an action pends; such service shall be accomplished at least 10 days prior to submission to such judge if service upon opposing counsel is other than personal. This time period may be waived if opposing counsel consents in writing to the application. This procedure permits opposing counsel to object or to consent to the grant of the application, but the application is addressed to the discretion of the court. Such application for leave of absence shall contain:

(A) A list of the actions to be protected, which shall include the file or estate number;

(B) The reason for the requested leave of absence; and

(C) The duration of the requested leave of absence.

A leave when granted shall relieve any attorney from all trials, hearings, depositions and other legal proceedings in that matter.

Publisher's Note

See Appendix A for Uniform Probate Court Rule amendments applicable to certain counties with a population of more than 96,000 persons.

RULE 15. CONFLICTS—STATE AND FEDERAL COURTS

15.1 Method of Resolution.

(A) An attorney shall not be deemed to have a conflict unless: (1) he is lead counsel in two or more of the actions affected; and, (2) he certifies that the matters cannot be adequately handled, and the client's interest adequately protected, by other counsel for the party in the action or by other attorneys in lead counsel's firm.

(B) When an attorney is scheduled to appear in two or more courts (trial or appellate; state or federal), at the same time and cannot arrange for other counsel to represent adequately his client's interests, the attorney shall give prompt written notice of the conflict to opposing counsel, to the clerk of each court and to the judge before whom each action is set for hearing. Attorneys confronted by such conflicts are expected to exercise diligence in giving such notice. The judges before whom such actions pend or the clerks of the respective courts shall confer, undertaking to resolve the conflict by agreement. Absent agreement, conflicts shall be promptly resolved by the judges or the clerk of each affected court in accordance with the following order of priorities:

(1) Criminal (felony) actions shall prevail over civil actions;

(2) Jury trials shall prevail over non-jury matters including trials and administrative proceedings;

(3) Trials shall prevail over appellate arguments, hearings and conferences;

(4) The action which was first filed shall take precedence.

15.2 Notice of Resolution. The judges or clerks of the courts in which such conflicts exist shall give prompt written notice to all counsel of the manner in which the conflicts have been resolved.

Publisher's Note

See Appendix A for Uniform Probate Court Rule amendments applicable to certain counties with a population of more than 96,000 persons.

RULE 16. TRANSFER/CHANGE OF VENUE

16.1 Procedure.

(A) Subject to the provisions of OCGA § 9–11–12 and section (C) of this rule, a timely motion in any pending action or proceeding (1) by any party, that jurisdiction is lacking or that venue is improper, or (2) by the court, sua sponte, that subject matter jurisdiction is lacking, shall be treated as a motion to transfer the action to another court, whether in the same or another county of this state.

(B) The moving party shall specify the court(s) having jurisdiction and in which venue properly would lie.

(C) If the basis of the motion is that a party necessary to the court's jurisdiction has been dismissed during or at the conclusion of the trial, the motion shall be made immediately and orally; any opposition shall be made orally. Should the motion to transfer be granted as to the remaining parties, the claim against the party dismissed shall be severed, so that the order of dismissal will be final for purposes of appeal.

(D) Unless otherwise ordered by the court, notice of a written motion to transfer shall be served upon all parties, including any who failed to file pleadings in the matter, at least 10 days before the motion is heard. A party opposing a written motion to transfer shall notify the court and all other parties in writing within 10 days after service upon that party of the motion to transfer; such notice shall designate the basis upon which it is claimed that the court in which the action pends has jurisdiction and upon which venue is claimed to be proper.

(E) When a motion to transfer is filed, the court may stay all other proceedings in the pending action until determination of the motion.

(F) No action or proceeding may be transferred except upon written order of the court in which the action pends (transferor court), reasonable notice of which shall be given to all parties. This order shall specify the court to which the matter is to be transferred (transferee court) and shall state that unless plaintiff pays all accrued court costs within 20 days of mailing or delivery of the cost bill to plaintiff, the action shall automatically stand dismissed without prejudice.

The court ruling upon a motion to transfer may award reasonable attorney fees to the prevailing party; if the court grants the motion, transfer costs of $50 shall be taxed, unless the court expressly determines otherwise, in its discretion.

(G) When an order transferring an action is filed with the clerk of the court entering such order, the clerk shall promptly compute the court costs, including the costs incident to preparing and transferring the record as provided in subparagraph (H) of this rule, and shall notify counsel for plaintiff (or, the plaintiff, if he has no counsel of record) in writing of the amount of the court costs. Plaintiff shall pay the costs within 20 days of mailing or delivery of the cost bill; if costs are not paid within that time, the action shall automatically stand dismissed, without prejudice.

(H) Upon timely payment of costs, the clerk of the transferor court shall make and retain copies of (1) the petition or initial pleading, (2) the motion to transfer if in writing, and (3) the order of transfer.

The originals of all pleadings, orders, depositions and other papers on file shall be indexed and certified by the clerk of the transferor court and transmitted, with the transfer cost (if applicable), to the clerk of the transferee court in the manner provided by law for transmittal of records to appellate courts.

(I) Upon receipt of the items specified in subparagraph (H) of this rule, the clerk of the transferee court shall assign the action an appropriate number and notify all parties and their respective counsel of record thereof. The action thereafter shall continue in the transferee court as though initially commenced there; all items specified in subparagraph (H) of this rule shall be deemed amended accordingly. It shall not be necessary that service of process be perfected a second time upon parties defendant, except that any publication required to be made in a newspaper in the proper venue shall be republished. Any interlocutory or other order theretofore entered in the action, upon the motion of any party, shall be reviewed, and thereafter reissued or vacated by the court to which the action was transferred.

Publisher's Note

See Appendix A for Uniform Probate Court Rule amendments applicable to certain counties with a population of more than 96,000 persons.

RULE 17. LIMITATION OF ACCESS TO COURT FILES

All court records are public and are to be available for public inspection unless public access is limited by law or by the procedure set forth below.

17.1 Motions and Orders. Upon motion by any party to any action, after hearing, the court may limit access to court files respecting that action. The order of limitation shall specify the part of the file to which access is limited, the nature and duration of the limitation, and the reason for limitation.

17.2 Finding of Harm. An order limiting access shall not be granted except upon a finding that the harm otherwise resulting to the privacy of a person in interest clearly outweighs the public interest.

17.3 Ex Parte Orders. Under compelling circumstances, a motion for temporary limitation of access, not to exceed 30 days, may be granted, ex parte, upon motion accompanied by supporting affidavit.

17.4 Review. A copy of an order limiting access shall be transmitted to and subject to review by the Supreme Court.

17.5 Amendments. Upon notice to all parties of record and after hearing, an order limiting access may be reviewed and amended by the court entering such order or by the Supreme Court at any time on its own motion or upon the motion of any person for good cause.

Publisher's Note

See Appendix A for Uniform Probate Court Rule amendments applicable to certain counties with a population of more than 96,000 persons.

RULE 18. ELECTRONIC AND PHOTOGRAPHIC NEWS COVERAGE OF JUDICIAL PROCEEDINGS

Unless otherwise provided by rule of the Supreme Court or otherwise ordered by the judge after appropriate hearing (conducted after notice to all parties and counsel of record) and findings, representatives of the print and electronic public media may be present at and unobtrusively make written notes and sketches pertaining to any judicial proceedings in the probate courts. However, due to the distractive nature of electronic or photographic equipment, representatives of the public media utilizing such equipment are subject to the following restrictions and conditions:

(A) Persons desiring to broadcast/record/photograph official court proceedings must file a timely written request (form attached as Exhibit "A") with the judge involved prior to the hearing or trial, specifying the particular case or proceedings for which such coverage is intended; the type equipment to be used in the courtroom; the trial, hearing or proceeding to be covered; and the person responsible for installation and operation of such equipment.

(B) Approval of the judge to broadcast/record/photograph a proceeding, if granted, shall be granted without partiality or preference to any person, news agency, or type of electronic or photographic coverage, who agrees to abide by and conform to these rules, up to the capacity of the space designated therefor in the courtroom. Violation of these rules will be grounds for a reporter/technician to be removed or excluded from the courtroom and held in contempt.

(C) The judge, in his discretion, may require pooled coverage which would allow only one still photographer, one television camera and attendant, and one radio or tape recorder outlet and attendant. Photographers, electronic reporters and technicians shall be expected to arrange among themselves pooled coverage if so directed by the judge and to present the judge with a schedule and description of the pooled coverage. If the covering persons cannot agree on such a schedule or arrangement, the judge may, in his discretion, designate the schedule and arrangements for pooled coverage.

(D) The positioning and removal of cameras and electronic devices shall be done quietly and, if possible, before or after the court session or during recesses; in no event shall such disturb the proceedings of the court. In every such case, equipment should be in place and ready to operate before the time court is scheduled to be called to order.

(E) Overhead lights in the courtroom shall be switched on and off only by court personnel. No other lights, flashbulbs, flashes or sudden light changes may be used unless the judge approves beforehand.

(F) No adjustment of central audio system shall be made except by persons authorized by the judge. Audio recordings of the court proceedings will be from one source, normally by connection to the court's central audio system. Upon prior approval of the court, other microphones may be added in an unobtrusive manner to the court's public address system.

(G) All television cameras, still cameras and tape recorders shall be assigned to a specific portion of the public area of the courtroom or specially designed access areas, and such equipment will not be permitted to be removed or relocated during the court proceedings.

(H) Still cameras, movie and television cameras and broadcasting and recording devices must operate quietly. If any equipment is determined by the judge to be of such noise as to be distractive to the court proceedings, then such equipment can be excluded from the courtroom by the judge.

(I) Photographs and televising of the public and the courtroom are allowed, if done without disruption to the court proceedings.

(J) Reporters, photographers, and technicians must have and produce upon request of court officials credentials identifying them and the media company for which they work.

(K) Court proceedings shall not be interrupted by a reporter or technician with a technical or an equipment problem.

(L) Reporters, photographers, and technicians should do everything possible to avoid attracting attention to themselves. Reporters, photographers, and technicians will be accorded full right of access to court proceedings for obtaining public information within the requirements of due process of law, so long as it is done without detracting from the dignity and decorum of the court.

(M) Other than as permitted by these rules and guidelines, there will be no photographing, radio or television broadcasting, including video taping pertaining to any judicial proceedings on the courthouse floor where the trial, hearing or proceeding is being held or any other courthouse floor whereon is located a probate court courtroom, whether or not the court is actually in session.

(N) No interviews pertaining to a particular judicial proceeding will be conducted in the courtroom except with the permission of the judge.

(O) All media plans heretofore approved by the Supreme Court for probate courts are hereby repealed.

Publisher's Note

See Appendix A for Uniform Probate Court Rule amendments applicable to certain counties with a population of more than 96,000 persons.

EXHIBIT A

IN THE PROBATE COURT OF ______ COUNTY
STATE OF GEORGIA

(STYLE OF CASE) ESTATE OR FILE NO. ______

<u>REQUEST TO INSTALL RECORDING AND/OR PHOTOGRAPHING EQUIPMENT PURSUANT TO RULES AND GUIDELINES FOR ELECTRONIC AND PHOTOGRAPHIC NEWS COVERAGE OF JUDICIAL PROCEEDINGS.</u>

Pursuant to Rule 18 of the Uniform Probate Court Rules, the undersigned hereby requests permission to install equipment in courtroom ______ in order to record, photograph or televise all or portions of the proceedings in the above-captioned case.

Consistent with the provisions of the rules and guidelines, the undersigned desires to install the following described equipment: ______ in the following locations: ______. The proceedings that the undersigned desires to record, photograph or televise commence on <u>(date)</u>. Subject to direction from the court regarding possible pooled coverage, the undersigned wishes to install this equipment in the courtroom on <u>(date)</u>. The personnel who will be responsible for the installation and operation of this equipment during its use are: <u>(identify appropriate personnel)</u>.

The undersigned hereby certifies that the equipment to be installed and the locations and operation of such equipment will be in conformity with the rules and guidelines issued by the court.

This ______ day of ______, 19__.

______
(Individual Signature)

______
(Representing/Firm)

______
(Position)

______
(Address)

______
(Telephone Number)

<u>Approved:</u>

______
Judge, Probate Court

______ County

RULE 19. RECUSAL

19.1 Motions. All motions to recuse or disqualify a judge presiding in a particular case or proceeding shall be in writing, accompanied by an affidavit asserting the facts upon which the motion is founded, and timely filed. Filing and presentation to the judge shall be not later than 5 days after the affiant first learned of the alleged grounds for disqualification, and not later than 10 days prior to the hearing or trial which is the subject of recusal or disqualification, unless good cause be shown for failure to meet such time requirements. In no event shall the motion be allowed to delay the trial or proceeding.

19.2 Duty of the Trial Judge. When a judge is presented with a motion to recuse, or disqualify, accompanied by an affidavit, he shall temporarily cease to act upon the merits of the matter and shall immediately determine the timeliness of the motion and the legal sufficiency of the affidavit, and make a determination, assuming any of the facts alleged in the affidavit to be true, whether recusal would be warranted. If it is found that the motion is timely, the affidavit sufficient and that recusal would be authorized if some or all of the facts set forth in the affidavit are true, the motion to recuse shall be heard by a state court judge of the same county if available, or if not, a superior court judge from the same circuit.

19.3 Procedure Upon a Motion for Disqualification. If the recusal motion is sustained, the probate judge shall be recused and a state court judge (other than the one who heard the motion) or an attorney with at least 2 years' experience shall be appointed by the judge who heard the recusal motion to sit in place of the recused judge.

19.4 Voluntary Recusal. If a judge, either on his own motion or that of one of the parties, voluntarily disqualifies himself, another person shall be assigned (by the judge who would have heard the motion under Rule 19.2) to hear the matter involved. Such judge shall be selected by the procedure set forth in Rule 19.3 above.

19.5 Selection of Judge. In the instance of any hearing on a motion to recuse or disqualify a judge, the challenged judge shall neither select nor participate in the selection of the judge to hear the motion. If recused or disqualified, the recused or disqualified judge shall not select nor participate in the selection of the person assigned to hear further proceedings in the involved action.

Publisher's Note

See Appendix A for Uniform Probate Court Rule amendments applicable to certain counties with a population of more than 96,000 persons.

RULE 20. FILING AND PROCESSING

20.1 Preparation of Documents. To the extent practical, all materials presented for filing in any probate court shall be typed, legibly written or printed in black ink suitable for reproduction, on opaque white paper measuring 8½″ × 11″ of a good quality, grade and weight. Manuscript covers and backings shall be omitted wherever practical. Preparation of wills on 8½″ × 11″ paper is encouraged but not mandatory.

20.2 Time of Docketing. Actions shall be entered by the clerk in the proper docket immediately or within a reasonable period after being received in the clerk's office.

20.3 Caption. Every document or pleading presented for filing in a probate court shall bear a caption which sets out the *exact* nature of the pleading or the type of petition.

20.4 Signatures. All judgments, orders, pleadings and other documents shall bear the signature of the responsible attorney or party who prepared the document, his name, proper address and telephone number typed or printed underneath.

20.5 Location of Original. All original documents, petitions and pleadings shall remain in the custody of the court except as provided by the judge, these rules, or as otherwise provided by law.

20.6 When Documents Considered Filed. A document is considered filed only when it is received by the court, regardless of whether the document is delivered by hand or by mail to the court.

20.7 Minutes and Final Record. There shall be one or more books or microfilm records kept in accordance with OCGA § 15–9–37. After recording, the original may be destroyed according to the state retention schedule or stored off premises as provided by law.

20.8 Filing of Transcripts. Any transcript requested by the probate judge shall be filed as directed by him, but the clerk shall not be required to record or preserve these in a bound book or on microfilm. See also Rule 9.3 concerning appeals.

20.9 File Categories. The categories of files to be established by the clerk shall be such that documents are reasonably accessible.

20.10 Identification. Each matter shall be identified by year of filing, type of case and consecutive estate number.

20.11 Filing Requirements. Pleadings or petitions presented to the clerk for filing shall be filed only when accompanied by the proper filing fee, fee for sheriff service or a pauper's affidavit, and, when applicable, any forms required by law or rule to be completed by the parties. The attorney or party filing the petition shall furnish the necessary service copies.

20.12 Return of Service. Entry of return of service shall be made by the sheriff or other authorized person on a form provided by the clerk and filed with the clerk.

20.13 Advance Costs. Advance costs paid upon filing shall be the minimum costs in a case.

Rule 20.1 effective January 1, 1986.

Publisher's Note

See Appendix A for Uniform Probate Court Rule amendments applicable to certain counties with a population of more than 96,000 persons.

RULE 21. STANDARD FORMS

(A) Standard forms will gradually be adopted for statewide use for as many probate court procedures as practicable.

(B) For purposes of this rule, the term probate court procedure is to be narrowly construed; thus, for example, a petition to probate a will in solemn form, a petition to probate a will in common form, a petition to probate a copy of a will in lieu of a lost original, and a combined petition to probate a will and to appoint an administrator with the will annexed, are each considered to involve a separate procedure which is appropriate for the promulgation of a standard form. Similarly, an application for letters of administration, an application for temporary letters of administration, and an application for letters of administration with the will annexed (where the will has already been probated pursuant to a separate probate petition), are each considered to involve such a separate procedure. Any such standard form is to be separately utilized unless any instructions thereon specifically provide otherwise. In cases where it is foreseeable that confusion might exist as to whether certain related matters constitute one procedure for purposes of utilizing a standard form, instructions on the form will specify the scope of its use.

(C) A form, including any instructions, shall be considered adopted when it has been approved by a majority of probate judges present at the spring or fall probate judges' seminar, or summer or winter county officers' association meeting and by a majority of a duly-appointed committee of the State Bar of Georgia Fiduciary Law Section. In lieu of the above requirement of a majority of judges present, a majority of judges at any such meeting may delegate authority to approve forms to a committee of probate judges named at such meeting.

(D) The effective date of any such standard form shall be July 1 immediately following notice as provided for in this paragraph of the form's adoption; provided, however, that a new or revised form which is based upon a new or amended statute or a recent case may become effective upon the effective date of the statute or decision or as soon thereafter as practicable, after notice of adoption of the form as provided in this paragraph. Prior to such effective date, notice of adoption of the form shall be published in an issue of the Official Advance Sheets of the Supreme Court of Georgia. Each newly-adopted form will either be published in full in an issue of such Advance Sheets and subsequently in the bound volume, or be available in each probate court of this state, at least one month prior to its effective date.

(E) These rules shall be construed to allow and facilitate the use of technology in document preparation such as by means of word processing. No standard forms or these rules shall require the filing party to mark or identify any changes in such forms unless they are material. Changes in such forms which are grammatical, changes in gender, changes from singular to plural, omission of optional or alternative language, and the inclusion of variable information such as names and addresses shall not be deemed material; however, the format and sequence of the forms shall be preserved as far as practicable.

(F) Each court will have a supply of printed copies of adopted standard forms. Each standard form will have a title and will contain numbered paragraphs. When an available standard form is not used for a probate court procedure, then the content of the substituted pleading or other document must conform to the standard form, indicating all material information added to or deleted from the standard form. Material additions must be underlined, placed in bold or all capital letters, or otherwise clearly indicated, and material deletions must be shown with a single strike through or otherwise clearly indicated. At the end of any such document, the attorney must sign the following statement: "I certify that the content of the foregoing is identical in all material respects with Georgia probate court standard form entitled, ______________, except for additions or deletions indicated as required by the Uniform Probate Court Rules." For purposes of this paragraph, instructions shall not be deemed to be a part of any standard form.

(G) With respect to any procedure for which a standard form has been adopted, the court may, in its discretion, process or decline to process any document not on an available standard form and which does not contain the certificate described above.

(H) Any document prepared in accordance with this rule and any other applicable rules shall be acceptable in any probate court in this state.

(I) For purposes of this rule, any change or modification of a standard form which changes only the format in which dates are set forth shall not be considered to be the adoption of a new form, and any existing standard form may be modified or amended solely for the purpose of changing the format in which dates are set forth without affecting the effective date or otherwise changing the standard form. In the event such changes are made to a standard form, newly printed or created forms may be distributed to and by probate courts in lieu of older forms without such changes; however, older versions of standard forms not containing such changes shall be acceptable for filing in all probate courts until existing supplies are depleted. Any change or modification of a standard form which changes only the format in which dates are set forth shall not be considered to be a substituted document such as to require the certificate required under subparagraph (F) of this rule.

Amended effective July 1, 1986; October 9, 1997; amended November 4, 1999, effective December 16, 1999.

Publisher's Note

See Appendix A for Uniform Probate Court Rule amendments applicable to certain counties with a population of more than 96,000 persons.

RULE 22. CITATIONS

(A) Unless the court specifically assumes the responsibility, it is the responsibility of the moving party to prepare a proper citation.

(B) Every citation shall include a statement that all objections to the petition must be in writing, setting forth the grounds of any such objections, and must be filed with the court at or before the time stated in the citation.

(C) Unless the court specifically assumes the responsibility, it is the responsibility of the moving party to see that all citations which must be personally served are delivered to the proper sheriff's office or special agent for service of process.

(D) Unless the court specifically assumes the responsibility otherwise, in connection with any citation which must be served by mail, including without limitation a citation concerning an application for year's support, a properly stamped envelope, addressed to each interested party, must be provided to the court by the petitioner.

(E) Unless the court directs otherwise, the court will deliver all citations which are to be published in the county where the petition is filed to the legal newspaper of that county.

(F) If a citation is to be published only one time, then it shall be published at least ten (10) days in advance of the date established as the deadline for filing objections.

(G) With respect to citations which are to be published, the court may set a deadline prior to which proposed citations must be delivered to the court, so that they can be checked by the court and delivered to the appropriate newspaper.

Publisher's Note

See Appendix A for Uniform Probate Court Rule amendments applicable to certain counties with a population of more than 96,000 persons.

RULE 23. GUARDIANS AD LITEM

Guardians ad litem may be nominated by parties to the case, but it remains the responsibility of the court, in its discretion, to choose an appropriate party to serve as a guardian ad litem. A guardian ad litem must either be disinterested or have an interest identical or similar to the person for whom he is appointed, but may not have an interest which could possibly conflict with the person for whom he is appointed.

Amended effective July 1, 1990.

Publisher's Note

See Appendix A for Uniform Probate Court Rule amendments applicable to certain counties with a population of more than 96,000 persons.

RULE 24. INVESTIGATION OF FIDUCIARIES

24.1 Criminal Background Information of Certain Nominated Temporary Administrators, Personal Representatives or Guardians. Any person requesting appointment by a probate court in this State as temporary administrator or personal representative of an estate of a decedent or as guardian of the person or property of an incapacitated adult or a minor may be required to first submit to a criminal background check by allowing the probate court in which the petition seeking such appointment is pending to access the criminal records information maintained by the Georgia Crime Information Center (GCIC) with reference to such person. The actual performance of a background check shall be in the discretion of the judge of the probate court before which the proceedings are pending, and there shall be no requirement that a criminal history be obtained for every such person. In order to allow access to the GCIC records, any person requesting such appointment shall, upon request by the probate court, sign a form consenting to the release of such information by GCIC to the probate court, which form shall be substantially the same as the consent form appended to the Georgia Probate Court Standard Form 31. All information received by a probate court pursuant to this Rule shall be considered confidential and shall be disclosed by the probate court or its staff only to the person seeking such appointment, any attorney representing such person, and any attorney and/or guardian-ad-litem representing the heirs or beneficiaries of the decedent, the alleged incapacitated adult or the minor involved in the proceedings. Any records so obtained by a probate court shall be destroyed within 30 days after the expiration of the time for filing of an appeal of the order of the probate court granting or denying such appointment; if an appeal is filed, such records shall be destroyed within 30 days after the appeal is dismissed or withdrawn or the remittitur is returned to the probate court.

Adopted effective July 1, 1999.

Publisher's Note

See Appendix A for Uniform Probate Court Rule amendments applicable to certain counties with a population of more than 96,000 persons.

APPENDIX A

The following amendments apply to the Uniform Probate Court Rules with respect to counties with a population of more than 96,000 persons according to the U.S. Decennial Census of 1990 or any future such census in which the judge thereof has been admitted to the practice of law for at least 7 years. In the material below, unless the context clearly indicates otherwise, "rule" means Uniform Probate Court Rule; "probate court" or "court" means a probate court of a county to which these amendments apply; "probate judge" or "judge" means the judge of the probate court of such a county.

Amended effective July 1, 1988; July 1, 1994.

Rule No.	Amendments
1.1	**Rule 1.1** (Repeal of Local Rules) is hereby amended to read as follows: "All local rules of the probate courts to which these amendments apply are hereby repealed."
1.2	**Rule 1.2** (Authority to Enact Local Rules) is hereby amended by adding the following sentence at the end of the second paragraph: "However, any such local rules shall not be inconsistent with this Appendix A."
1.2	The fourth paragraph of **Rule 1.2** is hereby amended by adding the following sentence at the end of such paragraph: "Likewise, any such probate court may, without specific Supreme Court approval, provide by local rule that any necessary jurors may be supplied by the superior court or state court serving that county."
3	With respect to **Rule 3,** the existing material shall be designated paragraph (A) and the following paragraph (B) shall be added: "(B) With respect to contested matters, any attorney appointed to act instead of a judge of the probate court pursuant to OCGA § 15–9–13(a), and any hearing officer appointed under any applicable law to hold a hearing in lieu of the judge of the probate court, shall have been admitted to the practice of law for at least 7 years. Such substitute need not be a resident of the same county as the judge of the probate court making such appointment."
5	**Rule 5** (Discovery) is deleted and the following is substituted in lieu thereof: "RULE 5. DISCOVERY In order for a party to utilize the court's compulsory process to compel discovery, any desired discovery procedures must first be commenced promptly, pursued diligently and completed without unnecessary delay and within six months after the filing of the answer, objection, or other response. At any time, the court, in its discretion, may extend, reopen or shorten the time to utilize the court's compulsory process to compel discovery." [Amended effective March 21, 1991.]
6.3	**Rule 6.3** (Hearing) is hereby deleted and the following is substituted in lieu thereof: **"Rule 6.3 Hearing.** Unless otherwise ordered by the court, all motions, including those for summary judgment, shall be decided by the court without oral hearing, except motions for new trial and motions for judgment notwithstanding the verdict. However, oral argument on any motion for summary judgment shall be permitted upon written request if such request is made not later than 5 days after the time for response."
6.8	With respect to **Rule 6,** the following section shall be added: **"Rule 6.8 Motions for New Trial** (A) *Time for Hearing.* In order to reduce delay between the conclusion of the trial and the filing of the notice of appeal, the trial court may hear motions for new trial immediately after filing and prior to the preparation of the transcript of proceedings. In any event, the motion for new trial shall be heard and decided as promptly as possible. (B) *Transcript Costs.* Except where leave to proceed in forma pauperis has been granted, an attorney who files a motion for new trial, or a notice of appeal which specifies that the transcript of evidence or hearing shall be included in the record, shall be personally responsible for compensating the court reporter for the cost of transcription. The filing of such motion or notice shall constitute a certificate by the attorney that the transcript has been ordered from the court reporter.

Rule No. **Amendments**

The filing of such motion or notice prior to ordering the transcript from the reporter shall subject the attorney to disciplinary action by the court."

7.2 **Rule 7.2** (Pre-Trial Order) is hereby deleted and the following is substituted in lieu thereof:

"Rule 7.2 Pre-Trial Order. At the pre-trial conference, or prior to that day as specified in the pre-trial calendar, counsel for each party shall have prepared and shall file with the court a proposed Pre-Trial Order in substantially the following form. The words 'plaintiff' and 'defendant' may be changed if other words are more appropriate.

IN THE PROBATE COURT OF
_______ COUNTY
STATE OF GEORGIA

(STYLE OF CASE) ESTATE NO. ____

PRE–TRIAL ORDER

The following constitutes a Pre-Trial Order entered in the above-styled case after conference with counsel for the parties:

(1) The name, address and phone number of the attorneys who will conduct the trial are as follows:
Plaintiff ____________
Defendant ____________
Other ____________

(2) The estimated time required for trial is ____________

(3) There are no motions or other matters pending for consideration by the court except as follows: ______

(4) The jury will be qualified as to relationship with the following: ______

(5) a. All discovery has been completed, unless otherwise noted, and the court will not consider any further motions to compel discovery except for good cause shown. The parties, however, shall be permitted to take depositions of any person(s) for the preservation of evidence for use at trial.

b. Unless otherwise noted, the names of the parties as shown in the caption to this order are correct and complete and there is no question by any party as to the misjoinder or nonjoinder of any parties.

(6) The following is the Plaintiff's brief and succinct outline of the case and contentions: (USE SPACE AS NEEDED)

(7) The following is the Defendant's brief and succinct outline of the case and contentions: (USE SPACE AS NEEDED) ____________

(8) The issues for determination are as follows: ____________

(9) The following facts are stipulated: ____________

(10) The following is a list of all documentary and physical evidence that will be tendered at the trial by the Plaintiff or Defendant. Unless noted, the parties have stipulated as to the authenticity of the documents listed and the exhibits listed may be admitted without further proof of authenticity. All exhibits shall be marked by counsel prior to trial so as not to delay the trial.
a. By the Plaintiff: ____________
b. By the Defendant: ____________

(11) Special authorities relied upon by Plaintiff relating to peculiar evidentiary or other legal questions are as follows: ____________

(12) Special authorities relied upon by Defendant relating to peculiar evidentiary or other legal questions are as follows: ____________

(13) Requests and exceptions to charge

All requests to charge shall be numbered consecutively on separate sheets of paper and submitted to the court in duplicate by counsel for all parties at the commencement of trial, unless otherwise provided by Pre-trial Order; provided, however, that additional requests may be submitted to cover unanticipated points that arise thereafter.

Rule No.	Amendments
	(14) The testimony of the following persons may be introduced by depositions: __________ Any objection to the depositions or questions or arguments in the depositions shall be called to the attention of the court prior to trial.
	(15) The following are lists of witnesses the
	a. Plaintiff *will* have present at trial: __________
	b. Plaintiff *may* have present at trial: __________
	c. Defendant *will* have present at trial: __________
	d. Defendant *may* have present at trial: __________
	Opposing counsel may rely on representation by the designated party that he *will* have a witness present unless notice to the contrary is given in sufficient time prior to trial to allow the other party to subpoena the witness or obtain his testimony by other means.
	(16) The form of all possible verdicts to be considered by the jury are as follows: __________
	(17) a. The possibilities of settling the case are: __________
	b. The parties do/do not want the case reported. If they do, __________ will arrange for the reporter.
	c. The cost of take-down will be paid by: __________
	d. Other matters:

Submitted by:

____

____

It is hereby ordered that the foregoing, including the attachments thereto, constitutes the PRE-TRIAL ORDER in the above case and supersedes the pleadings which may not be further amended except by order of the court to prevent manifest injustice.

This ______ day of ______, 19__.

____

Judge, Probate Court

Rule No.	Amendments
	__________ County"
9.2	**Rule 9.2** (Continuances) shall be deleted and the following shall be substituted: **"Rule 9.2 Continuance After Scheduled for Trial.** Continuances will not be granted merely by agreement of counsel. Actions will not be removed from a trial calendar after notice of such calendar has been duly given, except by court direction upon such terms as reasonably may be imposed, including the possible imposition of a penalty of up to $50 upon the moving party if, absent statutory grounds or good cause, a motion for continuance of an action is first made within 5 days of the trial week scheduled."
9.3	**Rule 9.3** (Appeals—Probate Court Transcript Not Transmitted) shall be deleted and the following shall be substituted: **"Rule 9.3 Appeals—Record.** The record which is transmitted to the appropriate appellate court on appeal shall be prepared in the same manner as appeals from the superior court are prepared, as nearly as practicable."
14	**Rule 14** (Leaves of Absence) shall be amended by adding the following after subsection (C): "(D) Whether any hearings or trials have been scheduled and, if so, the date of said hearing or trial."
19.3	**Rule 19.3** (Recusal—Procedure upon a Motion for Disqualification) shall be amended by deleting the present material and substituting the following: **"Rule 19.3 Procedure Upon a Motion for Disqualification.** If the recusal motion is sustained, the probate judge shall be recused and a state court judge (other than the one who heard the motion) or an attorney shall be appointed by the judge who heard the recusal motion to sit in place of the recused judge, provided that such state court judge or attorney appointed to hear the case shall have been admitted to the practice of law for at least 7 years."
20.8	**Rule 20.8** (Filing of Transcripts) is hereby amended by deleting the last sentence and substituting in lieu thereof the following

Rule No.	Amendments
	sentence: "See also Rule 9.3 in this Appendix A concerning appeals."
24	The following new **Rule 24** is added:

"RULE 24. JURY TRIALS

(A) *Right to Jury Trial.* The right to a jury trial must be asserted by a written demand within 30 days after the filing of the first pleading of the party or within 15 days after the filing of the first pleading of an opposing party, whichever is later, except that with respect to a petition pursuant to OCGA § 29–5–6, relating to guardianship of an incapacitated adult, if any interested party desires a trial by jury, such party must make such request for a jury within ten days after the date of mailing of the notice provided for by paragraph (1) of subsection (d) of OCGA § 29–5–6. If a party fails to assert the right to a jury trial, the right shall be deemed waived and may not thereafter be asserted.

(B) *Voir Dire.* The court may propound, or cause to be propounded by counsel, such questions of the jurors as provided in OCGA § 15–12–133; however, the form, time required and number of such questions is within the discretion of the court. The court may require that questions be asked once only to the full array of the jurors, rather than to every juror—one at a time—provided that the question be framed and the response given in a manner that will provide the propounder with an individual response prior to the interposition of challenge. Hypothetical questions are discouraged, but may be allowed in the discretion of the court. It is improper to examine a juror as to how he would act in certain contingencies or on a certain hypothetical state of facts. No question shall be framed so as to require a response from a juror which might amount to a prejudgment of the action. Questions calling for an opinion by a juror on matters of law are improper. The court will exclude questions which have been answered in substance previously by the same juror. It is discretionary with the court to permit examination of each juror without the presence of the remainder of the panel. Objections to the mode and conduct of voir dire must be raised promptly or they will be regarded as waived.

(C) *Selection of Juries.* After completion of the examination of jurors upon their voir dire, the parties and their counsel shall be entitled, upon request, to 15 minutes to prepare for jury selection; thereafter, during the selection of jurors, the judge in his discretion, upon first warning counsel, may restrict to not less than one minute the time within which each party may exercise a peremptory challenge; a party shall forfeit a challenge by failing to exercise it within the time allowed."

[Amended effective July 1, 1990.]

Rule No.	Amendments
25	The following new **Rule 25** is added:

"RULE 25. SETTLEMENT AGREEMENTS ALTERING TERMS OF WILL

With respect to approval of settlement agreements pursuant to OCGA § 53–3–22, the probate courts to which these amendments apply shall have the same powers that superior courts have on appeals from other probate courts."

Rule No.	Amendments
26	The following new **Rule 26** is added:

"RULE 26. COURT REPORTERS

Unless otherwise notified by the court, if any party desires that a hearing or trial be reported by a court reporter, then it shall be the duty of such party to arrange, at his own expense, for a court reporter to be present at the hearing or trial. Such party shall immediately notify the court and opposing counsel in writing when such arrangements have been made. No delay or continuance of any hearing or trial shall be granted in order to allow any party to make such arrangements, except for good cause shown. If the court will arrange for a court reporter to be present at a particular hearing or trial, then the court will so inform the parties in the notice of hearing, pre-trial order, or other appropriate notice."

GEORGIA PROBATE COURT STANDARD FORMS AND GENERAL INSTRUCTIONS

Table of Forms

GPCSF 1. GENERAL INSTRUCTIONS

GENERAL INSTRUCTIONS APPLICABLE TO ALL GEORGIA PROBATE COURT STANDARD FORMS

1. These instructions shall be construed to allow and facilitate the use of technology in document preparation such as by means of word processing. No standard forms or these instructions shall require the filing party to mark or identify any changes in such forms unless they are material. Changes in such forms which are grammatical, changes in gender, changes from singular to plural, omission of optional or alternative language, and the inclusion of variable information such as names and addresses shall not be deemed material; however, the format and sequence of the forms shall be preserved as far as practical.

2. When an available printed standard form is not used for a probate court procedure, then the content of the substituted pleading or other document must conform to the standard form, indicating all material information added to or deleted from the standard form. Material additions must be underlined, placed in bold or all capital letters, or otherwise clearly indicated, and material deletions must be shown with a single strike through or otherwise clearly indicated. At the end of any such document, the attorney must sign the following statement: "I certify that the content of the foregoing is identical in all material respects with Georgia probate court standard form entitled ______________, except for additions or deletions indicated as required by the Uniform Probate Court Rules." 1 For purposes of this paragraph, instructions shall not be deemed to be a part of any standard form.

3. Any material language on the form not considered applicable should be stricken with a single strike-through, or otherwise clearly indicated. Interlineations may be made if considered necessary and clearly indicated. This includes any change that might be appropriate due to a change in the law which occurs after a form has been adopted.

4. Except for optional or alternative language, any blank (other than extra signature lines) deemed not applicable should be marked "N/A" in the blank, except that if an entire paragraph or section is considered not applicable, it shall be marked "N/A" beside the paragraph number or section heading. If an entire page is not applicable, the page may be omitted, and beside the page number of the next page that is applicable there should be placed a notation similar to the following: page(s) ____ not applicable.

5. Words in parentheses should be left in the form if applicable, or stricken through if not applicable. However, where the letter "s" appears in parentheses to denote the plural, it is not necessary to strike the "s" where the singular applies, if otherwise clear from the context.

6. Whenever an instruction indicates that the petitioner should check a blank if applicable, any clear mark is acceptable.

7. If the space provided is not adequate, then additional sheets may be attached, so long as the name of the decedent, caption of the form, and appropriate paragraph number are shown on each additional sheet.

8. Words with Latin endings such as "executor", "administrator", "testator" and "caveator" include the plural and/or the feminine if the context so implies.

9. It is the responsibility of the filing party to complete all portions of the form, except for court signatures and dates, name and answer of any guardian ad litem, evaluator, or other person appointed by the court, and any other information which is not reasonably within the filing party's knowledge. The court may require that the guardian ad litem be an attorney licensed to practice in the State of Georgia.

10. If any other proceedings with respect to the minor, incapacitated adult, or decedent are pending, or have been completed, in any other probate court in this state, and the form states that none are pending, then strike the word "no" in the paragraph of the form dealing with this subject, and attach a sheet giving full details, including the information required by O.C.G.A. § 53–5–22(b) if applicable.

11. A form may only be reproduced by photocopying, offset printing, or some other method which does not involve any retyping or resetting of type, unless the certificate required by Paragraph 2 above is attached to the reproduction. Forms reproduced on word processors should contain such certificate.

Effective 1/98 GPCSF 1

Revised effective January 1, 1998.

1 Publisher's Note. Per Uniform Probate Court Rule 21(F).

GPCSF 2. PETITION FOR TEMPORARY LETTERS OF ADMINISTRATION

Petition for Temporary Letters of Administration

INSTRUCTIONS

I. Specific Instructions

1. This form is to be used for a petition for temporary letters of administration pursuant to O.C.G.A. §53-6-30.

II. General Instructions

General instructions applicable to all Georgia probate court standard forms are available in each probate court.

Effective 7/06 GPCSF 2 Complete

GEORGIA PROBATE COURT
STANDARD FORM

PROBATE COURT OF ________________ COUNTY

STATE OF GEORGIA

IN RE: ESTATE OF) ESTATE NO.
)
______________________________,) PETITION FOR TEMPORARY
DECEASED) LETTERS OF ADMINISTRATION

TO THE HONORABLE JUDGE OF THE PROBATE COURT:

The petition of ______________________________, whose domicile is/are ______________________________, and whose mailing address is/are ____________________ show(s) to the Court the following:

1.

______________________________, whose
First Middle Last Name

domicile was ______________________________
Street City County State

departed this life on ______________, 20____, leaving an estate of real property located in ______________________________ County(ies), Georgia having a total fair market value of approximately $__________ and personal property as follows (provide approximate value):

a. cash/bank accounts/certificates of deposit $

b. stocks/bonds/brokerage accounts $

c. other assets of significant value (list) $

APPROXIMATE TOTAL $

2.

Petitioner's(s') appointment is in the best interests of the estate by reason of the estate's being unrepresented and it is necessary for Temporary Letters of Administration to be granted for the sole purpose of collecting and preserving the assets of the decedent.

3.

Petitioner(s) is/are entitled to be appointed Temporary Administrator(s) by reason of (initial one):

____a. being the nominated executor(s) in decedent's purported will (a copy of which is attached hereto and made a part hereof).
____b. being unanimously selected by all the heirs.
____c. being the sole heir or being the surviving spouse.
____d. having been selected by a majority in interest of the heirs.
____e. being (an) eligible person(s) as defined in O.C.G.A. §53-6-1.
____f. being (a) creditor(s) of the decedent (evidence of the indebtedness is attached).
____g. being the county administrator.

4.

Listed below are the names of all the decedent's heirs with the age or majority status, address, and relationship to decedent set opposite the name of each:

Name	Age (Or over 18)	Address	Relationship

5.

Additional Data: Where full particulars are lacking, state here the reasons for any such omission. If any heirs listed above are cousins, grandchildren, nephews or nieces of the decedent, please indicate the deceased ancestor through whom they are related to the decedent.

6.

To the knowledge of the petitioner(s), no other proceedings with respect to this estate are pending, or have been completed, in any other probate court in this state.

WHEREFORE, petitioner(s) pray(s) for an order appointing petitioner(s) Temporary Administrator(s) of said estate.

Signature of first petitioner	Signature of second petitioner if any
Printed Name	Printed Name
Address	Address
Phone Number	Phone Number

Signature of Attorney: ______________________

Typed/printed name of Attorney: ______________________
Address: ______________________

Telephone: ______________________ State Bar # ______________________

VERIFICATION

GEORGIA, ______________________ COUNTY

Personally appeared before me the undersigned petitioner(s) who on oath state(s) that the facts set forth in the foregoing petition are true.

Sworn to and subscribed before
me this ______ day of ____________, 20____.

____
First Petitioner

____
NOTARY/CLERK OF PROBATE COURT

____
Printed Name

Sworn to and subscribed before
me this ______ day of ____________, 20____.

____
Second Petitioner, if any

____
NOTARY/CLERK OF PROBATE COURT

____
Printed Name

SELECTION BY HEIRS

GEORGIA, ______________________ COUNTY ESTATE NO. ________

IN RE: PETITION OF
FOR TEMPORARY LETTERS OF ADMINISTRATION

ESTATE OF ____, DECEASED

For the court's consideration in determining the person whose appointment would serve the best interests of the estate, (we) (all) (a majority in interest) of the heirs of ______________________, deceased, hereby select and request the appointment of ________________ to act as Temporary Administrator(s) of the estate of said decedent.

SIGNATURE(S)

Sworn to and subscribed before
me this _____ day of __________, 20____. ______________________________

______________________________ ______________________________
NOTARY/CLERK OF PROBATE COURT Printed Name

Sworn to and subscribed before
me this _____ day of __________, 20____. ______________________________

______________________________ ______________________________
NOTARY/CLERK OF PROBATE COURT Printed Name

Sworn to and subscribed before
me this _____ day of __________, 20____. ______________________________

______________________________ ______________________________
NOTARY/CLERK OF PROBATE COURT Printed Name

Sworn to and subscribed before
me this _____ day of __________, 20____. ______________________________

______________________________ ______________________________
NOTARY/CLERK OF PROBATE COURT Printed Name

Sworn to and subscribed before
me this _____ day of __________, 20____. ______________________________

______________________________ ______________________________
NOTARY/CLERK OF PROBATE COURT Printed Name

PROBATE COURT OF ______________ COUNTY

STATE OF GEORGIA

IN RE: ESTATE OF) ESTATE NO. ______________
)
______________,) PETITION FOR TEMPORARY
DECEASED) LETTERS OF ADMINISTRATION

ORDER

The petition of ______________ for Temporary Letters of Administration on the estate of ______________, deceased, has been duly filed. It appears that said decedent died domiciled in said county, that said petitioner(s) is/are lawfully qualified for said administration, that such appointment will be in the best interests of the estate, and that it is necessary that temporary letters should issue for the sole purpose of collecting and preserving the assets of said decedent until permanent letters are granted. It is, therefore,

ORDERED that the petitioner(s) be, and is/are hereby, appointed Temporary Administrator(s) of the estate, and that Letters be issued upon said Administrator's(s') giving bond with approved surety in the sum of $______________ dollars and taking the oath as the law requires.

IT IS FURTHER ORDERED that no disbursements from said estate may be made by said Temporary Administrator(s) unless permission is granted by further order of this Court for the purpose of preserving the estate.

SO ORDERED this ________ day of ______________, 20____.

Probate Judge

Effective 7/06 GPCSF 2 Complete

PROBATE COURT OF ____________________ COUNTY

STATE OF GEORGIA

IN RE: ESTATE OF) ESTATE NO. ____________________
)
____________________________________,) PETITION FOR TEMPORARY
DECEASED) LETTERS OF ADMINISTRATION

OATH

I do solemnly swear or affirm that
died with an estate that is currently unrepresented, so far as I know or believe, and that I will well and truly administer on all the estate of the decedent, and discharge to the best of my ability all my duties as Temporary Administrator. So help me God.

Temporary Administrator

Sworn to and subscribed before me

this ______ day of __________, 20____.

Probate Clerk/Deputy Clerk

Effective 7/06 GPCSF 2 Complete

STATE OF GEORGIA

COUNTY OF ______________________ ESTATE NO. __________

TEMPORARY LETTERS OF ADMINISTRATION

By ______________________, Judge of the Probate Court of said County.

WHEREAS, ______________________ died domiciled in this County, owning certain assets within this State; and the estate is unrepresented, and it appears necessary that such assets be collected and preserved until permanent letters are issued;

I do, therefore, hereby appoint ________ as Temporary Administrator(s) of the estate of the said decedent, for the sole purpose of collecting and preserving the assets of the said decedent until permanent letters are issued; and thereupon to deliver up such assets to whomsoever this Court shall commit the administration of the estate of said decedent, as provided by law.

Temporary administrators are authorized to carry out existing contracts of the decedent, to carry on the business of the decedent, and to do such acts as are necessary for the protection and preservation of the estate provided proper orders are secured from the probate court after due notice to all parties in interest.

IN TESTIMONY WHEREOF, I have hereunto affixed my signature as Judge of the Probate Court of said County and the seal of this office this ________ day of ______________, 20____.

Probate Judge

(SEAL)

NOTE: The following must be signed if the judge does not sign the original of this document:

Issued by:

PROBATE CLERK/DEPUTY CLERK

Effective 7/06 GPCSF 2 Complete

Instructions and form revised effective July, 1989; January 1, 1998; July 31, 2006.

GPCSF 3 PETITIONER. PETITION FOR LETTERS OF ADMINISTRATION

GEORGIA PROBATE COURT
STANDARD FORM

Petition for Letters of Administration

INSTRUCTIONS

I. Specific Instructions

1. This form is to be used for a petition for letters of administration pursuant to O.C.G.A. §53-6-20, et seq.

2. Use of this form is permissible, but not mandatory, in connection with a petition for appointment of a successor administrator, pursuant to O.C.G.A. §53-6-21(b). Appropriate interlineations must be made, and additional information must be given concerning the identity of the previous administrator, the reason for the vacancy in the office, and the date the office became vacant.

3. With respect to the conditions under which the judge may, pursuant to O.C.G.A. §53-7-1(b), waive bond and/or grant certain powers contained in O.C.G.A. §53-12-232, please note:

   (a) All of the heirs must consent, and

   (b) Notice must be published.

4. O.C.G.A. §53-11-2 provides that a party to a probate court proceeding concerning a decedent's estate who is unborn or unknown or is not sui juris must be represented by a guardian, provided that the court may appoint a guardian ad litem or determine that the natural guardian, guardian of the person or property, or testamentary guardian has no conflict and may serve. (See GPCSF 16). For purposes of the consent described in paragraph 3 above, with respect to any heir who is not sui juris, such consent may be given by such guardian. The personal representative of a deceased heir is authorized to consent on behalf of that heir.

II. General Instructions

General instructions applicable to all Georgia probate court standard forms are available in each probate court.

GEORGIA PROBATE COURT
STANDARD FORM

IN THE PROBATE COURT OF ______________ COUNTY

STATE OF GEORGIA

IN RE: ESTATE OF) ESTATE NO. ______________
)
______________________________,) PETITION FOR LETTERS OF
DECEASED) ADMINISTRATION

TO THE HONORABLE JUDGE OF THE PROBATE COURT:

The petition of ______________________________, whose domicile is/are ______________________________, and whose mailing address(es) is/are ______________________________, shows:

1.

______________________________, whose
First Middle Last Name

domicile was ______________________________,
Street City County State

departed this life on ______________, 20____, leaving an estate of real property located in ______________ County(ies), Georgia having a total fair market value of approximately $__________ and personal property as follows (provide approximate value):

a. cash/bank accounts/certificates of deposit $

b. stocks/bonds/brokerage accounts $

c. other assets of significant value (list) $

APPROXIMATE TOTAL $

2.

Under the law, it is necessary that said estate be administered; and ______________________________ should be appointed Administrator(s) by reason of (initial one):

____a. being unanimously selected by all the heirs. (This alternative does not apply if the surviving spouse is the sole heir and an action for divorce or separate maintenance was pending at the time of decedent's death.)
____b. being the surviving spouse where no action for divorce or separate maintenance was pending at the time of decedent's death.
____c. being (an) heir(s) and not the surviving spouse.
____d. having been selected by a majority in interest of the heirs.
____e. being (an) eligible person(s) as defined by O.C.G.A. §53-6-1.
____f. being (a) creditor(s) of the decedent (evidence of the indebtedness is attached).
____g. being the county administrator.

3.

Listed below are the names of all the decedent's heirs with the age or majority status, address, and relationship to decedent set opposite the name of each:

Name	Age (or over 18)	Address	Relationship

4.

Additional Data: Where full particulars are lacking, state here the reasons for any such omission. Also, state here all pertinent facts which may govern the method of giving notice to any party and which may determine whether or not a guardian ad litem should be appointed for any party. If any heirs listed above are cousins, grandchildren, nephews or nieces of the decedent, please indicate the deceased ancestor through whom they are related to the decedent.

5.

(Petitioner(s) MUST initial one):

____ All heirs have consented to the waiver of bond and/or grant of certain powers contained in O.C.G.A. §53-12-232 to the Administrator(s). Therefore, the Petitioner(s) hereby move(s) the Court to publish notice of the filing of the Petition and tender(s) with this Petition publication fees.

____ The identities and/or addresses of all heirs are not known. Therefore, the Petitioner(s) hereby move(s) the Court to publish notice of the filing of the Petition, and tender(s) with this Petition publication fees.

____ Notice of this Petition need not be published because the Petitioner(s) has/have listed all heirs at law and their addresses, and Petitioner(s) is/are not requesting a waiver of bond and returns or the grant of powers contained in O.C.G.A. § 53-12-232.

6.

To the knowledge of the petitioner(s), no other proceedings with respect to this estate are pending, or have been completed, in any other probate court in this state.

WHEREFORE, petitioner(s) pray(s) that
1. service be perfected and
2. that if no good cause is shown to the contrary, ______________________ be appointed Administrator(s) of the estate of said decedent.

______________________	______________________
Signature of first petitioner	Signature of second petitioner if any
______________________	______________________
Printed Name	Printed Name
______________________	______________________
Address	Address
______________________	______________________
______________________	______________________
Phone Number	Phone Number

Signature of Attorney: ______________________

Typed/printed name of Attorney: ______________________
Address: ______________________

Telephone: ______________________ State Bar # ______________________

VERIFICATION

GEORGIA, ____________________ COUNTY

Personally appeared before me the undersigned petitioner(s) who on oath state(s) that the facts set forth in the foregoing petition are true.

Sworn to and subscribed before
me this ______ day of ____________, 20____. ______________________________
First Petitioner

______________________________ ______________________________
NOTARY/CLERK OF PROBATE COURT Printed Name

Sworn to and subscribed before
me this ______ day of ____________, 20____. ______________________________
Second Petitioner, if any

______________________________ ______________________________
NOTARY/CLERK OF PROBATE COURT Printed Name

SELECTION BY HEIRS (AND CONSENT OF HEIRS TO WAIVER OF BOND AND/OR GRANT OF CERTAIN POWERS)

Note: If an heir is not sui juris, the guardian appointed by the Court or the person that the Court determined may act as guardian is authorized to consent for such non sui juris heir in accordance with the instruction page to this form.

GEORGIA, ______________________________ COUNTY ESTATE NO. __________

We, being (all of the) heirs of the estate of ______________________________, deceased, and being sui juris unless otherwise indicated, do hereby acknowledge service, waive all further notice, and select ______________________________ to act as Administrator(s) of the estate of said decedent. Further, *if so indicated below*, we hereby grant to the Administrator(s) the additional powers contained in (a) and/or (b) below.

____a. (optional; initial if applicable) In addition to selecting the above individual, I hereby consent to the waiver of bond for said Administrator(s) and the grant to said Administrator(s) the power to serve without making and filing inventory and without filing an annual or other returns or reports to any court.

____b. (optional; initial if applicable) In addition to selecting the above individual, I hereby consent to the grant to the Administrator(s) all of the powers contained in O.C.G.A. §53-12-232 not included in (a) above.

Sworn to and subscribed before
me this ______ day of ____________, 20____.

____
SIGNATURE OF HEIR

____
NOTARY/CLERK OF PROBATE COURT

____
PRINT NAME

____a. (optional; initial if applicable) In addition to selecting the above individual, I hereby consent to the waiver of bond for said Administrator(s) and the grant to said Administrator(s) the power to serve without making and filing inventory and without filing an annual or other returns or reports to any court.

____b. (optional; initial if applicable) In addition to selecting the above individual, I hereby consent to the grant to the Administrator(s) all of the powers contained in O.C.G.A. §53-12-232 not included in (a) above.

Sworn to and subscribed before
me this ______ day of ____________, 20____.

____
SIGNATURE OF HEIR

____
NOTARY/CLERK OF PROBATE COURT

____
PRINT NAME

Instructions and form revised effective July, 1989; July 1, 1990; July 1, 1992; January 1, 1998; July 1, 1998; July 31, 2006.

GPCSF 3 COURT. COURT FORMS FOR PETITION FOR LETTERS OF ADMINISTRATION

GEORGIA PROBATE COURT
STANDARD FORM

Petition for Letters of Administration

NOTICE: UNLESS OTHERWISE DIRECTED BY THE COURT, THE FOLLOWING FORMS ARE FOR PROBATE COURT STAFF TO COMPLETE

GEORGIA PROBATE COURT
STANDARD FORM

IN THE PROBATE COURT OF ____________________ COUNTY

STATE OF GEORGIA

IN RE: ESTATE OF) ESTATE NO. ____________________
)
____,) PETITION FOR LETTERS OF
DECEASED) ADMINISTRATION

ORDER FOR SERVICE OF NOTICE AND APPOINTING GUARDIAN AD LITEM, IF NECESSARY

(initial applicable:)

____a. Since the heirs have not made a unanimous selection, or the Petitioner(s) has/have requested the waiver of bond and/or grant of certain powers,

IT IS ORDERED that notice be issued and served as follows upon each heir who did not acknowledge service. Notice of this petition must be mailed by first-class mail to each heir with a known address at least 13 days prior to the date on or before which any objection is required to be filed. If there is any heir whose current address is unknown, or if the heirs have unanimously requested the waiver of bond and/or grant of certain powers, notice must be published once each week for four weeks prior to the week which includes the date on or before which any objection must be filed.

____b. IT IS FURTHER ORDERED that ______________________________________ is appointed guardian ad litem for __________ (minor) (unborn heir) (unknown heirs of the above decedent) and that said guardian ad litem be duly served with a copy of the foregoing notice, petition, and notice of this appointment, and that upon said guardian ad litem's acceptance of same, said guardian ad litem shall make answer hereto. This appointment is limited to this proceeding only and it shall cease when a final order is entered on this petition.

SO ORDERED this __________ day of ______________________________, 20____.

Probate Judge

NOTICE

NOTE: Strike the sentence in parenthesis below if not applicable.

GEORGIA, ______________________________ COUNTY PROBATE COURT

TO: (any heir whose current address is unknown) ______________________________

______________________________ has petitioned (for ______________________) to be appointed Administrator(s) of the estate of ______________, deceased, of said County. (The petitioner has also applied for waiver of bond and/or grant of certain powers contained in O.C.G.A. §53-12-232.) All interested parties are hereby notified to show cause why said petition should not be granted. All objections to the petition must be in writing, setting forth the grounds of any such objections, and must be filed with the court on or before __________, 20____. All pleadings/objections must be signed before a notary public or before a probate court clerk, and filing fees must be tendered with your pleadings/objections, unless you qualify to file as an indigent party. Contact probate court personnel at the following address/telephone number for the required amount of filing fees. If any objections are filed, a hearing will be (held on ________________ 20____) (scheduled at a later date). If no objections are filed, the petition may be granted without a hearing.

PROBATE JUDGE

By:
PROBATE CLERK/DEPUTY CLERK

ADDRESS

TELEPHONE NUMBER

CERTIFICATE OF MAILING

I do hereby certify that I have this day mailed by first-class mail a copy of the Notice in this matter to each heir with a known current address, as listed by the petitioner, who did not acknowledge service in an envelope, properly addressed and with adequate postage thereon, and deposited in the United States Mail, with the return address of this Court thereon.

_________________________ _________________________

DATE PROBATE CLERK/DEPUTY CLERK

IN THE PROBATE COURT OF ________________ COUNTY

STATE OF GEORGIA

IN RE: ESTATE OF) ESTATE NO. ________________

)

________________________________,) PETITION FOR LETTERS OF
DECEASED) ADMINISTRATION

ANSWER OF GUARDIAN AD LITEM

I hereby accept the foregoing appointment, acknowledge service and notice of the proceedings as provided by law, and for answer say:

________________________________ ________________________________

DATE GUARDIAN AD LITEM

ADDRESS ________________________

TELEPHONE ______________________

PROBATE COURT OF ______________ COUNTY

STATE OF GEORGIA

IN RE: ESTATE OF) ESTATE NO. ______________
)
______________,) PETITION FOR LETTERS OF
DECEASED) ADMINISTRATION

FINAL ORDER

The petition of ______________ for issuance of Letters of Administration on the estate of ______________, deceased, has been duly filed. Service was perfected according to law. It appears that said decedent died domiciled in said county, intestate; that ______ is/are lawfully qualified for said administration; and that no objection has been offered.

____ (Initial if applicable.) Such petition contained a request for waiver of bond and/or grant of certain powers contained in O.C.G.A. §53-12-232. The notice which was issued and published reflected this, and no objection to the request has been filed. Consent to such request was given by all heirs.

IT IS THEREFORE ORDERED that the undersigned judge does hereby:
(Initial all which apply):

____ a. waive the bond of the Administrator(s) and grant to the Administrator(s) the power to serve without making and filing inventory, and without filing any annual or other returns or reports to any court; but the fiduciary(ies) shall furnish to the income beneficiaries, at least annually, a statement of receipts and disbursements.

____ b. grant to the Administrator(s) all of the powers contained in O.C.G.A. §53-12-232 not included in (a) above.

IT IS THEREFORE ORDERED that the person(s) found above in this order to be qualified for such office be, and is/are hereby, appointed Administrator(s) of the estate of said decedent, and that appropriate Letters be issued upon said Administrator's(s') (giving bond with approved surety in the sum of $______________ and) taking the oath as provided by law.

(Initial if applicable)
____ IT IS FURTHER ORDERED that said Administrator(s) shall not make any distribution to a person for the benefit of a minor unless that person is qualified to receive such funds according to law.

SO ORDERED this ________ day of ______________, 20____.

Probate Judge

OATH

Georgia, ______________________________ County

I do solemnly swear or affirm that ______________________________, deceased, died intestate, so far as I know or believe, and that I will well and truly administer on all the estate of the decedent, and disburse the same as the law requires, and discharge to the best of my ability all my duties as Administrator. So help me God.

Sworn to and subscribed before me this _____ day of __________, 20____.

____
Administrator

____
NOTARY/CLERK OF PROBATE COURT

____
Printed Name

Sworn to and subscribed before me this _____ day of __________, 20____.

____
Administrator

____
NOTARY/CLERK OF PROBATE COURT

____
Printed Name

GEORGIA PROBATE COURT
STANDARD FORM

INSTRUCTIONS

1. Unless inventory has been waived, an inventory of the estate must be filed with this Court by the Administrator within six (6) months after these letters are issued and a copy of that inventory must be delivered to the heirs by first-class mail within the same period.

2. Within sixty (60) days after these letters are issued, notice must be given once a week for four (4) weeks by advertisement in the newspaper in this County in which sheriff's notices are published, requiring creditors of the estate to render in their demands and requiring debtors to make payment.

3. Unless returns have been waived, or a different accounting period has been approved, within sixty (60) days after the anniversary date of issuance of these letters, in each and every year, every Administrator must make a just and true account, under oath, of his receipts and expenditures on behalf of the estate during the preceding year, together with a note or memorandum of any other fact necessary to the exhibition of the true condition of the estate. The vouchers showing the correctness of each item must be retained by the Administrator.

4. The Administrator is allowed six (6) months from the date of his qualification to ascertain the condition of the estate, during which he is exempt from suit. He should collect all debts due the estate, and pay the debts of the estate, wholly or in part, at the end of the six-month period. Payment of the debts of the decedent shall be made in accordance with their rank in priority as provided in O.C.G.A. §53-7-40.

5. The Administrator may continue the business of the estate for the current year without a court order.

6. The normal commissions allowed the Administrator are two and one-half percent (2.5%) of all sums of money received, and a like commission on all sums of money paid out. In addition, upon petition, the Judge of the Probate Court may allow a commission of up to three percent (3%) of the value of all property distributed in kind. There are special rules concerning commissions on interest earned and extra compensation.

7. After the payment of all expenses of administration and other debts, the balance of the estate shall be promptly distributed to the heirs. The Administrator must then make a final return, showing the receipts and disbursements since the last annual accounting, unless returns have been waived.

For further information see O.C.G.A. Title 53, Chapters 6 & 7.

GEORGIA PROBATE COURT
STANDARD FORM

STATE OF GEORGIA

COUNTY OF ______________________ ESTATE NO. ________

LETTERS OF ADMINISTRATION

(Bond Waived and/or Certain Powers Granted at Time of Appointment)

By ______________________, Judge of the Probate Court of said County.

WHEREAS, ______________________ died intestate (check one:)

____ domiciled in this County;
____ not domiciled in this State, but owning property in this County;

and this Court granted an order appointing ______________________ as Administrator(s) of the estate of said decedent, on condition that said Administrator(s) give oath as required by law; and the said Administrator(s) having complied with said condition; the Court hereby grants unto said Administrator(s) full power to collect the assets of said decedent, and to pay the debts of said estate, so far as such assets will extend, according to law, and then to pay over the balance, if any, to the heirs of said decedent, and to do and perform all other duties as such Administrator(s), according to the laws of this State. In addition, this Court has:

(Initial all which apply:)

____ a. waived the bond of the Administrator(s) and granted to the Administrator(s) the power to serve without filing an inventory, and without filing any annual or other returns or reports to any court; but the fiduciary shall furnish to the income beneficiaries, at least annually, a statement of receipts and disbursements.

____ b. granted to the Administrator(s) all of the powers contained in O.C.G.A. §53-12-232 not included in (a) above.

IN TESTIMONY WHEREOF, I have hereunto affixed my signature as Judge of the Probate Court of said County and the seal of this office this ________ day of ______________, 20____.

Judge of the Probate Court

NOTE: The following must be signed if the judge does not sign the original of this document:

Issued by:

______________________ (Seal)

Clerk, Probate Court

(SEE INSTRUCTIONS ON REVERSE SIDE)

GEORGIA PROBATE COURT
STANDARD FORM

INSTRUCTIONS

1. An inventory of the estate must be filed with this Court by the Administrator within six (6) months after these letters are issued, and, subject to Instruction 8. below, a copy of that inventory must be delivered to the sui juris heirs by first-class mail within the same period.

2. Within sixty (60) days after these letters are issued, notice must be given once a week for four (4) weeks by advertisement in the newspaper in this County in which sheriff's notices are published, requiring creditors of the estate to render in their demands.

3. Unless a different accounting period has been approved, within sixty (60) days after the anniversary date of issuance of these letters, in each and every year, every Administrator must make a just and true account, under oath, of his receipts and expenditures on behalf of the estate during the preceding year, together with a note or memorandum of any other fact necessary to the exhibition of the true condition of the estate. The vouchers showing the correctness of each item must be retained by the Administrator. Subject to Instruction 8. below, a copy of each such return must be delivered to the sui juris heirs by first-class mail within the same period.

4. The Administrator is allowed six (6) months from the date of his qualification to ascertain the condition of the estate, during which he is exempt from suit. He should collect all debts due the estate, and pay the debts of the estate, wholly or in part, at the end of the six-month period. Payment of the debts of the decedent shall be made in accordance with their rank in priority as provided in O.C.G.A. §53-7-40.

5. The Administrator may continue the business of his intestate for the current year without a court order.

6. The normal commissions allowed the Administrator are two and one-half percent (2.5%) of all sums of money received, and a like commission on all sums of money paid out. In addition, the Judge of the Probate Court may allow a commission of up to three percent (3%) of the value of all property distributed in kind. There are special rules concerning commissions on interest earned and extra compensation.

7. After the payment of all expenses of administration and other debts, the balance of the estate shall be promptly distributed to the heirs. The Administrator must then make a final return, showing the receipts and disbursements since the last annual accounting. Subject to Instruction 8. below, a copy of the final return must be delivered to the sui juris heirs by first-class mail at the time of filing same.

8. It shall not be necessary for the Administrator to mail copies of any annual returns or the final return to any heir or beneficiary who has individually waived in writing the right to receive copies of same unless and until such waiver is revoked in writing.

For further information see O.C.G.A. Title 53, Chapters 6 &. 7.

GEORGIA PROBATE COURT
STANDARD FORM

STATE OF GEORGIA

COUNTY OF ______________________ ESTATE NO. ________

LETTERS OF ADMINISTRATION

(Bond, Inventory and Returns Required)

By ______________________, the Judge of the Probate Court of said County.

WHEREAS, ______________________ died intestate (check one:)
____ domiciled in this County;
____ not domiciled in this State, but owning property in this County;
and this Court granted an order appointing ______________________ as Administrator(s) of the estate of said decedent, on condition that said Administrator(s) give bond and security and give oath as required by law; and the said Administrator(s) having complied with said conditions; the Court hereby grants unto said Administrator(s) full power to collect the assets of said decedent, and to pay the debts of said estate, so far as such assets will extend, according to law, and then to pay over the balance, if any, to the legal heirs of said decedent, and to do and perform all other duties as such Administrator(s), according to the laws of this State.

IN TESTIMONY WHEREOF, I have hereunto affixed my signature as Judge of the Probate Court of said County and the seal of this office this ______ day of ____________, 20____.

Judge of the Probate Court

NOTE: The following must be signed if the judge does not sign the original of this document:

Issued by:

______________________ (Seal)
Clerk, Probate Court

(SEE INSTRUCTIONS ON REVERSE SIDE)

Effective 7/06 –10– GPCSF 3 Court

Form adopted effective July 31, 2006.

GPCSF 4. PETITION TO PROBATE WILL IN COMMON FORM

GEORGIA PROBATE COURT
STANDARD FORM

Petition to Probate Will in Common Form

INSTRUCTIONS

I. Specific Instructions

1. This form is to be used when filing a petition to probate will in common from pursuant to O.C.G.A. §53-5-16 et seq.

2. This form should not be used in connection with a petition to probate a copy of a will in lieu of a lost original without checking with the court in which the petition will be filed.

3. This form should not be used to file a combination petition to probate will and for letters of administration with the will annexed (see Petition to Probate Will in Solemn Form and For Letters of Administration with Will Annexed).

II. General Instructions

General instructions applicable to all Georgia probate court standard forms are available in each probate court.

GEORGIA PROBATE COURT
STANDARD FORM

IN THE PROBATE COURT OF ________________ COUNTY

STATE OF GEORGIA

IN RE: ESTATE OF	)	**ESTATE NO.**
	)	
____,	)	**PETITION TO PROBATE WILL IN**
DECEASED	)	**COMMON FORM**

TO THE HONORABLE JUDGE OF THE PROBATE COURT:

The petition of ____ whose mailing address is/are____, shows:

1.

On _____________, 20______,

First Middle Last Name

whose place of domicile was

Street City County State

departed this life owning property in Georgia.

2.

While alive, the decedent duly made and published a Last Will and Testament dated ________________________________ which is offered for probate in Common Form. Your petitioner(s) is/are named as the Executor(s).

3.

Listed below are all of decedent's heirs, with the age or majority status, address, and relationship to the decedent set opposite the name of each:

Name	Age (Or over 18)	Address	Relationship

4.

(initial if applicable)

_______ At the time of the decedent's death, and at this time, the decedent left/leaves (a) minor child(ren), and the Will names a Testamentary Guardian and/or Testamentary Conservator.

_______a. (initial if applicable). The Will names a Testamentary Guardian of (a) minor child(ren) of the decedent. At the time of the decedent' death, he/she had (a) minor child(ren) and there are no living parents; the following individual(s) is/are named as Testamentary Guardian in the decedent's Will:

Name Address

_______b. (initial if applicable). The Will names a Testamentary Conservator of (a) minor child(ren) of the decedent. At the time of the decedent's death, he/she had (a) minor child(ren) and there is/are no court-appointed Conservator(s); the following individual(s) is/are named as Testamentary Conservator(s) in the decedent's Will:

Name Address

_______c. (initial as applicable). The Will names a Testamentary Conservator of (a) minor child(ren) of the decedent. At the time of the decedent's death, he/she had (a) minor child(ren) and there is/are a court-appointed Conservator(s), who is/are identified as follows:

Name Address

5.

Additional Data: Where full particulars are lacking, state here the reasons for any such omission. If any persons listed above as heirs are cousins, grandchildren, nephews or nieces of the decedent, please list the deceased ancestor through whom they are related to the decedent. If any executor nominated in the will has a priority equal to or higher than the propounder but will not qualify, indicate the name and reasons.

6.

To the knowledge of the petitioner(s), no other proceedings with respect to this estate are pending, or have been completed, in any other probate court in this state.

WHEREFORE, petitioner(s) pray(s)

1. leave to prove said Will in Common Form,
2. that it be admitted to record on proper proof,
3. that Letters of Testamentary Guardianship and/or Letters of Testamentary Conservatorship issue, if applicable,
4. that Letters Testamentary issue, and
5. that this Court order such other relief as may be proper under the circumstances.

_______________________________ Signature of first petitioner

_______________________________ Signature of second petitioner if any

_______________________________ Printed Name

_______________________________ Printed Name

_______________________________ Address

_______________________________ Address

____

____

_______________________________ Phone Number

Phone Number

Signature of Attorney: _______________________________

Typed/printed name of Attorney: _______________________________

Address: _______________________________

Telephone: _______________________________ State Bar # __________

Effective 7/05 -3- GPCSF 4 Complete

VERIFICATION

GEORGIA, ______________________ COUNTY

Personally appeared before me the undersigned petitioner(s) who on oath state(s) that the facts set forth in the foregoing petition are true.

Sworn to and subscribed before
me this ____ day of ______________, 20____.

____
First Petitioner

____
NOTARY/CLERK OF PROBATE COURT

____
Printed Name

Sworn to and subscribed before
me this ____ day of ______________, 20____.

____
Second Petitioner, if any

____
NOTARY/CLERK OF PROBATE COURT

____
Printed Name

TESTAMENTARY GUARDIAN AND/OR TESTAMENTARY CONSERVATOR CONSENT TO SERVE

GEORGIA, ______________________________ COUNTY

IN RE: PETITION OF ____ TO PROBATE
THE WILL OF ____, DECEASED,
IN SOLEMN FORM

I/We, the undersigned, being 18 years of age or older, laboring under no legal disability and being named as Testamentary Guardian(s) and/or Testamentary Conservator(s), hereby consent to serve. I understand that once appointed, I will have the same rights, powers, and duties as set forth in O.C.G.A. §29-2-4 and 29-3-5.

SIGNATURE

Sworn to and subscribed before me this ____ day of ______________, 20____. ______________________________

______________________________ ______________________________
NOTARY/CLERK OF PROBATE COURT Printed Name

Sworn to and subscribed before me this ____ day of ______________, 20____. ______________________________

______________________________ ______________________________
NOTARY/CLERK OF PROBATE COURT Printed Name

Sworn to and subscribed before me this ____ day of ______________, 20____. ______________________________

______________________________ ______________________________
NOTARY/CLERK OF PROBATE COURT Printed Name

Sworn to and subscribed before me this ____ day of ______________, 20____. ______________________________

______________________________ ______________________________
NOTARY/CLERK OF PROBATE COURT Printed Name

PROBATE COURT OF ______________ COUNTY

STATE OF GEORGIA

IN RE: ESTATE OF	)	ESTATE NO.
	)	
________________________________,	)	PETITION TO PROBATE WILL IN
DECEASED	)	COMMON FORM

ORDER

It has been shown to the Court in the matter of the Last Will and Testament of ________________, deceased, propounded by ________________, named as Executor(s), that the said decedent died domiciled in said County; and that the said Will has been (self-proved) (proved by a witness) to be the Last Will and Testament of said decedent as alleged by the propounder.

IT IS, THEREFORE, ORDERED by this Court that said Will be established as the Last Will and Testament of ________________________, that the same be admitted to record as proved in Common Form, that the Executor(s) has/have leave to qualify as such by taking the required oath, and upon so doing, that Letters Testamentary be issued.

IT IS FURTHER ORDERED that the Executor(s), after payment of all debts, shall disburse property according to the terms of the Will and shall maintain all records of income and disbursements until they are discharged.

IT IS FURTHER ORDERED that the deputy clerk/clerk shall serve the Executor(s) with a copy of this Order by first class mail and shall file a certificate of service showing such service.

(initial if applicable)

_______ IT IS FURTHER ORDERED that Letters of Testamentary Guardianship and/or Conservatorship shall issue to the individuals so designated in said Will.

SO ORDERED this _____ day of ____________________, 20_____.

Probate Judge

PROBATE COURT OF ______________ COUNTY

STATE OF GEORGIA

IN RE: ESTATE OF) ESTATE NO. __________

)

__________________________,) PETITION TO PROBATE WILL IN

DECEASED) COMMON FORM

OATH

I do solemnly swear (or affirm) that this writing contains the true Last Will and Testament of __________________________, deceased, so far as I know or believe, and that I will well and truly execute the same in accordance with the laws of Georgia. So help me God.

Sworn to and subscribed before
me this ____ day of ____________, 20____. __________________________
Executor

__________________________ __________________________

NOTARY/CLERK OF PROBATE COURT Printed Name

Sworn to and subscribed before
me this ____ day of ____________, 20____. __________________________
Executor

__________________________ __________________________

NOTARY/CLERK OF PROBATE COURT Printed Name

Effective 7/05 GPCSF 4 Complete

STATE OF GEORGIA

COUNTY OF ______________________ ESTATE NO. ______________________

LETTERS TESTAMENTARY
Common Form
(Relieved of Filing Returns)

By ______________________, Judge of the Probate Court of said County.

KNOW ALL WHOM IT MAY CONCERN:

That on the ____ day of ____________, 20____, at a regular term of the Probate Court, the Last Will and Testament dated ____________, ______, of ______________________ deceased, at the time of his or her death a resident of said County, was legally proven in common form and was admitted to record by order, and it was further ordered that __________ named as Executor(s) in said Will, be allowed to qualify, and that upon so doing, Letters Testamentary be issued to such Executor(s).

NOW, THEREFORE, the said ______________________, having taken the oath of office and complied with all the necessary prerequisites of the law, is/are legally authorized to discharge all the duties and exercise all the powers of Executor(s) under the Will of said deceased, according to the Will and the law.

Given under my hand and official seal, the ______ day of ____________, 20____.

Probate Judge

NOTE: The following must be signed if the judge does not sign the original of this document:

Issued by: (Seal)

PROBATE CLERK/DEPUTY CLERK

STATE OF GEORGIA

COUNTY OF ____________________ ESTATE NO. ____________________

LETTERS TESTAMENTARY
Common Form
(Not Relieved of Filing Return)

By ____________________, Judge of the Probate Court of said County.

KNOW ALL WHOM IT MAY CONCERN:

That on the ____ day of ____________, 20____, at a regular term of the Probate Court, the Last Will and Testament dated ____________________, ________, of ____________________, deceased, at the time of his or her death a resident of said County, was legally proven in common form and was admitted to record by order, and it was further ordered that ____________________, named as Executor(s) in said Will, be allowed to qualify, and that upon so doing, Letters Testamentary be issued to such Executor(s).

NOW, THEREFORE, the said __________ having taken the oath of office and complied with all the necessary prerequisites of the law, is/are legally authorized to discharge all the duties and exercise all the powers of Executor(s) under the Will of said deceased, according to the Will and the law; and is/are hereby required to render a true and correct inventory of all the goods, chattels, rights and credits of said deceased, and make a return of them to this Court; and further, to file a proper annual or final return with this Court each year until the Executorship is fully discharged.

Given under my hand and official seal, the _____ day of ______________, 20_____.

Probate Judge

NOTE: The following must be signed if the judge does not sign the original of this document:

Issued by:

______________________________ (Seal)

PROBATE CLERK/DEPUTY CLERK

Effective 7/05 GPCSF 4 Complete

STATE OF GEORGIA
COUNTY OF ____________ ESTATE NO. ____________

LETTERS OF TESTAMENTARY GUARDIANSHIP OF MINOR

From the Judge of the Probate Court of said County.

TO: ______________________, Testamentary Guardian(s)
RE: ______________________, Minor

Pursuant to the Last Will and Testament of ______________________, deceased, you have been appointed Testamentary Guardian of the minor. You have assented to this appointment by taking your oath. In general, your duties as Testamentary Guardian are to protect and maintain the person of the minor and your power over the minor shall be the same as that of a parent over a child, the guardian(s) standing in place of the parent(s). A guardian shall at all times act as a fiduciary in the minor's best interest and exercise reasonable care, diligence, and prudence.

Special Instructions:

1. It is your duty to see that the minor is adequately fed, clothed, sheltered, educated, and cared for, and that the minor receives all necessary medical attention.
2. You must keep the Court informed of any change in your name or address.
3. You should inform the Court of any change of location of your minor.
4. You shall, within 60 days of appointment and within 60 days after each anniversary date of appointment, file with this Court and provide to the conservator of the minor, if any, a personal status report concerning the minor.
5. You shall promptly notify the court of any conflict of interest which may arise between you as guardian and the minor pursuant to O.C.G.A. §29-2-23.
6. The guardianship automatically terminates when the minor dies, reaches age 18, is adopted, or is emancipated.
7. You shall act in coordination and cooperation with the minor's conservator, if appointed, or if not, with others who have custody of the minor's property.
8. Please consult your attorney if you have any questions. Your authority to act pursuant to these Letters is subject to applicable statues[1] and to any special orders entered in this case.

Give under my hand and official seal, this _____ day of ______________, 20_____.

Probate Judge

NOTE: The following must be signed if the judge does not sign the original of this document:

Issued by:

____
PROBATE CLERK/DEPUTY CLERK (Seal)

Effective 7/05 GPCSF 4 Complete

1 So in original

STATE OF GEORGIA
COUNTY OF ______________________ ESTATE NO. ______________________

LETTERS OF TESTAMENTARY CONSERVATORSHIP OF MINOR

From the Judge of the Probate Court of said County.

TO: ______________________________, Testamentary Conservator(s)
RE: ______________________________, Minor

Pursuant to the Last Will and Testament of the below-named decedent, you have been appointed Testamentary Conservator of the minor's property. You have assented to this appointment by taking your oath. In general, your duties as Testamentary Conservator are to protect and maintain the property of the minor and utilize the minor's property solely for the benefit of the minor. Please consult your attorney if you have any questions.

These Letters of Testamentary Conservatorship empower the above testamentary conservator to hold, for the minor, only property which passed through the estate of

______________________________, Deceased.

Given under my hand and official seal, this _____ day of ________________, 20____.

Probate Judge

Note: The following must be signed if the judge does not sign the original of this document:

Issued by:

______________________________ (Seal)
PROBATE CLERK/DEPUTY CLERK

Effective 7/05 GPCSF 4 Complete

Instructions and form revised effective January 1, 1998; July 1, 1998; July 31, 2006.

GPCSF 5 PETITIONER. PETITION TO PROBATE WILL IN SOLEMN FORM

GEORGIA PROBATE COURT
STANDARD FORM

Petition to Probate Will in Solemn Form

INSTRUCTIONS

I. Specific Instructions

1. This form is to be used when filing a petition to probate will in solemn form pursuant to O.C.G.A. §53-5-20, et seq.

2. It is permissible, but not mandatory, to use this form in connection with a petition to probate a copy of a will in lieu of a lost original pursuant to O.C.G.A. §53-4-46, provided that appropriate interlineations are made, and additional information is given to overcome the presumption of revocation. Check with the court in which the petition will be filed.

3. This form may, but is not required to, be used where service by registered or certified mail with return receipt requested is requested by the petitioner in lieu of personal service, in accordance with O.C.G.A. §53-11-3(e). Appropriate changes would be required in the order for notice, notice and certificate of service.

4. Signatures of heirs who acknowledge service must be attested by a notary public or the clerk of any probate court of this state. It is not necessary that all acknowledgments appear on the same page. An attorney at law may acknowledge service on behalf of an heir; however, the attorney must certify that he or she currently represents that heir with regard to the pending matter and, in order to comply with O.C.G.A. §53-11-6, the attorney's signature must be attested as provided above. With respect to a power of attorney, the attorney-in-fact may acknowledge service on behalf of the donor of the power, provided that the power of attorney grants such authority, the signature of the attorney-in-fact is attested, a copy of the power of attorney is attached, and the attorney-in-fact certifies that the copy is a true copy and is still in effect.

5. O.C.G.A. §53-5-22(c) provides that service of notice, when made personally or by mail, shall include a copy of the petition and of the will for which probate is sought. The same is true when service is acknowledged.

II. General Instructions

General instructions applicable to all Georgia probate court standard forms are available in each probate court.

GEORGIA PROBATE COURT
STANDARD FORM

IN THE PROBATE COURT OF ____________________ COUNTY

STATE OF GEORGIA

IN RE: ESTATE OF	)	ESTATE NO. ________
	)	
______________________________,	)	PETITION TO PROBATE WILL
DECEASED	)	IN SOLEMN FORM

TO THE HONORABLE JUDGE OF THE PROBATE COURT:

The petition of ____, whose mailing address is/are ________________________________, shows:

1.

On ____, 20__________,
First Middle Last Name
whose place of domicile was
Street City County State
departed this life owning property in Georgia.

2.

While alive, decedent duly made and published a Last Will and Testament dated ______________, which is herewith offered for probate in Solemn Form. Your petitioner(s) is/are named as the Executor.

3.

Listed below are all of the decedent's heirs, with the age or majority status, address and relationship to the decedent set opposite the name of each:

Name	Age (Or over 18)	Address	Relationship

4.

(initial if applicable)

_____ As shown in paragraph 3. above, the decedent was survived by (a) minor child(ren), and:

_____a. (initial if applicable). The Will names a Testamentary Guardian of the minor child(ren) of the decedent. Petitioner shows there is no living parent of said child(ren). The following individual(s) who has/have consented to serve is/are named as Testamentary Guardian in the decedent's Will:

Name Address

_____b. (initial if applicable). The Will names a Testamentary Conservator of the minor child(ren) of the decedent for property passing under the decedent's Will. The following individual(s) who has/have consented to serve is/are named as Testamentary Conservator(s) in the decedent's Will:

Name Address

_____ i. (initial as applicable). There is/are now a court-appointed Conservator(s), who is/are identified as follows:

Name Address

5.

Additional Data: Where full particulars are lacking, state here the reasons for any such omission. Also, state here all pertinent facts which may govern the method of giving notice to any party and which may determine whether or not a guardian ad litem should be appointed for any party. If any heirs listed above are cousins, grandchildren, nephews or nieces of the decedent, please indicate the deceased ancestor through whom they are related to the decedent. If any executor nominated in the will has an equal or higher priority to the propounder, but will not qualify, indicate the name and reasons.

6.

(initial one)

_____ To the knowledge of the petitioner(s), no other proceedings with respect to this estate are pending, or have been completed, in any other probate court in this state.

_____ The probate of another purported Will of the decedent is pending in this state in the _______________ County Probate Court. The names and address(es) of the propounder(s) and the names, addresses and ages or majority status of the beneficiaries under the other purported Will to whom notice is required under O.C.G.A. §53-5-22(b) are listed on the attachment hereto, which is expressly made a part hereof, as if fully set forth herein.

WHEREFORE, petitioner(s) pray(s)

1. leave to prove said Will in solemn form,
2. that due and legal notice be given as the law requires,
3. that said Will be admitted to record on proper proof,
4. that Letters of Testamentary Guardianship and/or Letters of Testamentary Conservatorship issue, if applicable,
5. that Letters Testamentary issue, and
6. that this Court order such other relief as may be proper under the circumstances.

_______________	_______________
Signature of first petitioner	Signature of second petitioner if any
_______________	_______________
Printed Name	Printed Name
_______________	_______________
Address	Address
_______________	_______________
Phone Number	Phone Number

Signature of Attorney: _______________

Typed/printed name of Attorney: _______________

Address: _______________

Telephone: _______________ State Bar # _______________

VERIFICATION

GEORGIA, ______________________ COUNTY

Personally appeared before me the undersigned petitioner(s) who on oath state(s) that the facts set forth in the foregoing petition are true.

Sworn to and subscribed before
me this ____ day of ______________, 20____.

____
First Petitioner

____
NOTARY/CLERK OF PROBATE COURT

____
Printed Name

Sworn to and subscribed before
me this ____ day of ______________, 20____.

____
Second Petitioner, if any

____
NOTARY/CLERK OF PROBATE COURT

____
Printed Name

ACKNOWLEDGMENT OF SERVICE AND ASSENT TO PROBATE INSTANTER

GEORGIA, ______________________________ COUNTY

IN RE: PETITION OF ____ TO PROBATE
THE WILL OF ____, DECEASED,
IN SOLEMN FORM

We, the undersigned, being 18 years of age or older, laboring under no legal disability and being heirs of the above-named decedent, hereby acknowledge service of a copy of the petition to probate said Will in solemn form, purported Will, and notice, waive copies of same, waive further service and notice, and hereby assent to the probate of said Will in solemn form without further delay.

SIGNATURE(S) OF HEIRS

Sworn to and subscribed before
me this ____ day of ______________, 20____. ______________________________

______________________________ ______________________________
NOTARY/CLERK OF PROBATE COURT Printed Name

Sworn to and subscribed before
me this ____ day of ______________, 20____. ______________________________

______________________________ ______________________________
NOTARY/CLERK OF PROBATE COURT Printed Name

Sworn to and subscribed before
me this ____ day of ______________, 20____. ______________________________

______________________________ ______________________________
NOTARY/CLERK OF PROBATE COURT Printed Name

Sworn to and subscribed before
me this ____ day of ______________, 20____. ______________________________

______________________________ ______________________________
NOTARY/CLERK OF PROBATE COURT Printed Name

Sworn to and subscribed before
me this ____ day of ______________, 20____. ______________________________

______________________________ ______________________________
NOTARY/CLERK OF PROBATE COURT Printed Name

Sworn to and subscribed before
me this ____ day of ______________, 20____. ______________________________

______________________________ ______________________________
NOTARY/CLERK OF PROBATE COURT Printed Name

TESTAMENTARY GUARDIAN AND/OR TESTAMENTARY CONSERVATOR CONSENT TO SERVE

GEORGIA, ______________________________ COUNTY

IN RE: PETITION OF ______________________________ TO PROBATE
THE WILL OF ______________________________, DECEASED,
IN SOLEMN FORM

I/We, the undersigned, being 18 years of age or older, laboring under no legal disability and being named as Testamentary Guardian(s) and/or Testamentary Conservator(s), hereby consent to serve. I/We understand that once appointed, I/We will have the same rights, powers, and duties as set forth in O.C.G.A. §29-2-4 and 29-3-5.

SIGNATURE

Sworn to and subscribed before
me this ____ day of ______________, 20____. ______________________________

______________________________ ______________________________
NOTARY/CLERK OF PROBATE COURT Printed Name

Sworn to and subscribed before
me this ____ day of ______________, 20____. ______________________________

______________________________ ______________________________
NOTARY/CLERK OF PROBATE COURT Printed Name

Sworn to and subscribed before
me this ____ day of ______________, 20____. ______________________________

______________________________ ______________________________
NOTARY/CLERK OF PROBATE COURT Printed Name

Sworn to and subscribed before
me this ____ day of ______________, 20____. ______________________________

______________________________ ______________________________
NOTARY/CLERK OF PROBATE COURT Printed Name

Instructions and form revised effective January 1, 1998; July 1, 1998; July 31, 2006.

GPCSF 5 COURT. COURT FORMS FOR PETITION TO PROBATE WILL IN SOLEMN FORM

GEORGIA PROBATE COURT
STANDARD FORM

Petition to Probate Will in Solemn Form

NOTICE: UNLESS OTHERWISE DIRECTED BY THE COURT, THE FOLLOWING FORMS ARE FOR PROBATE COURT STAFF TO COMPLETE

GEORGIA PROBATE COURT
STANDARD FORM

PROBATE COURT OF ______________________ COUNTY

STATE OF GEORGIA

IN RE: ESTATE OF) ESTATE NO. ______________
)
______________________,) PETITION TO PROBATE WILL IN
DECEASED) SOLEMN FORM

ORDER FOR SERVICE OF NOTICE AND APPOINTMENT OF GUARDIAN AD LITEM, IF NECESSARY

The foregoing Petition to Probate Will in Solemn Form having been filed, and it appearing that the following heirs did not acknowledge service, it is Ordered that: (Initial any and all which apply:)

_____ Notice must be served personally, together with a copy of the petition and the purported Will, at least ten days before the Will can be probated on the following heirs who reside in Georgia:

_____ Notice must be served by registered or certified mail, return receipt requested, together with a copy of the petition and the purported Will, upon the following nonresident heirs whose current residence addresses are known:

_____ Notice must be published once a week for four weeks in the newspaper in which sheriff's advertisements are published in this county, before ______________________, in order to serve by publication the following heirs whose current residence addresses are unknown:

_____ **IT IS ORDERED** that ______________________ is appointed guardian ad litem for ______________________ (minor)(unborn heir)(and the unknown heir), and that said guardian ad litem be duly served with a copy of the foregoing Notice, petition, purported Will and notice of this appointment, and that upon said guardian ad litem's acceptance of same, said guardian ad litem shall make answer hereto. This appointment is limited to this proceeding only and it shall cease when a final order is entered on this petition.

SO ORDERED this _____ day of ______________, 20___.

Probate Judge

NOTICE

PROBATE COURT OF ______________________ COUNTY

RE: PETITION OF ______________________________ TO PROBATE IN SOLEMN FORM THE WILL OF ______________________, DECEASED, UPON WHICH AN ORDER FOR SERVICE WAS GRANTED BY THIS COURT ON ________, 20

(Strike the following paragraph if not applicable:)

TO: ____

(List here all heirs having known addresses in the continental U.S. to be served by certified or registered mail)

This is to notify you to file objection, if there is any, to the above referenced petition, in this Court on or before the thirteenth (13th) day after ______________, 20____ (the date of the mailing of this Notice to you by certified or registered mail, return receipt requested); provided, however, that if a return receipt for such Notice is actually received by the Court within such 13 days, the deadline for the filing of any objection shall be ten (10) days from the date of receipt shown on such return receipt.

(Strike the following paragraph if not applicable:)

TO: ____

(List here all heirs having known addresses outside the continental U.S. to be served by certified or registered mail)

This is to notify you to file objection, if there is any, to the above referenced petition, in this Court on or before the thirtieth (30th) day after ______________, 20____ (the date of the mailing of this Notice to you by certified or registered mail, return receipt requested); provided, however, that if a return receipt for such Notice is actually received by the Court within such 30 days, the deadline for the filing of any objection shall be ten (10) days from the date of receipt shown on such return receipt.

(Strike the following paragraph if not applicable:)

This is further to notify ______________________________________,

(List here all heirs who reside in Georgia to be served personally)

who are required to be served personally, to file objection, if there is any, to the above referenced petition, in this Court on or before the tenth (10th) day after the date you are personally served.

BE NOTIFIED FURTHER: All objections to the petition must be in writing, setting forth the grounds of any such objections. All pleadings/objections must be signed before a notary public or before a probate court clerk, and filing fees must be tendered with your pleadings/objections, unless you qualify to file as an indigent party. Contact probate court personnel at the following address/telephone number for the required amount of filing fees. If any objections are filed, a hearing will be (held on ______________ 20____) (scheduled at a later date). If no objections are filed, the petition may be granted without a hearing.

PROBATE JUDGE

By:
CLERK OF THE PROBATE COURT

ADDRESS

TELEPHONE NUMBER

Effective 7/06 GPCSF 5 Court

NOTICE

PROBATE COURT OF ______________________ COUNTY

RE: PETITION OF ______________________ TO PROBATE IN SOLEMN FORM THE WILL OF ______________________, DECEASED, UPON WHICH AN ORDER FOR SERVICE WAS GRANTED BY THIS COURT ON ________, 20 ___

(For use if an heir is required to be served by publication:)

TO: ______________________

(List here known heirs having unknown addresses to be served by publication)

______________________ all interested parties and all and singular the heirs of said decedent, and to whom it may concern:

This is to notify you to file objection, if there is any, to the above referenced petition, in this Court on or before ______________________, 20_____.

BE NOTIFIED FURTHER: All objections to the petition must be in writing, setting forth the grounds of any such objections. All pleadings/objections must be signed before a notary public or before a probate court clerk, and filing fees must be tendered with your pleadings/objections, unless you qualify to file as an indigent party. Contact probate court personnel at the following address/telephone number for the required amount of filing fees. If any objections are filed, a hearing will be (held on ______________________ 20_____) (scheduled at a later date). If no objections are filed, the petition may be granted without a hearing.

PROBATE JUDGE

By:
CLERK OF THE PROBATE COURT

ADDRESS

TELEPHONE NUMBER

Effective 7/06 GPCSF 5 Court

PROBATE COURT OF ______________________ COUNTY

STATE OF GEORGIA

IN RE: ESTATE OF ______________________) ESTATE NO. ______________
)
______________________________________,) PETITION TO PROBATE WILL IN
DECEASED) SOLEMN FORM

RETURN OF SHERIFF

I have this day served ____________________ personally with a copy of the foregoing petition, purported Will and notice.

______________________ ______________________________

Date

Deputy Sheriff, ________________ County

CERTIFICATE OF MAILING

This is to certify that I have this date forwarded by registered or certified mail, return receipt requested, in a stamped, addressed envelope, a copy of the foregoing petition, purported Will and the notice, to heirs who reside out of state at known current residence addresses.

DATE	PROBATE CLERK/DEPUTY CLERK

IN THE PROBATE COURT OF ________________ COUNTY

STATE OF GEORGIA

IN RE: ESTATE OF) ESTATE NO. ________________

)

________________,) PETITION TO PROBATE WILL

DECEASED) IN SOLEMN FORM

ANSWER OF GUARDIAN AD LITEM

I hereby accept the foregoing appointment, acknowledge service and notice of the proceedings as provided by law, and for answer say:

________________ ________________

DATE GUARDIAN AD LITEM

ADDRESS

____

TELEPHONE

PROBATE COURT OF ______________________ COUNTY

STATE OF GEORGIA

IN RE: ESTATE OF) ESTATE NO. ______________

)

______________________,) PETITION TO PROBATE WILL IN
DECEASED) SOLEMN FORM

ORDER

It being shown to the Court in the matter of the alleged Last Will and Testament of the above-named decedent, propounded by ______________________________________, named as Executor(s), that the said decedent died domiciled in said County; and that due notice of the intention of said propounder(s) to proceed with the proof in solemn form has been served on all of the heirs of said decedent, all in accordance with the laws of this State, and all other requirements of law having been fulfilled, and the said Will having been (self-proved) (proved by one of the witnesses) thereto to be the Last Will and Testament of said decedent as alleged by the propounder(s); and no objection having been filed;

IT IS ORDERED by this Court, that said Will be established as the Last Will and Testament of said decedent; that the same be admitted to record, as proved in solemn form; and that said Executor(s) have leave to qualify as such by taking the required oath, and upon so doing, that Letters Testamentary issue to said Executor(s).

IT IS FURTHER ORDERED that said Executor(s) shall disburse all property according to the terms of the Will and shall maintain all records of income and disbursements until they are discharged.

IT IS FURTHER ORDERED that the clerk/deputy clerk shall serve the Executor(s) with a copy of this Order by first class mail and shall file a certificate of service showing such service.

(initial if applicable)

_____ IT IS FURTHER ORDERED that Letters of Testamentary Guardianship and/or Conservatorship shall issue to the individuals so designated in said Will.

SO ORDERED this _____ day of __________________, 20____.

Probate Judge

PROBATE COURT OF ______________________ COUNTY

STATE OF GEORGIA

IN RE: ESTATE OF	)	ESTATE NO. ______________
	)	
______________________,	)	PETITION TO PROBATE WILL IN
DECEASED	)	SOLEMN FORM

OATH

I do solemnly swear (or affirm) that this writing contains the true Last Will and Testament of ______________________, deceased, so far as I know or believe, and that I will well and truly execute the same in accordance with the laws of Georgia. So help me God.

Sworn to and subscribed before
me this ____ day of ____________, 20____. ______________________
Executor

______________________ ______________________
NOTARY/CLERK OF PROBATE COURT Printed Name

Sworn to and subscribed before
me this ____ day of ____________, 20____. ______________________
Executor

______________________ ______________________
NOTARY/CLERK OF PROBATE COURT Printed Name

STATE OF GEORGIA

COUNTY OF ______________________ ESTATE NO.

LETTERS TESTAMENTARY

(Relieved of Filing Returns)

By ______________________, Judge of the Probate Court of said County.

KNOW ALL WHOM IT MAY CONCERN:

That on the ____ day of __________, 20____, at a regular term of the Probate Court, the Last Will and Testament dated ______________, ______, of ______________________ deceased, at the time of his or her death a resident of said County, was legally proven in ______________ form and was admitted to record by order, and it was further ordered that ____________ named as Executor(s) in said Will, be allowed to qualify, and that upon so doing, Letters Testamentary be issued to such Executor(s).

NOW, THEREFORE, the said ____, having taken the oath of office and complied with all the necessary prerequisites of the law, is/are legally authorized to discharge all the duties and exercise all the powers of Executor(s) under the Will of said deceased, according to the Will and the law.

Given under my hand and official seal, the ____ day of ______________, 20____.

Probate Judge

NOTE: The following must be signed if the judge does not sign the original of this document:

Issued by: (Seal)

PROBATE CLERK/DEPUTY CLERK

STATE OF GEORGIA

COUNTY OF ________________ ESTATE NO. ________________

LETTERS TESTAMENTARY
(Not Relieved of Filing Return)

By ________________, Judge of the Probate Court of said County.

KNOW ALL WHOM IT MAY CONCERN:

That on the ____ day of ____________, 20___, at a regular term of the Probate Court, the Last Will and Testament dated __________, ____, of ________________, deceased, at the time of his or her death a resident of said County, was legally proven in ______ form and was admitted to record by order, and it was further ordered that ____________, named as Executor(s) in said Will, be allowed to qualify, and that upon so doing, Letters Testamentary be issued to such Executor(s).

NOW, THEREFORE, the said ________ having taken the oath of office and complied with all the necessary prerequisites of the law, is/are legally authorized to discharge all the duties and exercise all the powers of Executor(s) under the Will of said deceased, according to the Will and the law; and is/are hereby required to render a true and correct inventory of all the goods, chattels, rights and credits of said deceased, and make a return of them to this Court; and further, to file a proper annual or final return with this Court each year until the Executorship is fully discharged.

Given under my hand and official seal, the ____ day of ____________, 20___.

Probate Judge

NOTE: The following must be signed if the judge does not sign the original of this document:

Issued by:

________________________ (Seal)

PROBATE CLERK/DEPUTY CLERK

Effective 7/06 GPCSF 5 Court

STATE OF GEORGIA

COUNTY OF ______________ ESTATE NO. ______________

LETTERS OF TESTAMENTARY GUARDIANSHIP OF MINOR

From the Judge of the Probate Court of said County.

TO: ______________________________, Testamentary Guardian(s)
RE: ______________________________, Minor

Pursuant to the Last Will and Testament of ______________________________, deceased, you have been appointed Testamentary Guardian of the minor. You have assented to this appointment by taking your oath. In general, your duties as Testamentary Guardian are to protect and maintain the person of the minor and your power over the minor shall be the same as that of a parent over a child, the guardian(s) standing in place of the parent(s). A guardian shall at all times act as a fiduciary in the minor's best interest and exercise reasonable care, diligence, and prudence.

Special Instructions:

1. It is your duty to see that the minor is adequately fed, clothed, sheltered, educated, and cared for, and that the minor receives all necessary medical attention.
2. You must keep the Court informed of any change in your name or address.
3. You should inform the Court of any change of location of your minor.
4. You shall, within 60 days of appointment and within 60 days after each anniversary date of appointment, file with this Court and provide to the conservator of the minor, if any, a personal status report concerning the minor.
5. You shall promptly notify the court of any conflict of interest which may arise between you as guardian and the minor pursuant to O.C.G.A. §29-2-23.
6. The guardianship automatically terminates when the minor dies, reaches age 18, is adopted, or is emancipated.
7. You shall act in coordination and cooperation with the minor's conservator, if appointed, or if not, with others who have custody of the minor's property.
8. Please consult your attorney if you have any questions. Your authority to act pursuant to these Letters is subject to applicable statues[1] and to any special orders entered in this case.

Give under my hand and official seal, this _____ day of ____________________, 20____.

Probate Judge

NOTE: The following must be signed if the judge does not sign the original of this document:

Issued by:

____
PROBATE CLERK/DEPUTY CLERK (Seal)

Effective 7/06 GPCSF 5 Court

[1] So in original

STATE OF GEORGIA

COUNTY OF ______________________ ESTATE NO. __________

LETTERS OF TESTAMENTARY CONSERVATORSHIP OF MINOR

From the Judge of the Probate Court of said County.

TO: ______________________________, Testamentary Conservator(s)
RE: ______________________________, Minor

Pursuant to the Last Will and Testament of the below-named decedent, you have been appointed Testamentary Conservator of the minor's property. You have assented to this appointment by taking your oath. In general, your duties as Testamentary Conservator are to protect and maintain the property of the minor and utilize the minor's property solely for the benefit of the minor. Please consult your attorney if you have any questions.

These Letters of Testamentary Conservatorship empower the above testamentary conservator to hold, for the minor, only property which passed through the estate of

______________________________, **Deceased.**

Given under my hand and official seal, this _____ day of ______________, 20_____.

Probate Judge

NOTE: The following must be signed if the judge does not sign the original of this document:

Issued by:

______________________________ (Seal)
PROBATE CLERK/DEPUTY CLERK

Effective 7/06 GPCSF 5 Court

Form adopted effective July 31, 2006.

GPCSF 6. INTERROGATORIES TO WITNESS TO WILL

INTERROGATORIES TO WITNESS TO WILL

PROBATE COURT OF ______________________________ COUNTY

Re: Petition of ______________________________ to probate in (Common) (Solemn) Form the purported Last Will and Testament dated ______________, _____, of ______________________________, deceased.

To: ______________________________
Name Address

The following interrogatories are submitted to you under the provisions of Official Code of Georgia Ann. §53-5-23 as amended, in connection with the petition referred to above.
(Initial A or B below:)

______ A. The original of said purported Will is exhibited to you herewith.

______ B. Attached hereto is a true photographic copy of said purported Will NOTE: said attachment must be filed with the Court.

You are hereby requested to answer the following questions in the space provided with respect to said purported Will:

1. Did YOU sign the purported Will as a witness? 1. Answer: __________
2. Did the above-named Decedent sign the purported Will? 2. Answer: __________
3. Did the decedent acknowledge that the purported Will was his/her Last Will and Testament at the time of signing? 3. Answer: __________
4. Did you witness this Will at the request of the decedent and in the presence of the decedent? 4. Answer: __________
5. Did the decedent know that he/she was executing his/her Last Will and Testament when he/she executed this instrument? 5. Answer: __________
6. Did the decedent execute this instrument voluntarily? 6. Answer: __________
7. Did the decedent appear to be of sound and disposing mind and memory at the time of execution of this instrument? 7. Answer: __________

Before me, the undersigned Notary Public or Clerk of the Probate Court, appeared ______________________________, who, under oath, stated that the answers (s)he has given to the foregoing interrogatories are true and correct.

This _____ day of ______________________________, _____.

Notary Public/Clerk of Probate Court

____
Signature of Witness to Will

Mailing Address:

Telephone Number:

Notes: (1) General instructions applicable to all Georgia probate court standard forms are available in each probate court. (2) If the interrogatories are submitted to a witness to a purported codicil, appropriate changes must be made in this form.

Effective 7/06 GPCSF 6

Revised effective January 1, 1998; July 31, 2006.

GPCSF 7 PETITIONER. PETITION TO PROBATE WILL IN SOLEMN FORM AND FOR LETTERS OF ADMINISTRATION WITH WILL ANNEXED

GEORGIA PROBATE COURT
STANDARD FORM

Petition to Probate Will in Solemn Form and for Letters of Administration With Will Annexed

INSTRUCTIONS

I. Specific Instructions

1. This form is to be used when filing a combined Petition to Probate Will in Solemn Form pursuant to O.C.G.A. §53-5-20, et seq., and for Letters of Administration with the Will Annexed (sometimes called Letters of Administration C.T.A.) pursuant to O.C.G.A. §53-6-13 et seq.

2. Signatures of heirs and beneficiaries who acknowledge service must be attested by a notary public or the clerk of any probate court of this state. An attorney at law may acknowledge service on behalf of an heir or beneficiary; however, the attorney must certify that he or she currently represents that heir or beneficiary with regard to the pending matter and, in order to comply with O.C.G.A. §53-11-6, the attorney's signature must be attested as provided above. With respect to a power of attorney, the attorney-in-fact may acknowledge service on behalf of the donor of the power, provided that the power of attorney grants such authority, the signature of the attorney-in-fact is attested, a copy of the power of attorney is attached, and the attorney-in-fact certifies that the copy is a true copy and is still in effect. It is not necessary that all acknowledgments appear on the same page.

3. O.C.G.A. §53-5-22(c) provides that service of notice, when made personally or by mail, shall include a copy of the petition and of the Will for which probate is sought. This form also provides for a copy of the purported Will to be served upon the beneficiaries, which, though not required by the statute, is of some practical benefit and simplifies several parts of this form.

II. General Instructions

General instructions applicable to all Georgia probate court standard forms are available in each probate court.

GEORGIA PROBATE COURT
STANDARD FORM

IN THE PROBATE COURT OF ______________________ COUNTY

STATE OF GEORGIA

IN RE: ESTATE OF	)	ESTATE NO. ____________________
	)	
______________________________,	)	PETITION TO PROBATE WILL IN
DECEASED	)	SOLEMN FORM AND FOR LETTERS
	)	OF ADMINISTRATION WITH WILL
	)	ANNEXED

TO THE HONORABLE JUDGE OF THE PROBATE COURT:

The petition of ______________________, whose mailing address(es) is/are ______________________, shows:

1.

On ______________, ____,
First Middle Last Name

whose place of domicile was ____
Street City County State

departed this life owning property in Georgia.

2.

While alive, decedent duly made and published a Last Will and Testament dated ____________, which is herewith offered for probate in Solemn Form.

3.

Listed below are all of the decedent's heirs, with the age or majority status, address and relationship to decedent set opposite the name of each:

Name	Age (or over 18)	Address	Relationship

4.

Listed below are all of the beneficiaries under said Will who have a present interest, including but not limited to a vested remainder interest but not including trust beneficiaries where there is a trustee who is not the nominated administrator with Will annexed, and whose identity and whereabouts are known or may be determined by reasonable diligence.

Name	Age (Or over 18)	Address

5.

Additional Data: Where full particulars are lacking, state here the reasons for any such omission. Also, state here all pertinent facts which may govern the method of giving notice to any party and which may determine whether or not a guardian ad litem should be appointed for any party. If any persons listed above as heirs are cousins, grandchildren, nephews or nieces of the decedent, please indicate the deceased ancestor through whom they are related to the decedent. If the propounder is not an heir or a beneficiary under the Will, state how the propounder is interested in the administration of the estate. If it is alleged that a nominated executor has failed to qualify, state here the name and address of such nominated executor.

6.

Petitioner(s) further show(s) that the circumstances giving rise to the need for an administrator with the Will annexed are as follows:

(initial all which apply:)

______ The decedent failed to name an Executor in the Will.
______ The named Executor is deceased.
______ The named Executor has renounced his/her right to serve as such.
______ Other reason a testate estate is unrepresented ______________________.

7.

(The Petitioner(s)) (______________________) is/are entitled to be appointed Administrator C.T.A. by reason of:

(initial (a) or (b) and complete (b) if initialed:)

______ a. having been unanimously selected by the beneficiaries of the Will who are capable of expressing a choice. If the sole beneficiary is the decedent's surviving spouse, no action for divorce or separate maintenance was pending at the time of death of the testator.

______ b. appointment of the proposed Administrator(s) C.T.A. named above will best serve the interest of the estate and the proposed Administrator(s) C.T.A. is/are:

______ (i) A beneficiary or the trustee of any trust that is a beneficiary under the Will.

______ (ii) An eligible person as defined in O.C.G.A. §53-6-1.

______ (iii) A creditor of the estate.

______ (iv) The county administrator.

8.

The proposed Administrator(s) C.T.A. should be allowed to qualify without the necessity of posting bond, since only personal representatives of intestate estates and temporary administrators are normally required to post bond. See O.C.G.A. §53-6-50(a).

9.

(initial if applicable)

______ As shown in paragraph 3. above, the decedent was survived by (a) minor child(ren), and:

______ a. (initial if applicable). The Will names a Testamentary Guardian of the minor child(ren) of the decedent. Petitioner shows there is no living parent of said child(ren). The following individual(s) who has/have consented to serve is/are named as Testamentary Guardian in the decedent's Will:

Name Address

______ b. (initial if applicable). The Will names a Testamentary Conservator of the minor child(ren) of the decedent for property passing under the decedent's Will. The following individual(s) who has/have consented to serve is/are named as Testamentary Conservator(s) in the decedent's Will:

Name Address

______ i. (initial as applicable). There is/are now a court-appointed Conservator(s), who is/are identified as follows:

Name Address

10.

(Initial one:)

______ To the knowledge of the petitioner, no other proceedings with respect to this estate are pending, or have been completed, in any other probate court in this state.

______ The probate of another purported Will of the decedent is pending in this state in the ______________________ County Probate Court. The names and address(es) of the propounder(s) and the names, addresses and ages or majority status of the beneficiaries under the other purported Will are listed on the attachment hereto, which is expressly made a part hereof, as if fully set forth herein.

WHEREFORE, Petitioner(s) pray(s):

1. That due and legal notice of this petition be given as the law requires.
2. That the Will be admitted to probate in solemn form and to record upon proper proof.
3. That Letters of Administration with Will Annexed issue to the proposed Administrator(s) C.T.A. named above.
4. That Letters of Testamentary Guardianship and/or Letters of Testamentary Conservatorship issue, if applicable,
5. That this Court grant such other and further relief as it deems proper under the circumstances.

Signature of first petitioner	Signature of second petitioner if any
Printed Name	Printed Name
Address	Address
Phone Number	Phone Number

Signature of Attorney: ______

Typed/printed name of Attorney: ______

Address: ______

Telephone: ______ State Bar # ______

VERIFICATION

GEORGIA, ______ COUNTY

Personally appeared before me the undersigned petitioner(s) who on oath state(s) that the facts set forth in the foregoing petition are true.

Sworn to and subscribed before me this ______ day of ______, 20____.

______
NOTARY/CLERK OF PROBATE COURT

______
First Petitioner

______
Printed Name

Sworn to and subscribed before me this ______ day of ______, 20____.

______
NOTARY/CLERK OF PROBATE COURT

______
Second Petitioner, if any

______
Printed Name

ACKNOWLEDGMENT OF SERVICE AND ASSENT TO PROBATE WILL IN SOLEMN FORM BY HEIRS AND BY BENEFICIARIES CAPABLE OF EXPRESSING A CHOICE

PROBATE COURT OF ______________________________ COUNTY

IN RE: PETITION OF ______________________________ TO PROBATE THE WILL OF ______________________________, DECEASED, IN SOLEMN FORM, AND FOR LETTERS OF ADMINISTRATION WITH WILL ANNEXED.

Each of the undersigned beneficiaries hereby acknowledges service of a copy of the petition referred to above and the purported Will, waives all further service and notice, selects the person proposed in said petition to be Administrator with Will Annexed and consents to the petition.

Each of the undersigned heirs of the above-named decedent being 18 years of age or older, and laboring under no legal disability, hereby acknowledges service of a copy of the petition referred to above, purported Will, and notice, waives all further service and notice, and hereby assent to the probate of said Will in Solemn Form without further delay.

SIGNATURE(S) OF HEIRS/BENEFICIARIES

Sworn to and subscribed before me this _____ day of ___________, 20_____. ______________________________

______________________________ ______________________________

NOTARY/CLERK OF PROBATE COURT Print Name

Sworn to and subscribed before me this _____ day of ___________, 20_____. ______________________________

______________________________ ______________________________

NOTARY/CLERK OF PROBATE COURT Print Name

Sworn to and subscribed before me this _____ day of ___________, 20_____. ______________________________

______________________________ ______________________________

NOTARY/CLERK OF PROBATE COURT Print Name

Sworn to and subscribed before me this _____ day of ___________, 20_____. ______________________________

______________________________ ______________________________

NOTARY/CLERK OF PROBATE COURT Print Name

Sworn to and subscribed before me this _____ day of ___________, 20_____. ______________________________

______________________________ ______________________________

NOTARY/CLERK OF PROBATE COURT Print Name

TESTAMENTARY GUARDIAN AND/OR TESTAMENTARY CONSERVATOR CONSENT TO SERVE

GEORGIA, ______________________ COUNTY

IN RE: PETITION OF ______________________ TO PROBATE THE WILL
OF ______________________, DECEASED, IN SOLEMN FORM

I/We, the undersigned, being 18 years of age or older, laboring under no legal disability and being named as Testamentary Guardian(s) and/or Testamentary Conservator(s), hereby consent to serve. I understand that once appointed, I will have the same rights, powers, and duties as set forth in O.C.G.A. §29-2-4 and 29-3-5.

SIGNATURE

Sworn to and subscribed before me this ____ day of __________, 20____. ______________________

______________________ ______________________
NOTARY/CLERK OF PROBATE COURT Printed Name

Sworn to and subscribed before me this ____ day of __________, 20____. ______________________

______________________ ______________________
NOTARY/CLERK OF PROBATE COURT Printed Name

Sworn to and subscribed before me this ____ day of __________, 20____. ______________________

______________________ ______________________
NOTARY/CLERK OF PROBATE COURT Printed Name

Sworn to and subscribed before me this ____ day of __________, 20____. ______________________

______________________ ______________________
NOTARY/CLERK OF PROBATE COURT Printed Name

Effective 7/06 -7- GPCSF 7 Petitioner

Instructions and form amended effective July 1, 1986; July 1, 1991; January 1, 1998; July 1, 1998; July 31, 2006.

GPCSF 7 COURT. COURT FORMS FOR PETITION TO PROBATE WILL IN SOLEMN FORM AND FOR LETTERS OF ADMINISTRATION WITH WILL ANNEXED

GEORGIA PROBATE COURT
STANDARD FORM

Petition to Probate Will in Solemn Form and for Letters of Administration With Will Annexed

NOTICE: UNLESS OTHERWISE DIRECTED BY THE COURT, THE FOLLOWING FORMS ARE FOR PROBATE COURT STAFF TO COMPLETE

IN THE PROBATE COURT OF ______________________ COUNTY

STATE OF GEORGIA

IN RE: ESTATE OF	)	ESTATE NO. ______________
	)	
______________________________,	)	PETITION TO PROBATE WILL IN
DECEASED	)	SOLEMN FORM AND FOR
	)	LETTERS OF ADMINISTRATION
	)	WITH WILL ANNEXED

ORDER FOR SERVICE OF NOTICE AND FOR APPOINTMENT OF GUARDIAN AD LITEM, IF NECESSARY

The foregoing Petition to Probate Will in Solemn Form and for Letters of Administration with Will Annexed having been filed, and all the heirs not having acknowledged service and/or the beneficiaries capable of expressing a choice not having made a unanimous selection and/or it being alleged that a nominated executor has failed to qualify, it is ordered that notice shall issue and be served upon the ((heirs) (beneficiaries) who have not acknowledged service of the petition) (upon any executor nominated in the Will who has failed to qualify), as follows:

(Initial any and all which apply:)

______ Notice must be served personally, together with a copy of the petition and purported Will, at least ten days before the deadline for filing objections upon the following interested parties who reside in Georgia:

______ Notice must be served by registered or certified mail, return receipt requested, together with a copy of the petition and purported Will, upon the following nonresident interested parties whose current residence addresses are known:

______ Notice must be published once a week for four weeks in the newspaper in which sheriff's advertisements are published in this county, before ______________________, in order to serve by publication the following interested parties whose current residence addresses are unknown:

______ IT IS ORDERED that ______________________ is appointed guardian ad litem for __________ (minor)(unborn heir)(and the unknown heir), and that said guardian ad litem be duly served with a copy of the foregoing Notice, petition, purported Will and notice of this appointment, and that upon said guardian ad litem's acceptance of the same, said guardian ad litem shall make answer hereto. This appointment is limited to this proceeding only and it shall cease when a final order is entered on this petition.

SO ORDERED this ________ day of ______________, 20____.

____
Probate Judge

Effective 7/06 GPCSF 7 Court

NOTICE

PROBATE COURT OF ______________________ COUNTY

RE: PETITION OF ______________________ TO PROBATE IN SOLEMN FORM THE WILL OF ______________________, DECEASED, AND FOR LETTERS OF ADMINISTRATION WITH WILL ANNEXED, UPON WHICH AN ORDER FOR SERVICE WAS GRANTED BY THIS COURT ON ______________________, ________.

(Strike the following paragraph if not applicable:)

TO: (List here all interested parties having known addresses in the continental U.S. to be served by certified or registered mail) ______________________

This is to notify you to file objection, if there is any, to the above referenced petition, in this Court on or before the thirteenth (13th) day after ______________________, 20____ (the date of the mailing of this Notice to you by certified or registered mail, return receipt requested); provided, however, that if a return receipt for such Notice is actually received by the Court within such 13 days, the deadline for the filing of any objection shall be ten (10) days from the date of receipt shown on such return receipt.

(Strike the following paragraph if not applicable:)

TO: (List here all interested parties having known addresses outside the continental U.S. to be served by certified or registered mail) ______________________

This is to notify you to file objection, if there is any, to the above referenced petition, in this Court on or before the thirtieth (30th) day after ______________________, 20____ (the date of the mailing of this Notice to you by certified or registered mail, return receipt requested); provided, however, that if a return receipt for such Notice is actually received by the Court within such 30 days, the deadline for the filing of any objection shall be ten (10) days from the date of receipt shown on such return receipt.

(Strike the following paragraph if not applicable:)

TO: (List here all interested parties who reside in Georgia to be served personally) __________, who are required to be served personally, to file objection, if there is any, to the above referenced petition, in this Court on or before the tenth (10th) day after the date you are personally served.

BE NOTIFIED FURTHER: All objections to the petition must be in writing, setting forth the grounds of any such objections. All pleadings must be signed before a notary public or probate court clerk, and filing fees must be tendered with your pleadings, unless you qualify to file as an indigent party. Contact probate court personnel at the below address/phone number for the required amount of filing fees. If any objections are filed, a hearing will be (held on ______________________) (scheduled at a later date). If no objections are filed, the petition may be granted without a hearing.

PROBATE JUDGE
By:
CLERK OF THE PROBATE COURT

ADDRESS

TELEPHONE NUMBER

Effective 7/06

GPCSF 7 Court

NOTICE

PROBATE COURT OF ________________ COUNTY

RE: PETITION OF ________________ TO PROBATE IN SOLEMN FORM THE WILL OF ________________, DECEASED, AND FOR LETTERS OF ADMINISTRATION WITH WILL ANNEXED, UPON WHICH AN ORDER FOR SERVICE WAS GRANTED BY THIS COURT ON ________________, ______.

(For use if an interested party is required to be served by publication:)

TO: (List here all known interested parties having unknown addresses to be served by publication)

All interested parties and all and singular the heirs of said decedent, the beneficiaries under the purported Will, and to whom it may concern: This is to notify you to file objection, if there is any, to the above referenced petition, in this Court on or before ________________, 20______.

BE NOTIFIED FURTHER: All objections to the petition must be in writing, setting forth the grounds of any such objections. All pleadings must be signed before a notary public or probate court clerk, and filing fees must be tendered with your pleadings, unless you qualify to file as an indigent party. Contact probate court personnel at the below address/phone number for the required amount of filing fees. If any objections are filed, a hearing will be (held on ________________) (scheduled at a later date). If no objections are filed, the petition may be granted without a hearing.

PROBATE JUDGE
By:
CLERK OF THE PROBATE COURT

ADDRESS

TELEPHONE NUMBER

Effective 7/06 GPCSF 7 Court

CERTIFICATE OF MAILING

This is to certify that I have this date forwarded by registered or certified mail, return receipt requested, in a stamped, addressed envelope, a copy of the foregoing petition, purported Will and the notice to all of the interested parties who reside out of state.

DATE	PROBATE CLERK/DEPUTY CLERK

Effective 7/06 GPCSF 7 Court

IN THE PROBATE COURT OF ______________________ COUNTY

STATE OF GEORGIA

IN RE: ESTATE OF) ESTATE NO. ____________________

)

__________________________,) PETITION TO PROBATE WILL IN
DECEASED) SOLEMN FORM AND FOR
) LETTERS OF ADMINISTRATION
) WITH WILL ANNEXED

RETURN OF SHERIFF

I have this day served __________________ personally with a copy of the foregoing petition, purported Will and notice.

____

Date

Deputy Sheriff, ________________________ County

Effective 7/06 GPCSF 7 Court

IN THE PROBATE COURT OF ____________________ COUNTY

STATE OF GEORGIA

IN RE: ESTATE OF) ESTATE NO. ____________

)

____________________,) PETITION TO PROBATE WILL IN
DECEASED) SOLEMN FORM AND FOR
) LETTERS OF ADMINISTRATION
) WITH WILL ANNEXED

ANSWER OF GUARDIAN AD LITEM

I hereby accept the foregoing appointment, acknowledge service and notice of the proceedings as provided by law, and for answer say:

____________________ Date

____________________ Guardian ad Litem

____
Address ____________________
Telephone ____________________

Effective 7/06

GPCSF 7 Court

PROBATE COURT OF ______________________ COUNTY

STATE OF GEORGIA

IN RE: ESTATE OF) ESTATE NO. ____________________

)

______________________,) PETITION TO PROBATE WILL IN
DECEASED) SOLEMN FORM AND FOR LETTERS
) OF ADMINISTRATION WITH WILL
) ANNEXED

ORDER

The Petition of ______________________________ to probate the Will of the above decedent in Solemn Form, and requesting that Letters of Administration with the Will Annexed be issued as set forth in the petition, having been duly filed;

And it appearing that the decedent died domiciled in this County, that notice was issued and duly served according to law, or was duly waived, and that notice of the petitioner's intention to proceed with the proof in Solemn Form has been duly served upon all of the heirs;

And said Will having been (self-proved)(proved by one of the witnesses thereto) to be the Last Will and Testament of said decedent, and it also appearing that ____________________ is/are lawfully qualified for said Administration, and all other requirements of law having been fulfilled; and no objection being offered thereto,

IT IS HEREBY ORDERED that said Will be established as the true Last Will and Testament of said decedent, that the same be admitted to record as proved in Solemn Form, and that Letters of Administration with the Will Annexed issue to the person(s) found above in this Order to be qualified for such office, upon his/her/their taking and subscribing the Oath as provided by law.

IT IS FURTHER ORDERED that said Administrator(s) with Will Annexed shall disburse all property according to the terms of the Will and shall maintain all records of income and disbursements until they are discharged.

IT IS FURTHER ORDERED that the clerk/deputy clerk shall serve the Administrator(s) with Will Annexed with a copy of this Order by first class mail and shall file a certificate of service showing such service.
(initial if applicable)

______ IT IS FURTHER ORDERED that Letters of Testamentary Guardianship and/or Conservatorship shall issue to the individuals so designated in said Will.

SO ORDERED this ________ day of ____________________________, 20_____.

Probate Judge

IN THE PROBATE COURT OF ______________________ COUNTY

STATE OF GEORGIA

IN RE: ESTATE OF	)	ESTATE NO. ______________
	)	
______________________,	)	PETITION TO PROBATE WILL IN
DECEASED	)	SOLEMN FORM AND FOR
	)	LETTERS OF ADMINISTRATION
	)	WITH WILL ANNEXED

OATH

I do solemnly swear (or affirm) that this writing contains the true Last Will and Testament of ______________________, deceased, so far as I know or believe, and that I will well and truly execute the same in accordance with the laws of Georgia. So help me God.

Sworn to and subscribed before me this ____ day of ______________, 20____.

____
NOTARY/CLERK OF PROBATE COURT

____
Administrator C.T.A.

____
Printed Name

Sworn to and subscribed before me this ____ day of ______________, 20____.

____
NOTARY/CLERK OF PROBATE COURT

____
Administrator C.T.A.

____
Printed Name

Effective 7/06

GPCSF 7 Court

GEORGIA PROBATE COURT
STANDARD FORM

STATE OF GEORGIA

COUNTY OF ______________________ ESTATE NO. ______________

LETTERS OF ADMINISTRATION WITH WILL ANNEXED
(Relieved of Filing Returns)

By ______________________________, Judge of the Probate Court of said County.

KNOW ALL WHOM IT MAY CONCERN:

That on the _____ day of ______________________________, 20_____, at a regular term of the Probate Court, the Last Will and Testament dated ______________________, of ______________________ deceased, at the time of his or her death a resident of said County, was legally proven in Solemn form and was admitted to record by order, and (on the _______ day of ______________________, ______________) it was (further) ordered that ______________________________ be allowed to qualify as Administrator with the Will Annexed, and that upon doing so, Letters of Administration with the Will Annexed be issued to said individual(s).

NOW, THEREFORE, the said ______________________, having taken the oath of office and complied with all the necessary prerequisites of the law, is/are legally authorized to discharge all the duties and exercise all the powers of Executor(s) under the Will of said deceased and of Administrator(s) with the Will Annexed according to the Will and the law.

Given under my hand and official seal, the ________ day of ______________________, 20_____.

Probate Judge

NOTE: The following must be signed if the judge does not sign the original of this document:

Issued by: ______________________________ (Seal)

PROBATE CLERK/DEPUTY CLERK

Effective 7/06 GPCSF 7 Court

GEORGIA PROBATE COURT
STANDARD FORM

STATE OF GEORGIA

COUNTY OF ____________________ ESTATE NO. ______________

LETTERS OF ADMINISTRATION WITH WILL ANNEXED

(Relieved of Filing Returns and/or Certain Powers Granted at Time of Appointment

By ______________________________, Judge of the Probate Court of said County.

KNOW ALL WHOM IT MAY CONCERN:

That on the ____ day of ______________________________, 20____, at a regular term of the Probate Court, the Last Will and Testament dated ______________, ________ of ______________________________ deceased, at the time of his or her death a resident of said County, was legally proven in Solemn form and was admitted to record by order, and (on the ____ day of ____________________, __________) it was (further) ordered that ____________________ be allowed to qualify as Administrator with the Will Annexed, and that upon doing so, Letters of Administration with the Will Annexed be issued to said individual(s).

NOW, THEREFORE, the said ____, having taken the oath of office and complied with all the necessary prerequisites of the law, is/are legally authorized to discharge all the duties and exercise all the powers of Executor(s) under the Will of said deceased and of Administrator(s) with the Will Annexed according to the Will and the law.

IT IS FURTHER ORDERED that the undersigned judge does hereby
(Initial all which apply:)

______ a. waive the bond of the Administrator(s) and granted to the Administrator(s) the power to serve without filing an inventory, and without filing any annual or other returns or reports to any court; but the fiduciary shall furnish to the income beneficiaries, at least annually, a statement of receipts and disbursements.

______ b. grant to the Administrator(s) all of the powers contained in O.C.G.A. §53-12-232 not included in (a) above.

Given under my hand and official seal, the ________ day of ____________________________, 20______.

Probate Judge

NOTE: The following must be signed if the judge does not sign the original of this document:

Issued by: (Seal)

PROBATE CLERK/DEPUTY CLERK

Effective 7/06 GPCSF 7 Court

GEORGIA PROBATE COURT
STANDARD FORM

STATE OF GEORGIA

COUNTY OF ______________________ ESTATE NO. ______________

LETTERS OF ADMINISTRATION WITH WILL ANNEXED

(Not Relieved of Filing Returns)

By ______________________________________, Judge of the Probate Court of said County.

KNOW ALL WHOM IT MAY CONCERN:

That on the _____ day of ______________________, 20_____, at a regular term of the Probate Court, the last Will and Testament dated ______________________, ____________ of ______________________ deceased, at the time of his or her death a resident of said County, was legally proven in Solemn form and was admitted to record by order, and (on the _____ day of ______________, ___________) it was (further) ordered that ______________________________ be allowed to qualify as Administrator with the Will Annexed, and that upon doing so, Letters of Administration with the Will Annexed be issued to said individual(s).

NOW, THEREFORE, the said ______________________________________, having taken the oath of office and complied with all the necessary prerequisites of the law, is/are legally authorized to discharge all the duties and exercise all the powers of Executor(s) under the Will of said deceased and of Administrator(s) with the Will Annexed according to the Will and the law and is/are hereby required to render a true and correct inventory of all the goods, chattels, rights and credits of said deceased, and make a return of them to this Court; and further, to file a proper annual or final return with this Court each year until the Administration with Will Annexed is fully discharged.

Given under my hand and official seal, the _______ day of ______________________, 20_____.

Probate Judge

NOTE: The following must be signed if the judge does not sign the original of this document:

Issued by: (Seal)

PROBATE CLERK/DEPUTY CLERK

Effective 7/06 GPCSF 7 Court

GEORGIA PROBATE COURT
STANDARD FORM

STATE OF GEORGIA

COUNTY OF ______________ ESTATE NO.

LETTERS OF TESTAMENTARY GUARDIANSHIP OF MINOR

From the Judge of the Probate Court of said County.

TO: ______________________________, Testamentary Guardian(s)
RE: ______________________________, Minor

Pursuant to the Last Will and Testament of ______________________, deceased, you have been appointed Testamentary Guardian of the minor. You have assented to this appointment by taking your oath. In general, your duties as Testamentary Guardian are to protect and maintain the person of the minor and your power over the minor shall be the same as that of a parent over a child, the guardian(s) standing in place of the parent(s). A guardian shall at all times act as a fiduciary in the minor's best interest and exercise reasonable care, diligence, and prudence.

Special Instructions:

1. It is your duty to see that the minor is adequately fed, clothed, sheltered, educated, and cared for, and that the minor receives all necessary medical attention.
2. You must keep the Court informed of any change in your name or address.
3. You should inform the Court of any change of location of your minor.
4. You shall, within 60 days of appointment and within 60 days after each anniversary date of appointment, file with this Court and provide to the conservator of the minor, if any, a personal status report concerning the minor.
5. You shall promptly notify the court of any conflict of interest which may arise between you as guardian and the minor pursuant to O.C.G.A. §29-2-23.
6. The guardianship automatically terminates when the minor dies, reaches age 18, is adopted, or is emancipated.
7. You shall act in coordination and cooperation with the minor's conservator, if appointed, or if not, with others who have custody of the minor's property.
8. Please consult your attorney if you have any questions. Your authority to act pursuant to these Letters is subject to applicable statues[1] and to any special orders entered in this case.

Give under my hand and official seal, this ________ day of ______________________, 20____.

Probate Judge

NOTE: The following must be signed if the judge does not sign the original of this document:

Issued by:

____

PROBATE CLERK/DEPUTY CLERK (Seal)

Effective 7/06 GPCSF 7 Court

1 So in original

GEORGIA PROBATE COURT
STANDARD FORM

STATE OF GEORGIA

COUNTY OF ______________________ ESTATE NO.

LETTERS OF TESTAMENTARY CONSERVATORSHIP OF MINOR

From the Judge of the Probate Court of said County.

TO: ____, Testamentary Conservator(s)
RE: ____, Minor

Pursuant to the Last Will and Testament of the below-named decedent, you have been appointed Testamentary Conservator of the minor's property. You have assented to this appointment by taking your oath. In general, your duties as Testamentary Conservator are to protect and maintain the property of the minor and utilize the minor's property solely for the benefit of the minor. Please consult your attorney if you have any questions.

These Letters of Testamentary Conservatorship empower the above testamentary conservator to hold, for the minor, only property which passed through the estate of ______________________________________, Deceased.

Given under my hand and official seal, this ________ day of ________________, 20______.

Probate Judge

NOTE: The following must be signed if the judge does not sign the original of this document:

Issued by:

____
PROBATE CLERK/DEPUTY CLERK (Seal)

Effective 7/06 GPCSF 7 Court

Form adopted effective July 31, 2006.

GPCSF 8 PETITIONER. PETITION FOR LETTERS OF ADMINISTRATION WITH WILL ANNEXED (WILL PREVIOUSLY PROBATED)

GEORGIA PROBATE COURT
STANDARD FORM

Petition for Letters of Administration with Will Annexed (Will Previously Probated)

INSTRUCTIONS

1. Specific Instructions

   1. This form is to be used in connection with a petition for letters of administration with the Will annexed (sometimes called letters of administration C.T.A.), when the Will has been previously probated pursuant to O.C.G.A. §53-6-15(b).

II. General Instructions

General instructions applicable to all Georgia probate court standard forms are available in each probate court.

Effective 7/06 GPCSF 8 Petitioner

IN THE PROBATE COURT OF ________________________ COUNTY

STATE OF GEORGIA

IN RE: ESTATE OF) ESTATE NO. ____________________

)

______________________________,) PETITION FOR LETTERS OF
DECEASED) ADMINISTRATION WITH WILL
) ANNEXED (WILL PREVIOUSLY
) PROBATED)

TO THE HONORABLE JUDGE OF THE PROBATE COURT:

The petition of ____,
whose mailing address is/are ____,
shows:

1.

On ____, ________, the Last Will and
Testament of ____,
First Middle Last Name
deceased, was probated in this Court in ______________________ Form.

2.

Listed below are all of the beneficiaries under said Will who have a present interest, including but not limited to a vested remainder interest but not including trust beneficiaries where there is a trustee who is not the nominated administrator with Will annexed, and whose identity and whereabouts are known or may be determined by reasonable diligence.

Name	Age (Or over 18)	Address

GEORGIA PROBATE COURT
STANDARD FORM

3.

Additional Data: Where full particulars are lacking, state here the reasons for any such omission. Also, state here all pertinent facts which may govern the method of giving notice to any party and which may determine whether or not a guardian ad litem should be appointed for any party. If the petitioner is not a beneficiary under the Will, state how the petitioner is interested in the administration of the estate. If it is alleged that a nominated executor has failed to qualify, state here the name and address of such nominated executor.

4.

To the knowledge of the petitioner(s), no other proceedings with respect to this estate are pending, or have been completed, in any other probate court in this state.

5.

Petitioner(s) further show(s) that the circumstances giving rise to the need for an administrator with the Will annexed are as follows:
(Initial all which apply:)

_____ The decedent failed to name an Executor in the Will.
_____ The named Executor is deceased.
_____ The named Executor has renounced his/her right to serve as such.
_____ Other reason a testate estate is unrepresented:

6.

(The Petitioner(s)) (____) is/are entitled to be appointed Administrator(s) C.T.A. by reason of:

_____ having been unanimously selected by the beneficiaries of the Will who are capable of expressing a choice. If the sole beneficiary is the decedent's surviving spouse, no action for divorce or separate maintenance was pending at the time of death.

_____ appointment of the proposed Administrator(s) C.T.A. named above will best serve the interest of the estate and the proposed Administrator(s) C.T.A. is/are:

_____ A beneficiary or the trustee of any trust that is a beneficiary under the Will.
_____ An eligible person as defined in O.C.G.A. §53-6-1.
_____ A creditor of the estate.
_____ The county administrator.

GEORGIA PROBATE COURT
STANDARD FORM

7.

The proposed Administrator(s) C.T.A. should be allowed to qualify without the necessity of posting bond, since only personal representatives of intestate estates and temporary administrators are normally required to post bond. See O.C.G.A. §53-6-50(a).

WHEREFORE, Petitioner(s) pray(s):

1. That due and legal notice of this petition be given as the law requires.

3. That Letters of Administration with Will Annexed issue to the proposed Administrator(s) C.T.A. named above.

3. That this Court grant such other and further relief as it deems proper under the circumstances.

______________________________	______________________________
Signature of first petitioner	Signature of second petitioner if any
Printed Name	Printed Name
Address	Address
Phone Number	Phone Number

Signature of Attorney: ______________________

Typed/printed name of Attorney: ______________________
Address: ______________________

Telephone: ______________________ State Bar # ________________

Effective 7/06 -3- GPCSF 8 Petitioner

GEORGIA PROBATE COURT
STANDARD FORM

VERIFICATION

GEORGIA, ____________________ COUNTY

Personally appeared before me the undersigned petitioner(s) who on oath state(s) that the facts set forth in the foregoing petition are true.

Sworn to and subscribed before
me this ____ day of ____________, 20____.

____
First Petitioner

____
NOTARY/CLERK OF PROBATE COURT

____
Printed Name

Sworn to and subscribed before
this ____ day of ____________, 20____.

____
Second Petitioner, if any

____
NOTARY/CLERK OF PROBATE COURT

____
Printed Name

ACKNOWLEDGMENT OF SERVICE AND
SELECTION BY BENEFICIARIES CAPABLE OF EXPRESSING A CHOICE

PROBATE COURT OF ____________________ COUNTY

IN RE: PETITION OF _ FOR LETTERS OF ADMINISTRATION WITH WILL ANNEXED ON THE ESTATE OF ____, DECEASED.

Each of the undersigned hereby acknowledges service of the petition referred to above, waives copies of same and all further service and notice, selects the person proposed in said petition to be Administrator with Will Annexed and consents to the petition.

SIGNATURE(S) OF BENEFICIARIES

Sworn to and subscribed before me this ___ day of __________, 20___. ______________________________

______________________________ ______________________________
NOTARY/CLERK OF PROBATE COURT Printed Name

Sworn to and subscribed before me this ___ day of __________, 20___. ______________________________

______________________________ ______________________________
NOTARY/CLERK OF PROBATE COURT Printed Name

Sworn to and subscribed before me this ___ day of __________, 20___. ______________________________

______________________________ ______________________________
NOTARY/CLERK OF PROBATE COURT Printed Name

Sworn to and subscribed before me this ___ day of __________, 20___. ______________________________

______________________________ ______________________________
NOTARY/CLERK OF PROBATE COURT Printed Name

Sworn to and subscribed before me this ___ day of __________, 20___. ______________________________

______________________________ ______________________________
NOTARY/CLERK OF PROBATE COURT Printed Name

Effective 7/06 -5- GPCSF 8 Petitioner

Instructions and form revised effective July 1, 1991; January 1, 1998; July 1, 1998; July 31, 2006.

GPCSF 8 COURT. COURT FORMS FOR PETITION FOR LETTERS OF ADMINISTRATION WITH WILL ANNEXED (WILL PREVIOUSLY PROBATED)

GEORGIA PROBATE COURT
STANDARD FORM

Petition for Letters of Administration with Will Annexed (Will Previously Probated)

NOTICE: UNLESS OTHERWISE DIRECTED BY THE COURT, THE FOLLOWING FORMS ARE FOR PROBATE COURT STAFF TO COMPLETE

Effective 7/06 GPCSF 8 Court

IN THE PROBATE COURT OF ____________________ COUNTY

STATE OF GEORGIA

IN RE: ESTATE OF) ESTATE NO. ____________________
)
____________________,) PETITION FOR LETTERS OF
DECEASED) ADMINISTRATION WITH WILL
) ANNEXED (WILL PREVIOUSLY
) PROBATED)

ORDER FOR SERVICE OF NOTICE AND FOR APPOINTMENT OF GUARDIAN AD LITEM, IF NECESSARY

The foregoing Petition for Letters of Administration with Will Annexed having been filed, and the beneficiaries capable of expressing a choice not having made a unanimous selection and/or it being alleged that a nominated executor has failed to qualify, it is ordered that notice shall issue and be served upon the beneficiaries who have not acknowledged service of the petition (upon the executor of the deceased executor whose death created the vacancy) (upon any executor nominated in the will who has failed to qualify), as follows: (Initial all which apply:)

______ Notice must be served personally, together with a copy of the petition, at least ten days before the deadline for filing objections on the following interested parties who reside in Georgia:

______ Notice must be served by registered or certified mail, return receipt requested, together with a copy of the petition, upon the following nonresident interested parties whose current residence addresses are known:

______ Notice must be published once a week for four weeks in the newspaper in which sheriff's advertisements are published in this county, before ____________________, 20____ in order to serve by publication the following interested parties whose current residence addresses are unknown or who are unknown:

______ IT IS ORDERED that ________ is appointed guardian ad litem for ____________________, and that said guardian ad litem be duly served with a copy of the foregoing petition, Notice, and notice of this appointment, and that upon said guardian ad litem's acceptance of same, said guardian ad litem shall make answer hereto. This appointment is limited to this proceeding only and it shall cease when a final order is entered on this petition.

SO ORDERED this ____ day of ________, 20____.

____
Probate Judge

Effective 7/06 GPCSF 8 Court

NOTICE

PROBATE COURT OF ________________ COUNTY
RE: PETITION OF ____ FOR LETTERS OF ADMINISTRATION WITH WILL ANNEXED, CONCERNING THE WILL OF ____, DECEASED.

(Strike the following paragraph if not applicable:)

TO: ____

(List here all interested parties having known addresses in the continental U.S. to be served by certified or registered mail)

This is to notify you to file objection, if there is any, to the above referenced petition, in this Court on or before the thirteenth (13th) day after ______________, 20______ (the date of the mailing of this Notice to you by certified or registered mail, return receipt requested); provided, however, that if a return receipt for such Notice is actually received by the Court within such 13 days, the deadline for the filing of any objection shall be ten (10) days from the date of receipt shown on such return receipt.

(Strike the following paragraph if not applicable:)

TO: ____

(List here all interested parties having known addresses outside the continental U.S. to be served by certified or registered mail)

This is to notify you to file objection, if there is any, to the above referenced petition, in this Court on or before the thirtieth (30th) day after ______________, ____ (the date of the mailing of this Notice to you by certified or registered mail, return receipt requested); provided, however, that if a return receipt for such Notice is actually received by the Court within such 30 days, the deadline for the filing of any objection shall be ten (10) days from the date of receipt shown on such return receipt.

(Strike the following paragraph if not applicable:)

To ____

(List here all interested parties who reside in Georgia to be served personally)

who are required to be served personally, to file objection, if there is any, to the above referenced petition, in this Court on or before the tenth (10th) day after the date you are personally served.

BE NOTIFIED FURTHER: All objections to the petition must be in writing, setting forth the grounds of any such objections. All pleadings/objections must be signed before a notary public or before a probate court clerk, and filing fees must be tendered with your pleadings/objections, unless you qualify to file as an indigent party. Contact probate court personnel at the following address/telephone number for the required amount of filing fees. If any objections are filed, a hearing will be (held on ______________________, 20______) (scheduled at a later date). If no objections are filed, the petition may be granted without a hearing.

PROBATE JUDGE

By: ______________________________
PROBATE CLERK/DEPUTY CLERK

ADDRESS

TELEPHONE

Effective 7/06

GPCSF 8 Court

NOTICE

PROBATE COURT OF ____________________ COUNTY
RE: PETITION OF ____ FOR LETTERS OF ADMINISTRATION WITH WILL ANNEXED, CONCERNING THE WILL OF ____, DECEASED.

(To be used if an interested party is required to be served by publication:)
TO:

___ (List here all unknown interested parties and known interested parties having unknown addresses to be served by publication)

and to whom it may concern: This is to notify you to file objection, if there is any, to the above referenced petition, in this Court on or before ______________________________, 20________.

BE NOTIFIED FURTHER: All objections to the petition must be in writing, setting forth the grounds of any such objections. All pleadings/objections must be signed before a notary public or before a probate court clerk, and filing fees must be tendered with your pleadings/objections, unless you qualify to file as an indigent party. Contact probate court personnel at the following address/telephone number for the required amount of filing fees. If any objections are filed, a hearing will be (held on ____________________, 20________) (scheduled at a later date). If no objections are filed, the petition may be granted without a hearing.

PROBATE JUDGE

By: ______________________________
PROBATE CLERK/DEPUTY CLERK

ADDRESS

TELEPHONE

IN THE PROBATE COURT OF ______________________ COUNTY

STATE OF GEORGIA

IN RE: ESTATE OF) ESTATE NO. ______________

)

______________________________,) PETITION FOR LETTERS OF

DECEASED) ADMINISTRATION WITH WILL

) ANNEXED (WILL PREVIOUSLY

) PROBATED)

RETURN OF SHERIFF

I have this day served ____ personally with a copy of the foregoing petition and notice.

____

Date

Deputy Sheriff, ____________________ County

Effective 7/06 GPCSF 8 Court

CERTIFICATE OF MAILING

This is to certify that I have this date forwarded by registered or certified mail, return receipt requested, in a stamped, addressed envelope, a copy of the foregoing petition and notice, to all interested parties who reside out of state at known current residence addresses.

____________________	______________________________
DATE	PROBATE CLERK/DEPUTY CLERK

Effective 7/06 GPCSF 8 Court

IN THE PROBATE COURT OF ______________________ COUNTY

STATE OF GEORGIA

IN RE: ESTATE OF) ESTATE NO. ____________________

)

_______________________________________,) PETITION FOR LETTERS OF
DECEASED) ADMINISTRATION WITH WILL
) ANNEXED (WILL PREVIOUSLY
) PROBATED)

ANSWER OF GUARDIAN AD LITEM

I hereby accept the foregoing appointment, acknowledge service and notice of the proceedings as provided by law, and for answer say:

_________________________ DATE

_________________________ GUARDIAN AD LITEM

ADDRESS

TELEPHONE

Effective 7/06 GPCSF 8 Court

PROBATE COURT OF ______________ COUNTY

STATE OF GEORGIA

IN RE: ESTATE OF) ESTATE NO. ______________
)
______________,) PETITION FOR LETTERS OF
DECEASED) ADMINISTRATION WITH WILL
) ANNEXED (WILL PREVIOUSLY
) PROBATED)

ORDER

The foregoing petition having been duly filed;

And it appearing that the Will of the decedent was previously probated in this Court, and that service was perfected according to law,

And it also appearing that ______________________________ is/are lawfully qualified for said Administration C.T.A., and all other requirements of law having been fulfilled; and no objection being offered thereto,

IT IS HEREBY ORDERED that Letters of Administration with the Will Annexed issue to the person(s) found above to be lawfully qualified, upon his/her/their taking and subscribing the Oath as provided by law.

SO ORDERED this ________ day of ____________________, 20____.

Probate Judge

Effective 7/06 GPCSF 8 Court

IN THE PROBATE COURT OF ______________________ COUNTY

STATE OF GEORGIA

IN RE: ESTATE OF) ESTATE NO. ______________________

)

______________________,) PETITION FOR LETTERS OF
DECEASED) ADMINISTRATION WITH WILL
) ANNEXED (WILL PREVIOUSLY
) PROBATED)

OATH

I do solemnly swear (or affirm) that this writing contains the true Last Will of ______________________, deceased, so far as I know or believe, and that I will well and truly execute the same in accordance with the laws of Georgia. So help me God.

Sworn to and subscribed before me
This ______ day of ______________,
20_____.

____
Administrator C.T.A.

____
Judge/Clerk of the Probate Court

____
Administrator C.T.A.

Effective 7/06 GPCSF 8 Court

STATE OF GEORGIA
COUNTY OF ______________________ ESTATE NO. ____________

LETTERS OF ADMINISTRATION WITH WILL ANNEXED
(Relieved of Filing Returns)

By ______________________________________, Judge of the Probate Court of said County.

KNOW ALL WHOM IT MAY CONCERN:

That on the ____ day of ____________________________, 20___, at a regular term of the Probate Court, the Last Will and Testament dated ______________________, ____________ of ______________________________ deceased, at the time of his or her death a resident of said County, was legally proven in ____________ form and was admitted to record by order, and (on the ______ day of ____________, ______) it was (further) ordered that ______________________________________ be allowed to qualify as Administrator with the Will Annexed, and that upon doing so, Letters of Administration with the Will Annexed be issued to said individual(s).

NOW, THEREFORE, the said ________ having taken the oath of office and complied with all the necessary prerequisites of the law, is/are legally authorized to discharge all the duties and exercise all the powers of Executor(s) under the Will of said deceased and of Administrator(s) with the Will Annexed according to the Will and the law.

Given under my hand and official seal, the ________ day of ____________, 20______.

Probate Judge

NOTE: The following must be signed if the judge does not sign the original of this document:

Issued by: (Seal)

Clerk, Probate Court

STATE OF GEORGIA
COUNTY OF ______________________ ESTATE NO. ______________

LETTERS OF ADMINISTRATION WITH WILL ANNEXED
(Relieved of Filing Returns and with additional Statutory Powers Granted)

By ______________________________________, Judge of the Probate Court of said County.

KNOW ALL WHOM IT MAY CONCERN:

That on the ____ day of ______________________________, 20___, at a regular term of the Probate Court, the Last Will and Testament dated ______________________, ____________ of ______________________________ deceased, at the time of his or her death a resident of said County, was legally proven in ____________ form and was admitted to record by order, and (on the ________ day of ______________,) it was (further) ordered that ______________________________________ be allowed to qualify as Administrator with the Will Annexed, and that upon doing so, Letters of Administration with the Will Annexed be issued to said individual(s).

NOW, THEREFORE, the said __________ having taken the oath of office and complied with all the necessary prerequisites of the law, is/are legally authorized to discharge all the duties and exercise all the powers of Executor(s) under the Will of said deceased and of Administrator(s) with the Will Annexed according to the Will and the law.

IT IS FURTHER ORDERED that the undersigned judge does hereby waive the bond of the Administrator and grant to the Administrator the power to serve without making and filing inventory, and without filing any annual or other returns or reports to any court; but the fiduciary shall furnish to the income beneficiaries, at leat annually, a statement of receipts and disbursements. Further, the undersigned judge grants to the Administrator all of the remaining power contained in O.C.G.S. § 53-12-232.

Given under my hand and official seal, the __________ day of ______________________, 20______.

Probate Judge

NOTE: The following must be signed if the judge does not sign the original of this document:

Issued by: (Seal)

Clerk, Probate Court

STATE OF GEORGIA
COUNTY OF ______________ ESTATE NO. ______________

LETTERS OF ADMINISTRATION WITH WILL ANNEXED
(Not Relieved of Filing Returns)

By ______________________________, Judge of the Probate Court of said County.

KNOW ALL WHOM IT MAY CONCERN:

That on the ____ day of ______________, 20____, at a regular term of the Probate Court, the Last Will and Testament dated ______________, ______________ of ______________ deceased, at the time of his or her death a resident of said County, was legally proven in ______ form and was admitted to record by order, and (on the ____ day of ______________, ____) it was (further) ordered that ______________________ be allowed to qualify as Administrator with the Will Annexed, and that upon doing so, Letters of Administration with the Will Annexed be issued to said individual(s).

NOW, THEREFORE, the said __________ having taken the oath of office and complied with all the necessary prerequisites of the law, is/are legally authorized to discharge all the duties and exercise all the powers of Executor(s) under the Will of said deceased and of Administrator(s) with the Will Annexed according to the Will and the law and is/are hereby required to render a true and correct inventory of all the goods, chattels, rights and credits of said deceased, and make a return of them to this Court; and further, to file a property annual or final return with this Court each year until the Administration with Will Annexed is fully discharged.

Given under my hand and official seal, the ________ day of ______________, 20_____.

Probate Judge

NOTE: The following must be signed if the judge does not sign the original of this document:

Issued by: (Seal)

Clerk, Probate Court

Form adopted effective July 31, 2006.

GPCSF 9. PETITION FOR ORDER DECLARING NO ADMINISTRATION NECESSARY

Re: Petition for Order Declaring No Administration Necessary

INSTRUCTIONS

I. Specific Instructions

1. This form is to be used when filing a petition for order declaring no administration necessary, pursuant to O.C.G.A. §53–2–40, et. seq.

2. O.C.G.A. §53–2–40(b) no longer requires that all heirs must be sui juris. O.C.G.A. §53–11–2 provides that a party to a probate proceeding who is not sui juris, must be represented by a guardian provided that the court may appoint a guardian ad litem or determine that the natural guardian, guardian of the person or property, or testamentary guardian has no conflict and may serve.

3. O.C.G.A. §53–2–40(c) provides that the personal representative of a deceased heir is authorized to agree to the division of property.

4. A signed original agreement setting out the heirs' agreed upon distribution of the estate must be attached to the petition.

5. The attached form consists of 8 pages.

II. General Instructions

General instructions applicable to all Georgia probate court standard forms are available in each probate court.

PETITION FOR ORDER DECLARING NO ADMINISTRATION NECESSARY

GEORGIA, ______________________ COUNTY

To the Honorable Judge of the Probate Court of said State and County:

The Petition of ______________________________________, whose mailing address is

____,
Street City State Zip

respectfully shows to the Court the following:

1.

____, whose domicile was
First Middle Last Name

____ died
Street City County State

intestate on ____________, 19___. Petitioner is an heir of the decedent.

2.

Listed below are all of the decedent's heirs, with the age or majority status, domicile and relationship to the decedent set opposite the name of each:

Name	Age (Or over 18)	Address	Relationship

3.

Additional information concerning the personal representative of any now deceased heir, the guardian of any incapacitated adult heir, and any information relative to whom the court should appoint as guardian, if one is needed, in this proceeding:

4.

The decedent owned the following described personal property in this state (include identifying account numbers, serial numbers, etc., where applicable):

5.

The decedent owned the following described real property in this state (include complete legal description and street address, if any):

6.

The estate of said decedent owes no debts
(Check any and all which apply)

___ A. except that there is an outstanding security deed held by ________________, who must be properly served in this matter unless such holder has consented in writing below to the petition.

___ B. except to such creditor(s) as have consented in writing to the petition, as shown on the consent below.

___ C. except the creditor(s) whose name(s) and address(es) are listed immediately below who have not consented in writing and must be served as provided by law:
____
____
____
____.

7.

The heirs have amicably agreed upon a division of the estate among themselves as shown by the written agreement attached hereto containing original signatures of all heirs, attested to by a notary public or probate court clerk.

8.

To the knowledge of the petitioner, no other proceedings with respect to this estate are pending, or have been completed, in any other probate court in this state.

WHEREFORE, Petitioner prays that this Court issue and serve any notice required by law in such matters, and that after ascertaining the legal sufficiency for granting this petition, this Court grant an Order that no administration is necessary in this estate, all as provided by law.

________________________________	________________________________
Signature of Attorney (or petitioner if pro se)	Signature of Attorney (or petitioner if pro se)
Address:	Address:
Telephone Number:	Telephone Number:
State Bar #:	State Bar #:

VERIFICATION

GEORGIA, ______________________ COUNTY

Personally appeared before me the undersigned petitioner(s) who on oath state(s) that the facts set forth in the foregoing petition are true.

______________________________	______________________________
Petitioner	Petitioner
Residence Address:	Residence Address:
Telephone Number:	Telephone Number:

Sworn to and subscribed before me, this ______ day of __________, 19___.

____
Clerk of Probate Court or Notary Public

ORDER FOR NOTICE
(NOT NEEDED IF ALL CREDITORS HAVE CONSENTED)

Upon reading and considering the foregoing petition, IT IS ORDERED that notice issue thereon as required by law, requiring all creditors who have not consented to the petition to show cause in writing filed in this Court on or before a day certain, if published, or within ten days of personal service, whichever is later, why the prayers of the petitioner should not be granted as prayed, and an Order granted that no administration is necessary in this estate. Further Ordered that any security deed holder or other creditor who has not consented in writing to the petition and whose current address is known be served with a copy of the Petition, this Order, and the following Notice, personally if a resident of this state, or by registered or certified mail, return receipt requested, if a nonresident with a known current address. Any creditor whose current address is not known must be served by publishing the notice once a week for four weeks.

______________________________	______________________________
DATE	JUDGE OF THE PROBATE COURT

NOTICE

Georgia, ______________________ County Probate Court

TO WHOM IT MAY CONCERN:

______________________ has petitioned for an order finding that no administration is necessary on the estate of ______________________, deceased. All creditors who have not consented to the petition are, therefore, required to show cause on or before __________, or within ten days after personal service, whichever is later, why such order should not be granted.

All objections to the petition must be in writing, setting forth the grounds of any such objections. If any objections are filed a hearing will be (held on __________)(scheduled for a later date). If no objections are filed, the petition may be granted without a hearing.

____
JUDGE OF THE PROBATE COURT

______________________________	By: ______________________________
DATE	CLERK OF THE PROBATE COURT

4

CERTIFICATE OF MAILING

This is to certify that I have this date forwarded by registered or certified mail, return receipt requested, in a stamped, addressed envelope supplied by the petitioner(s), a copy of the foregoing petition and the notice, to each of the following creditors who reside out of state at known current addresses:

____________________ ____________________

DATE CLERK, PROBATE COURT

RETURN OF SHERIFF

I do hereby certify that I have this day served ____________________ ____________, creditor in this matter, with a copy of the foregoing Petition for Order Declaring No Administration Necessary, Order for Notice and Notice.

____________________ ____________________

Date Deputy Sheriff, ____________ County

ACKNOWLEDGMENT OF SERVICE AND CONSENT

Each of the undersigned heirs of creditors (including any security deed holder) hereby acknowledges due and legal service of the foregoing Petition, waives copies of same and all further service and notice in this matter, and consents to the following Final Order declaring that no administration is necessary in the estate of ____________________, deceased.

SIGNATURE(S) OF HEIRS OR CREDITORS (INCLUDING ANY SECURITY DEED HOLDERS)

Sworn to and subscribed before me this _______ day of __________, 19___. ________________________________

________________________________ ________________________________

NOTARY/CLERK OF PROBATE COURT RELATIONSHIP TO ESTATE

Sworn to and subscribed before me this _______ day of __________, 19___. ________________________________

________________________________ ________________________________

NOTARY/CLERK OF PROBATE COURT RELATIONSHIP TO ESTATE

Sworn to and subscribed before me this _______ day of __________, 19___. ________________________________

________________________________ ________________________________

NOTARY/CLERK OF PROBATE COURT RELATIONSHIP TO ESTATE

Sworn to and subscribed before me this _______ day of __________, 19___. ________________________________

________________________________ ________________________________

NOTARY/CLERK OF PROBATE COURT RELATIONSHIP TO ESTATE

Sworn to and subscribed before me this _______ day of __________, 19___. ________________________________

________________________________ ________________________________

NOTARY/CLERK OF PROBATE COURT RELATIONSHIP TO ESTATE

Sworn to and subscribed before me this _______ day of __________, 19___. ________________________________

________________________________ ________________________________

NOTARY/CLERK OF PROBATE COURT RELATIONSHIP TO ESTATE

AGREEMENT

We, being all of the heirs of _______________, deceased, hereby agree to the division of the decedent's estate among ourselves in the amounts and portions determined in accordance with the rules of inheritance when a decedent dies without a will, or if different, as follows:

Sworn to and subscribed before
me this ______ day of _________, 19___. ____________________
HEIR

____
NOTARY/CLERK OF PROBATE COURT

Sworn to and subscribed before
me this ______ day of _________, 19___. ____________________
HEIR

____
NOTARY/CLERK OF PROBATE COURT

Sworn to and subscribed before
me this ______ day of _________, 19___. ____________________
HEIR

____
NOTARY/CLERK OF PROBATE COURT

Sworn to and subscribed before
me this ______ day of _________, 19___. ____________________
HEIR

____
NOTARY/CLERK OF PROBATE COURT

Sworn to and subscribed before
me this ______ day of _________, 19___. ____________________
HEIR

____
NOTARY/CLERK OF PROBATE COURT

7

PROBATE COURT OF ____________________ COUNTY

STATE OF GEORGIA

IN THE MATTER OF:) ESTATE NO. ________
)
ESTATE OF) RE: PETITION FOR ORDER
) DECLARING NO
______________________________,) ADMINISTRATION NECESSARY
DECEASED)

FINAL ORDER

A Petition stating that no administration is necessary on the above estate has been duly filed. It appearing that the decedent died intestate domiciled in this county or died intestate owning real property in this county if the decedent was not domiciled in this state; that all of the heirs of said decedent have agreed upon a division of the estate as evidenced by the Agreement attached to the petition and incorporated herein by reference; that the estate of said decedent owes no debts, except to creditors, if any, including any security deed holders, who have consented or been served in this matter; (that notice was issued and published once a week for four weeks in the newspaper in this county in which sheriff's advertisements appear); and that no written objections to the granting of an Order Declaring No Administration Necessary in said estate have been filed within the time required by law; now, therefore,

IT IS ORDERED AND DECREED that No Administration is Necessary on the above estate.

______________________________ ______________________________
DATE JUDGE OF THE PROBATE COURT

CERTIFICATE IN ACCORDANCE WITH UNIFORM PROBATE COURT RULE 21(F)

I certify that the content of the foregoing is identical in all material respects with Georgia probate court standard form entitled **Petition for Order Declaring No Administration Necessary,** except for additions or deletions indicated as required by the Uniform Probate Court Rules.

______________________________ ______________________________
Date Signature of Attorney
Address:

Telephone Number:
State Bar #:

8

Form amended effective July 1, 1986; revised effective July 1, 1992; instructions and form revised effective January 1, 1998.

GPCSF 10 PETITIONER. PETITION FOR YEAR'S SUPPORT

GEORGIA PROBATE COURT
STANDARD FORM

Petition for Year's Support

INSTRUCTIONS

I. Specific Instructions

1. This form is to be used for filing a petition for year's support pursuant to O.C.G.A. §53-3-1 et seq.

2. The amount set apart shall be an amount sufficient to maintain the standard of living that the surviving spouse and each minor child had prior to the death of the testator or intestate, for a period of 12 months, taking into consideration the following: (1) the support available to the individual for whom the property or money is to be set apart, from sources other than year's support, including but not limited to any separate estate and earning capacity of that individual; and (2) such other relevant criteria as the court deems equitable and proper, including the solvency of the estate.

3. This petition must be filed within 24 months after decedent's death.

4. The Petitioner or his/her/their attorney must prepare and file with the Court, no later than the date of the Final Order, a Georgia Department of Revenue Form PT-61 for each parcel of real property located in the State of Georgia shown on Exhibit "A."

II. General Instructions

General instructions applicable to all Georgia probate court standard forms are available in each probate court.

Effective 7/05 GPCSF 10 Petitioner

IN THE PROBATE COURT OF ______________ COUNTY

STATE OF GEORGIA

IN RE: ESTATE OF) ESTATE NO. ______________
)
______________________________,) PETITION FOR YEAR'S SUPPORT
DECEASED)

TO THE HONORABLE JUDGE OF THE PROBATE COURT:

The Petition of ____,
First Middle Last Name
whose mailing address is ____, shows that:

1.

The petitioner is:

_____ A. The surviving spouse.
_____ B. A guardian or other individual acting on behalf of the surviving spouse or minor child(ren) (state specific relationship): ______________________.

2.

The decedent, ____,
whose domicile was __________ departed this life on __________, 20_____.

____
(State full street address of decedent, including County of domicile)

3.

(Initial one:)

_____ A. There is not a Will.
_____ B. There is a Will, which has been offered for probate.
_____ C. There is a Will, which will be offered for probate.
_____ D. There is a Will, which will not be offered for probate but is attached to this Petition or is on file with this Court.

4.

The decedent's estate consists of real and/or personal property of the probable value of ______________________ dollars.

5.

Petitioner shows that the following named minor child ____ of said decedent, to wit:

____,
Name of Minor Child D.O.B. Name, Address of Parent or Guardian

____,
Name of Minor Child D.O.B. Name, Address of Parent or Guardian

____,
Name of Minor Child D.O.B. Name, Address of Parent or Guardian

____,
Name of Minor Child D.O.B. Name, Address of Parent or Guardian

____,
Name of Minor Child D.O.B. Name, Address of Parent or Guardian

(and ____________________ (Full Name of Surviving Spouse, if applicable) (is) (are) entitled, before the payment of debts of the decedent, to an allowance called Year's Support, which petitioner hereby claims for the individual(s) named above.

6.

A schedule of the property or a statement of the amount of money or both which the petitioner proposes to have set aside to the individuals listed in paragraph 5. above as year's support is attached hereto as "Exhibit A" and made a part hereof.

7.

(Select "A" or "B", and strike inapplicable words:)

_____ A. (There is no executor or administrator of this estate) (The petitioner is the executor or administrator of this estate) and therefore petitioner has set forth below by affidavit marked "Exhibit B" and made a part hereof a list of all interested persons, who must be mailed a copy of the notice not less than 21 days prior to the deadline shown in the notice by which objections, if any, must be filed.

_____ B. ______________________________________ (is) (are) the acting executor(s) or administrator(s) of this estate and must receive 21 days' notice by mail as described above. Note: "Exhibit B" is not required.

8.

In addition to all taxes and tax liens on real property accrued for years prior to the year of the decedent's death, petitioner elects to have property taxes on any real property set apart as year's support divested as follows:

_____1. Real property taxes accrued in the year of decedent's death;
_____2. Real property taxes accrued in the year in which this petition is filed; or
_____3. Real property taxes accrued in the year following the filing of this petition if this petition is filed in the year of the decedent's death.

9.

Additional Data: Where full particulars are lacking, state here the reasons for any such omission.

WHEREFORE, petitioner prays:

1. That this petition be accepted and filed.
2. That notice issue and be published and served as described above.
3. That any interested person who is a minor or an incapacitated adult have a guardian ad litem appointed for him or her, except for any minor child of decedent on whose behalf this petition has been filed by a guardian who is not the spouse of the decedent.
4. That this Court grant such other and further relief as it deems proper under the circumstances.

____
Signature of petitioner

____
Printed Name

____
Address

____

____
Telephone Number

Signature of Attorney: ______________________________

Typed/printed name of Attorney: ______________________________
Address: ______________________________

Telephone: ______________________ State Bar # ______________

VERIFICATION

GEORGIA, ____________________ COUNTY

Personally appeared before me the undersigned petitioner(s) who on oath state(s) that the facts set forth in the foregoing petition are true.

Sworn to and subscribed before
me this ___ day of __________, 20___.

____
Petitioner

____
NOTARY/CLERK OF PROBATE COURT

____
Printed Name

IN THE PROBATE COURT OF ____________________ COUNTY

STATE OF GEORGIA

IN RE: ESTATE OF	)	ESTATE NO. ______________
	)	
______________________________,	)	PETITION FOR YEAR'S SUPPORT
DECEASED	)	
	)	

EXHIBIT A

SCHEDULE OF PROPERTY

[NOTE: If the petitioner proposes to have set aside any interest in real property, then the complete legal description of the real property and the interest therein must appear in full on this schedule and on the proposed Certificate of Order of Year's Support (page 8).]

The following is a schedule of the property or a statement of the amount of money or both which the petitioner proposes to have set aside as year's support:

Petitioner

IN THE PROBATE COURT OF ________________ COUNTY

STATE OF GEORGIA

IN RE: ESTATE OF	)	ESTATE NO. ____________________
	)	
______________________________,	)	PETITION FOR YEAR'S SUPPORT
DECEASED	)	
	)	

EXHIBIT B

LIST OF INTERESTED PERSONS

(To be completed if (1) there is no appointed executor or administrator of the estate, or (2) if the petitioner has been appointed the executor or administrator of the decedent's estate)

Petitioner hereby certifies that petitioner has made reasonable inquiry to ascertain the names, last known addresses, and ages (if under 18) of all the interested persons with respect to the within matter. Petitioner understands that, for purposes of this affidavit, the term "interested person" refers to the above-named decedent's children, spouse, other heirs, beneficiaries, creditors, and any others having a property right or claim against the estate which may be affected by the above Year's Support proceeding. Petitioner hereby certifies that the following are all of the interested persons known to Petitioner with respect to this matter and that any incapacitated adults are identified as such:

Name	Last Known Address	Age (or over 18)	Relationship to Decedent

Sworn to and subscribed before
me this ___ day of __________, 20___.

____
Petitioner

Notary Public, or Clerk, Probate Court

ACKNOWLEDGMENT OF SERVICE AND CONSENT TO AWARD OF YEAR'S SUPPORT

GEORGIA, ____________________ COUNTY

IN RE: PETITION OF FOR YEAR'S SUPPORT
ESTATE OF ____, DECEASED

We, the undersigned, being over 18 years of age, laboring under no legal disability and being interested persons with respect to the within matter, hereby acknowledge service of the petition for year's support and notice, waive copies of same, waive all further service and notice, and hereby consent to the award of year's support as proposed in the petition.

SIGNATURE(S) OF INTERESTED PARTIES

Sworn to and subscribed before me this ___ day of __________, 20___.

______________________________ ______________________________

NOTARY/CLERK OF PROBATE COURT Print Name

Sworn to and subscribed before me this ___ day of __________, 20___.

______________________________ ______________________________

NOTARY/CLERK OF PROBATE COURT Print Name

Sworn to and subscribed before me this ___ day of __________, 20___.

______________________________ ______________________________

NOTARY/CLERK OF PROBATE COURT Print Name

Sworn to and subscribed before me this ___ day of __________, 20___.

______________________________ ______________________________

NOTARY/CLERK OF PROBATE COURT Print Name

Sworn to and subscribed before me this ___ day of __________, 20___.

______________________________ ______________________________

NOTARY/CLERK OF PROBATE COURT Print Name

Sworn to and subscribed before me this ___ day of __________, 20___.

______________________________ ______________________________

NOTARY/CLERK OF PROBATE COURT Print Name

Probate Court Return Mailing Address:

CERTIFICATE OF ORDER OF YEAR'S SUPPORT
(Pursuant to Ga. Code Ann. §53-3-11)

GEORGIA, ______________________ COUNTY

DATE ORDER GRANTED: ______

GRANTOR: (NAME OF DECEDENT) ______________________________

GRANTEE: (FULL NAME OF SURVIVING SPOUSE, AND EACH MINOR CHILD, AND DATE OF BIRTH OF EACH MINOR)

ADDRESS OF GRANTEE: ______________________________

Legal Description of Real Property and Interest Therein:

Also land in ______________________________, Count(y)(ies).

Original Certificate delivered or mailed to Clerk of Superior Court of ____________ County on ______________________, 20____.

Certificate prepared by:

SIGNATURE OF ATTORNEY
State Bar #: ______________________

I do hereby certify that the above information is based on the order of the Probate Court issued on the date set out above and that the above information is true and correct.

By: ______________________________

PROBATE CLERK/DEPUTY CLERK

Effective 7/05 8 GPCSF 10 Petitioner

Instructions and form amended effective July 1, 1986; revised effective January 1, 1998; July 1, 1998; July 31, 2006.

GPCSF 10 COURT. COURT FORMS FOR PETITION FOR YEAR'S SUPPORT

GEORGIA PROBATE COURT
STANDARD FORM

Petition for Year's Support

NOTICE: UNLESS OTHERWISE DIRECTED BY THE COURT, THE FOLLOWING FORMS ARE FOR PROBATE COURT STAFF TO COMPLETE

Effective 7/05 GPCSF 10 Court

GEORGIA PROBATE COURT
STANDARD FORM

IN THE PROBATE COURT OF ________________ COUNTY

STATE OF GEORGIA

IN RE: ESTATE OF	) ESTATE NO. ________________
	)
____________________________,	) PETITION FOR YEAR'S SUPPORT
DECEASED	)

ORDER FOR NOTICE AND APPOINTMENT OF GUARDIAN AD LITEM, WHERE NECESSARY

The Petition for Year's Support having been filed in this office, let notice issue and be published once a week for four weeks as required by law.

Further, it appearing that the estate (is) (is not) represented by a person other than the petitioner, let the clerk of this Court mail a copy of the notice in this matter to (such representative other than the petitioner) (all interested persons listed in "Exhibit B" to the petition).

Further ordered that the clerk of this Court must mail a copy of the petition within five days of its filing to the tax commissioner or tax collector of any county in this state in which real property proposed to be set apart is located.

Further Ordered, that any minors or incapacitated adults included in the petition or on Exhibit B shall have a guardian ad litem appointed for them, except when a guardian files on behalf of a minor or incapacitated adult and the guardian is not the surviving spouse.

(Note: Appoint more than one guardian ad litem if necessary to represent parties who are not sui juris and who may have adverse interests).

Further Ordered, that ________________________________ be appointed guardian ad litem for ________________________________ and that said guardian ad litem be duly served with a copy of the foregoing petition, Notice and notice of this appointment, and upon said guardian ad litem's acceptance of same, said guardian ad litem make answer hereto. This appointment is limited to this proceeding only and it shall cease when a final order is entered on this petition.

SO ORDERED this ______ day of ____________________, 20____.

Probate Judge

Effective 7/05 GPCSF 10 Court

NOTICE

GEORGIA, ________________ COUNTY PROBATE COURT

TO: ____

The petition of ____, for a year's support from the estate of ______________________________, deceased, for decedent's (surviving spouse) (and) (minor child ______), having been duly filed, all interested persons are hereby notified to show cause, if any they have, on or before _____, 20______, why said petition should not be granted.

All objections to the petition must be in writing, setting forth the grounds of any such objections, and must be filed on or before the time stated in the preceding sentence. All pleadings/objections must be signed before a notary public or before a probate court clerk, and filing fees must be tendered with your pleadings/objections, unless you qualify to file as an indigent party. Contact probate court personnel at the following address/telephone number for the required amount of filing fees. If any objections are filed, a hearing will be (held on ______________________ in the Probate Court of ________ County, courtroom __________, (address) ________________, Georgia) (scheduled at a later date). If no objections are filed, the petition may be granted without a hearing.

PROBATE JUDGE

By: ______________________

PROBATE CLERK/DEPUTY CLERK

ADDRESS

TELEPHONE

Effective 7/05

GPCSF 10 Court

IN THE PROBATE COURT OF ____________________ COUNTY

STATE OF GEORGIA

IN RE: ESTATE OF) ESTATE NO. ____________________

)

______________________________,) PETITION FOR YEAR'S SUPPORT

DECEASED)

CERTIFICATE OF MAILING

I do hereby certify that I have this day mailed a copy of the above notice in this matter to (initial one)

_____ the personal representative of the estate

_____ (all interested persons as listed by the petitioner on "Exhibit B" attached to the petition)

as follows:

in an envelope supplied by the petitioner for each person to be notified, properly addressed and with adequate postage thereon, and deposited in the United States Mail, with the return address of this Court thereon.

______________________________ ______________________________

DATE PROBATE CLERK/DEPUTY CLERK

Effective 7/05 GPCSF 10 Court

IN THE PROBATE COURT OF ______________ COUNTY

STATE OF GEORGIA

IN RE: ESTATE OF ______________) ESTATE NO. ______________
)
______________,) PETITION FOR YEAR'S SUPPORT
DECEASED)

ANSWER OF GUARDIAN AD LITEM

I hereby accept my said appointment, acknowledge service and notice of the proceedings as provided by law, and for answer say:

______________ DATE

______________ GUARDIAN AD LITEM

______________ ADDRESS ______________ TELEPHONE

PROBATE COURT OF ______________ COUNTY

STATE OF GEORGIA

IN RE: ESTATE OF) ESTATE NO.
)
______________________________,) PETITION FOR YEAR'S SUPPORT
DECEASED)

FINAL ORDER

The petition for a Year's Support for decedent's (surviving spouse) (minor child ______), setting forth the property sought to be set aside as a year's support, was filed; notice was issued, published, and served as required by law; and no objection was filed to the petition.

WHEREFORE IT IS ORDERED that the petition is granted and the schedule of property is made the award of this court, and further that property taxes on any real property awarded hereby shall be divested as elected in the petition.

SO ORDERED this _____ day of ______________, 20____.

Probate Judge

Effective 7/05 GPCSF 10 Court

Form adopted effective July 31, 2006.

GPCSF 11 PETITIONER. PETITION FOR THE APPOINTMENT OF AN EMERGENCY GUARDIAN AND/OR CONSERVATOR FOR A PROPOSED WARD

GEORGIA PROBATE COURT
STANDARD FORM

Petition for the Appointment of an Emergency Guardian and/or Conservator for a Proposed Ward

INSTRUCTIONS

I. Specific Instructions

1. This form is to be used for filing a Petition for the Appointment of an Emergency Guardian and/or Conservator for a Proposed Ward pursuant to O.C.G.A. §29-4-14 and/or 29-5-14

2. Regarding the need for the pre-hearing appointment of an Emergency Guardian and/or Conservator, O.C.G.A. §29-4-15-(c)(5) and 29-5-15 (c)(5) provide as follows: If the court determines that there is probable cause to believe that the proposed ward is in immediate need of an emergency guardian, the court shall appoint an emergency guardian to serve until the emergency hearing, with or without prior notice to the proposed ward, but only if the threatened risk is so immediate and the potential harm so irreparable that any delay is unreasonable and the existence of the threatened risk and potential for irreparable harm is certified by the affidavit of a physician licensed to practice medicine under Chapter 34 of Title 43, a psychologist licensed to practice under Chapter 39 of Title 43, or a licensed clinical social worker.

   If the court determines that there is probable cause to believe that the proposed ward is in immediate need of an emergency conservator, the court shall appoint an emergency conservator to serve until the emergency hearing, with or without prior notice to the proposed ward, but only if the threatened risk is so immediate and the potential harm so irreparable that any delay is unreasonable and the existence of the threatened risk and potential for irreparable harm is certified by the affidavit of a physician licensed to practice medicine under Chapter 34 of Title 43, a psychologist licensed to practice under Chapter 39 of Title 43, or licensed clinical social worker; provided, however, that, pending the emergency hearing, the court shall order that no withdrawals may be made from any account on the authority of the proposed ward's signature without the court's prior approval and that the emergency conservator shall not expend any funds of the proposed ward without prior court approval.

3. Further, if a pre-hearing emergency guardian and/or conservator is appointed to serve until the emergency hearing, then such guardian and/or conservator shall, prior to the issuance of Letters of Emergency Guardianship and/or Conservatorship, take an oath and post such bond as the court may require.

4. The burden of proof is on the petitioner to prove by clear and convincing evidence that the proposed ward lacks sufficient capacity to make or communicate significant responsible decisions concerning his/her health or safety and is in need of a guardian **AND** there is an immediate, clear, and substantial risk of death or serious physical injury, illness, or disease unless an emergency guardian is appointed and/or that the proposed ward lacks sufficient capacity to make or communicate significant responsible decisions concerning the management of his/her property and is in need of a conservator **AND** there is an immediate, substantial risk of irreparable waste or dissipation of the estate unless an emergency conservator is appointed.

5. In any case involving the appointment of a conservator when the proposed ward owns real property in Georgia, a certificate of creation of conservatorship will be completed by the clerk of the probate court and filed with the clerk of the superior court of each county in which the proposed ward owns real property.

II. General Instructions

General instructions applicable to all Georgia probate court standard forms appear in Volume 255 of the Georgia Reports and are available in each probate court.

GEORGIA PROBATE COURT
STANDARD FORM

PROBATE COURT OF ____________________ COUNTY

STATE OF GEORGIA

IN RE:) ESTATE NO.
)
______________________________,) PETITION FOR APPOINTMENT OF

PROPOSED WARD) AN EMERGENCY GUARDIAN AND/OR
) EMERGENCY CONSERVATOR FOR A
) PROPOSED WARD

TO THE HONORABLE JUDGE OF THE PROBATE COURT:

[NOTE: Unless there are two or more petitioners, the affidavit on page 8 must be completed by a physician, psychologist, or licensed clinical social worker based upon an examination within 15 days prior to the filing of this petition.]

1.

Petitioner, ____________________, is the (relationship) ____________________ of the proposed ward, and is domiciled at (address) ____ County of ____________________, State of __________, telephone number __________, and

(Initial either a. or b. below):

____ a. (Second Petitioner, if any)____________________, is the (relationship) ____________________ of the proposed ward, and is domiciled at (address) ____________________ County of ____________________, State of __________, telephone number __________, show that:

or

____ b. attached hereto as page 8 and made a part of this petition is the completed affidavit of ____, a physician, psychologist or licensed clinical social worker licensed to practice in Georgia, who has examined the proposed ward within fifteen days prior to the filing of this petition, show that:

2.

The proposed ward, age ______, date of birth ________________, social security no. ________________, is domiciled at (address) ________________ County, State of ________________, and is presently located at ________________, which is a (type of facility, if applicable) ________________ and can be contacted at (telephone number):________.

(initial if applicable)

_____ It is anticipated that the proposed ward will be moved within the next 3 days to the following address:
____,
telephone number ________

_____ The proposed ward is a citizen of a foreign country, being

(if a guardianship or conservatorship is granted, pursuant to The Vienna Convention, the Probate Court must notify the consul).

3.

The proposed ward is in need of an emergency guardian and/or conservator by reason of the following incapacity: ____ to the extent that the proposed ward: (initial all applicable)

____a. (for emergency guardianship:) lacks sufficient capacity to make or communicate significant responsible decisions concerning his/her health or safety, and there is an immediate, and substantial risk of death or serious physical injury, illness, or disease unless an emergency guardian is appointed,

____b. (for emergency conservatorship:) lacks sufficient capacity to make or communicate significant responsible decisions concerning the management of his/her property and there is an immediate, substantial risk of irreparable waste or dissipation of the estate unless an emergency conservator is appointed.

The facts which support the claim of the need for an emergency guardian and/or conservator are as follows:

(NOTE: pursuant to O.C.G.A. §29-4-15(b) and 29-5-14(b), the Court shall dismiss the petition if the petitioner does not allege facts which cause the Court to believe that the proposed ward is in need of an emergency guardian and/or conservator as stated above. The Petition cannot be granted unless sufficient facts are presented which support the claim for the need for the appointment of an emergency guardian and/or conservator. While an attached physician's/psychologist's/social worker's affidavit is permissible, the Petitioner(s) MUST specifically allege sufficient facts to support the granting of this Petition.)

4.

It is in the best interest of the proposed ward that ______________ be appointed emergency guardian and ______________ appointed emergency conservator.

5.

(Initial if applicable)

____a. In addition to the appointment of an emergency guardian after notice and a hearing, the Court immediately should appoint a pre-hearing emergency guardian for the following reasons:

Note: the court cannot appoint a pre-hearing emergency guardian unless the petition alleges sufficient specific facts showing that any delay is unreasonable and the existence of the threatened risk and potential for irreparable harm is certified by an affidavit of a physician, psychologist, or social worker.

and, the pre-hearing guardian should be granted the following specific powers and duties which do not exceed those absolutely necessary to respond to the immediate threatened risk(s) described above:

____b. In addition to the appointment of an emergency conservator after notice and a hearing, the Court immediately should appoint a pre-hearing emergency conservator for the following reasons:

Note: the court cannot appoint a pre-hearing emergency conservator unless the petition alleges sufficient specific facts showing that any delay is unreasonable and the existence of the threatened risk and potential for irreparable harm is certified by an affidavit of a physician, psychologist, or social worker.

and, the pre-hearing conservator should be granted the following specific powers and duties which do not exceed those absolutely necessary to respond to the immediate threatened risk(s) described above:

6.

The reason(s) why the procedures for the appointment of a non-emergency (permanent) guardianship and/or conservatorship are inadequate to protect the proposed ward and/or his/her property is/are:

(initial applicable)

____ A Petition for permanent guardianship/conservatorship was/is being/will be filed in conjunction with this Petition.

____ No Petition for permanent guardianship/conservatorship has been/will be filed, and a summary description of all known assets, income, other sources of funds, liabilities, and expenses of the proposed ward is shown on page 10.

7.

The foreseeable duration of the proposed ward's incapacity will be:
and the Court should grant the emergency guardian/conservator the following powers and duties which do not exceed those absolutely necessary to respond to the immediate threatened risk(s) described above: ____________________.

8.

(initial one:)

____a. No other person has authority to act in the circumstances, whether under a power of attorney, trust, or otherwise.

____b. The following individual(s) with the authority to act under a power of attorney, trust, or otherwise, appear(s) unwilling or unable to act: (name, address, and phone number):

9.

Additional Data: Where full particulars are lacking, state here the reasons for any such omission.

WHEREFORE, petitioner(s) pray(s):

1. that service be perfected as required by law;
2. that the court appoint legal counsel and an evaluator for the proposed ward and order an evaluation as required by law;
3. that the court order an emergency hearing to be conducted not sooner than 3 days nor later than 5 days after the filing of this petition;
4. that an emergency guardian and/or conservator be appointed for the proposed ward; and
5. that, if requested, the Court immediately appoint a pre-hearing emergency guardian and/or conservator with such powers and duties as the Court shall direct.

Signature of first petitioner	Signature of second petitioner, if any
Printed Name	Printed Name
Address	Address
Telephone Number	Telephone Number

Signature of Attorney:

Typed/printed name of Attorney:

Address: ______________________

Telephone: __________ State Bar # ______________

VERIFICATION

GEORGIA, ______________________________ COUNTY

Personally appeared before me the undersigned petitioner(s) who on oath state(s) that the facts set forth in the foregoing petition are true.

Sworn to and subscribed before
me this _____ day of __________, 20_____.

____
First Petitioner

____
NOTARY/CLERK OF PROBATE COURT

____
Printed Name

Sworn to and subscribed before
me this _____ day of __________, 20_____.

____
Second Petitioner, if any

____
NOTARY/CLERK OF PROBATE COURT

____
Printed Name

CONSENT TO SERVE AS EMERGENCY GUARDIAN AND/OR CONSERVATOR

RE: Petition for the appointment of an emergency guardian and/or conservator for ____________________, a proposed ward.

I/We, ____________________, having been nominated as emergency guardian(s) and I/we, ____________________, having been nominated as emergency conservator(s) of the above-named proposed ward, do hereby consent to serve as emergency guardian(s)/conservator(s) and pre-hearing emergency guardian(s)/conservator(s) if so appointed.

____________________	____________________
Proposed Emergency Guardian/Conservator	Proposed Emergency Guardian/Conservator
____________________	____________________
Print Name	Print Name
____________________	____________________
Address	Address
____________________	____________________
____________________	____________________
Telephone	Telephone

Proposed Emergency Guardian/Conservator

Print Name

____

Address

Telephone

STATE OF GEORGIA

COUNTY OF

PROBATE COURT OF ____________________ COUNTY

RE: Petition for appointment of an emergency guardian and/or conservator for ____________.

AFFIDAVIT OF PHYSICIAN, PSYCHOLOGIST, OR CLINICAL SOCIAL WORKER FOR EMERGENCY GUARDIANSHIP/CONSERVATORSHIP

I, being first duly sworn, depose and say that I am a physician licensed to practice under Chapter 34 of Title 43 of the Official Code of Georgia Annotated or a psychologist licensed to practice under Chapter 39 of Title 43 of the Official Code of Georgia Annotated, or a licensed clinical social worker; that my office address is ____________________, Georgia, and that I have examined the above-named proposed ward on the ______ day of __________, 20____. **NOTE: The examination on which this affidavit is based must occur WITHIN FIFTEEN DAYS prior to the filing of the petition.** I found him/her to be incapacitated by reason of:

to the extent that said proposed ward (initial all applicable):

____a. (re: emergency guardianship:) lacks sufficient capacity to make or communicate significant responsible decisions concerning his/her health or safety and there is an immediate and substantial risk of death or serious physical injury, illness, or disease unless an emergency guardian is appointed, and (if applicable)

____i. **the threatened risk is so immediate and the potential harm so irreparable that any delay is unreasonable and a pre-hearing guardian should be appointed.**

____b. (re: emergency conservatorship:) lacks sufficient capacity to make or communicate significant, responsible decisions concerning the management of his/her property and there is an immediate, substantial risk of irreparable waste or dissipation of the estate unless an emergency conservator is appointed, and (if applicable)

____i. **the threatened risk is so immediate and the potential harm so irreparable that any delay is unreasonable and a pre-hearing conservator should be appointed.**

The following facts support my opinion of incapacity and the existence of immediate threat(s) or risk(s) to the proposed ward:

The foreseeable limits on the duration of such incapacity are:

Based on available data, the proposed ward should retain the following rights which would be lost with the appointment of a guardian/conservator: (initial all applicable)

____a. contract marriage
____b. make, modify, or terminate other contracts
____c. consent to medical treatment
____d. establish a residence or dwelling place
____e. change domicile
____f. revoke a revocable trust established by the ward
____g. bring or defend any action at law or equity, except an action relating to the guardianship/conservatorship
____h. buy sell, or otherwise dispose of or encumber property
____i. enter into or conduct other business or commercial transactions
____j. none of the above

Optional: Affiant's opinions as to any other limitations on the emergency guardianship/conservatorship are:

WITNESS MY HAND AND SEAL this ________ day of ________________, 20____.

Sworn to and subscribed before me this
me this ____ day of __________, 20____.

____
Signature of Physician/Psychologist/Social Worker

____
Notary Public

____
Printed Name of Evaluator

My commission expires on the ____ day
of __________, 20____.
(NOTARIAL SEAL AFFIXED)

NOTE: If the appointment of an emergency conservator is sought and no petition for permanent conservatorship is being filed simultaneously, this form must be completed

ASSETS, INCOME, OTHER SOURCES OF FUNDS, LIABILITIES, AND EXPENSES OF PROPOSED WARD

PROPOSED WARD:

REAL PROPERTY

(Indicate if property is jointly owned and with whom)

Description	County	State	Approximate equity
Parcel_1			$
Parcel_2			$
Parcel_3			$

INCOME FROM ALL SOURCES

	Yearly Total
Social Security per year	$
SSI (Supplemental Security Income) per year	$
Retirement benefits per year	$
VA benefits per year	$
Other income per year, including, e.g., alimony, annuity, or trust distributions	$
Interest, dividend, or investment income_	$
YEARLY TOTAL OF ALL INCOME	$

PERSONAL AND INTANGIBLE PROPERTY

(Indicate if property is jointly owned and with whom)

Approximate Current Value

1. Checking/Savings/Money Market/Certificates of Deposit/Liquid Accounts:

Bank/Financial Institution/Broker	Acct. No.	Joint Owner (if any)	
			$
			$
			$
			$

2. Stocks/Bonds/Investments (including retirement and profit-sharing accounts):

a. held by brokers:

Brokerage Firm or Institution	Acct. No.	Joint Owner (if any)	
			$
			$
			$
			$
			$

b. privately held:

Company/Issuer	No. of Shares	Joint Owner (if any)	
			$
			$

3. Automobiles:

Year/Make/Model	V.I.N.	Joint owner (if any)	
			$
			$

4. Other assets of significant value:

Description	Joint owner (if any)	
		$
		$
		$

TOTAL VALUE OF PERSONAL AND INTANGIBLE PROPERTY $

DEBTS AND OTHER LIABILITIES

The proposed ward owes the following debts/liabilities:

1. Secured debts:

Obligor/Payee	Collateral	Solely/Jointly Owed	Approx. Current Balance
			$
			$
			$

2. Unsecured debts:

Obligor/Payee	Acct. No.	Solely/Jointly Owed	Approx. Current Balance
			$
			$
			$

TOTAL DEBTS AND OTHER LIABILITIES OF PROPOSED WARD $

AVERAGE MONTHLY LIABILITIES AND EXPENSES

Household:

Care Facility/Rent/Mortgage payments:	$
Property taxes/Insurance	$
Utilities/Lawn Care/Pest Control	$
Miscellaneous household food	$
Total credit account and other debt payments	$
Other (specify)	$

Automotive/Transportation

Fuel and Repairs	$
Tags and license fees, Insurance	$
Bus/Train/Taxi fares	$

Minors or Other Dependents of the Proposed Ward

Child Care	$
School Tuition/Supplies/Expenses/Lunches	$
Clothing/Diapers /Grooming/Hygiene	$
Medical/Dental/Prescription	$
Entertainment/Activities	$

Other Insurance
- Health $
- Life/Disability $
- Other (specify) $

Proposed Ward's Other Expenses
- Laundry/Clothing/Grooming/Hygiene $
- Medical/Dental/Prescriptions/Medications $
- Entertainment/Vacations/Subscriptions/Dues $
- Personal Caretakers/Cleaning personnel $
- Other (specify) $

Total Expenses $

Payments to Creditors:
Is the proposed ward behind in any debt payments? (yes) (no)
If so, payee and amount:

SUMMARY

1. Average Monthly Income $

2. Average Monthly Expenses $____________

Instructions and form adopted effective July 1, 1986; revised effective July 1, 1987; July 1, 1988; July, 1989; July 1, 1995; July 1, 2005; July 31, 2006.

GPCSF 11 COURT. COURT FORMS FOR THE APPOINTMENT OF AN EMERGENCY GUARDIAN AND/OR CONSERVATOR FOR A PROPOSED WARD

GEORGIA PROBATE COURT
STANDARD FORM

Petition for the Appointment of an Emergency Guardian and/or Conservator for a Proposed Ward

NOTICE: UNLESS OTHERWISE DIRECTED BY THE COURT, THE FOLLOWING FORMS ARE FOR PROBATE COURT STAFF TO COMPLETE

GEORGIA PROBATE COURT
STANDARD FORM

PROBATE COURT OF ____________ COUNTY

STATE OF GEORGIA

IN RE:) ESTATE NUMBER ____________
)
______________________________,) PETITION FOR APPOINTMENT OF
PROPOSED WARD) AN EMERGENCY GUARDIAN AND/OR
) CONSERVATOR FOR A
) PROPOSED WARD

ORDER FOR EVALUATION, APPOINTMENT OF COUNSEL, APPOINTMENT OF SPECIAL PROCESS SERVER, AND NOTICE OF HEARING

The above petition having been read and considered, and it appearing that there is probable cause to believe that the proposed ward is in need of an emergency guardian and/or emergency conservator within the meaning of O.C.G.A. §29-4-14 and/or 29-5-14, it is hereby ordered that ____________________, (physician) (psychologist) (licensed clinical social worker), is appointed to evaluate the above-named proposed ward at ____________ o'clock _____.M., on ____________________ at (location) ______________________________, telephone number ____________. In compliance with Georgia law and federal law, including HIPAA, healthcare providers shall permit the above evaluator to have access to the proposed ward's medical records.

IT IS FURTHER ORDERED that ____________________ is hereby appointed special agent to serve ____________________, proposed ward, with a copy of the petition for appointment of emergency guardian and/or conservator and this Order/Notice.

IT IS FURTHER ORDERED that the above-named proposed ward shall submit to an evaluation at the time and place stated above and that a written report shall be furnished to the Court and made available to the parties within 72 hours after the filing of the petition;

IT IS FURTHER ORDERED that an emergency hearing shall be conducted (in the Probate Court of ______________ County, courtroom ______________, (address) ____________________, Georgia) (at the following location: ______________________________) at ________ o'clock _____.M., on ______________ (which is not sooner than three days nor later than five days after the filing of the petition);

IT IS FURTHER ORDERED that the evaluator shall explain the purpose of the evaluation to the proposed ward;

IT IS FURTHER ORDERED that ______________________________, attorney at law, telephone number ____________________ is hereby appointed to represent the proposed ward;

GEORGIA PROBATE COURT
STANDARD FORM

IT IS FURTHER ORDERED that the Clerk /Deputy Clerk shall mail by first-class mail copies of the petition and this order to all interested individuals identified in paragraph 8 of the Petition, if any.

____a. IT IS FURTHER ORDERED that, based on the affidavit filed with the Petition, it appears that the threatened risk of death or serious physical injury, illness, or disease of the proposed ward is so immediate and the potential harm so irreparable that any delay is unreasonable, and ____________________ is named as pre-hearing emergency guardian of the proposed ward, to serve pending the hearing as scheduled above. Emergency Letters of Guardianship shall issued upon said emergency guardian taking the oath.

____b. IT IS FURTHER ORDERED that, based on the affidavit filed with the Petition, it appears that the threatened risk of waste or dissipation of the proposed ward's property is so immediate and the potential harm so irreparable that any delay is unreasonable, and ____________________ is named as pre-hearing emergency conservator of the proposed ward, to serve pending the hearing as scheduled above. Emergency Letters of Conservatorship shall issued upon said emergency conservator posting a surety bond in the amount of $________ and taking the oath.
(initial if applicable)

____(i) IT IS FURTHER ORDERED THAT, pending the emergency hearing, the court hereby orders that no withdrawals may be made from any account on the authority of the proposed ward's signature without the court's prior approval and that the emergency conservator shall not expend any funds of the proposed ward without prior court approval.

NOTICE TO PROPOSED WARD:

This is to notify you of a proceeding initiated in this court by ____________________ seeking to appoint (initial one or both)

a. ________ an emergency guardian for your person
b. ________ an emergency conservator for your property

BY THIS ORDER, THE COURT HAS APPOINTED AN ATTORNEY TO REPRESENT YOU AND HAS SCHEDULED A HEARING. YOU AND YOUR ATTORNEY HAVE THE RIGHT TO ATTEND ANY HEARING HELD ON THIS MATTER.

IF A GUARDIAN IS APPOINTED FOR YOU, YOU MAY LOSE IMPORTANT RIGHTS TO CONTROL AND MANAGE YOUR PERSON.

IF A CONSERVATOR IS APPOINTED FOR YOU, YOU MAY LOSE IMPORTANT RIGHTS TO CONTROL AND MANAGE YOUR PROPERTY.

ALTHOUGH YOU MUST ATTEND THE EVALUATION, YOU DO NOT HAVE TO RESPOND TO QUESTIONS.

So ordered this ______ day of ____________________, 20______.

Probate Judge

CERTIFICATE OF MAILING OF ORDER FOR EVALUATION; APPOINTMENT OF COUNSEL; APPOINTMENT OF SPECIAL PROCESS SERVER; AND NOTICE OF HEARING

ESTATE NO.

This is to certify that I have this day served the persons named in paragraph 8 of the petition, who were ordered to be served by first-class mail, with a copy of the foregoing petition and order, by placing a copy of same in an envelope addressed to each and depositing same in the U.S. Mail, first-class, with adequate postage thereon.

____
DATE PROBATE CLERK/DEPUTY CLERK

CERTIFICATE OF MAILING OF ORDER OF DISMISSAL

ESTATE NO.

This is to certify that I have this day served the proposed ward with a copy of the (petition, the medical affidavit, and) order for dismissal by placing a copy of same in an envelope addressed to the proposed ward and depositing same in the U.S. Mail, first-class, with adequate postage thereon. I have also served a copy of the order for dismissal in the same manner upon the persons required in said order to be so served.

____
DATE PROBATE CLERK/DEPUTY CLERK

* not necessary if dismissal is after evaluation.

PROBATE COURT OF ______________________ COUNTY

STATE OF GEORGIA

IN RE:) ESTATE NO. ______________________

)

______________________,) PETITION FOR APPOINTMENT OF

PROPOSED WARD) AN EMERGENCY GUARDIAN AND/OR
) CONSERVATOR FOR A
) PROPOSED WARD

ORDER FOR DISMISSAL

The above and foregoing petition having been read and considered pursuant to O.C.G.A. §29-4-15 and/or O.C.G.A. §29-5-15, and based on the petition and prior to the court-ordered evaluation, it appears that there is not probable cause to believe that the proposed ward is in need of an emergency guardian and/or conservator, therefore, it is hereby

ORDERED that the petition is dismissed.

IT IS FURTHER ORDERED that a copy of the Petition, the affidavit, if any, and this order be served on the proposed ward by first-class mail, and a copy of this order be served in the same manner upon the petitioner(s) or his/her/their attorney, if any.

SO ORDERED this _____ day of ______________, 20_____.

Probate Judge

PROBATE COURT OF ______________________ COUNTY

STATE OF GEORGIA

IN RE:) ESTATE NUMBER ______________

)

______________________,) PETITION FOR APPOINTMENT OF

PROPOSED WARD) AN EMERGENCY GUARDIAN AND/OR
) CONSERVATOR FOR A
) PROPOSED WARD

RETURN OF SHERIFF/SPECIAL AGENT

I have this day served the proposed ward, ______________________, personally with a copy of the petition for appointment of emergency guardian and/or conservator and Order for Evaluation, Appointment of Counsel, Appointment of Special Process Server, and Notice of Hearing.

This ______ day of ________________, 20______.

Deputy Sheriff ______ County, Georgia

Special Agent

Print Name

(If return is by special agent:)
Sworn to and subscribed before me, this
_____ day of ______________, 20_____.

Notary Public/Clerk, Probate Court
My commission expires ______________.

Effective 7/06 GPCSF 11Court

EVALUATOR'S REPORT AND RETURN OF SPECIAL AGENT, IF APPLICABLE

EMERGENCY GUARDIANSHIP AND/OR CONSERVATORSHIP PROCEEDINGS

ESTATE NO.

PETITIONER(S) ________

PROPOSED WARD ________

In compliance with the Order of the Probate Court of ________ County dated ________ 20____, I performed an evaluation of the above-named proposed ward on ________ 20________. This evaluation took place at ________ beginning at ________. The evaluation continued for ______ minutes. I explained the purpose of the evaluation to the proposed ward.

The following questions and tests were utilized in the evaluation:

Below is a list of all persons and other sources of information consulted in evaluating the proposed ward:

The following is a description of the proposed ward's mental and physical state and condition, including all observed facts considered by me:

The following is a description of the overall social condition of the proposed ward, including support, care, education, and well-being, and the functional capabilities of the proposed ward, if determined by the evaluator:

The following are my findings as to the needs of the proposed ward and their foreseeable duration:

(initial all applicable)

____a. I find the proposed ward to be incapacitated by reason of ____________________ to the extent that said proposed ward (initial all applicable):

____(i) (for emergency guardianship:) lacks sufficient capacity to make or communicate significant responsible decisions concerning his/her health or safety and there is an immediate, clear, and substantial risk of death or serious physical injury, illness, or disease unless an emergency guardian is appointed,

____(ii) (for emergency conservatorship:) lacks sufficient capacity to make or communicate significant responsible decisions concerning the management of his/her property and there is an immediate, substantial risk of irreparable waste or dissipation of the proposed ward's estate unless an emergency conservator is appointed,

____b. I do not find that the proposed ward meets the standards for emergency guardianship set out in a. (i) above.

____c. I do not find that the proposed ward meets the standards for emergency conservator set out in a. (ii) above.

Physician licensed under Chapter 34 of Title 43 of the
or
Psychologist licensed under Chapter 39 of Title 43 of the
Official Code of Georgia Annotated
or
Licensed Clinical Social Worker

Sworn to and subscribed before me
this ______ day of __________, 20_____.

Notary Public/Clerk, Probate Court

NOTE: This report must be filed with the Probate Court no later than 72 hours after the filing of the petition.

STIPULATION AND WAIVER BY PROPOSED WARD'S ATTORNEY

GEORGIA, ____________________ COUNTY ESTATE NO. ____________

TO THE PROBATE COURT OF SAID STATE AND COUNTY

IN RE: PETITION FOR THE APPOINTMENT OF AN EMERGENCY GUARDIAN AND/OR CONSERVATOR FOR ____________________, PROPOSED WARD

The undersigned, as the attorney representing the above-named proposed ward in these proceedings, (initial all applicable:)

____a. does hereby stipulate into evidence the affidavit prepared by (name of affiant evaluator) ____________________, being the evaluation report Ordered by the Court in this matter, and hereby waives the appearance of such affiant at any hearing concerning the said petition

____b. does hereby stipulate into evidence the affidavit(s) prepared by (name of affiant evaluator) ____________________, which is the affidavit referred to in Paragraph 1(b) of the petition, and hereby waives the appearance of such affiant at any hearing concerning the said petition.

____c. does further waive the appearance of my client the proposed ward at said hearing.

This __________ day of __________, 20____.

Attorney ______________________________

Typed/printed name of Attorney: ______________________________

Address: ______________________________

Telephone: ____________ State Bar # ____________

PROBATE COURT OF ____________________ COUNTY

STATE OF GEORGIA

IN RE:) ESTATE NO.
)
________________________________,) PETITION FOR APPOINTMENT OF
PROPOSED WARD) AN EMERGENCY GUARDIAN AND/OR
) CONSERVATOR FOR A
) PROPOSED WARD

FINAL ORDER

A hearing was held on the above-referenced petition on ____________________ 20______, and after considering the pleadings, the evaluation report and the evidence taken at the hearing, the Court makes the following:

FINDINGS OF FACT

1.

All procedural requirements of O.C.G.A. §29-4-14 and/or O.C.G.A. §29-5-15 have been met.

2.

The above-named proposed ward is in need of a guardian/conservator by reason of ____________________. Such need appears to be (permanent)(limited to the following number of days: __________).

3.

The current value of the personal property of the proposed ward is approximately $__________. The proposed ward has an interest in real property in the following locations:

a. ____________________ County, (state) ____________________;
b. ____________________ County, (state) ____________________;
c. ____________________ County, (state) ____________________.

The proposed ward has outstanding debts of $____________________ and average expenditures of $____________________ per month.

4.

Petitioner(s) moved the Court to appoint ________________ as emergency guardian and __________ as emergency conservator asserting those individual(s) should serve because _____.

(initial if applicable:)

____a. Another individual, being ____________________ was nominated/designated by the proposed ward to serve as guardian,

____ (i) and no good cause was shown to override such preference.

____ (ii) but good cause was shown not to appoint said individual, being: __________.

____b. Another individual with higher preference, being ________________ was nominated/designated to serve as guardian by someone other than the proposed ward, and/but it (is) (is not) in the best interest of the proposed ward to appoint him/her guardian because ____.

____c. Another individual, being ________________ was nominated/designated by the proposed ward to serve as conservator,

____ (i) and no good cause was shown to override such preference.

____ (ii) but good cause was shown not to appoint said individual, being: __________.

____d. Another individual with higher preference, being ________________ was nominated/designated to serve as conservator by someone other than the proposed ward, and/but it (is) (is not) in the best interest of the proposed ward to appoint him/her conservator because ____.

5.

The Petitioner asserted that the following additional powers pursuant to O.C.G.A. §29-4-23 (b) and O.C.G.A. §29-5-23(c) were absolutely necessary to respond to the immediate and threatened risks alleged in the petition: for the emergency guardian: ____________________ for the emergency conservator: ____

CONCLUSIONS OF LAW

The Court finds, by clear and convincing evidence, that the above-named proposed ward (hereinafter referred to as "the ward") is in need of:

____a. an emergency guardian because the ward lacks sufficient capacity to make or communicate significant responsible decisions concerning his/her health or safety and there is an immediate and substantial risk of death or serious physical injury, illness, or disease unless an emergency guardian is appointed.

____b. an emergency conservator because the ward lacks sufficient capacity to make or communicate significant responsible decisions concerning the management of his/her property and there is an immediate, substantial risk of irreparable waste or dissipation of the ward's property unless an emergency conservator is appointed.

The duration of the emergency guardianship/ conservatorship is for: (initial one)

____a. 60 days, or until the effective date of the appointment of permanent guardianship/conservatorship, or until the emergency guardian(s) and/or conservator(s) are removed, or the dismissal of a petition for the appointment of a guardian and/or conservator, whichever occurs first.

____b. a date certain prior to the time identified in (a) above, being ____________________, 20______.

Therefore it is

ORDERED that __________ should be, and hereby is/are, appointed emergency guardian(s) and ____ should be, and hereby is/are, appointed emergency conservator(s) of the ward. Letters of emergency guardianship and/or emergency conservatorship shall issue to such guardian(s) and/or conservator(s) upon taking the required oath and upon the emergency conservator's(s') posting bond in the amount of $__________. **The appointed emergency guardian(s)/conservator(s) shall have no authority to act on behalf of the ward until Letters of Emergency Guardianship/Conservatorship have issued.**

IT IS FURTHER ORDERED that the emergency guardian(s) shall have only the following powers and duties determined by the Court to be absolutely necessary to respond to the immediate threatened risk: ____

IT IS FURTHER ORDERED that the emergency conservator(s) shall have only the following powers and duties determined by the Court to be absolutely necessary to respond to the immediate threatened risk: ____

IT IS FURTHER ORDERED that the emergency guardian(s) shall file the following reports with the Court:

IT IS FURTHER ORDERED that the emergency conservator(s) shall file the following reports with the Court: ____

IT IS FURTHER ORDERED that a copy of this Order shall be hand delivered or mailed by first class mail to the ward, the ward's attorney; the guardian ad litem, if any; the guardian and/or conservator, the petitioner(s), and his/her/their attorney(s), if any.

IT IS FURTHER ORDERED that the ward's legal counsel shall make reasonable efforts to explain to the ward this Order and the ward's rights under this Order.

IT IS FURTHER ORDERED that, within 30 days of the date hereof, the clerk/deputy clerk shall file the certificate of creation of conservatorship in accordance with O.C.G.A. §29-5-13(d) with the Clerk of Superior Court of each county in this state in which the ward owns real property.

SO ORDERED this ________ day of ____________________, 20_____.

Probate Judge/Hearing Officer exercising the jurisdiction of the Probate Court pursuant to O.C.G.A. §29-4-12(d)(7) and/or 29-5-12(d)(7)

CERTIFICATE OF MAILING OF FINAL ORDER

I have this date mailed (or handed) a copy of the Final Order Appointing Emergency Guardian and/or Conservator to the ward, his/her attorney, (his/her guardian ad litem), (his/her representatives,) the guardian(s), the conservator(s), the petitioner(s) and petitioner's attorney(s).

____________________ ____________________

DATE PROBATE CLERK /DEPUTY CLERK

CERTIFICATE OF FILING CERTIFICATE OF CREATION OF CONSERVATORSHIP

ESTATE NO.

I have this date hand-delivered and/or mailed for filing a Certificate of Creation of Conservatorship to the Clerk of the Superior Court of each of the following counties, together with payment of any recording costs: ____________________

____________________ ____________________

DATE PROBATE CLERK/DEPUTY CLERK

ADDRESS

TELEPHONE

Effective 7/06 GPCSF 11Court

Probate Court Return Mailing Address:

CERTIFICATE OF CREATION OF EMERGENCY CONSERVATORSHIP

(Pursuant to O.C.G.A. § 29-5-13(d))

GEORGIA, ______________________________ County

PROBATE ESTATE NO.

DATE ORDER ISSUED:

GRANTOR: (NAME OF WARD) ______________________________

GRANTEE: (NAME OF EMERGENCY CONSERVATOR(S) OF ABOVE WARD)

An Emergency conservatorship of the property has been created for the above-named ward. Said emergency conservatorship expires (initial)

____a. in 60 days, or on the effective date of the appointment of a permanent conservator, or when the emergency conservator(s) is/are removed, or the dismissal of a petition for the appointment of a conservator, whichever occurs first.

____b. on a date certain, being ____________________, 20____.

Original Certificate delivered or mailed to Clerk of Superior Court of ______________ County on ____________________, 20____.

I do hereby certify that the above information is based on the Order of the Probate Court issued on the date set out above and that the above information is true and correct.

By: ______________________________

PROBATE CLERK /DEPUTY CLERK

Effective 7/06 GPCSF 11Court

GEORGIA PROBATE COURT
STANDARD FORM

STATE OF GEORGIA
COUNTY OF ______________ ESTATE NO. __________

LETTERS OF EMERGENCY GUARDIANSHIP OF ADULT WARD

From the Judge of the Probate Court of said County. Date of Birth ______

TO: ______________________________, Guardian(s)

RE: ______________________________, Adult Ward

This Court has found that the above-named ward is in need of an emergency guardian and has designated you as such guardian, and you have taken your oath. Your powers and duties as such emergency guardian which were declared by the Court to be those absolutely necessary to respond to the immediate threatened risk are ______________________________

These letters expire

____a. in 60 days, or on the effective date of the appointment of a permanent guardian, or when the emergency guardian(s) is/are removed, or upon the dismissal of a petition for the appointment of a permanent guardian, whichever occurs first.

____b. on a date certain, being

Given under my hand and official seal, the ______ day of ____________, 20____.

Probate Judge

NOTE: The following must be signed if the judge does not sign the original of this document:

Issued by:

______________________________(Seal)
PROBATE CLERK /DEPUTY CLERK

Effective 7/06 GPCSF 11Court

GEORGIA PROBATE COURT
STANDARD FORM

STATE OF GEORGIA
COUNTY OF ______________ ESTATE NO. ________

LETTERS OF EMERGENCY CONSERVATORSHIP OF ADULT WARD

From the Judge of the Probate Court of said County. Date of Birth ______

TO: ______________________________, Conservator(s)

RE: ______________________________, Adult Ward

This Court has found that the above-named ward is in need of an emergency conservator and has designated you as such conservator, and you have posted bond and taken your oath. Your powers and duties as such emergency conservator which were declared by the Court to be those absolutely necessary to respond to the immediate threatened risk are ______________________________

These letters expire (initial)

____a. in 60 days, or on the effective date of the appointment of a permanent conservator, or when the emergency conservator(s) is/are removed, or upon the dismissal of a petition for the appointment of a permanent guardian, whichever occurs first.

____b. on a date certain, being ______________, 20____.

Given under my hand and official seal, the _____ day of ______________, 20________.

Probate Judge

NOTE: The following must be signed if the judge does not sign the original of this document:

Issued by:

______________________________(Seal)
PROBATE CLERK /DEPUTY CLERK

Effective 7/06 GPCSF 11Court

GEORGIA PROBATE COURT
STANDARD FORM

STATE OF GEORGIA
COUNTY OF ________________ ESTATE NO. ________

LETTERS OF EMERGENCY GUARDIANSHIP AND CONSERVATORSHIP OF ADULT WARD

From the Judge of the Probate Court of said County. Date of Birth ________

TO: ______________________________, Guardian(s) and Conservator(s)

RE: ______________________________, Adult Ward,

This Court has found that the above-named ward is in need of an emergency guardian and conservator and has designated you as such guardian and conservator, and you have posted bond and taken your oath. Your powers and duties as such emergency guardian and conservator which were declared by the Court to be those absolutely necessary to respond to the immediate threatened risk are ____

These letters expire (initial)

____a. in 60 days, or on the effective date of the appointment of a permanent guardian and conservator, or when the emergency guardian(s) and conservator(s) is/are removed, or upon the dismissal of a petition for the appointment of a permanent guardian, whichever occurs first.

____b. on a date certain, being ________________, 20____.

Given under my hand and official seal, the ________ day of ____________________, 20____.

Probate Judge

NOTE: The following must be signed if the judge does not sign the original of this document:

Issued by:

____(Seal)
PROBATE CLERK /DEPUTY CLERK

Effective 7/06 GPCSF 11Court

Form adopted effective July 1, 2005; amended effective July 31, 2006.

GPCSF 12 PETITIONER. PETITION FOR THE APPOINTMENT OF A GUARDIAN AND/OR CONSERVATOR FOR A PROPOSED WARD

GEORGIA PROBATE COURT
STANDARD FORM

Petition for the Appointment of a Guardian and/or Conservator for a Proposed Ward

INSTRUCTIONS

I. Specific Instructions

1. This form is to be used for filing a Petition for the Appointment of a Guardian and/or Conservator for a Proposed Ward pursuant to O.C.G.A. §29-4-10 and O.C.G.A. §29-5-10.

2. In any case involving the creation of a conservatorship when the proposed ward owns real property, a certificate of creation of conservatorship will be completed by the clerk of the probate court and filed with the clerk of the superior court of each county of this state in which the proposed ward owns real property within 30 days of the date of such order.

3. The burden of proof is on the petitioner to present clear and convincing evidence that the proposed ward lacks sufficient capacity to make or communicate significant responsible decisions concerning his or her health or safety and is in need of a guardianship and/or that the proposed ward lacks sufficient capacity to make or communicate significant responsible decisions concerning the management of his or her property and is in need of a conservatorship.

II. General Instructions

General instructions applicable to all Georgia probate court standard forms appear in Volume 255 of the Georgia Reports and are available in each probate court.

GEORGIA PROBATE COURT
STANDARD FORM

PROBATE COURT OF ______________________________ COUNTY

STATE OF GEORGIA

IN RE:) ESTATE NO. ____________
)
______________________________,) PETITION FOR APPOINTMENT OF
PROPOSED WARD) A GUARDIAN AND/OR
) CONSERVATOR FOR A
) PROPOSED WARD

TO THE HONORABLE JUDGE OF THE PROBATE COURT:

[NOTE: Unless there are two or more petitioners, the affidavit on page 9 must be completed by a physician, psychologist, or licensed clinical social worker based upon an examination within 15 days prior to the filing of this petition.]

1.

Petitioner, ______________________________, is the (relationship) ______________ of the proposed ward, and is domiciled at (address) ______________ County of ______________, State of ______________, telephone number ______________, and

(Initial either a. or b. below):

_____ a. (Second Petitioner, if any) ______________________________, is the (relationship) ______________ of the proposed ward, and is domiciled at (address) ______________, County of ______________, State of ______________ telephone number ______________, show that:

or

_____ b. attached hereto as page 9 and made a part of this petition is the completed affidavit of ______________________________, a physician or psychologist licensed to practice in Georgia or a licensed clinical social worker, who has examined the proposed ward within fifteen days prior to the filing of this petition, show that:

GEORGIA PROBATE COURT
STANDARD FORM

2.

The proposed ward, age__________, date of birth____________________, social security no. ________________, is domiciled at (address) ________________________ County, State of ______________________, and is presently located at ____, which is a (type of facility, if applicable) ____ and can be contacted at (telephone number):______________________.

(initial if applicable)

_____ It is anticipated that the proposed ward will be moved within the next days to the following address: ____, telephone number __________________________.

_____ The proposed ward is a citizen of a foreign country, being ________________________ (if a guardianship or conservatorship is granted, pursuant to The Vienna Convention, the Probate Court must notify the consul).

3.

The proposed ward is in need of a guardian and/or conservator by reason of the following incapacity: ____ to the extent that the proposed ward (initial one or both):

_______a. (for guardianship:) lacks sufficient capacity to make or communicate significant responsible decisions concerning his/her health or safety.

_______b. (for conservatorship:) lacks sufficient capacity to make or communicate significant responsible decisions concerning the management of his/her property.

The facts which support the claim of the need for a guardian and/or conservator are as follows:

(NOTE: the Petition cannot be granted unless sufficient facts are presented which support the claim for the need for the appointment of a guardian or conservator. While an attached physician's/psychologist's/social worker's affidavit is permissible, the Petitioner(s) MUST specifically allege sufficient facts to support the granting of this Petition.)

GEORGIA PROBATE COURT
STANDARD FORM

4.

It is in the best interest of the proposed ward that ______________________________ be appointed guardian and ____ appointed conservator.

5.

The forseeable duration of the incapacity will be: ____________________ and the Court should allow the proposed ward to retain the following rights and powers: ____________________.

6.

(NOTE: The law requires notice to be given to the spouse, if any, and to all living children, if any, whose addresses are known. If there are no living adult children whose addresses are known, then list at least two adults in the following order of priority: lineal descendants of the proposed ward; parents and siblings of the proposed ward; and friends of the proposed ward. In determining the persons to whom notice is required to be given according to the foregoing rules, the petitioner(s) should not be counted as persons receiving notice.)

Pursuant to law, the names, addresses, telephone numbers and relationships of the persons to be notified are as follows:

NAME	AGE (or over 18)	ADDRESS TELEPHONE	RELATIONSHIP

GEORGIA PROBATE COURT
STANDARD FORM

7.

a. As to the guardianship, prior to the filing of this Petition, to the best of my/our knowledge, the following individual(s) has/have been nominated to serve under a living will, durable power of attorney for healthcare, order relating to cardiopulmonary resuscitation, or other instrument that deals with the management of the person of the proposed ward in the event of incapacity. If any, please provide their name(s), addresses(es), indicate the nature of their interest, whether they are willing to act or have failed to act under said appointment: ____________

b. As to the guardianship, prior to the filing of this Petition, to the best of my/our knowledge, the following individual(s) has/have been nominated in writing to serve as guardian by the proposed ward, his/her spouse, adult child, or parent. If any, please provide their name(s), addresses(es), indicate the nature of their interest, whether they are willing to act under said appointment, and whether the individual(s) is/are an owner, operator, or employee of a caregiving institution in which the proposed ward currently is receiving care: ____________

8.

a. As to the conservatorship, prior to the filing of this Petition, to the best of my/our knowledge, the following individual(s) has/have been nominated to serve under a power of attorney, trust, or other instrument that deals with the management of the property of the proposed ward in the event of incapacity. If any, please provide their name(s), addresses(es), the nature of their interest, and indicate whether they are willing to act or have failed to act under said appointment: ____________

b. As to the conservatorship, prior to the filing of this Petition, to the best of my/our knowledge, the following individual(s) has/have been nominated in writing to serve as conservator by the proposed ward, his/her spouse, adult child, or parent. If any, please provide their name(s), addresses(es), the nature of their interest, and indicate whether they are willing to act under said appointment, and whether the individual(s) is/are an owner, operator, or employee of a caregiving institution in which the proposed ward currently is receiving care: ____________

(initial if applicable)

____________ The above individual(s) may have the following ownership or financial conflict of interest in serving as conservator: NOTE: A CONFLICT OF INTEREST MAY EXIST IF THE PROPOSED CONSERVATOR IS A CO-OWNER OF A JOINT ACCOUNT OR REAL PROPERTY WITH THE PROPOSED WARD. (list) ____________

GEORGIA PROBATE COURT
STANDARD FORM

9.

Regarding other petitions for guardianship and/or conservatorship, (initial if applicable)

______a. (Name) ____, residing at ____, has been appointed as an emergency or permanent guardian/conservator for the proposed ward in the following county and state: ____.

______b. A ruling on a Petition for the appointment of an emergency or permanent guardian/conservator is pending in the following county and state: __________.

______c. A petition for emergency or permanent guardianship/conservatorship has been denied or dismissed within the prior two years by a court in the following county and state: ____

—.

______d. A petition for emergency or permanent guardianship/conservatorship has been denied or dismissed within the prior two years by a court in this state; however, there has been a significant change in the condition or circumstances of the proposed ward as shown by the affidavit or evaluation, attached as Exhibit "A."

10.

All known income and assets of the proposed ward are shown on page 11 attached hereto.

11.

A guardian ad litem should be appointed, because the following additional powers pursuant to O.C.G.A. §29-4-23 (b) and O.C.G.A. §29-5-23(c) are requested, with the reasons for such request:

GEORGIA PROBATE COURT
STANDARD FORM

12.

Additional Data: Where full particulars are lacking, state here the reasons for any such omission.

13.

It is in the best interest of the proposed ward that the within nominated guardian and/or conservator be appointed.

WHEREFORE, petitioner(s) pray(s):

1. that service be perfected as required by law;
2. that the court appoint legal counsel and an evaluator for the proposed ward and order an evaluation as required by law;
3. that upon receipt of the evaluation report, the court order a hearing to determine the need for a guardian and/or conservator for the proposed ward; and
4. that a guardian and/or conservator be appointed for the proposed ward.

Signature of first petitioner	Signature of second petitioner, if any
Printed Name	Printed Name
Address	Address
Telephone Number	Telephone Number

Signature of Attorney:

Typed/printed name of Attorney: ______________________

Address: ______________________

Telephone: ______________ State Bar # ______________

GEORGIA PROBATE COURT
STANDARD FORM

VERIFICATION

GEORGIA, ______________________________ COUNTY

Personally appeared before me the undersigned petitioner(s) who on oath state(s) that the facts set forth in the foregoing petition are true.

Sworn to and subscribed before me this ___ day of __________, 20___.

____
First Petitioner

____
NOTARY/CLERK OF PROBATE COURT

____
Printed Name

Sworn to and subscribed before me this ___ day of __________, 20 ___.

____
Second Petitioner, if any

____
NOTARY/CLERK OF PROBATE COURT

____
Printed Name

GEORGIA PROBATE COURT
STANDARD FORM

CONSENT TO SERVE AS GUARDIAN/CONSERVATOR

RE: Petition for the appointment of guardian and/or conservator for ____________________.

I/We, ________________________________ having been nominated as guardian and I/we, ____________________, having been nominated as conservator of the above-named proposed ward, do hereby consent to serve as such.

________________________	________________________
Proposed Guardian/Conservator	Proposed Guardian/Conservator
________________________	________________________
Print Name	Print Name
________________________	________________________
Address	Address
________________________	________________________
________________________	________________________
Telephone	Telephone

Proposed Guardian/Conservator

Print Name

____

Address

Telephone

GEORGIA PROBATE COURT
STANDARD FORM

STATE OF GEORGIA

COUNTY OF ____________________

PROBATE COURT OF ____________________ COUNTY

RE: Petition for appointment of a guardian and/or conservator for ____________________.

AFFIDAVIT OF PHYSICIAN, PSYCHOLOGIST, OR LICENSED CLINICAL SOCIAL WORKER

I, being first duly sworn, depose and say that I am a physician licensed to practice under Chapter 34 of Title 43 of the Official Code of Georgia Annotated, a psychologist licensed to practice under Chapter 39 of Title 43 of the Official Code of Georgia Annotated, or a Licensed Clinical Social Worker; that my office address is ____________________, Georgia, and that I have examined the above-named proposed ward on the ____ day of __________, 20 ____.
NOTE: The examination on which this affidavit is based must occur WITHIN FIFTEEN DAYS prior to the filing of the petition.
I found him/her to be incapacitated by reason of: ____________________

____________________ to the extent that said proposed ward (initial all applicable):

_____ a. (for guardianship:) lacks sufficient capacity to make or communicate significant responsible decisions concerning his/her health or safety.

_____ b. (for conservatorship:) lacks sufficient capacity to make or communicate significant responsible decisions concerning the management of his/her property.

The following facts support said diagnosis:

GEORGIA PROBATE COURT
STANDARD FORM

(cont.)

The foreseeable limits on the duration of such incapacity are:

WITNESS MY HAND AND SEAL this ________ day of ________________, 20____.

Sworn to and subscribed before me this ____ day of ________________, 20____.

____

Signature of (Physician)(Psychologist)(Social Worker)

Notary Public

My commission expires on the ____ day of ________________, 20 ______.

Typed Name ________________

(NOTARIAL SEAL AFFIXED)

NOTE: The examination on which this affidavit is based must occur WITHIN FIFTEEN DAYS prior to the filing of the petition.

GEORGIA PROBATE COURT
STANDARD FORM

ASSETS, INCOME, OTHER SOURCES OF FUNDS, LIABILITIES, AND EXPENSES OF PROPOSED WARD

PROPOSED WARD:

REAL PROPERTY

(Indicate if property is jointly owned and with whom)

Description	County	State	Approximate equity
Parcel_1 ______			$
Parcel_2 ______			$
Parcel_3 ______			$

INCOME FROM ALL SOURCES

	Yearly Total
Social Security per year	$
SSI (Supplemental Security Income)_ per year	$
Retirement benefits per year	$
VA benefits per year	$
Other income per year, including, e.g., alimony, annuity, or trust distributions	$
Interest, dividend, or investment income	$
YEARLY TOTAL OF ALL INCOME	$ ______

PERSONAL AND INTANGIBLE PROPERTY

(Indicate if property is jointly owned and with whom)

1. Checking/Savings/Money Market/Certificates of Deposit/Liquid Accounts:

Bank/Financial Institution/Broker	Acct. No.	Joint Owner (if any)	Approximate Current Value
			$
			$
			$
			$

GEORGIA PROBATE COURT
STANDARD FORM

2. Stocks/Bonds/Investments (including retirement and profit-sharing accounts):

a. held by brokers:

Brokerage Firm or Institution	Acct. No.	Joint Owner (if any)	
			$
			$
			$
			$
			$

b. privately held:

Company/Issuer	No. of Shares	Joint Owner (if any)	
			$
			$

3. Automobiles:

Year/Make/Model	V.I.N.	Joint owner (if any)	
			$
			$

4. Other assets of significant value:

Description	Joint owner (if any)	
		$
		$
		$

TOTAL VALUE OF PERSONAL AND INTANGIBLE PROPERTY $

GEORGIA PROBATE COURT
STANDARD FORM

DEBTS AND OTHER LIABILITIES

The proposed ward owes the following debts/liabilities:

1. Secured debts:

Obligor/Payee	Collateral	Solely/Jointly Owed	Approx. Current Balance
			$
			$
			$

2. Unsecured debts:

Obligor/Payee	Acct. No.	Solely/Jointly Owed	Approx. Current Balance
			$
			$
			$

TOTAL DEBTS AND OTHER LIABILITIES OF PROPOSED WARD $

AVERAGE MONTHLY LIABILITIES AND EXPENSES

Household:

Care Facility/Rent/Mortgage payments:	$
Property taxes/Insurance	$
Utilities/Lawn Care/Pest Control	$
Miscellaneous household/food	$
Total credit account and other debt payments	$
Other (specify)	$

Automotive/Transportation

Fuel and Repairs	$
Tags and license fees, Insurance	$
Bus/Train/Taxi fares	$

Minors or Other Dependents of the Proposed Ward

Child Care	$
School Tuition/Supplies/Expenses/Lunches	$

GEORGIA PROBATE COURT
STANDARD FORM

Clothing/Diapers /Grooming/Hygiene	$
Medical/Dental/Prescription	$
Entertainment/Activities	$
Other Insurance	
Health	$
Life/Disability	$
Other (specify)	$
Proposed Ward's Other Expenses	
Laundry/Clothing/Grooming/Hygiene	$
Medical/Dental/Prescriptions/Medications	$
Entertainment/Vacations/Subscriptions/Dues	$
Personal Caretakers/Cleaning personnel	$
Other (specify)	$
Total Expenses	$

Payments to Creditors:
Is the proposed ward behind in any debt payments? (yes) (no)
If so, payee and amount: ______________________________

SUMMARY

1. Average Monthly Income $
2. Average Monthly Expenses <$____________>

GEORGIA PROBATE COURT
STANDARD FORM

ACKNOWLEDGMENT OF SERVICE

PROPOSED WARD ______________________ ESTATE NO.

Due and legal service of the Petition for Appointment of a Guardian and/or Conservator is hereby acknowledged by the following interested persons as shown in paragraph 6, in addition to any nominated guardian(s) and/or conservator(s). The undersigned acknowledges that he/she has received a copy of the Petition and all further service and notice is waived.

SIGNATURE(S)

Sworn to and subscribed before me this ____ day of ____________, 20____. ______________________

______________________ ______________________

NOTARY/CLERK OF PROBATE COURT Printed Name

Sworn to and subscribed before me this ____ day of ____________, 20____. ______________________

______________________ ______________________

NOTARY/CLERK OF PROBATE COURT Printed Name

Sworn to and subscribed before me this ____ day of ____________, 20____. ______________________

______________________ ______________________

NOTARY/CLERK OF PROBATE COURT Printed Name

Sworn to and subscribed before me this ____ day of ____________, 20____. ______________________

______________________ ______________________

NOTARY/CLERK OF PROBATE COURT Printed Name

Sworn to and subscribed before me this ____ day of ____________, 20____. ______________________

______________________ ______________________

NOTARY/CLERK OF PROBATE COURT Printed Name

Instructions and form adopted effective July 1, 1986; revised effective July 1, 1987; July 1, 1988; July, 1989; July 1, 1990; July 1, 1995; July 1, 2005; July 31, 2006.

GPCSF 12 COURT. COURT FORMS FOR THE APPOINTMENT OF A GUARDIAN AND/OR CONSERVATOR FOR A PROPOSED WARD

GEORGIA PROBATE COURT
STANDARD FORM

Petition for the Appointment of a Guardian and/or Conservator for a Proposed Ward

NOTICE: UNLESS OTHERWISE DIRECTED BY THE COURT, THE FOLLOWING FORMS ARE FOR PROBATE COURT STAFF TO COMPLETE

GEORGIA PROBATE COURT
STANDARD FORM

PROBATE COURT OF ______________________________ COUNTY

STATE OF GEORGIA

IN RE:	)	ESTATE NO. ______________
	)	
______________________________,	)	PETITION FOR APPOINTMENT OF
PROPOSED WARD	)	A GUARDIAN AND/OR
	)	CONSERVATOR FOR A
	)	PROPOSED WARD

ORDER FOR EVALUATION

The above and foregoing petition having been read and considered, and it appearing that there is sufficient evidence to believe that the proposed ward is in need of a guardian and/or conservator within the meaning of O.C.G.A. §29-4-1 and/or 29-5-1, it is hereby ordered that ______________________________, (physician) (psychologist) (licensed clinical social worker), is appointed to evaluate the above-named proposed ward at _____ o'clock ___.M., on ______________________ 20______ at (location) ______________________________, telephone number ______________________________. In compliance with Georgia law and federal law, including HIPAA, healthcare providers shall permit the above evaluator to have access to the proposed ward's medical records.

IT IS FURTHER ORDERED that the above-named proposed ward shall submit to an evaluation at the time and place stated above;

IT IS FURTHER ORDERED that the evaluator shall explain the purpose of the evaluation to the proposed ward;

IT IS FURTHER ORDERED that a Clerk/deputy clerk shall immediately notify the proposed ward of these proceedings by having all pleadings, as well as this order and the notice of proceedings to appoint guardian and/or conservator, personally served on the proposed ward;

IT IS FURTHER ORDERED that a Clerk/deputy clerk shall mail by first-class mail copies of the petition, this order and the notice of evaluation to all interested individuals identified in paragraphs 6, 7, and 8 of the Petition.

SO ORDERED this ______ day of ______________________________, 20______.

Probate Judge

Effective 7/06 GPCSF 12Court

CERTIFICATE OF MAILING OF ORDER AND NOTICE OF PROCEEDINGS

ESTATE NO.

This is to certify that I have this day served the petitioner(s); the proposed ward's guardian ad litem (if any) and attorney; the spouse, family, and/or friends of the proposed ward as found in paragraphs 6, 7, and 8 of the Petition, who were ordered to be served by first-class mail, with a copy of the petition, order, and notice of proceedings to appoint guardian/conservator, by placing a copy of same in an envelope addressed to each and depositing same in the U.S. Mail, first-class, with adequate postage thereon.

This _____ day of ______________________, 20_____.

PROBATE CLERK/DEPUTY CLERK

CERTIFICATE OF MAILING OF ORDER FOR DISMISSAL

ESTATE NO.

This is to certify that I have this day served the proposed ward with a copy of the (petition and) order for dismissal by placing a copy of same in an envelope addressed to the proposed ward and depositing same in the U.S. Mail, first-class, with adequate postage thereon. I have also served a copy of the order for dismissal in the same manner upon the persons required in said order to be so served.

This _____ day of ______________________, 20_____.

PROBATE CLERK/DEPUTY CLERK

* not necessary if dismissal is after evaluation.

CERTIFICATE OF MAILING OF ORDER AND NOTICE OF HEARING

ESTATE NO.

This is to certify that I have this day served the persons show above in paragraphs 6, 7, and 8 of the Petition with a copy of the Order and Notice of Hearing and a copy of the evaluation report by placing copies of same in an envelope addressed to each and depositing same in the U.S. Mail, first-class, with adequate postage thereon.

This _____ day of ______________________, 20_____.

PROBATE CLERK/DEPUTY CLERK

Effective 7/06 GPCSF 12Court

PROBATE COURT OF ______________________ COUNTY

STATE OF GEORGIA

IN RE:) ESTATE NO. ______________
)
______________________,) PETITION FOR APPOINTMENT
PROPOSED WARD) OF A GUARDIAN AND/OR
) CONSERVATOR FOR A PROPOSED
) WARD

NOTICE TO PROPOSED WARD OF PROCEEDINGS TO APPOINT GUARDIAN AND/OR CONSERVATOR

TO: ______________________________________: this is to notify you of a proceeding initiated in this court by ______________________ seeking to appoint (initial one or both)

a. ______________ a guardian for your person
b. ______________ a conservator for your property

and to inform you of your right to independent counsel. If you wish to retain your own attorney, you must notify this court within two days; otherwise, an attorney will be appointed for you by the court.

You are further notified that ______________________________ has been appointed by the Court to evaluate you. You must submit to an evaluation by being present at: (location) ____
at o'clock ______.M. on ______________________, 20__________ which is not sooner than the fifth day after the service of notice on you.

Failure to present yourself for evaluation at the time and place above will authorize the court to order you transported directly to and from a medical facility or the office of the physician, psychologist, or licensed clinical social worker for the court-ordered evaluation.

YOU ARE FURTHER NOTIFIED:

YOU AND YOUR ATTORNEY HAVE THE RIGHT TO ATTEND ANY HEARING HELD ON THIS MATTER.

IF A GUARDIAN IS APPOINTED FOR YOU, YOU MAY LOSE IMPORTANT RIGHTS TO CONTROL AND MANAGE YOUR PERSON.

IF A CONSERVATOR IS APPOINTED FOR YOU, YOU MAY LOSE IMPORTANT RIGHTS TO CONTROL AND MANAGE YOUR PROPERTY.

ALTHOUGH YOU MUST ATTEND THE EVALUATION, YOU DO NOT HAVE TO RESPOND TO QUESTIONS.

Witness my hand and seal this ______ day of ________________, 20________________.

PROBATE CLERK/DEPUTY CLERK

Effective 7/06 GPCSF 12Court

PROBATE COURT OF ______________________ COUNTY

STATE OF GEORGIA

IN RE:	)	ESTATE NO. __________________
	)	
______________________,	)	PETITION FOR APPOINTMENT OF
PROPOSED WARD	)	A GUARDIAN AND/OR
	)	CONSERVATOR FOR A
	)	PROPOSED WARD

RETURN OF SHERIFF

I have this day served ______________________________ personally with a copy of the within petition, order and notice.

This ______ day of ________________, 20_____.

Deputy Sheriff ____________________ County, Georgia

PROBATE COURT OF ______________________ COUNTY

STATE OF GEORGIA

IN RE:) ESTATE NO. ______________________

)

______________________,) PETITION FOR APPOINTMENT OF

PROPOSED WARD) A GUARDIAN AND/OR
) CONSERVATOR FOR A
) PROPOSED WARD

APPOINTMENT OF ATTORNEY AND/OR GUARDIAN AD LITEM

(initial all applicable):

________ It appearing that this Court has not been notified of the retention of counsel by the proposed ward within the prescribed two-day period, ________ telephone number ______________________, is hereby appointed as attorney for the proposed ward in this matter.

________ IT IS FURTHER ORDERED that ______________________ is appointed as guardian ad litem for the proposed ward, and said individual shall

_____a. attend the guardianship hearing and make a recommendation to the Court.

_____b. file a written recommendation/report with the Court prior to the hearing and shall (be excused from appearing at) (attend) the hearing.

This ______ day of ______________________, 20_____.

Probate Judge

Effective 7/06 GPCSF 12Court

CERTIFICATE OF MAILING OF ORDER APPOINTING ATTORNEY AND/OR GUARDIAN AD LITEM

ESTATE NO.

This is to certify that I have this day served the petitioner(s); the proposed ward's guardian ad litem (if any) and attorney; the spouse, family, and/or friends of the proposed ward as found in paragraphs 6, 7, and 8 of the Petition, who were ordered to be served by first-class mail, with a copy of the above order, by placing a copy of same in an envelope addressed to each and depositing same in the U.S. Mail, first-class, with adequate postage thereon.

This _____ day of ____________________, 20_____.

PROBATE CLERK/DEPUTY CLERK

EVALUATOR'S REPORT

GUARDIANSHIP/CONSERVATORSHIP PROCEEDINGS ESTATE NO.

PETITIONER(S)

PROPOSED WARD

In compliance with the Order of the Probate Court of County dated ________________, 20________, I performed an evaluation of the above-named proposed ward on ________________________, 20 ____________. This evaluation took place at (location) ____ beginning at o'clock. The evaluation continued for ____________________________ minutes. I explained the purpose of the evaluation to the proposed ward.

The following questions, instruments, or tests were utilized in the evaluation:

Below is a list of all persons and other sources of information consulted in evaluating the proposed ward:

The following is a description of the proposed ward's mental and physical state and condition, including all observed facts considered by me:

The following is a description of the overall social condition of the proposed ward, including support, care, education, and well-being:

The following are my findings as to the needs of the proposed ward and their foreseeable duration:

____

(initial all applicable)

_______ a. I find the proposed ward to be incapacitated by reason of: ______________ to the extent that said proposed ward:

_______(i) (for guardianship:) lacks sufficient capacity to make or communicate significant responsible decisions concerning his/her health and safety.

_______(ii) (for conservatorship:) lacks sufficient capacity to make or communicate significant responsible decisions concerning the management of his/her property.

_______b. I do not find that the proposed ward meets the standards for guardianship set out in a. (i). above.

_______c. I do not find that the proposed ward meets the standards for conservatorship set out in a. (ii). above.

Physician licensed under Chapter 34 of Title 43 of the Official Code of Georgia Annotated
or
Psychologist licensed under Chapter 39 of Title 43 of the Official Code of Georgia Annotated
or
Licensed Clinical Social Worker

Sworn to and subscribed before me
This _____ day of _____________, 20____.

Notary Public/Clerk, Probate Court

NOTE: This report must be filed with the Probate Court no later than (7) days after the date of examination.

PROBATE COURT OF ______________________ COUNTY

STATE OF GEORGIA

IN RE:	)	ESTATE NO. ______________
	)	
______________________,	)	PETITION FOR APPOINTMENT OF
PROPOSED WARD	)	A GUARDIAN AND/OR
	)	CONSERVATOR FOR A
	)	PROPOSED WARD

ORDER FOR DISMISSAL

The above and foregoing petition having been read and considered pursuant to O.C.G.A. §29-4-11 and/or O.C.G.A. §29-5-11 of the Official Code of Georgia Annotated, and (initial one):

______ a. Based on the allegations made in the petition and prior to the court-ordered evaluation, it appears that there is not probable cause to believe that the proposed ward is in need of a guardian or conservator within the meaning of O.C.G.A. §29-4-1 and/or O.C.G.A. §29-5-1, therefore, it is

ORDERED that the petition is dismissed.

IT IS FURTHER ORDERED that a copy of the petition, the affidavit, if any, and this order be served on the proposed ward by first-class mail, and a copy of this order be served in the same manner upon the petitioner(s) or his/her/their attorney, if any.

______ b. Based on the allegations made in the petition and after review and consideration of the court-ordered evaluation report filed with this court, this court finds that there is not probable cause to support a finding that the proposed ward is in need of a guardian or a conservator within the meaning of O.C.G.A. §29-4-1 and/or O.C.G.A. §29-5-1; therefore, it is

ORDERED that the petition is dismissed.

IT IS FURTHER ORDERED that a copy of this order and the court-ordered evaluation report be served on the proposed ward, his attorney, his guardian ad litem, if any, and to the petitioner(s) or her/her/their attorney, if any, by first class mail.

SO ORDERED this ______ day of ______________________, 20____.

Probate Judge

Effective 7/06 GPCSF 12Court

PROBATE COURT OF ______________________ COUNTY

STATE OF GEORGIA

IN RE:) ESTATE NO. ______________

)

______________________,) PETITION FOR APPOINTMENT OF

PROPOSED WARD) A GUARDIAN AND/OR
) CONSERVATOR FOR A
) PROPOSED WARD

ORDER AND NOTICE OF HEARING

After review and consideration of the petition and the court-ordered evaluation report filed with this court, the court finds that there is probable cause to support a finding that the proposed ward is in need of a guardian and/or conservator within the meaning of O.C.G.A. §29-4-1 and/or O.C.G.A. §29-5-1,

THEREFORE, it is ordered and adjudged that:

1. A hearing shall be set for ________ o'clock __.M. on ______________, 20______, which is not less than 10 days from the date that this notice is mailed, to determine the need for the appointment of a (guardian) (and/or) (conservator) for the above-named proposed ward, to be held (in the Probate Court of ________ County, courtroom __________, (address) ______________________, Georgia) (at the following location: ______________). The proposed ward shall be represented by ______________, attorney, at such hearing.

2. A copy of this order and a copy of the evaluation report shall be sent to the proposed ward, his/her attorney and guardian ad litem, if any, to the interested persons shown in paragraphs 6, 7, and 8 of the petition, and to the petitioner(s) and his/her/their attorney, if any. These copies shall be sent by a Clerk/deputy clerk, first-class mail, as soon as practicable after the signing of this order.

SO ORDERED this ____ day of ______________, 20____.

Probate Judge

STIPULATION AND WAIVER BY PROPOSED WARD'S ATTORNEY

GEORGIA, ______________________ COUNTY ESTATE NO. ______________

TO THE PROBATE COURT OF SAID STATE AND COUNTY

IN RE: PETITION FOR THE APPOINTMENT OF A GUARDIAN AND/OR CONSERVATOR FOR ______________________, PROPOSED WARD

The undersigned, as the attorney representing the above-named proposed ward in these proceedings, (initial all applicable:)

_____ a. does hereby stipulate into evidence the affidavit prepared by (name of affiant evaluator) ______________________, being the evaluation report Ordered by the Court in this matter, and hereby waives the appearance of such affiant at any hearing concerning the said petition.

_____ b. does hereby stipulate into evidence the affidavit prepared by (name of affiant evaluator) ______________________, which is the affidavit referred to in Paragraph 1(b) of the petition), and hereby waives the appearance of such affiant at any hearing concerning the said petition.

_____ c. does further waive the appearance of my client the proposed ward at said hearing.

This _____ day of ______________________, 20_____.

____
Attorney

Typed/printed name of Attorney: ______________________

Address: ______________________

Telephone: ______________ State Bar # ______________

PROBATE COURT OF ______________________ COUNTY

STATE OF GEORGIA

IN RE:) ESTATE NO. ____________

)
______________________,) PETITION FOR APPOINTMENT OF
PROPOSED WARD) A GUARDIAN AND/OR
) CONSERVATOR FOR A
) PROPOSED WARD

FINAL ORDER

A hearing was held on the above-referenced petition on ______________________, 20 ___, and after considering the pleadings, the evaluation report and the evidence taken at the hearing, the Court makes the following:

FINDINGS OF FACT

1.

All procedural requirements of O.C.G.A. §29-4-11 and/or O.C.G.A. §29-5-11 have been met.

2.

The above-named proposed ward is in need of a guardian and/or conservator by reason of ______________________. Such need appears to be (permanent) (______________________).

3.

The approximate current value of the personal property of the proposed ward is $______________.

The proposed ward has an interest in real property in the following locations:

a. ______________________ County, (state) ______________________;
b. ______________________ County, (state) ______________________;
c. ______________________ County, (state) ______________________.

The proposed ward has outstanding debts of $______________________ and average expenditures of $______________________ per month.

4.

Petitioner(s) moved the Court to appoint ______________________ guardian and ______________________ conservator for the proposed ward asserting that/those individual(s) should serve because ______________________. (initial if applicable:)

______a. Another individual, being ______________________ was nominated/designated by the proposed ward to serve as guardian,

______ (i) and no good cause was shown to override such preference.

______ (ii) but good cause was shown not to appoint said individual, being: ______________________.

______b. Another individual with higher preference, being ______________ was nominated/designated to serve as guardian by someone other than the proposed ward, and/but it (is) (is not) in the best interest of the proposed ward to appoint him/her guardian because ______________________.

______c. Another individual, being ______________________ was nominated/designated by the proposed ward to serve as conservator,

______ (i) and no good cause was shown to override such preference.

______ (ii) but good cause was shown not to appoint said individual, being: ______________________.

______d. Another individual with higher preference, being ______________ was nominated/designated to serve as conservator by someone other than the proposed ward, and/but it (is) (is not) in the best interest of the proposed ward to appoint him/her conservator because ______________________.

5.

The Petitioner(s) requested that the guardian(s)/conservator(s) be granted the following additional powers pursuant to O.C.G.A. §29-4-23 (b) and/or O.C.G.A. §29-5-23(b) and/or (c): ______________

CONCLUSIONS OF LAW

The Court finds, by clear and convincing evidence, that the above-named proposed ward (hereinafter referred to as "the ward") is in need of (initial all applicable):

______ a. a guardian because the ward lacks sufficient capacity to make or communicate significant responsible decisions concerning his/her health or safety. The duration of the guardianship is (permanent) (______________).

______ b. a conservator because the ward lacks sufficient capacity to make or communicate significant responsible decisions concerning the management of his/her property. The duration of the conservatorship is (permanent) (______________).

Therefore it is

ORDERED that ____ should be, and hereby is, appointed guardian(s) and ______________ should be, and hereby is, appointed conservator(s) of the ward because ______________________. Letters of guardianship and/or conservatorship shall issue to such guardian(s) and/or conservator(s) upon taking the required oath and upon the conservator(s) posting bond in the amount of $______________________. **The appointed guardian(s)/conservator(s) shall have no authority to act on behalf of the ward until Letters of Guardianship and/or Conservatorship have issued.**

IT IS FURTHER ORDERED that due to the appointment of a guardian, this Order REMOVES from the ward the power to (initial all that are applicable):

______ a. Contract marriage;

______ b. Make, modify, or terminate other contracts;

______ c. Consent to medical treatment;

______ d. Establish a residence or dwelling place;

______ e. Change domicile;

______ f. Revoke a revocable trust established by the ward;

______ g. Bring or defend any action at law or equity, except an action relating to the guardianship.

IT IS FURTHER ORDERED that due to the appointment of a conservator, this Order REMOVES from the ward the power to (initial all that are applicable):

______a. Make, modify, or terminate contracts, other than the power to contract marriage;

______b. To buy, sell, or otherwise dispose of or encumber property;

______c. Enter into or conduct other business or commercial transactions;

______d. Revoke a revocable trust established by the ward;

______e. Bring or defend any action at law or equity, except an action relating to the conservatorship.

IT IS FURTHER ORDERED that the guardian(s) and/or conservator(s) shall have the following additional powers as set forth in O.C.G.A. §29-4-23(b) and O.C.G.A. §29-5-23(b)(1) and (c):

____

IT IS FURTHER ORDERED that, if only a guardian is appointed for the ward, or if different individuals are appointed guardian and conservator, the following reasonable sums of property shall be provided to the guardian to provide adequately for the ward's support, care, education, health, and welfare, until further Order of the Court: $______________________ per ______________________.

IT IS FURTHER ORDERED that the guardian shall file, in addition to the personal status report, the following supplemental reports: (monthly)(annually).

IT IS FURTHER ORDERED that a copy of this Order shall be served by first class mail on the ward, the ward's attorney; the guardian ad litem, if any; the guardian(s) and/or conservator(s); the petitioner(s); his/her/their attorney(s); and the individuals listed in paragraphs 6, 7, and 8 of the Petition.

IT IS FURTHER ORDERED that the ward's legal counsel shall make reasonable efforts to explain to the ward this Order and the ward's rights under this Order.

IT IS FURTHER ORDERED that, within 30 days of the date hereof, the clerk/deputy clerk shall file the certificate of creation of conservatorship in accordance with O.C.G.A. §29-5-13(d) with the Clerk of Superior Court of each county in this state in which the ward owns real property.

SO ORDERED this ________ day of ______________________, 20_____.

Probate Judge/Hearing Officer exercising the
jurisdiction of the Probate Court pursuant to O.C.G.A.
§29–4–12(d)(7) and/or 29–5–12(d)(7)

CERTIFICATE OF MAILING OF FINAL ORDER

ESTATE NO.

I have this date mailed (or handed) a copy of the above Order to the ward, his/her attorney, (his/her guardian ad litem), (his/her representatives,) the guardian(s), the conservator(s), the interested persons shown in paragraphs 6, 7, and 8 of the petition, the petitioner(s), and (petitioner's attorney).

______________________ ______________________

Date PROBATE CLERK/DEPUTY CLERK

CERTIFICATE OF FILING CERTIFICATE OF CREATION OF CONSERVATORSHIP

ESTATE NO.

I have this date hand-delivered and/or mailed for filing a Certificate of Creation of Conservatorship to the Clerk of the Superior Court of each of the following counties, together with payment of any recording costs: ______________________

PROBATE CLERK/DEPUTY CLERK

ADDRESS

TELEPHONE

Probate Court Return Mailing Address:

CERTIFICATE OF CREATION OF CONSERVATORSHIP
(Pursuant to O.C.G.A. §29-5-13(d))

GEORGIA, ______________________________ County

PROBATE ESTATE NO. ____________

DATE ORDER ISSUED: ____________

GRANTOR: (NAME OF WARD) ______________________________

GRANTEE: (NAME OF CONSERVATOR(S) OF ABOVE WARD) ______________________

A Conservatorship has been created for the above-named ward.

_________a. The Conservatorship is permanent.

_________b. The expiration date set by court order, is __________, 20____.

Original Certificate delivered or mailed to Clerk of Superior Court of ____________ County on ________________, 20_____.

I do hereby certify that the above information is based on the order of the Probate Court issued on the date set out above and that the above information is true and correct.

By: ______________________________
PROBATE CLERK/DEPUTY CLERK

Effective 7/06 GPCSF 12Court

GEORGIA PROBATE COURT
STANDARD FORM

STATE OF GEORGIA

COUNTY OF ______________________ ESTATE NO. __________

LETTERS OF GUARDIANSHIP OF ADULT WARD

From the Judge of the Probate Court of said County. Date of Birth:

TO: ______________________________, Guardian(s)

RE: ______________________________, Adult Ward

The above-named adult ward has been found by this Court to be in need of a guardian, and this Court has entered an order designating you as such guardian(s). You have assented to this appointment by taking your oath. In general, your duties as guardian are to protect and maintain the person of the ward.

Special Instructions:

1. It is your duty to see that the ward is adequately fed, clothed, sheltered and cared for, and that the ward receives all necessary medical attention.
2. You must keep the Court informed of any change in your name or address and promptly notify the Court of any conflict of interest arising between you and your ward.
3. Within 60 days after appointment and within 60 days after each anniversary date of appointment, you must file with the probate court a personal status report concerning your ward which shall include:
   (a) A description of the ward's general condition, changes since the last report, and needs;
   (b) Your recommendations for any alteration in the guardianship order;
   (c) All addresses of the ward during the reporting period and the living arrangements of the ward for all addresses;
   (d) A description of the amount of any funds received and expended by the guardian for the support of the ward.
4. Please consult your attorney if you have any questions.
5. Your authority to act pursuant to these Letters is subject to applicable statutes and to any special orders entered in this case.

Given under my hand and official seal, the ______ day of ____________________, 20______.

Probate Judge

NOTE: The following must be signed if the judge does not sign the original of this document:

Issued by:

______________________________ (Seal)
PROBATE CLERK/DEPUTY CLERK

Effective 7/06 GPCSF 12Court

GEORGIA PROBATE COURT
STANDARD FORM

STATE OF GEORGIA
COUNTY OF ______________________ ESTATE NO. __________

LETTERS OF CONSERVATORSHIP OF ADULT WARD

From the Judge of the Probate Court of said County. Date of Birth: __________

TO: ______________________, Conservator(s)
RE: ______________________, Adult Ward

The above-named adult ward has been found by this Court to be in need of a conservator, and this Court has entered an order designating you as such conservator(s). You have assented to this appointment by taking your oath and posting a bond. In general, your duties as conservator are to protect and maintain the property of the ward.

Special Instructions:

1. You must keep your ward's funds separate from your own. You should put your ward's funds in a separate checking or savings account, as appropriate, and make all payments by check.
2. You may not sell, mortgage, give away, or otherwise dispose of any of your ward's property without a court order.
3. You may not spend any of your ward's funds for any purpose except as set forth in the court approved budget without a court order.
4. You must file within two months of your appointment an inventory showing the ward's property and a plan for managing, expending, and distributing the property. Further, you must file, within 60 days of each anniversary date of these Letters an annual return, showing all receipts and disbursements, accompanied by an affidavit certifying that the original vouchers (checks) have been compared with the items listed on the return, and that the return is correct, together with an updated inventory and plan for managing the property. A copy of said return shall be sent by first class mail to the surety, the ward, and the guardian, if any.
5. The regular commissions allowed a conservator are 2.5% on all sums of money received, and 2.5% on all sums paid out, as shown by the annual or final return. There are special rules concerning commissions for property delivered in kind, interest earned, extraordinary services, and market value of property held as of the last day of your reporting period.
6. You must keep the Court informed of any change in your name or address and promptly notify the Court of any conflict of interest arising between you and your ward.
7. You should inform the Court of any change of location of your ward.
8. Please consult your attorney if you have any questions.
9. Your authority to act pursuant to these Letters is subject to applicable statutes and to any special orders entered in this case.

Given under my hand and official seal, the _____ day of ______________, 20_____.

Probate Judge

NOTE: The following must be signed if the judge does not sign the original of this document:
Issued by:

______________________________ (Seal)
PROBATE CLERK/DEPUTY CLERK

Effective 7/06 GPCSF 12Court

GEORGIA PROBATE COURT
STANDARD FORM

STATE OF GEORGIA
COUNTY OF ______________________ ESTATE NO. __________

LETTERS OF GUARDIANSHIP AND CONSERVATORSHIP OF ADULT WARD

From the Judge of the Probate Court of said County. Date of Birth:__________
TO: ______________________, Guardian(s) and Conservator(s)
RE: ______________________, Adult Ward

The above-named adult ward has been found by this Court to be in need of a guardian and conservator, and this Court has entered an order designating you as such guardian(s) and conservator(s). You have assented to this appointment by taking your oath and posting a bond. In general, your powers and duties are to protect and maintain the person and property of the ward.

Special Instructions:

1. It is your duty to see that your ward is adequately fed, clothed, sheltered and cared for, and that your ward receives all necessary medical attention.
2. You must keep your ward's funds separate from your own. You should put your ward's funds in a separate checking or savings account, as appropriate, and make all payments by check.
3. You may not sell, mortgage, give away, or otherwise dispose of any of your ward's property without a court order.
4. You may not spend any of your ward's funds for any purpose, except as set forth in the court approved budget, without a court order.
5. You must file within two months of your appointment an inventory showing the ward's property and a plan for managing, expending, and distributing the property. Further, you must file, within 60 days of each anniversary date of these Letters an annual return, showing all receipts and disbursements, accompanied by an affidavit certifying that the original vouchers (checks) have been compared with the items listed on the return, and that the return is correct, together with an updated inventory and plan for managing the property. A copy of said return shall be sent by first class mail to the surety, the ward, and the guardian, if any.
6. The regular commissions allowed a conservator are 2.5% on all sums of money received, and 2.5% on all sums paid out, as shown by the annual or final return. There are special rules concerning commissions for property delivered in kind, interest earned, extraordinary services, and market value of property held as of the last day of your reporting period.
7. You must keep the Court informed of any change in your name or address and promptly notify the Court of any conflict of interest arising between you and your ward.
8. Within 60 days after appointment and within 60 days after each anniversary date of appointment, you must file with the probate court a personal status report concerning your ward which shall include:
   (a) A description of your ward's general condition, changes since the last report, and needs;
   (b) Your recommendations for any alteration in the guardianship/conservatorship order;
   (c) All addresses of the ward during the reporting period and the living arrangements of the ward for all addresses.
9. Your authority to act pursuant to these Letters is subject to applicable statutes and to any special orders entered in this case.

Given under my hand and official seal, the ______ day of __________________, 20______.

NOTE: The following must be signed if the judge does not sign the original of this document
Issued by:

Probate Judge

______________________________ (Seal)
PROBATE CLERK/DEPUTY CLERK

Effective 7/06 GPCSF 12Court

Form adopted effective July 1, 2005; amended effective July 31, 2006.

GPCSF 13. PETITION OF PERSONAL REPRESENTATIVE FOR LEAVE TO SELL PROPERTY

GEORGIA PROBATE COURT
STANDARD FORM

Petition of Personal Representative for Leave to Sell Property

INSTRUCTIONS

I. Specific Instructions

1. This form is to be used when a personal representative or temporary administrator petitions for leave to sell real or personal property pursuant to O.C.G.A. §53-8-13. If the petition is by a temporary administrator, this form should be altered as follows: The term "temporary administrator" should be placed wherever the term "Personal Representative" or "Administrator" appears throughout the entire form.
2. With regard to paragraph 4 of the petition, a recent appraisal should be used if available; otherwise, a copy of the most recent ad valorem tax statement should be provided. If the appraised value or tax value is higher than the selling price, explain the discrepancy on an additional sheet, and add a reference to this in paragraph 4 of the petition.

II. General Instructions

General instructions applicable to all Georgia probate court standard forms are available in each probate court.

Effective 7/06 GPCSF 13 Complete

IN THE PROBATE COURT OF ______________________ COUNTY

STATE OF GEORGIA

IN RE: ESTATE OF) ESTATE NO. ______________

)

______________________________________,) PETITION OF PERSONAL

DECEASED) REPRESENTATIVE FOR

) LEAVE TO SELL PROPERTY

TO THE HONORABLE JUDGE OF THE PROBATE COURT:

The petition of _____, as duly appointed and qualified (Administrator(s)) (Executor(s)) of the Estate of ______________________________________, deceased, shows:

1.

Listed below or attached hereto as Exhibit 1 are all of decedent's (heirs) (beneficiaries), with the age or majority status, address and relationship to decedent set opposite the name of each:

Name	Age (Or over 18)	Address	Relationship

2.

Petitioner(s) desire(s) to sell certain real and/or personal property of said estate. The property and the estate's interest in said property are described as follows (give metes and bounds description, and street address if known, if real property):

3.

The specific purpose of said sale of said property is (check all which apply):

____ a. to pay the debts of the estate and/or

____ b. to make distributions to the (heirs)(beneficiaries)

____ c. other: ____

4.

The petitioner(s) desire(s) to sell said real and/or personal property upon the following terms and conditions [explain the proposed date, place and method of sale, including any minimum sales prices, and attach and label copies of any applicable contracts]: ______________________________

______________________ Attached hereto as Exhibit A is a copy of (the most recent ad valorem tax statement)(a recent appraisal) showing the current value of the property to be $__________.

5.

At present, the petitioner(s) has/have a bond on file in this Court in the amount of $_______. The net proceeds to the estate from the sale of the subject property will be approximately $_____. An additional bond in the amount of $ to cover the amount by which the net proceeds from the sale, plus the amount of personal property currently in the estate, will exceed the current bond amount will be posted prior to the deadline for objections set forth in the notice.

6.

The following (heirs)(beneficiaries) are not sui juris and require the appointment of a guardian ad litem to represent their interests in this matter:

7.

Additional Data: Where full particulars are lacking, state here the reasons for any such omission.

WHEREFORE, petitioner(s) pray(s)

1. an order directing notice be issued and served as the law requires, and
2. if no cause be shown to the contrary, your petitioner(s) be granted leave to sell said property as set forth above.

______________________________	______________________________
Signature of first petitioner	Signature of second petitioner if any
______________________________	______________________________
Printed Name	Printed Name
______________________________	______________________________
Address	Address
______________________________	______________________________
______________________________	______________________________
Phone Number	Phone Number

Signature of Attorney: ______________________________

Typed/printed name of Attorney: ______________________________

Address: ______________________________

____

Telephone: ____________ State Bar #____________

VERIFICATION

GEORGIA, ______________ COUNTY

Personally appeared before me the undersigned petitioner(s) who on oath state(s) that the facts set forth in the foregoing petition are true.

Sworn to and subscribed before
me this ___ day of __________, 20 ___.

____
First Petitioner

____
NOTARY/CLERK OF PROBATE COURT

____
Printed Name

Sworn to and subscribed before
me this ___ day of __________, 20 ___.

____
Second Petitioner, if any

____
NOTARY/CLERK OF PROBATE COURT

____
Printed Name

IN THE PROBATE COURT OF ____________________ COUNTY

STATE OF GEORGIA

IN RE: ESTATE OF) ESTATE NO. ____________________
)
____________________,) PETITION OF PERSONAL
DECEASED) REPRESENTATIVE FOR
) LEAVE TO SELL PROPERTY

ORDER FOR SERVICE OF NOTICE AND APPOINTING GUARDIAN AD LITEM IF NECESSARY

The foregoing petition of personal representative for leave to sell property having been filed, it is ordered that: (Initial any and all of the following which apply:)

____ Notice must be served personally, together with a copy of the petition, at least ten days before the deadline for objections on the following (heirs)(beneficiaries) who reside in Georgia and have not acknowledged service:

____ Notice must be served by registered or certified mail, return receipt requested, together with a copy of the petition, upon nonresident (heirs)(beneficiaries) whose current residence addresses are known:

____ Notice must be published once a week for four weeks in the newspaper in which sheriff's advertisements are published in this county, before ____________________, 20 __________ in order to serve by publication the following (heirs)(beneficiaries) whose current residence addresses are unknown or who are unknown:

____ IT IS ORDERED that __________ is appointed guardian ad litem for ____________________, and that said guardian ad litem be duly served with a copy of the foregoing petition, Notice and notice of this appointment, and that upon said guardian ad litem's acceptance of same, said guardian ad litem shall make answer hereto. This appointment is limited to this proceeding only and it shall cease when a final order is entered on this petition.

SO ORDERED this ______ day of ____________________, 20___.

____
Probate Judge

Effective 7/06 GPCSF 13 Complete

NOTICE

PROBATE COURT OF ____________________ COUNTY

RE: PETITION OF ____ FOR
LEAVE TO SELL PROPERTY OF ESTATE OF ______________________, DECEASED.

(Strike the following paragraph if not applicable:)

TO: ____

(List here all interested parties having known addresses in the continental U.S. to be served by certified or registered mail)

This is to notify you to file objection, if there is any, to the above referenced petition, in this Court on or before the thirteenth (13th) day after ______________, 20___ (the date of the mailing of this Notice to you by certified or registered mail, return receipt requested); provided, however, that if a return receipt for such Notice is actually received by the Court within such 13 days, the deadline for the filing of any objection shall be ten (10) days from the date of receipt shown on such return receipt.

(Strike the following paragraph if not applicable:)

TO: ____

(List here all interested parties having known addresses outside the continental U.S. to be served by certified or registered mail)

This is to notify you to file objection, if there is any, to the above referenced petition, in this Court on or before the thirtieth (30th) day after ____________________, 20 ________ (the date of the mailing of this Notice to you by certified or registered mail, return receipt requested); provided, however, that if a return receipt for such Notice is actually received by the Court within such 30 days, the deadline for the filing of any objection shall be ten (10) days from the date of receipt shown on such return receipt.

(Strike the following paragraph if not applicable:)

This is further to notify ____,

(List here all interested parties who reside in Georgia to be served personally)

who are required to be served personally, to file objection, if there is any, to the above referenced petition, in this Court on or before the tenth (10th) day after the date you are personally served.

BE NOTIFIED FURTHER: All objections to the petition must be in writing, setting forth the grounds of any such objections. All pleadings/objections must be signed before a notary public or before a probate court clerk, and filing fees must be tendered with your pleadings/objections, unless you qualify to file as an indigent party. Contact probate court personnel at the following address/telephone number for the required amount of filing fees. If any objections are filed, a hearing will be (held on ______________ 20___) (scheduled at a later date). If no objections are filed, the petition may be granted without a hearing.

PROBATE JUDGE

By: ______________________________
PROBATE CLERK/DEPUTY CLERK

ADDRESS

TELEPHONE

NOTICE

PROBATE COURT OF ______________ COUNTY

RE: PETITION OF ______________________________ FOR
LEAVE TO SELL PROPERTY OF ESTATE OF ______________________, DECEASED.

(For use if an interested party is required to be served by publication:)

TO: ____

(List here all unknown interested parties having known interested parties having unknown addresses to be served by publication)

All interested parties and to whom it may concern: This is to notify you to file objection, if there is any, to the above referenced petition, in this Court on or before ______________, 20___.

BE NOTIFIED FURTHER: All objections to the petition must be in writing, setting forth the grounds of any such objections. All pleadings/objections must be signed before a notary public or before a probate court clerk, and filing fees must be tendered with your pleadings/objections, unless you qualify to file as an indigent party. Contact probate court personnel at the following address/telephone number for the required amount of filing fees. If any objections are filed, a hearing will be (held on ______________ 20___) (scheduled at a later date). If no objections are filed, the petition may be granted without a hearing.

PROBATE JUDGE

By: ______________________________
PROBATE CLERK/DEPUTY CLERK

ADDRESS

TELEPHONE

Effective 7/06 7 GPCSF 13 Complete

CERTIFICATE OF MAILING

This is to certify that I have this date forwarded by registered or certified mail, return receipt requested, in a stamped, addressed envelope, a copy of the foregoing petition and the notice, to the (heirs)(beneficiaries) who reside out of state at known current residence addresses.

_________________________ DATE

_________________________ PROBATE CLERK/DEPUTY CLERK

IN THE PROBATE COURT OF ______________________ COUNTY

STATE OF GEORGIA

IN RE: ESTATE OF	)	ESTATE NO. ______________________
	)	
________________________________,	)	PETITION OF PERSONAL
DECEASED	)	REPRESENTATIVE FOR
	)	LEAVE TO SELL PROPERTY

RETURN OF SERVICE

I have this day served ____________________________ with a copy of the within notice and Petition of Personal Representative for Leave to Sell Property.

This ______ day of ________________, 20___.

Deputy Sheriff, ____________________ County

IN THE PROBATE COURT OF ____________________ COUNTY

STATE OF GEORGIA

IN RE: ESTATE OF	)	ESTATE NO. ____________
	)	
____________________________,	)	PETITION OF PERSONAL
DECEASED	)	REPRESENTATIVE FOR
	)	LEAVE TO SELL PROPERTY

ANSWER OF GUARDIAN AD LITEM

I hereby accept the foregoing appointment, acknowledge service and notice of the proceedings as provided by law, and for answer say:

______________________	______________________________
DATE	GUARDIAN AD LITEM
	ADDRESS
	TELEPHONE

ACKNOWLEDGMENT OF SERVICE AND CONSENT TO PETITION

PROBATE COURT OF ______________________ COUNTY

IN RE: PETITION OF ______________________ FOR LEAVE TO SELL PROPERTY OF THE ESTATE OF ______________________ DECEASED

We, the undersigned, being over 18 years of age, laboring under no legal disability and being heirs or beneficiaries of the above-named decedent, hereby acknowledge service of a copy of the petition and notice, waive copies of same, waive further service and notice, and hereby consent to the petition.

SIGNATURE(S) OF (HEIRS) (BENEFICIARIES)

Sworn to and subscribed before me this ___ day of ________, 20___.

______________________ ______________________

NOTARY/CLERK OF PROBATE COURT Printed Name

Sworn to and subscribed before me this ___ day of ________, 20___.

______________________ ______________________

NOTARY/CLERK OF PROBATE COURT Printed Name

Sworn to and subscribed before me this ___ day of ________, 20___.

______________________ ______________________

NOTARY/CLERK OF PROBATE COURT Printed Name

Sworn to and subscribed before me this ___ day of ________, 20___.

______________________ ______________________

NOTARY/CLERK OF PROBATE COURT Printed Name

Sworn to and subscribed before me this ___ day of ________, 20___.

______________________ ______________________

NOTARY/CLERK OF PROBATE COURT Printed Name

Sworn to and subscribed before me this ___ day of ________, 20___.

______________________ ______________________

NOTARY/CLERK OF PROBATE COURT Printed Name

PROBATE COURT OF ______________ COUNTY

STATE OF GEORGIA

IN RE: ESTATE OF	)	ESTATE NO. ______________
	)	
______________________,	)	PETITION OF PERSONAL
DECEASED	)	REPRESENTATIVE FOR
	)	LEAVE TO SELL PROPERTY

FINAL ORDER

The petition of ______________________, as Personal Representative of the estate of the above-named decedent, to sell certain property described as ______________ owned by said Estate for the purpose stated in the petition, coming on regularly to be heard; and

IT APPEARING that each (heir)(beneficiary) has been lawfully served with proper notice or has acknowledged service; and

IT APPEARING that the purpose of the transaction is lawful and that the proposed transaction is fair and is in the best interest of the Estate (and the guardian ad litem having filed an answer approving said transaction);

IT IS HEREBY ORDERED that the said Petitioner, as Personal Representative of said Estate, is authorized to sell the property described in the petition upon the terms set forth in said petition.

IT IS FURTHER ORDERED that a report of the sale authorized by this Order shall be furnished to this Court by the Petitioner. Said report shall specify the property sold, the purchasers, the amounts received, and the terms of the sale.

SO ORDERED this _______ day of ______________, 20___.

Probate Judge

Effective 7/06 12 GPCSF 13 Complete

Instructions and form adopted effective July 1, 1987; amended effective July 1, 1994; revised effective January 1, 1998; July 1, 1998; July 31, 2006.

GPCSF 14 PETITIONER. PETITION OF CONSERVATOR FOR LEAVE TO SELL PROPERTY OR RENT, LEASE, OR OTHERWISE DISPOSE OF PROPERTY

GEORGIA PROBATE COURT
STANDARD FORMS

Petition of Conservator for Leave to Sell Property or Rent, Lease, or Otherwise Dispose of Property

INSTRUCTIONS

I. Specific Instructions

1. This form is to be used when a conservator requests leave to sell, rent, lease, or otherwise dispose of real or personal property at public or private sale pursuant to O.C.G.A.§ 29–3–35(c) or 29–5–35(c).

2. With regard to paragraph 3 of the petition, a recent appraisal should be used if available; otherwise, a copy of the most recent ad valorem tax statement should be provided. If the appraised value or tax value is higher than the selling price, explain the discrepancy on an additional sheet, and add a reference to this in paragraph 3 of the petition.

3. This petition is to be filed by the conservator and not by a guardian. A guardian ad litem must be appointed for the minor/ward.

4. Service of the Petition and Notice on the minor/ward and guardian ad litem must be by personal service. If requested by the Petitioner(s) and approved by the Court, service may be made by registered or certified mail or statutory overnight delivery with return receipt requested and with delivery restricted to addressee only. See O.C.G.A. § 29–9–4(e) and/or O.C.G.A. § 15–9–17.

II. General Instructions

General instructions applicable to all Georgia probate court standard forms are available in each probate court.

Effective 7/05 GPCSF 14 Petitioner

GEORGIA PROBATE COURT
STANDARD FORM

IN THE PROBATE COURT OF ______________ COUNTY

STATE OF GEORGIA

IN RE:	)	ESTATE NO. ______________________
	)	
______________________________,	)	PETITION OF CONSERVATOR
MINOR/WARD	)	FOR LEAVE TO SELL REAL
	)	OR PERSONAL PROPERTY
______________________________,	)	OR RENT, LEASE, OR OTHERWISE
CONSERVATOR(S)	)	DISPOSE OF SAID PROPERTY

TO THE HONORABLE JUDGE OF THE PROBATE COURT:

The petition of ____,
Conservator(s) of the above minor/ward, whose address is: ______________________________
____shows that:

1.

Conservator(s) desire(s) to (initial one):

____a. sell ____d. exchange
____b. rent ____e. dispose of
____c. lease ____f. other:

Describe certain property belonging to the minor/ward's estate. The minor/ward owns a ________ % interest in said property, described as follows (if real property, give metes and bounds description, and street address if known):

2.

The purpose of said disposition of said property is: ______________________________
____
____

3.

Said transaction is believed to be in the best interest of the minor/ward, and

_____ a. The conservator(s) desire(s) to sell the property at public sale for no less than $________________.

_____ b. the conservator(s) desire(s) to sell the property at private sale for the sum of $____________________ because it is the belief of conservator(s) that said property will not bring that amount if sold at public sale. A copy of the contract for sale is attached to this petition as Exhibit "B."

_____ c. the conservator(s) desire to rent or lease the property for $________ per month. The property currently has mortgage payments of $__________ per month. A copy of the contract to rent or lease the property is attached to this petition as Exhibit "B."

_____ d. the conservator(s) desire to dispose of the property otherwise as follows: ________
____

Attached as Exhibit "A" is a copy of (a recent appraisal) (the most recent ad valorem tax statement) showing the current value of the property to be $____________________.

4.

At present, the conservator(s) has/have a bond on file in this Court in the amount of $______________. The net proceeds to the minor's/ward's estate from the sale of the subject property will be approximately $____________________. An additional bond in the amount of $____________________ to cover the amount by which the net proceeds from the sale, plus the amount of personal property currently in the estate, will exceed the current bond amount will be posted prior to the deadline for objections set forth in the citation.

5.

Conservator(s) request(s) that the minor/ward and guardian ad litem be personally served with citation and a copy of this petition.

6.

There is no relationship or connection between the Conservator(s) or members of their immediate family and the purchaser(s) except as follows: ____.

WHEREFORE, conservator(s) pray(s) that a guardian ad litem be appointed for said minor/ward, and prays for an order directing that citation be issued and personally served, together with a copy of this petition, upon the minor/ward and guardian ad litem, and if no cause be shown to the contrary, your conservator(s) be granted leave to sell, rent, lease, or otherwise dispose of said property as set forth above.

______________________________	______________________________
Signature of conservator	Signature of co–conservator, if any
______________________________	______________________________
Printed Name	Printed Name
______________________________	______________________________
Address	Address
______________________________	______________________________
______________________________	______________________________
Telephone Number	Telephone Number

Signature of Attorney: ______________________________

Typed/printed name of Attorney: ______________________________

Address: ______________________________

Telephone: ____________________ State Bar # ______________

VERIFICATION

GEORGIA, ____________________ COUNTY

Personally appeared before me the undersigned conservator(s) who on oath state(s) that the facts set forth in the foregoing petition are true.

Sworn to and subscribed before me this ___ day of __________, 20___.

____
Conservator

____
NOTARY/CLERK OF PROBATE COURT

____
Printed Name

Sworn to and subscribed before me this ___ day of __________, 20___.

____
Co–Conservator, if any

____
NOTARY/CLERK OF PROBATE COURT

____
Printed Name

Instructions and form adopted effective July 1, 1987; instruction and form revised effective January 1, 1998; form revised effective July 1, 1998; July 1, 2005.

GPCSF 14 COURT. COURT FORMS FOR THE PETITION OF CONSERVATOR FOR LEAVE TO SELL PROPERTY OR RENT, LEASE, OR OTHERWISE DISPOSE OF PROPERTY

GEORGIA PROBATE COURT
STANDARD FORMS

Petition of Conservator for Leave to Sell Property or Rent, Lease, or Otherwise Dispose of Property

NOTICE: UNLESS OTHERWISE DIRECTED BY THE COURT, THE FOLLOWING FORMS ARE FOR PROBATE COURT STAFF TO COMPLETE

Effective 7/06 GPCSF 14 Court

GEORGIA PROBATE COURT
STANDARD FORMS

IN THE PROBATE COURT OF ______________________ COUNTY

STATE OF GEORGIA

IN RE:) ESTATE NO. ______________________

)

______________________,) PETITION FOR LEAVE TO
MINOR/WARD) SELL PROPERTY OR RENT,
) LEASE, OR OTHERWISE DISPOSE
______________________,) OF SAID PROPERTY
CONSERVATOR(S))

ORDER FOR NOTICE, APPOINTING GUARDIAN AD LITEM, AND REQUIRING AN INCREASE IN BOND

The petition of ______________________ as conservator(s), requesting an Order from this Court authorizing the sale, rent, lease, or other disposition of certain real and/or personal property of the above-named minor/ward having been read and considered,

IT IS ORDERED that Citation issue and that a copy of the Petition, Citation and this Order be personally served on the minor/ward.

IT IS FURTHER ORDERED that ______________________ is appointed guardian ad litem for the minor/ward, and that said guardian ad litem be served personally with a copy of the foregoing petition, Citation, and this Order, and that upon said guardian ad litem's acceptance of same, said guardian ad litem shall make answer hereto. This appointment is limited to this proceeding only and it shall cease when a final order is entered on this petition.

(initial if applicable:)

____ IT IS FURTHER ORDERED that said conservator(s) shall increase his/her/their bond by $______________ within _____ days of the date of this Order.

SO ORDERED this _________ day of ______________________, 20___.

____
Probate Judge

Effective 7/06 GPCSF 14 Court

NOTICE

PROBATE COURT OF ______________________ COUNTY

RE: PETITION OF CONSERVATOR(S) FOR LEAVE TO SELL PROPERTY OR RENT LEASE OR OTHERWISE DISPOSE OF SAID PROPERTY

TO: ______________________________, Minor/Ward ESTATE NO. __________

Your conservator(s), has/have filed a petition to sell, rent, lease, or otherwise dispose of certain real and/or personal property from your estate. This is to notify you that objections to the petition, if any, must be filed within 30 days following the mailing of notice or service upon your guardian ad litem. All objections to the petition must be in writing, setting forth the grounds of any such objections and all pleadings must be signed before a notary public or probate court clerk. If any objections are filed, a hearing will be (held in the Probate Court of ______________ County, courtroom __________, (address) ______________________, Georgia on __________, 20___ at _____ o'clock ____.m.) (scheduled for a later date). If no objection is filed, the petition may be granted without a hearing.

TO: ______________________________, guardian ad litem

The conservator(s) of the above ward has/have filed a petition to sell, rent, lease, or otherwise dispose of certain real and/or personal property from the minor/ward's estate. This is to notify you that you must file your response to the petition with the Court within 30 days following the mailing of notice or service upon you. All objections to the petition must be in writing, setting forth the grounds of any such objections and all pleadings must be signed before a notary public or probate court clerk. If any objections are filed, a hearing will be (held in the Probate Court of ______________ County, courtroom __________, (address) ______________, Georgia on ______________________, 20___ at _____ o'clock ____.m.) (scheduled for a later date). If no objection is filed, the petition may be granted without a hearing.

PROBATE JUDGE

By: ______________________________
PROBATE CLERK/DEPUTY CLERK

ADDRESS

TELEPHONE

Effective 7/06 GPCSF 14 Court

IN THE PROBATE COURT OF ______________________ COUNTY

STATE OF GEORGIA

IN RE:	)	ESTATE NO. ______________
	)	
______________________________,	)	PETITION FOR LEAVE TO
MINOR/WARD	)	SELL PROPERTY OR RENT,
	)	LEASE, OR OTHERWISE DISPOSE
______________________________,	)	OF SAID PROPERTY
CONSERVATOR(S)	)	

ANSWER OF GUARDIAN AD LITEM

I hereby accept the foregoing appointment, acknowledge service and notice of said proceeding as provided by law, and for answer say:

____
GUARDIAN AD LITEM

ADDRESS: ______________________________
____

TELEPHONE: ______________________________

Effective 7/06 GPCSF 14 Court

CERTIFICATE OF MAILING

This is to certify that I have this date mailed copies of the foregoing, order for notice, appointing guardian ad litem, and requiring an increase in bond, and this certificate to the conservator(s) by first-class mail.

_______________ DATE

_______________ PROBATE CLERK/DEPUTY CLERK

Effective 7/06 GPCSF 14 Court

PROBATE COURT OF ______________________ COUNTY

STATE OF GEORGIA

IN RE:	) ESTATE NO. ______________
	)
______________________________,	) PETITION FOR LEAVE TO
MINOR/WARD	) SELL PROPERTY OR RENT,
	) LEASE, OR OTHERWISE DISPOSE
______________________________,	) OF SAID PROPERTY
CONSERVATOR(S)	)

FINAL ORDER

The petition of ____, as Conservator(s) of the above-named minor/ward, to sell at private sale, rent, lease, or otherwise dispose of certain property owned by said minor/ward described as:

for the purpose stated in the petition, coming on regularly to be heard; and

IT APPEARING that citation was duly issued and that copies of the petition and citation were duly served upon the minor/ward and guardian ad litem, and

IT APPEARING that the purpose of the transaction is lawful and that the proposed transaction is fair and is in the best interest of the minor/ward, and the guardian ad litem having filed an answer raising no objection to said transaction;

IT IS HEREBY ORDERED that the said Petitioner(s), as Conservator(s) of said minor/ward, is/are authorized to sell, rent, lease, or otherwise dispose of the property described above upon the terms set forth in said petition.

____ (initial if applicable:) Said authorization is conditioned upon the Conservator(s) having on file with this Court a surety bond in the amount of $______________.

IT IS FURTHER ORDERED that a return specifying the property sold, the purchasers, the amounts received, and the terms of the sale, or other terms of disposition of the property shall be furnished to this Court by the Conservator(s) within 30 days of the sale.

SO ORDERED this _____ day of ______________, 20____.

Probate Judge

Effective 7/06 GPCSF 14 Court

Form adopted effective July 1, 2005; amended effective July 31, 2006.

GPCSF 15. PETITION FOR LEAVE TO SELL PERISHABLE PROPERTY BY CONSERVATOR

GEORGIA PROBATE COURT
STANDARD FORMS

Petition for Leave to Sell Perishable Property by Conservator

INSTRUCTIONS

I. Specific Instructions

1. This form is to be used when filing a petition for leave to sell property which is perishable, liable to deteriorate from keeping, or expensive to keep, pursuant to O.C.G.A. §§ 29–3–35(a) and 29–5–35(a).

2. Under O.C.G.A. §§ 29–3–35(a) and 29–5–35(a), the order for sale may be granted only after such notice and opportunity for hearing, if any, as the judge deems practicable under the circumstances. Further, the sale shall be as soon as practicable and in such manner as the court determines to be in the best interest of the estate. Therefore, all notice provisions set forth in this form may be altered by the judge if necessary.

II. General Instructions

General instructions applicable to all Georgia probate court standard forms are available in each probate court.

GEORGIA PROBATE COURT
STANDARD FORMS

IN THE PROBATE COURT OF ______________ COUNTY

STATE OF GEORGIA

IN RE:	)	
	)	
______________________________,	)	**ESTATE NO.** ______________
MINOR/WARD	)	
	)	**PETITION FOR LEAVE TO SELL**
______________________________,	)	**PERISHABLE PROPERTY**
CONSERVATOR(S)	)	

TO THE HONORABLE JUDGE OF THE PROBATE COURT:

The petition of ______________________________ as conservator(s) of the estate of ______________________, whose address is ______________________ ____, shows that

1.

the following personal property: ____ ____ ____

is of perishable nature, or liable to deteriorate from keeping, or expensive to keep, and that it is in the best interest of said minor/ward that said property be sold as soon as practicable.

2.

The name(s), address(es), telephone number(s), of the guardian(s) of the minor/ward, if any, is/are: ____ ____.

If there are none or if the conservator(s) is/are also guardian(s) of the minor/ward, the names, addresses, telephone numbers, and relationship(s) of the heirs apparent of the minor/ward, is/are: ____ ____ ____ ____

3.

There is no relationship or connection between the Conservator(s) or members of their immediate family and the purchaser(s) except as follows: ______________________________
____.

THEREFORE, Petitioner(s) pray(s) for an order authorizing Petitioner(s) to sell said property for the highest valid offer received using the following method and terms of sale at the following time and location: ______________________________
____
____.

Signature of first petitioner	Signature of second petitioner, if any
Printed Name	Printed Name
Address	Address
Telephone Number	Telephone Number

Signature of Attorney: ______________________________

Typed/printed name of Attorney: ______________________________

Address: ______________________________

____

Telephone: ______________ State Bar #______________

VERIFICATION

GEORGIA, ______________________ COUNTY

Personally appeared before me the undersigned petitioner(s) who on oath state(s) that the facts set forth in the foregoing petition are true.

Sworn to and subscribed before
me this ___ day of __________, 20___.

____
First Petitioner

____
NOTARY/CLERK OF PROBATE COURT

____
Printed Name

Sworn to and subscribed before
me this ___ day of __________, 20___.

____
Second Petitioner, if any

____
NOTARY/CLERK OF PROBATE COURT

____
Printed Name

IN THE PROBATE COURT OF ______________ COUNTY

STATE OF GEORGIA

IN RE:	)	ESTATE NO. ______________
	)	
______________________________,	)	PETITION FOR LEAVE TO SELL
MINOR/WARD	)	PERISHABLE PROPERTY
	)	
______________________________,	)	
CONSERVATOR(S)	)	

ORDER CONCERNING NOTICE

(To be used only if the Judge of the Probate Court determines that it is practicable under the circumstances to afford notice or a hearing prior to ruling upon the petition.)

The clerk/deputy clerk shall serve (the guardian of the minor/ward) (the heirs apparent of the minor/ward) (the minor/ward) with notice of the filing of the above Petition; by ______________ ______________________ at least _____ days before the court rules upon the above petition.

SO ORDERED this _____ day of ______________, 20____.

____
Probate Judge

IN THE PROBATE COURT OF ______________ COUNTY

STATE OF GEORGIA

IN RE:	)	ESTATE NO. ______________
	)	
______________________________,	)	PETITION FOR LEAVE TO SELL
MINOR/WARD	)	PERISHABLE PROPERTY
	)	
______________________________,	)	
CONSERVATOR(S)	)	

NOTICE

(To be used only if the Judge of the Probate Court determines that it is practicable under the circumstances to afford notice or a hearing prior to ruling upon the petition.)

To: ____
____

The Petitioner(s), ______________________ as conservator(s) of the estate of ______________________, minor/ward has filed a petition for leave to sell property which is perishable, liable to deteriorate in value, or expensive to keep. If you have an objection, it must be filed on or before ______________, 20____. All objections to the petition must be in writing, setting forth the grounds of any such objections, and all pleadings/objections must be signed before a notary public or before a probate court clerk. If you are an heir–apparent of the minor/ward, filing fees must be tendered with your pleadings/objection, unless you qualify to file as an indigent party. Contact probate court personnel at the following address/telephone number for the required amount of filing fees. If any objections are filed, a hearing will be (held on______________________,20___ in the Probate Court of ______________________ County, courtroom __________, (address) ____, Georgia)(scheduled for a later date). If no objections are filed, the petition may be granted without a hearing.

____
PROBATE JUDGE

By: ______________________________
PROBATE CLERK/DEPUTY CLERK

____
ADDRESS

____
____
TELEPHONE NUMBER

IN THE PROBATE COURT OF ______________ COUNTY

STATE OF GEORGIA

IN RE:	)	ESTATE NO. ______________
	)	
______________,	)	PETITION FOR LEAVE TO SELL
MINOR/WARD	)	PERISHABLE PROPERTY
	)	
______________,	)	
CONSERVATOR(S)	)	

ORDER

Upon reading and considering the foregoing Petition, and it appearing that the facts stated therein are true, and (initial one:)

_____ a. it appearing that the provision of notice to interested parties prior to the sale is impractical,

_____ b. notice having been served as directed by the Court,

it is ORDERED that Petitioner(s) be, and is/are hereby, granted leave to sell the said property for the highest valid offer received using the method and terms of sale described in the petition.

SO ORDERED this _____ day of ______________, 20___.

____
Probate Judge

Instructions and form adopted effective July 1, 1987; revised effective January 1, 1998; July 1, 2005.

GPCSF 16 COURT. DETERMINATION BY COURT THAT A PERSON MAY ACT AS GUARDIAN OR APPOINTMENT OF GUARDIAN AD LITEM

GEORGIA PROBATE COURT
STANDARD FORM

Determination by Court that a Person May Act as Guardian or Appointment of Guardian ad Litem

INSTRUCTIONS

I. Specific Instructions

1. This form is to be used when the court determines, in accordance with O.C.G.A. §53-11-2(a) or O.C.G.A. §29-9-2(b), that for the purpose of a particular proceeding, the natural guardian, if any, or the testamentary guardian, if any, or the duly constituted conservator, if any, or the duly constituted guardian, if any, has no conflict of interest and thus may serve as guardian for purposes of the proceeding for a party who is not sui juris, who is unborn, or who is unknown.

2. This form may also be used whenever a Georgia Probate Court Standard Form does not contain a section concerning the appointment of a guardian ad litem, but the appointment of a guardian ad litem (or a determination by the Court that a person may act as guardian) is necessary.

II. General Instructions

General instructions applicable to all Georgia probate court standard forms are available in each probate court.

Effective 7/06 GPCSF 16 Court

GEORGIA PROBATE COURT
STANDARD FORM

PROBATE COURT OF ______________ COUNTY

STATE OF GEORGIA

IN RE:) **ESTATE NO.** ______________
)
______________________________,) **PETITION OF** ______________
MINOR/WARD/DECEASED) **TO/FOR** ______________
)
) **FILED ON** ______________

ORDER THAT A PERSON MAY ACT AS GUARDIAN OR APPOINTMENT OF GUARDIAN AD LITEM

(initial one:)

____ a. ______________________ who is (an adult ward/a minor/unborn/unknown, is in need of representation by a guardian in the above proceeding. This court hereby determines that ______________________, as (natural guardian)(testamentary guardian)(conservator)(guardian) has no conflict of interest and thus may serve as such guardian for the purpose of this proceeding.

____ b. ______________________ is appointed guardian ad litem for ______________________, in connection with the above proceeding.

Such guardian, conservator, or guardian ad litem shall be duly served with copies of this order and the above proceeding. (Such guardian/conservator)(Upon acceptance of such appointment, such guardian ad litem) shall make answer concerning the above proceeding. This determination or appointment is limited to this proceeding only and shall terminate when a final order is entered on the above proceeding.

SO ORDERED this ______ day of ______________, 20____.

Probate Judge

Effective 7/06 GPCSF 16 Court

PROBATE COURT OF ________________ COUNTY

STATE OF GEORGIA

IN RE:	)	ESTATE NO. ________________
	)	
________________________________,	)	PETITION OF ________________
MINOR/WARD/DECEASED	)	TO/FOR ________________
	)	
	)	FILED ON ________________

ANSWER OF GUARDIAN, CONSERVATOR, OR GUARDIAN AD LITEM

I hereby (accept the foregoing appointment,) acknowledge service and notice of the above proceeding and for answer say (attach additional sheet(s) if necessary):

________________________ ________________________

DATE (GUARDIAN/CONSERVATOR) (GUARDIAN AD LITEM)

ADDRESS ________________________

____

TELEPHONE ________________________

Effective 7/06 GPCSF 16 Court

Instructions and form adopted effective July 1, 1987; revised effective January 1, 1998; July 1, 2005; July 31, 2006.

GPCSF 17. PETITION FOR LEAVE TO CONVEY OR ENCUMBER PROPERTY PREVIOUSLY SET ASIDE AS YEAR'S SUPPORT

Re: Petition for Leave to Convey or Encumber Property Previously Set Aside as Year's Support

INSTRUCTIONS

I. Specific Instructions

1. This form is to be used when petitioning for leave to convey or encumber property set aside as year's support, pursuant to O.C.G.A. § 53–3–20.

2. This form is prepared on the assumption that the surviving spouse is the petitioner. If this is not the case, modify the form accordingly. The petition may be brought either by a surviving spouse who participated in the award or by the guardian of the property of a minor child who participated in the award.

3. Necessity for Filing; Venue
   a. Pursuant to O.C.G.A. § 53–3–19, it is not necessary to obtain probate court approval if the children for whom the award was made who are now sui juris will join in the conveyance or encumbrance, unless at least one of the children for whom the award was made is still a minor.
   b. Venue: The petition must be filed in the county where the year's support award was originally granted. O.C.G.A. § 53–3–19(b).

4. Method of Service
   a. Adult children for whose benefit the year's support was set apart with known addresses in this state who do not acknowledge service shall be served personally not less than ten days prior to the date set for hearing.
   b. Adult children for whose benefit the year's support was set apart with unknown addresses or residing out of state who do not acknowledge service shall be served by:
      1. Publication of notice in the legal organ one time not less than ten days prior to the date set for hearing;
      2. Posting of notice at the courthouse not less than ten days prior to the date set for hearing; and
      3. Mailing by first-class mail a copy of the notice to the last known address not less than ten days prior to the date set for hearing.
   c. A guardian ad litem, who shall accept the appointment in writing, must be appointed to represent any child for whose benefit the year's support was set apart who remains a minor at the time of filing this petition.

5. The attached form consists of 5 pages.

II. General Instructions

General instructions applicable to all Georgia probate court standard forms are available in each probate court.

Effective 7/98 GPCSF 17

GEORGIA PROBATE COURT
STANDARD FORM

PETITION FOR LEAVE TO CONVEY OR ENCUMBER PROPERTY PREVIOUSLY SET ASIDE AS YEAR'S SUPPORT

GEORGIA, ____________________ COUNTY

TO THE HONORABLE JUDGE OF THE PROBATE COURT:

The petition of ______________________________, surviving spouse [1] of ____________________, deceased, late of ______________________________ County, respectfully shows the Court the following:

1.

On ____________________, 19___, the Probate Court of this County awarded to the (petitioner) (and) (the following child____) of said decedent:

Name	Current Address	Last Known Address (if current unknown)	Present Age

as Year's Support from the estate of said decedent, the following described real estate located in ______________ County, Georgia (the same being recorded in ______________________ County Probate Court Minute Book ________, Page ________). A complete legal description of such real property is:

[1] **Note: The petition may be brought either by a surviving spouse who participated in the award or by the guardian of the property of a minor child who participated in the award.**

2.

It is necessary for petitioner to (convey) (encumber) said property for the purpose of: ________
____
____.

3.

The nature and terms of said (conveyance) (encumbrance) are as follows:

___ Sale according to the conditions and terms of the contract, a copy of which is attached hereto marked "Exhibit A" and made a part hereof.

___ Encumbrance of the real property to secure a loan in the principal amount of ________________ Dollars, the interest rate being _____% per annum, and to be repaid at the rate of ________________ Dollars per month for ________________ months. Petitioner will execute a deed to secure debt for the purpose of securing said loan.

4.

With respect to any child named in Paragraph "1" above whose current address is shown as "unknown", applicant certifies that the current address is unknown to petitioner and cannot be easily ascertained, and that the last known address for any such person is listed in Paragraph "1."

5.

Of the children named in Paragraph "1" above, ____ is/are still under the age of 18, and must have a guardian ad litem appointed to represent him/her/them.

WHEREFORE the petitioner prays, in accordance with O.C.G.A. § 53-3-20:

(a) that a hearing be set on this petition.
(b) that a guardian ad litem be appointed to represent the minor children concerned; and
(c) that the petition be granted after notice as required by law has been given.

____
Signature of Attorney
(or Petitioner if pro se)

Attorney's Address ______________________________
____
Telephone ______________________________
State Bar #: ______________________________

VERIFICATION

Personally appeared before me the undersigned petitioner who on oath states that the facts set forth in the foregoing petition are true.

____
Petitioner

Residence Address ______________________________
____
Telephone ______________________________

Sworn to and subscribed before me, this ______ day of ____________________, 19____.

____
Clerk, Probate Court/Notary Public

2

ORDER FOR SERVICE OF NOTICE

The foregoing application having been read and considered, let citation issue and be served personally upon all children with known addresses in Georgia who are under 18 or have not acknowledged service. If there are any children whose current addresses are unknown or outside Georgia who are under 18 or have not acknowledged service, then the following citation shall be published one time at least ten days prior to the hearing, and a copy of the notice shall be posted at the Courthouse and mailed by registered mail to the last known addresses of any such children at least ten days prior to the date set for the hearing. Further, ______________________________ is hereby appointed as guardian ad litem in this matter to represent the interests of the children named in the petition who are still under the age of 18, and to make answer as such to this Court; this appointment is limited to this proceeding only and it shall cease when a final order is entered on this petition.

______________________________ ______________________________
Date Judge of the Probate Court

NOTICE

GEORGIA, ______________________ COUNTY PROBATE COURT

To: ____
______________________________________ and to whom it may concern.

A petition has been filed seeking an Order of this Court granting leave to (convey) (encumber) certain property heretofore set apart from the estate of ______________, deceased as year's support. This is to notify those persons named above who are not required to be personally served that they must file their response to the petition with the Court on ______________, 19____, and the persons who are required to be personally served (namely [1] ______________________ ______________________) that they must file their response by the above date or the tenth day after they are personally served, whichever is later.

All objections to the petition must be in writing, setting forth the grounds of any such objections. If any objections are filed a hearing will be (held on ____________) (scheduled for a later date). If no objections are filed, the petition may be granted without a hearing.

____
Judge of the Probate Court

By: ______________________________
Clerk, of the Probate Court

Publication date: if necessary: ____________

[1] List children with known current addresses in this state.

CERTIFICATE OF MAILING

I do hereby certify that I have this day mailed, by first-class mail, a copy of the petition and notice herein to each child for whose benefit the year's support was set aside, whose current address is outside Georgia or is unknown, by placing same in an envelope for each, addressed and stamped by the petitioner with the return address of this Court thereon, and causing same to be placed in the United States Mail.

______________________________ ______________________________
Date Clerk, Probate Court

ACKNOWLEDGMENT OF SERVICE AND CONSENT BY ADULT CHILDREN

I hereby acknowledge service of the petition of ______________________ for leave to sell or encumber the property set apart as year's support to the persons shown in the petition. I am over 18 years of age and suffer no mental disability. I hereby consent to the granting of the petition, and will join with the petitioner in making the (encumbrance) (conveyance).

SIGNATURE(S) OF ADULT CHILDREN

Sworn to and subscribed before me this ______ day of ____________, 19____. ______________________

____
NOTARY/CLERK OF PROBATE COURT

Sworn to and subscribed before me this ______ day of ____________, 19____. ______________________

____
NOTARY/CLERK OF PROBATE COURT

Sworn to and subscribed before me this ______ day of ____________, 19____. ______________________

____
NOTARY/CLERK OF PROBATE COURT

Sworn to and subscribed before me this ______ day of ____________, 19____. ______________________

____
NOTARY/CLERK OF PROBATE COURT

Sworn to and subscribed before me this ______ day of ____________, 19____. ______________________

____
NOTARY/CLERK OF PROBATE COURT

Sworn to and subscribed before me this ______ day of ____________, 19____. ______________________

____
NOTARY/CLERK OF PROBATE COURT

Sworn to and subscribed before me this ______ day of ____________, 19____. ______________________

____
NOTARY/CLERK OF PROBATE COURT

4

RETURN OF SHERIFF

I have this day served ____
personally with a copy of the foregoing petition and notice.

______________________ ______________________
Date Deputy Sheriff, ______________ County

ACCEPTANCE AND ANSWER OF GUARDIAN AD LITEM

Having been appointed by the Court to represent the interests of the child____ interested herein who is/are still minor(s), I hereby accept my appointment as such, acknowledge service and notice of said proceeding as provided by law, and for answer say: I have made a careful investigation into this matter, find that the proceeding appears (to be) (not to be) regular, and I am of the opinion that it (would be) (would not be) in the best interests of the minor child____ to consummate the proposed (conveyance) (encumbrance) and I (do not object) (object) to the granting of the application.

______________________ ______________________
Date Guardian ad Litem

PROBATE COURT OF ______________________ COUNTY

STATE OF GEORGIA

ESTATE OF	)	ESTATE NO.______________
	)	
	)	RE: PETITION FOR LEAVE TO CONVEY
	)	OR ENCUMBER PROPERTY
______________________,	)	PREVIOUSLY SET ASIDE AS YEAR'S
DECEASED	)	SUPPORT

ORDER

The petition of ____,
praying for leave to (convey) (encumber) certain real property heretofore awarded from the estate of the above decedent as year's support, having been read and considered, and it appearing to the Court that notice was duly issued and served as required by law; it further appearing that a guardian ad litem was duly appointed to represent the interests of the minor child____ still under the age of 18, who has made answer thereto approving the proposed transaction; it also appearing that no objections have been filed in this matter, and that it is necessary and in the best interests of the minor child______ still under the age of 18 that said real property be (conveyed) (encumbered) as set forth in the petition;

IT IS ORDERED that said petition to (convey) (encumber) be, and the same is hereby, GRANTED.

______________________ ______________________
Date Judge of the Probate Court

CERTIFICATE IN ACCORDANCE WITH
UNIFORM PROBATE COURT RULE 21(F)

I certify that the content of the foregoing is identical in all material respects with Georgia probate court standard form entitled **Petition for Leave to Convey or Encumber Property Previously Set Aside as Year's support,** except for additions or deletions indicated as required by the Uniform Probate Court Rules.

____________________________ Date

____________________________ Signature of Attorney
Address:

Telephone Number:
State Bar #:

Instructions and form adopted effective July 1, 1987; revised effective January 1, 1998; July 1, 1998.

GPCSF 18. PETITION FOR PRESUMPTION OF DEATH OF MISSING INDIVIDUAL BELIEVED TO BE DEAD

Re: Petition for Presumption of Death of Missing Individual Believed to be Dead

INSTRUCTIONS

I. Specific Instructions

1. This form is to be used for petition for presumption of death of missing individual believed to be dead pursuant to O.C.G.A. § 53–9–1 et seq.

2. This form is to be used in conjunction with a petition for letters of administration, a petition to probate will in common or solemn form, a petition for a year's support or a petition for an order that no administration is necessary. Any of these other petitions may be granted at any time after the presumption of death is established, provided that all legal requirements for the granting of the other petition have been met.

3. The attached form consists of 7 pages.

II. General Instructions

General instructions applicable to all Georgia probate court standard forms are available in each probate court.

PETITION FOR PRESUMPTION OF DEATH OF MISSING INDIVIDUAL BELIEVED TO BE DEAD

GEORGIA, ________ COUNTY
TO THE HONORABLE JUDGE OF THE PROBATE COURT:
The petition of ________, whose mailing address is ________, respectfully shows to the Court:

1.

________________________ (hereinafter referred to as the "missing individual"), who was domiciled at ________________________ in ________________________, Georgia, is missing.
(County)

2.

(Check one:)
________ The missing individual has been missing from his/her last known place of domicile for a continuous period of four years or longer.
________ The missing individual has been missing from his/her last known place of domicile for a continuous period of twelve months or longer.
________ The missing individual was exposed to a specific peril or tragedy resulting in probable death under circumstances which may be proved by clear and convincing evidence. The specific peril or tragedy and the circumstances proving the death of the missing individual are fully explained in paragraph 7.

3.

The missing individual was last heard from on ________________________,
(Date)
at which time he/she was at ________________________.
(Location or Address)

4.

Listed below are the names of all the missing individual's heirs with the age or majority status, address, and relationship to the missing individual set opposite the name of each:

Name	Age (Or over 18)	Address	Relationship

5.

__________ Petitioner (has simultaneously filed) (will file) a petition concerning this estate for (check one):

__________ administration of the estate.
__________ probate of will in (common) (solemn) form.
__________ a year's support.
__________ an order that no administration is necessary.
OR __________ Petitioner does not presently intend to file any other proceedings.

6.

To the knowledge of the petitioner, no other proceedings with respect to this estate are pending, or have been completed, in any other probate court in this state.

7.

The petitioner shows the following facts in support of the belief that the missing individual is deceased **[If death is to be proved as a result of a specific peril or tragedy, please fully describe the specific peril or tragedy and the circumstances proving the decedent's exposure thereto and death as a result thereof]**:

Wherefore petitioner prays:

(a) that necessary notice be issued and served according to law; and
(b) that an order establishing a presumption of death be entered.

____________________		____________________	
Signature of Attorney (or petitioner if pro se)		Signature of Attorney (or petitioner if pro se)	
Printed Name:	__________	Printed Name:	__________
Address:	__________	Address:	__________
	__________		__________
Telephone:	__________	Telephone:	__________
State Bar #:	__________	State Bar #:	__________

VERIFICATION

Georgia, ________ County

Personally appeared before me the undersigned petitioner(s) who on oath state(s) that the facts set forth in the foregoing petition are true.

______________________________	______________________________
Petitioner	Petitioner
Printed Name: ______________	Printed Name: ______________
Address: ______________	Address: ______________
______________	______________
Telephone: ______________	Telephone: ______________

Sworn to and subscribed before me, this ___ day of _________, 20 ___.

____

Clerk of Probate Court or Notary Public

ACKNOWLEDGMENT OF SERVICE AND ASSENT TO PETITION

GEORGIA, ________ COUNTY
IN RE: PETITION OF ________ FOR THE PRESUMPTION OF DEATH OF ________, MISSING INDIVIDUAL BELIEVED TO BE DEAD

We, the undersigned, being over 18 years of age, laboring under no legal disability and being those who would be heirs if the missing individual were known to be dead, hereby acknowledge service of a copy of the petition for presumption of death of missing individual believed to be dead and notice, waive copies of same, waive further service and notice, and hereby assent to the petition without further delay

SIGNATURE(S) OF WOULD BE HEIRS

Sworn to and subscribed before me this __ day of ________, 20________.

________ Signature

________ NOTARY/CLERK OF PROBATE COURT ________ Print Name

Sworn to and subscribed before me this __ day of ________, 20________.

________ Signature

________ NOTARY/CLERK OF PROBATE COURT ________ Print Name

Sworn to and subscribed before me this __ day of ________, 20________.

________ Signature

________ NOTARY/CLERK OF PROBATE COURT ________ Print Name

Sworn to and subscribed before me this __ day of ________, 20________.

________ Signature

________ NOTARY/CLERK OF PROBATE COURT ________ Print Name

Sworn to and subscribed before me this __ day of ________, 20________.

________ Signature

________ NOTARY/CLERK OF PROBATE COURT ________ Print Name

Sworn to and subscribed before me this __ day of ________, 20________.

________ Signature

________ NOTARY/CLERK OF PROBATE COURT ________ Print Name

PROBATE COURT OF ________ COUNTY STATE OF GEORGIA

IN THE MATTER OF) ESTATE NUMBER ________
)
________________________________) RE: PETITION FOR PRESUMPTION OF
MISSING INDIVIDUAL BELIEVED DEAD) DEATH OF MISSING INDIVIDUAL
) BELIEVED TO BE DEAD

ORDER FOR SERVICE OF NOTICE (AND SEARCH FOR MISSING INDIVIDUAL)

[Note: If desired, the following Order for Service of Notice and Notice of Hearing may be combined with any other such Order and Notice required for the issuance of letters or an order for year's support or that no administration is necessary.]

On ________, 20 ___, ________ filed a petition to establish the presumption of death of the above-named missing individual believed to be dead (and a petition on the estate of such individual).

IT IS ORDERED that notice be published once a week for four weeks, in the official newspaper in this county in which sheriff's advertisements are published, giving notice that on a day stated, which must be at least 90 days after the first publication, evidence will be heard by this Court concerning the alleged absence of the missing individual and the circumstances and duration thereof.

IT IS FURTHER ORDERED that the notice be (initial any and all of the following which apply):

________ served personally, together with a copy of the petition, upon the following individuals who would be heirs if the missing individual were known to be dead, who reside within this state, who have not acknowledged service:

____

________ served by registered or certified mail, return receipt requested, together with a copy of the petition, upon nonresident individuals who would be heirs if the missing individual were known to be dead, whose current residence addresses are known and who have not acknowledged service:

____

________ served by publication upon the following individuals who would be heirs if the missing individual were known to be dead, whose current residence addresses are unknown and who have not acknowledged service:

____

________ (Optional) IT IS FURTHER ORDERED that the petitioner search for the missing individual in the following manner:

____

This ___ day of ________, 20 ___.

____

JUDGE OF THE PROBATE COURT

PROBATE COURT OF ________ COUNTY STATE OF GEORGIA

IN THE MATTER OF	)	ESTATE NUMBER ________
	)	
________,	)	RE: PETITION FOR PRESUMPTION OF
MISSING INDIVIDUAL BELIEVED DEAD	)	DEATH OF MISSING INDIVIDUAL
	)	BELIEVED TO BE DEAD

NOTICE OF HEARING

A petition for presumption of death of ________, a missing individual believed dead, has been filed by (in conjunction with a petition for ________). Notice is hereby given that at ____ o'clock ________.m., on the ____ day of ________, 20 ____, evidence will be heard by the probate court concerning the alleged absence of said missing individual and the circumstances and duration thereof. The missing individual, if alive, or any other individual having evidence that the missing individual is alive, is required to produce and present to the court evidence that the missing individual is still in life.

This ____ day of ________, 20 ____.

JUDGE OF THE PROBATE COURT

By: ________________

Clerk of the Probate Court

Publication dates: ________

CERTIFICATE OF MAILING

This is to certify that I have this date forwarded by registered or certified mail, return receipt requested, in a stamped, addressed envelope, a copy of the foregoing petition and the notice, to each of the following heirs-apparent who reside out of state at known current residence addresses: ____

________________________ ________________________

DATE CLERK, PROBATE COURT

PROBATE COURT OF ________ COUNTY STATE OF GEORGIA

IN THE MATTER OF	)	ESTATE NUMBER ____________
	)	
____________________________,	)	RE: PETITION FOR PRESUMPTION OF
MISSING INDIVIDUAL BELIEVED DEAD	)	DEATH OF MISSING INDIVIDUAL
	)	BELIEVED TO BE DEAD

ORDER ESTABLISHING PRESUMPTION OF DEATH AND DATE THEREOF

The petition of ________, for presumption of death of ________, a missing individual believed to be dead, having come before the Court for hearing on ________, 20 ___, and it appearing that notice of such hearing was duly published and served as required by law, and after hearing evidence in said case, it is the finding of the Court that a diligent and reasonable effort has been made to locate the missing individual and that a legal presumption of death of said missing individual has been established

________ by a preponderance of the evidence because the presumption of death has been proved by showing that the individual has been missing from his or her last known place of domicile for a continuous period of four years,

OR

________ by a preponderance of the evidence because the presumption of death has been proved by showing that the individual has been missing from his or her last known place of domicile for a continues period of twelve months or more,

OR

________ by clear and convincing evidence, because the presumption of death has been proved by showing that the individual was exposed to a specific peril or tragedy resulting in probable death, and this Court concludes that such missing individual may be declared dead.

WHEREUPON, IT IS ORDERED that ________ be and is hereby declared dead and the date of death is herby[1] established as ________.

SO ORDERED on ________.

____

Judge of the Probate Court

Instructions and form adopted effective July 1, 1987; revised effective January 1, 1998; August 12, 2004.

[1] So in original

GPCSF 19. PETITION TO COMPROMISE DOUBTFUL CLAIM OF MINOR/WARD

GEORGIA PROBATE COURT
STANDARD FORM

Petition to Compromise Doubtful Claim of Minor/Ward

INSTRUCTIONS

I. Specific Instructions

1. This form is to be used when petitioning the Probate Court for authorization to compromise a doubtful personal injury claim of a minor pursuant to O.C.G.A. §29-3-3 or adult ward pursuant to O.C.G.A. §29-5-23(c)(5). The terms "gross settlement", "net settlement", and "present value" are defined in O.C.G.A. §29-3-3. This form must be modified when a covenant not to sue, as opposed to a release, will be executed by the natural guardian or conservator.

2. This form may also be used when compromising other than personal injury claims pursuant to O.C.G.A. §29-3-3, provided appropriate changes are made in the form.

3. Even if there is a legally qualified conservator, it is not necessary to file a separate petition to encroach on corpus concerning the expenses listed in paragraph 11 of the form, unless the court so directs, in which case the prayers listed on page 6 and the provisions of the Order should be modified.

II. General Instructions

General instructions applicable to all Georgia probate court standard forms appear in Volume 255 of the Georgia Reports and are available in each probate court.

Effective 7/06 GPCSF 19 Complete

GEORGIA PROBATE COURT
STANDARD FORM

IN THE PROBATE COURT OF ____________________ COUNTY

STATE OF GEORGIA

IN RE:) ESTATE NO. ____________________

)

______________________________,) PETITION TO COMPROMISE
MINOR/WARD) DOUBTFUL CLAIM OF MINOR OR
) ADULT WARD

TO THE HONORABLE JUDGE OF THE PROBATE COURT:

The petition of ______________________________, shows to the Court:

1.

(Initial either a. or b. below):

____ a. Petitioner(s) has/have been appointed the conservator(s) of said minor/ward by Order of this Court, and brings this petition in such capacity.

or

____ b. Petitioner(s) is/are the natural guardian(s) of the above minor, the gross settlement amount is over $15,000.00 but the net settlement amount is less than $15,000.00, legal action has not been initiated (or, if initiated, has been dismissed with the approval of the trial judge).

(Initial if applicable:)

____ The minor/ward currently has cash/personal property in the amount of $ ______________ and will receive additional funds of $ __________. As a result of this settlement, the petitioner(s) will file an additional bond in the amount of $______________ to secure the minor/ward's estate.

2.

Petitioner(s) as natural guardian(s)/conservator(s) has/have claims against ______________ by virtue of an incident occurring on or about __________, 20___. Said minor/ward, whose birth date is __________ and who is __________ years old, received personal injuries as a result of the following occurrence:

and the minor/ward has potential claim(s) against the following adverse party(ies) not settled in this action: ____
____.

3.

____ A copy of the accident report is attached as Exhibit "A".
____ There was no accident report because ______________________________________.

4.

The minor/ward sustained the following injuries:

5.

The minor/ward has been treated by:

6.

The minor's/ward's physical, mental and emotional condition, as evidenced by the statement of the treating doctor attached as Exhibit "____", has returned to the condition of said minor/ward prior to such incident, except for:

7.

The following is a list of all medical expenses and other special damages incurred to date as a result of the injury to said minor/ward:

8.

The following is a list of all medical expenses and other special damages expected to be incurred in the future as a result of the injury to said minor/ward as evidenced by the statement of the treating doctor or doctors attached as Exhibit "____":

9.

Medical expenses have been paid as follows:

a. $________________ by ______________________________'s medical payment reimbursement insurance coverage. $______________________________ of such coverage remains and will not be released by this settlement.
b. $________________ from any group or private insurance sources.
c. $________________ as a result of workers' compensation coverage.
d. $________________ from any other source (identify).

10.

Petitioner(s) believe(s) this a fair, reasonable and just compromise because petitioner(s) has/have fully investigated the facts and circumstances surrounding the incident, and it is uncertain and doubtful that an amount could be recovered in excess of the settlement amount offered by ____, since the opposing party or parties contend that they are not responsible or liable in any way for whatever injuries might have been sustained by said minor/ward on the following grounds:

11.

Petitioner(s) and ____ have agreed upon a compromise settlement of all claims, which petitioner(s) believe(s) to be fair, reasonable, and just under the circumstances, upon the terms and conditions set forth below:

a. Expenses, if any, to be paid from settlement proceeds:
   (i) Attorney's fees $
   (ii) Expenses of litigation $
   (iii) Medical expenses now due $
   (iv) Other (explain below, if necessary) $
   (v) Total of such expenses $
b. Cash to conservatorship (not including above expenses, if any) $
c. (Value) (Cost) of annuity $
d. Gross settlement (total of a., b., and c.) $
e. Net settlement (total of b. and c.) $
f. Further explanation, if necessary:

12.

The following is a description and explanation of any amounts being paid to persons other than for the benefit of the minor/ward as a result of the injuries to said minor/ward:

13.

____ a. The adverse party's(ies') policy limits of insurance are ____________________.

____ b. Uninsured motorists coverage held by ______________________________ is contributing $______________ to the settlement.

____ c. There is no policy of insurance involved in this matter.

14.

[To be completed if the claim appears to be worth more than the insurance policy limits:]

Petitioner(s) has/have investigated the assets of the party or parties being released as part of this settlement, and has/have determined that it would not be worthwhile to decline this settlement offer because:

15.

Petitioner(s) has/have employed ______________________________ to represent Petitioner(s) in the prosecution of said minor's/ward's claim, and has/have agreed to pay the attorney's fees and expenses of litigation in paragraph 11 (a)(i) and (ii) above, which represents ________% of the total settlement.

16.

Petitioner(s) seek(s) to direct settlement proceeds into a structured settlement, and the Disclosures Regarding Structured Settlement is attached hereto as Exhibit ______.

17.

Additional Data: Where full particulars are lacking, state here the reasons for any such omission.

Effective 7/06 GPCSF 19 Completet

WHEREFORE. Petitioner(s) pray(s) for an Order approving, and allowing Petitioner(s) to accept, said offer to compromise and settle upon the terms set forth above; that Petitioner(s) be authorized to consummate the settlement and execute any and all agreements, receipts, releases and other documents necessary or proper to effect said settlement; and that Petitioner(s) be authorized to pay from the gross settlement amount all fees and expenses described in paragraph 11 above.

Signature of first petitioner	Signature of second petitioner if any
Printed Name	Printed Name
Address	Address
Telephone Number	Telephone Number

Signature of Attorney:

Typed/printed name of Attorney: ____________________

Address: ____________________

____

Telephone: __________ State Bar #__________

VERIFICATION

GEORGIA, ____________________ COUNTY

Personally appeared before me the undersigned petitioner(s) who on oath state(s) that the facts set forth in the foregoing petition are true.

Sworn to and subscribed before me this ___ day of __________, 20___.

____
First Petitioner

____
NOTARY/CLERK OF PROBATE COURT

____
Printed Name

Sworn to and subscribed before this ___ day of __________, 20___.

____
Second Petitioner, if any

____
NOTARY/CLERK OF PROBATE COURT

____
Printed Name

Disclosures Regarding Structured Settlement

MINOR/WARD ______________ ESTATE NO. ______________

1. Total Cost of Structured Settlement: ______________

2. Annuity
   a. Total payout over life of annuity: ______________
   b. Amount GUARANTEED: ______________ Rate of return: ___%
   c. Do payments terminate at death? ______________
   d. Amount of payments: ______________$
      i. If periodic,
         (1) state period (i.e. monthly)
         (2) Beginning date: ______________ Ending date: ______________
      ii. If lump sum distribution at date certain, list,
         (1) $______________ date ______________
         (2) $______________ date ______________
         (3) $______________ date ______________

   NOTE: THE ESTATE OF THE MINOR/WARD MUST BE THE NAMED BENEFICIARY TO RECEIVE ANY GUARANTEED PAYMENTS THAT WILL BE PAID AFTER THE DEATH OF THE MINOR/WARD. The Petitioner(s) may NOT name themselves as the beneficiary of any assets paid after a minor/ward's death, except with Court approval.

3. List any amounts attorneys will receive AFTER INITIAL SETTLEMENT, IF ANY:

   a. ______________ date ______________

   b. ______________ date ______________

4. Name, address, and telephone number of company underwriting the annuity:
   Name: ______________
   Address: ______________
   ____
   Telephone ______________

Effective 7/06 GPCSF 19 Complete

PROBATE COURT OF ____________________ COUNTY

STATE OF GEORGIA

IN RE:) ESTATE NO. ____________________

)
______________________________,) PETITION TO COMPROMISE
CLAIM)
MINOR/WARD)

ORDER APPOINTING GUARDIAN AD LITEM

(to be used if the Petitioner(s) is/are Conservator(s))

A Petition to Compromise Claim being filed by the conservator(s) of the above named minor/ward, it is hereby

ORDERED that ______________________________ is appointed guardian ad litem for the above minor/ward. The deputy clerk shall serve said guardian ad litem with a copy of this Order and the above Petition/Motion. Upon said guardian ad litem's acceptance of same, said guardian ad litem shall make answer hereto.

SO ORDERED this ________ day of ____________________, 20____.

Probate Judge

Effective 7/06 GPCSF 19 Complete

PROBATE COURT OF ____________________ COUNTY

STATE OF GEORGIA

IN RE: ____________________	)	ESTATE NO. ____________________
	)	
____________________,	)	PETITION TO COMPROMISE
CLAIM	)	
MINOR/WARD	)	

ANSWER OF GUARDIAN AD LITEM

I hereby accept the foregoing appointment, acknowledge service and notice of the proceedings as provided by law, and for answer say:

____________________ ____________________
DATE GUARDIAN AD LITEM

ADDRESS

TELEPHONE

Effective 7/06

GPCSF 19 Complete

PROBATE COURT OF ______________ COUNTY

STATE OF GEORGIA

IN RE:) ESTATE NO. ______________
)
______________,) PETITION TO COMPROMISE
CLAIM)
MINOR/WARD)

ORDER

The foregoing petition having been read and considered, and it appearing upon the hearing that the facts set out in the petition are true and that said settlement is fair, reasonable and just, that the same is made in good faith, and will be in the best interest of the said minor/ward and will advance the interests of said minor/ward;

(initial if applicable)

____ And no objection to the proposed compromise being raised by the guardian ad litem;

IT IS HEREBY ORDERED AND ADJUDGED that Petitioner(s) be and is/are hereby authorized to consummate said settlement as prayed in said petition, and to execute any and all agreements, receipts, releases or other documents necessary or proper to effect such settlement, and that such agreements, receipts, releases or other documents shall constitute the full, final and complete settlement of any and all actions, causes of action, claims or demands which the above-named minor/ward may have against those parties to the settlement named in the petition, as fully and completely as if said ward had executed said agreements, receipts, releases or other documents individually.

IT IS FURTHER ORDERED that Petitioner(s) be and is/are hereby authorized to pay all fees and expenses shown in paragraph 11 of the petition from the gross settlement amount.

SO ORDERED this ________ day of ______________, 20___.

Probate Judge

Effective 7/06 GPCSF 19 Complete

Instructions and form adopted effective July 1, 1987; revised effective July, 1989; July 1, 1995; July 1, 2005; July 31, 2006.

GPCSF 20. PETITION FOR LEAVE TO ENCROACH ON CORPUS

GEORGIA PROBATE COURT
STANDARD FORM

Petition for Leave to Encroach on Corpus

INSTRUCTIONS

I. Specific Instructions

1. This from is to be used for filing a Petition for Leave to Encroach on Corpus pursuant to O.C.G.A. §29-3-22 (c) and 29-5-23 (c).
2. A guardian ad litem must be appointed each time this Petition is filed.

II. General Instructions

General instructions applicable to all Georgia probate court standard forms appear in Volume 255 of the Georgia Reports and are available in each probate court.

GEORGIA PROBATE COURT
STANDARD FORM

IN THE PROBATE COURT OF ______________________ COUNTY

STATE OF GEORGIA

IN RE:) ESTATE NO. ______________________
)
______________________,) PETITION FOR LEAVE TO
MINOR/WARD) ENCROACH
) ON CORPUS
)
______________________,)
CONSERVATOR(S))

TO THE HONORABLE JUDGE OF THE PROBATE COURT:

The petition of ______________________, Conservator(s) of ______________________, (adult ward) (minor) shows:

1.

As such conservator(s), petitioner(s) has/have in hand assets valued at $______________. The conservator(s) expect(s) that the minor/ward will have income of $______________ during the next accounting period.

2.

The income from said assets or budget approved by the Court, if any, is insufficient for the maintenance, support and education of said minor/ward (and/or ______________________, who is/are legally dependent upon said ward).

3.

There are no other assets available to petitioner(s) to maintain, support and educate the person(s) indicated in Paragraph 2 above.

4.

By prior Court Order(s), the petitioner(s) was/were permitted to disburse $______________ per month for the benefit of the minor/ward.

GEORGIA PROBATE COURT
STANDARD FORM

5.

Since the inception of the conservatorship, petitioner(s) has/have previously encroached on the corpus of this estate in the total amount of approximately $____________________.

6.

The encroachment requested in this petition is needed for the following purpose(s) of maintenance, support or education of the person(s) indicated in Paragraph 2 above in order to provide the following specific items (attach separate sheet if necessary): ____________________.

WHEREFORE petitioner(s) pray(s) that the Court

1. appoint a guardian ad litem, and
2. grant an order allowing petitioner to expend from the corpus of the minor/ward's estate, the sum of $____________________ for the purposes set forth above.

____________________	____________________
Signature of first petitioner	Signature of second petitioner, if any
____________________	____________________
Printed Name	Printed Name
____________________	____________________
Address	Address
____________________	____________________
____________________	____________________
Telephone Number	Telephone Number

Signature of Attorney: ____________________

Typed/printed name of Attorney: ____________________

Address: ____________________

Telephone: ____________________ State Bar # ____________________

Effective 7/06 2 GPCSF 20 Complete

GEORGIA PROBATE COURT
STANDARD FORM

VERIFICATION

GEORGIA, ______________________ COUNTY

Personally appeared before me the undersigned petitioner(s) who on oath state(s) that the facts set forth in the foregoing petition are true.

Sworn to and subscribed before
me this ___ day of ________, 20___.

____
First Petitioner

____
NOTARY/CLERK OF PROBATE COURT

____
Printed Name

Sworn to and subscribed before
this ___ day of ________, 20___.

____
Second Petitioner, if any

____
NOTARY/CLERK OF PROBATE COURT

____
Printed Name

GEORGIA PROBATE COURT
STANDARD FORM

IN THE PROBATE COURT OF ______________________ COUNTY

STATE OF GEORGIA

IN RE:	)	ESTATE NO. ______________
	)	
______________________________,	)	PETITION TO ENCROACH
MINOR/WARD	)	
	)	
______________________________,	)	
CONSERVATOR(S)	)	

ORDER APPOINTING GUARDIAN AD LITEM

A Petition to Encroach being filed by the conservator(s) of the above named minor/ward, it is hereby

ORDERED that ______________________________ is appointed guardian ad litem for the above minor/ward. The deputy clerk shall serve said guardian ad litem with a copy of this Order and the above Petition. Upon said guardian ad litem's acceptance of same, said guardian ad litem shall make answer hereto.

SO ORDERED this ________ day of ______________________________, 20____.

Probate Judge

GEORGIA PROBATE COURT
STANDARD FORM

IN THE PROBATE COURT OF ______________________ COUNTY

STATE OF GEORGIA

IN RE:	)	ESTATE NO. ______________________
	)	
______________________________________,	)	PETITION TO ENCROACH
MINOR/WARD	)	
	)	
______________________________________,	)	
CONSERVATOR(S)	)	

ANSWER OF GUARDIAN AD LITEM

I hereby accept the foregoing appointment, acknowledge service and notice of the proceedings as provided by law, and for answer say:

______________________________	______________________________
DATE	GUARDIAN AD LITEM
	ADDRESS
	TELEPHONE

GEORGIA PROBATE COURT
STANDARD FORM

IN THE PROBATE COURT OF ______________________ COUNTY

STATE OF GEORGIA

IN RE:) ESTATE NO. ______________________
)
______________________________________,) PETITION TO ENCROACH
MINOR/WARD)
)
______________________________________,)
CONSERVATOR(S))

ORDER

Upon reading and considering the foregoing petition, and it appearing that the averments therein made are true, and the guardian ad litem for the minor/ward filing an answer to the petition which raised no objection to the grant of the Petition; it is ordered that, to the extent indicated below, the same be, and is hereby, granted; said conservator(s) is/are hereby (initial applicable):

____ a. allowed to expend from the corpus of said minor's/ward's estate up to the sum of $______________________ for the specific items set forth in said petition for the purpose of maintenance, support or education of the person(s) indicated in Paragraph 2 of the petition, and said Conservator(s) must show in his/her/their annual returns how such funds are actually spent.

____ b. allowed to increase his/her/their monthly budget to $______________________ per month and said Conservator(s) must show in his/her/their annual returns how such funds are actually spent.

SO ORDERED this ________ day of ______________________, 20____.

Probate Judge

Effective 7/06 6 GPCSF 20 Complete

Instructions and form adopted effective July 1, 1987; revised effective July 1, 2005; July 31, 2006.

GPCSF 21. BOND OF ADMINISTRATORS, CONSERVATORS, & EXECUTORS, ETC.

GEORGIA PROBATE COURT
STANDARD FORM

BOND OF ADMINISTRATORS, CONSERVATORS, & EXECUTORS, ETC.

GEORGIA ______________________ COUNTY BOND NO. ______________

Know all Men by these Presents:

That we, ____,
Principal, and ____,
Surety, are held and firmly bound unto ______________________________,
Judge of the Probate Court of said County, and the successors in said office, in the just and full sum of __________ Dollars, for the payment of which, well and truly to be made, we bind ourselves, our heirs, executors and administrators, jointly and severally, firmly by these presents.

The condition of the above bond or obligation is such, that whereas the said ______________ ____
has been named and appointed as (Administrator) (Conservator) (Executor) of the estate of _____ ____.

Now should the said ____
well and truly demean (himself) (herself) as such as aforesaid named, and faithfully discharge all of the duties required by law, then the above obligation to be satisfied and void, otherwise to remain in full force and effect.

Signed, sealed and dated, this ______ day of ______________, 20____.

Address and telephone number of Surety for Notices and Copies of Filings (Agent's address should not be used unless the agent is authorized by the issuer/underwriter to receive notices): ______________________
____
____
____

Initial Premium: $______________________

____
Principal (Seal)

____
Principal (Seal)

____
Corporate Surety
By: ______________________
Attorney–in–Fact (Seal)

Approved: ______________________
Probate Judge

Effective 7/05 GPCSF 21 Complete

Form adopted effective July 1, 1987; amended effective July 1, 2005.

GPCSF 22 PETITIONER. PETITION TO ESTABLISH CUSTODIAL ACCOUNT FOR MINOR OR INCAPACITATED ADULT

GEORGIA PROBATE COURT
STANDARD FORM

Petition to Establish Custodial Account for Minor or Incapacitated Adult

INSTRUCTIONS

I. Specific Instructions

1. This form is to be used when petitioning the court for authority to establish a custodial account for a minor or incapacitated adult pursuant to O.C.G.A. § 29–6–1, et seq.
2. It may be necessary for the petitioner to provide a social security number or taxpayer identification number to be used in connection with the bank account. Contact the appropriate probate court to determine whether this information is needed from petitioner.

II. General Instructions

General instructions applicable to all Georgia probate court standard forms appear in Volume 255 of the Georgia Reports and are available in each probate court.

Effective 7/05

GPCSF 22 Petitioner

IN THE PROBATE COURT OF ______________ COUNTY

STATE OF GEORGIA

IN RE: ______________________________) ESTATE NO. ______________________

______________________________,) PETITION TO ESTABLISH CUSTODIAL
MINOR/INCAPACITATED ADULT) ACCOUNT FOR MINOR OR
) INCAPACITATED ADULT

TO THE HONORABLE JUDGE OF THE PROBATE COURT:

The petition of ____ shows to the Court:

1.

____
is a minor/incapacitated adult who has no legal and qualified conservator.

2.

The minor/incapacitated adult is a resident of this County, residing at ______________
____.

3.

The minor's/incapacitated adult's age is __________ and date of birth is ____________.

4.

The minor/incapacitated adult is entitled to the sum of ____________________ arising from
____.

5.

The (parents of the minor, if any) (guardian(s) of the incapacitated adult, if any) are:

Name	address	telephone number

6.

The names and addresses of two people other than those listed in paragraph 5 who will likely be aware of the minor's/incapacitated adult's whereabouts in the future are:

____

____

WHEREFORE petitioner(s) pray(s) that the minor's/incapacitated adult's parents/guardian(s), if any, be served in accordance with Chapter 9 of Title 29 with a copy of this Petition and Notice, and that the petitioner(s) be allowed to pay over to the Judge of the Probate Court, as custodian, the money due and owing to the minor/incapacitated adult.

Signature of first petitioner	Signature of second petitioner, if any
Printed Name	Printed Name
Address	Address
Telephone Number	Telephone Number

Signature of Attorney: ______________________________

Typed/printed name of Attorney: ______________________________

Address: ______________________________

____

Telephone: ______________ State Bar # ____________

VERIFICATION

GEORGIA, ______________ COUNTY

Personally appeared before me the undersigned petitioner(s) who on oath state(s) that the facts set forth in the foregoing petition are true.

Sworn to and subscribed before me this ____ day of ________ 20___.

	First Petitioner
NOTARY/CLERK OF PROBATE COURT	Printed Name

Sworn to and subscribed before me this ____ day of ________, 20___.

	Second Petitioner, if any
NOTARY/CLERK OF PROBATE COURT	Printed Name

3

Instructions and form adopted effective July 1, 1987; amended effective July 1, 2001; July 1, 2005.

GPCSF 22 COURT. COURT FORMS FOR PETITION TO ESTABLISH CUSTODIAL ACCOUNT FOR MINOR OR INCAPACITATED ADULT

GEORGIA PROBATE COURT
STANDARD FORM

Petition to Establish Custodial Account for Minor or Incapacitated Adult

NOTICE: UNLESS OTHER WISE DIRECTED BY THE COURT, THE FOLLOWING FORMS ARE FOR PROBATE COURT STAFF TO COMPLETE

Effective 7/05 GPCSF 22 Court

GEORGIA PROBATE COURT
STANDARD FORM

IN THE PROBATE COURT OF ______ COUNTY

STATE OF GEORGIA

IN RE:	)	ESTATE NO. ____________
	)	
______________________,	)	PETITION TO ESTABLISH CUSTODIAL
MINOR/INCAPACITATED ADULT	)	ACCOUNT FOR MINOR OR
	)	INCAPACITATED ADULT

ORDER CONCERNING NOTICE

The above Petition being filed, it is hereby

ORDERED that the probate clerk/deputy clerk shall serve a copy of the Petition, this Order, and Notice of the filing of the above petition by first class mail, if domiciled outside Georgia, and by personal service, if domiciled in Georgia, on (initial applicable):

_____a. the parents of the minor

_____b. the guardian(s) of the incapacitated adult.

SO ORDERED this _____ day of ________________, 20 ___.

____
Probate Judge

IN THE PROBATE COURT OF ______________ COUNTY

STATE OF GEORGIA

IN RE:	)	ESTATE NO. ______________
	)	
______________,	)	PETITION TO ESTABLISH CUSTODIAL
MINOR/INCAPACITATED ADULT	)	ACCOUNT FOR MINOR OR
	)	INCAPACITATED ADULT

NOTICE

To: ____,
(the parents of the minor)(the guardian(s) of the incapacitated adult):

The Petitioner(s), ______________________, has/have filed the above Petition. If you have an objection, it must be filed on or before the tenth (10th) day after the date you are personally served with this Notice, or within 14 days from the date of mailing if you have been served by mail. All objections to the petition must be in writing, setting forth the grounds of any such objections, and all pleadings/objections must be signed before a notary public or before a Georgia probate court clerk. Filing fees must be tendered with your pleadings/objection, unless you qualify to file as an indigent party. Contact probate court personnel at the following address/telephone number for the required amount of filing fees. If any objections are filed, a hearing will be (held on ______________, 20____ in the Probate Court of ________________ County, courtroom ________, (address) ____ ________________________, Georgia)(scheduled for a later date). If no objections are filed, the petition may be granted without a hearing.

____
PROBATE JUDGE

By: ______________________________
PROBATE CLERK/DEPUTY CLERK

____
ADDRESS

____

____
TELEPHONE NUMBER

IN THE PROBATE COURT OF ____________ COUNTY

STATE OF GEORGIA

IN RE:	)	ESTATE NO. ____________
	)	
____________,	)	PETITION TO ESTABLISH CUSTODIAL
MINOR/INCAPACITATED ADULT	)	ACCOUNT FOR MINOR OR
	)	INCAPACITATED ADULT

ORDER

The foregoing petition having been read and considered, and it appearing that the facts set forth in the petition are true, and the above-named minor/incapacitated adult having no legal conservator,

IT IS ORDERED that the above Petition is GRANTED and pursuant to O.C.G.A. § 29-6-1, the undersigned is authorized to receive and collect all moneys arising from insurance policies, benefit societies, legacies, inheritances, or any other source and to deposit, manage, and expend same in accordance with Chapter 6 of Title 29.

SO ORDERED this _____ day of ____________, 20 ___.

____
Probate Judge

Instructions and form adopted effective July 1, 2005.

GPCSF 23 through GPCSF 27. [Reserved/Relocated]

GPCSF 28 PETITIONER. PETITION FOR TEMPORARY LETTERS OF GUARDIANSHIP OF MINOR

GEORGIA PROBATE COURT
STANDARD FORM

Petition for Temporary Letters of Guardianship of Minor

INSTRUCTIONS

I. Specific Instructions

1. This form is to be used for filing a Petition for Temporary Letters of Guardianship of a minor pursuant to O.C.G.A. §29-2-5.

2. Notice of the Petition must be given to the "parents" of the minor. If an objection to the establishment of the temporary guardianship is filed by a parent who is also a "natural guardian," the Court will dismiss the Petition without a hearing. If a parent who is not a natural guardian objects, a hearing on the matter will be scheduled.

   A "parent" is defined as the biological or adoptive father or mother whose parental rights have not been surrendered or terminated, except that in the case of a child born out of wedlock, the father shall be considered a "parent" only if he has legitimated the minor.

   A father of a child born out of wedlock has legitimated the minor if he took some legal action to be recognized as the legal or lawful father.

   A "natural guardian" is defined as each parent, unless the parents are divorced. If one parent has sole legal custody, that parent is the sole "natural guardian." If both parents have joint legal custody, then both parents are "natural guardians."

3. A temporary guardianship will be deemed to be a permanent guardianship for the purposes of obtaining medical insurance coverage for the minor if the guardian assumes in writing the obligation to support the minor while the guardianship is in effect to the extent that no other sources of support are available.

4. Unless otherwise permitted by the Probate Court in which filed, a separate Petition must be filed for each minor. Contact the Probate Court in which the Petition will be filed for its policy. If the filing of one petition for more than one minor is permitted by the Probate Court, modify the Petition accordingly.

II. General Instructions

General instructions applicable to all Georgia probate court standard forms appear in Volume 255 of the Georgia Reports and are available in each probate court.

GEORGIA PROBATE COURT
STANDARD FORM

IN THE PROBATE COURT OF ________________ COUNTY

STATE OF GEORGIA

IN RE:) ESTATE NO. ______________________________

)
______________________________________,) PETITION FOR TEMPORARY LETTERS
) OF GUARDIANSHIP OF MINOR
______________________________________,)
MINOR)

TO THE HONORABLE JUDGE OF THE PROBATE COURT:

The petition of ______________________________, who is/are domiciled at (physical address) ______________________________, ________________ County, who has/have actual physical custody of the minor named above, and whose mailing address(es) is/are ________ shows:

1.

The minor, ____________________, currently is located in the county in which this petition is being filed, is ______ years old with a date of birth of __________. The minor's current address is ______________________________. A copy of the minor's birth certificate is attached as exhibit "A."

2.

Said minor is in need of a temporary guardian. The Petitioner(s) has/have the following relationship with the minor: ____.

3.

The minor's mother, ______________________________, (initial all that apply)

______a. is not a natural guardian of the minor because her parental rights have been terminated or she has surrendered them;

______b. has sole legal custody of the minor:

______c. has joint legal custody of the minor:

______d. has selected petitioner(s) to serve as temporary guardian(s) (see attached notarized acknowledgment and consent);

______e. is deceased, and a copy of her death certificate is attached as exhibit "B;"

______f. has not consented to the creation of the temporary guardianship and her (current physical address county of residence is ______________________________, located in ______________ County) (current address is unknown).

4.

(initial either a., b or c:)

______a. The minor was born during a marriage. The father of the minor, ______________________________, (initial all that apply)

______(i) is not a natural guardian of the minor because his parental rights have been terminated or he has surrendered them;

______(ii) has sole legal custody of the minor;

______(iii) has joint legal custody of the minor;

______(iv) has selected petitioner to serve as temporary guardian (see attached notarized acknowledgment and consent);

______(v) is deceased, and a copy of his death certificate is attached as exhibit "C;"

______(vi) has not consented to the creation of the temporary guardianship and his (current physical address is ______________________________, located in ______________ County) (current address is unknown).

______b. The minor was born out of wedlock. The biological father of the minor, ______________________________, has not legitimated the minor.

______c. The minor was born out of wedlock AND the father of the minor legitimated the minor. The father of the minor, ______________________________, (initial all that apply)

______(i) is not a natural guardian of the minor because his parental rights have been terminated or he has surrendered them;

______(ii) has sole legal custody of the minor;

______(iii) has joint legal custody of the minor;

______(iv) has selected petitioner to serve as temporary guardian (see attached notarized acknowledgment and consent);

______(v) is deceased, and a copy of his death certificate is attached as exhibit "C;"

______(vi) has not consented to the creation of the temporary guardianship and his (current physical address is ______________________________ ______________________________, located in ______________ County) (current address is unknown).

5.

(initial if applicable)

______a. The minor, being over fourteen years of age, has selected the petitioner(s) to act as temporary guardian(s) as shown by the attached selection.

6.

NOTE: complete the following unless both parents have signed the attached notarized acknowledgment and consent:

The temporary guardianship is needed because ______________________________

7.

Additional Data: Where full particulars are lacking, state here the reasons for any such omission. Also, state here all pertinent facts which may govern the method of giving notice to any party and which may determine whether or not a guardian ad litem should be appointed for any party.

WHEREFORE, petitioner(s) pray(s) that
1. service be perfected as provided by law and
2. petitioner(s) be appointed temporary guardian(s) of the minor named above.

______________________________	______________________________
Signature of first petitioner	Signature of second petitioner, if any
______________________________	______________________________
Printed Name	Printed Name
______________________________	______________________________
Address	Address
______________________________	______________________________
______________________________	______________________________
Telephone Number	Telephone Number

Signature of Attorney: ______________________________

Typed/printed name of Attorney: ______________________________
Address: ______________________________

Telephone: ____________________ State Bar # ______________________________

VERIFICATION

GEORGIA, ______________________________ COUNTY

Personally appeared before me the undersigned petitioner(s) who on oath state(s) that the facts set forth in the foregoing petition are true.

Sworn to and subscribed before
me this ______ day of ____________, 20___.

____
First Petitioner

______________________________ ______________________________
NOTARY/CLERK OF PROBATE COURT Printed Name

Sworn to and subscribed before
me this ______ day of ____________, 20___.

____
Second Petitioner, if any

______________________________ ______________________________
NOTARY/CLERK OF PROBATE COURT Printed Name

IN THE PROBATE COURT OF ____________ COUNTY
STATE OF GEORGIA

IN RE:) ESTATE NO. ____________________
)
______________________________,) PETITION FOR TEMPORARY LETTERS
MINOR) OF GUARDIANSHIP OF MINOR

SELECTION BY MINOR IF AGED 14 OR OLDER

I, the undersigned minor resident of ____________ County select ______________________________ to be appointed temporary guardian(s) of my person, this _____ day of ____________, 20___.

Signature of Minor

____
Printed Name

ACKNOWLEDGMENT AND CONSENT TO CREATION OF TEMPORARY GUARDIANSHIP AND APPOINTMENT OF INDIVIDUAL(S) AS TEMPORARY GUARDIAN(S)

IN RE: ESTATE OF ______________________________ ESTATE NO. __________

I/We, ______________________________, the mother/father of ______________________________, minor, do hereby consent to the creation of a temporary guardianship and the appointment of (list all parties to whom you wish to grant temporary guardianship) ______________________, and also acknowledge service of the petition for appointment of a temporary guardian for said minor, and waive any and all further service and notice concerning said petition.

I/We further understand that pursuant to O.C.G.A. §29-2-8(b), upon application by a natural guardian (as defined in said statute; see Instructions), the court will remove the temporary guardian and dissolve the temporary guardianship unless an objection is timely filed by the temporary guardian. If an objection is timely filed to such an application, the juvenile court or the probate court shall determine, after notice and hearing, whether a continuation or dissolution of the temporary guardianship is in the best interest of the minor. I/We understand that nothing herein, including any optional assumption by the guardian of the obligation to support the minor to the extent that no other sources of support are available, affects my/our legal obligation to support and maintain said minor.

Mother

Sworn to and subscribed before
me this ______ day of ______________, 20____.

____
Printed Name

____
Notary Public/Clerk, Probate Court

____
Address

Telephone Number

____

Father

Sworn to and subscribed before
me this ______ day of ______________, 20____.

____
Printed Name

____
Notary Public/Clerk, Probate Court

____
Address

Telephone Number

ASSUMPTION OF OBLIGATION TO SUPPORT (OPTIONAL)

IN RE: ESTATE OF ______________________ ESTATE NO. __________

The undersigned, if appointed temporary guardian(s) of ______________________, minor, assume(s) the obligation to support the minor while the guardianship is in effect to the extent that no other sources of support are available.

Sworn to and subscribed before
me this ______ day of ____________, 20___.

____
Petitioner

____
Clerk, Probate Court/Notary Public

____
Printed Name

Sworn to and subscribed before
me this ______ day of ____________, 20___.

____
Co-Petitioner

____
Clerk, Probate Court/Notary Public

____
Printed Name

Effective 7/06 –7– GPCSF 28 Petitioner

Instructions and form adopted effective July, 1989; revised effective July 1, 1992; July 1, 1995; August 1, 2000; July 1, 2005; July 31, 2006.

GPCSF 28 COURT. COURT FORMS FOR TEMPORARY LETTERS OF GUARDIANSHIP OF MINOR

GEORGIA PROBATE COURT
STANDARD FORM

Petition for Temporary Letters of Guardianship of Minor

NOTICE: UNLESS OTHERWISE DIRECTED BY THE COURT, THE FOLLOWING FORMS ARE FOR PROBATE COURT STAFF TO COMPLETE

IN THE PROBATE COURT OF ________________ COUNTY

STATE OF GEORGIA

IN RE:) ESTATE NO. ____________________________

)

____,)

)

____,) PETITION FOR TEMPORARY LETTERS

MINOR) OF GUARDIANSHIP OF MINOR

ORDER FOR SERVICE

_______a. It appearing that the mother of the minor named in the petition has not acknowledged and consented to the Petition and that (initial):

_______(i) she resides at a known address in the State of Georgia, she must therefore be served by personal service.

_______(ii) she resides at a known address outside the State of Georgia, she must therefore be served by first class mail.

_______(iii) her current address is unknown, she must therefore be served by publication once a week for two weeks.

_______b. It appearing that the father of the minor named in the petition has not acknowledged and consented to the Petition and that (initial):

_______(i) he resides at a known address in the State of Georgia, he must therefore be served by personal service.

_______(ii) he resides at a known address outside the State of Georgia, he must therefore be served by first class mail.

_______(iii) his current address is unknown, he must therefore be served by publication once a week for two weeks.

THEREFORE, IT IS ORDERED that citation issue and be served as indicated above and in accordance with law.

SO ORDERED this __________ day of ____________________________, 20____.

Probate Judge

Effective 7/06 GPCSF 28 Court

CITATION

GEORGIA, ______________________ COUNTY ESTATE NO. __________

IN RE: PETITION OF ____

___ FOR TEMPORARY LETTERS OF GUARDIANSHIP

ESTATE OF ____,
MINOR

DATE OF MAILING, IF ANY __________

DATE OF SECOND PUBLICATION, IF ANY __________

TO: ____

You are hereby notified that a petition for the appointment of a temporary guardian has been filed regarding the above-named minor. All objections to the Petition described above either to the appointment of a temporary guardian or the appointment of the petitioner(s) as temporary guardian(s), must be in writing, setting forth the grounds of any such objections, and must be filed with this Court no later than 14 days after this notice is mailed, or 10 days after this notice is personally served upon you, or ten days after the second publication of this notice if you are served by publication. All pleadings must be signed before a notary public or Georgia probate court clerk, and filing fees must be tendered with your pleadings, unless you qualify to file as an indigent party. Contact probate court personnel at the below address/telephone number for the required amount of filing fees.

********* NOTE: If a natural guardian files an objection to the creation of the temporary guardianship, the Petition will be dismissed. If a natural guardian files an objection to the appointment of the petitioner(s) as guardian(s), or if a parent who is not a natural guardian files an objection to the petition, a hearing on the matter (shall be held on ______________ at ___.m. in the Probate Court of ______________ County, courtroom ______________, (address) ______________________, Georgia) (shall be scheduled at a later date).

PROBATE JUDGE

By: ______________________
PROBATE CLERK/DEPUTY CLERK

ADDRESS

TELEPHONE

Effective 7/06 GPCSF 28 Court

CERTIFICATE OF MAILING

I do hereby certify that I have this day mailed a copy of the above citation, petition and order for service to each party to whom the citation is directed who resides outside the State of Georgia at a known current address, in a properly addressed and stamped envelope, by first class mail.

______________________ ______________________

DATE PROBATE CLERK/DEPUTY CLERK

Effective 7/06 GPCSF 28 Court

GEORGIA PROBATE COURT
STANDARD FORM

IN THE PROBATE COURT OF ______________ COUNTY

STATE OF GEORGIA

IN RE: ESTATE OF) ESTATE NO. ______________

______________________________) PETITION FOR TEMPORARY LETTERS
) OF GUARDIANSHIP OF MINOR

______________________________,

MINOR

______________________________,

TEMPORARY GUARDIAN(S)

ORDER

Upon reading and considering the foregoing petition (and selection) and it appearing that each parent has acknowledged and consented to the Petition or been properly served with notice of this proceeding, and no objection having been filed,

IT IS ORDERED that the petitioner(s) be, and hereby is/are, appointed temporary guardian(s) of the above minor, and that temporary letters of guardianship issue to said petitioner(s) upon taking the oath as required by law.

(Initial if applicable:)

____ IT IS FURTHER ORDERED that the temporary guardian(s) shall file a personal status report with the Court annually.

____ IT IS FURTHER ORDERED that this guardianship shall be deemed to be a permanent guardianship for the purposes of the guardian's(s') obtaining medical insurance coverage for the minor because the guardian(s) has/have assumed in writing the obligation to support the minor while the guardianship is in effect to the extent that no other sources of support are available.

SO ORDERED this ________ day of ______________________, 20___.

Probate Judge

Effective 7/06 GPCSF 28 Court

GEORGIA PROBATE COURT
STANDARD FORM

IN THE PROBATE COURT OF ______________ COUNTY

STATE OF GEORGIA

IN RE: ESTATE OF) ESTATE NO. ______________
)
______________________________,) PETITION FOR TEMPORARY LETTERS
MINOR) OF GUARDIANSHIP OF MINOR
)
)
______________________________,)
TEMPORARY GUARDIAN(S))

OATH

I/We do solemnly swear (or affirm) that I/we will well and truly perform the duties required of me/us as temporary guardian(s) of the minor named above.

Sworn to and subscribed before
me this ______ day of ____________, 20___.

____
Temporary Guardian

____
JUDGE/CLERK OF PROBATE COURT

____
Printed Name

Sworn to and subscribed before
me this ______ day of ____________, 20___.

____
Co-Temporary Guardian, if any

____
JUDGE/CLERK OF PROBATE COURT

____
Printed Name

Effective 7/06 GPCSF 28 Court

GEORGIA PROBATE COURT
STANDARD FORM

STATE OF GEORGIA

COUNTY OF ______________________ ESTATE NO.

TEMPORARY LETTERS OF GUARDIANSHIP OF MINOR

From the Judge of the Probate Court of said County.

TO: ____, Guardian(s)

RE: ____, Minor

The above-named minor has been found by this Court to be in need of a guardian, and this Court has entered an order appointing you as such guardian. You have assented to this appointment by taking your oath. In general, your duties as guardian are to protect and maintain the person of the minor.

Special Instructions:

1. It is your duty to see that the minor is adequately fed, clothed, sheltered, educated and cared for, and that the minor receives all necessary medical attention.
2. You must keep the Court informed of any change in your name or address.
3. You should inform the Court of any change of location of the minor.
4. If the Order appointing you requires, you must file an annual Personal Status Report concerning the minor.
5. Please consult your attorney if you have any questions. Your authority to act pursuant to these Letters is subject to applicable statues[1] and to any special orders entered in this case.

(initial if applicable)

____ If initialed, the guardianship shall be deemed a permanent guardianship for the purposes of the guardian's(s') obtaining medical insurance coverage for the minor.

Given under my hand and official seal, the ______ day of ______________, 20___.

Probate Judge

NOTE: The following must be signed if the judge does not sign the original of this document:

Issued by:

PROBATE CLERK/DEPUTY CLERK (Seal)

[1] So in original

Effective 7/06 GPCSF 28 Court

Form adopted effective July 1, 2005; revised effective July 31, 2006.

GPCSF 29 PETITIONER. PETITION FOR LETTERS OF PERMANENT GUARDIANSHIP OF MINOR

GEORGIA PROBATE COURT
STANDARD FORM

Petition for Letters of Permanent Guardianship of Minor

INSTRUCTIONS

I. Specific Instructions

1. This form is to be used for filing a Petition for Letters of Guardianship of a minor by a person, pursuant to O.C.G.A. §29-2-14 when the minor has no natural guardian, testamentary guardian, or permanent guardian.

2. The minor's biological father (father of a minor born out of wedlock who has not legitimated the minor and whose rights regarding the minor have not been surrendered or terminated) is entitled to notice of the filing of the petition and is entitled to object to the Petition and request a continuance in order to legitimate the minor. If he objects, then legitimates the minor, the Petition will be dismissed. If he fails to legitimate the minor, the biological father will have no further rights to receive notice or object to the Petition. O.C.G.A. §29-2-15.

3. The petition should be filed in the county in which a minor is found or in which the proposed permanent guardian is domiciled. In its discretion, the probate court in which the petition is filed may transfer the case to another county in this state, if such transfer would serve the best interest of the minor.

4. The court may require the petitioner to submit additional information concerning the petitioner's qualifications to serve as guardian, in addition to the information required on this standard form.

5. As used in this form, a testamentary guardian is an individual named in a deceased parent's will. A nominated guardian is an individual nominated by a minor's parent to serve as guardian of the minor. A natural guardian, defined pursuant to O.C.G.A. §29-2-3, is each parent, unless the parents are divorced and one parent has sole custody of the minor, in which case the sole custodian is the sole natural guardian. If the parents have joint legal custody, both parents are the natural guardians of the minor.

II. General Instructions

General instructions applicable to all Georgia probate court standard forms appear in Volume 255 of the Georgia Reports and are available in each probate court.

GEORGIA PROBATE COURT
STANDARD FORM

IN THE PROBATE COURT OF ______________ COUNTY

STATE OF GEORGIA

IN RE:) ESTATE NO. ______________

)

________________________________,) PETITION FOR PERMANENT LETTERS
MINOR) OF GUARDIANSHIP OF MINOR

TO THE HONORABLE JUDGE OF THE PROBATE COURT:

The petition of ______________________, a resident of ______________ County, who is domiciled at _____, ______________ County, (state) ______________, whose mailing address is __________________________________, shows:

1.

The minor, ______________________ is domiciled in ______________ County and found in ______________ County, whose age is _____, date of birth is ________.

(initial if applicable)

________ The minor is a citizen of a foreign country, (if a guardianship or conservatorship is granted, pursuant to The Vienna Convention, the Probate Court must notify the consul).

2.

Attached hereto as Exhibit "A" is a copy of the minor's birth certificate.

3.

(initial if applicable)

________a. The minor, being over fourteen years of age, has selected the petitioner(s) to act as guardian(s) as shown by the attached selection.

4.

Said minor has no natural guardian, testamentary guardian, or permanent guardian.

5.

The Petitioner(s) is/are related to the minor as follows: The Petitioner(s) is/are the minor's: ________________________________.

6.

The mother of said minor, ________________________, (initial selection):

_____a. has had her parental rights terminated by court order, a copy of which is attached as exhibit "B," and is domiciled at

_____b. is deceased, and a copy of her death certificate is attached as exhibit "B."

7.

(initial and complete either a. or b.:)

_____a. The minor was born during a marriage. The father of the minor, ________________________, (initial selection):

_____(i) has had his parental rights terminated by court order, a copy of which is attached as exhibit "C," and is domiciled at: __________

_____(ii) is deceased, and a copy of his death certificate is attached as exhibit "C."

_____b. The minor was born out of wedlock. The biological father of the minor is ________________________ and his address is: ____________

and he (initial all applicable)

_____(i) has had his parental rights terminated by Court order, a copy of which is attached as exhibit "C."

_____(ii) has not legitimated the minor

_____(iii) is deceased.

_____(iv) is a registrant on the putative father registry who has acknowledged paternity; has indicated possible paternity of the minor's sibling born two years prior to this minor's date of birth; or has lived with the minor, contributed to the minor's support, made an attempt to legitimate the minor, or provided support or medical care for the minor's mother during her pregnancy or hospitalization during delivery.

8.

(initial if applicable)

______ There is a notarized or witnessed document, attached as exhibit "______," executed by a parent of the minor which addresses guardianship of the minor. That document nominates ____________________, whose address is ____________________, ________ County, as guardian.

9.

Regarding a conservator appointed for the minor (initial all that apply):

______a. No conservator has been appointed for the minor.

______b. There has been a conservator appointed for the minor, being ____________________ whose address is ____________________.

______c. There is a Petition for Conservatorship of the minor pending before the ____________ County Probate Court.

10.

The minor has (initial relevant paragraph):

______a. the following adult siblings (list up to three)

Name Address Telephone No.

______b. if no adult siblings, the following grandparents (list up to three)

Name Address Telephone No.

______c. if no adult siblings or grandparents, the following three nearest adult relatives of the minor:

Name Address Telephone No.

11.

The minor is entitled to personal property with a value of ______________ and real property with a value of ______________ by reason of ______________. The following reasonable sums of property are needed for the minor's support: $______________ per month.

12.

The Petitioner(s) (initial a. or b.)

______a. is/are seeking expanded powers under O.C.G.A. §29-2-22, and therefore moves the Court to appoint a guardian ad litem for the minor and set a hearing on the matter.

______b. is/are not seeking expanded powers under O.C.G.A. §29-2-22.

13.

If there is: (1) a court-appointed temporary guardian or a petition to appoint one pending; (2) another individual with court-ordered custody or guardianship; or (3) another individual with physical custody of the minor, provide the individual's(s') name(s), age(s) (or over 18), telephone number(s), address(es), nature of nomination or appointment, and court:

14.

Additional Data: Where full particulars are lacking, state the reasons for any such omission. Also, state all pertinent facts which may govern the method of giving notice to any party and which may determine whether or not a guardian ad litem should be appointed for any party.

WHEREFORE, petitioner(s) pray(s) that
1. ___ any required service be perfected and
2. petitioner(s) be appointed guardian(s) of the minor named above.

______________________ Signature of first petitioner	______________________ Signature of second petitioner, if any
______________________ Printed Name	______________________ Printed Name
______________________ Address	______________________ Address
______________________	______________________
______________________ Telephone Number	______________________ Telephone Number

Signature of Attorney: ______________________

Typed/printed name of Attorney: ______________________
Address: ______________________
Telephone: ____________ State Bar # ______________

VERIFICATION

GEORGIA, ______________________ COUNTY

Personally appeared before me the undersigned petitioner(s) who on oath state(s) that the facts set forth in the foregoing petition are true.

Sworn to and subscribed before
me this _____ day of ___________, 20___.

____
First Petitioner

______________________ ______________________
NOTARY/CLERK OF PROBATE COURT Printed Name

Sworn to and subscribed before
me this _____ day of ___________, 20___.

____
Second Petitioner, if any

______________________ ______________________
NOTARY/CLERK OF PROBATE COURT Printed Name

IN THE PROBATE COURT OF ______________ COUNTY

STATE OF GEORGIA

IN RE:) ESTATE NO. ________
)
______________________________,) PETITION FOR PERMANENT LETTERS
MINOR) OF GUARDIANSHIP OF MINOR

SELECTION BY MINOR IF AGED 14 OR OLDER

I, the undersigned minor resident of ______________ County select ____________________________ to be appointed guardian(s) of my person, this ______ day of ______________, 20____.

Signature of Minor

Printed Name

ACKNOWLEDGMENT OF SERVICE

IN RE: ESTATE OF ______________________ ESTATE NO. ________

We the undersigned being adult relatives and/or nominated designees as guardian(s) of the above minor hereby acknowledge service of a copy of the petition; waive further service and notice; and hereby consent to the appointment of the petitioner(s) as permanent guardian(s) of said minor.

SIGNATURE(S)

Sworn to and subscribed before me this ______ day of ____________, 20___. ________

______________________________ ______________________________

NOTARY/CLERK OF PROBATE COURT Printed Name

Sworn to and subscribed before me this ______ day of ____________, 20___. ________

______________________________ ______________________________

NOTARY/CLERK OF PROBATE COURT Printed Name

Sworn to and subscribed before me this ______ day of ____________, 20___. ________

______________________________ ______________________________

NOTARY/CLERK OF PROBATE COURT Printed Name

Sworn to and subscribed before me this ______ day of ____________, 20___. ________

______________________________ ______________________________

NOTARY/CLERK OF PROBATE COURT Printed Name

Sworn to and subscribed before me this ______ day of ____________, 20___. ________

______________________________ ______________________________

NOTARY/CLERK OF PROBATE COURT Printed Name

Instructions and form adopted effective July, 1989; revised effective July 1, 1992; July 1, 1995; July 1, 2005; July 31, 2006.

GPCSF 29 COURT. COURT FORMS FOR PETITION FOR PERMANENT LETTERS OF GUARDIANSHIP OF MINOR

GEORGIA PROBATE COURT
STANDARD FORM

Petition for Permanent Letters of Guardianship of Minor

NOTICE: UNLESS OTHERWISE DIRECTED BY THE COURT, THE FOLLOWING FORMS ARE FOR PROBATE COURT STAFF TO COMPLETE

GEORGIA PROBATE COURT
STANDARD FORM

PROBATE COURT OF __________ COUNTY

STATE OF GEORGIA

IN RE:) ESTATE NO. __________
______________________________,)
MINOR) PETITION FOR THE APPOINTMENT
) OF A GUARDIAN OF A MINOR
______________________________,)
PETITIONER(S))

ORDER FOR SERVICE, HEARING, AND APPOINTMENT OF GUARDIAN AD LITEM
(INITIAL ONE OR MORE OF THE FOLLOWING:)

______a. It appearing that the minor being born out of wedlock, the biological father of the minor is entitled to notice, therefore, IT IS ORDERED that citation issue and be served personally, if he resides in Georgia, by first class mail if he resides outside Georgia. or by publication if his address is unknown once per week for two weeks in the newspaper in this county in which sheriff's advertisements are published, together with a copy of the petition and this order, on said biological father.

______b. It appearing that one or more of the nearest adult relatives of the minor or one or more of the nominated guardian(s) residing *in* Georgia listed in the petition has/have not acknowledged service, IT IS ORDERED that citation issue and be served personally, together with a copy of the petition and this order, on each of the nearest adult blood relatives or nominated testamentary or permanent guardian(s) listed in the petition who has not acknowledged service.

______c. It appearing that one or more of the nearest adult relatives of the minor or one or more of the nominated testamentary or permanent guardian(s) residing *outside* Georgia listed in the petition has not acknowledged service, IT IS ORDERED that citation issue and be served by first class mail, together with a copy of the petition and this order, on each of the nearest adult blood relatives or nominated testamentary or permanent guardian(s) listed in the petition who has not acknowledged service.

______d. It appearing that the address of one or more of the adult relative(s) of the minor is unknown, IT IS ORDERED that citation issue and be published once per week for two weeks in the newspaper in this county in which sheriffs advertisements are published.

______e. The petitioner(s) seeking enhanced powers pursuant to O.C.G.A. §29-2-22(b), IT IS ORDERED that ______________________ is appointed guardian ad litem for the above minor. The clerk/deputy clerk shall serve said guardian ad litem with a copy of this Order and the above Petition. Upon said guardian ad litem's acceptance of same, said guardian ad litem shall make answer thereto.

IT IS FURTHER ORDERED that a hearing on the matter shall be held in this Probate Court in __________ County, courtroom __________, (address) ______________________________, Georgia on ____________________, 20___ at ______ o'clock ___m.

SO ORDERED this ________ day of ______________, 20___.

Probate Judge

Effective 7/06 GPCSF 29 Court

CITATION TO BIOLOGICAL FATHER

GEORGIA, ______________________ COUNTY ESTATE NO. ________

PROBATE COURT OF ______________________ COUNTY

Date of Mailing, or date of second publication:

TO: ____, biological father of ____, a minor: ____, Petitioner(s) has/have applied to be appointed permanent guardian(s) of the above minor

(initial if applicable)

________ and is/are seeking additional powers set forth in O.C.G.A. §29-2-22(b).

If you have any objection to the granting of this petition, you must: 1) file a written objection setting forth the grounds of any such objection with this Court within 14 days of the date you are personally served; the date that notice was mailed to you; or the day following the date of the second publication of this citation, AND you must 2) file a petition to legitimate the minor within 30 days of the hearing on your objection. If you fail to file a petition for legitimation within 30 days or your petition is dismissed for failure to prosecute, or if an order issues on your petition which does not name you as the father of the minor, you will have no further rights to receive notice or object to the appointment of a permanent guardian for the minor. All pleadings must be signed before a notary public or probate court clerk, and filing fees must be tendered with your pleadings, unless you qualify to file as an indigent party. Contact probate court personnel at the below address/telephone number for the required amount of filing fees. A hearing on this Petition shall be held in the Probate Court of ____________ County, courtroom ____________, (address) ________________________________, Georgia on ______________________, 20____ at ________ o'clock ____m.

PROBATE JUDGE

By:
PROBATE CLERK/DEPUTY CLERK

ADDRESS

TELEPHONE

CITATION TO INTERESTED PARTIES

GEORGIA, ____________________ COUNTY ESTATE NO. ________

PROBATE COURT OF ____________________ COUNTY

TO: (WHOM IT MAY CONCERN) AND (____________________)
____________________, Petitioner(s) has/have applied to be appointed permanent guardian(s) of ____________________, a minor:
Date of Second Publication, if any: __________ Date of Mailing, if any: ________
(initial if applicable)
________ and is/are seeking additional powers set forth in O.C.G.A. §29-2-22(b).

If you have any objection to either the establishment of a permanent guardianship, or to the selection of the Petitioner(s) as permanent guardians, or both, you must file a written objection setting forth the grounds of any such objection with this Court within ten days of the date you are personally served; or within 14 days of the date that notice was mailed to you; or within 10 days following the date of the second publication of this citation. All pleadings must be signed before a notary public or probate court clerk, and filing fees must be tendered with your pleadings, unless you qualify to file as an indigent party. Contact probate court personnel at the below address/telephone number for the required amount of filing fees. A hearing on this Petition shall be held in this Probate Court in __________ County, courtroom __________, (address) ____________________, Georgia on ________________, 20___ at _____ o'clock ___m.

PROBATE JUDGE

By:
PROBATE CLERK/DEPUTY CLERK

ADDRESS

TELEPHONE

Effective 7/06 GPCSF 29 Court

CERTIFICATE OF MAILING OF CITATION TO BIOLOGICAL FATHER

ESTATE NO.

This is to certify that I have this day served the biological father of the minor who resides outside Georgia, who was ordered to be served by first-class mail, with a copy of the petition, order, and citation, by placing a copy of same in an envelope addressed to him and depositing same in the U.S. Mail, first-class, with adequate postage thereon.

____________________ ________________________________

DATE PROBATE CLERK/DEPUTY CLERK

CERTIFICATE OF MAILING OF CITATION TO INTERESTED PARTIES

ESTATE NO.

This is to certify that I have this day served the interested party(ies) shown in paragraph 10 of the petitioner who reside(s) outside Georgia, who was/were ordered to be served by first-class mail, with a copy of the petition, order, and citation, by placing a copy of same in an envelope addressed to each and depositing same in the U.S. Mail, first-class, with adequate postage thereon.

____________________ ________________________________

DATE PROBATE CLERK/DEPUTY CLERK

PROBATE COURT OF ____________ COUNTY

STATE OF GEORGIA

IN RE:) ESTATE NO.
________________________________,)
MINOR) PETITION FOR THE APPOINTMENT
) OF A GUARDIAN OF A MINOR
________________________________,)
PETITIONER(S))

ORDER

Upon reading and considering the foregoing petition and it appearing that:

1.

there is no guardian of the minor, and notice was served upon the required adult relatives of the minor, and the biological father of the minor, if any, according to law, and no interested party has objected, and that:

2.

the following individual(s), being ____ ____________________, should be named as permanent guardian(s), who was/were selected because she/he/they petitioned to be appointed, and no objections to the appointment have been made, and it appears to be in the best interest of the minor that said individual(s) be appointed,

3.

(initial if applicable)
__________ and the minor, being fourteen years of age or older, selecting the petitioner(s) as guardian,

THEREFORE IT IS ORDERED that ____ ________________________________, be, and hereby is/are, appointed permanent guardian(s) of the minor named above and that letters of guardianship issue to him/her/them upon taking the oath (and posting bond in the amount of ______________), as required by law.

(initial if applicable)

_____a. IT IS FURTHER ORDERED that, no objection being filed by the guardian ad litem and notice being provided according to law, the guardian(s) shall have the following powers set forth in O.C.G.A. §29-2-22(b) (initial all applicable):

_____(i) to establish the minor's place of dwelling outside this state;

_____(ii) to change the jurisdiction of the guardianship to another Georgia county which is the county of the minor's place of dwelling;

_____(iii) to change the domicile of the minor to the minor's or guardian's place of dwelling based on the tax ramifications and the succession and inheritance rights of the minor and other parties;

_____(iv) to consent to the marriage of the minor;

_____(v) to receive reasonable compensation from the estate of the minor for services rendered to the minor;

_____(vi) if there is no conservator appointed for the minor, to disclaim or renounce property or interest in property of the minor in accordance with O.C.G.A. §53-1-20;

_____b. IT IS FURTHER ORDERED that, since the permanent guardian is not the conservator or there is not a conservator; the guardian(s) shall be permitted to utilize from the ward's property $_____________________ per month to provide adequately for the minor's support, care, education, health, and welfare, unless further Ordered by this Court.

IT IS FURTHER ORDERED that the guardian(s) shall promptly disclose to the Court any conflict of interest between himself/herself/themselves and the minor when such conflict of interest arises or becomes known to the guardian(s).

IT IS FURTHER ORDERED that the guardian(s) shall file personal status reports as required by law.

SO ORDERED this ________ day of ____________________, 20___.

Probate Judge

PROBATE COURT OF ______________ COUNTY

STATE OF GEORGIA

IN RE:	)	ESTATE NO. ______________
	)	
______________________________,	)	
MINOR	)	PETITION FOR THE APPOINTMENT
	)	OF A GUARDIAN OF A MINOR
______________________________,	)	
PETITIONER(S)	)	

OATH

I do solemnly swear (or affirm) that I will well and truly perform the duties required of me as guardian of the minor named above and faithfully account to my ward for my ward's estate.

Sworn to and subscribed before me this _____ day of ____________, 20___.

____
Guardian

____
JUDGE/CLERK OF PROBATE COURT

____
Printed Name

Sworn to and subscribed before me this _____ day of ____________, 20___.

____
Co-Guardian, if any

____
JUDGE/CLERK OF PROBATE COURT

____
Printed Name

GEORGIA PROBATE COURT
STANDARD FORM

STATE OF GEORGIA

COUNTY OF ______________________ ESTATE NO. ____________

LETTERS OF PERMANENT GUARDIANSHIP OF MINOR

From the Judge of the Probate Court of said County.

TO: ______________________________________, Guardian(s)

RE: ______________________________________, Minor

The above-named minor has been found by this Court to be in need of a guardian, and this Court has entered an order designating you as such guardian(s). You have assented to this appointment by taking your oath. In general, your duties as guardian are to protect and maintain the person of the minor and your power over the minor shall be the same as that of a parent over a child, the guardian(s) standing in place of the parent(s). A guardian shall at all times act as a fiduciary in the minor's best interest and exercise reasonable care, diligence, and prudence.

Special Instructions:

1. It is your duty to see that the minor is adequately fed, clothed, sheltered, educated, and cared for, and that the minor receives all necessary medical attention.
2. You must keep the Court informed of any change in your name or address.
3. You should inform the Court of any change of location of your minor.
4. You shall, within 60 days of appointment and within 60 days after each anniversary date of appointment, file with this Court and provide to the conservator of the minor, if any, a personal status report concerning the minor.
5. You shall promptly notify the court of any conflict of interest which may arise between you as guardian and the minor pursuant to O.C.G.A. §29-2-23.
6. The guardianship automatically terminates when the minor dies, reaches age 18, is adopted, or is emancipated.
7. You shall act in coordination and cooperation with the minor's conservator, if appointed, or if not, with others who have custody of the minor's property.
8. Please consult your attorney if you have any questions. Your authority to act pursuant to these Letters is subject to applicable statues[1] and to any special orders entered in this case.

Given under my hand and official seal, this ________ day of ____________________, 20___.

Probate Judge

NOTE: The following must be signed if the judge does not sign the original of this document:

Issued by:

____

PROBATE CLERK/DEPUTY CLERK (Seal)

[1] So in original

Effective 7/06 GPCSF 29 Court

Form adopted effective July 1, 2005; revised effective July 31, 2006.

GPCSF 30 PETITIONER. PETITION FOR LETTERS OF CONSERVATORSHIP OF MINOR

GEORGIA PROBATE COURT
STANDARD FORM

Petition for Letters of Conservatorship of Minor

INSTRUCTIONS

I. Specific Instructions

1. This form is to be used for filing a Petition for Letters of Conservatorship of Minor, with Bond, in the following situations:

   (a) A doubtful claim is being compromised by a natural guardian and the net settlement amount is more than $15,000.00. A natural guardian, defined pursuant to O.C.G.A. §29-2-3, is each parent, unless the parents are divorced and one parent has sole custody of the minor, in which case the sole custodian is the sole natural guardian. If the parents have joint legal custody, both parents are the natural guardians of the minor.

   (b) All other cases where a minor is receiving property which requires management by a conservator.

2. The court may require the petitioner to submit additional information concerning the petitioner's qualifications to serve as conservator, in addition to the information required on this standard form.

II. General Instructions

General instructions applicable to all Georgia probate court standard forms appear in Volume 255 of the Georgia Reports and are available in each probate court.

GEORGIA PROBATE COURT
STANDARD FORM

PROBATE COURT OF ________ COUNTY

STATE OF GEORGIA

IN RE:	)	ESTATE NO.
	)	
______________________________,	)	PETITION FOR LETTERS OF
MINOR	)	CONSERVATORSHIP OF MINOR

TO THE HONORABLE JUDGE OF THE PROBATE COURT:

1.

The Petition of ____________________, who is/are domiciled in ______________ county, and moves this Court to appoint a conservator/conservators for the above minor, age ______, whose date of birth is __________, whose social security number is ______________; and who is found at (address) ____________________ in ______________ County, Georgia,

(initial if applicable)

________ and who is a citizen of a foreign country, ______________(if a guardianship or conservatorship is granted, pursuant to The Vienna Convention, the Probate Court must notify the consul)

shows:

2.

Said minor is entitled to personal/real property with the approximate value of $______________ by reason of ____.

3.

Petitioner(s) move(s) the Court to appoint ____________________ as conservator(s), who is/are related to the minor as follows: ____________________ and who is/are domiciled at ______________________________, ______________ County, Georgia;

4.

(Initial if applicable:)

________ There is a notarized or witnessed document made by a parent of the minor that deals with the conservatorship of the minor, and the nominated conservator is ______________________________ whose address and telephone number are ____.

5.

Excluding the petitioner(s) and nominated conservator(s), the minor's nearest relatives whose whereabouts are known are as follows: (show parents whose rights have not been terminated; if none, adult siblings of the minor; if none, the grandparents of the minor; if none, any nearest relatives of the minor so that three individuals are named)

Name	Address	Telephone No.	Relationship to Minor
a.			
b.			
c.			

6.

Other than the assets shown in paragraph 2, the minor currently has the following assets (or "none"):
______________________________; has/will have the following income:
______________________________; has/will have the following sources of funds:
______________________________; and the following liabilities and expenses:
______________________________. The minor has an interest in real property located in ______________ County(ies), ______________.

7.

The proposed conservator(s) has/have the following financial interest in relation to the minor's estate: ______________________________; (i.e. joint ownership of property or any other type of financial interest in the minor's property or "n/a").

8.

The petitioner(s) request(s) that the proposed conservator(s) be granted the following powers pursuant to O.C.G.A. §29-3-22 (b) (initial those requested, and provide the reasons for the request below):

_______a. to invest the minor's property other than as authorized in Code Section 29-3-32 without further court approval in the following investments ______________________________;

_______b. to sell, rent, lease, exchange, or otherwise dispose of any or all of the minor's real or personal property without complying with the provisions of Code Section 29-3-35, other than the provisions for additional bond set forth in subsection (c) of Code Section 29-3-35;

_______c. to continue the operation of any farm or business in which the minor has an interest.

These powers are sought because ____.

9.

The petitioner(s) request(s) that a guardian ad litem be appointed because the following powers pursuant to O.C.G.A. §29-3-22 (c) are sought: ______________________

10.

A surety bond in the amount of $____________ issued by (name of surety) ______________________________ (agent's name, address, and telephone number) ______________________________ is being filed as part of this Petition or will be provided to the Court prior to the issuance of Letters of Conservatorship.

11.

Regarding a guardian appointed for the minor (initial all that apply):

______a. No guardian has been appointed for the minor.

______b. There has been a guardian appointed for the minor, being ______________________________ whose address is ____

______c. There is a Petition for Guardianship of the minor pending before the ______________ County Probate Court.

12.

Additional Data: Where full particulars are lacking, state here the reasons for any such omission.

WHEREFORE, petitioner(s) pray(s) that
1. said bond be duly filed, accepted and recorded.
2. service be perfected as required by law; and
3. the nominated conservator(s) be vested with authority as conservator(s) of said minor.

______________________	______________________
Signature of first petitioner	Signature of second petitioner, if any
______________________	______________________
Printed Name	Printed Name
______________________	______________________
Address	Address
______________________	______________________
______________________	______________________
Telephone Number	Telephone Number

Signature of Attorney: ______________________

Typed/printed name of Attorney: ______________________
Address: ______________________

Telephone: ______________ State Bar # ______________________

VERIFICATION

GEORGIA, ______________________ COUNTY

Personally appeared before me the undersigned petitioner(s) who on oath state(s) that the facts set forth in the foregoing petition are true.

Sworn to and subscribed before
me this _____ day of __________, 20___.

____
First Petitioner

____
NOTARY/CLERK OF PROBATE COURT

____
Printed Name

Sworn to and subscribed before
me this _____ day of __________, 20___.

____
Second Petitioner, if any

____
NOTARY/CLERK OF PROBATE COURT

____
Printed Name

PROBATE COURT OF ______________ COUNTY

STATE OF GEORGIA

IN RE:) ESTATE NO. ______________

)

______________________________,) PETITION FOR LETTERS OF

MINOR) CONSERVATORSHIP OF MINOR

SELECTION

I, the undersigned minor, being 14 years of age or older and a resident of __________ County, select __________ to be appointed my conservator(s), this __________ day of __________________, 20___.

Signature of Minor if age 14 or over

Printed Name

ACKNOWLEDGMENT OF SERVICE AND ASSENT TO PETITION FOR APPOINTMENT OF CONSERVATOR

IN RE: ESTATE OF ______________________________ ESTATE NO. __________

We, the undersigned, being over 18 years of age, laboring under no legal disability and being interested persons named in the foregoing Petition, hereby acknowledge service of a copy of the petition, waive further service and notice, and hereby assent to the appointment of the nominated conservator(s) for the above minor without further delay.

SIGNATURE OF INTERESTED PERSON

Sworn to and subscribed before
me this _____ day of ___________, 20___. ______________________________

______________________________ ______________________________
NOTARY/CLERK OF PROBATE COURT Printed Name

Sworn to and subscribed before
me this _____ day of ___________, 20___. ______________________________

______________________________ ______________________________
NOTARY/CLERK OF PROBATE COURT Printed Name

Sworn to and subscribed before
me this _____ day of ___________, 20___. ______________________________

______________________________ ______________________________
NOTARY/CLERK OF PROBATE COURT Printed Name

Effective 7/06 –6– GPCSF 30 Petitioner

Instructions and form adopted effective July, 1989; revised effective July 1, 1995; July 1, 2005; July 31, 2006.

GPCSF 30 COURT. COURT FORMS FOR LETTERS OF CONSERVATORSHIP OF MINOR

GEORGIA PROBATE COURT
STANDARD FORM

Petition for Letters of Conservatorship of Minor

NOTICE: UNLESS OTHERWISE DIRECTED BY THE COURT, THESE FORMS ARE FOR PROBATE COURT COMPLETION

GEORGIA PROBATE COURT
STANDARD FORM

IN THE PROBATE COURT OF ______________ COUNTY

STATE OF GEORGIA

IN RE:	)	ESTATE NO. ____________
	)	
______________________________,	)	PETITION FOR LETTERS OF
MINOR	)	CONSERVATORSHIP OF MINOR

ORDER FOR SERVICE OF NOTICE AND APPOINTMENT OF GUARDIAN AD LITEM

The foregoing petition for Letters of Conservatorship having been filed, and it appearing that the following interested parties did not acknowledge service, it is ORDERED that notice be served on the individuals listed in paragraphs 4 and 5 of the Petition:

(Initial any and all of the following which apply:)

______a. Notice must be served personally on the following individual(s) who reside in Georgia: ______________________________

______b. Notice must be served by first class mail, at least 14 days before the Petition can be granted, on the following individual(s) who reside outside this state at a known address: ______________________________

______c. Notice must be served by publication once per week for two weeks in the newspaper in this county in which sheriff's advertisements are published to the following individuals, whose addresses are unknown: ______________

______d. IT IS FURTHER ORDERED that, powers being sought pursuant to O.C.G.A. §29-3-22(c), ______________________ is appointed guardian ad litem for the above minor. The clerk/deputy clerk shall serve said guardian ad litem with a copy of this Order and the above Petition. Upon said guardian ad litem's acceptance of same, said guardian ad litem shall make answer hereto.

SO ORDERED this ______ day of ____________, 20___.

Probate Judge

Effective 7/06

GPCSF 30 Court

NOTICE

PROBATE COURT OF ______________________ COUNTY ESTATE NO. ____________

RE: PETITION FOR LETTERS OF CONSERVATORSHIP OF ______________________
______________________________, A MINOR, WITH BOND

Date of Second Publication, if any: ________ Date of Mailing, if any: ______________

(initial applicable):

______a. TO: (all interested persons having known addresses outside this state to be served by first class mail)

____This is to notify you to file objection, if there is any, either to the establishment of the conservatorship or to the selection of the identified individual as conservator or both, in this Court on or before the fourteenth (14th) day after ____________, 20____ (the date of the mailing of this Notice to you by first class mail);.

______b. TO: (all interested persons who reside in Georgia to be served personally) __________

____This is to notify you to file objection, if there is any, either to the establishment of the conservatorship or to the selection of the identified individual as conservator or both, in this Court on or before the tenth (10th) day after the date you are personally served.

______c. TO: (all interested persons whose addresses are unknown) ______________________

____This is to notify you to file objection, if there is any, either to the establishment of the conservatorship or to the selection of the identified individual as conservator or both, within 10 days following the date of the second publication of this citation.

BE NOTIFIED FURTHER: All pleadings must be signed before a notary public or probate court clerk, and filing fees must be tendered with your pleadings; unless you qualify to file as an indigent party. Contact probate court personnel at the below address/phone number for the required amount of filing fees. If an objection is filed, a hearing will be (held in the Probate Court of ______________ County, courtroom __________, (address) ______________________________, Georgia on __________ at ______ o'clock ____.m.) (scheduled at a later date). If no objection is filed, the petition may be granted without a hearing.

PROBATE JUDGE
By: ______________________________
PROBATE CLERK/DEPUTY CLERK

ADDRESS

TELEPHONE

PROBATE COURT OF ______________ COUNTY

STATE OF GEORGIA

IN RE:) ESTATE NO. ______________
)
______________,) PETITION FOR LETTERS OF
MINOR) CONSERVATORSHIP OF MINOR
______________,)
CONSERVATOR(S))

ORDER

The petition for Letters of Conservatorship of Minor having been read and considered, and it appearing that the facts stated therein are true, and that it is in the best interest of the minor to appoint the above conservator(s),

IT IS ORDERED that ______________ be vested with all the authority as Conservator(s) of said minor, to receive the minor's estate and manage it according to law and that Letters of Conservatorship issue upon the taking of the prescribed oath and upon the posting of bond in the amount of $__________. Said Conservator(s) should be appointed because ______________. The appointed conservator(s) shall have no authority to act on behalf of the ward until Letters of Conservatorship have issued.

IT IS FURTHER ORDERED that the Conservator(s) requested and shall have the following powers pursuant to O.C.G.A. §29-3-22(b): (initial those applicable)

______a. to invest the minor's property in the following investments, being investments other than those authorized in Code Section 29-3-32 without further court approval: ______;

______b. to sell, rent, lease, exchange, or otherwise dispose of the minor's following real or personal property without complying with the provisions of Code Section 29-3-35, other than the provisions for additional bond set forth in subsection (c) of Code Section 2-3-35: ______________;

______c. to continue the operation of the following farm or business in which the minor has an interest: ______________.

and after notice to the appointed guardian ad litem, the following powers pursuant to O.C.G.A. §29-3-22(c) (initial all applicable):

______a. to make disbursements that exceed the annual income or, if applicable, the annual budget amount which has been approved by the court pursuant to Code Section 29-3-30 by no more than $________ **per (month)(year)** for the support, care, education, health, and welfare of the minor; **subject to subsequent court order.**

______b. to enter into contracts for labor or services, being ____________, for which the compensation payable under the contracts when combined with other disbursements from the estate exceeds the annual income or, if applicable, the annual budget amount which has been approved by the court pursuant to Code Section 29-3-30;

______c. to compromise a contested or doubtful claim for or against the minor pursuant to the provisions of Code Section 29-3-3, being a claim made by/against ________;

______d. to release ____________, a debtor and compromise a debt when the collection of the debt is doubtful;

______e. to establish or add the following property to a trust for the benefit of the minor pursuant to Code Section 29-3-22: ____________________;

______f. to disclaim or renounce any property or interest in the following property of the minor in accordance with the provisions of Code Section 53-1-20 of the Revised Probate Code of 1998: ____________________;

______g. to engage in estate planning for the minor pursuant to the provisions of Code Section 29-3-36.

(initial if applicable:)

______ **IT IS FURTHER ORDERED** that, within 30 days of the date hereof, the clerk/deputy clerk shall file the certificate of creation of conservatorship in accordance with O.C.G.A. §29-3-10(b) with the Clerk of Superior Court of each county in this state in which the ward owns real property.

IT IS FURTHER ORDERED that the Conservator(s) shall:

1. keep the minor's funds separate from his/her/their own;
2. not sell or give away any of the minor's property without a court order;
3. not spend any of the minor's funds for any purpose except as set forth in the Court-approved budget;

4. file with this Court a management plan; an inventory of the minor's funds within two months of the date the Letters of Conservatorship issue; and an annual return within 60 days after each anniversary date of the issuance of Letters of Conservatorship, unless the Court has approved a different accounting period;
5. turn over to the minor any of the minor's property in his/her/their possession when the minor reaches 18;
6. not use the minor's funds for his/her/their own benefit;
7. keep the Court informed of any changes in his/her/their name(s), address(es), or the location of the minor;
8. not place his/her/their name(s) on the title of any funds and/or accounts belonging to the minor unless he/she/they specifically is/are designated in the title of the account as conservator(s) of the minor;
9. shall promptly disclose to the Court any conflict of interest between the conservator(s) and the minor when such conflict of interest arises or becomes known to the conservator(s).
10. keep accurate records, including adequate supporting data, as required by law.

(initial if applicable)

______ IT IS FURTHER ORDERED that the conservator(s) is/are authorized to spend or deliver to the guardian(s) of the minor the sum of $__________ per month for the benefit of the minor.

SO ORDERED this __________ day of ________________________, 20____.

Probate Judge

Probate Court Return Mailing Address:

CERTIFICATE OF CREATION OF CONSERVATORSHIP

(Pursuant to O.C.G.A. §29-3-10(b))

GEORGIA, ______________________________ County

PROBATE ESTATE NO.

DATE ORDER ISSUED:

GRANTOR: (NAME OF MINOR)

GRANTEE: (NAME OF CONSERVATOR(S) OF ABOVE MINOR)

A Conservatorship has been created for the above-named minor.

The minor attains the age of majority on __________ at which time the conservatorship shall automatically terminate.

Original Certificate delivered or mailed to Clerk of Superior Court of _______________ County on _______________, 20___.

I do hereby certify that the above information is based on the Order of the Probate Court issued on the date set out above and that the above information is true and correct.

By: ____
PROBATE CLERK/DEPUTY CLERK

Effective 7/06 GPCSF 30 Court

GEORGIA PROBATE COURT
STANDARD FORM

IN THE PROBATE COURT OF ________________ COUNTY

STATE OF GEORGIA

IN RE:) ESTATE NO. ________________________
)
____,) PETITION FOR LETTERS OF
MINOR) CONSERVATORSHIP OF MINOR

OATH

I do solemnly swear (or affirm) that I will well and truly perform the duties required of me as conservator of the minor named above, and faithfully account to my ward for my ward's estate.

Sworn to and subscribed before
me this ______ day of ____________, 20___.

____
Conservator

____
JUDGE/CLERK OF PROBATE COURT

____
Printed Name

Sworn to and subscribed before
me this ______ day of ____________, 20___.

____
Co-Conservator, if any

____
JUDGE/CLERK OF PROBATE COURT

____
Printed Name

Effective 7/06 GPCSF 30 Court

GEORGIA PROBATE COURT
STANDARD FORM

STATE OF GEORGIA

COUNTY OF ______________________ ESTATE NO. ______________

LETTERS OF CONSERVATORSHIP OF MINOR

From the Judge of the Probate Court of said County.

TO: ______________________________________, Conservator(s)

RE: ______________________________________, Minor

The above-named minor has been found by this Court to be in need of a conservator, and this Court has entered an order designating you as such conservator(s). You have assented to this appointment by taking your oath and posting bond. In general, your duties as conservator(s) are to protect and maintain the property of the above-named minor. Your authority to act pursuant to these Letters is subject to applicable statues[1] and to any special orders entered in this case.

Please consult your attorney if you have any questions.

Given under my hand and official seal, this ________ day of ____________________, 20___.

Probate Judge

Note: The following must be signed if the judge does not sign the original of this document:

Issued by:

____

PROBATE CLERK/DEPUTY CLERK (Seal)

[1] So in original

Effective 7/06 GPCSF 30 Court

Form adopted effective July 1, 2005; revised effective July 31, 2006.

GPCSF 31. [Reserved]

GPCSF 32 PETITIONER. PETITION BY PERSONAL REPRESENTATIVE FOR WAIVER OF BOND AND/OR GRANT OF CERTAIN POWERS

GEORGIA PROBATE COURT
STANDARD FORM

Petition by Personal Representative for Waiver of Bond and/or Grant of Certain Powers

INSTRUCTIONS

I. Specific Instructions

1. This form is to be used by an administrator or executor who has already been appointed when filing a petition for waiver of bond and/or grant of certain powers pursuant to O.C.G.A. §53-7-1(b).

2. Unanimous consent of the heirs to the administrator's petition is required, or the beneficiaries if the decedent died testate. O.C.G.A. §53-11-2 provides that a party to a probate court proceeding concerning a decedent's estate who is unborn or unknown or is not sui juris must be represented by a guardian, provided that the court may appoint a guardian ad litem or determine that the natural guardian, guardian of the person or property, or testamentary guardian has no conflict and may serve. (See GPCSF 16). For purposes of the consent required, with respect to any heir who is not sui juris, such consent may be given by such guardian. The personal representative of a deceased heir is authorized to consent on behalf of that heir.

3. Notice must be published once a week for four weeks.

4. The relief sought in this petition and provided in the order is not retroactive.

5. If bond has been posted, and waiver of bond is sought for the future, check with the bonding compan(y)(ies) to obtain the necessary bond description to be placed in the petition and order and to coordinate this matter with the bonding compan(y)(ies).

II. General Instructions

General instructions applicable to all Georgia probate court standard forms are available in each probate court.

GEORGIA PROBATE COURT
STANDARD FORM

IN THE PROBATE COURT OF ____________ COUNTY

STATE OF GEORGIA

IN RE: ESTATE OF	)	ESTATE NO. ____________
	)	
______________________________,	)	PETITION BY PERSONAL
	)	REPRESENTATIVE FOR
DECEASED	)	WAIVER OF BOND
	)	AND/OR GRANT OF
	)	CERTAIN POWERS

TO THE HONORABLE JUDGE OF THE PROBATE COURT:

The petition of __________, duly qualified personal representative(s) of the estate of ______________________, deceased, shows:

1.

Petitioner(s) was/were issued letters of administration/letters testamentary concerning the above-referenced estate by this Court on __________.

2.

Listed below are all of the names, ages, addresses of the heirs of the decedent if he/she died intestate, and the beneficiaries listed in the decedent's Will, if he/she died testate, and relationship to decedent:

Name	Age (or over 18) Relationship	Address

3.

All of the heirs/beneficiaries have consented that the judge of the probate court may waive the bond and/or grant certain powers as set forth in the Consent of Heirs/Beneficiaries attached hereto.

4.

WHEREFORE petitioner(s) pray(s) that the Court grant the relief requested in the Consent of Heirs/Beneficiaries attached hereto.

_______________________	_______________________
Signature of first petitioner	Signature of second petitioner if any
_______________________	_______________________
Printed Name	Printed Name
_______________________	_______________________
Address	Address
_______________________	_______________________
_______________________	_______________________
Phone Number	Phone Number

Signature of Attorney: _______________________

Typed/printed name of Attorney: _______________________

Address: _______________________

Telephone: _______________________ State Bar # ___________

VERIFICATION

GEORGIA, _______________________ COUNTY

Personally appeared before me the undersigned petitioner(s) who on oath state(s) that the facts set forth in the foregoing petition are true.

Sworn to and subscribed before me this ______ day of _______________, 20 _____.

____
First Petitioner

____
NOTARY/CLERK OF PROBATE COURT

____
Printed Name

Sworn to and subscribed before me this ______ day of _______________, 20 _____.

____
Second Petitioner, if any

____
NOTARY/CLERK OF PROBATE COURT

____
Printed Name

CONSENT OF HEIRS/BENEFICIARIES

IN RE: ESTATE OF ____________________ ESTATE NO. __________

Note: If an heir/beneficiary is not sui juris. indicate the relationship of the person who is authorized to consent for him in accordance with the instruction page to this form.

We, being all of the heirs of the above estate or being beneficiaries under the Will of the above deceased, being sui juris unless otherwise indicated, do hereby authorize the judge of the probate court to:

a. waive the necessity of bond of this personal representative from the date of the order on this petition forward, and grant to the personal representative the power to serve without making and filing inventory if not yet due, and without filing any annual or other returns or reports covering any period from the date of such order forward to any court. ____________________ **(initial if applicable)** SEE the Note below regarding applicable conditions/restrictions.

b. grant to the personal representative for the future all of the powers contained in O.C.G.A. §53-12-232 not included in (a) above. __________ **(initial if applicable)**

Sworn to and subscribed before me this ______ day of ______________, 20 _____.

______________________________ SIGNATURE OF HEIR/BENEFICIARY

______________________________ NOTARY/CLERK OF PROBATE COURT

______________________________ PRINT NAME

---

a. waive the necessity of bond of this personal representative from the date of the order on this petition forward, and grant to the personal representative the power to serve without making and filing inventory if not yet due, and without filing any annual or other returns or reports covering any period from the date of such order forward to any court. ____________________ **(initial if applicable)** SEE the Note below regarding applicable conditions/restrictions.

b. grant to the personal representative for the future all of the powers contained in O.C.G.A. §53-12-232 not included in (a) above. __________ **(initial if applicable)**

Sworn to and subscribed before me this ______ day of ______________, 20 _____.

______________________________ SIGNATURE OF HEIR/BENEFICIARY

______________________________ NOTARY/CLERK OF PROBATE COURT

______________________________ PRINT NAME

---

a. waive the necessity of bond of this personal representative from the date of the order on this petition forward, and grant to the personal representative the power to serve without making and filing inventory if not yet due, and without filing any annual or other returns or reports covering any period from the date of such order forward to any court. _____ **(initial if applicable)** SEE the Note below regarding applicable conditions/restrictions.

b. grant to the personal representative for the future all of the powers contained in O.C.G.A. §53-12-232 not included in (a) above. _____ **(initial if applicable)**

Sworn to and subscribed before me this _____ day of _____________, 20_____.

____
SIGNATURE OF HEIR/BENEFICIARY

____
NOTARY/CLERK OF PROBATE COURT

____
PRINT NAME

---

a. waive the necessity of bond of this personal representative from the date of the order on this petition forward, and grant to the personal representative the power to serve without making and filing inventory if not yet due, and without filing any annual or other returns or reports covering any period from the date of such order forward to any court. _____ **(initial if applicable)** SEE the Note below regarding applicable conditions/restrictions.

b. grant to the personal representative for the future all of the powers contained in O.C.G.A. §53-12-232 not included in (a) above. _____ **(initial if applicable)**

Sworn to and subscribed before me this _____ day of _____________, 20_____.

____
SIGNATURE OF HEIR/BENEFICIARY

____
NOTARY/CLERK OF PROBATE COURT

____
PRINT NAME

NOTE: if the Petition is granted, the following restrictions/conditions will apply: the fiduciary shall in the future furnish to the income beneficiaries, at least annually, a statement of receipts and disbursements. The present bond of the personal representative dated _______________, number ___________ written by ______________________________, surety, in the amount of $____________ may be reduced to zero ($0) as of the date of the order on this petition. The personal representative's surety shall be relieved of all liability from the date of the order on this petition forward, except liability for any waste or misconduct by the personal representative which occurred before the date of such order, and with respect to such continuing liability the surety shall not be relieved until the personal representative has been discharged as provided by law. Further, the personal representative must file a return with this court within 60 days from the date of such order covering the period from his most recent return, if any, up to the date of such order. A copy of such return shall be sent by first class mail by the personal representative to all of the heirs, if the decedent was intestate, and beneficiaries, if the decedent died testate. Objections to such return may be filed within 30 days after such return is filed with the court. If such notice is not given, or if any objection is made and sustained by the court, the court may withdraw from the date the personal representative failed to give such notice or from the date of its order on such objections any relief granted upon this petition.

Instructions and form adopted effective July 1, 1990; revised effective July 1, 1992; January 1, 1998; July 1, 1998; July 31, 2006.

GPCSF 32 COURT. COURT FORMS FOR PETITION BY PERSONAL REPRESENTATIVE FOR WAIVER OF BOND AND/OR GRANT OF CERTAIN POWERS

GEORGIA PROBATE COURT
STANDARD FORM

Petition by Personal Representative for Waiver of Bond and/or Grant of Certain Powers

NOTICE: UNLESS OTHERWISE DIRECTED BY THE COURT, THE FOLLOWING FORMS ARE FOR PROBATE COURT STAFF TO COMPLETE

Effective 7/06 GPCSF 32 Court

GEORGIA PROBATE COURT
STANDARD FORM

IN THE PROBATE COURT OF ____________________ COUNTY

STATE OF GEORGIA

IN RE: ESTATE OF	)	ESTATE NO. ____________________
	)	
______________________________,	)	PETITION BY PERSONAL
DECEASED	)	REPRESENTATIVE FOR WAIVER OF
	)	BOND AND/OR GRANT OF CERTAIN
	)	POWERS

ORDER FOR PUBLICATION AND APPOINTING GUARDIAN AD LITEM, IF NECESSARY

Upon reading the foregoing petition, it is ordered that notice be issued and published once a week for four weeks prior to the date on which objections must be filed.

(initial if applicable)

________ IT IS FURTHER ORDERED that ____________________ is appointed guardian ad litem for ______________________________, and that said guardian ad litem be duly served with a copy of the foregoing Notice, petition, purported Will if any, and notice of this appointment, and that upon said guardian ad litem's acceptance of same, said guardian ad litem shall make answer hereto. This appointment is limited to this proceeding only and it shall cease when a final order is entered on this petition.

SO ORDERED this ________ day of ____________________, 20______.

Probate Judge

IN THE PROBATE COURT OF ____________________ COUNTY

STATE OF GEORGIA

IN RE: ESTATE OF	)	ESTATE NO. ____________________
	)	
______________________________,	)	PETITION BY PERSONAL
DECEASED	)	REPRESENTATIVE FOR WAIVER OF
	)	BOND AND/OR GRANT OF CERTAIN
	)	POWERS

NOTICE

______________________________ has petitioned for waiver of bond and/or for the grant of certain powers contained in O.C.G.A. §53-12-232 in regard to the above estate. All interested parties are hereby notified to show cause why said petition should not be granted. All objections to the petition must be in writing, setting forth the grounds of any such objections, and must be filed with the court on or before ____________________, 20_____. All pleadings/objections must be signed before a notary public or before a probate court clerk, and filing fees must be tendered with your pleadings/objections, unless you qualify to file as an indigent party. Contact probate court personnel at the following address/telephone number for the required amount of filing fees. If any objections are filed, the Petition may be denied or a hearing will be (held on ____________________, 20 _____ in the Probate Court of ______________ County, courtroom ______________________________, (address) ____________________, Georgia) (scheduled for a later date). If no objections are filed, the petition may be granted without a hearing.

PROBATE CLERK/DEPUTY CLERK

ADDRESS

TELEPHONE NUMBER

Effective 7/06 GPCSF 32 Court

IN THE PROBATE COURT OF ______________ COUNTY

STATE OF GEORGIA

IN RE: ESTATE OF) ESTATE NO. ______________

)

______________________________,) PETITION BY PERSONAL
DECEASED) REPRESENTATIVE FOR WAIVER OF
) BOND AND/OR GRANT OF CERTAIN
) POWERS

ANSWER OF GUARDIAN AD LITEM

I hereby accept the foregoing appointment, acknowledge service and notice of the proceedings as provided by law, and for answer say:

______________________ ______________________
DATE GUARDIAN AD LITEM

____
ADDRESS

____
TELEPHONE

IN THE PROBATE COURT OF ____________________ COUNTY

STATE OF GEORGIA

IN RE: ESTATE OF	)	ESTATE NO. ____________________
	)	
____________________,	)	PETITION BY ADMINISTRATOR
DECEASED	)	PERSONAL REPRESENTATIVE
	)	FOR WAIVER OF BOND AND/OR
	)	GRANT OF CERTAIN POWERS

FINAL ORDER

The petition for waiver of bond and/or grant of certain powers contained in O.C.G.A. §53-12-232 to the personal representative of the estate of ____________________, deceased, has been duly filed. Consent to the petition was given by all heirs or beneficiaries under the Will, if testate. Notice was published according to law and no objection to the petition has been filed.

It is therefore ordered that the undersigned judge does hereby: (Initial all which apply):

______ a. waive the necessity of bond of this personal representative from the date of this order forward, and grant to the personal representative the power to serve without making and filing inventory if not yet due, and without filing any annual or other returns or reports covering any period from the date of this order forward to any court; but the fiduciary shall in the future furnish to the income beneficiaries, at least annually, a statement of receipts and disbursements. The present bond of the personal representative dated ________________, number ____________ written by ____________________, surety, in the amount of $ ____________ is hereby reduced to zero ($0) as of the date of this order. The foregoing relief is given upon the following conditions: The personal representative's surety shall be relieved of all liability from the date of this order forward, except liability for any waste or misconduct by the personal representative which occurred before the date of this order, and with respect to such continuing liability the surety shall not be relieved until the personal representative has been discharged as provided by law. Further, the personal representative must file a return with this court within 60 days from the date of this order covering the period from his most recent return, if any, up to the date of this order. A copy of such return shall be sent by first class mail by the personal representative to all of the heirs, if the decedent was intestate, and beneficiaries, if the decedent died testate. Objections to such return may be filed within 30 days after such return is filed with the court. If such notice is not given, or if any objection is made and sustained by the court, the court may withdraw from the date the personal representative failed to give such notice or from the date of its order on such objections any relief granted upon this petition.

______ b. grant to the personal representative from the date of this order forward all of the powers contained in O.C.G.A. §53-12-232 not included in (a) above.

FURTHER ORDERED that Letters of Administration or Testamentary reflecting the above be issued to the personal representative.

SO ORDERED this __________ day of ____________________, 20_____.

Probate Judge

GEORGIA PROBATE COURT
STANDARD FORM

INSTRUCTIONS

1. Unless inventory has been waived, an inventory of the estate must be filed with this Court by the Personal Representative within six (6) months after the date of qualification as Personal Representative , and a copy of that inventory must be delivered to the heirs by first-class mail within the same period.

2. Within sixty (60) days after the date of qualification as Personal Representative, notice must be given once a week for four (4) weeks by advertisement in the newspaper in this County in which sheriff's notices are published, requiring creditors of the estate to render in their demands and requiring debtors to make payment.

3. Unless returns have been waived, or a different accounting period has been approved, within sixty (60) days after the anniversary date of qualification as Personal Representative, in each and every year, every Personal Representative must make a just and true account, under oath, of his receipts and expenditures on behalf of the estate during the preceding year, together with a note or memorandum of any other fact necessary to the exhibition of the true condition of the estate. The vouchers showing the correctness of each item must be retained by the Personal Representative.

4. The Personal Representative is allowed six (6) months from the date of his qualification to ascertain the condition of the estate, during which he is exempt from suit. He should collect all debts due the estate, and pay the debts of the estate, wholly or in part, at the end of the six-month period. Payment of the debts of the decedent shall be made in accordance with their rank in priority as provided in O.C.G.A. §53-7-40.

5. The Personal Representative may continue the business of his intestate for the year of his qualification without a court order.

6. The normal commissions allowed the Personal Representative are two and one-half percent (2.5%) of all sums of money received, and a like commission on all sums of money paid out. In addition, the Judge of the Probate Court may allow a commission of up to three percent (3%) of the value of all property distributed in kind. There are special rules concerning commissions on interest earned and extra compensation.

7. After the payment of all expenses of administration and other debts, the balance of the estate shall be promptly distributed to the heirs. The Personal Representative must then make a final return, showing the receipts and disbursements since the last annual accounting, unless returns have been waived.

For further information see O.C.G.A. Title 53, Chapters 6 and 7.

GEORGIA PROBATE COURT
STANDARD FORM

STATE OF GEORGIA
COUNTY OF ______________________ ESTATE NO. ______________

LETTERS OF ADMINISTRATION

(Bond Waived and/or Certain Powers Granted Subsequent to Time of Appointment)

By ______________________________, Judge of the Probate Court of said County.

WHEREAS, ______________________ died intestate (check one:)

_____ domiciled in this County:

_____ not domiciled in this State, but owning property in this County:

and this Court granted an order appointing ______________ as Administrator of the estate of said decedent, and said Administrator did duly qualify for such office; the Court hereby grants unto said Administrator full power to collect the assets of said decedent, and to pay the debts of said estate, so far as such assets will extend, according to law, and then to pay over the balance, if any, to the legal heirs of said decedent, and to do and perform all other duties as such Administrator, according to the laws of this State. In addition, this Court has by order dated ______________:

(Check all which apply:)

_____ a. waived the necessity of bond of the Administrator from the date of such order forward, and granted to the administrator the power to serve without filing an inventory if not due prior to the date of such order, and without filing any annual or other returns or reports covering any period from the date of such order forward to any court; but the fiduciary shall in the future furnish to the income beneficiaries, at least annually, a statement of receipts and disbursements. Further, the Administrator must file a return with this court within 60 days from the date of such order covering the period from his most recent return, if any, up to the date of such order and a copy of such return must be sent by first class mail by the administrator to all of the heirs and known creditors of the estate at the time such return is filed.

_____ b. granted to the Administrator from the date of such order forward all of the powers contained in O.C.G.A. §53-12-232 not included in (a) above.

If Letters of Administration were previously issued to this Administrator, these Letters replace those.

IN TESTIMONY WHEREOF, I have hereunto affixed my signature as Judge of the Probate Court of said County and the seal of this office this _____ day of ______________, 20 ____.

Probate Judge

NOTE: The following must be signed if the judge does not sign the original of this document:

Issued by:

______________________________ (Seal)

PROBATE CLERK/DEPUTY CLERK

Effective 7/06 GPCSF 32 Court

GEORGIA PROBATE COURT
STANDARD FORM

STATE OF GEORGIA
COUNTY OF ______________________ ESTATE NO. ______________

LETTERS TESTAMENTARY

(Relieved of Filing Returns)

By ______________________________, Judge of the Probate Court of said County.

KNOW ALL WHOM IT MAY CONCERN:

That on the _____ day of ___________, 20 _____, at a regular term of the Probate Court, the Last Will and Testament dated ______________, ________, of ___________ deceased, at the time of his or her death a resident of said County, was legally proven in ____________ form and was admitted to record by order, and it was further ordered that ______________________, named as Executor(s) in said Will, be allowed to qualify, and that upon so doing, Letters Testamentary be issued to such Executor(s).

NOW, THEREFORE, the said ________________, having taken the oath of office and complied with all the necessary prerequisites of the law, is/are legally authorized to discharge all the duties and exercise all the powers of Executor(s) under the Will of said deceased, according to the Will and the law.

Given under my hand and official seal, the _____ day of ____________, _____.

Probate Judge

NOTE: The following must be signed if the judge does not sign the original of this document:

Issued by: (Seal)

PROBATE CLERK/DEPUTY CLERK

Effective 7/06 GPCSF 32 Court

Form adopted effective July 31, 2006.

GPCSF 33 PETITIONER. PETITION FOR DISCHARGE OF PERSONAL REPRESENTATIVE

GEORGIA PROBATE COURT
STANDARD FORM

Petition for Discharge of Personal Representative

INSTRUCTIONS

I. Specific Instructions

1. This form is to be used for a petition for discharge of a personal representative pursuant to O:C.G.A. §53-7-50 or discharge of a temporary administrator pursuant to O.C.G.A. §53-7-52. A personal representative may, pursuant to O.C.G.A. §53-7-50(e), petition the court solely for discharge from office but not from all liability.

2. If the petition is filed by a personal representative, the notice to creditors and/or debtors and creditors must have been published for four weeks, and three months must have elapsed from the date of the last publication. O.C.G.A. §§53-7-41, 53-11-4.

II. General Instructions

General instructions applicable to all Georgia probate court standard forms are available in each probate court.

GEORGIA PROBATE COURT
STANDARD FORM

IN THE PROBATE COURT OF ______________________ COUNTY

STATE OF GEORGIA

IN RE: ESTATE OF	)	ESTATE NO. ______________________
	)	
______________________,	)	PETITION FOR
DISCHARGE OF DECEASED	)	PERSONAL REPRESENTATIVE

TO THE HONORABLE JUDGE OF THE PROBATE COURT:

The petition of ______________, as (Executor(s)) (Administrator(s)) (Temporary Administrator(s)) of the above-referenced estate, shows:

1.

Petitioner(s) (initial one):

_______ a. has/have fully administered the estate of the decedent.
_______ b. was/were allowed to resign without fully administering said estate.
_______ c. has/have completely discharged all duties as temporary administrator(s).

2.

The names, age or majority status, and address of all known heirs of an intestate decedent or beneficiaries of a testate decedent, or persons who succeeded to the interest of any heir or beneficiary who died after the decedent died are:

Name	Relationship	Age (Or over 18)	Address

[**NOTE:** If discharge is sought solely from office and not from office and all liability, STRIKE paragraphs 3. and 4. below.]

GEORGIA PROBATE COURT
STANDARD FORM

3.

Of those named in paragraph 2. above, it is not necessary to notify the following heirs or beneficiaries (a) who have relieved the personal representative of all liability and as to each of whom a copy of the writing(s) granting such relief is/are attached hereto or (b) with respect to whom the personal representative has been relieved of all further liability in (a settlement of accounts) (an intermediate report)(other binding proceeding) pursuant to an order of this court dated ______________________________ and hereby incorporated herein:

4.

The following heirs or beneficiaries are represented or should be represented by a guardian (state names of heir/beneficiary and guardian, if one has already been appointed, and reason guardian needed/appointed):

5.

All claims against the estate have been paid (except for the following which have not been paid for the reasons set forth below):

6.

(initial one):

______ All necessary (inventories) (and) (returns) have been filed.
______ Petitioner was relieved of filing (inventories) (and) (returns).

GEORGIA PROBATE COURT
STANDARD FORM

7.

Additional Data: Where full particulars are lacking, state here the reasons for any such omission.

WHEREFORE, petitioner(s)
(initial one):

_____ (a) seek(s) discharge solely from office and, therefore, pray(s) that notice issue and be published one time in the official county newspaper with copies thereof being mailed by first-class mail to the creditors named in paragraph 5. above and that an order issue discharging the petitioner(s) from office.

OR

_____ (b) seek(s) discharge from office and all liability and, therefore, pray(s) that notice issue and be served and published as required by law and that an order issue releasing and discharging the petitioner(s) from office and from all liability.

______________________	______________________
Signature of first personal representative	Signature of second personal representative if any
______________________	______________________
Printed Name	Printed Name
______________________	______________________
Address	Address
______________________	______________________
______________________	______________________
Phone Number	Phone Number

Signature of Attorney: ______________________
Typed/printed name of Attorney: ______________________
Address: ______________________

Telephone: ______________________ State Bar # __________

GEORGIA PROBATE COURT
STANDARD FORM

VERIFICATION

GEORGIA, ________________ COUNTY

Personally appeared before me the undersigned petitioner(s) who on oath state(s) that the facts set forth in the foregoing petition are true.

Sworn to and subscribed before me this _____ day of ______________, 20 ____.

____
First Petitioner

____
NOTARY/CLERK OF PROBATE COURT

____
Printed Name

Sworn to and subscribed before me this _____ day of ______________, 20 ____.

____
Second Petitioner, if any

____
NOTARY/CLERK OF PROBATE COURT

____
Printed Name

GEORGIA PROBATE COURT
STANDARD FORM

ACKNOWLEDGMENT OF SERVICE AND CONSENT TO PETITION

GEORGIA, ________________ COUNTY
IN RE: PETITION OF ______________________ FOR DISCHARGE AS OF THE
ESTATE OF ______________, DECEASED.

We, the undersigned, being over 18 years of age, laboring under no legal disability and being heirs or beneficiaries or unpaid purported creditors of the above-named decedent, hereby acknowledge service of a copy of the above petition and notice, waive copies of same, waive further service and notice, and hereby consent to the petition.

SIGNATURE(S) OF INTERESTED PARTIES

Sworn to and subscribed before me this _____ day of ______________, 20 ____. ______________________________

______________________________ ______________________________
NOTARY/CLERK OF PROBATE COURT Print Name

Sworn to and subscribed before me this _____ day of ______________, 20 ____. ______________________________

______________________________ ______________________________
NOTARY/CLERK OF PROBATE COURT Print Name

Sworn to and subscribed before me this _____ day of ______________, 20 ____. ______________________________

______________________________ ______________________________
NOTARY/CLERK OF PROBATE COURT Print Name

Sworn to and subscribed before me this _____ day of ______________, 20 ____. ______________________________

______________________________ ______________________________
NOTARY/CLERK OF PROBATE COURT Print Name

Sworn to and subscribed before me this _____ day of ______________, 20 ____. ______________________________

______________________________ ______________________________
NOTARY/CLERK OF PROBATE COURT Print Name

Sworn to and subscribed before me this _____ day of ______________, 20 ____. ______________________________

______________________________ ______________________________
NOTARY/CLERK OF PROBATE COURT Print Name

Effective 7/06 - 5 - GPCSF 33 Petitioner

Instructions and forms adopted effective July 1, 1990; revised effective January 1, 1998; July 1, 1998; July 31, 2006.

GPCSF 33 COURT. COURT FORMS FOR PETITION FOR DISCHARGE OF PERSONAL REPRESENTATIVE

GEORGIA PROBATE COURT
STANDARD FORM

Petition for Discharge of Personal Representative

NOTICE: UNLESS OTHERWISE DIRECTED BY THE COURT, THE FOLLOWING FORMS ARE FOR PROBATE COURT STAFF TO COMPLETE

GEORGIA PROBATE COURT
STANDARD FORM

IN THE PROBATE COURT OF ____________________ COUNTY

STATE OF GEORGIA

IN RE: ESTATE OF	)	ESTATE NO.
	)	
______________________________,	)	PETITION FOR DISCHARGE OF
DECEASED	)	PERSONAL REPRESENTATIVE
	)	

ORDER FOR SERVICE OF NOTICE AND APPOINTING GUARDIAN AD LITEM, IF APPLICABLE

[Initial A. (discharge solely from office) or B. (discharge from office and all liability)]:

______ A. The foregoing petition having been filed, seeking discharge solely from office, it is ordered that Notice be published one time in the newspaper in which sheriff's advertisements are published in this county at least ten days before ______________________, 20 ______ and that a copy of the petition and Notice be mailed by first-class mail to the creditors whose claims have not been paid as set forth in paragraph 5. of the petition.

______ B. The foregoing petition having been filed, seeking discharge from office and all liability, it is ordered that all heirs or beneficiaries or unpaid creditors who did not acknowledge service and consent to the Petition be served as follows:

(Initial any and all of the following which apply:)

______ Notice must be served personally, together with a copy of the petition, at least ten days before the deadline for filing objections on the following interested parties who reside in Georgia and have not acknowledged service:

______ Notice must be served by registered or certified mail, return receipt requested, together with a copy of the petition, upon the following nonresident interested parties whose current residence addresses are known:

______ Notice must be published once a week for four weeks in the newspaper in which sheriff's advertisements are published in this county, before ______________________, 20______ in order to serve by publication the following interested parties whose current residence addresses are unknown or who are unknown:

_____ (Applies in all cases unless notice is published for four weeks:) Notice must be published one time in the newspaper in which sheriff's advertisements are published in this county at least ten days before ______________________, 20______ which is the date on or before which any objection is required to be filed.

_____ IT IS FURTHER ORDERED that ______________________ is appointed guardian ad litem for ______________________, and that said guardian ad litem be duly served with a copy of the foregoing Notice, petition, and notice of this appointment, and that upon said guardian ad litem's acceptance of same, said guardian ad litem shall make answer hereto. This appointment is limited to this proceeding only and it shall cease when a final order is entered on this petition.

SO ORDERED this __________ day of ______________________, 20 _____.

Probate Judge

NOTICE

(For Discharge Solely from Office)

PROBATE COURT OF ______________________ COUNTY
RE: PETITION OF ______________________ FOR DISCHARGE FROM OFFICE AS ______________________ OF THE ESTATE OF ______________________, DECEASED.

TO:

(List all creditors who did not acknowledge service whose claims have not been paid.)
and to whom it may concern:

This is to notify you to file objection, if there is any, to the above-referenced petition, in this Court on or before ______________________, 20 _____. All objections to the petition must be in writing, setting forth the grounds of any such objections. All pleadings/objections must be signed before a notary public or before a probate court clerk, and filing fees must be tendered with your pleadings/objections, unless you qualify to file as an indigent party. Contact probate court personnel at the following address/telephone number for the required amount of filing fees. If any objections are filed, a hearing will be (held on ______________________) (scheduled at a later date). If no objections are filed, the petition may be granted without a hearing.

PROBATE JUDGE

By: ______________________
PROBATE CLERK/DEPUTY CLERK

ADDRESS

TELEPHONE NUMBER

CERTIFICATE OF MAILING

This is to certify that I have this date forwarded by first-class mail, in a stamped, addressed envelope, a copy of the foregoing petition and notice, to each of the following creditors at the addresses given by petitioner(s) in paragraph 5. of the petition:

______________________ DATE

______________________ PROBATE CLERK/DEPUTY CLERK

NOTICE

(For Discharge from Office and all Liability)

PROBATE COURT OF ____________________ COUNTY

RE: PETITION OF ____________________ FOR DISCHARGE AS ____________________ OF THE ESTATE OF ____________________, DECEASED.

(Strike the following paragraph if no interested party is required to be served by publication:)

TO:

(List here all unknown interested parties and known interested parties having unknown addresses to be served by publication)

and (all and singular the heirs of said decedent,) (the beneficiaries under the will,) and to whom it may concern:

This is to notify you to file objection, if there is any, to the above referenced petition, in this Court on or before ______________, 20 _____.

(Strike the following paragraph if not applicable:)

TO:

(List here all interested parties having known addresses in the continental U.S. to be served by certified or registered mail)

This is to notify you to file objection, if there is any, to the above referenced petition, in this Court on or before the thirteenth (13th) day after ____________________, 20_____ (the date of the mailing of this Notice to you by certified or registered mail, return receipt requested); provided, however, that if a return receipt for such Notice is actually received by the Court within such 13 days, the deadline for the filing of any objection shall be ten (10) days from the date of receipt shown on such return receipt.

(Strike the following paragraph if not applicable:)

TO:

(List here all interested parties having known addresses outside the continental U.S. to be served by certified or registered mail)

This is to notify you to file objection, if there is any, to the above referenced petition, in this Court on or before the thirtieth (30th) day after ____________________, 20 _______ (the date of the mailing of this Notice to you by certified or registered mail, return receipt requested); provided, however, that if a return receipt for such Notice is actually received by the Court within such 30 days, the deadline for the filing of any objection shall be ten (10) days from the date of receipt shown on such return receipt.

(Strike the following paragraph if not applicable:)

This is further to: ____,

(List here all interested parties who reside in Georgia to be served personally)

who are required to be served personally, to file objection, if there is any, to the above referenced petition, in this Court on or before the tenth (10th) day after the date you are personally served.

BE NOTIFIED FURTHER: All objections to the petition must be in writing, setting forth the grounds of any such objections. All pleadings/objections must be signed before a notary public or before a probate court clerk, and filing fees must be tendered with your pleadings/objections, unless you qualify to file as an indigent party. Contact probate court personnel at the following address/telephone number for the required amount of filing fees. If any objections are filed, a hearing will be (held on ____________________, 20 _____) (scheduled at a later date). If no objections are filed, the petition may be granted without a hearing.

PROBATE JUDGE

By: ______________________________
PROBATE CLERK/DEPUTY CLERK

ADDRESS

TELEPHONE NUMBER

IN THE PROBATE COURT OF ____________________ COUNTY

STATE OF GEORGIA

IN RE: ESTATE OF	)	ESTATE NO.
	)	
______________________________,	)	PETITION FOR DISCHARGE OF
DECEASED	)	PERSONAL REPRESENTATIVE
	)	

RETURN OF SHERIFF

I have this day served ________ personally with a copy of the foregoing petition and the notice.

______________________________ ______________________________

Date Deputy Sheriff, ____________________ County

CERTIFICATE OF MAILING

This is to certify that I have this date forwarded by registered or certified mail, return receipt requested, in a stamped, addressed envelope, a copy of the foregoing petition and notice, to each of the following interested parties who reside out of state at known current residence addresses

______________________	______________________
DATE	CLERK, PROBATE COURT

Effective 7/06 GPCSF 33 Court

IN THE PROBATE COURT OF ________________ COUNTY

STATE OF GEORGIA

IN RE: ESTATE OF	)	ESTATE NO. ____________
	)	
______________________________,	)	PETITION FOR DISCHARGE OF
DECEASED	)	PERSONAL REPRESENTATIVE

ANSWER OF GUARDIAN AD LITEM

I hereby accept the foregoing appointment, acknowledge service and notice of the proceedings as provided by law, and for answer say:

____
DATE

____
GUARDIAN AD LITEM
ADDRESS: ______________________

TELEPHONE: ____________________

IN THE PROBATE COURT OF ____________________ COUNTY

STATE OF GEORGIA

IN RE: ESTATE OF	)	ESTATE NO.
	)	
______________________________,	)	PETITION FOR DISCHARGE OF
DECEASED	)	PERSONAL REPRESENTATIVE
	)	

FINAL ORDER

The foregoing petition for discharge of ______________________________ as ________________ was duly filed in this Court, notice was duly issued, served and published as required by law, and it appears that the petitioner(s) is/are legally entitled to discharge and no objection has been filed. Therefore,

IT IS ORDERED that petitioner(s) be, and is/are hereby, discharged

(initial one:)
_____ a. solely from office

_____ b. from office and all liability.

SO ORDERED this ________ day of ________________________, 20_____.

Probate Judge

Effective 7/06 GPCSF 33 Court

Form adopted effective July 31, 2006.

GPCSF 34 PETITIONER. PETITION OF CONSERVATOR FOR FINAL SETTLEMENT OF ACCOUNTS AND DISCHARGE FROM OFFICE AND LIABILITY

GEORGIA PROBATE COURT
STANDARD FORM

Petition of Conservator for Final Settlement of Accounts and Discharge from Office and Liability.

INSTRUCTIONS

I. Specific Instructions

1. This form is to be used by a conservator for a final settlement of accounts and discharge from office and liability pursuant to O.C.G.A. §29-3-71 (conservator of minor); and O.C.G.A. §29-5-81 (conservator of adult ward).

II. General Instructions

General instructions applicable to all Georgia probate court standard forms are available in each probate court.

GEORGIA PROBATE COURT
STANDARD FORM

IN THE PROBATE COURT OF ______________ COUNTY

STATE OF GEORGIA

IN RE:	)	ESTATE NO.
	)	
______________________________,	)	PETITION OF CONSERVATOR
MINOR/WARD	)	FOR FINAL SETTLEMENT
	)	OF ACCOUNTS AND DISCHARGE FROM
______________________________,	)	OFFICE AND LIABILITY
CONSERVATOR(S)	)	

TO THE HONORABLE JUDGE OF THE PROBATE COURT:

The petition of ____________________________, Conservator(s) of the estate of ______________________________, former (minor)(adult ward), shows:

1.

Conservator(s) has/have fully discharged all duties as such, and is/are entitled to be discharged from office and liability. Conservator(s) further show(s) that all required inventories and returns have been filed with this Court.

2.

Conservator(s) further show(s) (initial a or b:)

______ a. The former minor is now of age.

______ b. There is no longer a necessity to continue the conservatorship because

______ (i) the minor or adult ward is deceased

______ (ii) the ward's powers have been restored

______ (iii) the conservator(s) has/have filed a Petition to Resign

______ (iv) other: ____
____.

3.

Conservator(s) pray(s) that (initial applicable)

______ a. Since the ward is/was an adult ward,

______ (i) the Court waive the hearing requirements pursuant to O.C.G.A. §29-3-71 or O.C.G.A. §29-5-81 and discharge the conservator/s from office and liability because the former adult ward or the personal representative of his/her estate (being someone other than the conservator) has signed an acknowledgment of receipt of property and release of liability, attached hereto.

______ (ii) as Conservator(s) of an adult ward who is deceased, the Court cite the adult ward's personal representative for a final settlement of the conservator's accounts. The adult ward's personal representative, who is not the petitioner, is ______________________ and can be found at the following address: ______________________ ______________________ telephone: ______________________

______ (iii) as Conservator(s) of a deceased adult ward and also being personal representative(s) of the ward's estate, a guardian ad litem must be appointed to represent the deceased adult ward.

______ (iv.) as Conservator(s) of an adult ward who is living and has been restored to capacity, the Court cite the former adult ward for a final settlement of the conservator's accounts. The former adult ward can be found at the following address: ______________________ ______________________ telephone: ______________________

______ (v) as Conservator(s) of an adult ward who is living but has *not* been restored to capacity, the Court cite the adult ward for a final settlement of the conservator's accounts and appoint a guardian ad litem for the ward. The adult ward's successor conservator is ______________________ and can be found at the following address: ______________________ telephone: ______________________.
The adult ward can be found at the following address: ______________________ telephone: ______________________.
The ward's guardian, if any, can be found at the following address. ______________________ telephone: ______________________.

______ (vi) As Conservator(s) of a deceased adult ward, and there being no assets remaining in the estate, a guardian ad litem must be appointed to represent the deceased adult ward.

_____ b. since the ward is/was a minor,

_____ (i) the Court waive the hearing requirements pursuant to O.C.G.A. §29-3-71 or O.C.G.A. §29-5-81 and discharge the conservator/s from office and liability because the former minor or the personal representative of his/her estate (being someone other than the conservator) has signed an acknowledgment of receipt of property and release of liability, attached hereto.

_____ (ii) as Conservator(s) of a minor who is now 18 years of age, the Court cite the former minor for a final settlement of the conservator's accounts. The former minor can be found at the following address: _____________________________________
telephone: _____________________.

_____ (iii) as Conservator(s) of a minor who is deceased, the Court cite the minor's personal representative for a final settlement of the conservator's accounts. The minor's personal representative is _____________ _____________________ and can be found at the following address: _____________________________________
telephone: _____________________.

_____ (iv) as Conservator(s) of a minor who is deceased and also being the personal representative of the minor's estate, a guardian ad litem must be appointed to represent the minor's interest.

_____ (v) as Conservator(s) of a minor who is living, the Court cite the successor conservator(s) for a final settlement of the conservator's accounts. A guardian ad litem must be appointed to represent the minor. The minor's successor conservator is _____________ and can be found at the following address: _____________ _____________________________________
telephone: _____________________.
The minor can be found at the following address: _____________________________________
telephone: _____________________.

4.

Attached as Exhibit "A" is the final return showing to whom the estate assets have been disbursed.

5.

Additional Data: Where full particulars are lacking, state here the reasons for any such omission.

WHEREFORE, conservator(s) seek(s) discharge from office and all liability and, therefore, pray(s)

1. that the Court issue citation as requested above pursuant to O.C.G.A. §29-3-71(b) or O.C.G.A. §29-5-81(b);
2. that the Court examine all returns and accounts of the conservator(s) during the settlement period;
3. that notice be served and published as required by law and
4. that an order issue releasing and discharging the conservator(s) from office and from all liability.

Signature of conservator	Signature of co-conservator, if any
Printed Name	Printed Name
Address	Address
Telephone Number	Telephone Number

Signature of Attorney: ____________________

Typed/printed name of Attorney: ____________________

Address: ____________________

Telephone: ____________ State Bar # ____________

VERIFICATION

GEORGIA, ______________ COUNTY

Personally appeared before me the undersigned conservator(s) who on oath state(s) that the facts set forth in the foregoing petition are true.

Sworn to and subscribed before me this ____ day of ______________, 20 ____.

____
NOTARY/CLERK OF PROBATE COURT

____
Conservator

____
Printed Name

Sworn to and subscribed before me this ____ day of ______________, 20 ____.

____
NOTARY/CLERK OF PROBATE COURT

____
Co-Conservator, if any

____
Printed Name

Effective 7/06 GPCSF 34 Petitioner

ACKNOWLEDGEMENT OF RECEIPT OF PROPERTY AND RELEASE OF LIABILITY

IN RE: ESTATE OF ______________________________ ESTATE NO. ____________

The undersigned acknowledges that the conservator(s) has/have turned over all assets held in the conservatorship to the undersigned, being (initial one:)

______ a. the personal representative(s) of the former minor/ward's estate
______ b. the former minor ward upon reaching the age of eighteen or his or her emancipation
______ c. the former adult ward after restoration to competency
______ d. the successor conservator(s)

By signing this document, the undersigned acknowledges that he/she has received a copy of the Petition for Discharge from Office and Liability, the Final Return, and the receipt of $ ________ and all other property from the conservator(s); waives any hearing required under O.C.G.A. §29-3-71 or O.C.G.A. §29-5-81; and further consents that the conservator(s) may be discharged from office and from all liability.

Sworn to and subscribed before me this _____ day of ______________, 20 ___.

Personal Representative(s), Former Minor/Ward, or Successor Conservator(s)

____
Notary Public/Clerk of Probate Court

____
Print Name

Sworn to and subscribed before me this _____ day of ______________, 20_____.

____
Second, if any

____
Notary Public/Clerk of Probate Court

____
Print Name

Instructions and form adopted effective July 1, 1990; revised effective January 1, 1998; July 1, 2005; July 31, 2006.

GPCSF 34 COURT. COURT FORMS FOR PETITION OF CONSERVATOR FOR FINAL SETTLEMENT OF ACCOUNTS AND DISCHARGE FROM OFFICE AND LIABILITY

GEORGIA PROBATE COURT
STANDARD FORM

Petition of Conservator for Final Settlement of Accounts and Discharge from Office and Liability.

NOTICE: UNLESS OTHER WISE DIRECTED BY THE COURT, THE FOLLOWING FORMS ARE FOR PROBATE COURT STAFF TO COMPLETE

GEORGIA PROBATE COURT
STANDARD FORM

IN THE PROBATE COURT OF ______________________ COUNTY

STATE OF GEORGIA

IN RE:) ESTATE NO. ____________________

)

______________________________,) PETITION OF CONSERVATOR
(MINOR)(ADULT WARD)) FOR FINAL SETTLEMENT
) OF ACCOUNTS AND DISCHARGE FROM
______________________________,) OFFICE AND LIABILITY
CONSERVATOR(S))

ORDER FOR CITATION, PUBLICATION, AND
APPOINTMENT OF GUARDIAN AD LITEM, IF NECESSARY

The above petition having been read and considered, it is

Ordered that citation issue and be published one time at least 30 days before the deadline for objections.

(Initial any and all which apply:)

______ a. IT IS ORDERED that, discharge from liability being sought, and the former minor/ward or successor conservator(s) or representative(s) of the deceased ward's estate not waiving service, notice be served personally, together with a copy of the petition, at least ten days before the deadline for filing objections, on __________.

______ b. IT IS ORDERED that, discharge from liability being sought, notice be served by first class mail together with a copy of the petition and final return on the registered agent for service of process for ______________________________, the surety for the conservator (and the guardian of the above ward).

______ c. IT IS ORDERED that the ward being a minor still under the age of majority, or an adult ward still in need of a conservator, or the representative of the deceased ward's estate being the former conservator, that ______________________ is appointed guardian ad litem for the minor/ward, and that said guardian ad litem be personally served with a copy of the foregoing Citation and Petition for Discharge and notice of this appointment, and that upon said guardian ad litem's acceptance of same, said guardian ad litem shall make answer thereto. This appointment is limited to this proceeding only and shall cease when a final order is entered on this petition.

SO ORDERED this _____ day of _______________, 20 ____.

Probate Judge

Effective 7/06 GPCSF 34 Court

CITATION

PROBATE COURT OF ______________________________ COUNTY

RE: ESTATE OF ________________________________, (FORMER) MINOR/WARD.

Date of Publication, if any: ____________________

TO WHOM IT MAY CONCERN AND: ____:

The conservator(s) of the above estate, has/have applied for Discharge from said trust. This is to notify the above interested party(ies) to show cause, if any they can, why said conservator(s) should not be discharged from office and liability. All objections must be in writing, setting forth the grounds of any such objections, and filed with the above Probate Court. (address) ____________ ________________________________ on or before ________, 20 ___, said date being more than 30 days from the date of publication, or if personally served, then 10 days from the date of such service. All pleadings must be signed before a notary public or probate court clerk, and filing fees must be tendered with your pleadings, unless you qualify to file as an indigent party. Contact probate court personnel at the below address/telephone number for the required amount of filing fees.

If any objections are filed, a hearing will be (held on ______________________________ at _____ o'clock _____ m. at ____________________) (scheduled for a later date). If no objections are filed, the petition may be granted without a hearing.

PROBATE JUDGE

By: ____
PROBATE CLERK/DEPUTY CLERK

ADDRESS

TELEPHONE

Effective 7/06

GPCSF 34 Court

CERTIFICATE OF MAILING

This is to certify that I have this day served the registered agent for service of process as designated by the conservator's surety with a copy of the petition. Order for Citation, and Citation by placing a copy of same in an envelope addressed to the registered agent for service of process as designated by the conservator's surety and depositing same in the U.S. Mail. first-class, with adequate postage thereon.

____________________ DATE

____________________ PROBATE CLERK/DEPUTY CLERK

IN THE PROBATE COURT OF ____________________ COUNTY

STATE OF GEORGIA

IN RE:) ESTATE NO. ____________

)

______________________________,) PETITION OF CONSERVATOR
(MINOR)(ADULT WARD)) FOR FINAL SETTLEMENT OF
) ACCOUNTS AND DISCHARGE FROM
______________________________,) OFFICE AND LIABILITY
CONSERVATOR(S))

ORDER

The above petition, averring that the conservator(s) has/have fully discharged the duties of conservator's(s') trust, was duly filed in this Court, citation was duly issued and published as required by law, and no objection being filed, and it appears from an examination of the condition of the estate and the conduct and accounts of the conservator(s) that the conservator(s) has/have faithfully and honestly discharged the trust and confidence reposed in the conservator(s) and that conservator(s) is/are legally entitled to discharge therefrom, (initial applicable)

______ a. and that the former minor/ward has acknowledged receipt of all guardianship assets

______ b. and that the guardian ad litem has consented to said discharge

______ c. and all interested parties having consented to said discharge

and no good cause has been shown to the contrary. Therefore,

IT IS ORDERED that conservator(s) is/are hereby discharged from said trust and from office and all liability.

SO ORDERED this ________ day of ____________________, 20 ____.

Probate Judge

Effective 7/06 GPCSF 34 Court

Form adopted effective July 1, 2005; revised effective July 31, 2006.

GPCSF 35. GUARDIAN/CONSERVATOR/PERSONAL REPRESENTATIVE OATH

STATE OF GEORGIA

COUNTY OF ______________________ ESTATE NO. ______________________
Re: ESTATE OF ____,
(MINOR) (ADULT WARD) (DECEASED)

(initial oath given)

____ (TEMPORARY) GUARDIAN'S OATH

I do solemnly swear (or affirm) that I will well and truly perform the duties required of me as (temporary) guardian of the ward named above.

____ CONSERVATOR'S OATH

I do solemnly swear (or affirm) that I will well and truly perform the duties required of me as conservator of the minor/ward named above, and faithfully account to my ward for my ward's estate.

____ TEMPORARY ADMINISTRATOR'S OATH

I do solemnly swear or affirm that the above decedent died (testate)(intestate) and with an estate that is currently unrepresented, so far as I know or believe, and that I will well and truly administer on all the estate of the decedent, and discharge to the best of my ability all my duties as Temporary Administrator. So help me God.

____ ADMINISTRATOR'S OATH

I do solemnly swear (or affirm) that the above deceased died intestate, so far as I know or believe, and that I will well and truly administer on all the estate of the decedent, and disburse the same as the law requires, and discharge to the best of my ability all my duties as Administrator.

____ EXECUTOR'S OATH

I do solemnly swear (or affirm) that the propounded Will and Testament is the true Last Will and Testament of the above decedent, so far as I know or believe, and that I will well and truly execute the same in accordance with the laws of Georgia.

Sworn to and subscribed before
me this ____ day of __________, 20____.

____
Fiduciary

____
Judge / Clerk of Probate Court

____
Printed Name

....

Sworn to and subscribed before
me this ____ day of __________, 20____.

____
Co–Fiduciary, if any

____
Judge / Clerk of Probate Court

____
Printed Name

Form adopted effective July 1, 1990; amended effective July 1, 2005.

GPCSF 36 through GPCSF 51. [Reserved/Relocated]

GPCSF 52. DEFAULT CERTIFICATE

(To be prepared by attorney for petitioner, or by pro se petitioner, when required by Uniform Probate Court Rule 13.)

PROBATE COURT OF ________________ COUNTY
STATE OF GEORGIA

IN THE MATTER OF:) ESTATE NO. __________

______________________________,)

(DECEASED) (MINOR) (INCAPACITATED ADULT)) RE: (TYPE OF PETITION):

____

____

____

I hereby certify that according to court records all interested parties have been served with notice in the above-referenced matter, as required by law. Such parties were served as follows:

NAME OF PARTY	TYPE OF SERVICE	DATE OF SERVICE	DEADLINE FOR RESPONSE AS STATED IN NOTICE

I further certify that no objection or other defensive pleading has been filed by any interested party in this matter.

This ______ day of ______________________, 19[1] ____.

____
Signature

____
Printed Name

Effective 7/91 GPCSF 52

[1] So in original

CERTIFICATE IN ACCORDANCE WITH UNIFORM PROBATE COURT RULE 21(F)

I certify that the content of the foregoing is identical in all material respects with Georgia probate court standard form entitled **Default Certificate**, except for additions or deletions indicated as required by the Uniform Probate Court Rules.

Date	Signature of Attorney Address:
	Telephone Number: State Bar#:

Form adopted effective July 1, 1991.

GPCSF 53. COMMISSION TO ADMINISTER OATH

Re: Commission to Administer Oath

INSTRUCTIONS

I. Specific Instructions

1. This form is to be used when the judge of the probate court who appoints an administrator, executor or guardian desires to grant a commission to any judge or clerk of any court of record of any other state to administer the fiduciary's oath or affirmation. The form may be altered to grant the commission only to a specific judge or court if the appointing judge prefers. A commission from the county of appointment is not required in order for the fiduciary to be authorized to take the oath or affirmation before any judge or clerk of any probate court of this state. O.C.G.A. § 29–4–12(a), § 53–6–16(b), § 53–6–24(b).

2. If the oath or affirmation is made by an executor or administrator with will annexed, a certified copy of the probated will must be examined by the fiduciary at the time the oath or affirmation is taken. The oath or affirmation itself or the attestation of the attesting official should recite that this was done.

3. The attestation by the official who administers the oath or affirmation should contain the date, printed name and court of the official, and the official's signature.

4. The appropriate oath or affirmation to be taken should be provided by the judge granting the commission.

5. The attached form consists of 1 page.

II. General Instructions

General instructions applicable to all Georgia probate court standard forms are available in each probate court.

Effective 1/98 GPCSF 53

GEORGIA PROBATE COURT
STANDARD FORM

COMMISSION TO ADMINISTER OATH

GEORGIA, ______________________ COUNTY

To: Any Judge or Clerk of Any Court of Record of the State of ______________________:

______________ has been appointed by this Court as ______________ of ______________, (deceased) (minor) (incapacitated adult), and has requested to take the required oath or affirmation in your state. Pursuant to O.C.G.A. §29–4–12(a), §53–6–16(b), or §53–6–24(b), I hereby commission you to administer the attached oath or affirmation to said fiduciary. Please return the completed oath and attestation to this Court, together with your statement of costs, if any.

This ________ day of ______________, 19____.

____
Judge of the Probate Court of ____________
______________ County, Georgia

CERTIFICATE IN ACCORDANCE WITH UNIFORM PROBATE COURT RULE 21(F)

I certify that the content of the foregoing is identical in all material respects with Georgia probate court standard form entitled **Commission to Administer Oath**, except for additions or deletions indicated as required by the Uniform Probate Court Rules.

______________________ Date

____
Signature of Attorney
Address:

Telephone Number:
State Bar#:

Effective 1/98 1 GPCSF 53

Instructions and form adopted effective July 1, 1994; revised effective January 1, 1998.

GPCSF 54. SERVICE UPON MINOR OR ADULT WARD BY GUARDIAN

Service upon Minor or Adult Ward by Guardian.

INSTRUCTIONS

I. Specific Instructions

1. This form is to be used when serving a minor or adult ward pursuant to O.C.G.A. § 15–9–17. It will be inserted by the court at the appropriate place in the underlying proceedings.

2. With respect to service upon an adult ward, this form should only be used after the person has been adjudicated to be an incapacitated adult.

3. When this form is used, Uniform Probate Court Rule 22(D) applies. It provides, "Unless the court specifically assumes the responsibility otherwise, in connection with any citation which must be served by mail, including without limitation a citation concerning an application for year's support, a properly stamped envelope, addressed to each interested party, must be provided to the court by the petitioner." The envelope should show the return address of the court.

II. General Instructions

General instructions applicable to all Georgia probate court standard forms appear in Volume 255 of the Georgia Reports and are available in each probate court.

Effective 7/05 GPCSF 54 Complete

GEORGIA PROBATE COURT
STANDARD FORM

PROBATE COURT OF ________________ COUNTY

STATE OF GEORGIA

IN RE:	)	ESTATE NO. ____________
	)	
______________________________,	)	(TYPE OF PROCEEDING): ____________
DECEASED/MINOR/WARD	)	
	)	PETITION OF ____________
	)	(TO) (FOR) ____________
	)	____________

CERTIFICATE OF MAILING

This is to certify that I have this date forwarded by certified mail to ____________ ____________, minor/ward, a copy of the following document(s) concerning the above proceeding:

(Check one:)

___ the petition, order for citation and citation.

___ [list document(s)] ______________________________

______________________________ ______________________________
Date PROBATE CLERK/DEPUTY CLERK

ACKNOWLEDGMENT AND CERTIFICATE OF SERVICE

I hereby acknowledge service of a copy of the document(s) listed in the above certificate of mailing and certify that I have delivered a copy of such document(s) to said minor/ward.

______________________________ ______________________________
Date (Legal Guardian) (Guardian ad Litem)

Instructions and form adopted effective July 1, 1994; amended effective July 1, 2005.

GPCSF 55 through GPCSF 57. [Reserved/Relocated]

GPCSF 58. ADULT CONSERVATORSHIP INVENTORY AND ASSET MANAGEMENT PLAN

GEORGIA PROBATE COURT
STANDARD FORM

Adult Conservatorship Inventory and Asset Management Plan

INSTRUCTIONS

I. Specific Instructions

1. This form is to be used pursuant to O.C.G.A. §29-5-30.

II. General Instructions

General instructions applicable to all Georgia probate court standard forms are available in each probate court.

GEORGIA PROBATE COURT
STANDARD FORM

PROBATE COURT OF ______________________ COUNTY

STATE OF GEORGIA

ADULT CONSERVATORSHIP INVENTORY AND ASSET MANAGEMENT PLAN

WARD: ____ ESTATE NO. __________

CONSERVATOR(S):

REAL PROPERTY

(Indicate if property is jointly owned and with whom)

Description	County	State	Approximate equity
Parcel_1 ______________			$
Parcel_2 ______________			$
Parcel_3 ______________			$

INCOME FROM ALL SOURCES

	Yearly Total
Social Security per year	$
SSI (Supplemental Security Income)_per year	$
Retirement benefits per year (payor): ______________	$
Retirement benefits per year (payor): ______________	$
VA benefits per year	$
Other income per year, including, e.g., alimony, annuity, or trust distributions (payor): ______________	$
Interest, dividend, or investment income	$
YEARLY TOTAL OF ALL INCOME	$

If the Ward is a beneficiary of a Trust, please show the name of the Trust, the Trustee, his/her address, telephone number, and attach an outline showing when and how payments are required to be made under the Trust and the criteria for payment: ______________________________

PERSONAL AND INTANGIBLE PROPERTY
(Indicate if property is jointly owned and with whom)

Approximate Current Value

1. Checking/Savings/Money Market/Certificates of Deposit/Liquid Accounts:
   Bank/Financial Institution/Broker Acct. No. Joint Owner (if any)

   ____________________ $
   ____________________ $
   ____________________ $
   ____________________ $

2. Stocks/Bonds/Investments (including retirement and profit-sharing accounts):
   a. held by brokers:
   Brokerage Firm of Institution Acct. No. Joint Owner (if any)

   ____________________ $
   ____________________ $
   ____________________ $
   ____________________ $
   ____________________ $

   b. privately held:
   Company/Issuer No. of Shares Joint Owner (if any)

   ____________________ $
   ____________________ $

3. Automobiles:
   Year/Make/Model V.I.N. Joint owner (if any)

   ____________________ $
   ____________________ $

4. Other assets of significant value:
   Description Joint owner (if any)

   ____________________ $
   ____________________ $
   ____________________ $

TOTAL VALUE OF PERSONAL AND INTANGIBLE PROPERTY $

DEBTS AND OTHER LIABILITIES

The ward owes the following debts/liabilities:

1. Secured debts:

Obligor/Payee	Collateral	Solely/Jointly Owed	Approx. Current Balance
			$
			$

2. Unsecured debts:

Obligor/Payee	Acct. No.	Solely/Jointly Owed	Approx. Current Balance
			$
			$

TOTAL DEBTS AND OTHER LIABILITIES OF WARD $

AVERAGE MONTHLY LIABILITIES AND EXPENSES

Household:

Care Facility/Rent/Mortgage payments: $

Property taxes/Insurance $

Utilities/Lawn Care/Pest Control $

Miscellaneous household, food $

Total credit account and other debt payments $

Other (specify) $

Automotive/Transportation

Fuel and Repairs $

Tags and license fees, Insurance $

Bus/train/taxi fares $

Minors or Other Dependents of the Ward

Child Care $

School Tuition/Supplies/Expenses/Lunches $

Clothing/Diapers /Grooming/Hygiene $

Medical/Dental/Prescription $

Entertainment/Activities $

Other Insurance

Health/Life/Disability $

Other (specify) $

Ward's Other Expenses

Laundry/Clothing/grooming/hygiene $______

Medical/Dental/Prescriptions/medications $______

Entertainment/Vacations/Subscriptions/Dues $______

Personal Caretakers/cleaning personnel $______

Other (specify) $______

Total Expenses $______

Is the ward behind in any debt payments? (yes) (no)

If yes, payee and amount: ______

The following extraordinary purchases are anticipated next year: ______

SUMMARY

1. Average Monthly Income $______
2. Average Monthly Expenses <$______>

ASSET MANAGEMENT PLAN

Please describe how you plan to manage the ward's assets, including details regarding sale, refinancing, reallocation, investments, or other actions, if any: ______

(initial:)

______ a. Therefore, based upon the expenses shown above, the Conservator(s) hereby request(s) leave to disburse from the ward's estate the sum of $ ______ per month for the support, care, education, health, and welfare of the ward and those persons who are entitled to be supported by the Ward.

______ b. Therefore, based on the income of the Ward as shown above, the Conservator(s) hereby request(s) leave to disburse the ward's income as estimated above for the support of the ward and those persons who are entitled to be supported by the Ward.

______ c. Therefore, based on known one-time expenses, the Conservator(s) hereby request(s) leave to disburse from the Ward's estate $______ one time in the reporting year for the following purpose: ______

AFFIDAVIT

I/We, ______________________________, Conservator(s) of the above Ward, do swear that the foregoing Inventory and Asset Management Plan contains a just, true, and complete inventory and budget of all property belonging to said ward within my/our possession, control, or knowledge. This Inventory and Asset Management Plan has been provided to the Guardian of the ward, if any, by first class mail.

Sworn to and subscribed before me this _______ day of _______________, 20 ____.

____
NOTARY/CLERK OF PROBATE COURT

____
Conservator

____
Printed Name

Sworn to and subscribed before me this _______ day of _______________, 20 ____.

____
NOTARY/CLERK OF PROBATE COURT

____
Co-Conservator, if any

____
Printed Name

IN THE PROBATE COURT OF ______________________ COUNTY

STATE OF GEORGIA

IN RE:) ESTATE NO. ______________________

______________________________,) ASSET MANAGEMENT PLAN
WARD)

______________________________,)
CONSERVATOR(S))

ORDER

The Conservator(s) having filed an Asset Management Plan for the above estate, it is hereby ORDERED that the Conservator(s) is/are authorized to disburse from the Ward's estate: (initial applicable)

______ a. the sum of $____________________ per month for the support of the Ward and his/her dependents.

______ b. the income generated from the corpus of the Ward's estate for the benefit of the Ward and those persons who are entitled to be supported by the Ward.

______ c. the sum of $____________________ one time during the reporting period for the support of the Ward and those persons who are entitled to be supported by the Ward.

IT IS FURTHER ORDERED that said Conservator(s) shall show in the annual return how such funds actually were spent.

SO ORDERED this ______ day of ____________________, 20 ____.

Probate Judge

Effective 7/06 GPCSF 58 Complete

Instructions and form adopted effective July 1, 2005; revised effective July 31, 2006.

GPCSF 60 PETITIONER. PETITION FOR RECEIPT AND ACCEPTANCE OF FOREIGN GUARDIANSHIP AND/OR CONSERVATORSHIP

GEORGIA PROBATE COURT
STANDARD FORM

Petition for Receipt and Acceptance of Foreign Guardianship and/or Conservatorship

INSTRUCTIONS

I. Specific Instructions

1. This form is to be used by a guardian and/or conservator as appointed by another state to transfer the guardianship and/or conservatorship to a Georgia county pursuant to O.C.G.A. § 29-2-65 *et seq.;* O.C.G.A. §29-3-105 *et seq.;* O.C.G.A. §29-4-85 *et seq.;* and O.C.G.A. §29-5-125 *et seq.*

II. General Instructions

General instructions applicable to all Georgia probate court standard forms are available in each probate court.

GEORGIA PROBATE COURT
STANDARD FORM

IN THE PROBATE COURT OF ____________ COUNTY

STATE OF GEORGIA

IN RE:) ESTATE NO. ____________
)
____________,) PETITION FOR RECEIPT AND
MINOR/WARD) ACCEPTANCE OF FOREIGN
) GUARDIANSHIP AND/OR
) CONSERVATORSHIP

TO THE HONORABLE JUDGE OF THE PROBATE COURT:

The petition of ____________, Guardian(s) and/or Conservator(s), who reside(s) at ______, ______ County, Georgia, and who is/are domiciled at: ______ shows:

1.

Petitioner(s) was/were appointed Guardian(s) and/or Conservator(s) of the above minor/ward by Order dated ______, ___ as issued by the ______ Court of ______ County, State of ___. The clerk of said Court may be contacted as the following address: ______, telephone number ______.

2.

The minor/ward, age ___, date of birth ______, social security no. ______, is currently domiciled at (address) ______ County, State of ___, and is presently located at ______, which is a (type of facility, if applicable) ______ and can be contacted at (telephone number):______. Said minor/ward will be relocated to the following address: ____________

GEORGIA PROBATE COURT
STANDARD FORM

3.

Attached hereto as Exhibit "A" is an authenticated copy of:

a. the order establishing the guardianship and/or conservatorship, with all attachments describing the duties and powers of the guardian and/or conservator;

b. any orders modifying the order referenced in "a" above, including, if any, orders of transfer.

4.

Regarding other guardianship and/or conservatorship petitions pending, (initial one)

a._____ there are none

b._____ there is one; it has been filed in the _______________ Court of __________ County, State of ____, (address) ________________.

5.

(initial one):

a._____ The guardianship and/or conservatorship is of a minor. The following are the adult siblings of the minor:

NAME ADDRESS

b._____ The guardianship and/or conservatorship is of an adult ward. Pursuant to law, the names, addresses, and relationships of the persons to be notified are as follows: (NOTE: The law requires notice to be given to the spouse, if any, and to all living children, if any, whose addresses are known. If there are no living adult children whose addresses are known, then list at least two adults in the following order of priority: lineal descendants of the proposed ward; parents and siblings of the proposed ward; and friends of the proposed ward. In determining the persons to whom notice is required to be given according to the foregoing rules, the petitioner(s) should not be counted as persons receiving notice.)

NAME AGE (or over 18) ADDRESS RELATIONSHIP

GEORGIA PROBATE COURT
STANDARD FORM

6.

The following individuals, other than Petitioner(s), are caring for the minor/ward; have been appointed as guardian for the minor/ward; or have been appointed conservator for the minor/ward (or enter "not applicable"):

NAME ADDRESS RELATIONSHIP OR APPOINTED TITLE

7.

The following individual(s), other than Petitioner(s), is/are acting as legal representative, legal counsel, guardian ad litem, or court visitor by the court having jurisdiction over the current guardianship and/or conservatorship (or enter "not applicable")

NAME ADDRESS RELATIONSHIP OR APPOINTED TITLE

GEORGIA PROBATE COURT
STANDARD FORM

8.

If there is a conservatorship, the following is the name and address of the surety on the conservator's bond (or enter "not applicable")

NAME ADDRESS

9.

All known income and assets of the proposed ward are shown on page 6 attached hereto.

10.

The transfer of said guardianship and/or conservatorship to Georgia is in the best interest of the minor/ward because ______

11.

Additional Data: Where full particulars are lacking, state here the reasons for any such omission.

GEORGIA PROBATE COURT
STANDARD FORM

WHEREFORE, your Petitioner(s) pray(s) that
1. notice be served as required by law;
2. a hearing be held on the matter; and
3. this Court receive and accept the foreign guardianship and/or conservatorship.

______________________	______________________
Signature of Petitioner	Signature of second Petitioner, if any
______________________	______________________
Printed Name	Printed Name
______________________	______________________
Address	Address
______________________	______________________
______________________	______________________
Telephone Number	Telephone Number

Signature of Attorney:______________________

Typed/printed name of Attorney:______________________
Address: ______________________

Telephone: ______________ State Bar # ______________

VERIFICATION

GEORGIA, ______________________ COUNTY

Personally appeared before me the undersigned Petitioner(s) who on oath state(s) that the facts set forth in the foregoing petition are true.

Sworn to and subscribed before me this ___ day of ________, 20_____.	______________________ Petitioner
______________________ NOTARY/CLERK OF PROBATE COURT	______________________ Printed Name

____

Sworn to and subscribed before me this ___ day of ________, 20_____.	______________________ Second Petitioner, if any
______________________ NOTARY/CLERK OF PROBATE COURT	______________________ Printed Name

GEORGIA PROBATE COURT
STANDARD FORM

ASSETS, INCOME, OTHER SOURCES OF FUNDS OF WARD

WARD: __________

REAL PROPERTY
(Indicate if property is jointly owned and with whom)

	Description	County	State	Approximate equity
Parcel_1				$
Parcel_2				$
Parcel_3				$

INCOME FROM ALL SOURCES

	Yearly Total
Social Security per year	$
SSI (Supplemental Security Income)_ per year	$
Retirement benefits per year	$
VA benefits per year	$
Other income per year, including, e.g., alimony, annuity, or trust distributions	$
Interest, dividend, or investment income	$
YEARLY TOTAL OF ALL INCOME	$

PERSONAL AND INTANGIBLE PROPERTY

(Indicate if property is jointly owned and with whom)

Approximate Current Value

1. Checking/Savings/Money Market/Certificates of Deposit/Liquid Accounts:

Bank/Financial Institution/Broker	Acct. No.	Joint Owner (if any)	
			$
			$
			$
			$

GEORGIA PROBATE COURT
STANDARD FORM

2. Stocks/Bonds/Investments (including retirement and profit-sharing accounts):

a. held by brokers:

Brokerage Firm or Institution	Acct. No.	Joint Owner (if any)	
			$
			$
			$
			$
			$

b. privately held:

Company/Issuer	No. of Shares	Joint Owner (if any)	
			$
			$
			$

3. Automobiles:

Year/Make/Model	V.I.N.	Joint owner (if any)	
			$
			$

4. Other assets of significant value:

Description	Joint owner (if any)	
		$
		$
		$

TOTAL VALUE OF PERSONAL AND INTANGIBLE PROPERTY $

GEORGIA PROBATE COURT
STANDARD FORM

ACKNOWLEDGMENT OF SERVICE

IN RE: Estate of ______________________ ESTATE NO. ______________________

Due and legal service of the Petition for Receipt and Acceptance of Foreign Guardianship is hereby acknowledged by the following interested persons as shown in paragraphs 5, 6, 7, and 8. The undersigned acknowledges that he/she has received a copy of the Petition and all further service and notice is waived.

SIGNATURE(S)

Sworn to and subscribed before me this ___ day of __________, 20___.

______________________ ______________________

NOTARY/CLERK OF PROBATE COURT Printed Name

Sworn to and subscribed before me this ___ day of __________, 20______.

______________________ ______________________

NOTARY/CLERK OF PROBATE COURT Printed Name

Sworn to and subscribed before me this ___ day of __________, 20 ______.

______________________ ______________________

NOTARY/CLERK OF PROBATE COURT Printed Name

Sworn to and subscribed before me this ___ day of __________, 20 ______.

______________________ ______________________

NOTARY/CLERK OF PROBATE COURT Printed Name

Sworn to and subscribed before me this ___ day of __________, 20 ______.

______________________ ______________________

NOTARY/CLERK OF PROBATE COURT Printed Name

Instructions and form adopted effective July 31, 2006.

GPCSF 60 COURT. COURT FORMS FOR PETITION FOR RECEIPT AND ACCEPTANCE OF FOREIGN GUARDIANSHIP AND/OR CONSERVATORSHIP

GEORGIA PROBATE COURT
STANDARD FORM

Petition for the Receipt and Acceptance of a Foreign Guardianship/Conservatorship

NOTICE: UNLESS OTHERWISE DIRECTED BY THE COURT, THE FOLLOWING FORMS ARE FOR PROBATE COURT STAFF TO COMPLETE

GEORGIA PROBATE COURT
STANDARD FORM

PROBATE COURT OF ____________________ COUNTY

STATE OF GEORGIA

IN RE:) ESTATE NO. ____________
)
____________________,) PETITION FOR THE RECEIPT AND
WARD) ACCEPTANCE OF A FOREIGN
) GUARDIANSHIP/CONSERVATORSHIP

NOTICE OF PROCEEDINGS CONCERNING THE ACCEPTANCE OF TRANSFER OF GUARDIANSHIP AND/OR CONSERVATORSHIP FROM FOREIGN JURISDICTION TO THIS COUNTY AND REQUEST TO THE FOREIGN COURT

Date of Mailing of Notice:

TO THE MINOR/WARD: This is to notify you of a proceeding initiated in this court by ____________________ seeking to transfer to this County from the Court located in ____________ County, State of ____________ the guardianship/conservatorship created by Order dated ______ and to inform you of your right to independent counsel. If you wish to retain your own attorney, you must notify this court within two days; otherwise, an attorney will be appointed for you by the court. (If you wish a hearing scheduled in this matter, you must make a written request for hearing on or before the 30th day following the date you receive this notice) (A hearing on the matter will be scheduled by separate Order). YOU AND YOUR ATTORNEY HAVE THE RIGHT TO ATTEND ANY HEARING HELD ON THIS MATTER.

TO THE FOREIGN COURT: The undersigned hereby requests that you certify 1) whether you have any record that the guardian/conservator as shown above has engaged in malfeasance, misfeasance, or nonfeasance during his/her appointment; 2) whether periodic reports have been filed in a satisfactory manner; and 3) whether all bonds or other security requirements imposed under the guardianship/conservatorship have been performed. For your convenience, you may use the enclosed form if you wish.

Further, please forward to this Court a copy of all documents in your file, including but not limited to the initial petition for guardianship/conservatorship and other filings relevant to the appointment of a guardian / conservator; reports and recommendations of guardians ad litem, court visitors, or other individuals appointed by the foreign court to evaluate the appropriateness of the guardianship/conservatorship; if concerning an adult, reports of physical and mental health practitioners describing the capacity of the ward to care for himself or herself or to manage his or her affairs; periodic status reports on the condition of the minor/ward; and any order to transfer the guardianship/conservatorship. (A hearing on the matter will be held (in the Probate Court of ____________________ County, courtroom ____________________, (address) ______________________________ Georgia) (at the following location: ____________________).

TO THE INTERESTED PERSONS AS SHOWN IN THE PETITION: You have the right to object to the petition for receipt and acceptance of guardianship/conservatorship by this Court. (If you wish a hearing scheduled in this matter, you must make a written request for hearing on or before the 30th day following the date that this notice was mailed to you.)(A hearing on the matter will be held (in the Probate Court of ____________ County, courtroom ____________, (address) ____________, Georgia) (at the following location: ____________________).

Witness my hand and seal this _____ day of ______________, 20____.

PROBATE CLERK/DEPUTY CLERK

GEORGIA PROBATE COURT
STANDARD FORM

CERTIFICATE OF MAILING OF ORDER AND NOTICE OF HEARING

ESTATE NO. ______________________

This is to certify that I have this day served a copy of the Petition and this Order on the foreign Court, the minor/ward's attorney, and the interested persons identified in paragraphs 5, 6, 7, and 8 of the petition; and a copy of this Order on the petitioner(s) and his/her/their attorney by placing copies of same in an envelope addressed to each and depositing same in the U.S. Mail, first-class, with adequate postage thereon.

This _____ day of ________________, 20____.

PROBATE CLERK/DEPUTY CLERK

GEORGIA PROBATE COURT
STANDARD FORM

PROBATE COURT OF ________________________ COUNTY

STATE OF GEORGIA

IN RE:) ESTATE NO.
)
_______________________,) PETITION FOR THE RECEIPT AND
WARD) ACCEPTANCE OF A FOREIGN
) GUARDIANSHIP/CONSERVATORSHIP

ORDER AND NOTICE OF HEARING

The above Petition being filed with, and reviewed by, the Court, it is

ORDERED that a hearing shall be set for ____ o'clock ___.M. on ___________, 20 _____, which is not less than 10 days from the date that this notice is mailed, to hear evidence on the proposed transfer of the guardianship/conservatorship to this Court, to be held (in the Probate Court of _____________ County, courtroom _______, (address) ______________, Georgia) (at the following location: ______________________).

IT IS FURTHER ORDERED that attorney __________ is hereby appointed to represent the minor/ward at such hearing; said appointment will be rescinded if counsel retained by the ward files an entry of appearance.

IT IS FURTHER ORDERED that a copy of the Petition and this Order shall be personally served on the minor/ward as soon as practicable after the signing of this order.

IT IS FURTHER ORDERED that a copy of the Petition and this Order shall be sent to the foreign Court, to the minor/ward's attorney, and to the interested persons identified in paragraphs 5, 6, 7, and 8 of the petition by first class mail as soon as practicable after the signing of this order.

IT IS FURTHER ORDERED that a copy of this Order shall be sent to the petitioner(s) and his/her/their attorney by first-class mail, as soon as practicable after the signing of this order.

SO ORDERED this _____ day of __________________, 20____.

Probate Judge

Effective 7/06 GPCSF 60Court

GEORGIA PROBATE COURT
STANDARD FORM

CERTIFICATION BY FOREIGN COURT TO BE FILED IN THE PROBATE COURT OF ______________________ COUNTY, STATE OF GEORGIA

IN RE:	)	**ESTATE NO. ______________**
	)	
______________________________,	)	**PETITION FOR THE RECEIPT AND**
WARD	)	**ACCEPTANCE OF A FOREIGN**
	)	**GUARDIANSHIP/CONSERVATORSHIP**
	)	
	)	**FOREIGN COURT'S FILE NUMBER:**
	)	

COMES NOW ______, (JUDGE) (DEPUTY CLERK) (CLERK) (other: ______) OF THE ______ Court, ____________, and pursuant to the request made by the Probate Court of ________ County, Georgia, hereby certifies that (initial one):

_____a. There is no record that the guardian/conservator as shown above has engaged in malfeasance, misfeasance, or nonfeasance during his/her appointment; 2) periodic reports have been filed in a satisfactory manner; and 3) all bonds or other security requirements imposed under the guardianship/conservatorship have been performed.

_____b. There has been some record of malfeasance, misfeasance, or nonfeasance regarding the above estate and fiduciary, being __________________ as indicated in the attached records.

_____c. This Court declines to transfer the above matter to the above Georgia Probate Court.

Further, attached are copies of all documents relevant to the guardianship/conservatorship of the above ward.

JUDGE/COURT PERSONNEL

Title

Typed/printed name of Judge or Court Personnel:

Address:

Telephone number:

Effective 7/06 GPCSF 60Court

GEORGIA PROBATE COURT
STANDARD FORM

PROBATE COURT OF ______________________ COUNTY

STATE OF GEORGIA

IN RE:	) ESTATE NO. ______________
	)
______________________________,	) PETITION FOR THE RECEIPT AND
WARD	) ACCEPTANCE OF A FOREIGN
	) GUARDIANSHIP/CONSERVATORSHIP

RETURN OF SHERIFF

I have this day served ______________________ personally with a copy of the within petition, order and notice.

This _____ day of ______________, 20 ____.

Deputy Sheriff ______________ County, Georgia

GEORGIA PROBATE COURT
STANDARD FORM

WAIVER BY MINOR/WARD'S ATTORNEY

GEORGIA, ______________________ COUNTY ESTATE NO. ______________________

TO THE PROBATE COURT OF SAID STATE AND COUNTY

IN RE: PETITION FOR THE RECEIPT AND ACCEPTANCE OF A FOREIGN GUARDIANSHIP/CONSERVATORSHIP

The undersigned, as the attorney representing the above-named minor/ward in these proceedings, waives the appearance of my client at said hearing.

This _____ day of ______________________, 20 ____.

Attorney ____

Typed/printed name of Attorney: ____

Address: ____

Telephone: ____________________ State Bar # ____________________

GEORGIA PROBATE COURT
STANDARD FORM

PROBATE COURT OF ______________________ COUNTY

STATE OF GEORGIA

IN RE:	)	**ESTATE NO.**
	)	
______________________________,	)	**PETITION FOR THE RECEIPT AND**
WARD	)	**ACCEPTANCE OF A FOREIGN**
	)	**GUARDIANSHIP/CONSERVATORSHIP**

FINAL ORDER

A Petition for the Receipt and Acceptance of a Foreign Guardianship/Conservatorship being filed ____________________, 20 _____, and (initial one):

_____ a. a hearing being held _______________, 20_____,

_____ b. no hearing being requested, and based on the documentation submitted to the Court, it appearing that no hearing is necessary,

and it appearing that the fiduciary appointed in the foreign court has complied with the laws of the foreign state; and it appearing that the minor/ward has been relocated to this jurisdiction; and it appearing that it is in the best interest for the guardianship and/or conservatorship of the above minor/ward to be transferred to this jurisdiction, it is

ORDERED that the Petition for the Receipt and Acceptance of a Foreign Guardianship/Conservatorship is hereby GRANTED.

(initial all applicable):

_____ a. IT IS FURTHER ORDERED that if the fiduciary(ies) was/were appointed as guardian(s) of person, letters of guardianship shall issue to such guardian(s) upon taking the required oath. **The appointed guardian(s) shall have no authority to act on behalf of the ward until Letters of Guardianship have issued.**

_____ b. IT IS FURTHER ORDERED that if the fiduciary(ies) was/were appointed as guardian(s) of the property or conservator(s), letters of conservatorship shall issue to such conservator(s) upon taking the required oath and upon posting bond in the amount of $___________________. **The appointed conservator(s) shall have no authority to act on behalf of the ward until Letters of Conservatorship have issued.**

GEORGIA PROBATE COURT
STANDARD FORM

IT IS FURTHER ORDERED that, if only a guardian is appointed for the minor/ward, or if different individuals are appointed guardian and conservator, the following reasonable sums of property shall be provided to the guardian to provide adequately for the minor/ward's support, care, education, health, and welfare, until further Order of the Court: $______________ per ______________.

IT IS FURTHER ORDERED that the guardian shall file, in addition to the personal status report, the following supplemental reports: (monthly)(annually).

IT IS FURTHER ORDERED that a copy of this Order shall be served by first class mail on the foreign court, the minor/ward, the minor/ward's attorney; the guardian(s) and/or conservator(s); the petitioner(s); his/her/their attorney(s); and the individuals listed in paragraphs 5, 6, 7, and 8 of the Petition.

IT IS FURTHER ORDERED that, within 30 days of the date hereof, the clerk/deputy clerk shall file the certificate of creation of conservatorship in accordance with O.C.G.A. §29-5-13(d) with the Clerk of Superior Court of each county in this state in which the minor/ward owns real property.

SO ORDERED this ______ day of ______________, 20____.

Probate Judge/Hearing Officer exercising the
jurisdiction of the Probate Court pursuant
to O.C.G.A. §29-4-12(d)(7) and/or 29-5-12(d)(7)

GEORGIA PROBATE COURT
STANDARD FORM

CERTIFICATE OF MAILING OF FINAL ORDER

ESTATE NO.

I have this date mailed (or handed) a copy of the above Order to the foreign court, the minor/ward, his/her attorney, (his/her guardian ad litem), (his/her representatives,) the guardian(s), the conservator(s), the interested persons shown in paragraphs 5, 6, 7, and 8 of the petition, the petitioner(s), and (petitioner's attorney).

DATE PROBATE CLERK/DEPUTY CLERK

CERTIFICATE OF FILING CERTIFICATE OF CREATION OF CONSERVATORSHIP

ESTATE NO.

I have this date hand-delivered and/or mailed for filing a Certificate of Creation of Conservatorship to the Clerk of the Superior Court of each of the following counties, together with payment of any recording costs:

PROBATE CLERK/DEPUTY CLERK

ADDRESS

TELEPHONE

GEORGIA PROBATE COURT
STANDARD FORM

Probate Court Return Mailing Address:

CERTIFICATE OF CREATION OF CONSERVATORSHIP
(Pursuant to O.C.G.A. §29-5-13(d))

GEORGIA, ______________________________ County

PROBATE ESTATE NO. ____________________

DATE ORDER ISSUED: ____________________

GRANTOR: (NAME OF MINOR/WARD) ____
(If Minor, Date of Birth of Minor: ____________________)

GRANTEE: (NAME OF CONSERVATOR(S) OF ABOVE WARD)

A Conservatorship has been created for the above-named ward.

_____a. The Conservatorship is permanent.

_____b. The expiration date set by court order, is __________, 20 ____.

Original Certificate delivered or mailed to Clerk of Superior Court of ____________________ County on ______________________________, 20____.

I do hereby certify that the above information is based on the order of the Probate Court issued on the date set out above and that the above information is true and correct.

By: ____
PROBATE CLERK/DEPUTY CLERK

Effective 7/06

GPCSF 60Court

GEORGIA PROBATE COURT
STANDARD FORM

STATE OF GEORGIA

COUNTY OF ______________________________ ESTATE NO. ______________

LETTERS OF GUARDIANSHIP OF ADULT WARD

From the Judge of the Probate Court of said County. Date of Birth: ______________

TO: ______________________________, Guardian(s)

RE: ______________________________, Adult Ward

The above-named adult ward has been found by this Court to be in need of a guardian, and this Court has entered an order designating you as such guardian(s). You have assented to this appointment by taking your oath. In general, your duties as guardian are to protect and maintain the person of the ward.

Special Instructions:

1. It is your duty to see that the ward is adequately fed, clothed, sheltered and cared for, and that the ward receives all necessary medical attention.

2. You must keep the Court informed of any change in your name or address and promptly notify the Court of any conflict of interest arising between you and your ward.

3. Within 60 days after appointment and within 60 days after each anniversary date of appointment, you must file with the probate court a personal status report concerning your ward which shall include:
   (a) A description of the ward's general condition, changes since the last report, and needs;
   (b) Your recommendations for any alteration in the guardianship order;
   (c) All addresses of the ward during the reporting period and the living arrangements of the ward for all addresses;
   (d) A description of the amount of any funds received and expended by the guardian for the support of the ward.

4. Please consult your attorney if you have any questions.

5. Your authority to act pursuant to these Letters is subject to applicable statutes and to any special orders entered in this case.

Given under my hand and official seal, the ____ day of __________, 20____.

Probate Judge

NOTE: The following must be signed if the judge does not sign the original of this document:

Issued by:

______________________________ (Seal)
PROBATE CLERK/DEPUTY CLERK

Effective 7/06 GPCSF 60Court

GEORGIA PROBATE COURT
STANDARD FORM

STATE OF GEORGIA
COUNTY OF ______________________ ESTATE NO. ____________

LETTERS OF CONSERVATORSHIP OF ADULT WARD

From the Judge of the Probate Court of said County. Date of Birth: ____________

TO: ______________________, Conservator(s)

RE: ______________________, Adult Ward

The above-named adult ward has been found by this Court to be in need of a conservator, and this Court has entered an order designating you as such conservator(s). You have assented to this appointment by taking your oath and posting a bond. In general, your duties as conservator are to protect and maintain the property of the ward.

Special Instructions:

1. You must keep your ward's funds separate from your own. You should put your ward's funds in a separate checking or savings account, as appropriate, and make all payments by check.
2. You may not sell, mortgage, give away, or otherwise dispose of any of your ward's property without a court order.
3. You may not spend any of your ward's funds for any purpose except as set forth in the court approved budget without a court order.
4. You must file within two months of your appointment an inventory showing the ward's property and a plan for managing, expending, and distributing the property. Further, you must file, within 60 days of each anniversary date of these Letters an annual return, showing all receipts and disbursements, accompanied by an affidavit certifying that the original vouchers (checks) have been compared with the items listed on the return, and that the return is correct, together with an updated inventory and plan for managing the property. A copy of said return shall be sent by first class mail to the surety, the ward, and the guardian, if any.
5. The regular commissions allowed a conservator are 2.5% on all sums of money received, and 2.5% on all sums paid out, as shown by the annual or final return. There are special rules concerning commissions for property delivered in kind, interest earned, extraordinary services, and market value of property held as of the last day of your reporting period.
6. You must keep the Court informed of any change in your name or address and promptly notify the Court of any conflict of interest arising between you and your ward.
7. You should inform the Court of any change of location of your ward.
8. Please consult your attorney if you have any questions.
9. Your authority to act pursuant to these Letters is subject to applicable statutes and to any special orders entered in this case.

Given under my hand and official seal, the ____ day of ______________, 20____.

Probate Judge

NOTE: The following must be signed if the judge does not sign the original of this document:

Issued by:

______________________ (Seal)
PROBATE CLERK/DEPUTY CLERK

Effective 7/06 GPCSF 60Court

GEORGIA PROBATE COURT
STANDARD FORM

STATE OF GEORGIA
COUNTY OF ______________________________ ESTATE NO. ______________

LETTERS OF GUARDIANSHIP AND CONSERVATORSHIP OF ADULT WARD

From the Judge of the Probate Court of said County. Date of Birth: ______________
TO: ______________________________, Guardian(s) and Conservator(s)
RE: ______________________________, Adult Ward

The above-named adult ward has been found by this Court to be in need of a guardian and conservator, and this Court has entered an order designating you as such guardian(s) and conservator(s). You have assented to this appointment by taking your oath and posting a bond. In general, your powers and duties are to protect and maintain the person and property of the ward.

Special Instructions:

1. It is your duty to see that your ward is adequately fed, clothed, sheltered and cared for, and that your ward receives all necessary medical attention.
2. You must keep your ward's funds separate from your own. You should put your ward's funds in a separate checking or savings account, as appropriate, and make all payments by check.
3. You may not sell, mortgage, give away, or otherwise dispose of any of your ward's property without a court order.
4. You may not spend any of your ward's funds for any purpose, except as set forth in the court approved budget, without a court order.
5. You must file within two months of your appointment an inventory showing the ward's property and a plan for managing, expending, and distributing the property. Further, you must file, within 60 days of each anniversary date of these Letters an annual return, showing all receipts and disbursements, accompanied by an affidavit certifying that the original vouchers (checks) have been compared with the items listed on the return, and that the return is correct, together with an updated inventory and plan for managing the property. A copy of said return shall be sent by first class mail to the surety, the ward, and the guardian, if any.
6. The regular commissions allowed a conservator are 2.5% on all sums of money received, and 2.5% on all sums paid out, as shown by the annual or final return. There are special rules concerning commissions for property delivered in kind, interest earned, extraordinary services, and market value of property held as of the last day of your reporting period.
7. You must keep the Court informed of any change in your name or address and promptly notify the Court of any conflict of interest arising between you and your ward.
8. Within 60 days after appointment and within 60 days after each anniversary date of appointment, you must file with the probate court a personal status report concerning your ward which shall include:
   (a) A description of your ward's general condition, changes since the last report, and needs;
   (b) Your recommendations for any alteration in the guardianship/conservatorship order;
   (c) All addresses of the ward during the reporting period and the living arrangements of the ward for all addresses.
9. Your authority to act pursuant to these Letters is subject to applicable statutes and to any special orders entered in this case.

Given under my hand and official seal, the ____ day of ____________________, 20____.

Probate Judge

NOTE: The following must be signed if the judge does not sign the original of this document:

Issued by:

______________________________ (Seal)
PROBATE CLERK/DEPUTY CLERK

Effective 7/06 GPCSF 60Court

GEORGIA PROBATE COURT
STANDARD FORM

STATE OF GEORGIA

COUNTY OF ______________________ ESTATE NO. ______________

LETTERS OF CONSERVATORSHIP OF MINOR

From the Judge of the Probate Court of said County.

TO: ______________________________, Conservator(s)

RE: ______________________________, Minor

The above-named minor has been found by this Court to be in need of a conservator, and this Court has entered an order designating you as such conservator(s). You have assented to this appointment by taking your oath and posting bond. In general, your duties as conservator(s) are to protect and maintain the property of the above-named minor. Your authority to act pursuant to these Letters is subject to applicable statues[1] and to any special orders entered in this case.

Please consult your attorney if you have any questions.

Given under my hand and official seal, this ____ day of ________________, 20____.

Probate Judge

Note: The following must be signed if the judge does not sign the original of this document:

Issued by:

______________________________ (Seal)
PROBATE CLERK/DEPUTY CLERK

[1] So in original

Effective 7/06 GPCSF 60Court

GEORGIA PROBATE COURT
STANDARD FORM

STATE OF GEORGIA

COUNTY OF ______________________ ESTATE NO. ____________

LETTERS OF PERMANENT GUARDIANSHIP OF MINOR

From the Judge of the Probate Court of said County.

TO: ______________________, Guardian(s)

RE: ______________________, Minor

The above-named minor has been found by this Court to be in need of a guardian, and this Court has entered an order designating you as such guardian(s). You have assented to this appointment by taking your oath. In general, your duties as guardian are to protect and maintain the person of the minor and your power over the minor shall be the same as that of a parent over a child, the guardian(s) standing in place of the parent(s). A guardian shall at all times act as a fiduciary in the minor's best interest and exercise reasonable care, diligence, and prudence.

Special Instructions:

1. It is your duty to see that the minor is adequately fed, clothed, sheltered, educated, and cared for, and that the minor receives all necessary medical attention.
2. You must keep the Court informed of any change in your name or address.
3. You should inform the Court of any change of location of your minor.
4. You shall, within 60 days of appointment and within 60 days after each anniversary date of appointment, file with this Court and provide to the conservator of the minor, if any, a personal status report concerning the minor.
5. You shall promptly notify the court of any conflict of interest which may arise between you as guardian and the minor pursuant to O.C.G.A. §29-2-23.
6. The guardianship automatically terminates when the minor dies, reaches age 18, is adopted, or is emancipated.
7. You shall act in coordination and cooperation with the minor's conservator, if appointed, or if not, with others who have custody of the minor's property.
8. Please consult your attorney if you have any questions. Your authority to act pursuant to these Letters is subject to applicable statues[1] and to any special orders entered in this case.

Give under my hand and official seal, this ____ day of ________________, 20____.

Probate Judge

NOTE: The following must be signed if the judge does not sign the original of this document:

Issued by:

____
PROBATE CLERK/DEPUTY CLERK (Seal)

[1] So in original

Effective 7/06 GPCSF 60Court

Form adopted effective July 31, 2006.

GPCSF 65 PETITIONER. PETITION FOR THE RESTORATION OF AN INDIVIDUAL FOUND TO BE IN NEED OF A GUARDIAN AND/OR CONSERVATOR

GEORGIA PROBATE COURT
STANDARD FORM

Petition for the Restoration of an Individual Found to Be in Need of a Guardian and/or Conservator

INSTRUCTIONS

I. Specific Instructions

1. This form is to be used for filing a Petition for the Reinstatement of a Ward (formerly Incapacitated Adult) pursuant to O.C.G.A. §29- 4-42 and O.C.G.A. §29-5-72.
2. The burden of proof is on the petitioner to show by a preponderance of the evidence that there is no longer a need for a guardianship and/or conservatorship.

II. General Instructions

General instructions applicable to all Georgia probate court standard forms appear in Volume 255 of the Georgia Reports and are available in each probate court.

GEORGIA PROBATE COURT
STANDARD FORM

PROBATE COURT OF ______________________ COUNTY

STATE OF GEORGIA

IN RE:) ESTATE NO. ______________

)
______________________________,) PETITION FOR RESTORATION OF
WARD) AN INDIVIDUAL FORMERLY FOUND TO
) BE IN NEED OF A GUARDIAN AND/OR
) CONSERVATOR

TO THE HONORABLE JUDGE OF THE PROBATE COURT:

%ADNOTE: Unless there are two or more petitioners, the affidavit on page 9 must be completed by a physician, psychologist, or licensed clinical social worker based upon an examination within 15 days prior to the filing of this petition.]

1.

Petitioner, ____, is
______ a. the Ward
______ b. the (relationship) ____________________________ of the ward, and is domiciled at (address) ______________________________ County, State of ______________, telephone number ___________, and

(Initial either a. or b. below):

______ a. (Second Petitioner, if any) ______________________________, is the (relationship) ______________________________ of the ward, and is domiciled at (address) ______________________________ County, State of ___________________ telephone number ____________, show that

or

______ b. attached hereto as page 4 and made a part of this petition is the completed affidavit of ______________________________, a physician or psychologist licensed to practice in Georgia or a licensed clinical social worker, who has examined the ward within fifteen days prior to the filing of this petition, show that:

2.

The ward is domiciled at (address) ____________________ County, State of ____________________, and is presently located at ________________________________, and can be contacted at (telephone number): ____________________.

3.

The proposed ward no longer is in need of a guardian and/or conservator because:

(NOTE: the Petition cannot be granted unless sufficient facts are presented which support the claim for the restoration of the Ward. While an attached physician's/psychologist's/social worker's affidavit is permissible, the Petitioner(s) MUST specifically allege sufficient facts to support the granting of this Petition.)

4.

(Name(s) or n/a) ______________________________ currently serve(s) as the guardian and (Name(s) or n/a) ______________________________ as the conservator.

5.

Additional Data: Where full particulars are lacking, state here the reasons for any such omission.

WHEREFORE, petitioner(s) pray(s):

1. that service be perfected as required by law;
2. that the court appoint legal counsel and an evaluator for the ward and order an evaluation as required by law;
3. that upon receipt of the evaluation report, the court order a hearing to determine the continued need for a guardian and/or conservator for the ward; and
4. that the ward's rights be restored.

Signature of first petitioner	Signature of second petitioner, if any
Printed Name	Printed Name
Address	Address
Telephone Number	Telephone Number

Signature of Attorney: ____________

Typed/printed name of Attorney: ____________
Address: ____________

Telephone: ____________ State Bar # ___

VERIFICATION

GEORGIA, ____________ COUNTY

Personally appeared before me the undersigned petitioner(s) who on oath state(s) that the facts set forth in the foregoing petition are true.

Sworn to and subscribed before me this ______ day of __________, 20 ___.

First Petitioner

NOTARY/CLERK OF PROBATE COURT

Printed Name

Sworn to and subscribed before me this ______ day of __________, 20 ___.

Second Petitioner, if any

NOTARY/CLERK OF PROBATE COURT
STATE OF GEORGIA

Printed Name

STATE OF GEORGIA
COUNTY OF

PROBATE COURT OF ____________________ COUNTY

RE: Petition for RESTORATION of ____________________, a Ward.

AFFIDAVIT OF PHYSICIAN, PSYCHOLOGIST, OR LICENSED CLINICAL SOCIAL WORKER

I, being first duly sworn, depose and say that I am a physician licensed to practice under Chapter 34 of Title 43 of the Official Code of Georgia Annotated, a psychologist licensed to practice under Chapter 39 of Title 43 of the Official Code of Georgia Annotated, or a Licensed Clinical Social Worker; that my office address is ____________________, Georgia, that I have examined the above-named ward on the ______ day of __________, 20 ____, and that I found him/her to

(initial all applicable):

______ a. (for restoration regarding guardianship:) now have sufficient capacity to make or communicate significant responsible decisions concerning his/her health or safety.

______ b. (for restoration regarding conservatorship:) now have sufficient capacity to make or communicate significant responsible decisions concerning the management of his/her property.

______ c. (for retention of guardianship:) still lack sufficient capacity to make or communicate significant responsible decisions concerning his/her health or safety.

______ d. (for retention of conservatorship:) still lack sufficient capacity to make or communicate significant responsible decisions concerning the management of his/her property.

The following facts support said diagnosis:

(RESTORATION FORM, cont.)

WITNESS MY HAND AND SEAL this ________ day of ________________, 20 ___.

Sworn to and subscribed before me this ______ day of ________, 20 ___.

____

Signature of (Physician)(Psychologist)(Social Worker)

Notary Public

My commission expires on the ___ day of ________________, 20 ___.
(NOTARIAL SEAL AFFIXED)

Typed Name _______________________

NOTE: The examination on which this affidavit is based must occur WITHIN FIFTEEN DAYS prior to the filing of the petition.

Instructions and form adopted effective July 31, 2006.

GPCSF 65 COURT. COURT FORMS FOR PETITION FOR THE RESTORATION OF AN INDIVIDUAL FOUND TO BE IN NEED OF A GUARDIAN AND/OR CONSERVATOR

GEORGIA PROBATE COURT
STANDARD FORM

Petition for the Restoration of an Individual Found to Be in Need of a Guardian and/or Conservator

NOTICE: UNLESS OTHERWISE DIRECTED BY THE COURT, THE FOLLOWING FORMS ARE FOR PROBATE COURT STAFF TO COMPLETE

GEORGIA PROBATE COURT
STANDARD FORM

PROBATE COURT OF ____________________ COUNTY

STATE OF GEORGIA

IN RE:) ESTATE NO. ____________________
)
______________________________,) PETITION FOR RESTORATION OF
WARD) AN INDIVIDUAL FORMERLY FOUND TO
) BE IN NEED OF A GUARDIAN AND/OR
) CONSERVATOR

ORDER FOR EVALUATION

The above and foregoing petition having been read and considered, and it appearing that there is sufficient evidence to believe that the ward may no longer be in need of a guardian and/or conservator within the meaning of O.C.G.A. §29-4-1 and/or 29-5-1, it is hereby ordered that ______________, (physician) (psychologist) (licensed clinical social worker), is appointed to evaluate the above-named ward at ______ o'clock ___.M., on ______________ 20 ______ at (location) ______________________________.

IT IS FURTHER ORDERED that the above-named ward shall submit to an evaluation at the time and place stated above;

IT IS FURTHER ORDERED that the evaluator shall explain the purpose of the evaluation to the ward;

IT IS FURTHER ORDERED that a Clerk/deputy clerk shall immediately notify the ward of these proceedings by having all pleadings, as well as this order and the notice of proceedings to appoint guardian and/or conservator, personally served on the ward.

SO ORDERED this ______ day of ____________________, 20____.

Probate Judge

Effective 7/06 GPCSF 65Court

CERTIFICATE OF MAILING OF ORDER AND NOTICE OF PROCEEDINGS

ESTATE NO.

This is to certify that I have this day served the petitioner(s); the ward's guardian ad litem (if any) and attorney with a copy of the petition, order, and notice of proceedings to restore rights of ward by placing a copy of same in an envelope addressed to each and depositing same in the U.S. Mail, first-class, with adequate postage thereon.

This ______ day of ____________________, 20____.

PROBATE CLERK/DEPUTY CLERK

CERTIFICATE OF MAILING OF ORDER FOR DISMISSAL

ESTATE NO.

This is to certify that I have this day served the ward with a copy of the (petition and) order for dismissal by placing a copy of same in an envelope addressed to the ward and depositing same in the U.S. Mail, first-class, with adequate postage thereon. I have also served a copy of the order for dismissal in the same manner upon the persons required in said order to be so served.

This ______ day of ____________________, 20____.

PROBATE CLERK/DEPUTY CLERK

* not necessary if dismissal is after evaluation.

PROBATE COURT OF ____________________ COUNTY

STATE OF GEORGIA

IN RE:) ESTATE NO. ____________________
)
______________________________,) PETITION FOR RESTORATION OF
WARD) AN INDIVIDUAL FORMERLY FOUND TO
) BE IN NEED OF A GUARDIAN AND/OR
) CONSERVATOR

NOTICE TO WARD OF PROCEEDINGS TO RESTORE RIGHTS

TO: ________________________: this is to notify you of a proceeding initiated in this court by ________________________ seeking to restore your rights and to inform you of your right to independent counsel. If you wish to retain your own attorney, you must notify this court within two days; otherwise, an attorney will be appointed for you by the court.

You are further notified that ________________________ has been appointed by the Court to evaluate you. If you wish your rights restored, you must submit to an evaluation by being present at: (location) __________ at __________ o'clock ______.M. on ________________, 20____ which is not sooner than the fifth day after the service of notice on you.

YOU ARE FURTHER NOTIFIED:

YOU AND YOUR ATTORNEY HAVE THE RIGHT TO ATTEND ANY HEARING HELD ON THIS MATTER.

Witness my hand and seal this ______ day of ________________, 20____.

PROBATE CLERK/DEPUTY CLERK

Effective 7/06 GPCSF 65Court

PROBATE COURT OF ______________________ COUNTY

STATE OF GEORGIA

IN RE:) ESTATE NO. ________________________

)

__________________________________,) PETITION FOR RESTORATION OF
WARD) AN INDIVIDUAL FORMERLY FOUND TO
) BE IN NEED OF A GUARDIAN AND/OR
) CONSERVATOR

RETURN OF SHERIFF

I have this day served ______________________ personally with a copy of the within petition, order and notice.

This _____ day of ________________, 20____.

Deputy Sheriff ________________ County, Georgia

Effective 7/06 GPCSF 65Court

PROBATE COURT OF ______________________ COUNTY

STATE OF GEORGIA

IN RE:) ESTATE NO. ______________________
)
______________________________________,) PETITION FOR RESTORATION OF
WARD) AN INDIVIDUAL FORMERLY FOUND TO
) BE IN NEED OF A GUARDIAN AND/OR
) CONSERVATOR

APPOINTMENT OF ATTORNEY AND GUARDIAN AD LITEM, IF APPLICABLE

It appearing that this Court has not been notified of the retention of counsel by the ward within the prescribed two-day period, ______________________________ telephone number ____________________, is hereby appointed as attorney for the ward in this matter.

(initial if applicable)

______ IT IS FURTHER ORDERED that ______________________________ is appointed as guardian ad litem for the ward, and said individual shall

______ a. attend the restoration hearing and make a recommendation to the Court.

______ b. file a written recommendation/report with the Court prior to the hearing and shall (be excused from appearing at) (attend) the hearing.

This ______ day of ____________________, 20____.

Probate Judge

EVALUATOR'S REPORT REGARDING RESTORATION

GUARDIANSHIP/CONSERVATORSHIP PROCEEDINGS ESTATE NO. ______________

PETITIONER(S) ____

WARD ____

In compliance with the Order of the Probate Court of __________ County dated ____________________, 20 ____, I performed an evaluation of the above-named ward on ____________________, 20 ____________________. This evaluation took place at (location) ____ beginning at ________ o'clock. The evaluation continued for ____________________ minutes. I explained the purpose of the evaluation to the ward.

The following questions, instruments, or tests were utilized in the evaluation:

Below is a list of all persons and other sources of information consulted in evaluating the ward:

The following is a description of the ward's mental and physical state and condition, including all observed facts considered by me:

The following is a description of the overall social condition of the ward, including support, care, education, and well-being:

The following are my findings as to the needs of the ward and their foreseeable duration:

(initial all applicable)

_____ a. I find that the ward continues to be incapacitated by reason of: __________ ______________________ to the extent that said proposed ward lacks sufficient capacity to make or communicate significant responsible decisions concerning his/her health and safety.

_____ b. I find that the ward continues to be incapacitated by reason of: __________

to the extent that said proposed ward lacks sufficient capacity to make or communicate significant responsible decisions concerning the management of his/her property.

_____ c. I find that the ward now has sufficient capacity to make or communicate significant decisions concerning his/her health and safety.

_____ d. I find that the ward now has sufficient capacity to make or communicate significant responsible decisions concerning the management of his/her property.

Physician licensed under Chapter 34 of Title 43 of the Official Code of Georgia Annotated
or
Psychologist licensed under Chapter 39 of Title 43 of the Official Code of Georgia Annotated
or
Licensed Clinical Social Worker

Sworn to and subscribed before me
This _____ day of ____________________, 20____.

Notary Public/Clerk, Probate Court

NOTE: This report must be filed with the Probate Court no later than (7) days after the date of examination.

PROBATE COURT OF ____________________ COUNTY

STATE OF GEORGIA

IN RE:	) ESTATE NO. ____________________
	)
______________________________,	) PETITION FOR RESTORATION OF
WARD	) AN INDIVIDUAL FORMERLY FOUND TO
	) BE IN NEED OF A GUARDIAN AND/OR
	) CONSERVATOR

ORDER FOR DISMISSAL

The above and foregoing petition having been read and considered pursuant to O.C.G.A. §29-4-11 and/or O.C.G.A. §29-5-11 of the Official Code of Georgia Annotated, and (initial one):

________ a. Based on the allegations made in the petition and prior to the court-ordered evaluation, it appears that there is not probable cause to believe that the ward no longer is in need of a guardian or conservator within the meaning of O.C.G.A. §29-4-1 and/or O.C.G.A. §29-5-1, therefore, it is

ORDERED that the petition is dismissed.

IT IS FURTHER ORDERED that a copy of the petition, the affidavit, if any, and this order be served on the ward by first-class mail, and a copy of this order be served in the same manner upon the petitioner(s) or his/her/their attorney, if any.

________ b. Based on the allegations made in the petition and after review and consideration of the court-ordered evaluation report filed with this court, this court finds that there is not probable cause to support a finding that the ward no longer is in need of a guardian or a conservator within the meaning of O.C.G.A. §29-4-1 and/or O.C.G.A. §29-5-1; therefore, it is

ORDERED that the petition is dismissed.

IT IS FURTHER ORDERED that a copy of this order and the court-ordered evaluation report be served on the ward, his attorney, his guardian ad litem, if any, and to the petitioner(s) or her/her/their attorney, if any, by first class mail.

So ordered this _____ day of ____________________, 20 ____.

Probate Judge

Effective 7/06 GPCSF 65Court

PROBATE COURT OF ________________ COUNTY

STATE OF GEORGIA

IN RE:) ESTATE NO. ____________________

)

________________________________,) PETITION FOR RESTORATION OF

WARD) AN INDIVIDUAL FORMERLY FOUND TO

) BE IN NEED OF A GUARDIAN AND/OR

) CONSERVATOR

ORDER AND NOTICE OF HEARING

After review and consideration of the petition and the court-ordered evaluation report filed with this court, the court finds that there is probable cause to support a finding that the ward no longer is in need of a guardian and/or conservator within the meaning of O.C.G.A. §29-4-1 and/or O.C.G.A. §29-5-1,

THEREFORE, it is ordered and adjudged that:

1. A hearing shall be set for ________________ o'clock _____.M. on ________________, 20 ________, which is not less than 10 days from the date that this notice is mailed, to determine the need for the restoration of the ward's rights, to be held (in the Probate Court of __________ County, courtroom __________, (address) ________________, Georgia) (at the following location: __________). The ward shall be represented by _____, attorney, at such hearing.

2. A copy of this order and a copy of the evaluation report shall be sent to the ward, his/her attorney and guardian ad litem, if any, and to the petitioner(s) and his/her/their attorney, if any. These copies shall be sent by a Clerk/deputy clerk, first-class mail, as soon as practicable after the signing of this order.

So ordered this ______ day of ____________________, 20 ______.

Probate Judge

STIPULATION AND WAIVER BY WARD'S ATTORNEY

GEORGIA, ____________ COUNTY ESTATE NO. ________________

TO THE PROBATE COURT OF SAID STATE AND COUNTY

IN RE: PETITION FOR THE RESTORATION OF RIGHTS OF ____________________, WARD

The undersigned, as the attorney representing the above-named ward in these proceedings, (initial all applicable:)

______ a. does hereby stipulate into evidence the affidavit prepared by (name of affiant evaluator) ____________________, being the evaluation report Ordered by the Court in this matter, and hereby waives the appearance of such affiant at any hearing concerning the said petition.

______ b. does hereby stipulate into evidence the affidavit prepared by (name of affiant evaluator) ____________________, which is the affidavit referred to in Paragraph 1(b) of the petition), and hereby waives the appearance of such affiant at any hearing concerning the said petition.

______ c. does further waive the appearance of my client the ward at said hearing.

This ______ day of ____________________, 20 ____.

____
Attorney

Typed/printed name of Attorney: ____________________________________
Address: ____________________________________
____
Telephone: ________________ State Bar # ____________

PROBATE COURT OF ______________________ COUNTY

STATE OF GEORGIA

IN RE:) ESTATE NO. ______________

)

______________________,) PETITION FOR RESTORATION OF
WARD) AN INDIVIDUAL FORMERLY FOUND TO
) BE IN NEED OF A GUARDIAN AND/OR
) CONSERVATOR

FINAL ORDER

A hearing was held on the above-referenced petition on ______________________, 20 ____, and after considering the pleadings, the evaluation report and the evidence taken at the hearing, the Court makes the following:

FINDINGS OF FACT

1.

All procedural requirements of O.C.G.A. §29-4-11 and O.C.G.A. §29-4-42; and/or O.C.G.A. §29-5-11 and O.C.G.A. §29-5-72 have been met.

2.

The above-named ward is no longer in need of a guardian and/or conservator because ______ ____. The ward now has sufficient capacity to make or communicate significant decisions concerning his/her health and safety, and now has sufficient capacity to make or communicate significant responsible decisions concerning the management of his/her property.

CONCLUSIONS OF LAW

The Court finds, by clear and convincing evidence, that the above-named ward (hereinafter referred to as "former ward") is no longer in need of a guardian or conservator because the ward now has sufficient capacity to make or communicate significant responsible decisions concerning his/her health or safety, and now has sufficient capacity to make or communicate significant responsible decisions concerning the management of his/her property. Therefore it is

ORDERED that ______________________________ is hereby restored to full capacity and the guardianship/conservatorship of said former ward is hereby terminated.

IT IS FURTHER ORDERED that before any guardian and/or conservator, is released from his/her trust, that he/she file a Petition for Discharge and Final Return, with an acknowledgment as executed by the former ward.

IT IS FURTHER ORDERED that a Clerk of this Court shall record the restoration upon all records of this Court, including the previously issued letters of guardianship/conservatorship.

IT IS FURTHER ORDERED that the Clerk of this Court shall, within 30 days of this order, submit a certificate to the clerk of the superior court of each county of this state in which the restored ward owns real property, if any, notifying the clerk to record in the deed records that the ward has been restored to capacity.

IT IS FURTHER ORDERED that a copy of this Order shall be served by first class mail on the former ward, the former ward's attorney; the guardian ad litem, if any; the guardian(s) and/or conservator(s); the petitioner(s); and his/her/their attorney(s).

SO ORDERED this ________ day of ____________________, 20 ____.

Probate Judge/Hearing Officer exercising the
jurisdiction of the Probate Court pursuant
to O.C.G.A. §29-4-12(d)(7) and/or 29-5-12(d)(7)

CERTIFICATE OF MAILING OF FINAL ORDER

ESTATE NO.

I have this date mailed (or handed) a copy of the above Order to the former ward, his/her attorney, (his/her guardian ad litem), (his/her representatives,) the guardian(s), the conservator(s), the petitioner(s), and (petitioner's attorney).

______________________ ______________________

DATE PROBATE CLERK/DEPUTY CLERK

CERTIFICATE OF FILING CERTIFICATE OF RESTORATION OF RIGHTS

ESTATE NO.

I have this date hand-delivered and/or mailed for filing a Certificate of Restoration of Rights to the Clerk of the Superior Court of each of the following counties, together with payment of any recording costs: ______________________

PROBATE CLERK/DEPUTY CLERK

ADDRESS

TELEPHONE

Probate Court Return Mailing Address:

CERTIFICATE OF RESTORATION OF RIGHTS
(Pursuant to O.C.G.A. §29-5-13(d))

GEORGIA, ____________ County

PROBATE ESTATE NO. ________________ CROSS REFERENCE:
DEED BOOK ____________________
DATE ORDER ISSUED: ________________ PAGE NO. ____________________

GRANTOR: (NAME OF CONSERVATOR(S) OF FORMER WARD)

GRANTEE: (NAME OF FORMER WARD)

The rights of the above Former Ward being restored, the Conservatorship previously created for the above-named former ward is now DISSOLVED.

Original Certificate delivered or mailed to Clerk of Superior Court of ____________________ County on ____________________, 20 _____.

I do hereby certify that the above information is based on the order of the Probate Court issued on the date set out above and that the above information is true and correct.

By: ________________________________
PROBATE CLERK/DEPUTY CLERK

Effective 7/06 GPCSF 65Court

Form adopted effective July 31, 2006.

GPCSF 70. CERTIFICATE IN ACCORDANCE WITH UNIFORM PROBATE COURT RULE 21(F)

GEORGIA PROBATE COURT
STANDARD FORM

CERTIFICATE IN ACCORDANCE WITH UNIFORM PROBATE COURT RULE 21(F)

I certify that the content of the foregoing is identical in all material respects with Georgia probate court standard form entitled ______________________________, except for additions or deletions indicated as required by the Uniform Probate Court Rules.

______________________________ ______________________________

Date

Signature of Attorney
Address:

Telephone Number:
State Bar#:

INSTRUCTIONS

I. Specific Instructions

1. This form is to be used when an available standard form is not used; the content of the substituted pleading or other document must conform to the standard form, indicating all material information added to or deleted from the standard form. Material additions must be underlined, placed in bold or all capital letters, or otherwise clearly indicated, and material deletions must be shown with a single strike through or otherwise clearly indicated. This certificate must be attached to said form.

II. General Instructions

General instructions applicable to all Georgia probate court standard forms appear in Volume 255 of the Georgia Reports and are available in each probate court.

Effective 7/06 GPCSF 70 Complete

Form adopted effective July 31, 2006.

GPCSF 71. PETITION FOR LEAVE TO SELL PERISHABLE PROPERTY BY PERSONAL REPRESENTATIVE

GEORGIA PROBATE COURT
STANDARD FORM

Petition for Leave to Sell Perishable Property by Personal Representative

INSTRUCTIONS

I. Specific Instructions

1. This form is to be used when filing a petition for leave to sell property which is perishable, liable to deteriorate from keeping, or expensive to keep, pursuant to O.C.G.A. §53-8-11.

2. Under O.C.G.A. §53-8-11, the order for sale may be granted only after such notice and opportunity for hearing, if any, as the Court deems practicable under the circumstances. Further, the sale shall be as soon as practicable and in such manner as the Court determines to be in the best interest of the estate. Therefore, all notice provisions set forth in this form may be altered by the Court if necessary.

3. This form consists of four pages.

II. General Instructions

General instructions applicable to all Georgia probate court standard forms are available in each probate court.

Effective 7/06 GPCSF 71 Complete

GEORGIA PROBATE COURT
STANDARD FORM

PROBATE COURT OF ____________________ COUNTY

STATE OF GEORGIA

IN RE:) ESTATE NO. ____________________

)

______________________________,) PETITION FOR LEAVE TO SELL

DECEASED) PERISHABLE PROPERTY

TO THE HONORABLE JUDGE OF THE PROBATE COURT:

The petition of ________________________ as representative of the estate of ____________________________ shows that the following personal property:

____ is of perishable nature, or liable to deteriorate from keeping, or expensive to keep, and that it is in the best interest of said estate that said property be sold as soon as practicable. Petitioner therefore prays for an order authorizing Petitioner to sell said property for the highest valid offer received using the following method and terms of sale:

____________________________	____________________________
Signature of first petitioner	Signature of second petitioner if any
____________________________	____________________________
Printed Name	Printed Name
____________________________	____________________________
Address	Address
____________________________	____________________________
____________________________	____________________________
Phone Number	Phone Number

Signature of Attorney: ________________

Typed/printed name of Attorney: ________________

Address: ________________

____

Telephone: ________ State Bar # ___

Effective 7/06 GPCSF 71 Complete

VERIFICATION

GEORGIA, ______________________________ COUNTY

Personally appeared before me the undersigned petitioner(s) who on oath state(s) that the facts set forth in the foregoing petition are true.

Sworn to and subscribed before me this ______ day of __________, 20 ____.

____
First Petitioner

____
NOTARY/CLERK OF PROBATE COURT

____
Printed Name

Sworn to and subscribed before me this ______ day of __________, 20 ____.

____
Second Petitioner, if any

____
NOTARY/CLERK OF PROBATE COURT

____
Printed Name

Effective 7/06 GPCSF 71 Complete

PROBATE COURT OF ______________________ COUNTY

STATE OF GEORGIA

IN RE: ESTATE OF) ESTATE NO. ________________

)

________________________________,) PETITION FOR LEAVE TO SELL

DECEASED) PERISHABLE PROPERTY

ORDER

(Without opportunity to object)

Upon reading and considering the foregoing Petition, and it appearing that the facts stated therein are true, it is ORDERED that Petitioner(s) be, and is/are hereby, granted leave to sell the said property for the highest valid offer received using the method and terms of sale set forth in the petition, after giving notice of the property to be sold, the method and terms of such sale, the date and place of sale, and the means by which offers may be made as set forth below(check one)

_____ by ____

_____ by serving a copy of the petition and this order by first class mail at least thirteen (13) days in advance or in person on the sui juris (heirs of decedent) (beneficiaries who would have received such property under will of decedent).

_____ It is not practicable to afford notice or a hearing prior to ruling upon the above petition.

SO ORDERED, this __________ day of ______________, 20 ____.

Probate Judge

PROBATE COURT OF ____________________ COUNTY

STATE OF GEORGIA

IN RE: ESTATE OF) ESTATE NO. ____________________

)

____________________,) PETITION FOR LEAVE TO SELL

DECEASED) PERISHABLE PROPERTY

ORDER

(With opportunity to object)

Upon reading and considering the foregoing Petition, and it appearing that the facts stated therein are true, and it appearing to the Court that it is not practicable to afford notice or a hearing prior to ruling upon the petition;

IT IS ORDERED that the Petitioner(s) shall give notice of the property to be sold, the method and terms of such sale, the date and place of sale, and the means by which offers may be made as set forth below (check one or both:)

_____ by ____

__;

_____ by serving a copy of the petition and this order in person or by first class mail on the sui juris (heirs of decedent) (beneficiaries who would have received such property under will of decedent) at least thirteen (13) days prior to the date of the sale;

IT IS FURTHER ORDERED that any objection to the proposed sale, the method of sale, the date and place of the sale, and/or the means by which offers may be made must be filed **no later than** ____________________, 20 ___. **ANY OBJECTION** must be in writing and be signed before a notary public or probate court clerk, and filing fees must be tendered with the objection, unless the objecting party qualifies to file as an indigent party. Contact probate court personnel at the below address/phone number for the required amount of filing fees. If an objection is filed, a hearing will be (held in the Probate Court of ____________________ County, courtroom __________, (address) ____________________, Georgia on ____________________ at __________ o'clock ___.m.) (scheduled at a later date).

IT IS FURTHER ORDERED that, after giving such notice and if no objection is timely filed as set forth above, the Petitioner(s) be, and is/are hereby, granted leave to sell the said property for the highest valid offer received using the method and terms of sale set forth in the petition. The Petitioner(s) shall file a report of sale, within ten (10) days after the sale, certifying compliance with the notice requirements and reporting the results of the sale.

SO ORDERED, this __________ day of ____________________, 20 ____.

Probate Judge

Effective 7/06 GPCSF 71 Complete

Instructions and form adopted effective July 31, 2006.

INDEX TO UNIFORM PROBATE COURT RULES

*

UNIFORM MAGISTRATE COURT RULES

Effective July 1, 1985

Including Amendments Received Through November 1, 2006

Research Note

Use WESTLAW *to find cases citing a rule. In addition, use* WESTLAW *to search for specific terms or to update a rule; see the GA–RULES and GA–ORDERS Scope screens for further information.*

Amendments to these rules are published, as received, in the South Eastern Reporter 2d *and* Georgia Cases *advance sheets.*

Table of Rules

PART I. GENERAL AND ADMINISTRATIVE PROVISIONS

PART I. GENERAL AND ADMINISTRATIVE PROVISIONS

RULE 1. PREAMBLE

These rules are promulgated pursuant to the inherent powers of the Court and Article VI, Section IX, Paragraph I of the Georgia Constitution of 1983, in order to provide for the speedy, efficient and inexpensive resolution of disputes and prosecutions. It is not the intention, nor shall it be the effect, of these rules to conflict with the Constitution or substantive law, either per se or in individual actions and these rules shall be so construed and in case of conflict shall yield to substantive law.

1.1 Repeal of Local Rules. All local rules of the magistrate courts shall expire effective January 1, 1996. If any magistrate court by action of its chief magistrate proposes to prevent any local rule from expiring pursuant to Rule 1.1 then a proposal to prevent the local rule from expiring must be presented to the Supreme Court for approval 30 days prior to the expiration date as stated in Rule 1.1. Only those rules reapproved by the Supreme Court on or after January 1, 1996, shall remain in effect after that date. Rules timely resubmitted shall remain in effect until action by the Supreme Court.

1.2 Authority to Enact Rules Which Deviate From the Uniform Magistrate Court Rules.

(A) The term "local rules" will no longer be used in the context of the Uniform Magistrate Court Rules.

(B) Each magistrate court by action of its chief magistrate, from time to time, may propose to make and amend rules which deviate from the Uniform Magistrate Court Rules, provided such proposals are not inconsistent with general laws, these Uniform Magistrate Court Rules, or any directive of the Supreme Court of Georgia. Any such proposals shall be filed with the clerk of the Supreme Court; proposals so submitted shall take effect 30 days after approval by the Supreme Court. It is the intendment of these rules that rules which deviate from the Uniform Magistrate Court Rules be restricted in scope.

(C) Notwithstanding the expiration of previously approved local rules January 1, 1996, courts may continue to promulgate rules which relate only to internal procedure and do not affect the rights of any party substantially or materially, either to unreasonably delay or deny such rights. These rules, which will be designated "internal operating procedures," do not require the approval of the Supreme Court. "Internal operating procedures," as used in these Uniform Magistrate Court Rules, are defined as rules which relate to case management, administration, and operation of the court or govern programs which relate to filing costs in civil actions, costs in criminal matters, case management, administration, and operation of the court.

(D) Notwithstanding these uniform rules, the chief magistrate may promulgate experimental rules applicable to pilot projects, upon approval of the Supreme Court, adequately advertised to the local bar, with copies to the State Bar of Georgia, not to exceed a period of one year, subject to extension for one additional year upon approval of the Supreme Court. At the end of the second year, any such pilot projects will either be approved by the Supreme Court or will be allowed to sunset. Programs developed under the Alternative Dispute Resolution Rules of the Supreme Court will be approved by the Georgia Commission on Dispute Resolution before attaining permanent status under these rules.

(E) Rules which are approved as deviations from the Uniform Magistrate Court Rules and internal operating procedures of courts shall be published by the judicial circuit in which the rules are effective. Copies must be made available through the clerk of the magistrate court for the county where the rules are effective. Any amendments to deviations from the Uniform Magistrate Court Rules or to internal operating procedures must be published and made available through each magistrate court clerk's office within 15 days of the effective date of the amendment or change.

(F) Internal operating procedures effective in any court must be filed with the Supreme Court even though Supreme Court approval is not needed for these rules.

1.3 Matters of Statewide Concern. The following rules, to be known as "Uniform Magistrate Court Rules," are to be given statewide application.

1.4 Deviation. These rules are not subject to local deviation except as provided herein. A specific rule may be superseded in a specific action or case or by an order of the court entered in such case explaining the necessity for deviation and served upon the attorneys in the case.

1.5 Amendments. The Council of Magistrate Court Judges shall have a permanent committee to recommend to the Supreme Court such changes and additions to these rules as may from time to time appear necessary or desirable.

The State Bar of Georgia shall receive notice of the proposed changes and additions and be given the opportunity to comment.

1.6 Publication of Rules and Amendments. These rules and any amendments to these rules shall be published in the advance sheets to the Georgia Reports. Unless otherwise provided, the effective date of any amendment to these rules is the date of publication in the advance sheets to the Georgia Reports.

Amended effective June 7, 1990; October 28, 1993; November 9, 1995; July 15, 2004.

RULE 2. DEFINITIONS

2.1 Judge. The word "judge" as used in these rules refers to any person serving or acting as either a chief magistrate or magistrate in the Magistrate Courts of Georgia.

2.2 Clerk. The word "clerk" as used in these rules refers to the person designated as the clerk and to other members of the staff serving as deputy clerks. The chief magistrate may designate deputy clerks who shall have the same authority as the clerk.

2.3 Party(ies). The word "party" or "parties" as used in these rules shall include law enforcement officers participating in criminal proceedings and attorney(s) of record unless the context clearly indicates otherwise.

Amended effective October 28, 1993.

RULE 3. HOURS OF COURT OPERATION

The hours of court operation shall be set by the chief magistrate of each court and shall be recorded with the clerk of the magistrate court. Such information shall include the following:

(1) Normal hours and location of court.

(2) Emergency after-hours availability of judges and the names of such judges.

(3) Holidays during which the court will be closed and a plan for the availability of judges on such days.

(4) Days on which the court holds civil and criminal hearings (if not handled on the same day), and the times and locations of such hearing.

Amended effective October 28, 1993; November 9, 1995.

RULE 4. ASSIGNMENT OF CASES

4.1 Case Assignment. If the caseload is such, the chief magistrate shall assign cases among the magistrates.

4.2 Disqualification of Judge. If any judge is disqualified by law or judicial requirements from the hearing of any case or other matter, such case or matter shall be referred to the chief magistrate for assignment or disposition.

4.3 Disqualification of Chief Magistrate. If the chief magistrate is the judge disqualified, such case(s) shall be referred in rotation among the other magistrates in the county. The chief magistrate may provide by general order for the method of rotation and for selection of a court from which to request judicial assistance when all magistrates in a county are disqualified. Such general order shall apply only to cases where the disqualification arises after the date of the general order.

Amended effective October 28, 1993.

RULE 5. DOCKETS

5.1 Docket Categories. Each magistrate court shall keep a docket for criminal and search warrants, and a separate docket for all civil actions.

5.2 Time of Docketing. Actions shall be entered by the clerk, deputy clerk, or magistrate in the proper docket immediately or within a reasonable period after being received in the clerk's office.

RULE 6. WITHDRAWAL OF PAPERS FROM MAGISTRATE COURT

(A) *General Provisions*: No original papers may be withdrawn from the magistrate court.

(B) *Civil Cases*: Copies of documents in civil cases may be obtained upon payment of costs to the clerk.

(C) *Criminal Cases*: Copies of documents in criminal cases may be provided; however, the court may, at its discretion, remove from said copies information concerning the location addresses, phone numbers, and similar information, the disclosure of which would violate the Victim's Protection Act (OCGA § 17–17–10) or would expose alleged witnesses or victims of crimes to danger of assault and/or intimidation by criminal defendants, or their agents. Names of confidential informants of police officers shall not be released, except after court order requiring such release, which may only issue following motion and in camera review by the trial court under guidelines set out in statutory and case law.

(D) *Order to Limit Access*: Upon motion by any party to any civil action, after hearing, and for good cause shown, the court may limit access to court files respecting that action. The order of limitation shall specify the part of the file to which access is limited, the nature and duration of the limitation, and the reason for limitation.

An order limiting access shall not be granted except upon a finding that the harm otherwise resulting to the privacy of a person in interest clearly outweighs the public interest. Under compelling circumstances, a motion for temporary limitation of access, not to exceed 30 days, may be granted, ex parte, upon motion accompanied by supporting affidavit.

Upon notice to all parties of record and after hearing, an order limiting access may be reviewed and amended by the court entering such order or by the Superior Court of the Circuit where the magistrate court is located at any time, on the court's own motion, or upon the motion of any person for good cause.

(E) *Notes and Private Information*: This rule does not authorize release of papers containing a judge's application, trial or hearing notes or research notes pertaining to any case, civil or criminal. Further, this rule does not require release of any person's social security number, except to authorized state or federal authorities, as provided by applicable statutes.

(F) *Certification of Documents*: Upon request for certified copies of documents, the Court may provide the same, stating on the said certification what information was deleted as provided above.

Amended effective July 6, 2006.

RULE 7. DUTIES OF ATTORNEYS AND ALL PARTIES

7.1 Notification of Representation. No attorney shall appear in that capacity before a magistrate court until he or she has entered an appearance by filing a signed entry of appearance form or by filing a signed pleading in a pending action. An entry of appearance shall state (1) the style and number; (2) the identity of the party for whom the appearance is made; and (3) the name and current office address and telephone number of the attorney; and in criminal cases, the home telephone number of the attorney.

In criminal cases, immediately upon agreeing to represent the defendant in a criminal matter pending in magistrate court, each attorney shall notify the magistrate court orally, followed by written confirmation in conformity with the preceding paragraph.

7.2 Withdrawal of Counsel. The entry of an appearance or request for withdrawal by an attorney who is a member or an employee of a law firm or professional corporation shall relieve the other members or employees of the same law firm or professional corporation from the necessity of filing additional entries of appearance or requests for withdrawal in the same action.

7.3 Notification of Previous Presentation to Another Judge. Attorneys and parties shall not present to a judge any matter which has been previously presented to another judge without first advising the second judge of said fact and results of the previous presentation.

7.4 Prohibition on *Ex Parte* Communications. Except as authorized by law or by rule, judges shall not initiate, permit or consider *ex parte* communications by interested parties or their attorneys concerning a pending or impending proceeding. Where circumstances require, *ex parte* communications for scheduling, administrative purposes or emergencies that do not deal with substantive matters or the merits of the case are authorized, provided:

1. the judge reasonably believes that no party will gain a procedural or tactical advantage as a result of the *ex parte* communication, and

2. the judge takes reasonable steps to promptly notify all parties of the substance of the *ex parte* communication and allows an opportunity to respond.

Amended effective October 28, 1993; December 19, 2002.

RULE 8. RESOLUTION OF CONFLICTS—STATE AND FEDERAL COURTS

(A) An attorney shall not be deemed to have a conflict unless:

(1) the attorney is lead counsel in two or more of the actions affected; and,

(2) the attorney certifies that the matters cannot be adequately handled, and the client's interest adequately protected, by other counsel for the party in the action or by other attorneys in lead counsel's firm; certifies compliance with this rule and has nevertheless been unable to resolve the conflicts; and certifies in the notice a proposed resolution by list of such cases in the order of priority specified by this rule.

(B) When an attorney is scheduled for a day certain by trial calendar, special setting or court order to appear in two or more courts (trial or appellate; state or federal), the attorney shall give prompt written notice as specified in (A) above of the conflict to opposing counsel, to the clerk of each court and to the judge before whom each action is set for hearing (or, to an appropriate judge if there has been no designation of a presiding judge). The written notice shall contain the attorney's proposed resolution of the appearance conflicts in accordance with the priorities established by this rule and shall set forth the order of cases to be tried with a listing of the date and data required by (B)(1)–(4) as to each case arranged in the order in which the cases should prevail under this rule. In the absence of objection from opposing counsel or the courts affected, the proposed order of conflict resolution shall stand as offered. Should a judge wish to change the order of cases to be tried, such notice shall be given promptly after agreement is reached between the affected judges. Attorneys confronted by such conflicts are expected to give written notice such that it will be received at least seven (7) days prior to the date of conflict. Absent agreement, conflicts shall be promptly resolved by the judge or the clerk of each affected court in accordance with the following order of priorities:

(1) Criminal (felony) actions shall prevail over civil actions;

(2) Jury trials shall prevail over non-jury matters, including trials and administrative proceedings;

(3) Trials shall prevail over appellate arguments, hearings and conferences;

(4) Within each of the above categories only, the action which was first filed shall take precedence.

(C) Conflict resolution shall not require the continuance of the other matter or matters not having priority. In the event any matter listed in the letter notice is disposed of prior to the scheduled time set for any other matter listed or subsequent to the scheduled time set but prior to the end of the calendar, the attorney shall immediately notify all affected parties, including the court affected, of the disposal and shall, absent good cause shown to the court, proceed with the remaining case or cases in which the conflict was resolved by the disposal in the order of priorities as set forth heretofore.

Amended effective June 7, 1990.

RULE 9. LEAVES OF ABSENCE

Requests for leaves of absence shall be submitted in writing to the presiding magistrate or his or her designee accompanied by a listing of cases by case number, name, and hearing date for which protection is required.

Such request shall be accompanied by an appropriate order for signature if the petition is granted.

The request must be filed at least seven (7) business days prior to the date the requested leave is to commence.

Leave will not be granted merely by stipulation or agreement of parties.

Amended effective October 28, 1993.

RULE 10. TERMS OF COURT

Where statutes or case law of general application in this state require action within term of court, in the magistrate court this shall signify within thirty (30) days; where readiness is required by the next term of court, this shall signify after thirty (30) days.

Former Rule 10 renumbered as new Rule 22 effective October 28, 1993. New Rule 10 adopted effective October 28, 1993.

RULE 11. ELECTRONIC AND PHOTOGRAPHIC NEWS COVERAGE OF MAGISTRATE COURT PROCEEDINGS

Unless otherwise provided by rule of the Supreme Court or otherwise ordered by the assigned judge after appropriate hearing (conducted after notice to all parties and counsel of record) and findings, representatives of the print and electronic public media may be present at and unobtrusively make written notes and sketches pertaining to any judicial proceedings in the magistrate courts. However, due to the distractive nature of electronic or photographic equipment, representatives of the public media utilizing such equipment are subject to the following restrictions and conditions:

(A) Persons desiring to broadcast/record/photograph official court proceedings must file a timely written request with the judge involved prior to the hearing or trial, specifying the particular calendar/case or proceedings for which such coverage is intended; the type equipment to be used in the courtroom; the trial, hearing or proceeding to be covered; and the person responsible for installation and operation of such equipment.

(B) Approval of the judge to broadcast/record/photograph a proceeding, if granted, shall be granted without partiality or preference to any person, news agency, or type of electronic or photographic coverage, who agrees to abide by and conform to these rules, up to the capacity of the space designated therefor in the courtroom. Violation of these rules will be grounds for a reporter/technician to be removed or excluded from the courtroom and held in contempt.

(C) The judge may exercise discretion and require pooled coverage which would allow only one still photographer, one television camera and attendant, and one radio or tape recorder outlet and attendant. Photographers, electronic reporters and technicians shall be expected to arrange among themselves pooled coverage if so directed by the judge and to present the judge with a schedule and description of the pooled coverage. If the covering persons cannot agree on such a schedule or arrangement, the schedule and arrangements for pooled coverage may be designated at the judge's discretion.

(D) The positioning and removal of cameras and electronic devices shall be done quietly and, if possible, before or after the court session or during recesses; in no event shall such disturb the proceedings of the court. In every such case, equipment should be in place and ready to operate before the time court is scheduled to be called to order.

(E) Overhead lights in the courtroom shall be switched on and off only by court personnel. No other lights, flashbulbs, flashes or sudden light changes may be used unless the judge approves beforehand.

(F) No adjustment of central audio system shall be made except by persons authorized by the judge. Audio recordings of the court proceedings will be from one source, normally by connection to the court's central audio system. Upon prior approval of the court, other microphones may be added in an unobtrusive manner to the court's public address system.

(G) All television cameras, still cameras and tape recorders shall be assigned to a specific portion of the public area of the courtroom or specially designed access areas, and such equipment will not be permitted to be removed or relocated during the court proceedings.

(H) Still cameras must have quiet functioning shutters and advancers. Movie and television cameras and broadcasting and recording devices must be quiet running. If any equipment is determined by the judge to be of such noise as to be distractive to the court proceedings, then such equipment can be excluded from the courtroom by the judge.

(I) Reporters, photographers, and technicians must have and produce upon request of court officials credentials identifying them and the media company for which they work.

(J) Court proceedings shall not be interrupted by a reporter or technician with a technical or an equipment problem.

(K) Reporters, photographers, and technicians should do everything possible to avoid attracting attention to themselves. Reporters, photographers, and technicians will be accorded full right of access to court proceedings for obtaining public information within the requirements of due process of law, so long as it is done without detracting from the dignity and decorum of the court.

(L) Other than as permitted by these rules and guidelines, there will be no photographing, radio or television broadcasting, including video taping pertaining to any judicial proceedings on the floor where the trial, hearing or proceeding is being held or any other floor whereon is located a courtroom, whether or not the court is actually in session.

(M) No interviews pertaining to a particular judicial proceeding will be conducted in the courtroom except with the permission of the judge.

(N) A request for installation and use of electronic recording, transmission, videotaping or motion picture or still photography of any judicial proceeding shall be evaluated pursuant to the standards set forth in OCGA § 15–1–10.1.

(O) A request for media access to a court proceeding shall be in substantially the following form:

IN THE MAGISTRATE COURT OF ______
COUNTY
STATE OF GEORGIA

CASE NAME ______ CASE NO. ______

REQUEST FOR ELECTRONIC AND PHOTOGRAPHIC
MEDIA ACCESS TO COURT PROCEEDINGS

____

Pursuant to Uniform Magistrate Court Rule 11, the undersigned hereby requests permission to record, photograph or televise all or portions of the proceedings in the above-captioned case.

This request is for the following scheduled hearing (provide date, time, etc.):

____

The following equipment will be installed in the courtroom:

____

The person who will be responsible for the installation and operation of this equipment is:

____

The undersigned requests courtroom access prior to the scheduled event for the purpose of setting up equipment, as follows:

____

The undersigned hereby certifies that the equipment to be installed and the locations and operation of such equipment will be in conformity with the rules and guidelines issued by the court.

____
Signature and date

____
Print name, title, and organization/company name

____
Organization/company address and contact telephone number

APPROVED: ______________________________
Judge, Magistrate Court of ______ County

Former Rule 11 amended and renumbered as new Rule 23 effective October 28, 1993. Former Rule 23 amended and renumbered as new Rule 11 effective October 28, 1993; amended effective December 19, 2002.

RULE 12. COMPLETION OF QUARTERLY CASELOAD REPORTS

In order to compile accurate data on the operation of the magistrate courts, each chief magistrate shall insure the accurate completion and timely submission of the Quarterly Caseload Reports sent to them by the Administrative Office of the Courts.

Former Rule 12 amended and renumbered as new Rule 24 effective October 28, 1993. Former Rule 24 amended and renumbered as new Rule 12 effective October 28, 1993.

RULE 13. NOTICE OF SELECTION OF MAGISTRATES, CONSTABLES AND CLERKS OF MAGISTRATE COURTS

Whenever a magistrate, constable, or clerk (but not deputy clerks) of the magistrate court shall take the oath required for office in OCGA § 15–10–3, the chief magistrate shall forward to the Administrative Office of the Courts the name and title of the person taking the oath; the name of the person being succeeded; the term of the office, if appropriate; the date assuming duties; and the address and telephone number the official wishes to use for business correspondence.

Former Rule 13 amended and renumbered as new Rule 25 effective October 28, 1993. Former Rule 25 amended and renumbered as new Rule 13 effective October 28, 1993; amended effective June 10, 1999; March 22, 2001.

RULE 14. AT&T LANGUAGE LINE SERVICE

The AT&T Language Line Service is authorized for use in the magistrate courts whenever interpreting is needed in criminal and civil proceedings.

Adopted effective November 30, 1995.

RULE 15. TELEPHONE AND VIDEO CONFERENCING

15.1 Telephone Conferencing. The trial court on its own motion or upon the request of any party may in its discretion conduct pre–trial or post–trial proceedings in civil actions by telephone conference with attorneys for all affected parties. The trial judge may specify:

(A) The time and the person who will initiate the conference;

(B) The party which is to incur the initial expense of the conference call, or the apportionment of such costs among the parties, while retaining the discretion to make an adjustment of such costs upon final resolution of the case by taxing same as part of the costs; and

(C) Any other matter or requirement necessary to accomplish or facilitate the telephone conference.

15.2 Video–Conferencing.

(A) The following matters may be conducted by video–conference:

1. Determination of indigence and appointment of counsel;

2. Hearings on appearance and appeal bonds;

3. Initial appearance hearings and waiver of extradition hearings; subsection 15.2(E)(4) below not withstanding, public access to these hearings may provided by a video–conferencing system meeting the requirements of subsection 15.2(E)(2) and (3);

4. Probable cause hearings;

5. Applications for and issuance of arrest warrants;

6. Applications for and issuance of search warrants;

7. Arraignment or waiver of arraignment;

8. Pretrial diversion and post–sentencing compliance hearings;

9. Entry of pleas in criminal cases;

10. Impositions of sentences upon pleas of guilty or *nolo contendere*;

11. Probation revocation hearings in felony cases in which the probationer admits the violation and in all misdemeanor cases;

12. Post–sentencing proceedings in criminal cases;

13. Acceptance of special pleas of insanity (incompetency to stand trial);

14. Situations involving inmates with highly sensitive medical problems or who pose a high security risk: and

15. Testimony of youthful witnesses;

16. *Ex–parte* applications for Temporary Protective Orders under the Family Violence Act and the Stalking Statute;

17. Appearances of interpreters;

Notwithstanding any other provisions of this rule, a judge may order a defendant's personal appearance in court for any hearing.

(B) Confidential Attorney–Client Communication. Provision shall be made to preserve the confidentiality of attorney–client communications and privilege in accordance with Georgia law. In all criminal proceedings, the defendant and defense counsel shall be provided with a private means of communications when in different locations.

(C) Witnesses. In any pending matter, a witness may testify via video conference. Any party desiring to call a witness by video conference shall file a notice of intention to present testimony by video conference at least thirty (30) days prior to the date scheduled for such testimony. Any other party may file an objection to the testimony of a witness by video conference within ten (10) days of the filing of the notice of intention. In civil matters, the discretion to allow testimony via video conference shall rest with the trial judge. In any criminal matter, a timely objection shall be sustained; however, such objection shall act as a motion for continuance and a waiver of any speedy trial demand.

(D) Recording of Hearings. A record of any proceedings conducted by video conference shall be made in the same manner as all such similar proceedings not conducted by video conference. However, upon the consent of all parties, that portion of the proceedings conducted by video conference may be recorded by an audio–visual recording system and such recording shall be part of the record of the case and transmitted to courts of appeal as if part of a transcript.

(E) Technical Standards. Any video–conferencing system utilized under this rule must conform to the following minimum requirements:

1. All participants must be able to see, hear, and communicate with each other simultaneously;

2. All participants must be able to see, hear, and otherwise observe any physical evidence or exhibits presented during the proceeding, either by video, facsimile, or other method;

3. Video quality must be adequate to allow participants to observe each other's demeanor and nonverbal communications; and

4. The location from which the trial judge is presiding shall be accessible to the public to the same extent as such proceeding would if not conducted by video conference. The court shall accommodate any request by interested parties to observe the entire proceeding.

Adopted effective July 15, 2004.

PART II. CRIMINAL RULES

RULE 21. ADMINISTRATION OF OATHS

A clerk of the magistrate court may administer the oath and sign the jurat for affidavits, including those in support of arrest and search warrants and bad check citations. This rule shall not be interpreted as otherwise affecting the responsibilities of a judge in hearing applications for arrest and search warrants.

Adopted effective October 28, 1993.

RULE 22. HEARINGS ON ISSUANCE OF SEARCH WARRANTS

Whenever the hearing on the issuance of a search warrant is not recorded, the magistrate should make a written notation or memorandum of any oral testimony which is not included in the affidavit.

Former Rule 10 renumbered as new Rule 22 effective October 28, 1993.

RULE 23. BAIL IN CRIMINAL CASES

23.1 Misdemeanor Cases. Bail in misdemeanor cases shall be set as provided in OCGA §§ 17–6–1 and 17–6–2.

23.2 Felony Cases. Bail in felony cases shall be set by the magistrate court except for those offenses as to which OCGA §§ 17–6–1 or 17–10–1 provides that bail shall be set by the superior court or shall not be available. All defendants in custody must be transported and presented to this court for initial appearance within the time requirements of OCGA § 17–4–26 and § 17–4–62 for further consideration of bail.

23.3 Categories of Bail. The court may set bail which may be secured by:

(1) *Cash*—by a deposit with the sheriff of an amount equal to the required cash bail; or

(2) *Property*—by real estate located within the State of Georgia with unencumbered equity, not exempted, owned by the accused or surety, valued at double the amount of bail set in the bond; or

(3) *Recognizance*—in the discretion of the court;

(4) *Professional*—by a professional bail bondsman authorized by the sheriff and in compliance with the rules and regulations for execution of a surety bail bond.

Bail may be conditioned upon such other specified and reasonable conditions as the court may consider just and proper. The court may restrict the type of security permitted for the bond although the sheriff shall determine what sureties are acceptable when surety bond is permitted.

23.4 Amendment of Bail. The magistrate court has the authority to amend any bail previously authorized by the magistrate court under the provisions of OCGA § 17–6–18.

Former Rule 23 amended and renumbered as new Rule 11 effective October 28, 1993. Former Rule 11 amended and renumbered as new Rule 23 effective October 28, 1993.

RULE 24. DISMISSAL AND RETURN OF WARRANTS

24.1 Dismissal of Warrant. Any dismissal of a warrant of the magistrate court prior to the committal hearing and subsequent transfer to other courts shall be made exclusively by the magistrate court.

24.2 Return of Warrant to Magistrate Court. Once arrest of the defendant is effectuated, the original warrant shall be returned to the magistrate court or its designee for transfer to the appropriate prosecuting agency.

24.3 Assessment of Costs—Criminal. When, in a criminal action, costs are assessed by the Court upon the dismissal of a warrant the minimum amounts shall be $100.00 in felony cases and $50.00 in misdemeanor cases. Pursuant to OCGA § 17–11–4(a)(3), where prosecution of a criminal action is abandoned before trial, the prosecuting attorney of the trial court or his or her designee shall promptly notify the judge who issued the warrant of the fact of abandonment and of the amount of accrued costs. The judge shall enter a judgment for said costs against the prosecuting party.

Former Rule 24 amended and renumbered as new Rule 12 effective October 28, 1993. Former Rule 12 amended and renumbered as new Rule 24 effective October 28, 1993.

RULE 25. INITIAL APPEARANCE/COMMITMENT HEARINGS

25.1 Initial Appearance Hearing. Immediately following any arrest but no later than 48 hours if the arrest was without a warrant, or 72 hours following an arrest with a warrant, unless the accused has made bond in the meantime, the arresting officer or the law officer having custody of the accused shall present the accused in person before a magistrate or other judicial officer for first appearance.

At the first appearance, the judicial officer shall:

(1) Inform the accused of the charges;

(2) Inform the accused of the right to the presence and advice of an attorney, either retained or appointed, of the right to remain silent, and that any statement made may be used against him or her;

(3) Determine whether or not the accused desires and is in need of an appointed attorney and, if appropriate, advise the accused of the necessity for filing a written application;

(4) Inform the accused of the right to a pre-indictment commitment hearing, that the hearing will be postponed if the accused requests additional time to obtain counsel or subpoena witnesses or if state requests additional time to prepare its case, and inform the accused that giving a bond returnable to arraignment or trial shall be a waiver of the right to a commitment hearing although a magistrate may in his or her discretion hold a commitment hearing pursuant to Rule 25.2(A);

(5) Schedule a commitment hearing if authorized and if requested by the defendant and so notify the prosecuting attorney and the law officer having custody of the accused;

(6) In cases of warrantless arrest, unless a subsequent determination of probable cause has been made, make a fair and independent determination of probable cause for the arrest;

(7) Inform the accused of the right to grand jury indictment in felony cases, to accusation in misdemeanor cases, to uniform traffic citation in traffic cases, and the right to trial by jury, and, in felony cases, when the next grand jury will convene; in felony cases subject to OCGA § 17–7–70.1 (involving violations of OCGA §§ 16–8–2, 16–8–14, 16–8–18, 16–9–1, 16–9–2, 16–9–20, 16–9–31, 16–9–33, 16–9–37, 16–10–52, or 40–5–58), inform the accused that if the commitment hearing is expressly waived or the accused is bound over after the commitment hearing, the district attorney may prepare an accusation or seek an indictment;

(8) Inform the accused that the accused or his or her attorney may waive the right to a commitment hearing; and

(9) Set the amount of bail if the offense is not one bailable only by a superior court judge, or so inform the accused if it is.

25.2 Commitment Hearing.

A. A magistrate, in his or her discretion, may hold a commitment hearing even though the defendant has posted a bail bond as provided in Rule 23.

B. At the commitment hearing by the court of inquiry, the judicial officer shall perform the following duties:

(1) Explain the probable cause purpose of the hearing;

(2) Repeat to the accused the rights explained at the first appearance;

(3) Determine whether the accused waives the commitment hearing;

(4) If the accused waives the hearing, the court shall immediately bind the entire case over to the court having jurisdiction of the most serious offense charged;

(5) If the accused does not waive the hearing, the court shall immediately proceed to conduct the commitment hearing unless, for good cause shown, the hearing is continued to a later scheduled date;

(6) The judicial officer shall bind the entire case over to the court having jurisdiction of the most serious offense for which probable cause has been shown by sufficient evidence and dismiss any charge for which probable cause has not been shown;

(7) On each case which is bound over, a memorandum of the commitment shall be entered on the warrant by the judicial officer. The warrant, bail bond, and all other papers pertaining to the case shall be forwarded to the clerk of the appropriate court having jurisdiction over the offense for delivery to the prosecuting attorney.

Each bail bond shall contain the full name, residence, business and mailing address and telephone number of the accused and any surety;

(8) A copy of the record of any testimony and the proceedings of the first appearance and the commitment hearing, if available, shall be provided to the proper prosecuting officer and to the accused upon payment of the reasonable cost for preparation of the record;

(9) A judicial officer conducting a commitment hearing is without jurisdiction to make final disposition of the case or cases at the hearing by imposing any fine or punishment, except where the only charge arising out of the transaction at issue is the violation of a county or state authority ordinance.

C. At the commitment hearing, the following procedures shall be utilized:

(1) The rules of evidence shall apply except that hearsay may be allowed;

(2) The prosecuting entity shall have the burden of proving probable cause; and may be represented by a law enforcement officer, a district attorney, a solicitor, a private attorney or otherwise as is customary in that court;

(3) The accused may be represented by an attorney or may appear pro se; and

(4) The accused shall be permitted to introduce evidence.

25.3 Private citizen warrant application hearings.

A. Upon the filing of an application for an arrest warrant by a person other than a peace officer or law enforcement officer, and if the court determines that a hearing is appropriate pursuant to OCGA § 17–4–40, the court shall give notice of the date, time and location of the hearing to the applicant and to the person whose arrest is sought by personal service or by first class mail to the person's last known address or by any other means which is reasonably calculated to notify the person of the date, time and location of the hearing.

B. At the warrant application hearing the court shall:

a. Explain the probable cause purpose of the hearing;

b. Inform the accused of the charges;

c. Inform the accused of the right to hire and have the advise of an attorney, of the right to remain silent, and that any statement made may be used against him or her.

C. The warrant application hearing shall be conducted in accordance with OCGA § 17–4–40(4) and (5) and Rule 25.2(C) of these rules.

D. A copy of the record of any testimony and the proceedings of the warrant application hearing, if available, shall be provided to the proper prosecuting officer and to the accused upon payment of the reasonable cost for preparation of the record.

E. The judge conducting a warrant application hearing is without jurisdiction to make final disposition of the case or cases at the hearing by imposing any fine or punishment.

Former Rule 25 amended and renumbered as new Rule 13 effective October 28, 1993. Former Rule 13 amended and renumbered as new Rule 25 effective October 28, 1993; amended effective December 19, 2002.

RULE 26. APPOINTMENT OF COUNSEL FOR INDIGENT DEFENDANTS

26.1 Authority and Purpose. This rule is promulgated pursuant to OCGA § 17–12–4 in order to provide indigent persons with competent legal counsel in criminal proceedings.

26.2 Application For and Appointment of Counsel. When an accused person, contending to be financially unable to employ an attorney to defend against pending criminal charges or to appeal a conviction, desires to have an attorney appointed, the accused shall make a request in the form of an application for appointment of counsel and certificate of financial resources, made under oath and signed by the accused. This form shall contain information as to the accused's assets, liabilities, employment, earnings, other income, number and ages of dependents, the charges against the accused and such other information as shall be required by the court. The purpose of the application and certification is to provide the court or its designee with sufficient information from which to determine the financial ability of the accused to employ counsel.

Upon a determination of indigency the court shall, in writing, authorize the appointment of counsel for the indigent accused. The original authorization of appointment shall be filed with the clerk of court; a copy of the authorization shall be forwarded to the clerk, court administrator, public defender or such other person designated by the court to assign an attorney to an indigent defendant. Such person shall notify the accused, the appointed attorney, the sheriff and the prosecuting attorney of the appointment. The application for an attorney and certificate of financial resources shall be in substantially the following form:

IN THE MAGISTRATE COURT OF ______
COUNTY
STATE OF GEORGIA

STATE OF GEORGIA CASE NO.
CHARGE(S):
v.
____

APPLICATION FOR APPOINTMENT OF COUNSEL AND CERTIFICATE OF FINANCIAL RESOURCES

I am the defendant in the above-styled action. I cannot afford to hire a lawyer to assist me. I want the court to provide me with a lawyer. I understand that I am providing the following information in order for the court to determine my eligibility for a court-appointed lawyer to defend me on the above charges.

In jail ___ Out on bond ___ Arrest Date ______

1. Name ________ Telephone No. ______

Mailing address ______________

Birth date ___ Age ___ Soc.Sec.No. ______

Highest grade in school completed ______

2. If employed, employer is ______. My take home pay is ______

3. If unemployed, how long? ______ List other sources of income such as unemployment compensation, welfare or disability income and the amounts received per week or month: ______

4. Are you married ___ Is spouse employed? ___ If yes, by whom ______ Spouse's net income ______ (week)

5. Number of children living in home: ___ Ages ______

6. Dependents (other than spouse or children) in home, names, relationship, amount contributed to their support ______

7. Do you own a motor vehicle? ___ Year and model ______ How much do you owe on it? ______

8. Do you own a home? ___ Value __________ How much do you owe on it? __________

9. Amount of house payment or rent payment each month __________

10. List checking or savings accounts or other deposits with any bank or financial institution and the amount of deposits: __________________

11. List other assets or property, including real estate, jewelry, notes, bonds or stocks __________________

12. List indebtedness and amount of payments __________________

13. List any extraordinary living expenses and amount (such as regularly occurring medical expenses) __________________

14. Child support payable under any court order __________

15. Do you understand that whether you are convicted or acquitted __________ County may seek reimbursement of attorney's fees paid for you if you become financially able to pay or reimburse the county but refuse to do so? __________

I have read (had read to me) the above questions and answers and they are correct and true.

The undersigned swears that the information given herein is true and correct and understands that a false answer to any item may result in a charge of perjury.

The ___ day of __________, 20___.

____

Defendant's Signature

Sworn to and subscribed before me this ___ day of __________, 20___.

____

Notary Public

My Commission Expires __________

ORDER

Having considered the above matter, it is the finding of this court that the above-named defendant is/is not indigent under criteria of the Georgia Criminal Justice Act and appropriate court rules and is/is not entitled to have appointed counsel.

It is ordered that the clerk, panel administrator, or court administrator assign an attorney practicing in this county to represent the defendant in the above case.

Let the defendant and the assigned attorney be notified hereof and furnished a copy of this application and order.

This ___ day of __________, 20___.

Magistrate Court Judge

__________ County

26.3 Responsibility for Determination of Eligibility. The financial eligibility of a person for publicly provided counsel should be determined by the court. The court may appoint counsel in cases where the defendant does not qualify and cannot be provided counsel under provisions of the above.

26.4 Uniform Eligibility Guidelines. Income eligibility—Eligible accused persons include all applicants for an attorney with net income below a level set by the court as revised periodically.

The following special needs of a family unit may be deducted from net income in determining eligibility:

(1) Child care expenses for working custodial parents; and,

(2) Legally required support payments to dependents, including alimony for the support of a child/children.

"Net income" shall include only a client's take-home pay, which is the gross income earned by a client minus those deductions required by law or as a condition of employment.

"Family unit" includes the defendant, a spouse, if the couple lives together, any minors who are unemployed and unmarried, and any infirm or permanently disabled person living with the defendant and for whom the defendant has assumed financial responsibility. The income of a minor who is attending school full time, but has after-school employment or does odd jobs, shall not be attributed to that of the family unit. No other persons, even if living within the same household, will be deemed members of the family unit.

In the event an accused person is discovered to have been ineligible at the time of the appointment of an attorney, the court shall be notified. The court may discharge the appointed attorney and refer the matter to the private bar. The attorney should be paid for the time spent on the case and recoupment sought from the ineligible person.

Regardless of the prima facie eligibility on the basis of income, a person who has sufficient assets that are easily converted to cash by sale or mortgage may not be qualified for representation.

The court may appoint counsel for representation for any accused person who is unable to obtain counsel due to special circumstances such as emergency, hardship, or documented refusal of the case by members of the private bar because of financial inability to pay for counsel.

If the accused is determined to be eligible for defense services in accordance with approved financial eligibility criteria and procedures, and if, at the time that the determination is made, the accused is able to provide a cash contribution to offset defense costs without imposing a substantial financial hardship either personally or upon dependents, such contribution may be required as a condition of continued representation at public expense. The court should determine the amount to be contributed. The contribution shall be paid directly to the fund for indigent defense of the affected county.

26.5 County Selected Methods of Providing Counsel. The court shall, whenever practicable, use an available public defender system, legal aid and defender society, agency for indigent defense, a panel of private attorneys, a combination of the above, or other existing means, to provide adequate legal defense for indigents as required by these rules and the laws of this State.

26.6 Assignment of Cases to Private Attorneys.

(A) Appointments of private attorneys shall be made on an impartial and equitable basis;

(B) The cases shall be distributed among the attorneys to ensure balanced workloads through a rotation system;

(C) More difficult or complex cases shall be assigned to attorneys with sufficient levels of experience and competence to afford adequate representation;

(D) Less experienced attorneys should be assigned cases which are within their capabilities, but should be given the opportunity to expand their experience under supervision; and,

(E) Cases in which the death penalty is sought shall be assigned only to attorneys of sufficient experience, skill and competence to render effective assistance of counsel to defendants in such cases.

Adopted effective December 19, 2002.

RULE 27. ARRAIGNMENT

27.1 Calendar. The judge or the judge's designee, shall set the time of arraignment unless arraignment is waived either by the defendant or by operation of law. Notice of the date, time and place of arraignment shall be delivered to the clerk of the court and sent to attorneys of record, defendants and bondsmen.

27.2 Call for Arraignment. Before arraignment the court shall inquire whether the accused is represented by counsel and, if not, inquire into the defendant's desires and financial circumstances. If the defendant desires an attorney and is indigent, the court shall authorize the immediate appointment of counsel.

Upon the call of the case for arraignment, unless continued for good cause, the accused, or the attorney for the accused, shall answer whether the accused pleads "guilty," "not guilty" or desires to enter a plea of *nolo contendere* to the offense or offenses charged; a plea of not guilty shall constitute a joining of the issue.

Upon arraignment, the attorney, if any, who announces for or on behalf of an accused, or who is entered as counsel of record, shall represent the accused in that case throughout the trial, unless other counsel and the defendant notify the judge prior to trial that such other counsel represents the accused and is ready to proceed, or counsel is otherwise relieved by the judge.

Adopted effective December 19, 2002.

RULE 28. MOTIONS, DEMURRERS, SPECIAL PLEAS, AND SIMILAR ITEMS IN CRIMINAL MATTERS

28.1 Time for Filing. All motions, demurrers, and special pleas shall be made and filed at or before the time set by law, unless time therefor is extended by the judge in writing prior to trial. Notices of the state's intention to present evidence of similar transactions or occurrences and notices of the intention of the defense to raise the issue of insanity or mental illness shall be given and filed at least ten (10) days before trial unless the time is shortened or lengthened by the judge. Such filing shall be in accordance with the following procedures.

28.2 Time for Hearing. All such motions, demurrers, special pleas and notices shall be heard and considered at such time, date, and place as set by the judge. Generally, such will be heard at or after the time of arraignment and prior to the time at which such case is scheduled for trial.

28.3 Notice of Prosecution's Intent to Present Evidence of Similar Transactions.

(A) The prosecution may, upon notice filed in accordance with section 28.1 of these rules, request of the court in which the charging instrument is pending leave to present during the trial of the pending case evidence of similar transactions or occurrences.

(B) The notice shall be in writing, served upon the defendant's counsel, and shall state the transaction, date, county, and the name(s) of the victim(s) for each similar transaction or occurrence sought to be introduced. Copies of accusations or indictments, if any, and guilty pleas or verdicts, if any, shall be attached to the notice. The judge shall hold a hearing at such time as may be appropriate, and may receive evidence on any issue of fact necessary to determine the request. The burden of proving that the evidence of similar transactions or occurrences should be admitted shall be upon the prosecution. The state may present during the trial evidence of only those similar transactions or occurrences specifically approved by the judge.

(C) Evidence of similar transactions or occurrences not approved shall be inadmissible. In every case, the prosecuting attorney and defense attorney shall instruct their witnesses not to refer to similar crimes, transactions or occurrences, or otherwise place the defendant's character in issue, unless specifically authorized by the judge.

(D) If upon the trial of the case the defense places the defendant's character in issue, evidence of similar transactions or occurrences, as shall be admissible according to the rules of evidence, shall be admissible, the above provisions notwithstanding.

(E) Nothing in this rule is intended to prohibit the state from introducing evidence of similar transactions or occurrences which are lesser included alleged offenses of the charge being tried, or are immediately related in time and place to the charge being tried, as part of a single, continuous transaction. Nothing in this rule is intended to alter the rules of evidence relating to impeachment of witnesses.

(F) This rule shall not apply to sentencing hearings.

28.4 Notice of Intention of Defense to Raise Issue of Insanity, Mental Illness or Mental Competency.

(A) If, in any criminal proceeding, the defense intends to raise the issue that the defendant or accused was or is insane, mentally incompetent, or mentally ill at the time of act or acts charged against the accused, or at the time of trial, such intention must be stated, in writing, in a pleading denominated as "Notice of Intent of Defense to Raise Issue of Insanity or Mental Incompetence." This notice shall be filed and served upon the prosecuting attorney in accordance with section 28.1. of these rules. Upon the filing of such notice, the judge shall determine from the prosecuting attorney and the defense attorney whether such issue requires any further mental examination of the accused ahead of trial of the case on the merits.

(B) Except for good cause shown, the issue of insanity shall not be raised in the trial on the merits unless notice has been filed and served ahead of trial as provided in these rules.

28.5 Motions and Orders for Mental Examination at Public Expense. In pending cases where the mental competency of an accused is brought into question, the judge may, upon proper showing, exercise discretion and require a mental examination and evaluation at public expense. For a defendant who is represented by counsel, a motion for mental examination may be filed in writing by counsel setting out allegations and grounds for such motion, praying for a court-ordered evaluation. The judge may enter an order requiring psychiatric evaluation of the defendant for the purposes of competency to stand trial, degree of criminal responsibility at the time of the act in question and necessity of treatment. The judge may direct the Department of Human Resources (or any other forensic psychiatric service as may be necessary and available) to perform the examination at a time and place to be set by the department or service in cooperation with the county sheriff. A copy of the order shall be forwarded to the department or service accompanied by a copy of the accusation or specification of charges, a copy of the police arrest report, where available, and a brief summary of any known or alleged previous psychiatric treatment or hospitalization involving this particular person. Any other background information available to the court shall also be forwarded to the evaluating department or service to assist in performing adequately the requested services.

Copies of suggested orders requesting psychiatric examination are attached as Specimen Psychiatric Evaluation Order #1 and Specimen Psychiatric Evaluation Order #2. The department or service shall submit its report to the requesting judge, who shall provide copies of the report to the defendant's attorney and the prosecuting attorney.

SPECIMEN COMMITTAL ORDER AFTER SPECIAL PLEA OF MENTAL INCOMPETENCE TO STAND TRIAL

IN THE MAGISTRATE COURT OF ______
COUNTY
STATE OF GEORGIA

THE STATE OF GEORGIA CASE NO.
v. ______________ CHARGE(S):

JUDGMENT AND ORDER OF THE COURT ON THE
DEFENDANT'S SPECIAL PLEA OF MENTAL INCOMPETENCE TO STAND TRIAL

The above stated case came on regularly before the undersigned for trial this date. The defendant was represented by counsel.

After a hearing on defendant's special plea of insanity and due consideration, the plea of Mental Incompetence to Stand Trial is sustained.

IT IS, THEREFORE, THE ORDER of this court that the defendant be now delivered to the sheriff of County and that the defendant be delivered by the sheriff, or the sheriff's lawful deputy, to the Department of Human Resources, as provided by OCGA § 17–7–130.

IT IS FURTHER ORDERED that at such time as it is determined that the defendant is capable of understanding the nature and object of the proceedings, comprehends his or her own condition in reference to such proceedings, and is capable of rendering counsel assistance in providing a proper defense, the defendant be delivered by the Department of Human Resources to the sheriff of this county, or the sheriff's lawful deputy, with transportation costs to be borne by the county.

IT IS FURTHER ORDERED that, should it be determined in the light of present day medical knowledge that recovery of the defendant's legal mental competence to stand trial is not expected at any time in the foreseeable future, the defendant shall be dealt with by the Department of Human Resources as provided in OCGA § 17-7-130.

SO ORDERED, this the ___ day of _________, 20___.

____

Judge, Magistrate Court of _________ County, Georgia

SPECIMEN PSYCHIATRIC EVALUATION ORDER NO. 1

IN THE MAGISTRATE COURT OF _______ COUNTY
STATE OF GEORGIA

THE STATE OF GEORGIA CASE NO.
v.
CHARGE(S):
____

ORDER FOR MENTAL EVALUATION REGARDING COMPETENCY TO STAND TRIAL

WHEREAS the mental competency of the above defendant has been called into question, and evidence presented in the matter, and this court has found that it is appropriate for evaluation to be conducted by public expense;

IT IS HEREBY ORDERED that the Department of Human Resources (or Forensic Psychiatry Service) conduct an evaluative examination of said defendant, provide treatment of the defendant, if appropriate, and provide to this court a report of diagnosis, prognosis and its findings, with respect to: Competency to stand trial. Whether the accused is capable of understanding the nature and object of the proceedings; whether he comprehends his or her own condition in reference to such proceedings; and, whether the accused is capable of rendering counsel assistance in providing a proper defense.

IT IS FURTHER ORDERED that the department (or service) arrange with the county sheriff, or the sheriff's lawful deputies, for the prompt examination of said defendant, either at the county jail or at a designated hospital, with transportation of the defendant to be provided by the sheriff, where necessary, with transportation costs to be borne by the county. Upon completion of the examination, the examining facility shall notify the sheriff, who shall promptly reassume custody of the defendant.

Copies of documents supporting this request are attached hereto, as follows:

( ) Accusation

( ) Summary of previous mental health treatment

( ) Copy of arrest report

( ) Other

So ordered, this the ___ day of _________, 20___.

____

Judge, Magistrate Court of _________ County, Georgia

SPECIMEN PSYCHIATRIC EVALUATION ORDER NO. 2

IN THE MAGISTRATE COURT OF _______ COUNTY
STATE OF GEORGIA

THE STATE OF GEORGIA CASE NO.
v. _______________ CHARGE(S):

ORDER FOR MENTAL EVALUATION REGARDING COMPETENCY AT THE TIME OF THE ACT

WHEREAS, the mental competency of the above defendant has been called into question, and evidence presented in the matter, and this court has found that it is appropriate for an evaluation to be conducted at public expense;

IT IS HEREBY ORDERED that the Department of Human Resources (or Forensic Psychiatry Service) conduct an evaluative examination of the defendant, provide treatment of the defendant, if appropriate, and provide to this court a report of diagnosis, prognosis and its findings, with respect to:

1. Competency to Stand Trial. Whether the accused is capable of understanding the nature and object of the proceedings; whether the accused comprehends his or her own condition in reference to the proceedings, and, whether the accused is capable of rendering to counsel assistance in providing a proper defense.

2. Degree of Criminal Responsibility or Mental Competence at the Time of the Act. Whether or not the accused had the mental capacity to distinguish right from wrong in relation to the alleged act; whether or not the presence of a delusional compulsion overmastered the accused's will to resist committing the alleged act.

3. Any recommendations for disposition.

IT IS FURTHER ORDERED that the department or service arrange with the county sheriff, or the sheriff's lawful deputies, for the prompt examination of said defendant, either at the county jail or at a specified hospital, with transportation costs to be borne by the county. Upon completion of the examination, the examining facility shall notify the sheriff, who shall promptly reassume custody of the accused. Copies of documents supporting this request are attached hereto, as follows:

( ) Accusation

( ) Summary of previous mental health treatment

( ) Copy of arrest report

( ) Other

So ordered, this the ___ day of _________, 20___.

Judge, Magistrate Court of _________ County, Georgia

Adopted effective December 19, 2002; amended effective July 15, 2004.

RULE 29. CRIMINAL TRIAL CALENDAR

29.1 Calendar Preparation. All cases shall be set for trial within a reasonable time after arraignment. The judge or designee shall prepare a trial calendar, shall deliver a copy thereof to the clerk of court, and shall give notice in person or by mail to each counsel of record, the bondsman (if any) and the defendant at the last address indicated in court records, not less than 7 days before the trial date. The calendar shall list the dates that cases are set for trial, the cases to be tried at that session of court, the case numbers, the names of the defendants and the names of the defense counsel.

29.2 Removal From Calendar. No case shall be postponed or removed from the calendar except by the judge.

Adopted effective December 19, 2002.

RULE 30. PLEADING BY DEFENDANT

30.1 Alternatives.

(A) A defendant may plead guilty, not guilty, or in the discretion of the judge, nolo contendere. A plea of guilty or nolo contendere should be received only from the defendant personally in open court, except when the defendant is a corporation, in which case the plea may be entered by counselor a corporate officer. In misdemeanor cases, upon the request of a defendant who has made, in writing, a knowing, intelligent and voluntary waiver of his right to be present, the court may accept a plea of guilty in absentia.

(B) A defendant may plead nolo contendere only with the consent of the judge. Such a plea should be accepted by the judge only after due consideration of the views of the parties and the interest of the public in the effective administration of justice. Procedurally, a plea of nolo contendere should be handled under these rules in a manner similar to a plea of guilty.

30.2 Aid of Counsel—Time for Deliberation.

(A) A defendant shall not be called upon to plead before having an opportunity to retain counsel, or if defendant is eligible for appointment of counsel, until counsel has been appointed or right to counsel waived. A defendant with counsel shall not be required to enter a plea if counsel makes a reasonable request for additional time to represent the defendant's interest, or if the defendant has not had a reasonable time to consult with counsel.

(B) A defendant without counsel should not be called upon to plead to any offense without having had a reasonable time to consider this decision. When a defendant without counsel tenders a plea of guilty or nolo contendere to an offense, the court should not accept the plea unless it is reaffirmed by the defendant after a reasonable time for deliberation, following the advice from the court required in section 30.8.

30.3 Propriety of Plea Discussions and Plea Agreements.

(A) In cases in which it appears that the interests of the public in the effective administration of criminal justice (as stated in section 30.6) would thereby be served, the prosecuting attorney may engage in plea discussions for the purpose of reaching a plea agreement. The prosecuting attorney should engage in plea discussions or reach a plea agreement with the defendant only through defense counsel, except when the defendant is not eligible for or does not desire appointment of counsel and has not retained counsel.

(B) The prosecuting attorney, in reaching a plea agreement, may agree to one or more of the following, as dictated by the circumstances of the individual case:

(1) to make or not to oppose favorable recommendations as to the sentence which should be imposed if the defendant enters a plea of guilty or nolo contendere;

(2) to seek or not to oppose dismissal of the offense charged if the defendant enters a plea of guilty or nolo contendere to another offense reasonably related to defendant's conduct; or,

(3) to seek or not to oppose dismissal of other charges or potential charges against the defendant if the defendant enters a plea of guilty or nolo contendere.

30.4 Relationship Between Defense Counsel and Client.

(A) Defense counsel should conclude a plea agreement only with the consent of the defendant, and should ensure that the decision to enter or not enter a plea of guilty or nolo contendere is ultimately made by the defendant.

(B) To aid the defendant in reaching a decision, defense counsel, after appropriate investigation, should advise the defendant of the alternatives available and of considerations deemed important by him in reaching a decision.

30.5 Responsibilities of the Trial Judge.

(A) The trial judge should not participate in plea discussions.

(B) If a tentative plea agreement has been reached, upon request of the parties, the trial judge may permit the parties to disclose the tentative agreement and the reasons therefor in advance of the time for the tendering of the plea. The judge may then indicate to the prosecuting attorney and defense counsel whether the judge will likely concur in the proposed disposition if the information developed in the plea hearing or presented in the presentence report is consistent with the representations made by the parties. If the trial judge concurs but the final disposition differs from that contemplated by the plea agreement, then the judge shall state for the record what information in the presentence report or hearing contributed to the decision not to sentence in accordance with the plea agreement.

(C) When a plea of guilty or nolo contendere is tendered or received as a result of a plea agreement, the trial judge should give the agreement due consideration, but notwithstanding its existence, must reach an independent decision on whether to grant charge or sentence leniency under the principles set forth in section 30.6 of these rules.

30.6 Consideration of Plea in Final Disposition.

(A) It is proper for the judge to grant charge and sentence leniency to defendants who enter pleas of guilty or nolo contendere when the interests of the public in the effective administration of criminal justice are thereby served. Among the considerations which are appropriate in determining this question are:

(1) that the defendant by entering a plea has aided in ensuring the prompt and certain application of correctional measures;

(2) that the defendant has acknowledged guilt and shown a willingness to assume responsibility for conduct;

(3) that the leniency will make possible alternative correctional measures which are better adapted to achieving rehabilitative, protective, deterrent or other purposes of correctional treatment, or will prevent undue harm to the defendant from the form of conviction;

(4) that the defendant has made public trial unnecessary when there are good reasons for not having the case dealt with in a public trial;

(5) that the defendant has given or offered cooperation when such cooperation has resulted or may result in the successful prosecution of other offenders engaged in equally serious or more serious criminal conduct;

(6) that the defendant by entering a plea has aided in avoiding delay (including delay due to crowded dockets) in the disposition of other cases and thereby has increased the probability of prompt and certain application of correctional measures to other offenders.

(B) The judge should not impose upon a defendant any sentence in excess of that which would be justified by any of the rehabilitative, protective, deterrent or other purposes of the criminal law merely because the defendant has chosen to require the prosecution to prove the defendant's guilt at trial rather than to enter a plea of guilty or nolo contendere.

30.7 Determining Voluntariness of Plea. The judge shall not accept a plea of guilty or nolo contendere without first determining, on the record, that the plea is voluntary. By inquiry of the prosecuting attorney and defense counsel, the judge should determine whether the tendered plea is the result of prior plea discussions and a plea agreement, and, if it is, what agreement has been reached. If the prosecuting attorney has agreed to seek charge or sentence leniency which must be approved by the judge, the judge must advise the defendant personally that the recommendations of the prosecuting attorney are not binding on the judge. The judge should then address the defendant personally and determine whether any other promises or any force or threats were used to obtain the plea.

30.8 Defendant to Be Informed. The judge should not accept a plea of guilty or nolo contendere from a defendant without first:

(A) Determining on the record that the defendant understands the nature of the charge(s);

(B) Informing the defendant on the record that by entering a plea of guilty or nolo contendere one waives:

(1) the right to trial by jury;

(2) the presumption of innocence;

(3) the right to confront witnesses against oneself;

(4) the right to subpoena witnesses;

(5) the right to testify and to offer other evidence;

(6) the right to assistance of counsel during trial;

(7) the right not to incriminate oneself; and that by pleading not guilty or remaining silent and not entering a plea, one obtains a jury trial; and

(C) Informing the defendant on the record:

(1) of the terms of any negotiated plea;

(2) that a plea of guilty may have an impact on his or her immigration status if the defendant is not a citizen of the United States;

(3) of the maximum possible sentence on the charge, including that possible from consecutive sentences and enhanced sentences where provided by law; and/or

(4) of the mandatory minimum sentence, if any, on the charge. This information may be developed by questions from the judge, the district attorney or

the defense attorney, or a combination of any of these.

30.9 Determining Accuracy of Plea. Notwithstanding the acceptance of a plea of guilty, judgment should not be entered upon such plea without such inquiry on the record as may satisfy the judge that there is a factual basis for the plea.

30.10 Stating Intention to Reject the Plea Agreement. If the trial court intends to reject the plea agreement, the trial court shall, on the record, inform the defendant personally that (1) the trial court is not bound by any plea agreement; (2) the trial court intends to reject the plea agreement presently before it; (3) the disposition of the present case may be less favorable to the defendant than that contemplated by the plea agreement; and (4) that the defendant may then withdraw his or her guilty plea as a matter of right. If the plea is not then withdrawn, sentence may be pronounced.

30.11 Record of Proceedings. A verbatim record of the proceedings at which a defendant enters a plea of guilty or nolo contendere shall be made and preserved. The record should include:

(A) the inquiry into the voluntariness of the plea (as required in section 30.7);

(B) the advice to the defendant (as required in section 30.8);

(C) the inquiry into the accuracy of the plea (as required in section 30.9), and, if applicable;

(D) the notice to the defendant that the trial court intends to reject the plea agreement and the defendant's right to withdraw the guilty plea before sentence is pronounced.

30.12 Plea Withdrawal.

(A) After sentence is pronounced, the judge should allow the defendant to withdraw his plea of guilty or nolo contendere whenever the defendant, upon a timely motion for withdrawal, proves that withdrawal is necessary to correct a manifest injustice.

(B) In the absence of a showing that withdrawal is necessary to correct a manifest injustice, a defendant may not withdraw a plea of guilty or nolo contendere as a matter of right once sentence has been pronounced by the judge.

Adopted effective December 19, 2002.

PART III. CIVIL RULES

RULE 31. DESIGNATED AGENT FOR CIVIL ACTIONS

Any full-time officer or employee of a corporation, sole proprietorship, partnership or unincorporated association may be designated by such entity as agent for purposes of representing it in civil actions to which it is a party in magistrate court.

An action on behalf of a corporation, sole proprietorship, partnership, or unincorporated association, except affidavits in attachment, may be filed and presented by such designated agent.

Former Rule 14 renumbered as new Rule 31 effective October 28, 1993.

RULE 32. FILING OF CIVIL ACTIONS BY MAIL

Civil actions may be filed in magistrate court by mail providing such an action is properly verified by a notary or other attesting official. No magistrate court shall refuse to accept such mail filings.

Former Rule 15 renumbered as new Rule 32 effective October 28, 1993.

RULE 33. COMPUTING ANSWER DATES IN CIVIL ACTIONS

Except as otherwise provided by time period computations prescribed by statute, to compute the date an answer is due in civil actions, begin counting on the day following the day of service and count the number of days. If the last day falls on a Saturday, Sunday, or legal holiday, then the next regular business day becomes the day the answer is due. When the period of time is less than seven [7] days, intermediate Saturdays, Sundays, and legal holidays shall be excluded in the computation.

Former Rule 16 renumbered as new Rule 33 effective October 28, 1993.

RULE 34. ANSWER TO CIVIL ACTIONS

34.1 Oral answers and counterclaims to civil actions. Oral answers and counterclaims, if any, to civil actions must be given in person to a clerk or judge of the magistrate court. The clerk or judge shall reduce such answer to writing, have the defendant sign it and then file it with other papers in the case.

34.2 Setting hearing date in dispossessory proceedings. If a defendant in a dispossessory proceeding files an answer and/or counterclaim, a trial on the issues may be had within 7 days from the date the answer is filed.

Former Rule 17 amended and renumbered as new Rule 34 effective October 28, 1993; Former Rule 34 renumbered as subsection 34.1 and a new subsection 34.2 was added effective June 10, 1999; amended effective March 22, 2001.

RULE 35. OBJECTIONS TO PROCESS, JURISDICTION OR VENUE

Objections to sufficiency of process, service of process, personal jurisdiction or venue must be raised at the time of filing the answer or are waived. Where a valid objection to personal jurisdiction or venue was not raised when the answer was filed and thus is waived, the court may nevertheless in the interest of justice transfer the case to another Georgia court having jurisdiction if the present court is an inconvenient forum and the transfer would not unduly prejudice the opposing party. Objections to subject matter jurisdiction are never waived.

No special formula shall be required to raise an issue of jurisdiction or venue. In addition to answers explicitly raising the issue of lack of jurisdiction or venue, any motion to transfer or answer stating that the action was filed in the wrong court or asking that the case be transferred to another court, or words to that effect, shall be sufficient to raise an objection to jurisdiction or venue.

Adopted effective October 28, 1993.

RULE 36. TRANSFER/CHANGE OF VENUE

In all cases where it is determined by the court that the court in which a case is pending lacks jurisdiction, or venue, or both, the court shall by written order transfer the case in accordance with Article VI, Section 1, Paragraph 8, of the 1983 Constitution of the State of Georgia, or where this rule is not applicable, dismiss said case without prejudice.

36.1 Lack of Jurisdiction Over Counterclaim. Where the defendant asserts a legally sufficient counterclaim in good faith which is beyond the jurisdiction of the magistrate court but the entire case is within the jurisdiction of another Georgia court, the court shall transfer the case to a court with jurisdiction over the counterclaim. Where the parties agree on a transferee court with jurisdiction over the counterclaim, the court shall transfer the case to that court. Otherwise, the court shall select a proper court to which to transfer the case.

36.2 Transfer Between Magistrate Courts. Upon a judicial determination that the court lacks venue, the court shall transfer the case by written order to a magistrate court of proper venue. No court shall refuse to accept a transfer accompanied by the fees provided by paragraph 36.3. If it is later determined that the transferee court has no jurisdiction or venue to hear the case, it may in turn transfer the action pursuant to this rule.

36.3 Costs for Transfers Between Magistrate Courts.

A. The case shall be transferred with the initial filing fee, and the transferred filing fee shall be the filing fee in the transferee court. All surcharges, such as for local law library funds, retirement funds, and the like shall be retained and reported in the court of initial filing. No additional filing costs shall be required by the transferee court, no surcharges will be collected from the parties or be required to be paid by the transferee court, nor shall any refund be made to the parties if the filing fee is less in the transferee court.

B. If service upon the defendant has not been perfected, a service fee in the amount provided for in OCGA § 15–16–21(b)(1) for the transferee court shall be paid by the plaintiff prior to the transfer. If a service attempt (beyond a check of map, data base or index of addresses) has been made in the court where the action was originally filed, the original service fee shall be considered as expended and the entire service fee shall be billed to the plaintiff. If no service has been attempted, the plaintiff shall only be billed for the difference between the service fee originally paid and that required by this rule. A bill for the required service fee shall be sent to the plaintiff by regular mail and the case may be dismissed without prejudice for want of prosecution if the bill is not paid within thirty (30) days.

The service fee provided in OCGA § 15–16–21(b)(1) shall be the service fee in all transferred cases irrespective of whether the transferee court uses sheriff, marshal, or constable as the office for service of process in that county. The parties shall not be entitled to any refund of a portion of the fee.

36.4 Hearing Transfer Requests.

A. Where the defendant has not been served, the court may entertain a motion to transfer ex parte, either orally or upon written request and need not require a hearing.

B. Where the opposing party consents to a transfer, the court need not require a hearing. No transfer shall be made upon consent of the parties where no authorized factual grounds for transfer are asserted; however, the court may accept without further proof the factual assertions where the request is made by consent.

C. Where the defendant has been served and there is no consent to the request for transfer, the court may decide the request at the hearing regularly set in that case. Alternately, the court may, after reviewing the legal sufficiency of the request, notify the opposing party that the request will be granted unless a hearing is requested within ten days. Such notice shall be sent by regular mail to the address shown on the pleadings.

D. The transfer order shall not be entered until any required service fee is paid. The court shall transfer the case within 10 days of the entry of the order.

E. If an order allowing the plaintiff to proceed in forma pauperis has been entered in the court where the action was originally filed, it shall be honored in the transferee court unless and until successfully challenged by an opposing party.

Former Rule 18 amended and renumbered as new Rule 36 effective October 28, 1993.

RULE 37. AMENDMENTS

Amendments to pleadings in the magistrate court may be filed without leave of court. If the court finds that the opposite party is surprised and not prepared to go forward due to the lateness of notice of the amendment despite due diligence, the court shall continue the case. When the amending party has been negligent or dilatory in filing an amendment, the court may condition consideration of the amendment upon the payment of all or part of the costs to the opposing party attributable to the continuance of the case. The amending party may then elect to proceed immediately to trial in the magistrate court without consideration of the amendment or agree to pay the costs assessed by the court. Upon failure to pay those costs, the court may impose a default judgment or may hear the case on the merits and assess those costs as part of the final judgment.

Amendments filed at or prior to the hearing in the magistrate court shall be part of the pleadings upon de novo appeal even where such amendment was not considered in the magistrate court.

Adopted effective October 28, 1993.

RULE 38. MOTIONS AND REQUEST FOR RELIEF UNDER THE CIVIL PRACTICE ACT

No party or attorney shall be required to respond to a motion, including a request for relief under the Civil Practice Act (OCGA § 9–11–1 et seq.) prior to a scheduled hearing unless otherwise directed by the court. Unless otherwise provided by the court, prejudgment motions shall be ruled on at the first scheduled hearing for the case. Where a party contends that the grant or denial of the motion may require postponement of the hearing on the merits, the motion should so state. Post-judgment motions may be placed on a calendar for hearing. Motions may be denied without a hearing based upon the record of the court. Motions shall not be granted without a hearing unless hearing is waived by the respondent.

Parties and attorneys are reminded that the Georgia Civil Practice Act does not govern proceedings in Magistrate Court. Except as otherwise provided in these rules, any request for relief under that act will be considered under the standards of Howe v. Roberts, 259 Ga. 617 (1989).

No leave of court is required to file a suggestion, on the record, of death of a party.

Adopted effective October 28, 1993.

RULE 39. THIRD–PARTY PRACTICE

A defendant may file with the answer a statement of claim against a person who is not a party to the action who is or may be liable for all or part of the plaintiff's claim. All claims arising out of the same transaction or occurrence as the plaintiff's claim may be asserted. After the answer is filed, third-party claims may only be filed with permission of the court. A plaintiff defending a counterclaim may also file such a third-party claim with permission of the court. The procedures applicable to any other action shall apply to a statement of claim filed against a third-party defendant and the hearing on the entire case shall be set pursuant to OCGA § 15–10–43 calculating time limits from the day of the third-party defendant's answer.

The third-party defendant may assert a claim arising out of the same transaction or occurrence at the time of filing the answer against any other party to the action and may assert such related claims against non-parties with permission of the court. Existing parties other than the third-party plaintiff may file claims against the third-party defendant arising out of the same transaction or occurrence as the original action any time before the third-party defendant's answer is due.

Adopted effective October 28, 1993.

RULE 40. PRE–TRIAL DISCOVERY

Use of OCGA §§ 9–11–26 through 9–11–37 for purposes of pre-trial discovery in the magistrate court is not favored; however, requests for such discovery may be entertained when made by joint request of all parties. Requests for use of these provisions may also be allowed for preservation of testimony, obtaining evidence from out-of-state, minimizing expense and similar purposes in order to do substantial justice or lessen the expense to the parties.

No party or attorney may file any discovery request pursuant to OCGA §§ 9–11–26 through 9–11–37 without permission of the court; any such filing shall be a nullity.

Where discovery is permitted by the magistrate court, the magistrate may nevertheless decline to rule on a motion pursuant to OCGA § 9–11–37 in which case such motion may be renewed upon de novo appeal.

Adopted effective October 28, 1993.

RULE 41. SUMMARY JUDGMENT

Summary judgment motions in the magistrate court shall not be permitted and their filing shall be a nullity.

Adopted effective October 28, 1993.

RULE 42. BANKRUPTCY STAY

A party or attorney may file a signed notice of bankruptcy proceedings containing the bankruptcy case number; where the debtor in the bankruptcy case is the same as a party in the magistrate court, such a notice will stay proceedings in the magistrate court until further order of the court. Parties are encouraged to attach a copy of the first page of their bankruptcy filing to the notice. On the court's own motion, a judge or clerk may attempt to verify the filing with the U.S. Bankruptcy Court (which may be by telephone inquiry) and notify the parties to proceed with the case upon lack of verification.

Parties desiring to challenge the authenticity, scope, or continued duration of a bankruptcy stay shall file a written motion or request which shall be set for hearing before a magistrate.

Adopted effective October 28, 1993.

RULE 43. CONSENT JUDGMENTS IN CIVIL ACTIONS

Consent judgments must be reduced to writing, signed by the defendant and his or her attorney, if any, and filed with other papers in the case. If the consent judgment is for less than the amount of the claim as filed, then the plaintiff and his or her attorney, if any, shall also sign such consent judgment.

Former Rule 19 amended and renumbered as new Rule 43 effective October 28, 1993.

RULE 44. DEFERRED PARTIAL PAYMENTS OF JUDGMENTS BY DEFENDANTS

44.1 Clerical and Accounting Costs Due. Where plaintiff does not request partial payments be made to the court but the defendant requests to make such partial payments to the court rather than to the plaintiff, the judge may do so at the expense of the defendant and for the clerical and accounting costs incurred thereby, may charge 10%, but not less than $1.00 and not to exceed $10.00 for each payment.

44.2 Clerical and Accounting Costs Withheld. No clerical and accounting costs shall be deducted from monies received in the magistrate court in answer to a summons of garnishment, levy on property where such property is redeemed prior to public sale, when a defendant pays a claim in full, or when a defendant pays rent into court on a dispossessory action.

Former Rule 20 amended and renumbered as new Rule 44 effective October 28, 1993.

RULE 45. SATISFACTION OF FI. FA.

Upon sufficient showing, the judge or clerk shall indicate on the face of the fi. fa. that it has been satisfied, if such payment is made prior to public sale.

Former Rule 21 amended and renumbered as new Rule 45 effective October 28, 1993.

UNIFORM TRANSFER RULES

Effective April 1, 1984

Including Amendments Received Through November 1, 2006

Research Note

Use WESTLAW *to find cases citing a rule. In addition, use* WESTLAW *to search for specific terms or to update a rule; see the GA–RULES and GA–ORDERS Scope screens for further information.*

Amendments to these rules are published, as received, in the South Eastern Reporter 2d *and* Georgia Cases *advance sheets.*

These rules are adopted pursuant to the authority of Art. VI, Sec. IX, Par. I of the 1983 Constitution of the State of Georgia to implement Art. VI, Sec. I, Par. VIII of the 1983 Constitution which provides that: "Any court shall transfer to the appropriate court in this state any civil case in which it determines that jurisdiction or venue lies elsewhere."

T–1. These rules are applicable to Superior Courts, State Courts, Probate Courts, Magistrate Courts, and Juvenile Courts except when in conflict with the Juvenile Proceedings Code.

T–2. These rules are applicable only when the court in which the case is pending is alleged to lack jurisdiction or venue or both.

T–3. These rules are applicable to transfers of civil cases from a court within a county to another court within that county, and from a court within a county to a court in another county.

T–4. These rules shall become operative when a party makes a motion to dismiss, or any other motion or defense, on the basis that the court in which the case is pending lacks jurisdiction or venue or both. Such motion shall be treated as a motion to transfer pursuant to these rules. A motion to transfer shall be made only in the court in which the case is pending. These rules also become operative when a court on its own motion, after a hearing thereon, determines that it lacks subject matter jurisdiction.

T–5. A party making a motion to transfer on the basis that the court in which the case is pending lacks jurisdiction or venue or both shall do so in compliance with OCGA § 9–11–12, except as otherwise provided in rule T–6 (and except that a motion to transfer made in a Magistrate Court need not comply with OCGA § 9–11–12 but such motion shall be made pursuant to rules applicable to Magistrate Courts). Unless otherwise ordered by the court, notice of a written motion to transfer shall be served upon all parties, including any who failed to file pleadings in the matter, at least 10 days before the motion is heard.

T–6. If the basis for the motion to transfer is that a defendant necessary to the court's jurisdiction has been dismissed either during or at the conclusion of trial, such motion shall be made immediately and orally. If the motion to transfer the case against the remaining defendant is granted, the case against the dismissed defendant shall be severed from that case so that the order of dismissal will be final for purposes of appeal.

T–7. A party making a motion to transfer shall specify the court in which jurisdiction and venue lies (except in Magistrate Courts).

T–8. A party opposing a written motion to transfer shall notify the court of such opposition promptly and in no event more than ten days after the making and service of such motion. A motion required to be in writing shall be opposed in writing. A motion made orally, if opposed, shall be opposed orally and at the time of its being made. A party opposing a motion to transfer shall specify the basis on which the court in which the case is pending has jurisdiction, or venue, or both (except in Magistrate Courts).

T–9. After the filing of a motion to transfer, the court in which the case is pending may stay all other proceedings pending determination of the motion to transfer.

T–10. No action or proceeding shall be transferred except upon written order of the court in which the case is pending, notice of which shall be given to all parties. Such order shall specify the court to which the case is to be transferred. (a) Such order shall also provide notice to the plaintiff that if costs are not paid within twenty (20) days as provided in rule T–11, the case shall automatically stand dismissed without prejudice. The court granting (or denying) an order of transfer may impose reasonable attorney fees incurred in relation to such motion in favor of the prevailing party. Unless the court in its discretion expressly determines otherwise in such order of transfer, and except in Magistrate Courts (see OCGA § 15–10–80), a transfer fee of $50 shall automatically be imposed. (b) Where a party has filed a successful claim of indigence, the payment of costs shall not be a condition of transfer.

T–11. Upon the filing of an order transferring a case with the clerk of the court entering such order, the clerk shall promptly compute the court costs, including the costs incident to preparing and transferring the record as provided in rule T–12 and the $50 transfer fee provided for in rule T–10, and notify counsel for plaintiff (or the plaintiff if there be no counsel) in writing of the amount of the court costs. Plaintiff shall pay the unpaid costs within twenty (20) days of mailing or delivery of the cost bill. If costs are not paid within twenty (20) days, the case shall automatically stand dismissed, without prejudice, except where the plaintiff has filed as an indigent. Rule T–11 shall not be applicable in Magistrate Courts.

T–12. Upon timely payment of costs, the clerk of the court ordering transfer shall promptly make copies of (1) the complaint or initial pleading, (2) the motion to transfer if in writing, and (3) the order of transfer. The foregoing copies shall be retained by the clerk of the court ordering transfer. The originals of all pleadings, orders, depositions and other papers on file shall be indexed and certified by the clerk of the court ordering transfer and transmitted, with the $50 transfer fee (if applicable), to the clerk of the court to which the case is to be transferred in the manner provided by law for transmittal of records to appellate courts.

T–13. Upon receipt by the clerk of the court to which the case is transferred of the pleadings, orders, depositions and other papers specified above, such clerk shall assign the case the appropriate number. The case shall continue in the court to which transferred as though initially commenced there and all pleadings, orders, depositions and other papers shall be deemed to be amended accordingly. It shall not be necessary that service be perfected a second time upon the defendants, except that any publication which is required to be made in a newspaper in the proper venue shall be republished. Any interlocutory or other order already entered in the case shall, upon motion of any party, be reviewed and reissued or vacated by the court to which the case is transferred.

GEORGIA CODE OF JUDICIAL CONDUCT

Effective January 1, 1994

Including Amendments Received Through November 1, 2006

Research Note

Use WESTLAW *to find cases citing a rule. In addition, use* WESTLAW *to search for specific terms or to update a rule; see the GA–RULES and GA–ORDERS Scope screens for further information.*

Amendments to these rules are published, as received, in the South Eastern Reporter 2d *and* Georgia Cases *advance sheets.*

Table of Canons

PREAMBLE

Our legal system is based on the principle that an independent, fair and competent judiciary will interpret and apply the laws that govern us. The role of the judiciary is central to American concepts of justice and the rule of law. Intrinsic to all sections of this Code are the precepts that judges, individually and collectively, must respect and honor the judicial office as a public trust and strive to enhance and maintain confidence in our legal system.

Every judge should strive to maintain the dignity appropriate to the judicial office. The judge is an arbiter of facts and law for the resolution of disputes and a highly visible symbol of government under the rule of law. As a result, judges should be held to a higher standard, and should aspire to conduct themselves with the dignity accorded their esteemed position.

The Code of Judicial Conduct is intended to establish standards for ethical conduct of judges. It consists of broad statements called Canons, specific rules set forth in Sections under each Canon, a Terminology Section, an Application Section and Commentary. The text of the Canons and the Sections, including the Terminology and Application Sections, is authoritative. The Commentary, by explanation and example, provides guidance with respect to the purpose and meaning of the Canons and Sections. The Commentary is not intended as a statement of additional rules. When the text uses "shall" or "shall not," it is intended to impose binding obligations the violation of which can result in disciplinary action. When "should" or "should not" is used, the text is intended as advisory and as a statement of what is or is not appropriate conduct, but not as a binding rule under which a judge may be disciplined. When "may" is used, it denotes permissible discretion or, depending on the context, it refers to action that is not covered by specific proscriptions.

The Canons and Sections are rules of reason. They should be applied consistent with constitutional requirements, statutes, other court rules and decisional law, as well as in the context of all relevant circumstances. The Code is to be construed so as not to impinge on the essential independence of judges in making judicial decisions, or on judges' First Amendment rights of freedom of speech and association.

The Code is designed to provide guidance to judges and candidates for judicial office and to provide a structure for regulating conduct through disciplinary agencies. It is not designed for nor intended as a basis for civil liability or criminal prosecution. Furthermore, the purpose of the Code would be subverted if the Code were invoked by lawyers for mere tactical advantage in a proceeding.

The text of the Canons and Sections is intended to govern conduct of judges and to be binding upon them. It is not intended, however, that every transgression will result in disciplinary action. Whether disciplinary action is appropriate, and the degree of discipline to be imposed, should be determined through a reasonable and reasoned application of the text and should depend on such factors as the seriousness of the transgression, whether there is a pattern of improper activity, and the effect of the improper activity on others or on the judicial system.

The Code of Judicial Conduct is not intended as an exhaustive guide for the conduct of judges. They should also be governed in their judicial and personal conduct by general ethical standards. The mandatory provisions of the Canons and Sections describe the basic minimal ethical requirements of judicial conduct. Judges and candidates should strive to achieve the highest ethical standards, even if not required by this Code. As an example, a judge or candidate is permitted under Canon 7, Section B, to solicit campaign funds directly from potential donors. The Commentary, however, makes clear that the judge or candidate who wishes to exceed the minimal ethical requirements would choose to set up a campaign committee to raise and solicit contributions. The Code is intended to state only basic standards which should govern the conduct of all judges and to provide guidance to assist judges in establishing and maintaining high standards of judicial and personal conduct.

Adopted effective January 1, 1994; amended effective January 7, 2004.

TERMINOLOGY

Terms explained below are noted with an asterisk(*) in the Sections where they appear. In addition, the Sections where terms appear are referred to after the explanation of each term below.

"Appropriate authority" denotes the authority with responsibility for initiation of disciplinary process with respect to the violation to be reported. See Sections 3D(1) and 3D(2).

"Candidate." A candidate is a person seeking selection for or retention in judicial office by election or appointment. A person becomes a candidate for judicial office as soon as he or she appoints and/or forms a campaign committee, makes a public announcement of candidacy, declares or files as a candidate with the election or appointment authority, or authorizes solicitation or acceptance of contributions or support. The term "candidate" has the same meaning when applied to a judge seeking election or appointment to non-judicial office. See Preamble and Sections 7A(1), 7A(2), 7B(1), 7B(2) and 7C.

"Comment" in connection with a case refers to valuative statements judging the professional wisdom of specific lawyering tactics or the legal correctness of particular court decisions. In contrast, it does not mean the giving of generally informative explanations to describe litigation factors including: the prima facie legal elements of case types pending before the courts, legal concepts such as burden of proof and duty of persuasion or principles such as innocent until proven guilty and knowing waiver of constitutional rights, variable realities illustrated by hypothetical factual patterns of aggravating or mitigating conduct, procedural phases of unfolding lawsuits, the social policy goals behind the law subject to application in various cases, as well as competing theories about what the law should be. See Section 3B(9).

"Court personnel" does not include the lawyers in a proceeding before a judge. See Sections 3B(7)(c) and 3B(9).

"De minimis" denotes an insignificant interest that could not raise reasonable question as to a judge's impartiality. See Sections 3E(1)(c) and 3E(1)(d).

"Economic interest" denotes ownership of a more than de minimis legal or equitable interest, or a relationship as officer, director, advisor or other active participant in the affairs of a party, except that:

(i) ownership of an interest in a mutual or common investment fund that holds securities is not an economic interest in such securities unless the judge participates in the management of the fund or a proceeding pending or impending before the judge could substantially affect the value of the interest;

(ii) service by a judge as an officer, director, advisor or other active participant in an educational, religious, charitable, fraternal or civic organization, or service by a judge's spouse, parent or child as an officer, director, advisor or other active participant in any organization does not create an economic interest in securities held by that organization;

(iii) a deposit in a financial institution, the proprietary interest of a policy holder in a mutual insurance company, of a depositor in a mutual savings association, is not an economic interest in the organization unless a proceeding pending or impending before the judge could substantially affect the value of the interest;

(iv) ownership of government securities is not an economic interest in the issuer unless a proceeding pending or impending before the judge could substantially affect the value of the securities. See Sections 3E(1)(c) and 3E(2).

"Fiduciary" includes such relationships as executor, administrator, trustee, and guardian. See Sections 3E(1)(c), 3E(2) and 5D.

"Invidious discrimination" is any action by an organization that characterizes some immutable individual trait such as a person's race, gender or national origin, as well as religion, as odious or as signifying inferiority, which therefore is used to justify arbitrary exclusion of persons possessing those traits from membership, position or participation in the organization. See Section 2C.

"Knowingly," "knowledge," "known" or "knows" denotes actual knowledge of the fact in question. A person's knowledge may be inferred from circumstances. See Sections 3D(1), 3D(2) and 3E(1).

"Law" denotes court rules as well as statutes, constitutional provisions and decisional law. See Sections 2A, 3A, 3B(2), 3B(7), 4A, 4B, 4C, 5C(4) and 5G.

"Member of the judge's family residing in the judge's household" denotes any relative of a judge by blood or marriage, or a person treated by a judge as a member of the judge's family, who resides in the judge's household. See Sections 3E(1) and 4D(5).

"Non-public information" denotes information that, by law, is not available to the public. Non-public information may include but is not limited to: information that is sealed by statute or court order, impounded or communicated in camera; and information offered in grand jury proceedings, pre-sentencing reports, dependency cases or psychiatric reports. See Section 3B(11).

"Political organization" denotes a political party or other group, the principal purpose of which is to further the election or appointment of candidates to political office. See Sections 7A(1).

"Public election." This term includes primary and general elections; it includes partisan elections, nonpartisan elections and may include (as context demands) retention elections. See Sections 7A(1), 7A(2), 7B(1) and 7B(2).

"Require." The rules prescribing that a judge "require" certain conduct of others are, like all of the rules in this Code, rules of reason. The use of the term "require" in that context means a judge is to exercise reasonable direction and control over the conduct of those persons subject to the judge's direction and control. See Sections 3B(3), 3B(4), 3B(6), 3B(9) and 3C(2).

"Third degree of relationship." The following persons are relatives within the third degree of relationship: great-grandparent, grandparent, parent, uncle, aunt, brother, sister, child, grandchild, great-grandchild, nephew or niece. See Section 3E(1)(d).

Adopted effective January 1, 1994; amended effective January 1, 1998.

CANON 1 JUDGES SHALL UPHOLD THE INTEGRITY AND INDEPENDENCE OF THE JUDICIARY

An independent and honorable judiciary is indispensable to justice in our society. Judges shall participate in establishing, maintaining, and enforcing high standards of conduct and shall personally observe such standards of conduct so that the integrity and independence of the judiciary may be preserved. The provisions of this Code should be construed and applied to further that objective.

Commentary

Deference to the judgments and rulings of courts depends upon public confidence in the integrity and independence of judges. The integrity and independence of judges depends in turn upon their acting without fear or favor. Although judges should be independent, they must comply with the law, including the provisions of this Code. Public confidence in the impartiality of the judiciary is maintained by the adherence of each judge to this responsibility. Conversely, violation of this Code diminishes public confidence in the judiciary and thereby does injury to the system of government under law.

Adopted effective January 1, 1994.

CANON 2 JUDGES SHALL AVOID IMPROPRIETY AND THE APPEARANCE OF IMPROPRIETY IN ALL THEIR ACTIVITIES

A. Judges shall respect and comply with the law [1] and shall act at all times in a manner that promotes public confidence in the integrity and impartiality of the judiciary.

1 [Pub. Note: This term is explained in the section titled "Terminology", supra.]

Commentary

Public confidence in the judiciary is eroded by irresponsible or improper conduct of judges. Judges must avoid all impropriety and appearance of impropriety. Judges must expect to be the subject of constant public scrutiny. Judges must therefore accept restrictions on their conduct that might be viewed as burdensome by the ordinary citizen, and they should do so freely and willingly.

The prohibition against behaving with impropriety or the appearance of impropriety applies to both the professional and personal conduct of a judge. Because it is not practicable to list all prohibited acts, the proscription is necessarily cast in general terms that extend to conduct by judges that is harmful although not specifically mentioned in the Code.

Actual improprieties under this standard include violations of law, court rules, or other specific provisions of this Code. The test for appearance of impropriety is whether the conduct would create in reasonable minds a perception that the judge's ability to carry out judicial responsibilities with integrity, impartiality and competence is impaired.

See also, Commentary under Section 2C.

B. Judges shall not allow their family, social, political or other relationships to influence their judicial conduct or judgment. Judges shall not lend the prestige of judicial office to advance the private interests of the judge or others; nor should they convey or permit others to convey the impression that they are in a special position to influence them. Judges should not testify voluntarily as a character witness.

Commentary

Maintaining the prestige of judicial office is essential to a system of government in which the judiciary functions independently of the executive and legislative branches. Respect for the judicial office facilitates the orderly conduct of legitimate judicial functions. Judges should distinguish between proper and improper use of the prestige of office in all of their activities. For example, it would be improper for a judge to allude to his or her judgeship to gain a personal advantage such as deferential treatment when stopped by a police officer for a traffic offense. Similarly, judicial letterhead must not be used for conducting a judge's personal business.

A judge must avoid lending the prestige of judicial office for the advancement of the private interests of others. For example, a judge must not use the judge's position to gain advantage in a civil suit involving a member of the judge's family. In contracts for publication of a judge's writings, a judge should retain control over the advertising to avoid exploitation of the judge's office. As to the acceptance of awards, see Section 4D(5)(a) and Commentary.

Although a judge should be sensitive to possible abuse of the prestige of office, a judge may, based on the judge's personal knowledge, serve as a reference or provide a letter of recommendation. However, a judge must not initiate the communication of information to a sentencing judge or probation or corrections officer, but may provide to such person information for the record in response to a formal request.

Judges may participate in the process of judicial selection by cooperating with appointing authorities and screening committees seeking names for consideration, and by responding to official inquiries concerning a person being considered for a judgeship. See also Canon 5, regarding use of a judge's name in political activities.

A judge must not testify voluntarily as a character witness, because to do so may lend the prestige of the judicial office in support of a party for whom the judge testifies. Moreover, when a judge testifies as a witness, a lawyer who regularly appears before the judge may be placed in the awkward position of cross-examining the judge. A judge may, however, testify when properly summoned. Except in unusual circumstances where the demands of justice require, a judge should discourage a party from requiring the judge to testify as a character witness.

C. Judges shall not hold membership in any organization that practices invidious discrimination [1].

[1] [Pub. Note: This term is explained in the section titled "Terminology", supra.]

Commentary

Membership by a judge in an organization that practices invidious discrimination [1] may give rise to perceptions that the judge's impartiality is impaired. Section 2C refers to the current practices of the organization. Whether an organization practices invidious discrimination is often a complex question to which judges should be sensitive. The answer cannot be determined from a mere examination of an organization's current membership rolls, but rather depends on how the organization selects members and other relevant factors, such as whether the organization is dedicated to the preservation of religious, ethnic, or cultural values of legitimate common interest to its members, or whether it is in fact and effect an intimate, purely private organization whose membership limitations could not be constitutionally prohibited. Absent such factors, an organization is generally said to discriminate invidiously if it arbitrarily excludes from membership on the basis of race, religion, sex or national origin persons who would otherwise be admitted to membership. See New York State Club Ass'n, Inc. v. City of New York, *[487 U.S. 1] 108 S.Ct. 2225, 101 L.Ed.2d 1 (1988);* Board of Directors of Rotary International v. Rotary Club of Duarte, *481 U.S. 537, 107 S.Ct. 1940, 95 L.Ed.2d 474 (1987);* Roberts v. United States Jaycees, *468 U.S. 609, 104 S.Ct. 3244, 82 L.Ed.2d 462 (1984). Ultimately, each judge must determine in the judge's own conscience whether an organization of which the judge is a member practices invidious discrimination.*

Adopted effective January 1, 1994; amended effective January 1, 1998.

[1] [Pub. Note: This term is explained in the section titled "Terminology", supra.]

CANON 3 JUDGES SHALL PERFORM THE DUTIES OF JUDICIAL OFFICE IMPARTIALLY AND DILIGENTLY

A. Judicial Duties in General. The judicial duties of judges take precedence over all their other activities. Their judicial duties include all the duties of their office prescribed by law [1]. In the performance of these duties, the following standards apply:

B. Adjudicative Responsibilities.

(1) Judges shall hear and decide matters assigned to them, except those in which they are disqualified.

(2) Judges shall be faithful to the law [1] and maintain professional competence in it. Judges shall not be swayed by partisan interests, public clamor, or fear of criticism.

(3) Judges shall require [1] order and decorum in proceedings over which they preside.

(4) Judges shall be patient, dignified, and courteous to litigants, jurors, witnesses, lawyers, and others with whom they deal in their official capacity, and shall require [1] similar conduct of lawyers, and of staff, court officials, and others subject to their direction and control.

[1] [Pub. Note: These terms are explained in the section titled "Terminology", supra.]

Commentary

The duty to hear all proceedings fairly and with patience is not inconsistent with the duty to dispose promptly of the business of the court. Judges can be efficient and business-like while being patient and deliberate.

(5) Judges shall perform judicial duties without bias or prejudice. Judges shall not, in the performance of judicial duties, by words or conduct manifest bias or prejudice, including but not limited to bias or prejudice based upon race, sex, religion, national origin, disability, age, sexual orientation or socioeconomic status, and shall not permit staff, court officials and others subject to the judge's direction and control to do so.

Commentary

Judges must refrain from speech, gestures or other conduct that could reasonably be perceived as sexual harassment and must require the same standard of conduct of others subject to their direction and control.

Judges must perform judicial duties impartially and fairly. Judges who manifest bias on any basis in a proceeding impair the fairness of the proceeding and bring the judiciary into disrepute. Facial expression, body language, in addition to oral communication, can give to parties or lawyers in the proceeding, jurors, the media and others an appearance of judicial bias. Judges must be alert to avoid behavior that may be perceived as prejudicial.

(6) Judges shall require[1] lawyers in proceedings before the judge to refrain from manifesting, by words and conduct, bias or prejudice based upon race, sex, religion, national origin, disability, age, sexual orientation or socioeconomic status, against parties, witnesses, counsel or others. This Section, 3B(6), does not preclude legitimate advocacy when race, sex, religion, national origin, disability, age, sexual orientation or socioeconomic status, or other similar factors, are issues in the proceeding.

(7) Judges shall accord to every person who has a legal interest in a proceeding, or that person's lawyer, the right to be heard according to law[1]. Judges shall not initiate or consider ex parte communications, or consider other communications made to them outside the presence of the parties concerning a pending or impending proceeding, except that:

(a) Where circumstances require, ex parte communications for scheduling, administrative purposes or emergencies that do not deal with substantive matters or issues on the merits are authorized; provided:

(i) the judge reasonably believes that no party will gain procedural or tactical advantage as a result of the ex parte communication, and

(ii) the judge makes provision promptly to notify all other parties of the substance of the ex parte communication and allows an opportunity to respond.

(b) Judges may obtain the advice of a disinterested expert on the law[1] applicable to a proceeding before the judge, if the judge gives notice to the parties of the person consulted and the substance of the advice, and affords the parties reasonable opportunity to respond.

(c) Judges may consult with court personnel[1] whose function is to aid the judge in carrying out the judge's adjudicative responsibilities, or with other judges.

(d) Judges may, with the consent of the parties, confer separately with the parties or their lawyers in an effort to mediate or settle matters pending before the judge.

(e) Judges may initiate or consider any ex parte communications when expressly authorized by law[1] to do so.

[1] [Pub. Note: These terms are explained in the section titled "Terminology", supra.]

Commentary

The proscription against communications concerning a proceeding includes communications from lawyers, law teachers, and other persons who are not participants in the proceeding, except to the limited extent permitted.

To the extent reasonably possible, all parties or their lawyers shall be included in communications with a judge.

Whenever presence of a party or notice to a party is required by Section 3B(7), it is the party's lawyer, or if the party is unrepresented the party, who is to be present or to whom notice is given.

An appropriate and often desirable procedure for a court to obtain the advice of a disinterested expert on legal issues is to invite the expert to file a brief amicus curiae.

Certain ex parte communication is approved by Section 3B(7) to facilitate scheduling and other administrative purposes and to accommodate emergencies. In general, however, judges must discourage ex parte communication and allow it only if all the criteria stated in Section 3B(7) are clearly met. Judges must disclose to all parties all ex parte communications described in Section 3B(7)(a) and 3B(7)(b) regarding a proceeding pending or impending before them.

Judges must not independently investigate facts in a case and must consider only the evidence presented.

Judges may request a party to submit proposed findings of fact and conclusions of law, so long as the other parties are apprised of the request and are given an opportunity to respond to the proposed findings and conclusions.

Judges must make reasonable efforts, including the provision of appropriate supervision, to ensure that Section 3B(7) is not violated through law clerks or other personnel on their staff.

If communication between the trial judge and the appellate court with respect to a proceeding is permitted, a copy of any written communication or the substance of any oral communication should be provided to all parties.

(8) Judges shall dispose of all judicial matters fairly, promptly, and efficiently.

Commentary

In disposing of matters promptly, efficiently and fairly, judges must demonstrate due regard for the rights of the parties to be heard and to have issues resolved without unnecessary cost or delay. Containing costs while preserving fundamental rights of parties also protects the interests of witnesses and the general public. Judges should monitor and supervise cases so as to reduce or eliminate dilatory practices, avoidable delays and unnecessary costs. Judges should encourage and seek to facilitate settlement, but parties should not feel coerced into surrendering the right to have their controversy resolved by courts.

(a) The obligation of a judge to dispose of matters promptly and efficiently must not take precedence over the judge's obligation to dispose of matters fairly and with patience.

Commentary

Prompt disposition of the court's business requires judges to devote adequate time to their duties, to be punctual in attending court and expeditious in determining matters under submission, and to insist that court officials, litigants and their lawyers cooperate with them to that end.

(9) Judges shall not, while a proceeding is pending or impending in any court, make any public comment [1] that might reasonably be expected to affect its outcome or impair its fairness or make any non-public comment that might substantially interfere with a fair trial or hearing. Judges shall require [1] similar abstention on the part of court personnel [1] subject to their direction and control. This subsection does not prohibit judges from making public statements in the course of their official duties or from explaining for public information the procedures of the court. This Section does not apply to proceedings in which the judge is a litigant in a personal capacity.

1 [Pub. Note: These terms are explained in the section titled "Terminology", supra.]

Commentary

The requirement that judges abstain from public comment regarding a pending or impending proceeding continues during any appellate process and until final disposition. This Section does not prohibit judges from commenting on proceedings in which the judge is a litigant in a personal capacity, but in cases such as a writ of mandamus where a judge is a litigant in an official capacity, the judge must not comment publicly.

(10) Judges shall not commend or criticize jurors for their verdict other than in a court order or opinion in a proceeding, but may express appreciation to jurors for their service to the judicial system and the community.

Commentary

Commending or criticizing jurors for their verdict may imply a judicial expectation in future cases and may impair a juror's ability to be fair and impartial.

(11) Judges shall not disclose or use, for any purpose unrelated to judicial duties, non-public information [1] acquired in a judicial capacity.

C. Administrative Responsibilities.

(1) Judges shall diligently discharge their administrative responsibilities without bias or prejudice, maintain professional competence in judicial administration, and should cooperate with other judges and court officials in the administration of court business.

(2) Judges shall require [1] their staffs, court officials and others subject to their direction and control to observe the standards of fidelity and diligence that apply to the judges and to refrain from manifesting bias or prejudice in the performance of their official duties.

(3) Judges with supervisory authority for judicial performance of other judges should take reasonable measures to assure the prompt disposition of matters before them and the proper performance of their other judicial responsibilities.

(4) Judges shall not make unnecessary appointments. Judges shall exercise the power of appointment impartially and on the basis of merit. Judges shall avoid nepotism and favoritism. Judges shall not approve compensation of appointees beyond the fair value of services rendered.

1 [Pub. Note: These terms are explained in the section titled "Terminology", supra.]

Commentary

Appointees of judges include assigned counsel, officials such as referees, commissioners, special masters, receivers, guardians and personnel such as clerks, secretaries, and bailiffs. Consent by the parties to an appointment or an award of compensation does not relieve the judge of the obligation prescribed by Section 3C(4).

D. Disciplinary Responsibilities.

(1) Judges who receive information indicating a substantial likelihood that another judge has committed a violation of this Code should take appropriate action. Judges having knowledge [1] that another judge has committed a violation of this Code that raises a substantial question as to the other judge's fitness for office shall inform the appropriate authority [1].

(2) Judges who receive information indicating a substantial likelihood that a lawyer has committed a violation of the Standards of Conduct of the State Bar of Georgia should take appropriate action. Judges having knowledge [1] that a lawyer has committed a violation of the Standards of Conduct of the State Bar of Georgia that raises a substantial question as to the lawyer's honesty, trustworthiness or fitness as a lawyer in other respects shall inform the appropriate authority [1].

(3) Acts of judges, in the discharge of disciplinary responsibilities, required or permitted by Sections 3D(1) and 3D(2) are part of their judicial duties and shall be absolutely privileged, and no civil action predicated thereon may be instituted against these judges.

1 [Pub. Note: These terms are explained in the section titled "Terminology", supra.]

Commentary

Appropriate action may include direct communication with the judge or lawyer who has committed the violation, or other direct action if available, and reporting the violation to the appropriate authority or other agency or body.

Section 3D(1) requires judges to inform the Judicial Qualifications Commission of any other judge's violation of the Code of Judicial Conduct, if the violation raises a substantial question of fitness for office and if the violation is actually known to the reporting judge.

Section 3D(2) also requires judges to report to the State Bar of Georgia any violation by a lawyer of the Standards of Conduct, if the violation raises a substantial question of the lawyer's fitness as a lawyer and, again, if the violation is actually known to the reporting judge.

E. Disqualification.

(1) Judges shall disqualify themselves in any proceeding in which their impartiality might reasonably be questioned, including but not limited to instances where:

Commentary

Under this rule, judges are subject to disqualification whenever their impartiality might reasonably be questioned, regardless of whether any of the specific rules in Section 3E(1) apply. For example, if a judge were in the process of negotiating for employment with a law firm, the judge would be disqualified from any matters in which that firm appeared, unless the disqualification was waived by the parties after disclosure by the judge.

Judges should disclose on the record information that the court believes the parties or their lawyers might consider relevant to the question of disqualification, even if they believe there is no legal basis for disqualification.

The rule of necessity may override the rule of disqualification. For example, a judge might be required to participate in judicial review of a judicial salary statute, or might be the only judge available in a matter requiring immediate judicial action, such as a hearing on probable cause or a temporary restraining order. In the latter case, the judge must disclose on the record the basis for possible disqualification and use reasonable efforts to transfer the matter to another judge as soon as possible.

(a) the judge has a personal bias or prejudice concerning a party or a party's lawyer, or personal knowledge [1] of disputed evidentiary facts concerning the proceeding;

(b) the judge served as a lawyer in the matter in controversy, or a lawyer with whom the judge previously practiced law served during such association as a lawyer concerning the matter, or the judge has been a material witness concerning it;

1 [Pub. Note: This term is explained in the section titled "Terminology", supra.]

Commentary

A lawyer in a government agency does not ordinarily have an association with other lawyers employed by that agency within the meaning of Section 3E(1)(b); judges formerly employed by a governmental agency, however, should disqualify themselves in a proceeding if their impartiality might reasonably be questioned because of such association.

(c) the judge or the judge's spouse, or a person within the third degree of relationship [1] to either of them, or the spouse of such a person, or any other member of the judge's family residing in the judge's household [1]:

(i) is a party to the proceeding, or an officer, director, or trustee of a party;

(ii) is acting as a lawyer in the proceeding;

(iii) is known [1] by the judge to have a more than de minimis [1] interest that could be substantially affected by the proceeding;

(iv) is to the judge's knowledge [1] likely to be a material witness in the proceeding.

1 [Pub. Note: These terms are explained in the section titled "Terminology", supra.]

Commentary

The fact that a lawyer in a proceeding is affiliated with a law firm with which a relative of the judge is affiliated does not of itself disqualify the judge. Under appropriate circumstances, the fact that "the judge's impartiality might reasonably be questioned" under Section 3E(1), or that the relative is known by the judge to have an interest in the law firm that could be "substantially affected by the outcome of the proceeding" under Section 3E(1)(c)(iii) requires the judge's disqualification.

(2) Judges shall keep informed about their personal and fiduciary [1] economic interests [1], and make a reasonable effort to keep informed about the personal financial interests of their spouses and minor children residing in their households.

F. Remittal of Disqualification. Judges disqualified by the terms of Section 3E may disclose on the record the basis of their disqualification and may ask the parties and their lawyers to consider, out of the presence of the judge, whether to waive disqualification. If following disclosure of any basis for disqualification other than personal bias or prejudice concerning a party, the parties and lawyers, without participation by the judge, all agree that the judge should not be disqualified, and the judge is then willing to participate, the judge may participate in the proceeding. The agreement shall be incorporated in the record of the proceeding.

1 [Pub. Note: These terms are explained in the section titled "Terminology", supra.]

Commentary

A remittal procedure provides the parties an opportunity to proceed without delay if they wish to waive the disqualification. To assure that consideration of the question of remittal is made independently to the court, judges must not solicit, seek or hear comment on possible remittal or waiver of the disqualification, unless the lawyers jointly propose remittal after consultation as provided in Section 3F. A party may act through counsel, if counsel represents on the record that the party has been consulted and consents. As a practical matter, judges may wish to have all parties and their lawyers sign a remittal agreement.

Adopted effective January 1, 1994; amended effective January 1, 1998.

CANON 4 JUDGES MAY ENGAGE IN ACTIVITIES TO IMPROVE THE LAW, THE LEGAL SYSTEM, AND THE ADMINISTRATION OF JUSTICE

Judges, subject to the proper performance of their judicial duties, may not engage in the following quasi-judicial activities, if in doing they cast doubt on their capacity to decide impartially any issue that may come before them:

A. Judges may speak, write, lecture, teach, and participate in other activities concerning the law [1], the legal system, and the administration of justice.

B. Judges may appear at public hearings before an executive or legislative body or official on matters concerning the law [1], the legal system, and the administration of justice, and they may otherwise consult with an executive or legislative body or official, but only on matters concerning the administration of justice.

C. Judges may serve as members, officers, or directors of an organization or governmental agency devoted to the improvement of the law [1], the legal system, or the administration of justice. They may assist such organizations in raising funds and may participate in their management and investment, but should not personally participate in public fund raising activities. They may make recommendations to public and private fund-granting agencies on projects and programs concerning the law, the legal system, and the administration of justice.

[1] [Pub. Note: These terms are explained in the section titled "Terminology", supra.]

Commentary

As a judicial officer and person specially learned in the law, a judge is in a unique position to contribute to the improvement of the law, the legal system, and the administration of justice, including revision of substantive and procedural law and improvement of criminal and juvenile justice. To the extent that time permits, judges are encouraged to do so, either independently or through a bar association, judicial conference, or other organization dedicated to the improvement of the law.

Non quasi-judicial, or non law-related, extra-judicial activities are governed by Canon 5.

Adopted effective January 1, 1994.

CANON 5 JUDGES SHALL REGULATE THEIR EXTRA-JUDICIAL ACTIVITIES TO MINIMIZE THE RISK OF CONFLICT WITH THEIR JUDICIAL DUTIES

A. Avocational Activities. Judges may not engage in such avocational activities as detract from the dignity of their office or interfere with the performance of their judicial duties.

Commentary

Complete separation of judges from extra-judicial activities is neither possible nor wise; they should not become isolated from the society in which they live.

B. Civic and Charitable Activities. Judges may not participate in civic and charitable activities that reflect adversely upon their impartiality or interfere with the performance of their judicial duties. Judges may serve as officers, directors, trustees, or non-legal advisors of educational, religious, charitable, fraternal, or civic organizations not conducted for the economic or political advantage of their members, subject to the following limitations:

(1) Judges shall not serve if it is likely that the organization will be engaged in proceedings that would ordinarily come before them or will be regularly engaged in adversary proceedings in any court.

Commentary

The changing nature of some organizations and of their relationship to the law makes it necessary for judges regularly to re-examine the activities of each organization with which they are affiliated to determine if it is proper for them to continue their relationship with it. For example, in many jurisdictions charitable hospitals are now more frequently in court than in the past. Similarly, the boards of some legal aid organizations now make policy decisions that may have political significance or imply commitment to causes that may come before the courts for adjudication.

(2) Judges shall not solicit funds for any educational, religious, charitable, fraternal, or civic organization, or use or permit the use of the prestige of their office for that purpose, but they may be listed as officers, directors, or trustees of such organizations. A judge shall not be a speaker or the guest of honor at an organization's fund-raising event, but may attend such events.

(3) Judges shall not give investment advice to such an organization, but they may serve on its board of directors or trustees even though it has the responsibility for approving investment decisions.

Commentary

A judge's participation in an organization devoted to quasi-judicial, or law-related, extra-judicial activities is governed by Canon 4.

C. Financial Activities.

(1) Judges should refrain from financial and business dealings with lawyers, litigants, and others that tend to reflect adversely on their impartiality, interfere with the proper performance of their judicial duties, or exploit their judicial positions.

(2) Subject to the requirement of subsection (1), judges may hold and manage investments, including real estate and engage in other remunerative activity including the operation of a business.

(3) Judges should manage their investments and other financial interests to minimize the number of cases in which they are disqualified. As soon as they can do so without serious financial detriment they should divest themselves of investments and other financial interests that might require frequent disqualification.

(4) Neither judges nor members of their families residing in their households [1] should accept a substantial gift, bequest, favor, or loan from anyone except as follows:

(a) judges may accept gifts incident to a public testimonial to them; books supplied by publishers on a complimentary basis for official use; or invitations to judges and their spouses to attend bar-related functions or activities devoted to the improvement of the law [1], the legal system, or the administration of justice;

(b) judges or members of their families residing in their households may accept ordinary social hospitality; a gift, bequest, favor, or loan from a relative; a wedding or engagement gift; a loan from a lending institution in its regular course of business on the same terms generally available to persons who are not judges, or a scholarship or fellowship awarded on the same terms applied to other applicants;

(c) judges or members of their families residing in their households may accept any other gift, bequest, favor, or loan only if the donor is not a party or other person whose interests have come or are likely to come before them, and if its value exceeds $100, the judges report it in the same manner as they report compensation in Canon 6C.

1 [Pub. Note: These terms are explained in the section titled "Terminology", supra.]

Commentary

This subsection does not apply to contributions to a judge's campaign for judicial office, a matter governed by Canon 7.

(5) A judge is not required by this Code to disclose his income, debts, or investments, except as provided in this Canon and Canons 3 and 6.

Commentary

Canon 3 requires judges to disqualify themselves in any proceeding in which they have a financial interest; Canon 5 requires judges to refrain from financial activities that might interfere with the impartial performance of their judicial duties; Canon 6 requires them to report all compensation they receive for activities involving personal services outside their judicial office. Judges have the rights of an ordinary citizen, including the right to privacy in their financial affairs, except to the extent that limitations thereon are required to safeguard the proper performance of a judge's duties. Owning and receiving income from investments do not as such affect the performance of a judge's duties.

(6) Information acquired by judges in their judicial capacity should not be used or disclosed by them in financial dealings or for any other purpose not related to their judicial duties.

D. Fiduciary [1] Activities. Judges should not serve as executors, administrators, trustees, guardians, or other fiduciaries, except for the estates, trusts, or persons of members of their families and then only if such service will not interfere with the proper performance of their judicial duties. "Member of their families" includes a spouse, child, grandchild, parent, grandparent, or other relative or person with whom the judge maintains a close familiar [2] relationship. As family fiduciaries, judges are subject to the following restrictions:

(1) They should not serve if it is likely that as fiduciaries, they will be engaged in proceedings that would ordinarily come before them, or if the estates, trusts, or wards become involved in adversary proceedings in the court on which they serve or one under its appellate jurisdiction.

(2) While acting as fiduciaries, judges are subject to the same restrictions on financial activities that apply to them in their personal capacities.

1 [Pub. Note: This term is explained in the section titled "Terminology", supra.]

2 [Pub. Note: So in original.]

Commentary

Judges' obligations under this Canon and their obligations as fiduciaries may come into conflict. For example, a judge should resign as trustee if it would result in detriment to the trust to divest it of holdings whose retention would place the judge in violation of Canon 5C(3).

E. Arbitration. Judges shall not act as arbitrators or mediators for compensation. This prohibition does not apply to senior judges who serve as judges.

F. Practice of Law. Judges shall not practice law, unless allowed by law.

G. Extra-Judicial Appointments. A judge should not accept appointment to a governmental committee, commission, or other position that is concerned with issues of fact or policy on matters other than the improvement of the law [1], the legal system, or the administration of justice, if acceptance of such appointment might reasonably cast doubt upon the judge's impartiality or demean the judge's office.

1 [Pub. Note: This term is explained in the section titled "Terminology", supra.]

Commentary

Valuable services have been rendered in the past to the states and the nation by judges appointed by the executive to undertake important extra-judicial assignments. The appropriateness of conferring these assignments on judges must be reassessed, however, in light of the demands on judicial manpower created by today's crowded dockets and the need to protect the courts from involvement in extra-judicial matters that may prove to be controversial. Judges should not be expected or permitted to accept governmental appointments that could interfere with the effectiveness and independence of the judiciary.

Adopted effective January 1, 1994; amended effective January 1, 1998.

CANON 6 JUDGES SHOULD REGULARLY FILE REPORTS OF COMPENSATION RECEIVED FOR QUASI-JUDICIAL AND EXTRA-JUDICIAL ACTIVITIES

Judges may not receive compensation and reimbursement of expenses for the quasi-judicial and extra-judicial activities permitted by this Code, if the source of such payments gives the appearance of influencing the judge in his judicial duties or otherwise gives the appearance of impropriety. Such compensation is subject to the following restrictions:

A. Compensation. Compensation should not exceed a reasonable amount nor should it exceed what a person who is not a judge would receive for the same activity.

B. Expense Reimbursement. Expense reimbursement should be limited to the actual cost of travel, food, and lodging and other necessary expense reasonably incurred by the judge and, where appropriate to the occasion, by their spouses. Any payment in excess of such an amount is compensation.

C. Reports. Except as hereinafter provided to the contrary, full-time judges should report the dates, places, and nature of any activities involving personal services for which they received compensation, and the name of the payor and the amount of compensation so received. Compensation or income of a spouse attributed to the judge by operation of a community property law is not extra-judicial compensation to the judge. Judges' reports for each calendar year should be filed between January first and April fifteenth of the following year in the office of the Clerk of the Supreme Court of Georgia. A copy of a judge's federal income tax return shall be considered a sufficient compliance with this paragraph. Such report or tax return shall be filed under seal and shall be available for inspection only by the Justices of the Supreme Court of Georgia and the members of the Judicial Qualifications Commission.

Adopted effective January 1, 1994.

CANON 7 JUDGES SHALL REFRAIN FROM POLITICAL ACTIVITY INAPPROPRIATE TO THEIR JUDICIAL OFFICE

A. Political Conduct in General.

(1) A judge or a candidate[1] for public election[1] to judicial office shall not:

(a) act or hold himself or herself out as a leader or hold any office in a political organization[1];

(b) make speeches for a political organization or candidate or publicly endorse a candidate for public office;

1 [Pub. Note: These terms are explained in the section titled "Terminology", supra.]

Commentary

A candidate does not publicly endorse another candidate for public office by having his name on the same ticket.

(c) solicit funds for or pay an assessment or make a contribution to a political organization, or purchase tickets for political party dinners, or other functions, except as authorized in subsection A(2).

(2) Judges holding an office filled by public election[1] between competing candidates[1], or candidates for such office, may attend political gatherings and speak to such gatherings on their own behalf when they are candidates for election or re-election.

B. Campaign Conduct.

(1) Candidates[1], including an incumbent judge, for any judicial office that is filled by public election[1] between competing candidates:

(a) shall prohibit official or employees subject to their direction or control from doing for them what they are prohibited from doing under this Canon and shall not allow any other person to do for them what they are prohibited from doing under this Canon;

(b) shall not make statements that commit the candidate with respect to issues likely to come before the court;

1 [Pub. Note: These terms are explained in the section titled "Terminology", supra.]

Commentary

This Canon does not prohibit a judge or candidate from publicly stating his or her personal views on disputed issues, see Republican Party v. White, 536 U.S. 765 (2002). To ensure that voters understand a judge's duty to uphold the constitution and laws of Georgia where the law differs from his or her personal belief, however, judges and candidates are encouraged to emphasize in any public statement their duty to uphold the law regardless of their personal views.

(c) shall not use or participate in the publication of a false statement of fact concerning themselves or their candidacies, or concerning any opposing candidate or candidacy, with knowledge of the statement's falsity or with reckless disregard for the statement's truth or falsity;

Commentary:

The determination of whether a candidate knows of falsity or recklessly disregards the truth or falsity of his or her public communication is an objective one, from the viewpoint of a "reasonable attorney," using the standard of "objective malice." See In re Chmura, 608 N.W.2d 31 (Mich. 2000).

(d) shall be responsible for the content of any statement or advertisement published or communicated in any medium by a campaign committee if the candidate knew of or recklessly disregarded the content of said statement or advertisement prior to its release;

(e) and except where a statement or advertisement is published or communicated by a third party, shall be responsible for reviewing and approving the content of his or her statements and advertisements, and those of his or her campaign committee. Failure to do so will not be a defense to a complaint for violation of this Canon.

(2) Candidates[1], including an incumbent judge, for a judicial office that is filled by public election [1] between competing candidates, may personally solicit campaign contributions and publicly stated support. Candidates, including incumbent judges, should not use or permit the use of campaign contributions for the private benefit of themselves or members of their families.

1 [Pub. Note: These terms are explained in the section titled "Terminology", supra.]

Commentary:

Although judges and judicial candidates are free to personally solicit campaign contributions and publicly stated support, see Weaver v. Bonner, 309 F.3d 1312 (11th Cir. 2002), they are encouraged to establish campaign committees of responsible persons to secure and manage the expenditure of funds for their campaigns and to obtain public statements of support of their candidacies. The use of campaign committees is encouraged because they may better maintain campaign decorum and reduce campaign activity that may cause requests for recusal or the appearance of partisanship with respect to issues or the parties which require recusal.

C. Applicability.

(a) This Canon generally applies to all incumbent judges and judicial Candidates[1]. A successful candidate, whether or not an incumbent, is subject to judicial discipline by the Judicial Qualifications Commission for his or her campaign conduct.

(b) A lawyer who is a candidate [1] for judicial office shall comply with all provisions of the Code of Judicial Conduct applicable to candidates[1] for judicial office. An unsuccessful lawyer candidate[1] is subject to discipline for campaign conduct by the State Bar of Georgia pursuant to applicable standards of the State Bar of Georgia, and the Judicial Qualifications Commission shall immediately report any such alleged conduct to the office of the General Counsel of the State Bar of Georgia for such action as may be appropriate under applicable bar rules.

(c) An unsuccessful nonlawyer candidate[1] is subject to discipline for campaign misconduct by the Judicial Qualifications Commission, and in addition to any other sanctions authorized by the Rules of the Judicial Qualifications Commission, the Commission, after full hearing, is authorized to recommend that such individual be barred from seeking any elective or appointive judicial office in this State for a period not to exceed 10 years.

1 [Pub. Note: These terms are explained in the section titled "Terminology", supra.]

Adopted effective January 1, 1994; amended effective January 1, 1998; January 7, 2004.

APPLICATION OF THE CODE OF JUDICIAL CONDUCT

Anyone, whether or not a lawyer, who is an officer of a judicial system performing judicial functions, including an officer such as an administrative law judge of an executive branch agency or of the Board of Workers Compensation, an associate judge, special master, or magistrate, or any person who is a candidate for any such office is a judge for the purpose of this Code. All judges shall comply with this Code except as provided below.

A. Part-Time Judges. A part-time judge is a judge who serves on a continuing or periodic basis, but is permitted by law to devote time to some other profession or occupation and whose compensation for that reason is less than that of a full-time judge. Part-time judges:

(1) are not required to comply with Canon 5D [fiduciary activities], 5E [arbitration], 5F [practice of law], and 5G [extra-judicial appointments], and are not required to comply with Canon 6C [annual financial reporting] except as to compensation received for activity involving personal services other than the practice of law.

(2) should not practice law in the court on which they serve, or in any court subject to the appellate jurisdiction of the court on which they serve, or act as lawyers in proceedings in which they have served as judges or in any other proceeding related thereto.

B. Judge Pro Tempore. A judge pro tempore is a person who is appointed to act temporarily as a judge.

(1) While acting as such, a judge pro tempore is not required to comply with Canon 5C(3) [financial activities], 5D [fiduciary activities], 5E [arbitration and mediation], 5F [practice of law], and 5G [extra-judicial appointments], and Canon 6C [annual financial reporting].

(2) Persons who have been judges pro tempore should not act as lawyers in proceedings in which they have served as judges or in other proceedings related thereto.

C. Time for Compliance. A person to whom this Code becomes applicable shall comply immediately with all provisions of this Code except Sections 5C(1),

5C(2), 5C(3) [personal and family financial activities] and 5D [fiduciary activities], and shall comply with these Sections as soon as reasonably possible and shall do so in any event within the period of one year.

Commentary

If serving as a fiduciary when selected as judge, a new judge may, notwithstanding the prohibitions in Section 5D, continue to serve as fiduciary but only for that period of time necessary to avoid serious adverse consequences to the beneficiary of the fiduciary relationship and in no event longer than one year. Similarly, if engaged at the time of judicial selection in a business activity, a new judge may, notwithstanding the prohibitions in Section 5C(1), 5C(2) and 5C(3), continue in that activity for a reasonable period but in no event longer than one year.

D. Continuing Jurisdiction. In addition to the foregoing, the Commission shall have continuing jurisdiction over individuals to whom this Code is applicable regarding allegations of misconduct occurring during such individual's service as an officer of a judicial system if a complaint is filed no later than one (1) year following service of such judicial officer.

Adopted effective January 1, 1994; amended effective January 1, 1998.

EFFECTIVE DATE OF CODE

This Code shall become effective January 1, 1994.

Adopted effective January 1, 1994.

RULES OF THE JUDICIAL QUALIFICATIONS COMMISSION

Effective March 1, 1994

Including Amendments Received Through November 1, 2006

Research Note

Use WESTLAW *to find cases citing a rule. In addition, use* WESTLAW *to search for specific terms or to update a rule; see the GA–RULES and GA–ORDERS Scope screens for further information.*

Amendments to these rules are published, as received, in the South Eastern Reporter 2d *and* Georgia Cases *advance sheets.*

Table of Rules

INTRODUCTION

The Constitution of the State of Georgia of 1983 provides that "The Supreme Court shall adopt rules of implementation" for discipline, removal, and involuntary retirement of judges (OCGA Article VI, § VII, ¶ VII).

The following are rules adopted by the Supreme Court governing the functions of the Judicial Qualifications Commission:

Definition of Sanctions

The following working definition for disciplinary sanctions shall apply in all proceedings of the Commission, both formal and informal:

(a) Admonition. A private communication reminding a judge of ethical responsibilities and giving a gentle or friendly warning to avoid future misconduct or inappropriate practices. An admonition may be used to give authoritative advice and encouragement or to express disapproval of behavior that suggests the appearance of impropriety even though it meets minimum standards of judicial conduct.

(b) Private Reprimand. A private communication that declares a judge's conduct unacceptable under one of the grounds for judicial discipline but not so serious as to merit a public sanction.

(c) Public Reprimand. A public communication administered by a judicial officer which declares a judge's conduct unacceptable under one of the grounds for judicial discipline but not so serious as to warrant a censure.

(d) Censure. A public declaration by the Supreme Court that a judge is guilty of misconduct that does not require removal from office.

(e) Suspension. A decision by the Supreme Court to suspend a judge from office temporarily, with or without pay, for serious misconduct that merits more than a censure but less than removal. This sanction is flexible, and there are no restrictions on the length of a suspension.

(f) Removal. A decision by the Supreme Court to remove a judge permanently from office for serious misconduct.

(g) Retirement. A decision by the Supreme Court to retire a judge for a disability that seriously interferes with the performance of judicial duties that is or is likely to become permanent.

Effective March 1, 1994.

RULE 1. MEMBERS AND THEIR TERMS

(a) The power to discipline, remove and cause involuntary retirement of judges is vested in the Judicial Qualifications Commission, which consists of seven members, as follows:

(1) Two judges of any court of record, selected by the Supreme Court;

(2) Three members of the State Bar of Georgia, who have been active status members of the State Bar for at least ten years, and who shall be elected by the Board of Governors of the State Bar; and

(3) Two citizens, neither of whom shall be members of the State Bar, who shall be appointed by the Governor (Article VI, § VII, ¶ VI, Constitution of Georgia of 1983).

(b) All members of the Commission shall serve for terms of four years each and until their successors are elected or appointed and are qualified. Whenever any member ceases to hold the office or to possess the qualifications which entitle the member to be appointed a member, the member's membership shall terminate, and the appointing authority shall select a successor for the unexpired term. No member of the Commission shall receive any compensation for services, but shall be allowed necessary expenses for travel, board and lodging incurred in the performance of Commission duties. No member of the Commission, except judges, shall hold any other public office or be eligible for appointment to a State judiciary office while holding membership on the Commission. No member shall hold office in any political party or organization. No act of the Commission shall be valid unless concurred in by a majority of its membership.

(c) A vacancy shall occur when a Commission member becomes unable to continue service for any reason. An appointment to fill a vacancy for the duration of the unexpired term shall be made by the appropriate authority. If a vacancy is not filled at the end of sixty (60) days, the Commission shall appoint from the category to be represented a member who shall serve until such time as an appointment shall be made by the appropriate authority.

(d) A temporary vacancy shall occur when a Commission member becomes unable to attend a formal hearing for any reason. The Commission is authorized but not required to appoint a former member from the category to substitute at such formal hearing and subsequent action related to the hearing in lieu of such non-serving member.

Effective March 1, 1994.

RULE 2. OFFICERS AND THEIR DUTIES

(a) The Commission shall select from its members a Chairperson, a Vice Chairperson, and such other officers as the Commission may consider proper and helpful in carrying out its functions, who shall serve at the pleasure of the Commission. A member may be elected to more than one office.

(b) The Chairperson shall preside at all general meetings of the Commission as well as at formal hearings concerning the conduct or disability of a judge. If the Chairperson is not a lawyer, the Chairperson shall appoint a member of the Commission who is a lawyer to preside at any hearing held by the Commission. The Chairperson shall be responsible for the custody and safekeeping of all the records of the Commission, shall promptly furnish to members of the Commission copies of all complaints, notices, answers and other documents filed in connection with proceedings before the Commission, and shall perform such other duties as are indicated in these rules or as are customarily performed by a Chairperson. The Chairperson shall also annually make a report to the Supreme Court of the actions of the Commission but shall not set forth therein the name of or otherwise identify a judge with respect to matters which are confidential under the provisions of Rule 20.

(c) In the event the Chairperson is absent or is otherwise unable to attend a meeting or to perform the duties of office at a particular time, those duties shall be performed by the Vice Chairperson, and in the absence of the Vice Chairperson, by a member of the Commission designated by those present.

(d) The Director or, if the Director is absent, such member of the Commission as the Chairperson shall designate, shall have the duty of recording in the minute book, as a permanent record of the Commission, the action of the Commission at each meeting.

(e) The Commission may, at its discretion, designate a Director who shall serve at the pleasure of the Commission and shall have such duties, powers and authority as may be, from time to time, fixed, determined or delegated by the Commission. The Director may be authorized by the Commission to issue subpoenas on its behalf.

(f) Notwithstanding the foregoing provisions, the Chairperson, with the concurrence of a majority of the Commission, may at any time designate any judicial member of the Commission to preside at any formal hearing held by the Commission. Any such designation shall be made by written order signed by the Chairperson or the Director.

Effective March 1, 1994; amended effective September 8, 1994.

RULE 3. MEETINGS

(a) The Chairperson may, and upon the request of three members shall, call a meeting of the Commission. The Chairperson shall give reasonable notice to each member by telephone or other means of the time and place of the meeting.

(b) Decisions by the Commission to conduct an investigation of a judge, order a judge to submit to a physical examination, proceed against a person for contempt for failing to respond to a subpoena of the Commission, issue a public statement, institute contempt proceedings against a person for violation of the confidentiality provisions of the rules, hold or not to hold a formal hearing, hear additional evidence, make a report to the Supreme Court recommending removal, other discipline or retirement of a judge, or deciding after a formal hearing not to make such a report, shall be made at a formal meeting of the Commission. Decisions with respect to other matters may be arrived at through communications between the members of the Commission, but a report of such action shall be made by the Chairperson at the next meeting of the Commission and entered in the minutes of that meeting.

(c) Four members of the Commission shall constitute a quorum for the transaction of business at any formal meeting or for the conduct of a formal hearing, and if a quorum is present at a meeting, the vote of a majority of those in attendance shall be considered the official action of the Commission, except that a vote of a majority of the members of the Commission shall be required for a recommendation of discipline to the Supreme Court.

Effective March 1, 1994.

RULE 4. COMPLAINTS—INVESTIGATIONS

(a) The Commission shall require that all complaints shall be made to it in writing and the Commission, when it considers it appropriate, may require that the same be verified. A complaint shall not be a prerequisite to action by the Commission, but the Commission may act on its own motion in those cases where the Commission considers it appropriate.

(b) Upon receiving a complaint or otherwise receiving information indicating that a judge may have been guilty of willful misconduct in office, or willful and persistent failure to perform the duties of a judge, or habitual intemperance, or conduct prejudicial to the administration of justice which brings the judicial office into disrepute, or that a judge may have a disability that seriously interferes with the performance of the judge's duties which is or is likely to become permanent, the Commission may make an initial inquiry of the judge for such written comments with respect to the matters involved as the judge may wish to make; and, with or without making such initial inquiry, and with or without notice or other information being given to the judge, as the Commission may consider best, the Commission may conduct an investigation of the conduct or condition of the judge for the purpose of determining whether formal proceedings should be instituted and a hearing held. However, prior to any determination that a formal hearing will be held, the judge shall be sent a copy of the complaint or a synopsis of the matters to be or which have been investigated and the judge shall thereafter be given reasonable opportunity to make such statement to the Commission as the judge considers desirable. Such statement may be made, as the judge may elect, personally or by counsel, verbally or in writing, and may or may not be under oath. In exercising this right, the judge shall not have the right to call witnesses nor to confront nor cross-examine the person making the complaint or any person interviewed by the Commission or its duly authorized representative. If, after being notified by the Commission, the judge does not respond within a reasonable time or within the time fixed by the Commission, the right to make such statement shall thereupon terminate. In making an investigation, the Commission may issue subpoenas for witnesses to appear before the Commission's representative for the purpose of making a sworn statement and may likewise issue subpoenas for the production of books, papers and other evidentiary matter which are pertinent to the inquiry.

(c) Whenever the Commission reaches the conclusion that a complaint fails to state, or the facts developed upon an initial inquiry to the judge or an investigation fail to show, any reason for the institution of disciplinary proceedings, the Commission shall so advise the complainant. The Commission shall also so notify the judge, except that with respect to complaints which are rejected because they fail to state any grounds for disciplinary proceedings, the Commission may, but is not required to, advise the judge thereof.

(d) After receipt of a complaint or of information indicating that a judge may have been guilty of conduct which might warrant discipline, or that a judge may be disabled, the Commission, before voting to hold a formal hearing, may delegate to one or more of its members the authority and responsibility to personally and confidentially confer with the judge subject to the inquiry, and to make informal recommendations to the judge concerning the subject matter of the inquiry and a satisfactory disposition thereof; and if the judge agrees to the Commission's suggested disposition, the matter may be disposed of on the basis of the agreement reached. The Commission shall file a report of the disposition in the Supreme Court.

(e) The foregoing shall not be construed to mean that the Commission may not at any time entertain and act upon a proposal from a judge for disposition of any matter pending before the Commission concerning such a judge, provided that if such proposal is made after notice of formal hearing, and is found acceptable to the Commission, a report thereof shall be filed in the Supreme Court and such report shall not be considered confidential.

(f) At any time after receipt of a complaint or otherwise receiving information indicating that a judge may have been guilty of conduct which, while insufficient to warrant the institution of formal proceedings, nevertheless warrants sanctions, the Commission may informally: (i) admonish and/or reprimand a judge; (ii) direct professional counselling and assistance for a judge; (iii) impose conditions on a judge's future conduct or instruct a judge to make specific changes in particular matters of conduct; or (iv) adjust the complaint by any other appropriate means consistent with these rules.

Effective March 1, 1994; amended effective January 1, 1998; January 19, 2000.

RULE 5. INSTITUTION OF FORMAL PROCEEDINGS—NOTICE—JUDGE'S ANSWER

(a) When after receiving a complaint or otherwise obtaining information concerning the conduct or physical or mental condition of a judge, the Commission has made such investigation of the complaint or information as the Commission considers needful and proper, and the judge has been given the opportunity to make a statement to the Commission as stated in Rule 4(b), the Commission concludes that a formal hearing should be held, the Commission shall issue, as promptly as possible, a written notice to the judge advising the judge of the institution of formal proceedings to inquire into the charges against the judge. The proceedings shall be entitled: "Before the Commission on Judicial Qualifications, Inquiry Concerning Judge __________."

(b) The notice shall specify the charges against the judge with sufficient fullness to enable the judge to understand the nature thereof and shall advise the judge of the right to file a written answer to the charges; and a copy of such notice shall be filed in the Supreme Court.

(c) Within thirty (30) days after service of the notice of formal proceedings, the judge shall file with the Commission an original and six (6) copies of a verified answer. The notice of formal proceedings and the answer shall constitute the pleadings. No further pleadings shall be filed, except by way of amendment as provided for in Rule 9.

Effective March 1, 1994.

RULE 6. HEARING BEFORE COMMISSION OR A SPECIAL MASTER

Upon the filing of an answer or upon expiration of the time for its filing, the Commission shall promptly order a hearing to be held before it concerning the removal, other discipline or retirement of the judge, or the Commission may request the Supreme Court to appoint a Special Master to hear and take evidence in such matter and to report thereon to the Commission. The Commission shall set a time and place for the hearing, and shall give notice thereof to the judge at least twenty (20) days before the date thereof.

Effective March 1, 1994.

RULE 7. CONDUCT OF HEARING

(a) At the time and place set for the hearing, the Commission or the Special Master may proceed with the hearing whether or not the judge has filed an answer or appears at the hearing.

(b) The proceedings at the hearing shall be reported by a qualified reporter.

(c) At the hearing before the Commission or a Special Master appointed by the Supreme Court, legal evidence only shall be received, and oral evidence shall be taken on oath or affirmation.

(d) The Chairperson or presiding member of the Commission, if the hearing is held before the Commission, or the Special Master appointed to conduct the hearing, shall administer oaths or affirmations to witnesses, rule on the admissibility of evidence, and otherwise direct the manner or order of proceedings as a judge of a court of record.

(e) The Rules of Evidence applicable to civil cases shall apply at all hearings before the Commission or the Special Master, and the standard of proof shall be clear and convincing evidence. In all such hearings, the burden of proof shall be upon the counsel for the Commission.

Effective March 1, 1994.

RULE 8. RIGHTS OF JUDGE IN CONNECTION WITH HEARING

(a) Within fifteen (15) days after such notice of formal hearing has been mailed to or otherwise served upon the judge, it shall be the duty of the Commission to furnish to the judge as of the time of such notice the names of all persons and their addresses who have been interviewed by the Commission or its representative in investigating the charges set out in the notice of a formal hearing, as well as a copy or transcript of all statements of testimony, whether signed or unsigned, of any person so interviewed in connection with such charges and copies of all documents, writings, papers, records or other evidentiary material relevant to such charges which have been obtained by the Commission or its representative and reviewed by the Commission.

(b) If, after furnishing such information and prior to the date of the hearing, the Commission or its representative shall interview any other person or persons in connection with such charges, the Commission shall promptly inform the judge or the judge's counsel of the name and address of such other person or persons.

(c) If a witness is discovered or interviewed or any documentary or other tangible evidence is discovered or comes into the possession of the Commission or its representative after the hearing has begun, the Commission shall promptly inform the judge or the judge's counsel of the name and address of such witness and promptly furnish a copy of such documentary or other tangible evidence to the judge or the judge's counsel.

(d) The foregoing provisions shall not be construed as requiring that the Commission furnish to the judge any communications between members of the Commission or its representative or any other records of the Commission.

(e) In either of the situations described in Paragraphs (b) and (c), the Commission, upon compliance with the requirements of such paragraphs, shall be authorized to hear the testimony of any such witness or to admit into evidence any documentary or tangible evidence. However, the Commission may take such action with respect to the hearing either by way of postponement, recess or adjournment of the hearing to some future date as, upon a specific motion made by the judge therefor, may seem proper for the protection of the judge in the adequate presentation of a defense.

(f) At the hearing the judge shall have the right and reasonable opportunity to defend against the charges by the introduction of evidence; to be represented by counsel; to examine and cross-examine witnesses; and to have subpoenas issued for attendance of witnesses to testify or for the production of books, papers and other evidentiary matters.

(g) When a transcript of testimony has been prepared at the expense of the Commission, a copy thereof, upon request, shall be available for use by the judge and counsel in connection with the proceedings, or the judge may arrange to procure a copy at his or her expense. The judge shall have the right, without any order or approval, to have all or any portion of the testimony in the proceedings transcribed at the judge's expense.

(h) If, in a proceeding before the Commission, the Commission should be in doubt as to the competency of the judge, the Commission may appoint a guardian ad litem or take such other action as the Commission may consider appropriate.

Effective March 1, 1994.

RULE 9. AMENDMENTS TO NOTICE AND ANSWER

The Special Master, at any time prior to the conclusion of the hearing, or the Commission, at any time prior to its determination, may allow or require amendments to the notice of formal proceedings and may allow amendments to the answer. The notice may be amended to conform to proof or set forth additional facts and charges whether occurring before or after the commencement of the hearing. In case an amendment is allowed to the notice of formal hearing, the judge shall be given reasonable time both to answer the amendment and to prepare and present a defense against the matters set forth therein.

Effective March 1, 1994.

RULE 10. REPORT OF SPECIAL MASTER

(a) Within twenty (20) days after the conclusion of a hearing before a Special Master and the Master's receipt of a transcript of the evidence, the Special Master shall prepare and transmit to the Commission a report which shall contain a brief statement of the proceedings, findings of fact, any conclusions of law with respect to the issues presented by the notice of formal hearing and the answer thereto, or if there be no answer, findings of fact and any conclusions of law with respect to the allegations in the notice of formal hearing. The report shall also contain the Special Master's recommendation as to whether the Commission shall or shall not recommend discipline. The report shall be accompanied by a transcript of the evidence.

(b) Upon receiving the report of the Special Master, the Commission shall promptly serve a copy on the judge.

Effective March 1, 1994.

RULE 11. OBJECTIONS AND BRIEFS

(a) Within fifteen (15) days after a copy of the Special Master's report is served on the judge, the judge may file with the Commission an original and six (6) copies of a statement of objections to the findings of fact and conclusions of law contained in the report of the Special Master and may file an original and six (6) copies of a brief in support thereof.

(b) If the judge does not contest the findings of fact or conclusions of law as set forth in the Special Master's report, the judge may, nevertheless, within such time file an original and six (6) copies of a brief in support of a claim that such findings and conclusions are not sufficient to justify removal, other discipline or retirement.

(c) In making a report, the Commission, when there is a report of a Special Master, may accept, modify or reject any or all of the findings of fact and conclusions of law of the Special Master as well as the Special Master's recommendation to the Commission that it recommend or not recommend discipline.

(d) If a formal hearing is held by the Commission, the judge may, within a reasonable time after the termination of the hearing as may be fixed by the Commission, file an original and six (6) copies of a brief with the Commission in support of the judge's claim that the Commission should not recommend removal, other discipline or retirement.

Effective March 1, 1994.

RULE 12. ADDITIONAL EVIDENCE

In a proceeding pending before it, the Commission may, at any time after a formal hearing is held, order an additional hearing for the taking of additional evidence; provided that where a Special Master has been appointed, additional evidence shall be taken by the Special Master upon his or her own motion or by order of the Commission, and no such hearing for the taking of additional evidence shall be held by the Commission itself until after the Special Master has made a report. After the Special Master has made a report, the Commission may take additional evidence, or direct the Special Master to do so and report findings of fact and conclusions of law with respect thereto. The judge shall be given ten (10) days notice of the hearing to take additional evidence.

Effective March 1, 1994.

RULE 13. EXTENSIONS OF TIME

The Chairperson of the Commission may extend for periods not to exceed thirty (30) days in the aggregate the time for filing an answer, for the commencement of a hearing before the Commission, for the transmittal of the Special Master's report to the Commission, and for filing a statement of objections to the report of the Special Master, and a Special Master may similarly extend the time for the commencement of a hearing. The Commission may grant such additional extension of time as it may consider proper.

Effective March 1, 1994.

RULE 14. RECOMMENDATION OF COMMISSION OF REMOVAL, OTHER DISCIPLINE OR RETIREMENT

(a) The Commission may make a report recommending to the Supreme Court that a judge be (1) removed from office; (2) removed from office and prohibited from thereafter holding judicial office; (3) suspended from office for a specified period of time together with such other conditions and restrictions as the Commission may consider proper; (4) censured; (5) reprimanded; (6) retired; or (7) subjected to such other discipline as may seem to the Commission appropriate. In the case of a recommendation of censure, the same, if approved by the Supreme Court, shall be administered in open Court. If the Commission recommends a reprimand and such recommendation is approved by the Court, the same shall be administered by the Court at such place and in such manner as the Court may consider proper.

(b) The report shall be signed by the members of the Commission concurring therein and shall indicate if any member or members dissent from the report. Any member who does not agree with the report of the majority of the Commission may file a written dissent or special concurrence which shall be made a part of the record. The report shall be filed in the Supreme Court and shall be accompanied by the Special Master's report, if any, and a transcript of the evidence. A copy of the report as filed shall be promptly served upon the judge and evidence of such service shall be filed in the Supreme Court.

Effective March 1, 1994.

RULE 15. SUSPENSION BY THE COMMISSION FOR FELONY INDICTMENT

(a) Upon indictment for a felony by a grand jury of this State or by a grand jury of the United States of any judge, the Commission shall, subject to subparagraph (b) of this Rule, review the indictment, and if it determines that the indictment relates to, and adversely affects the administration of the office of this indicted judge, and that the rights and interests of the public are adversely affected thereby, the Commission shall suspend the judge immediately and without further action pending the final disposition of the case or until the expiration of the judge's term of office, whichever occurs first. During the term of office to which such judge was elected and in which the indictment occurred, if a nolle prosequi is entered, if the public official is acquitted, or if after conviction the conviction is later overturned as a result of any direct appeal or application for a writ of certiorari, the judge shall be immediately reinstated to the office from which he or she was suspended. While a judge is suspended under this subparagraph and until final conviction, the judge shall continue to receive compensation. For the duration of any suspension under this subparagraph, the Governor shall appoint a replacement judge. Upon a final conviction with no appeal or review pending, the office shall be declared vacant and a successor to that office shall be chosen as provided in the Constitution of the State of Georgia of 1983 or the laws enacted in pursuance thereof.

(b) The Commission shall not review the indictment for a period of fourteen (14) days from the day the indictment is received. This period of time may be extended by the Commission. During this period of time, the indicted judge may, in writing, authorize the Commission to suspend him or her from office. Any such voluntary suspension shall be subject to the same conditions for review, reinstatement or declaration of vacancy as are provided in this subparagraph for a nonvoluntary suspension.

(c) After any suspension is imposed under this subparagraph, the suspended judge may petition the Commission for a review. If the Commission determines that the judge should no longer be suspended, the judge shall immediately be reinstated to office.

(d) The findings and records of the Commission and the fact that the public official has or has not been suspended shall not be admissible in evidence in any court for any purpose. The finding and records of the Commission shall not be open to the public.

(e) The provisions of this subparagraph shall not apply to any indictment handed down prior to January 1, 1985.

(f) If a judge who is suspended from office under the provision of this subparagraph is not first tried at the next regular or special term following the indictment, the suspension shall be terminated and the judge shall be reinstated to office. The judge shall not be reinstated under this provision if he or she is not so tried based on a continuance granted upon a motion made only by the defendant.

Effective March 1, 1994.

RULE 16. PETITION TO MODIFY OR REJECT COMMISSION'S RECOMMENDATION

(a) A petition to the Supreme Court to modify or reject the recommendation of the Commission for removal, other discipline or retirement of a judge may be filed with six (6) copies within thirty (30) days after service of a copy of the Commission's report on the judge. The petition shall be verified, shall be based on the record, shall specify grounds relied on, and shall be accompanied by proof of service of seven (7) copies of the petition and of the brief on the Commission. Within twenty (20) days after service of the petition and brief, the Commission may serve and file a responsive brief. Within fifteen (15) days after service of such brief, the petitioner may file a reply brief, seven (7) copies of which shall be served on the Commission.

(b) Failure to file a petition within the time provided may be deemed a consent to a determination on the merits based upon the record filed by the Commission.

(c) A petition filed under this rule shall be heard in such manner as may be ordered by the Supreme Court.

Effective March 1, 1994.

RULE 17. COMMISSION'S POWER TO SECURE ASSISTANCE

(a) In conducting investigations, the preparation of notices, presentation of evidence at a formal hearing, preparation and filing of briefs and other documents, or in otherwise carrying out its functions, the Commission may utilize the services of the Attorney General of this State or one of the Attorney General's deputies or assistants, and in addition thereto, or in lieu thereof, may secure and pay for the services of a member of the Bar of this State in any or all of such matters.

(b) The Commission may also employ such assistants as it considers necessary for the performance of the duties and in the exercise of the powers conferred upon the Commission; subpoena or arrange for and compensate medical or other experts and reporters; subpoena witnesses; and arrange for the attendance of witnesses not subject to subpoena; and pay from funds available to it all expenses reasonably necessary for effectuating the purposes of Article VI, § VII, ¶ VII, of the 1983 Constitution of the State of Georgia.

Effective March 1, 1994.

RULE 18. POWERS OF COMMISSION—SUBPOENAS, DEPOSITIONS, CONTEMPT, PHYSICAL EXAMINATIONS, WITNESS FEES

(a) The Commission, through its Chairperson or Director, shall have the power to issue subpoenas for the attendance of witnesses at a formal hearing held before the Commission or a Special Master under Rule 7, for the production at such hearing of books, papers and other evidentiary matter.

(b) After notice is given to a judge that a formal hearing will be held under Rule 5, either the Commission or the judge may take the depositions of any witness upon reasonable written notice thereof given to the judge or the Commission of the time and place of taking of such depositions. The original of the deposition shall be returned to the Commission and at the hearing may be opened and used by either party under the same conditions and in the same manner and for the same purposes as depositions in civil cases.

In connection with the taking of such depositions, the Commission, through its Chairperson or Director, shall have the power to issue a subpoena for the attendance of the witness whose testimony is to be taken and for the production at the taking of the deposition of books, papers and other evidentiary matter.

(c) If any person refuses to attend, testify, or produce any writings or things required by a subpoena issued by the Commission, as authorized under subparagraph (b) of Rule 4 or under this rule, the Commission may petition the judge of the Superior Court of the circuit in which the person may be found, or if a judge of that circuit is involved in the proceedings, then to any judge of an adjoining circuit, for an order compelling the person to attend and testify or produce the writings or things required by the subpoena. The Court shall order the person to appear before it at a specified time and place and then and there shall consider why the person has not attended, testified or produced writings or things as required. A copy of said order shall be served upon the person to whom the subpoena of the Commission was directed. If it appears to the Court that the subpoena was regularly issued, the Court shall order the person to appear before the Commission, or a Special Master, at the time and place fixed in the order and to testify or produce the required writings or things. Failure to obey the order shall be punishable as contempt of court. The proceedings so instituted shall state in general terms, without identifying the judge, the nature of the pending matter, the name and residence of the person whose testimony is desired, and directions, if any, of the Commission requesting an order requiring the person to appear and testify and to produce writings or things as required by the Commission's subpoena. If the proceedings are instituted prior to the giving of notice of a formal hearing, the proceedings shall not identify the judge by name but only as a number.

(d) Each witness shall receive for attendance the same fees and allowances prescribed by OCGA § 24–10–24 for witnesses in civil cases.

(e) The Commission shall also have the authority after notice to the judge and a hearing to require that a judge involved in proceedings before the Commission submit to a physical or mental examination, or both, and specify the time, place, manner, conditions and scope of the examination and the physician or physicians by whom it is to be made.

Effective March 1, 1994.

RULE 19. NOTICES

(a) All notices provided for under these rules shall be in writing and shall be served upon the judge personally by a member of the Commission, or by a representative designated by the Chairperson, or may be served by registered or certified mail, return receipt requested.

(b) The initial notice sent to a judge with respect to an investigation to be or which has been conducted by the Commission shall be sent to the judge at such address as the Chairperson considers appropriate. Subsequent notices and mailed communications shall be sent to the judge at such address as he or she shall designate in writing filed with the Commission. If the judge is represented by counsel, all notices and papers to be sent to the judge under these rules may be served upon counsel.

(c) All notices mailed to a judge or counsel shall be enclosed in a sealed envelope marked on the face thereof, "Confidential—to be opened by addressee only."

Effective March 1, 1994.

RULE 20. CONFIDENTIALITY AND EXCEPTIONS

(a) The proceedings of the Commission, including, but not limited to, the fact of filing of complaints with the Commission, investigations to determine whether there is probable cause that judicial misconduct has occurred, conferences of the Commission with respect to matters pending before it, correspondence and other communications, information learned from any investigation by the Commission and all other papers and documents shall be kept confidential. Information obtained independently of any such complaint or investigation need not be maintained as confidential. Further, the requirement that participants maintain confidentiality shall cease at the time of the decision of the Commission on whether to initiate formal hearings against a judge, or at the time the complaint in question is resolved, closed, or otherwise settled through formal disposition. However, this confidentiality requirement shall not apply to notice of a formal hearing, a formal hearing, reports of the Commission to the Supreme Court recommending discipline, and decisions of the Commission made after a formal hearing that the judge with respect to whom the hearing was held was not guilty of misconduct justifying a recommendation of discipline. When, notwithstanding the rule of confidentiality set out in the first sentence of this subparagraph, the existence of a complaint filed with the Commission or any investigation of a judge whether or not based upon a complaint shall in some way become public, the Commission, at the request of the judge or upon its own motion if it considers such to be desirable, may make such statement with respect to the handling and status of the proceedings as the Commission may consider appropriate. When, in the exercise of its functions, the Commission has information concerning conduct of a member of the Bar which the Commission feels should be considered by the Disciplinary Board of The State Bar of Georgia for the purpose of determining whether such conduct constitutes a violation of the Code of Professional Responsibility, the Commission shall have the authority and it shall be its duty to refer the matter to the Board for such action as the Board may consider appropriate. The Commission shall be further authorized, in its discretion, to disclose to the Judicial Nominating Commission of the State of Georgia and to the Governor of the State, or any Commission, Board or Committee officially appointed to evaluate nominees for federal judgeships, including, but not limited to, a committee appointed by the American Bar Association for such purpose, any information involving any prospective nominee for judicial appointment which the Commission feels such Commission, Board or Committee should consider in passing upon the qualifications and fitness of the nominee for judicial appointment.

(b) All persons acting for the Commission in investigating a judge or participating in an official capacity in any proceedings relating thereto, including court reporters, shall be specifically advised by the Chairperson or by the Commission's representative of the requirement of confidentiality with respect to such matters as are confidential under subparagraph (a) of this Rule and shall be directed not to disclose any information acquired by them to any person not officially or formally connected with the investigation or proceedings.

(c) All subpoenas and other proceedings which may be issued or conducted by the Commission prior to service of a notice of formal hearing shall not name the judge against whom the charges are pending, but shall style the proceedings by number as set out in Rule 5.

(d) If there shall be probable cause for inquiry concerning, or prosecution of, a witness for perjury in proceedings before the Commission, the record of the proceedings or papers filed in connection therewith shall be disclosed to the extent required by the inquiry or prosecution.

(e) A judge about whom an inquiry or investigation is being made may request release of information concerning the complaint and investigation, and the Commission, if it considers appropriate, may comply with such request.

(f) Any person violating the rule of confidentiality as set forth in this section shall be subject to punishment for contempt of the Supreme Court.

(g) The rule of confidentiality as set forth in this section shall not apply to any information which the Commission considers to be relevant to any current or future civil or criminal action against a judge, and upon receipt of a duly issued subpoena or court order by any state or federal court of record, the Commission is authorized to comply with the same to the extent required by such subpoena or court order.

(h) The rule of confidentiality set forth in this section shall not apply to any complaint alleging a violation of Canon 7 of the Code of Judicial Conduct which the Commission, in its sole discretion, determine should be handled on an expedited basis in the manner set forth in Rule 27.

Effective March 1, 1994; amended effective January 1, 1998; January 19, 2000.

RULE 21. IMMUNITY

Complaints, reports or testimony in the course of proceedings under these rules shall be deemed to be made in the course of judicial proceedings. Members of the Commission, Commission counsel and the Commission staff shall be absolutely immune from suit for all conduct in the course of their official duties. All other participants shall be entitled to all rights, privileges and immunities afforded to participants in actions filed in the courts of this state, and shall be immune from civil liability with respect to all papers filed with, or statements made or testimony given to, the Commission or the Supreme Court or given in any investigation or proceeding pertaining to a complaint against a judge, when done in good faith.

Effective March 1, 1994.

RULE 22. ADVISORY OPINIONS

(a) The Commission shall be authorized to render official formal advisory opinions concerning a proper interpretation of the Code of Judicial Conduct, which advisory opinions the Commission shall publish and disseminate.

(b) The Commission shall examine and reconsider any of its advisory opinions upon the request of the Supreme Court.

(c) The Commission and the Supreme Court shall consider compliance with an advisory opinion to be evidence of a good faith effort to comply with the Code of Judicial Conduct, but only to the extent that the underlying facts are identical.

(d) The Supreme Court's determination of the propriety of particular conduct shall supersede any conflicting advisory opinion of the Commission.

Effective March 1, 1994; amended effective February 10, 2000.

RULE 23. OTHER POWERS

The Commission shall have such other powers and authority as may be reasonably necessary for the proper and efficient performance of its functions in carrying out the intent of the constitutional amendment creating the Commission.

Effective March 1, 1994.

RULE 24. COMPLAINT AGAINST A MEMBER OF THE SUPREME COURT

A complaint against a member of the Supreme Court shall proceed in the same manner as a complaint against any other judge except:

(a) If the Commission recommends a sanction and the respondent consents to the sanction, the Commission shall impose the sanction and there shall be no appeal or further review by the Court.

(b) If the Commission recommends a sanction and the respondent objects to the sanction, the Commission shall proceed in the manner outlined in Rule 14. However, all current members of the Court shall be automatically disqualified and a substitute Court consisting of the current Chairperson and the six (6) immediate past Chairpersons of the Council of Superior Court Judges shall be impaneled to decide the matter in lieu of the sitting members of the Supreme Court. If any such Chairperson shall be disqualified or otherwise fails or refuses to serve, the next preceding Chairperson of the Council shall serve as a member of the substitute Court.

Effective March 1, 1994.

RULE 25. EMERGENCY INTERIM RELIEF

(a) Incident to any preliminary investigation or formal proceeding conducted pursuant to these rules or upon receipt of sufficient evidence demonstrating that the continued service of any judge is causing immediate and substantial public harm and an erosion of public confidence in the orderly administration of justice and appears to be violative of the Georgia Code of Judicial Conduct, the Commission may petition the Supreme Court for injunctive or other relief, including temporary suspension or reassignment of the judge.

(b) The petition shall state the evidence justifying the emergency relief sought with particularity and shall be verified by the Chairperson and/or the Director of the Commission.

(c) Simultaneously with the filing of said petition, a copy shall be personally served upon the Respondent by any person approved by the Chairperson and/or the Director of the Commission. In the event personal service cannot be perfected, service may be perfected by registered or certified mail, return receipt requested, to the last known address of the Respondent as set forth in the most current issue of the Georgia Courts Directory published by the Administrative Office of the Courts.

(d) A written acknowledgment of service from the Respondent and/or his or her counsel shall constitute conclusive proof of service and eliminate the need to utilize any other form of service.

(e) Upon receipt of the verified petition for emergency relief, the Clerk of the Supreme Court shall immediately file the same; assign the matter a docket number; and notify the Chief Justice that the appointment of a Special Master is appropriate. Within 10 days after the docketing of said petition, the Court shall appoint a Special Master to conduct a hearing at which the Commission shall show cause why the relief sought by the Commission should be granted pending further disciplinary proceedings.

(f) Within 10 days after receipt of the Order of Appointment, the Special Master shall conduct a hearing at such time and place as may be designated by said Special Master or as may be mutually agreed upon by the parties.

(g) Within 10 days following the completion of said hearing, the Special Master shall file a report and recommendation with the Clerk of the Supreme Court and simultaneously serve copies thereof upon the Commission and the Respondent.

(h) The Supreme Court shall give expedited consideration to the report of the Special Master and may suspend the Respondent, with or without pay, pending final disposition of the disciplinary proceedings giving rise to the petition for emergency suspension or order such other action as it deems appropriate under all the circumstances.

Effective March 1, 1994.

RULE 26. INVOLUNTARY RETIREMENT OF JUDGES

In addition to other methods and causes provided in these Rules, a judge of any court in this State shall be subject to involuntary retirement for a mental or physical disability which constitutes a serious and likely permanent interference with the performance of the duties of office on the following terms and conditions:

(a) Upon receiving a complaint or otherwise receiving information indicating that a judge has been judicially declared incompetent; voluntarily committed by reason of incompetency or disability by a final judicial order after a judicial hearing; or may have a mental or physical disability that seriously impairs or interferes with the performance of the duties of office which is or is likely to become permanent, and after determining that said condition adversely affects the administration of the office of the disabled judge and the rights and interests of the public, the Commission shall, without further action, enter an order requiring the judge to show cause, within 10 days after service of said order, why said disabled judge should not be temporarily transferred to a disability inactive status pending the final disposition of the matter. A copy of said order shall be immediately served by hand delivery upon the judge, his or her guardian, or the director of the institution in which any such judge may be confined or otherwise receiving treatment.

Unless subsequently extended by consent, any such order shall automatically expire 90 calendar days after service upon the disabled judge, and during such time, said disabled judge shall continue to receive the compensation normally paid for such office.

(b) Simultaneously with the service of said order, the Commission shall request the judge to submit, within 10 days, all pertinent medical and other records to the Commission and shall designate one or more qualified medical, psychiatric or psychological experts to examine the disabled judge prior to any hearing on the matter. Said experts may or may not be agreed upon by the Commission and the disabled judge, but in any event, the written reports of all such experts shall be provided to the Commission and to the disabled judge as soon as medically feasible, and in any event, not less than 20 days prior to any hearing on the matter. The cost of any such examinations shall be borne solely by the Commission.

(c) The failure or refusal of a judge to submit the requested medical records or to submit to an independent medical examination, unless due to circumstances beyond the judge's control, shall preclude the judge from submitting reports of medical examinations done on his or her behalf, and the Commission may consider such failure or refusal as evidence that the judge has a disability.

(d) In the event the disabled judge shall desire independent medical examinations by experts other than those designated by the Commission, said judge shall have the absolute right to have such examinations conducted, provided, however, that any such examination shall be at the sole expense of the disabled judge and, provided further, that written reports of such examinations are provided to the Commission as soon as medically feasible and, in any event, not less than 20 days prior to any hearing on the matter.

(e) After receipt and review of the written reports of any and all such examinations and prior to any hearing on the matter, the Commission and the disabled judge may agree upon a proposed stipulated disposition of the matter. Said proposed stipulated disposition, which shall contain, as appropriate, (i) findings of fact, conclusions of law and recommended final disposition; (ii) copies of the original complaint or other material giving rise to the complaint; and (iii) all written reports of examinations received and reviewed by the Commission, shall be immediately filed with the Supreme Court for approval, rejection or modification. In such filing, the disabled judge shall not be identified, but the matter shall be captioned: "Stipulated Disposition Concerning Judge No. ______."

(f) The final decision on such stipulated disposition shall be made by the Supreme Court as soon as practicable, but in any event, not later than thirty (30) days after the matter is docketed in said Court, and the Court shall forthwith enter an appropriate order.

(g) In the event the proposed stipulated disposition is rejected and/or modified or revised in any substantial and material way, the disabled judge may, within ten (10) days of the receipt of the order of the Court, notify the Commission that he or she is withdrawing his or her agreement to the same, and said proposed stipulated disposition cannot thereafter be used against said disabled judge in any subsequent proceedings, nor shall the same be available for public inspection.

(h) If any such matter is not resolved by stipulated disposition, all such subsequent proceedings shall be conducted in the same manner as disciplinary proceedings, except:

(1) All such proceedings shall be and remain confidential until the final order of the Supreme Court;

(2) The Commission may appoint and compensate, if necessary, a lawyer to represent the disabled judge if the judge is without representation;

(3) If, after a formal hearing, the Commission concludes that the judge is incapacitated to continue to hold judicial office by reason of either physical or mental disability, it shall not be empowered to recommend any disciplinary action against said judge, but rather shall be limited to recommending a suspension from office, either temporary or permanent, on such terms and conditions as may appear just and proper under the circumstances, until such time as an appropriate petition for reinstatement to active status has been filed by the disabled judge and granted by the Supreme Court.

(4) For the duration of any suspension under this subparagraph, the Governor shall appoint a replacement judge who shall serve until the disabled judge is reinstated to active status or until the expiration of the disabled judge's term of office, whichever first occurs.

Effective March 1, 1994.

RULE 27. SPECIAL COMMITTEE ON JUDICIAL ELECTION CAMPAIGN INTERVENTION

(a) In every year in which a general election is held in this State and at such other times as the Commission may deem appropriate, the Chair shall name three (3) members to a Special Committee on Judicial Election Campaign Intervention ("Special Committee") whose responsibility shall be to deal expeditiously with allegations of ethical misconduct in campaigns for judicial office. The membership of such committee shall consist of the senior member of each of the three (3) categories of Commission membership if available, and if not, the next most senior member from that category. The Commission Director shall also serve as an ex-officio member. The objective of such committee shall be to alleviate unethical and unfair campaign practices in judicial elections, and to that end, the Special Committee shall have the following authority:

(b) Upon receipt of a complaint or otherwise receiving information facially indicating a violation by a judicial candidate of any provision of Canon 7 during the course of a campaign for judicial office, the Director shall immediately forward a copy of the same by facsimile and U.S. Mail to the Special Committee members and said Committee shall:

(1) seek, from the complainant and/or subject of the complaint, such further information on the allegation of the complaint as it deems necessary;

(2) conduct such additional investigation as the Committee may deem necessary;

(3) determine whether the allegations of the complaint warrant speedy intervention; if no intervention is needed, dismiss the complaint and so notify the complaining party;

(4) if further investigation is deemed necessary, request confidential written responses from the subject of the complaint and the complaining party on the following schedule:

(A) within 3 business days of receiving such a request from the Committee, a written response from the subject of the complaint;

(B) the Committee will share the subject's written response with the complaining party on a confidential basis, who shall be requested to provide a written response within 3 business days; and

(C) the Committee will share the complaining party's response with the subject of the complaint, who then shall be requested to submit a written rebuttal within one (1) business day.

In the event a complaint is filed within two (2) weeks before a judicial election, or if circumstances otherwise dictate, the Committee may accelerate the above schedule or eliminate the need for steps (B) and (C) as the Committee deems necessary. Each of the above papers must be served on the Committee only, and will be kept confidential except as described above. The identity of the complaining party will remain confidential until the Committee's decision is communicated to the parties unless that confidentiality is waived by the complaining party. Any party breaching the confidentiality of the above process shall be subject to a Public Statement as set forth in this Rule.

(5) if it is determined after the papers from the parties are reviewed that the allegations do warrant intervention, the Committee is authorized:

(A) to immediately release to the complaining party and the person and/or organization complained against, a non-confidential "Public Statement" setting out violations believed to exist; and/or

(B) to refer the matter to the full Commission for such action as may be appropriate under the applicable rules.

(6) if it is determined after the papers from the parties are reviewed that the allegations do not warrant intervention, the Committee shall dismiss the complaint and so notify the complaining party and the subject of the complaint.

(c) All proceedings under this Rule shall be informal and non-adversarial, and the Special Committee shall act on all complaints within ten (10) days of receipt, either in person; by facsimile; by U.S. Mail; or by teleconference.

(d) Except as hereinabove specifically authorized, the proceedings of the Special Committee shall remain confidential as provided in Rule 20, and in no event, shall the Committee have the authority to institute disciplinary action against any candidate for judicial office, which power is specifically reserved to the full Commission under applicable rules.

Adopted effective January 1, 1998; amended effective January 19, 2000; January 7, 2004.

RULE 28. RECUSAL OF COMMISSION MEMBERS

Commission Members shall recuse themselves in any proceeding in which their impartiality might reasonably be questioned, including, but not limited to instances where:

(a) the member is a party, or witness, or has a personal familial or financial relationship or interest involving the matter, any party or witness;

(b) the member is an attorney or party in any matter pending before the respondent;

(c) the member has personal knowledge or information which could interfere with that member impartially considering such matter;

(d) the member, as a judge similarly situated, would be required to recuse under the Code of Judicial Conduct; or

(e) the member believes that, for any reason, that member cannot render a fair and impartial decision.

If the propriety of a member's participation is raised, the issue shall be decided by a majority of the members present and voting. Temporary appointments to replace disqualified members, when necessary, shall be made in the same manner as authorized in Rule 1(d).

Adopted effective July 8, 1999.

RULES AND REGULATIONS FOR THE ORGANIZATION AND GOVERNMENT OF THE STATE BAR OF GEORGIA

Revised November 4, 1983

Including Amendments Received Through November 1, 2006

Research Note

Use WESTLAW *to find cases citing a rule. In addition, use* WESTLAW *to search for specific terms or to update a rule; see the GA–RULES and GA–ORDERS Scope screens for further information.*

Amendments to these rules are published, as received, in the South Eastern Reporter 2d *and* Georgia Cases *advance sheets.*

Table of Rules

PART I. CREATION AND ORGANIZATION

CHAPTER 1. CREATION AND PURPOSE

RULE 1–101. CREATION

Pursuant to the authority of this court and the Act of the General Assembly approved by the Governor on March 11, 1963 (Georgia Laws 1963, page 70) the State Bar of Georgia is hereby created and established.

RULE 1–102. POWERS

The State Bar of Georgia shall be a legal entity; may sue and be sued; shall have perpetual existence; may contract; may own real and personal property; may adopt and use an official seal; shall establish a principal office; and shall have such other powers, privileges and duties as may be reasonable and necessary for the proper fulfillment of its purposes.

RULE 1–103. PURPOSES

The purposes of the State Bar of Georgia shall be:

(a) to foster among the members of the bar of this State the principles of duty and service to the public;

(b) to improve the administration of justice; and

(c) to advance the science of law.

CHAPTER 2. MEMBERSHIP

RULE 1–201. MEMBERSHIP

All persons now or hereafter who are:

(1) authorized to practice law in this State or;

(2) authorized to act as a Foreign Law Consultant shall be members of the State Bar of Georgia.

Amended effective April 16, 1992.

RULE 1–202. CLASSES OF MEMBERS

Membership in the State Bar of Georgia shall consist of five classes: active, foreign law consultant, emeritus, disabled and inactive. The bylaws shall make provision for the registration of each active member and the location of his or her principal office for the practice of law, the registration of each foreign law consultant and the location of his or her principal office, and the registration of emeritus and inactive members and their mailing addresses.

(a) Inactive Members. All lawyers who are neither engaged in the practice of law nor holding themselves out as practicing attorneys nor occupying any public or private position in which they may be called upon to give legal advice or counsel or to examine the law or to pass upon the legal effect of any act, document, or law may be inactive members at their election. Members who are in military service may be inactive if they so elect.

(b) Active Members. Active members shall be all other lawyers including judges but excluding foreign law consultants. Only active members of the State Bar of Georgia in good standing may vote or hold office in the State Bar of Georgia.

(c) Foreign Law Consultants. Foreign law consultants shall be those persons who are licensed under Part D of the Rules Governing Admission to the Practice of Law as adopted by the Supreme Court of Georgia, Ga. Ct. & Bar Rules, p. 12–1 et seq.

(d) Emeritus Members. Any member in good standing of the State Bar of Georgia who shall have attained the age of 70 years and who shall have been admitted to the practice of law in the State of Georgia for 25 years, may retire from the State Bar upon petition to and approval by the Executive Committee. Such a retired member shall hold emeritus status and shall annually confirm in writing this emeritus status. An emeritus member of the State shall not be required to pay dues or annual fees. An emeritus member of the State shall not be privileged to practice law except that an emeritus member may handle pro bono cases referred by either an organized pro bono program recognized by the Pro Bono Project of the State Bar or a non-profit corporation that delivers legal services to the poor. An emeritus member may be reinstated to active membership upon application to the Executive Committee.

(e) Disabled Members. Any member of the State Bar of Georgia who is found to be permanently disabled by the Social Security Administration may retire from the State Bar of Georgia upon petition to and approval by the Board of Governors. Such a disabled member shall hold disabled status and shall annually confirm in writing this disabled status. A disabled member of the State Bar of Georgia holding disabled status under this paragraph shall not be privileged to practice law nor be required to pay dues or annual fees. A disabled member may be reinstated to active membership upon application to the State Bar of Georgia.

Amended February 19, 1987; amended effective April 16, 1992; July 1, 1997; June 5, 2002.

RULE 1–203. PRACTICE BY ACTIVE MEMBERS; NONRESIDENTS

No person shall practice law in this State unless such person is an active member of the State Bar of Georgia in good standing; except as provided below:

(1) A person who is not a member of the State Bar of Georgia, but who is licensed to practice in a state or states other than Georgia, and is in good standing in all states in which such person is licensed, may be permitted to appear in the courts of this state in isolated cases in the discretion of the judge of such court; or

(2) A person who is not a member of the State Bar of Georgia, but who is licensed to practice in a state or states other than Georgia, and is in good standing in all states in which such person is licensed, may be permitted to appear in the courts of this state if such person:

(i) is enrolled in a full time graduate degree program at an accredited law school in this state; and

(ii) is under the supervision of a resident attorney; and

(iii) limits his or her practice to the appearance in the courts of this state to the extent necessary to carry out the responsibilities of such graduate degree program.

(3) A person who is admitted to the Bar as a foreign law consultant pursuant to Part D of the Rules Governing Admission to the Practice of Law, [infra], may render legal services in the State of Georgia solely with respect to the laws of the foreign country (i.e., a country other than the United States of America, its possessions and territories) where such person is admitted to practice, to the extent provided by and in strict compliance with the provisions of Part D of the Rules Governing Admission to Practice, but shall not otherwise render legal services in this State.

(4) Persons who are authorized to practice law in this State are hereby authorized to practice law as sole proprietorships or as partners, shareholders, or members of:

(i) partnerships under OCGA § 14–8–1 et seq.; or

(ii) limited liability partnerships under OCGA § 14–8–1 et seq.; or

(iii) professional corporations under OCGA § 14–7–1 et seq.; or

(iv) professional associations under OCGA § 14–10–1 et seq.; or

(v) limited liability companies under OCGA § 14–11–100 et seq.

Amended October 3, 1985; amended effective April 16, 1992; August 29, 1996.

RULE 1–204. GOOD STANDING

No person shall be deemed a member in good standing:

(a) while delinquent after September 1 of any year for nonpayment of the license fee prescribed in Chapter 5 hereof;

(b) while suspended for disciplinary reasons;

(c) while disbarred;

(d) while suspended for failure to comply with continuing legal education requirements; or

(e) while in violation of Bar Rule 1–209 for failure to pay child support obligations.

Amended effective July 1, 1997.

RULE 1–205. BAR OF JUDICIAL CIRCUIT

Each member who is a resident of this State shall be considered a member of the bar of the judicial circuit in which his principal office for the practice of law is located, or, at his election, the circuit in which he resides, or if he has no office, the circuit in which he resides or last resided.

RULE 1–206. AFFILIATE MEMBERS

In addition to the membership and classes of membership provided in this Chapter, the State Bar may recognize as affiliates, without the rights and privileges of membership, members of the legal profession not authorized to practice law in Georgia, but who are licensed to practice law in another state or the District of Columbia, and are in good standing in all jurisdictions in which they are licensed. Affiliate members may be furnished copies of appropriate publications and may be entitled to attend and participate, without the right to vote or hold office, in those meetings and activities conducted by the State Bar and any of its component parts or sections.

Amended effective June 6, 1996.

RULE 1–206.1. LAW STUDENT MEMBERS

In addition to the membership and classes of membership provided in this Chapter, the State Bar may recognize as law student members, without the rights and privileges of membership, those law students currently enrolled in a law school approved by the American Bar Association or any law school approved by the Georgia Board of Bar Examiners. Law student members may be furnished copies of appropriate publications and may be entitled to attend and participate, without the right to vote or hold office, in those meetings and activities conducted by the State Bar and any of its component parts or sections.

Adopted effective June 6, 1996.

RULE 1–207. CHANGE OF ADDRESS

All members of the State Bar of Georgia shall keep the membership department, of the State Bar of Georgia informed of their current name, address and telephone number. It is incumbent upon those authorized to practice to keep the membership information current and accurate. The Court and the State Bar of Georgia may rely on the address carried by the membership department and failure on the part of a member to notify the membership department may have adverse consequences to a member. The choice of a member to use *only* a post office box address on the Bar membership records shall constitute an election to waive personal service in any proceedings between the Bar and the member. Notification given to any department of the Bar other than the Membership Department shall not satisfy this requirement.

Amended effective April 14, 1994.

RULE 1–208. RESIGNATION FROM MEMBERSHIP

(a) Resignation while in good standing: A member of the State Bar in good standing may, under oath, petition the Executive Committee for leave to resign from the State Bar. Upon acceptance of such petition by the Executive Committee by majority vote, such person shall not practice law in this state nor be entitled to any privileges and benefits accorded to active members of the State Bar in good standing unless such person complies with part (b) or (c) of this Rule.

(1) The petition for leave to resign while in good standing shall be filed, under oath, with the Executive Director of the State Bar and shall contain a statement that there are no disciplinary actions or criminal proceedings pending against the petitioner and that petitioner is a member in good standing. A copy of the petition shall be served upon the General Counsel of the State Bar.

(2) No petition for leave to resign while in good standing shall be accepted if there are disciplinary proceedings or criminal charges pending against the member or if the member is not a member in good standing.

(3) A petition filed under this paragraph shall constitute a waiver of the confidentiality provisions of Rule 4–221(d) as to any pending disciplinary proceedings.

(b) Readmission within five years after resignation: for a period of five years after the effective date of a voluntary resignation, the former member of the State Bar who has resigned while in good standing may apply for readmission to the State Bar upon completion of the following terms and conditions:

(1) payment in full of the current dues for the year in which readmission is sought;

(2) payment of a readmission fee to the State Bar equal to the amount the former member seeking readmission would have paid if he had instead elected inactive status; and

(3) submission to the membership section of the State Bar of a determination of fitness from the Board to Determine Fitness of Bar Applicants.

(c) Readmission after five years: after the expiration of five years from the effective date of a voluntary resignation, the former member must comply with the Rules governing admission to the practice of law in Georgia as adopted by the Supreme Court of Georgia.

Adopted effective March 21, 1991; amended effective November 7, 2001; June 5, 2002.

CHAPTER 3. BOARD OF GOVERNORS

RULE 1-301. GOVERNMENT BY BOARD OF GOVERNORS

The government of the State Bar of Georgia shall be vested in a Board of Governors.

Amended October 2, 1984.

RULE 1-302. COMPOSITION

(a) The Board of Governors shall be composed of the following:

(1) The President, the President-elect, the Immediate Past President, the Secretary, the Treasurer, the President of the Young Lawyers Division, the President-elect of the Young Lawyers Division, the Immediate Past President of the Young Lawyers Division, and the Attorney General of Georgia;

(2) the number of Board of Governors members for each Judicial Circuit as existed on January 1, 2001, plus an additional 7 Board of Governors members to be elected from the Atlanta Judicial Circuit.

(i) Each Judicial Circuit shall have an additional member for each additional five hundred active members of the State Bar added to that circuit after January 1, 2001. The size of the Board of Governors, excluding those designated in subsection (a)(1) above, shall not exceed 150, except as set out in subsection (b) below.

(ii) If the geographical limits of a judicial circuit are changed, and by reason of said change there is a reduction in the number of Superior Court judges to which that circuit was entitled on July 1, 1979, then and in that event, there shall be a corresponding reduction in the number of members of the Board of Governors representing that circuit provided there was more than one Board member representing that circuit. In the event that there is such a reduction, the last created post will be the first post eliminated.

(iii) If the change in the geographical limits of a judicial circuit does not result in a reduction in the number of Superior Court judges in such circuit, then such circuit shall retain at least as many members of the Board of Governors as it had on July 1, 1979. Additional Board representation will be determined by the number of active members of the State Bar residing in that circuit as provided above. A change in the name of a judicial circuit shall have no effect upon that circuit's Board of Governor's representatives, except as otherwise provided.

(3) two representatives of the active members of the State Bar of Georgia residing outside of the State of Georgia, who themselves must be residents of different states of the United States. The nonresident representatives shall be active members of the State Bar of Georgia in good standing residing outside of the State of Georgia.

(4) three members appointed as follows: The President-elect in office when this rule becomes effective shall appoint three members to the Board of Governors. Thereafter, the President-elect shall appoint the number of such members whose term expired at the annual meeting at which the President-elect assumed office. The appointed members shall be chosen in such a manner as to promote diversity within the Board of Governors.

(b) Upon the creation of a new circuit, such circuit shall be entitled to elect one member to the Board of Governors even if the cap of 150 Board of Governors members has been reached, and if the cap has not been reached, may be entitled to elect additional members depending on the number of active members of the State of Georgia residing in the circuit as provided above.

(c) A member of the Board of Governors must be an active member of the State Bar of Georgia in good standing. A member representing a judicial circuit shall be a member of the bar of that circuit.

(d) Members of the Board of Governors shall receive no compensation for their services.

Amended November 1, 1988; amended effective December 14, 1993; November 7, 2001.

RULE 1-303. MEETINGS

The Board of Governors shall hold at least three regular meetings in each year at such times and places as may be determined in accordance with the bylaws and upon such call and notice as may be set forth in the bylaws.

RULE 1-304. ELECTION OF MEMBERS OF BOARD OF GOVERNORS

The State Bar of Georgia shall, in its bylaws, establish the term of office and the method of election of the members of the Board of Governors representing judicial circuits and nonresident members. Such method of election shall ensure that:

(a) the election will be by secret written or secure electronic ballot;

(b) each active member of the State Bar of Georgia, in conjunction with a specified number of other active members, will have the right, upon compliance with reasonable conditions, to nominate a candidate from his judicial circuit (or candidates in circuits electing more than one member of the Board of Governors in such election) whose name will be placed on the ballot for his circuit;

(c) each active member of the State Bar of Georgia residing outside of the State, in conjunction with a specified number of other active nonresident members, will have the right, upon compliance with reasonable conditions, to nominate a candidate from the active members of the State Bar of Georgia residing outside of the State;

(d) any nominating petition shall bear or be accompanied by a statement signed by the nominee indicating his willingness to serve if elected;

(e) a ballot for his judicial circuit will be mailed to each active resident member and a ballot will be mailed to each active nonresident member in the case of election of nonresident board member, having printed thereon the names of all qualified nominees for such circuit or nonresident post and space for a write-in vote in ample time for the member to cast the ballot before the time fixed for the election. In lieu of a written ballot, a secure electronic ballot, which meets the requirements above, may be provided to members;

(f) each nominee shall be entitled to have at least one observer present at the counting of the written ballots from his judicial circuit; and,

(g) any change in the geographical limits of a judicial circuit or circuits shall automatically terminate the terms of all members elected to the Board of Governors, accordingly in such manners as the bylaws may provide. In the event the geographical limits of a circuit are changed after the notices of election have been distributed to the members of the State Bar of Georgia, then and in that event, the terms of the members of the Board of Governors from such circuits will remain as they were before the change in geographical limits until the election of the Board of Governors to be held the following year.

Amended November 1, 1988; amended effective January 8, 2004.

RULE 1–305. CHANGE IN GEOGRAPHICAL LIMITS OF JUDICIAL CIRCUITS

The number and terms of members of the Board of Governors from judicial circuits that have experienced a change in geographical limits shall be determined according to the provisions of Rules 1–302(b), 1–304(f) and as hereinafter provided by Rule 1–701 and the bylaws.

RULE 1–306. VACANCIES; TIES

The bylaws shall provide for filling vacancies in the Board of Governors and for deciding the outcome of tie votes.

CHAPTER 4. OFFICERS

RULE 1–401. DESIGNATION AND TERMS

The officers of the State Bar of Georgia shall include a President, a President-elect, a Secretary and a Treasurer and may include such other officers as may be specified in the bylaws. The President-elect, the Secretary and the Treasurer shall be elected by the membership in accordance with the bylaws and the results published at the annual meeting. The Secretary and Treasurer shall serve until the next annual meeting. The President-elect shall succeed to the presidency at the next annual meeting. If there is no President-elect, a President shall also be elected at the same time and in the same manner as the other officers. In the event of the death or resignation of the President, the President-elect shall succeed to the presidency, shall serve out the unexpired term, and shall continue to serve for the term during which he would regularly have served as President. The officers shall have such duties, rights, and powers as the bylaws may provide.

RULE 1–402. ELECTION OF OFFICERS

The State Bar of Georgia shall, in its bylaws, establish the method of election of the officers. Such method of election shall contain provisions equivalent to those required by Rule 1–304 relating to election of members of the Board of Governors. Officers may be nominated by the Board of Governors.

RULE 1–403. VACANCIES; TIES

The bylaws shall provide for filling vacancies in any office and for deciding the outcome of tie votes.

RULE 1–404. ELIGIBILITY OF PRESIDENT–ELECT

No person shall be eligible for election as President-elect if a member of the judicial circuit in which such person is a member was elected to the office of President-elect at any time within one year immediately prior to the election in which such person is a candidate.

Amended effective March 14, 1996.

CHAPTER 5. FINANCE

RULE 1-501. LICENSE FEES

(a) Annual license fees for membership in the State Bar shall be due and payable on July 1 of each year. Upon the failure of a member to pay the license fee by September 1, the member shall cease to be a member in good standing. When such license fees and late fees for the current and prior years have been paid, the member shall automatically be reinstated to the status of member in good standing, except as provided in section (b) of this Rule.

(b) In the event a member of the State Bar is delinquent without reasonable cause in the payment of license fees for a period of one (1) year, the member shall be automatically suspended, and shall not practice law in this state. The suspended member may thereafter lift such suspension only upon the successful completion of all of the following terms and conditions:

(i) payment of all outstanding dues, assessments, late fees, reinstatement fees, and any and all penalties due and owing before or accruing after the suspension of membership;

(ii) provide the membership section of the State Bar the following:

(A) a certificate from the Office of General Counsel of the State Bar that the suspended member is not presently subject to any disciplinary procedure;

(B) a certificate from the Commission on Continuing Lawyer Competency that the suspended member is current on all requirements for continuing legal education;

(C) a determination of fitness from the Board to Determine Fitness of Bar Applicants;

(iii) payment to the State Bar of a non-waivable reinstatement fee as follows:

(A) $150.00 for the first reinstatement paid within the first year of suspension, plus $150.00 for each year of suspension thereafter up to a total of five years;

(B) $250.00 for the second reinstatement paid within the first year of suspension, plus $250.00 for each year of suspension thereafter up to a total of five years;

(C) $500.00 for the third reinstatement paid within the first year of suspension, plus 500.00 for each year of suspension thereafter up to a total of five years; or

(D) $750.00 for each subsequent reinstatement paid within the first year of suspension, plus $750.00 for each year of suspension thereafter up to a total of five years.

The yearly increase in the reinstatement fee shall become due and owing in its entirety upon the first day of each next fiscal year and shall not be prorated for any fraction of the fiscal year in which it is actually paid.

(c) A member suspended for a license fee delinquency for a total of five years in succession shall be immediately terminated as a member without further action on the part of the State Bar. The terminated member shall not be entitled to a hearing as set out in section (d) below. The terminated member shall be required to apply for membership to the Office of Bar Admissions for readmission to the State Bar. Upon completion of the requirements for readmission, the terminated member shall be required to pay the total reinstatement fee due under subsection (b)(iii) above plus an additional $750.00 as a readmission fee to the State Bar.

(d) Prior to suspending membership for a license fee delinquency, the State Bar shall send by certified mail a notice thereof to the last known address of the member as contained in the official membership records. It shall specify the years for which the license fee is delinquent and state that either the fee and all penalties related thereto are paid within sixty (60) days or a hearing to establish reasonable cause is requested within sixty (60) days, the membership shall be suspended.

If a hearing is requested, it shall be held at State Bar Headquarters within ninety (90) days of receipt of the request by the Executive Committee. Notice of time and place of the hearing shall be mailed at least ten (10) days in advance. The party cited may be represented by counsel. Witnesses shall be sworn; and, if requested by the party cited, a complete electronic record or a transcript shall be made of all proceedings and testimony. The expense of the record shall be paid by the party requesting it and a copy thereof shall be furnished to the Executive Committee. The presiding member or special master shall have the authority to rule on all motions, objections, and other matters presented in connection with the Georgia Rules of Civil Procedure, and the practice in the trial of civil cases. The party cited may not be required to testify over his or her objection.

The Executive Committee shall (1) make findings of fact and conclusions of law and shall determine whether the party cited was delinquent in violation of this Rule 1-501; and (2) upon a finding of delinquency shall determine whether there was reasonable cause for the delinquency. Financial hardship short of adjudicated bankruptcy shall not constitute reasonable cause. A copy of the findings and the determination shall be sent to the party cited. If it is determined that no delinquency has occurred, the matter shall be dismissed. If it is determined that delinquency has occurred but that there was reasonable cause therefor, the matter shall be deferred for one (1) year at which time the matter will be reconsidered. If it is determined that delinquency has occurred without reasonable cause therefor, the membership shall be suspended immediately upon such determination. An appropriate notice of suspension shall be sent to the clerks of all Georgia courts and shall be published in an official publication of the State Bar. Alleged errors of law in the proceedings or findings of the Executive Committee or its delegate shall be reviewed by the Supreme Court. The Executive Committee may delegate to a special master any or all of its responsibilities and authority with respect to suspending membership for license fee delinquency in which event the special master shall make a report to the Committee of its findings for its approval or disapproval.

After a finding of delinquency, a copy of the finding shall be served upon the Respondent attorney. The Respondent attorney may file with the Court any written exceptions (supported by the written argument) said Respondent may have to the findings of the Executive Committee. All such exceptions shall be filed with the Clerk of the Supreme Court and served on the Executive Committee by service on the General Counsel within twenty (20) days of the date that the findings were served on the Respondent attorney. Upon the filing of exceptions by the Respondent attorney, the Executive Committee shall within twenty (20) days of said filing, file a report of its findings and the complete record and transcript of evidence with the Clerk of the Supreme Court. The Court may grant extensions of time for filing in appropriate cases. Findings of fact by the Executive Committee shall be conclusive if supported by any evidence. The Court may grant oral argument on any exception filed with it upon application for such argument by the Respondent attorney or the Executive Committee. The Court shall promptly consider the report of the Executive Committee, exceptions thereto, and the responses filed by any party to such exceptions, if any, and enter its judgment. A copy of the Court's judgment shall be transmitted to the Executive Committee and to the Respondent attorney by the Court.

Within thirty (30) days after a final judgment which suspends membership, the suspended member shall, under the supervision of the Supreme Court, notify all clients of said suspended member's inability to represent them and of the necessity for promptly retaining new counsel, and shall take all actions necessary to protect the interests of said suspended member's clients. Should the suspended member fail to notify said clients or fail to protect their interests as herein required, the Supreme Court, upon its motion, or upon the motion of the State Bar, and after ten (10) days' notice to the suspended member and proof of failure to notify or protect said clients, may hold the suspended member in contempt and order that a member or members of the State Bar take charge of the files and records of said suspended member and proceed to notify all clients and take such steps as seem indicated to protect their interests. Any member of the State Bar appointed by the Supreme Court to take charge of the files and records of the suspended member under these Rules shall not be permitted to disclose any information contained in the files and records in his or her care without the consent of the client to whom such file or record relates, except as clearly necessary to carry out the order of the court.

(e) Any member terminated solely for license fee delinquency after January 1, 1997 shall be eligible to apply for reinstatement on the same terms and conditions and in the same manner as a member suspended for license fee delinquency may apply for lifting of suspension pursuant to (b) above.

Amended October 3, 1985; amended effective June 6, 1996; amended effective October 26, 2000.

RULE 1-501.1. LICENSE FEES—LATE FEE

Any member who has not paid his or her license fee on or before August 1 shall be penalized in the amount of seventy-five dollars ($75.00). Any member who is delinquent in his or her license fee on or after January 1 of each year shall be penalized in the additional amount of one hundred dollars ($100) for a total of one hundred seventy-five dollars ($175).

Amended November 1, 1988; amended effective June 6, 1996; October 26, 2000.

RULE 1-502. AMOUNT OF LICENSE FEES

The amount of such license fees for active members shall not exceed $250.00, and shall annually be fixed by the Board of Governors for the ensuing year; provided, however, that except in the case of an emergency, such annual dues shall not be increased in any one year by more than $25.00 over those set for the next preceding year. The annual license fees for inactive members shall be in an amount not to exceed one-half (1/2) of those set for active members. Subject to the above limitations, license fees may be fixed in differing amounts for different classifications of active and inactive membership, as may be established in the bylaws.

Amended effective April 16, 1992; November 9, 1995; October 26, 2000.

RULE 1-502.1. FEES FOR ASSOCIATES

The amount of fees for associates as provided in Rule 1-206 shall be fixed by the Board of Governors at an amount less than the amount prescribed for active members pursuant to Rule 1-502, but for such amount as will reasonably cover the cost of the publications furnished; provided, however, law student association fees may be fixed at a nominal level.

Amended effective October 26, 2000.

RULE 1-503. DISBURSEMENTS

The Board of Governors shall have the power to direct the disbursement of funds of the State Bar. No officer named herein and no member of the Board of Governors shall receive any compensation for his or her services except that the Board of Governors may provide for the reimbursement of the actual and necessary expenses incurred by officers in the discharge of their duties.

Amended effective October 26, 2000.

RULE 1-504. BONDS

Every person having the duty or right to receive or disburse the funds of the State Bar shall be required to furnish bond conditioned on his or her faithful performance with such security as the bylaws or the Board of Governors may require.

Amended effective October 26, 2000.

RULE 1-505. AUDIT

The Board of Governors shall annually cause an audit of the financial affairs of the State Bar to be made, and the bylaws shall provide for the communication of the findings thereof to the membership.

Amended effective October 26, 2000.

RULE 1-506. CLIENTS' SECURITY FUND ASSESSMENT

(a) The State Bar is authorized to assess each member of the State Bar a fee of $100.00. This $100.00 fee may be paid in minimum annual installments of $20.00 for a period of five (5) years. Each new member of the State Bar will also be assessed a similar amount upon admission to the State Bar. This fee shall be used only to fund the Clients' Security Fund and shall be in addition to the annual license fee as provided in Rule 1-501 through Rule 1-502.

(b) For a member who joins the State Bar after taking the Georgia Bar Examination, the Clients' Security Fund assessment shall be due and payable in $20.00 installments on July 1 of each year until the balance of $100.00 is paid. The failure of a member to pay the minimum annual installments shall subject the member to the same penalty provisions, including late fees and suspension of membership, as pertain to the failure to pay the annual license fee as set forth in Bar Rules 1-501 and 1-501.1.

(c) For a member who is admitted as a Foreign Law Consultant or who joins without taking the Georgia Bar Examination, and who has not previously paid the Clients' Security Fund Assessment, the full assessment shall be due and payable prior to or upon registration with the State Bar.

Adopted effective May 7, 1992; amended effective October 26, 2000; November 8, 2003.

RULE 1-507. BAR FACILITY ASSESSMENT

(a) The State Bar is authorized to assess each member of the State Bar a fee of $200.00. This $200.00 fee may be paid in minimum annual installments of $50.00 for a period of four (4) years. This fee shall be used to purchase, maintain, and operate a facility for the State Bar offices and shall be in addition to the annual license fee as provided in Rule 1-501 through Rule 1-502 and the Clients' Security Fund Assessment as provided in Rule 1-506.

(b) For a member who joins the State Bar after taking the Georgia Bar Examination, the Bar Facility assessment shall be due and payable in $50.00 installments on July 1 of each year until the balance of $200.00 is paid. For members admitted to the Bar prior to July 1, 1997, such installments shall begin on July 1, 1997. For newly admitted members of the State Bar, such installments shall begin when a new member is admitted to the State Bar. The failure of a member to pay the minimum annual installments shall subject the member to the same penalty provisions, including late fees and suspension of membership, as pertain to the failure to pay the annual license fee as set forth in Bar Rules 1-501 and 1-501.1.

(c) For a member who is admitted as a Foreign Law Consultant or who joins the State Bar without taking the Georgia Bar Examination, and who has not previously paid the Bar Facility Assessment, the full assessment shall be due and payable prior to or upon registration with the State Bar.

Adopted effective October 26, 2000; amended effective November 8, 2003.

CHAPTER 6. BYLAWS

RULE 1-601. ADOPTION AND AMENDMENT

The State Bar of Georgia, at its first annual meeting shall adopt bylaws as directed herein, and at such meeting and any subsequent annual, annual midyear, or special meeting may adopt such other bylaws not inconsistent herewith as it may deem necessary and proper and may amend its bylaws from time to time.

RULE 1-602. PROPOSED BYLAWS AND AMENDMENTS

Bylaws and amendments thereto may be proposed by the Board of Governors or any ten members of the State Bar of Georgia by giving notice to the Secretary at least sixty days before the next annual meeting or annual midyear meeting. Written notice of such proposed bylaws and amendments shall be mailed to each member at least thirty days prior to the next annual meeting or annual midyear meeting and may be adopted by a majority of the members present and voting. The proposed bylaws and any amendments may be amended from the floor in any respect germane to the subject matter thereof. The notice by mail herein required may be by or through any one or more of the official publications of the State Bar of Georgia.

CHAPTER 7. COMMITTEES AND SECTIONS

RULE 1-701. EXECUTIVE COMMITTEE

There shall be an Executive Committee composed of such officers and members of the Board of Governors as may be designated in the bylaws, which shall exercise the powers and duties of the Board of Governors when it is not in session, subject to such limitations as the bylaws may provide. The Executive Committee shall also have the authority to supervise the election of the members of the Board of Governors as outlined in Rule 1-304 hereof, and, in particular, to ascertain on or after the first day of January of each year, the number of active members of the State Bar of Georgia who reside in each judicial circuit as of the last day of December of the preceding year; and thereupon to make a determination of whether any judicial circuit may be entitled to additional members of the Board of Governors as provided in Rule 1-302(b) hereof. In addition, whenever a new judicial circuit is created, the Executive Committee shall determine, under the provisions of Rule 1-302(b) and the bylaws, the number of members of the Board of Governors the new circuit is entitled to elect and shall supervise the elections of such members. In the event that the composition of the Board of Governors must be changed, as a result of an increase or decrease in the number of active members of the State Bar of Georgia who reside in each judicial circuit, as a result of the creation of a new judicial circuit, or as a result of a change in the geographical limits of a judicial circuit, the Executive Committee is empowered to take appropriate action to insure that the composition of the Board complies with the provisions of Rule 1-302(b), including but not limited to the implementing of the election of additional members and the designation of numerical posts. The Executive Committee shall generally have broad discretionary powers in the conduct of elections.

RULE 1-702. STANDING COMMITTEES; SPECIAL COMMITTEES

Unless otherwise provided in these Rules, there shall be standing and special committees, which shall be composed of such members, serving such terms, appointed in such manner, and having such duties as the bylaws may provide. A statement of the purpose of each committee shall be published annually in the State Bar Directory.

Amended effective December 8, 1994; June 6, 1996; July 1, 1997.

RULE 1-703. YOUNG LAWYERS DIVISION

There shall be a division of the State Bar composed of (1) all members of the State Bar who have not reached their thirty-sixth birthday prior to the close of the preceding Annual Meeting of the State Bar and (2) all members of the State Bar who have been admitted to their first bar less than three years. All persons holding an elective office or post in the Young Lawyers Division who are qualified by age to assume such office or post on the date of his or her election shall remain members of the Young Lawyers Division for the duration of their offices or posts. In the case of a President-elect of the Young Lawyers Division who is qualified by age to assume such office on the date of such person's election, such person shall remain a member of the Young Lawyers Division for the duration of the terms of President and Immediate Past President to which he or she succeeds.

The Young Lawyers Division shall have such organization, powers, and duties as may be prescribed by the Bylaws of the State Bar.

Amended effective December 8, 1994; May 28, 1998.

RULE 1-704. OTHER SECTIONS

Such additional sections may be created by the bylaws as may be deemed desirable.

RULE 1-705. SENIOR LAWYERS SECTION

There shall be a section of the State Bar composed from time to time of all members of the State Bar who have reached their 65th birthday prior to the close of the preceding Annual Meeting of the State Bar provided, however, that all those members of the State Bar who are between 60 and 65 years of age and are members in good standing of the Senior Section (sometimes called the Senior Law Section) at the time this amendment is adopted shall become members of the Senior Lawyers Section.

The Senior Lawyers Section shall have such organization, powers and duties as may be prescribed by the Bylaws of the State Bar.

Adopted effective August 18, 1994.

RULE 1-706. [RENUMBERED]

CHAPTER 8. MEETINGS

RULE 1-801. ANNUAL MEETING

An annual meeting of the State Bar of Georgia shall be held each year at such time and place as may be designated by the Board of Governors.

RULE 1-801.1. ANNUAL MIDYEAR MEETING

An annual midyear meeting of the State Bar of Georgia may be held each year at such time and place as may be designated by the Board of Governors.

RULE 1-802. SPECIAL MEETINGS

Special meetings of the State Bar of Georgia may be held at such times and places as may be determined by the Board of Governors. The Secretary shall call a special meeting of the State Bar of Georgia upon petition signed by not less than ten percent of the active members and such special meetings shall be held within sixty days after the petition is filed with the Secretary. The business to be transacted at special meetings shall be specified in the call.

RULE 1-803. NOTICE

At least thirty days notice of the time and place of each annual meeting, annual midyear meeting and any special meeting shall be given in writing by mail to each member at his address shown on the records of the State Bar of Georgia. The notice by mail herein required may be by or through any one or more of the official publications of the State Bar of Georgia.

PART II. ADMISSION TO THE BAR

CHAPTER 1. ADMISSION TO THE BAR

RULE 2-101. ADMISSION TO THE BAR

No person may be admitted to the State Bar as an active, emeritus or inactive member, or licensed as an attorney to practice law in this State without complying with the Rules Governing Admission to the Practice of Law as adopted by the Supreme Court of Georgia.

Amended October 21, 1987; amended effective April 16, 1992; November 8, 2003.

PART III. [RESERVED]

Deleted and reserved effective January 1, 2001.

PART IV. GEORGIA RULES OF PROFESSIONAL CONDUCT

CHAPTER 1. GEORGIA RULES OF PROFESSIONAL CONDUCT AND ENFORCEMENT THEREOF

RULE 4-101. ENFORCEMENT OF PROFESSIONAL STANDARDS

The State Bar of Georgia is hereby authorized to maintain and enforce, as set forth in rules hereinafter stated, Georgia Rules of Professional Conduct to be observed by the members of the State Bar of Georgia and those authorized to practice law in the State of Georgia and to institute disciplinary action in the event of the violation thereof.

Adopted effective January 1, 2001.

RULE 4-102. DISCIPLINARY ACTION; LEVELS OF DISCIPLINE; STANDARDS

(a) The Rules of Professional Conduct to be observed by the members of the State Bar of Georgia and those authorized to practice law in Georgia are set forth herein and any violation thereof; any assistance or inducement directed toward another for the purpose of producing a violation thereof; or any violation thereof through the acts of another, shall subject the offender to disciplinary action as hereinafter provided.

(b) The levels of discipline are set forth below. The power to administer a more severe level of discipline shall include the power to administer the lesser:

(1) *Disbarment*: A form of public discipline removing the respondent from the practice of law in Georgia. This level of discipline would be appropriate in cases of serious misconduct. This level of discipline includes publication as provided by Rule 4–219(b).

(2) *Suspension*: A form of public discipline which removes the respondent from the practice of law in Georgia for a definite period of time or until satisfaction of certain conditions imposed as a part of the suspension. This level of discipline would be appropriate in cases that merit more than a public reprimand but less than disbarment. This level of discipline includes publication as provided by Rule 4–219(b).

(3) *Public Reprimand*: A form of public discipline which declares the respondent's conduct to have been improper but does not limit the right to practice. A public reprimand shall be administered by a judge of a superior court in open court. This level of discipline would be appropriate in cases that merit more than a review panel reprimand but less than suspension.

(4) *Review Panel Reprimand*: A form of public discipline which declares the respondent's conduct to have been improper but does not limit the right to practice. A Review Panel Reprimand shall be administered by the Review Panel at a meeting of the Review Panel. This level of discipline would be appropriate in cases that merit more than an investigative panel reprimand but less than a public reprimand.

(5) *Investigative Panel Reprimand*: A form of confidential discipline which declares the respondent's conduct to have been improper but does not limit the right to practice. An Investigative Panel Reprimand shall be administered by the Investigative Panel at a meeting of the Investigative Panel. This level of discipline would be appropriate in cases that merit more than a formal admonition but less than a review panel reprimand.

(6) *Formal Admonition*: A form of confidential discipline which declares the respondent's conduct to have been improper but does not limit the right to practice. A formal admonition shall be administered by letter as provided in Rules 4–205 through 4–208. This level of discipline would be appropriate in cases that merit the lowest form of discipline.

(c)(1) The Supreme Court of Georgia may impose any of the levels of discipline set forth above following formal proceedings against a respondent; however, any case where discipline is imposed by the Court is a matter of public record despite the fact that the level of discipline would have been confidential if imposed by the Investigative Panel of the State Disciplinary Board.

(2) As provided in Part IV, Chapter 2 of the State Bar Rules, the Investigative Panel of the State Disciplinary Board may impose any of the levels of discipline set forth above provided that a respondent shall have the right to reject the imposition of discipline by the Investigative Panel pursuant to the provisions of Rule 4–208.3;

(d) The Table of Contents, Preamble, Scope, Terminology and Georgia Rules of Professional Conduct are as follows:

CONTENTS

PREAMBLE, SCOPE AND TERMINOLOGY

PREAMBLE: A LAWYER'S RESPONSIBILITIES

[1] A lawyer is a representative of clients, an officer of the legal system and a citizen having special responsibility for the quality of justice.

[2] As a representative of clients, a lawyer performs various functions. As advisor, a lawyer provides a client with an informed understanding of the client's legal rights and obligations and explains their practical implications. As advocate, a lawyer zealously asserts the client's position under the rules of the adversary system. As negotiator, a lawyer seeks a result advantageous to the client but consistent with requirements of honest dealing with others. As intermediary between clients, a lawyer seeks to reconcile their divergent interests as an advisor and, to a limited extent, as a spokesperson for each client. A lawyer acts as evaluator by examining a client's legal affairs and reporting about them to the client or to others.

[3] In all professional functions a lawyer should be competent, prompt and diligent. A lawyer should maintain communication with a client concerning the representation. A lawyer should keep in confidence information relating to representation of a client except so far as disclosure is required or permitted by these Rules or other law.

[4] A lawyer should use the law's procedures only for legitimate purposes and not to harass or intimidate others. A lawyer should demonstrate respect for the law, the legal system and for those who serve it, including judges, other lawyers and public officials. While it is a lawyer's duty, when necessary, to challenge the rectitude of official action, it is also a lawyer's duty to uphold legal process.

[5] As a citizen, a lawyer should seek improvement of the law, the administration of justice and the quality of service rendered by the legal profession. As a member of a learned profession, a lawyer should cultivate knowledge of the law beyond its use for clients, employ that knowledge in reform of the law and work to strengthen legal education. A lawyer should be mindful of deficiencies in the administration of justice and of the fact that the poor, and sometimes persons who are not poor, cannot afford adequate legal assistance, and should therefore devote professional time and civic influence in their behalf. A lawyer should aid the legal profession in pursuing these objectives and should help the bar regulate itself in the public interest.

[6] A lawyer's professional responsibilities are prescribed in the Rules of Professional Conduct, as well as by substantive and procedural law. A lawyer also is guided by conscience and the approbation of professional peers. A lawyer should strive to attain the highest level of skill, to improve the law and the legal profession and to exemplify the legal profession's ideals of public service.

[7] Reserved.

[8] In the nature of law practice conflicting responsibilities are encountered. Virtually all difficult ethical problems arise from conflict among a lawyer's responsibilities to clients, to the legal system and to the lawyer's own interest in remaining an upright person. The Rules of Professional Conduct prescribe terms for resolving such conflicts. Within the framework of these Rules, many difficult issues of professional discretion can arise. Such issues must be resolved through the exercise of sensitive professional and moral judgment guided by the basic principles underlying the Rules.

[9] The legal profession is largely self-governing. Although other professions also have been granted powers of self-government, the legal profession is unique in this respect because of the close relationship between the profession and the processes of government and law enforcement. This connection is manifested in the fact that ultimate authority over the legal profession is vested in the Supreme Court of Georgia.

[10] To the extent that lawyers meet the obligations of their professional calling, the occasion for government regulation is obviated. Self-regulation also helps maintain the legal profession's independence from government domination. An independent legal profession is an important force in preserving government under law, for abuse of legal authority is more readily challenged by a profession whose members are not dependent on government for the right to practice.

[11] The legal profession's relative autonomy carries with it special responsibilities of self-government. The profession has a responsibility to assure that its regulations are conceived in the public interest and not in furtherance of parochial or self-interested concerns of the bar. Every lawyer is responsible for observance of the Rules of Professional Conduct. A lawyer should also aid in securing their observance by other lawyers. Neglect of these responsibilities compromises the independence of the profession and the public interest which it serves.

[12] The fulfillment of a lawyer's professional responsibility role requires an understanding by them of their relationship to our legal system. The Rules of Professional Conduct, when properly applied, serve to define that relationship.

SCOPE

[13] The Rules of Professional Conduct are rules of reason. They should be interpreted with reference to the purposes of legal representation and of the law itself. Some of the Rules are imperatives, cast in the terms "shall" or "shall not." These define proper conduct for purposes of professional discipline. Others, generally cast in the terms "may" or "should," are permissive or aspirational and define areas under the Rules in which the lawyer has professional discretion. Disciplinary action shall not be taken when the lawyer's conduct falls within the bounds of such discretion. The Rules are thus partly obligatory and disciplinary and partly aspirational and descriptive. Together they define a lawyer's professional role. Comments do not add obligations to or expand the Rules but provide guidance for practicing in compliance with the Rules.

[14] The Rules presuppose a larger legal context shaping the lawyer's role. That context includes court

rules and statutes relating to matters of licensure, laws defining specific obligations of lawyers and substantive and procedural law in general. Compliance with the Rules, as with all law in an open society, depends primarily upon understanding and voluntary compliance, secondarily upon reinforcement by peer and public opinion and finally, when necessary, upon enforcement through disciplinary proceedings. The Rules do not, however, exhaust the moral and ethical considerations that should inform a lawyer, for no worthwhile human activity can be completely defined by legal rules. The Rules simply provide a framework for the ethical practice of law.

[15] Furthermore, for purposes of determining the lawyer's authority and responsibility, principles of substantive law external to these Rules determine whether a client-lawyer relationship exists. Most of the duties flowing from the client-lawyer relationship attach only after the client has requested the lawyer to render legal services and the lawyer has agreed to do so. But there are some duties, such as that of confidentiality under *Rule 1.6: Confidentiality of Information*, that may attach when the lawyer agrees to consider whether a client-lawyer relationship will be established. Whether a client-lawyer relationship exists for any specific purpose depends on the circumstances and may be a question of fact.

[16] Under various legal provisions, including constitutional, statutory and common law, the responsibilities of government lawyers may include authority concerning legal matters that ordinarily reposes in the client in private client-lawyer relationships. For example, a lawyer for a government entity may have authority on behalf of the government to decide upon settlement or whether to appeal from an adverse judgment. Such authority in various respects is generally vested in the attorney general and the state's attorney in state government, and their federal counterparts, and the same may be true of other government law officers. Also, lawyers under the supervision of these officers may be authorized by law to represent several government entities in intergovernmental legal controversies in circumstances where a private lawyer could not represent multiple private clients. They also may have authority to represent the "public interest" in circumstances where a private lawyer would not be authorized to do so. These Rules do not abrogate any such authority.

[17] Failure to comply with an obligation or prohibition imposed by a Rule is a basis for invoking the disciplinary process. The Rules presuppose that disciplinary assessment of a lawyer's conduct will be made on the basis of the facts and circumstances as they existed at the time of the conduct in question and in recognition of the fact that a lawyer often has to act upon uncertain or incomplete evidence of the situation. Moreover, the Rules presuppose that whether or not discipline should be imposed for a violation, and the severity of a sanction, depend on all the circumstances, such as the willfulness and seriousness of the violation, extenuating factors and whether there have been previous violations.

[18] The purpose of these Rules is not to give rise to a cause of action nor to create a presumption that a legal duty has been breached. These Rules are designed to provide guidance to lawyers and to provide a structure for regulating conduct through disciplinary agencies. They are not designed to be a basis for civil liability. Furthermore, the purpose of the Rules can be subverted when they are invoked by opposing parties as procedural weapons. The fact that a Rule is a just basis for a lawyer's self-assessment, or for sanctioning a lawyer under the administration of a disciplinary authority, does not imply that an antagonist in a collateral proceeding or transaction has standing to seek enforcement of the Rule. Accordingly, nothing in the Rules should be deemed to augment any substantive legal duty of lawyers or the extra-disciplinary consequences of violating such a duty.

[19] Moreover, these Rules are not intended to govern or affect judicial application of either the attorney-client or work product privilege. In reliance on the attorney-client privilege, clients are entitled to expect that communications within the scope of the privilege will be protected against compelled disclosure. The attorney-client privilege is that of the client and not of the lawyer. The fact that in exceptional situations the lawyer under the rules has a limited discretion to disclose a client confidence does not vitiate the proposition that, as a general matter, the client has a reasonable expectation that information relating to the client will not be voluntarily disclosed and that disclosure of such information may be judicially compelled only in accordance with recognized exceptions to the attorney-client and work product privileges.

[20] Reserved.

[21] The Comment accompanying each Rule explains and illustrates the meaning and purpose of the Rule. The Preamble and this note on Scope provide general orientation. The Comments are intended as guides to interpretation, but the text of each Rule is authoritative.

TERMINOLOGY

"Belief" or "believes" denotes that the person involved actually thought the fact in question to be true. A person's belief may be inferred from circumstances.

"Consult" or "consultation" denotes communication of information reasonably sufficient to permit the client to appreciate the significance of the matter in question.

"Domestic Lawyer" denotes a person authorized to practice law by the duly constituted and authorized governmental body of any State or Territory of the United States or the District of Columbia but not authorized by the Supreme Court of Georgia or its rules to practice law in the State of Georgia.

"Firm" or "law firm" denotes a lawyer or lawyers in a private firm, lawyers employed in the legal department of a corporation or other organization and lawyers employed in a legal services organization. See Comment, *Rule 1.10: Imputed Disqualification.*

"Foreign Lawyer" denotes a person authorized to practice law by the duly constituted and authorized governmental body of any foreign nation but not authorized by the Supreme Court of Georgia or its Rules to practice law in the State of Georgia.

"Fraud" or "fraudulent" denotes conduct having a purpose to deceive and not merely negligent misrepresentation or failure to apprise another of relevant information.

"Knowingly," "known," or "knows" denotes actual knowledge of the fact in question. A person's knowledge may be inferred from circumstances.

"Lawyer," denotes a person authorized by the Supreme Court of Georgia or its Rules to practice law in the State of Georgia including persons admitted to practice in this state pro hac vice.

"Nonlawyer" denotes a person not authorized to practice law by either the:

(a) Supreme Court of Georgia or its Rules (including pro hac vice admission), or

(b) duly constituted and authorized governmental body of any other State or Territory of the United States, or the District of Columbia, or

(c) duly constituted and authorized governmental body of any foreign nation.

"Partner" denotes a member of a partnership and a shareholder in a law firm organized as a professional corporation.

"Reasonable" or "reasonably" when used in relation to conduct by a lawyer denotes the conduct of a reasonably prudent and competent lawyer.

"Reasonable belief" or "reasonably believes" when used in reference to a lawyer denotes that the lawyer believes the matter in question and that the circumstances are such that the belief is reasonable.

"Reasonably should know" when used in reference to a lawyer denotes that a lawyer of reasonable prudence and competence would ascertain the matter in question.

"Substantial" when used in reference to degree or extent denotes a material matter of clear and weighty importance, or may refer to things of more than trifling value.

"Tribunal" denotes a court, an arbitrator in an arbitration proceeding or a legislative body, administrative agency or other body acting in an adjudicative capacity. A legislative body, administrative agency or other body acts in an adjudicative capacity when a neutral official, after the presentation of evidence or legal argument by a party or parties, will render a legal judgment directly affecting a party's interests in a particular matter.

Amended effective June 8, 2004.

PART ONE. CLIENT-LAWYER RELATIONSHIP

RULE 1.1 COMPETENCE

A lawyer shall provide competent representation to a client. Competent representation as used in this Rule means that a lawyer shall not handle a matter which the lawyer knows or should know to be beyond the lawyer's level of competence without associating another lawyer who the original lawyer reasonably believes to be competent to handle the matter in question. Competence requires the legal knowledge, skill, thoroughness and preparation reasonably necessary for the representation.

The maximum penalty for a violation of this Rule is disbarment.

Comment

Legal Knowledge and Skill

[1A] The purpose of these rules is not to give rise to a cause of action nor to create a presumption that a legal duty has been breached. These Rules are designed to provide guidance to lawyers and to provide a structure for regulating conduct through disciplinary agencies. They are not designed to be a basis for civil liability.

[1B] In determining whether a lawyer employs the requisite knowledge and skill in a particular matter, relevant factors include the relative complexity and specialized nature of the matter, the lawyer's general experience, the lawyer's training and experience in the field in question, the preparation and study the lawyer is able to give the matter and whether it is feasible to refer the matter to, or associate or consult with, a lawyer of established competence in the field in question. In many instances, the required proficiency is that of a general practitioner. Expertise in a particular field of law may be required in some circumstances.

[2] A lawyer need not necessarily have special training or prior experience to handle legal problems of a type with which the lawyer is unfamiliar. A newly admitted lawyer can be as competent as a practitioner with long experience. Some important legal skills, such as the analysis of precedent, the evaluation of evidence and legal drafting, are required in all legal problems. Perhaps the most fundamental legal skill consists of determining what kind of legal problems a situation may involve, a skill that necessarily transcends any particular specialized knowledge. A lawyer can provide adequate representation in a wholly novel field through necessary study. Competent representation can also be provided through the association of a lawyer of established competence in the field in question.

[3] In an emergency a lawyer may give advice or assistance in a matter in which the lawyer does not have the skill ordinarily required where referral to or consultation or association with another lawyer would be impractical. Even in an emergency, however, assistance should be limited to that reasonably necessary in the circumstances, for ill-considered action under emergency conditions can jeopardize the client's interest.

[4] A lawyer may accept representation where the requisite level of competence can be achieved by reasonable preparation. This applies as well to a lawyer who is appointed as counsel for an unrepresented person subject to *Rule 6.2: Accepting Appointments.*

Thoroughness and Preparation

[5] Competent handling of a particular matter includes inquiry into and analysis of the factual and legal elements of the problem, and use of methods and procedures meeting the standards of competent practitioners. It also includes adequate preparation. The required attention and preparation are determined in part by what is at stake; major litigation and complex transactions ordinarily require more elaborate treatment than matters of lesser consequence.

Maintaining Competence

[6] To maintain the requisite knowledge and skill, a lawyer should engage in continuing study and education.

RULE 1.2 SCOPE OF REPRESENTATION

(a) A lawyer shall abide by a client's decisions concerning the objectives of representation, subject to paragraphs (c), (d) and (e), and shall consult with the client as to the means by which they are to be pursued. A lawyer shall abide by a client's decision whether to accept an offer of settlement of a matter. In a criminal case, the lawyer shall abide by the client's decision, after consultation with the lawyer, as to a plea to be entered, whether to waive jury trial and whether the client will testify.

(b) A lawyer's representation of a client, including representation by appointment, does not constitute an endorsement of the client's political, economic, social or moral views or activities.

(c) A lawyer may limit the objectives of the representation if the client consents after consultation.

(d) A lawyer shall not counsel a client to engage in conduct that the lawyer knows is criminal or fraudulent, nor knowingly assist a client in such conduct, but a lawyer may discuss the legal consequences of any proposed course of conduct with a client and may counsel or assist a client to make a good faith effort to determine the validity, scope, meaning or application of the law.

(e) When a lawyer knows that a client expects assistance not permitted by the rules of professional conduct or other law, the lawyer shall consult with the client regarding the relevant limitations on the lawyer's conduct.

The maximum penalty for a violation of this Rule is disbarment.

Comment

Scope of Representation

[1] Both lawyer and client have authority and responsibility in the objectives and means of representation. The client has ultimate authority to determine the purposes to be served by legal representation, within the limits imposed by law and the lawyer's professional obligations. Within those limits, a client also has a right to consult with the lawyer about the means to be used in pursuing those objectives. At the same time, a lawyer is not required to pursue objectives or employ means simply because a client may wish that the lawyer do so. A clear distinction between objectives and means sometimes cannot be drawn, and in many cases the client-lawyer relationship partakes of a joint undertaking. In questions of means, the lawyer should assume responsibility for technical and legal tactical issues, but should defer to the client regarding such questions as the expense to be incurred and concern for third persons who might be adversely affected.

[2] In a case in which the client appears to be suffering mental disability, the lawyer's duty to abide by the client's decisions is to be guided by reference to *Rule 1.14: Client under a Disability.*

Independence from Client's Views or Activities

[3] Legal representation should not be denied to people who are unable to afford legal services, or whose cause is controversial or the subject of popular disapproval. By the same token, representing a client does not constitute approval of the client's views or activities.

Services Limited in Objectives or Means

[4] The objectives or scope of services provided by a lawyer may be limited by agreement with the client or by the terms under which the lawyer's services are made available to the client. For example, a retainer may be for a specifically defined purpose. Representation provided through a legal aid agency may be subject to limitations on the types of cases the agency handles. When a lawyer has been retained by an insurer to represent an insured, the representation may be limited to matters covered by the insurance policy. The terms upon which representation is undertaken may exclude specific objectives or means. Such limitations may include objectives or means that the lawyer regards as repugnant or imprudent.

[5] An agreement concerning the scope of representation must accord with the Rules of Professional Conduct and other law. Thus, the client may not be asked to agree to representation so limited in scope as to violate *Rule 1.1: Competence,* or to surrender the right to terminate the lawyer's services or the right to settle litigation that the lawyer might wish to continue. The agreement should be in writing.

Criminal, Fraudulent and Prohibited Transactions

[6] A lawyer is required to give an honest opinion about the actual consequences that appear likely to result from a client's conduct. The fact that a client uses advice in a course of action that is criminal or fraudulent does not, of itself, make a lawyer a party to the course of action. However, a lawyer may not knowingly assist a client in criminal or fraudulent conduct. There is a critical distinction between presenting an analysis of legal aspects of questionable conduct and recommending the means by which a crime or fraud might be committed with impunity.

[7] When the client's course of action has already begun and is continuing, the lawyer's responsibility is especially delicate. The lawyer is not permitted to reveal the client's wrongdoing, except where permitted by *Rule 1.6: Confidentiality of Information.* However, the lawyer is required to avoid furthering the purpose, for example, by suggesting how it might be concealed. A lawyer may not continue assisting a client in conduct that the lawyer originally supposes is legally proper but then discovers is criminal or fraudulent. Withdrawal from the representation, therefore, may be required.

[8] Where the client is a fiduciary, the lawyer may be charged with special obligations in dealings with a beneficiary.

[9] Paragraph (d) applies whether or not the defrauded party is a party to the transaction. Hence, a lawyer should not participate in a sham transaction; for example, a transaction to effectuate criminal or fraudulent escape of tax liability. Paragraph (d) does not preclude undertaking a criminal defense incident to a general retainer for legal services to a lawful enterprise. The last clause of paragraph (d) recognizes that determining the validity or interpretation of a statute or regulation may require a course of action involving disobedience of the statute or regulation or of the interpretation placed upon it by governmental authorities.

[10] Law defining the lawyer's scope of authority in litigation as well as the language of particular rules varies among jurisdictions. A lawyer should be mindful of the nuances and differences of the law and rules of each location in which he or she practices.

RULE 1.3 DILIGENCE

A lawyer shall act with reasonable diligence and promptness in representing a client. Reasonable diligence as used in this Rule means that a lawyer shall not without just cause to the detriment of the client in effect willfully abandon or willfully disregard a legal matter entrusted to the lawyer.

The maximum penalty for a violation of this Rule is disbarment.

Comment

[1] A lawyer should pursue a matter on behalf of a client despite opposition, obstruction or personal inconvenience to the lawyer, and may take whatever lawful and ethical measures are required to vindicate a client's cause or endeavor. A lawyer should act with commitment and dedication to the interests of the client and with zeal in advocacy upon the client's behalf. However, a lawyer is not bound to press for every advantage that might be realized for a client. A lawyer has professional discretion in determining the means by which a matter should be pursued. See *Rule 1.2: Scope of Representation.* A lawyer's work load should be controlled so that each matter can be handled adequately.

[2] Perhaps no professional shortcoming is more widely resented than procrastination. A client's interests often can be adversely affected by the passage of time or the change of conditions; in extreme instances, as when a lawyer overlooks a statute of limitations, the client's legal position may be destroyed. Even when the client's interests are not affected in substance, however, unreasonable delay can cause a client needless anxiety and undermine confidence in the lawyer's trustworthiness.

[3] Unless the relationship is terminated as provided in *Rule 1.16: Declining or Terminating Representation*, a lawyer should carry through to conclusion all matters undertaken for a client. If a lawyer's employment is limited to a specific matter, the relationship terminates when the matter has been resolved. If a lawyer has served a client over a substantial period in a variety of matters, the client sometimes may assume that the lawyer will serve on a continuing basis. Doubt about whether a client-lawyer relationship still exists should be clarified by the lawyer, preferably in writing, so that the client will not mistakenly suppose the lawyer is looking after the client's affairs when the lawyer has ceased to do so. For example, if a lawyer has handled a judicial or administrative proceeding that produced a result adverse to the client but has not been specifically instructed concerning pursuit of an appeal, the lawyer should advise the client of the possibility of appeal before relinquishing responsibility for the matter.

RULE 1.4 COMMUNICATION

A lawyer shall explain a matter to the extent reasonably necessary to permit the client to make informed decisions regarding the representation, shall keep the client reasonably informed about the status of matters and shall promptly comply with reasonable requests for information.

The maximum penalty for a violation of this Rule is a public reprimand.

Comment

[1A] The client should have sufficient information to participate intelligently in decisions concerning the objectives of the representation and the means by which they are to be pursued, to the extent the client is willing and able to do so. For example, a lawyer negotiating on behalf of a client should provide the client with facts relevant to the matter, inform the client of communications from another party and take other reasonable steps that permit the client to make a decision regarding a serious offer from another party. A lawyer who receives from opposing counsel an offer of settlement in a civil controversy or a proffered plea bargain in a criminal case should promptly inform the client of its substance unless prior discussions with the client have left it clear that the proposal will be unacceptable. See *Rule 1.2(a): Scope of Representation.* Even when a client delegates authority to the lawyer, the client should be kept advised of the status of the matter.

[1B] The timeliness of a lawyer's communication must be judged by all of the controlling factors. "Prompt" communication with the client does not equate to "instant" communication with the client and is sufficient if reasonable under the relevant circumstances.

[2] Adequacy of communication depends in part on the kind of advice or assistance involved. For example, in negotiations where there is time to explain a proposal, the lawyer should review all important provisions with the client before proceeding to an agreement. In litigation a lawyer should explain the general strategy and prospects of success and ordinarily should consult the client on tactics that might injure or coerce others. On the other hand, a lawyer ordinarily cannot be expected to describe trial or negotiation strategy in detail. The guiding principle is that the lawyer should fulfill reasonable client expectations for information consistent with the duty to act in the client's best interests,

and the client's overall requirements as to the character of representation.

[3] Ordinarily, the information to be provided is that which is appropriate for a client who is a comprehending and responsible adult. However, fully informing the client according to this standard may be impracticable, for example, where the client is a child or suffers from mental disability. See *Rule 1.14: Client under a Disability.* When the client is an organization or group, it is often impossible or inappropriate to inform every one of its members about its legal affairs; ordinarily, the lawyer should address communications to the appropriate officials of the organization. See *Rule 1.13: Organization as Client.* Where many routine matters are involved, a system of limited or occasional reporting may be arranged with the client. Practical exigency may also require a lawyer to act for a client without prior consultation.

Withholding Information

[4] In some circumstances, a lawyer may be justified in delaying transmission of information when the client would be likely to react imprudently to an immediate communication. Thus, a lawyer might withhold a psychiatric diagnosis of a client when the examining psychiatrist indicates that disclosure would harm the client. A lawyer may not withhold information to serve the lawyer's own interest or convenience. Rules or court orders governing litigation may provide that information supplied to a lawyer may not be disclosed to the client. *Rule 3.4(c): Fairness to Opposing Party and Counsel* directs compliance with such rules or orders.

RULE 1.5 FEES

(a) A lawyer's fee shall be reasonable. The factors to be considered in determining the reasonableness of a fee include the following:

(1) the time and labor required, the novelty and difficulty of the questions involved, and the skill requisite to perform the legal service properly;

(2) the likelihood that the acceptance of the particular employment will preclude other employment by the lawyer;

(3) the fee customarily charged in the locality for similar legal services;

(4) the amount involved and the results obtained;

(5) the time limitations imposed by the client or by the circumstances;

(6) the nature and length of the professional relationship with the client;

(7) the experience, reputation, and ability of the lawyer or lawyers performing the services; and

(8) whether the fee is fixed or contingent.

(b) When the lawyer has not regularly represented the client, the basis or rate of the fee shall be communicated to the client, preferably in writing, before or within a reasonable time after commencing the representation.

(c)(1) A fee may be contingent on the outcome of the matter for which the service is rendered, except in a matter in which a contingent fee is prohibited by paragraph (d) or other law. A contingent fee agreement shall be in writing and shall state the method by which the fee is to be determined, including the percentage or percentages that shall accrue to the lawyer in the event of settlement, trial or appeal, litigation and other expenses to be deducted from the recovery, and whether such expenses are to be deducted before or after the contingent fee is calculated.

(2) Upon conclusion of a contingent fee matter, the lawyer shall provide the client with a written statement stating the following:

(i) the outcome of the matter; and,

(ii) if there is a recovery, showing the:

(A) remittance to the client;

(B) the method of its determination;

(C) the amount of the attorney fee; and

(D) if the attorney's fee is divided with another lawyer who is not a partner in or an associate of the lawyer's firm or law office, the amount of fee received by each and the manner in which the division is determined.

(d) A lawyer shall not enter into an arrangement for, charge, or collect:

(1) any fee in a domestic relations matter, the payment or amount of which is contingent upon the securing of a divorce or upon the amount of alimony or support, or property settlement in lieu thereof; or

(2) a contingent fee for representing a defendant in a criminal case.

(e) A division of a fee between lawyers who are not in the same firm may be made only if:

(1) the division is in proportion to the services performed by each lawyer or, by written agreement with the client, each lawyer assumes joint responsibility for the representation;

(2) the client is advised of the share that each lawyer is to receive and does not object to the participation of all the lawyers involved; and

(3) the total fee is reasonable.

The maximum penalty for a violation of this Rule is a public reprimand.

Comment

Basis or Rate of Fee

[1] When the lawyer has regularly represented a client, they ordinarily will have evolved an understanding concerning the basis or rate of the fee. In a new client-lawyer relationship, however, an understanding as to the fee should be promptly established. It is not necessary to recite all the factors that underlie the basis of the fee but only those that are directly involved in its computation. It is sufficient, for example, to state that the basic rate is an hourly charge or a fixed amount or an estimated amount, or to identify the factors that may be taken into account in finally fixing the fee. When developments occur during the representation

that render an earlier estimate substantially inaccurate, a revised estimate should be provided to the client. A written statement concerning the fee reduces the possibility of misunderstanding. Furnishing the client with a simple memorandum or a copy of the lawyer's customary fee schedule is sufficient if the basis or rate of the fee is set forth.

Terms of Payment

[2] A lawyer may require advance payment of a fee, but is obliged to return any unearned portion. See *Rule 1.16(d): Declining or Terminating Representation.* A lawyer may accept property in payment for services, such as an ownership interest in an enterprise, providing this does not involve acquisition of a proprietary interest in the cause of action or subject matter of the litigation contrary to *Rule 1.8(j): Conflict of Interest.* However, a fee paid in property instead of money may be subject to special scrutiny because it involves questions concerning both the value of the services and the lawyer's special knowledge of the value of the property.

[3] An agreement may not be made, the terms of which might induce the lawyer improperly to curtail services for the client or perform them in a way contrary to the client's interest. For example, a lawyer should not enter into an agreement whereby services are to be provided only up to a stated amount when it is foreseeable that more extensive services probably will be required, unless the situation is adequately explained to the client. Otherwise, the client might have to bargain for further assistance in the midst of a proceeding or transaction. However, it is proper to define the extent of services in light of the client's ability to pay. A lawyer should not exploit a fee arrangement based primarily on hourly charges by using wasteful procedures.

Division of Fee

[4] A division of fee is a single billing to a client covering the fee of two or more lawyers who are not in the same firm. A division of fee facilitates association of more than one lawyer in a matter in which neither alone could serve the client as well. Joint responsibility for the representation entails the obligations stated in *Rule 5.1: Responsibilities of a Partner or Supervisory Lawyer* for purposes of the matter involved.

Disputes over Fees

[5] If a procedure has been established for resolution of fee disputes, such as an arbitration or mediation procedure established by the bar, the lawyer should conscientiously consider submitting to it. Law may prescribe a procedure for determining a lawyer's fee, for example, in representation of an executor or administrator, a class or a person entitled to a reasonable fee as part of the measure of damages. The lawyer entitled to such a fee and a lawyer representing another party concerned with the fee should comply with the prescribed procedure.

RULE 1.6 CONFIDENTIALITY OF INFORMATION

(a) A lawyer shall maintain in confidence all information gained in the professional relationship with a client, including information which the client has requested to be held inviolate or the disclosure of which would be embarrassing or would likely be detrimental to the client, unless the client consents after consultation, except for disclosures that are impliedly authorized in order to carry out the representation, or are required by these rules or other law, or by order of the Court.

(b)(1) A lawyer may reveal information covered by paragraph (a) which the lawyer reasonably believes necessary:

(i) to avoid or prevent harm or substantial financial loss to another as a result of client criminal conduct or third party criminal conduct clearly in violation of the law;

(ii) to prevent serious injury or death not otherwise covered by subparagraph (i) above;

(iii) to establish a claim or defense on behalf of the lawyer in a controversy between the lawyer and the client, to establish a defense to a criminal charge or civil claim against the lawyer based upon conduct in which the client was involved, or to respond to allegations in any proceeding concerning the lawyer's representation of the client.

(2) In a situation described in Subsection (1), if the client has acted at the time the lawyer learns of the threat of harm or loss to a victim, use or disclosure is permissible only if the harm or loss has not yet occurred.

(3) Before using or disclosing information pursuant to Subsection (1), if feasible, the lawyer must make a good faith effort to persuade the client either not to act or, if the client has already acted, to warn the victim.

(c) The lawyer may, where the law does not otherwise require, reveal information to which the duty of confidentiality does not apply under paragraph (b) without being subjected to disciplinary proceedings.

(d) The lawyer shall reveal information under paragraph (b) as the applicable law requires.

(e) The duty of confidentiality shall continue after the client-lawyer relationship has terminated.

The maximum penalty for a violation of this Rule is disbarment.

Comment

[1] The lawyer is part of a judicial system charged with upholding the law. One of the lawyer's functions is to advise clients so that they avoid any violation of the law in the proper exercise of their rights.

[2] The observance of the ethical obligation of a lawyer to hold inviolate confidential information of the client not only facilitates the full development of facts essential to proper representation of the client but also encourages people to seek early legal assistance.

[3] Almost without exception, clients come to lawyers in order to determine what their rights are and what is, in the maze of laws and regulations, deemed to be legal and correct. The common law recognizes that the client's confidences must be protected from disclosure. Based upon experience, lawyers know that almost all clients follow the advice given, and the law is upheld.

[4] A fundamental principle in the client-lawyer relationship is that the lawyer maintain confidentiality of information relating to the representation. The client is thereby encouraged to communicate fully and frankly with the lawyer even as to embarrassing or legally damaging subject matter.

[5] The principle of confidentiality is given effect in two related bodies of law, the attorney-client privilege (which includes the work product doctrine) in the law of evidence and the rule of confidentiality established in professional ethics. The attorney-client privilege applies in judicial and other proceedings in which a lawyer may be called as a witness or otherwise required to produce evidence concerning a client. The rule of client-lawyer confidentiality applies in situations other than those where evidence is sought from the lawyer through compulsion of law. *Rule 1.6: Confidentiality of Information* applies not merely to matters communicated in confidence by the client but also to all information relating to the representation, whatever its source. A lawyer may not disclose such information except as authorized or required by the Rules of Professional Conduct or other law. See also Scope. The requirement of maintaining confidentiality of information relating to representation applies to government lawyers who may disagree with the client's policy goals.

Authorized Disclosure

[6] A lawyer is impliedly authorized to make disclosures about a client when appropriate in carrying out the representation, except to the extent that the client's instructions or special circumstances limit that authority. In litigation, for example, a lawyer may disclose information by admitting a fact that cannot properly be disputed, or in negotiation by making a disclosure that facilitates a satisfactory conclusion.

[7] Lawyers in a firm may, in the course of the firm's practice, disclose to each other information relating to a client of the firm, unless the client has instructed that particular information be confined to specified lawyers.

Disclosure Adverse to Client

[8] The confidentiality rule is subject to limited exceptions. In becoming privy to information about a client, a lawyer may foresee that the client intends serious harm to another person. The public is better protected if full and open communication by the client is encouraged than if it is inhibited.

[9] Several situations must be distinguished. First, the lawyer may not knowingly assist a client in conduct that is criminal or fraudulent. See *Rule 1.2(d): Scope of Representation.* Similarly, a lawyer has a duty under *Rule 3.3(a)(4): Candor toward the Tribunal* not to use false evidence.

[10] Second, the lawyer may have been innocently involved in past conduct by the client that was criminal or fraudulent. In such a situation the lawyer has not violated *Rule 1.2(d): Scope of Representation*, because to "knowingly assist" criminal or fraudulent conduct requires knowing that the conduct is of that character.

[11] Third, the lawyer may learn that a client intends prospective conduct that is criminal and likely to result in death or substantial bodily harm. As stated in paragraph (b)(1), the lawyer has professional discretion to reveal information in order to prevent such consequences. The lawyer may make a disclosure in order to prevent death or serious bodily injury which the lawyer reasonably believes will occur. It is very difficult for a lawyer to "know" when such a heinous purpose will actually be carried out, for the client may have a change of mind.

[12] The lawyer's exercise of discretion requires consideration of such factors as the nature of the lawyer's relationship with the client and with those who might be injured by the client, the lawyer's own involvement in the transaction and factors that may extenuate the conduct in question. Where practical, the lawyer should seek to persuade the client to take suitable action. In any case, a disclosure adverse to the client's interest should be no greater than the lawyer reasonably believes necessary to the purpose. A lawyer's decision not to take preventive action permitted by paragraph (b)(1) does not violate this Rule.

Withdrawal

[13] If the lawyer's services will be used by the client in materially furthering a course of criminal or fraudulent conduct, the lawyer must withdraw, as stated in *Rule 1.16(a)(1): Declining or Terminating Representation.*

[14] After withdrawal the lawyer is required to refrain from making disclosure of the client's confidences, except as otherwise provided in *Rule 1.6: Confidentiality of Information.* Neither this rule nor *Rule 1.8(b): Conflict of Interest* nor *Rule 1.16(d): Declining or Terminating Representation* prevents the lawyer from giving notice of the fact of withdrawal, and the lawyer may also withdraw or disaffirm any opinion, document, affirmation, or the like.

[15] Where the client is an organization, the lawyer may be in doubt whether contemplated conduct will actually be carried out by the organization. Where necessary to guide conduct in connection with this Rule, the lawyer may make inquiry within the organization as indicated in *Rule 1.13(b): Organization as Client.*

Dispute Concerning a Lawyer's Conduct

[16] Where a legal claim or disciplinary charge alleges complicity of the lawyer in a client's conduct or other misconduct of the lawyer involving representation of the client, the lawyer may respond to the extent the lawyer reasonably believes necessary to establish a defense. The same is true with respect to a claim involving the conduct or representation of a former client. The lawyer's right to respond arises when an assertion of such complicity has been made. Paragraph (b)(1)(iii) does not require the lawyer to await the commencement of an action or proceeding that charges such complicity, so that the defense may be established by responding directly to a third party who has made such an assertion. The right to defend, of course, applies where a proceeding has been commenced. Where practicable and not prejudicial to the lawyer's ability to establish the defense, the lawyer should advise the client of the third party's assertion and request that the client respond appropriately. In any event, disclosure should be no greater than the lawyer reasonably believes is necessary to vindicate innocence, the disclosure should be made in a manner which limits access to the information to the tribunal or other persons having a need to know it, and appropriate protective orders or other arrangements should be sought by the lawyer to the fullest extent practicable.

[17] If the lawyer is charged with wrongdoing in which the client's conduct is implicated, the rule of confidentiality should not prevent the lawyer from defending against the charge. Such a charge can arise in a civil, criminal or professional disciplinary proceeding, and can be based on a wrong allegedly committed by the lawyer against the client,

or on a wrong alleged by a third person; for example, a person claiming to have been defrauded by the lawyer and client acting together. A lawyer entitled to a fee is permitted by paragraph (b)(1)(iii) to prove the services rendered in an action to collect it. This aspect of the rule expresses the principle that the beneficiary of a fiduciary relationship may not exploit it to the detriment of the fiduciary. As stated above, the lawyer must make every effort practicable to avoid unnecessary disclosure of information relating to a representation, to limit disclosure to those having the need to know it, and to obtain protective orders or make other arrangements minimizing the risk of disclosure.

Disclosures Otherwise Required or Authorized

[18] The attorney-client privilege is differently defined in various jurisdictions. If a lawyer is called as a witness to give testimony concerning a client, absent waiver by the client, paragraph (a) requires the lawyer to invoke the privilege when it is applicable. The lawyer must comply with the final orders of a court or other tribunal of competent jurisdiction requiring the lawyer to give information about the client.

[19] The Rules of Professional Conduct in various circumstances permit or require a lawyer to disclose information relating to the representation. See *Rules 2.2: Intermediary, 2.3: Evaluation for use by Third Persons, 3.3: Candor Toward the Tribunal and 4.1: Truthfulness in Statements to Others.* In addition to these provisions, a lawyer may be obligated or permitted by other provisions of law to give information about a client. Whether another provision of law supersedes *Rule 1.6: Confidentiality of Information* is a matter of interpretation beyond the scope of these Rules, but a presumption should exist against such a supersession.

RULE 1.7 CONFLICT OF INTEREST: GENERAL RULE

(a) A lawyer shall not represent or continue to represent a client if there is a significant risk that the lawyer's own interests or the lawyer's duties to another client, a former client, or a third person will materially and adversely affect the representation of the client, except as permitted in (b).

(b) If client consent is permissible a lawyer may represent a client notwithstanding a significant risk of material and adverse effect if each affected or former client consents, preferably in writing, to the representation after:

(1) consultation with the lawyer,

(2) having received in writing reasonable and adequate information about the material risks of the representation, and

(3) having been given the opportunity to consult with independent counsel.

(c) Client consent is not permissible if the representation:

(1) is prohibited by law or these rules;

(2) includes the assertion of a claim by one client against another client represented by the lawyer in the same or substantially related proceeding; or

(3) involves circumstances rendering it reasonably unlikely that the lawyer will be able to provide adequate representation to one or more of the affected clients.

The maximum penalty for a violation of this Rule is disbarment.

Comment

Loyalty to a Client

[1] Loyalty is an essential element in the lawyer's relationship to a client. If an impermissible conflict of interest exists before representation is undertaken the representation should be declined. The lawyer should adopt reasonable procedures, appropriate for the size and type of firm and practice, to determine in both litigation and non-litigation matters the parties and issues involved and to determine whether there are actual or potential conflicts of interest.

[2] If an impermissible conflict arises after representation has been undertaken, the lawyer should withdraw from the representation. See *Rule 1.16: Declining or Terminating Representation.* Where more than one client is involved and the lawyer withdraws because a conflict arises after representation, whether the lawyer may continue to represent any of the clients is determined by *Rule 1.9: Conflict of Interest: Former Client.* See also *Rule 2.2(b): Intermediary.* As to whether a client-lawyer relationship exists or, having once been established, is continuing, see Comment to *Rule 1.3: Diligence; and Scope.*

[3] As a general proposition, loyalty to a client prohibits undertaking representation directly adverse to that client without that client's consent. Paragraph (a) expresses that general rule. Thus, a lawyer ordinarily may not act as advocate against a person the lawyer represents in some other matter, even if it is wholly unrelated. On the other hand, simultaneous representation in unrelated matters of clients whose interests are only generally adverse, such as competing economic enterprises, does not require consent of the respective clients. Paragraph (a) applies only when the representation of one client would be directly adverse to the other.

[4] Loyalty to a client is also impaired when a lawyer cannot consider, recommend or carry out an appropriate course of action for the client because of the lawyer's other competing responsibilities or interests. The conflict in effect forecloses alternatives that would otherwise be available to the client. Paragraph (b) addresses such situations. A possible conflict does not itself preclude the representation. The critical questions are the likelihood that a conflict will eventuate and, if it does, whether it will materially interfere with the lawyer's independent professional judgment in considering alternatives or foreclose courses of action that reasonably should be pursued on behalf of the client. Consideration should be given to whether the client wishes to accommodate the other interest involved.

Consultation and Consent

[5] A client may consent to representation notwithstanding a conflict. However, as indicated in paragraph (a) with respect to representation directly adverse to a client, and paragraph (b) with respect to material limitations on representation of a client, when a disinterested lawyer would conclude that the client should not agree to the representation under the circumstances, the lawyer involved cannot properly ask for such agreement or provide representation

on the basis of the client's consent. When more than one client is involved, the question of conflict must be resolved as to each client. Moreover, there may be circumstances where it is impossible to make the disclosure necessary to obtain consent. For example, when the lawyer represents different clients in related matters and one of the clients refuses to consent to the disclosure necessary to permit the other client to make an informed decision, the lawyer cannot properly ask the latter to consent. If consent is withdrawn, the lawyer should consult *Rule 1.16: Declining or Terminating Representation* and *Rule 1.9: Conflict of Interest: Former Client.*

Lawyer's Interests

[6] The lawyer's personal or economic interests should not be permitted to have an adverse effect on representation of a client. See *Rules 1.1: Competence and 1.5: Fees.* If the propriety of a lawyer's own conduct in a transaction is in serious question, it may be difficult or impossible for the lawyer to give a client objective advice. A lawyer may not allow related business interests to affect representation, for example, by referring clients to an enterprise in which the lawyer has an undisclosed interest.

Conflicts in Litigation

[7] Paragraph (a) prohibits representation of opposing parties in litigation. Simultaneous representation of parties whose interests in litigation may conflict, such as coplaintiffs or codefendants, is governed by paragraph (b). An impermissible conflict may exist by reason of substantial discrepancy in the parties' testimony, incompatibility in positions in relation to an opposing party or the fact that there are substantially different possibilities of settlement of the claims or liabilities in question. Such conflicts can arise in criminal cases as well as civil. The potential for conflict of interest in representing multiple defendants in a criminal case is so grave that ordinarily a lawyer should decline to represent more than one codefendant. On the other hand, common representation of persons having similar interests is proper if the risk of adverse effect is minimal and the requirements of paragraph (b) are met. Compare *Rule 2.2: Intermediary* involving intermediation between clients.

[8] Ordinarily, a lawyer may not act as advocate against a client the lawyer represents in some other matter, even if the other matter is wholly unrelated. However, there are circumstances in which a lawyer may act as advocate against a client. For example, a lawyer representing an enterprise with diverse operations may accept employment as an advocate against the enterprise in an unrelated matter if doing so will not adversely affect the lawyer's relationship with the enterprise or conduct of the suit and if both clients consent upon consultation. By the same token, government lawyers in some circumstances may represent government employees in proceedings in which a government entity is the opposing party. The propriety of concurrent representation can depend on the nature of the litigation. For example, a suit charging fraud entails conflict to a degree not involved in a suit for a declaratory judgment concerning statutory interpretation.

[9] A lawyer may represent parties having antagonistic positions on a legal question that has arisen in different cases, unless representation of either client would be adversely affected. Thus, it is ordinarily not improper to assert such positions in cases while they are pending in different trial courts, but it may be improper to do so should one or more of the cases reach the appellate court.

Interest of Person Paying for a Lawyer's Service

[10] A lawyer may be paid from a source other than the client, if the client is informed of that fact and consents and the arrangement does not compromise the lawyer's duty of loyalty to the client. See *Rule 1.8(f): Conflict of Interest: Prohibited Transactions.* For example, when an insurer and its insured have conflicting interests in a matter arising from a liability insurance agreement, and the insurer is required to provide special counsel for the insured, the arrangement should assure the special counsel's professional independence. So also, when a corporation and its directors or employees are involved in a controversy in which they have conflicting interests, the corporation may provide funds for separate legal representation of the directors or employees, if the clients consent after consultation and the arrangement ensures the lawyer's professional independence.

Non-litigation Conflicts

[11] Conflicts of interest in contexts other than litigation sometimes may be difficult to assess. Relevant factors in determining whether there is potential for adverse effect include the duration and extent of the lawyer's relationship with the client or clients involved, the functions being performed by the lawyer, the likelihood that actual conflict will arise and the likely prejudice to the client from the conflict if it does arise.

[12] In a negotiation common representation is permissible where the clients are generally aligned in interest even though there is some difference of interest among them.

[13] Conflict questions may also arise in estate planning and estate administration. A lawyer may be called upon to prepare wills for several family members, such as husband and wife, and depending upon the circumstances, a conflict of interest may arise. In estate administration the identity of the client may be unclear under the law of a particular jurisdiction. Under one view, the client is the fiduciary; under another view the client is the estate or trust, including its beneficiaries. The lawyer should make clear the relationship to the parties involved.

[14] A lawyer for a corporation or other organization who is also a member of its board of directors should determine whether the responsibilities of the two roles may conflict. The lawyer may be called on to advise the corporation in matters involving actions of the directors. Consideration should be given to the frequency with which such situations may arise, the potential intensity of the conflict, the effect of the lawyer's resignation from the board and the possibility of the corporation's obtaining legal advice from another lawyer in such situations. If there is material risk that the dual role will compromise the lawyer's independence of professional judgment, the lawyer should not serve as a director.

Conflict Charged by an Opposing Party

[15] Resolving questions of conflict of interest is primarily the responsibility of the lawyer undertaking the representation. In litigation, a court may raise the question when there is reason to infer that the lawyer has neglected the responsibility. In a criminal case, inquiry by the court is generally required when a lawyer represents multiple defendants. Where the conflict is such as clearly to call into question the fair or efficient administration of justice, opposing counsel may properly raise the question. Such an objection should be viewed with caution, however, for it can be misused as a technique of harassment. See Scope.

RULE 1.8 CONFLICT OF INTEREST: PROHIBITED TRANSACTIONS

(a) A lawyer shall neither enter into a business transaction with a client if the client expects the lawyer to exercise the lawyer's professional judgment therein for the protection of the client, nor shall the lawyer knowingly acquire an ownership, possessory, security or other pecuniary interest adverse to a client unless:

(1) the transaction and terms on which the lawyer acquires the interest are fair and reasonable to the client and are fully disclosed and transmitted in writing to the client in a manner which can be reasonably understood by the client;

(2) the client is given a reasonable opportunity to seek the advice of independent counsel in the transaction; and

(3) the client consents in writing thereto.

(b) A lawyer shall not use information gained in the professional relationship with a client to the disadvantage of the client unless the client consents after consultation, except as allowed in Rule 1.6.

(c) A lawyer shall not prepare an instrument giving the lawyer or a person related to the lawyer as parent, child, sibling, or spouse any substantial gift from a client, including a testamentary gift, except where the client is related to the donee.

(d) Prior to the conclusion of representation of a client, a lawyer shall not make or negotiate an agreement giving the lawyer literary or media rights to a portrayal or account based in substantial part on information relating to the representation.

(e) A lawyer shall not provide financial assistance to a client in connection with pending or contemplated litigation, except that:

(1) a lawyer may advance court costs and expenses of litigation, the repayment of which may be contingent on the outcome of the matter; or

(2) a lawyer representing a client unable to pay court costs and expenses of litigation may pay those costs and expenses on behalf of the client.

(f) A lawyer shall not accept compensation for representing a client from one other than the client unless:

(1) the client consents after consultation;

(2) there is no interference with the lawyer's independence of professional judgment or with the client-lawyer relationship; and

(3) information relating to representation of a client is protected as required by Rule 1.6.

(g) A lawyer who represents two or more clients shall not participate in making an aggregate settlement of the claims for or against the clients, nor in a criminal case an aggregated agreement as to guilty or *nolo contendere* pleas, unless each client consents after consultation, including disclosure of the existence and nature of all claims or pleas involved and of the participation of each person in the settlement.

(h) A lawyer shall not make an agreement prospectively limiting the lawyer's liability to a client for malpractice unless permitted by law and the client is independently represented in making the agreement, or settle a claim for such liability with an unrepresented client or former client without first advising that person in writing that independent representation is appropriate in connection therewith.

(i) A lawyer related to another lawyer as parent, child, sibling or spouse shall not represent a client in a representation directly adverse to a person whom the lawyer has actual knowledge is represented by the other lawyer except upon consent by the client after consultation regarding the relationship. The disqualification stated in this paragraph is personal and is not imputed to members of firms with whom the lawyers are associated.

(j) A lawyer shall not acquire a proprietary interest in the cause of action or subject matter of litigation the lawyer is conducting for a client, except that the lawyer may:

(1) acquire a lien granted by law to secure the lawyer's fees or expenses as long as the exercise of the lien is not prejudicial to the client with respect to the subject of the representation; and

(2) contract with a client for a reasonable contingent fee in a civil case, except as prohibited by *Rule 1.5: Fees.*

The maximum penalty for a violation of Rule 1.8(b) is disbarment. The maximum penalty for a violation of Rule 1.8(a) and 1.8(c)-(j) is a public reprimand.

Comment

Transactions Between Client and Lawyer

[1A] As a general principle, all transactions between client and lawyer should be fair and reasonable to the client. The client should be fully informed of the true nature of the lawyer's interest or lack of interest in all aspects of the transaction. In such transactions a review by independent counsel on behalf of the client is often advisable. Furthermore, a lawyer may not exploit information relating to the representation to the client's disadvantage. For example, a lawyer who has learned that the client is investing in specific real estate may not, without the client's consent, seek to acquire nearby property where doing so would adversely affect the client's plan for investment. Paragraph (a) does not, however, apply to standard commercial transactions between the lawyer and the client for products or services that the client generally markets to others, for example, banking or brokerage services, medical services, products manufactured or distributed by the client, and utilities' services. In such transactions, the lawyer has no advantage in dealing with the client, and the restrictions in Paragraph (a) are unnecessary and impracticable.

Adverse Use of Information

[1B] It is a general rule that an attorney will not be permitted to make use of knowledge, or information, acquired by the attorney through the professional relationship with the client, or in the conduct of the client's business, to the disadvantage of the client. Paragraph (b) follows this general rule and provides that the client may waive this prohibition. However, if the waiver is conditional, the duty is on the attorney to comply with the condition.

Gifts from Clients

[2] A lawyer may accept a gift from a client, if the transaction meets general standards of fairness. For example, a simple gift such as a present given at a holiday or as a token of appreciation is permitted. If effectuation of a substantial gift requires preparing a legal instrument such as a will or conveyance, however, the client should have the objective advice that another lawyer can provide. Paragraph (c) recognizes an exception where the client is a relative of the donee or the gift is not substantial.

Literary Rights

[3] An agreement by which a lawyer acquires literary or media rights concerning the subject of the representation creates a conflict between the interest of the client and the personal interest of the lawyer. Measures suitable in the representation of the client may detract from the publication value of an account of the representation. Paragraph (d) does not prohibit a lawyer representing a client in a transaction concerning literary property from agreeing that the lawyer's fee shall consist of a share in ownership in the property, if the arrangement conforms to *Rule 1.5: Fees* and Paragraph (j) of this Rule.

Financial Assistance to Clients

[4] Paragraph (e) eliminates the former requirement that the client remain ultimately liable for financial assistance provided by the lawyer. It further limits permitted assistance to court costs and expenses directly related to litigation. Accordingly, permitted expenses would include expenses of investigation, medical diagnostic work connected with the matter under litigation and treatment necessary for the diagnosis, and the costs of obtaining and presenting evidence. Permitted expenses would not include living expenses or medical expenses other than those listed above.

Payment for a Lawyer's Services from One Other Than The Client

[5] When the client is a class, consent may be obtained on behalf of the class as provided by law.

Settlement of Aggregated Claims

[6] For example, Paragraph (g) requires consent after consultation. This requirement is not met by a blanket consent prior to settlement that the majority decision will rule.

Agreements to Limit Liability

[7] For example a lawyer may not condition an agreement to withdraw or the return of a client's documents on the client's release of claims. However, this paragraph is not intended to apply to customary qualifications and limitations in opinions and memoranda.

[8] A lawyer should not seek prospectively, by contract or other means, to limit the lawyer's individual liability to a client for the lawyer's malpractice. A lawyer who handles the affairs of a client properly has no need to attempt to limit liability for the lawyer's professional activities and one who does not handle the affairs of clients properly should not be permitted to do so. A lawyer may, however, practice law as a partner, member, or shareholder of a limited liability partnership, professional association, limited liability company, or professional corporation.

Family Relationships Between Lawyers

[9] Paragraph (i) applies to related lawyers who are in different firms. Related lawyers in the same firm are governed by *Rules 1.7: Conflict of Interest: General Rule, 1.9: Conflict of Interest: Former Client, and 1.10: Imputed Disqualification: General Rule.*

Acquisition of Interest in Litigation

[10] Paragraph (j) states the traditional general rule that lawyers are prohibited from acquiring a propriety interest in litigation. This general rule, which has its basis in the common law prohibition of champerty and maintenance, is subject to specific exceptions developed in decisional law and continued in these Rules, such as the exception for reasonable contingent fees set forth in *Rule 1.5: Fees* and the exception for lawyer's fees and for certain advances of costs of litigation set forth in Paragraph (e).

RULE 1.9 CONFLICT OF INTEREST: FORMER CLIENT

(a) A lawyer who has formerly represented a client in a matter shall not thereafter represent another person in the same or a substantially related matter in which that person's interests are materially adverse to the interests of the former client unless the former client consents after consultation.

(b) A lawyer shall not knowingly represent a person in the same or a substantially related matter in which a firm with which the lawyer formerly was associated had previously represented a client:

(1) whose interests are materially adverse to that person; and

(2) about whom the lawyer had acquired information protected by *Rules 1.6: Confidentiality and 1.9(c): Conflict of Interest: Former Client*, that is material to the matter, unless the former client consents after consultation.

(c) A lawyer who has formerly represented a client in a matter or whose present or former firm has formerly represented a client in a matter shall not thereafter:

(1) use information relating to the representation to the disadvantage of the former client except as *Rule 1.6: Confidentiality of Information* or *Rule 3.3: Candor Towards the Tribunal* would permit or require with respect to a client, or when the information has become generally known; or

(2) reveal information relating to the representation except as *Rule 1.6: Confidentiality of Information* or *Rule 3.3: Candor Towards the Tribunal* would permit or require with respect to a client.

The maximum penalty for a violation of this Rule is disbarment.

Comment

[1] The principles in *Rule 1.7: Conflict of Interest* determine whether, and to the extent the interests of a present and former client are adverse. Thus, a lawyer could not properly seek to rescind on behalf of a new client a contract drafted on behalf of the former client. A lawyer who has prosecuted an accused person could not properly represent the accused in a subsequent civil action against the government concerning the same transaction.

[2] The scope of a "matter" for purposes of this Rule may depend on the facts of a particular situation or transaction. The lawyer's involvement in a matter may be one of degree. The underlying question is whether the lawyer was so involved in the matter that the subsequent representation can be justly regarded as a changing of sides in the matter in question.

Lawyers Moving Between Firms

[3] *Reserved.*

[4] Reconciliation of these competing principles in the past has been attempted under two rubrics. One approach has been to seek per se rules of disqualification. For example, one view is that a partner in a law firm is conclusively presumed to have access to all confidences concerning all clients of the firm. Under this analysis, if a lawyer has been a partner in one law firm and then becomes a partner in another law firm, there may be a presumption that all confidences known by the partner in the first firm are known to all partners in the second firm. This presumption might properly be applied in some circumstances, especially where the client has been extensively represented, but may be unrealistic where the client was represented only for limited purposes. Furthermore, such a rigid rule exaggerates the difference between a partner and an associate in modern law firms.

[5] The other rubric formerly used for dealing with disqualification is the appearance of impropriety proscribed in Canon 9 of the ABA Model Code of Professional Responsibility. This rubric has a two-fold problem. First, the appearance of impropriety can be taken to include any new client-lawyer relationship that might make a former client feel anxious. If that meaning were adopted, disqualification would become little more than a question of subjective judgment by the former client. Second, since "impropriety" is undefined, the term "appearance of impropriety" is question-begging. It therefore has to be recognized that the problem of disqualification cannot be properly resolved either by simple analogy to a lawyer practicing alone or by the very general concept of appearance of impropriety.

Confidentiality

[6] Preserving confidentiality is a question of access to information. Access to information, in turn, is essentially a question of fact in particular circumstances, aided by inferences, deductions or working presumptions that reasonably may be made about the way in which lawyers work together. A lawyer may have general access to files of all clients of a law firm and may regularly participate in discussions of their affairs; yielding an inference that such a lawyer in fact is privy to all information about all the firm's clients. In contrast, another lawyer may have access to the files of only a limited number of clients and participate in discussions of the affairs of no other clients; yielding an inference that such a lawyer in fact is privy to information about the clients actually served but not that of other clients.

[7] Application of paragraph (b) depends on a situation's particular facts.

[8] Paragraph (b) operates to disqualify the lawyer only when the lawyer involved has actual knowledge of information protected by *Rules 1.6: Confidentiality and 1.9(b): Conflict of Interest: Former Client.* Thus, if a lawyer while with one firm acquired no knowledge or information relating to a particular client of the firm, and that lawyer later joined another firm, neither the lawyer individually nor the second firm is disqualified from representing another client in the same or a related matter even though the interests of the two clients conflict. See *Rule 1.10(b): Imputed Disqualification* for the restrictions on a firm once a lawyer has terminated association with the firm.

[9] Independent of the question of disqualification of a firm, a lawyer changing professional association has a continuing duty to preserve confidentiality of information about a client formerly represented. See *Rules 1.6: Confidentiality and 1.9: Conflict of Interest: Former Client.*

Adverse Positions

[10] The second aspect of loyalty to a client is the lawyer's obligation to decline subsequent representations involving positions adverse to a former client arising in substantially related matters. This obligation requires abstention from adverse representation by the individual lawyer involved, but does not properly entail abstention of other lawyers through imputed disqualification. Hence, this aspect of the problem is governed by *Rule 1.9(a): Conflict of Interest: Former Client.* Thus, if a lawyer left one firm for another, the new affiliation would not preclude the firms involved from continuing to represent clients with adverse interests in the same or related matters, so long as the conditions of paragraphs (b) and (c) concerning confidentiality have been met.

[11] Information acquired by the lawyer in the course of representing a client may not subsequently be used or revealed by the lawyer to the disadvantage of the client. However, the fact that a lawyer has once served a client does not preclude the lawyer from using generally known information about that client when later representing another client.

[12] Disqualification from subsequent representation is for the protection of former clients and can be waived by them. A waiver is effective only if there is disclosure of the circumstances, including the lawyer's intended role in behalf of the new client.

[13] With regard to an opposing party's raising a question of conflict of interest, see Comment to *Rule 1.7: Conflict of Interest.* With regard to disqualification of a firm with which a lawyer is or was formerly associated, see *Rule 1.10: Imputed Disqualification.*

RULE 1.10 IMPUTED DISQUALIFICATION: GENERAL RULE

(a) While lawyers are associated in a firm, none of them shall knowingly represent a client when any one of them practicing alone would be prohibited from doing so by *Rule 1.7: Conflict of Interest: General Rule, 1.8(c): Conflict of Interest: Prohibited Transactions, 1.9: Former Client or 2.2: Intermediary.*

(b) When a lawyer has terminated an association with a firm, the firm is not prohibited from thereafter representing a person with interests materially adverse to those of a client represented by the formerly associated lawyer unless:

(1) the matter is the same or substantially related to that in which the formerly associated lawyer represented the client; and

(2) any lawyer remaining in the firm has information protected by *Rules 1.6: Confidentiality of Information* and *1.9(c): Conflict of Interest: Former Client* that is material to the matter.

(c) A disqualification prescribed by this rule may be waived by the affected client under the conditions stated in *Rule 1.7: Conflict of Interest: General Rule.*

The maximum penalty for a violation of this Rule is disbarment.

Comment

Definition of "Firm"

[1] For purposes of these Rules, the term "firm" includes lawyers in a private firm, and lawyers in the legal department of a corporation or other organization, or in a legal services organization. Whether two or more lawyers constitute a firm within this definition can depend on the specific facts. For example, two practitioners who share office space and occasionally consult or assist each other ordinarily would not be regarded as constituting a firm. However, if they present themselves to the public in a way suggesting that they are a firm or conduct themselves as a firm, they should be regarded as a firm for the purposes of the Rules. The terms of any formal agreement between associated lawyers are relevant in determining whether they are a firm, as is the fact that they have mutual access to information concerning the clients they serve. Furthermore, it is relevant in doubtful cases to consider the underlying purpose of the Rule that is involved. A group of lawyers could be regarded as a firm for purposes of the rule that the same lawyer should not represent opposing parties in litigation, while it might not be so regarded for purposes of the rule that information acquired by one lawyer is attributed to the other.

[2] With respect to the law department of an organization, there is ordinarily no question that the members of the department constitute a firm within the meaning of the Rules of Professional Conduct. However, there can be uncertainty as to the identity of the client. For example, it may not be clear whether the law department of a corporation represents a subsidiary or an affiliated corporation, as well as the corporation by which the members of the department are directly employed. A similar question can arise concerning an unincorporated association and its local affiliates.

[3] Similar questions can also arise with respect to lawyers in legal aid. Lawyers employed in the same unit of a legal service organization constitute a firm, but not necessarily those employed in separate units. As in the case of independent practitioners, whether the lawyers should be treated as associated with each other can depend on the particular rule that is involved, and on the specific facts of the situation.

[4] Where a lawyer has joined a private firm after having represented the government, the situation is governed by *Rule 1.11(a) and (b): Successive Government and Private Employment;* where a lawyer represents the government after having served private clients, the situation is governed by *Rule 1.11(c)(1): Successive Government and Private Employment.* The individual lawyer involved is bound by the Rules generally, including *Rules 1.6: Confidentiality of Information, 1.7: Conflict of Interest: General Rule* and *1.9: Conflict of Interest: Former Client.*

[5] Different provisions are thus made for movement of a lawyer from one private firm to another and for movement of a lawyer between a private firm and the government. The government is entitled to protection of its client confidences and, therefore, to the protections provided in *Rules 1.6: Confidentiality of Information, 1.9: Conflict of Interest: Former Client,* and *1.11: Successive Government and Private Employment.* However, if the more extensive disqualification in *Rule 1.10: Imputed Disqualification* were applied to former government lawyers, the potential effect on the government would be unduly burdensome. The government deals with all private citizens and organizations and, thus, has a much wider circle of adverse legal interests than does any private law firm. In these circumstances, the government's recruitment of lawyers would be seriously impaired if *Rule 1.10: Imputed Disqualification* were applied to the government. On balance, therefore, the government is better served in the long run by the protections stated in *Rule 1.11: Successive Government and Private Employment.*

Principles of Imputed Disqualification

[6] The rule of imputed disqualification stated in paragraph (a) gives effect to the principle of loyalty to the client as it applies to lawyers who practice in a law firm. Such situations can be considered from the premise that a firm of lawyers is essentially one lawyer for purposes of the rules governing loyalty to the client, or from the premise that each lawyer is vicariously bound by the obligation of loyalty owed by each lawyer with whom the lawyer is associated. Paragraph (a) operates only among the lawyers currently associated in a firm. When a lawyer moves from one firm to another, the situation is governed by *Rules 1.9(b): Conflict of Interest: Former Client,* and *1.10(b): Imputed Disqualification: General Rule.*

[7] *Rule 1.10(b): Imputed Disqualification* operates to permit a law firm, under certain circumstances, to represent a person with interests directly adverse to those of a client represented by a lawyer who formerly was associated with the firm. The Rule applies regardless of when the formerly associated lawyer represented the client. However, the law firm may not represent a person with interests adverse to those of a present client of the firm, which would violate *Rule 1.7: Conflict of Interest.* Moreover, the firm may not represent the person where the matter is the same or substantially related to that in which the formerly associated lawyer represented the client and any other lawyer currently in the firm has material information protected by *Rules 1.6: Confidentiality of Information* and *1.9(c): Conflict of Interest: Former Client.*

RULE 1.11 SUCCESSIVE GOVERNMENT AND PRIVATE EMPLOYMENT

(a) Except as law may otherwise expressly permit, a lawyer shall not represent a private client in connection with a matter in which the lawyer participated personally and substantially as a public officer or employee, unless the appropriate government entity consents after consultation. No lawyer in a firm with which that lawyer is associated may knowingly undertake or continue representation in such a matter unless:

(1) the disqualified lawyer is screened from any participation in the matter and is apportioned no part of the fee therefrom; and

(2) written notice is duly given to the client and to the appropriate government entity to enable it to ascertain compliance with the provisions of this rule.

(b) Except as law may otherwise expressly permit, a lawyer having information that the lawyer knows is confidential government information about a person acquired when the lawyer was a public officer or employee, may not represent a private client whose interests are adverse to that person in a matter in which the information could be used to the material disadvantage of that person. A firm with which that lawyer is associated may undertake or continue representation in the matter only if the disqualified lawyer is screened from any participation in the matter and is apportioned no part of the fee therefrom.

(c) Except as law may otherwise expressly permit, a lawyer serving as a public officer or employee shall not:

(1) participate in a matter in which the lawyer participated personally and substantially while in private practice or nongovernmental employment, unless under applicable law no one is, or by lawful delegation may be, authorized to act in the lawyer's stead in the matter; or

(2) negotiate for private employment with any person who is involved as a party or as lawyer for a party in a matter in which the lawyer is participating personally and substantially, except that a lawyer serving as a law clerk to a judge, other adjudicative officer or arbitrator may negotiate for private employment as permitted by Rule 1.12(b) and subject to the conditions stated in Rule 1.12(b).

(d) As used in this Rule, the term "matter" includes:

(1) any judicial or other proceeding, application, request for a ruling or other determination, contract, claim, controversy, investigation, charge, accusation, arrest or other particular matter involving a specific party or parties; and

(2) any other matter covered by the conflict of interest rules of the appropriate government entity.

(e) As used in this Rule, the term "confidential government information" means information which has been obtained under governmental authority and which, at the time this rule is applied, the government is prohibited by law from disclosing to the public or has a legal privilege not to disclose, and which is not otherwise available to the public.

The maximum penalty for a violation of this Rule is disbarment.

Comment

[1] This Rule prevents a lawyer from exploiting public office for the advantage of a private client. It is a counterpart of *Rule 1.10(b): Imputed Disqualification*, which applies to lawyers moving from one firm to another.

[2] A lawyer representing a government entity, whether employed or specially retained by the government, is subject to the Rules of Professional Conduct, including the prohibition against representing adverse interests stated in *Rule 1.7: Conflict of Interest* and the protections afforded former clients in *Rule 1.9: Conflict of Interest: Former Client*. In addition, such a lawyer is subject to *Rule 1.11: Successive Government and Private Employment* and to statutes and government regulations regarding conflict of interest. Such statutes and regulations may circumscribe the extent to which the government entity may give consent under this Rule.

[3] Where the successive clients are a public entity and a private client, the risk exists that power or discretion vested in public authority might be used for the special benefit of a private client. A lawyer should not be in a position where benefit to a private client might affect performance of the lawyer's professional functions on behalf of public authority. Also, unfair advantage could accrue to the private client by reason of access to confidential government information about the client's adversary obtainable only through the lawyer's government service. However, the rules governing lawyers presently or formerly employed by a government entity should not be so restrictive as to inhibit transfer of employment to and from the government. The government has a legitimate need to attract qualified lawyers as well as to maintain high ethical standards. The provisions for screening and waiver are necessary to prevent the disqualification rule from imposing too severe a deterrent against entering public service.

[4] When the client is an agency of one government, that agency should be treated as a private client for purposes of this Rule if the lawyer thereafter represents an agency of another government, as when a lawyer represents a city and subsequently is employed by a federal agency.

[5] Paragraphs (a)(1) and (b) do not prohibit a lawyer from receiving a salary or partnership share established by prior independent agreement. They prohibit directly relating the lawyer's compensation to the fee in the matter in which the lawyer is disqualified.

[6] Paragraph (a)(2) does not require that a lawyer give notice to the government entity at a time when premature disclosure would injure the client; a requirement for premature disclosure might preclude engagement of the lawyer. Such notice is, however, required to be given as soon as practicable in order that the government entity will have a reasonable opportunity to ascertain that the lawyer is complying with *Rule 1.11: Successive Government and Private Employment* and to take appropriate action if it believes the lawyer is not complying.

[7] Paragraph (b) operates only when the lawyer in question has knowledge of the information, which means actual knowledge; it does not operate with respect to information that merely could be imputed to the lawyer.

[8] Paragraphs (a) and (c) do not prohibit a lawyer from jointly representing a private party and a government entity

when doing so is permitted by *Rule 1.7: Conflict of Interest* and is not otherwise prohibited by law.

[9] Paragraph (c) does not disqualify other lawyers in the entity with which the lawyer in question has become associated.

RULE 1.12 FORMER JUDGE OR ARBITRATOR

(a) Except as stated in paragraph (d), a lawyer shall not represent anyone in connection with a matter in which the lawyer participated personally and substantially as a judge or other adjudicative officer, arbitrator or law clerk to such a person, unless all parties to the proceeding consent after consultation.

(b) A lawyer shall not negotiate for employment with any person who is involved as a party or as lawyer for a party in a matter in which the lawyer is participating personally and substantially as a judge or other adjudicative officer or arbitrator. A lawyer serving as a law clerk to a judge, other adjudicative officer or arbitrator may negotiate for employment with a party or lawyer involved in a matter in which the clerk is participating personally and substantially, but only after the lawyer has notified the judge, other adjudicative officer or arbitrator. In addition, the law clerk shall promptly provide written notice of acceptance of employment to all counsel of record in all such matters in which the prospective employer is involved.

(c) If a lawyer is disqualified by paragraph (a), no lawyer in a firm with which that lawyer is associated may knowingly undertake or continue representation in the matter unless:

(1) the disqualified lawyer is screened from any participation in the matter and is apportioned no part of the fee therefrom; and

(2) written notice is promptly given to the appropriate tribunal to enable it to ascertain compliance with the provisions of this Rule.

(d) An arbitrator selected as a partisan of a party in a multimember arbitration panel is not prohibited from subsequently representing that party.

The maximum penalty for a violation of this Rule is a public reprimand.

Comment

This Rule generally parallels *Rule 1.11: Successive Government and Private Employment*. The term "personally and substantially" signifies that a judge who was a member of a multimember court, and thereafter left judicial office to practice law, is not prohibited from representing a client in a matter pending in the court, but in which the former judge did not participate. So also the fact that a former judge exercised administrative responsibility in a court does not prevent the former judge from acting as a lawyer in a matter where the judge had previously exercised remote or incidental administrative responsibility that did not affect the merits. The term "adjudicative officer" includes such officials as judges *pro tempore*, referees, special masters, hearing officers and other parajudicial officers, and also lawyers who serve as part-time judges. Compliance Canons A(2), B(2) and C of the Model Code of Judicial Conduct provide that a part-time judge, judge *pro tempore* or retired judge recalled to active service, may not "act as a lawyer in any proceeding in which he served as a judge or in any other proceeding related thereto." Although phrased differently from this Rule, those rules correspond in meaning.

RULE 1.13 ORGANIZATION AS CLIENT

(a) A lawyer employed or retained by an organization represents the organization acting through its duly authorized constituents.

(b) If a lawyer for an organization knows that an officer, employee or other person associated with the organization is engaged in action, intends to act or refuses to act in a matter related to the representation that is a violation of a legal obligation to the organization, or a violation of law which reasonably might be imputed to the organization, and is likely to result in substantial injury to the organization, the lawyer shall proceed as is reasonably necessary in the best interest of the organization. In determining how to proceed, the lawyer shall give due consideration to the seriousness of the violation and its consequences, the scope and nature of the lawyer's representation, the responsibility in the organization and the apparent motivation of the person involved, the policies of the organization concerning such matters and any other relevant considerations. Any measures taken shall be designed to minimize disruption of the organization and the risk of revealing information relating to the representation to persons outside the organization. Such measures may include among others:

(1) asking reconsideration of the matter;

(2) advising that a separate legal opinion on the matter be sought for presentation to appropriate authority in the organization; and

(3) referring the matter to higher authority in the organization, including, if warranted by the seriousness of the matter, referral to the highest authority that can act in behalf of the organization as determined by applicable law.

(c) If, despite the lawyer's efforts in accordance with paragraph (b), the highest authority that can act on behalf of the organization insists upon action, or a refusal to act, that is clearly a violation of law and is likely to result in substantial injury to the organization, the lawyer may resign in accordance with Rule 1.16.

(d) In dealing with an organization's directors, officers, employees, members, shareholders or other constituents, a lawyer shall explain the identity of the client when it is apparent that the organization's interests are adverse to those of the constituents with whom the lawyer is dealing.

(e) A lawyer representing an organization may also represent any of its directors, officers, employees, members, shareholders or other constituents, subject to the provisions of Rule 1.7. If the organization's consent to the dual representation is required by Rule 1.7, the consent shall be given by an appropriate official of the organization other than the individual who is to be represented, or by the shareholders.

(f) "Organization" as used herein includes governmental entities.

The maximum penalty for a violation of this Rule is a public reprimand.

Comment

The Entity as the Client

[1] An organizational client is a legal entity, but it cannot act except through its officers, directors, employees, shareholders and other constituents. Officers, directors, employees and shareholders are the constituents of the corporate organizational client. The duties defined in this Comment apply equally to unincorporated associations. "Other constituents" as used in this Comment also includes the positions equivalent to officers, directors, employees and shareholders held by persons acting for organizational clients that are not corporations.

[2] When one of the constituents of an organizational client communicates with the organization's lawyer in that person's organizational capacity, the communication is protected by *Rule 1.6: Confidentiality of Information.* Thus, by way of example, if an organizational client requests its lawyer to investigate allegations of wrongdoing, interviews made in the course of that investigation between the lawyer and the client's employees or other constituents are covered by *Rule 1.6: Confidentiality of Information.* This does not mean, however, that constituents of an organizational client are the clients of the lawyer. The lawyer may not disclose to such constituents information relating to the representation except for disclosures explicitly or impliedly authorized by the organizational client in order to carry out the representation or as otherwise permitted by *Rule 1.6: Confidentiality of Information.*

[3] When constituents of the organization make decisions for it, the decisions ordinarily must be accepted by the lawyer even if their utility or prudence is doubtful. Decisions concerning policy and operations, including ones entailing serious risk, are not as such in the lawyer's province. However, different considerations arise when the lawyer knows that the organization may be substantially injured by action of a constituent that is in violation of law. In such a circumstance, it may be reasonably necessary for the lawyer to ask the constituent to reconsider the matter. If that fails, or if the matter is of sufficient seriousness and importance to the organization, it may be reasonably necessary for the lawyer to take steps to have the matter reviewed by a higher authority in the organization. Clear justification should exist for seeking review over the head of the constituent normally responsible for it. The stated policy of the organization may define circumstances and prescribe channels for such review, and a lawyer should encourage the formulation of such a policy. Even in the absence of organization policy, however, the lawyer may have an obligation to refer a matter to higher authority, depending on the seriousness of the matter and whether the constituent in question has apparent motives to act at variance with the organization's interest. Review by the chief executive officer or by the board of directors may be required when the matter is of importance commensurate with their authority. At some point it may be useful or essential to obtain an independent legal opinion.

[4] In an extreme case, it may be reasonably necessary for the lawyer to refer the matter to the organization's highest authority. Ordinarily, that is the board of directors or similar governing body. However, applicable law may prescribe that under certain conditions highest authority reposes elsewhere, for example, in the independent directors of a corporation.

Relation to Other Rules

[5] The authority and responsibility provided in paragraph (b) are concurrent with the authority and responsibility provided in other Rules. In particular, this Rule does not limit or expand the lawyer's responsibility under *Rule 1.6: Confidentiality of Information*, 1.8, 1.16, 3.3 or 4.1. If the lawyer's services are being used by an organization to further a crime or fraud by the organization, *Rule 1.2(d): Scope of Representation* can be applicable.

Government Entity

[6] The duty defined in this Rule applies to governmental entities. However, when the client is a governmental entity, a different balance may be appropriate between maintaining confidentiality and assuring that the wrongful official act is prevented or rectified, for public business is involved. In addition, duties of lawyers employed by the government or lawyers in military service may be defined by statutes and regulation. Therefore, defining precisely the identity of the client and prescribing the resulting obligations of such lawyers may be more difficult in the government context. Although in some circumstances the client may be a specific agency, it is generally the government as a whole. For example, if the action or failure to act involves the head of a bureau, either the department of which the bureau is a part or the government as a whole may be the client for purpose of this Rule. Moreover, in a matter involving the conduct of government officials, a government lawyer may have authority to question such conduct more extensively than that of a lawyer for a private organization in similar circumstances. This Rule does not limit that authority. See note on Scope.

Clarifying the Lawyer's Role

[7] There are times when the organization's interest may be or become adverse to those of one or more of its constituents. In such circumstances the lawyer should advise any constituent, whose interest the lawyer finds adverse to that of the organization (1) of the conflict or potential conflict of interest, (2) that the lawyer can-not represent such constituent, and (3) that such person may wish to obtain independent representation. Care must be taken to assure that the individual understands that, when there is such adversity of interest, the lawyer for the organization cannot provide legal representation for that constituent individual, and that discussions between the lawyer for the organization and the individual may not be privileged.

[8] Whether such a warning should be given by the lawyer for the organization to any constituent individual may turn on the facts of each case.

Dual Representation

[9] Paragraph (e) recognizes that a lawyer for an organization may also represent a principal officer or major shareholder.

Derivative Actions

[10] Under generally prevailing law, the shareholders or members of a corporation may bring suit to compel the directors to perform their legal obligations in the supervision of the organization. Members of unincorporated associations have essentially the same right. Such an action may be brought nominally by the organization, but usually is, in fact, a legal controversy over management of the organization.

[11] The question can arise whether counsel for the organization may defend such an action. The proposition that the organization is the lawyer's client does not alone resolve the issue. Most derivative actions are a normal incident of an organization's affairs, to be defended by the organization's lawyer like any other suit. However, if the claim involves serious charges of wrongdoing by those in control of the organization, a conflict may arise between the lawyer's duty to the organization and the lawyer's relationship with the board. In those circumstances, *Rule 1.7: Conflict of Interest* governs who should represent the directors and the organization.

RULE 1.14 CLIENT UNDER A DISABILITY

(a) When a client's ability to make adequately considered decisions in connection with the representation is impaired, whether because of age, mental or medical disability or for some other reason, the lawyer shall, as far as reasonably possible, maintain a normal client-lawyer relationship with the client.

(b) A lawyer may seek the appointment of a guardian or take other protective action with respect to a client when the lawyer reasonably believes that the client cannot adequately act in the client's own interest.

The maximum penalty for a violation of this Rule is a public reprimand.

Comment

[1] The normal client-lawyer relationship is based on the assumption that the client, when properly advised and assisted, is capable of making decisions about important matters. When the client is a minor or suffers from a mental disorder or disability, however, maintaining the ordinary client-lawyer relationship may not be possible in all respects. In particular, an incapacitated person may have no power to make legally binding decisions. Nevertheless, a client lacking legal competence often has the ability to understand, deliberate upon, and reach conclusions about matters affecting the client's own well-being. Furthermore, to an increasing extent the law recognizes intermediate degrees of competence. For example, children as young as five or six years of age, and certainly those of ten or twelve, are regarded as having opinions that are entitled to weight in legal proceedings concerning their custody. So also, it is recognized that some persons of advanced age can be quite capable of handling routine financial matters while needing special legal protection concerning major transactions.

[2] The fact that a client suffers a disability does not diminish the lawyer's obligation to treat the client with attention and respect. If the person has no guardian or legal representative, the lawyer often must act as de facto guardian. Even if the person does have a legal representative, the lawyer should as far as possible accord the represented person the status of client, particularly in maintaining communication.

[3] If a legal representative has already been appointed for the client, the lawyer should ordinarily look to the representative for decisions on behalf of the client. If a legal representative has not been appointed, the lawyer should see to such an appointment where it would serve the client's best interests. Thus, if a disabled client has substantial property that should be sold for the client's benefit, effective completion of the transaction ordinarily requires appointment of a legal representative. In many circumstances, however, appointment of a legal representative may be expensive or traumatic for the client. Evaluation of these considerations is a matter of professional judgment on the lawyer's part.

[4] If the lawyer represents the guardian as distinct from the ward, and is aware that the guardian is acting adversely to the ward's interest, the lawyer may have an obligation to prevent or rectify the guardian's misconduct. See *Rule 1.2(d): Scope of Representation.*

Disclosure of the Client's Condition

[5] Rules of procedure in litigation generally provide that minors or persons suffering mental disability shall be represented by a guardian or next friend if they do not have a general guardian. However, disclosure of the client's disability can adversely affect the client's interests. For example, raising the question of disability could, in some circumstances, lead to proceedings for involuntary commitment. The lawyer's position in such cases is an unavoidably difficult one. The lawyer may seek guidance from an appropriate diagnostician.

RULE 1.15(I) SAFEKEEPING PROPERTY—GENERAL

(a) A lawyer shall hold property of clients or third persons that is in a lawyer's possession in connection with a representation separate from the lawyer's own property. Funds shall be kept in a separate account maintained in an approved institution as defined by Rule 1.15(III)(c)(1). Other property shall be identified as such and appropriately safeguarded. Complete records of such account funds and other property shall be kept by the lawyer and shall be preserved for a period of six years after termination of the representation.

(b) Upon receiving funds or other property in which a client or third person has an interest, a lawyer shall promptly notify the client or third person. Except as stated in this rule or otherwise permitted by law or by agreement with the client, a lawyer shall promptly deliver to the client or third person any funds or other property that the client or third person is entitled to receive and, upon request by the client or third person, shall promptly render a full accounting regarding such property.

(c) When in the course of representation a lawyer is in possession of property in which both the lawyer and another person claim interests, the property shall be kept separate by the lawyer until there is an accounting and severance of their interests. If a dispute arises concerning their respective interests, the portion in dispute shall be kept separate by the lawyer until the dispute is resolved.

The maximum penalty for a violation of this Rule is disbarment.

Comment

[1] A lawyer should hold property of others with the care required of a professional fiduciary. Securities should be kept in a safe deposit box, except when some other form of safekeeping is warranted by special circumstances. All property which is the property of clients or third persons should be kept separate from the lawyer's business and personal property and, if monies, in one or more trust accounts. Separate trust accounts may be warranted when administering estate monies or acting in similar fiduciary capacities.

[2] Lawyers often receive funds from third parties from which the lawyer's fee will be paid. If there is risk that the client may divert the funds without paying the fee, the lawyer is not required to remit the portion from which the fee is to be paid. However, a lawyer may not hold funds to coerce a client into accepting the lawyer's contention. The disputed portion of the funds should be kept in trust and the lawyer should suggest means for prompt resolution of the dispute, such as arbitration or interpleader. The undisputed portion of the funds shall be promptly distributed.

[3] Third parties, such as a client's creditors, may have just claims against funds or other property in a lawyer's custody. A lawyer may have a duty under applicable law to protect such third-party claims against wrongful interference by the client, and accordingly may refuse to surrender the property to the client. However, a lawyer should not unilaterally assume to arbitrate a dispute between the client and the third party. The obligations of a lawyer under this Rule are independent of those arising from activity other than rendering legal services. For example, a lawyer who serves as an escrow agent is governed by the applicable law relating to fiduciaries even though the lawyer does not render legal services in the transaction.

[4] A "clients' security fund" provides a means through the collective efforts of the bar to reimburse persons who have lost money or property as a result of dishonest conduct of a lawyer. Where such a fund has been established, a lawyer should participate.

RULE 1.15(II) SAFEKEEPING PROPERTY—TRUST ACCOUNT AND IOLTA

(a) Every lawyer who practices law in Georgia, whether said lawyer practices as a sole practitioner, or as a member of a firm, association, or professional corporation, and who receives money or property on behalf of a client or in any other fiduciary capacity, shall maintain or have available a trust account as required by these Rules. All funds held by a lawyer for a client and all funds held by a lawyer in any other fiduciary capacity shall be deposited in and administered from such account.

(b) No personal funds shall ever be deposited in a lawyer's trust account, except that unearned attorney's fees may be so held until the same are earned. Sufficient personal funds of the lawyer may be kept in the trust account to cover maintenance fees such as service charges on the account. Records on such trust accounts shall be so kept and maintained as to reflect at all times the exact balance held for each client or third person. No funds shall be withdrawn from such trust accounts for the personal use of the lawyer maintaining the account except earned attorney's fees debited against the account of a specific client and recorded as such.

(c) All client's funds shall be placed in either an interest-bearing account with the interest being paid to the client or an interest-bearing (IOLTA) account with the interest being paid to the Georgia Bar Foundation as hereinafter provided.

(1) With respect to funds which are not nominal in amount, or are not to be held for a short period of time, a lawyer shall, with notice to the clients, create and maintain an interest-bearing trust account in an approved institution as defined in Rule 1.15(III)(c)(1), with the interest to be paid to the client. No earnings from such an account shall be made available to a lawyer or law firm.

(2) With respect to funds which are nominal in amount or are to be held for a short period of time, a lawyer shall, with or without notice to the client, create and maintain an interest-bearing, government insured trust account (IOLTA) in compliance with the following provisions:

(i) No earnings from such an IOLTA account shall be made available to a lawyer or law firm.

(ii) The account shall include all clients' funds which are nominal in amount or which are to be held for a short period of time.

(iii) An interest-bearing trust account may be established with any approved institution as defined in Rule 1.15(III)(c)(1). Funds in each interest-bearing trust account shall be subject to withdrawal upon request and without delay.

(iv) The rate of interest payable on any interest-bearing trust account shall not be less than the rate paid by the depositor institution to regular, non-lawyer depositors. Higher rates offered by the institution to customers whose deposits exceed certain time or quantity minimum, such as those offered in the form of certificates of deposit, may be obtained by a lawyer or law firm on some or all of the deposit funds so long as there is no impairment of the right to withdraw or transfer principal immediately.

(v) Lawyers or law firms shall direct the depository institution:

(A) to remit to the Georgia Bar Foundation interest or dividends, net of any charges or fees on that account, on the average monthly balance in that account, or as otherwise computed in accordance with a financial institution's standard accounting practice, at least quarterly. Any bank fees or charges in excess of the interest earned on that account for any month shall be paid by the lawyer or law firm in whose names such account appears, if required by the bank;

(B) to transmit with each remittance to the Foundation a statement showing the name of the lawyer or law firm for whom the remittance is sent, the rate of interest applied, the average monthly balance against which the interest rate is applied, the service charges or fees applied, and the net interest remittance;

(C) to transmit to the depositing lawyer or law firm at the same time a report showing the amount paid to the Foundation, the rate of interest applied, the average account balance of the period for which the report is made, and such other information provided to non-lawyer customers with similar accounts.

(3) No charge of ethical impropriety or other breach of professional conduct shall attend the determination that such funds are nominal in amount or to be held for a short period of time, or to the decision to invest clients' funds in a pooled interest-bearing account.

(4) Whether the funds are designated short-term or nominal or not, a lawyer or law firm may elect to remit all interest earned, or interest earned net of charges, to the client or clients.

The maximum penalty for a violation of Rule 1.15(II)(a) and Rule 1.15(II)(b) is disbarment. The maximum penalty for a violation of Rule 1.15(II)(c) is a public reprimand.

Comment

[1] The personal money permitted to be kept in the lawyer's trust account by this Rule shall not be used for any purpose other than to cover the bank fees and if used for any other purpose the lawyer shall have violated this Rule. If the lawyer wishes to reduce the amount of personal money in the trust account, the change must be properly noted in the lawyer's financial records and the monies transferred to the lawyer's business account.

[2] Nothing in this Rule shall prohibit a lawyer from removing from the trust account fees which have been earned on a regular basis which coincides with the lawyer's billing cycles rather than removing the fees earned on an hour-by-hour basis.

RULE 1.15(III) RECORD KEEPING; TRUST ACCOUNT OVERDRAFT NOTIFICATION; EXAMINATION OF RECORDS

(a) Required Bank Accounts: Every lawyer who practices law in Georgia and who receives money or other property on behalf of a client or in any other fiduciary capacity shall maintain, in an approved financial institution as defined by this Rule, a trust account or accounts, separate from any business and personal accounts. Funds received by the lawyer on behalf of a client or in any other fiduciary capacity shall be deposited into this account. The financial institution shall be in Georgia or in the state where the lawyer's office is located, or elsewhere with the written consent and at the written request of the client or third person.

(b) Description of Accounts:

(1) A lawyer shall designate all trust accounts, whether general or specific, as well as all deposit slips and checks drawn thereon, as either an "Attorney Trust Account," "Attorney Escrow Account" or "Attorney Fiduciary Account."

(2) A lawyer shall designate all business accounts, as well as all deposit slips and all checks drawn thereon, as a "Business Account," a "Professional Account," an "Office Account," a "General Account," a "Payroll Account", "Operating Account" or a "Regular Account."

(3) Nothing in this Rule shall prohibit a lawyer from using any additional description or designation for a specific business or trust account including fiduciary accounts maintained by the lawyer as executor, guardian, trustee, receiver, agent or in any other fiduciary capacity.

(c) Procedure:

(1) *Approved Institutions*:

(i) A lawyer shall maintain his or her trust account only in a financial institution approved by the State Bar, which shall annually publish a list of approved institutions. Such institutions shall be located within the State of Georgia, within the state where the lawyer's office is located, or elsewhere with the written consent and at the written request of the client or fiduciary. The institution shall be authorized by federal or state law to do business in the jurisdiction where located and shall be federally insured. A financial institution shall be approved as a depository for lawyer trust accounts if it abides by an agreement to report to the State Disciplinary Board whenever any properly payable instrument is presented against a lawyer trust account containing insufficient funds, and the instrument is not honored. The agreement shall apply to all branches of the financial institution and shall not be canceled except upon thirty days notice in writing to the State Disciplinary Board. The agreement shall be filed with the Office of General Counsel on a form approved by the State Disciplinary Board. The agreement shall provide that all reports made by the financial institution shall be in writing and shall include the same information customarily forwarded to the depositor when an instrument is presented against insufficient funds. If the financial institution is located outside of the State of Georgia it shall also agree in writing to honor any properly issued State Bar of Georgia subpoena.

(ii) The State Disciplinary Board shall establish procedures for a lawyer or law firm to be excused from the requirements of this Rule if the lawyer or law firm has its principal office in a county where no bank, credit union, or savings and loan association will agree to comply with the provisions of this Rule.

(2) *Timing of Reports*:

(i) The financial institution shall file a report with the Office of General Counsel of the State Bar of Georgia in every instance where a properly payable instrument is presented against a lawyer trust account containing insufficient funds and said instrument is not honored within three business days of presentation.

(ii) The report shall be filed with the Office of General Counsel within fifteen days of the date of the presentation of the instrument, even if the instrument is subsequently honored after the three business days provided in (2)(i) above.

(3) Nothing shall preclude a financial institution from charging a particular lawyer or law firm for the reasonable cost of producing the reports and records required by this Rule.

(4) Every lawyer and law firm maintaining a trust account as provided by these Rules is hereby and shall be conclusively deemed to have consented to the reporting and production requirements mandated by this Rule and shall indemnify and hold harmless each financial institution for its compliance with the aforesaid reporting and production requirements.

(d) Effect on Financial Institution of Compliance: The agreement by a financial institution to offer accounts pursuant to this Rule shall be a procedure to advise the State Disciplinary Board of conduct by attorneys and shall not be deemed to create a duty to exercise a standard of care or a contract with third parties that may sustain a loss as a result of lawyers overdrawing attorney trust accounts.

(e) Availability of Records: A lawyer shall not fail to produce any of the records required to be maintained by these Standards at the request of the Investigative Panel of the State Disciplinary Board or the Supreme Court. This obligation shall be in addition to and not in lieu of the procedures contained in Part IV of these Rules for the production of documents and evidence.

(f) Audit for Cause: A lawyer shall not fail to submit to an Audit for Cause conducted by the State Disciplinary Board pursuant to Bar Rule 4–111.

The maximum penalty for a violation of this Rule is disbarment.

Comment

[1] Each financial institution wishing to be approved as a depository of client trust funds must file an overdraft notification agreement with the State Disciplinary Board of the State Bar of Georgia. The State Bar of Georgia will publish a list of approved institutions at least annually.

[2] The overdraft agreement requires that all overdrafts be reported to the Office of General Counsel of the State Bar of Georgia whether or not the instrument is honored. It is improper for a lawyer to accept "overdraft privileges" or any other arrangement for a personal loan on a client trust account, particularly in exchange for the institution's promise to delay or not to report an overdraft. The institution must notify the Office of General Counsel of all overdrafts even where the institution is certain that its own error caused the overdraft or that the matter could have been resolved between the institution and the lawyer within a reasonable period of time.

[3] The overdraft notification provision is not intended to result in the discipline of every lawyer who overdraws a trust account. The lawyer or institution may explain occasional errors. The provision merely intends that the Office of General Counsel receive an early warning of improprieties so that corrective action, including audits for cause, may be taken.

Audits

[4] Every lawyer's financial records and trust account records are required records and therefore are properly subject to audit for cause. The audit provisions are intended to uncover errors and omissions before the public is harmed, to deter those lawyers who may be tempted to misuse client's funds and to educate and instruct lawyers as to proper trust accounting methods. Although the auditors will be employed by the Office of General Counsel of the State Bar of Georgia, it is intended that disciplinary proceedings will be brought only when the auditors have reasonable cause to believe discrepancies or irregularities exist. Otherwise, the auditors should only educate the lawyer and the lawyer's staff as to proper trust accounting methods.

[5] An audit for cause may be conducted at any time and without advance notice if the Office of General Counsel receives sufficient evidence that a lawyer poses a threat of harm to clients or the public. The Office of General Counsel must have the written approval of the Chairman of the Investigative Panel of the State Disciplinary Board and the President-elect of the State Bar of Georgia to conduct an audit for cause.

RULE 1.16 DECLINING OR TERMINATING REPRESENTATION

(a) Except as stated in paragraph (c), a lawyer shall not represent a client or, where representation has commenced, shall withdraw from the representation of a client if:

(1) the representation will result in violation of the Georgia Rules of Professional Conduct or other law;

(2) the lawyer's physical or mental condition materially impairs the lawyer's ability to represent the client; or

(3) the lawyer is discharged.

(b) except as stated in paragraph (c), a lawyer may withdraw from representing a client if withdrawal can be accomplished without material adverse effect on the interests of the client, or if:

(1) the client persists in a course of action involving the lawyer's services that the lawyer reasonably believes is criminal or fraudulent;

(2) the client has used the lawyer's services to perpetrate a crime or fraud;

(3) the client insists upon pursuing an objective that the lawyer considers repugnant or imprudent;

(4) the client fails substantially to fulfill an obligation to the lawyer regarding the lawyer's services and has been given reasonable warning that the lawyer will withdraw unless the obligation is fulfilled;

(5) the representation will result in an unreasonable financial burden on the lawyer or has been rendered unreasonably difficult by the client; or

(6) other good cause for withdrawal exists.

(c) When a lawyer withdraws it shall be done in compliance with applicable laws and rules. When ordered to do so by a tribunal, a lawyer shall continue representation notwithstanding good cause for terminating the representation.

(d) Upon termination of representation, a lawyer shall take steps to the extent reasonably practicable to protect a client's interests, such as giving reasonable notice to the client, allowing time for employment of other counsel, surrendering papers and property to which the client is entitled and refunding any advance payment of fee that has not been earned.

The maximum penalty for a violation of this Rule is a public reprimand.

Comment

[1] A lawyer should not accept representation in a matter unless it can be performed competently, promptly, without improper conflict of interest and to completion. *But see Rule 1.2(c): Scope of Representation.*

Mandatory Withdrawal

[2] A lawyer ordinarily must decline or withdraw from representation if the client demands that the lawyer engage in conduct that is illegal or violates the Georgia Rules of Professional Conduct or other law. The lawyer is not obliged to decline or withdraw simply because the client suggests such a course of conduct; a client may make such a suggestion in the hope that a lawyer will not be constrained by a professional obligation.

[3] When a lawyer has been appointed to represent a client, withdrawal ordinarily requires approval of the appointing authority. See also *Rule 6.2: Accepting Appointments.* Difficulty may be encountered if withdrawal is based on the client's demand that the lawyer engage in unprofessional conduct. The court may wish an explanation for the withdrawal, while the lawyer may be bound to keep confidential the facts that would constitute such an explanation. The lawyer's statement that professional considerations require termination of the representation ordinarily should be accepted as sufficient.

Discharge

[4] A client has a right to discharge a lawyer at any time, with or without cause, subject to liability for payment for the lawyer's services. Where future dispute about the withdrawal may be anticipated, it may be advisable to prepare a written statement reciting the circumstances.

[5] Whether a client can discharge appointed counsel may depend on applicable law. To the extent possible, the lawyer should give the client an explanation of the consequences. These consequences may include a decision by the appointing authority that appointment of successor counsel is unjustified, thus requiring the client to be self-represented.

[6] If the client is mentally incompetent, the client may lack the legal capacity to discharge the lawyer, and in any event the discharge may be seriously adverse to the client's interests. The lawyer should make special effort to help the client consider the consequences and, in an extreme case, may initiate proceedings for a conservatorship or similar protection of the client. See *Rule 1.14: Client under a Disability.*

Optional Withdrawal

[7] The lawyer has the option to withdraw if it can be accomplished without material adverse effect on the client's interests. Withdrawal is also justified if the client persists in a course of action that the lawyer reasonably believes is criminal or fraudulent, for a lawyer is not required to be associated with such conduct even if the lawyer does not further it. Withdrawal is also permitted if the lawyer's services were misused in the past even if that would materially prejudice the client. The lawyer also may withdraw where the client insists on a repugnant or imprudent objective. The lawyer's statement that professional considerations require termination of the representation ordinarily should be accepted as sufficient.

[8] A lawyer may withdraw if the client refuses to abide by the terms of an agreement relating to the representation, such as an agreement concerning fees or court costs or an agreement limiting the objectives of the representation.

Assisting the Client upon Withdrawal

[9] Even if the lawyer has been unfairly discharged by the client, a lawyer must take all reasonable steps to mitigate the consequences to the client.

[10] Whether or not a lawyer for an organization may under certain unusual circumstances have a legal obligation to the organization after withdrawing or being discharged by the organization's highest authority is beyond the scope of these Rules.

RULE 1.17 SALE OF LAW PRACTICE

A lawyer or a law firm may sell or purchase a law practice, including good will, if the following conditions are satisfied:

(a) Reserved.

(b) The practice is sold as an entirety to another lawyer or law firm;

(c) Actual written notice is given to each of the seller's clients regarding;

(1) the proposed sale;

(2) the terms of any proposed change in the fee arrangement authorized by paragraph (d);

(3) the client's right to retain other counsel or to take possession of the file; and

(4) the fact that the client's consent to the sale will be presumed if the client does not take any action or does not otherwise object within ninety (90) days of receipt of the notice.

If a client cannot be given notice, the representation of that client may be transferred to the purchaser only upon entry of an order so authorizing by a court having jurisdiction. The seller may disclose to the court *in camera* information relating to the representation only to the extent necessary to obtain an order authorizing the transfer of a file.

(d) The fees charged clients shall not be increased by reason of the sale. The purchaser may, however, refuse to undertake the representation unless the client consents to pay the purchaser fees at a rate not exceeding the fees charged by the purchaser for rendering substantially similar services prior to the initiation of the purchase negotiations.

The maximum penalty for a violation of this Rule is a public reprimand.

Comment

[1] The practice of law is a profession, not merely a business. Clients are not commodities that can be purchased and sold at will. Pursuant to this Rule, when another lawyer or firm takes over the representation, the selling lawyer or firm may obtain compensation for the reasonable value of the practice as may withdrawing partners of law firms. See Rules 5.4: *Professional Independence of a Lawyer* and 5.6: *Restrictions on Right to Practice.*

Termination of Practice by the Seller

[2] The requirement that all of the private practice be sold is satisfied if the seller in good faith makes the entire practice available for sale to the purchaser. The fact that a number of the seller's clients decide not to be represented by the purchaser but take their matters elsewhere, therefore, does not result in a violation. Neither does a return to private practice as a result of an unanticipated change in circumstances result in a violation. For example, a lawyer who has sold the practice to accept an appointment to judicial office does not violate the requirement that the sale be attendant to cessation of practice if the lawyer later resumes private practice upon being defeated in a contested or a retention election for the office.

[3] *Reserved.*

[4] *Reserved.*

Single Purchaser

[5] The Rule requires a single purchaser. The prohibition against piecemeal sale of a practice protects those clients whose matters are less lucrative and who might find it difficult to secure other counsel if a sale could be limited to substantial fee-generating matters. The purchaser is required to undertake all client matters in the practice, subject to client consent. If, however, the purchaser is unable to undertake all client matters because of a conflict of interest in a specific matter respecting which the purchaser is not permitted by *Rule 1.7: Conflict of Interest* or another rule to represent the client, the requirement that there be a single purchaser is nevertheless satisfied.

Client Confidences, Consent and Notice

[6] Negotiations between seller and prospective purchaser prior to disclosure of information relating to a specific representation of an identifiable client no more violate the confidentiality provisions of *Rule 1.6: Confidentiality of Information* than do preliminary discussions concerning the possible association of another lawyer or mergers between firms, with respect to which client consent is not required. Providing the purchaser access to client-specific information relating to the representation and to the file, however, requires client consent. The Rule provides that before such information can be disclosed by the seller to the purchaser the client must be given actual written notice of the contemplated sale, including the identity of the purchaser and any proposed change in the terms of future representation, and must be told that the decision to consent or make other arrangements must be made within 90 days. If nothing is heard from the client within that time, consent to the sale is presumed.

[7] A lawyer or law firm ceasing to practice cannot be required to remain in practice because some clients cannot be given actual notice of the proposed purchase. Since these clients cannot themselves consent to the purchase or direct any other disposition of their files, the Rule requires an order from a court having jurisdiction authorizing their transfer or other disposition. The Court can be expected to determine whether reasonable efforts to locate the client have been exhausted, and whether the absent client's legitimate interests will be served by authorizing the transfer of the file so that the purchaser may continue the representation. Preservation of client confidences requires that the petition for a court order be considered *in camera.*

[8] All the elements of client autonomy, including the client's absolute right to discharge a lawyer and transfer the representation to another, survive the sale of the practice.

Fee Arrangements Between Client and Purchaser

[9] The sale may not be financed by increases in fees charged the clients of the practice. Existing agreements between the seller and the client as to fees and the scope of the work must be honored by the purchaser, unless the client consents. The purchaser may, however, advise the client that the purchaser will not undertake the representation unless the client consents to pay the higher fees the purchaser usually charges. To prevent client financing of the sale, the higher fee the purchaser may charge must not exceed the fees charged by the purchaser for substantially similar services rendered prior to the initiation of the purchase negotiations.

[10] The purchaser may not intentionally fragment the practice which is the subject of the sale by charging significantly different fees in substantially similar matters. Doing so would make it possible for the purchaser to avoid the obligation to take over the entire practice by charging arbitrarily higher fees for less lucrative matters, thereby increasing the likelihood that those clients would not consent to the new representation.

Other Applicable Ethical Standards

[11] Lawyers participating in the sale of a law practice are subject to the ethical standards applicable to involving another lawyer in the representation of a client. These include, for example, the seller's obligation to exercise competence in identifying a purchaser qualified to assume the practice and the purchaser's obligation to undertake the representation competently *(see Rule 1.1: Competence);* the obligation to avoid disqualifying conflicts, and to secure client

consent after consultation for those conflicts which can be agreed to *(see Rule 1.7: Conflict of Interest);* and the obligation to protect information relating to the representation *(see Rules 1.6 and 1.9)*.

[12] If approval of the substitution of the purchasing lawyer for the selling lawyer is required by the rules of any tribunal in which a matter is pending, such approval must be obtained before the matter can be included in the sale *(see Rule 1.16: Declining or Terminating Representation)*.

Applicability of the Rule

[13] This Rule applies to the sale of a law practice by representatives of a deceased, disabled or disappeared lawyer. Thus, the seller may be represented by a non-lawyer representative not subject to these Rules. Since, however, no lawyer may participate in a sale of a law practice which does not conform to the requirements of this Rule, the representatives of the seller as well as the purchasing lawyer can be expected to see to it that they are met.

[14] Admission to or retirement from a law partnership or professional association, retirement plans and similar arrangements, and a sale of tangible assets of a law practice, do not constitute a sale or purchase governed by this Rule.

[15] This Rule does not apply to the transfers of legal representation between lawyers when such transfers are unrelated to the sale of a practice.

PART TWO. COUNSELOR

RULE 2.1 ADVISOR

In representing a client, a lawyer shall exercise independent professional judgment and render candid advice. A lawyer should not be deterred from giving candid advice by the prospect that the advice will be unpalatable to the client.

The maximum penalty for a violation of this Rule is disbarment.

Comment

Scope of Advice

[1] A client is entitled to straightforward advice expressing the lawyer's honest assessment. Legal advice often involves unpleasant facts and alternatives that a client may be disinclined to confront. In presenting advice, a lawyer endeavors to sustain the client's morale and may put advice in as acceptable a form as honesty permits. However, a lawyer should not be deterred from giving candid advice by the prospect that the advice will be unpalatable to the client.

[2] In rendering advice, a lawyer may refer not only to law but to other considerations such as moral, economic, social and political factors that may be relevant to the client's situation. Advice couched in narrowly legal terms may be of little value to a client, especially where practical considerations, such as cost or effects on other people, are predominant. Purely technical legal advice, therefore, can sometimes be inadequate. It is proper for a lawyer to refer to relevant moral and ethical considerations in giving advice.

[3] A client may expressly or impliedly ask the lawyer for purely technical advice. When such a request is made by a client experienced in legal matters, the lawyer may accept it at face value. When such a request is made by a client inexperienced in legal matters, however, the lawyer's responsibility as advisor may include indicating that more may be involved than strictly legal considerations.

[4] Matters that go beyond strictly legal questions may also be in the domain of another profession. Family matters can involve problems within the professional competence of psychiatry, clinical psychology or social work; business matters can involve problems within the competence of the accounting profession or of financial specialists. Where consultation with a professional in another field is itself something a competent lawyer would recommend, the lawyer should make such a recommendation. At the same time, a lawyer's advice at its best often consists of recommending a course of action in the face of conflicting recommendations of experts.

Offering Advice

[5] In general, a lawyer is not expected to give advice until asked by the client. However, when a lawyer knows that a client proposes a course of action that is likely to result in substantial adverse legal consequences to the client, duty to the client under *Rule 1.4: Communication* may require that the lawyer act if the client's course of action is related to the representation. A lawyer ordinarily has no duty to initiate investigation of a client's affairs or to give advice that the client has indicated is unwanted, but a lawyer may initiate advice to a client when doing so appears to be in the client's interest.

RULE 2.2 INTERMEDIARY

(a) A lawyer acting as an intermediary by representing two or more parties with potentially conflicting interests shall withdraw if:

(1) any of the clients so request; or

(2) there comes into existence any of the conditions which would cause an attorney "not to accept or continue the representation" under the provisions of Rule 1.7.

(b) Upon withdrawal, the lawyer shall not continue to represent any of the clients in the matter that was the subject of the intermediation.

The maximum penalty for a violation of this Rule is disbarment.

Comment

[1] A lawyer acts as intermediary under this Rule when the lawyer represents two or more parties with potentially conflicting interests. A key factor in defining the relationship is whether the parties share responsibility for the lawyer's fee, but the common representation may be inferred from other circumstances. Because confusion can arise as to the lawyer's role where each party is not separately represented, it is important that the lawyer make clear the relationship.

[2] The Rule does not apply to a lawyer acting as arbitrator or mediator between or among parties who are not clients of the lawyer, even where the lawyer has been appointed with the concurrence of the parties. In performing such a

role the lawyer may be subject to applicable codes of ethics, such as the Code of Ethics for Arbitration in Commercial Disputes prepared by a joint Committee of the American Bar Association and the American Arbitration Association.

[3] A lawyer acts as intermediary in seeking to establish or adjust a relationship between clients on an amicable and mutually advantageous basis; for example, in helping to organize a business in which two or more clients are entrepreneurs, working out the financial reorganization of an enterprise in which two or more clients have an interest, arranging a property distribution in settlement of an estate or mediating a dispute between clients. The lawyer seeks to resolve potentially conflicting interests by developing the parties' mutual interests. The alternative can be that each party may have to obtain separate representation, with the possibility in some situations of incurring additional cost, complication or even litigation. Given these and other relevant factors, all the clients may prefer that the lawyer act as intermediary.

[4] In considering whether to act as intermediary between clients, a lawyer should be mindful that if the intermediation fails the result can be additional cost, embarrassment and recrimination. In some situations the risk of failure is so great that intermediation is plainly impossible. For example, a lawyer cannot undertake common representation of clients between whom contentious litigation is imminent or who contemplate contentious negotiations. More generally, if the relationship between the parties has already assumed definite antagonism, the possibility that the clients' interests can be adjusted by intermediation ordinarily is not very good.

[5] The appropriateness of intermediation can depend on its form. Forms of intermediation range from informal arbitration, where each client's case is presented by the respective client and the lawyer decides the outcome, to mediation, to common representation where the clients' interests are substantially though not entirely compatible. One form may be appropriate in circumstances where another would not. Other relevant factors are whether the lawyer subsequently will represent both parties on a continuing basis and whether the situation involves creating a relationship between the parties or terminating one. The lawyer must reasonably believe that the matter can be resolved on terms compatible with the clients' best interests, that each client will be able to make adequately informed decisions in the matter and that there is little risk of material prejudice to the interests of any of the clients if the contemplated resolution is unsuccessful; and the lawyer reasonably believes that the common representation can be undertaken impartially and without improper effect on other responsibilities the lawyer has to any of the clients.

Confidentiality and Privilege

[6] A particularly important factor in determining the appropriateness of intermediation is the effect on client-lawyer confidentiality and the attorney-client privilege. In a common representation, the lawyer is still required both to keep each client adequately informed and to maintain confidentiality of information relating to the representation. See Rules 1.4 and 1.6. Complying with both requirements while acting as intermediary requires a delicate balance. If the balance cannot be maintained, the common representation is improper. With regard to the attorney-client privilege, the prevailing rule is that as between commonly represented clients the privilege does not attach. Hence, it must be assumed that if litigation eventuates between the clients, the privilege will not protect any such communications, and the clients should be so advised.

[7] Since the lawyer is required to be impartial between commonly represented clients, intermediation is improper when that impartiality cannot be maintained. For example, a lawyer who has represented one of the clients for a long period and in a variety of matters might have difficulty being impartial between that client and one to whom the lawyer has only recently been introduced.

Consultation

[8] In acting as intermediary between clients, the lawyer is required to consult with the clients on the implications of doing so, and proceed only upon consent based on such a consultation. The consultation should make clear that the lawyer's role is not that of partisanship normally expected in other circumstances.

[9] Paragraph (b) is an application of the principle expressed in *Rule 1.4: Communication.* Where the lawyer is intermediary, the clients ordinarily must assume greater responsibility for decisions than when each client is independently represented.

Withdrawal

[10] Common representation does not diminish the rights of each client in the client-lawyer relationship. Each has the right to loyal and diligent representation, the right to discharge the lawyer as stated in *Rule 1.16: Declining or Terminating Representation,* and the protection of *Rule 1.9: Conflict of Interest: Former Client* concerning obligations to a former client.

RULE 2.3 EVALUATION FOR USE BY THIRD PERSONS

(a) A lawyer may undertake an evaluation of a matter affecting a client for the use of someone other than the client if:

(1) the lawyer reasonably believes that making the evaluation is compatible with other aspects of the lawyer's relationship with the client; and

(2) the client consents after consultation.

(b) Except as disclosure is required in connection with a report of an evaluation, information relating to the evaluation is otherwise protected by Rule 1.6.

The maximum penalty for a violation of this Rule is a public reprimand.

Comment

Definition

[1] An evaluation may be performed at the client's direction but for the primary purpose of establishing information for the benefit of third parties; for example, an opinion concerning the title of property rendered at the behest of a vendor for the information of a prospective purchaser, or at the behest of a borrower for the information of a prospective lender. In some situations, the evaluation may be required by a government entity; for example, an opinion concerning the legality of the securities registered for sale under the securities laws. In other instances, the evaluation may be required by a third person, such as a purchaser of a business.

[2] Lawyers for the government may be called upon to give a formal opinion on the legality of contemplated government entity action. In making such an evaluation, the government lawyer acts at the behest of the government as the client but for the purpose of establishing the limits of the agency's authorized activity. Such an opinion is to be distinguished from confidential legal advice given agency officials. The critical question is whether the opinion is to be made public.

[3] A legal evaluation should be distinguished from an investigation of a person with whom the lawyer does not have a client-lawyer relationship. For example, a lawyer retained by a purchaser to analyze a vendor's title to property does not have a client-lawyer relationship with the vendor. So also, an investigation into a person's affairs by a government lawyer, or by special counsel employed by the government, is not an evaluation as that term is used in this Rule. The question is whether the lawyer is retained by the person whose affairs are being examined. When the lawyer is retained by that person, the general rules concerning loyalty to client and preservation of confidences apply, which is not the case if the lawyer is retained by someone else. For this reason, it is essential to identify the person by whom the lawyer is retained. This should be made clear not only to the person under examination, but also to others to whom the results are to be made available.

Duty to Third Person

[4] When the evaluation is intended for the information or use of a third person, a legal duty to that person may or may not arise. That legal question is beyond the scope of this Rule. However, since such an evaluation involves a departure from the normal client-lawyer relationship, careful analysis of the situation is required. The lawyer must be satisfied as a matter of professional judgment that making the evaluation is compatible with other functions undertaken in behalf of the client. For example, if the lawyer is acting as advocate in defending the client against charges of fraud, it would normally be incompatible with that responsibility for the lawyer to perform an evaluation for others concerning the same or a related transaction. Assuming no such impediment is apparent, however, the lawyer should advise the client of the implications of the evaluation, particularly the lawyer's responsibilities to third persons and the duty to disseminate the findings.

Access to and Disclosure of Information

[5] The quality of an evaluation depends on the freedom and extent of the investigation upon which it is based. Ordinarily a lawyer should have whatever latitude of investigation seems necessary as a matter of professional judgment. Under some circumstances, however, the terms of the evaluation may be limited. For example, certain issues or sources may be categorically excluded, or the scope of search may be limited by time constraints or the noncooperation of persons having relevant information. Any such limitations which are material to the evaluation should be described in the report. If after a lawyer has commenced an evaluation, the client refuses to comply with the terms upon which it was understood the evaluation was to have been made, the lawyer's obligations are determined by law, having reference to the terms of the client's agreement and the surrounding circumstances.

Financial Auditors' Requests for Information

[6] When a question concerning the legal situation of a client arises at the instance of the client's financial auditor and the question is referred to the lawyer, the lawyer's response may be made in accordance with procedures recognized in the legal profession. Such a procedure is set forth in the American Bar Association Statement of Policy Regarding Lawyers' Responses to Auditors' Requests for Information, adopted in 1975.

PART THREE. ADVOCATE

RULE 3.1 MERITORIOUS CLAIMS AND CONTENTIONS

In the representation of a client, a lawyer shall not:

(a) file a suit, assert a position, conduct a defense, delay a trial, or take other action on behalf of the client when the lawyer knows or when it is obvious that such action would serve merely to harass or maliciously injure another;

(b) knowingly advance a claim or defense that is unwarranted under existing law, except that the lawyer may advance such claim or defense if it can be supported by good faith argument for an extension, modification or reversal of existing law.

The maximum penalty for a violation of this Rule is a public reprimand.

Comment

[1] The advocate has a duty to use legal procedure for the fullest benefit of the client's cause, but also a duty not to abuse legal procedure. The law, both procedural and substantive, establishes the limits within which an advocate may proceed. However, the law is not always clear and never is static. Accordingly, in determining the proper scope of advocacy, account must be taken of the law's ambiguities and potential for change.

[2] The filing of an action or defense or similar action taken for a client is not frivolous merely because the facts have not first been fully substantiated or because the lawyer expects to develop vital evidence only by discovery. Such action is not frivolous even though the lawyer believes that the client's position ultimately will not prevail. The action is frivolous, however, if the client desires to have the action taken primarily for the purpose of harassing or maliciously injuring a person, or, if the lawyer is unable either to make a good faith argument on the merits of the action taken or to support the action taken by a good faith argument for an extension, modification or reversal of existing law.

[3] It is not ethically improper for a lawyer to file a lawsuit before complete factual support for the claim has been established provided that the lawyer determines that a reasonable lawyer would conclude that there is a reasonable possibility that facts supporting the cause of action can be established after the filing of the claim; and provided future that the lawyer is not required by rules of procedure. or otherwise to represent that the cause of action has an adequate factual basis. If after filing it is discovered that

the lawsuit has no merit, the lawyer will dismiss the lawsuit or in the alternative withdraw.

[4] The decision of a court that a claim is not meritorious is not necessarily conclusive of a violation of this Rule.

RULE 3.2 EXPEDITING LITIGATION

A lawyer shall make reasonable efforts to expedite litigation consistent with the interests of the client.

The maximum penalty for a violation of this Rule is a public reprimand.

Comment

[1] Dilatory practices bring the administration of justice into disrepute.

[2] The reasonableness of a lawyer's effort to expedite litigation must be judged by all of the controlling factors. "Reasonable efforts" do not equate to "instant efforts" and are sufficient if reasonable under the relevant circumstances.

RULE 3.3 CANDOR TOWARD THE TRIBUNAL

(a) A lawyer shall not knowingly:

(1) make a false statement of material fact or law to a tribunal;

(2) fail to disclose a material fact to a tribunal when disclosure is necessary to avoid assisting a criminal or fraudulent act by the client;

(3) fail to disclose to the tribunal legal authority in the controlling jurisdiction known to the lawyer to be directly adverse to the position of the client and not disclosed by opposing counsel; or

(4) offer evidence that the lawyer knows to be false. If a lawyer has offered material evidence and comes to know of its falsity, the lawyer shall take reasonable remedial measures.

(b) The duties stated in paragraph (a) continue to the conclusion of the proceeding, and apply even if compliance requires disclosure of information otherwise protected by Rule 1.6.

(c) A lawyer may refuse to offer evidence that the lawyer reasonably believes is false.

(d) In an ex parte proceeding, other than grand jury proceedings, a lawyer shall inform the tribunal of all material facts known to the lawyer that the lawyer reasonably believes are necessary to enable the tribunal to make an informed decision, whether or not the facts are adverse.

The maximum penalty for a violation of this Rule is disbarment.

Comment

[1] The advocate's task is to present the client's case with persuasive force. Performance of that duty while maintaining confidences of the client is qualified by the advocate's duty of candor to the tribunal. However, an advocate does not vouch for the evidence submitted in a cause; the tribunal is responsible for assessing its probative value.

Representations by a Lawyer

[2] An advocate is responsible for pleadings and other documents prepared for litigation, but is usually not required to have personal knowledge of matters asserted therein, for litigation documents ordinarily present assertions by the client, or by someone on the client's behalf, and not assertions by the lawyer. Compare *Rule 3.1: Meritorious Claims and Contentions.* However, an assertion purporting to be on the lawyer's own knowledge, as in an affidavit by the lawyer or in a statement in open court, may properly be made only when the lawyer knows the assertion is true or believes it to be true on the basis of a reasonably diligent inquiry. There are circumstances where failure to make a disclosure is the equivalent of an affirmative misrepresentation. Whether disclosure is necessary shall be considered in light of all of the relevant circumstances. The obligation prescribed in *Rule 1.2(d): Scope of Representation* not to counsel a client to commit or assist the client in committing a fraud applies in litigation. Regarding compliance with *Rule 1.2(d): Scope of Representation*, see the Comment to that Rule. See also the Comment to *Rule 8.4(b): Misconduct.*

Misleading Legal Argument

[3] Legal argument based on a knowingly false representation of law constitutes dishonesty toward the tribunal. A lawyer is not required to make a disinterested exposition of the law, but must recognize the existence of pertinent legal authorities. Furthermore, as stated in paragraph (a)(3), an advocate has a duty to disclose directly adverse authority in the controlling jurisdiction which has not been disclosed by the opposing party. The underlying concept is that legal argument is a discussion seeking to determine the legal premises properly applicable to the case.

False Evidence

[4] When evidence that a lawyer knows to be false is provided by a person who is not the client, the lawyer must refuse to offer it regardless of the client's wishes.

[5] When false evidence is offered by the client, however, a conflict may arise between the lawyer's duty to keep the client's revelations confidential and the duty of candor to the court. Upon ascertaining that material evidence is false, the lawyer should seek to persuade the client that the evidence should not be offered or, if it has been offered, that its false character should immediately be disclosed. If the persuasion is ineffective, the lawyer must take reasonable remedial measures.

[6] Except in the defense of a criminal accused, the rule generally recognized is that, if necessary to rectify the situation, an advocate must disclose the existence of the client's deception to the court or to the other party. Such a disclosure can result in grave consequences to the client, including not only a sense of betrayal but also loss of the case and perhaps a prosecution for perjury. But the alternative is that the lawyer cooperate in deceiving the court, thereby subverting the truth-finding process which the adversary system is designed to implement. See *Rule 1.2(d): Scope of Representation.* Furthermore, unless it is clearly understood that the lawyer will act upon the duty to disclose the existence of false evidence, the client can simply reject the lawyer's advice to reveal the false evidence and insist that the lawyer keep silent.

Perjury by a Criminal Defendant

[7] Whether an advocate for a criminally accused has the same duty of disclosure has been intensely debated. While it

is agreed that the lawyer should seek to persuade the client to refrain from perjurious testimony, there has been dispute concerning the lawyer's duty when that persuasion fails. If the confrontation with the client occurs before trial, the lawyer ordinarily can withdraw. Withdrawal before trial may not be possible, however, either because trial is imminent, or because the confrontation with the client does not take place until the trial itself, or because no other counsel is available.

[8] The most difficult situation, therefore, arises in a criminal case where the accused insists on testifying when the lawyer knows that the testimony is perjurious. The lawyer's effort to rectify the situation can increase the likelihood of the client's being convicted as well as opening the possibility of a prosecution for perjury. On the other hand, if the lawyer does not exercise control over the proof, the lawyer participates, although in a merely passive way, in deception of the court.

[9] Three resolutions of this dilemma have been proposed. One is to permit the accused to testify by a narrative without guidance through the lawyer's questioning. This compromises both contending principles; it exempts the lawyer from the duty to disclose false evidence but subjects the client to an implicit disclosure of information imparted to counsel. Another suggested resolution, of relatively, recent origin, is that the advocate be entirely excused from the duty to reveal perjury if the perjury is that of the client. This is a coherent solution but makes the advocate a knowing instrument of perjury.

[10] The other resolution of the dilemma is that the lawyer must reveal the client's perjury if necessary to rectify the situation. A criminal accused has a right to the assistance of an advocate, a right to testify and a right of confidential communication with counsel. However, an accused should not have a right to assistance of counsel in committing perjury. Furthermore, an advocate has an obligation, not only in professional ethics but under the law as well, to avoid implication in the commission of perjury or other falsification of evidence. See *Rule 1.2(d): Scope of Representation.*

Remedial Measures

[11] If perjured testimony or false evidence has been offered, the advocate's proper course ordinarily is to remonstrate with the client confidentially. If that fails, the advocate should seek to withdraw if that will remedy the situation. If withdrawal will not remedy the situation or is impossible, the advocate should make disclosure to the court. It is for the court then to determine what should be done-making a statement about the matter to the trier of fact, ordering a mistrial or perhaps nothing. If the false testimony was that of the client, the client may controvert the lawyer's version of their communication when the lawyer discloses the situation to the court. If there is an issue whether the client has committed perjury, the lawyer cannot represent the client in resolution of the issue, and a mistrial may be unavoidable. An unscrupulous client might in this way attempt to produce a series of mistrials and thus escape prosecution. However, a second such encounter could be construed as a deliberate abuse of the right to counsel and as such a waiver of the right to further representation.

Constitutional Requirements

[12] The general rule—that an advocate must disclose the existence of perjury with respect to a material fact, even that of a client—applies to defense counsel in criminal cases, as well as in other instances. However, the definition of the lawyer's ethical duty in such a situation may be qualified by constitutional provisions for due process and the right to counsel in criminal cases. In some jurisdictions these provisions have been construed to require that counsel present an accused as a witness if the accused wishes to testify, even if counsel knows the testimony will be false. The obligation of the advocate under these Rules is subordinate to such a constitutional requirement.

Duration of Obligation

[13] A practical time limit on the obligation to rectify the presentation of false evidence has to be established. The conclusion of the proceeding is a reasonably definite point for the termination of the obligation.

Refusing to Offer Proof Believed to Be False

[14] Generally speaking, a lawyer has authority to refuse to offer testimony or other proof that the lawyer believes is untrustworthy. Offering such proof may reflect adversely on the lawyer's ability to discriminate in the quality of evidence and thus impair the lawyer's effectiveness as an advocate. In criminal cases, however, a lawyer may, in some jurisdictions, be denied this authority by constitutional requirements governing the right to counsel.

Ex Parte Proceedings

[15] Ordinarily, an advocate has the limited responsibility of presenting one side of the matters that a tribunal should consider in reaching a decision; the conflicting position is expected to be presented by the opposing party. However, in any *ex parte* proceeding, such as an application for a temporary restraining order, there is no balance of presentation by opposing advocates. The object of an *ex parte* proceeding is nevertheless to yield a substantially just result. The judge has an affirmative responsibility to accord the absent party just consideration. The lawyer for the represented party has the correlative duty to make disclosures of material facts known to the lawyer and that the lawyer reasonably believes are necessary to an informed decision.

RULE 3.4 FAIRNESS TO OPPOSING PARTY AND COUNSEL

A lawyer shall not:

(a) unlawfully obstruct another party's access to evidence or unlawfully alter, destroy or conceal a document or other material having potential evidentiary value. A lawyer shall not counsel or assist another person to do any such act;

(b)(1) falsify evidence;

(2) counsel or assist a witness to testify falsely;

(3) pay, offer to pay, or acquiesce in the payment of compensation to a witness contingent upon the content of the testimony or the outcome of the case. But a lawyer may advance, guarantee, or acquiesce in the payment of:

(i) expenses reasonably incurred by a witness in preparation, attending or testifying;

(ii) reasonable compensation to a witness for the loss of time in preparing, attending or testifying;

(iii) a reasonable fee for the professional services of an expert witness;

(c) Reserved.

(d) Reserved.

(e) Reserved.

(f) request a person other than a client to refrain from voluntarily giving relevant information to another party unless:

(1) the person is a relative or an employee or other agent of a client; or

(2) the information is subject to the assertion of a privilege by the client; and

(3) the lawyer reasonably believes that the person's interests will not be adversely affected by refraining from giving such information and the request is not otherwise prohibited by law;

(g) use methods of obtaining evidence that violate the legal rights of the opposing party or counsel; or

(h) present, participate in presenting or threaten to present criminal charges solely to obtain an advantage in a civil matter.

The maximum penalty for a violation of this Rule is disbarment.

Comment

[1] The procedure of the adversary system contemplates that the evidence in a case is to be marshaled competitively by the contending parties. Fair competition in the adversary system is secured by prohibitions against destruction or concealment of evidence, improperly influencing witnesses, obstructive tactics in discovery procedure, and the like.

[2] Documents and other items of evidence are often essential to establish a claim or defense. Subject to evidentiary privileges, the right of an opposing party, including the government, to obtain evidence through discovery or subpoena is an important procedural right. The exercise of that right can be frustrated if relevant material is altered, concealed or destroyed. Applicable law in many jurisdictions makes it an offense to destroy material for purpose of impairing its availability in a pending proceeding or one whose commencement can be foreseen. Falsifying evidence is also generally a criminal offense. Paragraph (a) applies to evidentiary material generally, including computerized information.

[3] *Reserved.*

[4] Paragraph (f) permits a lawyer to advise employees of a client to refrain from giving information to another party, for the employees may identify their interests with those of the client. See also *Rule 4.2: Communication with Persons Represented by Counsel.*

[5] As to paragraph (g), the responsibility to a client requires a lawyer to subordinate the interests of others to those of the client, but that responsibility does not imply that a lawyer may disregard the rights of the opposing party or counsel. It is impractical to catalogue all such rights, but they include legal restrictions on methods of obtaining evidence.

RULE 3.5 IMPARTIALITY AND DECORUM OF THE TRIBUNAL

A lawyer shall not, without regard to whether the lawyer represents a client in the matter:

(a) seek to influence a judge, juror, prospective juror or other official by means prohibited by law;

(b) communicate *ex parte* with such a person except as permitted by law; or

(c) engage in conduct intended to disrupt a tribunal.

The maximum penalty for a violation of part (a) of this Rule is disbarment. The maximum penalty for a violation of part (b) or part (c) of this Rule is a public reprimand.

Comment

[1] Many forms of improper influence upon the tribunal are proscribed by criminal law. All of those are specified in the *Georgia Code of Judicial Conduct* with which an advocate should be familiar. Attention is also directed to *Rule 8.4: Misconduct,* which governs other instances of improper conduct by a lawyer/candidate.

[2] If we are to maintain the integrity of the judicial process, it is imperative that an advocate's function be limited to the presentation of evidence and argument, to allow a cause to be decided according to law. The exertion of improper influence is detrimental to that process. Regardless of an advocate's innocent intention, actions which give the appearance of tampering with judicial impartiality are to be avoided. The activity proscribed by this Rule should be observed by the advocate in such a careful manner that there be no appearance of impropriety.

[3A] The Rule with respect to *ex parte* communications limits direct communications except as may be permitted by law. Thus, court rules or case law must be referred to in order to determine whether certain *ex parte* communications are legitimate. *Ex parte* communications may be permitted by statutory authorization.

[3B] A lawyer who obtains a judge's signature on a decree in the absence of the opposing lawyer where certain aspects of the decree are still in dispute, may have violated *Rule 3.5: Impartiality and Decorum of the Tribunal* regardless of the lawyer's good intentions or good faith.

[4] A lawyer may communicate as to the merits of the cause with a judge in the course of official proceedings in the case, in writing if the lawyer simultaneously delivers a copy of the writing to opposing counsel or to the adverse party if the party is not represented by a lawyer, or orally upon adequate notice to opposing counsel or to the adverse party if the party is not represented by a lawyer.

[5] If the lawyer knowingly instigates or causes another to instigate a communication proscribed by *Rule 3.5: Impartiality and Decorum of the Tribunal,* a violation may occur.

[6] Direct or indirect communication with a juror during the trial is clearly prohibited. A lawyer may not avoid the proscription of *Rule 3.5: Impartiality and Decorum of the Tribunal* by using agents to communicate improperly with jurors. A lawyer may be held responsible if the lawyer was aware of the client's desire to establish contact with jurors and assisted the client in doing so.

[7] *Reserved.*

[8] While a lawyer may stand firm against abuse by a judge, the lawyer's actions should avoid reciprocation. Fairness and impartiality of the trial process is strengthened by the lawyer's protection of the record for subsequent review and this preserves the professional integrity of the legal profession by patient firmness.

RULE 3.6 TRIAL PUBLICITY

(a) A lawyer who is participating or has participated in the investigation or litigation of a matter shall not make an extrajudicial statement that a person would reasonably believe to be disseminated by means of public communication if the lawyer knows or reasonably should know that it will have a substantial likelihood of materially prejudicing an adjudicative proceeding in the matter.

(b) Reserved.

(c) Notwithstanding paragraph (a), a lawyer may make a statement that a reasonable lawyer would believe is required to protect a client from the substantial undue prejudicial effect of recent publicity not initiated by the lawyer or the lawyer's client. A statement made pursuant to this paragraph shall be limited to such information as is necessary to mitigate the recent adverse publicity.

(d) No lawyer associated in a firm or government entity with a lawyer subject to paragraph (a) shall make a statement prohibited by paragraph (a).

The maximum penalty for a violation of this Rule is a public reprimand.

Comment

[1] It is difficult to strike a balance between protecting the right to a fair trial and safeguarding the right of free expression. Preserving the right to a fair trial necessarily entails some curtailment of the information that may be disseminated about a party prior to trial, particularly where trial by jury is involved. If there were no such limits, the result would be the practical nullification of the protective effect of the rules of forensic decorum and the exclusionary rules of evidence. On the other hand, there are vital social interests served by the free dissemination of information about events having legal consequences and about legal proceedings themselves. The public has a right to know about threats to its safety and measures aimed at assuring its security. It also has a legitimate interest in the conduct of judicial proceedings, particularly in matters of general public concern. Furthermore, the subject matter of legal proceedings is often of direct significance in debate and deliberation over questions of public policy.

[2] Special rules of confidentiality may validly govern proceedings in juvenile, domestic relations and mental disability proceedings, and perhaps other types of litigation. *Rule 3.4(c): Fairness to Opposing Party and Counsel* requires compliance with such rules.

[3] The Rule sets forth a basic general prohibition against a lawyer's making statements that the lawyer knows or should know will have a substantial likelihood of materially prejudicing an adjudicative proceeding. Recognizing that the public value of informed commentary is great and the likelihood of prejudice to a proceeding by the commentary of a lawyer who is not involved in the proceeding is small, the rule applies only to lawyers who are, or who have been involved in the investigation or litigation of a case, and their associates.

[4] *Reserved.*

[5A] There are, on the other hand, certain subjects which are more likely than not to have a material prejudicial effect on a proceeding, particularly when they refer to a civil matter triable to a jury, a criminal matter, or any other proceeding that could result in incarceration. These subjects relate to:

(a) the character, credibility, reputation or criminal record of a party, suspect in a criminal investigation or witness, or the identity of a witness, or the expected testimony of a party or witness;

(b) in a criminal case or proceeding that could result in incarceration, the possibility of a plea of guilty to the offense or the existence or contents of any confession, admission, or statement given by a defendant or suspect or that person's refusal or failure to make a statement;

(c) the performance or results of any examination or test or the refusal or failure of a person to submit to an examination or test, or the identity or nature of physical evidence expected to be presented;

(d) any opinion as to the guilt or innocence of a defendant or suspect in a criminal case or proceeding that could result in incarceration;

(e) information that the lawyer knows or reasonably should know is likely to be inadmissible as evidence in a trial and that would, if disclosed, create a substantial risk of prejudicing an impartial trial; or

(f) the fact that a defendant has been charged with a crime, unless there is included therein a statement explaining that the charge is merely an accusation and that the defendant is presumed innocent until and unless proven guilty.

[5B] In addition, there are certain subjects which are more likely than not to have no material prejudicial effect on a proceeding. Thus, a lawyer may usually state:

(a) the claim, offense or defense involved and, except when prohibited by law, the identity of the persons involved;

(b) information contained in a public record;

(c) that an investigation of a matter is in progress;

(d) the scheduling or result of any step in litigation;

(e) a request for assistance in obtaining evidence and information necessary thereto;

(f) a warning of danger concerning the behavior of a person involved, when there is reason to believe that there exists the likelihood of substantial harm to an individual or to the public interest; and

(g) in a criminal case, in addition to subparagraphs (1) through (6):

(i) the identity, residence, occupation and family status of the accused;

(ii) if the accused has not been apprehended, information necessary to aid in apprehension of that person;

(iii) the fact, time and place of arrest; and

(iv) the identity of investigating and arresting officers or agencies and the length of the investigation.

[6] Another relevant factor in determining prejudice is the nature of the proceeding involved. Criminal jury trials will be most sensitive to extrajudicial speech. Civil trials may be less sensitive. Non-jury hearings and arbitration proceedings may be even less affected. The Rule will still place limitations on prejudicial comments in these cases, but the likelihood of prejudice may be different depending on the type of proceeding.

[7] Finally, extrajudicial statements that might otherwise raise a question under this Rule may be permissible when they are made in response to statements made publicly by another party, another party's lawyer, or third persons, where a reasonable lawyer would believe a public response is required in order to avoid prejudice to the lawyer's client. When prejudicial statements have been publicly made by others, responsive statements may have the salutary effect of lessening any resulting adverse impact on the adjudicative proceeding. Such responsive statements should be limited to contain only such information as is necessary to mitigate undue prejudice created by the statements made by others.

RULE 3.7 LAWYER AS WITNESS

(a) A lawyer shall not act as advocate at a trial in which the lawyer is likely to be a necessary witness except where:

(1) the testimony relates to an uncontested issue;

(2) the testimony relates to the nature and value of legal services rendered in the case; or

(3) disqualification of the lawyer would work substantial hardship on the client.

(b) A lawyer may act as advocate in a trial in which another lawyer in the lawyer's firm is likely to be called as a witness unless precluded from doing so by Rule 1.7 or Rule 1.9.

The maximum penalty for a violation of this Rule is a public reprimand.

Comment

[1] Combining the roles of advocate and witness can prejudice the opposing party and can involve a conflict of interest between the lawyer and client.

[2] The opposing party has proper objection where the combination of roles may prejudice that party's rights in the litigation. A witness is required to testify on the basis of personal knowledge, while an advocate is expected to explain and comment on evidence given by others. It may not be clear whether a statement by an advocate-witness should be taken as proof or as an analysis of the proof.

[3] Paragraph (a)(1) recognizes that if the testimony will be uncontested, the ambiguities in the dual role are purely theoretical. Paragraph (a)(2) recognizes that where the testimony concerns the extent and value of legal services rendered in the action in which the testimony is offered, permitting the lawyers to testify avoids the need for a second trial with new counsel to resolve that issue. Moreover, in such a situation the judge has firsthand knowledge of the matter in issue; hence, there is less dependence on the adversary process to test the credibility of the testimony.

[4] Apart from these two exceptions, paragraph (a)(3) recognizes that a balancing is required between the interests of the client and those of the opposing party. Whether the opposing party is likely to suffer prejudice depends on the nature of the case, the importance and probable tenor of the lawyer's testimony, and the probability that the lawyer's testimony will conflict with that of other witnesses. Even if there is risk of such prejudice, in determining whether the lawyer should be disqualified, due regard must be given to the effect of disqualification on the lawyer's client. It is relevant that one or both parties could reasonably foresee that the lawyer would probably be a witness. The principle of imputed disqualification stated in *Rule 1.10: Imputed Disqualification* has no application to this aspect of the problem.

[5] Whether the combination of roles involves an improper conflict of interest with respect to the client is determined by *Rule 1.7: Conflict of Interest: General Rule* or *Rule 1.9: Conflict of Interest: Former Client*. For example, if there is likely to be substantial conflict between the testimony of the client and that of the lawyer or a member of the lawyer's firm, the representation is improper. The problem can arise whether the lawyer is called as a witness on behalf of the client or is called by the opposing party. Determining whether or not such a conflict exists is primarily the responsibility of the lawyer involved. See Comment to *Rule 1.7: Conflict of Interest*. If a lawyer who is a member of a firm may not act as both advocate and witness by reason of conflict of interest, *Rule 1.10: Imputed Disqualification* disqualifies the firm also.

RULE 3.8 SPECIAL RESPONSIBILITIES OF A PROSECUTOR

The prosecutor in a criminal case shall:

(a) refrain from prosecuting a charge that the prosecutor knows is not supported by probable cause;

(b) refrain from making any effort to prevent the accused from exercising a reasonable effort to obtain counsel;

(c) Reserved.

(d) make timely disclosure to the defense of all evidence or information known to the prosecutor that tends to negate the guilt of the accused or that mitigates the offense;

(e) exercise reasonable care to prevent persons who are under the direct supervision of the prosecutor from making an extrajudicial statement that the prosecutor would be prohibited from making under subsection (g) of this Rule;

(f) not subpoena a lawyer in a grand jury or other criminal proceeding to present evidence about a past or present client unless the prosecutor reasonably believes:

(1) the information sought is not protected from disclosure by any applicable privilege;

(2) the evidence sought is essential to the successful completion of an ongoing investigation or prosecution; and

(3) there is no other feasible alternative to obtain the information; and

(g) except for statements that are necessary to inform the public of the nature and extent of the prosecutor's action and that serve a legitimate law enforcement purpose, refrain from making extrajudicial comments that have a substantial likelihood of heightening public condemnation of the accused.

The maximum penalty for a violation of this Rule is a public reprimand.

Comment

[1] A prosecutor has the responsibility of a minister of justice and not simply that of an advocate. This responsibility carries with it specific obligations to see that the defendant is accorded procedural justice and that guilt is decided upon the basis of sufficient evidence. Precisely how far the prosecutor is required to go in this direction is a matter of debate and varies in different jurisdictions. Many jurisdictions have adopted the ABA Standards of Criminal Justice Relating to the Prosecution Function, which in turn are the product of prolonged and careful deliberation by lawyers experienced in both criminal prosecution and defense. Applicable law may require other measures by the prosecutor and knowing disregard of those obligations or a systematic abuse of prosecutorial discretion could constitute a violation of *Rule 8.4: Misconduct.*

[2] *Reserved.*

[3] *Reserved.*

[4] Paragraph (f) is intended to limit the issuance of lawyer subpoenas in grand jury and other criminal proceedings to those situations in which there is a genuine need to intrude into the client-lawyer relationship.

[5] Paragraph (g) supplements *Rule 3.6: Trial Publicity,* which prohibits extrajudicial statements that have a substantial likelihood of prejudicing an adjudicatory proceeding. In the context of a criminal prosecution, a prosecutor's extrajudicial statement can create the additional problem of increasing public condemnation of the accused. Although the announcement of an indictment, for example, will necessarily have severe consequences for the accused, a prosecutor can, and should, avoid comments which have no legitimate law enforcement purpose and have a substantial likelihood of increasing public opprobrium of the accused. Nothing in this Comment is intended to restrict the statements which a prosecutor may make which comply with *Rule 3.6(b)* or *3.6(c): Trial Publicity.*

RULE 3.9 ADVOCATE IN NONADJUDICATIVE PROCEEDINGS

A lawyer representing a client before a legislative or administrative tribunal in a nonadjudicative proceeding shall disclose that the appearance is in a representative capacity and shall conform to the provisions of Rules 3.3 (a) through (c), 3.4(a) through (c), and 3.5.

The maximum penalty for a violation of this Rule is a public reprimand.

Comment

[1] In representation before bodies such as legislatures, municipal councils, and executive and administrative agencies acting in a rule making or policy making capacity, lawyers present facts, formulate issues and advance argument in the matters under consideration. The decision making body, like a court, should be able to rely on the integrity of the submissions made to it. A lawyer appearing before such a body should deal with the tribunal honestly and in conformity with applicable rules of procedures.

[2] Lawyers have no exclusive right to appear before nonadjudicative bodies, as they do before a court. The requirements of this Rule therefore may subject lawyers to regulations inapplicable to advocates who are not lawyers. However, legislatures and administrative agencies have a right to expect lawyers to deal with them as they deal with courts.

[3] This Rule does not apply to representation of a client in a negotiation or other bilateral transaction with a governmental entity; representation in such a transaction is governed by Rules 4.1 through 4.4.

PART FOUR. TRANSACTIONS WITH PERSONS OTHER THAN CLIENTS

RULE 4.1 TRUTHFULNESS IN STATEMENTS TO OTHERS

In the course of representing a client a lawyer shall not knowingly:

(a) make a false statement of material fact or law to a third person; or

(b) fail to disclose a material fact to a third person when disclosure is necessary to avoid assisting a criminal or fraudulent act by a client, unless disclosure is prohibited by Rule 1.6.

The maximum penalty for a violation of this Rule is disbarment.

Comment

Misrepresentation

[1] A lawyer is required to be truthful when dealing with others on a client's behalf, but generally has no affirmative duty to inform an opposing party of relevant facts. A misrepresentation can occur if the lawyer incorporates or affirms a statement of another person that the lawyer knows is false. Misrepresentations can also occur by failure to act.

Statements of Fact

[2] This Rule refers to statements of fact. Whether a particular statement should be regarded as one of fact can depend on the circumstances. Under generally accepted conventions in negotiation, certain types of statements ordinarily are not taken as statements of material fact. Comments which fall under the general category of "puffing" do not violate this rule. Estimates of price or value placed on

the subject of a transaction and a party's intentions as to an acceptable settlement of a claim are in this category, and so is the existence of an undisclosed principal except where nondisclosure of the principal would constitute fraud.

Fraud by Client

[3] Paragraph (b) recognizes that substantive law may require a lawyer to disclose certain information to avoid being deemed to have assisted the client's crime or fraud. The requirement of disclosure created by this paragraph is, however, subject to the obligations created by *Rule 1.6: Confidentiality of Information.*

RULE 4.2 COMMUNICATION WITH PERSON REPRESENTED BY COUNSEL

(a) A lawyer who is representing a client in a matter shall not communicate about the subject of the representation with a person the lawyer knows to be represented by another lawyer in the matter, unless the lawyer has the consent of the other lawyer or is authorized to do so by constitutional law or statute.

(b) Attorneys for the State and Federal Government shall be subject to this Rule in the same manner as other attorneys in this State.

The maximum penalty for a violation of this Rule is disbarment.

Comment

[1] This Rule does not prohibit communication with a represented person, or an employee or agent of such a person, concerning matters outside the representation. For example, the existence of a controversy between a government entity and a private party, or between two organizations, does not prohibit a lawyer for either from communicating with nonlawyer representatives of the other regarding a separate matter. Also, parties to a matter may communicate directly with each other and a lawyer having independent justification or legal authorization for communicating with a represented person is permitted to do so. Communications authorized by law include, for example, the right of a party to a controversy with a government entity to speak with government officials about the matter.

[2] Communications authorized by law also include constitutionally permissible investigative activities of lawyers representing governmental entities, directly or through investigative agents, prior to the commencement of criminal or civil enforcement proceedings, when there is applicable judicial precedent that either has found the activity permissible under this Rule or has found this Rule inapplicable. However, the Rule imposes ethical restrictions that go beyond those imposed by constitutional provisions.

[3] This Rule applies to communications with any person, whether or not a party to a formal adjudicative proceeding, contract or negotiation, who is represented by counsel concerning the matter to which the communication relates.

[4A] In the case of an organization, this Rule prohibits communications by a lawyer for another person or entity concerning the matter in representation with persons having a managerial responsibility on behalf of the organization, and with any other person whose act or omission in connection with that matter may be imputed to the organization for purposes of civil or criminal liability or whose statement may constitute an admission on the part of the organization. If an agent or employee of the organization is represented in the matter by his or her own counsel, the consent by that counsel to a communication will be sufficient for purposes of this Rule. Compare *Rule 3.4(f): Fairness to Opposing Party and Counsel.*

[4B] In administering this Rule it should be anticipated that in many instances, prior to the beginning of the interview, the interviewing lawyer will not possess sufficient information to determine whether or not the relationship of the interviewee to the entity is sufficiently close to place the person in the "represented" category. In those situations the good faith of the lawyer in undertaking the interview should be considered. Evidence of good faith includes an immediate and candid statement of the interest of the person on whose behalf the interview is being taken, a full explanation of why that person's position is adverse to the interests of the entity with which the interviewee is associated, the exploration of the relationship issue at the outset of the interview and the cessation of the interview immediately upon determination that the interview is improper.

[5] The prohibition on communications with a represented person only applies, however, in circumstances where the lawyer knows that the person is in fact represented in the matter to be discussed. This means that the lawyer has actual knowledge of the fact of the representation; but such actual knowledge may be inferred from the circumstances. See Terminology. Such an inference may arise in circumstances where there is substantial reason to believe that the person with whom communication is sought is represented in the matter to be discussed. Thus, a lawyer cannot evade the requirement of obtaining the consent of counsel by ignoring the obvious.

[6] In the event the person with whom the lawyer communicates is not known to be represented by counsel in the matter, the lawyer's communications are subject to *Rule 4.3: Dealing with Unrepresented Person.*

[7] The anti-contact rule serves important public interests which preserve the proper functioning of the judicial system and the administration of justice by a) protecting against misuse of the imbalance of legal skill between a lawyer and layperson; b) safeguarding the client-attorney relationship from interference by adverse counsel; c) ensuring that all valid claims and defenses are raised in response to inquiry from adverse counsel; d) reducing the likelihood that clients will disclose privileged or other information that might harm their interests; and e) maintaining the lawyers ability to monitor the case and effectively represent the client.

[8] This Rule is not intended to affect communications between parties to an action entered into independent of and not at the request or direction of counsel.

RULE 4.3 DEALING WITH UNREPRESENTED PERSON

In dealing on behalf of a client with a person who is not represented by counsel, a lawyer shall not:

(a) state or imply that the lawyer is disinterested; when the lawyer knows or reasonably should know that the unrepresented person misunderstands the lawyer's role in the matter, the lawyer shall make reasonable efforts to correct the misunderstanding;

(b) give advice other than the advice to secure counsel; and

(c) initiate any contact with a potentially adverse party in a matter concerning personal injury or wrongful death or otherwise related to an accident or disaster involving the person to whom the contact is addressed or a relative of that person, unless the accident or disaster occurred more than 30 days prior to the contact.

The maximum penalty for a violation of this Rule is disbarment.

Comment

[1] An unrepresented person, particularly one not experienced in dealing with legal matters, might assume that a lawyer is disinterested in loyalties or is a disinterested authority on the law even when the lawyer represents a client.

[2] In some circumstances a lawyer must deal with a person who is unrepresented. In such an instance, a lawyer should not undertake to give advice to that person, other than the advice to obtain counsel.

RULE 4.4 RESPECT FOR RIGHTS OF THIRD PERSONS

In representing a client, a lawyer shall not use means that have no substantial purpose other than to embarrass, delay, or burden a third person, or use methods of obtaining evidence that violate the legal rights of such a person.

The maximum penalty for a violation of this Rule is a public reprimand.

Comment

[1] Responsibility to a client requires a lawyer to subordinate the interests of others to those of the client, but that responsibility does not imply that a lawyer may disregard the rights of third persons. It is impractical to catalogue all such rights, but they include legal restrictions on methods of obtaining evidence from third persons.

PART FIVE. LAW FIRMS AND ASSOCIATIONS

RULE 5.1 RESPONSIBILITIES OF A PARTNER OR SUPERVISORY LAWYER

(a) A partner in a law firm shall make reasonable efforts to ensure that the firm has in effect measures giving reasonable assurance that all lawyers in the firm conform to the Georgia Rules of Professional Conduct.

(b) A lawyer having direct supervisory authority over another lawyer shall make reasonable efforts to ensure that the other lawyer conforms to the Georgia Rules of Professional Conduct.

(c) A lawyer shall be responsible for another lawyer's violation of the Georgia Rules of Professional Conduct if:

(1) the partner or supervisory lawyer orders or, with knowledge of the specific conduct, ratifies the conduct involved; or

(2) the lawyer is a partner in the law firm in which the other lawyer practices or has direct supervisory authority over the other lawyer, and knows of the conduct at a time when its consequences can be avoided or mitigated but fails to take reasonable remedial action.

The maximum penalty for a violation of this Rule is disbarment.

Comment

[1] Paragraphs (a) and (b) refer to lawyers who have supervisory authority over the professional work of a firm or legal department of a government entity. This includes members of a partner-ship and the shareholders in a law firm organized as a professional corporation; lawyers having supervisory authority in the law department of an enterprise or government entity; and lawyers who have intermediate managerial responsibilities in a firm.

[2] The measures required to fulfill the responsibility prescribed in paragraphs (a) and (b) can depend on the firm's structure and the nature of its practice. In a small firm, informal supervision and occasional admonition ordinarily might be sufficient. In a large firm, or in practice situations in which intensely difficult ethical problems frequently arise, more elaborate procedures may be necessary. Some firms, for example, have a procedure whereby junior lawyers can make confidential referral of ethical problems directly to a designated senior partner or special committee. See *Rule 5.2: Responsibilities of a Subordinate Lawyer.* Firms, whether large or small, may also rely on continuing legal education in professional ethics. In any event, the ethical atmosphere of a firm can influence the conduct of all its members and a lawyer having authority over the work of another may not assume that the subordinate lawyer will inevitably conform to the Rules.

[3] Paragraph (c)(1) expresses a general principle of responsibility for acts of another. See also *Rule 8.4(a): Misconduct.*

[4] Paragraph (c)(2) defines the duty of a lawyer having direct supervisory authority over performance of specific legal work by another lawyer. Whether a lawyer has such supervisory authority in particular circumstances is a question of fact. Partners of a private firm have at least indirect responsibility for all work being done by the firm, while a partner in charge of a particular matter ordinarily has direct authority over other firm lawyers engaged in the matter. Appropriate remedial action by a partner would depend on the immediacy of the partner's involvement and the seriousness of the misconduct. The supervisor is required to intervene to prevent avoidable consequences of misconduct if the supervisor knows that the misconduct occurred. Thus, if a supervising lawyer knows that a subordinate misrepresented

a matter to an opposing party in negotiation, the supervisor as well as the subordinate has a duty to correct the resulting misapprehension.

[5] Professional misconduct by a lawyer under supervision could reveal a violation of paragraph (b) on the part of the supervisory lawyer even though it does not entail a violation of paragraph (c) because there was no direction, ratification or knowledge of the violation.

[6] Apart from this Rule and *Rule 8.4(a): Misconduct*, a lawyer does not have disciplinary liability for the conduct of a partner, associate or subordinate. Whether a lawyer may be liable civilly or criminally for another lawyer's conduct is a question of law beyond the scope of these Rules.

RULE 5.2 RESPONSIBILITIES OF A SUBORDINATE LAWYER

(a) A lawyer is bound by the Georgia Rules of Professional Conduct notwithstanding that the lawyer acted at the direction of another person.

(b) A subordinate lawyer does not violate the Georgia Rules of Professional Conduct if that lawyer acts in accordance with a supervisory lawyer's reasonable resolution of an arguable question of professional duty.

The maximum penalty for a violation of this Rule is disbarment.

Comment

[1] Although a lawyer is not relieved of responsibility for a violation by the fact that the lawyer acted at the direction of a supervisor, that fact may be relevant in determining whether a lawyer had the knowledge required to render conduct a violation of the Rules. For example, if a subordinate filed a frivolous pleading at the direction of a supervisor, the subordinate would not be guilty of a professional violation unless the subordinate knew of the document's frivolous character.

[2] When lawyers in a supervisor-subordinate relationship encounter a matter involving professional judgment as to ethical duty, the supervisor may assume responsibility for making the judgment. Otherwise a consistent course of action or position could not be taken. If the question can reasonably be answered only one way, the duty of both lawyers is clear and they are equally responsible for fulfilling it. However, if the question is reasonably arguable, someone has to decide upon the course of action. That authority ordinarily reposes in the supervisor and a subordinate may be guided accordingly. For example, if a question arises whether the interests of two clients conflict under *Rule 1.7: Conflict of Interest*, the supervisor's reasonable resolution of the question should protect the subordinate professionally if the resolution is subsequently challenged.

RULE 5.3 RESPONSIBILITIES REGARDING NONLAWYER ASSISTANTS

With respect to a nonlawyer employed or retained by or associated with a lawyer:

(a) a partner in a law firm shall make reasonable efforts to ensure that the firm has in effect measures giving reasonable assurance that the person's conduct is compatible with the professional obligations of the lawyer;

(b) a lawyer having direct supervisory authority over the non-lawyer shall make reasonable efforts to ensure that the person's conduct is compatible with the professional obligations of the lawyer; and

(c) a lawyer shall be responsible for conduct of such a person that would be a violation of the Georgia Rules of Professional Conduct if engaged in by a lawyer if:

(1) the lawyer orders or, with the knowledge of the specific conduct, ratifies the conduct involved; or

(2) the lawyer is a partner in the law firm in which the person is employed, or has direct supervisory authority over the person, and knows of the conduct at a time when its consequences can be avoided or mitigated but fails to take reasonable remedial action.

(d) a lawyer shall not allow any person who has been suspended or disbarred and who maintains a presence in an office where the practice of law is conducted by the lawyer, to:

(1) represent himself or herself as a lawyer or person with similar status;

(2) have any contact with the clients of the lawyer either in person, by telephone or in writing; or

(3) have any contact with persons who have legal dealings with the office either in person, by telephone or in writing.

The maximum penalty for a violation of this Rule is disbarment.

Comment

[1] Lawyers generally employ assistants in their practice, including secretaries, investigators, law student interns, and paraprofessionals. Such assistants, whether employees or independent contractors, act for the lawyer in rendition of the lawyer's professional services. A lawyer should give such assistants appropriate instruction and supervision concerning the ethical aspects of their employment, particularly regarding the obligation not to disclose information relating to representation of the client, and should be responsible for their work product. The measures employed in supervising nonlawyers should take account of the fact that they do not have legal training and are not subject to professional discipline.

[2] The prohibitions of paragraph (d) apply to professional conduct and not to social conversation unrelated to the representation of clients or legal dealings of the law office, or the gathering of general information in the course of working in a law office. The thrust of the restriction is to prevent the unauthorized practice of law in a law office by a person who has been suspended or disbarred.

RULE 5.4 PROFESSIONAL INDEPENDENCE OF A LAWYER

(a) A lawyer or law firm shall not share legal fees with a nonlawyer, except that:

(1) an agreement by a lawyer with the lawyer's firm, partner, or associate may provide for the payment of money, over a reasonable period of time after the lawyer's death, to the lawyer's estate or to one or more specified persons;

(2) a lawyer or law firm who purchases the practice of a deceased, disabled, or disappeared lawyer may, pursuant to the provisions of Rule 1.17, pay to the estate or other representative of that lawyer the agreed-upon purchase price; and

(3) a lawyer or law firm may include nonlawyer employees in a compensation or retirement plan, even though the plan is based in whole or in part on a profit-sharing arrangement; and

(4) a lawyer who undertakes to complete unfinished business of a deceased lawyer may pay to the estate of the deceased lawyer that proportion of the total compensation which fairly represents the services rendered by the deceased lawyer.

(5) a lawyer may pay a referral fee to a bar-operated non-profit lawyer referral service where such fee is calculated as a percentage of legal fees earned by the lawyer to whom the service has referred a matter pursuant to Rule 7.3. Direct Contact with Prospective Clients.

(b) A lawyer shall not form a partnership with a nonlawyer if any of the activities of the partnership consist of the practice of law.

(c) A lawyer shall not permit a person who recommends, employs, or pays the lawyer to render legal services for another to direct or regulate the lawyer's professional judgment in rendering such legal services.

(d) A lawyer shall not practice with or in the form of a professional corporation or association authorized to practice law for a profit, if:

(1) a nonlawyer owns any interest therein, except that a fiduciary representative of the estate of a lawyer may hold the stock or interest of the lawyer for a reasonable time during administration;

(2) a nonlawyer is a corporate director or officer thereof; or

(3) a nonlawyer has the right to direct or control the professional judgment of a lawyer.

The maximum penalty for a violation of this Rule is disbarment.

Amended effective June 9, 2004.

Comment

[1] The provisions of this Rule express traditional limitations on sharing fees. These limitations are to protect the lawyer's professional independence of judgment. Where someone other than the client pays the lawyer's fee or salary, or recommends employment of the lawyer, that arrangement does not modify the lawyer's obligation to the client. As stated in paragraph (c), such arrangements should not interfere with the lawyer's professional judgment.

RULE 5.5 UNAUTHORIZED PRACTICE OF LAW; MULTIJURISDICTIONAL PRACTICE OF LAW

(a) A lawyer shall not practice law in a jurisdiction in violation of the regulation of the legal profession in that jurisdiction, or assist another in doing so.

(b) A Domestic Lawyer shall not:

(1) except as authorized by these Rules or other law, establish an office or other systematic and continuous presence in this jurisdiction for the practice of law; or

(2) hold out to the public or otherwise represent that the Domestic Lawyer is admitted to practice law in this jurisdiction.

(c) A Domestic Lawyer, who is not disbarred or suspended from practice in any jurisdiction, may provide legal services on a temporary basis in this jurisdiction that:

(1) are undertaken in association with a lawyer who is admitted to practice in this jurisdiction and who actively participates in the matter;

(2) are in or reasonably related to a pending or potential proceeding before a tribunal in this or another jurisdiction, if the Domestic Lawyer, or a person the Domestic Lawyer is assisting, is authorized by law or order to appear in such proceeding or reasonably expects to be so authorized;

(3) are in or reasonably related to a pending or potential arbitration, mediation, or other alternative dispute resolution proceeding in this or another jurisdiction, if the services arise out of or are reasonably related to the Domestic Lawyer's practice in a jurisdiction in which the Domestic Lawyer is admitted to practice and are not services for which the forum requires pro hac vice admission; or

(4) are not within paragraphs (c)(2) or (c)(3) and arise out of or are reasonably related to the Domestic Lawyer's practice in a jurisdiction in which the Domestic Lawyer is admitted to practice.

(d) A Domestic Lawyer, who is not disbarred or suspended from practice in any jurisdiction, may provide legal services in this jurisdiction that:

(1) are provided to the Domestic Lawyer's employer or its organizational affiliates and are not services for which the forum requires pro hac vice admission; or

(2) are services that the Domestic Lawyer is authorized to provide by federal law or other law of this jurisdiction.

(e) A Foreign Lawyer shall not, except as authorized by this Rule or other law, establish an office or other systematic and continuous presence in this jurisdiction for the practice of law, or hold out to the public or otherwise represent that the lawyer is admitted to practice law in this jurisdiction. Such a Foreign Lawyer does not engage in the unauthorized practice of law in this jurisdiction when on a temporary basis the Foreign Lawyer performs services in this jurisdiction that:

(1) are undertaken in association with a lawyer who is admitted to practice in this jurisdiction and who actively participates in the matter;

(2) are in or reasonably related to a pending or potential proceeding before a tribunal held or to be held in a jurisdiction outside the United States if the Foreign Lawyer, or a person the Foreign Lawyer is assisting, is authorized by law or by order of the tribunal to appear in such proceeding or reasonably expects to be so authorized;

(3) are in or reasonably related to a pending or potential arbitration, mediation, or other alternative dispute resolution proceedings held or to be held in this or another jurisdiction, if the services arise out of or are reasonably related to the Foreign Lawyer's practice in a jurisdiction in which the Foreign Lawyer is admitted to practice;

(4) are not within paragraphs (2) or (3) and

(i) are performed for a client who resides or has an office in a jurisdiction in which the Foreign Lawyer is authorized to practice to the extent of that authorization; or

(ii) arise out of or are reasonably related to a matter that has a substantial connection to a jurisdiction in which the lawyer is authorized to practice to the extent of that authorization; or

(iii) are governed primarily by international law or the law of a non–United States jurisdiction.

(f) For purposes of this grant of authority, the Foreign Lawyer must be a member in good standing of a recognized legal profession in a foreign jurisdiction, the members of which are admitted to practice as lawyers or counselors at law or the equivalent and subject to effective regulation and discipline by a duly constituted professional body or a public authority.

The maximum penalty for a violation of this Rule is disbarment.

Amended effective June 8, 2004; amended February 2, 2005, nunc pro tunc June 8, 2004.

Comment

[1] A lawyer may practice law only in a jurisdiction in which the lawyer is authorized to practice. A lawyer may be admitted to practice law in a jurisdiction on a regular basis or may be authorized by court rule or order or by law to practice for a limited purpose or on a restricted basis. Paragraph (a) applies to unauthorized practice of law by a lawyer, whether through the lawyer's direct action or by the lawyer assisting another person.

[2] The definition of the practice of law is established by law and varies from one jurisdiction to another. Whatever the definition, limiting the practice of law to members of the bar protects the public against rendition of legal services by unqualified persons. This Rule does not prohibit a lawyer from employing the services of paraprofessionals and delegating functions to them, so long as the lawyer supervises the delegated work and retains responsibility for their work. See *Rule 5.3; Responsibilities Regarding Nonlawyer Assistants.*

[3] A lawyer may provide professional advice and instruction to nonlawyers whose employment requires knowledge of the law; for example, claims adjusters, employees of financial or commercial institutions, social workers, accountants and persons employed in government agencies. Lawyers also may assist independent nonlawyers, such as paraprofessionals, who are authorized by the law of a jurisdiction to provide particular law–related services. In addition, a lawyer may counsel nonlawyers who wish to proceed pro se.

[4] Other than as authorized by law or this Rule, a Domestic Lawyer violates paragraph (b) and a Foreign Lawyer violates paragraph (e) if the Domestic or Foreign Lawyer establishes an office or other systematic and continuous presence in this jurisdiction for the practice of law. Presence may be systematic and continuous even if the Domestic or Foreign Lawyer is not physically present here. Such Domestic or Foreign Lawyer must not hold out to the public or otherwise represent that the Domestic or Foreign Lawyer is admitted to practice law in this jurisdiction. See also Rules 7.1(a) and 7.5(b).

[5] There are occasions in which a Domestic or Foreign Lawyer, who is not disbarred or suspended from practice in any jurisdiction, may provide legal services on a temporary basis in this jurisdiction under circumstances that do not create an unreasonable risk to the interests of their clients, the public or the courts. Paragraph (c) identifies four such circumstances for the Domestic Lawyer. Paragraph (e) identifies five such circumstances for the Foreign Lawyer. The fact that conduct is not so identified does not imply that the conduct is or is not authorized. With the exception of paragraphs (d)(1) and (d)(2), this Rule does not authorize a Domestic Lawyer to establish an office or other systematic and continuous presence in this jurisdiction without being admitted to practice generally here.

[6] There is no single test to determine whether a Foreign or Domestic Lawyer's services are provided on a "temporary basis" in this jurisdiction, and may therefore be permissible under paragraph (c) or paragraph (e). Services may be "temporary" even though the Foreign or Domestic Lawyer provides services in this jurisdiction on a recurring basis, or for an extended period of time, as when the Domestic Lawyer is representing a client in a single lengthy negotiation or litigation.

[7] Paragraphs (c) and (d) apply to Domestic Lawyers. Paragraphs (e) and (f) apply to Foreign Lawyers. Paragraphs (c) and (e) contemplate that the Domestic or Foreign Lawyer is authorized to practice in the jurisdiction in which the Domestic or Foreign Lawyer is admitted and excludes a Domestic or Foreign Lawyer who while technically admitted is not authorized to practice, because, for example, the Domestic or Foreign Lawyer is on inactive status.

[8] Paragraph (c)(1) recognizes that the interests of clients and the public are protected if a Domestic Lawyer associates with a lawyer licensed to practice in this jurisdiction. Para-

graph (e)(1) recognizes that the interests of clients and the public are protected if a Foreign Lawyer associates with a lawyer licensed to practice in this jurisdiction. For these paragraphs to apply, however, the lawyer admitted to practice in this jurisdiction must actively participate in and share responsibility for the representation of the client.

[9] Domestic Lawyers not admitted to practice generally in a jurisdiction may be authorized by law or order of a tribunal or an administrative agency to appear before the tribunal or agency. This authority may be granted pursuant to formal rules governing admission pro hac vice or pursuant to informal practice of the tribunal or agency. Under paragraph (c)(2), a Domestic Lawyer does not violate this Rule when the Domestic Lawyer appears before a tribunal or agency pursuant to such authority. To the extent that a court rule or other law of this jurisdiction requires a Domestic Lawyer to obtain admission pro hac vice before appearing before a tribunal or administrative agency, this Rule requires the Domestic Lawyer to obtain that authority.

[10] Paragraph (c)(2) also provides that a Domestic Lawyer rendering services in this jurisdiction on a temporary basis does not violate this Rule when the Domestic Lawyer engages in conduct in anticipation of a proceeding or hearing in a jurisdiction in which the Domestic Lawyer is authorized to practice law or in which the Domestic Lawyer reasonably expects to be admitted pro hac vice. Examples of such conduct include meetings with the client, interviews of potential witnesses, and the review of documents. Similarly, a Domestic Lawyer may engage in conduct temporarily in this jurisdiction in connection with pending litigation in another jurisdiction in which the Domestic Lawyer is or reasonably expects to be authorized to appear, including taking depositions in this jurisdiction.

[11] When a Domestic Lawyer has been or reasonably expects to be admitted to appear before a court or administrative agency, paragraph (c)(2) also permits conduct by lawyers who are associated with that lawyer in the matter, but who do not expect to appear before the court or administrative agency. For example, subordinate Domestic Lawyers may conduct research, review documents, and attend meetings with witnesses in support of the Domestic Lawyer responsible for the litigation.

[12] Paragraph (c)(3) permits a Domestic Lawyer, and Paragraph (e)(3) permits a Foreign Lawyer, to perform services on a temporary basis in this jurisdiction if those services are in or reasonably related to a pending or potential arbitration, mediation, or other alternative dispute resolution proceeding in this or another jurisdiction, if the services arise out of or are reasonably related to the Domestic or Foreign Lawyer's practice in a jurisdiction in which the Domestic or Foreign Lawyer is admitted to practice. The Domestic Lawyer, however, must obtain admission pro hac vice in the case of a court-annexed arbitration or mediation or otherwise if court rules or law so require.

[13] Paragraph (c)(4) permits a Domestic Lawyer to provide certain legal services on a temporary basis in this jurisdiction that arise out of or are reasonably related to the Domestic Lawyer's practice in a jurisdiction in which the Domestic Lawyer is admitted but are not within paragraphs (c)(2) or (c)(3). These services include both legal services and services that nonlawyers may perform but that are considered the practice of law when performed by lawyers. Paragraph (e)(4)(i) permits a Foreign Lawyer to provide certain legal services in this jurisdiction on behalf of a client who resides or has an office in the jurisdiction in which the Foreign Lawyer is authorized to practice. Paragraph (e)(4)(ii) permits a Foreign Lawyer to provide certain legal services on a temporary basis in this jurisdiction that arise out of or are reasonably related to a matter that has a substantial connection to the jurisdiction in which the Foreign Lawyer is authorized to practice. These services include both legal services and services that nonlawyers may perform but that are considered the practice of law when performed by lawyers.

[14] Paragraphs (c)(3) and (c)(4) require that the services arise out of or be reasonably related to the Domestic Lawyer's practice in a jurisdiction in which the Domestic Lawyer is admitted. Paragraphs (e)(3) and (e)(4)(ii) require that the services arise out of or be reasonably related to the Foreign Lawyer's practice in a jurisdiction in which the Foreign Lawyer is admitted to practice. A variety of factors evidence such a relationship. The Domestic or Foreign Lawyer's client may have been previously represented by the Domestic or Foreign Lawyer, or may be resident in or have substantial contacts with the jurisdiction in which the Domestic or Foreign Lawyer is admitted. The matter, although involving other jurisdictions, may have a significant connection with that jurisdiction. In other cases, significant aspects of the Domestic or Foreign Lawyer's work might be conducted in that jurisdiction or a significant aspect of the matter may involve the law of that jurisdiction. The necessary relationship might arise when the client's activities or the legal issues involve multiple jurisdictions, such as when the officers of a multinational corporation survey potential business sites and seek the services of their Domestic or Foreign Lawyer in assessing the relative merits of each. In addition, the services may draw on the Domestic or Foreign Lawyer's recognized expertise developed through the regular practice of law on behalf of clients in matters involving a particular body of federal, nationally–uniform, foreign, or international law.

[15] Paragraph (d) identifies two circumstances in which a Domestic Lawyer, who is not disbarred or suspended from practice in any jurisdiction, may establish an office or other systematic and continuous presence in this jurisdiction for the practice of law as well as provide legal services on a temporary basis. Except as provided in paragraphs (d)(1) and (d)(2), a Domestic Lawyer who establishes an office or other systematic or continuous presence in this jurisdiction must become admitted to practice law generally in this jurisdiction.

[16] Paragraph (d)(1) applies to a Domestic Lawyer who is employed by a client to provide legal services to the client or its organizational affiliates, i.e., entities that control, are controlled by, or are under common control with the employer. This paragraph does not authorize the provision of personal legal services to the employer's officers or employees. The paragraph applies to in-house corporate lawyers, government lawyers and others who are employed to render legal services to the employer. The Domestic Lawyer's ability to represent the employer outside the jurisdiction in which the Domestic Lawyer is licensed generally serves the interests of the employer and does not create an unreasonable risk to the client and others because the employer is well situated to assess the Domestic Lawyer's qualifications and the quality of the Domestic Lawyer's work.

[17] If an employed Domestic Lawyer establishes an office or other systematic presence in this jurisdiction for the purpose of rendering legal services to the employer, the Domestic Lawyer may be subject to registration or other

requirements, including assessments for client protection funds and mandatory continuing legal education.

[18] Paragraph (d)(2) recognizes that a Domestic Lawyer may provide legal services in a jurisdiction in which the Domestic Lawyer is not licensed when authorized to do so by federal or other law, which includes statute, court rule, executive regulation or judicial precedent. Paragraph (e)(4)(iii) recognizes that a Foreign Lawyer may provide legal services when the services provided are governed by international law or the law of a foreign jurisdiction.

[19] A Domestic or Foreign Lawyer who practices law in this jurisdiction pursuant to paragraphs (c), (d) or (e) or otherwise is subject to the disciplinary authority of this jurisdiction. See Rule 8.5(a).

[20] In some circumstances, a Domestic Lawyer who practices law in this jurisdiction pursuant to paragraphs (c) or (d) may have to inform the client that the Domestic Lawyer is not licensed to practice law in this jurisdiction. For example, that may be required when the representation occurs primarily in this jurisdiction and requires knowledge of the law of this jurisdiction. See Rule 1.4.

[21] Paragraphs (c), (d) and (e) do not authorize communications advertising legal services to prospective clients in this jurisdiction by Domestic or Foreign Lawyers who are admitted to practice in other jurisdictions. Whether and how Domestic or Foreign Lawyers may communicate the availability of their services to prospective clients in this jurisdiction is governed by Rules 7.1 to 7.5.

RULE 5.6 RESTRICTIONS ON RIGHT TO PRACTICE

A lawyer shall not participate in offering or making:

(a) a partnership or employment agreement that restricts the right of a lawyer to practice after termination of the relationship, except an agreement concerning benefits upon retirement; or

(b) an agreement in which a restriction on the lawyer's right to practice is part of the settlement of a controversy between private parties.

The maximum penalty for a violation of this Rule is a public reprimand.

Comment

[1] An agreement restricting the right of partners or associates to practice after leaving a firm not only limits their professional autonomy but also limits the freedom of clients to choose a lawyer. Paragraph (a) prohibits such agreements except for restrictions incident to provisions concerning retirement benefits for service with the firm.

[2] Paragraph (b) prohibits a lawyer from agreeing not to represent other persons in connection with settling a claim on behalf of a client.

[3] This Rule does not apply to prohibit restrictions that may be included in the terms of the sale of a law practice pursuant to *Rule 1.17: Sale of Law Practice.*

RULE 5.7 RESPONSIBILITIES REGARDING LAW-RELATED SERVICES

(a) A lawyer shall be subject to the Georgia Rules of Professional Conduct with respect to the provision of law-related services, as defined in paragraph (b), if the law-related services are provided:

(1) by the lawyer in circumstances that are not distinct from the lawyer's provision of legal services to clients; or

(2) by a separate entity controlled by the lawyer individually or with others if the lawyer fails to take reasonable measures to assure that a person obtaining the law-related services knows that the services of the separate entity are not legal services and that the protections of the client-lawyer relationship do not exist.

(b) The term "law-related services" denotes services that might reasonably be performed in conjunction with and in substance are related to the provision of legal services, and that are not prohibited as unauthorized practice of law when provided by a nonlawyer.

The maximum penalty for a violation of this Rule is a public reprimand.

Comment

[1] When a lawyer performs law-related services or controls an organization that does so, there exists the potential for ethical problems. Principal among these is the possibility that the person for whom the law-related services are performed fails to understand that the services may not carry with them the protections normally afforded as part of the client-lawyer relationship. The recipient of the law-related services may expect, for example, that the protection of client confidences, prohibitions against representation of persons with conflicting interests, and obligations of a lawyer to maintain professional independence apply to the provision of law-related services when that may not be the case.

[2] *Rule 5.7: Restrictions Regarding Law-Related Services* applies to the provision of law-related services by a lawyer even when the lawyer does not provide any legal services to the person for whom the law-related services are performed. The Rule identifies the circumstances in which all of the Georgia Rules of Professional Conduct apply to the provision of law-related services. Even when those circumstances do not exist, however, the conduct of a lawyer involved in the provision of law-related services is subject to those Rules that apply generally to lawyer conduct, regardless of whether the conduct involves the provision of legal services. See, e.g., *Rule 8.4: Misconduct.*

[3] When law-related services are provided by a lawyer under circumstances that are distinct from the lawyer's provision of legal services to clients, the lawyer in providing the law-related services need not adhere to the requirements of the Georgia Rules of Professional Conduct as provided in *Rule 5.7(a)(1): Restrictions Regarding Law-Related Services.*

[4] Law-related services also may be provided through an entity that is distinct from that through which the lawyer provides legal services. If the lawyer individually or with others has control of such an entity's operations, the Rule requires the lawyer to take reasonable measures to assure that each person using the services of the entity knows that the services provided by the entity are not legal services and that the Georgia Rules of Professional Conduct that relate to the client-lawyer relationship do not apply. A lawyer's con-

trol of an entity extends to the ability to direct its operation. Whether a lawyer has such control will depend upon the circumstances of the particular case.

[5] When a client-lawyer relationship exists with a person who is referred by a lawyer to a separate law-related service entity controlled by the lawyer, individually or with others, the lawyer must comply with *Rule 1.8(a): Conflict of Interest.*

[6] In taking the reasonable measures referred to in paragraph (a)(2) to assure that a person using law-related services under-stands the practical effect or significance of the inapplicability of the Georgia Rules of Professional Conduct, the lawyer should communicate to the person receiving the law-related services, in a manner sufficient to assure that the person understands the significance of the fact, that the relationship of the person to the business entity will not be a client-lawyer relationship. The communication should be made before entering into an agreement for provision of or providing law-related services, and preferably should be in writing.

[7] The burden is upon the lawyer to show that the lawyer has taken reasonable measures under the circumstances to communicate the desired understanding. For instance, a sophisticated user of law-related services, such as a publicly held corporation, may require a lesser explanation than someone unaccustomed to making distinctions between legal services and law-related services, such as an individual seeking tax advice from a lawyer-accountant or investigative services in connection with a lawsuit.

[8] Regardless of the sophistication of potential recipients of law-related services, a lawyer should take special care to keep separate the provision of law-related and legal services in order to minimize the risk that the recipient will assume that the law-related services are legal services. The risk of such confusion is especially acute when the lawyer renders both types of services with respect to the same matter. Under some circumstances the legal and law-related services may be so closely entwined that they cannot be distinguished from each other, and the requirement of disclosure and consultation imposed by paragraph (a)(2) of the Rule cannot be met. In such a case a lawyer will be responsible for assuring that both the lawyer's conduct and, to the extent required by *Rule 5.3: Responsibilities Regarding Nonlawyer Assistants,* that of nonlawyer employees in the distinct entity which the lawyer controls complies in all respects with the Georgia Rules of Professional Conduct.

[9] A broad range of economic and other interests of clients may be served by lawyers' engaging in the delivery of law-related services. Examples of law-related services include providing title insurance, financial planning, accounting, trust services, real estate counseling, legislative lobbying, economic analysis, social work, psychological counseling, tax preparation, and patent, medical or environmental consulting.

[10] When a lawyer is obliged to accord the recipients of such services the protections of those Rules that apply to the client-lawyer relationship, the lawyer must take special care to heed the proscriptions of the Rules addressing conflict of interest (Rules 1.7 through 1.11, especially Rules 1.7(b) and 1.8(a),(b) and (f)), and to scrupulously adhere to the requirements of *Rule 1.6: Confidentiality of Information* relating to disclosure of confidential information. The promotion of the law-related services must also in all respects comply with Rules 7.1 through 7.3, dealing with advertising and solicitation. In that regard, lawyers should take special care to identify the obligations that may be imposed as a result of a jurisdiction's decisional law.

[11] When the full protections of all of the Georgia Rules of Professional Conduct do not apply to the provision of law-related services, principles of law external to the Rules, for example, the law of principal and agent, govern the legal duties owed to those receiving the services. Those other legal principles may establish a different degree of protection for the recipient with respect to confidentiality of information, conflicts of interest and permissible business relationships with clients. See also *Rule 8.4: Misconduct.*

PART SIX. PUBLIC SERVICE

RULE 6.1 VOLUNTARY *PRO BONO PUBLICO* SERVICE

A lawyer should aspire to render at least (50) hours of pro bono publico legal services per year. In fulfilling this responsibility, the lawyer should:

(a) provide a substantial portion of the (50) hours of legal services without fee or expectation of fee to:

(1) persons of limited means; or

(2) charitable, religious, civic, community, governmental and educational organizations in matters which are designed primarily to address the needs of persons of limited means; and

(b) provide any additional services through:

(1) delivery of legal services at no fee or substantially reduced fee to individuals, groups or organizations seeking to secure or protect civil rights, civil liberties or public rights, or charitable, religious, civic, community, governmental and educational organizations in matters in furtherance of their organizational purposes, where the payment of standard legal fees would significantly deplete the organization's economic resources or would be otherwise inappropriate;

(2) delivery of legal services at a substantially reduced fee to persons of limited means; or

(3) participation in activities for improving the law, the legal system or the legal profession.

In addition, a lawyer should voluntarily contribute financial support to organizations that provide legal services to persons of limited means.

No reporting rules or requirements may be imposed without specific permission of the Supreme Court granted through amendments to these Rules.

There is no disciplinary penalty for a violation of this Rule.

Comment

[1] Every lawyer, regardless of professional prominence or professional work load, has a responsibility to provide legal services to those unable to pay, and personal involvement in the problems of the disadvantaged can be one of the most rewarding experiences in the life of a lawyer. The American Bar Association urges all lawyers to provide a minimum of 50 hours of pro bono services annually. States, however, may decide to choose a higher or lower number of hours of annual service (which may be expressed as a percentage of a lawyer's professional time) depending upon local needs and local conditions. It is recognized that in some years a lawyer may render greater or fewer hours than the annual standard specified, but during the course of his or her legal career, each lawyer should render on average per year, the number of hours set forth in this Rule. Services can be performed in civil matters or in criminal or quasi-criminal matters for which there is no government obligation to provide funds for legal representation, such as post-conviction death penalty appeal cases.

[2] Paragraphs (a)(1) and (2) recognize the critical need for legal services that exists among persons of limited means by providing that a substantial majority of the legal services rendered annually to the disadvantaged be furnished without fee or expectation of fee. Legal services under these paragraphs consist of a full range of activities, including individual and class representation, the provision of legal advice, legislative lobbying, administrative rule making and the provision of free training or mentoring to those who represent persons of limited means. The variety of these activities should facilitate participation by government lawyers, even when restrictions exist on their engaging in the outside practice of law.

[3] Persons eligible for legal services under paragraphs (a)(1) and (2) are those who qualify for participation in programs funded by the Legal Services Corporation and those whose incomes and financial resources are slightly above the guidelines utilized by such programs but who nevertheless cannot afford counsel. Legal services can be rendered to individuals or to organizations such as homeless shelters, battered women's centers and food pantries that serve those of limited means. The term "governmental organizations" includes, but is not limited to, public protection programs and sections of governmental or public sector agencies.

[4] Because service must be provided without fee or expectation of fee, the intent of the lawyer to render free legal services is essential for the work performed to fall within the meaning of paragraphs (a)(1) and (2). Accordingly, services rendered cannot be considered pro bono if an anticipated fee is uncollected, but the award of statutory lawyers' fees in a case originally accepted as pro bono would not disqualify such services from inclusion under this section. Lawyers who do receive fees in such cases are encouraged to contribute an appropriate portion of such fees to organizations or projects that benefit persons of limited means.

[5] While it is possible for a lawyer to fulfill the annual responsibility to perform pro bono services exclusively through activities described in paragraphs (a)(1) and (2), to the extent that any hours of service remain unfulfilled, the remaining commitment can be met in a variety of ways as set forth in paragraph (b). Constitutional, statutory or regulatory restrictions may prohibit or impede government and public sector lawyers and judges from performing the pro bono services outlined in paragraphs (a)(1) and (2). Accordingly, where those restrictions apply, government and public sector lawyers and judges may fulfill their pro bono responsibility by performing services outlined in paragraph (b).

[6] Paragraph (b)(1) includes the provision of certain types of legal services to those whose incomes and financial resources place them above limited means. It also permits the pro bono lawyer to accept a substantially reduced fee for services. Examples of the types of issues that may be addressed under this paragraph include First Amendment claims, Title VII claims and environmental protection claims. Additionally, a wide range of organizations may be represented, including social service, medical research, cultural and religious groups.

[7] Paragraph (b)(2) covers instances in which lawyers agree to and receive a modest fee for furnishing legal services to persons of limited means. Participation in judicare programs and acceptance of court appointments in which the fee is substantially below a lawyer's usual rate are encouraged under this section.

[8] Paragraph (b)(3) recognizes the value of lawyers engaging in activities that improve the law, the legal system or the legal profession. Serving on bar association committees, serving on boards of pro bono or legal services programs, taking part in Law Day activities, acting as a continuing legal education instructor, a mediator or an arbitrator and engaging in legislative lobbying to improve the law, the legal system or the profession are a few examples of the many activities that fall within this paragraph.

[9] Because the provision of pro bono services is a professional responsibility, it is the individual ethical commitment of each lawyer. Nevertheless, there may be times when it is not feasible for a lawyer to engage in pro bono services. At such times a lawyer may discharge the pro bono responsibility by providing financial support to organizations providing free legal services to persons of limited means. Such financial support should be reasonably equivalent to the value of the hours of service that would have otherwise been provided. In addition, at times it may be more feasible to satisfy the pro bono responsibility collectively, as by a firm's aggregate pro bono activities.

[10] Because the efforts of individual lawyers are not enough to meet the need for free legal services that exists among persons of limited means, the government and the profession have instituted additional programs to provide those services. Every lawyer should financially support such programs, in addition to either providing direct pro bono services or making financial contributions when pro bono service is not feasible.

[11] The responsibility set forth in this Rule is not intended to be enforced through disciplinary process.

RULE 6.2 ACCEPTING APPOINTMENTS

For good cause a lawyer may seek to avoid appointment by a tribunal to represent a person.

There is no disciplinary penalty for a violation of this Rule.

Comment

[1] A lawyer ordinarily is not obliged to accept a client whose character or cause the lawyer regards as repugnant. The lawyer's freedom to select clients is, however, qualified. All lawyers have a responsibility to assist in providing pro bono publico service. See *Rule 6.1: Voluntary Pro Bono*

Publico Service. An individual lawyer fulfills this responsibility by accepting a fair share of unpopular matters or indigent or unpopular clients. A lawyer may also be subject to appointment by a court to serve unpopular clients or persons unable to afford legal services.

Appointed Counsel

[2] For good cause a lawyer may seek to decline an appointment to represent a person who cannot afford to retain counsel or whose cause is unpopular. Good cause exists if the lawyer could not handle the matter competently, see *Rule 1.1: Competence*, or if undertaking the representation would result in an improper conflict of interest, for example, when the client or the cause is so repugnant to the lawyer as to be likely to impair the client-lawyer relationship or the lawyer's ability to represent the client. A lawyer may also seek to decline an appointment if acceptance would be unreasonably burdensome, for example, when it would impose a financial sacrifice so great as to be unjust.

[3] An appointed lawyer has the same obligations to the client as retained counsel, including the obligations of loyalty and confidentiality, and is subject to the same limitations on the client-lawyer relationship, such as the obligation to refrain from assisting the client in violation of the Rules.

[4] This Rule is not intended to be enforced through disciplinary process.

RULE 6.3 MEMBERSHIP IN LEGAL SERVICES ORGANIZATION

A lawyer may serve as a director, officer or member of a legal services organization, apart from the law firm in which the lawyer practices, notwithstanding that the organization serves persons having interests adverse to a client of the lawyer. The lawyer shall not knowingly participate in a decision or action of the organization:

(a) if participating in the decision or action would be incompatible with the lawyer's obligations to a client under Rule 1.7; or

(b) where the decision or action could have a material adverse effect on the representation of a client of the organization whose interests are adverse to a client of the lawyer.

There is no disciplinary penalty for a violation of this Rule.

Comment

[1] Lawyers should be encouraged to support and participate in legal service organizations. A lawyer who is an officer or a member of such an organization does not thereby have a client-lawyer relationship with persons served by the organization. However, there is potential conflict between the interests of such persons and the interests of the lawyer's clients. If the possibility of such conflict disqualified a lawyer from serving on the board of a legal services organization, the profession's involvement in such organizations would be severely curtailed.

[2] It may be necessary in appropriate cases to reassure a client of the organization that the representation will not be affected by conflicting loyalties of a member of the board. Established, written policies in this respect can enhance the credibility of such assurances.

RULE 6.4 LAW REFORM ACTIVITIES AFFECTING CLIENT INTERESTS

A lawyer may serve as a director, officer or member of an organization involved in reform of the law or its administration not-withstanding that the reform may affect the interests of a client of the lawyer. When the lawyer knows that the interests of a client may be materially benefited by a decision in which the lawyer participates, the lawyer shall disclose that fact but need not identify the client.

There is no disciplinary penalty for a violation of this Rule.

Comment

[1] Lawyers involved in organizations seeking law reform generally do not have a client-lawyer relationship with the organization. See also *Rule 1.2(b): Scope of Representation.* Without this Rule, it might follow that a lawyer could not be involved in a bar association law reform program that might indirectly affect a client. For example, a lawyer specializing in antitrust litigation might be regarded as disqualified from participating in drafting revisions of rules governing that subject. In determining the nature and scope of participation in such activities, a lawyer should be mindful of obligations to clients under other Rules, particularly *Rule 1.7: Conflict of Interest.* A lawyer is professionally obligated to protect the integrity of the program by making an appropriate disclosure within the organization when the lawyer knows a private client might be materially benefited.

PART SEVEN. INFORMATION ABOUT LEGAL SERVICES

RULE 7.1 COMMUNICATIONS CONCERNING A LAWYER'S SERVICES

(a) A lawyer may advertise through all forms of public media and through written communication not involving personal contact so long as the communication is not false, fraudulent, deceptive or misleading. By way of illustration, but not limitation, a communication is false, fraudulent, deceptive or misleading if it:

(1) contains a material misrepresentation of fact or law or omits a fact necessary to make the statement considered as a whole not materially misleading;

(2) is likely to create an unjustified expectation about results the lawyer can achieve, or states or implies that the lawyer can achieve results by means that violate the Georgia Rules of Professional Conduct or other law;

(3) compares the lawyer's services with other lawyers' services unless the comparison can be factually substantiated;

(4) fails to include the name of at least one lawyer responsible for its content; or

(5) contains any information regarding contingent fees, and fails to conspicuously present the following disclaimer:

"Contingent attorneys' fees refers only to those fees charged by attorneys for their legal services. Such fees are not permitted in all types of cases. Court costs and other additional expenses of legal action usually must be paid by the client."

(6) contains the language "no fee unless you win or collect" or any similar phrase and fails to conspicuously present the following disclaimer:

"No fee unless you win or collect" (or insert the similar language used in the communication) refers only to fees charged by the attorney. Court costs and other additional expenses of legal action usually must be paid by the client. Contingent fees are not permitted in all types of cases.

(b) A public communication for which a lawyer has given value must be identified as such unless it is apparent from the context that it is such a communication.

(c) A lawyer retains ultimate responsibility to insure that all communications concerning the lawyer or the lawyer's services comply with the Georgia Rules of Professional Conduct.

The maximum penalty for a violation of this Rule is disbarment.

Comment

[1] This rule governs the content of all communications about a lawyer's services, including the various types of advertising permitted by Rules 7.3 through 7.5. Whatever means are used to make known a lawyer's services, statements about them should be truthful.

[2] The prohibition in sub-paragraph (a)(2) of this *Rule 7.1: Communications Concerning a Lawyer's Services* of statements that may create "unjustified expectations" would ordinarily preclude advertisements about results obtained on behalf of a client, such as the amount of a damage award or the lawyer's record in obtaining favorable verdicts, and advertisements containing client endorsements. Such information may create the unjustified expectation that similar results can be obtained for others without reference to the specific factual and legal circumstances.

Affirmative Disclosure

[3] In general, the intrusion on the First Amendment right of commercial speech resulting from rationally-based affirmative disclosure requirements is minimal, and is therefore a preferable form of regulation to absolute bans or other similar restrictions. For example, there is no significant interest in failing to include the name of at least one accountable attorney in all communications promoting the services of a lawyer or law firm as required by subparagraph (a)(5) of *Rule 7.1: Communications Concerning a Lawyer's Services.* Nor is there any substantial burden imposed as a result of the affirmative disclaimer requirement of sub-paragraph (a)(6) upon a lawyer who wishes to make a claim in the nature of "no fee unless you win." Indeed, the United States Supreme Court has specifically recognized that affirmative disclosure of a client's liability for costs and expenses of litigation may be required to prevent consumer confusion over the technical distinction between the meaning and effect of the use of such terms as "fees" and "costs" in an advertisement.

[4] Certain promotional communications of a lawyer may, as a result of content or circumstance, tend to mislead a consumer to mistakenly believe that the communication is something other than a form of promotional communication for which the lawyer has paid. Examples of such a communication might include advertisements for seminars on legal topics directed to the lay public when such seminars are sponsored by the lawyer, or a newsletter or newspaper column which appears to inform or to educate about the law. Paragraph (b) of this *Rule 7.1: Communications Concerning a Lawyer's Services* would require affirmative disclosure that a lawyer has given value in order to generate these types of public communications if such is in fact the case.

Accountability

[5] Paragraph (c) makes explicit an advertising attorney's ultimate responsibility for all the lawyer's promotional communications and would suggest that review by the lawyer prior to dissemination is advisable if any doubts exist concerning conformity of the end product with these Rules. Although prior review by disciplinary authorities is not required by these Rules, lawyers are certainly encouraged to contact disciplinary authorities prior to authorizing a promotional communication if there are any doubts concerning either an interpretation of these Rules or their application to the communication.

RULE 7.2 ADVERTISING

(a) Subject to the requirements of Rules 7.1 and 7.3, a lawyer may advertise services through:

(1) public media, such as a telephone directory, legal directory, newspaper or other periodical;

(2) outdoor advertising;

(3) radio or television;

(4) written, electronic or recorded communication.

(b) A copy or recording of an advertisement or communication shall be kept for two years after its last dissemination along with a record of when and where it was used.

The maximum penalty for a violation of this Rule is a public reprimand.

Comment

[1] To assist the public in obtaining legal services, lawyers should be allowed to make known their services not only through reputation but also through organized information campaigns in the form of advertising. Advertising involves an active quest for clients, contrary to the tradition that a lawyer should not seek clientele. However, the public's need to know about legal services can be fulfilled in part through advertising. This need is particularly acute in the case of persons of moderate means who have not made extensive use of legal services. The interest in expanding public information about legal services ought to prevail over considerations

of tradition. Nevertheless, advertising by lawyers entails the risk of practices that are misleading or overreaching.

[2] This Rule permits public dissemination of information concerning a lawyer's name or firm name, address and telephone number; the kinds of services the lawyer will undertake; the basis on which the lawyer's fees are determined, including prices for specific services and payment and credit arrangements; a lawyer's foreign language ability; names of references and, with their consent, names of clients regularly represented; and other information that might invite the attention of those seeking legal assistance.

[3] Questions of effectiveness and taste in advertising are matters of speculation and subjective judgment. Some jurisdictions have had extensive prohibitions against television advertising, against advertising going beyond specified facts about a lawyer, or against "undignified" advertising. Television is now one of the most powerful media for getting information to the public, particularly persons of low and moderate income; prohibiting television advertising, therefore, would impede the flow of information about legal services to many sectors of the public. Limiting the information that may be advertised has a similar effect and assumes that the bar can accurately forecast the kind of information that the public would regard as relevant.

[4] Neither this Rule nor *Rule 7.3: Direct Contact with Prospective Clients* prohibits communications authorized by law, such as notice to members of a class in class action litigation.

Record of Advertising

[5] Paragraph (b) requires that a record of the content and use of advertising be kept in order to facilitate enforcement of this Rule.

RULE 7.3 DIRECT CONTACT WITH PROSPECTIVE CLIENTS

(a) A lawyer shall not send, or knowingly permit to be sent, on behalf of the lawyer, the lawyer's firm, lawyer's partner, associate, or any other lawyer affiliated with the lawyer or the lawyer's firm, a written communication to a prospective client for the purpose of obtaining professional employment if:

(1) it has been made known to the lawyer that a person does not desire to receive communications from the lawyer;

(2) the communication involves coercion, duress, fraud, over-reaching, harassment, intimidation or undue influence;

(3) the written communication concerns an action for personal injury or wrongful death or otherwise relates to an accident or disaster involving the person to whom the communication is addressed or a relative of that person, unless the accident or disaster occurred more than 30 days prior to the mailing of the communication; or

(4) the lawyer knows or reasonably should know that the physical, emotional or mental state of the person is such that the person could not exercise reasonable judgment in employing a lawyer.

(b) Written communications to a prospective client, other than a close friend, relative, former client or one whom the lawyer reasonably believes is a former client, for the purpose of obtaining professional employment shall be plainly marked "Advertisement" on the face of the envelope and on the top of each page of the written communication in type size no smaller than the largest type size used in the body of the letter.

(c) A lawyer shall not compensate or give anything of value to a person or organization to recommend or secure the lawyer's employment by a client, or as a reward for having made a recommendation resulting in the lawyer's employment by a client; except that the lawyer may pay for public communications permitted by Rule 7.1 and except as follows:

(1) A lawyer may pay the usual and reasonable fees or dues charged by a bona fide lawyer referral service operated by an organization authorized by law and qualified to do business in this state provided, however, such organization has filed with the State Disciplinary Board, at least annually, a report showing its terms, its subscription charges, agreements with counsel, the number of lawyers participating, and the names and addresses of lawyers participating in the service;

(2) A lawyer may pay the usual and reasonable fees or dues charged by a bar–operated non–profit lawyer referral service, including a fee which is calculated as a percentage of the legal fees earned by the lawyer to whom the service has referred a matter, provided such bar–operated non–profit lawyer referral service meets the following criteria:

(i) the lawyer referral service shall be operated in the public interest for the purpose of referring prospective clients to lawyers, pro bono and public service legal programs, and government, consumer or other agencies who can provide the assistance the clients need. Such organization shall file annually with the State Disciplinary Board a report showing its rules and regulations, its subscription charges, agreements with counsel, the number of lawyers participating and the names and addresses of the lawyers participating in the service;

(ii) the sponsoring bar association for the lawyer referral service must be open to all lawyers licensed and eligible to practice in this state who maintain an office within the geographical area served, and who meet reasonable objectively determinable experience requirements established by the bar association;

(iii) The combined fees charged by a lawyer and the lawyer referral service to a client referred by such service shall not exceed the total charges which the client would have paid had no service been involved; and,

(iv) A lawyer who is a member of the qualified lawyer referral service must maintain in force a policy of errors and omissions insurance in an amount no less than $100,000 per occurrence and $300,000 in the aggregate.

(3) A lawyer may pay the usual and reasonable fees to a qualified legal services plan or insurer providing legal services insurance as authorized by law to promote the use of the lawyer's services, the lawyer's partner or associates services so long as the communications of the organization are not false, fraudulent, deceptive or misleading;

(4) A lawyer may pay the usual and reasonable fees charged by a lay public relations or marketing organization provided the activities of such organization on behalf of the lawyer are otherwise in accordance with these Rules;

(5) A lawyer may pay for a law practice in accordance with Rule 1.17: Sale of Law Practice.

(d) A lawyer shall not solicit professional employment as a private practitioner for the lawyer, a partner or associate through direct personal contact or through live telephone contact, with a non-lawyer who has not sought advice regarding employment of a lawyer.

(e) A lawyer shall not accept employment when the lawyer knows or it is obvious that the person who seeks to employ the lawyer does so as a result of conduct by any person or organization prohibited under Rules 7.3(c)(1), 7.3(c)(2) or 7.3(d): *Direct Contact with Prospective Clients.*

The maximum penalty for a violation of this Rule is disbarment.

Amended effective June 9, 2004.

Comment

Direct Personal Contact

[1] There is a potential for abuse inherent in solicitation through direct personal contact by a lawyer of prospective clients known to need legal services. It subjects the lay person to the private importuning of a trained advocate, in a direct interpersonal encounter. A prospective client often feels overwhelmed by the situation giving rise to the need for legal services, and may have an impaired capacity for reason, judgment and protective self-interest. Furthermore, the lawyer seeking the retainer is faced with a conflict stemming from the lawyer's own interest, which may color the advice and representation offered the vulnerable prospect.

[2] The situation is therefore fraught with the possibility of undue influence, intimidation, and overreaching. The potential for abuse inherent in solicitation of prospective clients through personal contact justifies its prohibition, particularly since the direct written contact permitted under paragraph (b) of this Rule offers an alternative means of communicating necessary information to those who may be in need of legal services. Also included in the prohibited types of personal contact are direct personal contact through an intermediary and live contact by telephone.

Direct Mail Solicitation

[3] Subject to the requirements of *Rule 7.1: Communications Concerning a Lawyer's Services* and paragraphs (b) and (c) of this *Rule 7.3: Direct Contact with Prospective Clients,* promotional communication by a lawyer through direct written contact is generally permissible. The public's need to receive information concerning their legal rights and the availability of legal services has been consistently recognized as a basis for permitting direct written communication since this type of communication may often be the best and most effective means of informing. So long as this stream of information flows cleanly, it will be permitted to flow freely.

[4] Certain narrowly-drawn restrictions on this type of communication are justified by a substantial state interest in facilitating the public's intelligent selection of counsel, including the restrictions of sub-paragraph (a)(3) & (4) which proscribe direct mailings to persons such as an injured and hospitalized accident victim or the bereaved family of a deceased.

[5] In order to make it clear that the communication is commercial in nature, paragraph (b) requires inclusion of an appropriate affirmative "advertisement" disclaimer. Again, the traditional exception for contact with close friends, relatives and former clients is recognized and permits elimination of the disclaimer in direct written contact with these persons.

[6] This Rule does not prohibit communications authorized by law, such as notice to members of a class in class action litigation.

Paying Others to Recommend a Lawyer

[7] A lawyer is allowed to pay for communications permitted by these Rules, but otherwise is not permitted to pay another person for channeling professional work. This restriction does not prevent an organization or person other than the lawyer from advertising or recommending the lawyer's services. Thus, a legal aid agency, a prepaid legal services plan or prepaid legal insurance organization may pay to advertise legal services provided under its auspices. Likewise, a lawyer may participate in lawyer referral programs and pay the usual fees charged by such programs, provided the programs are in compliance with the registration requirements of subparagraph (c)(1) or (c)(2) of this Rule 7.3: Direct Contact with Prospective Clients and the communications and practices of the organization are not deceptive or misleading.

[8] A lawyer may not indirectly engage in promotional activities through a lay public relations or marketing firm if such activities would be prohibited by these Rules if engaged in directly by the lawyer.

RULE 7.4 COMMUNICATION OF FIELDS OF PRACTICE

A lawyer may communicate the fact that the lawyer does or does not practice in particular fields of law. A lawyer who is a specialist in a particular field of law by experience, specialized training or education, or is certified by a recognized and bona fide professional entity, may communicate such specialty or certification so long as the statement is not false or misleading.

The maximum penalty for a violation of this Rule is a public reprimand.

Comment

[1] This Rule permits a lawyer to indicate areas of practice in communications about the lawyer's services. If a lawyer practices only in certain fields, or will not accept matters except in such fields, the lawyer is permitted to so indicate.

[2] A lawyer may truthfully communicate the fact that the lawyer is a specialist or is certified in a particular field of law by experience or as a result of having been certified as a "specialist" by successfully completing a particular program of legal specialization. An example of a proper use of the term would be "Certified as a Civil Trial Specialist by XYZ Institute" provided such was in fact the case, such statement would not be false or misleading and provided further that the Civil Trial Specialist program of XYZ Institute is a recognized and bona fide professional entity.

RULE 7.5 FIRM NAMES AND LETTERHEADS

(a) A lawyer shall not use a firm name, letterhead or other professional designation that violates Rule 7.1.

(b) A law firm with offices in more than one jurisdiction may use the same name in each jurisdiction, but identification of the lawyers in an office of the firm shall indicate the jurisdictional limitations on those not licensed to practice in the jurisdiction where the office is located.

(c) The name of a lawyer holding public office shall not be used in the name of a law firm, or in communications on its behalf, during any substantial period in which the lawyer is not actively and regularly practicing with the firm.

(d) Lawyers may state or imply that they practice in a partnership or other organization only when that is the fact.

(e) A trade name may be used by a lawyer in private practice if:

(1) the trade name includes the name of at least one of the lawyers practicing under said name. A law firm name consisting solely of the name or names of deceased or retired members of the firm does not have to include the name of an active member of the firm; and

(2) the trade name does not imply a connection with a government entity, with a public or charitable legal services organization or any other organization, association or institution or entity, unless there is, in fact, a connection.

The maximum penalty for a violation of this Rule is a public reprimand.

Comment

[1] Firm names and letterheads are subject to the general requirement of all advertising that the communication must not be false, fraudulent, deceptive or misleading. Therefore, lawyers sharing office facilities, but who are not in fact partners, may not denominate themselves as, for example, "Smith and Jones," for that title suggests partnership in the practice of law. Nor may a firm engage in practice in Georgia under more than one name. For example, a firm practicing as A, B and C may not set up a separate office called "ABC Legal Clinic."

[2] Trade names may be used so long as the name includes the name of at least one or more of the lawyers actively practicing with the firm. Firm names consisting entirely of the names of deceased or retired partners have traditionally been permitted and have proven a useful means of identification. Sub-paragraph (e)(1) permits their continued use as an exception to the requirement that a firm name include the name of at least one active member.

PART EIGHT. MAINTAINING THE INTEGRITY OF THE PROFESSION

RULE 8.1 BAR ADMISSION AND DISCIPLINARY MATTERS

An applicant for admission to the bar, or a lawyer in connection with a bar admission application or in connection with a disciplinary matter, shall not:

(a) knowingly make a false statement of material fact; or

(b) fail to disclose a fact necessary to correct a misapprehension known by the person to have arisen in the matter, or knowingly fail to respond to a lawful demand for information from an admissions or disciplinary authority, except that this rule does not require disclosure of information otherwise protected by Rule 1.6.

The maximum penalty for a violation of this Rule is disbarment.

Comment

[1] The duty imposed by this Rule extends to persons seeking admission to the bar as well as to lawyers. Hence, if a person makes a material false statement in connection with an application for admission, it may be the basis for subsequent disciplinary action if the person is admitted, and in any event may be relevant in a subsequent admission application. The duty imposed by this Rule applies to a lawyer's own admission or discipline as well as that of others. Thus, it is a separate professional offense for a lawyer to knowingly make a misrepresentation or omission in connection with a disciplinary investigation of the lawyer's own conduct. This Rule also requires affirmative clarification of any misunderstanding on the part of the admissions or disciplinary authority of which the person involved becomes aware.

[2] This Rule is subject to the provisions of the Fifth Amendment of the United States Constitution and corresponding provisions of state constitutions. A person relying on such a provision in response to a question, however, should do so openly and not use the right of nondisclosure as a justification for failure to comply with this Rule.

[3] A lawyer representing an applicant for admission to the bar, or representing a lawyer who is the subject of a disciplinary inquiry or proceeding, is governed by the rules applicable to the client-lawyer relationship.

RULE 8.2 JUDICIAL AND LEGAL OFFICIALS

(a) Reserved.

(b) A lawyer who is a candidate for judicial office shall comply with the applicable provisions of the Code of Judicial Conduct.

The maximum penalty for a violation of this Rule is disbarment.

Comment

[1] Assessments by lawyers are relied on in evaluating the professional or personal fitness of persons being considered for election or appointment to judicial office and to public legal offices, such as attorney general, prosecuting attorney and public defender. Expressing honest and candid opinions on such matters contributes to improving the administration of justice. Conversely, false statements by a lawyer can unfairly undermine public confidence in the administration of justice.

[2] When a lawyer seeks judicial office, the lawyer should be bound by applicable limitations on political activity.

[3] To maintain the fair and independent administration of justice, lawyers are encouraged to continue traditional efforts to defend judges and courts unjustly criticized.

RULE 8.3 REPORTING PROFESSIONAL MISCONDUCT

(a) A lawyer having knowledge that another lawyer has committed a violation of the Georgia Rules of Professional Conduct that raises a substantial question as to that lawyer's honesty, trustworthiness or fitness as a lawyer in other respects, should inform the appropriate professional authority.

(b) A lawyer having knowledge that a judge has committed a violation of applicable rules of judicial conduct that raises a substantial question as to the judge's fitness for office should inform the appropriate authority.

There is no disciplinary penalty for a violation of this Rule.

Comment

[1] Self-regulation of the legal profession requires that members of the profession initiate disciplinary investigations when they know of a violation of the Georgia Rules of Professional Conduct. Lawyers have a similar obligation with respect to judicial misconduct. An apparently isolated violation may indicate a pattern of misconduct that only a disciplinary investigation can uncover. Reporting a violation is especially important where the victim is unlikely to discover the offense.

RULE 8.4 MISCONDUCT

(a) It shall be a violation of the Georgia Rules of Professional Conduct for a lawyer to:

(1) violate or attempt to violate the Georgia Rules of Professional Conduct, knowingly assist or induce another to do so, or do so through the acts of another;

(2) be convicted of a felony;

(3) be convicted of a misdemeanor involving moral turpitude where the underlying conduct relates to the lawyer's fitness to practice law;

(4) engage in professional conduct involving dishonesty, fraud, deceit or misrepresentation;

(5) fail to pay any final judgment or rule absolute rendered against such lawyer for money collected by him or her as a lawyer within ten (10) days after the time appointed in the order or judgment. In such cases the record of the judgment is conclusive evidence unless obtained without valid service of process.

(b)(1) For purposes of this Rule, conviction shall include:

(i) a guilty plea;

(ii) a plea of nolo contendere;

(iii) a verdict of guilty; or

(iv) a verdict of guilty but mentally ill.

(2) The record of a conviction or disposition in any jurisdiction based upon a guilty plea, a plea of nolo contendere, a verdict of guilty, or a verdict of guilty but mentally ill, or upon the imposition of first offender probation shall be conclusive evidence of such conviction or disposition and shall be admissible in proceedings under these disciplinary rules.

(c) This Rule shall not be construed to cause any infringement of the existing inherent right of Georgia Superior Courts to suspend and disbar lawyers from practice based upon a conviction of a crime as specified in paragraphs (a)(1), (a)(2) and (a)(3) above.

(d) Rule 8.4(a)(1) does not apply to Part Six of the Georgia Rules of Professional Conduct.

The maximum penalty for a violation of Rule 8.4(a)(1) is the maximum penalty for the specific Rule violated. The maximum penalty for a violation of Rule 8.4(a)(2) through Rule 8.4(c) is disbarment.

Comment

[1] The prohibitions of this Rule as well as the prohibitions of Bar Rule 4–102 prohibit a lawyer from attempting to violate the Georgia Rules of Professional Conduct or from knowingly aiding or abetting, or providing direct or indirect assistance or inducement to another person who violates or attempts to violate a rule of professional conduct. A lawyer may not avoid a violation of the rules by instructing a nonlawyer, who is not subject to the rules, to act where the lawyer can not.

[2] This Rule, as its predecessor, is drawn in terms of acts involving "moral turpitude" with, however, a recognition

that some such offenses concern matters of personal morality and have no specific connection to fitness for the practice of law. Here the concern is limited to those matters which fall under both the rubric of "moral turpitude" and involve underlying conduct relating to the fitness of the lawyer to practice law.

[3] Many kinds of illegal conduct reflect adversely on fitness to practice law, such as offenses involving fraud and the offense of willful failure to file an income tax return. However, some kinds of offenses carry no such implication. Traditionally, the distinction was drawn in terms of offenses involving "moral turpitude." That concept can be construed to include offenses concerning some matters of personal morality, such as adultery and comparable offenses, that have no specific connection to fitness for the practice of law. Although a lawyer is personally answerable to the entire criminal law, a lawyer should be professionally answerable only for offenses that indicate lack of those characteristics relevant to law practice. Offenses involving violence, dishonesty, breach of trust, or serious interference with the administration of justice are in that category. A pattern of repeated offenses, even ones of minor significance when considered separately, can indicate indifference to legal obligation.

RULE 8.5 DISCIPLINARY AUTHORITY; CHOICE OF LAW

(a) Disciplinary Authority. A lawyer admitted to practice in this jurisdiction is subject to the disciplinary authority of this jurisdiction, regardless of where the lawyer's conduct occurs. A Domestic or Foreign Lawyer is also subject to the disciplinary authority of this jurisdiction if the Domestic or Foreign Lawyer provides or offers to provide any legal services in this jurisdiction. A lawyer or Domestic or Foreign Lawyer may be subject to the disciplinary authority of both this jurisdiction and another jurisdiction for the same conduct.

(b) Choice of Law. In any exercise of the disciplinary authority of this jurisdiction, the rules of professional conduct to be applied shall be as follows:

(1) for conduct in connection with a matter pending before a tribunal, the rules of the jurisdiction in which the tribunal sits, unless the rules of the tribunal provide otherwise; and

(2) for any other conduct, the rules of the jurisdiction in which the lawyer or Domestic or Foreign Lawyer's conduct occurred, or, if the predominant effect of the conduct is in a different jurisdiction, the rules of that jurisdiction shall be applied to the conduct. A lawyer or Domestic or Foreign Lawyer shall not be subject to discipline if the lawyer's or Domestic or Foreign Lawyer's conduct conforms to the rules of a jurisdiction in which the lawyer or Domestic or Foreign Lawyer reasonably believes the predominant effect of the lawyer or Domestic or Foreign Lawyer's conduct will occur.

Amended effective June 8, 2004.

Comment

Disciplinary Authority

[1] It is longstanding law that the conduct of a lawyer admitted to practice in this jurisdiction is subject to the disciplinary authority of this jurisdiction. Extension of the disciplinary authority of this jurisdiction to Domestic or Foreign Lawyers who provide or offer to provide legal services in this jurisdiction is for the protection of the citizens of this jurisdiction. Reciprocal enforcement of a jurisdiction's disciplinary findings and sanctions will further advance the purposes of this Rule. See, Rule 9.4: Jurisdiction and Reciprocal Discipline. A Domestic or Foreign Lawyer who is subject to the disciplinary authority of this jurisdiction under Rule 8.5(a) appoints an official to be designated by this Court to receive service of process in this jurisdiction. The fact that the Domestic or Foreign Lawyer is subject to the disciplinary authority of this jurisdiction may be a factor in determining whether personal jurisdiction may be asserted over the lawyer for civil matters.

Choice of Law

[2] A lawyer or Domestic or Foreign Lawyer may be potentially subject to more than one set of rules of professional conduct which impose different obligations. The lawyer or Domestic or Foreign Lawyer may be licensed to practice in more than one jurisdiction with differing rules, or may be admitted to practice before a particular court with rules that differ from those of the jurisdiction or jurisdictions in which the lawyer or Domestic or Foreign Lawyer is licensed to practice. Additionally, the lawyer or Domestic or Foreign Lawyer's conduct may involve significant contacts with more than one jurisdiction.

[3] Paragraph (b) seeks to resolve such potential conflicts. Its premise is that minimizing conflicts between rules, as well as uncertainty about which rules are applicable, is in the best interest of both clients and the profession (as well as the bodies having authority to regulate the profession). Accordingly, it takes the approach of (i) providing that any particular conduct of a lawyer or Domestic or Foreign Lawyer shall be subject to only one set of rules of professional conduct, (ii) making the determination of which set of rules applies to particular conduct as straightforward as possible, consistent with recognition of appropriate regulatory interests of relevant jurisdictions, and (iii) providing protection from discipline for lawyers or Domestic or Foreign Lawyers who act reasonably in the face of uncertainty.

[4] Paragraph (b)(1) provides that as to a lawyer or Domestic or Foreign Lawyer conduct relating to a proceeding pending before a tribunal, the lawyer or Domestic or Foreign Lawyer shall be subject only to the rules of the jurisdiction in which the tribunal sits unless the rules of the tribunal, including its choice of law rule, provide otherwise. As to all other conduct, including conduct in anticipation of a proceeding not yet pending before a tribunal, paragraph (b)(2) provides that a lawyer or Domestic or Foreign Lawyer shall be subject to the rules of the jurisdiction in which the lawyer or Domestic or Foreign Lawyer's conduct occurred, or, if the predominant effect of the conduct is in another jurisdiction, the rules of that jurisdiction shall be applied to the conduct. In the case of conduct in anticipation of a proceeding that is likely to be before a tribunal, the predominant effect of such conduct could be where the conduct occurred, where the tribunal sits or in another jurisdiction.

[5] When a lawyer or Domestic or Foreign Lawyer's conduct involves significant contacts with more than one jurisdiction, it may not be clear whether the predominant effect of the lawyer or Domestic or Foreign Lawyer's conduct will occur in a jurisdiction other than the one in which the conduct occurred. So long as the lawyer or Domestic or Foreign Lawyer's conduct conforms to the rules of a jurisdiction in which the lawyer or Domestic or Foreign Lawyer reasonably believes the predominant effect will occur, the lawyer or Domestic or Foreign Lawyer shall not be subject to discipline under this Rule.

[6] If two admitting jurisdictions were to proceed against a lawyer or Domestic or Foreign Lawyer for the same conduct, they should, applying this rule, identify the same governing ethics rules. They should take all appropriate steps to see that they do apply the same rule to the same conduct, and in all events should avoid proceeding against a lawyer or Domestic or Foreign Lawyer on the basis of two inconsistent rules.

[7] The choice of law provision applies to lawyers or Domestic or Foreign Lawyer engaged in transnational practice, unless international law, treaties or other agreements between competent regulatory authorities in the affected jurisdictions provide otherwise.

PART NINE. MISCELLANEOUS

RULE 9.1 REPORTING REQUIREMENTS

Members of the State Bar of Georgia shall notify the State Bar of Georgia of:

(a) all other jurisdictions in which the member is admitted to the practice of law and the dates of admission; and

(b) the conviction of any felony or of a misdemeanor involving moral turpitude where the underlying conduct relates to the lawyer's fitness to practice law, within sixty days of conviction.

The maximum penalty for a violation of this Rule is a public reprimand.

Comment

[1] The State Bar of Georgia is the regulatory authority created by the Supreme Court of Georgia to oversee the practice of law in Georgia. In order to provide effective disciplinary programs, the State Bar of Georgia needs information about its members.

RULE 9.2 SETTLEMENT OF CLAIMS

In connection with the settlement of a controversy or suit involving misuse of funds held in a fiduciary capacity, a lawyer shall not enter into an agreement that the person bringing the claim will be prohibited or restricted from filing a disciplinary complaint, or will be required to request the dismissal of a pending disciplinary complaint concerning that conduct.

The maximum penalty for a violation of this Rule is disbarment.

Comment

[1] The disciplinary system provides protection to the general public from those lawyers who are not morally fit to practice law. One problem in the past has been the lawyer who settles the civil claim/disciplinary complaint with the injured party on the basis that the injured party not bring a disciplinary complaint or request the dismissal of a pending disciplinary complaint. The lawyer is then is free to injure other members of the general public.

[2] To prevent such abuses in settlements, this rule prohibits a lawyer from settling any controversy or suit involving misuse of funds on any basis which prevents the person bringing the claim from pursuing a disciplinary complaint.

RULE 9.3 COOPERATION WITH DISCIPLINARY AUTHORITIES

During the investigation of a grievance filed under these Rules, the lawyer complained against shall respond to disciplinary authorities in accordance with State Bar Rules.

The maximum penalty for a violation of this Rule is a public reprimand.

Comment

[1] Much of the work in the disciplinary process is performed by volunteer lawyers and lay persons. In order to make good use of their valuable time, it is imperative that the lawyer complained against cooperate with the investigation. In particular, the lawyer must file a sworn response with the member of the Investigative Panel charged with the responsibility of investigating the complaint.

[2] Nothing in this Rule prohibits a lawyer from responding by making a Fifth Amendment objection, if appropriate. However, disciplinary proceedings are civil in nature and the use of a Fifth Amendment objection will give rise to a presumption against the lawyer.

RULE 9.4 JURISDICTION AND RECIPROCAL DISCIPLINE

(a) Jurisdiction. Any lawyer admitted to practice law in this jurisdiction, including any formerly admitted lawyer with respect to acts committed prior to resignation, suspension, disbarment, or removal from practice on any of the grounds provided in Rule 4–105 of the State Bar, or with respect to acts subsequent thereto which amount to the practice of law or constitute a violation of the Georgia Rules of Professional Conduct or any Rules or Code subsequently adopted by the court in lieu thereof, and any Domestic or Foreign Lawyer specially admitted by a court of this jurisdiction for a particular proceeding and any Domestic or Foreign Lawyer who practices law or renders or offers to render any legal services in this jurisdiction, is subject to the disciplinary jurisdiction of the State Bar of Georgia State Disciplinary Board.

(b) Reciprocal Discipline. Upon being disciplined in another jurisdiction, a lawyer admitted to practice in Georgia shall promptly inform the Office of General

Counsel of the State Bar of Georgia of the discipline. Upon notification from any source that a lawyer within the jurisdiction of the State Bar of Georgia has been disciplined in another jurisdiction, the Office of General Counsel shall obtain a certified copy of the disciplinary order and file it with the Investigative Panel of the State Disciplinary Board.

(1) Upon receipt of a certified copy of an order demonstrating that a lawyer admitted to practice in Georgia has been disciplined in another jurisdiction, the Investigative Panel of the State Disciplinary Board shall forthwith issue a notice directed to the lawyer containing:

(i) A copy of the order from the other jurisdiction; and

(ii) An order directing that the lawyer inform the Office of General Counsel and the Review Panel, within thirty days from service of the notice, of any claim by the lawyer predicated upon the grounds set forth in paragraph (b)(3) below, that the imposition of the identical discipline in this jurisdiction would be unwarranted and the reasons for that claim.

(2) In the event the discipline imposed in the other jurisdiction has been stayed there, any reciprocal discipline imposed in this jurisdiction shall be deferred until the stay expires.

(3) Upon the expiration of thirty days from service of the notice pursuant to the provisions of paragraph (b)(1), the Review Panel shall recommend to the Georgia Supreme Court the identical discipline, or removal from practice on the grounds provided in Rule 4–104, unless the Office of General Counsel or the lawyer demonstrates, or the Review Panel finds that it clearly appears upon the face of the record from which the discipline is predicated, that:

(i) The procedure was so lacking in notice or opportunity to be heard as to constitute a deprivation of due process; or

(ii) There was such infirmity of proof establishing the misconduct as to give rise to the clear conviction that the court could not, consistent with its duty, accept as final the conclusion on that subject; or

(iii) The discipline imposed would result in grave injustice or be offensive to the public policy of the jurisdiction; or

(iv) The reason for the original disciplinary status no longer exists; or

(v)(a) the conduct did not occur within the state of Georgia; and,

(b) the discipline imposed by the foreign jurisdiction exceeds the level of discipline allowed under these Rules.

If the Review Panel determines that any of those elements exists, the Review Panel shall make such other recommendation to the Georgia Supreme Court as it deems appropriate. The burden is on the party seeking different discipline in this jurisdiction to demonstrate that the imposition of the same discipline is not appropriate.

(4) In all other aspects, a final adjudication in another jurisdiction that a lawyer, whether or not admitted in that jurisdiction, has been guilty of misconduct, or has been removed from practice on any of the grounds provided in Rule 4–104 of the State Bar, shall establish conclusively the misconduct or the removal from practice for purposes of a disciplinary proceeding in this state.

The maximum penalty for a violation of this Rule is disbarment.

Amended effective June 8, 2004.

Comment

[1] If a lawyer suspended or disbarred in one jurisdiction is also admitted in another jurisdiction and no action can be taken against the lawyer until a new disciplinary proceeding is instituted, tried, and concluded, the public in the second jurisdiction is left unprotected against a lawyer who has been judicially determined to be unfit. Any procedure which so exposes innocent clients to harm cannot be justified. The spectacle of a lawyer disbarred in one jurisdiction yet permitted to practice elsewhere exposes the profession to criticism and undermines public confidence in the administration of justice.

[2] The Office of the General Counsel of the State Bar of Georgia should be notified by disciplinary counsel of the jurisdiction where the original discipline was imposed. Upon receipt of such information, the Office of General Counsel should promptly notify the Investigative Panel. The Panel should promptly obtain and serve upon the lawyer an order to show cause why identical discipline should not be imposed in Georgia. The certified copy of the order in the original jurisdiction should be incorporated into the order to show cause.

[3] The imposition of discipline in one jurisdiction does not mean that Georgia and every other jurisdiction in which the lawyer is admitted must necessarily impose discipline. The Review Panel has jurisdiction to recommend reciprocal discipline on the basis of public discipline imposed by a jurisdiction in which the respondent is licensed.

[4] A judicial determination of misconduct by the respondent in another jurisdiction is conclusive, and not subject to relitigation in the forum jurisdiction. The Review Panel should recommend identical discipline unless it determines, after review limited to the record of the proceedings in the foreign jurisdiction, that one of the grounds specified in paragraph (b)(3) exists. This Rule applies whether or not the respondent is admitted to practice in the foreign jurisdiction. See also, *Rule 8.5: Disciplinary Authority; Choice of Law*, Comment [1].

[5] For purposes of this Rule, the suspension or placement of a lawyer on inactive status in another jurisdiction because of want of sound mind, senility, habitual intoxication or drug addiction, to the extent of impairment of competency as an attorney shall be considered a disciplinary suspension under the Rules of the State Bar of Georgia.

RULE 9.5 LAWYER AS A PUBLIC OFFICIAL

(a) A lawyer who is a public official and represents the State, a municipal corporation in the State, the United States government, their agencies or officials, is bound by the provisions of these Rules.

(b) No provision of these Rules shall be construed to prohibit such a lawyer from taking a legal position adverse to the State, a municipal corporation in the State, the United States government, their agencies or officials, when such action is authorized or required by the U. S. Constitution, the Georgia Constitution or statutes of the United States or Georgia.

Rule 4-102. Adopted effective January 1, 2001; amended effective June 8, 2004; June 9, 2004.

RULE 4–103. MULTIPLE VIOLATIONS

A finding of a third or subsequent disciplinary infraction under these rules shall, in and of itself, constitute discretionary grounds for suspension or disbarment. The Review Panel may exercise this discretionary power when the question is appropriately before that Panel.

Amended July 1, 1986.

RULE 4–104. MENTAL INCAPACITY AND SUBSTANCE ABUSE

(a) Want of a sound mind, senility, habitual intoxication or drug addiction, to the extent of impairing competency as an attorney, when found to exist under the procedure outlined in Part IV, Chapter 2 of these rules, shall constitute grounds for removing the attorney from the practice of law. Notice of final judgment taking such action shall be given by the Review Panel as provided in Rule 4–220(a).

(b) Upon a finding by either panel of the State Disciplinary Board that an attorney may be impaired or incapacitated to practice law due to mental incapacity or substance abuse, that panel may, in its sole discretion, make a confidential referral of the matter to the Committee on Lawyer Impairment for the purposes of confrontation and referral of the attorney to treatment centers and peer support groups. Either panel may, in its discretion, defer disciplinary findings and proceedings based upon the impairment or incapacitation of an attorney pending attempts by the Committee on Lawyer Impairment to afford the attorney an opportunity to begin recovery. In such situations the committee shall report to the referring panel and Bar counsel concerning the attorney's progress toward recovery.

(c) In the event of a finding by the Supreme Court of Georgia that a lawyer is impaired or incapacitated, the Court may refer the matter to the Committee on Lawyer Impairment, before or after its entry of judgment under Bar Rules 4–219 or 4–220(a), so that rehabilitative aid may be provided to the impaired or incapacitated attorney. In such situations the committee shall be authorized to report to the Court, either panel of the State Disciplinary Board and Bar counsel concerning the attorney's progress toward recovery.

Amended July 1, 1986; March 15, 1989.

RULE 4–105. DECEASED, INCAPACITATED, IMPRISONED AND DISAPPEARING ATTORNEYS

When it appears to the Investigative Panel that an attorney's death, incapacity, imprisonment or disappearance poses a substantial threat of harm to his clients or the public, the Investigative Panel shall immediately investigate the matter. If the Investigative Panel determines that such threat exists and that no partner, associate or other appropriate representative is available to prevent the harm, it shall file its findings and recommendation of action in the Supreme Court and shall seek judgment as provided in Rule 4–219.

Amended July 1, 1986.

RULE 4–106. CONVICTION OF A CRIME: SUSPENSION AND DISBARMENT

(a) Upon receipt of information or evidence that an attorney has been convicted of any felony or misdemeanor involving moral turpitude, whether by verdict, plea of guilty, plea of nolo contendere or imposition of first offender probation, the Office of the General Counsel shall immediately assign the matter a State Disciplinary Board docket number and petition the Georgia Supreme Court for the appointment of a special master to conduct a show cause hearing.

(b) The petition shall show the date of the verdict or plea and the court in which the respondent was convicted, and shall be served upon the respondent pursuant to Bar Rule 4–203.1.

(c) Upon receipt of the Petition for Appointment of Special Master, the Clerk of the Georgia Supreme Court shall file the matter in the records of the Court, shall give the matter a docket number and notify the Court that appointment of a special master is appropriate.

(d) The Court will appoint a special master, pursuant to Rule 4–209(b).

(e) The show cause hearing should be held within fifteen days after service of the Petition for Appointment of Special Master upon the respondent or appointment of a special master, whichever is later. Within thirty days of the hearing, the special master shall file a recommendation with the Supreme Court of Georgia which shall be empowered to order such discipline as deemed appropriate.

(f)(1) If the Supreme Court of Georgia orders the respondent suspended pending the appeal of the conviction, upon the termination of the appeal the State Bar of Georgia may petition the special master to conduct a hearing for the purpose of determining whether the circumstances of the termination of the appeal indicate that the suspended respondent should:

(i) be disbarred under Standard 66, or

(ii) be reinstated, or

(iii) remain suspended pending retrial as a protection to the public, or

(iv) be reinstated while the facts giving rise to the conviction are investigated and, if proper, prosecuted under regular disciplinary procedures in these rules.

(2) Reports of the special master shall be filed with the Review Panel as provided hereafter in Rule 4–217. The Review Panel shall make its findings and recommendation as provided hereafter in Rule 4–218.

(g) For purposes of this rule, a certified copy of a conviction in any jurisdiction based upon a verdict, plea of guilty or plea of nolo contendere or the imposition of first offender treatment shall be prima facie evidence of an infraction of Standard 66 of Bar Rule 4–102 and shall be admissible in proceedings under the disciplinary rules.

Amended October 3, 1985; July 1, 1986; July 1, 1997.

RULE 4–107. [RESERVED]

RULE 4–108. CONDUCT CONSTITUTING THREAT OF HARM TO CLIENTS OR PUBLIC; EMERGENCY SUSPENSION

(a) Upon receipt of sufficient evidence demonstrating that an attorney's conduct poses a substantial threat of harm to his clients or the public and with the approval of the Immediate Past President of the State Bar of Georgia and the Chairperson of the Review Panel, or at the direction of the Chairperson of the Investigative Panel, the Office of General Counsel shall petition the Georgia Supreme Court for the suspension of the attorney pending disciplinary proceedings predicated upon the conduct causing such petition.

(b) The petition for emergency suspension shall state the evidence justifying the emergency suspension.

(c) The petition for emergency suspension shall be served upon the Respondent pursuant to Bar Rule 4–203.1.

(d) Upon receipt of the petition for emergency suspension, the Clerk of the Georgia Supreme Court shall file the matter in the records of the Court, shall assign the matter a docket number and shall notify the Court that appointment of a Special Master is appropriate.

(e) The Court will nominate a Special Master pursuant to Rule 4–209.2 to conduct a hearing where the State Bar shall show cause why the Respondent should be suspended pending disciplinary proceedings.

(f) Within fifteen days after service of the petition for emergency suspension upon the Respondent or appointment of a Special Master, whichever is later, the Special Master shall hold a hearing on the petition for emergency suspension.

(g) Within twenty days of the hearing, the Special Master shall file his or her recommendation with the Supreme Court of Georgia. The Court sitting en banc may suspend the Respondent pending final disposition of disciplinary proceedings predicated upon the conduct causing the emergency suspension, or order such other action as it deems appropriate.

Amended July 1, 1986; amended effective January 1, 1991; July 1, 1997.

RULE 4–109. REFUSAL OR FAILURE TO APPEAR FOR REPRIMAND; SUSPENSION

Either panel of the State Disciplinary Board based on the knowledge or belief that a respondent has refused, or failed without just cause, to appear in accordance with Bar Rule 4–220 before a panel or the superior court for the administration of a reprimand may file in the Supreme Court a motion for suspension of the respondent. A copy of the motion shall be sent to the respondent by registered mail. The Supreme Court may in its discretion, ten days after the filing of the motion, suspend the respondent until such time as the reprimand is administered.

Adopted February 26, 1986; amended July 1, 1986.

RULE 4–110. DEFINITIONS

(a) Respondent. A person whose conduct is the subject of any disciplinary investigation or proceeding.

(b) Confidential Proceedings. Any proceeding under these rules which occurs prior to a filing in the Supreme Court of Georgia.

(c) Public Proceedings. Any proceeding under these rules which has been filed with the Supreme Court of Georgia.

(d) Grievance/Memorandum of Grievance. An allegation of unethical conduct filed against an attorney.

(e) Probable Cause. A finding by the Investigative Panel that there is sufficient evidence to believe that the respondent has violated one or more of the provisions of Part IV, Chapter 1 of the Bar Rules.

(f) Petition for Voluntary Surrender of License. A Petition for Voluntary Discipline in which the respondent voluntarily surrenders his license to practice law in this State. A voluntary surrender of license is tantamount to disbarment.

(g) He, Him or His. Generic pronouns including both male and female.

(h) Attorney. A member of the State Bar of Georgia authorized by law to practice law in the State of Georgia.

(i) Notice of Discipline. A Notice by the Investigative Panel that the respondent will be subject to a disciplinary sanction for violation of one or more Standards of Conduct unless the respondent affirmatively rejects the notice.

Adopted July 1, 1986; amended effective January 1, 1991.

RULE 4-111. AUDIT FOR CAUSE

Upon receipt of sufficient evidence that a lawyer who practices law in this State poses a threat of harm to his clients or the public, the State Disciplinary Board may conduct an Audit for Cause with the written approval of the Chairman of the Investigative Panel of the State Disciplinary Board and the President-elect of the State Bar. Before approval can be granted, the lawyer shall be given notice that approval is being sought and be given an opportunity to appear and be heard. The sufficiency of the notice and opportunity to be heard shall be left to the sole discretion of the persons giving the approval. The State Disciplinary Board must inform the person being audited that the audit is an Audit for Cause. The failure of a lawyer to submit to an Audit for Cause shall be grounds for discipline pursuant to Standard 65.5.

Adopted effective January 1, 1996.

CHAPTER 2. DISCIPLINARY PROCEEDINGS

RULE 4-201. STATE DISCIPLINARY BOARD

The powers to investigate and discipline members of the State Bar of Georgia and those authorized to practice law in Georgia for violations of the Standards of Conduct set forth in Bar Rule 4-102 are hereby vested in a State Disciplinary Board and a Consumer Assistance Program. The State Disciplinary Board shall consist of two panels. The first panel shall be the Investigative Panel of the State Disciplinary Board (Investigative Panel). The second panel shall be the Review Panel of the State Disciplinary Board (Review Panel). The Consumer Assistance Program shall operate as described in Part XII of these Rules.

(a) The Investigative Panel shall consist of the President-elect of the State Bar of Georgia and the President-elect of the Younger Lawyers Section of the State Bar of Georgia, one member of the State Bar of Georgia from each judicial district of the State appointed by the President of the State Bar of Georgia with the approval of the Board of Governors of the State Bar of Georgia, one member of the State Bar of Georgia from each judicial district of the State appointed by the Supreme Court of Georgia, one at-large member of the State Bar of Georgia appointed by the Supreme Court, one at-large member of the State Bar of Georgia appointed by the President with the approval of the Board of Governors, and six public members appointed by the Supreme Court to serve as public members of the Panel.

(1) All members shall be appointed for three-year terms subject to the following exceptions:

(i) any person appointed to fill a vacancy caused by resignation, death, disqualification or disability shall serve only for the unexpired term of the member replaced unless reappointed;

(ii) ex-officio members shall serve during the term of their office; and

(iii) certain initial members as set forth in paragraph (2) below.

(2) It shall be the goal of the initial appointments that one-third (1/3) of the terms of the members appointed will expire annually.

(3) A member may be removed from the Panel pursuant to procedures set by the Panel for failure to attend regular meetings of the Panel. The vacancy shall be filled by appointment of the current President of the State Bar of Georgia.

(4) The Investigative Panel shall annually elect a chairperson, a vice-chairperson, or a vice-chairperson for any subcommittee for which the chairperson is not a member to serve as chairperson for that subcommittee, and such other officers as it may deem proper. The Panel shall meet in its entirety in July of each year to elect a chairperson. At any time the Panel may decide to divide itself into subcommittees or to consolidate after having divided. A majority shall constitute a quorum and a majority of a quorum shall be authorized to act. However, in any matter in which one or more Investigative Panel members are disqualified, the number of members constituting a quorum shall be reduced by the number of members disqualified from voting on the matter.

(5) The Investigative Panel is authorized to organize itself into as many subcommittees as the Panel

deems necessary to conduct the expeditious investigation of disciplinary matters referred to it by the Office of the General Counsel. However, no subcommittee shall consist of fewer than seven (7) members of the Panel and each such subcommittee shall include at least one (1) of the public members.

(b) The Review Panel shall consist of the Immediate Past President of the State Bar, the Immediate Past President of the Younger Lawyers Section or a member of the Younger Lawyers Section designated by its Immediate Past President, nine members of the State Bar, three from each of the three federal judicial districts of the State appointed as described below, and four public members appointed by the Supreme Court of Georgia.

(1) The nine members of the Bar from the federal judicial districts shall be appointed for three year terms so that the term of one Panel member from each district will expire each year. The three vacant positions will be filled in odd years by appointment by the President, with the approval of the Board of Governors, and in even years by appointment by the Supreme Court of Georgia.

(2) The Panel members serving at the time this rule goes into effect shall continue to serve until their respective terms expire. New Panel members shall be appointed as set forth above.

(3) Any person appointed to fill a vacancy caused by resignation, death, disqualification or disability shall serve only for the unexpired term of the member replaced unless reappointed.

(4) Ex-officio members shall serve during the term or terms of their offices.

(5) The Review Panel shall elect a chairperson and such other officers as it may deem proper in July of each year. A majority of the Panel shall constitute a quorum. A majority of a quorum shall be authorized to act except that a recommendation of the Review Panel to suspend or disbar shall require the affirmative vote of at least six members of the Review Panel, with not more than four negative votes. However, in any case in which one or more Review Panel members are disqualified, the number of members constituting a quorum and the number of members necessary to vote affirmatively for disbarment or suspension, shall be reduced by the number of members disqualified from voting on the case. No recommendation of disbarment or suspension may be made by fewer than four affirmative votes.

Amended July 1, 1986; November 1, 1988; amended effective July 1, 1991; December 14, 1993; December 8, 1994; July 1, 1997.

RULE 4–202. RECEIPT OF GRIEVANCES; INITIAL REVIEW BY BAR COUNSEL

(a) All grievances other than those initiated by the Supreme Court of Georgia, the Investigative Panel or inquiries which may be filed with the Consumer Assistance Program under Part XII of these Rules shall be first filed with the Office of the General Counsel of the State Bar of Georgia. The Office of the General Counsel shall require that oral grievances, and grievances illegibly or informally drawn, be reduced to a memorandum of grievance in such form as may be prescribed by the Investigative Panel.

(b) Upon receipt of a grievance in proper form, the Office of the General Counsel shall screen it to determine whether the grievance is unjustified, frivolous, patently unfounded or fails to state facts sufficient to invoke the disciplinary jurisdiction of the State Bar of Georgia. The Office of the General Counsel shall be empowered to collect evidence and information concerning any grievance and to add the findings and results of its investigation to the file containing such grievance. The screening process may include forwarding a copy of the grievance to the respondent in order that the respondent may respond to the grievance.

(c) Upon completion of its screening of a grievance, the Office of the General Counsel shall be empowered to dismiss those grievances which are unjustified, frivolous, patently unfounded or which fail to state facts sufficient to invoke the disciplinary jurisdiction of the State Bar of Georgia; provided, however, that a rejection of such grievance by the Office of the General Counsel shall not deprive the complaining party of any right of action he might otherwise have at law or in equity against the respondent. Those grievances which appear to allege any violation of Part IV, Chapter 1 of the State Bar Rules shall be forwarded to the Investigative Panel or a subcommittee of the Investigative Panel according to Rule 4–204.1.

Amended July 1, 1986; amended effective January 1, 1991; July 1, 1997.

RULE 4–203. POWERS AND DUTIES

(a) In accordance with these rules, the Investigative Panel shall have the following powers and duties:

(1) To receive and evaluate any and all written grievances against members of the State Bar and to frame such charges and grievances as shall conform to the requirements of these rules. A copy of any grievance serving as the basis for investigation or proceedings before the Panel shall be furnished to the respondent by the procedures set forth in Rule 4–204.2;

(2) To initiate grievances on its own motion, to require additional information from a complainant, where appropriate, and to dismiss and reject such grievances as to it may seem unjustified, frivolous, or patently unfounded. However, the rejection of a grievance by the Investigative Panel shall not deprive the complaining party of any right of action he or she

might otherwise have at law or in equity against the respondent;

(3) To issue letters of instruction when dismissing a grievance;

(4) To delegate the duties of the Panel enumerated in subparagraphs (1), (2), (11) and (12) hereof to the chairperson of the Panel or chairperson of any subcommittee of the Panel or such other members as the Panel or its chairperson may designate subject to review and approval by the Investigative Panel or subcommittee of the Panel;

(5) To conduct probable cause investigations, to collect evidence and information concerning grievances, to hold hearings where provided for in these rules, and to certify grievances to the Supreme Court for hearings by special masters as hereinafter provided;

(6) To pass upon petitions for protection of the clients of deceased, disappearing or incapacitated members of the State Bar;

(7) To adopt forms for formal complaints, subpoenas, notices, and any other written instruments necessary or desirable under these rules;

(8) To prescribe its own rules of conduct and procedure;

(9) To receive, investigate, and collect evidence and information; and to review and accept or reject such Petitions for Voluntary Discipline which request the imposition of confidential discipline and are filed with the Investigative Panel prior to the time of issuance of a formal complaint by Bar counsel. Each such petition shall contain admissions of fact and admissions of conduct in violation of Part IV, Chapter 1 of these rules sufficient to authorize the imposition of discipline. Bar counsel shall, upon filing of such petition, file with the Panel its recommendations as to acceptance or rejection of the petition by the Panel, giving the reasons therefor, and shall serve a copy of its recommendation upon the respondent presenting such petition;

(10) To sign and enforce, as hereinafter described, subpoenas for the appearance of persons and for the production of things and records at investigations and hearings;

(11) To extend the time within which a formal complaint may be filed;

(12) To issue letters of formal admonition and Investigative Panel Reprimands as hereinafter provided;

(13) To enter a Notice of Discipline providing that unless the respondent affirmatively rejects the notice, the respondent shall be sanctioned as ordered by the Investigative Panel;

(14) To use the investigators, auditors, and/or staff of the Office of the General Counsel in performing its duties.

(b) In accordance with these rules, the Review Panel or any subcommittee of the Panel shall have the following powers and duties:

(1) To receive reports from special masters, and to recommend to the Supreme Court the imposition of punishment and discipline;

(2) To adopt forms for subpoenas, notices, and any other written instruments necessary or desirable under these rules;

(3) To prescribe its own rules of conduct and procedure;

(4) (Reserved).

(5) Through the action of its chairperson or his or her designee and upon good cause shown, to allow a late filing of the respondent's answer where there has been no final selection of a special master within thirty days of service of the formal complaint upon the respondent;

(6) Through the action of its chairperson or his or her designee, to receive and pass upon challenges and objections to special masters.

Amended July 1, 1986; March 15, 1989; amended effective January 1, 1991; July 1, 1997; February 1, 2000.

RULE 4–203.1. UNIFORM SERVICE RULE

(a) Attorneys authorized to practice law in Georgia shall inform the Membership Department of the State Bar of Georgia, in writing, of their current name, address and telephone number. The Supreme Court of Georgia and the State Bar of Georgia may rely on the address file with the Membership Department in all efforts to contact, communicate with, and perfect service upon an attorney. The choice of an attorney to provide only a post office box address to the Membership Department of the State Bar of Georgia shall constitute an election to waive personal service. Notification of a change of address given to any department of the State Bar of Georgia other than the Membership Department shall not satisfy the requirement herein.

(b) In all matters requiring personal service under Part IV of the Bar Rules, service may be perfected in the following manner:

(1) *Acknowledgment of Service.* An acknowledgment of service from the Respondent shall constitute conclusive proof of service and shall eliminate the need to utilize any other form of service.

(2) *Written Response From Respondent.* A written response from the Respondent or Respondent's counsel shall constitute conclusive proof of service and shall eliminate the need to utilize any other form of service.

(3) In the absence of an acknowledgment of service, or a written response from the Respondent or Respondent's counsel, and subject to the provisions of

subparagraph (4) below, the Respondent shall be served in the following manner:

(i) Personal Service. Service may be accomplished by the Sheriff, or a Court approved agent for service of process, or any person approved by the Chairperson of the Investigative Panel or the Chair's designee. Receipt of a Return of Service Non Est Inventus from the Sheriff or any other person approved for service of the service documents, shall constitute conclusive proof that service cannot be perfected by personal service.

(ii) Service by Publication. In the event that personal service cannot be perfected, or when the Respondent has only provided a post office box to the Membership Department and Respondent has not acknowledged service within twenty (20) days of a mailing to Respondent's post office box, service May be accomplished by publication once a week for two weeks in the legal organ of the county of Respondent's address, as shown on the records of the Membership Department of the State Bar of Georgia, and, contemporaneously with the publication, mailing a copy of the service documents by first class mail to Respondent's address as shown on the records of the Membership Department of the State Bar of Georgia.

(4) When it appears from an affidavit made by the Office of General Counsel that the Respondent has departed from the state, or cannot, after due diligence, be found within the state, or seeks to avoid the service, the Chairperson of the Investigative Panel, or the chair's designee, may authorize service by publication without the necessity of first attempting personal service. The affidavit made by the Office of General Counsel must demonstrate recent unsuccessful attempts at personal service upon the Respondent regarding other or related disciplinary matters and that such personal service was attempted at Respondent's address as shown on the records of the Membership Department of the State Bar of Georgia.

(c) Whenever service of pleadings or other documents subsequent to the original complaint is required or permitted to be made upon a party represented by an attorney, the service shall be made upon the attorney unless service upon the party himself is otherwise required by these rules. Service upon the attorney or upon a party shall be made by delivering a copy to him or by mailing it to him at his last known address. As used in this rule, the term "delivery of a copy" means handing it to the attorney or to the party, or leaving it at his office with his clerk or other person in charge thereof or, if the office is closed or the person to be served has no office, leaving it at his dwelling house or usual place of abode with some person of suitable age and discretion then residing therein. Service by mail is complete upon mailing. Proof of service may be made by certificate of an attorney or of his employee, by written admission, by affidavit, or by other proof satisfactory to the court. Failure to make proof of service shall not affect the validity of the service.

Adopted effective July 1, 1997.

RULE 4–204. PRELIMINARY INVESTIGATION BY INVESTIGATIVE PANEL—GENERALLY

(a) Each grievance alleging conduct which appears to invoke the disciplinary jurisdiction of the State Disciplinary Board of the State Bar of Georgia shall be referred in accordance with Rule 4–204.1 by the Office of the General Counsel to the Investigative Panel or a subcommittee of the Investigative Panel for investigation and disposition in accordance with its rules. The Investigative Panel shall appoint one of its members to be responsible for the investigation. The Office of the General Counsel shall simultaneously assign a staff investigator to assist in the investigation. If the investigation of the Panel establishes probable cause to believe that the respondent has violated one or more of the provisions of Part IV, Chapter 1 of these rules, it shall:

(1) issue a letter of admonition;

(2) issue an Investigative Panel Reprimand;

(3) issue a Notice of Discipline; or

(4) refer the case to the Supreme Court of Georgia for hearing before a special master and file a formal complaint with the Supreme Court of Georgia, all as hereinafter provided.

All other cases may be either dismissed by the Investigative Panel or referred to the Fee Arbitration Committee or the Committee on Lawyer Impairment.

(b) The primary investigation shall be conducted by the staff investigators, the staff lawyers of the Office of the General Counsel, and the member of the Investigative Panel responsible for the investigation. The Board of Governors of the State Bar of Georgia shall fund the Office of the General Counsel so that the Office of the General Counsel will be able to adequately investigate and prosecute all cases.

Amended July 1, 1986; amended effective January 1, 1991.

RULE 4–204.1. NOTICE OF INVESTIGATION

(a) Upon completion of its screening of a grievance under Rule 4–202, the Office of the General Counsel shall forward those grievances which appear to invoke the disciplinary jurisdiction of the State Bar of Georgia to the Investigative Panel, or subcommittee of the Investigative Panel by serving a Notice of Investigation upon the Respondent.

(b) The Notice of Investigation shall accord the respondent reasonable notice of the charges against him and a reasonable opportunity to respond to the charges in writing and shall contain:

(1) a statement that the grievance is being transmitted to the Investigative Panel, or subcommittee of the Investigative Panel;

(2) a copy of the grievance;

(3) a list of the Standards of Conduct which appear to have been violated;

(4) the name and address of the Panel member assigned to investigate the grievance and a list of the Panel, or subcommittee of the Panel members;

(5) a statement of respondent's right to challenge the competency, qualifications or objectivity of any Panel member.

(c) The form for the Notice of Investigation shall be approved by the Investigative Panel.

Adopted March 15, 1989; amended effective January 1, 1991.

RULE 4-204.2. SERVICE OF THE NOTICE OF INVESTIGATION

The Office of the General Counsel shall cause the Notice of Investigation to be served upon the respondent pursuant to Bar Rule 4-203.1.

Adopted effective January 1, 1991; amended effective July 1, 1997.

RULE 4-204.3. ANSWER TO NOTICE OF INVESTIGATION REQUIRED

(a) The respondent shall file a written response under oath to the Notice of Investigation with the panel member assigned to investigate the grievance within thirty (30) days of service.

(b) The written response must address specifically all of the issues set forth in the Notice of Investigation.

(c) The panel member assigned to investigate the grievance may in the panel member's discretion grant extensions of time for respondent's answer. Any request for extension of time must be made in writing on or before the date on which the response was due and the grant of an extension of time must also be in writing. Extensions of time shall be reasonable in length and should not be routinely granted.

(d) In cases where the maximum sanction is disbarment or suspension, failure to respond by the respondent may authorize the Investigative Panel or subcommittee of the Panel to suspend the respondent until a response is filed.

(1) The determination that an adequate response has been filed is within the discretion of the Investigative Panel or subcommittee of the Panel.

(2) When the Investigative Panel or subcommittee of the Panel determines that a respondent has failed to respond in accordance with the rules of the Panel and that the respondent should be suspended, the Office of the General Counsel shall notify the Supreme Court of Georgia that the Panel has made such a recommendation. The Supreme Court shall enter an appropriate order.

(3) When the Investigative Panel or subcommittee of the Panel determines that a respondent who has been suspended for failure to respond in accordance with the rules of the Panel has filed an appropriate response and should be reinstated, the Office of the General Counsel shall notify the Supreme Court of Georgia that the Panel has made such a recommendation. The Supreme Court shall enter an appropriate order.

Adopted effective January 1, 1991; amended effective March 25, 1993.

RULE 4-204.4. FINDING OF PROBABLE CAUSE; REFERRAL TO SPECIAL MASTER

(a) In all cases wherein the Investigative Panel, or subcommittee of the Panel, finds probable cause of the respondent's violation of one or more of the provisions of Part IV, Chapter 1 of these rules and refers the matter to the Supreme Court for appointment of a special master, it shall file with the Clerk of the Supreme Court of Georgia the following documents in duplicate:

(1) notice of its finding of probable cause;

(2) a petition for the appointment of a special master and proposed order thereon;

(3) a formal complaint, as herein provided.

(b) The documents specified in paragraph (a) above shall be filed with the Clerk of the Supreme Court within thirty (30) days of the finding of probable cause unless the Investigative Panel, or subcommittee of the Panel, or its Chairperson grants an extension of time for the filing of the documents.

Adopted effective January 1, 1991.

RULE 4-204.5. LETTERS OF INSTRUCTION

(a) In addition to dismissing a complaint, the Investigative Panel, or subcommittee of the Panel, may issue a letter of instruction in any disciplinary case upon the following conditions:

(1) the case has been thoroughly investigated, the respondent has been notified of and has had an opportunity to answer the charges brought against him, and the case has been reported to the entire Panel, or

subcommittee of the Panel, assembled at a regularly scheduled meeting; and

(2) the Investigative Panel, or subcommittee of the Panel, as evidenced through the majority vote of its members present and voting, is of the opinion that the respondent either:

(i) has not engaged in conduct which is in violation of the provisions of Part IV, Chapter 1 of these rules; or

(ii) has engaged in conduct that although technically in violation of such rules is not reprehensible, and has resulted in no harm or injury to any third person, and is not in violation of the spirit of such rules; or

(iii) has engaged in conduct in violation of the Code of Professional Responsibility of Part III of these rules or any recognized voluntary creed of professionalism;

(b) Letters of instruction shall contain a statement of the conduct of the respondent which may have violated Part III of these rules or the voluntary creed of professionalism.

(c) A letter of instruction shall not constitute a finding of any disciplinary infraction.

Adopted effective January 1, 1991.

RULE 4-205. CONFIDENTIAL DISCIPLINE; IN GENERAL

In lieu of the imposition of any other discipline, the Investigative Panel or a subcommittee of the Investigative Panel may issue letters of formal admonition or an Investigative Panel Reprimand in any disciplinary case upon the following conditions:

(a) the case has been thoroughly investigated, the respondent has been notified of and has had an opportunity to answer the charges brought against him, and the case has been reported to the entire Panel or a subcommittee of the Panel assembled at a regularly scheduled meeting;

(b) the Panel or a subcommittee of the Panel, as evidenced through the majority vote of its members present and voting, is of the opinion that the respondent has engaged in conduct which is in violation of the provisions of Part IV, Chapter 1 of these rules;

(c) the Panel or a subcommittee of the Panel, as evidenced through the majority vote of its members present and voting, is of the opinion that the conduct referred to in sub-part (b) hereof was engaged in:

(1) inadvertently; or

(2) purposefully, but in ignorance of the applicable disciplinary rule or rules; or

(3) under such circumstances that it is the opinion of the Investigative Panel or a subcommittee of the Investigative Panel that the protection of the public and rehabilitation of the respondent would be best achieved by the issuance of a letter of admonition or an Investigative Panel Reprimand rather than by any other form of discipline.

Amended July 1, 1986; March 15, 1989; amended effective January 1, 1991.

RULE 4-206. CONFIDENTIAL DISCIPLINE; CONTENTS

(a) Letters of formal admonition and Investigative Panel Reprimands shall contain a statement of the specific conduct of the respondent which violates Part IV, Chapter 1 of these rules, shall state the name of the complainant and shall state the reasons for issuance of such confidential discipline.

(b) A letter of formal admonition shall also contain the following information:

(1) the right of the respondent to reject the letter of formal admonition under Rule 4-207;

(2) the procedure for rejecting the letter of formal admonition under Rule 4-207; and

(3) the effect of an accepted letter of formal admonition in the event of a third or subsequent imposition of discipline.

(c) An Investigative Panel Reprimand shall also contain information concerning the effect of the acceptance of such reprimand in the event of a third or subsequent imposition of discipline.

Amended July 1, 1986; March 15, 1989.

RULE 4-207. LETTERS OF FORMAL ADMONITION AND INVESTIGATIVE PANEL REPRIMANDS; NOTIFICATION AND RIGHT OF REJECTION

In any case where the Investigative Panel, or subcommittee of the Panel, votes to impose discipline in the form of a letter of formal admonition or an Investigative Panel Reprimand, such vote shall constitute the Panel's finding of probable cause. The respondent shall have the right to reject, in writing, the imposition of such discipline. A written rejection shall be deemed an election by the respondent to continue disciplinary proceedings under these rules and shall cause the Investigative Panel to proceed under Rule 4-204.4.

(a) Notification to respondent shall be as follows:

(1) in the case of letters of formal admonition, the letter of admonition;

(2) in the case of an Investigative Panel Reprimand, the letter notifying the respondent to appear for the administration of the reprimand;

(3) sent to the respondent at his address as reflected in State Bar records, via certified mail, return receipt requested.

(b) Rejection by respondent shall be as follows:

(1) in writing, within thirty (30) days of notification;

(2) sent to the Investigative Panel via certified mail, return receipt requested, directed to the Office of the General Counsel of the State Bar of Georgia at the current headquarters address of the State Bar.

(c) If the respondent rejects the imposition of a formal admonition or Investigative Panel Reprimand, the Office of the General Counsel shall file a formal complaint with the Clerk of the Supreme Court of Georgia within thirty (30) days of receipt of the rejection unless the Investigative Panel or its Chairperson grants an extension of time for the filing of the formal complaint.

(d) Investigative Panel Reprimands shall be administered before the Panel by the Chairperson or his or her designee.

Amended July 1, 1986; amended effective January 1, 1991.

RULE 4–208. CONFIDENTIAL DISCIPLINE; EFFECT IN EVENT OF SUBSEQUENT DISCIPLINE

An accepted letter of formal admonition or an Investigative Panel Reprimand shall be considered as a disciplinary infraction for the purpose of invoking the provisions of Rule 4–103. In the event of a subsequent disciplinary proceeding, the confidentiality of the imposition of confidential discipline shall be waived and the Office of the General Counsel may use such information as aggravation of discipline.

Amended July 1, 1986; March 15, 1989; amended effective January 1, 1991.

RULE 4–208.1. NOTICE OF DISCIPLINE

(a) In any case where the Investigative Panel or a subcommittee of the Panel finds probable cause, the Panel may issue a Notice of Discipline imposing any level of public discipline authorized by these rules.

(b) Unless the Notice of Discipline is rejected by the respondent as provided in Rule 4–208.3, (1) the respondent shall be in default; (2) the respondent shall have no right to any evidentiary hearing; and (3) the respondent shall be subject to such discipline and further proceedings as may be determined by the Supreme Court.

Adopted effective January 1, 1991; amended effective April 14, 1994.

RULE 4–208.2. NOTICE OF DISCIPLINE; CONTENTS; SERVICE

(a) The Notice of Discipline shall state the following:

(1) The Standards which the Investigative Panel found that the respondent violated,

(2) The facts, which if unrefuted, support the finding that such Standards have been violated,

(3) The level of public discipline recommended to be imposed,

(4) The reasons why such level of discipline is recommended, including matters considered in mitigation and matters considered in aggravation, and such other considerations deemed by the Investigative Panel to be relevant to such recommendation,

(5) The entire provisions of Rule 4–208.3 relating to rejection of Notice of Discipline. This may be satisfied by attaching a copy of the Rule to the Notice of Discipline and referencing same in the Notice.

(6) A copy of the Memorandum of Grievance.

(7) A statement of any prior discipline imposed upon the respondent, including confidential discipline under Rules 4–205 to 4–208.

(b) The original Notice of Discipline shall be filed with the Clerk of the Supreme Court of Georgia, and a copy of the Notice of Discipline shall be served upon the respondent pursuant to Bar Rule 4–203.1.

(c) [Reserved].

(d) [Reserved].

(e) [Reserved].

(f) [Reserved].

(g) The Office of General Counsel shall file the documents by which service was accomplished with the Clerk of the Supreme Court of Georgia.

(h) The level of disciplinary sanction in any Notice of Discipline rejected by the respondent or the Office of General Counsel shall not be binding on the Special Master, the Review Panel or the Supreme Court of Georgia.

Adopted effective January 1, 1991; amended effective April 14, 1994; July 1, 1997.

RULE 4–208.3. REJECTION OF NOTICE OF DISCIPLINE

(a) In order to reject the Notice of Discipline the respondent or the Office of the General Counsel must file a Notice of Rejection of the Notice of Discipline with the Clerk of the Supreme Court of Georgia within thirty (30) days following service of the Notice of Discipline. In the event service was accomplished by certified mail, the respondent shall have thirty-three (33) days from the date the Notice of Discipline was mailed to file the Notice of Rejection.

(b) Any Notice of Rejection by the respondent shall be served upon the Office of the General Counsel of the State Bar of Georgia. Any Notice of Rejection by the Office of the General Counsel of the State Bar of Georgia shall be served upon the respondent. No rejection by the respondent shall be considered valid unless the respondent files a written response to the pending grievance at or before the filing of the rejection. A copy of such written response must also be filed with the Clerk of the Supreme Court at the time of filing the Notice of Rejection.

(c) The timely filing of a Notice of Rejection shall constitute an election for the Supreme Court to appoint a special master and the matter shall thereafter proceed pursuant to Rules 4–209 through 4–225.

Adopted effective January 1, 1991; amended effective April 14, 1994.

RULE 4–208.4. FORMAL COMPLAINT FOLLOWING NOTICE OF REJECTION OF DISCIPLINE

(a) The Office of the General Counsel shall file a formal complaint within thirty days following the filing of a Notice of Rejection. At the same time, a Petition for Appointment of Special Master and proposed order thereon shall be filed. The Notice of Discipline shall operate as the notice of finding of probable cause by the Investigative Panel.

(b) The Office of the General Counsel may obtain extensions of time for the filing of the formal complaint from the Chairperson of the Investigative Panel or his or her designee.

(c) After the rejection of a Notice of Discipline and prior to the time of the filing of the formal complaint, the Investigative Panel may consider any new evidence regarding the grievance and take appropriate action.

Adopted effective January 1, 1991.

RULE 4–209. DOCKETING BY SUPREME COURT; APPOINTMENT OF SPECIAL MASTER; CHALLENGES TO SPECIAL MASTER

(a) Upon receipt of a finding of probable cause, a Petition for Appointment of a Special Master and proposed order thereon and a formal complaint from the Investigative Panel, the Clerk of the Georgia Supreme Court shall file the matter in the records of the Court, give the matter a docket number and notify the Court that appointment of a special master is appropriate. In those proceedings where a Notice of Discipline has been filed, the finding of probable cause need not be filed.

(b) Upon receipt of a petition/motion for appointment of a special master or notification that a special master previously appointed has been disqualified, the Court will nominate a special master to conduct formal disciplinary proceedings in such complaint within fourteen days. The Court shall select as special masters experienced members of the State Bar of Georgia who possess a reputation in the Bar for ethical practice; provided, that a special master may not be appointed to hear a complaint against a respondent who resides in the same circuit as that in which the special master resides.

(c) Upon being advised of appointment of a special master by the Court, the Clerk of the Court shall return the original notice of discipline, rejection of notice of discipline, if applicable, formal complaint, probable cause finding, petition for appointment of special master and the signed order thereon to the Office of General Counsel of the State Bar of Georgia. Upon notification of the appointment of a special master, the State Bar shall immediately serve the respondent with the order of appointment of a special master and with its formal complaint as hereinafter provided.

(d) Within ten days of service of the notice of appointment of a Special Master, the respondent and the State Bar shall lodge any and all objections or challenges they may have to the competency, qualifications or impartiality of the Special Master with the chairperson of the Review Panel. A copy of the objections or challenges shall be served upon the opposing counsel and the Special Master, who may respond to such objections or challenge. The chairperson of the Review Panel shall, within fifteen days, consider the challenges, the responses of counsel and of the Special Master, if any, determine whether the Special Master is disqualified and notify the parties and the Special Master of his decision. Exceptions to the chairperson's denial of disqualification are subject to review by the entire Review Panel and, thereafter, by the Supreme Court when exceptions arising during the evidentiary hearing and exceptions to the report of the Special Master and the Review Panel are properly before the Court. In the event of disqualification of a Special Master by the chairperson of the Review Panel, the Clerk of the Supreme Court, the Special Master and the parties shall be notified of the disqualification and nomination of a successor Special Master shall proceed as provided in this rule.

Amended July 1, 1986; amended effective January 1, 1991; July 1, 1997.

RULE 4–209.1. SPECIAL MASTERS

(a) The Supreme Court shall select and maintain a limited pool of qualified lawyers to serve as Special Masters. The names of those so selected shall be placed on a list maintained by the Supreme Court and shall be published annually in a regular State Bar publication. Although not mandatory, it is preferable that a lawyer so selected shall only remain on such list for five years, so that the term may generally be considered to be five years. Any lawyer whose name is removed from such list shall be eligible to be selected and placed on the list at any subsequent time.

(b) Training for Special Masters is required, subject to the terms of this Rule. Special Masters shall attend one Special Master training session within twelve months after selection by the Supreme Court to serve as Special Master. The Special Master training shall consist of a minimum of a six hour planned session conducted by ICJE or ICLE with input from the Office of General Counsel, the Respondent's Bar and the Supreme Court of Georgia. Special Masters who fail to attend such a minimum training session shall periodically be removed from consideration for appointment in future cases. Failure to attend such a training session shall not be the basis for a disqualification of any Special Master, as such qualifications shall remain in the sole discretion of the Supreme Court. Attorneys who are serving as Special Masters at the time this Rule is amended to require Special Master training shall be exempt from the provisions of this subparagraph; however, they are encouraged to participate in such training sessions.

(c) The Special Masters may be paid by the State Bar of Georgia from the general operating funds on a per case rate to be set by the Supreme Court.

(d) On or before the first day of March of each year, the Supreme Court may set the amount to be paid to the Special Masters during the fiscal year beginning the first day of July of that year, which rate shall continue until the conclusion of the fiscal year of the State Bar.

Former Rule 4-209.1 adopted effective July 1, 1991; stricken effective July 1, 1991; new Rule 4-209.1 adopted effective July 1, 1991; amended effective January 1, 1998.

RULE 4-209.2. SPECIAL MASTERS IN EMERGENCY SUSPENSION PROCEEDINGS; QUALIFICATIONS, TRAINING, TERMS, POWERS AND DUTIES

(a) In addition to the pool of Special Masters described in Rule 4-209.1, the Supreme Court shall appoint six members of the State Bar, and such additional number of members as the Court may feel to be desirable or necessary from time to time, to serve as Special Masters in emergency suspension show cause hearings and in such other matters as may be designated by the Supreme Court. Two (2) bar members shall be selected from each of the three federal judicial districts in Georgia, additional members shall be selected from appropriate federal judicial districts in Georgia as determined by the Court, and all appointees shall serve for five-year terms. A Special Master shall be eligible for reappointment.

(b) Training for Special Masters who serve in emergency suspension proceedings is required as provided in Bar Rule 4-209.1(b).

(c) A Special Master in an emergency suspension proceeding shall have the following powers and duties:

(1) to exercise general supervision over proceedings assigned to him or her and to perform all duties specifically enumerated in these Rules;

(2) to permit negotiations between the State Bar of Georgia and the Respondent;

(3) to receive and evaluate any Petition for Voluntary Discipline filed by a Respondent, to receive and evaluate responses to such petition from the Office of General Counsel and to make recommendations to the Supreme Court on such petition;

(4) to grant continuances and to extend any time limit provided for herein as to any matter pending before him or her;

(5) to apply to the Supreme Court of Georgia for an order naming a successor in the event that the Special Master becomes incapacitated to perform his or her duties;

(6) to sign subpoenas and exercise the powers described in Rule 4-221(b);

(7) to preside over evidential hearings and to decide questions of law and fact raised during such hearings; and

(8) to make a recommendation as to whether the Respondent should be suspended pending further disciplinary proceedings.

Adopted effective January 1, 1998.

RULE 4-210. POWERS AND DUTIES OF SPECIAL MASTERS

In accordance with these rules, a duly appointed special master shall have the following powers and duties:

(a) to exercise general supervision over disciplinary proceedings assigned to him and to perform all duties specifically enumerated in these Rules;

(b) to pass on all questions concerning the sufficiency of the formal complaint;

(c) to conduct the negotiations between the State Bar of Georgia and the respondent, whether at a pretrial meeting set by the special master or at any other time;

(d) To receive and evaluate any Petition for Voluntary Discipline;

(e) to grant continuances and to extend any time limit provided for herein as to any matter pending before him;

(f) to apply to the Supreme Court of Georgia for an order naming his successor in the event that he becomes incapacitated to perform his duties or in the event that he learns that he and the respondent reside in the same circuit;

(g) to defer action on any complaint pending before him when he learns of the docketing of another complaint against the same respondent and believes that the new complaint will be assigned to him by the Supreme Court;

(h) to hear and determine action on the complaints, where there are multiple complaints against a respondent growing out of different transactions, whether they involve one or more complainants, as separate counts, and may proceed to make recommendations on each count as constituting a separate offense;

(i) to sign subpoenas and exercise the powers described in Rule 4–221(b);

(j) to preside over evidentiary hearings and to decide questions of law and fact raised during such hearings;

(k) to make findings of fact and conclusions of law as hereinafter provided and to submit his findings for consideration by the Review Panel;

(*l*) to exercise general supervision over discovery by parties to disciplinary proceedings and to conduct such hearings and sign all appropriate pleadings and orders pertaining to such discovery as are provided for by the law of Georgia applicable to discovery in civil cases.

Amended July 1, 1986; amended effective January 1, 1991; July 1, 1997.

RULE 4–211. FORMAL COMPLAINT; SERVICE

(a) Within thirty days after a finding of probable cause, a formal complaint shall be prepared which shall specify with reasonable particularity the acts complained of and the grounds for disciplinary action. A formal complaint shall include the names and addresses of witnesses so far as then known. A copy of the formal complaint shall be served upon the respondent after nomination of a Special Master by the Supreme Court. In those cases where a Notice of Discipline has been filed and rejected, the filing of the formal complaint shall be governed by the time period set forth in Rule 4–208.4. The formal complaint shall be served pursuant to Bar Rule 4–203.1.

(b) [Reserved].

(c) At all stages of the proceeding both the respondent and the State Bar of Georgia may be represented by counsel. Counsel representing the State Bar of Georgia shall be authorized to prepare and sign notices, pleadings, motions, complaints, and certificates for and in behalf of the State Bar of Georgia and the State Disciplinary Board.

Amended July 1, 1986; amended effective January 1, 1991; July 1, 1997.

RULE 4–211.1. DISMISSAL AFTER FORMAL COMPLAINT

At any time after the Investigative Panel finds probable cause, the Office of General Counsel may dismiss the proceeding with the consent of the Chairperson or Vice Chairperson of the Investigative Panel or with the consent of any three members of the Investigative Panel.

Adopted effective November 9, 1995.

RULE 4–212. ANSWER OF RESPONDENT; DISCOVERY

(a) The respondent shall serve his answer to the formal complaint of the State Bar within thirty days after service of the formal complaint. In the event that respondent fails to answer or to obtain an extension of time for his answer, the facts alleged and violations charged in the formal complaint shall be deemed admitted. In the event the respondent's answer fails to address specifically the issues raised in the formal complaint, the facts alleged and violations charged in the formal complaint and not specifically addressed in the answer shall be deemed admitted. A respondent may obtain an extension of time not to exceed fifteen days to file the answer from the special master, or, when a challenge to the special master is pending, from the chairperson of the Review Panel. Extensions of time for the filing of an answer shall not be routinely granted.

(b) The pendency of objections or challenges to one or more special masters shall provide no justification for a respondent's failure to file his answer or for failure of the State Bar or the respondent to engage in discovery.

(c) Both parties to the disciplinary proceeding may engage in discovery under the rules of practice and procedure then applicable to civil cases in the State of Georgia.

(d) In lieu of filing an answer to the formal complaint of the State Bar, the respondent may submit to the special master a Petition for Voluntary Discipline; provided, however, that each such petition shall contain admissions of fact and admissions of conduct in violation of Part IV, Chapter 1 of these rules sufficient to authorize the imposition of discipline. As provided in Rule 4–210(d), the special master may solicit a response to such petition from Bar counsel.

Amended July 1, 1986; amended effective January 1, 1991.

RULE 4-213. EVIDENTIARY HEARING

(a) Within ninety days after the filing of respondent's answer to the formal complaint or the time for filing of the answer, whichever is later, the special master shall proceed to hear the case. The evidentiary hearing shall be stenographically reported and may be transcribed at the request and expense of the requesting party. When the hearing is complete, the special master shall proceed to make findings of fact and conclusions of law and file a report with the Review Panel as hereinafter provided. Alleged errors in the trial may be reviewed by the Supreme Court when the findings and recommendations of discipline of the Review Panel are filed with the Court. There shall be no direct appeal from such proceedings of the special master.

(b) Upon a showing of necessity and a showing of financial inability by the respondent to pay for the transcription, the special master shall order the State Bar of Georgia to provide the transcript.

Amended July 1, 1986.

RULES 4-214 TO 4-216. [RESERVED]

Deleted and reserved effective July 1, 1997.

RULE 4-217. REPORT OF THE SPECIAL MASTER

(a) Within thirty days from receipt of the transcript of the evidentiary hearing, the Special Master shall prepare a report which shall contain the following:

(1) findings of fact on the issues raised by the formal complaint;

(2) conclusions of law on the issues raised by the pleadings of the parties;

(3) a recommendation of discipline.

(b) The Special Master shall file his or her original report and recommendation with the Clerk of the State Disciplinary Board and shall serve a copy on the respondent and counsel for the State Bar pursuant to Rule 4-203.1.

(c) Thirty days after the Special Master's report and recommendation is filed, the Special Master shall direct the Clerk of the State Disciplinary Board to file the original record in the case directly with the Supreme Court unless either party requests review by the Review Panel as provided in Subsection (d) of this rule. In the event neither party requests review by the Review Panel and the matter goes directly to the Supreme Court, both parties shall be deemed to have waived any right they may have under the rules to file exceptions with or make request for oral argument to the Supreme Court. Any review undertaken by the Supreme Court shall be solely on the original record.

(d) Upon receipt of the Special Master's report, the parties may request review by the Review Panel as provided in Rule 4-218. The request shall be submitted in writing to the Special Master within thirty days after the Special Master's report is filed with the Clerk of the State Disciplinary Board. A copy of the request shall be served on the opposing party. Upon receipt of a timely written request, the Special Master shall direct the Clerk of the State Disciplinary Board to prepare and file the record and report with the Review Panel.

Amended July 1, 1986; amended effective January 1, 1991; July 1, 1997.

RULE 4-218. FINDINGS BY THE REVIEW PANEL

(a) Upon receipt of the report from a Special Master pursuant to Rule 4-217 (d), the Review Panel shall consider the record, make findings of fact and conclusions of law and determine whether a recommendation of disciplinary action will be made to the Supreme Court and the nature of such recommended discipline. The findings of fact and conclusions of law made by a Special Master shall not be binding on the Panel and may be reversed by it on the basis of the record submitted to the Panel by the Special Master.

(b) The respondent shall have the right to challenge the competency, qualifications, or objectivity of any member of the Review Panel considering the case against him under a procedure as provided for in the rules of the Panel.

(c) There shall be no de novo hearing before the Review Panel except by unanimous consent of the Panel.

(d) The Review Panel may grant rehearings, or new trials, for such reasons, in such manner, on such issues and within such times as the ends of justice may require.

(e) The Review Panel may consider exceptions to the report of the special master and may in its discretion grant oral argument. Exceptions and briefs shall be filed with the Review Panel, in accordance with Bar Rule 4-221(f), no later than twenty days prior to the next scheduled meeting. The responding party shall have ten days after service of the exceptions within which to respond.

(f) The Review Panel shall file its report and the complete record in the disciplinary proceeding with the Clerk of the Supreme Court. A copy of the Panel's report shall be served upon the respondent.

Amended July 1, 1986; amended effective January 1, 1991; July 1, 1997.

RULE 4–219. JUDGMENTS AND PROTECTIVE ORDERS

(a) After either the Review Panel's report or the Special Master's report is filed with the Supreme Court, the respondent and the State Bar may file with the Court any written exceptions, supported by written argument, each may have to the report subject to the provisions of Rule 4–217(c). All such exceptions shall be filed with the Court within twenty days of the date that the report is filed with the Court and a copy served upon the opposing party. The responding party shall have an additional twenty days to file its response with the Court. The Court may grant oral argument on any exception filed with it upon application for such argument by a party to the disciplinary proceedings. The Court will promptly consider the report of the Review Panel or the Special Master, any exceptions, and any responses filed by any party to such exceptions, and enter judgment upon the formal complaint. A copy of the Court's judgment shall be transmitted to the State Bar and the respondent by the Court.

(b) In cases in which the Supreme Court orders disbarment, voluntary surrender of license or suspension, or the respondent is disbarred or suspended on a Notice of Discipline, the Review Panel shall publish in a local newspaper or newspapers and on the official State Bar website, notice of the discipline, including the Respondent's full name and business address, the nature of the discipline imposed and the effective dates.

(c)(1) After a final judgment of disbarment or suspension, including a disbarment or suspension on a Notice of Discipline, the respondent shall immediately cease the practice of law in Georgia and shall, within thirty days, notify all clients of his inability to represent them and of the necessity for promptly retaining new counsel, and shall take all actions necessary to protect the interests of his clients. Within forty-five days after a final judgment of disbarment or suspension, the respondent shall certify to the Court that he has satisfied the requirements of this Rule. Should the respondent fail to comply with the requirements of this Rule, the Supreme Court, upon its own motion or upon motion of the Office of the General Counsel, and after ten days notice to the respondent and proof of his failure to notify or protect his clients, may hold the respondent in contempt and order that a member or members of the State Bar of Georgia take charge of the files and records of the respondent and proceed to notify all clients and to take such steps as seem indicated to protect their interests. Motions for reconsideration may be taken from the issuance or denial of such protective order by either the respondent or by the State Bar of Georgia.

(2) After a final judgment of disbarment or suspension under Part IV of these Rules, including a disbarment or suspension on a Notice of Discipline, the respondent shall take such action necessary to cause the removal of any indicia of the respondent as a lawyer, legal assistant, legal clerk or person with similar status. In the event the respondent should maintain a presence in an office where the practice of law is conducted, the respondent shall not:

(i) have any contact with the clients of the office either in person, by telephone, or in writing; or

(ii) have any contact with persons who have legal dealings with the office either in person, by telephone, or in writing.

(d) Upon a final determination by the Court that an attorney has disappeared, died, become physically or mentally incapacitated, or poses a substantial threat of harm to his clients or the public, and that no partner, associate or other appropriate representative is available to notify his clients of this fact, the Supreme Court may order that a member or members of the State Bar of Georgia be appointed as receiver to take charge of the attorney's files and records. Such receiver shall review the files, notify the attorney's clients and take such steps as seem indicated to protect the interests of the clients, the attorney and the public. A motion for reconsideration may be taken from the issuance or denial of such protective order by the respondent, his partners, associates or legal representatives or by the State Bar of Georgia.

(e) Any member of the State Bar of Georgia appointed by the Supreme Court as receiver to take charge of the files and records of a disciplined, deceased, incapacitated, imprisoned or disappearing attorney under these rules shall not be permitted to disclose any information contained in the files and records in his care without the consent of the client to whom such file or record relates, except as clearly necessary to carry out the order of the Court, or upon application by order of the Supreme Court.

(f) Any person serving as a receiver under these rules shall be immune from suit for any conduct in the course of their official duties.

Amended July 1, 1986; October 21, 1987; amended effective January 1, 1991; December 14, 1993; October 15, 1995; July 1, 1997; November 8, 2003.

RULE 4–220. NOTICE OF PUNISHMENT OR ACQUITTAL; ADMINISTRATION OF REPRIMANDS

(a) Upon a final judgment of disbarment or suspension, notice of the action taken shall be given by the Office of the General Counsel of the State Bar of Georgia to the clerks of all courts of record in this State and to the Secretary of the State Bar of Georgia, and the name of the respondent in question shall be stricken from the rolls of said courts and from the rolls of the State Bar of Georgia either permanently, in case of disbarment, or for the prescribed period, in case of suspension.

(b) Review Panel Reprimands shall be administered before the Panel by the chairperson or his or her designee.

(c) Public Reprimands shall be prepared by the Review Panel, the Chairperson of the Review Panel or his or her designee, and shall be read in open court, in the presence of the respondent, by the judge of the superior court in the county in which the respondent resides or in the county in which the disciplinary infraction occurred, with the location to be specified by the Review Panel, subject to the approval of the Supreme Court.

(d) After a Public or Review Panel Reprimand has been administered, a certificate reciting the fact of the administration of the reprimand and the date of its administration shall be filed with the Supreme Court. There shall be attached to such certificate a copy of the reprimand. Both the certificate and the copy of the reprimand shall become a part of the record in the disciplinary proceeding.

(e) In the event of a final judgment of acquittal, the State Bar of Georgia shall, if directed by the respondent, give notice thereof to the clerk of the superior court of the county in which the respondent resides. The respondent may give reasonable public notice of the judgment or acquittal.

Amended October 3, 1985; July 1, 1986; amended effective January 1, 1991.

RULE 4–221. PROCEDURES

(a) Oaths. Before entering upon his duties as herein provided, each member of the State Disciplinary Board and each special master shall subscribe to an oath to be administered by any person authorized to administer oaths under the laws of this State, such oath to be in writing and filed with the Executive Director of the State Bar of Georgia. The form of such oath shall be:

> I do solemnly swear that I will faithfully and impartially discharge and perform all of the duties incumbent upon me as a member of the State Disciplinary Board of the State Bar of Georgia/special master according to the best of my ability and understanding and agreeable to the laws and Constitution of this State and the Constitution of the United States so help me God.

(b) Witnesses and Evidence; Contempt.

(1) The respondent and the State Bar shall have the right to require the issuance of subpoenas for the attendance of witnesses to testify or to produce books and papers. The State Disciplinary Board or a special master shall have power to compel the attendance of witnesses and the production of books, papers, and documents, relevant to the matter under investigation, by subpoena, and as further provided by law in civil cases under the laws of Georgia.

(2) The following shall subject a person to rule for contempt of the special master or Panel:

(i) disregard, in any manner whatever, of a subpoena issued pursuant to Rule 4–221(b)(1),

(ii) refusal to answer any pertinent or proper question of a special master or Board member, or

(iii) willful or flagrant violation of a lawful directive of a special master or Board member.

It shall be the duty of the chairperson of the affected Panel or special master to report the fact to the Chief Judge of the superior court in and for the county in which said investigation, trial or hearing is being held. The superior court shall have jurisdiction of the matter and shall follow the procedures for contempt as are applicable in the case of a witness subpoenaed to appear and give evidence on the trial of a civil case before the superior court under the laws in Georgia.

(3) Any member of the State Disciplinary Board and any special master shall have power to administer oaths and affirmations and to issue any subpoena herein provided for.

(4) Depositions may be taken by the respondent or the State Bar in the same manner and under the same provisions as may be done in civil cases under the laws of Georgia, and such depositions may be used upon the trial or an investigation or hearing in the same manner as such depositions are admissible in evidence in civil cases under the laws of Georgia.

(5) All witnesses attending any hearing provided for under these rules shall be entitled to the same fees as are allowed by law to witnesses attending trials in civil cases in the superior courts of this State under subpoena, and said fees shall be assessed against the parties to the proceedings under the rule of law applicable to civil suits in the superior courts of this State.

(6) Whenever the deposition of any person is to be taken in this State pursuant to the laws of another state, territory, province or commonwealth, or of the United States or of another country, for use in attorney discipline, fitness or disability proceedings there, the chairperson of the Investigative Panel, or his or her designee upon petition, may issue a summons or subpoena as provided in this section to compel the attendance of witnesses and production of documents at such deposition.

(c) Venue of Hearings.

(1) The hearings on all complaints and charges against resident respondents shall be held in the county of residence of the respondent unless he otherwise agrees.

(2) Where the respondent is a nonresident of the State of Georgia and the complaint arose in the State of Georgia, the hearing shall be held in the county where the complaint arose.

(3) When the respondent is a nonresident of the State of Georgia and the offense occurs outside the State, the hearing may be held in the county of the State Bar of Georgia headquarters.

(d) Confidentiality of Investigations and Proceedings.

(1) The State Bar shall maintain as confidential all disciplinary investigations and proceedings pending at the screening or investigative stage, unless otherwise provided by these rules.

(2) After a proceeding under these rules is filed with the Supreme Court, all evidentiary and motions hearings shall be open to the public and all reports rendered shall be public documents.

(3) Nothing in these rules shall prohibit the complainant, respondent or third party from disclosing information regarding a disciplinary proceedings, unless otherwise ordered by the Supreme Court or a Special Master in proceedings under these rules.

(4) The Office of the General Counsel of the State Bar or the Investigative Panel of the State Disciplinary Board may reveal or authorize disclosure of information which would otherwise be confidential under this rule under the following circumstances:

(i) In the event of a charge of wrongful conduct against any member of the State Disciplinary Board or any person who is otherwise connected with the disciplinary proceeding in any way, either Panel of the Board or its Chairperson or his or her designee, may authorize the use of information concerning disciplinary investigations or proceedings to aid in the defense against such charge.

(ii) In the event the Office of the General Counsel receives information that suggests criminal activity, such information may be revealed to the appropriate criminal prosecutor.

(iii) In the event of subsequent disciplinary proceedings against a lawyer, the Office of the General Counsel may, in aggravation of discipline in the pending disciplinary case, reveal the imposition of confidential discipline under Rule 4-205 to 4-208 and facts underlying the imposition of discipline.

(iv) A complainant or lawyer representing the complainant may be notified of the status or disposition of the complaint.

(v) When public statements that are false or misleading are made about any otherwise confidential disciplinary case, the Office of the General Counsel may disclose all information necessary to correct such false or misleading statements.

(5) The Office of General Counsel may reveal confidential information to the following persona if it appears that the information may assist them in the discharge of their duties:

(i) The Committee on the Arbitration of Attorney Fee Disputes or the comparable body in other jurisdictions;

(ii) The Trustees of the Clients' Security Fund or the comparable body in other jurisdictions;

(iii) The Judicial Nominating Commission or the comparable body in other jurisdictions;

(iv) The Lawyer Assistance Program or the comparable body in other jurisdictions;

(v) The Board to Determine Fitness of Bar Applicants or the comparable body in other jurisdictions;

(vi) The Judicial Qualifications Commission or the comparable body in other jurisdictions;

(vii) The Executive Committee with the specific approval of the following representatives of the Investigative Panel of the State Disciplinary Board: the chairperson, the vice-chairperson and a third representative designated by chairperson;

(viii) The Formal Advisory Opinion Board;

(ix) The Consumer Assistance Program

(x) The General Counsel Overview Committee; and

(xi) An office or committee charged with discipline appointed by the United States Circuit or District Court or the highest court of any state, District of Columbia, commonwealth or possession of the United States.

(6) Any information used by the Office of the General Counsel in a proceeding under Rule 4-108 or in a proceeding to obtain a Receiver to administer the files of a member of the State Bar, shall not be confidential under this rule.

(7) The Office of General Counsel may reveal confidential information when required by law or court order.

(8) The authority or discretion to reveal confidential information under this rule shall not constitute a waiver of any evidentiary, statutory or other privilege which may be asserted by the State Bar or the State Disciplinary Board under Bar Rules or applicable law.

(9) Nothing in this rule shall prohibit the Office of the General Counsel or the Investigative Panel from interviewing potential witnesses or placing the Notice of Investigation out for service by sheriff or other authorized person.

(10) Members of the Office of General Counsel and State Disciplinary Board may respond to specific inquiries concerning matters that have been made public by the complainant, respondent or third parties but are otherwise confidential under these rules by acknowledging the existence and status of the proceeding.

(11) The State Bar shall not disclose information concerning discipline imposed on a lawyer under prior

Supreme Court Rules that was confidential when imposed, unless authorized to do so by said prior rules.

(e) Burden of Proof; Evidence.

(1) In all proceedings under this chapter, the burden of proof shall be on the State Bar of Georgia, except for proceedings under Rule 4–106.

(2) In all proceedings under this chapter occurring after a finding of probable cause as described in Rule 4–204.4, the procedures and rules of evidence applicable in civil cases under the laws of Georgia shall apply, except that the quantum of proof required of the State Bar shall be clear and convincing evidence.

(f) Pleadings and Copies. Original pleadings shall be filed with the appropriate Panel of the State Disciplinary Board at the headquarters of the State Bar of Georgia and copies served upon the special master and all parties to the disciplinary proceeding. Depositions and other original discovery shall be retained by counsel and shall not be filed except as permitted under the Uniform Rules of the Superior Court.

(g) Pleadings and Communications Privileged. Pleadings and oral and written statements of members of the State Disciplinary Board, members and designees of the Committee on Lawyer Impairment, special masters, Bar counsel and investigators, complainants, witnesses, and respondents and their counsel, made to one another or filed in the record during any investigation, intervention, hearing or other disciplinary proceeding under this Part IV, and pertinent to the disciplinary proceeding, are made in performance of legal and public duty, are absolutely privileged, and under no circumstances form the basis for a right of action.

Amended effective February 26, 1986; amended July 1, 1986; February 5, 1988; March 15, 1989; amended effective January 1, 1991; December 14, 1993; December 8, 1994; July 1, 1997; May 28, 1998; February 1, 2000; August 22, 2001.

RULE 4–222. LIMITATION

(a) No proceeding under Part IV, Chapter 2, shall be brought unless a Memorandum of Grievance has been received at State Bar of Georgia headquarters or instituted by the Investigative Panel within four years after the commission of the act. Provided, however, this limitation shall be tolled during any period of time, not to exceed two years, that the offender or the offense is unknown, the offender's whereabouts are unknown, or the offender's name is removed from the roll of those authorized to practice law in this State.

(b) Referral of a matter to the Investigative Panel by the Office of the General Counsel shall occur within twelve months of the receipt of the Memorandum of Grievance at State Bar of Georgia headquarters or institution of a Memorandum of Grievance by the Investigative Panel.

Amended July 1, 1986; amended effective January 1, 1991.

RULE 4–223. ADVISORY OPINIONS

(a) Any Formal Advisory Opinion issued pursuant to Rule 4–403 which is not thereafter disapproved by the Supreme Court of Georgia shall be binding on the State Bar of Georgia, the State Disciplinary Board, and the person who requested the opinion, in any subsequent disciplinary proceeding involving that person. Formal Advisory Opinions which have been approved or modified by the Supreme Court pursuant to Rule 4–403 shall also be binding in subsequent disciplinary proceedings which do not involve the person who requested the opinion.

(b) It shall be considered as mitigation to any grievance under these rules that the respondent has acted in accordance with and in reasonable reliance upon a written Informal Advisory Opinion requested by the respondent pursuant to Rule 4–401 or a Formal Advisory Opinion issued pursuant to Rule 4–403, but not reviewed by the Supreme Court of Georgia.

Amended July 1, 1986; amended effective January 1, 1991; July 1, 2002.

RULE 4–224. EXPUNGEMENT OF RECORDS

(a) The record of any grievance against a respondent under these rules which does not result in discipline against the respondent shall be expunged by the State Disciplinary Board in accordance with the following:

(1) those grievances closed by the Office of the General Counsel after screening pursuant to Rule 4–202(c) shall be expunged after one year;

(2) those grievances dismissed by the Investigative Panel of the State Disciplinary Board after a probable cause investigation pursuant to Rule 4–204(a) shall be expunged after two years; and

(3) those formal complaints dismissed by the Supreme Court after formal proceedings shall be expunged after two years.

(b) Definition. The terms "expunge" and "expunction" shall mean that all records or other evidence of the existence of the complaint shall be destroyed.

(c) Effect of Expungement. After a file has been expunged, any agency response to an inquiry requiring a reference to the matter shall state that any record the agency may have had of such matter has been expunged pursuant to court rule and, in addition, shall state that no inference adverse to the respondent is to be drawn on the basis of the incident in question. The respondent may answer any inquiry requiring a reference to an expunged matter by stating that the grievance or formal complaint was dismissed and thereafter expunged pursuant to court rule.

(d) Retention of Records. Upon application to the State Disciplinary Board by Bar counsel, for good cause shown and with notice to the respondent and opportunity to be heard, records which should otherwise be expunged under this Rule may be retained for such additional period of time, not exceeding three (3) years, as the State Disciplinary Board deems appropriate. Counsel may seek a further extension of the period for which retention of the records is authorized whenever a previous application has been granted for the maximum period permitted hereunder.

(e) A lawyer may respond in the negative when asked if there are any complaints against the lawyer if the matter has been expunged pursuant to this rule. Before making a negative response to any such inquiry, the lawyer shall confirm the expunction of the record and shall not presume that any matter has been expunged.

(f) A lawyer may respond in the negative when asked if he has ever been professionally disciplined or determined to have violated any professional disciplinary rules if all grievances filed against the lawyer have either been dismissed or dismissed with a letter of instruction.

Adopted November 1, 1988; amended March 1, 1989; amended effective January 1, 1991.

RULE 4-225. JURISDICTION

The State Disciplinary Board and any person who is connected with disciplinary proceedings in any way shall not be subject to the jurisdiction of any court other than the Supreme Court with respect thereto, except as provided in Rules 4-214, 4-215 and 4-216.

Adopted November 1, 1988; amended effective January 1, 1991.

RULE 4-226. IMMUNITY

The regulatory proceedings of the State Bar are judicial in nature. Therefore, members of the State Disciplinary Board, members and designees of the Committee on Lawyer Impairment, special masters, Bar counsel, special prosecutors, investigators and staff are entitled to judicial immunity when engaged in regulatory activities.

Adopted effective December 14, 1993.

RULE 4-227. PETITIONS FOR VOLUNTARY DISCIPLINE

(a) A petition for voluntary discipline shall contain admissions of fact and admissions of conduct in violation of Part IV, Chapter 1 of these rules sufficient to authorize the imposition of discipline.

(b) Prior to the issuance of a formal complaint, a respondent may submit a petition for voluntary discipline seeking any level of discipline authorized under these rules.

(1) Those petitions seeking private discipline shall be filed with the Office of General Counsel and assigned to a member of the Investigative Panel. The Investigative Panel of the State Disciplinary Board shall conduct an investigation and determine whether to accept or reject the petition as outlined at Bar Rule 4-203(a)(9).

(2) Those petitions seeking public discipline shall be filed directly with the Clerk of the Supreme Court. The Office of General Counsel shall have 30 days within which to file a response. The Court shall issue an appropriate order.

(c) After the issuance of a formal complaint a Respondent may submit a petition for voluntary discipline seeking any level of discipline authorized under these rules.

(1) The petition shall be filed with the Special Master who shall allow bar counsel 30 days within which to respond. The Office of General Counsel may assent to the petition or may file a response, stating objections and giving the reasons therefore. The Office of General Counsel shall serve a copy of its response upon the respondent.

(2) The Special Master shall consider the petition, the Bar's response and, the record as it then exists and may accept or reject the petition for voluntary discipline.

(3) The Special Master may reject a petition for such cause or causes as seem appropriate to the Special Master. Such causes may include but are not limited to a finding that:

(i) the petition fails to contain admissions of fact and admissions of conduct in violation of Part IV, Chapter 1 of these rules sufficient to authorize the imposition of discipline;

(ii) the petition fails to request appropriate discipline;

(iii) the petition fails to contain sufficient information concerning the admissions of fact and the admissions of conduct;

(iv) the record in the proceeding does not contain sufficient information upon which to base a decision to accept or reject.

(4) The Special Master's decision to reject a petition for voluntary discipline does not preclude the filing of a subsequent petition and is not subject to review by either the Review Panel or the Supreme Court. If the Special Master rejects a petition for voluntary discipline, the disciplinary case shall proceed as provided by these rules.

(5) If the Special Master accepts the petition for voluntary discipline, s/he shall enter a report making findings of fact and conclusions of law and deliver same to the Clerk of the State Disciplinary Board.

The Clerk of the State Disciplinary Board shall file the report and the complete record in the disciplinary proceeding with the Clerk of the Supreme Court. A copy of the Special Master's report shall be served upon the respondent. The Court shall issue an appropriate order.

(6) Pursuant to Bar Rule 4-210(e), the Special Master may in his or her discretion extend any of the time limits in these rules in order to adequately consider a petition for voluntary discipline.

Adopted effective July 1, 1997.

CHAPTER 3. RESERVED

RULE 4-301. [RESERVED]

Amended October 2, 1984; October 3, 1985; July 1, 1986; repealed and reinstated as reserved chapter effective March 1, 2000.

RULE 4-302. [RESERVED]

Amended October 3, 1985; October 8, 1985; July 1, 1986; repealed and reinstated as reserved chapter effective March 1, 2000.

RULE 4-303. [RESERVED]

Amended July 1, 1986; repealed and reinstated as reserved chapter effective March 1, 2000.

RULE 4-304. [RESERVED]

Amended July 1, 1986; repealed and reinstated as reserved chapter effective March 1, 2000.

RULE 4-305. [RESERVED]

Amended October 3, 1985; October 8, 1985; repealed and reinstated as reserved chapter effective March 1, 2000.

RULE 4-306. [RESERVED]

Adopted effective January 1, 1991; repealed and reinstated as reserved chapter effective March 1, 2000.

CHAPTER 4. ADVISORY OPINIONS

RULE 4-401. INFORMAL ADVISORY OPINIONS

The Office of the General Counsel of the State Bar of Georgia shall be authorized to render Informal Advisory Opinions concerning the Office of the General Counsel's interpretation of the Rules of Professional Conduct or any of the grounds for disciplinary action as applied to a given state of facts. The Informal Advisory Opinion should address prospective conduct and may be issued in oral or written form. An Informal Advisory Opinion is the personal opinion of the issuing attorney of the Office of the General Counsel and is neither a defense to any complaint nor binding on the State Disciplinary Board, the Supreme Court of Georgia, or the State Bar of Georgia. If the person requesting an Informal Advisory Opinion desires, the Office of the General Counsel will transmit the Informal Advisory Opinion to the Formal Advisory Opinion Board for discretionary consideration of the drafting of a Proposed Formal Advisory Opinion.

Adopted July 1, 1986; amended effective July 1, 2002.

RULE 4-402. THE FORMAL ADVISORY OPINION BOARD

(a) The Formal Advisory Opinion Board shall consist only of active members of the State Bar of Georgia who shall be appointed by the President of the State Bar of Georgia, with the approval of the Board of Governors of the State Bar of Georgia.

(b) The members of the Formal Advisory Opinion Board shall be selected as follows:

(1) Five members of the State Bar of Georgia At-Large;

(2) One member of the Georgia Trial Lawyers Association;

(3) One member of the Georgia Defense Lawyers Association;

(4) One member of the Georgia Association of Criminal Defense Lawyers;

(5) One member of the Young Lawyers Division of the State Bar of Georgia;

(6) One member of the Georgia District Attorneys Association;

(7) One member of the faculty of each American Bar Association Accredited Law School operating within the State of Georgia;

(8) One member of the Investigative Panel of the State Disciplinary Board; and

(9) One member of the Review Panel of the State Disciplinary Board.

(c) All members shall be appointed for terms of two years subject to the following exceptions:

(1) Any person appointed to fill a vacancy occasioned by resignation, death, disqualification, or disability shall serve only for the unexpired term of the member replaced unless reappointed;

(2) The members appointed from the Investigative Panel and Review Panel of the State Disciplinary Board shall serve for a term of one year;

(3) The terms of the current members of the Formal Advisory Opinion Board will terminate at the Annual Meeting of the State Bar following the amendment of this Rule regardless of the length of each member's current term; thereafter all appointments will be as follows to achieve staggered, two-year terms:

(i) Three of the initial Association members (including the Georgia Trial Lawyers Association, the Georgia Association of Defense Lawyers, the Georgia Association of Criminal Defense Lawyers, the Georgia District Attorneys Association and the Young Lawyers Division of the State Bar) shall be appointed to one-year terms; two of the initial Association members shall be appointed to two-year terms. As each initial term expires, the successor appointee shall be appointed for a term of two years;

(ii) Two of the initial members appointed from the State Bar of Georgia at-large (the "At-Large Members") shall be appointed to one-year terms; three of the initial At-Large members shall be appointed to two-year terms. As each initial term expires, the successor appointee shall be appointed for a term of two years;

(iii) Two of the initial Representatives from the American Bar Association Accredited Law Schools shall be appointed to one year terms; two of the initial law school representatives shall be appointed to two-year terms. As each initial term expires, the successor appointee shall be appointed for a term of two years;

(4) All members shall be eligible for immediate reappointment to one additional two-year term, unless the President of the State Bar of Georgia, with approval of the Board of Governors of the State Bar of Georgia, deems it appropriate to reappoint a member for one or more additional terms.

(d) The Formal Advisory Opinion Board shall have the authority to prescribe its own rules of conduct and procedure.

Adopted July 1, 1986; amended effective February 1, 2000.

RULE 4-403. FORMAL ADVISORY OPINIONS

(a) The Formal Advisory Opinion Board shall be authorized to draft Proposed Formal Advisory Opinions concerning a proper interpretation of the Rules of Professional Conduct or any of the grounds for disciplinary action as applied to a given state of facts. The Proposed Formal Advisory Opinion should address prospective conduct and may respond to a request for a review of an Informal Advisory Opinion or respond to a direct request for a Formal Advisory Opinion.

(b) When a Formal Advisory Opinion is requested, the Formal Advisory Opinion Board should review the request and make a preliminary determination whether a Proposed Formal Advisory Opinion should be drafted. Factors to be considered by the Formal Advisory Opinion Board include whether the issue is of general interest to the members of the Bar, whether a genuine ethical issue is presented, the existence of opinions on the subject from other jurisdictions, and the nature of the prospective conduct.

(c) When the Formal Advisory Opinion Board makes a preliminary determination that a Proposed Formal Advisory Opinion should be drafted, it shall publish the Proposed Formal Advisory Opinion in an official publication of the State Bar of Georgia and solicit comments from the members of the Bar. Following a reasonable period of time for receipt of comments from the members of the Bar, the Formal Advisory Opinion Board shall then make a final determination to either file the Proposed Formal Advisory Opinion as drafted or modified, or reconsider its decision and decline to draft and file the Proposed Formal Advisory Opinion.

(d) After the Formal Advisory Opinion Board makes a final determination that the Proposed Formal Advisory Opinion should be drafted and filed, the Formal Advisory Opinion shall then be filed with the Supreme Court of Georgia and republished in an official publication of the State Bar of Georgia. Unless the Supreme Court grants review as provided hereinafter, the opinion shall be binding only on the State Bar of Georgia and the person who requested the opinion, and not on the Supreme Court, which shall treat the opinion as persuasive authority only. Within 20 days of the filing of the Formal Advisory Opinion or the date the publication is mailed to the members of the Bar, whichever is later, the State Bar of Georgia or the person who requested the opinion may file a petition for discretionary review thereof with the Supreme Court of Georgia. The petition shall designate the Formal Advisory Opinion sought to be reviewed and shall concisely state the manner in which the petitioner is aggrieved. If the Supreme Court grants the petition for discretionary review or decides to review the opinion on its own motion, the record shall consist of the comments received by the Formal Advisory Opinion Board from members of the Bar. The State Bar of Georgia and the person requesting the opinion shall follow the briefing schedule set forth in Supreme Court Rule 10, counting from the date of the order granting review. The final determination may be either by written opinion or by order of the Supreme Court and shall state whether the Formal Advisory Opinion is approved, modified, or disapproved, or shall provide for such other final disposition as is appropriate.

(e) If the Supreme Court of Georgia declines to review the Formal Advisory Opinion, it shall be binding only on the State Bar of Georgia and the person who requested the opinion, and not on the Supreme Court, which shall treat the opinion as persuasive authority only. If the Supreme Court grants review and disapproves the opinion, it shall have absolutely no effect and shall not constitute either persuasive or binding authority. If the Supreme Court approves or modifies the opinion, it shall be binding on all members of the State Bar and shall be published in the official Georgia Court and Bar Rules manual. The Supreme Court shall accord such approved or modified opinion the same precedential authority given to the regularly published judicial opinions of the Court.

(f) The Formal Advisory Opinion Board may call upon the Office of the General Counsel for staff support in researching and drafting Proposed Formal Advisory Opinions.

(g) The name of a lawyer requesting an Informal Advisory Opinion or Formal Advisory Opinion will be held confidential unless the lawyer otherwise elects.

Adopted July 1, 1986; amended effective January 1, 1991; July 1, 2002.

RULE 4–404. IMMUNITY

The members of the Formal Advisory Opinion Board, as well as staff persons and counsel assisting the Board and its members, including, but not limited to staff counsel, advisors and the State Bar of Georgia, its officers and employees, members of the Executive Committee, and members of the Board of Governors, shall have absolute immunity from civil liability for all acts performed in the course of their official duties.

Adopted effective June 8, 2004.

PART V. AMENDMENT AND EFFECTIVE DATE

CHAPTER 1. AMENDMENT

RULE 5–101. AMENDMENT; FILING; NOTICE

The Supreme Court of Georgia may, on motion of the State Bar of Georgia, amend the rules of the State Bar of Georgia at any time; provided, however, that no motion to amend these rules may be filed until thirty (30) days after a notice setting forth the proposed amendment has been published in the *Georgia State Bar Journal*, the *Georgia State Bar News* or any other document of the State Bar of Georgia and the said publication or document mailed to the entire membership of the State Bar of Georgia. The said notice shall contain the following:

(a) the date upon which the motion to amend these rules shall be filed in the Supreme Court of Georgia;

(b) the verbatim text of the said motion as certified by the Executive Director of the State Bar of Georgia;

(c) a statement that the publication of the said motion to amend these rules is intended to comply with the notice requirement of this rule;

(d) a statement that any objection to the proposed amendment shall be made only in accordance with Rule 5–102.

At the same time that notice is sent to its membership, the State Bar of Georgia shall file a copy of such notice with the Clerk of the Supreme Court of Georgia.

RULE 5–102. OBJECTION TO AMENDMENT

Each member of the State Bar of Georgia shall be entitled to file a written objection to any motion to amend these rules by the State Bar of Georgia. Each objection shall contain the following:

(a) the grounds on which the objection is based;

(b) a request for oral argument on the proposed amendment if such argument is desired by the objecting member.

All written objections shall be filed with the Clerk of the Supreme Court of the State of Georgia before the date which the State Bar of Georgia has designated for filing its said motion to amend these rules under Rule 5–101. Any member filing a written objection shall serve the State Bar of Georgia with a copy thereof by mailing the same to the General Counsel of the State Bar of Georgia at the address of its headquarters.

RULE 5–103. ORAL ARGUMENT

The Supreme Court of Georgia may grant or refuse the objecting member's request for oral argument on the State Bar of Georgia's proposed amendment to these rules at its sole discretion. The Clerk of the Supreme Court of Georgia shall notify the General Counsel of the State Bar of Georgia and the objecting member of the date of any oral argument granted by the Supreme Court of Georgia under the provisions of Rule 23(b) of the Rules of the Supreme Court of the State of Georgia.

RULE 5–104. DUES INCREASE OR DECREASE; SPECIAL PROCEDURE

In addition to the procedures described in Rules 5–101 through 5–103, at least thirty (30) days notice shall be given to the membership of the State Bar of Georgia in the *Georgia State Bar Journal*, the *Georgia State Bar News* or any other document of the State Bar of Georgia of any meeting of the Board of Governors of the State Bar of Georgia at which amendment of Rule 1–502 (Amount of License Fees) will be considered and acted upon. The notice to the general membership of the State Bar of Georgia shall contain:

(a) a statement that the amendment of Rule 1–502 (Amount of License Fees) shall be considered by the Board of Governors of the State Bar of Georgia;

(b) a verbatim copy of the proposed amendment as certified by the Executive Director of the State Bar of Georgia;

(c) the date, time and location of the meeting of the Board of Governors of the State Bar of Georgia at which such amendment will be considered;

(d) a statement that each member of the State Bar of Georgia has a right to present his views concerning the proposed amendment either through his circuit representative to the Board of Governors or in person before such Board; and

(e) the address to which all written objections to the proposed amendment may be sent.

CHAPTER 2. EFFECTIVE DATE

RULE 5–201. EFFECTIVE DATE

These rules, as recodified, shall be effective January 1, 1977 except that Part IV, Chapter 2, Disciplinary Proceedings, shall be effective April 1, 1977; provided, however, any complaints pending before grievance tribunals on such date shall be handled to conclusion under the disciplinary proceedings now in effect.

PART VI. ARBITRATION OF FEE DISPUTES

PREAMBLE

The purpose of this program is to provide a convenient mechanism for (1) the resolution of disputes between lawyers and clients over fees, (2) the resolution of disputes between lawyers in connection with the withdrawal of a lawyer from a partnership or the dissolution and separation of a partnership, or (3) the resolution of disputes between lawyers concerning the entitlement to portions of fees earned from joint services. It is a process which may be invoked by either side after the parties have been unable to reach an agreement between themselves. Regardless of whether it is the lawyer or the client who takes the initiative of filing a petition requesting arbitration of the disputes, the petitioner must agree to be bound by the result of the arbitration. This is intended to discourage the filing of complaints which are frivolous or which seek to invoke the process simply to obtain an "advisory opinion." If the respondent also agrees to be bound, the resulting arbitration award will be enforceable under the general arbitration laws of the State.

A unique feature of this program provides that where the petitioner is a client whose claim after investigation appears to warrant a hearing, and the respondent lawyer refuses to be bound by any resulting award, the matter will not be dismissed, but an ex parte arbitration hearing may be held. If the outcome of this hearing is in the client's favor, the State Bar will provide a lawyer at no cost, other than actual litigation expenses, to the client to represent the client in subsequent litigation to adjust the fee in accordance with the arbitration award.

Amended October 21, 1987; amended effective January 5, 2005.

CHAPTER 1. COMMITTEE ON RESOLUTION OF FEE DISPUTES

RULE 6–101. COMMITTEE

The program will be administered by the State Bar Committee on the Arbitration of Attorney Fee Disputes ("Committee").

RULE 6–102. MEMBERSHIP

The Committee shall consist of six lawyer members and three public members who are not lawyers. The six lawyer members shall be appointed by the President of the State Bar, and the three public members shall be appointed by the Supreme Court of Georgia.

Amended effective January 5, 2005.

RULE 6–103. TERMS

Initially, two members of the Committee, including one of the public members, shall be appointed for a period of three years; two members, including the remaining public member, for a period of two years;

and one member for a period of one year. As each member's term of office on the Committee expires, his or her successor shall be appointed for a period of three years. The President of the State Bar shall appoint the Chairperson of the Committee each year from among the members. Vacancies in unexpired terms shall be filled by their respective appointing authorities.

RULE 6-104. RESPONSIBILITY

The Committee shall be responsible for determining jurisdiction to handle complaints which it receives, administering the selection of arbitrators, the conduct of the arbitration process, and the development and implementation of fee arbitration procedures.

RULE 6-105. STAFF

State Bar staff shall be assigned to assist the Committee. The staff so assigned will have the administrative responsibilities delegated by the Committee, which may include the following:

(a) receive and review complaints and discuss them with the parties if necessary;

(b) conduct inquiries to obtain any additional information required;

(c) make recommendations to the Committee to dismiss complaints or to accept jurisdiction;

(d) mail notices of arbitration hearings, arbitration awards and Committee correspondence.

The Committee shall review all of the available evidence, including the recommendations of the staff, and make a determination by majority vote whether to dismiss a complaint or to accept jurisdiction. All decisions of the Committee shall be final subject only to review by the Executive Committee of the State Bar of Georgia pursuant to its powers, functions and duties under the Rules governing the State Bar (241 Ga. 643).

Amended October 21, 1987.

RULE 6-106. WAITING PERIOD

If, following a preliminary investigation by the staff and review by the Committee, the Committee concludes that it has jurisdiction and that the petitioner's claim appears to have merit, the Committee shall notify the parties that it has assumed jurisdiction. The Committee will then delay any further steps until the expiration of thirty calendar days following such notice during which time the parties will be urged to exert their best efforts to resolve the dispute.

CHAPTER 2. JURISDICTIONAL GUIDELINES

RULE 6-201. JURISDICTION

The Committee may accept jurisdiction over a fee dispute only if all of the following requirements are satisfied:

(a) The fee in question, whether paid or unpaid, has been charged for legal services rendered by a lawyer who is or who at the time of rendition of the service had been licensed to practice law in the State of Georgia or who has been duly licensed as a foreign legal consultant in the State of Georgia.

(b) The services in question were performed either in the State of Georgia, or from an office located in the State of Georgia.

(c) At the time the legal services in question were performed there existed between the lawyer and the client an express or implied contract establishing between them a lawyer/client relationship. A relative or other person paying the legal fees of the client may request arbitration of disputes over those fees provided both the client and the payor join as co-petitioners or co-respondents and both agree to be bound by the result of the arbitration.

(d) The disputed fee:

(1) exceeds ($750) seven hundred and fifty dollars.

(2) is not one the amount of which is governed by statute or other law, nor one the full amount or all terms of which have already been fixed or approved by order of a court.

(e) A petition seeking arbitration of the dispute is filed with the Committee by the lawyer or the client no more than two years following the date on which the controversy arose. If this date is disputed, it shall be determined in the same manner as the commencement of a cause of action on the underlying contract.

(f) The client, whether petitioner or respondent, agrees to be bound by the result of the arbitration.

(g) The fee dispute is not the subject of litigation in court at the time the Petition for arbitration is filed.

(h) The petition contains the following elements:

(1) A statement of the nature of the dispute and the particulars of the petitioner's position, including relevant dates.

(2) The identities of both the client and the lawyer and the addresses of both.

(3) A statement that the petitioner has made a good faith effort to resolve the dispute and the details of that effort.

(4) The agreement of the petitioner to be bound by the result of the arbitration.

(5) The signature of the petitioner and date of the petition.

(6) The petition shall be filed on a form which will be supplied by the Committee. Such petition shall be served upon the opposite party at such party's last known address by certified mail, return receipt requested.

(i) In case of disputes between lawyers, the lawyers who are parties to the dispute are all members of the State Bar of Georgia, and all the lawyers involved agree to the arbitration.

Amended October 21, 1987; amended effective April 16, 1992; January 5, 2005.

RULE 6–202. TERMINATION OR SUSPENSION OF PROCEEDINGS

The Committee may decline, suspend, or terminate jurisdiction if the client, in addition to disputing the fee, claims any other form of relief against the lawyer arising out of the same set of circumstances, including any claim of malpractice or professional misconduct. Any claim or evidence of professional misconduct within the meaning of the Code of Professional Responsibility may be referred in a separate report by the arbitrators or the Committee to the General Counsel's Office for consideration under its normal procedures.

Amended October 21, 1987.

RULE 6–203. REVOCATION

After a petition has been filed, jurisdiction has been accepted by the Committee and the other party has agreed in writing to be bound by the award, the submission to arbitration shall be irrevocable except by consent of all parties to the dispute.

CHAPTER 3. SELECTION OF ARBITRATORS

RULE 6–301. ROSTER OF ARBITRATORS

(a) The Committee shall maintain a roster of lawyers available to serve as arbitrators on an "as needed" basis in appropriate geographical areas throughout the state. To the extent possible the arbitration should take place in the same geographical area where the services in question were performed; however, the final decision as to the location of the arbitration remains with the Committee.

(b) The Committee shall likewise maintain a roster of nonlawyer public members selected by the Supreme Court of Georgia.

RULE 6–302. NEUTRALITY OF ARBITRATORS

No person shall serve as an arbitrator in any matter in which that person has any financial or personal interest. Each arbitrator shall disclose to the Committee any bias that he or she may have in regard to the dispute in question, or any circumstances likely to create an appearance of bias which might disqualify that person as an impartial arbitrator. Either party may state any reason why he or she feels that an arbitrator should withdraw or be disqualified.

RULE 6–303. SELECTION OF ARBITRATORS

Except under special procedures outlined in Chapter 6, arbitrators shall be selected as follows:

(a) The lawyer arbitrators shall be selected by the following process: the Committee shall furnish the petitioner a list of the names of four possible lawyer arbitrators from which the petitioner shall strike one name; the Committee shall then supply the respondent with a list of the three remaining names from which the respondent shall strike one; the two persons whose names remain will be the lawyer members of the arbitration panel.

(b) The non-lawyer public members shall be selected by the following process: the Committee shall furnish a list of the names of three possible nonlawyer public arbitrators from which the petitioner shall strike one name; the Committee shall then supply the respondent with a list of the two remaining names from which the respondent shall strike one; the person whose name remains will be the nonlawyer member of the arbitration panel.

(c) If either party fails to exercise the foregoing strikes, the Committee is authorized to establish procedures to strike for that party.

(d) Petitioner and respondent by mutual agreement shall have the right to select the three arbitrators; and also mutually may agree to have the dispute determined by a sole arbitrator jointly selected by them, provided any such sole arbitrator shall be one of the persons on the roster of arbitrators or shall have been approved in advance by the Committee upon the joint request of petitioner and respondent.

Amended October 21, 1987.

RULE 6–304. QUALIFICATIONS

The lawyer arbitrators shall, in addition to being impartial, have the following qualifications:

(a) Have some experience in, or knowledge of, the field of law involved in the dispute.

(b) Have practiced law actively for at least five years.

(c) Be an active member of the State Bar of Georgia.

Amended October 21, 1987.

RULE 6-305. COMPENSATION

All arbitrators shall serve voluntarily and without fee or expense reimbursement. Provided, however, that arbitrators selected to serve in disputes in which all the parties are lawyers may at the discretion of the committee be compensated with such compensation to be paid by the lawyer parties as directed by the committee.

Amended October 21, 1987.

CHAPTER 4. RULES OF PROCEDURE

RULE 6-401. TIME AND PLACE OF HEARING

The arbitrators shall elect a chairperson and then shall fix a time [which shall be no more than sixty (60) days after the appointment of the last arbitrator] and place for each arbitration hearing. At least ten (10) calendar days prior thereto, the Committee shall mail notices, certified mail return receipt, of the time and place of the hearing to each party.

RULE 6-402. ATTENDANCE AT HEARING

If a lawyer will not agree to be bound by the arbitrators' decision, the lawyer waives the right to participate in the hearing. The lawyer shall have the right to attend the hearing. However, he or she may not participate in it without the express consent of the arbitrators.

It is the individual responsibility of each party to arrange for, at their own expense, the attendance of themselves, their witnesses, and, if desired, their counsel.

Amended October 21, 1987.

RULE 6-403. COUNSEL

Parties may be represented at the hearing by counsel at their own expense, or they may represent themselves.

RULE 6-404. STENOGRAPHIC RECORD

Any party may request the Committee to arrange for the taking of a stenographic record of the proceeding. If such a record is stipulated to be the official record of the proceedings by the parties, or in appropriate cases determined to be such by the arbitrators, it must be made available to the arbitrators and to the other party for inspection at a time and place determined by the arbitrators. The total cost of such a record shall be shared equally by those parties who ordered copies. However, it shall not be necessary to have a stenographic record of the hearing.

RULE 6-405. DEATH, DISABILITY OR RESIGNATION OF ARBITRATOR

If an arbitrator dies, resigns, or becomes unable to continue to act while a matter is pending, the Committee or its designee shall make a determination as to the course of further proceedings, and may appoint a substitute or replacement arbitrator, or by agreement of the parties, may proceed with one arbitrator. Two arbitrators shall not attempt to conduct the arbitration.

Amended October 21, 1987.

RULE 6-406. DISCOVERY AND WITNESSES

Discovery is limited in type and scope to that deemed necessary by the arbitrators in their sole discretion upon their own motion or the written request of either party. Persons having a direct interest in the arbitration shall be entitled to attend the hearing. The arbitrators shall have the power to require the retirement of any witness during the testimony of other witnesses. It shall be discretionary with the arbitrators to determine the propriety of the attendance of any other persons.

Amended October 21, 1987.

RULE 6-407. ADJOURNMENTS

The arbitrators for good cause shown may adjourn the hearing upon the request of either party or upon the arbitrators own initiative.

RULE 6-408. OATHS

Before proceeding with the hearing, the arbitrators shall take an oath of office. The arbitrators have the discretion to require witnesses to testify under oath or affirmation, and if requested by either party, shall so require.

RULE 6-409. ORDER OF PROCEEDINGS

(a) The hearing shall be opened by the filing of the oath of the arbitrators and by the recording of the place, time and date of the hearing, the names of the arbitrators and parties, and of witnesses or counsel if any are present.

(b) The normal order of proceedings shall be the same as in a trial with the petitioner first presenting his or her claim. However, the arbitrators shall have the discretion to vary the normal order of proceedings, and in any case shall afford full and equal opportunity to all parties for presentation of relevant proofs.

(c) The petitioner shall have the burden of proof by a preponderance of the evidence.

Amended October 21, 1987.

RULE 6–410. ARBITRATION IN THE ABSENCE OF A PARTY

The arbitration may proceed in the absence of a party who, after due notice, fails to be present. An award shall not be made solely on the default of a party; the arbitrators shall require the other party to present such evidence as the arbitrators may require for the making of an award.

RULE 6–411. EVIDENCE

(a) The parties may offer such evidence as they desire and shall produce such additional evidence as the arbitrators may deem necessary to an understanding and determination of the dispute. The arbitrators are authorized to subpoena witnesses and documents, and may do so either upon the arbitrators own initiative or upon the request of a party. These subpoenas shall be served and, upon application to the Superior Court in the county wherein the arbitration is pending by a party or the arbitrators, enforced in the same manner provided by law for the service and enforcement of subpoenas in a civil action, provided that the court shall not enforce subpoenas in the event that it determines that the effect of such subpoenas would be unduly burdensome or oppressive to any party or person. The arbitrators shall be the judge of the relevancy and materiality of the evidence offered. The rules of evidence shall be liberally interpreted and hearsay may be utilized at the discretion of the arbitrators and given such weight as the arbitrators deem appropriate.

(b) Exhibits, when offered by either party, may be received in evidence by the arbitrators. The names and addresses of all witnesses, and a listing of all exhibits in the order in which they were received shall be made a part of the record.

(c) The arbitrators may receive and consider the evidence of witnesses by affidavit (copies of which shall be served on the opposing party at least five (5) days prior to the hearing), but shall give such evidence only such weight as the arbitrators deem proper after consideration of any objections made to its admission.

(d) The petition, answer, other pleadings, and any documents attached thereto may be considered as evidence at the discretion of the arbitrators and given such weight as the arbitrators deem appropriate.

(e) The receipt of testimony by written interrogatories, conference telephone calls, and other procedures are within the discretion of the arbitrators upon their own motion or the written request of either party.

Amended October 21, 1987.

RULE 6–412. WRITTEN CONTRACT

No arbitrator shall have authority to enter an award contrary to terms of an executed written contract between the parties except on the grounds of fraud, accident, mistake or as being contrary to the laws of this state governing contracts.

Adopted October 21, 1987.

RULE 6–413. CLOSING OF HEARINGS

Prior to the closing of the hearing, the arbitrators shall inquire of all parties whether they have any further proofs to offer or additional witnesses to be heard. If they have none, the arbitrators shall declare the hearing closed and make a record of that fact.

Former Rule 6–412 redesignated as Rule 6–413 and further amended October 21, 1987.

RULE 6–414. REOPENING OF HEARINGS

The hearing may be reopened by the arbitrators either upon their own motion, or upon the motion of either party for good cause shown, at any time before an award is made. However, if the reopening of the hearing would prevent the making of an award within the time provided by these rules, the matter may not be reopened, unless both parties agree upon the extension of such time limit.

Former Rule 6–413 redesignated as Rule 6–414 October 21, 1987.

RULE 6–415. WAIVER OF RULES

Any party who proceeds with the arbitration after knowledge that any provision or requirement of these rules has not been complied with, and who fails to state an objection on the record or in writing prior to the closing of the hearing, shall be deemed to have waived any right to object.

Former Rule 6–414 redesignated as Rule 6–415 October 21, 1987.

RULE 6-416. WAIVER OF ORAL HEARINGS

The parties may provide by written agreement for the waiver of oral hearings.

Former Rule 6-415 redesignated as Rule 6-416 October 21, 1987.

RULE 6-417. AWARD

If both parties have agreed to be bound by the arbitration, the award of the arbitrators is final and binding upon them and may be enforced as provided by the general arbitration laws of the state.

Former Rule 6-416 redesignated as Rule 6-417 and further amended October 21, 1987.

RULE 6-418. TIME OF AWARD

The award shall be rendered promptly by the arbitrators not later than thirty (30) days from the date of the closing of the hearing, unless otherwise agreed upon by the parties with the consent of the arbitrators or an extension is obtained from the Committee or its chairman. If oral hearing has been waived, then the time period for rendering the award shall begin to run from the date of the receipt of final statements and proofs by the arbitrators.

Former Rule 6-417 redesignated as Rule 6-418 and further amended October 21, 1987.

RULE 6-419. FORM OF AWARD

The award shall be in writing and shall be signed by the arbitrators, or by a concurring majority. The parties shall so advise the arbitrators in writing prior to the close of the hearing if they request the arbitrators to accompany the award with an opinion.

Former Rule 6-418 redesignated as Rule 6-419 and further amended October 21, 1987.

RULE 6-420. AWARD UPON SETTLEMENT

If the parties settle their dispute during the course of the arbitration proceeding, the arbitrators, the Committee, or the Committee's designee, upon the written consent of all parties, may set forth the terms of the settlement in an award.

Former Rule 6-419 redesignated as Rule 6-420 and further amended October 21, 1987.

RULE 6-421. DELIVERY OF AWARD TO PARTIES

The parties shall accept as legal delivery of the award the placing of the award or a true copy thereof in the mail by the Committee addressed to each party at its last known address by certified mail with return receipt requested or to its counsel, or personal service of the award, or the filing of the award in any manner which may be prescribed by law.

Former Rule 6-420 redesignated as Rule 6-421 and further amended October 21, 1987.

RULE 6-422. COMMUNICATION WITH ARBITRATORS

There shall be no ex parte communication between the parties and the arbitrators.

Former Rule 6-421 redesignated as Rule 6-422 October 21, 1987.

RULE 6-423. INTERPRETATION AND APPLICATION OF RULES

The arbitrators shall interpret and apply these rules insofar as they relate to the arbitrators' powers and duties. Any dispute among the arbitrators on a panel shall be decided by a majority vote. If the dispute cannot be so resolved, either the arbitrators or a party may refer the question to the Committee for its determination. All other rules shall be interpreted and applied by the Committee and its decision shall be final subject only to review by the Executive Committee of the State Bar of Georgia pursuant to its powers, functions and duties under the Rules governing the State Bar.

Former Rule 6-422 redesignated as Rule 6-423 and further amended October 21, 1987.

CHAPTER 5. POST DECISION ACTIVITY

RULE 6-501. WHERE BOTH PARTIES AGREE

In cases where both parties agreed to be bound by the result of the arbitration and the award is not satisfied within thirty (30) days after the date of its mailing or other service by the Committee, either party may request the filing of the award on the records of the Superior Court of the county of residence of the party who has failed to satisfy the award. If not a Georgia resident, the award shall be entered in the county where the award was made. The said request shall be in writing with a copy mailed to the opposing party, shall be accompanied by all filing fees, and shall designate the appropriate county in which the award is to be entered. The Committee shall then mail the original award to the Clerk of the Superior Court of the designated county who shall file it in the same manner as the commencement of a new civil action and shall serve a copy bearing the civil action number and judge assignment by certified mail on all parties, with notice that if no objection under oath, including facts indicating that the award was the result of accident, or mistake or the fraud of some one or all of the arbitrators or parties, or is otherwise illegal, is filed within thirty (30) days, the award shall become final. Upon application of the party filing the award, the Clerk of the Superior Court shall issue a Writ of fi.fa. The fi.fa. may then be entered on the general execution docket in any jurisdiction.

All filing fees shall be furnished by the party or parties who requested that the award be so entered.

In the event an objection is properly filed, the Superior Court shall cause an issue to be made up which issue shall be tried by the court sitting without a jury under the same rules and regulations as are prescribed for the trials of appeals. Thus, the Superior Court shall render its decision from the record without a de novo trial on the merits and shall affirm the award, vacate the award, or return the award to the arbitrators with specific directions for further consideration. The decision of the Superior Court shall be final and not subject to appeal.

The General Counsel or an Assistant General Counsel of the State Bar of Georgia, or other volunteer lawyer may represent, assist, or advise any party in the collection of a final judgment or in the Superior Court's review of awards.

Amended October 21, 1987.

RULE 6–502. WHERE LAWYER REFUSES TO BE BOUND

If an award is made to the client and the respondent lawyer refuses to be bound thereby, the State Bar will provide the General Counsel, Assistant General Counsel, or other volunteer lawyer at no cost, other than actual litigation expenses, to the client to represent him or her in any litigation necessary to adjust the fee in accordance with the award.

(a) In such cases, the award rendered will be considered as prima facie evidence of the fairness of the award and the burden of proof shall shift to the lawyer to prove otherwise.

(b) In such cases, an award made in favor of the client will terminate the right of the lawyer to oppose the substitution of another lawyer designated by the client in any pending litigation pertaining to the subject matter of the arbitration.

Amended October 21, 1987.

CHAPTER 6. SPECIAL PROCEDURES

RULE 6–601. SPECIAL CASE PROCEDURE

After considering the complexity of the issues, the amount in controversy, the location of the arbitration, and all other factors, the Committee may upon its own motion or request of either party, assign any case to be arbitrated by the following special procedure:

(a) The waiting period of Rule 6–106, the arbitrator selection process of Rule 6–303, and the arbitrator qualifications of Rule 6–304, shall not apply.

(b) The arbitrator panel shall be selected by the Committee or its staff, and

(1) in cases involving amounts in dispute over $2,500 shall consist of two (2) attorneys who have practiced law actively for at least five (5) years and one (1) non–lawyer public member.

(2) in cases involving amounts in dispute of $2,500 or less, the arbitration panel may consist of one arbitrator who shall be a lawyer who has practiced law actively for at least five (5) years.

(c) All other rules of the Fee Arbitration program shall apply as in any other case.

Adopted October 21, 1987; amended effective January 5, 2005.

CHAPTER 7. CONFIDENTIALITY

RULE 6–701. CONFIDENTIALITY

With the exception of the award itself, all records, documents, files, proceedings and hearings pertaining to arbitrations of any fee disputes under these rules in which both the complainant and the attorney have consented to be bound by the result, shall not be opened to the public or any person not involved in the disputes without the written consent of both parties to the arbitration. However, the Committee, its staff, or representative may reveal confidential information in those circumstances in which the Office of General Counsel is authorized by Rule 4–221(d) to do so.

Former Rule 6–601 redesignated as Rule 6–701 and further amended October 21, 1987; amended February 5, 1988.

PART VII. LAWYER ASSISTANCE PROGRAM

PREAMBLE

The purpose of the Lawyer Assistance Program is to confidentially identify and assist Bar members who are experiencing problems which negatively impact their quality of life and their ability to function effectively as members of the Bar through education, intervention, peer support and professional clinical treatment.

Adopted effective November 8, 2003.

CHAPTER 1. LAWYER ASSISTANCE COMMITTEE

RULE 7–101. COMMITTEE

The program will be administered by the State Bar's Lawyer Assistance Committee ("Committee"). The Committee shall monitor and render advice to the staff, Executive Committee, and Board of Governors with respect to the rules, procedures, policies and operation of a Lawyer Assistance Program ("LAP").

Adopted effective November 8, 2003.

RULE 7–102. MEMBERSHIP

The Committee shall be appointed by the President of the State Bar in accordance with Article VIII, Section 1, of the bylaws of the State Bar of Georgia. In addition, the President, at his or her discretion, may appoint up to four non-lawyers to serve on the Committee, provided that such non-lawyers are licensed, certified addiction counselors, certified employee assistance professionals, licensed therapists, or other persons who have experience in conducting alcohol and drug rehabilitation intervention programs or mental health assistance programs. The term of such non-lawyer appointment shall be one year. Any member of the Committee who is a recovered chemical or alcohol dependent person must have a period of sobriety of at least five years.

Adopted effective November 8, 2003.

RULE 7–103. RESPONSIBILITY

The Committee shall be responsible for implementing an impairment program that provides education, referral and intervention.

Adopted effective November 8, 2003.

RULE 7–104. FUNDING

The work of the Committee and any treatment provider selected to assist the Committee in carrying out the work of the program shall be funded from the general budget of the State Bar and/or through donations and grants from the Georgia Bar Foundation or other public or private sources.

Adopted effective November 8, 2003.

RULE 7–105. STAFF AND FUNDING [DELETED]

Deleted effective November 8, 2003.

CHAPTER 2. GUIDELINES FOR OPERATION

RULE 7–201. EDUCATION, INFORMATION AND AWARENESS

The Committee shall promote and implement procedures to communicate to impaired attorneys and the Bar in general the fact that there is a program available and ready to assist in helping the impaired attorneys to overcome their problem.

Adopted effective November 8, 2003.

RULE 7–202. VOLUNTEERS

The Committee may establish a network of attorneys and lay persons throughout the State of Georgia, experienced or trained in impairment counseling, treatment, or rehabilitation, who can conduct education and awareness programs and assist in counseling and intervention programs and services.

Adopted effective November 8, 2003.

RULE 7–203. INTERVENTION AND COUNSELING

The members of the Committee shall establish, design and implement all procedures necessary to receive information concerning impaired attorneys. Upon a determination that an attorney is impaired, the Committee shall implement such resources as to the Committee appear appropriate in each individual case. In carrying out its duties under this rule, the Committee, subject to the approval of the Executive Committee, is authorized to outsource the clinical portion of the Lawyer Assistance Program to private sector health care professionals. Such health care professionals and their related staff, consultants and other designees shall be authorized to communicate with each other and with the Committee regarding the program or persons referred to the program by the Committee. Said communications shall not constitute a violation of the confidentiality rules established herein.

Adopted effective November 8, 2003.

RULE 7-204. DEFINITIONS

Attorney, as used in this Part VII, shall include active, inactive, emeritus and foreign law consultant members of the State Bar of Georgia.

An impaired attorney is an attorney who, in the opinion of the members of the Committee, the State Disciplinary Board, the Supreme Court of Georgia, or the members of the professional health care provider selected in accordance with Rule 7-302 above, who suffers from a psychological, emotional, or stress-related disease or problem, or who is actively abusing alcohol or other chemical substances, or has become dependent upon alcohol or such substances, such that the attorney poses a substantial threat of harm to the attorney or the attorney's clients, or the public.

Adopted effective November 8, 2003.

RULE 7-205. REFERRAL [DELETED]

Deleted effective November 8, 2003.

RULE 7-206. POWERS AND DUTIES OF SPECIAL MASTER [DELETED]

Deleted effective November 8, 2003.

RULE 7-207. DEFINITIONS [DELETED]

Deleted effective November 8, 2003.

CHAPTER 3. PROCEDURES

RULE 7-301. CONTACTS GENERALLY

The Committee shall be authorized to establish and implement procedures to handle all contacts from or concerning impaired attorneys, either through its chosen health care professional source, the statewide network established pursuant to Rule 7-102, or by any other procedure through which appropriate counseling or assistance to an impaired attorney may be provided.

Adopted effective November 8, 2003.

RULE 7-302. REFERRALS FROM THE STATE DISCIPLINARY BOARD

Upon the referral of any case to the Committee by the State Disciplinary Board of the State Bar of Georgia, the Committee shall provide assistance to the impaired attorney referred by the Disciplinary Board as otherwise authorized by these rules. The Committee shall report to the Board, from time to time, the progress or lack of progress of the attorney so referred.

Adopted effective November 8, 2003.

RULE 7-303. CONFIDENTIALITY

Except as provided in Bar Rule 4-104(b), Bar Rule 4-104(c), Bar Rule 4-108, and Bar Rule 7-203, all proceedings and records of the Committee, its members, staff, consultants and other designees shall be confidential unless the attorney who is the subject of the proceedings and records otherwise elects.

Adopted effective November 8, 2003.

RULE 7-304. REPORTS

The Committee shall implement and design such reports and documentation as it deems necessary or as is requested by the president of the State Bar, subject to the confidentiality provisions of Rule 7-303.

Adopted effective November 8, 2003.

RULE 7-305. EMERGENCY SUSPENSION

Upon receipt of sufficient evidence demonstrating that an impaired attorney's conduct poses a substantial threat of immediate or irreparable harm to the attorney's clients or the public, or if an impaired attorney refuses to cooperate with the Committee after an authorized intervention or referral, or refuses to take action recommended by the Committee, and said impaired attorney poses a substantial threat to the attorney, the attorney's clients, or the public, the Committee may request that the Office of General Counsel petition the Supreme Court of Georgia for the suspension of the attorney pursuant to Bar Rule 4-108. All proceedings under this part which occur prior to the filing of a petition in the Supreme Court of Georgia pursuant to this rule shall remain confidential and shall not be admissible against the attorney before the State Disciplinary Board of the State.

Adopted effective November 8, 2003.

RULE 7-306. IMMUNITY

The State Bar, its employees, and members of the Committee and its selected clinical outsource private health care professionals shall be absolutely immune from civil liability for all acts taken in the course of their official duties pursuant to this part.

Adopted effective November 8, 2003.

RULE 7–307. DEFINITIONS [DELETED]

Deleted effective November 8, 2003.

PART VIII. CONTINUING LAWYER COMPETENCY

CHAPTER 1. MINIMUM REQUIREMENTS FOR CONTINUING LEGAL EDUCATION

RULE 8–101. PURPOSE

It is of utmost importance to the members of the Bar and to the public that attorneys maintain their professional competence throughout their active practice of law. To that end these rules establish the minimum requirements for continuing legal education.

RULE 8–102. DEFINITIONS

(1) "Accredited sponsor" shall mean an organization whose entire continuing legal education program has been accredited by the Commission on Continuing Lawyer Competency. A specific, individual continuing legal education activity presented by such a sponsor constitutes an approved legal education activity.

(2) "Active member" shall include any person who is licensed to practice law in the State of Georgia and who is an active member of the State Bar of Georgia, but shall not include the Governor, Lieutenant Governor, Speaker of the House of Representatives, other Constitutional Executive Officers elected statewide, members of the Georgia Senate and the Georgia House of Representatives, United States Senators and Representatives, and shall not include judges who are prohibited by law, statute or ordinance from engaging in the practice of law.

(3) "Commission" shall mean the Commission on Continuing Lawyer Competency.

(4) "Inactive member" shall mean a member of the State Bar who is on inactive status.

(5) "Supreme Court" shall mean the Supreme Court of Georgia.

(6) "Year" shall mean the calendar year.

Amended October 2, 1984; March 2, 1988; March 22, 1989.

RULE 8–103. COMMISSION ON CONTINUING LAWYER COMPETENCY

(A) Membership, Appointment and Terms:

There is established a permanent commission of the State Bar of Georgia known as the Commission on Continuing Lawyer Competency. The Commission shall consist of sixteen (16) members, six (6) of whom shall be appointed by the Supreme Court of Georgia and six (6) by the Board of Governors of the State Bar of Georgia, one (1) shall be designated by the Executive Committee of the State Bar of Georgia, one (1) shall be the chair of the Board of Trustees of the Institute of Continuing Legal Education in Georgia or his or her designee, one (1) shall be designated by the Chief Justice's Commission on Professionalism, and one (1) shall be designated by the president of the Young Lawyers Division of the State Bar of Georgia. Members shall be members of the State Bar of Georgia. Members of the Commission appointed by the Supreme Court of Georgia and by the Board of Governors of the State Bar shall be appointed for staggered three (3) year terms and until their successors are appointed, except that the initial appointed members of the Commission shall consist of four (4) members appointed for a term of one (1) year, four (4) members appointed for a term of two (2) years, and four (4) members appointed for a term of three (3) years. The appointed members of the initial Commission shall be appointed half by the Supreme Court and half by the Board of Governors of the State Bar of Georgia. No member appointed by the Supreme Court or the Board of Governors may serve more than two (2) consecutive terms as a member of the Commission, and no such member may be reappointed otherwise to the Commission until he or she has been inactive as a Commission member for three (3) consecutive years. Members of the Commission designated by the Executive Committee, the chair of the Board of Trustees of the Institute of Continuing Legal Education, the Chief Justice's Commission on Professionalism, and the president of the Young Lawyers Division shall each serve for a term of one (1) year. No person so designated to the Commission may serve more than three (3) consecutive terms as a member of the Commission, and no such member may be redesignated otherwise to the Commission until he or she has been inactive as a Commission member for three (3) consecutive years.

The Commission shall designate each year one of its members to serve as Chairperson. The Executive Director of the State Bar of Georgia, the Executive Director of the Institute of Continuing Legal Education of Georgia, the Executive Director of the Chief Justice's Commission on Professionalism, and the Executive Director of the Commission shall serve as ex-officio members of the Commission, but shall have no vote. The Executive Director of the Commission shall serve as Secretary of the Commission.

(B) Powers and Duties of the Board:

(1) The Commission shall have general supervisory authority to administer these Rules.

(2) The Commission shall have specific duties and responsibilities:

(a) To approve all or portions of individual courses and programs of a sponsor which satisfy the educational requirements of Rule 8–106;

(b) To determine the number of credit hours allowed for each course or educational activity;

(c) To encourage courses and programs by established organizations, whether offered within or without the State;

(d) To educate the public about the legal profession;

(e) To adopt rules and regulations not inconsistent with these Rules;

(f) To establish an office or offices and to employ such persons as the Commission deems necessary for the proper administration of these Rules and to delegate to them appropriate authority, subject to the review of the Commission;

(g) To report at least annually to the State Bar and to the Supreme Court the activities and recommendations of the Commission and the effectiveness of the enforcement of these Rules;

(h) To report promptly to the Supreme Court any violation of these Rules.

(C) Finances:

(1) Purpose. The Commission should be adequately funded to enable it to perform its duties in a financially independent manner.

(2) Sources. Costs of administration of the Commission shall be derived from charges to members of the State Bar for continuing legal education activities.

(a) Sponsors of CLE programs to be held within the State of Georgia shall, as a condition of accreditation, agree to remit a list of Georgia attendees and to pay a fee for each active State Bar member who attends the program. This sponsor's fee shall be based on each day of attendance, with a proportional fee for programs lasting less than a whole day. The rate shall be set by the Commission.

(b) The Commission shall fix a reasonably comparable fee to be paid by individual attorneys who either (a) attend approved CLE programs outside the State of Georgia or (b) attend un–approved CLE programs within the State of Georgia that would have been approved for credit except for the failure of the sponsor to pay the fee described in the preceding paragraph. Such fee shall accompany the attorney's annual report.

(3) Uses. Funds may be expended for the proper administration of the Commission. However, the members of the Commission shall serve on a voluntary basis without expense reimbursement or compensation.

Amended November 1, 1988; amended effective February 10, 1994; February 2, 2005; December 9, 2005.

RULE 8–104. EDUCATION REQUIREMENTS AND EXEMPTIONS

(A) Minimum Continuing Legal Education Requirement.

Each active member shall complete a minimum of twelve (12) hours of actual instruction in an approved continuing legal education activity during each year. If a member completes more than twelve (12) hours in a year, the excess credit may be carried forward and applied to the education requirement for the succeeding year only

(B) Basic Legal Skills Requirement.

(1) Except as set out in subsections (a) and (b) below, any newly admitted active member admitted after June 30, 2005, must complete in the year of his or her admission or in the next calendar year the State Bar of Georgia Transition Into Law Practice Program, and such completion of the Transition Into Law Practice Program shall satisfy the mandatory continuing legal education requirements for such newly admitted active member for both the year of admission and the next succeeding year.

(a) Any newly admitted active member, who has practiced law in another United States jurisdiction other than Georgia for two or more years immediately prior to admission to practice in this state, may be exempted from completing the Transition Into Law Practice Program upon the submission, within three months of admission, of an affidavit to the Commission on Continuing Lawyer Competency. The affidavit shall provide the date or dates of admission in every other state in which the member is admitted to practice and a declaration that the newly admitted member has been actively engaged in the practice of law for two or more years immediately prior to admission in this state. Upon submission of a satisfactory affidavit, the newly admitted active member shall be required to complete the annual twelve hours of instruction in approved continuing legal education activity beginning at the start of the first full calendar year after the date of admission. Any newly admitted active member, who has practiced law in another United State jurisdiction other than Georgia for two or more years immediately prior to admission to practice in this state and who does not timely file the required affidavit, shall be required to complete the Transition Into Law Practice Program as set out above.

(b) Any newly admitted active member, who is a judicial law clerk or who begins a clerkship within three months of admission, shall not be subject to the requirement of completing the Transition Into

Law Practice Program during the period of the judicial clerkship. Within thirty days of admission to the State Bar or within thirty days of the beginning of the clerkship if said clerkship begins within three months after admission, the member shall provide written notice to the Commission on Continuing Lawyer Competency of the date of entry into the clerkship position. Judicial law clerks are required to complete the annual twelve hours of regular instruction in approved continuing legal education courses beginning at the start of the first full calendar year after the date of admission. Within thirty days of the completion of the clerkship, the member shall provide written notice to the Commission on Continuing Lawyer Competency of the date of such completion. The member must complete, in the year the clerkship was concluded, or the next calendar year, the Georgia Transition Into Law Practice Program. Such completion of the Transition Into Law Practice Program shall satisfy the mandatory continuing legal education requirements for such member for both the year of completion of the clerkship and the next succeeding calendar year.

(2) Each active member, except those participating in the Georgia Transition Into Law Practice Program, shall complete a minimum of one (1) hour of continuing legal education during each year in the area of ethics. This hour is to be included in, and not in addition to, the twelve-hour (12) requirement. If a member completes more than one (1) hour in ethics during the calendar year, the excess ethics credit may be carried forward up to a maximum of two (2) hours and applied to the ethics requirement for succeeding years.

(3) Each active member, except those participating in the Georgia Transition Into Law Practice Program, shall complete a minimum of one (1) hour of continuing legal education during each year in an activity of any sponsor approved by the Chief Justice's Commission on Professionalism in the area of professionalism. This hour is to be included in, and not in addition to, the twelve–hour (12) requirement. If a member completes more than one (1) hour in professionalism during the calendar year, the excess professionalism credit may be carried forward up to a maximum of two (2) hours and applied to the professionalism requirement for succeeding years.

(4) Confidentiality of proceedings.

(a) The confidentiality of all inquiries to, decisions of, and proceedings by the Transition Into Law Practice Program shall be respected. No disclosure of said inquiries, decisions and proceedings shall be made in the absence of the agreement of all participating.

(b) Except as expressly permitted by these rules, no person connected with the Transition Into Law Practice Program operated under the auspices of the Standards of the Profession Committee of the Commission on Continuing Lawyer Competency shall disclose any information concerning or comment on any proceeding under these rules.

(c) The Transition Into Law Practice Program operated under the auspices of the Standards of the Profession Committee of the Commission on Continuing Lawyer Competency may reveal private records when required by law, court rule, or court order.

(d) Any records maintained by the Transition Into Law Practice Program operated under the auspices of the Standards of the Profession Committee of the Commission on Continuing Lawyer Competency, as provided herein, shall be available to Counsel for the State Bar only in the event the State Bar or any department thereof receives a discovery request or properly executed subpoena requesting such records.

(C) Exemptions.

(1) An inactive member shall be exempt from the continuing legal education and the reporting requirements of this Rule.

(2) The Commission may exempt an active member from the continuing legal education, but not the reporting, requirements of this rule for a period of not more than one (1) year upon a finding by the Commission of special circumstances unique to that member constituting undue hardship.

(3) Any active member over the age of seventy (70) shall be exempt from the continuing legal education requirements of this rule, including the reporting requirements, unless the member notifies the Commission in writing that the member wishes to continue to be covered by the continuing legal education requirements of this rule.

(4) Any active member residing outside of Georgia who neither practices in Georgia nor represents Georgia clients shall be exempt, upon written application to the Commission, from the continuing legal education, but not the reporting, requirements of this rule during the year for which the written application is made. This application shall be filed with the annual report.

(5) Any active member of the Board of Bar Examiners shall be exempt from the continuing legal education but not the reporting requirement of this Rule.

(D) Requirements for Participation in Litigation.

(1) Prior to appearing as sole or lead counsel in the Superior or State Courts of Georgia in any contested civil case or in the trial of a criminal case, any participant in the Transition Into Law Practice Program admitted to practice after June 30, 2005, shall complete the mandatory Advocacy Experiences of the Transition Into Law Practice Program set forth in Regulation (5) hereunder. The mandatory Advocacy Experiences shall be completed as part of the Mentor-

ing Plan of Activities and Experiences, except that up to three (3) of the five (5) mandatory Advocacy Experiences may be obtained after completion of 60% of the credit hours required for law school graduation and prior to admission to practice. At least two (2) of the mandatory Advocacy Experiences must be completed as part of the Mentoring Plan of Activities and Experiences.

(2) Each active member who appears as sole or lead counsel in the Superior or State Courts of Georgia in any contested civil case or in the trial of a criminal case, shall complete for such year a minimum of three (3) hours of continuing legal education activity in the area of trial practice. A trial practice CLE activity is one exclusively limited to one or more of the following subjects: evidence, civil practice and procedure, criminal practice and procedure, ethics and professionalism in litigation, or trial advocacy. These hours are to be included in, and not in addition to, the 12–hour (twelve) requirement. If a member completes more than three (3) trial practice hours, the excess trial practice credit may be carried forward and applied to the trial practice requirement for the succeeding year only.

Amended October 2, 1984; October 21, 1987; November 1, 1988; May 4, 1989; December 14, 1989; amended effective July 4, 1991; February 22, 1996; April 4, 2001; June 9, 2004; February 2, 2005; December 9, 2005; April 7, 2006.

RULE 8–105. REPORTING REQUIREMENTS

On or before January 31 of each year, commencing in 1985, each active member shall make and file an Annual Report with the Commission in such form as the Commission shall prescribe, reporting compliance with Rule 8–104.

Amended effective December 9, 2005.

RULE 8–106. HOURS AND ACCREDITATION

(A) Hours. The Commission shall designate the number of hours to be earned by participation, including, but not limited to teaching, in continuing legal education activities approved by the Commission.

(B) Accreditation Standards. The Commission shall approve continuing legal education activities consistent with the following standards:

(1) They shall have significant intellectual or practical content and the primary objective shall be to increase the participant's professional competence as a lawyer.

(2) They shall constitute an organized program of learning dealing with matters directly related to the practice of law, professional responsibility or ethical obligations of lawyers.

(3) Credit may be given for continuing legal education activities where (a) live instruction is used or (b) mechanically or electronically recorded or reproduced material is used if a qualified instructor is available to comment and answer questions.

(4) Continuing legal education materials are to be prepared, and activities conducted, by an individual or group qualified by practical or academic experience in a setting physically suitable to the educational activity of the program.

(5) Thorough, high quality, and carefully prepared written materials should be distributed to all attendees at or before the time the course is presented. It is recognized that written materials are not suitable or readily available for some types of subjects; the absence of written materials for distribution should, however, be the exception and not the rule.

(6) The Commission may issue from time to time a list of approved accredited sponsors deemed by it to meet the requirements set forth in this rule. Any other sponsor desiring to be approved for accredited sponsor status must file an application with the Commission with such program material and information as the Commission may require.

(7) Any accredited sponsor must keep and maintain attendance records of each continuing legal education program sponsored by it, which shall be furnished to the Commission upon its request.

RULE 8–107. NON–COMPLIANCE

(A) Notice of Non–compliance.

(1) In the event an active member shall fail to complete the required units at the end of each applicable period, the Annual Report required under Rule 8–105 may be accompanied by a specific plan for making up the deficiency of necessary units within sixty (60) days after the date of the Annual Report. The plan shall be deemed accepted by the Commission unless within fifteen (15) days after the receipt of the Annual Report, the Commission notifies the lawyer to the contrary. Failure by the lawyer to complete the plan within the sixty (60) day period shall invoke the sanctions set forth in paragraph C.

(2) In the event that an active member shall fail to comply with these rules in any respect, the Commission shall promptly send notice of non–compliance. The notice shall specify the nature of the non–compliance and state that unless the non–compliance is corrected or a request for a hearing before the Commission is made within sixty (60) days, the statement of non–compliance shall be filed with the Supreme Court.

This notice, as well as any other notice or mailing required by Part VIII of these Rules, shall be mailed by first class mail to the member's current address contained in the membership records of the State Bar of Georgia. Service or actual receipt is not a prerequisite to actions authorized by these Rules.

(B) Hearing. If a hearing is requested, it shall be held within thirty (30) days by the full Commission, or one or more members designated by the Commission. Notice of the time and place of the hearing shall be given ten (10) days in advance. The party cited may be represented by counsel. Witnesses shall be sworn; and, if requested by the party cited, a complete electronic record or a transcript shall be made of all proceedings and testimony. The presiding member shall have the authority to rule on all motions, objections, and other matters presented in connection with the hearing. The hearing shall be conducted in conformity with the Georgia Rules of Civil Procedure, and the practice in the trial of civil cases. The party cited may not be required to testify over his or her objection. The chairman of the Commission who conducted the hearing shall (1) make findings of fact and determine whether the party cited has complied with the rules; and (2) upon a finding of noncompliance, shall determine whether there was reasonable cause for noncompliance. A copy of the findings and determination shall be sent to the party cited. If it is determined that compliance has occurred, the matter shall be dismissed and the Commission's records corrected to reflect compliance. If it is determined that compliance has not occurred, the Commission shall proceed as follows:

(i) If the Commission determines that there was reasonable cause for noncompliance, the party cited shall be allowed fifteen (15) days to file a specific plan for correcting the noncompliance within the next sixty (60) days following submission of the plan. The plan shall be deemed accepted by the Commission unless, within fifteen (15) days after receipt, the Commission notifies the party cited. Completion of the plan shall be reported by the lawyer in writing to the Commission not later than fifteen (15) days following the sixty (60) day period. If the party cited fails to file an acceptable plan, or fails to complete and certify completion within the sixty (60) day period, the Commission shall proceed as though there was not reasonable cause for noncompliance.

(ii) If the Commission determines that there was not reasonable cause for noncompliance, a record of the matter, including a copy of the findings, the determination, and the recommendation of the Commission for appropriate action, shall be filed promptly with the Supreme Court. If requested by the Commission, or the party cited, the record shall include a transcript of the hearing to be prepared at the expense of the requesting party.

(C) Supreme Court of Georgia Action. Upon receipt from the Commission of a statement of noncompliance or of the record of a Commission hearing, the Supreme Court shall enter an order it deems appropriate. In the case of active members it may include an order of summary suspension from the practice of law until further order of the court.

Amended November 1, 1988; amended effective December 9, 2005.

RULE 8–108. REINSTATEMENT

An active member suspended under the provisions of these rules may be reinstated by the court upon motion of the Commission and upon a showing that the delinquency has been corrected and payment to the Commission of a uniform reinstatement fee fixed by the Commission.

RULE 8–109. CONFIDENTIALITY

Records of the Commission are not confidential.

Amended November 1, 1988.

RULE 8–110. IMMUNITY

The State Bar, its employees, the Standards of the Profession Committee members and advisors, the Commission on Continuing Lawyer Competency, its employees, members and advisors, the Chief Justice's Commission on Professionalism, its employees, members, and advisors shall be absolutely immune from civil liability of all acts in the course of their official duties.

Adopted effective April 7, 2006.

RULE 8–111. COMPULSORY CONTINUING LEGAL EDUCATION OVERVIEW COMMITTEE

There is hereby created a Committee to be designated the Compulsory Continuing Legal Education Overview Committee. The Committee shall be composed of seven (7) persons who shall be members in good standing of the State Bar of Georgia and shall be named by the Supreme Court of Georgia to serve at the pleasure of the court. It shall be the duty of the Committee to monitor the administration of compulsory continuing legal education in Georgia, to evaluate its effectiveness and to report its findings to the Supreme Court of Georgia at least annually.

The Commission on Continuing Lawyer Competency shall cooperate with the Overview Committee.

RULE 8–112. FOREIGN LAW CONSULTANTS

Foreign law consultant members of the State Bar of Georgia shall be subject to and shall comply with the provisions of this Part VIII in the same manner and to the same extent as active members of the State Bar of Georgia.

Adopted effective April 16, 1992.

PART IX. PROFESSIONALISM

RULE 9–101. PURPOSE

This Part of the State Bar Rules is adopted in recognition of the importance of professionalism as the ultimate hallmark of the practice of law. The purpose of this Part is to create within the State Bar a Commission to identify, enunciate and encourage adherence to non–mandatory standards of professional conduct. These standards should involve aspirations higher than those required by the Georgia Rules of Professional Conduct in Part IV.

Adopted March 15, 1989; amended effective September 10, 2003; February 3, 2005.

RULE 9–102. CHIEF JUSTICE'S COMMISSION ON PROFESSIONALISM

(A) Membership, Appointment and Terms

There is established a permanent Commission of the State Bar of Georgia known as the Chief Justice's Commission on Professionalism. The Commission shall consist of twenty–one (21) members as follows: (1) the Chief Justice of the Supreme Court of Georgia or his or her designee, who shall serve as Chair of the Commission; (2) The Chief Judge of the Court of Appeals or his or her designee; (3) one superior court judge designated by the Council of Superior Court Judges; (4) one state court judge designated by the Council of State Court Judges; (5) four law school faculty members designated by the deans of the accredited law schools in the State of Georgia, one of whom must be a member of the State Bar Committee on Professionalism; provided, however, such faculty members shall not be from the same law school; (6) one non-lawyer former member of the State Disciplinary Board; (7) one non-lawyer citizen from the public at large; (8) the President of the State Bar of Georgia; (9) the President of the Young Lawyers Division of the State Bar of Georgia; (10) one Federal District Judge; and (11) eight members of the State Bar of Georgia actively engaged in the practice of law, one of whom must be employed by a unit of federal state, or local government, one must be engaged primarily in criminal defense practice, one must be a federal or state prosecutor, and one must be in–house counsel.

Three of the practicing lawyers and the non–lawyer former Disciplinary Board member shall be appointed by the Board of Governors of the State Bar of Georgia. The remaining members of the Commission, with the exception of the President of the State Bar of Georgia, the President of the Young Lawyers Division of the State Bar of Georgia, the superior court judge, and the state court judge, shall be appointed by the Supreme Court. The terms of the members of the Commission shall be staggered and that shall be accomplished by the initial appointments being as follows: two of the practicing lawyer members appointed by the Board of Governors shall serve until the conclusion of the State Bar Annual Meeting in 1990; the non-lawyer general public member shall serve until the conclusion of the State Bar Annual Meeting in 1990; the superior court judge member, one practicing lawyer member appointed by the Board of Governors and one law faculty member shall serve until the conclusion of the State Bar Annual Meeting in 1991. The remaining members of the Commission shall serve until the conclusion of the Annual Meeting of the State Bar in 1992. Thereafter, the superior court judge member shall serve for a two year term as designated by the Council of Superior Court Judges, the state court judge member shall serve for a two year term as designated by the Council of State Court Judges, and all other members of the Commission shall serve for three (3) year terms, and no member (except the Chief Justice, that member appointed by the Court of Appeals, and the law school representatives) may serve more than two (2) terms on the Commission.

(B) Powers and Duties of the Commission:

The Commission's major responsibilities shall be:

(1) To consider efforts by lawyers and judges to improve the administration of justice;

(2) To examine ways of making the system of justice more accessible to the public;

(3) To monitor and coordinate Georgia's professionalism efforts in such institutional settings as its bar, courts, law schools and law firms;

(4) To monitor professionalism efforts in jurisdictions outside Georgia;

(5) To conduct a study and issue a report on the present state of professionalism within Georgia;

(6) To plan the yearly Convocation on Professionalism;

(7) To promote various regional convocations on professionalism;

(8) To provide guidance and support to the Commission on Continuing Lawyer Competency in its implementation and execution of the continuing legal education professionalism requirement;

(9) To help implement a professionalism component in the Bridge–the–Gap program;

(10) To make recommendations to the Supreme Court and the State Bar concerning additional means by which professionalism can be enhanced;

(11) To receive and administer gifts and grants; and

(12) The Commission shall have no authority to impose sanctions of any kind upon any member of the State Bar of Georgia.

(C) Finances

Funding for the Chief Justice's Commission on Professionalism shall be provided by an additional surcharge for each active State Bar member who attends a course in professionalism sponsored by the Institute of Continuing Legal Education (ICLE) or by any other sponsor approved by the Commission. The rate shall be set annually by the Chief Justice's Commission on Professionalism, and the surcharge shall be remitted directly to it by ICLE, by any other such sponsor, or, in an appropriate case, by the individual State Bar member who attended a course in professionalism approved by the Commission.

Adopted March 15, 1989; amended May 4, 1989; December 1, 1989; May 23, 1990; amended effective November 8, 1990; March 26, 1992; July 9, 1992; December 29, 1994; December 19, 1996; September 10, 2003; February 3, 2005.

A LAWYER'S CREED

To my clients, I offer faithfulness, competence, diligence, and good judgment. I will strive to represent you as I would want to be represented and to be worthy of your trust.

To the opposing parties and their counsel, I offer fairness, integrity, and civility. I will seek reconciliation and, if we fail, I will strive to make our dispute a dignified one.

To the courts, and other tribunals, and to those who assist them, I offer respect, candor, and courtesy. I will strive to do honor to the search for justice.

To my colleagues in the practice of law, I offer concern for your welfare. I will strive to make our association a professional friendship.

To the profession, I offer assistance. I will strive to keep our business a profession and our profession a calling in the spirit of public service.

To the public and our systems of justice, I offer service. I will strive to improve the law and our legal system, to make the law and our legal system available to all, and to seek the common good through the representation of my clients.

Adopted October 9, 1992, nunc pro tunc July 3, 1990; amended effective September 10, 2003; February 3, 2005.

ASPIRATIONAL STATEMENT ON PROFESSIONALISM

The Court believes there are unfortunate trends of commercialization and loss of professional community in the current practice of law. These trends are manifested in an undue emphasis on the financial rewards of practice, a lack of courtesy and civility among members of our profession, a lack of respect for the judiciary and for our systems of justice, and a lack of regard for others and for the common good. As a community of professionals, we should strive to make the internal rewards of service, craft, and character, and not the external reward of financial gain, the primary rewards of the practice of law. In our practices we should remember that the primary justification for who we are and what we do is the common good we can achieve through the faithful representation of people who desire to resolve their disputes in a peaceful manner and to prevent future disputes. We should remember, and we should help our clients remember, that the way in which our clients resolve their disputes defines part of the character of our society and we should act accordingly.

As professionals, we need aspirational ideals to help bind us together in a professional community. Accordingly, the Court issues the following Aspirational Statement setting forth general and specific aspirational ideals of our profession. This statement is a beginning list of the ideals of our profession. It is primarily illustrative. Our purpose is not to regulate, and certainly not to provide a basis for discipline, but rather to assist the Bar's efforts to maintain a professionalism that can stand against the negative trends of commercialization and loss of community. It is the Court's hope that Georgia's lawyers, judges, and legal educators will use the following aspirational ideals to reexamine the justifications of the practice of law in our society and to consider the implications of those justifications for their conduct. The Court feels that enhancement of professionalism can be best brought about by the cooperative efforts of the organized bar, the courts, and the law schools with each group working independently, but also jointly in that effort.

GENERAL ASPIRATIONAL IDEALS

As a lawyer, I will aspire:

(a) To put fidelity to clients and, through clients, to the common good, before selfish interests.

(b) To model for others, and particularly for my clients, the respect due to those we call upon to resolve our disputes and the regard due to all participants in our dispute resolution processes.

(c) To avoid all forms of wrongful discrimination in all of my activities including discrimination on the basis of race, religion, sex, age, handicap, veteran status, or national origin. The social goals of equality and fairness will be personal goals for me.

(d) To preserve and improve the law, the legal system, and other dispute resolution processes as instruments for the common good.

(e) To make the law, the legal system, and other dispute resolution processes available to all.

(f) To practice with a personal commitment to the rules governing our profession and to encourage others to do the same.

(g) To preserve the dignity and the integrity of our profession by my conduct. The dignity and the integrity of our profession is an inheritance that must be maintained by each successive generation of lawyers.

(h) To achieve the excellence of our craft, especially those that permit me to be the moral voice of clients to the public in advocacy while being the moral voice of the public to clients in counseling. Good lawyering should be a moral achievement for both the lawyer and the client.

(i) To practice law not as a business, but as a calling in the spirit of public service.

SPECIFIC ASPIRATIONAL IDEALS

As to clients, I will aspire:

(a) To expeditious and economical achievement of all client objectives.

(b) To fully informed client decision–making. As a professional, I should:

(1) Counsel clients about all forms of dispute resolution;

(2) Counsel clients about the value of cooperation as a means towards the productive resolution of disputes;

(3) Maintain the sympathetic detachment that permits objective and independent advice to clients;

(4) Communicate promptly and clearly with clients; and,

(5) Reach clear agreements with clients concerning the nature of the representation.

(c) To fair and equitable fee agreements. As a professional, I should:

(1) Discuss alternative methods of charging fees with all clients;

(2) Offer fee arrangements that reflect the true value of the services rendered;

(3) Reach agreements with clients as early in the relationship as possible;

(4) Determine the amount of fees by consideration of many factors and not just time spent by the attorney;

(5) Provide written agreements as to all fee arrangements; and

(6) Resolve all fee disputes through the arbitration methods provided by the State Bar of Georgia.

(d) To comply with the obligations of confidentiality and the avoidance of conflicting loyalties in a manner designed to achieve the fidelity to clients that is the purpose of these obligations.

As to opposing parties and their counsel, I will aspire:

(a) To cooperate with opposing counsel in a manner consistent with the competent representation of all parties. As a professional, I should:

(1) Notify opposing counsel in a timely fashion of any canceled appearance;

(2) Grant reasonable requests for extensions or scheduling changes; and,

(3) Consult with opposing counsel in the scheduling of appearances, meetings, and depositions.

(b) To treat opposing counsel in a manner consistent with his or her professional obligations and consistent with the dignity of the search for justice. As a professional, I should:

(1) Not serve motions or pleadings in such a manner or at such a time as to preclude opportunity for a competent response;

(2) Be courteous and civil in all communications;

(3) Respond promptly to all requests by opposing counsel;

(4) Avoid rudeness and other acts of disrespect in all meetings including depositions and negotiations;

(5) Prepare documents that accurately reflect the agreement of all parties; and

(6) Clearly identify all changes made in documents submitted by opposing counsel for review.

As to the courts, other tribunals, and to those who assist them, I will aspire:

(a) To represent my clients in a manner consistent with the proper functioning of a fair, efficient, and humane system of justice. As a professional, I should:

(1) Avoid non–essential litigation and non–essential pleading in litigation;

(2) Explore the possibilities of settlement of all litigated matters;

(3) Seek non–coerced agreement between the parties on procedural and discovery matters;

(4) Avoid all delays not dictated by a competent presentation of a client's claims;

(5) Prevent misuses of court time by verifying the availability of key participants for scheduled appearances before the court and by being punctual; and

(6) Advise clients about the obligations of civility, courtesy, fairness, cooperation, and other proper behavior expected of those who use our systems of justice.

(b) To model for others the respect due to our courts. As a professional I should:

(1) Act with complete honesty;

(2) Know court rules and procedures;

(3) Give appropriate deference to court rulings;

(4) Avoid undue familiarity with members of the judiciary;

(5) Avoid unfounded, unsubstantiated, or unjustified public criticism of members of the judiciary;

(6) Show respect by attire and demeanor;

(7) Assist the judiciary in determining the applicable law; and,

(8) Seek to understand the judiciary's obligations of informed and impartial decision–making.

As to my colleagues in the practice of law, I will aspire:

(a) To recognize and to develop our interdependence;

(b) To respect the needs of others, especially the need to develop as a whole person; and,

(c) To assist my colleagues become better people in the practice of law and to accept their assistance offered to me.

As to our profession, I will aspire:

(a) To improve the practice of law. As a professional, I should:

(1) Assist in continuing legal education efforts;

(2) Assist in organized bar activities; and,

(3) Assist law schools in the education of our future lawyers.

(b) To protect the public from incompetent or other wrongful lawyering. As a professional, I should:

(1) Assist in bar admissions activities;

(2) Report violations of ethical regulations by fellow lawyers; and,

(3) Assist in the enforcement of the legal and ethical standards imposed upon all lawyers.

As to the public and our systems of justice, I will aspire:

(a) To counsel clients about the moral and social consequences of their conduct.

(b) To consider the effect of my conduct on the image of our systems of justice including the social effect of advertising methods.

(c) To provide the pro bono representation that is necessary to make our system of justice available to all.

(d) To support organizations that provide pro bono representation to indigent clients.

(e) To improve our laws and legal system by, for example:

(1) Serving as a public official;

(2) Assisting in the education of the public concerning our laws and legal system;

(3) Commenting publicly upon our laws; and,

(4) Using other appropriate methods of effecting positive change in our laws and legal system.

Adopted October 9, 1992, nunc pro tunc July 3, 1990; amended effective September 10, 2003; February 3, 2005.

PART X. CLIENTS' SECURITY FUND

PREAMBLE

The purpose of the Clients' Security Fund is to promote public confidence in the administration of justice and the integrity of the legal profession by providing monetary relief to persons who suffer reimbursable losses as a result of the dishonest conduct of Members of the State Bar of Georgia.

Adopted effective March 21, 1991.

RULE 10–101. FUND ESTABLISHED

There is established a separate fund of the State Bar of Georgia designated "Clients' Security Fund of the State Bar of Georgia." There is also established a Clients' Security Fund Board of Trustees which shall receive, hold, manage and disburse from the Fund such monies as may from time to time be appropriated to it by the State Bar of Georgia, or received through voluntary contributions, income from investments or other funding sources.

Adopted effective March 21, 1991.

RULE 10–102. DEFINITIONS

For this rule, the following terms shall have the following meanings:

(a) The "Board" means the Clients' Security Fund Board of Trustees.

(b) "Claimant" means one who files a claim for reimbursement with the Board of Trustees.

(c) The "Fund" means the Clients' Security Fund of the State Bar of Georgia.

(d) "Lawyer" means one who, at the time of the commencement of his or her handling of the matter in which the loss arose, was a Member of the State Bar of Georgia.

Adopted effective March 21, 1991.

RULE 10–103. FUNDING

(a) The State Bar of Georgia shall provide funding for the payment of claims and the costs of administering the Fund. In any year following a year in which the gross aggregate balance of the Fund falls below $1,000,000, the Bar shall assess and collect from each dues-paying member a pro rata share of the difference between the actual Fund balance and $1,000,000, provided that such assessments shall not exceed $25 in any single year. The aggregate amount paid to claimants from the Fund in any year shall not exceed $350,000. The Board of Governors may from time to time adjust the Fund's minimum aggregate balance, maximum annual payout, or maximum annual assessment to advance the purposes of the Fund or to preserve the fiscal integrity of the Fund.

(b) All monies or other assets of the Fund shall constitute a trust and shall be held in the name of the Fund, subject to the direction of the Board.

(c) No disbursements shall be made from the Fund except by the Board of Trustees.

Adopted effective March 21, 1991; amended effective July 1, 1997.

RULE 10–104. BOARD OF TRUSTEES

(a) The Board of Trustees shall consist of six (6) lawyers and one (1) non–lawyer appointed by the President of the State Bar. The initial appointments to the Board shall be of such terms as to result in the staggered expiration of the terms of all members of the Board. Thereafter, the appointments shall be for a term of five (5) years.

(b) Vacancies shall be filled by appointment of the President of the State Bar of Georgia for any unexpired term.

(c) The Board members shall select a chairperson, and such other officers as the Board members deem appropriate.

(d) A quorum for the transaction of business at any meeting of the Board shall consist of three current members in attendance.

(e) The Board may adopt a regulation to terminate Trustees who fail to regularly attend meetings and may adopt additional regulations for the administration of the Fund which are not otherwise inconsistent with these rules.

Adopted effective March 21, 1991; amended effective June 8, 2004.

RULE 10–105. INVESTIGATIONS

(a) The Board shall review every claim, and in its discretion, will investigate to the extent the Board deems appropriate those claims which appear to meet the requirements for payment as described in these rules.

(b) The Board may approve for payment from the fund such claims as are found, after investigation, to be meritorious and in accordance with these rules.

(c) Applications for relief shall be submitted on forms prescribed by the Board.

Adopted effective March 21, 1991.

RULE 10–106. ELIGIBLE CLAIMS

(a) The loss must be caused by the dishonest conduct of the lawyer and shall have arisen out of and by reason of a lawyer-client relationship, or a fiduciary relationship, between the lawyer and the claimant.

(b) As used in these Rules, "dishonest conduct" means wrongful acts committed by a lawyer in the nature of theft or embezzlement of money or the wrongful taking or conversion of money, property or other things of value.

(c) A complaint against the lawyer who caused or is alleged to have caused such loss shall have been filed with the State Disciplinary Board of the State Bar of Georgia and final disposition of such complaint has been made resulting in disciplinary action against the lawyer in the form of indefinite suspension, disbarment, or voluntary surrender of license.

(d) The claim shall be filed no later than two years after the date of final disciplinary action by the Supreme Court. In the event disciplinary action cannot be prosecuted due to the fact that the attorney is either deceased or cannot be located, the claim shall be filed no later than five years after the dishonest conduct was first discovered by the applicant; provided, however, the claim shall be filed no later than seven years after the dishonest conduct occurred.

(e) Except as provided by Section (f) of this Rule, the following losses shall not be reimbursable:

(1) Losses incurred by spouses, children, parents, grandparents, siblings, partners, associates and employees of lawyer(s) causing the losses;

(2) Losses covered by any bond, surety agreement, or insurance contract to the extent covered thereby, including any loss to which any bonding agent, surety or insurer is subrogated, to the extent of that subrogated interest;

(3) Losses incurred by any financial institution which are recoverable under a "banker's blanket bond" or similar commonly available insurance or surety contract;

(4) Losses incurred by any business entity controlled by the lawyer, or any person or entity described in Section (e)(1) hereof;

(5) Losses incurred by any governmental entity or agency;

(6) Losses incurred by corporations or partnerships, including general or limited.

(f) In cases of extreme hardship or special and unusual circumstances, the Board may, in its discretion, recognize a claim which otherwise would be excluded under these Rules in order to achieve the purpose of the Fund.

(g) In cases where it appears that there will be unjust enrichment, or the claimant unreasonably or knowingly contributed to the loss, the Board may, in its discretion, deny the claim.

(h) The Board shall require the applicant to exhaust his civil remedies unless the Board determines that the pursuit of the civil claim is not feasible or practical.

Adopted effective March 21, 1991; amended effective November 9, 1995.

RULE 10-107. PAYMENTS

(a) If, in the judgment of the Board, a reimbursable loss has been sustained by a claimant and the circumstances warrant relief, then, after taking into consideration the resources of the Fund and the priority to be assigned to such application in the discretion of the Board, the Board may, in the exercise of its discretion, as a matter of grace and not of right, grant monetary relief.

(b) Such monetary relief shall be in such an amount as the Board may determine and shall be payable in such a manner and upon such conditions and terms as the Board shall prescribe.

Adopted effective March 21, 1991.

RULE 10-108. NO LEGAL RIGHT TO PAYMENT

No person shall have any legal right to payment or reimbursement from the Fund whether as a claimant, third-party beneficiary, or otherwise.

Adopted effective March 21, 1991.

RULE 10-109. RESTITUTION AND SUBROGATION

(a) A lawyer whose dishonest conduct results in reimbursement to a claimant shall be liable to the Fund for restitution; the Board may bring such action as it deems advisable to enforce such obligation.

(b) As a condition of reimbursement, a claimant shall be required to provide the Fund with a pro tanto transfer of the claimant's rights against the lawyer, the lawyer's legal representative, estate or assigns, and the claimant's rights against any third party or entity who may be liable for the claimant's loss.

(c) No petition for reinstatement to practice law in the state of Georgia shall be granted until the petitioner has made restitution to the Clients' Security Fund for all amounts paid by the Fund as a result of the petitioner's conduct plus accrued interest.

Adopted effective March 21, 1991; amended effective February 1, 2000.

RULE 10-110. IMMUNITY

The Trustees, employees and agents of the Board shall be absolutely immune from civil liability for all acts in the course of their official duties. Absolute immunity shall also extend to claimants and lawyers who assist claimants for all communications to the Fund.

Adopted effective March 21, 1991.

RULE 10-111. CONFIDENTIALITY

(a) Claims, proceedings and reports involving claims for reimbursement are confidential until the Board authorizes reimbursement to the claimant, except as provided below. After payment of the reimbursement, the Board may publicize the nature of the claim, the amount of reimbursement, and the name of the lawyer. The name and the address of the claimant shall not be publicized by the Board unless specific permission has been granted by the claimant.

(b) This Rule shall not be construed to deny access to relevant information by professional discipline agencies or other law enforcement authorities as the Board shall authorize, or the release of statistical information which does not disclose the identity of the lawyer or the parties.

(c) In the event a lawyer whose conduct resulted in the payment of a claim files a petition for reinstatement to the practice of law, the Board shall release all information pertaining to the claim to the Board to Determine Fitness of Bar Applicants as may be pertinent to the reinstatement proceeding.

Adopted effective March 21, 1991; amended effective February 1, 2000.

RULE 10-112. REPEAL OF RESOLUTION

Any Resolution of the State Bar of Georgia currently in force and covering the subject matter of these Rules 10-101 through 10-112, shall be repealed upon adoption of these Rules by the Supreme Court of Georgia.

Adopted effective March 21, 1991.

PART XI. LAW PRACTICE MANAGEMENT PROGRAM

PREAMBLE

The purpose of the Law Practice Management Program is to provide law office management consulting services and materials to the members of the State Bar of Georgia, and thereby to facilitate and improve the delivery of legal services to the public.

Adopted effective February 22, 1996.

CHAPTER 1. CONFIDENTIALITY

RULE 11–101. CONFIDENTIALITY

Information obtained by the staff of the Law Practice Management Program shall be confidential unless the affected attorney otherwise elects or unless the information clearly shows the attorney intends to engage in criminal conduct in the future.

Adopted effective February 22, 1996.

CHAPTER 2. OVERSIGHT COMMITTEE

RULE 11–201. COMMITTEE

The advisory and oversight responsibility for this program will be vested in the Law Practice Management Committee ("Committee").

Adopted effective February 22, 1996.

RULE 11–202. MEMBERSHIP

The Committee shall consist of nine members, at least three of whom shall be members of the Board of Governors of the State Bar at the time of their appointment. The Director of the Law Practice Management Program, the Executive Director of the State Bar, or his or her designee, and the Executive Director of the Younger Lawyers Section of the State Bar shall be non-voting, ex-officio members of the Committee.

Adopted effective February 22, 1996.

RULE 11–203. TERMS

(a) Initially, three members of the Committee, including at least one member of the Board of Governors, shall be appointed by the Immediate Past President for one-year terms; three members of the Committee, including at least one member of the Board of Governors, shall be appointed by the President for two-year terms; and three members of the Committee, including at least one member of the Board of Governors, shall be appointed by the President-elect for three-year terms. The President of the State Bar shall appoint the chairperson of the Committee during the initial year from among the members. These appointments shall become effective July 1, 1995, and shall be made by those serving at that time in the offices of Immediate Past President, President and President-elect.

(b) In each year following the initial year, the President-elect shall appoint three members, at least one of whom shall be a member of the Board of Governors at the time of their appointment, to three-year terms.

(c) The Committee shall elect a chairperson and such other officers as the Committee members deem appropriate.

(d) Vacancies shall be filled by appointment of the President of the State Bar for any unexpired term.

Adopted effective February 22, 1996.

RULE 11–204. PURPOSE OF RESPONSIBILITY

The Committee shall meet for the purposes of oversight of the Law Practice Management Program, coordination of the Program's goals, and implementation of directives and resolutions from the Board of Governors. Additionally, the Committee will from time to time develop recommendations for submission to the Executive Committee and the Board of Governors with regard to the funding, staffing, administration, and operation of the program, which may include proposed changes to Bylaws or Rules of the State Bar.

Adopted effective February 22, 1996.

RULE 11–205. STAFF AND FUNDING

The State Bar may provide such staff as it deems necessary, including a Director and support staff. The work of the Director and staff shall be funded through the general budget of the State Bar or through donations and grants from foundations or other public or private sources. The income generated by this program through consultation fees, sales of materials, and other means shall be remitted directly to the State Bar by the Director and staff.

Adopted effective February 22, 1996.

RULE 11–206. CONSULTATION FEES

The Committee shall be authorized to charge consultation fees and costs for materials in conjunction with law practice management services.

Adopted effective February 22, 1996.

RULE 11–207. IMMUNITY

The State Bar, its employees, and members of the Committee shall be absolutely immune from civil liability for all acts in the course of their official duties.

Adopted effective February 22, 1996.

PART XII. CONSUMER ASSISTANCE PROGRAM

PREAMBLE

The purpose of the Consumer Assistance Program is to respond to inquiries from the public regarding State Bar members and to assist the public through informal methods including the resolution of inquiries which may involve minor violations of the disciplinary standards set forth in Part IV of these Rules.

Adopted effective July 1, 1997.

RULE 12–101. CONSUMER ASSISTANCE COMMITTEE

The advisory and oversight responsibility for this program will be vested in the Consumer Assistance Committee ("Committee").

Adopted effective July 1, 1997.

RULE 12–102. CONSUMER ASSISTANCE COMMITTEE; MEMBERSHIP AND TERMS

(a) The Committee shall consist of eight members including seven State Bar members and one public member. At least two-thirds of the State Bar members shall be members of the Board of Governors of the State Bar at the time of their appointment. Committee members shall serve staggered three-year terms. The number of members shall be subject to change by a majority vote of the Board of Governors but shall never be less than five.

(b) The public member shall be appointed by the Supreme Court for a three-year term. All other Committee members shall be appointed by the President of the Bar for three-year terms except, initially, two Committee members shall be appointed for one-year terms, two members shall be appointed for two-year terms, and two members shall be appointed for a three-year term. Committee terms shall begin with the operational year of the State Bar. Should additional members be approved, their three-year terms shall be assigned in such fashion as to best maintain uniformity in the number of members to be appointed each year.

(c) The Committee shall elect a chairperson and such other officers as the Committee members deem appropriate.

(d) Vacancies shall be filled by appointment of the President of the State Bar for any unexpired term.

Adopted effective July 1, 1997; amended effective February 24, 2000.

RULE 12–103. COMMITTEE PURPOSE AND RESPONSIBILITY

The Committee shall meet for the purposes of oversight of the Consumer Assistance Program, coordination of the program's goals and implementation of directives and resolutions from the Board of Governors. The Committee shall have authority to adopt additional regulations for the administration of the program which are not otherwise inconsistent with these rules. Additionally, the Committee will develop recommendations for submission to the Executive Committee and the Board of Governors with regard to the funding, staffing, administration, and operation of the program, which may include proposed changes to bylaws or Rules of the State Bar.

Adopted effective July 1, 1997.

RULE 12–104. STAFF AND FUNDING

The State Bar shall provide such staff as it deems necessary. The program shall be funded through the general budget of the State Bar and, when appropriate, through donations and grants from foundations and other public and private sources.

Adopted effective July 1, 1997.

RULE 12–105. SUPERVISION

The Consumer Assistance Program shall operate under the supervision of the Executive Director of the State Bar.

Adopted effective July 1, 1997.

RULE 12–106. PROCEDURES

Inquiries concerning State Bar members may be received by Consumer Assistance staff in writing, in person and by telephone. Consumer Assistance staff shall have the authority to contact the attorney involved and conduct other limited investigation necessary to determine if the inquiry can be resolved in an informal method either through communications with

Consumer Assistance staff or by referral to other State Bar programs including but not limited to Fee Arbitration, Clients' Security Fund, Law Practice Management Program, and the Lawyer Assistance Program.

If the conduct which is the subject of the inquiry appears to violate one of the standards of conduct set forth in Part IV of the Bar Rules, Consumer Assistance staff shall have independent authority to determine whether the matter can either be resolved informally or should be referred to the Office of General Counsel for further screening under Part IV of the Bar Rules.

Consumer Assistance staff shall follow written guidelines developed and established by the Consumer Assistance Committee with the advice and counsel of the General Counsel and Executive Director of the State Bar and approved by the Executive Committee and Board of Governors of the State Bar.

Regardless of any decision made by Consumer Assistance staff, any individual shall have the right to request grievance forms and file a grievance under Part IV of the Bar Rules.

In the event a bar member who is the subject of an inquiry disagrees with the voluntary resolution recommended by Consumer Assistance staff, staff may refer the matter to the Office of General Counsel for further screening under Part IV of the Bar Rules.

Adopted effective July 1, 1997.

RULE 12–107. CONFIDENTIALITY OF PROCEEDINGS

(a) All investigations and proceedings provided for herein shall be confidential unless the respondent otherwise elects or as hereinafter provided in this rule and Part IV of the Bar Rules.

(b) Except as expressly permitted by these rules, no person connected with the Consumer Assistance Program shall disclose information concerning or comment on any proceeding under Part XII of these rules.

(1) Nothing in the rules shall prohibit truthful and accurate public statements of fact about a proceeding under Part XII of these rules, provided however, that in the event of such statement any other person involved in the proceeding may make truthful and accurate public statements of fact regarding the proceeding, including information otherwise confidential under the provisions of Rule 4–102(d), Standard 28, as may be reasonably necessary to defend that person's reputation;

(2) Wilful and false statements of fact made by any person connected with a proceeding under Part XII of these rules may subject such person to rule for contempt by the Supreme Court.

(c) In the event the conduct of the attorney appears to violate one or more of the standards of conduct set forth in Part IV of the Bar Rules, and Consumer Assistance staff in its sole discretion makes a determination under Rule 12–106 that the matter cannot be resolved informally, then the Consumer Assistance staff shall inform callers of their option to file a grievance and shall advise the General Counsel's office to send the appropriate forms to the callers.

(d) The Consumer Assistance Committee and staff may reveal confidential information when required by law or court order.

Adopted effective July 1, 1997.

RULE 12–108. DISCLOSURE

Information obtained by the Consumer Assistance Committee and staff shall not be disclosed to the Office of General Counsel unless:

(a) the information clearly shows the attorney intends to engage in criminal conduct in the future;

(b) the information clearly shows the attorney has misappropriated funds or engaged in criminal conduct;

(c) the caller files a grievance and the affected attorney consents in writing to the release of the information; or

(d) as otherwise provided by Bar Rule 12–107.

Adopted effective July 1, 1997.

RULE 12–109. IMMUNITY

The State Bar, its employees, and members of the Committee shall be absolutely immune from civil liability for all acts in the course of their official duties.

Adopted effective July 1, 1997.

PART XIII. JUDICIAL DISTRICT PROFESSIONALISM PROGRAM

PREAMBLE

The purpose of the Judicial District Professionalism Program (hereinafter referred to as "JDPP") is to promote professionalism within the legal profession through increased communication, education and the informal use of local peer influence. The JDPP will be comprised of committees of Board of Governors members from each of Georgia's Judicial Districts. These committees shall be called *Judicial District*

Professionalism Committees (herein after referred to as "JDPC").

Adopted effective February 24, 2000.

RULE 13–101. VOLUNTARY NATURE OF PROGRAM

The JDPC seeks to use local peer influence on an informal basis to open channels of communication on a voluntary basis. No judge or lawyer is required to cooperate or counsel with the JDPC or any of its representatives. If the party against whom the inquiry is addressed refuses to cooperate by voluntarily meeting with JDPC representatives, the JDPC shall take no further action regarding the inquiry.

Adopted effective February 24, 2000.

RULE 13–102. PRIVACY OF PROCEEDINGS

(a) The privacy of all inquiries and proceedings provided herein shall be respected. The JDPC and staff shall not make disclosure of said inquiries and proceedings in the absence of the agreement of all participating.

(b) Except as expressly permitted by these Rules, the JDPC and staff shall not disclose information concerning or comment on any proceeding under these Rules.

(c) The JDPC and staff may reveal private records when required by law, court rule, or court order.

(d) Any records maintained by the JDPP, as provided herein, shall be available to counsel for the State Bar only in the event the State Bar or any department thereof receives a discovery request or properly executed subpoena requesting such records.

(e) The JDPP record of any inquiry against any lawyer or judge under these Rules shall not contain the name of the inquiring or responding party. Only information for raw statistical data shall be maintained by the JDPP or each JDPC.

(f) In order to preserve privacy, no lawyer or judge shall be required to respond when asked if there are any JDPP inquiries against the lawyer or judge.

Adopted effective February 24, 2000.

RULE 13–103. IMMUNITY

The State Bar, its employees, the JDPC members, the Chief Justice's Commission on Professionalism, its employees, the Bench and Bar Committee members and advisors of the JDPC shall be absolutely immune from civil liability for all acts in the course of their official duties.

Adopted effective February 24, 2000.

PART XIV. RULES GOVERNING THE INVESTIGATION AND PROSECUTION OF THE UNLICENSED PRACTICE OF LAW

CHAPTER 1. PREAMBLE

RULE 14–1.1. JURISDICTION

The Supreme Court of Georgia has the inherent authority to regulate the practice of law. *Wallace v. Wallace*, 225 Ga. 102, cert. denied, 396 U. S. 939 (1969); *Sams v. Olah*, 225 Ga. 497, cert. denied, 397 U. S. 914 (1970); *Fleming v. State*, 246 Ga. 90, cert. denied, 449 U. S. 904 (1980). This authority necessarily includes jurisdiction over the unlicensed practice of law.

Adopted effective February 7, 2001.

RULE 14–1.2. DUTY OF THE STATE BAR OF GEORGIA

The State Bar of Georgia, as an official arm of the Court, is charged with the duty of considering, investigating, and seeking the prohibition of matters pertaining to the unlicensed practice of law and the prosecution of alleged offenders. The Court hereby establishes a Standing Committee on the unlicensed practice of law and at least one District Committee on unlicensed practice of law in each judicial district.

Adopted effective February 7, 2001.

CHAPTER 2. DEFINITIONS

RULE 14–2.1. GENERALLY

Whenever used in these rules the following words or terms shall have the meaning herein set forth unless the use thereof shall clearly indicate a different meaning:

(a) Unlicensed Practice of Law. The unlicensed practice of law shall mean the practice of law, as prohibited by statute, court rule, and case law of the State of Georgia.

(b) Nonlawyer or Nonattorney. For purposes of this chapter, a nonlawyer or nonattorney is an individual who is not an active member of the State Bar of Georgia. This includes, but is not limited to, lawyers admitted in other jurisdictions, law students, law graduates, applicants to the State Bar of Georgia, inactive lawyers, disbarred lawyers, and suspended lawyers during the period of suspension.

(c) This Court or the Court. This Court or the Court shall mean the Supreme Court of Georgia.

(d) Counsel for the Bar. Counsel for the Bar is a member of the State Bar of Georgia other than Staff Counsel representing the Bar in any proceedings under these rules.

(e) Respondent. A respondent is a nonlawyer who is either accused of engaging in the unlicensed practice of law or whose conduct is under investigation.

(f) Judge. A Judge is the Superior Court Judge who conducts proceedings as provided under these rules.

(g) Standing Committee. The Standing Committee on UPL is the committee constituted according to the directives contained in these rules.

(h) District Committee. A District Committee is a local unlicensed practice of law District Committee.

(i) Staff Counsel. Staff counsel is an attorney employee of the State Bar of Georgia employed to perform such duties, as may be assigned.

(j) UPL. UPL is the unlicensed practice of law.

(k) The Board or Board of Governors. The Board or Board of Governors is the Board of Governors of the State Bar of Georgia.

(*l*) Executive Committee. The Executive Committee is the Executive Committee of the Board of Governors of the State Bar of Georgia, composed of such officers and members of the Board of Governors as may be designated in the bylaws, which shall exercise the powers and duties of the Board of Governors when it is not in session, subject to such limitations as the bylaws may provide.

Adopted effective February 7, 2001.

CHAPTER 3. STANDING COMMITTEE

RULE 14-3.1. GENERALLY

(a) Appointment and Terms. The Standing Committee shall be appointed by the Court, and shall consist of 23 members, 11 of whom shall be nonlawyers. The nonlawyer members should be geographically representative of the State. The lawyer members shall be appointed by the Court and shall include at least one member from each judicial district. The Court shall appoint a chair and at least 1 vice-chair of the Standing Committee, both of whom may be nonlawyers. Eight of the members of the Standing Committee shall constitute a quorum. All appointments to the Standing Committee shall be for a term of 3 years, except that it shall be the goal of the initial appointments that one-third (1/3) of the terms of the members appointed will expire annually. The members who initially serve terms of less than 3 years shall be eligible for immediate reappointment. No member shall be appointed to more than 2 full consecutive terms.

(b) Duties. It shall be the duty of the Standing Committee to receive and evaluate District Committee reports and to determine whether litigation should be instituted in Superior Court against any alleged offender. The Standing Committee may approve civil injunctive proceedings, civil or criminal contempt proceedings, a combination of injunctive and contempt proceedings, or such other action as may be appropriate. In addition, the duties of the Standing Committee shall include, but not be limited to:

(1) the consideration and investigation of activities that may, or do, constitute the unlicensed practice of law;

(2) the supervision of the District Committees, which shall include, but not be limited to:

(A) prescribing rules of procedure for District Committees;

(B) assigning reports of unlicensed practice of law for investigation;

(C) reassigning or withdrawing matters previously assigned, exercising final authority to close cases not deemed by the Standing Committee to then warrant further action by the State Bar of Georgia for unlicensed practice of law, and closing cases proposed to be resolved by a cease and desist affidavit where staff counsel objects to the closing of the case or the acceptance of a cease and desist affidavit by the District Committee;

(D) joining with a District Committee in a particular investigation; and

(E) request staff investigators, staff counsel, and voluntary bar counsel to conduct investigations on behalf of or in concert with the District Committees; and

(F) suspending District Committee members and chairs for cause and appointing a temporary District Committee chair where there has been a suspension, resignation, or removal, pending the appointment of a replacement chair by the Court;

(3) the initiation and supervision of litigation, including the delegation of responsibility to staff, or Counsel for the Bar to prosecute such litigation;

(4) the giving of advice regarding the unlicensed practice of law policy to the officers, Board of Governors, staff, sections, or committees of the State Bar of Georgia as requested; and

(5) furnishing any and all information, confidential records, and files regarding pending or closed investigations of unlicensed practice of law to any state or federal law enforcement or regulatory agency, United States Attorney, District Attorney, Solicitor, the Georgia Office of Bar Admissions and equivalent entities in other jurisdictions, the State Disciplinary Board of the State Bar of Georgia and equivalent entities in other jurisdictions where there is or may be a violation of state or federal law or the Rules of Professional Conduct of the State Bar of Georgia, or when required by law or court order.

Adopted effective February 7, 2001.

RULE 14–3.2. STAFF COUNSEL AND COUNSEL FOR THE BAR

(a) Staff Counsel. The State Bar of Georgia shall provide staff counsel and other employees sufficient to assist the Standing Committee and the District Committee in carrying out their responsibilities as prescribed elsewhere in these rules.

(b) Appointment of Counsel for the Bar. The President of the State Bar of Georgia may appoint one or more Counsel for the Bar to assist the State Bar of Georgia in meeting its duties as prescribed in (a) above.

Adopted effective February 7, 2001.

CHAPTER 4. DISTRICT COMMITTEES

RULE 14–4.1. GENERALLY

(a) Appointment and Terms. Each District Committee shall be appointed by the Court and shall consist of not fewer than 3 members, at least one-third of whom shall be nonlawyers. All appointees shall be residents of the judicial district or have their principal office in the district. The terms of the members of District Committees shall be for 3 years from the date of appointment by the Court or until such time as their successors are appointed, except that it shall be the goal of the initial appointments that one-third (1/3) of the terms of the members appointed will expire annually. The members who initially serve terms of less than 2 years shall be eligible for immediate reappointment. Continuous service of a member shall not exceed 6 years. The expiration of the term of any member shall not disqualify that member from concluding any investigations pending before that member. Any member of a District Committee may be removed from office by the Court.

(b) Committee Chair. For each District Committee there shall be a chair designated by the Court. A vice-chair and secretary may be designated by the chair of each District Committee. The chair shall be a member of the State Bar of Georgia.

(c) Quorum. Three members of the District Committee or a majority of the members, whichever is less, shall constitute a quorum.

(d) Panels. The Chair of a District Committee may divide that Committee into panels of not fewer than 3 members, 1 of whom must be a nonlawyer. The 3–member panel shall elect 1 of its members to preside over the panel's actions. If the chair or vice-chair of the District Committee is a member of a 3–member panel, the chair or vice-chair shall be the presiding officer.

(e) Duties. It shall be the duty of each District Committee to investigate, with dispatch, all reports of unlicensed practice of law and to make prompt written report of its investigation and findings to staff counsel. In addition, the duties of the District Committee shall include, but not be limited to:

(1) closing cases not deemed by the District Committee to warrant further action by the State Bar of Georgia;

(2) closing cases proposed to be resolved by a cease and desist affidavit; and

(3) forwarding to staff counsel recommendations for litigation to be reviewed by the Standing Committee.

(f) District Committee Meetings. District Committees should meet at regularly scheduled times. Either the chair or vice chair may call special meetings. District Committees should meet as often as necessary during any period when the Committee has 1 or more pending cases assigned for investigation and report. The time, date and place of scheduled meetings should be set in advance by agreement between each Committee and staff counsel. Meetings may be conducted by telephone conference or by any other technology available and agreed upon by the Committee. Any participant, including staff counsel, may participate in the meeting by telephone conference or any other technology agreed upon by the Committee.

Adopted effective February 7, 2001.

CHAPTER 5. COMPLAINT PROCESSING AND INITIAL INVESTIGATORY PROCEDURES

RULE 14-5.1. COMPLAINT PROCESSING

(a) Complaints. All complaints alleging unlicensed practice of law, except those initiated by the State Bar of Georgia, shall be in writing and signed by the complainant in such form as may be prescribed by the Standing Committee.

(b) Review by Staff Counsel. Staff counsel shall review the complaint and determine whether the alleged conduct, if proven, would constitute a violation of the prohibition against engaging in the unlicensed practice of law. Staff counsel may conduct a preliminary, informal investigation to aid in this determination and may use a State Bar of Georgia staff investigator to aid in the preliminary investigation. If staff counsel determines that the facts, if proven, would not constitute a violation, staff counsel may decline to pursue the complaint. A decision by staff counsel not to pursue a complaint shall not preclude further action or review under the rules regulating the State Bar of Georgia. The complainant shall be notified of a decision not to pursue a complaint.

(c) Referral to District Committee. Staff counsel may refer a UPL file to the appropriate District Committee for further investigation or action as authorized elsewhere in these rules.

(d) Closing by Staff Counsel and Committee Chair. If staff counsel and a District Committee chair concur in a finding that the case should be closed without a finding of unlicensed practice of law, the complaint may be closed on such finding without reference to the District Committee or Standing Committee.

(e) Referral to Staff Counsel for Opening. A complaint received by a District Committee or Standing Committee member directly from a complainant shall be reported to staff counsel for docketing and assignment of a case number. Should the District Committee or Standing Committee member decide that the facts, if proven, would not constitute the unlicensed practice of law, the District Committee or Standing Committee member shall forward this finding to staff counsel along with the complaint for notification to the complainant as outlined above. Formal investigation by a District Committee may proceed after the matter has been referred to staff counsel for docketing.

Adopted effective February 7, 2001.

CHAPTER 6. PROCEDURES FOR INVESTIGATION

RULE 14-6.1. HEARINGS

(a) Conduct of Proceedings. The proceedings of District Committees and the Standing Committee when hearings are held may be informal in nature and the committees shall not be bound by the rules of evidence. Committee deliberations shall be closed.

(b) Taking Testimony. Counsel for the Bar, Staff counsel, the Standing Committee, each District Committee, and members thereof conducting investigations are empowered to take and have transcribed the testimony and evidence of witnesses. If the testimony is recorded stenographically or otherwise, the witness shall be sworn by any person authorized by law to administer oaths.

(c) Rights and Responsibilities of Respondent. The respondent may be required to appear and to produce evidence as any other witness unless the respondent claims a privilege or right properly available to the respondent under applicable federal or state law. The respondent may be accompanied by counsel.

(d) Rights of Complaining Witness. The complaining witness is not a party to the investigative proceeding although the complainant may be called as a witness should the matter come before a Judge. The complainant may be granted the right to be present at any District Committee hearing when the respondent is present before the committee. The complaining witness shall have no right to appeal the finding of the District Committee.

Adopted effective February 7, 2001.

RULE 14-6.2. SUBPOENAS

(a) Issuance by Superior Court. Upon receiving a written application of the chair of the Standing Committee or of a District Committee or staff counsel alleging facts indicating that a person or entity is or may be practicing law without a license and that the issuance of a subpoena is necessary for the investigation of such unlicensed practice, the clerk of the Superior Court in which the committee is located shall issue subpoenas in the name of the Chief Judge of the Superior Court for the attendance of any person and production of books and records before staff counsel or the investigating District Committee or any member thereof at the time and place within its district designated in such application. Such subpoenas shall be returnable to the Superior Court of the residence or place of business of the person subpoenaed. A like subpoena shall issue upon application by any person or entity under investigation.

(b) Failure to Comply. Failure to comply with any subpoena shall constitute a contempt of court and may be punished by the Superior Court that issued the subpoena or where the contemnor may be found. The Superior Court shall have the power to enter such orders as may be necessary for the enforcement of the subpoena.

Adopted effective February 7, 2001.

RULE 14–6.3. RECOMMENDATIONS AND DISPOSITION OF COMPLAINTS

(a) District Committee Action. Upon concluding its investigation, the District Committee shall forward a report to staff counsel regarding the disposition of those cases closed, those cases where a cease and desist affidavit has been accepted, and those cases where litigation is recommended. A majority of those present is required for all District Committee recommendations; however, the vote may be taken by mail, telephone, fax, e-mail or other means rather than at a formal meeting. All recommendations for litigation under these rules shall be reviewed by the Standing Committee for final approval prior to initiating litigation.

(b) Action by Staff Counsel. Staff counsel shall review the disposition reports of the District Committee. If staff counsel objects to any action taken by the District Committee, staff counsel shall forward such objection to the District Committee within 10 business days of receipt of the District Committee report. Staff counsel shall place the action and objection before the Standing Committee for review at its next scheduled meeting. The Standing Committee shall review the District Committee action and the objection, and shall vote on the final disposition of the case. Once a case is closed or a cease and desist affidavit is accepted by the District Committee or by the Standing Committee, staff counsel shall inform the complainant and, if contacted, the respondent of the disposition of the complaint.

Adopted effective February 7, 2001.

CHAPTER 7. PROCEEDINGS BEFORE A JUDGE

RULE 14–7.1. PROCEEDINGS FOR INJUNCTIVE RELIEF

(a) Filing Complaints. In accordance with OCGA § 15–19–58, complaints for civil injunctive relief shall be by petition filed in the Superior Court in which the respondent resides or where venue might otherwise be proper by the State Bar of Georgia in its name.

(b) Petitions for Injunctive Relief. Except as provided in sub-paragraphs (1) through (7) of this Rule 14–7.1 (b), such petition shall be processed in the Superior Court in substantial compliance with Georgia law:

(1) The petition shall not be framed in technical language, but shall with reasonable clarity set forth the facts constituting the unlicensed practice of law. A demand for relief may be included in the petition but shall not be required.

(2) The Superior Court, upon consideration of any petition so filed, may issue its order to show cause directed to the respondent commanding the respondent to show cause, if there be any, why the respondent should not be enjoined from the unlicensed practice of law alleged, and further requiring the respondent to file with the Superior Court and serve upon staff counsel within 30 days after service on the respondent of the petition and order to show cause a written answer admitting or denying each of the matters set forth in the petition. The order and petition shall be served upon the respondent in the manner provided for service of process by Georgia law, and service of all other pleadings shall be governed by the procedures applicable under Georgia law.

(3) If no response or defense is filed within the time permitted, the allegations of the petition shall be taken as true for purposes of that action. The Superior Court will then, upon its motion or upon motion of any party, decide the case upon its merits, granting such relief and issuing such order as might be appropriate.

(4) If a response or defense filed by a respondent raises no issue of material fact, any party, upon motion, may request summary judgment and the Superior Court may rule thereon as a matter of law.

(5) The Superior Court may, upon its motion or upon motion of any party, enter a judgment on the pleadings or conduct a hearing with regard to the allegations contained in the petition.

(6) Subpoenas for the attendance of witnesses and the production of documentary evidence shall be issued in the name of the Superior Court upon request of a party. Failure or refusal to comply with any subpoena shall be contempt of court.

(7) The Georgia Rules of Civil Procedure, including those provisions pertaining to discovery, not inconsistent with these rules shall apply in injunctive proceedings before the Judge. The powers and jurisdiction generally reposed in the Superior Court under those rules may in this action be exercised by the Judge. The State Bar of Georgia may in every case amend its petition one time as a matter of right, within 60 days after the filing of the petition. All proceedings under these rules shall be heard by a Judge sitting without a jury. There shall be no right to a trial by jury with regard to any proceeding conducted under these rules.

(c) Judge's Order.

(1) At the conclusion of the hearing, the Judge shall determine as a matter of fact and law whether the respondent has engaged in the unlicensed practice of law, whether the respondent's activities should be enjoined by appropriate order, whether costs should be awarded, and whether further relief shall be granted. Copies of the Judge's order shall be served upon all parties.

(2) The Judge shall have discretion to recommend the assessment of costs. Taxable costs of the proceeding shall include only:

(A) investigative costs;

(B) court reporters' fees;

(C) copy costs;

(D) telephone charges;

(E) fees for translation services;

(F) witness expenses, including travel and out-of-pocket expenses;

(G) travel and out-of-pocket expenses of the Judge; and

(H) any other costs which may properly be taxed in civil litigation.

(3) Should the parties enter into a stipulated injunction prior to the hearing, the stipulation shall be filed with the Judge. The Judge may approve the stipulation or reject the stipulation and schedule a hearing as provided elsewhere in these rules.

(d) Review by the Supreme Court of Georgia.

(1) Objections to the order of the Judge shall be filed with the Court by any party aggrieved, within 30 days after the filing of the order. If the objector desires, a brief or memorandum of law in support of the objections may be filed at the time the objections are filed. Any other party may file a responsive brief or memorandum of law within 20 day of service of the objector's brief or memorandum of law. The objector may file a reply brief or memorandum of law within 10 days of service of the opposing party's responsive brief or memorandum of law. Oral argument will be allowed at the court's discretion.

(2) Upon the expiration of the time to file objections to the Judge's order, the Court shall review the order of the Judge, together with any briefs or memoranda of law or objections filed in support of or opposition to such order. After review, the Court shall determine as a matter of law whether the respondent has engaged in the unlicensed practice of law, whether the respondent's activities should be enjoined by appropriate order, whether costs should be awarded, and whether further relief shall be granted.

(e) Issuance of Preliminary or Temporary Injunction. Nothing set forth in this rule shall be construed to limit the authority of the Superior Court, upon proper application, to issue a preliminary or temporary injunction, or at any stage of the proceedings to enter any such order as the Superior Court deems proper when public harm or the possibility thereof is made apparent to the Superior Court, in order that such harm may be summarily prevented or speedily enjoined.

Adopted effective February 7, 2001.

CHAPTER 8. CONFIDENTIALITY

RULE 14–8.1. FILES

(a) Files Are Property of Bar. All matters, including files, preliminary investigation reports, interoffice memoranda, records of investigations, and the records in trials and other proceedings under these rules, except those unlicensed practice of law matters conducted in Superior Courts, are property of the State Bar of Georgia.

(b) Limitations on Disclosure. Any material provided to or promulgated by the State Bar of Georgia that is confidential under applicable law shall remain confidential and shall not be disclosed except as authorized by the applicable law.

Adopted effective February 7, 2001.

CHAPTER 9. ADVISORY OPINIONS

RULE 14–9.1. PROCEDURES FOR ISSUANCE OF ADVISORY OPINIONS ON THE UNLICENSED PRACTICE OF LAW

(a) Definitions.

(1) *Committee.* The Standing Committee as constituted according to the directives contained in these rules.

(2) *Petitioner.* An individual or organization seeking guidance as to the applicability, in a hypothetical situation, of the state's prohibitions against the unlicensed practice of law.

(3) *Public Notice.* Publication in a newspaper of general circulation in the county in which the hearing will be held and in the Georgia Bar Journal.

(4) *Court.* The Supreme Court of Georgia (or such other court in the state of Georgia as the Supreme Court may designate).

(b) Requests for Advisory Opinions. The Committee shall respond to written requests from all persons and entities seeking advisory opinions concerning activities that may constitute the unlicensed practice of law. Such requests shall be in writing and addressed to the State Bar of Georgia. The request for an advisory opinion shall state in detail all operative facts upon which the request for opinion is based and contain the name and address of the petitioner.

(c) Limitations on Opinions. No opinion shall be rendered with respect to any case or controversy pending in any court in this jurisdiction and no informal opinion shall be issued except as provided in Rule 14–9.1(g)(1).

(d) Services of Voluntary Counsel. The Committee shall be empowered to request and accept the voluntary services of a person licensed to practice in this state when the Committee deems it advisable to receive written or oral advice regarding the question presented by the petitioner.

(e) Conflict of Interest. Committee members shall not participate in any matter in which they have either a material pecuniary interest that would be affected by a proposed advisory opinion or Committee recommendation or any other conflict of interest that should prevent them from participating. However, no action of the Committee will be invalid where full disclosure has been made and the Committee has not decided that the member's participation was improper.

(f) Notice, Appearance, and Service.

(1) At least 30 days in advance of the Committee meeting at which initial action is to be taken with respect to a potential advisory opinion, the Committee shall give public notice of the date, time, and place of the meeting, state the question presented, and invite written comments on the question. On the announced date the Committee shall hold a public hearing at which any person affected shall be entitled to present oral testimony and be represented by counsel. Oral testimony by other persons may be allowed by the Committee at its discretion. At the time of or prior to the hearing any other person shall be entitled to file written testimony on the issue before the Committee. Additional procedures not inconsistent with this rule may be adopted by the Committee.

(2) The Committee shall issue either a written proposed advisory opinion, or a letter that declines to issue an opinion, or an informal opinion as provided in Rule 14–9.1(g)(1). No other form of communication shall be deemed to be an advisory opinion.

(3) A proposed advisory opinion shall be in writing and shall bear a date of issuance. The proposed opinion shall prominently bear a title indicating that it is a proposed advisory opinion and a disclaimer stating that it is only an interpretation of the law and does not constitute final court action. The Committee shall arrange for the publication of notice of filing the proposed advisory opinion and a summary thereof in the Georgia Bar Journal within a reasonable time. Interested parties shall be furnished a copy of the full opinion upon request.

(g) Service and Judicial Review of Proposed Advisory Opinions.

(1) In the case of any proposed advisory opinion in which the Standing Committee concludes that the conduct in question is not the unlicensed practice of law, it shall decide, by a vote of a majority of the Committee members present, either to publish the advisory opinion as provided in Rule 14–9.1(f)(3) as an informal advisory opinion, or to file a copy of the opinion with the Court as provided in Rule 14–9.1(g)(2).

(2) In the case of any proposed advisory opinion in which the Standing Committee concludes that the conduct in question constitutes or would constitute the unlicensed practice of law, the Committee shall file a copy of the opinion and all materials considered by the Committee in adopting the opinion with the clerk of the Court. The advisory opinion, together with notice of the filing thereof, shall be furnished by certified mail to the petitioner. Unless the Court grants review as provided hereinafter, the opinion shall be binding only on the Committee, the State Bar of Georgia, and the petitioner, and not on the Supreme Court, which shall treat the opinion as persuasive authority only.

(3) Within 20 days of the filing of the Advisory Opinion or the date the publication is mailed to the members of the Bar, whichever is later, the State Bar of Georgia or the petitioner may file a petition for discretionary review thereof with the Court, copies of which shall be served on the Committee. The petition shall designate the Advisory Opinion sought to be reviewed and shall concisely state the manner in which the petitioner is aggrieved. If the Court grants the petition for discretionary review or decides to review the opinion on its own motion, the record shall consist of the comments received by the, Committee. The State Bar of Georgia and the petitioner shall follow the briefing schedule set forth in Supreme Court Rule 10, counting from the date of the order granting review. The Committee may file a responsive brief, and any other interested person may seek leave of the Court to file and serve a brief, whether in support of or in opposition to the opinion. Oral argument will be allowed at the Court's discretion. The Rules of the Supreme Court of Georgia shall otherwise govern the methods of filing, service, and argument. The final determination may be either by written opinion or by order of the Supreme Court and

shall state whether the Advisory Opinion is approved, modified, or disapproved, or shall provide for such other final disposition as is appropriate.

(4) If the Court declines to review the Advisory Opinion, it shall be binding only on the Committee, the State Bar of Georgia, and the petitioner, and not on the Supreme Court, which shall treat the opinion as persuasive authority only. If the Court grants review and disapproves the opinion, it shall have absolutely no effect and shall not constitute either persuasive or binding authority. If the Court approves or modifies the opinion, it shall constitute binding precedent and shall be published in the official Georgia Court and Bar Rules manual. The Supreme Court shall accord such approved or modified opinion the same precedential authority given to the regularly published judicial opinions of the Court. There shall be no further review of the opinion except as granted by the Supreme Court in its discretion, upon petition to the Supreme Court.

Adopted effective February 7, 2001; amended effective July 1, 2002.

CHAPTER 10. IMMUNITY

RULE 14–10.1. GENERALLY

The members of the Standing Committee and District Committees, as well as staff persons and appointed voluntary counsel assisting those committees, including, but not limited to, staff counsel, Counsel for the Bar and investigators; and the State Bar of Georgia, its officers and employees, members of the Executive Committee, and members of the Board of Governors, shall have absolute immunity from civil liability for all acts in the course of their official duties.

Adopted effective February 7, 2001.

JDPP INTERNAL OPERATING PROCEDURES

1. Judicial District Professionalism Program Committees.

(a) The Judicial District Professionalism Program (hereinafter "JDPP") will be comprised of committees of Board of Governors members from each of Georgia's Judicial Districts.

(b) Each Judicial District Professionalism Committee (hereinafter "JDPC") shall consist of the current members of the Board (of Governors) of the State Bar, as described in Part I, Chapter 3 of the Bar Rules and Article III of the Bylaws, from a particular Judicial District.

(c) The JDPC members for each of the Judicial Districts will select one or more State and/or Superior Court judge to serve as JDPC advisors within each district.

(d) The longest serving member on the Board (of Governors) within each Judicial District shall serve as the chair for that district unless said representative declines to serve or a majority of the JDPC members vote to have someone else serve as chair.

(e) In the event there is a tie for the longest serving Board (of Governors) representative, the JDPC will elect a chair from among the members.

(f) Each JDPC may act through panels or subcommittees if it so elects.

2. Judicial Advisors.

(a) The judicial advisors shall be selected to serve at the beginning of the State Bar year during the first JDPC meeting following the Board of Governors meeting held in conjunction with the Annual Meeting of the State Bar.

(b) The judge's actual involvement in counseling with members of the bench and bar will be determined on a case by case basis. In some situations where appropriate, the JDPC might determine it best for the judicial advisor to approach other judges about questionable conduct or practices without the involvement of other JDPC members.

3. Oversight of the JDPP.

(a) The advisory and oversight responsibility for the JDPP shall be vested in the Bench and Bar Committee.

(b) The Committee shall have authority to adopt additional operating procedures for the administration of the program, which are not otherwise inconsistent with the Rules.

(c) The JDPP shall operate under the supervision of the Executive Director of the State Bar.

(d) The Bench and Bar Committee shall report as needed to the Board of Governors regarding the JDPP and present recommendations regarding its continued operation or modification. Each JDPC shall furnish statistical data to the Bench and Bar Committee to assist its evaluation of the JDPC.

4. Scope of JDPP.

(a) The JDPP shall promote professionalism within the legal profession through increased communication, education, and the informal use of local peer influence to alter unprofessional and uncivil conduct.

(b) The JDPP shall not deal with lawyer/client disputes, lawyer/employee disputes, lawyer/vendor disputes, or with violations of the Code of Judicial Conduct or of Part IV (Discipline) of the Rules and Regulations for the Organization and Government of the State Bar of Georgia.

(c) The JDPP should also serve the mentor function of providing guidance in "best practices" when approached by lawyers and judges.

(d) For purposes of these Rules, inquiry shall mean any inquiry concerning unprofessional conduct, as defined herein or in any Rules or operating procedures adopted by the Bench and Bar Committee, but shall not include any disciplinary charge, ethics violation, criminal conduct, or any other matter which falls under the provisions of Part IV (Discipline) of the Rules and Regulations for the organization and Government of the State Bar of Georgia or the Code of Judicial Conduct.

(e) JDPP committees may address the following conduct by State Bar members:

Unprofessional Judicial Conduct

(1) Incivility, bias or conduct unbecoming a judge;

(2) Lack of appropriate respect or deference;

(3) Failure to adhere to Uniform Rules;

(4) Excessive delay;

(5) Consistent lack of preparation;

(6) Other conduct deemed professionally inappropriate by each JDPC with the advice of the judicial advisors.

Unprofessional Lawyer Conduct

(1) Lack of appropriate respect or deference;

(2) Abusive discovery practices;

(3) Incivility, bias or conduct unbecoming a lawyer;

(4) Consistent lack of preparation;

(5) Communication problems;

(6) Deficient practice skills;

(7) Other conduct deemed professionally inappropriate by each JDPC with the advice of the judicial advisors.

(f) Inquiries from only lawyers or judges shall be referred to the JDPP. Inquiries from clients or other members of the public shall be handled by the Consumer Assistance Program or other appropriate State Bar programs. Inquiries or requests for assistance relating to pending litigation or current transactional matters are better left to the judicial process or the negotiations of the parties; consequently, any JDPC response to such requests should generally be delayed until the conclusion of the matter.

5. Procedures.

(a) Inquiries and requests for assistance shall be directed to a member of the JDPC or staff who shall forward the inquiry to the appropriate JDPC chair.

(b) Upon receiving an inquiry, the JDPC chair shall either call a committee meeting to address the inquiry or refer the matter to a subcommittee appointed by the chair for the purpose of considering the inquiry and determining whether to approach the inquiring party and the party against whom the inquiry is addressed in an effort to resolve the matter informally.

(c) The JDPC members shall have the authority to contact and counsel the lawyer or judge involved to determine if the inquiry can be resolved in an informal method either through communications with the JDPC members or by referral to other State Bar programs including, but not limited to, the Consumer Assistance Program, Fee Arbitration Program, Client's Security Fund, Law Practice Management Program, and the Lawyer Assistance Program or to the Judicial Qualifications Commission.

(d) Each JDPC shall have independent authority to consider whether to consider and how to resolve inquiries. The JDPC may determine that certain inquiries do not merit consideration or counseling while others may warrant extensive consideration and counseling.

(e) The actions of each JDPC as they relate to a specific inquiry are confidential and shall not be reported to the inquiring party or any other person or entity.

(f) JDPC members shall follow written guidelines developed and established by the Bench and Bar Committee, with the advice and counsel of the Bar Counsel and Executive Director of the State Bar, and approved by the Executive Committee, Board of Governors of the State Bar and Executive Committee of the Council of Superior Court Judges.

6. Inquiries Involving Lawyers and Judges Outside Their Judicial District.

A JDPC may encounter or receive an inquiry involving lawyers and judges from outside their Judicial District. In such situations, local committee members receiving the inquiry should refer the matter to the JDPC chair in the district where the lawyer or judge against whom the inquiry is addressed maintains his or her principal office.

7. Records.

Each JDPC shall maintain and report data about the types of matters and inquiries it receives and resolves to the Executive Director of the State Bar, the President of the Council of Superior Court Judges and Bench and Bar Committee. The purpose for maintaining such records is to identify problems that can be subjects of Continuing Legal Education or Continuing Judicial Education programming and other preventive programs. Furthermore, information on the results of the JDPCs efforts will help determine the program's effectiveness. JDPC records shall be kept for statistical purposes only and shall not contain the names of any person involved in a JDPC inquiry. Only file numbers and raw statistical data shall be maintained.

8. Promoting Professionalism.

(a) The JDPC members shall establish an annual professionalism award for the member in their local Judicial District who demonstrates the professionalism others should strive to emulate.

(b) Committee members shall also promote professionalism by preparing and publishing memorial tributes to lawyers and judges in their local area who pass away during the bar year. These tributes shall be published in local bar newsletters and/or forwarded to local newspapers recognizing our deceased colleagues for their positive contributions to our profession.

(c) The State Bar Communications Director and the Chief Justice's Commission on Professionalism shall work with each JDPC to help promote their activities, programs and awards.

9. Training for Judicial District Professionalism Committees.

An orientation program shall be developed by the State Bar and the Chief Justice's Commission on Professionalism for the purpose of training Board (of Governors) members on how to handle professionalism inquiries from members of the bench and bar. The training program may be given in conjunction with a Board of Governors meeting, and subsequent programs could be given each year following the annual meeting for all newly elected Board members.

Adopted effective February 24, 2000.

INDEX TO STATE BAR RULES AND REGULATIONS

*

RULES GOVERNING ADMISSION TO THE PRACTICE OF LAW

Effective October 5, 1988

Including Amendments Received Through November 1, 2006

Research Note

Use WESTLAW *to find cases citing a rule. In addition, use* WESTLAW *to search for specific terms or to update a rule; see the GA–RULES and GA–ORDERS Scope screens for further information.*

Amendments to these rules are published, as received, in the South Eastern Reporter 2d *and* Georgia Cases *advance sheets.*

Table of Rules

INTRODUCTION

In accordance with its statutory and inherent authority, the Supreme Court of Georgia hereby adopts the following Rules Governing Admission to the Practice of Law in Georgia.

PART A. BOARD TO DETERMINE FITNESS OF BAR APPLICANTS

SECTION 1. MEMBERS, TERMS, OATH

(a) The Board to Determine Fitness of Bar Applicants shall be composed of nine members, five attorney and three non-attorney members and the chair of the Board of Bar Examiners or his or her designee (who may be a current or past member of the Board of Bar Examiners) ex officio. The five attorney members and three non-attorney members shall be appointed by the Court for terms of five years each. The attorney members shall be learned and experienced members of the State Bar of Georgia of generally recognized ability and integrity. Appointments to fill vacancies other than by the expiration of a member's term shall be made for the unexpired term. The Court shall designate one member as chair. The chair shall be selected by the members of the Board to serve for a term of four years. The vice-chair shall be selected by the Board and serve for a term of four years. In the absence or disqualification of the chair, the vice-chair shall exercise the authority and duties of the chair. Each member of the Board shall take and subscribe an oath to faithfully, carefully and impartially perform all the duties imposed upon him or her, which oath shall be entered upon the minutes of the Court.

(b) Meetings of the Board shall be called by the chair at such place or places as may be convenient. Attorney members of the Board are excused from court engagements while in attendance at any meeting of the Board called by the chair provided reasonable and timely notice of such meeting is conveyed to the court and to opposing counsel.

Amended May 3, 1989; amended effective May 7, 1992.

SECTION 2. DUTIES

The Board shall inquire into the character and fitness of applicants for admission to the practice of law and shall certify as fit to practice law those applicants who have established to the Board's satisfaction that they possess the integrity and character requisite to be members of the Bar of Georgia. The Board shall pass upon applications at any special or regular meeting of the Board at which a quorum is present. A quorum shall consist of a majority of the members, and action on any matter may be taken by a majority vote of a quorum.

SECTION 3. APPLICATION FORMS

The Board shall prepare and publish application forms, shall prescribe the information which must be furnished by applicants and shall establish requirements for periodic updating of applications. It is the obligation of the applicant to submit a complete, accurate and timely application in conformity with these **Rules. Applications for Certification of Fitness to Practice Law must be typewritten.**

Amended effective August 8, 1996.

SECTION 4. APPLICATION DEADLINE

(a) Applications for Certification of Fitness to Practice Law must be filed with the Office of Bar Admissions no later than the first Wednesday of July for consideration for the bar examination to be administered the following February and no later than the first Wednesday of December for consideration for the bar examination to be administered the following July. Unless an applicant's fitness to practice law is called into question, he or she will be permitted to apply to the Board of Bar Examiners to take the bar examination as requested.

(b) Applications for Certification of Fitness to Practice Law filed between the first Wednesday in July and the first Wednesday in October for consideration for the bar examination to be administered the following February and applications filed between the first Wednesday in December and the first Wednesday in March for consideration for the bar examination to be administered the following July will be accepted for the requested examination if accompanied by a non-refundable late fee of $200, in addition to the regular fee prescribed by these **Rules**. Applications so filed will be placed for processing in order of receipt, but no processing will be begun until processing of all applications filed pursuant to the deadline set forth in subparagraph (a) above has begun. If appropriate, the Board may issue a temporary certification, valid for the requested examination only, which will permit the applicant to apply to the Board of Bar Examiners to take the examination while the investigation of the applicant's fitness to practice law is completed. An applicant who files pursuant to this subparagraph agrees that his or her bar examination results will not be released to him or her unless and until such time as the Board of Bar Examiners is informed by the Board to Determine Fitness of Bar Applicants that the applicant has been certified as fit to practice law.

(c) Applications filed after the first Wednesday in July for consideration for the bar examination to be administered the following February and applications filed after the first Wednesday in December for consideration for the bar examination to be administered the following July which are not accompanied by the fee described in subparagraph (b) above will be treated as if filed for the next succeeding examination.

Amended effective November 8, 1990; December 9, 1993; amended October 4, 2000, applicable to February 2002 bar examination.

SECTION 5. APPLICATION FEES

Late fees may be applicable; refer to Part B, Section 4 (b).

(a) Filings made prior to the award of the first professional degree in law.... $300
(b) Filings made between the award of the first professional degree in law and within one year thereof $450
(c) Filings made more than one year after the award of the first professional degree in law $600
(d) Applications for Attorneys' Examination $800
(e) Applications for Readmission following disbarment by the State Bar of Georgia.......................... $2500
(f) Applications for Readmission after voluntary resignation from the State Bar of Georgia $600
(g) Applications for Reinstatement following termination from State Bar of Georgia due to non-payment of dues $600
(h) Applications for renewal of certification $100

Provided a request in writing for withdrawal of his or her Application for Certification of Fitness to Practice Law is filed within 15 work days of the date of receipt of the application by the Office of Bar Admissions, the Board to Determine Fitness of Bar Applicants shall refund ⅔ of the filing fee paid by the applicant; provided, however, that no part of the late filing fees described in Section 4, above, may be refunded.

Amended effective July 1, 1989; November 8, 1990; amended effective March 1, 2000.

SECTION 6. INVESTIGATION OF APPLICANTS

(a) Prior to certifying an applicant as having the integrity and character requisite to be a member of the Bar of Georgia, the Board shall make such investigation as it deems necessary into his or her character, reputation and background. Each applicant shall provide written authority to the Board to conduct such investigation, and each applicant shall authorize all persons with information about him or her to furnish the Board with such information and documents as it may request. The authority granted by an applicant shall expire upon the applicant's admission to the practice of law in Georgia, denial of his or her application, or upon the applicant's written withdrawal of his or her application.

(b) The Board shall contact the Chief Judge of the superior courts of each judicial circuit in Georgia where an applicant has resided, attended school, or been employed during the five years next preceding the filing of his or her application and request information or recommendations concerning the applicant as the judge desires to furnish. Further, the Board may provide for the appointment of local committees on character and fitness to investigate the background of any applicant who has worked, resided or attended school in the judicial circuit. The reports of local committees shall include the facts found during their investigations but shall not include any recommendations.

(c) A fingerprint check may be made of all applicants.

Amended effective December 9, 1993.

SECTION 7. INFORMAL CONFERENCES, PERMISSIVE WITHDRAWAL OF APPLICATION, REAPPLICATION

(a) If, during the investigation of an applicant, information is obtained which raises a question as to the applicant's character or fitness to practice law, the Board may require the applicant to appear, together with his or her counsel if he or she so desires, before the Board or any designated member for an informal conference concerning such information.

(b) If after such a conference, the Board believes that certification of fitness to practice law would be inappropriate, it may, in lieu of denying certification, permit the applicant to withdraw his or her application upon the understanding that after a period of rehabilitation, to be no less than three years, it will accept a new application from the applicant, if it is accompanied by the appropriate initial filing fee.

Amended effective August 8, 1996.

SECTION 8. HEARINGS

(a) Prior to finally determining that an applicant shall not be certified as fit to practice law in this state, the Board shall notify the applicant by certified mail that it has entered a tentative order of denial of his or her Application for Certification and advise the applicant of his or her right to a formal hearing with respect to the reasons for the Board's tentative denial. Within ten business days of receipt of this notice, the applicant shall file his or her written request for a formal hearing with the Office of Bar Admissions. If no request is filed within ten business days, the Board's tentative order shall become final and non-appealable. If a request is filed, the Board shall prepare specifications of the reasons for the Board's tentative order and mail them by certified mail to the applicant. Within 20 days of receipt of the specifications the applicant shall file his or her answers thereto, and if any specification is not denied, it shall be deemed to have been admitted. In addition to answering the specifications, the applicant may assert any affirmative defenses he or she may have and/or any matters in mitigation he or she may wish to have considered. The hearing may be held before a single attorney member of the Board appointed by the chair or before the Board as a whole or before a member of the State Bar of Georgia appointed as hearing officer by the Court at the Board's request. The applicant may be represented by counsel, and the hearing shall be reported and transcribed by a certified court reporter.

(b) Witnesses may be subpoenaed by the Board and shall be subpoenaed by the Board upon the applicant's request as in civil cases in state courts of record. In case of a refusal of a witness to attend the hearing, to produce documentary or other evidence or to testify, the Board shall certify the failure to the Court, and the witness shall be dealt with as for a contempt. Witnesses shall be entitled to receive the fees and mileage provided for by law for witnesses in civil cases.

(c) Prior to the hearing, written interrogatories may be served upon any witness not within the state of Georgia. The answers to the written interrogatories and any exhibits submitted with them shall be admissible as evidence at the hearing. At the hearing, the hearing officer shall not be bound to strictly observe the rules of evidence but shall consider all evidence deemed relevant to the specifications and the answers, affirmative defenses and matters in mitigation raised by the Board and the applicant in an effort to discover the truth without undue embarrassment to the applicant; provided, however, the Board's investigatory file with respect to matters not placed in issue by the specifications, answers, affirmative defenses and matters in mitigation shall not be subject to discovery or introduction into evidence. The hearing officer shall make written findings of fact and recommendations to the Board, which, however, shall not be binding upon the Board.

(d) If after review of the recommendations of the hearing officer the Board determines not to certify the applicant as fit to practice law in Georgia, it shall so notify the applicant in writing by certified mail giving its reasons for its decision.

SECTION 9. REAPPLICATION AFTER DENIAL

The Board shall not accept a new application from an applicant who has been denied certification of fitness to practice law until three years have elapsed from the date a tentative order of denial becomes final, a final decision is issued after a hearing and not appealed or a final decision is affirmed by the Court, whichever date is applicable.

Renumbered from Pt. A, § 10, effective March 22, 2001.

SECTION 10. READMISSION OF DISBARRED LAWYERS

(a) Any applicant who was formerly a member of the State Bar of Georgia and who was disbarred, voluntarily surrendered his or her license or was removed from membership in the State Bar of Georgia pursuant to Bar Rule 4–104 may apply for readmission five years after the date of the court order of disbarment or the court order accepting the surrender of the license.

(b) The applicant seeking readmission shall file a Fitness Application as provided in Part A, Sections 3 and 4. The fee required for such application shall be $2500.

(c) The applicant seeking readmission shall also file with the Fitness Application a full and complete copy of the proceedings in the disciplinary matter which led to the disbarment or voluntary surrender of the license.

(d) The Fitness Board, in considering the applicant's fitness for readmission shall:

(1) provide notice to the State Bar of Georgia of the application for readmission and provide an opportunity for the State Bar to present information it deems relevant to the applicant's fitness for readmission;

(2) give notice to the membership of the local bar where the applicant formerly practiced (through notice to an official of the local bar association) and to the Chief Judge of that Circuit of the applicant's intention to seek readmission;

(3) give notice to the public in the area where the applicant formerly practiced by placing a notice in a newspaper serving that locality;

(4) confirm with the Client Security Fund that restitution has been made of the amounts paid as a result of the applicant's conduct; and

(5) follow all the other procedures for certification designated in this Part.

(e) An applicant who is seeking reinstatement to the State Bar of Georgia pursuant to Bar Rule 1–501 (b) shall file a fitness application after completing the requirements contained in that Bar Rule and shall not be required to take the bar examination. An applicant who has been terminated by the State Bar pursuant to Bar Rule 1–501 (c) is required to comply with the provisions of that Bar Rule and is required to take and pass the bar examination before being readmitted.

Adopted effective March 1, 2000; renumbered from Pt. A, §11, effective March 22, 2001.

SECTION 11. CERTIFICATIONS OF FITNESS TO PRACTICE LAW

Upon being satisfied that an applicant possesses the integrity and character requisite to be a member of the Bar of Georgia, the Board shall certify the applicant as fit to practice law. Certifications may be in the form of a letter to the applicant which shall include the certification's expiration date, which shall be five (5) years after the date issued; however, certifications issued by the Board prior to January 1, 1984 or by judges of the superior courts prior to July 1, 1977 shall be valid for a period of five (5) years from the date issued and until a date specified by the Board in its notification to the applicant that he or she must apply for renewal. Certifications may be renewed upon application to the Board not less than three months prior to the certificate's stated expiration date or, in case of certifications issued prior to January 1, 1984, not less than three months prior to the date specified by the Board in its renewal notification. Applications for renewal of certification shall be on such forms, including an original application form, as the Board may determine and shall be accompanied by a fee of $100. The Board shall conduct such investigation as it deems appropriate in the circumstances, and the Board may renew, decline to renew or take such other action with respect to renewal as it might take with an original application. An applicant for renewal shall have the same rights with respect to conferences, hearings and appeals as would an original applicant. If application for renewal of certification is not made in accordance with the deadlines specified in this section and the applicant thereafter wishes to apply to take the bar examination, he or she, to be eligible to apply to the Board of Bar Examiners to take the examination, must file a new, initial Application for Certification with the Board to Determine Fitness of Bar Applicants and must pay the appropriate fee required by these **Rules**.

Renumbered from Pt. A, § 12, effective March 22, 2001.

SECTION 12. REVIEW OF CERTIFICATIONS PRIOR TO ADMISSION TO THE PRACTICE OF LAW

Certifications of fitness to practice law shall be tentative until an applicant is actually admitted to the practice of law and may be reviewed by the Board upon its own motion or upon receiving a request for further review from the Board of Bar Examiners. In any case where a further review is deemed necessary, the Board shall suspend the applicant's certification and shall so notify by certified mail the applicant and the Board of Bar Examiners which thereafter shall not admit the applicant to an examination, or release the result of an examination taken prior to the receipt of such notice until the Board to Determine Fitness of Bar Applicants notifies it that the applicant's certification of fitness to practice law has been reinstated.

Renumbered from Pt. A, § 13, effective March 22, 2001.

SECTION 13. AUTHORITY OF THE CHAIR

Any action which may be taken by the Board may, when the Board is not in session and time is of the essence, be taken by the chair alone who shall promptly notify the members of the Board of such action, which action shall be subject to confirmation at the next following regular meeting of the Board.

Renumbered from Pt. A, § 14, effective March 22, 2001.

SECTION 14. COMPENSATION AND EXPENSES

The members of the Board, attorneys appointed as hearing officers by the Court and members of local committees on character and fitness appointed by the Board shall receive a reasonable fee as established by order of the Supreme Court and shall be reimbursed for their necessary travel, meal and lodging expenses incurred in the performance of their duties.

Amended effective December 10, 1997; renumbered from Pt. A, § 15, effective March 22, 2001.

PART B. BOARD OF BAR EXAMINERS

SECTION 1. BOARD OF BAR EXAMINERS

(a) The Board of Bar Examiners shall be composed of six members of the State Bar of Georgia who are learned and experienced and of generally recognized ability and integrity appointed by the Court for terms of six years each. Appointments to fill vacancies occurring other than by expiration of a term shall be for the unexpired term. Each member of the Board shall take and subscribe an oath to faithfully, carefully and impartially perform all of the duties imposed upon him or her as a member of the Board of Bar Examiners, which oath shall be entered upon the minutes of the Court. The Board shall designate one of its members as Chair.

(b) Meetings of the Board shall be called by the chair at such place or places as may be convenient. Members of the Board are excused from court engagements while in attendance at any meeting of the Board duly called by its chair provided reasonable and timely notice of such meeting is conveyed to the court and to opposing counsel.

(c) Each member of the Board shall receive a fee of $5,000 per examination. Out of this sum, members shall pay their necessary traveling and other expenses incurred in performing the duties of their office. Any reasonable and necessary expenses incurred by Examiners or Graders as a result of participating in grading workshops sponsored by the National Conference of Bar Examiners shall be reimbursed by the Office of Bar Admissions.

Amended effective December 9, 1993; May 16, 1996; August 8, 1996; amended effective with the February 2000 bar examination; amended effective September 13, 2005.

SECTION 2. APPLICATIONS FOR EXAMINATIONS

(a) An application to take the February administration of the Georgia Bar Examination must be filed with the Office of Bar Admissions not later than the first Friday of the preceding January; an application to take the July administration of the Georgia Bar Examination must be filed with the Office of Bar Admissions not later than the first Friday of the preceding June. However, any person who was unsuccessful on any examination shall be allowed ten business days from the date of the general announcement of examination results in which to file an application to take the next examination if such announcement falls on, after or within five business days prior to the application deadline provided above, and in those instances where the Board to Determine Fitness of Bar Applicants certifies an applicant as fit to practice law after the deadline for filing an application to take the examination as described above, the applicant shall be allowed ten business days from the date of his or her notification of certification in which to file an application to take the examination.

(b) Applications to take the bar examination shall be filed with the Office of Bar Admissions on a form prescribed by the Board of Bar Examiners and shall be accompanied by a fee of $75.00 payable to the Board of Bar Examiners and an additional fee payable to the National Conference of Bar Examiners. **Prior to filing such application, each applicant must obtain from the Board to Determine Fitness of Bar Applicants a certificate of fitness to practice law.** An applicant will not be allowed to file an application or take the examination who has not first received such a certificate.

Further, evidence that the applicant meets the educational requirements set forth in these Rules must be submitted contemporaneously with his or her application.

(c) All fees for the Multistate Bar Examination or the Multistate Performance Test shall be paid by the applicant to the National Conference of Bar Examiners (NCBE) as instructed by the Office of Bar Admissions.

(d) An applicant who is unsuccessful on an examination may file an application to take a subsequent bar examination without obtaining a new certificate of fitness from the Board to Determine Fitness of Bar Applicants if the certificate has not expired. Further, applicants who wish to take a subsequent examination need not resubmit evidence of meeting the educational requirements set forth in these **Rules**.

(e) An applicant who fails to timely file an application to take the bar examination or fails to submit fees to the NCBE as provided above shall nevertheless be permitted to take the examination if, within 30 days of the deadline as provided above, he or she files an application to do so and pays a late fee of $200 (for a total of $275) and submits all applicable fees to the NCBE; provided, however, that no bar examination application shall be accepted unless it is received in the Office of Bar Admissions not less than fourteen days prior to the date of the bar examination.

Amended effective June 28, 1989; amended February 15, 1990; amended effective November 8, 1990; May 16, 1996.

SECTION 3. REFUNDS

Refunds of the bar examination application fee will be made in the event an applicant is found to be ineligible to take an examination. Further, an applicant who withdraws not less than fourteen (14) days prior to an examination shall be refunded 50% of the bar application fee paid. Fees submitted to the NCBE are not refundable.

Amended effective May 16, 1996.

SECTION 4. EDUCATIONAL REQUIREMENTS

The educational requirements to take the bar examination are as follows:

(a)(1) Prior to taking the bar examination, an applicant must have been awarded an undergraduate degree (BA, BS, BBA or their equivalent) by an institution of higher learning which has been accredited by an accrediting body recognized by the Commission on Recognition of Postsecondary Accreditation (CORPA).

(2) An applicant who has been awarded an undergraduate degree (BA, BS, BBA or their equivalent) by an institution of higher learning which has not been accredited by an accrediting body recognized by CORPA shall be considered as satisfying the undergraduate educational requirement of these **Rules** if the applicant has received the first professional degree in law (JD or LLB) from a law school approved by the American Bar Association. If, however, the applicant is a graduate of a law school certified by the Georgia Board of Bar Examiners and the applicant has been awarded an undergraduate degree from an institution not recognized by CORPA, the applicant shall be considered to have satisfied the undergraduate degree requirements of these **Rules** if, prior to the date of the examination he or she wishes to take, he or she has the College Board certify to the Board of Bar Examiners that he or she has passed the College Level Examination Program (CLEP) all multiple-choice version of the General Examination in English Composition and any two of the following CLEP examinations: General Examination in Humanities; General Examination in Mathematics; General Examination in Natural Sciences; and General Examination in Social Sciences and History. The passing score for each of the general examinations shall be that scaled score which represents the 50th percentile of achievement as reported by the College Board for its 1978 reference group or such later reference group as may be established by the College Board.

(b)(1) Prior to taking the bar examination an applicant must have been awarded the first professional degree in law (JD or LLB) by a law school approved by the American Bar Association.

(2) Graduates of law schools approved by the Georgia Board of Bar Examiners but not by the American Bar Association who have been certified as fit to practice law, who satisfy the undergraduate educational requirement of these **Rules**, and who graduate from law school prior to January 1, 1998, shall be eligible to take the bar examination in the same manner and under the same conditions as are graduates of American Bar Association approved law schools.

(c) An applicant shall not be permitted to take the examination unless evidence is first received directly from the schools involved showing that he or she meets the educational requirements of these Rules. It is the responsibility of the applicant alone to insure that the evidence is received prior to the examination. The form of evidence shall be an **official transcript** from the college or university that awarded the undergraduate degree and a transcript from the law school that awarded the J.D. degree; in lieu of an official transcript of legal studies an applicant who has graduated within the six months prior to the date of the examination he or she wishes to take shall cause his or her law school to submit a certification to the effect that he or she has graduated within the six months prior to the date of the examination he or she seeks to take. However, a final transcript indicating the award of the JD degree and the date awarded must be received prior to the release of grades.

Amended effective March 3, 1994; April 25, 1994; July 1, 1995; August 8, 1996; October 4, 2000; September 26, 2002.

SECTION 5. APPROVAL AND DISAPPROVAL OF APPLICATIONS

Applications to take the bar examination which show on their face that the applicant has been certified as fit to practice law and that he or she satisfies the undergraduate and legal educational requirements of these **Rules** shall be approved by the Board of Bar Examiners or, if so designated by the Board, by the Director of Bar Admissions. Applications to take the bar examination which show on their face that the applicant has not been certified as fit to practice law and/or that he or she does not satisfy the undergraduate and/or legal educational requirements of these **Rules** shall be disapproved by the Board of Bar Examiners or, if so designated by the Board, by the Director of Bar Admissions.

SECTION 6. EXAMINATIONS

(a) The Board of Bar Examiners shall conduct two examinations each year, each of which shall be held in Atlanta or such other location as the Board may designate at least 60 days in advance of the examination. Each shall be conducted on any two or three consecutive days and may be scheduled so as to coincide with the administration of multistate examinations prepared by the National Conference of Bar Examiners.

(b) The exam shall consist of three parts: (1) four essay questions prepared by the Board of Bar Examiners; (2) the Multistate Bar Examination prepared and graded by the National Conference of Bar Examiners; and (3) the Multistate Performance Test prepared by the National Conference of Bar Examiners and graded by the Board of Bar Examiners.

(c) Essay questions prepared by the Board of Bar Examiners shall be drawn from the following list of subjects, to wit: Business Organizations; Civil Procedure; Constitutional Law; Contracts; Criminal Law and Procedure; Evidence; Family Law; Federal Practice and Procedure; Georgia Practice and Procedure; Non–Monetary Remedies; Professional Ethics; Property; Torts; Trusts, Wills and Estates; and the Uniform Commercial Code (Articles 2, 3, & 9). Applicants will be provided forty-five minutes to answer each question.

(d) The Multistate Bar Examination (MBE) shall consist of 200 multiple choice questions in the following six substantive areas of law, to wit: Constitutional Law, Contracts, Criminal Law, Evidence, Torts and Real Property.

(e) The Multistate Performance Test (MPT) shall consist of two 90 minute tasks, and the areas of law may involve any subject matter whether covered in the essay questions, Multistate Bar Examination or otherwise.

(f) Further, the Board of Bar Examiners shall require each applicant to pass the separately administered Multistate Professional Responsibility Examination (MPRE) with a scaled score of 75 or greater prior to certifying the applicant as eligible for admission to the practice of law.

(g) Copies of the Multistate Bar Examination (MBE) and the Multistate Performance Test (MPT) shall not be made public in any manner unless authorized by the National Conference of Bar Examiners. Copies of the essay questions prepared by the Board of Bar Examiners may be made public in such manner as deemed proper by said Board.

Amended effective March 26, 1992; July 1, 1995; May 16, 1996; January 1, 1999; October 1, 2003.

SECTION 7. RE–EXAMINATION

There shall be no limit on the number of times an applicant may take the examination. However, once an applicant fails the bar examination three (3) times, the applicant will not be eligible to sit for the next available examination.

If this applicant fails any subsequent examination, the applicant must sit out the next available examination.

Adopted effective July 1, 1995; amended effective July 7, 2005.

SECTION 8. GRADING OF THE EXAMINATION AND NOTIFICATION OF RESULTS

(a) An applicant shall have passed the Georgia Bar Examination if he or she obtains a total score of 270 on the exam. This score shall be the sum of the scaled score achieved on the Multistate Bar Examination (MBE), the scaled score achieved on the Multistate Performance Test (MPT) and the scaled score achieved on the essay questions prepared by the Board of Bar Examiners. If an applicant does not achieve a scaled score of 115 on the MBE, he or she will be deemed to have failed the exam and the essay and MPT answers will not be graded by the Board of Bar Examiners.

In determining whether an applicant has achieved 270 on the examination, the Board shall not use an MBE score from any prior examination, or an MBE score from an examination taken in any other jurisdiction. If an applicant achieves a total score of 265 or higher but not 270, his or her essay and MPT papers shall be regraded by the Board of Bar Examiners prior to the release of grades.

(b) Answers to the essay part of the examination and the Multistate Performance Test shall be graded by or under the direction of the Board, which shall pass upon the merits of papers submitted in answer to questions on those parts of the bar examination. If the Multistate Performance Test is used as part of the examination and if grading standards or a grading service for questions on the Multistate Performance Test are provided by or are made available under the auspices of the National Conference of Bar Examiners, the Board may rely upon such standards or service in passing upon the merits of the answers to those questions.

(c) The Board shall individually notify each bar applicant whether or not he or she passed the examination as promptly as feasible. The Board may disclose to applicants their grades on any or all parts of the examination, including, if calculated, their percentile ranking on any part of the examination. Applicant grades shall not be disclosed to any person other than the applicant except that upon the written request of an applicant, the Board may disclose the applicant's scaled and raw MBE scores to the bar examining authority of any United States jurisdiction.

(d) A bar applicant who receives a passing score on the Georgia Bar Examination, but who has not met all of the requirements of these Rules at the time of the notification of the passing score, shall have three years from the date of the notification to complete the requirements of these Rules in order to qualify for certification of eligibility for admission to the practice of law. The Board of Bar Examiners shall not issue a certificate of eligibility for admission to the practice of law to an applicant who has not completed all of the requirements of these Rules within three years of the notification that the applicant received a passing score on the Georgia Bar Examination.

Former Part B, Section 7 renumbered as Part B, Section 8 effective July 1, 1995; amended effective May 16, 1996; September 10, 2006.

SECTION 9. ANONYMITY OF EXAMINEES

The examination of each applicant shall be done in such a manner that his or her examination paper is not identifiable by name to the members of the Board of Bar Examiners or the staff of the Office of Bar Admissions. The Board shall develop, and publish before each examination, a plan to insure the anonymity of each applicant's paper, which plan shall be approved by the Supreme Court.

Former Part B, Section 8 renumbered as Part B, Section 9 effective July 1, 1995.

SECTION 10. MONITORS

The Board of Bar Examiners shall appoint a sufficient number of monitors to insure the examination is conducted in an orderly and expeditious manner and to insure no applicant gives or receives aid in taking the examination.

Former Part B, Section 9 renumbered as Part B, Section 10 effective July 1, 1995.

SECTION 11. OATH OF APPLICANT

Each applicant shall, by taking the examination, be deemed to have sworn the following with respect to each question:

> "I solemnly swear or affirm that I have no previous information as to the contents of the questions upon which I have been examined and that I have not received directly or indirectly, from any source whatever, any assistance, but that I wrote the answer exclusively from my knowledge."

Former Part B, Section 11 deleted effective August 1, 1994; former Part B, Section 10 renumbered as Section 11 effective July 1, 1995.

SECTION 12. MISCONDUCT BY APPLICANTS DURING EXAMINATION

If, during an examination, the Board has brought to its attention conduct by an applicant which may violate any law or rule governing the examination, the Board shall cause an immediate investigation to be made. If the Board determines that an applicant has violated the law or rules governing the examination, it shall immediately disqualify the applicant from the examination and certify the violations and the disqualification to the Board to Determine Fitness of Bar Applicants for its investigation. Thereafter, the Board to Determine Fitness of Bar Applicants shall determine whether the applicant's certification of fitness to practice law shall remain valid.

SECTION 13. REVIEW OF EXAMINATION ANSWERS

Neither the Board of Bar Examiners nor any member thereof shall conduct post examination interviews with applicants nor shall the Board or any member thereof regrade any applicant's answers to examination questions after the general release of grades nor shall any applicant's answers be retained beyond the commencement date of the succeeding examination. The Director of Bar Admissions may conduct post examination interviews with applicants but he shall not review examination questions or answers with an applicant, nor shall he allow inspection of either questions or answers following the giving of an examination, but an applicant may make duplicate copies of his or her answers at the time of taking the examination and may retain copies of questions with the exception of questions and answers on those portions of any examination prepared for the Board by or under the supervision of the National Conference of Bar Examiners.

SECTION 14. CERTIFICATES OF ELIGIBILITY FOR ADMISSION TO THE BAR

Upon an applicant's passing the bar examination and provided that his or her certification of fitness to practice law is current and that he or she has met all of the educational and testing requirements of these **Rules**, the Board shall issue a certification of eligibility for admission to the practice of law to the applicant. Certification may be in such form as the Board prescribes, including a letter bearing the seal of the Board and signed by the chair of the Board of Bar Examiners, or any member of the Board designated by the chair or by the Director of Bar Admissions. The applicant shall deliver the certificate to the Chief Judge of the circuit in which he or she wishes to be admitted to the Bar. Such certificate shall be valid for one year from the date of its issuance.

SECTION 15. DUTY OF JUDGES AFTER RECEIVING CERTIFICATE OF THE BOARD

The judge of the superior court, upon receiving the Board's certificate that an applicant is eligible for admission to the Bar, shall enter an order in substantially the following form:

> "At Chambers, ___ day of _________ 20 ___. It appearing from a certificate issued by the Board of Bar Examiners, that _________ is entitled to be licensed to practice law in this State upon taking the oath prescribed by law and paying the usual fee to the clerk of this court, it is ordered that upon doing so, the clerk issue a license,

authorizing such applicant to plead and practice law in all the courts of this State, except the Supreme Court and the Court of Appeals, upon compliance with the Rules of the State Bar of Georgia. It is further ordered that the certificate of the Board of Bar Examiners be filed with the Clerk, and this order and the oath as attorney be entered upon the minutes of this court.

____

Judge, Superior Court."

SECTION 16. ATTORNEY'S OATH FORM: ENTRY ON MINUTES

The oath of an attorney is as follows:

"I, __________, swear that I will truly and honestly, justly and uprightly conduct myself as a member of this learned profession and in accordance with the Georgia Rules of Professional Conduct, as an attorney and counselor, and that I will support and defend the Constitution of the United States and the Constitution of the State of Georgia. So help me God."

The oath may be taken in open court or in chambers or, if the applicant resides outside the state, before any officer authorized to administer oaths. The completed oath shall be entered on the minutes of the court as provided above.

Amended effective April 22, 2002.

SECTION 17. DUTY OF THE CLERK OF SUPERIOR COURT

Whenever there is delivered to the Clerk of the Superior Court an order for admission and the proper papers, described in Section 15, supra, the Clerk shall proceed as directed. The entries upon the minutes of the Superior Court may be made in term or in vacation.

PART C. ADMISSION ON MOTION WITHOUT EXAMINATION

SECTION 1. GENERAL

The Board of Bar Examiners may admit on motion without examination any attorney licensed in a United States jurisdiction other than Georgia if that attorney satisfies the criteria set out in Section 2 of this Part. The attorney must also be certified for fitness, pursuant to Part A of these Rules, before petitioning the Board of Bar Examiners to be admitted on motion without examination.

Adopted effective January 1, 2003.

SECTION 2. ELIGIBILITY

In order to petition the Board of Bar Examiners to be admitted without examination, an attorney licensed in a state other than Georgia must meet the following eligibility criteria. The attorney:

(a) Must meet the educational eligibility requirements established in Part B, Section 4 of these Rules, including holding a first professional degree in law (JD or LL.B) from a law school approved by the American Bar Association at the time the graduate matriculated;

(b) Has been admitted by examination to membership in the bar of the highest court of another United States jurisdiction which has comity for bar admissions purposes with the State of Georgia;

(c) Has never been denied certification of fitness to practice law in Georgia or any other state;

(d) Has never taken and failed the Georgia Bar Examination or the Georgia Attorneys' Examination;

(e) Has been primarily engaged in the active practice of law for five of the seven years immediately preceding the date upon which the application is filed;

(f) Has at all times been in good professional standing in every jurisdiction in which the applicant has been licensed to practice law;

(g) Has never been the subject of private or public professional discipline of any nature, including formal letters of admonition, in any United States jurisdiction; and

(h) Has received Certification of Fitness to Practice Law in Georgia from the Board to Determine Fitness of Bar Applicants.

Adopted effective January 1, 2003; amended effective September 10, 2006.

SECTION 3. DEFINITION OF PRACTICE OF LAW

(a) For the purposes of this Rule, the "active practice of law" shall include the following activities, if performed in a jurisdiction in which the applicant is admitted, or if performed in a jurisdiction that affirmatively permits such activity by a lawyer not admitted to practice:

(1) representation of one or more clients in the practice of law;

(2) service as a lawyer with a local, state or federal agency, including military service;

(3) teaching law at a law school approved by the American Bar Association;

(4) service as a judge in a federal, state or local court of record;

(5) service as a judicial law clerk; or

(6) service as corporate counsel.

(b) For purposes of this Rule, the "active practice of law" shall not include work that, as undertaken, constituted the unauthorized practice of law in the jurisdiction in which it was performed or in the jurisdiction in which the clients receiving the unauthorized services were located.

Adopted effective January 1, 2003.

SECTION 4. FEES AND FILING INSTRUCTIONS

(a) Applications for Certification of Fitness to Practice Law for admission pursuant to this Rule shall be made in accordance with the requirements established in Part A of these Rules and shall be accompanied by a non-refundable fee of $800.

(b) Once certified for fitness, the applicant must file a petition with the Board of Bar Examiners requesting admission on motion without examination. The petition from the applicant must contain a statement that the applicant intends to engage in the practice of law in Georgia and must be accompanied by a non-refundable fee of $500. Such petition will be approved if the applicant documents to the satisfaction of the Board compliance with Section 2 of this Part and satisfies the Board that the jurisdiction in which the applicant has been admitted and practiced will admit Georgia lawyers without examination.

(c) Once the Board of Bar Examiners has approved the petition, the applicant shall be issued a Certification of Eligibility for Admission to the Practice of Law. The applicant shall follow the procedures specified in Part B, Sections 14, 15, 16 and 17 of these Rules in order to be sworn in by a judge of the Superior Court.

Adopted effective January 1, 2003.

PART D. ATTORNEYS' EXAMINATION

SECTION 1. GENERAL

The Board of Bar Examiners may offer an Attorneys' Examination in lieu of the general bar examination to those attorneys who satisfy the criteria described in Section 2, below. Attorney examinees shall be subject to and have the benefit of all of the provisions of these **Rules** which are not inconsistent with the provisions of this Part C[1].

Adopted effective November 8, 1990; former Part C, § 1 redesignated as Part D, § 1 effective January 1, 2003.

[1] So in original

SECTION 2. ELIGIBILITY

A person who:

(a) Has been awarded an undergraduate degree by a college or university which has been accredited by an accrediting body recognized by the Commission on Recognition of Postsecondary Accreditation and who has been awarded the first professional degree in law (JD or LLB) by a law school approved by the American Bar Association; and who

(b) Is not now and never has been admitted to the practice of law in Georgia but who has been admitted by examination to membership in the Bar of the highest court of another United States jurisdiction at least twelve months prior to the date of taking the Attorneys' Examination in Georgia and who is currently a member in good standing thereof; and who

(c) Has received certification of fitness to practice law from the Board to Determine Fitness of Bar Applicants; and who

(d) Has never been denied certification of fitness to practice law in Georgia, who has not been allowed to withdraw an Application for Certification of Fitness to Practice Law in lieu of denial of certification of fitness to practice law; and who

(e) Has never taken and failed the Georgia Bar Examination; and who

(f) Has never been the subject of private or public lawyer discipline of any nature including a letter of admonition in any United States jurisdiction

may in conformity with the application deadlines established in Parts A and B of these **Rules** apply to the Board of Bar Examiners to be admitted to the Attorneys' Examination.

Adopted effective November 8, 1990; amended effective March 26, 1992; October 4, 2000; former Part C, § 2 redesignated as Part D, § 2 effective January 1, 2003.

SECTION 3. EXAMINATION CONTENT

The Attorneys' Examination shall be composed of the essay portion of the Georgia Bar Examination and the Multistate Performance Test, if it is a part of the regular examination. It shall not include the Multistate Bar Examination.

Adopted effective November 8, 1990; amended effective May 16, 1996; former Part C, § 3 redesignated as Part D, § 3 effective January 1, 2003.

SECTION 4. GRADING

The Attorneys' Examination shall be graded by the Board of Bar Examiners in accordance with procedures established by the Board. An examination score of 135 shall be required to pass the Attorneys' Examination.

Adopted effective November 8, 1990; amended effective January 1, 1997; former Part C, § 4 redesignated as Part D, § 4 effective January 1, 2003.

SECTION 5. FEES AND FILING DEADLINES

(a) Applications for Certification of Fitness to Practice Law shall be made in accordance with the deadlines established in Part A, Section 4 (a) of these **Rules** and shall be accompanied by a non-refundable fee of $800. Late filing of Applications for Certification of Fitness to Practice Law shall be accepted if made in accordance with the deadlines established in Part A, Section 4 of these **Rules** and if accompanied by the late filing fees specified therein.

(b) Applications to take the Attorneys' Examination shall be made in accordance with the deadlines established in Part B, Section 2 of these **Rules** and shall be accompanied by the fees specified therein.

Adopted effective November 8, 1990; former Part C, § 5 redesignated as Part D, § 5 effective January 1, 2003.

PART E. LICENSURE OF FOREIGN LAW CONSULTANTS

SECTION 1. GENERAL REGULATION AS TO LICENSING OF LEGAL CONSULTANTS

A person who meets the following qualifications may apply to the Office of Bar Admissions for licensing as a Foreign Law Consultant. The applicant must:

(a) be a member in good standing of a recognized legal profession in a foreign country, the members of which are admitted to practice as attorneys or counselors at law or the equivalent and are subject to effective regulation and discipline by a duly constituted professional body or a public authority;

(b) for at least five of the seven years immediately preceding his or her application have been a member in good standing of such legal profession and has actually been engaged in the practice of law in the said foreign country or elsewhere substantially involving or relating to the rendering of advice or the provision of legal services concerning the law of the said foreign country;

(c) possess the good moral character and general fitness requisite for a member of the bar of this State;

(d) intends to practice as a legal consultant in this State.

Adopted effective March 26, 1992; former Part D, § 1 redesignated as Part E, § 1 effective January 1, 2003; amended effective September 3, 2004.

SECTION 2. PROOF REQUIRED

(a) An applicant under this Rule shall file with the Office of Bar Admissions:

(1) a certificate from the professional body or public authority in such foreign country having final jurisdiction over professional discipline, certifying as to the applicant's admission to practice and the date thereof, as to his or her good standing as such attorney or counselor at law or the equivalent, and as to whether any charge or complaint has ever been filed against the applicant with such authority, and, if so, the substance of each charge or complaint and the adjudication or resolution thereof;

(2) a letter of recommendation from one of the members of the executive body of such professional body or public authority or from one of the judges of the highest law court or court of original jurisdiction of such foreign country;

(3) a duly authenticated English translation of such certificate and such letter i in either case, it is not in English;

(4) a letter of recommendation from at least two (2) active members of the State Bar of Georgia setting forth the length of time, when, and under what circumstances they have known the applicant, and their appraisal of the applicant's moral character; and

(5) such other evidence as to the applicant's educational and professional qualifications, good moral character and general fitness, and compliance with the requirements of Section 1 of the **Rules** as the Office of Bar Admissions may require.

(b) The fee for filing an original application to determine the character and fitness of an applicant shall be determined from time to time by the Fitness Board, but in no event shall such fee be less than $1,000.

(c) The review of the moral character and fitness of an applicant for a license to practice law as a foreign law consultant shall be conducted in compliance with the provisions of Sections 6 through 10 of Part A of the **Rules**.

(d) Upon showing that strict compliance with the provisions of Sections 2(a)(1) and 2(a)(2) of this Part E of these **Rules** is impossible for reasons beyond the control of an applicant, the Fitness Board may, in its discretion, waive or vary the application of such provisions and permit the applicant to submit other comparable evidence of the applicant's qualifications and moral character and fitness.

(e) If the Fitness Board determines that an applicant possesses the integrity and character requisite to be a member of the State Bar of Georgia, the Fitness Board shall certify the applicant as fit to practice as a foreign law consultant. Certification may be in the form of a letter to the applicant which shall include the certification's expiration date, which shall be one (1) year after the date issued.

(f) Certification of fitness issued to foreign law consultant applicants may be renewed upon application to the Fitness Board not less than one (1) month prior to the certificate's expiration date. Applications for renewal of certification shall be on such forms as the Fitness Board may determine and shall be accompanied by a fee of $100.00. Applications for renewal of certification by foreign law consultant applicants shall otherwise be governed by the provisions in Section 11 of Part A of the **Rules Governing Admission to the Practice of Law** in Georgia.

Adopted effective March 26, 1992; former Part D, § 2 redesignated as Part E, § 2 effective January 1, 2003; amended effective September 3, 2004.

SECTION 3. CERTIFICATION OF ELIGIBILITY

(a) Upon receiving the Fitness Board's certificate of fitness to practice law, an applicant shall file an application for admission to practice as a foreign law consultant with the Board of Bar Examiners on a form furnished by the Board of Bar Examiners, or, if so designated by the Board, by the Director of Bar Admissions, accompanied by the requisite fee, the certificate of fitness to practice law and the following documents, together with duly authenticated English translations if they are not in English:

(1) the documents referred to in Sections 2(a)(1) and 2(a)(2) or Section 2(d) of Part E of these **Rules;** and

(2) such other evidence as to the applicant's educational and professional qualifications and required practice as the Board of Bar Examiners may require.

(b) The fee for filing an original application to be licensed to practice as a foreign law consultant shall be the fee determined from time to time by the Board of Bar Examiners, but in no event shall such fee be less than $75.00.

(c) If the Board of Bar Examiners determines that an applicant possesses all of the qualifications and has satisfied all the requirements set forth in Sections 1 and 3 of this Part E of these **Rules,** the Board shall issue to the applicant a certification of eligibility for admission to practice as a foreign law consultant. Certification may be in such form as the Board of Bar Examiners prescribes, including a letter, bearing the seal of the Board and signed by the chair of the Board, or any member of the Board designated by the chair or by the Director of Bar Admissions. Such certificate shall be valid for one year from the date of its issuance. Upon application being made to the Office of Bar Admissions, a certificate of eligibility shall be subject to renewal in the same manner as outlined in Section 2(f) of Part E of these **Rules.**

(d) Upon receiving the certificate of the Office of Bar Admissions that an applicant is eligible for admission to practice as a foreign law consultant, the applicant shall deliver the certificate to the Chief Judge of the circuit in which he or she wishes a license to practice as a foreign law consultant.

(e) Upon receiving the certificate of eligibility for admission, the superior court shall enter an order that, upon payment of the usual fee to the Clerk of the superior court, the Clerk issue a license authorizing such applicant to render legal services and give professional legal advice as a foreign law consultant.

Adopted effective March 26, 1992; former Part D, § 3 redesignated as Part E, § 3 effective January 1, 2003; amended effective September 3, 2004.

SECTION 4. LIMITED SCOPE OF PRACTICE

(a) A person licensed to practice as a legal consultant under this Rule may render legal services in this State subject, however, to the limitations that he or she shall not:

(i) appear for a person other than himself or herself as attorney in any court, or before any magistrate or other judicial officer, in this State;

(ii) prepare any instrument effecting the transfer or registration of title to real estate located in the United States of America;

(iii) prepare:

(a) any will or trust instrument effecting the disposition on death of any property located in the United States of America and owned by a resident thereof, or

(b) any instrument relating to the administration of a decedent's estate in the United States of America;

(iv) prepare any instrument in respect of the marital or parental relations, rights or duties of a resident of the United States of America, or the custody or care of the children of such a resident;

(v) render professional legal advice on the law of this State, or of any other United States jurisdiction, or of the United States of America (whether rendered incident to the preparation of legal instruments or otherwise) except on the basis of advice from a person duly qualified and entitled (otherwise than by virtue of having been licensed under this Rule) to render professional legal advice in this State;

(vi) be, or in any way hold himself or herself out as, a member of the bar of this State; or

(vii) carry on his or her practice under, or utilize in connection with such practice, any name, title or designation other than one or more of the following:

(a) his or her own name;

(b) the name of the law firm with which he or she is affiliated;

(c) his or her authorized title in the foreign country of his or her admission to practice, which may be used in conjunction with the name of such country; and

(d) the title "legal consultant," which may be used in conjunction with the words "admitted to the practice of law in [name of the foreign country of his or her admission to practice]."

(b) A person licensed to practice as a legal consultant under this Rule may render legal advice regarding matters which are governed by international law, the law of the foreign country where the applicant is admitted to practice, or the law of a non–United States jurisdiction.

Adopted effective March 26, 1992; former Part D, § 4 redesignated as Part E, § 4 effective January 1, 2003; amended effective September 3, 2004.

SECTION 5. DISCIPLINARY PROVISIONS

A person licensed to practice as a legal consultant under this Rule shall be subject to professional discipline in the same manner and to the same extent as members of the bar of this State and to this end:

(a) Every person licensed to practice as a legal consultant under these **Rules** shall be subject to control by the Supreme Court and the State Bar of Georgia and to censure, suspension, removal or revocation of his or her license to practice by the Supreme Court;

(b) An applicant for licensure to practice as a foreign law consultant shall execute and file with the Office of Bar Admissions, in such form and manner as the Office of Bar Admissions may prescribe:

(1) his or her commitment to observe the Georgia Rules of Professional Conduct and the Rules of the State Bar of Georgia to the extent applicable to the legal services authorized under Section 5 of this Rule;

(2) a duly acknowledged instrument, in writing, setting forth his or her address in this State and designating the Clerk of the Supreme Court as his or her agent upon whom process may be served, with like effect as if served personally upon him or her, in any action or proceeding thereafter brought against him or her and arising out of or based upon any legal services rendered or offered to be rendered by him or her within or to residents of this State, whenever after due diligence service cannot be made upon him or her at such address or at such new address in this State as he or she shall have filed in the office of the Clerk of the Supreme Court by means of a duly acknowledged supplemental instrument in writing;

(3) a written undertaking to notify the Office of Bar Admissions of any change in such person's good standing as a member of the foreign legal profession referred to in Section 1(a) of this Rule and of any final action of the professional body or public authority referred to in Section 2(a)(1) of this Rule imposing any disciplinary censure, suspension, or other sanction upon such person; and

(4) a commitment to notify the Office of Bar Admissions of any lawsuit brought against the consultant which arises out of or is based upon any legal services rendered or offered to be rendered by the consultant within this State or any other jurisdiction.

(c) Service of process on the Clerk of the Supreme Court, pursuant to the designation filed as aforesaid, shall be made by personally delivering to and leaving with the Clerk, or with a deputy or assistant authorized by him or her to receive such service, at his or her office, duplicate copies of such process together with a fee of $10. Service of process shall be complete when such attorney has been so served. Such clerk shall promptly send one of such copies to the legal consultant to whom the process is directed, by certified mail, return receipt requested, addressed to such legal consultant at the address specified by him or her as aforesaid.

Adopted effective March 26, 1992; former Part D, § 5 redesignated as Part E, § 5 effective January 1, 2003; amended effective September 3, 2004.

SECTION 6. REVOCATION OF LICENSE

In the event that the Office of Bar Admissions determines that a person licensed as a legal consultant under this Rule no longer meets the requirements for licensure set forth in Section 1(a) or Section 1(c) of this Rule, it shall revoke the license granted to such person hereunder.

Adopted effective March 26, 1992; former Part D, § 6 redesignated as Part E, § 6 effective January 1, 2003; amended effective September 3, 2004.

SECTION 7. ADMISSION TO BAR

In the event that a person licensed as a legal consultant under this Rule is subsequently admitted as a member of the bar of this State under the provisions Part C or Part D of the Rules governing such admission, the license granted to such person hereunder shall be deemed superseded by the license granted to such person to practice law as a member of the bar of this State.

Adopted effective March 26, 1992; former Part D, § 7 redesignated as Part E, § 7 effective January 1, 2003; amended effective September 3, 2004.

PART F. GENERAL PROVISIONS

SECTION 1. OFFICE OF BAR ADMISSIONS

The Office of Bar Admissions shall serve as office of the Board to Determine Fitness of Bar Applicants and of the Board of Bar Examiners; shall perform all administrative duties for the Boards, including the acceptance of applications and fees, the investigation of applicants and their educational qualifications, the payment of expenses and other such matters as may be provided for by the Boards or the Court.

Former Part C, § 1 redesignated as Part D, § 1 effective November 8, 1990; redesignated as Part E, § 1 effective March 26, 1992; redesignated as Part F, § 1 effective January 1, 2003.

SECTION 2. DIRECTOR OF BAR ADMISSIONS

The Director of Bar Admissions shall be appointed by and serve at the pleasure of the Court. In addition to such other duties as may be assigned by the Court, he shall serve as liaison officer between the Court and the Board to Determine Fitness of Bar Applicants, between the Court and the Board of Bar Examiners and between the Boards; shall serve as chief administrative officer of the Office of Bar Admissions; shall supervise the investigations of applicants and the administration of bar examinations; and shall perform such other duties as may be authorized by these **Rules** or as may be specified by the Court or by the Boards.

Former Part C, § 2 redesignated as Part D, § 2 effective November 8, 1990; redesignated as Part E, § 2 effective March 26, 1992; redesignated as Part F, § 2 effective January 1, 2003.

SECTION 3. RECORDS

(a) The Office of Bar Admissions shall maintain such records as are generated in the course of accepting and processing Applications for Certification of Fitness to Practice Law and as are generated in accepting and processing applications to stand bar examinations and of results of taking the bar examination. The following records, and no others, shall be maintained as public records:

(1) With respect to Applications for Certification of Fitness to Practice Law: Name and address of each applicant;

(2) With respect to applications to stand the bar examination: Name and address of each applicant;

(3) With respect to each bar examination:

(i) The names and addresses of the persons who took the bar examination;

(ii) The names and addresses of persons who passed the examination; and

(iii) Such statistical summaries as may be specifically authorized by the Supreme Court.

(b) All other information provided by or obtained with respect to an applicant for certification of fitness to practice law or to stand a bar examination, including examination results except as specifically provided for herein, shall be considered confidential and privileged communications and shall not be released to any person or agency except in those instances where a hearing with respect to an Application for Certification of Fitness to Practice Law is to be held pursuant to Part A, Section 8 of these **Rules**, information and documents obtained by the Board pursuant to its investigation and relevant to the specifications issued by the Board may be disclosed to the applicant and his or her counsel and to a hearing officer appointed to conduct the hearing. Further, information provided by or obtained with respect to an applicant for certification of fitness to practice law may be disclosed to the bar admissions authority of any United States jurisdiction where the applicant may apply for admission to the practice of law but then only on the written request of the applicant that such information be supplied to such other authority and only on the understanding that such information will not be released to the applicant; and the name, address, date of birth and social security number of each applicant for certification of fitness to practice law may be furnished to the National Conference of Bar Examiners for dissemination to the bar admissions authority of any United States jurisdiction upon request; and applications for certification of fitness to practice law and applications to take the bar examination may be released to the General Counsel of the State Bar of Georgia in disciplinary matters; and information and records may be disclosed as provided by order of the Court.

Former Part C, § 3 redesignated as Part D, § 3 effective November 8, 1990; amended and redesignated as Part E, § 3 effective March 26, 1992; redesignated as Part F, § 3 effective January 1, 2003.

SECTION 4. WAIVERS

The Board to Determine Fitness, with respect to rules contained herein pertaining to it and the Board of Bar Examiners with respect to rules contained herein pertaining to it may, for good cause shown by clear and convincing evidence, waive any rule contained herein; provided, however, neither Board shall waive filing fees, including late fees, nor shall the Board of Bar Examiners waive the prohibition on regrading of essay or MPT answers after the general release of grades. The decision of either the Board to Determine Fitness of Bar Applicants or the Board of Bar Examiners not to waive any rules herein subject to waiver may be appealed to the Court in accordance with the procedures set forth in Part A, Section 9(b) of the **Rules**.

Former Part C, § 4 amended effective June 28, 1989; redesignated as Part D, § 4 effective November 8, 1990; redesignated as Part E, § 4 effective March 26, 1992; amended effective October 5, 1999; redesignated as Part F, § 4 effective January 1, 2003.

SECTION 5. COMMUNICATIONS WITH BOARD MEMBERS

All communications to or with the Board to Determine Fitness of Bar Applicants or any member thereof relating to pending Applications for Certification of Fitness to Practice Law and all communications to or with the Board of Bar Examiners or any member thereof relating to pending applications to take the bar examination or to the results thereof or to eligibility for admission to the bar examination or to certificates of eligibility for admission to the practice of law and all communications with either Board or any member thereof relating to waiver of any part of these **Rules**, whether by an applicant or by any person or agent acting for or on the behalf of an applicant shall be transmitted through the Office of Bar Admissions unless otherwise directed in writing by the Chair of the appropriate board or by the Director of Bar Admissions.

Former Part C, § 5 redesignated as Part D, § 5 effective November 8, 1990; redesignated as Part E, § 5 effective March 26, 1992; redesignated as Part F, § 5 effective January 1, 2003.

SECTION 6. FILINGS

All filings required to be made with the Board to Determine Fitness of Bar Applicants and with the Board of Bar Examiners by these **Rules** shall be made with the Office of Bar Admissions. Unless otherwise indicated, filings must be *received* by the Office of Bar Admissions on or before the appropriate filing deadline in order to be timely filed. Mailings which are *received* after a deadline or which, if *received* by or on a deadline date, are incomplete or which do not include required fees or which include a check in payment of required fees which is not honored by the drawee bank will not be considered as timely filed.

Former Part C, § 6 redesignated as Part D, § 6 effective November 8, 1990; former Part D, § 6 redesignated as Part E, § 6 effective March 26, 1992; amended effective July 1, 1994; redesignated as Part F, § 6 effective January 1, 2003.

SECTION 7. APPEALS

(a) Upon being notified by the Board to Determine Fitness of Bar Applicants that his or her application has been denied or by the Board of Bar Examiners of any final determination by that Board (with the exception of bar exam results), an applicant may appeal the decision to the Court for review. To secure the appeal, the applicant must, within thirty days of notification that his or her application has been denied, file a written notice of appeal with the Office of Bar Admissions and with the Clerk of the Supreme Court and must serve a copy of the notice of appeal on the Attorney General of Georgia. The Office of Bar Admissions shall then prepare the complete file, which shall be confidential, for delivery to the Clerk.

(b) The Clerk shall docket the appeal, which shall be a public record, and shall notify the applicant or the applicant's attorney, the Office of Bar Admissions and the Attorney General of Georgia that the appeal has been docketed. Within 20 days the applicant or his or her attorney may submit written argument (an original and seven copies) in support of his or her appeal, a copy of which must be served on the Office of Bar Admissions and on the Attorney General of Georgia. Arguments of the Board in support of its decision shall be filed within 40 days after the appeal is docketed or 20 days after the filing of the applicant's arguments, whichever is later. Although the bar admissions file shall be a confidential record during the appeal process, the docketing information shall be a public record.

(c) The Court, upon review of the arguments, shall issue an order affirming or reversing the decision of the Board or remanding the application for further consideration by the Board. Written opinions may be rendered and may be based upon facts contained in the confidential record. Oral arguments will not be had unless requested by the Court.

Adopted effective March 22, 2001; former Part E, § 7 redesignated as Part F, § 7 effective January 1, 2003.

SECTION 8. CIVIL IMMUNITY

(a) The Board of Bar Examiners and the Board to Determine Fitness of Bar Applicants, and their members, employees, and agents are immune from all civil liability for conduct and communications occurring in the performance of their official duties relating to the examination, the character and fitness qualification, and licensing of persons seeking to be admitted to the practice of law.

(b) Records, statements of opinion, and other information regarding an applicant for admission to the bar communicated by any entity including any person, firm, or institution, without malice, to the Board of Bar Examiners or the Board to Determine Fitness of Bar Applicants, or their members, employees, or agents are privileged, and civil suits predicated thereon may not be instituted.

Adopted effective May 15, 1997; renumbered from Pt. E, § 7, effective March 22, 2001; former Part E, § 8 redesignated as Part F, § 8, effective January 1, 2003.

USE OF INTERPRETERS FOR NON-ENGLISH SPEAKING PERSONS

Effective October 10, 2001

Including Amendments Received Through November 1, 2006

Research Note

Use WESTLAW *to find cases citing a rule. In addition, use* WESTLAW *to search for specific terms or to update a rule; see the GA–RULES and GA–ORDERS Scope screens for further information.*

Amendments to these rules are published, as received, in the South Eastern Reporter 2d *and* Georgia Cases *advance sheets.*

Table of Rules

INTRODUCTION

Pursuant to the inherent powers of the Court and the Georgia Constitution of 1983, and in order to secure the rights of non-English speaking persons, this Court now promulgates the following rules to establish a statewide plan for the use of Interpreters by the Courts of Georgia.

Adopted effective October 10, 2001; amended effective January 13, 2003.

RULE I. DEFINITIONS

(A) "Non-English Speaker" means any party or witness who cannot readily understand or communicate in spoken English and who consequently cannot equally participate in or benefit from the proceedings unless an interpreter is available to assist him or her. The fact that a person for whom English is a second language knows some English should not prohibit that individual from being allowed to have an interpreter;

(B) "Interpreter" means any person certified as an interpreter by the Georgia Commission on Interpreters; any person on the registered interpreters' list; or any person authorized by a Court to translate or interpret oral or written communication in a foreign language during court proceedings.

(C) "Court Proceedings" means a proceeding before any court of this State or a Grand Jury hearing.

(D) Uniform Rule for Use of Interpreters is found in Appendix A.

(E) Requirements for Certification, Registration and Training of Interpreters are found in Appendix B.

(F) Ethical Standards for Interpreters are found in Appendix C.

Commentary

Courts should make a diligent effort to appoint a Certified Interpreter. If a Certified Interpreter is unavailable, a Registered Interpreter is to be given preference. There will be occasions when it is necessary to utilize a telephonic language service or a less qualified interpreter. Faced with a need, where no interpreter is available locally, courts should weigh the need for immediacy in conducting a hearing against the potential compromise of due process, or the potential of substantive injustice, if interpreting is inadequate. Unless immediacy is a primary concern, some delay might be more appropriate than the use of a telephonic language service.

Adopted effective October 10, 2001; amended effective January 13, 2003.

RULE II. CENTRAL ORGANIZATION

There is hereby created the Georgia Commission on Interpreters for Non–English Speakers:

(A) The Georgia Commission on Interpreters for Non–English speakers will consist of: the current Chief Justice of the Georgia Supreme Court or the Chief Justice's designee, a judge of the Court of Appeals, a Superior Court Judge, a State Court Judge, a Juvenile Court Judge, a Probate Court Judge, a Magistrate Court Judge, a Municipal Court Judge, a designee of the State Bar of Georgia, one member from the Georgia General Assembly, four members of the State Bar of Georgia, and three non-lawyer public members. All members of the Commission shall be appointed by the Georgia Supreme Court. The chair of the Commission shall be designated by the Georgia Supreme Court.

(B) The first Commission will be appointed to serve terms as follows: the first term for three members will be one year, the first term for three members will be two years, the first term for four members will be three years, the first term for three members will be four years, the first term for three members will be five years. Thereafter, the term for Commission members will be five years. A Commission member shall not succeed himself or herself, except that Commission members originally appointed to a term of two years or less would be eligible for reappointment to one additional five-year term. If the status of a Commission member chosen to represent a particular category changes during his or her term, the member will continue to serve out his or her term.

(C) Members of the Commission shall receive no compensation for their services but shall be entitled to reimbursement for expenses and mileage for travel in connection with Commission business.

(D) The Commission is charged as follows:

1. To administer a statewide comprehensive interpreter program;

2. To oversee the development and ensure the quality of all interpreters;

3. To approve court interpreter programs;

4. To develop guidelines for interpreter programs;

5. To designate languages for which certification programs shall be established;

6. To develop criteria for training and certification of interpreters;

7. To establish standards of conduct for interpreters;

(E) The responsibilities of the Georgia Commission on Interpreters will include the following:

1. To serve as a resource for interpreter education and research;

2. To provide technical assistance to new and existing interpreter programs;

3. To develop the capability of providing training to interpreters in courts throughout the state;

4. To implement the Commission's policies regarding qualifications of interpreters and quality of programs;

5. To register interpreters and remove interpreters from the registry if necessary;

6. To collect statistics from interpreter programs in order to monitor the effectiveness of various programs throughout the state.

Adopted effective October 10, 2001; amended effective January 13, 2003.

RULE III. CERTIFICATION PROGRAMS

The Commission shall establish programs for the purpose of certifying interpreters. The Commission shall have the authority to establish the requirements and procedures for interpreter certification. Fees for certification will be established by the Georgia Commission on Interpreters and interpreters seeking certification shall be required to pay the fee established by said Commission.

Adopted effective October 10, 2001; amended effective January 13, 2003.

RULE IV. DISCIPLINE

(A) **Suspension or Revocation of Certification**

Certified or Registered status issued by the Georgia Commission on Interpreters may be suspended or revoked for any of the following reasons:

1. Conviction of a felony or a misdemeanor involving moral turpitude, dishonesty, or false statements;

2. Fraud, dishonesty, or corruption which is related to the functions and duties of a court interpreter;

3. Continued false or deceptive advertising after receipt of notification to discontinue;

4. Knowingly and willfully disclosing confidential or privileged information obtained while serving in an official capacity;

5. Gross incompetence or unprofessional or unethical conduct;

6. Failing to appear as scheduled without good cause;

7. Noncompliance with any existing continuing education requirements;

8. Nonpayment of any required renewal fees; or

9. Violation of the Code of Professional Responsibility for Court Interpreters.

Commentary

The appropriateness of disciplinary action and the degree of discipline to be imposed should depend upon factors such as the seriousness of the violation, the intent of the interpreter, whether there is a pattern of improper activity, and the effect of the improper activity on others or on the judicial system.

(B) **Disciplinary Procedures**

1. **Initiation of a Complaint.** Disciplinary proceedings may be initiated by a standard form asserting a ground for discipline. The complaint shall be in writing and filed with the Georgia Commission on Interpreters. The Commission may initiate disciplinary proceedings on its own motion.

2. **Probable Cause; Notification.** If a majority of the Commission finds probable cause to believe that a ground for discipline has occurred, it shall sent written notification thereof, identifying the rule or rules alleged to have been violated, to the court interpreter. If the complaint is found to be facially insufficient, the complaint shall be dismissed without prejudice and the complainant and interpreter shall be so notified.

3. **Response.** Within 30 days of the issuance of a finding of probable cause, the court interpreter shall file a written response with the Commission. If no response is filed, the violations identified in the finding of probable cause shall be deemed admitted.

4. **Identity of Complainant.** Upon written request filed with the Commission, the Commission shall promptly reveal to the court interpreter the identity of the complaining party.

5. **Informal Resolution of Complaint.** Efforts to resolve the complaint informally may be initiated by any of the parties to the complaint at any time. Any resolution reached must be submitted to the Commission for approval. Upon approval of any resolution reached informally, the Commission will notify the complainant and the court interpreter of its decision in writing.

6. **Review.** Within 60 days after receipt of a written response to the finding of probable cause or within 60 days following the expiration of the time within which to file a response if none is filed, the Commission shall review the complaint, the finding of probable cause, and the response, if any. The Commission shall decide whether to (i) dismiss the proceeding, (ii) issue a proposed disposition, or (iii) set a hearing.

(a) No Hearing Demanded. A proposed disposition issued pursuant to subdivision 6 (ii) shall become final unless the court interpreter demands a hearing within 30 days of the date on which the proposed disposition was issued.

(b) Hearing Demanded. If the court interpreter demands a hearing in a timely manner, the hearing shall take place no less than 30 days nor more than 90 days from the date of notice pursuant to subdivision (6)(iii).

(c) Legal Representation. The court interpreter may be represented by an attorney at any stage of the proceeding. The court interpreter shall be responsible for all of his or her costs and expenses, including attorney's fees.

7. **Hearings.**

(a) Pre-Hearing Discovery. Pre-hearing discovery shall not be permitted unless expressly authorized by the Commission, in response to a written request.

(b) Rules of Evidence. Strict rules of evidence shall not apply. The Commission may, in its discretion, consider any evidence presented, including affidavits, giving such evidence the weight it deems appropriate.

(c) Reporting of Hearings. The Commission shall ensure that all hearings are reported or electronically recorded.

(d) Hearing Procedure. At the hearing, both the Commission and the court interpreter shall be afforded the opportunity to introduce documents and other relevant evidence, and to elicit sworn testimony.

(e) Commission Deliberations. Following the presentation of evidence, the Commission shall deliberate regarding its decision. Such deliberations shall take place in private.

(f) Finality of Decision and Rehearing Requests. Unless the court interpreter files a request for rehearing within 30 days of the date of the decision, the decision shall become final without further action. If a timely request for rehearing is filed, the decision shall not become final until the request has been disposed of by written decision, a copy of which shall be sent to the court interpreter.

(C) **Disciplinary Dispositions**

1. **Burden of Proof.** If the Commission finds that there is clear and convincing evidence that the court interpreter has violated one or more of these rules, it shall impose such discipline as it may deem appropriate, consistent with these rules.

2. **Vote Required; Notification.** All decisions of the Commission shall be by majority vote, in writing and, if adverse to the court interpreter, shall contain factual findings supporting the decision. A copy of the decision shall be sent to the court interpreter.

3. **Sanctions.** Sanctions may consist of but are not limited to one or more of the following:

(a) A private reprimand;

(b) Requiring that specified education courses be taken;

(c) Requiring that one or more parts of the interpreter certification examination be retaken;

(d) Limiting the scope of practice or interpreting services, which may include removal or suspension from any registry, including the Registry of Certified and Registered Foreign Language Interpreters;

(e) Requiring that work be supervised;

(f) Suspension or revocation of Certified or Registered status.

(D) **Confidentiality**

When a disciplinary proceeding is either dismissed or results in a private reprimand, all records of the proceeding shall remain confidential; otherwise, all such records shall become public when the Commission's decision becomes final.

(E) **Appeal**

The interpreter may appeal the Commission's decision to the Judicial Council of Georgia no later than 20 days after the decision is mailed to the interpreter. The appeal shall include the interpreter's written objections to the decision. The Judicial Council shall review the record of the hearing to determine whether the decision reached and sanctions imposed were appropriate, or whether the Commission abused its discretion.

(F) **Reinstatement**

A court interpreter whose Certified or Registered status has been suspended or revoked may apply in writing for reinstatement. This request shall explain why the applicant believes the reinstatement should occur. The Commission shall have the sole discretion whether to grant or deny reinstatement, or to impose conditions upon reinstatement as it deems appropriate.

Adopted effective October 10, 2001; amended effective January 13, 2003.

RULE V. COMPENSATION OF INTERPRETERS

There shall be no uniform, state-wide compensation system at this time. Local courts will have the responsibility for developing and testing a variety of approaches to compensation consistent with guidelines that may be established by the Commission and by Statute (O.C.G.A. § 17–12–40). The Commission shall evaluate the approaches to compensation developed by the local courts and determine the need for a statewide flexible compensation system. Subject to Supreme Court approval, the Commission shall implement such a system.

Commentary

Although the contribution of volunteers to interpreter programs throughout the country is inestimable, the Georgia Supreme Court believes that the comprehensive system of statewide interpreter services envisioned by these rules cannot be handled entirely by unpaid volunteers. This court is convinced that in order to build and maintain a statewide system of interpreter services of the extent and quality desired, there must be mechanisms for compensating interpreters at appropriate levels. This court also believes that the Georgia interpreter program will require a combination of volunteers, salaried in-house interpreters, and free market interpreters in order to meet the highly varied demands and circumstances of courts in urban, rural, and suburban areas.

Adopted effective October 10, 2001; amended effective January 13, 2003.

RULE VI. OATH, CONFIDENTIALITY AND PUBLIC COMMENT

(A) Prior to providing any service to a non-English speaking person, the interpreter shall subscribe to an oath that he or she shall interpret all communications in an accurate manner to the best of his or her skill and knowledge.

(B) The oath shall conform substantially to the following form:

INTERPRETER'S OATH

> Do you solemnly swear or affirm that you will faithfully interpret from (state the language) into English and from English into (state the language) the proceedings before this Court in an accurate manner to the best of your skill and knowledge?

(C) Interpreter shall not voluntarily disclose any admission or communication that is declared to be confidential or privileged under state law. Out of court disclosures made by a non-English speaker communicating through an interpreter shall be treated by the interpreter as confidential and/or privileged unless the Court orders the interpreter to disclose such communications or the non-English speaker waives such confidentiality or privilege.

(D) Interpreters shall not publicly discuss, report, or offer an opinion concerning a matter in which they are engaged, even when that information is not privileged or required by law to be confidential.

(E) Prior to service, every interpreter serving in the courts of the State of Georgia shall agree in writing to comply with the Code of Professional Responsibility for Court Interpreters.

(F) The presence of an interpreter shall not affect the privileged nature of any discussion.

Adopted effective October 10, 2001; amended effective January 13, 2003.

RULE VII. RECORD OF INTERPRETER TESTIMONY

(A) Where a certified interpreter is used, no record shall generally be made of the non-English testimonial statements. Where a challenge is made to the accuracy of a translation, the court shall first determine whether the interpreter is able to communicate accurately with and translate information to and from the non-English speaking person. If it is determined that the interpreter cannot perform these functions, arrangements for another interpreter should be made, unless ***testimony*** that is cumulative, irrelevant, or immaterial is involved. Where the court determines that the interpreter has the ability to communicate effectively with the non-English speaker, the court shall resolve the issue of the contested translation and the record to be made of the contested testimony in its discretion. Any transcript prepared shall consist only of the English language spoken in court.

(B) In criminal cases, whenever a certified interpreter is not utilized, the court shall make an audio or audio-visual recording of any testimony given in a language other than English. This includes any colloquies between the court and any non-English speaking persons, statements or testimony made to the court given by a non-English speaking person, as well as all translations provided by the interpreter of such proceedings. This recording shall become part of the record of the proceeding. There is no requirement to record any translation for a non-English speaking defendant of other proceedings where the defendant does not directly participate, such as the translation of testimony of an English speaking witness when the defendant is represented by counsel. Nor shall a record be made of private conversations between defendant and counsel.

(C) In civil cases, whenever a certified interpreter is not utilized and a party was denied the right to use an interpreter of his or her own choosing, the court shall make an audio or audio-visual recording of any testimony given in a language other than English. This includes any colloquies between the court and any non-English speaking persons, statements or testimony made to the court given by a non-English speaking person, as well as all translations provided by the interpreter in the proceedings. This recording shall become part of the record of the proceeding. There is no requirement to record the translation for a non-English speaking party of other proceedings where the party does not directly participate, such as the translation of testimony of an English speaking witness when the party is represented by counsel. Nor shall a record be made of private conversations between parties and counsel.

(D) In all cases where an audio or audio-visual recording is not required, the court shall have the discretion to authorize the making of such a recording.

Adopted effective October 10, 2001; amended effective January 13, 2003.

APPENDIX A. UNIFORM RULE FOR INTERPRETER PROGRAMS

I. *General Rule.* The following rules apply to all proceedings in Georgia where there are non-English speaking persons in need of interpreters.

(A) An interpreter is needed and a court interpreter shall be appointed when the judge determines, after an examination of a party or witness, that: (1) the party cannot understand and speak English well enough to participate fully in the proceedings and to assist counsel; or (2) the witness cannot speak English so as to be understood directly by counsel, court, and jury.

(B) The court should examine a party or witness on the record to determine whether an interpreter is needed if: (1) a party or counsel requests such an examination; or (2) it appears to the court that the party or witness may not understand and speak English well enough to participate fully in the proceedings, or (3) if the party or witness requests an interpreter. The fact that a person for whom English is a second language knows some English should not prohibit that individual from being allowed to have an interpreter.

(C) To determine if an interpreter is needed the court should normally include questions on the following:

1. Identification (for example: name, address, birth date, age, place of birth);

2. Active vocabulary in vernacular English (for example: "How did you come to the court today?" "What kind of work do you do?", "Where did you go to school?", "What was the highest grade you completed?", "Describe what you see in the courtroom." "What have you eaten today?"). Questions should be phrased to avoid "yes or no" replies;

3. The court proceedings (for example: the nature of the charge or the type of case before the court, the purpose of the proceedings and function of the court, the rights of a party or criminal defendant, and the responsibilities of a witness).

(D) After the examination, the court should state its conclusion on the record, and the file in the case should be clearly marked and data entered electronically when appropriate by court personnel to ensure that an interpreter will be present when needed in any subsequent proceeding.

(E) For good cause, the court should authorize a pre-appearance interview between the interpreter and the party or witness. Good cause exists if the interpreter needs clarification on any interpreting issues, including but not limited to: colloquialisms, culturalisms, dialects, idioms, linguistic capabilities and traits, regionalisms, register, slang, speech patterns, or technical terms.

(F) When a Certified or Registered interpreter is not being used, the court or the court's designee should give instructions to interpreters, either orally or in writing, that substantially conform to the following:

1. Do not discuss the pending proceedings with a party or witness, outside of professional employment in the same case.

2. Do not disclose communications between counsel and client.

3. Do not give legal advice to a party or witness. Refer legal questions to the attorney or to the court.

4. Inform the court if you are unable to interpret a word, expression, special terminology, or dialect, or have doubts about your linguistic expertise or ability to perform adequately in a particular case.

5. Interpret all words, including slang, vulgarisms, and epithets, to convey the intended meaning.

6. Use the first person when interpreting statements made in the first person. (For example, a statement or question should not be introduced with the words, "He says ....")

7. Direct all inquiries or problems to the court and not to the witness or counsel. If necessary you may request permission to approach the bench with counsel to discuss a problem.

8. Position yourself near the witness or party without blocking the view of the judge, jury, or counsel.

9. Inform the court if you become fatigued during the proceedings.

10. When interpreting for a party at counsel table, speak loudly enough to be heard by the party or counsel but not so loudly as to interfere with the proceedings.

11. Interpret everything including objections.

12. If the court finds good cause under section (E), hold a pre- appearance interview with the party or witness to become familiar with speech patterns and linguistic traits and to determine what technical or special terms may be used. Counsel may be present at the pre-appearance interview.

13. During the pre-appearance interview with a non-English speaking witness, give the witness the following instructions on the procedure to be followed when the witness is testifying:

(a) The witness must speak in a loud, clear voice so that the entire court and not just the interpreter can hear.

(b) The witness must direct all responses to the person asking the question, not to the interpreter.

(c) The witness must direct all questions to counsel or to the court and not to the interpreter. The witness may not seek advice from or engage in any discussion with the interpreter.

(d) During the pre-appearance interview with a non-English speaking party, give the following instructions on the procedure to be used when the non-English speaking party is not testifying: (i) The interpreter will interpret all statements made in open court. (ii) The party must direct any questions to counsel. The interpreter will interpret all questions to counsel and the responses. The party may not seek advice from or engage in discussion with the interpreter.

Commentary

A model written form for performing this procedure may be obtained from the Georgia Commission on Interpreters. It is recommended that when a non-professional interpreter is used that the Court personally verify a basic understanding of the interpreter's role on the record.

(G) The court or the court's designee should give the following instructions to counsel, either orally or in writing:

1. When examining a non-English speaking witness, direct all questions to the witness and not to the interpreter. (For example, do not say to the interpreter, "Ask him if . . .");

2. If there is a disagreement with the interpretation, direct any objection to the court and not to the interpreter. Ask permission to approach the bench to discuss the problem;

3. If you have a question regarding the qualifications of the interpreter, you may request permission to conduct a supplemental examination on the interpreter's qualifications.

II. *Criminal Cases.*

(A) Each non-English speaking defendant will be provided with an interpreter at each step of the proceedings; within the judge's discretion, costs can be assessed upon a defendant when appropriate.

(B) A non-English speaking person may waive the right to the use of an interpreter. Such a waiver shall be in writing and approved by the court. The court shall determine, on the record, that the right to an interpreter has been waived knowingly and voluntarily utilizing the services of the most available interpreter. Additionally, counsel may waive the presence of an interpreter in bond hearings.

(C) The court shall provide an interpreter to any non-English speaking person whenever the non-English speaking person is a party, or has been subpoenaed, or summoned or has otherwise been compelled to appear in a court proceeding. Within the judge's discretion, costs can be assessed upon a defendant when appropriate.

III. *Civil Cases.*

(A) Upon request, each non-English speaking person shall be provided with the fee schedule and a list of the interpreters who have been approved for providing services within that particular court.

(B) Each non-English speaking party shall have the right to an interpreter at each step of the proceedings at the expense of the non-English speaking person. If a fee schedule exists then one shall be given. Advanced notice of use of an interpreter shall be provided to all parties and to the court.

(C) In the event the court has approved a pauper's affidavit in any civil case and the person filing said affidavit requires the use of in interpreter, one will be provided at no cost to said person.

IV. ***Juvenile Cases.***

(A) Each non-English speaking person in a delinquency proceeding or whose parental rights to full custody of any minor child are challenged by any governmental unit or agency such as DFCS, shall be provided with an interpreter at each step of the proceedings;

(B) The court shall provide a qualified interpreter to any non-English speaking person whenever such person's rights to full custody of any minor child is challenged for allegedly causing a child to be dependent or delinquent or neglected in violation of the Georgia Juvenile Court Code of 1971, as amended, and the rules established by this court;

(C) The provided interpreter shall be present at all times when the non- English speaking person is consulting with legal counsel should said legal counsel not be able to communicate with the non-English speaking person;

(D) A non-English speaking person may waive the right to the use of an interpreter. Such a waiver shall be in writing and approved by the court. The court shall determine, on the record, that the right to an interpreter has been waived knowingly and voluntarily utilizing the services of the most available interpreter. In no event shall the failure to request an interpreter be deemed to be a waiver.

V. ***Replacement of Interpreter.*** Upon a request by the non-English speaking person, by his or her counsel, or by any other officer of the court, the court shall determine whether the interpreter so provided is able to communicate accurately with and translate information to and from the non- English speaking person. If it is determined that the interpreter cannot perform these functions, the court shall provide the non-English speaking person with another interpreter.

VI. ***Interpreter's fees and expenses.***

(A) Any interpreter providing service under this rule shall be compensated as directed by these rules.

(B) The expenses of providing an interpreter in any court proceeding may be assessed by the court as costs in such proceeding.

Adopted effective October 10, 2001; amended effective January 13, 2003.

APPENDIX B. POWERS AND DUTIES OF THE GEORGIA COMMISSION ON INTERPRETERS; REQUIREMENT FOR CERTIFICATION, REGISTRATION AND TRAINING OF INTERPRETERS

The Georgia Commission on Interpreters shall administer the training and discipline of courtroom interpreters and provide regulations that:

I. Shall mandate classroom training for interpreters, which initially shall be no less than sixteen hours.

II. Shall designate the languages for which interpreting skill can be tested and certified.

III. Shall result in certification under a multi-state program for simultaneous, consecutive, and sight-reading interpretation.

IV. A "Certified Interpreter List" shall be comprised of individuals competent in court interpretation as demonstrated by successful completion of an oral and written examination demonstrating competence in interpreting as provided for by the Georgia Commission on Interpreters and the completion of required continuing education providing familiarity with the Georgia court system and the roles and responsibilities of interpreters within that system. In lieu of the examination, the Commission may recognize federal certification or certification of states participating in the national Consortium for State Court Interpreter Certification.

V. A "Registered Interpreter List" shall be comprised of individuals appearing competent in court interpretation that have completed mandatory classroom training and passed a written examination demonstrating familiarity with the Georgia court system and the roles and responsibilities of interpreters within that system. This list may include those interpreters interpreting a language for which no examination is given. Qualification tests for this list may also test language and interpretation skills. It is intended that a court will choose an interpreter from this category only if a Certified Interpreter is not available.

VI. The Commission is authorized to maintain other classification and resource lists as it deems necessary.

VII. The Commission shall have the authority to set expiration dates for any qualification category, to establish fees, tests, and other requirements, including continuing education requirements, for any qualification category.

VIII. The Georgia Commission on Interpreters is dedicated to the principle that interpreters serving in court programs should be of the highest possible caliber in training and experience. All interpreters serving in Georgia programs should be of good moral character. The Commission is authorized to enact reasonable regulations to ensure these ends.

IX. The Commission is authorized to pass regulations governing the procedure in disciplining interpreters, including revocation of any qualification status.

X. All other persons interpreting court proceedings shall be required to comply with the standards for interpreting of the Georgia Commission on Interpreters to the **best of their ability.** It is intended that such persons be selected by the court for interpretation only where no Certified or Registered interpreters are available.

Adopted effective October 10, 2001; amended effective January 13, 2003.

APPENDIX C. ETHICAL STANDARDS FOR INTERPRETERS

Requirements for Ethical Standards for Interpreters:

Rules of fair practice for interpreters shall include acknowledging the need to refer a particular case to another interpreter as a result of technical difficulties, cultural biases or personal interests.

Interpreters are permitted to advertise. Interpreters have an obligation to the integrity of the interpretation process. In that regard, all statements as to qualifications must be truthful. Interpreters may never claim that they will guarantee a specific result. It is important to the public perception of interpreters that advertisements by interpreters are not only accurate, clear, and truthful, but that they are in no way misleading.

Pending adoption of a Code of Professional Responsibility for Court Interpreters by the Georgia Commission on Interpreters for Non-English Speakers the following shall be the interim Code of Professional Responsibility governing all court interpreters serving in Georgia's Courts upon which discipline under these rules may be based.

I. Act strictly in the interest of the court during proceedings before the court and with fidelity to the non-English speaker for whom they are interpreting;

II. Reflect proper court decorum and act with dignity and respect to the officials and staff of the court;

III. Avoid professional or personal conduct which could discredit the court;

IV. Work unobtrusively so that attention is focused on the parties rather than the interpreter;

V. Accurately state their qualifications as a court interpreter;

VI. Refuse any assignment for which they are not qualified or under conditions which substantially impair their effectiveness;

VII. Disclose to the court and parties in any prior involvement with a case, private involvement with the parties or with others significantly involved in the case;

VIII. Interpret accurately and faithfully without indicating any personal bias, avoiding even the appearance of partiality;

IX. Preserve the level of language used and the ambiguities and nuances of the speaker without editing;

X. Inform the judge or counsel if the non-English speaker cannot understand the language level and ask for simplification;

XI. Request clarification of ambiguous statements or unfamiliar vocabulary from the judge or counsel;

XII. Promptly notify the court of any error in their interpretation;

XIII. Continually improve their skills and knowledge through such activities as professional training and education;

XIV. Maintain impartiality by avoiding undue contact with witnesses, attorneys, interested parties, and jurors before, during and until the case is concluded;

XV. Never take advantage of knowledge obtained in the performance of official duties, for their own or another's personal gain;

XVI. Not disclose any information pertaining to court cases unless ordered otherwise by the court;

XVII. Inform the presiding judge should the interpreter feel harassed or intimidated by an officer of the court;

XVIII. Immediately report to the court any solicitations or efforts by another to induce or encourage the interpreter to violate any law, standard, or any part of this Code of Professional Responsibility;

XIX. Accept no money, gift or other benefit in excess of the authorized compensation for the performance of interpretation duties;

XX. Refrain from expressing personal opinion in a matter before the court;

XXI. Not give any kind of legal advice whether solicited or not. In all instances, the non-English speaker shall be referred to the judge or counsel;

XXII. Never act as an individual referral service for any attorney. If asked by a non-English speaker to refer the speaker to an attorney, an interpreter shall direct such individual to the local bar or to the indigent defense office;

XXIII. Agree to be bound by this Code. Violations of this Code may result in the interpreter's removal from the interpreter registry maintained by the Commission on Interpreters, and willful violation may also result in other appropriate sanctions.

Adopted effective October 10, 2001; amended effective January 13, 2003.

†